The National Hockey League

Official Guide & Record Book

1994-95

TRIUMPH
B O O K S

CHICAGO

THE NATIONAL HOCKEY LEAGUE
Official Guide & Record Book/1994-95

Staff

For the NHL: Michael Berger; Supervising Editor: Greg Inglis; Statistician: Benny Ercolani; Editorial Staff: David Keon, Sherry McKeown, Justin Sanft

Managing Editors: Ralph Dinger, James Duplacey

Contributing Editor: Igor Kuperman

All-Time Club vs. Club Statistics: Neil McDonald

Contributors:
Kevin Bixby, Jack Blum, Ray Bolen, Sharon Corder, Nick Debennaro, Luca Del-Vita, Mel Foster, Elliotte Freedman, Lisa Ickles, David Ilderton, Joe Lowes (Brantford Smoke), Sam Malkin, Mike Meyers (IHL), Herb Morell (OHL), NHL Broadcasters' Association, NHL Central Registry, NHL Players' Association, Jari-Pekka Niemi, Larry Parnes, Bruce Plante, Douglas Reynolds, Valentina Riazanova, Renato Rossi, Hellen M. Schroeder (AHL), Steven Siegal, Michael Stojakovic, Will Sutton, Louis-Robert Tackoor, Clark M. Topper, Stale Volleng, Jeff Weiss (CCHA).

Consulting Publisher: Dan Diamond

Photo Credits

Historical and special event photos: Bruce Bennett, David Bier, Michael Burns, Graphic Artists Collection, New York Rangers, Rice Studio, Robert Shaver, Imperial Oil Turofsky Collection, Hockey Hall of Fame.

Current photos: Graig Abel, Toronto; Joe Angeles, St. Louis; Steve Babineau, Boston; Sol Benjamin, Chicago, Bruce Bennett, NY Islanders, Tony Biegun, Winnipeg, Denis Brodeur, Montreal; Mark Buckner, St. Louis; Denny Cavanaugh, Pittsburgh; Steve Crandall, New Jersey; Bill Cunningham, Vancouver; Willie Dagenais, Montreal; Edmonton Northlands; Bob Fisher, Montreal; Ray Grabowski, Chicago; John Hartman, Detroit; Jonathan Hayt, Tampa Bay; J. Henson Photographics, Washington; The Ice Age, Toronto; George Kalinsky, NY Rangers; Deborah King, Washington; V.J. Lovero, Anaheim; Jim Mackey, Detroit; Doug MacLellan; McElligott-Teckles Sports Focus Imaging, Ottawa; Bill McKeown, Edmonton; Al Messerschmidt, Florida; Jack Murray, Vancouver; Tim Parker, St. Louis; Photography Ink, Los Angeles; Andre Pichette, Montreal and Quebec; Richard Pilling, New Jersey; Len Redkoles, Philadelphia; Wen Roberts, Los Angeles, Al Ruelle, Boston; Harry Scull, Jr., Buffalo; Don Smith, San Jose; Diane Sobolewski, Hartford; Gerry Thomas, Edmonton; Jim Turner, New Jersey; Brad Watson, Calgary; Westfile, Edmonton; Rocky Widner, San Jose; Bill Wippert, Buffalo.

Distribution

Canadian representatives:
North 49 Books, 193 Bartley Drive, Toronto, Ontario M4A 1E6
416/750-7777; FAX 416/750-2049
NHL Publishing, 194 Dovercourt Road, Toronto, Ontario M6J 3C8
416/531-6535; FAX 416/531-3939

U.S. representatives: Triumph Books,
644 South Clark Street, Chicago, Illinois 60605   312/939-3330; FAX 312/663-3557

International representatives: Barkers Worldwide Publications,
155 Maybury Road, Woking, Surrey, England GU21 5JR
Tel. and FAX: 011/44/483/776-141

Data Management and Typesetting: Caledon Data Management, Caledon, Ontario
Additional Typesetting: Moveable Type, Toronto, Ontario
Film Output and Process Camera: Stafford Graphics, Toronto, Ontario
Printing: Web Offset Publications Limited, Pickering, Ontario
Production Management: Dan Diamond and Associates, Inc., Toronto, Ontario

The National Hockey League
1251 Avenue of the Americas, 47th Floor, New York, New York 10020-1198
1800 McGill College Avenue, Suite 2600, Montreal, Quebec H3A 3J6
75 International Boulevard, Suite 300, Rexdale, Ontario M9W 6L9

Table of Contents

Introduction   **5**
NHL Directory   **6**
Referees and Linesmen   **8**

11 CLUBS   records, rosters, management

Mighty Ducks of Anaheim	11
Boston Bruins	15
Buffalo Sabres	19
Calgary Flames	23
Chicago Blackhawks	27
Dallas Stars	31
Detroit Red Wings	35
Edmonton Oilers	39
Florida Panthers	45
Hartford Whalers	47
Los Angeles Kings	51
Montreal Canadiens	55
New Jersey Devils	59
New York Islanders	63
New York Rangers	67
Ottawa Senators	71
Philadelphia Flyers	75
Pittsburgh Penguins	79
Quebec Nordiques	83
St. Louis Blues	87
San Jose Sharks	91
Tampa Bay Lightning	95
Toronto Maple Leafs	99
Vancouver Canucks	103
Washington Capitals	107
Winnipeg Jets	111

115 FINAL STATISTICS 1993-94

Standings	115
Individual Leaders	116
Rookie Leaders	117
Three-or-More Goal Games	118
Goaltending Leaders	119
Team Statistics	120
Penalty and Power-Play Statistics	121
Regular Season Overtime	122
Penalty Shots	122

Table of Contents *continued*

123 NHL RECORD BOOK

All-Time Standings of NHL Teams	123
Year-by-Year Final Standings and Leading Scorers	123
NHL History	136
Major Rule Changes	137
TEAM RECORDS	
Winning and Losing Streaks	139
Team Goaltending Records	140
Team Scoring Records	141
INDIVIDUAL RECORDS	**145**
WAYNE GRETZKY'S ALL-TIME GOAL-SCORING RECORD	**156**
Top 100 Scoring Leaders	158
All-Time Games Played Leaders	164
Goaltending Records	166
Coaching Records	168
One Season Scoring Records	172
Active Players' Three-or-More Goal Games	175
Rookie Scoring Records	176
50-Goal Seasons	177
100-Point Seasons	179
Five-or-more Goal Games	181
500th Goal, 1,000th Point	182
Trophies and Awards	**183**
AMATEUR AND ENTRY DRAFT	
First Selections	190
Summary by Player Sources	190
Detailed Draft Breakdown, OHL, WHL, QMJHL	191
Detailed Draft Breakdown, NCAA, High Schools	192
Detailed Draft Breakdown, International	193
Analysis by Origin, Position, Age	193
Notes on 1994 First Round Selections	195
1994 Entry Draft	196
First two rounds, 1993-69	198
NHL ALL-STARS	
All-Star Selection Records	202
All-Star Teams	203
All-Star Game Results	206
All-Star Game Records	207
HOCKEY HALL OF FAME	**210**

213 STANLEY CUP GUIDE & RECORD BOOK

1994 STANLEY CUP PLAYOFFS	
Results	213
Playoff Leaders	214
Team Statistics	215
STANLEY CUP RECORD BOOK	
Championship Trophy Winners	216
Stanley Cup Winners — rosters and final series scores	217
All-Time Playoff Format History	225
Playoff Records	226
Leading Playoff Scorers	237
Three-or-More-Goal Playoff Games	238
Leading Scorers and Playoff Standings, 1918-94	239
Overtime Games since 1918	240
Stanley Cup Coaching Records	243
Stanley Cup Penalty Shots, Longest Overtime Games	244

245 PLAYER REGISTER

Key to Player and Goaltender Registers	**245**
Late Additions	246
Year-by-year records of forwards and defensemen	247
Retired NHL Player Index	**397**

423 GOALTENDING REGISTER

Year-by-year records of goaltenders	423
Retired NHL Goaltender Index	**443**

446 1993-94 NHL PLAYER TRANSACTIONS

(1994-95 NHL Schedule begins inside front cover)

Introduction

WELCOME TO *THE NHL OFFICIAL GUIDE & RECORD BOOK FOR 1994-95.* Since 1984, when the *Guide* was first produced in its present large format, new features and other improvements have been added to each edition of the book, but in no instance have changes been as significant as those incorporated into this year's 448-page version.

The book's typeface and paper stock have both changed. The new typeface – Frutiger – gives the book a clean, open look and is easily read in the small sizes used in the Guide's tables. The new paper is 12% heavier and is more opaque, reducing show through.

The NHL's All-Time Standings now list the League's early franchises. Previously, these clubs weren't included, leaving the all-time standings chart incomplete. The expanded chart is found on page 123.

Wayne Gretzky's numerous milestone goals are listed on page 156. Gretzky surpassed Gordie Howe's longstanding NHL career mark of 801 goals on March 23, 1994, giving #99 a complete set of career scoring records. He now holds the all-time NHL records for goals, assists and points in both regular-season and playoff competition.

The NHL's Active Top 100 goal scorers, assist leaders and points scorers are listed on pages 159, 161 and 163. Each one of these new tables faces the corresponding All-Time Top 100 list, making for easy comparison.

An All-Time NHL Coaching Register is found on page 168. The regular-season record for every NHL coach from 1917 to 1994 is included.

Draft coverage – always one of the most-read sections of the *Guide* – is improved with the addition of a listing of those U.S. high schools and prep schools that have contributed 10-or-more players to the NHL Entry Draft. In addition, Major Junior clubs have been sorted to separate out those clubs no longer in operation.

The Guide & Record Book's Player and Goaltender Registers have been enhanced by the addition of NHL affiliation to each data panel. Affiliation is usually apparent for players already established in the NHL, but the situation for players signed as free agents or playing junior, college, minor-pro or European hockey can be less clear. This affiliation provides another way for users of the *Guide* to evaluate the depth of each organization's farm system. Affiliation information is current to August 19, 1994. As well, information provided by the NHL Broadcasters' Association has been used to add phonetic pronunciations of the names of more than 350 players. Player Register listings begin on page 245. The Goaltender Register begins on page 423. Late additions to the registers are found on page 246.

As always, our thanks to readers, correspondents and members of the media who take the time to comment on the *Guide & Record Book*. Thanks as well to the people working in the communications departments of the NHL's member clubs and to their counterparts in the AHL, IHL, ECHL, Central, Colonial and junior leagues as well as in college athletic conferences and European hockey federations.

Best wishes for an enjoyable 1994-95 NHL season.

ACCURACY REMAINS THE GUIDE & RECORD BOOK'S TOP PRIORITY.
We appreciate comments and clarification from our readers. Please direct these to:

Greg Inglis   1251 Avenue of the Americas, New York, New York 10020-1198 . . . or

David Keon   75 International Blvd., Suite 300, Rexdale, Ontario M9W 6L9.

Your involvement makes a better book.

NATIONAL HOCKEY LEAGUE
Established Novermber 22, 1917

Board of Governors

Mighty Ducks of Anaheim
Disney Sports Enterprises, Inc.
Michael D. Eisner......................................Governor
Tony Tavares............................Alternate Governor

Boston Bruins
Boston Professional Hockey Association, Inc.
Jeremy M. Jacobs................................. Governor
Louis Jacobs............................ Alternate Governor
Harry J. Sinden.......................Alternate Governor

Buffalo Sabres
Niagara Frontier Hockey, L.P.
Seymour H. Knox III...........................Governor
Seymour H. Knox, IV................Alternate Governor
Gerard M. Meehan....................Alternate Governor
John J. Rigas...........................Alternate Governor
Robert O. Swados.....................Alternate Governor

Calgary Flames
Calgary Flames Limited Partnership
Harley N. Hotchkiss................................Governor
William C. Hay.........................Alternate Governor
Byron J. Seaman......................Alternate Governor

Chicago Blackhawks
Chicago Blackhawks Hockey Team, Inc.
William W. Wirtz.................................. Governor
Gene Gozdecki.........................Alternate Governor
Thomas N. Ivan........................Alternate Governor
Robert J. Pulford......................Alternate Governor
Arthur M. Wirtz, Jr. ....Alternate Governor
W. Rockwell Wirtz....................Alternate Governor

Dallas Stars
Dallas Hockey Club, Inc.
Norman Green..Governor
John W. G. Donahue.................Alternate Governor
James R. Lites..........................Alternate Governor

Detroit Red Wings
Detroit Red Wings, Inc.
Michael Ilitch..Governor
Jay A. Bielfield.........................Alternate Governor
Jim Devellano..........................Alternate Governor
Atanas Ilitch...........................Alternate Governor
Christopher Ilitch......................Alternate Governor
John A. Ziegler, Jr. ....Alternate Governor

Edmonton Oilers
Edmonton Oilers Hockey Corp.
Peter Pocklington......................................Governor
Lorne J. Ruzicka......................Alternate Governor
Glen Sather.............................Alternate Governor

Florida Panthers
Florida Panthers Hockey Club, Ltd.
William A. Torrey.....................................Governor
Dean Jordan............................Alternate Governor

Hartford Whalers
KTR Hockey Limited Partnership
Peter Karmanos, Jr.....................................Governor
Jim Rutherford.........................Alternate Governor

Los Angeles Kings
LAK Acquisition Corp.
Bruce P. McNall.......................................Governor
Joe Cohen..............................Alternate Governor
Jeffrey Sudikoff........................Alternate Governor
Rogie Vachon..........................Alternate Governor

Montréal Canadiens
Le Club de Hockey Canadien, Inc.
Ronald L. Corey..Governor
A. Barry Joslin.........................Alternate Governor
Serge Savard...........................Alternate Governor

New Jersey Devils
Meadowlanders, Inc.
Dr. John J. McMullen...............................Governor
Louis A. Lamoriello....................Alternate Governor
Peter McMullen........................Alternate Governor

New York Islanders
New York Islanders Hockey Club, L.P.
Steve Walsh..Governor
John H. Krumpe.......................Alternate Governor
Don Maloney...........................Alternate Governor
Ralph F. Palleschi......................Alternate Governor
Robert Rosenthal......................Alternate Governor

New York Rangers
The New York Rangers Hockey Club
A Division of
Madison Square Garden Center, Inc.
Kenneth W. Munoz................................Governor
Robert M. Gutkowski...............Alternate Governor
Neil Smith...............................Alternate Governor

Ottawa Senators
Ottawa Senators Hockey Club
Limited Partnership
Roderick M. Bryden...............................Governor
Bernard J. Ashe.......................Alternate Governor
Cyril Leeder............................Alternate Governor
Randy J. Sexton.......................Alternate Governor

Philadelphia Flyers
Philadelphia Flyers Limited Partnership
Edward M. Snider..................................Governor
Bob Clarke.............................Alternate Governor
Ronald K. Ryan........................Alternate Governor
Jay T. Snider...........................Alternate Governor

Pittsburgh Penguins
Pittsburgh Hockey Associates
Howard L. Baldwin................................Governor
Morris Belzberg.......................Alternate Governor
John H. Kelley..........................Alternate Governor
Roy Mlakar.............................Alternate Governor
Craig Patrick...........................Alternate Governor
Thomas V. Ruta.......................Alternate Governor

Québec Nordiques
Le Club de Hockey les Nordiques
Societe en Commandite
Marcel Aubut.. Governor
Pierre Lacroix..........................Alternate Governor
Sherwood Bassin......................Alternate Governor

St. Louis Blues
Kiel Center Partners, L.P.
Michael F. Shanahan...............................Governor
Ron Caron..............................Alternate Governor
Thomas J. Guilfoil....................Alternate Governor
Jack Quinn..............................Alternate Governor

San Jose Sharks
San Jose Sharks Corp.
George Gund III...................................... Governor
Gordon Gund..........................Alternate Governor
Irvin A. Leonard.......................Alternate Governor
Arthur L. Savage......................Alternate Governor

Tampa Bay Lightning
Lightning Partners, Inc.
David E. LeFevre......................................Governor
Phil Esposito...........................Alternate Governor
Mel Lowell..............................Alternate Governor

Toronto Maple Leafs
Maple Leaf Gardens Ltd.
Steve A. Stavro...................................... Governor
Brian P. Bellmore.....................Alternate Governor
Cliff Fletcher...........................Alternate Governor

Vancouver Canucks
Vancouver Hockey Club Ltd.
Arthur R. Griffiths....................................Governor
Frank W. Griffiths....................Alternate Governor
George McPhee........................Alternate Governor
J. B. Patrick Quinn...................Alternate Governor

Washington Capitals
Washington Hockey Limited Partnership
Richard M. Patrick...................................Governor
Abe Pollin..............................Alternate Governor
Peter O'Malley........................ Alternate Governor
David Osnos............................Alternate Governor
David R. Poile.........................Alternate Governor

Winnipeg Jets
Jets Hockey Ventures
(A Limited Partnership)
Barry L. Shenkarow................................Governor
Bill Davis...............................Alternate Governor

League Offices

New York	**Montreal**	**Toronto**
1251 Avenue of the Americas	1800 McGill College Avenue	75 International Blvd.
47th Floor	Suite 2600	Suite 300
New York, NY 10020-1198	Montreal, Quebec H3A 3J6	Rexdale, Ontario M9W 6L9
(212) 789-2000	(514) 288-9220	(416) 798-0809
Fax: (212) 789-2020	Fax: (514) 284-0300	Fax: (416) 798-0819

National Hockey League Staff Directory

Commissioner...Gary B. Bettman
Senior VP and Chief Operating Officer.....................................Stephen J. Solomon
Senior VP and General Counsel.....................................Jeffrey Pash
Senior VP and Director of Hockey Operations.....................Brian P. Burke
VP Hockey Operations (Toronto).....................................Jim Gregory
VP Public Relations.....................................Arthur Pincus
VP Corporate Communications.....................................Bernadette Mansur
VP Broadcasting.....................................Glenn Adamo
VP Television and Team Services.....................Ellis T. "Skip" Prince III
VP and Chief Financial Officer.....................................John Huston
VP Event Marketing.....................................Frank Supovitz
Director of Security.....................................Dennis Cunningham
Associate General Counsel.....................................David Zimmerman
Executive Assistant to the Commissioner.....................Debbie Walsh

Administration

Director (Montreal).....................................Phil Scheuer
Director.....................................Janet A. Meyers
Assistant Director (Montreal).....................................Steve Hatzepetros

Broadcasting

VP Broadcasting.....................................Glenn Adamo
Manager, Broadcasting.....................................Ward Glassmeyer
Manager, Video Services, NHL Productions ....Mott Linn
Analyst, Broadcast Research.....................................Samuel Esposito, Jr.

Corporate Communications

VP Corporate Communications.....................................Bernadette Mansur
Director, Corporate Communications.....................................Mary Pat Clarke
Director, Special Projects.....................................John Halligan
Director, Creative Services.....................................David F. Haney

Event Marketing / Special Events

VP Special Events.....................................Frank Supovitz
Director, Special Events.....................................Lori Boesch
Director, Event Marketing.....................................Karen Hovsepian
Manager, Event Marketing.....................................Patricia L. Conrad
Manager, Special Events.....................................Ann Collette Devney
Manager, Special Events.....................................Anne I. Grotefeld
Manager, Special Events.....................................Michael Santos
Manager, Special Events.....................................Maria Sutherland

Finance

VP and Chief Financial Officer.....................................John Huston
Controller (Montreal).....................................Joseph DeSousa
Controller.....................................Phil Litwinoff
Assistant Controller (Montreal).....................................Olivia Pietrantonio
Assistant Controller.....................................Patricia Cooper
Accounting Supervisor (Montreal).....................................Donna Gillman

Hockey Operations

Senior VP and Director of Hockey Operations.....................Brian P. Burke
Vice President, Hockey Operations (Toronto).....................Jim Gregory
Director, Central Registry (Montreal).....................................Garry Lovegrove
Assistant Director, Central Registry (Montreal).....................Madeleine Supino
Director of Central Scouting (Toronto).....................................Frank Bonello
Director of Officiating (Toronto).....................................Bryan Lewis
Assistant Director of Officiating (Toronto).....................................Wally Harris
NHL Officiating Coach.....................................Dave Newell
Hockey Operations Coordinator.....................................David Nonis
Consultant (Montreal).....................................Brian F. O'Neill

Information Systems

Director (Montreal).....................................Mario Carangi
Assistant Director (Montreal).....................................Luc Coulombe

Pension

Director (Montreal).....................................Yvon Chamberland
Controller, Pension (Montreal).....................................Mary Skiadopoulos
Manager, Pension (Montreal).....................................Lise DeJocas

Public Relations

VP Public Relations.....................................Arthur Pincus
Director, Public Relations (Toronto).....................................Gary Meagher
Chief Statistician (Toronto).....................................Benny Ercolani
Manager, Media Relations.....................................Susan Aglietti
Manager, News Services.....................................Greg Inglis
Manager, Public Relations and News Services.....................Andrew McGowan
Public Relations Assistant (Toronto).....................................David Keon

Security

Director.....................................Dennis Cunningham

Television and Team Services

VP Television and Team Services.....................Ellis T. "Skip" Prince III
Director, New Business Development.....................................Bryant S. McBride

NHL Enterprises, Inc.

New York	**Toronto**
1251 Avenue of the Americas	75 International Blvd.
47th Floor	Suite 301
New York, NY 10020-1198	Rexdale, Ontario M9W 6L9
(212) 789-2000	(416) 798-9388
Fax: (212) 789-2020	Fax: (416) 798-9395

Senior VP and Chief Operating Officer.....................................Rick Dudley
Senior Assistant.....................................Bonnie Harner

Corporate Marketing

VP Corporate Marketing.....................................Ed Horne
Director, Corporate Marketing.....................................Dina Gilbertie
Director, Corporate Marketing (Toronto).....................................Paul McLaren
Marketing Manager.....................................Jim Haskins

Fan Development

Director.....................................Ken Yaffe
Manager.....................................Alysse Soll

Finance

Controller, Retail Licensing.....................................Mary C. McCarthy
Assistant Controller, Marketing.....................................Donna MacPhee
Assistant Controller, Corporate.....................................Pamela Weiner
Manager, Accounts Payable.....................................Evelyn Torres
Manager, Information Systems.....................................John Ho

Legal

Senior VP and General Counsel.....................................Richard Zahnd
Associate General Counsel.....................................Adam Helfant
Staff Attorney.....................................Leslie Gittess

Legal,
continued

Director, Licensing and Trademark Compliance.....................Ruth Gruhin
Manager of Contract Administration.....................................Heather Bell

Retail Licensing

VP Licensing.....................................Fred Scalera
Director, Apparel Licensing.....................................Brian Jennings
Director, Children's Licensing.....................................Tina Ellis
Director, Collectibles and Trading Card Licensing.....................Ilene Kent
Director, Licensing and Trademark Compliance.....................Ruth Gruhin
Director, Non-Apparel Licensing.....................................Judith Salsberg
Managing Director, Canadian Licensing (Toronto).....................Bob McLaughlin
National Sales Manager.....................................Bill Tighe
Sales Manager, Mid-Western Region.....................................Christopher Agnew
Sales Manager, Western Region.....................................Mark Cordon
Sales Manager, Eastern Region.....................................Brendan P. McQuillan

International Licensing

Manager.....................................Brad Kwong

Publishing

General Manager.....................................Michael Berger

Commissioner and League Presidents

Gary B. Bettman

Gary B. Bettman took office as the NHL's first Commissioner on February 1, 1993. Since the League was formed in 1917, there have been five League Presidents.

NHL President	Years in office
Frank Calder	1917 to 1943
Mervyn "Red" Dutton	1943 to 1946
Clarence Campbell	1946 to 1977
John A. Ziegler, Jr.	1977 to 1992
Gil Stein	1992 to 1993

NHL Enterprises Canada, Inc.
75 International Blvd. Suite 301
Rexdale, Ont. M9W 6L9
Phone: 416/798-9388
FAX: 416/798-9395

Bob McLaughlin – Managing Director
Paul McLaren – Director, Corporate Sponsorship
Karen Hanson – Licensing Manager, Apparel
Fiona Hastie – Licensing Manager, Collectibles
Barry Monaghan – Retail Merchandising Manager

NHL Enterprises B.V.
Polakweg 14
2288 GG Rijswijk
Nederland
Phone: 31-(0)70-390-7797
FAX: 31-(0)70-390-7625

Stephen J. Solomon – Director
Richard Zahnd – Director
Cyril Speijer – Director

Hockey Hall of Fame
BCE Place
30 Yonge Street
Toronto, Ont. M5E 1X8
Phone: 416/360-7735
FAX: 416/360-1501

Ian "Scotty" Morrison – Chairman
David Taylor – President
Phil Denyes – Vice President, Marketing
Jeff Denomme – Vice President, Finance/Treasurer
Ray Paquet – Manager, Facility Systems & Exhibit
    Development
Philip Pritchard – Manager, Resource Centre &
    Acquisitions
Ron Ellis – Education and Group Program Co-ordinator
Sue Bolender – Manager, Facility Sales
Scott North – Manager, Special Events
Christine Simpson – Marketing Manager
Bryan McDermott – Retail and Merchandise Manager

National Hockey League Players' Association
One Dundas Street West
Suite 2300
Toronto, Ontario
M5G 1Z3
Phone: 416/408-4040
FAX: 416/408-3685

Bob Goodenow – Executive Director, General Counsel
Ted Saskin – Senior Director, Business Affairs & Licensing
Barbara Larcina – Director of Benefits &
    Business Administration
Ian Pulver – Associate Counsel
Chris Malone – Director of Licensing Operations
Steve McAllister – Manager, Media Relations
Bruce Newton – Manager, Special Projects

Referees and Linesmen

BLAINE ANGUS . . . Referee . . . Born: Sept. 25, 1961 in Shawville, Que. . . . Hired by the NHL in 1991, Angus worked his first NHL game Oct. 17, 1992. Total NHL games: 15 . . . enjoys golf, running and carpentry in the off-season . . . is a registered x-ray technologist . . . resides in Barrie, Ontario with his wife and three children.

RON ASSELSTINE . . . Linesman . . . Born: Nov. 6, 1946 in Toronto, Ont. . . . First NHL game: Oct. 10, 1979 . . . Total NHL games: 1,175 . . . Worked 1,000th NHL game on January 4, 1992 at New Jersey. Ron is very active in his community as chairman of the "Make-A-Wish" Foundation. He was the recipient of the Prime Minister's Commendation and was awarded the "Golden Whistle" Award in 1994. He is married and has two children.

WAYNE BONNEY . . . Linesman . . . Born: May 27, 1953 in Ottawa, Ont. . . . First NHL game: Oct. 10, 1979 . . . Total NHL games: 1,073 . . . Joined the NHL in 1979. Bonney worked the 1989 All-Star Game in Edmonton and the Stanley Cup championship series in 1990, 1991 and 1993. He missed the entire 1993-94 season due to an injury. He currently resides in Redwood, WA., with his wife and daughter. He is an avid baseball player.

GORD BROSEKER . . . Linesman . . . Born: July 8, 1950 in Baltimore, MD . . . First NHL game: Jan 14, 1975 . . . Total NHL games: 1,407 . . . Joined the NHL in 1973 and officiated in his 1,250th NHL game in 1991-92. Before beginning his officiating career, he played baseball in the Texas Rangers' organization. Broseker was selected to officiate in the 1991 Stanley Cup championship series and the 1994 All-Star Game. He currently resides in Richmond, VA, with his wife and daughter.

PIERRE CHAMPOUX . . . Linesman . . . Born: Apr. 18, 1963 in Ville St. Pierre, Que. . . . First NHL game: Oct. 8, 1988 . . . Total NHL games: 385 . . . Began officiating minor league games at the age of 12 in the Quebec pee wee league. Since then he has worked in two international competitions, having officiated in an exhibition game between the United States and Canada at the Forum and in Canada Cup 1987. During the off-season, Champoux enjoys golf, tennis and cycling. Champoux is single.

KEVIN COLLINS . . . Linesman . . . Born: Dec. 15,1950 in Springfield, MA . . . First NHL game: Oct. 13, 1977 . . . Total NHL games: 1,348 . . . Joined the NHL in 1977. He was selected to officiate in the 1993 NHL All-Star Game and officiated in the 1993 Stanley Cup finals. He also worked Game Seven of the 1994 Stanley Cup Finals. Currently residing in Springfield, MA, Collins is married and has three children.

MICHAEL CVIK . . . Linesman . . . Born: July 6, 1962 in Calgary, Alta. . . . First NHL game: Oct. 8, 1987 . . . Total NHL games: 465 . . . The tallest of the officials at 6'9", began his officiating career in the AAHA in 1978. After working his way through the WHL, he joined the NHL in 1987. During the off-season, Mike is an instructor at the WHL School of Officiating. He volunteers for S.T.A.R.S. — a medical helicopter for trauma patients. Sells real estate in the off-season. He enjoys weightlifting, cycling, music, reading, yoga and golf. He is single.

PAT DAPUZZO . . . Linesman . . . Born: Dec. 29, 1958 in Hoboken, NJ . . . First NHL game: Dec. 5, 1984 . . . Total NHL games: 718 . . . Officiated in his first NHL game on Dec. 5, 1984, in Madison Square Garden. He worked six games in the 1991 Canada Cup and the 1994 All-Star Game. Pat resides in North Bergen, NJ. He is married and has one child. He is an avid weightlifter and karate enthusiast.

BERNARD DEGRACE . . . Referee . . . Born: May 1, 1967 in Lameque, N.B. . . . First NHL game: Oct. 15, 1991 . . . Total NHL games: 157 . . . Began his career as a linesman. Worked the 1992 Calder Cup Finals . . . During the off-season he enjoys golf, tennis and waterskiing . . . He is single.

GREG DEVORSKI . . . Linesman . . . Born: Aug. 3, 1969 in Guelph, Ont . . . First NHL game: Oct. 9, 1993 . . . Total NHL games: 54 . . . Worked 1993 Memorial Cup and CIAU finals . . . Worked in AHL in 1993 . . . Continuing his education in the off-season. Enjoys swimming and hiking. He is married.

PAUL DEVORSKI . . . Referee . . . Born: Aug. 18, 1958 in Guelph, Ont. . . . First NHL game: Oct. 14, 1989 . . . Total NHL games: 210 . . . Joined the NHL in 1987 . . . Total NHL games: 145 . . . Devorski enjoys golf and mountain biking. He is single.

SCOTT DRISCOLL . . . Linesman . . . Born: May 2, 1968 in Seaforth, Ont. . . . Hired by the NHL in 1991 . . . Began refereeing minor hockey at the age of 13 . . . First NHL game: Oct. 10, 1992 . . . Total NHL games: 118 . . . Worked 1993 AHL finals . . . Enjoys playing several sports in the off-season . . . He is married.

MARK FAUCETTE . . . Referee . . . Born: June 9, 1958 in Springfield, MA . . . Now resides in Largo, FL . . . First NHL game: 1985 . . . Total NHL games: 335 . . . Joined the NHL in 1985. First playoff game was 6-5 overtime win by Los Angeles over Vancouver in 1991. Enjoys boating. He is single.

RON FINN . . . Linesman . . . Born: Dec. 1, 1940 in Toronto, Ont. . . . First NHL game: October 11, 1969 . . . Total NHL games: 1,893 . . . Has worked in more games than any other active official. . . . A resident of Brampton, Ont. He has worked in two All-Star Games including 1977 (Vancouver) and 1982 (Washington, D.C.). He also worked during Rendez-Vous '87 in Quebec City. Finn set an NHL playoff record for officials by working in his 252nd career playoff game on April 23, 1991 and holds the record for regular season games by an official (1,893). He is an instructor at various officiating schools in Ontario. Ron is married and has four children.

KERRY FRASER . . . Referee . . . Born: May 30, 1952 in Sarnia, Ont. . . . Total NHL games: 886 . . . After playing minor league hockey as a youngster, attended the NHL training camp for officials in 1972. Fraser has become one of the League's most experienced and respected referees, as proven by his selection to referee five Stanley Cup championship series (1985, 1986, 1989-91). During the off-season, Fraser assists in numerous charitable fundraisers, does Public relations work for a financial institution and works with amateur hockey officials' groups. Fraser enjoys sailing and golf. He is married and has seven children.

GERARD GAUTHIER . . . Linesman . . . Born: Sept. 5, 1948 in Montreal, Que. . . . First NHL game: Oct. 16, 1971 . . . Total NHL games: 1,743 . . . Attended his first NHL training camp in 1971 after two years in junior hockey. He has been selected to work at two NHL All-Star Games in his career; Los Angeles (1981) and Calgary (1985). In addition, he has worked in the 1984 Canada Cup and in four Stanley Cup Championship series. On January 25, 1991, Gauthier became the fifth linesman in NHL history to reach 1,500 career games. During the off-season, Gauthier enjoys golfing and tennis. He is married and has two children.

TERRY GREGSON . . . Referee . . . Born: Nov. 7 1953 in Guelph, Ont. . . . Now resides in Erin, Ont. . . . First NHL game: Dec. 19, 1981 . . . Total NHL games: 753 . . . Joined the NHL in 1979. Gregson was selected to officiate his second career All-Star Game in 1991 at Chicago. Worked the 1992 and 1993 Stanley Cup Championship as well as Game Seven of the 1994 Stanley Cup Final. President of the National Hockey League Officials' Association, Gregson also organizes the NHLOA's Golf Classic for the Children's Wish Foundation. During the off-season he is an avid traveller. Gregson is married.

CONRAD HACHÉ . . . Linesman . . . Born: May 15, 1972 in Sudbury Ont. . . . now resides in Oakville, Ont. . . . Began officiating at age 13. Has worked in the OHL since 1991, including the 1994 playoffs. He is currently completing a business degree from Laurentian University. In the off-season he enjoys softball, squash and in-line skating. He is single.

DON HENDERSON . . . Linesman . . . Born: Sept. 23, 1968 in Calgary, Alta. . . . Has worked the Mac's Tournament Final, as well as the WHL Playoffs. Operates a hockey school with his brother. Enjoys golf, carpentry, and working on cars. He is single.

SHANE HEYER . . . Linesman . . . Born: Feb. 7,1964 in Summerland, B.C. . . . First NHL game: Oct. 5, 1988 . . . Total NHL games: 435 . . . Began officiating in Penticton, B.C., at the age of 10 and was invited to join the NHL program in 1988. In his first year of service, Heyer was selected to work in the December 31 game between the Los Angeles Kings and the Dynamo Riga club during Super Series '88-89. Heyer is single and enjoys softball, tennis and golf.

BOB HODGES . . . Linesman . . . Born: Aug. 16, 1944 in Hespeler, Ont. . . . First NHL game: Oct. 14, 1972 . . . Total NHL games: 1,535 . . . Hired by the NHL in 1972-73 season at the age of 28, Hodges is one of the NHL's senior officials. He has been chosen to work in the Stanley Cup Finals three times (1982, 1986 and 1987) and officiated at the All-Star Game in Calgary (1985) and Pittsburgh (1990). He worked his 1,500th regular season game on Dec. 15, 1993. During the off-season he works with various charities and enjoys gardening, hunting, fishing and golf. Hodges is married and has two children.

DAVE JACKSON . . . Referee . . . Born: Nov. 28, 1964 in Montreal, Que. . . . Total NHL games: 83 . . . One of two officials to join the NHL in 1989, he was an NHL trainee at the age of 21. He made his first NHL appearance in the 1990-91 season. Worked Calder Cup finals in 1993. During the off-season, he enjoys golf, softball, biking, carpentry, reading and cooking. Jackson is married and has one child.

GREG KIMMERLY . . . Referee . . . Born: Dec. 8, 1964 in North York, Ont . . . Began officiating at age 16 . . . NHL trainee since 1990 . . . Ten years experience in minor hockey . . . Three years experience in OHL . . . He worked the 1994 Calder Cup and Turner Cup Playoffs. He is married and has one daughter.

SWEDE KNOX . . . Linesman . . . Born: Mar. 2, 1948 in Edmonton, Alta. . . . First NHL game: Oct. 14, 1972 . . . Total NHL games: 1,695 . . . Joined the NHL in 1971. In 1982, he was selected to work in the NHL All-Star Game in Washington, D.C. He has also worked in five Stanley Cup championship series. Worked his 1,500th game October 26, 1991. A full-time resident of Edmonton, Swede is married and has two children. He enjoys squash and golf during the off-season.

DON KOHARSKI . . . Referee . . . Born: Dec. 2, 1955 in Halifax, N.S. . . . Now resides in St. Louis, MO . . . First NHL game: Oct. 14, 1977 . . . Total NHL games: 881 (163 as a linesman) . . . Hired as an official in the WHA at the age of 18. He joined the NHL in 1977 as a linesman, becoming a referee after 163 games. Koharski gained international experience in Canada Cup 1987 and has worked in six Stanley Cup Finals (1986-88, 1990-92). He refereed his first NHL All-Star Game in 1992. He is married and has two sons.

DENNIS LaRUE . . . Referee . . . Born: July 14, 1959 in Savannah, GA . . . Total NHL games: 37 . . . Attended the USA Hockey Referee Development Camp in 1983 and joined the NHL in 1988. He made his NHL debut on March 26, 1991. During the off-season he is a youth baseball coach and an instructor at the USA Hockey Referee Development Camp. He is an avid golfer. Dennis is married and has two children.

BRAD LAZAROWICH . . . Linesman . . . Born: Aug. 4, 1962 in Vancouver, B.C. . . . First NHL game: Oct. 9, 1986 . . . Total NHL games: 574 . . . Joined the NHL in 1986. Worked his 500th NHL game in March, 1993. During the off-season, studies business management and is an instructor at an officiating school. He is an avid bicyclist, golfer and weightlifter. He is married and has two children.

DAN MAROUELLI . . . Referee . . . Born: July 16, 1955 in Edmonton, Alta. . . . First NHL game: Nov. 2, 1984 . . . Total NHL games: 604 . . . Began his officiating career at the age of 13 with the Knights of Columbus. He joined the NHL in 1982. During the summer, Marouelli works at a number of refereeing schools and owns a small construction business in addition to participating in many charity fundraising events. He is an avid golfer. Dan is married and has three children.

ROB MARTELL . . . Referee . . . Born: October 21, 1963 in Winnipeg, Man. . . . First NHL game: Mar. 14, 1984 . . . Began officiating minor hockey at the age of 14 . . . Off-season he works in a landscaping business and drives tractor trailers . . . Enjoys golf, biking and summer hockey . . . He is married.

DAN McCOURT . . . Linesman . . . Born: Aug. 14, 1954 in Falconbridge, Ont. . . . First NHL game: Dec. 27, 1980 . . . Total NHL games: 950 . . . Joined the NHL in 1979. . . . Worked the 1990 All-Star Game in Pittsburgh. During the off-season, he works with the Easter Seals Society. He enjoys golf, baseball, boating and waterskiing. McCourt is married and has two daughters.

BILL McCREARY . . . Referee . . . Born: Nov. 17, 1955 in Guelph, Ont. . . . First NHL game: Nov. 3, 1984 . . . Total NHL games: 624 . . . Joined the NHL in 1982. He was selected to referee in the 1991 Canada Cup and the 1994 All-Star Game. During the off-season also enjoys golfing and fishing. He is married and has two sons and a daughter.

ANDY McELMAN . . . Linesman . . . Born: Feb. 24, 1961 in Chicago Heights, IL . . . First NHL game: Oct. 7, 1993 . . . Total NHL games: 60 . . . Graduate of USA Hockey Officiating Program . . . Worked two U.S. National Junior Championships, one IIHF World Junior Championship . . . Also worked IHL All-Star Game in Atlanta . . . Designs printed circuit boards in the off-season . . . Plays volleyball, ball hockey. He is married and has a son.

MIKE McGEOUGH . . . Referee . . . Born: June 20, 1957 in Regina, Sask. . . . First NHL game: Jan. 15, 1989 . . . Total NHL games: 211 . . . Began his NHL career in 1987. During the off-season, McGeough enjoys golf and horseback riding. He instructs at various refereeing schools. He is married and has three children.

RANDY MITTON . . . Linesman . . . Born: Sept. 22, 1950 in Fredericton, N.B. . . . First NHL game: Dec. 26, 1973 . . . Total NHL games: 1,497 . . . Became involved in NHL officiating in 1972 after working in the WHL and AHL for two years. He gained international experience as a linesman for the 1987 Canada Cup and was selected to officiate in the 1988 NHL All-Star Game in St. Louis. During the off-season, Mitton teaches at a number of officiating schools in Western Canada. He is married and has two children.

JEAN MORIN . . . Linesman . . . Born: August 10, 1963 in Sorel, Que. . . . First NHL game: Oct. 5, 1991 . . . Total NHL games: 168. Worked three games during the 1991-92 series between the U.S. or Canadian National Team and NHL teams . . . Enjoys golf, reading, softball and volleyball . . . He is married and has one child.

BRIAN MURPHY . . . Linesman . . . Born: Dec. 13, 1964 in Dover, NH . . . First NHL game: Oct. 7, 1988 . . . Total NHL games: 394 . . . Joined the League in 1988-89 after graduating from the University of New Hampshire with a degree in Business Administration. During his years at University, he worked in the NCAA officiating ranks, including the 1988 NCAA Division I National Championship Game in Lake Placid. During the off-season, Murphy enjoys golf and landscaping. Murphy is married and has one child.

THOR NELSON . . . Linesman . . . Born: Jan. 6, 1968 in Westminister, CA . . . now resides in Minot, ND . . . Has worked for USA Hockey since 1990, including two national championships. Also worked the Gold Medal game of the 1994 U.S. Olympic Festival. In the off-season, he works in a construction materials testing laboratory. He also enjoys golf, hiking and biking. He is married.

TIM NOWAK . . . Linesman . . . Born: Sept. 6, 1967 in Buffalo, N.Y. . . . First NHL game: Oct. 8, 1993 . . . Total NHL games: 48 . . . On-ice official since age 12 . . . Four years in AHL semi-finals . . . He worked the 1994 Turner Cup (IHL) Finals . . . In the off-season he is an instructor for USA Hockey's referee development program. He enjoys golf and collecting sports cards. He is single.

DAN O'HALLORAN . . . Referee . . . Born: March 25, 1964 at Leamington, Ont. . . . Worked the 1992 IHL All-Star Game, the 1992 Turner Cup (IHL) Finals and the 1994 Calder Cup (AHL) Finals . . . Enjoys carpentry, golf and cooking . . . He is married and has one child.

MARK PARE . . . Linesman . . . Born: July 26, 1957 in Windsor, Ont. . . . First NHL Game: Oct. 11, 1979 . . . Total NHL games: 1,146 . . . Joined the NHL in 1979 after working minor leagues in Windsor. Pare worked his 1,000th game in 1991-92. He made his NHL All-Star Game debut in 1992. He enjoys golfing. Pare is married and has three children.

BARON PARKER . . . Linesman . . . Born: March 5, 1967 in Vancouver, B.C. . . . Began officiating minor hockey at age 12 . . . Worked in the WHL playoffs in 1993 and 1994. Enjoys playing several sports during the off-season. He is married.

STÉPHANE PROVOST . . . Linesman . . . Born: May 5, 1967 in Montreal, Que. . . . Worked in the Memorial Cup and the AHL Playoffs in 1994. Also worked in the QMJHL and the CHL All-Star Game in 1992-93. In the off-season he is a part-time firefighter. He also enjoys golf and softball. He is single.

PIERRE RACICOT . . . Linesman . . . Born: Feb. 15, 1967 in Verdun, Que . . . First NHL game: Oct. 12, 1993 . . . Total NHL games: 54 . . . On-ice official since age 14 . . . Worked QMJHL finals in 1992 and 1993 and CIAU finals in 1993 . . . Works with young offenders in the off-season . . . Hobbies include softball, golf and computers . . . He is single.

LANCE ROBERTS . . . Referee . . . Born: May 28, 1957 in Edmonton, Alta. . . . First NHL game: Nov. 3, 1989 . . . Total NHL games: 110 . . . Began his career at the age of 15 in the minor leagues of Alberta. Worked AHL finals in 1992 and 1993. Roberts takes business courses during the summer and works in real estate. He is married with three daughters and enjoys golf and baseball.

RAY SCAPINELLO . . . Linesman . . . Born: Nov. 5, 1946 in Guelph, Ont. . . . First NHL Game in 1971 in Buffalo . . . Total NHL games: 1,831 . . . Joined NHL in 1971 . . . Has worked three All-Star Games, 13 consecutive Stanley Cup Finals plus the Canada Cup, Challenge Cup and Rendez-Vous 87 . . . He worked Game 7 of the 1994 Stanley Cup Final . . . In the off-season, Ray is a two-handicap golfer and works with the "Make-A-Wish" chapter in Guelph . . . He is married and has a son.

DAN SCHACHTE . . . Linesman . . . Born: July 13, 1958 in Madison, WI . . . First NHL game: October 8, 1982 . . . Total NHL games: 876 . . . Joined the NHL in 1982. He was chosen to officiate in the 1991 All-Star Game in Chicago. Also worked in the 1991 Canada Cup. He enjoys hunting, fishing and boating. He is married and has three children.

LYLE SEITZ . . . Referee . . . Born: Jan. 22, 1969 in Brooks, Alta. . . . Began officiating minor hockey at the age of 9 . . . Began his NHL career as a linesman . . . First NHL game: Oct. 6, 1992 . . . Total NHL games: 102 . . . Worked AHL finals, 1993 . . . Worked the 1991 WHL All-Star Game and the 1992 Memorial Cup Finals . . . Off-season activities include cattle and grain farming . . . Enjoys racquet sports, golf, cycling and weightlifting. He is single.

JAY SHARRERS . . . Linesman . . . Born: July 3, 1967 in New Westminster, B.C. . . . Joined the NHL in 1990 . . . First NHL game: Oct. 6, 1990 . . . Total NHL games: 244 . . . Has also worked Canadian college games and, in 1985-86, a tournament involving college teams from the U.S., Canada and Japan . . . Teaches at an officiating school. Enjoys camping, fishing, baseball and golf. He is single.

ROB SHICK . . . Referee . . . Born: Dec. 4, 1957, in Port Alberni, B.C. . . . First NHL game: Apr. 6, 1986 . . . Total NHL games: 441 . . . Joined the NHL in 1984. He is married. Instructs at a referees' school in the off-season . . . Runs a charity golf tournament in Port Alberni for the Children's Hospital. Enjoys golf, fishing and travelling.

PAUL STEWART . . . Referee . . . Born: Mar. 21, 1955 in Boston, MA . . . First NHL game: Mar. 27, 1987 . . . Total NHL games: 454 . . . Joined the NHL in 1985. Worked 1987 and 1991 Canada Cup. Stewart is the only former NHL player on the active officiating staff. During the off-season, Stewart is involved in a clothing company and assists several charities. Stewart is single and enjoys model trains, World War II history and golf.

LEON STICKLE . . . Linesman . . . Born: Apr. 20, 1948 in Toronto, Ont. . . . First NHL game: Oct. 17, 1970 . . . Total NHL games: 1,786 . . . Joined the NHL in 1969 after four years in the minor leagues. In his career, he has worked in three NHL All-Star Games (Montreal, 1975; Buffalo,1978 and Long Island, 1983). He also was selected as an official for the Canada Cup tournament in 1981 and 1984. He has worked in the Stanley Cup Finals six times (1977, 1978, 1980, 1981, 1984 and 1985). During the off-season, Stickle is active with the Ontario and Canadian Special Olympics, hosting a summer golf tournament. He is married and has three children.

RICHARD TROTTIER . . . Referee . . . Born: Feb. 28, 1957 in Laval, Que. . . . First NHL game: Dec 13, 1989 . . . Total NHL games: 122 . . . During his career, he has served as the executive vice-president for the Quebec Esso Cup in 1987-88 and 1988-89 and has been the referee-in-chief for the Quebec Ice Hockey Federation since 1986. He has worked CIAU, Memorial Cup and World Junior tournaments. During the off-season, he enjoys golf.

ANDY Van HELLEMOND . . . Referee . . . Born: Feb. 16, 1948 in Winnipeg, Man. . . . First NHL game: Nov. 22, 1972 . . . Total NHL games: 1,373 . . . Joined the NHL in 1971 and has become one of the senior NHL officials. He worked in two NHL All-Star Games and in Rendez-Vous '87 in Quebec City. He has been selected to work in the Stanley Cup Final series 17 consecutive years since 1977. During the off-season, vanHellemond enjoys hiking, gardening and horseback riding.

DON VAN MASSENHOVEN . . . Referee . . . Born: July 17, 1960 in London, Ont. . . . First NHL game: Nov. 11, 1993 . . . Total NHL games: 13 . . . Began officiating at the age of 15 . . . Worked the 1990 Memorial Cup Final in Hamilton. Also worked OHL finals 1991 and 1992. Is a police officer in the off-season. He is married and has two children. Coaches minor baseball in off-season.

MARK VINES . . . Linesman . . . Born: Dec. 3, 1960 in Elmira, Ont. . . . First NHL game: Oct. 13, 1984 . . . Total NHL games: 780 . . . Joined the NHL in 1984. Worked the 1991 Canada Cup and at the 1992 NHL All-Star game in Philadelphia. Involved with Tim Horton Memorial Children's Foundation and Core Literacy in Kitchener. He attends university during the off-season and is single.

STEPHEN WALKOM . . . Referee . . . Born: Aug. 8, 1963 in North Bay, Ontario. . . . First NHL game: Oct. 18, 1992 . . . Total NHL games: 20 . . . Has also worked OHL, minor pro, Canadian college, Northern OHA, senior and junior B . . . Honors degree in Commerce from Laurentian U . . . Lives in Kitchener, Ont. . . . Enjoys running, cycling, racquet sports and sailing . . . Power-skating instructor. He is married with one daughter.

BRAD WATSON . . . Referee . . . Born: Oct. 4, 1961 in Regina, Sask . . . Now resides in Westfield, MA . . . First NHL game: Feb. 5, 1994 . . . Officiated junior hockey since 1984 . . . Worked 1989 IIHF World Junior Championships, 1991 Izvestia Tournament, 1991 Canada Cup exhibition game and 1992 Spengler Cup . . . He is married.

MARK WHELER . . . Linesman . . . Born: Sept. 20, 1965 in North Battleford, Sask. . . . First NHL game: Oct. 10, 1992 . . . Total NHL games: 134 . . . Began officiating at the age of 12. Worked the 1989 and 1992 Memorial Cup Finals. He works as an instructor at the WHL's officiating schools. Has Bachelor of Commerce degree. Enjoys playing golf, cycling and other outdoor activities. He is married and has one son.

SCOTT ZELKIN . . . Referee . . . Born: Sept. 12, 1968, in Wilmette, IL . . . Now resides in Boston, MA . . . Began officiating minor hockey at age 12. Has worked in the NCAA Finals (1990), the IIHF World Championship (1991), and the IHL All-Star Game (1994). In the off-season, he teaches at USA Hockey Officials Development Camps. He also enjoys golf and cycling. He holds a Bachelor's degree in Finance from the University of Denver. He is single.

Notes

NHL Attendance

Season	Regular Season Games	Regular Season Attendance	Playoffs Games	Playoffs Attendance	Total Attendance
1960-61	210	2,317,142	17	242,000	2,559,142
1961-62	210	2,435,424	18	277,000	2,712,424
1962-63	210	2,590,574	16	220,906	2,811,480
1963-64	210	2,732,642	21	309,149	3,041,791
1964-65	210	2,822,635	20	303,859	3,126,494
1965-66	210	2,941,164	16	249,000	3,190,184
1966-67	210	3,084,759	16	248,336	3,333,095
1967-68[1]	444	4,938,043	40	495,089	5,433,132
1968-69	456	5,550,613	33	431,739	5,982,352
1969-70	456	5,992,065	34	461,694	6,453,759
1970-71[2]	546	7,257,677	43	707,633	7,965,310
1971-72	546	7,609,368	36	582,666	8,192,034
1972-73[3]	624	8,575,651	38	624,637	9,200,288
1973-74	624	8,640,978	38	600,442	9,241,420
1974-75[4]	720	9,521,536	51	784,181	10,305,717
1975-76	720	9,103,761	48	726,279	9,830,040
1976-77	720	8,563,890	44	646,279	9,210,169
1977-78	720	8,526,564	45	686,634	9,213,198
1978-79	680	7,758,053	45	694,521	8,452,574
1979-80[5]	840	10,533,623	63	976,699	11,510,322
1980-81	840	10,726,198	68	966,390	11,692,588
1981-82	840	10,710,894	71	1,058,948	11,769,842
1982-83	840	11,020,610	66	1,088,222	12,028,832
1983-84	840	11,359,386	70	1,107,400	12,466,786
1984-85	840	11,633,730	70	1,107,500	12,741,230
1985-86	840	11,621,000	72	1,152,503	12,773,503
1986-87	840	11,855,880	87	1,383,967	13,239,847
1987-88	840	12,117,512	83	1,336,901	13,454,413
1988-89	840	12,417,969	83	1,327,214	13,745,183
1989-90	840	12,579,651	85	1,355,593	13,935,244
1990-91	840	12,343,897	92	1,442,203	13,786,100
1991-92[6]	880	12,769,676	86	1,327,920	14,097,596
1992-93[7]	1,008	14,158,177[8]	83	1,346,034	15,504,211
1993-94[9]	1,092	16,105,604[10]	90	1,440,095	17,545,699

[1] First expansion: Los Angeles, Pittsburgh, California (Cleveland), Philadelphia, St. Louis and Minnesota (Dallas)
[2] Second expansion: Buffalo and Vancouver
[3] Third expansion: Atlanta (Calgary) and New York Islanders
[4] Fourth expansion: Kansas City (Colorado, New Jersey) and Washington
[5] Fifth expansion: Edmonton, Hartford, Quebec and Winnipeg
[6] Sixth expansion: San Jose
[7] Seventh expansion: Ottawa and Tampa Bay
[8] Includes 24 neutral site games
[9] Eighth espansion: Anaheim and Florida
[10] Includes 26 neutral site games

Mighty Ducks of Anaheim
1993-94 Results: 33w-46l-5t 71pts. Fourth, Pacific Division

Schedule

Oct. Sat. 1 at Dallas
Wed. 5 at Edmonton
Fri. 7 at Vancouver
Sun. 9 Calgary
Wed. 12 Vancouver
Fri. 14 Boston
Mon. 17 Edmonton
Wed. 19 at Edmonton
Thur. 20 at Calgary
Sun. 23 at Winnipeg
Tues. 25 at Detroit
Thur. 27 at Chicago
Sun. 30 St. Louis
Nov. Wed. 2 NY Rangers
Fri. 4 New Jersey
Tues. 8 at Los Angeles
Thur. 10 at San Jose
Fri. 11 Vancouver
Sun. 13 Calgary
Tues. 15 Buffalo
Thur. 17 at Vancouver
Sun. 20 Chicago
Wed. 23 San Jose
Fri. 25 at Boston*
Sat. 26 at Hartford*
Tues. 29 at Pittsburgh
Wed. 30 at Toronto
Dec. Fri. 2 at NY Rangers
Sun. 4 at Chicago
Wed. 7 Washington
Fri. 9 at San Jose
Sun. 11 Toronto
Tues. 13 Pittsburgh
Fri. 16 San Jose
Sun. 18 NY Islanders
Wed. 21 at Winnipeg
Thur. 22 at Calgary
Mon. 26 Los Angeles
Wed. 28 at Los Angeles
Fri. 30 Chicago
Jan. Mon. 2 Montreal*
Fri. 6 at Buffalo
Sat. 7 at New Jersey

Mon. 9 at Philadelphia
Wed. 11 at Detroit
Thur. 12 at Toronto
Sun. 15 at Ottawa
Tues. 17 at Quebec
Wed. 18 at Montreal
Wed. 25 Dallas
Fri. 27 Winnipeg
Tues. 31 at St. Louis
Feb. Fri. 3 Detroit
Sun. 5 Edmonton*
Wed. 8 Calgary
Thur. 9 St. Louis
(in Las Vegas)
Sun. 12 at Edmonton*
Mon. 13 at Calgary
Wed. 15 Quebec
Fri. 17 Ottawa
Sun. 19 Los Angeles
Tues. 21 at Los Angeles
Wed. 22 Philadelphia
Fri. 24 at San Jose
Sun. 26 Vancouver*
Mar. Wed. 1 Tampa Bay
Fri. 3 at Dallas
Sun. 5 at Florida
Mon. 6 at Tampa Bay
Thur. 9 Detroit
Sat. 11 at Dallas
(in San Antonio)
Wed. 15 Hartford
Fri. 17 Toronto
Sun. 19 St. Louis*
Tues. 21 Florida
Thur. 23 at St. Louis
Sat. 25 at Washington*
Sun. 26 at NY Islanders*
Wed. 29 Winnipeg
Fri. 31 at Vancouver
Apr. Sun. 2 San Jose*
Wed. 5 Edmonton
Fri. 7 Dallas
Sun. 9 Los Angeles*

* Denotes afternoon game.

Home Starting Times:
Weeknights . . . . 7:30 p.m.
Sundays . . . . 5:00 p.m.
Matinees . . . . 1:00 p.m.
Except Fri. Dec. 16 . . . . 6:00 p.m.
Mon. Jan. 2 . . . . 11:00 a.m.
Sun. Apr. 2, Apr. 9 . . . . . 12:00 p.m.
Wed. Apr. 5 . . . . 8:00 p.m.
Fri. Apr. 7 . . . . 8:00 p.m.

Franchise date: June 15, 1993

2nd NHL Season

PACIFIC DIVISION

Year-by-Year Record

Season	GP	Home W	L	T	Road W	L	T	Overall W	L	T	GF	GA	Pts.	Finished	Playoff Result
1993-94	84	14	26	2	19	20	3	33	46	5	229	251	71	4th, Pacific Div.	Out of Playoffs

Joe Sacco was one of the Mighty Ducks' most effective players, contributing 19 goals, killing penalties and working on the powerplay.

1994-95 Player Personnel

FORWARDS	HT	WT	S	Place of Birth	Date	1993-94 Club
BETS, Maxim	6-1	185	L	Chelyabinsk, USSR	1/31/74	Spokane-Anaheim-San Diego
CARNBACK, Patrik	6-0	187	L	Goteborg, Sweden	2/1/68	Anaheim
CORKUM, Bob	6-2	212	R	Salisbury, MA	12/18/67	Anaheim
DOURIS, Peter	6-1	195	R	Toronto, Ont.	2/19/66	Anaheim
EWEN, Dean	6-2	225	L	St. Albert, Alta.	2/28/69	San Diego
EWEN, Todd	6-2	220	R	Saskatoon, Sask.	3/22/66	Anaheim
GRIMSON, Stu	6-5	227	L	Kamloops, B.C.	5/20/65	Anaheim
JOMPHE, Jean-Francois	6-1	193	L	Harve' St. Pierre, Que.	12/28/72	San Diego-Greensboro
KARIYA, Paul	5-11	175	L	Vancouver, B.C.	10/16/74	U. of Maine-Cdn. National-Cdn. Olympic
KARPOV, Valeri	5-10	176	L	Chelyabinsk, USSR	8/5/71	Chelyabinsk
KING, Steven	6-0	195	R	Greenwich, RI	7/22/69	Anaheim
LAMBERT, Denny	5-11	200	L	Wawa, Ont.	1/7/70	San Diego
LEBEAU, Stephan	5-10	173	R	St. Jerome, Que.	2/28/68	Montreal-Anaheim
LILLEY, John	5-9	170	R	Wakefield, MA	8/3/72	U.S. National-U.S. Olympic-Anaheim-San Diego
MANELUK, Mike	5-11	188	R	Winnipeg, Man.	10/1/73	Brandon
MCKAY, Scott	5-11	200	R	Burlington, Ont.	1/26/72	Anaheim-San Diego
REICHERT, Craig	6-1	196	R	Winnipeg, Man.	5/11/74	Red Deer
RUCCHIN, Steve	6-3	210	L	London, Ont.	7/4/71	Western Ont.
SACCO, Joe	6-1	195	L	Medford, MA	2/4/69	Anaheim
SEMENOV, Anatoli	6-2	190	L	Moscow, USSR	3/5/62	Anaheim
STEVENSON, Jeremy	6-1	208	L	San Bernadino, CA	7/28/74	Newmarket-S.S. Marie
SWEENEY, Tim	5-11	185	L	Boston, MA	4/12/67	Anaheim
THOMSON, Jim	6-1	220	R	Edmonton, Alta.	12/30/65	Anaheim
VALK, Garry	6-1	205	L	Edmonton, Alta.	11/27/67	Anaheim
VAN ALLEN, Shaun	6-1	200	L	Shaunavon, Sask.	8/29/67	Anaheim
YAKE, Terry	5-11	190	R	New Westminster, B.C.	10/22/68	Anaheim

DEFENSEMEN						
BRISKE, Byron	6-2	194	R	Humboldt, Sask.	1/23/76	Red Deer
CHARTIER, Scott	6-1	200	R	St. Lazare, Man.	1/19/72	San Diego
DESANTIS, Mark	6-0	205	R	Brampton, Ont.	1/12/72	San Diego
DIRK, Robert	6-4	218	L	Regina, Sask.	8/20/66	Vancouver-Chicago
DOLLAS, Bobby	6-2	212	L	Montreal, Que.	1/31/65	Anaheim
FEDOTOV, Anatoli	5-11	178	L	Saratov, USSR	5/11/66	Anaheim-San Diego
FERNER, Mark	6-0	193	L	Regina, Sask.	9/5/65	Anaheim
KURVERS, Tom	6-2	195	L	Minneapolis, MN	9/14/62	NY Islanders
LADOUCEUR, Randy	6-2	220	L	Brockville, Ont.	6/30/60	Anaheim
MARSHALL, Jason	6-2	195	R	Cranbrook, B.C.	2/22/71	Cdn. National-Peoria
McSWEEN, Don	5-11	197	L	Detroit, MI	6/9/64	San Diego-Anaheim
O'CONNOR, Myles	5-11	190	L	Calgary, Alta.	4/2/67	Anaheim-San Diego
TSULYGIN, Nikolai	6-3	196	R	Ufa, USSR	6/29/75	Yulayev
TVERDOVSKY, Oleg	6-0	183	L	Donetsk, USSR	5/18/76	Soviet Wings
WILLIAMS, David	6-2	195	R	Plainfield, NJ	8/25/67	Anaheim-San Diego

GOALTENDERS	HT	WT	C	Place of Birth	Date	1993-94 Club
BESTER, Allan	5-7	155	L	Hamilton, Ont.	3/26/64	San Diego
HEBERT, Guy	5-11	185	L	Troy, NY	1/7/67	Anaheim
SHTALENKOV, Mikhail	6-2	180	L	Moscow, USSR	10/20/65	Anaheim-San Diego
TANNER, John	6-3	182	L	Cambridge, Ont.	3/17/71	Cornwall-San Diego

A seventh round draft selection of the Montreal Canadiens in 1988, Patrik Carnback led all Anaheim rookies in scoring, collecting 12 goals and 11 assists in 73 games.

1993-94 Scoring

* – rookie

Regular Season

Pos	#	Player	Team	GP	G	A	Pts	+/–	PIM	PP	SH	GW	GT	S	%
C	25	Terry Yake	ANA	82	21	31	52	2	44	5	0	2	0	188	11.2
R	20	Bob Corkum	ANA	76	23	28	51	4	18	3	3	0	1	180	12.8
L	18	Garry Valk	ANA	78	18	27	45	8	100	4	1	5	0	165	10.9
L	8	Tim Sweeney	ANA	78	16	27	43	3	49	6	1	2	0	114	14.0
D	23	Bill Houlder	ANA	80	14	25	39	18–	40	3	0	3	0	187	7.5
R	14	Joe Sacco	ANA	84	19	18	37	11–	61	3	1	2	1	206	9.2
L	16	Peter Douris	ANA	74	12	22	34	5–	21	1	0	1	0	142	8.5
C	22	Shaun Van Allen	ANA	80	8	25	33	0	64	2	2	1	0	104	7.7
C	19	Anatoli Semenov	ANA	49	11	19	30	4–	12	4	0	2	0	103	10.7
D	6	Sean Hill	ANA	68	7	20	27	12–	78	2	1	1	0	165	4.2
C	47	Stephan Lebeau	MTL	34	9	7	16	1	8	4	0	2	1	61	14.8
			ANA	22	6	4	10	5–	14	2	0	1	0	37	16.2
			TOTAL	56	15	11	26	4–	22	6	0	3	1	98	15.3
C	21	* Patrik Carnback	ANA	73	12	11	23	8–	54	3	0	2	0	81	14.8
D	2	Bobby Dollas	ANA	77	9	11	20	20	55	1	0	1	0	121	7.4
D	4	David Williams	ANA	56	5	15	20	8	42	2	0	0	0	74	6.8
L	24	Troy Loney	ANA	62	13	6	19	5–	88	6	0	1	0	93	14.0
R	36	Todd Ewen	ANA	76	9	9	18	7–	272	0	0	2	0	59	15.3
D	39	Don McSween	ANA	32	3	9	12	4	39	1	0	2	0	43	7.0
R	17	* Steven King	ANA	36	8	3	11	7–	44	3	0	1	0	50	16.0
D	29	Randy Ladouceur	ANA	81	1	9	10	7	74	0	0	0	0	66	1.5
C	10	Jarrod Skalde	ANA	20	5	4	9	3–	10	2	0	2	0	25	20.0
D	3	Mark Ferner	ANA	50	3	5	8	16–	30	0	0	0	0	44	6.8
R	48	* John Lilley	ANA	13	1	6	7	1	8	0	0	1	0	20	5.0
L	32	Stu Grimson	ANA	77	1	5	6	6–	199	0	0	0	0	34	2.9
D	44	Myles O'Connor	ANA	5	0	1	1	0	6	0	0	0	0	7	.0
C	26	Robin Bawa	ANA	12	0	1	1	3–	7	0	0	0	0	1	.0
C	45	* Scott McKay	ANA	1	0	0	0	0	0	0	0	0	0	1	.0
L	27	Lonnie Loach	ANA	3	0	0	0	2–	2	0	0	0	0	8	.0
D	34	Anatoli Fedotov	ANA	3	0	0	0	1–	0	0	0	0	0	1	.0
L	43	* Maxim Bets	ANA	3	0	0	0	3–	0	0	0	0	0	1	.0
R	33	Jim Thomson	ANA	6	0	0	0	0	5	0	0	0	0	1	.0
G	35	Mikhail Shtalenkov	ANA	10	0	0	0	0	0	0	0	0	0	0	.0
G	31	Guy Hebert	ANA	52	0	0	0	0	2	0	0	0	0	0	.0

Goaltending

No.	Goaltender	GPI	Mins	Avg	W	L	T	EN	SO	GA	SA	S%
35	Mikhail Shtalenkov	10	543	2.65	3	4	1	1	0	24	265	.909
31	Guy Hebert	52	2991	2.83	20	27	3	5	2	141	1513	.907
1	Ron Tugnutt	28	1520	3.00	10	15	1	4	1	76	828	.908
	Totals	**84**	**5079**	**2.97**	**33**	**46**	**5**	**10**	**3**	**251**	**2616**	**.904**

General Manager

FERREIRA, JACK
General Manager, The Mighty Ducks of Anaheim.
Born in Providence, R.I., June 9, 1944.

In his role as the first general manager in the history of The Mighty Ducks of Anaheim, Jack Ferreira brings with him more than 20 years of professional hockey experience, including vital experience in assembling an expansion team.

Following a four-year college hockey career as a goaltender at Boston University, where he received All-American honors while earning a bachelor's degree in history, Ferreira began his coaching career at Princeton University, serving as the school's assistant hockey coach in 1969. From 1970 to 1972 he was assistant hockey coach at Brown University.

His professional career began in 1972 with the New England Whalers of the World Hockey Association, where he served as head scout, assistant coach and assistant general manager through 1977.

From 1977 to 1980 he was a New England scout for the National Hockey League Central Scouting Bureau, and from 1980 to 1986 he was a U.S. and college scout for the Calgary Flames.

From there he took a post as director of player development for the New York Rangers, serving in that capacity from 1986 to 1988. From 1988 to 1990 he was vice president and general manager of the Minnesota North Stars and in 1990 he helped start the San Jose Sharks expansion franchise as that team's executive vice president and general manager.

Prior to joining The Mighty Ducks of Anaheim, he was director of pro scouting for the Montreal Canadiens, where he kept tabs on talent in the NHL, the International Hockey League and the American Hockey League throughout the 1992-93 season.

Ferreira was a member of the USA Hockey Committee for the 1992 Winter Olympics and served as general manager for the U.S. team at the 1991 World Hockey Championship in Finland.

General Managers' History

Jack Ferreira, 1993-94 to date.

Coaching History

Ron Wilson, 1993-94 to date.

Captains' History

Troy Loney, 1993-94.

Club Records

Team

(Figures in brackets for season records are games played)

Most Points	71	1993-94 (84)
Most Wins	33	1993-94 (84)
Most Ties	5	1993-94 (84)
Most Losses	46	1993-94 (84)
Most Goals	229	1993-94 (84)
Most Goals Against	251	1993-94 (84)
Fewest Points	71	1993-94 (84)
Fewest Wins	33	1993-94 (84)
Fewest Ties	5	1993-94 (84)
Fewest Losses	46	1993-94 (84)
Fewest Goals	229	1993-94 (84)
Fewest Goals Against	251	1993-94 (84)

Longest Winning Streak
Over-all ... 4 Nov. 19-24/93
Home ... 2 Jan. 26/94-Jan. 28/94; Mar. 13-Mar. 16/94
Away ... 4 Nov. 19-24/93

Longest Undefeated Streak
Over-all ... 4 Oct. 13-19/93 (2 wins, 2 ties); Nov. 19-24/93 (4 wins)
Home ... 3 Oct. 13-17/93 (1 win, 2 ties)
Away ... 5 Jan. 2-19/94 (3 wins, 2 ties)

Longest Losing Streak
Over-all ... 6 Oct. 20-31/93
Home ... 4 Dec. 22/93-Jan. 12/94
Away ... 6 Oct. 20-Nov. 14/93

Longest Winless Streak
Over-all ... 6 Oct. 20-31/93 (6 losses)
Home ... 4 Oct. 15-31/93 (2 losses, 2 ties); Dec. 22/93-Jan. 12/94 (4 losses)
Away ... 6 Oct. 20-Nov. 14/93 (6 losses)
Most Shutouts, Season ... 2 1993-94 (84)
Most PIM, Season ... 1,507 1993-94 (84)
Most Goals, Game ... 7 Dec. 20/93 (Ana. 7 at Wpg. 5)

Individual

Most Seasons	1	Numerous
Most Games	84	Joe Sacco
Most Goals, Career	23	Bob Corkum
Most Assists, Career	31	Terry Yake
Most Points, Career	52	Terry Yake
Most PIM, Career	272	Todd Ewen
Most Shutouts, Career	2	Guy Hebert

Longest Consecutive Games Streak ... 84 Joe Sacco
Most Goals, Season ... 23 Bob Corkum (1993-94)
Most Assists, Season ... 31 Terry Yake (1993-94)
Most Points, Season ... 52 Terry Yake (1993-94) (21 goals, 31 assists)
Most PIM, Season ... 272 Todd Ewen (1993-94)
Most Points, Defenseman Season ... 39 Bill Houlder (1993-94) (14 goals, 25 assists)
Most Points, Center Season ... 52 Terry Yake (1993-94) (21 goals, 31 assists)
Most Points, Right Wing Season ... 51 Bob Corkum (1993-94) (23 goals, 28 assists)
Most Points, Left Wing Season ... 45 Garry Valk (1993-94) (18 goals, 27 assists)
Most Points, Rookie Season ... 23 Patrik Carnback (1993-94) (12 goals, 11 assists)
Most Shutouts, Season ... 2 Guy Hebert (1993-94)
Most Goals, Game ... 3 Terry Yake (Oct. 19/93)
Most Assists, Game ... 3 3 times, most recent Alexei Kasatonov (Jan. 6/94)
Most Points, Game ... 4 4 times, most recent Joe Sacco (Feb. 16/94)

© Disney

Right winger Todd Ewen scored two game-winning goals for the Mighty Ducks in 1993-94.

All-time Record vs. Other Clubs

Regular Season

	At Home							On Road							Total						
	GP	W	L	T	GF	GA	PTS	GP	W	L	T	GF	GA	PTS	GP	W	L	T	GF	GA	PTS
Boston	1	0	0	1	1	1	1	1	0	1	0	3	5	0	2	0	1	1	4	6	1
Buffalo	1	0	1	0	0	3	0	1	0	1	0	2	4	0	2	0	2	0	2	7	0
Calgary	3	0	2	1	4	9	1	3	1	2	0	8	10	2	6	1	4	1	12	19	3
Chicago	2	0	2	0	4	6	0	3	1	2	0	6	7	2	5	1	4	0	10	13	2
Dallas	3	2	1	0	11	9	4	2	1	1	0	6	6	2	5	3	2	0	17	15	6
Detroit	2	0	2	0	6	13	0	2	0	1	1	6	9	1	4	0	3	1	12	22	1
Edmonton	3	2	1	0	10	7	4	3	3	0	0	13	6	6	6	5	1	0	23	13	10
Florida	1	0	1	0	2	3	0	1	1	0	0	4	1	2	2	1	1	0	6	4	2
Hartford	1	1	0	0	6	3	2	1	1	0	0	3	2	2	2	2	0	0	9	5	4
Los Angeles	3	1	2	0	10	10	2	3	1	2	0	8	10	2	6	2	4	0	18	20	4
Montreal	1	0	1	0	2	5	0	1	0	1	0	1	4	0	2	0	2	0	3	9	0
New Jersey	1	0	1	0	3	6	0	1	0	1	0	0	4	0	2	0	2	0	3	10	0
NY Islanders	1	0	1	0	3	4	0	1	1	0	0	3	0	2	2	1	1	0	6	4	2
NY Rangers	1	1	0	0	3	2	2	1	1	0	0	4	2	2	2	2	0	0	7	4	4
Ottawa	1	1	0	0	5	1	2	1	0	1	0	1	4	0	2	1	1	0	6	5	2
Philadelphia	1	1	0	0	6	3	2	1	1	0	0	3	2	2	2	2	0	0	9	5	4
Pittsburgh	1	0	1	0	4	5	0	1	0	0	1	2	2	1	2	0	1	1	6	7	1
Quebec	1	0	1	0	0	1	0	1	1	0	0	6	3	2	2	1	1	0	6	4	2
St. Louis	2	1	1	0	4	4	2	2	1	1	0	6	7	2	4	2	2	0	10	11	4
San Jose	3	0	3	0	6	11	0	3	0	3	0	3	11	0	6	0	6	0	9	22	0
Tampa Bay	1	0	1	0	2	4	0	1	1	0	0	4	1	2	2	1	1	0	6	5	2
Toronto	2	1	1	0	6	5	2	2	1	0	1	4	3	3	4	2	1	1	10	8	5
Vancouver	4	2	2	0	13	9	4	2	0	2	0	2	6	0	6	2	4	0	15	15	4
Washington	1	0	1	0	2	5	0	1	0	1	0	0	3	0	2	0	2	0	2	8	0
Winnipeg	2	2	0	0	8	3	4	2	2	0	0	9	6	4	4	4	0	0	17	9	8
Totals	**42**	**14**	**26**	**2**	**115**	**129**	**30**	**42**	**19**	**20**	**3**	**114**	**122**	**41**	**84**	**33**	**46**	**5**	**229**	**251**	**71**

1993-94 Results

Date	Opponent	Score	Date	Opponent	Score
Oct. 8	Detroit	2-7	8 at	St. Louis	5-3
10	NY Islanders	3-4	10	Detroit	4-6
13	Edmonton	4-3	12	San Jose	2-5
15	Boston	1-1	14	Hartford	6-3
17	Calgary	2-2	16	Vancouver	3-4
19 at	NY Rangers	4-2	18 at	Toronto	3-3
20 at	New Jersey	0-4	19 at	Detroit	4-4
23 at	Montreal	1-4	24	St. Louis	2-3
25 at	Ottawa	1-4	26	Winnipeg	3-1
28 at	San Jose	3-4	28	NY Rangers	3-2
29	Washington	2-5	29 at	Los Angeles	1-5
31	San Jose	1-2	Feb. 2	Calgary	2-4
Nov. 3	Dallas	5-4	4	Vancouver	3-0
5	New Jersey	3-6	6	Chicago	2-3
7	Pittsburgh	4-5	11	Los Angeles	3-5
9	Dallas	4-2	13 at	Edmonton	6-3
11 at	Calgary	4-5	16	Philadelphia	6-3
14 at	Vancouver	2-3	18	Quebec	0-1
17	Toronto	3-4	20 at	St. Louis	1-4
19	Vancouver	6-3	23 at	Buffalo	2-4
21 at	Edmonton	4-2	24 at	Pittsburgh	2-2
22 at	Calgary	2-1	26 at	Quebec	6-3
24 at	Winnipeg	2-1	Mar. 2	Montreal	2-5
26	San Jose	3-4	4	Edmonton	4-1
27 at	San Jose	0-1	6 at	San Jose	0-6
Dec. 1	Winnipeg	5-2	8 at	Chicago	0-3
2 at	Los Angeles	2-3	9	Buffalo	0-3
5	Tampa Bay	2-4	11	Chicago	2-3
7	Florida	2-3	13	Ottawa	5-1
12	St. Louis	2-1	16	Los Angeles	5-2
14 at	Detroit	2-5	22 at	Dallas	3-4
15 at	Toronto	1-0	24 at	Boston	3-5
17	Dallas	3-2	26 at	Hartford	3-2
19 at	Chicago	0-2	27 at	Philadelphia	3-2
20 at	Winnipeg	7-5	30 at	Los Angeles	5-2
22	Dallas	2-3	31	Edmonton	2-3
26	Los Angeles	2-3	Apr. 2	Toronto	3-1
28 at	NY Islanders	3-0	6 at	Calgary	2-4
30 at	Washington	0-3	8 at	Edmonton	3-1
Jan. 1 at	Florida	4-1	9 at	Vancouver	0-3
2 at	Tampa Bay	4-1	11	Calgary	0-3
6 at	Chicago	6-2	13	Vancouver	1-2

Entry Draft
Selections 1994-93

1994 Pick		1993 Pick	
2	Oleg Tverdovsky	4	Paul Kariya
28	Johan Davidsson	30	Nikolai Tsulygin
67	Craig Reichert	56	Valeri Karpov
80	Byron Briske	82	Joel Gagnon
106	Pavel Trnka	108	Mikhail Shtalenkov
132	Jon Battaglia	134	Antti Aalto
158	Mark (Rocky) Welsing	160	Matt Peterson
184	John Brad Englehart	186	Tom Askey
236	Tommi Miettinen	212	Vitaly Kozel
262	Jeremy Stevenson	238	Anatoli Fedotov
		264	David Penney

Coach

WILSON, RON
Head Coach, The Mighty Ducks of Anaheim.
Born in Windsor, Ont., May 28, 1955.

On June 30, 1993 Disney Sports Enterprises, Inc., introduced Ron Wilson as the first head coach in Mighty Ducks history. In his first year as a head coach in the NHL, Wilson led Anaheim to a 33-46-5 record and 71 points as the Mighty Ducks made a substantial run at a playoff berth in the Western Conference. Anaheim's 33 wins tied the Florida Panthers for most-ever by an NHL first-year franchise while the Mighty Ducks' 71 points were the fourth-highest total for an NHL first-year club. Under Wilson's guidance, the Mighty Ducks achieved 19 of their 33 victories away from home, the most-ever road wins by an NHL first-year squad. Wilson received 12 points in the voting for the Jack Adams NHL coach of the year Award, including one first-place vote.

Wilson, 39, came to the Mighty Ducks after serving the previous three seasons as an assistant coach to Pat Quinn for the Vancouver Canucks. During Wilson's three seasons in Vancouver, the Canucks posted a 116-98-30 record (.537) and qualified for the Stanley Cup playoffs all three years.

Prior to becoming an assistant coach with Vancouver, Wilson was an assistant coach for the Milwaukee Admirals (IHL) under Ron LaPointe.

Wilson has significant playing experience in professional, amateur and international hockey. He played four years at Providence College where he was a two-time All-American and four-time All-Hockey East. Wilson was Hockey East Player of the Year in 1975 when he led the nation in scoring with 26-61-87 points in 26 games. He remains Providence's all-time leading scorer and ranks as the all-time NCAA leading scorer among defensemen with 250 points. Wilson received a Bachelor of Arts Degree in economics from Providence College.

Drafted by the Toronto Maple Leafs (132nd overall) in 1975, Wilson began his professional hockey career in 1976-77 with the Dallas Blackhawks in the old Central Hockey League. He joined the Toronto Maple Leafs in 1977-78, playing in 64 NHL contests over three seasons. Wilson then moved to Switzerland in 1980 and competed for the Swiss teams Klöten and Davos for six seasons. The former defenseman/winger signed with the Minnesota North Stars as a free agent in 1985 where he played through 1988, closing out his pro career.

Though he was born in Canada, Wilson was raised in the United States. He is a four-time player for U.S. National Teams (1975, 1981, 1983, 1987) and coached the 1994 squad at the World Championships in Italy, leading Team USA to a 4-4-0 record with a fourth-place finish – its highest ranking since 1991. Wilson led the U.S. team to its first victory over Russia in international competition since the 1980 "miracle on ice" game during the 1980 Winter Olympics at Lake Placid, NY. Wilson was assisted by Mighty Ducks Assistant Coach Tim Army on the 1994 U.S. squad that included six players from the Mighty Ducks' inaugural season.

The Windsor, Ontario native also has some family ties to the NHL. His father, Larry, played six NHL seasons with the Detroit Red Wings and Chicago Blackhawks and coached pro hockey for 11 seasons, including one with Detroit. Ron Wilson's uncle, Johnny, played 13 years in the NHL and also coached for Detroit, Los Angeles, Colorado and Pittsburgh. Johnny Wilson once played 580 consecutive games in the NHL, a record at that time. Ron Wilson's brothers, Brad and Randy, played at Providence.

Wilson is active in all Disney GOALS charity events and is part of the Mighty Ducks' Speakers Bureau. He is known for his keen sense of humor and is an avid golfer. Wilson and his wife Maureen reside in Orange, CA. They have two daughters, Kristen, 17, and Lauren, 14.

Coaching Record

Season	Team	Games	Regular Season W	L	T	%	Playoffs Games	W	L	%
1993-94	Anaheim (NHL)	84	33	46	5	.423	....	....	....	....
	NHL Totals	84	33	46	5	.423	....	....	....	....

Club Directory

Disney Sports Enterprises Inc.
Arrowhead Pond of Anaheim
2695 Katella Ave.
P.O. Box 61077
Anaheim, CA 92803-6177
Phone **714/704-2700**
FAX 714/704-2753
Capacity: 17,174

Officers and Head Management
Governor	Michael Eisner
President and Alternate Governor	Tony Tavares
Vice President/General Manager	Jack Ferreira
Assistant General Manager	Pierre Gauthier
Vice President of Finance/Administration	Andy Roundtree

Hockey & Administrative Staff
Head Coach	Ron Wilson
Director of Hockey Operations	Kevin Gilmore
Director of Player Personnel	David McNab
Assistant Coaches	Al Sims, Tim Army
Coordinator of Computer Scouting and Video	Angela Gorgone
Pro Scout	Paul Fenton
Amateur Scouts	Thommie Bergman, Alain Chainey, Al Godfrey, Richard Green
Scouting Staff	Jim Benning, Mike McGraw, Mark Odnokon, Vern Stenlund, Ed Wright
Trainer	Blynn DeNiro
Equipment Manager	Mark O'Neill
Assistant Equipment Manager	John Allaway
Director of Sales and Marketing	Bill Holford
Director of Public Relations	Bill Robertson
Director of Advertising Sales & Service	Bob Wagner
Director of Broadcasting	Lisa Seltzer
Controller	Martin Greenspun
Senior Accountant	Melody Martin
Manager of Administration	Jenny Price
Season Ticket Manager	Don Boudreau
Manager of Premium Ticket Services	Anne McNiff
Merchandise Manager	Shelley Gartner
Media Services Coordinator	Rob Scichili
Junior Accountant	Shelly Baker
Marketing Services Representative	Michele Amiro
Sponsorship Services Coordinator	Matthew Stys
Ticket Account Executives	Patti Conklin, Jeanice Scott
Administrative Assistant to the President	Susan Jackson
Administrative Assistant to the General Manager	Barbara Potts
Administrative Assistant to Hockey Operations	Debbie Blanchard
Administrative Assistant	Cindy Williams
Sales and Marketing Administrative Assistant	Janet Conley
Ticket Sales Assistant	Debbie Nielander
Team Store Manager	Mike Laverty
Associate Producers	Mark Vittorio, Tim Davis
Receptionist	Anne Mason
Hockey Operations Intern	Will Gillespie
Promotions Intern	Kerry Fopma
Public Relations Intern	Marc Simon
Sponsorship Sales Intern	Heather Holter
Team Physicians	Dr. Ronald Glousman, Dr. Craig Milhouse
Oral Surgeon	Dr. Jeff Pulver
Strength and Conditioning Coach	Jamie Yanchar

Miscellaneous
Colors	Purple, Jade, Silver and White
Television KCAL (Ch. 9) & Prime Ticket	Chris Madsen and Brian Hayward
Radio KEZY (95.9 FM)	Matt McConnell and Charlie Simmer
Minor League Affiliations	San Diego Gulls (IHL) and Greensboro Monarchs (ECHL)

Leftwinger Peter Douris had 34 points in 74 games played in 1993-94.

Boston Bruins

1993-94 Results: 42w-29L-13T 97PTS. Second, Northeast Division

Bruin captain Ray Bourque became the first NHL player to be named to the League's post-season All-Star Teams in 15 consecutive seasons.

Schedule

Oct.	Sat.	1	at Montreal	Wed. 11	at Ottawa
	Mon.	3	at Ottawa	Thur. 12	Winnipeg
	Thur.	6	Quebec	Sat. 14	at Quebec
	Sat.	8	Toronto	Mon. 16	Washington*
	Mon.	10	Florida*	Wed. 18	Pittsburgh
	Wed.	12	at San Jose	Wed. 25	at NY Rangers
	Fri.	14	at Anaheim	Thur. 26	New Jersey
	Sat.	15	at Los Angeles	Sat. 28	at Philadelphia*
	Wed.	19	at Vancouver	Mon. 30	Florida
	Fri.	21	at Edmonton	**Feb.** Thur. 2	Ottawa
	Sat.	22	at Calgary	Sat. 4	NY Islanders*
	Thur.	27	Montreal	Tues. 7	NY Rangers
	Sat.	29	Buffalo	Thur. 9	San Jose
Nov.	Thur.	3	Pittsburgh	Sat. 11	Los Angeles*
	Sat.	5	Chicago	Sun. 12	at Buffalo
	Mon.	7	at Ottawa	Wed. 15	at Dallas
	Thur.	10	Quebec	Fri. 17	at Tampa Bay
	Sat.	12	at New Jersey*	Sun. 19	at Florida
	Sun.	13	at Florida	Wed. 22	at Hartford
	Thur.	17	St. Louis	Fri. 25	at Quebec
	Sat.	19	Washington	Tues. 28	Quebec
	Mon.	21	Pittsburgh	**Mar.** Thur. 2	New Jersey
	Wed.	23	at Buffalo	Sat. 4	Ottawa*
	Fri.	25	Anaheim*	Sun. 5	at Hartford
	Sun.	27	Vancouver*	Thur. 9	at Tampa Bay
	Tues.	29	at NY Islanders		(in Minneapolis)
Dec.	Thur.	1	Hartford	Sun. 12	at Washington*
	Sat.	3	at Pittsburgh	Tues. 14	Buffalo
	Sun.	4	at Hartford		(in Hamilton)
	Tues.	6	at Detroit	Thur. 16	Montreal
	Thur.	8	Edmonton	Sat. 18	Buffalo*
	Sat.	10	Calgary	Sun. 19	at New Jersey
	Wed.	14	at Montreal	Wed. 22	at Montreal
	Fri.	16	at Washington	Fri. 24	at Tampa Bay
	Sat.	17	Buffalo	Sun. 26	at St. Louis
	Wed.	21	at NY Rangers	Tues. 28	NY Islanders
	Thur.	22	Dallas	Thur. 30	at Pittsburgh
	Mon.	26	Hartford	**Apr.** Sat. 1	NY Rangers*
	Thur.	29	at Winnipeg	Sun. 2	at Philadelphia*
	Sat.	31	at Toronto	Tues. 4	Philadelphia
Jan.	Mon.	2	Tampa Bay*	Thur. 6	at NY Islanders
	Thur.	5	Philadelphia	Sat. 8	Tampa Bay*
	Sat.	7	Detroit	Sun. 9	at Chicago*

* Denotes afternoon game.

Home Starting Times:

Weeknights	. . . .	7:30 p.m.
Saturdays and Sundays	. . . .	7:00 p.m.
Matinees	. . . .	1:30 p.m.
Except	Sat. Oct. 8	7:30 p.m.
	Fri. Nov. 25	1:00 p.m.

Franchise date: November 1, 1924

NORTHEAST DIVISION

71st NHL Season

Year-by-Year Record

		Home			Road			Overall							
Season	GP	W	L	T	W	L	T	W	L	T	GF	GA	Pts.	Finished	Playoff Result
1993-94	84	20	14	8	22	15	5	42	29	13	289	252	97	2nd, Northeast Div.	Lost Conf. Semi-Final
1992-93	84	29	10	3	22	16	4	51	26	7	332	268	109	1st, Adams Div.	Lost Div. Semi-Final
1991-92	80	23	11	6	13	21	6	36	32	12	270	275	84	2nd, Adams Div.	Lost Conf. Championship
1990-91	80	26	9	5	18	15	7	44	24	12	299	264	100	1st, Adams Div.	Lost Conf. Championship
1989-90	80	23	13	4	23	12	5	46	25	9	289	232	101	1st, Adams Div.	Lost Final
1988-89	80	17	15	8	20	14	6	37	29	14	289	256	88	2nd, Adams Div.	Lost Div. Final
1987-88	80	24	13	3	20	17	3	44	30	6	300	251	94	2nd, Adams Div.	Lost Final
1986-87	80	25	11	4	14	23	3	39	34	7	301	276	85	3rd, Adams Div.	Lost Div. Semi-Final
1985-86	80	24	9	7	13	22	5	37	31	12	311	288	86	3rd, Adams Div.	Lost Div. Semi-Final
1984-85	80	21	15	4	15	19	6	36	34	10	303	287	82	4th, Adams Div.	Lost Div. Semi-Final
1983-84	80	25	12	3	24	13	3	49	25	6	336	261	104	1st, Adams Div.	Lost Div. Semi-Final
1982-83	80	28	6	6	22	14	4	50	20	10	327	228	110	1st, Adams Div.	Lost Conf. Championship
1981-82	80	24	12	4	19	15	6	43	27	10	323	285	96	2nd, Adams Div.	Lost Div. Final
1980-81	80	26	10	4	11	20	9	37	30	13	316	272	87	2nd, Adams Div.	Lost Prelim. Round
1979-80	80	27	9	4	19	12	9	46	21	13	310	234	105	2nd, Adams Div.	Lost Quarter-Final
1978-79	80	25	10	5	18	13	9	43	23	14	316	270	100	1st, Adams Div.	Lost Semi-Final
1977-78	80	29	6	5	22	12	6	51	18	11	333	218	113	1st, Adams Div.	Lost Final
1976-77	80	27	7	6	22	16	2	49	23	8	312	240	106	1st, Adams Div.	Lost Final
1975-76	80	27	5	8	21	10	9	48	15	17	313	237	113	1st, Adams Div.	Lost Semi-Final
1974-75	80	29	5	6	11	21	8	40	26	14	345	245	94	2nd, Adams Div.	Lost Prelim. Round
1973-74	78	33	4	2	19	13	7	52	17	9	349	221	113	1st, East Div.	Lost Final
1972-73	78	27	10	2	24	12	3	51	22	5	330	235	107	2nd, East Div.	Lost Quarter-Final
1971-72	78	28	4	7	26	9	4	54	13	11	330	204	119	**1st, East Div.**	**Won Stanley Cup**
1970-71	78	33	4	2	24	10	5	57	14	7	399	207	121	1st, East Div.	Lost Quarter-Final
1969-70	76	27	3	8	13	14	11	40	17	19	277	216	99	**2nd, East Div.**	**Won Stanley Cup**
1968-69	76	29	3	6	13	15	10	42	18	16	303	221	100	2nd, East Div.	Lost Semi-Final
1967-68	74	22	9	6	15	18	4	37	27	10	259	216	84	3rd, East Div.	Lost Quarter-Final
1966-67	70	10	21	4	7	22	6	17	43	10	182	253	44	6th,	Out of Playoffs
1965-66	70	15	17	3	6	26	3	21	43	6	174	275	48	5th,	Out of Playoffs
1964-65	70	12	17	6	9	26	0	21	43	6	166	253	48	6th,	Out of Playoffs
1963-64	70	13	15	7	5	25	5	18	40	12	170	212	48	6th,	Out of Playoffs
1962-63	70	7	18	10	7	21	7	14	39	17	198	281	45	6th,	Out of Playoffs
1961-62	70	9	22	4	6	25	4	15	47	8	177	306	38	6th,	Out of Playoffs
1960-61	70	13	17	5	2	25	8	15	42	13	176	254	43	6th,	Out of Playoffs
1959-60	70	21	11	3	7	23	5	28	34	8	220	241	64	5th,	Out of Playoffs
1958-59	70	21	11	3	11	18	6	32	29	9	205	215	73	2nd,	Lost Semi-Final
1957-58	70	15	14	6	12	14	9	27	28	15	199	194	69	4th,	Lost Final
1956-57	70	20	9	6	14	15	6	34	24	12	195	174	80	3rd,	Lost Final
1955-56	70	14	14	7	9	20	6	23	34	13	147	185	59	5th,	Out of Playoffs
1954-55	70	16	10	9	7	16	12	23	26	21	169	188	67	4th,	Lost Semi-Final
1953-54	70	22	8	5	10	20	5	32	28	10	177	181	74	4th,	Lost Semi-Final
1952-53	70	19	10	6	9	19	7	28	29	13	152	172	69	3rd,	Lost Final
1951-52	70	15	12	8	10	17	8	25	29	16	162	176	66	4th,	Lost Semi-Final
1950-51	70	13	12	10	9	18	8	22	30	18	178	197	62	4th,	Lost Semi-Final
1949-50	70	15	12	8	7	20	8	22	32	16	198	228	60	5th,	Out of Playoffs
1948-49	60	18	10	2	11	13	6	29	23	8	178	163	66	2nd,	Lost Semi-Final
1947-48	60	12	8	10	11	16	3	23	24	13	167	168	59	3rd,	Lost Semi-Final
1946-47	60	18	7	5	8	16	6	26	23	11	190	175	63	3rd,	Lost Semi-Final
1945-46	50	11	5	4	13	13	4	24	18	8	167	156	56	2nd,	Lost Final
1944-45	50	11	12	2	5	18	2	16	30	4	179	219	36	4th,	Lost Semi-Final
1943-44	50	15	8	2	4	18	3	19	26	5	223	268	43	5th,	Out of Playoffs
1942-43	50	17	3	5	7	14	4	24	17	9	195	176	57	2nd,	Lost Final
1941-42	48	17	4	3	8	13	3	25	17	6	160	118	56	3rd,	Lost Semi-Final
1940-41	48	15	4	5	12	4	8	27	8	13	168	102	67	1st,	**Won Stanley Cup**
1939-40	48	20	3	1	11	9	4	31	12	5	170	98	67	1st,	Lost Semi-Final
1938-39	48	20	2	2	16	8	0	36	10	2	156	76	74	1st,	**Won Stanley Cup**
1937-38	48	18	3	3	12	8	4	30	11	7	142	89	67	1st, Amn. Div.	Lost Semi-Final
1936-37	48	9	11	4	14	7	3	23	18	7	120	110	53	2nd, Amn. Div.	Lost Quarter-Final
1935-36	48	15	8	1	7	12	5	22	20	6	92	83	50	2nd, Amn. Div.	Lost Quarter-Final
1934-35	48	17	7	0	9	9	6	26	16	6	129	112	58	1st, Amn. Div.	Lost Semi-Final
1933-34	48	11	11	2	7	14	3	18	25	5	111	130	41	4th, Amn. Div.	Out of Playoffs
1932-33	48	20	2	2	5	13	6	25	15	8	124	88	58	1st, Amn. Div.	Lost Semi-Final
1931-32	48	11	10	3	4	11	9	15	21	12	122	117	42	4th, Amn. Div.	Out of Playoffs
1930-31	44	17	1	4	11	9	2	28	10	6	143	90	62	1st, Amn. Div.	Lost Semi-Final
1929-30	44	23	1	0	15	4	1	38	5	1	179	98	77	1st, Amn. Div.	Lost Final
1928-29	44	16	6	1	10	7	4	26	13	5	89	52	57	**1st, Amn. Div.**	**Won Stanley Cup**
1927-28	44	13	5	4	7	9	6	20	13	11	77	70	51	1st, Amn. Div.	Lost Semi-Final
1926-27	44	15	7	0	6	13	3	21	20	3	97	89	45	2nd, Amn. Div.	Lost Final
1925-26	36	10	7	1	7	8	3	17	15	4	92	85	38	4th,	Out of Playoffs
1924-25	30	3	12	0	3	12	0	6	24	0	49	119	12	6th,	Out of Playoffs

1994-95 Player Personnel

FORWARDS	HT	WT	S	Place of Birth	Date	1993-94 Club
BEDDOES, Clayton	5-11	190	L	Bentley, Alta.	11/10/70	Lake Superior
BODNARCHUK, Michael	6-1	175	R	Bramalea, Ont.	3/26/70	Albany-Phoenix
CZERKAWSKI, Mariusz	6-0	195	R	Radomsko, Poland	4/13/72	Djurgarden-Boston
DONATO, Ted	5-10	180	L	Dedham, MA	4/28/69	Boston
GONEAU, Daniel	6-1	196	L	Montreal, Que.	1/16/76	Laval
HEINZE, Stephen	5-11	192	R	Lawrence, MA	1/30/70	Boston
HOLLAND, Dennis	5-10	165	L	Vernon, B.C.	1/30/69	Providence (AHL)
HUGHES, Brent	5-11	195	L	New Westminster, B.C.	4/5/66	Boston-Providence (AHL)
KNIPSCHEER, Fred	5-11	185	L	Ft. Wayne, IN	9/3/69	Boston-Providence (AHL)
LACROIX, Daniel	6-2	188	L	Montreal, Que.	3/11/69	NY Rangers-Binghamton
LEACH, Stephen	5-11	197	R	Cambridge, MA	1/16/66	Boston
LOMBARDI, Stephen	6-1	180	L	South Easton, MA	4/14/73	Yale
MAKELA, Mikko	6-1	194	L	Tampere, Finland	2/28/65	Malmo
MOGER, Sandy	6-3	215	R	100 Mile House, B.C.	3/21/69	Hamilton
MURRAY, Glen	6-2	213	R	Halifax, N.S.	11/1/72	Boston
NEELY, Cam	6-1	217	R	Comox, B.C.	6/6/65	Boston
OATES, Adam	5-11	185	R	Weston, Ont.	8/27/62	Boston
PANTELEEV, Grigori	5-9	190	L	Gastello, USSR	11/13/72	Boston-Providence (AHL)
REID, David	6-1	217	L	Toronto, Ont.	5/15/64	Boston
ROY, Andre	6-3	178	L	Port Chester, NY	2/8/75	Chicoutimi
SMOLINSKI, Bryan	6-1	200	R	Toledo, OH	12/27/71	Boston
STEWART, Cameron	5-11	196	L	Kitchener, Ont.	9/18/71	Boston-Providence (AHL)
STUMPEL, Jozef	6-1	208	R	Nitra, Czech.	6/20/72	Boston-Providence (AHL)
ZHOLTOK, Sergei	6-0	190	R	Riga, Latvia	12/2/72	Boston-Providence (AHL)
DEFENSEMEN						
ARMSTRONG, Bill	6-5	220	L	Richmond Hill, Ont.	5/18/70	Providence (AHL)
BOURQUE, Ray	5-11	215	L	Montreal, Que.	12/28/60	Boston
CHERVYAKOV, Denis	6-0	185	L	Leningrad, USSR	4/20/70	Providence (AHL)
FOSTER, Stephen	6-3	210	R	Brockton, MA	3/21/71	Boston U.
GRUDEN, John	6-0	189	L	Hastings, MN	4/6/70	Ferris State-Boston
IAFRATE, Al	6-3	235	L	Dearborn, MI	3/21/66	Washington-Boston
KASATONOV, Alexei	6-1	215	L	Leningrad, USSR	10/14/59	Anaheim-St. Louis
KIENASS, Torsten	5-11	180	L	Berlin, East Germany	2/23/71	Dusseldorf
MACKEY, James	6-4	225	R	Saratoga Springs, NY	1/20/72	Yale
MASTAD, Milt	6-3	205	L	Regina, Sask.	3/5/75	Seattle-Moose Jaw
PAQUETTE, Charles	6-1	193	L	Lachute, Que.	6/17/75	Sherbrooke
ROHLOFF, Jon	5-11	220	R	Mankato, MN	10/3/69	Providence (AHL)
SAPOZHNIKOV, Andrei	6-1	185	L	Chelyabinsk, USSR	6/15/71	Chelyabinsk
SEROWIK, Jeff	6-1	210	R	Manchester, NH	1/10/67	Cincinnati
SHAW, David	6-2	205	R	St. Thomas, Ont.	5/25/64	Boston
SIMPSON, Geoff	6-1	180	R	Victoria, B.C.	3/6/69	Charlotte-Huntington
STOLK, Darren	6-4	210	L	Tabler, Alta.	7/22/68	Providence (AHL)
SWEENEY, Don	5-10	188	L	St. Stephen, N.B.	8/17/66	Boston
TIMANDER, Mattias	6-1	194	L	Solleftea, Sweden	4/16/74	MoDo
WETHERILL, Darren	6-0	180	L	Regina, Sask.	1/28/70	Lake Superior
WRIGHT, Darren	6-1	182	L	Duncan, B.C.	5/22/76	Prince Albert

GOALTENDERS	HT	WT	C	Place of Birth	Date	1993-94 Club
BAILEY, Scott	6-0	195	L	Calgary, Alta.	5/2/72	Providence (AHL)-Charlotte
BLUE, John	5-10	185	L	Huntington Beach, CA	2/19/66	Boston-Providence (AHL)
LACHER, Blaine	6-1	205	L	Medicine Hat, Alta.	9/5/70	Lake Superior
PERSSON, Joakim	5-11	176	L	Ostervala, Sweden	5/4/70	Hammarby-Providence (AHL)
RIENDEAU, Vincent	5-10	185	L	St. Hyacinthe, Que.	4/20/66	Detroit-Adirondack-Boston
RYABCHIKOV, Evgeny	5-11	167	L	Yaroslavl, Soviet Union	1/16/74	Molot Perm

General Managers' History

Arthur H. Ross, 1924-25 to 1953-54; Lynn Patrick, 1954-55 to 1964-65; Leighton "Hap" Emms, 1965-66 to 1966-67; Milt Schmidt, 1967-68 to 1971-72; Harry Sinden, 1972-73 to date.

Captains' History

No Captain, 1924-25 to 1926-27; Lionel Hitchman, 1927-28 to 1930-31; George Owen, 1931-32; Dit Clapper, 1932-33 to 1937-38; Cooney Weiland, 1938-39; Dit Clapper, 1939-40 to 1945-46; Dit Clapper, John Crawford, 1946-47; John Crawford 1947-48 to 1949-50; Milt Schmidt, 1950-51 to 1953-54; Milt Schmidt, Ed Sanford, 1954-55; Fern Flaman, 1955-56 to 1960-61; Don McKenney, 1961-62, 1962-63; Leo Boivin, 1963-64 to 1965-66; John Bucyk, 1966-67; no captain, 1967-68 to 1972-73; John Bucyk, 1973-74 to 1976-77; Wayne Cashman, 1977-78 to 1982-83; Terry O'Reilly, 1983-84, 1984-85; Ray Bourque, Rick Middleton (co-captains) 1985-86 to 1987-88; Ray Bourque, 1988-89 to date.

Coaching History

Arthur H. Ross, 1924-25 to 1927-28; Cy Denneny, 1928-29; Arthur H. Ross, 1929-30 to 1933-34; Frank Patrick, 1934-35 to 1935-36; Arthur H. Ross, 1936-37 to 1938-39; Ralph (Cooney) Weiland, 1939-40 to 1940-41; Arthur H. Ross, 1941-42 to 1944-45; Aubrey V. (Dit) Clapper, 1945-46 to 1948-49; George (Buck) Boucher, 1949-50; Lynn Patrick, 1950-51 to 1953-54; Lynn Patrick and Milt Schmidt, 1954-55; Milt Schmidt, 1955-56 to 1960-61; Phil Watson, 1961-62; Phil Watson and Milt Schmidt, 1962-63; Milt Schmidt, 1963-64 to 1965-66; Harry Sinden, 1966-67 to 1969-70; Tom Johnson, 1970-71 to 1971-72; Tom Johnson and Bep Guidolin, 1972-73; Bep Guidolin, 1973-74; Don Cherry, 1974-75 to 1978-79; Fred Creighton and Harry Sinden, 1979-80; Gerry Cheevers, 1980-81 to 1983-84; Gerry Cheevers and Harry Sinden, 1984-85; Butch Goring, 1985-86; Butch Goring and Terry O'Reilly, 1986-87; Terry O'Reilly, 1987-88 to 1988-89; Mike Milbury, 1989-90 to 1990-91; Rick Bowness, 1991-92; Brian Sutter, 1992-93 to date.

1993-94 Scoring

* – rookie

Regular Season

Pos	#	Player	Team	GP	G	A	Pts	+/-	PIM	PP	SH	GW	GT	S	%
C	12	Adam Oates	BOS	77	32	80	112	10	45	16	2	3	0	197	16.2
D	77	Ray Bourque	BOS	72	20	71	91	26	58	10	3	1	1	386	5.2
R	8	Cam Neely	BOS	49	50	24	74	12	54	20	0	13	1	185	27.0
D	43	Al Iafrate	WSH	67	10	35	45	10	143	4	0	3	0	252	4.0
			BOS	12	5	8	13	6	20	2	0	1	0	47	10.6
			TOTAL	79	15	43	58	16	163	6	0	4	0	299	5.0
D	26	Glen Wesley	BOS	81	14	44	58	1	64	6	1	1	1	265	5.3
C	21	Ted Donato	BOS	84	22	32	54	0	59	9	2	1	1	158	13.9
C	20	* Bryan Smolinski	BOS	83	31	20	51	4	82	4	3	5	0	179	17.3
R	44	Glen Murray	BOS	81	18	13	31	1–	48	0	0	4	2	114	15.8
L	18	Brent Hughes	BOS	77	13	11	24	10	143	1	0	1	0	100	13.0
R	22	* Jozef Stumpel	BOS	59	8	15	23	4	14	0	0	1	0	62	12.9
L	17	Dave Reid	BOS	83	6	17	23	10	25	0	2	1	0	145	4.1
R	23	Stephen Heinze	BOS	77	10	11	21	2–	32	0	2	1	0	183	5.5
D	32	Don Sweeney	BOS	75	6	15	21	29	50	1	2	2	0	136	4.4
L	10	Dmitri Kvartalnov	BOS	39	12	7	19	9–	10	4	0	0	0	68	17.6
R	27	Stephen Leach	BOS	42	5	10	15	10–	74	1	0	1	1	89	5.6
R	33	Dan Marois	BOS	22	7	3	10	4–	18	3	0	0	0	32	21.9
D	25	Paul Stanton	BOS	71	3	7	10	7–	54	1	0	1	0	136	2.2
D	34	David Shaw	BOS	55	1	9	10	11–	85	0	0	0	0	107	.9
C	16	* Cameron Stewart	BOS	57	3	6	9	6–	66	0	0	1	0	55	5.5
D	6	Glen Featherstone	BOS	58	1	8	9	5–	152	0	0	1	0	55	1.8
D	14	Gordie Roberts	BOS	59	1	6	7	13–	40	0	0	0	0	19	5.3
L	48	* Fred Knipscheer	BOS	11	3	2	5	3	14	0	0	1	0	15	20.0
R	19	* Mariusz Czerkawski	BOS	4	2	1	3	2–	0	1	0	0	0	11	18.2
R	11	* Sergei Zholtok	BOS	24	2	1	3	7–	2	1	0	0	0	25	8.0
G	30	Jon Casey	BOS	57	0	2	2	0	14	0	0	0	0	0	.0
L	56	Darren Banks	BOS	4	0	1	1	0	9	0	0	0	0	3	.0
D	29	* John Gruden	BOS	7	0	1	1	3–	2	0	0	0	0	8	.0
G	37	Vincent Riendeau	DET	8	0	0	0	0	0	0	0	0	0	0	.0
			BOS	18	0	1	1	0	0	0	0	0	0	0	.0
			TOTAL	26	0	1	1	0	0	0	0	0	0	0	.0
C	45	* Andrew McKim	BOS	29	0	1	1	10–	4	0	0	0	0	22	.0
D	28	Jamie Huscroft	BOS	36	0	1	1	2–	144	0	0	0	0	13	.0
D	28	Mikhail Tatarinov	BOS	2	0	0	0	0	2	0	0	0	0	4	.0
C	29	Jon Morris	BOS	4	0	0	0	2–	0	0	0	0	0	3	.0
D	36	Jim Wiemer	BOS	4	0	0	0	3–	2	0	0	0	0	8	.0
L	13	Grigori Panteleev	BOS	10	0	0	0	2–	0	0	0	0	0	8	.0
G	39	John Blue	BOS	18	0	0	0	0	7	0	0	0	0	0	.0

Goaltending

No.	Goaltender	GPI	Mins	Avg	W	L	T	EN	SO	GA	SA	S%
30	Jon Casey	57	3192	2.88	30	15	9	1	4	153	1289	.881
39	John Blue	18	944	2.99	5	8	3	1	0	47	407	.885
37	Vincent Riendeau	18	976	3.07	7	6	1	0	1	50	415	.880
	Totals	**84**	**5116**	**2.96**	**42**	**29**	**13**	**2**	**5**	**252**	**2113**	**.881**

Playoffs

Pos	#	Player	Team	GP	G	A	Pts	+/-	PIM	PP	SH	GW	GT	S	%
C	12	Adam Oates	BOS	13	3	9	12	3–	8	2	0	0	0	42	7.1
D	77	Ray Bourque	BOS	13	2	8	10	5–	0	1	0	0	0	64	3.1
C	20	* Bryan Smolinski	BOS	13	5	4	9	1–	4	2	0	0	0	30	16.7
R	44	Glen Murray	BOS	13	4	5	9	2–	14	0	0	0	0	28	14.3
R	22	* Jozef Stumpel	BOS	13	1	7	8	0	4	0	0	0	0	22	4.5
C	21	Ted Donato	BOS	13	4	2	6	1–	10	2	0	1	0	18	22.2
D	26	Glen Wesley	BOS	13	3	3	6	0	12	1	0	0	0	35	8.6
R	19	* Mariusz Czerkawski	BOS	13	3	3	6	1–	4	1	0	0	0	22	13.6
R	23	Stephen Heinze	BOS	13	2	3	5	6	7	0	0	0	0	16	12.5
D	43	Al Iafrate	BOS	13	3	1	4	2–	6	1	0	1	0	49	6.1
D	32	Don Sweeney	BOS	12	2	1	3	2–	4	0	0	1	1	11	18.2
L	48	* Fred Knipscheer	BOS	12	2	1	3	0	6	0	0	1	0	9	22.2
L	18	Brent Hughes	BOS	13	2	1	3	3–	27	0	0	1	0	17	11.8
L	17	Dave Reid	BOS	13	2	1	3	1–	2	0	1	0	0	23	8.7
D	34	David Shaw	BOS	13	1	2	3	4	16	0	0	1	0	19	5.3
C	16	* Cameron Stewart	BOS	8	0	3	3	0	7	0	0	0	0	4	.0
R	27	Stephen Leach	BOS	5	0	1	1	2–	2	0	0	0	0	3	.0
R	33	Dan Marois	BOS	11	0	1	1	1–	16	0	0	0	0	18	.0
D	14	Gordie Roberts	BOS	12	0	1	1	0	8	0	0	0	0	9	.0
D	6	Glen Featherstone	BOS	1	0	0	0	1	0	0	0	0	0	0	.0
G	37	Vincent Riendeau	BOS	2	0	0	0	0	0	0	0	0	0	0	.0
D	28	Jamie Huscroft	BOS	4	0	0	0	1	9	0	0	0	0	3	.0
G	30	Jon Casey	BOS	11	0	0	0	0	0	0	0	0	0	0	.0

Goaltending

No.	Goaltender	GPI	Mins	Avg	W	L	EN	SO	GA	SA	S%
30	Jon Casey	11	698	2.92	5	6	0	0	34	308	.890
37	Vincent Riendeau	2	120	4.00	1	1	0	0	8	42	.810
	Totals	**13**	**821**	**3.07**	**6**	**7**	**0**	**0**	**42**	**350**	**.880**

Retired Numbers

2	Eddie Shore	1926-1940
3	Lionel Hitchman	1925-1934
4	Bobby Orr	1966-1976
5	Dit Clapper	1927-1947
7	Phil Esposito	1967-1975
9	John Bucyk	1957-1978
15	Milt Schmidt	1936-1955

Club Records

Team

(Figures in brackets for season records are games played; records for fewest points, wins, ties, losses, goals, goals against are for 70 or more games)

Most Points	121	1970-71 (78)
Most Wins	57	1970-71 (78)
Most Ties	21	1954-55 (70)
Most Losses	47	1961-62 (70)
Most Goals	399	1970-71 (78)
Most Goals Against	306	1961-62 (70)
Fewest Points	38	1961-62 (70)
Fewest Wins	14	1962-63 (70)
Fewest Ties	5	1972-73 (78)
Fewest Losses	13	1971-72 (78)
Fewest Goals	147	1955-56 (70)
Fewest Goals Against	172	1952-53 (70)

Longest Winning Streak

Over-all	14	Dec. 3/29-Jan. 9/30
Home	*20	Dec. 3/29-Mar. 18/30
Away	8	Feb. 17-Mar. 8/72; Mar. 15-Apr. 14/93

Longest Undefeated Streak

Over-all	23	Dec. 22/40-Feb. 23/41 (15 wins, 8 ties)
Home	27	Nov. 22/70-Mar. 20/71 (26 wins, 1 tie)
Away	15	Dec. 22/40-Mar. 16/41 (9 wins, 6 ties)

Longest Losing Streak

Over-all	11	Dec. 3/24-Jan. 5/25
Home	*11	Dec. 8/24-Feb. 17/25
Away	14	Dec. 27/64-Feb. 21/65

Longest Winless Streak

Over-all	20	Jan. 28-Mar. 11/62 (16 losses, 4 ties)
Home	11	Dec. 8/24-Feb. 17/25 (11 losses)
Away	14	Three times
Most Shutouts, Season	15	1927-28 (44)
Most PIM, Season	2,443	1987-88 (80)
Most Goals, Game	14	Jan. 21/45 (NYR 3 at Bos. 14)

Individual

Most Seasons	21	John Bucyk
Most Games	1,436	John Bucyk
Most Goals, Career	545	John Bucyk
Most Assists, Career	877	Ray Bourque
Most Points, Career	1,339	John Bucyk (545 goals, 794 assists)
Most PIM, Career	2,095	Terry O'Reilly
Most Shutouts, Career	74	Tiny Thompson

Longest Consecutive

Games Streak	418	John Bucyk (Jan. 23/69-Mar. 2/75)
Most Goals, Season	76	Phil Esposito (1970-71)
Most Assists, Season	102	Bobby Orr (1970-71)
Most Points, Season	152	Phil Esposito (1970-71) (76 goals, 76 assists)
Most PIM, Season	304	Jay Miller (1987-88)

Most Points, Defenseman

Season	*139	Bobby Orr (1970-71) (37 goals, 102 assists)

Most Points, Center

Season	152	Phil Esposito (1970-71) (76 goals, 76 assists)

Most Points, Right Wing

Season	105	Ken Hodge (1970-71) (43 goals, 62 assists) Ken Hodge (1973-74) (50 goals, 55 assists) Rick Middleton (1983-84) (47 goals, 58 assists)

Most Points, Left Wing

Season	116	John Bucyk (1970-71) (51 goals, 65 assists)

Most Points, Rookie

Season	102	Joe Juneau (1992-93) (32 goals, 70 assists)
Most Shutouts, Season	15	Hal Winkler (1927-28)
Most Goals, Game	4	Several players
Most Assists, Game	6	Ken Hodge (Feb. 9/71) Bobby Orr (Jan. 1/73)
Most Points, Game	7	Bobby Orr (Nov. 15/73) Phil Esposito (Dec. 19/74) Barry Pederson (Apr. 4/82) Cam Neely (Oct. 16/88)

* NHL Record.

All-time Record vs. Other Clubs

Regular Season

	At Home							On Road							Total						
	GP	W	L	T	GF	GA	PTS	GP	W	L	T	GF	GA	PTS	GP	W	L	T	GF	GA	PTS
Anaheim	1	1	0		5	3	2	1	0	1		1	1	1	2	1	1	0	6	4	3
Buffalo	81	47	24	10	336	251	104	82	27	41	14	255	310	68	163	74	65	24	591	561	172
Calgary	39	24	10	5	138	107	53	38	20	15	3	140	144	43	77	44	25	8	278	251	96
Chicago	276	159	85	32	1003	778	350	278	93	141	44	745	896	230	554	252	226	76	1748	1674	580
Dallas	53	38	6	9	239	125	85	53	29	13	11	198	145	69	106	67	19	20	437	270	154
Detroit	279	151	85	43	986	739	345	278	76	150	52	699	930	204	557	227	235	95	1685	1669	549
Edmonton	23	17	4	2	107	63	36	22	11	8	3	76	76	25	45	28	12	5	183	139	61
Florida	2	1	0		5	4	3	2	1	1		2	4	2	4	2	1		7	8	5
Hartford	55	38	12	5	226	146	81	53	23	23	7	192	188	53	108	61	35	12	418	334	134
Los Angeles	54	41	10	3	261	149	85	53	30	18	5	203	185	65	107	71	28	8	464	334	150
Montreal	309	142	114	53	911	836	337	308	84	179	45	713	1052	213	617	226	293	98	1624	1888	550
New Jersey	36	23	10	3	162	118	49	33	19	6	8	124	90	46	69	42	16	11	286	208	95
NY Islanders	40	22	9	9	157	112	53	41	22	15	4	142	129	48	81	44	24	13	299	241	101
NY Rangers	278	150	88	40	1009	774	340	282	106	122	54	792	857	266	560	256	210	94	1801	1631	606
Ottawa	7	7	0		37	17	14	5	5	0		24	8	10	12	12	0		61	25	24
Philadelphia	56	36	13	7	233	165	79	53	25	22	6	164	178	56	109	61	35	13	397	343	135
Pittsburgh	56	40	10	6	259	161	86	58	26	21	11	222	198	63	114	66	31	17	481	359	149
Quebec	53	29	16	8	220	166	66	55	33	17	5	249	201	71	108	62	33	13	469	367	137
St. Louis	51	33	11	7	225	138	73	52	22	21	9	181	163	53	103	55	32	16	406	301	126
San Jose	3	3	0		14	10	6	3	2	0	1	13	4	5	6	5	0	1	27	14	11
Tampa Bay	3	1	1	1	6	7	3	3	1	0	2	10	8	4	6	2	1	3	16	15	7
Toronto	280	151	82	47	924	749	349	280	86	147	47	728	953	219	560	237	229	94	1652	1702	568
Vancouver	43	35	4	4	194	96	74	44	22	14	8	187	149	52	87	57	18	12	381	245	126
Washington	36	23	9	4	156	103	50	36	19	9	8	140	110	46	72	42	18	12	296	213	96
Winnipeg	22	16	3	3	105	70	35	23	12	9	2	86	83	26	45	28	12	5	191	153	61
Defunct Clubs	164	112	39	13	525	306	237	164	79	67	18	496	440	176	328	191	106	31	1021	746	413
Totals	**2300**	**1340**	**645**	**315**	**8443**	**6193**	**2995**	**2300**	**873**	**1059**	**368**	**6782**	**7502**	**2114**	**4600**	**2213**	**1704**	**683**	**15225**	**13695**	**5109**

Calgary totals include Atlanta, 1972-73 to 1979-80. Dallas totals include Minnesota, 1967-68 to 1992-93. New Jersey totals include Kansas City, 1974-75 to 1975-76, and Colorado, 1976-77 to 1981-82.

Playoffs

	Series	W	L	GP	W	L	T	GF	GA	Last Mtg.	Round	Result
Buffalo	6	5	1	33	19	14	0	132	113	1993	DSF	L 0-4
Chicago	6	5	1	22	16	5	1	97	63	1978	QF	W 4-0
Dallas	1	0	1	3	0	3	0	13	20	1981	PR	L 0-3
Detroit	7	4	3	33	19	14	0	96	98	1957	SF	W 4-1
Edmonton	2	0	2	9	1	8	0	20	41	1990	F	L 1-4
Hartford	2	2	0	13	8	5	0	24	17	1991	DSF	W 4-2
Los Angeles	2	2	0	13	8	5	0	56	38	1977	QF	W 4-2
Montreal	28	7	21	139	52	87	0	339	430	1994	CQF	W 4-3
New Jersey	2	1	1	13	6	7	0	47	41	1994	CSF	L 2-4
NY Islanders	2	0	2	11	3	8	0	35	49	1983	CF	L 2-4
NY Rangers	9	6	3	42	22	18	2	114	104	1973	QF	L 1-4
Philadelphia	4	2	2	20	11	9	0	60	57	1978	SF	W 4-1
Pittsburgh	4	2	2	19	9	10	0	62	67	1992	CF	L 0-4
Quebec	2	1	1	11	6	5	0	37	36	1983	DSF	W 3-1
St. Louis	2	2	0	8	4	4	0	48	15	1972	SF	W 4-0
Toronto	13	5	8	62	30	31	1	153	150	1974	QF	W 4-0
Washington	1	0	1	4	0	4	0	15	6	1990	CF	W 4-0
Defunct Clubs	3	1	2	11	4	5	2	20	20			
Totals	**96**	**46**	**50**	**466**	**226**	**234**	**6**	**1384**	**1386**			

Playoff Results 1994-90

Year	Round	Opponent	Result	GF	GA
1994	CSF	New Jersey	L 2-4	17	22
	CQF	Montreal	W 4-3	22	20
1993	DSF	Buffalo	L 0-4	12	19
1992	CF	Pittsburgh	L 0-4	7	19
	DF	Montreal	W 4-0	14	8
	DSF	Buffalo	W 4-3	19	24
1991	CF	Pittsburgh	L 2-4	18	27
	DF	Montreal	W 4-3	18	18
	DSF	Hartford	W 4-2	24	17
1990	F	Edmonton	L 1-4	8	20
	CF	Washington	W 4-0	15	6
	DF	Montreal	W 4-1	16	12
	DSF	Hartford	W 4-3	23	21

Abbreviations: Round: F – Final; **CF** – conference final; **CQF** – conference quarter-final; **CSF** – conference semi-final; **DF** – division final; **DSF** – division semi-final; **SF** – semi-final; **QF** – quarter-final; **PR** – preliminary round.

1993-94 Results

Oct.	5	at	NY Rangers	4-3	15	Detroit	2-3
	7		Buffalo	3-5	17	Hartford	5-3
	9		Quebec	7-3	19 at	Montreal	3-3
	11		Montreal	1-1	24 at	Hartford	2-1
	15	at	Anaheim	1-1	25 at	Washington	3-1
	16	at	San Jose	1-1	28 at	NY Islanders	3-0
	19	at	Vancouver	4-5	29	NY Islanders	2-1
	22	at	Edmonton	3-1	31	Quebec	4-3
	23	at	Calgary	3-3	Feb. 3	NY Rangers	0-3
	28		Ottawa	6-2	5	Philadelphia	4-0
	30		St. Louis	1-2	6 at	Florida	0-3
Nov.	2	at	Detroit	1-6	8 at	Quebec	6-1
	4		Calgary	6-3	10	Buffalo	3-3
	6		Tampa Bay	1-1	12	New Jersey	5-3
	7	at	Buffalo	4-3	14 at	Los Angeles	3-2
	11		Edmonton	5-1	16 at	Dallas	3-0
	13	at	NY Islanders	5-18	18 at	St. Louis	1-3
	17		Hartford	4-2	20 at	Tampa Bay	2-2
	18		San Jose	3-1	23 at	NY Rangers	6-3
	20		Philadelphia	5-5	25 at	Winnipeg	7-6
	24	at	Pittsburgh	3-7	27 at	Chicago	4-0
	26		Florida	3-2	Mar. 3	Los Angeles	6-4
	27		Toronto	2-4	5	Ottawa	6-1
	30	at	Quebec	5-2	7	Washington	6-3
Dec.	2		NY Islanders	7-3	8 at	Pittsburgh	3-7
	4		Montreal	1-8	10	NY Rangers	2-2
	5	at	Buffalo	1-3	12	New Jersey	1-2
	9		Vancouver	2-3	14 at	Montreal	4-5
	11		Chicago	4-5	17	Pittsburgh	2-4
	12		Hartford	2-2	19	New Jersey	6-8
	15	at	New Jersey	5-4	22 at	Quebec	3-5
	18	at	Tampa Bay	5-3	24	Anaheim	5-3
	19	at	Florida	2-1	26	Montreal	6-3
	23		Pittsburgh	3-4	27 at	Washington	6-4
	27	at	Ottawa	5-3	31	Dallas	2-2
	31		Philadelphia	3-4	Apr. 1 at	Buffalo	0-5
Jan.	2		Washington	8-2	3 at	Pittsburgh	2-6
	6		Winnipeg	5-2	7	Ottawa	5-4
	8		Florida	5-2	9	Tampa Bay	0-3
	10		Toronto	0-3	10 at	Philadelphia	4-3
	11	at	Pittsburgh	4-5	13 at	Ottawa	8-0
	13	at	Philadelphia	2-6	14	Hartford	2-3

Entry Draft
Selections 1994-80

1994
Pick
- 21 Evgeni Ryabchikov
- 47 Daniel Goneau
- 99 Eric Nickulas
- 125 Darren Wright
- 151 Andre Roy
- 177 Jeremy Schaefer
- 229 Neil Savary
- 255 Neil Savary
- 281 Andrei Yakhanov

1993
Pick
- 25 Kevyn Adams
- 51 Matt Alvey
- 88 Charles Paquette
- 103 Shawn Bates
- 129 Andrei Sapozhnikov
- 155 Milt Mastad
- 181 Ryan Golden
- 207 Hal Gill
- 233 Joel Prpic
- 259 Joakim Persson

1992
Pick
- 16 Dmitri Kvartalnov
- 55 Sergei Zholtok
- 112 Scott Bailey
- 133 Jiri Dopita
- 136 Grigori Panteleev
- 184 Kurt Seher
- 208 Mattias Timander
- 232 Chris Crombie
- 256 Denis Chervyakov
- 257 Evgeny Pavlov

1991
Pick
- 18 Glen Murray
- 40 Jozef Stumpel
- 62 Marcel Cousineau
- 84 Brad Tiley
- 106 Mariusz Czerkawski
- 150 Gary Golczewski
- 172 John Moser
- 194 Daniel Hodge
- 216 Steve Norton
- 238 Stephen Lombardi
- 260 Torsten Kienass

1990
Pick
- 21 Bryan Smolinski
- 63 Cameron Stewart
- 84 Jerome Buckley
- 105 Mike Bales
- 126 Mark Woolf
- 147 Jim Mackey
- 168 John Gruden
- 189 Darren Wetherill
- 210 Dean Capuano
- 231 Andy Bezeau
- 252 Ted Miskolczi

1989
Pick
- 17 Shayne Stevenson
- 38 Mike Parson
- 57 Wes Walz
- 80 Jackson Penney
- 101 Mark Montanari
- 122 Stephen Foster
- 143 Otto Hascak
- 164 Rick Allain
- 185 James Lavish
- 206 Geoff Simpson
- 227 David Franzosa

1988
Pick
- 18 Robert Cimetta
- 60 Stephen Heinze
- 81 Joe Juneau
- 102 Daniel Murphy
- 123 Derek Geary
- 165 Mark Krys
- 186 Jon Rohloff
- 228 Eric Reisman
- 249 Doug Jones

1987
Pick
- 3 Glen Wesley
- 14 Stephane Quintal
- 56 Todd Lalonde
- 67 Darwin McPherson
- 77 Matt Delguidice
- 98 Ted Donato
- 119 Matt Glennon
- 140 Rob Cheevers
- 161 Chris Winnes
- 182 Paul Ohman
- 203 Casey Jones
- 224 Eric Lemarque
- 245 Sean Gorman

1986
Pick
- 13 Craig Janney
- 34 Pekka Tirkkonen
- 76 Dean Hall
- 97 Matt Pesklewis
- 118 Garth Premak
- 139 Paul Beraldo
- 160 Brian Ferreira
- 181 Jeff Flaherty
- 202 Greg Hawgood
- 223 Staffan Malmqvist
- 244 Joel Gardner

1985
Pick
- 31 Alain Cote
- 52 Bill Ranford
- 73 Jaime Kelly
- 94 Steve Moore
- 115 Gord Hynes
- 136 Per Martinelle
- 157 Randy Burridge
- 178 Gord Cruickshank
- 199 Dave Buda
- 210 Bob Beers
- 220 John Byce
- 241 Marc West

1984
Pick
- 19 Dave Pasin
- 40 Ray Podloski
- 61 Jeff Cornelius
- 82 Robert Joyce
- 103 Mike Bishop
- 124 Randy Oswald
- 145 Mark Thietke
- 166 Don Sweeney
- 186 Kevin Heffernan
- 207 J.D. Urbanic
- 227 Bill Kopecky
- 248 Jim Newhouse

1983
Pick
- 21 Nevin Markwart
- 42 Greg Johnston
- 62 Greg Puhalski
- 82 Alain Larochelle
- 102 Allen Pederson
- 122 Terry Taillefer
- 142 Ian Armstrong
- 162 Francois Olivier
- 182 Harri Laurilla
- 202 Paul Fitzsimmons
- 222 Norm Foster
- 242 Greg Murphy

1982
Pick
- 1 Gord Kluzak
- 22 Brian Curran
- 39 Lyndon Byers
- 60 Dave Reid
- 102 Bob Nicholson
- 123 Bob Sweeney
- 144 John Meulenbroeks
- 165 Tony Fiore
- 186 Doug Kostynski
- 207 Tony Gilliard
- 228 Tommy Lehmann
- 249 Bruno Campese

1981
Pick
- 14 Normand Leveille
- 35 Luc Dufour
- 77 Scott McLellan
- 98 Joe Mantione
- 119 Bruce Milton
- 140 Mats Thelin
- 161 Armel Parisee
- 182 Don Sylvestri
- 203 Richard Bourque

1980
Pick
- 18 Barry Pederson
- 60 Tom Fergus
- 81 Steve Kasper
- 102 Randy Hillier
- 123 Steve Lyons
- 144 Tony McMurchy
- 165 Mike Moffat
- 186 Michael Thelven
- 207 Jens Ohling

Club Directory

Boston Garden
150 Causeway Street
Boston, Massachusetts 02114
Phone **617/227-3206**
FAX 617/523-7184
Capacity: 14,448

Executive
Owner and Governor	Jeremy M. Jacobs
Alternative Governor	Louis Jacobs
President, General Manager and Alternative Governor	Harry Sinden
Vice President	Tom Johnson
Assistant General Manager	Mike O'Connell
Sr. Assistant to the President	Nate Greenberg
General Counsel	Barbara Macon
Director of Administration	Dale Hamilton
Assistant to the President	Joe Curnane
Administrative Assistant	Carol Gould
Receptionist	Karen Leonard

Coaching Staff
Coach	Brian Sutter
Assistant Coach	Tom McVie
Coach, Providence Bruins	Steve Kasper
Coach, Charlotte Checkers	John Marks

Scouting Staff
Director of Player Evaluation	Bart Bradley
Director of Scouting	Bob Tindall
Director of European Scouting	Svenake Svenson
Assistant Directors of Scouting	Jim Morrison, Gordie Clark
Scouting Staff	Don Saatzer, Joe Lyons, Harvey Keck, Yuri Karmanov, Jean Ratelle, Zbenek Kusy, Jiri Hamel, Marcel Pelletier

Communications Staff
Director of Media Relations	Heidi Holland
Assistant Director of Media Relations	Jeff Gorton
Director of Community Relations, Marketing Services	Sue Byrne
Assistant Director of Community Relations & Marketing Services	Kevin Lyons
Director of Alumni Relations	John Bucyk
Administrative Assistant	Mal Viola

Medical and Training Staff
Athletic Trainer	Don Del Negro
Physical Therapist	Tim Trahant
Equipment Manager	Ken Fleger
Assistant Equipment Manager	Keith Robinson
Team Physicians	Dr. Bertram Zarins, Dr. Ashby Moncure, Dr. John J. Boyle
Team Dentists	Dr. John Kelly and Dr. Bruce Donoff
Team Psychologist	Dr. Fred Neff

Ticketing and Finance Staff
Director of Ticket Operations	Matt Brennan
Assistant Director of Ticket Operations	Jim Foley
Receptionist	Linda Bartlett
Controller	Bob Vogel
Accounting Manager	Richard McGlinchey
Accounts Payable	Barbara Johnson

Television and Radio
Broadcasters (WSBK-TV 38)	Fred Cusick and Derek Sanderson
Broadcasters (NESN)	Fred Cusick, Derek Sanderson and Dave Shea
Broadcasters (Radio)	Bob Wilson and John Bucyk
TV Channels	New England Sports Network (NESN) and WSBK-TV 38
Radio Station	WBNW (590 AM) and Bruins Radio Network
Dimensions of Rink	191 feet by 83 feet
Club Colors	Gold, Black and White

General Manager

SINDEN, HARRY JAMES
President and General Manager, Boston Bruins.
Born in Collins Bay, Ont., September 14, 1932.

Harry Sinden never played a game in the NHL but stepped into the Bruins' organization with an impressive coaching background in minor professional hockey and his continued excellence has earned him a place in the Hockey Hall of Fame as one of the true builders in hockey history. In 1965-66 as playing-coach of Oklahoma City Blazers in the CPHL, Sinden led the club to second place in the regular standings and then to eight straight playoff victories for the Jack Adams Trophy. After five years in OHA Senior hockey — including 1958 with the IIHF World Amateur Champion Whitby Dunlops — Sinden became a playing-coach in the old Eastern Professional League and its successor, the Central Professional League.

Under his guidance, the Bruins of 1967-68 made the playoffs for the first time in nine seasons, finishing third in the East Division, and were nosed out of first place in 1968-69 by Montreal. In 1969-70, Sinden led the Bruins to their first Stanley Cup win since 1940-41.

The following season he went into private business but returned to the hockey scene in the summer of 1972 when he was appointed coach of Team Canada. He molded that group of NHL stars into a powerful unit and led them into an exciting eight-game series against the Soviet national team in September of 1972. Team Canada emerged the winner by a narrow margin with a record of four wins, three losses and one tie.

Sinden then returned to the Bruins organization early in the 1972-73 season. Sinden last took over as the Bruins' coach in February 1985, after replacing Gerry Cheevers. Boston finished 11-10-3 with Sinden behind the bench before being defeated by Montreal in five games in the Adams Division semi-finals.

NHL Coaching Record

Season	Team	Regular Season					Playoffs			
		Games	W	L	T	%	Games	W	L	%
1966-67	Boston	70	17	43	10	.314				
1967-68	Boston	74	37	27	10	.568	4	0	4	.000
1968-69	Boston	76	42	18	16	.658	10	6	4	.600
1969-70	Boston	76	40	17	19	.651	14	12	2	.857*
1979-80	Boston	10	4	6	0	.400	9	4	5	.444
1984-85	Boston	24	11	10	3	.521	5	2	3	.400
	NHL Totals	**330**	**151**	**121**	**58**	**.545**	**42**	**24**	**18**	**.571**

Coach

SUTTER, BRIAN
Coach, Boston Bruins. Born in Viking, Alta., October 7, 1956.

In his second season as coach of the Boston Bruins, Brian Sutter guided the team to a second place finish in the Northeast Division. Brian Sutter became the 20th coach in the history of the Boston Bruins, joining the organization after four successful seasons as head coach of the St. Louis Blues. Sutter, who received the Jack Adams Award as the NHL's coach of the year in 1990-91 after directing the Blues to a club-record 47 wins, led the Blues to an above-.500 record in three of his four seasons behind the St. Louis bench. A second round draft selection in 1976, Sutter spent his entire playing career with the Blues, and ranks second in franchise history in games (779), goals (303), assists (333) and points (636).

Coaching Record

Season	Team	Regular Season					Playoffs			
		Games	W	L	T	%	Games	W	L	%
1988-89	St. Louis (NHL)	80	33	35	12	.488	10	5	5	.500
1989-90	St. Louis (NHL)	80	37	34	9	.519	12	7	5	.583
1990-91	St. Louis (NHL)	80	47	22	11	.656	13	6	7	.462
1991-92	St. Louis (NHL)	80	36	33	11	.519	6	2	4	.333
1992-93	Boston (NHL)	84	51	26	7	.649	4	0	4	.000
1993-94	Boston (NHL)	84	42	29	13	.577	13	6	7	.462
	NHL Totals	**488**	**246**	**179**	**63**	**.569**	**58**	**26**	**32**	**.448**

Buffalo Sabres

1993-94 Results: 43W-32L-9T 95PTS. Fourth, Northeast Division

Schedule

Oct.	Sat.	1	at Quebec	Wed.	11	Washington
	Wed.	5	at Pittsburgh	Fri.	13	at Calgary
	Fri.	7	Montreal	Sun.	15	at Edmonton
	Sat.	8	at Montreal	Wed.	18	at Vancouver
	Mon.	10	Toronto	Mon.	23	Ottawa
	Wed.	12	at Detroit	Wed.	25	New Jersey
	Fri.	14	Hartford	Fri.	27	Quebec
	Sat.	15	at Washington	Sat.	28	at Ottawa
	Fri.	21	Florida	Feb. Thur.	2	at New Jersey
	Sun.	23	Quebec	Sat.	4	at Philadelphia*
	Thur.	27	at Florida	Tues.	7	Dallas
	Sat.	29	at Boston	Thur.	9	Florida
Nov.	Wed.	2	Chicago	Sat.	11	at Toronto
	Fri.	4	Philadelphia	Sun.	12	Boston
	Sat.	5	at Philadelphia	Wed.	15	NY Rangers
	Tues.	8	Tampa Bay	Fri.	17	at Florida
	Thur.	10	Ottawa	Sat.	18	at Tampa Bay
	Sat.	12	at San Jose	Mon.	20	Winnipeg
	Tues.	15	at Anaheim	Wed.	22	NY Islanders
	Thur.	17	at Los Angeles	Sat.	25	at Hartford
	Mon.	21	at Dallas	Sun.	26	NY Rangers
	Wed.	23	Boston	Tues.	28	San Jose
	Fri.	25	Vancouver	Mar. Thur.	2	at Chicago
	Sun.	27	NY Islanders	Sat.	4	at Quebec
	Wed.	30	at NY Rangers	Sun.	5	Calgary
Dec.	Fri.	2	Los Angeles	Wed.	8	at NY Rangers
	Sat.	3	at NY Islanders	Fri.	10	at Winnipeg
	Wed.	7	Pittsburgh	Sun.	12	at St. Louis
	Fri.	9	Hartford	Tues.	14	at Boston
	Sat.	10	at Pittsburgh			(in Hamilton)
	Wed.	14	at Tampa Bay	Thur.	16	Detroit
	Fri.	16	Montreal	Sat.	18	at Boston*
	Sat.	17	at Boston	Sun.	19	Tampa Bay*
	Mon.	19	at Ottawa	Tues.	21	Pittsburgh
	Wed.	21	at Montreal	Fri.	24	Quebec
	Fri.	23	Hartford	Sat.	25	at Montreal
	Mon.	26	at New Jersey	Wed.	29	Edmonton
	Tues.	27	New Jersey	Apr. Sat.	1	at NY Islanders*
	Thur.	29	at Pittsburgh	Sun.	2	Ottawa*
	Sat.	31	Philadelphia	Tues.	4	St. Louis
Jan.	Fri.	6	Anaheim	Fri.	7	Washington
	Sat.	7	at Hartford	Sat.	8	at Washington
	Mon.	9	NY Islanders			
			(in Minneapolis)			

* Denotes afternoon game.

Home Starting Times:
Tuesdays through Saturdays . . . . . . 7:30 p.m.
Sundays and Mondays . . . . 7:00 p.m.
Matinees . . . . 2:00 p.m.

Franchise date: May 22, 1970

NORTHEAST DIVISION

25th NHL Season

Donald Audette made a dramatic recovery from a serious knee injury to collect 29 goals for the Buffalo Sabres, the third highest total on the squad.

Year-by-Year Record

Season	GP	Home W	L	T	Road W	L	T	Overall W	L	T	GF	GA	Pts.	Finished		Playoff Result
1993-94	84	22	17	3	21	15	6	43	32	9	282	218	95	4th,	Northeast Div.	Lost Conf. Quarter-Final
1992-93	84	25	15	2	13	21	8	38	36	10	335	297	86	4th,	Adams Div.	Lost Div. Final
1991-92	80	22	13	5	9	24	7	31	37	12	289	299	74	3rd,	Adams Div.	Lost Div. Semi-Final
1990-91	80	15	13	12	16	17	7	31	30	19	292	278	81	3rd,	Adams Div.	Lost Div. Semi-Final
1989-90	80	27	11	2	18	16	6	45	27	8	286	248	98	2nd,	Adams Div.	Lost Div. Semi-Final
1988-89	80	25	12	3	13	23	4	38	35	7	291	299	83	3rd,	Adams Div.	Lost Div. Semi-Final
1987-88	80	19	14	7	18	18	4	37	32	11	283	305	85	3rd,	Adams Div.	Lost Div. Semi-Final
1986-87	80	18	18	4	10	26	4	28	44	8	280	308	64	5th,	Adams Div.	Out of Playoffs
1985-86	80	23	16	1	14	21	5	37	37	6	296	291	80	5th,	Adams Div.	Out of Playoffs
1984-85	80	23	10	7	15	18	7	38	28	14	290	237	90	3rd,	Adams Div.	Lost Div. Semi-Final
1983-84	80	25	9	6	23	16	1	48	25	7	315	257	103	2nd,	Adams Div.	Lost Div. Semi-Final
1982-83	80	25	7	8	13	22	5	38	29	13	318	285	89	3rd,	Adams Div.	Lost Div. Final
1981-82	80	23	8	9	16	18	6	39	26	15	307	273	93	3rd,	Adams Div.	Lost Div. Semi-Final
1980-81	80	21	7	12	18	13	9	39	20	21	327	250	99	1st,	Adams Div.	Lost Quarter-Final
1979-80	80	27	5	8	20	12	8	47	17	16	318	201	110	1st,	Adams Div.	Lost Semi-Final
1978-79	80	19	13	8	17	15	8	36	28	16	280	263	88	2nd,	Adams Div.	Lost Prelim. Round
1977-78	80	25	7	8	19	12	9	44	19	17	288	215	105	2nd,	Adams Div.	Lost Quarter-Final
1976-77	80	27	8	5	21	16	3	48	24	8	301	220	104	2nd,	Adams Div.	Lost Quarter-Final
1975-76	80	28	7	5	18	14	8	46	21	13	339	240	105	2nd,	Adams Div.	Lost Quarter-Final
1974-75	80	28	6	6	21	10	9	49	16	15	354	240	113	1st,	Adams Div.	Lost Final
1973-74	78	24	10	5	9	24	6	32	34	12	242	250	76	5th,	East Div.	Out of Playoffs
1972-73	78	30	6	3	7	21	11	37	27	14	257	219	88	4th,	East Div.	Lost Quarter-Final
1971-72	78	11	19	9	5	24	10	16	43	19	203	289	51	6th,	East Div.	Out of Playoffs
1970-71	78	16	13	10	8	26	5	24	39	15	217	291	63	5th,	East Div.	Out of Playoffs

1994-95 Player Personnel

FORWARDS	HT	WT	S	Place of Birth	Date	1993-94 Club
AMBROZIAK, Peter	6-0	206	L	Toronto, Ont.	9/15/71	Rochester
AUDETTE, Donald	5-8	175	R	Laval, Que.	9/23/69	Buffalo
BARNABY, Matthew	6-0	170	L	Ottawa, Ont.	5/4/73	Buffalo-Rochester
BARRIE, Mike	6-1	170	R	Kelowna, B.C.	3/16/74	Red Deer-Seattle-Rochester
BROWN, Curtis	6-0	182	L	Unity, Sask.	2/12/76	Moose Jaw
DAWE, Jason	5-10	195	L	North York, Ont.	5/29/73	Buffalo-Rochester
GAGE, Jody	6-0	190	R	Toronto, Ont.	11/29/59	Rochester
GORDIOUK, Viktor	5-10	176	R	Odintsovo, USSR	4/11/70	Rochester
HANNAN, Dave	5-10	185	L	Sudbury, Ont.	11/26/61	Buffalo
HAWERCHUK, Dale	5-11	190	L	Toronto, Ont.	4/4/63	Buffalo
HOLZINGER, Brian	5-11	180	R	Parma, OH	10/10/72	Bowling Green
KHMYLEV, Yuri	6-1	189	R	Moscow, USSR	8/9/64	Buffalo
LaFONTAINE, Pat	5-10	177	R	St. Louis, MO	2/22/65	Buffalo
MACDONALD, Doug	6-0	192	L	Assiniboia, Sask.	2/8/69	Buffalo-Rochester
MAY, Brad	6-1	210	L	Toronto, Ont.	11/29/71	Buffalo
McCARTHY, Brian	6-2	190	L	Salem, MA	12/6/71	St. Lawrence
MOGILNY, Alexander	5-11	187	L	Khabarovsk, USSR	2/18/69	Buffalo
MOORE, Barrie	6-0	195	L	London, Ont.	5/22/75	Sudbury
NICHOL, Scott	5-9	175	R	Calgary, Alta.	12/31/74	Portland (WHL)
PETRENKO, Sergei	6-0	176	L	Kharkov, USSR	9/10/68	Buffalo-Rochester
PHILPOTT, Ethan	6-4	230	R	Rochester, MN	2/11/75	Harvard
PLANTE, Derek	5-11	180	L	Cloquet, MN	1/17/71	Buffalo-U.S. National
PRESLEY, Wayne	5-11	180	R	Dearborn, MI	3/23/65	Buffalo
PRIMEAU, Wayne	6-3	193	L	Scarborough, Ont.	6/4/76	Owen Sound
RAY, Rob	6-0	203	L	Belleville, Ont.	6/8/68	Buffalo
RUSHFORTH, Paul	6-0	189	R	Prince George, B.C.	4/22/74	Belleville
SAFARIK, Richard	6-3	194	L	Nova Zamky, Czech.	2/26/75	Hull
SIMON, Todd	5-10	188	R	Toronto, Ont.	4/21/72	Buffalo-Rochester
SIMPSON, Craig	6-2	195	R	London, Ont.	2/15/67	Buffalo
STEINER, Ondrej	6-1	176	L	Plzen, Czech.	2/12/74	Skoda Plzen
SWEENEY, Bob	6-3	200	R	Concord, MA	1/25/64	Buffalo
THOMAS, Scott	6-2	195	R	Buffalo, NY	1/18/70	Buffalo-Rochester
VOLKOV, Mikhail	5-10	174	L	Voronezh, USSR	3/9/72	Rochester
WOOD, Randy	6-0	195	L	Princeton, NJ	10/12/63	Buffalo
YOUNG, Jason	5-10	197	L	Sudbury, Ont.	12/16/72	Rochester
DEFENSEMEN						
ASTLEY, Mark	5-11	185	L	Calgary, Alta.	3/30/69	Cdn. National-Cdn. Olympic-Buf
BENAZIC, Cal	6-3	187	L	Mackenzie, B.C.	9/29/75	Medicine Hat
BODGER, Doug	6-2	213	L	Chemainus, B.C.	6/18/66	Buffalo
BOUCHER, Philippe	6-2	189	R	St. Apollinaire, Que.	3/24/73	Buffalo-Rochester
COOPER, David	6-2	204	L	Ottawa, Ont.	11/2/73	Rochester
HOUDA, Doug	6-2	190	R	Blairmore, Alta.	6/3/66	Hartford-Los Angeles
KLIMENTJEV, Sergei	5-11	200	L	Kiev, USSR	4/5/75	Medicine Hat
KUNTOS, Jiri	5-11	207	L	Vlasim, Czech.	12/11/71	Olomouc
MELANSON, Dean	5-11	211	R	Antigonish, N.S.	11/19/73	Rochester
MUNI, Craig	6-3	208	L	Toronto, Ont.	7/19/62	Chicago-Buffalo
NDUR, Ruman	6-2	200	L	Zaria, Nigeria	7/7/75	Guelph
NEDOMA, Milan	5-10	180	L	Brno, Czech.	3/29/72	Stadion
SMEHLIK, Richard	6-3	208	L	Ostrava, Czech.	1/23/70	Buffalo
SUTTON, Ken	6-0	198	L	Edmonton, Alta.	11/5/69	Buffalo
SVOBODA, Petr	6-1	174	L	Most, Czech.	2/14/66	Buffalo
TSYGUROV, Denis	6-3	198	L	Chelyabinsk, USSR	2/26/71	Buffalo-Rochester
GOALTENDERS	**HT**	**WT**	**C**	**Place of Birth**	**Date**	**1993-94 Club**
DAVIS, Chris	6-3	177	L	Calgary, Alta.	12/1/74	Alaska-Anch.
FUHR, Grant	5-9	190	R	Spruce Grove, Alta.	9/28/62	Buffalo-Rochester
HASEK, Dominik	5-11	165	L	Pardubice, Czech.	1/29/65	Buffalo
KETTERER, Markus	5-11	167	L	Helsinki, Finland	8/23/67	Rochester
SHIELDS, Steve	6-3	210	L	Toronto, Ont.	7/19/72	U. of Michigan

Coach and General Manager

MUCKLER, JOHN
Coach and General Manager, Buffalo Sabres.
Born in Midland, Ont., April 3, 1934.

In his second full season behind the Buffalo bench, and first as the general manager, John helped guide a Sabres team that suffered 291 man-games lost to injury to a 95-point season. In the wake of the injuries which kept many of his offensive weapons sidelined, Muckler substituted a solid defensive style which resulted in a Jennings Trophy. The award goes to the team with the lowest goals-against. Buffalo's two netminders surrendered just 218 goals for a 2.57 per game average. The defensive-minded Sabres set a new team record in 1993-94 for short-handed goals in one season by totalling 21, second in the NHL in that category.

Muckler reached a few significant numbers of his own during the season. He reached the 100 wins plateau in his Buffalo coaching career on April 1, becoming just the third coach in team history to reach that mark. He is also just the fourth Buffalo coach to surpass the 200 games coached mark, currently ranking third in club history. On the overall list, "Muck" hit the 400 NHL games coached plateau on March 9.

In 1994-95, Muckler enters his fourth season with the Sabres. He was hired as the director of hockey operations in the summer of 1991 and also took over as coach in December of that season. His first full season behind the Buffalo bench came in 1992-93 when he helped lead Buffalo to its first appearance in the second round of the playoffs since 1983. John added G.M.'s duties to his job in the summer of 1993.

In two seasons as head coach in Edmonton prior to joining the Sabres, Muckler led the Oilers to the Stanley Cup in 1989-90, and to the Conference Finals in 1990-91.

1993-94 Scoring

* – rookie

Regular Season

Pos	#	Player	Team	GP	G	A	Pts	+/–	PIM	PP	SH	GW	GT	S	%
C	10	Dale Hawerchuk	BUF	81	35	51	86	10	91	13	1	7	0	227	15.4
R	89	Alexander Mogilny	BUF	66	32	47	79	8	22	17	0	7	1	258	12.4
R	28	Donald Audette	BUF	77	29	30	59	2	41	16	1	4	0	207	14.0
L	13	Yuri Khmylev	BUF	72	27	31	58	13	49	11	0	4	0	171	15.8
C	26 *	Derek Plante	BUF	77	21	35	56	4	24	8	1	2	0	147	14.3
L	27	Brad May	BUF	84	18	27	45	6–	171	3	0	3	0	166	10.8
D	42	Richard Smehlik	BUF	84	14	27	41	22	69	3	3	1	1	106	13.2
D	8	Doug Bodger	BUF	75	7	32	39	8	76	5	1	1	0	144	4.9
L	19	Randy Wood	BUF	84	22	16	38	11	71	2	2	5	0	161	13.7
R	18	Wayne Presley	BUF	65	17	8	25	18	103	1	5	1	0	93	18.3
C	20	Bob Sweeney	BUF	60	11	14	25	3	94	3	3	1	0	76	14.5
D	41	Ken Sutton	BUF	78	4	20	24	6–	71	1	0	0	0	95	4.2
C	14	Dave Hannan	BUF	83	6	15	21	10	53	0	3	1	0	40	15.0
C	16	Pat LaFontaine	BUF	16	5	13	18	4–	2	1	0	0	0	40	12.5
L	22	Craig Simpson	BUF	22	8	8	16	3–	8	2	0	2	0	28	28.6
D	7	Petr Svoboda	BUF	60	2	14	16	11	89	1	0	0	0	80	2.5
D	4 *	Philippe Boucher	BUF	38	6	8	14	1–	29	4	0	1	0	67	9.0
D	5	Craig Muni	CHI	9	0	4	4	3	4	0	0	0	0	6	.0
			BUF	73	2	8	10	28	62	0	1	2	0	39	5.1
			TOTAL	82	2	12	14	31	66	0	1	2	0	45	4.4
L	43 *	Jason Dawe	BUF	32	6	7	13	1	12	3	0	1	0	35	17.1
D	24	Randy Moller	BUF	78	2	11	13	5–	154	0	0	0	0	77	2.6
L	32	Rob Ray	BUF	82	3	4	7	2	274	0	0	0	0	34	8.8
L	36 *	Matthew Barnaby	BUF	35	2	4	6	7–	106	1	0	0	0	13	15.4
C	40	James Black	DAL	13	2	3	5	4–	2	2	0	0	0	16	12.5
			BUF	2	0	0	0	0	0	0	0	0	0	2	.0
			TOTAL	15	2	3	5	4–	2	2	0	0	0	18	11.1
R	21 *	Scott Thomas	BUF	32	2	2	4	6–	8	1	0	0	0	26	7.7
L	15 *	Sergei Petrenko	BUF	14	0	4	4	3–	0	0	0	0	0	7	.0
G	31	Grant Fuhr	BUF	32	0	4	4	0	16	0	0	0	0	0	.0
G	39	Dominik Hasek	BUF	58	0	3	3	0	6	0	0	0	0	0	.0
C	17 *	Todd Simon	BUF	15	0	1	1	3–	0	0	0	0	0	14	.0
D	33 *	Mark Astley	BUF	1	0	0	0	1–	0	0	0	0	0	2	.0
L	44 *	Doug Macdonald	BUF	4	0	0	0	2–	0	0	0	0	0	3	.0
D	29 *	Denis Tsygurov	BUF	8	0	0	0	1–	8	0	0	0	0	3	.0

Goaltending

No.	Goaltender	GPI	Mins	Avg	W	L	T	EN	SO	GA	SA	S%
39	Dominik Hasek	58	3358	1.95	30	20	6	3	7	109	1552	.930
31	Grant Fuhr	32	1726	3.68	13	12	3	0	2	106	907	.883
	Totals	**84**	**5097**	**2.57**	**43**	**32**	**9**	**3**	**9**	**218**	**2462**	**.911**

Playoffs

Pos	#	Player	Team	GP	G	A	Pts	+/–	PIM	PP	SH	GW	GT	S	%
C	10	Dale Hawerchuk	BUF	7	0	7	7	1–	4	0	0	0	0	16	.0
R	89	Alexander Mogilny	BUF	7	4	2	6	1	6	1	0	0	0	22	18.2
L	13	Yuri Khmylev	BUF	7	3	1	4	1–	8	0	0	0	0	22	13.6
R	18	Wayne Presley	BUF	7	2	1	3	1–	14	1	0	1	0	19	10.5
D	8	Doug Bodger	BUF	7	0	3	3	0	6	0	0	0	0	15	.0
D	4 *	Philippe Boucher	BUF	7	1	1	2	2	2	1	0	0	0	10	10.0
D	24	Randy Moller	BUF	7	0	2	2	2	8	0	0	0	0	12	.0
L	27	Brad May	BUF	7	0	2	2	2	9	0	0	0	0	11	.0
D	42	Richard Smehlik	BUF	7	0	2	2	1–	10	0	0	0	0	2	.0
C	17 *	Todd Simon	BUF	5	1	0	1	1	0	1	0	1	0	5	20.0
C	14	Dave Hannan	BUF	7	1	0	1	1	6	0	0	1	1	8	12.5
L	32	Rob Ray	BUF	7	1	0	1	1	43	0	0	0	0	4	25.0
C	26 *	Derek Plante	BUF	7	1	0	1	1	0	0	0	0	0	14	7.1
L	43 *	Jason Dawe	BUF	6	0	1	1	1	6	0	0	0	0	3	.0
R	28	Donald Audette	BUF	7	0	1	1	1–	6	0	0	0	0	8	.0
C	20	Bob Sweeney	BUF	1	0	0	0	0	0	0	0	0	0	1	.0
D	7	Petr Svoboda	BUF	3	0	0	0	1–	4	0	0	0	0	2	.0
L	36 *	Matthew Barnaby	BUF	3	0	0	0	2	17	0	0	0	0	0	.0
D	41	Ken Sutton	BUF	4	0	0	0	2	2	0	0	0	0	8	.0
L	19	Randy Wood	BUF	6	0	0	0	2–	0	0	0	0	0	7	.0
G	39	Dominik Hasek	BUF	7	0	0	0	0	2	0	0	0	0	0	.0
D	5	Craig Muni	BUF	7	0	0	0	1	4	0	0	0	0	6	.0

Goaltending

No.	Goaltender	GPI	Mins	Avg	W	L	EN	SO	GA	SA	S%
39	Dominik Hasek	7	484	1.61	3	4	1	2	13	261	.950
	Totals	**7**	**486**	**1.73**	**3**	**4**	**1**	**2**	**14**	**262**	**.947**

Coaching Record

		Regular Season					Playoffs			
Season	Team	Games	W	L	T	%	Games	W	L	%
1959-60	N.Y. Rovers (EHL)	60	18	41	1	.308	....	....	....	....
1960-61	N.Y. Rovers (EHL)	64	18	45	1	.289	....	....	....	....
1961-62	Long Island (EHL)	68	26	41	1	.390	....	....	....	....
1962-63	Long Island (EHL)	68	36	28	4	.559	7	4	3	.571
1963-64	Long Island (EHL)	72	32	34	6	.486	....	....	....	....
1964-65	Long Island (EHL)	72	42	29	1	.590	15	11	4	.733
1965-66	Long Island (EHL)	72	46	23	3	.660	12	7	5	.583
1968-69	**Minnesota (NHL)**	**35**	**6**	**23**	**6**	**.257**	....	....	....	....
1971-72	Cleveland (AHL)	76	32	34	10	.487	6	2	4	.333
1972-73	*Cleveland (AHL)	76	23	44	9	.362	....	....	....	....
1973-74	Providence (AHL)	76	38	26	12	.579	15	9	6	.600
1974-75	Providence (AHL)	76	43	21	12	.645	6	2	4	.333
1975-76	Providence (AHL)	76	34	34	8	.500	3	0	3	.000
1976-77	Providence (AHL)	53	21	30	2	.415	....	....	....	....
1978-79	Dallas (CHL)	76	45	28	3	.612	9	8	1	.889
1981-82	Wichita (CHL)	80	44	33	3	.569	7	3	4	.423
1989-90	**Edmonton (NHL)**	**80**	**38**	**28**	**14**	**.563**	**22**	**16**	**6**	**.727****
1990-91	**Edmonton (NHL)**	**80**	**37**	**37**	**6**	**.500**	**18**	**9**	**9**	**.500**
1991-92	**Buffalo (NHL)**	**52**	**22**	**22**	**8**	**.500**	**7**	**3**	**4**	**.429**
1992-93	**Buffalo (NHL)**	**84**	**38**	**36**	**10**	**.512**	**8**	**4**	**4**	**.500**
1993-94	**Buffalo (NHL)**	**84**	**43**	**32**	**9**	**.565**	**7**	**3**	**4**	**.429**
	NHL Totals	**415**	**184**	**178**	**53**	**.507**	**62**	**35**	**27**	**.565**

* Club moved to Jacksonville during regular season. ** Won Stanley Cup.

Club Records

Team

(Figures in brackets for season records are games played)

Most Points **113** 1974-75 (80)
Most Wins **49** 1974-75 (80)
Most Ties **21** 1980-81 (80)
Most Losses **44** 1986-87 (80)
Most Goals **354** 1974-75 (80)
Most Goals Against **308** 1986-87 (80)
Fewest Points **51** 1971-72 (78)
Fewest Wins **16** 1971-72 (78)
Fewest Ties **6** 1985-86 (80)
Fewest Losses **16** 1974-75 (80)
Fewest Goals **203** 1971-72 (78)
Fewest Goals Against **201** 1979-80 (80)

Longest Winning Streak
Over-all .... **10** Jan. 4-23/84
Home .... **12** Nov. 12/72-Jan. 7/73; Oct. 13-Dec. 10/89
Away .... ***10** Dec. 10/83-Jan. 23/84

Longest Undefeated Streak
Over-all .... **14** March 6-April 6/80 (8 wins, 6 ties)
Home .... **21** Oct. 8/72-Jan. 7/73 (18 wins, 3 ties)
Away .... ***10** Dec. 10/83-Jan. 23/84 (10 wins)

Longest Losing Streak
Over-all .... **7** Oct. 25-Nov. 8/70; Apr. 3-15/93; Oct. 9-22/93
Home .... **6** Oct. 10-Nov. 10/93
Away .... **7** Oct. 14-Nov. 7/70; Feb. 6-27/71

Longest Winless Streak
Over-all .... **12** Nov. 23-Dec. 20/91 (8 losses, 4 ties)
Home .... **12** Jan. 27-Mar. 10/91 (7 losses, 5 ties)
Away .... **23** Oct. 30/71-Feb. 19/72 (15 losses, 8 ties)

Most Shutouts, Season **9** 1993-94 (84)
Most PIM, Season **2,712** 1991-92 (80)
Most Goals, Game .... **14** Jan. 21/75 (Wsh. 2 at Buf. 14) Mar. 19/81 (Tor. 4 at Buf. 14)

Individual

Most Seasons .... **17** Gilbert Perreault
Most Games .... **1,191** Gilbert Perreault
Most Goals, Career .... **512** Gilbert Perreault
Most Assists, Career .... **814** Gilbert Perreault
Most Points, Career .... **1,326** Gilbert Perreault
Most PIM, Career .... **1,450** Mike Foligno
Most Shutouts, Career .... **14** Don Edwards
Longest Consecutive Games Streak .... **776** Craig Ramsay (Mar. 27/73-Feb. 10/83)
Most Goals, Season .... **76** Alexander Mogilny (1992-93)
Most Assists, Season .... **95** Pat LaFontaine (1992-93)
Most Points, Season .... **148** Pat LaFontaine (1992-93) (53 goals, 95 assists)
Most PIM, Season .... **354** Rob Ray (1991-92)
Most Points, Defenseman Season .... **81** Phil Housley (1989-90) (21 goals, 60 assists)
Most Points, Center Season .... **148** Pat LaFontaine (1992-93) (53 goals, 95 assists)
Most Points, Right Wing Season .... **127** Alexander Mogilny (1992-93) (76 goals, 51 assists)
Most Points, Left Wing Season .... **95** Richard Martin (1974-75) (52 goals, 43 assists)
Most Points, Rookie Season .... **74** Richard Martin (1971-72) (44 goals, 30 assists)
Most Shutouts, Season .... **7** Dominik Hasek (1993-94)
Most Goals, Game .... **5** Dave Andreychuk (Feb. 6/86)
Most Assists, Game .... **5** Gilbert Perreault (Feb. 1/76; Mar. 9/80; Jan. 4/84) Dale Hawerchuk (Jan. 15/92); Pat LaFontaine (Dec. 31/92; Feb. 10/93)
Most Points, Game .... **7** Gilbert Perreault (Feb. 1/76)

* NHL Record.

Coaching History

"Punch" Imlach, 1970-71; "Punch" Imlach, Floyd Smith and Joe Crozier, 1971-72; Joe Crozier, 1972-73 to 1973-74; Floyd Smith, 1974-75 to 1976-77; Marcel Pronovost, 1977-78; Marcel Pronovost and Bill Inglis, 1978-79; Scott Bowman, 1979-80; Roger Neilson, 1980-81; Jim Roberts and Scott Bowman, 1981-82; Scott Bowman 1982-83 to 1984-85; Jim Schoenfeld and Scott Bowman, 1985-86; Scott Bowman, Craig Ramsay and Ted Sator, 1986-87; Ted Sator, 1987-88 to 1988-89; Rick Dudley, 1989-90 to 1990-91; Rick Dudley and John Muckler, 1991-92; John Muckler, 1992-93 to date.

Captains' History

Floyd Smith, 1970-71; Gerry Meehan, 1971-72 to 1973-74; Gerry Meehan and Jim Schoenfeld, 1974-75; Jim Schoenfeld, 1975-76 to 1976-77; Danny Gare, 1977-78 to 1980-81; Danny Gare and Gil Perreault, 1981-82; Gil Perreault, 1982-83 to 1985-86; Gil Perreault and Lindy Ruff, 1986-87; Lindy Ruff, 1987-88; Lindy Ruff and Mike Foligno, 1988-89; Mike Foligno, 1989-90. Mike Foligno and Mike Ramsey, 1990-91; Mike Ramsey, 1991-92; Mike Ramsey and Pat LaFontaine, 1992-93; Pat LaFontaine and Alexander Mogilny, 1993-94; Pat LaFontaine, 1994-95.

All-time Record vs. Other Clubs

Regular Season

	At Home							On Road							Total						
	GP	W	L	T	GF	GA	PTS	GP	W	L	T	GF	GA	PTS	GP	W	L	T	GF	GA	PTS
Anaheim	1	1	0	0	4	2	2	1	1	0	0	3	0	2	2	2	0	0	7	2	4
Boston	82	41	27	14	310	255	96	81	24	47	10	251	336	58	163	65	74	24	561	591	154
Calgary	38	22	12	4	160	115	48	38	15	13	10	133	137	40	76	37	25	14	293	252	88
Chicago	45	28	11	6	174	116	62	43	15	22	6	120	138	36	88	43	33	12	294	254	98
Dallas	45	23	12	10	168	124	56	46	20	20	6	144	144	46	91	43	32	16	312	268	102
Detroit	45	31	7	7	209	124	69	47	18	24	5	145	176	41	92	49	31	12	354	300	110
Edmonton	23	9	9	5	95	90	23	22	4	16	2	59	97	10	45	13	25	7	154	187	33
Florida	2	1	1	0	6	4	2	2	1	1	0	8	4	2	4	2	2	0	14	8	4
Hartford	54	29	18	7	229	177	65	56	28	19	9	179	168	65	110	57	37	16	408	345	130
Los Angeles	45	22	15	8	183	141	52	46	21	17	8	162	158	50	91	43	32	16	345	299	102
Montreal	77	36	23	18	244	221	90	77	21	48	8	229	323	50	154	57	71	26	473	544	140
New Jersey	34	24	6	4	159	105	52	35	20	8	7	138	110	47	69	44	14	11	297	215	99
NY Islanders	41	23	13	5	147	119	51	41	17	17	7	119	122	41	82	40	30	12	266	241	92
NY Rangers	48	30	12	6	223	160	66	46	14	21	11	129	164	39	94	44	33	17	352	324	105
Ottawa	5	5	0	0	30	9	10	7	5	1	1	31	15	11	12	10	1	1	61	24	21
Philadelphia	44	21	17	6	155	136	48	47	11	28	8	128	175	30	91	32	45	14	283	311	78
Pittsburgh	49	24	11	14	214	140	62	48	15	21	12	169	185	42	97	39	32	26	383	325	104
Quebec	54	31	15	8	218	172	70	54	18	27	9	175	207	45	108	49	42	17	393	379	115
St. Louis	44	28	12	4	183	138	60	43	11	26	6	111	165	28	87	39	38	10	294	303	88
San Jose	4	4	0	0	21	16	8	3	1	1	1	16	12	3	7	5	1	1	37	28	11
Tampa Bay	3	1	1	1	10	10	3	3	2	1	0	6	5	4	6	3	2	1	16	15	7
Toronto	50	31	16	3	212	145	65	49	23	18	8	183	152	54	99	54	34	11	395	297	119
Vancouver	45	23	14	8	164	130	54	44	13	21	10	146	168	36	89	36	35	18	310	298	90
Washington	37	27	6	4	165	98	58	36	21	8	7	146	102	49	73	48	14	11	311	200	107
Winnipeg	22	19	1	2	104	53	40	22	11	9	2	82	71	24	44	30	10	4	186	124	64
Defunct Clubs	23	13	5	5	94	63	31	23	12	8	3	97	76	27	46	25	13	8	191	139	58
Totals	**960**	**547**	**264**	**149**	**3881**	**2863**	**1243**	**960**	**362**	**442**	**156**	**3109**	**3410**	**880**	**1920**	**909**	**706**	**305**	**6990**	**6273**	**2123**

Calgary totals include Atlanta, 1972-73 to 1979-80. Dallas totals include Minnesota, 1970-71 to 1992-93.
New Jersey totals include Kansas City, 1974-75 to 1975-76, and Colorado, 1976-77 to 1981-82.

Playoffs

	Series	W	L	GP	W	L	T	GF	GA	Last Mtg.	Round	Result
Boston	6	1	5	33	14	19	0	113	132	1993	DSF	W 4-0
Chicago	2	2	0	9	8	1	0	36	17	1980	QF	W 4-0
Dallas	2	1	1	7	3	4	0	28	26	1981	QF	L 1-4
Montreal	6	2	4	31	13	18	0	94	114	1993	DF	L 0-4
New Jersey	1	0	1	7	3	4	0	14	14	1994	CQF	L 3-4
NY Islanders	3	0	3	16	4	12	0	45	59	1980	SF	L 2-4
NY Rangers	1	1	0	3	2	1	0	11	6	1978	PR	W 2-1
Philadelphia	2	0	2	11	3	8	0	23	35	1978	QF	L 1-4
Pittsburgh	1	0	1	3	1	2	0	9	9	1979	PR	L 1-2
Quebec	2	0	2	8	2	6	0	27	35	1985	DSF	L 2-3
St. Louis	1	1	0	3	2	1	0	7	8	1976	PR	W 2-1
Vancouver	2	2	0	7	6	1	0	28	14	1981	PR	W 3-0
Totals	**29**	**10**	**19**	**138**	**61**	**77**	**0**	**435**	**462**			

Playoff Results 1994-90

Year	Round	Opponent	Result	GF	GA
1994	CQF	New Jersey	L 3-4	14	14
1993	DF	Montreal	L 0-4	12	16
	DSF	Boston	W 4-0	19	12
1992	DSF	Boston	L 3-4	24	19
1991	DSF	Montreal	L 2-4	24	29
1990	DSF	Montreal	L 2-4	13	17

Abbreviations: Round: F – Final; **CF** – conference final; **CQF** – conference quarter-final; **CSF** – conference semi-final; **DF** – division final; **DSF** – division semi-final; **SF** – semi-final; **QF** – quarter-final; **PR** – preliminary round.

1993-94 Results

Oct.	7	at	Boston	5-3		12	at	Winnipeg	2-3
	9	at	Montreal	4-7		15	at	St. Louis	1-2
	10		Hartford	2-3		16	at	Dallas	4-2
	12	at	Philadelphia	3-5		19		Edmonton	1-1
	15		NY Rangers	2-5		24	at	Tampa Bay	0-4
	16	at	Washington	3-4		27		Washington	7-2
	18		Detroit	4-6		29	at	Montreal	3-2
	22		Pittsburgh	2-4		30		Florida	2-3
	23	at	Hartford	3-3	**Feb.**	2	at	New Jersey	3-2
	27	at	Calgary	5-3		4	at	Florida	7-2
	29	at	Edmonton	6-3		6		NY Islanders	4-1
	30	at	Vancouver	6-3		8	at	NY Islanders	1-3
Nov.	3		Pittsburgh	2-6		10	at	Boston	3-3
	7		Boston	3-4		11		Montreal	5-1
	10		Philadelphia	3-5		13		Dallas	3-5
	13	at	Philadelphia	7-2		16	at	Hartford	5-3
	17	at	New Jersey	0-4		18		Florida	4-1
	19		Winnipeg	6-0		20	at	Washington	3-3
	21		San Jose	6-5		21		Quebec	2-1
	22	at	Ottawa	5-2		23		Anaheim	4-2
	24		New Jersey	3-5		25		Chicago	1-3
	26		Ottawa	5-2		26	at	Pittsburgh	3-4
	27	at	Quebec	2-2	**Mar.**	2	at	Ottawa	7-2
	29	at	Toronto	3-0		4		Pittsburgh	2-1
Dec.	1	at	Tampa Bay	3-0		6	at	Detroit	3-2
	2	at	Florida	1-2		8	at	San Jose	4-4
	5		Boston	3-1		9	at	Anaheim	3-0
	8	at	Ottawa	3-1		12	at	Los Angeles	5-3
	10		Calgary	6-2		17		New Jersey	1-6
	11	at	Hartford	3-0		18	at	NY Islanders	2-2
	13	at	NY Rangers	0-2		20		Ottawa	6-2
	16	at	Pittsburgh	1-2		23		St. Louis	2-3
	17		Los Angeles	2-0		25		Hartford	6-3
	19		Tampa Bay	3-3		27		NY Islanders	4-1
	23		Montreal	5-0		30		Tampa Bay	2-3
	26	at	NY Islanders	3-4	**Apr.**	1		Boston	5-0
	27		Philadelphia	0-2		2	at	Quebec	6-2
	31		NY Rangers	4-1		4	at	Quebec	4-6
Jan.	2		Toronto	3-3		8		Montreal	1-0
	7		Pittsburgh	3-4		10		Quebec	4-1
	9		Vancouver	5-3		12	at	NY Rangers	2-3
	11	at	Chicago	5-2		14		Washington	2-3

Entry Draft Selections 1994-80

1994

Pick	
17	Wayne Primeau
43	Curtis Brown
69	Rumun Ndur
121	Sergei Klimentjev
147	Cal Benazic
168	Steve Plouffe
173	Shane Hnidy
176	Steve Webb
199	Bob Westerby
225	Craig Millar
251	Mark Polak
277	Shayne Wright

1993

Pick	
38	Denis Tsygurov
64	Ethan Philpott
116	Richard Safarik
142	Kevin Pozzo
168	Sergei Petrenko
194	Mike Barrie
220	Barrie Moore
246	Chris Davis
272	Scott Nichol

1992

Pick	
11	David Cooper
35	Jozef Cierny
59	Ondrej Steiner
80	Dean Melanson
83	Matthew Barnaby
107	Markus Ketterer
108	Yuri Khmylev
131	Paul Rushforth
179	Dean Tiltgen
203	Todd Simon
227	Rick Kowalsky
251	Chris Clancy

1991

Pick	
13	Philippe Boucher
35	Jason Dawe
57	Jason Young
72	Peter Ambroziak
101	Steve Shields
123	Sean O'Donnell
124	Brian Holzinger
145	Chris Snell
162	Jiri Kuntos
189	Tony Iob
211	Spencer Meany
233	Mikhail Volkov
255	Michael Smith

1990

Pick	
14	Brad May
82	Brian McCarthy
97	Richard Smehlik
100	Todd Bojcun
103	Brad Pascall
142	Viktor Gordiyuk
166	Milan Nedoma
187	Jason Winch
208	Sylvain Naud
229	Kenneth Martin
250	Brad Rubachuk

1989

Pick	
14	Kevin Haller
56	John (Scott) Thomas
77	Doug MacDonald
98	Ken Sutton
107	Bill Pye
119	Mike Barkley
161	Derek Plante
183	Donald Audette
194	Mark Astley
203	John Nelson
224	Todd Henderson
245	Michael Bavis

1988

Pick	
13	Joel Savage
55	Darcy Loewen
76	Keith E. Carney
89	Alexander Mogilny
97	Robert Ray
106	David Di Vita
118	Mike McLaughlin
139	Mike Griffith
160	Daniel Ruoho
181	Wade Flaherty
223	Thomas Nieman
244	Robert Wallwork

1987

Pick	
1	Pierre Turgeon
22	Brad Miller
53	Andrew MacVicar
84	John Bradley
85	David Pergola
106	Chris Marshall
127	Paul Flanagan
148	Sean Dooley
153	Tim Roberts
169	Grant Tkachuk
190	Ian Herbers
211	David Littman
232	Allan MacIsaac

1986

Pick	
5	Shawn Anderson
26	Greg Brown
47	Bob Corkum
56	Kevin Kerr
68	David Baseggio
89	Larry Rooney
110	Miguel Baldris
131	Mike Hartman
152	Francois Guay
173	Shawn Whitham
194	Kenton Rein
215	Troy Arndt

1985

Pick	
14	Calle Johansson
35	Benoit Hogue
56	Keith Gretzky
77	Dave Moylan
98	Ken Priestlay
119	Joe Reekie
140	Petri Matikainen
161	Trent Kaese
182	Jiri Sejba
203	Boyd Sutton
224	Guy Larose
245	Ken Baumgartner

1984

Pick	
18	Mikael Andersson
39	Doug Trapp
60	Ray Sheppard
81	Bob Halkidis
102	Joey Rampton
123	James Gasseau
144	Darcy Wakaluk
165	Orvar Stambert
206	Brian McKinnon
226	Grant Delcourt
247	Sean Baker

1983

Pick	
5	Tom Barrasso
10	Normand Lacombe
11	Adam Creighton
31	John Tucker
34	Richard Hajdu
74	Daren Puppa
94	Jayson Meyer
114	Jim Hofford
134	Christian Ruutlu
154	Don McSween
174	Tim Hoover
194	Mark Ferner
214	Uwe Krupp
234	Marc Hamelin
235	Kermit Salfi

1982

Pick	
6	Phil Housley
9	Paul Cyr
16	Dave Andreychuk
26	Mike Anderson
30	Jens Johansson
68	Timo Jutila
79	Jeff Hamilton
100	Bob Logan
111	Jeff Parker
121	Jacob Gustavsson
142	Allen Bishop
163	Claude Verret
184	Rob Norman
205	Mike Craig
226	Jim Plankers

1981

Pick	
17	Jiri Dudacek
38	Hannu Virta
59	Jim Aldred
60	Colin Chisholm
80	Jeff Eatough
83	Anders Wikberg
101	Mauri Eivola
122	Ali Butorac
143	Heikki Leime
164	Gates Orlando
185	Venci Sebek
206	Warren Harper

1980

Pick	
20	Steve Patrick
41	Mike Moller
56	Sean McKenna
62	Jay North
83	Jim Wiemer
104	Dirk Rueter
125	Daniel Naud
146	Jari Paavola
167	R. Cunneyworth
188	Dave Beckon
209	John Bader

Club Directory

Memorial Auditorium
Buffalo, NY 14202
Phone **716/856-7300**
Outside Buffalo: **800/333-PUCK**
Ticket Office: 716/856-8100
FAX 716/856-2104
Capacity: 16,284

Board of Directors

Chairman of the Board and President	Seymour H. Knox, III
Vice-Chairman of the Board and Counsel	Robert O. Swados
Vice-Chairman of the Board	Robert E. Rich, Jr.
Treasurer	Joseph T.J. Stewart
Board of Directors. **Niagara Frontier Hockey, L.P.** (includes above listed officers)	Edwin C. Andrews, Peter C. Andrews, George L. Collins, Jr. M.D., William C. Cox, III, John B. Fisher, George T. Gregory, John B. Houghton, Seymour H. Knox, IV, John J. Rigas, Michael J. Rigas, Richard W. Rupp, Howard T. Saperston, Jr., Paul A. Schoellkopf, George Strawbridge, Jr., William H. Weeks

Administration

Assistant to the President	Seymour H. Knox, IV
Executive Vice-President of Sports Operations	Gerry Meehan
Senior Vice-President/Administration and Marketing	George Bergantz
Senior Vice-President/Finance and Chief Financial Officer	Dan DiPofi
Consultant	Northrup R. Knox
Consultant/Administration	Mitchell Owen
Administrative Assistants: President	Elaine Burzynski
General Manager	Debbie Bonner
Administration	Verna B. Wojcik
Receptionists	Olive Anticola, Evelyn Battleson

Hockey Department

General Manager/Head Coach	John Muckler
Director of Player Personnel	Don Luce
Director of Player Evaluation	Larry Carriere
Assistant Coach	Don Lever
Assistant Coach	John Tortorella
Goaltender Consultant	Mitch Korn
Director of Scouting	Rudy Migay
Scouting Staff	Don Barrie, Jim Benning, Jack Bowman, Baris Janicek, Paul Merritt, Mike Racicot, Gleb Tchistyakov, Frank Zywiec
Information Manager	Ken Bass
Administrative Assistant	Cyndi Dyll

Training/Medical

Head Athletic Trainer	Jim Pizzutelli
Trainer	Rip Simonick
Equipment Supervisor	George Babcock
Club Doctor	John L. Butsch, M.D.
Orthopedic Consultant	John Marzo, M.D.
Club Dentist	Daniel Yustin, D.D.S., M.S.

Public Relations

Director of Public Relations	Steve Rossi
Public Relations Assistant	Bruce R. Wawrzyniak
Media Relations Assistant	Jeff Holbrook
Coordinator of Community Relations	TBA
Administrative Assistant	Barb Blendowski
Team Photographer	Bill Wippert

Sales & Marketing

Director of Ticket Sales	Tom Pokel
Executive Administrative Assistants	Cheryl Reukuf, Ann Miller
Sales & Marketing Administrative Assistant	Sue Smith
Director of Merchandising	Julie Scully
Merchandise Manager	Mike Kaminska
Merchandise Assistant	Rob Lescarbeau
Director of Ticket Operations	John Sinclair
Ticket Administrators	Carm Glebe, Jennifer Glowny, Christopher Makowski, Rose Thompson, Mike Trout
Empire Sports Sales: Vice President/General Manager	Dave Recher
General Sales Manager	Kerry Atkinson
Director of Sponsorship Sales	Bob Russell
Director of Sponsor Television	Jim DiMino
Sponsorship Sales Managers	Heidi Puff, Tim Jehle
Regional Sponsorship Sales Managers	Rich Chiano, Nick DiVico
Account Executive	Nick Turano
Ticket Sales Representatives	Craig Cieplinski, Jim Meissner, Andrew White, Gary Rabinowitz

Operations & Promotions

Director of Operations	Stan Makowski
Director of Corporate Relations	Larry Playfair
Promotions Manager	Matt Rabinowitz
Staff Assistant	Gerry Magill
Public Address Announcer	Milt Ellis
Administrative Assistant	Pat Chimera

Finance

Controller	John Cudmore
Assistant Controller	Elizabeth McPartland
Accounting Manager	Chris Ivansitz
Finance Assistants	Robert Dahar, Birgid Haensel, Mary Jones, Sally Lippert, Terese Melber, Toni Jaruszewski

Sabreland

Manager	Cliff Smith

Crossroads Arena Corporation

Executive Vice-President	Larry Quinn
Director of Sales and Marketing/ Suite and Club Seating	Karen Marsch
Suite Sales Manager	David Aston
Project Director	Carolyn Hoyt
Administrative Assistants	Deidre Daniels, Debbie Driscoll

Legal

Associate Counsel	Helen Drew
Adminstrative Assistant	Eleanor MacKenzie

TV & Radio

Director of Communications	Paul Wieland
Television Producer	Joe Guarnieri
TV Stations	Empire Sports Network and WUTV Fox 29
TV Broadcast Team	John Gurtler, Jim Lorentz
Radio Flagship Station	WGR AM-550
Radio Broadcast Team	Rick Jeanneret, Larry Playfair

General Information

Dimensions of Rink	193 feet by 84 feet
Location of Press Box	Suspended from ceiling on west side
Club Colors	Blue, Gold & White
Training Camp/Practice Site	Sabreland/Wheatfield, NY
AHL Affiliate	Rochester Americans

General Managers' History

George "Punch" Imlach, 1970-71 to 1977-78; John Anderson (acting), 1978-79; Scott Bowman, 1979-80 to 1985-86; Scott Bowman and Gerry Meehan, 1986-87; Gerry Meehan, 1987-88 to 1992-93; John Muckler, 1993-94 to date.

Retired Numbers

11	Gilbert Perreault	1970-1987

Calgary Flames

1993-94 Results: 42W-29L-13T 97PTS. First, Pacific Division

Schedule

Oct.	Sat.	1	Vancouver	Tues.	10	Tampa Bay

Oct. Sat. 1 Vancouver — Tues. 10 Tampa Bay
Tues. 4 at Dallas — Thur. 12 Chicago
Sat. 8 at Los Angeles — Fri. 13 Buffalo
Sun. 9 at Anaheim — Mon. 16 Los Angeles
Wed. 12 at Edmonton — Wed. 18 Winnipeg
Fri. 14 San Jose — Mon. 23 Edmonton
Sun. 16 Philadelphia — Wed. 25 at Tampa Bay
Tues. 18 Winnipeg — Thur. 26 at Florida
Thur. 20 Anaheim — Sat. 28 at St. Louis
Sat. 22 Boston — **Feb.** Wed. 1 Detroit
Mon. 24 at Toronto — Fri. 3 Hartford
Wed. 26 at New Jersey — Sat. 4 Toronto
Fri. 28 at NY Rangers — Wed. 8 at Anaheim
Sat. 29 at NY Islanders — Fri. 10 at Dallas
Nov. Tues. 1 Washington — Sat. 11 at St. Louis
Fri. 4 Edmonton — Mon. 13 Anaheim
Sun. 6 Florida — Wed. 15 at Winnipeg
Tues. 8 St. Louis — Sat. 18 Dallas
Thur. 10 at Los Angeles — Mon. 20 Dallas
Sun. 13 at Anaheim — Wed. 22 San Jose
Tues. 15 at San Jose — (in Phoenix)
Fri. 18 at Edmonton — Sat. 25 at Los Angeles
Sat. 19 at Vancouver — Tues. 28 Edmonton
Tues. 22 Los Angeles — **Mar.** Thur. 2 Pittsburgh
Thur. 24 Chicago — Sat. 4 at Toronto
Sat. 26 at Edmonton — Sun. 5 at Buffalo
Dec. Fri. 2 at Detroit — Tues. 7 at Washington
Sun. 4 at Ottawa — Thur. 9 at Philadelphia
Tues. 6 at Quebec — Sat. 11 at Pittsburgh*
Wed. 7 at Montreal — Sun. 12 at Chicago*
Sat. 10 at Boston — Wed. 15 Ottawa
Mon. 12 at Hartford — Fri. 17 San Jose
Thur. 15 Toronto — Sun. 19 NY Islanders
Sun. 18 NY Rangers — Tues. 21 Detroit
Tues. 20 St. Louis — Thur. 23 at NY Rangers
Thur. 22 Anaheim — (in Phoenix)
Tues. 27 at Winnipeg — Fri. 24 New Jersey
Thur. 29 at Vancouver — Sun. 26 Vancouver
Sat. 31 Montreal — Fri. 31 San Jose
Jan. Tues. 3 at Detroit — **Apr.** Sun. 2 at Vancouver*
Thur. 5 at Chicago — Wed. 5 at San Jose
Sat. 7 at San Jose* — Fri. 7 Los Angeles
Sun. 8 Quebec — Sat. 8 Vancouver

* Denotes afternoon game.

Home Starting Times:
Weeknights . . . . 7:30 p.m.
Saturdays . . . . 8:30 p.m.
Sundays . . . . 6:00 p.m.
Except Sat. Dec. 31 . . . . 5:30 p.m.

Franchise date: June 24, 1980
Transferred from Atlanta to Calgary.

PACIFIC DIVISION

23rd NHL Season

Gary Roberts led the Flames with 41 goals in 1993-94.

Year-by-Year Record

Season	GP	Home W	L	T	Road W	L	T	Overall W	L	T	GF	GA	Pts.	Finished		Playoff Result
1993-94	84	25	12	5	17	17	8	42	29	13	302	256	97	1st,	Pacific Div.	Lost Conf. Quarter-Final
1992-93	84	23	14	5	20	16	6	43	30	11	322	282	97	2nd,	Smythe Div.	Lost Div. Semi-Final
1991-92	80	19	14	7	12	23	5	31	37	12	296	305	74	5th,	Smythe Div.	Out of Playoffs
1990-91	80	29	8	3	17	18	5	46	26	8	344	263	100	2nd,	Smythe Div.	Lost Div. Semi-Final
1989-90	80	28	7	5	14	16	10	42	23	15	348	265	99	1st,	Smythe Div.	Lost Div. Semi-Final
1988-89	**80**	**32**	**4**	**4**	**22**	**13**	**5**	**54**	**17**	**9**	**354**	**226**	**117**	**1st,**	**Smythe Div.**	**Won Stanley Cup**
1987-88	80	26	11	3	22	12	6	48	23	9	397	305	105	1st,	Smythe Div.	Lost Div. Final
1986-87	80	25	13	2	21	18	1	46	31	3	318	289	95	2nd,	Smythe Div.	Lost Div. Semi-Final
1985-86	80	23	11	6	17	20	3	40	31	9	354	315	89	2nd,	Smythe Div.	Lost Final
1984-85	80	23	11	6	18	16	6	41	27	12	363	302	94	3rd,	Smythe Div.	Lost Div. Semi-Final
1983-84	80	22	11	7	12	21	7	34	32	14	311	314	82	2nd,	Smythe Div.	Lost Div. Final
1982-83	80	21	12	7	11	22	7	32	34	14	321	317	78	2nd,	Smythe Div.	Lost Div. Final
1981-82	80	20	11	9	9	23	8	29	34	17	334	345	75	3rd,	Smythe Div.	Lost Div. Semi-Final
1980-81	80	25	5	10	14	22	4	39	27	14	329	298	92	3rd,	Patrick Div.	Lost Semi-Final
1979-80*	80	18	15	7	17	17	6	35	32	13	282	269	83	4th,	Patrick Div.	Lost Prelim. Round
1978-79*	80	25	11	4	16	20	4	41	31	8	327	280	90	4th,	Patrick Div.	Lost Prelim. Round
1977-78*	80	20	13	7	14	14	12	34	27	19	274	252	87	3rd,	Patrick Div.	Lost Prelim. Round
1976-77*	80	22	11	7	12	23	5	34	34	12	264	265	80	3rd,	Patrick Div.	Lost Prelim. Round
1975-76*	80	19	14	7	16	19	5	35	33	12	262	237	82	3rd,	Patrick Div.	Lost Prelim. Round
1974-75*	80	24	9	7	10	22	8	34	31	15	243	233	83	4th,	Patrick Div.	Out of Playoffs
1973-74*	78	17	15	7	13	19	7	30	34	14	214	238	74	4th,	West Div.	Lost Quarter-Final
1972-73*	78	16	16	7	9	22	8	25	38	15	191	239	65	7th,	West Div.	Out of Playoffs

* Atlanta Flames

1994-95 Player Personnel

FORWARDS	HT	WT	S	Place of Birth	Date	1993-94 Club
BUCZKOWSKI, Paul	5-11	190	L	Saskatoon, Sask.	3/20/75	Saskatoon
DINGMAN, Chris	6-3	231	L	Edmonton, Alta.	7/6/76	Brandon
DUTHIE, Ryan	5-10	180	R	Red Deer, Alta.	9/2/74	Spokane
EISENHUT, Neil	6-1	190	L	Osoyoos, B.C.	2/9/67	Vancouver-Hamilton
FLEURY, Theoren	5-6	160	R	Oxbow, Sask.	6/29/68	Calgary
GREIG, Mark	5-11	190	R	High River, Alta.	1/25/70	Hfd-Springfield-Tor-St. John's
HARPER, Kelly	6-2	180	R	Sudbury, Ont.	5/9/72	Michigan State
HLUSHKO, Todd	5-11	195	L	Toronto, Ont.	2/7/70	Cdn. National-Cdn. Olympic-Philadelphia-Hershey
JONSSON, Jorgen	6-0	185	L	Angelholm, Sweden	9/29/72	Rogle
KISIO, Kelly	5-10	185	R	Peace River, Alta.	9/18/59	Calgary
KOHN, Ladislav	5-10	175	L	Uherske Hradiste, Czech.	3/4/75	Brandon-Swift Current
KRUSE, Paul	6-0	202	L	Merritt, B.C.	3/15/70	Calgary
KUSHNER, Dale	6-1	195	L	Terrace, B.C.	6/13/66	Saint John
McCARTHY, Sandy	6-3	225	R	Toronto, Ont.	6/15/72	Calgary
MORROW, Scott	6-1	185	L	Chicago, IL	6/18/69	Springfield-Saint John
MURRAY, Marty	5-9	170	L	Deloraine, Man.	2/16/75	Brandon
MURRAY, Michael	6-1	200	R	Cumberland, RI	4/18/71	Lowell
NIEUWENDYK, Joe	6-1	195	L	Oshawa, Ont.	9/10/66	Calgary
NYLANDER, Michael	5-11	190	L	Stockholm, Sweden	10/3/72	Hartford-Springfield-Calgary
OTTO, Joel	6-4	220	R	Elk River, MN	10/29/61	Calgary
PERRY, Jeff	6-0	195	L	Sarnia, Ont.	4/12/71	Saint John
REICHEL, Robert	5-10	185	L	Litvinov, Czech.	6/25/71	Calgary
ROBERTS, Gary	6-1	190	L	North York, Ont.	5/23/66	Calgary
ST. PIERRE, David	6-0	185	R	Montreal, Que.	3/22/72	Saint John
SMART, Jason	6-4	212	L	Prince George, B.C.	1/23/70	Columbus
STERN, Ronnie	6-0	195	R	Ste. Agathe, Que.	1/11/67	Calgary
STILLMAN, Cory	6-0	180	L	Peterborough, Ont.	12/20/73	Saint John
STRUCH, David	5-10	180	L	Flin Flon, Man.	2/11/71	Calgary-Saint John
SULLIVAN, Mike	6-2	190	L	Marshfield, MA	2/27/68	S.J.-Kansas City-Cgy-Saint John
SUNDBLAD, Niklas	6-1	200	R	Stockholm, Sweden	1/3/73	Saint John
TITOV, German	6-1	190	L	Moscow, USSR	10/16/65	Calgary
VIITAKOSKI, Vesa	6-3	215	L	Lappeenranta, Finland	2/13/71	Calgary-Saint John
WALZ, Wes	5-10	185	R	Calgary, Alta.	5/15/70	Calgary-Saint John
DEFENSEMEN						
ALLISON, Jamie	6-1	190	L	Lindsay, Ont.	5/13/75	Detroit (OHL)
APPEL, Frank	6-4	207	L	Dusseldorf, West Germany	5/12/76	Dusseldorf
BOUCHARD, Joel	6-0	190	L	Montreal, Que.	1/23/74	Verdun-Saint John
CHIASSON, Steve	6-1	205	L	Barrie, Ont.	4/14/67	Detroit
DAHL, Kevin	5-11	190	R	Regina, Sask.	12/30/68	Calgary-Saint John
ESAU, Leonard	6-3	190	R	Meadow Lake, Sask.	6/3/68	Calgary-Saint John
GROLEAU, Francois	6-0	200	L	Longueuil, Que.	1/23/73	Saint John
HELENIUS, Sami	6-5	225	L	Helsinki, Finland	1/22/74	Reipas
HOUSLEY, Phil	5-10	185	L	St. Paul, MN	3/9/64	St. Louis
JOHANSSON, Roger	6-1	190	L	Ljungby, Sweden	4/17/67	Leksand
KECZMER, Dan	6-1	190	L	Mt. Clemens, MI	5/25/68	Hartford-Springfield-Calgary
MARSHALL, Bobby	6-1	190	L	North York, Ont.	4/11/72	Miami-Ohio
McCAMBRIDGE, Keith	6-2	205	L	Thompson, Man.	2/1/74	Swift Current
MUSIL, Frank	6-3	215	L	Pardubice, Czech.	12/17/64	Calgary
PATRICK, James	6-2	198	R	Winnipeg, Man.	6/14/63	NY Rangers-Hartford-Calgary
PERREAULT, Nicolas	6-3	200	L	Loretteville, Que.	4/24/72	Michigan State
SIMPSON, Todd	6-3	215	L	Edmonton, Alta.	5/28/73	Tri-City-Saskatoon
YAWNEY, Trent	6-3	195	L	Hudson Bay, Sask.	9/29/65	Calgary
ZALAPSKI, Zarley	6-1	211	L	Edmonton, Alta.	4/22/68	Hartford-Calgary

GOALTENDERS	HT	WT	C	Place of Birth	Date	1993-94 Club
KIDD, Trevor	6-2	190	L	Dugald, Man.	3/29/72	Calgary
MUZZATTI, Jason	6-1	190	L	Toronto, Ont.	2/3/70	Calgary-Saint John
ROLOSON, Dwayne	6-1	180	L	Simcoe, Ont.	10/12/69	Lowell
TREFILOV, Andrei	6-0	180	L	Kirovo-Chepetsk, USSR	8/31/69	Calgary-Saint John

General Manager

RISEBROUGH, DOUG

General Manager, Calgary Flames. Born in Guelph, Ont., January 29, 1954.

Doug Risebrough enters his fourth full NHL season as general manager of the Calgary Flames. After ending his 14-year NHL playing career with the Flames in 1987, Risebrough was named an assistant coach with Calgary and joined Terry Crisp behind the bench. Risebrough was appointed head coach of the Flames on May 18, 1990 and on May 16, 1991, he also assumed the role of general manager. Late in the 1991-92 campaign he directed his energies full-time to general manager, handing the coaching responsibilities over to Guy Charron for the balance of the season.

During his first season as an NHL head coach, Risebrough led the Flames to a fourth place overall finish in the NHL standings. Risebrough was Montreal's first selection, seventh overall, in the 1974 Amateur Draft. During his nine years with the Canadiens, he helped his club to four consecutive Stanley Cup championships between 1976 and 1979. He joined the Flames prior to the start of the club's 1982 training camp. During his NHL career, his clubs have won five Stanley Cup titles (1976-1979 and 1989 with Calgary) and two Presidents' Trophies (1987-88 and 1988-89).

NHL Coaching Record

		Regular Season					Playoffs			
Season	Team	Games	W	L	T	%	Games	W	L	%
1990-91	Calgary	80	46	26	8	.625	7	3	4	.429
1991-92	Calgary	64	25	30	9	.461	....	....	....	....
	NHL Totals	**144**	**71**	**56**	**17**	**.522**	**7**	**3**	**4**	**.429**

General Managers' History

Cliff Fletcher, 1972-73 to 1990-91; Doug Risebrough, 1991-92 to date.

1993-94 Scoring

* – rookie

Regular Season

Pos	#	Player	Team	GP	G	A	Pts	+/–	PIM	PP	SH	GW	GT	S	%
C	26	Robert Reichel	CGY	84	40	53	93	20	58	14	0	6	0	249	16.1
R	14	Theoren Fleury	CGY	83	40	45	85	30	186	16	1	6	0	278	14.4
L	10	Gary Roberts	CGY	73	41	43	84	37	145	12	3	5	1	202	20.3
D	2	Al MacInnis	CGY	75	28	54	82	35	95	12	1	5	0	324	8.6
C	25	Joe Nieuwendyk	CGY	64	36	39	75	19	51	14	1	7	1	191	18.8
C	92	Michael Nylander	HFD	58	11	33	44	2–	24	4	0	1	2	74	14.9
			CGY	15	2	9	11	10	6	0	0	0	0	21	9.5
			TOTAL	73	13	42	55	8	30	4	0	1	2	95	13.7
D	33	Zarley Zalapski	HFD	56	7	30	37	6–	56	0	0	0	0	121	5.8
			CGY	13	3	7	10	0	18	1	0	1	0	35	8.6
			TOTAL	69	10	37	47	6–	74	1	0	1	0	156	6.4
C	13	German Titov	CGY	76	27	18	45	20	28	8	3	2	0	153	17.6
C	17	Wes Walz	CGY	53	11	27	38	20	16	1	0	0	0	79	13.9
D	6	James Patrick	NYR	6	0	3	3	1	2	0	0	0	0	6	.0
			HFD	47	8	20	28	12–	32	4	1	2	1	65	12.3
			CGY	15	2	2	4	6	6	1	0	0	0	20	10.0
			TOTAL	68	10	25	35	5–	40	5	1	2	1	91	11.0
C	11	Kelly Kisio	CGY	51	7	23	30	6–	28	1	0	1	0	62	11.3
R	22	Ronnie Stern	CGY	71	9	20	29	6	243	0	1	3	0	105	8.6
C	29	Joel Otto	CGY	81	11	12	23	17–	92	3	1	1	0	108	10.2
D	7	Michel Petit	CGY	63	2	21	23	5	110	0	0	0	0	103	1.9
D	39	Dan Keczmer	HFD	12	0	1	1	6–	12	0	0	0	0	12	.0
			CGY	57	1	20	21	2–	48	0	0	0	0	104	1.0
			TOTAL	69	1	21	22	8–	60	0	0	0	0	116	.9
D	18	Trent Yawney	CGY	58	6	15	21	21	60	1	1	1	1	62	9.7
D	5	Chris Dahlquist	CGY	77	1	11	12	5	52	0	0	0	0	57	1.8
L	12	Paul Kruse	CGY	68	3	8	11	6–	185	0	0	0	0	52	5.8
R	15	* Sandy McCarthy	CGY	79	5	5	10	3–	173	0	0	0	0	39	12.8
C	32	Mike Sullivan	S.J.	26	2	2	4	3–	4	0	2	1	0	21	9.5
			CGY	19	2	3	5	2	6	0	0	0	0	27	7.4
			TOTAL	45	4	5	9	1–	10	0	2	1	0	48	8.3
D	3	Frank Musil	CGY	75	1	8	9	38	50	0	0	0	0	65	1.5
D	21	Brad Schlegel	CGY	26	1	6	7	4–	4	0	0	0	0	24	4.2
C	42	Guy Larose	TOR	10	1	2	3	2–	10	0	0	0	0	9	11.1
			CGY	7	0	1	1	3–	4	0	0	0	0	3	.0
			TOTAL	17	1	3	4	5–	14	0	0	0	0	12	8.3
G	37	* Trevor Kidd	CGY	31	0	4	4	0	4	0	0	0	0	0	.0
L	19	* Vesa Viitakoski	CGY	8	1	2	3	0	0	1	0	0	0	15	6.7
D	36	* Leonard Esau	CGY	6	0	3	3	1–	7	0	0	0	0	4	.0
D	4	Kevin Dahl	CGY	33	0	3	3	2–	23	0	0	0	0	20	.0
R	23	Greg Paslawski	CGY	15	2	0	2	4–	2	0	0	1	0	13	15.4
L	19	* David Haas	CGY	2	1	1	2	2	7	0	0	0	0	3	33.3
D	34	Brad Miller	CGY	8	0	1	1	2–	14	0	0	0	0	2	.0
D	6	Lee Norwood	CGY	16	0	1	1	3	16	0	0	0	0	10	.0
G	31	* Jason Muzzatti	CGY	1	0	0	0	0	0	0	0	0	0	0	.0
C	16	Mark Freer	CGY	2	0	0	0	0	4	0	0	0	0	0	.0
D	38	Peter Ahola	CGY	2	0	0	0	0	0	0	0	0	0	1	.0
C	33	* David Struch	CGY	4	0	0	0	2–	4	0	0	0	0	3	.0
D	34	* Kevin Wortman	CGY	5	0	0	0	1	2	0	0	0	0	2	.0
G	1	* Andrei Trefilov	CGY	11	0	0	0	0	4	0	0	0	0	0	.0
G	30	Mike Vernon	CGY	48	0	0	0	0	14	0	0	0	0	0	.0

Goaltending

No.	Goaltender	GPI	Mins	Avg	W	L	T	EN	SO	GA	SA	S%
1	* Andrei Trefilov	11	623	2.50	3	4	2	1	2	26	305	.915
30	Mike Vernon	48	2798	2.81	26	17	5	4	3	131	1209	.892
37	* Trevor Kidd	31	1614	3.16	13	7	6	0	0	85	752	.887
35	Jeff Reese	1	13	4.62	0	0	0	0	0	1	5	.800
31	* Jason Muzzatti	1	60	8.00	0	1	0	0	0	8	35	.771

Playoffs

Pos	#	Player	Team	GP	G	A	Pts	+/–	PIM	PP	SH	GW	GT	S	%
R	14	Theoren Fleury	CGY	7	6	4	10	1	5	1	0	2	0	23	26.1
D	2	Al MacInnis	CGY	7	2	6	8	5	12	1	0	0	0	32	6.3
L	10	Gary Roberts	CGY	7	2	6	8	3	24	1	0	1	0	18	11.1
C	26	Robert Reichel	CGY	7	0	5	5	3	0	0	0	0	0	24	.0
C	25	Joe Nieuwendyk	CGY	6	2	2	4	0	0	1	0	0	0	8	25.0
C	17	Wes Walz	CGY	6	3	0	3	1–	2	0	0	0	0	7	42.9
C	13	German Titov	CGY	7	2	1	3	4–	4	1	0	0	0	16	12.5
D	33	Zarley Zalapski	CGY	7	0	3	3	1	2	0	0	0	0	23	.0
R	22	Ronnie Stern	CGY	7	2	0	2	1–	12	0	0	0	0	11	18.2
C	32	Mike Sullivan	CGY	7	1	1	2	0	8	0	1	0	0	7	14.3
C	11	Kelly Kisio	CGY	7	0	2	2	1–	8	0	0	0	0	5	.0
C	29	Joel Otto	CGY	3	0	1	1	2–	4	0	0	0	0	0	.0
D	3	Frank Musil	CGY	7	0	1	1	2	4	0	0	0	0	6	.0
D	6	James Patrick	CGY	7	0	1	1	1–	6	0	0	0	0	4	.0
D	5	Chris Dahlquist	CGY	1	0	0	0	3–	0	0	0	0	0	1	.0
D	39	Dan Keczmer	CGY	3	0	0	0	0	4	0	0	0	0	6	.0
C	92	Michael Nylander	CGY	3	0	0	0	1–	0	0	0	0	0	3	.0
D	4	Kevin Dahl	CGY	6	0	0	0	3–	4	0	0	0	0	4	.0
G	30	Mike Vernon	CGY	7	0	0	0	0	2	0	0	0	0	0	.0
D	18	Trent Yawney	CGY	7	0	0	0	5–	16	0	0	0	0	11	.0
L	12	Paul Kruse	CGY	7	0	0	0	3–	14	0	0	0	0	11	.0
R	15	* Sandy McCarthy	CGY	7	0	0	0	2–	34	0	0	0	0	3	.0

Goaltending

No.	Goaltender	GPI	Mins	Avg	W	L	EN	SO	GA	SA	S%
30	Mike Vernon	7	466	2.96	3	4	0	0	23	220	.895
	Totals	**7**	**466**	**2.96**	**3**	**4**	**0**	**0**	**23**	**220**	**.895**

Club Records

Team

(Figures in brackets for season records are games played)

Most Points	117	1988-89 (80)
Most Wins	54	1988-89 (80)
Most Ties	19	1977-78 (80)
Most Losses	38	1972-73 (78)
Most Goals	397	1987-88 (80)
Most Goals Against	345	1981-82 (80)
Fewest Points	65	1972-73 (78)
Fewest Wins	25	1972-73 (78)
Fewest Ties	3	1986-87 (80)
Fewest Losses	17	1988-89 (80)
Fewest Goals	191	1972-73 (78)
Fewest Goals Against	226	1988-89 (80)

Longest Winning Streak

Overall .... 10 Oct. 14-Nov. 3/78

Home .... 9 Oct. 17-Nov. 15/78
Jan. 3-Feb. 5/89
Mar. 3-Apr. 1/90
Feb. 21-Mar. 14/91

Away .... 7 Nov. 10-Dec. 4/88

Longest Undefeated Streak

Over-all .... 13 Nov. 10-Dec. 8/88 (12 wins, 1 tie)

Home .... 18 Dec. 29/90-Mar. 14/91 (17 wins, 1 tie)

Away .... 9 Feb. 20-Mar. 21/88 (6 wins, 3 ties)
Nov. 11-Dec. 16/90 (6 wins, 3 ties)

Longest Losing Streak

Over-all .... 11 Dec. 14/85-Jan. 7/86

Home .... 4 Seven times

Away .... 9 Dec. 1/85-Jan. 12/86

Longest Winless Streak

Over-all .... 11 Dec. 14/85-Jan. 7/86 (11 losses)
Jan. 5-26/93 (9 losses, 2 ties)

Home .... 6 Nov. 25-Dec. 18/82 (5 losses, 1 tie)

Away .... 13 Feb. 3-Mar. 29/73 (10 losses, 3 ties)

Most Shutouts, Season	8	1974-75 (80)
Most PIM, Season	2,655	1991-92 (80)
Most Goals, Game	13	Feb. 10/93 (San Jose 1 at Calgary 13)

Individual

Most Seasons	11	Al MacInnis
Most Games	803	Al MacInnis
Most Goals, Career	293	Joe Nieuwendyk
Most Assists, Career	609	Al MacInnis
Most Points, Career	822	Al MacInnis (213 goals, 609 assists)
Most PIM, Career	2,405	Tim Hunter
Most Shutouts, Career	20	Dan Bouchard

Longest Consecutive

Games Streak .... 257 Brad Marsh (Oct. 11/78-Nov. 10/81)

Most Goals, Season .... 66 Lanny McDonald (1982-83)

Most Assists, Season .... 82 Kent Nilsson (1980-81)

Most Points, Season .... 131 Kent Nilsson (1980-81) (49 goals, 82 assists)

Most PIM, Season .... 375 Tim Hunter (1988-89)

Most Points, Defenseman

Season .... 103 Al MacInnis (1990-91) (28 goals, 75 assists)

Most Points, Center

Season .... 131 Kent Nilsson (1980-81) (49 goals, 82 assists)

Most Points, Right Wing

Season .... 110 Joe Mullen (1988-89) (51 goals, 59 assists)

Most Points, Left Wing

Season .... 90 Gary Roberts (1991-92) (53 goals, 37 assists)

Most Points, Rookie

Season .... 92 Joe Nieuwendyk (1987-88) (51 goals, 41 assists)

Most Shutouts, Season .... 5 Dan Bouchard (1973-74)
Phil Myre (1974-75)

Most Goals, Game .... 5 Joe Nieuwendyk (Jan. 11/89)

Most Assists, Game .... 6 Guy Chouinard (Feb. 25/81)
Gary Suter (Apr. 4/86)

Most Points, Game .... 7 Sergei Makarov (Feb. 25/90)

Retired Numbers

9 Lanny McDonald 1981-1989

All-time Record vs. Other Clubs

Regular Season

	At Home						On Road						Total					
	GP	W	L	T	GF	GA	PTS	GP	W	L	T	GF	GA	PTS	GP	W	L	T	GF	GA	PTS
Anaheim	3	2	1	0	10	8	4	3	2	0	1	9	4	5	6	4	1	1	19	12	9
Boston	38	15	20	3	144	140	33	39	10	24	5	107	138	25	77	25	44	8	251	278	58
Buffalo	38	13	15	10	137	133	36	38	13	22	4	115	160	28	76	25	37	14	252	293	64
Chicago	43	20	16	7	142	133	47	41	12	20	9	124	149	33	84	32	36	16	266	282	80
Dallas	42	26	5	11	173	112	63	42	16	21	5	137	158	37	84	42	26	16	310	270	100
Detroit	40	24	11	5	178	129	53	39	12	20	7	128	153	31	79	36	31	12	306	282	84
Edmonton	54	29	19	6	254	198	64	54	18	28	8	197	231	44	108	47	47	14	451	429	108
Florida	1	1	0	0	4	2	2	1	0	1	0	1	2	0	2	1	1	0	5	4	2
Hartford	22	17	4	1	118	75	35	22	12	7	3	90	75	27	44	29	11	4	208	150	62
Los Angeles	71	44	18	9	341	239	97	69	26	37	6	258	283	58	140	70	55	15	599	522	155
Montreal	37	11	21	5	120	135	27	38	11	21	6	94	135	28	75	22	42	11	214	270	55
New Jersey	36	27	4	5	172	93	59	37	23	11	3	144	109	49	73	50	15	8	316	202	108
NY Islanders	43	19	13	11	154	134	49	43	10	24	9	114	178	29	86	29	37	20	268	312	78
NY Rangers	43	24	10	9	196	134	57	44	20	19	5	160	156	45	87	44	29	14	356	290	102
Ottawa	2	2	0	0	18	4	4	2	1	1	0	7	9	2	4	3	1	0	25	6	6
Philadelphia	45	23	13	9	188	148	55	44	12	30	2	120	180	26	89	35	43	11	308	328	81
Pittsburgh	38	22	9	7	163	114	51	38	10	18	10	125	139	30	76	32	27	17	288	253	81
Quebec	23	13	4	6	103	72	32	22	9	7	6	90	93	24	45	22	11	12	193	165	56
St. Louis	42	21	18	3	151	125	45	43	18	18	7	138	152	43	85	39	36	10	289	277	88
San Jose	10	8	2	0	55	22	16	12	9	2	1	45	32	19	22	17	4	1	100	54	35
Tampa Bay	2	1	1	0	3	6	2	3	2	1	0	16	13	4	5	3	2	0	19	19	6
Toronto	42	26	12	4	189	140	56	40	17	16	7	160	157	41	82	43	28	11	349	297	97
Vancouver	71	50	12	9	324	201	109	72	31	26	15	247	259	77	143	81	38	24	571	460	186
Washington	32	22	6	4	140	77	48	33	13	15	5	121	127	31	65	35	21	9	261	204	79
Winnipeg	51	34	10	7	247	162	75	50	20	22	8	185	207	48	101	54	32	15	432	369	123
Defunct Clubs	13	8	4	1	51	34	17	13	7	3	3	43	33	17	26	15	7	4	94	67	34
Totals	**882**	**502**	**248**	**132**	**3775**	**2770**	**1136**	**882**	**333**	**413**	**136**	**2975**	**3325**	**802**	**1764**	**835**	**661**	**268**	**6750**	**6095**	**1938**

Calgary totals include Atlanta, 1972-73 to 1979-80. Dallas totals include Minnesota, 1972-73 to 1992-93.
New Jersey totals include Kansas City, 1974-75 to 1975-76, and Colorado, 1976-77 to 1981-82.

Playoffs

	Series	W	L	GP	W	L	T	GF	GA	Last Mtg.	Round	Result
Chicago	2	2	0	8	7	1	0	30	17	1989	CF	W 4-1
Dallas	1	0	1	6	2	4	0	18	25	1981	SF	L 2-4
Detroit	1	0	1	2	0	2	0	5	8	1978	PR	L 0-2
Edmonton	5	1	4	30	11	19	0	96	132	1991	DSF	L 3-4
Los Angeles	6	2	4	26	13	13	0	102	105	1993	DSF	L 2-4
Montreal	2	1	1	11	5	6	0	32	31	1989	F	W 4-2
NY Rangers	1	0	1	4	1	3	0	8	14	1980	PR	L 1-3
Philadelphia	2	1	1	11	4	7	0	28	43	1981	QF	W 4-3
St. Louis	1	1	0	7	4	3	0	28	22	1986	CF	W 4-3
Toronto	1	0	1	2	0	2	0	5	9	1979	PR	L 0-2
Vancouver	5	3	2	25	13	12	0	82	80	1994	CQF	L 3-4
Winnipeg	3	1	2	13	6	7	0	43	45	1987	DSF	L 2-4
Totals	**30**	**12**	**18**	**145**	**66**	**79**	**0**	**487**	**531**			

Playoff Results 1994-90

Year	Round	Opponent	Result	GF	GA
1994	CQF	Vancouver	L 3-4	20	23
1993	DSF	Los Angeles	L 2-4	28	33
1991	DSF	Edmonton	L 3-4	20	22
1990	DSF	Los Angeles	L 2-4	24	29

Abbreviations: Round: F – Final;
CF – conference final; **CQF** – conference quarter-final;
CSF – conference semi-final; **DF** – division final;
DSF – division semi-final; **SF** – semi-final;
QF – quarter-final; **PR** – preliminary round.

1993-94 Results

Oct.	5		NY Islanders	2-1	7	at	NY Islanders	2-6
	7		San Jose	6-2	8	at	Pittsburgh	2-2
	9	at	Vancouver	5-1	11		Quebec	1-0
	14	at	San Jose	2-1	15		Ottawa	10-0
	16	at	Los Angeles	4-8	17	at	San Jose	2-3
	17	at	Anaheim	2-2	19	at	Vancouver	4-3
	20	at	Edmonton	5-3	24		Los Angeles	3-3
	21		Vancouver	3-6	26		Dallas	2-3
	23		Boston	3-3	28		New Jersey	2-3
	25		Washington	3-2	29		St. Louis	3-5
	27		Buffalo	3-5	Feb. 2	at	Anaheim	4-2
	30		Edmonton	4-1	5	at	Los Angeles	5-4
	31	at	Winnipeg	4-3	7		Edmonton	4-3
Nov.	3	at	Hartford	6-3	9	at	Edmonton	6-1
	4	at	Boston	3-6	11		Hartford	4-1
	6	at	Montreal	4-3	12		Toronto	3-2
	9		Los Angeles	3-2	14		Chicago	2-4
	11		Anaheim	5-4	18	at	Dallas	2-4
	13		Vancouver	4-3	20	at	Winnipeg	5-2
	15		Winnipeg	7-2	22	at	Vancouver	4-4
	18	at	St. Louis	3-3	24		Tampa Bay	0-4
	20	at	Dallas	3-4	26		Los Angeles	4-2
	22		Anaheim	1-2	Mar. 1	at	Detroit	2-5
	24		Toronto	5-3	3	at	Chicago	2-4
	26		Chicago	3-6	5	at	New Jersey	3-6
	30		Dallas	2-2	6	at	Washington	4-2
Dec.	4		Philadelphia	6-0	9		Detroit	1-5
	6	at	Ottawa	6-1	11		Florida	4-2
	7	at	Quebec	4-4	12		San Jose	2-0
	10	at	Buffalo	2-6	15	at	Tampa Bay	7-3
	11	at	Toronto	1-3	16	at	Florida	1-2
	14		Vancouver	8-4	20	at	Toronto	6-3
	17		St. Louis	3-4	22		NY Rangers	4-4
	18		Winnipeg	5-4	26		Pittsburgh	2-5
	20		Los Angeles	4-5	31	at	Philadelphia	4-1
	22	at	Edmonton	3-7	Apr. 2	at	Detroit	3-3
	23	at	Vancouver	3-4	3	at	Chicago	1-2
	28	at	San Jose	3-3	6		Anaheim	4-2
	30		Edmonton	7-1	8		San Jose	5-2
	31		Montreal	2-5	9		Detroit	4-2
Jan.	2	at	St. Louis	3-4	11	at	Anaheim	3-0
	5	at	NY Rangers	4-1	13	at	Los Angeles	4-6

Entry Draft Selections 1994-80

1994
Pick
19 Chris Dingman
45 Dmitri Ryabykin
77 Chris Clark
91 Ryan Duthie
97 Johan Finnstrom
107 Nils Ekman
123 Frank Appel
149 Patrick Haltia
175 Ladislav Kohn
201 Keith McCambridge
227 Jorgen Jonsson
253 Mike Peluso
279 Pavel Torgayev

1993
Pick
18 Jesper Mattsson
44 Jamie Allison
70 Dan Tompkins
95 Jason Smith
96 Marty Murray
121 Darryl Lafrance
122 John Emmons
148 Andreas Karlsson
200 Derek Sylvester
252 German Titov
278 Burke Murphy

1992
Pick
6 Cory Stillman
30 Chris O'Sullivan
54 Mathias Johansson
78 Robert Svehla
102 Sami Helenius
126 Ravil Yakubov
129 Joel Bouchard
150 Pavel Rajnoha
174 Ryan Mulhern
198 Brandon Carper
222 Jonas Hoglund
246 Andrei Potaichuk

1991
Pick
19 Niklas Sundblad
41 Francois Groleau
52 Sandy McCarthy
63 Brian Caruso
85 Steven Magnusson
107 Jerome Butler
129 Bobby Marshall
140 Matt Hoffman
151 Kelly Harper
173 David St. Pierre
195 David Struch
217 Sergei Zolotov
239 Marko Jantunen
261 Andrei Trefilov

1990
Pick
11 Trevor Kidd
26 Nicolas P. Perreault
32 Vesa Viitakoski
41 Etienne Belzile
62 Glen Mears
83 Paul Kruse
125 Chris Tschupp
146 Dmitri Frolov
167 Shawn Murray
188 Mike Murray
209 Rob Sumner
230 invalid claim
251 Leo Gudas

1989
Pick
24 Kent Manderville
42 Ted Drury
50 Veli-Pekka Kautonen
63 Corey Lyons
70 Robert Reichel
84 Ryan O'Leary
105 F. (Toby) Kearney
147 Alex Nikolic
168 Kevin Wortman
189 Sergei Gomolyako
210 Dan Sawyer
231 Alexander Yudin
252 Kenneth Kennholt

1988
Pick
21 Jason Muzzatti
42 Todd Harkins
84 Gary Socha
85 Thomas Forslund
90 Scott Matusovich
126 Jonas Bergqvist
147 Stefan Nilsson
168 Troy Kennedy
189 Brett Peterson
210 Guy Darveau
231 Dave Tretowicz
252 Sergei Priakhan

1987
Pick
19 Bryan Deasley
25 Stephane Matteau
40 Kevin Grant
61 Scott Mahoney
70 Tim Harris
103 Tim Corkery
124 Joe Aloi
145 Peter Ciavaglia
166 Theoren Fleury
187 Mark Osiecki
208 William Sedergren
229 Peter Hasselblad
250 Magnus Svensson

1986
Pick
16 George Pelawa
37 Brian Glynn
79 Tom Quinlan
100 Scott Bloom
121 John Parker
142 Rick Lessard
163 Mark Olsen
184 Warren Sharples
205 Doug Pickell
226 Anders Lindstrom
247 Antonin Stavjana

1985
Pick
17 Chris Biotti
27 Joe Nieuwendyk
38 Jeff Wenaas
59 Lane MacDonald
80 Roger Johansson
101 Esa Keskinen
122 Tim Sweeney
143 Stu Grimson
164 Nate Smith
185 Darryl Olsen
206 Peter Romberg
227 Alexander Kozhevnikov
248 Bill Gregoire

1984
Pick
12 Gary Roberts
33 Ken Sabourin
38 Paul Ranheim
75 Petr Rosol
96 Joel Paunio
117 Brett Hull
138 Kevan Melrose
159 Jiri Hrdina
180 Gary Suter
200 Petr Rucka
221 Stefan Jonsson
241 Rudolf Suchanek

1983
Pick
13 Dan Quinn
51 Brian Bradley
55 Perry Berezan
66 John Bekkers
71 Kevan Guy
77 Bill Claviter
91 Igor Liba
111 Grant Blair
131 Jeff Hogg
151 Chris MacDonald
171 Rob Kivell
191 Tom Pratt
211 Jaroslav Benak
231 Sergei Makarov

1982
Pick
29 Dave Reierson
37 Richard Kromm
51 Jim Laing
65 Dave Meszaros
72 Mark Lamb
93 Lou Kiriakou
114 Jeff Vaive
118 Mats Kihlstrom
135 Brad Ramsden
156 Roy Myllari
177 Ted Pearson
198 Jim Uens
219 Rick Erdall
240 Dale Thompson

1981
Pick
15 Allan MacInnis
56 Mike Vernon
78 Peter Madach
99 Mario Simioni
120 Todd Hooey
141 Rick Heppner
162 Dale Degray
183 George Boudreau
204 Bruce Eakin

1980
Pick
13 Denis Cyr
31 Tony Curtale
32 Kevin LaVallee
39 Steve Konroyd
76 Marc Roy
97 Randy Turnbull
118 John Multan
139 Dave Newsom
160 Claude Drouin
181 Hakan Loob
202 Steve Fletcher

Coach

KING, DAVE
Coach, Calgary Flames. Born in Saskatoon, Sask., December 22, 1947.

Dave King, who is entering his 23rd season as a coach, brings a wealth of experience to the Calgary Flames' organization. Long respected for his outstanding contribution to the Canadian National Team program, King started his coaching career with the University of Saskatchewan in 1972-73, eventually moving on to the WHL before returning to Saskatchewan and leading the Huskies to the CIAU title in 1983. King first attracted nation-wide attention when he led the Canadian National Junior Team to the gold medal at the 1982 World Junior Championships. Since that time, he has directed the National and Olympic Teams in both the World Championships and the Olympics. Under his guidance, Canada captured the silver medal at the 1992 Games, the country's first Olympic hockey medal since 1968.

Coaching Record

		Regular Season or World Championships					Playoffs or Olympics				
Year	Team	Games	W	L	T	%	Games	W	L	T	%
1984	Canadian National	....	....	....	....	....	7	4	3	0	.571
1987	Canadian National	10	3	5	2	.400	....	....	....	....	....
1988	Canadian National	....	....	....	....	....	8	5	2	1	.688
1989	Canadian National	10	7	3	0	.700	....	....	....	....	....
1990	Canadian National	10	6	3	1	.650	....	....	....	....	....
1991	Canadian National	10	5	2	3	.650	....	....	....	....	....
1992	Canadian National	6	2	3	1	.417	8	6	2	0	.750
1992-93	**Calgary (NHL)**	**84**	**43**	**30**	**11**	**.577**	**6**	**2**	**4**	**0**	**.333**
1993-94	**Calgary (NHL)**	**84**	**42**	**29**	**13**	**.577**	**7**	**3**	**4**	**0**	**.429**
	NHL Totals	**168**	**85**	**59**	**24**	**.577**	**13**	**5**	**8**	**0.385**	

Club Directory

Olympic Saddledome
P.O. Box 1540 Station M
Calgary, Alberta T2P 3B9
Phone **403/261-0475**
FAX 403/261-0470
Capacity: 20,230

Owners Harley N. Hotchkiss, Byron J. Seaman, Daryl K. Seaman, Grant A. Bartlett, N. Murray Edwards, Ronald V. Joyce, Alvin G. Libin, Allan P. Markin, J.R. (Bud) McCaig

Management
President / Alternate Governor . . . . W.C. (Bill) Hay
Vice-President, General Manager . . . . Doug Risebrough
Vice-President, Business and Finance . . . . Clare Rhyasen
Vice-President, Marketing and Broadcasting. . . . . Lanny McDonald

Hockey Club Personnel
Director of Hockey Operations . . . . Al MacNeil
Assistant General Manager. . . . . Al Coates
Head Coach . . . . Dave King
Assistant Coaches. . . . . Guy Charron, Jamie Hislop, Slavomir Lener
Goaltending Consultant . . . . Glenn Hall
St. John Head Coach . . . . Bob Francis
St. John Assistant Coach. . . . . Rick Carriere
Director of Amateur Scouting. . . . . Tom Thompson
Scouts. . . . . Ray Clearwater, Jiri Hrdina, Guy Lapointe, Ian McKenzie
Pro Scout . . . . Nick Polano
Scouting Staff. . . . . Ron Ferguson, Glen Giovanucci, Larry Popein, Ernie Vargas, Paul McIntosh, Jarmo Tolvanen, Andres Steen
Secretary to President and Finance . . . . Yvette Mutcheson
Secretary to General Manager . . . . June Yeates
Secretary to Hockey Operations/Coaches . . . . Brenda Koyich

Administration
Controller. . . . . Michael Holditch
Assistant Controller . . . . Dorothy Stuart
Manager, Accounting. . . . . Marilyn Oliver

Marketing
Director, Advertising and Publishing . . . . Pat Halls
Manager, Marketing and Special Events. . . . . Roger Lemire
Manager, Corporate Services . . . . Bob White
Manager, Retail Stores . . . . Mark Mason

Public Relations
Director, Public Relations . . . . Rick Skaggs
Assistant Public Relations Director . . . . Mike Burke

Ticketing
Manager, Tickets . . . . Ann-Marie Malarchuk
Assistant Ticket Manager . . . . Linda Forrest

Medical/Training Staff
Head Trainer. . . . . Jim (Bearcat) Murray
Equipment Manager. . . . . Bobby Stewart
Physiotherapist and Fitness Coordinator . . . . James Gattinger
Dressing Room Attendants. . . . . Ernie Minhinnett, Cliff Stewart, Craig Forester, Les Jarvis
Director of Medicine. . . . . Dr. Terry Groves
Orthopedic Surgeon . . . . Dr. Lowell Van Zuiden
Team Dentist . . . . Dr. Bill Blair
Consulting . . . . Dr. Hap Davis

Olympic Saddledome Operations
General Manager . . . . Jay Green
Assistant Manager . . . . Libby Raines
Operations Manager. . . . . George Greenwood
Food Services Manager. . . . . Art Hernandez

Facility
Location of Press Boxes. . . . . Print – north side
Radio – south side
TV – concourse
Dimensions of Rink. . . . . 200 feet by 85 feet

Broadcast Stations
Radio . . . . 66 CFR Radio (660 AM)
Television . . . . Channels 2 & 7

Coaching History

Bernie Geoffrion, 1972-73 to 1973-74; Bernie Geoffrion and Fred Creighton, 1974-75; Fred Creighton, 1975-76 to 1978-79; Al MacNeil, 1979-80 (Atlanta); 1980-81 to 1981-82 (Calgary); Bob Johnson, 1982-83 to 1986-87; Terry Crisp, 1987-88 to 1989-90; Doug Risebrough, 1990-91; Doug Risebrough and Guy Charron, 1991-92; Dave King, 1992-93 to date.

Captains' History

Keith McCreary, 1972-73 to 1974-75; Pat Quinn, 1975-76, 1976-77; Tom Lysiak, 1977-78, 1978-79; Jean Pronovost, 1979-80; Brad Marsh, 1980-81; Phil Russell, 1981-82, 1982-83; Lanny McDonald, Doug Risebrough (co-captains), 1983-84; Lanny McDonald, Doug Risebrough, Jim Peplinski (tri-captains), 1984-85 to 1986-87; Lanny McDonald, Jim Peplinski (co-captains), 1987-88; Lanny McDonald, Jim Peplinski, Tim Hunter (tri-captains), 1988-89; Brad McCrimmon, 1989-90; alternating captains, 1990-91; Joe Nieuwendyk, 1991-92 to date.

Chicago Blackhawks

1993-94 Results: 39w-36L-9T 87PTS. Fifth, Central Division

A two-time winner of the Norris Trophy, Chris Chelios, far left, registered 60 points for the Blackhawks in 1993-94. Tony Amonte, left, was acquired by Chicago from the New York Rangers on March 21, 1994 in exchange for Stephane Matteau and Brian Noonan.

Schedule

Oct.	Sat.	1	at Pittsburgh		Fri.	6	at Detroit
	Sun.	2	St. Louis		Sun.	8	Los Angeles
	Thur.	6	New Jersey		Wed.	11	at Vancouver
	Sat.	8	at Dallas		Thur.	12	at Calgary
	Sun.	9	Edmonton		Sun.	15	Hartford
	Tues.	11	at St. Louis		Tues.	17	at Toronto
	Thur.	13	Winnipeg		Wed.	25	Edmonton
	Sat.	15	at Quebec		Fri.	27	Toronto
	Mon.	17	at Montreal		Sun.	29	at Washington*
	Thur.	20	San Jose		Tues.	31	at Philadelphia
	Sat.	22	at Winnipeg	Feb.	Thur.	2	at NY Rangers
	Sun.	23	Los Angeles		Sat.	4	at New Jersey*
	Thur.	27	Anaheim		Wed.	8	at Edmonton
	Sun.	30	Tampa Bay		Thur.	9	at Vancouver
Nov.	Wed.	2	at Buffalo		Wed.	15	at Toronto
	Sat.	5	at Boston		Thur.	16	Pittsburgh
	Sun.	6	Dallas		Sun.	19	Winnipeg*
	Thur.	10	Toronto		Tues.	21	Ottawa
	Sat.	12	at Winnipeg		Thur.	23	Washington
	Sun.	13	St. Louis		Sat.	25	at St. Louis
	Tues.	15	at Los Angeles		Sun.	26	Detroit
	Sun.	20	at Anaheim		Tues.	28	at Ottawa
	Tues.	22	at San Jose	Mar.	Thur.	2	Buffalo
	Thur.	24	at Calgary		Sat.	4	at Hartford*
	Fri.	25	at Edmonton		Sun.	5	St. Louis*
Dec.	Thur.	1	at Montreal		Tues.	7	Winnipeg
	Sat.	3	at Florida		Thur.	9	Ottawa
	Sun.	4	Anaheim				(in Phoenix)
	Thur.	8	Vancouver		Sun.	12	Calgary*
	Fri.	9	at Dallas		Tues.	14	at Detroit
	Sun.	11	Florida		Thur.	16	Vancouver
	Wed.	14	Dallas		Sat.	18	Hartford
	Fri.	16	at Tampa Bay				(in Phoenix)
	Sun.	18	Philadelphia		Tues.	21	at San Jose
	Tues.	20	NY Islanders		Thur.	23	at Los Angeles
	Wed.	21	at Toronto		Sun.	26	Dallas*
	Fri.	23	at Detroit		Mon.	27	at Dallas
	Mon.	26	Detroit		Wed.	29	Detroit
	Tues.	27	at St. Louis		Fri.	31	Quebec
	Fri.	30	at Anaheim	Apr.	Sun.	2	NY Rangers*
Jan.	Sun.	1	San Jose		Wed.	5	at Winnipeg
	Tues.	3	at NY Islanders		Thur.	6	Toronto
	Thur.	5	Calgary		Sun.	9	Boston*

* Denotes afternoon game.

Home Starting Times:
Night games . . . . 7:30 p.m.
Matinees . . . . 1:30 p.m.
Except Sun. Jan. 8, Feb. 26 . . . . 7:00 p.m.
Sun. Apr. 2, Apr. 9 . . . . . 12:00 p.m.

Franchise date: September 25, 1926

CENTRAL DIVISION

69th NHL Season

Year-by-Year Record

Season	GP	Home W	L	T	Road W	L	T	Overall W	L	T	GF	GA	Pts.	Finished		Playoff Result
1993-94	84	21	16	5	18	20	4	39	36	9	254	240	87	5th,	Central Div.	Lost Conf. Quarter-Final
1992-93	84	25	11	6	22	14	6	47	25	12	279	230	106	1st,	Norris Div.	Lost Div. Semi-Final
1991-92	80	23	9	8	13	20	7	36	29	15	257	236	87	2nd,	Norris Div.	Lost Final
1990-91	80	28	8	4	21	15	4	49	23	8	284	211	106	1st,	Norris Div.	Lost Div. Semi-Final
1989-90	80	25	13	2	16	20	4	41	33	6	316	294	88	1st,	Norris Div.	Lost Conf. Championship
1988-89	80	16	14	10	11	27	2	27	41	12	297	335	66	4th,	Norris Div.	Lost Conf. Championship
1987-88	80	21	17	2	9	24	7	30	41	9	284	326	69	3rd,	Norris Div.	Lost Div. Semi-Final
1986-87	80	18	13	9	11	24	5	29	37	14	290	310	72	3rd,	Norris Div.	Lost Div. Semi-Final
1985-86	80	23	12	5	16	21	3	39	33	8	351	349	86	1st,	Norris Div.	Lost Div. Semi-Final
1984-85	80	22	16	2	16	19	5	38	35	7	309	299	83	2nd,	Norris Div.	Lost Conf. Championship
1983-84	80	25	13	2	5	29	6	30	42	8	277	311	68	4th,	Norris Div.	Lost Div. Semi-Final
1982-83	80	29	8	3	18	15	7	47	23	10	338	268	104	1st,	Norris Div.	Lost Conf. Championship
1981-82	80	20	13	7	10	25	5	30	38	12	332	363	72	4th,	Norris Div.	Lost Conf. Championship
1980-81	80	21	11	8	10	22	8	31	33	16	304	315	78	2nd,	Smythe Div.	Lost Prelim. Round
1979-80	80	21	12	7	13	15	12	34	27	19	241	250	87	1st,	Smythe Div.	Lost Quarter-Final
1978-79	80	18	12	10	11	24	5	29	36	15	244	277	73	1st,	Smythe Div.	Lost Quarter-Final
1977-78	80	19	16	5	7	27	6	26	43	11	240	298	63	3rd,	Smythe Div.	Lost Prelim. Round
1976-77	80	17	15	8	15	15	10	32	30	18	254	261	82	1st,	Smythe Div.	Lost Quarter-Final
1975-76	80	24	12	4	13	23	4	37	35	8	268	241	82	1st,	Smythe Div.	Lost Quarter-Final
1974-75	78	20	6	13	21	8	10	41	14	23	272	164	105	2nd,	West Div.	Lost Semi-Final
1973-74	78	26	9	4	16	18	5	42	27	9	284	225	93	1st,	West Div.	Lost Final
1972-73	78	28	3	8	18	14	7	46	17	15	256	166	107	1st,	West Div.	Lost Semi-Final
1971-72	78	30	6	3	19	14	6	49	20	9	277	184	107	1st,	West Div.	Lost Final
1970-71	76	26	7	5	19	15	4	45	22	9	250	170	99	1st,	East Div.	Lost Semi-Final
1969-70	76	20	14	4	14	19	5	34	33	9	280	246	77	6th,	East Div.	Out of Playoffs
1968-69	74	20	13	4	12	13	12	32	26	16	212	222	80	4th,	East Div.	Lost Semi-Final
1967-68	70	24	5	6	17	12	6	41	17	12	264	170	94	1st,		Lost Semi-Final
1966-67	70	21	8	6	16	17	2	37	25	8	240	187	82	2nd,		Lost Semi-Final
1965-66	70	20	13	2	14	15	6	34	28	8	224	176	76	3rd,		Lost Final
1964-65	70	26	4	5	10	18	7	36	22	12	218	169	84	2nd,		Lost Semi-Final
1963-64	70	17	9	9	15	12	8	32	21	17	194	178	81	2nd,		Lost Semi-Final
1962-63	70	20	10	5	11	16	8	31	26	13	217	186	75	3rd,		Lost Final
1961-62	70	20	6	9	9	18	8	29	24	17	198	180	75	3rd,		Won Stanley Cup
1960-61	**70**	**20**	**6**	**9**	**9**	**18**	**8**	**29**	**24**	**17**	**198**	**180**	**75**	**3rd,**		**Won Stanley Cup**
1959-60	70	18	11	6	10	18	7	28	29	13	191	180	69	3rd,		Lost Semi-Final
1958-59	70	14	12	9	14	17	4	28	29	13	197	208	69	3rd,		Lost Semi-Final
1957-58	70	15	17	3	9	22	4	24	39	7	163	202	55	5th,		Out of Playoffs
1956-57	70	12	15	8	4	24	7	16	39	15	169	225	47	6th,		Out of Playoffs
1955-56	70	9	19	7	10	20	5	19	39	12	155	216	50	6th,		Out of Playoffs
1954-55	70	6	21	8	7	19	9	13	40	17	161	235	43	6th,		Out of Playoffs
1953-54	70	8	21	6	4	30	1	12	51	7	133	242	31	6th,		Out of Playoffs
1952-53	70	14	11	10	13	17	5	27	28	15	169	175	69	4th,		Lost Semi-Final
1951-52	70	9	19	7	8	25	2	17	44	9	158	241	43	6th,		Out of Playoffs
1950-51	70	8	22	5	5	25	5	13	47	10	171	280	36	6th,		Out of Playoffs
1949-50	70	13	18	4	9	20	6	22	38	10	203	244	54	6th,		Out of Playoffs
1948-49	60	13	12	5	8	19	3	21	31	8	173	211	50	5th,		Out of Playoffs
1947-48	60	10	17	3	10	17	3	20	34	6	195	225	46	6th,		Out of Playoffs
1946-47	60	10	17	3	9	20	1	19	37	4	193	274	42	6th,		Out of Playoffs
1945-46	50	15	5	5	8	15	2	23	20	7	200	178	53	3rd,		Lost Semi-Final
1944-45	50	9	14	2	4	16	5	13	30	7	141	194	33	5th,		Out of Playoffs
1943-44	50	15	6	4	7	17	1	22	23	5	178	187	49	4th,		Lost Final
1942-43	50	14	3	8	3	15	7	17	18	15	179	180	49	5th,		Out of Playoffs
1941-42	48	15	8	1	7	15	2	22	23	3	145	155	47	4th,		Lost Quarter-Final
1940-41	48	11	10	3	5	15	4	16	25	7	112	139	39	5th,		Lost Semi-Final
1939-40	48	15	7	2	8	12	4	23	19	6	112	120	52	4th,		Lost Quarter-Final
1938-39	48	5	13	6	7	15	2	12	28	8	91	132	32	7th,		Out of Playoffs
1937-38	**48**	**10**	**10**	**4**	**4**	**15**	**5**	**14**	**25**	**9**	**97**	**139**	**37**	**3rd,**	**Amn. Div.**	**Won Stanley Cup**
1936-37	48	8	13	3	6	14	4	14	27	7	99	131	35	4th,	Amn. Div.	Out of Playoffs
1935-36	48	15	7	2	6	12	6	21	19	8	93	92	50	3rd,	Amn. Div.	Lost Quarter-Final
1934-35	48	12	9	3	14	8	2	26	17	5	118	88	57	2nd,	Amn. Div.	Lost Quarter-Final
1933-34	**48**	**13**	**4**	**7**	**7**	**13**	**4**	**20**	**17**	**11**	**88**	**83**	**51**	**2nd,**	**Amn. Div.**	**Won Stanley Cup**
1932-33	48	12	7	5	4	13	7	16	20	12	88	101	44	4th,	Amn. Div.	Out of Playoffs
1931-32	48	13	5	6	5	14	5	18	19	11	86	101	47	2nd,	Amn. Div.	Lost Quarter-Final
1930-31	44	14	7	1	10	10	2	24	17	3	108	78	51	2nd,	Amn. Div.	Lost Final
1929-30	44	12	9	1	9	9	4	21	18	5	117	111	47	2nd,	Amn. Div.	Lost Quarter-Final
1928-29	44	3	13	6	4	16	2	7	29	8	33	85	22	5th,	Amn. Div.	Out of Playoffs
1927-28	44	2	18	2	5	16	1	7	34	3	68	134	17	5th,	Amn. Div.	Out of Playoffs
1926-27	44	12	8	2	7	14	1	19	22	3	115	116	41	3rd,	Amn. Div.	Lost Quarter-Final

1994-95 Player Personnel

FORWARDS	HT	WT	S	Place of Birth	Date	1993-94 Club
AMONTE, Tony	6-0	190	L	Hingham, MA	8/2/70	NY Rangers-Chicago
BELANGER, Hugo	6-1	190	L	St. Herbert, Que.	5/28/70	Indianapolis
CONN, Rob	6-2	200	R	Calgary, Alta.	9/3/68	Indianapolis
DAZE, Eric	6-4	202	L	Montreal, Que.	7/2/75	Beauport
DUBINSKY, Steve	6-0	190	L	Montreal, Que.	7/9/70	Chicago-Indianapolis
ELVENAS, Stefan	6-1	183	L	Lund, Sweden	3/30/70	Rogle
ENSON, Jim	6-3	191	L	Oshawa, Ont.	8/24/76	North Bay
FISHER, Craig	6-3	180	L	Oshawa, Ont.	6/30/70	Cape Breton-Winnipeg-Moncton
GAUTHIER, Daniel	6-1	190	L	Charlemagne, Que.	5/17/70	Cincinnati
GOULET, Michel	6-1	195	L	Peribonka, Que.	4/21/60	Chicago
GRAHAM, Dirk	5-11	198	R	Regina, Sask.	7/29/59	Chicago
GRIEVE, Brent	6-1	202	L	Oshawa, Ont.	5/9/69	NYI-Salt Lake-Edm-Cape Breton
HORACEK, Tony	6-4	210	L	Vancouver, B.C.	2/3/67	Chicago-Indianapolis
HOUSE, Bobby	6-1	200	R	Whitehorse, Yukon	1/7/73	Indianapolis-Flint
HUSKA, Ryan	6-2	194	L	Cranbrook, B.C.	7/2/75	Kamloops
HYMOVITZ, David	5-11	170	L	Boston, MA	5/30/74	Boston College
JOSEPHSON, Mike	5-11	195	L	Vancouver, B.C.	4/6/76	Kamloops
KIMBLE, Darin	6-2	210	R	Lucky Lake, Sask.	11/22/68	Chicago
KIRTON, Scott	6-4	215	R	Penetanguishene, Ont.	10/4/71	North Dakota
KLIMOVICH, Sergei	6-3	189	R	Novosibirsk, USSR	3/8/74	Moscow D'amo
KRIVOKRASOV, Sergei	5-10	174	L	Angarsk, USSR	4/15/74	Chicago-Indianapolis
LeCOMPTE, Eric	6-4	190	L	Montreal, Que.	4/4/75	Hull
LEROUX, Jean-Yves	6-2	193	L	Montreal, Que.	6/24/76	Beauport
MacINTYRE, Andy	6-1	190	L	Thunder Bay, Ont.	4/16/74	Saskatoon
MANLOW, Eric	6-0	190	L	Belleville, Ont.	4/7/75	Kitchener
MARA, Rob	6-1	175	R	Boston, MA	9/25/75	Belmont Hill
MCGHAN, Mike	6-1	177	L	Prince Albert, Alta.	7/11/75	Prince Albert
MOREAU, Ethan	6-2	205	L	Huntsville, Ont.	9/22/75	Niagara Falls
MURPHY, Joe	6-1	190	L	London, Ont.	10/16/67	Chicago
NICHOLLS, Bernie	6-1	185	R	Haliburton, Ont.	6/24/61	New Jersey
OATES, Matt	6-3	208	L	Evanston, IL	12/20/72	Miami-Ohio
PETERSON, Erik	6-0	185	L	Boston, MA	3/31/72	Providence
PETROV, Sergei	5-11	185	L	Leningrad, USSR	1/22/75	Minn.-Duluth
POMICHTER, Michael	6-1	222	L	New Haven, CT	9/10/73	Boston U.
POULIN, Patrick	6-1	208	L	Vanier, Que.	4/23/73	Hartford-Chicago
PROBERT, Bob	6-3	225	L	Windsor, Ont.	6/5/65	Detroit
PROKOPEC, Mike	6-2	190	R	Toronto, Ont.	5/17/74	Guelph
PROSOFSKY, Tyler	5-11	175	L	Saskatoon, Sask.	2/19/76	Tacoma
PULLOLA, Tommi	6-5	202	L	Vaasa, Finland	5/18/71	Lukko-Tuto
PYSZ, Patrik	5-11	187	L	Novy Targ, Poland	1/15/75	Augsburg
ROENICK, Jeremy	6-0	170	R	Boston, MA	1/17/70	Chicago
RUUTTU, Christian	5-11	194	L	Lappeenranta, Finland	2/20/64	Chicago
ST. JACQUES, Kevin	5-11	190	R	Edmonton, Alta.	2/25/71	Indianapolis-Flint
SAVENKO, Bogdan	6-1	192	R	Kiev, USSR	11/20/74	Niagara Falls
SHANTZ, Jeff	6-0	184	R	Duchess, Alta.	10/10/73	Chicago-Indianapolis
SUTTER, Brent	5-11	180	R	Viking, Alta.	6/10/62	Chicago
SUTTER, Rich	5-11	188	R	Viking, Alta.	12/2/63	Chicago
TUCKER, Chris	5-11	183	L	White Plains, NY	2/9/72	U. Wisconsin
VAUHKONEN, Jonni	6-2	189	L	Suonenjoki, Finland	1/1/75	Reipas
WHITE, Tom	6-1	185	L	Chicago, IL	8/25/75	Miami
YSEBAERT, Paul	6-1	190	L	Sarnia, Ont.	5/15/66	Winnipeg-Chicago
DEFENSEMEN						
BALKOVEC, Maco	6-2	200	L	New Westminster, B.C.	1/17/71	U. Wisconsin
CARNEY, Keith E.	6-2	205	L	Providence, RI	2/3/70	Buffalo-Chicago-Indianapolis
CHELIOS, Chris	6-1	186	R	Chicago, IL	1/25/62	Chicago
DROPPA, Ivan	6-2	209	L	Liptovsky Mikulas, Czech.	2/1/72	Chicago-Indianapolis
DUPUIS, Marc	5-11	176	L	Cornwall, Ont.	4/22/76	Belleville
DYKHUIS, Karl	6-3	195	L	Sept-Iles, Que.	7/8/72	Indianapolis
HOGAN, Tim	6-2	180	R	Oshawa, Ont.	1/7/74	U. of Michigan
JANDERA, Lubomir	5-11	180	L	Chomutov, Czech.	4/21/76	Litvinov
KELLOGG, Bob	6-4	210	L	Springfield, MA	2/16/71	Indianapolis
LARKIN, Mike	6-1	180	R	Boston, MA	3/15/73	U. of Vermont
MCLAREN, Steve	6-0	194	L	Owen Sound, Ont.	2/3/75	North Bay
RICCIARDI, Jeff	5-10	203	L	Thunder Bay, Ont.	6/22/71	Indianapolis
RUSK, Mike	6-1	175	L	Milton, Ont.	4/26/75	Guelph
RUSSELL, Cam	6-4	174	L	Halifax, N.S.	1/12/69	Chicago
SKRYPEC, Gerry	6-0	190	L	Kitchener, Ont.	6/21/74	Nmkt-Niag. Falls-Det (OHL)
SMITH, Steve	6-4	215	L	Glasgow, Scotland	4/30/63	Chicago
SMYTH, Greg	6-3	212	R	Oakville, Ont.	4/23/66	Florida-Toronto-Chicago
SUTER, Gary	6-0	190	L	Madison, WI	6/24/64	Calgary-Chicago
THIESSEN, Travis	6-3	203	L	North Battleford, Sask.	7/11/72	Cleveland
WEINRICH, Eric	6-1	210	L	Roanoke, VA	12/19/66	Hartford-Chicago

GOALTENDERS	HT	WT	C	Place of Birth	Date	1993-94 Club
BELFOUR, Ed	5-11	182	L	Carman, Man.	4/21/65	Chicago
HACKETT, Jeff	6-1	180	L	London, Ont.	6/1/68	Chicago
NOBLE, Tom	5-10	165	L	Quincy, MA	3/21/75	Catholic Mem.
ROGLES, Chris	5-11	175	L	St. Louis, MO	1/22/69	Indianapolis
SOUCY, Christian	5-11	160	L	Gatineau, Que.	9/14/70	Chicago-Indianapolis
WEIBEL, Lars	6-0	178	L	Rapperswil, Switz.	5/20/74	Lugano

Captains' History

Dick Irvin, 1926-27 to 1928-29; Duke Dutkowski, 1929-30; Ty Arbour, 1930-31 Cy Wentworth, 1931-32; Helge Bostrom, 1932-33; Chuck Gardiner, 1933-34; no captain, 1934-35; Johnny Gottselig, 1935-36 to 1939-40; Earl Seibert, 1940-41, 1941-42; Doug Bentley, 1942-43, 1943-44; Clint Smith 1944-45; John Mariucci, 1945-46; Red Hamill, 1946-47; John Mariucci, 1947-48; Gaye Stewart, 1948-49; Doug Bentley, 1949-50; Jack Stewart, 1950-51, 1951-52; Bill Gadsby, 1952-53, 1953-54; Gus Mortson, 1954-55 to 1956-57; no captain, 1957-58; Eddie Litzenberger, 1958-59 to 1960-61; Pierre Pilote, 1961-62 to 1967-68, no captain, 1968-69; Pat Stapleton, 1969-70; no captain, 1970-71 to 1974-75; Stan Mikita, Pit Martin, 1975-76; Stan Mikita, Pit Martin, Keith Magnuson, 1976-77; Keith Magnuson, 1977-78, 1978-79; Keith Magnuson, Terry Ruskowski, 1979-80; Terry Ruskowski, 1980-81, 1981-82; Darryl Sutter, 1982-83 to 1986-87; Keith Brown, Troy Murray, Denis Savard, 1987-88; Dirk Graham, 1988-89 to date.

1993-94 Scoring

* – rookie

Regular Season

Pos	#	Player	Team	GP	G	A	Pts	+/-	PIM	PP	SH	GW	GT	S	%
C	27	Jeremy Roenick	CHI	84	46	61	107	21	125	24	5	5	1	281	16.4
R	17	Joe Murphy	CHI	81	31	39	70	1	111	7	4	4	0	222	14.0
D	7	Chris Chelios	CHI	76	16	44	60	12	212	7	1	2	0	219	7.3
R	10	Tony Amonte	NYR	72	16	22	38	5	31	3	0	4	0	179	8.9
			CHI	7	1	3	4	5–	6	1	0	0	0	16	6.3
			TOTAL	79	17	25	42	0	37	4	0	4	0	195	8.7
C	12	Brent Sutter	CHI	73	9	29	38	17	43	3	2	0	0	127	7.1
L	14	Paul Ysebaert	WPG	60	9	18	27	8–	18	1	0	0	0	120	7.5
			CHI	11	5	3	8	1	8	2	0	1	0	31	16.1
			TOTAL	71	14	21	35	7–	26	3	0	1	0	151	9.3
R	33	Dirk Graham	CHI	67	15	18	33	13	45	0	2	5	0	122	12.3
L	16	Michel Goulet	CHI	56	16	14	30	1	26	3	0	6	0	120	13.3
C	22	Christian Ruuttu	CHI	54	9	20	29	4–	68	1	1	1	0	96	9.4
L	44	Patrick Poulin	HFD	9	2	1	3	8–	11	1	0	0	0	13	15.4
			CHI	58	12	13	25	0	40	1	0	3	0	83	14.5
			TOTAL	67	14	14	28	8–	51	2	0	3	0	96	14.6
D	2	Eric Weinrich	HFD	8	1	1	2	5–	2	1	0	0	0	10	10.0
			CHI	54	3	23	26	6	31	1	0	2	0	105	2.9
			TOTAL	62	4	24	28	1	33	2	0	2	0	115	3.5
D	5	Steve Smith	CHI	57	5	22	27	5–	174	1	0	1	0	89	5.6
R	15	Rich Sutter	CHI	83	12	14	26	8–	108	0	0	2	0	122	9.8
L	19	Randy Cunneyworth	HFD	63	9	8	17	2–	87	0	1	1	0	121	7.4
			CHI	16	4	3	7	1	13	0	0	1	0	33	12.1
			TOTAL	79	13	11	24	1–	100	0	1	2	0	154	8.4
D	20	Gary Suter	CGY	25	4	9	13	3–	20	2	1	0	0	51	7.8
			CHI	16	2	3	5	9–	18	2	0	0	0	35	5.7
			TOTAL	41	6	12	18	12–	38	4	1	0	0	86	7.0
C	11	* Jeff Shantz	CHI	52	3	13	16	14–	30	0	0	0	0	56	5.4
D	4	Keith Carney	BUF	7	1	3	4	1–	4	0	0	0	0	6	16.7
			CHI	30	3	5	8	15	35	0	0	0	0	31	9.7
			TOTAL	37	4	8	12	14	39	0	0	0	0	37	10.8
D	23	Neil Wilkinson	CHI	72	3	9	12	2	116	1	0	0	0	72	4.2
C	32	* Steve Dubinsky	CHI	27	2	6	8	1	16	0	0	0	0	20	10.0
D	8	Cam Russell	CHI	67	1	7	8	10	200	0	0	0	0	41	2.4
R	29	Darin Kimble	CHI	65	4	2	6	2	133	0	0	0	0	17	23.5
D	6	Robert Dirk	VAN	65	2	3	5	18	105	0	0	0	0	38	5.3
			CHI	6	0	0	0	0	26	0	0	0	0	4	.0
			TOTAL	71	2	3	5	18	131	0	0	0	0	42	4.8
G	30	Ed Belfour	CHI	70	0	4	4	0	61	0	0	0	0	0	.0
R	25	Dave Christian	CHI	9	0	3	3	0	0	0	0	0	0	6	.0
D	3	Greg Smyth	FLA	12	1	0	1	0	37	0	0	0	0	4	25.0
			TOR	11	0	1	1	2–	38	0	0	0	0	3	.0
			CHI	38	0	0	0	2–	108	0	0	0	0	29	.0
			TOTAL	61	1	1	2	4–	183	0	0	0	0	36	2.8
R	55	* Sergei Krivokrasov	CHI	9	1	0	1	2–	4	0	0	0	0	7	14.3
D	58	* Ivan Droppa	CHI	12	0	1	1	2	12	0	0	0	0	13	.0
G	31	Jeff Hackett	CHI	22	0	1	1	0	2	0	0	0	0	0	.0
G	50	* Christian Soucy	CHI	1	0	0	0	0	0	0	0	0	0	0	.0
L	34	Tony Horacek	CHI	7	0	0	0	1	53	0	0	0	0	2	.0

Goaltending

No.	Goaltender	GPI	Mins	Avg	W	L	T	EN	SO	GA	SA	S%
50	* Christian Soucy	1	3	0.00	0	0	0	0	0	0	0	.000
30	Ed Belfour	70	3998	2.67	37	24	6	0	7	178	1892	.906
31	Jeff Hackett	22	1084	3.43	2	12	3	0	0	62	566	.890

Playoffs

Pos	#	Player	Team	GP	G	A	Pts	+/-	PIM	PP	SH	GW	GT	S	%
C	27	Jeremy Roenick	CHI	6	1	6	7	4	2	0	0	1	1	15	6.7
R	10	Tony Amonte	CHI	6	4	2	6	4	4	1	0	1	0	21	19.0
D	20	Gary Suter	CHI	6	3	2	5	0	6	2	0	0	0	16	18.8
R	17	Joe Murphy	CHI	6	1	3	4	2	25	0	0	0	0	12	8.3
D	7	Chris Chelios	CHI	6	1	1	2	0	8	1	0	0	0	29	3.4
D	2	Eric Weinrich	CHI	6	0	2	2	2	6	0	0	0	0	4	.0
R	33	Dirk Graham	CHI	6	0	1	1	0	4	0	0	0	0	11	.0
D	4	Keith Carney	CHI	6	0	1	1	2	4	0	0	0	0	3	.0
R	25	Dave Christian	CHI	1	0	0	0	0	0	0	0	0	0	0	.0
R	29	Darin Kimble	CHI	1	0	0	0	1–	5	0	0	0	0	0	.0
D	6	Robert Dirk	CHI	2	0	0	0	1–	15	0	0	0	0	1	.0
D	23	Neil Wilkinson	CHI	4	0	0	0	1–	0	0	0	0	0	1	.0
L	44	Patrick Poulin	CHI	4	0	0	0	0	0	0	0	0	0	3	.0
G	30	Ed Belfour	CHI	6	0	0	0	0	2	0	0	0	0	0	.0
L	19	Randy Cunneyworth	CHI	6	0	0	0	1–	8	0	0	0	0	7	.0
C	22	Christian Ruuttu	CHI	6	0	0	0	2–	2	0	0	0	0	5	.0
D	3	Greg Smyth	CHI	6	0	0	0	2–	0	0	0	0	0	2	.0
R	15	Rich Sutter	CHI	6	0	0	0	1–	2	0	0	0	0	15	.0
C	12	Brent Sutter	CHI	6	0	0	0	0	2	0	0	0	0	7	.0
L	14	Paul Ysebaert	CHI	6	0	0	0	2–	8	0	0	0	0	9	.0
C	32	* Steve Dubinsky	CHI	6	0	0	0	1–	10	0	0	0	0	2	.0
C	11	* Jeff Shantz	CHI	6	0	0	0	2–	6	0	0	0	0	3	.0

Goaltending

No.	Goaltender	GPI	Mins	Avg	W	L	EN	SO	GA	SA	S%
30	Ed Belfour	6	360	2.50	2	4	0	0	15	191	.921
	Totals	**6**	**364**	**2.47**	**2**	**4**	**0**	**0**	**15**	**191**	**.921**

General Managers' History

Major Frederic McLaughlin, 1926-27 to 1941-42; Bill Tobin, 1942-43 to 1953-54; Tommy Ivan, 1954-55 to 1976-77; Bob Pulford, 1977-78 to 1989-90; Mike Keenan, 1990-91 to 1991-92; Mike Keenan and Bob Pulford, 1992-93; Bob Pulford, 1993-94 to date.

Club Records

Team

(Figures in brackets for season records are games played; records for fewest points, wins, ties, losses, goals, goals against are for 70 or more games)

Most Points	**107**	1970-71 (78) 1971-72 (78)
Most Wins	**49**	1970-71 (78) 1990-91 (80)
Most Ties	**23**	1973-74 (78)
Most Losses	**51**	1953-54 (70)
Most Goals	**351**	1985-86 (80)
Most Goals Against	**363**	1981-82 (80)
Fewest Points	**31**	1953-54 (70)
Fewest Wins	**12**	1953-54 (70)
Fewest Ties	**6**	1989-90 (80)
Fewest Losses	**14**	1973-74 (78)
Fewest Goals	***133**	1953-54 (70)
Fewest Goals Against	**164**	1973-74 (78)
Longest Winning Streak		
Over-all	**8**	Dec. 9-26/71; Jan. 4-21/81
Home	**13**	Nov. 11- Dec. 20/70
Away	**7**	Dec. 9-29/64
Longest Undefeated Streak		
Over-all	**15**	Jan. 14- Feb. 16/67 (12 wins, 3 ties)
Home	**18**	Oct. 11- Dec. 20/70 (16 wins, 2 ties)
Away	**12**	Oct. 29- Dec. 3/75 (6 wins, 9 ties)
Longest Losing Streak		
Over-all	**13**	Feb. 25- Oct. 11/51
Home	**11**	Feb. 8- Nov. 22/28
Away	**17**	Jan. 2- Oct. 7/54
Longest Winless Streak		
Over-all	**21**	Dec. 17/50- Jan. 28/51 (18 losses, 3 ties)
Home	***15**	Dec. 16/28- Feb. 28/29 (11 losses, 4 ties)
Away	**23**	Dec. 19/50- Oct. 11/51 (15 losses, 8 ties)
Most Shutouts, Season	**15**	1969-70 (76)
Most PIM, Season	**2,663**	1991-92 (80)
Most Goals, Game	**12**	Jan. 30/69 (Chi. 12 at Phil. 0)

Individual

Most Seasons	**22**	Stan Mikita
Most Games	**1,394**	Stan Mikita
Most Goals, Career	**604**	Bobby Hull
Most Assists, Career	**926**	Stan Mikita
Most Points, Career	**1,467**	Stan Mikita (541 goals, 926 assists)
Most PIM, Career	**1,442**	Keith Magnuson
Most Shutouts, Career	**74**	Tony Esposito
Longest Consecutive Games Streak	**884**	Steve Larmer (1982-83 to 1992-93)
Most Goals, Season	**58**	Bobby Hull (1968-69)
Most Assists, Season	**87**	Denis Savard (81-82, 87-88)
Most Points, Season	**131**	Denis Savard (1987-88) (44 goals, 87 assists)
Most PIM, Season	**408**	Mike Peluso (1991-92)
Most Points, Defenseman Season	**85**	Doug Wilson (1981-82) (39 goals, 46 assists)
Most Points, Center, Season	**131**	Denis Savard (1987-88) (44 goals, 87 assists)
Most Points, Right Wing, Season	**101**	Steve Larmer (1990-91) (44 goals, 57 assists)
Most Points, Left Wing, Season	**107**	Bobby Hull (1968-69) (58 goals, 49 assists)
Most Points, Rookie, Season	**90**	Steve Larmer (1982-83) (43 goals, 47 assists)
Most Shutouts, Season	**15**	Tony Esposito (1969-70)
Most Goals, Game	**5**	Grant Mulvey (Feb. 3/82)
Most Assists, Game	**6**	Pat Stapleton (Mar. 30/69)
Most Points, Game	**7**	Max Bentley (Jan. 28/43) Grant Mulvey (Feb. 3/82)

* NHL Record.

Coaching History

Pete Muldoon, 1926-27; Barney Stanley and Hugh Lehman, 1927-28; Herb Gardiner, 1928-29; Tom Shaughnessy and Bill Tobin, 1929-30; Dick Irvin, 1930-31; Dick Irvin and Bill Tobin, 1931-32; Godfrey Matheson, Emil Iverson and Tommy Gorman, 1932-33; Tommy Gorman, 1933-34; Clem Loughlin, 1934-35 to 1936-37; Bill Stewart, 1937-38; Bill Stewart and Paul Thompson, 1938-39; Paul Thompson, 1939-40 to 1943-44; Paul Thompson and Johnny Gottselig, 1944-45; Johnny Gottselig, 1945-46 to 1946-47; Johnny Gottselig and Charlie Conacher, 1947-48; Charlie Conacher, 1948-49 to 1949-50; Ebbie Goodfellow, 1950-51 to 1951-52; Sid Abel, 1952-53 to 1953-54; Frank Eddolls, 1954-55; Dick Irvin, 1955-56; Tommy Ivan, 1956-57; Tommy Ivan and Rudy Pilous, 1957-58; Rudy Pilous, 1958-59 to 1962-63; Billy Reay, 1963-64 to 1975-76; Billy Reay and Bill White, 1976-77; Bob Pulford, 1977-78 to 1978-79; Eddie Johnston, 1979-80; Keith Magnuson, 1980-81; Keith Magnuson and Bob Pulford, 1981-82; Orval Tessier, 1982-83 to 1983-84; Orval Tessier and Bob Pulford, 1984-85; Bob Pulford, 1985-86 to 1986-87; Bob Murdoch, 1987-88; Mike Keenan, 1988-89 to 1991-92; Darryl Sutter, 1992-93 to date.

All-time Record vs. Other Clubs

Regular Season

	At Home							On Road							Total						
	GP	W	L	T	GF	GA	PTS	GP	W	L	T	GF	GA	PTS	GP	W	L	T	GF	GA	PTS
Anaheim	3	2	1	0	7	6	4	2	2	0	0	6	4	4	5	4	1	0	13	10	8
Boston	278	141	93	44	896	745	326	276	85	159	32	778	1003	202	554	226	252	76	1674	1748	528
Buffalo	43	22	15	6	138	120	50	45	11	28	6	116	174	28	88	33	43	12	254	294	78
Calgary	41	20	12	9	149	124	49	43	16	20	7	133	142	39	84	36	32	16	282	266	88
Dallas	87	57	20	10	362	228	124	88	38	38	12	292	302	88	175	95	58	22	654	530	212
Detroit	309	144	117	48	935	853	336	309	91	190	28	762	1062	210	618	235	307	76	1697	1915	546
Edmonton	24	12	9	3	101	101	27	25	10	14	1	93	112	21	49	22	23	4	194	213	48
Florida	1	0	0	1	4	4	1	1	1	0	0	3	2	2	2	1	0	1	7	6	3
Hartford	22	13	6	3	99	64	29	23	11	10	2	80	80	24	45	24	16	5	179	144	53
Los Angeles	55	28	19	8	214	168	64	54	24	24	6	183	185	54	109	52	43	14	397	353	118
Montreal	267	91	121	55	722	747	237	267	51	168	48	629	1037	150	534	142	289	103	1351	1784	387
New Jersey	39	22	9	8	163	112	52	38	14	15	9	115	114	37	77	36	24	17	278	226	89
NY Islanders	41	20	16	5	135	143	45	39	11	16	12	118	142	34	80	31	32	17	253	285	79
NY Rangers	278	125	111	42	848	777	292	279	108	117	54	790	827	270	557	233	228	96	1638	1604	562
Ottawa	2	1	0	1	7	5	3	2	2	0	0	5	2	4	4	3	0	1	12	7	7
Philadelphia	53	24	11	18	191	150	66	54	15	28	11	145	178	41	107	39	39	29	336	328	107
Pittsburgh	52	35	8	9	221	144	79	51	22	24	5	170	181	49	103	57	32	14	391	325	128
Quebec	23	14	7	2	94	74	30	22	9	9	4	89	94	22	45	23	16	6	183	168	52
St. Louis	91	55	25	11	370	280	121	88	28	44	16	271	307	72	179	83	69	27	641	587	193
San Jose	5	4	0	1	23	12	9	6	2	4	0	14	17	4	11	6	4	1	37	29	13
Tampa Bay	5	3	0	2	16	9	8	4	2	2	0	15	14	4	9	5	2	2	31	23	12
Toronto	299	152	108	39	927	779	343	299	89	159	51	769	1028	229	598	241	267	90	1696	1807	572
Vancouver	51	33	13	5	192	121	71	52	15	25	12	148	163	42	103	48	38	17	340	284	113
Washington	32	20	7	5	134	97	45	33	10	19	4	102	127	24	65	30	26	9	236	224	69
Winnipeg	27	20	4	3	138	80	43	27	10	14	3	98	107	23	54	30	18	6	236	187	66
Defunct Clubs	139	79	40	20	408	268	178	140	52	67	21	316	346	125	279	131	107	41	724	614	303
Totals	**2267**	**1137**	**772**	**358**	**7494**	**6211**	**2632**	**2267**	**729**	**1194**	**344**	**6240**	**7750**	**1802**	**4534**	**1866**	**1966**	**702**	**13734**	**13961**	**4434**

Calgary totals include Atlanta, 1972-73 to 1979-80. Dallas totals include Minnesota, 1967-68 to 1992-93.
New Jersey totals include Kansas City, 1974-75 to 1975-76, and Colorado, 1976-77 to 1981-82.

Playoffs

	Series	W	L	GP	W	L	T	GF	GA	Last Mtg.	Round	Result
Boston	6	1	5	22	5	16	1	63	97	1978	QF	L 0-4
Buffalo	2	0	2	9	1	8	0	17	36	1980	QF	L 0-4
Calgary	2	0	2	8	1	7	0	17	30	1989	CF	L 1-4
Dallas	6	4	2	33	19	14	0	119	119	1991	DSF	L 2-4
Detroit	13	8	5	64	37	27	0	198	177	1992	DF	W 4-0
Edmonton	4	1	3	20	8	12	0	77	102	1992	CF	W 4-0
Los Angeles	1	1	0	5	4	1	0	10	7	1974	QF	W 4-1
Montreal	17	5	12	81	29	50	2	185	261	1976	QF	L 0-4
NY Islanders	2	0	2	6	0	6	0	6	21	1979	QF	L 0-4
NY Rangers	5	4	1	24	14	10	0	66	54	1973	SF	W 4-1
Philadelphia	1	1	0	4	4	0	0	20	8	1971	QF	W 4-0
Pittsburgh	2	1	1	8	4	4	0	24	23	1992	F	L 0-4
St. Louis	9	7	2	45	27	18	0	166	129	1993	DSF	L 0-4
Toronto	8	2	6	31	11	19	1	67	91	1994	CQF	L 2-4
Vancouver	1	0	1	5	1	4	0	13	18	1982	CF	L 1-4
Defunct Clubs	4	2	2	9	5	3	1	16	15			
Totals	**83**	**37**	**46**	**374**	**170**	**199**	**5**	**1064**	**1188**			

Playoff Results 1994-90

Year	Round	Opponent	Result	GF	GA
1994	CQF	Toronto	L 2-4	10	15
1993	DSF	St. Louis	L 0-4	6	13
1992	F	Pittsburgh	L 0-4	10	15
	CF	Edmonton	W 4-0	21	8
	DF	Detroit	W 4-0	11	6
	DSF	St. Louis	W 4-2	23	19
1991	DSF	Minnesota	L 2-4	16	23
1990	CF	Edmonton	L 2-4	20	25
	DF	St. Louis	W 4-3	28	22
	DSF	Minnesota	W 4-3	21	18

Abbreviations: Round: F – Final;
CF – conference final; **CQF** – conference quarter-final;
CSF – conference semi-final; **DF** – division final;
DSF – division semi-final; **SF** – semi-final;
QF – quarter-final; **PR** – preliminary round.

1993-94 Results

Oct.	6		Florida	4-4		13		Tampa Bay	1-0
	9	at	Toronto	1-2		15	at	NY Islanders	5-5
	10		Winnipeg	4-3		16		NY Rangers	1-5
	12	at	Dallas	3-3		25	at	Detroit	5-0
	14		Hartford	2-6		27		Detroit	3-4
	16	at	Winnipeg	0-1		29		Ottawa	3-3
	18		Dallas	3-5		31	at	Ottawa	1-0
	21		Quebec	3-2	**Feb.**	2	at	Vancouver	4-6
	23		Detroit	4-2		4	at	Edmonton	3-1
	26		St. Louis	9-2		6	at	Anaheim	3-2
	28		Toronto	2-4		8	at	San Jose	3-4
	30	at	Pittsburgh	3-4		9	at	Los Angeles	2-4
	31		Philadelphia	6-9		11	at	San Jose	3-4
Nov.	4		NY Islanders	4-2		13	at	San Jose	0-1
	7		Edmonton	3-0		14	at	Calgary	4-2
	11		Pittsburgh	4-1		17		Vancouver	2-4
	13	at	Toronto	3-2		18	at	Winnipeg	7-2
	14		Dallas	4-1		20		New Jersey	1-1
	18	at	Florida	3-2		24		Winnipeg	6-3
	20	at	Tampa Bay	3-4		25	at	Buffalo	3-1
	24	at	Edmonton	3-1		27		Boston	0-4
	26	at	Calgary	6-3	**Mar.**	3		Calgary	4-2
	29	at	Vancouver	1-2		6		Los Angeles	3-3
Dec.	4	at	New Jersey	2-2		8		Anaheim	3-0
	7	at	St. Louis	2-3		9	at	Los Angeles	4-0
	11	at	Boston	5-4		11	at	Anaheim	3-2
	12		San Jose	2-1		13		Vancouver	5-2
	15	at	Dallas	3-2		14	at	Quebec	1-5
	18	at	Philadelphia	2-2		16	at	Montreal	3-5
	19		Anaheim	2-0		18	at	NY Rangers	7-3
	21	at	Detroit	1-5		20		St. Louis	3-4
	23		San Jose	5-3		22	at	Detroit	1-3
	26	at	St. Louis	2-3		24		Montreal	5-5
	27		Toronto	5-2		27		Detroit	1-3
	29	at	Winnipeg	2-3		30	at	Hartford	2-3
	31		Dallas	2-5		31		Washington	3-6
Jan.	2		Winnipeg	5-1	**Apr.**	3		Calgary	2-1
	4	at	Dallas	2-1		5	at	St. Louis	1-5
	6		Anaheim	2-6		8		St. Louis	6-1
	8	at	Washington	1-4		10		Los Angeles	2-1
	9		Edmonton	2-4		12	at	Toronto	4-3
	11		Buffalo	2-5		14		Toronto	4-6

Entry Draft
Selections 1994-80

1994
Pick
14 Ethan Moreau
40 Jean-Yves Leroux
85 Steve McLaren
118 Marc Dupuis
144 Jim Enson
170 Tyler Prosofsky
196 Mike Josephson
222 Lubomir Jandera
248 Lars Weibel
263 Rob Mara

1993
Pick
24 Eric Lecompte
50 Eric Manlow
54 Bogdan Savenko
76 Ryan Huska
90 Eric Daze
102 Patrik Pysz
128 Jonni Vauhkonen
180 Tom White
206 Sergei Petrov
232 Mike Rusk
258 Mike McGhan
284 Tom Noble

1992
Pick
12 Sergei Krivokrasov
36 Jeff Shantz
41 Sergei Klimovich
89 Andy Macintyre
113 Tim Hogan
137 Gerry Skrypec
161 Mike Prokopec
185 Layne Roland
209 David Hymovitz
233 Richard Raymond

1991
Pick
22 Dean McAmmond
39 Michael Pomichter
44 Jamie Matthews
66 Bobby House
71 Igor Kravchuk
88 Zac Boyer
110 Maco Balkovec
112 Kevin St. Jacques
132 Jacques Auger
154 Scott Kirton
176 Roch Belley
198 Scott MacDonald
220 A. Andriyevsky
242 Mike Larkin
264 Scott Dean

1990
Pick
16 Karl Dykhuis
37 Ivan Droppa
79 Chris Tucker
121 Brett Stickney
124 Derek Edgerly
163 Hugo Belanger
184 Owen Lessard
205 Erik Peterson
226 Steve Dubinsky
247 Dino Grossi

1989
Pick
6 Adam Bennett
27 Michael Speer
48 Bob Kellogg
111 Tommi Pullola
132 Tracy Egeland
153 Milan Tichy
174 Jason Greyerbiehl
195 Matt Saunders
216 Mike Kozak
237 Michael Doneghey

1988
Pick
8 Jeremy Roenick
50 Trevor Dam
71 Stefan Elvenas
92 Joe Cleary
113 Justin Lafayette
134 Craig Woodcroft
155 Jon Pojar
176 Mathew Hentges
197 Daniel Maurice
218 Dirk Tenzer
239 Andreas Lupzig

1987
Pick
8 Jimmy Waite
29 Ryan McGill
50 Cam Russell
60 Mike Dagenais
92 Ulf Sandstrom
113 Mike McCormick
134 Stephen Tepper
155 John Reilly
176 Lance Werness
197 Dale Marquette
218 Bill Lacouture
239 Mike Lappin

1986
Pick
14 Everett Sanipass
35 Mark Kurzawski
77 Frantisek Kucera
98 Lonnie Loach
119 Mario Doyon
140 Mike Hudson
161 Marty Nanne
182 Geoff Benic
203 Glen Lowes
224 Chris Thayer
245 Sean Williams

1985
Pick
11 Dave Manson
53 Andy Helmuth
74 Dan Vincellette
87 Rick Herbert
95 Brad Belland
116 Jonas Heed
137 Victor Posa
158 John Reid
179 Richard LaPlante
200 Brad Hamilton
221 Ian Pound
242 Rick Braccia

1984
Pick
3 Ed Olczyk
45 Trent Yawney
66 Tommy Eriksson
90 Timo Lehkonen
101 Darin Sceviour
111 Chris Clifford
132 Mike Stapleton
153 Glen Greenough
174 Ralph DiFiorie
194 Joakim Persson
215 Bill Brown
224 David Mackey
235 Dan Williams

1983
Pick
18 Bruce Cassidy
39 Wayne Presley
59 Marc Bergevin
79 Tarek Howard
99 Kevin Robinson
115 Jari Torkki
119 Mark Lavarre
139 Scot Birnie
159 Kevin Paynter
179 Brian Noonan
199 Dominik Hasek
219 Steve Pepin

1982
Pick
7 Ken Yaremchuk
28 Rene Badeau
49 Tom McMurchy
70 Bill Watson
91 Brad Beck
112 Mark Hatcher
133 Jay Ness
154 Jeff Smith
175 Phil Patterson
196 Jim Camazzola
217 Mike James
238 Bob Andrea

1981
Pick
12 Tony Tanti
25 Kevin Griffin
54 Darrell Anholt
75 Perry Pelensky
96 Doug Chessell
117 Bill Schafhauser
138 Marc Centrone
159 Johan Mellstrom
180 John Benns
201 Sylvain Roy

1980
Pick
3 Denis Savard
15 Jerome Dupont
28 Steve Ludzik
30 Ken Solheim
36 Len Dawes
57 Troy Murray
58 Marcel Frere
67 Carey Wilson
78 Brian Shaw
99 Kevin Ginnell
120 Steve Larmer
141 Sean Simpson
162 Jim Ralph
183 Don Dietrich
204 Dan Frawley

Club Directory

United Center
1901 W. Madison St.
Chicago, IL 60612
Phone **312/455-7000**
Capacity: 20,500

President . . . . William W. Wirtz
Vice President & Assistant to the President . . . . Thomas N. Ivan
Senior Vice President/General Manager . . . . Robert J. Pulford
Vice President . . . . Jack Davison
Director of Player Personnel . . . . Bob Murray
Head Coach . . . . Darryl Sutter
Assistant Coach . . . . Rich Preston
Assistant Coach . . . . Paul Baxter
Player Development Coach . . . . Phil Myre
Goaltending Consultant . . . . Vladislav Tretiak
Video Coach . . . . Rob Pulford
Pro Scout . . . . Jim Pappin
Chief Amateur Scout . . . . Michel Dumas
Amateur Scouting Staff . . . . Kerry Davison, Bruce Franklin, Dave Lucas,
Steve Lyons, Jim Walker
European Scouts . . . . Jan Blomgren, Lars Norrman
Director of Team Services . . . . Phil Thibodeau
Executive Assistant . . . . Cindy Bodnarchuk
Receptionist/Secretary . . . . Vicki Littleton

Medical Staff
Club Doctors . . . . Louis Kolb, Howard Baim
Club Dentist . . . . Robert Duresa
Head Trainer . . . . Michael Gapski
Equipment Manager/Asst. Trainer . . . . Lou Varga
Fitness Consultant . . . . Mark Kling
Massage Therapist . . . . Pawel Prylinski

Finance
Controller . . . . Robert Rinkus
Assistant to the Controller . . . . Penny Swenson
Staff Accountant . . . . Dave Jorns
Accounting Secretary . . . . Pat Dema

Public Relations/Marketing
Vice President of Marketing . . . . Peter R. Wirtz
Director of Public Relations/Sales . . . . Jim DeMaria
Director of Marketing/Merchandising . . . . Jim Sofranko
Marketing Associate . . . . Kelly Bodnarchuk
Director of Community Relations/PR Assistant . . . . . Barbara Davidson
Director of Publications/PR Assistant . . . . Brad Freeman
Director of Game Night Operations/Special Events . . Tom Finks

Ticketing
Ticket Manager . . . . Jim Bare
Switchboard Operators . . . . Esther Cox, Mary Joiner
Team Photographers . . . . Ray Grabowski, Rob Grabowski
Organist . . . . Frank Pellico
Location of Press Box . . . . North Side of United Center
Dimensions of Rink . . . . 200 feet by 85 feet
Club Colors . . . . Red,Black & White
Uniforms . . . . Home – Base color white trimmed with black & red;
Away – Base color red trimmed with black &
white
Radio Station . . . . WMVP (AM 1000)
Television Station . . . . SportsChannel
Broadcasters . . . . Pat Foley, Dale Tallon, Darren Pang, Brian Davis,
Jim Blaney

General Manager

PULFORD, ROBERT JESSE (BOB)
General Manager, Chicago Blackhawks.
Born in Newton Robinson, Ont., March 31, 1936.

A member of the Chicago Blackhawks organization since 1977, Bob Pulford has served as coach, general manager and senior vice president in his 17-year affiliation with the team. In 1992, Pulford resumed the general manager's duties, replacing Mike Keenan, who had served in that capacity since 1990.

A member of the Hockey Hall of Fame as a player and an accomplished hockey executive, Pulford was named as the NHL's Coach of the Year in 1974-75 when he led the Los Angeles Kings to their best record in franchise history. Since joining the Blackhawks family on July 6, 1977, the team has never failed to make the playoffs.

Pulford is also recognized for his outstanding contributions to hockey in the United States, coaching the Team USA entry at the 1976 Canada Cup tournament and serving as the co-General Manager for the 1991 U.S. team at the 1991 Tournament.

NHL Coaching Record

			Regular Season				Playoffs			
Season	Team	Games	W	L	T	%	Games	W	L	%
1972-73	Los Angeles	78	31	36	11	.468	....	....	....	....
1973-74	Los Angeles	78	33	33	12	.500	5	1	4	.200
1974-75	Los Angeles	80	42	17	21	.656	3	1	2	.333
1975-76	Los Angeles	80	38	33	9	.531	9	5	4	.556
1976-77	Los Angeles	80	34	31	15	.519	9	4	5	.444
1977-78	Chicago	80	32	29	19	.519	4	0	4	.000
1978-79	Chicago	80	29	36	15	.456	4	0	4	.000
1981-82	Chicago	28	13	13	2	.500	15	8	7	.533
1984-85	Chicago	27	16	7	4	.667	15	9	6	.600
1985-86	Chicago	80	39	33	8	.538	3	0	3	.000
1986-87	Chicago	80	29	37	14	.450	4	0	4	.000
	NHL Totals	**771**	**336**	**305**	**130**	**.520**	**71**	**28**	**43**	**.394**

Retired Numbers

1	Glenn Hall	1957-1967
9	Bobby Hull	1957-1972
21	Stan Mikita	1958-1980
35	Tony Esposito	1969-1984

Coach

SUTTER, DARRYL JOHN
Coach, Chicago Blackhawks. Born in Viking, Alberta, August 19, 1958.

Darryl Sutter was appointed as the 29th coach in Chicago Blackhawks' history on June 11, 1992. Sutter, who spent his entire eight-year playing career with Chicago before injuries forced him to retire in 1987, served as an associate coach to Mike Keenan for two seasons. Following his retirement, Sutter spent a year as an assistant coach under Bob Murdoch before taking over the head coaching reins of the Blackhawks' top IHL farm affiliate in Saginaw. In his first season as head coach, Sutter led the squad to 46-26-10 record, the best in the league. When the Saginaw franchise was shifted to Indianapolis for the following season, Sutter guided the team to the IHL's Turner Cup championship, earning IHL coach of the year honors.

Coaching Record

			Regular Season				Playoffs			
Season	Team	Games	W	L	T	%	Games	W	L	%
1988-89	Saginaw (IHL)	82	46	26	10	.560	6	2	4	.333
1989-90	Indianapolis (IHL)	82	53	21	8	.646	14	12	2	.857
1992-93	**Chicago (NHL)**	**84**	**47**	**25**	**12**	**.631**	**4**	**0**	**4**	**.000**
1993-94	**Chicago (NHL)**	**84**	**39**	**36**	**9**	**.518**	**6**	**2**	**4**	**.333**
	NHL Totals	**168**	**86**	**61**	**21**	**.574**	**10**	**2**	**8**	**.200**

Dallas Stars

1993-94 Results: 42W-29L-13T 97PTS. Third, Central Division

Schedule

Oct.	Sat.	1	Anaheim		
	Tues.	4	Calgary		
	Sat.	8	Chicago		
	Tues.	11	Winnipeg		
	Sat.	15	Ottawa		
	Mon.	17	at Detroit		
	Wed.	19	at Winnipeg		
	Fri.	21	Vancouver		
	Sun.	23	Edmonton*		
	Tues.	25	at Pittsburgh		
	Wed.	26	at NY Rangers		
	Sat.	29	at Quebec		
Nov.	Tues.	1	NY Islanders		
	Fri.	4	Winnipeg		
	Sun.	6	at Chicago		
	Mon.	7	at NY Islanders		
	Thur.	10	Pittsburgh		
	Sat.	12	Detroit		
	Sun.	13	at Philadelphia		
	Tues.	15	at Washington		
	Wed.	16	at New Jersey		
	Fri.	18	San Jose		
	Mon.	21	Buffalo		
	Wed.	23	Quebec		
	Sat.	26	St. Louis		
	Mon.	28	Toronto		
Dec.	Fri.	2	at Vancouver		
	Mon.	5	San Jose		
	Wed.	7	St. Louis		
	Fri.	9	Chicago		
	Sat.	10	at St. Louis		
	Tues.	13	at Detroit		
	Wed.	14	at Chicago		
	Sat.	17	New Jersey		
	Mon.	19	at Toronto		
	Wed.	21	at Hartford		
	Thur.	22	at Boston		
	Mon.	26	St. Louis		
	Wed.	28	at Detroit*		
	Thur.	29	at Toronto		
	Sat.	31	at St. Louis		
Jan.	Mon.	2	Los Angeles		
	Fri.	6	at Tampa Bay		
	Sat.	7	Winnipeg		
	Mon.	9	at Edmonton		
	Wed.	11	at San Jose		
	Sat.	14	at Los Angeles		
	Mon.	16	Hartford		
	Wed.	18	at Hartford (in Denver)		
	Tues.	24	at Los Angeles		
	Wed.	25	at Anaheim		
	Sat.	28	at San Jose*		
Feb.	Thur.	2	Tampa Bay		
	Sat.	4	at St. Louis		
	Sun.	5	at Florida		
	Tues.	7	at Buffalo		
	Fri.	10	Calgary		
	Sat.	11	Detroit		
	Mon.	13	Toronto		
	Mon.	13	Boston		
	Wed.	15	Boston		
	Fri.	17	at Winnipeg		
	Sat.	18	at Calgary		
	Mon.	20	at Calgary		
	Wed.	22	at Edmonton		
	Fri.	24	Vancouver		
Mar.	Wed.	1	Montreal		
	Fri.	3	Anaheim		
	Mon.	6	Los Angeles		
	Wed.	8	at Winnipeg		
	Sat.	11	Anaheim (in San Antonio)		
	Mon.	13	Toronto		
	Wed.	15	Philadelphia		
	Sat.	18	at Montreal		
	Sun.	19	at Ottawa		
	Tues.	21	NY Rangers		
	Thur.	23	Edmonton		
	Sun.	26	at Chicago*		
	Mon.	27	Chicago		
	Wed.	29	at Toronto		
Apr.	Sat.	1	Detroit*		
	Sun.	2	Washington*		
	Tues.	4	at Vancouver		
	Fri.	7	at Anaheim		
	Sun.	9	Florida*		

* Denotes afternoon game.

Home Starting Times:
Weeknights . . . . 7:30 p.m.
Saturday and Sunday nights . . . . . . 7:00 p.m.
Saturday matinees . . . . 1:00 p.m.
Sunday matinees . . . . 12:00 p.m.

Franchise date: June 5, 1967
Transferred from Minnesota to Dallas beginning with 1993-94 season.

28th NHL Season

CENTRAL DIVISION

Mike Modano reached the 50-goal plateau for the first time in his career during the 1993-94 campaign, leading all Dallas marksmen with 50 goals and 93 points.

Year-by-Year Record

Season	GP	Home W	L	T	Road W	L	T	Overall W	L	T	GF	GA	Pts.	Finished		Playoff Result
1993-94	84	23	12	7	19	17	6	42	29	13	286	265	97	3rd,	Central Div.	Lost Conf. Semi-Final
1992-93*	84	18	17	7	18	21	3	36	38	10	272	293	82	5th,	Norris Div.	Out of Playoffs
1991-92*	80	20	16	4	12	26	2	32	42	6	246	278	70	4th,	Norris Div.	Lost Div. Semi-Final
1990-91*	80	19	15	6	8	24	8	27	39	14	256	266	68	4th,	Norris Div.	Lost Final
1989-90*	80	26	12	2	10	28	2	36	40	4	284	291	76	4th,	Norris Div.	Lost Div. Semi-Final
1988-89*	80	17	15	8	10	22	8	27	37	16	258	278	70	3rd,	Norris Div.	Lost Div. Semi-Final
1987-88*	80	10	24	6	9	24	7	19	48	13	242	349	51	5th,	Norris Div.	Out of Playoffs
1986-87*	80	17	20	3	13	20	7	30	40	10	296	314	70	5th,	Norris Div.	Out of Playoffs
1985-86*	80	21	15	4	17	18	5	38	33	9	327	305	85	2nd,	Norris Div.	Lost Div. Semi-Final
1984-85*	80	14	19	7	11	24	5	25	43	12	268	321	62	4th,	Norris Div.	Lost Div. Final
1983-84*	80	22	14	4	17	17	6	39	31	10	345	344	88	1st,	Norris Div.	Lost Conf. Championship
1982-83*	80	23	6	11	17	18	5	40	24	16	321	290	96	2nd,	Norris Div.	Lost Div. Final
1981-82*	80	21	7	12	16	16	8	37	23	20	346	288	94	1st,	Norris Div.	Lost Div. Semi-Final
1980-81*	80	23	10	7	12	18	10	35	28	17	291	263	87	3rd,	Adams Div.	Lost Final
1979-80*	80	25	8	7	11	20	9	36	28	16	311	253	88	3rd,	Adams Div.	Lost Semi-Final
1978-79*	80	19	15	6	9	25	6	28	40	12	257	289	68	4th,	Adams Div.	Out Of Playoffs
1977-78*	80	12	24	4	6	29	5	18	53	9	218	325	45	5th,	Smythe Div.	Out of Playoffs
1976-77*	80	17	14	9	6	25	9	23	39	18	240	310	64	2nd,	Smythe Div.	Lost Prelim. Round
1975-76*	80	15	22	3	5	31	4	20	53	7	195	303	47	4th,	Smythe Div.	Out of Playoffs
1974-75*	80	17	20	3	6	30	4	23	50	7	221	341	53	4th,	Smythe Div.	Out of Playoffs
1973-74	78	18	15	6	5	23	11	23	38	17	235	275	63	7th,	West Div.	Out of Playoffs
1972-73*	78	26	8	5	11	22	6	37	30	11	254	230	85	3rd,	West Div.	Lost Quarter-Final
1971-72*	78	22	11	6	15	18	6	37	29	12	212	191	86	2nd,	West Div.	Lost Quarter-Final
1970-71*	78	16	15	8	12	19	8	28	34	16	191	223	72	4th,	West Div.	Lost Semi-Final
1969-70*	76	11	16	11	8	19	11	19	35	22	224	257	60	3rd,	West Div.	Lost Quarter-Final
1968-69*	76	11	21	6	7	22	9	18	43	15	189	270	51	6th,	West Div.	Out of Playoffs
1967-68*	74	17	12	8	10	20	7	27	32	15	191	226	69	4th,	West Div.	Lost Semi-Final

* Minnesota North Stars

1994-95 Player Personnel

FORWARDS

	HT	WT	S	Place of Birth	Date	1993-94 Club
BES, Jeff	6-0	186	L	Tillsonburg, Ont.	7/31/73	Dayton-Kalamazoo
BOYER, Zac	6-1	185	R	Inuvik, N.W.T.	10/25/71	Indianapolis
BROTEN, Neal	5-9	170	L	Roseau, MN	11/29/59	Dallas
BROTEN, Paul	5-11	188	R	Roseau, MN	10/27/65	Dallas
CHURLA, Shane	6-1	200	R	Fernie, B.C.	6/24/65	Dallas
COURTNALL, Russ	5-11	185	L	Duncan, B.C.	6/2/65	Dallas
EVASON, Dean	5-10	180	R	Flin Flon, Man.	8/22/64	Dallas
GAGNER, Dave	5-10	180	L	Chatham, Ont.	12/11/64	Dallas
GILCHRIST, Brent	5-11	181	L	Moose Jaw, Sask.	4/3/67	Dallas
HARVEY, Todd	5-11	190	R	Hamilton, Ont.	2/17/75	Detroit (OHL)
KENNEDY, Mike	6-1	170	R	Vancouver, B.C.	4/13/72	Kalamazoo
KLATT, Trent	6-1	205	R	Robbinsdale, MN	1/30/71	Dallas-Kalamazoo
LAWRENCE, Mark	6-4	212	R	Burlington, Ont.	1/27/72	Kalamazoo
MARSHALL, Grant	6-1	185	R	Mississauga, Ont.	6/9/73	St. John's
MAY, Alan	6-1	200	R	Swan Hills, Alta.	1/14/65	Washington-Dallas
McGOWAN, Cal	6-1	185	L	Sydney, N.S.	6/19/70	Kalamazoo
McPHEE, Mike	6-1	203	L	Sydney, N.S.	7/14/60	Dallas
MODANO, Mike	6-3	190	L	Livonia, MI	6/7/70	Dallas
NEEDHAM, Mike	5-10	185	R	Calgary, Alta.	4/4/70	Pittsburgh-Cleveland-Dallas
VARVIO, Jarkko	5-9	175	R	Tampere, Finland	4/28/72	Dallas-Kalamazoo
ZEZEL, Peter	5-11	200	L	Toronto, Ont.	4/22/65	Toronto

DEFENSEMEN

	HT	WT	S	Place of Birth	Date	1993-94 Club
CAVALLINI, Paul	6-1	210	L	Toronto, Ont.	10/13/65	Dallas
DONNELLY, Gord	6-1	202	R	Montreal, Que.	4/5/62	Buffalo-Dallas
HATCHER, Derian	6-5	225	L	Sterling Heights, MI	6/4/72	Dallas
HERTER, Jason	6-1	190	R	Hafford, Sask.	10/2/70	Kalamazoo
LALOR, Mike	6-0	200	L	Buffalo, NY	3/8/63	San Jose-Dallas
LEDYARD, Grant	6-2	195	L	Winnipeg, Man.	11/19/61	Dallas
LUDWIG, Craig	6-3	222	L	Rhinelander, WI	3/15/61	Dallas
MATVICHUK, Richard	6-2	190	L	Edmonton, Alta.	2/5/73	Dallas-Kalamazoo
RICHARDS, Travis	6-1	185	L	Crystal, MN	3/22/70	U.S. National-U.S. Olympic-Kalamazoo
TINORDI, Mark	6-4	205	L	Red Deer, Alta.	5/9/66	Dallas
ZMOLEK, Doug	6-2	225	L	Rochester, MN	11/3/70	San Jose-Dallas

GOALTENDERS

	HT	WT	C	Place of Birth	Date	1993-94 Club
FERNANDEZ, Emmanuel	6-0	173	L	Etobicoke, Ont.	8/27/74	Laval
LEVY, Jeff	5-11	160	L	Salt Lake City, UT	12/9/70	U.S. National-Dayton-Kalamazoo
MOOG, Andy	5-8	170	L	Penticton, B.C.	2/18/60	Dallas
TORCHIA, Mike	5-11	215	L	Toronto, Ont.	2/23/72	Kalamazoo
WAKALUK, Darcy	5-11	180	L	Pincher Creek, Alta.	3/14/66	Dallas

General Managers' History

Wren A. Blair, 1967-68 to 1973-74; Jack Gordon, 1974-75 to 1976-77; Lou Nanne, 1977-78 to 1987-88; Jack Ferreira, 1988-89 to 1989-90; Bob Clarke 1990-91 to 1991-92; Bob Gainey, 1992-93 to date.

Coaching History

Wren Blair, 1967-68; John Muckler and Wren Blair, 1968-69; Wren Blair and Charlie Bruns, 1969-70; Jackie Gordon, 1970-71 to 1972-73; Jackie Gordon and Parker MacDonald, 1973-74; Jackie Gordon and Charlie Burns, 1974-75; Ted Harris, 1975-76 to 1976-77; Ted Harris, André Beaulieu, Lou Nanne, 1977-78; Harry Howell and Glen Sonmor, 1978-79; Glen Sonmor, 1979-80 to 1981-82; Glen Sonmor and Murray Oliver, 1982-83; Bill Mahoney, 1983-84 to 1984-85; Lorne Henning, 1985-86; Lorne Henning and Glen Sonmor, 1986-87; Herb Brooks, 1987-88; Pierre Page, 1988-89 to 1989-90; Bob Gainey, 1990-91 to date.

Captains' History

Bob Woytowich, 1967-68; Elmer Vasko, 1968-69; Claude Larose, 1969-70; Ted Harris, 1970-71 to 1973-74; Bill Goldsworthy, 1974-75, 1975-76; Bill Hogaboam, 1976-77; Nick Beverly, 1977-78; J.P. Parise, 1978-79; Paul Shmyr, 1979-80, 1980-81; Tim Young, 1981-82; Craig Hartsburg, 1982-83; Brian Bellows, Craig Hartsburg, 1983-84; Craig Hartsburg, 1984-85 to 1987-88; Curt Fraser, Bob Rouse and Curt Giles, 1988-89; Curt Giles, 1989-90 to 1990-91; Mark Tinordi, 1991-92 to date.

Retired Numbers

8	Bill Goldsworthy	1967-1976
19	Bill Masterton	1967-1968

1993-94 Scoring

– rookie

Regular Season

Pos	#	Player	Team	GP	G	A	Pts	+/-	PIM	PP	SH	GW	GT	S	%
C	9	Mike Modano	DAL	76	50	43	93	8–	54	18	0	4	2	281	17.8
R	26	Russ Courtnall	DAL	84	23	57	80	6	59	5	0	4	0	231	10.0
C	15	Dave Gagner	DAL	76	32	29	61	13	83	10	0	6	1	213	15.0
C	7	Neal Broten	DAL	79	17	35	52	10	62	2	1	1	0	153	11.1
D	12	Grant Ledyard	DAL	84	9	37	46	7	42	6	0	1	0	177	5.1
D	14	Paul Cavallini	DAL	74	11	33	44	13	82	6	0	3	0	145	7.6
C	16	Dean Evason	DAL	80	11	33	44	12–	66	3	2	2	1	118	9.3
R	29	Trent Klatt	DAL	61	14	24	38	13	30	3	0	2	0	86	16.3
R	20	Mike Craig	DAL	72	13	24	37	14–	139	3	0	2	0	150	8.7
L	17	Mike McPhee	DAL	79	20	15	35	8	36	1	3	1	1	115	17.4
C	41	Brent Gilchrist	DAL	76	17	14	31	0	31	3	1	5	0	103	16.5
D	2	Derian Hatcher	DAL	83	12	19	31	19	211	2	1	2	0	132	9.1
R	21	Paul Broten	DAL	64	12	12	24	18	30	0	0	3	0	76	15.8
D	24	Mark Tinordi	DAL	61	6	18	24	6	143	1	0	0	0	112	5.4
C	6	Pelle Eklund	PHI	48	1	16	17	1–	8	0	0	0	0	49	2.0
			DAL	5	2	1	3	1–	2	0	0	0	0	4	50.0
			TOTAL	53	3	17	20	2–	10	0	0	0	0	53	5.7
D	3	Craig Ludwig	DAL	84	1	13	14	1–	123	1	0	0	0	65	1.5
R	27	Shane Churla	DAL	69	6	7	13	8–	333	3	0	1	0	62	9.7
L	23	Alan May	WSH	43	4	7	11	2–	97	0	0	0	0	33	12.1
			DAL	8	1	0	1	1–	18	0	0	1	0	7	14.3
			TOTAL	51	5	7	12	3–	115	0	0	1	0	40	12.5
R	10	Dave Barr	DAL	20	2	5	7	6–	21	0	0	0	0	20	10.0
R	11	* Jarkko Varvio	S.J.	8	2	3	5	1	4	0	0	1	0	17	11.8
D	5	Doug Zmolek	S.J.	68	0	4	4	9–	122	0	0	0	0	29	.0
			DAL	7	1	0	1	1	11	0	0	0	0	3	33.3
			TOTAL	75	1	4	5	8–	133	0	0	0	0	32	3.1
C	18	Chris Tancill	DAL	12	1	3	4	7–	8	0	0	0	0	18	5.6
D	4	Richard Matvichuk	DAL	25	0	3	3	1	22	0	0	0	0	18	.0
D	18	Mike Lalor	S.J.	23	0	2	2	5–	8	0	0	0	0	19	.0
			DAL	12	0	1	1	5–	6	0	0	0	0	3	.0
			TOTAL	35	0	3	3	10–	14	0	0	0	0	22	.0
G	34	Darcy Wakaluk	DAL	36	0	2	2	0	34	0	0	0	0	0	.0
R	33	Mike Needham	PIT	25	1	0	1	0	2	0	0	1	0	6	16.7
			DAL	5	0	0	0	2–	0	0	0	0	0	3	.0
			TOTAL	30	1	0	1	2–	2	0	0	1	0	9	11.1
C	37	Neil Brady	DAL	5	0	1	1	1–	21	0	0	0	0	1	.0
D	43	Gord Donnelly	BUF	7	0	0	0	0	31	0	0	0	0	2	.0
			DAL	18	0	1	1	4–	66	0	0	0	0	5	.0
			TOTAL	25	0	1	1	3–	97	0	0	0	0	7	.0
G	35	Andy Moog	DAL	55	0	1	1	0	16	0	0	0	0	0	.0
R	25	Rob Brown	DAL	1	0	0	0	1–	0	0	0	0	0	1	.0
L	23	Derrick Smith	DAL	1	0	0	0	1–	0	0	0	0	0	1	.0
D	23	Duane Joyce	DAL	3	0	0	0	0	0	0	0	0	0	1	.0
D	5	Brad Berry	DAL	8	0	0	0	2–	12	0	0	0	0	4	.0

Goaltending

No.	Goaltender	GPI	Mins	Avg	W	L	T	EN	SO	GA	SA	S%
34	Darcy Wakaluk	36	2000	2.64	18	9	6	0	3	88	978	.910
35	Andy Moog	55	3121	3.27	24	20	7	7	2	170	1604	.894

Playoffs

Pos	#	Player	Team	GP	G	A	Pts	+/-	PIM	PP	SH	GW	GT	S	%
C	9	Mike Modano	DAL	9	7	3	10	2–	16	2	0	2	0	48	14.6
D	14	Paul Cavallini	DAL	9	1	8	9	4–	4	1	0	1	1	20	5.0
R	26	Russ Courtnall	DAL	9	1	8	9	3–	0	0	0	0	0	41	2.4
C	15	Dave Gagner	DAL	9	5	1	6	3–	2	3	0	0	0	36	13.9
C	41	Brent Gilchrist	DAL	9	3	1	4	3–	2	1	0	0	0	20	15.0
R	27	Shane Churla	DAL	9	1	3	4	1	35	1	0	0	0	10	10.0
C	7	Neal Broten	DAL	9	2	1	3	1	6	0	0	1	0	23	8.7
L	17	Mike McPhee	DAL	9	2	1	3	0	2	0	0	0	0	16	12.5
R	29	Trent Klatt	DAL	9	2	1	3	1–	4	1	0	0	0	14	14.3
D	12	Grant Ledyard	DAL	9	1	2	3	0	6	0	0	1	0	23	4.3
C	6	Pelle Eklund	DAL	9	0	3	3	2–	4	0	0	0	0	9	.0
D	3	Craig Ludwig	DAL	9	0	3	3	3	8	0	0	0	0	15	.0
D	4	Richard Matvichuk	DAL	7	1	1	2	2	12	1	0	0	0	14	7.1
R	21	Paul Broten	DAL	9	1	1	2	0	2	0	0	0	0	15	6.7
C	16	Dean Evason	DAL	9	0	2	2	1	12	0	0	0	0	4	.0
D	2	Derian Hatcher	DAL	9	0	2	2	2–	14	0	0	0	0	17	.0
R	10	Dave Barr	DAL	9	0	1	1	1	4	0	0	0	0	3	.0
D	5	Doug Zmolek	DAL	7	0	1	1	2–	4	0	0	0	0	2	.0
L	23	Alan May	DAL	1	0	0	0	0	0	0	0	0	0	1	.0
R	20	Mike Craig	DAL	4	0	0	0	1–	2	0	0	0	0	6	.0
G	35	Andy Moog	DAL	4	0	0	0	0	0	0	0	0	0	0	.0
D	18	Mike Lalor	DAL	5	0	0	0	0	6	0	0	0	0	4	.0
G	34	Darcy Wakaluk	DAL	5	0	0	0	0	0	0	0	0	0	0	.0

Goaltending

No.	Goaltender	GPI	Mins	Avg	W	L	EN	SO	GA	SA	S%
35	Andy Moog	4	246	2.93	1	3	0	0	12	121	.901
34	Darcy Wakaluk	5	307	2.93	4	1	1	0	15	168	.911
	Totals	**9**	**560**	**3.00**	**5**	**4**	**1**	**0**	**28**	**290**	**.903**

Club Records

Team

(Figures in brackets for season records are games played)

Most Points	97	1993-94 (84)
Most Wins	42	1993-94 (84)
Most Ties	22	1969-70 (76)
Most Losses	53	1975-76, 1977-78 (80)
Most Goals	346	1981-82 (80)
Most Goals Against	349	1987-88 (80)
Fewest Points	45	1977-78 (80)
Fewest Wins	18	1968-69 (76)
		1977-78 (80)
Fewest Ties	4	1989-90 (80)
Fewest Losses	23	1981-82 (80)
Fewest Goals	189	1968-69 (76)
Fewest Goals Against	191	1971-72 (78)

Longest Winning Streak

Over-all	7	Mar. 16-28/80
Home	11	Nov. 4-Dec. 27/72
Away	7	Nov. 18-Dec. 5/92; Jan. 26-Feb. 21/94

Longest Undefeated Streak

Over-all	12	Feb. 18-Mar. 15/82 (9 wins, 3 ties)
Home	13	Oct. 28-Dec. 27/72 (12 wins, 1 tie) Nov. 21-Jan. 9/80 (10 wins, 3 ties) Jan. 17-Mar. 17/91 (11 wins, 2 ties)
Away	8	Jan. 26-Feb. 21/94 (7 wins, 1 tie)

Longest Losing Streak

Over-all	10	Feb. 1-20/76
Home	6	Jan. 17-Feb. 4/70
Away	8	Oct. 19-Nov. 13/75; Jan. 28-Mar. 3/88

Longest Winless Streak

Over-all	20	Jan. 15-Feb. 28/70 (15 losses, 5 ties)
Home	12	Jan. 17-Feb. 25/70 (8 losses, 4 ties)
Away	23	Oct. 25/74-Jan. 28/75 (19 losses, 4 ties)

Most Shutouts, Season	7	1972-73 (78)
Most PIM, Season	2,313	1987-88 (80)
Most Goals, Game	15	Nov. 11/81 (Wpg. 2 at Minn. 15)

Individual

Most Seasons	14	Neal Broten
Most Games	955	Neal Broten
Most Goals, Career	342	Brian Bellows
Most Assists, Career	582	Neal Broten
Most Points Career	848	Neal Broten (266 goals, 582 assists)
Most PIM, Career	1,567	Basil McRae
Most Shutouts, Career	26	Cesare Maniago
Longest Consecutive Games Streak	442	Danny Grant (Dec. 4/68-Apr. 7/74)
Most Goals, Season	55	Dino Ciccarelli (1981-82) Brian Bellows (1989-90)
Most Assists, Season	76	Neal Broten (1985-86)
Most Points, Season	114	Bobby Smith (1981-82) (43 goals, 71 assists)
Most PIM, Season	382	Basil McRae (1987-88)
Most Points, Defenseman Season	77	Craig Hartsburg (1981-82) (17 goals, 60 assists)
Most Points, Center, Season	114	Bobby Smith (1981-82) (43 goals, 71 assists)
Most Points, Right Wing, Season	107	Dino Ciccarelli (1981-82) (55 goals, 52 assists)
Most Point, Left Wing, Season	99	Brian Bellows (1989-90) (55 goals, 44 assists)
Most Points, Rookie, Season	98	Neal Broten (1981-82) (38 goals, 60 assists)
Most Shutouts, Season	6	Cesare Maniago (1967-68)
Most Goals, Game	5	Tim Young (Jan. 15/79)
Most Assists, Game	5	Murray Oliver (Oct. 24/71) Larry Murphy (Oct. 17/89)
Most Points, Game	7	Bobby Smith (Nov. 11/81)

Records include Minnesota North Stars 1967-68 through 1992-93.

All-time Record vs. Other Clubs

Regular Season

	At Home						On Road						Total					
	GP	W	L	T	GF	GA	PTS	GP	W	L	T	GF	GA	PTS	GP	W	L	T	GF	GA	PTS
Anaheim	2	1	1	0	6	6	2	3	1	2	0	9	11	2	5	2	3	0	15	17	4
Boston	53	13	29	11	145	198	37	53	6	38	9	125	239	21	106	19	67	20	270	437	58
Buffalo	46	20	20	6	144	144	46	45	12	23	10	124	168	34	91	32	43	16	268	312	80
Calgary	42	21	16	5	158	137	47	42	5	26	11	112	173	21	84	26	42	16	270	310	68
Chicago	88	38	38	12	302	292	88	87	20	57	10	228	362	50	175	58	95	22	530	654	138
Detroit	84	45	25	14	320	254	104	82	30	40	12	282	334	72	166	75	65	26	602	588	176
Edmonton	25	8	12	5	91	91	21	24	3	15	6	79	122	12	49	11	27	11	170	213	33
Florida	1	0	0	1	4	4	1	1	1	0	0	5	4	2	2	1	0	1	9	8	3
Hartford	22	12	9	1	93	72	25	23	11	9	3	87	84	25	45	23	18	4	180	156	50
Los Angeles	59	35	15	9	243	168	79	58	17	26	15	174	211	49	117	52	41	24	417	379	128
Montreal	52	14	27	11	135	186	39	51	9	35	7	125	230	25	103	23	62	18	260	416	64
New Jersey	37	22	9	6	150	100	50	37	16	18	3	115	123	35	74	38	27	9	265	223	85
NY Islanders	39	14	19	6	114	148	34	39	9	22	8	111	154	26	78	23	41	14	225	302	60
NY Rangers	53	16	29	8	162	205	40	54	11	33	10	148	194	32	107	27	62	18	310	399	72
Ottawa	3	2	1	0	17	8	4	2	2	0	0	9	6	4	5	4	1	0	26	14	8
Philadelphia	59	24	22	13	197	196	61	59	9	40	10	136	235	28	118	33	62	23	333	431	89
Pittsburgh	57	32	20	5	218	192	69	56	17	34	5	158	216	39	113	49	54	10	376	408	108
Quebec	22	13	7	2	88	72	28	23	5	16	2	62	107	12	45	18	23	4	150	179	40
St. Louis	92	42	32	18	321	270	102	95	25	52	18	269	350	68	187	67	84	36	590	620	170
San Jose	5	4	1	0	26	16	8	5	4	1	0	26	14	8	10	8	2	0	52	30	16
Tampa Bay	4	3	1	0	15	12	6	5	3	0	2	13	7	8	9	6	1	2	28	19	14
Toronto	84	42	31	11	327	280	95	86	29	43	14	278	317	72	170	71	74	25	605	597	167
Vancouver	51	30	13	8	207	148	68	51	19	24	8	163	201	46	102	49	37	16	370	349	114
Washington	32	14	10	8	122	94	36	33	13	13	7	105	106	33	65	27	23	15	227	200	69
Winnipeg	28	16	8	4	123	87	36	27	13	13	1	98	99	27	55	29	21	5	221	186	63
Defunct Clubs	33	19	8	6	123	86	44	32	10	16	6	84	105	26	65	29	24	12	207	191	70
Totals	**1073**	**500**	**403**	**170**	**3851**	**3466**	**1170**	**1073**	**300**	**596**	**177**	**3125**	**4172**	**777**	**2146**	**800**	**999**	**347**	**6976**	**7638**	**1947**

Calgary totals include Atlanta, 1972-73 to 1979-80. Dallas totals include Minnesota, 1967-68 to 1992-93.
New Jersey totals include Kansas City, 1974-75 to 1975-76, and Colorado, 1976-77 to 1981-82.

Playoffs

	Series	W	L	GP	W	L	T	GF	GA	Last Mtg.	Round	Result
Boston	1	1	0	3	3	0	0	20	13	1981	PR	W 3-0
Buffalo	2	1	1	7	4	3	0	26	28	1981	QF	W 4-1
Calgary	1	1	0	6	4	2	0	25	18	1981	SF	W 4-2
Chicago	6	2	4	33	14	19	0	119	119	1991	DSF	W 4-2
Detroit	1	0	1	7	3	4	0	19	23	1992	DSF	L 3-4
Edmonton	2	1	1	9	4	5	0	30	36	1991	CF	W 4-1
Los Angeles	1	1	0	7	4	3	0	26	21	1968	QF	W 4-3
Montreal	2	1	1	13	6	7	0	37	48	1980	QF	W 4-3
NY Islanders	1	0	1	5	1	4	0	16	26	1981	F	L 1-4
Philadelphia	2	0	2	11	3	8	0	26	41	1980	SF	L 1-4
Pittsburgh	1	0	1	6	2	4	0	16	28	1991	F	L 2-4
St. Louis	10	5	5	56	30	26	0	174	162	1994	CQF	W 4-2
Toronto	2	2	0	7	6	1	0	35	26	1983	DSF	W 3-1
Vancouver	1	0	1	5	1	4	0	11	18	1994	CSF	L 1-4
Totals	**33**	**15**	**18**	**175**	**85**	**90**	**0**	**580**	**607**			

Playoff Results 1994-90

Year	Round	Opponent	Result	GF	GA
1994	CSF	Vancouver	L 1-4	11	18
	CQF	St. Louis	W 4-0	16	10
1992	DSF	Detroit	L 3-4	19	23
1991	F	Pittsburgh	L 2-4	16	28
	CF	Edmonton	W 4-1	20	14
	DF	St. Louis	W 4-2	22	17
	DSF	Chicago	W 4-2	23	16
1990	DSF	Chicago	L 3-4	18	21

Abbreviations: Round: F – Final;
CF – conference final; **CQF** – conference quarter-final;
CSF – conference semi-final; **DF** – division final;
DSF – division semi-final; **SF** – semi-final;
QF – quarter-final; **PR** – preliminary round.

1993-94 Results

Oct.	5		Detroit	6-4	6	Philadelphia	8-0
	7	at	Toronto	3-6	9	St. Louis	2-1
	9		Winnipeg	3-3	11	Edmonton	5-2
	12		Chicago	3-3	13 at	Toronto	3-4
	16		St. Louis	4-0	14 at	Detroit	3-9
	18	at	Chicago	5-3	16	Buffalo	2-4
	20	at	Montreal	2-5	18	Los Angeles	5-3
	21	at	Ottawa	6-5	24	New Jersey	2-6
	23	at	Quebec	2-3	26 at	Calgary	3-2
	25	at	Detroit	5-3	27 at	Vancouver	3-2
	27		Hartford	5-1	29 at	Edmonton	5-3
	30		Ottawa	4-5	Feb. 2 at	Winnipeg	7-3
Nov.	1		Toronto	3-3	6	San Jose	1-7
	3	at	Anaheim	4-5	9	Winnipeg	4-2
	5	at	San Jose	2-4	12	Pittsburgh	9-3
	7		Winnipeg	1-1	13 at	Buffalo	5-3
	9	at	Anaheim	2-4	16	Boston	0-3
	11		San Jose	4-0	18	Calgary	4-2
	13	at	Winnipeg	3-2	21 at	San Jose	6-3
	14	at	Chicago	1-4	23 at	Los Angeles	0-0
	17		Tampa Bay	4-3	26	NY Rangers	3-1
	20		Calgary	4-3	Mar. 2 at	Winnipeg	2-4
	21		Los Angeles	7-4	4	Vancouver	1-4
	24		NY Islanders	2-2	6	Montreal	2-2
	27	at	Detroit	4-10	8 at	Philadelphia	4-3
	29	at	Edmonton	6-5	9 at	Toronto	2-4
	30	at	Calgary	2-2	12 at	Hartford	0-4
Dec.	4	at	St. Louis	3-4	13 at	New Jersey	0-4
	5		Edmonton	4-3	18	Washington	6-2
	8		Pittsburgh	3-2	20	Vancouver	2-1
	9		Ottawa	6-1	22	Anaheim	4-3
	12		Florida	4-4	25 at	St. Louis	3-5
	15		Chicago	2-3	27 at	Tampa Bay	2-2
	17		Anaheim	2-3	28 at	Florida	5-4
	19	at	Vancouver	3-1	31 at	Boston	2-2
	22		Anaheim	3-2	Apr. 1 at	NY Rangers	0-3
	23	at	Los Angeles	2-1	3 at	Washington	6-3
	27		Detroit	0-6	5	Toronto	4-6
	29		Toronto	4-0	8 at	NY Islanders	1-5
	31	at	Chicago	5-2	10 at	St. Louis	9-5
Jan.	2		Quebec	4-6	12	St. Louis	9-5
	4		Chicago	1-2	14	Detroit	4-3

Entry Draft
Selections 1994-80

1994
Pick
20	Jason Botterill
46	Lee Jinman
98	Jamie Wright
124	Marty Turco
150	Yevgeny Petrochinin
228	Marty Flichel
254	Jimmy Roy
280	Chris Szysky

1993
Pick
9	Todd Harvey
35	Jamie Langenbrunner
87	Chad Lang
136	Rick Mrozik
139	Per Svartvadet
165	Jeremy Stasiuk
191	Rob Lurtsema
243	Jordan Willis
249	Bill Lang
269	Cory Peterson

1992
Pick
34	Jarkko Varvio
58	Jeff Bes
88	Jere Lehtinen
130	Michael Johnson
154	Kyle Peterson
178	Juha Lind
202	Lars Edstrom
226	Jeff Romfo
250	Jeffrey Moen

1991
Pick
8	Richard Matvichuk
74	Mike Torchia
97	Mike Kennedy
118	Mark Lawrence
137	Geoff Finch
174	Michael Burkett
184	Derek Herlofsky
206	Tom Nemeth
228	Shayne Green
250	Jukka Suomalainen

1990
Pick
8	Derian Hatcher
50	Laurie Billeck
70	Cal McGowan
71	Frank Kovacs
92	Enrico Ciccone
113	Roman Turek
134	Jeff Levy
155	Doug Barrault
176	Joe Biondi
197	Troy Binnie
218	Ole-Eskild Dahlstrom
239	John McKersie

1989
Pick
7	Doug Zmolek
28	Mike Craig
60	Murray Garbutt
75	Jean-François Quintin
87	Pat MacLeod
91	Bryan Schoen
97	Rhys Hollyman
112	Scott Cashman
154	Jonathan Pratt
175	Kenneth Blum
196	Arturs Irbe
217	Tom Pederson
238	Helmut Balderis

1988
Pick
1	Mike Modano
40	Link Gaetz
43	Shaun Kane
64	Jeffrey Stop
148	Ken MacArthur
169	Travis Richards
190	Ari Matilainen
211	Grant Bischoff
232	Trent Andison

1987
Pick
6	David Archibald
35	Scott McCrady
48	Kevin Kaminski
73	John Weisbrod
88	Teppo Kivela
109	Darcy Norton
130	Timo Kulonen
151	Don Schmidt
172	Jarmo Myllys
193	Larry Olimb
214	Mark Felicio
235	Dave hields

1986
Pick
12	Warren Babe
30	Neil Wilkinson
33	Dean Kolstad
54	Eric Bennett
55	Rob Zettler
58	Brad Turner
75	Kirk Tomlinson
96	Jari Gronstrand
159	Scott Mathias
180	Lance Pitlick
201	Dan Keczmer
222	Garth Joy
243	Kurt Stahura

1985
Pick
51	Stephane Roy
69	Mike Berger
90	Dwight Mullins
111	MikeMullowney
132	Mike Kelfer
153	Ross Johnson
174	Tim Helmer
195	Gordon Ernst
216	Ladislav Lubina
237	Tommy Sjodin

1984
Pick
13	David Quinn
46	Ken Hodge
76	Miroslav Maly
89	Jiri Poner
97	Kari Takko
118	Gary McColgan
139	Vladimir Kyhos
160	Darin MacInnis
181	Duane Wahlin
201	Mike Orn
222	Tom Terwilliger
242	Mike Nightenale

1983
Pick
1	Brian Lawton
36	Malcolm Parks
38	Frantisek Musil
56	Mitch Messier
76	Brian Durand
96	Rich Geist
116	Tom McComb
136	Sean Toomey
156	Don Biggs
176	Paul Pulis
196	Milos Riha
212	Oldrich Valek
236	Paul Roff

1982
Pick
2	Brian Bellows
59	Wally Chapman
80	Rob Rouse
81	Dusan Pasek
101	Marty Wiitala
122	Todd Carlile
143	Victor Zhluktov
164	Paul Miller
185	Pat Micheletti
206	Arnold Kadlec
227	Scott Knutson

1981
Pick
13	Ron Meighan
27	Dave Donnelly
31	Mike Sands
33	Tom Hirsch
34	Dave Preuss
41	Jali Wahlsten
69	Terry Tait
76	Jim Malwitz
97	Kelly Hubbard
118	Paul Guay
139	Jim Archibald
160	Kari Kaervo
181	Scott Bjugstad
202	Steve Kudebeh

1980
Pick
16	Brad Palmer
37	Don Beaupre
53	Randy Velischek
79	Mark Huglen
100	Dave Jensen
121	Dan Zavarise
142	Bill Stewart
163	Jeff Walters
184	Bob Lakso
205	Dave Richter

Coach and General Manager

GAINEY, BOB
Coach and General Manager, Dallas Stars.
Born in Peterborough, Ont., December 13, 1953.

Bob Gainey led the Dallas Stars to a record-setting season in the club's first year in Texas. The Stars set franchise records in wins (42) and points (97) in 1993-94, advancing to the Western Conference Semi-finals. Gainey has been the general manager of the Stars since June, 1992 after being appointed head coach on June 19, 1990. The Stars have improved their regular-season record in each of Gainey's four seasons as coach, improving from 27 wins and 68 points his first season to the 42 wins and 97 points in 1993-94. In his first season in 1990-91, Gainey led the Stars through stunning playoff upsets of the League's top two teams and all the way to the Stanley Cup Finals. After surprising Chicago and St. Louis in the first two rounds, the Stars eliminated the defending champion Edmonton Oilers before bowing in six games to Pittsburgh in the Finals.

Elected to the Hockey Hall of Fame in 1992, Gainey was Montreal's first choice (eighth overall) in the 1973 Amateur Draft. During his 16-year career with the Canadiens, Gainey was a member of five Stanley Cup-winning teams and was named the Conn Smythe Trophy winner in 1979. He was a four-time recipient of the Frank Selke Trophy (1978-81), awarded to the League's top defensive forward, and participated in four NHL All-Star Games (1977, 1978, 1980 and 1981). He served as team captain for eight seasons (1981-89). During his career, he played in 1,160 regular-season games, registering 239 goals and 262 assists for 501 points. In addition, he tallied 73 points (25-48-73) in 182 post-season games. He coached in Epinal, France in the 1989-90 season before joining the Stars.

Coaching Record

| Season | Team | | Regular Season | | | | | Playoffs | | | |
		Games	W	L	T	%	Games	W	L	%
1989-90	Epinal (France)	....				....				....
1990-91	Minnesota (NHL)	80	27	39	14	.425	23	14	9	.643
1991-92	Minnesota (NHL)	80	32	42	6	.438	7	3	4	.429
1992-93	Minnesota (NHL)	84	36	38	10	.488	....	....	....	....
1993-94	Dallas (NHL)	84	42	29	13	.577	9	5	4	.556
	NHL Totals	**328**	**137**	**148**	**43**	**.483**	**39**	**22**	**17**	**.564**

Club Directory

Reunion Arena

Dallas Stars Hockey Club, Inc.
901 Main Street, Suite 2301
Dallas, TX 75202
Phone **214/712-2890**
FAX 214/712-2860
Capacity: 16,914

Executive
Owner and Governor	Norman N. Green
President	James Lites
Director, Board of Directors	Denise Ilitch Lites
Vice President of Hockey Operations	Bob Gainey
Vice President of Marketing	William C. Strong
Vice President of Advertising and Promotion	Jeff Cogen
Vice President of Business Operations/ General Counsel	Len Perna
Vice President of Finance	Rick McLaughlin
Director of Operations	Geoff Moore
Executive Assistant/Office Manager	Rene Marshall
Executive Assistant	Lesa Moake

Hockey
General Manager and Head Coach	Bob Gainey
Assistant General Manager	Les Jackson
Assistant Coaches	Doug Jarvis, Rick Wilson
Assistant to the General Manager	Doug Armstrong
Director of Amateur Scouting	Craig Button
Chief Scout	Bob Gernander
Scout	Tim Bernhardt
Pro Scout	Doug Overton
Regional Scouts	Brad Robson, Jeff Twohey, Bob Atrill, Ray Robson, Tom Osiecki, Kevin Pottle, David Korol, Jim Pederson, Bob Richardson, Alain Rioux, Hans Edlund, Evgeny Larionov
Head Athletic Trainer	Dave Suprenant
Assistant Trainer	Dave Smith
Strength Coach	Norm Temnograd
Equipment Manager	Lance Vogt
Assistant to the Hockey Department/Team Video	Dan Stuchal
Executive Assistant	Sally Turnbull

Public Relations
Director of Public Relations	Larry Kelly
Assistant Director of Public Relations	Kurt Daniels
Director of Publications	Jacqueline Grisez

Ticket Sales
Director of Ticket Sales	Brian Byrnes
Senior Account Executive	Paul Hart
Manager of Group Sales	Renay Hodson
Sales and Marketing Assistant	Shannon Cockrell
Sales Representatives	Tom Fireovid, Frank Hubach, Brad Huff, Ed Hunt, Laurie Krist, Jamie Norman, Laura Radwanski, Nicole Wilder
Season Ticket & Group Ticket Assistant	Devin Fogleman

Advertising and Promotion
Director of Advertising & Promotions	Christy Martinez
Director of Promotions	Cookie Lehman
Promotions Manager	Jeff Buch
Director of Community Relations	Tracy Long

Merchandising
Director of Merchandising	Jason Siegel
Retail Manager	Tiffani McCallon
Operations Manager	Brad Eckensberger

Corporate Sales
Director of Corporate Sales	Dana Summers
Director of Corporate Hospitality	Jill Cogen
Assistant Director of Corporate Hospitality	Barbara Patton

Broadcasting
Producer/Director	Kevin Spivey
Announcers	Mike Fornes, Ralph Strangis
Director, Broadcast Sales Services	Rebecca Whitehead

Finance
Controller	Therese M. Baird
Director of Ticket Operations	Augie Manfredo
Senior Accountant	Mike Brooks
Senior Accountant	Tim Montrose
Box Office Manager	Jenny Cauhorn
Assistant Box Office Manager	Stacey Lesanto
Box Office Assistant	Miriam Blaiweiss
Phone Room Supervisors	Beth Marthaler, Juan Ramirez
Accounting Assistant	Cliff Johnson

Operations
Receptionist	Tara Dosch
Office Assistant	Tracy Issacs
Practice Facility	Star Center
Television	KTXA–21, KTVT–11, HSE (cable)
Radio	WBAP–820 AM
Colors	Black, Green, Gold and White

Detroit Red Wings

1993-94 Results: 46w-30L-8T 100pts. First, Central Division

Schedule

Oct.	Sat.	1	St. Louis		Wed.	11	Anaheim
	Wed.	5	at Los Angeles		Fri.	13	Winnipeg
	Fri.	7	at San Jose		Sat.	14	at Toronto
	Wed.	12	Buffalo		Tues.	17	at NY Rangers
	Fri.	14	Florida		Wed.	18	Toronto
	Sat.	15	at NY Islanders		Tues.	24	Vancouver
	Mon.	17	Dallas		Sat.	28	Edmonton*
	Wed.	19	Montreal		Mon.	30	at Edmonton
	Fri.	21	Pittsburgh	**Feb.**	Wed.	1	at Calgary
	Sat.	22	at Quebec		Fri.	3	at Anaheim
	Tues.	25	Anaheim		Sat.	4	at Los Angeles
	Fri.	28	Los Angeles		Mon.	6	Tampa Bay
	Sat.	29	at Ottawa				(in Hamilton)
Nov.	Tues.	1	Hartford		Thur.	9	Los Angeles
	Fri.	4	Toronto		Sat.	11	at Dallas
	Sat.	5	at Toronto		Sun.	12	at St. Louis
	Tues.	8	Winnipeg		Wed.	15	Edmonton
	Sat.	12	at Dallas		Fri.	17	Washington
	Wed.	16	at Tampa Bay		Sat.	18	at Washington
	Thur.	17	at Florida		Mon.	20	NY Islanders
	Sun.	20	at Philadelphia		Wed.	22	Tampa Bay
	Wed.	23	St. Louis		Fri.	24	at Winnipeg
	Sat.	26	New Jersey*		Sun.	26	at Chicago
	Mon.	28	San Jose	**Mar.**	Wed.	1	Ottawa
	Wed.	30	Philadelphia		Fri.	3	Toronto
Dec.	Fri.	2	Calgary		Sun.	5	at Edmonton*
	Sat.	3	at Montreal		Mon.	6	at Vancouver
	Tues.	6	Boston		Thur.	9	at Anaheim
	Wed.	7	at Hartford		Fri.	10	at San Jose
	Fri.	9	at New Jersey		Sun.	12	at Florida
	Sun.	11	at St. Louis				(in Denver)
	Tues.	13	Dallas		Tues.	14	Chicago
	Thur.	15	Quebec		Thur.	16	at Buffalo
	Sat.	17	Winnipeg*		Fri.	17	Vancouver
	Sun.	18	at Winnipeg		Tues.	21	at Calgary
	Tues.	20	at Pittsburgh		Wed.	22	at Winnipeg
	Fri.	23	Chicago		Sat.	25	at Vancouver
	Mon.	26	at Chicago		Tues.	28	NY Rangers
	Wed.	28	Dallas		Wed.	29	at Chicago
	Sat.	31	San Jose	**Apr.**	Sat.	1	at Dallas*
Jan.	Tues.	3	Calgary		Sun.	2	St. Louis*
	Fri.	6	Chicago		Thur.	6	at St. Louis
	Sat.	7	at Boston		Sat.	8	at Toronto

* Denotes afternoon game.

Home Starting Times:
Night Games . . . . 7:30 p.m.
Matinees . . . . 1:00 p.m.

Franchise date: September 25, 1926

69th NHL Season

CENTRAL DIVISION

Sergei Fedorov, who recorded a career-high 56 goals and 64 assists in 1993-94, became the first Russian-trained player to win the Hart Trophy as League MVP.

Year-by-Year Record

		Home			Road			Overall						
Season	GP	W	L	T	W	L	T	W	L	T	GF	GA	Pts.	Finished	Playoff Result
1993-94	84	23	13	6	23	17	2	46	30	8	356	275	100	1st, Central Div.	Lost Conf. Quarter-Final
1992-93	84	25	14	3	22	14	6	47	28	9	369	280	103	2nd, Norris Div.	Lost Div. Semi-Final
1991-92	80	24	12	4	19	13	8	43	25	12	320	256	98	1st, Norris Div.	Lost Div. Final
1990-91	80	26	14	0	8	24	8	34	38	8	273	298	76	3rd, Norris Div.	Lost Div. Semi-Final
1989-90	80	20	14	6	8	24	8	28	38	14	288	323	70	5th, Norris Div.	Out of Playoffs
1988-89	80	20	14	6	14	20	6	34	34	12	313	316	80	1st, Norris Div.	Lost Div. Semi-Final
1987-88	80	24	10	6	17	18	5	41	28	11	322	269	93	1st, Norris Div.	Lost Conf. Championship
1986-87	80	20	14	6	14	22	4	34	36	10	260	274	78	2nd, Norris Div.	Lost Conf. Championship
1985-86	80	10	26	4	7	31	2	17	57	6	266	415	40	5th, Norris Div.	Out of Playoffs
1984-85	80	19	14	7	8	27	5	27	41	12	313	357	66	3rd, Norris Div.	Lost Div. Semi-Final
1983-84	80	18	20	2	13	22	5	31	42	7	298	323	69	3rd, Norris Div.	Lost Div. Semi-Final
1982-83	80	14	19	7	7	25	8	21	44	15	263	344	57	5th, Norris Div.	Out of Playoffs
1981-82	80	15	19	6	6	28	6	21	47	12	270	351	54	6th, Norris Div.	Out of Playoffs
1980-81	80	16	15	9	3	28	9	19	43	18	252	339	56	5th, Norris Div.	Out of Playoffs
1979-80	80	14	21	5	12	22	6	26	43	11	268	306	63	5th, Norris Div.	Out of Playoffs
1978-79	80	15	17	8	8	24	8	23	41	16	252	295	62	5th, Norris Div.	Out of Playoffs
1977-78	80	22	11	7	10	23	7	32	34	14	252	266	78	2nd, Norris Div.	Lost Quarter-Final
1976-77	80	12	22	6	4	33	3	16	55	9	183	309	41	5th, Norris Div.	Out of Playoffs
1975-76	80	17	15	8	9	29	2	26	44	10	226	300	62	4th, Norris Div.	Out of Playoffs
1974-75	80	17	17	6	6	28	6	23	45	12	259	335	58	4th, Norris Div.	Out of Playoffs
1973-74	78	21	12	6	8	27	4	29	39	10	255	319	68	6th, East Div.	Out of Playoffs
1972-73	78	22	12	5	15	17	7	37	29	12	265	243	86	5th, East Div.	Out of Playoffs
1971-72	78	25	11	3	8	24	7	33	35	10	261	262	76	5th, East Div.	Out of Playoffs
1970-71	78	17	15	7	5	30	4	22	45	11	209	308	55	7th, East Div.	Out of Playoffs
1969-70	76	20	11	7	20	10	8	40	21	15	246	199	95	3rd, East Div.	Lost Quarter-Final
1968-69	76	23	8	7	10	23	5	33	31	12	239	221	78	5th, East Div.	Out of Playoffs
1967-68	74	18	15	4	9	20	8	27	35	12	245	257	66	6th, East Div.	Out of Playoffs
1966-67	70	21	11	3	6	28	1	27	39	4	212	241	58	5th,	Out of Playoffs
1965-66	70	20	8	7	11	19	5	31	27	12	221	194	74	4th,	Lost Final
1964-65	70	25	7	3	15	16	4	40	23	7	224	175	87	1st,	Lost Semi-Final
1963-64	70	23	9	3	7	20	8	30	29	11	191	204	71	4th,	Lost Final
1962-63	70	19	10	6	13	15	7	32	25	13	200	194	77	4th,	Lost Final
1961-62	70	17	11	7	6	22	7	23	33	14	184	219	60	5th,	Out of Playoffs
1960-61	70	15	13	7	10	16	9	25	29	16	195	215	66	4th,	Lost Final
1959-60	70	18	14	3	8	15	12	26	29	15	186	197	67	4th,	Lost Semi-Final
1958-59	70	13	17	5	12	20	3	25	37	8	167	218	58	6th,	Out of Playoffs
1957-58	70	16	11	8	13	18	4	29	29	12	176	207	70	3rd,	Lost Semi-Final
1956-57	70	23	7	5	15	13	7	38	20	12	198	157	88	1st,	Lost Semi-Final
1955-56	70	21	6	8	9	18	8	30	24	16	183	148	76	2nd,	Lost Final
1954-55	70	25	5	5	17	12	6	42	17	11	204	134	95	1st,	**Won Stanley Cup**
1953-54	70	24	4	7	13	15	7	37	19	14	191	132	88	1st,	**Won Stanley Cup**
1952-53	70	20	5	10	16	11	8	36	16	18	222	133	90	1st,	Lost Semi-Final
1951-52	70	24	7	4	20	7	8	44	14	12	215	133	100	1st,	**Won Stanley Cup**
1950-51	70	25	3	7	19	10	6	44	13	13	236	139	101	1st,	Lost Semi-Final
1949-50	70	19	9	7	18	10	7	37	19	14	229	164	88	1st,	**Won Stanley Cup**
1948-49	60	21	6	3	13	13	4	34	19	7	195	145	75	1st,	Lost Final
1947-48	60	16	9	5	14	9	7	30	18	12	187	148	72	2nd,	Lost Final
1946-47	60	14	10	6	8	17	5	22	27	11	190	193	55	4th,	Lost Semi-Final
1945-46	50	16	5	4	4	15	6	20	20	10	146	159	50	4th,	Out of Playoffs
1944-45	50	19	5	1	12	9	4	31	14	5	218	161	67	2nd,	Lost Final
1943-44	50	18	5	2	8	13	4	26	18	6	214	177	58	2nd,	Lost Semi-Final
1942-43	50	16	4	5	9	10	6	25	14	11	169	124	61	1st,	**Won Stanley Cup**
1941-42	48	14	7	3	5	18	1	19	25	4	140	147	42	5th,	Lost Final
1940-41	48	14	5	5	7	11	6	21	16	11	112	102	53	3rd,	Lost Final
1939-40	48	11	10	3	5	16	3	16	26	6	90	126	38	5th,	Lost Semi-Final
1938-39	48	14	8	2	4	16	4	18	24	6	107	128	42	5th,	Lost Semi-Final
1937-38	48	8	10	6	4	15	5	12	25	11	99	133	35	4th, Amn. Div.	Out of Playoffs
1936-37	48	14	5	5	11	9	4	25	14	9	128	102	59	1st, Amn. Div.	**Won Stanley Cup**
1935-36	48	14	5	5	10	11	3	24	16	8	124	103	56	1st, Amn. Div.	**Won Stanley Cup**
1934-35	48	11	8	5	8	14	2	19	22	7	127	114	45	4th, Amn. Div.	Out of Playoffs
1933-34	48	15	5	4	9	9	6	24	14	10	113	98	58	1st, Amn. Div.	Lost Final
1932-33*	48	17	3	4	8	12	4	25	15	8	111	93	58	2nd, Amn. Div.	Lost Semi-Final
1931-32	48	15	3	6	3	17	4	18	20	10	95	108	46	3rd, Amn. Div.	Lost Quarter-Final
1930-31**	44	10	7	5	6	14	2	16	21	7	102	105	39	4th, Amn. Div.	Out of Playoffs
1929-30	44	11	6	5	3	14	3	14	24	6	117	133	34	4th, Amn. Div.	Out of Playoffs
1928-29	44	11	6	5	8	10	4	19	16	9	72	63	47	3rd, Amn. Div.	Lost Quarter-Final
1927-28	44	9	10	3	10	9	3	19	19	6	88	79	44	4th, Amn. Div.	Out of Playoffs
1926-27***	44	6	15	1	6	13	3	12	28	4	76	105	28	5th, Amn. Div.	Out of Playoffs

* Team name changed to Red Wings. ** Team name changed to Falcons. *** Team named Cougars.

1994-95 Player Personnel

FORWARDS	HT	WT	S	Place of Birth	Date	1993-94 Club
AIVAZOFF, Micah	6-0	195	L	Powell River, B.C.	5/4/69	Detroit
BOWEN, Curtis	6-1	195	L	Kenora, Ont.	3/24/74	Ottawa (OHL)
BURR, Shawn	6-1	195	L	Sarnia, Ont.	7/1/66	Detroit
CASSELMAN, Mike	5-11	190	L	Morrisburg, Ont.	8/23/68	Adirondack
CICCARELLI, Dino	5-10	185	R	Sarnia, Ont.	2/8/60	Detroit
CLOUTIER, Sylvain	6-0	195	L	Mont-Laurier, Que.	2/13/74	Guelph-Adirondack
DRAPER, Kris	5-11	185	L	Toronto, Ont.	5/24/71	Detroit-Adirondack
FEDOROV, Sergei	6-1	200	L	Pskov, USSR	12/13/69	Detroit
FREDERICK, Joseph	6-1	190	R	St. Hubert, Que.	8/6/69	Adirondack
JOHNSON, Greg	5-10	185	L	Thunder Bay, Ont.	3/16/71	Det-Cdn. National-Cdn. Olympic-Adirondack
KOZLOV, Vyacheslav	5-10	180	L	Voskresensk, USSR	5/3/72	Detroit-Adirondack
KRUSHELNYSKI, Mike	6-2	200	L	Montreal, Que.	4/27/60	Toronto
LAPOINTE, Martin	5-11	200	R	Lachine, Que.	9/12/73	Detroit-Adirondack
MacDONALD, Jason	6-0	195	R	Charlottetown, P.E.I.	4/1/74	Owen Sound
MARTIN, Craig	6-2	215	R	Amherst, N.S.	1/21/71	Adirondack
McCARTY, Darren	6-1	210	R	Burnaby, B.C.	4/1/72	Detroit
MILLER, Jason	6-1	190	L	Edmonton, Alta.	3/1/71	Albany
MILLER, Kurtis	5-11	190	L	Bemidji, MN	6/1/70	Lake Superior
PRIMEAU, Keith	6-4	210	L	Toronto, Ont.	11/24/71	Detroit
SHEPPARD, Ray	6-1	195	R	Pembroke, Ont.	5/27/66	Detroit
SILLINGER, Mike	5-10	190	R	Regina, Sask.	6/29/71	Detroit
SPITZIG, Tim	6-0	195	R	Goderich, Ont.	4/15/74	Kitchener
TAYLOR, Tim	6-1	188	L	Stratford, Ont.	2/6/69	Detroit-Adirondack
YZERMAN, Steve	5-11	185	R	Cranbrook, B.C.	5/9/65	Detroit
DEFENSEMEN						
BAUTIN, Sergei	6-3	200	L	Rogachev, USSR	3/11/67	Winnipeg-Detroit-Adirondack
CARKNER, Terry	6-3	210	L	Smiths Falls, Ont.	3/7/66	Detroit
COFFEY, Paul	6-0	190	L	Weston, Ont.	6/1/61	Detroit
ERIKSSON, Anders	6-3	218	L	Bollnas, Sweden	1/9/75	MoDo
GOLUBOVSKY, Yan	6-3	183	R	Novosibirsk, USSR	3/9/76	Mosc. D'amo 2
HALKIDIS, Bob	5-11	205	L	Toronto, Ont.	3/5/66	Detroit-Adirondack
HOWE, Mark	5-11	185	L	Detroit, MI	5/28/55	Detroit
KONSTANTINOV, Vladimir	5-11	190	R	Murmansk, USSR	3/19/67	Detroit
KRUPPKE, Gord	6-1	215	R	Slave Lake, Alta.	4/2/69	Detroit-Adirondack
LAROSE, Benoit	6-0	200	L	Ottawa, Ont.	5/31/73	Shawinigan
LIDSTROM, Nicklas	6-2	185	L	Vasteras, Sweden	4/28/70	Detroit
MOTKOV, Dmitri	6-3	191	L	Moscow, USSR	2/23/71	Adirondack
PUSHOR, Jamie	6-3	205	R	Lethbridge, Alta.	2/11/73	Adirondack
RAMSEY, Mike	6-3	195	L	Minneapolis, MN	12/3/60	Pittsburgh
ROUSE, Bob	6-1	210	R	Surrey, B.C.	6/18/64	Toronto
WARD, Aaron	6-2	200	R	Windsor, Ont.	1/17/73	Detroit-Adirondack
YORK, Jason	6-1	192	R	Ottawa, Ont.	5/20/70	Detroit-Adirondack

GOALTENDERS	HT	WT	C	Place of Birth	Date	1993-94 Club
ESSENSA, Bob	6-0	185	L	Toronto, Ont.	1/14/65	Winnipeg-Detroit
HODSON, Kevin	6-0	178	L	Winnipeg, Man.	3/27/72	Adirondack
ING, Peter	6-2	170	L	Toronto, Ont.	4/28/69	Detroit-Adirondack-Las Vegas
MARACLE, Norm	5-9	175	L	Belleville, Ont.	10/2/74	Saskatoon
OSGOOD, Chris	5-10	175	L	Peace River, Alta.	11/26/72	Detroit-Adirondack
VERNON, Mike	5-9	165	L	Calgary, Alta.	2/24/63	Calgary

Director of Player Personnel/Coach

BOWMAN, WILLIAM, SCOTT (SCOTTY)
Director of Player Personnel/Coach, Detroit Red Wings.
Born in Montreal, Que. September 18, 1933.

Scotty Bowman is in his second year behind the Red Wings' bench. 1994-95 will be his first season as Detroit's director of player personnel. This is the third time that Bowman has held a front-office position while working as an NHL head coach. Bowman holds the NHL regular-season record for coaching wins (880) and winning percentage (.654) and has also recorded more post-season victories than any other coach, compiling a 140-86 mark in playoff encounters.

One of only two coaches to guide three different teams into the Stanley Cup Finals, Bowman's six Cup victories are second only to Montreal's Toe Blake. After guiding the St. Louis Blues into the championship round in three consecutive seasons from 1968-70, Bowman was appointed head coach of the Montreal Canadiens, who captured five Stanley Cup titles under Bowman's supervision.

Following an eight season term as the general manager of the Buffalo Sabres, and a brief stint as a commentator for CBC Television, Bowman joined the Pittsburgh Penguins as director of player development, but returned to coaching when head coach Bob Johnson became ill in September, 1991. Bowman was elected to the Hockey Hall of Fame as a builder in 1991.

NHL Coaching Record

		Regular Season					Playoffs			
Season	Team	Games	W	L	T	%	Games	W	L	%
1967-68	St. Louis	58	23	21	14	.517	18	8	10	.444
1968-69	St. Louis	76	37	25	14	.579	12	8	4	.667
1969-70	St. Louis	76	37	27	12	.566	16	8	8	.500
1970-71	St. Louis	28	13	10	5	.554	6	2	4	.333
1971-72	Montreal	78	46	16	16	.692	6	2	4	.333
1972-73	Montreal	78	52	10	16	.769	17	12	5	.706*
1973-74	Montreal	78	45	24	9	.635	6	2	4	.333
1974-75	Montreal	80	47	14	19	.706	11	6	5	.545
1975-76	Montreal	80	58	11	11	.794	13	12	1	.923*
1976-77	Montreal	80	60	8	12	.825	14	12	2	.857*
1977-78	Montreal	80	59	10	11	.806	15	12	3	.800*
1978-79	Montreal	80	52	17	11	.719	16	12	4	.750*
1979-80	Buffalo	80	47	17	16	.688	14	9	5	.643
1981-82	Buffalo	35	18	10	7	.614	4	1	3	.250
1982-83	Buffalo	80	38	29	13	.556	10	6	4	.600
1983-84	Buffalo	80	48	25	7	.644	3	0	3	.000

1993-94 Scoring

* – rookie

Regular Season

Pos	#	Player	Team	GP	G	A	Pts	+/–	PIM	PP	SH	GW	GT	S	%
C	91	Sergei Fedorov	DET	82	56	64	120	48	34	13	4	10	0	337	16.6
R	26	Ray Sheppard	DET	82	52	41	93	13	26	19	0	5	0	260	20.0
C	19	Steve Yzerman	DET	58	24	58	82	11	36	7	3	3	1	217	11.1
D	77	Paul Coffey	DET	80	14	63	77	28	106	5	0	3	0	278	5.0
C	13	Vyacheslav Kozlov	DET	77	34	39	73	27	50	8	2	6	0	202	16.8
L	55	Keith Primeau	DET	78	31	42	73	34	173	7	3	4	2	155	20.0
R	22	Dino Ciccarelli	DET	66	28	29	57	10	73	12	0	1	2	153	18.3
D	5	Nicklas Lidstrom	DET	84	10	46	56	43	26	4	0	3	0	200	5.0
D	3	Steve Chiasson	DET	82	13	33	46	17	122	4	1	2	0	238	5.5
D	16	Vlad. Konstantinov	DET	80	12	21	33	30	138	1	3	3	0	97	12.4
C	12	Mike Sillinger	DET	62	8	21	29	2	10	0	1	1	0	91	8.8
R	25 *	Darren McCarty	DET	67	9	17	26	12	181	0	0	2	0	81	11.1
D	4	Mark Howe	DET	44	4	20	24	16	8	1	0	0	0	72	5.6
L	11	Shawn Burr	DET	51	10	12	22	12	31	0	1	1	0	64	15.6
R	24	Bob Probert	DET	66	7	10	17	1–	275	1	0	0	0	105	6.7
C	23 *	Greg Johnson	DET	52	6	11	17	7–	22	1	1	0	0	48	12.5
R	20 *	Martin Lapointe	DET	50	8	8	16	7	55	2	0	0	0	45	17.8
R	15	Sheldon Kennedy	DET	61	6	7	13	2–	30	0	1	0	0	60	10.0
C	33	Kris Draper	DET	39	5	8	13	11	31	0	1	0	0	55	9.1
C	27 *	Micah Aivazoff	DET	59	4	4	8	1–	38	0	0	0	0	52	7.7
D	2	Terry Carkner	DET	68	1	6	7	13	130	0	0	0	0	32	3.1
D	29	Sergei Bautin	WPG	59	0	7	7	13–	78	0	0	0	0	39	.0
			DET	1	0	0	0	1	0	0	0	0	0	0	.0
			TOTAL	60	0	7	7	12–	78	0	0	0	0	39	.0
D	21	Bob Halkidis	DET	28	1	4	5	1–	93	0	0	0	0	35	2.9
D	38 *	Jason York	DET	7	1	2	3	0	2	0	0	0	0	9	11.1
G	35	Bob Essensa	WPG	56	0	0	0	0	6	0	0	0	0	0	.0
			DET	13	0	2	2	0	0	0	0	0	0	0	.0
			TOTAL	69	0	2	2	0	6	0	0	0	0	0	.0
C	38 *	Tim Taylor	DET	1	1	0	1	1–	0	0	0	0	0	4	25.0
D	29 *	Aaron Ward	DET	5	1	0	1	2	4	0	0	0	0	3	33.3
L	34	Steve Maltais	DET	4	0	1	1	1–	0	0	0	0	0	2	.0
L	18	Mark Pederson	DET	2	0	0	0	1–	2	0	0	0	0	0	.0
G	31	Peter Ing	DET	3	0	0	0	0	0	0	0	0	0	0	.0
D	44 *	Gord Kruppke	DET	9	0	0	0	4–	12	0	0	0	0	5	.0
G	30 *	Chris Osgood	DET	41	0	0	0	0	2	0	0	0	0	0	.0

Goaltending

No.	Goaltender	GPI	Mins	Avg	W	L	T	EN	SO	GA	SA	S%
35	Bob Essensa	13	778	2.62	4	7	2	3	1	34	337	.899
30	* Chris Osgood	41	2206	2.86	23	8	5	0	2	105	999	.895
29	Tim Cheveldae	30	1572	3.47	16	9	1	3	1	91	727	.875
37	Vincent Riendeau	8	345	4.00	2	4	0	1	0	23	131	.824
31	Peter Ing	3	170	5.29	1	2	0	0	0	15	102	.853
	Totals	**84**	**5094**	**3.24**	**46**	**30**	**8**	**7**	**4**	**275**	**2303**	**.881**

Playoffs

Pos	#	Player	Team	GP	G	A	Pts	+/–	PIM	PP	SH	GW	GT	S	%
C	91	Sergei Fedorov	DET	7	1	7	8	1–	6	0	0	0	0	19	5.3
R	22	Dino Ciccarelli	DET	7	5	2	7	1	14	1	0	0	0	22	22.7
C	13	Vyacheslav Kozlov	DET	7	2	5	7	3	12	0	0	0	0	16	12.5
D	77	Paul Coffey	DET	7	1	6	7	6	8	0	0	0	0	23	4.3
D	5	Nicklas Lidstrom	DET	7	3	2	5	4	0	1	1	0	0	20	15.0
D	3	Steve Chiasson	DET	7	2	3	5	3	2	2	0	1	0	13	15.4
C	33	Kris Draper	DET	7	2	2	4	5	4	0	1	0	0	15	13.3
C	23 *	Greg Johnson	DET	7	2	2	4	2–	2	1	0	0	0	7	28.6
R	25 *	Darren McCarty	DET	7	2	2	4	3	8	0	0	0	0	6	33.3
C	19	Steve Yzerman	DET	3	1	3	4	4	0	0	0	0	0	8	12.5
R	26	Ray Sheppard	DET	7	2	1	3	0	4	0	0	0	0	15	13.3
R	15	Sheldon Kennedy	DET	7	1	2	3	3	0	0	0	0	0	8	12.5
L	11	Shawn Burr	DET	7	2	0	2	3	6	0	0	2	0	13	15.4
R	24	Bob Probert	DET	7	1	1	2	1	8	0	0	0	0	10	10.0
L	55	Keith Primeau	DET	7	0	2	2	0	6	0	0	0	0	12	.0
D	16	Vladimir Konstantinov	DET	7	0	2	2	3	4	0	0	0	0	4	.0
D	4	Mark Howe	DET	6	0	1	1	0	0	0	0	0	0	2	.0
D	21	Bob Halkidis	DET	1	0	0	0	1–	2	0	0	0	0	0	.0
G	35	Bob Essensa	DET	2	0	0	0	0	0	0	0	0	0	0	.0
R	20 *	Martin Lapointe	DET	4	0	0	0	0	6	0	0	0	0	2	.0
G	30 *	Chris Osgood	DET	6	0	0	0	0	0	0	0	0	0	0	.0
D	2	Terry Carkner	DET	7	0	0	0	1–	4	0	0	0	0	3	.0

Goaltending

No.	Goaltender	GPI	Mins	Avg	W	L	EN	SO	GA	SA	S%
30	* Chris Osgood	6	307	2.35	3	2	0	1	12	110	.891
35	Bob Essensa	2	109	4.95	0	2	0	0	9	43	.791
	Totals	**7**	**420**	**3.00**	**3**	**4**	**0**	**1**	**21**	**153**	**.863**

NHL Coaching Record — *continued*

		Regular Season					Playoffs			
Season	Team	Games	W	L	T	%	Games	W	L	%
1984-85	Buffalo	80	38	28	14	.563	5	2	3	.400
1985-86	Buffalo	37	18	18	1	.500	....	....	....	....
1986-87	Buffalo	12	3	7	2	.333	....	....	....	....
1991-92	Pittsburgh	80	39	32	9	.544	21	16	5	.762*
1992-93	Pittsburgh	84	56	21	7	.708	12	7	5	.583
1993-94	Detroit	84	46	30	8	.595	7	3	4	.429
	NHL Totals	**1524**	**880**	**410**	**234**	**.654**	**226**	**140**	**86**	**.619**

* Won Stanley Cup

Club Records

Team

(Figures in brackets for season records are games played; records for fewest points, wins, ties, losses, goals, goals against are for 70 or more games)

Most Points	103	1992-93 (84)
Most Wins	47	1992-93 (84)
Most Ties	18	1952-53 (70)
		1980-81 (80)
Most Losses	57	1985-86 (80)
Most Goals	369	1992-93 (84)
Most Goals Against	415	1985-86 (80)
Fewest Points	40	1985-86 (80)
Fewest Wins	16	1976-77 (80)
Fewest Ties	4	1966-67 (70)
Fewest Losses	13	1950-51 (70)
Fewest Goals	167	1958-59 (70)
Fewest Goals Against	132	1953-54 (70)

Longest Winning Streak

Over-all	9	Mar. 3-21/51; Feb. 27-Mar. 20/55
Home	14	Jan. 21-Mar. 25/65
Away	6	Jan. 6-27/94

Longest Undefeated Streak

Over-all	15	Nov. 27-Dec. 28/52 (8 wins, 7 ties)
Home	18	Dec. 26/54-Mar. 20/55 (13 wins, 5 ties)
Away	15	Oct. 18-Dec. 20/51 (10 wins, 5 ties)

Longest Losing Streak

Over-all	14	Feb. 24-Mar. 25/82
Home	7	Feb. 20-Mar. 25/82
Away	14	Oct. 19-Dec. 21/66

Longest Winless Streak

Over-all	19	Feb. 26-Apr. 3/77 (18 losses, 1 tie)
Home	10	Dec. 11/85-Jan. 18/86 (9 losses, 1 tie)
Away	26	Dec. 15/76-Apr. 3/77 (23 losses, 3 ties)

Most Shutouts, Season	13	1953-54 (70)
Most. PIM, Season	2,393	1985-86 (80)
Most Goals, Game	15	Jan. 23/44 (NYR 0 at Det. 15)

Individual

Most Seasons	25	Gordie Howe
Most Games	1,687	Gordie Howe
Most Goals, Career	786	Gordie Howe
Most Assists, Career	1,023	Gordie Howe
Most Points, Career	1,809	Gordie Howe (786 goals, 1,023 assists)
Most PIM, Career	2,090	Bob Probert
Most Shutouts, Career	85	Terry Sawchuk

Longest Consecutive

Games Streak	548	Alex Delvecchio (Dec. 13/56-Nov. 11/64)
Most Goals, Season	65	Steve Yzerman (1988-89)
Most Assists, Season	90	Steve Yzerman (1988-89)
Most Points, Season	155	Steve Yzerman (1988-89) (65 goals, 90 assists)
Most PIM, Season	398	Bob Probert (1987-88)

Most Points, Defenseman

Season	77	Paul Coffey (1993-94) (14 goals, 63 assists)

Most Points, Center

Season	155	Steve Yzerman (1988-89) (65 goals, 90 assists)

Most Points, Right Wing

Season	103	Gordie Howe (1968-69) (44 goals, 59 assists)

Most Points, Left Wing

Season	105	John Ogrodnick (1984-85) (55 goals, 50 assists)

Most Points, Rookie

Season	87	Steve Yzerman (1983-84) (39 goals, 48 assists)

Most Shutouts, Season	12	Terry Sawchuk (1951-52; 1953-54; 1954-55) Glenn Hall (1955-56)
Most Goals, Game	6	Syd Howe (Feb. 3/44)
Most Assists, Game	*7	Billy Taylor (Mar. 16/47)
Most Points, Game	7	Carl Liscombe (Nov. 5/42) Don Grosso (Feb. 3/44) Billy Taylor (Mar. 16/47)

* NHL Record

Retired Numbers

1	Terry Sawchuk	1949-55, 57-64, 68-69
6	Larry Aurie	1927-1939
7	Ted Lindsay	1944-57, 64-65
9	Gordie Howe	1946-1971
10	Alex Delvecchio	1951-1973

All-time Record vs. Other Clubs

Regular Season

	GP	W	L	T	GF	GA	PTS	GP	W	L	T	GF	GA	PTS	GP	W	L	T	GF	GA	PTS
			At Home							On Road							Total				
Anaheim	2	1	0	1	9	6	3	2	2	0	0	13	6	4	4	3	0	1	22	12	7
Boston	278	150	76	52	930	699	352	279	85	151	43	739	986	213	557	235	227	95	1669	1685	565
Buffalo	47	24	18	5	176	145	53	45	7	31	7	124	209	21	92	31	49	12	300	354	74
Calgary	39	20	12	7	153	128	47	40	11	24	5	129	178	27	79	31	36	12	282	306	74
Chicago	309	190	91	28	1062	762	408	309	117	144	48	853	935	282	618	307	235	76	1915	1697	690
Dallas	82	40	30	12	334	282	92	84	25	45	14	254	320	64	166	65	75	26	588	602	156
Edmonton	24	9	13	2	92	107	20	24	7	13	4	98	120	18	48	16	26	6	190	227	38
Florida	1	1	0	0	7	3	2	1	1	0	0	4	3	2	2	2	0	0	11	6	4
Hartford	23	10	7	6	88	68	26	22	7	14	1	60	85	15	45	17	21	7	148	153	41
Los Angeles	59	24	27	8	238	225	56	60	16	33	11	187	260	43	119	40	60	19	425	485	99
Montreal	274	125	96	53	782	703	303	274	62	169	43	608	978	167	548	187	265	96	1390	1681	470
New Jersey	32	18	12	2	138	114	38	33	10	15	8	95	118	28	65	28	27	10	233	232	66
NY Islanders	37	19	16	2	131	123	40	38	14	22	2	109	148	30	75	33	38	4	240	271	70
NY Rangers	278	158	75	45	978	689	361	276	87	131	58	710	852	232	554	245	206	103	1688	1541	593
Ottawa	2	2	0	0	13	5	4	2	1	1	0	7	7	2	4	3	1	0	20	12	6
Philadelphia	51	24	18	9	184	168	57	52	12	29	11	156	210	35	103	36	47	20	340	378	92
Pittsburgh	58	36	11	11	232	164	83	57	14	39	4	169	254	32	115	50	50	15	401	418	115
Quebec	22	12	9	1	88	77	25	23	8	12	3	85	96	19	45	20	21	4	173	173	44
St. Louis	83	35	36	12	304	274	82	83	23	47	13	231	308	59	166	58	83	25	535	582	141
San Jose	5	5	0	0	28	10	10	6	4	1	1	32	20	9	11	9	1	1	60	30	19
Tampa Bay	4	3	1	0	20	13	6	6	5	1	0	39	21	10	10	8	2	0	59	34	16
Toronto	302	157	100	45	900	738	359	301	96	161	44	796	1007	236	603	253	261	89	1696	1745	595
Vancouver	46	27	13	6	195	137	60	45	14	24	7	145	186	35	91	41	37	13	340	323	95
Washington	40	16	13	11	142	118	43	38	14	20	4	120	152	32	78	30	33	15	262	270	75
Winnipeg	28	15	10	3	118	101	33	26	7	11	8	78	90	22	54	22	21	11	196	191	55
Defunct Clubs	141	76	40	25	430	307	177	141	49	63	29	364	375	127	282	125	103	54	794	682	304
Totals	**2267**	**1197**	**724**	**346**	**7772**	**6166**	**2740**	**2267**	**698**	**1201**	**368**	**6205**	**7924**	**1764**	**4534**	**1895**	**1925**	**714**	**13977**	**14090**	**4504**

Calgary totals include Atlanta, 1972-73 to 1979-80. Dallas totals include Minnesota, 1967-68 to 1992-93.
New Jersey totals include Kansas City, 1974-75 to 1975-76, and Colorado, 1976-77 to 1981-82.

Playoffs

	Series	W	L	GP	W	L	T	GF	GA	Last Mtg.	Round	Result
Boston	7	3	4	33	14	19	0	98	96	1957	SF	L 1-4
Calgary	1	1	0	2	2	0	0	8	5	1978	PR	W 2-0
Chicago	13	5	8	64	27	37	0	177	198	1992	DF	L 0-4
Dallas	1	1	0	7	4	3	0	23	19	1992	DSF	W 4-3
Edmonton	2	0	2	10	2	8	0	26	39	1988	CF	L 1-4
Montreal	12	7	5	62	29	33	0	149	161	1978	QF	L 1-4
NY Rangers	5	4	1	23	13	10	0	57	49	1950	F	W 4-3
St. Louis	3	1	2	16	8	8	0	53	51	1991	DF	L 3-4
San Jose	1	0	1	7	3	4	0	27	21	1994	CQF	L 3-4
Toronto	23	11	12	117	59	58	0	321	311	1993	DSF	L 3-4
Defunct Clubs	4	3	1	10	7	2	1	21	13			
Totals	**72**	**36**	**36**	**351**	**168**	**182**	**1**	**960**	**963**			

Playoff Results 1994-90

Year	Round	Opponent	Result	GF	GA
1994	CQF	San Jose	L 3-4	27	21
1993	DSF	Toronto	L 3-4	30	24
1992	DF	Chicago	L 0-4	6	11
	DSF	Minnesota	W 4-3	23	19
1991	DSF	St. Louis	L 3-4	20	24

Abbreviations: Round: F – Final;
CF – conference final; **CQF** – conference quarter-final;
CSF – conference semi-final; **DF** – division final;
DSF – division semi-final; **SF** – semi-final;
QF – quarter-final; **PR** – preliminary round.

1993-94 Results

Oct.	5	at	Dallas	4-6		15	at	Boston	3-2
	8	at	Anaheim	7-2		17	at	Tampa Bay	6-3
	9	at	Los Angeles	3-10		19		Anaheim	4-4
	13		St. Louis	2-5		25		Chicago	0-5
	15	at	Toronto	3-6		27	at	Chicago	4-3
	16		Toronto	1-2		29		Winnipeg	7-1
	18	at	Buffalo	6-4		30	at	Washington	3-6
	21		Winnipeg	6-2	Feb.	2	at	Tampa Bay	3-1
	23	at	Chicago	2-4		4		Pittsburgh	3-6
	25		Dallas	3-5		5	at	Toronto	4-3
	27		Los Angeles	8-3		8		Vancouver	3-6
	30	at	Quebec	3-5		11		Philadelphia	6-3
Nov.	2		Boston	6-1		12	at	St. Louis	5-4
	4		Toronto	3-3		15	at	Toronto	4-5
	9		Edmonton	2-4		16		Florida	7-3
	13	at	Pittsburgh	7-3		18		Edmonton	5-1
	17	at	Winnipeg	1-2		20	at	Florida	4-3
	20	at	New Jersey	4-3		23		New Jersey	2-7
	21	at	St. Louis	2-2		24		Hartford	3-0
	23	at	San Jose	4-6		26		San Jose	2-0
	24	at	Vancouver	5-4	Mar.	1		Calgary	5-2
	27		Dallas	10-4		4		Toronto	5-6
	28	at	NY Islanders	4-1		6		Buffalo	2-3
Dec.	1	at	Hartford	3-5		7	at	NY Rangers	6-3
	3		Ottawa	8-1		9	at	Calgary	5-1
	5	at	Winnipeg	4-6		11	at	Edmonton	2-4
	6		Winnipeg	6-2		15		Vancouver	5-2
	9		St. Louis	3-2		17		NY Islanders	1-3
	11		San Jose	5-3		19	at	Winnipeg	2-4
	14		Anaheim	5-3		22		Chicago	3-1
	17		NY Rangers	6-4		23	at	Ottawa	4-5
	18	at	Montreal	1-8		25		Washington	2-2
	21		Chicago	5-1		27	at	Chicago	3-1
	23	at	Philadelphia	3-1		29		Hartford	6-2
	27	at	Dallas	6-0		31		Quebec	2-4
	31		Los Angeles	4-4	Apr.	2		Calgary	3-3
Jan.	4	at	St. Louis	4-4		3		St. Louis	3-3
	6	at	San Jose	10-3		5	at	Vancouver	8-3
	8	at	Los Angeles	6-3		9	at	Calgary	2-4
	10	at	Anaheim	6-4		10	at	Edmonton	3-4
	12		Tampa Bay	2-4		13		Montreal	9-0
	14		Dallas	9-3		14	at	Dallas	3-4

Entry Draft
Selections 1994-80

1994
Pick
23	Yan Golubovsky
49	Mathieu Dandenault
75	Sean Gillam
114	Frederic Deschenes
127	Doug Battaglia
153	Pavel Agarkov
205	Jason Elliot
231	Jeff Mikesch
257	Tomas Holmstrom
283	Toivo Suursoo

1993
Pick
22	Anders Eriksson
48	Jonathan Coleman
74	Kevin Hilton
97	John Jakopin
100	Benoit Larose
126	Norm Maracle
152	Tim Spitzig
178	Yuri Yeresko
204	Vitezslav Skuta
230	Ryan Shanahan
256	James Kosecki
282	Gordon Hunt

1992
Pick
22	Curtis Bowen
46	Darren McCarty
70	Sylvain Cloutier
118	Mike Sullivan
142	Jason MacDonald
166	Greg Scott
183	Justin Krall
189	C.J. Denomme
214	Jeff Walker
238	Daniel McGillis
262	Ryan Bach

1991
Pick
10	Martin Lapointe
32	Jamie Pushor
54	Chris Osgood
76	Michael Knuble
98	Dmitri Motkov
142	Igor Malykhin
186	Jim Bermingham
208	Jason Firth
230	Bart Turner
252	Andrew Miller

1990
Pick
3	Keith Primeau
45	Vyacheslav Kozlov
66	Stewart Malgunas
87	Tony Burns
108	Claude Barthe
129	Jason York
150	Wes McCauley
171	Anthony Gruba
192	Travis Tucker
213	Brett Larson
234	John Hendry

1989
Pick
11	Mike Sillinger
32	Bob Boughner
53	Nicklas Lidstrom
74	Sergei Fedorov
95	Shawn McCosh
116	Dallas Drake
137	Scott Zygulski
158	Andy Suhy
179	Bob Jones
200	Greg Bignell
204	Rick Judson
221	Vladimir Konstantinov
242	Joseph Frederick
246	Jason Glickman

1988
Pick
17	Kory Kocur
38	Serge Anglehart
47	Guy Dupuis
59	Petr Hrbek
80	Sheldon Kennedy
143	Kelly Hurd
164	Brian McCormack
185	Jody Praznik
206	Glen Goodall
227	Darren Colbourne
248	Donald Stone

1987
Pick
11	Yves Racine
32	Gordon Kruppke
41	Bob Wilkie
52	Dennis Holland
74	Mark Reimer
95	Radomir Brazda
116	Sean Clifford
137	Mike Gober
158	Kevin Scott
179	Mikko Haapakoski
200	Darin Bannister
221	Craig Quinlan
242	Tomas Jansson

1986
Pick
1	Joe Murphy
22	Adam Graves
43	Derek Mayer
64	Tim Cheveldae
85	Johan Garpenlov
106	Jay Stark
127	Per Djoos
148	Dean Morton
169	Marc Potvin
190	Scott King
211	Tom Bissett
232	Peter Ekroth

1985
Pick
8	Brent Fedyk
29	Jeff Sharples
50	Steve Chiasson
71	Mark Gowans
92	Chris Luongo
113	Randy McKay
134	Thomas Bjur
155	Mike Luckraft
176	Rob Schenna
197	Erik Hamalainen
218	Bo Svanberg
239	Mikael Lindman

1984
Pick
7	Shawn Burr
28	Doug Houda
49	Milan Chalupa
91	Mats Lundstrom
112	Randy Hansch
133	Stefan Larsson
152	Lars Karlsson
154	Urban Nordin
175	Bill Shibicky
195	Jay Rose
216	Tim Kaiser
236	Tom Nickolau

1983
Pick
4	Steve Yzerman
25	Lane Lambert
46	Bob Probert
68	David Korol
86	Petr Klima
88	Joey Kocur
106	Chris Pusey
126	Bob Pierson
146	Craig Butz
166	Dave Sikorski
186	Stuart Grimson
206	Jeff Frank
226	Charles Chiatto

1982
Pick
17	Murray Craven
23	Yves Courteau
44	Carmine Vani
66	Craig Coxe
86	Brad Shaw
107	Claude Vilgrain
128	Greg Hudas
149	Pat Lahey
170	Gary Cullen
191	Brent Meckling
212	Mike Stern
233	Shaun Reagan

1981
Pick
23	Claude Loiselle
44	Corrado Micalef
86	Larry Trader
107	Gerard Gallant
128	Greg Stefan
149	Rick Zombo
170	Don Leblanc
191	Robert Nordmark

1980
Pick
11	Mike Blaisdell
46	Mark Osborne
88	Mike Corrigan
109	Wayne Crawford
130	Mike Braun
151	John Beukeboom
172	Dave Miles
193	Brian Rorabeck

Dino Ciccarelli scored 12 powerplay goals for the Red Wings in 1993-94.

Club Directory

Joe Louis Arena
600 Civic Center Drive
Detroit, Michigan 48226
Phone **(313) 396-7544**
FAX PR: (313) 567-0296
Capacity: 19,275

Owner/President	Mike Ilitch
Owner/Secretary-Treasurer	Marian Ilitch
Vice-Presidents	Atanas Ilitch, Christopher Ilitch
Senior Vice-President	Jim Devellano
Director of Player Personnel/Head Coach	Scotty Bowman
Assistant General Manager	Ken Holland
Assistant Coaches	Barry Smith, Dave Lewis
Pro Scouting Director	Dan Belisle
Amateur Scouting Director	Jim Nill
Scouts	Billy Dea, Wayne Meier, Chris Coury, Paul Crowley, Ken Hoodikoff, Tim Murray, Hakan Andersson, Vladimir Havlug, Mark Leach
Controller	Paul MacDonald
Public Relations Director	Bill Jamieson
General Sales Manager	Jack Johnson
Broadcast Print/Sales Director	Amy Goan
Marketing Director	Ted Speers
Public Relations Coordinator	Howard Berlin
Public Relations Assistants	Kathy Best, Karen Davis
Box Office Manager	Bob Kerlin
Season Ticket Sales Director	Tina Lasley
Executive Assistant	Nancy Beard
Accounting Assistant	Cathy Witzke
Administrative Assistant	Kristin Armstrong
Athletic Trainer	John Wharton
Equipment Manager/Trainer	Paul Boyer
Assistant Equipment Manager	Tim Abbott
Team Physicians	Dr. John Finley, D.O., Dr. David Collon, M.D.
Team Dentist	Dr. C.J. Regula, D.M.D.
Team Ophthalmologist	Dr. Charles Slater, M.D.
Home Ice/Training Camp Site	Joe Louis Arena
Press Box & Radio-TV Booths	Jefferson Avenue side of arena, top of seats
Media Lounge	First-floor hallway near Red Wings' dressing room, riv
Rink Dimensions	200 feet by 85 feet
Uniforms	Home: Base color white, trimmed in red
	Road: Base color red, trimmed in white
Radio flagship station	WJR-AM (760)
TV stations	WKBD (Channel 50); PASS Cable; Special Order Sports
Radio announcers	Bruce Martyn, Paul Woods
TV announcers	Dave Strader, Mickey Redmond

General Managers' History

Art Duncan, 1926-27; Jack Adams, 1927-28 to 1961-62; Sid Abel, 1962-63 to 1969-70; Sid Abel and Ned Harkness, 1970-71; Ned Harkness, 1971-72 to 1973-74; Alex Delvecchio, 1974-75 to 1975-76; Alex Delvecchio and Ted Lindsay, 1976-77; Ted Lindsay, 1977-78 to 1979-80; Jimmy Skinner, 1980-81 to 1981-82; Jim Devellano, 1982-83 to 1989-90; Bryan Murray, 1990-91 to 1993-94.

Coaching History

Art Duncan, 1926-27; Jack Adams, 1927-28 to 1946-47; Tommy Ivan, 1947-48 to 1953-54; Jimmy Skinner, 1954-55 to 1956-57; Jimmy Skinner and Sid Abel, 1957-58; Sid Abel, 1958-59 to 1967-68; Bill Gadsby, 1968-69; Bill Gadsby and Sid Abel, 1969-70; Ned Harkness and Doug Barkley, 1970-71; Doug Barkley and John Wilson, 1971-72; John Wilson, 1972-73; Ted Garvin and Alex Delvecchio, 1973-74; Alex Delvecchio, 1974-75; Doug Barkley and Alex Delvecchio, 1975-76; Alex Delvecchio and Larry Wilson, 1976-77; Bobby Kromm, 1977-78 to 1978-79; Bobby Kromm and Ted Lindsay, 1979-80; Ted Lindsay and Wayne Maxner, 1980-81; Wayne Maxner and Billy Dea, 1981-82; Nick Polano, 1982-83 to 1984-85; Harry Neale and Brad Park, 1985-86; Jacques Demers, 1986-87 to 1989-90; Bryan Murray, 1990-91 to 1992-93; Scotty Bowman, 1993-94 to date.

Captains' History

Art Duncan, 1926-27; Reg Noble, 1927-28 to 1929-30; George Hay, 1930-31; Carson Cooper, 1931-32; Larry Aurie, 1932-33; Herbie Lewis, 1933-34; Ebbie Goodfellow, 1934-35; Doug Young, 1935-36 to 1937-38; Ebbie Goodfellow, 1938-39 to 1940-41; Ebbie Goodfellow and Sid Abel, 1941-42; Sid Abel, 1942-43; Mud Bruneteau, Bill Hollett (co-captains), 1943-44; Bill Hollett, 1944-45; Bill Hollett, Sid Abel, 1945-46; Sid Abel, 1946-47 to 1951-52; Ted Lindsay, 1952-53 to 1955-56; Red Kelly, 1956-57, 1957-58; Gordie Howe, 1958-59 to 1961-62; Alex Delvecchio, 1962-63 to 1972-73; Alex Delvecchio, Nick Libett, Red Berenson, Gary Bergman, Ted Harris, Mickey Redmond, Larry Johnston, 1973-74; Marcel Dionne, 1974-75; Danny Grant, Terry Harper, 1975-76; Danny Grant, Dennis Polonich, 1976-77; Dan Maloney, Dennis Hextall, 1977-78; Dennis Hextall, Nick Libett, Paul Woods, 1978-79; Dale McCourt, 1979-80; Errol Thompson, Reed Larson, 1980-81; Reed Larson, 1981-82; Danny Gare, 1982-83 to 1985-86; Steve Yzerman, 1986-87 to date.

Edmonton Oilers

1993-94 Results: 25W-45L-14T 64PTS. Sixth, Pacific Division

Schedule

Oct.	Sun.	2	Vancouver		Wed.	11	Tampa Bay
	Wed.	5	Anaheim		Sat.	14	at Vancouver
	Fri.	7	at Winnipeg		Sun.	15	Buffalo
	Sun.	9	at Chicago		Tues.	17	Los Angeles
	Wed.	12	Calgary		Mon.	23	at Calgary
	Sat.	15	at Vancouver		Wed.	25	at Chicago
	Mon.	17	at Anaheim		Thur.	26	at St. Louis
	Wed.	19	Anaheim		Sat.	28	at Detroit*
	Fri.	21	Boston		Mon.	30	Detroit
	Sun.	23	at Dallas*	Feb.	Wed.	1	Hartford
	Tues.	25	at Quebec		Fri.	3	Toronto
	Wed.	26	at Montreal		Sun.	5	at Anaheim*
	Fri.	28	at Toronto		Mon.	6	at Los Angeles
	Sun.	30	Washington		Wed.	8	Chicago
Nov.	Wed.	2	Florida		Fri.	10	Winnipeg
	Fri.	4	at Calgary		Sun.	12	Anaheim*
	Tues.	8	at Washington		Tues.	14	at Pittsburgh
	Fri.	11	at Florida		Wed.	15	at Detroit
	Sat.	12	at Tampa Bay		Sat.	18	at Philadelphia*
	Mon.	14	at Winnipeg		Mon.	20	at St. Louis
	Wed.	16	Vancouver		Wed.	22	Dallas
	Fri.	18	Calgary		Sat.	25	Philadelphia
	Sun.	20	San Jose		Tues.	28	at Calgary
	Wed.	23	Los Angeles	Mar.	Wed.	1	Vancouver
	Fri.	25	Chicago		Fri.	3	Pittsburgh
	Sat.	26	Calgary		Sun.	5	Detroit*
	Wed.	30	Winnipeg		Wed.	8	at San Jose
Dec.	Sat.	3	at New Jersey*		Thur.	9	at Vancouver
	Sun.	4	at NY Rangers		Sun.	12	Ottawa
	Tues.	6	at NY Islanders		Tues.	15	St. Louis
	Thur.	8	at Boston		Fri.	17	NY Islanders
	Sat.	10	at Hartford		Mon.	20	Toronto
	Tues.	13	Toronto				(in Saskatoon)
	Sat.	17	NY Rangers		Tues.	21	New Jersey
	Sun.	18	St. Louis		Thur.	23	at Dallas
	Tues.	20	at San Jose		Sun.	26	at Ottawa
	Thur.	22	at Los Angeles		Mon.	27	at Toronto
	Tues.	27	San Jose		Wed.	29	at Buffalo
	Fri.	30	Montreal		Fri.	31	Los Angeles
Jan.	Mon.	2	at Winnipeg	Apr.	Mon.	3	at Los Angeles
			(in Saskatoon)		Wed.	5	at Anaheim
	Sat.	7	Quebec		Fri.	7	at San Jose
	Mon.	9	Dallas		Sun.	9	San Jose

* Denotes afternoon game.

Home Starting Times:
Weeknights	7:30 p.m.
Saturdays	8:30 p.m.
Sundays	6:00 p.m.
Matinees	2:00 p.m.

Franchise date: June 22, 1979

PACIFIC DIVISION

16th NHL Season

Year-by-Year Record

		Home			Road			Overall							
Season	GP	W	L	T	W	L	T	W	L	T	GF	GA	Pts.	Finished	Playoff Result
1993-94	84	17	22	3	8	23	11	25	45	14	261	305	64	6th, Pacific Div.	Out of Playoffs
1992-93	84	16	21	5	10	29	3	26	50	8	242	337	60	5th, Smythe Div.	Out of Playoffs
1991-92	80	22	13	5	14	21	5	36	34	10	295	297	82	3rd, Smythe Div.	Lost Conf. Championship
1990-91	80	22	15	3	15	22	3	37	37	6	272	272	80	3rd, Smythe Div.	Lost Conf. Championship
1989-90	80	23	11	6	15	17	8	38	28	14	315	283	90	**2nd, Smythe Div.**	**Won Stanley Cup**
1988-89	80	21	16	3	17	18	5	38	34	8	325	306	84	3rd, Smythe Div.	Lost Div. Semi-Final
1987-88	80	28	8	4	16	17	7	44	25	11	363	288	99	**2nd, Smythe Div.**	**Won Stanley Cup**
1986-87	80	29	6	5	21	18	1	50	24	6	372	284	106	**1st, Smythe Div.**	**Won Stanley Cup**
1985-86	80	32	6	2	24	11	5	56	17	7	426	310	119	1st, Smythe Div.	Lost Div. Final
1984-85	80	26	7	7	23	13	4	49	20	11	401	298	109	**1st, Smythe Div.**	**Won Stanley Cup**
1983-84	80	31	5	4	26	13	1	57	18	5	446	314	119	**1st, Smythe Div.**	**Won Stanley Cup**
1982-83	80	25	9	6	22	12	6	47	21	12	424	315	106	1st, Smythe Div.	Lost Final
1981-82	80	31	5	4	17	12	11	48	17	15	417	295	111	1st, Smythe Div.	Lost Div. Semi-Final
1980-81	80	17	13	10	12	22	6	29	35	16	328	327	74	4th, Smythe Div.	Lost Quarter-Final
1979-80	80	17	14	9	11	25	4	28	39	13	301	322	69	4th, Smythe Div.	Lost Prelim. Round

A former NCAA All-Star with Lake Superior State, Doug Weight had his finest NHL season in 1993-94, leading the Oilers in assists (50) and points (74).

1994-95 Player Personnel

FORWARDS

	HT	WT	S	Place of Birth	Date	1993-94 Club
ALLISON, Scott	6-4	194	L	St. Boniface, Man.	4/22/72	Cape Breton
ARNOTT, Jason	6-3	195	R	Collingwood, Ont.	10/11/74	Edmonton
BONSIGNORE, Jason	6-4	208	R	Rochester, NY	4/15/76	Newmarket-Niagara Falls
BREEN, George	6-2	200	R	Webster, MA	8/3/73	Providence
BUCHBERGER, Kelly	6-2	210	L	Langenburg, Sask.	12/2/66	Edmonton
CIERNY, Jozef	6-2	185	L	Zvolen, Czech.	5/13/74	Edmonton-Cape Breton
CIGER, Zdeno	6-1	190	L	Martin, Czech.	10/19/69	Edmonton
CORSON, Shayne	6-1	200	L	Midland, Ont.	8/13/66	Edmonton
HOLDEMAN, Tom	6-2	205	R	Columbus, IN	11/8/70	South Carolina-Roanoke
HULBIG, Joe	6-3	212	L	Norwood, MA	9/29/73	Providence
INTRANUOVO, Ralph	5-8	185	L	East York, Ont.	12/11/73	Cape Breton
KERCH, Alexander	5-10	185	R	Arkhangelsk, USSR	3/16/67	Edmonton-Cape Breton
MALTBY, Kirk	6-0	180	L	Guelph, Ont.	12/22/72	Edmonton
MARCHANT, Todd	6-0	190	L	Buffalo, NY	8/12/73	U.S. National-U.S. Olympic-NYR-Edmonton-Cape Breton
McAMMOND, Dean	5-11	185	L	Grand Cache, Alta.	6/15/73	Edmonton-Cape Breton
OKSIUTA, Roman	6-3	229	L	Murmansk, USSR	8/21/70	Edmonton-Cape Breton
OLIVER, David	5-11	185	R	Sechelt, B.C.	4/17/71	U. of Michigan
PADEN, Kevin	6-3	175	L	Woodhaven, MI	2/12/75	Detroit (OHL)-Windsor
PEARSON, Scott	6-1	205	L	Cornwall, Ont.	12/19/69	Edmonton
SMYTH, Ryan	6-1	185	L	Banff, Alta.	2/21/76	Moose Jaw
THORNTON, Scott	6-2	200	L	London, Ont.	1/9/71	Edmonton-Cape Breton
VUJTEK, Vladimir	6-1	190	L	Ostrava, Czech.	2/17/72	Edmonton
VYBORNY, David	5-10	174	L	Jihlava, Czech.	1/22/75	Sparta Praha
WEIGHT, Doug	5-11	191	L	Warren, MI	1/21/71	Edmonton
WHITE, Peter	5-11	200	L	Montreal, Que.	3/15/69	Edmonton-Cape Breton
WRIGHT, Tyler	5-11	175	R	Canora, Sask.	4/6/73	Edmonton-Cape Breton
ZAVISHA, Brad	6-2	205	L	Hines Creek, Alta.	1/4/72	Edmonton-Cape Breton

DEFENSEMEN

	HT	WT	S	Place of Birth	Date	1993-94 Club
BAKULA, Martin	6-1	190	L	Kladno, Czech.	6/23/70	Cape Breton
BENNETT, Adam	6-4	206	R	Georgetown, Ont.	3/30/71	Edmonton-Cape Breton
DeVRIES, Greg	6-3	218	L	Sundridge, Ont.	1/4/73	Niagara Falls-Cape Breton
FERGUSON, Scott	6-1	195	L	Camrose, Alta.	1/6/73	Kamloops
HERBERS, Ian	6-4	225	L	Jasper, Alta.	7/18/67	Edmonton-Cape Breton
MARCHMENT, Bryan	6-1	198	L	Scarborough, Ont.	5/1/69	Chicago-Hartford
MARK, Gordon	6-4	218	R	Edmonton, Alta.	9/10/64	Cape Breton-Edmonton
MARTINI, Darcy	6-4	220	L	Castlegar, B.C.	1/30/69	Edmonton-Cape Breton
MIRONOV, Boris	6-3	196	R	Moscow, USSR	3/21/72	Winnipeg-Edmonton
NEILSON, Corey	6-5	207	R	Oromocto, N.B.	8/22/76	North Bay
OLAUSSON, Fredrik	6-2	195	R	Dadesjo, Sweden	10/5/66	Winnipeg-Edmonton
POPE, Brent	6-3	214	R	Hamilton, Ont.	2/20/73	Wheeling
STAJDUHAR, Nick	6-2	195	L	Kitchener, Ont.	12/6/74	London
SYMES, Brad	6-2	210	L	Edmonton, Alta.	4/26/76	Portland (WHL)
ZHURIK, Alexander	6-3	195	L	Minsk, USSR	5/29/75	Kingston

GOALTENDERS

	HT	WT	C	Place of Birth	Date	1993-94 Club
BRATHWAITE, Fred	5-7	170	L	Ottawa, Ont.	11/24/72	Edmonton-Cape Breton
COWLEY, Wayne	6-0	185	L	Scarborough, Ont.	12/4/64	Edmonton-Cape Breton
GAGE, Joaquin	6-0	200	L	Vancouver, B.C.	10/19/73	Prince Albert
LOUDER, Greg	6-1	185	L	Concord, MA	11/16/71	Notre Dame
PASSMORE, Steve	5-9	165	L	Thunder Bay, Ont.	1/29/73	Kamloops
RANFORD, Bill	5-10	170	L	Brandon, Man.	12/14/66	Edmonton
VERNER, Andrew	6-0	194	L	Weston, Ont.	11/20/72	Cape Breton

1993-94 Scoring

* – rookie

Regular Season

Pos	#	Player	Team	GP	G	A	Pts	+/–	PIM	PP	SH	GW	GT	S	%
C	39	Doug Weight	EDM	84	24	50	74	22–	47	4	1	1	0	188	12.8
C	7 *	Jason Arnott	EDM	78	33	35	68	1	104	10	0	4	1	194	17.0
R	8	Zdeno Ciger	EDM	84	22	35	57	11–	8	8	0	1	2	158	13.9
L	9	Shayne Corson	EDM	64	25	29	54	8–	118	11	0	3	1	171	14.6
D	21	Igor Kravchuk	EDM	81	12	38	50	12–	16	5	0	2	0	197	6.1
D	2	Bob Beers	T.B.	16	1	5	6	11–	12	1	0	0	0	35	2.9
			EDM	66	10	27	37	11–	74	5	0	0	1	152	6.6
			TOTAL	82	11	32	43	22–	86	6	0	0	1	187	5.9
L	33	Scott Pearson	EDM	72	19	18	37	4–	165	3	0	7	0	160	11.9
D	15	Fredrik Olausson	WPG	18	2	5	7	3–	10	1	0	0	0	41	4.9
			EDM	55	9	19	28	4–	20	6	0	1	0	85	10.6
			TOTAL	73	11	24	35	7–	30	7	0	1	0	126	8.7
R	12	Steven Rice	EDM	63	17	15	32	10–	36	6	0	1	1	129	13.2
D	20 *	Boris Mironov	WPG	65	7	22	29	29–	96	5	0	0	1	122	5.7
			EDM	14	0	2	2	4–	14	0	0	0	0	23	.0
			TOTAL	79	7	24	31	33–	110	5	0	0	1	145	4.8
D	10	Ilya Byakin	EDM	44	8	20	28	3–	30	6	0	3	0	51	15.7
C	37 *	Dean McAmmond	EDM	45	6	21	27	12	16	2	0	0	0	52	11.5
C	25	Mike Stapleton	PIT	58	7	4	11	4–	18	3	0	0	0	59	11.9
			EDM	23	5	9	14	1–	28	1	0	0	1	43	11.6
			TOTAL	81	12	13	25	5–	46	4	0	0	1	102	11.8
R	16	Kelly Buchberger	EDM	84	3	18	21	20–	199	0	0	0	0	93	3.2
R	18 *	Kirk Maltby	EDM	68	11	8	19	2–	74	0	1	1	0	89	12.4
L	23	Vladimir Vujtek	EDM	40	4	15	19	7–	14	1	0	0	0	66	6.1
L	34 *	Brent Grieve	NYI	3	0	0	0	0	7	0	0	0	0	1	.0
			EDM	24	13	5	18	4	14	4	0	0	1	53	24.5
			TOTAL	27	13	5	18	4	21	4	0	0	1	54	24.1
C	17	Scott Thornton	EDM	61	4	7	11	15–	104	0	0	0	0	65	6.2
L	29	Louie Debrusk	EDM	48	4	6	10	9–	185	0	0	0	0	27	14.8
D	35 *	Adam Bennett	EDM	48	3	6	9	8–	49	1	0	0	0	57	5.3
L	27 *	Peter White	EDM	26	3	5	8	1	2	0	0	0	0	17	17.6
R	26	Shjon Podein	EDM	28	3	5	8	3–	8	0	0	0	0	26	11.5
D	22	Luke Richardson	EDM	69	2	6	8	13–	131	0	0	0	0	92	2.2
R	28 *	Roman Oksiuta	EDM	10	1	2	3	1–	4	0	0	0	0	18	5.6
D	6	Ian Herbers	EDM	22	0	2	2	6–	32	0	0	0	0	16	.0
G	30	Bill Ranford	EDM	71	0	2	2	0	2	0	0	0	0	0	.0
C	36 *	Todd Marchant	NYR	1	0	0	0	1–	0	0	0	0	0	1	.0
			EDM	3	0	1	1	1–	2	0	0	0	0	5	.0
			TOTAL	4	0	1	1	2–	2	0	0	0	0	6	.0
D	32	Gordon Mark	EDM	12	0	1	1	2–	43	0	0	0	0	8	.0
G	1	Wayne Cowley	EDM	1	0	0	0	0	0	0	0	0	0	0	.0
R	20 *	Jozef Cierny	EDM	1	0	0	0	1–	0	0	0	0	0	1	.0
D	20	Jeff Chychrun	EDM	2	0	0	0	1	0	0	0	0	0	2	.0
D	34 *	Darcy Martini	EDM	2	0	0	0	1–	6	0	0	0	0	1	.0
L	20 *	Bradley Zavisha	EDM	2	0	0	0	2–	0	0	0	0	0	1	.0
L	20 *	Marc Laforge	EDM	5	0	0	0	2–	21	0	0	0	0	0	.0
C	19 *	Tyler Wright	EDM	5	0	0	0	4–	2	0	0	0	0	2	.0
R	34	Alexander Kerch	EDM	5	0	0	0	8–	0	0	0	0	0	4	.0
G	31 *	Fred Brathwaite	EDM	19	0	0	0	0	0	0	0	0	0	0	.0

Goaltending

No.	Goaltender	GPI	Mins	Avg	W	L	T	EN	SO	GA	SA	S%
1	Wayne Cowley	1	57	3.16	0	1	0	0	0	3	35	.914
30	Bill Ranford	71	4070	3.48	22	34	11	8	1	236	2325	.898
31	* Fred Brathwaite	19	982	3.54	3	10	3	0	0	58	523	.889
	Totals	**84**	**5121**	**3.57**	**25**	**45**	**14**	**8**	**1**	**305**	**2891**	**.895**

Coach

BURNETT, STEPHEN GEORGE
Coach, Edmonton Oilers. Born in Port Perry, Ont., March 25, 1962.

George Burnett became the fifth head coach in Edmonton Oilers' history on August 2, 1994. Burnett spent the past two seasons as coach of the Oilers' AHL affiliate, the Cape Breton Oilers, and led the Maritime team to the Calder Cup championship in 1992-93.

After graduating from McGill University in 1985, where he compiled 146 points in 84 games as an All-Canadian center, Burnett began his coaching career in Port Perry and, later, Seneca College in Toronto. In 1989-90, he became an assistant coach with the Oshawa Generals and midway through the season, he was hired as the head coach of the OHL's Niagara Falls Thunder. After three seasons and two second place finishes with the Thunder, Burnett joined the Oilers organization as coach of the Cape Breton franchise.

At age 32, Burnett is the youngest coach in the NHL.

Coaching Record

			Regular Season					Playoffs			
Season	Team	Games	W	L	T	%	Games	W	L	%
1989-90	Niagara Falls (OHL)	46	19	25	2	.435	16	9	7	.563
1990-91	Niagara Falls (OHL)	66	39	18	9	.659	14	8	6	.571
1991-92	Niagara Falls (OHL)	66	39	23	4	.621	17	9	8	.529
1992-93	Cape Breton (AHL)	80	36	32	12	.525	16	14	2	.875
1993-94	Cape Breton (AHL)	80	32	35	13	.481	5	1	4	.200

General Managers' History

Larry Gordon, 1979-80; Glen Sather, 1980-81 to date.

Coaching History

Glen Sather, 1979-80; Bryan Watson and Glen Sather, 1980-81; Glen Sather, 1981-82 to 1988-89; John Muckler, 1989-90 to 1990-91; Ted Green, 1991-92 to 1992-93; Ted Green and Glen Sather, 1993-94; George Burnett, 1994-95.

Captains' History

Ron Chipperfield, 1979-80; Blair MacDonald and Lee Fogolin, 1980-81; Lee Fogolin, 1981-82 to 1982-83; Wayne Gretzky, 1983-84 to 1987-88; Mark Messier, 1988-89 to 1990-91; Kevin Lowe, 1991-92; Craig MacTavish, 1992-93 to 1993-94.

Retired Numbers

3	Al Hamilton	1972-1980

Club Records

Team

(Figures in brackets for season records are games played)

Most Points	119	1983-84 (80) 1985-86 (80)
Most Wins	57	1983-84 (80)
Most Ties	16	1980-81 (80)
Most Losses	50	1992-93 (84)
Most Goals	*446	1983-84 (80)
Most Goals Against	327	1980-81 (80)
Fewest Points	60	1992-93 (84)
Fewest Wins	25	1993-94 (84)
Fewest Ties	5	1983-84 (80)
Fewest Losses	17	1981-82 (80) 1985-86 (80)
Fewest Goals	242	1992-93 (84)
Fewest Goals Against	272	1990-91 (80)

Longest Winning Streak

Over-all	8	Five times
Home	8	Jan. 19-Feb. 22/85; Feb. 24-Apr. 2/86
Away	8	Dec. 9/86-Jan. 17/87

Longest Undefeated Streak

Over-all	15	Oct. 11-Nov. 9/84 (12 wins, 3 ties)
Home	14	Nov. 15/89-Jan. 6/90 (11 wins, 3 ties)
Away	9	Jan. 17-Mar. 2/82 (6 wins, 3 ties) Nov. 23/82-Jan. 18/83 (7 wins, 2 ties)

Longest Losing Streak

Over-all	11	Oct. 16-Nov. 7/93
Home	9	Oct. 16-Nov. 24/93
Away	9	Nov. 25-Dec. 30/80

Longest Winless Streak

Over-all	14	Oct. 11-Nov. 7/93 (13 losses, 1 tie)
Home	9	Oct. 16-Nov. 24/93 (9 losses)
Away	9	Three times
Most Shutouts, Season	4	1987-88 (80)
Most PIM, Season	2,173	1987-88 (80)
Most Goals, Game	13	Nov. 19/83 (NJ 4 at Edm. 13) Nov. 8/85 (Van. 0 at Edm. 13)

Individual

Most Seasons	13	Kevin Lowe
Most Games	966	Kevin Lowe
Most Goals, Career	583	Wayne Gretzky
Most Assists, Career	1,086	Wayne Gretzky
Most Points, Career	1,669	Wayne Gretzky (583 goals, 1,086 assists)
Most PIM, Career	1,291	Kevin McClelland
Most Shutouts, Career	9	Grant Fuhr
Longest Consecutive Games Streak	521	Craig MacTavish (Oct. 11/86-Jan. 2/93)
Most Goals, Season	*92	Wayne Gretzky (1981-82)
Most Assists, Season	*163	Wayne Gretzky (1985-86)
Most Points, Season	*215	Wayne Gretzky (1985-86) (52 goals, 163 assists)
Most PIM, Season	286	Steve Smith (1987-88)
Most Points, Defenseman, Season	138	Paul Coffey (1985-86) (48 goals, 90 assists)
Most Points, Center, Season	*215	Wayne Gretzky (1985-86) (52 goals, 163 assists)
Most Points, Right Wing, Season	135	Jari Kurri (1984-85) (71 goals, 64 assists)
Most Points, Left Wing, Season	106	Mark Messier (1982-83) (48 goals, 58 assists)
Most Points, Rookie, Season	75	Jari Kurri (1980-81) (32 goals, 43 assists)
Most Shutouts, Season	4	Grant Fuhr (1987-88)
Most Goals, Game	5	Wayne Gretzky (Feb. 18/81, Dec. 30/81, Dec. 15/84, Dec. 6/87) Jari Kurri (Nov. 19/83) Pat Hughes (Feb. 3/84)
Most Assists, Game	*7	Wayne Gretzky (Feb. 15/80; Dec. 11/85; Feb. 14/86)
Most Points, Game	8	Wayne Gretzky (Nov. 19/83) Paul Coffey (Mar. 14/86) Wayne Gretzky (Jan. 4/84)

* NHL Record.

All-time Record vs. Other Clubs

Regular Season

	At Home						On Road						Total					
	GP	W	L	T	GF	GA	PTS	GP	W	L	T	GF	GA	PTS	GP	W	L	T	GF	GA	PTS
Anaheim	3	0	3	0	6	13	0	3	1	2	0	7	10	2	6	1	5	0	13	23	2
Boston	22	8	11	3	76	76	19	23	4	17	2	63	107	10	45	12	28	5	139	183	29
Buffalo	22	16	4	2	97	59	34	23	9	9	5	90	95	23	45	25	13	7	187	154	57
Calgary	54	28	18	8	231	197	64	54	19	29	6	198	254	44	108	47	47	14	429	451	108
Chicago	25	14	10	1	112	93	29	24	9	12	3	101	101	21	49	23	22	4	213	194	50
Dallas	24	15	3	6	122	79	36	25	12	8	5	91	91	29	49	27	11	11	213	170	65
Detroit	24	13	7	4	120	98	30	24	13	9	2	107	92	28	48	26	16	6	227	190	58
Florida	1	0	1	0	3	5	0	1	0	1	0	4	4	1	2	0	1	1	7	9	1
Hartford	23	17	3	3	102	67	37	22	9	9	4	83	94	22	45	26	12	7	185	161	59
Los Angeles	55	28	14	13	282	220	69	54	22	21	11	242	234	55	109	50	35	24	524	454	124
Montreal	23	13	10	0	82	71	26	22	6	13	3	67	79	15	45	19	23	3	149	150	41
New Jersey	25	13	7	5	124	97	31	25	12	11	2	88	88	26	50	25	18	7	212	185	57
NY Islanders	23	14	5	4	93	70	32	23	5	10	8	92	99	18	46	19	15	12	185	169	50
NY Rangers	22	10	11	1	86	77	21	22	12	6	4	90	87	28	44	22	17	5	176	164	49
Ottawa	2	1	1	0	10	9	2	2	0	2	0	5	7	0	4	1	3	0	15	16	2
Philadelphia	22	13	5	4	83	63	30	23	6	16	1	67	102	13	45	19	21	5	150	165	43
Pittsburgh	23	18	4	1	125	80	37	23	12	10	1	110	90	25	46	30	14	2	235	170	62
Quebec	22	17	5	0	125	66	34	22	13	7	2	107	88	28	44	30	12	2	232	154	62
St. Louis	24	13	8	3	105	93	29	24	10	10	4	104	99	24	48	23	18	7	209	192	53
San Jose	10	8	0	2	47	22	18	10	2	7	1	24	41	5	20	10	7	3	71	63	23
Tampa Bay	3	3	0	0	9	6	6	3	0	2	1	6	13	1	6	3	2	1	15	19	7
Toronto	24	14	5	5	123	81	33	24	12	10	2	118	99	26	48	26	15	7	241	180	59
Vancouver	54	39	11	4	279	168	82	55	28	21	6	235	211	62	109	67	32	10	514	379	144
Washington	22	9	9	4	88	78	22	22	8	12	2	81	96	18	44	17	21	6	169	174	40
Winnipeg	52	33	16	3	242	174	69	51	27	20	4	236	210	58	103	60	36	7	478	384	127
Totals	**604**	**357**	**171**	**76**	**2772**	**2062**	**790**	**604**	**251**	**273**	**80**	**2416**	**2491**	**582**	**1208**	**608**	**444**	**156**	**5188**	**4553**	**1372**

Calgary totals include Atlanta, 1979-80. Dallas totals include Minnesota, 1979-80 to 1992-93.
New Jersey totals include Colorado, 1979-80 to 1981-82.

Playoffs

	Series	W	L	GP	W	L	T	GF	GA	Last Mtg.	Round	Result
Boston	2	2	0	9	8	1	0	41	20	1990	F	W 4-1
Calgary	5	4	1	30	19	11	0	132	96	1991	DSF	W 4-3
Chicago	4	3	1	20	12	8	0	102	77	1992	CF	L 0-4
Dallas	2	1	1	9	5	4	0	36	30	1991	CF	L 1-4
Detroit	2	2	0	10	8	2	0	39	26	1988	CF	W 4-1
Los Angeles	7	5	2	36	24	12	0	154	127	1992	DSF	W 4-2
Montreal	1	1	0	3	3	0	0	15	6	1981	PR	W 3-0
NY Islanders	3	1	2	15	6	9	0	47	58	1984	F	W 4-1
Philadelphia	3	2	1	15	8	7	0	49	44	1987	F	W 4-3
Vancouver	2	2	0	9	7	2	0	35	20	1992	DF	W 4-2
Winnipeg	6	6	0	26	22	4	0	120	75	1990	DSF	W 4-3
Totals	**37**	**29**	**8**	**180**	**120**	**60**	**0**	**770**	**579**			

Playoff Results 1994-90

Year	Round	Opponent	Result	GF	GA
1992	CF	Chicago	L 0-4	8	21
	DF	Vancouver	W 4-2	18	15
	DSF	Los Angeles	W 4-2	23	18
1991	CF	Minnesota	L 1-4	14	20
	DF	Los Angeles	W 4-2	21	20
	DSF	Calgary	W 4-3	22	20
1990	**F**	**Boston**	**W 4-1**	**20**	**8**
	DF	Chicago	W 4-2	25	20
	DF	Los Angeles	W 4-0	24	10
	DSF	Winnipeg	W 4-3	24	22

Abbreviations: Round: F – Final;
CF – conference final; **CQF** – conference quarter-final;
CSF – conference semi-final; **DF** – division final;
DSF – division semi-final; **SF** – semi-final;
QF – quarter-final; **PR** – preliminary round.

1993-94 Results

Oct.	6		San Jose	3-2		9	at	Chicago	4-2
	8		NY Islanders	5-1		11	at	Dallas	2-5
	11	at	Vancouver	1-4		13	at	St. Louis	4-6
	13	at	Anaheim	3-4		15	at	Pittsburgh	3-4
	14	at	Los Angeles	4-4		18	at	Ottawa	3-4
	16		Vancouver	2-3		19	at	Buffalo	1-1
	18	at	Winnipeg	3-6		24		Vancouver	4-5
	20		Calgary	3-5		26		New Jersey	3-3
	22		Boston	1-3		28		St. Louis	2-3
	24		Washington	2-3		29		Dallas	3-5
	26	at	San Jose	1-3	Feb.	2		Los Angeles	6-4
	29		Buffalo	3-6		4		Chicago	1-3
	30	at	Calgary	1-4		6		Winnipeg	5-2
Nov.	3		Ottawa	5-7		7	at	Calgary	3-4
	6	at	St. Louis	5-6		9		Calgary	1-6
	7	at	Chicago	0-3		12		Hartford	2-5
	9	at	Detroit	4-2		13		Anaheim	3-6
	11	at	Boston	1-5		15	at	Washington	2-2
	13	at	Hartford	4-4		18	at	Detroit	1-5
	15	at	Toronto	5-5		19	at	Toronto	2-3
	17	at	Montreal	1-3		20		Toronto	6-3
	20		Toronto	2-3		25		Los Angeles	5-5
	21		Anaheim	2-4		27		Tampa Bay	3-2
	24		Chicago	1-3	Mar.	1	at	Vancouver	7-4
	27		Vancouver	2-1		3	at	San Jose	2-4
	29		Dallas	2-5		6	at	Anaheim	1-4
Dec.	1		Philadelphia	3-1		9		Florida	3-5
	5	at	Dallas	3-4		11		Detroit	4-2
	7	at	NY Islanders	4-4		16	at	Tampa Bay	4-4
	8	at	NY Rangers	1-1		18	at	Florida	4-4
	11		New Jersey	2-5		20	at	Quebec	5-3
	12	at	Philadelphia	2-1		23		NY Rangers	3-5
	15		Vancouver	7-2		25		Los Angeles	3-4
	17		San Jose	4-2		27	at	Pittsburgh	5-3
	19		St. Louis	1-4		31	at	Anaheim	3-2
	21	at	Vancouver	3-6	Apr.	2	at	Los Angeles	5-3
	22		Calgary	7-3		3	at	Los Angeles	1-6
	27		Winnipeg	6-0		6	at	Winnipeg	4-3
	29		Montreal	6-3		8		Anaheim	4-3
	30	at	Calgary	1-7		10		Detroit	4-3
Jan.	2		San Jose	4-4		13	at	San Jose	2-2
	7		Quebec	6-4		14	at	Los Angeles	2-2

Entry Draft
Selections 1994-80

1994
Pick
- 4 Jason Bonsignore
- 6 Ryan Smyth
- 32 Mike Watt
- 53 Corey Neilson
- 60 Brad Symes
- 79 Adam Copeland
- 95 Jussi Tarvainen
- 110 Jon Gaskins
- 136 Terry Marchant
- 160 Curtis Sheptak
- 162 Dmitri Shulga
- 179 Chris Wickenheiser
- 185 Rob Guinn
- 188 Jason Reid
- 214 Jeremy Jablonski
- 266 Ladislav Benysek

1993
Pick
- 7 Jason Arnott
- 16 Nick Stajduhar
- 33 David Vyborny
- 59 Kevin Paden
- 60 Alexander Kerch
- 111 Miroslav Satan
- 163 Alexander Zhurik
- 189 Martin Bakula
- 215 Brad Norton
- 241 Oleg Maltsev
- 267 Ilja Byakin

1992
Pick
- 13 Joe Hulbig
- 37 Martin Reichel
- 61 Simon Roy
- 65 Kirk Maltby
- 96 Ralph Intranuovo
- 109 Joaquin Gage
- 157 Steve Gibson
- 181 Kyuin Shim
- 190 Colin Schmidt
- 205 Marko Tuomainen
- 253 Bryan Rasmussen

1991
Pick
- 12 Tyler Wright
- 20 Martin Rucinsky
- 34 Andrew Verner
- 56 George Breen
- 78 Mario Nobili
- 93 Ryan Haggerty
- 144 David Oliver
- 166 Gary Kitching
- 210 Vegar Barlie
- 232 Evgeny Belosheikin
- 254 Juha Riihijarvi

1989
Pick
- 17 Scott Allison
- 38 Alexandre Legault
- 59 Joe Crowley
- 67 Joel Blain
- 101 Greg Louder
- 122 Keijo Sailynoja
- 143 Mike Power
- 164 Roman Mejzlik
- 185 Richard Zemlicka
- 206 Petr Korinek
- 227 invalid claim
- 248 Sami Nuutinen

1989
Pick
- 15 Jason Soules
- 36 Richard Borgo
- 78 Josef Beranek
- 92 Peter White
- 120 Anatoli Semenov
- 140 Davis Payne
- 141 Sergei Yashin
- 162 Darcy Martini
- 225 Roman Bozek

1988
Pick
- 19 Francois Leroux
- 39 Petro Koivunen
- 53 Trevor Sim
- 61 Collin Bauer
- 82 Cam Brauer
- 103 Don Martin
- 124 Len Barrie
- 145 Mike Glover
- 166 Shjon Podein
- 187 Tom Cole
- 208 Vladimir Zubkov
- 229 Darin MacDonald
- 250 Tim Tisdale

1987
Pick
- 21 Peter Soberlak
- 42 Brad Werenka
- 63 Geoff Smith
- 64 Peter Eriksson
- 105 Shaun Van Allen
- 126 Radek Toupal
- 147 Tomas Srsen
- 168 Age Ellingsen
- 189 Gavin Armstrong
- 210 Mike Tinkham
- 231 Jeff Pauletti
- 241 Jesper Duus
- 252 Igor Vyazmikin

1986
Pick
- 21 Kim Issel
- 42 Jamie Nichols
- 63 Ron Shudra
- 84 Dan Currie
- 105 David Haas
- 126 Jim Ennis
- 147 Ivan Matulik
- 168 Nicolas Beaulieu
- 189 Mike Greenlay
- 210 Matt Lanza
- 231 Mojmir Bozik
- 252 Tony Hand

1985
Pick
- 20 Scott Metcalfe
- 41 Todd Carnelley
- 62 Mike Ware
- 104 Tomas Kapusta
- 125 Brian Tessier
- 146 Shawn Tyers
- 167 Tony Fairfield
- 188 Kelly Buchberger
- 209 Mario Barbe
- 230 Peter Headon
- 251 John Haley

1984
Pick
- 21 Selmar Odelein
- 42 Daryl Reaugh
- 63 Todd Norman
- 84 Rich Novak
- 105 Richard Lambert
- 106 Emanuel Viveiros
- 126 Ivan Dornic
- 147 Heikki Riihijarvi
- 168 Todd Ewen
- 209 Joel Curtis
- 229 Simon Wheeldon
- 250 Darren Gani

1983
Pick
- 19 Jeff Beukeboom
- 40 Mike Golden
- 60 Mike Flanagan
- 80 Esa Tikkanen
- 120 Don Barber
- 140 Dale Derkatch
- 160 Ralph Vos
- 180 Dave Roach
- 200 Warren Yadlowski
- 220 John Miner
- 240 Steve Woodburn

1982
Pick
- 20 Jim Playfair
- 41 Steve Graves
- 62 Brent Loney
- 83 Jaroslav Pouzar
- 104 Dwayne Boettger
- 125 Raimo Summanen
- 146 Brian Small
- 167 Dean Clark
- 188 Ian Wood
- 209 Grant Dion
- 230 Chris Smith
- 251 Jeff Crawford

1981
Pick
- 8 Grant Fuhr
- 29 Todd Strueby
- 71 Paul Houck
- 92 Phil Drouillard
- 111 Steve Smith
- 113 Marc Habscheid
- 155 Mike Sturgeon
- 176 Miloslav Horava
- 197 Gord Sherven

1980
Pick
- 6 Paul Coffey
- 48 Shawn Babcock
- 69 Jari Kurri
- 90 Walt Poddubny
- 111 Mike Winther
- 132 Andy Moog
- 153 Rob PolmanTuin
- 174 Lars-Gunnar Pettersson

Club Directory

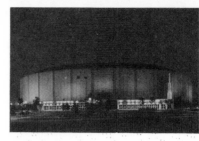

Edmonton Coliseum
7424 – 118 Avenue
Edmonton, Alberta T5B 4M9
Phone **403/474-8561**
Ticketing 403/471-2191
FAX 403/477-9625
Capacity: TBA

Owner/Governor . . . . Peter Pocklington
Alternate Governor . . . . Glen Sather
General Counsel . . . . Lorne Ruzicka
President/General Manager . . . . Glen Sather
Exec. Vice-President/Assistant G.M. . . . . Bruce MacGregor
Assistant to the President . . . . Ted Green
Coach . . . . George Burnett
Assistant Coaches . . . . Ron Low, Kevin Primeau
Director of Player Personnel/Chief Scout . . . . Barry Fraser
Hockey Operations . . . . Kevin Prendergast
Coordinator of Development . . . . Curtis Brackenbury
Scouting Staff . . . . Ed Chadwick, Lorne Davis, Bob Freeman,
Harry Howell, Curly Reeves, Brad Smith,
Kent Nilsson, Bob McCammon
Executive Secretary . . . . Betsy Freedman
Receptionist/Secretary . . . . Melahna Matan

Medical and Training Staff
Athletic Trainer/Therapist . . . . Ken Lowe
Athletic Trainer . . . . Barrie Stafford
Assistant Trainer . . . . Lyle Kulchisky
Massage Therapist . . . . Stewart Poirier
Team Medical Chief of Staff / Director of Glen
Sather Sports Medicine Clinic . . . . Dr. David C. Reid
Team Physicians . . . . Dr. Don Groot, Dr. Boris Boyko
Team Dentists . . . . Dr. Tony Sneazwell, Dr. Brian Nord
Fitness Consultant . . . . Dr. Art Quinney
Physical Therapy Consultant . . . . Dr. Dave Magee
Team Acupuncturist . . . . Dr. Steven Aung
Sports Psychologist Consultant . . . . Dr. Murray Smith

Finance
Vice-President, Finance . . . . Werner Baum
Accountants . . . . Ellie Merrick, Allison Coward
Executive Secretary . . . . Lisa Colby

Public Relations
Director of Public Relations . . . . Bill Tuele
Coordinator of Publications and Statistics . . . . Steve Knowles
Director of Community Relations/Special Events . . . . Trish Kerr
Public Relations Secretary . . . . Fiona Liew

Marketing
Director of Marketing . . . . Stew MacDonald
Marketing Representative/Properties Mgr. . . . . Darrell Holowaychuk
Marketing Representative . . . . Brad MacGregor
Sales Representative . . . . Dave Semenko
Marketing Representative . . . . Skip Krake
Marketing Secretary . . . . Heather Hansch
Merchandising Clerks . . . . Julia Slade, Kerri Hill
Warehouse Supervisor . . . . Ray MacDonald
Warehouse Assistant . . . . Jim Groff

Ticketing
Director of Ticketing Operations . . . . Sheila MacDonald
Ticketing Operations . . . . Sheila McCaskill, Marcia Godwin,
Marcella Kinsman

Miscellaneous
Team Administration Offices . . . . Edmonton Coliseum, Edmonton, Alta.,
Canada T5B 4M9
Location of Press Box . . . . East Side at top (Radio/TV)
West Side at top (Media)
Dimensions of Rink . . . . 200 feet by 85 feet
Club Colours . . . . Blue, Orange, White
Team Uniforms . . . . Home: Base colour white, trimmed with
blue and orange
Away: Base colour blue, trimmed with
white and orange
Training Camp Site . . . . Banff Recreation Centre, Banff, Alberta;
Northlands Agricom, Edmonton, Alberta
Television Channel . . . . CFRN (Channel 3, Cable 2)
CBXT TV (Channel 5, Cable 4)
Radio Station . . . . CFCW (790 AM)

General Manager

SATHER, GLEN CAMERON
President and General Manager, Edmonton Oilers.
Born in High River, Alta., Sept. 2, 1943.

The architect of the Edmonton Oilers' five Stanley Cup championships, Glen Sather is one of the most respected administrators in the NHL. The 1994-95 season is his 15th as general manager of the Oilers and his 19th with Edmonton since joining the organization in August of 1976.

Sather was the Oilers' coach and general manager for nine of the team's first ten seasons and returned to the coaching ranks in 1993-94, relieving Ted Green in late November. In 60 games, Sather guided the team to a 22-27-11 record. In 842 regular season games as coach, Sather has compiled a 464-268-110 record for a .616 winning percentage. He ranks seventh on the NHL's all-time coaching list while his .706 winning percentage in the playoffs is the best mark in NHL history.

Sather played for six different teams during his nine-year NHL career, registering 80 goals, 113 points in 660 games.

NHL Coaching Record

			Regular Season				Playoffs			
Season	Team	Games	W	L	T	%	Games	W	L	%
1979-80	Edmonton (NHL)	80	28	39	13	.431	3	0	3	.000
1980-81	Edmonton (NHL)	62	25	26	11	.492	9	5	4	.555
1981-82	Edmonton (NHL)	80	48	17	15	.694	5	2	3	.400
1982-83	Edmonton (NHL)	80	47	21	12	.663	16	11	5	.687
1983-84	Edmonton (NHL)	80	57	18	5	.744	19	15	4	.789*
1984-85	Edmonton (NHL)	80	49	20	11	.681	18	15	3	.833*
1985-86	Edmonton (NHL)	80	56	17	7	.744	10	6	4	.600
1986-87	Edmonton (NHL)	80	50	24	6	.663	21	16	5	.762*
1987-88	Edmonton (NHL)	80	44	25	11	.619	18	16	2	.889*
1988-89	Edmonton (NHL)	80	38	34	8	.538	7	3	4	.429
1993-94	Edmonton (NHL)	60	22	27	11	.458	....	....	....	....
	NHL Totals	**842**	**464**	**268**	**110**	**.616**	**126**	**89**	**37**	**.706**

* Stanley Cup win.

Florida Panthers

1993-94 Results: 33W-34L-17T 83PTS. Fifth, Atlantic Division

Schedule

Oct.	Tues.	4	Philadelphia		Mon.	9	at NY Rangers
	Thur.	6	St. Louis		Wed.	11	at NY Islanders
	Sat.	8	NY Rangers*		Thur.	12	at Philadelphia
	Mon.	10	at Boston*		Sat.	14	at Montreal
	Wed.	12	at Hartford		Tues.	17	New Jersey
	Fri.	14	at Detroit		Mon.	23	Tampa Bay
	Sun.	16	New Jersey		Thur.	26	Calgary
	Wed.	19	Toronto		Sat.	28	at Hartford*
	Fri.	21	at Buffalo		Mon.	30	at Boston
	Sat.	22	at NY Islanders		Tues.	31	NY Islanders
	Tues.	25	Los Angeles	Feb.	Thur.	2	Montreal
	Thur.	27	Buffalo		Sat.	4	at Washington
Nov.	Wed.	2	at Edmonton		Sun.	5	Dallas
	Sat.	5	at Vancouver		Tues.	7	at Pittsburgh
	Sun.	6	at Calgary		Thur.	9	at Buffalo
	Wed.	9	NY Islanders		Sat.	11	Hartford
	Fri.	11	Edmonton		Sun.	12	Pittsburgh
	Sun.	13	Boston		Wed.	15	NY Islanders
	Thur.	17	Detroit		Fri.	17	Buffalo
	Sat.	19	Winnipeg		Sun.	19	Boston
	Mon.	21	at Quebec		Thur.	23	Montreal
	Wed.	23	at Montreal		Sat.	25	at Ottawa
	Sat.	26	at Ottawa		Mon.	27	at Montreal
	Sun.	27	at NY Rangers				(in Hamilton)
	Wed.	30	at Tampa Bay		Tues.	28	at NY Rangers
Dec.	Thur.	1	San Jose	Mar.	Thur.	2	at Philadelphia
	Sat.	3	Chicago		Sat.	4	at New Jersey*
	Mon.	5	Tampa Bay		Sun.	5	Anaheim
	Thur.	8	Ottawa		Wed.	8	Quebec
	Sat.	10	Quebec		Fri.	10	at Washington
	Sun.	11	at Chicago		Sun.	12	Detroit
	Tues.	13	at Quebec				(in Denver)
	Thur.	15	at New Jersey		Wed.	15	Washington
	Sat.	17	at Toronto		Sat.	18	Philadelphia
	Tues.	20	Washington		Mon.	20	at Los Angeles
	Thur.	22	Pittsburgh		Tues.	21	at Anaheim
	Tues.	27	Philadelphia		Thur.	23	at San Jose
	Thur.	29	at Washington		Sun.	26	Tampa Bay*
	Fri.	30	at New Jersey		Wed.	29	Hartford
Jan.	Sun.	1	NY Rangers*	Apr.	Sun.	2	at Tampa Bay*
	Tues.	3	Vancouver		Wed.	5	Ottawa
	Thur.	5	at Pittsburgh		Fri.	7	at Winnipeg
	Sat.	7	at St. Louis		Sun.	9	at Dallas*

* Denotes afternoon game.

Home Starting Times:

Weeknights	7:30 p.m.
Saturday nights	7:30 p.m.
Saturday matinees	1:00 p.m.
Sunday nights	6:00 p.m.
Sunday matinees	12:00 p.m.
Except Sat. Dec. 10	7:00 p.m.
Sun. Feb. 5	8:00 p.m.
Sun. Mar. 5	7:30 p.m.

Franchise date: June 14, 1993

2nd NHL Season

ATLANTIC DIVISION

Year-by-Year Record

Season	GP	Home			Road			Overall					Pts.	Finished		Playoff Result
		W	L	T	W	L	T	W	L	T	GF	GA				
1993-94	84	15	18	9	18	16	8	33	34	17	233	233	83	5th,	Atlantic Div.	Out of Playoffs

The excellent goaltending of John Vanbiesbrouck (21 wins, 2.53 GAA) kept the Florida Panthers in the playoff hunt until the final days of the 1993-94 season.

1994-95 Player Personnel

FORWARDS	HT	WT	S	Place of Birth	Date	1993-94 Club
BARNES, Stu	5-11	180	R	Edmonton, Alta.	12/25/70	Winnipeg-Florida
BARRAULT, Doug	6-2	205	R	Golden, B.C.	4/21/70	Florida-Cincinnati
BELANGER, Jesse	6-0	170	R	St. Georges de Beauce, Que	6/15/69	Florida
BOUDRIAS, Jasson	6-0	200	R	Val D'or, Que.	2/16/76	Laval
CABANA, Chad	6-1	200	L	Bonnyville, Alta.	10/1/74	Tri-City
CIRONE, Jason	5-9	185	L	Toronto, Ont.	2/21/71	Cincinnati-Birmingham
DANIELS, Jeff	6-1	200	L	Oshawa, Ont.	6/24/68	Pittsburgh-Florida
FITZGERALD, Tom	6-1	195	R	Melrose, MA	8/28/68	Florida
GREENLAW, Jeff	6-1	230	L	Toronto, Ont.	2/28/68	Florida-Cincinnati
HOUGH, Mike	6-1	192	L	Montreal, Que.	2/6/63	Florida
HULL, Jody	6-2	200	R	Cambridge, Ont.	2/2/69	Florida
KUDELSKI, Bob	6-1	200	R	Springfield, MA	3/3/64	Ottawa-Florida
LEACH, Jamie	6-1	205	R	Winnipeg, Man.	8/25/69	Florida-Cincinnati
LEHTERA, Tero	6-1	185	R	Finland	4/21/72	Espoo
LINDEN, Jamie	6-3	185	R	Medicine Hat, Alta.	7/19/72	Cincinnati-Birmingham
LINDSAY, Bill	5-11	185	L	Big Fork, MT	5/17/71	Florida
LOMAKIN, Andrei	5-10	175	L	Voskresensk, USSR	4/3/64	Florida
LOWRY, Dave	6-1	195	L	Sudbury, Ont.	2/14/65	Florida
McCAULEY, Bill	6-0	173	L	Detroit, MI	4/20/75	Detroit (OHL)
MELLANBY, Scott	6-1	205	R	Montreal, Que.	6/11/66	Florida
MONTREUIL, Eric	6-1	170	L	Verdun, Que.	5/18/75	Beauport
NEMIROVSKY, David	6-2	176	R	Toronto, Ont.	8/1/76	Ottawa (OHL)
NIEDERMAYER, Rob	6-2	200	L	Cassiar, B.C.	12/28/74	Florida
PODOLLAN, Jason	6-1	181	R	Vernon, B.C.	2/18/76	Spokane
SKRUDLAND, Brian	6-0	196	L	Peace River, Alta.	7/31/63	Florida
SMYTH, Brad	6-0	200	R	Ottawa, Ont.	3/13/73	Cincinnati-Birmingham
TOMLINSON, Dave	5-11	177	L	North Vancouver, B.C.	5/8/69	Winnipeg-Moncton
WASHBURN, Steve	6-2	185	L	Ottawa, Ont.	4/10/75	Ottawa (OHL)
DEFENSEMEN						
ANDERSSON, Peter	6-0	196	L	Orebro, Sweden	8/29/65	NY Rangers-Florida
ARMSTRONG, Chris	6-0	184	L	Regina, Sask.	6/26/75	Moose Jaw-Cincinnati
BENNING, Brian	6-0	195	L	Edmonton, Alta.	6/10/66	Florida
BOUGHNER, Bob	6-0	201	R	Windsor, Ont.	3/8/71	Adirondack
BROWN, Keith	6-1	192	R	Corner Brook, Nfld.	5/6/60	Florida
CIRELLA, Joe	6-3	210	R	Hamilton, Ont.	5/9/63	Florida
DOYLE, Trevor	6-3	204	R	Ottawa, Ont.	1/1/74	Kingston
EAKINS, Dallas	6-2	195	L	Dade City, FL	2/27/67	Florida-Cincinnati
GERIS, Dave	6-5	221	L	North Bay, Ont.	6/7/76	Windsor
GUSTAFFSON, Per	6-1	187	L	Sweden	4/6/70	HV-71
JOVANOVSKI, Ed	6-2	205	L	Windsor, Ont.	6/26/76	Windsor
LAUS, Paul	6-1	212	R	Beamsville, Ont.	9/26/70	Florida
MOLLER, Randy	6-2	207	R	Red Deer, Alta.	8/23/63	Buffalo
MURPHY, Gord	6-2	195	R	Willowdale, Ont.	3/23/67	Florida
NASREDDINE, Alain	6-1	201	L	Montreal, Que.	7/10/75	Chicoutimi
O'DETTE, Matt	6-4	205	R	East York, Ont.	11/9/75	Kitchener
RICHER, Stephane J. G.	5-11	190	R	Hull, Que.	4/28/66	Florida-Cincinnati
SEVERYN, Brent	6-2	210	L	Vegreville, Alta.	2/22/66	Florida
SMITH, Geoff	6-3	200	L	Edmonton, Alta.	3/7/69	Edmonton-Florida
TJALLDEN, Mikael	6-2	194	L	Ornskoldsvik, Sweden	2/16/75	Sundsvall-Timra
WARRENER, Rhett	6-1	209	L	Shaunavon, Sask.	1/27/76	Saskatoon

GOALTENDERS	HT	WT	C	Place of Birth	Date	1993-94 Club
CHABOT, Frederic	5-11	177	R	Hebertville-Station, Que.	2/12/68	Mtl-Fred-Vegas-Phi-Her
FITZPATRICK, Mark	6-2	190	L	Toronto, Ont.	11/13/68	Florida
LORENZ, Danny	5-10	183	L	Murrayville, B.C.	12/12/69	Salt Lake-Springfield
MacDONALD, Todd	6-0	155	L	Charlottetown, P.E.I.	7/5/75	Tacoma
VANBIESBROUCK, John	5-8	172	L	Detroit, MI	9/4/63	Florida
WEEKES, Kevin	6-0	158	L	Toronto, Ont.	4/4/75	Owen Sound

1993-94 Scoring

* – rookie

Regular Season

Pos	#	Player	Team	GP	G	A	Pts	+/–	PIM	PP	SH	GW	GT	S	%
R	22	Bob Kudelski	OTT	42	26	15	41	25–	14	12	0	1	0	127	20.5
			FLA	44	14	15	29	8–	10	5	0	2	1	124	11.3
			TOTAL	86	40	30	70	33–	24	17	0	3	1	251	15.9
R	27	Scott Mellanby	FLA	80	30	30	60	0	149	17	0	4	1	204	14.7
C	26	* Jesse Belanger	FLA	70	17	33	50	4–	16	11	0	3	1	104	16.3
C	14	Stu Barnes	WPG	18	5	4	9	1–	8	2	0	0	0	24	20.8
			FLA	59	18	20	38	5	30	6	1	3	0	148	12.2
			TOTAL	77	23	24	47	4	38	8	1	3	0	172	13.4
L	19	Andrei Lomakin	FLA	76	19	28	47	1	26	3	0	2	0	139	13.7
D	5	Gord Murphy	FLA	84	14	29	43	11–	71	9	0	2	3	172	8.1
C	20	Brian Skrudland	FLA	79	15	25	40	13	136	0	2	1	0	110	13.6
L	10	Dave Lowry	FLA	80	15	22	37	4–	64	3	0	3	1	122	12.3
R	21	Tom Fitzgerald	FLA	83	18	14	32	3–	54	0	3	1	0	144	12.5
D	7	Brian Benning	FLA	73	6	24	30	7–	107	2	0	0	0	112	5.4
L	18	Mike Hough	FLA	78	6	23	29	3	62	0	1	1	0	106	5.7
R	12	Jody Hull	FLA	69	13	13	26	6	8	0	1	5	1	100	13.0
C	44	* Rob Niedermayer	FLA	65	9	17	26	11–	51	3	0	2	0	67	13.4
L	11	Bill Lindsay	FLA	84	6	6	12	2–	97	0	0	0	0	90	6.7
D	4	Keith Brown	FLA	51	4	8	12	11	60	1	0	0	0	52	7.7
D	24	Brent Severyn	FLA	67	4	7	11	1–	156	1	0	1	0	93	4.3
D	2	Joe Cirella	FLA	63	1	9	10	8	99	0	0	0	0	63	1.6
R	17	Mike Foligno	TOR	4	0	0	0	0	4	0	0	0	0	3	.0
			FLA	39	4	5	9	7	49	0	0	0	0	32	12.5
			TOTAL	43	4	5	9	7	53	0	0	0	0	35	11.4
D	25	Geoff Smith	EDM	21	0	3	3	10–	12	0	0	0	0	23	.0
			FLA	56	1	5	6	3–	38	0	0	0	0	44	2.3
			TOTAL	77	1	8	9	13–	50	0	0	0	0	67	1.5
L	23	Jeff Daniels	PIT	63	3	5	8	1–	20	0	0	1	0	46	6.5
			FLA	7	0	0	0	0	0	0	0	0	0	6	.0
			TOTAL	70	3	5	8	1–	20	0	0	1	0	52	5.8
D	6	Peter Andersson	NYR	8	1	1	2	3–	2	0	1	1	0	10	10.0
			FLA	8	1	1	2	5–	0	0	0	0	0	11	9.1
			TOTAL	16	2	2	4	8–	2	0	1	1	0	21	9.5
D	3	* Paul Laus	FLA	39	2	0	2	9	109	0	0	1	0	15	13.3
L	28	* Patrick Lebeau	FLA	4	1	1	2	0	4	1	0	0	0	4	25.0
G	30	Mark Fitzpatrick	FLA	28	0	2	2	0	4	0	0	0	0	0	.0
R	9	Jamie Leach	FLA	2	1	0	1	2–	0	0	0	0	0	2	50.0
D	41	Stephane Richer	FLA	2	0	1	1	1–	0	0	0	0	0	3	.0
L	29	Jeff Greenlaw	FLA	4	0	1	1	1–	2	0	0	0	0	6	.0
D	8	Dallas Eakins	FLA	1	0	0	0	0	0	0	0	0	0	2	.0
C	16	* Len Barrie	FLA	2	0	0	0	2–	0	0	0	0	0	0	.0
G	33	Eldon Reddick	FLA	2	0	0	0	0	0	0	0	0	0	0	.0
R	15	* Doug Barrault	FLA	2	0	0	0	2–	0	0	0	0	0	2	.0
G	34	John Vanbiesbrouck	FLA	57	0	0	0	0	38	0	0	0	0	0	.0

Goaltending

No.	Goaltender	GPI	Mins	Avg	W	L	T	EN	SO	GA	SA	S%
34	John Vanbiesbrouck	57	3440	2.53	21	25	11	4	1	145	1912	.924
30	Mark Fitzpatrick	28	1603	2.73	12	8	6	3	1	73	844	.914
33	Eldon Reddick	2	80	6.00	0	1	0	0	0	8	45	.822
	Totals	**84**	**5144**	**2.72**	**33**	**34**	**17**	**7**	**2**	**233**	**2808**	**.917**

Right winger Scott Mellanby fired 30 goals and led the Panthers with 17 powerplay goals in 1993-94.

General Manager

MURRAY, BRYAN CLARENCE
General Manager, Florida Panthers.
Born in Shawville, Que., December 5, 1942.

Murray, 51, joins the Panthers after serving with the Detroit Red Wings from July 13, 1990 until June 3, 1994. When Murray first joined the Red Wings, he held the dual roles of coach and general manager, but on May 26, 1993, Murray relinquished his coaching duties to concentrate on his general manager's responsibilities.

During Murray's four-year stay in Detroit, the Red Wings finished first in their division twice, second once and third once. Last season, the Red Wings finished first in the newly created Central Division with a record of 46-30-8, good for a total of 100 points. It was the second season in a row in which the Wings reached the 100-point plateau.

In 328 games under Murray's control, the Wings won a total of 170 games while losing only 121 and tying 37 for an average of 43 wins and 93 points per season. In 1989-90, the season before Murray's arrival, the Wings failed to make the playoffs, posting a record of 28-38-14 and 70 points. In the four seasons before Murray, the Wings averaged only 34 wins in a season.

Prior to joining the Wings, Murray spent parts of nine seasons as head coach of the Washington Capitals. Murray began his coaching reign with the Caps on November 11, 1981 when he replaced Gary Green. Murray remained the head coach until January 15, 1990, when he was replaced by his brother Terry (currently the Flyers head coach). During his stay in Washington, Murray coached a total of 672 regular season games. He won 343, lost 246 and tied 83 for a winning percentage of .574.

In his seven full seasons behind the Capitals' bench (1982-83 through 1988-89) Murray's team finished first in the Patrick Division once, second five times and third once. His third place finish was in his first full season. His first place finish was the season before he was replaced.

In all, Murray has coached a total of 916 regular-season NHL games. His record is 467-337-112 with a winning percentage of .571.

NHL Coaching Record

		Regular Season					Playoffs			
Season	Team	Games	W	L	T	%	Games	W	L	%
1981-82	Washington (NHL)	76	25	28	13	.477	....	....	....	....
1982-83	Washington (NHL)	80	39	25	16	.588	4	1	3	.250
1983-84	Washington (NHL)	80	48	27	5	.631	8	4	4	.500
1984-85	Washington (NHL)	80	46	25	9	.631	5	2	3	.400
1985-86	Washington (NHL)	80	50	23	7	.669	9	5	4	.556
1986-87	Washington (NHL)	80	38	32	10	.538	7	3	4	.429
1987-88	Washington (NHL)	80	38	33	9	.531	14	7	7	.500
1988-89	Washington (NHL)	80	41	29	10	.575	6	2	4	.333
1989-90	Washington (NHL)	46	18	24	4	.435	....	....	....	....
1990-91	Detroit (NHL)	80	34	38	8	.475	7	3	4	.429
1991-92	Detroit (NHL)	80	43	25	12	.613	11	4	7	.364
1992-93	Detroit (NHL)	84	47	28	9	.613	7	3	4	.429
	NHL Totals	**916**	**467**	**337**	**112**	**.571**	**78**	**34**	**44**	**.436**

Club Records

Team

(Figures in brackets for season records are games played)

Most Points	83	1993-94 (84)
Most Wins	33	1993-94 (84)
Most Ties	17	1993-94 (84)
Most Losses	34	1993-94 (84)
Most Goals	233	1993-94 (84)
Most Goals Against	233	1993-94 (84)
Fewest Points	83	1993-94 (84)
Fewest Wins	33	1993-94 (84)
Fewest Ties	17	1993-94 (84)
Fewest Losses	34	1993-94 (84)
Fewest Goals	233	1993-94 (84)
Fewest Goals Against	233	1993-94 (84)

Longest Winning Streak

Over-all	4	Jan. 16-Jan. 24/94
Home	2	Oct. 28-Oct. 30/93
		Jan. 19-Jan. 24/94
Away	3	Nov. 7-Nov. 10/93
		Dec. 7-Dec. 10/93

Longest Undefeated Streak

Over-all	9	Jan. 8-Jan. 30/94
Home	5	Mar. 14-Mar. 21/94
		(3 wins, 2 ties)
Away	7	Dec. 7-Dec. 29/93
		(5 wins, 2 ties)

Longest Losing Streak

Over-all	4	Feb. 24-Mar. 3/94
Home	5	Feb. 20-Mar. 4/94
Away	3	Nov. 26-Dec. 5/93

Longest Winless Streak

Over-all	8	Mar. 28-Apr. 12/94
		(4 losses, 4 ties)
Home	6	Mar. 21-Apr. 12/94
		(3 losses, 3 ties)
Away	4	Jan. 3-Jan. 13/94
		(2 losses, 2 ties)

Most Shutouts, Season	2	1993-94 (84)
Most PIM, Season	1,620	1993-94 (84)
Most Goals, Game	8	Jan. 24/94
		(Mtl. 3 at Fla. 8)

Individual

Most Seasons	1	Several Players
Most Games	84	Gord Murphy
		Bill Lindsay
Most Goals, Career	30	Scott Mellanby
Most Assists, Career	33	Jesse Belanger
Most Points, Career	60	Scott Mellanby
		(30 goals, 30 assists)
Most PIM, Career	156	Brent Severyn
Most Shutouts, Career	1	John Vanbiesbrouck
		Mark Fitzpatrick
Longest Consecutive		
Games Streak	84	Gord Murphy
		Bill Lindsay
Most Goals, Season	30	Scott Mellanby
		(1993-94)
Most Assists, Season	33	Jesse Belanger
		(1993-94)
Most Points, Season	60	Scott Mellanby
		(1993-94)
		(30 goals, 30 assists)
Most PIM, Season	156	Brent Severyn
		(1993-94)
Most Shutouts, Season	1	John Vanbiesbrouck
		Mark Fitzpatrick
		(1993-94)

Most Points, Defenseman

Season	43	Gord Murphy
		(1993-94)
		(14 goals, 29 assists)

Most Points, Center

Season	50	Jesse Belanger
		(1993-94)
		(17 goals, 33 assists)

Most Points, Right Wing

Season	60	Scott Mellanby
		(1993-94)
		(30 goals, 30 assists)

Most Points, Left Wing

Season	47	Andrei Lomakin
		(1993-94)
		(19 goals, 28 assists)

Most Points, Rookie

Season	50	Jesse Belanger
		(1993-94)
		(17 goals, 33 assists)

Most Goals, Game	2	Eleven players
Most Assists, Game	3	Four players
Most Points, Game	4	Jesse Belanger
		(Jan. 19/94)

Reliable rearguard Brent Severyn bolstered the Panthers' defence, collecting 11 points in 67 games while delivering solid bodychecks along the blueline.

1993-94 Results

Oct.	6	at	Chicago	4-4		17	at NY Islanders	2-1
	7	at	St. Louis	3-5		19	Washington	5-1
	9	at	Tampa Bay	2-0		24	Montreal	8-3
	12		Pittsburgh	1-2		26	at Tampa Bay	1-1
	14		Ottawa	5-4		28	San Jose	3-3
	17		Tampa Bay	3-3		30	at Buffalo	3-2
	19		Los Angeles	2-2	Feb.	1	at Pittsburgh	1-2
	21		Toronto	3-4		2	at Ottawa	4-1
	23		New Jersey	1-2		4	Buffalo	2-7
	26		Winnipeg	2-5		6	Boston	3-0
	28		NY Islanders	5-2		10	at Philadelphia	3-4
	30		Tampa Bay	2-1		12	at NY Islanders	4-3
Nov.	2		Philadelphia	3-4		13	Vancouver	2-1
	3	at	Toronto	3-6		16	at Detroit	3-7
	7	at	Quebec	3-1		18	at Buffalo	1-4
	10	at	Montreal	3-1		20	Detroit	3-4
	11	at	Ottawa	5-4		22	at Winnipeg	3-2
	14		Quebec	2-5		24	Washington	1-2
	16		NY Rangers	2-4		26	at Washington	2-4
	18		Chicago	2-3		28	Pittsburgh	3-4
	20		Washington	4-3	Mar.	2	New Jersey	2-3
	23		Hartford	1-2		4	Hartford	1-2
	26	at	Boston	2-3		7	at Vancouver	2-1
	27	at	Hartford	0-4		9	at Edmonton	5-3
Dec.	2		Buffalo	2-1		11	at Calgary	2-4
	5	at	San Jose	1-2		14	NY Rangers	2-1
	7	at	Anaheim	3-2		16	Calgary	2-1
	8	at	Los Angeles	6-5		18	Edmonton	4-4
	10	at	Winnipeg	5-2		20	Philadelphia	5-3
	12	at	Dallas	4-4		21	New Jersey	3-3
	15		Montreal	3-3		23	Toronto	1-1
	19		Boston	1-2		24	at Philadelphia	3-4
	22		NY Rangers	3-2		26	at NY Islanders	3-1
	26	at	Tampa Bay	3-3		28	Dallas	4-5
	28	at	Washington	3-3		30	St. Louis	1-3
	29	at	Hartford	5-3	Apr.	2	Ottawa	2-2
Jan.	1		Anaheim	4-2		4	at NY Rangers	2-3
	3	at	NY Rangers	3-3		5	at Quebec	3-3
	7	at	New Jersey	1-4		7	at Philadelphia	3-3
	8	at	Boston	2-2		10	New Jersey	2-2
	13	at	Pittsburgh	2-2		12	Quebec	2-5
	15	at	Montreal	5-2		14	NY Islanders	4-1

All-time Record vs. Other Clubs

Regular Season

	At Home							On Road							Total						
	GP	W	L	T	GF	GA	PTS	GP	W	L	T	GF	GA	PTS	GP	W	L	T	GF	GA	PTS
Anaheim	1	1	0	0	4	2	2	1	1	0	0	3	2	2	2	2	0	0	7	4	4
Boston	2	1	1	0	4	2	2	2	0	1	1	4	5	1	4	1	2	1	8	7	3
Buffalo	2	1	1	0	4	8	2	2	1	0	1	4	6	2	4	2	1	0	8	14	4
Calgary	1	1	0	0	2	1	2	1	0	1	0	2	4	0	2	1	1	0	4	5	2
Chicago	1	0	1	0	2	3	0	1	0	0	1	4	4	1	2	0	1	1	6	7	1
Dallas	1	0	1	0	4	5	0	1	0	1	0	4	4	1	2	0	2	0	8	9	1
Detroit	1	0	1	0	3	4	0	1	0	1	0	3	7	0	2	0	2	0	6	11	0
Edmonton	1	0	0	1	4	4	1	1	0	0	1	5	3	2	2	0	0	2	9	7	3
Hartford	2	0	2	0	2	4	0	2	1	1	0	5	7	2	4	1	3	0	7	11	2
Los Angeles	1	0	0	1	2	2	1	1	1	0	0	6	5	2	2	1	0	1	8	7	3
Montreal	2	1	0	1	11	6	3	2	2	0	0	8	3	4	4	3	0	1	19	9	7
New Jersey	3	0	1	2	7	8	2	2	0	2	0	6	0	5	5	0	3	2	9	14	2
NY Islanders	2	2	0	0	9	3	4	3	3	0	0	9	5	6	5	5	0	0	18	8	10
NY Rangers	3	2	1	0	7	7	4	2	0	2	0	4	6	0	5	2	3	0	11	13	4
Ottawa	2	1	0	1	7	6	3	2	2	0	0	9	5	4	4	3	0	1	16	11	7
Philadelphia	2	1	1	0	8	7	2	3	0	2	1	9	11	1	5	1	3	1	17	18	3
Pittsburgh	2	0	2	0	4	6	0	2	0	1	1	3	4	1	4	0	3	1	7	10	1
Quebec	2	0	2	0	4	10	0	2	1	0	1	6	4	3	4	1	2	1	10	14	3
St. Louis	1	0	1	0	1	3	0	1	0	1	0	3	5	0	2	0	2	0	4	8	0
San Jose	1	0	0	1	3	3	1	1	1	0	0	1	2	2	2	1	0	1	4	5	1
Tampa Bay	2	1	0	1	5	4	3	3	2	1	0	6	5	5	5	3	0	2	11	6	8
Toronto	2	0	1	1	4	5	1	1	0	1	0	3	6	0	3	0	3	0	7	11	1
Vancouver	1	1	0	0	2	1	2	1	0	1	0	2	1	2	2	2	0	0	4	2	4
Washington	3	2	1	0	10	6	4	2	2	0	0	8	7	1	5	2	2	2	11	15	5
Winnipeg	1	0	1	0	2	5	0	2	2	0	0	8	4	4	3	2	1	0	10	9	4
Totals	**42**	**15**	**18**	**9**	**115**	**115**	**39**	**42**	**18**	**16**	**8**	**118**	**118**	**44**	**84**	**33**	**34**	**17**	**233**	**233**	**83**

Entry Draft Selections 1994-93

1994 Pick		**1993** Pick	
1	Ed Jovanovski	5	Rob Niedermayer
27	Rhett Warrener	41	Kevin Weekes
31	Jason Podollan	57	Chris Armstrong
36	Ryan Johnson	67	Mikael Tjallden
84	David Nemirovsky	78	Steve Washburn
105	Dave Geris	83	Bill McCauley
157	Matt O'Dette	109	Todd MacDonald
183	Jasson Boudrias	135	Alain Nasreddine
235	Tero Lehtera	161	Trevor Doyle
261	Per Gustafsson	187	Briane Thompson
		213	Chad Cabana
		239	John Demarco
		265	Eric Montreuil

Coach

NEILSON, ROGER PAUL
Coach, Florida Panthers. Born in Toronto, Ont., June 16, 1934.

After being named head coach on June 2, 1993, Roger Neilson enjoyed one of the most successful seasons by an expansion team in all of professional sports. Neilson's defensive style of coaching fit perfectly with the type of players suiting up for the Panthers. His neutral zone ''Trap'' was effective in bringing this young club to NHL records in wins (33) and points (83) by a first-year club.

Prior to joining the Panthers, Neilson, 60, coached the NY Rangers from the beginning of the 1989-90 season until being replaced on January 4, 1993. In his three-plus seasons with the Rangers, Neilson led the team to two regular season Patrick Division championships ('90 & '92) and he was twice a finalist for NHL Coach of the Year honors ('90 & '92). In 280 regular season games behind the Rangers bench, Neilson posted a record of 141-104-35 for a winning percentage of .566.

Neilson began his hockey coaching career in 1966-67 when he became the head coach of the Peterborough Petes of the Ontario Hockey Association. Neilson spent 10 seasons with the Petes. During his tenure, his teams captured one OHA championship and finished lower than third only twice.

Neilson left the Petes in 1976-77 to take his first professional-level coaching job with the Dallas Blackhawks of the Central Hockey League. After spending only one season in Dallas, Neilson joined the NHL coaching ranks with the Toronto Maple Leafs. Neilson coached the Leafs for two seasons ('77-78 & '78-79) and he led his team to two winning seasons. In 1977-78, Neilson led the Leafs to the NHL semi-finals.

Following his two-year stay in Toronto, and prior to joining the Rangers in 1989, Neilson coached with the Buffalo Sabres (1979-81), the Vancouver Canucks (1982-83), the Los Angeles Kings (1983-84), and the Chicago Blackhawks (co-coach 1984-85 through 1986-87).

Coaching Record

Season	Team	Games	Regular Season W	L	T	%	Playoffs Games	W	L	%
1966-67	Peterborough (OHA)					UNAVAILABLE				
1967-68	Peterborough (OHA)	54	13	30	11	.342	....	....	....	....
1968-69	Peterborough (OHA)	54	27	18	9	.583	10	4	6	.400
1969-70	Peterborough (OHA)	54	29	13	12	.648	....	....	....	....
1970-71	Peterborough (OHA)	62	41	13	8	.726	....	....	....	....
1971-72	Peterborough (OHA)	63	34	20	9	.611	....	....	....	....
1972-73	Peterborough (OHA)	63	42	13	8	.730	....	....	....	....
1973-74	Peterborough (OHA)	70	35	21	14	.600	....	....	....	....
1974-75	Peterborough (OHA)	70	37	20	13	.621	....	....	....	....
1975-76	Peterborough (OHA)	66	18	37	11	.356	....	....	....	....
1976-77	Dallas (CHL)	76	35	25	16	.566	....	....	....	....
1977-78	**Toronto (NHL)**	80	41	29	10	.575	13	6	7	.462
1978-79	**Toronto (NHL)**	80	34	33	13	.506	6	2	4	.333
1979-80	**Buffalo (NHL)**	26	14	6	6	.654	....	....	....	....
1980-81	**Buffalo (NHL)**	80	39	20	21	.619	8	4	4	.500
1981-82	**Vancouver (NHL)**	5	4	0	1	.900	17	11	6	.647
1982-83	**Vancouver (NHL)**	80	30	35	15	.469	4	1	3	.250
1983-84	**Vancouver (NHL)**	48	17	26	5	.406	....	....	....	....
1983-84	**Los Angeles (NHL)**	28	8	17	3	.339	....	....	....	....
1989-90	**NY Rangers (NHL)**	80	36	31	13	.531	10	5	5	.500
1990-91	**NY Rangers (NHL)**	80	36	31	13	.531	6	2	4	.333
1991-92	**NY Rangers (NHL)**	80	50	25	5	.656	13	6	7	.462
1992-93	**NY Rangers (NHL)**	40	19	17	4	.525	....	....	....	....
1993-94	**Florida (NHL)**	84	33	34	17	.494	....	....	....	....
	NHL Totals	791	361	304	126	.536	77	37	40	.481

Club Directory

Miami Arena
100 Northeast Third Avenue
Tenth Floor
Fort Lauderdale, FL 33301
Phone **305/768-1900**
FAX 305/768-9870
Capacity: 14,503

Chairman and CEO	H. Wayne Huizenga
President & Governor	William A. Torrey
Vice President, Business/Mktg. & Alt. Governor	Dean Jordan
Vice President, Finance and Administration	Jonathan D. Mariner
General Manager	Bryan Murray
Special Counsel	James J. Blosser
Special Consultant	Richard C. Rochon
Consultant	Gary Green
Director, Finance and Administration	Steve Dauria
Accounting Manager	Evelyn Lopez
Staff Accountant	Laura Barrera
Executive Assistants to President	Deanna Cocozzelli, Cathy Stevenson
Executive Assistant/Business & Marketing	Laurie Sharkey Scott
Executive Assistant/Finance & Administration	Sally Rose
Executive Assistant to General Manager	Diana Marchand
Receptionist	Marilyn Klees

Hockey Operations

Director of Player Personnel	John Chapman
Assistant General Manager	Chuck Fletcher
Head Coach	Roger Neilson
Associate Coach	Craig Ramsay
Assistant Coach	Lindy Ruff
Goaltending Coach	Bill Smith
Eastern Scout	Ron Harris
European Scout	Matti Vaisanen
Video Coordinator/Director, Team Services	Jon Christiano
Assistant, Team Services	Scott Krady
Athletic Trainer	David Smith
Equipment Manager	Mark Brennan
Associate Equipment Manager	Tim Leroy
Assistant to the Equipment Manager	Scott Tinkler
Internist	Charles Posternack, M.D.
Orthopedic Surgeons	David E. Attarian, M.D., Stephen R. Southworth, M.D.
Plastic Surgeon	Harry K. Moon
Minor League Affiliates	Cincinnati (IHL) and Birmingham (ECHL)

Communications Department

Director, Public/Media Relations	Greg Bouris
Public/Media Relations Associates	Kevin Dessart, Ron Colangelo
Manager of Archives	Ed Krajewski
Secretary, Public/Media Relations	Aza Krotz
Broadcast Intern	Marni Share

Marketing Department

Director, Promotions & Special Projects	Declan J. Bolger
Director, Corporate Sales and Sponsorship	Kimberly Terranova
Director, Merchandise	Ron Dennis
Coordinator, Corporate Sales and Sponsorship	Sam Ambrose
Coordinator, Promotions/Community Projects	Alan Keystone
Marketing Assistant	Brette Zalkin
Secretary, Corporate Sales and Sponsorship	Susan Gonzalez
Secretary, Promotions & Special Projects	Lauren Devine
Secretary, Merchandise	Mary Lou Poag

Ticket Operations

Director, Ticket and Game Day Operations	Steve Dangerfield
Manager, Ticket Operations	Scott Wampold
Sales Managers	Greg Hanessian, Barry Cohen, Jose Velasco, Jeff Moss
Ticket Operations	Julian Smyle, Matt Coyne
Secretary, Sales/Ticket Operations	Janine Shea
Office Services Coordinator	Paul Seal
Mailroom Clerk	Brian Mejia

General Information

Arena Phone Number	(305) 530-4444
Location of Press Box	Mezzanine, Sec. 211
Dimensions of Rink	200 feet by 85 feet
Practice Arena	Gold Coast Ice Arena (305) 784-5500
Team Colors	Red, Navy Blue, Yellow-Gold
Television Station	Sunshine Network & WBFS Channel 33
Television Announcers	Jeff Rimer, Denis Potvin, Paul Kennedy
Panthers Radio Network	WQAM, 560 AM
Radio Announcers	Chris Moore, Denis Potvin
Panthers Spanish Radio	WCMQ, 1210 AM
Spanish Announcers	Arley Londono, Manalo Alvarez

General Managers' History

Bob Clarke, 1993-94; Bryan Murray, 1994-95.

Coaching History

Roger Neilson, 1993-94 to date.

Captains' History

Brian Skrudland, 1993-94 to date.

Hartford Whalers

1993-94 Results: 27W-48L-9T 63PTS. Sixth, Northeast Division

Year-by-Year Record

Season	GP	Home W	L	T	Road W	L	T	Overall W	L	T	GF	GA	Pts.	Finished		Playoff Result
1993-94	84	14	22	6	13	26	3	27	48	9	227	288	63	6th,	Northeast Div.	Out of Playoffs
1992-93	84	12	25	5	14	27	1	26	52	6	284	369	58	5th,	Adams Div.	Out of Playoffs
1991-92	80	13	17	10	13	24	3	26	41	13	247	283	65	4th,	Adams Div.	Lost Div. Semi-Final
1990-91	80	18	16	6	13	22	5	31	38	11	238	276	73	4th,	Adams Div.	Lost Div. Semi-Final
1989-90	80	17	18	5	21	15	4	38	33	9	275	268	85	4th,	Adams Div.	Lost Div. Semi-Final
1988-89	80	21	17	2	16	21	3	37	38	5	299	290	79	4th,	Adams Div.	Lost Div. Semi-Final
1987-88	80	21	14	5	14	24	2	35	38	7	249	267	77	4th,	Adams Div.	Lost Div. Semi-Final
1986-87	80	26	9	5	17	21	2	43	30	7	287	270	93	1st,	Adams Div.	Lost Div. Semi-Final
1985-86	80	21	17	2	19	19	2	40	36	4	332	302	84	4th,	Adams Div.	Lost Div. Final
1984-85	80	17	18	5	13	23	4	30	41	9	268	318	69	5th,	Adams Div.	Out of Playoffs
1983-84	80	19	16	5	9	26	5	28	42	10	288	320	66	5th,	Adams Div.	Out of Playoffs
1982-83	80	13	22	5	6	32	2	19	54	7	261	403	45	5th,	Adams Div.	Out of Playoffs
1981-82	80	13	17	10	8	24	8	21	41	18	264	351	60	5th,	Adams Div.	Out of Playoffs
1980-81	80	14	17	9	7	24	9	21	41	18	292	372	60	4th,	Norris Div.	Out of Playoffs
1979-80	80	22	12	6	5	22	13	27	34	19	303	312	73	4th,	Norris Div.	Lost Prelim. Round

Schedule

Oct.						
Sat.	1	at Philadelphia		Fri.	13	at Pittsburgh
Tues.	4	at Toronto		Sun.	15	at Chicago
Sat.	8	Quebec		Mon.	16	at Dallas
Wed.	12	Florida		Wed.	18	at Dallas
Fri.	14	at Buffalo				(in Denver)
Sat.	15	NY Rangers		Mon.	23	at Montreal
Wed.	19	Ottawa		Wed.	25	Ottawa
Fri.	21	at Washington		Thur.	26	at Philadelphia
Sat.	22	Washington		Sat.	28	Florida*
Thur.	27	Quebec		Mon.	30	at Vancouver
Sat.	29	Winnipeg		**Feb.** Wed.	1	at Edmonton
Nov. Tues.	1	at Detroit		Fri.	3	at Calgary
Sat.	5	at Pittsburgh		Sat.	4	at Winnipeg
Tues.	8	Montreal		Wed.	8	San Jose
Wed.	9	at NY Rangers		Fri.	10	at Tampa Bay
Sat.	12	at NY Islanders		Sat.	11	at Florida
Sun.	13	at Ottawa		Mon.	13	at Montreal
Wed.	16	St. Louis		Wed.	15	Montreal
Sat.	19	NY Islanders		Sat.	18	Pittsburgh*
Mon.	21	at Montreal		Sun.	19	at Pittsburgh*
Wed.	23	Philadelphia		Wed.	22	Boston
Sat.	26	Anaheim*		Fri.	24	at NY Rangers
Sun.	27	Tampa Bay		Sat.	25	Buffalo
Tues.	29	NY Rangers		Tues.	28	at NY Islanders
Dec. Thur.	1	at Boston		**Mar.** Wed.	1	New Jersey
Sat.	3	at Quebec		Sat.	4	Chicago*
Sun.	4	Boston		Sun.	5	Boston
Wed.	7	Detroit		Wed.	8	Philadelphia
Fri.	9	at Buffalo		Thur.	9	at St. Louis
Sat.	10	Edmonton		Sun.	12	at San Jose*
Mon.	12	Calgary		Tues.	14	at Los Angeles
Wed.	14	Ottawa		Wed.	15	at Anaheim
Sat.	17	Washington		Sat.	18	at Chicago
Tues.	20	at New Jersey				(in Phoenix)
Wed.	21	Dallas		Wed.	22	Quebec
Fri.	23	at Buffalo		Sat.	25	NY Islanders*
Mon.	26	at Boston		Sun.	26	at Washington*
Wed.	28	Pittsburgh		Wed.	29	at Florida
Thur.	29	at Quebec		Fri.	31	at Tampa Bay
Sat.	31	at Ottawa		**Apr.** Tues.	4	at New Jersey
Jan. Wed.	4	Los Angeles		Wed.	5	Toronto
Fri.	6	Vancouver		Sat.	8	New Jersey*
Sat.	7	Buffalo		Sun.	9	Tampa Bay*

* Denotes afternoon game.

Home Starting Times:
Night Games . . . . 7:00 p.m.
Matinees . . . . 1:30 p.m.

Franchise date: June 22, 1979

EASTERN CONFERENCE NHL

16th NHL Season

NORTHEAST DIVISION

After a slow start, Sean Burke rebounded to record 17 victories and an excellent 2.99 goals-against average for the Whalers in 1993-94.

1994-95 Player Personnel

FORWARDS

	HT	WT	S	Place of Birth	Date	1993-94 Club
BENNETT, Rick	6-4	215	L	Springfield, MA	7/24/67	Springfield
CARSON, Jimmy	6-1	200	R	Southfield, MI	7/20/68	Los Angeles-Vancouver
CASSELS, Andrew	6-0	192	L	Bramalea, Ont.	7/23/69	Hartford
CHIBIREV, Igor	6-0	180	L	Kiev, USSR	4/19/68	Hartford-Springfield
DANIELS, Scott	6-3	200	L	Prince Albert, Sask.	9/19/69	Springfield
DOMENICHELLI, Hnat	5-11	173	L	Edmonton, Alta.	2/17/76	Kamloops
DRURY, Ted	6-0	185	L	Boston, MA	9/13/71	Cgy-U.S. National-U.S. Olympic-Hfd
JANSSENS, Mark	6-3	216	L	Surrey, B.C.	5/19/68	Hartford
KRON, Robert	5-10	180	L	Brno, Czech.	2/27/67	Hartford
LEMIEUX, Jocelyn	5-10	200	L	Mont-Laurier, Que.	11/18/67	Chicago-Hartford
MacPHERSON, Billy Jo	6-2	200	L	Toronto, Ont.	9/23/73	North Bay
NIKOLISHIN, Andrei	5-11	180	L	Vorkuta, USSR	3/25/73	Moscow D'amo
O'NEILL, Jeff	6-1	183	R	Richmond Hill, Ont.	2/23/76	Guelph
OSMAK, Corey	5-11	173	L	Edmonton, Alta.	8/20/70	Minn.-Duluth
PETROVICKY, Robert	5-11	172	L	Kosice, Czech.	10/26/73	Hartford-Springfield
POTVIN, Marc	6-1	200	R	Ottawa, Ont.	1/29/67	Los Angeles-Hartford
RANHEIM, Paul	6-0	195	R	St. Louis, MO	1/25/66	Calgary-Hartford
REID, Jarrett	5-10	180	R	Sault Ste. Marie, Ont.	3/10/73	Belleville-Springfield-Raleigh
RICE, Steven	6-0	215	R	Kitchener, Ont.	5/26/71	Edmonton
SANDERSON, Geoff	6-0	185	L	Hay River, N.W.T.	2/1/72	Hartford
SANDLAK, Jim	6-4	219	R	Kitchener, Ont.	12/12/66	Hartford
SMYTH, Kevin	6-2	217	L	Banff, Alta.	11/22/73	Hartford-Springfield
STORM, Jim	6-2	200	L	Milford, MI	2/5/71	Hartford
TURCOTTE, Darren	6-0	178	L	Boston, MA	3/2/68	NY Rangers-Hartford
VERBEEK, Pat	5-9	190	R	Sarnia, Ont.	5/24/64	Hartford
VOLOGJANINOV, Ivan	5-10	174	L	Ukhta, USSR	3/9/72	Lethbridge

DEFENSEMEN

	HT	WT	S	Place of Birth	Date	1993-94 Club
AGNEW, Jim	6-1	190	L	Hartney, Man.	3/21/66	Did Not Play
BURT, Adam	6-0	190	L	Detroit, MI	1/15/69	Hartford
CHYCHRUN, Jeff	6-4	215	L	LaSalle, Que.	5/3/66	Edmonton-Cape Breton
GODYNYUK, Alexander	6-0	207	L	Kiev, Ukraine	1/27/70	Florida-Hartford
KUCERA, Frantisek	6-2	205	L	Prague, Czech.	2/3/68	Chicago-Hartford
MALIK, Marek	6-5	185	L	Ostrava, Czech.	6/24/75	TJ Vitkovice
McBAIN, Jason	6-2	178	L	Ilion, NY	4/12/74	Portland (WHL)
McCOSH, Shayne	6-0	183	L	Oshawa, Ont.	1/27/74	Windsor-Detroit (OHL)
McCRIMMON, Brad	5-11	197	L	Dodsland, Sask.	3/29/59	Hartford
PETERS, Rob	6-6	205	L	North Tonowanda, NY	5/15/72	Ohio State
PRATT, Nolan	6-2	190	L	Fort McMurray, Alta.	8/14/75	Portland (WHL)
PRONGER, Chris	6-5	190	L	Dryden, Ont.	10/10/74	Hartford
RISODORE, Ryan	6-4	192	L	Hamilton, Ont.	4/4/76	Guelph
STEVENS, John	6-1	195	L	Campbellton, N.B.	5/4/66	Hartford-Springfield
SWINSON, Wes	6-2	183	L	Peterborough, Ont.	5/26/75	Kitchener
TILEY, Brad	6-1	185	L	Markdale, Ont.	7/5/71	Binghamton-Phoenix
VOPAT, Jan	6-0	198	L	Most, Czech.	3/22/73	Litvinov
WESLEY, Glen	6-1	201	L	Red Deer, Alta.	10/2/68	Boston
YULE, Steve	6-0	210	R	Gleichen, Alta.	5/27/72	Springfield

GOALTENDERS

	HT	WT	C	Place of Birth	Date	1993-94 Club
BURKE, Sean	6-4	210	L	Windsor, Ont.	1/29/67	Hartford
CURRIE, Jason	5-10	170	R	Brampton, Ont.	4/26/72	Clarkson
GOSSELIN, Mario	5-8	160	L	Thetford Mines, Que.	6/15/63	Hartford-Springfield
LEGACE, Emmanuel	5-9	162	L	Toronto, Ont.	2/4/73	Cdn. National
MULLIN, Matt	5-3	150	L	Guelph, Ont.	11/9/74	Windsor-Sudbury
REESE, Jeff	5-9	170	L	Brantford, Ont.	3/24/66	Calgary-Hartford

1993-94 Scoring

– rookie

Regular Season

Pos	#	Player	Team	GP	G	A	Pts	+/–	PIM	PP	SH	GW	GT	S	%
R	16	Pat Verbeek	HFD	84	37	38	75	15–	177	15	1	3	1	226	16.4
C	8	Geoff Sanderson	HFD	82	41	26	67	13–	42	15	1	6	2	266	15.4
C	21	Andrew Cassels	HFD	79	16	42	58	21–	37	8	1	3	0	126	12.7
C	18	Robert Kron	HFD	77	24	26	50	0	8	2	1	3	0	194	12.4
D	44	* Chris Pronger	HFD	81	5	25	30	3–	113	2	0	0	0	174	2.9
L	26	Brian Propp	HFD	65	12	17	29	3	44	3	1	2	0	108	11.1
L	23	Jocelyn Lemieux	CHI	66	12	8	20	5	63	0	0	1	1	129	9.3
			HFD	16	6	1	7	8–	19	0	0	2	0	22	27.3
			TOTAL	82	18	9	27	3–	82	0	0	2	1	151	11.9
L	14	Paul Ranheim	CGY	67	10	14	24	7–	20	0	2	2	0	110	9.1
			HFD	15	0	3	3	11–	2	0	0	0	0	21	.0
			TOTAL	82	10	17	27	18–	22	0	2	2	0	131	7.6
D	5	Alexander Godynyuk	FLA	26	0	10	10	5	35	0	0	0	0	43	.0
			HFD	43	3	9	12	8	40	0	0	1	0	67	4.5
			TOTAL	69	3	19	22	13	75	0	0	1	0	110	2.7
D	4	Frantisek Kucera	CHI	60	4	13	17	9	34	2	0	0	0	90	4.4
			HFD	16	1	3	4	12–	14	1	0	0	0	32	3.1
			TOTAL	76	5	16	21	3–	48	3	0	0	0	122	4.1
C	89	Darren Turcotte	NYR	13	2	4	6	2–	13	0	0	0	0	17	11.8
			HFD	19	2	11	13	11–	4	0	0	0	0	43	4.7
			TOTAL	32	4	15	19	13–	17	0	0	0	0	60	6.7
C	17	* Ted Drury	CGY	34	5	7	12	5–	26	0	1	1	1	43	11.6
			HFD	16	1	5	6	10–	10	0	0	0	0	37	2.7
			TOTAL	50	6	12	18	15–	36	0	1	1	1	80	7.5
D	6	Adam Burt	HFD	63	1	17	18	4–	75	0	0	0	0	91	1.1
L	24	* Jim Storm	HFD	68	6	10	16	4	27	1	0	0	0	84	7.1
C	32	Igor Chibirev	HFD	37	4	11	15	7	2	0	0	0	0	30	13.3
D	27	Bryan Marchment	CHI	13	1	4	5	2–	42	0	0	0	0	18	5.6
			HFD	42	3	7	10	12–	124	0	1	1	0	74	4.1
			TOTAL	55	4	11	15	14–	166	0	1	1	0	92	4.3
C	22	Mark Janssens	HFD	84	2	10	12	3–	137	0	0	0	0	52	3.8
C	39	Robert Petrovicky	HFD	33	6	5	11	1–	39	1	0	0	0	33	18.2
R	14	Jim Sandlak	HFD	27	6	2	8	6	32	2	0	1	0	32	18.8
D	10	Brad McCrimmon	HFD	65	1	5	6	7–	72	0	0	0	0	39	2.6
L	20	* Kevin Smyth	HFD	21	3	2	5	1–	10	0	0	0	0	8	37.5
R	29	Marc Potvin	L.A.	3	0	0	0	3–	26	0	0	0	0	1	.0
			HFD	51	2	3	5	8–	246	0	0	1	0	25	8.0
			TOTAL	54	2	3	5	8–	272	0	0	1	0	26	7.7
D	33	* Ted Crowley	HFD	21	1	2	3	1–	10	1	0	0	0	28	3.6
D	45	John Stevens	HFD	9	0	3	3	4	4	0	0	0	0	3	.0
D	25	Bob McGill	NYI	3	0	0	0	0	5	0	0	0	0	0	.0
			HFD	30	0	3	3	7–	41	0	0	0	0	14	.0
			TOTAL	33	0	3	3	7–	46	0	0	0	0	14	.0
R	15	* Todd Harkins	HFD	28	1	0	1	4–	49	0	0	0	0	15	6.7
G	35	Jeff Reese	CGY	1	0	0	0	0	0	0	0	0	0	0	.0
			HFD	19	0	1	1	0	0	0	0	0	0	0	.0
			TOTAL	20	0	1	1	0	0	0	0	0	0	0	.0
C	28	Mike Tomlak	HFD	1	0	0	0	0	0	0	0	0	0	2	.0
G	35	* Mike Lenarduzzi	HFD	1	0	0	0	0	0	0	0	0	0	0	.0
L	11	Yvon Corriveau	HFD	3	0	0	0	0	0	0	0	0	0	0	.0
G	31	Mario Gosselin	HFD	7	0	0	0	0	0	0	0	0	0	0	.0
D	41	Allen Pedersen	HFD	7	0	0	0	1–	0	0	0	0	1	0	.0
G	40	Frank Pietrangelo	HFD	19	0	0	0	0	0	0	0	0	0	0	.0
G	1	Sean Burke	HFD	47	0	0	0	0	16	0	0	0	0	0	.0

Goaltending

No.	Goaltender	GPI	Mins	Avg	W	L	T	EN	SO	GA	SA	S%
35	* Mike Lenarduzzi	1	21	2.86	0	0	0	0	1	1	12	.917
1	Sean Burke	47	2750	2.99	17	24	5	7	2	137	1458	.906
35	Jeff Reese	19	1086	3.09	5	9	3	4	1	56	524	.893
40	Frank Pietrangelo	19	984	3.60	5	11	1	1	0	59	473	.875
31	Mario Gosselin	7	239	5.27	0	4	0	2	0	21	107	.804
	Totals	84	5099	3.39	27	48	9	14	3	288	2588	.889

Pat Verbeek topped all Hartford scorers with 75 points in the 1993-94 season, including 15 powerplay and three game-winning goals.

General Managers' History

Jack Kelly, 1979-80 to 1980-81; Larry Pleau, 1981-82 to 1982-83; Emile Francis, 1983-84 to 1988-89; Ed Johnston, 1989-90 to 1991-92; Brian Burke, 1992-93; Paul Holmgren, 1993-94; Jim Rutherford, 1994-95.

Coaching History

Don Blackburn, 1979-80; Don Blackburn and Larry Pleau, 1980-81; Larry Pleau, 1981-82; Larry Kish, Larry Pleau and John Cuniff, 1982-83; Jack "Tex" Evans, 1983-84 to 1986-87; Jack "Tex" Evans and Larry Pleau, 1987-88; Larry Pleau, 1988-89; Rick Ley, 1989-90 to 1990-91; Jim Roberts, 1991-92; Paul Holmgren, 1992-93; Paul Holmgren and Pierre Maguire, 1993-94; Paul Holmgren, 1994-95.

Captains' History

Rick Ley, 1979-80; Rick Ley, Mark Howe and Mike Rogers, 1980-81. Dave Keon, 1981-82; Russ Anderson, 1982-83; Mark Johnson, 1983-84; Mark Johnson and Ron Francis, 1984-85; Ron Francis, 1985-86 to 1990-91; Randy Ladouceur, 1991-92; Pat Verbeek, 1992-93 to date.

Club Records

Team

(Figures in brackets for season records are games played)

Most Points	93	1986-87 (80)	
Most Wins	43	1986-87 (80)	
Most Ties	19	1979-80 (80)	
Most Losses	54	1982-83 (80)	
Most Goals	332	1985-86 (80)	
Most Goals Against	403	1982-83 (80)	
Fewest Points	45	1982-83 (80)	
Fewest Wins	19	1982-83 (80)	
Fewest Ties	4	1985-86 (80)	
Fewest Losses	30	1986-87 (80)	
Fewest Goals	227	1993-94 (84)	
Fewest Goals Against	267	1987-88 (80)	

Longest Winning Streak

Over-all	7	Mar. 16-29/85
Home	5	Mar. 17-29/85
Away	6	Nov. 10-Dec. 7/90

Longest Undefeated Streak

Over-all	10	Jan. 20-Feb. 10/82 (6 wins, 4 ties)
Home	7	Mar. 15-Apr. 5/86 (5 wins, 2 ties)
Away	6	Jan. 23-Feb. 10/82 (3 wins, 3 ties); Nov. 30-Dec. 26/89 (5 wins, 1 tie); Nov. 10-Dec. 7/90 (6 wins)

Longest Losing Streak

Over-all	9	Feb. 19/83-Mar. 8/83
Home	6	Feb. 19/83-Mar. 12/83; Feb. 10-Mar. 3/85
Away	13	Dec. 18/82-Feb. 5/83

Longest Winless Streak

Over-all	14	Jan. 4/92-Feb. 9/92 (8 losses, 6 ties)
Home	13	Jan. 15-Mar. 10/85 (11 losses, 2 ties)
Away	15	Nov. 11/79-Jan. 9/80 (11 losses, 4 ties)

Most Shutouts, Season	5	1986-87 (80)
Most PIM, Season	2,354	1992-93 (84)
Most Goals, Game	11	Feb. 12/84 (Edm. 0 at Hfd. 11) Oct. 19/85 (Mtl. 6 at Hfd. 11) Jan. 17/86 (Que. 6 at Hfd. 11) Mar. 15/86 (Chi. 4 at Hfd. 11)

Individual

Most Seasons	10	Ron Francis
Most Games	714	Ron Francis
Most Goals, Career	264	Ron Francis
Most Assists, Career	557	Ron Francis
Most Points, Career	821	Ron Francis (264 goals, 557 assists)
Most PIM, Career	1,368	Torrie Robertson
Most Shutouts, Career	13	Mike Liut

Longest Consecutive

Games Streak	419	Dave Tippett (Mar. 3/84-Oct. 7/89)
Most Goals, Season	56	Blaine Stoughton (1979-80)
Most Assists, Season	69	Ron Francis (1989-90)
Most Points, Season	105	Mike Rogers (1979-80) (44 goals, 61 assists) (1980-81) (40 goals, 65 assists)
Most PIM, Season	358	Torrie Robertson (1985-86)

Most Points, Defenseman

Season	69	Dave Babych (1985-86) (14 goals, 55 assists)

Most Points, Center,

Season	105	Mike Rogers (1979-80) (44 goals, 61 assists) (1980-81) (40 goals, 65 assists)

Most Points, Right Wing,

Season	100	Blaine Stoughton (1979-80) (56 goals, 44 assists)

Most Points, Left Wing,

Season	89	Geoff Sanderson (1992-93) (46 goals, 43 assists)

Most Points, Rookie,

Season	72	Sylvain Turgeon (1983-84) (40 goals, 32 assists)

Most Shutouts, Season	4	Mike Liut (1986-87) Peter Sidorkiewicz (1988-89)
Most Goals, Game	4	Jordy Douglas (Feb. 3/80) Ron Francis (Feb. 12/84)
Most Assists, Game	6	Ron Francis (Mar. 5/87)
Most Points, Game	6	Paul Lawless (Jan. 4/87) Ron Francis (Mar. 5/87, Oct. 8/89)

All-time Record vs. Other Clubs

Regular Season

	At Home							On Road							Total						
	GP	W	L	T	GF	GA	PTS	GP	W	L	T	GF	GA	PTS	GP	W	L	T	GF	GA	PTS
Anaheim	1	0	1	0	2	3	0	1	0	1	0	3	6	0	2	0	2	0	5	9	0
Boston	53	23	23	7	188	192	53	55	12	38	5	146	226	29	108	35	61	12	334	418	82
Buffalo	56	19	28	9	168	179	47	54	18	29	7	177	229	43	110	37	57	16	345	408	90
Calgary	22	7	12	3	75	90	17	22	4	17	1	75	118	9	44	11	29	4	150	208	26
Chicago	23	10	11	2	80	80	22	22	6	13	3	64	99	15	45	16	24	5	144	179	37
Dallas	23	9	11	3	84	87	21	22	9	12	1	72	93	19	45	18	23	4	156	180	40
Detroit	22	14	7	1	85	60	29	23	7	10	6	68	88	20	45	21	17	7	153	148	49
Edmonton	22	9	9	4	94	83	22	23	3	17	3	67	102	9	45	12	26	7	161	185	31
Florida	2	1	1	0	7	5	2	2	2	0	0	4	4	4	4	3	1	0	11	7	6
Los Angeles	23	12	8	3	90	94	27	22	6	13	3	87	100	15	45	18	21	6	177	194	42
Montreal	55	18	29	8	168	210	44	53	10	37	6	158	248	26	108	28	66	14	326	458	70
New Jersey	24	12	7	5	90	75	29	25	10	13	2	96	98	22	49	22	20	7	186	173	51
NY Islanders	25	10	11	4	90	97	24	24	7	14	3	63	93	17	49	17	25	7	153	190	41
NY Rangers	24	13	8	3	94	86	29	24	7	15	2	71	109	16	48	20	23	5	165	195	45
Ottawa	5	5	0	0	24	11	10	7	5	1	1	24	13	11	12	10	1	1	48	24	21
Philadelphia	24	9	11	4	98	103	22	24	7	16	1	71	101	15	48	16	27	5	169	204	37
Pittsburgh	25	13	11	1	113	101	27	24	9	12	3	100	113	21	49	22	23	4	213	214	48
Quebec	53	22	20	11	185	189	55	55	16	32	7	171	239	39	108	38	52	18	356	428	94
St. Louis	24	9	13	2	74	76	20	23	8	13	2	77	91	18	47	17	26	4	151	167	38
San Jose	4	2	2	0	13	10	4	3	1	2	0	14	19	2	7	3	4	0	27	29	6
Tampa Bay	3	3	0	0	13	6	6	3	1	2	0	7	11	2	6	4	2	0	20	17	8
Toronto	22	12	6	4	102	74	28	22	12	8	2	90	82	26	44	24	14	6	192	156	54
Vancouver	22	9	9	4	73	79	22	23	8	9	6	66	82	22	45	17	18	10	139	161	44
Washington	25	9	13	3	80	96	21	24	9	14	1	73	84	19	49	18	27	4	153	180	40
Winnipeg	22	11	6	5	92	71	27	24	11	12	1	88	86	23	46	22	18	6	180	157	50
Totals	**604**	**261**	**257**	**86**	**2182**	**2157**	**608**	**604**	**188**	**350**	**66**	**1932**	**2532**	**442**	**1208**	**449**	**607**	**152**	**4114**	**4689**	**1050**

Calgary totals include Atlanta, 1979-80. Dallas totals include Minnesota, 1979-80 to 1992-93.
New Jersey totals include Colorado, 1979-80 to 1981-82.

Playoffs

	Series	W	L	GP	W	L	T	GF	GA	Last Mtg.	Round	Result
Boston	2	0	2	13	5	8	0	38	47	1991	DSF	L 2-4
Montreal	5	0	5	27	8	19	0	70	96	1992	DSF	L 3-4
Quebec	2	1	1	9	5	4	0	35	34	1987	DSF	L 2-4
Totals	**9**	**1**	**8**	**49**	**18**	**31**	**0**	**143**	**177**			

Playoff Results 1994-90

Year	Round	Opponent	Result	GF	GA
1992	DSF	Montreal	L 3-4	18	21
1991	DSF	Boston	L 2-4	17	24
1990	DSF	Boston	L 3-4	21	23

Abbreviations: Round: F – Final;
CF – conference final; **CQF** – conference quarter-final;
CSF – conference semi-final; **DF** – division final;
DSF – division semi-final; **SF** – semi-final;
QF – quarter-final; **PR** – preliminary round.

1993-94 Results

Oct.	6	at	Montreal	3-4		12	at	Los Angeles	4-6
	9		Philadelphia	2-5		14	at	Anaheim	3-6
	10	at	Buffalo	3-2		15	at	San Jose	2-8
	13		Montreal	4-3		17	at	Boston	3-5
	14	at	Chicago	6-2		19		Toronto	3-3
	16	at	Pittsburgh	3-5		24		Boston	1-2
	19	at	Toronto	2-7		26		Montreal	0-3
	20		Quebec	2-5		27	at	Ottawa	1-1
	23		Buffalo	3-3		29		Quebec	2-3
	27	at	Dallas	1-5	Feb.	1		Quebec	2-1
	28	at	St. Louis	1-2		2	at	Montreal	2-9
	30		NY Rangers	1-4		4	at	Winnipeg	2-2
Nov.	1		Calgary	2-4		6	at	Vancouver	4-2
	3		Calgary	3-6		11	at	Calgary	1-4
	6	at	NY Islanders	3-5		12	at	Edmonton	5-2
	10		Ottawa	4-3		16		Buffalo	3-5
	13		Edmonton	4-4		17	at	Pittsburgh	4-6
	17		Boston	2-4		19		NY Rangers	4-2
	18	at	Philadelphia	3-6		24	at	Detroit	0-3
	20		San Jose	2-3		26		New Jersey	1-1
	23	at	Florida	2-1		27		Washington	1-3
	24	at	Tampa Bay	1-4	Mar.	1		Los Angeles	1-4
	27		Florida	4-0		4	at	Florida	2-1
	29	at	Ottawa	4-2		5	at	Tampa Bay	2-4
Dec.	1		Detroit	5-3		9		Tampa Bay	4-1
	4		Pittsburgh	6-7		10	at	New Jersey	0-4
	7	at	Washington	6-1		12		Dallas	2-2
	8		Vancouver	1-4		13		Pittsburgh	2-3
	11		Buffalo	0-3		16	at	NY Rangers	0-4
	12	at	Boston	2-2		17	at	Quebec	0-4
	15	at	NY Rangers	2-5		19	at	Philadelphia	5-3
	18		Washington	4-1		22	at	Washington	1-4
	22		New Jersey	6-3		25	at	Buffalo	3-6
	23	at	Ottawa	2-1		26		Anaheim	2-3
	26		Ottawa	3-2		29	at	Detroit	2-6
	28	at	New Jersey	2-4		30		Chicago	3-2
	29		Florida	3-5	Apr.	2		Philadelphia	5-6
Jan.	1	at	NY Islanders	4-3		6		NY Islanders	3-3
	2		Pittsburgh	7-2		7	at	Quebec	2-5
	5		Winnipeg	4-0		10		Tampa Bay	6-4
	6		St. Louis	1-2		11		Montreal	1-3
	8		NY Islanders	6-0		14	at	Boston	3-2

Entry Draft
Selections 1994-80

1994 Pick		**1990** Pick		**1986** Pick		**1982** Pick	
5	Jeff O'Neill	15	Mark Greig	11	Scott Young	14	Paul Lawless
83	Hnat Domenichelli	36	Geoff Sanderson	32	Marc Laforge	35	Mark Paterson
109	Ryan Risidore	57	Mike Lenarduzzi	74	Brian Chapman	56	Kevin Dineen
187	Tom Buckley	78	Chris Bright	95	Bill Horn	67	Ulf Samuelsson
213	Ashlin Halfnight	120	Cory Keenan	116	Joe Quinn	88	Ray Ferraro
230	Matt Ball	141	Jergus Baca	137	Steve Torrel	109	Randy Gilhen
239	Brian Regan	162	Martin D'Orsonnens	158	Ron Hoover	130	Jim Johannson
265	Steve Nimigon	183	Corey Osmak	179	Robert Glasgow	151	Mickey Kramptoich
1993 Pick		204	Espen Knutsen	200	Sean Evoy	172	Kevin Skilliter
2	Chris Pronger	225	Tommie Eriksen	221	Cal Brown	214	Martin Linse
72	Marek Malik	246	Denis Chalifoux	242	Brian Verbeek	235	Randy Cameron
84	Trevor Roenick	**1989** Pick		**1985** Pick		**1981** Pick	
115	Nolan Pratt	10	Robert Holik	5	Dana Murzyn	4	Ron Francis
188	Emmanuel Legace	52	Blair Atcheynum	26	Kay Whitmore	61	Paul MacDermid
214	Dmitri Gorenko	73	Jim McKenzie	68	Gary Callaghan	67	Michael Hoffman
240	Wes Swinson	94	James Black	110	Shane Churla	93	Bill Maguire
266	Igor Chibirev	115	Jerome Bechard	131	Chris Brant	103	Dan Bourbonnais
1992 Pick		136	Scott Daniels	152	Brian Puhalsky	130	John Mokosak
9	Robert Petrovicky	157	Raymond Saumier	173	Greg Dornbach	151	Denis Dore
47	Andrei Nikolishin	178	Michel Picard	194	Paul Tory	172	Jeff Poeschl
57	Jan Vopat	199	Trevor Buchanan	215	Jerry Pawlowski	193	Larry Power
79	Kevin Smyth	220	John Battice	236	Bruce Hill	**1980** Pick	
81	Jason McBain	241	Peter Kasowski	**1984** Pick		8	Fred Arthur
143	Jarret Reid	**1988** Pick		11	Sylvain Cote	29	Michel Galarneau
153	Ken Belanger	11	Chris Govedaris	110	Mike Millar	50	Mickey Volcan
177	Konstantin Korotkov	32	Barry Richter	131	Mike Vellucci	71	Kevin McClelland
201	Greg Zwakman	74	Dean Dyer	173	John Devereaux	92	Darren Jensen
225	Steven Halko	95	Scott Morrow	193	Brent Regan	113	Mario Cerri
249	Joacim Esbjors	116	Corey Beaulieu	214	Jim Culhane	134	Mike Martin
1991 Pick		137	Kerry Russell	234	Pete Abric	155	Brent Denat
9	Patrick Poulin	158	Jim Burke	**1983** Pick		176	Paul Fricker
31	Martin Hamrlik	179	Mark Hirth	2	Sylvain Turgeon	197	Lorne Bokshowan
53	Todd Hall	200	Wayde Bucsis	20	David Jensen		
59	Mikael Nylander	221	Rob White	23	Ville Siren		
75	Jim Storm	242	Dan Slatalla	61	Leif Carlsson		
119	Mike Harding	**1987** Pick		64	Dave MacLean		
141	Brian Mueller	18	Jody Hull	72	Ron Chyzowski		
163	Steve Yule	39	Adam Burt	104	Brian Johnson		
185	Chris Belanger	81	Terry Yake	124	Joe Reekie		
207	Jason Currie	102	Marc Rousseau	143	Chris Duperron		
229	Mike Santonelli	123	Jeff St. Cyr	144	James Falle		
251	Rob Peters	144	Greg Wolf	164	Bill Fordy		
		165	John Moore	193	Reine Karlsson		
		186	Joe Day	204	Allan Acton		
		228	Kevin Sullivan	224	Darcy Kaminski		
		249	Steve Laurin				

Club Directory

Hartford Whalers
242 Trumbull Street
Eighth Floor
Hartford, Connecticut 06103
Phone **203/728-3366**
GM FAX 203/493-2423
FAX 203/522-7707
Capacity: 15,635

Ownership
Chief Executive Officer/Governor	Peter Karmanos Jr.
General Partner	Thomas Thewes
Chief Operating Officer/President/General Manager	Jim Rutherford

Hockey Operations
Vice President of Hockey Operations	Terry McDonnell
Director of Hockey Operations	Kevin Maxwell
Head Coach	Paul Holmgren
Assistant Coach	Ted Nolan
Assistant Coach	Kevin McCarthy
Strength and Conditioning Instructor	Doug McKenney
Goaltending Consultant	Steve Weeks
Scouting Staff	Bruce Haralson, Ken Schinkel, Tom Rowe, Claude Larose, Larry Johnson, Yves Sansfacon, Willy Langer
Medical Trainer	Bud Gouveia
Equipment Managers	Skip Cunningham, Wally Tatimor
Assistant Equipment Managers	Bob Gorman, Todd MacGowan
Executive Secretary, Hockey Operations	Anne Sullivan
Secretary, Hockey Operations	Cathy Merrick

Administration
Senior Vice President of Marketing and P.R.	Russ Gregory
Vice President of Finance and Administration	Michael J. Amendola
Vice President of Marketing and Sales	Rick Francis
Advertising Sales Manager	Kevin Bauer
Senior Account Executive	Bill McMinn
Director of Public and Media Relations	John Forslund
Community Relations Director	Mary Lynn Gorman
Director of Publications/Chief Statistician/Archivist	Frank Polnaszek
Director of Amateur Hockey Development	Mike Veisor
Director of Ticket Sales	Jim Baldwin
Ticket Office Supervisors	Mike Barnes, Chris O'Connor
Group Sales Manager	Brian Dooley

General Information
Radio Play-by-Play	Chuck Kaiton
Radio Color	John Forslund
TV/Cable Play-by-Play	Rick Peckham
TV/Cable Commentator	Gerry Cheevers
Cable TV Outlet	SportsChannel - New England
Radio Network Flagship Station	WTIC-AM (1080)
Home Ice	Hartford Civic Center, Veterans Memorial Coliseum
Dimensions of Rink	200 feet by 85 feet

General Manager

RUTHERFORD, JIM
General Manager, Hartford Whalers. Born in Beeton, Ont., February 17, 1949.

Years of work by Jim Rutherford and the KTR Limited Partnership were rewarded on June 28 when the Detroit, Michigan group was approved by the National Hockey League Board of Governors as the owners of the Hartford Whalers. KTR completed a $50 million deal with the Connecticut Development Authority to keep the only major professional sports team in the state.

Rutherford has extensive experience in youth hockey and junior programs, serving as Director of Hockey Operations for Compuware Sports Corporation. As a former player, coach, and general manager, he earned much respect in the hockey world for his ability to develop players and produce winning programs.

As KTR Limited Partnership's point man over the past 10 years, Rutherford led efforts to land an NHL expansion franchise. Based on Rutherford's experience in the sport and Compuware's success at the junior hockey level, the CDA and the State of Connecticut elected to sell the Whalers to KTR Limited Partnership.

Rutherford, 45, began his professional goaltending career in 1969, as a first-round selection of the Detroit Red Wings. He collected 14 career shutouts in his 13 seasons in the NHL for Pittsburgh, Toronto, Los Angeles and Detroit, serving as the Red Wings' player representative for five seasons. Rutherford also played for Team Canada in the World Championships in Vienna in 1977 and Moscow in 1979.

After his playing days with the Red Wings, Rutherford joined Compuware and guided Compuware Sports Corporation's purchase of the Windsor Spitfires of the Ontario Hockey League in April, 1984. Rutherford served as G.M. of the Spitfires from that season until 1987-88, and spent the 1986-87 season behind the bench as head coach. He was instrumental in guiding the Spitfires to the 1988 Memorial Cup finals.

On December 11, 1989, Rutherford brought the first American-based OHL franchise to Detroit, as the Ambassadors donned Compuware's orange and brown colors. Two seasons later, Rutherford renamed the club the Detroit Jr. Red Wings, in coordination with the NHL Red Wings, to further promote youth hockey in Detroit and the United States.

With Detroit, Rutherford took over as coach for the 1991-92 season, leading the Ambassadors to their first-ever playoff berth. As Director of Hockey Operations, he then put together the 1993-94 Jr. Red Wings that won the Emms Division championship. Rutherford won the 1993 Executive of the Year Award in both the OHL and the Canadian Hockey League. He again won the OHL Executive of the Year Award in 1994.

Coach

HOLMGREN, PAUL
Coach, Hartford Whalers. Born in St. Paul, MN, December 2, 1955.

Paul Holmgren was reappointed coach of the Hartford Whalers, succeeding Pierre McGuire, on June 28, 1994. A sixth round draft selection of the Philadelphia Flyers in 1975, Holmgren spent nine years with the team before finishing his career with the Minnesota North Stars in 1985. The next season, he was named as an assistant to Mike Keenan, spending three years in that role. In 1988, Holmgren became the first former-Flyer to be named head coach, serving in that capacity for four seasons. In Philadelphia, Holmgren compiled a 107-126-31 record before being replaced by Bill Dineen on December 4, 1991. He resigned as Whalers' coach on November 16, 1993 to concentrate on his duties as the club's general manager.

Coaching Record

| Season | Team | Regular Season | | | | | Playoffs | | | |
		Games	W	L	T	%	Games	W	L	%
1988-89	Philadelphia (NHL)	80	36	36	8	.500	19	10	9	.526
1989-90	Philadelphia (NHL)	80	30	39	11	.444	....	....	....	....
1990-91	Philadelphia (NHL)	80	33	37	10	.475	....	....	....	....
1991-92	Philadelphia (NHL)	24	8	14	2	.375	....	....	....	....
1992-93	Hartford (NHL)	84	26	52	6	.345	....	....	....	....
1993-94	Hartford (NHL)	17	4	11	2	.294	....	....	....	....
	NHL Totals	**365**	**137**	**189**	**39**	**.429**	**19**	**10**	**9**	**.526**

Los Angeles Kings

1993-94 Results: 27W-45L-12T 66PTS. Fifth, Pacific Division

Part of the Kings' solid corps of young, mobile defencemen, rearguard Darryl Sydor appeared in all 84 games for Los Angeles, collecting 35 points.

Schedule

Oct.	Sat.	1	at San Jose		Sat.	14	Dallas
	Wed.	5	Detroit		Mon.	16	at Calgary
	Sat.	8	Calgary		Tues.	17	at Edmonton
	Tues.	11	San Jose		Mon.	23	at San Jose
	Thur.	13	Vancouver		Tues.	24	Dallas
	Sat.	15	Boston		Thur.	26	San Jose
	Tues.	18	at NY Islanders		Sat.	28	Winnipeg
	Thur.	20	at NY Rangers		Tues.	31	Winnipeg
	Sat.	22	at Pittsburgh				(in Phoenix)
	Sun.	23	at Chicago	Feb.	Thur.	2	at St. Louis
	Tues.	25	at Florida		Sat.	4	Detroit
	Wed.	26	at Tampa Bay		Mon.	6	Edmonton
	Fri.	28	at Detroit		Wed.	8	at New Jersey
Nov.	Tues.	1	NY Rangers		Thur.	9	at Detroit
	Fri.	4	at Vancouver		Sat.	11	at Boston*
	Sun.	6	New Jersey		Mon.	13	at Philadelphia
	Tues.	8	Anaheim		Thur.	16	Quebec
	Thur.	10	Calgary		Sat.	18	Ottawa
	Sat.	12	Vancouver		Sun.	19	at Anaheim
	Tues.	15	Chicago		Tues.	21	Anaheim
	Thur.	17	Buffalo		Thur.	23	Philadelphia
	Tues.	22	at Calgary		Sat.	25	Calgary
	Wed.	23	at Edmonton		Tues.	28	Tampa Bay
	Sat.	26	at Montreal	Mar.	Thur.	2	at St. Louis
	Mon.	28	at Ottawa				(in Las Vegas)
	Tues.	29	at Quebec		Sat.	4	Montreal
Dec.	Fri.	2	at Buffalo		Mon.	6	at Dallas
	Sat.	3	at Toronto		Thur.	9	at Toronto
	Thur.	8	Washington		Sat.	11	at Winnipeg
	Sat.	10	Toronto		Tues.	14	Hartford
	Mon.	12	at Vancouver		Thur.	16	St. Louis
	Thur.	15	Pittsburgh		Sat.	18	Toronto
	Sat.	17	NY Islanders		Mon.	20	Florida
	Thur.	22	Edmonton		Thur.	23	Chicago
	Mon.	26	at Anaheim		Sat.	26	San Jose*
	Wed.	28	Anaheim		Sun.	26	at San Jose*
	Sat.	31	at Winnipeg*		Wed.	29	at Vancouver
Jan.	Mon.	2	at Dallas		Fri.	31	at Edmonton
	Wed.	4	at Hartford	Apr.	Sat.	1	Winnipeg
	Fri.	6	at Washington		Mon.	3	Edmonton
	Sun.	8	at Chicago		Thur.	6	Vancouver
	Tues.	10	at St. Louis		Fri.	7	at Calgary
	Thur.	12	St. Louis		Sun.	9	at Anaheim*

* Denotes afternoon game.

Home Starting Times:
Night Games . . . . 7:30 p.m.
Matinees . . . . 1:00 p.m.

Franchise date: June 5, 1967

28th NHL Season

PACIFIC DIVISION

Year-by-Year Record

		Home			Road			Overall						
Season	GP	W	L	T	W	L	T	W	L	T	GF	GA	Pts.	Finished	Playoff Result
1993-94	84	18	19	5	9	26	7	27	45	12	294	322	66	5th, Pacific Div.	Out of Playoffs
1992-93	84	22	15	5	17	20	5	39	35	10	338	340	88	3rd, Smythe Div.	Lost Final
1991-92	80	20	11	9	15	20	5	35	31	14	287	296	84	2nd, Smythe Div.	Lost Div. Semi-Final
1990-91	80	26	9	5	20	15	5	46	24	10	340	254	102	1st, Smythe Div.	Lost Div. Final
1989-90	80	21	16	3	13	23	4	34	39	7	338	337	75	4th, Smythe Div.	Lost Div. Final
1988-89	80	25	12	3	17	19	4	42	31	7	376	335	91	2nd, Smythe Div.	Lost Div. Final
1987-88	80	19	18	3	11	24	5	30	42	8	318	359	68	4th, Smythe Div.	Lost Div. Semi-Final
1986-87	80	20	17	3	11	24	5	31	41	8	318	341	70	4th, Smythe Div.	Lost Div. Semi-Final
1985-86	80	9	27	4	14	22	4	23	49	8	284	389	54	5th, Smythe Div.	Out of Playoffs
1984-85	80	20	14	6	14	18	8	34	32	14	339	326	82	4th, Smythe Div.	Lost Div. Semi-Final
1983-84	80	13	19	8	10	25	5	23	44	13	309	376	59	5th, Smythe Div.	Out of Playoffs
1982-83	80	20	13	7	7	28	5	27	41	12	308	365	66	5th, Smythe Div.	Out of Playoffs
1981-82	80	19	15	6	5	26	9	24	41	15	314	369	63	4th, Smythe Div.	Lost Div. Final
1980-81	80	22	11	7	21	13	6	43	24	13	337	290	99	2nd, Norris Div.	Lost Prelim. Round
1979-80	80	18	13	9	12	23	5	30	36	14	290	313	74	2nd, Norris Div.	Lost Prelim. Round
1978-79	80	20	13	7	14	21	5	34	34	12	292	286	80	3rd, Norris Div.	Lost Prelim. Round
1977-78	80	18	16	6	13	18	9	31	34	15	243	245	77	3rd, Norris Div.	Lost Prelim. Round
1976-77	80	20	13	7	14	18	8	34	31	15	271	241	83	2nd, Norris Div.	Lost Quarter-Final
1975-76	80	22	13	5	16	20	4	38	33	9	263	265	85	2nd, Norris Div.	Lost Quarter-Final
1974-75	80	22	7	11	20	10	10	42	17	21	269	185	105	2nd, Norris Div.	Lost Prelim. Round
1973-74	78	22	13	4	11	20	8	33	33	12	233	231	78	3rd, West Div.	Lost Quarter-Final
1972-73	78	21	11	7	10	25	4	31	36	11	232	245	73	6th, West Div.	Out of Playoffs
1971-72	78	14	23	2	6	26	7	20	49	9	206	305	49	7th, West Div.	Out of Playoffs
1970-71	78	17	14	8	8	26	5	25	40	13	239	303	63	5th, West Div.	Out of Playoffs
1969-70	76	12	22	4	2	30	6	14	52	10	168	290	38	6th, West Div.	Out of Playoffs
1968-69	76	19	14	5	5	28	5	24	42	10	185	260	58	4th, West Div.	Lost Semi-Final
1967-68	74	20	13	4	11	20	6	31	33	10	200	224	72	2nd, West Div.	Lost Quarter-Final

1994-95 Player Personnel

FORWARDS	HT	WT	S	Place of Birth	Date	1993-94 Club
BROWN, Kevin	6-1	212	R	Birmingham, England	5/11/74	Detroit (OHL)
BROWN, Rob	5-11	185	L	Kingston, Ont.	4/10/68	Dallas-Kalamazoo
BYLSMA, Dan	6-2	215	L	Grand Rapids, MI	9/19/70	Greensboro-Albany-Moncton
CONACHER, Pat	5-8	190	L	Edmonton, Alta.	5/1/59	Los Angeles
DONNELLY, Mike	5-11	185	L	Detroit, MI	10/10/63	Los Angeles
DRUCE, John	6-2	195	R	Peterborough, Ont.	2/23/66	Los Angeles-Phoenix
GRANATO, Tony	5-10	185	R	Downers Grove, IL	7/25/64	Los Angeles
GRETZKY, Wayne	6-0	180	L	Brantford, Ont.	1/26/61	Los Angeles
JOHNSON, Matt	6-5	230	L	Welland, Ont.	11/23/75	Peterborough
KURRI, Jari	6-1	195	R	Helsinki, Finland	5/18/60	Los Angeles
LANG, Robert	6-2	189	R	Teplice, Czech.	12/19/70	Los Angeles-Phoenix
LEVEQUE, Guy	6-1	180	R	Kingston, Ont.	12/28/72	Los Angeles-Phoenix
McREYNOLDS, Brian	6-1	192	L	Penetanguishene, Ont.	1/5/65	Los Angeles-Phoenix
PERREAULT, Yanic	5-11	182	L	Sherbrooke, Que.	4/4/71	Toronto-St. John's
POTOMSKI, Barry	6-2	215	L	Windsor, Ont.	11/24/72	Toledo-Adirondack
REDMOND, Keith	6-3	208	L	Richmond Hill, Ont.	10/25/72	Los Angeles-Phoenix
RYCHEL, Warren	6-0	202	L	Tecumseh, Ont.	5/12/67	Los Angeles
SHEVALIER, Jeff	5-11	185	L	Mississauga, Ont.	3/14/74	North Bay
SHUCHUK, Gary	5-11	190	R	Edmonton, Alta.	2/17/67	Los Angeles
SOULLIERE, Stephane	5-11	180	L	Greenfield Park, Que.	5/30/75	Oshawa
THOMLINSON, Dave	6-1	215	L	Edmonton, Alta.	10/22/66	Los Angeles-Phoenix
TOCCHET, Rick	6-0	205	R	Scarborough, Ont.	4/9/64	Pittsburgh
TODD, Kevin	5-10	180	L	Winnipeg, Man.	5/4/68	Chicago-Los Angeles
WARD, Dixon	6-0	200	R	Leduc, Alta.	9/23/68	Vancouver-Los Angeles

DEFENSEMEN						
BLAKE, Rob	6-3	215	R	Simcoe, Ont.	12/10/69	Los Angeles
COWIE, Rob	6-0	195	L	Toronto, Ont.	11/3/67	Springfield
DUFRESNE, Donald	6-1	206	R	Quebec City, Que.	4/10/67	Tampa Bay-Los Angeles
HOCKING, Justin	6-4	205	R	Stettler, Alta.	1/9/74	L.A.-Medicine Hat-Phoenix
HUDDY, Charlie	6-0	210	L	Oshawa, Ont.	6/2/59	Los Angeles
McSORLEY, Marty	6-1	225	R	Hamilton, Ont.	5/18/63	Pittsburgh-Los Angeles
O'DONNELL, Sean	6-2	224	L	Ottawa, Ont.	10/13/71	Rochester
PETIT, Michel	6-1	205	R	St. Malo, Que.	2/12/64	Calgary
SYDOR, Darryl	6-0	205	L	Edmonton, Alta.	5/13/72	Los Angeles
WATTERS, Tim	5-11	185	L	Kamloops, B.C.	7/25/59	Los Angeles
ZHITNIK, Alexei	5-11	190	L	Kiev, USSR	10/10/72	Los Angeles

GOALTENDERS	HT	WT	C	Place of Birth	Date	1993-94 Club
HRUDEY, Kelly	5-10	189	L	Edmonton, Alta.	1/13/61	Los Angeles
JAKS, Pauli	6-0	194	L	Schaffhausen, Switz.	1/25/72	Phoenix
STAUBER, Robb	5-11	180	L	Duluth, MN	11/25/67	Los Angeles-Phoenix
STORR, Jamie	6-1	192	L	Brampton, Ont.	12/28/75	Owen Sound

Defenceman Alexei Zhitnik had another impressive year for the Los Angeles Kings, recording 12 goals and 52 points in 81 games.

1993-94 Scoring

* – rookie

Regular Season

Pos	#	Player	Team	GP	G	A	Pts	+/–	PIM	PP	SH	GW	GT	S	%
C	99	Wayne Gretzky	L.A.	81	38	92	130	25–	20	14	4	0	1	233	16.3
L	20	Luc Robitaille	L.A.	83	44	42	86	20–	86	24	0	3	0	267	16.5
L	17	Jari Kurri	L.A.	81	31	46	77	24–	48	14	4	3	1	198	15.7
D	4	Rob Blake	L.A.	84	20	48	68	7–	137	7	0	6	0	304	6.6
D	2	Alexei Zhitnik	L.A.	81	12	40	52	11–	101	11	0	1	1	227	5.3
L	11	Mike Donnelly	L.A.	81	21	21	42	2	34	4	2	3	0	177	11.9
D	25	Darryl Sydor	L.A.	84	8	27	35	9–	94	1	0	0	0	146	5.5
R	19	John Druce	L.A.	55	14	17	31	16	50	1	1	0	0	104	13.5
D	33	Marty McSorley	PIT	47	3	18	21	9–	139	0	0	0	1	122	2.5
			L.A.	18	4	6	10	3–	55	1	0	1	0	38	10.5
			TOTAL	65	7	24	31	12–	194	1	0	1	1	160	4.4
L	15	Pat Conacher	L.A.	77	15	13	28	0	71	0	3	1	0	98	15.3
C	12	Kevin Todd	CHI	35	5	6	11	2–	16	1	0	1	0	49	10.2
			L.A.	12	3	8	11	1–	8	3	0	0	0	16	18.8
			TOTAL	47	8	14	22	3–	24	4	0	1	0	65	12.3
L	21	Tony Granato	L.A.	50	7	14	21	2–	150	2	0	0	0	117	6.0
L	10	Warren Rychel	L.A.	80	10	9	19	19–	322	0	0	3	0	105	9.5
C	13	* Robert Lang	L.A.	32	9	10	19	7	10	0	0	0	0	41	22.0
D	22	Charlie Huddy	L.A.	79	5	13	18	4	71	1	0	0	0	134	3.7
R	9	Dixon Ward	VAN	33	6	1	7	14–	37	2	0	1	0	46	13.0
			L.A.	34	6	2	8	8–	45	2	0	0	0	44	13.6
			TOTAL	67	12	3	15	22–	82	4	0	1	0	90	13.3
D	5	Tim Watters	L.A.	60	1	9	10	11–	67	0	1	0	0	38	2.6
D	29	Donald Dufresne	T.B.	51	2	6	8	2–	48	0	0	0	0	49	4.1
			L.A.	9	0	0	0	5–	10	0	0	0	0	7	.0
			TOTAL	60	2	6	8	7–	58	0	0	0	0	56	3.6
D	6	Doug Houda	HFD	7	0	0	0	4–	23	0	0	0	0	1	.0
			L.A.	54	2	6	8	15–	165	0	0	0	0	31	6.5
			TOTAL	61	2	6	8	19–	188	0	0	0	0	32	6.3
R	18	Dave Taylor	L.A.	33	4	3	7	1	28	0	1	2	0	39	10.3
C	14	Gary Shuchuk	L.A.	56	3	4	7	8–	30	0	0	1	0	55	5.5
D	42	Dominic Lavoie	L.A.	8	3	3	6	2–	2	2	0	1	0	21	14.3
D	7	Jim Paek	PIT	41	0	4	4	7–	8	0	0	0	0	24	.0
			L.A.	18	1	1	2	1–	10	0	0	0	0	11	9.1
			TOTAL	59	1	5	6	8–	18	0	0	0	0	35	2.9
C	26	Brian McReynolds	L.A.	20	1	3	4	2–	4	0	0	0	0	10	10.0
D	24	Mark Hardy	L.A.	16	0	3	3	5–	27	0	0	0	0	8	.0
L	37	* Dan Currie	L.A.	5	1	1	2	1–	0	0	0	0	0	12	8.3
L	23	Philip Crowe	L.A.	31	0	2	2	4	77	0	0	0	0	5	.0
L	45	* Keith Redmond	L.A.	12	1	0	1	3–	20	0	0	0	0	9	11.1
D	3	Brent Thompson	L.A.	24	1	0	1	1–	81	0	0	0	0	9	11.1
D	50	Bob Jay	L.A.	3	0	1	1	0	0	0	0	0	0	2	.0
C	28	* Guy Leveque	L.A.	5	0	1	1	1	2	0	0	0	0	3	.0
C	8	Rob Murphy	L.A.	8	0	1	1	3–	22	0	0	0	0	4	.0
G	32	Kelly Hrudey	L.A.	64	0	1	1	0	6	0	0	0	0	0	.0
G	41	* David Goverde	L.A.	1	0	0	0	0	0	0	0	0	0	0	.0
D	51	* Justin Hocking	L.A.	1	0	0	0	0	0	0	0	0	0	0	.0
G	1	Rick Knickle	L.A.	4	0	0	0	0	0	0	0	0	0	0	.0
L	27	Dave Thomlinson	L.A.	7	0	0	0	6–	21	0	0	0	0	6	.0
G	35	Robb Stauber	L.A.	22	0	0	0	0	18	0	0	0	0	0	.0

Goaltending

No.	Goaltender	GPI	Mins	Avg	W	L	T	EN	SO	GA	SA	S%
1	Rick Knickle	4	174	3.10	1	2	0	2	0	9	71	.873
35	Robb Stauber	22	1144	3.41	4	11	5	2	1	65	706	.908
32	Kelly Hrudey	64	3713	3.68	22	31	7	9	1	228	2219	.897
41	* David Goverde	1	60	7.00	0	1	0	0	0	7	37	.811
	Totals	84	5124	3.77	27	45	12	13	2	322	3046	.894

General Managers' History

Larry Regan, 1967-68 to 1972-73; Larry Regan and Jake Milford, 1973-74; Jake Milford, 1974-75 to 1976-77; George Maguire, 1977-78 to 1982-83; George Maguire and Rogatien Vachon, 1983-84; Rogatien Vachon, 1984-85 to 1991-92; Nick Beverley, 1992-93 to 1993-94; Sam McMaster, 1994-95.

Coaching History

Leonard "Red" Kelly, 1967-68 to 1968-69; Hal Laycoe and John Wilson, 1969-70; Larry Regan, 1970-71; Larry Regan and Fred Glover, 1971-72; Bob Pulford, 1972-73 to 1976-77; Ron Stewart, 1977-78; Bob Berry, 1978-79 to 1980-81; Parker MacDonald and Don Perry, 1981-82; Don Perry, 1982-83; Don Perry, Rogatien Vachon and Roger Neilson, 1983-84; Pat Quinn, 1984-85 to 1985-86; Pat Quinn and Mike Murphy 1986-87; Mike Murphy and Robbie Ftorek, 1987-88; Robbie Ftorek, 1988-89; Tom Webster, 1989-90 to 1991-92; Barry Melrose, 1992-93 to date.

Captains' History

Bob Wall, 1967-68, 1968-69; Larry Cahan, 1969-70, 1970-71; Bob Pulford, 1971-72, 1972-73; Terry Harper, 1973-74, 1974-75; Mike Murphy, 1975-76 to 1980-81; Dave Lewis, 1981-82, 1982-83; Terry Ruskowski, 1983-84, 1984-85; Dave Taylor, 1985-86 to 1988-89; Wayne Gretzky, 1989-90 to 1991-92; Wayne Gretzky and Luc Robitaille, 1992-93; Wayne Gretzky, 1993-94 to date.

Retired Numbers

16	Marcel Dionne	1975-1987
30	Rogatien Vachon	1971-1978

Club Records

Team

(Figures in brackets for season records are games played)

Most Points	105	1974-75 (80)
Most Wins	46	1990-91 (80)
Most Ties	21	1974-75 (80)
Most Losses	52	1969-70 (76)
Most Goals	376	1988-89 (80)
Most Goals Against	389	1985-86 (80)
Fewest Points	38	1969-70 (76)
Fewest Wins	14	1969-70 (76)
Fewest Ties	7	1988-89 (80)
		1989-90 (80)
Fewest Losses	17	1974-75 (80)
Fewest Goals	168	1969-70 (76)
Fewest Goals Against	185	1974-75 (80)

Longest Winning Streak

Over-all	8	Oct. 21-Nov. 7/72
Home	12	Oct. 10-Dec. 5/92
Away	8	Dec. 18/74-Jan. 16/75

Longest Undefeated Streak

Over-all	11	Feb. 28-Mar. 24/74 (9 wins, 2 ties)
Home	13	Oct. 10-Dec. 8/92 (12 wins, 1 tie)
Away	11	Oct. 10-Dec. 11/74 (6 wins, 5 ties)

Longest Losing Streak

Over-all	10	Feb. 22-Mar. 9/84
Home	9	Feb. 8-Mar. 12/86
Away	12	Jan. 11-Feb. 15/70

Longest Winless Streak

Over-all	17	Jan. 29-Mar. 5/70 (13 losses, 4 ties)
Home	9	Jan. 29-Mar. 5/70 (8 losses, 1 tie)
		Feb. 8-Mar. 12/86 (9 losses)
Away	21	Jan. 11-Apr. 3/70 (17 losses, 4 ties)

Most Shutouts, Season	9	1974-75 (80)
Most PIM, Season	2,228	1990-91 (80)
Most Goals, Game	12	Nov. 28/84 (Van. 1 at L.A. 12)

Individual

Most Seasons	17	Dave Taylor
Most Games	1,111	Dave Taylor
Most Goals, Career	550	Marcel Dionne
Most Assists, Career	757	Marcel Dionne
Most Points Career	1,307	Marcel Dionne
Most PIM, Career	1,615	Marty McSorley
Most Shutouts, Career	32	Rogie Vachon

Longest Consecutive

Games Streak	324	Marcel Dionne (Jan. 7/78-Jan. 9/82)
Most Goals, Season	70	Bernie Nicholls (1988-89)
Most Assists, Season	122	Wayne Gretzky (1990-91)
Most Points, Season	168	Wayne Gretzky (1988-89) (54 goals, 114 assists)
Most PIM, Season	399	Marty McSorley (1992-93)

Most Points, Defenseman

Season	76	Larry Murphy (1980-81) (16 goals, 60 assists)

Most Points, Center,

Season	168	Wayne Gretzky (1988-89) (54 goal, 114 assists)

Most Points, Right Wing,

Season	112	Dave Taylor (1980-81) (47 goals, 65 assists)

Most Points, Left Wing,

Season	*125	Luc Robitaille (1992-93) (63 goals, 62 assists)

Most Points, Rookie,

Season	84	Luc Robitaille (1986-87) (45 goals, 39 assists)

Most Shutouts, Season	8	Rogie Vachon (1976-77)
Most Goals, Game	4	Several players
Most Assists, Game	6	Bernie Nicholls (Dec. 1/88)
		Tomas Sandstrom (Oct. 9/93)
Most Points, Game	8	Bernie Nicholls (Dec. 1/88)

* NHL Record

All-time Record vs. Other Clubs

Regular Season

			At Home						On Road						Total				
	GP	W	L	T	GF	GA	PTS	GP	W	L	T	GF	GA	PTS	GP	W	L	T	GF	GA	PTS
Anaheim	3	2	1	0	10	8	4	3	2	1	0	10	10	4	6	4	2	0	20	18	8
Boston	53	18	30	5	185	203	41	54	10	41	3	149	261	23	107	28	71	8	334	464	64
Buffalo	46	17	21	8	158	162	42	45	15	22	8	141	183	38	91	32	43	16	299	345	80
Calgary	69	37	26	6	283	258	80	71	18	44	9	239	341	45	140	55	70	15	522	599	125
Chicago	54	24	24	6	185	183	54	55	19	28	8	168	214	46	109	43	52	14	353	397	100
Dallas	58	26	17	15	211	174	67	59	15	35	9	168	243	39	117	41	52	24	379	417	106
Detroit	60	33	16	11	260	187	77	59	27	24	8	225	238	62	119	60	40	19	485	425	139
Edmonton	54	21	22	11	234	242	53	55	14	28	13	220	282	41	109	35	50	24	454	524	94
Florida	1	0	1	0	5	6	0	1	0	0	1	2	2	1	2	0	1	1	7	8	1
Hartford	22	13	6	3	100	87	29	23	8	12	3	94	90	19	45	21	18	6	194	177	48
Montreal	58	15	34	9	178	234	39	57	7	39	11	147	265	25	115	22	73	20	325	499	64
New Jersey	35	26	3	6	189	107	58	35	15	15	5	130	121	35	70	41	18	11	319	228	93
NY Islanders	37	16	14	7	132	125	39	37	13	20	4	108	140	30	74	29	34	11	240	265	69
NY Rangers	52	20	23	9	174	187	49	51	15	31	5	150	207	35	103	35	54	14	324	394	84
Ottawa	2	2	0	0	15	6	4	2	1	1	0	5	7	2	4	3	1	0	20	13	6
Philadelphia	58	17	34	7	171	204	41	56	15	34	7	145	217	37	114	32	68	14	316	421	78
Pittsburgh	62	40	14	8	245	161	88	64	19	37	8	203	243	46	126	59	51	16	448	404	134
Quebec	22	13	8	1	102	77	27	22	9	10	3	91	94	21	44	22	18	4	193	171	48
St. Louis	58	31	19	8	218	167	70	58	14	38	6	153	225	34	116	45	57	14	371	392	104
San Jose	10	8	1	1	41	23	17	10	4	4	2	36	39	10	20	12	5	3	77	62	27
Tampa Bay	3	0	3	0	9	21	0	2	2	0	0	9	5	4	5	2	3	0	18	19	4
Toronto	56	31	18	7	203	161	69	55	15	30	10	184	231	40	111	46	48	17	387	392	109
Vancouver	77	41	26	10	321	253	92	75	25	38	12	254	298	62	152	66	64	22	575	551	154
Washington	39	23	12	4	159	123	50	38	15	17	6	140	166	36	77	38	29	10	299	289	86
Winnipeg	49	18	22	9	207	206	45	52	18	25	9	193	227	45	101	36	47	18	400	433	90
Defunct Clubs	35	27	6	2	141	76	56	34	11	14	9	91	109	31	69	38	20	11	232	185	87
Totals	**1073**	**519**	**401**	**153**	**4136**	**3634**	**1191**	**1073**	**326**	**588**	**159**	**3455**	**4458**	**811**	**2146**	**845**	**989**	**312**	**7591**	**8092**	**2002**

Calgary totals include Atlanta, 1972-73 to 1979-80. Dallas totals include Minnesota, 1967-68 to 1992-93.
New Jersey totals include Kansas City, 1974-75 to 1975-76, and Colorado, 1976-77 to 1981-82.

Playoffs

										Last		
	Series	W	L	GP	W	L	T	GF	GA	Mtg.	Round	Result
Boston	2	0	2	13	5	8	0	38	56	1977	QF	L 2-4
Calgary	6	4	2	26	13	13	0	105	112	1993	DSF	W 4-2
Chicago	1	0	1	5	1	4	0	7	10	1974	QF	L 1-4
Dallas	1	0	1	7	3	4	0	21	26	1968	QF	L 3-4
Edmonton	7	2	5	36	12	24	0	124	150	1992	DSF	L 2-4
Montreal	1	0	1	5	1	4	0	12	15	1993	F	L 1-4
NY Islanders	1	0	1	4	1	3	0	10	21	1980	PR	L 1-3
NY Rangers	2	0	2	5	1	5	0	14	32	1981	PR	L 1-3
St. Louis	1	0	1	4	0	4	0	5	16	1969	SF	L 0-4
Toronto	3	1	2	12	5	7	0	31	41	1993	CF	W 4-3
Vancouver	3	2	1	17	9	8	0	66	60	1993	DF	W 4-2
Defunct Clubs	1	1	0	7	4	3	0	23	25			
Totals	**29**	**10**	**19**	**142**	**55**	**87**	**0**	**459**	**568**			

Playoff Results 1994-90

Year	Round	Opponent	Result	GF	GA
1993	F	Montreal	L 1-4	12	15
	CF	Toronto	W 4-3	22	23
	DF	Vancouver	W 4-2	26	25
	DSF	Calgary	W 4-2	33	28
1992	DSF	Edmonton	L 2-4	18	23
1991	DF	Edmonton	L 2-4	20	21
	DSF	Vancouver	W 4-2	26	16
1990	DF	Edmonton	L 0-4	10	24
	DSF	Calgary	W 4-2	29	24

Abbreviations: Round: F – Final;
CF – conference final; **CQF** – conference quarter-final;
CSF – conference semi-final; **DF** – division final;
DSF – division semi-final; **SF** – semi-final;
QF – quarter-final; **PR** – preliminary round.

1993-94 Results

Oct.	6		Vancouver	2-5		15	at	New Jersey	5-3
	9		Detroit	10-3		16	at	Philadelphia	2-5
	10		San Jose	5-2		18	at	Dallas	3-5
	12		NY Islanders	7-5		24	at	Calgary	3-3
	14		Edmonton	4-4		25		Winnipeg	4-4
	16		Calgary	8-4		27		NY Rangers	4-5
	19	at	Florida	2-2		29		Anaheim	5-1
	20	at	Tampa Bay	4-3		31	at	Vancouver	1-3
	22	at	Washington	3-6	Feb.	2	at	Edmonton	4-6
	24	at	NY Rangers	2-3		5		Calgary	4-5
	26	at	NY Islanders	0-7		9		Chicago	4-2
	27	at	Detroit	3-8		11	at	Anaheim	5-3
	29	at	Winnipeg	4-3		12		Washington	1-6
Nov.	3		New Jersey	3-2		14		Boston	2-5
	6		Pittsburgh	8-3		18		Philadelphia	3-4
	9	at	Calgary	2-3		19	at	San Jose	3-4
	10	at	Vancouver	0-4		21		Toronto	4-6
	13		St. Louis	6-3		23		Dallas	0-0
	18		Toronto	2-3		25	at	Edmonton	5-5
	20	at	St. Louis	1-4		26	at	Calgary	2-4
	21	at	Dallas	4-7		28		Montreal	3-3
	25	at	Quebec	6-8	Mar.	2	at	Hartford	4-1
	27	at	Montreal	0-4		3	at	Boston	4-6
	30		Winnipeg	6-8		6	at	Chicago	3-3
Dec.	2		Anaheim	3-2		9		Chicago	0-4
	4		Tampa Bay	4-5		12		Buffalo	3-5
	8		Florida	5-6		15		Ottawa	7-0
	11		St. Louis	9-1		16	at	Anaheim	2-5
	13	at	Ottawa	2-5		19		San Jose	2-1
	14	at	Pittsburgh	2-4		20	at	San Jose	6-6
	17	at	Buffalo	0-2		23		Vancouver	3-6
	18	at	Toronto	1-4		25	at	Edmonton	4-3
	20	at	Calgary	5-4		27	at	Vancouver	3-4
	23		Dallas	1-2	Apr.	2		Anaheim	2-5
	26	at	Anaheim	3-2		2		Edmonton	3-5
	28	at	Vancouver	6-5		3		Edmonton	6-1
	31	at	Detroit	4-4		5		San Jose	1-2
Jan.	1	at	Toronto	7-4		7	at	St. Louis	2-6
	4		Quebec	5-1		9	at	Winnipeg	3-4
	8		Detroit	3-6		10	at	Chicago	1-2
	11	at	San Jose	2-2		13		Calgary	6-4
	12		Hartford	6-4		14		Edmonton	2-2

Entry Draft
Selections 1994-80

1994
Pick
- 7 Jamie Storr
- 33 Matt Johnson
- 59 Vitali Yachmenev
- 111 Chris Schmidt
- 163 Luc Gagne
- 189 Andrew Dale
- 215 Jan Nemecek
- 241 Sergei Shalomai

1993
Pick
- 42 Shayne Toporowski
- 68 Jeffrey Mitchell
- 94 Bob Wren
- 105 Frederick Beaubien
- 117 Jason Saal
- 120 Tomas Vlasak
- 146 Jere Karalahti
- 172 Justin Martin
- 198 John-Tra Dillabough
- 224 Martin Strbak
- 250 Kimmo Timonen
- 276 Patrick Howald

1992
Pick
- 39 Justin Hocking
- 63 Sandy Allan
- 87 Kevin Brown
- 111 Jeff Shevalier
- 135 Raymond Murray
- 207 Magnus Wernblom
- 231 Ryan Pisiak
- 255 Jukka Tiilikainen

1991
Pick
- 42 Guy Leveque
- 79 Keith Redmond
- 81 Alexei Zhitnik
- 108 Pauli Jaks
- 130 Brett Seguin
- 152 Kelly Fairchild
- 196 Craig Brown
- 218 Mattias Olsson
- 240 Andre Bouliane
- 262 Michael Gaul

1990
Pick
- 7 Darryl Sydor
- 28 Brandy Semchuk
- 49 Bob Berg
- 91 David Goverde
- 112 Erik Andersson
- 133 Robert Lang
- 154 Dean Hulett
- 175 Denis LeBlanc
- 196 Patrik Ross
- 217 K.J. (Kevin) White
- 238 Troy Mohns

1989
Pick
- 39 Brent Thompson
- 81 Jim Maher
- 102 Eric Ricard
- 103 Thomas Newman
- 123 Daniel Rydmark
- 144 Ted Kramer
- 165 Sean Whyte
- 182 Jim Giacin
- 186 Martin Maskarinec
- 207 Jim Hiller
- 228 Steve Jaques
- 249 Kevin Sneddon

1988
Pick
- 7 Martin Gelinas
- 28 Paul Holden
- 49 John Van Kessel
- 70 Rob Blake
- 91 Jeff Robison
- 109 Micah Aivazoff
- 112 Robert Larsson
- 133 Jeff Kruesel
- 154 Timo Peltomaa
- 175 Jim Larkin
- 196 Brad Hyatt
- 217 Doug Laprade
- 238 Joe Flanagan

1987
Pick
- 4 Wayne McBean
- 27 Mark Fitzpatrick
- 43 Ross Wilson
- 90 Mike Vukonich
- 111 Greg Batters
- 132 Kyosti Karjalainen
- 174 Jeff Gawlicki
- 195 John Preston
- 216 Rostislav Vlach
- 237 Mikael Lindholm

1986
Pick
- 2 Jimmy Carson
- 44 Denis Larocque
- 65 Sylvain Couturier
- 86 Dave Guden
- 107 Robb Stauber
- 128 Sean Krakiwsky
- 149 Rene Chapdelaine
- 170 Trevor Pochipinski
- 191 Paul Kelly
- 212 Russ Mann
- 233 Brian Hayton

1985
Pick
- 9 Craig Duncanson
- 10 Dan Gratton
- 30 Par Edlund
- 72 Perry Florio
- 93 Petr Prajsler
- 135 Tim Flannigan
- 156 John Hyduke
- 177 Steve Horner
- 219 Trent Ciprick
- 240 Marian Horwath

1984
Pick
- 6 Craig Redmond
- 24 Brian Wilks
- 48 John English
- 69 Tom Glavine
- 87 Dave Grannis
- 108 Greg Strome
- 129 Tim Hanley
- 150 Shannon Deegan
- 171 Luc Robitaille
- 191 Jeff Crossman
- 212 Paul Kenny
- 232 Brian Martin

1983
Pick
- 47 Bruce Shoebottom
- 67 Guy Benoit
- 87 Bob LaForest
- 100 Garry Galley
- 107 Dave Lundmark
- 108 Kevin Stevens
- 127 Tim Burgess
- 147 Ken Hammond
- 167 Bruce Fishback
- 187 Thomas Ahlen
- 207 Miroslav Blaha
- 227 Chad Johnson

1982
Pick
- 27 Mike Heidt
- 48 Steve Seguin
- 64 Dave Gans
- 82 Dave Ross
- 90 Darcy Roy
- 95 Ulf Isaksson
- 132 Victor Nechaev
- 153 Peter Helander
- 174 Dave Chartier
- 195 John Franzosa
- 216 Ray Shero
- 237 Mats Ulander

1981
Pick
- 2 Doug Smith
- 39 Dean Kennedy
- 81 Marty Dallman
- 123 Brad Thompson
- 134 Craig Hurley
- 144 Peter Sawkins
- 165 Dan Brennan
- 186 Allan Tuer
- 207 Jeff Baikie

1980
Pick
- 4 Larry Murphy
- 10 Jim Fox
- 33 Greg Terrion
- 34 Dave Morrison
- 52 Steve Bozek
- 73 Bernie Nicholls
- 94 Alan Graves
- 115 Darren Eliot
- 136 Mike O'Connor
- 157 Bill O'Dwyer
- 178 Daryl Evans
- 199 Kim Collins

Coach

MELROSE, BARRY
Coach, Los Angeles Kings. Born in Kelvington, Sask., July 15, 1956.

Barry Melrose enters his third season as head coach of the Los Angeles Kings in 1994-95. Melrose became the 17th head coach of the Los Angeles Kings on June 25, 1992, replacing Tom Webster. In 1993, Melrose guided the Kings to their first appearance in the Stanley Cup Finals. Melrose, who started his professional playing career at the age of 20 with the Cincinnati Stingers of the WHA, spent eight years in the NHL with Toronto, Winnipeg and Detroit. Following his successful playing career, Melrose turned his attention to coaching and led the WHL's Medicine Hat Tigers to the Memorial Cup title in 1988. For the following three seasons, he was the coach of the AHL's Adirondack Red Wings, Detroit's top farm affiliate. In 1991-92, Melrose guided the Wings to the AHL's Calder Cup championship, the fourth title for the Adirondack franchise since 1981.

Coaching Record

			Regular Season				Playoffs			
Season	Team	Games	W	L	T	%	Games	W	L	%
1987-88	Medicine Hat (WHL)	72	44	22	6	.653	16	12	4	.750
1988-89	Seattle (WHL)	72	33	35	4	.486	....	....	....	....
1989-90	Adirondack (AHL)	80	42	27	11	.594	6	2	4	.333
1990-91	Adirondack (AHL)	80	33	37	10	.475	....	....	....	....
1991-92	Adirondack (AHL)	80	40	36	4	.525	19	14	5	.737
1992-93	**Los Angeles (NHL)**	**84**	**39**	**35**	**10**	**.524**	**24**	**13**	**11**	**.542**
1993-94	**Los Angeles (NHL)**	**84**	**27**	**45**	**12**	**.393**	....	....	....	....
	NHL Totals	**168**	**66**	**80**	**22**	**.458**	**24**	**13**	**11**	**.542**

Club Directory

The Great Western Forum
3900 West Manchester Blvd.
Inglewood, California 90305
Phone **310/419-3160**
GM FAX 310/672-1490
PR FAX 310/673-8927
Capacity: 16,005

Executive
Owners	Joseph M. Cohen, Bruce P. McNall, Jeffrey P. Sudlkoff
Chairman/Alternate Governor	Joseph M. Cohen
President/Governor	Bruce McNall
Assistant to the President	Rogatien Vachon
Executive Vice President	Lester M. Wintz
Vice President, Finance	Michael Handelman, CPA
Vice President, Marketing	Gregory McElroy
Vice President, Broadcasting & Communications	Scott Carmichael
Executive Administrative Assistant to President	Carmen Garcia
Executive Secretary to Chairman	Celeste Grant

Hockey Operations
General Manager	Sam McMaster
Assistant to the General Manager	Dave Taylor
Administrative Assistant to General Manager	John Wolf
Executive Secretary to General Manager	Marcia Galloway
Head Coach	Barry Melrose
Assistant Coaches	Cap Raeder, John Perpich
Director of Pro Scouting	Ace Bailey
Director of Amateur Scouting	Al Murray
Scouting Staff	Serge Aubry, Peter Brill, Gary Harker, Jan Lindegren, Vaclav Nedomansky, Don Perry, John Stanton
Video Coordinator	Bill Gurney

Medical Staff
Trainer	Pete Demers
Equipment Manager	Peter Millar
Massage Therapist/Physical Therapist	Robert Zolg
Assistant Equipment Manager	Rick Garcia
Team Physicians	Kerlan/Jobe Orthopaedic Clinic directed by Dr. Ronald Kvitne
Internist	Dr. Michael Mellman
Team Dentist	Dr. Gordon Knuth

Communications
Director, Media Relations	Rick Minch
Director, Publications	Nick Salata
Communications Coordinator	Angela Ladd
Fundraising Coordinator	Jim Fox
Media Relations	Tami Cole, Jill Berke
Receptionist	Elizabeth Tutt

Personnel/Accounting
Director, Human Resources	Barbara Mendez
Controller	Pete Mazur
Accounts Payable	Emma Harris

Marketing/Advertising/Sales
Executive Director, Merchandising	Harvey Boles
Executive Director, Sales	Dennis Metz
Advertising Account Executives	Sergio del Prado, John Covarrubias
Season Seat Account Executives	Keith Jacobson, Andrew Silverman
Manager, Marketing Services	Susan Long
Marketing Coordinator	Shawn Kallan
Assistant to the Executive Vice President	Charlie Jacobs

Broadcasting
Play-by-Play Announcer, Television	Bob Miller
Color Commentator, Television	Jim Fox
Play-by-Play Announcer, Radio	Nick Nickson
Color Commentator, Radio	Brian Engblom
Television	Prime Ticket Cable Network & KTLA Channel 5
Radio Station	XTRA (690 AM)
Spanish Radio	KWIZ (1480 AM)

Home Ice	The Great Western Forum
Dimensions of Rink	200 feet by 85 feet
Supervisor of Off-Ice Officials	Bill Meuris
Public Address Announcer	David Courtney
Organist	Dan Stein
Colors	Black, White and Silver
Training Camp	Iceoplex, North Hills, CA
Location of Press Box	West Colonnade, Sec. 28, Rows 1-12

General Manager

McMASTER, SAM
General Manager, Los Angeles Kings. Born in Vancouver, B.C., March 3, 1944.

Sam McMaster was named the sixth general manager in the history of the Los Angeles Kings on May 24, 1994. He spent the six years prior to his appointment as general manager and director of hockey operations for the Sudbury Wolves of the Ontario Hockey League (OHL), earning league Executive of the Year honors in 1991. Prior to his tenure at Sudbury, McMaster served as assistant director of player personnel for the Washington Capitals from 1985-88. He was also general manager of the OHL's Sault Ste. Marie Greyhounds (1980-85), where the club won over 70 percent of its games and captured three OHL titles.

Montreal Canadiens

1993-94 Results: 41W-29L-14T 96PTS. Third, Northeast Division

For the fourth consecutive season, Vincent Damphousse led his team in scoring. Damphousse led Toronto in points in 1990-91 and Edmonton in scoring in 1991-92. He has topped all Montreal scorers in each of his two seasons with the club.

Schedule

Oct.	Sat.	1	Boston		Thur.	5	at Quebec
	Wed.	5	at Winnipeg				(in Phoenix)
	Fri.	7	at Buffalo		Mon.	9	Ottawa
	Sat.	8	Buffalo		Thur.	12	at Quebec
	Wed.	12	NY Islanders		Sat.	14	Florida
	Fri.	14	at Washington		Wed.	18	Anaheim
	Sat.	15	at Pittsburgh		Mon.	23	Hartford
	Mon.	17	Chicago		Sat.	28	New Jersey*
	Wed.	19	at Detroit		Sun.	29	Philadelphia*
	Sat.	22	NY Rangers	**Feb.**	Wed.	1	at Tampa Bay
	Mon.	24	New Jersey		Thur.	2	at Florida
	Wed.	26	Edmonton		Sat.	4	Vancouver
	Thur.	27	at Boston		Mon.	6	San Jose
	Sat.	29	Pittsburgh		Wed.	8	at Ottawa
Nov.	Wed.	2	Tampa Bay		Sat.	11	at Pittsburgh
	Sat.	5	at Ottawa		Mon.	13	Hartford
	Tues.	8	at Hartford		Wed.	15	at Hartford
	Thur.	10	at New Jersey		Thur.	16	at NY Rangers
	Sat.	12	at Toronto		Sat.	18	St. Louis
	Wed.	16	NY Islanders		Mon.	20	at Washington*
	Thur.	17	at Quebec		Thur.	23	at Florida
	Sat.	19	Quebec		Sat.	25	Toronto
	Mon.	21	Hartford		Mon.	27	Florida
	Wed.	23	Florida				(in Hamilton)
	Sat.	26	Los Angeles	**Mar.**	Wed.	1	at Dallas
	Mon.	28	Washington		Sat.	4	at Los Angeles
	Wed.	30	at St. Louis		Wed.	8	Washington
Dec.	Thur.	1	at Chicago		Thur.	9	at NY Islanders
	Sat.	3	Detroit		Sat.	11	NY Rangers
	Wed.	7	Calgary		Wed.	15	Winnipeg
	Thur.	8	at Philadelphia		Thur.	16	at Boston
	Sat.	10	Philadelphia		Sat.	18	Dallas
	Wed.	14	Boston		Mon.	20	at Philadelphia
	Fri.	16	at Buffalo		Wed.	22	Boston
	Sat.	17	Ottawa		Fri.	24	at Pittsburgh
	Mon.	19	Tampa Bay		Sat.	25	Buffalo
	Wed.	21	Buffalo		Mon.	27	at Tampa Bay
	Fri.	23	at NY Rangers		Thur.	30	at NY Islanders
	Tues.	27	at Vancouver	**Apr.**	Sat.	1	at New Jersey
	Fri.	30	at Edmonton		Mon.	3	at Ottawa
	Sat.	31	at Calgary		Wed.	5	Quebec
Jan.	Mon.	2	at Anaheim*		Thur.	6	at Quebec
	Wed.	4	at San Jose		Sat.	8	Pittsburgh

* Denotes afternoon game.

Home Starting Times:
Night Games . . . . 7:30 p.m.
Matinees . . . . 1:30 p.m.

Franchise date: November 22, 1917

NORTHEAST DIVISION

78th NHL Season

Year-by-Year Record

		Home			Road			Overall							
Season	**GP**	**W**	**L**	**T**	**W**	**L**	**T**	**W**	**L**	**T**	**GF**	**GA**	**Pts.**	**Finished**	**Playoff Result**
1993-94	84	26	12	4	15	17	10	41	29	14	283	248	96	3rd, Northeast Div.	Lost Conf. Quarter-Final
1992-93	**84**	**27**	**13**	**2**	**21**	**17**	**4**	**48**	**30**	**6**	**326**	**280**	**102**	**3rd, Adams Div.**	**Won Stanley Cup**
1991-92	80	27	8	5	14	20	6	41	28	11	267	207	93	1st, Adams Div.	Lost Div. Final
1990-91	80	23	12	5	16	18	6	39	30	11	273	249	89	2nd, Adams Div.	Lost Div. Final
1989-90	80	26	8	6	15	20	5	41	28	11	288	234	93	3rd, Adams Div.	Lost Div. Final
1988-89	80	30	6	4	23	12	5	53	18	9	315	218	115	1st, Adams Div.	Lost Final
1987-88	80	26	8	6	19	14	7	45	22	13	298	238	103	1st, Adams Div.	Lost Div. Final
1986-87	80	27	9	4	14	20	6	41	29	10	277	241	92	2nd, Adams Div.	Lost Conf. Championship
1985-86	**80**	**25**	**11**	**4**	**15**	**22**	**3**	**40**	**33**	**7**	**330**	**280**	**87**	**2nd, Adams Div.**	**Won Stanley Cup**
1984-85	80	24	10	6	17	17	6	41	27	12	309	262	94	1st, Adams Div.	Lost Div. Final
1983-84	80	19	19	2	16	21	3	35	40	5	286	295	75	4th, Adams Div.	Lost Conf. Championship
1982-83	80	25	6	9	17	18	5	42	24	14	350	286	98	2nd, Adams Div.	Lost Div. Semi-Final
1981-82	80	25	6	9	21	11	8	46	17	17	360	223	109	1st, Adams Div.	Lost Div. Semi-Final
1980-81	80	31	7	2	14	15	11	45	22	13	332	232	103	1st, Norris Div.	Lost Prelim. Round
1979-80	80	30	7	3	17	13	10	47	20	13	328	240	107	1st, Norris Div.	Lost Quarter-Final
1978-79	**80**	**29**	**6**	**5**	**23**	**11**	**6**	**52**	**17**	**11**	**337**	**204**	**115**	**1st, Norris Div.**	**Won Stanley Cup**
1977-78	**80**	**32**	**4**	**4**	**27**	**6**	**7**	**59**	**10**	**11**	**359**	**183**	**129**	**1st, Norris Div.**	**Won Stanley Cup**
1976-77	**80**	**33**	**1**	**6**	**27**	**7**	**6**	**60**	**8**	**12**	**387**	**171**	**132**	**1st, Norris Div.**	**Won Stanley Cup**
1975-76	**80**	**32**	**3**	**5**	**26**	**8**	**6**	**58**	**11**	**11**	**337**	**174**	**127**	**1st, Norris Div.**	**Won Stanley Cup**
1974-75	80	27	8	5	20	6	14	47	14	19	374	225	113	1st, Norris Div.	Lost Semi-Final
1973-74	78	24	12	3	21	12	6	45	24	9	293	240	99	2nd, East Div.	Lost Quarter-inal
1972-73	**78**	**29**	**4**	**6**	**23**	**6**	**10**	**52**	**10**	**16**	**329**	**184**	**120**	**1st, East Div.**	**Won Stanley Cup**
1971-72	78	29	3	7	17	13	9	46	16	16	307	205	108	3rd, East Div.	Lost Quarter-Final
1970-71	**78**	**29**	**7**	**3**	**13**	**16**	**10**	**42**	**23**	**13**	**291**	**216**	**97**	**3rd, East Div.**	**Won Stanley Cup**
1969-70	76	21	9	8	17	13	8	38	22	16	244	201	92	5th, East Div.	Out of Playoffs
1968-69	**76**	**26**	**7**	**5**	**20**	**12**	**6**	**46**	**19**	**11**	**271**	**202**	**103**	**1st, East Div.**	**Won Stanley Cup**
1967-68	**74**	**26**	**5**	**6**	**16**	**17**	**4**	**42**	**22**	**10**	**236**	**167**	**94**	**1st, East Div.**	**Won Stanley Cup**
1966-67	70	19	9	7	13	16	6	32	25	13	202	188	77	2nd,	Lost Final
1965-66	**70**	**23**	**11**	**1**	**18**	**10**	**7**	**41**	**21**	**8**	**239**	**173**	**90**	**1st,**	**Won Stanley Cup**
1964-65	**70**	**20**	**8**	**7**	**16**	**15**	**4**	**36**	**23**	**11**	**211**	**185**	**83**	**2nd,**	**Won Stanley Cup**
1963-64	70	22	7	6	14	14	7	36	21	13	209	167	85	1st,	Lost Semi-Final
1962-63	70	15	10	10	13	9	13	28	19	23	225	183	79	3rd,	Lost Semi-Final
1961-62	70	26	2	7	16	12	7	42	14	14	259	166	98	1st,	Lost Semi-Final
1960-61	70	24	6	5	17	13	5	41	19	10	254	188	92	1st,	Lost Semi-Final
1959-60	**70**	**23**	**4**	**8**	**17**	**14**	**4**	**40**	**18**	**12**	**255**	**178**	**92**	**1st,**	**Won Stanley Cup**
1958-59	**70**	**21**	**8**	**6**	**18**	**10**	**7**	**39**	**18**	**13**	**58**	**158**	**91**	**1st,**	**Won Stanley Cup**
1957-58	**70**	**23**	**8**	**4**	**20**	**9**	**6**	**43**	**17**	**10**	**250**	**158**	**96**	**1st,**	**Won Stanley Cup**
1956-57	**70**	**23**	**6**	**6**	**12**	**17**	**6**	**35**	**23**	**12**	**210**	**155**	**82**	**2nd,**	**Won Stanley Cup**
1955-56	**70**	**29**	**5**	**1**	**16**	**10**	**9**	**45**	**15**	**10**	**222**	**131**	**100**	**1st,**	**Won Stanley Cup**
1954-55	70	26	5	4	15	13	7	41	18	11	228	157	93	2nd,	Lost Final
1953-54	70	27	5	3	8	19	8	35	24	11	195	141	81	2nd,	Lost Final
1952-53	**70**	**18**	**12**	**5**	**10**	**11**	**14**	**28**	**23**	**19**	**155**	**148**	**75**	**2nd,**	**Won Stanley Cup**
1951-52	70	22	8	5	12	18	5	34	26	10	195	164	78	2nd,	Lost Final
1950-51	70	17	10	8	8	20	7	25	30	15	173	184	65	3rd,	Lost Final
1949-50	70	17	8	10	12	14	9	29	22	19	172	150	77	2nd,	Lost Semi-Final
1948-49	60	19	8	3	9	15	6	28	23	9	152	126	65	3rd,	Lost Semi-Final
1947-48	60	13	13	4	7	16	7	20	29	11	147	169	51	5th,	Out of Playoffs
1946-47	60	19	6	5	15	10	5	34	16	10	189	138	78	1st,	Lost Final
1945-46	**50**	**16**	**6**	**3**	**12**	**11**	**2**	**28**	**17**	**5**	**172**	**134**	**61**	**1st,**	**Won Stanley Cup**
1944-45	50	21	2	2	17	6	2	38	8	4	228	121	80	1st,	Lost Semi-Final
1943-44	**50**	**22**	**0**	**3**	**16**	**5**	**4**	**38**	**5**	**7**	**234**	**109**	**83**	**1st,**	**Won Stanley Cup**
1942-43	50	14	4	7	5	15	5	19	19	12	181	191	50	4th,	Lost Semi-Final
1941-42	48	12	10	2	6	17	1	18	27	3	134	173	39	6th,	Lost Quarter-Final
1940-41	48	11	9	4	5	17	2	16	26	6	121	147	38	6th,	Lost Quarter-Final
1939-40	48	5	14	5	5	19	0	10	33	5	90	167	25	7th,	Out of Playoffs
1938-39	48	8	11	5	7	13	4	15	24	9	115	146	39	6th,	Lost Quarter-Final
1937-38	48	13	4	7	5	13	6	18	17	13	123	128	49	3rd, Cdn. Div.	Lost Quarter-Final
1936-37	48	16	8	0	8	10	6	24	18	6	115	111	54	1st, Cdn. Div.	Lost Semi-Final
1935-36	48	5	11	8	6	15	3	11	26	11	82	123	33	4th, Cdn. Div.	Out of Playoffs
1934-35	48	11	11	2	8	12	4	19	23	6	110	145	44	3rd, Cdn. Div.	Lost Quarter-Final
1933-34	48	16	6	2	6	14	4	22	20	6	99	101	50	2nd, Cdn. Div.	Lost Quarter-Final
1932-33	48	15	5	4	3	20	1	18	25	5	92	115	41	3rd, Cdn. Div.	Lost Quarter-Final
1931-32	48	18	3	3	7	13	4	25	16	7	128	111	57	1st, Cdn. Div.	Lost Semi-Final
1930-31	**44**	**15**	**3**	**4**	**11**	**7**	**4**	**26**	**10**	**8**	**129**	**89**	**60**	**1st, Cdn. Div.**	**Won Stanley Cup**
1929-30	**44**	**13**	**5**	**4**	**8**	**9**	**5**	**21**	**14**	**9**	**142**	**114**	**51**	**2nd, Cdn. Div.**	**Won Stanley Cup**
1928-29	44	12	4	6	10	3	9	22	7	15	71	43	59	1st, Cdn. Div.	Lost Semi-Final
1927-28	44	12	7	3	14	4	4	26	11	7	116	48	59	1st, Cdn. Div.	Lost Semi-Final
1926-27	44	15	5	2	13	9	0	28	14	2	99	67	58	2nd, Cdn. Div.	Lost Semi-Final
1925-26	36	5	12	1	6	12	0	11	24	1	79	108	23	7th,	Out of Playoffs
1924-25	30	10	5	0	7	6	2	17	11	2	93	56	36	3rd,	Lost Final
1923-24	**24**	**10**	**2**	**0**	**3**	**9**	**0**	**13**	**11**	**0**	**59**	**48**	**26**	**2nd,**	**Won Stanley Cup**
1922-23	24	10	2	0	3	7	2	13	9	2	73	61	28	2nd,	Lost NHL Final
1921-22	24	8	3	1	4	8	0	12	11	1	88	94	25	3rd,	Out of Playoffs
1920-21	24	16	8	0	8	10	6	13	11	0	112	99	26	3rd and 2nd*	Out of Playoffs
1919-20	24	8	4	0	5	7	0	13	11	0	129	113	26	2nd and 3rd*	Out of Playoffs
1918-19	18	7	2	0	3	6	0	10	8	0	88	78	20	1st and 2nd*	Cup Final but no Decision
1917-18	22	8	3	0	5	6	0	13	9	0	115	84	26	1st and 3rd*	Lost NHL Final

* Season played in two halves with no combined standing at end.
From 1917-18 through 1925-26, NHL champions played against PCHA champions for Stanley Cup.

1994-95 Player Personnel

FORWARDS	HT	WT	S	Place of Birth	Date	1993-94 Club
BELLOWS, Brian	5-11	209	R	St. Catharines, Ont.	9/1/64	Montreal
BRASHEAR, Donald	6-3	214	L	Bedford, IN	1/7/72	Montreal-Fredericton
BRUNET, Benoit	5-11	193	L	Pointe-Claire, Que.	8/24/68	Montreal
BURE, Valeri	5-11	164	R	Moscow, USSR	6/13/74	Spokane
CAMPBELL, Jim	6-1	175	R	Worcester, MA	4/3/73	U.S. National-U.S. Olympic-Fred
CONROY, Craig	6-2	190	R	Potsdam, NY	9/4/71	Clarkson
CORPSE, Keli	5-11	176	L	London, Ont.	5/14/74	Kingston
DAMPHOUSSE, Vincent	6-1	199	L	Montreal, Que.	12/17/67	Montreal
DARBY, Craig	6-3	180	R	Oneida, NY	9/26/72	Fredericton
DI PIETRO, Paul	5-9	181	R	Sault Ste. Marie, Ont.	9/8/70	Montreal
DIONNE, Gilbert	6-0	194	L	Drummondville, Que.	9/19/70	Montreal
DUCHESNE, Alexandre	6-0	212	L	Val d'Or, Que.	1/4/74	Drummondville
FERGUSON, Craig	6-0	185	L	Castro Valley, CA	4/8/70	Montreal-Fredericton
FLEMING, Gerry	6-5	240	L	Montreal, Que.	10/16/67	Montreal-Fredericton
FRASER, Scott	6-1	200	R	Moncton, N.B.	5/3/72	Dartmouth-Cdn. National
GUILLET, Robert	5-11	189	R	Montreal, Que.	2/22/72	Fredericton
KEANE, Mike	5-10	180	R	Winnipeg, Man.	5/29/67	Montreal
LeCLAIR, John	6-2	219	L	St. Albans, VT	7/5/69	Montreal
MAJIC, Xavier	6-0	190	L	Fernie, B.C.	3/10/73	RPI
MONTGOMERY, Jim	5-10	185	R	Montreal, Que.	6/30/69	St. Louis-Peoria
MULLER, Kirk	6-0	205	L	Kingston, Ont.	2/8/66	Montreal
PETROV, Oleg	5-9	166	L	Moscow, USSR	4/18/71	Montreal-Fredericton
PRPIC, Tony	6-4	207	R	Euclid, OH	6/16/73	Fredericton-Wheeling
ROBERGE, Mario	5-11	193	L	Quebec City, Que.	1/25/64	Montreal
RONAN, Edward	6-0	197	R	Quincy, MA	3/21/68	Montreal
SARAULT, Yves	6-1	170	L	Valleyfield, Que.	12/23/72	Fredericton
SAVAGE, Brian	6-2	191	L	Sudbury, Ont.	2/24/71	Cdn. National-Cdn. Olympic-Montreal-Fredericton
SEVIGNY, Pierre	6-0	189	L	Trois-Rivières, Que.	9/8/71	Montreal
STEVENSON, Turner	6-3	200	R	Prince George, B.C.	5/18/72	Montreal-Fredericton
SYCHRA, Martin	6-1	180	L	Brno, Czech.	6/19/74	Kingston
DEFENSEMEN						
BERNARD, Louis	6-2	205	R	Victoriaville, Que.	7/10/74	Sherbrooke
BILODEAU, Brent	6-4	215	L	Dallas, TX	3/27/73	Fredericton
BRISEBOIS, Patrice	6-2	192	R	Montreal, Que.	1/27/71	Montreal
DAIGNEAULT, Jean-Jacques	5-11	199	L	Montreal, Que.	10/12/65	Montreal
DARLING, Dion	6-3	205	L	Edmonton, Alta.	10/22/74	Spokane-Moose Jaw-Wheeling
DESJARDINS, Eric	6-1	200	R	Rouyn, Que.	6/14/69	Montreal
FOGARTY, Bryan	6-2	206	L	Brantford, Ont.	6/11/69	Atl-Vegas-K.C.-Mtl
MAGUIRE, Derek	6-0	185	R	Delbarton, NJ	12/9/71	Harvard
O'SULLIVAN, Kevin	6-0	197	L	Dorchester, MA	11/13/70	Fredericton
ODELEIN, Lyle	5-10	206	R	Quill Lake, Sask.	7/21/68	Montreal
POPOVIC, Peter	6-5	241	R	Koping, Sweden	2/10/68	Montreal
PROULX, Christian	6-1	190	L	Sherbrooke, Que.	12/10/73	Montreal-Fredericton
RACINE, Yves	6-0	200	L	Matane, Que.	2/7/69	Philadelphia
RIVET, Craig	6-2	178	R	North Bay, Ont.	9/13/74	Kingston-Fredericton
SCHNEIDER, Mathieu	5-11	189	L	New York, NY	6/12/69	Montreal
WILKIE, David	6-3	215	R	Ellensburgh, WA	5/30/74	Kamloops-Regina

GOALTENDERS	HT	WT	C	Place of Birth	Date	1993-94 Club
BROCHU, Martin	5-11	195	L	Anjou, Que.	3/10/73	Fredericton
KUNTAR, Les	6-2	195	L	Elma, NY	7/28/69	Montreal-Fredericton
LABRECQUE, Patrick	6-0	190	L	Laval, Que.	3/6/71	Cornwall-Greensboro
LAMOTHE, Marc	6-2	187	L	New Liskeard, Ont.	2/27/74	Kingston
ROY, Patrick	6-0	192	L	Quebec City, Que.	10/5/65	Montreal
TUGNUTT, Ron	5-11	155	L	Scarborough, Ont.	10/22/67	Anaheim-Montreal

Coach

DEMERS, JACQUES
Coach, Montreal Canadiens. Born in Montreal, Que., August 25, 1944.

Named as the 21st head coach in the history of the Montreal Canadiens in July, 1992, Jacques Demers guided the Habs to their 24th Stanley Cup title in 1992-93, defeating the Los Angeles Kings in five games in the championship finals. Demers, who is the only man in NHL history to win coach of the year honors in back-to-back seasons when he was with Detroit, began his coaching career in the QMJHL before making his professional coaching debut with the WHA's Chicago Cougars in 1972-73. Eventually, Demers joined the Quebec Nordiques' organization and was the team's first coach when the club joined the NHL in 1979-80. In 1981, Demers was appointed as the head of the Nordiques' AHL farm affiliate in Fredericton, where he earned Executive of the Year honors in 1983. The following season, Demers returned to the NHL with the St. Louis Blues, where he spent three seasons as head coach.

Coaching Record

		Regular Season					Playoffs			
Season	Team	Games	W	L	T	%	Games	W	L	%
1975-76	Indianapolis (WHA)	80	35	39	6	.475	7	3	4	.429
1976-77	Indianapolis (WHA)	81	36	37	8	.494	9	5	4	.556
1977-78	Cincinnati (WHA)	80	35	42	3	.456	....	....	....	....
1978-79	Quebec (WHA)	80	41	34	5	.544	4	0	4	.000
1979-80	**Quebec (NHL)**	**80**	**25**	**44**	**11**	**.381**	....	....	....	....
1981-82	Fredericton (AHL)	80	20	55	5	.281	....	....	....	....
1982-83	Fredericton (AHL)	80	45	27	8	.544	12	6	6	.500
1983-84	**St. Louis (NHL)**	**80**	**32**	**41**	**7**	**.444**	**11**	**6**	**5**	**.545**
1984-85	**St. Louis (NHL)**	**80**	**37**	**31**	**12**	**.538**	**3**	**0**	**3**	**.000**
1985-86	**St. Louis (NHL)**	**80**	**37**	**34**	**9**	**.519**	**19**	**10**	**9**	**.526**
1986-87	**Detroit (NHL)**	**80**	**34**	**36**	**10**	**.488**	**16**	**9**	**7**	**.563**
1987-88	**Detroit (NHL)**	**80**	**41**	**28**	**11**	**.581**	**16**	**9**	**7**	**.563**
1988-89	**Detroit (NHL)**	**80**	**34**	**34**	**12**	**.500**	**6**	**2**	**4**	**.333**
1989-90	**Detroit (NHL)**	**80**	**28**	**38**	**14**	**.437**	....	....	....	....
1992-93	**Montreal (NHL)**	**84**	**48**	**30**	**6**	**.607**	**20**	**16**	**4**	**.800***
1993-94	**Montreal (NHL)**	**84**	**41**	**29**	**14**	**.571**	**7**	**3**	**4**	**.429**
	NHL Totals	**808**	**357**	**345**	**106**	**.507**	**98**	**55**	**43**	**.561**

* Stanley Cup win.

1993-94 Scoring

* – rookie

Regular Season

Pos	#	Player	Team	GP	G	A	Pts	+/–	PIM	PP	SH	GW	GT	S	%
L	25	Vincent Damphousse	MTL	84	40	51	91	0	75	13	0	10	1	274	14.6
L	23	Brian Bellows	MTL	77	33	38	71	9	36	13	0	2	1	251	13.1
L	11	Kirk Muller	MTL	76	23	34	57	1–	96	9	2	3	0	168	13.7
D	27	Matt Schneider	MTL	75	20	32	52	15	62	11	0	4	0	193	10.4
R	12	Mike Keane	MTL	80	16	30	46	6	119	6	2	2	1	129	12.4
L	45	Gilbert Dionne	MTL	74	19	26	45	9–	31	3	0	5	2	162	11.7
C	17	John LeClair	MTL	74	19	24	43	17	32	1	0	1	0	153	12.4
D	24	Lyle Odelein	MTL	79	11	29	40	8	276	6	0	2	0	116	9.5
C	21	Guy Carbonneau	MTL	79	14	24	38	16	48	0	0	1	0	120	11.7
D	28	Eric Desjardins	MTL	84	12	23	35	1–	97	6	1	3	0	193	6.2
C	15	Paul Di Pietro	MTL	70	13	20	33	2–	37	2	0	0	0	115	11.3
L	22	Benoit Brunet	MTL	71	10	20	30	14	20	0	3	1	0	92	10.9
R	6 *	Oleg Petrov	MTL	55	12	15	27	7	2	1	0	1	1	107	11.2
D	43	Patrice Brisebois	MTL	53	2	21	23	5	63	1	0	0	0	71	2.8
R	26	Gary Leeman	MTL	31	4	11	15	5	17	0	0	0	0	53	7.5
R	31	Ed Ronan	MTL	61	6	8	14	3	42	0	0	1	0	49	12.2
D	34 *	Peter Popovic	MTL	47	2	12	14	10	26	1	0	0	0	58	3.4
D	48	J.J. Daigneault	MTL	68	2	12	14	16	73	0	0	1	0	61	3.3
D	14	Kevin Haller	MTL	68	4	9	13	3	118	0	0	1	0	72	5.6
C	8	Ron Wilson	MTL	48	2	10	12	2–	12	0	0	0	0	39	5.1
L	20 *	Pierre Sevigny	MTL	43	4	5	9	6	42	1	0	1	0	19	21.1
L	35 *	Donald Brashear	MTL	14	2	2	4	0	34	0	0	0	0	15	13.3
D	5 *	Christian Proulx	MTL	7	1	2	3	0	20	0	0	0	0	11	9.1
D	44	Bryan Fogarty	MTL	13	1	2	3	4–	10	0	0	0	0	22	4.5
L	32	Mario Roberge	MTL	28	1	2	3	2–	55	0	0	0	0	5	20.0
C	49 *	Brian Savage	MTL	3	1	0	1	0	0	0	0	0	0	3	33.3
C	46 *	Craig Ferguson	MTL	2	0	1	1	1	0	0	0	0	0	0	.0
G	33	Patrick Roy	MTL	68	0	1	1	0	30	0	0	0	0	0	.0
R	42 *	Lindsay Vallis	MTL	1	0	0	0	0	0	0	0	0	0	0	.0
R	30 *	Turner Stevenson	MTL	2	0	0	0	2–	2	0	0	0	0	0	.0
L	36	Gerry Fleming	MTL	5	0	0	0	4–	25	0	0	0	0	4	.0
G	40 *	Les Kuntar	MTL	6	0	0	0	0	2	0	0	0	0	0	.0
G	37	Andre Racicot	MTL	11	0	0	0	0	0	0	0	0	0	0	.0
G	1	Ron Tugnutt	ANA	28	0	0	0	0	2	0	0	0	0	0	.0
			MTL	8	0	0	0	0	0	0	0	0	0	0	.0
			TOTAL	36	0	0	0	0	2	0	0	0	0	0	.0

Goaltending

No.	Goaltender	GPI	Mins	Avg	W	L	T	EN	SO	GA	SA	S%
33	Patrick Roy	68	3867	2.50	35	17	11	4	7	161	1956	.918
40	* Les Kuntar	6	302	3.18	2	2	0	1	0	16	130	.877
1	Ron Tugnutt	8	378	3.81	2	3	1	0	0	24	172	.860
37	Andre Racicot	11	500	4.44	2	6	2	0	0	37	246	.850
35	* Frederic Chabot	1	60	5.00	0	1	0	0	0	5	24	.792
	Totals	**84**	**5122**	**2.91**	**41**	**29**	**14**	**5**	**7**	**248**	**2533**	**.902**

Playoffs

Pos	#	Player	Team	GP	G	A	Pts	+/–	PIM	PP	SH	GW	GT	S	%
L	11	Kirk Muller	MTL	7	6	2	8	0	4	3	0	2	1	16	37.5
C	15	Paul Di Pietro	MTL	7	2	4	6	3–	2	2	0	1	0	12	16.7
L	22	Benoit Brunet	MTL	7	1	4	5	1	16	0	0	0	0	13	7.7
R	12	Mike Keane	MTL	6	3	1	4	1	4	0	0	0	0	8	37.5
C	21	Guy Carbonneau	MTL	7	1	3	4	4	4	0	0	0	0	4	25.0
D	43	Patrice Brisebois	MTL	7	0	4	4	3–	6	0	0	0	0	11	.0
C	17	John Leclair	MTL	7	2	1	3	1–	8	1	0	0	0	13	15.4
L	45	Gilbert Dionne	MTL	5	1	2	3	1–	0	0	0	0	0	8	12.5
L	23	Brian Bellows	MTL	6	1	2	3	2–	2	0	0	0	0	16	6.3
L	25	Vincent Damphousse	MTL	7	1	2	3	1–	8	0	0	0	0	14	7.1
D	14	Kevin Haller	MTL	7	1	1	2	3–	19	0	0	0	0	8	12.5
R	30 *	Turner Stevenson	MTL	3	0	2	2	1	0	0	0	0	0	2	.0
C	49 *	Brian Savage	MTL	3	0	2	2	0	0	0	0	0	0	6	.0
D	28	Eric Desjardins	MTL	7	0	2	2	1–	4	0	0	0	0	9	.0
R	31	Ed Ronan	MTL	7	1	0	1	1–	0	0	0	0	0	7	14.3
L	20 *	Pierre Sevigny	MTL	3	0	1	1	1–	0	0	0	0	0	1	.0
D	34 *	Peter Popovic	MTL	6	0	1	1	3	0	0	0	0	0	5	.0
D	48	J.J. Daigneault	MTL	7	0	1	1	1	12	0	0	0	0	14	.0
R	26	Gary Leeman	MTL	1	0	0	0	0	0	0	0	0	0	0	.0
D	27	Matt Schneider	MTL	1	0	0	0	0	0	0	0	0	0	1	.0
G	1	Ron Tugnutt	MTL	1	0	0	0	0	0	0	0	0	0	0	.0
R	6 *	Oleg Petrov	MTL	2	0	0	0	1–	0	0	0	0	0	1	.0
L	35 *	Donald Brashear	MTL	2	0	0	0	1–	0	0	0	0	0	2	.0
C	8	Ron Wilson	MTL	4	0	0	0	1–	0	0	0	0	0	1	.0
G	33	Patrick Roy	MTL	6	0	0	0	0	0	0	0	0	0	0	.0
D	24	Lyle Odelein	MTL	7	0	0	0	3	17	0	0	0	0	7	.0

Goaltending

No.	Goaltender	GPI	Mins	Avg	W	L	EN	SO	GA	SA	S%
33	Patrick Roy	6	375	2.56	3	3	0	0	16	228	.930
1	Ron Tugnutt	1	59	5.08	0	1	1	0	5	25	.800
	Totals	**7**	**437**	**3.02**	**3**	**4**	**1**	**0**	**22**	**254**	**.913**

Captains' History

Newsy Lalonde, 1917-18 to 1920-21; Sprague Cleghorn, 1921-22 to 1924-25; Bill Couture, 1925-26; Sylvio Mantha, 1926-27 to 1931-32; George Hainsworth, 1932-33; Sylvio Mantha, 1933-34 to 1935-36; Babe Seibert, 1936-37 to 1938-39; Walter Buswell, 1939-40; Toe Blake, 1940-41 to 1946-47; Toe Blake, Bill Durnan (co-captains) 1947-48; Emile Bouchard, 1948-49 to 1955-56; Maurice Richard, 1956-57 to 1959-60; Doug Harvey, 1960-61; Jean Beliveau, 1961-62 to 1970-71; Henri Richard, 1971-72 to 1974-75; Yvan Cournoyer, 1975-76 to 1978-79; Serge Savard, 1979-80, 1980-81; Bob Gainey, 1981-82 to 1988-89, Guy Carbonneau and Chris Chelios (co-captains), 1989-90; Guy Carbonneau, 1990-91 to 1993-94; Kirk Muller, 1994-95.

Club Records

Team

(Figures in brackets for season records are games played; records for fewest points, wins, ties, losses, goals, goals against are for 70 or more games)

Most Points .... *132 — 1976-77 (80)
Most Wins .... *60 — 1976-77 (80)
Most Ties .... 23 — 1962-63 (70)
Most Losses .... 40 — 1983-84 (80)
Most Goals .... 387 — 1976-77 (80)
Most Goals Against .... 295 — 1983-84 (80)
Fewest Points .... 65 — 1950-51 (70)
Fewest Wins .... 25 — 1950-51 (70)
Fewest Ties .... 5 — 1983-84 (80
Fewest Losses .... *8 — 1976-77 (80)
Fewest Goals .... 155 — 1952-53 (70)
Fewest Goals Against ...... *131 — 1955-56 (70)

Longest WinningStreak
Over-all .... 12 — Jan. 6-Feb. 3/68
Home .... 13 — Nov. 2/43-Jan. 8/44; Jan. 30-Mar. 26/77
Away .... 8 — Dec. 18/77-Jan. 18/78; Jan. 21-Feb. 21/82

Longest Undefeated Streak
Over-all .... 28 — Dec. 18/77-Feb. 23/78 (23 wins, 5 ties)
Home .... *34 — Nov. 1/76-Apr. 2/77 (28 wins, 6 ties)
Away .... *23 — Nov. 27/74-Mar. 12/75 (14 wins, 9 ties)

Longest Losing Streak
Over-all .... 12 — Feb. 13/26-Mar. 13/26
Home .... 7 — Dec. 16/39-Jan. 18/40
Away .... 10 — Dec. 1/25-Feb. 2/26

Longest Winless Streak
Over-all .... 12 — Feb. 13-Mar. 13/26 (12 losses); Nov. 28-Dec. 29/35 (8 losses, 4 ties)
Home .... *15 — Dec. 16/39-Mar. 7/40 (12 losses, 3 ties)
Away .... 12 — Oct. 20-Dec. 13/51 (8 losses, 4 ties)

Most Shutouts, Season ...... *22 — 1928-29 (44)
Most PIM, Season .... 1,842 — 1987-88 (80)
Most Goals, Game .... *16 — Mar. 3/20 (Mt. 16 at Que. 3)

Individual

Most Seasons .... 20 — Henri Richard, Jean Beliveau
Most Games .... 1,256 — Henri Richard
Most Goals Career .... 544 — Maurice Richard
Most Assists, Career .... 728 — Guy Lafleur
Most Points Career .... 1,246 — Guy Lafleur (518 goals, 728 assists)
Most PIM, Career .... 2,248 — Chris Nilan
Most Shutouts, Career .... 75 — George Hainsworth
Longest Consecutive Games Streak .... 560 — Doug Jarvis (Oct. 8/75-Apr. 4/82)
Most Goals, Season .... 60 — Steve Shutt (1976-77); Guy Lafleur (1977-78)
Most Assists, Season .... 82 — Peter Mahovlich (1974-75)
Most Points, Season .... 136 — Guy Lafleur (1976-77) (56 goals, 80 assists)
Most PIM, Season .... 358 — Chris Nilan (1984-85)
Most Points, Defenseman Season .... 85 — Larry Robinson (1976-77) (19 goals, 66 assists)
Most Points, Center, Season .... 117 — Peter Mahovlich (1974-75) (35 goals, 82 assists)
Most Points, Right Wing, Season .... 136 — Guy Lafleur (1976-77) (56 goals, 80 assists)
Most Points, Left Wing, Season .... 110 — Mats Naslund (1985-86) (43 goals, 67 assists)
Most Points, Rookie, Season .... 71 — Mats Naslund (1982-83) (26 goals, 45 assists); Kjell Dahlin (1985-86) (32 goals, 39 assists)
Most Shutouts, Season ...... *22 — George Hainsworth (1928-29)
Most Goals, Game .... 6 — Newsy Lalonde (Jan. 10/20)
Most Assists, Game .... 6 — Elmer Lach (Feb. 6/43)
Most Points, Game .... 8 — Maurice Richard 5G-3A (Dec. 28/44); Bert Olmstead 4G-4A (Jan. 9/54)

* NHL Record.

Retired Numbers

2	Doug Harvey	1947-1961
4	Aurèle Joliat	1922-1938
	Jean Béliveau	1950-1971
7	Howie Morenz	1923-1937
9	Maurice Richard	1942-1960
10	Guy Lafleur	1971-1984
16	Elmer Lach	1942-1954
	Henri Richard	1955-1975

All-time Record vs. Other Clubs

Regular Season

	At Home							On Road							Total						
	GP	W	L	T	GF	GA	PTS	GP	W	L	T	GF	GA	PTS	GP	W	L	T	GF	GA	PTS
Anaheim	1	1	0	0	4	1	2	1	1	0	0	5	2	2	2	2	0	0	9	3	4
Boston	308	179	84	45	1052	713	403	309	114	142	53	836	911	281	617	293	226	98	1888	1624	684
Buffalo	77	48	21	8	323	229	104	77	23	36	18	221	244	64	154	71	57	26	544	473	168
Calgary	38	21	11	6	135	94	48	37	21	11	5	135	120	47	75	42	22	11	270	214	95
Chicago	267	168	51	48	1037	629	384	267	121	91	55	747	722	297	534	289	142	103	1784	1351	681
Dallas	51	35	9	7	230	125	77	52	27	14	11	186	135	65	103	62	23	18	416	260	142
Detroit	274	169	62	43	978	608	381	274	96	125	53	703	782	245	548	265	187	96	1681	1390	626
Edmonton	22	13	6	3	79	67	29	23	10	13	0	71	82	20	45	23	19	3	150	149	49
Florida	2	0	2	0	3	8	0	2	0	1	1	6	11	1	4	0	3	1	9	19	1
Hartford	53	37	10	6	248	158	80	55	29	18	8	210	168	66	108	66	28	14	458	326	146
Los Angeles	57	39	7	11	265	147	89	58	34	15	9	234	178	77	115	73	22	20	499	325	166
New Jersey	34	24	6	4	141	88	52	34	24	10	0	159	94	48	68	48	16	4	300	182	100
NY Islanders	40	22	11	7	155	126	51	41	19	18	4	127	139	42	81	41	29	11	282	265	93
NY Rangers	270	181	55	34	1066	623	396	270	109	109	52	789	782	270	540	290	164	86	1855	1405	666
Ottawa	7	5	2	0	25	22	10	5	4	1	0	20	14	8	12	9	3	0	45	36	18
Philadelphia	54	29	14	11	209	159	69	53	21	19	13	162	154	55	107	50	33	24	371	313	124
Pittsburgh	60	49	4	7	307	142	105	59	30	20	9	217	177	69	119	79	24	16	524	319	174
Quebec	54	34	12	8	231	167	76	55	26	26	3	204	187	55	109	60	38	11	435	354	131
St. Louis	52	38	8	6	235	134	82	51	27	10	14	183	129	68	103	65	18	20	418	263	150
San Jose	4	4	0	0	21	7	8	4	2	0	2	8	6	6	8	6	0	2	29	13	14
Tampa Bay	3	2	1	0	6	6	4	3	0	2	1	5	8	1	6	2	3	1	11	14	5
Toronto	314	191	83	40	1119	773	422	315	111	160	44	824	954	266	629	302	243	84	1943	1727	688
Vancouver	45	35	8	2	226	120	72	43	28	7	8	172	107	64	88	63	15	10	398	227	136
Washington	40	27	7	6	181	83	60	40	18	15	7	136	104	43	80	45	22	13	317	187	103
Winnipeg	22	20	2	0	119	51	40	22	9	8	5	84	71	23	44	29	10	5	203	122	63
Defunct Clubs	231	148	58	25	779	469	321	230	98	97	35	586	606	231	461	246	155	60	1365	1075	552
Totals	**2380**	**1519**	**534**	**327**	**9174**	**5749**	**3365**	**2380**	**1002**	**968**	**410**	**7030**	**6887**	**2414**	**4760**	**2521**	**1502**	**737**	**16204**	**12636**	**5779**

Calgary totals include Atlanta, 1972-73 to 1979-80. Dallas totals include Minnesota, 1967-68 to 1992-93.
New Jersey totals include Kansas City, 1974-75 to 1975-76, and Colorado, 1976-77 to 1981-82.

Playoffs

	Series	W	L	GP	W	L	T	GF	GA	Last Mtg.	Round	Result
Boston	28	21	7	139	87	52	0	430	339	1994	CQF	L 3-4
Buffalo	6	4	2	31	18	13	0	114	94	1993	DF	W 4-0
Calgary	2	1	1	11	6	5	0	31	32	1989	F	L 2-4
Chicago	17	12	5	81	50	29	2	261	185	1976	QF	W 4-0
Dallas	2	1	1	13	7	6	0	48	37	1980	QF	L 3-4
Detroit	12	5	7	62	33	29	0	161	149	1978	QF	W 4-1
Edmonton	1	0	1	3	0	3	0	6	15	1981	PR	L 0-3
Hartford	5	5	0	27	19	8	0	96	70	1992	DSF	W 4-3
Los Angeles	1	1	0	5	4	1	0	15	12	1993	F	W 4-1
NY Islanders	4	3	1	22	14	8	0	64	55	1993	CF	W 4-1
NY Rangers	13	7	6	55	32	21	2	171	139	1986	CF	W 4-1
Philadelphia	4	3	1	21	14	7	0	72	52	1989	CF	W 4-2
Quebec	5	3	2	31	17	14	0	105	85	1993	DSF	W 4-2
St. Louis	3	3	0	12	12	0	0	42	14	1977	QF	W 4-0
Toronto	13	7	6	67	39	28	0	203	148	1979	QF	W 4-0
Vancouver	1	1	0	5	4	1	0	20	9	1975	QF	W 4-1
Defunct Clubs	12	7	5	32	18	10	4	82	83			
Totals	**130***	**84**	**45**	**617**	**374**	**235**	**8**	**1921**	**1518**			

* 1919 Final incomplete due to influenza epidemic.

Playoff Results 1994-90

Year	Round	Opponent	Result	GF	GA
1994	CQF	Boston	L 3-4	20	22
1993	**F**	**Los Angeles**	**W 4-1**	**15**	**12**
	CF	NY Islanders	W 4-1	16	11
	DF	Buffalo	W 4-0	16	12
	DSF	Quebec	W 4-2	19	16
1992	DF	Boston	L 0-4	8	14
	DSF	Hartford	W 4-3	21	18
1991	DF	Boston	L 3-4	18	18
	DSF	Buffalo	W 4-2	29	24
1990	DF	Boston	L 1-4	12	16
	DSF	Buffalo	W 4-2	17	13

Abbreviations: Round: F – Final; **CF** – conference final; **CQF** – conference quarter-final; **CSF** – conference semi-final; **DF** – division final; **DSF** – division semi-final; **SF** – semi-final; **QF** – quarter-final; **PR** – preliminary round.

1993-94 Results

Oct.	6		Hartford	4-3
	7	at	Pittsburgh	1-2
	9		Buffalo	7-4
	11	at	Boston	1-1
	13	at	Hartford	3-4
	16		Quebec	2-5
	18	at	Quebec	4-2
	20		Dallas	5-2
	23		Anaheim	4-1
	26	at	New Jersey	2-0
	28	at	NY Rangers	3-3
	30		Toronto	5-2
Nov.	3		Tampa Bay	1-0
	6		Calgary	3-4
	10		Florida	1-3
	13		Ottawa	2-3
	15	at	Ottawa	4-2
	17		Edmonton	3-1
	18		NY Islanders	1-5
	20		Pittsburgh	2-2
	23	at	NY Rangers	4-5
	24	at	Philadelphia	2-9
	27		Los Angeles	4-0
Dec.	1		Ottawa	3-6
	3	at	Washington	2-2
	4	at	Boston	8-1
	6		Vancouver	4-3
	8		New Jersey	2-4
	11		Washington	3-5
	14	at	Tampa Bay	1-1
	15	at	Florida	3-3
	18		Detroit	8-1
	22		NY Islanders	3-5
	23	at	Buffalo	0-5
	27	at	St. Louis	5-2
	29	at	Edmonton	3-6
	31	at	Calgary	5-2
Jan.	2	at	Vancouver	3-2
	4	at	San Jose	2-2
	5	at	Quebec	4-0
	8		NY Rangers	3-2
	10		Winnipeg	4-2
	12		New Jersey	3-2
	14	at	NY Islanders	2-5
	15		Florida	2-5
	17		Washington	3-1
	19		Boston	3-3
	24	at	Florida	3-8
	26	at	Hartford	3-0
	29		Buffalo	2-3
	30		Philadelphia	5-4
Feb.	2		Hartford	9-2
	4	at	Washington	4-0
	5	at	Ottawa	4-3
	7	at	Pittsburgh	4-1
	9		NY Rangers	4-3
	11	at	Buffalo	1-5
	12		Quebec	5-2
	17	at	Tampa Bay	3-4
	19		Pittsburgh	4-1
	21	at	Philadelphia	7-8
	23		San Jose	3-1
	26	at	Toronto	3-0
	28	at	Los Angeles	3-3
Mar.	2	at	Anaheim	5-2
	6	at	Dallas	2-2
	9		St. Louis	7-2
	10	at	Quebec	4-4
	12		Philadelphia	4-4
	14		Boston	5-4
	16		Chicago	5-3
	19		Quebec	5-2
	23	at	Winnipeg	1-3
	24	at	Chicago	5-5
	26	at	Boston	3-6
	28		Ottawa	3-2
	29	at	New Jersey	2-5
Apr.	1	at	NY Islanders	2-5
	2		NY Islanders	3-3
	6		Tampa Bay	1-3
	8	at	Buffalo	0-1
	9		Pittsburgh	9-1
	11	at	Hartford	3-1
	13	at	Detroit	0-9

Entry Draft
Selections 1994-80

1994 Pick		1990 Pick		1986 Pick		1982 Pick	
18	Brad Brown	12	Turner Stevenson	15	Mark Pederson	19	Alain Heroux
44	Jose Theodore	39	Ryan Kuwabara	27	Benoit Brunet	31	Jocelyn Gauvreau
54	Chris Murray	58	Charles Poulin	57	Jyrki Lumme	32	Kent Carlson
70	Marko Kiprusoff	60	Robert Guillet	78	Brent Bobyck	33	David Maley
74	Martin Belanger	81	Gilbert Dionne	94	Eric Aubertin	40	Scott Sandelin
96	Arto Kuki	102	Paul DiPietro	99	Mario Milani	61	Scott Harlow
122	Jimmy Drolet	123	Craig Conroy	120	Steve Bisson	69	John Devoe
148	Joel Irving	144	Stephen Rohr	141	Lyle Odelein	103	Kevin Houle
174	Jessie Rezansoff	165	Brent Fleetwood	162	Rick Hayward	117	Ernie Vargas
200	Peter Strom	186	Derek Maguire	183	Antonin Routa	124	Michael Dark
226	Tomas Vokoun	207	Mark Kettelhut	204	Eric Bohemier	145	Hannu Jarvenpaa
252	Chris Aldous	228	John Uniac	225	Charlie Moore	150	Steve Smith
278	Ross Parsons	249	Sergei Martynyuk	246	Karel Svoboda	166	Tom Kolioupoulos
						187	Brian Williams
						208	Bob Emery

1993 Pick		1989 Pick		1985 Pick		229	Darren Acheson
21	Saku Koivu	13	Lindsay Vallis	12	Jose Charbonneau	250	Bill Brauer
47	Rory Fitzpatrick	30	Patrice Brisebois	16	Tom Chorske		
73	Sebastien Bordeleau	41	Steve Larouche	33	Todd Richards	**1981** Pick	
85	Adam Wiesel	51	Pierre Sevigny	47	Rocky Dundas	7	Mark Hunter
99	Jean-Francois Houle	83	Andre Racicot	75	Martin Desjardins	18	Gilbert Delorme
113	Jeff Lank	104	Marc Deschamps	79	Brent Gilchrist	19	Jan Ingman
125	Dion Darling	146	Craig Ferguson	96	Tom Sagissor	32	Lars Eriksson
151	Darcy Tucker	167	Patrick Lebeau	117	Donald Dufresne	40	Chris Chelios
177	David Ruhly	188	Roy Mitchell	142	Ed Cristofoli	46	Dieter Hegen
203	Alan Letang	209	Ed Henrich	163	Mike Claringbull	82	Kjell Dahlin
229	Alexandre Duchesne	230	Justin Duberman	184	Roger Beedon	88	Steve Rooney
255	Brian Larochelle	251	Steve Cadieux	198	Maurice Mansi	124	Tom Anastos
281	Russell Guzior			205	Chad Arthur	145	Tom Kurvers
		1988 Pick		226	Mike Bishop	166	Paul Gess
1992 Pick		20	Eric Charron	247	John Ferguson Jr.	187	Scott Ferguson
20	David Wilkie	34	Martin St. Amour			208	Danny Burrows
33	Valeri Bure	46	Neil Carnes	**1984** Pick			
44	Keli Corpse	83	Patrik Kjellberg	5	Petr Svoboda	**1980** Pick	
68	Craig Rivet	93	Peter Popovic	8	Shayne Corson	1	Doug Wickenheiser
82	Louis Bernard	104	Jean-Claude Bergeron	29	Stephane Richer	27	Ric Nattress
92	Marc Lamothe	125	Patrik Carnback	51	Patrick Roy	40	John Chabot
116	Don Chase	146	Tim Chase	54	Graeme Bonar	45	John Newberry
140	Martin Sychra	167	Sean Hill	65	Lee Brodeur	61	Craig Ludwig
164	Christian Proulx	188	Harijs Vitolinsh	95	Gerald Johannson	82	Jeff Teal
188	Michael Burman	209	Yuri Krivokhizha	116	Jim Nesich	103	Remi Gagne
212	Earl Cronan	230	Kevin Dahl	137	Scott MacTavish	124	Mike McPhee
236	Trent Cavicchi	251	Dave Kunda	158	Brad McCughey	145	Bill Norton
260	Hiroyuki Miura			179	Eric Demers	166	Steve Penney
		1987 Pick		199	Ron Annear	187	John Schmidt
1991 Pick		17	Andrew Cassels	220	Dave Tanner	208	Scott Robinson
17	Brent Bilodeau	33	John LeClair	240	Troy Crosby		
28	Jim Campbll	38	Eric Desjardins				
43	Craig Darby	44	Mathieu Schneider	**1983** Pick			
61	Yves Sarault	58	Francois Gravel	17	Alfie Turcotte		
73	Vladimir Vujtek	80	Kris Miller	26	Claude Lemieux		
83	Sylvain Lapointe	101	Steve McCool	27	Sergio Momesso		
100	Brad Layzell	122	Les Kuntar	35	Todd Francis		
105	Tony Prpic	143	Rob Kelley	45	Daniel Letendre		
127	Oleg Petrov	164	Will Geist	78	John Kordic		
149	Brady Kramer	185	Eric Tremblay	98	Dan Wurst		
171	Brian Savage	206	Barry McKinlay	118	Arto Javanainen		
193	Scott Fraser	227	Ed Ronan	138	Vladislav Tretiak		
215	Greg MacEachern	248	Bryan Herring	158	Rob Bryden		
237	Paul Lepler			178	Grant MacKay		
259	Dale Hooper			198	Thomas Rundqvist		
				218	Jeff Perpich		
				238	Jean-Guy Bergeron		

General Managers' History

Joseph Cattarinich, 1909-1910; George Kennedy, 1910-11 to 1919-20; Leo Dandurand, 1920-21 to 1934-35; Ernest Savard, 1935-36; Cecil Hart, 1936-37 to 1938-39; Jules Dugal, 1939-40; Tom P. Gorman, 1941-42 to 1945-46; Frank J. Selke, 1946-47 to 1963-64; Sam Pollock, 1964-65 to 1977-78; Irving Grundman, 1978-79 to 1982-83; Serge Savard, 1983-84 to date.

Coaching History

George Kennedy, 1917-18 to 1919-20; Léo Dandurand, 1920-21 to 1924-25; Cecil Hart, 1925-26 to 1931-32; Newsy Lalonde, 1932-33 to 1933-34; Newsy Lalonde and Léo Dandurand, 1934-35; Sylvio Mantha, 1935-36; Cecil Hart, 1936-37 to 1937-38; Cecil Hart and Jules Dugal, 1938-39; ''Babe'' Siebert, 1939*; Pit Lepine, 1939-40; Dick Irvin 1940-41 to 1954-55; Toe Blake, 1955-56 to 1967-68; Claude Ruel, 1968-69 to 1969-70; Claude Ruel and Al MacNeil, 1970-71; Scott Bowman, 1971-72 to 1978-79; Bernie Geoffrion and Claude Ruel, 1979-80; Claude Ruel, 1980-81; Bob Berry, 1981-82 to 1982-83; Bob Berry and Jacques Lemaire, 1983-84; Jacques Lemaire, 1984-85; Jean Perron, 1985-86 to 1987-88; Pat Burns, 1988-89 to 1991-92; Jacques Demers, 1992-93 to date.

* Named coach in summer but died before 1939-40 season began.

Club Directory

Montreal Forum
2313 St. Catherine Street West
Montreal, Quebec H3H 1N2
Phone **514/932-2582**
FAX (Hockey) 514/932-8736
Team Services 514/989-2717
P.R. 514/932-9296
Media 514/932-8285
Capacity: 16,259 (standing 1,700)

Owner: The Molson Companies Limited

Chairman of the Board, President and Governor	Ronald Corey
Vice-President Hockey, Managing Director and Alternate Governor	Serge Savard
Vice-President, Forum Operations	Aldo Giampaolo
Vice-President, Finance and Administration	Fred Steer
Vice-President, Communications and Marketing Services	Bernard Brisset
Assistant Managing Director, Director of Scouting and Managing Director of the Fredericton Canadiens	André Boudrias
Head Coach	Jacques Demers
Assistant Coaches	Jacques Laperrière, Charles Thiffault, Steve Shutt
Goaltending Instructor	François Allaire
Director of Team Services	Michele Lapointe
Pro Scout	Carol Vadnais
Director of Player Development and Scout	Claude Ruel
Chief Scout	Doug Robinson
Scouting Staff	Neil Armstrong, Scott Baker, Elmer Benning, Pat Flannery, Pierre Mondou, Gerry O'Flaherty, Richard Scammell, Eric Taylor, Jean-Claude Tremblay, Del Wilson

AHL Affiliation Fredericton Canadiens

Head Coach	Paulin Bordeleau
Assistant Coach	Luc Gauthier
Director of Operations	Wayne Gamble

Medical and Training Staff

Club Physician	Dr. D.G. Kinnear
Athletic Trainer	Gaétan Lefebvre
Assistant to the Athletic Trainer	John Shipman
Equipment Manager	Eddy Palchak
Assistants to the Equipment Manager	Pierre Gervais, Robert Boulanger, Pierre Ouellette

Marketing

EFFIX Inc.	François-Xavier Seigneur

Communications

Director of Communications	Donald Beauchamp
Assistant to the Director of Communications	Denis Dessureault

Finance

Director of Finance	François Trudel
Controller	Dennis McKinley
Administrative Supervisor	Dave Poulton
Manager of Finance Analysis and Control	Françoise Brault
Accountants	Gilles Viens, Paule Jolicoeur

Forum

Forum Superintendent	Alain Gauthier
Director of Security	Pierre Sauvé
Director of Events	Louise Laliberté
Director of Computer, Operations	Sylvain Roy
Director of Concessions	Monique Lacas
Director of Purchasing	Robert Loiseau
Director, Souvenir Boutiques	Yves Renaud

Ticketing

Box Office Manager	Richard Primeau
Assistant to the Box Office Manager	Caterina D'Ascoli

Executive Assistants
President, Lise Beaudry; Managing Director, Donna Stuart; V.P. Forum Operations, Vicky Mercuri; V.P. Finance, Susan Cryans; Public Rel., Normande Herget; Media Rel., Frédérique Cardinal; Hockey, Claudine Crépin

Location of Press Box	Suspended above ice — West side
Location of Radio and TV booth	Suspended above ice — East side
Dimensions of rink	200 feet by 85 feet
Club colors	Red, White and Blue
Club trains at	Montreal Forum
Play-by-Play — Radio/TV	Dick Irvin, Jim Corsi (English) Claude Quenneville, René Pothier, Benoit Lévesque, Pierre Houde (French)
TV Channels	CBMT (6), TQS (35), CBFT (2)
Cable TV	RDS (25)
Radio Stations	CBF (690) (French), CJAD (800) (English)

General Manager

SAVARD, SERGE A.
Managing Director, Montreal Canadiens.
Born in Montreal, Que., January 22, 1946.

Serge Savard who was elected to the Hockey Hall of Fame in 1986, following a brilliant 16 year career as a defenseman, was appointed Managing Director of the Canadiens on April 28, 1983. Since then, the team has never missed the playoffs and has won its first playoff round in 11 of 12 seasons. Under the direction of Serge Savard, the Canadiens have won two Stanley Cups (1986, 1993), three Conference and four Division Championships. As a player with Montreal, he was a member of eight Stanley Cup-winning teams. He won the Conn Smythe Trophy as MVP of the 1969 playoffs and the Bill Masterton Trophy in 1978-79. He was selected to the 1978-79 Second All-Star Team. He ended his playing career in Winnipeg in 1982-83. In 1994, Serge Savard was named an Officer of the Order of Canada.

New Jersey Devils

1993-94 Results: 47W-25L-12T 106PTS. Second, Atlantic Division

Schedule

Oct.	Sat.	1	NY Rangers
	Thur.	6	at Chicago
	Sat.	8	Ottawa
	Wed.	12	Philadelphia
	Sat.	15	at Tampa Bay
	Sun.	16	at Florida
	Wed.	19	Washington
	Sat.	22	San Jose*
	Mon.	24	at Montreal
	Wed.	26	Calgary
	Sat.	29	Vancouver
	Sun.	30	Winnipeg
Nov.	Tues.	1	at San Jose
	Fri.	4	at Anaheim
	Sun.	6	at Los Angeles
	Tues.	8	at Pittsburgh
	Thur.	10	Montreal
	Sat.	12	Boston*
	Sun.	13	at Quebec*
	Wed.	16	Dallas
	Fri.	18	NY Islanders
	Sat.	19	at Tampa Bay
	Wed.	23	at Ottawa
	Fri.	25	at Philadelphia*
	Sat.	26	at Detroit*
Dec.	Thur.	1	Quebec
	Sat.	3	Edmonton*
	Sun.	4	at St. Louis
	Wed.	7	at Winnipeg
	Fri.	9	Detroit
	Sun.	11	at Philadelphia
	Tues.	13	at Ottawa
	Thur.	15	Florida
	Sat.	17	at Dallas
	Tues.	20	Hartford
	Fri.	23	Ottawa
	Mon.	26	Buffalo
	Tues.	27	at Buffalo
	Fri.	30	Florida
	Sat.	31	at Washington
Jan.	Wed.	4	Pittsburgh
	Sat.	7	Anaheim
	Mon.	9	Pittsburgh
			(in Denver)

	Wed.	11	Philadelphia
	Fri.	13	NY Islanders
	Sun.	15	at NY Rangers
	Tues.	17	at Florida
	Wed.	18	at Tampa Bay
	Wed.	25	at Buffalo
	Thur.	26	at Boston
	Sat.	28	at Montreal*
	Tues.	31	Washington
Feb.	Thur.	2	Buffalo
	Sat.	4	Chicago*
	Sun.	5	at Quebec*
	Wed.	8	Los Angeles
	Fri.	10	Toronto
	Sun.	12	at Washington*
			(in Halifax)
	Wed.	15	St. Louis
	Fri.	17	NY Islanders
	Sat.	18	at NY Islanders
	Tues.	21	Pittsburgh
	Thur.	23	Tampa Bay
	Sat.	25	Washington*
	Sun.	26	at Washington*
Mar.	Wed.	1	at Hartford
	Thur.	2	at Boston
	Sat.	4	Florida*
	Mon.	6	at NY Rangers
	Tues.	7	at NY Islanders
	Sat.	11	at Toronto
	Tues.	14	Quebec
	Wed.	15	at NY Rangers
	Sat.	18	Tampa Bay*
	Sun.	19	Boston
	Tues.	21	at Edmonton
	Thur.	23	at Vancouver
	Fri.	24	at Calgary
	Thur.	30	at Philadelphia
Apr.	Sat.	1	Montreal
	Tues.	4	Hartford
	Wed.	5	at Pittsburgh
	Sat.	8	at Hartford*
	Sun.	9	NY Rangers*

* Denotes afternoon game.

Home Starting Times:
Night Games . . . . 7:30 p.m.
Matinees . . . . 1:00 p.m.
Except   Sun. Mar. 19 . . . . 8:00 p.m.

Franchise date: June 30, 1982
Transferred from Denver to New Jersey,
previously transferred from Kansas City
to Denver, Colorado.

EASTERN
NHL CONFERENCE

ATLANTIC DIVISION

21st NHL Season

Year-by-Year Record

Season	GP	Home W	L	T	Road W	L	T	Overall W	L	T	GF	GA	Pts.	Finished		Playoff Result
1993-94	84	29	11	2	18	14	10	47	25	12	306	220	106	2nd,	Atlantic Div.	Lost Conf. Championship
1992-93	84	24	14	4	16	23	3	40	37	7	308	299	87	4th,	Patrick Div.	Lost Div. Semi-Final
1991-92	80	24	12	4	14	19	3	38	31	11	289	259	87	4th,	Patrick Div.	Lost Div. Semi-Final
1990-91	80	23	10	7	9	23	8	32	33	15	272	264	79	4th,	Patrick Div.	Lost Div. Semi-Final
1989-90	80	22	15	3	15	19	6	37	34	9	295	288	83	2nd,	Patrick Div.	Lost Div. Semi-Final
1988-89	80	17	18	5	10	23	7	27	41	12	281	325	66	5th,	Patrick Div.	Out of Playoffs
1987-88	80	23	16	1	15	20	5	38	36	6	295	296	82	4th,	Patrick Div.	Lost Conf. Championship
1986-87	80	20	17	3	9	28	3	29	45	6	293	368	64	6th,	Patrick Div.	Out of Playoffs
1985-86	80	17	21	2	11	28	1	28	49	3	300	374	59	6th,	Patrick Div.	Out of Playoffs
1984-85	80	13	21	6	9	27	4	22	48	10	264	346	54	5th,	Patrick Div.	Out of Playoffs
1983-84	80	10	28	2	7	28	5	17	56	7	231	350	41	5th,	Patrick Div.	Out of Playoffs
1982-83	80	11	20	9	6	29	5	17	49	14	230	338	48	5th,	Patrick Div.	Out of Playoffs
1981-82**	80	14	21	5	4	28	8	18	49	13	241	362	49	5th,	Smythe Div.	Out of Playoffs
1980-81**	80	15	16	9	7	29	4	22	45	13	258	344	57	5th,	Smythe Div.	Out of Playoffs
1979-80**	80	12	20	8	7	28	5	19	48	13	234	308	51	6th,	Smythe Div.	Out of Playoffs
1978-79**	80	8	24	8	7	29	4	15	53	12	210	331	42	4th,	Smythe Div.	Out of Playoffs
1977-78**	80	17	14	9	2	26	12	19	40	21	257	305	59	2nd,	Smythe Div.	Lost Prelim. Round
1976-77**	80	12	20	8	8	26	6	20	46	14	226	307	54	5th,	Smythe Div.	Out of Playoffs
1975-76*	80	8	24	8	4	32	4	12	56	12	190	351	36	5th,	Smythe Div.	Out of Playoffs
1974-75*	80	12	20	8	3	34	3	15	54	11	184	328	41	5th,	Smythe Div.	Out of Playoffs

* Kansas City Scouts. ** Colorado Rockies.

Bill Guerin reached the 25-goal mark for the first time in his career in helping the New Jersey Devils set franchise records in wins (47) and points (106).

1994-95 Player Personnel

FORWARDS	HT	WT	S	Place of Birth	Date	1993-94 Club
ARMSTRONG, Bill H.	6-2	195	L	London, Ont.	6/25/66	Albany
BERTRAND, Eric	6-1	195	L	St. Ephrem, Que.	4/16/75	Granby
BRULE, Steve	5-11	184	R	Montreal, Que.	1/15/75	St-Jean
BRYLIN, Sergei	5-9	176	L	Moscow, USSR	1/13/74	CSKA-Russian Pen's
CARPENTER, Bob	6-0	200	L	Beverly, MA	7/13/63	New Jersey
CHORSKE, Tom	6-1	205	R	Minneapolis, MN	9/18/66	New Jersey
DOWD, Jim	6-1	190	R	Brick, NJ	12/25/68	New Jersey-Albany
ELIAS, Patrik	6-0	176	L	Trebic, Czech.	4/13/76	Kladno
EMMA, David	5-11	180	L	Cranston, RI	1/14/69	New Jersey-Albany
GUERIN, Bill	6-2	200	R	Wilbraham, MA	11/9/70	New Jersey
HANKINSON, Ben	6-2	210	R	Edina, MN	5/1/69	New Jersey-Albany
HOLIK, Bobby	6-3	220	R	Jihlava, Czech.	1/1/71	New Jersey
LEMIEUX, Claude	6-1	215	R	Buckingham, Que.	7/16/65	New Jersey
MacLEAN, John	6-0	200	R	Oshawa, Ont.	11/20/64	New Jersey
McKAY, Randy	6-1	205	R	Montreal, Que.	1/25/67	New Jersey
MILLEN, Corey	5-7	170	L	Cloquet, MN	3/30/64	New Jersey
OLIWA, Krzysztof	6-5	220	L	Tychy, Poland	4/12/73	Albany-Raleigh
PEDERSON, Denis	6-2	190	R	Prince Albert, Sask.	9/10/75	Prince Albert
PELLERIN, Scott	5-11	180	L	Shediac, N.B.	1/9/70	New Jersey-Albany
PELUSO, Mike	6-4	220	L	Pengilly, MN	11/8/65	New Jersey
PROVENCHER, Jimmy	6-3	200	R	Kitchener, Ont.	3/22/75	St-Jean
REGNIER, Curt	6-2	220	L	Prince Albert, Sask.	1/24/72	Albany-Raleigh
RHEAUME, Pascal	6-1	185	L	Quebec, Que.	6/21/73	Albany
RICHER, Stephane J. J.	6-2	215	R	Ripon, Que.	6/7/66	New Jersey
ROLSTON, Brian	6-2	185	L	Flint, MI	2/21/73	U.S. National-U.S. Olympic-Alb
RUCHTY, Matthew	6-1	210	L	Kitchener, Ont.	11/27/69	Albany
SEMAK, Alexander	5-10	180	R	Ufa, USSR	2/11/66	New Jersey
SIMPSON, Reid	6-1	211	L	Flin Flon, Man.	5/21/69	Kalamazoo-Albany
SULLIVAN, Steve	5-9	155	R	Timmons, Ont.	7/6/74	S.S. Marie
WILLIAMS, Jeff	6-0	175	L	Pointe-Claire, Que.	2/11/76	Guelph
ZELEPUKIN, Valeri	5-11	190	L	Voskresensk, USSR	9/17/68	New Jersey

DEFENSEMEN	HT	WT	S	Place of Birth	Date	1993-94 Club
ALBELIN, Tommy	6-1	190	L	Stockholm, Sweden	5/21/64	New Jersey-Albany
BOMBARDIR, Brad	6-2	190	L	Powell River, B.C.	5/5/72	North Dakota
DANEYKO, Ken	6-0	210	L	Windsor, Ont.	4/17/64	New Jersey
DEAN, Kevin	6-2	195	L	Madison, WI	4/1/69	Albany
DRIVER, Bruce	6-0	185	L	Toronto, Ont.	4/29/62	New Jersey
GOSSELIN, Christian	6-4	205	L	St. Redempteur, Que.	8/21/76	St-Hyacinthe
HELMER, Bryan	6-1	190	R	Sault Ste. Marie, Ont.	7/15/72	Albany
HULSE, Cale	6-3	210	R	Edmonton, Alta.	11/10/73	Albany
KINNEAR, Geordie	6-1	200	L	Simcoe, Ont.	7/9/73	Albany
MALKOC, Dean	6-3	200	L	Vancouver, B.C.	1/26/70	Albany
McALPINE, Chris	6-0	190	R	Roseville, MN	12/1/71	U. Minnesota
MODRY, Jaroslav	6-2	195	L	Ceske-Budejovice, Czech.	2/27/71	New Jersey-Albany
NIEDERMAYER, Scott	6-0	200	L	Edmonton, Alta.	8/31/73	New Jersey
REIRDEN, Todd	6-4	175	L	Arlington Heights, IL	6/25/71	Bowling Green
SMITH, Jason	6-3	185	R	Calgary, Alta.	11/2/73	New Jersey-Albany
SOURAY, Sheldon	6-2	210	L	Elk Point, Alta.	7/13/76	Tri-City
STEVENS, Scott	6-2	210	L	Kitchener, Ont.	4/1/64	New Jersey

GOALTENDERS	HT	WT	C	Place of Birth	Date	1993-94 Club
BRODEUR, Martin	6-1	205	L	Montreal, Que.	5/6/72	New Jersey
DUNHAM, Michael	6-3	185	L	Johnson City, NY	6/1/72	U.S. National-U.S. Olympic-Alb
ERICKSON, Chad	5-10	175	R	Minneapolis, MN	8/21/70	Albany-Raleigh
SCHWAB, Corey	6-0	180	L	North Battleford, Sask.	11/4/70	Albany
SIDORKIEWICZ, Peter	5-9	180	L	Dabrowa Bialostocka, Pol.	6/29/63	New Jersey-Albany-Fort Wayne
TERRERI, Chris	5-8	160	L	Providence, RI	11/15/64	New Jersey

Stephane Richer scored nine game-winning goals for the Devils in 1993-94.

1993-94 Scoring
*– rookie

Regular Season

Pos	#	Player	Team	GP	G	A	Pts	+/-	PIM	PP	SH	GW	GT	S	%
D	4	Scott Stevens	N.J.	83	18	60	78	53	112	5	1	4	0	215	8.4
R	44	Stephane Richer	N.J.	80	36	36	72	31	16	7	3	9	3	217	16.6
R	15	John MacLean	N.J.	80	37	33	70	30	95	8	0	4	0	277	13.4
L	25	Valeri Zelepukin	N.J.	82	26	31	57	36	70	8	0	0	0	155	16.8
C	10	Corey Millen	N.J.	78	20	30	50	24	52	4	0	3	1	132	15.2
C	9	Bernie Nicholls	N.J.	61	19	27	46	24	86	3	0	1	1	142	13.4
D	27	Scott Niedermayer	N.J.	81	10	36	46	34	42	5	0	2	1	135	7.4
R	12	Bill Guerin	N.J.	81	25	19	44	14	101	2	0	3	0	195	12.8
R	22	Claude Lemieux	N.J.	79	18	26	44	13	86	5	0	5	0	185	9.9
L	17	Tom Chorske	N.J.	76	21	20	41	14	32	1	1	4	0	131	16.0
L	16	Bobby Holik	N.J.	70	13	20	33	28	72	2	0	3	0	130	10.0
L	19	Bob Carpenter	N.J.	76	10	23	33	7	51	0	2	1	0	125	8.0
D	23	Bruce Driver	N.J.	66	8	24	32	29	63	3	1	0	1	109	7.3
D	20	Alexander Semak	N.J.	54	12	17	29	6	22	2	2	2	0	88	13.6
R	21	Randy McKay	N.J.	78	12	15	27	24	244	0	0	1	1	77	15.6
L	8	Mike Peluso	N.J.	69	4	16	20	19	238	0	0	0	0	44	9.1
D	6	Tommy Albelin	N.J.	62	2	17	19	20	36	1	0	1	0	62	3.2
D	5 *	Jaroslav Modry	N.J.	41	2	15	17	10	18	2	0	0	0	35	5.7
C	11 *	Jim Dowd	N.J.	15	5	10	15	8	0	2	0	0	0	26	19.2
D	2	Viacheslav Fetisov	N.J.	52	1	14	15	14	30	0	0	0	0	36	2.8
R	24 *	David Emma	N.J.	15	5	5	10	0	2	1	0	2	0	24	20.8
D	3	Ken Daneyko	N.J.	78	1	9	10	27	176	0	0	0	0	60	1.7
D	26 *	Jason Smith	N.J.	41	0	5	5	7	43	0	0	0	0	47	.0
G	31	Chris Terreri	N.J.	44	0	2	2	0	4	0	0	0	0	0	.0
R	14 *	Ben Hankinson	N.J.	13	1	0	1	0	23	0	0	1	0	14	7.1
R	18	Scott Pellerin	N.J.	1	0	0	0	0	2	0	0	0	0	0	.0
G	1	Peter Sidorkiewicz	N.J.	3	0	0	0	0	0	0	0	0	0	0	.0
G	30 *	Martin Brodeur	N.J.	47	0	0	0	0	2	0	0	0	0	0	.0

Goaltending

No.	Goaltender	GPI	Mins	Avg	W	L	T	EN	SO	GA	SA	S%
30 *	Martin Brodeur	47	2625	2.40	27	11	8	0	3	105	1238	.915
31	Chris Terreri	44	2340	2.72	20	11	4	2	2	106	1141	.907
1	Peter Sidorkiewicz	3	130	2.77	0	3	0	1	0	6	55	.891
	Totals	84	5104	2.59	47	25	12	3	5	220	2437	.910

Playoffs

Pos	#	Player	Team	GP	G	A	Pts	+/-	PIM	PP	SH	GW	GT	S	%
R	22	Claude Lemieux	N.J.	20	7	11	18	4	44	0	0	2	0	50	14.0
R	15	John MacLean	N.J.	20	6	10	16	2–	22	2	0	1	0	65	9.2
C	9	Bernie Nicholls	N.J.	16	4	9	13	3	28	2	1	0	0	37	10.8
R	44	Stephane Richer	N.J.	20	7	5	12	2	6	3	0	2	2	72	9.7
D	4	Scott Stevens	N.J.	20	2	9	11	1–	42	2	0	1	0	56	3.6
D	23	Bruce Driver	N.J.	20	3	5	8	4	12	2	0	0	0	33	9.1
C	11 *	Jim Dowd	N.J.	19	2	6	8	3–	8	0	0	0	0	30	6.7
L	19	Bob Carpenter	N.J.	20	1	7	8	1–	20	0	0	0	0	39	2.6
L	25	Valeri Zelepukin	N.J.	20	5	2	7	1	14	1	0	0	0	40	12.5
L	17	Tom Chorske	N.J.	20	4	3	7	0	0	1	0	1	0	32	12.5
D	6	Tommy Albelin	N.J.	20	2	5	7	5	14	1	1	0	0	30	6.7
D	27	Scott Niedermayer	N.J.	20	2	2	4	1–	8	1	0	0	0	29	6.9
R	12	Bill Guerin	N.J.	17	2	1	3	1	35	0	0	0	0	49	4.1
R	21	Randy McKay	N.J.	20	1	2	3	1–	24	0	0	0	0	15	6.7
L	16	Bobby Holik	N.J.	20	0	3	3	0	6	0	0	0	0	23	.0
R	14 *	Ben Hankinson	N.J.	2	1	0	1	1	4	0	0	0	0	3	33.3
C	10	Corey Millen	N.J.	7	1	0	1	0	2	0	0	1	0	7	14.3
D	2	Viacheslav Fetisov	N.J.	14	1	0	1	1–	8	0	0	0	0	14	7.1
L	8	Mike Peluso	N.J.	17	1	0	1	2–	64	0	0	1	0	7	14.3
G	30 *	Martin Brodeur	N.J.	17	0	1	1	0	0	0	0	0	0	0	.0
D	3	Ken Daneyko	N.J.	20	0	1	1	6–	45	0	0	0	0	8	.0
C	20	Alexander Semak	N.J.	2	0	0	0	0	0	0	0	0	0	0	.0
G	31	Chris Terreri	N.J.	4	0	0	0	0	0	0	0	0	0	0	.0
D	26 *	Jason Smith	N.J.	6	0	0	0	1–	0	0	0	0	0	2	.0

Goaltending

No.	Goaltender	GPI	Mins	Avg	W	L	EN	SO	GA	SA	S%
30 *	Martin Brodeur	17	1171	1.95	8	9	2	1	38	531	.928
31	Chris Terreri	4	200	2.70	3	0	0	0	9	111	.919
	Totals	20	1375	2.14	11	9	2	1	49	644	.924

General Managers' History

(Kansas City) Sidney Abel, 1974-75 to 1975-76; (Colorado) Ray Miron, 1976-77 to 1980-81; Billy MacMillan, 1981-82 to 1982-83; Billy MacMillan and Max McNab, 1983-84; Max McNab 1984-85 to 1986-87; Lou Lamoriello, 1987-88 to date.

Coaching History

(Kansas City) Bep Guidolin, 1974-75; Bep Guidolin, Sid Abel, and Eddie Bush, 1975-76; (Colorado) John Wilson, 1976-77; Pat Kelly, 1977-78; Pat Kelly, Aldo Guidolin, 1978-79; Don Cherry, 1979-80; Bill MacMillan, 1980-81; Bert Marshall and Marshall Johnston, 1981-82; (New Jersey) Bill MacMillan, 1982-83; Bill MacMillan and Tom McVie, 1983-84; Doug Carpenter, 1984-85 to 1986-87; Doug Carpenter and Jim Schoenfeld, 1987-88; Jim Schoenfeld, 1988-89; Jim Schoenfeld and John Cunniff, 1989-90; John Cunniff and Tom McVie, 1990-91; Tom McVie, 1991-92; Herb Brooks, 1992-93; Jacques Lemaire, 1993-94 to date.

Captains' History

Simon Nolet, 1974-75 to 1976-77; Wilf Paiement, 1977-78; Gary Croteau, 1978-79; Mike Christie, Rene Robert, Lanny McDonald, 1979-80; Lanny McDonald, 1980-81; Lanny McDonald, Rob Ramage, 1981-82; Don Lever, 1982-83; Don Lever, Mel Bridgman, 1983-84; Mel Bridgman, 1984-85, 1985-86; Kirk Muller, 1987-88 to 1990-91; Bruce Driver, 1991-92; Scott Stevens, 1992-93 to date.

Club Records

Team

(Figures in brackets for season records are games played)

Most Points	106	1993-94 (84)
Most Wins	47	1993-94 (84)
Most Ties	21	1977-78 (80)
Most Losses	56	1983-84 (80)
		1975-76 (80)
Most Goals	308	1992-93 (84)
Most Goals Against	374	1985-86 (80)
Fewest Points	*36	1975-76 (80)
	41	1983-84 (80)
Fewest Wins	*12	1975-76 (80)
	17	1982-83 (80)
		1983-84 (80)
Fewest Ties	3	1985-86 (80)
Fewest Losses	25	1993-94 (84)
Fewest Goals	*184	1974-75 (80)
	230	1982-83 (80)
Fewest Goals Against	220	1993-94 (84)

Longest Winning Streak

Over-all	7	Oct. 6-Oct. 23/93
Home	8	Oct. 9-Nov. 7/87
Away	4	Oct. 5-23/89 Dec. 31/91-Jan. 31/92 Nov. 5-Nov. 18/93

Longest Undefeated Streak

Over-all	9	Feb. 26-Mar. 13/94 (7 wins, 2 ties)
Home	10	Feb. 28-Mar. 29/94 (9 wins, 1 tie)
Away	8	Nov. 5-Dec. 2/93 (5 wins, 3 ties)

Longest Losing Streak

Over-all	*14	Dec. 30/75-Jan. 29/76
	10	Oct. 14-Nov. 4/83

Home	9	Dec. 22/85-Feb. 6/86
Away	12	Oct. 19/83-Dec. 1/83

Longest Winless Streak

Over-all	*27	Feb. 12-Apr. 4/76 (21 losses, 6 ties)
	18	Oct. 20-Nov. 26/82 (14 losses 4 ties)
Home	*14	Feb. 12-Mar. 30/76 (10 losses, 4 ties)
		Feb. 4-Mar. 31/79 (12 losses, 2 ties)
	9	Dec. 22/85-Feb. 6/86 (9 losses)
Away	*32	Nov. 12/77-Mar. 15/78 (22 losses, 10 ties)
	14	Dec. 26/82-Mar. 5/83 (13 losses, 1 tie)

Most Shutouts, Season	5	1993-94 (84)
Most PIM, Season	2,494	1988-89 (80)
Most Goals, Game	9	Seven times.

Individual

Most Seasons	10	Ken Daneyko, John MacLean, Bruce Driver
Most Games	706	John MacLean
Most Goals, Career	278	John MacLean
Most Assists, Career	335	Kirk Muller
Most Points, Career	559	John MacLean (278 goals, 281 assists)
Most PIM, Career	1,882	Ken Daneyko
Most Shutouts, Career	6	Chris Terreri
Longest Consecutive Games Streak	388	Ken Daneyko (Nov. 4/89-Mar. 29/94)
Most Goals, Season	46	Pat Verbeek (1987-88)
Most Assists, Season	60	Scott Stevens (1993-94)

Most Points, Season	94	Kirk Muller (1987-88; 37G, 57A)
Most PIM, Season	283	Ken Daneyko (1988-89)
Most Points, Defenseman Season	78	Scott Stevens (1993-94; 18G, 60A)
Most Points, Center Season	94	Kirk Muller (1987-88; 37G, 57A)
Most Points, Right Wing, Season	*87	Wilf Paiement (1977-78; 31G, 56A)
	87	John MacLean (1988-89; 42G, 45A)
Most Points, Left Wing, Season	86	Kirk Muller (1989-90; 30G, 56A)
Most Points, Rookie, Season	63	Kevin Todd (1991-92; 21G, 42A)
Most Shutouts, Season	3	Sean Burke (1988-89) Martin Brodeur (1993-94)
Most Goals, Game	4	Bob MacMillan (Jan. 8/82) Pat Verbeek (Feb. 28/88)
Most Assists, Game	5	Kirk Muller (Mar. 25/87) Greg Adams (Oct. 10/86) Tom Kurvers (Feb. 13/89)
Most Points, Game	6	Kirk Muller (Nov. 29/86; 3G, 3A)

* Records include Kansas City Scouts and Colorado Rockies from 1974-75 through 1981-82

All-time Record vs. Other Clubs

Regular Season

		At Home							On Road							Total					
	GP	W	L	T	GF	GA	PTS	GP	W	L	T	GF	GA	PTS	GP	W	L	T	GF	GA	PTS
Anaheim	1	1	0	0	4	0	2	1	1	0	0	6	3	2	2	2	0	0	10	3	4
Boston	33	6	19	8	90	124	20	36	10	23	3	118	162	23	69	16	42	11	208	286	43
Buffalo	35	8	20	7	110	138	23	34	6	24	4	105	159	16	69	14	44	11	215	297	39
Calgary	37	11	23	3	109	144	25	36	4	27	5	93	172	13	73	15	50	8	202	316	38
Chicago	38	15	14	9	114	115	39	39	9	22	8	112	163	26	77	24	36	17	226	278	65
Dallas	37	18	16	3	123	115	39	37	9	22	6	100	150	24	74	27	38	9	223	265	63
Detroit	33	15	10	8	118	95	38	32	12	18	2	114	138	26	65	27	28	10	232	233	64
Edmonton	25	11	12	2	88	88	24	25	7	13	5	97	124	19	50	18	25	7	185	212	43
Florida	2	2	0	0	6	2	4	3	1	0	2	8	7	4	5	3	0	2	14	9	8
Hartford	25	13	10	2	98	96	28	24	7	12	5	75	90	19	49	20	22	7	173	186	47
Los Angeles	35	15	15	5	121	130	35	35	3	26	6	107	189	12	70	18	41	11	228	319	47
Montreal	34	10	24	0	94	159	20	34	6	24	4	88	141	16	68	16	48	4	182	300	36
NY Islanders	59	19	31	9	194	240	47	59	6	45	8	165	283	20	118	25	76	17	359	523	67
NY Rangers	60	25	31	4	206	233	54	59	15	36	8	185	263	38	119	40	67	12	391	496	92
Ottawa	4	4	0	0	20	9	8	4	2	1	1	16	9	5	8	6	1	1	36	18	13
Philadelphia	58	29	25	4	216	224	62	59	11	41	7	143	255	29	117	40	66	11	359	479	91
Pittsburgh	57	29	19	9	226	198	67	57	19	34	4	203	242	42	114	48	53	13	429	440	109
Quebec	26	12	12	2	109	96	26	24	9	12	3	80	98	21	50	21	24	5	189	194	47
St. Louis	39	17	15	7	128	114	41	38	8	25	5	118	172	21	77	25	40	12	246	286	62
San Jose	4	3	1	0	20	7	6	3	2	1	0	10	5	4	7	5	2	0	30	12	10
Tampa Bay	4	4	0	0	18	9	8	3	2	0	1	10	7	5	7	6	0	1	28	16	13
Toronto	32	13	10	9	120	103	35	33	6	24	3	107	151	15	65	19	34	12	227	254	50
Vancouver	41	18	17	6	130	137	42	41	6	24	11	118	160	23	82	24	41	17	248	297	65
Washington	56	23	27	6	180	182	52	57	14	40	3	173	254	31	113	37	67	9	353	436	83
Winnipeg	21	6	9	6	66	70	18	23	4	16	3	61	92	11	44	10	25	9	127	162	29
Defunct Clubs	8	4	2	2	25	19	10	8	2	3	3	19	27	7	16	6	5	5	44	46	17
Totals	**804**	**331**	**362**	**111**	**2733**	**2847**	**773**	**804**	**181**	**513**	**110**	**2431**	**3516**	**472**	**1608**	**512**	**875**	**221**	**5164**	**6363**	**1245**

Calgary totals include Atlanta, 1974-75 to 1979-80. Dallas totals include Minnesota, 1974-75 to 1992-93. New Jersey totals include Kansas City, 1974-75 to 1975-76, and Colorado, 1976-77 to 1981-82.

Playoffs

	Series	W	L	GP	W	L	T	GF	GA	Last Mtg.	Round	Result
Boston	2	1	1	13	7	6	0	41	47	1994	CSF	W 4-2
Buffalo	1	1	0	7	4	3	0	14	14	1994	CQF	W 4-3
NY Islanders	1	1	0	6	4	2	0	23	18	1988	DSF	W 4-2
NY Rangers	2	0	2	14	6	8	0	41	46	1994	CF	L 3-4
Philadelphia	1	0	1	2	0	2	0	3	8	1978	PR	L 0-2
Pittsburgh	2	0	2	12	4	8	0	30	48	1993	DSF	L 1-4
Washington	2	1	1	13	6	7	0	43	44	1990	DSF	L 2-4
Totals	**11**	**4**	**7**	**67**	**31**	**36**	**0**	**195**	**223**			

Playoff Results 1994-90

Year	Round	Opponent	Result	GF	GA
1994	CF	NY Rangers	L 3-4	16	18
	CSF	Boston	W 4-2	22	17
	CQF	Buffalo	W 4-3	14	14
1993	DSF	Pittsburgh	L 1-4	13	23
1992	DSF	NY Rangers	L 3-4	25	28
1991	DSF	Pittsburgh	L 3-4	17	25
1990	DSF	Washington	L 2-4	18	21

Abbreviations: Round: F – Final;
CF – conference final; **CQF** – conference quarter-final;
CSF – conference semi-final; **DF** – division final;
DSF – division semi-final; **SF** – semi-final;
QF – quarter-final; **PR** – preliminary round.

1993-94 Results

Oct.	6		Tampa Bay	2-1	14	at	Washington	5-2
	8	at	Washington	6-3	15		Los Angeles	3-5
	9		Washington	6-4	19	at	Winnipeg	4-0
	12		Winnipeg	7-4	24	at	Dallas	6-2
	16	at	NY Islanders	6-3	26	at	Edmonton	3-3
	20		Anaheim	4-0	28	at	Calgary	2-2
	23		Florida	2-1	29	at	Vancouver	3-6
	26		Montreal	0-2	Feb. 2		Buffalo	2-3
	30		Philadelphia	5-3	4		Ottawa	2-3
	31	at	NY Rangers	1-4	5		Pittsburgh	7-3
Nov.	3	at	Los Angeles	2-3	10		Vancouver	7-3
	5	at	Anaheim	6-3	12	at	Boston	3-5
	7	at	San Jose	2-1	13	at	Tampa Bay	3-3
	10		NY Islanders	5-3	17	at	Toronto	1-2
	11	at	Philadelphia	5-3	19		Tampa Bay	5-4
	13		San Jose	2-4	20	at	Chicago	1-1
	17		Buffalo	4-0	23	at	Detroit	7-2
	18	at	Ottawa	5-2	24		NY Rangers	1-3
	20		Detroit	3-4	26	at	Hartford	1-1
	23	at	Quebec	1-1	28		St. Louis	5-1
	24	at	Buffalo	5-3	Mar. 2	at	Florida	3-2
	26	at	St. Louis	6-6	3	at	Tampa Bay	5-2
	30		NY Rangers	1-3	5		Calgary	6-3
Dec.	2	at	Pittsburgh	2-2	7		Quebec	2-2
	4		Chicago	2-2	10		Hartford	4-0
	5	at	NY Rangers	1-2	12		Boston	2-1
	8	at	Montreal	4-2	13		Dallas	4-0
	9		Quebec	2-3	15	at	NY Islanders	2-3
	11		Edmonton	5-2	17	at	Buffalo	6-1
	14	at	NY Islanders	1-4	19	at	Boston	8-6
	15		Boston	4-5	21	at	Florida	3-3
	18	at	Quebec	6-2	24		Tampa Bay	2-1
	19		Philadelphia	4-2	26		Philadelphia	7-2
	22	at	Hartford	3-6	27		Quebec	5-2
	23		Toronto	3-2	29		Montreal	5-2
	26	at	NY Rangers	3-8	Apr. 1	at	Washington	1-2
	28		Hartford	4-2	2		NY Rangers	2-4
Jan.	1	at	Pittsburgh	7-1	6	at	Pittsburgh	1-3
	4		NY Islanders	5-3	8		Pittsburgh	7-2
	7		Florida	4-1	10	at	Florida	2-2
	9		Washington	0-4	12	at	Philadelphia	2-4
	12	at	Montreal	2-3	14		Ottawa	4-1

Entry Draft
Selections 1994-80

1994		1990		1986		1982	
Pick		**Pick**		**Pick**		**Pick**	
25	Vadim Sharifijanov	20	Martin Brodeur	3	Neil Brady	8	Rocky Trottier
51	Patrik Elias	24	David Harlock	24	Todd Copeland	18	Ken Daneyko
71	Sheldon Souray	29	Chris Gotziaman	45	Janne Ojanen	43	Pat Verbeek
103	Zdenek Skorepa	53	Michael Dunham	62	Marc Laniel	54	Dave Kasper
129	Christian Gosselin	56	Brad Bombardir	66	Anders Carlsson	5	Scott Brydges
134	Ryan Smart	64	Mike Bodnarchuk	108	Troy Crowder	106	Mike Moher
155	Luciano Caravaggio	95	Dean Malkoc	129	Kevin Todd	127	Paul Fulcher
181	Jeff Williams	104	Petr Kuchyna	150	Ryan Pardoski	148	John Hutchings
207	Eric Bertrand	116	Lubomir Kolnik	171	Scott McCormack	169	Alan Hepple
233	Steve Sullivan	137	Chris McAlpine	192	Frederic Chabot	190	Brent Shaw
259	Scott Swanjord	179	Jaroslav Modry	213	John Andersen	207	Tony Gilliard
269	Mike Hanson	200	Corey Schwab	236	Doug Kirton	211	Scott Fusco
		221	Valeri Zelepukin			232	Dan Dorion
1993		242	Todd Reirden	**1985**			
Pick				**Pick**		**1981**	
13	Denis Pederson	**1989**		3	Craig Wolanin	**Pick**	
32	Jay Pandolfo	**Pick**		24	Sean Burke	5	Joe Cirella
39	Brendan Morrison	5	Bill Guerin	32	Eric Weinrich	26	Rich Chernomaz
65	Krzysztof Oliwa	18	Jason Miller	45	Myles O'Connor	48	Uli Hiemer
110	John Guirestante	26	Jarrod Skalde	66	Gregg Polak	66	Gus Greco
143	Steve Brule	47	Scott Pellerin	108	Bill McMillan	87	Doug Speck
169	Nikolai Zavarukhin	89	Mike Heinke	129	Kevin Schrader	108	Bruce Driver
195	Thomas Cullen	110	David Emma	150	Ed Krayer	129	Jeff Larmer
221	Judd Lambert	152	Sergei Starikov	171	Jamie Huscroft	150	Tony Arima
247	Jimmy Provencher	173	Andre Faust	192	Terry Shold	171	Tim Army
273	Michael Legg	215	Jason Simon	213	Jamie McKinley	192	John Johannson
		236	Peter Larsson	234	David Williams		
1992						**1980**	
Pick		**1988**		**1984**		**Pick**	
18	Jason Smith	**Pick**		**Pick**		19	Paul Gagne
42	Sergei Brylin	12	Corey Foster	2	Kirk Muller	22	Joe Ward
64	Cale Hulse	23	Jeff Christian	23	Craig Billington	64	Rick LaFerriere
90	Vitali Tomilin	54	Zdeno Ciger	44	Neil Davey	85	Ed Cooper
94	Scott McCabe	65	Matt Ruchty	74	Paul Ysebaert	106	Aaron Broten
114	Ryan Black	75	Scott Luik	86	Jon Morris	127	Dan Fascinato
138	Daniel Trebil	96	Chris Nelson	107	Kirk McLean	148	Andre Hidi
162	Geordie Kinnear	117	Chad Johnson	128	Ian Ferguson	169	Shawn MacKenzie
186	Stephane Yelle	138	Chad Erickson	149	Vladimir Kames	190	Bob Jansch
210	Jeff Toms	159	Bryan Lafort	170	Mike Roth		
234	Heath Weenk	180	Sergei Svetlov	190	Mike Peluso		
258	Vladislav Yakovenko	201	Bob Woods	211	Jarkko Piiparinen		
		207	Alexander Semak	231	Chris Kiene		
1991		222	Charles Hughes				
Pick		243	Michael Pohl	**1983**			
3	Scott Niedermayer			**Pick**			
11	Brian Rolston	**1987**		6	John MacLean		
33	Donevan Hextall	**Pick**		24	Shawn Evans		
55	Fredrik Lindqvist	2	Brendan Shanahan	85	Chris Terreri		
77	Bradley Willner	23	Rickard Persson	105	Gordon Mark		
121	Curt Regnier	65	Brian Sullivan	125	Greg Evtushevski		
143	David Craievich	86	Kevin Dean	145	Viacheslav Fetisov		
165	Paul Wolanski	107	Ben Hankinson	165	Jay Octeau		
187	Daniel Reimann	128	Tom Neziol	185	Alexander Chernykh		
231	Kevin Riehl	149	Jim Dowd	205	Allan Stewart		
253	Jason Hehr	170	John Blessman	225	Alexei Kasatonov		
		191	Peter Fry				
		212	Alain Charland				

Club Directory

Meadowlands Arena
P.O. Box 504
East Rutherford, NJ 07073
Phone **201/935-6050**
GM FAX 201/935-6898
FAX 201/935-2127
Capacity: 19,040

Chairman	John J. McMullen
President & General Manager	Louis A. Lamoriello
Executive Vice President	Max McNab
Senior Vice President, Finance	Chris Modrzynski
Vice President, Sales & Marketing	Michael G. McCall
Vice President, Operations & Human Resources	Peter McMullen
Administrative Assistants to the President/GM	Marie Carnevale, Charlotte Smaldone
General Counsel	Joseph Benedetti

Hockey Club Personnel

Head Coach	Jacques Lemaire
Assistant Coaches	Larry Robinson, Dennis Gendron
Goaltending Coach	Jacques Caron
Strength & Conditioning Coach	Michael Vasalani
Director of Scouting	David Conte
Scouting Staff	Claude Carrier, Marcel Pronovost, Milt Fisher, Ed Thomlinson, Dan Labraaten, Glen Dirk, Les Widdifield, Joe Mahoney, Ferny Flaman, Larry Perris, Lou Reycroft, Dimitri Goryachkin, Yvon Lemaire
Pro Scouting Staff	John Cunniff, Bob Hoffmeyer, Jan Ludvig
Scouting Staff Assistant	Callie A. Smith
Medical Trainer	Ted Schuch
Equipment Manager	Dave Nichols
Assistant Equipment Manager	Alex Abasto
Massage Therapist	Bob Huddleston
Team Cardiologist	Dr. Joseph Niznik
Team Dentist	Dr. H. Hugh Gardy
Team Internist	Dr. Richard Commentucci
Team Orthopedists	Dr. Barry Fisher, Dr. Len Jaffe
Exercise Physiologist	Dr. Garret Caffrey
Physical Therapist	David Feniger

Communications Department

Director, Public Relations	TBA
Director, Media Relations	Mike Levine
Receptionists	Jelsa Belotta, Pat Maione
Staff Assistant	Wayne Rose

Finance Department

Director of Finance	Scott Struble
Staff Accountants	Chuck Meyers, Tina Pampanin, Bill Rodriguez
Secretary	Eileen Musikant

Marketing Department

Director, Promotional Marketing	Ken Ferriter
Coordinator, Game Entertainment	Carol Kolbus
Account Managers	David Beck, Alan Concha, Megan Gardner, Mike Kozak, Holly Meyer, Ken Scala, Mark Truhan, Christine Turk
Group Account Managers	Neil Desormeaux, John Glynn, Liz Greco, Bob Marks
Secretaries	Karen Pietz, Mary K. Morrison
Merchandising Assistants	Stan Smith, David Perricone
Merchandising Secretary	Maryanne Spangenberg

Ticket Department

Senior Director, Ticket Operations	Terry Farmer
Assistant Director, Ticket Operations	Scott Tanfield
Gold Circle Customer Service Representative	Gail DeRisi

Television Outlet	SportsChannel
Broadcasters	Mike Emrick, Play-by-Play; Peter McNab, Color
Radio Outlet	WABC (770 AM)
Broadcasters	Mike Miller, Play-by-Play; Sherry Ross, Color
Team Photographer	Jim Turner
Video Consultant	Mitch Kaufman
Dimensions of Rink	200 feet by 85 feet
Club Colors	Red, Black and White

Coach

LEMAIRE, JACQUES GERARD
Coach, New Jersey Devils. Born in LaSalle, Quebec, September 7, 1945.

Jacques Lemaire is entering his second season as head coach of the New Jersey Devils. In 1993-94, his first season behind the Devils bench, Lemaire led the team to a franchise record 106 points and guided the team to the Conference Finals for the first time since 1988. Lemaire was named the winner of the Jack Adams Award as the NHL's outstanding coach and was also honored by The Sporting News and The Hockey News. Lemaire, who served as the Assistant to the Managing Director of the Montreal Canadiens for seven years, coached the Canadiens from February 24, 1984 to the end of the 1984-85 season. During his successful term as the Habs' coach, he led the team to the Conference Finals in 1984 and to a first place finish in the Adams Division in 1984-85.

A member of the Hockey Hall of Fame as a player, Lemaire coached Sierre of the Swiss League and Longueuil of the Quebec Major Junior Hockey League before joining the Canadiens' organization in 1983.

Coaching Record

		Regular Season					Playoffs			
Season	**Team**	**Games**	**W**	**L**	**T**	**%**	**Games**	**W**	**L**	**%**
1979-80	Sierre (Switzerland)					UNAVAILABLE				
1980-81	Sierre (Switzerland)					UNAVAILABLE				
1982-83	Longueuil (QMJHL)	70	37	29	4	.557	15	9	6	.600
1983-84	**Montreal (NHL)**	17	7	10	0	.412	15	9	6	.600
1984-85	**Montreal (NHL)**	80	41	27	12	.588	12	6	6	.500
1993-94	**New Jersey (NHL)**	84	47	25	12	.631	20	11	9	.550
	NHL Totals	181	95	62	24	.591	47	26	21	.553

General Manager

LAMORIELLO, LOU
President and General Manager, New Jersey Devils.
Born in Providence, Rhode Island, October 21, 1942.

Lou Lamoriello's life-long dedication to the game of hockey was rewarded in 1992 when he was named a recipient of the Lester Patrick Trophy for outstanding service to hockey in the United States. Lamoriello is entering his eighth season as president and general manager of the Devils following more than 20 years with Providence College as a player, coach and administrator. A member of the varsity hockey Friars during his undergraduate days, he became an assistant coach with the college club after graduating in 1963. Lamoriello was later named head coach and in the ensuing 15 years, led his teams to a 248-179-13 record, a .578 winning percentage and appearances in 10 post-season tournaments, including the 1983 NCAA Final Four. Lamoriello also served a five-year term as athletic director at Providence and was a co-founder of Hockey East, one of the strongest collegiate hockey conferences in the U.S. He remained as athletic director until he was hired as president of the Devils on April 30, 1987. He assumed the dual responsibility of general manager on September 10, 1987.

New York Islanders

1993-94 Results: 36w-36l-12t 84pts. Fourth, Atlantic Division

Schedule

Oct.	Sat.	1	Tampa Bay	Wed. 11	Florida
	Fri.	7	Ottawa	Fri. 13	at New Jersey
	Sat.	8	at Washington	Sat. 14	at Pittsburgh
	Wed.	12	at Montreal	Mon. 16	Philadelphia*
	Sat.	15	Detroit	Wed. 18	Quebec
	Tues.	18	Los Angeles	Tues. 24	St. Louis
	Sat.	22	Florida	Thur. 26	Washington
	Tues.	25	Vancouver	Sat. 28	Tampa Bay
	Sat.	29	Calgary	Mon. 30	at NY Rangers
Nov.	Tues.	1	at Dallas	Tues. 31	at Florida
	Wed.	2	at St. Louis	**Feb.** Thur. 2	at Philadelphia
	Sat.	5	at Tampa Bay	Sat. 4	at Boston*
	Mon.	7	Dallas	Tues. 7	Winnipeg
	Wed.	9	at Florida	Sat. 11	San Jose*
	Fri.	11	at NY Rangers	Mon. 13	at Tampa Bay
	Sat.	12	Hartford	Wed. 15	at Florida
	Wed.	16	at Montreal	Fri. 17	at New Jersey
	Fri.	18	at New Jersey	Sat. 18	New Jersey
	Sat.	19	at Hartford	Mon. 20	at Detroit
	Wed.	23	Tampa Bay	Wed. 22	at Buffalo
	Sat.	26	Toronto	Fri. 24	at Toronto
	Sun.	27	at Buffalo	Sat. 25	Pittsburgh
	Tues.	29	Boston	Tues. 28	Hartford
Dec.	Thur.	1	at Philadelphia	**Mar.** Thur. 2	at Washington
	Sat.	3	Buffalo	Sat. 4	NY Rangers
	Tues.	6	Edmonton	Sun. 5	at Ottawa
	Thur.	8	at NY Rangers	Tues. 7	New Jersey
	Sat.	10	Ottawa	Thur. 9	Montreal
	Tues.	13	NY Rangers	Sat. 11	at Quebec
			(in Portland, OR)	Tues. 14	at Vancouver
	Wed.	14	at San Jose	Fri. 17	at Edmonton
	Sat.	17	at Los Angeles	Sun. 19	at Calgary
	Sun.	18	at Anaheim	Thur. 23	Philadelphia
	Tues.	20	at Chicago	Sat. 25	at Hartford*
	Fri.	23	Quebec	Sun. 26	Anaheim*
	Mon.	26	Washington	Tues. 28	at Boston
	Wed.	28	at Ottawa	Thur. 30	Montreal
	Fri.	30	Philadelphia	**Apr.** Sat. 1	Buffalo*
	Sat.	31	at Pittsburgh	Sun. 2	at Quebec*
Jan.	Tues.	3	Chicago	Tues. 4	Pittsburgh
	Thur.	5	NY Rangers	Thur. 6	Boston
	Sat.	7	Washington	Sun. 9	at Winnipeg*
	Mon.	9	at Buffalo		
			(in Minneapolis)		

* Denotes afternoon game.

Home Starting Times:

Weeknights	7:30 p.m.
Saturday and Sunday nights	7:00 p.m.
Matinees	1:00 p.m.
Except Sat. Nov. 26	7:30 p.m.
Mon. Jan. 16	1:00 p.m.

Franchise date: June 6, 1972

EASTERN NHL **CONFERENCE**

ATLANTIC DIVISION

23rd NHL Season

Although he missed 15 games because of injury, Pierre Turgeon still powered the Islanders' offense, collecting 38 goals and 56 assists in 69 games.

Year-by-Year Record

Season	GP	Home W	L	T	Road W	L	T	Overall W	L	T	GF	GA	Pts.	Finished		Playoff Result
1993-94	84	23	15	4	13	21	8	36	36	12	282	264	84	4th,	Atlantic Div.	Lost Conf. Quarter-Final
1992-93	84	20	19	3	20	18	4	40	37	7	335	297	87	3rd,	Patrick Div.	Lost Conf. Championship
1991-92	80	20	15	5	14	20	6	34	35	11	291	299	79	5th,	Patrick Div.	Out of Playoffs
1990-91	80	15	19	6	10	26	4	25	45	10	223	290	60	6th,	Patrick Div.	Out of Playoffs
1989-90	80	15	17	8	16	21	3	31	38	11	281	288	73	4th,	Patrick Div.	Lost Div. Semi-Final
1988-89	80	19	18	3	9	29	2	28	47	5	265	325	61	6th,	Patrick Div.	Out of Playoffs
1987-88	80	24	10	6	15	21	4	39	31	10	308	267	88	1st,	Patrick Div.	Lost Div. Semi-Final
1986-87	80	20	15	5	15	18	7	35	33	12	279	281	82	3rd,	Patrick Div.	Lost Div. Final
1985-86	80	22	11	7	17	18	5	39	29	12	327	284	90	3rd,	Patrick Div.	Lost Div. Semi-Final
1984-85	80	26	11	3	14	23	3	40	34	6	345	312	86	3rd,	Patrick Div.	Lost Div. Final
1983-84	80	28	11	1	22	15	3	50	26	4	357	269	104	1st,	Patrick Div.	Lost Final
1982-83	**80**	**26**	**11**	**3**	**16**	**15**	**9**	**42**	**26**	**12**	**302**	**226**	**96**	**2nd,**	**Patrick Div.**	**Won Stanley Cup**
1981-82	**80**	**33**	**3**	**4**	**21**	**13**	**6**	**54**	**16**	**10**	**385**	**250**	**118**	**1st,**	**Patrick Div.**	**Won Stanley Cup**
1980-81	**80**	**23**	**6**	**11**	**25**	**12**	**3**	**48**	**18**	**14**	**355**	**260**	**110**	**1st,**	**Patrick Div.**	**Won Stanley Cup**
1979-80	**80**	**26**	**9**	**5**	**13**	**19**	**8**	**39**	**28**	**13**	**281**	**247**	**91**	**2nd,**	**Patrick Div.**	**Won Stanley Cup**
1978-79	80	31	3	6	20	12	8	51	15	14	358	214	116	1st,	Patrick Div.	Lost Semi-Final
1977-78	80	29	3	8	19	14	7	48	17	15	334	210	111	1st,	Patrick Div.	Lost Quarter-Final
1976-77	80	24	11	5	23	10	7	47	21	12	288	193	106	2nd,	Patrick Div.	Lost Semi-Final
1975-76	80	24	8	8	18	13	9	42	21	17	297	190	101	2nd,	Patrick Div.	Lost Semi-Final
1974-75	80	22	6	12	11	19	10	33	25	22	264	221	88	3rd,	Patrick Div.	Lost Semi-Final
1973-74	78	13	17	9	6	24	9	19	41	18	182	247	56	8th,	East Div.	Out of Playoffs
1972-73	78	10	25	4	2	35	2	12	60	6	170	347	30	8th,	East Div.	Out of Playoffs

1994-95 Player Personnel

FORWARDS	HT	WT	S	Place of Birth	Date	1993-94 Club
ARMSTRONG, Derek	5-11	180	R	Ottawa, Ont.	4/23/73	NY Islanders-Salt Lake
BERTUZZI, Todd	6-3	227	L	Sudbury, Ont.	2/2/75	Guelph
BRICKLEY, Andy	5-11	200	L	Melrose, MA	8/9/61	Winnipeg-Moncton
CHYZOWSKI, David	6-1	190	L	Edmonton, Alta.	7/11/71	NY Islanders-Salt Lake
DALGARNO, Brad	6-3	215	R	Vancouver, B.C.	8/11/67	NY Islanders
DEULING, Jarrett	5-11	194	L	Vernon, B.C.	3/4/74	Kamloops
FERRARO, Ray	5-10	185	L	Trail, B.C.	8/23/64	NY Islanders
FLATLEY, Pat	6-2	197	R	Toronto, Ont.	10/3/63	NY Islanders
GREEN, Travis	6-2	200	R	Castlegar, B.C.	12/20/70	NY Islanders
JUNKER, Steve	6-0	184	L	Castlegar, B.C.	6/26/72	NY Islanders-Salt Lake
KAMINSKY, Yan	6-1	176	L	Penza, USSR	7/28/71	Winnipeg-NY Islanders
KING, Derek	6-1	203	L	Hamilton, Ont.	2/11/67	NY Islanders
LINDROS, Brett	6-4	215	R	London, Ont.	12/2/75	Cdn. National-Kingston
LOACH, Lonnie	5-10	181	L	New Liskeard, Ont.	4/14/68	Anaheim-San Diego
LOACH, Mike	6-1	181	R	New Liskeard, Ont.	9/8/76	Windsor
LONEY, Troy	6-3	209	L	Bow Island, Alta.	9/21/63	Anaheim
MARINUCCI, Chris	6-0	175	L	Grand Rapids, MN	12/29/71	Minn.-Duluth
McINNIS, Marty	6-0	185	R	Hingham, MA.	6/2/70	NY Islanders
MILLER, Kip	5-10	190	L	Lansing, MI	6/11/69	San Jose-Kansas City
MULLEN, Brian	5-10	180	L	New York, NY	3/16/62	NY Islanders
PALFFY, Zigmund	5-10	169	L	Skalica, Czech.	5/5/72	NY Islanders-Salt Lake
PLANTE, Dan	5-11	198	R	St. Louis, MO	10/5/71	NY Islanders-Salt Lake
SCISSONS, Scott	6-1	201	L	Saskatoon, Sask.	10/29/71	NY Islanders-Salt Lake
SIMON, Jason	6-1	190	L	Sarnia, Ont.	3/21/69	NYI-Salt Lake-Detroit (ColHL)
SUTTER, Ron	6-0	180	R	Viking, Alta.	12/2/63	St. Louis-Quebec
TAYLOR, Chris	6-0	185	L	Stratford, Ont.	3/6/72	Salt Lake-Raleigh
THOMAS, Steve	5-11	185	L	Stockport, England	7/15/63	NY Islanders
TURGEON, Pierre	6-1	202	L	Rouyn, Que.	8/29/69	NY Islanders
VUKOTA, Mick	6-2	195	R	Saskatoon, Sask.	9/14/66	NY Islanders
ZENT, Jason	5-11	180	L	Buffalo, NY	4/15/71	U. Wisconsin
DEFENSEMEN						
BEERS, Bob	6-2	200	R	Pittsburgh, PA	5/20/67	Tampa Bay-Edmonton
CHEBATURKIN, Vladimir	6-2	189	L	Tyumen, USSR	4/23/75	Elektrostal
CHYNOWETH, Dean	6-2	190	R	Calgary, Alta.	10/30/68	NY Islanders-Salt Lake
DINEEN, Gord	6-0	195	R	Quebec City, Que.	9/21/62	Ottawa-San Diego
GUY, Kevan	6-3	202	R	Edmonton, Alta.	7/16/65	Salt Lake
KASPARAITIS, Darius	5-11	187	L	Elektrenai, USSR	10/16/72	NY Islanders
LACHANCE, Scott	6-1	197	L	Charlottesville, VA	10/22/72	NY Islanders
LUONGO, Chris	6-0	180	R	Detroit, MI	3/17/67	NY Islanders-Salt Lake
MALAKHOV, Vladimir	6-2	207	L	Sverdlovsk, USSR	8/30/68	NY Islanders
MCCABE, Bryan	6-1	200	L	St. Catharines, Ont.	6/8/75	Spokane
PILON, Richard	6-0	202	L	Saskatoon, Sask.	4/30/68	NY Islanders-Salt Lake
TICHY, Milan	6-3	198	L	Plzen, Czech.	9/22/69	Moncton
VASKE, Dennis	6-2	210	L	Rockford, IL	10/11/67	NY Islanders
WIDMER, Jason	6-0	205	L	Calgary, Alta.	8/1/73	Lethbridge

GOALTENDERS	HT	WT	C	Place of Birth	Date	1993-94 Club
HEXTALL, Ron	6-3	192	L	Brandon, Man.	5/3/64	NY Islanders
HNILICKA, Milan	6-0	180	L	Litomerice, Czech.	6/25/73	Richmond-Salt Lake
McLENNAN, Jamie	6-0	190	L	Edmonton, Alta.	6/30/71	NY Islanders-Salt Lake
PIETRANGELO, Frank	5-10	185	L	Niagara Falls, Ont.	12/17/64	Hartford-Springfield
SALO, Tommy	5-11	161	L	Surahammar, Sweden	2/1/71	Vasteras

Coach

HENNING, LORNE
Coach, New York Islanders. Born in Melfort, Sask., February 23, 1952.

Lorne Henning, an original Islander and a member of the organization for 18 of its 22 years, was named the fifth head coach in club history on June 20, 1994.

The Islanders' second draft pick ever (17th overall in 1972), Henning enjoyed a nine-year playing career with the team, posting statistics of 73-111-184 in 544 games and earning a reputation as one of the League's top penalty killers. He made his mark on Islander history when he and John Tonnelli set up Bob Nystrom's Stanley Cup-winning overtime goal in 1980.

After one year as a player/assistant, Henning became Al Arbour's full-time aide in 1981. After playing a major part of four straight Stanley Cups and an appearance in the 1984 finals, he was named head coach of the Springfield Indians, the Islanders' AHL affiliate, in 1984-85.

The following season, he was named head coach of the Minnesota North Stars. In his first year the Saskatchewan native led the North Stars to a 23-point improvement, the biggest one-season jump in club history. He finished third in the voting for the Jack Adams Award as coach of the year behind Glen Sather and Jacques Demers. After his dismissal in 1987 and two seasons out of hockey, he re-joined Arbour and the Islanders for the 1989-90 season.

Lorne and his wife Cathye have three children: Brett (14), Garrett (12) and Marissa (8) and reside in Huntington, New York.

Coaching Record

		Regular Season					Playoffs			
Season	**Team**	**Games**	**W**	**L**	**T**	**%**	**Games**	**W**	**L**	**%**
1985-86	Minnesota (NHL)	80	38	33	9	.531	5	2	3	.400
1986-87	Minnesota (NHL)	78	30	39	9	.422	....	....	....	....
	NHL Totals	158	68	72	18	.487	5	2	3	.400

1993-94 Scoring

* – rookie

Regular Season

Pos	#	Player	Team	GP	G	A	Pts	+/–	PIM	PP	SH	GW	GT	S	%
C	77	Pierre Turgeon	NYI	69	38	56	94	14	18	10	4	6	0	254	15.0
L	32	Steve Thomas	NYI	78	42	33	75	9–	139	17	0	5	2	249	16.9
L	27	Derek King	NYI	78	30	40	70	18	59	10	0	7	1	171	17.5
C	33	Benoit Hogue	NYI	83	36	33	69	7–	73	9	5	3	0	218	16.5
D	23	Vladimir Malakhov	NYI	76	10	47	57	29	80	4	0	2	0	235	4.3
C	18	Marty McInnis	NYI	81	25	31	56	31	24	3	5	3	1	136	18.4
C	20	Ray Ferraro	NYI	82	21	32	53	1	83	5	0	3	3	136	15.4
R	26	Patrick Flatley	NYI	64	12	30	42	12	40	2	1	2	0	112	10.7
C	39	Travis Green	NYI	83	18	22	40	16	44	1	0	2	1	164	11.0
D	28	Tom Kurvers	NYI	66	9	31	40	7	47	5	0	1	0	141	6.4
R	15	Brad Dalgarno	NYI	73	11	19	30	14	62	3	0	1	0	97	11.3
D	4	Uwe Krupp	NYI	41	7	14	21	11	30	3	0	0	0	82	8.5
L	25	Dave Volek	NYI	32	5	9	14	0	10	2	0	0	0	56	8.9
D	7	Scott Lachance	NYI	74	3	11	14	5–	70	0	0	1	0	59	5.1
D	37	Dennis Vaske	NYI	65	2	11	13	21	76	0	0	0	0	71	2.8
D	11	Darius Kasparaitis	NYI	76	1	10	11	6–	142	0	0	0	0	81	1.2
C	24	Keith Acton	WSH	6	0	0	0	4–	21	0	0	0	0	2	.0
			NYI	71	2	7	9	1–	50	0	0	0	0	33	6.1
			TOTAL	77	2	7	9	5–	71	0	0	0	0	35	5.7
L	8	David Maley	S.J.	19	0	0	0	1–	30	0	0	0	0	4	.0
			NYI	37	0	6	6	6–	74	0	0	0	0	19	.0
			TOTAL	56	0	6	6	7–	104	0	0	0	0	23	.0
D	47	Richard Pilon	NYI	28	1	4	5	4–	75	0	0	0	0	20	5.0
R	12	Mick Vukota	NYI	72	3	1	4	5–	237	0	0	0	0	26	11.5
D	2	Chris Luongo	NYI	17	1	3	4	1–	13	0	0	0	0	16	6.3
D	3	Dean Chynoweth	NYI	39	0	4	4	3	122	0	0	0	0	26	.0
L	17	* Yan Kaminsky	WPG	1	0	0	0	1	0	0	0	0	0	0	.0
			NYI	23	2	1	3	4	4	0	0	0	0	23	8.7
			TOTAL	24	2	1	3	5	4	0	0	0	0	23	8.7
G	72	Ron Hextall	NYI	65	0	3	3	0	52	0	0	0	0	0	.0
C	10	Claude Loiselle	NYI	17	1	1	2	2–	49	0	0	0	0	14	7.1
L	9	Dave Chyzowski	NYI	3	1	0	1	1–	4	0	0	0	0	4	25.0
R	34	* Dan Plante	NYI	12	0	1	1	2–	4	0	0	0	0	9	.0
G	29	* Jamie McLennan	NYI	22	0	1	1	0	6	0	0	0	0	0	.0
C	14	* Scott Scissons	NYI	1	0	0	0	0	0	0	0	0	0	0	.0
C	38	* Derek Armstrong	NYI	1	0	0	0	0	0	0	0	0	0	2	.0
L	38	* Jason Simon	NYI	4	0	0	0	0	34	0	0	0	0	0	.0
L	68	* Zigmund Palffy	NYI	5	0	0	0	6–	0	0	0	0	0	5	.0
L	17	* Steve Junker	NYI	5	0	0	0	0	0	0	0	0	0	2	.0
G	35	Tom Draper	NYI	7	0	0	0	0	0	0	0	0	0	0	.0
L	14	Joe Day	NYI	24	0	0	0	7–	30	0	0	0	0	16	.0

Goaltending

No.	Goaltender	GPI	Mins	Avg	W	L	T	EN	SO	GA	SA	S%
29	* Jamie McLennan	22	1287	2.84	8	7	6	0	0	61	639	.905
72	Ron Hextall	65	3581	3.08	27	26	6	3	5	184	1801	.898
35	Tom Draper	7	227	4.23	1	3	0	0	0	16	118	.864
	Totals	**84**	**5119**	**3.09**	**36**	**36**	**12**	**3**	**5**	**264**	**2561**	**.897**

Playoffs

Pos	#	Player	Team	GP	G	A	Pts	+/–	PIM	PP	SH	GW	GT	S	%
R	34	* Dan Plante	NYI	1	1	0	1	0	2	0	0	0	0	3	33.3
C	20	Ray Ferraro	NYI	4	1	0	1	2–	6	0	0	0	0	8	12.5
L	32	Steve Thomas	NYI	4	1	0	1	5–	8	1	0	0	0	9	11.1
C	33	Benoit Hogue	NYI	4	0	1	1	3–	4	0	0	0	0	5	.0
R	15	Brad Dalgarno	NYI	4	0	1	1	2–	4	0	0	0	0	8	.0
L	27	Derek King	NYI	4	0	1	1	3–	0	0	0	0	0	6	.0
D	4	Uwe Krupp	NYI	4	0	1	1	3–	4	0	0	0	0	4	.0
C	77	Pierre Turgeon	NYI	4	0	1	1	4–	0	0	0	0	0	7	.0
D	37	Dennis Vaske	NYI	4	0	1	1	1–	2	0	0	0	0	0	.0
L	9	Dave Chyzowski	NYI	2	0	0	0	1–	0	0	0	0	0	3	.0
D	3	Dean Chynoweth	NYI	2	0	0	0	1–	2	0	0	0	0	0	.0
G	29	* Jamie McLennan	NYI	2	0	0	0	0	0	0	0	0	0	0	.0
L	17	* Yan Kaminsky	NYI	2	0	0	0	1–	4	0	0	0	0	0	.0
G	72	Ron Hextall	NYI	3	0	0	0	0	4	0	0	0	0	0	.0
D	28	Tom Kurvers	NYI	3	0	0	0	4–	2	0	0	0	0	5	.0
L	8	David Maley	NYI	3	0	0	0	2–	0	0	0	0	0	3	.0
D	7	Scott Lachance	NYI	3	0	0	0	5–	0	0	0	0	0	3	.0
C	24	Keith Acton	NYI	4	0	0	0	0	8	0	0	0	0	1	.0
R	12	Mick Vukota	NYI	4	0	0	0	0	17	0	0	0	0	1	.0
C	39	Travis Green	NYI	4	0	0	0	5–	2	0	0	0	0	7	.0
D	23	Vladimir Malakhov	NYI	4	0	0	0	5–	6	0	0	0	0	7	.0
C	18	Marty McInnis	NYI	4	0	0	0	5–	0	0	0	0	0	7	.0
D	11	Darius Kasparaitis	NYI	4	0	0	0	6–	8	0	0	0	0	3	.0

Goaltending

No.	Goaltender	GPI	Mins	Avg	W	L	EN	SO	GA	SA	S%
29	* Jamie McLennan	2	82	4.39	0	1	0	0	6	47	.872
72	Ron Hextall	3	158	6.08	0	3	0	0	16	80	.800
	Totals	**4**	**240**	**5.50**	**0**	**4**	**0**	**0**	**22**	**127**	**.827**

Club Records

Team

(Figures in brackets for season records are games played)

Most Points	118	1981-82 (80)
Most Wins	54	1981-82 (80)
Most Ties	22	1974-75 (80)
Most Losses	60	1972-73 (78)
Most Goals	385	1981-82 (80)
Most Goals Against	347	1972-73 (78)
Fewest Points	30	1972-73 (78)
Fewest Wins	12	1972-73 (78)
Fewest Ties	4	1983-84 (80)
Fewest Losses	15	1978-79 (80)
Fewest Goals	170	1972-73 (78)
Fewest Goals Against	190	1975-76 (80)

Longest Winning Streak

Over-all	15	Jan. 21/82- Feb. 20/82
Home	14	Jan. 2/82- Feb. 27/82
Away	8	Feb. 27/81 Mar. 31/81

Longest Undefeated Streak

Over-all	15	Jan. 21- Feb. 20/82 (15 wins) Nov. 4- Dec. 4/80 (13 wins, 2 ties)
Home	23	Oct. 17/78- Jan. 27/79 (19 wins, 4 ties) Jan. 2/82- Apr. 3/82 (21 wins, 2 ties)
Away	8	Four times

Longest Losing Streak

Over-all	12	Dec. 27/72- Jan. 18/73 Nov. 22- Dec. 17/88
Home	5	Jan. 2-23/33 Feb. 28- Mar. 19/74 Nov. 22- Dec. 17/88
Away	15	Jan. 20- Apr. 1/73

Longest Winless Streak

Over-all	15	Nov. 22- Dec. 23/72 (12 losses, 3 ties)
Home	7	Oct. 14- Nov. 21/72 (6 losses, 1 tie) Nov. 28- Dec. 23/72 (5 losses, 2 ties) Feb. 13- Mar. 13/90 (4 losses, 3 ties)
Away	20	Nov. 3/72- Jan. 13/73 (19 losses, 1 tie)

Most Shutouts, Season	10	1975-76 (80)
Most PIM, Season	1,857	1986-87 (80)
Most Goals, Game	11	Dec. 20/83 (Pit. 3 at NYI 11) Mar. 3/84 (NYI 11 at Tor. 6)

Individual

Most Seasons	17	Billy Smith
Most Games	1,123	Bryan Trottier
Most Goals, Career	573	Mike Bossy
Most Assists, Career	853	Bryan Trottier
Most Points, Career	1,353	Bryan Trottier (500 goals, 853 assists)
Most PIM, Career	1,466	Garry Howatt
Most Shutouts, Career	25	Glenn Resch
Longest Consecutive Games Streak	576	Bill Harris (Oct. 7/72-Nov. 30/79)
Most Goals, Season	69	Mike Bossy (1978-79)
Most Assists, Season	87	Bryan Trottier (1978-79)
Most Points, Season	147	Mike Bossy (1981-82) (64 goals, 83 assists)
Most PIM, Season	356	Brian Curran (1986-87)
Most Points, Defenseman, Season	101	Denis Potvin (1978-79) (31 goals, 70 assists)
Most Points, Center, Season	134	Bryan Trottier (1978-79) (47 goals, 87 assists)
Most Points, Right Wing, Season	*147	Mike Bossy (1981-82) (64 goals, 83 assists)
Most Points, Left Wing, Season	100	John Tonelli (1984-85) (42 goals, 58 assists)
Most Points, Rookie, Season	95	Bryan Trottier (1975-76) (32 goals, 63 assists)
Most Shutouts, Season	7	Glenn Resch (1975-76)
Most Goals, Game	5	Bryan Trottier (Dec. 23/78; Feb. 13/82) John Tonelli (Jan. 6/81)
Most Assists, Game	6	Mike Bossy (Jan. 6/81)
Most Points, Game	8	Bryan Trottier (Dec. 23/78)

* NHL Record.

Retired Numbers

5	Denis Potvin	1973-1988
22	Mike Bossy	1977-1987
31	Billy Smith	1972-1989

All-time Record vs. Other Clubs

Regular Season

	At Home							On Road							Total						
	GP	W	L	T	GF	GA	PTS	GP	W	L	T	GF	GA	PTS	GP	W	L	T	GF	GA	PTS
Anaheim	1	0	1	0	0	3	0	1	1	0	0	4	2	2	2	1	1	0	4	6	2
Boston	41	15	22	4	129	142	34	40	9	22	9	112	157	27	81	24	44	13	241	299	61
Buffalo	41	17	17	7	122	119	41	41	13	23	5	119	147	31	82	30	40	12	241	266	72
Calgary	43	24	10	9	178	114	57	43	13	19	11	134	154	37	86	37	29	20	312	268	94
Chicago	39	16	11	12	142	118	44	41	16	20	5	143	135	37	80	32	31	17	285	253	81
Dallas	39	22	9	8	154	111	52	39	19	14	6	148	114	44	78	41	23	14	302	225	96
Detroit	38	22	14	2	148	109	46	37	16	19	2	123	131	34	75	38	33	4	271	240	80
Edmonton	23	10	5	8	99	92	28	23	5	14	4	70	93	14	46	15	19	12	169	185	42
Florida	3	0	3	0	5	9	0	2	0	2	0	3	9	0	5	0	5	0	8	18	0
Hartford	24	14	7	3	93	63	31	25	11	10	4	97	90	26	49	25	17	7	190	153	57
Los Angeles	37	20	13	4	140	108	44	37	14	16	7	125	132	35	74	34	29	11	265	240	79
Montreal	41	18	19	4	139	127	40	40	11	22	7	126	155	29	81	29	41	11	265	282	69
New Jersey	59	45	6	8	283	165	98	59	31	19	9	240	194	71	118	76	25	17	523	359	169
NY Rangers	71	48	17	6	311	220	102	70	19	43	8	211	281	46	141	67	60	14	522	501	148
Ottawa	4	2	1	1	21	13	5	3	2	0	1	18	6	5	7	4	1	2	39	19	10
Philadelphia	72	40	21	11	290	211	91	70	20	42	8	215	271	48	142	60	63	19	505	482	139
Pittsburgh	63	34	21	8	265	205	76	64	24	29	11	226	247	59	127	58	50	19	491	452	135
Quebec	23	14	8	1	101	78	29	25	10	13	2	83	98	22	48	24	21	3	184	176	51
St. Louis	41	23	8	10	161	98	56	40	17	16	7	134	146	41	81	40	24	17	295	244	97
San Jose	4	4	0	0	27	15	8	3	3	1	2	12	8	2	7	5	2	0	39	23	10
Tampa Bay	3	2	1	0	12	11	4	4	3	1	0	15	7	6	7	5	2	0	27	18	10
Toronto	38	22	13	3	166	117	47	40	20	17	3	149	135	43	78	42	30	6	315	252	90
Vancouver	39	22	9	8	150	102	52	41	20	18	3	138	135	43	80	42	27	11	288	237	95
Washington	59	37	21	1	245	184	75	59	27	23	9	199	184	63	118	64	44	10	444	368	138
Winnipeg	23	11	6	6	87	71	28	22	13	7	2	87	70	28	45	24	13	8	174	141	56
Defunct Clubs	13	11	0	2	75	33	24	13	4	5	4	35	41	12	26	15	5	6	110	74	36
Totals	**882**	**493**	**263**	**126**	**3543**	**2638**	**1112**	**882**	**339**	**416**	**127**	**2966**	**3143**	**805**	**1764**	**832**	**679**	**253**	**6509**	**5781**	**1917**

Calgary totals include Atlanta, 1972-73 to 1979-80. Dallas totals include Minnesota, 1972-73 to 1992-93.
New Jersey totals include Kansas City, 1974-75 to 1975-76, and Colorado, 1976-77 to 1981-82.

Playoffs

	Series	W	L	GP	W	L	T	GF	GA	Last Mtg.	Round	Result
Boston	2	2	0	11	8	3	0	49	35	1983	CF	W 4-2
Buffalo	3	3	0	16	12	4	0	59	45	1980	SF	W 4-2
Chicago	2	2	0	6	6	0	0	21	6	1979	QF	W 4-0
Dallas	1	1	0	5	4	1	0	26	16	1981	F	W 4-1
Edmonton	3	2	1	15	9	6	0	58	47	1984	F	L 1-4
Los Angeles	1	1	0	4	3	1	0	21	10	1980	PR	W 3-1
Montreal	4	1	3	22	8	14	0	55	64	1993	CF	L 1-4
New Jersey	1	0	1	6	2	4	0	18	23	1988	DSF	L 2-4
NY Rangers	8	5	3	39	20	19	0	129	132	1994	CQF	L 0-4
Philadelphia	4	1	3	25	11	14	0	69	83	1987	DF	L 3-4
Pittsburgh	3	3	0	19	11	8	0	67	58	1993	DF	W 4-3
Quebec	1	1	0	4	4	0	0	18	9	1982	CF	W 4-0
Toronto	2	1	1	10	6	4	0	33	20	1981	PR	W 3-0
Vancouver	2	2	0	6	6	0	0	26	14	1982	F	W 4-0
Washington	6	5	1	30	18	12	0	99	88	1993	DSF	W 4-2
Totals	**43**	**30**	**13**	**218**	**128**	**90**	**0**	**748**	**650**			

Playoff Results 1994-90

Year	Round	Opponent	Result	GF	GA
1994	CQF	NY Rangers	L 0-4	3	22
1993	CF	Montreal	L 1-4	11	16
	DF	Pittsburgh	W 4-3	23	21
	DSF	Washington	W 4-2	23	22
1990	DSF	NY Rangers	L 1-4	13	22

Abbreviations: Round: F – Final;
CF – conference final; **CQF** – conference quarter-final;
CSF – conference semi-final; **DF** – division final;
DSF – division semi-final; **SF** – semi-final;
QF – quarter-final; **PR** – preliminary round.

Entry Draft
Selections 1994-80

1994
Pick
9	Brett Lindros
38	Jason Holland
63	Jason Strudwick
90	Brad Lukowich
112	Mark McArthur
116	Albert O'Connell
142	Jason Stewart
194	Mike Loach
203	Peter Hogardh
220	Gord Walsh
246	Kirk Dewaele
272	Dick Tarnstrom

1993
Pick
23	Todd Bertuzzi
40	Bryan McCabe
66	Vladim Chebaturkin
92	Warren Luhning
118	Tommy Salo
144	Peter Leboutillier
170	Darren Van Impe
196	Rod Hinks
222	Daniel Johansson
248	Stephane Larocque
274	Carl Charland

1992
Pick
5	Darius Kasparaitis
56	Jarrett Deuling
104	Tomas Klimt
105	Ryan Duthie
128	Derek Armstrong
152	Vladimir Grachev
159	Steve O'Rourke
176	Jason Widmer
200	Daniel Paradis
224	David Wainwright
248	Andrei Vasiljev

1991
Pick
4	Scott Lachance
26	Zigmund Palffy
48	Jamie McLennan
70	Milan Hnilicka
92	Steve Junker
114	Robert Valicevic
136	Andreas Johansson
158	Todd Sparks
180	John Johnson
202	Robert Canavan
224	Marcus Thuresson
246	Marty Schriner

1990
Pick
6	Scott Scissons
27	Chris Taylor
48	Dan Plante
90	Chris Marinucci
111	Joni Lehto
132	Michael Guilbert
153	Sylvain Fleury
174	John Joyce
195	Richard Enga
216	Martin Lacroix
237	Andy Shirr

1989
Pick
2	Dave Chyzowski
23	Travis Green
44	Jason Zent
65	Brent Grieve
86	Jace Reed
90	Steve Young
99	Kevin O'Sullivan
128	Jon Larson
133	Brett Harkins
149	Phil Huber
170	Matthew Robbins
191	Vladimir Malakhov
212	Kelly Ens
233	Iain Fraser

1988
Pick
16	Kevin Cheveldayoff
29	Wayne Doucet
37	Sean LeBrun
58	Danny Lorenz
79	Andre Brassard
100	Paul Rutherford
111	Pavel Gross
121	Jason Rathbone
142	Yves Gaucher
163	Marty McInnis
184	Jeff Blumer
205	Jeff Kampersal
226	Phillip Neururer
247	Joe Capprini

1987
Pick
13	Dean Chynoweth
34	Jeff Hackett
55	Dean Ewen
76	George Maneluk
97	Petr Vlk
118	Rob DiMaio
139	Knut Walbye
160	Jeff Saterdalen
181	Shawn Howard
202	John Herlihy
223	Michael Erickson
244	Will Averill

1986
Pick
17	Tom Fitzgerald
38	Dennis Vaske
59	Bill Berg
80	Shawn Byram
101	Dean Sexsmith
104	Todd McLellan
122	Tony Schmalzbauer
138	Will Anderson
143	Richard Pilon
164	Peter Harris
185	Jeff Jablonski
206	Kerry Clark
227	Dan Beaudette
248	Paul Thompson

1985
Pick
6	Brad Dalgarno
13	Derek King
34	Brad Lauer
55	Jeff Finley
76	Kevin Herom
89	Tommy Hedlund
97	Jeff Sveen
118	Rod Dallman
139	Kurt Lackten
160	Hank Lammens
181	Rich Wiest
202	Real Arsenault
223	Mike Volpe
244	Tony Grenier

1984
Pick
20	Duncan MacPherson
41	Bruce Melanson
62	Jeff Norton
70	Doug Wieck
83	Ari Haanpaa
104	Mike Murray
125	Jim Wilharm
146	Kelly Murphy
167	Franco Desantis
187	Tom Warden
208	David Volek
228	Russ Becker
249	Allister Brown

1983
Pick
3	Pat LaFontaine
16	Gerald Diduck
37	Garnet McKechney
57	Mike Neill
65	Mikko Makila
84	Bob Caulfield
97	Ron Viglasi
117	Darin Illikainen
137	Jim Sprenger
157	Dale Henry
177	Kevin Vescio
197	Dave Shellington
217	John Bjorkman
237	Peter McGeough

1982
Pick
21	Patrick Flatley
42	Vern Smith
63	Garry Lacey
84	Alan Kerr
105	Rene Breton
126	Roger Kortko
147	John Tiano
168	Todd Okerlund
189	Gord Paddock
210	Eric Faust
231	Pat Goff
252	Jim Koudys

1981
Pick
21	Paul Boutilier
42	Gord Dineen
57	Ron Handy
63	Neal Coulter
84	Todd Lumbard
94	Jacques Sylvestre
126	Chuck Brimmer
147	Teppo Virta
168	Bill Dowd
189	Scott MacLellan
210	Dave Randerson

1980
Pick
17	Brent Sutter
38	Kelly Hrudey
59	Dave Simpsn
68	Monty Trottier
80	Greg Gilbert
101	Ken Leiter
122	Dan Revell
143	Mark Hamway
164	Morrison Gare
185	Peter Steblyk
206	Glen Johannesen

General Manager

MALONEY, DON
General Manager, New York Islanders.
Born in Lindsay, Ont., September 5, 1958.

Don Maloney became the second general manager in New York Islanders' history on August 17, 1992. After a 13-year playing career that included stays with the Rangers, Islanders and Whalers, Maloney joined the Islanders' organization in January, 1991 as a part-time assistant to coach Al Arbour and general manager Bill Torrey. The following season, he became assistant general manager, representing the team in contract discussions and organizing the Islanders' training camp itinerary. In his playing career, Maloney compiled 214 goals and 350 assists in 765 games.

General Managers' History

William A. Torrey, 1972-73 to 1991-92; Don Maloney, 1992-93 to date.

Coaching History

Phil Goyette and Earl Ingarfield, 1972-73; Al Arbour, 1973-74 to 1985-86; Terry Simpson, 1986-87 to 1987-88; Terry Simpson and Al Arbour, 1988-89; Al Arbour, 1989-90 to 1993-94; Lorne Henning, 1994-95.

Captains' History

Ed Westfall, 1972-73 to 1975-76; Ed Westfall, Clark Gillies, 1976-77; Clark Gillies, 1977-78, 1978-79; Denis Potvin, 1979-80 to 1986-87; Brent Sutter, 1987-88 to 1990-91; Brent Sutter and Patrick Flatley, 1991-92; Patrick Flatley, 1992-93 to date.

Club Directory

Nassau Veterans'
Memorial Coliseum
Uniondale, NY 11553
Phone **516/794-4100**
GM FAX 516/542-9350
FAX 516/542-9348
Capacity: 16,297

Co-Chairmen	Robert Rosenthal, Stephen Walsh
Chief Operating Officer	Ralph Palleschi
Executive Vice-President	Paul Greenwood
Senior Vice-President & CFO	Arthur McCarthy
Consultant	John Krumpe
General Counsel	William Skehan

Hockey Staff
Vice-President/General Manager	Don Maloney
Vice-President of Hockey Operations	Al Arbour
Assistant General Manager/ Director of Player Personnel	Darcy Regier
Assistant to the General Manager	Gerry Ehman
Head Coach	Lorne Henning
Assistant Coaches	Rick Green, Ron Kennedy
Goaltending Coach	Bob Froese
Strength and Conditioning Coach	Chris Pryor
Director of Pro Scouting	Ken Morrow
Scouting Staff	Harry Boyd, Earl Ingarfield, Gord Lane, Bert Marshall, Jim Madigan, Mario Saraceno
Administrative Assistants to the General Manager	Joanne Holewa, Pam Kamvakis
Video Coordinator	Bob Smith

Communications Staff
Vice-President/Communications	Pat Calabria
Director of Amateur Hockey Development/ Alumni Relations	Bob Nystrom
Director of Community Relations	Maureen Brady
Director of Game Events	Tim Beach
Director of Media Relations	Ginger Killian Serby
Director of Publications	Chris Botta
Media Relations Assistant	Eric Mirlis

Sales and Administration
Vice-President/Media Sales	Arthur Adler
Controller	Ralph Sellitti
Assistant Controller	Ginna Cotton
Director of Administration	Joseph Dreyer
Director of Corporate Sales	Bill Kain
Director of Executive Suites	Tracy F. Matthews
Director of Merchandising	Mike Walsh
Director of Ticket Sales	Jim Johnson
Executive Suite Services	Sam Buonogura
Ticket Manager	Cathy Henning
Ticket Sales Representatives	Tom Engel, Ken Gray, Susan Kelly, Brian Rabinowitz, Andy Smith
Accountants	Christine Blazak, Vincent Diorio, Sue Meares
Assistant Ticket Manager	Joy Rusciano
Administrative Assistants	Priscilla Dehaven, Tracy Levy, Kathleen Maloney
Receptionists	Anne Beauchamp, Suzanne Mauro

Medical and Training Staff
Athletic Trainer	Ed Tyburski
Equipment Manager	John Doolan
Assistant Trainer	Jerry Iannarelli
Assistant Equipment Manager	Joe McMahon
Team Orthopedists	Jeffrey Minkoff, M.D., Barry Simonson, M.D.
Team Internists	Gerald Cordani, M.D., Larry Smith, M.D.
Physical Therapist	Steve Wirth
Team Dentists	Bruce Michnick, D.D.S., Jan Sherman, D.D.S.

Team Information
Colors	Blue, Orange and White
Television Coverage	SportsChannel
Announcers	Jiggs McDonald, Ed Westfall, Stan Fischler
Radio	WRCN – 94.3 & 103.9
Announcers	Barry Landers, Bob Nystrom

New York Rangers

1993-94 Results: 52W-24L-8T 112PTS. First, Atlantic Division

Schedule

Oct.
- Sat. 1 at New Jersey
- Mon. 3 Pittsburgh
- Thur. 6 Philadelphia
- Sat. 8 at Florida*
- Tues. 11 Tampa Bay
- Thur. 13 at St. Louis
- Sat. 15 at Hartford
- Tues. 18 at Quebec
- Thur. 20 Los Angeles
- Sat. 22 at Montreal
- Sun. 23 San Jose
- Wed. 26 Dallas
- Fri. 28 Calgary
- Sun. 30 Vancouver

Nov.
- Tues. 1 at Los Angeles
- Wed. 2 at Anaheim
- Sat. 5 at San Jose
- Wed. 9 Hartford
- Fri. 11 NY Islanders
- Sun. 13 Washington
- Thur. 17 at Philadelphia
- Sat. 19 at Ottawa
- Wed. 23 at Pittsburgh
- Fri. 25 at Winnipeg
- Sun. 27 Florida
- Tues. 29 at Hartford
- Wed. 30 Buffalo

Dec.
- Fri. 2 Anaheim
- Sun. 4 Edmonton
- Tues. 6 at Pittsburgh
- Thur. 8 NY Islanders
- Tues. 13 at NY Islanders (in Portland, OR)
- Wed. 14 at Vancouver
- Sat. 17 at Edmonton
- Sun. 18 at Calgary
- Wed. 21 Boston
- Fri. 23 Montreal
- Mon. 26 Ottawa
- Tues. 27 at Washington
- Fri. 30 at Tampa Bay

Jan.
- Sun. 1 at Florida*
- Tues. 3 St. Louis
- Thur. 5 at NY Islanders
- Sat. 7 at Tampa Bay
- Mon. 9 Florida
- Wed. 11 Pittsburgh
- Sat. 14 at Washington
- Sun. 15 New Jersey
- Tues. 17 Detroit
- Mon. 23 Quebec
- Wed. 25 Boston
- Fri. 27 Tampa Bay
- Sat. 28 at Quebec
- Mon. 30 NY Islanders

Feb.
- Thur. 2 Chicago
- Sat. 4 at Ottawa
- Mon. 6 Winnipeg
- Tues. 7 at Boston
- Thur. 9 at Philadelphia
- Sat. 11 at Tampa Bay
- Wed. 15 at Buffalo
- Thur. 16 Montreal
- Sat. 18 at Toronto
- Mon. 20 Toronto*
- Fri. 24 Hartford
- Sun. 26 at Buffalo
- Tues. 28 Florida

Mar.
- Fri. 3 Philadelphia
- Sat. 6 at NY Islanders
- Mon. 6 New Jersey
- Wed. 8 Buffalo
- Sat. 11 at Montreal
- Mon. 13 at Philadelphia
- Wed. 15 New Jersey
- Sat. 18 at Washington
- Tues. 21 at Dallas
- Thur. 23 Calgary (in Phoenix)
- Tues. 28 at Detroit
- Thur. 30 Quebec

Apr.
- Sat. 1 at Boston*
- Sun. 2 at Chicago*
- Wed. 5 Washington
- Fri. 7 Ottawa
- Sun. 9 at New Jersey*

* Denotes afternoon game.

Home Starting Times:
- Weeknights .... 7:30 p.m.
- Sundays .... 7:00 p.m.
- Except Sun. Jan. 15 .... 8:00 p.m.
- Mon. Feb. 20 .... 1:30 p.m.

Franchise date: May 15, 1926

EASTERN CONFERENCE

ATLANTIC DIVISION

69th NHL Season

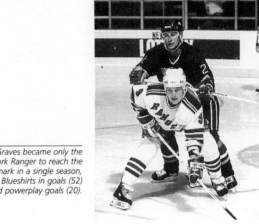

Adam Graves became only the second New York Ranger to reach the 50-goal mark in a single season, leading the Blueshirts in goals (52) and powerplay goals (20).

Year-by-Year Record

Season	GP	Home W	L	T	Road W	L	T	Overall W	L	T	GF	GA	Pts.	Finished	Playoff Result
1993-94	**84**	**28**	**8**	**6**	**24**	**16**	**2**	**52**	**24**	**8**	**299**	**231**	**112**	**1st, Atlantic Div.**	**Won Stanley Cup**
1992-93	84	20	17	5	14	22	6	34	39	11	304	308	79	6th, Patrick Div.	Out of Playoffs
1991-92	80	28	8	4	22	17	1	50	25	5	321	246	105	1st, Patrick Div.	Lost Div. Final
1990-91	80	22	11	7	14	20	6	36	31	13	297	265	85	2nd, Patrick Div.	Lost Div. Semi-Final
1989-90	80	20	11	9	16	20	4	36	31	13	279	267	85	1st, Patrick Div.	Lost Div. Final
1988-89	80	21	17	2	16	18	6	37	35	8	310	307	82	3rd, Patrick Div.	Lost Div. Semi-Final
1987-88	80	22	13	5	14	21	5	36	34	10	300	283	82	5th, Patrick Div.	Out of Playoffs
1986-87	80	18	18	4	16	20	4	34	38	8	307	323	76	4th, Patrick Div.	Lost Div. Semi-Final
1985-86	80	20	18	2	16	20	4	36	38	6	280	276	78	4th, Patick Div.	Lost Conf. Championship
1984-85	80	16	18	6	10	26	4	26	44	10	295	345	62	4th, Patrick Div.	Lost Div. Semi-Final
1983-84	80	27	12	1	15	17	8	42	29	9	314	304	93	4th, Patrick Div.	Lost Div. Semi-Final
1982-83	80	24	13	3	11	22	7	35	35	10	306	287	80	4th, Patrick Div.	Lost Div. Final
1981-82	80	19	15	6	20	12	8	39	27	14	316	306	92	2nd, Patrick Div.	Lost Div. Final
1980-81	80	17	13	10	13	23	4	30	36	14	312	317	74	4th, Patrick Div.	Lost Semi-Final
1979-80	80	22	10	8	16	22	2	38	32	10	308	284	86	3rd, Patrick Div.	Lost Quarter-Final
1978-79	80	19	13	8	21	16	3	40	29	11	316	292	91	3rd, Patrick Div.	Lost Final
1977-78	80	18	15	7	12	22	6	30	37	13	279	280	73	4th, Patrick Div.	Lost Prelim. Round
1976-77	80	17	18	5	12	19	9	29	37	14	272	310	72	4th, Patrick Div.	Out of Playoffs
1975-76	80	16	16	8	13	26	1	29	42	9	262	333	67	4th, Patrick Div.	Out of Playoffs
1974-75	80	21	11	8	16	18	6	37	29	14	319	276	88	2nd, Patrick Div.	Lost Prelim. Round
1973-74	78	26	7	6	14	17	8	40	24	14	300	251	94	3rd, East Div.	Lost Semi-Final
1972-73	78	26	8	5	21	15	3	47	23	8	297	208	102	3rd, East Div.	Lost Semi-Final
1971-72	78	26	6	7	22	11	6	48	17	13	317	192	109	2nd, East Div.	Lost Final
1970-71	78	30	2	7	19	16	4	49	18	11	259	177	109	2nd, East Div.	Lost Semi-Final
1969-70	76	22	8	8	16	14	8	38	22	16	246	189	92	4th, East Div.	Lost Quarter-Final
1968-69	76	27	7	4	14	19	5	41	26	9	231	196	91	3rd, East Div.	Lost Quarter-Final
1967-68	74	22	8	7	17	15	5	39	23	12	226	183	90	2nd, East Div.	Lost Quarter-Final
1966-67	70	18	12	5	12	16	7	30	28	12	188	189	72	4th,	Lost Semi-Final
1965-66	70	12	16	7	6	25	4	18	41	11	195	261	47	6th,	Out of Playoffs
1964-65	70	8	19	8	12	19	4	20	38	12	179	246	52	5th,	Out of Playoffs
1963-64	70	14	13	8	8	25	2	22	38	10	186	242	54	5th,	Out of Playoffs
1962-63	70	12	17	6	10	19	6	22	36	12	211	233	56	5th,	Out of Playoffs
1961-62	70	16	11	8	10	21	4	26	32	12	195	207	64	4th,	Lost Semi-Final
1960-61	70	15	15	5	7	23	5	22	38	10	204	248	54	5th,	Out of Playoffs
1959-60	70	10	15	10	7	23	5	17	38	15	187	247	49	6th,	Out of Playoffs
1958-59	70	14	16	5	12	16	7	26	32	12	201	217	64	5th,	Out of Playoffs
1957-58	70	14	15	6	18	10	7	32	25	13	195	188	77	2nd,	Lost Semi-Final
1956-57	70	15	12	8	11	18	6	26	30	14	184	227	66	4th,	Lost Semi-Final
1955-56	70	20	7	8	12	21	2	32	28	10	204	203	74	3rd,	Lost Semi-Final
1954-55	70	10	12	13	7	23	5	17	35	18	150	210	52	5th,	Out of Playoffs
1953-54	70	18	12	5	11	19	5	29	31	10	161	182	68	5th,	Out of Playoffs
1952-53	70	11	14	10	6	23	6	17	37	16	152	211	50	6th,	Out of Playoffs
1951-52	70	16	13	6	7	21	7	23	34	13	192	219	59	5th,	Out of Playoffs
1950-51	70	14	11	10	6	18	11	20	29	21	169	201	61	5th,	Out of Playoffs
1949-50	70	19	12	4	9	19	7	28	31	11	170	189	67	4th,	Lost Final
1948-49	60	13	12	5	5	19	6	18	31	11	133	172	47	6th,	Out of Playoffs
1947-48	60	11	12	7	10	14	6	21	26	13	176	201	55	4th,	Lost Semi-Final
1946-47	60	11	14	5	11	18	1	22	32	6	167	186	50	5th,	Out of Playoffs
1945-46	50	8	12	5	5	16	4	13	28	9	144	191	35	6th,	Out of Playoffs
1944-45	50	7	11	7	4	18	3	11	29	10	154	247	32	6th,	Out of Playoffs
1943-44	50	4	17	4	2	22	1	6	39	5	162	310	17	6th,	Out of Playoffs
1942-43	50	7	13	5	4	18	3	11	31	8	161	253	30	6th,	Out of Playoffs
1941-42	48	15	8	1	14	9	1	29	17	2	177	143	60	1st,	Lost Semi-Final
1940-41	48	13	7	4	8	12	4	21	19	8	143	125	50	4th,	Lost Quarter-Final
1939-40	**48**	**17**	**4**	**3**	**10**	**7**	**7**	**27**	**11**	**10**	**136**	**77**	**64**	**2nd,**	**Won Stanley Cup**
1938-39	48	13	8	3	13	8	3	26	16	6	149	105	58	2nd,	Lost Semi-Final
1937-38	48	15	5	4	12	10	2	27	15	6	149	96	60	2nd, Amn. Div.	Lost Div. Semi-Final
1936-37	48	9	7	8	10	13	1	19	20	9	117	106	49	3rd, Amn. Div.	Lost Final
1935-36	48	11	6	7	8	11	5	19	17	12	91	96	50	4th, Amn. Div.	Out of Playoffs
1934-35	48	11	8	5	11	13	1	22	20	6	137	139	50	3rd, Amn. Div.	Lost Semi-Final
1933-34	48	11	6	7	10	12	2	21	19	8	120	113	50	3rd, Amn. Div.	Lost Semi-Final
1932-33	**48**	**12**	**7**	**5**	**11**	**10**	**3**	**23**	**17**	**8**	**135**	**107**	**54**	**3rd, Amn. Div.**	**Won Stanley Cup**
1931-32	48	13	7	4	10	10	4	23	17	8	134	112	54	1st,	Lost Final
1930-31	44	10	9	3	9	7	6	19	16	9	106	87	47	3rd, Amn. Div.	Lost Semi-Final
1929-30	44	11	5	6	6	12	4	17	17	10	136	143	44	3rd, Amn. Div.	Lost Semi-Final
1928-29	44	12	6	4	9	5	8	21	13	10	72	65	52	2nd, Amn. Div.	Lost Final
1927-28	**44**	**10**	**8**	**4**	**9**	**8**	**5**	**19**	**16**	**9**	**94**	**79**	**47**	**2nd, Amn. Div.**	**Won Stanley Cup**
1926-27	44	13	5	4	12	8	2	25	13	6	95	72	56	1st, Amn. Div.	Lost Quarter-Final

1994-95 Player Personnel

FORWARDS	HT	WT	S	Place of Birth	Date	1993-94 Club
DUNCANSON, Craig	6-0	190	L	Sudbury, Ont.	3/17/67	Binghamton
GERNANDER, Ken	5-10	175	L	Coleraine, MN	6/30/69	Moncton
GILBERT, Greg	6-1	191	L	Mississauga, Ont.	1/22/62	NY Rangers
GRAVES, Adam	6-0	207	L	Toronto, Ont.	4/12/68	NY Rangers
HARTMAN, Mike	6-0	190	L	Detroit, MI	2/7/67	NY Rangers
HILLER, Jim	6-0	190	R	Port Alberni, B.C.	5/15/69	NY Rangers-Binghamton
HUDSON, Mike	6-1	205	L	Guelph, Ont.	2/6/67	NY Rangers
KENNY, Rob	6-1	205	L	New York, NY	9/19/68	Binghamton
KOCUR, Joey	6-0	205	R	Calgary, Alta.	12/21/64	NY Rangers
KOVALEV, Alexei	6-0	200	L	Togliatti, USSR	2/24/73	NY Rangers
KUDINOV, Andrei	6-0	185	L	Chelyabinsk, USSR	6/28/70	Chelyabinsk-Binghamton
KYPREOS, Nick	6-0	205	L	Toronto, Ont.	6/4/66	Hartford-NY Rangers
LANGDON, Darren	6-1	200	L	Deer Lake, Nfld.	1/8/71	Binghamton
LARMER, Steve	5-11	185	L	Peterborough, Ont.	6/16/61	NY Rangers
MATTEAU, Stephane	6-3	200	L	Rouyn-Noranda, Que.	9/2/69	Chicago-NY Rangers
McCOSH, Shawn	6-0	188	R	Oshawa, Ont.	6/5/69	Binghamton
McLAUGHLIN, Michael	6-1	175	L	Longmeadow, MA	3/29/70	Binghamton
MESSIER, Mark	6-1	205	L	Edmonton, Alta.	1/18/61	NY Rangers
NEDVED, Petr	6-3	185	L	Liberec, Czech.	12/9/71	Cdn. National-Cdn. Olympic-StL
NEMCHINOV, Sergei	6-0	201	L	Moscow, USSR	1/14/64	NY Rangers
NIELSEN, Jeff	6-0	170	R	Grand Rapids, MN	9/20/71	U. Minnesota
NOONAN, Brian	6-1	200	R	Boston, MA	5/29/65	Chicago-NY Rangers
OLCZYK, Eddie	6-1	205	L	Chicago, IL	8/16/66	NY Rangers
OSBORNE, Mark	6-2	205	L	Toronto, Ont.	8/13/61	Toronto
ROY, Jean-Yves	5-10	185	L	Rosemere, Que.	2/17/69	Bing-Cdn. National-Cdn. Olympic
SMITH, David	6-1	180	L	Arthur, Ont.	11/21/68	Ft. Wayne
STAROSTENKO, Dmitri	6-0	185	L	Minsk, USSR	3/18/73	CSKA-Binghamton
DEFENSEMEN						
BEUKEBOOM, Jeff	6-5	225	R	Ajax, Ont.	3/28/65	NY Rangers
BRIERLEY, Dan	6-2	185	L	Nashua, NH	1/23/74	Yale
CAIRNS, Eric	6-5	217	L	Oakville, Ont.	6/27/74	Detroit (OHL)
FEATHERSTONE, Glen	6-4	215	L	Toronto, Ont.	7/8/68	Boston
FIORENTINO, Peter	6-1	205	R	Niagara Falls, Ont.	12/22/68	Binghamton
KARPOVTSEV, Alexander	6-1	205	R	Moscow, USSR	4/7/70	NY Rangers
LEETCH, Brian	5-11	195	L	Corpus Christi, TX	3/3/68	NY Rangers
LOWE, Kevin	6-2	195	L	Lachute, Que.	4/15/59	NY Rangers
MALONE, Scott	6-0	180	L	Boston, MA	1/16/71	N. Hampshire
MESSIER, Joby	6-0	200	R	Regina, Sask.	3/2/70	NY Rangers-Binghamton
NORSTROM, Mattias	6-1	205	L	Mora, Sweden	1/2/72	NY Rangers-Binghamton
REID, Shawn	6-0	195	L	Toronto, Ont.	9/21/70	Colorado
RICHTER, Barry	6-2	203	L	Madison, WI	9/11/70	U.S. National-U.S. Olympic-Bing
SILVERMAN, Andrew	6-3	210	L	Beverly, MA	8/23/72	U. of Maine
STEWART, Michael	6-2	210	L	Calgary, Alta.	5/30/72	Binghamton
WELLS, Jay	6-1	210	L	Paris, Ont.	5/18/59	NY Rangers
WERENKA, Darcy	6-1	210	R	Edmonton, Alta.	5/13/73	Binghamton
ZUBOV, Sergei	6-1	195	R	Moscow, USSR	7/22/70	NY Rangers-Binghamton

GOALTENDERS	HT	WT	C	Place of Birth	Date	1993-94 Club
HEALY, Glenn	5-10	183	L	Pickering, Ont.	8/23/62	NY Rangers
HILLEBRANDT, Jon	5-10	160	L	Cottage Grove, WI	12/18/71	U.S. National-Binghamton-Erie
HIRSCH, Corey	5-10	160	L	Medicine Hat, Alta.	7/1/72	Cdn. National-Cdn. Olympic-Bing
RAM, Jamie	5-11	164	L	Scarborough, Ont.	1/18/71	Michigan Tech
RICHTER, Mike	5-11	182	L	Abington, PA	9/22/66	NY Rangers

General Managers' History

Lester Patrick, 1927-28 to 1945-46; Frank Boucher, 1946-47 to 1954-55; Murray "Muzz" Patrick, 1955-56 to 1963-64; Emile Francis, 1964-65 to 1974-75; Emile Francis and John Ferguson, 1975-76; John Ferguson, 1976-77 to 1977-78; John Ferguson and Fred Shero, 1978-79; Fred Shero, 1979-80; Fred Shero and Craig Patrick, 1980-81; Craig Patrick, 1981-82 to 1985-86; Phil Esposito, 1986-87 to 1988-89; Neil Smith, 1989-90 to date.

Coaching History

Lester Patrick, 1926-27 to 1938-39; Frank Boucher, 1939-40 to 1947-48; Frank Boucher and Lynn Patrick, 1948-49; Lynn Patrick, 1949-50; Neil Colville, 1950-51; Neil Colville and Bill Cook, 1951-52; Bill Cook, 1952-53; Frank Boucher and Murray Patrick, 1953-54; Murray Patrick, 1954-55; Phil Watson, 1955-56 to 1958-59; Phil Watson and Alf Pike, 1959-60; Alf Pike, 1960-61; Doug Harvey, 1961-62; Murray Patrick and George Sullivan, 1962-63; George Sullivan, 1963-64 to 1964-65; George Sullivan and Emile Francis, 1965-66; Emile Francis, 1966-67 to 1967-68; Bernie Geoffrion and Emile Francis, 1968-69; Emile Francis, 1969-70 to 1972-73; Larry Popein and Emile Francis, 1973-74; Emile Francis, 1974-75; Ron Stewart and John Ferguson, 1975-76; John Ferguson, 1976-77; Jean-Guy Talbot, 1977-78; Fred Shero, 1978-79 to 1979-80; Fred Shero and Craig Patrick, 1980-81; Herb Brooks, 1981-82 to 1983-84; Herb Brooks and Craig Patrick, 1984-85; Ted Sator, 1985-86; Ted Sator, Tom Webster, Phil Esposito 1986-87; Michel Bergeron, 1987-88; Michel Bergeron and Phil Esposito, 1988-89; Roger Neilson, 1989-90 to 1991-92; Roger Neilson and Ron Smith, 1992-93; Mike Keenan, 1993-94; Colin Campbell, 1994-95.

Captains' History

Bill Cook, 1926-27 to 1936-37; Art Coulter, 1937-38 to 1941-42; Ott Heller, 1942-43 to 1944-45; Neil Colville 1945-46 to 1948-49; Buddy O'Connor, 1949-50; Frank Eddolls, 1950-51; Frank Eddolls, Allan Stanley, 1951-52; Allan Stanley, 1952-53; Allan Stanley, Don Raleigh, 1953-54; Don Raleigh, 1954-55; Harry Howell, 1955-56, 1956-57; George Sullivan, 1957-58 to 1960-61; Andy Bathgate, 1961-61, 1962-63; Andy Bathgate, Camille Henry, 1963-64; Camille Henry, Bob Nevin, 1964-65; Bob Nevin 1965-66 to 1970-71; Vic Hadfield, 1971-72 to 1973-74; Brad Park, 1974-75; Brad Park, Phil Esposito, 1975-76; Phil Esposito, 1976-77, 1977-78; Dave Maloney, 1978-79, 1979-80; Dave Maloney, Walt Tkaczuk, Barry Beck, 1980-81; Barry Beck, 1981-82 to 1985-86; Ron Greschner, 1986-87; Ron Greschner and Kelly Kisio, 1987-88; Kelly Kisio, 1988-89 to 1990-91; Mark Messier, 1991-92 to date.

1993-94 Scoring

* – rookie

Regular Season

Pos	#	Player	Team	GP	G	A	Pts	+/–	PIM	PP	SH	GW	GT	S	%
D	21	Sergei Zubov	NYR	78	12	77	89	20	39	9	0	1	0	222	5.4
C	11	Mark Messier	NYR	76	26	58	84	25	76	6	2	5	0	216	12.0
L	9	Adam Graves	NYR	84	52	27	79	27	127	20	4	4	1	291	17.9
D	2	Brian Leetch	NYR	84	23	56	79	28	67	17	1	4	0	328	7.0
R	28	Steve Larmer	NYR	68	21	39	60	14	41	6	4	7	0	146	14.4
C	27	Alexei Kovalev	NYR	76	23	33	56	18	154	7	0	3	0	184	12.5
L	10	Esa Tikkanen	NYR	83	22	32	54	5	114	5	3	4	0	257	8.6
C	13	Sergei Nemchinov	NYR	76	22	27	49	13	36	4	0	6	0	144	15.3
R	36	Glenn Anderson	TOR	73	17	18	35	6–	50	5	0	3	0	127	13.4
			NYR	12	4	2	6	1	12	2	0	0	0	22	18.2
			TOTAL	85	21	20	41	5–	62	7	0	3	0	149	14.1
R	16	Brian Noonan	CHI	64	14	21	35	2	57	8	0	3	1	134	10.4
			NYR	12	4	2	6	5	12	2	0	3	0	26	15.4
			TOTAL	76	18	23	41	7	69	10	0	6	1	160	11.3
L	32	Stephane Matteau	CHI	65	15	16	31	10	55	2	0	2	0	113	13.3
			NYR	12	4	3	7	5	2	1	0	0	1	22	18.2
			TOTAL	77	19	19	38	15	57	3	0	2	1	135	14.1
C	14	Craig MacTavish	EDM	66	16	10	26	20–	80	0	0	1	0	97	16.5
			NYR	12	4	2	6	6	11	1	0	1	1	25	16.0
			TOTAL	78	20	12	32	14–	91	1	0	2	1	122	16.4
D	4	Kevin Lowe	NYR	71	5	14	19	4	70	0	0	1	0	50	10.0
D	25 *	A. Karpovtsev	NYR	67	3	15	18	12	58	1	0	1	0	78	3.8
D	23	Jeff Beukeboom	NYR	68	8	8	16	18	170	1	0	0	0	58	13.8
L	17	Greg Gilbert	NYR	76	4	11	15	3–	29	1	0	0	1	64	6.3
C	15	Mike Hudson	NYR	48	4	7	11	5–	47	0	0	1	0	48	8.3
D	24	Jay Wells	NYR	79	2	7	9	4	110	0	0	0	0	64	3.1
C	12	Ed Olczyk	NYR	37	3	5	8	1–	28	0	0	1	0	40	7.5
L	19	Nick Kypreos	HFD	10	0	0	0	8–	37	0	0	0	0	5	.0
			NYR	46	3	5	8	8–	102	0	0	1	0	29	10.3
			TOTAL	56	3	5	8	16–	139	0	0	1	0	34	8.8
R	26	Joey Kocur	NYR	71	2	1	3	9–	129	0	0	0	0	43	4.7
L	18	Mike Hartman	NYR	35	1	1	2	5–	70	0	0	0	0	19	5.3
D	8 *	Joby Messier	NYR	4	0	2	2	1–	0	0	0	0	0	7	.0
D	5 *	Mattias Norstrom	NYR	9	0	2	2	0	6	0	0	0	0	3	.0
G	30	Glenn Healy	NYR	29	0	2	2	0	2	0	0	0	0	0	.0
D	6	Doug Lidster	NYR	34	0	2	2	12–	33	0	0	0	0	25	.0
R	16	Jim Hiller	NYR	2	0	0	0	1	7	0	0	0	0	0	.0
L	32 *	Dan Lacroix	NYR	4	0	0	0	0	0	0	0	0	0	0	.0
G	35	Mike Richter	NYR	68	0	0	0	0	2	0	0	0	0	0	.0

Goaltending

No.	Goaltender	GPI	Mins	Avg	W	L	T	EN	SO	GA	SA	S%
35	Mike Richter	68	3710	2.57	42	12	6	1	5	159	1758	.910
30	Glenn Healy	29	1368	3.03	10	12	2	2	2	69	567	.878
	Totals	**84**	**5089**	**2.72**	**52**	**24**	**8**	**3**	**7**	**231**	**2328**	**.901**

Playoffs

Pos	#	Player	Team	GP	G	A	Pts	+/–	PIM	PP	SH	GW	GT	S	%
D	2	Brian Leetch	NYR	23	11	23	34	19	6	4	0	4	0	88	12.5
C	11	Mark Messier	NYR	23	12	18	30	14	33	2	1	4	0	75	16.0
C	27	Alexei Kovalev	NYR	23	9	12	21	5	18	5	0	2	0	71	12.7
D	21	Sergei Zubov	NYR	22	5	14	19	10	0	2	0	0	0	60	8.3
L	9	Adam Graves	NYR	23	10	7	17	12	24	3	0	0	0	93	10.8
R	28	Steve Larmer	NYR	23	9	7	16	8	14	3	0	0	0	54	16.7
R	16	Brian Noonan	NYR	22	4	7	11	2	17	2	0	1	0	45	8.9
L	32	Stephane Matteau	NYR	23	6	3	9	5	20	1	0	2	2	36	16.7
L	10	Esa Tikkanen	NYR	23	4	4	8	1	34	0	0	1	0	56	7.1
C	13	Sergei Nemchinov	NYR	23	2	5	7	1	6	0	0	0	0	33	6.1
R	36	Glenn Anderson	NYR	23	3	3	6	5	42	0	1	2	0	31	9.7
D	23	Jeff Beukeboom	NYR	22	0	6	6	17	50	0	0	0	0	22	.0
C	14	Craig MacTavish	NYR	23	1	4	5	0	22	0	0	0	0	15	6.7
L	17	Greg Gilbert	NYR	23	1	3	4	2–	8	0	0	0	0	23	4.3
D	25 *	A. Karpovtsev	NYR	17	0	4	4	6–	12	0	0	0	0	14	.0
D	6	Doug Lidster	NYR	9	2	0	2	4–	10	0	0	0	0	9	22.2
R	26	Joey Kocur	NYR	20	1	1	2	1–	17	0	0	0	0	16	6.3
D	4	Kevin Lowe	NYR	22	1	0	1	6	20	0	0	0	0	15	6.7
C	12	Ed Olczyk	NYR	1	0	0	0	1–	0	0	0	0	0	1	.0
G	30	Glenn Healy	NYR	2	0	0	0	0	0	0	0	0	0	0	.0
L	19	Nick Kypreos	NYR	3	0	0	0	1–	2	0	0	0	0	0	.0
G	35	Mike Richter	NYR	23	0	0	0	0	2	0	0	0	0	0	.0
D	24	Jay Wells	NYR	23	0	0	0	6–	20	0	0	0	0	12	.0

Goaltending

No.	Goaltender	GPI	Mins	Avg	W	L	EN	SO	GA	SA	S%
30	Glenn Healy	2	68	.88	0	0	0	0	1	17	.941
35	Mike Richter	23	1417	2.07	16	7	0	4	49	623	.921
	Totals	**23**	**1485**	**2.02**	**16**	**7**	**0**	**4**	**50**	**640**	**.922**

Retired Numbers

1	Eddie Giacomin	1965-1976
7	Rod Gilbert	1960-1978

Club Records

Team

(Figures in brackets for season records are games played; records for fewest points, wins, ties, losses, goals, goals against are for 70 or more games)

Most Points 112 1993-94 (84)
Most Wins 52 1993-94 (84)
Most Ties 21 1950-51 (70)
Most Losses 44 1984-85 (80)
Most Goals 371 1991-92 (80)
Most Goals Against 345 1984-85 (80)
Fewest Points 47 1965-66 (70)
Fewest Wins 17 1952-53; 54-55; 59-60 (70)
Fewest Ties 5 1991-92 (80)
Fewest Losses 17 1971-72 (78)
Fewest Goals 150 1954-55 (70)
Fewest Goals Against 177 1970-71 (78)

Longest Winning Streak
Over-all .... 10 Dec. 19/39-
Jan. 13/40
Jan. 19-
Feb. 10/73
Home .... 14 Dec. 19/39-
Feb. 25/40
Away .... 7 Jan. 12-
Feb. 12/35
Oct. 28-
Nov. 29/78

Longest Undefeated Streak
Over-all .... 19 Nov. 23/39-
Jan. 13/40
(14 wins, 5 ties)
Home .... 26 Mar. 29/70-
Feb. 2/71
(19 wins, 7 ties)
Away .... 11 Nov. 5/39-
Jan. 13/40
(6 wins, 5 ties)

Longest Losing Streak
Over-all .... 11 Oct. 30-
Nov. 27/43
Home .... 7 Oct. 20-
Nov. 14/76;
Mar. 24-
Apr. 14/93

Away .... 10 Oct. 30-
Dec. 23/43

Longest Winless Streak
Over-all .... 21 Jan. 23-
Mar. 19/44
(17 losses, 4 ties)
Home .... 10 Jan. 30-
Mar. 19/44
(7 losses, 3 ties)
Away .... 16 Oct. 9-
Dec. 20/52
(12 losses, 4 ties)

Most Shutouts, Season 13 1928-29 (44)
Most PIM, Season 2,018 1989-90 (80)
Most Goals, Game .... 12 Nov. 21/71
(Cal. 1 at NYR 12)

Individual

Most Seasons .... 17 Harry Howell
Most Games .... 1,160 Harry Howell
Most Goals, Career .... 406 Rod Gilbert
Most Assists, Career ...... 615 Rod Gilbert
Most Points, Career ...... 1,021 Rod Gilbert
(406 goals, 615 assists)
Most PIM, Career .... 1,226 Ron Greschner
Most Shutouts, Career .... 49 Ed Giacomin
Longest Consecutive
Games Streak .... 560 Andy Hebenton
(Oct. 7/55-Mar. 24/63)
Most Goals, Season .... 52 Adam Graves
(1993-94)
Most Assists, Season .... 80 Brian Leetch
(1991-92)
Most Points, Season .... 109 Jean Ratelle
(1971-72)
(46 goals, 63 assists)
Most PIM, Season .... 305 Troy Mallette
(1989-90)
Most Points, Defenseman
Season................... 102 Brian Leetch
(1991-92)
(22 goals, 80 assists)
Most Points, Center,
Season................... 109 Jean Ratelle
(1971-72)
(46 goals, 63 assists)

Most Points, Right Wing,
Season .... 97 Rod Gilbert
(1971-72)
(43 goals, 54 assists)
Rod Gilbert
(1974-75)
(36 goals, 61 assists)
Most Points, Left Wing,
Season .... 106 Vic Hadfield
(1971-72)
(50 goals, 56 assists)
Most Points, Rookie,
Season .... 76 Mark Pavelich
(1981-82)
(33 goals, 43 assists)
Most Shutouts, Season .... 13 John Ross Roach
(1928-29)
Most Goals, Game .... 5 Don Murdoch
(Oct. 12/76)
Mark Pavelich
(Feb. 23/83)
Most Assists, Game .... 5 Walt Tkaczuk
(Feb. 12/72)
Rod Gilbert
(Mar. 2/75; Mar. 30/75;
Oct. 8/76)
Don Maloney
(Jan. 3/87)
Most Points, Game........... 7 Steve Vickers
(Feb. 18/76)

All-time Record vs. Other Clubs

Regular Season

	At Home						On Road						Total					
	GP	W	L	T	GF	GA	PTS	GP	W	L	T	GF	GA	PTS	GP	W	L	T	GF	GA	PTS
Anaheim	1	0	1	0	2	4	0	1	0	1	0	2	3	0	2	0	2	0	4	7	0
Boston	282	122	106	54	857	792	298	278	88	150	40	774	1009	216	560	210	256	94	1631	1801	514
Buffalo	46	21	14	11	164	129	53	48	12	30	6	160	223	30	94	33	44	17	324	352	83
Calgary	44	19	20	5	156	160	43	43	10	24	9	134	196	29	87	29	44	14	290	356	72
Chicago	279	117	108	54	827	790	288	278	111	125	42	777	848	264	557	228	233	96	1604	1638	552
Dallas	54	33	11	10	194	148	76	53	19	16	8	205	162	66	107	62	27	18	399	310	142
Detroit	276	131	87	58	852	710	320	278	75	158	45	689	978	195	554	206	245	103	1541	1688	515
Edmonton	22	6	12	4	87	90	16	22	11	10	1	77	86	23	44	17	22	5	164	176	39
Florida	2	2	0	0	6	4	4	3	1	2	0	7	7	2	5	3	2	0	13	11	6
Hartford	24	15	7	2	109	71	32	24	8	13	3	86	94	19	48	23	20	5	195	165	51
Los Angeles	51	31	15	5	207	150	67	52	15	20	9	187	174	55	103	54	35	14	394	324	122
Montreal	270	109	109	52	782	789	270	270	55	181	34	623	1066	144	540	164	290	86	1405	1855	414
New Jersey	59	36	15	8	263	185	80	60	31	25	4	233	206	66	119	67	40	12	496	391	146
NY Islanders	70	43	19	8	281	211	94	71	17	48	6	220	311	40	141	60	67	14	501	522	134
Ottawa	3	3	0	0	15	5	6	4	4	0	0	19	10	8	7	7	0	0	34	15	14
Philadelphia	85	39	26	20	285	246	98	83	29	41	13	243	291	71	168	68	67	33	528	537	169
Pittsburgh	78	41	30	7	320	273	89	77	36	30	11	289	278	83	155	77	60	18	609	551	172
Quebec	24	16	5	3	103	66	35	25	10	12	3	106	110	23	49	26	17	6	209	176	58
St. Louis	53	42	6	5	228	120	89	55	26	21	8	183	163	60	108	68	27	13	411	283	149
San Jose	3	2	0	1	15	7	5	4	4	0	0	22	9	8	7	6	0	1	37	16	13
Tampa Bay	5	3	2	0	20	22	6	3	2	1	0	11	11	4	8	5	3	0	31	33	10
Toronto	268	111	101	56	821	785	278	267	78	151	38	692	920	194	535	189	252	94	1513	1705	472
Vancouver	47	35	5	7	215	117	75	45	31	11	3	187	144	65	92	66	18	8	402	261	140
Washington	60	30	24	6	246	217	66	61	24	29	8	210	237	56	121	54	53	14	456	454	122
Winnipeg	22	12	8	2	104	89	26	23	12	9	2	87	84	26	45	24	17	4	191	173	52
Defunct Clubs	139	87	30	22	460	290	196	139	82	34	23	441	291	187	278	169	64	45	901	581	383
Totals	**2267**	**1106**	**763**	**398**	**7619**	**6470**	**2610**	**2267**	**809**	**1142**	**316**	**6664**	**7911**	**1934**	**4534**	**1915**	**1905**	**714**	**14283**	**14381**	**4544**

Calgary totals include Atlanta, 1972-73 to 1979-80. Dallas totals include Minnesota, 1967-68 to 1992-93.
New Jersey totals include Kansas City, 1974-75 to 1975-76, and Colorado, 1976-77 to 1981-82.

Playoffs

	Series	W	L	GP	W	L	T	GF	GA	Last Mtg.	Round	Result
Boston	9	3	6	42	18	22	2	104	114	1973	QF	W 4-1
Buffalo	1	0	1	3	1	2	0	6	11	1978	PR	L 1-2
Calgary	1	1	0	4	3	1	0	14	8	1980	PR	W 3-1
Chicago	5	1	4	24	10	14	0	54	66	1973	SF	L 1-4
Detroit	5	1	4	23	10	13	0	49	57	1950	F	L 3-4
Los Angeles	2	2	0	6	5	1	0	32	14	1981	PR	W 3-1
Montreal	13	6	7	55	21	32	2	139	171	1986	CF	L 1-4
New Jersey	2	2	0	14	8	6	0	46	41	1994	CF	W 4-3
NY Islanders	8	3	5	39	19	20	0	132	129	1994	CQF	W 4-0
Philadelphia	8	4	4	38	19	19	0	130	119	1987	DSF	L 2-4
Pittsburgh	2	0	2	10	2	8	0	30	44	1992	DF	L 2-4
St. Louis	1	1	0	6	4	2	0	29	22	1981	QF	W 4-2
Toronto	8	5	3	35	19	16	0	86	86	1971	QF	W 4-2
Vancouver	1	1	0	7	4	3	0	21	19	1994	F	W 4-3
Washington	4	2	2	22	11	11	0	71	75	1994	CSF	W 4-1
Defunct	9	6	3	22	11	7	4	43	29			
Totals	**79**	**38**	**41**	**350**	**165**	**177**	**8**	**986**	**1004**			

Playoff Results 1994-90

Year	Round	Opponent	Result	GF	GA
1994	F	Vancouver	W 4-3	21	19
	CF	New Jersey	W 4-3	18	16
	CSF	Washington	W 4-1	20	12
	CQF	NY Islanders	W 4-0	22	3
1992	DF	Pittsburgh	L 2-4	19	24
	DSF	New Jersey	W 4-3	28	25
1991	DSF	Washington	L 2-4	16	16
1990	DF	Washington	L 1-4	15	22
	DSF	NY Islanders	W 4-1	22	13

Abbreviations: Round: **F** – Final;
CF – conference final; **CQF** – conference quarter-final;
CSF – conference semi-final; **DF** – division final;
DSF – division semi-final; **SF** – semi-final;
QF – quarter-final; **PR** – preliminary round.

1993-94 Results

Oct.	5		Boston	3-4	14		Philadelphia	5-2
	7		Tampa Bay	5-4	16	at	Chicago	5-1
	9	at	Pittsburgh	2-3	18		St. Louis	4-1
	11		Washington	5-2	25	at	San Jose	8-3
	13		Quebec	6-4	27	at	Los Angeles	5-4
	15	at	Buffalo	5-2	28	at	Anaheim	2-3
	16	at	Philadelphia	3-4	31		Pittsburgh	5-3
	19		Anaheim	2-4	Feb. 2		NY Islanders	4-4
	22	at	Tampa Bay	1-4	3	at	Boston	2-4
	24		Los Angeles	3-2	7		Washington	1-4
	28		Montreal	3-3	9	at	Montreal	3-4
	30	at	Hartford	4-1	12	at	Ottawa	4-3
	31		New Jersey	4-1	14	at	Quebec	4-2
Nov.	3		Vancouver	6-3	18		Ottawa	3-0
	6	at	Quebec	4-2	19	at	Hartford	2-4
	8		Tampa Bay	6-3	21		Pittsburgh	4-3
	10		Winnipeg	2-1	23		Boston	3-0
	13	at	Washington	2-0	24	at	New Jersey	3-1
	14		San Jose	3-3	26	at	Dallas	1-3
	16	at	Florida	4-2	28		Philadelphia	4-1
	19	at	Tampa Bay	5-3	Mar. 2		Quebec	3-3
	23		Montreal	5-4	4		NY Islanders	3-3
	24	at	Ottawa	7-1	5	at	NY Islanders	5-4
	27	at	NY Islanders	4-6	7		Detroit	3-6
	28		Washington	3-1	9	at	Washington	7-5
	30	at	New Jersey	3-1	10	at	Boston	3-2
Dec.	4	at	Toronto	4-3	12	at	Pittsburgh	2-6
	5		New Jersey	2-1	14	at	Florida	1-2
	8		Edmonton	1-1	16		Hartford	4-0
	13		Buffalo	2-0	18		Chicago	3-7
	15		Hartford	5-2	22	at	Calgary	4-4
	17	at	Detroit	4-6	23	at	Edmonton	5-3
	19		Ottawa	6-3	25	at	Vancouver	5-2
	22	at	Florida	2-3	27	at	Winnipeg	5-2
	23	at	Washington	1-0	29	at	Philadelphia	4-3
	26		New Jersey	8-3	Apr. 1		Dallas	3-0
	29	at	St. Louis	4-3	2	at	New Jersey	4-2
	31	at	Buffalo	1-4	4		Florida	3-2
Jan.	3		Florida	3-2	8		Toronto	5-3
	5		Calgary	1-4	10	at	NY Islanders	4-5
	8	at	Montreal	2-3	12		Buffalo	3-2
	10		Tampa Bay	2-5	14		Philadelphia	2-2

Entry Draft Selections 1994-80

1994			
Pick			
26	Dan Cloutier		
52	Rudolf Vercik		
78	Adam Smith		
100	Alexander Korobolin		
104	Sylvain Blouin		
130	Martin Ethier		
135	Yuri Litvinov		
156	David Brosseau		
182	Alexei Lazarenko		
208	Craig Anderson		
209	Vitali Yeremeyev		
234	Eric Boulton		
260	Radoslav Kropac		
267	Jamie Butt		
286	Kim Johnsson		

1993
Pick
8 Niklas Sundstrom
34 Lee Sorochan
61 Maxim Galanov
86 Sergei Olimpiyev
112 Gary Roach
138 Dave Trofimenkoff
162 Sergei Kondrashkin
164 Todd Marchant
190 Eddy Campbell
216 Ken Shepard
242 Andrei Kudinov
261 Pavel Komarov
268 Maxim Smelnitsky

1992
Pick
24 Peter Ferraro
48 Mattias Norstrom
72 Eric Cairns
85 Chris Ferraro
120 Dmitri Starostenko
144 David Dal Grande
168 Matt Oates
192 Mickey Elick
216 Dan Brierley
240 Vladimir Vorobjev

1991
Pick
15 Alexei Kovalev
37 Darcy Werenka
96 Corey Machanic
125 Fredrik Jax
128 Barry Young
147 John Rushin
169 Corey Hirsch
191 Viacheslav Uvayev
213 Jamie Ram
235 Vitali Chinakhov
257 Brian Wiseman

1990
Pick
13 Michael Stewart
34 Doug Weight
55 John Vary
69 Jeff Nielsen
76 Rick Willis
85 Sergei Zubov
99 Lubos Rob
118 Jason Weinrich
139 Bryan Lonsinger
160 Todd Hedlund
181 Andrew Silverman
202 Jon Hillebrandt
223 Brett Lievers
244 Sergei Nemchinov

1989
Pick
20 Steven Rice
40 Jason Prosofsky
45 Rob Zamuner
49 Louie DeBrusk
67 Jim Cummins
88 Aaron Miller
118 Joby Messier
139 Greg Leahy
160 Greg Spenrath
181 Mark Bavis
202 Roman Oksyuta
223 Steve Locke
244 Ken MacDermid

1988
Pick
22 Troy Mallette
26 Murray Duval
68 Tony Amonte
99 Martin Bergeron
110 Dennis Vial
131 Mike Rosati
152 Eric Couvrette
173 Shorty Forrest
194 Paul Cain
202 Eric Fenton
215 Peter Fiorentino
236 Keith Slifstien

1987
Pick
10 Jayson More
31 Daniel Lacroix
46 Simon Gagne
69 Michael Sullivan
94 Eric O'Borsky
115 Ludek Cajka
136 Clint Thomas
157 Charles Wiegand
178 Eric Burrill
199 David Porter
205 Brett Barnett
220 Lance Marciano

1986
Pick
9 Brian Leetch
51 Bret Walter
53 Shawn Clouston
72 Mark Janssens
93 Jeff Bloemberg
114 Darren Turcotte
135 Robb Graham
156 Barry Chyzowski
177 Pat Scanlon
198 Joe Ranger
219 Russell Parent
240 Soren True

1985
Pick
7 Ulf Dahlen
28 Mike Richter
49 Sam Lindstahl
70 Pat Janostin
91 Brad Stephan
112 Brian McReynolds
133 Neil Pilon
154 Larry Bernard
175 Stephane Brochu
196 Steve Nemeth
217 Robert Burakowsky
238 Rudy Poeschek

1984
Pick
14 Terry Carkner
35 Raimo Helminen
77 Paul Broten
98 Clark Donatelli
119 Kjell Samuelsson
140 Thomas Hussey
161 Brian Nelson
182 Ville Kentala
188 Heinz Ehlers
202 Kevin Miller
223 Tom Lorentz
243 Scott Brower

1983
Pick
12 Dave Gagner
33 Randy Heath
49 Vesa Salo
53 Gordie Walker
73 Peter Andersson
93 Jim Andonoff
113 Bob Alexander
133 Steve Orth
153 Peter Marcov
173 Paul Jerrard
213 Bryan Walker
233 Ulf Nilsson

1982
Pick
15 Chris Kontos
36 Tomas Sandstrom
57 Corey Millen
78 Chris Jensen
120 Tony Granato
141 Sergei Kapustin
160 Brian Glynn
162 Jan Karlsson
183 Kelly Miller
193 Simo Saarinen
204 Bob Lowes
225 Andy Otto
246 Dwayne Robinson

1981
Pick
9 James Patrick
30 Jan Erixon
50 Peter Sundstrom
51 Mark Morrison
72 John Vanbiesbrouck
114 Eric Magnuson
135 Mike Guentzel
156 Ari Lahteenmaki
177 Paul Reifenberger
198 Mario Proulx

1980
Pick
14 Jim Malone
35 Mike Allison
77 Kurt Kleinendorst
98 Scot Kleinendorst
119 Reijo Ruotsalainen
140 Bob Scurfield
161 Bart Wilson
182 Chris Wray
203 Anders Backstrom

Club Directory

Madison Square Garden
4 Pennsylvania Plaza
New York, New York 10001
Phone **212/465-6000**
PR FAX 212/465-6494
Capacity: 18,200

Executive Management
President and General Manager . . . . Neil Smith
Vice-President and General Counsel . . . . Kenneth W. Munoz
Vice-President, Finance . . . . Jim Abry
Governor . . . . TBA
Alternate Governors . . . . Neil Smith, Robert M. Gutkowski,
Kenneth W. Munoz

Hockey Club Personnel
Assistant General Manager/Player Development . . . . Larry Pleau
Head Coach . . . . Colin Campbell
Assistant Coach . . . . Dick Todd
Assistant Coach . . . . Mike Murphy
Development Coach . . . . Al Hill
Assistant Development Coach . . . . Mike Busniak
Scouting Staff . . . . Darwin Bennett, Tony Feltrin, Herb Hammond,
Martin Madden, Christer Rockstrom
Director of Business Administration . . . . John Gentile
Director of Hockey Administration . . . . Kevin McDonald
Director of Team Operations . . . . Matthew Loughran
Scouting Manager . . . . Bill Short
Executive Administrative Assistant . . . . Barbara Dand
Senior Secretary . . . . Nicole Wetzold

Medical/Training Staff
Team Physician and Orthopedic Surgeon . . . . Dr. Barton Nisonson
Assistant Team Physician . . . . Dr. Tony Maddalo
Medical Consultants . . . . Dr. Howard Chester, Dr. Frank Gardner,
Dr. Ronald Weissman
Team Dentists . . . . Dr. Irwin Miller, Dr. Don Soloman
Sports Physiologist . . . . Dr. Howie Wenger
Medical Trainer . . . . TBA
Equipment Manager . . . . Mike Folga
Equipment Trainer . . . . Joe Murphy
Massage Therapist . . . . Bruce Lifrieri
Lockerroom Assistant . . . . Benny Petrizzi
Staff Assistant . . . . Brad Kolodny

Communications Department
Director of Communications. . . . . Barry Watkins
Assistant to the Director of Communications . . . . . . John Rosasco
Manager of Community Relations . . . . Rod Gilbert
Communications Assistant . . . . Rob Koch
Administrative Assistant . . . . Ann Marie Gilmartin

Marketing Department
Director of Marketing. . . . . Kevin Kennedy
Promotions Manager . . . . Caroline Calabrese
Manager of Marketing Operations . . . . Jim Pfeifer
Manager of Event Presentation. . . . . Jeannie Baumgartner

Home Ice . . . . Madison Square Garden
Press Facilities . . . . 33rd Street
Television Facilities . . . . 31st Street
Radio Facilities . . . . 33rd Street
Rink Dimensions . . . . 200 feet by 85 feet
Ends and Sides of Rink . . . . Plexiglass (8 feet)
Club Colors. . . . . Blue, Red and White
Practice Facility . . . . Rye, New York
TV Announcers . . . . Bruce Beck, John Davidson, Sam Rosen,
Al Trautwig
Radio Announcers . . . . Marv Albert, Sal Messina, Howie Rose
Television Outlets . . . . Madison Square Garden Cable Network
Radio Outlet . . . . MSG Radio – WFAN (66 AM), WEVD (1050
AM), WXPS (107.1 FM)

The New York Rangers Hockey Club is part of Madison Square Garden

Coach

CAMPBELL, COLIN
Coach, New York Rangers. Born in London, Ontario, January 28, 1953.

Campbell, 41, began his coaching career in 1985-86 with Detroit, following his retirement as a player after the 1984-85 season. He worked a total of five seasons as a Red Wings assistant coach, one season under coach Harry Neale and four seasons under coach Jacques Demers.

The native of London, Ontario, joined the Rangers organization in August of 1990 as an assistant coach to Roger Neilson. He served in that role until January 4, 1993, when he became head coach of the Binghamton Rangers, New York's American Hockey League affiliate. He guided Binghamton to a record of 29-8-5, helping the club set AHL records for wins (57) and points (124) in a single season.

On June 21, 1993, Campbell was promoted to associate coach of New York, under head coach Mike Keenan, helping the Rangers capture the Presidents' Trophy, given to the team with the best regular-season record, and the Stanley Cup.

Before joining the coaching ranks, Campbell played 12 seasons of professional hockey as a defensive defenseman. After being drafted by the Pittsburgh Penguins in the second round of the 1973 Amateur Draft, he opted to join the Vancouver Blazers of the World Hockey Association. Following one season in the WHA, he went on to play 11 seasons in the National Hockey League for the Penguins, Colorado Rockies, Edmonton Oilers (where he was a teammate of Mark Messier and Kevin Lowe), Vancouver Canucks and the Red Wings.

He played in a total of 636 NHL contests, collecting 25 goals and 103 assists for 128 points along with 1,292 penalty minutes.

Coaching Record

			Regular Season				Playoffs			
Season	Team	Games	W	L	T	%	Games	W	L	%
1992-93	Binghamton (AHL)	42	29	8	5	.750	14	7	7	.500

General Manager

SMITH, NEIL
General Manager, New York Rangers. Born in Toronto, Ont., January 9, 1954.

Entering his sixth season as the team's general manager, Neil Smith has one of the most successful tenures at the helm of the Rangers in franchise history. In his first five seasons with the club, the team has finished in first place three times, won two Presidents' Trophies and won the Stanley Cup this past season. Smith, 40, joined the Rangers on July 17, 1989 after seven seasons with the Detroit Red Wings where he held several different positions, including director of scouting and general manager/governor of the Adirondack Red Wings where he won two Calder Cup championships in 1985-86 and 1988-89. Smith began his career as a scout with the Islanders in 1980-81 and 1981-82.

A former All-American defenseman from Western Michigan University, Smith was drafted in 1974 by the New York Islanders. After receiving his degree in communications and business, Smith played two seasons in the IHL. He spent 1978-79 with the Kalamazoo Wings and Saginaw Gears and 1979-80 with the Dayton Gems, Milwaukee Admirals and Muskegon Mohawks.

Ottawa Senators

1993-94 Results: 14W-61L-9T 37PTS. Seventh, Northeast Division

Year-by-Year Record

		Home			Road			Overall							
Season	GP	W	L	T	W	L	T	W	L	T	GF	GA	Pts.	Finished	Playoff Result
1993-94	84	8	30	4	6	31	5	14	61	9	201	397	37	7th, Northeast Div.	Out of Playoffs
1992-93	84	9	29	4	1	41	0	10	70	4	202	395	24	6th, Adams Div.	Out of Playoffs

Schedule

Oct. Sat. 1 Winnipeg
Mon. 3 Boston
Wed. 5 Washington
Fri. 7 at NY Islanders
Sat. 8 at New Jersey
Tues. 11 at Toronto
Sat. 15 at Dallas
Wed. 19 at Hartford
Sat. 22 at Philadelphia*
Sun. 23 Tampa Bay*
Wed. 26 Pittsburgh
Sat. 29 Detroit
Nov. Tues. 1 at Pittsburgh
Wed. 2 Philadelphia
Sat. 5 Montreal
Mon. 7 Boston
Thur. 10 at Buffalo
Sat. 12 at Quebec*
Sun. 13 Hartford
Wed. 16 Pittsburgh
Thur. 17 at Pittsburgh
Sat. 19 NY Rangers
Wed. 23 New Jersey
Sat. 26 Florida
Mon. 28 Los Angeles
Wed. 30 Washington
Dec. Sat. 3 Philadelphia
Sun. 4 Calgary
Wed. 7 at Tampa Bay
Thur. 8 at Florida
Sat. 10 at NY Islanders
Tues. 13 New Jersey
Wed. 14 at Hartford
Sat. 17 at Montreal
Mon. 19 Buffalo
Wed. 21 Tampa Bay
Fri. 23 at New Jersey
Mon. 26 at NY Rangers
Wed. 28 NY Islanders
Sat. 31 Hartford
Jan. Mon. 2 at Toronto
(in Hamilton)
Thur. 5 at Winnipeg

Sat. 7 Toronto
Mon. 9 at Montreal
Wed. 11 Boston
Sat. 14 at Philadelphia
Sun. 15 Anaheim
Mon. 23 at Buffalo
Wed. 25 at Hartford
Fri. 27 at Washington
Sat. 28 Buffalo
Feb. Wed. 1 San Jose
Thur. 2 at Boston
Sat. 4 NY Rangers
Mon. 6 Vancouver
Wed. 8 Montreal
Sat. 11 at Quebec
Wed. 15 at San Jose
Fri. 17 at Anaheim
Sat. 18 at Los Angeles
Tues. 21 at Chicago
Thur. 23 Quebec
Sat. 25 Florida
Tues. 28 Chicago
Mar. Wed. 1 at Detroit
Sat. 4 at Boston*
Sun. 5 NY Islanders
Tues. 7 at St. Louis
Thur. 9 at Chicago
(in Phoenix)
Sat. 11 at Vancouver
Sun. 12 at Edmonton
Wed. 15 at Calgary
Sat. 18 Pittsburgh*
Sun. 19 Dallas
Tues. 21 at Washington
Wed. 22 at Tampa Bay
Sat. 25 at Quebec
Sun. 26 Edmonton
Wed. 29 St. Louis
Apr. Sun. 2 at Buffalo*
Mon. 3 Montreal
Wed. 5 at Florida
Fri. 7 at NY Rangers
Sat. 8 Quebec

* Denotes afternoon game.

Home Starting Times:
Mondays through Saturdays . . . . . . 7:30 p.m.
Sundays . . . . 7:00 p.m.
Matinees . . . . 1:30 p.m.

Franchise date: December 16, 1991

3rd NHL Season

NORTHEAST DIVISION

The play of rookie Alexei Yashin was a highlight of the Ottawa Senators' second NHL season. Yashin led all Senator scorers with 30 goals and 49 assists.

1994-95 Player Personnel

FORWARDS	HT	WT	S	Place of Birth	Date	1993-94 Club
ARCHIBALD, Dave	6-1	210	L	Chilliwack, B.C.	4/14/69	Ottawa
BOIVIN, Claude	6-2	200	L	Ste. Foy, Que.	3/1/70	Philadelphia-Hershey-Ottawa
BONK, Radek	6-3	215	L	Krnov, Czech.	1/9/76	Las Vegas
BOURQUE, Phil	6-1	196	L	Chelmsford, MA	6/8/62	NY Rangers-Ottawa
CUNNEYWORTH, Randy	6-0	180	L	Etobicoke, Ont.	5/10/61	Hartford-Chicago
DAIGLE, Alexandre	6-0	185	L	Montreal, Que.	2/7/75	Ottawa
DAVYDOV, Evgeny	6-0	200	R	Chelyabinsk, USSR	5/27/67	Florida-Ottawa
DEMITRA, Pavol	6-0	189	L	Dubnica, Czech.	11/29/74	Ottawa-P.E.I.
ELYNUIK, Pat	6-0	185	R	Foam Lake, Sask.	10/30/67	Washington-Tampa Bay
GARDINER, Bruce	6-1	185	R	Barrie, Ont.	2/11/71	Colgate-Peoria
GRIMES, Jake	6-1	196	L	Montreal, Que.	9/13/72	Thunder Bay-PEI
GUERARD, Daniel	6-4	215	L	LaSalle, Que.	4/9/74	Verdun-PEI
HUARD, Bill	6-1	215	L	Welland, Ont.	6/24/67	Ottawa
LEVINS, Scott	6-4	210	R	Spokane, WA	1/30/70	Florida-Ottawa
MALLETTE, Troy	6-2	210	L	Sudbury, Ont.	2/25/70	Ottawa
MCCLEARY, Trent	6-0	180	R	Swift Current, Sask.	10/10/72	P.E.I.-Thunder Bay
McILWAIN, Dave	6-0	185	L	Seaforth, Ont.	1/9/67	Ottawa
MURRAY, Troy	6-1	195	R	Calgary, Alta.	7/31/62	Chicago-Indianapolis-Ottawa
PANKEWICZ, Greg	6-0	185	R	Dray Valley, Alta.	10/6/70	Ottawa-PEI
PARSON, Steve	6-0	180	L	Elmira, Ont.	3/14/73	Kingston
PENNEY, Chad	6-0	195	L	Labrador City, Nfld.	9/18/73	Ottawa-PEI
PICARD, Michel	5-11	190	L	Beauport, Que.	11/7/69	Portland (AHL)
ROWLAND, Chris	6-1	188	R	Calgary, Alta.	3/30/71	PEI-Thunder Bay
ST. CYR, Gerry	6-1	188	R	North Vancouver, B.C.	8/18/71	Thunder Bay
SAVOIE, Claude	5-11	200	R	Montreal, Que.	3/12/73	PEI
SCHNEIDER, Andy	5-9	170	L	Edmonton, Alta.	3/29/72	Ottawa-PEI
TURGEON, Sylvain	6-0	200	L	Noranda, Que.	1/17/65	Ottawa
YASHIN, Alexei	6-3	215	R	Sverdlovsk, USSR	11/5/73	Ottawa

DEFENSEMEN	HT	WT	S	Place of Birth	Date	1993-94 Club
BICANEK, Radim	6-1	195	L	Uherske Hradiste, Czech.	1/18/75	Belleville
DAHLQUIST, Chris	6-1	195	L	Fridley, MN	12/14/62	Calgary
FILIMONOV, Dmitri	6-4	220	R	Perm, USSR	10/14/71	Ottawa-PEI
FOSTER, Corey	6-3	204	L	Ottawa, Ont.	10/27/69	Hershey
HAMR, Radek	5-11	175	L	Usti-Nad-Labem, Czech.	6/15/74	Ottawa-PEI
HILL, Sean	6-0	195	L	Duluth, MN	2/14/70	Anaheim
HUFFMAN, Kerry	6-2	200	L	Peterborough, Ont.	1/3/68	Quebec-Ottawa
KONROYD, Steve	6-1	195	L	Scarborough, Ont.	2/10/61	Detroit-Ottawa
LEROUX, Francois	6-6	225	L	Ste.-Adele, Que.	4/18/70	Ottawa
MACIVER, Norm	5-11	180	L	Thunder Bay, Ont.	9/8/64	Ottawa
MAYER, Derek	6-0	200	R	Rossland, B.C.	5/21/67	Cdn. National-Cdn. Olympic-Ott
NECKAR, Stanislav	6-1	196	L	Ceske Budejovice, Czech.	12/22/75	Budejovice
PAEK, Jim	6-1	195	L	Seoul, South Korea	4/7/67	Pittsburgh-Los Angeles
PITLICK, Lance	6-0	190	R	Minneapolis, MN	11/5/67	Hershey
RUMBLE, Darren	6-1	200	L	Barrie, Ont.	1/23/69	Ottawa-PEI
SHAW, Brad	6-0	190	R	Cambridge, Ont.	4/28/64	Ottawa
TRAVERSE, Patrick	6-3	200	L	Montreal, Que.	3/14/74	St-Jean-PEI
VIAL, Dennis	6-2	218	L	Sault Ste. Marie, Ont.	4/10/69	Ottawa

GOALTENDERS	HT	WT	C	Place of Birth	Date	1993-94 Club
BALES, Michael	6-1	180	L	Prince Albert, Sask.	8/6/71	Providence (AHL)
BILLINGTON, Craig	5-10	170	L	London, Ont.	9/11/66	Ottawa
LABBE, Jean-Francois	5-9	170	L	Sherbrooke, Que.	6/15/72	Thunder Bay-P.E.I.
LESLIE, Lance	5-10	160	L	Dawson Creek, B.C.	6/21/74	Tri-City
MADELEY, Darrin	5-11	170	L	Holland Landing, Ont.	2/25/68	Ottawa-PEI

1993-94 Scoring

* – rookie

Regular Season

Pos	#	Player	Team	GP	G	A	Pts	+/-	PIM	PP	SH	GW	GT	S	%
C	19 *	Alexei Yashin	OTT	83	30	49	79	49—	22	11	2	3	0	232	12.9
C	91 *	Alexandre Daigle	OTT	84	20	31	51	45—	40	4	0	2	0	168	11.9
C	17	Dave McIlwain	OTT	66	17	26	43	40—	48	1	1	1	0	115	14.8
L	61	Sylvain Turgeon	OTT	47	11	15	26	25—	52	7	0	2	2	116	9.5
L	18	Troy Mallette	OTT	82	7	16	23	33—	166	0	0	0	0	100	7.0
D	4	Brad Shaw	OTT	66	4	19	23	41—	59	1	0	0	0	113	3.5
D	22	Norm Maciver	OTT	53	3	20	23	26—	26	0	0	0	0	88	3.4
D	6	Gord Dineen	OTT	77	0	21	21	52—	89	0	0	0	0	62	.0
R	11	Evgeny Davydov	FLA	21	2	6	8	3—	8	1	0	0	0	22	9.1
			OTT	40	5	7	12	6—	38	0	0	0	1	44	11.4
			TOTAL	61	7	13	20	9—	46	1	0	0	1	66	10.6
R	20	Andrew McBain	OTT	55	11	8	19	41—	64	8	0	0	0	91	12.1
C	26 *	Scott Levins	FLA	29	5	6	11	0	69	2	0	1	0	38	13.2
			OTT	33	3	5	8	26—	93	2	0	0	0	39	7.7
			TOTAL	62	8	11	19	26—	162	4	0	1	0	77	10.4
C	15	David Archibald	OTT	33	10	8	18	7—	14	2	0	1	0	65	15.4
C	38	Vladimir Ruzicka	OTT	42	5	13	18	21—	14	4	0	0	1	64	7.8
D	5	Kerry Huffman	QUE	28	0	6	6	2	28	0	0	0	0	44	.0
			OTT	34	4	8	12	30—	12	2	1	0	1	68	5.9
			TOTAL	62	4	14	18	28—	40	2	1	0	1	112	3.6
D	34	Darren Rumble	OTT	70	6	9	15	50—	116	0	0	0	0	95	6.3
C	7	Dan Quinn	OTT	13	7	0	7	0	6	2	0	3	0	31	22.6
R	16	Brad Lauer	OTT	30	2	5	7	15—	6	0	0	0	0	45	4.4
L	21	Dennis Vial	OTT	55	2	5	7	9—	214	0	0	0	0	37	5.4
L	27	Phil Bourque	NYR	16	0	1	1	2—	8	0	0	0	0	2	.0
			OTT	11	2	3	5	2—	11	0	0	0	1	19	10.5
			TOTAL	27	2	4	6	4—	8	0	2	0	1	21	9.5
C	33	Troy Murray	CHI	12	0	1	1	1	6	0	0	0	0	7	.0
			OTT	15	2	3	5	2	4	0	0	0	0	14	14.3
			TOTAL	27	2	4	6	2	10	0	1	0	0	21	9.5
C	11	Jarmo Kekalainen	OTT	28	1	5	6	8—	14	0	0	0	0	18	5.6
R	24	Robert Burakowsky	OTT	23	2	3	5	7—	6	0	0	0	0	40	5.0
D	55 *	Dimitri Filimonov	OTT	30	1	4	5	10—	18	0	0	0	0	15	6.7
D	9 *	Derek Mayer	OTT	17	2	2	4	16—	8	1	0	0	0	29	6.9
L	28	Bill Huard	OTT	63	2	2	4	4—	162	0	0	0	0	24	8.3
L	23	Claude Boivin	PHI	26	1	1	2	11—	57	0	0	0	0	11	9.1
			OTT	15	1	0	1	6—	38	0	0	0	0	6	16.7
			TOTAL	41	2	1	3	7—	95	0	0	0	0	17	11.8
D	27	Hank Lammens	OTT	27	1	2	3	20—	22	0	0	0	0	6	16.7
L	10	Darcy Loewen	OTT	44	0	3	3	11—	52	0	0	0	0	39	.0
L	78 *	Pavol Demitra	OTT	12	1	1	2	7—	4	1	0	0	0	10	10.0
D	24	Steve Konroyd	DET	19	0	0	0	1	10	0	0	0	0	12	.0
			OTT	8	0	2	2	4—	2	0	0	0	0	9	.0
			TOTAL	27	0	2	2	3—	12	0	0	0	0	21	.0
D	3	Kent Paynter	OTT	9	0	1	1	6—	8	0	0	0	0	8	.0
D	29 *	Francois Leroux	OTT	23	0	1	1	4—	70	0	0	0	0	8	.0
G	32	Daniel Berthiaume	OTT	1	0	0	0	0	0	0	0	0	0	0	.0
D	2	Kevin MacDonald	OTT	1	0	0	0	2—	2	0	0	0	0	0	.0
L	25 *	Chad Penney	OTT	3	0	0	0	2—	0	0	0	0	0	2	.0
R	33 *	Greg Pankewicz	OTT	3	0	0	0	1—	4	0	0	0	0	0	.0
G	35	Mark Laforest	OTT	5	0	0	0	0	0	0	0	0	0	0	.0
D	5 *	Radek Hamr	OTT	7	0	0	0	10—	0	0	0	0	0	5	.0
R	9 *	Andy Schneider	OTT	10	0	0	0	6—	15	0	0	0	0	4	.0
L	12	Graeme Townshend	OTT	14	0	0	0	7—	19	0	0	0	0	6	.0
R	25	Herb Raglan	OTT	29	0	0	0	13—	52	0	0	0	0	13	.0
G	30 *	Darrin Madeley	OTT	32	0	0	0	0	0	0	0	0	0	1	.0
G	1	Craig Billington	OTT	63	0	0	0	0	8	0	0	0	0	1	.0

Goaltending

No.	Goaltender	GPI	Mins	Avg	W	L	T	EN	SO	GA	SA	S%
30 *	Darrin Madeley	32	1583	4.36	3	18	5	3	0	115	868	.868
1	Craig Billington	63	3319	4.59	11	41	4	6	0	254	1801	.859
35	Mark LaForest	5	182	5.60	0	2	0	0	0	17	96	.823
32	Daniel Berthiaume	1	1	20.00	0	0	0	0	0	2	2	.000
	Totals	84	5105	4.67	14	61	9	9	0	397	2776	.857

General Manager

SEXTON, RANDY JOHN
General Manager, Ottawa Senators. Born in Brockville, Ont., July 24, 1959.

Randy Sexton was appointed general manager of the Ottawa Senators in April 1993, adding to his responsibilities of president and alternate governor. Sexton became chief executive officer and alternate governor of the club. In January 1993, Sexton was appointed president and chief operating officer.

He is ultimately responsible for the business and hockey operations of the organization, providing overall direction and management to all operating units: Hockey Operations, Sales, Marketing, Finance, Media and Community Relations and Guest Services.

As the club's general manager, Sexton quickly signed seven draft picks from 1992, including Alexei Yashin, the club's first draft pick, as well as the signing of Alexandre Daigle, the first pick overall in 1993, to a unique multi-year contract in June, 1993.

During the course of 1994, he solidified the team's defensive squad by trading for Sean Hill and Jim Paek, and by acquiring free agent Chris Dahlquist. Sexton also added depth to the club's offense by signing free agents Pat Elynuik and Randy Cunneyworth.

His post secondary education began at St. Lawrence University where he obtained a Bachelor of Science degree. He played for the St. Lawrence University varsity hockey team from 1979 to 1982, and served as the team captain for his last two seasons. He acted as assistant coach and scout with St. Lawrence from 1983 to 1985. Sexton later received his Master degree in Business Administration from Clarkson University, Potsdam, New York.

Craig Billington was a workhorse for the Ottawa Senators in 1993-94, appearing in 63 games and winning a franchise record 11 games.

Club Records

Team

(Figures in brackets for season records are games played)

Most Points	37	1993-94 (84)	
Most Wins	14	1993-94 (84)	
Most Ties	9	1993-94 (84)	
Most Losses	70	1992-93 (84)	
Most Goals	202	1992-93 (84)	
Most Goals Against	397	1993-94 (84)	
Fewest Points	24	1992-93 (84)	
Fewest Wins	10	1992-93 (84)	
Fewest Ties	4	1992-93 (84)	
Fewest Losses	61	1993-94 (84)	
Fewest Goals	201	1993-94 (84)	
Fewest Goals Against	395	1992-93 (84)	

Longest Winning Streak

Over-all	3	Oct. 30/93-Nov. 5/93
Home	3	Mar. 23/94-Apr. 6/94
Away	3	Oct. 30/93-Nov. 5/93

Longest Undefeated Streak

Over-all	3	Three times
Home	4	Jan. 28/93-Feb. 8/93 (3-0-1)
Away	3	Oct. 30-Nov. 5/93

Longest Losing Streak

Over-all	14	Mar. 2/93-Apr. 7/93
Home	*11	Oct. 27-Dec. 8/93
Away	*38	Oct. 10/92-Apr. 3/93**

Longest Winless Streak

Over-all	21	Oct. 10/92-Nov. 23/92 (0-20-1)
Home	11	Oct. 27-Dec. 8/93
Away	*38	Oct. 10/92-Apr. 3/93 (0-39-0)**

** NHL records do not include neutral site games

Most Shutouts, Season	None	
Most PIM, Season	1,716	1992-93 (84)
Most Goals, Game	7	Nov. 3/93 (Ott. 7 at Edm. 5)
		Nov. 5/93 (Ott. 7 at Wpg. 6-OT)

Individual

Most Seasons	2	Ten players
Most Games, Career	147	Brad Shaw
Most Goals, Career	47	Bob Kudelski
Most Assists, Career	66	Norm Maciver
Most Points, Career	86	Norm Maciver
		(20 goals, 66 assits)
Most PIM, Career	318	Mike Peluso
Most Shutouts, Career	None	

Longest Consecutive

Games Streak	103	Brad Shaw
		(Oct. 31/92-Dec. 9/93)
Most Goals, Season	30	Alexei Yashin
		(1993-94)
Most Assists, Season	49	Alexei Yashin
		(1993-94)
Most Points, Season	79	Alexei Yashin
		(1993-94)
		(30 goals, 49 assists)
Most PIM, Season	318	Mike Peluso
		(1992-93)

Most Shutouts, Season .... None

Most Points, Defenseman

Season	63	Norm Maciver
		(1992-93)
		(17 goals, 46 assists)

Most Points, Center

Season	79	Alexei Yashin
		(1993-94)
		(30 goals, 49 assists)

Most Points, Right Wing

Season	43	Dave McLlwain
		(1993-94)
		(17 goals, 26 assists)

Most Points, Left Wing

Season	43	Sylvain Turgeon
		(1992-93)
		(25 goals, 18 assists)

Most Points, Rookie

Season	79	Alexei Yashin
		(1993-94)
		(30 goals, 49 assists)
Most Goals, Game	3	Five times
Most Assists, Game	4	Alexei Yashin
		(Nov. 5/93)
Most Points, Game	5	Alexei Yashin
		(Nov. 3/93)

* NHL Record.

Although he was hampered by injuries in 1993-94, Sylvain Turgeon still notched seven powerplay goals and 26 points in 47 games for the second-year Senators.

General Managers' History

Mel Bridgman, 1992-93; Randy Sexton, 1993-94 to date.

Coaching History

Rick Bowness, 1992-93 to date.

Captains' History

Laurie Boschman, 1992-93; Brad Shaw, Mark Lamb and Gord Dineen, 1993-94.

Retired Numbers

8   Frank Finnigan   1924-1934

All-time Record vs. Other Clubs

Regular Season

	At Home							On Road							Total					
	GP	W	L	T	GF	GA	PTS	GP	W	L	T	GF	GA	PTS	GP	W	L	T	GF	GA	PTS
Anaheim	1	1	0	0	4	1	2	1	0	1	0	1	5	0	2	1	1	0	5	6	2
Boston	5	0	5	0	8	24	0	7	0	7	0	17	37	0	12	0	12	0	25	61	0
Buffalo	7	1	5	1	15	31	3	5	0	5	0	9	30	0	12	1	10	1	24	61	3
Calgary	2	0	1	1	2	7	1	2	0	2	0	4	18	0	4	0	3	1	6	25	1
Chicago	2	0	2	0	5	6	0	2	1	1	0	5	7	1	4	0	3	1	7	12	1
Dallas	2	0	2	0	6	9	0	3	1	2	0	8	17	2	5	1	4	0	14	26	2
Detroit	2	1	1	0	7	7	2	2	0	5	0	5	13	0	3	1	3	0	12	20	2
Edmonton	2	2	0	0	7	5	4	2	1	1	0	9	10	2	4	3	1	0	16	15	6
Florida	2	0	2	0	5	9	0	1	1	0	0	6	7	1	4	0	3	1	11	16	1
Hartford	7	1	5	1	13	24	3	5	0	5	0	11	24	0	12	1	10	1	24	48	3
Los Angeles	2	1	1	0	7	5	2	2	0	2	0	6	15	0	4	1	3	0	13	20	2
Montreal	5	1	4	0	14	20	2	7	2	5	0	22	25	4	12	3	9	0	36	45	6
New Jersey	4	1	2	1	9	16	3	4	0	4	0	9	20	0	8	1	6	1	18	36	3
NY Islanders	3	0	2	1	6	18	1	4	1	2	1	13	21	3	7	1	4	2	19	39	4
NY Rangers	4	0	4	0	10	19	0	3	0	5	0	5	15	0	7	0	15	0	15	34	0
Philadelphia	3	1	1	1	8	10	3	4	0	4	0	6	27	0	7	1	5	1	14	37	3
Pittsburgh	4	1	3	0	5	16	2	5	0	4	1	10	23	1	9	1	7	1	15	39	3
Quebec	8	3	4	1	27	36	7	6	0	6	0	14	35	0	14	3	10	1	41	71	7
St. Louis	2	0	2	0	2	15	0	2	0	2	0	6	12	0	4	0	4	0	8	27	0
San Jose	2	2	0	0	9	6	4	2	1	1	0	4	4	2	4	3	1	0	13	10	6
Tampa Bay	3	0	3	0	4	12	0	3	0	3	0	4	9	0	6	0	6	0	8	21	0
Toronto	2	0	2	0	2	7	0	3	0	7	0	16	0	0	5	0	9	0	3	23	0
Vancouver	2	0	2	0	2	10	0	1	1	0	0	3	6	1	4	0	3	1	5	16	1
Washington	4	1	3	0	15	21	2	4	0	4	0	11	30	0	7	0	7	0	26	51	2
Winnipeg	4	0	3	1	9	21	1	1	0	10	0	12	6	1	4	1	4	1	19	33	3
Totals	**84**	**17**	**59**	**8**	**198**	**354**	**42**	**84**	**7**	**72**	**5**	**205**	**438**	**19**	**168**	**24**	**131**	**13**	**403**	**792**	**61**

Dallas totals include Minnesota, 1992-93.

1993-94 Results

Oct.	6		Quebec	5-5		6	at	Toronto	3-6
	9	at	St. Louis	5-7		8		Winnipeg	2-3
	14	at	Florida	4-5		10		NY Islanders	3-3
	16	at	Tampa Bay	1-4		11	at	Philadelphia	1-4
	21		Dallas	5-6		14	at	Vancouver	2-2
	23	at	NY Islanders	5-5		15	at	Calgary	0-10
	25		Anaheim	4-1		18		Edmonton	4-3
	27		Philadelphia	2-5		25	at	Pittsburgh	2-4
	28	at	Boston	2-6		27		Hartford	1-1
	30		Dallas	5-4		29	at	Chicago	3-3
Nov.	3	at	Edmonton	7-5		31		Chicago	0-1
	5	at	Winnipeg	7-6	Feb.	2		Florida	1-4
	10	at	Hartford	3-4		4	at	New Jersey	2-5
	11		Florida	4-5		5		Montreal	3-4
	13	at	Montreal	3-2		8		Philadelphia	3-3
	15		Montreal	2-4		10		Tampa Bay	2-6
	17		NY Islanders	1-8		12		NY Rangers	3-4
	18		New Jersey	2-5		18	at	NY Rangers	0-3
	22		Buffalo	2-5		19	at	NY Islanders	0-4
	24		NY Rangers	1-7		24		San Jose	6-4
	26	at	Buffalo	2-5		26	at	St. Louis	1-11
	27	at	Pittsburgh	2-2		28		Toronto	2-7
	29		Hartford	2-4	Mar.	2		Buffalo	2-7
Dec.	1	at	Montreal	6-3		4		Winnipeg	1-6
	3	at	Detroit	1-8		5	at	Boston	1-6
	4		Washington	1-6		8	at	Quebec	2-5
	6		Calgary	1-6		10	at	Philadelphia	2-8
	8		Buffalo	1-3		13	at	Anaheim	1-5
	9	at	Dallas	1-6		15	at	Los Angeles	0-7
	11	at	Quebec	2-5		17	at	San Jose	2-1
	13		Los Angeles	5-2		20	at	Buffalo	2-6
	15	at	Tampa Bay	3-4		23		Detroit	5-4
	17	at	Washington	2-11		24	at	Pittsburgh	1-5
	19	at	NY Rangers	3-6		28	at	Montreal	2-3
	21		Quebec	2-1		30		Quebec	6-4
	23		Hartford	1-2	Apr.	2	at	Florida	2-2
	26	at	Hartford	2-3		6		Washington	6-5
	27		Boston	3-5		7	at	Boston	4-5
	30		Tampa Bay	0-3		9	at	Washington	4-8
Jan.	1		New Jersey	1-7		11		Pittsburgh	0-4
	3		Pittsburgh	1-4		13		Boston	0-8
	5		Vancouver	2-7		14	at	New Jersey	1-4

Entry Draft
Selections 1994-92

1994 Pick		1993 Pick		1992 Pick	
3	Radek Bonk	1	Alexandre Daigle	2	Alexei Yashin
29	Stanislav Neckar	27	Radim Bicanek	25	Chad Penney
81	Bryan Masotta	53	Patrick Charbonneau	50	Patrick Traverse
131	Mike Gaffney	91	Cosmo Dupaul	73	Radek Hamr
133	Daniel Alfredsson	131	Rick Bodkin	98	Daniel Guerard
159	Doug Sproule	157	Sergei Poleschuk	121	Al Sinclair
210	Frederic Cassivi	183	Jason Disher	146	Jaroslav Miklenda
211	Danny Dupont	209	Toby Kvalevog	169	Jay Kenney
237	Stephen MacKinnon	227	Pavol Demitra	194	Claude Savoie
274	Antti Tormanen	235	Rick Schuwerk	217	Jake Grimes
				242	Tomas Jelinek
				264	Petter Ronnqvist

Alexander Daigle scored 20 goals and added 31 assists and 51 points as a rookie in 1993-94.

Coach

BOWNESS, RICK
Coach, Ottawa Senators. Born in Moncton, N.B., January 25, 1955.

Rick Bowness is entering his third season behind the Senators' bench. He was appointed the club's first head coach on June 15, 1992. Posting a 24-129-13 record in 166 games with the club (.184), Rick coached his 250th NHL game on February 10, 1994 vs Tampa Bay. Prior to joining the Senators, Bowness coached the Boston Bruins in 1991-92, guiding the team to a 39-32-12 record and a berth in the Conference Finals. The Moncton native began his coaching career with the AHL's Sherbrooke Jets as a player/coach in 1981, and returned to his hometown in 1987 as the coach and general manager of the Moncton Hawks, the Jets' AHL farm team. In February 1989, Bowness took over as interim coach of the Winnipeg Jets (28 games). He then joined the Bruins' organization, coaching the AHL's Maine Mariners for two seasons before assuming head coaching duties for the Bruins for 1991-92.

Coaching Record

Season	Team	Regular Season					Playoffs			
		Games	W	L	T	%	Games	W	L	%
1987-88	Moncton (AHL)	80	27	45	8	.388	....	....	....	....
1988-89	Moncton (AHL)	53	28	20	5	.576	....	....	....	....
	Winnipeg (NHL)	**28**	**8**	**17**	**3**	**.340**	....	....	....	....
1989-90	Maine (AHL)	80	31	38	11	.457	....	....	....	....
1990-91	Maine (AHL)	80	34	34	12	.500	2	0	2	.000
1991-92	**Boston (NHL)**	**80**	**36**	**32**	**12**	**.525**	**15**	**8**	**7**	**.533**
1992-93	**Ottawa (NHL)**	**84**	**10**	**70**	**4**	**.143**				
1993-94	**Ottawa (NHL)**	**84**	**14**	**61**	**9**	**.220**				
	NHL Totals	**276**	**68**	**180**	**28**	**.297**	**15**	**8**	**7**	**.533**

Club Directory

Ottawa Civic Centre

Ottawa Senators
301 Moodie Drive
Suite 200
Nepean, Ontario
K2H 9C4
Phone **613/721-0115**
FAX 613/726-1419
Capacity: 10,575

Governor, Chairman and Chief Executive Officer	Rod Bryden
President, G.M. and Alternate Governor	Randy Sexton
Senior V.P., Commercial Operations & C.F.O.	Bernie Ashe
President, Palladium Corporation	Cyril Leeder
Assistant General Manager	Ray Shero
Director, Hockey Operations	Brian McKenna
Director, Player Personnel	John Ferguson
Head Coach	Rick Bowness
Assistant Coach	E.J. McGuire
Assistant Coach	Alain Vigneault
Goaltender Coach and Scout	Glenn "Chico" Resch
Head Coach, Development Team	Dave Allison
Head Equipment Trainer	Ed Georgica
Athletic Trainer	Conrad Lackten
Assistant Trainer	John Gervais
Massage Therapist	Lori Lee
Director, Team Services	Trevor Timmins
Executive Secretary to the President	Allison Vaughan
Secretary, Hockey Department	Erin Galloway
US Eastern Amateur Scout	Paul Castron
Quebec Amateur Scout	André Dupont
Ontario Amateur Scout	Tim Higgins
Professional Scout	Barry Long
Western Canada Scout	Bruce Southern
Team Doctor	Jamie Kissick M.D.
Strength and Conditioning Coach	Mark Slater
Vice President, Finance	Jim Ablett
Controller	Mark Goudie
Senior Accountant	Lynda Rozon
Senior Accountant	David Spooner
Accounts Payable	Anne Hersey
Payroll Supervisor	Sandi Horner
Junior Accountant	Lisa Saumure
Junior Accountant	Lorrie Laurin
Vice-President, Corporate Communications	John Owens
Executive Secretary to the Governor	Sharry Dozois
Executive Secretary, Commercial Operations	Cheryl Blake
Director, Team and Business Development	Brad Marsh
Vice-President, Sales	Mark Bonneau
Director, Outaouais Business Development	Enrico Valente
Senior Account Manager	Brian Jokat
Senior Account Manager	Chris Knight
Senior Account Manager	Darren MacCartney
Senior Account Manager	Dan Quinn
Corporate Sales Coodinator	Kelly MacCallum
Vice-President, Marketing	Jim Steel
Secretary, Marketing	Krista Pogue
Director of Publications	Carl Lavigne
Graphic Designer	Kevin Caradonna
Art Director	Jean-Guy Brunet
Vice President, Ticket & Game-Day Operations	Jeff Kyle
Secretary, Ticket & Game-Day Operations	Paulette Surette
Director of Operations, Guests Services	David Dakers
Guest Services Representative	Cindy Rodrigue
Ticket Account Executive	Susan Ferguson
Ticket Account Executive	Shawn Williams
Ticket Coordinator	Tracey Drennan
Ticket and Jr. Fan Club Coordinator	Jody Thorson
Director, Promotions	Patti Zebchuck
Game & Event Producer	Randy Burgess
Director, Community Relations	Lisa Brazeau
Community Relations Coordinator	Marie Olney
Community Relations Coordinator	Sylvie Guénette-Craig
Manager, Computer Services & Administration	Chris Whiting
Office Coordinator	Renée Keays
Receptionist	Christine Clancy
Director, Media Relations	Laurent Benoit
Media Relations Assistant	Dominick Saillant
Media Relations Secretary	Vivianne Dumais
Club Historian	Jim McAuley

Philadelphia Flyers

1993-94 Results: 35W-39L-10T 80PTS. Sixth, Atlantic Division

Schedule

Oct.	Sat.	1	Hartford	Mon.	9	Anaheim	
	Tues.	4	at Florida	Wed.	11	at New Jersey	
	Thur.	6	at NY Rangers	Thur.	12	Florida	
	Sat.	8	Tampa Bay	Sat.	14	Ottawa	
	Wed.	12	at New Jersey	Mon.	16	at NY Islanders*	
	Fri.	14	at Winnipeg	Wed.	18	Washington	
	Sun.	16	at Calgary	Mon.	23	at Pittsburgh	
	Mon.	17	at Vancouver	Thur.	26	Hartford	
	Thur.	20	Quebec	Sat.	28	Boston*	
	Sat.	22	Ottawa*	Sun.	29	at Montreal*	
	Thur.	27	Vancouver	Tues.	31	Chicago	
	Sat.	29	Toronto	**Feb.** Thur.	2	NY Islanders	
Nov.	Wed.	2	at Ottawa	Sat.	4	Buffalo*	
	Fri.	4	at Buffalo	Tues.	7	at Toronto	
	Sat.	5	Buffalo	Thur.	9	NY Rangers	
	Tues.	8	at Quebec	Fri.	10	Washington	
	Thur.	10	Washington			(in Halifax)	
	Sat.	12	at Washington	Mon.	13	Los Angeles	
	Sun.	13	Dallas	Thur.	16	St. Louis	
	Thur.	17	NY Rangers	Sat.	18	Edmonton*	
	Sat.	19	Pittsburgh	Mon.	20	at San Jose*	
	Sun.	20	Detroit	Wed.	22	at Anaheim	
	Wed.	23	at Hartford	Thur.	23	at Los Angeles	
	Fri.	25	New Jersey*	Sat.	25	at Edmonton	
	Sat.	26	Tampa Bay*	**Mar.** Thur.	2	Florida	
	Wed.	30	at Detroit	Fri.	3	at NY Rangers	
Dec.	Thur.	1	NY Islanders	Sun.	5	San Jose	
	Sat.	3	at Ottawa	Wed.	8	at Hartford	
	Thur.	8	Montreal	Thur.	9	Calgary	
	Sat.	10	at Montreal	Sat.	11	at Tampa Bay	
	Sun.	11	New Jersey	Mon.	13	NY Rangers	
	Thur.	15	Winnipeg	Wed.	15	at Dallas	
	Sat.	17	at Quebec*	Sat.	18	at Florida	
	Sun.	18	at Chicago	Mon.	20	Montreal	
	Wed.	21	Quebec	Thur.	23	at NY Islanders	
	Fri.	23	at Washington	Sun.	26	Pittsburgh	
	Mon.	26	at Tampa Bay	Tues.	28	at Pittsburgh	
	Tues.	27	at Florida	Thur.	30	New Jersey	
	Fri.	30	at NY Islanders	Fri.	31	at Washington	
	Sat.	31	at Buffalo	**Apr.** Sun.	2	Boston*	
Jan.	Thur.	5	at Boston	Tues.	4	at Boston	
	Sat.	7	at Pittsburgh	Thur.	6	Tampa Bay	
			(in San Antonio)	Sun.	9	at St. Louis*	

* Denotes afternoon game.

Home Starting Times:
Mondays through Saturdays . . . . . 7:30 p.m.
Sundays . . . . 7:00 p.m.
Matinees . . . . 1:00 p.m.
Except   Wed. Dec. 21 . . . . 7:00 p.m.
         Sat. Feb. 4 . . . . 12:00 p.m.
         Thu. Feb. 9, Mar. 2 . . . . . 7:00 p.m.
         Sun. Mar. 26 . . . . 8:00 p.m.

Franchise date: June 5, 1967

28th NHL Season

ATLANTIC DIVISION

A key member of the Philadelphia Flyers attack, Rod Brind'Amour led all Flyer scorers with 14 powerplay goals on his way to a 35 goals and 62 assists in 1993-94.

Year-by-Year Record

Season	GP	Home W	L	T	Road W	L	T	Overall W	L	T	GF	GA	Pts.	Finished		Playoff Result
1993-94	84	19	20	3	16	19	7	35	39	10	294	314	80	6th,	Atlantic Div.	Out of Playoffs
1992-93	84	23	14	5	13	23	6	36	37	11	319	319	83	5th,	Patrick Div.	Out of Playoffs
1991-92	80	22	11	7	10	26	4	32	37	11	252	273	75	6th,	Patrick Div.	Out of Playoffs
1990-91	80	18	16	6	15	21	4	33	37	10	252	267	76	5th,	Patrick Div.	Out of Playoffs
1989-90	80	17	19	4	13	20	7	30	39	11	290	297	71	6th,	Patrick Div.	Out of Playoffs
1988-89	80	22	15	3	14	21	5	36	36	8	307	285	80	4th,	Patrick Div.	Lost Conf. Championship
1987-88	80	20	14	6	18	19	3	38	33	9	292	292	85	3rd,	Patrick Div.	Lost Div. Semi-Final
1986-87	80	29	9	2	17	17	6	46	26	8	310	245	100	1st,	Patrick Div.	Lost Final
1985-86	80	33	6	1	20	17	3	53	23	4	335	241	110	1st,	Patrick Div.	Lost Div. Semi-Final
1984-85	80	32	4	4	21	16	3	53	20	7	348	241	113	1st,	Patrick Div.	Lost Final
1983-84	80	25	10	5	19	16	5	44	26	10	350	290	98	3rd,	Patrick Div.	Lost Div. Semi-Final
1982-83	80	29	8	3	20	15	5	49	23	8	326	240	106	1st,	Patrick Div.	Lost Div. Semi-Final
1981-82	80	25	10	5	13	21	6	38	31	11	325	313	87	3rd,	Patrick Div.	Lost Div. Semi-Final
1980-81	80	23	9	8	18	15	7	41	24	15	313	249	97	2nd,	Patrick Div.	Lost Quarter-Final
1979-80	80	27	5	8	21	7	12	48	12	20	327	254	116	1st,	Patrick Div.	Lost Final
1978-79	80	26	10	4	14	15	11	40	25	15	281	248	95	2nd,	Patrick Div.	Lost Quarter-Final
1977-78	80	29	6	5	16	14	10	45	20	15	296	200	105	2nd,	Patrick Div.	Lost Semi-Final
1976-77	80	33	6	1	15	10	15	48	16	16	323	213	112	1st,	Patrick Div.	Lost Semi-Final
1975-76	80	36	2	2	15	11	14	51	13	16	348	209	118	1st,	Patrick Div.	Lost Final
1974-75	**80**	**32**	**6**	**2**	**19**	**12**	**9**	**51**	**18**	**11**	**293**	**181**	**113**	**1st,**	**Patrick Div.**	**Won Stanley Cup**
1973-74	**78**	**28**	**6**	**5**	**22**	**10**	**7**	**50**	**16**	**12**	**273**	**164**	**112**	**1st,**	**West Div.**	**Won Stanley Cup**
1972-73	78	27	8	4	10	22	7	37	30	11	296	256	85	2nd,	West Div.	Lost Semi-Final
1971-72	78	19	13	7	7	25	7	26	38	14	200	236	66	5th,	West Div.	Out of Playoffs
1970-71	78	20	10	9	8	23	8	28	33	17	207	225	73	3rd,	West Div.	Lost Quarter-Final
1969-70	76	11	14	13	6	21	11	17	35	24	197	225	58	5th,	West Div.	Out of Playoffs
1968-69	76	14	16	8	6	19	13	20	35	21	174	225	61	3rd,	West Div.	Lost Quarter-Final
1967-68	74	17	13	7	14	19	4	31	32	11	173	179	73	1st,	West Div.	Lost Quarter-Final

1994-95 Player Personnel

FORWARDS

Name	HT	WT	S	Place of Birth	Date	1993-94 Club
BERANEK, Josef	6-2	185	L	Litvinov, Czechoslovakia	10/25/69	Philadelphia
BRIND'AMOUR, Rod	6-1	202	L	Ottawa, Ont.	8/9/70	Philadelphia
BROWN, David	6-5	222	R	Saskatoon, Sask.	10/12/62	Philadelphia
CROWE, Philip	6-2	220	L	Nanton, Alta.	4/14/70	Phoenix-Los Angeles
DiMAIO, Rob	5-10	190	R	Calgary, Alta.	2/19/68	Tampa Bay-Philadelphia
DINEEN, Kevin	5-11	190	R	Quebec City, Que.	10/28/63	Philadelphia
DUPRE, Yanick	6-0	189	L	Montreal, Que.	11/20/72	Hershey
EGELAND, Tracy	6-1	197	R	Lethbridge, Alta.	8/20/70	Hershey
FAUST, Andre	5-11	191	L	Joliette, Que.	10/7/69	Philadelphia-Hershey
FEDYK, Brent	6-0	195	R	Yorkton, Sask.	3/8/67	Philadelphia
HERPERGER, Chris	6-0	190	L	Esterhazy, Sask.	2/24/74	Seattle
JUHLIN, Patrik	6-0	194	L	Huddinge, Sweden	4/24/70	Vasteras
KRECHIN, Vladimir	5-11	190	L	Chelyabinsk, USSR	3/23/75	Windsor
LAMB, Mark	5-9	180	L	Ponteix, Sask.	8/3/64	Ottawa-Philadelphia
LINDROS, Eric	6-4	229	R	London, Ont.	2/28/73	Philadelphia
LIPIANSKY, Jan	6-2	187	L	Bratislava, Czech.	7/23/74	Bratislava
MacTAVISH, Craig	6-1	195	L	London, Ont.	8/15/58	Edmonton-NY Rangers
METLYUK, Denis	6-0	183	L	Togliatti, USSR	1/30/72	Hershey
NORRIS, Clayton	6-2	205	R	Edmonton, Alta.	3/8/72	Hershey
PAQUIN, Patrice	6-2	192	L	St. Jerome, Que.	6/26/74	Beauport
PODEIN, Shjon	6-2	200	L	Rochester, MN	3/5/68	Edmonton-Cape Breton
PROSPAL, Vaclav	6-2	173	L	Ceske-Budejovice, Czech.	2/17/75	Hershey
RECCHI, Mark	5-10	185	L	Kamloops, B.C.	2/1/68	Philadelphia
RENBERG, Mikael	6-1	218	L	Pitea, Sweden	5/5/72	Philadelphia
SELIVANOV, Alexander	6-1	187	L	Moscow, USSR	3/23/71	Spartak
VALLEE, Sebastien	6-4	180	L	Thetford Mines, Que.	1/2/76	Victoriaville
WINNES, Chris	6-0	201	R	Ridgefield, CT	2/12/68	Philadelphia-Hershey

DEFENSEMEN

Name	HT	WT	S	Place of Birth	Date	1993-94 Club
ANDERSON, Shawn	6-1	200	L	Montreal, Que.	2/7/68	Washington
BOULIN, Vladislav	6-4	196	L	Penza, USSR	5/18/72	Moscow D'amo
BOWEN, Jason	6-4	215	L	Port Alice, B.C.	11/9/73	Philadelphia
BRIMANIS, Aris	6-3	210	R	Cleveland, OH	3/14/72	Philadelphia-Hershey
FINLEY, Jeff	6-2	204	L	Edmonton, Alta.	4/14/67	Philadelphia
GALLEY, Garry	6-0	204	L	Montreal, Que.	4/16/63	Philadelphia
HALLER, Kevin	6-2	183	L	Trochu, Alta.	12/5/70	Montreal
HOLAN, Milos	5-11	196	L	Bilovec, Czech.	4/22/71	Philadelphia-Hershey
KORDIC, Dan	6-5	220	L	Edmonton, Alta.	4/18/71	Philadelphia-Hershey
MacDONALD, Garett	6-0	183	L	Burnaby, B.C.	1/12/71	N. Michigan
MALGUNAS, Stewart	6-0	200	L	Prince George, B.C.	4/21/70	Philadelphia
McGILL, Ryan	6-2	210	R	Prince Albert, Sask.	2/28/69	Philadelphia
SANDWITH, Terran	6-4	210	L	Edmonton, Alta.	4/17/72	Hershey
STAPLES, Jeff	6-2	207	L	Kitimat, B.C.	3/4/75	Brandon
THERIEN, Chris	6-3	230	L	Ottawa, Ont.	12/14/71	Cdn. National-Cdn. Olympic-Her
WILKIE, Bob	6-2	215	R	Calgary, Alta.	2/11/69	Philadelphia
YUSHKEVICH, Dimitri	5-11	208	R	Yaroslavl, USSR	11/19/71	Philadelphia
ZETTLER, Rob	6-3	200	L	Sept Iles, Que.	3/8/68	San Jose-Philadelphia

GOALTENDERS

Name	HT	WT	C	Place of Birth	Date	1993-94 Club
ISRAEL, Aaron	6-2	176	L	Boston, MA	6/4/73	Harvard
LaGRAND, Scott	6-0	165	L	Potsdam, NY	2/11/70	Hershey
LITTLE, Neil	6-1	175	L	Medicine Hat, Alta.	12/18/71	RPI-Hershey
ROUSSEL, Dominic	6-1	191	L	Hull, Que.	2/22/70	Philadelphia
SODERSTROM, Tommy	5-9	165	L	Stockholm, Sweden	7/17/69	Philadelphia-Hershey

1993-94 Scoring

* – rookie

Regular Season

Pos	#	Player	Team	GP	G	A	Pts	+/−	PIM	PP	SH	GW	GT	S	%
R	8	Mark Recchi	PHI	84	40	67	107	2−	46	11	0	5	0	217	18.4
C	88	Eric Lindros	PHI	65	44	53	97	16	103	13	2	9	1	197	22.3
C	17	Rod Brind'Amour	PHI	84	35	62	97	9−	85	14	1	4	0	230	15.2
L	19	* Mikael Renberg	PHI	83	38	44	82	8	36	9	0	1	0	195	19.5
D	3	Garry Galley	PHI	81	10	60	70	11−	91	5	1	0	1	186	5.4
D	29	Yves Racine	PHI	67	9	43	52	11−	48	5	1	1	1	142	6.3
L	42	Josef Beranek	PHI	80	28	21	49	2−	85	6	0	2	0	182	15.4
R	11	Kevin Dineen	PHI	71	19	23	42	9−	113	5	1	2	1	156	12.2
R	18	Brent Fedyk	PHI	72	20	18	38	14−	74	5	0	1	0	104	19.2
C	22	Mark Lamb	OTT	66	11	18	29	41−	56	4	1	1	0	105	10.5
			PHI	19	1	6	7	3−	16	0	0	1	0	19	5.3
			TOTAL	85	12	24	36	44−	72	4	1	2	0	124	9.7
D	2	Dimitri Yushkevich	PHI	75	5	25	30	8−	86	1	0	2	0	136	3.7
C	20	Rob Dimaio	T.B.	39	8	7	15	5−	40	2	0	1	0	51	15.7
			PHI	14	3	5	8	1	6	0	0	1	0	30	10.0
			TOTAL	53	11	12	23	4−	46	2	0	2	0	81	13.6
C	14	Dave Tippett	PHI	73	4	11	15	20−	38	0	2	1	0	45	8.9
C	36	* Andre Faust	PHI	37	8	5	13	1−	10	0	0	1	0	33	24.2
D	25	Jeff Finley	PHI	55	1	8	9	16	24	0	0	0	0	43	2.3
R	15	Allan Conroy	PHI	62	4	3	7	12−	65	0	1	0	0	40	10.0
D	26	Rob Zettler	S.J.	42	0	3	3	7−	65	0	0	0	0	28	.0
			PHI	33	0	4	4	19−	69	0	0	0	0	27	.0
			TOTAL	75	0	7	7	26−	134	0	0	0	0	55	.0
D	28	* Jason Bowen	PHI	56	1	5	6	12	87	0	0	1	0	50	2.0
R	21	Dave Brown	PHI	71	1	4	5	12−	137	0	0	0	0	16	6.3
D	24	* Bob Wilkie	PHI	10	1	3	4	2−	8	0	0	0	0	10	10.0
D	27	Ryan McGill	PHI	50	1	3	4	5−	112	0	0	0	0	53	1.9
D	23	* Stewart Malgunas	PHI	67	1	3	4	2	86	0	0	0	0	54	1.9
D	41	* Milos Holan	PHI	8	1	1	2	4−	4	1	0	0	0	26	3.8
R	32	Chris Winnes	PHI	4	0	2	2	1	0	0	0	0	0	4	.0
D	5	Rob Ramage	MTL	6	0	1	1	1−	2	0	0	0	0	5	.0
			PHI	15	0	1	1	11−	14	0	0	0	0	18	.0
			TOTAL	21	0	2	2	12−	16	0	0	0	0	23	.0
C	10	* Todd Hlushko	PHI	2	1	0	1	1	0	0	0	0	0	2	50.0
G	33	Dominic Roussel	PHI	60	0	1	1	0	4	0	0	0	0	0	.0
D	40	* Aris Brimanis	PHI	1	0	0	0	0	0	0	0	0	0	1	.0
L	43	Claude Vilgrain	PHI	2	0	0	0	1−	0	0	0	0	0	0	.0
D	6	Dan Kordic	PHI	4	0	0	0	0	5	0	0	0	0	0	.0
G	35	* Frederic Chabot	MTL	1	0	0	0	0	0	0	0	0	0	0	.0
			PHI	4	0	0	0	0	0	0	0	0	0	0	.0
			TOTAL	5	0	0	0	0	0	0	0	0	0	0	.0
G	30	Tommy Soderstrom	PHI	34	0	0	0	0	0	0	0	0	0	0	.0

Goaltending

No.	Goaltender	GPI	Mins	Avg	W	L	T	EN	SO	GA	SA	S%
33	Dominic Roussel	60	3285	3.34	29	20	5	3	1	183	1762	.896
30	Tommy Soderstrom	34	1736	4.01	6	18	4	7	2	116	851	.864
35	* Frederic Chabot	4	70	4.29	0	1	1	0	0	5	40	.875
	Totals	**84**	**5102**	**3.69**	**35**	**39**	**10**	**10**	**3**	**314**	**2663**	**.882**

General Managers' History

Bud Poile, 1967-68 to 1968-69; Bud Poile and Keith Allen, 1969-70; Keith Allen, 1970-71 to 1982-83; Bob McCammon, 1983-84; Bob Clarke, 1984-85 to 1989-90; Russ Farwell, 1990-91 to 1993-94; Bob Clarke, 1994-95.

Coaching History

Keith Allen, 1967-68 to 1968-69; Vic Stasiuk, 1969-70 to 1970-71; Fred Shero, 1971-72 to 1977-78; Bob McCammon and Pat Quinn, 1978-79; Pat Quinn, 1979-80 to 1980-81; Pat Quinn and Bob McCammon, 1981-82; Bob McCammon, 1982-83 to 1983-84; Mike Keenan, 1984-85 to 1987-88; Paul Holmgren, 1988-89 to 1990-91; Paul Holmgren and Bill Dineen, 1991-92; Bill Dineen, 1992-93; Terry Simpson, 1993-94; Terry Murray, 1994-95.

Captains' History

Lou Angotti, 1967-68; Ed Van Impe, 1968-69 to 1971-72; Ed Van Impe and Bobby Clarke, 1972-73; Bobby Clarke, 1973-74 to 1978-79; Mel Bridgman, 1979-80, 1980-81; Bill Barber, 1981-82; Bill Barber and Bobby Clarke, 1982-83; Bobby Clarke, 1983-84; Dave Poulin, 1984-85 to 1988-89; Dave Poulin and Ron Sutter, 1989-90; Ron Sutter, 1990-91; Rick Tocchet, 1991-92; no captain, 1992-93; Kevin Dineen, 1993-94.

Retired Numbers

1	Bernie Parent	1967-1971
		and 1973-1979
4	Barry Ashbee	1970-1974
7	Bill Barber	1972-1985
16	Bobby Clarke	1969-1984

Former Flyer captain and superstar center Bob Clarke returns to Philadelphia in the dual role of club president and general manager for 1994-95.

Club Records

Team

(Figures in brackets for season records are games played)

Most Points	118	1975-76 (80)
Most Wins	53	1984-85 (80)
		1985-86 (80)
Most Ties	*24	1969-70 (76)
Most Losses	39	1993-94 (84)
Most Goals	350	1983-84 (80)
Most Goals Against........	319	1992-93 (84)
Fewest Points.............	58	1969-70 (76)
Fewest Wins..............	17	1969-70 (76)
Fewest Ties	4	1985-86 (80)
Fewest Losses	12	1979-80 (80)
Fewest Goals	173	1967-68 (74)
Fewest Goals Against	164	1973-74 (78)

Longest Winning Streak

Over-all	13	Oct. 19-Nov. 17/85
Home.....................	*20	Jan. 4- Apr. 3/76
Away	8	Dec. 22/82- Jan. 16/83

Longest Undefeated Streak

Over-all	*35	Oct. 14/79- Jan. 6/80 (25 wins, 10 ties)
Home....................	26	Oct. 11/79- Feb. 3/80 (19 wins, 7 ties)
Away	16	Oct. 20/79- Jan. 6/80 (11 wins, 5 ties)

Longest Losing Streak

Over-all	6	Mar. 25- Apr. 4/70; Dec. 5- Dec. 17/92; Jan. 25- Feb. 5/94
Home....................	5	Jan. 30- Feb. 15/69
Away	8	Oct. 25- Nov. 26/72

Longest Winless Streak

Over-all	11	Nov. 21- Dec. 14/69 (9 losses, 2 ties) Dec. 10/70- Jan. 3/71 (9 losses, 2 ties)
Home.....................	8	Dec. 19/68- Jan. 18/69 (4 losses, 4 ties)
Away	19	Oct. 23/71- Jan. 27/72 (15 losses, 4 ties)
Most Shutouts, Season	13	1974-75 (80)
Most PIM, Season........	2,621	1980-81 (80)
Most Goals, Game	13	Mar. 22/84 (Pit. 4 at Phi. 13) Oct. 18/84 (Van. 2 at Phil. 13)

Individual

Most Seasons	15	Bobby Clarke
Most Games	1,144	Bobby Clarke
Most Goals, Career.........	420	Bill Barber
Most Assists, Career........	852	Bobby Clarke
Most Points, Career........	1,210	Bobby Clarke (358 goals, 852 assists)
Most PIM, Career	1,683	Rick Tocchet
Most Shutouts, Career.......	50	Bernie Parent

Longest Consecutive

Game Streak..............	287	Rick MacLeish (Oct. 6/72-Feb. 5/76)
Most Goals, Season	61	Reggie Leach (1975-76)
Most Assists, Season	89	Bobby Clarke (1974-75; 1975-76)
Most Points, Season........	123	Mark Recchi (1992-93) (53 goals, 70 assists)
Most PIM, Season	*472	Dave Schultz (1974-75)

Most Points, Defenseman,

Season....................	82	Mark Howe (1985-86) (24 goals, 58 assists)

Most Points, Center,

Season	119	Bobby Clarke (1975-76) (30 goals, 89 assists)

Most Points, Right Wing,

Season	123	Mark Recchi (1992-93) (53 goals, 70 assists)

Most Points, Left Wing,

Season	112	Bill Barber (1975-76) (50 goals, 62 assists)

Most Points, Rookie,

Season	82	Mikael Renberg (1983-84) (38 goals, 44 assists)
Most Shutouts, Season	12	Bernie Parent (1973-74; 1974-75)
Most Goals, Game	4	Rick MacLeish (Feb. 13/73; Mar. 4/73) Tom Bladon (Dec. 11/77) Tim Kerr (Oct. 25/84, Jan. 17/85, Feb. 9/85, Nov. 20/86) Brian Propp (Dec. 2/86) Rick Tocchet (Feb. 27/88; Jan. 25/90) Kevin Dineen (Oct. 31/93)
Most Assists, Game	5	Bobby Clarke (Apr. 1/76) Eric Lindros (Mar. 10/94)
Most Points, Game............	8	Tom Bladon (Dec. 11/77)

* NHL Record.

All-time Record vs. Other Clubs

Regular Season

				At Home						On Road						Total			
	GP	W	L	T	GF	GA	PTS	GP	W	L	T	GF	GA	PTS	GP	W	L	T	GF	GA	PTS
Anaheim	1	0	1	0	2	3	0	1	0	1	0	3	6	0	2	0	2	0	5	9	0
Boston	53	22	25	6	178	164	50	56	13	36	7	165	233	33	109	35	61	13	343	397	83
Buffalo	47	28	11	8	175	128	64	44	17	21	6	136	155	40	91	45	32	14	311	283	104
Calgary	44	30	12	2	180	120	62	45	13	23	9	148	188	35	89	43	35	11	328	308	97
Chicago	54	28	15	11	178	145	67	53	11	24	18	150	191	40	107	39	39	29	328	336	107
Dallas	59	40	9	10	235	136	90	59	22	24	13	196	197	57	118	62	33	23	431	333	147
Detroit	52	29	12	11	210	156	69	51	18	24	9	168	184	45	103	47	36	20	378	340	114
Edmonton	23	16	6	1	102	67	33	22	5	13	4	63	83	14	45	21	19	5	165	150	47
Florida	3	2	0	1	11	9	5	2	1	1	0	7	8	2	5	3	1	1	18	17	7
Hartford	24	16	7	1	101	71	33	24	11	9	4	103	98	26	48	27	16	5	204	169	59
Los Angeles	56	34	15	7	217	145	75	58	34	17	7	204	171	75	114	68	32	14	421	316	150
Montreal	53	19	21	13	154	162	51	54	14	29	11	159	209	39	107	33	50	24	313	371	90
New Jersey	59	41	11	7	255	143	89	58	25	29	4	224	216	54	117	66	40	11	479	359	143
NY Islanders	70	42	20	8	271	215	92	72	21	40	11	211	290	53	142	63	60	19	482	505	145
NY Rangers	83	41	29	13	291	243	95	85	26	39	20	246	285	72	168	67	68	33	537	528	167
Ottawa	4	4	0	0	27	6	8	3	1	1	1	10	8	3	7	5	1	1	37	14	11
Pittsburgh	83	61	15	7	360	214	129	83	31	35	17	268	286	79	166	92	50	24	628	500	208
Quebec	25	20	3	2	103	64	42	24	9	8	7	89	88	25	49	29	11	9	192	152	67
St. Louis	59	40	10	9	237	135	89	59	29	23	7	183	173	65	118	69	33	16	420	308	154
San Jose	3	2	1	0	12	7	4	4	3	1	0	14	9	6	7	5	2	0	26	16	10
Tampa Bay	3	2	0	1	14	7	5	4	2	2	0	10	12	4	7	4	2	1	24	19	9
Toronto	52	33	11	8	211	133	74	52	20	19	13	177	180	53	104	53	30	21	388	303	127
Vancouver	45	30	14	1	202	135	61	45	24	10	11	174	131	59	90	54	24	12	376	266	120
Washington	61	35	22	4	233	177	74	58	26	22	10	210	208	62	119	61	44	14	443	385	136
Winnipeg	23	17	6	0	107	69	34	22	11	9	2	78	72	24	45	28	15	2	185	141	58
Defunct Clubs	34	24	4	6	137	67	54	35	13	14	8	102	89	34	69	37	18	14	239	156	88
Totals	**1073**	**656**	**280**	**137**	**4203**	**2911**	**1449**	**1073**	**400**	**474**	**199**	**3498**	**3770**	**999**	**2146**	**1056**	**754**	**336**	**7701**	**6681**	**2448**

Calgary totals include Atlanta, 1972-73 to 1979-80. Dallas totals include Minnesota, 1967-68 to 1992-93.
New Jersey totals include Kansas City, 1974-75 to 1975-76, and Colorado, 1976-77 to 1981-82.

Playoffs

	Series	W	L	GP	W	L	T	GF	GA	Last Mtg.	Round	Result
Boston	4	2	2	20	9	11	0	57	60	1978	QF	L 1-4
Buffalo	2	2	0	11	8	3	0	35	23	1978	QF	W 4-1
Calgary	2	1	1	11	7	4	0	43	28	1981	QF	L 3-4
Chicago	1	0	1	4	0	4	0	8	20	1971	QF	L 0-4
Dallas	2	2	0	11	8	3	0	41	26	1980	SF	W 4-1
Edmonton	3	1	2	15	7	8	0	44	49	1987	F	L 3-4
Montreal	4	1	3	21	6	15	0	52	72	1989	CF	L 2-4
New Jersey	1	1	0	2	2	0	0	6	3	1978	PR	W 2-0
NY Islanders	4	3	1	25	14	11	0	83	69	1987	DF	W 4-3
NY Rangers	8	4	4	38	19	19	0	119	130	1987	DSF	W 4-2
Pittsburgh	1	1	0	7	4	3	0	31	24	1989	DF	W 4-3
Quebec	2	2	0	11	7	4	0	39	29	1985	CF	W 4-2
St. Louis	2	1	1	11	3	8	0	20	34	1969	QF	L 0-4
Toronto	3	3	0	17	12	5	0	67	47	1977	QF	W 4-2
Vancouver	1	1	0	3	2	1	0	15	9	1979	PR	W 2-1
Washington	3	1	2	16	7	9	0	55	65	1989	DSF	W 4-2
Totals	**43**	**25**	**18**	**223**	**116**	**107**	**0**	**715**	**688**			

Abbreviations: Round: F – Final;
CF – conference final; **CQF** – conference quarter-final;
CSF – conference semi-final; **DF** – division final;
DSF – division semi-final; **SF** – semi-final;
QF – quarter-final; **PR** – preliminary round.

1993-94 Results

Oct.	5		Pittsburgh	4-3	11		Ottawa	4-1
	9	at	Hartford	5-2	13		Boston	6-2
	10		Toronto	4-5	14	at	NY Rangers	2-5
	12		Buffalo	5-3	16		Los Angeles	5-2
	15	at	Washington	3-0	19		St. Louis	8-3
	16		NY Rangers	4-3	25	at	Quebec	4-6
	22		NY Islanders	4-3	29		Washington	2-4
	23		Winnipeg	6-9	30	at	Montreal	4-5
	26	at	Quebec	4-2	Feb. 2		Washington	2-5
	27	at	Ottawa	5-2	3		San Jose	2-3
	30	at	New Jersey	3-5	5	at	Boston	0-4
	31	at	Chicago	9-6	8	at	Ottawa	3-3
Nov.	2	at	Florida	4-3	10		Florida	4-3
	4		Quebec	4-1	11	at	Detroit	3-6
	6	at	Toronto	3-5	13		Pittsburgh	0-3
	7		Vancouver	2-5	15	at	San Jose	6-4
	10	at	Buffalo	5-3	16	at	Anaheim	3-6
	11		New Jersey	3-5	18	at	Los Angeles	4-3
	13		Buffalo	2-7	21		Montreal	8-7
	16	at	Pittsburgh	5-11	24		NY Islanders	5-4
	18		Hartford	6-3	25	at	NY Islanders	0-2
	20	at	Boston	5-5	28	at	NY Rangers	1-4
	21		NY Islanders	4-5	Mar. 4	at	Washington	3-3
	24		Montreal	9-2	6	at	Tampa Bay	3-1
	26		Tampa Bay	3-0	8		Dallas	3-4
	27	at	Tampa Bay	4-3	10		Ottawa	8-2
Dec.	1	at	Edmonton	1-3	12	at	Montreal	4-4
	2	at	Vancouver	6-3	13		Tampa Bay	5-5
	4	at	Calgary	0-6	19		Hartford	3-5
	9		Washington	2-4	20	at	Florida	3-5
	11	at	NY Islanders	2-5	22	at	St. Louis	6-3
	12		Edmonton	1-2	24		Florida	4-3
	16		Quebec	3-2	26	at	New Jersey	2-7
	18		Chicago	3-2	27		Anaheim	2-3
	19	at	New Jersey	2-4	29		NY Rangers	3-4
	21		Washington	1-4	31		Calgary	1-4
	23		Detroit	1-3	Apr. 2	at	Hartford	6-5
	27	at	Buffalo	2-0	4	at	Winnipeg	2-2
	28	at	Pittsburgh	4-4	7		Florida	3-3
	31	at	Boston	4-3	10		Boston	3-4
Jan.	6	at	Dallas	0-8	12		New Jersey	4-2
	8	at	Tampa Bay	2-4	14	at	NY Rangers	2-2

Entry Draft
Selections 1994-80

1994
Pick
62	Artem Anisimov
88	Adam Magarrell
101	Sebastien Vallee
140	Alexander Selivanov
166	Colin Forbes
192	Derek Diener
202	Raymond Giroux
218	Johan Hedberg
244	Andre Payette
270	Jan Lipiansky

1993
Pick
36	Janne Niinimaa
71	Vaclav Prospal
77	Milos Holan
114	Vladimir Krechin
140	Mike Crowley
166	Aaron Israel
192	Paul Healey
218	Tripp Tracy
226	E.J. Bradley
244	Jeffrey Staples
270	Kenneth Hemmenway

1992
Pick
7	Ryan Sittler
15	Jason Bowen
31	Denis Metlyuk
103	Vladislav Buljin
127	Roman Zolotov
151	Kirk Daubenspeck
175	Claude Jutras Jr.
199	Jonas Hakansson
223	Chris Herperger
247	Patrice Paquin

1991
Pick
6	Peter Forsberg
50	Yanick Dupre
86	Aris Brimanis
94	Yanick Degrace
116	Clayton Norris
122	Dmitri Yushkevich
138	Andrei Lomakin
182	James Bode
204	Josh Bartell
226	Neil Little
248	John Porco

1990
Pick
4	Mike Ricci
25	Chris Simon
40	Mikael Renberg
42	Terran Sandwith
44	Kimbi Daniels
46	Bill Armstrong
47	Chris Therien
52	Al Kinisky
88	Dan Kordic
109	Viacheslav Butsayev
151	Patrik Englund
172	Toni Porkka
193	Greg Hanson
214	Tommy Soderstrom
235	William Lund

1989
Pick
33	Greg Johnson
34	Patrik Juhlin
72	Reid Simpson
117	Niklas Eriksson
138	John Callahan Jr.
159	Sverre Sears
180	Glen Wisser
201	Al Kummu
222	Matt Brait
243	James Pollio

1988
Pick
14	Claude Boivin
35	Pat Murray
56	Craig Fisher
63	Dominic Roussel
77	Scott Lagrand
98	Edward O'Brien
119	Gordie Frantti
140	Jamie Cooke
161	Johan Salle
182	Brian Arthur
203	Jeff Dandreta
224	Scott Billey
245	Drahomir Kadlec

1987
Pick
20	Darren Rumble
30	Jeff Harding
62	Martin Hostak
83	Tomaz Eriksson
104	Bill Gall
125	Tony Link
146	Mark Strapon
167	Darryl Ingham
188	Bruce McDonald
209	Steve Morrow
230	Darius Rusnak
251	Dale Roehl

1986
Pick
20	Kerry Huffman
23	Jukka Seppo
28	Kent Hawley
83	Mark Bar
125	Steve Scheifele
146	Sami Wahlsten
167	Murray Baron
188	Blaine Rude
209	Shawn Sabol
230	Brett Lawrence
251	Daniel Stephano

1985
Pick
21	Glen Seabrooke
42	Bruce Rendall
48	Darryl Gilmour
63	Shane Whelan
84	Paul Marshall
105	Daril Holmes
126	Ken Alexander
147	Tony Horacek
168	Mike Cusack
189	Gordon Murphy
231	Rod Williams
252	Paul Maurice

1984
Pick
22	Greg Smyth
27	Scott Mellanby
37	Jeff Chychrun
43	Dave McLay
47	John Stevens
79	Dave Hanson
100	Brian Dobbin
121	John Dzikowski
142	Tom Allen
163	Luke Vitale
184	Bill Powers
204	Daryn Fersovitch
245	Juraj Bakos

1983
Pick
41	Peter Zezel
44	Derrick Smith
81	Alan Bourbeau
101	Jerome Carrier
121	Rick Tocchet
141	Bobby Mormina
161	Per-Erik Eklund
181	Rob Nichols
201	William McCormick
221	Brian Jopling
241	Harold Duvall

1982
Pick
4	Ron Sutter
46	Miroslav Dvorak
47	Bill Campbell
77	Mikael Hjalm
98	Todd Bergen
119	Ron Hextall
140	Dave Brown
161	Alain Lavigne
182	Magnus Roupe
203	Tom Allen
224	Rick Gal
245	Mark Vichorek

1981
Pick
16	Steve Smith
37	Rich Costello
47	Barry Tabobondung
58	Ken Strong
5	David Michayluk
79	Ken Latta
100	Justin Hanley
121	Andre Villeneuve
137	Vladimir Svitek
142	Gil Hudon
163	Steve Taylor
184	Len Hachborn
205	Steve Tsujiura

1980
Pick
21	Mike Stothers
42	Jay Fraser
63	Paul Mercier
84	Taras Zytynsky
105	Daniel Held
126	Brian Tutt
147	Ross Fitzpatrick
168	Mark Botell
189	Peter Dineen
195	Bob O'Brien
210	Andy Brickley

Club Directory

The Spectrum
3601 South Broad St.
Philadelphia, PA 19148
Phone **215/465-4500**
PR FAX 215/389-9403
Pres. & GM FAX 215/389-9409
Capacity: 17,380

Board of Directors
Ed Snider, Jay Snider, Joe Scott, Keith Allen, Fred Shabel, Sylvan Tobin, Carl Hirsh, Sanford Lipstein, Ron Ryan

Majority Ownership	Ed Snider and family
Limited Partners	Sylvan and Fran Tobin
President and General Manager	Bob Clarke
Chairman of the Board, Emeritus	Joe Scott
Chief Operating Officer	Ron Ryan
Executive Vice-President	Keith Allen
Head Coach	Terry Murray
Assistant General Manager	John Blackwell
Assistant Coaches	Keith Acton, Tom Webster
Director of Pro Scouting	Bill Barber
Chief Scout	Jerry Melnyk
Scouts	Bill Dineen, Inge Hammarstrom, Simon Nolet, Vaclav Slansky, Evgeny Zimin
Head Trainer	Dave Settlemyre
Trainers	Jim Evers, Harry Bricker, Derek Settlemyre
Medical Trainer	John Worley
Medical Staff	Arthur Bartolozzi, M.D., Gary Dorshimer, M.D., Jeff Hartzell, M.D.
Director of Team Services	Joe Kadlec
Computer Analyst	David Gelberg
Executive VP, Sales/Marketing	Dick Deleguardia
Vice-President, Finance	Dan Clemmens
Vice-President, Public Relations	Mark Piazza
Vice-President, Sales	Jack Betson
Director of Finance	Jeff Niessen
Controller	Michelle Hay
Director of Marketing	Eileen Smith
Manager, Season Ticket Sales	Steve Schiff
Manager, Publications	Jill Vogel
Manager, Media Relations	Zack Hill
Assistant Director of Public Relations	Joe Klueg
Public Relations Assistants	Jennifer Corey, Linda Held
Director of Community Relations	Linda Panasci
Director of Youth Hockey	Greg Scott
Ticket Manager	Cecilia Baker
Ticket Office Assistant	Wade Clarke
Sales/Marketing Assistant	Helen Hubbard
Flyers Sales Staff	Dave Resnick, Ivan Shlichtman, Joe Watson, Carolyn Wollman
Executive Assistants	Suzanne Carlin, Kim Clayton, Dena Felici, Peggy Kwapinski, Dianna Taylor
Receptionist	Aggie Preston
Television Announcers	Gene Hart, Gary Dornhoefer
Radio Announcers	Jim Jackson, Steve Coates
Broadcast Consultant	Mike Finocchiaro
Public Address Announcer	Lou Nolan
Television Outlets	WPHL-TV (Ch. 17), PRISM, SportsChannel Philadelphia
Radio Station (Flagship)	WIP-AM (610 AM)

Coach

MURRAY, TERRY RODNEY
Coach, Philadelphia Flyers. Born in Shawville, Que., July 20, 1950.

Terry Murray was named as the tenth coach of the Philadelphia Flyers on June 23, 1994. He is the second former Flyer player to return to the team as head coach, joining Paul Holmgren, who coached the team from 1988-91. Prior to joining the Flyers, Murray served as the head coach of the Washington Capitals for five seasons from January 20, 1990 to January 27, 1994. As coach of the Capitals, Murray's team posted an overall record of 163-134-28 for a .545 winning percentage. After leaving the Capitals, Murray served as head coach of the Cincinnati Cyclones, the Florida Panthers' IHL affiliate, leading the team to a 17-7-4 record in 28 games. The Shawville, Quebec native also spent six seasons as the head coach of the AHL's Baltimore Skipjacks.

Murray was selected 88th overall by California in the 1970 Amateur Draft. He enjoyed a successful playing career in both the NHL and American Hockey League. He led the Maine Mariners to two Calder Cup championships in 1977-78 and 1978-79, and was awarded the AHL's Eddie Shore Plaque as the outstanding defenseman in both seasons. He was an AHL First Team All-Star in three seasons, 1975-76, 1977-78 and 1978-79. Terry played in 302 NHL games over 8 seasons, concluding his career with the Capitals in 1981-82. He was the first ex-Capital to coach the club.

Coaching Record

| Season | Team | | Regular Season | | | | | Playoffs | | | |
		Games	W	L	T	%	Games	W	L	%
1988-89	Baltimore (AHL)	80	30	46	4	.400	....	....	....	....
1989-90	Baltimore (AHL)	44	26	17	1	.603	....	....	....	....
1989-90	Washington (NHL)	34	18	14	2	.559	15	8	7	.533
1990-91	Washington (NHL)	80	37	36	7	.506	11	5	6	.455
1991-92	Washington (NHL)	80	45	27	8	.613	7	3	4	.429
1992-93	Washington (NHL)	84	43	34	7	.554	6	2	4	.333
1993-94	Washington (NHL)	47	20	23	4	.468	....	....	....	....
	Cincinnati (IHL)	28	17	7	4	.679	11	6	5	.545
	NHL Totals	**325**	**163**	**134**	**28**	**.545**	**39**	**18**	**21**	**.462**

General Manager

CLARKE, ROBERT EARLE (BOB)
General Manager, Philadelphia Flyers. Born in Flin Flon, Man., August 13, 1949.

Bob Clarke was named as the president and general manager of the Philadelphia Flyers on June 15, 1994. Prior to joining the Flyers' family, Clarke served as vice president and general manager of the Florida Panthers. In 1993-94, their first season in the NHL, the Panthers established NHL records for wins (33) and points (83) by an expansion franchise. Clarke also served as the vice president and general manager of the Minnesota North Stars from 1990-92, guiding the team to the Stanley Cup finals in 1990-91.

Clarke's appointment marks the second time he has served as the Flyers' general manager. The Flin Flon native was the Flyers' vice president and general manager from 1984-90, when the team posted a 256-177-47 record. During his six years as general manager, the Flyers won three divisional titles, two conference championships, reached the Stanley Cup semifinals three times and the Finals twice.

As a player, the former Philadelphia captain led his club to Stanley Cup championships in 1974 and 1975 and captured numerous individual awards, including the Hart Trophy as the League's most valuable player in 1973, 1975 and 1976. The four-time All-Star also received the Masterton Memorial Trophy (perseverance and dedication) in 1972 and the Frank J. Selke Trophy (top defensive forward) in 1983. He appeared in nine All-Star Games and was elected to the Hockey Hall of Fame in 1987. He was awarded the Lester Patrick Trophy in 1979-80 in recognition of his contribution to hockey in the United States. Clarke appeared in 1,144 regular-season games, recording 358 goals and 852 assists for 1,210 points. He also added 119 points in 136 playoff games.

Pittsburgh Penguins

1993-94 Results: 44W-27L-13T 101PTS. First, Northeast Division

Schedule

Oct.	Sat.	1	Chicago	Sat.	7	Philadelphia
	Mon.	3	at NY Rangers			(in San Antonio)
	Wed.	5	Buffalo	Mon.	9	at New Jersey
	Fri.	7	at Washington			(in Denver)
	Tues.	11	at Quebec	Wed.	11	at NY Rangers
	Wed.	12	Washington	Fri.	13	Hartford
	Sat.	15	Montreal	Sat.	14	NY Islanders
	Tues.	18	at Tampa Bay	Wed.	18	at Boston
	Fri.	21	at Detroit	Mon.	23	Philadelphia
	Sat.	22	Los Angeles	Fri.	27	Vancouver
	Tues.	25	Dallas	Sat.	28	Toronto
	Wed.	26	at Montreal	Feb. Thur.	2	at Winnipeg
	Sat.	29	at Montreal	Sat.	4	Tampa Bay
Nov.	Tues.	1	Ottawa	Tues.	7	Florida
	Thur.	3	at Boston	Thur.	9	Quebec
	Sat.	5	Hartford	Sat.	11	Montreal
	Tues.	8	New Jersey	Sun.	12	at Florida
	Thur.	10	at Dallas	Tues.	14	Edmonton
	Sat.	12	at St. Louis	Thur.	16	at Chicago
	Wed.	16	at Ottawa	Sat.	18	at Hartford*
	Thur.	17	Ottawa	Sun.	19	Hartford*
	Sat.	19	at Philadelphia	Tues.	21	at New Jersey
	Mon.	21	at Boston	Fri.	24	St. Louis
	Wed.	23	NY Rangers	Sat.	25	at NY Islanders
	Fri.	25	at Washington	Tues.	28	at Vancouver
	Sat.	26	San Jose	Mar. Thur.	2	at Calgary
	Tues.	29	Anaheim	Fri.	3	at Edmonton
Dec.	Thur.	1	Washington	Mon.	6	at Quebec
	Sat.	3	Boston	Thur.	9	Quebec
	Tues.	6	NY Rangers	Sat.	11	Calgary*
	Wed.	7	at Buffalo	Mon.	13	Winnipeg
	Sat.	10	Buffalo	Thur.	16	Tampa Bay
	Tues.	13	at Anaheim	Sat.	18	at Ottawa*
	Thur.	15	at Los Angeles	Sun.	19	at Quebec*
	Sat.	17	at San Jose	Tues.	21	at Buffalo
	Tues.	20	Detroit	Fri.	24	Montreal
	Thur.	22	at Florida	Sun.	26	at Philadelphia
	Fri.	23	at Tampa Bay	Tues.	28	Philadelphia
	Wed.	28	at Hartford	Thur.	30	Boston
	Thur.	29	Buffalo	Apr. Sun.	2	at Toronto*
	Sat.	31	NY Islanders	Tues.	4	at NY Islanders
Jan.	Wed.	4	at New Jersey	Wed.	5	New Jersey
	Thur.	5	Florida	Sat.	8	at Montreal

* Denotes afternoon game.

Home Starting Times:

Night Games . . . . 7:30 p.m.
Matinees . . . . 1:30 p.m.
Except   Sat. Dec. 31 . . . . 6:30 p.m.

Franchise date: June 5, 1967

**NORTHEAST
DIVISION**

**28th
NHL
Season**

Year-by-Year Record

		Home			Road			Overall						
Season	GP	W	L	T	W	L	T	W	L	T	GF	GA	Pts.	Finished	Playoff Result
1993-94	84	25	9	8	19	18	5	44	27	13	299	285	101	1st, Northeast Div.	Lost Conf. Quarter-Final
1992-93	84	32	6	4	24	15	3	56	21	7	367	268	119	1st, Patrick Div.	Lost Div. Final
1991-92	**80**	**21**	**13**	**6**	**18**	**19**	**3**	**39**	**32**	**9**	**343**	**308**	**87**	**3rd, Patrick Div.**	**Won Stanley Cup**
1990-91	**80**	**25**	**12**	**3**	**16**	**21**	**3**	**41**	**33**	**6**	**342**	**305**	**88**	**1st, Patrick Div.**	**Won Stanley Cup**
1989-90	80	22	15	3	10	25	5	32	40	8	318	359	72	5th, Patrick Div.	Out of Playoffs
1988-89	80	24	13	3	16	20	4	40	33	7	347	349	87	2nd, Patrick Div.	Lost Div. Final
1987-88	80	22	12	6	14	23	3	36	35	9	319	316	81	6th, Patrick Div.	Out of Playoffs
1986-87	80	19	15	6	11	23	6	30	38	12	297	290	72	5th, Patrick Div.	Out of Playoffs
1985-86	80	20	15	5	14	23	3	34	38	8	313	305	76	5th, Patrick Div.	Out of Playoffs
1984-85	80	17	20	3	7	31	2	24	51	5	276	385	53	6th, Patrick Div.	Out of Playoffs
1983-84	80	7	29	4	9	29	2	16	58	6	254	390	38	6th, Patrick Div.	Out of Playoffs
1982-83	80	14	22	4	4	31	5	18	53	9	257	394	45	6th, Patrick Div.	Out of Playoffs
1981-82	80	21	11	8	10	25	5	31	36	13	310	337	75	4th, Patrick Div.	Lost Div. Semi-Final
1980-81	80	21	16	3	9	21	10	30	37	13	302	345	73	3rd, Norris Div.	Lost Prelim. Round
1979-80	80	20	13	7	10	24	6	30	37	13	251	303	73	3rd, Norris Div.	Lost Prelim. Round
1978-79	80	23	12	5	13	19	8	36	31	13	281	279	85	2nd, Norris Div.	Lost Quarter-Final
1977-78	80	16	15	9	9	22	9	25	37	18	254	321	68	4th, Norris Div.	Out of Playoffs
1976-77	80	22	12	6	12	21	7	34	33	13	240	252	81	3rd, Norris Div.	Lost Prelim. Round
1975-76	80	23	11	6	12	22	6	35	33	12	339	303	82	3rd, Norris Div.	Lost Prelim. Round
1974-75	80	25	5	10	12	23	5	37	28	15	326	289	89	3rd, Norris Div.	Lost Quarter-Final
1973-74	78	15	18	6	13	23	3	28	41	9	242	273	65	5th, West Div.	Out of Playoffs
1972-73	78	24	11	4	8	26	5	32	37	9	257	265	73	5th, West Div.	Out of Playoffs
1971-72	78	18	15	6	8	23	8	26	38	14	220	258	66	4th, West Div.	Lost Quarter-Final
1970-71	78	18	12	9	3	25	11	21	37	20	221	240	62	6th, West Div.	Out of Playoffs
1969-70	76	17	13	8	9	25	4	26	38	12	182	238	64	2nd, West Div.	Lost Semi-Final
1968-69	76	12	20	6	8	25	5	20	45	11	189	252	51	5th, West Div.	Out of Playoffs
1967-68	74	15	12	10	12	22	3	27	34	13	195	216	67	5th, West Div.	Out of Playoffs

Ron Francis, who reached the 1,000-point plateau on October 23, 1993, finished second in team scoring for the Penguins in 1993-94, amassing 93 points in 82 games.

1994-95 Player Personnel

FORWARDS	HT	WT	S	Place of Birth	Date	1993-94 Club
BARRIE, Len	6-0	200	L	Kimberley, B.C.	6/4/69	Florida-Cincinnati
BLACK, Jamie	6-0	185	L	Calgary, Alta.	4/4/72	Cleveland
BROWN, Doug	5-10	185	R	Southborough, MA	6/12/64	Pittsburgh
CHRISTIAN, Jeff	6-1	195	L	Burlington, Ont.	7/30/70	Albany
CULLEN, John	5-10	180	R	Puslinch, Ont.	8/2/64	Toronto
DUBERMAN, Justin	6-1	185	R	New Haven, CT	3/23/70	Pittsburgh-Cleveland
DZIEDZIC, Joe	6-3	200	L	Minneapolis, MN	12/18/71	U. Minnesota
FARRELL, Brian	5-11	190	L	West Hartford, CT	4/16/72	Harvard
FITZGERALD, Rusty	6-1	190	L	Minneapolis, MN	10/4/72	Minn.-Duluth
FRANCIS, Ron	6-2	200	L	Sault Ste. Marie, Ont.	3/1/63	Pittsburgh
HAWKINS, Todd	6-1	195	R	Kingston, Ont.	8/2/66	Cleveland
JAGR, Jaromir	6-2	208	L	Kladno, Czech.	2/15/72	Pittsburgh
KARABIN, Ladislav	6-1	189	L	Spisska Nova Ves, Czech.	2/16/70	Pittsburgh-Cleveland
LEMIEUX, Mario	6-4	210	R	Montreal, Que.	10/5/65	Pittsburgh
McEACHERN, Shawn	5-11	195	L	Waltham, MA	2/28/69	Los Angeles-Pittsburgh
McKENZIE, Jim	6-3	205	L	Gull Lake, Sask.	11/3/69	Hartford-Dallas-Pittsburgh
MULLEN, Joe	5-9	180	R	New York, NY	2/26/57	Pittsburgh
NASLUND, Markus	6-0	186	L	Ornskoldsvik, Sweden	7/30/73	Pittsburgh-Cleveland
PARK, Richard	5-11	176	R	Seoul, S. Korea	5/27/76	Belleville
PATTERSON, Ed	6-2	213	R	Delta, B.C.	11/14/72	Pittsburgh-Cleveland
PITTIS, Domenic	5-11	180	L	Calgary, Alta.	10/1/74	Lethbridge
ROBITAILLE, Luc	6-1	195	L	Montreal, Que.	2/17/66	Los Angeles
ROCHE, Dave	6-4	224	L	Lindsay, Ont.	6/13/75	Peterborough-Windsor
SANDSTROM, Tomas	6-2	200	L	Jakobstad, Finland	9/4/64	Los Angeles-Pittsburgh
SELMSER, Sean	6-1	180	L	Calgary, Alta.	11/10/74	Red Deer
STEVENS, Kevin	6-3	217	L	Brockton, MA	4/15/65	Pittsburgh
STRAKA, Martin	5-10	178	L	Plzen, Czech.	9/3/72	Pittsburgh
TOROPCHENKO, Leonid	6-4	220	R	Moscow, USSR	8/28/68	Cleveland
WELLS, Chris	6-6	215	L	Calgary, Alta.	11/12/75	Seattle
DEFENSEMEN						
ANDRUSAK, Greg	6-1	190	R	Cranbrook, B.C.	11/14/69	Pittsburgh-Cleveland
BANCROFT, Steve	6-1	214	L	Toronto, Ont.	10/6/70	Cleveland
BERGQVIST, Stefan	6-3	216	L	Leksand, Sweden	3/10/75	Leksand
BROWN, Greg	6-0	185	R	Hartford, CT	3/7/68	Pittsburgh-San Diego
BUTENSCHON, Sven	6-5	201	L	Itzehoe, West Germany	3/22/76	Brandon
DAGENAIS, Mike	6-3	200	L	Gloucester, Ont.	7/22/69	Cleveland
DYCK, Paul	6-1	192	L	Steinbach, Man.	4/20/71	Cleveland
HAWGOOD, Greg	5-10	190	L	Edmonton, Alta.	8/10/68	Philadelphia-Florida-Pittsburgh
JENNINGS, Grant	6-3	210	L	Hudson Bay, Sask.	5/5/65	Pittsburgh
MORAN, Ian	5-11	180	R	Cleveland, OH	8/24/72	U.S. National-Cleveland
MURPHY, Larry	6-2	210	R	Scarborough, Ont.	3/8/61	Pittsburgh
NEATON, Pat	6-0	180	L	Redford, MI	5/21/71	Pittsburgh-Cleveland
SAMUELSSON, Kjell	6-6	235	R	Tingsryd, Sweden	10/18/58	Pittsburgh
SAMUELSSON, Ulf	6-1	195	L	Fagersta, Sweden	3/26/64	Pittsburgh
TAGLIANETTI, Peter	6-2	200	L	Framingham, MA	8/15/63	Pittsburgh
TAMER, Chris	6-2	185	L	Dearborn, MI	11/17/70	Pittsburgh-Cleveland
GOALTENDERS	**HT**	**WT**	**C**	**Place of Birth**	**Date**	**1993-94 Club**
BARRASSO, Tom	6-3	211	R	Boston, MA	3/31/65	Pittsburgh
DeROUVILLE, Philippe	6-1	183	L	Victoriaville, Que.	8/7/74	Verdun
LALIME, Patrick	6-2	170	L	St. Bonaventure, Que.	7/7/74	Shawinigan
WREGGET, Ken	6-1	195	L	Brandon, Man.	3/25/64	Pittsburgh

Coach

JOHNSTON, ED

Coach, Pittsburgh Penguins. Born in Montreal, Que., November 24, 1935.

Ed Johnston led the Penguins to the Northeast Division title in 1993-94 and their second best record in club history. He began his second stint as coach of the Penguins in 1993-94 having previously coached the team for three seasons from 1980-81 to 1982-83 compiling a record of 79-126-35. He was named general manager of the team on May 27, 1983, a position he held for five seasons. During the 1988-89 season, his last with the Penguins, Johnston served as the assistant general manager. In 1989, Johnston was named vice president and general manager of the Hartford Whalers, a position he held for three seasons. During Johnston's first season in Hartford (1989-90), the Whalers recorded the second best record (38-33-9) in their NHL history.

Johnston played in the NHL for 16 seasons with Boston, Toronto, St. Louis and Chicago. He was a member of two Stanley Cup Championship teams with the Boston Bruins, and was the last goaltender to play every minute of a season, when he played all 70 games in 1963-64 for the Bruins. Overall, Johnston played in 592 games, recording 236 wins, 32 shutouts and a 3.25 goals against average.

Coaching Record

		Regular Season					Playoffs			
Season	Team	Games	W	L	T	%	Games	W	L	%
1979-80	Chicago (NHL)	80	34	27	19	.544	7	3	4	.429
1980-81	Pittsburgh (NHL)	80	30	37	13	.456	5	2	3	.400
1981-82	Pittsburgh (NHL)	80	31	36	13	.469	5	2	3	.400
1982-83	Pittsburgh (NHL)	80	18	53	9	.281	....	....	....	....
1993-94	Pittsburgh (NHL)	84	44	27	13	.601	6	2	4	.333
	NHL Totals	404	157	180	67	.472	23	9	14	.391

Coaching History

George Sullivan, 1967-68 to 1968-69; Red Kelly, 1969-70 to 1971-72; Red Kelly and Ken Schinkel, 1972-73; Ken Schinkel and Marc Boileau, 1973-74; Marc Boileau, 1974-75; Marc Boileau and Ken Schinkel, 1975-76; Ken Schinkel, 1976-77; John Wilson, 1977-78 to 1979-80; Eddie Johnston, 1980-81 to 1982-83; Lou Angotti, 1983-84; Bob Berry, 1984-85 to 1986-87; Pierre Creamer, 1987-88; Gene Ubriaco, 1988-89; Gene Ubriaco and Craig Patrick, 1989-90; Bob Johnson, 1990-91 to 1991-92; Scotty Bowman, 1991-92 to 1992-93; Eddie Johnston, 1993-94 to date.

1993-94 Scoring

* – rookie

Regular Season

Pos	#	Player	Team	GP	G	A	Pts	+/–	PIM	PP	SH	GW	GT	S	%
R	68	Jaromir Jagr	PIT	80	32	67	99	15	61	9	0	6	2	298	10.7
C	10	Ron Francis	PIT	82	27	66	93	3–	62	8	0	2	1	216	12.5
L	25	Kevin Stevens	PIT	83	41	47	88	24–	155	21	0	4	0	284	14.4
D	55	Larry Murphy	PIT	84	17	56	73	10	44	7	0	4	0	236	7.2
R	7	Joe Mullen	PIT	84	38	32	70	9	41	6	2	9	0	231	16.5
C	82	Martin Straka	PIT	84	30	34	64	24	24	2	0	6	1	130	23.1
R	17	Tomas Sandstrom	L.A.	51	17	24	41	12–	59	4	0	2	1	121	14.0
			PIT	27	6	11	17	5	24	0	0	1	0	72	8.3
			TOTAL	78	23	35	58	7–	83	4	0	3	1	193	11.9
R	24	Doug Brown	PIT	77	18	37	55	19	18	2	0	1	0	152	11.8
C	15	Shawn McEachern	L.A.	49	8	13	21	1	24	0	3	0	0	81	9.9
			PIT	27	12	9	21	13	10	0	2	1	0	78	15.4
			TOTAL	76	20	22	42	14	34	0	5	1	0	159	12.6
R	22	Rick Tocchet	PIT	51	14	26	40	15–	134	5	1	2	1	150	9.3
C	66	Mario Lemieux	PIT	22	17	20	37	2–	32	7	0	4	0	92	18.5
D	4	Greg Hawgood	PHI	19	3	12	15	2	19	3	0	0	0	37	8.1
			FLA	33	2	14	16	8	9	0	0	1	0	55	3.6
			PIT	12	1	2	3	1–	8	1	0	1	0	20	5.0
			TOTAL	64	6	28	34	9	36	4	0	2	0	112	5.4
D	5	Ulf Samuelsson	PIT	80	5	24	29	23	199	1	0	0	1	106	4.7
C	19	Bryan Trottier	PIT	41	4	11	15	12–	36	0	0	0	0	45	8.9
D	32	Peter Taglianetti	PIT	60	2	12	14	5	142	0	0	0	0	57	3.5
D	28	Kjell Samuelsson	PIT	59	5	8	13	18	118	1	0	0	0	57	8.8
R	29 *	Markus Naslund	PIT	71	4	7	11	3–	27	1	0	0	0	80	5.0
D	34	Greg Brown	PIT	36	3	8	11	1	28	1	0	0	0	37	8.1
L	33	Jim McKenzie	HFD	26	1	2	3	6–	67	0	0	0	0	9	11.1
			DAL	34	2	3	5	4	63	0	0	1	0	18	11.1
			PIT	11	0	0	0	5–	16	0	0	0	0	6	.0
			TOTAL	71	3	5	8	7–	146	0	0	1	0	33	9.1
D	3	Grant Jennings	PIT	61	2	4	6	10–	126	0	1	1	0	49	4.1
R	44 *	Ed Patterson	PIT	27	3	1	4	5–	10	0	0	0	0	15	20.0
D	6	Mike Ramsey	PIT	65	2	2	4	4–	22	0	0	0	0	31	6.5
D	36 *	Pat Neaton	PIT	9	1	1	2	3	12	1	0	0	0	11	9.1
C	12	Larry Depalma	PIT	7	1	0	1	1	5	0	0	0	0	2	50.0
G	31	Ken Wregget	PIT	42	0	1	1	0	8	0	0	0	0	0	.0
G	35	Tom Barrasso	PIT	44	0	1	1	0	42	0	0	0	0	0	.0
G	30	Roberto Romano	PIT	2	0	0	0	0	0	0	0	0	0	0	.0
G	1	Rob Dopson	PIT	2	0	0	0	0	0	0	0	0	0	0	.0
D	4 *	Greg Andrusak	PIT	3	0	0	0	1–	2	0	0	0	0	4	.0
R	37 *	Justin Duberman	PIT	4	0	0	0	0	0	0	0	0	0	2	.0
L	14 *	Ladislav Karabin	PIT	9	0	0	0	0	2	0	0	0	0	3	.0
D	2 *	Chris Tamer	PIT	12	0	0	0	3	9	0	0	0	0	10	.0

Goaltending

No.	Goaltender	GPI	Mins	Avg	W	L	T	EN	SO	GA	SA	S%
30	Roberto Romano	2	125	1.44	1	0	1	0	0	3	56	.946
35	Tom Barrasso	44	2482	3.36	22	15	5	2	2	139	1304	.893
31	Ken Wregget	42	2456	3.37	21	12	7	0	1	138	1291	.893
1	Rob Dopson	2	45	4.00	0	0	0	0	0	3	23	.870
	Totals	**84**	**5118**	**3.34**	**44**	**27**	**13**	**2**	**3**	**285**	**2676**	**.893**

Playoffs

Pos	#	Player	Team	GP	G	A	Pts	+/–	PIM	PP	SH	GW	GT	S	%
C	66	Mario Lemieux	PIT	6	4	3	7	4–	2	1	0	0	0	23	17.4
R	68	Jaromir Jagr	PIT	6	2	4	6	3–	16	0	0	1	0	16	12.5
R	22	Rick Tocchet	PIT	6	2	3	5	2–	20	1	0	1	0	14	14.3
D	55	Larry Murphy	PIT	6	0	5	5	6–	0	0	0	0	0	13	.0
L	25	Kevin Stevens	PIT	6	1	1	2	5–	10	0	0	0	0	20	5.0
D	32	Peter Taglianetti	PIT	5	0	2	2	2	16	0	0	0	0	0	.0
C	10	Ron Francis	PIT	6	0	2	2	2–	6	0	0	0	0	9	.0
R	7	Joe Mullen	PIT	6	1	0	1	1–	2	0	0	0	0	6	16.7
C	15	Shawn McEachern	PIT	6	1	0	1	2–	2	0	0	0	0	10	10.0
C	82	Martin Straka	PIT	6	1	0	1	3–	2	0	0	0	0	3	33.3
D	34	Greg Brown	PIT	6	0	1	1	2–	4	0	0	0	0	3	.0
D	5	Ulf Samuelsson	PIT	6	0	1	1	3–	18	0	0	0	0	6	.0
C	12	Larry Depalma	PIT	1	0	0	0	0	0	0	0	0	0	0	.0
D	4	Greg Hawgood	PIT	1	0	0	0	0	0	0	0	0	0	1	.0
D	6	Mike Ramsey	PIT	1	0	0	0	0	0	0	0	0	0	2	.0
C	19	Bryan Trottier	PIT	2	0	0	0	0	0	0	0	0	0	1	.0
D	3	Grant Jennings	PIT	3	0	0	0	1–	2	0	0	0	0	2	.0
L	33	Jim McKenzie	PIT	3	0	0	0	0	0	0	0	0	0	0	.0
D	2 *	Chris Tamer	PIT	5	0	0	0	1	2	0	0	0	0	2	.0
G	35	Tom Barrasso	PIT	6	0	0	0	0	4	0	0	0	0	0	.0
R	24	Doug Brown	PIT	6	0	0	0	0	2	0	0	0	0	3	.0
D	28	Kjell Samuelsson	PIT	6	0	0	0	0	26	0	0	0	0	3	.0
R	17	Tomas Sandstrom	PIT	6	0	0	0	4–	4	0	0	0	0	10	.0

Goaltending

No.	Goaltender	GPI	Mins	Avg	W	L	EN	SO	GA	SA	S%
35	Tom Barrasso	6	356	2.87	2	4	3	0	17	162	.895
	Totals	**6**	**360**	**3.33**	**2**	**4**	**3**	**0**	**20**	**165**	**.879**

Captains' History

Ab McDonald, 1967-68; no captain, 1968-69 to 1972-73; Ron Schock, 1973-74 to 1976-77; Jean Pronovost, 1977-78; Orest Kindrachuk, 1978-79 to 1980-81; Randy Carlyle, 1981-82 to 1983-84; Mike Bullard, 1984-85, 1985-86; Mike Bullard and Terry Ruskowski, 1986-87; Dan Frawley and Mario Lemieux, 1987-88; Mario Lemieux, 1988-89 to date.

Club Records

Team

(Figures in brackets for season records are games played)

Most Points	**119**	1992-93 (84)
Most Wins	**56**	1992-93 (84)
Most Ties	**20**	1970-71 (78)
Most Losses	**58**	1983-84 (80)
Most Goals	**367**	1992-93 (84)
Most Goals Against	**394**	1982-83 (80)
Fewest Points	**38**	1983-84 (80)
Fewest Wins	**16**	1983-84 (80)
Fewest Ties	**5**	1984-85 (80)
Fewest Losses	**28**	1974-75 (80)
Fewest Goals	**182**	1969-70 (76)
Fewest Goals Against	**216**	1967-68 (74)
Longest Winning Streak		
Over-all	***17**	Mar. 9-Apr. 10/93
Home	**11**	Jan. 5-Mar. 7/91
Away	**6**	Mar. 14-Apr. 9/93
Longest Undefeated Streak		
Over-all	**18**	Mar. 9-Apr. 14/93 (17 wins, 1 tie)
Home	**20**	Nov. 30/74-Feb. 22/75 (12 wins, 8 ties)
Away	**7**	Twice
Longest Losing Streak		
Over-all	**11**	Jan. 22/83-Feb. 10/83
Home	**7**	Oct. 8-29/83
Away	**18**	Dec. 23/82-Mar. 4/83
Longest Winless Streak		
Over-all	**18**	Jan. 2-Feb. 10/83 (17 losses, 1 tie)
Home	**11**	Oct. 8-Nov. 19/83 (9 losses, 2 ties)
Away	**18**	Oct. 25/70-Jan. 14/71 (11 losses, 7 ties) Dec. 23/82-Mar. 4/83 (18 losses)
Most Shutouts, Season	**6**	1967-68 (74) 1976-77 (80)
Most PIM, Season	***2,670**	1988-89 (80)
Most Goals, Game	**12**	Mar. 15/75 (Wash. 1 at Pit. 12) Dec. 26/91 (Tor. 1 at Pit. 12)

Individual

Most Seasons	**11**	Rick Kehoe
Most Games	**753**	Jean Pronovost
Most Goals, Career	**494**	Mario Lemieux
Most Assists, Career	**717**	Mario Lemieux
Most Points, Career	**1,211**	Mario Lemieux (494 goals, 717 assists)
Most PIM, Career	**980**	Troy Loney
Most Shutouts, Career	**11**	Les Binkley
Longest Consecutive Games Streak	**320**	Ron Schock (Oct. 24/73-Apr. 3/77)
Most Goals, Season	**85**	Mario Lemieux (1988-89)
Most Assists, Season	**114**	Mario Lemieux (1988-89)
Most Points, Season	**199**	Mario Lemieux (1988-89)
Most PIM, Season	**409**	Paul Baxter (1981-82)
Most Points, Defenseman, Season	**113**	Paul Coffey (1988-89) (30 goals, 83 assists)
Most Points, Center, Season	**199**	Mario Lemieux (1988-89) (85 goals, 114 assists)
Most Points, Right Wing, Season	**115**	Rob Brown (1988-89) (49 goals, 66 assists)
Most Points, Left Wing, Season	**123**	Kevin Stevens (1991-92) (54 goals, 69 assists)
Most Points, Rookie, Season	**100**	Mario Lemieux (1984-85) (43 goals, 57 assists)
Most Shutouts, Season	**6**	Les Binkley (1967-68)
Most Goals, Game	**5**	Mario Lemieux (Dec. 31/88)
Most Assists, Game	**6**	Ron Stackhouse (Mar. 8/75) Greg Malone (Nov. 28/79) Mario Lemieux (Oct. 15/88, Dec. 5/92)
Most Points, Game	**8**	Mario Lemieux (Oct. 15/88, Dec. 31/88)

* NHL Record.

Retired Numbers

21	Michel Brière	1969-1970

All-time Record vs. Other Clubs

Regular Season

	At Home							On Road							Total						
	GP	W	L	T	GF	GA	PTS	GP	W	L	T	GF	GA	PTS	GP	W	L	T	GF	GA	PTS
Anaheim	1	0	0	1	2	2	1	1	1	0	0	5	4	2	2	1	0	1	7	6	3
Boston	58	21	26	11	198	222	53	56	10	40	6	161	259	26	114	31	66	17	359	481	79
Buffalo	48	21	15	12	185	169	54	49	11	24	14	140	214	36	97	32	39	26	325	383	90
Calgary	38	18	10	10	139	125	46	38	9	22	7	114	163	25	76	27	32	17	253	288	71
Chicago	51	24	22	5	181	170	53	52	8	35	9	144	221	25	103	32	57	14	325	391	78
Dallas	56	34	17	5	216	158	73	57	20	32	5	192	218	45	113	54	49	10	408	376	118
Detroit	57	39	14	4	254	169	82	58	11	36	11	164	232	33	115	50	50	15	418	401	115
Edmonton	23	10	12	1	90	110	21	23	4	18	1	80	125	9	46	14	30	2	170	235	30
Florida	2	1	0	1	4	3	3	2	2	0	0	6	4	4	4	3	0	1	10	7	7
Hartford	24	12	9	3	113	100	27	25	11	13	1	101	113	23	49	23	22	4	214	213	50
Los Angeles	64	37	19	8	243	203	82	62	14	40	8	161	245	36	126	51	59	16	404	448	118
Montreal	59	20	30	9	177	217	49	60	4	49	7	142	307	15	119	24	79	16	319	524	64
New Jersey	57	34	19	4	242	203	72	57	19	29	9	198	226	47	114	53	48	13	440	429	119
NY Islanders	64	29	24	11	247	226	69	63	21	34	8	205	265	50	127	50	58	19	452	491	119
NY Rangers	77	30	36	11	278	289	71	78	30	41	7	273	320	67	155	60	77	18	551	609	138
Ottawa	5	4	0	1	23	10	9	4	3	1	0	16	5	6	9	7	1	1	39	15	15
Philadelphia	83	35	31	17	286	268	87	83	15	61	7	214	360	37	166	50	92	24	500	628	124
Quebec	26	14	8	4	116	105	32	23	11	12	0	92	106	22	49	25	20	4	208	211	54
St. Louis	56	25	19	12	209	172	62	57	13	38	6	154	228	32	113	38	57	18	363	400	94
San Jose	3	2	0	1	19	6	5	4	3	0	1	27	10	7	7	5	0	2	46	16	12
Tampa Bay	3	2	0	1	13	7	5	3	2	1	0	13	10	4	6	4	1	1	26	17	9
Toronto	54	28	20	6	223	176	62	53	17	25	11	178	220	45	107	45	45	17	401	396	107
Vancouver	43	28	8	7	194	144	63	43	20	20	3	165	159	43	86	48	28	10	359	303	106
Washington	63	32	25	6	257	220	70	66	26	34	6	252	291	58	129	58	59	12	509	511	128
Winnipeg	23	16	7	0	96	69	32	22	12	9	1	83	83	25	45	28	16	1	179	152	57
Defunct Clubs	35	22	6	7	148	93	51	34	13	10	11	108	101	37	69	35	16	18	256	194	88
Totals	**1073**	**538**	**377**	**158**	**4153**	**3636**	**1234**	**1073**	**310**	**624**	**139**	**3388**	**4489**	**759**	**2146**	**848**	**1001**	**297**	**7541**	**8125**	**1993**

Calgary totals include Atlanta, 1972-73 to 1979-80. Dallas totals include Minnesota, 1967-68 to 1992-93.
New Jersey totals include Kansas City, 1974-75 to 1975-76, and Colorado, 1976-77 to 1981-82.

Playoffs

	Series	W	L	GP	W	L	T	GF	GA	Last Mtg.	Round	Result
Boston	4	2	2	19	10	9	0	67	62	1992	CF	W 4-0
Buffalo	1	1	0	3	2	1	0	9	9	1979	PR	W 2-1
Chicago	2	1	1	8	4	4	0	23	24	1992	F	W 4-0
Dallas	1	1	0	6	4	2	0	28	16	1991	F	W 4-2
New Jersey	2	2	0	12	8	4	0	48	30	1993	DSF	W 4-1
NY Islanders	3	0	3	19	8	11	0	58	67	1993	DF	L 3-4
NY Rangers	2	2	0	10	8	2	0	43	30	1992	DF	W 4-2
Philadelphia	1	0	1	7	3	4	0	24	31	1989	DF	L 3-4
St. Louis	3	1	2	13	6	7	0	40	45	1981	PR	L 2-3
Toronto	2	0	2	6	2	4	0	13	21	1977	PR	L 1-2
Washington	3	2	1	18	10	8	0	56	60	1994	CQF	L 2-4
Defunct Clubs	1	1	0	4	4	0	0	13	6			
Totals	**25**	**13**	**12**	**125**	**69**	**56**	**0**	**422**	**401**			

Playoff Results 1994-90

Year	Round	Opponent	Result	GF	GA
1994	CQF	Washington	L 2-4	12	20
1993	DF	NY Islanders	L 3-4	27	24
	DSF	New Jersey	W 4-1	23	13
1992	**F**	**Chicago**	**W 4-0**	**15**	**10**
	CF	Boston	W 4-0	19	7
	DF	NY Rangers	W 4-2	24	19
	DSF	Washington	W 4-3	25	27
1991	**F**	**Minnesota**	**W 4-2**	**28**	**16**
	CF	Boston	W 4-2	27	18
	DF	Washington	W 4-1	19	13
	DSF	New Jersey	W 4-3	25	17

Abbreviations: Round: F – Final;
CF – conference final; **CQF** – conference quarter-final;
CSF – conference semi-final; **DF** – division final;
DSF – division semi-final; **SF** – semi-final;
QF – quarter-final; **PR** – preliminary round.

1993-94 Results

Oct.	5	at	Philadelphia	3-4
	7		Montreal	2-1
	9		NY Rangers	3-2
	10	at	Quebec	4-7
	12	at	Florida	2-1
	14	at	Tampa Bay	2-3
	16		Hartford	5-3
	19	at	NY Islanders	3-2
	22	at	Buffalo	4-2
	23		St. Louis	3-3
	28		Quebec	3-7
	30		Chicago	4-3
Nov.	2	at	San Jose	3-3
	3	at	Buffalo	6-2
	6	at	Los Angeles	3-8
	7	at	Anaheim	5-4
	9	at	St. Louis	3-3
	11	at	Chicago	1-4
	13		Detroit	3-7
	16		Philadelphia	11-5
	18		Washington	3-2
	20	at	Montreal	2-2
	24		Boston	7-3
	26	at	Washington	4-4
	27		Ottawa	2-2
Dec.	2		New Jersey	2-2
	4	at	Hartford	7-6
	8	at	Dallas	2-3
	11	at	Tampa Bay	6-3
	14		Los Angeles	4-2
	16		Buffalo	2-1
	19		NY Islanders	3-6
	21		Tampa Bay	8-3
	23	at	Boston	4-3
	26	at	Washington	3-7
	28		Philadelphia	4-4
	31		Quebec	4-5
Jan.	2	at	Hartford	2-7
	3	at	Ottawa	4-1
	7	at	Buffalo	4-3
	8		Calgary	2-2
	11		Boston	5-4
	13		Florida	2-2
	15		Edmonton	4-3
	18	at	Quebec	3-6
	25		Ottawa	4-2
	27		Quebec	3-0
	29	at	Toronto	4-4
	31	at	NY Rangers	3-5
Feb.	1		Florida	2-1
	4	at	Detroit	6-3
	5	at	New Jersey	3-7
	7		Montreal	1-4
	10		NY Islanders	3-5
	12		Dallas	3-9
	13	at	Philadelphia	3-0
	15		Winnipeg	5-3
	17		Hartford	6-4
	19	at	Montreal	1-4
	21	at	NY Rangers	3-4
	24		Anaheim	2-2
	26		Buffalo	4-3
	28	at	Florida	4-3
Mar.	4	at	Buffalo	1-2
	6	at	Winnipeg	5-3
	8		Boston	7-3
	10		Toronto	2-4
	12		NY Rangers	6-2
	13	at	Hartford	3-2
	15		Washington	4-5
	17	at	Boston	4-2
	19		Vancouver	5-4
	20	at	NY Islanders	2-1
	22		San Jose	2-2
	24		Ottawa	5-1
	26	at	Calgary	3-5
	27	at	Edmonton	3-5
	30	at	Vancouver	3-1
Apr.	3		Boston	6-2
	4		Tampa Bay	2-1
	6		New Jersey	3-1
	8	at	New Jersey	2-7
	9	at	Montreal	1-9
	11	at	Ottawa	4-0

Entry Draft
Selections 1994-80

1994
Pick
24 Chris Wells
50 Richard Park
57 Sven Butenschon
73 Greg Crozier
76 Alexei Krivchenkov
102 Thomas O'Connor
128 Clint Johnson
154 Valentin Morozov
161 Serge Aubin
180 Drew Palmer
206 Boris Zelenko
232 Jason Godbout
258 Mikhail Kazakevich
284 Brian Leitza

1993
Pick
26 Stefan Bergqvist
52 Domenic Pittis
62 Dave Roche
104 Jonas Andersson-Junkka
130 Chris Kelleher
156 Patrick Lalime
182 Sean Selmser
208 Larry McMorran
234 Timothy Harberts
260 Leonid Toropchenko
286 Hans Jonsson

1992
Pick
19 Martin Straka
43 Marc Hussey
67 Travis Thiessen
91 Todd Klassen
115 Philipp De Rouville
139 Artem Kopot
163 Jan Alinc
187 Fran Bussey
211 Brian Bonin
235 Brian Callahan

1991
Pick
16 Markus Naslund
38 Rusty Fitzgerald
60 Shane Peacock
82 Joe Tamminen
104 Robert Melanson
126 Brian Clifford
148 Ed Patterson
170 Peter McLaughlin
192 Jeff Lembke
214 Chris Tok
236 Paul Dyck
258 Pasi Huura

1990
Pick
5 Jaromir Jagr
61 Joe Dziedzic
68 Chris Tamer
89 Brian Farrell
107 Ian Moran
110 Denis Casey
130 Mika Valila
131 Ken Plaquin
145 Pat Neaton
152 Petteri Koskimaki
173 Ladislav Karabin
194 Timothy Fingerhut
215 Michael Thompson
236 Brian Bruininks

1989
Pick
16 Jamie Heward
37 Paul Laus
58 John Brill
79 Todd Nelson
100 Tom Nevers
121 Mike Markovich
126 Mike Needham
142 Patrick Schafhauser
163 Dave Shute
184 Andrew Wolf
205 Greg Hagen
226 Scott Farrell
247 Jason Smart

1988
Pick
4 Darrin Shannon
25 Mark Major
62 Daniel Gauthier
67 Mark Recchi
88 Greg Andrusak
130 Troy Mick
151 Jeff Blaeser
172 Rob Gaudreau
193 Donald Pancoe
214 Cory Laylin
235 Darren Stolk

1987
Pick
5 Chris Joseph
26 Richard Tabaracci
47 Jamie Leach
68 Risto Kurkinen
89 Jeff Waver
110 Shawn McEachern
131 Jim Bodden
152 Jiri Kucera
173 Jack MacDougall
194 Daryn McBride
215 Mark Carlson
236 Ake Lilljebjorn

1986
Pick
4 Zarley Zalapski
25 Dave Capuano
46 Brad Aitken
67 Rob Brown
88 Sandy Smith
109 Jeff Daniels
130 Doug Hobson
151 Steve Rohlik
172 Dave McLlwain
193 Kelly Cain
214 Stan Drulia
235 Rob Wilson

1985
Pick
2 Craig Simpson
23 Lee Giffin
58 Bruce Racine
86 Steve Gotaas
107 Kevin Clemens
114 Stuart Marston
128 Steve Titus
149 Paul Stanton
170 Jim Paek
191 Steve Shaunessy
212 Doug Greschuk
233 Gregory Choules

1984
Pick
1 Mario Lemieux
9 Doug Bodger
16 Roger Belanger
64 Mark Teevens
85 Arto Javanainen
127 Tom Ryan
169 John Del Col
189 Steve Hurt
210 Jim Steen
230 Mark Ziliotto

1983
Pick
15 Bob Errey
22 Todd Charlesworth
58 Mike Rowe
63 Frank Pietrangelo
103 Patrick Emond
123 Paul Ames
163 Marty Ketola
183 Alec Haidy
203 Garth Hildebrand
223 Dave Goertz

1982
Pick
10 Rich Sutter
38 Tim Hrynewich
52 Troy Loney
94 Grant Sasser
136 Grant Couture
157 Peter Derksen
178 Greg Gravel
199 Stu Wenaas
220 Chris McCauley
241 Stan Bautch

1981
Pick
28 Steve Gatzos
49 Tom Thornbury
70 Norm Schmidt
109 Paul Edwards
112 Rod Buskas
133 Geoff Wilson
154 Mitch Lamoureux
175 Dean Defazio
196 David Hannan

1980
Pick
9 Mike Bullard
51 Randy Boyd
72 Tony Feltrin
93 Doug Shedden
114 Pat Graham
156 Robert Geale
177 Brian Lundberg
198 Steve McKenzie

General Manager

PATRICK, CRAIG
General Manager, Pittsburgh Penguins. Born in Detroit, MI, May 20, 1946.

Appointed general manager of the Penguins on December 5, 1989, Patrick's teams have since won two Stanley Cup titles (1991 and 1992), and the Presidents' Trophy (1993). Patrick has laid the groundwork for success through shrewd acquisitions and drafts; his trades for Ulf Samuelsson, Ron Francis, Rick Tocchet and Ken Wregget, and the drafting of Jaromir Jagr are all moves considered crucial to Pittsburgh's recent success.

A 1969 graduate of the University of Denver, Patrick was captain of the Pioneers' NCAA Championship hockey team that year. He returned to his alma mater in 1986 where he served as director of athletics and recreation for two years. Patrick served as administrative assistant to the president of the Amateur Hockey Association of the United States in 1980 and as an assistant coach/assistant general manager for the 1980 gold-medal winning U.S. Olympic hockey team. Before pursuing a coaching career, Patrick played professional hockey with Washington, Kansas City, St. Louis, Minnesota and California from 1971-79. In eight seasons, Patrick tallied 163 points (72-91-163) in 401 games.

NHL Coaching Record

Season	Team	Regular Season					Playoffs			
		Games	W	L	T	%	Games	W	L	%
1980-81	NY Rangers	59	26	23	10	.525	14	7	7	.500
1984-85	NY Rangers	35	11	22	2	.343	3	0	3	.000
1989-90	Pittsburgh	54	22	26	6	.463	...	...	...	...
	NHL Totals	**148**	**59**	**71**	**18**	**.459**	**17**	**7**	**10**	**.412**

General Managers' History

Jack Riley, 1967-68 to 1969-70; Leonard "Red" Kelly, 1970-71 to 1971-72; Jack Riley, 1972-73 to 1973-74; Jack Button, 1974-75; Wren A. Blair, 1975-76; Wren A. Blair and Baz Bastien, 1976-77; Baz Bastien, 1977-78 to 1982-83; Ed Johnston, 1983-84 to 1987-88; Tony Esposito, 1988-89; Tony Esposito and Craig Patrick, 1989-90; Craig Patrick, 1990-91 to date.

Club Directory

Civic Arena
Pittsburgh, PA 15219
Phone **412/642-1800**
FAX 412/642-1859
Capacity: TBA

Pittsburgh Hockey Associates Directory
Ownership . . . . Howard Baldwin, Morris Belzberg, Thomas Ruta
Chairman of the Board & Governor . . . . Howard Baldwin

Administration
Chief Operating Officer – PGH Sports Associates . . . Roy Mlakar
President & Alternate Governor . . . . Jack Kelley
Senior Executive Vice-President. . . . . Bill Barnes
Executive Vice-President & Chief Financial Officer. . . . . Donn Patton
Executive Vice-President of Advertising/ PHA Sports Marketing Ltd. . . . . Richard Chmura
General Counsel . . . . The law firm of Eckert, Seamans, Cherin & Mellott
Executive Assistants . . . . Elaine Heufelder, Paula Nichols
Receptionist . . . . Mary Ann Dayton

Hockey Operations
Executive Vice-President & General Manager . . . . . . Craig Patrick
Head Coach . . . . Ed Johnston
Assistant Coaches. . . . . Rick Kehoe, Bryan Trottier
Goaltending Coach and Scout . . . . Gilles Meloche
Head Scout . . . . Greg Malone
Scouting Staff. . . . . Les Binkley, John Gill, Charlie Hodge, Mark Kelley, Ralph Cox
Professional Scout . . . . Phil Russell
Strength and Conditioning Coach . . . . John Welday
Equipment Manager. . . . . Steve Latin
Trainer . . . . Charles "Skip" Taylor
Team Video Coordinator . . . . Howard Baldwin, Jr.
Team Physician . . . . Dr. Charles Burke
Team Dentists. . . . . Dr. David Donatelli
Executive Assistant . . . . Tracey Botsford
Assistant Equipment Manager . . . . Kevin Greenway

Public and Community Relations
Vice-President, Public & Community Relations . . . . . Phil Langan
Director of Public Relations . . . . Cindy Himes
Director of Media Relations . . . . Harry Sanders
Director of Amateur Hockey Development . . . . George Kirk
Director of Special Events . . . . Jamie Belo
Assistant Media Relations Director . . . . Steve Bovino
Public Relations Administrative Assistant . . . . Renee Petrichevich

Finance
Controller . . . . Kevin Hart
Accounting Staff. . . . . Eric Brandenberg, Tracey Clontz, Barb Manion, Rick Patterson

Ticketing
Director of Ticket Sales . . . . Jeff Mercer
Choice Seat Operations . . . . Mark Watkins
Box Office Manager . . . . Carol Coulson
Assistant Box Office Manager . . . . Debbie Campbell
Ticket Sales Representatives . . . . Terri Dobos Young, Linda Gallentine, Fred Traynor
Choice Seat Staff . . . . Edna Greeley, Julie Kapples, Tony Miller, Tim Porco

Sales and Communications
Director of Advertising Sales . . . . Taylor Baldwin
Director of Suite Sales and Service . . . . Chuck Saller
Director of Promotions & Advertising Sales Coordinator . . . . Amy Novak
Advertising Sales Representatives . . . . Chris Clark, Bruce Weber, Steve Violetta
Director of Penvision . . . . Bill Miller

Merchandising
Director of Merchandising & Memorabilia . . . . Mark Willand
Assistant Director of Merchandising . . . . Bill Cox
Assistant Director of Memorabilia. . . . . Nick Ruta
Retail Manager . . . . Jeff Butler
Office Manager/Customer Relations Coordinator . . . Jill Murtha
Warehouse Manager . . . . Louise Stock
Marketing Representative . . . . David Lacenere
Administrative Assistant . . . . Christine Black

Summer Teams
General Manager – Phantoms & Stingers . . . . Jeff Barrett
Coach – Phantoms . . . . Rick Kehoe
Assistant Coach & Dir. of Player Personnel – Phantoms . . . . Warren Young
Coach – Stingers. . . . . Paul Child
Assistant Coach & Dir. of Player Personnel – Stingers . . . . Denny Kohlmyer
Consultant – Stingers . . . . John Kowalski
Marketing and Promotions . . . . Steve Warshaw
Director of Operations . . . . Arden Robbins
Senior Sales Representative . . . . Rich Nixon
Assistant Director of Operations . . . . Vikki Hultquist

General Information
Home Ice . . . . Civic Arena
Dimensions of Rink. . . . . 200 feet by 85 feet
Location of Press Box . . . . West Side of Building
Team Colors . . . . Black, Gold and White
Flagship Radio Station. WTAE (1250 AM)
TV Stations . . . . KBL and KDKA-TV
Announcers . . . . Mike Lange, Paul Steigerwald, Stan Savran, Doug McLeod

Quebec Nordiques

1993-94 Results: 34W-42L-8T 76PTS. Fifth, Northeast Division

Joe Sakic's 64 assists, 92 points and nine game-winning goals were all team-leading totals for the Quebec Nordiques in 1993-94.

Schedule

Oct.	Sat.	1	Buffalo
	Tues.	4	at Tampa Bay
	Thur.	6	at Boston
	Sat.	8	at Hartford
	Tues.	11	Pittsburgh
	Thur.	13	at Toronto
	Sat.	15	Chicago
	Tues.	18	NY Rangers
	Thur.	20	at Philadelphia
	Sat.	22	Detroit
	Sun.	23	at Buffalo
	Tues.	25	Edmonton
	Thur.	27	at Hartford
	Sat.	29	Dallas
Nov.	Tues.	1	Tampa Bay
	Sat.	5	at Washington
	Tues.	8	Philadelphia
	Thur.	10	at Boston
	Sat.	12	Ottawa*
	Sun.	13	New Jersey*
	Thur.	17	Montreal
	Sat.	19	at Montreal
	Mon.	21	Florida
	Wed.	23	at Dallas
	Thur.	24	at St. Louis
	Sat.	26	Washington
	Tues.	29	Los Angeles
Dec.	Thur.	1	at New Jersey
	Sat.	3	Hartford
	Tues.	6	Calgary
	Fri.	9	at Tampa Bay
	Sat.	10	at Florida
	Tues.	13	Florida
	Thur.	15	at Detroit
	Sat.	17	Philadelphia*
	Sun.	18	Tampa Bay*
	Wed.	21	at Philadelphia
	Fri.	23	at NY Islanders
	Tues.	27	Toronto
	Thur.	29	Hartford
	Sat.	31	at Vancouver
Jan.	Thur.	5	Montreal
			(in Phoenix)

	Sat.	7	at Edmonton
	Sun.	8	at Calgary
	Thur.	12	Montreal
	Sat.	14	Boston
	Tues.	17	Anaheim
	Wed.	18	at NY Islanders
	Mon.	23	at NY Rangers
	Tues.	24	Washington
	Fri.	27	at Buffalo
	Sat.	28	NY Rangers
Feb.	Thur.	2	at Washington
	Sat.	4	San Jose*
	Sun.	5	New Jersey*
	Tues.	7	Vancouver
	Thur.	9	at Pittsburgh
	Sat.	11	Ottawa
	Wed.	15	at Anaheim
	Thur.	16	at Los Angeles
	Sat.	18	at San Jose
	Mon.	20	at Vancouver
			(in Saskatoon)
	Thur.	23	at Ottawa
	Sat.	25	Boston
	Tues.	28	at Boston
Mar.	Thur.	2	at Winnipeg
	Sat.	4	at Buffalo
	Mon.	6	Pittsburgh
	Wed.	8	at Florida
	Thur.	9	at Pittsburgh
	Sat.	12	NY Islanders
	Tues.	14	at New Jersey
	Thur.	16	Winnipeg
	Sun.	19	Pittsburgh*
	Wed.	22	at Hartford
	Fri.	24	at Buffalo
	Sat.	25	Ottawa
	Tues.	28	St. Louis
	Thur.	30	at NY Rangers
	Fri.	31	at Chicago
Apr.	Sun.	2	NY Islanders*
	Wed.	5	at Montreal
	Thur.	6	Montreal
	Sat.	8	at Ottawa

* Denotes afternoon game.

Home Starting Times:

Weeknights . . . . 7:30 p.m.
Saturdays . . . . 7:00 p.m.
Matinees . . . . 1:30 p.m.
Except   Sat. Jan. 28 . . . . 7:30 p.m.

Franchise date: June 22, 1979

NORTHEAST DIVISION

16th NHL Season

Year-by-Year Record

Season	GP	Home			Road			Overall			GF	GA	Pts.	Finished		Playoff Result
		W	L	T	W	L	T	W	L	T						
1993-94	84	19	17	6	15	25	2	34	42	8	277	292	76	5th,	Northeast Div.	Out of Playoffs
1992-93	84	23	17	2	24	10	8	47	27	10	351	300	104	2nd,	Adams Div.	Lost Div. Semi-Final
1991-92	80	18	19	3	2	29	9	20	48	12	255	318	52	5th,	Adams Div.	Out of Playoffs
1990-91	80	9	23	8	7	27	6	16	50	14	236	354	46	5th,	Adams Div.	Out of Playoffs
1989-90	80	8	26	6	4	35	1	12	61	7	240	407	31	5th,	Adams Div.	Out of Playoffs
1988-89	80	16	20	4	11	26	3	27	46	7	269	342	61	5th,	Adams Div.	Out of Playoffs
1987-88	80	15	23	2	17	20	3	32	43	5	271	306	69	5th,	Adams Div.	Out of Playoffs
1986-87	80	20	13	7	11	26	3	31	39	10	267	276	72	4th,	Adams Div.	Lost Div. Final
1985-86	80	23	13	4	20	18	2	43	31	6	330	289	92	1st,	Adams Div.	Lost Div. Semi-Final
1984-85	80	24	12	4	17	18	5	41	30	9	323	275	91	2nd,	Adams Div.	Lost Conf. Championship
1983-84	80	24	11	5	18	17	5	42	28	10	360	278	94	3th,	Adams Div.	Lost Div. Final
1982-83	80	23	10	7	11	24	5	34	34	12	343	336	80	4th,	Adams Div.	Lost Div. Semi-Final
1981-82	80	24	13	3	9	18	13	33	31	16	356	345	82	4th,	Adams Div.	Lost Conf. Championship
1980-81	80	18	11	11	12	21	7	30	32	18	314	318	78	4th,	Adams Div.	Lost Prelim. Round
1979-80	80	17	16	7	8	28	4	25	44	11	248	313	61	5th,	Adams Div.	Out of Playoffs

1994-95 Player Personnel

FORWARDS	HT	WT	S	Place of Birth	Date	1993-94 Club
BASSEN, Bob	5-10	180	L	Calgary, Alta.	5/6/65	St. Louis-Quebec
BROUSSEAU, Paul	6-2	203	R	Pierrefonds, Que.	9/18/73	Cornwall
CLARK, Wendel	5-11	194	L	Kelvington, Sask.	10/25/66	Toronto
CORBET, Rene	6-0	187	L	Victoriaville, Que.	6/25/73	Quebec-Cornwall
DEADMARSH, Adam	6-0	195	R	Trail, B.C.	5/10/75	Portland (WHL)
FORSBERG, Peter	6-0	190	L	Ornskoldsvik, Sweden	7/20/73	MoDo
FRASER, Iain	5-10	175	L	Scarborough, Ont.	8/10/69	Quebec
FRIEDMAN, Doug	6-1	189	L	Cape Elizabeth, ME	9/1/71	Boston U.
HUGHES, Ryan	6-2	196	L	Montreal, Que.	1/17/72	Cornwall
KAMENSKY, Valeri	6-2	198	R	Voskresensk, USSR	4/18/66	Quebec
KLIPPENSTEIN, Wade	6-3	219	L	Boissevain, Man.	5/9/70	Cornwall-Greensboro
KOVALENKO, Andrei	5-10	200	L	Balakovo, USSR	6/7/70	Quebec
LAPOINTE, Claude	5-9	181	L	Lachine, Que.	10/11/68	Quebec
MacDERMID, Paul	6-1	205	R	Chesley, Ont.	4/14/63	Quebec
McKEE, Mike	6-3	203	R	Toronto, Ont.	6/18/69	Quebec-Cornwall
NOLAN, Owen	6-1	201	R	Belfast, Ireland	9/22/71	Quebec
NORRIS, Dwayne	5-10	175	R	St. John's, Nfld.	1/8/70	Cdn. National-Cdn. Olympic-Que-Corw'll
RICCI, Mike	6-0	190	L	Scarborough, Ont.	10/27/71	Quebec
RUCINSKY, Martin	6-0	178	L	Most, Czech.	3/11/71	Quebec
SAKIC, Joe	5-11	185	L	Burnaby, B.C.	7/7/69	Quebec
SAVAGE, Reggie	5-10	192	L	Montreal, Que.	5/1/70	Quebec-Cornwall
SCHULTE, Paxton	6-2	217	L	Ionaway, Alta.	7/16/72	Quebec-Cornwall
SIMON, Chris	6-3	219	L	Wawa, Ont.	1/30/72	Quebec
VEILLEUX, Eric	5-7	148	L	Quebec, Que.	2/20/72	Cornwall
WARD, Ed	6-3	205	R	Edmonton, Alta.	11/10/69	Quebec-Cornwall
YELLE, Stephane	6-1	162	L	Ottawa, Ont.	5/9/74	Oshawa
YOUNG, Scott	6-0	190	L	Clinton, MA	10/1/67	Quebec

DEFENSEMEN						
BREKKE, Brent	6-1	175	L	Minot, ND	8/16/71	W. Michigan
FINN, Steven	6-0	191	L	Laval, Que.	8/20/66	Quebec
FOOTE, Adam	6-0	202	R	Toronto, Ont.	7/10/71	Quebec
GUSAROV, Alexei	6-3	185	L	Leningrad, USSR	7/8/64	Quebec
HURLBUT, Mike	6-2	200	L	Massena, NY	10/7/66	Quebec-Cornwall
KARPA, Dave	6-1	202	R	Regina, Sask.	5/7/71	Quebec-Cornwall
KLEMM, Jon	6-3	200	R	Cranbrook, B.C.	1/8/70	Quebec-Cornwall
KRUPP, Uwe	6-6	235	R	Cologne, West Germany	6/24/65	NY Islanders
LAUKKANEN, Janne	6-0	180	L	Lahti, Finland	3/19/70	HPK
LEFEBVRE, Sylvain	6-2	205	L	Richmond, Que.	10/14/67	Toronto
LESCHYSHYN, Curtis	6-1	205	L	Thompson, Man.	9/21/69	Quebec
MATIER, Mark	6-1	209	L	St. Catharines, Ont.	12/14/73	Cornwall
MILLER, Aaron	6-3	197	R	Buffalo, NY	8/11/71	Quebec-Cornwall
PARROTT, Jeff	6-1	195	R	The Pas, Man.	4/6/71	Cornwall
SCOTT, Blair	6-0	202	L	Winnipeg, Man.	2/25/72	Cornwall
WOLANIN, Craig	6-3	205	L	Grosse Pointe, MI	7/27/67	Quebec

GOALTENDERS	HT	WT	C	Place of Birth	Date	1993-94 Club
ELLIS, Aaron	6-1	170	L	Indianapolis, IN	5/13/74	Detroit (OHL)
FISET, Stephane	6-1	195	L	Montreal, Que.	6/17/70	Quebec-Cornwall
KRAKE, Paul	6-0	183	L	Lloydminster, Sask.	3/25/69	Cornwall
SHULMISTRA, Richard	6-2	186	R	Sudbury, Ont.	4/1/71	Miami-Ohio
SNOW, Garth	6-3	200	L	Wrentham, MA	7/28/69	U.S. National-U.S. Olympic-Que-Corw'll
THIBAULT, Jocelyn	5-11	170	L	Montreal, Que.	1/12/75	Quebec-Cornwall

1993-94 Scoring

*– rookie

Regular Season

Pos	#	Player	Team	GP	G	A	Pts	+/-	PIM	PP	SH	GW	GT	S	%
C	19	Joe Sakic	QUE	84	28	64	92	8-	18	10	1	9	1	279	10.0
C	13	Mats Sundin	QUE	84	32	53	85	1	60	6	2	4	0	226	14.2
L	31	Valeri Kamensky	QUE	76	28	37	65	12	42	6	0	1	0	170	16.5
C	9	Mike Ricci	QUE	83	30	21	51	9-	113	13	3	6	1	138	21.7
R	48	Scott Young	QUE	76	26	25	51	4-	14	6	1	1	0	236	11.0
C	22	Ron Sutter	STL	36	6	12	18	1-	46	1	0	2	0	42	14.3
			QUE	37	9	13	22	3	44	4	0	0	0	66	13.6
			TOTAL	73	15	25	40	2	90	5	0	2	0	108	13.9
C	38	*Iain Fraser	QUE	60	17	20	37	5-	23	2	0	2	0	109	15.6
R	51	Andrei Kovalenko	QUE	58	16	17	33	5-	46	5	0	4	0	92	17.4
L	25	Martin Rucinsky	QUE	60	9	23	32	4	58	4	0	1	0	96	9.4
C	28	Bob Bassen	STL	46	2	7	9	14-	44	0	1	0	0	73	2.7
			QUE	37	11	8	19	3-	55	1	0	0	1	56	19.6
			TOTAL	83	13	15	28	17-	99	1	1	0	1	129	10.1
C	47	Claude Lapointe	QUE	59	11	17	28	2	70	1	1	1	0	73	15.1
D	5	Alexei Gusarov	QUE	76	5	20	25	3	38	0	1	0	0	84	6.0
D	7	Curtis Leschyshyn	QUE	72	5	17	22	2-	65	3	0	2	0	97	5.2
D	55	Garth Butcher	STL	43	1	6	7	6-	76	0	1	0	0	37	2.7
			QUE	34	3	9	12	1-	67	0	1	1	0	29	10.3
			TOTAL	77	4	15	19	7-	143	0	2	1	0	66	6.1
D	59	*Dave Karpa	QUE	60	5	12	17	0	148	2	0	0	0	48	10.4
D	29	Steven Finn	QUE	80	4	13	17	9-	159	0	0	1	0	74	5.4
D	6	Craig Wolanin	QUE	63	6	10	16	16	80	0	0	0	0	78	7.7
D	45	*Mike McKee	QUE	48	3	12	15	5	41	2	0	0	0	60	5.0
L	17	Chris Lindberg	QUE	37	6	8	14	1-	12	0	0	0	0	42	14.3
D	2	Tommy Sjodin	DAL	7	0	2	2	1-	4	0	0	0	0	8	.0
			QUE	22	1	9	10	5	18	1	0	0	0	46	2.2
			TOTAL	29	1	11	12	4	22	1	0	0	0	54	1.9
D	27	Brad Werenka	EDM	15	0	4	4	1-	14	0	0	0	0	11	.0
			QUE	11	0	7	7	4	8	0	0	0	0	17	.0
			TOTAL	26	0	11	11	3	22	0	0	0	0	28	.0
L	12	*Chris Simon	QUE	37	4	4	8	2-	132	0	0	1	0	39	10.3
D	52	Adam Foote	QUE	45	2	6	8	3	67	0	0	0	0	42	4.8
C	33	*Reggie Savage	QUE	17	3	4	7	3	16	1	0	0	0	25	12.0
R	23	Paul MacDermid	QUE	44	2	3	5	3-	35	0	0	0	0	16	12.5
R	11	Owen Nolan	QUE	6	2	2	4	2	8	0	0	0	0	15	13.3
L	15	Tony Twist	QUE	49	0	4	4	1-	101	0	0	0	0	15	.0
G	35	Stephane Fiset	QUE	50	0	3	3	0	6	0	0	0	0	0	.0
R	14	*Dwayne Norris	QUE	4	1	1	2	1	4	0	0	0	0	7	14.3
L	55	*Rene Corbet	QUE	9	1	1	2	1	0	0	0	0	0	14	7.1
R	54	*Ed Ward	QUE	7	1	0	1	0	5	0	0	0	0	3	33.3
D	4	Mike Hurlbut	QUE	1	0	0	0	1-	0	0	0	0	0	1	.0
D	44	*Aaron Miller	QUE	1	0	0	0	1-	0	0	0	0	0	0	.0
L	24	*Paxton Schulte	QUE	1	0	0	0	0	0	0	0	0	0	0	.0
G	1	*Garth Snow	QUE	5	0	0	0	0	2	0	0	0	0	0	.0
D	73	Alain Cote	QUE	6	0	0	0	2-	4	0	0	0	0	4	.0
D	42	*Jon Klemm	QUE	7	0	0	0	1-	4	0	0	0	0	11	.0
G	32	Jacques Cloutier	QUE	14	0	0	0	0	2	0	0	0	0	0	.0
G	41	*Jocelyn Thibault	QUE	29	0	0	0	0	0	0	0	0	0	0	.0

Goaltending

No.	Goaltender	GPI	Mins	Avg	W	L	T	EN	SO	GA	SA	S%
32	Jacques Cloutier	14	475	3.03	3	2	1	1	0	24	232	.897
41	*Jocelyn Thibault	29	1504	3.31	8	13	3	3	0	83	768	.892
35	Stephane Fiset	50	2798	3.39	20	25	4	7	2	158	1434	.890
1	*Garth Snow	5	279	3.44	3	2	0	0	0	16	127	.874
	Totals	**84**	**5080**	**3.45**	**34**	**42**	**8**	**11**	**2**	**292**	**2572**	**.886**

General Manager

LACROIX, PIERRE
General Manager, Quebec Nordiques.
Born in Montreal, Que., August 3, 1948.

Pierre Lacroix was appointed as the fourth General Manager in the Quebec Nordiques franchise history on May 24, 1994.

Following a 20-year career in world of hockey as a players' agent, he knows and understands the National Hockey League and he also knows the needs of today's young athletes.

General Managers' History

Maurice Filion, 1979-80 to 1987-88; Martin Madden 1988-89; Martin Madden and Maurice Filion, 1989-90; Pierre Page, 1990-91 to 1993-94; Pierre Lacroix, 1994-95.

Coaching History

Jacques Demers, 1979-80; Maurice Filion and Michel Bergeron, 1980-81; Michel Bergeron, 1981-82 to 1986-87; André Savard and Ron Lapointe, 1987-88; Ron Lapointe, and Jean Perron, 1988-89; Michel Bergeron, 1989-90; Dave Chambers, 1990-91; Dave Chambers and Pierre Page, 1991-92; Pierre Page, 1992-93 to 1993-94; Marc Crawford, 1994-95.

Captains' History

Marc Tardif, 1979-80, 1980-81; Robbie Ftorek and Andre Dupont, 1981-82; Mario Marois, 1982-83 to 1984-85; Mario Marois, Peter Stastny, 1985-86; Peter Stastny, 1986-87 to 1989-90; Joe Sakic and Steven Finn, 1990-91; Mike Hough, 1991-92; Joe Sakic, 1992-93 to date.

Retired Numbers

3	J.C. Tremblay	1972-1979
8	Marc Tardif	1979-1983

Club Records

Team

(Figures in brackets for season records are games played)

Most Points	104	1992-93 (84)
Most Wins	47	1992-93 (84)
Most Ties	18	1980-81 (80)
Most Losses	61	1989-90 (80)
Most Goals	360	1983-84 (80)
Most Goals Against	407	1989-90 (80)
Fewest Points	31	1989-90 (80)
Fewest Wins	12	1989-90 (80)
Fewest Ties	5	1987-88 (80)
Fewest Losses	27	1992-93 (84)
Fewest Goals	236	1990-91 (80)
Fewest Goals Against	275	1984-85 (80)

Longest Winning Streak

Over-all .... 7 Nov. 24-
Dec. 10/83
Oct. 10-21/85
Dec. 31/85-
Jan. 11/86

Home .... 10 Nov. 26/83-
Jan. 10/84

Away .... 5 Feb. 28-
Mar. 24, 1986

Longest Undefeated Streak

Over-all .... 11 Mar. 10-31/81
(7 wins, 4 ties)

Home .... 14 Nov. 19/83
Jan. 21/84
(11 wins, 3 ties)

Away .... 8 Feb. 17/81-
Mar. 22/81
(6 wins, 2 ties)

Longest Losing Streak

Over-all .... 14 Oct. 21-
Nov. 19/90

Home .... 8 Oct. 21-
Nov. 24/90

Away .... 18 Jan. 18-
Apr. 1/90

Longest Winless Streak

Over-all .... 17 Oct. 21-
Nov. 25/90
(15 losses, 2 ties)

Home .... 11 Nov. 14-
Dec. 26/89
(7 losses, 4 ties)

Away .... 33 Oct. 8/91-
Feb. 27/92
(25 losses, 8 ties)

Most Shutouts, Season 6 1985-86 (80)
Most PIM, Season 2,104 1989-90 (80)
Most Goals, Game .... 12 Feb. 1/83
(Hfd. 3 at Que. 12)
Oct. 20/84
(Que. 12 at Tor. 3)

Individual

Most Seasons .... 11 Michel Goulet
Most Games .... 813 Michel Goulet
Most Goals, Career .... 456 Michel Goulet
Most Assists, Career .... 668 Peter Stastny
Most Points, Career ..... 1,048 Peter Stastny
(380 goals, 668 assists)
Most PIM, Career ...... 1,545 Dale Hunter
Most Shutouts, Career ... 6 Mario Gosselin

Longest Consecutive
Games Streak .... 312 Dale Hunter
(Oct. 9/80-Mar. 13/84)

Most Goals, Season .... 57 Michel Goulet
(1982-83)

Most Assists, Season .... 93 Peter Stastny
(1981-82)

Most Points, Season .... 139 Peter Stastny
(1981-82)
(46 goals, 93 assists)

Most PIM, Season .... 301 Gord Donnelly
(1987-88)

Most Points, Defenseman,
Season .... 82 Steve Duchesne
(1992-93)
(20 goals, 62 assists)

Most Points, Center,
Season .... 139 Peter Stastny
(1981-82)
(46 goals, 93 assists)

Most Points, Right Wing,
Season .... 103 Jacques Richard
(1980-81)
(52 goals, 51 assists)

Most Points, Left Wing,
Season .... 121 Michel Goulet
(1983-84)
(56 goals, 65 assists)

Most Points, Rookie,
Season .... 109 Peter Stastny
(1980-81)
(39 goals, 70 assists)

Most Shutouts, Season .... 4 Clint Malarchuk
(1985-86)

Most Goals, Game .... 5 Mats Sundin
(Mar. 5/92)
Mike Ricci
(Feb. 17/94)

Most Assists, Game .... 5 Anton Stastny
(Feb. 22/81)
Michel Goulet
(Jan. 3/84)
Owen Nolan
(Mar. 5/92)
Mike Ricci
(Dec. 12/92)

Most Points, Game .... 8 Peter Stastny
(Feb. 22/81)
Anton Stastny
(Feb. 22/81)

All-time Record vs. Other Clubs

Regular Season

			At Home							On Road							Total				
	GP	W	L	T	GF	GA	PTS	GP	W	L	T	GF	GA	PTS	GP	W	L	T	GF	GA	PTS
Anaheim	1	0	1	0	3	6	0	1	0	1	0	2	2	1	1	0	4	6	2
Boston	55	17	33	5	201	249	39	53	16	29	8	166	220	40	108	33	62	13	367	469	79
Buffalo	54	27	18	9	207	175	63	54	15	31	8	172	218	38	108	42	49	17	379	393	101
Calgary	22	7	9	6	93	90	20	23	4	13	6	72	103	14	45	11	22	12	165	193	34
Chicago	22	9	9	4	94	89	22	23	7	14	2	74	94	16	45	16	23	6	168	183	38
Dallas	23	16	5	2	107	62	34	22	7	13	2	72	88	16	45	23	18	4	179	150	50
Detroit	23	12	8	3	96	85	27	22	9	12	1	77	88	19	45	21	20	4	173	173	46
Edmonton	22	7	13	2	88	107	16	22	5	17	0	66	125	10	44	12	30	2	154	232	26
Florida	2	0	1	1	4	6	1	2	2	0	0	10	4	4	4	2	1	1	14	10	5
Hartford	55	32	16	7	239	171	71	53	20	22	11	189	185	51	108	52	38	18	428	356	122
Los Angeles	22	10	9	3	94	91	23	22	8	13	1	77	102	17	44	18	22	4	171	193	40
Montreal	55	26	26	3	187	204	55	54	12	34	8	167	231	32	109	38	60	11	354	435	87
New Jersey	24	12	9	3	98	80	27	26	12	12	2	96	109	26	50	24	21	5	194	189	53
NY Islanders	25	13	10	2	98	83	28	23	8	14	1	78	101	17	48	21	24	3	176	184	45
NY Rangers	25	12	10	3	110	106	27	24	5	16	3	66	103	13	49	17	26	6	176	209	40
Ottawa	6	6	0	0	35	14	12	8	4	3	1	36	27	9	14	10	3	1	71	41	21
Philadelphia	24	8	9	7	88	89	23	25	3	20	2	64	103	8	49	11	29	9	152	192	31
Pittsburgh	23	12	11	0	106	92	24	26	8	14	4	105	116	20	49	20	25	4	211	208	44
St. Louis	22	10	9	3	82	74	23	22	4	16	2	74	105	10	44	14	25	5	156	179	33
San Jose	3	3	0	0	17	9	6	4	2	2	0	21	20	4	7	5	2	0	38	29	10
Tampa Bay	3	2	1	0	13	9	4	4	1	3	0	12	14	2	7	3	4	0	25	23	6
Toronto	23	13	5	5	94	73	31	23	10	11	2	99	84	22	46	23	16	7	193	157	53
Vancouver	23	9	10	4	67	68	22	22	7	11	4	88	93	18	45	16	21	8	155	161	40
Washington	24	8	12	4	77	98	20	24	9	12	3	80	97	21	48	17	24	7	157	195	41
Winnipeg	23	10	10	3	93	95	23	22	7	10	5	87	94	19	45	17	20	8	180	189	42
Totals	**604**	**281**	**244**	**79**	**2391**	**2225**	**641**	**604**	**186**	**342**	**76**	**2049**	**2524**	**448**	**1208**	**467**	**586**	**155**	**4440**	**4749**	**1089**

Calgary totals include Atlanta, 1979-80. Dallas totals include Minnesota, 1979-80 to 1992-93.
New Jersey totals include Colorado, 1979-80 to 1981-82.

Playoffs

	Series	W	L	GP	W	L	T	GF	GA	Last Mtg.	Round	Result
Boston	2	1	1	11	5	6	0	36	37	1983	DSF	L 1-3
Buffalo	2	2	0	8	6	2	0	35	27	1985	DSF	W 3-2
Hartford	2	1	1	9	4	5	0	34	35	1987	DSF	W 4-2
Montreal	5	2	3	31	14	17	0	85	105	1993	DSF	L 2-4
NY Islanders	1	0	1	4	0	4	0	9	18	1982	CF	L 0-4
Philadelphia	2	0	2	11	4	7	0	29	39	1985	CF	L 2-4
Totals	**14**	**6**	**8**	**74**	**33**	**41**	**0**	**228**	**261**			

Playoff Results 1994-90

Year	Round	Opponent	Result	GF	GA
1993	DSF	Montreal	L 2-4	16	19

Abbreviations: Round: F – Final;
CF – conference final; **CQF** – conference quarter-final;
CSF – conference semi-final; **DF** – division final;
DSF – division semi-final; **SF** – semi-final;
QF – quarter-final; **PR** – preliminary round.

1993-94 Results

Oct.	6	at	Ottawa	5-5		11	at	Calgary	0-1
	9	at	Boston	3-7		12	at	Vancouver	3-4
	10		Pittsburgh	7-4		15		Washington	0-4
	13	at	NY Rangers	4-6		18		Pittsburgh	6-3
	16	at	Montreal	5-2		25		Philadelphia	6-4
	18		Montreal	2-4		27	at	Pittsburgh	0-3
	20	at	Hartford	5-2		29	at	Hartford	3-2
	21	at	Chicago	2-3		31	at	Boston	3-4
	23		Dallas	3-2	**Feb.**	1		Hartford	1-2
	26		Philadelphia	2-4		3	at	St. Louis	4-3
	28	at	Pittsburgh	7-3		5		NY Islanders	2-3
	30		Detroit	3-5		8		Boston	1-6
Nov.	2		Tampa Bay	8-2		12	at	Montreal	2-5
	4	at	Philadelphia	1-4		14		NY Rangers	2-4
	6		NY Rangers	2-4		17	at	San Jose	8-2
	7		Florida	1-3		18	at	Anaheim	1-0
	9	at	Washington	1-2		21	at	Buffalo	1-2
	13		Tampa Bay	3-4		24		St. Louis	6-0
	14		Florida	5-2		26		Anaheim	3-6
	20		Winnipeg	5-5		27	at	NY Islanders	2-5
	23		New Jersey	1-1	**Mar.**	2	at	NY Rangers	2-5
	25		Los Angeles	8-6		5		Toronto	4-1
	27		Buffalo	2-2		7	at	New Jersey	2-2
	30		Boston	2-5		8		Ottawa	5-2
Dec.	3		NY Islanders	3-2		10		Montreal	4-4
	4		Vancouver	3-1		12	at	Washington	4-3
	7		Calgary	4-4		14		Chicago	5-1
	9	at	New Jersey	3-2		17		Hartford	4-1
	11		Ottawa	5-2		19	at	Montreal	2-5
	13		Washington	2-5		20		Edmonton	3-5
	16	at	Philadelphia	2-3		22		Boston	5-3
	18		New Jersey	2-6		26	at	Toronto	3-6
	19		San Jose	7-5		27	at	New Jersey	2-5
	21	at	Ottawa	1-2		30	at	Ottawa	4-6
	23	at	Winnipeg	2-5		31	at	Detroit	4-2
	28		Tampa Bay	1-4	**Apr.**	2		Buffalo	2-6
	29		NY Islanders	5-3		4		Buffalo	6-4
	31	at	Pittsburgh	5-4		5		Florida	3-3
Jan.	2	at	Dallas	6-4		7		Hartford	5-2
	4	at	Los Angeles	1-5		10	at	Buffalo	1-4
	5		Montreal	0-4		12	at	Florida	5-2
	7	at	Edmonton	4-6		14	at	Tampa Bay	2-5

Entry Draft
Selections 1994-80

1994
Pick
12	Wade Belak
22	Jeffrey Kealty
35	Josef Marha
61	Sebastien Bety
72	Chris Drury
87	Milan Hejduk
113	Tony Tuzzolino
139	Nicholas Windsor
165	Calvin Elfring
191	Jay Bertsch
217	Tim Thomas
243	Chris Pittman
285	Steven Low

1993
Pick
10	Jocelyn Thibault
14	Adam Deadmarsh
49	Ashley Buckberger
75	Bill Pierce
101	Ryan Tocher
127	Anders Myrvold
137	Nicholas Checco
153	Christian Matte
179	David Ling
205	Petr Franek
231	Vincent Auger
257	Mark Pivetz
283	John Hillman

1992
Pick
4	Todd Warriner
28	Paul Brousseau
29	Tuomas Gronman
52	Emmanuel Fernandez
76	Ian McIntyre
100	Charlie Wasley
124	Paxton Schulte
148	Martin LePage
172	Mike Jickling
196	Steve Passmore
220	Anson Carter
244	Aaron Ellis

1991
Pick
1	Eric Lindros
24	Rene Corbet
46	Richard Brennan
68	Dave Karpa
90	Patrick Labrecque
103	Bill Lindsay
134	Mikael Johansson
156	Janne Laukkanen
157	Aaron Asp
178	Adam Bartell
188	Brent Brekke
200	Paul Koch
222	Doug Friedman
244	Eric Meloche

1990
Pick
1	Owen Nolan
22	Ryan Hughes
43	Bradley Zavisha
106	Jeff Parrott
127	Dwayne Norris
148	Andrei Kovalenko
158	Alexander Karpovtsev
169	Pat Mazzoli
190	Scott Davis
211	Mika Stromberg
232	Wade Klippenstein

1989
Pick
1	Mats Sundin
22	Adam Foote
43	Stephane Morin
54	John Tanner
68	Niclas Andersson
76	Eric Dubois
85	Kevin Kaiser
106	Dan Lambert
127	Sergei Mylnikov
148	Paul Krake
169	Viacheslav Bykov
190	Andrei Khomutov
211	Byron Witkowski
232	Noel Rahn

1988
Pick
3	Curtis Leschyshyn
5	Daniel Dore
24	Stephane Fiset
45	Petri Aaltonen
66	Darin Kimble
87	Stephane Venne
108	Ed Ward
129	Valeri Kamensky
150	Sakari Lindfors
171	Dan Wiebe
213	Alexei Gusarov
234	Claude Lapointe

1987
Pick
9	Bryan Fogarty
15	Joe Sakic
51	Jim Sprott
72	Kip Miller
93	Rob Mendel
114	Garth Snow
135	Tim Hanus
156	Jake Enebak
177	Jaroslav Sevcik
183	Ladislav Tresl
198	Darren Nauss
219	Mike Williams

1986
Pick
18	Ken McRae
39	Jean-Marc Routhier
41	Stephane Guerard
81	Ron Tugnutt
102	Gerald Bzdel
117	Scott White
123	Morgan Samuelsson
134	Mark Vermette
144	Jean-Francois Nault
165	Keith Miller
186	Pierre Millier
207	Chris Lappin
228	Martin Latreille
249	Sean Boudreault

1985
Pick
15	David Latta
36	Jason Lafreniere
57	Max Middendorf
65	Peter Massey
78	David Espe
99	Bruce Major
120	Andy Akervik
141	Mike Oliverio
162	Mario Brunetta
183	Brit Peer
204	Tom Sasso
225	Gary Murphy
246	Jean Bois

1984
Pick
15	Trevor Stienburg
36	Jeff Brown
57	Steve Finn
78	Terry Perkins
120	Darren Cota
141	Henrik Cedergren
162	Jyrki Maki
183	Guy Ouellette
203	Ken Quinney
244	Peter Loob

1983
Pick
32	Yves Heroux
52	Bruce Bell
54	Iiro Jarvi
92	Luc Guenette
112	Brad Walcott
132	Craig Mack
152	Tommy Albelin
172	Wayne Groulx
192	Scott Shaunessy
232	Bo Berglund
239	Jindrich Kokrment

1982
Pick
13	David Shaw
34	Paul Gillis
55	Mario Gosselin
76	Jiri Lala
97	Phil Stanger
131	Daniel Poudrier
181	Mike Hough
202	Vincent Lukac
223	Andre Martin
244	Jozef Lukac
248	Jan Jasko

1981
Pick
11	Randy Moller
53	Jean-Marc Gaulin
74	Clint Malarchuk
95	Ed Lee
116	Mike Eagles
158	Andre Cote
179	Marc Brisebois
200	Kari Takko

1980
Pick
24	Normand Rochefort
66	Jay Miller
87	Basil McRae
108	Mark Kumpel
129	Gaston Therrien
150	Michel Bolduc
171	Christian Tanguay
192	William Robinson

Coach

CRAWFORD, MARC
Coach, Quebec Nordiques. Born in Belleville, Ont., February 13, 1961.

Marc Crawford became the 10th head coach in the history of the Quebec Nordiques on July 6, 1994, taking charge behind the bench of an NHL team for the first time in his coaching career.

After serving as the general manager and coach of the Cornwall Royals for two seasons, Crawford joined the Toronto Maple Leafs' organization as head coach of the St. John's Maple Leafs in 1991. In three seasons, he recorded 125 wins, 78 losses and 37 ties for a winning percentage of .598. In 1991-92 he led his team to the finals of the AHL before losing in seven games. The same season, he received the Louis A.R. Pieri Memorial Award presented by the AHL's coaches, as coach of the year. In 1992-93, his team finished with 41 wins and a total of 95 points while winning the Atlantic Division title.

Marc Crawford has been associated with professional hockey since the early 1980s. He played 176 games in the NHL, all with the Vancouver Canucks.

Coaching Record

Season	Team	Games	Regular Season W	L	T	%	Playoffs Games	W	L	%
1989-90	Cornwall (OHL)	66	24	38	4	.394	6	2	4	.333
1990-91	Cornwall (OHL)	66	23	42	1	.356	....	....	....	....
1991-92	St. John's (AHL)	80	39	29	12	.562	16	11	5	.688
1992-93	St. John's (AHL)	80	41	26	13	.594	9	4	5	.444
1993-94	St. John's (AHL)	80	45	23	12	.638	11	6	5	.545

Club Directory

Colisée de Québec
2205 Ave du Colisée
Québec City, Québec
G1L 4W7
Phone 418/529-8441
FAX 418/529-1052
Capacity: 15,399

President and Governor	Marcel Aubut
Assistants to the President	Luc Ouellet, Diane Thivierge
Alternate Governor	Pierre Lacroix
Executive Secretaries to the President	Louise Marois, Jeanne Simard
Coordinator – President's Agenda	Sylvie Fiset

Hockey Club Personnel
General Manager	Pierre Lacroix
Assistant to the General Manager – Hockey operations	Sherwood Bassin
Administrative Assistant to the General Manager	François Giguère
Head Coach	Marc Crawford
Assistant Coaches	Jacques Martin, Joel Quenneville
Goaltending Coach	Jacques Cloutier
Strength and Conditioning Coach	Lorne Goldenberg
Director of Player Development and Pro Scout	André Savard
Chief Scout	Dave Draper
Scouts	Shannon Currie, Lucien Deblois, Yvon Gendron, Jan Janda, Bengt Lundholm, Brian MacDonald, Don McKenney, Lewis A. Mongelluzzo, Don Paarup, Orval Tessier
Physiotherapist	Jacques Lavergne
Assistant to the Physiotherapist	Matthew Sokolowski
Trainers	René Lacasse, René Lavigueur, Jean-René Lavigueur, Brian Turpin
Team Physician	Dr. Pierre Beauchemin
Executive Secretary – hockey department	Martine Bélanger
Secretary – hockey department and Travel Coordinator	Nathalie Paquet

Administration and Finance
Vice-President/Administration and Finance	Jean Laflamme
Controller	François Bilodeau
Supervisor of Special Projects	Louis Parent
Assistant to the Controller	Rémi Bolduc
Accountants	Danielle Bhérer, Lucette Lemieux, Sylvie Jacques
Supervisor of Computer Systems Development	André Demers
Archivist	Gaétan Simard
Executive Secretary	P. Huguette Gauthier
Receptionist	Edith Murphy
Messangers	Raymond Boulianne, François Fournier

Sales, Marketing and Communications
Sales and Marketing
Director of Marketing	Bernard Thiboutot
Director of Sales	André Lestourneau
Representatives – National sales	Jacques Beauchesne, Mark Charest
Representatives – Local sales	Charles Langlois, Reynald Roberge
Supervisor-Promotional agreements coordination	Jean-François Drolet
Account Assistants – Promotional agreements coordination	Kevin Donnelly, Chantal Poirier, Anne-Cécile Piraux
Assistant to the Director of Sales	Nicolas Labbé
Supervisor of Nordtel Service	Josée Métivier
Supervisor of Telemarketing	Hélène Dion
Supervisor of Group Sales	Christine Côté
Sales Representatives	Jean Frenette, Luc Gagné, Nathalie Gauthier, Bernard Nadeau, Gérald Veilleux
Supervisor of Novelties & Souvenirs	Anne Latouche
Executive Secretary – Marketing and Promotions	Barbara Sévier
Telephonist – Nordtel Service	Marie-Claude Létourneau
Secretaries – Marketing and Promotions	Jacinthe Côté, Josée Bédard
Executive Secretary – Sales	Guylaine Poirier
Secretary – Sales	Kathia Gagnon

Communications
Director of Public Relations	Jacques Labrie
Director of Press Relations	Jean Martineau
Coordinator of Public Relations	Nicole Bouchard
Graphic Communications Coordinator	Pierre Masson
Computer Graphists	Hélène Foley, Stéphane Caron
Executive Secretary – Public Relations	Francine Racette
Team Photographer	Jean-Yves Michaud

Location of Press Box	East & West side of building, upper level
Dimensions of Rink	200 feet by 85 feet
Club Colors	Blue, White & Red
Uniforms	Home: Base color white trimmed with blue & red
	Away: Base color blue trimmed with white & red
Training Camp Site	Québec City
Radio Station	CJRP 1060
Radio Announcers	Alain Crête, Mario Marois
TV Station	CFAP (2) Quatre Saisons
TV Announcers	André Côté, Claude Bédard

St. Louis Blues

1993-94 Results: 40W-33L-11T 91PTS. Fourth, Central Division

Schedule

Oct.				Sun.	8	Winnipeg
Sat.	1	at Detroit		Tues.	10	Los Angeles
Sun.	2	at Chicago		Thur.	12	at Los Angeles
Thur.	6	at Florida		Sat.	14	at San Jose
Fri.	7	at Tampa Bay		Tues.	17	at Winnipeg
Tues.	11	Chicago		Tues.	24	at NY Islanders
Thur.	13	NY Rangers		Thur.	26	Edmonton
Sat.	15	at Toronto		Sat.	28	Calgary
Sun.	16	Tampa Bay		Tues.	31	Anaheim
Tues.	18	San Jose	Feb.	Thur.	2	Los Angeles
Sat.	22	Toronto				(in Las Vegas)
Sun.	23	Vancouver		Sat.	4	Dallas
Tues.	25	Washington		Thur.	9	at Anaheim
Sat.	29	at San Jose				(in Las Vegas)
Sun.	30	at Anaheim		Sat.	11	Calgary
Nov.	Wed.	2	NY Islanders	Sun.	12	Detroit
Sat.	5	Winnipeg		Wed.	15	at New Jersey
Tues.	8	at Calgary		Thur.	16	at Philadelphia
Thur.	10	at Winnipeg		Sat.	18	at Montreal
Sat.	12	Pittsburgh		Mon.	20	Edmonton
Sun.	13	at Chicago		Wed.	22	Toronto
Wed.	16	at Hartford		Fri.	24	at Pittsburgh
Thur.	17	at Boston		Sat.	25	Chicago
Sat.	19	at Toronto		Mon.	27	at Toronto
Wed.	23	at Detroit	Mar.	Thur.	2	Los Angeles
Thur.	24	Quebec				(in Las Vegas)
Sat.	26	at Dallas		Sat.	4	at Winnipeg*
Mon.	28	Winnipeg		Sun.	5	at Chicago*
Wed.	30	Montreal		Tues.	7	Ottawa
Dec.	Sun.	4	New Jersey	Thur.	9	Hartford
Wed.	7	at Dallas		Sun.	12	Buffalo
Sat.	10	Dallas		Tues.	14	at Edmonton
Sun.	11	Detroit		Thur.	16	at Los Angeles
Fri.	16	at Vancouver		Sun.	19	at Anaheim*
Sun.	18	at Edmonton		Tues.	21	at Vancouver
Tues.	20	at Calgary		Thur.	23	Anaheim
Fri.	23	Vancouver		Sun.	26	Boston
Mon.	26	at Dallas		Tues.	28	at Quebec
Tues.	27	Chicago		Wed.	29	at Ottawa
Thur.	29	San Jose		Fri.	31	Toronto
Sat.	31	Dallas	Apr.	Sun.	2	at Detroit*
Jan.	Mon.	2	at Washington*	Tues.	4	at Buffalo
Tues.	3	at NY Rangers		Thur.	6	Detroit
Sat.	7	Florida		Sun.	9	Philadelphia*

* Denotes afternoon game.

Home Starting Times:
Mondays through Saturdays . . . . . 7:30 p.m.
Sundays . . . . 6:00 p.m.
Matinees . . . . 12:00 p.m.
Except   Sat. Oct. 22 . . . . 6:30 p.m.
              Sun. Feb. 12 . . . . 7:00 p.m.

Franchise date: June 5, 1967

28th NHL Season

CENTRAL DIVISION

Year-by-Year Record

		Home			Road			Overall							
Season	GP	W	L	T	W	L	T	W	L	T	GF	GA	Pts.	Finished	Playoff Result
1993-94	84	23	11	8	17	22	3	40	33	11	270	283	91	4th, Central Div.	Lost Conf. Quarter-Final
1992-93	84	22	13	7	15	23	4	37	36	11	282	278	85	4th, Norris Div.	Lost Div. Final
1991-92	80	25	12	3	11	21	8	36	33	11	279	266	83	3rd, Norris Div.	Lost Div. Semi-Final
1990-91	80	24	9	7	23	13	4	47	22	11	310	250	105	2nd, Norris Div.	Lost Div. Final
1989-90	80	20	15	5	17	19	4	37	34	9	295	279	83	2nd, Norris Div.	Lost Div. Final
1988-89	80	22	11	7	11	24	5	33	35	12	275	285	78	2nd, Norris Div.	Lost Div. Final
1987-88	80	18	17	5	16	21	3	34	38	8	278	294	76	2nd, Norris Div.	Lost Div. Final
1986-87	80	21	12	7	11	21	8	32	33	15	281	293	79	1st, Norris Div.	Lost Div. Semi-Final
1985-86	80	23	11	6	14	23	3	37	34	9	302	291	83	3rd, Norris Div.	Lost Conf. Championship
1984-85	80	21	12	7	16	19	5	37	31	12	299	288	86	1st, Norris Div.	Lost Div. Semi-Final
1983-84	80	23	14	3	9	27	4	32	41	7	293	316	71	2nd, Norris Div.	Lost Div. Final
1982-83	80	16	16	8	9	24	7	25	40	15	285	316	65	4th, Norris Div.	Lost Div. Semi-Final
1981-82	80	22	14	4	10	26	4	32	40	8	315	349	72	3rd Norris Div.	Lost Div. Final
1980-81	80	29	7	4	16	11	13	45	18	17	352	281	107	1st, Smythe Div.	Lost Quarter-Final
1979-80	80	20	13	7	14	21	5	34	34	12	266	278	80	2nd, Smythe Div.	Lost Prelim. Round
1978-79	80	14	20	6	4	30	6	18	50	12	249	348	48	3rd, Smythe Div.	Out of Playoffs
1977-78	80	12	20	8	8	27	5	20	47	13	195	304	53	4th, Smythe Div.	Out of Playoffs
1976-77	80	22	13	5	10	26	4	32	39	9	239	276	73	1st, Smythe Div.	Lost Quarter-Final
1975-76	80	20	12	8	9	25	6	29	37	14	249	290	72	3rd, Smythe Div.	Lost Prelim. Round
1974-75	80	23	13	4	12	18	10	35	31	14	269	267	84	2nd, Smythe Div.	Lost Prelim. Round
1973-74	78	16	16	7	10	24	5	26	40	12	206	248	64	6th, West Div.	Out of Playoffs
1972-73	78	21	11	7	11	23	5	32	34	12	233	251	76	4th, West Div.	Lost Quarter-Final
1971-72	78	17	17	5	11	22	6	28	39	11	208	247	67	3rd, West Div.	Lost Semi-Final
1970-71	78	23	7	9	11	18	10	34	25	19	223	208	87	2nd, West Div.	Lost Quarter-Final
1969-70	76	24	9	5	13	18	7	37	27	12	224	179	86	1st, West Div.	Lost Final
1968-69	76	21	8	9	16	17	5	37	25	14	204	157	88	1st, West Div.	Lost Final
1967-68	74	18	12	7	9	19	9	27	31	16	177	191	70	3rd, West Div.	Lost Final

One of the NHL's most dynamic goal-scorers, Brett Hull reached the 50-goal mark for the fifth consecutive season, collecting 57 goals for St. Louis in the 1993-94 campaign.

1994-95 Player Personnel

FORWARDS	HT	WT	S	Place of Birth	Date	1993-94 Club
BOZON, Philippe	5-10	185	L	Chamonix, France	11/30/66	St. Louis
CARBONNEAU, Guy	5-11	184	R	Sept-Iles, Que.	3/18/60	Montreal
CHASE, Kelly	5-11	195	R	Porcupine Plain, Sask.	10/25/67	St. Louis
CHASSE, Denis	6-2	190	R	Montreal, Que.	2/7/70	Cornwall-St. Louis
FELSNER, Denny	6-0	195	L	Warren, MI	4/29/70	St. Louis-Peoria
HULL, Brett	5-10	201	R	Belleville, Ont.	8/9/64	St. Louis
JANNEY, Craig	6-1	190	L	Hartford, CT	9/26/67	St. Louis
JOHNSON, Craig	6-2	197	L	St. Paul, MN	3/18/72	U.S. National-U.S. Olympic
KARAMNOV, Vitali	6-2	185	L	Moscow, USSR	7/6/68	St. Louis-Peoria
KENADY, Christopher	6-2	195	R	Mound, MN	4/10/73	U. of Denver
KOROLEV, Igor	6-1	187	L	Moscow, USSR	9/6/70	St. Louis
LACHANCE, Bob	5-11	180	R	Northampton, MA	2/1/74	Boston U.
LAPERRIERE, Ian	6-0	191	R	Montreal, Que.	1/19/74	St. Louis-Drummondville-Peoria
McRAE, Basil	6-2	205	L	Beaverton, Ont.	1/5/61	St. Louis
MIEHM, Kevin	6-2	200	L	Kitchener, Ont.	9/10/69	St. Louis-Peoria
MILLER, Kevin	5-11	190	L	Lansing, MI	9/2/65	St. Louis
PROKHOROV, Vitali	5-9	185	L	Moscow, USSR	12/25/66	St. Louis-Peoria
ROBERTS, David	6-0	185	L	Alameda, CA	5/28/70	U.S. National-U.S. Olympic-St. Louis-Peoria
ROY, Stephane	5-10	173	L	Ste-Martine, Que.	1/26/76	Val D'or
SHANAHAN, Brendan	6-3	215	R	Mimico, Ont.	1/23/69	St. Louis
STASTNY, Peter	6-1	200	L	Bratislava, Czech.	9/18/56	Bratislava-Slov. Olympic-StL
TARDIF, Patrice	6-2	185	L	Thetford Mines, Que.	10/30/70	U. of Maine-Peoria
TIKKANEN, Esa	6-1	200	L	Helsinki, Finland	1/25/65	NY Rangers
TWIST, Tony	6-0	208	L	Sherwood Park, Alta.	5/9/68	Quebec
VASILEVSKY, Alexander	5-11	190	L	Kiev, USSR	1/8/75	Victoria

DEFENSEMEN						
BARON, Murray	6-3	215	L	Prince George, B.C.	6/1/67	St. Louis
BATTERS, Jeff	6-2	215	R	Victoria, B.C.	10/23/70	St. Louis-Peoria
DUCHESNE, Steve	5-11	195	L	Sept-Iles, Que.	6/30/65	St. Louis
HAMRLIK, Martin	5-11	185	R	Gottwaldov, Czech.	5/6/73	Springfield-Peoria
HOLLINGER, Terry	6-1	200	L	Regina, Sask.	2/24/71	St. Louis-Peoria
HOULDER, Bill	6-3	218	L	Thunder Bay, Ont.	3/11/67	Anaheim
LAPERRIERE, Daniel	6-1	195	L	Laval, Que.	3/28/69	St. Louis-Peoria
LIDSTER, Doug	6-1	200	R	Kamloops, B.C.	10/18/60	NY Rangers
MacINNIS, Al	6-2	196	R	Inverness, N.S.	7/11/63	Calgary
RIVERS, Jamie	6-0	180	L	Ottawa, Ont.	3/16/75	Sudbury
STAIOS, Steve	6-0	185	R	Hamilton, Ont.	7/28/73	Peoria
TILLEY, Tom	6-0	190	R	Trenton, Ont.	3/28/65	St. Louis
ZOMBO, Rick	6-1	195	R	Des Plaines, IL	5/8/63	St. Louis

GOALTENDERS	HT	WT	C	Place of Birth	Date	1993-94 Club
CASEY, Jon	5-10	155	L	Grand Rapids, MN	3/29/62	Boston
DUFFUS, Parris	6-2	192	L	Denver, CO	1/27/70	Peoria
JOSEPH, Curtis	5-10	182	L	Keswick, Ont.	4/29/67	St. Louis
SARJEANT, Geoff	5-9	180	L	Newmarket, Ont.	11/30/69	Peoria

General Managers' History

Lynn Patrick, 1967-68 to 1968-69; Scotty Bowman, 1969-70 to 1970-71; Lynn Patrick, 1971-72; Sid Abel, 1972-73; Charles Catto, 1973-74; Gerry Ehman, 1974-75; Dennis Ball, 1975-76; Emile Francis, 1976-77 to 1982-83; Ron Caron, 1983-84 to 1993-94; Mike Keenan, 1994-95.

Coaching History

Lynn Patrick and Scott Bowman, 1967-68; Scott Bowman, 1968-69 to 1969-70; Al Arbour and Scott Bowman, 1970-71; Sid Abel, Bill McCreary, Al Arbour, 1971-72; Al Arbour and Jean-Guy Talbot, 1972-73; Jean-Guy Talbot and Lou Angotti, 1973-74; Lou Angotti, Lynn Patrck and Garry Young, 1974-75; Garry Young, Lynn Patrick and Leo Boivin, 1975-76; Emile Francis, 1976-77; Leo Boivin and Barclay Plager, 1977-78; Barclay Plager, 1978-79; Barclay Plager and Red Berenson, 1979-80; Red Berenson, 1980-81; Red Berenson and Emile Francis, 1981-82; Barclay Plager and Emile Francis, 1982-83; Jacques Demers, 1983-84 to 1985-86; Jacques Martin, 1986-87 to 1987-88; Brian Sutter, 1988-89 to 1991-92; Bob Plager and Bob Berry, 1992-93; Bob Berry, 1993-94; Mike Keenan, 1994-95.

Captains' History

Al Arbour, 1967-68 to 1969-70; Red Berenson, Barclay Plager, 1970-71; Barclay Plager, 1971-72 to 1975-76; no captain, 1976-77; Red Berenson, 1977-78; Barry Gibbs, 1978-79; Brian Sutter, 1979-80 to 1987-88; Bernie Federko, 1988-89; Rick Meagher, 1989-90; Scott Stevens, 1990-91; Garth Butcher, 1991-92; Brett Hull, 1992-93 to date.

Retired Numbers

3	Bob Gassoff	1973-1977
8	Barclay Plager	1967-1977
11	Brian Sutter	1976-1988
24	Bernie Federko	1976-1989

1993-94 Scoring

* – rookie

Regular Season

Pos	#	Player	Team	GP	G	A	Pts	+/–	PIM	PP	SH	GW	GT	S	%
L	19	Brendan Shanahan	STL	81	52	50	102	9–	211	15	7	8	1	397	13.1
R	16	Brett Hull	STL	81	57	40	97	3–	38	25	3	6	1	392	14.5
C	15	Craig Janney	STL	69	16	68	84	14–	24	8	0	1	0	95	16.8
R	14	Kevin Miller	STL	75	23	25	48	6	83	6	3	5	0	154	14.9
D	28	Steve Duchesne	STL	36	12	19	31	1	14	8	0	1	0	115	10.4
L	25	Vitali Prokhorov	STL	55	15	10	25	6–	20	3	0	1	0	85	17.6
C	36	Philippe Bozon	STL	80	9	16	25	4	42	0	1	1	0	118	7.6
D	7	Alexei Kasatonov	ANA	55	4	18	22	8–	43	1	0	1	0	81	4.9
			STL	8	0	2	2	5	19	0	0	0	0	6	.0
			TOTAL	63	4	20	24	3–	62	1	0	1	0	87	4.6
D	6	Phil Housley	STL	26	7	15	22	5–	12	4	0	1	1	60	11.7
L	12	* Vitali Karamnov	STL	59	9	12	21	3–	51	2	0	1	0	66	13.6
C	93	Petr Nedved	STL	19	6	14	20	2	8	2	0	1	0	63	9.5
C	10	* Jim Montgomery	STL	67	6	14	20	1–	44	0	0	1	0	67	9.0
C	38	Igor Korolev	STL	73	6	10	16	12–	40	0	0	1	0	93	6.5
C	26	Peter Stastny	STL	17	5	11	16	2–	4	2	0	1	0	30	16.7
D	34	Murray Baron	STL	77	5	9	14	14–	123	0	0	0	0	73	6.8
L	18	Tony Hrkac	STL	36	6	5	11	11–	8	1	1	1	0	43	14.0
D	4	Rick Zombo	STL	74	2	8	10	15–	85	0	0	0	0	53	3.8
D	32	Doug Crossman	STL	50	2	7	9	1	10	1	0	0	0	30	6.7
D	20	Tom Tilley	STL	48	1	7	8	3	32	0	0	0	0	41	2.4
R	39	Kelly Chase	STL	68	2	5	7	5–	278	0	0	0	0	57	3.5
L	23	Dave Mackey	STL	30	2	3	5	4–	56	0	0	1	0	21	9.5
L	41	* Daniel Laperriere	STL	20	1	3	4	1–	8	1	0	0	0	20	5.0
L	17	Basil McRae	STL	40	1	2	3	7–	103	0	0	0	0	23	4.3
G	31	Curtis Joseph	STL	71	0	3	3	0	4	0	0	0	0	0	.0
R	9	* Denny Felsner	STL	6	1	0	1	1	2	0	0	0	0	6	16.7
R	27	Denis Chasse	STL	3	0	1	1	1	15	0	0	0	0	4	.0
C	37	* Kevin Miehm	STL	14	0	1	1	3–	4	0	0	0	0	5	.0
C	29	Jim Hrivnak	STL	23	0	1	1	0	2	0	0	0	0	0	.0
L	21	* David Roberts	STL	1	0	0	0	2	0	0	0	0	0	1	.0
C	22	* Ian Laperriere	STL	1	0	0	0	1–	0	0	0	0	0	1	.0
C	44	* Terry Hollinger	STL	2	0	0	0	1	0	0	0	0	0	0	.0
D	43	* Jeff Batters	STL	6	0	0	0	1	7	0	0	0	0	1	.0

Goaltending

No.	Goaltender	GPI	Mins	Avg	W	L	T	EN	SO	GA	SA	S%
31	Curtis Joseph	71	4127	3.10	36	23	11	0	1	213	2382	.911
29	Jim Hrivnak	23	970	4.27	4	10	0	1	0	69	563	.877
	Totals	84	5107	3.32	40	33	11	1	1	283	2946	.904

Playoffs

Pos	#	Player	Team	GP	G	A	Pts	+/–	PIM	PP	SH	GW	GT	S	%
L	19	Brendan Shanahan	STL	4	2	5	7	6	0	1	0	0	0	20	10.0
C	15	Craig Janney	STL	4	1	3	4	3	0	0	0	0	0	8	12.5
D	6	Phil Housley	STL	4	2	1	3	3–	4	2	0	0	0	10	20.0
R	16	Brett Hull	STL	4	2	1	3	1	0	1	0	0	0	22	9.1
D	7	Alexei Kasatonov	STL	4	2	0	2	2–	2	0	0	0	0	7	28.6
D	28	Steve Duchesne	STL	4	0	2	2	1–	2	0	0	0	0	11	.0
R	14	Kevin Miller	STL	3	1	0	1	0	4	0	0	1	0	5	20.0
R	39	Kelly Chase	STL	4	0	1	1	0	6	0	0	0	0	3	.0
C	93	Petr Nedved	STL	4	0	1	1	2–	4	0	0	0	0	13	.0
C	20	Tom Tilley	STL	4	0	1	1	0	2	0	0	0	0	1	.0
L	23	Dave Mackey	STL	2	0	0	0	1–	2	0	0	0	0	2	.0
L	17	Basil McRae	STL	2	0	0	0	0	12	0	0	0	0	0	.0
R	38	Igor Korolev	STL	2	0	0	0	2–	0	0	0	0	0	4	.0
L	21	* David Roberts	STL	3	0	0	0	1–	12	0	0	0	0	2	.0
D	34	Murray Baron	STL	4	0	0	0	1–	10	0	0	0	0	5	.0
C	36	Philippe Bozon	STL	4	0	0	0	2–	4	0	0	0	0	5	.0
C	18	Tony Hrkac	STL	4	0	0	0	3–	0	0	0	0	0	10	.0
G	31	Curtis Joseph	STL	4	0	0	0	0	0	0	0	0	0	0	.0
C	26	Peter Stastny	STL	4	0	0	0	4–	2	0	0	0	0	3	.0
D	4	Rick Zombo	STL	4	0	0	0	1	11	0	0	0	0	4	.0
L	25	Vitali Prokhorov	STL	4	0	0	0	5–	0	0	0	0	0	1	.0

Goaltending

No.	Goaltender	GPI	Mins	Avg	W	L	EN	SO	GA	SA	S%
31	Curtis Joseph	4	246	3.66	0	4	1	0	15	158	.905
	Totals	4	249	3.86	0	4	1	0	16	159	.899

Club Records

Team

(Figures in brackets for season records are games played)

Most Points	107	1980-81 (80)
Most Wins	47	1990-91 (80)
Most Ties	19	1970-71 (78)
Most Losses	50	1978-79 (80)
Most Goals	352	1980-81 (80)
Most Goals Against	349	1981-82 (80)
Fewest Points	48	1978-79 (80)
Fewest Wins	18	1978-79 (80)
Fewest Ties	7	1983-84 (80)
Fewest Losses	18	1980-81 (80)
Fewest Goals	177	1967-68 (74)
Fewest Goals Against	157	1968-69 (76)

Longest Winning Streak

Over-all .... 7 Jan. 21-
Feb. 3/88;
Mar. 19-31/91

Home .... 9 Jan. 26-
Feb. 26/91

Away .... 4 Four times

Longest Undefeated Streak

Over-all .... 12 Nov. 10-
Dec. 8/68
(5 wins, 7 ties)

Home .... 11 Feb. 12-
Mar. 19/69
(5 wins, 6 ties);
Feb. 7-
Mar. 29/75
(9 wins, 2 ties);
Oct. 7-
Nov. 26/93
(7 wins, 4 ties)

Away .... 7 Dec. 9-26/87
(4 wins, 3 ties)

Longest Losing Streak

Over-all .... 7 Nov. 12-26/67;
Feb. 12-25/89

Home .... 5 Nov. 19-
Dec. 6/77

Away .... 10 Jan. 20/82-
Mar. 8/82

Longest Winless Streak

Over-all .... 12 Jan. 17-
Feb. 15/78
(10 losses, 2 ties)

Home .... 7 Dec. 28/82-
Jan. 25/83
(5 losses, 2 ties)

Away .... 17 Jan. 23-
Apr. 7/74
(14 losses, 3 ties)

Most Shutouts, Season	13	1968-69 (76)
Most PIM, Season	2,041	1990-91 (80)
Most Goals, Game	11	Feb. 26/94
		(St. L. 11 at Ott. 1)

Individual

Most Seasons	13	Bernie Federko
Most Games	927	Bernie Federko
Most Goals, Career	386	Brett Hull
Most Assists, Career	721	Bernie Federko
Most Points, Career	1,073	Bernie Federko
Most PIM, Career	1,786	Brian Sutter
Most Shutouts, Career	16	Glenn Hall

Longest Consecutive
Games Streak .... 662 Garry Unger
(Feb. /71-Apr. 8/79)

Most Goals, Season .... 86 Brett Hull
(199 91)

Most Assists, Season .... 90 Adam Oates
(19 91)

Most Points, Season .... 131 Brett Hull
(19 -91)
(8 goals, 45 assists)

Most PIM, Season .... 306 Bob Gassoff
(1 5-76)

Most Points, Defenseman
Season .... 78 J Brown
(92-93)
(goals, 53 assists)

Most Points, Center,
Season .... 115 am Oates
(90-91)
5 goals, 90 assists)

Most Points, Right Wing,
Season .... 131 rett Hull
(1990-91)
86 goals, 45 assists)

Most Points, Left Wing,
Season .... 102 Brendan Shanahan
(1993-94)
(52 goals, 50 assists)

Most Points, Rookie,
Season .... 73 Jorgen Pettersson
(1980-81)
(37 goals, 36 assists)

Most Shutouts, Season	8	Glenn Hall
		(1968-69)
Most Goals, Game	6	Red Berenson
		(Nov. 7/68)
Most Assists, Game	5	Brian Sutter
		(Nov. 22/88)
		Bernie Federko
		(Feb. 27/88)
		Adam Oates
		(Jan. 26/91)
Most Points, Game	7	Red Berenson
		(Nov. 7/68)
		Garry Unger
		(Mar. 13/71)

All-time Record vs. Other Clubs

Regular Season

		At Home						On Road						Total					
	GP	W	L	T	GF	GA	PTS	GP	W	L	T	GF	GA	PTS	GP	W	L	T	GF	GA	PTS
Anaheim	2	1	1	0	7	6	2	2	1	1	0	4	4	2	4	2	2	0	11	10	4
Boston	52	21	22	9	163	181	51	51	11	33	7	138	225	29	103	32	55	16	301	406	80
Buffalo	43	26	11	6	165	111	58	44	12	28	4	138	183	28	87	38	39	10	303	294	86
Calgary	43	18	18	7	152	138	43	42	18	21	3	125	151	39	85	36	39	10	277	289	82
Chicago	88	44	28	16	307	271	104	91	25	55	11	280	370	61	179	69	83	27	587	641	165
Dallas	95	52	25	18	350	269	122	92	32	42	18	270	321	82	187	84	67	36	620	590	204
Detroit	83	47	23	13	308	231	107	83	36	35	12	274	304	84	166	83	58	25	582	535	191
Edmonton	24	10	10	4	99	104	24	24	8	13	3	93	105	19	48	18	23	7	192	209	43
Florida	1	1	0	0	5	3	2	1	1	0	0	3	1	2	2	2	0	0	8	4	4
Hartford	23	13	8	2	91	77	28	24	13	9	2	76	74	28	47	26	17	4	167	151	56
Los Angeles	58	38	14	6	225	153	82	58	19	31	8	167	218	46	116	57	45	14	392	371	128
Montreal	51	10	27	14	129	183	34	52	8	38	6	134	235	22	103	18	65	20	263	418	56
New Jersey	38	25	8	5	172	118	55	39	15	17	7	114	128	37	77	40	25	12	286	246	92
NY Islanders	40	16	17	7	146	134	39	41	8	23	10	98	161	26	81	24	40	17	244	295	65
NY Rangers	55	21	26	8	163	183	50	53	6	42	5	120	228	17	108	27	68	13	283	411	67
Ottawa	2	2	0	0	12	6	4	2	2	0	0	15	2	4	4	4	0	0	27	8	8
Philadelphia	59	23	29	7	173	183	53	59	17	40	2	135	237	29	118	33	69	16	308	420	82
Pittsburgh	57	38	13	6	228	154	82	56	19	25	12	172	209	50	113	57	38	18	400	363	132
Quebec	22	16	4	2	105	74	34	22	9	10	3	74	82	21	44	25	14	5	179	156	55
San Jose	7	6	1	0	31	15	12	4	4	0	0	14	6	8	11	10	1	0	45	21	20
Tampa Bay	4	3	1	0	18	13	6	5	2	2	1	18	17	5	9	5	3	1	36	30	11
Toronto	83	48	23	12	293	240	108	83	21	52	10	241	322	52	166	69	75	22	534	562	160
Vancouver	51	29	15	7	198	155	65	52	23	23	6	160	164	52	103	52	38	13	358	319	117
Washington	33	14	11	8	139	111	36	32	12	17	3	98	118	27	65	26	28	11	237	229	63
Winnipeg	27	13	6	8	109	83	34	28	7	15	6	83	97	20	55	20	21	14	192	180	54
Defunct Clubs	32	25	4	3	131	55	53	33	11	10	12	95	100	34	65	36	14	15	226	155	87
Totals	**1073**	**560**	**345**	**168**	**3919**	**3251**	**1288**	**1073**	**333**	**582**	**158**	**3139**	**4062**	**824**	**2146**	**893**	**927**	**326**	**7058**	**7313**	**2112**

Calgary totals include Atlanta, 1972-73 to 1979-80. Dallas totals include Minnesota, 1967-68 to 1992-93.
New Jersey totals include Kansas City, 1974-75 to 1975-76, and Colorado, 1976-77 to 1981-82.

Playoffs

	Series	W	L	GP	W	L	T	GF	GA	Last Mtg.	Round	Result
Boston	2	0	2	8	0	8	0	15	48	1972	SF	L 0-4
Buffalo	1	0	1	3	1	2	0	8	7	1976	PR	L 1-2
Calgary	1	0	1	7	3	4	0	22	28	1986	CF	L 3-4
Chicago	9	2	7	45	18	27	0	129	166	1993	DSF	W 4-0
Detroit	3	2	1	16	8	8	0	51	53	1991	DSF	W 4-3
Los Angeles	1	1	0	4	4	0	0	16	5	1969	SF	W 4-0
Dallas	10	5	5	56	26	30	0	162	174	1994	CQF	L 0-4
Montreal	3	0	3	12	0	12	0	14	42	1977	QF	L 0-4
NY Rangers	1	0	1	6	2	4	0	22	29	1981	QF	L 2-4
Philadelphia	2	2	0	11	8	3	0	34	20	1969	QF	W 4-0
Pittsburgh	3	2	1	13	7	6	0	45	40	1981	PR	W 3-2
Toronto	4	2	2	25	13	12	0	67	75	1993	DF	L 3-4
Winnipeg	1	1	0	4	4	0	0	20	13	1982	DSF	W 3-1
Totals	**41**	**17**	**24**	**210**	**93**	**117**	**0**	**605**	**700**			

Playoff Results 1994-90

Year	Round	Opponent	Result	GF	GA
1994	CQF	Dallas	L 0-4	10	16
1993	DF	Toronto	L 3-4	11	22
	DSF	Chicago	W 4-0	13	6
1992	DSF	Chicago	L 2-4	19	23
1991	DF	Minnesota	L 2-4	17	22
	DSF	Detroit	W 4-3	24	20
1990	DF	Chicago	L 3-4	22	28
	DSF	Toronto	W 4-1	20	16

Abbreviations: Round: F – Final;
CF – conference final; **CQF** – conference quarter-final;
CSF – conference semi-final; **DF** – division final;
DSF – division semi-final; **SF** – semi-final;
QF – quarter-final; **PR** – preliminary round.

1993-94 Results

Oct.	7		Florida	5-3		9	at	Dallas	1-2
	9		Ottawa	7-5		13		Edmonton	6-4
	13	at	Detroit	5-2		15		Buffalo	2-1
	16	at	Dallas	0-4		18	at	NY Rangers	1-4
	19	at	San Jose	4-1		19	at	Philadelphia	3-8
	21		San Jose	5-2		24	at	Anaheim	3-2
	23	at	Pittsburgh	3-3		25	at	Vancouver	3-3
	26	at	Chicago	2-9		28	at	Edmonton	3-2
	28		Hartford	2-1		29	at	Calgary	5-3
	30	at	Boston	2-1	Feb. 1		Toronto	4-4
Nov.	1		Hartford	4-2		3		Quebec	3-4
	3	at	Winnipeg	3-0		5		San Jose	4-3
	6		Edmonton	6-5		8		Winnipeg	6-5
	9		Pittsburgh	3-3		10		Washington	3-4
	11		Toronto	3-2		12		Detroit	4-5
	13	at	Los Angeles	3-6		15		Vancouver	3-2
	16	at	Vancouver	0-3		18		Boston	3-3
	18		Calgary	3-3		20		Anaheim	4-1
	20		Los Angeles	4-1		24	at	Quebec	0-6
	21		Detroit	2-2		26	at	Ottawa	11-1
	24	at	Washington	2-5		28	at	New Jersey	1-5
	26		New Jersey	6-6	Mar. 1	at	NY Islanders	2-4
	28		Winnipeg	3-4		3	at	Vancouver	0-4
Dec.	1		Toronto	2-4		7	at	Toronto	3-2
	2		Toronto	4-5		9	at	Montreal	2-7
	4		Dallas	4-3		12	at	NY Islanders	5-5
	7		Chicago	3-2		16	at	Winnipeg	0-4
	9	at	Detroit	2-3		18	at	Toronto	2-4
	11	at	Los Angeles	1-9		20	at	Chicago	4-3
	12	at	Anaheim	1-2		22		Philadelphia	3-6
	15	at	San Jose	3-1		23	at	Buffalo	3-2
	17	at	Calgary	4-3		25		Dallas	5-3
	19	at	Edmonton	4-1		27		San Jose	3-4
	23		Tampa Bay	7-4		30	at	Florida	3-1
	26		Chicago	3-2	Apr. 1	at	Tampa Bay	2-4
	27		Montreal	2-5		3	at	Detroit	3-3
	29		NY Rangers	3-4		5		Chicago	5-1
	31	at	Winnipeg	1-2		7		Los Angeles	6-2
Jan.	2		Calgary	4-3		8	at	Chicago	1-6
	4		Detroit	4-4		10		Dallas	2-2
	6	at	Hartford	2-1		12	at	Dallas	5-9
	8		Anaheim	3-5		14		Winnipeg	3-1

Entry Draft
Selections 1994-80

1994		1990		1987		1984	
Pick		**Pick**		**Pick**		**Pick**	
68	Stephane Roy	33	Craig Johnson	12	Keith Osborne	26	Brian Benning
94	Tyler Harlton	54	Patrice Tardif	54	Kevin Miehm	32	Tony Hrkac
120	Edvin Frylen	96	Jason Ruff	59	Robert Nordmark	50	Toby Ducolon
172	Roman Vopat	117	Kurtis Miller	75	Darin Smith	53	Robert Dirk
198	Steve Noble	138	Wayne Conlan	82	Andy Rymsha	56	Alan Perry
224	Marc Stephan	180	Parris Duffus	117	Rob Robinson	71	Graham Herring
250	Kevin Harper	201	Steve Widmeyer	138	Todd Crabtree	92	Scott Paluch
276	Scott Fankhouser	222	Joe Hawley	159	Guy Hebert	113	Steve Tuttle
		243	Joe Fleming	180	Robert Dumas	134	Cliff Ronning
1993				201	David Marvin	148	Don Porter
Pick		**1989**		207	Andy Cesarski	155	Jim Vesey
37	Maxim Bets	**Pick**		222	Dan Rolfe	176	Daniel Jomphe
63	Jamie Rivers	9	Jason Marshall	243	Ray Savard	196	Tom Tilley
89	Jamal Mayers	31	Rick Corriveau			217	Mark Cupolo
141	Todd Kelman	55	Denny Felsner	**1986**		237	Mark Lanigan
167	Mike Buzak	93	Daniel Laperriere	**Pick**			
193	Eric Boguniecki	114	David Roberts	10	Jocelyn Lemieux	**1983**	
219	Michael Grier	124	Derek Frenette	31	Mike Posma	DID NOT DRAFT	
245	Libor Prochazka	135	Jeff Batters	52	Tony Hejna		
271	Alexander Vasilevsky	156	Kevin Plager	73	Glen Featherstone	**1982**	
275	Christer Olsson	177	John Roderick	87	Michael Wolak	**Pick**	
		198	John Valo	115	Mike O'Toole	50	Mike Posavad
1992		219	Brian Lukowski	136	Andy May	92	Scott Machej
Pick				157	Randy Skarda	113	Perry Ganchar
38	Igor Korolev	**1988**		178	Martyn Ball	134	Doug Gilmour
62	Vitali Karamnov	**Pic**		199	Rod Thacker	155	Chris Delaney
64	Vitali Prokhorov	9	Rod Brind' Amour	220	Terry MacLean	176	Matt Christensen
86	Lee J. Leslie	30	Adrien Plavsic	234	Bill Butler	197	John Shumski
134	Bob Lachance	51	Rob Fournier	241	David O'Brien	218	Brian Ahern
158	Ian LaPerriere	72	Jaan Luik			239	Peter Smith
160	Lance Burns	105	Dave Lacouture	**1985**			
180	Igor Boldin	114	Dan Fowler	**Pick**		**1981**	
182	Nicholas Naumenko	135	Matt Hayes	37	Herb Raglan	**Pick**	
206	Todd Harris	156	John McCoy	44	Nelson Emerson	20	Marty Ruff
230	Yuri Gunko	177	Tony Twist	54	Ned Desmond	36	Hakan Nordin
259	Wade Salzman	198	Bret Hedican	100	Dan Brooks	62	Gordon Donnelly
		219	Heath DeBoer	121	Rich Burchill	104	Mike Hickey
1991		240	Michael Francis	138	Pat Jablonski	125	Peter Aslin
Pick				159	Scott Brickey	146	Erik Holmberg
27	Steve Staios			180	Jeff Urban	167	Alain Vigneault
64	Kyle Reeves			201	Vince Guidotti	188	Dan Wood
65	Nathan Lafayette			222	Ron Saatzer	209	Richard Zemlak
87	Grayden Reid			243	Dave Jecha		
109	Jeff Callinan					**1980**	
131	Bruce Gardiner					**Pick**	
153	Terry Hollinger					12	Rik Wilson
175	Christopher Kenady					54	Jim Pavese
197	Jed Fiebelkorn					75	Bob Brooke
219	Chris MacKenzie					96	Alain Lemieux
241	Kevin Rappana					117	Perry Anderson
263	Mike Veisor					138	Roger Hagglund
						159	Pat Rabbitt
						180	Peter Lindgren
						201	John Smyth

Club Directory

Kiel Center
1401 Clark Avenue
St. Louis, MO 63103
Phone **314/622-2500**
FAX 314/622-2582
Capacity: 19,260

Board of Directors
Michael F. Shanahan, Jud Perkins, Andrew Craig,
John J. Quinn, Edwin Trusheim, Horace Wilkins, Alfred Kerth

Chairman of the Board . . . . Michael F. Shanahan
President . . . . John J. Quinn
Executive Vice-President . . . . Ronald Caron
General Manager/Head Coach . . . . Mike Keenan
Vice-President/Director of Sales . . . . Bruce Affleck
Vice-President/Director of Player
Personnel and Scouting . . . . Ted Hampson
Vice-President/Director of Broadcast Sales . . . . Matt Hyland
Vice-President/Director of Finance and
Administration . . . . Jerry Jasiek
Vice-President/Director of Public Relations
and Marketing . . . . Susie Mathieu
Vice-President/Director of Player Development . . . . . Bob Plager
Associate Coaches . . . . Bob Berry, Ted Sator
Head Coach – Peoria Rivermen . . . . Paul MacLean
Assistant Coach – Peoria Rivermen . . . . Mark Reeds
Assistant Director of Scouting . . . . Jack Evans
Western Canada/United States Scout . . . . Pat Ginnell
Eastern Scout . . . . Matt Keator
Midwest Scout . . . . Ken Williamson
Director of Promotions/Community Relations . . . . . . Tracy Lovasz
Director of Team Services . . . . Rick Meagher
Assistant Director of Public Relations . . . . Jeff Trammel
Assistant Director of Public Relations . . . . Michael Caruso
Accounting . . . . Craig Bryant, Marsha McBride, Jim Bergman
Sales . . . . John Casson, Wes Edwards, Tammy Iuli,
Jill Mann
Merchandise Manager . . . . George Pavlik
Trainers . . . . Ron DuBuque, Tom Nash
Conditioning Consultant . . . . Mackie Shilstone
Equipment Managers . . . . Frank Burns, Terry Roof
Executive Secretary . . . . Lynn Diederichsen
Administrative Assistant Hockey Department . . . . . . Sue Profeta
Marketing/Public Relations Secretary . . . . Donna Quirk
Receptionist . . . . Pam Barrett
Orthopedic Surgeon . . . . Dr. Jerome Gilden
Internist . . . . Dr. Aaron Birenbaum
Dentist . . . . Dr. Ron Sherstoff
Dentist Emeritus . . . . Dr. Leslie Rich
Optometrist/Contact Lens Consultant . . . . Dr. N. Rex Ghormley
Team Colors . . . . Blue, Gold & Red
Television Station . . . . KPLR-TV Channel 11
Radio Station . . . . KMOX 1120 AM
Broadcasters . . . . Ken Wilson, Joe Micheletti, Bruce Affleck,
Rick Meagher, Ron Jacober
Public Address Announcer . . . . Tom Calhoun

General Manager and Coach

KEENAN, MICHAEL (MIKE)
General Manager and Coach, St. Louis Blues.
Born in Toronto, Ontario, October 21, 1949.

Mike Keenan became the eighteenth head coach and ninth general manager in St.
Louis Blues' history on July 18, 1994, only a month after winning his first Stanley Cup.
Keenan coached the New York Rangers to their first cup in 54 years in only his first
season in New York.

Keenan has a career coaching record of 395-252-77 in 724 career games. He has a
career playoff record of 81-59 in 140 games and has coached in the Stanley Cup
Finals four times. He has won his division six times and had the best record in the
National Hockey League three times with three different teams. Keenan has averaged
44 wins and 96 points per season throughout his NHL coaching career.

He started in the NHL with Philadelphia in 1984-85 taking the Flyers from a third place
finish the previous season to the best record in the NHL with 113 points. He coached
the Flyers for three more seasons and posted a mark of 190-102-28 in 320 games. He
then moved to Chicago in 1988-89 and coached the Blackhawks for four seasons and
320 games. He left in 1991-92 with a record of 153-126-41 having coached the
Hawks to the NHL's best record in 1990-91 with 106 points and a Stanley Cup Final
appearance the next season. Keenan also served as the Blackhawks general manager
in 1989-90 through his departure in 1991-92.

Keenan then joined the New York Rangers on April 17, 1993 and guided the Rangers
to their best record ever (52-24-8, 113PTS) and his first Stanley Cup Championship.

Mike has one daughter, Gayla and resides in St. Louis.

Coaching Record

Season	Team	Regular Season					Playoffs			
		Games	W	L	T	%	Games	W	L	%
1979-80	Peterborough (OHL)	68	47	20	1	.699	18	15	3	.833
1980-81	Rochester (AHL)	80	30	42	8	.425	....	....	....	....
1981-82	Rochester (AHL)	80	40	31	9	.556	9	4	5	.444
1982-83	Rochester (AHL)	80	46	25	9	.631	16	12	4	.750
1983-84	U. of Toronto (CIAU)	49	41	5	3	.867	....	....	....	....
1984-85	**Philadelphia (NHL)**	80	53	20	7	.706	19	12	7	.632
1985-86	**Philadelphia (NHL)**	80	53	23	4	.688	5	2	3	.400
1986-87	**Philadelphia (NHL)**	80	46	26	8	.625	26	15	11	.577
1987-88	**Philadelphia (NHL)**	80	38	33	9	.531	7	3	4	.429
1988-89	**Chicago (NHL)**	80	27	41	12	.413	16	9	7	.563
1989-90	**Chicago (NHL)**	80	41	33	6	.550	20	10	10	.500
1990-91	**Chicago (NHL)**	80	49	23	8	.663	6	2	4	.333
1991-92	**Chicago (NHL)**	80	36	29	15	.544	18	12	6	.667
1993-94	**NY Rangers (NHL)**	84	52	24	8	.667	23	16	7	.696*
	NHL Totals	724	395	252	77	.599	140	81	59	.579

* Won Stanley Cup.

San Jose Sharks

1993-94 Results: 33W-35L-16T 82PTS. Third, Pacific Division

Year-by-Year Record

Season	GP	Home W	L	T	Road W	L	T	Overall W	L	T	GF	GA	Pts.	Finished		Playoff Result
1993-94	84	19	13	10	14	22	6	33	35	16	252	265	82	3rd,	Pacific Div.	Lost Conf. Semi-Final
1992-93	84	8	33	1	3	38	1	11	71	2	218	414	24	6th,	Smythe Div.	Out of Playoffs
1991-92	80	14	23	3	3	35	2	17	58	5	219	359	39	6th,	Smythe Div.	Out of Playoffs

Schedule

Oct.	Sat.	1	Los Angeles		Sat.	7	Calgary*
	Wed.	5	at Vancouver		Wed.	11	Dallas
	Fri.	7	Detroit		Sat.	14	St. Louis
	Sun.	9	Vancouver*		Mon.	16	Vancouver
	Tues.	11	at Los Angeles		Mon.	23	Los Angeles
	Wed.	12	Boston		Wed.	25	Winnipeg
	Fri.	14	at Calgary		Thur.	26	at Los Angeles
	Sun.	16	at Winnipeg		Sat.	28	Dallas*
	Tues.	18	at St. Louis		Mon.	30	at Toronto
	Thur.	20	at Chicago	Feb.	Wed.	1	at Ottawa
	Sat.	22	at New Jersey*		Sat.	4	at Quebec*
	Sun.	23	at NY Rangers		Mon.	6	at Montreal
	Sat.	29	St. Louis		Wed.	8	at Hartford
Nov.	Tues.	1	New Jersey		Thur.	9	at Boston
	Sat.	5	NY Rangers		Sat.	11	at NY Islanders*
	Mon.	7	at Vancouver		Wed.	15	Ottawa
	Tues.	8	Vancouver		Thur.	16	at Vancouver
	Thur.	10	Anaheim		Sat.	18	Quebec
	Sat.	12	Buffalo		Mon.	20	Philadelphia*
	Tues.	15	Calgary		Wed.	22	at Calgary
	Fri.	18	at Dallas				(in Phoenix)
	Sun.	20	at Edmonton		Fri.	24	Anaheim
	Tues.	22	Chicago		Sun.	26	Tampa Bay*
	Wed.	23	at Anaheim		Tues.	28	at Buffalo
	Sat.	26	at Pittsburgh	Mar.	Wed.	1	at Toronto
	Mon.	28	at Detroit		Sat.	4	at Washington
Dec.	Thur.	1	at Florida		Sun.	5	at Philadelphia
	Fri.	2	at Tampa Bay		Wed.	8	Edmonton
	Mon.	5	at Dallas		Fri.	10	Detroit
	Wed.	7	Toronto		Sun.	12	Hartford*
	Fri.	9	Anaheim		Wed.	15	Toronto
	Sat.	10	Washington		Fri.	17	at Calgary
	Wed.	14	NY Islanders		Sun.	19	at Winnipeg*
	Fri.	16	at Anaheim		Tues.	21	Chicago
	Sat.	17	Pittsburgh		Thur.	23	Florida
	Tues.	20	Edmonton		Sat.	25	at Los Angeles*
	Wed.	21	Vancouver		Sun.	26	Los Angeles*
			(in Portland, OR)		Tues.	28	Winnipeg
	Tues.	27	at Edmonton		Fri.	31	at Calgary
	Thur.	29	at St. Louis	Apr.	Sun.	2	at Anaheim*
	Sat.	31	at Detroit		Wed.	6	Calgary
Jan.	Sun.	1	at Chicago		Fri.	7	Edmonton
	Wed.	4	Montreal		Sun.	9	at Edmonton

* Denotes afternoon game.

Home Starting Times:
Night Games . . . . 7:30 p.m.
Matinees . . . . 2:00 p.m.
Except   Fri. Oct. 7 . . . . 6:00 p.m.

Franchise date: May 9, 1990

PACIFIC DIVISION

4th NHL Season

The surprising rise of the San Jose Sharks was led by a rejuvenated Sergei Makarov, who led the club with 30 goals in 1993-94.

1994-95 Player Personnel

FORWARDS	HT	WT	S	Place of Birth	Date	1993-94 Club
BAKER, Jamie	6-0	190	L	Ottawa, Ont.	8/31/66	San Jose
BRUCE, David	5-11	190	R	Thunder Bay, Ont.	10/7/64	San Jose-Kansas City
BUTSAYEV, Vyacheslav	6-2	200	L	Togliatti, USSR	6/13/70	Philadelphia-San Jose
CALOUN, Jan	5-10	175	R	Usti-Nad-Labem, Czech.	12/20/72	Litvinov
CHERBAYEV, Alexander	6-1	190	L	Voskresensk, USSR	8/13/73	Kansas City
COURTENAY, Edward	6-4	215	R	Verdun, Que.	2/2/68	Kansas City
CRAIGWELL, Dale	5-11	180	L	Toronto, Ont.	4/24/71	San Jose-Kansas City
DAHLEN, Ulf	6-2	195	L	Ostersund, Sweden	1/12/67	Dallas-San Jose
DONOVAN, Shean	6-2	190	R	Timmins, Ont.	1/22/75	Ottawa (OHL)
DUCHESNE, Gaetan	5-11	200	L	Les Saulles, Que.	7/11/62	San Jose
ELIK, Todd	6-2	195	L	Brampton, Ont.	4/15/66	Edmonton-San Jose
ERREY, Bob	5-10	185	L	Montreal, Que.	9/21/64	San Jose
FALLOON, Pat	5-11	198	R	Foxwarren, Man.	9/22/72	San Jose
FRIESEN, Jeff	6-0	185	L	Meadow Lake, Sask.	8/5/76	Regina
GARPENLOV, Johan	5-11	185	L	Stockholm, Sweden	3/21/68	San Jose
GAUDREAU, Rob	5-11	185	R	Lincoln, RI	1/20/70	San Jose
HOLT, Todd	5-7	155	R	Estevan, Sask.	1/20/73	Swift Current
KOZLOV, Viktor	6-5	225	R	Togliatti, USSR	2/14/75	Moscow D'amo
LARIONOV, Igor	5-9	170	L	Voskresensk, USSR	12/3/60	San Jose
LESLIE, Lee	6-4	190	L	Prince George, B.C.	8/15/72	Kansas City
MAKAROV, Sergei	5-11	185	L	Chelyabinsk, USSR	6/19/58	San Jose
MATTHEWS, Jamie	6-1	215	R	Amherst, N.S.	5/25/73	Sudbury
NAZAROV, Andrei	6-5	230	R	Chelyabinsk, USSR	5/22/74	Moscow D'amo-S.J.-Kansas City
NILSSON, Fredrik	6-1	200	L	Stockholm, Sweden	4/16/71	Kansas City
ODGERS, Jeff	6-0	195	R	Spy Hill, Sask.	5/31/69	San Jose
PELTONEN, Ville	5-11	172	L	Vantaa, Finland	5/24/73	HIFK
QUINTIN, Jean-Francois	6-0	187	L	St. Jean, Que.	5/28/69	Kansas City
VARADA, Vaclav	6-0	198	L	Vseyin, Czech.	4/26/76	Vitkovice
WHITNEY, Ray	5-9	160	R	Fort Saskatchewan, Alta.	5/8/72	San Jose
WOOD, Dody	5-11	181	L	Chetwynd, B.C.	3/10/72	Kansas City
YEGOROV, Alexei	5-11	185	L	St. Petersburg, USSR	5/21/75	SKA St. Peterburg
DEFENSEMEN						
BUSCHAN, Andrei	6-2	200	L	Kiev, USSR	8/21/70	Kansas City
CRONIN, Shawn	6-2	225	L	Joliet, IL	8/20/63	San Jose
KROUPA, Vlastimil	6-2	185	L	Most, Czech.	4/27/75	San Jose-Kansas City
MORE, Jayson	6-1	200	R	Souris, Man.	1/12/69	San Jose-Kansas City
NIKOLOV, Angel	6-1	176	L	Most, Czech.	11/18/75	Litvinov
NORTON, Jeff	6-2	190	L	Acton, MA	11/25/65	San Jose
ODUYA, Fredrik	6-2	185	L	Stockholm, Sweden	5/31/75	Ottawa (OHL)
OZOLINSH, Sandis	6-1	195	L	Riga, Latvia	8/3/72	San Jose
PEDERSON, Tom	5-9	175	R	Bloomington, MN	1/14/70	San Jose-Kansas City
RAGNARSSON, Marcus	6-1	200	L	Ostervala, Sweden	8/13/71	Djurgarden
RATHJE, Mike	6-6	220	L	Mannville, Alta.	5/11/74	San Jose-Kansas City
SYKORA, Michal	6-5	225	L	Pardubice, Czech.	7/5/73	San Jose-Kansas City

GOALTENDERS	HT	WT	C	Place of Birth	Date	1993-94 Club
FLAHERTY, Wade	6-0	170	R	Terrace, B.C.	1/11/68	Kansas City
IRBE, Arturs	5-7	180	L	Riga, Latvia	2/2/67	San Jose
ROBINS, Trevor	5-11	190	L	Brandon, Man.	5/31/72	Kansas City-Fort Worth
RYDER, Dan	6-1	200	L	Kitchener, Ont.	10/24/72	Kansas City-Roanoke
SALAJKO, Jeff	6-0	175	L	Kitchener, Ont.	4/18/75	Ottawa (OHL)
SAURDIFF, Corwin	5-11	168	L	Warroad, MN	10/17/72	Kansas City-Fort Worth
SCHOEN, Bryan	6-2	180	L	St. Paul, MN	9/9/70	Fort Worth-Roanoke-Louisville
WAITE, Jimmy	6-1	180	L	Sherbrooke, Que.	4/15/69	San Jose

Coach

CONSTANTINE, KEVIN
Head Coach, San Jose Sharks.
Born in International Falls, MN, December 27, 1958.

Having been successful at every previous level in his young coaching career, it should have come as no surprise that Kevin Constantine would quickly make his mark in the NHL. But few predicted that as a rookie head coach in 1993-94, he would lead the Sharks to a league-record 58-point improvement over the previous season and their first playoff berth.

Constantine was runner-up for the Jack Adams Award as NHL coach of the year. He also received honorable mention as coach of the year in annual awards presented by *The Hockey News*, in which he finished third in that voting behind Jacques Lemaire and Mike Keenan. In late June, Constantine was named recipient of USA Hockey's Distinguished Achievement Award.

Constantine was named Sharks head coach on June 16, 1993 after two seasons as coach of the Kansas City Blades, San Jose's development affiliate and champion in 1991-92.

The International Falls, MN, native led Kansas City to a combined record of 102-48-14 (.659) from 1991 to 1993. His club recorded professional hockey's best mark of 56-22-4 in 1991-92, earning him IHL coach of the year honors.

Before being hired by the Sharks to coach at Kansas City, Constantine was an assistant coach with the IHL Kalamazoo Wings from 1988 to 1991. His coaching resume also includes experience in international competition. He coached the U.S. National Junior Team to a fourth-place finish and a record of 4-2-1 at the 1991 IIHF World Junior Championships.

Coaching Record

		Regular Season					Playoffs			
Season	Team	Games	W	L	T	%	Games	W	L	%
1985-86	North Iowa (USHL)	48	17	31	0	.354	....	....	....	....
1987-88	Rochester (USHL)	48	39	7	2	.833	15	9 (2 ties)	4	.692
1991-92	Kansas City (IHL)	82	56	22	4	.707	15	12	3	.800
1992-93	Kansas City (IHL)	82	46	26	10	.622	12	6	6	.500
1993-94	**San Jose (NHL)**	**84**	**33**	**35**	**16**	**.488**	**14**	**7**	**7**	**.500**
	NHL Totals	**84**	**33**	**35**	**16**	**.488**	**14**	**7**	**7**	**.500**

1993-94 Scoring

* – rookie

Regular Season

Pos	#	Player	Team	GP	G	A	Pts	+/–	PIM	PP	SH	GW	GT	S	%
R	22	Ulf Dahlen	DAL	65	19	38	57	1–	10	12	0	3	1	147	12.9
			S.J.	13	6	6	12	0	0	3	0	2	0	43	14.0
			TOTAL	78	25	44	69	1–	10	15	0	5	1	190	13.2
R	24	Sergei Makarov	S.J.	80	30	38	68	11	78	10	0	5	0	155	19.4
C	27	Todd Elik	EDM	4	0	0	0	0	6	0	0	0	0	5	.0
			S.J.	75	25	41	66	3–	89	9	0	4	1	180	13.9
			TOTAL	79	25	41	66	3–	95	9	0	4	1	185	13.5
D	6	Sandis Ozolinsh	S.J.	81	26	38	64	16	24	4	0	3	0	157	16.6
C	7	Igor Larionov	S.J.	60	18	38	56	20	40	3	2	2	1	72	25.0
R	17	Pat Falloon	S.J.	83	22	31	53	3–	18	6	0	1	0	193	11.4
L	10	Johan Garpenlov	S.J.	80	18	35	53	9	28	7	0	3	0	125	14.4
L	14	Ray Whitney	S.J.	61	14	26	40	2	14	1	0	0	1	82	17.1
D	8	Jeff Norton	S.J.	64	7	33	40	16	36	1	0	0	0	92	7.6
R	37	Rob Gaudreau	S.J.	84	15	20	35	10–	28	6	0	4	0	151	9.9
L	12	Bob Errey	S.J.	64	12	18	30	11–	126	5	0	2	0	89	13.5
L	11	Gaetan Duchesne	S.J.	84	12	18	30	8	28	0	1	3	0	121	9.9
D	41	Tom Pederson	S.J.	74	6	19	25	3	31	3	0	1	1	185	3.2
C	9	V. Butsayev	PHI	47	12	9	21	2	58	2	0	3	0	79	15.2
			S.J.	12	0	2	2	2–	10	0	0	0	0	6	.0
			TOTAL	59	12	11	23	0	68	2	0	3	0	85	14.1
R	36	Jeff Odgers	S.J.	81	13	8	21	13–	222	7	0	0	1	73	17.8
C	13	Jamie Baker	S.J.	65	12	5	17	2	38	0	0	2	0	68	17.6
D	40	* Mike Rathje	S.J.	47	1	9	10	9–	59	1	0	0	0	30	3.3
C	33	Dale Craigwell	S.J.	58	3	6	9	13–	16	0	1	0	0	35	8.6
D	4	Jay More	S.J.	49	1	6	7	5–	63	0	0	0	0	38	2.6
C	50	* Jaroslav Otevrel	S.J.	9	3	2	5	5–	2	1	0	0	0	11	27.3
D	38	* Michal Sykora	S.J.	22	1	4	5	4–	14	0	0	0	0	22	4.5
C	20	Kip Miller	S.J.	11	2	2	4	1–	6	0	0	0	0	21	9.5
D	26	* Vlastimil Kroupa	S.J.	27	1	3	4	6–	20	0	0	0	0	16	6.3
D	44	Shawn Cronin	S.J.	34	0	2	2	2	76	0	0	0	0	14	.0
G	32	Arturs Irbe	S.J.	74	0	2	2	0	16	0	0	0	0	0	.0
C	9	Gary Emmons	S.J.	3	1	0	1	4–	0	1	0	0	0	6	16.7
C	43	Jeff McLean	S.J.	6	1	0	1	1	0	0	0	0	0	5	20.0
L	27	Dave Capuano	S.J.	4	0	1	1	5–	0	0	0	0	0	5	.0
R	23	* Andrei Nazarov	S.J.	1	0	0	0	0	0	0	0	0	0	0	.0
R	15	David Bruce	S.J.	2	0	0	0	2–	0	0	0	0	0	5	.0
G	29	Jim Waite	S.J.	15	0	0	0	0	6	0	0	0	0	0	.0

Goaltending

No.	Goaltender	GPI	Mins	Avg	W	L	T	EN	SO	GA	SA	S%
32	Arturs Irbe	74	4412	2.84	30	28	16	4	3	209	2064	.899
29	Jim Waite	15	697	4.30	3	7	0	2	0	50	319	.843
	Totals	**84**	**5125**	**3.10**	**33**	**35**	**16**	**6**	**3**	**265**	**2389**	**.889**

Playoffs

Pos	#	Player	Team	GP	G	A	Pts	+/–	PIM	PP	SH	GW	GT	S	%
C	7	Igor Larionov	S.J.	14	5	13	18	1–	10	0	0	0	0	27	18.5
R	24	Sergei Makarov	S.J.	14	8	2	10	2	4	3	0	2	0	26	30.8
C	27	Todd Elik	S.J.	14	5	5	10	5–	12	1	0	0	0	45	11.1
L	10	Johan Garpenlov	S.J.	14	4	6	10	0	6	0	0	2	0	23	17.4
D	6	Sandis Ozolinsh	S.J.	14	0	10	10	3	8	0	0	0	0	23	.0
R	22	Ulf Dahlen	S.J.	14	6	2	8	3–	0	3	0	1	0	36	16.7
D	41	Tom Pederson	S.J.	14	1	6	7	7–	2	0	1	0	0	34	2.9
D	8	Jeff Norton	S.J.	14	1	5	6	4	20	0	0	0	0	24	4.2
C	13	Jamie Baker	S.J.	14	3	2	5	1–	30	0	0	1	0	13	23.1
L	12	Bob Errey	S.J.	14	3	2	5	3–	10	1	0	0	0	12	25.0
L	11	Gaetan Duchesne	S.J.	14	1	4	5	2–	12	0	0	0	0	17	5.9
L	14	Ray Whitney	S.J.	14	0	4	4	4–	8	0	0	0	0	16	.0
R	17	Pat Falloon	S.J.	14	1	2	3	2–	6	0	0	0	0	8	12.5
D	26	* Vlastimil Kroupa	S.J.	14	1	2	3	8–	21	0	0	1	0	6	16.7
R	37	Rob Gaudreau	S.J.	14	2	0	2	1–	0	1	1	0	0	14	14.3
D	4	Jay More	S.J.	13	0	2	2	3–	32	0	0	0	0	5	.0
D	44	Shawn Cronin	S.J.	14	1	0	1	4–	20	0	0	0	0	5	20.0
D	40	* Mike Rathje	S.J.	1	0	0	0	1	0	0	0	0	0	0	.0
G	29	Jim Waite	S.J.	2	0	0	0	0	0	0	0	0	0	0	.0
R	36	Jeff Odgers	S.J.	11	0	0	0	2–	11	0	0	0	0	6	.0
G	32	Arturs Irbe	S.J.	14	0	0	0	0	6	0	0	0	0	0	.0

Goaltending

No.	Goaltender	GPI	Mins	Avg	W	L	EN	SO	GA	SA	S%
32	Arturs Irbe	14	806	3.72	7	7	0	0	50	399	.875
29	Jim Waite	2	40	4.50	0	0	0	0	3	17	.824
	Totals	**14**	**849**	**3.75**	**7**	**7**	**0**	**0**	**53**	**416**	**.873**

General Managers' History

Jack Ferreira, 1991-92; Office of the General Manager: Chuck Grillo (V.P. Director of Player Personnel) and Dean Lombardi (V.P. Director of Hockey Operations), 1992-93 to date.

Coaching History

George Kingston, 1991-92 to 1992-93; Kevin Constantine, 1993-94 to date.

Captains' History

Doug Wilson, 1991-92 to 1992-93; Bob Errey, 1993-94 to date.

Club Records

Team

(Figures in brackets for season records are games played)

Most Points	82	1993-94 (84)
Most Wins	33	1993-94 (84)
Most Ties	16	1993-94 (84)
Most Losses	*71	1992-93 (84)
Most Goals	252	1993-94 (84)
Most Goals Against	414	1992-93 (84)
Fewest Points	24	1992-93 (84)
Fewest Wins	11	1992-93 (84)
Fewest Ties	*2	1992-93 (84)
Fewest Losses	35	1993-94 (84)
Fewest Goals	218	1992-93 (84)
Fewest Goals Against	265	1993-94 (84)

Longest Winning Streak
Overall .... 7 Mar. 24-Apr. 5/94
Home .... 4 Mar. 29-Apr. 10/94
Away .... 4 Mar. 24-Apr. 5/94

Longest Undefeated Streak
Overall .... 9 Mar. 20-
Apr. 5/94
(7 wins, 2 ties)
Home .... 6 Mar. 20-
Apr. 13/94
(4 wins, 2 ties)
Away .... 5 Two times

Longest Losing Streak
Overall .... *17 Jan. 4/93-Feb. 12/93
Home .... 9 Nov. 19/92-Dec. 19/92
Away .... 19 Nov. 27/92-Feb. 12/93

Longest Winless Streak
Overall .... 20 Dec. 29/92-
Feb. 12/93 (0-19-1)
Home .... 9 Nov. 19/92-
Dec. 18/92 (0-9-0)
Away .... 19 Nov. 27/92-
Feb. 12/93 (0-19-0)

Most Shutouts, Season	3	1993-94 (84)
Most PIM, Season	2134	1992-93 (84)
Most Goals, Game	9	Mar. 29/94 (Wpg. 4 at S.J. 9)

Individual

Most Seasons	3	Pat Falloon, Jayson More
Most Games, Career	208	Jeff Odgers
Most Goals, Career	61	Pat Falloon
Most Assists, Career	85	Johan Garpenlov
Most Points, Career	140	Pat Falloon (61 goals, 79 assists)
Most PIM, Career	692	Jeff Odgers
Most Shutouts, Career	4	Arturs Irbe

Longest Consecutive
Games Streak .... 117 Doug Zmolek
(Oct. 8/92-Dec. 15/93)

Most Goals, Season .... 30 Sergei Makarov
(1993-94)

Most Assists, Season .... 52 Kelly Kisio
(1992-93)

Most Points, Season .... 78 Kelly Kisio
(1992-93)
(26 goals, 52 assists)

Most PIM, Season .... 326 Link Gaetz
(1991-92)

Most Shutouts, Season ...... 3 Arturs Irbe
(1993-94)

Most Points, Defenseman Season ... 64 Sandis Ozolnish
(1993-94)
(26 goals, 38 assists)

Most Points, Center, Season ... 78 Kelly Kisio
(1992-93)
(26 goals, 52 assists)

Most Points, Right Wing, Season ... 68 Sergei Makarov
(1993-94)
(30 goals, 38 assists)

Most Points, Left Wing, Season ... 66 Johan Garpenlov
(1992-93)
(22 goals, 44 assists)

Most Points, Rookie, Season ... 59 Pat Falloon
(1991-92)
(25 goals, 34 assists)

Most Goals, Game	3	Eight times
Most Assists, Game	4	Two times
Most Points, Game	4	Seventeen times

* NHL Record.

Entry Draft Selections 1994-91

1994
Pick
11 Jeff Friesen
37 Angel Nikolov
66 Alexei Yegorov
89 Vaclav Varada
115 Brian Swanson
141 Alexander Korolyuk
167 Sergei Gorbachev
193 Eric Landry
219 Yevgeny Nabokov
240 Tomas Pisa
245 Aniket Dhadphale
271 David Beauregard

1993
Pick
6 Viktor Kozlov
28 Shean Donovan
45 Vlastimil Kroupa
58 Ville Peltonen
80 Alexander Osadchy
106 Andrei Buschan
132 Petri Varis
154 Fredrik Oduya
158 Anatoli Filatov
184 Todd Holt
210 Jonas Forsberg
236 Jeff Salajko
262 Jamie Matthews

1992
Pick
3 Mike Rathje
10 Andrei Nazarov
51 Alexander Cherbajev
75 Jan Caloun
99 Marcus Ragnarsson
123 Michal Sykora
147 Eric Bellerose
171 Ryan Smith
195 Chris Burns
219 A. Kholomeyev
243 Victor Ignatjev

1991
Pick
2 Pat Falloon
23 Ray Whitney
30 Sandis Ozolinsh
45 Dody Wood
67 Kerry Toporowski
89 Dan Ryder
111 Fredrik Nilsson
133 Jaroslav Otevrel
155 Dean Grillo
177 Corwin Saurdiff
199 Dale Craigdell
221 Aaron Kriss
243 Mikhail Kravets

All-time Record vs. Other Clubs

Regular Season

		At Home							On Road							Total				
	GP	W	L	T	GF	GA	PTS	GP	W	L	T	GF	GA	PTS	GP	W	L	T	GF	GA	PTS
Anaheim	3	3	0	0	11	3	6	3	3	0	0	11	6	6	6	6	0	0	22	9	12
Boston	3	0	2	1	4	13	1	3	1	3	0	3	0	10	14	0	6	0	5	1	14	27	1
Buffalo	3	1	1	1	12	16	3	4	0	4	0	16	21	0	7	1	5	1	28	37	3
Calgary	12	2	9	1	32	45	5	10	2	8	0	22	55	4	22	4	17	1	54	100	9
Chicago	6	4	2	0	17	14	8	5	0	4	1	12	23	1	11	4	6	1	29	37	9
Dallas	5	1	4	0	14	26	2	5	1	4	0	16	26	2	10	2	8	0	30	52	4
Detroit	6	1	4	1	20	32	3	5	0	5	0	10	28	0	11	1	9	1	30	60	3
Edmonton	10	7	2	1	41	24	15	10	0	8	2	22	47	2	20	7	10	3	63	71	17
Florida	1	1	0	0	2	1	2	1	0	1	0	3	3	1	2	1	1	0	5	4	3
Hartford	3	2	1	0	19	14	4	2	2	0	0	10	13	4	5	4	1	0	29	27	8
Los Angeles	10	4	4	2	39	36	10	10	1	8	1	23	41	3	20	5	12	3	62	77	13
Montreal	4	0	2	2	6	8	2	4	0	4	0	7	21	0	8	0	6	2	13	29	2
New Jersey	3	1	2	0	5	10	2	4	0	4	1	7	20	2	7	1	6	1	12	30	4
NY Islanders	3	2	1	0	8	12	4	4	0	4	0	15	27	0	7	2	5	0	23	39	4
NY Rangers	4	0	4	0	9	22	0	3	0	2	1	7	15	1	7	0	6	1	16	37	1
Ottawa	2	1	1	0	4	4	2	2	2	0	0	6	9	4	4	3	1	0	10	13	2
Philadelphia	4	1	3	0	9	14	2	3	0	2	1	7	12	2	7	2	5	0	16	26	4
Pittsburgh	4	0	3	1	10	27	1	3	0	2	1	6	19	1	7	0	5	2	16	46	2
Quebec	4	2	2	0	20	21	4	3	0	3	0	9	17	0	7	2	5	0	29	38	4
St. Louis	4	0	4	0	6	14	0	7	1	6	0	15	31	2	11	1	10	0	21	45	2
Tampa Bay	3	0	3	0	9	13	0	3	2	1	0	5	7	4	6	2	4	0	14	20	4
Toronto	6	2	3	1	12	16	5	5	1	3	1	7	17	3	11	3	6	2	19	33	8
Vancouver	10	3	6	1	32	38	7	10	1	9	0	22	46	2	20	4	15	1	54	84	9
Washington	3	0	3	0	7	12	0	3	0	1	2	7	12	2	6	1	4	2	14	24	2
Winnipeg	8	3	3	2	36	35	8	10	3	6	1	30	38	7	18	6	9	3	66	73	15
Totals	**124**	**41**	**69**	**14**	**384**	**470**	**96**	**124**	**20**	**95**	**9**	**305**	**568**	**49**	**248**	**61**	**164**	**23**	**689**	**1038**	**145**

Dallas totals include Minnesota, 1991-92 to 1992-93.

Playoffs

	Series	W	L	GP	W	L	T	GF	GA	Last Mtg.	Round	Result
Detroit	1	1	0	7	4	3	0	21	27	1994	CQF	W 4-3
Toronto	1	0	1	7	3	4	0	21	26	1994	CSF	L 3-4
Totals	**2**	**1**	**1**	**14**	**7**	**7**	**0**	**42**	**53**			

Playoff Results 1994-90

Year	Round	Opponent	Result	GF	GA
1994	CSF	Toronto	L 3-4	21	26
	CQF	Detroit	W 4-3	21	27

Abbreviations: Round: F – Final;
CF – conference final; **CQF** – conference quarter-final;
CSF – conference semi-final; **DF** – division final;
DSF – division semi-final; **SF** – semi-final;
QF – quarter-final; **PR** – preliminary round.

1993-94 Results

Oct.	6	at	Edmonton	2-3	11	Los Angeles	2-2
	7	at	Calgary	2-6	12	at Anaheim	5-2
	10	at	Los Angeles	2-5	15	Hartford	8-2
	14		Calgary	1-2	17	Calgary	3-2
	16		Boston	1-1	25	NY Rangers	3-8
	19		St. Louis	1-4	28	at Florida	3-3
	21	at	St. Louis	2-5	29	at Tampa Bay	2-1
	23		Vancouver	4-6	Feb. 1	at NY Islanders	4-5
	24	at	Vancouver	4-3	3	at Philadelphia	3-2
	26		Edmonton	3-1	5	at St. Louis	3-4
	28		Anaheim	4-3	6	at Dallas	7-1
	30		Washington	2-4	8	Chicago	4-3
	31	at	Anaheim	2-1	11	Chicago	4-3
Nov.	2		Pittsburgh	3-3	13	Chicago	1-0
	5		Dallas	4-2	15	Philadelphia	4-6
	7		New Jersey	1-2	17	Quebec	2-8
	9		Toronto	3-3	19	Los Angeles	2-8
	11	at	Dallas	0-4	21	Dallas	3-6
	13	at	New Jersey	4-2	23	at Montreal	1-3
	14	at	NY Rangers	3-3	24	at Ottawa	4-6
	16	at	Washington	2-1	26	at Detroit	2-3
	18	at	Boston	1-3	28	at Winnipeg	3-3
	20	at	Hartford	3-2	Mar. 3	Edmonton	4-2
	21	at	Buffalo	5-6	6	Anaheim	6-0
	23		Detroit	6-4	8	Buffalo	4-4
	26	at	Anaheim	4-3	10	NY Islanders	4-3
	27		Anaheim	1-0	12	at Calgary	0-2
Dec.	3		Winnipeg	3-3	17	Ottawa	1-2
	5		Florida	2-1	19	at Los Angeles	1-2
	7		Tampa Bay	1-3	20	Los Angeles	6-6
	11	at	Detroit	3-5	22	at Pittsburgh	2-2
	12	at	Chicago	1-2	24	at Toronto	2-1
	15		St. Louis	1-3	25	at Winnipeg	8-3
	17	at	Edmonton	3-3	27	at St. Louis	1-3
	19	at	Quebec	5-7	29	Winnipeg	9-4
	22	at	Toronto	2-2	31	Toronto	5-3
	23	at	Chicago	3-5	Apr. 2	Vancouver	7-4
	28		Calgary	3-3	5	at Los Angeles	2-1
	31	at	Vancouver	3-2	7	at Vancouver	2-2
Jan.	2	at	Edmonton	4-4	8	at Calgary	2-5
	4		Montreal	2-2	10	Vancouver	3-1
	7		Detroit	3-10	13	Edmonton	2-2

Office of the General Manager

LOMBARDI, DEAN
Vice President and Director of Hockey Operations, San Jose Sharks.
Born in Holyoke, Massachusetts, March 5, 1958.

Dean Lombardi enters his seventh year in the National Hockey League and his fifth with the Sharks organization. After two seasons as assistant general manager, he was named to his present position on June 26, 1992. Before joining the Sharks, he spent two seasons, 1988-89 and 1989-90, as assistant general manager with the Minnesota North Stars.

Lombardi, 36, utilizes his skills in contract negotiations and knowledge of the NHL's business and legal workings to benefit the Sharks and works closely with Chuck Grillo in the club's player evaluation process.

He has successfully negotiated contracts with several players in the Sharks system and has also been instrumental in constructing key trades, including the 1993 draft day deal with Hartford which brought Sergei Makarov to the Sharks and led to the drafting of Viktor Kozlov and Vlastimil Kroupa.

Lombardi was mentioned in many circles as one of the NHL's top executives in 1993-94 (he finished third in *The Hockey News* award voting for executive of the year) by helping shape the club that posted the greatest single-season turnaround in league history. Among his key moves in 1993-94 were picking up Todd Elik via waivers from Edmonton and acquiring Ulf Dahlen in a trading-deadline deal with Dallas.

On the ice, Lombardi was captain during his final two seasons at the University of New Haven where he received a full athletic scholarship and earned the school's student/athlete of the year award. He also was named to the Junior All-America team in 1978 while playing for the Springfield (MA) Olympics.

GRILLO, CHUCK
Vice President and Director of Player Personnel, San Jose Sharks.
Born in Hibbing, Minnesota, July 24, 1939.

Moving into his 15th NHL season and fifth with the Sharks is Chuck Grillo, the vice president and director of player personnel for the Sharks. Grillo supervises the club's scouting department and player development program, having held that position since 1990, when the vice president's title — along with some duties of the office of general manager — were added on June 26, 1992. Grillo, a native of Hibbing, MN, served as director of pro scouting from 1988 to 1990 with the Minnesota North Stars, preceded by eight years as a scout for the New York Rangers.

One of only two U.S.-born player personnel directors in the NHL, Grillo is noted for his ability to distinguish talent and implement innovative ideas for player development. Since joining the Sharks, Grillo and his scouting staff have already seen 11 of their 37 Entry Draft selections play with the parent club. Seven of the 13 players taken in the initial draft in 1991 have NHL experience, including Pat Falloon, Ray Whitney, Sandis Ozolinsh and Dale Craigwell from last season's playoff club. Many players who contributed to the 1991-92 International Hockey League champion Kansas City Blades (Sharks development affiliate) were acquired and developed by Grillo and his staff while with Minnesota.

Grillo has participated in the NHL draft process since 1981. His contributions have led to the selection of 39 players who are established NHL performers, and nearly 30 others who either have NHL experience or are on the verge of breaking into the league. Out of 13 first-round selections for whom he has been responsible, 11 have become NHL regulars, including James Patrick, Dave Gagner, Ulf Dahlen, Brian Leetch (1994 playoff MVP), Jayson More, Falloon and Mike Rathje. Viktor Kozlov, taken first (6th overall) by the Sharks in 1993, and 1992 first round selection (10th overall) Andrei Nazarov, are projected to join that group.

Grillo, 55, also is owner and operator of a successful hockey camp in Nisswa, MN. Many athletes at the camp have gone on to become players, coaches and trainers in the NHL. In addition, many NHL clubs send their players to the camp for off-season development.

Grillo spent 16 years as a high school hockey and baseball coach, taking teams to the Minnesota state tournament 11 times including 1973 when he was named Minnesota State High School League coach of the year at Bemidji High School.

Owner of a master's degree in guidance and counseling from Bemidji State University, Grillo is working toward a doctorate in educational administration, also from Bemidji State.

Club Directory

San Jose Arena
525 West Santa Clara Street
P.O. Box 1240
San Jose, California 95113
Phone **408/287-7070**
FAX 408/999-5797
Capacity: 17,190

Executive Staff

Majority Owner & Chairman	George Gund III
Co-Owner	Gordon Gund
President & Chief Executive Officer	Arthur L. Savage
Vice-President, Director of Player Personnel	Chuck Grillo
Exec. Vice President, Chief Operating Officer	Greg Jamison
Exec. Vice President, Building Operations	Frank Jirik
Exec. Vice President, Development	Matt Levine
Vice-President, Director of Hockey Operations	Dean Lombardi
Vice Chairman	Tom McEnery
Interim Chief Financial Officer	Harry M. Stokes
Chief of Staff to President & CEO	Karen C. Shiraki
Executive Assistant to President & CEO	Dawn Beres

Hockey

Head Coach	Kevin Constantine
Assistant Coach & Ass't to the Dir. of Hockey Oper.	Wayne Thomas
Assistant Coach	Vasily Tikhonov
Assistant Coach	Drew Remenda
Strength Coach	Steve Millard
Head Coach, Kansas City Blades	Jim Wiley
Scouting Coordinator	Joe Will
Exec. Assistant to V.P., Dir. of Hockey Operations	Brenda Will
Eastern Regional Scout	Ray Payne
Professional/Amateur Scout	Tim Burke
Scout and Player Development	Pat Funk
Scout and Player Development	Rob Grillo
Area Scouts	Jim Bzdel (Saskatchewan), Tim Gorski (Alaska), Randy Joevenazzo (Alberta), Konstantin Krylov (Russia), Karel Masopust (Czech. Republic), Jack Morganstern (New England), Larry Ross (Minnesota), Joe Rowley (Ontario), Dan Summers (Manitoba)
Video Scouting Coordinator	Bob Friedlander
Head Trainer	Tom Woodcock
Equipment Manager	Bob Crocker, Jr.
Assistant Trainer/Massage Therapist	Sergei Tchekmarev
Travel Coordinator	Steve Perry
Team Physician	Arthur J. Ting, M.D.
Team Dentist	Robert Bonahoom, D.D.S.
Medical Staff	Warren King, M.D., James Klint, M.D., Will Straw, M.D.
Team Vision Specialist	Vincent S. Zuccaro, O.D., F.A.A.O.

Business Operations

Vice President, Broadcast & Media Marketing	Malcolm Bordelon
Director of Media Relations	Ken Arnold
Director of Executive Suite Services	Ted Atlee
Director of Ticket Sales	Rich Muschell
Director of Community Development	Lori Smith
Director of Broadcasting	Mark Stulberger
Director of Marketing	Elaine Sullivan-Digre
Manager of Event Services	Diane Bloom
Executive Assistant	Michelle Simmons
Account Service Managers	Annie Chan-Zien, Elizabeth Sabatino, Paul Solby, Gene Wiggins
Sponsorship Services Coordinator	Valerie Bigelow
Ticket Manager	Mary Enriquez
Media Marketing Managers	Jim Josel, Don Olvarado
Manager, Educational Marketing	J.D. Kershaw
Group Sales Manager	Mary Ross
Suite Hospitality Managers	Pat Swan, Coleen Duncan
Promotions and Broadcast Coordinator	Martha Baumgartner
Tour Administrator	Dianna Carthew
Assistant Ticket Manager	Walt Dethlefs
Assistant, Community Development	Roger Ross
Assistant Director of Media Relations	Paul Turner
S.J. Arena Administrative Marketing Assistant	Beth Brigino
Assistant, Executive Suite Services	Kimberly Brown
Ticket Sales Assistant	Kris Lyon
Assistant, Event Services	Anna Saalfield
Mascot Coordinator	Jason Minsky
Mascot	S.J. Sharkie

Finance

Director of Finance and Accounting	Brent M. Billinger
Manager of Finance	Mike Cain
Manager, Information Systems	Alex Ignacio
Systems Support Analyst	Wee Yap
Accounting Associates	Colleen Baker, Sue Feachen, Beth Ganeff, Sara McEnery

Building Operations

Vice President, Arena Project Manager	Jim Goddard
Director of Booking & Operations	Jack Larson
Manager of Guest Services	Mike Kolatski
Director of Ticket Operations	Daniel DeBoer
Executive Assistant	Chris Palmer
Administrative Ass't & Arena Project Coordinator	Colleen Reilly
Assistant Box Office Manager	Judy Jones
Senior Technical Advisor	Bob McCrobie
Building Services Managers	Bruce Tharaldson, John Jordan, Blair Engelbrekt
Mailroom Coordinator	Hunter Van Pelt
Receptionist	Marcia Cady
Administrative Assistants	Cathy Hancock, Helen Matz

Development

Director of Special Projects	Herb Briggin
Executive Assistant	Joyce Coppola

Miscellaneous

Team Colors	Pacific Teal, Gray, Black, White
Dimensions of Rink	200 feet by 85 feet
Television Stations	KICU-TV 36, SportsChannel
Radio Network Flagship	KFRC (610-AM)
Play-By-Play (Radio)	Dan Rusanowsky
Play-By-Play (Television)	Randy Hahn
Color Commentator (Television)	Pete Stemkowski
Color Commentator (Radio)	Chris Collins
P.A. Announcer	Sam Player
Organist	Dieter Ruehle

Tampa Bay Lightning

1993-94 Results: 30w-43L-11T 71PTS. Seventh, Atlantic Division

Year-by-Year Record

	Home			Road			Overall							
Season	GP	W	L	T	W	L	T	W	L	T	GF	GA	Pts.	Finished	Playoff Result
1993-94	84	14	22	6	16	21	5	30	43	11	224	251	71	7th, Atlantic Div.	Out of Playoffs
1992-93	84	12	27	3	11	27	4	23	54	7	245	332	53	6th, Norris Div.	Out of Playoffs

First-year center Chris Gratton led all Tampa Bay rookies in games (84), goals (13), assists (29) and points (42).

Schedule

Oct.	Sat.	1	at NY Islanders
	Tues.	4	Quebec
	Fri.	7	St. Louis
	Sat.	8	at Philadelphia
	Tues.	11	at NY Rangers
	Sat.	15	New Jersey
	Sun.	16	at St. Louis
	Tues.	18	Pittsburgh
	Thur.	20	Toronto
	Sun.	23	at Ottawa*
	Wed.	26	Los Angeles
	Sun.	30	at Chicago
Nov.	Tues.	1	at Quebec
	Wed.	2	at Montreal
	Sat.	5	NY Islanders
	Tues.	8	at Buffalo
	Wed.	9	at Toronto
	Sat.	12	Edmonton
	Wed.	16	Detroit
	Fri.	18	Winnipeg
	Sat.	19	New Jersey
	Wed.	23	at NY Islanders
	Sat.	26	at Philadelphia*
	Sun.	27	at Hartford
	Wed.	30	Florida
Dec.	Fri.	2	San Jose
	Sat.	3	at Washington
	Mon.	5	at Florida
	Wed.	7	Ottawa
	Fri.	9	Quebec
	Wed.	14	Buffalo
	Fri.	16	Chicago
	Sun.	18	at Quebec*
	Mon.	19	at Montreal
	Wed.	21	at Ottawa
	Fri.	23	Pittsburgh
	Mon.	26	Philadelphia
	Fri.	30	NY Rangers
Jan.	Mon.	2	at Boston*
	Wed.	4	Vancouver
	Fri.	6	Dallas
	Sat.	7	NY Rangers
	Tues.	10	at Calgary

	Wed.	11	at Edmonton
	Fri.	13	at Vancouver
	Sun.	15	at Winnipeg
	Wed.	18	New Jersey
	Mon.	23	at Florida
	Wed.	25	Calgary
	Fri.	27	at NY Rangers
	Sat.	28	at NY Islanders
Feb.	Wed.	1	Montreal
	Thur.	2	at Dallas
	Sat.	4	at Pittsburgh
	Mon.	6	at Detroit (in Hamilton)
	Wed.	8	Washington
	Fri.	10	Hartford
	Sat.	11	NY Rangers
	Mon.	13	NY Islanders
	Wed.	15	at Washington
	Fri.	17	Boston
	Sat.	18	Buffalo
	Wed.	22	at Detroit
	Thur.	23	at New Jersey
	Sun.	26	at San Jose*
	Tues.	28	at Los Angeles
Mar.	Wed.	1	at Anaheim
	Mon.	6	Anaheim
	Thur.	9	Boston (in Minneapolis)
	Sat.	11	Philadelphia
	Mon.	13	Washington
	Thur.	16	at Pittsburgh
	Sat.	18	at New Jersey*
	Sun.	19	at Buffalo*
	Wed.	22	Ottawa
	Fri.	24	Boston
	Sun.	26	at Florida*
	Mon.	27	Montreal
	Wed.	29	Washington
	Fri.	31	Hartford
Apr.	Sun.	2	Florida*
	Thur.	6	at Philadelphia
	Sat.	8	at Boston*
	Sun.	9	at Hartford*

* Denotes afternoon game.

Home Starting Times:
Night Games . . . . 7:30 p.m.
Matinees . . . . 1:30 p.m.

Franchise date: December 16, 1991

3rd NHL Season

ATLANTIC DIVISION

1994-95 Player Personnel

FORWARDS	HT	WT	S	Place of Birth	Date	1993-94 Club
ANDERSSON, Mikael	5-11	185	L	Malmo, Sweden	5/10/66	Tampa Bay
BRADLEY, Brian	5-10	177	R	Kitchener, Ont.	1/21/65	Tampa Bay
BUREAU, Marc	6-1	198	R	Trois-Rivières, Que.	5/19/66	Tampa Bay
CAMPEAU, Christian	5-10	180	R	Verdun, Que.	6/2/71	Atlanta
CLOUTIER, Colin	6-3	224	L	Winnipeg, Man.	1/27/76	Brandon
COLE, Danton	5-11	185	R	Pontiac, MI	1/10/67	Tampa Bay
CREIGHTON, Adam	6-5	210	L	Burlington, Ont.	6/2/65	Tampa Bay
CUMMINS, Jim	6-2	203	R	Dearborn, MI	5/17/70	Phi-Hershey-T.B.-Atlanta
EGELAND, Allan	6-0	184	L	Lethbridge, Alta.	1/31/73	Tacoma
GALLANT, Gerard	5-10	190	L	Summerside, P.E.I.	9/2/63	Tampa Bay
GAVEY, Aaron	6-1	170	L	Sudbury, Ont.	2/22/74	S.S. Marie
GRATTON, Chris	6-3	202	L	Brantford, Ont.	7/5/75	Tampa Bay
GRETZKY, Brent	5-10	160	L	Brantford, Ont.	2/20/72	Tampa Bay-Atlanta
KACIR, Marian	6-1	183	L	Hodonin, Czech.	9/29/74	Owen Sound
KLIMA, Petr	6-0	190	R	Chomutov, Czech.	12/23/64	Tampa Bay
MACDONALD, Tom	5-11	190	L	Toronto, Ont.	4/14/74	S.S. Marie
MILLER, Colin	6-0	188	R	Grimsby, Ont.	8/21/71	Atlanta
MYHRES, Brantt	6-3	195	R	Edmonton, Alta.	3/18/74	Lethbridge-Spokane-Atlanta
POESCHEK, Rudy	6-2	210	R	Kamloops, B.C.	9/29/66	Tampa Bay
RUFF, Jason	6-2	192	L	Kelowna, B.C.	1/27/70	Tampa Bay-Atlanta
SAVARD, Denis	5-10	175	R	Pointe Gatineau, Que.	2/4/61	Tampa Bay
TANGUAY, Martin	5-11	185	L	Ste-Julie, Que.	1/12/73	Knoxville-Atlanta
TARDIF, Marc	6-1	199	L	Montreal, Que.	1/6/73	Atlanta
TOMS, Jeff	6-3	180	L	Swift Current, Sask.	6/4/74	S.S. Marie
TUCKER, John	6-0	200	R	Windsor, Ont.	9/29/64	Tampa Bay
WIEMER, Jason	6-1	215	L	Kimberley, B.C.	4/14/76	Portland (WHL)
ZAMUNER, Rob	6-2	202	L	Oakville, Ont.	9/17/69	Tampa Bay
DEFENSEMEN						
BANNISTER, Drew	6-1	193	R	Belleville, Ont.	9/4/74	S.S. Marie
BERGEVIN, Marc	6-1	197	L	Montreal, Que.	8/11/65	Tampa Bay
BROWN, Ryan	6-3	215	R	Boyle, Alta.	9/19/74	Swift Current
BUCHANAN, Jeff	5-10	165	R	Swift Current, Sask.	5/23/71	Atlanta
CHAMBERS, Shawn	6-2	200	L	Royal Oaks, MI	10/11/66	Tampa Bay
CHARRON, Eric	6-3	192	L	Verdun, Que.	1/14/70	Tampa Bay-Atlanta
CICCONE, Enrico	6-4	200	L	Montreal, Que.	4/10/70	Wsh-Portland (AHL)-T.B.
CROSS, Cory	6-5	212	L	Lloydminster, Alta.	1/3/71	Tampa Bay-Atlanta
DUBOIS, Eric	6-0	195	R	Montreal, Que.	5/9/70	Atlanta
HAMRLIK, Roman	6-2	202	L	Gottwaldov, Czech.	4/12/74	Tampa Bay
JOSEPH, Chris	6-2	210	R	Burnaby, B.C.	9/10/69	Edmonton-Tampa Bay
LAPORTE, Alexandre	6-3	210	R	Cowansville, Que.	5/1/75	Victoriaville
LIPUMA, Chris	6-0	183	L	Bridgeview, IL	3/23/71	Tampa Bay-Atlanta
MAILLET, Chris	6-5	188	L	Moncton, NB	1/28/76	Red Deer
RABY, Mathieu	6-2	204	R	Hull, Que.	1/19/75	Victoriaville

GOALTENDERS	HT	WT	C	Place of Birth	Date	1993-94 Club
BERGERON, Jean-Claude	6-2	192	L	Hauterive, Que.	10/14/68	Tampa Bay-Atlanta
GREENLAY, Mike	6-3	200	L	Vitoria, Brazil	9/15/68	Atlanta
MOSS, Tyler	6-0	168	R	Ottawa, Ont.	6/29/75	Kingston
PUPPA, Daren	6-3	205	R	Kirkland Lake, Ont.	3/23/65	Tampa Bay
WILKINSON, Derek	6-0	160	L	Lasalle, Que.	7/29/74	Belleville
YOUNG, Wendell	5-9	181	L	Halifax, N.S.	8/1/63	Tampa Bay-Atlanta

1993-94 Scoring

* – rookie

Regular Season

Pos	#	Player	Team	GP	G	A	Pts	+/–	PIM	PP	SH	GW	GT	S	%
C	19	Brian Bradley	T.B.	78	24	40	64	8–	56	6	0	2	0	180	13.3
R	85	Petr Klima	T.B.	75	28	27	55	15–	76	10	0	2	0	167	16.8
C	9	Denis Savard	T.B.	74	18	28	46	1–	106	2	1	2	0	181	9.9
R	24	Danton Cole	T.B.	81	20	23	43	7	32	8	1	4	0	149	13.4
C	77 *	Chris Gratton	T.B.	84	13	29	42	25–	123	5	1	2	1	161	8.1
R	14	John Tucker	T.B.	66	17	23	40	9	28	2	0	6	1	126	13.5
D	22	Shawn Chambers	T.B.	66	11	23	34	6–	23	6	1	1	0	142	7.7
D	23	Chris Joseph	EDM	10	1	1	2	8–	28	1	0	0	0	25	4.0
			T.B.	66	10	19	29	13–	108	7	0	0	0	154	6.5
			TOTAL	76	11	20	31	21–	136	8	0	0	0	179	6.1
R	15	Pat Elynuik	WSH	4	1	1	2	3–	0	1	0	0	0	8	12.5
			T.B.	63	12	14	26	18–	64	3	1	1	0	103	11.7
			TOTAL	67	13	15	28	21–	64	4	1	1	0	111	11.7
L	34	Mikael Andersson	T.B.	76	13	12	25	8	23	1	1	2	1	136	9.6
D	44	Roman Hamrlik	T.B.	64	3	18	21	14–	135	0	0	0	0	158	1.9
C	10	Adam Creighton	T.B.	53	10	10	20	7–	37	2	0	1	0	77	13.0
D	25	Marc Bergevin	T.B.	83	1	15	16	5–	87	0	0	1	0	76	1.3
C	28	Marc Bureau	T.B.	75	8	7	15	9–	30	0	1	1	0	110	7.3
L	17	Gerard Gallant	T.B.	51	4	9	13	6–	74	1	0	2	0	45	8.9
L	7	Rob Zamuner	T.B.	59	6	6	12	9–	42	0	0	1	0	109	5.5
D	20	Rudy Poeschek	T.B.	71	3	6	9	3	118	0	0	1	1	46	6.5
C	11	Bill McDougall	T.B.	22	3	3	6	4–	8	1	0	0	1	26	11.5
D	26 *	Chris Lipuma	T.B.	27	0	4	4	1	77	0	0	0	0	20	.0
L	8 *	Jason Ruff	T.B.	6	1	2	3	2	2	0	0	0	0	14	7.1
C	49 *	Brent Gretzky	T.B.	10	1	2	3	0	2	0	0	0	0	14	7.1
R	12 *	Jim Cummins	PHI	22	1	2	3	0	71	0	0	0	0	17	5.9
			T.B.	4	0	0	0	1–	13	0	0	0	0	3	.0
			TOTAL	26	1	2	3	1–	84	0	0	0	0	20	5.0
D	39	Enrico Ciccone	WSH	46	1	1	2	2–	174	0	0	0	0	23	4.3
			T.B.	11	0	1	1	2–	52	0	0	0	0	10	.0
			TOTAL	57	1	2	3	4–	226	0	0	0	0	33	3.0
G	93	Daren Puppa	T.B.	63	0	1	1	0	2	0	0	0	0	0	.0
C	16	Jason Lafreniere	T.B.	1	0	0	0	1–	0	0	0	0	0	2	.0
G	30	J.C. Bergeron	T.B.	3	0	0	0	0	0	0	0	0	0	0	.0
D	3 *	Eric Charron	T.B.	4	0	0	0	0	2	0	0	0	0	1	.0
D	4 *	Cory Cross	T.B.	5	0	0	0	3–	6	0	0	0	0	5	.0
D	5	Normand Rochefort	T.B.	6	0	0	0	1–	10	0	0	0	0	4	.0
G	1	Wendell Young	T.B.	9	0	0	0	0	4	0	0	0	0	0	.0

Goaltending

No.	Goaltender	GPI	Mins	Avg	W	L	T	EN	SO	GA	SA	S%
1	Wendell Young	9	480	2.50	2	3	1	1	1	20	211	.905
93	Daren Puppa	63	3653	2.71	22	33	6	4	4	165	1637	.899
30	J.C. Bergeron	3	134	3.13	1	1	1	0	0	7	69	.899
35	Pat Jablonski	15	834	3.88	5	6	3	0	0	54	374	.856
	Totals	**84**	**5116**	**2.94**	**30**	**43**	**11**	**5**	**5**	**251**	**2296**	**.891**

General Manager

ESPOSITO, PHIL
General Manager, Tampa Bay Lightning.
Born in Sault Ste. Marie, Ont., February 20, 1942.

Phil Esposito, who headed up Tampa Bay's successful campaign to obtain an NHL franchise, was rewarded for his hard work when the Lightning were granted a berth in the NHL, beginning with the 1992-93 season. After an 18-year Hall-of-Fame career that included eight All-Star selections as well as winning the Hart Trophy twice and the Art Ross Trophy five times, Esposito was named vice president and general manager of the NY Rangers in 1986, remaining in that role until the start of the 1989-90 season. He also doubled as coach during the 1986-87 campaign and took over the bench duties again at the conclusion of 1988-89. Esposito, who began his career with Chicago and finished his playing days with the NY Rangers, had his most productive days with the Boston Bruins, winning a pair of Stanley Cup titles while establishing numerous team records, including most goals (76) and points (152) in a single season. In 1968-69, he became the first NHL player to record 100 points in a season.

NHL Coaching Record

		Regular Season					Playoffs			
Season	Team	Games	W	L	T	%	Games	W	L	%
1986-87	NY Rangers (NHL)	43	24	19	0	.558	6	2	4	.333
1988-89	NY Rangers (NHL)	2	0	2	0	.000	4	0	4	.000
	NHL Totals	**45**	**24**	**21**	**0**	**.533**	**10**	**2**	**8**	**.200**

General Managers' History

Phil Esposito, 1992-93 to date.

Coaching History

Terry Crisp, 1992-93 to date.

Captains' History

No captain

Coach

CRISP, TERRY
Coach, Tampa Bay Lightning. Born in Parry Sound, Ont., May 28, 1943.

After a two-year absence, Terry Crisp returned to the NHL's coaching ranks to become the first coach of the Tampa Bay Lightning. Crisp, who won two Stanley Cups as a member of the Philadelphia Flyers, played 11 years in the NHL for the Bruins, Blues, Islanders and Flyers. After retiring in 1976, he joined the Flyers' organization as an assistant coach, serving two terms before leaving to coach the OHL's Sault Ste. Marie Greyhounds. With the Greyhounds, Crisp won three regular-season crowns and twice earned the nod as the league's coach of the year. In 1985, Crisp accepted a coaching position with the Calgary Flames' top AHL farm affiliate in Moncton and spent two seasons with the Golden Flames before being elevated to the head coaching position with their parent club. Crisp led Calgary to its best finish in 1988-89, winning 54 games and capturing the franchise's first Stanley Cup championship after a six-game final series win over the Montreal Canadiens. After being released by the Flames, Crisp joined the Canadian National Team program as an assistant coach and was with the club when Team Canada won a silver medal at the 1992 Olympics.

Coaching Record

			Regular Season				Playoffs				
Season	Team	Games	W	L	T	%	Games	W	L	T	%
1979-80	S.S. Marie (OHL)	68	22	45	1	.331	....	....	....	....	....
1980-81	S.S. Marie (OHL)	68	47	19	2	.706	19	8	7	4	.526
1981-82	S.S. Marie (OHL)	68	40	25	3	.610	13	4	6	3	.423
1982-83	S.S. Marie (OHL)	70	48	21	1	.693	16	7	6	3	.531
1983-84	S.S. Marie (OHL)	70	38	28	4	.571	16	8	4	4	.625
1984-85	S.S. Marie (OHL)	66	54	11	1	.826	16	12	2	2	.813
1985-86	Moncton (AHL)	80	34	34	12	.500	10	5	5	0	.500
1986-87	Moncton (AHL)	80	43	31	6	.575	6	2	4	0	.333
1987-88	**Calgary (NHL)**	**80**	**48**	**23**	**9**	**.656**	**9**	**4**	**5**	**0**	**.444**
1988-89	**Calgary (NHL)**	**80**	**54**	**17**	**9**	**.731**	**22**	**16**	**6**	**0**	**.727***
1989-90	**Calgary (NHL)**	**80**	**42**	**23**	**15**	**.619**	**6**	**2**	**4**	**0**	**.333**
1992-93	**Tampa Bay (NHL)**	**84**	**23**	**54**	**7**	**.315**	....	....	....	....	....
1993-94	**Tampa Bay (NHL)**	**84**	**30**	**43**	**11**	**.423**	....	....	....	....	....
	NHL Totals	**408**	**197**	**160**	**51**	**.545**	**37**	**22**	**15**		**0.595**

* Stanley Cup win.

Club Records

Team

(Figures in brackets for season records are games played)

Most Points	71	1993-94 (84)
Most Wins	30	1993-94 (84)
Most Ties	11	1993-94 (84)
Most Losses	54	1992-93 (84)
Most Goals	245	1992-93 (84)
Most Goals Against	332	1992-93 (84)
Fewest Points	53	1992-93 (84)
Fewest Wins	23	1992-93 (84)
Fewest Ties	7	1992-93 (84)
Fewest Losses	43	1993-94 (84)
Fewest Goals	224	1993-94 (84)
Fewest Goals Against	251	1993-94 (84)

Longest Winning Streak
Overall . . . . 4 Nov. 7-13/92
Home . . . . 3 Nov. 3-13/92
Away . . . . 3 Dec. 3-7/93

Longest Undefeated Streak
Overall . . . . 6 Nov. 3-13/92
(5 wins, 1 tie)
Home . . . . 3 Nov. 3-13/92
(3 wins)
Away . . . . 6 Dec. 28/93-Jan. 12/94
(5 wins, 1 tie)

Longest Losing Streak
Overall . . . . 8 Mar. 9-28/93
Home . . . . 6 Mar. 9-Apr. 11/93
Away . . . . 5 Dec. 22/92-Jan. 4/93

Longest Winless Streak
Overall . . . . 8 Mar. 9-28/93
(8 losses)
Home . . . . 9 Mar. 9-Apr. 10/93
(8 losses, 1 tie)
Away . . . . 8 Feb. 3-Mar. 23/93
Most Shutouts, Season 5 1993-94 (84)
Most PIM, Season 1,625 1992-93 (84)
Most Goals, Game . . . . 7 Three times

Individual

Most Seasons	2	Several players
Most Games, Career	161	Marc Bergevin
Most Goals, Career	66	Brian Bradley
Most Assists, Career	84	Brian Bradley
Most Points, Career	150	Brian Bradley
Most PIM, Career	206	Roman Hamrlik
Most Shutouts, Career	4	Daren Puppa (1993-94)

Longest Consecutive
Games Streak . . . . 95 Rob Zamuner
Most Goals, Season . . . . 42 Brian Bradley (1992-93)
Most Assists, Season . . . . . 44 Brian Bradley (1992-93)
Most Points, Season . . . . . . 86 Brian Bradley (1992-93)
Most PIM, Season . . . . 154 Mike Hartman (1992-93)
Most Shutouts, Season . . . . . 4 Daren Puppa (1993-94)
Most Points, Defenseman Season . . . . . 39 Shawn Chambers (1992-93)
Most Points, Center, Season . . . . 86 Brian Bradley (1992-93)
Most Points, Right Wing, Season . . . . 56 John Tucker (1992-93)
Most Points, Left Wing, Season . . . . 51 Chris Kontos (1992-93)
Most Points, Rookie, Season . . . . 43 Rob Zamuner (1992-93) Chris Gratton (1993-94)
Most Goals, Game . . . . 4 Chris Kontos (Oct. 7/92)
Most Assists, Game . . . . 4 Joe Reekie (Oct. 7/92) Marc Bureau (Dec. 16/92)
Most Points, Game . . . . 6 Doug Crossman (Nov. 11/92)

Veteran Denis Savard contributed 18 goals and 28 assists to the Lightning's offensive totals.

Danton Cole reached career-highs in goals (20), assists (23) and points (43) during the 1993-94 season.

All-time Record vs. Other Clubs

Regular Season

	At Home						On Road						Total					
	GP	W	L	T	GF	GA	PTS	GP	W	L	T	GF	GA	PTS	GP	W	L	T	GF	GA	PTS
Anaheim	1	0	1	0	1	4	0	1	1	0	0	4	2	2	2	1	1	0	5	6	2
Boston	3	0	1	2	8	10	2	3	1	1	1	7	6	3	6	1	2	3	15	16	5
Buffalo	3	1	2	0	5	6	2	3	1	1	1	10	10	3	6	2	3	1	15	16	5
Calgary	3	1	2	0	13	16	2	2	1	1	0	6	3	2	5	2	3	0	19	19	4
Chicago	4	2	2	0	14	15	4	5	0	3	2	9	16	2	9	2	5	2	23	31	6
Dallas	5	0	3	2	7	13	2	4	1	3	0	12	15	2	9	1	6	2	19	28	4
Detroit	6	1	5	0	21	39	2	4	1	3	0	13	20	2	10	2	8	0	34	59	4
Edmonton	3	2	0	1	13	6	5	3	0	3	0	6	9	0	6	2	3	1	19	15	5
Florida	3	0	2	1	2	6	1	2	0	1	1	4	5	1	5	0	3	2	6	11	2
Hartford	3	2	1	0	11	7	4	3	0	3	0	6	13	0	6	2	4	0	17	20	4
Los Angeles	2	0	2	0	5	9	0	3	3	0	0	14	9	6	5	3	2	0	19	18	6
Montreal	3	2	0	1	8	5	5	3	1	2	0	6	6	2	6	3	2	1	14	11	7
New Jersey	3	0	2	1	7	10	1	4	0	4	0	9	18	0	7	0	6	1	16	28	1
NY Islanders	4	1	3	0	7	15	2	3	1	1	2	11	12	2	7	2	5	0	18	27	4
NY Rangers	3	1	2	0	11	11	2	5	2	3	0	22	20	4	8	3	5	0	33	31	6
Ottawa	3	3	0	0	9	4	6	3	0	3	0	12	4	6	6	3	3	0	21	8	12
Philadelphia	4	2	2	0	12	10	4	3	0	2	1	7	14	1	7	2	4	1	19	24	5
Pittsburgh	3	1	2	0	10	13	2	3	0	2	1	7	13	1	6	1	4	1	17	26	3
Quebec	4	3	1	0	14	12	6	3	1	2	0	9	13	2	7	4	3	0	23	25	8
St. Louis	5	2	2	1	17	18	5	4	1	3	0	13	18	2	9	3	5	1	30	36	7
San Jose	3	1	2	0	7	5	2	3	0	3	0	13	9	0	6	1	5	0	20	14	2
Toronto	5	1	4	0	18	6	2	3	1	2	0	14	24	6	12	4	8	0	32	42	8
Vancouver	2	0	2	0	5	8	0	3	3	0	0	14	5	0	5	0	5	0	8	22	0
Washington	3	0	3	0	4	12	0	4	1	2	1	16	16	4	7	1	4	2	28	28	4
Winnipeg	3	0	3	0	10	14	0	1	1	1	0	9	8	4	4	2	4	0	19	22	4
Totals	**84**	**26**	**49**	**9**	**229**	**286**	**61**	**84**	**27**	**48**	**9**	**240**	**297**	**63**	**168**	**53**	**97**	**18**	**469**	**583**	**124**

Dallas totals include Minnesota, 1992-93.

1993-94 Results

Oct.	6	at	New Jersey	1-2		10	at	NY Rangers	5-2
	7	at	NY Rangers	4-5		12	at	Detroit	4-2
	9		Florida	0-2		13	at	Chicago	0-1
	14		Pittsburgh	3-2		16	at	Winnipeg	3-2
	16		Ottawa	4-1		17		Detroit	3-6
	17	at	Florida	3-3		19		NY Islanders	4-3
	20		Los Angeles	3-4		24		Buffalo	4-0
	22		NY Rangers	4-1		26		Florida	1-1
	23		Toronto	0-2		29		San Jose	1-2
	27		Winnipeg	3-4	**Feb.**	2		Detroit	1-3
	29		NY Islanders	2-4		5	at	Washington	3-6
	30	at	Florida	1-2		7	at	Toronto	2-3
Nov.	2	at	Quebec	2-8		10	at	Ottawa	6-2
	3	at	Montreal	0-1		12		Vancouver	2-3
	6	at	Boston	1-1		13		New Jersey	3-3
	8	at	NY Rangers	3-6		15	at	NY Islanders	1-2
	11		Washington	1-4		17		Montreal	4-3
	13		Quebec	4-3		19	at	New Jersey	4-5
	17	at	Dallas	3-4		20		Boston	2-2
	19		NY Rangers	3-5		24	at	Calgary	4-0
	20		Chicago	4-3		26	at	Vancouver	3-4
	24		Hartford	4-1		27	at	Edmonton	2-3
	26	at	Philadelphia	0-3	**Mar.**	1	at	Washington	4-3
	27		Philadelphia	3-4		3		New Jersey	4-5
Dec.	1		Buffalo	0-3		5		Hartford	4-3
	4	at	Los Angeles	5-4		6		Philadelphia	1-3
	5	at	Anaheim	4-2		9	at	Hartford	1-4
	7	at	San Jose	3-1		13	at	Philadelphia	5-5
	11		Pittsburgh	3-6		15		Calgary	3-7
	14		Montreal	1-1		16		Edmonton	1-3
	15		Ottawa	4-3		20		Washington	0-3
	18		Boston	3-5		22	at	NY Islanders	4-5
	19	at	Buffalo	3-3		24	at	New Jersey	1-2
	21	at	Pittsburgh	3-8		27		Dallas	2-2
	23	at	St. Louis	4-7		30	at	Buffalo	3-2
	26		Florida	1-3	**Apr.**	1		St. Louis	4-3
	28	at	Quebec	4-1		4	at	Pittsburgh	1-2
	30	at	Ottawa	3-0		6	at	Montreal	3-1
Jan.	1	at	Washington	5-5		9	at	Boston	3-0
	2		Anaheim	1-4		10	at	Hartford	4-6
	4	at	Toronto	1-0		13		NY Islanders	0-2
	8		Philadelphia	4-2		14		Quebec	5-2

Entry Draft
Selections 1994-92

1994 Pick		1993 Pick		1992 Pick	
8	Jason Wiemer	3	Chris Gratton	1	Roman Hamrlik
34	Colin Cloutier	29	Tyler Moss	26	Drew Bannister
55	Vadim Epanchintsev	55	Allan Egeland	49	Brent Gretzky
86	Dmitri Klevakin	81	Marian Kacir	74	Aaron Gavey
137	Daniel Juden	107	Ryan Brown	97	Brantt Myhres
138	Bryce Salvador	133	Kiley Hill	122	Martin Tanguay
164	Chris Maillet	159	Mathieu Raby	145	Derek Wilkinson
190	Alexei Baranov	185	Ryan Nauss	170	Dennis Maxwell
216	Yuri Smirnov	211	Alexandre Laporte	193	Andrew Kemper
242	Shawn Gervais	237	Brett Duncan	218	Marc Tardif
268	Brian White	263	Mark Szoke	241	Tom MacDonald

Although he made his NHL debut in 1987-88, defenceman Rudy Poeschek spent his first full season in the NHL in 1993-94, appearing in 71 games and collecting nine points for the Lightning.

Club Directory

ThunderDome

501 East Kennedy Boulevard
Suite 175
Tampa, FL 33602
Phone **813/229-2658**
FAX 813/229-3350

Capacity: 28,000

Lightning Partners, Ltd
General Partner .... Lightning Partners, Inc.
Limited Partners .... Lightning International, Inc.
Tokyo Tower Development Co., Ltd
Nippon Meat Packers, Inc.
John Chase
Equity Resources Group of
Indian River County, Inc.
James Murphy
Tampa Bay Hockey Group Partners, Ltd.
Board of Directors. .... Yoshio Nakamura, Chairman,
Phil Esposito, David LeFevre, Fukusaboro
Maeda, Dr. Fujio Matsuda, Mushao Miyake,
Chris Phillips, Reece Smith, Jr., Yoshiuki Sugioka

Executive Staff
President. .... Yoshio Nakamura
Governor .... David LeFevre
General Manager and Alternate Governor .... Phil Esposito
Executive Vice President and Alternate Governor ... Chris Phillips
Executive Vice President and Alternate Governor ... Mel Lowell

Hockey Operations
President, Tampa Bay Lightning Hockey Club ...... Phil Esposito
Director of Hockey Operations .... Tony Esposito
Counsel .... Henry Lee Paul – Lazzara & Paul, P.A.
Head Coach .... Terry Crisp
Assistant Coach .... Wayne Cashman, Danny Gare
Head Scout .... Don Murdoch
Scouting Staff. .... Angelo Bumbacco, Jacques Campeau,
Jake Goertzen, Doug Macauley, Richard
Rose, Luke Williams
Head Trainer. .... Larry Ness
Equipment Manager. .... Jocko Cayer
Assistant Trainer .... Bill Cronin
Strength and Conditioning .... Chris Reichert
Director of Team Services .... Carrie Esposito Wall
Administrative Assistant .... Teresa P. Huffam

Administrative Assistant .... Kathy Skelton
Ice System Supervisors .... Michael Wall, Tim Friedenberger
Video Coordinator .... Duncan McMillian

Finance
Chief Financial Officer .... Mark Anderson
Accounting Manager .... Vincent Ascanio
Accounting Assistant .... Irene Canino
Administrative Assistant .... Angela Gard

Marketing and Sales
Director of Sales .... Paul D'Aiuto
Director of Promotions .... Mark Myron
Sales Representative .... Karl Nickel
Marketing Assistant .... Marlene Eskine
Director of Fan Services .... Steve Woznick
Director of Merchandising .... Kevin L. Murphy
Manager/Lightning Locker .... Dan Cohen

Ticket Operations
Director of Ticket Operations .... Jeff Morander
Box Office Manager .... Karen McKenzie
Ticket Office Representatives .... April Blackmon, Mark Arata
Season Ticket Service Manager .... Steve Ross
Group Sales Manager. .... Bill Makris, Ray Mihara
Senior Sales Representative .... Mike Eagan
Regional Sales Representative. .... Jon Roman
Sales Representatives .... Keith Brennan, Nigel Kirwan, Jason Baumgarten,
Brendan Cunningham, Nicole Reckner

Communications
Vice President/Communications .... Gerry Helper
Media Relations Manager. .... Barry Hanrahan
Publications Manager .... Becky D'Aiuto
Communications Assistant .... Carrie Schuldt
Receptionist .... Kim Pryor

Medical Staff
Team Physician .... Dr. David Leffers
Team Dentist .... Dr. Joseph Spoto

Game Night Staff
Team Photographer .... Jonathan Hayt
Off-ice Officials. .... Jim Galluzzi, Ron Brace, Gerry Dollmont,
Ralph Emery, Chuck Fontana, Rich Galipault,
Mark Losier, Tony Mancuso, Jeff Maust, Mike
Rees, Gary Reilly, Bill Shapiro, John Supak, Rich
Wasilewski
Media Interface .... Rick Pratt
NHL Commercial Coordinator. .... David Rice
P.A. Announcer .... Paul Porter
Scoreboard Operation .... Bill Heald, John Watts

Television and Radio
Television Stations .... Sunshine Network, WTOG-TV 44 &
Lightning Television Network
Broadcasters .... John Kelly and Bobby Taylor
Radio Station .... WFNS 910 AM
Broadcasters .... John Kelly, Bobby Taylor and Larry Hirsch

Team Information
Rink Dimensions .... 200 feet by 85 feet
Team Colors .... Black, Blue, Silver and White
Training Camp Site .... Lakeland Civic Center, Lakeland, Florida

Toronto Maple Leafs

1993-94 Results: 43W-29L-12T 98PTS. Second, Central Division

TORONTO MAPLE LEAFS ®

The first player in NHL history to record at least 30 goals in each of his first 15 seasons in the League, Mike Gartner joined the Toronto Maple Leafs in late March.

Schedule

Month	Day	Date	Opponent
Oct.	Sat.	1	Washington
	Tues.	4	Hartford
	Sat.	8	at Boston
	Mon.	10	at Buffalo
	Tues.	11	Ottawa
	Thur.	13	Quebec
	Sat.	15	St. Louis
	Wed.	19	at Florida
	Thur.	20	at Tampa Bay
	Sat.	22	at St. Louis
	Mon.	24	Calgary
	Fri.	28	Edmonton
	Sat.	29	at Philadelphia
Nov.	Wed.	2	at Winnipeg
	Fri.	4	at Detroit
	Sat.	5	Detroit
	Wed.	9	Tampa Bay
	Thur.	10	at Chicago
	Sat.	12	Montreal
	Wed.	16	Winnipeg
	Fri.	18	at Washington
	Sat.	19	St. Louis
	Mon.	21	Vancouver
	Wed.	23	at Winnipeg
	Sat.	26	at NY Islanders
	Mon.	28	at Dallas
	Wed.	30	Anaheim
Dec.	Sat.	3	Los Angeles
	Tues.	6	at Vancouver
	Wed.	7	at San Jose
	Sat.	10	at Los Angeles
	Sun.	11	at Anaheim
	Tues.	13	at Edmonton
	Thur.	15	at Calgary
	Sat.	17	Florida
	Mon.	19	Dallas
	Wed.	21	Chicago
	Tues.	27	at Quebec
	Thur.	29	Dallas
	Sat.	31	Boston
Jan.	Mon.	2	Ottawa (in Hamilton)
	Sat.	7	at Ottawa
	Tues.	10	Winnipeg
	Thur.	12	Anaheim
	Sat.	14	Detroit
	Tues.	17	Chicago
	Wed.	18	at Detroit
	Wed.	25	Vancouver
	Fri.	27	at Chicago
	Sat.	28	at Pittsburgh
	Mon.	30	San Jose
Feb.	Wed.	1	at Vancouver
	Fri.	3	at Edmonton
	Sat.	4	at Calgary
	Tues.	7	Philadelphia
	Fri.	10	at New Jersey
	Sat.	11	Buffalo
	Mon.	13	at Dallas
	Wed.	15	Chicago
	Sat.	18	NY Rangers
	Mon.	20	at NY Rangers*
	Wed.	22	at St. Louis
	Fri.	24	NY Islanders
	Sat.	25	at Montreal
	Mon.	27	St. Louis
Mar.	Wed.	1	San Jose
	Fri.	3	at Detroit
	Sat.	4	Calgary
	Thur.	9	Los Angeles
	Sat.	11	New Jersey
	Mon.	13	at Dallas
	Wed.	15	at San Jose
	Fri.	17	at Anaheim
	Sat.	18	at Los Angeles
	Mon.	20	at Edmonton (in Saskatoon)
	Fri.	24	Winnipeg
	Sat.	25	at Winnipeg
	Mon.	27	Edmonton
	Wed.	29	Dallas
	Fri.	31	at St. Louis
Apr.	Sun.	2	Pittsburgh*
	Wed.	5	at Hartford
	Thur.	6	at Chicago
	Sat.	8	Detroit

* Denotes afternoon game.

Home Starting Times:

Night Games	7:30 p.m.
Matinees	1:30 p.m.
Except Sat. Dec. 31	5:00 p.m.

Franchise date: November 22, 1917

WESTERN NHL CONFERENCE

CENTRAL DIVISION

78th NHL Season

Year-by-Year Record

		Home			Road			Overall							
Season	GP	W	L	T	W	L	T	W	L	T	GF	GA	Pts.	Finished	Playoff Result
1993-94	84	23	15	4	20	14	8	43	29	12	280	243	98	2nd, Central Div.	Lost Conf. Championship
1992-93	84	25	11	6	19	18	5	44	29	11	288	241	99	3rd, Norris Div.	Lost Conf. Championship
1991-92	80	21	16	3	9	27	4	30	43	7	234	294	67	5th, Norris Div.	Out of Playoffs
1990-91	80	15	21	4	8	25	7	23	46	11	241	318	57	5th, Norris Div.	Out of Playoffs
1989-90	80	24	14	2	14	24	2	38	38	4	337	358	80	3rd, Norris Div.	Lost Div. Semi-Final
1988-89	80	15	20	5	13	26	1	28	46	6	259	342	62	5th, Norris Div.	Out of Playoffs
1987-88	80	14	20	6	7	29	4	21	49	10	273	345	52	4th, Norris Div.	Lost Div. Semi-Final
1986-87	80	22	14	4	10	28	2	32	42	6	286	319	70	4th, Norris Div.	Lost Div. Final
1985-86	80	16	21	3	9	27	4	25	48	7	311	386	57	4th, Norris Div.	Lost Div. Final
1984-85	80	10	28	2	10	24	6	20	52	8	253	358	48	5th, Norris Div.	Out of Playoffs
1983-84	80	17	16	7	9	29	2	26	45	9	303	387	61	5th, Norris Div.	Out of Playoffs
1982-83	80	20	15	5	8	25	7	28	40	12	293	330	68	3rd, Norris Div.	Lost Div. Semi-Final
1981-82	80	12	20	8	8	24	8	20	44	16	298	380	56	5th, Norris Div.	Out of Playoffs
1980-81	80	14	21	5	14	16	10	28	37	15	322	367	71	5th, Adams Div.	Lost Prelim. Round
1979-80	80	17	19	4	18	21	1	35	40	5	304	327	75	4th, Adams Div.	Lost Prelim. Round
1978-79	80	20	12	8	14	21	5	34	33	13	267	252	81	3rd, Adams Div.	Lost Quarter-Final
1977-78	80	21	13	6	20	16	4	41	29	10	271	237	92	3rd, Adams Div.	Lost Semi-Final
1976-77	80	18	13	9	15	19	6	33	32	15	301	285	81	3rd, Adams Div.	Lost Quarter-Final
1975-76	80	23	12	5	11	19	10	34	31	15	294	276	83	3rd, Adams Div.	Lost Quarter-Final
1974-75	80	19	12	9	12	21	7	31	33	16	280	309	78	3rd, Adams Div.	Lost Quarter-Final
1973-74	78	21	11	7	14	16	9	35	27	16	274	230	86	4th, East Div.	Lost Quarter-Final
1972-73	78	20	12	7	7	29	3	27	41	10	247	279	64	6th, East Div.	Out of Playoffs
1971-72	78	21	11	7	12	20	7	33	31	14	209	208	80	4th, East Div.	Lost Quarter-Final
1970-71	78	24	9	6	13	24	2	37	33	8	248	211	82	4th, East Div.	Lost Quarter-Final
1969-70	76	18	13	7	11	21	6	29	34	13	222	242	71	6th, East Div.	Out of Playoffs
1968-69	76	20	8	10	15	18	5	35	26	15	234	217	85	4th, East Div.	Lost Quarter-Final
1967-68	74	24	9	4	9	22	6	33	31	10	209	176	76	5th, East Div.	Out of Playoffs
1966-67	**70**	**21**	**8**	**6**	**11**	**19**	**5**	**32**	**27**	**11**	**204**	**211**	**75**	**3rd,**	**Won Stanley Cup**
1965-66	70	22	9	4	12	16	7	34	25	11	208	187	79	3rd,	Lost Semi-Final
1964-65	70	17	15	3	13	11	11	30	26	14	204	173	74	4th,	Lost Semi-Final
1963-64	**70**	**22**	**7**	**6**	**11**	**18**	**6**	**33**	**25**	**12**	**192**	**172**	**78**	**3rd,**	**Won Stanley Cup**
1962-63	**70**	**21**	**8**	**6**	**14**	**15**	**6**	**35**	**23**	**12**	**221**	**180**	**82**	**1st,**	**Won Stanley Cup**
1961-62	**70**	**25**	**5**	**5**	**12**	**17**	**6**	**37**	**22**	**11**	**232**	**180**	**85**	**2nd,**	**Won Stanley Cup**
1960-61	70	21	6	8	18	13	4	39	19	12	234	176	90	2nd,	Lost Semi-Final
1959-60	70	20	9	6	15	17	3	35	26	9	199	195	79	2nd,	Lost Final
1958-59	70	17	13	5	10	19	6	27	32	11	189	201	65	4th,	Lost Final
1957-58	70	12	16	7	9	22	4	21	38	11	192	226	53	6th,	Out of Playoffs
1956-57	70	12	16	7	9	18	8	21	34	15	174	192	57	5th,	Out of Playoffs
1955-56	70	19	10	6	5	23	7	24	33	13	153	181	61	4th,	Lost Semi-Final
1954-55	70	14	10	11	10	14	11	24	24	22	147	135	70	3rd,	Lost Semi-Final
1953-54	70	22	6	7	10	18	7	32	24	14	152	131	78	3rd,	Lost Semi-Final
1952-53	70	17	12	6	10	18	7	27	30	13	156	167	67	5th,	Out of Playoffs
1951-52	70	17	10	8	12	15	8	29	25	16	168	157	74	3rd,	Lost Semi-Final
1950-51	**70**	**22**	**8**	**5**	**19**	**8**	**8**	**41**	**16**	**13**	**212**	**138**	**95**	**2nd,**	**Won Stanley Cup**
1949-50	70	18	9	8	13	18	4	31	27	12	176	173	74	3rd,	Lost Semi-Final
1948-49	**60**	**12**	**8**	**10**	**10**	**17**	**3**	**22**	**25**	**13**	**147**	**161**	**57**	**4th,**	**Won Stanley Cup**
1947-48	**60**	**22**	**3**	**5**	**10**	**12**	**8**	**32**	**15**	**13**	**182**	**143**	**77**	**1st,**	**Won Stanley Cup**
1946-47	**60**	**20**	**8**	**2**	**11**	**11**	**8**	**31**	**19**	**10**	**209**	**172**	**72**	**2nd,**	**Won Stanley Cup**
1945-46	50	10	13	2	9	11	5	19	24	7	174	185	45	5th,	Out of Playoffs
1944-45	**50**	**13**	**9**	**3**	**11**	**13**	**1**	**24**	**22**	**4**	**183**	**161**	**52**	**3rd,**	**Won Stanley Cup**
1943-44	50	13	11	1	10	12	3	23	23	4	214	174	50	3rd,	Lost Semi-Final
1942-43	50	17	6	2	5	13	7	22	19	9	198	159	53	3rd,	Lost Semi-Final
1941-42	**48**	**18**	**6**	**0**	**9**	**12**	**3**	**27**	**18**	**3**	**158**	**136**	**57**	**2nd,**	**Won Stanley Cup**
1940-41	48	16	5	3	12	9	3	28	14	6	145	99	62	2nd,	Lost Semi-Final
1939-40	48	15	3	6	10	14	0	25	17	6	134	110	56	3rd,	Lost Final
1938-39	48	13	8	3	6	12	6	19	20	9	114	107	47	3rd,	Lost Final
1937-38	48	13	6	5	11	9	4	24	15	9	151	127	57	1st, Cdn. Div.	Lost Final
1936-37	48	14	9	1	8	12	4	22	21	5	119	115	49	3rd, Cdn. Div.	Lost Quarter-Final
1935-36	48	15	4	5	8	15	1	23	19	6	126	106	52	2nd, Cdn. Div.	Lost Final
1934-35	48	16	6	2	14	8	2	30	14	4	157	111	64	1st, Cdn. Div.	Lost Final
1933-34	48	19	2	3	7	11	6	26	13	9	174	119	61	1st, Cdn. Div.	Lost Semi-Final
1932-33	48	16	4	4	8	14	2	24	18	6	119	111	54	1st, Cdn. Div.	Lost Final
1931-32	**48**	**17**	**4**	**3**	**6**	**14**	**4**	**23**	**18**	**7**	**155**	**127**	**53**	**2nd, Cdn. Div.**	**Won Stanley Cup**
1930-31	44	15	4	3	7	9	6	22	13	9	118	99	53	2nd, Cdn. Div.	Lost Quarter-Final
1929-30	44	10	8	4	7	13	2	17	21	6	116	124	40	4th, Cdn. Div.	Out of Playoffs
1928-29	44	15	5	2	6	13	3	21	18	5	85	69	47	3rd, Cdn. Div.	Lost Semi-Final
1927-28	44	9	8	5	9	10	3	18	18	8	89	88	44	4th, Cdn. Div.	Out of Playoffs
1926-27*	44	10	10	2	5	14	3	15	24	5	79	94	35	5th, Cdn. Div.	Out of Playoffs
1925-26	36	11	5	2	1	16	1	12	21	3	92	114	27	6th,	Out of Playoffs
1924-25	30	10	5	0	9	6	0	19	11	0	90	84	38	2nd,	Lost NHL S-Final
1923-24	24	7	5	0	3	9	0	10	14	0	59	85	20	3rd,	Out of Playoffs
1922-23	24	10	1	1	3	9	0	13	10	1	82	88	27	3rd,	Out of Playoffs
1921-22	**24**	**8**	**4**	**0**	**5**	**6**	**1**	**13**	**10**	**1**	**98**	**97**	**27**	**2nd,**	**Won Stanley Cup**
1920-21	24	9	3	0	6	6	0	15	9	0	105	100	30	2nd and 1st***	Lost NHL Final
1919-20**	24	8	4	0	4	8	0	12	12	0	119	106	24	3rd and 2nd***	Lost NHL Final
1918-19	18	5	4	0	0	9	0	5	13	0	64	92	10	3rd and 3rd***	Out of Playoffs
1917-18	**22**	**10**	**1**	**0**	**3**	**8**	**0**	**13**	**9**	**0**	**108**	**109**	**26**	**2nd and 1st*** **	**Won Stanley Cup**

* Name changed from St. Patricks to Maple Leafs. ** Name changed from Arenas to St. Patricks.
*** Season played in two halves with no combined standing at end.

1994-95 Player Personnel

FORWARDS	HT	WT	S	Place of Birth	Date	1993-94 Club
ANDREWS, Jeff	6-4	200	L	Lindsay, Ont.	5/10/75	North Bay-Oshawa
ANDREYCHUK, Dave	6-3	220	R	Hamilton, Ont.	9/29/63	Toronto
AUGUSTA, Patrik	5-10	170	L	Jihlava, Czech.	11/13/69	Toronto-St. John's
BAUMGARTNER, Ken	6-1	205	L	Flin Flon, Man.	3/11/66	Toronto
BELANGER, Ken	6-4	220	L	Sault Ste. Marie, Ont.	5/14/74	Guelph
BERG, Bill	6-1	205	L	St. Catharines, Ont.	10/21/67	Toronto
BIALOWAS, Frank	5-11	220	L	Winnipeg, Man.	9/25/70	St. John's-Toronto
BORSCHEVSKY, Nikolai	5-9	180	L	Tomsk, USSR	1/12/65	Toronto
BUTZ, Rob	6-3	195	L	Dewberry, Alta.	2/24/75	Victoria-St. John's
CHEBATOR, Bob	6-0	190	L	Arlington, MA	12/1/70	N. Hampshire
CHITARONI, Terry	5-11	200	R	Haileybury, Ont.	12/9/72	St. John's
CLARKE, Wayne	6-1	187	R	Sterling, Ont.	8/30/72	RPI
CONVERY, Brandon	6-1	182	R	Kingston, Ont.	2/4/74	Nmkt.-Niag. Falls-Det (OHL)
CRAIG, Mike	6-1	185	R	St. Mary, Ont.	6/6/71	Dallas
DE RUITER, Chris	6-2	190	R	Kingston, Ont.	2/27/74	Clarkson
DEYELL, Mark	5-11	170	R	Winnipeg, Man.	3/26/76	Saskatoon
EASTWOOD, Mike	6-3	205	R	Ottawa, Ont.	7/1/67	Toronto
FERGUSON, Kyle	6-3	215	R	Toronto, Ont.	8/12/73	Michigan Tech
GARTNER, Mike	6-0	190	R	Ottawa, Ont.	10/29/59	NY Rangers-Toronto
GILMOUR, Doug	5-11	172	L	Kingston, Ont.	6/25/63	Toronto
HAGGERTY, Sean	6-1	186	L	Rye, NY	2/11/76	Detroit (OHL)
HAKANSSON, Mikael	6-1	196	L	Stockholm, Sweden	5/31/74	Djurgarden
HENDRICKSON, Darby	6-0	185	L	Richfield, MN	8/28/72	U.S. National-U.S. Olympic-St. John's-Toronto
KELLEY, Jonathan	6-1	180	R	Brighton, MA	6/25/73	Princeton
KOLESAR, Mark	6-1	188	R	Brampton, Ont.	1/23/73	Brandon
KUCHARCIK, Tomas	6-2	200	L	Vlasim, Czech.	5/10/70	Skoda Plzen
KUDASHOV, Alexei	6-0	183	R	Elektrostal, USSR	7/21/71	Soviet Wings-Toronto-Russian Olympic-St. John's
LACROIX, Eric	6-1	200	L	Montreal, Que.	7/15/71	Toronto-St. John's
MALLGRAVE, Matthew	6-0	180	R	Washington, D.C.	5/3/70	St. John's-South Carolina
MANDERVILLE, Kent	6-3	207	L	Edmonton, Alta.	4/12/71	Toronto
McINTYRE, Robb	6-1	190	L	Royal Oak, MI	4/27/72	Ferris State
MODIN, Fredrik	6-3	202	L	Sundsvall, Sweden	10/8/74	Sundsvall
NEDVED, Zdenek	6-0	180	L	Lany, Czech.	3/3/75	Sudbury
PROCHAZKA, Martin	5-11	180	R	Slany, Czech.	3/3/72	Kladno
RIDLEY, Mike	6-0	195	L	Winnipeg, Man.	7/8/63	Washington
SACCO, David	6-0	190	R	Malden, MA	7/31/70	U.S. National-U.S. Olympic-Toronto-St. John's
SUNDIN, Mats	6-4	204	R	Bromma, Sweden	2/13/71	Quebec
TOMBERLIN, Justin	6-1	195	L	Grand Rapids, MN	11/15/70	U. of Maine
VANDENBUSSCHE, Ryan	5-11	187	R	Simcoe, Ont.	2/28/73	St. John's-Springfield
VINCENT, Paul	6-4	200	L	Utica, NY	1/4/75	Seattle
WALBY, Steffon	6-1	190	R	Madison, WI	11/22/72	St. John's
WARRINER, Todd	6-1	182	L	Blenheim, Ont.	1/3/74	Cdn. National-Cdn. Olympic-Kitchener-Cornwall
DEFENSEMEN						
BEREHOWSKY, Drake	6-2	211	R	Toronto, Ont.	1/3/72	Toronto-St. John's
BUTCHER, Garth	6-0	204	R	Regina, Sask.	1/8/63	St. Louis-Quebec
CULL, Trent	6-3	210	L	Brampton, Ont.	9/27/73	Kingston
DEMPSEY, Nathan	6-0	170	L	Spruce Grove, Alta.	7/14/74	Regina
ELLETT, Dave	6-2	200	L	Cleveland, OH	3/30/64	Toronto
GILL, Todd	6-0	185	L	Brockville, Ont.	11/9/65	Toronto
GODBOUT, Daniel	6-2	195	L	Grand Falls, N.B.	3/20/75	Belleville
GRONVALL, Janne	6-3	195	L	Rauma, Finland	7/17/73	Tappara-St. John's
HARLOCK, David	6-2	195	L	Toronto, Ont.	3/16/71	Cdn. National-Cdn. Olympic-Toronto-St. John's
JONSSON, Kenny	6-3	195	L	Angelholm, Sweden	10/6/74	Rogle
LAPIN, Mikhail	6-2	190	L	Moscow, USSR	5/12/75	W. Michigan
MACOUN, Jamie	6-2	200	L	Newmarket, Ont.	8/17/61	Toronto
MARTIN, Matt	6-3	190	L	Hamden, CT	4/30/71	U.S. National-U.S. Olympic-Toronto-St. John's
MCMURTRY, Chris	6-4	190	L	Hamilton, Ont.	7/13/74	Guelph-Sudbury
MIRONOV, Dmitri	6-2	214	R	Moscow, USSR	12/25/65	Toronto
MULLIN, Kory	6-2	200	L	Lethbridge, Alta.	5/24/75	Tri-City-Tacoma
SIMONOV, Sergei	6-3	194	L	Saratov, USSR	5/20/74	CSKA
SNELL, Chris	5-11	200	L	Regina, Sask.	5/12/71	Toronto-St. John's
WHITE, Kam	6-3	195	L	Chicago, IL	2/13/76	Newmarket

GOALTENDERS	HT	WT	C	Place of Birth	Date	1993-94 Club
BRUMBY, David	6-1	172	L	Victoria, B.C.	6/23/75	Tri-City
COUSINEAU, Marcel	5-9	180	L	Delson, Que.	4/30/73	St. John's
FICHAUD, Eric	5-11	165	L	Montreal, Que.	11/4/75	Chicoutimi
JABLONSKI, Pat	6-0	178	R	Toledo, OH	6/20/67	Tampa Bay-St. John's
POTVIN, Felix	6-1	183	L	Anjou, Que.	6/23/71	Toronto
RACINE, Bruce	6-0	178	L	Cornwall, Ont.	8/9/66	St. John's
RHODES, Damian	6-0	175	L	St. Paul, MN	5/28/69	Toronto

General Managers' History

Conn Smythe, 1927-28 to 1956-57; Hap Day, 1957-58; George "Punch" Imlach, 1958-59 to 1968-69; Jim Gregory, 1969-70 to 1978-79; Punch Imlach, 1979-80 to 1980-81; Punch Imlach and Gerry McNamara, 1981-82; Gerry McNamara, 1982-83 to 1987-88; Gord Stellick, 1988-89; Floyd Smith, 1989-90 to 1990-91; Cliff Fletcher, 1991-92 to date.

Coaching History

Conn Smythe, 1927-28 to 1929-30; Conn Smythe and Art Duncan, 1930-31; Art Duncan and Dick Irvin, 1931-32; Dick Irvin, 1932-33 to 1939-40; Hap Day, 1940-41 to 1949-50; Joe Primeau, 1950-51 to 1952-53; "King" Clancy, 1953-54 to 1955-56; Howie Meeker, 1956-57; Billy Reay, 1957-58; Billy Reay and "Punch" Imlach, 1958-59; "Punch" Imlach, 1959-60 to 1968-69; John McLellan, 1969-70 to 1970-71; John McLellan and "King" Clancy, 1971-72; John McLellan, 1972-73; Red Kelly, 1973-74 to 1976-77; Roger Neilson, 1977-78 to 1978-79; Floyd Smith, Dick Duff and "Punch" Imlach, 1979-80; "Punch" Imlach, Joe Crozier and Mike Nykoluk, 1980-81; Mike Nykoluk, 1981-82 to 1983-84; Dan Maloney, 1984-85 to 1985-86; John Brophy, 1986-87 to 1987-88; John Brophy and George Armstrong, 1988-89; Doug Carpenter, 1989-90; Doug Carpenter and Tom Watt, 1990-91; Tom Watt, 1991-92; Pat Burns, 1992-93 to date.

1993-94 Scoring

* – rookie

Regular Season

Pos	#	Player	Team	GP	G	A	Pts	+/–	PIM	PP	SH	GW	GT	S	%
C	93	Doug Gilmour	TOR	83	27	84	111	25	105	10	1	3	2	167	16.2
L	14	Dave Andreychuk	TOR	83	53	46	99	22	98	21	5	8	0	333	15.9
L	17	Wendel Clark	TOR	64	46	30	76	10	115	21	0	8	0	275	16.7
R	11	Mike Gartner	NYR	71	28	24	52	11	58	10	5	4	0	245	11.4
			TOR	10	6	6	12	9	4	1	0	0	0	30	20.0
			TOTAL	81	34	30	64	20	62	11	5	4	0	275	12.4
D	4	Dave Ellett	TOR	68	7	36	43	6	42	5	0	1	1	146	4.8
D	15	Dmitri Mironov	TOR	76	9	27	36	5	78	3	0	0	2	147	6.1
R	16	Nikolai Borschevsky	TOR	45	14	20	34	6	10	7	0	1	0	105	13.3
C	19	John Cullen	TOR	53	13	17	30	2–	67	2	0	4	1	80	16.3
R	12	Rob Pearson	TOR	67	12	18	30	6–	189	1	0	4	0	119	10.1
D	34	Jamie Macoun	TOR	82	3	27	30	5–	115	1	0	1	0	122	2.5
D	23	Todd Gill	TOR	45	4	24	28	8	44	2	0	1	0	74	5.4
L	21	Mark Osborne	TOR	73	9	15	24	2	145	1	1	2	0	103	8.7
L	10	Bill Berg	TOR	83	8	11	19	3–	93	0	0	1	0	99	8.1
C	32	Mike Eastwood	TOR	54	8	10	18	2	28	1	0	2	0	41	19.5
C	25	Peter Zezel	TOR	41	8	8	16	5	19	0	0	0	0	47	17.0
L	18	Kent Manderville	TOR	67	7	9	16	5	63	0	0	1	0	81	8.6
D	3	Bob Rouse	TOR	63	5	11	16	8	101	1	1	0	0	77	6.5
R	11	Mark Greig	HFD	31	4	5	9	6–	31	0	0	0	0	41	9.8
			TOR	13	2	2	4	1	10	0	0	0	0	14	14.3
			TOTAL	44	6	7	13	5–	41	0	0	0	0	55	10.9
C	26	Mike Krushelnyski	TOR	54	5	6	11	5–	28	1	0	1	0	71	7.0
D	2	Sylvain Lefebvre	TOR	84	2	9	11	33	79	0	0	0	1	96	2.1
D	55	Drake Berehowsky	TOR	49	2	8	10	3–	63	2	0	2	0	29	6.9
L	22	Ken Baumgartner	TOR	64	4	4	8	6–	185	0	0	0	0	34	11.8
C	44	* Yanic Perreault	TOR	13	3	3	6	1	0	2	0	0	0	24	12.5
L	8	Chris Govedaris	TOR	12	2	2	4	4	14	0	0	0	1	16	12.5
G	29	Felix Potvin	TOR	66	0	4	4	0	4	0	0	0	0	0	.0
D	7	* David Sacco	TOR	4	1	1	2	2–	4	1	0	0	0	4	25.0
C	40	Ken McRae	TOR	9	1	1	2	1	36	0	0	0	0	11	9.1
C	20	* Alexei Kudashov	TOR	25	1	0	1	3–	4	0	0	0	0	24	4.2
D	33	* Matt Martin	TOR	12	0	1	1	0	6	0	0	0	0	6	.0
D	38	* Chris Snell	TOR	2	0	0	0	1–	2	0	0	0	0	4	.0
R	24	* Patrik Augusta	TOR	2	0	0	0	0	0	0	0	0	0	3	.0
L	41	* Eric Lacroix	TOR	3	0	0	0	0	2	0	0	0	0	3	.0
L	36	Frank Bialowas	TOR	3	0	0	0	0	12	0	0	0	0	1	.0
D	28	* David Harlock	TOR	6	0	0	0	2–	0	0	0	0	0	2	.0
G	35	Pat Jablonski	T.B.	15	0	0	0	0	0	0	0	0	0	0	.0
			TOR	0	0	0	0	0	0	0	0	0	0	0	.0
			TOTAL	15	0	0	0	0	0	0	0	0	0	0	.0
G	1	* Damian Rhodes	TOR	22	0	0	0	0	2	0	0	0	0	0	.0

Goaltending

No.	Goaltender	GPI	Mins	Avg	W	L	T	EN	SO	GA	SA	S%
1	* Damian Rhodes	22	1213	2.62	9	7	3	0	0	53	541	.902
29	Felix Potvin	66	3883	2.89	34	22	9	3	3	187	2010	.907
	Totals	**84**	**5115**	**2.85**	**43**	**29**	**12**	**3**	**3**	**243**	**2554**	**.905**

Playoffs

Pos	#	Player	Team	GP	G	A	Pts	+/–	PIM	PP	SH	GW	GT	S	%
C	93	Doug Gilmour	TOR	18	6	22	28	3	42	5	0	1	0	31	19.4
D	4	Dave Ellett	TOR	18	3	15	18	1	31	3	0	0	0	33	9.1
L	17	Wendel Clark	TOR	18	9	7	16	0	24	2	0	1	0	72	12.5
D	15	Dmitri Mironov	TOR	18	6	9	15	3–	6	6	0	0	0	29	20.7
R	11	Mike Gartner	TOR	18	5	6	11	3	14	1	0	3	1	53	9.4
L	14	Dave Andreychuk	TOR	18	5	5	10	3–	16	3	1	0	0	50	10.0
L	21	Mark Osborne	TOR	18	4	2	6	1	52	0	2	1	0	23	17.4
C	25	Peter Zezel	TOR	18	2	4	6	2–	8	0	0	1	1	32	6.3
D	23	Todd Gill	TOR	18	1	5	6	1	37	0	0	1	1	20	5.0
C	32	Mike Eastwood	TOR	18	3	2	5	5–	12	1	0	1	0	22	13.6
R	16	Nikolai Borschevsky	TOR	15	2	2	4	5–	4	1	0	0	0	26	7.7
L	10	Bill Berg	TOR	18	1	2	3	1–	10	0	0	0	0	26	3.8
D	2	Sylvain Lefebvre	TOR	18	0	3	3	3–	16	0	0	0	0	26	.0
D	3	Bob Rouse	TOR	18	0	3	3	4–	29	0	0	0	0	30	.0
D	34	Jamie Macoun	TOR	18	1	1	2	4–	12	0	0	0	0	35	2.9
L	18	Kent Manderville	TOR	12	1	0	1	1–	4	0	1	0	0	13	7.7
R	12	Rob Pearson	TOR	14	1	0	1	5–	32	0	0	0	0	21	4.8
G	1	* Damian Rhodes	TOR	1	0	0	0	0	0	0	0	0	0	0	.0
L	8	Chris Govedaris	TOR	2	0	0	0	1–	0	0	0	0	0	2	.0
C	9	* Darby Hendrickson	TOR	2	0	0	0	1–	0	0	0	0	0	1	.0
L	41	* Eric Lacroix	TOR	2	0	0	0	1–	0	0	0	0	0	0	.0
C	19	John Cullen	TOR	3	0	0	0	0	0	0	0	0	0	3	.0
C	26	Mike Krushelnyski	TOR	6	0	0	0	2–	0	0	0	0	0	4	.0
C	40	Ken McRae	TOR	6	0	0	0	2–	4	0	0	0	0	3	.0
L	22	Ken Baumgartner	TOR	10	0	0	0	1–	18	0	0	0	0	3	.0
G	29	Felix Potvin	TOR	18	0	0	0	0	4	0	0	0	0	0	.0

Goaltending

No.	Goaltender	GPI	Mins	Avg	W	L	EN	SO	GA	SA	S%
1	* Damian Rhodes	1	0	0.00	0	0	0	0	0	0	.000
29	Felix Potvin	18	1124	2.46	9	9	1	3	46	520	.912
	Totals	**18**	**1130**	**2.50**	**9**	**9**	**1**	**3**	**47**	**521**	**.910**

Captains' History

Hap Day, 1927-28 to 1936-37; Charlie Conacher, 1937-38; Red Horner, 1938-39, 1939-40; Syl Apps, 1940-41 to 1942-43; Bob Davidson, 1943-44, 1944-45; Syl Apps, 1945-46 to 1947-48; Ted Kennedy, 1948-49 to 1954-55; Sid Smith, 1955-56; Ted Kennedy, Jim Thomson, 1956-57; George Armstrong, 1957-58 to 1968-69; Dave Keon, 1969-70 to 1974-75; Darryl Sittler, 1975-76 to 1980-81; Rick Vaive, 1981-82 to 1985-86; no captain, 1986-87 to 1988-89; Rob Ramage, 1989-90 to 1990-91; Wendel Clark, 1991-92 to 1993-94; Doug Gilmour, 1994-95.

Club Records

Team

(Figures in brackets for season records are games played; records for fewest points, wins, ties, losses, goals, goals against are for 70 or more games)

Most Points	99	1992-93 (84)
Most Wins	44	1992-93 (84)
Most Ties	22	1954-55 (70)
Most Losses	52	1984-85 (80)
Most Goals	337	1989-90 (80)
Most Goals Against	387	1983-84 (80)
Fewest Points	48	1984-85 (80)
Fewest Wins	20	1981-82, 1984-85 (80)
Fewest Ties	4	1989-90 (80)
Fewest Losses	16	1950-51 (70)
Fewest Goals	147	1954-55 (70)
Fewest Goals Against	*131	1953-54 (70)

Longest Winning Streak
Over-all .... 10 Oct. 7-28/93
Home .... 9 Nov. 11-
Dec. 26/53
Away .... 7 Nov. 14-
Dec. 15/40
Dec. 4/60-
Jan. 5/61

Longest Undefeated Streak
Over-all .... 11 Oct. 15-
Nov. 8/50
(8 wins, 3 ties)
Jan. 6-
Feb. 1/94
(7 wins, 4 ties)
Home .... 18 Nov. 28/33-
Mar. 10/34
(15 wins, 3 ties)
Oct. 31/53-
Jan. 23/54
(16 wins, 2 ties)
Away .... 9 Nov. 30/47-
Jan. 11/48
(4 wins, 5 ties)

Longest Losing Streak
Over-all .... 10 Jan. 15-
Feb. 8/67
Home .... 7 Nov. 10-
Dec. 5/84
Jan. 26-
Feb. 25/85
Feb. 20/-
Apr. 1/88
Away .... 11 Feb. 20/-
Apr. 1/88

Longest Winless Streak
Over-all .... 15 Dec. 26/87-
Jan. 25/88
(11 losses, 4 ties)
Home .... 11 Dec. 19/87-
Jan. 25/88
(7 losses, 4 ties)
Away .... 18 Oct. 6/82-
Jan. 5/83
(13 losses, 5 ties)

Most Shutouts, Season	13	1953-54 (70)
Most PIM, Season	2,419	1989-90 (80)
Most Goals, Game	14	Mar. 16/57

(NYR 1 at Tor. 14)

Individual

Most Seasons	21	George Armstrong
Most Games	1,187	George Armstrong
Most Goals, Career	389	Darryl Sittler
Most Assists, Career	620	Borje Salming
Most Points, Career	916	Darryl Sittler
		(389 goals, 527 assists)
Most PIM, Career	1,670	Dave Williams
Most Shutouts, Career	62	Turk Broda

Longest Consecutive
Games Streak .... 486 Tim Horton
(Feb. 11/61-Feb. 4/68)
Most Goals, Season .... 54 Rick Vaive
(1981-82)
Most Assists, Season .... 95 Doug Gilmour
(1992-93)
Most Points, Season .... 127 Doug Gilmour
(1992-93)
(32 goals, 95 assists)
Most PIM, Season .... 351 Dave Williams
(1977-78)
Most Points, Defenseman
Season .... 79 Ian Turnbull
(1976-77)
(22 goals, 57 assists)

Most Points, Center
Season .... 127 Doug Gilmour
(1992-93)
(32 goals, 95 assists)
Most Points, Right Wing,
Season .... 97 Wilf Paiement
(1980-81)
(40 goals, 57 assists)
Most Points, Left Wing,
Season .... 99 Dave Andreychuk
(1993-94)
(53 goals, 46 assists)
Most Points, Rookie,
Season .... 66 Peter Ihnacak
(1982-83)
(28 goals, 38 assists)
Most Shutouts, Season .... 13 Harry Lumley
(1953-54)
Most Goals, Game .... 6 Corb Denneny
(Jan. 26/21)
Darryl Sittler
(Feb. 7/76)
Most Assists, Game .... 6 Babe Pratt
(Jan. 8/44)
Doug Gilmour
(Feb. 13/93)
Most Points, Game .... *10 Darryl Sittler
(Feb. 7/76)

* NHL Record.

Retired Numbers

5	Bill Barilko	1946-1951
6	Irvine "Ace" Bailey	1927-1934

Honored Numbers

9	Ted Kennedy	1942-1955, 56-57
10	Syl Apps	1936-1948

All-time Record vs. Other Clubs

Regular Season

			At Home							On Road							Total				
	GP	W	L	T	GF	GA	PTS	GP	W	L	T	GF	GA	PTS	GP	W	L	T	GF	GA	PTS
Anaheim	2	0	1	1	3	4	1	2	1	1	0	5	6	2	4	1	2	1	8	10	3
Boston	280	147	86	47	953	728	341	280	82	151	47	749	924	211	560	229	237	94	1702	1652	552
Buffalo	49	18	23	8	152	183	44	50	16	31	3	145	212	35	99	34	54	11	297	395	79
Calgary	40	16	17	7	157	160	39	42	12	26	4	140	189	28	82	28	43	11	297	349	67
Chicago	299	159	89	51	1028	769	369	299	108	152	39	779	927	255	598	267	241	90	1807	1696	624
Dallas	86	43	29	14	317	278	100	84	31	42	11	280	327	73	170	74	71	25	597	605	173
Detroit	301	161	96	44	1007	796	366	300	100	157	45	738	900	245	603	261	253	89	1745	1696	611
Edmonton	24	10	12	2	99	118	22	24	5	14	5	81	123	15	48	15	26	7	180	241	37
Florida	1	1	0	0	6	3	2	2	1	0	1	5	4	3	3	2	0	1	11	7	5
Hartford	22	8	12	2	82	90	18	22	6	12	4	74	102	16	44	14	24	6	156	192	34
Los Angeles	55	30	15	10	231	184	70	56	18	31	7	161	203	43	111	48	46	17	392	387	113
Montreal	315	160	111	44	954	824	364	314	83	191	40	773	1119	206	629	243	302	84	1727	1943	570
New Jersey	33	24	6	3	151	107	51	32	10	13	9	103	120	29	65	34	19	12	254	227	80
NY Islanders	40	17	20	3	135	149	37	38	13	22	3	117	166	29	78	30	42	6	252	315	66
NY Rangers	267	151	78	38	920	692	340	268	101	111	56	785	821	258	535	252	189	94	1705	1513	598
Ottawa	3	3	0	0	16	7	6	2	2	0	0	7	2	4	5	5	0	0	23	9	10
Philadelphia	52	19	20	13	180	177	51	52	11	33	8	123	211	30	104	30	53	21	303	388	81
Pittsburgh	53	25	17	11	220	178	61	54	20	28	6	176	223	46	107	45	45	17	396	401	107
Quebec	23	11	10	2	84	99	24	23	5	13	5	73	94	15	46	16	23	7	157	193	39
St. Louis	83	52	21	10	322	241	114	83	23	48	12	240	293	58	166	75	69	22	562	534	172
San Jose	5	3	1	1	17	7	7	6	3	2	1	16	12	7	11	6	3	2	33	19	14
Tampa Bay	7	4	3	0	24	14	8	5	4	1	0	18	8	8	12	8	4	0	42	22	16
Vancouver	47	20	18	9	177	165	49	45	14	24	7	147	154	35	92	34	42	16	324	319	84
Washington	34	19	11	4	164	122	42	35	12	21	2	96	132	26	69	31	32	6	260	254	68
Winnipeg	27	10	16	1	104	115	21	27	10	13	4	113	122	24	54	20	29	5	217	237	45
Defunct Clubs	232	158	53	21	860	515	337	233	84	120	29	607	745	197	465	242	173	50	1467	1260	534
Totals	**2380**	**1269**	**765**	**346**	**8363**	**6725**	**2884**	**2380**	**775**	**1257**	**348**	**6551**	**8139**	**1898**	**4760**	**2044**	**2022**	**694**	**14914**	**14864**	**4782**

Calgary totals include Atlanta, 1972-73 to 1979-80. Dallas totals include Minnesota, 1967-68 to 1992-93.
New Jersey totals include Kansas City, 1974-75 to 1975-76, and Colorado, 1976-77 to 1981-82.

Playoffs

	Series	W	L	GP	W	L	T	GF	GA	Last Mtg.	Round	Result
Boston	13	8	5	62	31	30	1	150	153	1974	QF	L 0-4
Calgary	1	1	0	2	2	0	0	9	5	1979	PR	W 2-0
Chicago	8	6	2	31	19	11	1	91	67	1994	CQF	W 4-2
Dallas	2	0	2	7	1	6	0	26	35	1983	DSF	L 1-3
Detroit	23	12	11	117	58	59	0	311	321	1993	DSF	W 4-3
Los Angeles	3	2	1	12	7	5	0	41	31	1993	CF	L 3-4
Montreal	13	6	7	67	28	39	0	148	203	1979	QF	L 0-4
NY Islanders	2	1	1	10	4	6	0	20	33	1981	PR	L 0-3
NY Rangers	8	3	5	35	16	19	0	86	86	1971	QF	L 2-4
Philadelphia	3	0	3	17	5	12	0	47	67	1977	QF	L 2-4
Pittsburgh	2	2	0	6	4	2	0	21	13	1977	PR	W 2-1
St. Louis	4	2	2	25	12	13	0	75	67	1993	DF	W 4-3
San Jose	1	1	0	7	4	3	0	26	21	1994	CSF	W 4-3
Vancouver	1	0	1	5	1	4	0	9	16	1994	CF	L 1-4
Defunct	4	3	1	10	5	4	1	20	16			
Totals	**88**	**47**	**41**	**413**	**197**	**213**	**3**	**1080**	**1134**			

Playoff Results 1994-90

Year	Round	Opponent	Result	GF	GA
1994	CF	Vancouver	L 1-4	9	16
	CSF	San Jose	W 4-3	26	21
	CQF	Chicago	W 4-2	15	10
1993	CF	Los Angeles	L 3-4	23	22
	DF	St. Louis	W 4-3	22	11
	DSF	Detroit	W 4-3	24	30
1990	DSF	St. Louis	L 1-4	16	20

Abbreviations: Round: F – Final;
CF – conference final; **CQF** – conference quarter-final;
CSF – conference semi-final; **DF** – division final;
DSF – division semi-final; **SF** – semi-final;
QF – quarter-final; **PR** – preliminary round.

1993-94 Results

Oct.	7	Dallas	6-3		6	Ottawa	6-3
	9	Chicago	2-1		8	Vancouver	5-3
	10	at Philadelphia	5-4		10	at Boston	3-0
	13	Washington	7-1		11	at Washington	2-1
	15	Detroit	6-3		13	Dallas	4-3
	16	at Detroit	2-1		15	at Winnipeg	5-1
	19	Hartford	7-2		18	Anaheim	3-3
	21	at Florida	4-3		19	at Hartford	3-3
	23	at Tampa Bay	2-0		26	NY Islanders	4-3
	28	at Chicago	4-2		29	Pittsburgh	4-4
	30	at Montreal	2-5	Feb. 1	at St. Louis	4-4
Nov.	1	at Dallas	3-3		5	Detroit	3-4
	3	Florida	6-3		7	Tampa Bay	1-2
	4	at Detroit	3-3		11	at Winnipeg	3-1
	6	Philadelphia	5-3		12	at Calgary	2-3
	9	at San Jose	2-2		15	Detroit	5-4
	11	at St. Louis	2-3		17	New Jersey	2-1
	13	Chicago	2-3		19	Edmonton	3-2
	15	Edmonton	5-5		21	at Los Angeles	6-4
	17	at Anaheim	4-3		23	at Edmonton	3-6
	18	at Los Angeles	3-2		26	Montreal	0-3
	20	at Edmonton	3-2		28	at Ottawa	4-1
	22	at Vancouver	5-2	Mar. 4	at Detroit	6-5
	24	at Calgary	3-5		5	at Quebec	1-4
	27	Boston	4-2		7	St. Louis	2-3
	29	Buffalo	0-3		9	Dallas	4-2
Dec.	1	St. Louis	4-2		10	at Pittsburgh	4-2
	2	at St. Louis	5-4		12	Winnipeg	3-1
	4	NY Rangers	3-4		16	Vancouver	1-4
	8	Winnipeg	4-5		18	St. Louis	4-2
	11	Calgary	3-1		20	Calgary	3-6
	12	at Winnipeg	3-3		23	at Florida	1-1
	15	Anaheim	0-1		24	San Jose	1-2
	17	at NY Islanders	2-6		26	Quebec	6-3
	18	Los Angeles	4-1		28	at Vancouver	2-3
	22	San Jose	2-2		31	at San Jose	3-5
	23	at New Jersey	2-3	Apr. 2	at Anaheim	1-3
	27	at Chicago	2-5		5	at Dallas	5-6
	29	at Dallas	0-4		8	at NY Rangers	3-5
Jan.	1	Los Angeles	4-7		10	at Winnipeg	7-0
	2	at Buffalo	3-3		12	Chicago	3-4
	4	Tampa Bay	0-1		14	at Chicago	6-4

Entry Draft
Selections 1994-80

1994
Pick
16	Eric Fichaud
48	Sean Haggerty
64	Fredrik Modin
126	Mark Deyell
152	Kam White
178	Tommi Rajamaki
204	Rob Butler
256	Sergei Berezin
282	Doug Nolan

1993
Pick
12	Kenny Jonsson
19	Landon Wilson
123	Zdenek Nedved
149	Paul Vincent
175	Jeff Andrews
201	David Brumby
253	Kyle Ferguson
279	Mikhail Lapin

1992
Pick
8	Brandon Convery
23	Grant Marshall
77	Nikolai Borschevsky
95	Mark Raiter
101	Janne Gronvall
106	Chris Deruiter
125	Mikael Hakansson
149	Patrik Augusta
173	Ryan Vandenbussche
197	Wayne Clarke
221	Sergei Simonov
245	Nathan Dempsey

1991
Pick
47	Yanic Perreault
69	Terry Chitaroni
102	Alexei Kudashov
113	Jeff Perry
120	Alexander Kuzminsky
135	Martin Prochazka
160	Dmitri Mironov
164	Robb McIntyre
167	Tomas Kucharcik
179	Guy Lehoux
201	Gary Miller
223	Jonathan Kelley
245	Chris O'Rourke

1990
Pick
10	Drake Berehowsky
31	Felix Potvin
73	Darby Hendrickson
80	Greg Walters
115	Alexander Godynyuk
136	Eric Lacroix
157	Dan Stiver
178	Robert Horyna
199	Rob Chebator
220	Scott Malone
241	Nick Vachon

1989
Pick
3	Scott Thornton
12	Rob Pearson
21	Steve Bancroft
66	Matt Martin
96	Keith Carney
108	David Burke
125	Michael Doers
129	Keith Merkler
150	Derek Langille
171	Jeffrey St. Laurent
192	Justin Tomberlin
213	Mike Jackson
234	Steve Chartrand

1988
Pick
6	Scott Pearson
27	Tie Domi
48	Peter Ing
69	Ted Crowley
88	Leonard Esau
132	Matt Mallgrave
153	Roger Elvenas
174	Mike Delay
195	David Sacco
216	Mike Gregorio
237	Peter DeBoer

1987
Pick
7	Luke Richardson
28	Daniel Marois
49	John McIntyre
71	Joe Sacco
91	Mike Eastwood
112	Damian Rhodes
133	Trevor Jobe
154	Chris Jensen
175	Brian Blad
196	Ron Bernacci
217	Ken Alexander
238	Alex Weinrich

1986
Pick
6	Vincent Damphousse
36	Darryl Shannon
48	Sean Boland
69	Kent Hulst
90	Scott Taylor
111	Stephane Giguere
132	Danny Hie
153	Stephen Brennan
174	Brian Bellefeuille
195	Sean Davidson
216	Mark Holick
237	Brian Hoard

1985
Pick
1	Wendel Clark
22	Ken Spangler
43	Dave Thomlinson
64	Greg Vey
85	Jeff Serowik
106	Jiri Latal
127	Tim Bean
148	Andy Donahue
169	Todd Whittemore
190	Bob Reynolds
211	Tim Armstrong
232	Mitch Murphy

1984
Pick
4	Al Iafrate
25	Todd Gill
67	Jeff Reese
88	Jack Capuano
109	Joseph Fabian
130	Joe McInnis
151	Derek Laxdal
172	Dan Turner
192	David Buckley
213	Mikael Wurst
233	Peter Slanina

1983
Pick
7	Russ Courtnall
28	Jeff Jackson
48	Allan Bester
83	Dan Hodgson
128	Cam Plante
148	Paul Bifano
168	Cliff Albrecht
184	Greg Rolston
188	Brian Ross
208	Mike Tomlak
228	Ron Choules

1982
Pick
3	Gary Nylund
24	Gary Leeman
25	Peter Ihnacak
45	Ken Wregget
73	Vladimir Ruzicka
87	Eduard Uvira
99	Sylvain Charland
108	Ron Dreger
115	Craig Kales
129	Dom Campedelli
139	Jeff Triano
171	Miroslav Ihnacak
192	Leigh Verstraete
213	Tim Loven
234	Jim Appleby

1981
Pick
6	Jim Benning
24	Gary Yaremchuk
55	Ernie Godden
90	Normand LeFrancois
102	Barry Brigley
132	Andrew Wright
153	Richard Turmel
174	Greg Barber
195	Marc Magnan

1980
Pick
25	Craig Muni
26	Bob McGill
43	Fred Boimistruck
74	Stewart Gavin
95	Hugh Larkin
116	Ron Dennis
137	Russ Adam
158	Fred Perlini
179	Darwin McCutcheon
200	Paul Higgins

Club Directory

Maple Leaf Gardens
60 Carlton Street
Toronto, Ontario M5B 1L1
Phone **416/977-1641**
FAX 416/977-5364
Capacity: 15,642 (standing 200)

Board of Directors
Brian P. Bellmore, J. Donald Crump, Terence V. Kelly, Q.C., Ted Nikolaou,
W. Ron Pringle, Steve A. Stavro, George E. Whyte, Q.C.

Chairman of the Board and CEO	Steve A. Stavro
President, Chief Operating Officer and General Manager	Cliff Fletcher
Secretary-Treasurer	J. Donald Crump
Alternate Governors	Cliff Fletcher, Brian P. Bellmore
Assistant General Manager	Bill Watters
Special Consultant to the President	Darryl Sittler
Director of Business Operations and Communications	Bob Stellick
Head Coach	Pat Burns
Assistant Coach	Mike Kitchen
Assistant Coach	Rick Wamsley
Director of Scouting	TBA
Director of Professional Development	Floyd Smith
Scouts	George Armstrong, Anders Hedberg, Peter Johnson, Garth Malarchuk, Dan Marr, Dick Bouchard, Jack Gardiner, Bob Johnson, Ernie Gare, Doug Woods
Public Relations Coordinator	Pat Park
Administrative Assistants	Mary Speck, Aimee Houston
Public Relations Assistants	Kristy Fletcher, Casey VandenHeuvel
Executive Secretary to the President and G.M.	Shelley Bernardo
Head Athletic Therapist	Chris Broadhurst
Athletic Therapist	Brent Smith
Trainers	Brian Papineau, Jim Carey
Vice President of Building Operations	Brian Conacher
Director of Marketing	Bill Cluff
Controller	Ian Clarke
Assistant Controller	Paul Franck
Marketing Representatives	Denis Cordick, Chris Reed
Marketing Coordinator	Nancy McIlveen
Marketing Assistant	Angela McManus
Retail Operations Manager	Jeff Newman
Box Office Manager	Donna Henderson
Building Superintendent	Wayne Gillespie
Team Doctors	Dr. Michael Clarfield, Dr. Darrell Ogilvie-Harris, Dr. Leith Douglas, Dr. Michael Easterbrook, Dr. Simon McGrail
Team Dentist	Dr. Ernie Lewis
Team Psychologist	Robert Offenberger, Ph.D.
Head Off Ice Official	Joe Lamantia
AHL Affiliate	St. John's Maple Leafs

Coach

BURNS, PAT
Coach, Toronto Maple Leafs. Born in St-Henri, Que., April 4, 1952.

In just two seasons behind the bench in Toronto, Pat Burns' club has become one of the NHL's most competitive teams. Last season, the Maple Leafs fell just one win and one point shy of club records set in 1992-93, Burns' first season as the team's coach. Toronto surpassed 40 wins in consecutive seasons for the first time, and the Leafs were the only NHL team to reach the Conference Championships in both 1993 and 1994. A league-record 10-game winning streak to start last season vaulted the team to the top of the NHL's overall standings for most of the first half of the schedule.

Under Burns' guidance, Toronto established club records in 1992-93 for most wins (44), points (99), home ice wins in one season (25), playoff victories in one season (11), and playoff games in one season (21). The Maple Leafs dramatic improvement of 32 points from the previous season was the largest single-season improvement in the club's history. Burns was named winner of the 1992-93 Jack Adams Award as coach of the year.

He is just the third multiple Jack Adams winner, joining Pat Quinn of the Canucks and Jacques Demers of the Canadiens. Burns also joins Quinn as the only coaches to win the award with two different teams. He was also recognized by readers of *The Hockey News* as their choice for 1992-93 NHL coach of the year.

Before joining the Leafs, Burns served four seasons as the coach of the Hull Olympiques of the QMJHL, one season with the Sherbrooke Canadiens of the AHL and four seasons with the Montreal Canadiens. Burns has never missed the post-season in his NHL career.

Coaching Record

Season	Team	Regular Season					Playoffs			
		Games	W	L	T	%	Games	W	L	%
1983-84	Hull (QMJHL)	70	25	45	0	.357	....	....	....	....
1984-85	Hull (QMJHL)	68	33	34	1	.493	5	1	4	.200
1985-86	Hull (QMJHL)	72	54	18	0	.750	15	15	0	1.000
1986-87	Hull (QMJHL)	70	26	39	5	.407	8	4	4	.500
1987-88	Sherbrooke (AHL)	80	42	34	4	.550	6	2	4	.333
1988-89	Montreal (NHL)	80	53	18	9	.719	21	14	7	.667
1989-90	Montreal (NHL)	80	41	28	11	.581	11	5	6	.455
1990-91	Montreal (NHL)	80	39	30	11	.556	13	7	6	.538
1991-92	Montreal (NHL)	80	41	28	11	.581	11	4	7	.364
1992-93	Toronto (NHL)	84	44	29	11	.589	21	11	10	.524
1993-94	Toronto (NHL)	84	43	29	12	.583	18	9	9	.500
	NHL Totals	**488**	**261**	**162**	**65**	**.601**	**95**	**50**	**45**	**.526**

General Manager

FLETCHER, CLIFF
President, General Manager and Chief Operating Officer, Toronto Maple Leafs. Born in Montreal, Que., August 16, 1935.

The revival of the Maple Leafs over the past two seasons can be traced to the appointment of Cliff Fletcher on July 1, 1991. By combining the tasks of chief operating officer, president and general manager, Cliff has restored the winning traditions of one of hockey's most fabled franchises. The club set regular season records with 44 wins and 99 points en route to the Norris Division playoff championship in 1992-93. The appearance in the NHL Conference Championship in 1993 was the team's first since 1978 and fans were treated to the most memorable hockey at Maple Leaf Gardens in years.

Fletcher was named *The Hockey News* NHL 1992-93 executive of the year, by a panel of scouts, GMs, coaches, and journalists. He was also selected *The Hockey News* man of the year, awarded annually to a person who has worked for the betterment of the game. In just three years, Fletcher has obtained accomplished personnel including Mats Sundin, Grant Fuhr (later traded to Buffalo), Doug Gilmour, Mike Gartner, Dave Andreychuk, and coach Pat Burns. Fletcher's shaping of the franchise has renewed fan interest in Toronto.

Fletcher was the first general manager to sign and bring a player from the Soviet Union to the NHL with official consent. Sergei Priakin joined the Flames in 1988 and Sergei Makarov was added the following year.

Cliff and his wife Boots make their home in Rosedale, Ontario. The couple have a son, Chuck, and a daughter, Kristy.

Vancouver Canucks

1993-94 Results: 41w-40l-3t 85pts. Second, Pacific Division

Year-by-Year Record

		Home			Road			Overall						
Season	GP	W	L	T	W	L	T	W	L	T	GF	GA	Pts.	Finished	Playoff Result
1993-94	84	20	19	3	21	21	0	41	40	3	279	276	85	2nd, Pacific Div.	Lost Final
1992-93	84	27	11	4	19	18	5	46	29	9	346	278	101	1st, Smythe Div.	Lost Div. Final
1991-92	80	23	10	7	19	16	5	42	26	12	285	250	96	1st, Smythe Div.	Lost Div. Final
1990-91	80	18	17	5	10	26	4	28	43	9	243	315	65	4th, Smythe Div.	Lost Div. Semi-Final
1989-90	80	13	16	11	12	25	3	25	41	14	245	306	64	5th, Smythe Div.	Out of Playoffs
1988-89	80	19	15	6	14	24	2	33	39	8	251	253	74	4th, Smythe Div.	Lost Div. Semi-Final
1987-88	80	15	20	5	10	26	4	25	46	9	272	320	59	5th, Smythe Div.	Out of Playoffs
1986-87	80	17	19	4	12	24	4	29	43	8	282	314	66	5th, Smythe Div.	Out of Playoffs
1985-86	80	17	18	5	6	26	8	23	44	13	282	333	59	4th, Smythe Div.	Lost Div. Semi-Final
1984-85	80	15	21	4	10	25	5	25	46	9	284	401	59	5th, Smythe Div.	Out of Playoffs
1983-84	80	20	16	4	12	23	5	32	39	9	306	328	73	3rd, Smythe Div.	Lost Div. Semi-Final
1982-83	80	20	12	8	10	23	7	30	35	15	303	309	75	3rd, Smythe Div.	Lost Div. Semi-Final
1981-82	80	20	8	12	10	25	5	30	33	17	290	286	77	2nd, Smythe Div.	Lost Final
1980-81	80	17	12	11	11	20	9	28	32	20	289	301	76	3rd, Smythe Div.	Lost Prelim. Round
1979-80	80	14	17	9	13	20	7	27	37	16	256	281	70	3rd, Smythe Div.	Lost Prelim. Round
1978-79	80	15	18	7	10	24	6	25	42	13	217	291	63	2nd, Smythe Div.	Lost Prelim. Round
1977-78	80	13	15	12	7	28	5	20	43	17	239	320	57	3rd, Smythe Div.	Out of Playoffs
1976-77	80	13	21	6	12	21	7	25	42	13	235	294	63	4th, Smythe Div.	Out of Playoffs
1975-76	80	22	11	7	11	21	8	33	32	15	271	272	81	2nd, Smythe Div.	Lost Prelim. Round
1974-75	80	23	12	5	15	20	5	38	32	10	271	254	86	1st, Smythe Div.	Lost Quarter-Final
1973-74	78	14	18	7	10	25	4	24	43	11	224	296	59	7th, East Div.	Out of Playoffs
1972-73	78	17	18	4	5	29	5	22	47	9	233	339	53	7th, East Div.	Out of Playoffs
1971-72	78	14	20	5	6	30	3	20	50	8	203	297	48	7th, East Div.	Out of Playoffs
1970-71	78	17	18	4	7	28	4	24	46	8	229	296	56	6th, East Div.	Out of Playoffs

Schedule

Oct.	Sat.	1	at Calgary		Sat.	31	Quebec
	Sun.	2	at Edmonton	Jan.	Tues.	3	at Florida
	Wed.	5	San Jose		Wed.	4	at Tampa Bay
	Fri.	7	Anaheim		Fri.	6	at Hartford
	Sun.	9	at San Jose*		Wed.	11	Chicago
	Wed.	12	at Anaheim		Fri.	13	Tampa Bay
	Thur.	13	at Los Angeles		Sat.	14	Edmonton
	Sat.	15	Edmonton		Mon.	16	at San Jose
	Mon.	17	Philadelphia		Wed.	18	Buffalo
	Wed.	19	Boston		Tues.	24	at Detroit
	Fri.	21	at Dallas		Wed.	25	at Toronto
	Sun.	23	at St. Louis		Fri.	27	at Pittsburgh
	Tues.	25	at NY Islanders		Mon.	30	Hartford
	Thur.	27	at Philadelphia	Feb.	Wed.	1	Toronto
	Sat.	29	at New Jersey		Sat.	4	at Montreal
	Sun.	30	at NY Rangers		Mon.	6	at Ottawa
Nov.	Wed.	2	Washington		Tues.	7	at Quebec
	Fri.	4	Los Angeles		Thur.	9	Chicago
	Sat.	5	Florida		Sat.	11	Winnipeg
	Mon.	7	San Jose		Thur.	16	San Jose
	Tues.	8	at San Jose		Mon.	20	Quebec
	Fri.	11	at Anaheim				(in Saskatoon)
	Sat.	12	at Los Angeles		Wed.	22	at Winnipeg
	Wed.	16	at Edmonton		Fri.	24	at Dallas
	Thur.	17	Anaheim		Sun.	26	at Anaheim*
	Sat.	19	Calgary		Tues.	28	Pittsburgh
	Mon.	21	at Toronto	Mar.	Wed.	1	at Edmonton
	Wed.	23	at Washington		Mon.	6	Detroit
	Fri.	25	at Buffalo		Thur.	9	Edmonton
	Sun.	27	at Boston*		Sat.	11	Ottawa
Dec.	Fri.	2	Dallas		Tues.	14	NY Islanders
	Sat.	3	Winnipeg		Thur.	16	at Chicago
	Tues.	6	Toronto		Fri.	17	at Detroit
	Thur.	8	at Chicago		Tues.	21	St. Louis
	Sat.	10	at Winnipeg		Thur.	23	New Jersey
	Mon.	12	Los Angeles		Sat.	25	Detroit
	Wed.	14	NY Rangers		Sun.	26	at Calgary
	Fri.	16	St. Louis		Wed.	29	Los Angeles
	Wed.	21	at San Jose		Fri.	31	Anaheim
			(in Portland, OR)	Apr.	Sun.	2	Calgary*
	Fri.	23	at St. Louis		Tues.	4	Dallas
	Tues.	27	Montreal		Thur.	6	at Los Angeles
	Thur.	29	Calgary		Sat.	8	at Calgary

* Denotes afternoon game.

Home Starting Times:
Night Games . . . . 7:30 p.m.
Matinees . . . . 2:00 p.m.
Except Sat. Dec. 31 . . . . 5:00 p.m.

Franchise date: May 22, 1970

25th NHL Season

PACIFIC DIVISION

Vancouver captain Trevor Linden guided the Canucks to the Stanley Cup finals, collecting 25 points in 24 playoff games.

1994-95 Player Personnel

FORWARDS	HT	WT	S	Place of Birth	Date	1993-94 Club
ADAMS, Greg	6-3	198	L	Nelson, B.C.,	8/1/63	Vancouver
ANTOSKI, Shawn	6-4	235	L	Brantford, Ont.	3/25/70	Vancouver
BADDUKE, John	6-2	195	R	Watson, Sask.	6/21/72	Hamilton-Columbus-Brantford
BOHONOS, Lonny	5-11	190	R	Winnipeg, Man.	5/20/73	Portland (WHL)
BURE, Pavel	5-10	189	L	Moscow, USSR	3/31/71	Vancouver
CHARBONNEAU, Jose	6-0	195	R	Ferme-Neuve, Que.	11/21/66	Vancouver-Hamilton
COURTNALL, Geoff	6-1	195	L	Duncan, B.C.	8/18/62	Vancouver
CRAVEN, Murray	6-2	185	L	Medicine Hat, Alta.	7/20/64	Vancouver
GELINAS, Martin	5-11	195	L	Shawinigan, Que.	6/5/70	Quebec-Vancouver
GIRARD, Rick	5-11	175	L	Edmonton, Alta.	5/1/74	Swift Current-Hamilton
HUNTER, Tim	6-2	202	R	Calgary, Alta.	9/10/60	Vancouver
JACKSON, Dane	6-1	200	R	Castlegar, B.C.	5/17/70	Vancouver-Hamilton
KESA, Danny	6-0	198	R	Vancouver, B.C.	11/23/71	Vancouver-Hamilton
La FAYETTE, Nathan	6-1	194	R	New Westminster, B.C.	2/17/73	St. Louis-Peoria-Vancouver
LINDEN, Trevor	6-4	210	R	Medicine Hat, Alta.	4/11/70	Vancouver
LONEY, Brian	6-2	200	R	Winnipeg, Man.	8/9/72	Hamilton
McINTYRE, John	6-1	190	L	Ravenswood, Ont.	4/29/69	Vancouver
MOMESSO, Sergio	6-3	215	L	Montreal, Que.	9/4/65	Vancouver
ODJICK, Gino	6-3	210	L	Maniwaki, Que.	9/7/70	Vancouver
PECA, Michael	5-11	180	R	Toronto, Ont.	3/26/74	Vancouver-Ottawa (OHL)
RONNING, Cliff	5-8	170	L	Burnaby, B.C.	10/1/65	Vancouver
STOJANOV, Alek	6-4	220	L	Windsor, Ont.	4/25/73	Hamilton
DEFENSEMEN						
AUCOIN, Adrian	6-1	194	R	Ottawa, Ont.	7/3/73	Cdn. National-Cdn. Olympic-Ham
BABYCH, Dave	6-2	215	L	Edmonton, Alta.	5/23/61	Vancouver
BROWN, Jeff	6-1	204	R	Ottawa, Ont.	4/30/66	St. Louis-Vancouver
CULLIMORE, Jassen	6-5	225	L	Simcoe, Ont.	12/4/72	Hamilton
DIDUCK, Gerald	6-2	207	R	Edmonton, Alta.	4/6/65	Vancouver
GLYNN, Brian	6-4	220	L	Iserlohn, West Germany	11/23/67	Ottawa-Vancouver
HEDICAN, Bret	6-2	195	L	St. Paul, MN	8/10/70	St. Louis-Vancouver
LUMME, Jyrki	6-1	205	L	Tampere, Finland	7/16/66	Vancouver
MURZYN, Dana	6-2	200	L	Calgary, Alta.	12/9/66	Vancouver
NAMESTNIKOV, Yevgeny	5-11	190	R	Arzamis-Ig, USSR	10/9/71	Vancouver
ROHLIN, Leif	6-1	198	L	Vasteras, Sweden	2/26/68	Vasteras
SLEGR, Jiri	6-1	205	L	Jihlava, Czech.	5/30/71	Vancouver
TULLY, Brent	6-3	195	R	Peterborough, Ont.	3/26/74	Ptrboro-Cdn. National-Ham
WALKER, Scott	5-9	180	R	Montreal, Que.	7/19/73	Hamilton

GOALTENDERS	HT	WT	C	Place of Birth	Date	1993-94 Club
FOUNTAIN, Mike	6-1	176	L	North York, Ont.	1/26/72	Hamilton
McLEAN, Kirk	6-0	195	L	Willowdale, Ont.	6/26/66	Vancouver
TKACHENKO, Sergei	6-2	198	L	Kiev, USSR	6/6/71	Hamilton-Columbus
WHITMORE, Kay	5-11	175	L	Sudbury, Ont.	4/10/67	Vancouver

General Manager

QUINN, PAT
President and General Manager, Vancouver Canucks.
Born in Hamilton, Ont., January 29, 1943.

After guiding the Vancouver Canucks to their third straight season with 40+ wins and a berth in the 1994 Stanley Cup finals, Pat Quinn stepped down as the most successful coach in Canuck history. In his three and one-half seasons as head coach, Quinn posted a .554 winning percentage and a record of 138-108-28, four victories shy of the team record. In 1992-93 he directed the Canucks to a 46-29-9 record, the best in franchise history. A charter member of the inaugural Vancouver Canucks team, Quinn re-joined the organization as president and general manager in 1987-88 and three years later, on January 31, 1991, added the coaching responsibilities to his portfolio. In 1991-92 Quinn won the Jack Adams Award as NHL coach of the year for the second time in his career, and is one of only two coaches to win the award with two different teams. Quinn previously coached Los Angeles from 1984 to 1987 and in Philadelphia from 1978 to 1982. In 1979-80, his first full season behind the Flyers' bench, Quinn guided the team to a Campbell Conference title and the best record in the NHL at 48-12-20. That season he authored an NHL record 35-game undefeated streak and was named coach of the year. After leaving the Flyers organization, Quinn remained out of hockey for two years, earning a Law Degree from Delaware Law School. An NHL defenseman himself, Quinn played in more than 600 games over nine years.

NHL Coaching Record

		Regular Season					Playoffs			
Season	Team	Games	W	L	T	%	Games	W	L	%
1978-79	Philadelphia	30	18	8	4	.667	8	3	5	.375
1979-80	Philadelphia	80	48	12	20	.725	19	13	6	.684
1980-81	Philadelphia	80	41	24	15	.606	12	6	6	.500
1981-82	Philadelphia	72	34	29	9	.535	....	....	....	....
1984-85	Los Angeles	80	34	32	14	.513	3	0	3	.000
1985-86	Los Angeles	80	23	49	8	.338	....	....	....	....
1986-87	Los Angeles	42	18	20	4	.476	....	....	....	....
1990-91	Vancouver	26	9	13	4	.423	6	2	4	.333
1991-92	Vancouver	80	42	26	12	.600	13	6	7	.462
1992-93	Vancouver	84	46	29	9	.601	12	6	6	.500
1993-94	Vancouver	84	41	40	3	.506	24	15	9	.625
	NHL Totals	**738**	**354**	**282**	**102**	**.549**	**97**	**51**	**46**	**.526**

General Managers' History

Normand Robert Poile, 1970-71 to 1972-73; Hal Laycoe, 1973-74; Phil Maloney, 1974-75 to 1976-77; Jake Milford, 1977-78 to 1981-82; Harry Neale, 1982-83 to 1984-85; Jack Gordon, 1985-86 to 1986-87; Pat Quinn, 1987-88 to date.

1993-94 Scoring

* – rookie

Regular Season

Pos	#	Player	Team	GP	G	A	Pts	+/-	PIM	PP	SH	GW	GT	S	%
R	10	Pavel Bure	VAN	76	60	47	107	1	86	25	4	9	0	374	16.0
L	14	Geoff Courtnall	VAN	82	26	44	70	15	123	12	1	2	0	264	9.8
C	7	Cliff Ronning	VAN	76	25	43	68	7	42	10	0	4	1	197	12.7
D	22	Jeff Brown	STL	63	13	47	60	13–	46	7	0	3	1	196	6.6
			VAN	11	1	5	6	2	10	0	0	0	0	41	2.4
			TOTAL	74	14	52	66	11–	56	7	0	3	1	237	5.9
R	16	Trevor Linden	VAN	84	32	29	61	6	73	10	2	3	0	234	13.7
L	32	Murray Craven	VAN	78	15	40	55	5	30	2	1	3	0	115	13.0
D	21	Jyrki Lumme	VAN	83	13	42	55	3	50	1	3	3	0	161	8.1
D	24	Jiri Slegr	VAN	78	5	33	38	0	86	1	0	0	0	160	3.1
L	8	Greg Adams	VAN	68	13	24	37	1–	20	5	1	2	0	139	9.4
D	44	Dave Babych	VAN	73	4	28	32	0	52	0	0	2	0	96	4.2
L	29	Gino Odjick	VAN	76	16	13	29	13	271	4	0	5	0	121	13.2
L	23	Martin Gelinas	QUE	31	6	6	12	2–	8	0	0	0	1	53	11.3
			VAN	33	8	8	16	6–	26	3	0	1	1	54	14.8
			TOTAL	64	14	14	28	8–	34	3	0	1	2	107	13.1
C	17	Jimmy Carson	L.A.	25	4	7	11	2–	2	1	0	0	0	47	8.5
			VAN	34	7	10	17	13–	22	2	0	1	0	82	8.5
			TOTAL	59	11	17	28	15–	24	3	0	1	0	129	8.5
L	27	Sergio Momesso	VAN	68	14	13	27	2–	149	4	0	1	0	112	12.5
D	5	Dana Murzyn	VAN	80	6	14	20	4	109	0	1	0	0	79	7.6
D	28	Brian Glynn	OTT	48	2	13	15	15–	41	1	0	0	0	66	3.0
			VAN	16	0	0	0	4–	12	0	0	0	0	5	.0
			TOTAL	64	2	13	15	19–	53	1	0	0	0	71	2.8
R	20	Jose Charbonneau	VAN	30	7	7	14	3–	49	1	0	0	0	28	25.0
D	3	Bret Hedican	STL	61	0	11	11	8–	64	0	0	0	0	78	.0
			VAN	8	0	1	1	1	0	0	0	0	0	10	.0
			TOTAL	69	0	12	12	7–	64	0	0	0	0	88	.0
D	4	Gerald Diduck	VAN	55	1	10	11	2	72	0	0	0	0	50	2.0
D	6	Adrien Plavsic	VAN	47	1	9	10	5–	6	0	0	1	0	41	2.4
C	15	John McIntyre	VAN	62	3	6	9	9–	38	0	0	0	0	30	10.0
C	25	* Nathan Lafayette	STL	38	2	3	5	9–	14	0	0	0	0	23	8.7
			VAN	11	1	1	2	2	4	0	0	0	0	11	9.1
			TOTAL	49	3	4	7	7–	18	0	0	0	0	34	8.8
R	19	Tim Hunter	VAN	56	3	4	7	7–	171	0	1	1	0	41	7.3
R	36	* Dane Jackson	VAN	12	5	1	6	3	9	0	0	0	0	18	27.8
R	25	* Dan Kesa	VAN	19	2	4	6	3–	18	1	0	1	0	18	11.1
D	2	* Yevgeny Namestnikov	VAN	17	0	5	5	2–	10	0	0	0	0	11	.0
C	23	Neil Eisenhut	VAN	13	1	3	4	0	21	0	0	0	0	13	7.7
G	1	Kirk McLean	VAN	52	0	4	4	0	2	0	0	0	0	0	.0
L	18	* Shawn Antoski	VAN	55	1	2	3	11–	190	0	0	1	0	25	4.0
C	25	Stephane Morin	VAN	5	1	1	2	0	6	0	0	0	0	6	16.7
C	33	* Mike Peca	VAN	4	0	0	0	1–	2	0	0	0	0	5	.0
G	35	Kay Whitmore	VAN	32	0	0	0	0	6	0	0	0	0	0	.0

Goaltending

No.	Goaltender	GPI	Mins	Avg	W	L	T	EN	SO	GA	SA	S%
1	Kirk McLean	52	3128	2.99	23	26	3	5	3	156	1430	.891
35	Kay Whitmore	32	1921	3.53	18	14	0	2	0	113	848	.867
	Totals	**84**	**5070**	**3.27**	**41**	**40**	**3**	**7**	**3**	**276**	**2285**	**.879**

Playoffs

Pos	#	Player	Team	GP	G	A	Pts	+/-	PIM	PP	SH	GW	GT	S	%
R	10	Pavel Bure	VAN	24	16	15	31	8	40	3	0	2	1	101	15.8
R	16	Trevor Linden	VAN	24	12	13	25	3	18	5	1	1	1	67	17.9
L	14	Geoff Courtnall	VAN	24	9	10	19	10	51	0	1	3	1	77	11.7
D	22	Jeff Brown	VAN	24	6	9	15	7	37	3	0	0	0	76	7.9
C	7	Cliff Ronning	VAN	24	5	10	15	2–	16	2	0	2	0	69	7.2
L	8	Greg Adams	VAN	23	6	8	14	1	2	2	0	2	2	46	13.0
L	32	Murray Craven	VAN	22	4	9	13	10	18	0	0	1	0	38	10.5
D	21	Jyrki Lumme	VAN	24	2	11	13	8	16	2	0	1	0	53	3.8
L	23	Martin Gelinas	VAN	24	5	4	9	1–	14	2	0	1	0	35	14.3
C	25	* Nathan Lafayette	VAN	20	2	7	9	13	4	0	0	0	0	24	8.3
D	44	Dave Babych	VAN	24	3	5	8	4	12	0	0	1	0	26	11.5
D	4	Gerald Diduck	VAN	24	1	7	8	1	22	0	0	0	0	32	3.1
L	27	Sergio Momesso	VAN	24	3	4	7	7	56	0	0	1	1	38	7.9
D	3	Bret Hedican	VAN	24	1	6	7	13	16	0	0	0	0	22	4.5
D	28	Brian Glynn	VAN	17	0	3	3	5	10	0	0	0	0	11	.0
R	20	Jose Charbonneau	VAN	3	1	0	1	1	4	0	0	0	0	4	25.0
C	17	Jimmy Carson	VAN	2	0	1	1	1	0	0	0	0	0	2	.0
L	18	* Shawn Antoski	VAN	16	0	1	1	3–	36	0	0	0	0	4	.0
C	15	John McIntyre	VAN	24	0	1	1	3–	16	0	0	0	0	12	.0
G	1	Kirk McLean	VAN	24	0	1	1	0	0	0	0	0	0	0	.0
D	5	Dana Murzyn	VAN	7	0	0	0	4–	4	0	0	0	0	7	.0
L	29	Gino Odjick	VAN	10	0	0	0	0	18	0	0	0	0	3	.0
R	19	Tim Hunter	VAN	24	0	0	0	3–	26	0	0	0	0	8	.0

Goaltending

No.	Goaltender	GPI	Mins	Avg	W	L	EN	SO	GA	SA	S%
1	Kirk McLean	24	1544	2.29	15	9	2	4	59	820	.928
	Totals	**24**	**1554**	**2.36**	**15**	**9**	**2**	**4**	**61**	**822**	**.926**

Club Records

Team

(Figures in brackets for season records are games played)

Most Points	101	1992-93 (84)
Most Wins	46	1992-93 (84)
Most Ties	20	1980-81 (80)
Most Losses	50	1971-72 (78)
Most Goals	346	1992-93 (84)
Most Goals Against	401	1984-85 (80)
Fewest Points	48	1971-72 (78)
Fewest Wins	20	1971-72 (78)
		1977-78 (80)
Fewest Ties	3	1993-94 (84)
Fewest Losses	26	1991-92 (84)
Fewest Goals	203	1971-72 (78)
Fewest Goals Against	250	1991-92 (80)

Longest Winning Streak

Over-all	7	Feb. 10-23/89
Home	9	Nov. 6-Dec. 9/92
Away	5	Jan. 14-25/92

Longest Undefeated Streak

Over-all	10	Mar. 5-25/77 (5 wins, 5 ties)
Home	18	Oct. 30/92 Jan. 18/93 (16 wins, 2 ties)
Away	5	Four times

Longest Losing Streak

Over-all	9	Four times
Home	6	Dec. 18/70-Jan. 20/71 Nov. 3-18/78
Away	12	Nov. 28/81-Feb. 6/82

Longest Winless Streak

Over-all	13	Nov. 9-Dec. 7/73 (10 losses, 3 ties)
Home	11	Dec. 18/70-Feb. 6/71 (10 losses, 1 tie)
Away	20	Jan. 2/86-Apr. 2/86 (14 losses, 6 ties)

Most Shutouts, Season	8	1974-75 (80)
Most PIM, Season	2,326	1992-93 (84)
Most Goals, Game	11	Mar. 28/71 (Cal. 5 at Van. 11) Nov. 25/86 (L.A. 5 at Van. 11) Mar. 1/92 (Cgy. 0 at Van. 11)

Individual

Most Seasons	13	Stan Smyl
Most Games	896	Stan Smyl
Most Goals, Career	262	Stan Smyl
Most Assists, Career	411	Stan Smyl
Most Points, Career	673	Stan Smyl (262 goals, 411 assists)
Most PIM, Career	1,668	Garth Butcher
Most Shutouts, Career	16	Kirk McLean

Longest Consecutive Games Streak . . . 437 Don Lever (Oct. 7/72-Jan. 14/78)

Most Goals, Season	60	Pavel Bure (1992-93, 1993-94)
Most Assists, Season	62	André Boudrias (1974-75)
Most Points, Season	110	Pavel Bure (1992-93) (60 goals, 50 assists)
Most PIM, Season	370	Gino Odjick (1992-93)

Most Points, Defenseman, Season . . . 63 Doug Lidster (1986-87) (12 goals, 51 assists)

Most Points, Center, Season	91	Patrik Sundstrom (1983-84) (38 goals, 53 assists)
Most Points, Right Wing, Season	110	Pavel Bure (1992-93) (60 goals, 50 assists)
Most Points, Left Wing, Season	81	Darcy Rota (1982-83) (42 goals, 39 assists)
Most Points, Rookie, Season	60	Ivan Hlinka (1981-82) (23 goals, 37 assists) Pavel Bure (1991-92) (34 goals, 26 assists)
Most Shutouts, Season	6	Gary Smith (1974-75)
Most Goals, Game	4	Several players
Most Assists, Game	6	Patrik Sundstrom (Feb. 29/84)
Most Points, Game	7	Patrik Sundstrom (Feb. 29/84)

All-time Record vs. Other Clubs

Regular Season

	At Home							On Road							Total						
	GP	W	L	T	GF	GA	PTS	GP	W	L	T	GF	GA	PTS	GP	W	L	T	GF	GA	PTS
Anaheim	3	1	2	0	7	11	2	3	2	1	0	6	7	4	6	3	0	13	18	6	
Boston	44	14	22	8	149	187	36	43	4	35	4	96	194	12	87	18	57	12	245	381	48
Buffalo	44	21	13	10	168	146	52	45	14	23	8	130	164	36	89	35	36	18	298	310	88
Calgary	72	26	31	15	259	247	67	71	12	50	9	201	324	33	143	38	81	24	460	571	100
Chicago	52	25	15	12	163	148	62	51	13	33	5	121	192	31	103	38	48	17	284	340	93
Dallas	51	24	19	8	201	163	56	51	13	30	8	148	207	34	102	37	49	16	349	370	90
Detroit	45	24	14	7	186	145	55	46	13	27	6	137	195	32	91	37	41	13	323	340	87
Edmonton	55	21	28	6	211	235	48	54	11	39	4	168	279	26	109	32	67	10	379	514	74
Florida	1	0	1	0	1	2	0	1	0	1	0	1	2	0	2	0	2	0	2	4	0
Hartford	23	9	8	6	82	66	24	22	9	9	4	79	73	22	45	18	17	10	161	139	46
Los Angeles	75	38	25	12	298	254	88	77	26	41	10	253	321	62	152	64	66	22	551	575	150
Montreal	43	7	28	8	107	172	22	45	8	35	2	120	226	18	88	15	63	10	227	398	40
New Jersey	41	24	6	11	160	118	59	41	17	18	6	137	130	40	82	41	24	17	297	248	99
NY Islanders	41	18	20	3	135	138	39	39	9	22	8	102	150	26	80	27	42	11	237	288	65
NY Rangers	45	11	31	3	144	187	25	47	7	35	5	117	215	19	92	18	66	8	261	402	44
Ottawa	2	1	0	1	6	3	3	2	2	0	0	10	2	4	4	3	0	1	16	5	7
Philadelphia	45	10	24	11	131	174	31	45	14	30	1	135	202	29	90	24	54	12	266	376	60
Pittsburgh	43	20	20	3	159	165	43	43	8	28	7	144	194	23	86	28	48	10	303	359	66
Quebec	22	11	7	4	93	88	26	23	10	9	4	68	67	24	45	21	16	8	161	155	50
St. Louis	52	23	23	6	164	160	52	51	15	29	7	155	198	37	103	38	52	13	319	358	89
San Jose	10	9	1	0	46	22	18	10	6	3	1	38	32	13	20	15	4	1	84	54	31
Tampa Bay	3	3	0	0	14	3	6	2	2	0	0	8	5	4	5	5	0	0	22	8	10
Toronto	45	24	14	7	154	147	55	47	18	20	9	165	177	45	92	42	34	16	319	324	100
Washington	32	15	13	4	109	103	34	33	11	18	4	103	111	26	65	26	31	8	212	214	60
Winnipeg	52	30	14	8	205	151	68	49	18	24	7	188	192	43	101	48	38	15	393	343	111
Defunct Clubs	19	14	3	2	82	48	30	19	10	7	1	71	68	21	38	24	11	3	153	116	51
Totals	**960**	**423**	**382**	**155**	**3434**	**3283**	**1001**	**960**	**272**	**568**	**120**	**2901**	**3927**	**664**	**1920**	**695**	**950**	**275**	**6335**	**7210**	**1665**

Calgary totals include Atlanta, 1972-73 to 1979-80. Dallas totals include Minnesota, 1970-71 to 1992-93.
New Jersey totals include Kansas City, 1974-75 to 1975-76, and Colorado, 1976-77 to 1981-82.

Playoffs

	Series	W	L	GP	W	L	T	GF	GA	Last Mtg.	Round	Result
Buffalo	2	0	2	7	1	6	0	14	28	1981	PR	L 0-3
Calgary	5	2	3	25	12	13	0	80	82	1994	CQF	W 4-3
Chicago	1	1	0	5	4	1	0	18	13	1982	CF	W 4-1
Dallas	1	1	0	5	4	1	0	18	11	1994	CSF	W 4-1
Edmonton	2	0	2	9	2	7	0	20	35	1992	DF	L 2-4
Los Angeles	3	1	2	17	10	7	0	60	66	1993	DF	L 2-4
Montreal	1	0	1	5	1	4	0	9	20	1975	QF	L 1-4
NY Islanders	2	0	2	6	0	6	0	14	26	1982	F	L 0-4
NY Rangers	1	0	1	7	3	4	0	19	21	1994	F	L 3-4
Philadelphia	1	0	1	3	1	2	0	9	15	1979	PR	L 1-2
Toronto	1	1	0	5	4	1	0	16	9	1994	CF	W 4-1
Winnipeg	2	2	0	13	8	5	0	50	34	1993	DSF	W 4-2
Totals	**22**	**8**	**14**	**107**	**48**	**59**	**0**	**327**	**360**			

Playoff Results 1994-90

Year	Round	Opponent	Result	GF	GA
1994	F	NY Rangers	L 3-4	19	21
	CF	Toronto	W 4-1	16	9
	CSF	Dallas	W 4-1	18	11
	CQF	Calgary	W 4-3	23	20
1993	DF	Los Angeles	L 2-4	25	26
	DSF	Winnipeg	W 4-2	21	17
1992	DF	Edmonton	L 2-4	15	18
	DSF	Winnipeg	W 4-3	29	17
1991	DSF	Los Angeles	L 2-4	16	26

Abbreviations: Round: F – Final;
CF – conference final; **CQF** – conference quarter-final;
CSF – conference semi-final; **DF** – division final;
DSF – division semi-final; **SF** – semi-final;
QF – quarter-final; **PR** – preliminary round.

1993-94 Results

Oct.								
Oct.	6	at	Los Angeles	5-2	14		Ottawa	2-2
	9		Calgary	1-5	16	at	Anaheim	4-3
	11		Edmonton	4-1	19		Calgary	3-4
	16	at	Edmonton	3-2	24	at	Edmonton	5-4
	19		Boston	5-4	25		St. Louis	3-3
	21	at	Calgary	6-3	27		Dallas	2-3
	23	at	San Jose	6-4	29		New Jersey	6-3
	24		San Jose	3-2	31		Los Angeles	3-1
	27		Washington	2-4	Feb. 2		Chicago	6-4
	30		Buffalo	3-6	4	at	Anaheim	0-3
Nov.	2	at	NY Islanders	2-1	6		Hartford	2-4
	3	at	NY Rangers	3-6	8	at	Detroit	6-3
	5	at	Washington	2-3	10	at	New Jersey	3-7
	7	at	Philadelphia	5-2	12	at	Tampa Bay	3-2
	10		Los Angeles	4-0	13	at	Florida	1-2
	13	at	Calgary	3-4	15	at	St. Louis	2-3
	14		Anaheim	3-2	17	at	Chicago	4-2
	16		St. Louis	3-0	22		Calgary	4-4
	19		Anaheim	3-6	26		Tampa Bay	3-1
	22		Toronto	2-5	Mar. 1		Edmonton	4-7
	24		Detroit	4-5	3	at	St. Louis	4-0
	26	at	Winnipeg	5-3	4	at	Dallas	4-1
	27	at	Edmonton	1-2	7		Florida	1-2
	29		Chicago	2-1	9		NY Islanders	5-4
Dec.	2		Philadelphia	3-6	11	at	Winnipeg	8-4
	4	at	Quebec	1-3	13	at	Chicago	2-5
	6	at	Montreal	3-4	15	at	Detroit	2-5
	8	at	Hartford	4-1	16	at	Toronto	4-1
	9	at	Boston	3-2	19	at	Pittsburgh	4-5
	14	at	Calgary	4-8	20	at	Dallas	1-2
	15	at	Edmonton	2-7	23	at	Los Angeles	6-3
	17		Winnipeg	6-1	25		NY Rangers	2-5
	19		Dallas	1-3	27		Los Angeles	4-3
	21		Edmonton	6-3	28		Toronto	3-2
	23		Calgary	4-3	30		Pittsburgh	1-3
	28	at	Los Angeles	5-6	Apr. 1		Winnipeg	5-1
	31		San Jose	2-3	2	at	San Jose	4-7
Jan.	2		Montreal	2-3	5		Detroit	3-8
	5	at	Ottawa	7-2	7		San Jose	3-2
	8	at	Toronto	3-5	9		Anaheim	1-3
	9	at	Buffalo	3-5	10	at	San Jose	1-3
	12		Quebec	4-3	13	at	Anaheim	2-1

Entry Draft
Selections 1994-80

1994
Pick
13	Mattias Ohlund
39	Robb Gordon
42	Dave Scatchard
65	Chad Allan
92	Mike Dubinsky
117	Yanick Dube
169	Yuri Kuznetsov
195	Rob Trumbley
221	Bill Muckalt
247	Tyson Nash
273	Robert Longpre

1993
Pick
20	Mike Wilson
46	Rick Girard
98	Dieter Kochan
124	Scott Walker
150	Troy Creurer
176	Yevgeny Babariko
202	Sean Tallaire
254	Bert Robertsson
280	Sergei Tkachenko

1992
Pick
21	Libor Polasek
40	Mike Peca
45	Michael Fountain
69	Jeff Connolly
93	Brent Tully
110	Brian Loney
117	Adrian Aucoin
141	Jason.Clark
165	Scott Hollis
213	Sonny Mignacca
237	Mark Wotton
261	Aaron Boh

1991
Pick
7	Alex Stojanov
29	Jassen Cullimore
51	Sean Pronger
95	Danny Kesa
117	Evgeny Namestnikov
139	Brent Thurston
161	Eric Johnson
183	David Neilson
205	Brad Barton
227	Jason Fitzsimmons
249	Xavier Majic

1990
Pick
2	Petr Nedved
18	Shawn Antoski
23	Jiri Slegr
65	Darin Bader
86	Gino Odjick
128	Daryl Filipek
149	Paul O'Hagan
170	Mark Cipriano
191	Troy Neumier
212	Tyler Ertel
233	Karri Kivi

1989
Pick
8	Jason Herter
29	Robert Woodward
71	Brett Hauer
113	Pavel Bure
134	James Revenberg
155	Rob Sangster
176	Sandy Moger
197	Gus Morschauser
218	Hayden O'Rear
239	Darcy Cahill
248	Jan Bergman

1988
Pick
2	Trevor Linden
33	Leif Rohlin
44	Dane Jackson
107	Corrie D'Alessio
122	Phil Von Stefenelli
128	Dixon Ward
149	Greg Geldart
170	Roger Akerstrom
191	Paul Constantin
212	Chris Wolanin
233	Stefan Nilsson

1987
Pick
24	Rob Murphy
45	Steve Veilleux
66	Doug Torrel
87	Sean Fabian
108	Garry Valk
129	Todd Fanning
150	Viktor Tumenev
171	Craig Daly
192	John Fletcher
213	Roger Hansson
233	Neil Eisenhut
234	Matt Evo

1986
Pick
7	Dan Woodley
49	Don Gibson
70	Ronnie Stern
91	Eric Murano
112	Steve Herniman
133	Jon Helgeson
154	Jeff Noble
175	Matt Merton
196	Marc Lyons
217	Todd Hawkins
238	Vladimir Krutov

1985
Pick
4	Jim Sandlak
25	Troy Gamble
46	Shane Doyle
67	Randy Siska
88	Robert Kron
109	Martin Hrstka
130	Brian McFarlane
151	Hakan Ahlund
172	Curtis Hunt
193	Carl Valimont
214	Igor Larionov
235	Darren Taylor

1984
Pick
10	J.J. Daigneault
31	Jeff Rohlicek
52	Dave Saunders
55	Landis Chaulk
58	Mike Stevens
73	Brian Bertuzzi
94	Brett MacDonald
115	Jeff Korchinski
136	Blaine Chrest
157	Jim Agnew
178	Rex Grant
198	Ed Lowney
219	Doug Clarke
239	Ed Kister

1983
Pick
9	Cam Neely
30	Dave Bruce
50	Scott Tottle
70	Tim Lorentz
90	Doug Quinn
110	Dave Lowry
130	Terry Maki
150	John Labatt
170	Allan Measures
190	Roger Grillo
210	Steve Kayser
230	Jay Mazur

1982
Pick
11	Michel Petit
53	Yves Lapointe
71	Shawn Kilroy
116	Taylor Hall
137	Parie Proft
158	Newell Brown
179	Don McLaren
200	Al Raymond
221	Steve Driscoll
242	Shawn Green

1981
Pick
10	Garth Butcher
52	Jean-Marc Lanthier
73	Wendell Young
105	Moe Lemay
115	Stu Kulak
136	Bruce Holloway
157	Petri Skriko
178	Frank Caprice
199	Rejean Vignola

1980
Pick
7	Rick Lanz
49	Andy Schliebener
70	Marc Crawford
91	Darrell May
112	Ken Berry
133	Doug Lidster
154	John O'Connor
175	Patrik Sundstrom
196	Grant Martin

Coach

LEY, RICK
Coach, Vancouver Canucks. Born in Orillia, Ont., November 2, 1948.

After serving three years as an assistant coach under Pat Quinn, Rick Ley was promoted to head coach of the Vancouver Canucks on August 10, 1994. He is the 12th head coach in franchise history. He inherits a team that has won 40+ games each of the past three seasons and, in 1994, advanced to the Stanley Cup finals for the first time since 1982.

Ley was previously head coach of the Hartford Whalers for two seasons, where he posted records of 31-38-11 in 1991 and 38-33-9 in 1990, the best winning percentage in Whaler history. In nine seasons as a head coach in professional hockey, Ley has posted a lifetime record of 378-255-55 for a .589 winning percentage. Four times under his direction, teams have posted 50-or-more wins in a single season.

Prior to coaching Hartford, Ley was with the Canuck organization as head coach of the team's IHL affiliate, Milwaukee Admirals, in 1988-89, guiding them to a 54-23-5 record. Ley also coached the IHL's Muskegon Lumberjacks to four first place finishes from 1984 to 1988. In 1984-85, after guiding the Lumberjacks to the Turner Cup championship, Ley shared IHL coach of the year honors.

A former player in the NHL, Ley retired in 1981 after 13 seasons with Toronto and Hartford, including six as Whalers captain. Ley is one of only three players in Hartford Whalers history to have his jersey (#2) retired. Gordie Howe and John McKenzie are the others.

Coaching Record

Season	Team	Games	Regular Season W	L	T	%	Playoffs Games	W	L	%
1982-83	Binghamton (AHL)	44	22	17	5	.534	5	1	4	.200
1983-84	Mohawk Valley (ACHL)	75	29	39	7	.433	5	1	4	.200
1984-85	Muskegon (IHL)	82	50	29	3	.628	17	11	6	.647
1985-86	Muskegon (IHL)	82	50	32	0	.610	14	12	2	.857
1986-87	Muskegon (IHL)	82	47	30	5	.604	15	10	5	.667
1987-88	Muskegon (IHL)	82	58	14	10	.768	6	2	4	.333
1988-89	Milwaukee (IHL)	82	54	23	5	.689	11	5	6	.455
1989-90	Hartford (NHL)	80	38	33	9	.531	7	3	4	.429
1990-91	Hartford (NHL)	80	31	38	11	.456	6	2	4	.333
	NHL Totals	160	69	71	20	.494	13	5	8	.385

Club Directory

Pacific Coliseum
100 North Renfrew Street
Vancouver, B.C. V5K 3N7
Phone **604/254-5141**
FAX 604/251-5123
Capacity: 16,150

Chairman and Governor	Arthur R. Griffiths
Deputy Chairman, C.O.O., General Counsel	Mike Korenberg
President	Pat Quinn
Vice-President, Marketing and Communications	Glen Ringdal
Vice President, Finance and Administration	Carlos Mascarenhas
Executive Assistant	Melodi Kitagawa, Lisa Roenisch

Hockey Operations
General Manager	Pat Quinn
Director of Hockey Operations	George McPhee
Director of Player Development/Scouting	Mike Penny
Head Coach	Rick Ley
Assistant Coaches	Stan Smyl, Ron Smith
Goaltending Coach	Glen Hanlon
Head Coach, Syracuse Crunch	Jack McIlhargey
Assistant Coach, Syracuse Crunch	Mario Marois
Strength and Conditioning Coach	Peter Twist
Director of Pro Scouting	Murray Oliver
Scouting Staff	Jack Birch, Ron Delorme, Jack McCartan, Noel Price, Ken Slater
Part-time Scouting Staff	Mike Backman, Sergei Chibisov, Jimmy Eagle, Thomas Gradin, Ross Mahoney, Ed McColgan, Al McDonald, Ray Miron
Executive Assistant, G.M. and Marketing	Susan Bain
Executive Assistant, Hockey Oper. and Finance	Patti Timms

Medical/Training Staff
Medical Trainer	Larry Ashley
Equipment Trainers	Pat O'Neill, Darren Granger
Massage Therapist	Dave Schima
Doctors	Dr. Ross Davidson, Dr. Doug Clement
Dentist	Dr. David Lawson
Chiropractic Consultant	Dr. Sid Sheard

Media and Public Relations
Director of Media and Public Relations	Steve Tambellini
Public Relations Assistant	Veronica Bateman
Director of Hockey Information	Steve Frost
Manager of Special Events	Suzanne Campbell-Clement
Receptionist	Brenda Baldwin, Lisa Ryan

Marketing
Director of Publishing	Norm Jewison
Managing Director, Winnipeg Spirit	Larry Donen
Corporate Sales Manager	Eric Thomsen
Corporate Sales/Promotions	Jane Bremner
Ticket Manager	Denise McDonald

Finance
Controller	Dave Cobb
Accountant	Mindy Chochan

Centre Ice Club
Club Manager	Dale Vaux
Sales, Marketing Manager	Silveria Roselli
Operations Manager	Giselle Wagner
Beverage Supervisor	Shane Clark

Miscellaneous Information
Pacific Coliseum seating capacity	16,150
Rink Dimensions	200 feet by 85 feet
Club Colors	Red, Black, White and Gold
Television	BCTV (8), CHEK (6), CBC (3)
Radio	CKNW (980 AM) and WIN Network
Radio Broadcasters	Jim Hughson (play-by-play), Tom Larscheid (color)
TV Broadcasters	TBA
Public Address	John Ashbridge
Team Photographer	Jack Murray
Canucks' Booster Club	Box 4183, Vancouver, BC V6B 3Z6; Tel: (604) 524-1593
Pavel Bure Fan Club	Box 23661, Richmond, BC V7B 1X8; Tel: (604) 431-0634

Coaching History

Hal Laycoe, 1970-71 to 1971-72; Vic Stasiuk, 1972-73; Bill McCreary and Phil Maloney, 1973-74; Phil Maloney, 1974-75 to 1975-76; Phil Maloney and Orland Kurtenbach, 1976-77; Orland Kurtenbach, 1977-78; Harry Neale, 1978-79 to 1980-81; Harry Neale and Roger Neilson, 1981-82; Roger Neilson 1982-83; Roger Neilson and Harry Neale, 1983-84; Harry Neale and Bill Laforge, 1984-85; Tom Watt, 1985-86, 1986-87; Bob McCammon, 1987-88 to 1989-90. Bob McCammon and Pat Quinn, 1990-91; Pat Quinn, 1991-92 to 1993-94; Rick Ley, 1994-95.

Captains' History

Orland Kurtenbach, 1970-71 to 1973-74; no captain, 1974-75; Andre Boudrias, 1975-76; Chris Oddleifson, 1976-77; Don Lever, 1977-78; Don Lever, Kevin McCarthy, 1978-79; Kevin McCarthy, 1979-80 to 1981-82; Stan Smyl, 1982-83 to 1989-90; Dan Quinn, Doug Lidster and Trevor Linden, 1990-91; Trevor Linden, 1991-92 to date.

Retired Numbers

12	Stan Smyl	1978-1991

Washington Capitals

1993-94 Results: 39W-35L-10T 88PTS. Third, Atlantic Division

Schedule

Oct.	Sat.	1	at Toronto	Fri.	6	Los Angeles	
	Wed.	5	at Ottawa	Sat.	7	at NY Islanders	
	Fri.	7	Pittsburgh	Wed.	11	at Buffalo	
	Sat.	8	NY Islanders	Sat.	14	NY Rangers	
	Wed.	12	at Pittsburgh	Mon.	16	at Boston*	
	Fri.	14	Montreal	Wed.	18	at Philadelphia	
	Sat.	15	Buffalo	Tues.	24	at Quebec	
	Wed.	19	at New Jersey	Thur.	26	at NY Islanders	
	Fri.	21	Hartford	Fri.	27	Ottawa	
	Sat.	22	at Hartford	Sun.	29	Chicago*	
	Tues.	25	at St. Louis	Tues.	31	at New Jersey	
	Thur.	27	at Winnipeg	**Feb.** Thur.	2	Quebec	
	Sun.	30	at Edmonton	Sat.	4	Florida	
Nov.	Tues.	1	at Calgary	Wed.	8	at Tampa Bay	
	Wed.	2	at Vancouver	Fri.	10	at Philadelphia	
	Sat.	5	Quebec			(in Halifax)	
	Tues.	8	Edmonton	Sun.	12	New Jersey*	
	Thur.	10	at Philadelphia			(in Halifax)	
	Sat.	12	Philadelphia	Wed.	15	Tampa Bay	
	Sun.	13	at NY Rangers	Fri.	17	at Detroit	
	Tues.	15	Dallas	Sat.	18	Detroit	
	Fri.	18	Toronto	Mon.	20	Montreal*	
	Sat.	19	at Boston	Thur.	23	at Chicago	
	Wed.	23	Vancouver	Sat.	25	at New Jersey*	
	Fri.	25	Pittsburgh	Sun.	26	New Jersey*	
	Sat.	26	at Quebec	**Mar.** Thur.	2	NY Islanders	
	Mon.	28	at Montreal	Sat.	4	San Jose	
	Wed.	30	at Ottawa	Tues.	7	Calgary	
Dec.	Thur.	1	at Pittsburgh	Wed.	8	at Montreal	
	Sat.	3	Tampa Bay	Fri.	10	Florida	
	Wed.	7	at Anaheim	Sun.	12	Boston*	
	Thur.	8	at Los Angeles	Mon.	13	at Tampa Bay	
	Sat.	10	at San Jose	Wed.	15	at Florida	
	Tues.	13	Winnipeg	Sat.	18	NY Rangers	
	Fri.	16	Boston	Tues.	21	Ottawa	
	Sat.	17	at Hartford	Sat.	25	Anaheim*	
	Tues.	20	at Florida	Sun.	26	Hartford*	
	Fri.	23	Philadelphia	Wed.	29	at Tampa Bay	
	Mon.	26	at NY Islanders	Fri.	31	Philadelphia	
	Tues.	27	NY Rangers	**Apr.** Sun.	2	at Dallas*	
	Thur.	29	Florida	Wed.	5	at NY Rangers	
	Sat.	31	New Jersey	Fri.	7	at Buffalo	
Jan.	Mon.	2	St. Louis*	Sat.	8	Buffalo	

* Denotes afternoon game.

Home Starting Times:
Mondays through Thursday . . . . . . 7:30 p.m.
Fridays . . . . 8:00 p.m.
Saturdays. . . . . 7:30 p.m.
Matinees. . . . . 1:30 p.m.
Except   Fri. Oct. 14 . . . . 7:30 p.m.
          Sat. Nov. 5 . . . . 7:00 p.m.
          Wed. Nov. 23. . . . . 8:00 p.m.
          Fri. Nov. 25. . . . . 7:30 p.m.
          Sun. Jan. 29 . . . . 12:00 p.m.

Franchise date: June 11, 1974

21st NHL Season

ATLANTIC DIVISION

The Washington Capitals obtained playmaker Joé Juneau from the Boston Bruins on March 21, 1994.

Year-by-Year Record

		Home			Road			Overall							
Season	GP	W	L	T	W	L	T	W	L	T	GF	GA	Pts.	Finished	Playoff Result
1993-94	84	17	16	9	22	19	1	39	35	10	277	263	88	3rd, Atlantic Div.	Lost Conf. Semi-Final
1992-93	84	21	15	6	22	19	1	43	34	7	325	286	93	2nd, Patrick Div.	Lost Div. Semi-Final
1991-92	80	25	12	3	20	15	5	45	27	8	330	275	98	2nd, Patrick Div.	Lost Div. Semi-Final
1990-91	80	21	14	5	16	22	2	37	36	7	258	258	81	3rd, Patrick Div.	Lost Div. Final
1989-90	80	19	18	3	17	20	3	36	38	6	284	275	78	3rd, Patrick Div.	Lost Conf. Championship
1988-89	80	25	12	3	16	17	7	41	29	10	305	259	92	1st, Patrick Div.	Lost Div. Semi-Final
1987-88	80	22	14	4	16	19	5	38	33	9	281	249	85	2nd, Patrick Div.	Lost Div. Final
1986-87	80	22	15	3	16	17	7	38	32	10	285	278	86	2nd, Patrick Div.	Lost Div. Semi-Final
1985-86	80	30	8	2	20	15	5	50	23	7	315	272	107	2nd, Patrick Div.	Lost Div. Final
1984-85	80	27	11	2	19	14	7	46	25	9	322	240	101	2nd, Patrick Div.	Lost Div. Semi-Final
1983-84	80	26	11	3	22	16	2	48	27	5	308	226	101	2nd, Patrick Div.	Lost Div. Final
1982-83	80	22	12	6	17	13	10	39	25	16	306	283	94	3rd, Patrick Div.	Lost Div. Semi-Final
1981-82	80	16	16	8	10	25	5	26	41	13	319	338	65	5th, Patrick Div.	Out of Playoffs
1980-81	80	16	17	7	10	19	11	26	36	18	286	317	70	5th, Patrick Div.	Out of Playoffs
1979-80	80	20	14	6	7	26	7	27	40	13	261	293	67	5th, Patrick Div.	Out of Playoffs
1978-79	80	15	19	6	9	22	9	24	41	15	273	338	63	4th, Norris Div.	Out of Playoffs
1977-78	80	10	23	7	7	26	7	17	49	14	195	321	48	5th, Norris Div.	Out of Playoffs
1976-77	80	17	15	8	7	27	6	24	42	14	221	307	62	4th, Norris Div.	Out of Playoffs
1975-76	80	6	26	8	5	33	2	11	59	10	224	394	32	5th, Norris Div.	Out of Playoffs
1974-75	80	7	28	5	1	39	0	8	67	5	181	446	21	5th, Norris Div.	Out of Playoffs

1994-95 Player Personnel

FORWARDS	HT	WT	S	Place of Birth	Date	1993-94 Club
ALLISON, Jason	6-3	200	R	North York, Ont.	5/29/75	Wsh-London-Portland (AHL)
BERUBE, Craig	6-1	205	L	Calahoo, Alta.	12/17/65	Washington
BOBACK, Michael	5-11	180	R	Mt. Clemens, MI	8/13/70	Portland (AHL)
BONDRA, Peter	6-0	200	L	Lutsk, USSR	2/7/68	Washington
BURRIDGE, Randy	5-9	185	L	Fort Erie, Ont.	1/7/66	Washington
CHERREY, Scott	6-1	199	L	Drayton, Ont.	5/27/76	North Bay
GENDRON, Martin	5-8	182	R	Valleyfield, Que.	2/15/74	Cdn. National-Hull
HUNTER, Dale	5-10	198	L	Petrolia, Ont.	7/31/60	Washington
JONES, Keith	6-2	190	L	Brantford, Ont.	11/8/68	Washington-Portland (AHL)
JUNEAU, Joe	6-0	195	R	Pont-Rouge, Que.	1/5/68	Boston-Washington
KAMINSKI, Kevin	5-9	170	L	Churchbridge, Sask.	3/13/69	Washington-Portland (AHL)
KHARLAMOV, Alexander	5-11	183	L	Moscow, USSR	9/23/75	CSKA
KHRISTICH, Dimitri	6-2	195	R	Kiev, USSR	7/23/69	Washington
KONOWALCHUK, Steve	6-0	180	L	Salt Lake City, UT	11/11/72	Washington-Portland (AHL)
KRYGIER, Todd	5-11	180	L	Chicago Heights, MI	10/12/65	Washington
LONGO, Chris	5-10	180	R	Belleville, Ont.	1/5/72	Portland (AHL)
MILLER, Kelly	5-11	197	L	Lansing, MI	3/3/63	Washington
NELSON, Jeff	6-0	180	L	Prince Albert, Sask.	12/18/72	Portland (AHL)
PEAKE, Pat	6-0	195	R	Rochester, MI	5/28/73	Washington-Portland (AHL)
PEARSON, Rob	6-3	198	R	Oshawa, Ont.	3/8/71	Toronto
PIVONKA, Michal	6-2	198	L	Kladno, USSR	1/28/66	Washington
POIRIER, Joel	6-1	190	L	Richmond Hill, Ont.	1/15/75	Sudbury-Windsor
POULIN, Dave	5-11	190	L	Timmins, Ont.	12/17/58	Washington
USTORF, Stefan	5-11	190	L	Kaufbeuren, Germany	1/3/74	Kaufbeuren
VARGA, John	5-9	172	L	Chicago, IL	1/31/74	Tacoma
DEFENSEMEN						
BAUMGARTNER, Nolan	6-1	187	R	Calgary, Alta.	3/23/76	Kamloops
BOILEAU, Patrick	6-0	184	R	Montreal, Que.	2/22/75	Laval
COTE, Sylvain	5-11	185	R	Quebec City, Que.	1/19/66	Washington
GONCHAR, Sergei	6-2	212	L	Chelyabinsk, USSR	4/13/74	Moscow D'amo-Portland (AHL)
HATCHER, Kevin	6-4	225	R	Detroit, MI	9/9/66	Washington
JEAN, Yanick	6-1	198	L	Alma, Que.	11/26/75	Chicoutimi
JOHANSSON, Calle	5-11	205	L	Goteborg, Sweden	2/14/67	Washington
JOHNSON, Jim	6-1	190	L	New Hope, MN	8/9/62	Dallas-Washington
KLEE, Ken	6-1	200	R	Indianapolis, IN	4/24/71	Portland (AHL)
MEKESHKIN, Dmitri	6-1	174	L	Izhevsk, USSR	1/29/76	Avangard Omsk
NELSON, Todd	6-0	201	L	Prince Albert, Sask.	5/11/69	Washington-Portland (AHL)
REEKIE, Joe	6-3	215	L	Victoria, B.C.	2/22/65	Tampa Bay-Washington
SLANEY, John	6-0	185	L	St. John's, Nfld.	2/7/72	Washington-Portland (AHL)
TERTYSHNY, Sergei	6-0	187	L	Chelyabinsk, USSR	6/3/70	Chelyabinsk
WITT, Brendan	6-1	205	L	Humbolt, Sask.	2/20/75	Seattle
WOOLLEY, Jason	6-0	186	L	Toronto, Ont.	7/27/69	Washington-Portland (AHL)

GOALTENDERS	HT	WT	C	Place of Birth	Date	1993-94 Club
BEAUPRE, Don	5-10	172	L	Waterloo, Ont.	9/19/61	Washington
DAFOE, Byron	5-11	175	L	Sussex, England	2/25/71	Washington-Portland (AHL)
DERKSEN, Duane	6-1	180	L	St. Boniface, Man.	7/7/68	Rochester-Adirondack-Milwaukee
KOLZIG, Olaf	6-3	205	L	Johannesburg, South Africa	4/9/70	Washington-Portland (AHL)
TABARACCI, Rick	5-11	179	L	Toronto, Ont.	1/2/69	Washington-Portland (AHL)

General Manager

POILE, DAVID
Vice-President and General Manager, Washington Capitals.
Born in Toronto, Ont., February 14, 1949.

Thirteen years and 500 wins ago, the Washington Capitals were a struggling franchise that had never made the playoffs. Today, the franchise can look back on twelve consecutive playoff appearances as one of the NHL's most successful clubs. Washington has recorded a 500-367-104 mark in the David Poile era, fifth among all NHL teams in that span.

Poile became the Capitals general manager on August 30, 1982, and immediately turned the team into a perennial contender. In his initial season, the Capitals made the playoffs for the first time in club history, and had their first winning season. He was named *The Sporting News* executive of the year following that season, and again after the 1984-85 season. He was named *Inside Hockey* man of the year in 1992 after leading the team to a 45-27-8 mark, and championing the instant replay rule. Poile, a graduate of Northeastern University, began his professional hockey management career as an administrative assistant with the Atlanta Flames organization, where he served until joining the Washington franchise.

General Managers' History

Milt Schmidt, 1974-75 to 1975-76; Max McNab, 1976-77 to 1980-81; Roger Crozier, 1981-82; David Poile, 1982-83 to date.

Captains' History

Doug Mohns, 1974-75; Bill Clement and Yvon Labre, 1975-76; Yvon Labre, 1976-77, 1977-78; Guy Charron, 1978-79; Ryan Walter, 1979-80 to 1981-82; Rod Langway, 1982-83 to 1991-92; Rod Langway and Kevin Hatcher, 1992-93; Kevin Hatcher, 1993-94 to date.

1993-94 Scoring

* – rookie

Regular Season

Pos	#	Player	Team	GP	G	A	Pts	+/–	PIM	PP	SH	GW	GT	S	%
C	90	Joe Juneau	BOS	63	14	58	72	11	35	4	0	2	1	142	9.9
			WSH	11	5	8	13	0	6	2	0	0	0	22	22.7
			TOTAL	74	19	66	85	11	41	6	0	2	1	164	11.6
C	17	Mike Ridley	WSH	81	26	44	70	15	24	10	2	4	3	144	18.1
C	8	Dimitri Khristich	WSH	83	29	29	58	2–	73	10	0	4	1	195	14.9
D	3	Sylvain Cote	WSH	84	16	35	51	30	66	3	2	2	0	212	7.5
C	20	Michal Pivonka	WSH	82	14	36	50	2	38	5	0	4	0	138	10.1
R	12	Peter Bondra	WSH	69	24	19	43	22	40	4	0	2	0	200	12.0
L	18	Randy Burridge	WSH	78	25	17	42	1–	73	8	1	5	0	150	16.7
D	6	Calle Johansson	WSH	84	9	33	42	3	59	4	0	1	0	141	6.4
D	4	Kevin Hatcher	WSH	72	16	24	40	13–	108	6	0	3	0	217	7.4
L	10	Kelly Miller	WSH	84	14	25	39	8	32	0	1	3	0	138	10.1
C	32	Dale Hunter	WSH	52	9	29	38	4–	131	1	0	1	0	61	14.8
R	26	Keith Jones	WSH	68	16	19	35	4	149	5	0	1	0	97	16.5
L	21	Todd Krygier	WSH	66	12	18	30	4–	60	0	1	3	0	146	8.2
C	14	* Pat Peake	WSH	49	11	18	29	1	39	3	0	1	1	91	12.1
C	22	Steve Konowalchuk	WSH	62	12	14	26	9	33	0	0	0	0	63	19.0
C	9	Dave Poulin	WSH	63	6	19	25	1–	52	0	1	0	0	64	9.4
D	29	Joe Reekie	T.B.	73	1	11	12	8	127	0	0	0	0	88	1.1
			WSH	12	0	5	5	7	29	0	0	0	0	10	.0
			TOTAL	85	1	16	17	15	156	0	0	0	0	98	1.0
D	28	* John Slaney	WSH	47	7	9	16	3	27	3	0	1	0	70	10.0
L	27	Craig Berube	WSH	84	7	7	14	4–	305	0	0	0	0	48	14.6
R	11	Tim Bergland	T.B.	51	6	5	11	14–	6	0	0	0	0	61	9.8
			WSH	3	0	0	0	1–	4	0	0	0	0	4	.0
			TOTAL	54	6	5	11	15–	10	0	0	0	0	65	9.2
D	36	Shawn Anderson	WSH	50	0	9	9	1–	12	0	0	0	0	31	.0
D	2	Jim Johnson	DAL	53	0	7	7	6–	51	0	0	0	0	44	.0
			WSH	8	0	0	0	1–	12	0	0	0	0	5	.0
			TOTAL	61	0	7	7	7–	63	0	0	0	0	49	.0
C	23	* Kevin Kaminski	WSH	13	0	5	5	2	87	0	0	0	0	9	.0
D	25	Jason Woolley	WSH	10	1	2	3	2	4	0	0	0	0	15	6.7
D	40	* Todd Nelson	WSH	2	1	0	1	1	2	1	0	1	0	1	100.0
D	38	Brian Curran	WSH	26	1	0	1	2–	61	0	0	0	0	11	9.1
C	41	* Jason Allison	WSH	2	0	1	1	1	0	0	0	0	0	5	.0
G	33	Don Beaupre	WSH	53	0	1	1	0	16	0	0	0	0	0	.0
G	35	* Byron Dafoe	WSH	5	0	0	0	0	0	0	0	0	0	0	.0
G	37	* Olaf Kolzig	WSH	7	0	0	0	0	0	0	0	0	0	0	.0
G	31	Rick Tabaracci	WSH	32	0	0	0	0	6	0	0	0	0	0	.0

Goaltending

No.	Goaltender	GPI	Mins	Avg	W	L	T	EN	SO	GA	SA	S%
33	Don Beaupre	53	2853	2.84	24	16	8	3	2	135	1122	.880
31	Rick Tabaracci	32	1770	3.08	13	14	2	0	2	91	817	.889
35	* Byron Dafoe	5	230	3.39	2	2	0	0	0	13	101	.871
37	* Olaf Kolzig	7	224	5.36	0	3	0	1	0	20	128	.844
	Totals	**84**	**5099**	**3.09**	**39**	**35**	**10**	**4**	**4**	**263**	**2172**	**.879**

Playoffs

Pos	#	Player	Team	GP	G	A	Pts	+/–	PIM	PP	SH	GW	GT	S	%
C	17	Mike Ridley	WSH	11	4	6	10	7	6	0	0	0	0	17	23.5
C	90	Joe Juneau	WSH	11	4	5	9	2–	6	2	0	1	0	25	16.0
L	10	Kelly Miller	WSH	11	2	7	9	3	0	1	1	0	0	11	18.2
D	3	Sylvain Cote	WSH	9	1	8	9	3	6	0	0	0	0	30	3.3
C	20	Michal Pivonka	WSH	7	4	4	8	0	4	1	0	0	0	16	25.0
D	4	Kevin Hatcher	WSH	11	3	4	7	2–	37	0	1	0	0	40	7.5
R	12	Peter Bondra	WSH	9	2	4	6	2	4	0	0	1	0	26	7.7
C	8	Dimitri Khristich	WSH	11	2	3	5	0	10	0	0	0	0	14	14.3
C	9	Dave Poulin	WSH	11	2	2	4	3–	19	0	0	0	0	13	15.4
D	6	Calle Johansson	WSH	6	1	3	4	4	4	0	0	1	0	12	8.3
D	29	Joe Reekie	WSH	11	2	1	3	1	29	0	1	1	0	11	18.2
C	32	Dale Hunter	WSH	7	0	3	3	2–	14	0	0	0	0	7	.0
L	21	Todd Krygier	WSH	5	2	0	2	2–	10	0	0	0	0	6	33.3
D	28	* John Slaney	WSH	11	1	1	2	1–	2	1	0	0	0	16	6.3
L	18	Randy Burridge	WSH	11	0	2	2	3–	12	0	0	0	0	11	.0
D	25	Jason Woolley	WSH	4	1	0	1	0	4	0	0	1	0	2	50.0
D	36	Shawn Anderson	WSH	8	1	0	1	1–	12	0	0	0	0	9	11.1
C	14	* Pat Peake	WSH	8	0	1	1	2–	8	0	0	0	0	8	.0
R	26	Keith Jones	WSH	11	0	1	1	1	36	0	0	0	0	14	.0
C	22	Steve Konowalchuk	WSH	11	0	1	1	1–	10	0	0	0	0	6	.0
G	31	Rick Tabaracci	WSH	2	0	0	0	0	0	0	0	0	0	0	.0
G	35	* Byron Dafoe	WSH	2	0	0	0	0	0	0	0	0	0	0	.0
D	40	* Todd Nelson	WSH	4	0	0	0	1–	0	0	0	0	0	0	.0
G	33	Don Beaupre	WSH	8	0	0	0	0	2	0	0	0	0	0	.0
L	27	Craig Berube	WSH	8	0	0	0	1–	21	0	0	0	0	0	.0

Goaltending

No.	Goaltender	GPI	Mins	Avg	W	L	EN	SO	GA	SA	S%
35	* Byron Dafoe	2	118	2.54	0	2	0	0	5	39	.872
33	Don Beaupre	8	429	2.94	5	2	0	1	21	191	.890
31	Rick Tabaracci	2	111	3.24	0	2	0	0	6	50	.880
	Totals	**11**	**660**	**2.91**	**5**	**6**	**0**	**1**	**32**	**280**	**.886**

Retired Numbers

7 Yvon Labre 1973-1981

Club Records

Team

(Figures in brackets for season records are games played)

Most Points	107	1985-86 (80)
Most Wins	50	1985-86 (80)
Most Ties	18	1980-81 (80)
Most Losses	67	1974-75 (80)
Most Goals	330	1991-92 (80)
Most Goals Against	*446	1974-75 (80)
Fewest Points	*21	1974-75 (80)
Fewest Wins	*8	1974-75 (80)
Fewest Ties	5	1974-75 (80)
		1983-84 (80)
Fewest Losses	23	1985-86 (80)
Fewest Goals	181	1974-75 (80)
Fewest Goals Against	226	1983-84 (80)

Longest Winning Streak

Over-all	10	Jan. 27- Feb. 18/84
Home	8	Feb. 1- Mar. 11/86 Mar. 3- April 1/89
Away	6	Feb. 26- Apr. 1/84

Longest Undefeated Streak

Over-all	14	Nov. 24- Dec. 23/82 (9 wins, 5 ties)
Home	13	Nov. 25/92- Feb. 2/93 (9 wins, 4 ties)
Away	10	Nov. 24/82- Jan. 8/83 (6 wins, 4 ties)

Longest Losing Streak

Over-all	*17	Feb. 18- Mar. 26/75
Home	*11	Feb. 18- Mar. 30/75
Away	37	Oct. 9/74- Mar. 26/75

Longest Winless Streak

Over-all	25	Nov. 29/75- Jan. 21/76 (22 losses, 3 ties)
Home	14	Dec. 3/75- Jan. 21/76 (11 losses, 3 ties)
Away	37	Oct. 9/74- Mar. 26/75 (37 losses)

Most Shutouts, Season	8	1983-84 (80)
Most PIM, Season	2,204	1989-90 (80)
Most Goals, Game	12	Feb. 6/90 (Que. 2 at Wash. 12)

Individual

Most Seasons	11	Rod Langway
Most Games	758	Mike Gartner
Most Goals, Career	397	Mike Gartner
Most Assists, Career	392	Mike Gartner
Most Points, Career	789	Mike Gartner (397 goals, 392 assists)
Most PIM, Career	1,630	Scott Stevens
Most Shutouts, Career	12	Don Beaupre
Longest Consecutive Games Streak	422	Bob Carpenter
Most Goals, Season	60	Dennis Maruk (1981-82)
Most Assists, Season	76	Dennis Maruk (1981-82)
Most Points, Season	136	Dennis Maruk (1981-82) (60 goals, 76 assists)
Most PIM, Season	339	Alan May (1989-90)
Most Points, Defenseman, Season	81	Larry Murphy (1986-87) (23 goals, 58 assists)
Most Points, Center, Season	136	Dennis Maruk (1981-82) (60 goals, 76 assists)
Most Points, Right Wing, Season	102	Mike Gartner (1984-85) (50 goals, 52 assists)
Most Points, Left Wing, Season	87	Ryan Walter (1981-82) (38 goals, 49 assists)
Most Points, Rookie, Season	67	Bobby Carpenter (1981-82) (32 goals, 35 assists) Chris Valentine (1981-82) (30 goals, 37 assists)
Most Shutouts, Season	5	Don Beaupre (1990-91)
Most Goals, Game	5	Bengt Gustafsson (Jan. 8/84) Peter Bondra (Feb. 5/94)
Most Assists, Game	6	Mike Ridley (Jan. 7/89)
Most Points, Game	7	Dino Ciccarelli (Mar. 18/89)

* NHL Record.

All-time Record vs. Other Clubs

Regular Season

	At Home						On Road						Total					
	GP	W	L	T	GF	GA	PTS	GP	W	L	T	GF	GA	PTS	GP	W	L	T	GF	GA	PTS
Anaheim	1	1	0		3	0	2	1	1	0	0	5	2	2	2	2	0	0	8	2	4
Boston	36	9	19	8	110	140	26	36	9	23	4	103	156	22	72	18	42	12	213	296	48
Buffalo	36	8	21	7	102	146	23	37	6	27	4	98	165	16	73	14	48	11	200	311	39
Calgary	33	15	13	5	127	121	35	32	6	22	4	77	140	16	65	21	35	9	204	261	51
Chicago	33	19	10	4	127	102	42	32	7	20	5	97	134	19	65	26	30	9	224	236	61
Dallas	33	13	13	7	106	105	33	32	10	14	8	94	122	28	65	23	27	15	200	227	61
Detroit	38	20	14	4	152	120	44	40	13	16	11	118	142	37	78	33	30	15	270	262	81
Edmonton	22	12	8	2	96	81	26	22	9	9	4	78	88	22	44	21	17	6	174	169	48
Florida	2	1	0	1	7	5	3	3	1	2	0	6	10	2	5	2	2	1	13	15	5
Hartford	24	14	9	1	84	73	29	25	13	9	3	96	80	29	49	27	18	4	180	153	58
Los Angeles	38	17	15	6	166	140	40	39	12	23	4	123	159	28	77	29	38	10	289	299	68
Montreal	40	15	18	7	104	136	37	40	7	27	6	83	181	20	80	22	45	13	187	317	57
New Jersey	57	40	14	3	254	173	83	56	27	23	6	182	180	60	113	67	37	9	436	353	143
NY Islanders	59	23	27	9	184	199	55	59	21	37	1	184	245	43	118	44	64	10	368	444	98
NY Rangers	61	29	24	8	237	210	66	60	24	30	6	217	246	54	121	53	54	14	454	456	120
Ottawa	4	4	0	0	30	11	8	4	3	1	0	21	15	6	8	7	1	0	51	26	14
Philadelphia	58	22	26	10	208	210	54	61	22	35	4	177	233	48	119	44	61	14	385	443	102
Pittsburgh	66	34	26	6	291	250	74	63	25	32	6	220	257	56	129	59	58	12	511	509	130
Quebec	24	12	9	3	97	80	27	24	12	8	4	98	77	28	48	24	17	7	195	157	55
St. Louis	32	17	12	3	118	98	37	33	11	14	8	111	139	30	65	28	26	11	229	237	67
San Jose	3	2	1	0	12	7	4	3	3	0	0	12	7	6	6	5	1	0	24	14	10
Tampa Bay	4	1	1	2	16	14	4	3	3	0	0	12	4	6	7	4	1	2	28	18	10
Toronto	35	21	12	2	132	96	44	34	11	19	4	122	164	26	69	32	31	6	254	260	70
Vancouver	33	18	11	4	111	103	40	32	13	15	4	103	109	30	65	31	26	8	214	212	70
Winnipeg	22	15	5	2	104	70	32	23	6	12	5	83	90	17	45	21	17	7	187	160	49
Defunct Clubs	10	2	8	0	28	42	4	10	4	5	1	30	39	9	20	6	13	1	58	81	13
Totals	**804**	**384**	**316**	**104**	**3006**	**2734**	**872**	**804**	**279**	**423**	**102**	**2550**	**3184**	**660**	**1608**	**663**	**739**	**206**	**5556**	**5918**	**1532**

Calgary totals include Atlanta, 1974-75 to 1979-80. Dallas totals include Minnesota, 1974-75 to 1992-93.
New Jersey totals include Kansas City, 1974-75 to 1975-76, and Colorado, 1976-77 to 1981-82.

Playoffs

	Series	W	L	GP	W	L	T	GF	GA	Last Mtg.	Round	Result
Boston	1	0	1	4	0	4	0	6	15	1990	CF	L 0-4
New Jersey	2	1	1	13	7	6	0	44	43	1990	DSF	W 4-2
NY Islanders	6	1	5	30	12	18	0	88	89	1993	DSF	L 2-4
NY Rangers	4	3	1	22	11	11	0	75	71	1994	CSF	L 1-4
Philadelphia	3	2	1	16	9	7	0	65	55	1989	DSF	L 2-4
Pittsburgh	3	1	2	18	8	10	0	60	56	1994	CQF	W 4-2
Totals	**19**	**7**	**12**	**103**	**47**	**56**	**0**	**338**	**339**			

Playoff Results 1994-90

Year	Round	Opponent	Result	GF	GA
1994	CSF	NY Rangers	L 1-4	12	20
	CQF	Pittsburgh	W 4-2	20	12
1993	DSF	NY Islanders	L 2-4	22	23
1992	DSF	Pittsburgh	L 3-4	27	25
1991	DF	Pittsburgh	L 1-4	13	19
	DSF	NY Rangers	W 4-2	16	16
1990	CF	Boston	L 0-4	6	15
	DF	NY Rangers	W 4-1	22	17
	DSF	New Jersey	W 4-2	21	18

Abbreviations: Round: F – Final;
CF – conference final; **CQF** – conference quarter-final;
CSF – conference semi-final; **DF** – division final;
DSF – division semi-final; **SF** – semi-final;
QF – quarter-final; **PR** – preliminary round.

1993-94 Results

Oct.	6	at	Winnipeg	4-6	14		New Jersey	2-5
	8		New Jersey	3-6	15	at	Quebec	4-0
	9	at	New Jersey	4-6	17	at	Montreal	1-3
	11	at	NY Rangers	2-5	19	at	Florida	1-5
	13	at	Toronto	1-7	25		Boston	1-3
	15		Philadelphia	0-3	27	at	Buffalo	2-7
	16		Buffalo	4-3	29	at	Philadelphia	4-2
	22		Los Angeles	6-3	30		Detroit	6-3
	24	at	Edmonton	3-2	Feb. 2	at	Philadelphia	5-2
	25	at	Calgary	2-3	4		Montreal	0-4
	27	at	Vancouver	4-2	5		Tampa Bay	6-3
	29	at	Anaheim	5-2	7	at	NY Rangers	4-1
	30	at	San Jose	4-2	10	at	St. Louis	4-3
Nov.	5		Vancouver	3-2	12	at	Los Angeles	6-1
	9		Quebec	2-1	15		Edmonton	2-2
	11	at	Tampa Bay	4-1	18		NY Islanders	3-1
	13		NY Rangers	0-2	20		Buffalo	3-3
	16		San Jose	1-2	21	at	NY Islanders	0-4
	18	at	Pittsburgh	2-3	24	at	Florida	2-1
	20	at	Florida	3-4	26		Florida	4-2
	24		St. Louis	5-2	27	at	Hartford	2-3
	26		Pittsburgh	4-4	Mar. 1		Tampa Bay	3-4
	28	at	NY Rangers	1-3	4		Philadelphia	3-3
	30	at	NY Islanders	4-6	6		Calgary	4-4
Dec.	3		Montreal	2-2	7	at	Boston	3-6
	4	at	Ottawa	6-1	9		NY Rangers	5-7
	7		Hartford	1-6	12		Quebec	3-4
	9	at	Philadelphia	4-2	15	at	Pittsburgh	5-4
	11	at	Montreal	5-3	18	at	Dallas	2-6
	13	at	Quebec	3-5	20	at	Tampa Bay	3-0
	17		Ottawa	11-2	22		Hartford	4-1
	18	at	Hartford	1-4	25	at	Detroit	2-2
	21	at	Philadelphia	4-1	27		Boston	4-6
	23		NY Rangers	0-1	29		NY Islanders	2-2
	26		Pittsburgh	7-3	31	at	Chicago	6-3
	28		Florida	3-3	Apr. 1		New Jersey	2-1
	30		Anaheim	3-0	3		Dallas	3-6
Jan.	1		Tampa Bay	5-5	5		NY Islanders	3-4
	2	at	Boston	2-8	6	at	Ottawa	5-6
	8		Chicago	4-1	9		Ottawa	8-4
	9	at	New Jersey	4-0	12		Winnipeg	4-3
	11		Toronto	1-2	14	at	Buffalo	3-2

Entry Draft
Selections 1994-80

1994
Pick
10 Nolan Baumgartner
15 Alexander Kharlamov
41 Scott Cherrey
93 Matthew Herr
119 Yanick Jean
145 Dmitri Mekeshkin
171 Daniel Reja
197 Chris Patrick
223 John Tuohy
249 Richard Zednik
275 Sergei Tertyshny

1993
Pick
11 Brendan Witt
17 Jason Allison
69 Patrick Boileau
147 Frank Banham
173 Daniel Hendrickson
174 Andrew Brunette
199 Joel Poirier
225 Jason Gladney
251 Mark Seliger
277 Dany Bousquet

1992
Pick
14 Sergei Gonchar
32 Jim Carey
53 Stefan Ustorf
71 Martin Gendron
119 John Varga
167 Mark Matier
191 Mike Mathers
215 Brian Stagg
239 Gregory Callahan
263 Billy Jo MacPherson

1991
Pick
14 Pat Peake
21 Trevor Halverson
25 Eric Lavigne
36 Jeff Nelson
58 Steve Konowalchuk
80 Justin Morrison
146 Dave Morissette
168 Rick Corriveau
190 Trevor Duhaime
209 Rob Leask
212 Carl LeBlanc
234 Rob Puchniak
256 Bill Kovacs

1990
Pick
9 John Slaney
30 Rod Pasma
51 Chris Longo
72 Randy Pearce
93 Brian Sakic
94 Mark Ouimet
114 Andrei Kovalev
135 Roman Kontsek
156 Peter Bondra
159 Steve Martell
177 Ken Klee
198 Michael Boback
219 Alan Brown
240 Todd Hlushko

1989
Pick
19 Olaf Kolzig
35 Byron Dafoe
59 Jim Mathieson
61 Jason Woolley
82 Trent Klatt
145 Dave Lorentz
166 Dean Holoien
187 Victor Gervais
208 Jiri Vykoukal
229 Andrei Sidorov
250 Ken House

1988
Pick
15 Reginald Savage
36 Tim Taylor
41 Wade Bartley
57 Duane Derksen
78 Rob Krauss
120 Dmitri Khristich
141 Keith Jones
144 Brad Schlegel
162 Todd Hilditch
183 Petr Pavlas
192 Mark Sorensen
204 Claudio Scremin
225 Chris Venkus
246 Ron Pascucci

1987
Pick
36 Jeff Ballantyne
57 Steve Maltais
78 Tyler Larter
99 Pat Beauchesne
120 Rich Defreitas
141 Devon Oleniuk
162 Thomas Sjogren
204 Chris Clarke
225 Milos Vanik
240 Dan Brettschneider
246 Ryan Kummu

1986
Pick
19 Jeff Greenlaw
40 Steve Seftel
60 Shawn Simpson
61 Jimmy Hrivnak
82 Erin Ginnell
103 John Purves
124 Stefan Nilsson
145 Peter Choma
166 Lee Davidson
187 Tero Toivola
208 Bobby Bobcock
229 John Schratz
250 Scott McCrory

1985
Pick
19 Yvon Corriveau
40 John Druce
61 Rob Murray
82 Bill Houlder
83 Larry Shaw
103 Claude Dumas
124 Doug Stromback
145 Jamie Nadjiwan
166 Mark Haarmann
187 Steve Hollett
208 Dallas Eakins
229 Steve Hrynewich
250 Frank DiMuzio

1984
Pick
17 Kevin Hatcher
34 Steve Leach
59 Michal Pivonka
80 Kris King
122 Vito Cramarossa
143 Timo Iljina
164 Frank Joo
185 Jim Thomson
205 Paul Cavallini
225 Mikhail Tatarinov
246 Per Schedrin

1983
Pick
75 Tim Bergland
95 Martin Bouliane
135 Dwaine Hutton
155 Marty Abrams
175 David Cowan
195 Yves Beaudoin
215 Alain Raymond
216 Anders Huss

1982
Pick
5 Scott Stevens
58 Milan Novy
89 Dean Evason
110 Ed Kastelic
152 Wally Schreiber
173 Jamie Reeve
194 Juha Nurmi
215 Wayne Prestage
236 Jon Holden
247 Marco Kallas

1981
Pick
3 Bob Carpenter
45 Eric Calder
68 Tony Kellin
89 Mike Siltala
91 Peter Sidorkiewicz
110 Jim McGeough
131 Risto Jalo
152 Gaetan Duchesne
173 George White
194 Chris Valentine

1980
Pick
5 Darren Veitch
47 Dan Miele
55 Torrie Robertson
89 Timo Blomqvist
110 Todd Bidner
131 Frank Perkins
152 Bruce Raboin
173 Peter Andersson
194 Tony Camazzola

Coach

SCHOENFELD, JAMES GRANT (JIM)
Coach, Washington Capitals. Born in Galt, Ont., September 4, 1952.

Jim Schoenfeld was named the tenth head coach of the Washington Capitals on January 27, 1994. Under his leadership, the Capitals recorded a 19-12-6 record, finishing seventh in the Conference. Prior to joining the Capitals, Schoenfeld had coached the Buffalo Sabres (1985-86) and the New Jersey Devils (1988-90).

The 42-year old native of Galt, Ontario began his coaching career in 1984-85 by leading the AHL's Rochester Americans to a League record 11 straight wins to start the season. He spent 43 games behind the Sabres' bench 1985-86 and guided the New Jersey Devils to the Wales Conference Finals in 1988.

The lead analyst for ESPN's National Hockey Night for two years (1992-94), Schoenfeld spent 13 seasons in the NHL with Buffalo, Detroit and Boston.

Coaching Record

Season	Team	Games	W	L	T	%	Games	W	L	%
1984-85	Rochester (AHL)	25	17	6	2	.720	....	....	....	....
1985-86	**Buffalo (NHL)**	43	19	19	5	.500	....	....	....	....
1987-88	New Jersey (NHL)	30	17	12	1	.583	20	11	9	.550
1988-89	New Jersey (NHL)	80	27	41	12	.413	....	....	....	....
1989-90	New Jersey (NHL)	14	6	6	2	.500	....	....	....	....
1993-94	Washington (NHL)	37	19	12	6	.595	11	5	6	.455
	NHL Totals	204	88	90	26	.495	31	16	15	.516

Coaching History

Jim Anderson, George Sullivan and Milt Schmidt, 1974-75; Milt Schmidt and Tom McVie, 1975-76; Tom McVie, 1976-77 to 1977-78; Danny Belisle, 1978-79; Danny Belisle and Gary Green, 1979-80; Gary Green, 1980-81; Gary Green and Bryan Murray, 1981-82; Bryan Murray, 1982-83 to 1988-89; Bryan Murray and Terry Murray, 1989-90; Terry Murray, 1990-91 to 1992-93; Terry Murray and Jim Schoenfeld, 1993-94; Jim Schoenfeld, 1994-95.

Club Directory

U.S. Air Arena
1 Harry S Truman Drive
Landover, Maryland 20785
Phone **301/386-7000**
PR FAX 301/386-7012
Capacity: 18,130

Board of Directors
David P. Bindeman, Stuart L. Bindeman, James A. Cafritz, A. James Clark, Albert Cohen, J. Martin Irving, R. Robert Linowes, Arthur K. Mason, Dr. Jack Meshel, David M. Osnos, Richard M. Patrick

Management
Chairman . . . . Abe Pollin
President and Governor . . . . Richard M. Patrick
Legal Counsel and Alternate Governors . . . . David M. Osnos, Peter O'Malley
Vice-President of Finance . . . . Edmund Stelzer

Hockey Department
Vice-President, G.M. and Alternate Governor . . . . . . David Poile
Director of Player Personnel . . . . Jack Button
Head Coach . . . . Jim Schoenfeld
Assistant Coaches . . . . Keith Allain, Tod Button
Head Coach, Portland Pirates . . . . Barry Trotz
Assistant Coach, Portland Pirates . . . . Paul Gardner
Admin. Assistant to the V.P. and G.M. . . . . Pat Young
Assistant to the Hockey Department . . . . Todd Warren
Piney Orchard Staff . . . . Alex Walker
Chief Eastern Scout . . . . Hugh Rogers
Chief Western Scout . . . . Craig Channell
Chief Quebec Scout . . . . Gilles Cote
Scouts . . . . Fred Devereaux, Eje Johansson, Bud Quinn, Bob Schmidt, Shawn Simpson, Dan Sylvester, Niklas Wikegard, Darryl Young

Medical and Training Staff
Head Trainer . . . . Stan Wong
Assistant Trainer/Head Equipment Manager . . . . . . Doug Shearer
Assistant Equipment Manager . . . . Craig Leydig
Assistant to the Equipment Manager . . . . Rick Harper
Strength and Conditioning Coach . . . . Frank Costello
Massage Therapist . . . . Curt Millar
Team Nutritionist . . . . Pat Mann
Team Physicians . . . . Dr. Richard Grossman, Dr. Stephen Haas, Dr. Carl MacCartee, Dr. Frank Melograna
Team Ophthamologist . . . . Dr. Michael Herr
Team Dentist . . . . Dr. Howard Salob

Communications Department
Vice President of Communications . . . . Ed Quinlan
Director of Community Relations . . . . Yvon Labre
Communications Manager . . . . Dan Kaufman
Assistant Director of Community Relations . . . . Gary Bingham
Communications Assistant . . . . Rick Braunstein
Admin. Assistant to Communications Dept. . . . . . . Julie Hensley

Accounting Department
Controller . . . . Aggie Ballard
Accounting Assistants . . . . Kathleen Brady, Crystal Coffren, Deborah Kostakos, Melanie Loveless

Marketing and Sales Department
Vice-President of Marketing . . . . Lew Strudler
Assistant Director of Marketing . . . . Debi Angus
Director of Promotions and Advertising . . . . Charles Copeland
Director of Season Subscriptions . . . . Joanne Kowalski
Ticket Operations . . . . Kerry Gregg
Sponsorship Sales Manager . . . . Don Gore
Merchandising Coordinator . . . . Kim Moyer
Assistant Merchandising Coordinator . . . . Amy Hobbs
Game Presentation Coordinator . . . . Gina Hoagland
Admin. Assistant to the V.P. of Marketing . . . . Janice Toepper
Administrative Assistant to Marketing . . . . Kathy Moriarty
Receptionist . . . . Nancy Woodall

Director of Sales . . . . Jerry Murphy
Regional Sales Managers . . . . Scott Bershadsky, Darren Bruening, Bryan Maust, John Oakes, Sherri Petti, Ron Potter
Corporate Sales Managers . . . . David Abrutyn, Annemarie Henning
Sales Representatives . . . . Ben Bouma, Tim Bronaugh, Todd Freundlich, Steve Salm, Scott Tippins, Brian Walsh
Admin. Assistants to the Sales Department . . . . . . Shelly Finkel, Tonya Turner

Winnipeg Jets

1993-94 Results: 24W-51L-9T 57PTS. Sixth, Central Division

Schedule

Oct.	Sat.	1	at Ottawa
	Wed.	5	Montreal
	Fri.	7	Edmonton
	Tues.	11	at Dallas
	Thur.	13	at Chicago
	Fri.	14	Philadelphia
	Sun.	16	San Jose
	Tues.	18	at Calgary
	Wed.	19	Dallas
	Sat.	22	Chicago
	Sun.	23	Anaheim
	Thur.	27	Washington
	Sat.	29	at Hartford
	Sun.	30	at New Jersey
Nov.	Wed.	2	Toronto
	Fri.	4	at Dallas
	Sat.	5	at St. Louis
	Tues.	8	at Detroit
	Thur.	10	St. Louis
	Sat.	12	Chicago
	Mon.	14	Edmonton
	Wed.	16	at Toronto
	Fri.	18	at Tampa Bay
	Sat.	19	at Florida
	Wed.	23	Toronto
	Fri.	25	NY Rangers
	Mon.	28	at St. Louis
	Wed.	30	at Edmonton
Dec.	Sat.	3	at Vancouver
	Wed.	7	New Jersey
	Sat.	10	Vancouver
	Tues.	13	at Washington
	Thur.	15	at Philadelphia
	Sat.	17	at Detroit*
	Sun.	18	Detroit
	Wed.	21	Anaheim
	Tues.	27	Calgary
	Thur.	29	Boston
	Sat.	31	Los Angeles*
Jan.	Mon.	2	Edmonton
			(in Saskatoon)
	Thur.	5	Ottawa
	Sat.	7	at Dallas

	Sun.	8	at St. Louis
	Tues.	10	at Toronto
	Thur.	12	at Boston
	Fri.	13	at Detroit
	Sun.	15	Tampa Bay
	Tues.	18	St. Louis
	Wed.	18	at Calgary
	Wed.	25	at San Jose
	Fri.	27	at Anaheim
	Sat.	28	at Los Angeles
	Tues.	31	at Los Angeles
			(in Phoenix)
Feb.	Thur.	2	Pittsburgh
	Sat.	4	Hartford
	Mon.	6	at NY Rangers
	Tues.	7	at NY Islanders
	Fri.	10	at Edmonton
	Sat.	11	at Vancouver
	Wed.	15	Calgary
	Fri.	17	Dallas
	Sun.	19	at Chicago*
	Mon.	20	at Buffalo
	Wed.	22	Vancouver
	Fri.	24	Detroit
Mar.	Thur.	2	Quebec
	Sat.	4	St. Louis*
	Tues.	7	at Chicago
	Wed.	8	Dallas
	Fri.	10	Buffalo
	Sat.	11	Los Angeles
	Mon.	13	at Pittsburgh
	Wed.	15	at Montreal
	Thur.	16	at Quebec
	Sun.	19	San Jose*
	Wed.	22	Detroit
	Fri.	24	at Toronto
	Sat.	25	Toronto
	Tues.	28	at San Jose
	Wed.	29	at Anaheim
Apr.	Sat.	1	at Los Angeles
	Wed.	5	Chicago
	Fri.	7	Florida
	Sun.	9	NY Islanders*

* Denotes afternoon game.

Home Starting Times:

Weeknights	....	7:30 p.m.
Saturdays and Sundays	....	6:30 p.m.
Matinees	....	2:00 p.m.
Except Sat. Dec. 31	....	4:30 p.m.
Sun. Mar. 19	....	1:00 p.m.

Franchise date: June 22, 1979

CENTRAL
DIVISION

16th
NHL
Season

Veteran Thomas Steen is the first European-trained player since Borje Salming to spend 13 NHL seasons with one team.

Year-by-Year Record

		Home			Road			Overall							
Season	GP	W	L	T	W	L	T	W	L	T	GF	GA	Pts.	Finished	Playoff Result
1993-94	84	15	23	4	9	28	5	24	51	9	245	344	57	6th, Central Div.	Out of Playoffs
1992-93	84	23	16	3	17	21	4	40	37	7	322	320	87	4th, Smythe Div.	Lost Div. Semi-Final
1991-92	80	20	14	6	13	18	9	33	32	15	251	244	81	4th, Smythe Div.	Lost Div. Semi-Final
1990-91	80	17	18	5	9	25	6	26	43	11	260	288	63	5th, Smythe Div.	Out of Playoffs
1989-90	80	22	13	5	15	19	6	37	32	11	298	290	85	3rd, Smythe Div.	Lost Div. Semi-Final
1988-89	80	17	18	5	9	24	7	26	42	12	300	355	64	5th, Smythe Div.	Out of Playoffs
1987-88	80	20	14	6	13	22	5	33	36	11	292	310	77	3rd, Smythe Div.	Lost Div. Semi-Final
1986-87	80	25	12	3	15	20	5	40	32	8	279	271	88	3rd, Smythe Div.	Lost Div. Final
1985-86	80	18	19	3	8	28	4	26	47	7	295	372	59	3rd, Smythe Div.	Lost Div. Semi-Final
1984-85	80	21	13	6	22	14	4	43	27	10	358	332	96	2nd, Smythe Div.	Lost Div. Final
1983-84	80	17	15	8	14	23	3	31	38	11	340	374	73	4th, Smythe Div.	Lost Div. Semi-Final
1982-83	80	22	16	2	11	23	6	33	39	8	311	333	74	4th, Smythe Div.	Lost Div. Semi-Final
1981-82	80	18	13	9	15	20	5	33	33	14	319	332	80	2nd, Norris Div.	Lost Div. Semi-Final
1980-81	80	7	25	8	2	32	6	9	57	14	246	400	32	6th, Smythe Div.	Out of Playoffs
1979-80	80	13	19	8	7	30	3	20	49	11	214	314	51	5th, Smythe Div.	Out of Playoffs

1994-95 Player Personnel

FORWARDS	HT	WT	S	Place of Birth	Date	1993-94 Club
BORSATO, Luciano	5-11	190	R	Richmond Hill, Ont.	1/7/66	Winnipeg
COURVILLE, Larry	6-1	180	L	Timmins, Ont.	4/2/75	Newmarket-Moncton
DEAZELEY, Mark	6-4	240	L	North York, Ont.	4/8/72	Toledo-Fort Wayne
DOMI, Tie	5-10	200	R	Windsor, Ont.	11/1/69	Winnipeg
DRAKE, Dallas	6-0	180	L	Trail, B.C.	2/4/69	Detroit-Adirondack-Winnipeg
EAGLES, Mike	5-10	190	L	Sussex, N.B.	3/7/63	Winnipeg
EMERSON, Nelson	5-11	175	R	Hamilton, Ont.	8/17/67	Winnipeg
GILHEN, Randy	6-0	190	L	Zweibrucken, W. Germany	6/13/63	Florida-Winnipeg
GROSEK, Michal	6-2	180	R	Vyskov, Czech.	6/1/75	Winnipeg-Tacoma-Moncton
GUSMANOV, Ravil	6-3	185	L	Naberezhnye Chelny, USSR	7/25/72	Chelyabinsk
KENNEDY, Sheldon	5-10	175	R	Elkhorn, Man.	6/15/69	Detroit
KING, Kris	5-11	208	L	Bracebridge, Ont.	2/18/66	Winnipeg
LeBLANC, John	6-1	190	L	Campbellton, N.B.	1/21/64	Winnipeg-Moncton
MURRAY, Rob	6-1	180	R	Toronto, Ont.	4/4/67	Winnipeg-Moncton
ROMANIUK, Russell	6-0	195	L	Winnipeg, Man.	6/9/70	Cdn. National-Wpg-Moncton
SELANNE, Teemu	6-0	200	L	Helsinki, Finland	7/3/70	Winnipeg
SHANNON, Darrin	6-2	210	L	Barrie, Ont.	12/8/69	Winnipeg
STEEN, Thomas	5-11	190	L	Grums, Sweden	6/8/60	Winnipeg
TKACHUK, Keith	6-2	210	L	Melrose, MA	3/28/72	Winnipeg
VITOLINSH, Harijs	6-3	212	L	Riga, Latvia	4/30/68	Winnipeg-Moncton
ZHAMNOV, Alexei	6-1	195	L	Moscow, USSR	10/1/70	Winnipeg

DEFENSEMEN	HT	WT	S	Place of Birth	Date	1993-94 Club
BLOMSTEN, Arto	6-3	210	L	Vaasa, Finland	3/16/65	Winnipeg-Moncton
KENNEDY, Dean	6-2	208	R	Redvers, Sask.	1/18/63	Winnipeg
MANSON, Dave	6-2	202	L	Prince Albert, Sask.	1/27/67	Edmonton-Winnipeg
McBEAN, Wayne	6-2	185	L	Calgary, Alta.	2/21/69	NY Islanders-Salt Lake-Winnipeg
MIKULCHIK, Oleg	6-2	200	R	Minsk, USSR	6/27/64	Winnipeg-Moncton
MULLER, Mike	6-2	205	L	Fairview, Minn.	9/18/71	Moncton
NUMMINEN, Teppo	6-1	190	R	Tampere, Finland	7/3/68	Winnipeg
QUINT, Deron	6-1	182	L	Durham, NH	3/12/76	Seattle
QUINTAL, Stephane	6-3	215	R	Boucherville, Que.	10/22/68	Winnipeg
SHANNON, Darryl	6-2	200	L	Barrie, Ont.	6/21/68	Winnipeg-Moncton
THOMPSON, Brent	6-2	200	L	Calgary, Alta.	1/9/71	Los Angeles-Phoenix
ULANOV, Igor	6-2	205	L	Krasnokamsk, USSR	10/1/69	Winnipeg
VISHEAU, Mark	6-4	200	R	Burlington, Ont.	6/27/73	Winnipeg-Moncton
WILKINSON, Neil	6-3	190	R	Selkirk, Man.	8/15/67	Chicago

GOALTENDERS	HT	WT	C	Place of Birth	Date	1993-94 Club
BEAUREGARD, Stephane	5-11	190	R	Cowansville, Que.	1/10/68	Winnipeg-Moncton
CHEVELDAE, Tim	5-10	195	L	Melville, Sask.	2/15/68	Detroit-Adirondack-Winnipeg
GAUTHIER, Sean	5-11	202	L	Sudbury, Ont.	3/28/71	Moncton-Fort Wayne
KHABIBULIN, Nikolai	6-1	176	L	Sverdlovsk, USSR	1/13/73	CSKA-Russian Pen's
LANGKOW, Scott	5-11	190	L	Sherwood Park, Alta.	4/21/75	Portland (WHL)
O'NEILL, Mike	5-7	160	L	LaSalle, Que.	11/3/67	Winnipeg-Moncton-Fort Wayne

1993-94 Scoring

* – rookie

Regular Season

Pos	#	Player	Team	GP	G	A	Pts	+/-	PIM	PP	SH	GW	GT	S	%
L	7	Keith Tkachuk	WPG	84	41	40	81	12-	255	22	3	3	1	218	18.8
C	19	Nelson Emerson	WPG	83	33	41	74	38-	80	4	5	6	1	282	11.7
C	10	Alexei Zhamnov	WPG	61	26	45	71	20-	62	7	0	1	1	196	13.3
L	34	Darrin Shannon	WPG	77	21	37	58	18-	87	9	0	2	0	124	16.9
R	13	Teemu Selanne	WPG	51	25	29	54	23-	22	11	0	2	0	191	13.1
C	25	Thomas Steen	WPG	76	19	32	51	38-	32	6	0	1	1	137	13.9
C	18	Dallas Drake	DET	47	10	22	32	5	37	0	1	2	0	78	12.8
			WPG	15	3	5	8	6-	12	1	1	1	0	34	8.8
			TOTAL	62	13	27	40	1-	49	1	2	3	0	112	11.6
D	4	Stephane Quintal	WPG	81	8	18	26	25-	119	1	1	1	0	154	5.2
D	27	Teppo Numminen	WPG	57	5	23	28	23-	28	4	0	1	0	89	5.6
D	3	Dave Manson	EDM	57	3	13	16	4-	140	0	0	0	0	144	2.1
			WPG	13	1	4	5	10-	51	0	0	0	0	36	2.8
			TOTAL	70	4	17	21	14-	191	1	0	0	0	180	2.2
R	20	Tie Domi	WPG	81	8	11	19	8-	347	0	0	0	0	98	8.2
C	38	Luciano Borsato	WPG	75	5	13	18	11-	28	1	1	2	0	65	7.7
D	5	Igor Ulanov	WPG	74	0	17	17	11-	165	0	0	0	0	46	.0
D	6	Wayne McBean	NYI	19	1	4	5	13-	16	0	0	0	0	33	3.0
			WPG	31	2	9	11	21-	24	2	0	0	0	81	2.5
			TOTAL	50	3	13	16	34-	40	2	0	0	0	114	2.6
C	15	Randy Gilhen	FLA	20	4	4	8	1	16	0	0	0	0	52	7.7
			WPG	40	3	3	6	13-	34	0	0	0	0	43	7.0
			TOTAL	60	7	7	14	12-	50	0	0	0	0	95	7.4
L	21	Russ Romaniuk	WPG	24	4	8	12	11-	6	3	0	0	0	36	11.1
C	36	Mike Eagles	WPG	73	4	8	12	20-	96	0	1	0	0	53	7.5
L	17	Kris King	WPG	83	4	8	12	22-	205	0	0	1	0	86	4.7
R	26	Dean Kennedy	WPG	76	2	8	10	22-	164	0	0	1	0	38	5.3
R	37	John Leblanc	WPG	17	6	2	8	2-	2	1	1	1	0	29	20.7
C	11	* Dave Tomlinson	WPG	31	1	3	4	12-	24	0	0	0	0	29	3.4
D	24	Darryl Shannon	WPG	20	0	4	4	6-	18	0	0	0	0	14	.0
D	55	* Arto Blomsten	WPG	18	0	2	2	6-	6	0	0	0	0	15	.0
L	60	* Michal Grosek	WPG	3	0	1	1	1-	0	0	0	0	0	4	25.0
D	42	Oleg Mikulchik	WPG	4	0	1	1	2-	17	0	0	0	0	3	.0
G	29	Tim Cheveldae	DET	30	0	1	1	0	0	0	0	0	0	0	.0
			WPG	14	0	0	0	0	2	0	0	0	0	0	.0
			TOTAL	44	0	1	1	0	2	0	0	0	0	0	.0
D	39	* Mark Visheau	WPG	1	0	0	0	0	0	0	0	0	0	1	.0
L	23	Andy Brickley	WPG	2	0	0	0	2-	0	0	0	0	0	0	.0
C	50	* Craig Fisher	WPG	4	0	0	0	1-	2	0	0	0	0	5	.0
R	28	Kevin McClelland	WPG	6	0	0	0		19	0	0	0	0	1	.0
C	12	Rob Murray	WPG	6	0	0	0		2	0	0	0	0	1	.0
C	14	* Harijs Vitolinsh	WPG	8	0	0	0		4	0	0	0	0	7	.0
G	30	Steph Beauregard	WPG	13	0	0	0		0	0	0	0	0	0	.0
C	18	Bryan Erickson	WPG	16	0	0	0	7-	6	0	0	0	0	8	.0
G	1	* Michael O'Neill	WPG	17	0	0	0		0	0	0	0	0	0	.0

Goaltending

No.	Goaltender	GPI	Mins	Avg	W	L	T	EN	SO	GA	SA	S%
35	Bob Essensa	56	3136	3.85	19	30	6	5	1	201	1714	.883
29	Tim Cheveldae	14	788	3.96	5	8	1	0	1	52	485	.893
1	* Michael O'Neill	17	738	4.15	0	9	1	1	0	51	382	.866
30	Steph Beauregard	13	418	4.88	0	4	1	0	0	34	211	.839
	Totals	84	5098	4.05	24	51	9	6	2	344	2798	.877

Keith Tkachuk became one of the youngest team captains in NHL history when he was given the "C" by the Winnipeg Jets during the 1993-94 campaign.

General Managers' History

John Ferguson, 1979-80 to 1987-88; John Ferguson and Mike Smith, 1988-89; Mike Smith, 1989-90 to 1992-93; Mike Smith and John Paddock, 1993-94; John Paddock, 1994-95.

Coaching History

Tom McVie, 1979-80; Tom McVie and Bill Sutherland, 1980-81; Tom Watt, 1981-82 to 1982-83; Tom Watt, John Ferguson and Barry Long, 1983-84; Barry Long, 1984-85; Barry Long and John Ferguson, 1985-86. Dan Maloney, 1986-87 to 1987-88, Dan Maloney and Rick Bowness 1988-89; Bob Murdoch, 1989-90 to 1990-91; John Paddock, 1991-92 to date.

Captains' History

Lars-Erik Sjoberg, 1979-80; Morris Lukowich, 1980-81; Dave Christian, 1981-82; Dave Christian and Lucien DeBlois, 1982-83; Lucien DeBlois, 1983-84; Dale Hawerchuk, 1984-85 to 1988-89; Randy Carlyle, Dale Hawerchuk and Thomas Steen, 1989-90; Randy Carlyle and Thomas Steen, 1990-91; Troy Murray, 1991-92; Troy Murray and Dean Kennedy, 1992-93; Dean Kennedy and Keith Tkachuk, 1993-94; Keith Tkachuk, 1994-95.

Retired Numbers

9	Bobby Hull	1972-1980

Club Records

Team

(Figures in brackets for season records are games played)

Most Points	96	1984-85 (80)
Most Wins	43	1984-85 (80)
Most Ties	15	1991-92 (80)
Most Losses	57	1980-81 (80)
Most Goals	358	1984-85 (80)
Most Goals Against	400	1980-81 (80)
Fewest Points	32	1980-81 (80)
Fewest Wins	9	1980-81 (80)
Fewest Ties	7	1985-86 (80)
Fewest Losses	27	1984-85 (80)
Fewest Goals	214	1979-80 (80)
Fewest Goals Against	244	1991-92 (80)

Longest Winning Streak
Over-all ... 9 Mar. 8-27/85
Home ... 9 Dec. 27/92-Jan. 23/93
Away ... 8 Feb. 25-Apr. 6/85

Longest Undefeated Streak
Over-all ... 13 Mar. 8-Apr. 7/85 (10 wins, 3 ties)
Home ... 11 Dec. 23/83 Feb. 5/84 (6 wins, 5 ties)
Away ... 9 Feb. 25-Apr. 7/85 (8 wins, 1 tie)

Longest Losing Streak
Over-all ... 10 Nov. 30-Dec. 20/80 Feb. 6-25/94
Home ... 5 Oct. 29-Nov. 13/93
Away ... 13 Jan. 26-Apr. 14/94

Longest Winless Streak
Over-all ... *30 Oct. 19-Dec. 20/80 (23 losses, 7 ties)
Home ... 14 Oct. 19-Dec. 14/80 (9 losses, 5 ties)

Away ... 18 Oct. 10-Dec. 20/80 (16 losses, 2 ties)
Most Shutouts, Season ... 7 1991-92 (80)
Most PIM, Season ... 2,278 1987-88 (80)
Most Goals, Game ... 12 Feb. 25/85 (Wpg. 12 at NYR. 5)

Individual

Most Seasons	13	Thomas Steen
Most Games	919	Thomas Steen
Most Goals, Career	379	Dale Hawerchuk
Most Assists, Career	550	Dale Hawerchuk
Most Points, Career	929	Dale Hawerchuk (379 goals, 550 assists)
Most PIM, Career	1,338	Laurie Boschman
Most Shutouts, Career	14	Bob Essensa

Longest Consecutive Games Streak ... 475 Dale Hawerchuk (Dec. 19/82-Dec. 10/88)
Most Goals, Season ... 76 Teemu Selanne (1992-93)
Most Assists, Season ... 79 Phil Housley (1992-93)
Most Points, Season ... 132 Teemu Selanne (1992-93) (76 goals, 56 assists)
Most PIM, Season ... 347 Tie Domi (1993-94)
Most Points, Defenseman Season ... 97 Phil Housley (1992-93) (18 goals, 79 assists)
Most Points, Center, Season ... 130 Dale Hawerchuk (1984-85) (53 goals, 77 assists)
Most Points, Right Wing, Season ... 132 Teemu Selanne (1992-93) (76 goals, 56 assists)
Most Points, Left Wing, Season ... 92 Morris Lukowich (1981-82) (43 goals, 49 assists)

Most Points, Rookie, Season ... *132 Teemu Selanne (1992-93) (76 goals, 56 assists)
Most Shutouts, Season ... 5 Bob Essensa (1991-92)
Most Goals, Game ... 5 Willy Lindstrom (Mar. 2/82)
Most Assists, Game ... 5 Dale Hawerchuk (Mar. 6/84, Mar. 18/89, Mar. 4/90) Phil Housley (Jan. 18/93)
Most Points, Game ... 6 Willy Lindstrom (Mar. 2/82) Dale Hawerchuk (Dec. 14/83, Mar. 5/88, Mar. 18/89) Thomas Steen (Oct. 24/84) Eddie Olczyk (Dec. 21/91)

* NHL Record.

1993-94 Results

Oct.	6		Washington	6-4		6	at	Boston	4-5
	9	at	Dallas	3-3		8	at	Ottawa	3-2
	10	at	Chicago	3-4		10	at	Montreal	2-4
	12	at	New Jersey	4-7		12		Buffalo	3-2
	16		Chicago	1-0		15		Toronto	1-5
	18		Edmonton	6-3		16		Tampa Bay	2-3
	21	at	Detroit	2-6		19		New Jersey	0-4
	23	at	Philadelphia	9-6		25	at	Los Angeles	4-4
	26	at	Florida	5-2		26	at	Anaheim	1-3
	27	at	Tampa Bay	4-3		29	at	Detroit	1-7
	29		Los Angeles	3-4	Feb.	2		Dallas	3-7
	31		Calgary	3-4		4		Hartford	2-2
Nov.	3		St. Louis	0-3		6	at	Edmonton	2-5
	5		Ottawa	6-7		8	at	St. Louis	5-6
	7	at	Dallas	1-1		9	at	Dallas	2-4
	9	at	NY Islanders	5-2		11		Toronto	1-3
	10	at	NY Rangers	1-2		15	at	Pittsburgh	3-5
	13		Dallas	2-3		18		Chicago	2-7
	15	at	Calgary	2-7		20		Calgary	2-5
	17		Detroit	2-1		22		Florida	2-3
	19	at	Buffalo	0-6		24	at	Chicago	3-6
	20	at	Quebec	5-5		25		Boston	6-7
	24		Anaheim	1-2		28		San Jose	3-3
	26		Vancouver	3-5	Mar.	2		Dallas	4-2
	28	at	St. Louis	4-3		4	at	Ottawa	6-1
	30	at	Los Angeles	8-6		6		Pittsburgh	3-5
Dec.	1	at	Anaheim	2-5		7		NY Islanders	2-7
	3	at	San Jose	3-3		11		Vancouver	4-8
	5		Detroit	6-4		12	at	Toronto	1-3
	6	at	Detroit	2-6		16		St. Louis	4-0
	8	at	Toronto	5-4		19		Detroit	4-2
	10		Florida	2-5		23		Montreal	3-1
	12		Toronto	3-3		25		San Jose	3-8
	17	at	Vancouver	1-6		27		NY Rangers	3-1
	18	at	Calgary	4-5		29	at	San Jose	4-9
	20		Anaheim	5-7	Apr.	1	at	Vancouver	1-5
	23		Quebec	5-2		4		Philadelphia	2-2
	27	at	Edmonton	0-6		6		Edmonton	3-4
	29		Chicago	3-2		9		Los Angeles	4-3
	31		St. Louis	2-1		10	at	Toronto	0-7
Jan.	2	at	Chicago	1-5		12	at	Washington	3-4
	5	at	Hartford	0-4		14	at	St. Louis	1-3

All-time Record vs. Other Clubs

Regular Season

		At Home							On Road							Total					
	GP	W	L	T	GF	GA	PTS	GP	W	L	T	GF	GA	PTS	GP	W	L	T	GF	GA	PTS
Anaheim	2	0	2	0	6	9	0	2	0	2	0	3	8	0	4	0	4	0	9	17	0
Boston	23	9	12	2	83	86	20	22	3	16	3	70	105	9	45	12	28	5	153	191	29
Buffalo	22	9	11	2	71	82	20	22	1	19	2	53	104	4	44	10	30	4	124	186	24
Calgary	50	22	20	8	207	185	52	51	10	34	7	162	247	27	101	32	54	15	369	432	79
Chicago	27	14	10	3	107	98	31	27	4	20	3	80	138	11	54	18	30	6	187	236	42
Dallas	27	13	13	1	99	98	27	28	8	16	4	87	123	20	55	21	29	5	186	221	47
Detroit	26	11	7	8	90	78	30	28	10	15	3	101	118	23	54	21	22	11	191	196	53
Edmonton	51	20	27	4	210	236	44	52	16	33	3	174	242	35	103	36	60	7	384	478	79
Florida	2	0	2	0	4	8	0	1	1	0	0	5	2	2	3	1	2	0	9	10	2
Hartford	24	12	11	1	86	88	25	22	6	11	5	71	92	17	46	18	22	6	157	180	42
Los Angeles	52	25	18	9	227	193	59	49	22	18	9	206	207	53	101	47	36	18	433	400	112
Montreal	22	8	9	5	71	84	21	22	2	20	0	51	119	4	44	10	29	5	122	203	25
New Jersey	23	16	4	3	92	61	35	21	9	6	6	70	66	24	44	25	10	9	162	127	59
NY Islanders	22	7	13	2	70	87	16	23	6	11	6	71	87	18	45	13	24	8	141	174	34
NY Rangers	23	9	12	2	84	87	20	22	8	12	2	89	104	18	45	17	24	4	173	191	38
Ottawa	2	1	1	0	12	10	2	4	3	0	1	21	9	7	6	4	1	1	33	19	9
Philadelphia	22	9	11	2	72	78	20	23	6	17	0	69	107	12	45	15	28	2	141	185	32
Pittsburgh	22	9	12	1	83	83	19	23	7	16	0	69	96	14	45	16	28	1	152	179	33
Quebec	22	10	7	5	94	87	25	23	10	10	3	95	93	23	45	20	17	8	189	180	48
St. Louis	28	15	7	6	97	83	36	27	6	13	8	83	109	20	55	21	20	14	180	192	56
San Jose	10	6	3	1	38	30	13	8	3	3	2	35	36	8	18	9	6	3	73	66	21
Tampa Bay	3	1	2	0	8	9	2	2	3	0	0	14	10	6	6	4	2	0	22	19	8
Toronto	27	13	10	4	122	113	30	27	16	10	1	115	104	33	54	29	20	5	237	217	63
Vancouver	49	24	18	7	192	188	55	52	14	30	8	151	205	36	101	38	48	15	343	393	91
Washington	23	12	6	5	90	83	29	22	5	15	2	70	104	12	45	17	21	7	160	187	41
Totals	**604**	**275**	**248**	**81**	**2315**	**2244**	**631**	**604**	**179**	**347**	**78**	**2015**	**2635**	**436**	**1208**	**454**	**595**	**159**	**4330**	**4879**	**1067**

Calgary totals include Atlanta, 1979-80. Dallas totals include Minnesota, 1979-80 to 1992-93.
New Jersey totals include Colorado, 1979-80 to 1981-82.

Playoffs

	Series	W	L	GP	W	L	T	GF	GA	Last Mtg.	Round	Result
Calgary	3	2	1	13	7	6	0	45	43	1987	DSF	W 4-2
Edmonton	6	0	6	26	4	22	0	75	120	1990	DSF	L 3-4
St. Louis	1	0	1	4	1	3	0	13	20	1982	DSF	L 1-3
Vancouver	2	0	2	13	5	8	0	34	50	1993	DSF	L 2-4
Totals	**12**	**2**	**10**	**56**	**17**	**39**	**0**	**167**	**233**			

Playoff Results 1994-90

Year	Round	Opponent	Result	GF	GA
1993	DSF	Vancouver	L 2-4	17	21
1992	DSF	Vancouver	L 3-4	17	29
1990	DSF	Edmonton	L 3-4	22	24

Abbreviations: Round: F – Final;
CF – conference final; **CQF** – conference quarter-final;
CSF – conference semi-final; **DF** – division final;
DSF – division semi-final; **SF** – semi-final;
QF – quarter-final; **PR** – preliminary round.

Entry Draft
Selections 1994-80

1994
Pick
30 Deron Quint
56 Dorian Anneck
58 Tavis Hansen
82 Steve Cheredaryk
108 Craig Mills
143 Steve Vezina
146 Chris Kibermanis
186 Ramil Saifullin
212 Henrik Smangs
238 Mike Mader
264 Jason Issel

1993
Pick
15 Mats Lindgren
31 Scott Langkow
43 Alexei Budayev
79 Ruslan Batyrshin
93 Ravil Gusmanov
119 Larry Courville
145 Michal Grosek
171 Martin Woods
197 Adrian Murray
217 Vladimir Potapov
223 Ilja Stashenkov
228 Harijs Vitolinsh
285 Russell Hewson

1992
Pick
17 Sergei Bautin
27 Boris Mironov
60 Jeremy Stevenson
84 Mark Visheau
132 Alexander Alexeyev
155 Artur Oktyabrev
156 Andrei Raisky
204 Nikolai Khaibulin
228 Yevgeny Garanin
229 Teemu Numminen
252 Andrei Karpovtsev
254 Ivan Vologzhaninov

1991
Pick
5 Aaron Ward
49 Dmitri Filimonov
91 Juha Ylonen
99 Yan Kaminsky
115 Jeff Sebastian
159 Jeff Ricciardi
181 Sean Gauthier
203 Igor Ulanov
225 Jason Jennings
247 Sergei Sorokin

1990
Pick
19 Keith Tkachuk
35 Mike Muller
74 Roman Meluzin
75 Scott Levins
77 Alexei Zhamnov
98 Craig Martin
119 Daniel Jardemyr
140 John Lilley
161 Henrik Andersson
182 Rauli Raitanen
203 Mika Alatalo
224 Sergei Selyanin
245 Keith Morris

1989
Pick
4 Stu Barnes
25 Dan Ratushny
46 Jason Cirone
62 Kris Draper
64 Mark Brownschidle
69 Alain Roy
109 Dan Bylsma
130 Pekka Peltola
131 Doug Evans
151 Jim Solly
172 Stephane Gauvin
193 Joe Larson
214 Bradley Podiak
235 Evgeny Davydov
240 Sergei Kharin

1988
Pick
10 Teemu Selanne
31 Russell Romaniuk
52 Stephane Beauregard
73 Brian Hunt
94 Anthony Joseph
101 Benoit Lebeau
115 Ronald Jones
127 Markus Akerblom
136 Jukka Marttila
157 Mark Smith
178 Mike Helber
199 Pavel Kostichkin
220 Kevin Heise
241 Kyle Galloway

1987
Pick
16 Bryan Marchment
37 Patrik Erickson
79 Don McLennan
96 Ken Gernander
100 Darrin Amundson
121 Joe Harwell
142 Tod Hartje
163 Markku Kyllonen
184 Jim Fernholz
226 Roger Rougelot
247 Hans Goran Elo

1986
Pick
8 Pat Elynuik
29 Teppo Numminen
50 Esa Palosaari
71 Hannu Jarvenpaa
92 Craig Endean
113 Robertson Bateman
155 Frank Furlan
176 Mark Green
197 John Blue
218 Matt Cote
239 Arto Blomsten

1985
Pick
18 Ryan Stewart
39 Roger Ohman
60 Daniel Berthiaume
81 Fredrik Olausson
102 John Borrell
123 Danton Cole
144 Brent Mowery
165 Tom Draper
186 Nevin Kardum
207 Dave Quigley
228 Chris Norton
249 Anssi Melametsa

1984
Pick
30 Peter Douris
68 Chris Mills
72 Sean Clement
93 Scott Schneider
99 Brent Severyn
114 Gary Lorden
135 Luciano Borsato
156 Brad Jones
177 Gord Whitaker
197 Rick Forst
218 Mike Warus
238 Jim Edmonds

1983
Pick
8 Andrew McBain
14 Bobby Dollas
29 Brad Berry
43 Peter Taglianetti
69 Bob Essensa
89 Harry Armstrong
109 Joel Baillargeon
129 Iain Duncan
149 Ron Pessetti
169 Todd Flichel
189 Cory Wright
209 Eric Cormier
229 Jamie Husgen

1982
Pick
12 Jim Kyte
74 Tom Martin
75 Dave Ellett
96 Tim Mishler
138 Derek Ray
159 Guy Gosselin
180 Tom Ward
201 Mike Savage
222 Bob Shaw
243 Jan Urban Ericson

1981
Pick
1 Dale Hawerchuk
22 Scott Arniel
43 Jyrki Seppa
64 Kirk McCaskill
85 Marc Behrend
106 Bob O'Connor
127 Peter Nilsson
148 Dan McFaul
169 Greg Dick
190 Vladimir Kadlec
211 Dave Kirwin

1980
Pick
2 David Babych
23 Moe Mantha
44 Murray Eaves
65 Guy Fournier
86 Glen Ostir
107 Ron Loustel
128 Brian Mullen
135 Mike Lauen
149 Sandy Beadle
170 Ed Christian
191 Dave Chartier

General Manager and Coach

PADDOCK, JOHN
General Manager and Coach, Winnipeg Jets.
Born in Brandon, Man., June 9, 1954.

John Paddock, who was named as the 10th head coach of the Winnipeg Jets on June 17, 1991, enters his fourth season as coach of the Winnipeg Jets in 1994-95. Paddock has also assumed the duties of general manager, taking over from Mike Smith on an interim basis on January 19, 1994. He officially became general manager on June 3, 1994. Paddock joined the Jets after serving one season as head coach of the Binghamton Rangers of the American Hockey League.

His coaching career began in the AHL in 1983. Paddock, then playing for the Maine Mariners, succeeded Tom McVie behind the Mariners bench when McVie was summoned to New Jersey; the Mariners won the AHL Calder Cup Championship that season. Paddock later joined the Hershey Bears, where he won another Calder Cup and two coach of the year awards. Paddock served one season as assistant general manager for the Philadelphia Flyers before joining the New York Rangers organization in 1990.

Paddock played 87 NHL games as a right wing, drafted by the Washington Capitals, and recorded eight goals and 14 assists during his career.

Coaching Record

Season	Team	Games	Regular Season W	L	T	%	Games	Playoffs W	L	%
1983-84	Maine (AHL)	80	33	36	11	.481	17	12	5	.706
1984-85	Maine (AHL)	80	38	32	10	.538	11	5	6	.454
1985-86	Hershey (AHL)	80	48	29	3	.619	18	10	8	.555
1986-87	Hershey (AHL)	80	43	36	1	.544	5	1	4	.200
1987-88	Hershey (AHL)	80	50	27	3	.644	12	12	0	1.000
1988-89	Hershey (AHL)	80	40	30	10	.563	12	7	5	.583
1990-91	Binghamton (AHL)	80	44	30	6	.588	10	4	6	.400
1991-92	**Winnipeg (NHL)**	**80**	**33**	**32**	**15**	**.506**	**7**	**3**	**4**	**.429**
1992-93	**Winnipeg (NHL)**	**84**	**40**	**37**	**7**	**.518**	**6**	**2**	**4**	**.333**
1993-94	**Winnipeg (NHL)**	**84**	**24**	**51**	**9**	**.339**	...	...	...	....
	NHL Totals	248	97	120	31	.454	13	5	8	.385

Club Directory

Winnipeg Arena
15-1430 Maroons Road
Winnipeg, Manitoba R3G 0L5
Phone 204/982-5387
FAX 204/788-4668
Capacity: 15,393

Board of Directors
Barry L. Shenkarow, Bill Davis, Marvin Shenkarow, Harvey Secter, Steve Bannatyne, Dick Archer, Barry McQueen

President & Governor . . . . Barry L. Shenkarow
Alternate Governor. . . . . Bill Davis

Hockey Operations
General Manager & Head Coach . . . . John Paddock
Assistant General Manager/VP of Communications . Mike O'Hearn
Director of Player Development . . . . Randy Carlyle
Assistant Coaches . . . . Andy Murray, Terry Simpson,
  Zinetula Bilyaletdinov
Goaltending Coach. . . . . Pete Peeters
Coordinator of Coaching Services. . . . . Glen Williamson
Director of Scouting. . . . . Bill Lesuk
Assistant Director of Scouting. . . . . Joe Yannetti
Scouts. . . . . Tom Savage, Connie Broden, Sean Coady,
  Charlie Burroughs, Boris Yemeljanov, Larry
  Hornung, Vaughn Karpan
Executive Assistant to General Manager . . . . Brenda Thompson
Executive Assistant to Assistant GM/
  Director of Community Relations. . . . . Pat MacDonald

Communications
Director, Hockey Information . . . . Igor Kuperman
Media/Public Relations . . . . Richard Nairn
Special Events Director/Executive Director of
  Winnipeg Jets Goals For Kids . . . . Lori Summers
Administrative Assistant – Winnipeg
  Jets Goals For Kids . . . . Michelle McCrea

Finance and Administration
Vice-President, Finance & Administration . . . . Don Binda
Director of Ticket Operations . . . . Dianne Gabbs
Director of Information System. . . . . Doug Bergman
Ticket Operations Assistant . . . . Georgie Jorowski
Director of Team Services . . . . Murray Harding
Controller . . . . Joe Leibfried
Accounting/Ticketing Assistant . . . . Sacha Palmer
Accounting Assistants . . . . Bryan Braun, Robert Thorsten, Lynda Sweetland
Jets' All Sports Store Managers . . . . Jennifer Zalnasky, Dave Blackmore
Administrative Consultant . . . . Laurence Gilman
Receptionist . . . . Maryann Mazepa

Marketing
Manager of Retail Operations. . . . . Val Brakel
Marketing Manager . . . . Sherri Wilson
Graphic Design/Desktop Publishing . . . . Roberta Rackal
Manager of Ticket Sales . . . . Hartley Miller
Group Sales Coordinator . . . . Patti Peters
Director of Corporate Sales. . . . . Dave Baker
National Accounts Manager . . . . Gord Dmytriw
Account Executive . . . . Laurie Kepron
Account Executive . . . . Ian Bergman
Account Executive . . . . Dave MacLean
Administration Assistant/Corporate Sales . . . . Teresa Bastian

Dressing Room
Athletic Trainers . . . . Phil Walker, Gord Hart
Equipment Managers . . . . Craig Heisinger, Stan Wilson, Mike Romani
Team Physician . . . . Dr. Brian Lukie
Team Dentist . . . . Dr. Gene Solmundson

Team Information
Office Address . . . . 10th floor – 1661 Portage Ave.
  Winnipeg, Manitoba
  R3J 3T7
Team Colors . . . . Blue, Red and White
Dimensions of Rink . . . . 200 feet by 85 feet
Training Camp . . . . Winnipeg
Press Box Location . . . . East Side
TV Channel. . . . . CKND TV (Channel 9 – Cable 12)
Radio Station . . . . CJOB AM 680
Play-by-Play (Radio). . . . . Kelly Moore

1993-94 Final Statistics

Standings

Abbreviations: GA – goals against; **GF** – goals for; **GP** – games played; **L** – losses; **PTS** – points; **T** – ties; **W** – wins; **%** – percentage of games won.

EASTERN CONFERENCE
Northeast Division

	GP	W	L	T	GF	GA	PTS	%
Pittsburgh	84	44	27	13	299	285	101	.601
Boston	84	42	29	13	289	252	97	.577
Montreal	84	41	29	14	283	248	96	.571
Buffalo	84	43	32	9	282	218	95	.565
Quebec	84	34	42	8	277	292	76	.452
Hartford	84	27	48	9	227	288	63	.375
Ottawa	84	14	61	9	201	397	37	.220

Atlantic Division

	GP	W	L	T	GF	GA	PTS	%
NY Rangers	84	52	24	8	299	231	112	.667
New Jersey	84	47	25	12	306	220	106	.631
Washington	84	39	35	10	277	263	88	.524
NY Islanders	84	36	36	12	282	264	84	.500
Florida	84	33	34	17	233	233	83	.494
Philadelphia	84	35	39	10	294	314	80	.476
Tampa Bay	84	30	43	11	224	251	71	.423

WESTERN CONFERENCE
Central Division

	GP	W	L	T	GF	GA	PTS	%
Detroit	84	46	30	8	356	275	100	.595
Toronto	84	43	29	12	280	243	98	.583
Dallas	84	42	29	13	286	265	97	.577
St. Louis	84	40	33	11	270	283	91	.542
Chicago	84	39	36	9	254	240	87	.518
Winnipeg	84	24	51	9	245	344	57	.339

Pacific Division

	GP	W	L	T	GF	GA	PTS	%
Calgary	84	42	29	13	302	256	97	.577
Vancouver	84	41	40	3	279	276	85	.506
San Jose	84	33	35	16	252	265	82	.488
Anaheim	84	33	46	5	229	251	71	.423
Los Angeles	84	27	45	12	294	322	66	.393
Edmonton	84	25	45	14	261	305	64	.381

One of the NHL's finest playmakers, Adam Oates led all Boston skaters in assists (80) and points (112) during the 1993-94 campaign.

INDIVIDUAL LEADERS

Goal Scoring

Player	Team	GP	G
Pavel Bure	Van.	76	60
Brett Hull	St. L.	81	57
Sergei Fedorov	Det.	82	56
Dave Andreychuk	Tor.	83	53
Brendan Shanahan	St. L.	81	52
Ray Sheppard	Det.	82	52
Adam Graves	NYR	84	52
Cam Neely	Bos.	49	50
Mike Modano	Dal.	76	50
Wendel Clark	Tor.	64	46
Jeremy Roenick	Chi.	84	46

Assists

Player	Team	GP	A
Wayne Gretzky	L.A.	81	92
Doug Gilmour	Tor.	83	84
Adam Oates	Bos.	77	80
Sergei Zubov	NYR	78	77
Ray Bourque	Bos.	72	71
Craig Janney	St. L.	69	68
Jaromir Jagr	Pit.	80	67
Mark Recchi	Phi.	84	67

Power-play Goals

Player	Team	GP	PP
Pavel Bure	Van.	76	25
Brett Hull	St. L.	81	25
Luc Robitaille	L.A.	83	24
Jeremy Roenick	Chi.	84	24
Keith Tkachuk	Wpg.	84	22
Wendel Clark	Tor.	64	21
Dave Andreychuk	Tor.	83	21
Kevin Stevens	Pit.	83	21

Short-handed Goals

Player	Team	GP	SH
Brendan Shanahan	St. L.	81	7
Wayne Presley	Buf.	65	5
Shawn McEachern	L.A.-Pit.	76	5
Mike Gartner	NYR-Tor.	81	5
Marty McInnis	NYI	81	5
Dave Andreychuk	Tor.	83	5
Benoit Hogue	NYI	83	5
Nelson Emerson	Wpg.	83	5
Jeremy Roenick	Chi.	84	5

Game-winning Goals

Player	Team	GP	GW
Cam Neely	Bos.	49	13
Sergei Fedorov	Det.	82	10
Vincent Damphousse	Mtl.	84	10
Eric Lindros	Phi.	65	9
Pavel Bure	Van.	76	9
Stephane Richer	N.J.	80	9
Joe Mullen	Pit.	84	9
Joe Sakic	Que.	84	9

Game-tying Goals

Player	Team	GP	GT
Stephane Richer	N.J.	80	3
Mike Ridley	Wsh.	81	3
Ray Ferraro	NYI	82	3
Gord Murphy	Fla.	84	3

Shots

Player	Team	GP	S
Brendan Shanahan	St. L.	81	397
Brett Hull	St. L.	81	392
Ray Bourque	Bos.	72	386
Pavel Bure	Van.	76	374
Sergei Fedorov	Det.	82	337

Shooting Percentage
(minimum 84 shots)

Player	Team	GP	G	S	%
Cam Neely	Bos.	49	50	185	27.0
Martin Straka	Pit.	84	30	130	23.1
Eric Lindros	Phi.	65	44	197	22.3
Mike Ricci	Que.	83	30	138	21.7
Gary Roberts	Cgy.	73	41	202	20.3

Penalty Minutes

Player	Team	GP	PIM
Tie Domi	Wpg.	81	347
Shane Churla	Dal.	69	333
Warren Rychel	L.A.	80	322
Craig Berube	Wsh.	84	305
Kelly Chase	St. L.	68	278

Plus/Minus

Player	Team	GP	+/-
Scott Stevens	N.J.	83	53
Sergei Fedorov	Det.	82	48
Nicklas Lidstrom	Det.	84	43
Frank Musil	Cgy.	75	38
Gary Roberts	Cgy.	73	37

Individual Leaders

Abbreviations: * – rookie eligible for Calder Trophy; **A** – assists; **G** – goals; **GP** – games played; **GT** – game-tying goals; **GW** – game-winning goals; **PIM** – penalties in minutes; **PP** – power play goals; **Pts** – points; **S** – shots on goal; **SH** – short-handed goals; **%** – percentage shots resulting in goals; **+/–** – difference between Goals For (**GF**) scored when a player is on the ice with his team at even strength or short-handed and Goals Against (**GA**) scored when the same player is on the ice with his team at even strength or on a power play.

Individual Scoring Leaders for Art Ross Trophy

Player	Team	GP	G	A	Pts	+/–	PIM	PP	SH	GW	GT	S	%
Wayne Gretzky	Los Angeles	81	38	92	130	25 –	20	14	4	0	1	233	16.3
Sergei Fedorov	Detroit	82	56	64	120	48	34	13	4	10	0	337	16.6
Adam Oates	Boston	77	32	80	112	10	45	16	2	3	0	197	16.2
Doug Gilmour	Toronto	83	27	84	111	25	105	10	1	3	2	167	16.2
Pavel Bure	Vancouver	76	60	47	107	1	86	25	4	9	0	374	16.0
Jeremy Roenick	Chicago	84	46	61	107	21	125	24	5	5	1	281	16.4
Mark Recchi	Philadelphia	84	40	67	107	2 –	46	11	0	5	0	217	18.4
Brendan Shanahan	St. Louis	81	52	50	102	9 –	211	15	7	8	1	397	13.1
Dave Andreychuk	Toronto	83	53	46	99	22	98	21	5	8	0	333	15.9
Jaromir Jagr	Pittsburgh	80	32	67	99	15	61	9	0	6	2	298	10.7
Brett Hull	St. Louis	81	57	40	97	3 –	38	25	3	6	1	392	14.5
Eric Lindros	Philadelphia	65	44	53	97	16	103	13	2	9	1	197	22.3
Rod Brind'Amour	Philadelphia	84	35	62	97	9 –	85	14	1	4	0	230	15.2
Pierre Turgeon	NY Islanders	69	38	56	94	14	18	10	4	6	0	254	15.0
Ray Sheppard	Detroit	82	52	41	93	13	26	19	0	5	0	260	20.0
Mike Modano	Dallas	76	50	43	93	8 –	54	18	0	4	2	281	17.8
Robert Reichel	Calgary	84	40	53	93	20	58	14	0	6	0	249	16.1
Ron Francis	Pittsburgh	82	27	66	93	3 –	62	8	0	2	1	216	12.5
Joe Sakic	Quebec	84	28	64	92	8 –	18	10	1	9	1	279	10.0
Vincent Damphousse	Montreal	84	40	51	91	0	75	13	0	10	1	274	14.6
Ray Bourque	Boston	72	20	71	91	26	58	10	3	1	1	386	5.2
Sergei Zubov	NY Rangers	78	12	77	89	20	39	9	0	1	0	222	5.4
Kevin Stevens	Pittsburgh	83	41	47	88	24 –	155	21	0	4	0	284	14.4
Luc Robitaille	Los Angeles	83	44	42	86	20 –	86	24	0	3	0	267	16.5
Dale Hawerchuk	Buffalo	81	35	51	86	10	91	13	1	7	0	227	15.4
Theoren Fleury	Calgary	83	40	45	85	30	186	16	1	6	0	278	14.4

Defensemen Scoring Leaders

Player	Team	GP	G	A	Pts	+/–	PIM	PP	SH	GW	GT	S	%
Ray Bourque	Boston	72	20	71	91	26	58	10	3	1	1	386	5.2
Sergei Zubov	NY Rangers	78	12	77	89	20	39	9	0	1	0	222	5.4
Al MacInnis	Calgary	75	28	54	82	35	95	12	1	5	0	324	8.6
Brian Leetch	NY Rangers	84	23	56	79	28	67	17	1	4	0	328	7.0
Scott Stevens	New Jersey	83	18	60	78	53	112	5	1	4	0	215	8.4
Paul Coffey	Detroit	80	14	63	77	28	106	5	0	3	0	278	5.0
Larry Murphy	Pittsburgh	84	17	56	73	10	44	7	0	4	0	236	7.2
Garry Galley	Philadelphia	81	10	60	70	11 –	91	5	1	0	1	186	5.4
Rob Blake	Los Angeles	84	20	48	68	7 –	137	7	0	6	0	304	6.6
Jeff Brown	St. L.-Van.	74	14	52	66	11 –	56	7	0	3	1	237	5.9
Sandis Ozolinsh	San Jose	81	26	38	64	16	24	4	0	3	0	157	16.6
Chris Chelios	Chicago	76	16	44	60	12	212	7	1	2	0	219	7.3
Al Iafrate	Wsh.-Bos.	79	15	43	58	16	163	6	0	4	0	299	5.0

CONSECUTIVE SCORING STREAKS

Goals

Games	Player	Team	G
8	Pavel Bure	Vancouver	11
8	Josef Beranek	Philadelphia	10
7	Dave Andreychuk	Toronto	8
7	Wendel Clark	Toronto	8
7	Eric Lindros	Philadelphia	8
6	Keith Tkachuk	Winnipeg	9
6	Wendel Clark	Toronto	8
6	Dave Andreychuk	Toronto	7
6	Bob Kudelski	Ottawa	7
6	Nelson Emerson	Winnipeg	6
6	*Mikael Renberg	Philadelphia	6

Assists

Games	Player	Team	A
11	Garry Galley	Philadelphia	15
11	Steve Yzerman	Detroit	12
10	Darrin Shannon	Winnipeg	13
9	Steve Yzerman	Detroit	14
8	Paul Coffey	Detroit	13
8	Mark Recchi	Philadelphia	13
8	Mark Recchi	Philadelphia	11
8	Andrew Cassels	Hartford	10
8	Todd Elik	Edm.-S.J.	9
8	Murray Craven	Vancouver	8

Points

Games	Player	Team	G	A	PTS
16	Dave Andreychuk	Toronto	14	13	27
13	Adam Oates	Boston	7	16	23
13	Pierre Turgeon	NY Islanders	13	10	23
13	Rod Brind'Amour	Philadelphia	4	18	22
13	Dave Gagner	Dallas	7	9	16
12	Pavel Bure	Vancouver	16	8	24
12	Pavel Bure	Vancouver	11	10	21
12	Eric Lindros	Philadelphia	12	9	21
12	Scott Stevens	New Jersey	4	14	18
12	Pat Verbeek	Hartford	7	9	16

Sophomore rearguard, below, Sergei Zubov led the NY Rangers in scoring and finished second among NHL defencemen with 12 goals and 77 assists. Doug Gilmour, right, who finished fourth in NHL scoring with 111 points in 1993-94, was second to Wayne Gretzky in assists with 84.

Individual Rookie Scoring Leaders

Rookie	Team	GP	G	A	Pts	+/−	PIM	PP	SH	GW	GT	S	%
Mikael Renberg	Philadelphia	83	38	44	82	8	36	9	0	1	0	195	19.5
Alexei Yashin	Ottawa	83	30	49	79	49−	22	11	2	3	0	232	12.9
Jason Arnott	Edmonton	78	33	35	68	1	104	10	0	4	1	194	17.0
Derek Plante	Buffalo	77	21	35	56	4	24	8	1	2	0	147	14.3
Bryan Smolinski	Boston	83	31	20	51	4	82	4	3	5	0	179	17.3
Alexandre Daigle	Ottawa	84	20	31	51	45−	40	4	0	2	0	168	11.9
Jesse Belanger	Florida	70	17	33	50	4−	16	11	0	3	1	104	16.3
Chris Gratton	Tampa Bay	84	13	29	42	25−	123	5	1	2	1	161	8.1
Iain Fraser	Quebec	60	17	20	37	5−	23	2	0	2	0	109	15.6
Boris Mironov	Wpg.-Edm.	79	7	24	31	33−	110	5	0	0	1	145	4.8

Edmonton Oilers newcomer Jason Arnott, left, finished third in rookie scoring in 1993-94, collecting 68 points. Boris Mironov, who split the 1993-94 season between Winnipeg and Edmonton, scored five powerplay goals. Both players earned a blueline spot on the NHL/Upper Deck All-Rookie Team.

Goal Scoring

Name	Team	GP	G
Mikael Renberg	Philadelphia	83	38
Jason Arnott	Edmonton	78	33
Bryan Smolinski	Boston	83	31
Alexei Yashin	Ottawa	83	30
Derek Plante	Buffalo	77	21
Alexandre Daigle	Ottawa	84	20
Iain Fraser	Quebec	60	17
Jesse Belanger	Florida	70	17

Assists

Name	Team	GP	A
Alexei Yashin	Ottawa	83	49
Mikael Renberg	Philadelphia	83	44
Derek Plante	Buffalo	77	35
Jason Arnott	Edmonton	78	35
Jesse Belanger	Florida	70	33
Alexandre Daigle	Ottawa	84	31
Chris Gratton	Tampa Bay	84	29
Chris Pronger	Hartford	81	25

Power Play Goals

Name	Team	GP	PP
Jesse Belanger	Florida	70	11
Alexei Yashin	Ottawa	83	11
Jason Arnott	Edmonton	78	10
Mikael Renberg	Philadelphia	83	9
Derek Plante	Buffalo	77	8
Boris Mironov	Wpg.-Edm.	79	5
Chris Gratton	Tampa Bay	84	5
Brent Grieve	NYI-Edm.	27	4
Philippe Boucher	Buffalo	38	4
Scott Levins	Fla.-Ott.	62	4
Bryan Smolinski	Boston	83	4
Alexandre Daigle	Ottawa	84	4

Short Hand Goals

Name	Team	GP	SH
Bryan Smolinski	Boston	83	3
Alexei Yashin	Ottawa	83	2
Ted Drury	Cgy.-Hfd.	50	1
Greg Johnson	Detroit	52	1
Kirk Maltby	Edmonton	68	1
Derek Plante	Buffalo	77	1
Chris Gratton	Tampa Bay	84	1

Game Winning Goals

Name	Team	GP	GW
Bryan Smolinski	Boston	83	5
Jason Arnott	Edmonton	78	4
Jesse Belanger	Florida	70	3
Alexei Yashin	Ottawa	83	3
David Emma	New Jersey	15	2
Iain Fraser	Quebec	60	2
Rob Niedermayer	Florida	65	2
Darren McCarty	Detroit	67	2
Patrik Carnback	Anaheim	73	2
Derek Plante	Buffalo	77	2
Alexandre Daigle	Ottawa	84	2
Chris Gratton	Tampa Bay	84	2

Game Tying Goals

Name	Team	GP	GT
Brent Grieve	NYI-Edm.	27	1
Pat Peake	Washington	49	1
Ted Drury	Cgy.-Hfd.	50	1
Oleg Petrov	Montreal	55	1
Jesse Belanger	Florida	70	1
Jason Arnott	Edmonton	78	1
Boris Mironov	Wpg.-Edm.	79	1
Chris Gratton	Tampa Bay	84	1

Shots

Name	Team	GP	S
Alexei Yashin	Ottawa	83	232
Mikael Renberg	Philadelphia	83	195
Jason Arnott	Edmonton	78	194
Bryan Smolinski	Boston	83	179
Chris Pronger	Hartford	81	174
Alexandre Daigle	Ottawa	84	168
Chris Gratton	Tampa Bay	84	161
Derek Plante	Buffalo	77	147

Shooting Percentage
(minimum 84 shots)

Name	Team	GP	G	S	%
Mikael Renberg	Philadelphia	83	38	195	19.5
Bryan Smolinski	Boston	83	31	179	17.3
Jason Arnott	Edmonton	78	33	194	17.0
Jesse Belanger	Florida	70	17	104	16.3
Iain Fraser	Quebec	60	17	109	15.6
Derek Plante	Buffalo	77	21	147	14.3
Alexei Yashin	Ottawa	83	30	232	12.9
Kirk Maltby	Edmonton	68	11	89	12.4

Plus/Minus

Name	Team	GP	+/−
Dean McAmmond	Edmonton	45	12
Jason Bowen	Philadelphia	56	12
A. Karpovtsev	NY Rangers	67	12
Darren McCarty	Detroit	67	12
Jaroslav Modry	New Jersey	41	10
Peter Popovic	Montreal	47	10

Three-or-More-Goal Games

Player	Team	Date	Final Score	G
Dave Andreychuk	Toronto	Dec. 01	St. L. 2 Tor. 4	3
Peter Bondra	Washington	Feb. 05	T.B. 3 Wsh. 6	5
Pavel Bure	Vancouver	Jan. 24	Van. 5 Edm. 4	3
Pavel Bure	Vancouver	Mar. 11	Van. 8 Wpg. 4	3
Pavel Bure	Vancouver	Mar. 27	L.A. 3 Van. 4	3
Shawn Burr	Detroit	Oct. 18	Det. 6 Buf. 4	3
Randy Burridge	Washington	Oct. 22	L.A. 3 Wsh. 6	3
Randy Burridge	Washington	Mar. 15	Wsh. 7 Pit. 4	3
V. Butsayev	Philadelphia	Dec. 02	Phi. 6 Van. 3	3
Guy Carbonneau	Montreal	Dec. 27	Mtl. 5 St. L. 2	3
Dino Ciccarelli	Detroit	Apr. 05	Det. 8 Van. 3	4
Wendel Clark	Toronto	Feb. 28	Tor. 4 Ott. 1	3
Wendel Clark	Toronto	Mar. 04	Tor. 6 Det. 5	3
Shayne Corson	Edmonton	Nov. 15	Edm. 5 Tor. 5	3
Ulf Dahlen	San Jose	Apr. 02	Van. 4 S.J. 7	3
Vincent Damphousse	Montreal	Oct. 30	Tor. 2 Mtl. 5	3
Vincent Damphousse	Montreal	Feb. 04	Mtl. 4 Wpg. 5	3
Kevin Dineen	Philadelphia	Oct. 31	Phi. 9 Chi. 6	4
Kevin Dineen	Philadelphia	Nov. 24	Mtl. 2 Phi. 9	3
Mike Donnelly	Los Angeles	Nov. 13	St. L. 3 L.A. 6	3
John Druce	Los Angeles	Apr. 13	Cgy. 4 L.A. 6	3
Steve Duchesne	St. Louis	Mar. 07	St. L. 3 Tor. 2	3
Sergei Fedorov	Detroit	Mar. 01	Cgy. 2 Det. 5	3
Patrick Flatley	NY Islanders	Feb. 01	S.J. 4 NYI 5	3
Theoren Fleury	Calgary	Mar. 31	Cgy. 4 Phi. 1	3
Dave Gagner	Dallas	Apr. 12	St. L. 5 Dal. 9	4
Mike Gartner	NY Rangers	Jan. 31	Pit. 3 NYR 5	3
Rob Gaudreau	San Jose	Feb. 06	S.J. 7 Dal. 1	3
Doug Gilmour	Toronto	Oct. 15	Det. 3 Tor. 6	3
Adam Graves	NY Rangers	Feb. 02	NYI 4 NYR 4	3
Travis Green	NY Islanders	Nov. 30	Wsh. 4 NYI 6	3
*Brent Grieve	Edmonton	Feb. 25	L.A. 5 Edm. 5	3
Brett Hull	St. Louis	Dec. 19	St. L. 4 Edm. 1	3
Brett Hull	St. Louis	Feb. 01	Tor. 4 St. L. 4	3
Brett Hull	St. Louis	Mar. 25	Dal. 3 St. L. 5	3
Derek King	NY Islanders	Oct. 23	Ott. 5 NYI 5	3
Vyacheslav Kozlov	Detroit	Jan. 06	Det. 10 S.J. 3	3
Todd Krygier	Washington	Apr. 09	Ott. 4 Wsh. 8	3
Bob Kudelski	Ottawa	Nov. 05	Ott. 7 Wpg. 6	3
Igor Larionov	San Jose	Jan. 15	Wpg. 2 S.J. 8	3
Igor Larionov	San Jose	Mar. 25	S.J. 8 Wpg. 3	3
Dominic Lavoie	Los Angeles	Oct. 09	Det. 3 L.A. 10	3
Jocelyn Lemieux	Chicago	Jan. 02	Wpg. 1 Chi. 5	3
Eric Lindros	Philadelphia	Jan. 19	St. L. 3 Phi. 8	3
Sergei Makarov	San Jose	Mar. 29	Wpg. 4 S.J. 9	3
Kevin Miller	St. Louis	Oct. 21	S.J. 2 St. L. 5	3
Mike Modano	Dallas	Feb. 21	Dal. 6 S.J. 3	3
Alexander Mogilny	Buffalo	Nov. 19	Wpg. 0 Buf. 6	3
Cam Neely	Boston	Nov. 04	Cgy. 3 Bos. 6	3
Cam Neely	Boston	Jan. 02	Wsh. 2 Bos. 8	3
Cam Neely	Boston	Feb. 12	N.J. 1 Bos. 5	3
Bernie Nicholls	New Jersey	Jan. 01	N.J. 7 Ott. 1	3
Joe Nieuwendyk	Calgary	Dec. 14	Van. 4 Cgy. 8	3
Adam Oates	Boston	Oct. 09	Que. 3 Bos. 7	3
Adam Oates	Boston	Feb. 08	Bos. 6 Que. 1	3
Lyle Odelein	Montreal	Mar. 09	St. L. 2 Mtl. 7	3
Joel Otto	Calgary	Nov. 03	Cgy. 6 Hfd. 3	3
*Oleg Petrov	Montreal	Dec. 18	Det. 1 Mtl. 8	3
*Derek Plante	Buffalo	Dec. 01	Buf. 3 T.B. 0	3
Robert Reichel	Calgary	Jan. 15	Ott. 0 Cgy. 10	3
Robert Reichel	Calgary	Mar. 20	Cgy. 6 Tor. 3	3
*Mikael Renberg	Philadelphia	Feb. 15	Phi. 6 S.J. 4	3
Mike Ricci	Quebec	Feb. 17	Que. 8 S.J. 2	5
Gary Roberts	Calgary	Dec. 06	Cgy. 6 Ott. 1	3
Gary Roberts	Calgary	Mar. 15	Cgy. 7 T.B. 3	4
Luc Robitaille	Los Angeles	Nov. 25	L.A. 6 Que. 8	4
Jeremy Roenick	Chicago	Feb. 24	Wpg. 3 Chi. 6	4
Teemu Selanne	Winnipeg	Oct. 06	Wsh. 4 Wpg. 6	3
Teemu Selanne	Winnipeg	Dec. 23	Que. 2 Wpg. 5	3
Alexander Semak	New Jersey	Oct. 16	N.J. 6 NYI 3	3
Brendan Shanahan	St. Louis	Oct. 07	Fla. 3 St. L. 5	3
Brendan Shanahan	St. Louis	Dec. 26	Chi. 2 St. L. 3	3
Brendan Shanahan	St. Louis	Jan. 29	Wpg. 1 Det. 7	3
Brendan Shanahan	St. Louis	Apr. 12	St. L. 5 Dal. 9	3
Ray Sheppard	Detroit	Jan. 06	Det. 10 S.J. 3	3
Ray Sheppard	Detroit	Jan. 29	Wpg. 1 Det. 7	3
Kevin Stevens	Pittsburgh	Jan. 11	Bos. 4 Pit. 5	3
Martin Straka	Pittsburgh	Mar. 08	Bos. 3 Pit. 7	3
Steve Thomas	NY Islanders	Nov. 27	NYR 4 NYI 6	3
Keith Tkachuk	Winnipeg	Oct. 23	Wpg. 9 Phi. 6	3
Pierre Turgeon	NY Islanders	Nov. 17	NYI 8 Ott. 1	3
Pierre Turgeon	NY Islanders	Mar. 09	NYI 4 Van. 5	3
Sylvain Turgeon	Ottawa	Oct. 23	Ott. 5 NYI 5	3
Pat Verbeek	Hartford	Oct. 14	Hfd. 6 Chi. 2	3
Pat Verbeek	Hartford	Dec. 07	Hfd. 6 Wsh. 1	3
Glen Wesley	Boston	Dec. 15	Bos. 5 N.J. 4	3
Terry Yake	Anaheim	Oct. 19	Ana. 4 NYR 2	3
*Alexei Yashin	Ottawa	Nov. 03	Ott. 7 Edm. 5	3
Scott Young	Quebec	Dec. 19	S.J. 5 Que. 7	3
Alexei Zhamnov	Winnipeg	Nov. 09	Wpg. 5 NYI 2	3
Alexei Zhamnov	Winnipeg	Nov. 30	Wpg. 8 L.A. 6	3

NOTE: 91 Three-or-more-goal games recorded in 1993-94.

Washington sharpshooter Peter Bondra (#12), below, registered a five-goal game against Tampa Bay in a 6-3 victory by the the Capitals on February 5, 1994. Mike Richter, right, who assumed the New York Rangers' number-one goaltending job in 1993-94, led all NHL netminders with 42 wins.

Goaltending Leaders

Minimum 27 games

Goals Against Average

Goaltender	Team	GPI	Mins	GA	Avg.
Dominik Hasek	Buffalo	58	3358	109	1.95
*Martin Brodeur	New Jersey	47	2625	105	2.40
Patrick Roy	Montreal	68	3867	161	2.50
John Vanbiesbrouck	Florida	57	3440	145	2.53
Mike Richter	NY Rangers	68	3710	159	2.57

Save Percentage

Goaltender	Team	GPI	Mins	GA	SA	S%	W	L	T
Dominik Hasek	Buffalo	58	3358	109	1552	.930	30	20	6
John Vanbiesbrouck	Florida	57	3440	145	1912	.924	21	25	11
Patrick Roy	Montreal	68	3867	161	2.50	.918	35	17	11
*Martin Brodeur	New Jersey	47	2625	105	2.40	.915	27	11	8
Mark Fitzpatrick	Florida	28	1603	73	844	.913	12	8	6

Wins

Goaltender	Team	GPI	Mins	W	L	T
Mike Richter	NY Rangers	68	3710	42	12	6
Ed Belfour	Chicago	70	3998	37	24	6
Curtis Joseph	St. Louis	71	4127	36	23	11
Patrick Roy	Montreal	68	3867	35	17	11
Felix Potvin	Toronto	66	3883	34	22	9

Shutouts

Goaltender	Team	GPI	Mins	SO	W	L	T
Dominik Hasek	Buffalo	58	3358	7	30	20	6
Patrick Roy	Montreal	68	3867	7	35	17	11
Ed Belfour	Chicago	70	3998	7	37	24	6
Ron Hextall	NY Islanders	65	3581	5	27	26	6
Mike Richter	NY Rangers	68	3710	5	42	12	6

Team-by-Team Point Totals

1989-90 to 1993-94

(Ranked by five-year average)

	93-94	92-93	91-92	90-91	89-90	Average
Boston	97	109	84	100	101	98.2
Chicago	87	106	87	106	88	94.8
Montreal	96	102	93	89	93	94.6
Pittsburgh	101	119	87	88	72	93.4
Calgary	97	97	74	100	99	93.4
NY Rangers	112	79	105	85	85	93.2
St. Louis	91	85	83	105	83	89.4
Detroit	100	103	98	76	70	89.4
New Jersey	106	87	87	79	83	88.4
Washington	88	93	98	81	78	87.6
Buffalo	95	86	74	81	98	86.8
Florida	83	–	–	–	–	83.0
Los Angeles	66	88	84	102	75	83.0
Vancouver	85	101	96	65	64	82.2
Toronto	98	99	67	57	80	80.2
Dallas	97	82	70	68	76	78.6
Philadelphia	80	83	75	76	71	77.0
NY Islanders	84	87	79	60	73	76.6
Edmonton	64	60	82	80	90	75.2
Winnipeg	57	87	81	63	85	74.6
Anaheim	71	–	–	–	–	71.0
Hartford	63	58	65	73	85	68.8
Tampa Bay	71	53	–	–	–	62.0
Quebec	76	104	52	46	31	61.8
San Jose	82	24	39	–	–	48.3
Ottawa	37	24	–	–	–	30.5

Team Record When Scoring First Goal of a Game

Team	GP	FG	W	L	T
NY Rangers	84	55	38	13	4
Detroit	84	51	36	10	5
Florida	84	54	30	12	12
New Jersey	84	46	33	8	5
Buffalo	84	49	31	12	6
Chicago	84	49	31	12	6
Washington	84	46	29	10	7
Montreal	84	42	29	7	6
Pittsburgh	84	42	29	8	5
St. Louis	84	42	28	8	6
Calgary	84	45	29	14	2
NY Islanders	84	42	27	10	5
Boston	84	41	26	10	5
Toronto	84	40	26	10	4
Quebec	84	41	25	11	5
Dallas	84	40	23	9	8
Vancouver	84	44	25	16	3
San Jose	84	39	21	8	10
Philadelphia	84	34	21	6	7
Tampa Bay	84	37	22	14	1
Anaheim	84	35	20	12	3
Winnipeg	84	36	19	13	4
Hartford	84	32	19	10	3
Edmonton	84	41	16	18	7
Los Angeles	84	38	16	15	7
Ottawa	84	30	9	18	3

Team Plus/Minus Differential

Team	GF	PPGF	Net GF	GA	PPGA	Net GA	Goal Differential
New Jersey	306	61	**245**	220	71	149	+ 96
Detroit	356	85	**271**	275	73	202	+ 69
Calgary	302	87	**215**	256	90	166	+ 49
NY Rangers	299	96	**203**	231	67	164	+ 39
Buffalo	282	96	**186**	218	58	160	+ 26
Montreal	283	78	**205**	248	68	180	+ 25
NY Islanders	282	74	**208**	264	79	185	+ 23
Toronto	280	88	**192**	283	74	169	+ 23
Chicago	254	67	**187**	240	71	169	+ 18
Washington	277	70	**207**	263	74	189	+ 18
Boston	289	84	**205**	252	58	194	+ 11
Pittsburgh	299	76	**223**	285	72	213	+ 10
Dallas	286	81	**205**	265	68	197	+ 8
Quebec	277	67	**210**	292	87	205	+ 5
Florida	233	65	**168**	233	69	164	+ 4
Vancouver	279	83	**196**	276	84	192	+ 4
San Jose	252	68	**184**	265	77	188	– 4
Anaheim	229	54	**175**	251	67	184	– 9
Philadelphia	294	80	**214**	314	80	234	– 20
St. Louis	270	86	**184**	283	73	210	– 26
Tampa Bay	224	57	**167**	251	58	193	– 26
Los Angeles	294	92	**202**	322	90	232	– 30
Hartford	227	61	**166**	288	88	200	– 34
Edmonton	261	74	**187**	305	78	227	– 40
Winnipeg	245	82	**163**	344	91	253	– 90
Ottawa	201	63	**138**	397	110	287	–149

Team Record when Leading, Trailing, Tied

	Leading after						Trailing after						Tied after					
	1 period			2 periods			1 period			2 periods			1 period			2 periods		
Team	W	L	T	W	L	T	W	L	T	W	L	T	W	L	T	W	L	T
Anaheim	15	5	1	24	6	2	10	22	2	2	33	0	8	19	2	7	7	3
Boston	24	4	4	35	2	2	9	17	4	4	25	5	9	8	5	3	2	6
Buffalo	23	8	3	38	7	7	4	11	1	0	18	2	15	13	5	5	7	0
Calgary	22	3	3	32	3	1	9	16	7	5	24	5	11	10	3	5	2	7
Chicago	25	5	7	30	3	5	2	19	1	2	27	0	12	12	1	7	6	4
Dallas	22	5	6	30	3	3	7	15	0	3	23	3	13	9	7	9	3	7
Detroit	29	8	4	39	2	2	3	15	4	2	21	2	14	7	0	5	7	4
Edmonton	14	10	3	15	1	2	6	19	2	1	32	8	5	16	9	9	12	4
Florida	21	6	7	30	0	5	1	16	5	0	22	3	11	12	5	3	12	9
Hartford	16	4	1	17	5	1	5	31	2	1	37	3	6	13	6	9	6	5
Los Angeles	11	10	4	21	4	6	3	24	4	3	37	1	13	11	4	3	4	5
Montreal	25	3	4	33	2	5	9	18	3	4	24	5	7	8	7	3	4	4
New Jersey	26	2	1	35	1	2	8	11	5	3	21	3	13	12	6	9	3	7
NY Islanders	24	8	4	30	4	3	4	15	5	4	25	4	8	13	3	2	7	5
NY Rangers	29	6	2	40	0	4	9	11	2	4	18	3	14	7	4	8	6	1
Ottawa	7	9	3	8	5	2	3	36	4	4	46	3	4	16	2	2	10	4
Philadelphia	20	4	5	24	2	4	6 ·	25	4	4	25	3	9	10	1	7,	12	3
Pittsburgh	21	5	5	32	2	3	11	13	6	4	18	4	12	9	2	2	7	6
Quebec	17	6	3	23	2	3	3	23	3	1	37	4	14	13	2	10	3	1
St. Louis	16	4	5	23	4	2	5	21	5	5	24	5	19	11	1	12	5	4
San Jose	16	2	4	22	2	6	7	28	3	4	28	3	10	5	9	7	5	7
Tampa Bay	16	6	3	22	5	2	4	24	4	4	31	1	10	13	4	4	7	8
Toronto	16	7	2	35	4	1	8	12	5	5	20	7	19	10	5	3	5	4
Vancouver	25	5	0	31	3	0	6	26	1	5	30	0	10	9	2	5	7	3
Washington	25	4	4	27	1	4	4	21	4	3	27	3	10	10	2	9	7	3
Winnipeg	12	10	2	15	5	5	3	28	4	1	38	2	9	13	3	8	8	2

Team Statistics

TEAMS' HOME-AND-ROAD RECORD

Northeast Division

			Home								Road				
	GP	W	L	T	GF	GA	PTS	%	GP	W	L	T	GF	GA	PTS	%
PIT	42	25	9	8	161	130	58	.690	42	19	18	5	138	155	43	.512
BOS	42	20	14	8	151	125	48	.571	42	22	15	5	138	127	49	.583
MTL	42	26	12	4	159	114	56	.667	42	15	17	10	124	134	40	.476
BUF	42	22	17	3	140	107	47	.560	42	21	15	6	142	111	48	.571
QUE	42	19	17	6	151	143	44	.524	42	15	25	2	126	149	32	.381
HFD	42	14	22	6	123	139	34	.405	42	13	26	3	104	159	29	.345
OTT	42	8	30	4	98	190	20	.238	42	6	31	5	103	207	17	.202
Total	**294**	**134**	**121**	**39**	**983**	**938**	**307**	**.522**	**294**	**111**	**147**	**36**	**875**	**1042**	**258**	**.439**

Atlantic Division

	GP	W	L	T	GF	GA	PTS	%	GP	W	L	T	GF	GA	PTS	%
NYR	42	28	8	6	153	111	62	.738	42	24	16	2	146	120	50	.595
N.J.	42	29	11	2	160	99	60	.714	42	18	14	10	146	121	46	.548
WSH	42	17	16	9	140	128	43	.512	42	22	19	1	137	135	45	.536
NYI	42	23	15	4	148	116	50	.595	42	13	21	8	134	148	34	.405
FLA	42	15	18	9	115	115	39	.464	42	18	16	8	118	118	44	.524
PHI	42	19	20	3	155	147	41	.488	42	16	19	7	139	167	39	.464
T.B.	42	14	22	6	107	126	34	.405	42	16	21	5	117	125	37	.440
Total	**294**	**145**	**110**	**39**	**978**	**842**	**329**	**.560**	**294**	**127**	**126**	**41**	**937**	**934**	**295**	**.502**

Central Division

	GP	W	L	T	GF	GA	PTS	%	GP	W	L	T	GF	GA	PTS	%
DET	42	23	13	6	182	122	52	.619	42	23	17	2	174	153	48	.571
TOR	42	23	15	4	148	115	50	.595	42	20	14	8	132	128	48	.571
DAL	42	23	12	7	148	119	53	.631	42	19	17	6	138	146	44	.524
ST.L.	42	23	11	8	160	136	54	.643	42	17	22	3	110	147	37	.440
CHI	42	21	16	5	137	126	47	.560	42	18	20	4	117	114	40	.476
WPG	42	15	23	4	125	154	34	.405	42	9	28	5	120	190	23	.274
Total	**252**	**128**	**90**	**34**	**900**	**772**	**290**	**.575**	**252**	**106**	**118**	**28**	**791**	**878**	**240**	**.476**

Pacific Division

	GP	W	L	T	GF	GA	PTS	%	GP	W	L	T	GF	GA	PTS	%
CGY	42	25	12	5	156	116	55	.655	42	17	17	8	146	140	42	.500
VAN	42	20	19	3	133	135	43	.512	42	21	21	0	146	141	42	.500
S.J.	42	19	13	10	137	133	48	.571	42	14	22	6	115	132	34	.405
ANA	42	14	26	2	115	129	30	.357	42	19	20	3	114	122	41	.488
L.A.	42	18	19	5	172	148	41	.488	42	9	26	7	122	174	25	.298
EDM	42	17	22	3	147	147	37	.440	42	8	23	11	114	158	27	.321
Total	**252**	**113**	**111**	**28**	**860**	**808**	**254**	**.504**	**252**	**88**	**129**	**35**	**757**	**867**	**211**	**.419**
Total	**1092**	**520**	**432**	**140**	**3721**	**3360**	**1180**	**.540**	**1092**	**432**	**520**	**140**	**3360**	**3721**	**1004**	**.460**

TEAMS' DIVISIONAL RECORD

Northeast Division

			Against Own Division								Against Other Divisions				
	GP	W	L	T	GF	GA	PTS	%	GP	W	L	T	GF	GA	PTS	%
PIT	32	21	9	2	120	103	44	.688	52	23	18	11	179	182	57	.548
BOS	31	14	13	4	113	107	32	.516	53	28	16	9	176	145	65	.613
MTL	31	17	10	4	112	81	38	.613	53	24	19	10	171	167	58	.547
BUF	31	19	9	3	113	75	41	.661	53	24	23	6	169	143	54	.509
QUE	31	13	15	3	104	110	29	.468	53	21	27	5	173	182	47	.443
HFD	30	9	18	3	78	106	21	.350	54	18	30	6	149	182	42	.389
OTT	30	4	23	3	67	125	11	.183	54	10	38	6	134	272	26	.241
Total	**216**	**97**	**97**	**22**	**707**	**707**	**216**	**.500**	**372**	**148**	**171**	**53**	**1151**	**1273**	**349**	**.469**

Atlantic Division

	GP	W	L	T	GF	GA	PTS	%	GP	W	L	T	GF	GA	PTS	%
NYR	32	21	8	3	113	85	45	.703	52	31	16	5	186	146	67	.644
N.J.	31	17	11	3	101	91	37	.597	53	30	14	9	205	129	69	.651
WSH	32	13	15	4	93	95	30	.469	52	26	20	6	184	168	58	.558
NYI	30	14	13	3	98	96	31	.517	54	22	23	9	184	168	53	.491
FLA	30	13	11	6	81	72	32	.533	54	20	23	11	152	161	51	.472
PHI	31	11	16	4	89	110	26	.419	53	24	23	6	205	204	54	.509
T.B.	30	5	20	5	75	101	15	.250	54	25	23	6	149	150	56	.519
Total	**216**	**94**	**94**	**28**	**650**	**650**	**216**	**.500**	**372**	**178**	**142**	**52**	**1265**	**1126**	**408**	**.548**

Central Division

	GP	W	L	T	GF	GA	PTS	%	GP	W	L	T	GF	GA	PTS	%
DET	30	13	13	4	117	99	30	.500	54	33	17	4	239	176	70	.648
TOR	30	18	8	4	113	87	40	.667	54	25	21	8	167	156	58	.537
DAL	30	13	12	5	101	107	29	.483	54	30	16	8	185	158	68	.630
ST.L.	30	12	13	5	89	102	29	.483	54	28	20	6	181	181	62	.574
CHI	30	14	15	1	98	84	29	.483	54	25	21	8	156	156	58	.537
WPG	30	10	17	3	72	111	23	.383	54	14	34	6	173	233	34	.315
Total	**180**	**79**	**79**	**22**	**590**	**590**	**180**	**.500**	**324**	**155**	**129**	**40**	**1101**	**1060**	**350**	**.540**

Pacific Division

	GP	W	L	T	GF	GA	PTS	%	GP	W	L	T	GF	GA	PTS	%
CGY	32	20	8	4	126	94	44	.688	52	22	21	9	176	162	53	.510
VAN	32	17	14	1	109	111	35	.547	52	24	26	2	170	165	50	.481
S.J.	30	14	11	5	88	83	33	.550	54	19	24	11	164	182	49	.454
ANA	30	11	18	1	80	87	23	.383	54	22	28	4	149	164	48	.444
L.A.	32	12	14	6	112	115	30	.469	52	15	31	6	182	207	36	.346
EDM	32	9	18	5	97	122	23	.359	52	16	27	9	164	183	41	.394
Total	**188**	**83**	**83**	**22**	**612**	**612**	**188**	**.500**	**316**	**118**	**157**	**41**	**1005**	**1063**	**277**	**.438**

TEAM STREAKS

Consecutive Wins

Games	Team	From	To
10	Toronto	Oct. 7	Oct. 28
7	New Jersey	Oct. 6	Oct. 23
7	NY Rangers	Oct. 30	Nov. 13
7	San Jose	Mar. 24	Apr. 5
6	Vancouver	Oct. 11	Oct. 24
6	Washington	Oct. 27	Nov. 11
6	Chicago	Nov. 4	Nov. 18
6	NY Islanders	Dec. 11	Dec. 26
6	Toronto	Jan. 6	Jan. 15
6	Montreal	Jan. 30	Feb. 9
6	Calgary	Feb. 2	Feb. 12
6	Boston	Feb. 23	Mar. 7

Consecutive Home Wins

Games	Team	From	To
8	Chicago	Nov. 4	Dec.27
8	Detroit	Nov. 27	Dec.21
7	Toronto	Oct. 7	Nov.6
7	Montreal	Jan. 30	Mar.9
7	New Jersey	Mar. 10	Mar.29
6	NY Islanders	Feb. 15	Mar.1
5	New Jersey	Oct. 6	Oct.23
5	St. Louis	Oct. 7	Nov.6
5	Calgary	Oct. 30	Nov.15
5	NY Rangers	Dec. 13	Jan.3
5	New Jersey	Dec. 19	Jan.7

Consecutive Road Wins

Games	Team	From	To
7	Dallas	Jan. 26	Feb. 21
6	NY Rangers	Oct. 30	Nov. 24
6	Detroit	Jan. 6	Jan. 27
5	Vancouver	Oct. 6	Nov. 2
5	Toronto	Oct. 10	Oct. 28
5	Washington	Jan. 29	Feb. 12
5	Chicago	Feb. 14	Mar. 11

Consecutive Undefeated

Games	Team	W	T	From	To
14	NY Rangers	12	2	Oct. 24	Nov. 24
11	Toronto	7	4	Jan. 6	Feb. 1
11	Montreal	7	4	Feb. 23	Mar. 19
10	Toronto	10	0	Oct. 7	Oct. 28
9	Florida	5	4	Jan. 8	Jan. 30
9	New Jersey	7	2	Feb. 26	Mar. 13
9	San Jose	7	2	Mar. 20	Apr. 5
8	Boston	6	2	Nov. 4	Nov. 20
8	Pittsburgh	4	4	Nov. 16	Dec. 4
8	Detroit	6	2	Dec. 21	Jan. 10
8	NY Islanders	5	3	Mar. 29	Apr. 13

Consecutive Home Undefeated

Games	Team	W	T	From	To
16	NY Rangers	13	3	Oct. 24	Jan. 3
13	Montreal	11	2	Jan. 30	Apr. 2
11	St. Louis	7	4	Oct. 7	Nov. 26
11	Dallas	7	4	Nov. 1	Dec. 12
10	New Jersey	9	1	Feb. 28	Mar. 29
9	Detroit	8	1	Nov. 27	Dec. 31
8	Los Angeles	7	1	Oct. 9	Nov. 13
8	Chicago	8	0	Nov. 4	Dec. 27
7	Toronto	7	0	Oct. 7	Nov. 6
7	Boston	5	2	Nov. 4	Dec. 2
7	Pittsburgh	5	2	Nov. 16	Dec. 16
7	Pittsburgh	5	2	Jan. 8	Feb. 1
7	Boston	5	2	Feb. 5	Mar. 10
7	Calgary	6	1	Mar. 11	Apr. 9

Consecutive Road Undefeated

Games	Team	W	T	From	To
9	Detroit	8	1	Dec. 23	Jan. 27
8	New Jersey	5	3	Nov. 5	Dec. 2
8	Dallas	7	1	Jan. 26	Feb. 23
7	Florida	5	2	Dec. 7	Dec. 29
7	Toronto	4	3	Jan. 2	Feb. 11
7	Buffalo	5	2	Mar. 2	Apr. 2
6	NY Rangers	6	0	Oct. 30	Nov. 24
6	Los Angeles	4	2	Dec. 20	Jan. 15
6	Tampa Bay	5	1	Dec. 28	Jan. 12
6	Florida	3	3	Jan. 8	Jan. 30

TEAM PENALTIES

Abbreviations: GP – games played; **PEN** – total penalty minutes including bench minutes; **BMI** – total bench minor minutes; **AVG** – average penalty minutes/game calculated by dividing total penalty minutes by games played

Team	GP	PEN	BMI	AVG
S.J.	84	1343	26	16.0
BOS	84	1442	14	17.2
ANA	84	1507	24	17.9
MTL	84	1524	12	18.1
T.B.	84	1579	6	18.8
FLA	84	1620	6	19.3
PIT	84	1624	20	19.3
QUE	84	1625	18	19.3
ST. L.	84	1659	20	19.8
NYR	84	1688	20	20.1
PHI	84	1697	32	20.2
OTT	84	1710	22	20.4
N.J.	84	1734	16	20.6
BUF	84	1760	16	21.0
DET	84	1775	18	21.1
NYI	84	1787	8	21.3
HFD	84	1809	22	21.5
CGY	84	1847	16	22.0
EDM	84	1858	12	22.1
TOR	84	1877	8	22.3
DAL	84	1919	24	22.8
VAN	84	1923	16	22.9
WSH	84	2007	24	23.9
L.A.	84	2017	14	24.0
CHI	84	2125	24	25.3
WPG	84	2143	8	25.5
TOTAL	**1092**	**45599**	**446**	**41.8**

Seven-year veteran Glen Wesley helped the Boston Bruins tie the Buffalo Sabres for the League lead in penalty-killing with a efficiency rate of 84.7%

TEAMS' POWER PLAY RECORD

Abbreviations: ADV – total advantages; **PPGF** – power-play goals for; **%** – calculated by dividing number of power-play goals by total advantages.

			Home						Road						Overall		
	Team	GP	ADV	PPGF	%	Team	GP	ADV	PPGF	%	Team	GP	ADV	PPGF	%
1	ST. L.	42	219	57	26.0	VAN	42	211	51	24.2	NYR	84	417	96	23.0
2	PHI	42	214	55	25.7	NYR	42	207	49	23.7	BUF	84	424	96	22.6
3	L.A.	42	229	58	25.3	CGY	42	198	44	22.2	BOS	84	387	84	21.7
4	BUF	42	235	58	24.7	DET	42	189	39	20.6	CGY	84	410	87	21.2
5	BOS	42	209	48	23.0	BOS	42	178	36	20.2	PHI	84	385	80	20.8
6	WPG	42	211	48	22.7	BUF	42	189	38	20.1	DET	84	408	85	20.8
7	NYR	42	210	47	22.4	NYI	42	175	33	18.9	L.A.	84	444	92	20.7
8	MTL	42	193	43	22.3	PIT	42	193	36	18.7	ST. L.	84	420	86	20.5
9	N.J.	42	164	36	22.0	DAL	42	179	33	18.4	NYI	84	369	74	20.1
10	NYI	42	194	41	21.1	TOR	42	221	40	18.1	MTL	84	388	78	20.1
11	DET	42	219	46	21.0	EDM	42	188	34	18.1	WPG	84	423	82	19.4
12	CGY	42	212	43	20.3	MTL	42	195	35	17.9	TOR	84	459	88	19.2
13	TOR	42	238	48	20.2	CHI	42	170	30	17.6	PIT	84	404	76	18.8
14	WSH	42	203	39	19.2	WSH	42	183	31	16.9	VAN	84	441	83	18.8
15	PIT	42	211	40	19.0	T.B.	42	179	29	16.2	DAL	84	440	81	18.4
16	EDM	42	214	40	18.7	S.J.	42	188	30	16.0	EDM	84	402	74	18.4
17	DAL	42	261	48	18.4	WPG	42	212	34	16.0	N.J.	84	333	61	18.3
18	CHI	42	213	37	17.4	FLA	42	190	30	15.8	WSH	84	386	70	18.1
19	QUE	42	218	37	17.0	L.A.	42	215	34	15.8	CHI	84	383	67	17.5
20	S.J.	42	236	38	16.1	HFD	42	197	30	15.2	S.J.	84	424	68	16.0
21	FLA	42	219	35	16.0	OTT	42	210	32	15.2	FLA	84	409	65	15.9
22	HFD	42	211	31	14.7	N.J.	42	169	25	14.8	QUE	84	430	67	15.6
23	ANA	42	205	29	14.1	PHI	42	171	25	14.6	HFD	84	408	61	15.0
24	VAN	42	230	32	13.9	ANA	42	171	25	14.6	T.B.	84	388	57	14.7
25	OTT	42	225	31	13.8	ST. L.	42	201	29	14.4	OTT	84	435	63	14.5
26	T.B.	42	209	28	13.4	QUE	42	212	30	14.2	ANA	84	376	54	14.4
	TOTAL	**1092**	**5602**	**1093**	**19.5**		**1092**	**4991**	**882**	**17.7**		**1092**	**10593**	**1975**	**18.6**

SHORT HAND GOALS FOR

		Home			Road			Overall	
	Team	GP	SHGF	Team	GP	SHGF	Team	GP	SHGF
1	DET	42	11	BUF	42	13	DET	84	22
2	L.A.	42	10	ST. L.	42	12	BUF	84	21
3	NYR	42	9	BOS	42	11	NYR	84	20
4	NYI	42	9	DET	42	11	L.A.	84	19
5	BUF	42	8	NYR	42	11	BOS	84	17
6	CGY	42	7	VAN	42	9	ST. L.	84	17
7	DAL	42	6	CHI	42	9	CGY	84	16
8	N.J.	42	6	WPG	42	9	NYI	84	15
9	CHI	42	6	CGY	42	9	CHI	84	15
10	BOS	42	6	L.A.	42	9	VAN	84	14
11	HFD	42	6	NYI	42	6	WPG	84	13
12	PHI	42	6	MTL	42	6	QUE	84	10
13	ST. L.	42	5	OTT	42	6	N.J.	84	10
14	VAN	42	5	ANA	42	6	PHI	84	9
15	QUE	42	5	QUE	42	5	OTT	84	9
16	WPG	42	5	T.B.	42	5	ANA	84	9
17	TOR	42	4	FLA	42	5	DAL	84	8
18	OTT	42	3	WSH	42	5	MTL	84	8
19	PIT	42	3	N.J.	42	4	HFD	84	8
20	WSH	42	3	PHI	42	4	FLA	84	8
21	ANA	42	3	TOR	42	4	WSH	84	8
22	FLA	42	3	PIT	42	3	TOR	84	8
23	S.J.	42	3	S.J.	42	3	T.B.	84	7
24	MTL	42	2	HFD	42	2	PIT	84	6
25	EDM	42	2	DAL	42	2	S.J.	84	6
26	T.B.	42	2	EDM	42	0	EDM	84	2
	TOTAL	**1092**	**136**		**1092**	**169**		**1092**	**305**

TEAMS' PENALTY KILLING RECORD

Abbreviations: TSH – total times short-handed; **PPGA** – power-play goals against; **%** – calculated by dividing times short minus power-play goals against by times short.

			Home						Road						Overall		
	TEAM	GP	TSH	PPGA	%	TEAM	GP	TSH	PPGA	%	TEAM	GP	TSH	PPGA	%
1	NYR	42	202	26	87.1	CHI	42	209	31	85.2	BOS	84	378	58	84.7
2	FLA	42	176	23	86.9	BOS	42	196	32	83.7	BUF	84	380	58	84.7
3	BUF	42	182	25	86.3	VAN	42	240	40	83.3	NYR	84	435	67	84.6
4	BOS	42	182	26	85.7	BUF	42	198	33	83.3	DAL	84	428	68	84.1
5	DAL	42	231	34	85.3	T.B.	42	176	30	83.0	CHI	84	427	71	83.4
6	NYI	42	204	31	84.8	TOR	42	215	37	82.8	T.B.	84	335	58	82.7
7	ST. L.	42	182	30	83.5	DAL	42	197	34	82.7	ANA	84	388	67	82.7
8	MTL	42	180	30	83.3	ANA	42	200	35	82.5	MTL	84	390	68	82.6
9	L.A.	42	219	37	83.1	NYR	42	233	41	82.4	FLA	84	396	69	82.6
10	PIT	42	176	30	83.0	MTL	42	210	38	81.9	PIT	84	401	72	82.0
11	ANA	42	188	32	83.0	WSH	42	220	40	81.8	TOR	84	409	74	81.9
12	T.B.	42	159	28	82.4	PIT	42	225	42	81.3	VAN	84	458	84	81.7
13	HFD	42	170	31	81.8	N.J.	42	194	37	80.9	WSH	84	403	74	81.6
14	DET	42	181	33	81.8	PHI	42	221	43	80.5	ST. L.	84	388	73	81.2
15	CHI	42	218	40	81.7	DET	42	202	40	80.2	NYI	84	417	79	81.1
16	CGY	42	206	38	81.6	EDM	42	211	42	80.1	N.J.	84	376	71	81.1
17	WPG	42	205	38	81.5	CGY	42	259	52	79.9	DET	84	383	73	80.9
18	WSH	42	183	34	81.4	S.J.	42	179	37	79.3	PHI	84	414	80	80.7
19	N.J.	42	182	34	81.3	FLA	42	220	46	79.1	CGY	84	465	90	80.6
20	EDM	42	190	36	81.1	ST. L.	42	206	43	79.1	EDM	84	401	78	80.5
21	TOR	42	194	37	80.9	QUE	42	208	45	78.4	L.A.	84	462	90	80.5
22	PHI	42	193	37	80.8	L.A.	42	243	53	78.2	QUE	84	426	87	79.6
23	QUE	42	218	42	80.7	WPG	42	240	53	77.9	WPG	84	445	91	79.6
24	VAN	42	218	44	79.8	NYI	42	213	48	77.5	HFD	84	416	88	78.8
25	S.J.	42	181	40	77.9	HFD	42	246	57	76.8	S.J.	84	360	77	78.6
26	OTT	42	171	46	73.1	OTT	42	241	64	73.4	OTT	84	412	110	73.3
	TOTAL	**1092**	**4991**	**882**	**82.3**		**1092**	**5602**	**1093**	**80.5**		**1092**	**10593**	**1975**	**81.4**

SHORT HAND GOALS AGAINST

		Home			Road			Overall	
	Team	GP	SHGA	Team	GP	SHGA	Team	GP	SHGA
1	NYR	42	2	EDM	42	1	NYR	84	5
2	HFD	42	2	N.J.	42	2	N.J.	84	8
3	MTL	42	4	TOR	42	2	L.A.	84	8
4	L.A.	42	4	PIT	42	3	BUF	84	8
5	CGY	42	5	BUF	42	3	BOS	84	8
6	BOS	42	5	NYR	42	3	CGY	84	9
7	ST. L.	42	5	CHI	42	3	NYI	84	9
8	BUF	42	5	BOS	42	4	HFD	84	9
9	NYI	42	5	NYI	42	4	EDM	84	9
10	PHI	42	6	OTT	42	4	TOR	84	9
11	N.J.	42	6	CGY	42	4	MTL	84	10
12	ANA	42	6	L.A.	42	4	CHI	84	10
13	VAN	42	6	WSH	42	5	PIT	84	11
14	CHI	42	7	S.J.	42	5	VAN	84	11
15	TOR	42	7	VAN	42	5	WSH	84	12
16	WSH	42	7	DAL	42	5	S.J.	84	13
17	WPG	42	8	DET	42	6	ANA	84	13
18	EDM	42	8	FLA	42	6	PHI	84	14
19	PIT	42	8	MTL	42	6	DET	84	14
20	T.B.	42	8	HFD	42	7	OTT	84	14
21	DET	42	8	ANA	42	7	ST. L.	84	14
22	S.J.	42	8	PHI	42	8	FLA	84	15
23	QUE	42	9	QUE	42	9	DAL	84	16
24	FLA	42	9	WPG	42	9	WPG	84	17
25	OTT	42	10	ST. L.	42	9	QUE	84	18
26	DAL	42	11	T.B.	42	12	T.B.	84	20
	TOTAL	**1092**	**169**		**1092**	**136**		**1092**	**305**

Overtime Results

1993-94 to 1984-85

Team	1993-94 GP	W	L	T	1992-93 GP	W	L	T	1991-92 GP	W	L	T	1990-91 GP	W	L	T	1989-90 GP	W	L	T	1988-89 GP	W	L	T	1987-88 GP	W	L	T	1986-87 GP	W	L	T	1985-86 GP	W	L	T	1984-85 GP	W	L	T
ANA	12	2	5	5																																				
BOS	17	2	2	13	15	5	3	7	9	3	0	6	17	5	0	12	14	3	2	9	19	3	2	14	14	4	4	6	12	2	3	7	17	2	3	12	18	4	4	10
BUF	13	0	4	9	18	4	4	10	7	1	1	5	24	3	2	19	15	4	3	8	13	2	4	7	12	0	1	11	13	1	4	8	9	1	2	6	17	0	3	14
CGY	18	3	2	13	19	4	4	11	11	1	3	7	15	3	4	8	21	3	3	15	17	5	3	9	15	2	4	9	4	1	0	3	12	1	2	9	14	1	1	12
CHI	16	2	5	9	16	1	3	12	8	0	0	8	12	3	1	8	10	2	2	6	17	2	3	12	15	4	2	9	15	1	0	14	12	3	1	8	12	2	3	7
DAL	22	6	3	13	10	0	0	10	5	0	1	4	17	0	3	14	11	3	4	4	17	0	1	16	16	1	2	13	14	2	2	10	15	4	2	9	15	1	2	12
DET	15	5	2	8	11	2	0	9	5	1	0	4	14	2	4	8	17	2	1	14	16	3	1	12	16	2	3	11	17	2	5	10	13	2	5	6	14	0	2	12
EDM	21	1	6	14	17	5	4	8	5	0	0	5	15	4	5	6	20	5	1	14	15	4	3	8	16	3	2	11	14	5	3	6	14	5	2	7	12	0	1	11
FLA	24	2	5	17																																				
HFD	14	4	1	9	18	3	9	6	11	0	1	10	18	2	5	11	9	0	0	9	10	1	4	5	12	3	2	7	9	2	0	7	7	1	2	4	17	4	4	9
L.A.	18	3	3	12	13	2	1	10	9	0	0	9	16	4	2	10	12	3	2	7	14	6	1	7	12	1	3	8	12	2	2	8	14	3	3	8	19	3	2	14
MTL	19	3	2	14	14	5	3	6	10	4	1	5	17	3	3	11	17	4	2	11	11	2	0	9	16	1	2	13	16	2	4	10	14	1	6	7	18	3	3	12
N.J.	14	1	1	12	11	4	0	7	8	2	2	4	17	1	1	15	16	3	4	9	17	1	4	12	12	4	2	6	13	3	4	6	10	4	3	3	12	0	1	10
NYI	19	5	2	12	13	3	3	7	8	1	2	5	15	2	3	10	16	3	2	11	11	3	3	5	13	3	0	10	20	5	3	12	17	4	1	12	15	1	8	6
NYR	12	3	1	8	17	2	4	11	7	0	3	4	16	1	2	13	17	2	2	13	10	1	1	8	11	0	1	10	19	5	6	8	13	0	7	6	17	2	5	10
OTT	17	4	4	9	10	0	6	4																																
PHI	18	3	5	10	17	4	2	11	10	2	1	7	11	1	0	10	18	2	5	11	14	1	5	8	13	1	3	9	10	1	1	8	9	4	1	4	9	1	1	7
PIT	19	4	2	13	10	3	0	7	8	1	1	6	12	4	2	6	14	3	3	8	10	2	1	7	16	5	2	9	21	5	4	12	14	3	3	8	8	3	0	5
QUE	8	0	0	8	15	4	1	10	6	0	3	3	18	1	3	14	8	0	1	7	10	2	1	7	9	2	2	5	14	0	4	10	11	4	1	6	14	3	2	9
ST.L	17	4	2	11	17	2	4	11	6	2	1	3	18	3	4	11	15	2	4	9	16	3	1	12	14	2	4	8	21	4	2	15	17	5	3	9	15	2	1	12
S.J.	19	2	1	16	10	3	5	2	6	1	2	3																												
T.B.	18	3	4	11	14	3	4	7																																
TOR	17	4	1	12	13	1	1	11	7	4	0	3	17	4	2	11	11	3	4	4	11	1	4	6	13	1	2	10	13	3	4	6	17	4	6	7	15	5	2	8
VAN	12	5	4	3	10	1	0	9	10	2	1	7	15	3	3	9	21	2	5	14	14	2	4	8	11	0	2	9	16	1	2	13	17	7	1	9				
WSH	14	2	2	10	11	2	2	7	4	1	0	3	14	4	3	7	9	2	1	6	16	2	4	10	15	2	4	9	17	5	2	10	11	4	0	7	12	3	0	9
WPG	15	1	5	9	11	2	2	7	9	1	2	6	14	1	2	11	19	4	4	11	20	6	2	12	21	8	2	11	11	2	1	8	8	0	1	7	14	3	1	10
Totals	**214**	**74**		**140**	**165**	**65**		**100**	**169**	**30**		**139**	**166**	**54**		**112**	**155**	**55**		**100**	**149**	**52**		**97**	**146**	**49**		**97**	**148**	**55**		**93**	**135**	**56**		**79**	**152**	**48**		**104**

1993-94
Home Team Wins: 30
Visiting Team Wins: 44

1993-94 Penalty Shots

Scored

Bob Kudelski (Ottawa) scored against Darcy Wakaluk (Dallas), October 30. Final score: Ottawa 5 at Dallas 4.

Paul Ranheim (Calgary) scored against Bob Essensa (Winnipeg), October 31. Final score: Calgary 4 at Winnipeg 3.

Wendel Clark (Toronto) scored against Trevor Kidd (Calgary), November 24. Final score: Toronto 3 at Calgary 5.

Andrei Kovalenko (Quebec) scored against Kirk McLean (Vancouver), December 4. Final score: Vancouver 1 at Quebec 3.

Sergei Fedorov (Detroit) scored against Andy Moog (Dallas), December 27. Final score: Detroit 6 at Dallas 0.

Randy Wood (Buffalo) scored against Jeff Hackett (Chicago), January 11. Final score: Buffalo 5 at Chicago 2.

Steve Larmer (NY Rangers) scored against Ed Belfour (Chicago), January 16. Final score: NY Rangers 5 at Chicago 1.

Robert Reichel (Calgary) scored against Bill Ranford (Edmonton), February 7. Final score: Edmonton 3 at Calgary 4.

Ray Bourque (Boston) scored against Chris Terreri (New Jersey), March 19. Final score: New Jersey 8 at Boston 6.

Sergei Makarov (San Jose) scored against Tim Cheveldae (Winnipeg), March 29. Final score: Winnipeg 4 at San Jose 9.

Andrew Cassels (Hartford) scored against Ron Hextall (NY Islanders), April 6. Final score: NY Islanders 3 at Hartford 3.

Stopped

Jon Casey (Boston) stopped Alexei Kovalev (NY Rangers), October 5. Final score: Boston 4 at NY Rangers 3.

Kelly Hrudey (Los Angeles) stopped Pavel Bure (Vancouver), October 6. Final score: Vancouver 5 at Los Angeles 2.

Ron Tugnutt (Anaheim) stopped Cam Neely (Boston), October 15. Final score: Boston 1 at Anaheim 1.

Bob Essensa (Winnipeg) stopped Philippe Bozon (St. Louis), November 3. Final score: St. Louis 3 at Winnipeg 0.

Damian Rhodes (Toronto) stopped Scott Pearson (Edmonton), November 20. Final score: Toronto 3 at Edmonton 2.

Jocelyn Thibault (Quebec) stopped Tony Granato (Los Angeles), November 25. Final score: Los Angeles 6 at Quebec 8.

Robb Stauber (Los Angeles) stopped Alexander Mogilny (Buffalo), December 17. Final score: Los Angeles 0 at Buffalo 2.

Mike Vernon (Calgary) stopped Kevin Miller (St. Louis), December 17. Final score: St. Louis 4 at Calgary 3.

Kirk McLean (Vancouver) stopped Brent Gilchrist (Dallas), January 27. Final score: Dallas 3 at Vancouver 2.

Kelly Hrudey (Los Angeles) stopped Tony Amonte (NY Rangers), January 27. Final score: NY Rangers 5 at Los Angeles 4.

Ed Belfour (Chicago) stopped Roman Oksiuta (Edmonton), February 4. Final score: Chicago 3 at Edmonton 1.

Vincent Riendeau (Boston) stopped Wayne Presley (Buffalo), February 10. Final score: Buffalo 3 at Boston 3.

Chris Osgood (Detroit) stopped Peter Zezel (Toronto), March 4. Final score: Toronto 6 at Detroit 5.

Ed Belfour (Chicago) stopped Mark Howe (Detroit), March 22. Final score: Chicago 1 at Detroit 3.

Curtis Joseph (St. Louis) stopped Mike Donnelly (Los Angeles), April 7. Final score: Los Angeles 2 at St. Louis 6.

Ed Belfour set an NHL record by facing three penalty shots in one season in 1993-94. The Blackhawks goalie blanked Edmonton's Roman Oksiuta and Detroit's Mark Howe before allowing a goal to Ranger forward Steve Larmer.

John Vanbiesbrouck (Florida) stopped Zigmund Palffy (NY Islanders), April 14. Final score: NY Islanders 1 at Florida 4.

Summary

27 penalty shots resulted in 11 goals.

NHL Record Book

Year-by Year Final Standings & Leading Scorers

* Stanley Cup winner

1917-18

Team	GP	W	L	T	GF	GA	PTS
Montreal	22	13	9	0	115	84	26
*Toronto	22	13	9	0	108	109	26
Ottawa	22	9	13	0	102	114	18
**Mtl. Wanderers	6	1	5	0	17	35	2

**Montreal Arena burned down and Wanderers forced to withdraw from League. Canadiens and Toronto each counted a win for defaulted games with Wanderers.

Leading Scorers

Player	Club	GP	G	A	PTS
Malone, Joe	Montreal	20	44	—	44
Denneny, Cy	Ottawa	22	36	—	36
Noble, Reg	Toronto	20	28	—	28
Lalonde, Newsy	Montreal	14	23	—	23
Denneny, Corbett	Toronto	21	20	—	20
Pitre, Didier	Montreal	19	17	—	17
Cameron, Harry	Toronto	20	17	—	17
Darragh, Jack	Ottawa	18	14	—	14
Hyland, Harry	Mtl.W., Ott.	16	14	—	14
Skinner, Alf	Toronto	19	13	—	13
Gerard, Eddie	Ottawa	21	13	—	13

1918-19

Team	GP	W	L	T	GF	GA	PTS
Ottawa	18	12	6	0	71	53	24
Montreal	18	10	8	0	88	78	20
Toronto	18	5	13	0	64	92	10

Leading Scorers

Player	Club	GP	G	A	PTS	PIM
Lalonde, Newsy	Montreal	17	21	9	30	40
Cleghorn, Odie	Montreal	17	23	6	29	33
Denneny, Cy	Ottawa	18	18	4	22	43
Nighbor, Frank	Ottawa	18	18	4	22	27
Pitre, Didier	Montreal	17	14	4	18	9
Skinner, Alf	Toronto	17	12	3	15	26
Cameron, Harry	Tor., Ott.	14	11	3	14	35
Noble, Reg	Toronto	17	11	3	14	35
Darragh, Jack	Ottawa	14	12	1	13	27
Randall, Ken	Toronto	14	7	6	13	27

1919-20

Team	GP	W	L	T	GF	GA	PTS
*Ottawa	24	19	5	0	121	64	38
Montreal	24	13	11	0	129	113	26
Toronto	24	12	12	0	119	106	24
Quebec	24	4	20	0	91	177	8

Leading Scorers

Player	Club	GP	G	A	PTS	PIM
Malone, Joe	Quebec	24	39	9	48	12
Lalonde, Newsy	Montreal	23	36	6	42	33
Denneny, Corbett	Toronto	23	23	12	35	18
Nighbor, Frank	Ottawa	23	26	7	33	18
Noble, Reg	Toronto	24	24	7	31	51
Darragh, Jack	Ottawa	22	22	5	27	22
Arbour, Amos	Montreal	20	22	4	26	10
Wilson, Cully	Toronto	23	21	5	26	79
Broadbent, Punch	Ottawa	20	19	4	23	39
Cleghorn, Odie	Montreal	21	19	3	22	30
Pitre, Didier	Montreal	22	15	7	22	6

All-Time Standings of NHL Teams

(ranked by percentage)

Active Clubs

Team	Games	Wins	Losses	Ties	Goals For	Goals Against	Points	%	First Season
Montreal	4760	2521	1502	737	16204	12636	5779	.607	1917-18
Philadelphia	2146	1056	754	336	7701	6681	2448	.570	1967-68
Edmonton	1208	608	444	156	5188	4553	1372	.568	1967-68
Boston	4600	2213	1704	683	15225	13695	5109	.555	1924-25
Buffalo	1920	909	706	305	6990	6273	2123	.553	1970-71
Calgary	1764	835	661	268	6750	6095	1938	.549	1972-73
NY Islanders	1764	832	679	253	6509	5781	1917	.543	1972-73
Toronto	4760	2044	2022	694	14914	14864	4782	.502	1917-18
NY Rangers	4534	1915	1905	714	14283	14381	4544	.501	1926-27
Detroit	4534	1895	1925	714	13977	14090	4504	.497	1926-27
Florida	84	33	34	17	233	233	83	.494	1993-94
St. Louis	2146	893	927	326	7058	7313	2112	.492	1967-68
Chicago	4534	1866	1966	702	13734	13961	4434	.489	1926-27
Washington	1608	663	739	206	5556	5918	1532	.476	1974-75
Los Angeles	2146	845	989	312	7591	8092	2002	.466	1967-68
Pittsburgh	2146	848	1001	297	7541	8125	1993	.464	1967-68
Dallas	2146	800	999	347	6976	7638	1947	.454	1967-68
Quebec	1208	467	586	155	4440	4749	1089	.451	1979-80
Winnipeg	1208	454	595	159	4330	4879	1067	.442	1979-80
Hartford	1208	449	607	152	4114	4689	1050	.435	1979-80
Vancouver	1920	695	950	275	6335	7210	1665	.434	1970-71
Anaheim	84	33	46	5	229	251	71	.423	1993-94
New Jersey	1608	512	875	221	5164	6363	1245	.387	1974-75
Tampa Bay	168	53	97	18	469	583	124	.369	1992-93
San Jose	248	61	164	23	689	1038	145	.292	1991-92
Ottawa	168	24	131	13	403	792	61	.182	1992-93

Defunct Clubs

Team	Games	Wins	Losses	Ties	Goals For	Goals Against	Points	%	First Season	Last Season
Ottawa Senators	542	258	221	63	1458	1333	579	.534	1917-18	1933-34
Montreal Maroons	622	271	260	91	1474	1405	633	.509	1924-25	1937-38
NY/Brooklyn Americans	784	255	402	127	1643	2182	637	.406	1925-26	1941-42
Hamilton Tigers	126	47	78	1	414	475	95	.377	1920-21	1924-25
Cleveland Barons	160	47	87	26	470	617	120	.375	1976-77	1977-78
Pittsburgh Pirates	212	67	122	23	376	519	157	.370	1925-26	1929-30
Calif./Oakland Seals	698	182	401	115	1826	2580	479	.343	1967-68	1975-76
St. Louis Eagles	48	11	31	6	86	144	28	.292	1934-35	1934-35
Quebec Bulldogs	24	4	20	0	91	177	8	.167	1919-20	1919-20
Montreal Wanderers	6	1	5	0	17	35	2	.167	1917-18	1917-18
Philadelphia Quakers	44	4	36	4	76	184	12	.136	1930-31	1930-31

Calgary totals include Atlanta, 1972-73 to 1979-80.
Dallas totals include Minnesota, 1967-68 to 1992-93.
Detroit totals include Cougars, 1926-27 to 1928-29, and Falcons, 1929-30 to 1931-32.
New Jersey totals include Kansas City, 1974-75 to 1975-76, and Colorado, 1976-77 to 1981-82.
Toronto totals include Arenas, 1917-18 to 1918-19, and St. Patricks, 1919-20 to 1925-56.

1920-21

Team	GP	W	L	T	GF	GA	PTS
Toronto	24	15	9	0	105	100	30
*Ottawa	24	14	10	0	97	75	28
Montreal	24	13	11	0	112	99	26
Hamilton	24	6	18	0	92	132	12

Leading Scorers

Player	Club	GP	G	A	PTS	PIM
Lalonde, Newsy	Montreal	24	33	8	41	36
Denneny, Cy	Ottawa	24	34	5	39	0
Dye, Babe	Ham., Tor.	24	35	2	37	32
Malone, Joe	Hamilton	20	30	4	34	2
Cameron, Harry	Toronto	24	18	9	27	35
Noble, Reg	Toronto	24	20	6	26	54
Prodgers, Goldie	Hamilton	23	18	8	26	8
Denneny, Corbett	Toronto	20	17	6	23	27
Nighbor, Frank	Ottawa	24	18	3	21	10
Berlinquette, Louis	Montreal	24	12	9	21	24

1921-22

Team	GP	W	L	T	GF	GA	PTS
Ottawa	24	14	8	2	106	84	30
*Toronto	24	13	10	1	98	97	27
Montreal	24	12	11	1	88	94	25
Hamilton	24	7	17	0	88	105	14

Leading Scorers

Player	Club	GP	G	A	PTS	PIM
Broadbent, Punch	Ottawa	24	32	14	46	24
Denneny, Cy	Ottawa	22	27	12	39	18
Dye, Babe	Toronto	24	30	7	37	18
Malone, Joe	Hamilton	24	25	7	32	4
Cameron, Harry	Toronto	24	19	8	27	18
Denneny, Corbett	Toronto	24	19	7	26	28
Noble, Reg	Toronto	24	17	8	25	10
Cleghorn, Odie	Montreal	23	21	3	24	26
Cleghorn, Sprague	Montreal	24	17	7	24	63
Reise, Leo	Hamilton	24	9	14	23	8

1922-23

Team	GP	W	L	T	GF	GA	PTS
*Ottawa	24	14	9	1	77	54	29
Montreal	24	13	9	2	73	61	28
Toronto	24	13	10	1	82	88	27
Hamilton	24	6	18	0	81	110	12

Leading Scorers

Player	Club	GP	G	A	PTS	PIM
Dye, Babe	Toronto	22	26	11	37	19
Denneny, Cy	Ottawa	24	21	10	31	20
Adams, Jack	Toronto	23	19	9	28	42
Boucher, Billy	Montreal	24	23	4	27	52
Cleghorn, Odie	Montreal	24	19	7	26	14
Roach, Mickey	Hamilton	23	17	8	25	8
Boucher, George	Ottawa	23	15	9	24	44
Joliat, Aurel	Montreal	24	13	9	22	31
Noble, Reg	Toronto	24	12	10	22	41
Wilson, Cully	Hamilton	23	16	3	19	46

1923-24

Team	GP	W	L	T	GF	GA	PTS
Ottawa	24	16	8	0	74	54	32
*Montreal	24	13	11	0	59	48	26
Toronto	24	10	14	0	59	85	20
Hamilton	24	9	15	0	63	68	18

Leading Scorers

Player	Club	GP	G	A	PTS	PIM
Denneny, Cy	Ottawa	21	22	1	23	10
Boucher, Billy	Montreal	23	16	6	22	33
Joliat, Aurel	Montreal	24	15	5	20	19
Dye, Babe	Toronto	19	17	2	19	23
Boucher, George	Ottawa	21	14	5	19	28
Burch, Billy	Hamilton	24	16	2	18	4
Clancy, King	Ottawa	24	9	8	17	18
Adams, Jack	Toronto	22	13	3	16	49
Morenz, Howie	Montreal	24	13	3	16	20
Noble, Reg	Toronto	23	12	3	15	23

1924-25

Team	GP	W	L	T	GF	GA	PTS
Hamilton	30	19	10	1	90	60	39
Toronto	30	19	11	0	90	84	38
Montreal	30	17	11	2	93	56	36
Ottawa	30	17	12	1	83	66	35
Mtl. Maroons	30	9	19	2	45	65	20
Boston	30	6	24	0	49	119	12

Leading Scorers

Player	Club	GP	G	A	PTS	PIM
Dye, Babe	Toronto	29	38	6	44	41
Denneny, Cy	Ottawa	28	27	15	42	16
Joliat, Aurel	Montreal	24	29	11	40	85
Morenz, Howie	Montreal	30	27	7	34	31
Boucher, Billy	Montreal	30	18	13	31	92
Adams, Jack	Toronto	27	21	8	29	66
Burch, Billy	Hamilton	27	20	4	24	10
Green, Red	Hamilton	30	19	4	23	63
Herberts, Jimmy	Boston	30	17	5	22	50
Day, Hap	Toronto	26	10	12	22	27

1925-26

Team	GP	W	L	T	GF	GA	PTS
Ottawa	36	24	8	4	77	42	52
*Mtl. Maroons	36	20	11	5	91	73	45
Pittsburgh	36	19	16	1	82	70	39
Boston	36	17	15	4	92	85	38
NY Americans	36	12	20	4	68	89	28
Toronto	36	12	21	3	92	114	27
Montreal	36	11	24	1	79	108	23

Leading Scorers

Player	Club	GP	G	A	PTS	PIM
Stewart, Nels	Mtl. Maroons	36	34	8	42	119
Denneny, Cy	Ottawa	36	24	12	36	18
Cooper, Carson	Boston	36	28	3	31	10
Herberts, Jimmy	Boston	36	26	5	31	47
Morenz, Howie	Montreal	31	23	3	26	39
Adams, Jack	Toronto	36	21	5	26	52
Joliat, Aurel	Montreal	35	17	9	26	52
Burch, Billy	NY Americans	36	22	3	25	33
Smith, Hooley	Ottawa	28	16	9	25	53
Nighbor, Frank	Ottawa	35	12	13	25	40

1926-27

Canadian Division

Team	GP	W	L	T	GF	GA	PTS
*Ottawa	44	30	10	4	86	69	64
Montreal	44	28	14	2	99	67	58
Mtl. Maroons	44	20	20	4	71	68	44
NY Americans	44	17	25	2	82	91	36
Toronto	44	15	24	5	79	94	35

American Division

Team	GP	W	L	T	GF	GA	PTS
New York	44	25	13	6	95	72	56
Boston	44	21	20	3	97	89	45
Chicago	44	19	22	3	115	116	41
Pittsburgh	44	15	26	3	79	108	33
Detroit	44	12	28	4	76	105	28

Leading Scorers

Player	Club	GP	G	A	PTS	PIM
Cook, Bill	New York	44	33	4	37	58
Irvin, Dick	Chicago	43	18	18	36	34
Morenz, Howie	Montreal	44	25	7	32	49
Fredrickson, Frank	Det., Bos.	41	18	13	31	46
Dye, Babe	Chicago	41	25	5	30	14
Bailey, Ace	Toronto	42	15	13	28	82
Boucher, Frank	New York	44	13	15	28	17
Burch, Billy	NY Americans	43	19	8	27	40
Oliver, Harry	Boston	42	18	6	24	17
Keats, Gordon	Bos., Det.	42	16	8	24	52

1927-28

Canadian Division

Team	GP	W	L	T	GF	GA	PTS
Montreal	44	26	11	7	116	48	59
Mtl. Maroons	44	24	14	6	96	77	54
Ottawa	44	20	14	10	78	57	50
Toronto	44	18	18	8	89	88	44
NY Americans	44	11	27	6	63	128	28

American Division

Team	GP	W	L	T	GF	GA	PTS
Boston	44	20	13	11	77	70	51
*New York	44	19	16	9	94	79	47
Pittsburgh	44	19	17	8	67	76	46
Detroit	44	19	19	6	88	79	44
Chicago	44	7	34	3	68	134	17

Leading Scorers

Player	Club	GP	G	A	PTS	PIM
Morenz, Howie	Montreal	43	33	18	51	66
Joliat, Aurel	Montreal	44	28	11	39	105
Boucher, Frank	New York	44	23	12	35	15
Hay, George	Detroit	42	22	13	35	20
Stewart, Nels	Mtl. Maroons	41	27	7	34	104
Gagne, Art	Montreal	44	20	10	30	75
Cook, Fred	New York	44	14	14	28	45
Carson, Bill	Toronto	32	20	6	26	36
Finnigan, Frank	Ottawa	38	20	5	25	34
Cook, Bill	New York	43	18	6	24	42
Keats, Gordon	Det., Chi..	38	14	10	24	60

1928-29

Canadian Division

Team	GP	W	L	T	GF	GA	PTS
Montreal	44	22	7	15	71	43	59
NY Americans	44	19	13	12	53	53	50
Toronto	44	21	18	5	85	69	47
Ottawa	44	14	17	13	54	67	41
Mtl. Maroons	44	15	20	9	67	65	39

American Division

Team	GP	W	L	T	GF	GA	PTS
*Boston	44	26	13	5	89	52	57
New York	44	21	13	10	72	65	52
Detroit	44	19	16	9	72	63	47
Pittsburgh	44	9	27	8	46	80	26
Chicago	44	7	29	8	33	85	22

Leading Scorers

Player	Club	GP	G	A	PTS	PIM
Bailey, Ace	Toronto	44	22	10	32	78
Stewart, Nels	Mtl. Maroons	44	21	8	29	74
Cooper, Carson	Detroit	43	18	9	27	14
Morenz, Howie	Montreal	42	17	10	27	47
Blair, Andy	Toronto	44	12	15	27	41
Boucher, Frank	New York	44	10	16	26	8
Oliver, Harry	Boston	43	17	6	23	24
Cook, Bill	New York	43	15	8	23	41
Ward, Jimmy	Mtl. Maroons	43	14	8	22	46

Seven players tied with 19 points

1929-30

Canadian Division

Team	GP	W	L	T	GF	GA	PTS
Mtl. Maroons	44	23	16	5	141	114	51
*Montreal	44	21	14	9	142	114	51
Ottawa	44	21	15	8	138	118	50
Toronto	44	17	21	6	116	124	40
NY Americans	44	14	25	5	113	161	33

American Division

Team	GP	W	L	T	GF	GA	PTS
Boston	44	38	5	1	179	98	77
Chicago	44	21	18	5	117	111	47
New York	44	17	17	10	136	143	44
Detroit	44	14	24	6	117	133	34
Pittsburgh	44	5	36	3	102	185	13

Leading Scorers

Player	Club	GP	G	A	PTS	PIM
Weiland, Cooney	Boston	44	43	30	73	27
Boucher, Frank	New York	42	26	36	62	16
Clapper, Dit	Boston	44	41	20	61	48
Cook, Bill	New York	44	29	30	59	56
Kilrea, Hec	Ottawa	44	36	22	58	72
Stewart, Nels	Mtl. Maroons	44	39	16	55	81
Morenz, Howie	Montreal	44	40	10	50	72
Himes, Norm	NY Americans	44	28	22	50	15
Lamb, Joe	Ottawa	44	29	20	49	119
Gainor, Norm	Boston	42	18	31	49	39

1930-31

Canadian Division

Team	GP	W	L	T	GF	GA	PTS
*Montreal	44	26	10	8	129	89	60
Toronto	44	22	13	9	118	99	53
Mtl. Maroons	44	20	18	6	105	106	46
NY Americans	44	18	16	10	76	74	46
Ottawa	44	10	30	4	91	142	24

American Division

Team	GP	W	L	T	GF	GA	PTS
Boston	44	28	10	6	143	90	62
Chicago	44	24	17	3	108	78	51
New York	44	19	16	9	106	87	47
Detroit	44	16	21	7	102	105	39
Philadelphia	44	4	36	4	76	184	12

Leading Scorers

Player	Club	GP	G	A	PTS	PIM
Morenz, Howie	Montreal	39	28	23	51	49
Goodfellow, Ebbie	Detroit	44	25	23	48	32
Conacher, Charlie	Toronto	37	31	12	43	78
Cook, Bill	New York	43	30	12	42	39
Bailey, Ace	Toronto	40	23	19	42	46
Primeau, Joe	Toronto	38	9	32	41	18
Stewart, Nels	Mtl. Maroons	42	25	14	39	75
Boucher, Frank	New York	44	12	27	39	20
Weiland, Cooney	Boston	44	25	13	38	14
Cook, Fred	New York	44	18	17	35	72
Joliat, Aurel	Montreal	43	13	22	35	73

1931-32

Canadian Division

Team	GP	W	L	T	GF	GA	PTS
Montreal	48	25	16	7	128	111	57
*Toronto	48	23	18	7	155	127	53
Mtl. Maroons	48	19	22	7	142	139	45
NY Americans	48	16	24	8	95	142	40

American Division

Team	GP	W	L	T	GF	GA	PTS
New York	48	23	17	8	134	112	54
Chicago	48	18	19	11	86	101	47
Detroit	48	18	20	10	95	108	46
Boston	48	15	21	12	122	117	42

Leading Scorers

Player	Club	GP	G	A	PTS	PIM
Jackson, Harvey	Toronto	48	28	25	53	63
Primeau, Joe	Toronto	46	13	37	50	25
Morenz, Howie	Montreal	48	24	25	49	46
Conacher, Charlie	Toronto	44	34	14	48	66
Cook, Bill	New York	48	34	14	48	33
Trottier, Dave	Mtl. Maroons	48	26	18	44	94
Smith, Reg	Mtl. Maroons	43	11	33	44	49
Siebert, Albert	Mtl. Maroons	48	21	18	39	64
Clapper, Dit	Boston	48	17	22	39	21
Joliat, Aurel	Montreal	48	15	24	39	46

Red Green, who finished eighth in scoring with Hamilton in 1924-25, scores on Canadiens netminder Harry Rheaume during this game between the New York Americans and Montreal in 1925-26.

1932-33

Canadian Division

Team	GP	W	L	T	GF	GA	PTS
Toronto	48	24	18	6	119	111	54
Mtl. Maroons	48	22	20	6	135	119	50
Montreal	48	18	25	5	92	115	41
NY Americans	48	15	22	11	91	118	41
Ottawa	48	11	27	10	88	131	32

American Division

Team	GP	W	L	T	GF	GA	PTS
Boston	48	25	15	8	124	88	58
Detroit	48	25	15	8	111	93	58
*New York	48	23	17	8	135	107	54
Chicago	48	16	20	12	88	101	44

Leading Scorers

Player	Club	GP	G	A	PTS	PIM
Cook, Bill	New York	48	28	22	50	51
Jackson, Harvey	Toronto	48	27	17	44	43
Northcott, Lawrence	Mtl. Maroons	48	22	21	43	30
Smith, Reg	Mtl. Maroons	48	20	21	41	66
Haynes, Paul	Mtl. Maroons	48	16	25	41	18
Joliat, Aurel	Montreal	48	18	21	39	53
Barry, Marty	Boston	48	24	13	37	40
Cook, Fred	New York	48	22	15	37	35
Stewart, Nels	Boston	47	18	18	36	62
Morenz, Howie	Montreal	46	14	21	35	32
Gagnon, Johnny	Montreal	48	12	23	35	64
Shore, Eddie	Boston	48	8	27	35	102
Boucher, Frank	New York	47	7	28	35	4

1933-34

Canadian Division

Team	GP	W	L	T	GF	GA	PTS
Toronto	48	26	13	9	174	119	61
Montreal	48	22	20	6	99	101	50
Mtl. Maroons	48	19	18	11	117	122	49
NY Americans	48	15	23	10	104	132	40
Ottawa	48	13	29	6	115	143	32

American Division

Team	GP	W	L	T	GF	GA	PTS
Detroit	48	24	14	10	113	98	58
*Chicago	48	20	17	11	88	83	51
New York	48	21	19	8	120	113	50
Boston	48	18	25	5	111	130	41

Leading Scorers

Player	Club	GP	G	A	PTS	PIM
Conacher, Charlie	Toronto	42	32	20	52	38
Primeau, Joe	Toronto	45	14	32	46	8
Boucher, Frank	New York	48	14	30	44	4
Barry, Marty	Boston	48	27	12	39	12
Dillon, Cecil	New York	48	13	26	39	10
Stewart, Nels	Boston	48	21	17	38	68
Jackson, Harvey	Toronto	38	20	18	38	38
Joliat, Aurel	Montreal	48	22	15	37	27
Smith, Reg	Mtl. Maroons	47	18	19	37	58
Thompson, Paul	Chicago	48	20	16	36	17

1934-35

Canadian Division

Team	GP	W	L	T	GF	GA	PTS
Toronto	48	30	14	4	157	111	64
*Mtl. Maroons	48	24	19	5	123	92	53
Montreal	48	19	23	6	110	145	44
NY Americans	48	12	27	9	100	142	33
St. Louis	48	11	31	6	86	144	28

American Division

Team	GP	W	L	T	GF	GA	PTS
Boston	48	26	16	6	129	112	58
Chicago	48	26	17	5	118	88	57
New York	48	22	20	6	137	139	50
Detroit	48	19	22	7	127	114	45

Leading Scorers

Player	Club	GP	G	A	PTS	PIM
Conacher, Charlie	Toronto	47	36	21	57	24
Howe, Syd	St.L., Det.	50	22	25	47	34
Aurie, Larry	Detroit	48	17	29	46	24
Boucher, Frank	New York	48	13	32	45	2
Jackson, Harvey	Toronto	42	22	22	44	27
Lewis, Herb	Detroit	47	16	27	43	26
Chapman, Art	NY Americans	47	9	34	43	4
Barry, Marty	Boston	48	20	20	40	33
Schriner, Sweeney	NY Americans	48	18	22	40	6
Stewart, Nels	Boston	47	21	18	39	45
Thompson, Paul	Chicago	48	16	23	39	20

1935-36

Canadian Division

Team	GP	W	L	T	GF	GA	PTS
Mtl. Maroons	48	22	16	10	114	106	54
Toronto	48	23	19	6	126	106	52
NY Americans	48	16	25	7	109	122	39
Montreal	48	11	26	11	82	123	33

American Division

Team	GP	W	L	T	GF	GA	PTS
*Detroit	48	24	16	8	124	103	56
Boston	48	22	20	6	92	83	50
Chicago	48	21	19	8	93	92	50
New York	48	19	17	12	91	96	50

Leading Scorers

Player	Club	GP	G	A	PTS	PIM
Schriner, Sweeney	NY Americans	48	19	26	45	8
Barry, Marty	Detroit	48	21	19	40	16
Thompson, Paul	Chicago	45	17	23	40	19
Thoms, Bill	Toronto	48	23	15	38	29
Conacher, Charlie	Toronto	44	23	15	38	74
Smith, Reg	Mtl. Maroons	47	19	19	38	75
Romnes, Doc	Chicago	48	13	25	38	6
Chapman, Art	NY Americans	47	10	28	38	14
Lewis, Herb	Detroit	45	14	23	37	25
Northcott, Lawrence	Mtl. Maroons	48	15	21	36	41

1936-37

Canadian Division

Team	GP	W	L	T	GF	GA	PTS
Montreal	48	24	18	6	115	111	54
Mtl. Maroons	48	22	17	9	126	110	53
Toronto	48	22	21	5	119	115	49
NY Americans	48	15	29	4	122	161	34

American Division

Team	GP	W	L	T	GF	GA	PTS
*Detroit	48	25	14	9	128	102	59
Boston	48	23	18	7	120	110	53
New York	48	19	20	9	117	106	47
Chicago	48	14	27	7	99	131	35

Leading Scorers

Player	Club	GP	G	A	PTS	PIM
Schriner, Sweeney	NY Americans	48	21	25	46	17
Apps, Syl	Toronto	48	16	29	45	10
Barry, Marty	Detroit	48	17	27	44	6
Aurie, Larry	Detroit	45	23	20	43	20
Jackson, Harvey	Toronto	46	21	19	40	12
Gagnon, Johnny	Montreal	48	20	16	36	38
Gracie, Bob	Mtl. Maroons	47	11	25	36	18
Stewart, Nels	Bos., NYA	43	23	12	35	37
Thompson, Paul	Chicago	47	17	18	35	28
Cowley, Bill	Boston	46	13	22	35	4

1937-38

Canadian Division

Team	GP	W	L	T	GF	GA	PTS
Toronto	48	24	15	9	151	127	57
NY Americans	48	19	18	11	110	111	49
Montreal	48	18	17	13	123	128	49
Mtl. Maroons	48	12	30	6	101	149	30

American Division

Team	GP	W	L	T	GF	GA	PTS
Boston	48	30	11	7	142	89	67
New York	48	27	15	6	149	96	60
*Chicago	48	14	25	9	97	139	37
Detroit	48	12	25	11	99	133	35

Leading Scorers

Player	Club	GP	G	A	PTS	PIM
Drillon, Gord	Toronto	48	26	26	52	4
Apps, Syl	Toronto	47	21	29	50	9
Thompson, Paul	Chicago	48	22	22	44	14
Mantha, Georges	Montreal	47	23	19	42	12
Dillon, Cecil	New York	48	21	18	39	6
Cowley, Bill	Boston	48	17	22	39	8
Schriner, Sweeney	NY Americans	49	21	17	38	22
Thoms, Bill	Toronto	48	14	24	38	14
Smith, Clint	New York	48	14	23	37	0
Stewart, Nels	NY Americans	48	19	17	36	29
Colville, Neil	New York	45	17	19	36	11

1938-39

Team	GP	W	L	T	GF	GA	PTS
*Boston	48	36	10	2	156	76	74
New York	48	26	16	6	149	105	58
Toronto	48	19	20	9	114	107	47
NY Americans	48	17	21	10	119	157	44
Detroit	48	18	24	6	107	128	42
Montreal	48	15	24	9	115	146	39
Chicago	48	12	28	8	91	132	32

Leading Scorers

Player	Club	GP	G	A	PTS	PIM
Blake, Hector	Montreal	48	24	23	47	10
Schriner, Sweeney	NY Americans	48	13	31	44	20
Cowley, Bill	Boston	34	8	34	42	2
Smith, Clint	New York	48	21	20	41	2
Barry, Marty	Detroit	48	13	28	41	4
Apps, Syl	Toronto	44	15	25	40	4
Anderson, Tom	NY Americans	48	13	27	40	14
Gottselig, Johnny	Chicago	48	16	23	39	15
Haynes, Paul	Montreal	47	5	33	38	27
Conacher, Roy	Boston	47	26	11	37	12
Carr, Lorne	NY Americans	46	19	18	37	16
Colville, Neil	New York	48	18	19	37	12
Watson, Phil	New York	48	15	22	37	42

1939-40

Team	GP	W	L	T	GF	GA	PTS
Boston	48	31	12	5	170	98	67
*New York	48	27	11	10	136	77	64
Toronto	48	25	17	6	134	110	56
Chicago	48	23	19	6	112	120	52
Detroit	48	16	26	6	90	126	38
NY Americans	48	15	29	4	106	140	34
Montreal	48	10	33	5	90	167	25

Leading Scorers

Player	Club	GP	G	A	PTS	PIM
Schmidt, Milt	Boston	48	22	30	52	37
Dumart, Woody	Boston	48	22	21	43	16
Bauer, Bob	Boston	48	17	26	43	2
Drillon, Gord	Toronto	43	21	19	40	13
Cowley, Bill	Boston	48	13	27	40	24
Hextall, Bryan	New York	48	24	15	39	52
Colville, Neil	New York	48	19	19	38	22
Howe, Syd	Detroit	46	14	23	37	17
Blake, Hector	Montreal	48	17	19	36	48
Armstrong, Murray	NY Americans	48	16	20	36	12

1940-41

Team	GP	W	L	T	GF	GA	PTS
*Boston	48	27	8	13	168	102	67
Toronto	48	28	14	6	145	99	62
Detroit	48	21	16	11	112	102	53
New York	48	21	19	8	143	125	50
Chicago	48	16	25	7	112	139	39
Montreal	48	16	26	6	121	147	38
NY Americans	48	8	29	11	99	186	27

Leading Scorers

Player	Club	GP	G	A	PTS	PIM
Cowley, Bill	Boston	46	17	45	62	16
Hextall, Bryan	New York	48	26	18	44	16
Drillon, Gord	Toronto	42	23	21	44	2
Apps, Syl	Toronto	41	20	24	44	6
Patrick, Lynn	New York	48	20	24	44	12
Howe, Syd	Detroit	48	20	24	44	8
Colville, Neil	New York	48	14	28	42	28
Wiseman, Eddie	Boston	48	16	24	40	10
Bauer, Bobby	Boston	48	17	22	39	2
Schriner, Sweeney	Toronto	48	24	14	38	6
Conacher, Roy	Boston	40	24	14	38	7
Schmidt, Milt	Boston	44	13	25	38	23

1941-42

Team	GP	W	L	T	GF	GA	PTS
New York	48	29	17	2	177	143	60
*Toronto	48	27	18	3	158	136	57
Boston	48	25	17	6	160	118	56
Chicago	48	22	23	3	145	155	47
Detroit	48	19	25	4	140	147	42
Montreal	48	18	27	3	134	173	39
Brooklyn	48	16	29	3	133	175	35

Leading Scorers

Player	Club	GP	G	A	PTS	PIM
Hextall, Bryan	New York	48	24	32	56	30
Patrick, Lynn	New York	47	32	22	54	18
Grosso, Don	Detroit	48	23	30	53	13
Watson, Phil	New York	48	15	37	52	48
Abel, Sid	Detroit	48	18	31	49	45
Blake, Hector	Montreal	47	17	28	45	19
Thoms, Bill	Chicago	47	15	30	45	8
Drillon, Gord	Toronto	48	23	18	41	6
Apps, Syl	Toronto	38	18	23	41	0
Anderson, Tom	Brooklyn	48	12	29	41	54

1942-43

Team	GP	W	L	T	GF	GA	PTS
*Detroit	50	25	14	11	169	124	61
Boston	50	24	17	9	195	176	57
Toronto	50	22	19	9	198	159	53
Montreal	50	19	19	12	181	191	50
Chicago	50	17	18	15	179	180	49
New York	50	11	31	8	161	253	30

Leading Scorers

Player	Club	GP	G	A	PTS	PIM
Bentley, Doug	Chicago	50	33	40	73	18
Cowley, Bill	Boston	48	27	45	72	10
Bentley, Max	Chicago	47	26	44	70	2
Patrick, Lynn	New York	50	22	39	61	28
Carr, Lorne	Toronto	50	27	33	60	15
Taylor, Billy	Toronto	50	18	42	60	2
Hextall, Bryan	New York	50	27	32	59	28
Blake, Hector	Montreal	48	23	36	59	28
Lach, Elmer	Montreal	45	18	40	58	14
O'Connor, Herb	Montreal	50	15	43	58	2

1943-44

Team	GP	W	L	T	GF	GA	PTS
*Montreal	50	38	5	7	234	109	83
Detroit	50	26	18	6	214	177	58
Toronto	50	23	23	4	214	174	50
Chicago	50	22	23	5	178	187	49
Boston	50	19	26	5	223	268	43
New York	50	6	39	5	162	310	17

Leading Scorers

Player	Club	GP	G	A	PTS	PIM
Cain, Herb	Boston	48	36	46	82	4
Bentley, Doug	Chicago	50	38	39	77	22
Carr, Lorne	Toronto	50	36	38	74	9
Liscombe, Carl	Detroit	50	36	37	73	17
Lach, Elmer	Montreal	48	24	48	72	23
Smith, Clint	Chicago	50	23	49	72	4
Cowley, Bill	Boston	36	30	41	71	12
Mosienko, Bill	Chicago	50	32	38	70	10
Jackson, Art	Boston	49	28	41	69	8
Bodnar, Gus	Toronto	50	22	40	62	18

Billy Taylor, who finished as the League's sixth-leading scorer with Toronto in 1942-43, joined Detroit Red Wings in 1946-47 and topped the League with 46 assists.

1944-45

Team	GP	W	L	T	GF	GA	PTS
Montreal	50	38	8	4	228	121	80
Detroit	50	31	14	5	218	161	67
*Toronto	50	24	22	4	183	161	52
Boston	50	16	30	4	179	219	36
Chicago	50	13	30	7	141	194	33
New York	50	11	29	10	154	247	32

Leading Scorers

Player	Club	GP	G	A	PTS	PIM
Lach, Elmer	Montreal	50	26	54	80	37
Richard, Maurice	Montreal	50	50	23	73	36
Blake, Hector	Montreal	49	29	38	67	15
Cowley, Bill	Boston	49	25	40	65	2
Kennedy, Ted	Toronto	49	29	25	54	14
Mosienko, Bill	Chicago	50	28	26	54	0
Carveth, Joe	Detroit	50	26	28	54	6
DeMarco, Albert	New York	50	24	30	54	10
Smith, Clint	Chicago	50	23	31	54	0
Howe, Syd	Detroit	46	17	36	53	6

1945-46

Team	GP	W	L	T	GF	GA	PTS
*Montreal	50	28	17	5	172	134	61
Boston	50	24	18	8	167	156	56
Chicago	50	23	20	7	200	178	53
Detroit	50	20	20	10	146	159	50
Toronto	50	19	24	7	174	185	45
New York	50	13	28	9	144	191	35

Leading Scorers

Player	Club	GP	G	A	PTS	PIM
Bentley, Max	Chicago	47	31	30	61	6
Stewart, Gaye	Toronto	50	37	15	52	8
Blake, Hector	Montreal	50	29	21	50	2
Smith, Clint	Chicago	50	26	24	50	2
Richard, Maurice	Montreal	50	27	21	48	50
Mosienko, Bill	Chicago	40	18	30	48	12
DeMarco, Albert	New York	50	20	27	47	20
Lach, Elmer	Montreal	50	13	34	47	34
Kaleta, Alex	Chicago	49	19	27	46	17
Taylor, Billy	Toronto	48	23	18	41	14
Horeck, Pete	Chicago	50	20	21	41	34

1946-47

Team	GP	W	L	T	GF	GA	PTS
Montreal	60	34	16	10	189	138	78
*Toronto	60	31	19	10	209	172	72
Boston	60	26	23	11	190	175	63
Detroit	60	22	27	11	190	193	55
New York	60	22	32	6	167	186	50
Chicago	60	19	37	4	193	274	42

Leading Scorers

Player	Club	GP	G	A	PTS	PIM
Bentley, Max	Chicago	60	29	43	72	12
Richard, Maurice	Montreal	60	45	26	71	69
Taylor, Billy	Detroit	60	17	46	63	35
Schmidt, Milt	Boston	59	27	35	62	40
Kennedy, Ted	Toronto	60	28	32	60	27
Bentley, Doug	Chicago	52	21	34	55	18
Bauer, Bob	Boston	58	30	24	54	4
Conacher, Roy	Detroit	60	30	24	54	6
Mosienko, Bill	Chicago	59	25	27	52	2
Dumart, Woody	Boston	60	24	28	52	12

1947-48

Team	GP	W	L	T	GF	GA	PTS
*Toronto	60	32	15	13	182	143	77
Detroit	60	30	18	12	187	148	72
Boston	60	23	24	13	167	168	59
New York	60	21	26	13	176	201	55
Montreal	60	20	29	11	147	169	51
Chicago	60	20	34	6	195	225	46

Leading Scorers

Player	Club	GP	G	A	PTS	PIM
Lach, Elmer	Montreal	60	30	31	61	72
O'Connor, Buddy	New York	60	24	36	60	8
Bentley, Doug	Chicago	60	20	37	57	16
Stewart, Gaye	Tor., Chi.	61	27	29	56	83
Bentley, Max	Chi., Tor.	59	26	28	54	14
Poile, Bud	Tor., Chi.	58	25	29	54	17
Richard, Maurice	Montreal	53	28	25	53	89
Apps, Syl	Toronto	55	26	27	53	12
Lindsay, Ted	Detroit	60	33	19	52	95
Conacher, Roy	Chicago	52	22	27	49	4

1948-49

Team	GP	W	L	T	GF	GA	PTS
Detroit	60	34	19	7	195	145	75
Boston	60	29	23	8	178	163	66
Montreal	60	28	23	9	152	126	65
*Toronto	60	22	25	13	147	161	57
Chicago	60	21	31	8	173	211	50
New York	60	18	31	11	133	172	47

Leading Scorers

Player	Club	GP	G	A	PTS	PIM
Conacher, Roy	Chicago	60	26	42	68	8
Bentley, Doug	Chicago	58	23	43	66	38
Abel, Sid	Detroit	60	28	26	54	49
Lindsay, Ted	Detroit	50	26	28	54	97
Conacher, Jim	Det., Chi.	59	26	23	49	43
Ronty, Paul	Boston	60	20	29	49	11
Watson, Harry	Toronto	60	26	19	45	0
Reay, Billy	Montreal	60	22	23	45	33
Bodnar, Gus	Chicago	59	19	26	45	14
Peirson, John	Boston	59	22	21	43	45

1949-50

Team	GP	W	L	T	GF	GA	PTS
*Detroit	70	37	19	14	229	164	88
Montreal	70	29	22	19	172	150	77
Toronto	70	31	27	12	176	173	74
New York	70	28	31	11	170	189	67
Boston	70	22	32	16	198	228	60
Chicago	70	22	38	10	203	244	54

Leading Scorers

Player	Club	GP	G	A	PTS	PIM
Lindsay, Ted	Detroit	69	23	55	78	141
Abel, Sid	Detroit	69	34	35	69	46
Howe, Gordie	Detroit	70	35	33	68	69
Richard, Maurice	Montreal	70	43	22	65	114
Ronty, Paul	Boston	70	23	36	59	8
Conacher, Roy	Chicago	70	25	31	56	16
Bentley, Doug	Chicago	64	20	33	53	28
Peirson, John	Boston	57	27	25	52	49
Prystai, Metro	Chicago	65	29	22	51	31
Guidolin, Bep	Chicago	70	17	34	51	42

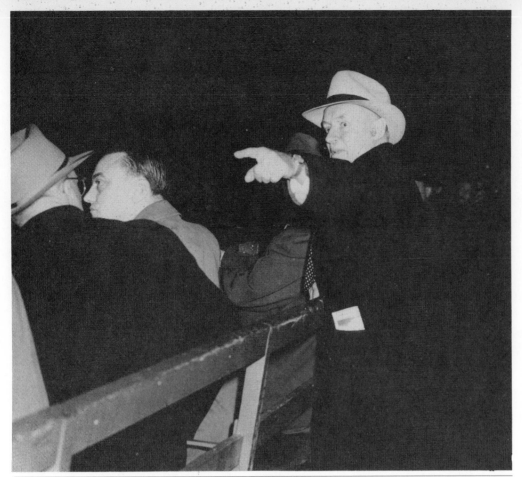

Canny Conn Smythe, who helped form the Toronto Maple Leafs in February, 1927, managed the Leafs to seven Stanley Cup titles in his 30-year association with the club.

1950-51

Team	GP	W	L	T	GF	GA	PTS
Detroit	70	44	13	13	236	139	101
*Toronto	70	41	16	13	212	138	95
Montreal	70	25	30	15	173	184	65
Boston	70	22	30	18	178	197	62
New York	70	20	29	21	169	201	61
Chicago	70	13	47	10	171	280	36

Leading Scorers

Player	Club	GP	G	A	PTS	PIM
Howe, Gordie	Detroit	70	43	43	86	74
Richard, Maurice	Montreal	65	42	24	66	97
Bentley, Max	Toronto	67	21	41	62	34
Abel, Sid	Detroit	69	23	38	61	30
Schmidt, Milt	Boston	62	22	39	61	33
Kennedy, Ted	Toronto	63	18	43	61	32
Lindsay, Ted	Detroit	67	24	35	59	110
Sloan, Tod	Toronto	70	31	25	56	105
Kelly, Red	Detroit	70	17	37	54	24
Smith, Sid	Toronto	70	30	21	51	10
Gardner, Cal	Toronto	66	23	28	51	42

1951-52

Team	GP	W	L	T	GF	GA	PTS
*Detroit	70	44	14	12	215	133	100
Montreal	70	34	26	10	195	164	78
Toronto	70	29	25	16	168	157	74
Boston	70	25	29	16	162	176	66
New York	70	23	34	13	192	219	59
Chicago	70	17	44	9	158	241	43

Leading Scorers

Player	Club	GP	G	A	PTS	PIM
Howe, Gordie	Detroit	70	47	39	86	78
Lindsay, Ted	Detroit	70	30	39	69	123
Lach, Elmer	Montreal	70	15	50	65	36
Raleigh, Don	New York	70	19	42	61	14
Smith, Sid	Toronto	70	27	30	57	6
Geoffrion, Bernie	Montreal	67	30	24	54	66
Mosienko, Bill	Chicago	70	31	22	53	10
Abel, Sid	Detroit	62	17	36	53	32
Kennedy, Ted	Toronto	70	19	33	52	33
Schmidt, Milt	Boston	69	21	29	50	57
Peirson, John	Boston	68	20	30	50	30

1952-53

Team	GP	W	L	T	GF	GA	PTS
Detroit	70	36	16	18	222	133	90
*Montreal	70	28	23	19	155	148	75
Boston	70	28	29	13	152	172	69
Chicago	70	27	28	15	169	175	69
Toronto	70	27	30	13	156	167	67
New York	70	17	37	16	152	211	50

Leading Scorers

Player	Club	GP	G	A	PTS	PIM
Howe, Gordie	Detroit	70	49	46	95	57
Lindsay, Ted	Detroit	70	32	39	71	111
Richard, Maurice	Montreal	70	28	33	61	112
Hergesheimer, Wally	New York	70	30	29	59	10
Delvecchio, Alex	Detroit	70	16	43	59	28
Ronty, Paul	New York	70	16	38	54	20
Prystai, Metro	Detroit	70	16	34	50	12
Kelly, Red	Detroit	70	19	27	46	8
Olmstead, Bert	Montreal	69	17	28	45	83
Mackell, Fleming	Boston	65	27	17	44	63
McFadden, Jim	Chicago	70	23	21	44	29

1953-54

Team	GP	W	L	T	GF	GA	PTS
*Detroit	70	37	19	14	191	132	88
Montreal	70	35	24	11	195	141	81
Toronto	70	32	24	14	152	131	78
Boston	70	32	28	10	177	181	74
New York	70	29	31	10	161	182	68
Chicago	70	12	51	7	133	242	31

Leading Scorers

Player	Club	GP	G	A	PTS	PIM
Howe, Gordie	Detroit	70	33	48	81	109
Richard, Maurice	Montreal	70	37	30	67	112
Lindsay, Ted	Detroit	70	26	36	62	110
Geoffrion, Bernie	Montreal	54	29	25	54	87
Olmstead, Bert	Montreal	70	15	37	52	85
Kelly, Red	Detroit	62	16	33	49	18
Reibel, Earl	Detroit	69	15	33	48	18
Sandford, Ed	Boston	70	16	31	47	42
Mackell, Fleming	Boston	67	15	32	47	60
Mosdell, Ken	Montreal	67	22	24	46	64
Ronty, Paul	New York	70	13	33	46	18

1954-55

Team	GP	W	L	T	GF	GA	PTS
*Detroit	70	42	17	11	204	134	95
Montreal	70	41	18	11	228	157	93
Toronto	70	24	24	22	147	135	70
Boston	70	23	26	21	169	188	67
New York	70	17	35	18	150	210	52
Chicago	70	13	40	17	161	235	43

Leading Scorers

Player	Club	GP	G	A	PTS	PIM
Geoffrion, Bernie	Montreal	70	38	37	75	57
Richard, Maurice	Montreal	67	38	36	74	125
Beliveau, Jean	Montreal	70	37	36	73	58
Reibel, Earl	Detroit	70	25	41	66	15
Howe, Gordie	Detroit	64	29	33	62	68
Sullivan, George	Chicago	69	19	42	61	51
Olmstead, Bert	Montreal	70	10	48	58	103
Smith, Sid	Toronto	70	33	21	54	14
Mosdell, Ken	Montreal	70	22	32	54	82
Lewicki, Danny	New York	70	29	24	53	8

1955-56

Team	GP	W	L	T	GF	GA	PTS
*Montreal	70	45	15	10	222	131	100
Detroit	70	30	24	16	183	148	76
New York	70	32	28	10	204	203	74
Toronto	70	24	33	13	153	181	61
Boston	70	23	34	13	147	185	59
Chicago	70	19	39	12	155	216	50

Leading Scorers

Player	Club	GP	G	A	PTS	PIM
Beliveau, Jean	Montreal	70	47	41	88	143
Howe, Gordie	Detroit	70	38	41	79	100
Richard, Maurice	Montreal	70	38	33	71	89
Olmstead, Bert	Montreal	70	14	56	70	94
Sloan, Tod	Toronto	70	37	29	66	100
Bathgate, Andy	New York	70	19	47	66	59
Geoffrion, Bernie	Montreal	59	29	33	62	66
Reibel, Earl	Detroit	68	17	39	56	10
Delvecchio, Alex	Detroit	70	25	26	51	24
Creighton, Dave	New York	70	20	31	51	43
Gadsby, Bill	New York	70	9	42	51	84

1956-57

Team	GP	W	L	T	GF	GA	PTS
Detroit	70	38	20	12	198	157	88
*Montreal	70	35	23	12	210	155	82
Boston	70	34	24	12	195	174	80
New York	70	26	30	14	184	227	66
Toronto	70	21	34	15	174	192	57
Chicago	70	16	39	15	169	225	47

Leading Scorers

Player	Club	GP	G	A	PTS	PIM
Howe, Gordie	Detroit	70	44	45	89	72
Lindsay, Ted	Detroit	70	30	55	85	103
Beliveau, Jean	Montreal	69	33	51	84	105
Bathgate, Andy	New York	70	27	50	77	60
Litzenberger, Ed	Chicago	70	32	32	64	48
Richard, Maurice	Montreal	63	33	29	62	74
McKenney, Don	Boston	69	21	39	60	31
Moore, Dickie	Montreal	70	29	29	58	56
Richard, Henri	Montreal	63	18	36	54	71
Ullman, Norm	Detroit	64	16	36	52	47

1957-58

Team	GP	W	L	T	GF	GA	PTS
*Montreal	70	43	17	10	250	158	96
New York	70	32	25	13	195	188	77
Detroit	70	29	29	12	176	207	70
Boston	70	27	28	15	199	194	69
Chicago	70	24	39	7	163	202	55
Toronto	70	21	38	11	192	226	53

Leading Scorers

Player	Club	GP	G	A	PTS	PIM
Moore, Dickie	Montreal	70	36	48	84	65
Richard, Henri	Montreal	67	28	52	80	56
Bathgate, Andy	New York	65	30	48	78	42
Howe, Gordie	Detroit	64	33	44	77	40
Horvath, Bronco	Boston	67	30	36	66	71
Litzenberger, Ed	Chicago	70	32	30	62	63
Mackell, Fleming	Boston	70	20	40	60	72
Beliveau, Jean	Montreal	55	27	32	59	93
Delvecchio, Alex	Detroit	70	21	38	59	22
McKenney, Don	Boston	70	28	30	58	22

1958-59

Team	GP	W	L	T	GF	GA	PTS
*Montreal	70	39	18	13	258	158	91
Boston	70	32	29	9	205	215	73
Chicago	70	28	29	13	197	208	69
Toronto	70	27	32	11	189	201	65
New York	70	26	32	12	201	217	64
Detroit	70	25	37	8	167	218	58

Leading Scorers

Player	Club	GP	G	A	PTS	PIM
Moore, Dickie	Montreal	70	41	55	96	61
Beliveau, Jean	Montreal	64	45	46	91	67
Bathgate, Andy	New York	70	40	48	88	48
Howe, Gordie	Detroit	70	32	46	78	57
Litzenberger, Ed	Chicago	70	33	44	77	37
Geoffrion, Bernie	Montreal	59	22	44	66	30
Sullivan, George	New York	70	21	42	63	56
Hebenton, Andy	New York	70	33	29	62	8
McKenney, Don	Boston	70	32	30	62	20
Sloan, Tod	Chicago	59	27	35	62	79

1959-60

Team	GP	W	L	T	GF	GA	PTS
*Montreal	70	40	18	12	255	178	92
Toronto	70	35	26	9	199	195	79
Chicago	70	28	29	13	191	180	69
Detroit	70	26	29	15	186	197	67
Boston	70	28	34	8	220	241	64
New York	70	17	38	15	187	247	49

Leading Scorers

Player	Club	GP	G	A	PTS	PIM
Hull, Bobby	Chicago	70	39	42	81	68
Horvath, Bronco	Boston	68	39	41	80	60
Beliveau, Jean	Montreal	60	34	40	74	57
Bathgate, Andy	New York	70	26	48	74	28
Richard, Henri	Montreal	70	30	43	73	66
Howe, Gordie	Detroit	70	28	45	73	46
Geoffrion, Bernie	Montreal	59	30	41	71	36
McKenney, Don	Boston	70	20	49	69	28
Stasiuk, Vic	Boston	69	29	39	68	121
Prentice, Dean	New York	70	32	34	66	43

1960-61

Team	GP	W	L	T	GF	GA	PTS
Montreal	70	41	19	10	254	188	92
Toronto	70	39	19	12	234	176	90
*Chicago	70	29	24	17	198	180	75
Detroit	70	25	29	16	195	215	66
New York	70	22	38	10	204	248	54
Boston	70	15	42	13	176	254	43

Leading Scorers

Player	Club	GP	G	A	PTS	PIM
Geoffrion, Bernie	Montreal	64	50	45	95	29
Béliveau, Jean	Montreal	69	32	58	90	57
Mahovlich, Frank	Toronto	70	48	36	84	131
Bathgate, Andy	New York	70	29	48	77	22
Howe, Gordie	Detroit	64	23	49	72	30
Ullman, Norm	Detroit	70	28	42	70	34
Kelly, Red	Toronto	64	20	50	70	12
Moore, Dickie	Montreal	57	35	34	69	62
Richard, Henri	Montreal	70	24	44	68	91
Delvecchio, Alex	Detroit	70	27	35	62	26

1961-62

Team	GP	W	L	T	GF	GA	PTS
Montreal	70	42	14	14	259	166	98
*Toronto	70	37	22	11	232	180	85
Chicago	70	31	26	13	217	186	75
New York	70	26	32	12	195	207	64
Detroit	70	23	33	14	184	219	60
Boston	70	15	47	8	177	306	38

Leading Scorers

Player	Club	GP	G	A	PTS	PIM
Hull, Bobby	Chicago	70	50	34	84	35
Bathgate, Andy	New York	70	28	56	84	44
Howe, Gordie	Detroit	70	33	44	77	54
Mikita, Stan	Chicago	70	25	52	77	97
Mahovlich, Frank	Toronto	70	33	38	71	87
Delvecchio, Alex	Detroit	70	26	43	69	18
Backstrom, Ralph	Montreal	66	27	38	65	29
Ullman, Norm	Detroit	70	26	38	64	54
Hay, Bill	Chicago	60	11	52	63	34
Provost, Claude	Montreal	70	33	29	62	22

Gordie Howe attempts to corral a loose puck as Maple Leaf defenders Allan Stanley and Cesare Maniago sprawl to prevent him from scoring in this Toronto-Detroit matchup on February 25, 1961. Howe is wearing a helmet to protect an injury he sustained in a game against Toronto on January 4, 1961.

1962-63

Team	GP	W	L	T	GF	GA	PTS
*Toronto	70	35	23	12	221	180	82
Chicago	70	32	21	17	194	178	81
Montreal	70	28	19	23	225	183	79
Detroit	70	32	25	13	200	194	77
New York	70	22	36	12	211	233	56
Boston	70	14	39	17	198	281	45

Leading Scorers

Player	Club	GP	G	A	PTS	PIM
Howe, Gordie	Detroit	70	38	48	86	100
Bathgate, Andy	New York	70	35	46	81	54
Mikita, Stan	Chicago	65	31	45	76	69
Mahovlich, Frank	Toronto	67	36	37	73	56
Richard, Henri	Montreal	67	23	50	73	57
Beliveau, Jean	Montreal	69	18	49	67	68
Bucyk, John	Boston	69	27	39	66	36
Delvecchio, Alex	Detroit	70	20	44	64	8
Hull, Bobby	Chicago	65	31	31	62	27
Oliver, Murray	Boston	65	22	40	62	38

1963-64

Team	GP	W	L	T	GF	GA	PTS
Montreal	70	36	21	13	209	167	85
Chicago	70	36	22	12	218	169	84
*Toronto	70	33	25	12	192	172	78
Detroit	70	30	29	11	191	204	71
New York	70	22	38	10	186	242	54
Boston	70	18	40	12	170	212	48

Leading Scorers

Player	Club	GP	G	A	PTS	PIM
Mikita, Stan	Chicago	70	39	50	89	146
Hull, Bobby	Chicago	70	43	44	87	50
Beliveau, Jean	Montreal	68	28	50	78	42
Bathgate, Andy	NYR, Tor.	71	19	58	77	34
Howe, Gordie	Detroit	69	26	47	73	70
Wharram, Ken	Chicago	70	39	32	71	18
Oliver, Murray	Boston	70	24	44	68	41
Goyette, Phil	New York	67	24	41	65	15
Gilbert, Rod	New York	70	24	40	64	62
Keon, Dave	Toronto	70	23	37	60	6

1964-65

Team	GP	W	L	T	GF	GA	PTS
Detroit	70	40	23	7	224	175	87
*Montreal	70	36	23	11	211	185	83
Chicago	70	34	28	8	224	176	76
Toronto	70	30	26	14	204	173	74
New York	70	20	38	12	179	246	52
Boston	70	21	43	6	166	253	48

Leading Scorers

Player	Club	GP	G	A	PTS	PIM
Mikita, Stan	Chicago	70	28	59	87	154
Ullman, Norm	Detroit	70	42	41	83	70
Howe, Gordie	Detrot	70	29	47	76	104
Hull, Bobby	Chicago	61	39	32	71	32
Delvecchio, Alex	Detroit	68	25	42	67	16
Provost, Claude	Montreal	70	27	37	64	28
Gilbert, Rod	New York	70	25	36	61	52
Pilote, Pierre	Chicago	68	14	45	59	162
Bucyk, John	Boston	68	26	29	55	24
Backstrom, Ralph	Montreal	70	25	30	55	41
Esposito, Phil	Chicago	70	23	32	55	44

1965-66

Team	GP	W	L	T	GF	GA	PTS
*Montreal	70	41	21	8	239	173	90
Chicago	70	37	25	8	240	187	82
Toronto	70	34	25	11	208	187	79
Detroit	70	31	27	12	221	194	74
Boston	70	21	43	6	174	275	48
New York	70	18	41	11	195	261	47

Leading Scorers

Player	Club	GP	G	A	PTS	PIM
Hull, Bobby	Chicago	65	54	43	97	70
Mikita, Stan	Chicago	68	30	48	78	58
Rousseau, Bobby	Montreal	70	30	48	78	20
Beliveau, Jean	Montreal	67	29	48	77	50
Howe, Gordie	Detroit	70	29	46	75	83
Ullman, Norm	Detroit	70	31	41	72	35
Delvecchio, Alex	Detroit	70	31	38	69	16
Nevin, Bob	New York	69	29	33	62	10
Richard, Henri	Montreal	62	22	39	61	47
Oliver, Murray	Boston	70	18	42	60	30

1966-67

Team	GP	W	L	T	GF	GA	PTS
Chicago	70	41	17	12	264	170	94
Montreal	70	32	25	13	202	188	77
*Toronto	70	32	27	11	204	211	75
New York	70	30	28	12	188	189	72
Detroit	70	27	39	4	212	241	58
Boston	70	17	43	10	182	253	44

Leading Scorers

Player	Club	GP	G	A	PTS	PIM
Mikita, Stan	Chicago	70	35	62	97	12
Hull, Bobby	Chicago	66	52	28	80	52
Ullman, Norm	Detroit	68	26	44	70	26
Wharram, Ken	Chicago	70	31	34	65	21
Howe, Gordie	Detroit	69	25	40	65	53
Rousseau, Bobby	Montreal	68	19	44	63	58
Esposito, Phil	Chicago	69	21	40	61	40
Goyette, Phil	New York	70	12	49	61	6
Mohns, Doug	Chicago	61	25	35	60	58
Richard, Henri	Montreal	65	21	34	55	28
Delvecchio, Alex	Detroit	70	17	38	55	10

Jean Béliveau finished among the NHL's top-ten scorers in nine of ten seasons, from 1954-55 to 1963-64. In 1961-62, Béliveau suffered a severe knee injury and missed 17 games, finished out of the scoring race with 41 points in 47 games.

1967-68

East Division

Team	GP	W	L	T	GF	GA	PTS
*Montreal	74	42	22	10	236	167	94
New York	74	39	23	12	226	183	90
Boston	74	37	27	10	259	216	84
Chicago	74	32	26	16	212	222	80
Toronto	74	33	31	10	209	176	76
Detroit	74	27	35	12	245	257	66

West Division

Team	GP	W	L	T	GF	GA	PTS
Philadelphia	74	31	32	11	173	179	73
Los Angeles	74	31	33	10	200	224	72
St. Louis	74	27	31	16	177	191	70
Minnesota	74	27	32	15	191	226	69
Pittsburgh	74	27	34	13	195	216	67
Oakland	74	15	42	17	153	219	47

Leading Scorers

Player	Club	GP	G	A	PTS	PIM
Mikita, Stan	Chicago	72	40	47	87	14
Esposito, Phil	Boston	74	35	49	84	21
Howe, Gordie	Detroit	74	39	43	82	53
Ratelle, Jean	New York	74	32	46	78	18
Gilbert, Rod	New York	73	29	48	77	12
Hull, Bobby	Chicago	71	44	31	75	39
Ullman, Norm	Det., Tor.	71	35	37	72	28
Delvecchio, Alex	Detroit	74	22	48	70	14
Bucyk, John	Boston	72	30	39	69	8
Wharram, Ken	Chicago	74	27	42	69	18

1968-69

East Division

Team	GP	W	L	T	GF	GA	PTS
*Montreal	76	46	19	11	271	202	103
Boston	76	42	18	16	303	221	100
New York	76	41	26	9	231	196	91
Toronto	76	35	26	15	234	217	85
Detroit	76	33	31	12	239	221	78
Chicago	76	34	33	9	280	246	77

West Division

Team	GP	W	L	T	GF	GA	PTS
St. Louis	76	37	25	14	204	157	88
Oakland	76	29	36	11	219	251	69
Philadelphia	76	20	35	21	174	225	61
Los Angeles	76	24	42	10	185	260	58
Pittsburgh	76	20	45	11	189	252	51
Minnesota	76	18	43	5	189	270	51

Leading Scorers

Player	Club	GP	G	A	PTS	PIM
Esposito, Phil	Boston	74	49	77	126	79
Hull, Bobby	Chicago	74	58	49	107	48
Howe, Gordie	Detroit	76	44	59	103	58
Mikita, Stan	Chicago	74	30	67	97	52
Hodge, Ken	Boston	75	45	45	90	75
Cournoyer, Yvan	Montreal	76	43	44	87	31
Delvecchio, Alex	Detroit	72	25	58	83	8
Berenson, Red	St. Louis	76	35	47	82	43
Beliveau, Jean	Montreal	69	33	49	82	55
Mahovlich, Frank	Detroit	76	49	29	78	38
Ratelle, Jean	New York	75	32	46	78	26

1969-70

East Division

Team	GP	W	L	T	GF	GA	PTS
Chicago	76	45	22	9	250	170	99
*Boston	76	40	17	19	277	216	99
Detroit	76	40	21	15	246	199	95
New York	76	38	22	16	246	189	92
Montreal	76	38	22	16	244	201	92
Toronto	76	29	34	13	222	242	71

West Division

Team	GP	W	L	T	GF	GA	PTS
St. Louis	76	37	27	12	224	179	86
Pittsburgh	76	26	38	12	182	238	64
Minnesota	76	19	35	22	224	257	60
Oakland	76	22	40	14	169	243	58
Philadelphia	76	17	35	24	197	225	58
Los Angeles	76	14	52	10	168	290	38

Leading Scorers

Player	Club	GP	G	A	PTS	PIM
Orr, Bobby	Boston	76	33	87	120	125
Esposito, Phil	Boston	76	43	56	99	50
Mikita, Stan	Chicago	76	39	47	86	50
Goyette, Phil	St. Louis	72	29	49	78	16
Tkaczuk, Walt	New York	76	27	50	77	38
Ratelle, Jean	New York	75	32	42	74	28
Berenson, Red	St. Louis	67	33	39	72	38
Parise, Jean-Paul	Minnesota	74	24	48	72	72
Howe, Gordie	Detroit	76	31	40	71	58
Mahovlich, Frank	Detroit	74	38	32	70	59
Balon, Dave	New York	76	33	37	70	00
McKenzie, John	Boston	72	29	41	70	114

1970-71

East Division

Team	GP	W	L	T	GF	GA	PTS
Boston	78	57	14	7	399	207	121
New York	78	49	18	11	259	177	109
*Montreal	78	42	23	13	291	216	97
Toronto	78	37	33	8	248	211	82
Buffalo	78	24	39	15	217	291	63
Vancouver	78	24	46	8	229	296	56
Detroit	78	22	45	11	209	308	55

West Division

Team	GP	W	L	T	GF	GA	PTS
Chicago	78	49	20	9	277	184	107
St. Louis	78	34	25	19	223	208	87
Philadelphia	78	28	33	17	207	225	73
Minnesota	78	28	34	16	191	223	72
Los Angeles	78	25	40	13	239	303	63
Pittsburgh	78	21	37	20	221	240	62
California	78	20	53	5	199	320	45

Leading Scorers

Player	Club	GP	G	A	PTS	PIM
Esposito, Phil	Boston	78	76	76	152	71
Orr, Bobby	Boston	78	37	102	139	91
Bucyk, John	Boston	78	51	65	116	8
Hodge, Ken	Boston	78	43	62	105	113
Hull, Bobby	Chicago	78	44	52	96	32
Ullman, Norm	Toronto	73	34	51	85	24
Cashman, Wayne	Boston	77	21	58	79	100
McKenzie, John	Boston	65	31	46	77	120
Keon, Dave	Toronto	76	38	38	76	4
Beliveau, Jean	Montreal	70	25	51	76	40
Stanfield, Fred	Boston	75	24	52	76	12

1971-72

East Division

Team	GP	W	L	T	GF	GA	PTS
*Boston	78	54	13	11	330	204	119
New York	78	48	17	13	317	192	109
Montreal	78	46	16	16	307	205	108
Toronto	78	33	31	14	209	208	80
Detroit	78	33	35	10	261	262	76
Buffalo	78	16	43	19	203	289	51
Vancouver	78	20	50	8	203	297	48

West Division

Team	GP	W	L	T	GF	GA	PTS
Chicago	78	46	17	15	256	166	107
Minnesota	78	37	29	12	212	191	86
St. Louis	78	28	39	11	208	247	67
Pittsburgh	78	26	38	14	220	258	66
Philadelphia	78	26	38	14	200	236	66
California	78	21	39	18	216	288	60
Los Angeles	78	20	49	9	206	305	49

Leading Scorers

Player	Club	GP	G	A	PTS	PIM
Esposito, Phil	Boston	76	66	67	133	76
Orr, Bobby	Boston	76	37	80	117	106
Ratelle, Jean	New York	63	46	63	109	4
Hadfield, Vic	New York	78	50	56	106	142
Gilbert, Rod	New York	73	43	54	97	64
Mahovlich, Frank	Montreal	76	43	53	96	36
Hull, Bobby	Chicago	78	50	43	93	24
Cournoyer, Yvan	Montreal	73	47	36	83	15
Bucyk, John	Boston	78	32	51	83	4
Clarke, Bobby	Philadelphia	78	35	46	81	87
Lemaire, Jacques	Montreal	77	32	49	81	26

1972-73

East Division

Team	GP	W	L	T	GF	GA	PTS
*Montreal	78	52	10	16	329	184	120
Boston	78	51	22	5	330	235	107
NY Rangers	78	47	23	8	297	208	102
Buffalo	78	37	27	14	257	219	88
Detroit	78	37	29	12	265	243	86
Toronto	78	27	41	10	247	279	64
Vancouver	78	22	47	9	233	339	53
NY Islanders	78	12	60	6	170	347	30

West Division

Team	GP	W	L	T	GF	GA	PTS
Chicago	78	42	27	9	284	225	93
Philadelphia	78	37	30	11	296	256	85
Minnesota	78	37	30	11	254	230	85
St. Louis	78	32	34	12	233	251	76
Pittsburgh	78	32	37	9	257	265	73
Los Angeles	78	31	36	11	232	245	73
Atlanta	78	25	38	15	191	239	65
California	78	16	46	16	213	323	48

Leading Scorers

Player	Club	GP	G	A	PTS	PIM
Esposito, Phil	Boston	78	55	75	130	87
Clarke, Bobby	Philadelphia	78	37	67	104	80
Orr, Bobby	Boston	63	29	72	101	99
MacLeish, Rick	Philadelphia	78	50	50	100	69
Lemaire, Jacques	Montreal	77	44	51	95	16
Ratelle, Jean	NY Rangers	78	41	53	94	12
Redmond, Mickey	Detroit	76	52	41	93	24
Bucyk, John	Boston	78	40	53	93	12
Mahovlich, Frank	Montreal	78	38	55	93	51
Pappin, Jim	Chicago	76	41	51	92	82

1973-74

East Division

Team	GP	W	L	T	GF	GA	PTS
Boston	78	52	17	9	349	221	113
Montreal	78	45	24	9	293	240	99
NY Rangers	78	40	24	14	300	251	94
Toronto	78	35	27	16	274	230	86
Buffalo	78	32	34	12	242	250	76
Detroit	78	29	39	10	255	319	68
Vancouver	78	24	43	11	224	296	59
NY Islanders	78	19	41	18	182	247	56

West Division

Team	GP	W	L	T	GF	GA	PTS
*Philadelphia	78	50	16	12	273	164	112
Chicago	78	41	14	23	272	164	105
Los Angeles	78	33	33	12	233	231	78
Atlanta	78	30	34	14	214	238	74
Pittsburgh	78	28	41	9	242	273	65
St. Louis	78	26	40	12	206	248	63
Minnesota	78	23	38	17	235	275	63
California	78	13	55	10	195	342	36

Leading Scorers

Player	Club	GP	G	A	PTS	PIM
Esposito, Phil	Boston	78	68	77	145	58
Orr, Bobby	Boston	74	32	90	122	82
Hodge, Ken	Boston	76	50	55	105	43
Cashman, Wayne	Boston	78	30	59	89	111
Clarke, Bobby	Philadelphia	77	35	52	87	113
Martin, Rick	Buffalo	78	52	34	86	38
Apps, Syl	Pittsburgh	75	24	61	85	37
Sittler, Darryl	Toronto	78	38	46	84	55
MacDonald, Lowell	Pittsburgh	78	43	39	82	14
Park, Brad	NY Rangers	78	25	57	82	148
Hextall, Dennis	Minnesota	78	20	62	82	138

1974-75

PRINCE OF WALES CONFERENCE
Norris Division

Team	GP	W	L	T	GF	GA	PTS
Montreal	80	47	14	19	374	225	113
Los Angeles	80	42	17	21	269	185	105
Pittsburgh	80	37	28	15	326	289	89
Detroit	80	23	45	12	259	335	58
Washington	80	8	67	5	181	446	21

Adams Division

Buffalo	80	49	16	15	354	240	113
Boston	80	40	26	14	345	245	94
Toronto	80	31	33	16	280	309	78
California	80	19	48	13	212	316	51

CLARENCE CAMPBELL CONFERENCE
Patrick Division

*Philadelphia	80	51	18	11	293	181	113
NY Rangers	80	37	29	14	319	276	88
NY Islanders	80	33	25	22	264	221	88
Atlanta	80	34	31	15	243	233	83

Smythe Division

Vancouver	80	38	32	10	271	254	86
St. Louis	80	35	31	14	269	267	84
Chicago	80	37	35	8	268	241	82
Minnesota	80	23	50	7	221	341	53
Kansas City	80	15	54	11	184	328	41

Leading Scorers

Player	Club	GP	G	A	PTS	PIM
Orr, Bobby	Boston	80	46	89	135	101
Esposito, Phil	Boston	79	61	66	127	62
Dionne, Marcel	Detroit	80	47	74	121	14
Lafleur, Guy	Montreal	70	53	66	119	37
Mahovlich, Pete	Montreal	80	35	82	117	64
Clarke, Bobby	Philadelphia	80	27	89	116	125
Robert, Rene	Buffalo	74	40	60	100	75
Gilbert, Rod	NY Rangers	76	36	61	97	22
Perreault, Gilbert	Buffalo	68	39	57	96	36
Martin, Rick	Buffalo	68	52	43	95	72

1975-76

PRINCE OF WALES CONFERENCE
Norris Division

Team	GP	W	L	T	GF	GA	PTS
*Montreal	80	58	11	11	337	174	127
Los Angeles	80	38	33	9	263	265	85
Pittsburgh	80	35	33	12	339	303	82
Detroit	80	26	44	10	226	300	62
Washington	80	11	59	10	224	394	32

Adams Division

Boston	80	48	15	17	313	237	113
Buffalo	80	46	21	13	339	240	105
Toronto	80	34	31	15	294	276	83
California	80	27	42	11	250	278	65

CLARENCE CAMPBELL CONFERENCE
Patrick Division

Philadelphia	80	51	13	16	348	209	118
NY Islanders	80	42	21	17	297	190	101
Atlanta	80	35	33	12	262	237	82
NY Rangers	80	29	42	9	262	333	67

Smythe Division

Chicago	80	32	30	18	254	261	82
Vancouver	80	33	32	15	271	272	81
St. Louis	80	29	37	14	249	290	72
Minnesota	80	20	53	7	195	303	47
Kansas City	80	12	56	12	190	351	36

Leading Scorers

Player	Club	GP	G	A	PTS	PIM
Lafleur, Guy	Montreal	80	56	69	125	36
Clarke, Bobby	Philadelphia	76	30	89	119	13
Perreault, Gilbert	Buffalo	80	44	69	113	36
Barber, Bill	Philadelphia	80	50	62	112	104
Larouche, Pierre	Pittsburgh	76	53	58	111	33
Ratelle, Jean	NYR, Bos.	80	36	69	105	18
Mahovlich, Pete	Montreal	80	34	71	105	76
Pronovost, Jean	Pittsburgh	80	52	52	104	24
Sittler, Darryl	Toronto	79	41	59	100	90
Apps, Syl	Pittsburgh	80	32	67	99	24

1976-77

PRINCE OF WALES CONFERENCE
Norris Division

Team	GP	W	L	T	GF	GA	PTS
*Montreal	80	60	8	12	387	171	132
Los Angeles	80	34	31	15	271	241	83
Pittsburgh	80	34	33	13	240	252	81
Washington	80	24	42	14	221	307	62
Detroit	80	16	55	9	183	309	41

Adams Division

Boston	80	49	23	8	312	240	106
Buffalo	80	48	24	8	301	202	104
Toronto	80	33	32	15	301	285	81
Cleveland	80	25	42	13	240	292	63

CLARENCE CAMPBELL CONFERENCE
Patrick Division

Philadelphia	80	48	16	16	323	213	112
NY Islanders	80	47	21	12	288	193	106
Atlanta	80	34	34	12	264	265	80
NY Rangers	88	29	37	14	272	310	72

Smythe Division

St. Louis	80	32	39	9	239	276	73
Minnesota	80	23	39	18	240	310	64
Chicago	80	26	43	11	240	298	63
Vancouver	80	25	42	13	235	294	63
Colorado	80	20	46	14	226	307	54

Leading Scorers

Player	Club	GP	G	A	PTS	PIM
Lafleur, Guy	Montreal	80	56	80	136	20
Dionne, Marcel	Los Angeles	80	53	69	122	12
Shutt, Steve	Montreal	80	60	45	105	28
MacLeish, Rick	Philadelphia	79	49	48	97	42
Perreault, Gilbert	Buffalo	80	39	56	95	30
Young, Tim	Minnesota	80	29	66	95	58
Ratelle, Jean	Boston	78	33	61	94	2
McDonald, Lanny	Toronto	80	46	44	90	77
Sittler, Darryl	Toronto	73	38	52	90	89
Clarke, Bobby	Philadelphia	80	27	63	90	71

1977-78

PRINCE OF WALES CONFERENCE
Norris Division

Team	GP	W	L	T	GF	GA	PTS
*Montreal	80	59	10	11	359	183	129
Detroit	80	32	34	14	252	266	78
Los Angeles	80	31	34	15	243	245	77
Pittsburgh	80	25	37	18	254	321	68
Washington	80	17	49	14	195	321	48

Adams Division

Boston	80	51	18	11	333	218	113
Buffalo	80	44	19	17	288	215	105
Toronto	80	41	29	10	271	237	92
Cleveland	80	22	45	13	230	325	57

CLARENCE CAMPBELL CONFERENCE
Patrick Division

NY Islanders	80	48	17	15	334	210	111
Philadelphia	80	45	20	15	296	200	105
Atlanta	80	34	27	19	274	252	87
NY Rangers	80	30	37	13	279	280	73

Smythe Division

Chicago	80	32	29	19	230	220	83
Colorado	80	19	40	21	257	305	59
Vancouver	80	20	43	17	239	320	57
St. Louis	80	20	47	13	195	304	53
Minnesota	80	18	53	9	218	325	45

Leading Scorers

Player	Club	GP	G	A	PTS	PIM
Lafleur, Guy	Montreal	79	60	72	132	26
Trottier, Bryan	NY Islanders	77	46	77	123	46
Sittler, Darryl	Toronto	80	45	72	117	100
Lemaire, Jacques	Montreal	76	36	61	97	14
Potvin, Denis	NY Islanders	80	30	64	94	81
Bossy, Mike	NY Islanders	73	53	38	91	6
O'Reilly, Terry	Boston	77	29	61	90	211
Perreault, Gilbert	Buffalo	79	41	48	89	20
Clarke, Bobby	Philadelphia	71	21	68	89	83
McDonald, Lanny	Toronto	74	47	40	87	54
Paiement, Wilf	Colorado	80	31	56	87	114

1978-79

PRINCE OF WALES CONFERENCE
Norris Division

Team	GP	W	L	T	GF	GA	PTS
*Montreal	80	52	17	11	337	204	115
Pittsburgh	80	36	31	13	281	279	85
Los Angeles	80	34	34	12	292	286	80
Washington	80	24	41	15	273	338	63
Detroit	80	23	41	16	252	295	62

Adams Division

Boston	80	43	23	14	316	270	100
Buffalo	80	36	28	16	280	263	88
Toronto	80	34	33	13	267	252	81
Minnesota	80	28	40	12	257	289	68

CLARENCE CAMPBELL CONFERENCE
Patrick Division

NY Islanders	80	51	15	14	358	214	116
Philadelphia	80	40	25	15	281	248	95
NY Rangers	80	40	29	11	316	292	91
Atlanta	80	41	31	8	327	280	90

Smythe Division

Chicago	80	29	36	15	244	277	73
Vancouver	80	25	42	13	217	291	63
St. Louis	80	18	50	12	249	348	48
Colorado	80	15	53	12	210	331	42

Leading Scorers

Player	Club	GP	G	A	PTS	PIM
Trottier, Bryan	NY Islanders	76	47	87	134	50
Dionne, Marcel	Los Angeles	80	59	71	130	30
Lafleur, Guy	Montreal	80	52	77	129	28
Bossy, Mike	NY Islanders	80	69	57	126	25
MacMillan, Bob	Atlanta	79	37	71	108	14
Chouinard, Guy	Atlanta	80	50	57	107	14
Potvin, Denis	NY Islanders	73	31	70	101	58
Federko, Bernie	St. Louis	74	31	64	95	14
Taylor, Dave	Los Angeles	78	43	48	91	124
Gillies, Clark	NY Islanders	75	35	56	91	68

Although his career as a best-selling author began after he retired in 1979, Ken Dryden rewrote the NHL record book in the 1970s, scripting five Vezina Trophy wins and six Stanley Cup titles in his eight-year NHL career.

1979-80

PRINCE OF WALES CONFERENCE

Norris Division

Team	GP	W	L	T	GF	GA	PTS
Montreal	80	47	20	13	328	240	107
Los Angeles	80	30	36	14	290	313	74
Pittsburgh	80	30	37	13	251	303	73
Hartford	80	27	34	19	303	312	73
Detroit	80	26	43	11	268	306	63

Adams Division

Team	GP	W	L	T	GF	GA	PTS
Buffalo	80	47	17	16	318	201	110
Boston	80	46	21	13	310	234	105
Minnesota	80	36	28	16	311	253	88
Toronto	80	35	40	5	304	327	75
Quebec	80	25	44	11	248	313	61

CLARENCE CAMPBELL CONFERENCE

Patrick Division

Team	GP	W	L	T	GF	GA	PTS
Philadelphia	80	48	12	20	327	254	116
*NY Islanders	80	39	28	13	281	247	91
NY Rangers	80	38	32	10	308	284	86
Atlanta	80	35	32	13	282	269	83
Washington	80	27	40	13	261	293	67

Smythe Division

Team	GP	W	L	T	GF	GA	PTS
Chicago	80	34	27	19	241	250	87
St. Louis	80	34	34	12	266	278	80
Vancouver	80	27	37	16	256	281	70
Edmonton	80	28	39	13	301	322	69
Winnipeg	80	20	49	11	214	314	51
Colorado	80	19	48	13	234	308	51

Leading Scorers

Player	Club	GP	G	A	PTS	PIM
Dionne, Marcel	Los Angeles	80	53	84	137	32
Gretzky, Wayne	Edmonton	79	51	86	137	21
Lafleur, Guy	Montreal	74	50	75	125	12
Perreault, Gilbert	Buffalo	80	40	66	106	57
Rogers, Mike	Hartford	80	44	61	105	10
Trottier, Bryan	NY Islanders	78	42	62	104	68
Simmer, Charlie	Los Angeles	64	56	45	101	65
Stoughton, Blaine	Hartford	80	56	44	100	16
Sittler, Darryl	Toronto	73	40	57	97	62
MacDonald, Blair	Edmonton	80	46	48	94	6
Federko, Bernie	St. Louis	79	38	56	94	24

The Toronto Maple Leafs main offensive catalyst throughout the 1970s, Darryl Sittler finished among the League's top scorers four times, including a 45-goal, 117-point effort in 1977-78.

1980-81

PRINCE OF WALES CONFERENCE

Norris Division

Team	GP	W	L	T	GF	GA	PTS
Montreal	80	45	22	13	332	232	103
Los Angeles	80	43	24	13	337	290	99
Pittsburgh	80	30	37	13	302	345	73
Hartford	80	21	41	18	292	372	60
Detroit	80	19	43	18	252	339	56

Adams Division

Team	GP	W	L	T	GF	GA	PTS
Buffalo	80	39	20	21	327	250	99
Boston	80	37	30	13	316	272	87
Minnesota	80	35	28	17	291	263	87
Quebec	80	30	32	18	314	318	78
Toronto	80	28	37	15	322	367	71

CLARENCE CAMPBELL CONFERENCE

Patrick Division

Team	GP	W	L	T	GF	GA	PTS
*NY Islanders	80	48	18	14	355	260	110
Philadelphia	80	41	24	15	313	249	97
Calgary	80	39	27	14	329	298	92
NY Rangers	80	30	36	14	312	317	74
Washington	80	26	36	18	286	317	70

Smythe Division

Team	GP	W	L	T	GF	GA	PTS
St. Louis	80	45	18	17	352	281	107
Chicago	80	31	33	16	304	315	78
Vancouver	80	28	32	20	289	301	76
Edmonton	80	29	35	16	328	327	74
Colorado	80	22	45	13	258	344	57
Winnipeg	80	9	57	14	246	400	32

Leading Scorers

Player	Club	GP	G	A	PTS	PIM
Gretzky, Wayne	Edmonton	80	55	109	164	28
Dionne, Marcel	Los Angeles	80	58	77	135	70
Nilsson, Kent	Calgary	80	49	82	131	26
Bossy, Mike	NY Islanders	79	68	51	119	32
Taylor, Dave	Los Angeles	72	47	65	112	130
Stastny, Peter	Quebec	77	39	70	109	37
Simmer, Charlie	Los Angeles	65	56	49	105	62
Rogers, Mike	Hartford	80	40	65	105	32
Federko, Bernie	St. Louis	78	31	73	104	47
Richard, Jacques	Quebec	78	52	51	103	39
Middleton, Rick	Boston	80	44	59	103	16
Trottier, Bryan	NY Islanders	73	31	72	103	74

1981-82

CLARENCE CAMPBELL CONFERENCE

Norris Division

Team	GP	W	L	T	GF	GA	PTS
Minnesota	80	37	23	20	346	288	94
Winnipeg	80	33	33	14	319	332	80
St. Louis	80	32	40	8	315	349	72
Chicago	80	30	38	12	332	363	72
Toronto	80	20	44	16	298	380	56
Detroit	80	21	47	12	270	351	54

Smythe Division

Team	GP	W	L	T	GF	GA	PTS
Edmonton	80	48	17	15	417	295	111
Vancouver	80	30	33	17	290	286	77
Calgary	80	29	34	17	334	345	75
Los Angeles	80	24	41	15	314	369	63
Colorado	80	18	49	13	241	362	49

PRINCE OF WALES CONFERENCE

Adams Division

Team	GP	W	L	T	GF	GA	PTS
Montreal	80	46	17	17	360	223	109
Boston	80	43	27	10	323	285	96
Buffalo	80	39	26	15	307	273	93
Quebec	80	33	31	16	356	345	82
Hartford	80	21	41	18	264	351	60

Patrick Division

Team	GP	W	L	T	GF	GA	PTS
*NY Islanders	80	54	16	10	385	250	118
NY Rangers	80	39	27	14	316	306	92
Philadelphia	80	38	31	11	325	313	87
Pittsburgh	80	31	36	13	310	337	75
Washington	80	26	41	13	319	338	65

Leading Scorers

Player	Club	GP	G	A	PTS	PIM
Gretzky, Wayne	Edmonton	80	92	120	212	26
Bossy, Mike	NY Islanders	80	64	83	147	22
Stastny, Peter	Quebec	80	46	93	139	91
Maruk, Dennis	Washington	80	60	76	136	128
Trottier, Bryan	NY Islanders	80	50	79	129	88
Savard, Denis	Chicago	80	32	87	119	82
Dionne, Marcel	Los Angeles	78	50	67	117	50
Smith, Bobby	Minnesota	80	43	71	114	82
Ciccarelli, Dino	Minnesota	76	55	51	106	138
Taylor, Dave	Los Angeles	78	39	67	106	130

1982-83

CLARENCE CAMPBELL CONFERENCE

Norris Division

Team	GP	W	L	T	GF	GA	PTS
Chicago	80	47	23	10	338	268	104
Minnesota	80	40	24	16	321	290	96
Toronto	80	28	40	12	293	330	68
St. Louis	80	25	40	15	285	316	65
Detroit	80	21	44	15	263	344	57

Smythe Division

Team	GP	W	L	T	GF	GA	PTS
Edmonton	80	47	21	12	424	315	106
Calgary	80	32	34	14	321	317	78
Vancouver	80	30	35	15	303	309	75
Winnipeg	80	33	39	8	311	333	74
Los Angeles	80	27	41	12	308	365	66

PRINCE OF WALES CONFERENCE

Adams Division

Team	GP	W	L	T	GF	GA	PTS
Boston	80	50	20	10	327	228	110
Montreal	80	42	24	14	350	286	98
Buffalo	80	38	29	13	318	285	89
Quebec	80	34	34	12	343	336	80
Hartford	80	19	54	7	261	403	45

Patrick Division

Team	GP	W	L	T	GF	GA	PTS
Philadelphia	80	49	23	8	32	240	106
*NY Islanders	80	42	26	12	302	226	96
Washington	80	39	25	16	306	283	94
NY Rangers	80	35	35	10	306	287	80
New Jersey	80	17	49	14	230	338	48
Pittsburgh	80	18	53	9	257	394	45

Leading Scorers

Player	Club	GP	G	A	PTS	PIM
Gretzky, Wayne	Edmonton	80	71	125	196	59
Stastny, Peter	Quebec	75	47	77	124	78
Savard, Denis	Chicago	78	35	86	121	99
Bossy, Mike	NY Islanders	79	60	58	118	20
Dionne, Marcel	Los Angeles	80	56	51	107	22
Pederson, Barry	Boston	77	46	61	107	47
Messier, Mark	Edmonton	77	48	58	106	72
Goulet, Michel	Quebec	80	57	48	105	51
Anderson, Glenn	Edmonton	72	48	56	104	70
Nilsson, Kent	Calgary	80	46	58	104	10
Kurri, Jari	Edmonton	80	45	59	104	22

For ten consecutive seasons, Denis Savard finished either first or second in team scoring for the Chicago Blackhawks, including a franchise-record 131-point effort in 1987-88.

1983-84
CLARENCE CAMPBELL CONFERENCE
Norris Division

Team	GP	W	L	T	GF	GA	PTS
Minnesota	80	39	31	10	345	344	88
St. Louis	80	32	41	7	293	316	71
Detroit	80	31	42	7	298	323	69
Chicago	80	30	42	8	277	311	68
Toronto	80	26	45	9	303	387	61

Smythe Division

Team	GP	W	L	T	GF	GA	PTS
*Edmonton	80	57	18	5	446	314	119
Calgary	80	34	32	14	311	314	82
Vancouver	80	32	39	9	306	328	73
Winnipeg	80	31	38	11	340	374	73
Los Angeles	80	23	44	13	309	376	59

PRINCE OF WALES CONFERENCE
Adams Division

Team	GP	W	L	T	GF	GA	PTS
Boston	80	49	25	6	336	261	104
Buffalo	80	48	25	7	315	257	103
Quebec	80	42	28	10	360	278	94
Montreal	80	35	40	5	286	295	75
Hartford	80	28	42	10	288	320	66

Patrick Division

Team	GP	W	L	T	GF	GA	PTS
NY Islanders	80	50	26	4	357	269	104
Washington	80	48	27	5	308	226	101
Philadelphia	80	44	26	10	350	290	98
NY Rangers	80	42	29	9	314	304	93
New Jersey	80	17	56	7	231	350	41
Pittsburgh	80	16	58	6	254	390	38

Leading Scorers

Player	Club	GP	G	A	PTS	PIM
Gretzky, Wayne	Edmonton	74	87	118	205	39
Coffey, Paul	Edmonton	80	40	86	126	104
Goulet, Michel	Quebec	75	56	65	121	76
Stastny, Peter	Quebec	80	46	73	119	73
Bossy, Mike	NY Islanders	67	51	67	118	8
Pederson, Barry	Boston	80	39	77	116	64
Kurri, Jari	Edmonton	64	52	61	113	14
Trottier, Bryan	NY Islanders	68	40	71	111	59
Federko, Bernie	St. Louis	79	41	66	107	43
Middleton, Rick	Boston	80	47	58	105	14

1984-85
CLARENCE CAMPBELL CONFERENCE
Norris Division

Team	GP	W	L	T	GF	GA	PTS
St. Louis	80	37	31	12	299	288	86
Chicago	80	38	35	7	309	299	83
Detroit	80	27	41	12	313	357	66
Minnesota	80	25	43	12	268	321	62
Toronto	80	20	52	8	253	358	48

Smythe Division

Team	GP	W	L	T	GF	GA	PTS
*Edmonton	80	49	20	11	401	298	109
Winnipeg	80	43	27	10	358	332	96
Calgary	80	41	27	12	363	302	94
Los Angeles	80	34	32	14	339	326	82
Vancouver	80	25	46	9	284	401	59

PRINCE OF WALES CONFERENCE
Adams Division

Team	GP	W	L	T	GF	GA	PTS
Montreal	80	41	27	12	309	262	94
Quebec	80	41	30	9	323	275	91
Buffalo	80	38	28	14	290	237	90
Boston	80	36	34	10	303	287	82
Hartford	80	30	41	9	268	318	69

Patrick Division

Team	GP	W	L	T	GF	GA	PTS
Philadelphia	80	53	20	7	348	241	113
Washington	80	46	25	9	322	240	101
NY Islanders	80	40	34	6	345	312	86
NY Rangers	80	26	44	10	295	345	62
New Jersey	80	22	48	10	264	346	54
Pittsburgh	80	24	51	5	276	385	53

Leading Scorers

Player	Club	GP	G	A	PTS	PIM
Gretzky, Wayne	Edmonton	80	73	135	208	52
Kurri, Jari	Edmonton	73	71	64	135	30
Hawerchuk, Dale	Winnipeg	80	53	77	130	74
Dionne, Marcel	Los Angeles	80	46	80	126	46
Coffey, Paul	Edmonton	80	37	84	121	97
Bossy, Mike	NY Islanders	76	58	59	117	38
Ogrodnick, John	Detroit	79	55	50	105	30
Savard, Denis	Chicago	79	38	67	105	56
Federko, Bernie	St. Louis	76	30	73	103	27
Gartner, Mike	Washington	80	50	52	102	7

1985-86
CLARENCE CAMPBELL CONFERENCE
Norris Division

Team	GP	W	L	T	GF	GA	PTS
Chicago	80	39	33	8	351	349	86
Minnesota	80	38	33	9	327	305	85
St. Louis	80	37	34	9	302	291	83
Toronto	80	25	48	7	311	386	57
Detroit	80	17	57	6	266	415	40

Smythe Division

Team	GP	W	L	T	GF	GA	PTS
Edmonton	80	56	17	7	426	310	119
Calgary	80	40	31	9	354	315	89
Winnipeg	80	26	47	7	295	372	59
Vancouver	80	23	44	13	282	333	59
Los Angeles	80	23	49	8	284	389	54

PRINCE OF WALES CONFERENCE
Adams Division

Team	GP	W	L	T	GF	GA	PTS
Quebec	80	43	31	6	330	289	92
*Montreal	80	40	33	7	330	280	87
Boston	80	37	31	12	311	288	86
Hartford	80	40	36	4	332	302	84
Buffalo	80	37	37	6	296	291	80

Patrick Division

Team	GP	W	L	T	GF	GA	PTS
Philadelphia	80	53	23	4	335	241	110
Washington	80	50	23	7	315	272	107
NY Islanders	80	39	29	12	327	284	90
NY Rangers	80	36	38	6	280	276	78
Pittsburgh	80	34	38	8	313	305	76
New Jersey	80	28	49	3	300	374	59

Leading Scorers

Player	Club	GP	G	A	PTS	PIM
Gretzky, Wayne	Edmonton	80	52	163	215	52
Lemieux, Mario	Pittsburgh	79	48	93	141	43
Coffey, Paul	Edmonton	79	48	90	138	120
Kurri, Jari	Edmonton	78	68	63	131	22
Bossy, Mike	NY Islanders	80	61	62	123	14
Stastny, Peter	Quebec	76	41	81	122	60
Savard, Denis	Chicago	80	47	69	116	111
Naslund, Mats	Montreal	80	43	67	110	16
Hawerchuk, Dale	Winnipeg	80	46	59	105	44
Broten, Neal	Minnesota	80	29	76	105	47

1986-87
CLARENCE CAMPBELL CONFERENCE
Norris Division

Team	GP	W	L	T	GF	GA	PTS
St. Louis	80	32	33	15	281	293	79
Detroit	80	34	36	10	260	274	78
Chicago	80	29	37	14	290	310	72
Toronto	80	32	42	6	286	319	70
Minnesota	80	30	40	10	296	314	70

Smythe Division

Team	GP	W	L	T	GF	GA	PTS
*Edmonton	80	50	24	6	372	284	106
Calgary	80	46	31	3	318	289	95
Winnipeg	40	40	32	8	279	271	88
Los Angeles	80	31	41	8	318	341	70
Vancouver	80	29	43	8	282	314	66

PRINCE OF WALES CONFERENCE
Adams Division

Team	GP	W	L	T	GF	GA	PTS
Hartford	80	43	30	7	287	270	93
Montreal	80	41	29	10	277	241	92
Boston	80	39	34	7	301	276	85
Quebec	80	31	39	10	267	276	72
Buffalo	80	28	44	8	280	308	64

Patrick Division

Team	GP	W	L	T	GF	GA	PTS
Philadelphia	80	46	26	8	310	245	100
Washington	80	38	32	10	285	278	86
NY Islanders	80	35	33	12	279	281	82
NY Rangers	80	34	38	8	307	323	76
Pittsburgh	80	30	38	12	297	290	72
New Jersey	80	29	45	6	293	368	64

Leading Scorers

Player	Club	GP	G	A	PTS	PIM
Gretzky, Wayne	Edmonton	79	62	121	183	28
Kurri, Jari	Edmonton	79	54	54	108	41
Lemieux, Mario	Pittsburgh	63	54	53	107	57
Messier, Mark	Edmonton	77	37	70	107	73
Gilmour, Doug	St. Louis	80	42	63	105	58
Ciccarelli, Dino	Minnesota	80	52	51	103	92
Hawerchuk, Dale	Winnipeg	80	47	53	100	54
Goulet, Michel	Quebec	75	49	47	96	61
Kerr, Tim	Philadelphia	75	58	37	95	57
Bourque, Ray	Boston	78	23	72	95	36

1987-88
CLARENCE CAMPBELL CONFERENCE
Norris Division

Team	GP	W	L	T	GF	GA	PTS
Detroit	80	41	28	11	322	269	93
St. Louis	80	34	38	8	278	294	76
Chicago	80	30	41	9	284	326	69
Toronto	80	21	49	10	273	345	52
Minnesota	80	19	48	13	242	349	51

Smythe Division

Team	GP	W	L	T	GF	GA	PTS
Calgary	80	48	23	9	397	305	105
*Edmonton	80	44	25	11	363	288	99
Winnipeg	80	33	36	11	292	310	77
Los Angeles	80	30	42	8	318	359	68
Vancouver	80	25	46	9	272	320	59

PRINCE OF WALES CONFERENCE
Adams Division

Team	GP	W	L	T	GF	GA	PTS
Montreal	80	45	22	13	298	238	103
Boston	80	44	30	6	300	251	94
Buffalo	80	37	32	11	283	305	85
Hartford	80	35	38	7	249	267	77
Quebec	80	32	43	5	271	306	69

Patrick Division

Team	GP	W	L	T	GF	GA	PTS
NY Islanders	80	39	31	10	308	267	88
Washington	80	38	33	9	281	249	85
Philadelphia	80	38	33	9	292	282	85
New Jersey	80	38	36	6	295	296	82
NY Rangers	80	36	34	10	300	283	82
Pittsburgh	80	36	35	9	319	316	81

Leading Scorers

Player	Club	GP	G	A	PTS	PIM
Lemieux, Mario	Pittsburgh	76	70	98	168	92
Gretzky, Wayne	Edmonton	64	40	109	149	24
Savard, Denis	Chicago	80	44	87	131	95
Hawerchuk, Dale	Winnipeg	80	44	77	121	59
Robitaille, Luc	Los Angeles	80	53	58	111	82
Stastny, Peter	Quebec	76	46	65	111	69
Messier, Mark	Edmonton	77	37	74	111	103
Carson, Jimmy	Los Angeles	80	55	52	107	45
Loob, Hakan	Calgary	80	50	56	106	47
Goulet, Michel	Quebec	80	48	58	106	56

1988-89
CLARENCE CAMPBELL CONFERENCE
Norris Division

Team	GP	W	L	T	GF	GA	PTS
Detroit	80	34	34	12	313	316	80
St. Louis	80	33	35	12	275	285	78
Minnesota	80	27	37	16	258	278	70
Chicago	80	27	41	12	297	335	66
Toronto	80	28	46	6	259	342	62

Smythe Division

Team	GP	W	L	T	GF	GA	PTS
*Calgary	80	54	17	9	354	226	117
Los Angeles	80	42	31	7	376	335	91
Edmonton	80	38	34	8	325	306	84
Vancouver	80	33	39	8	251	253	74
Winnipeg	80	26	42	12	300	355	64

PRINCE OF WALES CONFERENCE
Adams Division

Team	GP	W	L	T	GF	GA	PTS
Montreal	80	53	18	9	315	218	115
Boston	80	37	29	14	289	256	88
Buffalo	80	38	35	7	291	299	83
Hartford	80	37	38	5	299	290	79
Quebec	80	27	46	7	269	342	61

Patrick Division

Team	GP	W	L	T	GF	GA	PTS
Washington	80	41	29	10	305	259	92
Pittsburgh	80	40	33	7	347	349	87
NY Rangers	80	37	35	8	310	307	82
Philadelphia	80	36	36	8	307	285	80
New Jersey	80	27	41	12	281	325	66
NY Islanders	80	28	47	5	265	325	61

Leading Scorers

Player	Club	GP	G	A	PTS	PIM
Lemieux, Mario	Pittsburgh	76	85	114	199	100
Gretzky, Wayne	Los Angeles	78	54	114	168	26
Yzerman, Steve	Detroit	80	65	90	155	61
Nicholls, Bernie	Los Angeles	79	70	80	150	96
Brown, Rob	Pittsburgh	68	49	66	115	118
Coffey, Paul	Pittsburgh	75	30	83	113	193
Mullen, Joe	Calgary	79	51	59	110	16
Kurri, Jari	Edmonton	76	44	58	102	69
Carson, Jimmy	Edmonton	80	49	51	100	36
Robitaille, Luc	Los Angeles	78	46	52	98	65

Hakan Loob became only the second European-trained player to score 50 goals in a single season when he reached the half-century plateau for the Calgary Flames on March 4, 1988 in a 4-1 victory over the Minnesota North Stars.

1989-90
CLARENCE CAMPBELL CONFERENCE
Norris Division

Team	GP	W	L	T	GF	GA	PTS
Chicago	80	41	33	6	316	294	88
St. Louis	80	37	34	9	295	279	83
Toronto	80	38	38	4	337	358	80
Minnesota	80	36	40	4	284	291	76
Detroit	80	28	38	14	288	323	70

Smythe Division

Team	GP	W	L	T	GF	GA	PTS
Calgary	80	42	23	15	348	265	99
*Edmonton	80	38	28	14	315	283	90
Winnipeg	80	37	32	11	298	290	85
Los Angeles	80	34	39	7	338	337	75
Vancouver	80	25	41	14	245	306	64

PRINCE OF WALES CONFERENCE
Adams Division

Team	GP	W	L	T	GF	GA	PTS
Boston	80	46	25	9	289	232	101
Buffalo	80	45	27	8	286	248	98
Montreal	80	41	28	11	288	234	93
Hartford	80	38	33	9	275	268	85
Quebec	80	12	61	7	240	407	31

Patrick Division

Team	GP	W	L	T	GF	GA	PTS
NY Rangers	80	36	31	13	279	267	85
New Jersey	80	37	34	9	295	288	83
Washington	80	36	38	6	284	275	78
NY Islanders	80	31	38	11	281	288	73
Pittsburgh	80	32	40	8	318	359	72
Philadelphia	80	30	39	11	290	297	71

Leading Scorers

Player	Club	GP	G	A	PTS	PIM
Gretzky, Wayne	Los Angeles	73	40	102	142	42
Messier, Mark	Edmonton	79	45	84	129	79
Yzerman, Steve	Detroit	79	62	65	127	79
Lemieux, Mario	Pittsburgh	59	45	78	123	78
Hull, Brett	St. Louis	80	72	41	113	24
Nicholls, Bernie	L.A., NYR	79	39	73	112	86
Turgeon, Pierre	Buffalo	80	40	66	106	29
LaFontaine, Pat	NY Islanders	74	54	51	105	38
Coffey, Paul	Pittsburgh	80	29	74	103	95
Sakic, Joe	Quebec	80	39	63	102	27
Oates, Adam	St. Louis	80	23	79	102	30

1990-91
CLARENCE CAMPBELL CONFERENCE
Norris Division

Team	GP	W	L	T	GF	GA	PTS
Chicago	80	49	23	8	284	211	106
St. Louis	80	47	22	11	310	250	105
Detroit	80	34	38	8	273	298	76
Minnesota	80	27	39	14	256	266	68
Toronto	80	23	46	11	241	318	57

Smythe Division

Team	GP	W	L	T	GF	GA	PTS
Los Angeles	80	46	24	10	340	254	102
Calgary	80	46	26	8	344	263	100
Edmonton	80	37	37	6	272	272	80
Vancouver	80	28	43	9	243	315	65
Winnipeg	80	26	43	11	260	288	63

PRINCE OF WALES CONFERENCE
Adams Division

Team	GP	W	L	T	GF	GA	PTS
Boston	80	44	24	12	299	264	100
Montreal	80	39	30	11	273	249	89
Buffalo	80	31	30	19	292	278	81
Hartford	80	31	38	11	238	276	73
Quebec	80	16	50	14	236	354	46

Patrick Division

Team	GP	W	L	T	GF	GA	PTS
*Pittsburgh	80	41	33	6	342	305	88
NY Rangers	80	36	31	13	297	265	85
Washington	80	37	36	7	258	258	81
New Jersey	80	32	33	15	272	264	79
Philadelphia	80	33	37	10	252	267	76
NY Islanders	80	25	45	10	223	290	60

Leading Scorers

Player	Club	GP	G	A	PTS	PIM
Gretzky, Wayne	Los Angeles	78	41	122	163	16
Hull, Brett	St. Louis	78	86	45	131	22
Oates, Adam	St. Louis	61	25	90	115	29
Recchi, Mark	Pittsburgh	78	40	73	113	48
Cullen, John	Pit., Hfd.	78	39	71	110	101
Sakic, Joe	Quebec	80	48	61	109	24
Yzerman, Steve	Detroit	80	51	57	108	34
Fleury, Theo	Calgary	79	51	53	104	136
MacInnis, Al	Calgary	78	28	75	103	90
Larmer, Steve	Chicago	80	44	57	101	79

1991-92
CLARENCE CAMPBELL CONFERENCE
Norris Division

Team	GP	W	L	T	GF	GA	PTS
Detroit	80	43	25	12	320	256	98
Chicago	80	36	29	15	257	236	87
St. Louis	80	36	33	11	279	266	83
Minnesota	80	32	42	6	246	278	70
Toronto	80	30	43	7	234	294	67

Smythe Division

Team	GP	W	L	T	GF	GA	PTS
Vancouver	80	42	26	12	285	250	96
Los Angeles	80	35	31	14	287	296	84
Edmonton	80	36	34	10	295	297	82
Winnipeg	80	33	32	15	251	244	81
Calgary	80	31	37	12	296	305	74
San Jose	80	17	58	5	219	359	39

PRINCE OF WALES CONFERENCE
Adams Division

Team	GP	W	L	T	GF	GA	PTS
Montreal	80	41	28	11	267	207	93
Boston	80	36	32	12	270	275	84
Buffalo	80	31	37	12	289	299	74
Hartford	80	26	41	13	247	283	65
Quebec	80	20	48	12	255	318	52

Patrick Division

Team	GP	W	L	T	GF	GA	PTS
NY Rangers	80	50	25	5	321	246	105
Washington	80	45	27	8	330	275	98
*Pittsburgh	80	39	32	9	343	308	87
New Jersey	80	38	31	11	289	259	87
NY Islanders	80	34	35	11	291	299	79
Philadelphia	80	32	37	11	252	273	75

Leading Scorers

Player	Club	GP	G	A	PTS	PIM
Lemieux, Mario	Pittsburgh	64	44	87	131	94
Stevens, Kevin	Pittsburgh	80	54	69	123	254
Gretzky, Wayne	Los Angeles	74	31	90	121	34
Hull, Brett	St. Louis	73	70	39	109	48
Robitaille, Luc	Los Angeles	80	44	63	107	95
Messier, Mark	NY Rangers	79	35	72	107	76
Roenick, Jeremy	Chicago	80	53	50	103	23
Yzerman, Steve	Detroit	79	45	58	103	64
Leetch, Brian	NY Rangers	80	22	80	102	26
Oates, Adam	St. L., Bos.	80	20	79	99	22

1992-93
CLARENCE CAMPBELL CONFERENCE
Norris Division

Team	GP	W	L	T	GF	GA	PTS
Chicago	84	47	25	12	279	230	106
Detroit	84	47	28	9	369	280	103
Toronto	84	44	29	11	288	241	99
St. Louis	84	37	36	11	282	278	85
Minnesota	84	36	38	10	272	293	82
Tampa Bay	84	23	54	7	245	332	53

Smythe Division

Team	GP	W	L	T	GF	GA	PTS
Vancouver	84	46	29	9	346	278	101
Calgary	84	43	30	11	322	282	97
Los Angeles	84	39	35	10	338	340	88
Winnipeg	84	40	37	7	322	320	87
Edmonton	84	26	50	8	242	337	60
San Jose	84	11	71	2	218	414	24

PRINCE OF WALES CONFERENCE
Adams Division

Team	GP	W	L	T	GF	GA	PTS
Boston	84	51	26	7	332	268	109
Quebec	84	47	27	10	351	300	104
*Montreal	84	48	30	6	326	280	102
Buffalo	84	38	36	10	335	297	86
Hartford	84	26	52	6	284	369	58
Ottawa	84	10	70	4	202	395	24

Patrick Division

Team	GP	W	L	T	GF	GA	PTS
Pittsburgh	84	56	21	7	367	268	119
Washington	84	43	34	7	325	286	93
NY Islanders	84	40	37	7	335	297	87
New Jersey	84	40	37	7	308	299	87
Philadelphia	84	36	37	11	319	319	83
NY Rangers	84	34	39	11	304	308	79

Leading Scorers

Player	Club	GP	G	A	PTS	PIM
Lemieux, Mario	Pittsburgh	60	69	91	160	38
LaFontaine, Pat	Buffalo	84	53	95	148	63
Oates, Adam	Boston	84	45	97	142	32
Yzerman, Steve	Detroit	84	58	79	137	44
Selanne, Teemu	Winnipeg	84	76	56	132	45
Turgeon, Pierre	NY Islanders	83	58	74	132	26
Mogilny, Alexander	Buffalo	77	76	51	127	40
Gilmour, Doug	Toronto	83	32	95	127	100
Robitaille, Luc	Los Angeles	84	63	62	125	100
Recchi, Mark	Philadelphia	84	53	70	123	95

1993-94
EASTERN CONFERENCE
Northeast Division

Team	GP	W	L	T	GF	GA	PTS
Pittsburgh	84	44	27	13	299	285	101
Boston	84	42	29	13	289	252	97
Montreal	84	41	29	14	283	248	96
Buffalo	84	43	32	9	282	218	95
Quebec	84	34	42	8	277	292	76
Hartford	84	27	48	9	227	288	63
Ottawa	84	14	61	9	201	397	37

Atlantic Division

Team	GP	W	L	T	GF	GA	PTS
*NY Rangers	84	52	24	8	299	231	112
New Jersey	84	47	25	12	306	220	106
Washington	84	39	35	10	277	263	88
NY Islanders	84	36	36	12	282	264	84
Florida	84	33	34	17	233	233	83
Philadelphia	84	35	39	10	294	314	80
Tampa Bay	84	30	43	11	224	251	71

WESTERN CONFERENCE
Central Division

Team	GP	W	L	T	GF	GA	PTS
Detroit	84	46	30	8	356	275	100
Toronto	84	43	29	12	280	243	98
Dallas	84	42	29	13	286	265	97
St. Louis	84	40	33	11	270	283	91
Chicago	84	39	36	9	254	240	87
Winnipeg	84	24	51	9	245	344	57

Pacific Division

Team	GP	W	L	T	GF	GA	PTS
Calgary	84	42	29	13	302	256	97
Vancouver	84	41	40	3	279	276	85
San Jose	84	33	35	16	252	265	82
Anaheim	84	33	46	5	229	251	71
Los Angeles	84	27	45	12	294	322	66
Edmonton	84	25	45	14	261	305	64

Leading Scorers

Player	Club	GP	G	A	PTS	PIM
Gretzky, Wayne	Los Angeles	81	38	92	130	20
Fedorov, Sergei	Detroit	82	56	64	120	34
Oates, Adam	Boston	77	32	80	112	45
Gilmour, Doug	Toronto	83	27	84	111	105
Bure, Pavel	Vancouver	76	60	47	107	86
Roenick, Jeremy	Chicago	84	46	61	107	125
Recchi, Mark	Philadelphia	84	40	67	107	46
Shanahan, Brendan	St. Louis	81	52	50	102	211
Andreychuk, Dave	Toronto	83	53	46	99	98
Jagr, Jaromir	Pittsburgh	80	32	67	99	61

Note: Detailed statistics for 1993-94 are listed in the Final Statistics, 1993-94 section of the **NHL Guide & Record Book.**

Jeremy Roenick became the first Blackhawk to record three consecutive 100-point seasons, collecting 107 points in 1993-94.

NHL History

1917 — National Hockey League organized November 22 in Montreal following suspension of operations by the National Hockey Association of Canada Limited (NHA). Montreal Canadiens, Montreal Wanderers, Ottawa Senators and Quebec Bulldogs attended founding meeting. Delegates decided to use NHA rules.

Toronto Arenas were later admitted as fifth team; Quebec decided not to operate during the first season. Quebec players allocated to remaining four teams.

Frank Calder elected president and secretary-treasurer.

First NHL games played December 19, with Toronto only arena with artificial ice. Clubs played 22-game split schedule.

1918 — Emergency meeting held January 3 due to destruction by fire of Montreal Arena which was home ice for both Canadiens and Wanderers.

Wanderers withdrew, reducing the NHL to three teams; Canadiens played remaining home games at 3,250-seat Jubilee rink.

Quebec franchise sold to P.J. Quinn of Toronto on October 18 on the condition that the team operate in Quebec City for 1918-19 season. Quinn did not attend the November League meeting and Quebec did not play in 1918-19.

1919-20 — NHL reactivated Quebec Bulldogs franchise. Former Quebec players returned to the club. New Mount Royal Arena became home of Canadiens. Toronto Arenas changed name to St. Patricks. Clubs played 24-game split schedule.

1920-21 — H.P. Thompson of Hamilton, Ontario made application for the purchase of an NHL franchise. Quebec franchise shifted to Hamilton with other NHL teams providing players to strengthen the club.

1921-22 — Split schedule abandoned. First and second place teams at the end of full schedule to play for championship.

1922-23 — Clubs agreed that players could not be sold or traded to clubs in any other league without first being offered to all other clubs in the NHL. In March, Foster Hewitt broadcasts radio's first hockey game.

1923-24 — Ottawa's new 10,000-seat arena opened. First U.S. franchise granted to Boston for following season.

Dr. Cecil Hart Trophy donated to NHL to be awarded to the player judged most useful to his team.

1924-25 — Canadian Arena Company of Montreal granted a franchise to operate Montreal Maroons. NHL now six team league with two clubs in Montreal. Inaugural game in new Montreal Forum played November 29, 1924 as Canadiens defeated Toronto 7-1. Forum was home rink for the Maroons, but no ice was available in the Canadiens arena November 29, resulting in shift to Forum.

Hamilton finished first in the standings, receiving a bye into the finals. But Hamilton players, demanding $200 each for additional games in the playoffs, went on strike. The NHL suspended all players, fining them $200 each. Stanley Cup finalist to be the winner of NHL semi-final between Toronto and Canadiens.

Prince of Wales and Lady Byng trophies donated to NHL.

Clubs played 30-game schedule.

1925-26 — Hamilton club dropped from NHL. Players signed by new New York Americans franchise. Franchise granted to Pittsburgh.

Clubs played 36-game schedule.

1926-27 — New York Rangers granted franchise May 15, 1926. Chicago Black Hawks and Detroit Cougars granted franchises September 25, 1926. NHL now ten-team league with an American and a Canadian Division.

Stanley Cup came under the control of NHL. In previous seasons, winners of the now-defunct Western or Pacific Coast leagues would play NHL champion in Cup finals.

Toronto franchise sold to a new company controlled by Hugh Aird and Conn Smythe. Name changed from St. Patricks to Maple Leafs.

Clubs played 44-game schedule.

The Montreal Canadiens donated the Vezina Trophy to be awarded to the team allowing the fewest goals-against in regular season play. The winning team would, in turn, present the trophy to the goaltender playing in the greatest number of games during the season.

1929-30 — Detroit franchise changed name from Cougars to Falcons.

1930-31 — Pittsburgh transferred to Philadelphia for one season. Pirates changed name to Philadelphia Quakers. Trading deadline for teams set at February 15 of each year. NHL approved operation of farm teams by Rangers, Americans, Falcons and Bruins. Four-sided electric arena clock first demonstrated.

1931-32 — Philadelphia dropped out. Ottawa withdrew for one season. New Maple Leaf Gardens completed. Clubs played 48-game schedule.

1932-33 — Detroit franchise changed name from Falcons to Red Wings. Franchise application received from St. Louis but refused because of additional travel costs. Ottawa team resumed play.

1933-34 — First All-Star Game played as a benefit for injured player Ace Bailey. Leafs defeated All-Stars 7-3 in Toronto.

1934-35 — Ottawa franchise transferred to St. Louis. Team called St. Louis Eagles and consisted largely of Ottawa's players.

1935-36 — Ottawa-St. Louis franchise terminated. Montreal Canadiens finished season with very poor record. To strengthen the club, NHL gave Canadiens first call on the services of all French-Canadian players for three seasons.

1937-38 — Second benefit all-star game staged November 2 in aid of the family of the late Canadiens star Howie Morenz.

Montreal Maroons withdrew from the NHL on June 22, 1938, leaving seven clubs in the League.

1938-39 — Expenses for each club regulated at $5 per man per day for meals and $2.50 per man per day for accommodation.

1939-40 — Benefit All-Star Game played October 29, 1939 in Montreal for the children of the late Albert (Babe) Siebert.

1940-41 — Ross-Tyer puck adopted as the official puck of the NHL. Early in the season it was apparent that this puck was too soft. The Spalding puck was adopted in its place.

After the playoffs, Arthur Ross, NHL governor from Boston, donated a perpetual trophy to be awarded annually to the player voted outstanding in the league.

1941-42 — New York Americans changed name to Brooklyn Americans.

1942-43 — Brooklyn Americans withdrew from NHL, leaving six teams: Boston, Chicago, Detroit, Montreal, New York and Toronto. Playoff format saw first-place team play third-place team and second play fourth.

Clubs played 50-game schedule.

Frank Calder, president of the NHL since its inception, died in Montreal. Meryn "Red" Dutton, former manager of the New York Americans, became president. The NHL commissioned the Calder Memorial Trophy to be awarded to the League's outstanding rookie each year.

1945-46 — Philadelphia, Los Angeles and San Francisco applied for NHL franchises.

The Philadelphia Arena Company of the American Hockey League applied for an injunction to prevent the possible operation of an NHL franchise in that city.

1946-47 — Mervyn Dutton retired as president of the NHL prior to the start of the season. He was succeeded by Clarence S. Campbell.

Individual trophy winners and all-star team members to receive $1,000 awards.

Playoff guarantees for players introduced.

Clubs played 60-game schedule.

1947-48 — The first annual All-Star Game for the benefit of the players' pension fund was played when the All-Stars defeated the Stanley Cup Champion Toronto Maple Leafs 4-3 in Toronto on October 13, 1947.

Ross Trophy, awarded to the NHL's outstanding player since 1941, to be awarded annually to the League's scoring leader.

Philadelphia and Los Angeles franchise applications refused.

National Hockey League Pension Society formed.

1949-50 — Clubs played 70-game schedule.

First intra-league draft held April 30, 1950. Clubs allowed to protect 30 players. Remaining players available for $25,000 each.

1951-52 — Referees included in the League's pension plan.

1952-53 — In May of 1952, City of Cleveland applied for NHL franchise. Application denied. In March of 1953, the Cleveland Barons of the AHL challenged the NHL champions for the Stanley Cup. The NHL governors did not accept this challenge.

1953-54 — The James Norris Memorial Trophy presented to the NHL for annual presentation to the League's best defenseman.

Intra-league draft rules amended to allow teams to protect 18 skaters and two goaltenders, claiming price reduced to $15,000.

1954-55 — Each arena to operate an "out-of-town" scoreboard. Referees and linesmen to wear shirts of black and white vertical stripes. Teams agree to wear colored uniforms at home and white uniforms on the road.

1956-57 — Standardized signals for referees and linesmen introduced.

1960-61 — Canadian National Exhibition, City of Toronto and NHL reach agreement for the construction of a Hockey Hall of Fame on the CNE grounds. Hall opens on August 26, 1961.

Bryan Hextall is congratulated by coach Frank Boucher after scoring the Stanley Cup-winning goal for the New York Rangers in their six-game victory over the Toronto Maple Leafs in the 1940 finals.

1963-64 — Player development league established with clubs operated by NHL franchises located in Minneapolis, St. Paul, Indianapolis, Omaha and, beginning in 1964-65, Tulsa. First universal amateur draft took place. All players of qualifying age (17) unaffected by sponsorship of junior teams available to be drafted.

1964-65 — Conn Smythe Trophy presented to the NHL to be awarded annually to the outstanding player in the Stanley Cup playoffs.

Minimum age of players subject to amateur draft changed to 18.

1965-66 — NHL announced expansion plans for a second six-team division to begin play in 1967-68.

1966-67 — Fourteen applications for NHL franchises received.

Lester Patrick Trophy presented to the NHL to be awarded annually for outstanding service to hockey in the United States.

NHL sponsorship of junior teams ceased, making all players of qualifying age not already on NHL-sponsored lists eligible for the amateur draft.

1967-68 — Six new teams added: California Seals, Los Angeles Kings, Minnesota North Stars, Philadelphia Flyers, Pittsburgh Penguins, St. Louis Blues. New teams to play in West Division. Remaining six teams to play in East Division.

Minimum age of players subject to amateur draft changed to 20.

Clubs played 74-game schedule.

Clarence S. Campbell Trophy awarded to team finishing the regular season in first place in West Division.

California Seals changed name to Oakland Seals on December 8, 1967.

1968-69 — Clubs played 76-game schedule.

Amateur draft expanded to cover any amateur player of qualifying age throughout the world.

1970-71 — Two new teams added: Buffalo Sabres and Vancouver Canucks. These teams joined East Division: Chicago switched to West Division.

Clubs played 78-game schedule.

1971-72 — Playoff format amended. In each division, first to play fourth; second to play third.

1972-73 — Soviet Nationals and Canadian NHL stars play eight-game pre-season series. Canadians win 4-3-1.

Two new teams added. Atlanta Flames join West Division; New York Islanders join East Division.

1974-75 — Two new teams added: Kansas City Scouts and Washington Capitals. Teams realigned into two nine-team conferences, the Prince of Wales made up of the Norris and Adams Divisions, and the Clarence Campbell made up of the Smythe and Patrick Divisions.

Clubs played 80-game schedule.

1976-77 — California franchise transferred to Cleveland. Team named Cleveland Barons. Kansas City franchise transferred to Denver. Team named Colorado Rockies.

1977-78 — Clarence S. Campbell retires as NHL president. Succeeded by John A. Ziegler, Jr.

1978-79 — Cleveland and Minnesota franchises merge, leaving NHL with 17 teams. Merged team placed in Adams Division, playing home games in Minnesota.

Minimum age of players subject to amateur draft changed to 19.

1979-80 — Four new teams added: Edmonton Oilers, Hartford Whalers, Quebec Nordiques and Winnipeg Jets.

Minimum age of players subject to entry draft changed to 18.

1980-81 — Atlanta franchise shifted to Calgary, retaining "Flames" name.

1981-82 — Teams realigned within existing divisions. New groupings based on geographical areas. Unbalanced schedule adopted.

1982-83 — Colorado Rockies franchise shifted to East Rutherford, New Jersey. Team named New Jersey Devils. Franchise moved to Patrick Division from Smythe; Winnipeg moved to Smythe Division from Norris.

1991-92 — San Jose Sharks added, making the NHL a 22-team league. NHL celebrates 75th Anniversary Season. The 1991-92 regular season suspended due to a strike by members of the NHL Players' Association on April 1, 1992. Play resumed April 12, 1992.

1992-93 — Gil Stein named NHL president (October, 1992). Gary Bettman named first NHL Commissioner (February, 1993). Ottawa Senators and Tampa Bay Lightning added, making the NHL a 24-team league. NHL celebrates Stanley Cup Centennial. Clubs played 84-game schedule.

1993-94 — Mighty Ducks of Anaheim and Florida Panthers added, making the NHL a 26-team league. Minnesota franchise shifted to Dallas, team named Dallas Stars. Prince of Wales and Clarence Campbell Conferences renamed Eastern and Western. Adams, Patrick, Norris and Smythe Divisions renamed Northeast, Atlantic, Central and Pacific. Winnipeg moved to Central Division from Pacific; Tampa Bay moved to Atlantic Division from Central; Pittsburgh moved to Northeast Division from Atlantic.

Major Rule Changes

1910-11 — Game changed from two 30-minute periods to three 20-minute periods.

1911-12 — National Hockey Association (forerunner of the NHL) originated six-man hockey, replacing seven-man game.

1917-18 — Goalies permitted to fall to the ice to make saves. Previously a goaltender was penalized for dropping to the ice.

1918-19 — Penalty rules amended. For minor fouls, substitutes not allowed until penalized player had served three minutes. For major fouls, no substitutes for five minutes. For match fouls, no substitutes allowed for the remainder of the game.

With the addition of two lines painted on the ice twenty feet from center, three playing zones were created, producing a forty-foot neutral center ice area in which forward passing was permitted. Kicking the puck was permitted in this neutral zone.

Tabulation of assists began.

1921-22 — Goaltenders allowed to pass the puck forward up to their own blue line.

Overtime limited to twenty minutes.

Minor penalties changed from three minutes to two minutes.

1923-24 — Match foul defined as actions deliberately injuring or disabling an opponent. For such actions, a player was fined not less than $50 and ruled off the ice for the balance of the game. A player assessed a match penalty may be replaced by a substitute at the end of 20 minutes. Match penalty recipients must meet with the League president who can assess additional punishment.

1925-26 — Delayed penalty rules introduced. Each team must have a minimum of four players on the ice at all times.

Two rules were amended to encourage offense: No more than two defensemen permitted to remain inside a team's own blue line when the puck has left the defensive zone. A faceoff to be called for ragging the puck unless short-handed.

Team captains only players allowed to talk to referees.

Goaltender's leg pads limited to 12-inch width.

Timekeeper's gong to mark end of periods rather than referee's whistle. Teams to dress a maximum of 12 players for each game from a roster of no more than 14 players.

1926-27 — Blue lines repositioned to sixty feet from each goal-line, thereby enlarging the neutral zone and standardizing distance from blueline to goal.

Uniform goal nets adopted throughout NHL with goal posts securely fastened to the ice.

1927-28 — To further encourage offense, forward passes allowed in defending and neutral zones and goaltender's pads reduced in width from 12 to 10 inches.

Game standardized at three twenty-minute periods of stop-time separated by ten-minute intermissions.

Teams to change ends after each period.

Ten minutes of sudden-death overtime to be played if the score is tied after regulation time.

Minor penalty to be assessed to any player other than a goaltender for deliberately picking up the puck while it is in play. Minor penalty to be assessed for deliberately shooting the puck out of play.

The Art Ross goal net adopted as the official net of the NHL.

Maximum length of hockey sticks limited to 53 inches measured from heel of blade to end of handle. No minimum length stipulated.

Home teams given choice of goals to defend at start of game.

1928-29 — Forward passing permitted in defensive and neutral zones and into attacking zone if pass receiver is in neutral zone when pass is made. No forward passing allowed inside attacking zone.

Minor penalty to be assessed to any player who delays the game by passing the puck back into his defensive zone.

Ten-minute overtime without sudden-death provision to be played in games tied after regulation time. Games tied after this overtime period declared a draw.

Exclusive of goaltenders, team to dress at least 8 and no more than 12 skaters.

After starting the 1947-48 season with the AHL's Buffalo Bisons, Doug Harvey was promoted to the Montreal Canadiens, where he went on to win six Norris Trophies in 14 seasons with the Habs.

Major Rule Changes — *continued*

1929-30 — Forward passing permitted inside all three zones but not permitted across either blue line.

Kicking the puck allowed, but a goal cannot be scored by kicking the puck in.

No more than three players including the goaltender may remain in their defensive zone when the puck has gone up ice. Minor penalties to be assessed for the first two violations of this rule in a game; major penalties thereafter.

Goaltenders forbidden to hold the puck. Pucks caught must be cleared immediately. For infringement of this rule, a faceoff to be taken ten feet in front of the goal with no player except the goaltender standing between the faceoff spot and the goal-line.

Highsticking penalties introduced.

Maximum number of players in uniform increased from 12 to 15.

December 21, 1929 — Forward passing rules instituted at the beginning of the 1929-30 season more than doubled number of goals scored. Partway through the season, these rules were further amended to read, "No attacking player allowed to precede the play when entering the opposing defensive zone." This is similar to modern offside rule.

1930-31 — A player without a complete stick ruled out of play and forbidden from taking part in further action until a new stick is obtained. A player who has broken his stick must obtain a replacement at his bench.

A further refinement of the offside rule stated that the puck must first be propelled into the attacking zone before any player of the attacking side can enter that zone; for infringement of this rule a faceoff to take place at the spot where the infraction took place.

1931-32 — Though there is no record of a team attempting to play with two goaltenders on the ice, a rule was instituted which stated that each team was allowed only one goaltender on the ice at one time.

Attacking players forbidden to impede the movement or obstruct the vision of opposing goaltenders.

Defending players with the exception of the goaltender forbidden from falling on the puck within 10 feet of the net.

1932-33 — Each team to have captain on the ice at all times.

If the goaltender is removed from the ice to serve a penalty, the manager of the club to appoint a substitute.

Match penalty with substitution after five minutes instituted for kicking another player.

1933-34 — Number of players permitted to stand in defensive zone restricted to three including goaltender.

Visible time clocks required in each rink.

Two referees replace one referee and one linesman.

1934-35 — Penalty shot awarded when a player is tripped and thus prevented from having a clear shot on goal, having no player to pass to other than the offending player. Shot taken from inside a 10-foot circle located 38 feet from the goal. The goaltender must not advance more than one foot from his goal-line when the shot is taken.

1937-38 — Rules introduced governing icing the puck.

Penalty shot awarded when a player other than a goaltender falls on the puck within 10 feet of the goal.

1938-39 — Penalty shot modified to allow puck carrier to skate in before shooting.

One referee and one linesman replace two referee system.

Blue line widened to 12 inches.

Maximum number of players in uniform increased from 14 to 15.

1939-40 — A substitute replacing a goaltender removed from ice to serve a penalty may use a goaltender's stick and gloves but no other goaltending equipment.

1940-41 — Flooding ice surface between periods made obligatory.

1941-42 — Penalty shots classified as minor and major. Minor shot to be taken from a line 28 feet from the goal. Major shot, awarded when a player is tripped with only the goaltender to beat, permits the player taking the penalty shot to skate right into the goalkeeper and shoot from point-blank range.

One referee and two linesmen employed to officiate games.

For playoffs, standby minor league goaltenders employed by NHL as emergency substitutes.

1942-43 — Because of wartime restrictions on train scheduling, regular-season overtime was discontinued on November 21, 1942.

Player limit reduced from 15 to 14. Minimum of 12 men in uniform abolished.

1943-44 — Red line at center ice introduced to speed up the game and reduce offside calls. This rule is considered to mark the beginning of the modern era in the NHL.

Delayed penalty rules introduced.

1945-46 — Goal indicator lights synchronized with official time clock required at all rinks.

1946-47 — System of signals by officials to indicate infractions introduced.

Linesmen from neutral cities employed for all games.

1947-48 — Goal awarded when a player with the puck has an open net to shoot at and a thrown stick prevents the shot on goal. Major penalty to any player who throws his stick in any zone other than defending zone. If a stick is thrown by a player in his defending zone but the thrown stick is not considered to have prevented a goal, a penalty shot is awarded.

All playoff games played until a winner determined, with 20-minute sudden-death overtime periods separated by 10-minute intermissions.

1949-50 — Ice surface painted white.

Clubs allowed to dress 17 players exclusive of goaltenders.

Major penalties incurred by goaltenders served by a member of the goaltender's team instead of resulting in a penalty shot.

1950-51 — Each team required to provide an emergency goaltender in attendance with full equipment at each game for use by either team in the event of illness or injury to a regular goaltender.

1951-52 — Home teams to wear basic white uniforms; visiting teams basic colored uniforms.

Goal crease enlarged from 3 × 7 feet to 4 × 8 feet.

Number of players in uniform reduced to 15 plus goaltenders.

Faceoff circles enlarged from 10-foot to 15-foot radius.

1952-53 — Teams permitted to dress 15 skaters on the road and 16 at home.

1953-54 — Number of players in uniform set at 16 plus goaltenders.

1954-55 — Number of players in uniform set at 18 plus goaltenders up to December 1 and 16 plus goaltenders thereafter.

1956-57 — Player serving a minor penalty allowed to return to ice when a goal is scored by opposing team.

1959-60 — Players prevented from leaving their benches to enter into an altercation. Substitutions permitted providing substitutes do not enter into altercation.

1960-61 — Number of players in uniform set at 16 plus goaltenders.

1961-62 — Penalty shots to be taken by the player against whom the foul was committed. In the event of a penalty shot called in a situation where a particular player hasn't been fouled, the penalty shot to be taken by any player on the ice when the foul was committed.

1964-65 — No bodily contact on faceoffs.

In playoff games, each team to have its substitute goaltender dressed in his regular uniform except for leg pads and body protector. All previous rules governing standby goaltenders terminated.

1965-66 — Teams required to dress two goaltenders for each regular-season game.

1966-67 — Substitution allowed on coincidental major penalties.

Between-periods intermissions fixed at 15 minutes.

1967-68 — If a penalty incurred by a goaltender is a co-incident major, the penalty to be served by a player of the goaltender's team on the ice at the time the penalty was called.

1970-71 — Home teams to wear basic white uniforms; visiting teams basic colored uniforms.

Limit of curvature of hockey stick blade set at ½ inch.

Minor penalty for deliberately shooting the puck out of the playing area.

1971-72 — Number of players in uniform set at 17 plus 2 goaltenders.

Third man to enter an altercation assessed an automatic game misconduct penalty.

1972-73 — Minimum width of stick blade reduced to 2 inches from 2-½ inches.

1974-75 — Bench minor penalty imposed if a penalized player does not proceed directly and immediately to the penalty box.

1976-77 — Rule dealing with fighting amended to provide a major and game misconduct penalty for any player who is clearly the instigator of a fight.

1977-78 — Teams requesting a stick measurement to be assessed a minor penalty in the event that the measured stick does not violate the rules.

1981-82 — If both of a team's listed goaltenders are incapacitated, the team can dress and play any eligible goaltender who is available.

1982-83 — Number of players in uniform set at 18 plus 2 goaltenders.

1983-84 — Five-minute sudden-death overtime to be played in regular-season games that are tied at the end of regulation time.

1985-86 — Substitutions allowed in the event of co-incidental minor penalties.

1986-87 — Delayed off-side is no longer in effect once the players of the offending team have cleared the opponents' defensive zone.

1991-92 — Video replays employed to assist referees in goal/no goal situations. Size of goal crease increased. Crease changed to semi-circular configuration. Time clock to record tenths of a second in last minute of each period and overtime. Major and game misconduct penalty for checking from behind into boards. Penalties added for crease infringement and unnecessary contact with goaltender. Goal disallowed if puck enters net while a player of the attacking team is standing on the goal crease line, is in the goal crease or places his stick in the goal crease.

1992-93 — No substitutions allowed in the event of coincidental minor penalties called when both teams are at full strength. Wearing of helmets made optional for forwards and defensemen. Minor penalty for attempting to draw a penalty ("diving"). Major and game misconduct penalty for checking from behind into goal frame. Game misconduct penalty for instigating a fight. Highsticking redefined to include any use of the stick above waist-height. Previous rule stipulated shoulder-height.

1993-94 — High sticking redefined to allow goals scored with a high stick below the height of the crossbar of the goal frame.

The fortunes of the Chicago Black Hawk franchise began to turn when defenceman Pierre Pilote joined the team during the 1955-56 season. Pilote went on to win the Norris Trophy in three consecutive seasons beginning in 1962-63.

Team Records

BEST WINNING PERCENTAGE, ONE SEASON:
.875 — **Boston Bruins,** 1929-30. 38w-5L-1T. 77PTS in 44GP
.830 — Montreal Canadiens, 1943-44. 38w-5L-7T. 83PTS in 50GP
.825 — Montreal Canadiens, 1976-77. 60w-8L-12T. 132PTS in 80GP
.806 — Montreal Canadiens, 1977-78. 59w-10L-11T. 129PTS in 80GP
.800 — Montreal Canadiens, 1944-45. 38w-8L-4T. 80PTS in 50GP

MOST POINTS, ONE SEASON:
132 — **Montreal Canadiens,** 1976-77. 60w-8L-12T. 80GP
129 — Montreal Canadiens, 1977-78. 59w-10L-11T. 80GP
127 — Montreal Canadiens, 1975-76. 58w-11L-11T. 80GP

FEWEST POINTS, ONE SEASON:
8 — **Quebec Bulldogs,** 1919-20. 4w-20L-0T. 24GP
10 — Toronto Arenas, 1918-19. 5w-13L-0T. 18GP
12 — Hamilton Tigers, 1920-21. 6w-18L-0T. 24GP
— Hamilton Tigers, 1922-23. 6w-18L-0T. 24GP
— Boston Bruins, 1924-25. 6w-24L-0T. 30GP
— Philadelphia Quakers, 1930-31. 4w-36L-4T. 44GP

FEWEST POINTS, ONE SEASON (MINIMUM 70-GAME SCHEDULE):
21 — **Washington Capitals,** 1974-75. 8w-67L-5T. 80GP
24 — Ottawa Senators, 1992-93. 10w-70L-4T. 84GP
— San Jose Sharks, 1992-93. 11w-71L-2T. 84GP
30 — NY Islanders, 1972-73. 12w-60L-6T. 78GP

WORST WINNING PERCENTAGE, ONE SEASON:
.131 — **Washington Capitals,** 1974-75. 8w-67L-5T. 21PTS in 80GP
.136 — Philadelphia Quakers, 1930-31. 4w-36L-4T. 12PTS in 44GP
.143 — Ottawa Senators, 1992-93. 10w-70L-4T. 24PTS in 84GP
.143 — San Jose Sharks, 1992-93. 11w-71L-2T. 24PTS in 84GP
.148 — Pittsburgh Pirates, 1929-30. 5w-36L-3T. 13PTS in 44GP

MOST WINS, ONE SEASON:
60 — **Montreal Canadiens,** 1976-77. 80GP
59 — Montreal Canadiens, 1977-78. 80GP
58 — Montreal Canadiens, 1975-76. 80GP

FEWEST WINS, ONE SEASON:
4 — **Quebec Bulldogs,** 1919-20. 24GP
— **Philadelphia Quakers,** 1930-31. 44GP
5 — Toronto Arenas, 1918-19. 18GP
— Pittsburgh Pirates, 1929-30. 44GP

FEWEST WINS, ONE SEASON (MINIMUM 70-GAME SCHEDULE):
8 — **Washington Capitals,** 1974-75. 80GP
9 — Winnipeg Jets, 1980-81. 80GP
10 — Ottawa Senators, 1992-93. 84GP

MOST LOSSES, ONE SEASON:
71 — **San Jose Sharks,** 1992-93. 84GP
70 — Ottawa Senators, 1992-93. 84GP
67 — Washington Capitals, 1974-75. 80GP
61 — Quebec Nordiques, 1989-90. 80GP
— Ottawa Senators, 1993-94. 84GP

FEWEST LOSSES, ONE SEASON:
5 — **Ottawa Senators,** 1919-20. 24GP
— **Boston Bruins,** 1929-30. 44GP
— **Montreal Canadiens,** 1943-44. 50GP

FEWEST LOSSES, ONE SEASON (MINIMUM 70-GAME SCHEDULE):
8 — **Montreal Canadiens,** 1976-77. 80GP
10 — Montreal Canadiens, 1972-73. 78GP
— Montreal Canadiens, 1977-78. 80GP
11 — Montreal Canadiens, 1975-76. 80GP

MOST TIES, ONE SEASON:
24 — **Philadelphia Flyers,** 1969-70. 76GP
23 — Montreal Canadiens, 1962-63. 70GP
— Chicago Blackhawks, 1973-74. 78GP

FEWEST TIES, ONE SEASON (Since 1926-27):
1 — **Boston Bruins,** 1929-30. 44GP
2 — NY Americans, 1926-27. 44GP
— Montreal Canadiens, 1926-27. 44GP
— Boston Bruins, 1938-39. 48GP
— NY Rangers, 1941-42. 48GP
— San Jose Sharks, 1992-93. 84GP

FEWEST TIES, ONE SEASON (MINIMUM 70-GAME SCHEDULE):
2 — **San Jose Sharks,** 1992-93. 84GP
3 — New Jersey Devils, 1985-86. 80GP
— Calgary Flames, 1986-87. 80GP
— Vancouver Canucks, 1993-94. 84GP

MOST HOME WINS, ONE SEASON:
36 — **Philadelphia Flyers,** 1975-76. 40GP
33 — Boston Bruins, 1970-71. 39GP
— Boston Bruins, 1973-74. 39GP
— Montreal Canadiens, 1976-77. 40GP
— Philadelphia Flyers, 1976-77. 40GP
— NY Islanders, 1981-82. 40GP
— Philadelphia Flyers,1985-86. 40GP

MOST ROAD WINS, ONE SEASON:
27 — **Montreal Canadiens,** 1976-77. 40GP
— **Montreal Canadiens,** 1977-78. 40GP
26 — Boston Bruins, 1971-72. 39GP
— Montreal Canadiens, 1975-76. 40GP
— Edmonton Oilers, 1983-84. 40GP

MOST HOME LOSSES, ONE SEASON:
*32 — **San Jose Sharks,** 1992-93. 41GP
29 — Pittsburgh Penguins, 1983-84. 40GP
* — Ottawa Senators, 1993-94. 41GP

MOST ROAD LOSSES, ONE SEASON:
*40 — **Ottawa Senators,** 1992-93. 41GP
39 — Washington Capitals, 1974-75. 40GP
37 — California Seals, 1973-74. 39GP
* — San Jose Sharks, 1992-93. 41GP

MOST HOME TIES, ONE SEASON:
13 — **NY Rangers,** 1954-55. 35GP
— **Philadelphia Flyers,** 1969-70. 38GP
— **California Seals,** 1971-72. 39GP
— **California Seals,** 1972-73. 39GP
— **Chicago Blackhawks,** 1973-74. 39GP

MOST ROAD TIES, ONE SEASON:
15 — **Philadelphia Flyers,** 1976-77. 40GP
14 — Montreal Canadiens, 1952-53. 35GP
— Montreal Canadiens, 1974-75. 40GP
— Philadelphia Flyers, 1975-76. 40GP

FEWEST HOME WINS, ONE SEASON:
2 — **Chicago Blackhawks,** 1927-28. 22GP
3 — Boston Bruins, 1924-25. 15GP
— Chicago Blackhawks, 1928-29. 22GP
— Philadelphia Quakers, 1930-31. 22GP

FEWEST HOME WINS, ONE SEASON (MINIMUM 70-GAME SCHEDULE):
6 — **Chicago Blackhawks,** 1954-55. 35GP
— **Washington Capitals,** 1975-76. 40GP
7 — Boston Bruins, 1962-63. 35GP
— Washington Capitals, 1974-75. 40GP
— Winnipeg Jets, 1980-81. 40GP
— Pittsburgh Penguins, 1983-84. 40GP

FEWEST ROAD WINS, ONE SEASON:
0 — **Toronto Arenas,** 1918-19. 9GP
— **Quebec Bulldogs,** 1919-20. 12GP
— **Pittsburgh Pirates,** 1929-30. 22GP
1 — Hamilton Tigers, 1921-22. 12GP
— Toronto St. Patricks, 1925-26. 18GP
— Philadelphia Quakers, 1930-31. 22GP
— NY Americans, 1940-41. 24GP
— Washington Capitals, 1974-75. 40GP
* — Ottawa Senators, 1992-93. 41GP

FEWEST ROAD WINS, ONE SEASON (MINIMUM 70-GAME SCHEDULE):
1 — **Washington Capitals,** 1974-75. 40GP
* — **Ottawa Senators,** 1992-93. 41GP
2 — Boston Bruins, 1960-61. 35GP
— Los Angeles Kings, 1969-70. 38GP
— NY Islanders, 1972-73. 39GP
— California Seals, 1973-74. 39GP
— Colorado Rockies, 1977-78. 40GP
— Winnipeg Jets, 1980-81. 40GP
— Quebec Nordiques, 1991-92. 40GP

FEWEST HOME LOSSES, ONE SEASON:
0 — **Ottawa Senators,** 1922-23. 12GP
— **Montreal Canadiens,** 1943-44. 25GP
1 — Toronto Arenas, 1917-18. 11GP
— Ottawa Senators, 19. 9GP
— Ottawa Senators, 1919-20. 12GP
— Toronto St. Patricks, 1922-23. 12GP
— Boston Bruins, 1929-30 and 1930-31. 22GP
— Montreal Canadiens, 1976-77. 40GP

FEWEST HOME LOSSES, ONE SEASON (MINIMUM 70-GAME SCHEDULE):
1 — **Montreal Canadiens,** 1976-77. 40GP
2 — Montreal Canadiens, 1961-62. 35GP
— NY Rangers, 1970-71. 39GP
— Philadelphia Flyers, 1975-76. 40GP

* Does not include neutral site games

FEWEST ROAD LOSSES, ONE SEASON:
3 — Montreal Canadiens, 1928-29. 22GP
4 — Ottawa Senators, 1919-20. 12GP
— Montreal Canadiens, 1927-28. 22GP
— Boston Bruins, 1929-30. 20GP
— Boston Bruins, 1940-41. 24GP

FEWEST ROAD LOSSES, ONE SEASON (MINIMUM 70-GAME SCHEDULE):
6 — Montreal Canadiens, 1972-73. 39GP
— Montreal Canadiens, 1974-75. 40GP
— Montreal Canadiens, 1977-78. 40GP
7 — Detroit Red Wings, 1951-52. 35GP
— Montreal Canadiens, 1976-77. 40GP
— Philadelphia Flyers, 1979-80. 40GP

LONGEST WINNING STREAK:
17 Games — Pittsburgh Penguins, Mar. 9, 1993 - Apr. 10, 1993.
15 Games — NY Islanders, Jan. 21, 1982 - Feb. 20, 1982.
14 Games — Boston Bruins, Dec. 3, 1929 - Jan. 9, 1930.
13 Games — Boston Bruins, Feb. 23, 1971 - Mar. 20, 1971.
— Philadelphia Flyers, Oct. 19, 1985 - Nov. 17, 1985.

LONGEST WINNING STREAK FROM START OF SEASON:
10 Games — Toronto Maple Leafs, 1993-94.
8 Games — Toronto Maple Leafs, 1934-35.
— Buffalo Sabres, 1975-76.
7 Games — Edmonton Oilers, 1983-84.
— Quebec Nordiques, 1985-86.
— Pittsburgh Penguins, 1986-87.

LONGEST WINNING STREAK, INCLUDING PLAYOFFS:
15 Games — Detroit Red Wings, Feb. 27, 1955 - Apr. 5, 1955. Nine regular-season games, six playoff games.

LONGEST HOME WINNING STREAK FROM START OF SEASON:
11 Games — Chicago Blackhawks, 1963-64
10 Games — Ottawa Senators, 1925-26
9 Games — Montreal Canadiens, 1953-54
— Chicago Blackhawks, 1971-72
8 Games — Boston Bruins, 1983-84
— Philadelphia Flyers, 1986-87
— New Jersey Devils, 1987-88

LONGEST HOME WINNING STREAK (ONE SEASON):
20 Games — Boston Bruins, Dec. 3, 1929 - Mar. 18, 1930.
— Philadelphia Flyers, Jan. 4, 1976 - Apr. 3, 1976.

LONGEST HOME WINNING STREAK, INCLUDING PLAYOFFS:
24 Games — Philadelphia Flyers, Jan. 4, 1976 - Apr. 25, 1976. 20 regular-season games, 4 playoff games.

LONGEST ROAD WINNING STREAK (ONE SEASON):
10 Games — Buffalo Sabres, Dec. 10, 1983 - Jan. 23, 1984.
8 Games — Boston Bruins, Feb. 17, 1972 - Mar. 8, 1972.
— Los Angeles Kings, Dec. 18, 1974 - Jan. 16, 1975.
— Montreal Canadiens, Dec. 18, 1977 - Jan. 18. 1978.
— NY Islanders, Feb. 27, 1981 - Mar. 29, 1981.
— Montreal Canadiens, Jan. 21, 1982 - Feb. 21, 1982.
— Philadelphia Flyers, Dec. 22, 1982 - Jan. 16, 1983.
— Winnipeg Jets, Feb. 25, 1985 - Apr. 6, 1985.
— Edmonton Oilers, Dec. 9, 1986 - Jan. 17, 1987.
— Boston Bruins, Mar. 15, 1993 - Apr. 14, 1993.

LONGEST UNDEFEATED STREAK (ONE SEASON):
35 Games — Philadelphia Flyers, Oct. 14, 1979 - Jan. 6, 1980. 25w-10T.
28 Games — Montreal Canadiens, Dec. 18, 1977 - Feb. 23, 1978. 23w-5T.
23 Games — Boston Bruins, Dec. 22, 1940 - Feb. 23, 1941. 15w-8T.
— Philadelphia Flyers, Jan. 29, 1976 - Mar. 18, 1976. 17w-6T.

LONGEST UNDEFEATED STREAK FROM START OF SEASON:
15 Games — Edmonton Oilers, 1984-85. 12w-3T
14 Games — Montreal Canadiens, 1943-44. 11w-3T
13 Games — Montreal Canadiens, 1972-73. 9w-4T

LONGEST HOME UNDEFEATED STREAK (ONE SEASON):
34 Games — Montreal Canadiens, Nov. 1, 1976 - Apr. 2, 1977. 28w-6T.
27 Games — Boston Bruins, Nov. 22, 1970 - Mar. 20, 1971. 26w-1T.

LONGEST HOME UNDEFEATED STREAK, INCLUDING PLAYOFFS:
38 Games — Montreal Canadiens, Nov. 1, 1976 - Apr. 26, 1977. 28w-6T in regular season and 4w in playoffs).

LONGEST ROAD UNDEFEATED STREAK (ONE SEASON):
23 Games — Montreal Canadiens, Nov. 27, 1974 - Mar. 12, 1975. 14w-9T.
17 Games — Montreal Canadiens, Dec. 18, 1977 - Mar. 1, 1978. 14w-3T.
16 Games — Philadelphia Flyers, Oct. 20, 1979 - Jan. 6, 1980. 11w-5T.

LONGEST LOSING STREAK (ONE SEASON):
17 Games — Washington Capitals, Feb. 18, 1975 - Mar. 26, 1975.
— San Jose Sharks, Jan. 4, 1993 - Feb. 12, 1993.
15 Games — Philadelphia Quakers, Nov. 29, 1930 - Jan. 8, 1931.

LONGEST LOSING STREAK FROM START OF SEASON:
11 Games — NY Rangers, 1943-44.
7 Games — Montreal Canadiens, 1938-39.
— Chicago Blackhawks, 1947-48.
— Washington Capitals, 1983-84.

LONGEST HOME LOSING STREAK (ONE SEASON):
11 Games — Boston Bruins, Dec. 8, 1924 - Feb. 17; 1925.
— Washington Capitals, Feb. 18, 1975 - Mar. 30, 1975.
— Ottawa Senators, Oct. 27, 1993 - Dec. 8, 1993.

LONGEST ROAD LOSING STREAK (ONE SEASON):
***38 Games — Ottawa Senators,** Oct. 10, 1992 - Apr. 3, 1993.
37 Games — Washington Capitals, Oct. 9, 1974 - Mar. 26, 1975.
* – Does not include neutral site games.

LONGEST WINLESS STREAK (ONE SEASON):
30 Games — Winnipeg Jets, Oct. 19, 1980 - Dec. 20, 1980. 23L-7T.
27 Games — Kansas City Scouts, Feb. 12, 1976 - Apr. 4, 1976. 21L-6T.
25 Games — Washington Capitals, Nov. 29, 1975 - Jan. 21, 1976. 22L-3T.

LONGEST WINLESS STREAK FROM START OF SEASON:
15 Games — NY Rangers, 1943-44. 14L-1T
12 Games — Pittsburgh Pirates, 1927-28. 9L-3T
11 Games — Minnesota North Stars, 1973-74. 5L-6T.

LONGEST HOME WINLESS STREAK (ONE SEASON):
15 Games — Chicago Blackhawks, Dec. 16, 1928 - Feb. 28, 1929. 11L-4T.
— Montreal Canadiens, Dec. 16, 1939 - Mar. 7, 1940. 12L-3T.

LONGEST ROAD WINLESS STREAK (ONE SEASON):
***38 Games — Ottawa Senators,** Oct. 10, 1992 - Apr. 3, 1993. 38L-0T.
37 Games — Washington Capitals, Oct. 9, 1974 - Mar. 26, 1975. 37L-0T.
* – Does not include neutral site games.

LONGEST NON-SHUTOUT STREAK:
264 Games — Calgary Flames, Nov. 12, 1981 - Jan. 9, 1985.
262 Games — Los Angeles Kings, Mar. 15, 1986 - Oct. 25, 1989.
244 Games — Washington Capitals, Oct. 31, 1989 - Nov. 11, 1993.
230 Games — Quebec Nordiques, Feb. 10, 1980 - Jan. 13, 1983.
229 Games — Edmonton Oilers, Mar. 15, 1981 - Feb. 11, 1984.

LONGEST NON-SHUTOUT STREAK INCLUDING PLAYOFFS:
264 Games — Los Angeles Kings, Mar. 15 1986 - Apr. 6, 1989. (5 playoff games in 1987; 5 in 1988; 2 in 1989)
262 Games — Chicago Blackhawks, Mar. 14, 1970 - Feb. 21, 1973. (8 playoff games in 1970; 18 in 1971; 8 in 1972).
251 Games — Quebec Nordiques, Feb. 10, 1980 - Jan. 13, 1983. (5 playoff games in 1981; 16 in 1982).
245 Games — Pittsburgh Penguins, Jan. 7, 1989 - Oct. 26, 1991. (11 playoff games in 1989; 23 in 1991).

MOST CONSECUTIVE GAMES SHUT OUT:
8 — Chicago Blackhawks, 1928-29.

MOST SHUTOUTS, ONE SEASON:
22 — Montreal Canadiens, 1928-29. All by George Hainsworth. 44GP
16 — NY Americans, 1928-29. Roy Worters had 13; Flat Walsh 3. 44GP
15 — Ottawa Senators, 1925-26. All by Alex Connell. 36GP
— Ottawa Senators, 1927-28. All by Alex Connell. 44GP
— Boston Bruins, 1927-28. All by Hal Winkler. 44GP
— Chicago Blackhawks, 1969-70. All by Tony Esposito. 76GP

MOST GOALS, ONE SEASON:
446 — Edmonton Oilers, 1983-84. 80GP
426 — Edmonton Oilers, 1985-86. 80GP
424 — Edmonton Oilers, 1982-83. 80GP
417 — Edmonton Oilers, 1981-82. 80GP
401 — Edmonton Oilers, 1984-85. 80GP

HIGHEST GOALS-PER-GAME AVERAGE, ONE SEASON:
5.58 — Edmonton Oilers, 1983-84. 446G in 80GP.
5.38 — Montreal Canadiens, 1919-20. 129G in 24GP.
5.33 — Edmonton Oilers, 1985-86. 426G in 80GP.
5.30 — Edmonton Oilers, 1982-83. 424G in 80GP.
5.23 — Montreal Canadiens, 1917-18. 115G in 22GP.

FEWEST GOALS, ONE SEASON:
33 — Chicago Blackhawks, 1928-29. 44GP
45 — Montreal Maroons, 1924-25. 30GP
46 — Pittsburgh Pirates, 1928-29. 44GP

FEWEST GOALS, ONE SEASON (MINIMUM 70-GAME SCHEDULE):
133 — Chicago Blackhawks, 1953-54. 70GP
147 — Toronto Maple Leafs, 1954-55. 70GP
— Boston Bruins, 1955-56. 70GP
150 — NY Rangers, 1954-55. 70GP

LOWEST GOALS-PER-GAME AVERAGE, ONE SEASON:
.75 — Chicago Blackhawks, 1928-29, 33G in 44GP.
1.05 — Pittsburgh Pirates, 1928-29. 46G in 44GP.
1.20 — NY Americans, 1928-29. 53G in 44GP.

MOST GOALS AGAINST, ONE SEASON:
446 — Washington Capitals, 1974-75. 80GP
415 — Detroit Red Wings, 1985-86. 80GP
414 — San Jose Sharks, 1992-93. 84GP
407 — Quebec Nordiques, 1989-90. 80GP
403 — Hartford Whalers, 1982-83. 80GP

HIGHEST GOALS-AGAINST-PER-GAME AVERAGE, ONE SEASON:
7.38 — Quebec Bulldogs, 1919-20, 177GA vs. in 24GP.
6.20 — NY Rangers, 1943-44, 310GA vs. in 50GP.
5.58 — Washington Capitals, 1974-75, 446GA vs. in 80GP.

FEWEST GOALS AGAINST, ONE SEASON:
  42 — Ottawa Senators, 1925-26. 36GP
  43 — Montreal Canadiens, 1928-29. 44GP
  48 — Montreal Canadiens, 1923-24. 24GP
     — Montreal Canadiens, 1927-28. 44GP

FEWEST GOALS AGAINST, ONE SEASON (MINIMUM 70-GAME SCHEDULE):
  131 — Toronto Maple Leafs, 1953-54. 70GP
     — Montreal Canadiens, 1955-56. 70GP
  132 — Detroit Red Wings, 1953-54. 70GP
  133 — Detroit Red Wings, 1951-52. 70GP
     — Detroit Red Wings, 1952-53. 70GP

LOWEST GOALS-AGAINST-PER-GAME AVERAGE, ONE SEASON:
  .98 — Montreal Canadiens, 1928-29. 43GA vs. in 44GP.
  1.09 — Montreal Canadiens, 1927-28. 48GA vs. in 44GP.
  1.17 — Ottawa Senators, 1925-26. 42GA vs. in 36GP.

MOST POWER-PLAY GOALS, ONE SEASON:
  119 — Pittsburgh Penguins, 1988-89. 80GP
  113 — Detroit Red Wings, 1992-93. 84GP
  111 — NY Rangers, 1987-88. 80GP
  110 — Pittsburgh Penguins, 1987-88. 80GP
     — Winnipeg Jets, 1987-88, 80GP

MOST POWER-PLAY GOALS AGAINST, ONE SEASON:
  122 — Chicago Blackhawks, 1988-89. 80GP
  120 — Pittsburgh Penguins, 1987-88. 80GP
  115 — New Jersey Devils, 1988-89. 80GP
     — Ottawa Senators, 1992-93. 84GP
  114 — Los Angeles Kings, 1992-93. 84GP
  113 — San Jose Sharks, 1992-93. 84GP

MOST SHORTHAND GOALS, ONE SEASON:
  36 — Edmonton Oilers, 1983-84. 80GP
  28 — Edmonton Oilers, 1986-87. 80GP
  27 — Edmonton Oilers, 1985-86. 80GP
     — Edmonton Oilers, 1988-89. 80GP

MOST SHORTHAND GOALS AGAINST, ONE SEASON:
  22 — Pittsburgh Penguins, 1984-85. 80GP
     — Minnesota North Stars, 1991-92. 80GP
  21 — Calgary Flames, 1984-85. 80GP
     — Pittsburgh Penguins, 1989-90. 80GP
  20 — Minnesota North Stars, 1982-83. 80GP
     — Quebec Nordiques, 1985-86. 80GP
     — Tampa Bay Lightning, 1993-94. 84GP

MOST ASSISTS, ONE SEASON:
  737 — Edmonton Oilers, 1985-86. 80GP
  736 — Edmonton Oilers, 1983-84. 80GP
  706 — Edmonton Oilers, 1981-82. 80GP

FEWEST ASSISTS, ONE SEASON:
  45 — NY Rangers, 1926-27. 44GP

FEWEST ASSISTS, ONE SEASON (MINIMUM 70-GAME SCHEDULE):
  206 — Chicago Blackhawks, 1953-54. 70GP

Pete Mahovlich had the finest season of his career in 1974-75, compiling 117 points in helping the Montreal Canadiens establish a new NHL mark with a 23-game road unbeaten streak. The Habs won 14 games and tied nine during their record run on the road.

MOST SCORING POINTS, ONE SEASON:
  1,182 — Edmonton Oilers, 1983-84. 80GP
  1,163 — Edmonton Oilers, 1985-86. 80GP
  1,123 — Edmonton Oilers, 1981-82. 80GP

MOST 50-OR-MORE-GOAL SCORERS, ONE SEASON:
  3 — Edmonton Oilers, 1983-84. Wayne Gretzky, 87; Glenn Anderson, 54; Jari Kurri, 52 80GP.
     — Edmonton Oilers, 1985-86. Jari Kurri, 68; Glenn Anderson, 54; Wayne Gretzky, 52. 80GP.
  2 — Boston Bruins, 1970-71. Phil Esposito, 76; John Bucyk, 51. 78GP
     — Boston Bruins, 1973-74. Phil Esposito, 68; Ken Hodge, 50. 78GP
     — Philadelphia Flyers, 1975-76. Reggie Leach, 61; Bill Barber, 50. 80GP
     — Pittsburgh Penguins, 1975-76. Pierre Larouche, 53; Jean Pronovost, 52. 80GP
     — Montreal Canadiens, 1976-77. Steve Shutt, 60; Guy Lafleur, 56. 80GP
     — Los Angeles Kings, 1979-80. Charlie Simmer, 56; Marcel Dionne, 53. 80GP
     — Montreal Canadiens, 1979-80. Pierre Larouche, 50; Guy Lafleur, 50. 80GP
     — Los Angeles Kings, 1980-81. Marcel Dionne, 58; Charlie Simmer, 56. 80GP
     — Edmonton Oilers, 1981-82. Wayne Gretzky, 92; Mark Messier, 50. 80GP
     — NY Islanders, 1981-82. Mike Bossy, 64; Bryan Trottier, 50. 80GP
     — Edmonton Oilers, 1984-85. Wayne Gretzky, 73; Jari Kurri, 71. 80GP
     — Washington Capitals, 1984-85. Bob Carpenter, 53; Mike Gartner, 50. 80GP
     — Edmonton Oilers, 1986-87. Wayne Gretzky, 62; Jari Kurri, 54. 80GP
     — Calgary Flames, 1987-88. Joe Nieuwendyk, 51; Hakan Loob, 50. 80GP
     — Los Angeles Kings, 1987-88. Jimmy Carson, 55; Luc Robitaille, 53. 80GP
     — Los Angeles Kings, 1988-89. Bernie Nicholls, 70; Wayne Gretzky, 54. 80GP
     — Calgary Flames, 1988-89. Joe Nieuwendyk, 51; Joe Mullen, 51. 80GP
     — Buffalo Sabres, 1992-93. Alexander Mogilny, 76; Pat Lafontaine, 53. 84GP
     — Pittsburgh Penguins, 1992-93. Mario Lemieux, 69; Kevin Stevens, 55. 84GP
     — St. Louis Blues, 1992-93. Brett Hull, 54; Brendan Shanahan, 51. 84GP
     — St. Louis Blues, 1993-94. Brett Hull, 57; Brendan Shanahan, 52. 84GP
     — Detroit Red Wings, 1993-94. Sergei Fedorov, 56; Ray Sheppard, 52. 84GP

MOST 40-OR-MORE-GOAL SCORERS, ONE SEASON:
  4 — Edmonton Oilers, 1982-83. Wayne Gretzky, 71; Glenn Anderson, 48; Mark Messier, 48; Jari Kurri, 45. 80GP
     — Edmonton Oilers, 1983-84. Wayne Gretzky, 87; Glenn Anderson, 54; Jari Kurri, 52; Paul Coffey, 40. 80GP
     — Edmonton Oilers, 1984-85. Wayne Gretzky, 73; Jari Kurri, 71; Mike Krushelnyski, 43; Glenn Anderson, 42. 80GP
     — Edmonton Oilers, 1985-86. Jari Kurri, 68; Glenn Anderson, 54; Wayne Gretzky, 52; Paul Coffey, 48. 80GP
     — Calgary Flames, 1987-88. Joe Nieuwendyk, 51; Hakan Loob, 50; Mike Bullard, 48; Joe Mullen, 40. 80GP
  3 — Boston Bruins, 1970-71. Phil Esposito, 76; John Bucyk, 51; Ken Hodge, 43. 78GP
     — NY Rangers, 1971-72. Vic Hadfield, 50; Jean Ratelle, 46; Rod Gilbert, 43. 78GP
     — Buffalo Sabres, 1975-76. Danny Gare, 50; Rick Martin, 49; Gilbert Perreault, 44. 80GP
     — Montreal Canadiens, 1979-80. Guy Lafleur, 50; Pierre Larouche, 50; Steve Shutt, 47. 80GP
     — Buffalo Sabres, 1979-80. Danny Gare, 56; Rick Martin, 45; Gilbert Perreault, 40. 80GP
     — Los Angeles Kings, 1980-81. Marcel Dionne, 58; Charlie Simmer, 56; Dave Taylor, 47. 80GP
     — Los Angeles Kings, 1984-85. Marcel Dionne, 46; Bernie Nicholls, 46; Dave Taylor, 41. 80GP
     — NY Islanders, 1984-85. Mike Bossy, 58; Brent Sutter, 42; John Tonelli, 42. 80GP
     — Chicago Blackhawks, 1985-86. Denis Savard, 47; Troy Murray, 45; Al Secord, 40. 80GP
     — Chicago Blackhawks, 1987-88. Denis Savard, 44; Rick Vaive, 43; Steve Larmer, 41. 80GP
     — Edmonton Oilers, 1987-88. Craig Simpson, 43; Jari Kurri, 43; Wayne Gretzky, 40. 80GP
     — Los Angeles Kings, 1988-89. Bernie Nicholls, 70; Wayne Gretzky 54; Luc Robitaille, 46. 80GP
     — Los Angeles Kings, 1990-91. Luc Robitaille, 45; Tomas Sandstrom, 45; Wayne Gretzky 41. 80GP
     — Pittsburgh Penguins, 1991-92. Kevin Stevens, 54; Mario Lemieux, 44; Joe Mullen, 42. 80GP
     — Pittsburgh Penguins, 1992-93. Mario Lemieux, 69; Kevin Stevens, 55; Rick Tocchet, 48. 84GP
     — Calgary Flames, 1993-94. Gary Roberts, 41; Robert Reichel, 40; Theoren Fleury, 40. 84GP

MOST 30-OR-MORE GOAL SCORERS, ONE SEASON:

6 —Buffalo Sabres, 1974-75. Rick Martin, 52; Rene Robert, 40; Gilbert Perreault, 39; Don Luce, 33; Rick Dudley, Danny Gare, 31 each. 80GP

—**NY Islanders,** 1977-78, Mike Bossy, 53; Bryan Trottier, 46; Clark Gillies, 35; Denis Potvin, Bob Nystrom, Bob Bourne, 30 each. 80GP

—**Winnipeg Jets,** 1984-85, Dale Hawerchuk, 53; Paul MacLean, 41; Laurie Boschman, 32; Brian Mullen, 32; Doug Smail, 31; Thomas Steen, 30. 80GP

5 —Chicago Blackhawks, 1968-69. 76GP
—Boston Bruins, 1970-71. 78GP
—Montreal Canadiens, 1971-72. 78GP
—Philadelphia Flyers, 1972-73. 78GP
—Boston Bruins, 1973-74. 78GP
—Montreal Canadiens, 1974-75. 80GP
—Montreal Canadiens, 1975-76. 80GP
—Pittsburgh Penguins, 1975-76. 80GP
—NY Islanders, 1978-79. 80GP
—Detroit Red Wings, 1979-80. 80GP
—Philadelphia Flyers, 1979-80. 80GP
—NY Islanders, 1980-81. 80GP
—St. Louis Blues, 1980-81. 80GP
—Chicago Blackhawks, 1981-82. 80GP
—Edmonton Oilers, 1981-82. 80GP
—Montreal Canadiens, 1981-82. 80GP
—Quebec Nordiques, 1981-82. 80GP
—Washington Capitals, 1981-82. 80GP
—Edmonton Oilers, 1982-83. 80GP
—Edmonton Oilers, 1983-84. 80GP
—Edmonton Oilers, 1984-85. 80GP
—Los Angeles Kings, 1984-85. 80GP
—Edmonton Oilers, 1985-86. 80GP
—Edmonton Oilers, 1986-87. 80GP
—Edmonton Oilers, 1987-88. 80GP
—Edmonton Oilers, 1988-89. 80GP
—Detroit Red Wings, 1991-92. 80GP
—NY Rangers, 1991-92. 80GP
—Pittsburgh Penguins, 1991-92. 80GP
—Detroit Red Wings, 1992-93. 84GP
—Pittsburgh Penguins, 1992-93. 84GP

MOST 20-OR-MORE GOAL SCORERS, ONE SEASON:

11 —Boston Bruins, 1977-78; Peter McNab, 41; Terry O'Reilly, 29; Bobby Schmautz, Stan Jonathan, 27 each; Jean Ratelle, Rick Middleton, 25 each; Wayne Cashman, 24; Gregg Sheppard, 23; Brad Park, 22; Don Marcotte, Bob Miller, 20 each. 80GP

10 —Boston Bruins, 1970-71. 78GP
—Montreal Canadiens, 1974-75. 80GP
—St. Louis Blues, 1980-81. 80GP

MOST 100 OR-MORE-POINT SCORERS, ONE SEASON:

4 —Boston Bruins, 1970-71, Phil Esposito, 76G-76A-152PTS; Bobby Orr, 37G-102A-139PTS; John Bucyk, 51G-65A-116PTS; Ken Hodge, 43G-62A-105PTS. 78GP

—**Edmonton Oilers,** 1982-83, Wayne Gretzky, 71G-125A-196PTS; Mark Messier, 48G-58A-106PTS; Glenn Anderson, 48G-56A-104PTS; Jari Kurri, 45G-59A-104PTS. 80GP.

—**Edmonton Oilers,** 1983-84, Wayne Gretzky, 87G-118A-205PTS; Paul Coffey, 40G-86A-126PTS; Jari Kurri, 52G-61A-113PTS; Mark Messier, 37G-64A-101PTS. 80GP.

—**Edmonton Oilers,**1985-86, Wayne Gretzky, 52G-163A-215PTS; Paul Coffey, 48G-90A-138PTS; Jari Kurri, 68G-63A-131PTS; Glenn Anderson, 54G-48A-102PTS. 80GP

—**Pittsburgh Penguins,**1992-93, Mario Lemieux, 69G-91A-160PTS; Kevin Stevens, 55G-56A-111PTS; Rick Tocchet, 48G-61A-109PTS; Ron Francis, 24G-76A-100PTS. 84GP

3 —Boston Bruins, 1973-74, Phil Esposito, 68G-77A-145PTS; Bobby Orr, 32G-90A-122PTS; Ken Hodge, 50G-55A-105PTS. 78GP
—NY Islanders, 1978-79, Bryan Trottier, 47G-87A-134PTS; Mike Bossy, 69G-57A-126PTS; Denis Potvin, 31G-70A-101PTS. 80GP
—Los Angeles Kings, 1980-81, Marcel Dionne, 58G-77A-135PTS; Dave Taylor, 47 G-65A-112PTS; Charlie Simmer, 56G-49A-105PTS. 80GP
—Edmonton Oilers, 1984-85, Wayne Gretzky, 73G-135A-208PTS; Jari Kurri, 71G-64A-135PTS; Paul Coffey, 37G-84A-121PTS. 80GP
—NY Islanders, 1984-85. Mike Bossy, 58G-59A-117PTS; Brent Sutter, 42G-60A-102PTS; John Tonelli, 42G-58A-100PTS. 80GP
—Edmonton Oilers, 1986-87, Wayne Gretzky, 62G-121A-183PTS; Jari Kurri, 54G-54A-108PTS; Mark Messier, 37G-70A-107PTS. 80GP
—Pittsburgh Penguins, 1988-89, Mario Lemieux, 85G-114A-199PTS; Rob Brown, 49G-66A-115PTS; Paul Coffey, 30G-83A-113PTS. 80GP

MOST PENALTY MINUTES, ONE SEASON:

2,713 —Buffalo Sabres, 1991-92. 80GP
2,670 —Pittsburgh Penguins, 1988-89. 80GP
2,663 —Chicago Blackhawks, 1991-92. 80GP
2,643 —Calgary Flames, 1991-92. 80GP
2,621 —Philadelphia Flyers, 1980-81. 80GP

MOST GOALS, BOTH TEAMS, ONE GAME:

21 —Montreal Canadiens, Toronto St. Patricks, at Montreal, Jan. 10, 1920. Montreal won 14-7.

—**Edmonton Oilers, Chicago Blackhawks,** at Chicago, Dec. 11, 1985. Edmonton won 12-9.

20 —Edmonton Oilers, Minnesota North Stars, at Edmonton, Jan. 4, 1984. Edmonton won 12-8.
—Toronto Maple Leafs, Edmonton Oilers, at Toronto, Jan. 8, 1986. Toronto won 11-9.

19 —Montreal Wanderers, Toronto Arenas, at Montreal, Dec. 19, 1917. Montreal won 10-9.
—Montreal Canadiens, Quebec Bulldogs, at Quebec, Mar. 3, 1920, Montreal won 16-3.
—Montreal Canadiens, Hamilton Tigers, at Montreal, Feb. 26, 1921. Montreal won 13-6.
—Boston Bruins, NY Rangers, at Boston, Mar. 4, 1944, Boston won 10-9.
—Boston Bruins, Detroit Red Wings, at Detroit, Mar. 16, 1944. Detroit won 10-9.
—Vancouver Canucks, Minnesota North Stars, at Vancouver, Oct. 7, 1983. Vancouver won 10-9.

MOST GOALS, ONE TEAM, ONE GAME:

16 —Montreal Canadiens, Mar. 3, 1920, at Quebec. Defeated Quebec Bulldogs 16-3.

MOST CONSECUTIVE GOALS, ONE TEAM, ONE GAME:

15 —Detroit Red Wings, Jan. 23, 1944, at Detroit. Defeated NY Rangers 15-0.

MOST POINTS, BOTH TEAMS, ONE GAME:

62 —Edmonton Oilers, Chicago Blackhawks, at Chicago, Dec. 11, 1985. Edmonton won 12-9. Edmonton had 24A, Chicago, 17.

53 —Quebec Nordiques, Washington Capitals, at Washington, Feb. 22, 1981. Quebec won 11-7. Quebec had 22A, Washington, 13.
—Edmonton Oilers, Minnesota North Stars, at Edmonton, Jan. 4, 1984. Edmonton won 12-8. Edmonton had 20A, Minnesota 13.
—Minnesota North Stars, St. Louis Blues, at St. Louis, Jan. 27, 1984. Minnesota won 10-8. Minnesota had 19A, St. Louis 16.
—Toronto Maple Leafs, Edmonton Oilers, at Toronto, Jan. 8, 1986. Toronto won 11-9. Toronto had 17A, Edmonton 16.

52 —Mtl. Maroons, NY Americans, at New York, Feb. 18, 1936. 8-8 tie. New York had 20A, Montreal 16. (3A allowed for each goal.)
—Vancouver Canucks, Minnesota North Stars, at Vancouver, Oct. 7, 1983. Vancouver won 10-9. Vancouver had 16A, Minnesota 17.

Steve Thomas scored a pair of goals as the Toronto Maple Leafs and Edmonton Oilers combined for 20 goals in the Leafs' 11-9 win over Edmonton on January 8, 1988.

MOST POINTS, ONE TEAM, ONE GAME:
 40 — **Buffalo Sabres,** Dec. 21, 1975, at Buffalo. Buffalo defeated Washington 14-2, receiving 26A.
 39 — Minnesota North Stars, Nov. 11, 1981, at Minnesota. Minnesota defeated Winnipeg 15-2, receiving 24A.
 37 — Detroit Red Wings, Jan. 23, 1944, at Detroit. Detroit defeated NY Rangers 15-0, receiving 22A.
    — Toronto Maple Leafs, Mar. 16, 1957, at Toronto. Toronto defeated NY Rangers 14-1, receiving 23A.
    — Buffalo Sabres, Feb. 25, 1978, at Cleveland. Buffalo defeated Cleveland 13-3, receiving 24A.
    — Calgary Flames, Feb. 10, 1993, at Calgary. Calgary defeated San Jose 13-1, receiving 24A.

MOST SHOTS, BOTH TEAMS, ONE GAME:
 141 — **NY Americans, Pittsburgh Pirates,** Dec. 26, 1925, at New York. NY Americans, who won game 3-1, had 73 shots; Pit. Pirates, 68 shots.

MOST SHOTS, ONE TEAM, ONE GAME:
 83 — **Boston Bruins,** March 4, 1941, at Boston. Boston defeated Chicago 3-2.
 73 — NY Americans, Dec. 26, 1925, at New York. NY Americans defeated Pit. Pirates 3-1.
    — Boston Bruins, March 21, 1991, at Boston. Boston tied Quebec 3-3.
 72 — Boston Bruins, Dec. 10, 1970, at Boston. Boston defeated Buffalo 8-2.

MOST PENALTIES, BOTH TEAMS, ONE GAME:
85 Penalties — **Edmonton Oilers (44), Los Angeles Kings (41)** at Los Angeles, Feb. 28, 1990. Edmonton received 26 minors, 7 majors, 6 10-minute misconducts, 4 game misconducts and 1 match penalty; Los Angeles received 26 minors, 9 majors, 3 10-minute misconducts and 3 game misconducts.

MOST PENALTY MINUTES, BOTH TEAMS, ONE GAME:
406 Minutes — **Minnesota North Stars, Boston Bruins** at Boston, Feb. 26, 1981. Minnesota received 18 minors, 13 majors, 4 10-minute misconducts and 7 game misconducts; a total of 211PIM. Boston received 20 minors, 13 majors, 3 10-minute misconducts and six game misconducts; a total of 195PIM.

MOST PENALTIES, ONE TEAM, ONE GAME:
 44 — **Edmonton Oilers,** Feb. 28, 1990, at Los Angeles. Edmonton received 26 minors, 7 majors, 6 10-minute misconducts, 4 game misconducts and 1 match penalty.
 42 — Minnesota North Stars, Feb. 26, 1981, at Boston. Minnesota received 18 minors, 13 majors, 4 10-minute misconducts and 7 game misconducts.
    — Boston Bruins, Feb. 26, 1981, at Boston vs. Minnesota. Boston received 20 minors, 13 majors, 3 10-minute misconducts and 7 game misconducts.

MOST PENALTY MINUTES, ONE TEAM, ONE GAME:
 211 — **Minnesota North Stars,** Feb. 26, 1981, at Boston. Minnesota received 18 minors, 13 majors, 4 10-minute misconducts and 7 game misconducts.

MOST GOALS, BOTH TEAMS, ONE PERIOD:
 12 — **Buffalo Sabres, Toronto Maple Leafs,** at Buffalo, March 19, 1981, second period. Buffalo scored 9 goals, Toronto 3. Buffalo won 14-4.
    — **Edmonton Oilers, Chicago Blackhawks,** at Chicago, Dec. 11, 1985, second period. Edmonton scored 6 goals, Chicago 6. Edmonton won 12-9.
 10 — NY Rangers, NY Americans, at NY Americans, March 16, 1939, third period. NY Rangers scored 7 goals, NY Americans 3. NY Rangers won 11-5.
    — Toronto Maple Leafs, Detroit Red Wings, at Detroit, March 17, 1946, third period. Toronto scored 6 goals, Detroit 4. Toronto won 11-7.
    — Vancouver Canucks, Buffalo Sabres, at Buffalo, Jan. 8, 1976, third period. Buffalo scored 6 goals, Vancouver 4. Buffalo won 8-5.
    — Buffalo Sabres, Montreal Canadiens, at Montreal, Oct. 26, 1982, first period. Montreal scored 5 goals, Buffalo 5. 7-7 tie.
    — Boston Bruins, Quebec Nordiques, at Quebec, Dec. 7, 1982, second period. Quebec scored 6 goals, Boston 4. Quebec won 10-5.
    — Calgary Flames, Vancouver Canucks, at Vancouver, Jan. 16, 1987, first period. Vancouver scored 6 goals, Calgary 4. Vancouver won 9-5.
    — Winnipeg Jets, Detroit Red Wings, at Detroit, Nov. 25, 1987, third period. Detroit scored 7 goals, Winnipeg 3. Detroit won 10-8.
    — Chicago Blackhawks, St. Louis Blues, at St. Louis, March 15, 1988, third period. Chicago scored 5 goals, St. Louis 5. 7-7 tie.

MOST GOALS, ONE TEAM, ONE PERIOD:
 9 — **Buffalo Sabres,** March 19, 1981, at Buffalo, second period during 14-4 win over Toronto.
 8 — Detroit Red Wings, Jan. 23, 1944, at Detroit, third period during 15-0 win over NY Rangers.
    — Boston Bruins, March 16, 1969, at Boston, second period during 11-3 win over Toronto.
    — NY Rangers, Nov. 21, 1971, at New York, third period during 12-1 win over California.
    — Philadelphia Flyers, March 31, 1973, at Philadelphia, second period during 10-2 win over NY Islanders.
    — Buffalo Sabres, Dec. 21, 1975, at Buffalo, third period during 14-2 win over Washington.
    — Minnesota North Stars, Nov. 11, 1981, at Minnesota, second period during 15-2 win over Winnipeg.
    — Pittsburgh Penguins, Dec. 17, 1991, at Pittsburgh, second period during 10-2 win over San Jose.

MOST POINTS, BOTH TEAMS, ONE PERIOD:
 35 — **Edmonton, Oilers, Chicago Blackhawks,** at Chicago, Dec. 11, 1985, second period. Edmonton had 6G, 12A; Chicago, 6G, 11A. Edmonton won 12-9.
 31 — Buffalo Sabres, Toronto Maple Leafs, at Buffalo, March 19, 1981, second period. Buffalo had 9G, 14A; Toronto, 3G, 5A. Buffalo won 14-4.
 29 — Winnipeg Jets, Detroit Red Wings, at Detroit, Nov. 25, 1987, third period. Detroit had 7G, 13A; Winnipeg had 3G, 6A. Detroit won 10-8.
    — Chicago Blackhawks, St. Louis Blues, at St. Louis, March 15, 1988, third period. St. Louis had 5G, 10A; Chicago had 5G, 9A. 7-7 tie.

Ric Seiling collected a goal and two assists in Buffalo's record-breaking nine-goal second period as the Sabres defeated the Toronto Maple Leafs 14-4 on March 19, 1981.

MOST POINTS, ONE TEAM, ONE PERIOD:
23 —**NY Rangers,** Nov. 21, 1971, at New York, third period during 12-1 win over California. NY Rangers scored 8G and 15A.
—**Buffalo Sabres,** Dec. 21, 1975, at Buffalo, third period during 14-2 win over Washington. Buffalo scored 8G and 15A.
—**Buffalo Sabres,** March 19, 1981, at Buffalo, second period, during 14-4 win over Toronto. Buffalo scored 9G and 14A.
22 —Detroit Red Wings, Jan. 23, 1944, at Detroit, third period during 15-0 win over NY Rangers. Detroit scored 8G and 14A.
—Boston Bruins, March 16, 1969, at Boston, second period during 11-3 win over Toronto Maple Leafs. Boston scored 8G and 14A.
—Minnesota North Stars, Nov. 11, 1981, at Minnesota, second period during 15-2 win over Winnipeg. Minnesota scored 8G and 14A.
—Pittsburgh Penguins, Dec. 17, 1991, at Pittsburgh, second period during 10-2 win over San Jose. Pittsburgh scored 8G and 14A.

MOST SHOTS, ONE TEAM, ONE PERIOD:
33 —**Boston Bruins,** March 4, 1941, at Boston, second period. Boston defeated Chicago 3-2.

MOST PENALTIES, BOTH TEAMS, ONE PERIOD:
67 —**Minnesota North Stars, Boston Bruins,** at Boston, Feb. 26, 1981, first period. Minnesota received 15 minors, 8 majors, 4 10-minute misconducts and 7 game misconducts, a total of 34 penalties. Boston had 16 minors, 8 majors, 3 10-minute misconducts and 6 game misconducts, a total of 33 penalties.

MOST PENALTY MINUTES, BOTH TEAMS, ONE PERIOD:
372 —**Los Angeles Kings, Philadelphia Flyers** at Philadelphia, March 11, 1979, first period. Philadelphia received 4 minors, 8 majors, 6 10-minute misconducts and 8 game misconducts for 188 minutes. Los Angeles received 2 minors, 8 majors, 6 10-minute misconducts and 8 game misconducts for 184 minutes.

MOST PENALTIES, ONE TEAM, ONE PERIOD:
34 —**Minnesota North Stars,** Feb. 26, 1981, at Boston, first period. 15 minors, 8 majors, 4 10-minute misconducts, 7 game misconducts.

MOST PENALTY MINUTES, ONE TEAM, ONE PERIOD:
188 —**Philadelphia Flyers,** March 11, 1979, at Philadelphia vs. Los Angeles, first period. Flyers received 4 minors, 8 majors, 6 10-minute misconducts and 8 game misconducts.

FASTEST SIX GOALS, BOTH TEAMS
3 Minutes, 15 Seconds — **Montreal Canadiens, Toronto Maple Leafs,** at Montreal, Jan. 4, 1944, first period. Montreal scored 4G, Toronto 2. Montreal won 6-3.

FASTEST FIVE GOALS, BOTH TEAMS:
1 Minute, 24 Seconds — **Chicago Blackhawks, Toronto Maple Leafs,** at Toronto, Oct. 15, 1983, second period. Scorers were: Gaston Gingras, Toronto, 16:49; Denis Savard, Chicago, 17:12; Steve Larmer, Chicago, 17:27; Savard, 17:42; and John Anderson, Toronto, 18:13. Toronto won 10-8.
1 Minute, 39 Seconds — Detroit Red Wings, Toronto Maple Leafs, at Toronto, Nov. 15, 1944, third period. Scorers were: Ted Kennedy, Toronto, 10:36 and 10:55; Hal Jackson, Detroit, 11:48; Steve Wochy, Detroit, 12:02; Don Grosso, Detroit, 12:15. Detroit won 8-4.

FASTEST FIVE GOALS, ONE TEAM:
2 Minutes, 7 Seconds — **Pittsburgh Penguins,** at Pittsburgh, Nov. 22, 1972, third period. Scorers: Bryan Hextall, 12:00; Jean Pronovost, 12:18; Al McDonough, 13:40; Ken Schinkel, 13:49; Ron Schock, 14:07. Pittsburgh defeated St. Louis 10-4.
2 Minutes, 37 seconds — NY Islanders, at New York, Jan. 26, 1982, first period. Scorers: Duane Sutter, 1:31; John Tonelli, 2:30; Bryan Trottier, 2:46; Bryan Trottier, 3:31; Duane Sutter, 4:08. NY Islanders defeated Pittsburgh 9-2.
2 Minutes, 55 Seconds — Boston Bruins, at Boston, Dec. 19, 1974. Scorers: Bobby Schmautz, 19:13 (first period); Ken Hodge, 0:18; Phil Esposito, 0:43; Don Marcotte, 0:58; John Bucyk, 2:08 (second period). Boston defeated NY Rangers 11-3.

FASTEST FOUR GOALS, BOTH TEAMS:
53 Seconds — **Chicago Blackhawks, Toronto Maple Leafs,** at Toronto, Oct. 15, 1983, second period. Scorers were: Gaston Gingras, Toronto, 16:49; Denis Savard, Chicago, 17:12; Steve Larmer, Chicago, 17:27; and Savard at 17:42. Toronto won 10-8.
57 Seconds — Quebec Nordiques, Detroit Red Wings, at Quebec, Jan. 27, 1990, first period. Scorers were: Paul Gillis, Quebec, 18:01; Claude Loiselle, Quebec, 18:12; Joe Sakic, Quebec, 18:27; and Jimmy Carson, Detroit, 18:58. Detroit won 8-6.
1 Minute, 1 Second — Colorado Rockies, NY Rangers, at New York, Jan. 15, 1980, first period. Scorers were: Doug Sulliman, NY Rangers, 7:52; Ed Johnstone, NY Rangers, 7:57; Warren Miller, NY Rangers, 8:20; Rob Ramage, Colorado, 8:53. 6-6 tie.
— Chicago Blackhawks, Toronto Maple Leafs, at Toronto, Oct. 15, 1983, second period. Scorers were: Denis Savard, Chicago, 17:12; Steve Larmer, Chicago, 17:27; Savard, 17:42; John Anderson, Toronto, 18:13. Toronto won 10-8.

FASTEST FOUR GOALS, ONE TEAM:
1 Minute, 20 Seconds — **Boston Bruins,** at Boston, Jan. 21, 1945, second period. Scorers were: Bill Thoms at 6:34; Frank Mario at 7:08 and 7:27; and Ken Smith at 7:54. Boston defeated NY Rangers 14-3.

FASTEST THREE GOALS, BOTH TEAMS:
15 Seconds — **Minnesota North Stars, NY Rangers,** at Minnesota, Feb. 10, 1983, second period. Scorers were: Mark Pavelich, NY Rangers, 19:18; Ron Greschner, NY Rangers, 19:27; Willi Plett, Minnesota, 19:33. Minnesota won 7-5.
18 Seconds — Montreal Canadiens, NY Rangers, at Montreal, Dec. 12, 1963, first period. Scorers were: Dave Balon, Montreal, 0:58; Gilles Tremblay, Montreal, 1:04; Camille Henry, NY Rangers, 1:16. Montreal won 6-4.
18 Seconds — California Golden Seals, Buffalo Sabres, at California, Feb. 1, 1976, third period. Scorers were: Jim Moxey, California, 19:38; Wayne Merrick, California, 19:45; Danny Gare, Buffalo, 19:56. Buffalo won 9-5.

FASTEST THREE GOALS, ONE TEAM:
20 Seconds — **Boston Bruins,** at Boston, Feb. 25, 1971, third period. John Bucyk scored at 4:50, Ed Westfall at 5:02 and Ted Green at 5:10. Boston defeated Vancouver 8-3.
21 Seconds — Chicago Blackhawks, at New York, March 23, 1952, third period. Bill Mosienko scored all three goals, at 6:09, 6:20 and 6:30. Chicago defeated NY Rangers 7-6.
21 Seconds — Washington Capitals, at Washington, Nov. 23, 1990, first period. Michal Pivonka scored at 16:18 and Stephen Leach at 16:29 and 16:39. Washington defeated Pittsburgh 7-3.

FASTEST THREE GOALS FROM START OF PERIOD, BOTH TEAMS:
1 Minute, 5 seconds — **Hartford Whalers, Montreal Canadiens,** at Montreal, March 11, 1989, second period. Scorers were: Kevin Dineen, Hartford, 0:11; Guy Carbonneau, Montreal, 0:36; Petr Svoboda, Montreal, 1:05. Montreal won 5-3.

FASTEST THREE GOALS FROM START OF PERIOD, ONE TEAM:
53 Seconds — **Calgary Flames,** at Calgary, Feb. 10, 1993, third period. Scorers were: Gary Suter at 0:17, Chris Lindbergh at 0:40, Ron Stern at 0:53. Calgary defeated San Jose 13-1.

FASTEST TWO GOALS, BOTH TEAMS:
2 Seconds — **St. Louis Blues, Boston Bruins,** at Boston, Dec. 19, 1987, third period. Scorers were: Ken Linseman, Boston, at 19:50; Doug Gilmour, St. Louis, at 19:52. St. Louis won 7-5.
3 Seconds — Chicago Blackhawks, Minnesota North Stars, at Minnesota, November 5, 1988, third period. Scorers were: Steve Thomas, Chicago, at 6:03; Dave Gagner, Minnesota, at 6:06. 5-5 tie.

FASTEST TWO GOALS, ONE TEAM:
4 Seconds — **Montreal Maroons,** at Montreal, Jan. 3, 1931, third period. Nels Stewart scored both goals, at 8:24 and 8:28. Mtl. Maroons defeated Boston 5-3.
— **Buffalo Sabres,** at Buffalo, Oct. 17, 1974, third period. Scorers were: Lee Fogolin at 14:55 and Don Luce at 14:59. Buffalo defeated California 6-1.
— **Toronto Maple Leafs,** at Quebec, December 29, 1988, third period. Scorers were: Ed Olczyk at 5:24 and Gary Leeman at 5:28. Toronto defeated Quebec 6-5.
— **Calgary Flames,** at Quebec, October 17, 1989, third period. Scorers were: Doug Gilmour at 19:45 and Paul Ranheim at 19:49. Calgary and Quebec tied 8-8.

FASTEST TWO GOALS FROM START OF PERIOD, BOTH TEAMS:
14 Seconds — **NY Rangers, Quebec Nordiques,** at Quebec, Nov. 5, 1983, third period. Scorers: Andre Savard, Quebec, 0:08; Pierre Larouche, NY Rangers, 0:14. 4-4 tie.
26 Seconds — Buffalo Sabres, St. Louis Blues, at Buffalo, Jan. 3, 1993, third period. Scorers: Alexander Mogilny, Buffalo, 0:08; Phillippe Bozon, St. Louis, 0:26. Buffalo won 6-5.
28 Seconds — Boston Bruins, Montreal Canadiens, at Montreal, Oct. 11, 1989, third period. Scorers: Jim Wiemer, Boston 0:10; Tom Chorske, Montreal 0:28. Montreal won 4-2.

FASTEST TWO GOALS FROM START OF GAME, ONE TEAM:
24 Seconds — **Edmonton Oilers,** March 28, 1982, at Los Angeles. Mark Messier, at 0:14 and Dave Lumley, at 0:24, scored in first period. Edmonton defeated Los Angeles 6-2.
29 Seconds — Pittsburgh Penguins, Dec. 6, 1981, at Pittsburgh. George Ferguson, at 0:17 and Greg Malone at 0:29, scored in first period. Pittsburgh defeated Chicago 6-4.
32 Seconds — Calgary Flames, March 11, 1987, at Hartford. Doug Risebrough at 0:09, and Colin Patterson, at 0:32, in first period. Calgary defeated Hartford 6-1.

FASTEST TWO GOALS FROM START OF PERIOD, ONE TEAM:
21 Seconds — **Chicago Blackhawks,** Nov. 5, 1983, at Minnesota, second period. Ken Yaremchuk scored at 0:12 and Darryl Sutter at 0:21. Minnesota defeated Chicago 10-5.
30 Seconds — Washington Capitals, Jan. 27, 1980, at Washington, second period. Mike Gartner scored at 0:08 and Bengt Gustafsson at 0:30. Washington defeated NY Islanders 7-1.
31 Seconds —Buffalo Sabres, Jan. 10, 1974, at Buffalo, third period. Rene Robert scored at 0:21 and Rick Martin at 0:30. Buffalo defeated NY Rangers 7-2.
— NY Islanders, Feb. 22, 1986, at New York, third period. Roger Kortko scored at 0:10 and Bob Bourne at 0:31. NY Islanders defeated Detroit 5-2.

Individual Records

Career

MOST SEASONS:
26 —Gordie Howe, Detroit, 1946-47 – 1970-71; Hartford, 1979-80.
24 —Alex Delvecchio, Detroit, 1950-51 – 1973-74.
—Tim Horton, Toronto, NY Rangers, Pittsburgh, Buffalo, 1949-50, 1951-52 – 1973-74.
23 —John Bucyk, Detroit, Boston, 1955-56 – 1977-78.
22 —Dean Prentice, NY Rangers, Boston, Detroit, Pittsburgh, Minnesota, 1952-53 – 1973-74.
—Doug Mohns, Boston, Chicago, Minnesota, Atlanta, Washington, 1953-54 – 1974-75.
—Stan Mikita, Chicago, 1958-59 – 1979-80.

MOST GAMES:
1,767 —Gordie Howe, Detroit, 1946-47 – 1970-71; Hartford, 1979-80.
1,549 —Alex Delvecchio, Detroit, 1950-51 – 1973-74.
1,540 —John Bucyk, Detroit, Boston, 1955-56 – 1977-78.

MOST GOALS:
803 —Wayne Gretzky, Edmonton, Los Angeles, in 15 seasons, 1,125GP.
801 —Gordie Howe, Detroit, Hartford, in 26 seasons, 1,767GP.
731 —Marcel Dionne, Detroit, Los Angeles, NY Rangers, in 18 seasons, 1,348GP.
717 —Phil Esposito, Chicago, Boston, NY Rangers, in 18 seasons, 1,282GP.
617 —Mike Gartner, Washington, Minnesota, NY Rangers, Toronto, in 15 seasons, 1,170GP.

HIGHEST GOALS-PER-GAME AVERAGE, CAREER
(AMONG PLAYERS WITH 200 OR MORE GOALS):
.825 —Mario Lemieux, Pittsburgh, 494G, 599GP, from 1984-85 – 1993-94.
.767 —Cy Denneny, Ottawa, Boston, 250G, 326GP, from 1917-18 – 1928-29.
.765 —Brett Hull, Calgary, St. Louis, 413G, 540GP, from 1986-87 – 1993-94.
.762 —Mike Bossy, NY Islanders, 573G, 752GP, from 1977-78 – 1986-87.
.714 —Wayne Gretzky, Edmonton, Los Angeles, 803G, 1,125GP, from 1979-80 – 1993-94.

MOST ASSISTS:
1,655 —Wayne Gretzky, Edmonton, Los Angeles, in 15 seasons, 1,125GP.
1,049 —Gordie Howe, Detroit, Hartford in 26 seasons, 1,767GP.
1,040 —Marcel Dionne, Detroit, Los Angeles, NY Rangers in 18 seasons, 1,348GP.
934 —Paul Coffey, Edmonton, Pittsburgh, Los Angeles, Detroit, in 14 seasons, 1,033GP.
926 —Stan Mikita, Chicago, in 22 seasons, 1,394GP.

HIGHEST ASSIST-PER-GAME AVERAGE, CAREER
(AMONG PLAYERS WITH 300 OR MORE ASSISTS):
1.471 —Wayne Gretzky, Edmonton, Los Angeles, 1,655A, 1,125GP from 1979-80 – 1993-94.
1.197 —Mario Lemieux, Pittsburgh, 717A, 599GP from 1984-85 – 1993-94.
.982 —Bobby Orr, Boston, Chicago, 645A, 657GP from 1966-67 – 1978-79.
.908 —Adam Oates, Detroit, St. Louis, Boston, 570A, 628GP from 1984-85 – 1993-94.
.904 —Paul Coffey, Edmonton, Pittsburgh, Los Angeles, Detroit, 934A, 1,033GP from 1980-81 – 1993-94.

MOST POINTS:
2,458 —Wayne Gretzky, Edmonton, Los Angeles, in 15 seasons, 1,125GP (803G-1,655A).
1,850 —Gordie Howe, Detroit, Hartford, in 26 seasons, 1,767GP (801G-1049A).
1,771 —Marcel Dionne, Detroit, Los Angeles, NY Rangers, in 18 seasons, 1,348GP (731G-1,040A).
1,590 —Phil Esposito, Chicago, Boston, NY Rangers in 18 seasons, 1,282GP (717G-873A).
1,467 —Stan Mikita, Chicago in 22 seasons, 1,394GP (541G-926A).

HIGHEST POINTS-PER-GAME AVERAGE, CAREER:
(AMONG PLAYERS WITH 500 OR MORE POINTS):
2.185 —Wayne Gretzky, Edmonton, Los Angeles, 2,458PTS (803G-1,655A), 1,125GP from 1979-80 – 1993-94.
2.022 —Mario Lemieux, Pittsburgh, 1,211PTS (494G-717A), 599GP from 1984-85 – 1993-94.
1.497 —Mike Bossy, NY Islanders, 1,126PTS (573G-553A), 752GP from 1978-79 – 1986-87.
1.393 —Bobby Orr, Boston, Chicago, 915PTS (270G-645A), 657GP from 1966-67 – 1978-79.
1.377 —Steve Yzerman, Detroit, 1,122PTS (469G-653A), 815GP from 1983-84 – 1993-94.

MOST GOALS BY A CENTER, CAREER
803 —Wayne Gretzky, Edmonton, Los Angeles, in 15 seasons.
731 —Marcel Dionne, Detroit, Los Angeles, NY Rangers, in 18 seasons
717 —Phil Esposito, Chicago, Boston, NY Rangers, in 18 seasons.
541 —Stan Mikita, Chicago, in 22 seasons.
524 —Bryan Trottier, NY Islanders, Pittsburgh, in 18 seasons.

MOST ASSISTS BY A CENTER, CAREER;
1,655 —Wayne Gretzky, Edmonton, Los Angeles, in 15 seasons.
1,040 —Marcel Dionne, Detroit, Los Angeles, NY Rangers, in 18 seasons.
926 —Stan Mikita, Chicago, in 22 seasons.
901 —Bryan Trottier, NY Islanders, Pittsburgh, in 18 seasons.
873 —Phil Esposito, Chicago, Boston, NY Rangers, in 18 seasons.

Mike Bossy, who scored 573 goals in his decade with the New York Islanders, ranks third all-time among right-wingers in goals.

MOST POINTS BY A CENTER, CAREER:
2,458 —Wayne Gretzky, Edmonton, Los Angeles, in 15 seasons.
1,771 —Marcel Dionne, Detroit, Los Angeles, NY Rangers, in 18 seasons.
1,590 —Phil Esposito, Chicago, Boston, NY Rangers, in 18 seasons.
1,467 —Stan Mikita, Chicago, in 22 seasons
1,425 —Bryan Trottier, NY Islanders, Pittsburgh, in 18 seasons.

MOST GOALS BY A LEFT WING, CAREER:
610 —Bobby Hull, Chicago, Winnipeg, Hartford, in 16 seasons.
556 —John Bucyk, Detroit, Boston, in 23 seasons.
548 —Michel Goulet, Quebec, Chicago, in 15 seasons.
533 —Frank Mahovlich, Toronto, Detroit, Montreal, in 18 seasons.
426 —Dave Andreychuk, Buffalo, Toronto, in 12 seasons.

MOST ASSISTS BY A LEFT WING, CAREER:
813 —John Bucyk, Detroit, Boston, in 23 seasons.
604 —Michel Goulet, Quebec, Chicago, in 15 seasons.
579 —Brian Propp, Philadelphia, Boston, Minnesota, Hartford, in 15 seasons.
570 —Frank Mahovlich, Toronto, Detroit, Montreal, in 18 seasons.
560 —Bobby Hull, Chicago, Winnipeg, Hartford, in 16 seasons.

MOST POINTS BY A LEFT WING, CAREER:
1,369 —John Bucyk, Detroit, Boston, in 23 seasons.
1,170 —Bobby Hull, Chicago, Winnipeg, Hartford, in 16 seasons.
1,152 —Michel Goulet, Quebec, Chicago, in 15 seasons.
1,103 —Frank Mahovlich, Toronto, Detroit, Montreal, in 18 seasons.
1,004 —Brian Propp, Philadelphia, Boston, Minnesota, Hartford, in 15 seasons.

MOST GOALS BY A RIGHT WING, CAREER:
801 —Gordie Howe, Detroit, Hartford, in 26 seasons.
617 —Mike Gartner, Washington, Minnesota, NY Rangers, Toronto, in 15 seasons.
573 —Mike Bossy, NY Islanders, in 10 seasons.
560 —Guy Lafleur, Montreal, NY Rangers, Quebec, in 17 seasons.
555 —Jari Kurri, Edmonton, Los Angeles, in 13 seasons.

MOST ASSISTS BY A RIGHT WING, CAREER:
1,049 —Gordie Howe, Detroit, Hartford, in 26 seasons.
793 —Guy Lafleur, Montreal, NY Rangers, Quebec, in 17 seasons.
712 —Jari Kurri, Edmonton, Los Angeles, in 13 seasons.
638 —Dave Taylor, Los Angeles, in 17 seasons.
624 —Andy Bathgate, NY Rangers, Toronto, Detroit, Pittsburgh in 17 seasons.

MOST POINTS BY A RIGHT WING, CAREER:
1,850 —Gordie Howe, Detroit, Hartford, in 26 seasons.
1,353 —Guy Lafleur, Montreal, NY Rangers, Quebec, in 17 seasons.
1,267 —Jari Kurri, Edmonton, Los Angeles, in 13 seasons.
1,171 —Mike Gartner, Washington, Minnesota, NY Rangers, Toronto, in 15 seasons.

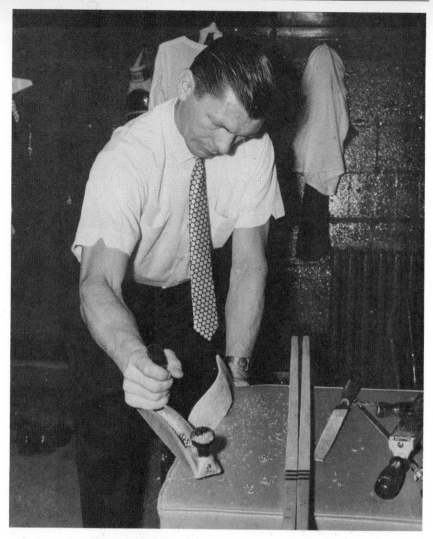

Stan Mikita, seen here putting the finishing touches on one of his famous "banana-blade" sticks, collected 926 regular-season and 96 playoff assists in his illustrious 22-year career with the Chicago Blackhawks.

MOST GOALS BY A DEFENSEMAN, CAREER:
344 — Paul Coffey, Edmonton, Pittsburgh, Los Angeles, Detroit, in 14 seasons.
311 — Ray Bourque, Boston, in 15 seasons.
310 — Denis Potvin, NY Islanders, in 15 seasons.
270 — Bobby Orr, Boston, Chicago, in 12 seasons.
249 — Phil Housley, Buffalo, Winnipeg, St. Louis, in 12 seasons.

MOST ASSISTS BY A DEFENSEMAN, CAREER:
934 — Paul Coffey, Edmonton, Pittsburgh, Los Angeles, Detroit, in 14 seasons.
877 — Ray Bourque, Boston, in 15 seasons.
750 — Larry Robinson, Montreal, Los Angeles, in 20 seasons.
742 — Denis Potvin, NY Islanders, in 15 seasons.
687 — Larry Murphy, Los Angeles, Washington, Minnesota, Pittsburgh, in 14 seasons.

MOST POINTS BY A DEFENSEMAN, CAREER:
1,278 — Paul Coffey, Edmonton, Pittsburgh, Los Angeles, Detroit, in 14 seasons.
1,188 — Ray Bourque, Boston, in 15 seasons.
1,052 — Denis Potvin, NY Islanders, in 15 seasons.
958 — Larry Robinson, Montreal, Los Angeles, in 20 seasons.
915 — Bobby Orr, Boston, Chicago, in 12 seasons.

MOST OVERTIME GOALS, CAREER:
7 — Mario Lemieux, Pittsburgh.
— **Jari Kurri,** Edmonton.
— **Tomas Sandstrom,** NY Rangers, Los Angeles.
— **Bob Sweeney,** Boston, Buffalo.

MOST OVERTIME ASSISTS, CAREER:
12 — Wayne Gretzky, Edmonton, Los Angeles.
10 — Mario Lemieux, Pittsburgh.
— Mark Messier, Edmonton, NY Rangers.
9 — Bernie Federko, St. Louis.
— Dale Hawerchuk, Winnipeg, Buffalo.
— Doug Gilmour, St. Louis, Calgary, Toronto.

MOST OVERTIME POINTS, CAREER:
17 — Mario Lemieux, Pittsburgh, 7G-10A
15 — Mark Messier, Edmonton, NY Rangers. 5G-10A
14 — Wayne Gretzky, Edmonton, Los Angeles. 2G-12A
13 — Jari Kurri, Edmonton, Los Angeles. 7G-6A
— Paul MacLean, Winnipeg, Detroit, St. Louis. 6G-7A
— Dale Hawerchuk, Winnipeg, Buffalo. 4G-9A

MOST PENALTY MINUTES:
3,966 — Dave Williams, Toronto, Vancouver, Detroit, Los Angeles, Hartford, in 14 seasons, 962GP.
3,043 — Chris Nilan, Monteal, NY Rangers, Boston, in 13 seasons, 688GP.
3,005 — Dale Hunter, Quebec, Washington, in 14 seasons, 1,054GP.
2,769 — Tim Hunter, Calgary, Quebec, Vancouver, in 13 seasons, 675GP.
2,572 — Willi Plett, Atlanta, Calgary, Minnesota, Boston, in 13 seasons, 834GP.

MOST GAMES, INCLUDING PLAYOFFS:
1,924 — Gordie Howe, Detroit, Hartford, 1,767 regular-season and 157 playoff games.
1,670 — Alex Delvecchio, Detroit, 1,549 regular-season and 121 playoff games.
1,664 — John Bucyk, Detroit, Boston, 1,540 regular-season and 124 playoff games.

MOST GOALS, INCLUDING PLAYOFFS:
913 — Wayne Gretzky, Edmonton, Los Angeles, 803 regular-season and 110 playoff goals.
869 — Gordie Howe, Detroit, Hartford, 801 regular-season goals and 68 playoff goals.
778 — Phil Esposito, Chicago, Boston, NY Rangers, 717 regular-season and 61 playoff goals.
752 — Marcel Dionne, Detroit, Los Angeles, NY Rangers, 731 regular-season and 21 playoff goals.

MOST ASSISTS, INCLUDING PLAYOFFS:
1,891 — Wayne Gretzky, Edmonton, Los Angeles, 1,655 regular-season and 236 playoff assists.
1,141 — Gordie Howe, Detroit, Hartford, 1,049 regular-season and 92 playoff assists.
1,064 — Marcel Dionne, Detroit, Los Angeles, NY Rangers, 1,040 regular-season and 24 playoff assists.
1,041 — Paul Coffey, Edmonton, Pittsburgh, Los Angeles, Detroit, 934 regular-season and 107 playoff assists.
1,017 — Stan Mikita, Chicago, 926 regular-season and 91 playoff assists.

MOST POINTS, INCLUDING PLAYOFFS:
2,804 — Wayne Gretzky, Edmonton, Los Angeles, 2,458 regular-season and 346 playoff points.
2,010 — Gordie Howe, Detroit, Hartford, 1,850 regular-season and 160 playoff assists.
1,816 — Marcel Dionne, Detroit, Los Angeles, NY Rangers, 1,771 regular-season and 45 playoff points.
1,727 — Phil Esposito, Chicago, Boston, NY Rangers, 1,590 regular-season and 137 playoff points.
1,617 — Stan Mikita, Chicago, 1,467 regular-season and 150 playoff points.

MOST PENALTY MINUTES, INCLUDING PLAYOFFS:
4,421 — Dave Williams, Toronto, Vancouver, Detroit, Los Angeles, Hartford, 3,966 in regular season; 455 in playoffs.
3,618 — Dale Hunter, Quebec, Washington, 3,005 in regular-season; 613 in playoffs.
3,584 — Chris Nilan, Montreal, NY Rangers, Boston, 3,043 in regular-season; 541 in playoffs.
3,173 — Tim Hunter, Calgary, Quebec, Vancouver, 2,769 regular-season; 404 in playoffs.
3,038 — Willi Plett, Atlanta, Calgary, Minnesota, Boston, 2,572 in regular-season; 466 in playoffs.

MOST CONSECUTIVE GAMES:
964 — Doug Jarvis, Montreal, Washington, Hartford, from Oct. 8, 1975 – Oct. 10, 1987.
914 — Garry Unger, Toronto, Detroit, St. Louis, Atlanta from Feb. 24, 1968, – Dec. 21, 1979.
884 — Steve Larmer, Chicago, from Oct. 6, 1982 to April 16, 1993.
776 — Craig Ramsay, Buffalo, from March 27, 1973, – Feb. 10, 1983.
630 — Andy Hebenton, NY Rangers, Boston, nine complete 70-game seasons from 1955-56 – 1963-64.

MOST GAMES APPEARED IN BY A GOALTENDER, CAREER:
971 — Terry Sawchuk, Detroit, Boston, Toronto, Los Angeles, NY Rangers from 1949-50 – 1969-70.
906 — Glenn Hall, Detroit, Chicago, St. Louis from 1952-53 – 1970-71.
886 — Tony Esposito, Montreal, Chicago from 1968-69 – 1983-84.
860 — Lorne "Gump" Worsley, NY Rangers, Montreal, Minnesota from 1952-53 – 1973-74.

MOST CONSECUTIVE COMPLETE GAMES BY A GOALTENDER:
502 — Glenn Hall, Detroit, Chicago. Played 502 games from beginning of 1955-56 season - first 12 games of 1962-63. In his 503rd straight game, Nov. 7, 1962, at Chicago, Hall was removed from the game against Boston with a back injury in the first period.

MOST SHUTOUTS BY A GOALTENDER, CAREER:
103 — Terry Sawchuk, Detroit, Boston, Toronto, Los Angeles, NY Rangers in 21 seasons.
94 — George Hainsworth, Montreal Canadiens, Toronto in 10 seasons.
84 — Glenn Hall, Detroit, Chicago, St. Louis in 16 seasons.

MOST THREE-OR-MORE GOAL GAMES, CAREER:
49 — Wayne Gretzky, Edmonton, Los Angeles, in 15 seasons, 36 three-goal games, 9 four-goal games, 4 five-goal games.
39 — Mike Bossy, NY Islanders, in 10 seasons, 30 three-goal games, 9 four-goal games.
32 — Phil Esposito, Chicago, Boston, NY Rangers, in 18 seasons, 27 three-goal games, 5 four-goal games.
31 — Mario Lemieux, Pittsburgh, in 10 seasons, 21 three-goal games, 8 four-goal games and 2 five-goal games.
28 — Bobby Hull, Chicago, Winnipeg, Hartford, in 16 seasons, 24 three-goal games, 4 four-goal games.
— Marcel Dionne, Detroit, Los Angeles, NY Rangers, in 18 seasons, 25 three-goal games, 3 four-goal games.
26 — Cy Denneny, Ottawa in 12 seasons. 20 three-goal games, 5 four-goal games, 1 six-goal game.
— Maurice Richard, Montreal, in 18 seasons, 23 three-goal games, 2 four-goal games, 1 five-goal game.

MOST 20-OR-MORE GOAL SEASONS:
22 — Gordie Howe, Detroit, Hartford in 26 seasons.
17 — Marcel Dionne, Detroit, Los Angeles, NY Rangers, in 18 seasons.
16 — Phil Esposito, Chicago, Boston, NY Rangers, in 18 seasons.
— Norm Ullman, Detroit, Toronto, in 19 seasons.
— John Bucyk, Detroit, Boston, in 22 seasons.
15 — Frank Mahovlich, Toronto, Detroit, Montreal in 17 seasons.
— Gilbert Perreault, Buffalo, in 17 seasons.
— Mike Gartner, Washington, Minnesota, NY Rangers, Toronto, in 15 seasons.

MOST CONSECUTIVE 20-OR-MORE GOAL SEASONS:
22 — Gordie Howe, Detroit, 1949-50 – 1970-71.
17 — Marcel Dionne, Detroit, Los Angeles, NY Rangers, 1971-72 – 1987-88.
16 — Phil Esposito, Chicago, Boston, NY Rangers, 1964-65 – 1979-80.
15 — Mike Gartner, Washington, Minnesota, NY Rangers, Toronto, 1979-80 – 1993-94.
14 — Maurice Richard, Montreal, 1943-44 – 1956-57.
— Stan Mikita, Chicago, 1961-62 – 1974-75.
— Michel Goulet, Quebec, Chicago, 1979-80 – 1992-93.
13 — Bobby Hull, Chicago, 1959-60 – 1971-72.
— Guy Lafleur, Montreal, 1971-72 – 1983-84.
— Bryan Trottier, NY Islanders, 1975-76 – 1987-88.
— Wayne Gretzky, Edmonton, Los Angeles, 1979-80 – 1991-92.
— Ron Francis, Hartford, Pittsburgh, 1981-82 – 1993-94.

MOST 30-OR-MORE GOAL SEASONS:
15 — Mike Gartner, Washington, Minnesota, NY Rangers, Toronto in 15 seasons.
14 — Gordie Howe, Detroit, Hartford in 26 seasons.
— Marcel Dionne, Detroit, Los Angeles, NY Rangers in 18 seasons.
— Wayne Gretzky, Edmonton, Los Angeles in 15 seasons.
13 — Bobby Hull, Chicago, Winnipeg, Hartford in 16 seasons.
— Phil Esposito, Chicago, Boston, NY Rangers in 18 seasons.

Joe Mullen (left), the highest-scoring American-born player in NHL history, had six consecutive 40-goal seasons from 1983-84 to 1988-89.

MOST CONSECUTIVE 30-OR-MORE GOAL SEASONS:
15 — Mike Gartner, Washington, Minnesota, NY Rangers, Toronto, 1979-80 – 1993-94.
13 — Bobby Hull, Chicago, 1959-60 – 1971-72.
— Phil Esposito, Boston, NY Rangers, 1967-68 – 1979-80.
— Wayne Gretzky, Edmonton, Los Angeles, 1979-80 – 1991-92.
12 — Marcel Dionne, Detroit, Los Angeles, 1974-75 – 1985-86.
10 — Darryl Sittler, Toronto, Philadelphia, 1973-74 – 1982-83.
— Mike Bossy, NY Islanders, 1977-78 – 1986-87.
— Jari Kurri, Edmonton, 1980-81 – 1989-90.

MOST 40-OR-MORE GOAL SEASONS:
12 — Wayne Gretzky, Edmonton, Los Angeles, in 15 seasons.
10 — Marcel Dionne, Detroit, Los Angeles, NY Rangers, in 18 seasons.
9 — Mike Bossy, NY Islanders, in 10 seasons.
— Mike Gartner, Washington, Minnesota, NY Rangers, in 15 seasons.
8 — Bobby Hull, Chicago, Winnipeg, Hartford, in 16 seasons.
— Phil Esposito, Chicago, Boston, NY Rangers, in 18 seasons.
— Jari Kurri, Edmonton, Los Angeles, in 13 seasons.
— Dale Hawerchuk, Winnipeg, Buffalo, in 11 seasons.
— Luc Robitaille, Los Angeles, in 8 seasons.

MOST CONSECUTIVE 40-OR-MORE GOAL SEASONS:
12 — Wayne Gretzky, Edmonton, Los Angeles, 1979-80 – 1990-91.
9 — Mike Bossy, NY Islanders, 1977-78 – 1985-86.
8 — Luc Robitaille, Los Angeles, 1986-87 – 1993-94.
7 — Phil Esposito, Boston, 1968-69 – 1974-75.
— Michel Goulet, Quebec, 1981-82 – 1987-88.
— Jari Kurri, Edmonton, 1982-83 – 1988-89.
6 — Guy Lafleur, Montreal, 1974-75 – 1979-80.
— Joe Mullen, St. Louis, Calgary, 1983-84 – 1988-89.
— Mario Lemieux, Pittsburgh, 1984-85 – 1989-90.
— Steve Yzerman, Detroit, 1987-88 – 1992-93.
— Brett Hull, St. Louis, 1988-89 – 1993-94.

MOST 50-OR-MORE GOAL SEASONS:
9 — Mike Bossy, NY Islanders, in 11 seasons.
— **Wayne Gretzky,** Edmonton, Los Angeles, in 15 seasons.
6 — Guy Lafleur, Montreal, NY Rangers, Quebec, in 17 seasons.
— Marcel Dionne, Detroit, Los Angeles, NY Rangers, in 18 seasons.
5 — Bobby Hull, Chicago, Winnipeg, Hartford, in 16 seasons.
— Phil Esposito, Chicago, Boston, NY Rangers, in 18 seasons.
— Brett Hull, Calgary, St. Louis, in 8 seasons.

MOST CONSECUTIVE 50-OR-MORE GOAL SEASONS:
9 — Mike Bossy, NY Islanders, 1977-78 – 1985-86.
8 — Wayne Gretzky, Edmonton, 1979-80 – 1986-87.
6 — Guy Lafleur, Montreal, 1974-75 – 1979-80.
5 — Phil Esposito, Boston, 1970-71 – 1974-75.
— Marcel Dionne, Los Angeles, 1978-79 – 1982-83.
— Brett Hull, St. Louis, 1989-90 – 1993-94.

MOST 60-OR-MORE GOAL SEASONS:
5 — Mike Bossy, NY Islanders, in 10 seasons.
— **Wayne Gretzky,** Edmonton, Los Angeles, in 15 seasons.
4 — Phil Esposito, Chicago, Boston, NY Rangers, in 18 seasons.

MOST CONSECUTIVE 60-OR-MORE GOAL SEASONS:
4 — Wayne Gretzky, Edmonton, 1981-82 – 1984-85.
3 — Mike Bossy, NY Islanders, 1980-81 – 1982-83.
— Brett Hull, St. Louis, 1989-90 – 1991-92.
2 — Phil Esposito, Boston, 1970-71 – 1971-72, 1973-74 – 1974-75.
— Jari Kurri, Edmonton, 1984-85 – 1985-86.
— Mario Lemieux, Pittsburgh, 1987-88 – 1988-89.
— Steve Yzerman, Detroit, 1988-89 – 1989-90.
— Pavel Bure, Vancouver, 1992-93 – 1993-94.

MOST 100-OR-MORE POINT SEASONS:
14 —**Wayne Gretzky,** Edmonton, Los Angeles, 1979-80 – 1991-92; 1993-94.
8 —Marcel Dionne, Detroit, 1974-75; Los Angeles, 1976-77; 1978-79 – 1982-83; 1984-85.
—Mario Lemieux, Pittsburgh, 1984-85 – 1989-90; 1991-92; 1992-93.
7 —Mike Bossy, NY Islanders, 1978-79; 1980-81 – 1985-86.
—Peter Stastny, Quebec, 1980-81 – 1985-86; 1987-88.
6 —Phil Esposito, Boston, 1968-69; 1970-71 – 1974-75.
—Bobby Orr, Boston, 1969-70 – 1974-75.
—Guy Lafleur, Montreal, 1974-75 – 1979-80.
—Bryan Trottier, NY Islanders, 1977-78 – 1981-82; 1983-84.
—Dale Hawerchuk, Winnipeg, 1981-82; 1983-84 – 1987-88.
—Jari Kurri, Edmonton, 1982-83 – 1986-87; 1988-89.
—Mark Messier, Edmonton, 1982-83 – 1983-84; 1986-87 – 1987-88; 1989-90; NY Rangers, 1991-92.
—Steve Yzerman, Detroit, 1987-88 – 1992-93.

MOST CONSECUTIVE 100-OR-MORE POINT SEASONS:
13 —**Wayne Gretzky,** Edmonton, Los Angeles, 1979-80 – 1991-92.
6 —Bobby Orr, Boston, 1969-70 – 1974-75.
—Guy Lafleur, Montreal, 1974-75 – 1979-80.
—Mike Bossy, NY Islanders,1980-81 – 1985-86.
—Peter Stastny, Quebec, 1980-81 – 1985-86.
—Mario Lemieux, Pittsburgh, 1984-85 – 1989-90.
—Steve Yzerman, Detroit, 1987-88 – 1992-93.

MOST 40-OR-MORE WIN SEASONS BY A GOALTENDER:
3 —**Jacques Plante,** Montreal, NY Rangers, St. Louis, Toronto, Boston in 18 seasons.
2 —Terry Sawchuck, Detroit, Boston, Toronto, Los Angeles, NY Rangers in 21 seasons.
—Bernie Parent, Boston, Philadelphia, Toronto in 13 seasons.
—Ken Dryden, Montreal, in 8 seasons.
—Ed Belfour, Chicago, in 5 seasons.

MOST CONSECUTIVE 40-OR-MORE WIN SEASONS BY A GOALTENDER:
2 —**Terry Sawchuk,** Detroit, 1950-51 – 1951-52.
—**Bernie Parent,** Philadelphia, 1973-74 – 1974-75.
—**Ken Dryden,** Montreal, 1975-76 – 1976-77.

MOST 30-OR-MORE WIN SEASONS BY A GOALTENDER:
8 —**Tony Esposito,** Montreal, Chicago in 16 seasons.
7 —Jacques Plante, Montreal, NY Rangers, St. Louis, Toronto, Boston in 18 seasons.
—Ken Dryden, Montreal, in 8 seasons.
6 —Glenn Hall, Detroit, Chicago, St. Louis in 18 seasons.

MOST CONSECUTIVE 30-OR-MORE WIN SEASONS BY A GOALTENDER:
7 —**Tony Esposito,** Chicago, 1969-70 – 1975-76.
6 —Jacques Plante, Montreal, 1954-55 – 1959-60.
5 —Ken Dryden, Montreal, 1974-75 – 1978-79.
4 —Terry Sawchuk, Detroit, 1950-51 – 1953-54.
—Ed Giacomin, NY Rangers, 1966-67 – 1969-70.

Single Season

MOST GOALS, ONE SEASON:
92 —**Wayne Gretzky,** Edmonton, 1981-82. 80 game schedule.
87 —Wayne Gretzky, Edmonton, 1983-84. 80 game schedule.
86 —Brett Hull, St. Louis, 1990-91. 80 game schedule.
85 —Mario Lemieux, Pittsburgh, 1988-89. 80 game schedule.
76 —Phil Esposito, Boston, 1970-71. 78 game schedule.
—Alexander Mogilny, Buffalo, 1992-93. 84 game schedule.
—Teemu Selanne, Winnipeg, 1992-93. 84 game schedule.
73 —Wayne Gretzky, Edmonton, 1984-85. 80 game schedule.
72 —Brett Hull, St. Louis, 1989-90. 80 game schedule.
71 —Jari Kurri, Edmonton, 1984-85 80 game schedule.
—Wayne Gretzky, Edmonton, 1982-83. 80 game schedule.
70 —Mario Lemieux, Pittsburgh, 1987-1988. 80 game schedule.
—Bernie Nicholls, Los Angeles, 1988-89. 80 game schedule.
—Brett Hull, St. Louis, 1991-92. 80 game schedule.

MOST ASSISTS, ONE SEASON:
163 —**Wayne Gretzky,** Edmonton , 1985-86. 80 game schedule.
135 —Wayne Gretzky, Edmonton, 1984-85. 80 game schedule.
125 —Wayne Gretzky, Edmonton, 1982-83. 80 game schedule.
122 —Wayne Gretzky, Los Angeles, 1990-91. 80 game schedule.
121 —Wayne Gretzky, Edmonton, 1986-87. 80 game schedule.
120 —Wayne Gretzky, Edmonton, 1981-82. 80 game schedule.
118 —Wayne Gretzky, Edmonton, 1983-84. 80 game schedule.
114 —Wayne Gretzky, Los Angeles, 1988-89. 80 game schedule.
—Mario Lemieux, Pittsburgh, 1988-89. 80 game schedule.
109 —Wayne Gretzky, Edmonton, 1980-81. 80 game schedule.
—Wayne Gretzky, Edmonton, 1987-88. 80 game schedule.
102 —Bobby Orr, Boston, 1970-71. 78 game schedule.
—Wayne Gretzky, Los Angeles, 1989-90. 80 game schedule.

MOST POINTS, ONE SEASON:
215 —**Wayne Gretzky,** Edmonton, 1985-86. 80 game schedule.
212 —Wayne Gretzky, Edmonton, 1981-82. 80 game schedule.
208 —Wayne Gretzky, Edmonton, 1984-85. 80 game schedule.
205 —Wayne Gretzky, Edmonton, 1983-84. 80 game schedule.
199 —Mario Lemieux, Pittsburgh, 1988-89. 80 game schedule.
196 —Wayne Gretzky, Edmonton, 1982-83. 80 game schedule.
183 —Wayne Gretzky, Edmonton, 1986-87. 80 game schedule.
168 —Mario Lemieux, Pittsburgh, 1987-88, 80 game schedule.
—Wayne Gretzky, Los Angeles, 1988-89. 80 game schedule.
164 —Wayne Gretzky, Edmonton, 1980-81. 80 game schedule.
163 —Wayne Gretzky, Los Angeles, 1990-91. 80 game schedule.
160 —Mario Lemieux, Pittsburgh, 1992-93. 84 game schedule.
155 —Steve Yzerman, Detroit, 1988-89. 80 game schedule.

MOST THREE-OR-MORE GOAL GAMES, ONE SEASON:
10 —**Wayne Gretzky,** Edmonton, 1981-82. 6 three-goal games, 3 four-goal games, 1 five-goal game.
—**Wayne Gretzky,** Edmonton, 1983-84. 6 three-goal games, 4 four-goal games.
9 —Mike Bossy, NY Islanders, 1980-81. 6 three-goal games, 3 four-goal games.
—Mario Lemieux, Pittsburgh, 1988-89. 7 three-goal games, 1 four-goal game, 1 five-goal game.
8 —Brett Hull, St. Louis, 1991-92. 8 three-goal games.
7 —Joe Malone, Montreal, 1917-18. 2 three-goal games, 2 four-goal games, 3 five-goal games.
—Phil Esposito, Boston, 1970-71. 7 three-goal games.
—Rick Martin, Buffalo, 1975-76. 6 three-goal games, 1 four-goal game.
—Alexander Mogilny, Buffalo, 1992-93. 5 three-goal games, 2 four-goal games.

HIGHEST GOALS-PER-GAME AVERAGE, ONE SEASON
(AMONG PLAYERS WITH 20-OR-MORE GOALS):
2.20 —**Joe Malone,** Montreal, 1917-18, with 44G in 20GP.
1.64 —Cy Denneny, Ottawa, 1917-18, with 36G in 22GP.
—Newsy Lalonde, Montreal, 1917-18, with 23G in 14GP.
1.63 —Joe Malone, Qebec, 1919-20, with 39G in 24GP.
1.57 —Newsy Lalonde, Montreal, 1919-20, with 36G in 23GP.
1.50 —Joe Malone, Hamilton, 1920-21, with 30G in 20GP.

HIGHEST GOALS-PER-GAME AVERAGE, ONE SEASON
(AMONG PLAYERS WITH 50-OR-MORE GOALS):
1.18 —**Wayne Gretzky,** Edmonton, 1983-84, with 87G in 74GP.
1.15 —Wayne Gretzky, Edmonton, 1981-82, with 92G in 80GP.
—Mario Lemieux, Pittsburgh, 1992-93, with 69G in 60GP.
1.12 —Mario Lemieux, Pittsburgh, 1988-89, with 85G in 76GP.
1.10 —Brett Hull, St. Louis, 1990-91, with 86G in 78GP.
1.02 —Cam Neely, Boston, 1993-94, with 50G in 49GP.
1.00 —Maurice Richard, Montreal, 1944-45, with 50G in 50GP.
.99 —Alexander Mogilny, Buffalo, 1992-93, with 76G in 77GP.
.97 —Phil Esposito, Boston, 1970-71, with 76G in 78GP.
—Jari Kurri, Edmonton, 1984-85, with 71G in 73GP.

Buffalo superstar Alexander Mogilny became the second Sabre player to register seven three-or-more-goal games in a single season. He recorded five hat-tricks and two four-goal games in 1992-93.

**HIGHEST ASSISTS-PER-GAME AVERAGE, ONE SEASON
(AMONG PLAYERS WITH 35-OR-MORE ASSISTS):**
2.04 —**Wayne Gretzky,** Edmonton, 1985-86, with 163A in 80GP.
1.70 —Wayne Grezky, Edmonton, 1987-88, with 109A in 64GP.
1.69 —Wayne Gretzky, Edmonton, 1984-85, with 135A in 80GP.
1.59 —Wayne Gretzky, Edmonton, 1983-84, with 118A in 74GP.
1.56 —Wayne Gretzky, Edmonton, 1982-83, with 125A in 80GP.
1.56 —Wayne Gretzky, Los Angeles, 1990-91, with 122A in 78GP.
1.53 —Wayne Gretzky, Edmonton, 1986-87, with 121A in 79GP.
1.52 —Mario Lemieux, Pittsburgh, 1992-93, with 91A in 60GP.
1.50 —Wayne Gretzky, Edmonton, 1981-82, with 120A in 80GP.
1.50 —Mario Lemieux, Pittsburgh, 1988-89, with 114A in 76GP.

**HIGHEST POINTS-PER-GAME AVERAGE, ONE SEASON
(AMONG PLAYERS WITH 50-OR-MORE POINTS):**
2.77 —**Wayne Gretzky,** Edmonton, 1983-84, with 205PTS in 74GP.
2.69 —Wayne Gretzky, Edmonton, 1985-86, with 215PTS in 80GP.
2.67 —Mario Lemieux, Pittsburgh, 1992-93, with 160PTS in 60GP.
2.65 —Wayne Gretzky, Edmonton, 1981-82, with 212PTS in 80GP.
2.62 —Mario Lemieux, Pittsburgh, 1988-89, with 199PTS in 78GP.
2.60 —Wayne Gretzky, Edmonton, 1984-85, with 208PTS in 80GP.
2.45 —Wayne Gretzky, Edmonton, 1982-83, with 196PTS in 80GP.
2.33 —Wayne Gretzky, Edmonton, 1987-88, with 149PTS in 64GP.
2.32 —Wayne Gretzky, Edmonton, 1986-87, with 183PTS in 79GP.
2.18 —Mario Lemieux, Pittsburgh, 1987-88 with 168PTS in 77GP.
2.15 —Wayne Gretzky, Los Angeles, 1988-89, with 168PTS in 78GP.
2.09 —Wayne Gretzky, Los Angeles, 1990-91, with 163 PTS in 78GP.
2.08 —Mario Lemieux, Pittsburgh, 1989-90, with 123 PTS in 59GP.
2.05 —Wayne Gretzky, Edmonton, 1980-81, with 164PTS in 80GP.

MOST GOALS, ONE SEASON, INCLUDING PLAYOFFS:
100 —**Wayne Gretzky,** Edmonton, 1983-84, 87G in 74 regular-season games and 13G in 19 playoff games.
 97 —Wayne Gretzky, Edmonton, 1981-82, 92G in 80 regular-season games and 5G in 5 playoff games.
   —Mario Lemieux, Pittsburgh, 1988-89, 85G in 76 regular-season games and 12G in 11 playoff games.
   —Brett Hull, St. Louis, 1990-91, 86G in 78 regular-season games and 11G in 13 playoff games.
 90 —Wayne Gretzky, Edmonton, 1984-85, 73G in 80 regular season games and 17G in 18 playoff games.
   —Jari Kurri, Edmonton, 1984-85, 71G in 80 regular season games and 19G in 18 playoff games.
 85 —Mike Bossy, NY Islanders, 1980-81, 68G in 79 regular-season games and 17G in 18 playoff games.
   —Brett Hull, St. Louis, 1989-90, 72G in 80 regular season games and 13G in 12 playoff games.
 83 —Wayne Gretzky, Edmonton, 1982-83, 71G in 73 regular-season games and 12G in 16 playoff games.
   —Alexander Mogilny, Buffalo, 1992-93, 76G in 77 regular-season games and 7G in 7 playoff games.
 81 —Mike Bossy, NY Islanders, 1981-82, 64G in 80 regular-season games and 17G in 19 playoff games.

MOST ASSISTS, ONE SEASON, INCLUDING PLAYOFFS:
174 —**Wayne Gretzky,** Edmonton, 1985-86, 163A in 80 regular-season games and 11A in 10 playoff games.
165 —Wayne Gretzky, Edmonton, 1984-85, 135A in 80 regular-season games and 30A in 18 playoff games.
151 —Wayne Gretzky, Edmonton, 1982-83, 125A in 80 regular-season games and 26A in 16 playoff games.
150 —Wayne Gretzky, Edmonton, 1986-87, 121A in 79 regular-season games and 29A in 21 playoff games.
140 —Wayne Gretzky, Edmonton, 1983-84, 118A in 74 regular-season games and 22A in 19 playoff games.
   —Wayne Gretzky, Edmonton, 1987-88, 109A in 64 regular-season games and 31A in 19 playoff games.
133 —Wayne Gretzky, Los Angeles, 1990-91, 122A in 78 regular-season games and 11A in 12 playoff games.
131 —Wayne Gretzky, Los Angeles, 1988-89, 114A in 78 regular-season games and 17A in 11 playoff games.
127 —Wayne Gretzky, Edmonton, 1981-82, 120A in 80 regular-season games and 7A in 5 playoff games.
123 —Wayne Gretzky, Edmonton, 1980-81, 109A in 80 regular-season games and 14A in 9 playoff games.
121 —Mario Lemieux, Pittsburgh, 1988-89, 114A in 76 regular-season games and 7A in 11 playoff games.

MOST POINTS, ONE SEASON, INCLUDING PLAYOFFS:
255 —**Wayne Gretzky,** Edmonton, 1984-85, 208PTS in 80 regular-season games and 47PTS in 18 playoff games.
240 —Wayne Gretzky, Edmonton, 1983-84, 205PTS in 74 regular-season games and 35PTS in 19 playoff games.
234 —Wayne Gretzky, Edmonton, 1982-83, 196PTS in 80 regular-season games and 38PTS in 16 playoff games.
   —Wayne Gretzky, Edmonton, 1985-86, 215PTS in 80 regular-season games and 19PTS in 10 playoff games.
224 —Wayne Gretzky, Edmonton, 1981-82, 212PTS in 80 regular-season games and 12PTS in 5 playoff games.
218 —Mario Lemieux, Pittsburgh, 1988-89, 199PTS in 76 regular-season games and 19PTS in 11 playoff games.
217 —Wayne Gretzky, Edmonton, 1986-87, 183PTS in 79 regular-season games and 34PTS in 21 playoff games.
192 —Wayne Gretzky, Edmonton, 1987-88, 149PTS in 64 regular-season games and 43PTS in 19 playoff games.
190 —Wayne Gretzky, Los Angeles, 1988-89, 168PTS in 78 regular-season games and 22PTS in 11 playoff games.
185 —Wayne Gretzky, Edmonton, 1980-81, 164PTS in 80 regular-season games and 21PTS in 9 playoff games.

MOST GOALS, ONE SEASON, BY A DEFENSEMAN:
48 —**Paul Coffey,** Edmonton, 1985-86. 80 game schedule.
46 —Bobby Orr, Boston, 1974-75. 80 game schedule.
40 —Paul Coffey, Edmonton, 1983-84. 80 game schedule.
39 —Doug Wilson, Chicago, 1981-82. 80 game schedule.
37 —Bobby Orr, Boston, 1970-71. 78 game schedule.
   —Bobby Orr, Boston, 1971-72. 78 game schedule.
   —Paul Coffey, Edmonton, 1984-85 80 game schedule..
34 —Kevin Hatcher, Washington, 1992-93. 84 game schedule.
33 —Bobby Orr, Boston, 1969-70. 76 game schedule.
32 —Bobby Orr, Boston, 1973-74. 78 game schedule.

MOST GOALS, ONE SEASON, BY A CENTER:
92 —**Wayne Gretzky,** Edmonton, 1981-82. 80 game schedule.
87 —Wayne Gretzky, Edmonton, 1983-84. 80 game schedule.
85 —Mario Lemieux, Pittsburgh, 1988-89. 80 game schedule.
76 —Phil Esposito, Boston, 1970-71. 78 game schedule.
73 —Wayne Gretzky, Edmonton, 1984-85. 80 game schedule.
71 —Wayne Gretzky, Edmonton, 1982-83. 80 game schedule.
70 —Mario Lemieux, Pittsburgh, 1987-88. 80 game schedule.
   —Bernie Nicholls, Los Angeles, 1988-89. 80 game schedule.

Despite being sidelined by injury in each of the past five seasons, Mario Lemieux's name is still a fixture in the individual records section of the NHL Official Guide and Record Book.

MOST GOALS, ONE SEASON, BY A RIGHT WINGER:
86 — Brett Hull, St. Louis, 1990-91. 80 game schedule.
76 — Alexander Mogilny, Buffalo, 1992-93. 84 game schedule.
— Teemu Selanne, Winnipeg, 1992-93. 84 game schedule.
72 — Brett Hull, St. Louis, 1989-90. 80 game schedule.
71 — Jari Kurri, Edmonton, 1984-85. 80 game schedule.
70 — Brett Hull, St. Louis, 1991-92. 80 game schedule.
69 — Mike Bossy, NY Islanders, 1978-79. 80 game schedule.
68 — Jari Kurri, Edmonton, 1985-86. 80 game schedule..
— Mike Bossy, NY Islanders, 1980-81. 80 game schedule.
66 — Lanny McDonald, Calgary, 1982-83. 80 game schedule.
64 — Mike Bossy, NY Islanders, 1981-82. 80 game schedule.
61 — Reggie Leach, Philadelphia, 1975-76. 80 game schedule.
— Mike Bossy, NY Islanders, 1985-86. 80 game schedule.

MOST GOALS, ONE SEASON, BY A LEFT WINGER:
63 — Luc Robitaille, Los Angeles, 1992-93. 84 game schedule.
60 — Steve Shutt, Montreal, 1976-77. 80 game schedule.
58 — Bobby Hull, Chicago, 1968-69. 76 game schedule.
57 — Michel Goulet, Quebec, 1982-83. 80 game schedule.
56 — Charlie Simmer, Los Angeles, 1979-80. 80 game schedule.
— Charlie Simmer, Los Angeles, 1980-81. 80 game schedule.
— Michel Goulet, Quebec, 1983-84. 80 game schedule.
55 — Michel Goulet, Quebec, 1984-85. 80 game schedule.
— John Ogrodnick, Detroit, 1984-85. 80 game schedule.
— Kevin Stevens, Pittsburgh, 1992-93. 84 game schedule.

MOST GOALS, ONE SEASON, BY A ROOKIE:
76 — Teemu Selanne, Winnipeg, 1992-93. 84 game schedule.
53 — Mike Bossy, NY Islanders, 1977-78. 80 game schedule.
51 — Joe Nieuwendyk, Calgary, 1987-88. 80 game schedule.
45 — Dale Hawerchuk, Winnipeg, 1981-82. 80 game schedule.
— Luc Robitaille, Los Angeles, 1986-87. 80 game schedule.
44 — Richard Martin, Buffalo, 1971-72. 78 game schedule.
— Barry Pederson, Boston, 1981-82. 80 game schedule.
43 — Steve Larmer, Chicago, 1982-83. 80 game schedule.
— Mario Lemieux, Pittsburgh, 1984-85. 80 game schedule.

MOST GOALS, ONE SEASON, BY A ROOKIE DEFENSEMAN:
23 — Brian Leetch, NY Rangers, 1988-89. 80 game schedule.
22 — Barry Beck, Colorado, 1977-78. 80 game schedule.
19 — Reed Larson, Detroit, 1977-78. 80 game schedule.
— Phil Housley, Buffalo, 1982-83. 80 game schedule.

MOST ASSISTS, ONE SEASON, BY A DEFENSEMAN:
102 — Bobby Orr, Boston, 1970-71. 78 game schedule.
90 — Paul Coffey, Edmonton, 1985-86. 80 game schedule.
90 — Bobby Orr, Boston, 1973-74. 78 game schedule.
89 — Bobby Orr, Boston, 1974-75. 80 game schedule.

MOST ASSISTS, ONE SEASON, BY A CENTER:
163 — Wayne Gretzky, Edmonton, 1985-86. 80 game schedule.
135 — Wayne Gretzky, Edmonton, 1984-85. 80 game schedule.
125 — Wayne Gretzky, Edmonton, 1982-83. 80 game schedule.
122 — Wayne Gretzky, Los Angeles, 1990-91. 80 game schedule.
121 — Wayne Gretzky, Edmonton, 1986-87. 80 game schedule.
120 — Wayne Gretzky, Edmonton, 1981-82. 80 game schedule.
118 — Wayne Gretzky, Edmonton, 1983-84. 80 game schedule.
114 — Wayne Gretzky, Edmonton, 1988-89. 80 game schedule.
— Mario Lemieux, Pittsburgh, 1988-89. 80 game schedule.
109 — Wayne Gretzky, Edmonton, 1980-81. 80 game schedule.
— Wayne Gretzky, Edmonton, 1987-88. 80 game schedule.

MOST ASSISTS, ONE SEASON, BY A RIGHT WINGER:
83 — Mike Bossy, NY Islanders, 1981-82. 80 game schedule.
80 — Guy Lafleur, Montreal, 1976-77. 80 game schedule.
77 — Guy Lafleur, Montreal, 1978-79. 80 game schedule.

MOST ASSISTS, ONE SEASON, BY A LEFT WINGER:
70 — Joe Juneau, Boston, 1992-93. 84 game schedule.
69 — Kevin Stevens, Pittsburgh, 1991-92. 80 game schedule.
67 — Mats Naslund, Montreal, 1985-86. 80 game schedule.
65 — John Bucyk, Boston, 1970-71. 78 game schedule.
— Michel Goulet, Quebec, 1983-84. 80 game schedule.
64 — Mark Messier, Edmonton, 1983-84. 80 game schedule.
63 — Luc Robitaille, Los Angeles, 1991-92. 80 game schedule.

Barry "Bubba" Beck, below, established an NHL record for goals by a rookie defenceman when he connected 22 times during the 1977-78 season. The record stood for eleven seasons until Brian Leetch of the Rangers set a new mark with 23 goals in 1988-89. Jari Kurri, right, became the first right winger to record a 70-goal season, finishing with 71 in 1984-85

MOST ASSISTS, ONE SEASON, BY A ROOKIE:
 70 — Peter Stastny, Quebec, 1980-81. 80 game schedule.
  — Joe Juneau, Boston, 1992-93. 84 game schedule.
 63 — Bryan Trottier, NY Islanders, 1975-76. 80 game schedule.
 62 — Sergei Makarov, Calgary, 1989-90. 80 game schedule.
 60 — Larry Murphy, Los Angeles, 1980-81. 80 game schedule.

MOST ASSISTS, ONE SEASON, BY A ROOKIE DEFENSEMAN:
 60 — Larry Murphy, Los Angeles, 1980-81. 80 game schedule.
 55 — Chris Chelios, Montreal, 1984-85. 80 game schedule.
 50 — Stefan Persson, NY Islanders, 1977-78. 80 game schedule.
  — Gary Suter, Calgary, 1985-86, 80 game schedule..
 49 — Nicklas Lidstrom, Detroit, 1991-92. 80 game schedule.
 48 — Raymond Bourque, Boston, 1979-80. 80 game schedule.
  — Brian Leetch, NY Rangers, 1988-89. 80 game schedule.

MOST POINTS, ONE SEASON, BY A DEFENSEMAN:
 139 — Bobby Orr, Boston, 1970-71. 78 game schedule.
 138 — Paul Coffey, Edmonton,1985-86. 80 game schedule.
 135 — Bobby Orr, Boston, 1974-75. 80 game schedule.
 126 — Paul Coffey, Edmonton, 1983-84. 80 game schedule.
 122 — Bobby Orr, Boston, 1973-74. 78 game schedule.

MOST POINTS, ONE SEASON, BY A CENTER:
 215 — Wayne Gretzky, Edmonton, 1985-86. 80 game schedule.
 212 — Wayne Gretzky, Edmonton, 1981-82. 80 game schedule.
 208 — Wayne Gretzky, Edmonton, 1984-85. 80 game schedule.
 205 — Wayne Gretzky, Edmonton, 1983-84. 80 game schedule.
 199 — Mario Lemieux, Pittsburgh, 1988-89. 80 game schedule.
 196 — Wayne Gretzky, Edmonton, 1982-83. 80 game schedule.
 183 — Wayne Gretzky, Edmonton, 1986-87. 80 game schedule.
 168 — Mario Lemieux, Pittsburgh, 1987-88. 80 game schedule.
  — Wayne Gretzky, Los Angeles, 1988-89. 80 game schedule.
 164 — Wayne Gretzky, Edmonton, 1980-81. 80 game schedule.
 163 — Wayne Gretzky, Los Angeles, 1990-91. 80 game schedule.

MOST POINTS, ONE SEASON, BY A RIGHT WINGER:
 147 — Mike Bossy, NY Islanders, 1981-82. 80 game schedule.
 136 — Guy Lafleur, Montreal, 1976-77. 80 game schedule.
 135 — Jari Kurri, Edmonton, 1984-85. 80 game schedule.
 132 — Guy Lafleur, Montreal, 1977-78. 80·game schedule.
  — Teemu Selanne, Winnipeg, 1992-93. 84 game schedule.

MOST POINTS, ONE SEASON, BY A LEFT WINGER:
 125 — Luc Robitaille, Los Angeles, 1992-93. 84 game schedule.
 123 — Kevin Stevens, Pittsburgh, 1991-92. 80 game schedule.
 121 — Michel Goulet, Quebec, 1983-84. 80 game schedule.
 116 — John Bucyk, Boston, 1970-71. 78 game schedule.
 112 — Bill Barber, Philadelphia, 1975-76. 80 game schedule.

MOST POINTS, ONE SEASON, BY A ROOKIE:
 132 — Teemu Selanne, Winnipeg, 1992-93. 84 game schedule.
 109 — Peter Stastny, Quebec, 1980-81. 80 game schedule.
 103 — Dale Hawerchuk, Winnipeg, 1981-82. 80 game schedule.
 102 — Joe Juneau, Boston, 1992-93. 84 game schedule.
 100 — Mario Lemieux, Pittsburgh, 1984-85. 80 game schedule.

MOST POINTS, ONE SEASON, BY A ROOKIE DEFENSEMAN:
 76 — Larry Murphy, Los Angeles, 1980-81. 80 game schedule.
 71 — Brian Leetch, NY Rangers, 1988-89. 80 game schedule.
 68 — Gary Suter, Calgary, 1985-86. 80 game schedule.
 66 — Phil Housley, Buffalo, 1982-83. 80 game schedule.
 65 — Raymond Bourque, Boston, 1979-80. 80 game schedule.
 64 — Chris Chelios, Montreal, 1984-85. 80 game schedule.

MOST POINTS, ONE SEASON, BY A GOALTENDER:
 14 — Grant Fuhr, Edmonton, 1983-84. (14A)
  9 — Curtis Joseph, St. Louis, 1991-92. (9A)
  8 — Mike Palmateer, Washington, 1980-81. (8A)
   — Grant Fuhr, Edmonton, 1987-88. (8A)
   — Ron Hextall, Philadelphia, 1988-89. (8A)
   — Tom Barrasso, Pittsburgh, 1992-93. (8A)
  7 — Ron Hextall, Philadelphia, 1987-88. (1G-6A)
   — Mike Vernon, Calgary, 1987-88. (7A)

MOST POWER-PLAY GOALS, ONE SEASON:
 34 — Tim Kerr, Philadelphia, 1985-86. 80 game schedule.
 32 — Dave Andreychuk, Buffalo, Toronto, 1992-93. 84 game schedule.
 31 — Joe Nieuwendyk, Calgary, 1987-88. 80 game schedule.
  — Mario Lemieux, Pittsburgh, 1988-89. 80 game schedule.
 29 — Michel Goulet, Quebec, 1987-88. 80 game schedule.
  — Brett Hull, St. Louis, 1990-91. 80 game schedule.
  — Brett Hull, St. Louis, 1992-93. 84 game schedule.

MOST SHORTHAND GOALS, ONE SEASON:
 13 — Mario Lemieux, Pittsburgh, 1988-89. 80 game schedule.
 12 — Wayne Gretzky, Edmonton, 1983-84. 80 game schedule.
 11 — Wayne Gretzky, Edmonton, 1984-85. 80 game schedule.
 10 — Marcel Dionne, Detroit, 1974-75. 80 game schedule.
  — Mario Lemieux, Pittsburgh, 1987-88. 80 game schedule.
  — Dirk Graham, Chicago, 1988-89. 80 game schedule.

Chris Chelios, a standout blueliner with the 1984 U.S. Olympic Team and the University of Wisconsin, collected 64 points as a rookie defenceman with the Montreal Canadiens in 1984-85.

MOST SHOTS ON GOAL, ONE SEASON:
550 — Phil Esposito, Boston, 1970-71. 78 game schedule.
426 — Phil Esposito, Boston, 1971-72. 78 game schedule.
414 — Bobby Hull, Chicago, 1968-69. 76 game schedule.

MOST PENALTY MINUTES, ONE SEASON:
472 — Dave Schultz, Philadelphia, 1974-75.
409 — Paul Baxter, Pittsburgh, 1981-82.
408 — Mike Peluso, Chicago, 1991-92.
405 — Dave Schultz, Los Angeles, Pittsburgh, 1977-78.

MOST SHUTOUTS, ONE SEASON:
22 — George Hainsworth, Montreal, 1928-29. 44GP
15 — Alex Connell, Ottawa, 1925-26. 36GP
— Alex Connell, Ottawa, 1927-28. 44GP
— Hal Winkler, Boston, 1927-28. 44GP
— Tony Esposito, Chicago, 1969-70. 63GP
14 — George Hainsworth, Montreal, 1926-27. 44GP

LONGEST WINNING STREAK, ONE SEASON, BY A GOALTENDER:
17 — Gilles Gilbert, Boston, 1975-76.
14 — Don Beaupre, Minnesota, 1985-86.
— Ross Brooks, Boston, 1973-74.
— Tiny Thompson, Boston, 1929-30.
— Tom Barrasso, Pittsburgh, 1992-93.

LONGEST UNDEFEATED STREAK BY A GOALTENDER:
32 Games — Gerry Cheevers, Boston, 1971-72. 24w-8T.
31 Games — Pete Peeters, Boston, 1982-83. 26w-5T.
27 Games — Pete Peeters, Philadelphia, 1979-80. 22w-5T.
23 Games — Frank Brimsek, Boston, 1940-41. 15w-8T.
— Glenn Resch, NY Islanders, 1978-79. 15w-8T.
— Grant Fuhr, Edmonton, 1981-82. 15w-8T.

MOST GAMES, ONE SEASON, BY A GOALTENDER:
75 — Grant Fuhr, Edmonton, 1987-88.
74 — Ed Belfour, Chicago, 1990-91.
— Arturs Irbe, San Jose, 1993-94.
73 — Bernie Parent, Philadelphia, 1973-74.
72 — Gary Smith, Vancouver, 1974-75.
— Don Edwards, Buffalo, 1977-78.
— Tim Cheveldae, Detroit, 1991-92.

Detroit's Ted Hampson and Toronto's Bob Pulford collide in the crease as goalie Terry Sawchuk keeps a close eye on the action. Sawchuk is one of only three goalies in NHL history to compile back-to-back 40-win seasons.

MOST WINS, ONE SEASON, BY A GOALTENDER:
47 — Bernie Parent, Philadelphia, 1973-74.
44 — Bernie Parent, Philadelphia, 1974-75.
— Terry Sawchuk, Detroit, 1950-51.
— Terry Sawchuk, Detroit, 1951-52.

LONGEST SHUTOUT SEQUENCE BY A GOALTENDER:
461 Minutes, 29 Seconds — Alex Connell, Ottawa, 1927-28, six consecutive
shutouts. (Forward passing not permitted in attacking zones in 1927-1928.)
343 Minutes, 5 Seconds — George Hainsworth, Montreal, 1928-29, four consecutive
shutouts.
324 Minutes, 40 Seconds — Roy Worters, NY Americans, 1930-31, four consecutive
shutouts.
309 Minutes, 21 Seconds — Bill Durnan, Montreal, 1948-49, four consecutive shutouts.

MOST GOALS, 50 GAMES FROM START OF SEASON:
61 — Wayne Gretzky, Edmonton, 1981-82. Oct. 7, 1981 - Jan. 22, 1982.
(80-game schedule)
— **Wayne Gretzky,** Edmonton, 1983-84. Oct. 5, 1983 - Jan. 25, 1984.
(80-game schedule)
54 — Mario Lemieux, Pittsburgh, 1988-89. Oct. 7, 1988 - Jan. 31, 1989. (80-game
schedule)
53 — Wayne Gretzky, Edmonton, 1984-85. Oct. 11, 1984 - Jan. 28, 1985.
(80-game schedule).
52 — Brett Hull, St. Louis, 1990-91. Oct. 4, 1990 - Jan. 26, 1991. (80-game
schedule)
50 — Maurice Richard, Montreal, 1944-45. Oct. 28, 1944 - March 18, 1945.
(50-game schedule)
— Mike Bossy, NY Islanders, 1980-81. Oct. 11, 1980 - Jan. 24, 1981. (80-game
schedule)
— Brett Hull, St. Louis, 1991-92. Oct. 5, 1991 – Jan 28, 1992. (80 game
schedule)

LONGEST CONSECUTIVE POINT-SCORING STREAK
FROM START OF SEASON:
51 Games — Wayne Gretzky, Edmonton, 1983-84. 61G-92A-153PTS during
streak which was stopped by goaltender Markus Mattsson and
Los Angeles on Jan. 28, 1984.

LONGEST CONSECUTIVE POINT SCORING STREAK:
51 Games — Wayne Gretzky, Edmonton, 1983-84. 61G-92A-153PTS during streak.
46 Games — Mario Lemieux, Pittsburgh, 1989-90. 39G-64A-103PTS during streak.
39 Games — Wayne Gretzky, Edmonton, 1985-86. 33G-75A-108PTS during streak.
30 Games — Wayne Gretzky, Edmonton, 1982-83. 24G52A76PTS during streak.
— Mats Sundin, Quebec, 1992-93. 21G-25A-46PTS during streak.
28 Games — Guy Lafleur, Montreal, 1976-77. 19G-42A-61PTS during streak.
— Wayne Gretzky, Edmonton, 1984-85. 20G-43A-63PTS during streak.
— Mario Lemieux, Pittsburgh, 1985-86. 21G-38A-59PTS during streak.
— Paul Coffey, Edmonton, 1985-86. 16G-39A-55PTS during streak.
— Steve Yzerman, Detroit, 1988-89. 29G-36A-65PTS during streak.

LONGEST CONSECUTIVE POINT-SCORING STREAK BY A DEFENSEMAN:
28 Games — Paul Coffey, Edmonton, 1985-86. 16G-39A-55PTS during streak.
19 Games — Ray Bourque, Boston, 1987-88. 6G-21A-27PTS during streak.
17 Games — Ray Bourque, Boston, 1984-85. 4G-24A-28PTS during streak.
— Brian Leetch, NY Rangers, 1991-92. 5G-24A-29PTS during streak.
16 Games — Gary Suter, Calgary, 1987-88. 8G-17A-25PTS during streak.
15 Games — Bobby Orr, Boston, 1970-71. 10G-23A-33PTS during streak.
— Bobby Orr, Boston, 1973-74. 8G-15A-23PTS during streak.
— Steve Duchesne, Quebec, 1992-93. 4G-17A-21PTS during streak.

LONGEST CONSECUTIVE GOAL-SCORING STREAK:
16 Games — Harry (Punch) Broadbent, Ottawa, 1921-22.
25 goals during streak.
14 Games — Joe Malone, Montreal, 1917-18. 35 goals during streak.
13 Games — Newsy Lalonde, Montreal, 1920-21. 24 goals during streak.
— Charlie Simmer, Los Angeles, 1979-80. 17 goals during streak.
12 Games — Cy Denneny, Ottawa, 1917-18. 23 goals during streak.
— Dave Lumley, Edmonton, 1981-82. 15 goals during streak.
— Mario Lemieux, Pittsburgh, 1992-93. 18 goals during streak.

LONGEST CONSECUTIVE ASSIST-SCORING STREAK:
23 Games — Wayne Gretzky, Los Angeles, 1990-91. 48A during streak.
18 Games — Adam Oates, Boston, 1992-93. 28A during streak.
17 Games — Wayne Gretzky, Edmonton, 1983-84. 38A during streak.
— Paul Coffey, Edmonton, 1985-86. 27A during streak.
— Wayne Gretzky, Los Angeles, 1989-90. 35A during streak.
15 Games — Jari Kurri, Edmonton, 1983-84. 21A during streak.
— Brian Leetch, NY Rangers, 1991-92. 23A during streak.

Single Game

MOST GOALS, ONE GAME:
7 — Joe Malone, Quebec Bulldogs, Jan. 31, 1920, at Quebec. Quebec 10,
Toronto 6.
6 — Newsy Lalonde, Montreal, Jan. 10, 1920, at Montreal. Montreal 14,
Toronto 7.
— Joe Malone, Quebec Bulldogs, March 10, 1920, at Quebec. Quebec 10,
Ottawa 4.
— Corb Denneny, Toronto, Jan. 26, 1921, at Toronto. Toronto 10, Hamilton 3.
— Cy Denneny, Ottawa, March 7, 1921, at Ottawa. Ottawa 12, Hamilton 5.
— Syd Howe, Detroit, Feb. 3, 1944, at Detroit. Detroit 12, NY Rangers 2.
— Red Berenson, St. Louis, Nov. 7, 1968, at Philadelphia. St. Louis 8,
Philadelphia 0.
— Darryl Sittler, Toronto, Feb. 7, 1976, at Toronto. Toronto 11, Boston 4.

MOST GOALS, ONE ROAD GAME:

6 — **Red Berenson,** St. Louis, Nov. 7, 1968, at Philadelphia. St. Louis 8, Philadelphia 0.

5 — Joe Malone, Montreal, Dec. 19, 1917, at Ottawa. Montreal 9, Ottawa 4.
— Redvers Green, Hamilton, Dec. 5, 1924, at Toronto. Hamilton 10, Toronto 3.
— Babe Dye, Toronto, Dec. 22, 1924, at Boston. Toronto 10, Boston 2.
— Harry Broadbent, Mtl. Maroons, Jan. 7, 1925, at Hamilton. Mtl. Maroons 6, Hamilton 2.
— Don Murdoch, NY Rangers, Oct. 12, 1976, at Minnesota. NY Rangers 10, Minnesota 4.
— Tim Young, Minnesota, Jan. 15, 1979, at NY Rangers. Minnesota 8, NY Rangers 1.
— Willy Lindstrom, Winnipeg, March 2, 1982, at Philadelphia. Winnipeg 7, Philadelphia 6.
— Bengt Gustafsson, Washington, Jan. 8, 1984, at Philadelphia. Washington 7, Philadelphia 1.
— Wayne Gretzky, Edmonton, Dec. 15, 1984, at St. Louis. Edmonton 8, St. Louis 2.
— Dave Andreychuk, Buffalo, Feb. 6, 1986, at Boston. Buffalo 8, Boston 6.
— Mats Sundin, Quebec, Mar. 5, 1992, at Hartford. Quebec 10, Hartford 4.
— Mario Lemieux, Pittsburgh, Apr. 9, 1993, at New York. Pittsburgh 10, NY Rangers 4.
— Mike Ricci, Quebec, Feb. 17, 1994, at San Jose. Quebec 8, San Jose 2.

MOST ASSISTS, ONE GAME:

7 — **Billy Taylor,** Detroit, March 16, 1947, at Chicago. Detroit 10, Chicago 6.
— **Wayne Gretzky,** Edmonton, Feb. 15, 1980, at Edmonton. Edmonton 8, Washington 2.
— **Wayne Gretzky,** Edmonton, Dec. 11, 1985, at Chicago. Edmonton 12, Chicago 9.
— **Wayne Gretzky,** Edmonton, Feb. 14, 1986, at Edmonton. Edmonton 8, Quebec 2.

6 — Elmer Lach, Montreal, Feb. 6, 1943.
— Walter (Babe) Pratt, Toronto, Jan. 8, 1944.
— Don Grosso, Detroit, Feb. 3, 1944.
— Pat Stapleton, Chicago, March 30, 1969.
— Ken Hodge, Boston, Feb. 9, 1971.
— Bobby Orr, Boston, Jan. 1, 1973.
— Ron Stackhouse, Pittsburgh, March 8, 1975.
— Greg Malone, Pittsburgh, Nov. 28, 1979.
— Mike Bossy, NY Islanders, Jan. 6, 1981.
— Guy Chouinard, Calgary, Feb. 25, 1981.
— Mark Messier, Edmonton, Jan. 4, 1984.
— Patrik Sundstrom, Vancouver, Feb 29, 1984.
— Wayne Gretzky, Edmonton, Dec. 20, 1985.
— Paul Coffey, Edmonton, March 14, 1986.
— Gary Suter, Calgary, Apr. 4, 1986.
— Ron Francis, Hartford, March 5, 1987.
— Mario Lemieux, Pittsburgh, Oct. 15, 1988.
— Bernie Nicholls, Los Angeles, Dec. 1, 1988.
— Mario Lemieux, Pittsburgh, Dec. 31, 1988.
— Mario Lemieux, Pittsburgh, Dec. 5, 1992.
— Doug Gilmour, Toronto, Feb. 13, 1993.
— Tomas Sandstrom, Los Angeles, Oct. 9, 1993.

MOST ASSISTS, ONE ROAD GAME:

7 — **Billy Taylor,** Detroit, March 16, 1947, at Chicago. Detroit 10, Chicago 6.
— **Wayne Gretzky,** Edmonton, Dec. 11, 1985, at Chicago. Edmonton 12, Chicago 9.

6 — Bobby Orr, Boston, Jan. 1, 1973, at Vancouver. Boston 8, Vancouver 2.
— Patrik Sundstrom, Vancouver, Feb. 29, 1984, at Pittsburgh. Vancouver 9, Pittsburgh 5.
— Mario Lemieux, Pittsburgh, Dec. 5, 1992, at San Jose. Pittsburgh 9, San Jose 4.

MOST POINTS, ONE GAME:

10 — **Darryl Sittler,** Toronto, Feb. 7, 1976, at Toronto, 6G-4A. Toronto 11, Boston 4.

8 — Maurice Richard, Montreal, Dec. 28, 1944, at Montreal, 5G-3A. Montreal 9, Detroit 1.
— Bert Olmstead, Montreal, Jan. 9, 1954, at Montreal, 4G-4A. Montreal 12, Chicago 1.
— Tom Bladon, Philadelphia, Dec. 11, 1977, at Philadelphia, 4G-4A. Philadelphia 11, Cleveland 1.
— Bryan Trottier, NY Islanders, Dec. 23, 1978, at New York, 5G-3A. NY Islanders 9, NY Rangers 4.
— Peter Stastny, Quebec, Feb. 22, 1981, at Washington, 4G-4A. Quebec 11, Washington 7.
— Anton Stastny, Quebec, Feb. 22, 1981, at Washington, 3G-5A. Quebec 11, Washington 7.
— Wayne Gretzky, Edmonton, Nov. 19, 1983, at Edmonton, 3G-5A. Edmonton 13, New Jersey 4.
— Wayne Gretzky, Edmonton, Jan. 4, 1984, at Edmonton, 4G-4A. Edmonton 12 Minnesota 8.
— Paul Coffey, Edmonton, March 14, 1986, at Edmonton, 2G-6A. Edmonton 12, Detroit 3.
— Mario Lemieux, Pittsburgh, Oct. 15, 1988, at Pittsburgh, 2G-6A. Pittsburgh 9, St. Louis 2.
— Mario Lemieux, Pittsburgh, Dec. 31, 1988, at Pittsburgh, 5G-3A. Pittsburgh 8, New Jersey 6.
— Bernie Nicholls, Los Angeles, Dec. 1, 1988, at Los Angeles, 2G-6A. Los Angeles 9, Toronto 3.

Calgary defenseman Gary Suter recorded six assists in one game late in the 1985-86 season.

High-flying Stephane Richer had a five-point first period in 1989-90.

MOST POINTS, ONE ROAD GAME:
8 —**Peter Stastny,** Quebec, Feb. 22, 1981, at Washington, 4G-4A. Quebec 11, Washington 7.
—**Anton Stastny,** Quebec, Feb. 22, 1981, at Washington, 3G-5A. Quebec 11, Washington 7.
7 —Billy Taylor, Detroit, March 16, 1947, at Chicago, 7A. Detroit 10, Chicago 6.
—Red Berenson, St. Louis, Nov. 7, 1968, at Philadelphia, 6G-1A. St. Louis 8, Philadelphia 0.
—Gilbert Perreault, Buffalo, Feb. 1, 1976, at California, 2G-5A. Buffalo 9, California 5.
—Peter Stastny, Quebec, April 1, 1982, at Boston, 3G-4A. Quebec 8, Boston 5.
—Wayne Gretzky, Edmonton, Nov. 6, 1983, at Winnipeg, 4G-3A. Edmonton 8, Winnipeg 5.
—Patrik Sundstrom, Vancouver, Feb. 29, 1984, at Pittsburgh, 1G-6A. Vancouver 9, Pittsburgh 5.
—Wayne Gretzky, Edmonton, Dec. 11, 1985, at Chicago. 7A, Edmonton 12, Chicago 9.
—Mario Lemieux, Pittsburgh, Jan. 21, 1989, at Edmonton, 2G, 5A. Pittsburgh 7, Edmonton 4.
—Cam Neely, Boston, Oct. 16, 1988, at Chicago, 3G, 4A. Boston 10, Chicago 3.
—Dino Ciccarelli, Washington, March 18, 1989, at Hartford, 4G, 3A. Washington 8, Hartford 2.
—Mats Sundin, Quebec, Mar. 5, 1992, at Hartford, 5G, 2A. Quebec 10, Hartford 4.
—Mario Lemieux, Pittsburgh, Dec. 5, 1992, at San Jose, 1G, 6A. Pittsburgh 9, San Jose 4.

MOST GOALS, ONE GAME, BY A DEFENSEMAN:
5 —**Ian Turnbull,** Toronto, Feb. 2, 1977, at Toronto. Toronto 9, Detroit 1.
4 —Harry Cameron, Toronto, Dec. 26, 1917, at Toronto. Toronto 7, Montreal 5.
—Harry Cameron, Montreal, March 3, 1920, at Quebec City. Montreal 16, Que. Bulldogs 3.
—Sprague Cleghorn, Montreal, Jan. 14, 1922, at Montreal. Montreal 10, Hamilton 6.
—Johnny McKinnon, Pit. Pirates, Nov. 19, 1929, at Pittsburgh. Pit. Pirates 10, Toronto 5.
—Hap Day, Toronto, Nov. 19, 1929, at Pittsburgh. Pit. Pirates 10, Toronto 5.
—Tom Bladon, Philadelphia, Dec. 11, 1977, at Philadelphia. Philadelphia 11, Cleveland 1.
—Ian Turnbull, Los Angeles, Dec. 12, 1981, at Los Angeles. Los Angeles 7, Vancouver 5.
—Paul Coffey, Edmonton, Oct. 26, 1984, at Calgary. Edmonton 6, Calgary 5.

MOST GOALS BY ONE PLAYER IN HIS FIRST NHL GAME:
3 —**Alex Smart,** Montreal, Jan. 14, 1943, at Montreal. Montreal 5, Chicago 1.
—**Real Cloutier,** Quebec, Oct. 10, 1979, at Quebec. Atlanta 5, Quebec 3.

MOST GOALS, ONE GAME, BY A PLAYER IN HIS FIRST NHL SEASON:
5 —**Howie Meeker,** Toronto, Jan. 8, 1947, at Toronto. Toronto 10, Chicago 4.
—**Don Murdoch,** NY Rangers, Oct. 12, 1976, at Minnesota. NY Rangers 10, Minnesota 4.

MOST ASSISTS, ONE GAME, BY A DEFENSEMAN:
6 —**Babe Pratt,** Toronto, Jan. 8, 1944, at Toronto. Toronto 12, Boston 3.
—**Pat Stapleton,** Chicago, March 30, 1969, at Chicago. Chicago 9, Detroit 5.
—**Bobby Orr,** Boston, Jan. 1, 1973, at Vancouver, Boston 8, Vancouver 2.
—**Ron Stackhouse,** Pittsburgh, March 8, 1975, at Pittsburgh. Pittsburgh 8, Philadelphia 2.
—**Paul Coffey,** Edmonton, Mar. 14, 1986, at Edmonton. Edmonton 12, Detroit 3.
—**Gary Suter,** Calgary, Apr. 4, 1986, at Calgary. Calgary 9, Edmonton 3.

MOST ASSISTS BY ONE PLAYER IN HIS FIRST NHL GAME:
4 —**Earl (Dutch) Reibel,** Detroit, Oct. 8, 1953, at Detroit. Detroit 4, NY Rangers 1.
—**Roland Eriksson,** Minnesota, Oct. 6, 1976, at New York. NY Rangers 6, Minnesota 5.
3 —Al Hill, Philadelphia, Feb. 14, 1977, at Philadelphia. Philadelphia 6, St. Louis 4.

MOST ASSISTS, ONE GAME, BY A PLAYER IN HIS FIRST NHL SEASON:
7 —**Wayne Gretzky,** Edmonton, Feb. 15, 1980, at Edmonton. Edmonton 8, Washington 2.
6 —Gary Suter, Calgary, Apr. 4, 1986, at Calgary. Calgary 9, Edmonton 3.

MOST ASSISTS, ONE GAME, BY A GOALTENDER:
3 —**Jeff Reese,** Calgary, Feb. 10, 1993, at Calgary. Calgary 13, San Jose 1.

MOST POINTS, ONE GAME, BY A DEFENSEMAN:
8 —**Tom Bladon,** Philadelphia, Dec. 11, 1977, at Philadelphia. 4G-4A. Philadelphia 11, Cleveland 1.
—**Paul Coffey,** Edmonton, Mar. 14, 1986, at Edmonton. 2G-6A. Edmonton 12, Detroit 3.
7 —Bobby Orr, Boston, Nov. 15, 1973, at Boston, 3G-4A. Boston 10, NY Rangers 2.

MOST POINTS BY ONE PLAYER IN HIS FIRST NHL GAME:
5 —**Al Hill,** Philadelphia, Feb. 14, 1977, at Philadelphia. 2G-3A. Philadelphia 6, St. Louis 4.
4 —Alex Smart, Montreal, Jan. 14, 1943, at Montreal, 3G-1A. Montreal 5, Chicago 1.
—Earl (Dutch) Reibel, Detroit, Oct. 8, 1953, at Detroit. 4A. Detroit 4, NY Rangers 1.
—Roland Eriksson, Minnesota, Oct. 6, 1976 at New York. 4A. NY Rangers 6, Minnesota 5.

MOST POINTS, ONE GAME, BY A PLAYER IN HIS FIRST NHL SEASON:
8 —**Peter Stastny,** Quebec, Feb. 22, 1981, at Washington. 4G-4A. Quebec 11, Washington 7.
— **Anton Stastny,** Quebec, Feb. 22, 1981, at Washington. 3G-5A. Quebec 11, Washington 7.
7 —Wayne Gretzky, Edmonton, Feb. 15, 1980, at Edmonton. 7A. Edmonton 8, Washington 2.
— Sergei Makarov, Calgary, Feb. 25, 1990, at Calgary, 2G-5A. Calgary 10, Edmonton 4.
6 —Wayne Gretzky, Edmonton, March 29, 1980, at Toronto. 2G-4A. Edmonton 8, Toronto 5.
— Gary Suter, Calgary, Apr. 4, 1986, at Calgary. 6A. Calgary 9, Edmonton 3.

MOST PENALTIES, ONE GAME:
10 —**Chris Nilan,** Boston, March 31, 1991, at Boston against Hartford. 6 minors, 2 majors, 1 10-minute misconduct, 1 game misconduct.
9 —Jim Dorey, Toronto, Oct. 16, 1968, at Toronto against Pittsburgh. 4 minors, 2 majors, 2 10-minute misconducts, 1 game misconduct.
— Dave Schultz, Pittsburgh, Apr. 6, 1978, at Detroit. 5 minors, 2 majors, 2 10-minute misconducts.
— Randy Holt, Los Angeles, Mar. 11, 1979, at Philadelphia. 1 minor, 3 majors, 2 10-minute misconducts, 3 game misconducts.
— Russ Anderson, Pittsburgh, Jan. 19, 1980, at Pittsburgh. 3 minors, 3 majors, 3 game misconducts.
— Kim Clackson, Quebec, March 8, 1981, at Quebec. 4 minors, 3 majors, 2 game misconducts.
— Terry O'Reilly, Boston, Dec. 19, 1984 at Hartford. 5 minors, 3 majors, 1 game misconduct.
— Larry Playfair, Los Angeles, Dec. 9, 1986, at NY Islanders. 6 minors, 2 majors, 1 10-minute misconduct.
— Marty McSorley, Los Angeles, Apr. 14, 1992, at Vancouver. 5 minors, 2 majors, 1 10-minute misconduct, 1 game misconduct.

MOST PENALTY MINUTES, ONE GAME:
67 —**Randy Holt,** Los Angeles, Mar. 11, 1979, at Philadelphia. 1 minor, 3 majors, 2 10-minute misconducts, 3 game misconducts.
55 —Frank Bathe, Philadelphia, Mar. 11, 1979, at Philadelphia. 3 majors, 2 10-minute misconducts, 2 game misconducts.
51 —Russ Anderson, Pittsburgh, Jan. 19, 1980, at Pittsburgh. 3 minors, 3 majors, 3 game misconducts.

MOST GOALS, ONE PERIOD:
4 —**Harvey (Busher) Jackson,** Toronto, Nov. 20, 1934, at St. Louis, third period. Toronto 5, St. Louis Eagles 2.
— **Max Bentley,** Chicago, Jan. 28, 1943, at Chicago, third period. Chicago 10, NY Rangers 1.
— **Clint Smith,** Chicago, March 4, 1945, at Chicago, third period. Chicago 6, Montreal 4.
— **Red Berenson,** St. Louis, Nov. 7, 1968, at Philadelphia, second period. St. Louis 8, Philadelphia 0.
— **Wayne Gretzky,** Edmonton, Feb. 18, 1981, at Edmonton, third period. Edmonton 9, St. Louis 2.
— **Grant Mulvey,** Chicago, Feb. 3, 1982, at Chicago, first period. Chicago 9, St. Louis 5.
— **Bryan Trottier,** NY Islanders, Feb. 13, 1982, at New York, second period. NY Islanders 8, Philadelphia 2.
— **Al Secord,** Chicago, Jan. 7, 1987 at Chicago, second period. Chicago 6, Toronto 4.
— **Joe Nieuwendyk,** Calgary, Jan. 11, 1989, at Calgary, second period. Calgary 8, Winnipeg 3.
— **Peter Bondra,** Washington, Feb. 5, 1994, at Washington, first period. Washington 6, Tampa Bay 3.

MOST ASSISTS, ONE PERIOD:
5 —**Dale Hawerchuk,** Winnipeg, Mar. 6, 1984, at Los Angeles, second period. Winnipeg 7, Los Angeles 3.
4 —Four assists have been recorded in one period on 44 occasions since Buddy O'Connor of Montreal first accomplished the feat vs. NY Rangers on Nov. 8, 1942. Most recent player, Adam Oates of Boston (Mar. 24, 1994 vs Anaheim).

MOST POINTS, ONE PERIOD:
6 —**Bryan Trottier,** NY Islanders, Dec. 23, 1978, at NY Islanders, second period. 3G, 3A. NY Islanders 9, NY Rangers 4.
5 —Les Cunningham, Chicago, Jan. 28, 1940, at Chicago, third period. 2G, 3A. Chicago 8, Montreal 1.
— Max Bentley, Chicago, Jan. 28, 1943, at Chicago, third period. 4G, 1A, Chicago 10, NY Rangers 1.
— Leo Labine, Boston, Nov. 28, 1954, at Boston, second period, 3G, 2A. Boston 6, Detroit 2.
— Darryl Sittler, Toronto, Feb. 7, 1976, at Toronto, second period. 3G, 2A. Toronto 11, Boston 4.
— Dale Hawerchuk, Winnipeg, Mar. 6, 1984, at Los Angeles, second period. 5A. Winnipeg 7, Los Angeles 3.
— Jari Kurri, Edmonton, October 26, 1984 at Edmonton, second period. Edmonton 8, Los Angeles 2.
— Pat Elynuik, Winnipeg, Jan. 20, 1989, at Winnipeg, second period. 2G, 3A. Winnipeg 7, Pittsburgh 3.
— Ray Ferraro, Hartford, Dec. 9, 1989, at Hartford, first period. 3G, 2A. Hartford 7, New Jersey 3.
— Stephane Richer, Montreal, Feb. 14, 1990, at Montreal, first period. 2G, 3A. Montreal 10, Vancouver 1.
— Cliff Ronning, Vancouver, Apr. 15, 1993, at Los Angeles, third period. 3G, 2A. Vancouver 8, Los Angeles 6.

MOST PENALTIES, ONE PERIOD:
9 —**Randy Holt,** Los Angeles, Mar. 11, 1979, at Philadelphia, first period. 1 minor, 3 majors, 2 10-minute misconducts, 3 game misconducts.

MOST PENALTY MINUTES, ONE PERIOD:
67 —**Randy Holt,** Los Angeles, Mar. 11, 1979, at Philadelphia, first period. 1 minor, 3 majors, 2 10-minute misconducts, 3 game misconducts.

FASTEST GOAL BY A ROOKIE IN HIS FIRST NHL GAME:
15 Seconds — Gus Bodnar, Toronto, Oct. 30, 1943. Toronto 5, NY Rangers 2.
18 Seconds — Danny Gare, Buffalo, Oct. 10, 1974. Buffalo 9, Boston 5.
20 Seconds — Alexander Mogilny, Buffalo, Oct. 5, 1989. Buffalo 4, Quebec 3.

FASTEST GOAL FROM START OF A GAME:
5 Seconds — Doug Smail, Winnipeg, Dec. 20, 1981, at Winnipeg. Winnipeg 5, St. Louis 4.
— **Bryan Trottier,** NY Islanders, Mar. 22, 1984, at Boston. NY Islanders 3, Boston 3
— **Alexander Mogilny,** Buffalo, Dec. 21, 1991, at Toronto. Buffalo 4, Toronto 1.
6 Seconds — Henry Boucha, Detroit, Jan. 28, 1973, at Montreal. Detroit 4, Montreal 2
— Jean Pronovost, Pittsburgh, March 25, 1976, at St. Louis. St. Louis 5, Pittsburgh 2
7 Seconds — Charlie Conacher, Toronto, Feb. 6, 1932, at Toronto. Toronto 6, Boston 0
— Danny Gare, Buffalo, Dec. 17, 1978, at Buffalo. Buffalo 6, Vancouver 3
— Dave Williams, Los Angeles, Feb. 14, 1987 at Los Angeles. Los Angeles 5, Harford 2.
8 Seconds — Ron Martin, NY Americans, Dec. 4, 1932, at New York. NY Americans 4, Montreal 2
— Chuck Arnason, Colorado, Jan. 28, 1977, at Atlanta. Colorado 3, Atlanta 3
— Wayne Gretzky, Edmonton, Dec. 14, 1983, at New York. Edmonton 9, NY Rangers 4
— Gaetan Duchesne, Washington, Mar. 14, 1987, at St. Louis. Washington 3, St. Louis 3.
— Tim Kerr, Philadelphia, March 7, 1989, at Philadelphia. Philadelphia 4, Edmonton 3.
— Grant Ledyard, Buffalo, Dec. 4, 1991, at Winnipeg. Buffalo 4, Winnipeg 4.

FASTEST GOAL FROM START OF A PERIOD:
4 Seconds — Claude Provost, Montreal, Nov. 9, 1957, at Montreal, second period. Montreal 4, Boston 2.
— **Denis Savard,** Chicago, Jan. 12, 1986, at Chicago, third period. Chicago 4, Hartford 2.

FASTEST TWO GOALS:
4 Seconds — Nels Stewart, Mtl. Maroons, Jan. 3, 1931, at Montreal at 8:24 and 8:28, third period. Mtl. Maroons 5, Boston 3.
5 Seconds — Pete Mahovlich, Montreal, Feb. 20, 1971, at Montreal at 12:16 and 12:21, third period. Montreal 7, Chicago 1.
6 Seconds — Jim Pappin, Chicago, Feb. 16, 1972, at Chicago at 2:57 and 3:03, third period. Chicago 3, Philadelphia 3.
— Ralph Backstrom, Los Angeles, Nov. 2, 1972, at Los Angeles at 8:30 and 8:36, third period. Los Angeles 5, Boston 2.
— Lanny McDonald, Calgary, Mar. 22, 1984, at Calgary at 16:23 and 16:29, first period. Detroit 6, Calgary 4.
— Sylvain Turgeon, Hartford, Mar. 28, 1987, at Hartford at 13:59 and 14:05, second period. Hartford 5, Pittsburgh 4.

FASTEST THREE GOALS:
21 Seconds — Bill Mosienko, Chicago, March 23, 1952, at New York, against goaltender Lorne Anderson. Mosienko scored at 6:09, 6:20 and 6:30 of third period, all with both teams at full strength. Chicago 7, NY Rangers 6.
44 Seconds — Jean Béliveau, Montreal, Nov. 5, 1955, at Montreal, against goaltender Terry Sawchuk. Béliveau scored at :42, 1:08 and 1:26 of second period, all with Montreal holding a 6-4 man advantage. Montreal 4, Boston 2.

FASTEST THREE ASSISTS:
21 Seconds — Gus Bodnar, Chicago, March 23, 1952, at New York, Bodnar assisted on Bill Mosienko's three goals at 6:09, 6:20, 6:30 of third period. Chicago 7, NY Rangers 6.
44 Seconds — Bert Olmstead, Montreal, Nov. 5, 1955, at Montreal against Boston. Olmstead assisted on Jean Béliveau's three goals at :42, 1:08 and 1:26 of second period. Montreal 4, Boston 2.

MOST PENALTY MINUTES, ONE PERIOD:
67 —**Randy Holt,** Los Angeles, Mar. 11, 1979, at Philadelphia, first period. 1 minor, 3 majors, 2 10-minute misconducts, 3 game misconducts.

Wayne Gretzky Milestone Review

On March 23, 1994, Wayne Gretzky became the NHL's all-time leading goal scorer, surpassing Gordie Howe's long-standing regular-season goal total of 801. Gretzky's milestone goal gave him an unprecedented complete set of NHL career scoring records. He is now the NHL's all-time leader in goals, assists and points in both regular-season and playoff competition. Highlights of Gretzky's goal-scoring log and photographs of some record-setting moments follow.

Career Goal #	Date		Opponent	Goaltender	Notes
1	Oct. 14	1979	Vancouver	Glen Hanlon	First NHL goal
50	Apr. 2	1980	Minnesota	Gary Edwards	First of eight consecutive 50-goal seasons
100	Mar. 7	1981	Philadelphia	empty net	
156	Dec. 30	1981	Philadelphia	empty net	50 goals in 39 games
183	Feb. 24	1982	Buffalo	Don Edwards	77th goal of '81-82 season, breaking Phil Esposito's single-season record
198	Mar. 26	1982	Los Angeles	Mike Blake	92nd goal of '81-82. NHL's highest single-season total
200	Oct. 9	1982	Vancouver	Richard Brodeur	Fastest 200 goals in NHL history
300	Dec. 13	1983	NY Islanders	Billy Smith	First Oiler in team history to score 300 goals
325	Jan. 18	1984	Vancouver	Richard Brodeur	Surpassed Nels Stewart's career total which topped the NHL from 1940 to 1952
400	Jan. 13	1985	Buffalo	Tom Barrasso	
500	Nov. 22	1986	Vancouver	empty net	Surpassed Mike Bossy's record for fastest 500 goals
545	Oct. 14	1987	Calgary	Mike Vernon	Surpassed Maurice Richard's career total which topped the NHL from 1952 to 1963
600	Nov. 23	1988	Detroit	Greg Stefan	
611	Dec. 23	1988	Vancouver	empty net	Surpassed Bobby Hull's career total
641	Oct. 15	1989	Edmonton	Bill Ranford	Set all-time point scoring record: 1,851 points
700	Jan. 3	1991	NY Islanders	Glenn Healy	
718	Mar. 28	1991	Minnesota	Jon Casey	Surpassed Phil Esposito's career total
732	Dec. 21	1991	Detroit	Tim Cheveldae	Surpassed Marcel Dionne's career total
800	Mar. 20	1994	San Jose	Arturs Irbe	Second player to reach 800-goal plateau
801	Mar. 20	1994	San Jose	Arturs Irbe	Tied Gordie Howe's career total which had topped the NHL since 1963
802	Mar. 23	1994	Vancouver	Kirk McLean	Surpassed Gordie Howe's career total

FAST START • *Edmonton vs. Vancouver, October 14, 1979*

Wayne Gretzky made his NHL debut with the Edmonton Oilers on October 10, 1979. He scored his first NHL goal four days later to help the Oilers earn a 3-3 tie with the Vancouver Canucks.

Edmonton vs. Buffalo, February 24, 1982

Wayne Gretzky fired his 77th goal of the season past Buffalo goaltender Don Edwards late in the third period, breaking Phil Esposito's record for goals in a single season. In 1970-71, Esposito needed 550 shots to establish his milestone mark of 76 goals, but Gretzky broke Espo's 11-year old record on his 300th shot of the 1981-82 season. He finished the season with a record 92 goals.

GOAL-SCORING RECORD • *Los Angeles vs. Vancouver, March 23, 1994*

Post-game celebration. With less than six minutes remaining in the second period, Gretzky took a pass from Marty McSorley and one-timed a shot that eluded Vancouver's Kirk McLean to set the new mark. Gretzky's first 802 goals were scored on 135 NHL goaltenders. In his 1,125 game career. Gretzky has scored two-or-more goals in a game 190 times for a total of 446 goals.

POINT-SCORING RECORD • *Los Angeles vs. Edmonton, October 15, 1989*

With less than a minute remaining in the Kings-Oilers game and the Kings' goaltender on the bench for an extra attacker, Gretzky flipped a pass from Dave Taylor over Bill Ranford's shoulder to break Gordie Howe's mark of 1,850 regular-season points. This game took place in Edmonton's Northlands Coliseum where Gretzky had led the Oilers to four Stanley Cup championships prior to the 1988 trade that brought him to Los Angeles.

ALL-TIME ASSIST RECORD • *Edmonton vs. Los Angeles, March 1, 1988.*

Midway through the first period of the Los Angeles-Edmonton match on March 1, 1988, Wayne Gretzky slipped a pass to Jari Kurri to register his 1,050th NHL assist and eclipse Gordie Howe's record of 1,049.

Top 100 All-Time Goal-Scoring Leaders

* active player

(figures in parentheses indicate ranking of top 10 by goals per game)

Player	Seasons	Games	Goals	Goals per game
*1. Wayne Gretzky, Edm., L.A.	15	1125	**803**	.714 (4)
2. Gordie Howe, Det., Hfd.	26	1767	**801**	.453
3. Marcel Dionne, Det., L.A., NYR	18	1348	**731**	.542
4. Phil Esposito, Chi., Bos., NYR.	18	1282	**717**	.559
*5. Mike Gartner, Wsh., Min., NYR, Tor.	15	1170	**617**	.527
6. Bobby Hull, Chi., Wpg., Hfd.	16	1063	**610**	.574 (7)
7. Mike Bossy, NYI.	10	752	**573**	.762 (3)
8. Guy Lafleur, Mtl., NYR, Que.	17	1126	**560**	.497
9. John Bucyk, Det., Bos.	23	1540	**556**	.361
*10. Jari Kurri, Edm., L.A.	13	990	**555**	.561(10)
*11. Michel Goulet, Que., Chi.	15	1089	**548**	.503
12. Maurice Richard, Mtl.	18	978	**544**	.556
13. Stan Mikita, Chi.	22	1394	**541**	.388
14. Frank Mahovlich, Tor., Det., Mtl.	18	1181	**533**	.451
*15. Bryan Trottier, NYI, Pit.	18	1279	**524**	.410
*16. Dino Ciccarelli, Min., Wsh., Det.	14	973	**513**	.527
17. Gilbert Perreault, Buf.	17	1191	**512**	.430
18. Jean Beliveau, Mtl.	20	1125	**507**	.451
19. Lanny McDonald, Tor., Col., Cgy.	16	1111	**500**	.450
*20. Mario Lemieux, Pit.	10	599	**494**	.825 (1)
21. Jean Ratelle, NYR, Bos.	21	1281	**491**	.383
22. Norm Ullman, Det., Tor.	20	1410	**490**	.348
*23. Dale Hawerchuk, Wpg., Buf.	13	1032	**484**	.469
24. Darryl Sittler, Tor., Phi., Det.	15	1096	**484**	.442
*25. Glenn Anderson, Edm., Tor., NYR	14	1061	**480**	.452
*26. Mark Messier, Edm., NYR	15	1081	**478**	.442
*27. Joey Mullen, St.L., Cgy., Pit.	14	926	**471**	.509
*28. Steve Yzerman, Det.	11	815	**469**	.575 (6)
29. Alex Delvecchio, Det.	24	1549	**456**	.294
*30. Peter Stastny, Que., N.J., St.L.	14	971	**449**	.462
31. Rick Middleton, NYR, Bos.	14	1005	**448**	.446
32. Rick Vaive, Van., Tor., Chi., Buf.	13	876	**441**	.503
*33. Denis Savard, Chi., Mtl., T.B.	14	1020	**441**	.432
34. Dave Taylor, L.A.	17	1111	**431**	.388
35. Yvan Cournoyer, Mtl.	16	968	**428**	.442
*36. Steve Larmer, Chi., NYR.	14	959	**427**	.445
*37. Dave Andreychuk, Buf., Tor.	12	877	**426**	.486
*38. Brian Propp, Phi., Bos., Min., Hfd.	15	1016	**425**	.418
39. Steve Shutt, Mtl., L.A.	13	930	**424**	.456
40. Bill Barber, Phi.	12	903	**420**	.465
*41. Bernie Nicholls, L.A., NYR, Edm., N.J.	13	885	**416**	.470
*42. Brian Bellows, Min., Mtl.	12	912	**415**	.455
*43. Brett Hull, Cgy., St.L.	9	540	**413**	.765 (2)
44. Garry Unger, Tor., Det., St.L., Atl., L.A., Edm.	16	1105	**413**	.374
45. Rod Gilbert, NYR	18	1065	**406**	.381
46. John Ogrodnick, Det., Que., NYR	14	928	**402**	.433
47. Dave Keon, Tor., Hfd.	18	1296	**396**	.306
48. Pierre Larouche, Pit., Mtl., Hfd., NYR.	14	812	**395**	.486
49. Bernie Geoffrion, Mtl., NYR	16	883	**393**	.445
*50. Luc Robitaille, L.A.	8	640	**392**	.613 (5)
*51. Pat LaFontaine, NYI, Buf.	11	687	**391**	.569 (8)
52. Jean Pronovost, Pit., Atl., Wsh.	14	998	**391**	.392
53. Dean Prentice, NYR, Bos., Det., Pit., Min.	22	1378	**391**	.284
54. Richard Martin, Buf., L.A.	11	685	**384**	.561
55. Reggie Leach, Bos., Cal., Phi., Det.	13	934	**381**	.408
56. Ted Lindsay, Det., Chi.	17	1068	**379**	.355
57. Butch Goring, L.A., NYI, Bos.	16	1107	**375**	.339
58. Rick Kehoe, Tor., Pit.	14	906	**371**	.409
59. Tim Kerr, Phi., NYR, Hfd.	13	655	**370**	.565 (9)
60. Bernie Federko, St.L., Det.	14	1000	**369**	.369
61. Jacques Lemaire, Mtl.	12	853	**366**	.429
62. Peter McNab, Buf., Bos., Van., N.J.	14	954	**363**	.381
63. Ivan Boldirev, Bos., Cal., Chi., Atl., Van., Det.	15	1052	**361**	.343
64. Bobby Clarke, Phi.	15	1144	**358**	.313
65. Henri Richard, Mtl.	20	1256	**358**	.285
66. Bobby Smith, Min., Mtl.	15	1077	**357**	.331
67. Dennis Maruk, Cal., Cle., Wsh., Min.	13	882	**356**	.404
68. Wilf Paiement, K.C., Col., Tor., Que., NYR, Buf., Pit.	14	946	**356**	.376
*69. Pat Verbeek, N.J., Hfd.	12	867	**355**	.409
*70. Mike Foligno, Det., Buf., Tor., Fla.	15	1018	**355**	.349
71. Danny Gare, Buf., Det., Edm.	13	827	**354**	.428
72. Rick MacLeish, Phi., Hfd., Pit., Det.	14	846	**349**	.413
73. Andy Bathgate, NYR, Tor., Det., Pit.	17	1069	**349**	.326
*74. Paul Coffey, Edm., Pit., L.A., Det.	14	1033	**344**	.333
*75. Cam Neely, Van., Bos.	11	635	**342**	.539
76. Charlie Simmer, Cal., Cle., L.A., Bos., Pit.	14	712	**342**	.480
*77. Dave Christian, Wpg., Wsh., Bos., St.L., Chi.	15	1009	**340**	.337

Rick Vaive, who patrolled right wing for Vancouver, Toronto, Chicago and Buffalo before retiring after the 1993-94 season, recorded 441 goals in his 13-season career in the NHL.

Player	Seasons	Games	Goals	Goals per game
*78. Ron Francis, Hfd., Pit.	13	964	**338**	.351
*79. Brent Sutter, NYI, Chi.	14	893	**334**	.374
80. Ron Ellis, Tor.	16	1034	**332**	.321
81. Mike Bullard, Pit., Cgy., St.L., Phi., Tor.	11	727	**329**	.453
82. Ken Hodge, Chi., Bos., NYR	13	881	**328**	.372
83. John Tonelli, NYI, Cgy., L.A., Chi., Que.	14	1028	**325**	.316
84. Nels Stewart, Mtl. M., Bos., NYA	15	654	**324**	.495
85. Paul MacLean, St.L., Wpg., Det.	11	719	**324**	.451
86. Pit Martin, Det., Bos., Chi., Van.	17	1101	**324**	.294
87. Vic Hadfield, NYR, Pit.	16	1002	**323**	.322
88. Tony McKegney, Buf., Que., Min., St.L., Det., Chi.	14	912	**320**	.351
89. Clark Gillies, NYI, Buf.	14	958	**319**	.333
90. Don Lever, Van., Atl., Cgy., Col., N.J., Buf.	15	1020	**313**	.307
*91. Ray Bourque, Bos.	15	1100	**311**	.283
92. Denis Potvin, NYI	15	1060	**310**	.292
93. Bob Nevin, Tor., NYR, Min., L.A.	18	1128	**307**	.272
*94. Doug Gilmour, St.L., Cgy., Tor.	11	856	**304**	.355
95. Brian Sutter, St.L.	12	779	**303**	.389
96. Dennis Hull, Chi., Det.	14	959	**303**	.316
*97. Stephane Richer, Mtl., N.J.	10	645	**301**	.467
*98. Tomas Sandstrom, NYR, L.A., Pit.	10	669	**296**	.442
99. George Armstrong, Tor.	21	1187	**296**	.249
*100. Bob Carpenter, Wsh., NYR, L.A., Bos., N.J.	13	901	**295**	.327

Top 100 Active Goal-Scoring Leaders

	Player	Games	Goals	Goals per game
1.	**Wayne Gretzky**, Edm., L.A.	1125	803	.714
2.	**Mike Gartner**, Wsh., Min., NYR, Tor.	1170	617	.527
3.	**Jari Kurri**, Edm., L.A.	990	555	.561
4.	**Michel Goulet**, Que., Chi.	1089	548	.503
5.	**Bryan Trottier**, NYI, Pit.	1279	524	.410
6.	**Dino Ciccarelli**, Min., Wsh., Det.	973	513	.527
7.	**Mario Lemieux**, Pit.	599	494	.825
8.	**Dale Hawerchuk**, Wpg., Buf.	1032	484	.469
9.	**Glenn Anderson**, Edm., Tor., NYR	1061	480	.452
10.	**Mark Messier**, Edm., NYR	1081	478	.442
11.	**Joe Mullen**, St.L., Cgy., Pit.	926	471	.509
12.	**Steve Yzerman**, Det.	815	469	.575
13.	**Peter Stastny**, Que., N.J., St.L.	971	449	.462
14.	**Denis Savard**, Chi., Mtl., T.B.	1020	441	.432
15.	**Dave Taylor**, L.A.	1111	431	.388
16.	**Steve Larmer**, Chi., NYR	959	427	.445
17.	**Dave Andreychuk**, Buf., Tor.	877	426	.486
18.	**Brian Propp**, Phi., Bos., Min., Hfd.	1016	425	.418
19.	**Bernie Nicholls**, L.A., NYR, Edm., N.J.	885	416	.470
20.	**Brian Bellows**, Min., Mtl.	912	415	.455
21.	**Brett Hull**, Cgy., St.L.	540	413	.765
22.	**Luc Robitaille**, L.A.	640	392	.613
23.	**Pat LaFontaine**, NYI, Buf.	687	391	.569
24.	**Pat Verbeek**, N.J., Hfd.	867	355	.409
25.	**Mike Foligno**, Det., Buf., Tor., Fla.	1018	355	.349
26.	**Paul Coffey**, Edm., Pit., L.A., Det.	1033	344	.333
27.	**Cam Neely**, Van., Bos.	635	342	.539
28.	**Dave Christian**, Wpg., Wsh., Bos., St.L., Chi.	1009	340	.337
29.	**Ron Francis**, Hfd., Pit.	964	338	.351
30.	**Brent Sutter**, NYI, Chi.	893	334	.374
31.	**Mike Bullard**, Pit., Cgy., St.L., Phi., Tor.	727	329	.453
32.	**Ray Bourque**, Bos.	1100	311	.283
33.	**Doug Gilmour**, St.L., Cgy., Tor.	856	304	.355
34.	**Stephane Richer**, Mtl., N.J.	645	301	.467
35.	**Tomas Sandstrom**, NYR, L.A., Pit.	669	296	.442
36.	**Bob Carpenter**, Wsh., NYR, L.A., Bos., N.J.	901	295	.327
37.	**Kevin Dineen**, Hfd., Phi.	707	294	.416
38.	**Joe Nieuwendyk**, Cgy.	531	293	.552
39.	**Rick Tocchet**, Phi., Pit.	681	291	.427
40.	**Tony Tanti**, Chi., Van., Pit., Buf.	697	287	.412
41.	**Brent Ashton**, Van., Colorado, N.J., Min., Que., Det., Wpg., Bos., Cgy.	998	284	.285
42.	**John Anderson**, Tor., Que., Hfd.	814	282	.346
43.	**Kirk Muller**, N.J., Mtl.	790	281	.356
44.	**John MacLean**, N.J.	706	278	.394
45.	**Dale Hunter**, Que., Wsh.	1054	278	.264
46.	**Petr Klima**, Det., Edm., T.B.	626	275	.439
47.	**Geoff Courtnall**, Bos., Edm., Wsh., St.L., Van.	743	272	.366
48.	**Neal Broten**, Min., Dal.	955	266	.279
49.	**Jimmy Carson**, L.A., Edm., Det., Van.	577	265	.459
50.	**Eddie Olczyk**, Chi., Tor., Wpg., NYR	718	263	.366
51.	**Brian Mullen**, Wpg., NYR, S.J., NYI	832	260	.313
52.	**Thomas Steen**, Wpg.	919	259	.282
53.	**Steve Thomas**, Tor., Chi., NYI	620	258	.416
54.	**Sylvain Turgeon**, Hfd., N.J., Mtl., Ott.	636	258	.406
55.	**Pierre Turgeon**, Buf., NYI	543	256	.471
56.	**Mike Ridley**, NYR, Wsh.	706	256	.363
57.	**Ray Ferraro**, Hfd., NYI	711	251	.353
58.	**Phil Housley**, Buf., Wpg., St.L.	866	249	.288
59.	**Craig Simpson**, Pit., Edm., Buf.	610	243	.398
60.	**Greg Adams**, N.J., Van.	644	241	.374
61.	**Dan Quinn**, Cgy., Pit., Van., St.L., Phi., Min., Ott.	682	239	.350
62.	**Mike Krushelnyski**, Bos., Edm., L.A., Tor.	877	239	.273
63.	**Kevin Stevens**, Pit.	431	236	.548
64.	**Vincent Damphousse**, Tor., Edm., Mtl.	642	235	.366
65.	**Gary Roberts**, Cgy.	542	233	.430
66.	**Russ Courtnall**, Tor., Mtl., Min., Dal.	727	231	.318
67.	**Dave Gagner**, NYR, Min., Dal.	596	230	.386
68.	**Keith Acton**, Mtl., Min., Edm., Phi., Wsh., NYI	1023	226	.221
69.	**Jeremy Roenick**, Chi.	425	225	.529
70.	**Brendan Shanahan**, N.J., St.L.	513	224	.437
71.	**Kelly Kisio**, Det., NYR, S.J., Cgy.	749	222	.296
72.	**Guy Carbonneau**, Mtl.	912	221	.242
73.	**Murray Craven**, Det., Phi., Hfd., Van.	785	220	.280
74.	**Larry Murphy**, L.A., Wsh., Min., Pit.	1104	220	.199
75.	**Troy Murray**, Chi., Wpg., Ott.	806	219	.272
76.	**Claude Lemieux**, Mtl., N.J.	589	216	.367
77.	**Joe Sakic**, Que.	461	215	.466
78.	**Dirk Graham**, Min., Chi.	732	215	.294
79.	**Al MacInnis**, Cgy.	803	213	.265
80.	**Gerard Gallant**, Det., T.B.	614	211	.344
81.	**Mark Osborne**, Det., NYR, Tor., Wpg.	882	211	.239
82.	**Ray Sheppard**, Buf., NYR, Det.	444	208	.468

Michel Goulet's 548 goals rank fourth among active NHLers.

	Player	Games	Goals	Goals per game
83.	**Wendel Clark**, Tor.	463	208	.449
84.	**Mark Recchi**, Pit., Phi.	415	207	.499
85.	**Theoren Fleury**, Cgy.	441	203	.460
86.	**Craig MacTavish**, Bos., Edm., NYR	930	203	.218
87.	**Esa Tikkanen**, Edm., NYR	620	202	.326
88.	**Dave Poulin**, Phi., Bos., Wsh.	695	201	.289
89.	**Mike McPhee**, Mtl., Min., Dal.	744	200	.269
90.	**Adam Oates**, Det., St.L., Bos.	628	199	.317
91.	**Gary Leeman**, Tor., Cgy., Mtl.	655	197	.301
92.	**Mark Howe**, Hfd., Phi., Det.	911	196	.215
93.	**Alexander Mogilny**, Buf.	337	192	.570
94.	**Ulf Dahlen**, NYR, Min., Dal., S.J.	508	190	.374
95.	**Peter Zezel**, Phi., St.L., Wsh., Tor.	662	190	.287
96.	**Greg Paslawski**, Mtl., St.L., Wpg., Buf., Que., Phi., Cgy.	650	187	.288
97.	**Ron Sutter**, Phi., St.L., Que.	755	183	.242
98.	**Trevor Linden**, Van.	481	180	.374
99.	**Gaetan Duchesne**, Wsh., Que., Min., S.J.	982	176	.179
100.	**Mike Modano**, Min., Dal.	393	173	.440

Top 100 All-Time Assist Leaders

* active player

(figures in parentheses indicate ranking of top 10 in order of assists per game)

	Player	Seasons	Games	Assists	Assists per game
*1.	**Wayne Gretzky**, Edm., L.A.	15	1125	**1655**	1.471 (1)
2.	**Gordie Howe**, Det., Hfd.	26	1767	**1049**	.594
3.	**Marcel Dionne**, Det., L.A., NYR	18	1348	**1040**	.772
*4.	**Paul Coffey**, Edm., Pit., L.A., Det.	14	1033	**934**	.904 (5)
5.	**Stan Mikita**, Chi.	22	1394	**926**	.664
*6.	**Bryan Trottier**, NYI, Pit.	18	1279	**901**	.704
*7.	**Ray Bourque**, Bos.	15	1100	**877**	.797 (8)
8.	**Phil Esposito**, Chi., Bos., NYR	18	1282	**873**	.681
9.	**Bobby Clarke**, Phi.	15	1144	**852**	.745
*10.	**Mark Messier**, Edm., NYR	15	1081	**838**	.775
11.	**Alex Delvecchio**, Det.	24	1549	**825**	.533
*12.	**Dale Hawerchuk**, Wpg., Buf.	13	1032	**814**	.789 (9)
13.	**Gilbert Perreault**, Buf.	17	1191	**814**	.683
14.	**John Bucyk**, Det., Bos.	23	1540	**813**	.528
*15.	**Denis Savard**, Chi., Mtl., T.B.	14	1020	**797**	.781(10)
16.	**Guy Lafleur**, Mtl., NYR, Que.	17	1126	**793**	.704
*17.	**Peter Stastny**, Que., N.J., St.L.	14	971	**788**	.812 (6)
18.	**Jean Ratelle**, NYR, Bos.	21	1281	**776**	.606
19.	**Bernie Federko**, St.L., Det.	14	1000	**761**	.761
20.	**Larry Robinson**, Mtl., L.A.	20	1384	**750**	.542
21.	**Denis Potvin**, NYI.	15	1060	**742**	.700
*22.	**Ron Francis**, Hfd., Pit.	13	964	**741**	.769
23.	**Norm Ullman**, Det., Tor.	20	1410	**739**	.524
*24.	**Mario Lemieux**, Pit.	10	599	**717**	1.197 (2)
*25.	**Jari Kurri**, Edm., L.A.	13	990	**712**	.719
26.	**Jean Beliveau**, Mtl.	20	1125	**712**	.633
27.	**Henri Richard**, Mtl.	20	1256	**688**	.548
*28.	**Larry Murphy**, L.A., Wsh., Min., Pit.	14	1104	**687**	.622
29.	**Brad Park**, NYR, Bos., Det.	17	1113	**683**	.614
30.	**Bobby Smith**, Min., Mtl.	15	1077	**679**	.630
*31.	**Steve Yzerman**, Det.	11	815	**653**	.801 (7)
32.	**Bobby Orr**, Bos., Chi.	12	657	**645**	.982 (3)
33.	**Dave Taylor**, L.A.	17	1111	**638**	.574
34.	**Darryl Sittler**, Tor., Phi., Det.	15	1096	**637**	.581
35.	**Borje Salming**, Tor., Det.	17	1148	**637**	.555
*36.	**Doug Gilmour**, St.L., Cgy., Tor.	11	856	**632**	.738
37.	**Andy Bathgate**, NYR, Tor., Det., Pit.	17	1069	**624**	.584
38.	**Rod Gilbert**, NYR	18	1065	**615**	.577
*39.	**Al MacInnis**, Cgy.	13	803	**609**	.758
*40.	**Bernie Nicholls**, L.A., NYR, Edm., N.J.	13	885	**607**	.686
*41.	**Michel Goulet**, Que., Chi.	15	1089	**604**	.555
*42.	**Dale Hunter**, Que., Wsh.	14	1054	**599**	.568
*43.	**Phil Housley**, Buf., Wpg., St.L.	12	866	**590**	.681
44.	**Doug Wilson**, Chi., S.J.	16	1024	**590**	.576
45.	**Dave Keon**, Tor., Hfd.	18	1296	**590**	.455
*46.	**Neal Broten**, Min., Dal.	14	955	**582**	.609
*47.	**Brian Propp**, Phi., Bos., Min., Hfd.	15	1016	**579**	.570
*48.	**Glenn Anderson**, Edm., Tor., NYR	14	1061	**579**	.546
*49.	**Adam Oates**, Det., St.L., Bos.	9	628	**570**	.908 (4)
50.	**Frank Mahovlich**, Tor., Det., Mtl.	18	1181	**570**	.483
51.	**Bobby Hull**, Chi., Wpg., Hfd.	16	1063	**560**	.527
*52.	**Steve Larmer**, Chi., NYR.	14	959	**556**	.580
*53.	**Mike Gartner**, Wsh., Min., NYR, Tor.	15	1170	**554**	.474
54.	**Mike Bossy**, NYI.	10	752	**553**	.735
55.	**Ken Linseman**, Phi., Edm., Bos., Tor.	14	860	**551**	.641
56.	**Tom Lysiak**, Atl., Chi.	13	919	**551**	.600
*57.	**Thomas Steen**, Wpg.	13	919	**543**	.591
58.	**Red Kelly**, Det., Tor.	20	1316	**542**	.412
*59.	**Mark Howe**, Hfd., Phi., Det.	15	911	**540**	.593
60.	**Rick Middleton**, NYR, Bos.	14	1005	**540**	.537
*61.	**Scott Stevens**, Wsh., St.L., N.J.	12	911	**522**	.573
62.	**Dennis Maruk**, Cal., Cle., Wsh., Min.	13	882	**521**	.591
*63.	**Joey Mullen**, St.L., Cgy., Pit.	14	926	**518**	.559
64.	**Wayne Cashman**, Bos.	17	1027	**516**	.502
65.	**Butch Goring**, L.A., NYI, Bos.	16	1107	**513**	.463
*66.	**Dave Babych**, Wpg., Hfd., Van.	14	930	**512**	.551
67.	**John Tonelli**, NYI, Cgy., L.A., Chi., Que.	14	1028	**511**	.497
68.	**Lanny McDonald**, Tor., Col., Cgy.	16	1111	**506**	.455
69.	**Ivan Boldirev**, Bos., Cal., Chi., Atl., Van., Det.	15	1052	**505**	.480
*70.	**Dino Ciccarelli**, Min., Wsh., Det.	14	973	**501**	.515
71.	**Randy Carlyle**, Tor., Pit., Wpg.	17	1055	**499**	.473
72.	**Peter Mahovlich**, Det., Mtl., Pit.	16	884	**485**	.549
73.	**Pit Martin**, Det., Bos., Chi., Van.	17	1101	**485**	.441
*74.	**Dave Andreychuk**, Buf., Tor.	12	877	**482**	.550
75.	**Ken Hodge**, Chi., Bos., NYR	13	881	**472**	.536
76.	**Ted Lindsay**, Det., Chi.	17	1068	**472**	.442
77.	**Jacques Lemaire**, Mtl.	12	853	**469**	.550

From his office on the blueline in New York, Boston and Detroit, Brad Park set-up his teammates 683 times in his 17 NHL seasons.

	Player	Seasons	Games	Assists	Assists per game
78.	**Dean Prentice**, NYR, Bos., Det., Pit., Min.	22	1378	**469**	.340
*79.	**Kirk Muller**, N.J., Mtl.	10	790	**467**	.591
80.	**Phil Goyette**, Mtl., NYR, St.L., Buf.	16	941	**467**	.496
*81.	**Brian Bellows**, Min., Mtl.	12	912	**466**	.511
82.	**Bill Barber**, Phi.	12	903	**463**	.513
83.	**Reed Larson**, Det., Bos., Edm., NYI, Min., Buf.	14	904	**463**	.512
84.	**Doug Mohns**, Bos., Chi., Min., Atl., Wsh.	22	1390	**462**	.332
85.	**Bobby Rousseau**, Mtl., Min., NYR.	15	942	**458**	.486
86.	**Wilf Paiement**, K.C., Col., Tor., Que., NYR, Buf., Pit.	14	946	**458**	.484
87.	**Murray Oliver**, Det., Bos., Tor., Min.	17	1127	**454**	.403
88.	**Doug Harvey**, Mtl., NYR, Det., St.L.	19	1113	**452**	.406
89.	**Guy Lapointe**, Mtl., St.L., Bos.	16	884	**451**	.510
90.	**Walt Tkachuk**, NYR.	14	945	**451**	.477
91.	**Peter McNab**, Buf., Bos., Van., N.J.	14	954	**450**	.472
92.	**Mel Bridgman**, Phi., Chi., N.J., Det., Van.	14	977	**449**	.460
*93.	**Gary Suter**, Cgy.	9	633	**440**	.695
*94.	**Chris Chelios**, Mtl., Chi.	11	719	**438**	.609
95.	**Bill Gadsby**, Chi., NYR, Det.	20	1248	**437**	.350
96.	**Yvan Cournoyer**, Mtl.	16	968	**435**	.449
*97.	**Pat LaFontaine**, NYI, Buf.	11	687	**434**	.632
*98.	**Dave Christian**, Wpg., Wsh., Bos., St.L., Chi.	15	1009	**433**	.429
99.	**Ron Greschner**, NYR.	16	982	**431**	.439
100.	**Bernie Geoffrion**, Mtl., NYR.	16	883	**429**	.486

Top 100 Active Assist Leaders

	Player	Games	Assists	Assists per game
1.	**Wayne Gretzky**, Edm., L.A.	1125	**1655**	1.471
2.	**Paul Coffey**, Edm., Pit., L.A., Det.	1033	**934**	.904
3.	**Bryan Trottier**, NYI, Pit.	1279	**901**	.704
4.	**Ray Bourque**, Bos.	1100	**877**	.797
5.	**Mark Messier**, Edm., NYR	1081	**838**	.775
6.	**Dale Hawerchuk**, Wpg., Buf.	1032	**814**	.789
7.	**Denis Savard**, Chi., Mtl., T.B.	1020	**797**	.781
8.	**Peter Stastny**, Que., N.J., St.L.	971	**788**	.812
9.	**Ron Francis**, Hfd., Pit.	964	**741**	.769
10.	**Mario Lemieux**, Pit.	599	**717**	1.197
11.	**Jari Kurri**, Edm., L.A.	990	**712**	.719
12.	**Larry Murphy**, L.A., Wsh., Min., Pit.	1104	**687**	.622
13.	**Steve Yzerman**, Det.	815	**653**	.801
14.	**Dave Taylor**, L.A.	1111	**638**	.574
15.	**Doug Gilmour**, St.L., Cgy., Tor.	856	**632**	.738
16.	**Al MacInnis**, Cgy.	803	**609**	.758
17.	**Bernie Nicholls**, L.A., NYR, Edm., N.J.	885	**607**	.686
18.	**Michel Goulet**, Que., Chi.	1089	**604**	.555
19.	**Dale Hunter**, Que., Wsh.	1054	**599**	.568
20.	**Phil Housley**, Buf., Wpg., St.L.	866	**590**	.681
21.	**Neal Broten**, Min., Dal.	955	**582**	.609
22.	**Brian Propp**, Phi., Bos., Min., Hfd.	1016	**579**	.570
23.	**Glenn Anderson**, Edm., Tor., NYR	1061	**579**	.546
24.	**Adam Oates**, Det., St.L., Bos.	628	**570**	.908
25.	**Steve Larmer**, Chi., NYR	959	**556**	.580
26.	**Mike Gartner**, Wsh., Min., NYR, Tor.	1170	**554**	.474
27.	**Thomas Steen**, Wpg.	919	**543**	.591
28.	**Mark Howe**, Hfd., Phi., Det.	911	**540**	.593
29.	**Scott Stevens**, Wsh., St.L., N.J.	911	**522**	.573
30.	**Joe Mullen**, St.L., Cgy., Pit.	926	**518**	.559
31.	**Dave Babych**, Wpg., Hfd., Van.	930	**512**	.551
32.	**Dino Ciccarelli**, Min., Wsh., Det.	973	**501**	.515
33.	**Dave Andreychuk**, Buf., Tor.	877	**482**	.550
34.	**Kirk Muller**, N.J., Mtl.	790	**467**	.591
35.	**Brian Bellows**, Min., Mtl.	912	**466**	.511
36.	**Gary Suter**, Cgy., Chi.	633	**440**	.695
37.	**Chris Chelios**, Mtl., Chi.	719	**438**	.609
38.	**Pat LaFontaine**, NYI, Buf.	687	**434**	.632
39.	**Dave Christian**, Wpg., Wsh., Bos., St.L., Chi.	1009	**433**	.429
40.	**Kelly Kisio**, Det., NYR, S.J., Cgy.	749	**425**	.567
41.	**Rob Ramage**, Colorado, St.L., Cgy., Tor., Min., T.B., Mtl., Phi.	1044	**425**	.407
42.	**Brent Sutter**, NYI, Chi.	893	**418**	.468
43.	**Luc Robitaille**, L.A.	640	**411**	.642
44.	**Murray Craven**, Det., Phi., Hfd., Van.	785	**405**	.516
45.	**Mike Ridley**, NYR, Wsh.	706	**392**	.555
46.	**James Patrick**, NYR, Hfd., Cgy.	733	**385**	.525
47.	**Pierre Turgeon**, Buf., NYI	543	**380**	.700
48.	**Craig Janney**, Bos., St.L.	440	**378**	.859
49.	**Mike Foligno**, Det., Buf., Tor., Fla.	1018	**372**	.365
50.	**Vincent Damphousse**, Tor., Edm., Mtl.	642	**371**	.578
51.	**Dan Quinn**, Cgy., Pit., Van., St.L., Phi., Min., Ott.	682	**367**	.538
52.	**Eddie Olczyk**, Chi., Tor., Wpg., NYR	718	**363**	.506
53.	**Brian Mullen**, Wpg., NYR, S.J., NYI	832	**362**	.435
54.	**Bob Carpenter**, Wsh., NYR, L.A., Bos., N.J.	901	**360**	.400
55.	**Doug Crossman**, Chi., Phi., L.A., NYI, Hfd., Det., T.B., St.L.	914	**359**	.393
56.	**Gordie Roberts**, Hfd., Min., Phi., St.L., Pit., Bos.	1097	**359**	.327
57.	**Keith Acton**, Mtl., Min., Edm., Phi., Wsh., NYI	1023	**358**	.350
58.	**Tomas Sandstrom**, NYR, L.A., Pit.	669	**355**	.531
59.	**Pat Verbeek**, N.J., Hfd.	867	**351**	.405
60.	**Rick Tocchet**, Phi., Pit.	681	**350**	.514
61.	**Joe Sakic**, Que.	461	**349**	.757
62.	**John Anderson**, Tor., Que., Hfd.	814	**349**	.429
63.	**Mike Bullard**, Pit., Cgy., St.L., Phi., Tor.	727	**345**	.475
64.	**Brent Ashton**, Van., Colorado, N.J., Min., Que., Det., Wpg., Bos., Cgy.	998	**345**	.346
65.	**Charlie Huddy**, Edm., L.A.	911	**344**	.378
66.	**Brian Leetch**, NYR	437	**343**	.785
67.	**Doug Bodger**, Pit., Buf.	718	**343**	.478
68.	**Russ Courtnall**, Tor., Mtl., Min., Dal.	727	**341**	.469
69.	**Dave Ellett**, Wpg., Tor.	752	**337**	.448
70.	**Jeff Brown**, Que., St.L., Van.	577	**336**	.582
71.	**Peter Zezel**, Phi., St.L., Wsh., Tor.	662	**336**	.508
72.	**Per-Erik Eklund**, Phi., Dal.	594	**335**	.564
73.	**Troy Murray**, Chi., Wpg., Ott.	806	**328**	.407
74.	**Guy Carbonneau**, Mtl.	912	**326**	.357
75.	**Tom Kurvers**, Mtl., Buf., N.J., Tor., Van., NYI	637	**325**	.510
76.	**Mike Krushelnyski**, Bos., Edm., L.A., Tor.	877	**325**	.371
77.	**Kevin Lowe**, Edm., NYR	1086	**322**	.297
78.	**Dave Poulin**, Phi., Bos., Wsh.	695	**320**	.460

The prototypical offensive defenseman, Paul Coffey has recorded 934 assists in 14 NHL seasons.

	Player	Games	Assists	Assists per game
79.	**Geoff Courtnall**, Bos., Edm., Wsh., St.L., Van.	743	**318**	.428
80.	**Steve Duchesne**, L.A., Phi., Que., St.L.	578	**316**	.547
81.	**Mark Osborne**, Det., NYR, Tor., Wpg.	882	**316**	.358
82.	**Kevin Dineen**, Hfd., Phi.	707	**313**	.443
83.	**Brad McCrimmon**, Bos., Phi., Cgy., Det., Hfd.	1094	**310**	.283
84.	**Mark Hardy**, L.A., NYR, Min.	915	**306**	.334
85.	**Bruce Driver**, N.J.	661	**304**	.460
86.	**Mark Recchi**, Pit., Phi.	415	**302**	.728
87.	**Michal Pivonka**, Wsh.	583	**302**	.518
88.	**Pat Flatley**, NYI	611	**299**	.489
89.	**Esa Tikkanen**, Edm., NYR	620	**295**	.476
90.	**Ray Ferraro**, Hfd., NYI	711	**295**	.415
91.	**Al Iafrate**, Tor., Wsh., Bos.	740	**295**	.399
92.	**Steve Thomas**, Tor., Chi., NYI	620	**293**	.473
93.	**Garry Galley**, L.A., Wsh., Bos., Phi.	693	**292**	.421
94.	**Ron Sutter**, Phi., St.L., Que.	755	**289**	.383
95.	**Brett Hull**, Cgy., St.L.	540	**287**	.531
96.	**Christian Ruuttu**, Buf., Chi.	576	**287**	.498
97.	**John MacLean**, N.J.	706	**281**	.398
98.	**Kevin Hatcher**, Wsh.	685	**277**	.404
99.	**Jimmy Carson**, L.A., Edm., Det., Van.	577	**276**	.478
100.	**Stephane Richer**, Mtl., N.J.	645	**274**	.425

Top 100 All-Time Point Leaders

* active player

(figures in parentheses indicate ranking of top 10 by points per game)

The first defenceman in NHL history to reach the 1,000-point plateau, Denis Potvin's career total of 1,052 career points rank him 34th among the NHL's all-time leading scorers.

Player	Seasons	Games	Goals	Assists	Points	Points per game
*1. **Wayne Gretzky**, Edm., L.A.	15	1125	803	1655	**2458**	2.185 (1)
2. **Gordie Howe**, Det., Hfd.	26	1767	801	1049	**1850**	1.047
3. **Marcel Dionne**, Det., L.A., NYR	18	1348	731	1040	**1771**	1.314 (6)
4. **Phil Esposito**, Chi., Bos., NYR	18	1282	717	873	**1590**	1.240
5. **Stan Mikita**, Chi.	22	1394	541	926	**1467**	1.052
*6. **Bryan Trottier**, NYI, Pit.	18	1279	524	901	**1425**	1.114
7. **John Bucyk**, Det., Bos.	23	1540	556	813	**1369**	.889
8. **Guy Lafleur**, Mtl., NYR, Que.	17	1126	560	793	**1353**	1.202
9. **Gilbert Perreault**, Buf.	17	1191	512	814	**1326**	1.113
*10. **Mark Messier**, Edm., NYR	15	1081	478	838	**1316**	1.217
*11. **Dale Hawerchuk**, Wpg., Buf.	13	1032	484	814	**1298**	1.258 (9)
12. **Alex Delvecchio**, Det.	24	1549	456	825	**1281**	.827
*13. **Paul Coffey**, Edm., Pit., L.A., Det.	14	1033	344	934	**1278**	1.237
*14. **Jari Kurri**, Edm., L.A.	13	990	555	712	**1267**	1.280 (7)
15. **Jean Ratelle**, NYR, Bos.	21	1281	491	776	**1267**	.989
16. **Denis Savard**, Chi., Mtl., T.B.	14	1020	441	797	**1238**	1.214
*17. **Peter Stastny**, Que., N.J., St.L.	14	971	449	788	**1237**	1.274 (8)
18. **Norm Ullman**, Det., Tor.	20	1410	490	739	**1229**	.872
19. **Jean Beliveau**, Mtl.	20	1125	507	712	**1219**	1.084
*20. **Mario Lemieux**, Pit.	10	599	494	717	**1211**	2.022 (2)
21. **Bobby Clarke**, Phi.	15	1144	358	852	**1210**	1.058
*22. **Ray Bourque**, Bos.	15	1100	311	877	**1188**	1.080
*23. **Mike Gartner**, Wsh., Min., NYR, Tor.	15	1170	617	554	**1171**	1.001
24. **Bobby Hull**, Chi., Wpg., Hfd.	16	1063	610	560	**1170**	1.101
*25. **Michel Goulet**, Que., Chi.	15	1089	548	604	**1152**	1.058
26. **Bernie Federko**, St.L., Det.	14	1000	369	761	**1130**	1.130
27. **Mike Bossy**, NYI	10	752	573	553	**1126**	1.497 (3)
*28. **Steve Yzerman**, Det.	11	815	469	653	**1122**	1.377 (5)
29. **Darryl Sittler**, Tor., Phi., Det.	15	1096	484	637	**1121**	1.023
30. **Frank Mahovlich**, Tor., Det., Mtl.	18	1181	533	570	**1103**	.934
*31. **Ron Francis**, Hfd., Pit.	13	964	338	741	**1079**	1.119
*32. **Dave Taylor**, L.A.	17	1111	431	638	**1069**	.962
*33. **Glenn Anderson**, Edm., Tor., NYR	14	1061	480	579	**1059**	.998
34. **Denis Potvin**, NYI	15	1060	310	742	**1052**	.992
35. **Henri Richard**, Mtl.	20	1256	358	688	**1046**	.833
36. **Bobby Smith**, Min., Mtl.	15	1077	357	679	**1036**	.962
*37. **Bernie Nicholls**, L.A., NYR, Edm., N.J.	13	885	416	607	**1023**	1.156
38. **Rod Gilbert**, NYR	18	1065	406	615	**1021**	.959
*39. **Dino Ciccarelli**, Min., Wsh., Det.	14	973	513	501	**1014**	1.042
40. **Lanny McDonald**, Tor., Col., Cgy.	16	1111	500	506	**1006**	.905
*41. **Brian Propp**, Phi., Bos., Min., Hfd.	15	1016	425	579	**1004**	.988
*42. **Joey Mullen**, St.L., Cgy., Pit.	14	926	471	518	**989**	1.068
43. **Rick Middleton**, NYR, Bos.	14	1005	448	540	**988**	.983
44. **Dave Keon**, Tor., Hfd.	18	1296	396	590	**986**	.761
*45. **Steve Larmer**, Chi., NYR	14	959	427	556	**983**	1.025
46. **Andy Bathgate**, NYR, Tor., Det., Pit.	17	1069	349	624	**973**	.910
47. **Maurice Richard**, Mtl.	18	978	544	421	**965**	.987
48. **Larry Robinson**, Mtl., L.A.	20	1384	208	750	**958**	.692
*49. **Doug Gilmour**, St.L., Cgy., Tor.	11	856	304	632	**936**	1.093
50. **Bobby Orr**, Bos., Chi.	12	657	270	645	**915**	1.393 (4)
*51. **Dave Andreychuk**, Buf., Tor.	12	877	426	482	**908**	1.035
*52. **Larry Murphy**, L.A., Wsh., Min., Pit.	14	1104	220	687	**907**	.822
53. **Brad Park**, NYR, Bos., Det.	17	1113	213	683	**896**	.805
54. **Butch Goring**, L.A., NYI, Bos.	16	1107	375	513	**888**	.802
55. **Bill Barber**, Phi.	12	903	420	463	**883**	.978
*56. **Brian Bellows**, Min., Mtl.	12	912	415	466	**881**	.966
57. **Dennis Maruk**, Cal., Cle., Wsh., Min.	13	882	356	521	**877**	.994
*58. **Dale Hunter**, Que., Wsh.	14	1054	278	599	**877**	.832
59. **Ivan Boldirev**, Bos., Cal., Chi., Atl., Van., Det.	15	1052	361	505	**866**	.823
60. **Yvan Cournoyer**, Mtl.	16	968	428	435	**863**	.892
61. **Dean Prentice**, NYR, Bos., Det., Pit., Min.	22	1378	391	469	**860**	.624
62. **Ted Lindsay**, Det., Chi.	17	1068	379	472	**851**	.797
*63. **Neal Broten**, Min., Dal.	14	955	266	582	**848**	.888
64. **Tom Lysiak**, Atl., Chi.	13	919	292	551	**843**	.917
*65. **Phil Housley**, Buf., Wpg., St.L.	12	866	249	590	**839**	.969

Player	Seasons	Games	Goals	Assists	Points	Points per game
66. **John Tonelli**, NYI, Cgy., L.A., Chi., Que.	14	1028	325	511	**836**	.813
67. **Jacques Lemaire**, Mtl.	12	853	366	469	**835**	.979
68. **John Ogrodnick**, Det., Que., NYR	14	928	402	425	**827**	.891
69. **Doug Wilson**, Chi., S.J.	16	1024	237	590	**827**	.808
*70. **Pat LaFontaine**, NYI, Buf.	11	687	391	434	**825**	1.201
71. **Red Kelly**, Det., Tor.	20	1316	281	542	**823**	.625
*72. **Al MacInnis**, Cgy.	13	803	213	609	**822**	1.024
73. **Pierre Larouche**, Pit., Mtl., Hfd., NYR	14	812	395	427	**822**	1.012
74. **Bernie Geoffrion**, Mtl., NYR	16	883	393	429	**822**	.931
75. **Steve Shutt**, Mtl., L.A.	13	930	424	393	**817**	.878
76. **Wilf Paiment**, K.C., Col., Tor., Que., NYR, Buf., Pit.	14	946	356	458	**814**	.860
77. **Peter McNab**, Buf., Bos., Van., N.J.	14	954	363	450	**813**	.852
78. **Pit Martin**, Det., Bos., Chi., Van.	17	1101	324	485	**809**	.735
79. **Ken Linseman**, Phi., Edm., Bos., Tor.	14	860	256	551	**807**	.938
80. **Garry Unger**, Tor., Det., St.L., Atl., L.A., Edm.	16	1105	413	391	**804**	.728
*81. **Luc Robitaille**, L.A.	8	640	392	411	**803**	1.255 (10)
*82. **Thomas Steen**, Wpg.	13	919	259	543	**802**	.873
83. **Ken Hodge**, Chi., Bos., NYR	13	881	328	472	**800**	.908
84. **Wayne Cashman**, Bos.	17	1027	277	516	**793**	.772
85. **Rick Vaive**, Van., Tor., Chi., Buf.	13	876	441	347	**788**	.900
86. **Borje Salming**, Tor., Det.	17	1148	150	637	**787**	.686
*87. **Dave Christian**, Wpg., Wsh., Bos., St.L., Chi.	15	1009	340	443	**773**	.766
88. **Jean Pronovost**, Pit., Atl., Wsh.	14	998	391	383	**774**	.776
89. **Peter Mahovlich**, Det., Mtl., Pit.	16	884	288	485	**773**	.874
*90. **Adam Oates**, Det., St.L., Bos.	9	628	199	570	**769**	1.225
91. **Rick Kehoe**, Tor., Pit.	14	906	371	396	**767**	.847
92. **Rick MacLeish**, Phi., Hfd., Pit., Det.	14	846	349	410	**759**	.897
*93. **Brent Sutter**, NYI, Chi.	14	893	334	418	**752**	.842
*94. **Kirk Muller**, N.J., Mtl.	10	790	281	467	**748**	.947
*95. **Mark Howe**, Hfd., Phi., Det.	15	911	196	540	**736**	.808
96. **Murray Oliver**, Det., Bos., Tor., Min.	17	1127	274	454	**728**	.646
*97. **Mike Foligno**, Det., Buf., Tor., Fla.	15	1018	355	372	**727**	.714
98. **Bob Nevin**, Tor., NYR, Min., L.A.	18	1128	307	419	**726**	.644
99. **George Armstrong**, Tor.	21	1187	296	417	**713**	.601
100. **Vic Hadfield**, NYR, Pit.	16	1002	323	389	**712**	.711

Top 100 Active Point Leaders

	Player	Games	Goals	Assists	Points	Points per game
1.	**Wayne Gretzky**, Edm., L.A.	1125	803	1655	**2458**	2.185
2.	**Bryan Trottier**, NYI, Pit.	1279	524	901	**1425**	1.114
3.	**Mark Messier**, Edm., NYR	1081	478	838	**1316**	1.217
4.	**Dale Hawerchuk**, Wpg., Buf.	1032	484	814	**1298**	1.258
5.	**Paul Coffey**, Edm., Pit., L.A., Det.	1033	344	934	**1278**	1.237
6.	**Jari Kurri**, Edm., L.A.	990	555	712	**1267**	1.280
7.	**Denis Savard**, Chi., Mtl., T.B.	1020	441	797	**1238**	1.214
8.	**Peter Stastny**, Que., N.J., St.L.	971	449	788	**1237**	1.274
9.	**Mario Lemieux**, Pit.	599	494	717	**1211**	2.022
10.	**Ray Bourque**, Bos.	1100	311	877	**1188**	1.080
11.	**Mike Gartner**, Wsh., Min., NYR, Tor.	1170	617	554	**1171**	1.001
12.	**Michel Goulet**, Que., Chi.	1089	548	604	**1152**	1.058
13.	**Steve Yzerman**, Det.	815	469	653	**1122**	1.377
14.	**Ron Francis**, Hfd., Pit.	964	338	741	**1079**	1.119
15.	**Dave Taylor**, L.A.	1111	431	638	**1069**	.962
16.	**Glenn Anderson**, Edm., Tor., NYR	1061	480	579	**1059**	.998
17.	**Bernie Nicholls**, L.A., NYR, Edm., N.J.	885	416	607	**1023**	1.156
18.	**Dino Ciccarelli**, Min., Wsh., Det.	973	513	501	**1014**	1.042
19.	**Brian Propp**, Phi., Bos., Min., Hfd.	1016	425	579	**1004**	.988
20.	**Joe Mullen**, St.L., Cgy., Pit.	926	471	518	**989**	1.068
21.	**Steve Larmer**, Chi., NYR	959	427	556	**983**	1.025
22.	**Doug Gilmour**, St.L., Cgy., Tor.	856	304	632	**936**	1.093
23.	**Dave Andreychuk**, Buf., Tor.	877	426	482	**908**	1.035
24.	**Larry Murphy**, L.A., Wsh., Min., Pit.	1104	220	687	**907**	.822
25.	**Brian Bellows**, Min., Mtl.	912	415	466	**881**	.966
26.	**Dale Hunter**, Que., Wsh.	1054	278	599	**877**	.832
27.	**Neal Broten**, Min., Dal.	955	266	582	**848**	.888
28.	**Phil Housley**, Buf., Wpg., St.L.	866	249	590	**839**	.969
29.	**Pat LaFontaine**, NYI, Buf.	687	391	434	**825**	1.201
30.	**Al MacInnis**, Cgy.	803	213	609	**822**	1.024
31.	**Luc Robitaille**, L.A.	640	392	411	**803**	1.255
32.	**Thomas Steen**, Wpg.	919	259	543	**802**	.873
33.	**Dave Christian**, Wpg., Wsh., Bos., St.L., Chi.	1009	340	433	**773**	.766
34.	**Adam Oates**, Det., St.L., Bos.	628	199	570	**769**	1.225
35.	**Brent Sutter**, NYI, Chi.	893	334	418	**752**	.842
36.	**Kirk Muller**, N.J., Mtl.	790	281	467	**748**	.947
37.	**Mark Howe**, Hfd., Phi., Det.	911	196	540	**736**	.808
38.	**Mike Foligno**, Det., Buf., Tor., Fla.	1018	355	372	**727**	.714
39.	**Pat Verbeek**, N.J., Hfd.	867	355	351	**706**	.814
40.	**Brett Hull**, Cgy., St.L.	540	413	287	**700**	1.296
41.	**Mike Bullard**, Pit., Cgy., St.L., Phi., Tor.	727	329	345	**674**	.927
42.	**Scott Stevens**, Wsh., St.L., N.J.	911	150	522	**672**	.738
43.	**Bob Carpenter**, Wsh., NYR, L.A., Bos., N.J.	901	295	360	**655**	.727
44.	**Tomas Sandstrom**, NYR, L.A., Pit.	669	296	355	**651**	.973
45.	**Mike Ridley**, NYR, Wsh.	706	256	392	**648**	.918
46.	**Kelly Kisio**, Det., NYR, S.J., Cgy.	749	222	425	**647**	.864
47.	**Rick Tocchet**, Phi., Pit.	681	291	350	**641**	.941
48.	**Dave Babych**, Wpg., Hfd., Van.	930	129	512	**641**	.689
49.	**Pierre Turgeon**, Buf., NYI	543	256	380	**636**	1.171
50.	**John Anderson**, Tor., Que., Hfd.	814	282	349	**631**	.775
51.	**Brent Ashton**, Van., Colorado, N.J., Min., Que., Det., Wpg., Bos., Cgy.	998	284	345	**629**	.630
52.	**Eddie Olczyk**, Chi., Tor., Wpg., NYR	718	263	363	**626**	.872
53.	**Murray Craven**, Det., Phi., Hfd., Van.	785	220	405	**625**	.796
54.	**Brian Mullen**, Wpg., NYR, S.J., NYI	832	260	362	**622**	.748
55.	**Cam Neely**, Van., Bos.	635	342	265	**607**	.956
56.	**Kevin Dineen**, Hfd., Phi.	707	294	313	**607**	.859
57.	**Vincent Damphousse**, Tor., Edm., Mtl.	642	235	371	**606**	.944
58.	**Dan Quinn**, Cgy., Pit., Van., St.L., Phi., Min., Ott.	682	239	367	**606**	.889
59.	**Geoff Courtnall**, Bos., Edm., Wsh., St.L., Van.	743	272	318	**590**	.794
60.	**Keith Acton**, Mtl., Min., Edm., Phi., Wsh., NYI	1023	226	358	**584**	.571
61.	**Stephane Richer**, Mtl., N.J.	645	301	274	**575**	.891
62.	**Russ Courtnall**, Tor., Mtl., Min., Dal.	727	231	341	**572**	.787
63.	**Gary Suter**, Cgy., Chi.	633	130	440	**570**	.900
64.	**Joe Nieuwendyk**, Cgy.	531	293	273	**566**	1.066
65.	**Joe Sakic**, Que.	461	215	349	**564**	1.223
66.	**Mike Krushelnyski**, Bos., Edm., L.A., Tor.	877	239	325	**564**	.643
67.	**Rob Ramage**, Colorado, St.L., Cgy., Tor., Min., T.B., Mtl., Phi.	1044	139	425	**564**	.540
68.	**Chris Chelios**, Mtl., Chi.	719	124	438	**562**	.782
69.	**Tony Tanti**, Chi., Van., Pit., Buf.	697	287	273	**560**	.803
70.	**John MacLean**, N.J.	706	278	281	**559**	.792
71.	**Steve Thomas**, Tor., Chi., NYI	620	258	293	**551**	.889
72.	**Troy Murray**, Chi., Wpg., Ott.	806	219	328	**547**	.679
73.	**Guy Carbonneau**, Mtl.	912	221	326	**547**	.600
74.	**Ray Ferraro**, Hfd., NYI	711	251	295	**546**	.768
75.	**Jimmy Carson**, L.A., Edm., Det., Van.	577	265	276	**541**	.938

Boston's Ray Bourque is the tenth-leading scorer and the second highest scoring defenseman among active NHLers.

	Player	Games	Goals	Assists	Points	Points per game
76.	**Mark Osborne**, Det., NYR, Tor., Wpg.	882	211	316	**527**	.598
77.	**Peter Zezel**, Phi., St.L., Wsh., Tor.	662	190	336	**526**	.795
78.	**Dave Poulin**, Phi., Bos., Wsh.	695	201	320	**521**	.750
79.	**Mark Recchi**, Pit., Phi.	415	207	302	**509**	1.227
80.	**Craig Janney**, Bos., St.L.	440	131	378	**509**	1.157
81.	**Kevin Stevens**, Pit.	431	236	264	**500**	1.160
82.	**Greg Adams**, N.J., Van.	644	241	258	**499**	.775
83.	**James Patrick**, NYR, Hfd., Cgy.	733	114	385	**499**	.681
84.	**Esa Tikkanen**, Edm., NYR	620	202	295	**497**	.802
85.	**Jeremy Roenick**, Chi.	425	225	270	**495**	1.165
86.	**Dave Gagner**, NYR, Min., Dal.	596	230	262	**492**	.826
87.	**Craig Simpson**, Pit., Edm., Buf.	610	243	243	**486**	.797
88.	**Gerard Gallant**, Det., T.B.	614	211	269	**480**	.782
89.	**Petr Klima**, Det., Edm., T.B.	626	275	205	**480**	.767
90.	**Brendan Shanahan**, N.J., St.L.	513	224	255	**479**	.934
91.	**Sylvain Turgeon**, Hfd., N.J., Mtl., Ott.	636	258	218	**476**	.748
92.	**Dirk Graham**, Min., Chi.	732	215	261	**476**	.650
93.	**Ron Sutter**, Phi., St.L., Que.	755	183	289	**472**	.625
94.	**Dave Ellett**, Wpg., Tor.	752	134	337	**471**	.626
95.	**Jeff Brown**, Que., St.L., Van.	577	134	336	**470**	.815
96.	**Doug Crossman**, Chi., Phi., L.A., NYI, Hfd., Det., T.B., St.L.	914	105	359	**464**	.508
97.	**Gary Leeman**, Tor., Cgy., Mtl.	655	197	266	**463**	.707
98.	**Theoren Fleury**, Cgy.	441	203	259	**462**	1.048
99.	**Steve Duchesne**, L.A., Phi., Que., St.L.	578	145	316	**461**	.798
100.	**Gary Roberts**, Cgy.	542	233	226	**459**	.847

All-Time Games Played Leaders

Regular Season

* active player

	Player	Team	Seasons	GP
1.	Gordie Howe	Detroit	25	1,687
		Hartford	1	80
		Total	**26**	**1,767**
2.	Alex Delvecchio	Detroit	24	1,549
3.	John Bucyk	Detroit	2	104
		Boston	21	1,436
		Total	**23**	**1,540**
4.	Tim Horton	Toronto	19¾	1,185
		NY Rangers	1¼	93
		Pittsburgh	1	44
		Buffalo	2	124
		Total	**24**	**1,446**
5.	Harry Howell	NY Rangers	17	1,160
		California	1½	83
		Los Angeles	2½	168
		Total	**21**	**1,411**
6.	Norm Ullman	Detroit	12½	875
		Toronto	7½	535
		Total	**20**	**1,410**
7.	Stan Mikita	Chicago	22	1,394
8.	Doug Mohns	Boston	11	710
		Chicago	6½	415
		Minnesota	2½	162
		Atlanta	1	28
		Washington	1	75
		Total	**22**	**1,390**
9.	Larry Robinson	Montreal	17	1,202
		Los Angeles	3	182
		Total	**20**	**1,384**
10.	Dean Prentice	NY Rangers	10½	666
		Boston	3	170
		Detroit	3½	230
		Pittsburgh	2	144
		Minnesota	3	168
		Total	**22**	**1,378**
11.	Ron Stewart	Toronto	13	838
		Boston	2	126
		St. Louis	½	19
		NY Rangers	4	306
		Vancouver	1	42
		NY Islanders	½	22
		Total	**21**	**1,353**
12.	Marcel Dionne	Detroit	4	309
		Los Angeles	11¾	921
		NY Rangers	2¼	118
		Total	**18**	**1,348**
13.	Red Kelly	Detroit	12½	846
		Toronto	7½	470
		Total	**20**	**1,316**
14.	Dave Keon	Toronto	15	1,062
		Hartford	3	234
		Total	**18**	**1,296**
15.	Phil Esposito	Chicago	4	235
		Boston	8¼	625
		NY Rangers	5¾	422
		Total	**18**	**1,282**
16.	Jean Ratelle	NY Rangers	15¼	862
		Boston	5¾	419
		Total	**21**	**1,281**
*17.	Bryan Trottier	NY Islanders	15	1,123
		Pittsburgh	3	156
		Total	**18**	**1,279**
18.	Henri Richard	Montreal	20	1,256
19.	Bill Gadsby	Chicago	8½	468
		NY Rangers	6½	457
		Detroit	5	323
		Total	**20**	**1,248**
20.	Allan Stanley	NY Rangers	6¼	307
		Chicago	1¾	111
		Boston	2	129
		Toronto	9	633
		Philadelphia	1	64
		Total	**21**	**1,244**
21.	Eddie Westfall	Boston	11	734
		NY Islanders	7	493
		Total	**18**	**1,227**
22.	Eric Nesterenko	Toronto	5	206
		Chicago	16	1,013
		Total	**21**	**1,219**
23.	Marcel Pronovost	Detroit	16	983
		Toronto	5	223
		Total	**21**	**1,206**
24.	Gilbert Perreault	Buffalo	17	1,191
25.	George Armstrong	Toronto	21	1,187
26.	Frank Mahovlich	Toronto	11¾	720
		Detroit	2¾	198
		Montreal	3½	263
		Total	**18**	**1,181**

	Player	Team	Seasons	GP
27.	Don Marshall	Montreal	10	585
		NY Rangers	7	479
		Buffalo	1	62
		Toronto	1	50
		Total	**19**	**1,176**
*28.	Mike Gartner	Washington	9¾	758
		Minnesota	1	80
		NY Rangers	4	251
		Toronto	¼	10
		Total	**15**	**1,170**
29.	Bob Gainey	Montreal	16	1,160
30.	Leo Boivin	Toronto	3¼	137
		Boston	11½	717
		Detroit	1¼	85
		Pittsburgh	1½	114
		Minnesota	1½	97
		Total	**19**	**1,150**
31.	Borje Salming	Toronto	16	1,099
		Detroit	1	49
		Total	**17**	**1,148**
32.	Bobby Clarke	Philadelphia	15	1,144
33.	Bob Nevin	Toronto	5¾	250
		NY Rangers	7¼	505
		Minnesota	2	138
		Los Angeles	3	235
		Total	**18**	**1,128**
34.	Murray Oliver	Detroit	2½	101
		Boston	6½	429
		Toronto	3	226
		Minnesota	5	371
		Total	**17**	**1,127**
35.	Guy Lafleur	Montreal	14	961
		NY Rangers	1	67
		Quebec	2	98
		Total	**17**	**1,126**
36.	Jean Beliveau	Montreal	20	1,125
*37.	Wayne Gretzky	Edmonton	9	696
		Los Angeles	6	429
		Total	**15**	**1,125**
38.	Doug Harvey	Montreal	14	890
		NY Rangers	3	151
		Detroit	1	2
		St. Louis	1	70
		Total	**19**	**1,113**

	Player	Team	Seasons	GP
39.	Brad Park	NY Rangers	7½	465
		Boston	7½	501
		Detroit	2	147
		Total	**17**	**1,113**
40.	Lanny McDonald	Toronto	6½	477
		Colorado	1¾	142
		Calgary	7¾	441
		Total	**16**	**1,111**
41.	Dave Taylor	Los Angeles	17	1,111
42.	Butch Goring	Los Angeles	10¾	736
		NY Islanders	4¾	332
		Boston	½	39
		Total	**16**	**1,107**
43.	Garry Unger	Toronto	½	15
		Detroit	3	216
		St. Louis	8½	662
		Atlanta	1	79
		Los Angeles	¾	58
		Edmonton	2¼	75
		Total	**16**	**1,105**
*44.	Larry Murphy	Los Angeles	3¼	242
		Washington	5½	453
		Minnesota	1¾	121
		Pittsburgh	3½	288
		Total	**14**	**1,104**
45.	Pit Martin	Detroit	3¼	119
		Boston	1¾	111
		Chicago	10¾	740
		Vancouver	1¾	131
		Total	**17**	**1,101**
*46.	Ray Bourque	Boston	15	1,100
*47.	Gordie Roberts	Hartford	1½	107
		Minnesota	7	555
		Philadelphia	¼	11
		St. Louis	2½	166
		Pittsburgh	1¾	134
		Boston	2	124
		Total	**15**	**1,097**
48.	Darryl Sittler	Toronto	11½	844
		Philadelphia	2½	191
		Detroit	1	61
		Total	**15**	**1,096**

Mike Foligno, the third player chosen in the 1979 Entry Draft, played his 1,000th game on January 7, 1994 as the Florida Panthers – Foligno's fourth NHL club – lost 4-1 to the New Jersey Devils.

Player	Team	Seasons	GP
*49. Brad McCrimmon	Boston	3	228
	Philadelphia	5	367
	Calgary	3	231
	Detroit	3	203
	Hartford	1	65
	Total	**15**	**1,094**
*50. Michel Goulet	Quebec	10¾	813
	Chicago	4¼	276
	Total	**15**	**1,089**
51. Carol Vadnais	Montreal	2	42
	Oakland	2	152
	California	1¾	94
	Boston	3½	263
	NY Rangers	6¾	485
	New Jersey	1	51
	Total	**17**	**1,087**
52. Brad Marsh	Atlanta	2	160
	Calgary	1¼	97
	Philadelphia	6¾	514
	Toronto	2¾	181
	Detroit	1¼	75
	Ottawa	1	59
	Total	**15**	**1,086**
*53. Kevin Lowe	Edmonton	13	966
	NY Rangers	2	120
	Total	**15**	**1,086**
*54. Mark Messier	Edmonton	12	851
	NY Rangers	3	230
	Total	**15**	**1,081**
55. Bob Pulford	Toronto	14	947
	Los Angeles	2	132
	Total	**16**	**1,079**
56. Bobby Smith	Minnesota	8¼	572
	Montreal	6¾	505
	Total	**15**	**1,077**
57. Craig Ramsay	**Buffalo**	**14**	**1,070**
58. Andy Bathgate	NY Rangers	11¾	719
	Toronto	1¼	70
	Detroit	2	130
	Pittsburgh	2	150
	Total	**17**	**1,069**
59. Ted Lindsay	Detroit	14	862
	Chicago	3	206
	Total	**17**	**1,068**
60. Terry Harper	Montreal	10	554
	Los Angeles	3	234
	Detroit	4	252
	St. Louis	1	11
	Colorado	1	15
	Total	**19**	**1,066**
61. Rod Gilbert	**NY Rangers**	**18**	**1,065**
62. Bobby Hull	Chicago	15	1,036
	Winnipeg	⅔	18
	Hartford	⅓	9
	Total	**16**	**1,063**
*63. Glenn Anderson	Edmonton	11	828
	Toronto	2¾	221
	NY Rangers	¼	12
	Total	**14**	**1,061**
64. Denis Potvin	**NY Islanders**	**15**	**1,060**
65. Jean Guy Talbot	Montreal	13	791
	Minnesota	¼	4
	Detroit	½	32
	St. Louis	2½	172
	Buffalo	¾	57
	Total	**17**	**1,056**
66. Randy Carlyle	Toronto	2	94
	Pittsburgh	5¾	397
	Winnipeg	9¼	564
	Total	**17**	**1,055**
*67. Dale Hunter	Quebec	7	523
	Washington	7	531
	Total	**14**	**1,054**
68. Ivan Boldirev	Boston	1¼	13
	California	2¾	191
	Chicago	4¾	384
	Atlanta	1	65
	Vancouver	2¾	216
	Detroit	2½	183
	Total	**15**	**1,052**
69. Eddie Shack	NY Rangers	2¼	141
	Toronto	8¾	504
	Boston	2	120
	Los Angeles	1¼	84
	Buffalo	1½	111
	Pittsburgh	1¼	87
	Total	**17**	**1,047**

Player	Team	Seasons	GP
*70. Rob Ramage	Colorado	3	234
	St. Louis	5¾	441
	Calgary	1¼	80
	Toronto	2	160
	Minnesota	1	34
	Tampa Bay	¾	66
	Montreal	½	14
	Philadelphia	¾	15
	Total	**15**	**1,044**
71. Serge Savard	Montreal	15	917
	Winnipeg	2	123
	Total	**17**	**1,040**
72. Ron Ellis	**Toronto**	**16**	**1,034**
73. Harold Snepsts	Vancouver	11¾	781
	Minnesota	1	71
	Detroit	3	120
	St. Louis	1¼	61
	Total	**17**	**1,033**
*74. Paul Coffey	Edmonton	7	532
	Pittsburgh	4¾	331
	Los Angeles	¾	60
	Detroit	1½	110
	Total	**14**	**1,033**
75. Ralph Backstrom	Montreal	14½	844
	Los Angeles	2¼	172
	Chicago	¼	16
	Total	**17**	**1,032**
*76. Dale Hawerchuk	Winnipeg	9	713
	Buffalo	4	319
	Total	**13**	**1,032**
77. Dick Duff	Toronto	9¾	582
	NY Rangers	¾	43
	Montreal	5	305
	Los Angeles	¾	39
	Buffalo	1¾	61
	Total	**18**	**1,030**
78. John Tonelli	NY Islanders	7¾	584
	Calgary	2¼	161
	Los Angeles	3	231
	Chicago	¾	33
	Quebec	¼	19
	Total	**14**	**1,028**
79. Wayne Cashman	**Boston**	**17**	**1,027**
80. Doug Wilson	Chicago	14	938
	San Jose	2	86
	Total	**16**	**1,024**

Player	Team	Seasons	GP
81. Jim Neilson	NY Rangers	12	810
	California	2	98
	Cleveland	2	115
	Total	**16**	**1,023**
*82. Keith Acton	Montreal	4¼	228
	Minnesota	4¼	343
	Edmonton	1	72
	Philadelphia	4½	303
	Washington	¼	6
	NY Islanders	¾	71
	Total	**15**	**1,023**
83. Don Lever	Vancouver	7⅔	593
	Atlanta	⅓	28
	Calgary	1¼	85
	Colorado	¾	59
	New Jersey	3	216
	Buffalo	2	39
	Total	**15**	**1,020**
*84. Denis Savard	Chicago	10	736
	Montreal	3	210
	Tampa Bay	1	74
	Total	**14**	**1,020**
*85. Mike Foligno	Detroit	2½	186
	Buffalo	9	664
	Toronto	2¾	129
	Florida	¾	39
	Total	**15**	**1,018**
86. Phil Russell	Chicago	6¾	504
	Atlanta	1¼	93
	Calgary	3	229
	New Jersey	2¾	172
	Buffalo	1¼	18
	Total	**15**	**1,016**
*87. Brian Propp	Philadelphia	10¾	790
	Boston	¼	14
	Minnesota	3	147
	Hartford	1	65
	Total	**15**	**1,016**
88. Laurie Boschman	Toronto	2¾	187
	Edmonton	1	73
	Winnipeg	7¼	526
	New Jersey	2	153
	Ottawa	1	70
	Total	**14**	**1,009**
*89. Dave Christian	Winnipeg	4	230
	Washington	6½	504
	Boston	1½	128
	St. Louis	1	78
	Chicago	2	69
	Total	**15**	**1,009**
90. Dave Lewis	NY Islanders	6¾	514
	Los Angeles	3¼	221
	New Jersey	3	209
	Detroit	2	64
	Total	**15**	**1,008**
91. Bob Murray	**Chicago**	**15**	**1,008**
92. Jim Roberts	Montreal	9⅔	611
	St. Louis	5⅓	395
	Total	**15**	**1,006**
93. Claude Provost	**Montreal**	**15**	**1,005**
94. Rick Middleton	NY Rangers	2	124
	Boston	12	881
	Total	**14**	**1,005**
95. Ryan Walter	Washington	4	307
	Montreal	9	604
	Vancouver	2	92
	Total	**15**	**1,003**
96. Vic Hadfield	NY Rangers	13	839
	Pittsburgh	3	163
	Total	**16**	**1,002**
97. Bernie Federko	St. Louis	14	927
	Detroit	1	73
	Total	**15**	**1,000**

Bob Gainey donned the bleu, blanc et rouge of the Montreal Canadiens 1,160 times in his 17-year career. Among players who spent their entire careers with one franchise, only Alex Delvecchio, Stan Mikita, Henri Richard, Gilbert Perreault and George Armstrong played more games than Gainey.

Goaltending Records

All-Time Shutout Leaders

Goaltender	Team	Seasons	Games	Shutouts
Terry Sawchuk	Detroit	14	734	85
(1949-1970)	Boston	2	102	11
	Toronto	3	91	4
	Los Angeles	1	36	2
	NY Rangers	1	8	1
	Total	21	971	**103**
George Hainsworth	Montreal	7½	318	75
(1926-1937)	Toronto	3½	146	19
	Total	11	464	**94**
Glenn Hall	Detroit·	4	148	17
(1952-1971)	Chicago	10	618	51
	St. Louis	4	140	16
	Total	18	906	**84**
Jacques Plante	Montreal	11	556	58
(1952-1973)	NY Rangers	2	98	5
	St. Louis	2	69	10
	Toronto	2¾	106	7
	Boston	¼	8	2
	Total	18	837	**82**
Tiny Thompson	Boston	10¼	468	74
(1928-1940)	Detroit	1¾	85	7
	Total	12	553	**81**
Alex Connell	Ottawa	8	293	64
(1924-1937)	Detroit	1	48	6
	NY Americans	1	1	0
	Mtl. Maroons	2	75	11
	Total	12	417	**81**
Tony Esposito	Montreal	1	13	2
(1968-1984)	Chicago	15	873	74
	Total	16	886	**76**
Lorne Chabot	NY Rangers	2	80	21
(1926-1937)	Toronto	5	214	33
	Montreal	1	47	8
	Chicago	1	48	8
	Mtl. Maroons	1	16	2
	NY Americans	1	6	1
	Total	11	411	**73**
Harry Lumley	Detroit	6½	324	26
(1943-1960)	NY Rangers	½	1	0
	Chicago	2	134	5
	Toronto	4	267	34
	Boston	3	78	6
	Total	16	804	**71**
Roy Worters	Pittsburgh Pirates	3	123	22
(1925-1937)	NY Americans	9	360	44
	* Montreal		1	0
	Total	12	484	**66**
Turk Broda	Toronto	14	629	**62**
(1936-1952)				
John Roach	Toronto	7	223	13
(1921-1935)	NY Rangers	4	89	30
	Detroit	3	180	15
	Total	14	492	**58**

Goaltender	Team	Seasons	Games	Shutouts
Clint Benedict	Ottawa	7	158	19
(1917-1930)	Mtl. Maroons	6	204	38
	Total	13	362	**57**
Bernie Parent	Boston	2	57	1
(1965-1979)	Philadelphia	9½	486	50
	Toronto	1½	65	4
	Total	13	608	**55**
Ed Giacomin	NY Rangers	10¼	539	49
(1965-1978)	Detroit	2¾	71	5
	Total	13	610	**54**
David Kerr	Mtl. Maroons	3	101	11
(1930-1941)	NY Americans	1	1	0
	NY Rangers	7	324	40
	Total	11	426	**51**
Rogie Vachon	Montreal	5¼	206	13
(1966-1982)	Los Angeles	6¾	389	32
	Detroit	2	109	4
	Boston	2	91	2
	Total	16	795	**51**
Ken Dryden	Montreal	8	397	**46**
(1970-1979)				
Gump Worsley	NY Rangers	10	583	24
(1952-1974)	Montreal	6½	172	16
	Minnesota	4½	107	3
	Total	21	862	**43**
Charlie Gardiner	Chicago	7	316	**42**
(1927-1934)				
Frank Brimsek	Boston	9	444	35
(1938-1950)	Chicago	1	70	5
	Total	10	514	**40**
Johnny Bower	NY Rangers	3	77	5
(1953-1970)	Toronto	12	475	32
	Total	15	552	**37**
Bill Durnan	Montreal	7	383	**34**
(1943-1950)				
Eddie Johnston	Boston	11	444	27
(1962-1978)	Toronto	1	26	1
	St. Louis	3⅔	118	4
	Chicago	⅓	4	0
	Total	16	592	**32**
Roger Crozier	Detroit	7	313	20
(1963-1977)	Buffalo	6	202	10
	Washington	1	3	0
	Total	14	518	**30**
Cesare Maniago	Toronto	1	7	0
(1960-1978)	Montreal	1	14	0
	NY Rangers	2	34	2
	Minnesota	9	420	26
	Vancouver	2	93	2
	Total	15	568	**30**

*Played 1 game for Canadiens in 1929-30.

Ten or More Shutouts, One Season

Number of Shutouts	Goaltender	Team	Season	Length of Schedule
22	George Hainsworth	Montreal	1928-29	44
15	Alex Connell	Ottawa	1925-26	36
	Alex Connell	Ottawa	1927-28	44
	Hal Winkler	Boston	1927-28	44
	Tony Esposito	Chicago	1969-70	76
14	George Hainsworth	Montreal	1926-27	44
13	Clint Benedict	Mtl. Maroons	1926-27	44
	Alex Connell	Ottawa	1926-27	44
	George Hainsworth	Montreal	1927-28	44
	John Roach	NY Rangers	1928-29	44
	Roy Worters	NY Americans	1928-29	44
	Harry Lumley	Toronto	1953-54	70
12	Tiny Thompson	Boston	1928-29	44
	Lorne Chabot	Toronto	1928-29	44
	Chuck Gardiner	Chicago	1930-31	44
	Terry Sawchuk	Detroit	1951-52	70
	Terry Sawchuk	Detroit	1953-54	70
	Terry Sawchuk	Detroit	1954-55	70
	Glenn Hall	Detroit	1955-56	70
	Bernie Parent	Philadelphia	1973-74	78
	Bernie Parent	Philadelphia	1974-75	80

Number of Shutouts	Goaltender	Team	Season	Length of Schedule
11	Lorne Chabot	NY Rangers	1927-28	44
	Harry Holmes	Detroit	1927-28	44
	Clint Benedict	Mtl. Maroons	1928-29	44
	Joe Miller	Pittsburgh Pirates	1928-29	44
	Tiny Thompson	Boston	1932-33	48
	Terry Sawchuk	Detroit	1950-51	70
10	Lorne Chabot	NY Rangers	1926-27	44
	Roy Worters	Pittsburgh Pirates	1927-28	44
	Clarence Dolson	Detroit	1928-29	44
	John Roach	Detroit	1932-33	48
	Chuck Gardiner	Chicago	1933-34	48
	Tiny Thompson	Boston	1935-36	48
	Frank Brimsek	Boston	1938-39	48
	Bill Durnan	Montreal	1948-49	60
	Gerry McNeil	Montreal	1952-53	70
	Harry Lumley	Toronto	1952-53	70
	Tony Esposito	Chicago	1973-74	78
	Ken Dryden	Montreal	1976-77	80

All-Time Win Leaders

(Minimum 200 Wins)

Wins	Goaltender	GP	Decisions	Mins.	Losses	Ties	%
435	Terry Sawchuk	971	960	57,154	337	188	.551
434	Jacques Plante	837	817	49,553	246	137	.615
423	Tony Esposito	886	881	52,585	307	151	.566
407	Glenn Hall	906	899	53,484	327	165	.544
355	Rogie Vachon	795	761	46,298	291	115	.542
335	Gump Worsley	862	838	50,232	353	150	.489
332	Harry Lumley	804	799	48,097	324	143	.505
305	Billy Smith	680	643	38,431	233	105	.556
303	* Andy Moog	551	515	31,078	148	64	.650
302	Turk Broda	629	627	38,173	224	101	.562
293	Mike Liut	663	651	38,155	271	74	.507
289	Ed Giacomin	610	592	35,693	206	97	.570
288	* Grant Fuhr	579	542	32,769	186	68	.594
286	Dan Bouchard	655	631	37,919	232	113	.543
284	Tiny Thompson	553	553	34,174	194	75	.581
270	Bernie Parent	608	588	35,136	197	121	.562
270	Gilles Meloche	788	752	45,401	351	131	.446
266	* Tom Barrasso	546	522	31,430	196	60	.567
260	* Patrick Roy	486	465	28,092	146	59	.623
258	Ken Dryden	397	389	23,352	57	74	.758
254	* Don Beaupre	585	547	33,019	221	72	.530
252	Frank Brimsek	514	514	31,210	182	80	.568
251	Johnny Bower	549	537	32,016	196	90	.551
248	* Mike Vernon	467	406	26,578	155	51	.674
247	George Hainsworth	464	467	29,415	146	74	.608
246	Pete Peeters	489	461	27,699	155	51	.589
236	Rejean Lemelin	507	461	28,006	162	63	.580
236	Eddie Johnston	592	579	34,209	256	87	.483
231	Glenn Resch	571	537	32,279	224	82	.507
230	Gerry Cheevers	418	398	24,394	94	74	.671
230	* Kelly Hrudey	530	493	30,122	197	66	.533
221	* John Vanbiesbrouck	506	481	28,820	202	58	.520
218	John Roach	491	491	30,423	204	69	.514
215	Greg Millen	604	588	35,377	284	89	.441
208	Bill Durnan	383	382	22,945	112	62	.626
208	Don Edwards	459	440	26,181	155	77	.560
206	Lorne Chabot	411	411	25,309	140	65	.580
206	Roger Crozier	518	477	28,566	197	74	.509
204	Rick Wamsley	407	381	23,123	131	46	.596
203	David Kerr	426	426	26,519	148	75	.565

Active Shutout Leaders

Goaltender	Teams	Seasons	Games	Shutouts
Patrick Roy	Montreal	10	486	**27**
Ed Belfour	Chicago	6	290	**23**
Tom Barrasso	Buffalo, Pittsburgh	11	546	**21**
Andy Moog	Edmonton, Boston	14	551	**19**
John Vanbiesbrouck	NY Rangers, Florida	12	506	**17**
Kirk McLean	New Jersey, Vancouver	9	364	**16**
Jon Casey	Minnesota, Boston	9	382	**16**
Kelly Hrudey	NY Islanders, Los Angeles	11	530	**16**
Bob Essensa	Winnipeg, Detroit	6	294	**15**
Don Beaupre	Minnesota, Washington	14	585	**15**
Grant Fuhr	Edm., Tor., Buf.	13	579	**14**
Clint Malarchuk	Que., Wsh., Buf.	10	338	**12**
Daren Puppa	Buf., Tor., T.B.	9	286	**11**
Tim Cheveldae	Detroit, Winnipeg	6	278	**10**

Active Goaltending Leaders

(Ranked by winning percentage; minimum 250 games played)

Goaltender	Teams	Seasons	GP	Decisions	W	L	T	Winning %
Andy Moog	Edm., Bos., Dal.	14	551	515	303	148	64	.650
Patrick Roy	Montreal	10	486	465	260	146	59	.623
Mike Vernon	Calgary	11	467	454	248	155	51	.602
Ed Belfour	Chicago	6	290	274	146	91	37	.600
Grant Fuhr	Edm., Tor., Buf.	13	579	542	288	186	68	.594
Tom Barrasso	Buffalo, Pittsburgh	11	546	522	266	196	60	.567
Tim Cheveldae	Detroit, Winnipeg	6	278	265	133	101	31	.560
Ron Hextall	Phi., Que., NYI	8	400	380	186	152	42	.545
Daren Puppa	Buf., Tor., T.B.	9	286	261	124	103	34	.540
Kelly Hrudey	NY Islanders, Los Angeles	11	530	493	230	197	66	.533
Don Beaupre	Minnesota, Washington	14	585	547	254	221	72	.530
Jon Casey	Minnesota, Boston	9	382	350	158	141	51	.524
J. Vanbiesbrouck	NY Rangers, Florida	12	506	481	221	202	58	.520
Clint Malarchuk	Que., Wsh., Buf.	10	338	316	141	130	45	.517
Bob Essensa	Winnipeg, Detroit	6	294	275	120	121	34	.498
Kirk McLean	New Jersey, Vancouver	9	364	351	153	162	36	.487
Bill Ranford	Boston, Edmonton	9	401	369	154	170	45	.478
Glenn Healy	L.A., NYI, NYR	8	288	267	113	128	26	.472
Sean Burke	New Jersey, Hartford	6	259	243	95	117	31	.455
Jacques Cloutier	Buf., Chi., Que.	12	255	208	82	102	24	.452
Ken Wregget	Tor., Phi., Pit.	11	383	352	136	181	35	.436

Goals Against Average Leaders

(minimum 27 games played, 1992-93 to 1993-94; 25 games played, 1926–27 to 1991-92; 15 games played, 1917–18 to 1925–26.)

Season	Goaltender and Club	GP	Mins.	GA	SO	AVG.
1993-94	Dominik Hasek, Buffalo	58	3,358	109	7	1.95
1992-93	Felix Potvin, Toronto	48	2,781	116	2	2.50
1991-92	Patrick Roy, Montreal	67	3,935	155	5	2.36
1990-91	Ed Belfour, Chicago	74	4,127	170	4	2.47
1989-90	Mike Liut, Hartford, Washington	37	2,161	91	4	2.53
1988-89	Patrick Roy, Montreal	48	2,744	113	4	2.47
1987-88	Pete Peeters, Washington	35	1,896	88	2	2.78
1986-87	Brian Hayward, Montreal	37	2,178	102	1	2.81
1985-86	Bob Froese, Philadelphia	51	2,728	116	5	2.55
1984-85	Tom Barrasso, Buffalo	54	3,248	144	5	2.66
1983-84	Pat Riggin, Washington	41	2,299	102	4	2.66
1982-83	Pete Peeters, Boston	62	3,611	142	8	2.36
1981-82	Denis Herron, Montreal	27	1,547	68	3	2.64
1980-81	Richard Sevigny, Montreal	33	1,777	71	2	2.40
1979-80	Bob Sauve, Buffalo	32	1,880	74	4	2.36
1978-79	Ken Dryden, Montreal	47	2,814	108	5	2.30
1977-78	Ken Dryden, Montreal	52	3,071	105	5	2.05
1976-77	Michel Larocque, Montreal	26	1,525	53	4	2.09
1975-76	Ken Dryden, Montreal	62	3,580	121	8	2.03
1974-75	Bernie Parent, Philadelphia	68	4,041	137	12	2.03
1973-74	Bernie Parent, Philadelphia	73	4,314	136	12	1.89
1972-73	Ken Dryden, Montreal	54	3,165	119	6	2.26
1971-72	Tony Esposito, Chicago	48	2,780	82	9	1.77
1970-71	Jacques Plante, Toronto	40	2,329	73	4	1.88
1969-70	Ernie Wakely, St. Louis	30	1,651	58	4	2.11
1968-69	Jacques Plante, St. Louis	37	2,139	70	5	1.96
1967-68	Gump Worsley, Montreal	40	2,213	73	6	1.98
1966-67	Glenn Hall, Chicago	32	1,664	66	2	2.38
1965-66	Johnny Bower, Toronto	35	1,998	75	3	2.25
1964-65	Johnny Bower, Toronto	34	2,040	81	3	2.38
1963-64	Johnny Bower, Toronto	51	3,009	106	5	2.11
1962-63	Jacques Plante, Montreal	56	3,320	138	5	2.49
1961-62	Jacques Plante, Montreal	70	4,200	166	4	2.37
1960-61	Johnny Bower, Toronto	58	3,480	145	2	2.50
1959-60	Jacques Plante, Montreal	69	4,140	175	3	2.54
1958-59	Jacques Plante, Montreal	67	4,000	144	9	2.16
1957-58	Jacques Plante, Montreal	57	3,386	119	9	2.11
1956-57	Jacques Plante, Montreal	61	3,660	123	9	2.02
1955-56	Jacques Plante, Montreal	64	3,840	119	7	1.86
1954-55	Terry Sawchuk, Detroit	68	4,080	132	12	1.94
1953-54	Harry Lumley, Toronto	69	4,140	128	13	1.86
1952-53	Terry Sawchuk, Detroit	63	3,780	120	9	1.90
1951-52	Terry Sawchuk, Detroit	70	4,200	133	12	1.90
1950-51	Al Rollins, Toronto	40	2,367	70	5	1.77
1949-50	Bill Durnan, Montreal	64	3,840	141	8	2.20
1948-49	Bill Durnan, Montreal	60	3,600	126	10	2.10
1947-48	Turk Broda, Toronto	60	3,600	143	5	2.38
1946-47	Bill Durnan, Montreal	60	3,600	138	4	2.30
1945-46	Bill Durnan, Montreal	40	2,400	104	4	2.60
1944-45	Bill Durnan, Montreal	50	3,000	121	1	2.42
1943-44	Bill Durnan, Montreal	50	3,000	109	2	2.18
1942-43	Johnny Mowers, Detroit	50	3,010	124	6	2.47
1941-42	Frank Brimsek, Boston	47	2,930	115	3	2.35
1940-41	Turk Broda, Toronto	48	2,970	99	5	2.00
1939-40	Dave Kerr, NY Rangers	48	3,000	77	8	1.54
1938-39	Frank Brimsek, Boston	43	2,610	68	10	1.56
1937-38	Tiny Thompson, Boston	48	2,970	89	7	1.80
1936-37	Normie Smith, Detroit	48	2,980	102	6	2.05
1935-36	Tiny Thompson, Boston	48	2,930	82	10	1.68
1934-35	Lorne Chabot, Chicago	48	2,940	88	8	1.80
1933-34	Wilf Cude, Detroit, Montreal	30	1,920	47	5	1.47
1932-33	Tiny Thompson, Boston	48	3,000	88	11	1.76
1931-32	Chuck Gardiner, Chicago	48	2,989	92	4	1.85
1930-31	Roy Worters, NY Americans	44	2,760	74	8	1.61
1929-30	Tiny Thompson, Boston	44	2,680	98	3	2.19
1928-29	George Hainsworth, Montreal	44	2,800	43	22	0.92
1927-28	George Hainsworth, Montreal	44	2,730	48	13	1.05
1926-27	Clint Benedict, Mtl. Maroons	43	2,748	65	13	1.42
1925-26	Alex Connell, Ottawa	36	2,251	42	15	1.12
1924-25	Georges Vezina, Montreal	30	1,860	56	5	1.81
1923-24	Georges Vezina, Montreal	24	1,459	48	3	1.97
1922-23	Clint Benedict, Ottawa	24	1,478	54	4	2.19
1921-22	Clint Benedict, Ottawa	24	1,508	84	2	3.34
1920-21	Clint Benedict, Ottawa	24	1,457	75	2	3.09
1919-20	Clint Benedict, Ottawa	24	1,444	64	5	2.66
1918-19	Clint Benedict, Ottawa	18	1,113	53	2	2.86
1917-18	Georges Vezina, Montreal	21	1,282	84	1	3.93

All-Time NHL Coaching Register

Regular Season, 1917-94

(figures in parentheses indicate ranking of top 25 in order of games coached)

Name	NHL Teams	Games	Wins	Losses	Ties	%	Cup Wins	Seasons
Abel, Sid (6)	Chicago	140	39	79	22	.357	0	1952-54
	Detroit	810	340	338	132	.501	0	1957-68
	St. Louis	10	3	6	1	.350	0	1970-71
	Kansas City	3	0	3	0	.000	0	1975-76
	Total	**963**	**382**	**426**	**155**	**.477**	**0**	**1952-76**
Adams, Jack (5)	Toronto St. Pats	18	10	7	1	.583	0	1922-23
	Detroit	964	413	390	161	.328	3	1927-44
	Total	**982**	**423**	**397**	**162**	**.513**	**3**	**1922-44**
Allen, Keith	Philadelphia	150	51	67	32	.544	0	1967-69
Anderson, Jim	Washington	54	4	45	5	.516	0	1974-75
	St. Louis	32	6	20	6	.281	0	1973-75
	Pittsburgh	80	16	58	6	.238	0	1983-84
	Total	**112**	**22**	**78**	**12**	**.250**	**0**	**1973-84**
Arbour, Al (1)	St. Louis	107	42	40	25	.509	0	1970-73
	NY Islanders	1499	739	537	223	.567	4	1973-86, 1988-94
	Total	**1606**	**781**	**577**	**248**	**.564**	**4**	**1970-94**
Armstrong, George	Toronto	47	17	26	4	.404	0	1988-89
Barkley, Doug	Detroit	96	23	61	12	.302	0	1970-72, 1975-76
Beaulieu, André	Minnesota	31	6	22	3	.242	0	1977-78
Belisle, Danny	Washington	96	28	51	17	.380	0	1978-79
Berenson, Red	St. Louis	204	100	72	32	.569	0	1979-82
Bergeron, Michel (13)	Quebec	634	265	283	86	.486	0	1980-87, 1989-90
	NY Rangers	158	73	67	18	.519	0	1987-89
	Total	**792**	**338**	**350**	**104**	**.492**	**0**	**1980-89**
Berry, Bob (10)	Los Angeles	240	107	94	39	.527	0	1978-81
	Montreal	223	116	71	36	.601	0	1981-84
	Pittsburgh	240	88	127	25	.419	0	1984-87
	St. Louis	157	73	63	21	.532	0	1992-94
	Total	**860**	**384**	**355**	**121**	**.517**	**0**	**1978-94**
Blackburn, Don	Hartford	140	42	63	35	.425	0	1979-81
Blair, Wren	Minnesota	147	48	65	34	.442	0	1967-70
Blake, Toe (9)	Montreal	914	500	255	159	.634	8	1955-68
Bolieau, Marc	Pittsburgh	151	66	61	24	.517	0	1973-76
Boivin, Leo	St. Louis	97	28	53	16	.371	0	1975-76, 1977-78
Boucher, Frank	NY Rangers	525	179	263	83	.420	1	1939-49, 1953-54
Boucher, George	Mtl. Maroons	12	6	5	1	.542	0	1930-31
	Ottawa	48	13	29	6	.333	0	1933-34
	St.L. Eagles	35	9	20	6	.343	0	1934-35
	Boston	70	22	32	16	.429	0	1949-50
	Total	**165**	**50**	**86**	**29**	**.391**	**0**	**1930-50**
Bowman, Scott (2)	St. Louis	238	110	83	45	.557	0	1967-71
	Montreal	634	419	110	105	.744	5	1971-79
	Buffalo	404	210	134	60	.594	0	1979-87
	Pittsburgh	164	95	53	16	.628	1	1991-93
	Detroit	84	46	30	8	.595	0	1993-94
	Total	**1524**	**880**	**410**	**234**	**.654**	**6**	**1967-94**
Bowness, Rick	Winnipeg	28	8	17	3	.339	0	1988-89
	Boston	80	36	32	12	.525	0	1991-92
	Ottawa	168	24	131	13	.182	0	1992-94
	Total	**276**	**68**	**180**	**28**	**.297**	**0**	**1991-94**
Brooks, Herb	NY Rangers	295	131	113	41	.514	0	1981-85
	Minnesota	80	19	48	13	.319	0	1987-88
	New Jersey	84	40	37	7	.518	0	1992-93
	Total	**449**	**190**	**198**	**61**	**.491**	**0**	**1981-93**
Brophy, John	Toronto	160	53	91	16	.381	0	1986-93
Burns, Charlie	Minnesota	86	22	50	14	.337	0	1969-75
Burns, Pat	Montreal	320	174	104	42	.609	0	1988-92
	Toronto	168	87	58	23	.586	0	1992-94
	Total	**488**	**261**	**162**	**65**	**.601**	**0**	**1988-94**
Bush, Eddie	Kansas City	32	1	23	8	.156	0	1975-76
Carpenter, Doug	New Jersey	290	100	166	24	.386	0	1984-88
	Toronto	91	39	47	5	.456	0	1989-90
	Total	**381**	**139**	**213**	**29**	**.403**	**0**	**1984-90**
Carroll, Dick	Toronto Arenas	40	18	22	0	.450	1	1917-19
	Toronto St. Pats	24	15	9	0	.625	0	1920-21
	Total	**64**	**33**	**31**	**0**	**.516**	**1**	**1917-21**
Cashman, Wayne	NY Rangers	2	0	2	0	.000	0	1986-87
Chambers, Dave	Quebec	98	19	64	15	.270	0	1990-91
Charron, Guy	Calgary	16	6	7	3	.469	0	1991-92
Cheevers, Gerry	Boston	376	204	126	46	.604	0	1980-85
Cherry, Don	Boston	400	231	105	64	.658	0	1974-79
	Colorado	80	19	48	13	.319	0	1979-80
	Total	**480**	**250**	**153**	**77**	**.601**	**0**	**1974-80**
Clancy, King	Mtl. Maroons	18	6	11	1	.361	0	1937-38
	Toronto	235	96	94	45	.504	0	1953-56, 1966-67, 1971-72
	Total	**253**	**102**	**105**	**46**	**.494**	**0**	**1937-72**
Clapper, Dit	Boston	230	102	88	40	.530	0	1945-49
Cleghorn, Odie	Pit. Pirates	168	62	86	20	.429	0	1925-29
Colville, Neil	NY Rangers	93	26	41	26	.419	0	1950-52
Conacher, Charlie	Chicago	162	56	84	22	.414	0	1947-50
Conacher, Lionel	NY Americans	44	14	25	5	.375	0	1929-30
Constantine, Kevin	San Jose	84	33	46	5	.423	0	1993-94
Cook, Bill	NY Rangers	117	34	59	24	.393	0	1951-53
Creamer, Pierre	Pittsburgh	80	36	35	9	.506	0	1987-88
Creighton, Fred	Atlanta	348	156	136	56	.529	0	1974-79
	Boston	73	40	20	13	.637	0	1979-80
	Total	**421**	**196**	**156**	**69**	**.548**	**0**	**1974-80**
Crisp, Terry	Calgary	240	144	63	33	.669	1	1987-90
	Tampa Bay	168	53	97	18	.369	0	1992-94
	Total	**408**	**197**	**160**	**51**	**.545**	**1**	**1987-94**
Crozier, Joe	Buffalo	192	77	80	35	.492	0	1971-74
	Toronto	40	13	22	5	.388	0	1980-81
	Total	**232**	**90**	**102**	**40**	**.474**	**0**	**1971-81**
Crozier, Roger	Washington	1	0	1	0	.000	0	1981-82
Cunniff, John	Hartford	13	3	9	1	.269	0	1982-83
	New Jersey	133	59	56	18	.511	0	1990-91
	Total	**146**	**62**	**65**	**19**	**.490**	**0**	**1983-91**
Dandurand, Leo	Montreal	158	82	68	8	.544	1	1920-25, 1934-35
Day, Hap	Toronto	546	259	206	81	.549	5	1940-50
Dea, Bill	Detroit	100	32	57	11	.375	0	1975-76, 1976-77, 1881-82
Delvecchio, Alex	Detroit	156	53	82	21	.407	0	1973-77
Demers, Jacques (12)	Quebec	80	25	44	11	.381	0	1979-80
	St. Louis	240	106	106	28	.500	0	1983-86
	Detroit	320	137	136	47	.502	0	1986-90
	Montreal	168	89	59	20	.589	1	1992-94
	Total	**808**	**357**	**345**	**106**	**.507**	**1**	**1979-94**
Denneny, Cy	Boston	44	26	13	5	.648	1	1928-29
	Ottawa	48	11	27	10	.333	0	1932-33
	Total	**92**	**37**	**40**	**15**	**.484**	**1**	**1928-33**
Dineen, Bill	Philadelphia	140	60	60	20	.500	0	1991-93
Dudley, Rick	Buffalo	188	85	72	31	.535	0	1989-91
Duff, Dick	Toronto	2	0	2	0	.000	0	1979-80
Dugal, Jules	Montreal	18	9	6	3	.583	0	1938-39

King Clancy, who coached 253 games in the NHL, chats with George "Punch" Imlach, the master motivator who won four Stanley Cup championships with Toronto in the 1960s. In addition to his stints with the Leafs, Imlach coached the expansion Buffalo Sabres from 1970 to 1972.

Name	NHL Teams	Games	Wins	Losses	Ties	%	Cup Wins	Seasons
Duncan, Art	Detroit	44	12	28	4	.318	0	1926-27
	Toronto	47	21	16	10	.553	0	1930-32
	Total	**91**	**33**	**44**	**14**	**.440**	**0**	**1926-32**
Dutton, Red	NY Americans	336	106	180	50	.390	0	1935-42
Eddolls, Frank	Chicago	70	13	40	17	.307	0	1954-55
Esposito, Phil	NY Rangers	45	24	19	0	.533	0	1986-87, 1988-89
Evans, Jack (23)	California	80	27	42	11	.406	0	1975-76
	Cleveland	160	47	87	26	.375	0	1976-78
	Hartford	374	163	174	37	.485	0	1983-88
	Total	**614**	**237**	**303**	**74**	**.446**	**0**	**1975-88**
Fashoway, Gordie	Oakland	10	4	5	1	.450	0	1967-688
Ferguson, John	NY Rangers	121	43	59	19	.434	0	1975-77
	Winnipeg	14	7	6	1	.536	0	1985-86
	Total	**135**	**50**	**65**	**20**	**.444**	**0**	**1975-86**
Filion, Maurice	Quebec	6	1	3	2	.333	0	1980-81
Francis, Emile (15)	NY Rangers	654	347	209	98	.606	0	1965-75
	St. Louis	124	46	64	14	.427	0	1976-77, 1981-83
	Total	**778**	**393**	**273**	**112**	**.577**	**0**	**1965-83**
Frederickson, Frank	Pit. Pirates	44	5	36	3	.148	0	1929-30
Ftorek, Robbie	Los Angeles	132	65	56	11	.534	0	1987-89
Gadsby, Bill	Detroit	79	35	32	12	.519	0	1968-70
Gainey, Bob	Minnesota	244	95	119	30	.451	0	1990-93
	Dallas	84	42	29	13	.577	0	1993-94
	Total	**328**	**137**	**148**	**43**	**.483**	**0**	**1990-94**
Gardiner, Herb	Chicago	44	7	29	8	.250	0	1928-29
Gardner, Jimmy	Hamilton	30	19	10	1	.650	0	1924-25
Garvin, Ted	Detroit	11	2	8	1	.227	0	1973-74
Geoffrion, Bernie	NY Rangers	43	22	18	3	.547	0	1968-69
	Atlanta	208	77	92	39	.464	0	1972-75
	Montreal	30	15	9	6	.600	0	1979-80
	Total	**281**	**114**	**119**	**48**	**.491**	**0**	**1968-80**
Gerard, Eddie	Ottawa	22	9	13	0	.409	0	1917-18
	Mtl. Maroons	294	129	112	43	.512	1	1924-29, 1932-34
	NY Americans	92	34	50	18	.467	0	1930-32
	St.L. Eagles	13	2	11	0	.154	0	1934-35
	Total	**421**	**174**	**186**	**61**	**.486**	**1**	**1917-35**
Gill, David	Ottawa	132	64	41	27	.587	1	1926-29
Glover, Fred	California	356	96	207	53	.344	0	1968-71, 1972-74
	Los Angeles	68	18	42	8	.324	0	1971-72
	Total	**424**	**114**	**249**	**61**	**.341**	**0**	**1968-74**
Goodfellow, Ebbie	Chicago	140	30	91	19	.282	0	1950-52
Gordon, Jackie	Minnesota	289	116	123	50	.488	0	1970-75
Goring, Butch	Boston	93	42	38	13	.522	0	1985-87
Gorman, Tommy	NY Americans	80	31	33	16	.488	0	1925-26, 1928-29
	Chicago	73	28	28	17	.500	1	1932-34
	Mtl. Maroons	174	74	71	29	.509	1	1934-38
	Total	**327**	**133**	**132**	**62**	**.502**	**2**	**1925-38**
Gottselig, Johnny	Chicago	187	62	104	21	.388	0	1944-48
Goyette, Phil	NY Islanders	48	6	38	4	.167	0	1972-73
Green, Gary	Washington	157	50	78	29	.411	0	1979-82
Green, Pete	Ottawa	186	117	61	8	.651	3	1919-26
Green, Wilf	NY Americans	44	11	27	6	.318	0	1927-28
Green, Ted	Edmonton	188	65	102	21	.402	0	1991-93
Guidolin, Aldo	Colorado	59	12	39	8	.271	0	1978-79
Guidolin, Bep	Boston	104	72	23	9	.736	0	1972-74
	Kansas City	125	26	84	15	.268	0	1974-76
	Total	**229**	**98**	**107**	**24**	**.480**	**0**	**1972-76**
Harkness, Ned	Detroit	19	9	7	3	.553	0	1970-71
Harris, Ted	Minnesota	179	48	104	27	.344	0	1975-78
Hart, Cecil	Montreal	430	207	149	74	.567	2	1925-39
Harvey, Doug	NY Rangers	70	26	32	12	.457	0	1961-62
Heffernan, Frank	Toronto St. Pats	12	5	7	0	.417	0	1919-20
Henning, Lorne	Minnesota	158	68	72	18	.487	0	1985-87
Holmgren, Paul	Philadelphia	264	107	126	31	.464	0	1988-92
	Hartford	101	30	63	8	.337	0	1992-93
	Total	**365**	**137**	**189**	**39**	**.429**	**0**	**1988-93**
Howell, Harry	Minnesota	11	3	6	2	.364	0	1978-79
Imlach, Punch (7)	Toronto	760	363	274	123	.559	4	1958-69, 1979-80
	Buffalo	119	32	62	25	.374	0	1970-72
	Total	**879**	**395**	**336**	**148**	**.534**	**4**	**1958-80**
Ingarfield, Earl	NY Islanders	30	6	22	2	.233	0	1972-73
Inglis, Bill	Buffalo	56	28	18	10	.589	0	1978-79
Irvin, Dick (3)	Chicago	114	43	56	15	.443	0	1930-31, 1955-56
	Toronto	427	216	152	59	.575	1	1931-40
	Montreal	896	431	313	152	.566	3	1940-55
	Total	**1437**	**690**	**521**	**226**	**.559**	**4**	**1930-55**
Ivan, Tommy (24)	Detroit	470	262	118	90	.653	3	1947-54
	Chicago	140	40	78	22	.364	0	1956-58
	Total	**610**	**302**	**196**	**112**	**.587**	**3**	**1947-58**
Iverson, Emil	Chicago	71	26	28	17	.486	0	1931-33
Johnson, Bob	Calgary	400	193	155	52	.548	0	1982-87
	Pittsburgh	80	41	33	6	.550	1	1990-91
	Total	**480**	**234**	**188**	**58**	**.548**	**1**	**1982-91**
Johnson, Tom	Boston	208	142	43	23	.738	1	1970-73
Johnston, Eddie	Chicago	80	34	27	19	.544	0	1979-80
	Pittsburgh	324	123	153	48	.454	0	1980-83, 1993-94
	Total	**404**	**157**	**180**	**67**	**.472**	**0**	**1979-94**
Johnston, Marshall	California	69	13	45	11	.268	0	1973-75
	Colorado	56	15	32	9	.348	0	1981-82
	Total	**125**	**28**	**77**	**20**	**.304**	**0**	**1973-82**

Name	NHL Teams	Games	Wins	Losses	Ties	%	Cup Wins	Seasons
Keats, Duke	Detroit	11	2	7	2	.273	0	1926-27
Keenan, Mike (22)	Philadelphia	320	190	102	28	.638	0	1984-88
	Chicago	320	153	126	41	.542	0	1988-92
	NY Rangers	84	52	24	8	.667	1	1993-94
	Total	**724**	**395**	**252**	**77**	**.599**	**1**	**1984-94**
Kelly, Pat	Colorado	101	22	54	25	.342	0	1977-79
Kelly, Red (18)	Los Angeles	150	55	75	20	.433	0	1967-69
	Pittsburgh	274	90	132	52	.423	0	1969-73
	Toronto	318	133	123	62	.516	0	1973-77
	Total	**742**	**278**	**330**	**134**	**.465**	**0**	**1967-77**
Kennedy, George	Montreal	64	36	28	0	.563	0	1917-20
King, Dave	Calgary	168	85	59	24	.577	0	1992-94
Kingston, George	San Jose	164	28	129	7	.192	0	1991-93
Kish, Larry	Hartford	49	12	32	5	.296	0	1982-83
Kromm, Bobby	Detroit	231	79	111	41	.431	0	1977-80
Kurtenbach, Orland	Vancouver	125	36	62	27	.396	0	1976-78
LaForge, Bill	Vancouver	20	4	14	2	.250	0	1984-85
Lalonde, Newsy	NY Americans	44	17	25	2	.409	0	1926-27
	Ottawa	88	31	45	12	.420	0	1929-31
	Montreal	112	45	53	14	.464	0	1932-35
	Total	**244**	**93**	**123**	**28**	**.439**	**0**	**1926-35**
Lapointe, Ron	Quebec	89	33	50	6	.404	0	1987-88
Laycoe, Hal	Los Angeles	24	5	18	1	.229	0	1969-70
	Vancouver	156	44	96	16	.333	0	1970-72
	Total	**180**	**49**	**114**	**17**	**.319**	**0**	**1969-72**
Lehman, Hugh	Chicago	21	3	17	1	.167	0	1927-28
Lemaire, Jacques	Montreal	97	48	37	12	.557	0	1983-85
	New Jersey	84	47	25	12	.631	0	1993-94
	Total	**181**	**95**	**62**	**24**	**.591**	**0**	**1983-94**
Lepine, Pit	Montreal	48	10	33	5	.260	0	1939-40
LeSueur, Percy	Hamilton	24	9	15	0	.375	0	1923-24
Ley, Rick	Hartford	160	69	71	20	.494	0	1989-91
Lindsay, Ted	Detroit	20	3	14	3	.225	0	1980-81
Long, Barry	Winnipeg	205	87	93	25	.485	0	1983-86
Loughlin, Clem	Chicago	144	61	63	20	.493	0	1934-37
MacDonald, Parker	Minnesota	61	20	30	11	.418	0	1973-74
	Los Angeles	42	13	24	5	.369	0	1981-82
	Total	**103**	**33**	**54**	**16**	**.398**	**0**	**1973-82**
MacMillan, Billy	Colorado	80	22	45	13	.356	0	1980-81
	New Jersey	100	19	67	14	.260	0	1982-84
	Total	**180**	**41**	**112**	**27**	**.303**	**0**	**1980-83**
MacNeil, Al	Montreal	55	31	15	9	.645	1	1970-71
	Atlanta	80	35	32	13	.519	0	1979-80
	Calgary	160	68	61	31	.522	0	1980-82
	Total	**295**	**134**	**108**	**53**	**.544**	**1**	**1970-82**
Mahoney, Bill	Minnesota	93	42	39	12	.516	0	1983-85
Magnuson, Keith	Chicago	132	49	57	26	.470	0	1980-82
Maloney, Dan	Toronto	160	45	100	15	.328	0	1984-86
	Winnipeg	212	91	93	28	.495	0	1986-90
	Total	**372**	**136**	**193**	**43**	**.423**	**0**	**1984-90**
Maloney, Phil	Vancouver	232	95	105	32	.478	0	1973-77
Mantha, Sylvio	Montreal	48	11	26	11	.344	0	1935-36
Marshall, Bert	Colorado	24	3	17	4	.208	0	1981-82
Martin, Jacques	St. Louis	160	66	71	23	.484	0	1986-88
Maxner, Wayne	Detroit	129	34	68	27	.368	0	1980-82
McCammon, Bob	Philadelphia	218	119	68	31	.617	0	1978-79, 1981-84
	Vancouver	293	102	155	36	.410	0	1987-91
	Total	**511**	**221**	**223**	**67**	**.498**	**0**	**1978-91**
McCreary, Bill	St. Louis	24	6	14	4	.333	0	1971-72
	Vancouver	41	9	25	7	.305	0	1973-74
	California	32	8	20	4	.313	0	1974-75
	Total	**97**	**23**	**59**	**15**	**.314**	**0**	**1971-75**
McLellan, John	Toronto	295	117	136	42	.468	0	1969-73
McVie, Tom	Washington	204	49	122	33	.321	0	1975-78
	Winnipeg	105	20	67	18	.276	0	1979-80, 1980-81
	New Jersey	153	57	74	22	.444	0	1990-92
	Total	**462**	**126**	**263**	**73**	**.352**	**0**	**1975-92**
Meeker, Howie	Toronto	70	21	34	15	.407	0	1956-57
Melrose, Barry	Los Angeles	168	66	80	22	.458	0	1992-94
Milbury, Mike	Boston	160	90	49	21	.628	0	1989-91
Muckler, John	Minnesota	35	6	23	6	.257	0	1968-69
	Edmonton	160	75	65	20	.531	1	1989-91
	Buffalo	220	103	90	27	.530	0	1992-94
	Total	**415**	**184**	**178**	**53**	**.507**	**1**	**1968-94**
Muldoon, Pete	Chicago	44	19	22	3	.466	0	1926-27
Munro, Dunc	Mtl. Maroons	76	37	29	10	.553	0	1929-31
Murdoch, Bob	Chicago	80	30	41	9	.431	0	1987-88
	Winnipeg	160	59	75	26	.450	0	1989-91
	Total	**240**	**89**	**116**	**35**	**.444**	**0**	**1987-91**
Murphy, Mike	Los Angeles	65	20	37	8	.369	0	1987-88
Murray, Bryan (8)	Washington	672	343	246	83	.572	0	1981-90
	Detroit	244	124	91	29	.568	0	1990-93
	Total	**916**	**467**	**337**	**112**	**.571**	**0**	**1981-93**
Murray, Terry	Washington	325	163	134	28	.545	0	1989-94
Nanne, Lou	Minnesota	29	7	18	4	.310	0	1977-78
Neale, Harry	Vancouver	407	142	189	76	.442	0	1978-82, 1983-84, 1984-85
	Detroit	35	8	23	4	.286	0	1985-86
	Total	**442**	**150**	**212**	**80**	**.430**	**0**	**1978-86**

All-Time Coaching Register *continued*

Name	NHL Teams	Games	Wins	Losses	Ties	%	Cup Wins	Seasons
Neilson, Roger (14)	Toronto	160	75	62	23	.541	0	1977-79
	Buffalo	106	53	26	27	.627	0	1979-81
	Vancouver	133	51	61	21	.462	0	1982-84
	Los Angeles	28	8	17	3	.339	0	1983-84
	NY Rangers	280	141	104	35	.566	0	1989-93
	Florida	84	33	34	17	.494	0	1993-94
	Total	**791**	**361**	**304**	**126**	**.536**	**0**	**1977-94**
Nykoluk, Mike	Toronto	200	63	99	38	.410	0	1980-83
Oliver, Murray	Minnesota	40	21	11	8	.625	0	1983-84
Olmstead, Bert	Oakland	64	11	37	16	.297	0	1967-68
O'Reilly, Terry	Boston	227	115	86	26	.564	0	1986-89
Paddock, John	Winnipeg	248	97	120	31	.454	0	1991-94
Pagé, Pierre	Minnesota	160	63	77	20	.456	0	1988-90
	Quebec	230	98	103	29	.489	0	1991-94
	Total	**390**	**161**	**180**	**49**	**.476**	**0**	**1988-94**
Park, Brad	Detroit	45	9	34	2	.222	0	1985-86
Patrick, Craig	NY Rangers	94	37	45	12	.457	0	1980-81, 1984-85
	Pittsburgh	54	22	26	6	.463	0	1989-90
	Total	**148**	**59**	**71**	**18**	**.459**	**0**	**1980-89**
Patrick, Frank	Boston	96	48	36	12	.563	0	1934-36
Patrick, Lester (25)	NY Rangers	604	281	216	107	.554	2	1926-39
Patrick, Lynn	NY Rangers	107	40	51	16	.449	0	1948-50
	Boston	310	117	120	63	.479	0	1950-55
	St. Louis	26	8	15	3	.365	0	1967-68, 1974-76
	Total	**443**	**165**	**186**	**82**	**.465**	**0**	**1948-76**
Patrick, Muzz	NY Rangers	136	45	65	26	.426	0	1953-55, 1962-63
Perron, Jean	Montreal	240	126	84	30	.588	1	1985-88
	Quebec	47	16	26	5	.394	0	1988-89
	Total	**287**	**142**	**110**	**35**	**.556**	**1**	**1985-89**
Perry, Don	Los Angeles	168	52	85	31	.402	0	1982-83
Pike, Alf	NY Rangers	125	36	67	22	.376	0	1959-61
Pilous, Rudy	Chicago	420	172	168	80	.505	1	1957-63
Plager, Barclay	St. Louis	178	49	96	33	.368	0	1977-80, 1982-83
Plager, Bob	St. Louis	11	4	6	1	.409	0	1992-93
Pleau, Larry	Hartford	224	81	117	26	.420	0	1981-83, 1988-89
Polano, Nick	Detroit	240	79	127	34	.400	0	1982-85
Popein, Larry	NY Rangers	41	18	14	9	.549	0	1973-74
Powers, Eddie	Toronto St. Pats	114	54	56	4	.491	1	1921-26
Primeau, Joe	Toronto	210	97	71	42	.562	1	1950-53
Pronovost, Marcel	Buffalo	104	52	29	23	.611	0	1977-79
	Detroit	9	2	7	0	.222	0	1979-80
	Total	**113**	**54**	**36**	**23**	**.580**	**0**	**1977-80**
Pulford, Bob (16)	Los Angeles	396	178	150	68	.535	0	1972-77
	Chicago	375	158	155	62	.504	0	1977-87
	Total	**771**	**336**	**305**	**130**	**.520**	**0**	**1972-87**
Querrie, Charlie	Toronto St. Pats	6	3	3	0	.500	0	1922-23
Quinn, Mike	Que. Bulldogs	24	4	20	0	.167	0	1919-20
Quinn, Pat (19)	Philadelphia	262	141	73	48	.630	0	1978-82
	Los Angeles	202	75	101	26	.436	0	1984-87
	Vancouver	274	138	108	28	.555	0	1990-94
	Total	**738**	**354**	**282**	**102**	**.549**	**0**	**1978-94**
Ramsay, Craig	Buffalo	21	4	15	2	.238	0	1986-87
Reay, Billy (4)	Toronto	90	26	50	14	.367	0	1957-59
	Chicago	1012	516	335	161	.589	0	1963-77
	Total	**1102**	**542**	**385**	**175**	**.571**	**0**	**1957-77**
Regan, Larry	Los Angeles	88	27	47	14	.386	0	1970-72
Risebrough, Doug	Calgary	144	71	56	11	.531	0	1990-92
Roberts, Jim	Buffalo	45	21	15	9	.567	0	1981-82
	Hartford	80	26	41	13	.406	0	1991-92
	Total	**125**	**47**	**56**	**22**	**.464**	**0**	**1981-92**
Ross, Art (21)	Mtl. Wanderers	6	1	5	0	.167	0	1917-18
	Hamilton	24	6	18	0	.250	0	1922-23
	Boston	698	354	254	90	.572	1	1924-28, 1929-34, 1936-39, 1941-45
	Total	**728**	**361**	**277**	**90**	**.558**	**1**	**1917-45**
Ruel, Claude	Montreal	305	172	82	51	.648	1	1968-71, 1979-81
Sather, Glen (11)	Edmonton	842	464	268	110	.616	4	1979-89, 1993-94
Sator, Ted	NY Rangers	99	41	48	10	.465	0	1985-86
	Buffalo	207	96	89	22	.517	0	1986-88
	Total	**306**	**137**	**137**	**32**	**.500**	**0**	**1985-88**
Savard, André	Quebec	24	10	13	1	.438	0	1987-88
Schinkel, Ken	Pittsburgh	203	83	92	28	.478	0	1972-77
Schmidt, Milt (17)	Boston	726	245	360	121	.421	0	1954-61, 1962-66
	Washington	43	5	33	5	.174	0	1974-76
	Total	**769**	**250**	**393**	**126**	**.407**	**0**	**1954-66**
Schoenfeld, Jim	Buffalo	43	19	19	5	.500	0	1985-86
	New Jersey	124	50	59	15	.464	0	1987-90
	Washington	37	19	12	6	.595	0	1993-94
	Total	**161**	**69**	**71**	**21**	**.494**	**0**	**1985-94**
Shaughnessy, Tom	Chicago	21	10	8	3	.548	0	1929-30
Shero, Fred (20)	Philadelphia	554	308	151	95	.642	2	1971-78
	NY Rangers	180	82	74	24	.522	0	1978-81
	Total	**734**	**390**	**225**	**119**	**.612**	**2**	**1971-81**
Simpson, Joe	NY Americans	144	42	72	30	.396	0	1932-35
Simpson, Terry	NY Islanders	187	81	82	24	.497	0	1986-89
	Winnipeg	1*	0	1	0	.000	0	1992-93
	Philadelphia	84	35	39	10	.476	0	1993-94
	Total	**271**	**116**	**121**	**34**	**.491**	**0**	**1986-93**
Sinden, Harry	Boston	330	151	121	58	.545	1	1966-70, 1979-80, 1984-85
Skinner, Jimmy	Detroit	247	123	78	46	.591	1	1954-58
Smeaton, Cooper	Phil. Quakers	44	4	36	4	.136	0	1930-31
Smith, Alf	Ottawa	18	12	6	0	.667	0	1918-19
Smith, Floyd	Buffalo	241	143	62	36	.668	0	1974-77
	Toronto	68	30	33	5	.478	0	1979-80
	Total	**309**	**173**	**95**	**41**	**.626**	**0**	**1971-80**
Smith, Mike	Winnipeg	23	2	17	4	.174	0	1980-81
Smith, Ron	NY Rangers	44	15	22	7	.420	0	1992-93
Smythe, Conn	Toronto	178	72	81	25	.475	0	1926-30
Sonmor, Glen	Minnesota	416	174	161	81	.516	0	1978-83
Sproule, Harry	Toronto St. Pats	12	7	5	0	.583	0	1919-20
Stanley, Barney	Chicago	23	4	17	2	.217	0	1927-28
Stasiuk, Vic	Philadelphia	154	45	68	41	.425	0	1969-71
	California	75	21	38	16	.387	0	1971-72
	Vancouver	78	22	47	9	.340	0	1972-73
	Total	**307**	**88**	**153**	**66**	**.394**	**0**	**1969-73**
Stewart, Bill	Chicago	69	22	35	12	.406	1	1937-39
Stewart, Ron	NY Rangers	39	15	20	4	.436	0	1975-76
	Los Angeles	80	31	34	15	.481	0	1977-78
	Total	**119**	**46**	**54**	**19**	**.466**	**0**	**1975-78**
Sullivan, Red	NY Rangers	196	58	103	35	.385	0	1962-65
	Pittsburgh	150	47	79	24	.393	0	1967-69
	Washington	19	2	17	0	.105	0	1974-75
	Total	**365**	**107**	**199**	**59**	**.374**	**0**	**1962-75**
Sutherland, Bill	Winnipeg	32	7	22	7	.328	0	1979-80, 1980-81
Sutter, Brian	St. Louis	320	153	124	43	.545	0	1988-92
	Boston	168	93	55	20	.613	0	1992-94
	Total	**488**	**246**	**179**	**63**	**.569**	**0**	**1988-94**
Sutter, Darryl	Chicago	168	86	61	21	.574	0	1992-94
Talbot, Jean-Guy	St. Louis	120	52	53	15	.496	0	1972-74
	NY Rangers	80	30	37	13	.456	0	1977-78
	Total	**200**	**82**	**90**	**28**	**.480**	**0**	**1972-78**
Tessier, Orval	Chicago	213	99	93	21	.514	0	1982-85
Thompson, Paul	Chicago	272	104	127	41	.458	0	1938-45
Thompson, Percy	Hamilton	48	14	34	0	.292	0	1920-22
Tobin, Bill	Chicago	23	11	10	2	.522	0	1929-30
Ubriaco, Gene	Pittsburgh	106	50	47	9	.514	0	1988-90
Vachon, Rogie	Los Angeles	3	1	1	1	.500	0	1983-84, 1987-88
Watson, Bryan	Edmonton	18	4	9	5	.361	0	1980-81
Watson, Phil	NY Rangers	294	118	124	52	.490	0	1955-59
	Boston	84	16	55	13	.268	0	1961-63
	Total	**378**	**134**	**179**	**65**	**.440**	**0**	**1955-64**
Watt, Tom	Winnipeg	181	72	85	24	.464	0	1981-84
	Vancouver	160	52	87	21	.391	0	1985-87
	Toronto	149	52	80	17	.406	0	1990-92
	Total	**490**	**176**	**252**	**62**	**.422**	**0**	**1981-92**
Webster, Tom	NY Rangers	16	5	7	4	.438	0	1986-87
	Los Angeles	240	115	94	31	.544	0	1989-92
	Total	**256**	**120**	**101**	**35**	**.537**	**0**	**1986-92**
Weiland, Cooney	Boston	96	58	20	18	.698	1	1939-41
White, Bill	Chicago	46	16	24	6	.413	0	1976-77
Wilson, Johnny	Los Angeles	52	9	34	9	.260	0	1969-70
	Detroit	145	67	56	22	.538	0	1971-73
	Colorado	80	20	46	14	.338	0	1976-77
	Pittsburgh	240	91	105	44	.471	0	1977-80
	Total	**517**	**187**	**241**	**89**	**.448**	**0**	**1969-80**
Wilson, Larry	Detroit	36	3	29	4	.139	0	1976-77
Wilson, Ron	Anaheim	84	33	46	5	.423	0	1993-94
Young, Garry	California	12	2	7	3	.292	0	1972-73
	St. Louis	98	41	41	16	.500	0	1974-76
	Total	**110**	**43**	**48**	**19**	**.477**	**0**	**1972-76**

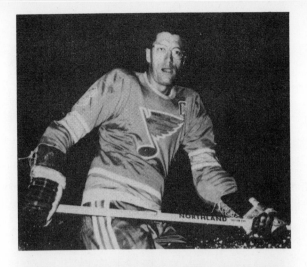

Stanley Cup-winning coaches: Opposite page, left: Terry Crisp, Calgary 1989; right: John Muckler, Edmonton, 1990. This page, top: Al Arbour, New York Islanders, 1980-83; middle: Toe Blake, Montreal, 1956-60, 65, 66, 68; bottom: Fred Shero, Philadelphia, 1974-75.

All-Time Penalty-Minute Leaders

* active player
(Regular season. Minimum 1,500 minutes)

Player	Teams	Seasons	Games	Penalty Minutes	Mins. per game
Dave Williams,	Tor., Van., Det., L.A., Hfd.	14	962	**3,966**	4.12
Chris Nilan,	Mtl., NYR, Bos.	13	688	**3,043**	4.42
*Dale Hunter,	Que., Wsh.	14	1,054	**3,005**	2.85
*Tim Hunter,	Cgy., Que., Van.	13	675	**2,769**	4.10
*Marty McSorley,	Pit., Edm., L.A.	11	666	**2,640**	3.96
Willi Plett,	Atl., Cgy., Min., Bos.	13	834	**2,572**	3.08
*Basil McRae,	Que., Tor., Det., Min., St.L.	13	529	**2,333**	4.41
Dave Schultz,	Phi., L.A., Pit., Buf.	9	535	**2,294**	4.29
Laurie Boschman,	Tor., Edm., Wpg., N.J., Ott.	14	1,009	**2,265**	2.24
*Garth Butcher,	Van., St.L., Que.	13	852	**2,243**	2.63
*Jay Wells,	L.A., Phi., Buf., NYR	15	958	**2,243**	2.34
*Rob Ramage,	Col., St.L., Cgy., Tor., Min., T.B., Mtl., Phi.	15	1,044	**2,226**	2.13
Bryan Watson,	Mtl., Det., Cal., Pit., St.L., Wsh.	16	878	**2,212**	2.52
*Scott Stevens,	Wsh., St.L., N.J.	12	911	**2,134**	2.34
*Joey Kocur,	Det., NYR.	10	591	**2,131**	3.61
*Rick Tocchet,	Phi., Pit.	10	681	**2,120**	3.11
Terry O'Reilly,	Boston.	14	891	**2,095**	2.35
Al Secord,	Chi., Tor., Phi.	12	766	**2,093**	2.73
*Bob Probert,	Detroit.	9	474	**2,090**	4.41
*Mike Foligno,	Det., Buf., Tor., Fla.	15	1,018	**2,049**	2.01
Phil Russell,	Chi., Atl., Cgy., N.J., Buf.	15	1,016	**2,038**	2.01
*Pat Verbeek,	N.J., Hfd.	12	867	**2,034**	2.35
*Gord Donnelly,	Que., Wpg., Buf., Dal.	11	538	**2,017**	3.75
Harold Snepsts,	Van., Min., Det., St.L.	17	1,033	**2,009**	1.94
Andre Dupont,	NYR, St.L., Phi., Que.	13	810	**1,986**	2.45
*Ken Daneyko,	N.J.	11	691	**1,879**	2.72
Garry Howatt,	NYI, Hfd., N.J.	12	720	**1,836**	2.55
Carol Vadnais,	Mtl., Oak., Cal., Bos., NYR, N.J.	17	1,087	**1,813**	1.67
Larry Playfair,	Buf., L.A.	11	688	**1,812**	2.63
Ted Lindsay,	Det., Chi.	17	1,068	**1,808**	1.69
Jim Korn,	Det., Tor., Buf., N.J., Cgy.	10	597	**1,801**	3.02
*Ulf Samuelsson,	Hfd., Pit.	10	696	**1,801**	2.59
*Dave Manson,	Chi., Edm., Wpg.	8	562	**1,796**	3.20
Brian Sutter,	St. Louis.	12	779	**1,786**	2.29
*Shane Churla,	Hfd., Cgy., Min., Dal.	8	361	**1,778**	4.93
*Steve Smith,	Edm., Chi.	10	596	**1,772**	2.97
*Bob McGill,	Tor., Chi., S.J., Det., NYI, Hfd.	13	705	**1,766**	2.50
Wilf Paiment,	K.C., Col., Tor., Que., NYR, Buf., Pit.	14	946	**1,757**	1.86
Torrie Robertson,	Wsh., Hfd., Det.	10	442	**1,751**	3.96
Mario Marois,	NYR, Van., Que., Win., St.L.	15	955	**1,746**	1.83
Ken Linseman,	Phi., Edm., Bos., Tor.	14	860	**1,727**	2.01
*Craig Berube,	Phi., Tor., Cgy.	8	472	**1,726**	3.66
Jay Miller,	Bos., L.A.	7	446	**1,723**	3.86
*Chris Chelios,	Mtl., Chi.	11	719	**1,714**	2.38
*Dave Brown,	Phi., Edm.	12	664	**1,690**	2.55
Gordie Howe,	Det., Hfd.	26	1,767	**1,685**	.95
Paul Holmgren,	Phi., Min.	10	527	**1,684**	3.20
*Randy Moller,	Que., NYR, Buf.	13	798	**1,676**	2.10
*Gerard Gallant,	Det., T.B.	10	614	**1,674**	2.73
*Kevin McClelland,	Pit., Edm., Det., Tor., Wpg.	12	588	**1,672**	2.84
Jerry Korab,	Chi., Van., Buf., L.A.	15	975	**1,629**	1.67
Mel Bridgman,	Phi., Cgy., N.J., Det., Van.	14	977	**1,625**	1.66
*Gary Roberts,	Calgary	8	542	**1,615**	2.98
Tim Horton,	Tor., NYR, Pit., Buf.	24	1,446	**1,611**	1.11
*Mick Vukota,	NY Islanders	7	421	**1,593**	3.78
*Gordie Roberts,	Hfd., Min., Phi., St.L., Pit., Bos.	15	1,097	**1,582**	1.44
Paul Baxter,	Que., Pit., Cgy.	8	472	**1,564**	3.31
Dave Taylor,	Los Angeles	17	1,111	**1,589**	1.43
Glen Cochrane,	Phi., Van., Chi., Edm.	9	411	**1,556**	3.79
Stan Smyl,	Vancouver	13	896	**1,556**	1.74
Mike Milbury,	Boston.	12	754	**1,552**	2.06
Dave Hutchison,	L.A., Tor., Chi., N.J.	10	584	**1,550**	2.65
*Ken Baumgartner,	L.A., NYI, Tor.	7	404	**1,546**	3.83
Doug Risebrough,	Mtl., Cgy.	14	740	**1,542**	2.08
Bill Gadsby,	Chi., NYR, Det.	20	1,248	**1,539**	1.23
*Joel Otto,	Calgary	10	683	**1,512**	2.21

One Season Scoring Records

Goals-Per-Game Leaders, One Season

(Among players with 20 goals or more in one season)

Player	Team	Season	Games	Goals	Average
Joe Malone	Montreal	1917-18	20	44	2.20
Cy Denneny	Ottawa	1917-18	22	36	1.64
Newsy Lalonde	Montreal	1917-18	14	23	1.64
Joe Malone	Quebec	1919-20	24	39	1.63
Newsy Lalonde	Montreal	1919-20	23	36	1.57
Joe Malone	Hamilton	1920-21	20	30	1.50
Babe Dye	Ham., Tor.	1920-21	24	35	1.46
Cy Denneny	Ottawa	1920-21	24	34	1.42
Reg Noble	Toronto	1917-18	20	28	1.40
Newsy Lalonde	Montreal	1920-21	24	33	1.38
Odie Cleghorn	Montreal	1918-19	17	23	1.35
Harry Broadbent	Ottawa	1921-22	24	32	1.33
Babe Dye	Toronto	1924-25	29	38	1.31
Babe Dye	Toronto	1921-22	24	30	1.25
Newsy Lalonde	Montreal	1918-19	17	21	1.24
Cy Denneny	Ottawa	1921-22	22	27	1.23
Aurel Joliat	Montreal	1924-25	24	29	1.21
Wayne Gretzky	Edmonton	1983-84	74	87	1.18
Babe Dye	Toronto	1922-23	22	26	1.18
Wayne Gretzky	Edmonton	1981-82	80	92	1.15
Mario Lemieux	Pittsburgh	1992-93	60	69	1.15
Frank Nighbor	Ottawa	1919-20	23	26	1.13
Mario Lemieux	Pittsburgh	1988-89	76	85	1.12
Brett Hull	St. Louis	1990-91	78	86	1.10
Amos Arbour	Montreal	1919-20	20	22	1.10
Cy Denneny	Ottawa	1923-24	21	22	1.05
Joe Malone	Hamilton	1921-22	24	25	1.04
Billy Boucher	Montreal	1922-23	24	25	1.04
Cam Neely	Boston	**1993-94**	49	50	1.02
Maurice Richard	Montreal	1944-45	50	50	1.00
Howie Morenz	Montreal	1924-25	30	30	1.00
Reg Noble	Toronto	1919-20	24	24	1.00
Corbett Denneny	Toronto	1919-20	23	23	1.00
Jack Darragh	Ottawa	1919-20	22	22	1.00
Alexander Mogilny	Buffalo	1992-93	77	76	.99
Cooney Weiland	Boston	1929-30	44	43	.98
Phil Esposito	Boston	1970-71	78	76	.97
Jari Kurri	Edmonton	1984-85	73	71	.97

With 50 goals in 49 games played, Cam Neely became the fifth player of the modern era to average more than one goal per game.

Penalty Leaders

* Match Misconduct penalty not included in total penalty minutes.
** Three Match Misconduct penalties not included in total penalty minutes.
1946-47 was the first season that a Match penalty was automatically written into the player's total penalty minutes as 20 minutes. Now all penalties, Match, Game Misconduct, and Misconduct, are written as 10 minutes. Penalty minutes not calculated in 1917-18.

Season	Player and Club	GP	PIM	Season	Player and Club	GP	PIM	Season	Player and Club	GP	PIM
1993-94	Tie Domi, Winnipeg	81	347	1967-68	Barclay Plager, St. Louis	49	153	1941-42	Jimmy Orlando, Detroit	48	81**
1992-93	Marty McSorley, Los Angeles	81	399	1966-67	John Ferguson, Montreal	67	177	1940-41	Jimmy Orlando, Detroit	48	99
1991-92	Mike Peluso, Chicago	63	408	1965-66	Reg Fleming, Bos., NYR	69	166	1939-40	Red Horner, Toronto	30	87
1990-91	Rob Ray, Buffalo	66	350	1964-65	Carl Brewer, Toronto	70	177	1938-39	Red Horner, Toronto	48	85
1989-90	Basil McRae, Minnesota	66	351	1963-64	Vic Hadfield, NY Rangers	69	151	1937-38	Red Horner, Toronto	47	82*
1988-89	Tim Hunter, Calgary	75	375	1962-63	Howie Young, Detroit	64	273	1936-37	Red Horner, Toronto	48	124
1987-88	Bob Probert, Detroit	74	398	1961-62	Lou Fontinato, Montreal	54	167	1935-36	Red Horner, Toronto	43	167
1986-87	Tim Hunter, Calgary	73	361	1960-61	Pierre Pilote, Chicago	70	165	1934-35	Red Horner, Toronto	46	125
1985-86	Joey Kocur, Detroit	59	377	1959-60	Carl Brewer, Toronto	67	150	1933-34	Red Horner, Toronto	42	126*
1984-85	Chris Nilan, Montreal	77	358	1958-59	Ted Lindsay, Chicago	70	184	1932-33	Red Horner, Toronto	48	144
1983-84	Chris Nilan, Montreal	76	338	1957-58	Lou Fontinato, NY Rangers	70	152	1931-32	Red Dutton, NY Americans	47	107
1982-83	Randy Holt, Washington	70	275	1956-57	Gus Mortson, Chicago	70	147	1930-31	Harvey Rockburn, Detroit	42	118
1981-82	Paul Baxter, Pittsburgh	76	409	1955-56	Lou Fontinato, NY Rangers	70	202	1929-30	Joe Lamb, Ottawa	44	119
1980-81	Dave Williams, Vancouver	77	343	1954-55	Fern Flaman, Boston	70	150	1928-29	Red Dutton, Mtl. Maroons	44	139
1979-80	Jimmy Mann, Winnipeg	72	287	1953-54	Gus Mortson, Chicago	68	132	1927-28	Eddie Shore, Boston	44	165
1978-79	Dave Williams, Toronto	77	298	1952-53	Maurice Richard, Montreal	70	112	1926-27	Nels Stewart, Mtl. Maroons	44	133
1977-78	Dave Schultz, L.A., Pit.	74	405	1951-52	Gus Kyle, Boston	69	127	1925-26	Bert Corbeau, Toronto	36	121
1976-77	Dave Williams, Toronto	77	338	1950-51	Gus Mortson, Toronto	60	142	1924-25	Billy Boucher, Montreal	30	92
1975-76	Steve Durbano, Pit., K.C.	69	370	1949-50	Bill Ezinicki, Toronto	67	144	1923-24	Bert Corbeau, Toronto	24	55
1974-75	Dave Schultz, Philadelphia	76	472	1948-49	Bill Ezinicki, Toronto	52	145	1922-23	Billy Boucher, Montreal	24	52
1973-74	Dave Schultz, Philadelphia	73	348	1947-48	Bill Barilko, Toronto	57	147	1921-22	Sprague Cleghorn, Montreal	24	63
1972-73	Dave Schultz, Philadelphia	76	259	1946-47	Gus Mortson, Toronto	60	133	1920-21	Bert Corbeau, Montreal	24	86
1971-72	Bryan Watson, Pittsburgh	75	212	1945-46	Jack Stewart, Detroit	47	73	1919-20	Cully Wilson, Toronto	23	79
1970-71	Keith Magnuson, Chicago	76	291	1944-45	Pat Egan, Boston	48	86	1918-19	Joe Hall, Montreal	17	85
1969-70	Keith Magnuson, Chicago	76	213	1943-44	Mike McMahon, Montreal	42	98				
1968-69	Forbes Kennedy, Phi., Tor.	77	219	1942-43	Jimmy Orlando, Detroit	40	89*				

Assists-Per-Game Leaders, One Season

(Among players with 35 assists or more in one season)

Player	Team	Season	Games	Assists	Average	Player	Team	Season	Games	Assists	Average
Wayne Gretzky	Edmonton	1985-86	80	163	2.04	Bobby Clarke	Philadelphia	1974-75	80	89	1.11
Wayne Gretzky	Edmonton	1987-88	64	109	1.70	Paul Coffey	Pittsburgh	1988-89	75	83	1.11
Wayne Gretzky	Edmonton	1984-85	80	135	1.69	Wayne Gretzky	Los Angeles	1992-93	45	49	1.11
Wayne Gretzky	Edmonton	1983-84	74	118	1.59	Denis Savard	Chicago	1982-83	78	86	1.10
Wayne Gretzky	Edmonton	1982-83	80	125	1.56	Denis Savard	Chicago	1981-82	80	87	1.09
Wayne Gretzky	Los Angeles	1990-91	78	122	1.56	Denis Savard	Chicago	1987-88	80	87	1.09
Wayne Gretzky	Edmonton	1986-87	79	121	1.53	Wayne Gretzky	Edmonton	1979-80	79	86	1.09
Mario Lemieux	Pittsburgh	1992-93	60	91	1.52	Paul Coffey	Edmonton	1983-84	80	86	1.08
Wayne Gretzky	Edmonton	1981-82	80	120	1.50	Elmer Lach	Montreal	1944-45	50	54	1.08
Mario Lemieux	Pittsburgh	1988-89	76	114	1.50	Peter Stastny	Quebec	1985-86	76	81	1.07
Adam Oates	St. Louis	1990-91	61	90	1.48	Mark Messier	Edmonton	1989-90	79	84	1.06
Wayne Gretzky	Los Angeles	1988-89	78	114	1.46	Paul Coffey	Edmonton	1984-85	80	84	1.05
Wayne Gretzky	Los Angeles	1989-90	73	102	1.40	Marcel Dionne	Los Angeles	1979-80	80	84	1.05
Wayne Gretzky	Edmonton	1980-81	80	109	1.36	Bobby Orr	Boston	1971-72	76	80	1.05
Mario Lemieux	Pittsburgh	1991-92	64	87	1.36	Mike Bossy	NY Islanders	1981-82	80	83	1.04
Mario Lemieux	Pittsburgh	1989-90	59	78	1.32	Adam Oates	Boston	**1993-94**	77	80	1.04
Bobby Orr	Boston	1970-71	78	102	1.31	Phil Esposito	Boston	1968-69	74	77	1.04
Mario Lemieux	Pittsburgh	1987-88	77	98	1.27	Bryan Trottier	NY Islanders	1983-84	68	71	1.04
Bobby Orr	Boston	1973-74	74	90	1.22	Pete Mahovlich	Montreal	1974-75	80	82	1.03
Wayne Gretzky	Los Angeles	1991-92	74	90	1.22	Kent Nilsson	Calgary	1980-81	80	82	1.03
Mario Lemieux	Pittsburgh	1985-86	79	93	1.18	Peter Stastny	Quebec	1982-83	75	77	1.03
Bobby Clarke	Philadelphia	1975-76	76	89	1.17	Doug Gilmour	Toronto	**1993-94**	83	84	1.01
Peter Stastny	Quebec	1981-82	80	93	1.16	Bernie Nicholls	Los Angeles	1988-89	79	80	1.01
Adam Oates	Boston	1992-93	84	97	1.15	Guy Lafleur	Montreal	1979-80	74	75	1.01
Doug Gilmour	Toronto	1992-93	83	95	1.14	Guy Lafleur	Montreal	1976-77	80	80	1.00
Wayne Gretzky	Los Angeles	**1993-94**	81	92	1.14	Marcel Dionne	Los Angeles	1984-85	80	80	1.00
Paul Coffey	Edmonton	1985-86	79	90	1.14	Brian Leetch	NY Rangers	1991-92	80	80	1.00
Bobby Orr	Boston	1969-70	76	87	1.14	Bryan Trottier	NY Islanders	1977-78	77	77	1.00
Bryan Trottier	NY Islanders	1978-79	76	87	1.14	Mike Bossy	NY Islanders	1983-84	67	67	1.00
Bobby Orr	Boston	1972-73	63	72	1.14	Jean Ratelle	NY Rangers	1971-72	63	63	1.00
Bill Cowley	Boston	1943-44	36	41	1.14	Steve Yzerman	Detroit	**1993-94**	58	58	1.00
Pat LaFontaine	Buffalo	1992-93	84	95	1.13	Ron Francis	Hartford	1985-86	53	53	1.00
Steve Yzerman	Detroit	1988-89	80	90	1.13	Guy Chouinard	Calgary	1980-81	52	52	1.00
Paul Coffey	Pittsburgh	1987-88	46	52	1.13	Elmer Lach	Montreal	1943-44	48	48	1.00
Bobby Orr	Boston	1974-75	80	89	1.11						

Bernie Nicholls registered 80 assists in 79 games for the Kings in 1988-89.

Points-Per-Game Leaders, One Season

(Among players with 50 points or more in one season)

Player	Team	Season	Games	Points	Average
Wayne Gretzky	Edmonton	1983-84	74	205	2.77
Wayne Gretzky	Edmonton	1985-86	80	215	2.69
Mario Lemieux	Pittsburgh	1992-93	60	160	2.67
Wayne Gretzky	Edmonton	1981-82	80	212	2.65
Mario Lemieux	Pittsburgh	1988-89	76	199	2.62
Wayne Gretzky	Edmonton	1984-85	80	208	2.60
Wayne Gretzky	Edmonton	1982-83	80	196	2.45
Wayne Gretzky	Edmonton	1987-88	64	149	2.33
Wayne Gretzky	Edmonton	1986-87	79	183	2.32
Mario Lemieux	Pittsburgh	1987-88	77	168	2.18
Wayne Gretzky	Los Angeles	1988-89	78	168	2.15
Wayne Gretzky	Los Angeles	1990-91	78	163	2.09
Mario Lemieux	Pittsburgh	1989-90	59	123	2.08
Wayne Gretzky	Edmonton	1980-81	80	164	2.05
Mario Lemieux	Pittsburgh	1991-92	64	131	2.05
Bill Cowley	Boston	1943-44	36	71	1.97
Phil Esposito	Boston	1970-71	78	152	1.95
Wayne Gretzky	Los Angeles	1989-90	73	142	1.95
Steve Yzerman	Detroit	1988-89	80	155	1.94
Bernie Nicholls	Los Angeles	1988-89	79	150	1.90
Adam Oates	St. Louis	1990-91	61	115	1.89
Phil Esposito	Boston	1973-74	78	145	1.86
Jari Kurri	Edmonton	1984-85	73	135	1.85
Mike Bossy	NY Islanders	1981-82	80	147	1.84
Mario Lemieux	Pittsburgh	1985-86	79	141	1.78
Bobby Orr	Boston	1970-71	78	139	1.78
Jari Kurri	Edmonton	1983-84	64	113	1.77
Pat LaFontaine	Buffalo	1992-93	84	148	1.76
Bryan Trottier	NY Islanders	1978-79	76	134	1.76
Mike Bossy	NY Islanders	1983-84	67	118	1.76
Paul Coffey	Edmonton	1985-86	79	138	1.75
Phil Esposito	Boston	1971-72	76	133	1.75
Peter Stastny	Quebec	1981-82	80	139	1.74
Wayne Gretzky	Edmonton	1979-80	79	137	1.73
Jean Ratelle	NY Rangers	1971-72	63	109	1.73
Marcel Dionne	Los Angeles	1979-80	80	137	1.71
Herb Cain	Boston	1943-44	48	82	1.71
Guy Lafleur	Montreal	1976-77	80	136	1.70
Dennis Maruk	Washington	1981-82	80	136	1.70
Phil Esposito	Boston	1968-69	74	126	1.70
Guy Lafleur	Montreal	1974-75	70	119	1.70
Mario Lemieux	Pittsburgh	1986-87	63	107	1.70
Adam Oates	Boston	1992-93	84	142	1.69
Bobby Orr	Boston	1974-75	80	135	1.69
Marcel Dionne	Los Angeles	1980-81	80	135	1.69
Guy Lafleur	Montreal	1977-78	78	132	1.69
Guy Lafleur	Montreal	1979-80	74	125	1.69
Rob Brown	Pittsburgh	1988-89	68	115	1.69
Jari Kurri	Edmonton	1985-86	78	131	1.68
Brett Hull	St. Louis	1990-91	78	131	1.68
Phil Esposito	Boston	1972-73	78	130	1.67
Cooney Weiland	Boston	1929-30	44	73	1.66
Alexander Mogilny	Buffalo	1992-93	77	127	1.65
Peter Stastny	Quebec	1982-83	75	124	1.65
Bobby Orr	Boston	1973-74	74	122	1.65
Kent Nilsson	Calgary	1980-81	80	131	1.64
Wayne Gretzky	Los Angeles	1991-92	74	121	1.64
Denis Savard	Chicago	1987-88	80	131	1.64
Steve Yzerman	Detroit	1992-93	84	137	1.63
Marcel Dionne	Los Angeles	1978-79	80	130	1.63
Dale Hawerchuk	Winnipeg	1984-85	80	130	1.63
Mark Messier	Edmonton	1989-90	79	129	1.63
Bryan Trottier	NY Islanders	1983-84	68	111	1.63
Pat LaFontaine	Buffalo	1991-92	57	93	1.63
Charlie Simmer	Los Angeles	1980-81	65	105	1.62
Guy Lafleur	Montreal	1978-79	80	129	1.61
Bryan Trottier	NY Islanders	1981-82	80	129	1.61
Phil Esposito	Boston	1974-75	79	127	1.61
Steve Yzerman	Detroit	1989-90	79	127	1.61
Peter Stastny	Quebec	1985-86	76	122	1.61
Michel Goulet	Quebec	1983-84	75	121	1.61
Wayne Gretzky	Los Angeles	**1993-94**	81	130	1.60
Bryan Trottier	NY Islanders	1977-78	77	123	1.60
Bobby Orr	Boston	1972-73	63	101	1.60
Guy Chouinard	Calgary	1980-81	52	83	1.60
Elmer Lach	Montreal	1944-45	50	80	1.60
Pierre Turgeon	NY Islanders	1992-93	83	132	1.59
Steve Yzerman	Detroit	1987-88	64	102	1.59
Mike Bossy	NY Islanders	1978-79	80	126	1.58
Paul Coffey	Edmonton	1983-84	80	126	1.58
Marcel Dionne	Los Angeles	1984-85	80	126	1.58
Bobby Orr	Boston	1969-70	76	120	1.58
Charlie Simmer	Los Angeles	1979-80	64	101	1.58
Teemu Selanne	Winnipeg	1992-93	84	132	1.57
Bobby Clarke	Philadelphia	1975-76	76	119	1.57
Guy Lafleur	Montreal	1975-76	80	125	1.56
Dave Taylor	Los Angeles	1980-81	72	112	1.56
Denis Savard	Chicago	1982-83	78	121	1.55
Mike Bossy	NY Islanders	1985-86	80	123	1.54
Bobby Orr	Boston	1971-72	76	117	1.54
Kevin Stevens	Pittsburgh	1991-92	80	123	1.54
Mike Bossy	NY Islanders	1984-85	76	117	1.54
Kevin Stevens	Pittsburgh	1992-93	72	111	1.54
Doug Bentley	Chicago	1943-44	50	77	1.54
Doug Gilmour	Toronto	1992-93	83	127	1.53
Marcel Dionne	Los Angeles	1976-77	80	122	1.53
Marcel Dionne	Detroit	1974-75	80	121	1.51
Paul Coffey	Pittsburgh	1988-89	75	113	1.51
Cam Neely	Boston	**1993-94**	49	74	1.51

Bobby Orr, right, averaged better than a point-per-game in six of his nine NHL seasons, including a 1.78 point-per-game average in 1970-71, the highest rating by a defenceman in NHL history. Charlie Simmer, below, seen here in the uniform of the Cleveland Barons, averaged 1.58 points-per-game as a member of the Los Angeles Kings' Triple Crown Line in 1979-80.

Active NHL Players' Three-or-More-Goal Games

Regular Season

Teams named are the ones the players were with at the time of their multiple-scoring games. Players listed alphabetically.

Wendel Clark, who was traded to the Quebec Nordiques on June 28, 1994, recorded seven three-or-more-goal games for the Maple Leafs in his nine seasons in Toronto.

Player	Team	3-Goals	4-Goals	5-Goals
Acton, Keith	Mtl., Min.	3	—	—
Adams, Greg	Vancouver	1	1	—
Amonte, Tony	NY Rangers	1	—	—
Anderson, Glenn	Edm., Tor.	18	3	—
Andersson, Mikael	Tampa Bay	1	—	—
Andreychuk, Dave	Buf., Tor.	7	2	1
Arniel, Scott	Winnipeg	1	—	—
Ashton, Brent	Que., Wpg.	6	—	—
Babych, Dave	Vancouver	1	—	—
Barnes, Stu	Winnipeg	1	—	—
Barr, Dave	St. L., Det.	2	—	—
Bellows, Brian	Min., Mtl.	5	3	—
Bondra, Peter	Washington	1	—	1
Bourque, Phil	Pittsburgh	1	—	—
Bourque, Ray	Boston	1	—	—
Bradley, Brian	Tampa Bay	1	—	—
Brickley, Andy	Pit., Bos.	2	—	—
Brind'Amour, Rod	Philadelphia	1	—	—
Broten, Neal	Minnesota	6	—	—
Broten, Paul	NY Rangers	1	—	—
Brown, Rob	Pittsburgh	7	—	—
Buchberger, Kelly	Edmonton	1	—	—
Bullard, Mike	Pit., Tor.	8	—	—
Bure, Pavel	Vancouver	4	1	—
Burr, Shawn	Detroit	3	—	—
Burridge, Randy	Bos., Wsh.	4	—	—
Butsayev, Viacheslav	Philadelphia	1	—	—
Carbonneau, Guy	Montreal	1	1	—
Carpenter, Bob	Wsh., Bos.	2	1	—
Carson, Jimmy	L.A., Edm., Det.	9	1	—
Cavallini, Gino	St. Louis	1	—	—
Chabot, John	Pittsburgh	1	—	—
Christian, Dave	Wpg., Wsh.	2	—	—
Ciccarelli, Dino	Min., Wsh.	14	4	1
Clark, Wendel	Toronto	6	1	—
Coffey, Paul	Edmonton	4	1	—
Corson, Shayne	Mtl., Edm.	3	—	—
Courtnall, Geoff	Bos., Wsh.	2	—	—
Courtnall, Russ	Tor., Mtl., Min.	3	—	—
Craven, Murray	Philadelphia	3	—	—
Creighton, Adam	Buf., Chi.	2	—	—
Crossman, Doug	Tampa Bay	1	—	—
Cullen, John	Pit., Hfd.	3	—	—
Cunneyworth, R.	Pittsburgh	1	1	—
Dahlen, Ulf	NYR, Min., S.J.	4	—	—
Damphousse, V.	Tor., Edm., Mtl.	7	1	—
Davydov, Evgeny	Winnipeg	1	—	—
Dineen, Kevin	Hfd., Phi.	9	1	—
Dionne, Gilbert	Montreal	1	—	—
Donnelly, Mike	Los Angeles	2	—	—
Druce, John	Wsh., L.A.	2	—	—
Duchesne, Steve	L.A., Phi., St.L.	3	—	—
Eklund, Pelle	Philadelphia	1	—	—
Errey, Bob	Pittsburgh	1	—	—
Evason, Dean	Hartford	1	—	—
Fedorov, Sergei	Detroit	1	—	—
Fergus, Tom	Toronto	4	—	—
Ferraro, Ray	Hfd., NYI	6	1	—
Flatley, Patrick	NY Islanders	2	1	—
Fleury, Theo	Calgary	7	—	—
Fogarty, Bryan	Quebec	1	—	—
Foligno, Mike	Det., Buf.	8	—	—
Francis, Ron	Hartford	8	1	—
Gagner, Dave	Min., Dal.	3	1	—
Gallant, Gerard	Detroit	4	—	—
Garpenlov, Johan	Det., S.J.	1	1	—
Gartner, Mike	Wsh., Min., NYR	14	2	—
Gaudreau, Rob	San Jose	3	—	—
Gelinas, Martin	Edmonton	1	—	—
Gilbert, Greg	NY Islanders	2	—	—
Gilchrist, Brent	Montreal	1	—	—
Gilmour, Doug	St.L., Tor.	3	—	—
Goulet, Michel	Que., Chi.	14	2	—
Graham, Dirk	Minnesota	1	—	—
Granato, Tony	NYR, L.A.	3	1	—
Graves, Adam	Edm., NYR	4	—	—
Green, Travis	NY Islanders	1	—	—
Gretzky, Wayne	Edm., L.A.	36	9	4
Grieve, Brent	Edmonton	1	—	—
Hannan, Dave	Edmonton	1	—	—
Hatcher, Kevin	Washington	1	—	—
Hawerchuk, Dale	Wpg., Buf.	13	—	—
Heinze, Stephen	Boston	1	—	—
Hodge, Ken	Boston	2	—	—
Hogue, Benoit	NY Islanders	1	—	—
Holik, Bobby	New Jersey	2	—	—
Horacek, Tony	Philadelphia	1	—	—
Housley, Phil	Buffalo	2	—	—

Player	Team	3-Goal	4-Goal	5-Goal
Howe, Mark	Hartford	1	—	—
Hull, Brett	Cgy., St. L.	21	—	—
Hull, Jody	Hartford	1	—	—
Jagr, Jaromir	Pittsburgh	1	—	—
Janney, Craig	Bos., St. L.	3	—	—
Juneau, Joe	Boston	1	—	—
Khmylev, Yuri	Buffalo	1	—	—
Khristich, Dimitri	Washington	2	—	—
King, Derek	NY Islanders	4	1	—
Klima, Petr	Det., Edm.	6	—	—
Kontos, Chris	Tampa Bay	—	1	—
Kovalenko, Andrei	Quebec	1	—	—
Kovalev, Alexei	NY Rangers	1	—	—
Kozlov, Vyacheslav	Detroit	1	—	—
Krushelnyski, Mike	Edmonton	1	—	—
Krygier, Todd	Washington	1	—	—
Kudelski, Robert	L.A., Ott.	4	—	—
Kurri, Jari	Edm., L.A.	20	1	1
LaFontaine, Pat	NYI, Buf.	12	—	—
Larionov, Igor	Van., S.J.	4	—	—
Larmer, Steve	Chicago	9	—	—
Lavoie, Dominic	Los Angeles	1	—	—
Lebeau, Stephan	Montreal	1	—	—
Leeman, Gary	Tor., Cgy.	5	—	—
Lemieux, Claude	Mtl., N.J.	4	—	—
Lemieux, Jocelyn	Chicago	2	—	—
Lemieux, Mario	Pittsburgh	21	8	2
Linden, Trevor	Vancouver	3	—	—
Lindros, Eric	Philadelphia	4	—	—
MacInnis, Al	Calgary	1	—	—
MacLean, John	New Jersey	6	—	—
MacTavish, Craig	Edmonton	2	—	—
Makarov, Sergei	Cgy., S.J.	4	—	—
Makela, Mikko	NY Islanders	1	—	—
Maley, David	New Jersey	1	—	—
Marois, Daniel	Toronto	3	—	—
McBain, Andrew	Winnipeg	1	—	—
McPhee, Mike	Montreal	3	—	—
Messier, Mark	Edm., NYR	12	4	—
Miller, Kevin	Det., St.L.	3	—	—
Modano, Mike	Min., Dal.	2	—	—
Mogilny, Alexander	Buffalo	8	2	—
Momesso, Sergio	Montreal	1	—	—
Mullen, Brian	Wpg., NYR	2	—	—
Mullen, Joe	St. L., Cgy., Pit.	7	4	—
Muller, Kirk	N.J., Mtl.	6	—	—
Murray, Troy	Chicago	4	—	—
Murzyn, Dana	Calgary	1	—	—
Neely, Cam	Boston	11	—	—
Nemchinov, Sergei	NY Rangers	1	—	—
Nicholls, Bernie	L.A., N.J.	13	2	—
Nieuwendyk, Joe	Calgary	6	2	1
Noonan, Brian	Chicago	2	1	—
Nolan, Owen	Quebec	4	—	—
Nylander, Michael	Hartford	1	—	—
Oates, Adam	Boston	5	—	—
Odelein, Lyle	Montreal	1	—	—
Olczyk, Ed	Tor., NYR	3	—	—
Osborne, Mark	Detroit	1	—	—
Otto, Joel	Calgary	2	—	—
Paslawski, Greg	St.L., Phi.	3	—	—
Petrov, Oleg	Montreal	1	—	—

Player	Team	3-Goal	4-Goal	5-Goal
Pivonka, Michal	Washington	1	—	—
Plante, Derek	Buffalo	1	—	—
Poulin, Dave	Philadelphia	5	—	—
Presley, Wayne	Chicago	1	—	—
Probert, Bob	Detroit	1	—	—
Prokhorov, Vitali	St. Louis	1	—	—
Propp, Brian	Philadelphia	3	1	—
Quinn, Dan	Pit., Van.	4	—	—
Ranheim, Paul	Calgary	1	—	—
Recchi, Mark	Pittsburgh	1	—	—
Reichel, Robert	Calgary	3	—	—
Renberg, Mikael	Philadelphia	1	—	—
Ricci, Mike	Quebec	—	—	1
Richer, Stephane	Mtl., N.J.	7	1	—
Ridley, Mike	NYR, Wsh.	3	1	—
Roberts, Gary	Calgary	6	1	—
Robitaille, Luc	Los Angeles	9	2	—
Roenick, Jeremy	Chicago	4	3	—
Ronning, Cliff	St.L., Van.	2	—	—
Ruzicka, Vladimir	Boston	3	—	—
Sakic, Joe	Quebec	5	—	—
Sanderson, Geoff	Hartford	2	—	—
Sandlak, Jim	Vancouver	1	—	—
Sandstrom, Tomas	NYR, L.A.	7	1	—
Savard, Denis	Chi., Mtl.	12	—	—
Selanne, Teemu	Winnipeg	6	1	—
Semak, Alexander	New Jersey	1	—	—
Shanahan, Brendan	N.J., St.L.	6	—	—
Sheppard, Ray	Buf., Det.	5	—	—
Simpson, Craig	Pit., Edm.	3	—	—
Smith, Derrick	Philadelphia	1	—	—
Stastny, Peter	Que., N.J.	15	2	—
Steen, Thomas	Winnipeg	4	—	—
Stern, Ronnie	Calgary	2	—	—
Stevens, Kevin	Pittsburgh	8	2	—
Straka, Martin	Pittsburgh	1	—	—
Sundin, Mats	Quebec	3	—	1
Sutter, Brent	NY Islanders	6	—	—
Sutter, Rich	Vancouver	1	—	—
Sweeney, Bob	Boston	1	—	—
Tanti, Tony	Van., Pit., Buf.	11	1	—
Thomas, Steve	Chi., NYI	4	2	—
Tikkanen, Esa	Edmonton	3	—	—
Tkachuk, Keith	Winnipeg	1	—	—
Tocchet, Rick	Phi., Pit.	9	2	—
Trottier, Bryan	NY Islanders	13	1	2
Tucker, John	Buffalo	1	—	—
Turcotte, Darren	NY Rangers	4	—	—
Turgeon, Pierre	Buf., NYI	10	—	—
Turgeon, Sylvain	Hfd., N.J., Ott.	5	—	—
Verbeek, Pat	N.J., Hfd.	8	1	—
Volek, Dave	NY Islanders	1	—	—
Vukota, Mick	NY Islanders	1	—	—
Wesley, Glen	Boston	1	—	—
Wood, Randy	NY Islanders	1	—	—
Yake, Terry	Anaheim	1	—	—
Yashin, Alexei	Ottawa	1	—	—
Young, Scott	Quebec	2	—	—
Yzerman, Steve	Detroit	17	1	—
Ysebaert, Paul	Detroit	1	—	—
Zezel, Peter	Philadelphia	1	—	—
Zhamnov, Alexei	Winnipeg	2	—	—

Alexei Zhamnov, who spent four seasons with Moscow Dynamo before joining the Winnipeg Jets, collected 72 points as a rookie in 1992-93.

Rookie Scoring Records

All-Time Top 50 Goal-Scoring Rookies

	Rookie	Team	Position	Season	GP	G	A	PTS
1.	* Teemu Selanne	Winnipeg	Right wing	1992-93	84	76	56	132
2.	* Mike Bossy	NY Islanders	Right wing	1977-78	73	53	38	91
3.	* Joe Nieuwendyk	Calgary	Center	1987-88	75	51	41	92
4.	* Dale Hawerchuk	Winnipeg	Center	1981-82	80	45	58	103
	* Luc Robitaille	Los Angeles	Left wing	1986-87	79	45	39	84
6.	Rick Martin	Buffalo	Left wing	1971-72	73	44	30	74
	Barry Pederson	Boston	Center	1981-82	80	44	48	92
8.	* Steve Larmer	Chicago	Right wing	1982-83	80	43	47	90
	* Mario Lemieux	Pittsburgh	Center	1984-85	73	43	57	100
10.	Eric Lindros	Philadelphia	Center	1992-93	61	41	34	75
11.	Darryl Sutter	Chicago	Left wing	1980-81	76	40	22	62
	Sylvain Turgeon	Hartford	Left wing	1983-84	76	40	32	72
	Warren Young	Pittsburgh	Left wing	1984-85	80	40	32	72
14.	* Eric Vail	Atlanta	Left wing	1974-75	72	39	21	60
	Anton Stastny	Quebec	Left wing	1980-81	80	39	46	85
	* Peter Stastny	Quebec	Center	1980-81	77	39	70	109
	Steve Yzerman	Detroit	Center	1983-84	80	39	48	87
18.	* Gilbert Perreault	Buffalo	Center	1970-71	78	38	34	72
	Neal Broten	Minnesota	Center	1981-82	73	38	60	98
	Ray Sheppard	Buffalo	Right wing	1987-88	74	38	27	65
	Mikael Renberg	Philadelphia	Left wing	**1993-94**	83	38	44	82
22.	Jorgen Pettersson	St. Louis	Left wing	1980-81	62	37	36	73
	Jimmy Carson	Los Angeles	Centre	1986-87	80	37	42	79
24.	Mike Foligno	Detroit	Right wing	1979-80	80	36	35	71
	Mike Bullard	Pittsburgh	Center	1981-82	75	36	27	63
	Paul MacLean	Winnipeg	Right wing	1981-82	74	36	25	61
	Tony Granato	NY Rangers	Right wing	1988-89	78	36	27	63
28.	Marian Stastny	Quebec	Right wing	1981-82	74	35	54	89
	Brian Bellows	Minnesota	Right wing	1982-83	78	35	30	65
	Tony Amonte	NY Rangers	Right wing	1991-92	79	35	34	69
31.	Nels Stewart	Mtl. Maroons	Center	1925-26	36	34	8	42
	* Danny Grant	Minnesota	Left wing	1968-69	75	34	31	65
	Norm Ferguson	Oakland	Right wing	1968-69	76	34	20	54
	Brian Propp	Philadelphia	Left wing	1979-80	80	34	41	75
	Wendel Clark	Toronto	Left wing	1985-86	66	34	11	45
	* Pavel Bure	Vancouver	Right wing	1991-92	65	34	26	60
37.	* Willi Plett	Atlanta	Right wing	1976-77	64	33	23	56
	Dale McCourt	Detroit	Center	1977-78	76	33	39	72
	Mark Pavelich	NY Rangers	Center	1981-82	79	33	43	76
	Ron Flockhart	Philadelphia	Center	1981-82	72	33	39	72
	Steve Bozek	Los Angeles	Center	1981-82	71	33	23	56
	Jason Arnott	Edmonton	Center	**1993-94**	78	33	35	68
43.	Bill Mosienko	Chicago	Right wing	1943-44	50	32	38	70
	Michel Bergeron	Detroit	Right wing	1975-76	72	32	27	59
	* Bryan Trottier	NY Islanders	Center	1975-76	80	32	63	95
	Don Murdoch	NY Rangers	Right wing	1976-77	59	32	24	56
	Jari Kurri	Edmonton	Left wing	1980-81	75	32	43	75
	Bobby Carpenter	Washington	Center	1981-82	80	32	35	67
	Kjell Dahlin	Montreal	Right wing	1985-86	77	32	39	71
	Petr Klima	Detroit	Left wing	1985-86	74	32	24	56
	Darren Turcotte	NY Rangers	Right wing	1989-90	76	32	34	66
	Joe Juneau	Boston	Center	1992-93	84	32	70	102

* Calder Trophy Winner

All-Time Top 50 Point-Scoring Rookies

	Rookie	Team	Position	Season	GP	G	A	PTS
1.	* Teemu Selanne	Winnipeg	Right wing	1992-93	84	76	56	132
2.	* Peter Stastny	Quebec	Center	1980-81	77	39	70	109
3.	* Dale Hawerchuk	Winnipeg	Center	1981-82	80	45	58	103
4.	Joe Juneau	Boston	Center	1992-93	84	32	70	102
5.	* Mario Lemieux	Pittsburgh	Center	1984-85	73	43	57	100
6.	Neal Broten	Minnesota	Center	1981-82	73	38	60	98
7.	* Bryan Trottier	NY Islanders	Center	1975-76	80	32	63	95
8.	Barry Pederson	Boston	Center	1981-82	80	44	48	92
	* Joe Nieuwendyk	Calgary	Center	1987-88	75	51	41	92
10.	* Mike Bossy	NY Islanders	Right wing	1977-78	73	53	38	91
11.	* Steve Larmer	Chicago	Right wing	1982-83	80	43	47	90
12.	Marian Stastny	Quebec	Right wing	1981-82	74	35	54	89
13.	Steve Yzerman	Detroit	Center	1983-84	80	39	48	87
14.	* Sergei Makarov	Calgary	Right wing	1989-90	80	24	62	86
15.	Anton Stastny	Quebec	Left wing	1980-81	80	39	46	85
16.	* Luc Robitaille	Los Angeles	Left wing	1986-87	79	45	39	84
17.	Mikael Renberg	Philadelphia	Left wing	**1993-94**	83	38	44	82
18.	Jimmy Carson	Los Angeles	Center	1986-87	80	37	42	79
	Sergei Fedorov	Detroit	Center	1990-91	77	31	48	79
	Alexei Yashin	Ottawa	Center	**1993-94**	83	30	49	79
21.	Marcel Dionne	Detroit	Center	1971-72	78	28	49	77
22.	Larry Murphy	Los Angeles	Defense	1980-81	80	16	60	76
	Mark Pavelich	NY Rangers	Center	1981-82	79	33	43	76
	Dave Poulin	Philadelphia	Center	1983-84	73	31	45	76
25.	Brian Propp	Philadelphia	Left wing	1979-80	80	34	41	75
	Jari Kurri	Edmonton	Left wing	1980-81	75	32	43	75
	Denis Savard	Chicago	Center	1980-81	76	28	47	75
	Mike Modano	Minnesota	Center	1989-90	80	29	46	75
	Eric Lindros	Philadelphia	Center	1992-93	61	41	34	75
30.	Rick Martin	Buffalo	Left wing	1971-72	73	44	30	74
	* Bobby Smith	Minnesota	Center	1978-79	80	30	44	74
	Jorgen Pettersson	St. Louis	Left wing	1980-81	62	37	36	73
33.	* Gilbert Perreault	Buffalo	Center	1970-71	78	38	34	72
	Dale McCourt	Detroit	Center	1977-78	76	33	39	72
	Ron Flockhart	Philadelphia	Center	1981-82	72	33	39	72
	Sylvain Turgeon	Hartford	Left wing	1983-84	76	40	32	72
	Warren Young	Pittsburgh	Left wing	1984-85	80	40	32	72
	Carey Wilson	Calgary	Center	1984-85	74	24	48	72
	Alexei Zhamnov	Winnipeg	Center	1992-93	68	25	47	72
40.	Mike Foligno	Detroit	Right wing	1979-80	80	36	35	71
	Dave Christian	Winnipeg	Center	1980-81	80	28	43	71
	Mats Naslund	Montreal	Left wing	1982-83	74	26	45	71
	Kjell Dahlin	Montreal	Right wing	1985-86	77	32	39	71
	* Brian Leetch	NY Rangers	Defense	1988-89	68	23	48	71
45.	Bill Mosienko	Chicago	Right wing	1943-44	50	32	38	70
46.	Roland Eriksson	Minnesota	Center	1976-77	80	25	44	69
	Tony Amonte	NY Rangers	Right wing	1991-92	79	35	34	69
48.	Jude Drouin	Minnesota	Center	1970-71	75	16	52	68
	Pierre Larouche	Pittsburgh	Center	1974-75	79	31	37	68
	Ron Francis	Hartford	Center	1981-82	59	25	43	68
	* Gary Suter	Calgary	Defense	1985-86	80	18	50	68
	Jason Arnott	Edmonton	Center	1993-94	84	33	35	68

* Calder Trophy Winner

50-Goal Seasons

50th Player	Team	Date of Player's Goal	Team Score	Total		Total Goaltender	Scored Game No.	Game No.	Goals	Games	Age When First 50th (Yrs. & Mos.)
Maurice Richard	Mtl.	18-3-45	Mtl. 4	at Bos. 2		Harvey Bennett	50	50	50	50	23.7
Bernie Geoffrion	Mtl.	16-3-61	Tor. 2	at Mtl. 5		Cesare Maniago	62	68	50	64	30.1
Bobby Hull	Chi.	25-3-62	Chi. 1	at NYR 4		Gump Worsley	70	70	50	70	23.2
Bobby Hull	Chi.	2-3-66	Det. 4	at Chi. 5		Hank Bassen	52	57	54	65	
Bobby Hull	Chi.	18-3-67	Chi. 5	at Tor. 9		Bruce Gamble	63	66	52	66	
Bobby Hull	Chi.	5-3-69	NYR 4	at Chi. 4		Ed Giacomin	64	66	58	74	
Phil Esposito	Bos.	20-2-71	Bos. 4	at L.A. 5		Denis DeJordy	58	58	76	78	29.0
John Bucyk	Bos.	16-3-71	Bos. 11	at Det. 4		Roy Edwards	69	69	51	78	35.1
Phil Esposito	Bos.	20-2-72	Bos. 3	at Chi. 1		Tony Esposito	60	60	66	76	
Bobby Hull	Chi.	2-4-72	Det. 1	at Chi. 6		Andy Brown	78	78	50	78	
Vic Hadfield	NYR	2-4-72	Mtl. 6	at NYR 5		Denis DeJordy	78	78	50	78	31.6
Phil Esposito	Bos.	25-3-73	Buf. 1	at Bos. 6		Roger Crozier	75	75	55	78	
Mickey Redmond	Det.	27-3-73	Det. 8	at Tor. 1		Ron Low	73	75	52	76	25.3
Rick MacLeish	Phi.	1-4-73	Phi. 4	at Pit. 5		Cam Newton	78	78	50	78	23.2
Phil Esposito	Bos.	20-2-74	Bos. 5	at Min. 5		Cesare Maniago	56	56	68	78	
Mickey Redmond	Det.	23-3-74	NYR 3	at Det 5		Ed Giacomin	69	71	51	76	
Ken Hodge	Bos.	6-4-74	Bos. 2	at Mtl. 6		Michel Larocque	75	77	50	76	29.10
Rick Martin	Buf.	7-4-74	St. L. 2	at Buf. 5		Wayne Stephenson	78	78	52	78	22.9
Phil Esposito	Bos.	8-2-75	Bos. 8	at Det. 5		Jim Rutherford	54	54	61	79	
Guy Lafleur	Mtl.	29-3-75	K.C. 1	at Mtl. 4		Denis Herron	66	76	53	70	23.6
Danny Grant	Det.	2-4-75	Wsh. 3	at Det. 8		John Adams	78	78	50	80	29.2
Rick Martin	Buf.	3-4-75	Bos. 2	at Buf. 4		Ken Broderick	67	79	52	68	
Reggie Leach	Phi.	14-3-76	Atl. 1	at Phi. 6		Daniel Bouchard	69	69	61	80	25.11
Jean Pronovost	Pit.	24-3-76	Bos. 5	at Pit. 5		Gilles Gilbert	74	74	52	80	31.3
Guy Lafleur	Mtl.	27-3-76	K.C. 2	at Mtl. 8		Denis Herron	76	76	56	80	
Bill Barber	Phi.	3-4-76	Buf. 2	at Phi. 5		Al Smith	79	79	50	80	23.9
Pierre Larouche	Pit.	3-4-76	Wsh. 5	at Pit. 4		Ron Low	75	79	53	76	20.5
Danny Gare	Buf.	4-4-76	Tor. 2	at Buf. 5		Gord McRae	79	80	50	79	21.11
Steve Shutt	Mtl.	1-3-77	Mtl. 5	at NYI 4		Glenn Resch	65	65	60	80	24.8
Guy Lafleur	Mtl.	6-3-77	Mtl. 1	at Buf. 4		Don Edwards	68	68	56	80	
Marcel Dionne	L.A.	2-4-77	Min. 2	at L.A. 7		Pete LoPresti	79	79	53	80	25.8
Guy Lafleur	Mtl.	8-3-78	Wsh. 3	at Mtl. 4		Jim Bedard	63	65	60	78	
Mike Bossy	NYI	1-4-78	Wsh. 2	at NYI 3		Bernie Wolfe	69	76	53	73	21.2
Mike Bossy	NYI	24-2-79	Det. 1	at NYI 3		Rogie Vachon	58	58	69	80	
Marcel Dionne	L.A.	11-3-79	L.A. 3	at Phi. 6		Wayne Stephenson	68	68	59	80	
Guy Lafleur	Mtl.	31-3-79	Pit. 3	at Mtl. 5		Denis Herron	76	76	52	80	
Guy Chouinard	Atl.	6-4-79	NYR 2	at Atl. 9		John Davidson	79	79	50	80	22.5
Marcel Dionne	L.A.	12-3-80	L.A. 2	at Pit. 4		Nick Ricci	70	70	53	80	
Mike Bossy	NYI	16-3-80	NYI 6	at Chi. 1		Tony Esposito	68	71	51	75	
Charlie Simmer	L.A.	19-3-80	Det. 3	at L.A. 4		Jim Rutherford	57	73	56	64	26.0
Pierre Larouche	Mtl.	25-3-80	Chi. 4	at Mtl. 8		Tony Esposito	72	75	50	73	
Danny Gare	Buf.	27-3-80	Det. 1	at Buf. 10		Jim Rutherford	71	75	56	76	
Blaine Stoughton	Hfd.	28-3-80	Hfd. 4	at Van. 4		Glen Hanlon	75	75	56	80	27.0
Guy Lafleur	Mtl.	2-4-80	Mtl. 7	at Det. 2		Rogie Vachon	72	78	50	74	
Wayne Gretzky	Edm.	2-4-80	Min. 1	at Edm. 1		Gary Edwards	78	79	51	79	19.2
Reggie Leach	Phi.	3-4-80	Wsh. 2	at Phi. 4		(empty net)	75	79	50	76	
Mike Bossy	NYI	24-1-81	Que. 3	at NYI 7		Ron Grahame	50	50	68	79	
Charlie Simmer	L.A.	26-1-81	L.A. 7	at Que. 5		Michel Dion	51	51	56	65	
Marcel Dionne	L.A.	8-3-81	L.A. 4	at Wpg. 1		Markus Mattsson	68	68	58	80	
Wayne Babych	St. L.	12-3-81	St. L. 3	at Mtl. 4		Richard Sevigny	70	70	54	78	22.9
Wayne Gretzky	Edm.	15-3-81	Edm. 3	at Cgy. 3		Pat Riggin	69	69	55	80	
Rick Kehoe	Pit.	16-3-81	Pit. 7	at Edm. 6		Eddie Mio	70	70	55	80	29.7
Jacques Richard	Que.	29-3-81	Mtl. 0	at Que. 4		Richard Sevigny	76	75	52	78	28.6
Dennis Maruk	Wsh.	5-4-81	Det. 2	at Wsh. 7		Larry Lozinski	80	80	50	80	25.3
Wayne Gretzky	Edm.	30-12-81	Phi. 5	at Edm. 7		(empty net)	39	39	92	80	
Dennis Maruk	Wsh.	21-2-82	Wpg. 3	at Wsh. 6		Doug Soetaert	61	61	60	80	
Mike Bossy	NYI	4-3-82	Tor. 1	at NYI 10		Michel Larocque	66	66	64	80	
Dino Ciccarelli	Min.	8-3-82	St. L. 1	at Min. 8		Mike Liut	67	68	55	76	21.7
Rick Vaive	Tor.	24-3-82	St. L. 3	at Tor. 4		Mike Liut	72	75	54	77	22.10
Rick Middleton	Bos.	28-3-82	Bos. 5	at Buf. 9		Paul Harrison	72	77	51	75	28.11
Blaine Stoughton	Hfd.	28-3-82	Min. 5	at Hfd. 2		Gilles Meloche	76	76	52	80	28.3
Marcel Dionne	L.A.	30-3-82	Cgy. 7	at L.A. 5		Pat Riggin	75	77	50	78	
Mark Messier	Edm.	31-3-82	L.A. 3	at Edm. 7		Mario Lessard	78	79	50	78	21.3
Bryan Trottier	NYI	3-4-82	Phi. 3	at NYI 6		Pete Peeters	79	79	50	80	25.9
Lanny McDonald	Cgy.	18-2-83	Cgy. 1	at Buf. 5		Bob Sauve	60	60	66	80	30.0
Wayne Gretzky	Edm.	19-2-83	Edm. 10	at Pit. 7		Nick Ricci	60	60	71	80	
Michel Goulet	Que.	5-3-83	Que. 7	at Hfd. 3		Mike Veisor	67	67	57	80	22.11
Mike Bossy	NYI	12-3-83	Wsh. 2	at NYI 6		Al Jensen	70	71	60	79	
Marcel Dionne	L.A.	17-3-83	Que. 3	at L.A. 4		Daniel Bouchard	71	71	56	80	
Al Secord	Chi.	20-3-83	Tor. 3	at Chi. 7		Mike Palmateer	73	73	54	80	25.0
Rick Vaive	Tor.	30-3-83	Tor. 4	at Det. 2		Gilles Gilbert	76	78	51	78	
Wayne Gretzky	Edm.	7-1-84	Hfd. 3	at Edm. 5		Greg Millen	42	42	87	74	
Michel Goulet	Que.	8-3-84	Que. 8	at Pit. 6		Denis Herron	63	69	56	75	
Rick Vaive	Tor.	14-3-84	Min. 3	at Tor. 3		Gilles Meloche	69	72	52	76	
Mike Bullard	Pit.	14-3-84	Pit. 6	at L.A. 7		Markus Mattsson	71	72	51	76	23.0

Maurice Richard

Kent Nilsson

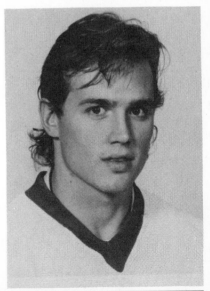

Steve Yzerman

50-Goal Seasons – *continued*

Dave Andreychuk

Gary Roberts

Player	Team	Date of 50th Goal	Score		Goaltender	Player's Game No.	Team Game No.	Total Goals	Total Games	Age When First 50th Scored (Yrs. & Mos.)
Jari Kurri	Edm.	15-3-84	Edm. 2	at Mtl. 3	Rick Wamsley	57	73	52	64	23.10
Glenn Anderson	Edm.	21-3-84	Hfd. 3	at Edm. 5	Greg Millen	76	76	54	80	23.6
Tim Kerr	Phi.	22-3-84	Pit. 4	at Phi. 13	Denis Herron	74	75	54	79	24.3
Mike Bossy	NYI	31-3-84	NYI 3	at Wsh. 1	Pat Riggin	67	79	51	67	
Wayne Gretzky	Edm.	26-1-85	Pit. 3	at Edm. 6	Denis Herron	49	49	73	80	
Jari Kurri	Edm.	3-2-85	Hfd. 3	at Edm. 6	Greg Millen	50	53	71	73	
Mike Bossy	NYI	5-3-85	Phi. 5	at NYI 4	Bob Froese	61	65	58	76	
Tim Kerr	Phi.	7-3-85	Wsh. 6	at Phi. 9	Pat Riggin	63	65	54	74	
John Ogrodnick	Det.	13-3-85	Det. 6	at Edm. 7	Grant Fuhr	69	69	55	79	25.9
Bob Carpenter	Wsh.	21-3-85	Wsh. 2	at Mtl. 3	Steve Penney	72	72	53	80	21.9
Michel Goulet	Que.	6-3-85	Buf. 3	at Que. 4	Tom Barrasso	62	73	55	69	
Dale Hawerchuk	Wpg.	29-3-85	Chi. 5	at Wpg. 5	W. Skorodenski	77	77	53	80	21.1
Mike Gartner	Wsh.	7-4-85	Pit. 3	at Wsh. 7	Brian Ford	80	80	50	80	25.5
Jari Kurri	Edm.	4-3-86	Edm. 6	at Van. 2	Richard Brodeur	63	65	68	78	
Mike Bossy	NYI	11-3-86	Cgy. 4	at NYI 8	Rejean Lemelin	67	67	61	80	
Glenn Anderson	Edm.	14-3-86	Det. 3	at Edm. 12	Greg Stefan	63	71	54	72	
Michel Goulet	Que.	17-3-86	Que. 8	at Mtl. 6	Patrick Roy	67	72	53	75	
Wayne Gretzky	Edm.	18-3-86	Wpg. 2	at Edm. 6	Brian Hayward	72	72	52	80	
Tim Kerr	Phi.	20-3-86	Pit. 1	at Phi. 5	Roberto Romano	68	72	58	76	
Wayne Gretzky	Edm.	4-2-87	Edm. 6	at Min. 5	Don Beaupre	55	55	62	79	
Tim Kerr	Phi.	17-3-87	NYR 1	at Phi. 4	J. Vanbiesbrouck	67	71	58	75	
Jari Kurri	Edm.	17-3-87	N.J. 4	at Edm. 7	Craig Billington	69	70	54	79	
Mario Lemieux	Pit.	12-3-87	Que. 3	at Pit. 6	Mario Gosselin	53	70	54	63	21.5
Dino Ciccarelli	Min.	7-3-87	Pit. 7	at Min. 3	Gilles Meloche	66	66	52	80	
Mario Lemieux	Pit.	2-2-88	Wsh. 2	at Pit. 3	Pete Peeters	51	54	70	77	
Steve Yzerman	Det.	1-3-88	Buf. 0	at Det. 4	Tom Barrasso	64	64	50	64	22.10
Joe Nieuwendyk	Cgy.	12-3-88	Buf. 4	at Cgy. 10	Tom Barrasso	66	70	51	75	21.5
Craig Simpson	Edm.	15-3-88	Buf. 4	at Edm. 6	Jacques Cloutier	71	71	56	80	21.1
Jimmy Carson	L.A.	26-3-88	Chi. 5	at L.A. 9	Darren Pang	77	77	55	88	19.7
Luc Robitaille	L.A.	1-4-88	L.A. 6	at Cgy. 3	Mike Vernon	79	79	53	80	21.10
Hakan Loob	Cgy.	3-4-88	Min. 1	at Cgy. 4	Don Beaupre	80	80	50	80	27.9
Stephane Richer	Mtl.	3-4-88	Mtl. 4	at Buf. 4	Tom Barrasso	72	80	50	72	21.10
Mario Lemieux	Pit.	20-1-89	Pit. 3	at Wpg. 7	Eldon Reddick	44	46	85	76	
Bernie Nicholls	L.A.	28-1-89	Edm. 7	at L.A. 6	Grant Fuhr	51	51	70	79	27.7
Steve Yzerman	Det.	5-2-89	Det. 6	at Wpg. 2	Eldon Reddick	55	55	65	80	
Wayne Gretzky	L.A.	4-3-89	Phi. 2	at L.A. 6	Ron Hextall	66	67	54	78	
Joe Nieuwendyk	Cgy.	21-3-89	NYI 1	at Cgy. 4	Mark Fitzpatrick	72	74	51	77	
Joe Mullen	Cgy.	31-3-89	Wpg. 1	at Cgy. 4	Bob Essensa	78	79	51	79	32.1
Brett Hull	St. L.	6-2-90	Tor. 4	at St. L. 6	Jeff Reese	54	54	72	80	25.6
Steve Yzerman	Det.	24-2-90	Det. 3	at NYI 3	Glenn Healy	63	63	62	79	
Cam Neely	Bos.	10-3-90	Bos. 3	at NYI 3	Mark Fitzpatrick	69	71	55	76	24.9
Brian Bellows	Min.	22-3-90	Min. 5	at Det. 1	Tim Cheveldae	75	75	55	80	25.
Pat LaFontaine	NYI	24-3-90	NYI 5	at Edm. 5	Bill Ranford	71	77	54	74	25.1
Luc Robitaille	L.A.	21-3-90	L.A. 3	at Van. 6	Kirk McLean	79	79	52	80	
Stephane Richer	Mtl.	24-3-90	Mtl. 4	at Hfd. 7	Peter Sidorkiewicz	75	77	51	75	
Gary Leeman	Tor.	28-3-90	NYI 6	at Tor. 3	Mark Fitzpatrick	78	78	51	80	26.1
Brett Hull	St. L.	25-1-91	St. L. 9	at Det. 4	Dave Gagnon	49	49	86	78	
Cam Neely	Bos.	26-3-91	Bos. 7	at Que. 4	empty net	67	78	51	69	
Theoren Fleury	Cgy.	26-3-91	Van. 2	at Cgy. 7	Bob Mason	77	77	51	79	22.9
Steve Yzerman	Det.	30-3-91	NYR 5	at Det. 6	Mike Richter	79	79	51	80	
Brett Hull	St. L.	28-1-92	St. L. 3	at L.A. 3	Kelly Hrudey	50	50	70	73	
Kevin Stevens	Pit.	24-3-92	Pit. 3	at Det. 4	Tim Cheveldae	74	74	54	80	26.11
Gary Roberts	Cgy.	31-3-92	Edm. 2	at Cgy. 5	Bill Ranford	73	77	53	76	25.10
Jeremy Roenick	Chi.	7-3-92	Chi. 2	at Bos. 1	Daniel Berthiaume	67	67	53	80	22.2
Alexander Mogilny	Buf.	3-2-93	Hfd. 2	at Buf. 3	Sean Burke	46	53	76	77	23.11
Teemu Selanne	Wpg.	28-2-93	Min. 6	at Wpg. 7	Darcy Wakaluk	63	63	76	84	22.6
Pavel Bure	Van.	1-3-93	Van. 5	at Buf. 2*	Grant Fuhr	63	63	60	83	21.11
Steve Yzerman	Det.	10-3-93	Det. 6	at Edm. 3	Bill Ranford	70	70	58	84	
Luc Robitaille	L.A.	15-3-93	L.A. 4	at Buf. 2	Grant Fuhr	69	69	63	84	
Brett Hull	St. L.	20-3-93	St. L. 2	at L.A. 3	Robb Stauber	73	73	54	80	
Mario Lemieux	Pit.	21-3-93	Pit. 6	at Edm. 4**	Ron Tugnutt	48	72	69	60	
Kevin Stevens	Pit.	21-3-93	Pit. 6	at Edm. 4**	Ron Tugnutt	62	72	55	72	
Dave Andreychuk	Tor.	23-3-93	Tor. 5	at Wpg. 4	Bob Essensa	72	73	54	83	29.6
Pat LaFontaine	Buf.	28-3-93	Ott. 1	at Buf. 3	Peter Sidorkiewicz	75	75	53	84	
Pierre Turgeon	NYI	2-4-93	NYI 3	at NYR 2	Mike Richter	75	76	58	83	23.8
Mark Recchi	Phi.	3-4-93	T.B. 2	at Phi. 6	J-C Bergeron	77	77	53	84	25.2
Jeremy Roenick	Chi.	15-4-93	Tor. 2	at Chi. 3	Felix Potvin	84	84	50	84	
Brendan Shanahan	St. L.	15-4-93	T.B. 5	at St. L. 6	Pat Jablonski	71	84	51	71	24.3
Cam Neely	Bos.	7-3-94	Wsh. 3	at Bos. 6	Don Beaupre	44	66	50	49	
Sergei Fedorov	Det.	15-3-94	Van. 2	at Det. 5	Kirk McLean	67	69	56	82	24.3
Pavel Bure	Van.	23-3-94	Van. 6	at L.A. 3	empty net	65	73	60	76	
Adam Graves	NYR	23-3-94	NYR 5	at Edm. 3	Bill Ranford	74	74	51	84	25.11
Dave Andreychuk	Tor	24-3-94	S.J. 2	at Tor. 1	Arturs Irbe	73	74	53	83	
Brett Hull	St.L.	25-3-94	Dal. 3	at St.L. 5	Andy Moog	71	74	52	81	
Ray Sheppard	Det.	29-3-94	Hfd. 2	at Det. 6	Sean Burke	74	76	52	82	27.10
Brendan Shanahan	St.L.	12-4-94	St.L. 5	at Dal. 9	Andy Moog	80	83	52	81	
Mike Modano	Dal.	12-4-94	St.L. 5	at Dal. 9	Curtis Joseph	75	83	50	76	23.11

* neutral site game played at Hamilton; ** neutral site game played at Cleveland

Ray Sheppard

100-Point Seasons

Player	Team	Date of 100th Point	G or A	Score		Player's Game No.	Team Game No.	Points G - A PTS	Total Games	Age when first 100th point scored (Yrs. & Mos.)
Phil Esposito	Bos.	2-3-69	(G)	Pit. 0	at Bos. 4	60	62	49-77 — 126	74	27.1
Bobby Hull	Chi.	20-3-69	(G)	Chi. 5	at Bos. 5	71	71	58-49 — 107	76	30.2
Gordie Howe	Det.	30-3-69	(G)	Det. 5	at Chi. 9	76	76	44-59 — 103	76	41.0
Bobby Orr	Bos.	15-3-70	(G)	Det. 5	at Bos. 5	67	67	33-87 — 120	76	22.11
Phil Esposito	Bos.	6-2-71	(A)	Buf. 3	at Bos. 4	51	51	76-76 — 152	78	
Bobby Orr	Bos.	22-2-71	(A)	Bos. 4	at L.A. 5	58	58	37-102 — 139	78	
John Bucyk	Bos.	13-3-71	(G)	Bos. 6	at Van. 3	68	68	51-65 — 116	78	35.10
Ken Hodge	Bos.	21-3-71	(A)	Buf. 7	at Bos. 5	72	72	43-62 — 105	78	269
Jean Ratelle	NYR	18-2-72	(A)	NYR 2	at Cal. 2	58	58	46-63 — 109	63	31.4
Phil Esposito	Bos.	19-2-72	(A)	Bos. 6	at Min. 4	59	59	66-67 — 133	76	
Bobby Orr	Bos.	2-3-72	(A)	Van. 3	at Bos. 7	64	64	37-80 — 117	76	
Vic Hadfield	NYR	25-3-72	(A)	NYR 3	at Mtl. 3	74	74	50-56 — 106	78	31.5
Phil Esposito	Bos.	3-3-73	(A)	Bos. 1	at Mtl. 5	64	64	55-75 — 130	78	
Bobby Clarke	Phi.	29-3-73	(G)	Atl. 2	at Phi. 4	76	76	37-67 — 104	78	23.7
Bobby Orr	Bos.	31-3-73	(G)	Bos. 3	at Tor. 7	62	77	29-72 — 101	63	
Rick MacLeish	Phi.	1-4-73	(G)	Phi. 4	at Pit. 5	78	78	50-50 — 100	78	23.3
Phil Esposito	Bos.	13-2-74	(A)	Bos. 9	at Cal. 6	53	53	68-77 — 145	78	
Bobby Orr	Bos.	12-3-74	(A)	Buf. 0	at Bos. 4	62	66	32-90 — 122	74	
Ken Hodge	Bos.	24-3-74	(A)	Mtl. 3	at Bos. 6	72	72	50-55 — 105	76	
Phil Esposito	Bos.	8-2-75	(A)	Bos. 8	at Det. 5	54	54	61-66 — 127	79	
Bobby Orr	Bos.	13-2-75	(A)	Bos. 1	at Buf. 3	57	57	46-89 — 135	80	
Guy Lafleur	Mtl.	7-3-75	(G)	Wsh. 4	at Mtl. 8	56	66	53-66 — 119	70	24.6
Pete Mahovlich	Mtl.	9-3-75	(G)	Mtl. 5	at NYR 3	67	67	35-82 — 117	80	29.5
Marcel Dionne	Det.	9-3-75	(A)	Det. 5	at Phi. 8	67	67	47-74 — 121	80	23.7
Bobby Clarke	Phi.	22-3-75	(A)	Min. 0	at Phi. 4	72	72	27-89 — 116	80	
Rene Robert	Buf.	5-4-75	(A)	Buf. 4	at Tor. 2	74	80	40-60 — 100	74	26.4
Guy Lafleur	Mtl.	10-3-76	(G)	Mtl. 5	at Chi. 1	69	69	56-69 — 125	80	
Bobby Clarke	Phi.	11-3-76	(A)	Buf. 1	at Phi. 6	64	68	30-89 — 119	76	
Bill Barber	Phi.	18-3-76	(A)	Van. 2	at Phi. 3	71	71	50-62 — 112	80	23.8
Gilbert Perreault	Buf.	21-3-76	(A)	K.C. 1	at Buf. 3	73	73	44-69 — 113	80	25.4
Pierre Larouche	Pit.	24-3-76	(G)	Bos. 5	at Pit. 5	70	74	53-58 — 111	76	20.4
Pete Mahovlich	Mtl.	28-3-76	(A)	Mtl. 2	at Bos. 2	77	77	34-71 — 105	80	
Jean Ratelle	Bos.	30-3-76	(G)	Buf. 4	at Bos. 4	77	77	36-69 — 105	80	
Jean Pronovost	Pit.	3-4-76	(A)	Wsh. 5	at Pit. 4	79	79	52-52 — 104	80	30.4
Darryl Sittler	Tor.	3-4-76	(A)	Bos. 4	at Tor. 2	78	79	41-59 — 100	79	26.7
Guy Lafleur	Mtl.	26-2-77	(A)	Clev. 3	at Mtl. 5	63	63	56-80 — 136	80	
Marcel Dionne	L.A.	5-3-77	(G)	Pit. 3	at L.A. 3	67	67	53-69 — 122	80	
Steve Shutt	Mtl.	27-3-77	(A)	Mtl. 6	at Det. 0	77	77	60-45 — 105	80	24.9
Bryan Trottier	NYI	25-2-78	(A)	Chi. 1	at NYI 7	59	60	46-77 — 123	77	21.7
Guy Lafleur	Mtl.	28-2-78	(G)	Det. 3	at Mtl. 9	69	61	60-72 — 132	78	
Darryl Sittler	Tor.	12-3-78	(A)	Tor. 7	at Pit. 1	67	67	45-72 — 117	80	
Guy Lafleur	Mtl.	27-2-79	(A)	Mtl. 3	at NYI 7	61	61	52-77 — 129	80	
Bryan Trottier	NYI	6-3-79	(A)	Buf. 3	at NYI 2	59	63	47-87 — 134	76	
Marcel Dionne	L.A.	8-3-79	(G)	L.A. 4	at Buf. 6	66	66	59-71 — 130	80	
Mike Bossy	NYI	11-3-79	(G)	NYI 4	at Bos. 4	66	66	69-57 — 126	80	22.2
Bob MacMillan	Atl.	15-3-79	(A)	Atl. 4	at Phi. 5	68	69	37-71 — 108	79	26.6
Guy Chouinard	Atl.	30-3-79	(G)	L.A. 3	at Atl. 5	75	75	50-57 — 107	80	22.5
Denis Potvin	NYI	8-4-79	(A)	NYI 5	at NYR 2	73	80	31-70 — 101	73	25.5
Marcel Dionne	L.A.	6-2-80	(A)	L.A. 3	at Hfd. 7	53	53	53-84 — 137	80	
Guy Lafleur	Mtl.	10-2-80	(A)	Mtl. 3	at Bos. 2	55	55	50-75 — 125	74	
Wayne Gretzky	Edm.	24-2-80	(A)	Bos. 4	at Edm. 2	61	62	51-86 — 137	79	19.2
Bryan Trottier	NYI	30-3-80	(A)	NYI 9	at Que. 6	75	77	42-62 — 104	78	
Gilbert Perreault	Buf.	1-4-80	(A)	Buf. 5	at Atl. 2	77	77	40-66 — 106	80	
Mike Rogers	Hfd.	4-4-80	(A)	Que. 2	at Hfd. 9	79	79	44-61 — 105	80	25.5
Charlie Simmer	L.A.	5-4-80	(G)	Van. 3	at L.A. 3	64	80	56-45 — 101	64	26.0
Blaine Stoughton	Hfd.	6-4-80	(A)	Det. 3	at Hfd. 5	80	80	56-44 — 100	80	27.0
Wayne Gretzky	Edm.	6-2-81	(G)	Wpg. 4	at Edm. 10	53	53	55-109 — 164	80	
Marcel Dionne	L.A.	12-2-81	(A)	L.A. 5	at Chi. 5	58	58	58-77 — 135	80	
Charlie Simmer	L.A.	14-2-81	(A)	Bos. 5	at L.A. 4	59	59	56-49 — 105	65	
Kent Nilsson	Cgy.	27-2-81	(G)	Hfd. 1	at Cgy. 5	64	64	49-82 — 131	80	24.6
Mike Bossy	NYI	3-3-81	(G)	Edm. 8	at NYI 8	65	66	68-51 — 119	79	
Dave Taylor	L.A.	14-3-81	(G)	Min. 4	at L.A. 10	63	70	47-65 — 112	72	25.3
Mike Rogers	Hfd.	22-3-81	(G)	Tor. 3	at Hfd. 3	74	74	40-65 — 105	80	
Bernie Federko	St. L.	28-3-81	(A)	Buf. 4	at St. L. 7	74	76	31-73 — 104	78	24.10
Rick Middleton	Bos.	28-3-81	(A)	Chi. 2	at Bos. 5	76	76	44-59 — 103	80	27.4
Jacques Richard	Que.	29-3-81	(G)	Mtl. 0	at Que. 4	75	76	52-51 — 103	78	28.6
Bryan Trottier	NYI	29-3-81	(A)	NYI 5	at Wsh. 4	69	76	31-72 — 103	73	
Peter Stastny	Que.	29-3-81	(A)	Mtl. 0	at Que. 4	73	76	39-70 — 109	77	24.6
Wayne Gretzky	Edm.	27-12-81	(G)	L.A. 3	at Edm. 10	38	38	92-120 — 212	80	
Mike Bossy	NYI	13-2-82	(A)	Phi. 2	at NYI 8	55	55	64-83 — 147	80	
Peter Stastny	Que.	16-2-82	(A)	Wpg. 3	at Que. 7	60	60	46-93 — 139	80	
Dennis Maruk	Wsh.	20-2-82	(A)	Wsh. 3	at Min. 7	60	60	60-76 — 136	80	26.3
Bryan Trottier	NYI	23-2-82	(G)	Chi. 1	at NYI 5	61	61	50-79 — 129	80	
Denis Savard	Chi.	27-2-82	(A)	Chi. 5	at L.A. 3	64	64	32-87 — 119	80	21.1
Bobby Smith	Min.	3-3-82	(A)	Det. 4	at Min. 6	66	66	43-71 — 114	80	24.1
Marcel Dionne	L.A.	6-3-82	(G)	L.A. 6	at Hfd. 7	64	66	50-67 — 117	78	
Dave Taylor	L.A.	20-3-82	(A)	Pit. 5	at L.A. 7	71	72	39-67 — 106	78	
Dale Hawerchuk	Wpg.	24-3-82	(A)	L.A. 3	at Wpg.	74	74	45-58 — 103	80	18.11
Dino Ciccarelli	Min.	27-3-82	(A)	Min. 6	at Bos. 5	72	76	55-52 — 107	76	21.8
Glenn Anderson	Edm.	28-3-82	(G)	Edm. 6	at L.A. 2	78	78	38-67 — 105	80	21.7
Mike Rogers	NYR	2-4-82	(G)	Pit. 7	at NYR 5	79	79	38-65 — 103	80	

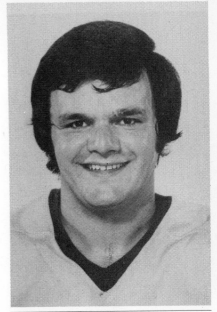

Marcel Dionne

Bryan Trottier

Glenn Anderson

100-Point Seasons — *continued*

Neal Broten

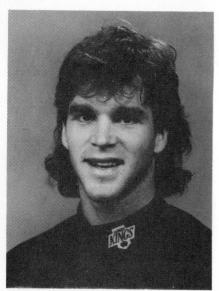

Luc Robitaille

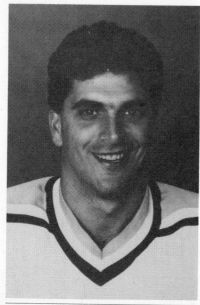

Kevin Stevens

Player	Team	Date of 100th Point	G or A	Score	Player's Game No.	Team Game No.	Points G - A	PTS	Total Games	Age when first 100th point scored (Yrs. & Mos.)
Wayne Gretzky	Edm.	5-1-83	(A)	Edm. 8 at Wpg. 3	42	42	71-125	196	80	
Mike Bossy	NYI	3-3-83	(A)	Tor. 1 at NYI. 5	66	67	60-58	118	79	
Peter Stastny	Que.	3-3-83	(A)	Hfd. 3 at Que. 10	62	67	47-77	124	75	
Denis Savard	Chi.	6-3-83	(G)	Mtl. 4 at Chi. 5	65	67	35-86	121	78	
Mark Messier	Edm.	23-3-83	(G)	Edm. 4 at Wpg. 7	73	76	48-58	106	77	22.2
Barry Pederson	Bos.	26-3-83	(A)	Hfd. 4 at Bos. 7	73	76	46-61	107	77	22.0
Marcel Dionne	L.A.	26-3-83	(A)	Edm. 9 at L.A. 3	75	75	56-51	107	77	
Michel Goulet	Que.	27-3-83	(A)	Que. 6 at Buf. 6	77	77	57-48	105	80	22.11
Glenn Anderson	Edm.	29-3-83	(A)	Edm. 7 at Van. 4	70	78	48-56	104	72	
Jari Kurri	Edm.	29-3-83	(A)	Edm. 7 at Van. 4	78	78	45-59	104	80	22.10
Kent Nilsson	Cgy.	29-3-83	(G)	L.A. 3 at Cgy. 5	78	78	46-58	104	80	
Wayne Gretzky	Edm.	18-12-83	(G)	Edm. 7 at Wpg. 5	34	34	87-118	205	74	
Paul Coffey	Edm.	4-3-84	(A)	Mtl. 1 at Edm. 6	68	68	40-86	126	80	22.9
Michel Goulet	Que.	4-3-84	(A)	Que. 1 at Buf. 1	62	67	56-65	121	75	
Jari Kurri	Edm.	7-3-84	(G)	Chi. 4 at Edm. 7	53	69	52-61	113	64	
Peter Stastny	Que.	8-3-84	(A)	Que. 8 at Pit. 6	69	69	46-73	119	80	
Mike Bossy	NYI	8-3-84	(A)	Tor. 5 at NYI 4	56	68	51-67	118	67	
Barry Pederson	Bos.	14-3-84	(A)	Bos. 4 at Det. 2	71	71	39-77	116	80	
Bryan Trottier	NYI	18-3-84	(A)	NYI 4 at Hfd. 5	62	73	40-71	111	68	
Bernie Federko	St. L.	20-3-84	(A)	Wpg. 3 at St. L. 9	75	76	41-66	107	79	
Rick Middleton	Bos.	27-3-84	(G)	Bos. 6 at Que. 4	77	77	47-58	105	80	
Dale Hawerchuk	Wpg.	27-3-84	(G)	Wpg. 3 at L.A. 3	77	77	37-65	102	80	
Mark Messier	Edm.	27-3-84	(G)	Edm. 9 at Cgy. 2	72	79	37-64	101	73	
Wayne Gretzky	Edm.	29-12-84	(A)	Det. 3 at Edm. 6	35	35	73-135	208	80	
Jari Kurri	Edm.	29-1-85	(G)	Edm. 4 at Cgy. 2	48	51	71-64	135	73	
Mike Bossy	NYI	23-2-85	(A)	Bos. 1 at NYI 7	56	60	58-59	117	76	
Dale Hawerchuk	Wpg.	25-2-85	(A)	Wpg. 12 at NYR 5	64	64	53-77	130	80	
Marcel Dionne	L.A.	5-3-85	(A)	Pit. 0 at L.A. 6	66	66	46-80	126	80	
Brent Sutter	NYI	12-3-85	(A)	NYI 6 at St. L. 5	68	68	42-60	102	72	22.10
John Ogrodnick	Det.	22-3-85	(A)	NYR 3 at Det. 5	73	73	55-50	105	79	25.9
Paul Coffey	Edm.	26-3-85	(G)	Edm. 7 at NYI 5	74	74	37-84	121	80	
Denis Savard	Chi.	29-3-8	(A)	Chi. 5 at Wpg. 5	75	76	38-67	105	79	
Peter Stastny	Que.	2-4-85	(A)	Bos. 4 at Que. 6	74	77	32-68	100	75	
Bernie Federko	St. L.	4-4-85	(A)	NYR 5 at St. L. 4	74	78	30-73	103	76	
John Tonelli	NYI	6-4-85	(A)	NJ 5 at NYI 5	80	80	42-58	100	80	28.1
Paul MacLean	Wpg.	6-4-85	(A)	Wpg. 6 at Edm. 5	78	79	41-60	101	79	27.1
Mike Gartner	Wsh.	7-4-85	(G)	Pit. 3 at Wsh. 7	80	80	50-52	102	80	25.6
Bernie Nicholls	L.A.	6-4-85	(A)	Van. 4 at L.A. 4	80	80	46-54	100	80	22.9
Mario Lemieux	Pit.	7-4-85	(G)	Pit. 3 at Wsh. 7	73	80	43-57	100	73	19.6
Wayne Gretzky	Edm.	4-1-86	(A)	Hfd. 3 at Edm. 4	39	39	52-163	215	80	
Mario Lemieux	Pit.	15-2-86	(G)	Van. 4 at Pit. 9	55	56	48-93	141	79	
Paul Coffey	Edm.	19-2-86	(A)	Tor. 5 at Edm. 9	59	60	48-90	138	79	
Jari Kurri	Edm.	2-3-86	(A)	Phi. 1 at Edm. 2	62	64	68-63	131	78	
Peter Stastny	Que.	1-3-86	(A)	Buf. 8 at Que. 4	66	68	41-81	122	76	
Mike Bossy	NYI	8-3-86	(G)	Wsh. 6 at NYI 2	65	65	61-62	123	80	
Denis Savard	Chi.	12-3-86	(A)	Buf. 7 at Chi. 6	69	69	47-69	116	80	
Mats Naslund	Mtl.	13-3-86	(A)	Mtl. 2 at Bos. 3	70	70	43-67	110	80	26.4
Michel Goulet	Que.	24-3-86	(A)	Que. 1 at Min. 0	70	75	53-50	103	75	
Glenn Anderson	Edm.	25-3-86	(G)	Edm. 7 at Det. 2	66	74	54-48	102	72	
Neal Broten	Min.	26-3-86	(A)	Min. 6 at Tor. 1	76	76	29-76	105	80	26.4
Dale Hawerchuk	Wpg.	31-3-86	(A)	Wpg. 5 at L.A. 2	78	78	46-59	105	80	
Bernie Federko	St. L.	5-4-86	(G)	Chi. 5 at St. L. 7	79	79	34-68	102	80	
Wayne Gretzky	Edm.	11-1-87	(A)	Cgy. 3 at Edm. 5	42	42	62-121	183	79	
Jari Kurri	Edm.	14-3-87	(A)	Buf. 3 at Edm. 5	67	68	54-54	108	79	
Mario Lemieux	Pit.	18-3-87	(A)	St. L. 4 at Pit. 5	55	72	54-53	107	63	
Mark Messier	Edm.	19-3-87	(A)	Edm. 4 at Cgy. 5	71	71	37-70	107	77	
Doug Gilmour	St. L.	2-4-87	(A)	Buf. 3 at St. L. 5	78	78	42-63	105	80	23.10
Dino Ciccarelli	Min.	30-3-87	(A)	NYR 6 at Min. 5	78	78	52-51	103	80	
Dale Hawerchuk	Wpg.	5-4-87	(A)	Wpg. 3 at Cgy. 1	80	80	47-53	100	80	
Mario Lemieux	Pit.	20-1-88	(G)	Pit. 8 at Chi. 3	45	48	70-98	168	77	
Wayne Gretzky	Edm.	11-2-88	(A)	Edm. 7 at Van. 2	43	56	40-109	149	64	
Denis Savard	Chi.	12-2-88	(A)	St. L. 3 at Chi. 4	57	57	44-87	131	80	
Dale Hawerchuk	Wpg.	23-2-88	(G)	Wpg. 4 at Pit. 3	61	61	44-77	121	80	
Steve Yzerman	Det.	27-2-88	(A)	Det. 4 at Que. 5	63	63	50-52	102	64	22.10
Peter Stastny	Que.	8-3-88	(A)	Hfd. 4 at Que. 6	63	67	46-65	111	76	
Mark Messier	Edm.	15-3-88	(A)	Buf. 4 at Edm. 6	68	71	37-74	111	77	
Jimmy Carson	L.A.	26-3-88	(A)	Chi. 5 at L.A. 9	77	77	55-52	107	80	19.8
Hakan Loob	Cgy.	26-3-88	(A)	Van. 1 at Cgy. 6	76	76	50-56	106	80	27.9
Mike Bullard	Cgy.	26-3-88	(A)	Van. 1 at Cgy. 6	76	76	48-55	103	79	27.1
Michel Goulet	Que.	27-3-88	(A)	Pit. 6 at Que. 3	76	76	48-58	106	80	
Luc Robitaille	L.A.	30-3-88	(G)	Cgy. 7 at L.A. 9	78	78	53-58	111	80	22.1
Mario Lemieux	Pit.	31-12-88	(A)	N.J. 6 at Pit. 8	36	38	85-114	199	76	
Wayne Gretzky	L.A.	21-1-89	(A)	L.A. 4 at Hfd. 5	47	48	54-114	168	78	
Steve Yzerman	Det.	27-1-89	(G)	Tor. 1 at Det. 8	50	50	65-90	155	80	
Bernie Nicholls	L.A.	21-1-89	(A)	L.A. 4 at Hfd. 5	48	48	70-80	150	79	
Rob Brown	Pit.	16-3-89	(A)	Pit. 2 at N.J. 1	60	72	49-66	115	68	20.11
Paul Coffey	Pit.	20-3-89	(A)	Pit. 2 at Min. 7	69	74	30-83	113	75	
Joe Mullen	Cgy.	23-3-89	(A)	L.A. 2 at Cgy. 4	74	75	51-59	110	79	32.1
Jari Kurri	Edm.	29-3-89	(A)	Edm. 5 at Van. 2	75	79	44-58	102	76	
Jimmy Carson	Edm.	2-4-89	(A)	Edm. 2 at Cgy. 4	80	80	49-51	100	80	
Mario Lemieux	Pit.	28-1-90	(G)	Pit. 2 at Buf. 7	50	50	45-78	123	59	
Wayne Gretzky	L.A.	30-1-90	(A)	N.J. 2 at L.A. 5	51	51	40-102	142	73	
Steve Yzerman	Det.	19-2-90	(A)	Mtl. 5 at Det. 5	61	61	62-65	127	79	
Mark Messier	Edm.	20-2-90	(A)	Edm. 4 at Van. 2	62	62	45-84	129	79	
Brett Hull	St. L.	3-3-90	(A)	NYI 4 at St. L. 5	67	67	72-41	113	80	25.7
Bernie Nicholls	NYR	12-3-90	(A)	L.A. 6 at NYR 2	70	71	39-73	112	79	
Pierre Turgeon	Buf.	25-3-90	(G)	N.J. 4 at Buf. 3	76	76	40-66	106	80	20.7

Player	Team	Date of 100th Point	G or A	Score			Player's Game No.	Team Game No.	Points G - A PTS	Total Games	Age when first 100th point scored (Yrs. & Mos.)
Pat LaFontaine	NYI	27-3-90	(G)	Cgy. 4	at	NYI 2	72	78	54-51 — 105	74	25.1
Adam Oates	St. L.	29-3-90	(G)	Pit 4	at	St. L. 5	79	79	23-79 — 102	80	27.7
Joe Sakic	Que.	31-3-90	(G)	Hfd. 3	at	Que. 2	79	79	39-63 — 102	80	20.8
Ron Francis	Hfd.	31-3-90	(G)	Hfd. 3	at	Que. 2	79	79	32-69 — 101	80	27.0
Luc Robitaille	L.A.	1-4-90	(A)	L.A. 4	at	Cgy. 8	80	80	52-49 — 101	80	
Wayne Gretzky	L.A.	30-1-91	(A)	N.J. 4	at	L.A. 2	50	51	41-122 — 163	78	
Brett Hull	St. L.	23-2-91	(G)	Bos. 2	at	St. L. 9	60	62	86-45 — 131	78	
Mark Recchi	Pit.	5-3-91	(G)	Van. 1	at	Pit. 4	66	67	40-73 — 113	78	23.1
Steve Yzerman	Det.	10-3-91	(G)	Det. 4	at	St. L. 1	72	72	51-57 — 108	80	
John Cullen	Hfd.	16-3-91	(G)	N.J. 2	at	Hfd. 6	71	71	39-71 — 110	78	26.7
Adam Oates	St. L.	17-3-91	(A)	St. L. 4	at	Chi. 6	54	73	25-90 — 115	61	
Joe Sakic	Que.	19-3-91	(G)	Edm. 7	at	Que. 6	74	74	48-61 — 109	80	
Steve Larmer	Chi.	24-3-91	(A)	Min. 4	at	Chi. 5	76	76	44-57 — 101	80	29.9
Theoren Fleury	Cgy.	26-3-91	(A)	Van. 3	at	Cgy. 7	77	77	51-53 — 104	78	22.9
Al MacInnis	Cgy.	28-3-91	(A)	Edm. 4	at	Cgy. 4	78	78	28-75 — 103	78	27.8
Brett Hull	St. L.	2-3-92	(G)	St. L. 5	at	Van. 3	66	66	70-39 — 109	73	
Wayne Gretzky	L.A.	3-3-92	(A)	Phi. 1	at	L.A. 4	60	66	31-90 — 121	74	
Kevin Stevens	Pit.	7-3-92	(A)	Pit. 3	at	L.A. 5	66	66	54-69 — 123	80	26.11
Mario Lemieux	Pit.	10-03-92	(A)	Cgy. 4	at	Pit. 5	53	67	44-87 — 131	64	
Luc Robitaille	L.A.	17-3-92	(A)	Wpg. 4	at	L.A. 5	73	73	44-63 — 107	80	
Mark Messier	NYR	22-3-92	(A)	N.J. 3	at	NYR 6	74	75	35-72 — 107	79	
Jeremy Roenick	Chi.	29-3-92	(A)	Tor. 1	at	Chi. 5	77	77	53-50 — 103	80	22.2
Steve Yzerman	Det.	14-4-92	(A)	Det. 7	at	Min. 4	79	80	45-58 — 103	79	
Brian Leetch	NYR	16-4-92	(G)	Pit. 1	at	NYR 7	80	80	22-80 — 102	80	24.1
Mario Lemieux	Pit.	31-12-92	(G)	Tor. 3	at	Pit. 3	38	39	69-91 — 160	60	
Pat LaFontaine	Buf.	10-2-93	(A)	Buf. 6	at	Wpg. 2	55	55	53-95 — 148	84	
Adam Oates	Bos.	14-2-93	(A)	Bos. 3	at	T.B. 3	58	58	45-97 — 142	84	
Steve Yzerman	Det.	24-2-93	(A)	Det. 7	at	Buf. 10	64	64	58-79 — 137	84	
Pierre Turgeon	NYI	28-2-93	(G)	NYI 7	at	Hfd. 6	62	63	58-74 — 132	83	
Doug Gilmour	Tor.	3-3-93	(A)	Min. 1	at	Tor. 3	64	64	32-95 — 127	83	
Alexander Mogilny	Buf.	5-3-93	(A)	Hfd. 4	at	Buf. 2	58	65	76-51 — 127	77	24.1
Mark Recchi	Phi.	7-3-93	(G)	Phi. 3	at	N.J. 7	66	66	53-70 — 123	84	22.7
Teemu Selanne	Wpg.	9-3-93	(A)	Wpg. 4	at	T.B. 2	68	68	76-56 — 132	84	22.7
Luc Robitaille	L.A.	15-3-93	(A)	L.A. 4	at	Buf. 2	69	69	63-62 — 125	84	
Kevin Stevens	Pit.	23-3-93	(A)	S.J. 2	at	Pit. 7	63	73	55-56 — 111	72	
Mats Sundin	Que.	27-3-93	(A)	Phi. 3	at	Que. 8	71	75	47-67 — 114	80	22.1
Pavel Bure	Van.	1-4-93	(G)	Van. 5	at	T.B. 3	77	77	60-50 — 110	83	22.0
Jeremy Roenick	Chi.	4-4-93	(G)	St. L. 4	at	Chi. 5	79	79	50-57 — 107	84	
Craig Janney	St. L.	4-4-93	(A)	St. L. 4	at	Chi. 5	79	79	24-82 — 106	84	25.7
Rick Tocchet	Pit.	7-4-93	(G)	Mtl. 3	at	Pit. 4	77	81	48-61 — 109	80	28.11
Joe Sakic	Que.	8-4-93	(A)	Que. 2	at	Bos. 6	75	81	48-57 — 105	78	
Ron Francis	Pit.	9-4-93	(A)	Pit. 10	at	NYR 4	82	82	24-76 — 100	84	
Brett Hull	St. L.	11-4-93	(G)	Min. 1	at	St. L. 5	78	82	54-47 — 101	80	
Theoren Fleury	Cgy.	11-4-93	(G)	Cgy. 3	at	Van. 6	82	82	34-66 — 100	83	
Joe Juneau	Bos.	14-4-93	(A)	Bos. 4	at	Ott. 2	84	84	32-70 — 102	84	25.3
Wayne Gretzky	L.A.	14-2-94	(A)	Bos. 3	at	L.A. 2	56	56	38-92 — 130	81	
Sergei Fedorov	Det.	1-3-94	(A)	Cgy. 2	at	Det. 5	63	63	56-64 — 120	82	24.2
Doug Gilmour	Tor.	23-3-94	(A)	Tor. 1	at	Fla. 1	74	74	27-84 — 111	83	
Adma Oates	Bos.	26-3-94	(A)	Mtl. 3	at	Bos. 6	68	75	32-80 — 112	77	
Mark Recchi	Phi.	27-3-94	(A)	Ana. 3	at	Phi. 2	76	76	40-67 — 107	84	
Pavel Bure	Van.	28-3-94	(G)	Tor. 2	at	Van. 3	68	76	60-47 — 107	76	
Brendan Shanahan	St.L.	12-4-94	(G)	St.L. 5	at	Dal. 9	80	83	52-50 — 102	81	25.2

Ron Francis

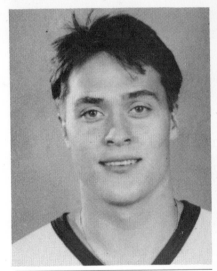

Teemu Selanne

Five-or-more-Goal Games

Player	Team	Date	Score			Opposing Goaltender
SEVEN GOALS						
Joe Malone	Quebec Bulldogs	Jan. 31/20	Tor. 6	at	Que. 10	Ivan Mitchell
SIX GOALS						
Newsy Lalonde	Montreal	Jan. 10/20	Tor. 7	at	Mtl. 14	Ivan Mitchell
Joe Malone	Quebec Bulldogs	Mar. 10/20	Ott. 4	at	Que. 10	Clint Benedict
Corb Denneny	Toronto St. Pats	Jan. 26/21	Ham. 3	at	Tor. 10	Howard Lockhart
Cy Denneny	Ottawa Senators	Mar. 7/21	Ham. 5	at	Ott. 12	Howard Lockhart
Syd Howe	Detroit	Feb. 3/44	NYR 2	at	Det. 12	Ken McAuley
Red Berenson	St. Louis	Nov. 7/68	St. L. 8	at	Phil 0	Doug Favell
Darryl Sittler	Toronto	Feb. 7/76	Bos. 4	at	Tor. 11	Dave Reece
FIVE GOALS						
Joe Malone	Montreal	Dec. 19/17	Mtl. 7	at	Ott. 4	Clint Benedict
Harry Hyland	Mtl. Wanderers	Dec. 19/17	Tor. 9	at	Mtl. W. 10	Arthur Brooks
Joe Malone	Montreal	Jan. 12/18	Ott. 4	at	Mtl. 9	Clint Benedict
Joe Malone	Montreal	Feb. 2/18	Tor. 2	at	Mtl. 11	Harry Holmes
Mickey Roach	Toronto St. Pats	Mar. 6/20	Que. 2	at	Tor. 11	Frank Brophy
Newsy Lalonde	Montreal	Feb. 16/21	Ham. 5	at	Mtl. 10	Howard Lockhart
Babe Dye	Toronto St. Pats	Dec. 16/22	Mtl. 2	at	Tor. 7	Georges Vezina
Redvers Green	Hamilton Tigers	Dec. 5/24	Ham. 10	at	Tor. 3	John Roach
Babe Dye	Toronto St. Pats	Dec. 22/24	Tor. 10	at	Bos. 1	Charlie Stewart
Harry Broadbent	Mtl. Maroons	Jan. 7/25	Mtl. 6	at	Ham. 2	Vernon Forbes
Pit Lepine	Montreal	Dec. 14/29	Ott. 4	at	Mtl. 6	Alex Connell
Howie Morenz	Montreal	Mar. 18/30	NYA 3	at	Mtl. 8	Roy Worters
Charlie Conacher	Toronto	Jan. 19/32	NYA 3	at	Tor. 11	Roy Worters
Ray Getliffe	Montreal	Feb. 6/43	Bos. 3	at	Mtl. 8	Frank Brimsek
Maurice Richard	Montreal	Dec. 28/44	Det. 1	at	Mtl. 9	Harry Lumley
Howie Meeker	Toronto	Jan. 8/47	Chi. 4	at	Tor. 10	Paul Bibeault
Bernie Geoffrion	Montreal	Feb. 19/55	NYR 2	at	Mtl. 4	Gump Worsley
Bobby Rousseau	Montreal	Feb. 1/64	Det. 3	at	Mtl. 9	Roger Crozier
Yvan Cournoyer	Montreal	Feb. 15/75	Chi. 3	at	Mtl. 12	Mike Veisor
Don Murdoch	NY Rangers	Oct. 12/76	NYR 10	at	Min. 4	Gary Smith
Ian Turnbull	Toronto	Feb. 2/77	Det. 1	at	Tor. 9	Ed Giacomin (2) Jim Rutherford (3)
Bryan Trottier	NY Islanders	Dec. 23/78	NYR 4	at	NYI 9	Wayne Thomas (4) John Davidson (1)

Player	Team	Date	Score			Opposing Goaltender
Tim Young	Minnesota	Jan. 15/79	Min. 8	at	NYR 1	Doug Soetaert (3) Wayne Thomas (2) empty net (1)
John Tonelli	NY Islanders	Jan. 6/81	Tor. 3	at	NYI 6	Jiri Crha (4) empty net (1)
Wayne Gretzky	Edmonton	Feb. 18/81	St. L. 2	at	Edm. 9	Mike Liut (3) Ed Staniowski (2)
Wayne Gretzky	Edmonton	Dec. 30/81	Phi. 5	at	Edm. 7	Pete Peeters (4) empty net (1)
Grant Mulvey	Chicago	Feb. 3/82	St. L. 5	at	Chi. 9	Mike Liut (4) Gary Edwards (1)
Bryan Trottier	NY Islanders	Feb. 13/82	Phi. 2	at	NYI 8	Pete Peeters
Willy Lindstrom	Winnipeg	Mar. 2/82	Wpg. 7	at	Phi. 6	Pete Peeters
Mark Pavelich	NY Rangers	Feb. 23/83	Hfd. 3	at	NYR 11	Greg Millen
Jari Kurri	Edmonton	Nov. 19/83	N.J. 4	at	Edm. 13	Glenn Resch (3) Ron Low (2)
Bengt Gustafsson	Washington	Jan. 8/84	Wsh. 7	at	Phi. 1	Pelle Lindbergh
Pat Hughes	Edmonton	Feb. 3/84	Cgy. 5	at	Edm. 10	Don Edwards (3) Rejean Lemelin (2)
Wayne Gretzky	Edmonton	Dec. 15/84	Edm. 8	at	St. L. 2	Rick Wamsley (4) Mike Liut (1)
Dave Andreychuk	Buffalo	Feb. 6/86	Buf. 8	at	Bos. 6	Pat Riggin (1) Doug Keans (4)
Wayne Gretzky	Edmonton	Dec. 6/87	Min. 4	at	Edm. 10	Don Beaupre (4) Kari Takko (1)
Mario Lemieux	Pittsburgh	Dec. 31/88	N.J. 6	at	Pit. 8	Bob Sauve (3) Chris Terreri (2)
Joe Nieuwendyk	Calgary	Jan. 11/89	Wpg. 3	at	Cgy. 8	Daniel Berthiaume (2) Peter Sidorkiewicz (3)
Mats Sundin	Quebec	Mar. 5/92	Que. 10	at	Hfd. 4	Kay Whitmore (2)
Mario Lemieux	Pittsburgh	Apr. 9/93	Pit. 10	at	NYR 4	Corey Hirsch (3) Mike Richter (2)
Peter Bondra	Washington	Feb. 5/94	T.B. 3	at	Wsh. 6	Darren Puppa (4) Pat Jablonski (1)
Mike Ricci	Quebec	Feb. 17/94	S.J. 2	at	Que. 8	Arturs Irbe (3) Jimmy Waite (2)

Players' 500th Goals

Player	Team	Date	Game No.	Score		Opposing Goaltender	Total Goals	Total Games
Maurice Richard	Montreal	Oct. 19/57	863	Chi. 1	at Mtl. 3	Glenn Hall	544	978
Gordie Howe	Detroit	Mar. 14/62	1,045	Det. 2	at NYR 3	Gump Worsley	801	1,767
Bobby Hull	Chicago	Feb. 21/70	861	NYR. 2	at Chi. 4	Ed Giacomin	610	1,063
Jean Béliveau	Montreal	Feb. 11/71	1,101	Min. 2	at Mtl. 6	Gilles Gilbert	507	1,125
Frank Mahovlich	Montreal	Mar. 21/73	1,105	Van. 2	at Mtl. 3	Dunc Wilson	533	1,181
Phil Esposito	Boston	Dec. 22/74	803	Det. 4	at Bos. 5	Jim Rutherford	717	1,282
John Bucyk	Boston	Oct. 30/75	1,370	St. L. 2	at Bos. 3	Yves Bélanger	556	1,540
Stan Mikita	Chicago	Feb. 27/77	1,221	Van. 4	at Chi. 3	Cesare Maniago	541	1,394
Marcel Dionne	Los Angeles	Dec. 14/82	887	L.A. 2	at Wsh. 7	Al Jensen	731	1,348
Guy Lafleur	Montreal	Dec. 20/83	918	Mtl. 6	at N.J. 0	Glenn Resch	560	1,126
Mike Bossy	NY Islanders	Jan. 2/86	647	Bos. 5	at NYI 7	empty net	573	752
Gilbert Perreault	Buffalo	Mar. 9/86	1,159	NJ 3	at Buf. 4	Alain Chevrier	512	1,191
*Wayne Gretzky	Edmonton	Nov. 22/86	575	Van. 2	at Edm. 5	empty net	803	1,125
Lanny McDonald	Calgary	Mar. 21/89	1,107	NYI 1	at Cgy. 4	Mark Fitzpatrick	500	1,111
*Bryan Trottier	NY Islanders	Feb. 13/90	1,104	Cgy. 4	at NYI 2	Rick Wamsley	524	1,279
*Mike Gartner	NY Rangers	Oct. 14/91	936	Wsh. 5	at NYR 3	Mike Liut	617	1,170
*Michel Goulet	Chicago	Feb. 16/92	951	Cgy. 5	at Chi. 5	Jeff Reese	548	1,089
*Jari Kurri	Los Angeles	Oct. 17/92	833	Bos. 6	at L.A. 8	empty net	555	990
*Dino Ciccarelli	Detroit	Jan. 8/94	946	Det. 6	at L.A. 3	Kelly Hrudey	513	973

*Active

Mike Bossy

Players' 1,000th Points

Player	Team	Date	Game No.	G or A	Score		Total Points G A PTS	Total Games
Gordie Howe	Detroit	Nov. 27/60	938	(A)	Tor. 0	at Det. 2	801–1,049–1,850	1,767
Jean Béliveau	Montreal	Mar. 3/68	911	(G)	Mtl. 2	at Det. 5	507–712–1,219	1,125
Alex Delvecchio	Detroit	Feb. 16/69	1,143	(A)	LA 3	at Det. 6	456–825–1,281	1,549
Bobby Hull	Chicago	Dec. 12/70	909	(A)	Minn. 3	at Chi. 5	610–560–1,170	1,063
Norm Ullman	Toronto	Oct. 16/71	1,113	(A)	NYR 5	at Tor. 3	490–739–1,229	1,410
Stan Mikita	Chicago	Oct. 15/72	924	(A)	St.L. 3	at Chi. 1	541–926–1,467	1,394
John Bucyk	Boston	Nov. 9/72	1,144	(A)	Det. 3	at Bos. 8	556–813–1,369	1,540
Frank Mahovlich	Montreal	Feb. 13/73	1,090	(A)	Phi. 7	at Mtl. 6	533–570–1,103	1,181
Henri Richard	Montreal	Dec. 20/73	1,194	(A)	Mtl. 2	at Buf. 2	358–688–1,046	1,256
Phil Esposito	Boston	Feb. 15/74	745	(A)	Bos. 4	at Van. 2	717–873–1,590	1,282
Rod Gilbert	NY Rangers	Feb. 19/77	1,027	(G)	NYR 2	at NYI 5	406–615–1,021	1,065
Jean Ratelle	Boston	Apr. 3/77	1,007	(A)	Tor. 4	at Bos. 7	491–776–1,267	1,281
Marcel Dionne	Los Angeles	Jan. 7/81	740	(G)	L.A. 5	at Hfd. 3	731–1,040–1,771	1,348
Guy Lafleur	Montreal	Mar. 4/81	720	(G)	Mtl. 9	at Wpg. 3	560–793–1,353	1,126
Bobby Clarke	Philadelphia	Mar. 19/81	922	(G)	Bos. 3	at Phi. 5	358–852–1,210	1,144
Gilbert Perreault	Buffalo	Apr. 3/82	871	(G)	Buf. 5	at Mtl.4	512–814–1,326	1,191
Darryl Sittler	Philadelphia	Jan. 20/83	927	(G)	Cgy 2	at Phi. 5	484–637–1,121	1,096
*Wayne Gretzky	Edmonton	Dec. 19/84	424	(A)	L.A. 3	at Edm. 7	803–1,655–2,458	1,125
*Bryan Trottier	NY Islanders	Jan. 29/85	726	(A)	Min. 4	at NYI 4	524–901–1,425	1,279
Mike Bossy	NY Islanders	Jan. 24/86	656	(A)	NYI 7	at Wsh. 5	573–553–1,126	752
Denis Potvin	NY Islanders	Apr. 4/87	987	(G)	Buf. 6	at NYI 6	310–742–1,052	1,060
Bernie Federko	St. Louis	Mar 19/88	855	(G)	Hfd. 5	at St.L. 3	369–761–1,130	1,000
Lanny McDonald	Calgary	Mar. 7/89	1,101	(G)	Wpg. 5	at Cgy. 9	500–506–1,006	1,111
*Peter Stastny	Quebec	Oct. 19/89	682	(G)	Que. 5	at Chi. 3	449–788–1,237	971
*Jari Kurri	Edmonton	Jan. 2/90	716	(A)	Edm. 6	at St.L. 4	555–712–1,267	990
*Denis Savard	Chicago	Mar. 11/90	727	(A)	St.L. 6	at Chi. 4	441–797–1,238	1,020
*Paul Coffey	Pittsburgh	Dec. 22/90	770	(A)	Pit. 4	at NYI 3	344–934–1,278	1,033
*Mark Messier	Edmonton	Jan. 13/91	822	(A)	Edm. 5	at Phi. 3	478–838–1,316	1,081
Dave Taylor	Los Angeles	Feb. 5/91	930	(A)	L.A. 3	at Phi. 2	431–638–1,069	1,111
*Michel Goulet	Chicago	Feb. 23/91	878	(G)	Chi. 3	at Min. 3	548–604–1,152	1,089
*Dale Hawerchuk	Buffalo	Mar. 8/91	781	(G)	Chi. 5	at Buf. 3	484–814–1,298	1,032
Bobby Smith	Minnesota	Nov. 30/91	986	(A)	Min. 4	at Tor. 3	357–679–1,036	1,077
*Mike Gartner	NY Rangers	Jan. 4/92	971	(G)	NYR 4	at N.J. 6	617–554–1,171	1,170
*Ray Bourque	Boston	Feb. 29/92	933	(G)	Wsh. 5	at Bos. 5	311–877–1,188	1,100
*Mario Lemieux	Pittsburgh	Mar. 24/92	513	(A)	Pit. 3	at Det. 4	494–717–1,211	599
*Glenn Anderson	Toronto	Feb. 22/93	954	(G)	Tor. 8	at Van. 1	480–579–1,059	1,061
*Steve Yzerman	Detroit	Feb. 24/93	737	(A)	Det. 7	at Buf. 10	469–653–1,122	815
*Ron Francis	Pittsburgh	Oct. 28/93	893	(G)	Que. 7	at Pit. 3	338–741–1079	964
*Bernie Nicholls	New Jersey	Feb. 13/94	858	(G)	N.J. 3	at T.B. 3	416–607–1,023	885
*Dino Ciccarelli	Detroit	Mar. 9/94	957	(G)	Det. 5	at Cgy. 1	513–501–1014	973
*Brian Propp	Hartford	Mar. 19/94	1,008	(G)	Hfd. 5	at Phi. 3	425–578–1003	1016

*Active

Lanny McDonald

Individual Awards

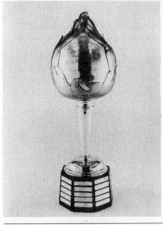

Hart Memorial Trophy

Art Ross Trophy

Calder Memorial Trophy

James Norris Memorial Trophy

HART MEMORIAL TROPHY

An annual award "to the player adjudged to be the most valuable to his team". Winner selected in poll by Professional Hockey Writers' Association in the 26 NHL cities at the end of the regular schedule. The winner receives $10,000 and the runners-up $6,000 and $4,000.

History: The Hart Memorial Trophy was presented by the National Hockey League in 1960 after the original Hart Trophy was retired to the Hockey Hall of Fame. The original Hart Trophy was donated to the NHL in 1923 by Dr. David A. Hart, father of Cecil Hart, former manager-coach of the Montreal Canadiens.

1993-94 Winner: Sergei Fedorov, Detroit Red Wings
Runners-up: Dominik Hasek, Buffalo Sabres
John Vanbiesbrouck, Florida Panthers

Detroit Red Wings center Sergei Fedorov received 31 of 54 first place votes and was named on 48 of 54 ballots, earning 194 points. Goaltenders finished second and third in the balloting, with Buffalo's Dominik Hasek taking the runner-up position with 86 points and Florida's John Vanbiesbrouck placing third with 74 points.

Fedorov's fourth NHL season was his best ever, as he established career highs in goals (56), assists (64) and points (120) en route to finishing second in the NHL scoring race behind Wayne Gretzky. His plus-minus rating of +48 was the League's second-best, behind New Jersey's Scott Stevens (+53). The Red Wings finished the regular season with the best record in the Western Conference, posting a 46-30-8 mark for 100 points.

Fedorov is the first Detroit Red Wing to win the Hart Trophy since Gordie Howe captured the last of his six Hart Trophies in 1963. Other Red Wings to have won the award are Sid Abel in 1949 and Ebbie Goodfellow in 1940.

ART ROSS TROPHY

An annual award "to the player who leads the league in scoring points at the end of the regular season." The winner receives $10,000 and the runners-up $6,000 and $4,000.

History: Arthur Howie Ross, former manager-coach of Boston Bruins, presented the trophy to the National Hockey League in 1947. If two players finish the schedule with the same number of points, the trophy is awarded in the following manner: 1. Player with most goals. 2. Player with fewer games played. 3. Player scoring first goal of the season.

1993-94 Winner: Wayne Gretzky, Los Angeles Kings
Runners-up: Sergei Fedorov, Detroit Red Wings
Adam Oates, Boston Bruins

Wayne Gretzky of the Los Angeles Kings won the tenth Art Ross Trophy of his career in 1993-94. Gretzky recorded 38 goals and 92 assists for 130 points to win his first scoring title in three seasons. Sergei Fedorov of the Detroit Red Wings finished second to Gretzky with 56 goals and 64 assists for 120 points. Adam Oates of the Boston Bruins finished third in scoring with 32 goals and 80 assists for 112 points.

CALDER MEMORIAL TROPHY

An annual award "to the player selected as the most proficient in his first year of competition in the National Hockey League". Winner selected in poll by Professional Hockey Writers' Association at the end of the regular schedule. The winner receives $10,000 and the runners-up $6,000 and $4,000.

History: From 1936-37 until his death in 1943, Frank Calder, NHL President, bought a trophy each year to be given permanently to the outstanding rookie. After Calder's death, the NHL presented the Calder Memorial Trophy in his memory and the trophy is to be kept in perpetuity. To be eligible for the award, a player cannot have played more than 25 games in any single preceding season nor in six or more games in each of any two preceding seasons in any major professional league. Beginning in 1990-91, to be eligible for this award a player must not have attained his twenty-sixth birthday by September 15th of the season in which he is eligible.

1993-94 Winner: Martin Brodeur, New Jersey Devils
Runners-up: Jason Arnott, Edmonton Oilers
Mikael Renberg, Philadelphia Flyers

Goaltender Martin Brodeur of the New Jersey Devils received 21 of 54 first-place ballots for a 164 point total, slightly ahead of second place finisher Jason Arnott of the Edmonton Oilers (137 points). Mikael Renberg of the Philadelphia Flyers finished in third place with 109 points.

Brodeur, who turned 22 in May, appeared in 47 games for New Jersey in 1993-94 and posted a 27-11-8 record, 2.40 goals-against average and .915 save percentage. He finished second among all NHL goaltenders in goals-against average and fourth overall in save percentage. Brodeur is just the third goaltender in the last 20 years to win the Calder Trophy, joining Tom Barrasso (Buffalo, 1984) and Ed Belfour (Chicago, 1991).

JAMES NORRIS MEMORIAL TROPHY

An annual award "to the defense player who demonstrates throughout the season the greatest all-round ability in the position." Winner selected in poll by Professional Hockey Writers' Association at the end of the regular schedule. The winner receives $10,000 and the runners-up $6,000 and $4,000.

History: The James Norris Memorial Trophy was presented in 1953 by the four children of the late James Norris in memory of the former owner-president of the Detroit Red Wings.

1993-94 Winner: Ray Bourque, Boston Bruins
Runners-up: Scott Stevens, New Jersey Devils
Al MacInnis, Calgary Flames

Ray Bourque of the Boston Bruins won his fifth career Norris Trophy in 1993-94

Bourque, who finished as runner-up in Norris voting for the past two seasons, polled 199 points to edge second place Scott Stevens of the New Jersey Devils (195 points), the smallest winning margin in Norris Trophy history. Al MacInnis of the Calgary Flames was third in the voting with 60 points.

Bourque finished second on the Bruins in scoring with 91 points (20-71-91 in 72 games), the ninth time in the last 11 seasons that he has reached 80-or-more points. His plus-minus rating of +26 was also second on Bruins and among the best in the League. Bourque helped the Bruins post a 42-29-13 record for 97 points, fourth in the Eastern Conference.

Bourque became the third defenseman in NHL history to win the Norris Trophy at least five times, joining Bobby Orr (eight times) and Doug Harvey (seven). His five Norris Trophy wins have all come in the last eight years, having previously won the award in 1987, 1988, 1990 and 1991.

Vezina Trophy

Lady Byng Memorial Trophy

Frank J. Selke Trophy

Conn Smythe Trophy

VEZINA TROPHY

An annual award "to the goalkeeper adjudged to be the best at his position" as voted by the general managers of each of the 26 clubs. Over-all winner receives $10,000, runners-up $6,000 and $4,000.

History: Leo Dandurand, Louis Letourneau and Joe Cattarinich, former owners of the Montreal Canadiens, presented the trophy to the National Hockey League in 1926-27 in memory of Georges Vezina, outstanding goalkeeper of the Canadiens who collapsed during an NHL game November 28, 1925, and died of tuberculosis a few months later. Until the 1981-82 season, the goalkeeper(s) of the team allowing the fewest number of goals during the regular-season were awarded the Vezina Trophy.

1993-94 Winner: Dominik Hasek, Buffalo Sabres
   Runners-up: John Vanbiesbrouck, Florida Panthers
     Patrick Roy, Montreal Canadiens

Buffalo Sabres goaltender Dominik Hasek received 15 of 26 first-place votes and tallied 99 of a possible 130 points in the balloting to edge second place finisher John Vanbiesbrouck of the Florida Panthers, who earned 64 points. Patrick Roy of the Montreal Canadiens finished in third place with 34 points.

In 1993-94, Hasek led all goaltenders in goals-against average with a 1.95 mark in 58 games, becoming the first goaltender to post a sub-2.00 goals-against average since Philadelphia's Bernie Parent in 1973-74. He also led the League in save percentage (.930), shared the lead in shutouts (seven) and posted a 30-20-6 record. He teamed with Grant Fuhr to win the William Jennings Trophy, as the Sabres allowed just 218 goals in 84 regular season games for a 2.57 average.

This represents Hasek's first career Vezina Trophy win. He joins Tom Barrasso (1984) as Buffalo Sabres goaltenders to have won the Vezina Trophy since the award's criterion was modified in 1981-82.

LADY BYNG MEMORIAL TROPHY

An annual award "to the player adjudged to have exhibited the best type of sportsmanship and gentlemanly conduct combined with a high standard of playing ability." Winner selected in poll by Professional Hockey Writers' Association at the end of the regular schedule. The winner receives $10,000 and the runners-up $6,000 and $4,000.

History: Lady Byng, wife of Canada's Governor-General at the time, presented the Lady Byng Trophy in 1925. After Frank Boucher of New York Rangers won the award seven times in eight seasons, he was given the trophy to keep and Lady Byng donated another trophy in 1936. After Lady Byng's death in 1949, the National Hockey League presented a new trophy, changing the name to Lady Byng Memorial Trophy.

1993-94 Winner: Wayne Gretzky, Los Angeles Kings
   Runners-up: Adam Oates, Boston Bruins
     Pierre Turgeon, New York Islanders

Los Angeles Kings center Wayne Gretzky received 23 of 54 first place votes, was named on 39 of 54 ballots and posted 145 total points to win the Lady Byng Trophy for the fourth time in his 15-year NHL career. Boston Bruins' center Adam Oates was second in the voting for the second consecutive year with 81 points, followed by last year's winner, center Pierre Turgeon of the New York Islanders (71 points).

Gretzky captured his 10th career Art Ross Trophy in 1993-94 as the NHL's scoring leader, amassing 130 points (38-92-130) in 81 games. On March 23, he notched his 802nd career goal to pass Gordie Howe as the NHL's all-time leading goal-scorer. Throughout the regular season Gretzky accumulated just 20 minutes in penalties. In addition to winning the award four times, Gretzky has finished second in Lady Byng voting five times and in third place once.

FRANK J. SELKE TROPHY

An annual award "to the forward who best excels in the defensive aspects of the game." Winner selected in poll by Professional Hockey Writers' Association at the end of the regular schedule. The winner receives $10,000 and the runners-up $6,000 and $4,000.

History: Presented to the National Hockey League in 1977 by the Board of Governors of the NHL in honour of Frank J. Selke, one of the great architects of NHL championship teams.

1993-94 Winner: Sergei Fedorov, Detroit Red Wings
   Runners-up: Doug Gilmour, Toronto Maple Leafs
     Brian Skrudland, Florida Panthers

Center Sergei Fedorov of the Detroit Red Wings received 32 of a possible 54 first place votes and was named on 41 of 54 ballots, totalling 181 points. Toronto Maple Leafs center Doug Gilmour, last year's winner, finished in the runner-up position with 107 points, while center Brian Skrudland of the Florida Panthers took third place with 37 points.

Fedorov posted a +48 rating this season, the best plus-minus rating among all NHL forwards and second in the League overall to New Jersey's Scott Stevens (+53). He finished second in the League scoring race, tallying a career-high 120 points (56-64-120) to help the Red Wings post the best record in the Western Conference with a 46-30-8 mark for 100 points.

This represents Fedorov's first Frank Selke Trophy win in his second year as a finalist, having previously finished second to Montreal's Guy Carbonneau in 1992. He becomes the first member of the Red Wings to win the Selke Trophy since the award was introduced in 1978.

CONN SMYTHE TROPHY

An annual award "to the most valuable player for his team in the playoffs." Winner selected by the Professional Hockey Writers' Association at the conclusion of the final game in the Stanley Cup Finals. The winner receives $10,000.

History: Presented by Maple Leaf Gardens Limited in 1964 to honor Conn Smythe, the former coach, manager, president and owner-governor of the Toronto Maple Leafs.

1993-94 Winner: Brian Leetch, New York Rangers

New York Rangers defenseman Brian Leetch topped all playoff scorers with 34 points in 23 post-season games en route to the Stanley Cup in 1994. Leetch finished with a +/– rating of +19 for the playoffs and scored four power-play and four game-winning goals. He logged considerable ice time in every game, rushed the puck and scored five goals in the Ranger's seven-gmae final series victory over the Vancouver Canucks.

WILLIAM M. JENNINGS TROPHY

An annual award "to the goalkeeper(s) having played a minimum of 25 games for the team with the fewest goals scored against it." Winners selected on regular-season play. Overall winner receives $10,000, runners-up $6,000 and $4,000.

History: The Jennings Trophy was presented in 1981-82 by the National Hockey League's Board of Governors to honor the late William M. Jennings, longtime governor and president of the New York Rangers and one of the great builders of hockey in the United States.

1993-94 Winner: Dominik Hasek, Grant Fuhr, Buffalo Sabres
   Runners-up: Martin Brodeur, Chris Terreri, New Jersey Devils
     Mike Richter, Glenn Healy, New York Rangers

The Buffalo Sabres goaltending tandem of Dominek Hasek and Grant Fuhr combined for nine shutouts in 1993-94 and led the NHL with a combined goals-agiainst average of 2.57 and 218 goals against.

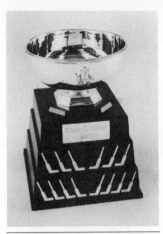

William M. Jennings Trophy

Jack Adams Award

Bill Masterton Trophy

Lester Patrick Trophy

Lester B. Pearson Award

JACK ADAMS AWARD

An annual award presented by the National Hockey League Broadcasters' Association to "the NHL coach adjudged to have contributed the most to his team's success." Winner selected by poll among members of the NHL Broadcasters' Association at the end of the regular season. The winner receives $1,000 from the NHLBA.

History: The award was presented by the NHL Broadcasters' Association in 1974 to commemorate the late Jack Adams, coach and general manager of the Detroit Red Wings, whose lifetime dedication to hockey serves as an inspiration to all who aspire to further the game.

1993-94 Winner: Jacques Lemaire, New Jersey Devils
        Runners-up: Kevin Constantine, San Jose Sharks
                John Muckler, Buffalo Sabres

New Jersey Devils head coach Jacques Lemaire received 28 of 66 first place votes, was named on 54 of 66 ballots and totalled 202 points to finish ahead of second place Kevin Constantine of the San Jose Sharks, who tallied 136 points. Buffalo Sabres head coach John Muckler was third, with 98 points.

Lemaire guided the Devils to a team-record 106 point finish in the regular-season, his first season with the club. The Devils finished with the NHL's second-best record behind their Atlantic Division rival New York Rangers with a 47-25-12 mark in 84 games and registered the NHL's second-best defensive record, allowing 220 goals for a 2.59 average per game.

Lemaire becomes the first coach of the New Jersey Devils to capture the Jack Adams Award since its establishment in 1974.

BILL MASTERTON MEMORIAL TROPHY

An annual award under the trusteeship of the Professional Hockey Writers' Association to "the National Hockey League player who best exemplifies the qualities of perseverance, sportsmanship and dedication to hockey." Winner selected by poll among the 26 chapters of the PHWA at the end of the regular season. A $2,500 grant from the PHWA is awarded annually to the Bill Masterton Scholarship Fund, based in Bloomington, MN, in the name of the Masterton Trophy winner.

History: The trophy was presented by the NHL Writers' Association in 1968 to commemorate the late William Masterton, a player of the Minnesota North Stars, who exhibited to a high degree the qualities of perseverance, sportsmanship and dedication to hockey, and who died January 15, 1968.

1993-94 Winner: Cam Neely, Boston Bruins
        Runners-up: Garry Galley, Philadelphia Flyers
                Mark Howe, Detroit Red Wings

Cam Neely enjoyed one of the greatest comeback seasons in NHL history in 1993-94. A serious thigh injury suffered in the 1991 Wales Conference Final versus Pittsburgh sidelined Neely for the first half of the 1991-92 season and a subsequent knee injury required him to miss the balance of that season and all but 13 games of the 1992-93 season. Neely's tireless rehabilitation work paid off in 1993-94 when he returned to regular action with the Bruins, reaching the 50-goal mark for the third time in his career in just his 44th game of the season. Only Wayne Gretzky had scored 50 goals in fewer games from the start of a season. He tallied goals in 33 of 49 games and points in 40 of 49 games prior to suffering a season-ending knee injury on March 19.

LESTER PATRICK TROPHY

An annual award "for outstanding service to hockey in the United States." Eligible recipients are players, officials, coaches, executives and referees. Winner selected by an award committee consisting of the President of the NHL, an NHL Governor, a representative of the New York Rangers, a member of the Hockey Hall of Fame Builder's section, a member of the Hockey Hall of Fame Player's section, a member of the U.S. Hockey Hall of Fame, a member of the NHL Broadcasters' Association and a member of the Professional Hockey Writers' Association. Each except the League President is rotated annually. The winner receives a miniature of the trophy.

History: Presented by the New York Rangers in 1966 to honor the late Lester Patrick, longtime general manager and coach of the New York Rangers, whose teams finished out of the playoffs only once in his first 16 years with the club.

1993-94 Winners: Wayne Gretzky
                Robert Ridder

Los Angeles Kings superstar center Wayne Gretzkly and long-time hockey administrator Robert (Bob) Ridder are the 1994 recipients of the Lester Patrick Trophy. Gretzky is the holder of more than 60 NHL records and has been a leading force in establishing hockey as a national sport in the United States. Gretzky began his NHL career with the Edmonton Oilers in 1979. He joined the Los Angeles Kings in 1988, and solidified the Kings and hockey as a prime attraction in southern California. The success of the Gretzky-era Kings paved the way for four new franchises in warm weather climates: San Jose, Tampa Bay, Anaheim and Florida.

Robert Ridder began his hockey involvement in the 1940s with a senior team in Duluth, MN. In 1947, he became one of the founders of the Minnesota Amateur Hockey Association. The MAHA has grown into one of hockey's largest and most successful amateur organizations and has produced many players who have gone on to productive careers in professional hockey. Ridder also served as manager of the silver-medal winning U.S. Olympic Hockey Team in 1952 and 1956. He is a member and director of the U.S. Hockey Hall of Fame and was a part of the original group that brought the Minnesota North Stars to Minneapolis-St. Paul in 1967.

LESTER B. PEARSON AWARD

An annual award presented to the NHL's outstanding player as selected by the members of the National Hockey League Players' Association. The winner receives $10,000.

History: The award was presented in 1970-71 by the NHLPA in honor of the late Lester B. Pearson, former Prime Minister of Canada.

1993-94 Winner: Sergei Fedorov, Detroit Red Wings

Sergei Fedorov led the Red Wings with strong two-way play in 1993-94. Simultaneously one of the NHL's premiere defensive forwards and a 50-goal scorer, Fedorov scored 10 game-winning goals and recorded 11 short-handed points for Detroit.

King Clancy Memorial Trophy

Alka-Seltzer Plus Award

Presidents' Trophy

KING CLANCY MEMORIAL TROPHY

An annual award "to the player who best exemplifies leadership qualities on and off the ice and has made a noteworthy humanitarian contribution in his community". The winner receives $3,000 and the runner-up $1,000.

History: The King Clancy Memorial Trophy was presented to the National Hockey League by the Board of Governors in 1988 to honor the late Frank "King" Clancy.

1993-94 Winner: Adam Graves, New York Rangers
Runner-up: Sean Burke, Hartford Whalers

For the last two seasons New York Rangers left wing Adam Graves has received the "Players Player Award", selected by the Rangers players themselves in recognition of the outstanding team player with team spirit. For three consecutive years he has been named winner of the prestigious Steven McDonald "Extra Effort" Award by the fans, awarded to the Rangers player who "went above and beyond the call of duty."

Graves makes numerous guest appearances and conducts clinics for various youth hockey organizations, including the "Ice Hockey in Harlem" program, and has been actively involved with the Prevention of Child Abuse, The leukemia Society, Multiple Sclerosis and March of Dimes. He is the celebrity chairman of Family Dynamics, a New York City-based agency that helps children who have been abused by their parents, and is chairman of the Greater New York City Ice Hockey League, which involves youth hockey groups throughout New York's five boroughs.

ALKA-SELTZER PLUS AWARD

An annual award "to the player, having played a minimum of 60 games, who leads the League in plus/minus statistics" at the end of the regular season. Miles, Inc. will contribute $5,000 on behalf of the winner to the charity of his choice and $1000 on behalf of each individual team winner.

History: The award was presented to the NHL in 1989-90 by Miles, Inc., to recognize the League leader in plus-minus statistics. Plus-minus statistics are calculated by giving a player a "plus" when on-ice for an even-strength or shorthand goal scored by his team. He receives a "minus" when on-ice for an even-strength or shorthand goal scored by the opposing team. A plus-minus award has been presented since the 1982-83 season.

1993-94 Winner: Scott Stevens, New Jersey Devils

New Jersey defenseman Scott Stevens was the NHL's leader in +/− rankings in 1993-94 with a total of +53 in 83 games played. The second and third-highest +/− figures belonged to members of the Detroit Red Wings: Sergei Fedorov (+48) and Nicklas Lidstrom (+43). Team +/− leaders for 1993-94 were: Anaheim, Bobby Dollas; Boston, Don Sweeney; Buffalo, Craig Muni; Calgary, Gary Roberts; Chicago, Jeremy Roenick; Dallas, Derian Hatcher; Detroit, Sergei Fedorov; Edmonton, Dean McAmmond; Florida, Keith Brown; Hartford, Alexander Godynyuk; Los Angeles, John Druce; Montreal, John LeClair; New Jersey, Scott Stevens; NY Islanders, Marty McInnis; NY Rangers, Brian Leetch; Ottawa, Evgeny Davydov; Philadelphia, Jeff Finley and Eric Lindros; Pittsburgh, Martin Straka; Quebec, Craig Wolanin; St. Louis, Kevin Miller; San Jose, Igor Larionov; Tampa Bay, John Tucker; Toronto, Sylvain Lefebvre; Vancouver, Geoff Courtnall; Washington, Sylvain Cote; Winnipeg, Tie Domi.

NHL AWARD MONEY BREAKDOWN

(Players on each club determine how team award money is divided.)

TEAM AWARDS

Stanley Cup Playoffs	Number of Clubs	Share Per Club	Total
Conference Quarter-Final Losers	8	$ 175,000	$1,400,000
Conference Semi-Final Losers	4	350,000	1,400,000
Conference Championship Losers	2	550,000	1,100,000
Stanley Cup Loser	1	825,000	825,000
Stanley Cup Winners	1	1,250,000	1,250,000
TOTAL PLAYOFF AWARD MONEY			$5,975,000

Final Standings, Regular Season	Number of Clubs	Share Per Club	Total
Presidents' Trophy			
Club's Share	1	$ 100,000	$ 100,000
Players' Share	1	250,000	250,000
Division Winners	4	425,000	1,700,000
Division Second Place	4	200,000	800,000
TOTAL REGULAR-SEASON AWARD MONEY			$2,850,000

INDIVIDUAL AWARDS	Winner	First Runner-up	Second Runner-up
Hart, Calder, Norris, Ross, Vezina, Byng, Selke, Jennings, Masterton Trophies	$10,000	$6,000	$4,000
Conn Smythe Trophy	$10,000		
King Clancy Memorial Award	$ 3,000	$1,000	
TOTAL INDIVIDUAL AWARD MONEY			$194,000

ALL-STARS	Number of winners	Per Player	Total
First Team All-Stars	6	$10,000	$ 60,000
Second Team All-Stars	6	5,000	$ 30,000
All-Star Game Winners	22	5,000	$110,000
TOTAL ALL-STAR AWARD MONEY			$200,000
TOTAL ALL AWARDS			**$9,219,000**

PRESIDENTS' TROPHY

An annual award to the club finishing the regular-season with the best overall record. The winner receives $200,000, to be split evenly between the team and its players.

History: Presented to the National Hockey League in 1985-86 by the NHL Board of Governors to recognize the team compiling the top regular-season record.

1993-94 Winner: New York Rangers
Runners-up: New Jersey Devils
Pittsburgh Penguins

The New York Rangers won their second Presidents' Trophy in three seasons in 1993-94, compiling the NHL's best regular-season record of 52-24-8 for 112 points. The New Jersey Devils finished second with a 47-25-12 record for 106 points while the Pittsburgh Penguins had the third best regular season mark with a record of 44-27-13 for 101 points.

1993-94 NHL Player of the Week Award Winners

Player of the Week

Week Ending	Player	Team
Oct. 12	**Adam Oates**	Boston
Oct. 18	**Felix Potvin**	Toronto
Oct. 25	**Teemu Selanne**	Winnipeg
Nov. 1	**Patrick Roy**	Montreal
Nov. 8	**Alexei Yashin**	Ottawa
Nov. 15	**Brett Hull**	St. Louis
Nov. 22	**Pierre Turgeon**	NY Islanders
Nov. 29	**Arturs Irbe**	San Jose
	Jeff Reese	Hartford
Dec. 6	**Keith Tkachuk**	Winnipeg
Dec. 13	**Dominek Hasek**	Buffalo
Dec. 20	**Ray Bourque**	Boston
	Curtis Joseph	St. Louis
Dec. 27	**Joe Mullen**	
Jan. 3	**Wayne Gretzky**	Los Angeles
Jan. 10	**Daren Puppa**	Tampa Bay
Jan. 17	**Felix Potvin**	Toronto
Jan. 24	**Ray Sheppard**	Detroit
Jan. 31	**Jesse Belanger**	Florida
Feb. 7	**Vincent Damphousse**	Montreal
Feb. 14	**Mike Vernon**	Calgary
Feb. 21	**Steve Yzerman**	Detroit
Feb. 28	**Ron Hextall**	NY Islanders
Mar. 7	**Sergei Makarov**	San Jose
Mar. 14	**Ed Belfour**	Chicago
Mar. 21	**John Vanbiesbrouck**	Florida
Mar. 28	**Adam Oates**	Boston
	Scott Stevens	New Jersey
Apr. 4	**Mike Richter**	NY Rangers
Apr. 11	**Benoit Hogue**	NY Islanders

Player of the Month

Month	Player	Team
Oct.	**Felix Potvin**	Toronto
Nov.	**Mike Richter**	NY Rangers
Dec.	**Sergei Fedorov**	Detroit
	Dominek Hasek	Buffalo
Jan.	**Cam Neely**	Boston
Feb.	**Patrick Roy**	Montreal
Mar.	**Pavel Bure**	Vancouver
Apr.	**Brendan Shanahan**	St. Louis

1993-94 Upper Deck/NHL Rookie of the Month Award

Month	Player	Team
Oct.	**Alexandre Daigle**	Ottawa
Nov.	**Alexei Yashin**	Ottawa
Dec.	**Jesse Belanger**	Florida
Jan.	**Martin Brodeur**	New Jersey
Feb.	**Chris Osgood**	Detroit
Mar.	**Martin Brodeur**	New Jersey

NATIONAL HOCKEY LEAGUE INDIVIDUAL AWARD WINNERS

ART ROSS TROPHY

	Winner	Runner-up
1994	Wayne Gretzky, L.A.	Sergei Fedorov, Det.
1993	Mario Lemieux, Pit.	Pat LaFontaine, Buf.
1992	Mario Lemieux, Pit.	Kevin Stevens, Pit.
1991	Wayne Gretzky, L.A.	Brett Hull, St.L.
1990	Wayne Gretzky, L.A.	Mark Messier, Edm.
1989	Mario Lemieux, Pit.	Wayne Gretzky, L.A.
1988	Mario Lemieux, Pit.	Wayne Gretzky, Edm.
1987	Wayne Gretzky, Edm.	Jari Kurri, Edm.
1986	Wayne Gretzky, Edm.	Mario Lemieux, Pit.
1985	Wayne Gretzky, Edm.	Jari Kurri, Edm.
1984	Wayne Gretzky, Edm.	Paul Coffey, Edm.
1983	Wayne Gretzky, Edm.	Peter Stastny, Que.
1982	Wayne Gretzky, Edm.	Mike Bossy, NYI
1981	Wayne Gretzky, Edm.	Marcel Dionne, L.A.
1980	Marcel Dionne, L.A.	Wayne Gretzky, Edm.
1979	Bryan Trottier, NYI	Marcel Dionne, L.A.
1978	Guy Lafleur, Mtl.	Bryan Trottier, NYI
1977	Guy Lafleur, Mtl.	Marcel Dionne, L.A.
1976	Guy Lafleur, Mtl.	Bobby Clarke, Phi.
1975	Bobby Orr, Bos.	Phil Esposito, Bos.
1974	Phil Esposito, Bos.	Bobby Orr, Bos.
1973	Phil Esposito, Bos.	Bobby Clarke, Phi.
1972	Phil Esposito, Bos.	Bobby Orr, Bos.
1971	Phil Esposito, Bos.	Bobby Orr, Bos.
1970	Bobby Orr, Bos.	Phil Esposito, Bos.
1969	Phil Esposito, Bos.	Bobby Hull, Chi.
1968	Stan Mikita, Chi.	Phil Esposito, Bos.
1967	Stan Mikita, Chi.	Bobby Hull, Chi.
1966	Bobby Hull, Chi.	Stan Mikita, Chi.
1965	Stan Mikita, Chi.	Norm Ullman, Det.
1964	Stan Mikita, Chi.	Bobby Hull, Chi.
1963	Gordie Howe, Det.	Andy Bathgate, NYR
1962	Bobby Hull, Chi.	Andy Bathgate, NYR
1961	Bernie Geoffrion, Mtl.	Jean Beliveau, Mtl.
1960	Bobby Hull, Chi.	Bronco Horvath, Bos.
1959	Dickie Moore, Mtl.	Jean Beliveau, Mtl.
1958	Dickie Moore, Mtl.	Henri Richard, Mtl.
1957	Gordie Howe, Det.	Ted Lindsay, Det.
1956	Jean Beliveau, Mtl.	Gordie Howe, Det.
1955	Bernie Geoffrion, Mtl.	Maurice Richard, Mtl.
1954	Gordie Howe, Det.	Maurice Richard, Mtl.
1953	Gordie Howe, Det.	Ted Lindsay, Det.
1952	Gordie Howe, Det.	Ted Lindsay, Det.
1951	Gordie Howe, Det.	Maurice Richard, Mtl.
1950	Ted Lindsay, Det.	Sid Abel, Det.
1949	Roy Conacher, Chi.	Doug Bentley, Chi.
1948	Elmer Lach, Mtl.	Buddy O'Connor, NYR
1947*	Max Bentley, Chi.	Maurice Richard, Mtl.
1946	Max Bentley, Chi.	Gaye Stewart, Tor.
1945	Elmer Lach, Mtl.	Maurice Richard, Mtl.
1944	Herbie Cain, Bos.	Doug Bentley, Chi.
1943	Doug Bentley, Chi.	Bill Cowley, Bos.
1942	Bryan Hextall, NYR	Lynn Patrick, NYR
1941	Bill Cowley, Bos.	Bryan Hextall, NYR
1940	Milt Schmidt, Bos.	Woody Dumart, Bos.
1939	Toe Blake, Mtl.	Dave Schriner, NYA
1938	Gordie Drillon, Tor.	Syl Apps, Tor.
1937	Dave Schriner, NYA	Syl Apps, Tor.
1936	Dave Schriner, NYA	Marty Barry, Det.
1935	Charlie Conacher, Tor.	Syd Howe, St.L-Det.
1934	Charlie Conacher, Tor.	Joe Primeau, Tor
1933	Bill Cook, NYR	Harvey Jackson, Tor.
1932	Harvey Jackson, Tor.	Joe Primeau, Tor.
1931	Howie Morenz, Mtl.	Ebbie Goodfellow, Det.
1930	Cooney Weiland, Bos.	Frank Boucher, NYR
1929	Ace Bailey, Tor.	Nels Stewart, Mtl.M
1928	Howie Morenz, Mtl.	Aurel Joliat, Mtl.
1927	Bill Cook, NYR	Dick Irvin, Chi.
1926	Nels Stewart, Mtl.M.	Cy Denneny, Ott.
1925	Babe Dye, Tor.	Cy Denneny, Ott.
1924	Cy Denneny, Ott.	Billy Boucher, Mtl.
1923	Babe Dye, Tor.	Cy Denneny, Ott.
1922	Punch Broadbent, Ott.	Cy Denneny, Ott.
1921	Newsy Lalonde, Mtl.	Cy Denneny, Ott.
1920	Joe Malone, Que.	Newsy Lalonde, Mtl.
1919	Newsy Lalonde, Mtl.	Odie Cleghorn, Mtl.
1918	Joe Malone, Mtl.	Cy Denneny, Ott.

* Trophy first awarded in 1948.
Scoring leaders listed from 1918 to 1947.

KING CLANCY MEMORIAL TROPHY

1994	Adam Graves	NY Rangers
1993	Dave Poulin	Boston
1992	Ray Bourque	Boston
1991	Dave Taylor	Los Angeles
1990	Kevin Lowe	Edmonton
1989	Bryan Trottier	NY Islanders
1988	Lanny McDonald	Calgary

HART TROPHY

	Winner	Runner-up
1994	Sergei Fedorov, Det.	Dominik Hasek, Buf.
1993	Mario Lemieux, Pit.	Doug Gilmour, Tor.
1992	Mark Messier, NYR	Patrick Roy, Mtl.
1991	Brett Hull, St.L.	Wayne Gretzky, L.A.
1990	Mark Messier, Edm.	Ray Bourque, Bos.
1989	Wayne Gretzky, L.A.	Mario Lemieux, Pit.
1988	Mario Lemieux, Pit.	Grant Fuhr, Edm.
1987	Wayne Gretzky, Edm.	Ray Bourque, Bos.
1986	Wayne Gretzky, Edm.	Mario Lemieux, Pit.
1985	Wayne Gretzky, Edm.	Dale Hawerchuk, Wpg.
1984	Wayne Gretzky, Edm.	Rod Langway, Wsh.
1983	Wayne Gretzky, Edm.	Pete Peeters, Bos.
1982	Wayne Gretzky, Edm.	Bryan Trottier, NYI
1981	Wayne Gretzky, Edm.	Mike Liut, St.L.
1980	Wayne Gretzky, Edm.	Marcel Dionne, L.A.
1979	Bryan Trottier, NYI	Guy Lafleur, Mtl
1978	Guy Lafleur, Mtl.	Bryan Trottier, NYI
1977	Guy Lafleur, Mtl.	Bobby Clarke, Phi.
1976	Bobby Clarke, Phi.	Denis Potvin, NYI
1975	Bobby Clarke, Phi.	Rogatien Vachon, L.A.
1974	Phil Esposito, Bos.	Bernie Parent, Phi.
1973	Bobby Clarke, Phi.	Phil Esposito, Bos.
1972	Bobby Orr, Bos.	Ken Dryden, Mtl.
1971	Bobby Orr, Bos.	Phil Esposito, Bos.
1970	Bobby Orr, Bos.	Tony Esposito, Chi.
1969	Phil Esposito, Bos.	Jean Beliveau, Mtl.
1968	Stan Mikita, Chi.	Jean Beliveau, Mtl.
1967	Stan Mikita, Chi.	Ed Giacomin, NYR
1966	Bobby Hull, Chi.	Jean Beliveau, Mtl.
1965	Bobby Hull, Chi.	Norm Ullman, Det.
1964	Jean Beliveau, Mtl.	Bobby Hull, Chi.
1963	Gordie Howe, Det.	Stan Mikita, Chi.
1962	Jacques Plante, Mtl.	Doug Harvey, NYR
1961	Bernie Geoffrion, Mtl.	Johnny Bower, Tor.
1960	Gordie Howe, Det.	Bobby Hull, Chi.
1959	Andy Bathgate, NYR	Gordie Howe, Det.
1958	Gordie Howe, Det.	Andy Bathgate, NYR
1957	Gordie Howe, Det.	Jean Beliveau, Mtl.
1956	Jean Beliveau, Mtl.	Tod Sloan, Tor.
1955	Ted Kennedy, Tor.	Harry Lumley, Tor.
1954	Al Rollins, Chi.	Red Kelly, Det.
1953	Gordie Howe, Det.	Al Rollins, Chi.
1952	Gordie Howe, Det.	Elmer Lach, Mtl.
1951	Milt Schmidt, Bos.	Maurice Richard, Mtl.
1950	Charlie Rayner, NYR	Ted Kennedy, Tor.
1949	Sid Abel, Det.	Bill Durnan, Mtl.
1948	Buddy O'Connor, NYR	Frank Brimsek, Bos.
1947	Maurice Richard, Mtl.	Milt Schmidt, Bos.
1946	Max Bentley, Chi.	Gaye Stewart, Tor.
1945	Elmer Lach, Mtl.	Maurice Richard, Mtl.
1944	Babe Pratt, Tor.	Bill Cowley, Bos.
1943	Bill Cowley, Bos.	Doug Bentley, Chi.
1942	Tom Anderson, Bro.	Syl Apps, Tor.
1941	Bill Cowley, Bos.	Dit Clapper, Bos.
1940	Ebbie Goodfellow, Det.	Syl Apps, Tor.
1939	Toe Blake, Mtl.	Syl Apps, Tor.
1938	Eddie Shore, Bos.	Paul Thompson, Chi.
1937	Babe Siebert, Mtl.	Lionel Conacher, Mtl.M
1936	Eddie Shore, Bos.	Hooley Smith, Mtl.M
1935	Eddie Shore, Bos.	Charlie Conacher, Tor.
1934	Aurel Joliat, Mtl.	Lionel Conacher, Chi.
1933	Eddie Shore, Bos.	Bill Cook, NYR
1932	Howie Morenz, Mtl.	Ching Johnson, NYR
1931	Howie Morenz, Mtl.	Eddie Shore, Bos.
1930	Nels Stewart, Mtl.M.	Lionel Hitchman, Bos.
1929	Roy Worters, NYA	Ace Bailey, Tor.
1928	Howie Morenz, Mtl.	Roy Worters, Pit.
1927	Herb Gardiner, Mtl.	Bill Cook, NYR
1926	Nels Stewart, Mtl.M.	Sprague Cleghorn, Bos.
1925	Billy Burch, Ham.	Howie Morenz, Mtl.
1924	Frank Nighbor, Ott.	Sprague Cleghorn, Mtl.

FRANK J. SELKE TROPHY

	Winner	Runner-up
1994	Sergei Fedorov, Det.	Doug Gilmour, Tor.
1993	Doug Gilmour, Tor.	Dave Poulin, Bos.
1992	Guy Carbonneau, Mtl.	Sergei Fedorov, Det.
1991	Dirk Graham, Chi.	Esa Tikkanen, Edm.
1990	Rick Meagher, St.L.	Guy Carbonneau, Mtl.
1989	Guy Carbonneau, Mtl.	Esa Tikkanen, Edm.
1988	Guy Carbonneau, Mtl.	Steve Kasper, Bos.
1987	Dave Poulin, Phi.	Guy Carbonneau, Mtl.
1986	Troy Murray, Chi.	Ron Sutter, Phi.
1985	Craig Ramsay, Buf.	Doug Jarvis, Wsh.
1984	Doug Jarvis, Wsh.	Bryan Trottier, NYI
1983	Bobby Clarke, Phi.	Jari Kurri, Edm.
1982	Steve Kasper, Bos.	Bob Gainey, Mtl.
1981	Bob Gainey, Mtl.	Craig Ramsay, Buf.
1980	Bob Gainey, Mtl.	Craig Ramsay, Buf.
1979	Bob Gainey, Mtl.	Don Marcotte, Bos.
1978	Bob Gainey, Mtl.	Craig Ramsay, Buf.

LADY BYNG TROPHY

	Winner	Runner-up
1994	Wayne Gretzky, L.A.	Adam Oates, Bos.
1993	Pierre Turgeon, NYI	Adam Oates, Bos.
1992	Wayne Gretzky, L.A.	Joe Sakic, Que.
1991	Wayne Gretzky, L.A.	Brett Hull, St.L.
1990	Brett Hull, St.L.	Wayne Gretzky, L.A.
1989	Joe Mullen, Cgy.	Wayne Gretzky, L.A.
1988	Mats Naslund, Mtl.	Wayne Gretzky, Edm.
1987	Joe Mullen, Cgy.	Wayne Gretzky, Edm.
1986	Mike Bossy, NYI	Jari Kurri, Edm.
1985	Jari Kurri, Edm.	Joe Mullen, St.L.
1984	Mike Bossy, NYI	Rick Middleton, Bos.
1983	Mike Bossy, NYI	Rick Middleton, Bos.
1982	Rick Middleton, Bos.	Mike Bossy, NYI
1981	Rick Kehoe, Pit.	Wayne Gretzky, Edm.
1980	Wayne Gretzky, Edm.	Marcel Dionne, L.A.
1979	Bob MacMillan, Atl.	Marcel Dionne, L.A.
1978	Butch Goring, L.A.	Peter McNab, Bos.
1977	Marcel Dionne, L.A.	Jean Ratelle, Bos.
1976	Jean Ratelle, NYR-Bos.	Jean Pronovost, Pit.
1975	Marcel Dionne, Det.	John Bucyk, Bos.
1974	John Bucyk, Bos.	Lowell MacDonald, Pit.
1973	Gilbert Perreault, Buf.	Jean Ratelle, NYR
1972	Jean Ratelle, NYR	John Bucyk, Bos.
1971	John Bucyk, Bos.	Dave Keon, Tor.
1970	Phil Goyette, St.L.	John Bucyk, Bos.
1969	Alex Delvecchio, Det.	Ted Hampson, Oak.
1968	Stan Mikita, Chi.	John Bucyk, Bos.
1967	Stan Mikita, Chi.	Dave Keon, Tor.
1966	Alex Delvecchio, Det.	Bobby Rousseau, Mtl.
1965	Bobby Hull, Chi.	Alex Delvecchio, Det.
1964	Ken Wharram, Chi.	Dave Keon, Tor.
1963	Dave Keon, Tor.	Camille Henry, NYR
1962	Dave Keon, Tor.	Claude Provost, Mtl.
1961	Red Kelly, Tor.	Norm Ullman, Det.
1960	Don McKenney, Bos.	Andy Hebenton, NYR
1959	Alex Delvecchio, Det.	Andy Hebenton, NYR
1958	Camille Henry, NYR	Don Marshall, Mtl.
1957	Andy Hebenton, NYR	Earl Reibel, Det.
1956	Earl Reibel, Det.	Floyd Curry, Mtl.
1955	Sid Smith, Tor.	Danny Lewicki, NYR
1954	Red Kelly, Det.	Don Raleigh, NYR
1953	Red Kelly, Det.	Wally Hergesheimer, NYR
1952	Sid Smith, Tor.	Red Kelly, Det.
1951	Red Kelly, Det.	Woody Dumart, Bos.
1950	Edgar Laprade, NYR	Red Kelly, Det.
1949	Bill Quackenbush, Det.	Harry Watson, Tor.
1948	Buddy O'Connor, NYR	Syl Apps, Tor.
1947	Bobby Bauer, Bos.	Syl Apps, Tor.
1946	Toe Blake, Mtl.	Clint Smith, Chi.
1945	Bill Mosienko, Chi.	Syd Howe, Det.
1944	Clint Smith, Chi.	Herb Cain, Bos.
1943	Max Bentley, Chi.	Buddy O'Connor, Mtl.
1942	Syl Apps, Tor.	Gordie Drillon, Tor.
1941	Bobby Bauer, Bos.	Gordie Drillon, Tor.
1940	Bobby Bauer, Bos.	Clint Smith, NYR
1939	Clint Smith, NYR	Marty Barry, Det.
1938	Gordie Drillon, Tor.	Clint Smith, NYR
1937	Marty Barry, Det.	Gordie Drillon, Tor.
1936	Doc Romnes, Chi.	Dave Schriner, NYA
1935	Frank Boucher, NYR	Russ Blinco, Mtl.M
1934	Frank Boucher, NYR	Joe Primeau, Tor.
1933	Frank Boucher, NYR	Joe Primeau, Tor.
1932	Joe Primeau, Tor.	Frank Boucher, NYR
1931	Frank Boucher, NYR	Normie Himes, NYA
1930	Frank Boucher, NYR	Normie Himes, NYA
1929	Frank Boucher, NYR	Harry Darragh, Pit.
1928	Frank Boucher, NYR	George Hay, Det.
1927	Billy Burch, NYA	Dick Irvin, Chi.
1926	Frank Nighbor, Ott.	Billy Burch, NYA
1925	Frank Nighbor, Ott.	none

WILLIAM M. JENNINGS TROPHY

	Winner	Runner-up
1994	Dominik Hasek, Buf.	Martin Brodeur, N.J.
	Grant Fuhr	Chris Terreri
1993	Ed Belfour, Chi.	Felix Potvin, Tor.
		Grant Fuhr
1992	Patrick Roy, Mtl.	Ed Belfour, Chi.
1991	Ed Belfour, Chi.	Patrick Roy, Mtl.
1990	Andy Moog, Bos.	Patrick Roy, Mtl.
	Rejean Lemelin	Brian Hayward
1989	Patrick Roy, Mtl.	Mike Vernon, Cgy.
	Brian Hayward	Rick Wamsley
1988	Patrick Roy, Mtl.	Clint Malarchuk, Wsh.
	Brian Hayward	Pete Peeters
1987	Patrick Roy, Mtl.	Ron Hextall, Phi.
	Brian Hayward	
1986	Bob Froese, Phi.	Al Jensen, Wsh.
	Darren Jensen	Pete Peeters
1985	Tom Barrasso, Buf.	Pat Riggin, Wsh.
	Bob Sauve	
1984	Al Jensen, Wsh.	Tom Barrasso, Buf.
	Pat Riggin	Bob Sauve
1983	Roland Melanson, NYI	Pete Peeters, Bos.
	Bill Smith	
1982	Rick Wamsley, Mtl.	Billy Smith, NYI
	Denis Herron	Roland Melanson

VEZINA TROPHY

	Winner	Runner-up
1994	Dominik Hasek, Buf.	John Vanbiesbrouck, Fla.
1993	Ed Belfour, Chi.	Tom Barrasso, Pit.
1992	Patrick Roy, Mtl.	Kirk McLean, Van.
1991	Ed Belfour, Chi.	Patrick Roy, Mtl.
1990	Patrick Roy, Mtl.	Daren Puppa, Buf.
1989	Patrick Roy, Mtl.	Mike Vernon, Cgy.
1988	Grant Fuhr, Edm.	Tom Barrasso, Buf.
1987	Ron Hextall, Phi.	Mike Liut, Hfd.
1986	John Vanbiesbrouck, NYR	Bob Froese, Phi.
1985	Pelle Lindbergh, Phi.	Tom Barrasso, Buf.
1984	Tom Barrasso, Buf.	Rejean Lemelin, Cgy.
1983	Pete Peeters, Bos.	Roland Melanson, NYI
1982	Bill Smith, NYI	Grant Fuhr, Edm.
1981	Richard Sevigny, Mtl.	Pete Peeters, Phi.
	Denis Herron, Mtl.	Rick St. Croix, Phi.
	Michel Larocque, Mtl.	
1980	Bob Sauve, Buf.	Gerry Cheevers, Bos.
	Don Edwards, Buf.	Gilles Gilbert, Bos.
1979	Ken Dryden, Mtl.	Glenn Resch, NYI
	Michel Larocque, Mtl.	Bill Smith, NYI
1978	Ken Dryden, Mtl.	Bernie Parent, Phi.
	Michel Larocque	Wayne Stephenson, Phi.
1977	Ken Dryden, Mtl.	Glenn Resch, NYI
	Michel Larocque, Mtl.	Bill Smith, NYI
1976	Ken Dryden, Mtl.	Glenn Resch, NYI
		Bill Smith, NYI
1975	Bernie Parent, Phi.	Rogie Vachon, L.A.
		Gary Edwards, L.A.
1974	Bernie Parent, Phi. (tie)	Gilles Gilbert, Bos.
	Tony Esposito, Chi. (tie)	
1973	Ken Dryden, Mtl.	Ed Giacomin, NYR
		Gilles Villemure, NYR
1972	Tony Esposito, Chi.	Cesare Maniago, Min.
	Gary Smith, Chi.	Lorne Worsley, Min.
1971	Ed Giacomin, NYR	Tony Esposito, Chi.
	Gilles Villemure, NYR	
1970	Tony Esposito, Chi.	Jacques Plante, St.L.
		Ernie Wakely, St.L.
1969	Jacques Plante, St.L.	Ed Giacomin, NYR
	Glenn Hall, St.L.	
1968	Lorne Worsley, Mtl.	Johnny Bower, Tor.
	Rogatien Vachon, Mtl.	Bruce Gamble, Tor.
1967	Glenn Hall, Chi.	Charlie Hodge, Mtl.
	Denis Dejordy, Chi.	
1966	Lorne Worsley, Mtl.	Glenn Hall, Chi.
	Charlie Hodge, Mtl.	
1965	Terry Sawchuk, Tor.	Roger Crozier, Det.
	Johnny Bower, Tor.	
1964	Charlie Hodge, Mtl.	Glenn Hall, Chi.
1963	Glenn Hall, Chi.	Johnny Bower, Tor.
		Don Simmons, Tor.
1962	Jacques Plante, Mtl.	Johnny Bower, Tor.
1961	Johnny Bower, Tor.	Glenn Hall, Chi.
1960	Jacques Plante, Mtl.	Glenn Hall, Chi.
1959	Jacques Plante, Mtl.	Johnny Bower, Tor.
		Ed Chadwick, Tor.
1958	Jacques Plante, Mtl.	Lorne Worsley, NYR
		Marcel Paille, NYR
1957	Jacques Plante, Mtl.	Glenn Hall, Det.
1956	Jacques Plante, Mtl.	Glenn Hall, Det.
1955	Terry Sawchuk, Det.	Harry Lumley, Tor.
1954	Harry Lumley, Tor.	Terry Sawchuk, Det.
1953	Terry Sawchuk, Det.	Gerry McNeil, Mtl.
1952	Terry Sawchuk, Det.	Al Rollins, Tor.
1951	Al Rollins, Tor.	Terry Sawchuk, Det.
1950	Bill Durnan, Mtl.	Harry Lumley, Det.
1949	Bill Durnan, Mtl.	Harry Lumley, Det.
1948	Turk Broda, Tor.	Harry Lumley, Det.
1947	Bill Durnan, Mtl.	Turk Broda, Tor.
1946	Bill Durnan, Mtl.	Frank Brimsek, Bos.
1945	Bill Durnan, Mtl.	Frank McCool, Tor. (tie)
		Harry Lumley, Det. (tie)
1944	Bill Durnan, Mtl.	Paul Bibeault, Tor.
1943	Johnny Mowers, Det.	Turk Broda, Tor.
1942	Frank Brimsek, Bos.	Turk Broda, Tor.
1941	Turk Broda, Tor.	Frank Brimsek, Bos. (tie)
		Johnny Mowers, Det. (tie)
1940	Dave Kerr, NYR	Frank Brimsek, Bos.
1939	Frank Brimsek, Bos.	Dave Kerr, NYR
1938	Tiny Thompson, Bos.	Dave Kerr, NYR
1937	Normie Smith, Det.	Dave Kerr, NYR
1936	Tiny Thompson, Bos.	Mike Karakas, Chi.
1935	Lorne Chabot, Chi.	Alex Connell, Mtl.M
1934	Charlie Gardiner, Chi.	Wilf Cude, Det.
1933	Tiny Thompson, Bos.	John Roach, Det.
1932	Charlie Gardiner, Chi.	Alex Connell, Det.
1931	Roy Worters, NYA	Charlie Gardiner, Chi.
1930	Tiny Thompson, Bos.	Charlie Gardiner, Chi.
1929	George Hainsworth, Mtl.	Tiny Thompson, Bos.
1928	George Hainsworth, Mtl.	Alex Connell, Ott.
1927	George Hainsworth, Mtl.	Clint Benedict, Mtl.M

BILL MASTERTON TROPHY

1994	Cam Neely	Boston
1993	Mario Lemieux	Pittsburgh
1992	Mark Fitzpatrick	NY Islanders
1991	Dave Taylor	Los Angeles
1990	Gord Kluzak	Boston
1989	Tim Kerr	Philadelphia
1988	Bob Bourne	Los Angeles
1987	Doug Jarvis	Hartford
1986	Charlie Simmer	Boston
1985	Anders Hedberg	NY Rangers
1984	Brad Park	Detroit
1983	Lanny McDonald	Calgary
1982	Glenn Resch	Colorado
1981	Blake Dunlop	St. Louis
1980	Al MacAdam	Minnesota
1979	Serge Savard	Montreal
1978	Butch Goring	Los Angeles
1977	Ed Westfall	NY Islanders
1976	Rod Gilbert	NY Rangers
1975	Don Luce	Buffalo
1974	Henri Richard	Montreal
1973	Lowell MacDonald	Pittsburgh
1972	Bobby Clarke	Phiiladelphia
1971	Jean Ratelle	NY Rangers
1970	Pit Martin	Chicago
1969	Ted Hampson	Oakland
1968	Claude Provost	Montreal

CALDER MEMORIAL TROPHY

	Winner	Runner-up
1994	Martin Brodeur, N.J.	Jason Arnott, Edm.
1993	Teemu Selanne, Wpg.	Joe Juneau, Bos.
1992	Pavel Bure, Van.	Nicklas Lidstrom, Det
1991	Ed Belfour, Chi.	Sergei Fedorov, Det.
1990	Sergei Makarov, Cgy.	Mike Modano, Min.
1989	Brian Leetch, NYR	Trevor Linden, Van.
1988	Joe Nieuwendyk, Cgy.	Ray Sheppard, Buf.
1987	Luc Robitaille, L.A.	Ron Hextall, Phi.
1986	Gary Suter, Cgy.	Wendel Clark, Tor.
1985	Mario Lemieux, Pit.	Chris Chelios, Mtl.
1984	Tom Barrasso, Buf.	Steve Yzerman, Det.
1983	Steve Larmer, Chi.	Phil Housley, Buf.
1982	Dale Hawerchuk, Wpg.	Barry Pederson, Bos.
1981	Peter Stastny, Que.	Larry Murphy, L.A.
1980	Ray Bourque, Bos.	Mike Foligno, Det.
1979	Bobby Smith, Min	Ryan Walter, Wsh.
1978	Mike Bossy, NYI	Barry Beck, Col.
1977	Willi Plett, Atl.	Don Murdoch, NYR
1976	Bryan Trottier, NYI	Glenn Resch, NYI
1975	Eric Vail, Atl.	Pierre Larouche, Pit.
1974	Denis Potvin, NYI	Tom Lysiak, Atl.
1973	Steve Vickers, NYR	Bill Barber, Phi.
1972	Ken Dryden, Mtl.	Rick Martin, Buf.
1971	Gilbert Perreault, Buf.	Jude Drouin, Min.
1970	Tony Esposito, Chi.	Bill Fairbairn, NYR
1969	Danny Grant, Min.	Norm Ferguson, Oak.
1968	Derek Sanderson, Bos.	Jacques Lemaire, Mtl.
1967	Bobby Orr, Bos.	Ed Van Impe, Chi.
1966	Brit Selby, Tor.	Bert Marshall, Det.
1965	Roger Crozier, Det.	Ron Ellis, Tor.
1964	Jacques Laperriere, Mtl.	John Ferguson, Mtl.
1963	Kent Douglas, Tor.	Doug Barkley, Det.
1962	Bobby Rousseu, Mtl.	Cliff Pennington, Bos.
1961	Dave Keon, Tor.	Bob Nevin, Tor.
1960	Bill Hay, Chi.	Murray Oliver, Det.
1959	Ralph Backstrom, Mtl.	Carl Brewer, Tor.
1958	Frank Mahovlich, Tor.	Bobby Hull, Chi.
1957	Larry Regan, Bos.	Ed Chadwick, Tor.
1956	Glenn Hall, Det.	Andy Hebenton, NYR
1955	Ed Litzenberger, Chi.	Don McKenney, Bos.
1954	Camille Henry, NYR	Earl Reibel, Det.
1953	Lorne Worsley, NYR	Gordie Hannigan, Tor.
1952	Bernie Geoffrion, Mtl.	Hy Buller, NYR
1951	Terry Sawchuk, Det.	Al Rollins, Tor.
1950	Jack Gelineau, Bos.	Phil Maloney, Bos.
1949	Pentti Lund, NYR	Allan Stanley, NYR
1948	Jim McFadden, Det.	Pete Babando, Bos.
1947	Howie Meeker, Tor.	Jimmy Conacher, Det.
1946	Edgar Laprade, NYR	George Gee, Chi.
1945	Frank McCool, Tor.	Ken Smith, Bos.
1944	Gus Bodnar, Tor.	Bill Durnan, Mtl.
1943	Gaye Stewart, Tor.	Glen Harmon, Mtl.
1942	Grant Warwick, NYR	Buddy O'Connor, Mtl.
1941	Johnny Quilty, Mtl.	Johnny Mowers, Det.
1940	Kilby MacDonald, NYR	Wally Stanowski, Tor.
1939	Frank Brimsek, Bos.	Roy Conacher, Bos.
1938	Cully Dahlstrom, Chi.	Murph Chamberlain, Tor.
1937	Syl Apps, Tor.	Gordie Drillon, Tor.
1936	Mike Karakas, Chi.	Bucko McDonald, Det.
1935	Dave Schriner, NYA	Bert Connolly, NYR
1934	Russ Blinko, Mtl.M.	
1933	Carl Voss, Det.	

CONN SMYTHE TROPHY

1994	Brian Leetch	NY Rangers
1993	Patrick Roy	Montreal
1992	Mario Lemieux	Pittsburgh
1991	Mario Lemieux	Pittsburgh
1990	Bill Ranford	Edmonton
1989	Al MacInnis	Calgary
1988	Wayne Gretzky	Edmonton
1987	Ron Hextall	Philadelphia
1986	Patrick Roy	Montreal
1985	Wayne Gretzky	Edmonton
1984	Mark Messier	Edmonton
1983	Bill Smith	NY Islanders
1982	Mike Bossy	NY Islanders
1981	Butch Goring	NY Islanders
1980	Bryan Trottier	NY Islanders
1979	Bob Gainey	Montreal
1978	Larry Robinson	Montreal
1977	Guy Lafleur	Montreal
1976	Reggie Leach	Philadelphia
1975	Bernie Parent	Philadelphia
1974	Bernie Parent	Philadelphia
1973	Yvan Cournoyer	Montreal
1972	Bobby Orr	Boston
1971	Ken Dryden	Montreal
1970	Bobby Orr	Boston
1969	Serge Savard	Montreal
1968	Glenn Hall	St. Louis
1967	Dave Keon	Toronto
1966	Roger Crozier	Detroit
1965	Jean Béliveau	Montreal

JAMES NORRIS TROPHY

	Winner	Runner-up
1994	Ray Bourque, Bos.	Scott Stevens, N.J.
1993	Chris Chelios, Chi.	Ray Bourque, Bos.
1992	Brian Leetch, NYR	Ray Bourque, Bos.
1991	Ray Bourque, Bos.	Al MacInnis, Cgy.
1990	Ray Bourque, Bos.	Al MacInnis, Cgy.
1989	Chris Chelios, Mtl	Paul Coffey, Pit.
1988	Ray Bourque, Bos.	Scott Stevens, Wsh.
1987	Ray Bourque, Bos.	Mark Howe, Phi.
1986	Paul Coffey, Edm.	Mark Howe, Phi.
1985	Paul Coffey, Edm.	Ray Bourque, Bos.
1984	Rod Langway, Wsh.	Paul Coffey, Edm.
1983	Rod Langway, Wsh.	Mark Howe, Phi.
1982	Doug Wilson, Chi.	Ray Bourque, Bos.
1981	Randy Carlyle, Pit.	Denis Potvin, NYI
1980	Larry Robinson, Mtl.	Borje Salming, Tor.
1979	Denis Potvin, NYI	Larry Robinson, Mtl.
1978	Denis Potvin, NYI	Brad Park, Bos.
1977	Larry Robinson, Mtl.	Borje Salming, Tor.
1976	Denis Potvin, NYI	Brad Park, NYR-Bos.
1975	Bobby Orr, Bos.	Denis Potvin, NYI
1974	Bobby Orr, Bos.	Brad Park, NYR
1973	Bobby Orr, Bos.	Guy Lapointe, Mtl.
1972	Bobby Orr, Bos.	Brad Park, NYR
1971	Bobby Orr, Bos.	Brad Park, NYR
1970	Bobby Orr, Bos.	Brad Park, NYR
1969	Bobby Orr, Bos.	Tim Horton, Tor.
1968	Bobby Orr, Bos.	J.C. Tremblay, Mtl
1967	Harry Howell, NYR	Pierre Pilote, Chi.
1966	Jacques Laperriere, Mtl.	Pierre Pilote, Chi.
1965	Pierre Pilote, Chi.	Jacques Laperriere, Mtl.
1964	Pierre Pilote, Chi.	Tim Horton, Tor.
1963	Pierre Pilote, Chi.	Carl Brewer, Tor.
1962	Doug Harvey, NYR	Pierre Pilote, Chi.
1961	Doug Harvey, Mtl.	Marcel Pronovost, Det.
1960	Doug Harvey, Mtl.	Allan Stanley, Tor.
1959	Tom Johnson, Mtl.	Bill Gadsby, NYR
1958	Doug Harvey, Mtl.	Bill Gadsby, NYR
1957	Doug Harvey, Mtl.	Red Kelly, Det.
1956	Doug Harvey, Mtl.	Bill Gadsby, NYR
1955	Doug Harvey, Mtl.	Red Kelly, Det.
1954	Red Kelly, Det.	Doug Harvey, Mtl.

JACK ADAMS AWARD

	Winner	Runner-up
1994	Jacques Lemaire, N.J.	Kevin Constantine, S.J.
1993	Pat Burns, Tor.	Brian Sutter, Bos.
1992	Pat Quinn, Van.	Roger Neilson, NYR
1991	Brian Sutter, St.L.	Tom Webster, L.A.
1990	Bob Murdoch, Wpg.	Mike Milbury, Bos.
1989	Pat Burns, Mtl.	Bob McCammon, Van.
1988	Jacques Demers, Det.	Terry Crisp, Cgy.
1987	Jacques Demers, Det.	Jack Evans, Hfd.
1986	Glen Sather, Edm.	Jacques Demers, St.L.
1985	Mike Keenan, Phi.	Barry Long, Wpg.
1984	Bryan Murray, Wsh.	Scott Bowman, Buf.
1983	Orval Tessier, Chi.	
1982	Tom Watt, Wpg.	
1981	Red Berenson, St.L.	Bob Berry, L.A.
1980	Pat Quinn, Phi.	
1979	Al Arbour, NYI	Fred Shero, NYR
1978	Bobby Kromm, Det.	Don Cherry, Bos.
1977	Scott Bowman, Mtl.	Tom McVie, Wsh.
1976	Don Cherry, Bos.	
1975	Bob Pulford, L.A.	
1974	Fred Shero, Phi.	

LESTER PATRICK TROPHY

1994	Wayne Gretzky
	Robert Ridder
1993	Frank Boucher
	Mervyn (Red) Dutton
	Bruce McNall
	Gil Stein
1992	Al Arbour
	Art Berglund
	Lou Lamoriello
1991	Rod Gilbert
	Mike Illitch
1990	Len Ceglarski
1989	Dan Kelly
	Lou Nanne
	*Lynn Patrick
	Bud Poile
1988	Keith Allen
	Fred Cusick
	Bob Johnson
1987	*Hobey Baker
	Frank Mathers
1986	John MacInnes
	Jack Riley
1985	Jack Butterfield
	Arthur M. Wirtz
1984	John A. Ziegler Jr.
	*Arthur Howie Ross
1983	Bill Torrey
1982	Emile P. Francis
1981	Charles M. Schulz
1980	Bobby Clarke
	Edward M. Snider
	Frederick A. Shero
	1980 U.S. Olympic Hockey Team
1979	Bobby Orr
1978	Philip A. Esposito
	Tom Fitzgerald
	William T. Tutt
	William W. Wirtz
1977	John P. Bucyk
	Murray A. Armstrong
	John Mariucci
1976	Stanley Mikita
	George A. Leader
	Bruce A. Norris
1975	Donald M. Clark
	William L. Chadwick
	Thomas N. Ivan
1974	Alex Delvecchio
	Murray Murdoch
	*Weston W. Adams, Sr.
	*Charles L. Crovat
1973	Walter L. Bush, Jr.
1972	Clarence S. Campbell
	John Kelly
	Ralph "Cooney" Weiland
	*James D. Norris
1971	William M. Jennings
	*John B. Sollenberger
	*Terrance G. Sawchuk
1970	Edward W. Shore
	*James C. V. Hendy
1969	Robert M. Hull
	*Edward J. Jeremiah
1968	Thomas F. Lockhart
	*Walter A. Brown
	*Gen. John R. Kilpatrick
1967	Gordon Howe
	*Charles F. Adams
	*James Norris, Sr.
1966	J.J. "Jack" Adams
	* awarded posthumously

LESTER B. PEARSON AWARD

1994	Sergei Fedorov	Detroit
1993	Mario Lemieux	Pittsburgh
1992	Mark Messier	NY Rangers
1991	Brett Hull	St. Louis
1990	Mark Messier	Edmonton
1989	Steve Yzerman	Detroit
1988	Mario Lemieux	Pittsburgh
1987	Wayne Gretzky	Edmonton
1986	Mario Lemieux	Pittsburgh
1985	Wayne Gretzky	Edmonton
1984	Wayne Gretzky	Edmonton
1983	Wayne Gretzky	Edmonton
1982	Wayne Gretzky	Edmonton
1981	Mike Liut	St. Louis
1980	Marcel Dionne	Los Angeles
1979	Marcel Dionne	Los Angeles
1978	Guy Lafleur	Montreal
1977	Guy Lafleur	Montreal
1976	Guy Lafleur	Montreal
1975	Bobby Orr	Boston
1974	Phil Esposito	Boston
1973	Bobby Clarke	Philadelphia
1972	Jean Ratelle	NY Rangers
1971	Phil Esposito	Boston

Frank "Mr. Zero" Brimsek won the Calder Trophy and the Vezina Trophy in 1938-39 after leading the League in goals-against average (1.58), victories (33) and shutouts (10) for the Stanley Cup champion Boston Bruins. Brimsek repeated as the Vezina Trophy winner in 1941-42.

ALKA-SELTZER PLUS AWARD

1994	Scott Stevens	New Jersey
1993	Mario Lemieux	Pittsburgh
1992	Paul Ysebaert	Detroit
1991	Marty McSorley	Los Angeles
	Theoren Fleury	Calgary
1990	Paul Cavallini	St. Louis

NHL Amateur and Entry Draft

Ed Jovanovski was chosen first overall by the Florida Panthers in the 1994 NHL Entry Draft. Jovanovski, a member of the gold medal-winning 1994 Canadian National Junior Team, finished tenth among OHL defencemen in scoring during the 1993-94 season, collecting 51 points in 62 games for the Windsor Spitfires.

History

Year	Site	Date	Total Players Drafted
1963	Queen Elizabeth Hotel	June 5	21
1964	Queen Elizabeth Hotel	June 11	24
1965	Queen Elizabeth Hotel	April 27	11
1966	Mount Royal Hotel	April 25	24
1967	Queen Elizabeth Hotel	June 7	18
1968	Queen Elizabeth Hotel	June 13	24
1969	Queen Elizabeth Hotel	June 12	84
1970	Queen Elizabeth Hotel	June 11	115
1971	Queen Elizabeth Hotel	June 10	117
1972	Queen Elizabeth Hotel	June 8	152
1973	Mount Royal Hotel	May 15	168
1974	NHL Montreal Office	May 28	247
1975	NHL Montreal Office	June 3	217
1976	NHL Montreal Office	June 1	135
1977	NHL Montreal Office	June 14	185
1978	Queen Elizabeth Hotel	June 15	234
1979	Queen Elizabeth Hotel	August 9	126
1980	Montreal Forum	June 11	210
1981	Montreal Forum	June 10	211
1982	Montreal Forum	June 9	252
1983	Montreal Forum	June 8	242
1984	Montreal Forum	June 9	250
1985	Toronto Convention Centre	June 15	252
1986	Montreal Forum	June 21	252
1987	Joe Louis Sports Arena	June 13	252
1988	Montreal Forum	June 11	252
1989	Metropolitan Sports Center	June 17	252
1990	B. C. Place	June 16	250
1991	Memorial Auditorium	June 9	264
1992	Montreal Forum	June 20	264
1993	Colisée de Québec	June 26	286
1994	Hartford Civic Center	June 28-29	286

* The NHL Amateur Draft became the NHL Entry Draft in 1979

First Selections

Year	Player	Pos	Drafted By	Drafted From	Age
1969	Rejean Houle	LW	Montreal	Jr. Canadiens	19.8
1970	Gilbert Perreault	C	Buffalo	Jr. Canadiens	19.7
1971	Guy Lafleur	RW	Montreal	Quebec Remparts	19.9
1972	Billy Harris	RW	NY Islanders	Toronto Marlboros	20.4
1973	Denis Potvin	D	NY Islanders	Ottawa 67's	19.7
1974	Greg Joly	D	Washington	Regina Pats	20.0
1975	Mel Bridgman	C	Philadelphia	Victoria Cougars	20.1
1976	Rick Green	D	Washington	London Knights	20.3
1977	Dale McCourt	C	Detroit	St. Catharines Fincups	20.4
1978	Bobby Smith	C	Minnesota	Ottawa 67's	20.4
1979	Bob Ramage	D	Colorado	London Knights	20.5
1980	Doug Wickenheiser	C	Montreal	Regina Pats	19.2
1981	Dale Hawerchuk	C	Winnipeg	Cornwall Royals	18.2
1982	Gord Kluzak	D	Boston	Nanaimo Islanders	18.3
1983	Brian Lawton	C	Minnesota	Mount St. Charles HS	18.11
1984	Mario Lemieux	C	Pittsburgh	Laval Voisins	18.8
1985	Wendel Clark	LW/D	Toronto	Saskatoon Blades	18.7
1986	Joe Murphy	C	Detroit	Michigan State	18.8
1987	Pierre Turgeon	C	Buffalo	Granby Bisons	17.10
1988	Mike Modano	C	Minnesota	Prince Albert Raiders	18.0
1989	Mats Sundin	RW	Quebec	Nacka (Sweden)	18.4
1990	Owen Nolan	RW	Quebec	Cornwall Royals	18.4
1991	Eric Lindros	C	Quebec	Oshawa Generals	18.3
1992	Roman Hamrlik	D	Tampa Bay	ZPS Zlin (Czech.)	18.2
1993	Alexandre Daigle	C	Ottawa	Victoriaville Tigres	18.5
1994	Ed Jovanovski	D	Florida	Windsor Spitfires	18.0

Draft Summary

Following is a summary of the number of players drafted from the Ontario Hockey League (OHL), Western Hockey League (WHL), Quebec Major Junior Hockey League (QMJHL), United States Colleges, United States High Schools, European Leagues and other Leagues throughout North America since 1969:

	OHL	WHL	QMJHL	US Coll.	US HS	International	Other
1969	36	20	11	7	0	1	9
1970	51	22	13	16	0	0	13
1971	41	28	13	22	0	0	13
1972	46	44	30	21	0	0	11
1973	56	49	24	25	0	0	14
1974	69	66	40	41	0	6	25
1975	55	57	28	59	0	6	12
1976	47	33	18	26	0	8	3
1977	42	44	40	49	0	5	5
1978	59	48	22	73	0	16	16
1979	48	37	19	15	0	6	1
1980	73	41	24	42	7	13	10
1981	59	37	28	21	17	32	17
1982	60	55	17	20	47	35	18
1983	57	41	24	14	35	34	37
1984	55	38	16	22	44	40	36
1985	59	47	15	20	48	31	31
1986	66	32	22	22	40	28	42
1987	32	36	17	40	69	38	20
1988	32	30	22	48	56	39	25
1989	39	44	16	48	47	38	20
1990	39	33	14	38	57	53	16
1991	43	40	25	43	37	55	21
1992	57	45	22	9	25	84	22
1993	60	44	23	17	33	78	31
1994	45	66	28	6	28	80	33
Total	**1326**	**1077**	**571**	**764**	**590**	**726**	**501**

Total Drafted, 1969-1994: 5,555

Ontario Hockey League

Club	'69	'70	'71	'72	'73	'74	'75	'76	'77	'78	'79	'80	'81	'82	'83	'84	'85	'86	'87	'88	'89	'90	'91	'92	'93	'94	Total
Peterborough	5	5	4	5	9	4	8	1	4	6	9	10	3	5	7	3	9	2	5	2	2	4	3	4	4	2	125
Oshawa	5	4	3	5	5	7	6	6	1	3	3	2	9	5	5	6	6	6	3	2	4	2	4	4	4	1	111
Kitchener	1	6	2	8	4	13	3	1	3	4	4	4	5	5	8	4	6	3	2	1	7	5	3	1	4	2	109
Ottawa	2	4	3	4	6	5	6	5	5	5	3	8	4	9	2	2	3	3	2	1	–	5	5	6	4	1	103
London	4	9	1	5	6	6	3	5	4	3	6	2	5	5	3	7	1	3	2	6	3	3	1	3	4	1	101
S.S. Marie	–	–	–	–	4	5	2	5	1	5	3	3	8	1	6	4	5	7	1	2	3	1	2	7	3	4	82
Sudbury	–	–	–	–	6	6	4	5	4	4	3	7	2	4	–	2	5	3	1	–	1	2	8	2	10	2	81
Kingston	–	–	–	–	–	4	4	6	4	9	2	8	5	2	1	3	3	4	1	1	–	2	2	3	5	2	71
Niagara Falls	4	2	1	4	–	–	–	–	2	3	5	8	6	6	–	–	–	–	–	–	4	4	4	4	4	3	64
Windsor	–	–	–	–	–	–	–	2	1	4	2	3	5	3	2	2	3	7	–	5	2	1	–	3	–	3	48
North Bay	–	–	–	–	–	–	–	–	–	–	–	–	–	–	4	4	3	3	3	3	1	4	2	5	2	7	41
Guelph	–	–	–	–	–	–	–	–	–	–	–	–	–	–	1	5	3	8	2	–	4	–	–	2	2	7	34
Belleville	–	–	–	–	–	–	–	–	–	–	–	–	–	–	3	4	4	5	2	–	4	2	1	4	–	3	32
Detroit	–	–	–	–	–	–	–	–	–	–	–	–	–	–	–	–	–	–	–	–	–	–	2	2	7	2	13
Owen Sound	–	–	–	–	–	–	–	–	–	–	–	–	–	–	–	–	–	–	–	–	–	1	1	2	4	3	11
Newmarket	–	–	–	–	–	–	–	–	–	–	–	–	–	–	–	–	–	–	–	–	–	–	–	–	3	2	5

Teams no longer operating

Club	'69	'70	'71	'72	'73	'74	'75	'76	'77	'78	'79	'80	'81	'82	'83	'84	'85	'86	'87	'88	'89	'90	'91	'92	'93	'94	Total
Toronto	3	7	6	5	6	8	4	4	7	5	4	10	2	6	4	4	3	4	1	2	2	–	–	–	–	–	97
Hamilton	2	3	5	4	6	4	7	3	–	8	1	–	–	–	–	–	3	6	4	4	–	–	2	–	–	–	62
St. Catharines	5	5	8	5	4	7	8	4	6	–	–	–	–	–	–	–	–	–	–	–	–	–	–	–	–	–	52
Cornwall	–	–	–	–	–	–	–	–	–	–	–	–	–	7	4	3	2	2	3	3	2	3	3	5	–	–	37
Brantford	–	–	–	–	–	–	–	–	–	–	3	8	5	2	7	2	–	–	–	–	–	–	–	–	–	–	27
Montreal	5	6	8	1	–	–	–	–	–	–	–	–	–	–	–	–	–	–	–	–	–	–	–	–	–	–	20

Year	Total Ontario Drafted	Total Players Drafted	Ontario %
1969	36	84	42.9
1970	51	115	44.3
1971	41	117	35.0
1972	46	152	30.3
1973	56	168	33.3
1974	69	247	27.9
1975	55	217	25.3
1976	47	135	34.8
1977	42	185	22.7
1978	59	234	25.2
1979	48	126	38.1
1980	73	210	34.8
1981	59	211	28.0
1982	60	252	23.8
1983	57	242	23.6
1984	55	250	22.0
1985	59	252	23.4
1986	66	252	26.2
1987	32	252	12.7
1988	32	252	12.7
1989	39	252	15.5
1990	39	250	15.6
1991	43	264	16.3
1992	57	264	21.6
1993	60	286	21.0
1994	45	286	15.7
Total	**1326**	**5555**	**23.8**

Western Hockey League

Club	'69	'70	'71	'72	'73	'74	'75	'76	'77	'78	'79	'80	'81	'82	'83	'84	'85	'86	'87	'88	'89	'90	'91	'92	'93	'94	Total
Regina	–	–	5	5	1	8	5	3	1	4	1	3	5	6	8	4	4	3	2	–	5	1	–	4	–	3	81
Saskatoon	1	–	1	3	8	4	5	3	4	1	2	2	3	5	5	3	1	5	4	4	3	2	2	3	2	4	80
Portland	–	–	–	–	–	–	–	–	4	8	7	8	6	7	7	5	2	4	3	1	4	1	1	4	4	3	79
Medicine Hat	–	–	–	4	6	4	5	3	5	4	–	4	2	1	2	1	6	2	5	1	4	1	3	3	1	6	73
Victoria	–	–	–	2	2	5	7	4	3	3	1	8	6	2	3	4	2	1	2	4	4	2	–	1	2	2	70
Brandon	–	3	1	5	2	7	4	–	3	1	10	5	2	2	1	3	2	1	3	3	–	1	1	1	2	5	68
Kamloops	–	–	–	–	–	4	4	4	4	–	–	–	–	2	4	4	4	4	3	1	5	4	6	3	2	9	67
Lethbridge	–	–	–	–	–	–	3	2	3	5	4	1	4	7	2	1	5	1	–	3	3	4	7	3	4	3	65
Seattle	–	–	–	–	–	–	–	–	–	4	2	3	–	6	–	1	3	1	2	4	2	6	3	2	4	5	48
Prince Albert	–	–	–	–	–	–	–	–	–	–	–	–	–	4	2	2	6	6	1	3	3	4	6	2	5	3	47
Swift Current	1	–	1	–	3	6	–	–	–	–	–	–	–	–	–	–	–	–	5	2	2	2	1	1	5	4	33
Spokane	–	–	–	–	–	–	–	–	–	–	–	–	1	–	–	–	–	–	1	3	2	1	5	7	4	4	28
Moose Jaw	–	–	–	–	–	–	–	–	–	–	–	–	–	–	–	–	4	1	3	–	3	1	2	3	2	3	22
Tri-Cities	–	–	–	–	–	–	–	–	–	–	–	–	–	–	–	–	–	–	–	–	4	3	3	5	2	2	19
Tacoma	–	–	–	–	–	–	–	–	–	–	–	–	–	–	–	–	–	–	–	–	–	–	–	3	2	5	10
Red Deer	–	–	–	–	–	–	–	–	–	–	–	–	–	–	–	–	–	–	–	–	–	–	–	–	3	5	8

Teams no longer operating

Club	'69	'70	'71	'72	'73	'74	'75	'76	'77	'78	'79	'80	'81	'82	'83	'84	'85	'86	'87	'88	'89	'90	'91	'92	'93	'94	Total
Calgary	3	5	2	7	4	8	4	4	4	3	–	2	5	4	3	3	3	2	–	–	–	–	–	–	–	–	66
New Westm'r	–	–	–	6	8	7	9	5	8	6	5	1	–	–	–	2	1	1	2	1	–	–	–	–	–	–	62
Flin Flon	4	4	5	2	4	7	4	3	1	5	–	–	–	–	–	–	–	–	–	–	–	–	–	–	–	–	39
Winnipeg	3	2	4	2	5	4	4	–	4	–	–	–	1	4	1	–	–	–	–	–	–	–	–	–	–	–	34
Edmonton	4	4	5	6	6	2	3	2	–	–	2	–	–	–	–	–	–	–	–	–	–	–	–	–	–	–	34
Billings	–	–	–	–	–	–	–	–	–	4	3	4	2	–	–	–	–	–	–	–	–	–	–	–	–	–	13
Estevan	4	4	4	–	–	–	–	–	–	–	–	–	–	–	–	–	–	–	–	–	–	–	–	–	–	–	12
Kelowna	–	–	–	–	–	–	–	–	–	–	–	–	–	–	2	4	5	–	–	–	–	–	–	–	–	–	11
Nanaimo	–	–	–	–	–	–	–	–	–	–	–	–	–	5	1	–	–	–	–	–	–	–	–	–	–	–	6
Vancouver	–	–	–	2	–	–	–	–	–	–	–	–	–	–	–	–	–	–	–	–	–	–	–	–	–	–	2

Year	Total Western Drafted	Total Players Drafted	Western %
1969	20	84	23.8
1970	22	115	19.1
1971	28	117	23.9
1972	44	152	28.9
1973	49	168	29.2
1974	66	247	26.7
1975	57	217	26.3
1976	33	135	24.4
1977	44	185	23.8
1978	48	234	20.5
1979	37	126	29.4
1980	41	210	19.5
1981	37	211	17.5
1982	55	252	21.8
1983	41	242	16.9
1984	37	250	14.8
1985	48	252	19.0
1986	32	252	12.7
1987	36	252	14.3
1988	30	252	11.9
1989	44	252	17.5
1990	33	250	13.2
1991	40	264	15.2
1992	45	264	17.0
1993	44	286	15.4
1994	66	286	23.0
Total	**1077**	**5555**	**19.3**

Quebec Major Junior Hockey League

Club	'69	'70	'71	'72	'73	'74	'75	'76	'77	'78	'79	'80	'81	'82	'83	'84	'85	'86	'87	'88	'89	'90	'91	'92	'93	'94	Total
Shawinigan	3	2	1	6	1	5	3	–	3	–	–	2	2	5	5	2	–	2	1	–	2	–	2	3	1	1	52
Sherbrooke	–	–	2	2	4	3	7	5	6	3	4	1	5	2	–	–	–	–	–	–	–	–	–	–	3	2	49
Hull	–	–	–	–	–	–	3	2	2	3	–	3	1	–	3	1	–	4	3	2	2	3	3	3	3	1	42
Laval	–	–	–	1	–	2	1	1	4	2	1	–	–	2	1	2	–	5	3	1	3	3	4	1	2	5	44
Chicoutimi	–	–	–	–	–	1	–	–	5	1	1	3	6	1	3	–	3	1	2	2	1	1	–	1	1	3	36
Drummondville	2	4	1	4	2	1	–	–	–	–	–	–	–	–	–	1	2	2	2	4	1	–	4	2	2	1	35
Verdun	–	1	1	2	–	–	–	–	–	1	3	3	–	–	3	3	–	3	0	3	1	–	–	3	–	–	27
Granby	–	–	–	–	–	–	–	–	–	–	–	–	–	2	1	3	2	2	4	–	2	–	2	–	1	5	24
St. Jean	–	–	–	–	–	–	–	–	–	–	–	–	–	–	2	–	1	1	0	3	1	–	3	1	2	1	15
Victoriaville	–	–	–	–	–	–	–	–	–	–	–	–	–	–	–	–	–	–	–	4	–	1	–	2	6	1	14
St. Hyacinthe	–	–	–	–	–	–	–	–	–	–	–	–	–	–	–	–	–	–	–	–	–	3	1	2	1	4	11
Beauport	–	–	–	–	–	–	–	–	–	–	–	–	–	–	–	–	–	–	–	–	–	–	1	3	1	3	8
Val D'Or	–	–	–	–	–	–	–	–	–	–	–	–	–	–	–	–	–	–	–	–	–	–	–	–	–	1	1

Teams no longer operating

Club	'69	'70	'71	'72	'73	'74	'75	'76	'77	'78	'79	'80	'81	'82	'83	'84	'85	'86	'87	'88	'89	'90	'91	'92	'93	'94	Total
Quebec	1	1	2	4	6	6	1	3	7	1	3	2	2	1	2	2	3	–	–	–	–	–	–	–	–	–	47
Trois Rivieres	–	1	2	2	2	2	3	2	6	3	2	2	2	1	3	–	3	–	1	3	3	1	2	1	–	–	47
Cornwall	2	1	2	6	4	8	1	3	1	6	1	5	5	–	–	–	–	–	–	–	–	–	–	–	–	–	45
Montreal	–	–	–	–	4	4	8	1	3	2	4	3	–	3	–	–	–	–	–	–	–	–	–	–	–	–	32
Sorel	2	3	1	3	1	8	1	1	3	–	–	–	5	–	–	–	–	–	–	–	–	–	–	–	–	–	28
Longueuil	–	–	–	–	–	–	–	–	–	–	–	–	–	–	1	2	1	2	1	–	–	2	3	–	–	–	12
St. Jerome	1	–	1	–	–	–	–	–	–	–	–	–	–	–	–	–	–	–	–	–	–	–	–	–	–	–	2

Year	Total Quebec Drafted	Total Players Drafted	Quebec %
1969	11	84	13.1
1970	13	115	11.3
1971	13	117	11.1
1972	30	152	19.7
1973	24	168	14.3
1974	40	247	16.2
1975	28	217	12.9
1976	18	135	13.3
1977	40	185	21.6
1978	22	234	9.4
1979	19	126	15.1
1980	24	210	11.4
1981	28	211	13.3
1982	17	252	6.7
1983	24	242	9.9
1984	16	250	6.4
1985	15	252	5.9
1986	22	252	8.7
1987	17	252	6.7
1988	22	252	8.7
1989	16	252	6.3
1990	14	250	5.6
1991	25	264	9.5
1992	22	264	8.3
1993	23	286	8.0
1994	28	286	9.7
Total	**571**	**5555**	**10.2**

United States Colleges

Club	'69	'70	'71	'72	'73	'74	'75	'76	'77	'78	'79	'80	'81	'82	'83	'84	'85	'86	'87	'88	'89	'90	'91	'92	'93	'94	Total
Minnesota	1	3	2	–	–	9	4	4	5	5	2	3	1	1	–	–	2	1	1	1	–	–	–	–	–	–	46
Michigan Tech	–	–	3	1	2	5	4	4	1	2	1	4	–	1	–	2	2	2	1	1	2	1	2	–	1	2	44
Michigan	1	–	–	–	2	2	3	3	1	6	–	4	–	–	–	1	1	–	1	2	3	5	4	2	1	1	43
Wisconsin	–	1	2	4	5	4	4	2	3	–	1	–	3	2	–	1	1	–	1	–	1	–	–	–	–	–	36
Denver	1	3	2	4	2	3	1	2	2	2	2	1	–	1	–	–	1	2	4	1	1	–	–	–	–	–	35
Boston U.	–	4	–	–	1	1	1	1	4	5	1	–	1	–	–	1	1	2	2	3	1	2	2	1	1	–	35
Michigan State	–	–	1	–	1	1	1	1	–	–	–	2	–	2	–	2	–	1	1	4	4	5	4	1	1	1	33
North Dakota	2	3	3	1	4	2	1	–	1	2	3	3	1	–	1	–	–	–	2	1	1	–	–	–	–	–	31
Providence	–	–	–	–	–	3	2	3	4	–	5	4	1	2	–	1	1	–	–	–	1	–	–	–	–	–	27
Clarkson	–	–	2	2	1	–	2	–	2	2	1	1	1	1	1	1	–	–	1	1	1	3	2	1	1	–	27
New Hampshire	–	–	–	1	1	3	6	–	4	1	2	1	1	1	2	–	–	–	1	–	–	–	–	–	–	–	25
Cornell	–	–	–	2	1	1	–	1	1	1	–	1	1	1	–	1	2	–	1	2	5	2	–	–	–	–	23
Bowling Green	–	–	–	–	–	1	3	2	1	1	1	1	–	–	1	–	–	–	3	2	1	3	1	–	–	–	21
Colorado	2	1	–	–	1	3	1	2	2	–	1	–	–	–	3	–	1	–	1	2	–	–	–	–	–	–	20
W. Michigan	–	–	–	–	–	–	–	2	–	–	2	–	–	2	2	–	2	1	1	1	1	4	–	2	–	–	20
Lake Superior	–	–	–	1	1	1	–	3	–	–	–	–	1	3	–	3	2	3	1	–	1	–	1	–	–	–	20
Notre Dame	–	–	2	3	–	7	2	–	3	1	1	–	–	–	–	–	–	–	–	–	–	–	–	–	–	–	19
RPI	–	–	–	1	–	–	1	3	–	1	2	1	1	–	1	–	2	2	–	–	3	1	–	–	–	–	19
St. Lawrence	–	–	–	–	1	1	4	–	–	–	3	–	1	1	1	1	1	1	1	1	2	–	–	2	1	–	19
Harvard	–	–	2	–	–	–	2	–	2	2	–	–	1	1	–	2	–	1	1	2	–	–	–	2	1	–	19
Boston College	–	1	–	–	–	1	1	–	5	–	2	1	1	–	–	–	1	2	–	2	–	–	–	–	–	–	17
Northern Mich.	–	–	–	–	–	–	–	4	–	1	2	1	–	–	–	4	1	2	–	1	–	–	–	–	–	–	16
Vermont	–	–	–	1	–	4	–	1	1	1	–	1	1	2	–	–	1	–	1	1	–	–	–	1	–	–	16
Miami of Ohio	–	–	–	–	–	–	–	–	–	–	–	1	–	2	4	2	–	–	2	1	1	–	–	–	–	–	13
Minn.-Duluth	–	–	2	1	–	–	–	1	1	–	–	1	–	–	–	1	1	–	2	1	2	1	–	–	–	–	12
Ohio State	–	–	–	–	–	2	1	–	–	1	–	–	–	2	2	–	–	1	1	1	1	–	–	–	–	–	12
Brown	–	–	–	1	2	1	–	3	2	–	–	1	–	–	–	–	1	–	–	–	–	–	–	–	–	–	11
Colgate	–	–	–	–	1	–	–	2	1	–	–	–	1	1	2	2	–	–	1	–	–	–	–	–	–	–	10
Yale	–	–	1	–	1	–	2	–	1	–	–	–	1	2	–	1	–	–	1	–	–	–	–	–	–	–	10
Maine	–	–	–	–	–	–	1	1	–	1	–	3	2	1	–	–	1	–	–	–	–	–	–	–	–	–	10
Northeastern	–	–	–	–	1	–	–	1	–	1	–	1	1	–	1	–	1	–	–	–	–	–	–	–	–	–	8
Princeton	–	–	–	1	–	1	–	1	1	1	–	1	–	1	–	–	1	–	–	–	–	–	–	–	–	–	8
Ferris State	–	–	–	–	–	–	–	–	–	–	–	–	–	–	2	1	1	1	2	–	–	–	–	–	–	–	7
St. Louis	–	–	–	–	1	2	–	1	2	–	–	–	–	–	–	–	–	–	–	–	–	–	–	–	–	–	6
U. of Ill.-Chi.	–	–	–	–	–	–	–	–	–	–	1	–	2	1	2	–	–	–	–	–	–	–	–	–	–	–	6
Pennsylvania	–	–	1	2	1	–	–	1	–	–	–	–	–	–	–	–	–	–	–	–	–	–	–	–	–	–	5
Dartmouth	–	–	1	–	–	–	1	1	–	–	1	–	–	–	–	1	–	–	–	–	–	–	–	–	–	–	5
Union College	–	–	–	–	–	4	–	–	–	–	–	–	–	–	–	–	–	–	–	–	–	–	–	–	–	–	4
Lowell	–	–	–	–	–	1	1	1	–	1	–	–	–	–	–	–	–	–	–	–	–	–	–	–	–	–	4
Merrimack	–	–	–	–	–	–	–	–	–	–	–	–	1	–	1	–	1	–	1	–	–	–	–	–	–	–	4
Alaska-Anchorage	–	–	–	–	–	–	–	–	–	–	–	–	–	–	–	–	–	2	1	–	1	–	–	–	–	–	4
Babson College	–	–	–	–	–	–	–	–	–	–	–	–	1	–	1	1	–	–	–	–	–	–	–	–	–	–	3
Alaska-Fairbanks	–	–	–	–	–	–	–	–	–	–	–	–	–	–	–	–	–	–	–	–	1	1	–	–	–	–	2
Salem State	–	–	–	–	–	–	1	–	–	–	–	–	–	–	–	–	–	–	–	–	–	–	–	–	–	–	1
Bemidji State	–	1	–	–	–	–	–	–	–	–	–	–	–	–	–	–	–	–	–	–	–	–	–	–	–	–	1
San Diego U.	–	–	–	–	–	–	–	–	–	–	–	–	1	–	–	–	–	–	–	–	–	–	–	–	–	–	1
Greenway	–	–	–	–	–	–	–	–	–	–	–	–	–	–	–	–	–	1	–	–	–	–	–	–	–	–	1
St. Anselen College	–	–	–	–	–	–	–	–	–	–	–	–	–	–	–	–	–	1	–	–	–	–	–	–	–	–	1
Hamilton College	–	–	–	–	–	–	–	–	–	–	–	–	–	–	–	–	–	1	–	–	–	–	–	–	–	–	1
St. Thomas	–	–	–	–	–	–	–	–	–	–	–	–	–	–	–	–	–	–	1	–	–	–	–	–	–	–	1
St. Cloud State	–	–	–	–	–	–	–	–	–	–	–	–	–	–	–	–	–	–	1	–	–	–	–	–	–	–	1
Amer. Int'l College	–	–	–	–	–	–	–	–	–	–	–	–	–	–	–	–	–	–	–	1	–	–	–	–	–	–	1

Year	Total College Drafted	Total Players Drafted	College %
1969	7	84	8.3
1970	16	115	13.9
1971	22	117	18.8
1972	21	152	13.8
1973	25	168	14.9
1974	41	247	16.6
1975	59	217	26.7
1976	26	135	19.3
1977	49	185	26.5
1978	73	234	31.2
1979	15	126	11.9
1980	42	210	20.0
1981	21	211	10.0
1982	20	252	7.9
1983	14	242	5.8
1984	22	250	8.8
1985	20	252	7.9
1986	22	252	8.7
1987	40	252	15.9
1988	48	252	19.0
1989	48	252	19.0
1990	38	250	15.2
1991	43	264	16.3
1992	9	264	3.4
1993	17	286	5.9
1994	6	286	2.1
Total	**764**	**5555**	**13.7**

United States High Schools

Schools with 10-or-more players drafted are listed.

Club	'80	'81	'82	'83	'84	'85	'86	'87	'88	'89	'90	'91	'92	'93	'94	Total
Northwood Prep (NY)	–	–	2	1	–	2	2	4	1	1	3	1	–	1	1	19
Belmont Hill (MA)	–	–	–	1	–	2	1	2	1	3	2	1	2	–	–	16
Edina (MN)	–	1	4	2	2	–	–	1	2	2	1	–	1	–	–	16
Hill-Murray (MN)	–	–	–	–	3	–	3	3	–	3	–	–	1	–	–	15
Cushing Acad. (MA)	–	–	–	–	–	1	–	–	3	2	3	1	–	2	2	14
Mount St. Charles (RI)	–	1	–	3	1	–	2	1	2	1	1	–	–	–	–	12
Culver Mil. Acad. (IN)	–	–	–	–	–	–	2	1	2	2	1	2	2	–	–	12
Catholic Memorial (MA)	–	–	–	–	2	–	1	1	2	–	2	1	2	1	2	11
Canterbury (CT)	–	–	–	–	–	2	–	3	–	2	–	2	1	–	–	10
Matignon (MA)	1	1	1	–	3	–	–	3	–	–	–	1	–	–	–	10
Roseau (MN)	1	–	1	1	1	–	1	–	–	1	3	1	–	–	–	10

Year	Total USHS Drafted	Total Players Drafted	USHS %
1980	7	210	3.3
1981	17	211	8.1
1982	47	252	18.6
1983	35	242	14.5
1984	44	250	17.6
1985	48	252	19.1
1986	40	252	15.9
1987	69	252	27.4
1988	56	252	22.2
1989	47	252	18.7
1990	57	250	22.8
1991	37	264	14.0
1992	25	264	9.5
1993	33	286	11.5
1994	28	286	9.7
Total	**590**	**5555**	**10.6**

International

Country	'69	'70	'71	'72	'73	'74	'75	'76	'77	'78	'79	'80	'81	'82	'83	'84	'85	'86	'87	'88	'89	'90	'91	'92	'93	'94	Total
Sweden	–	–	–	–	–	5	2	5	2	8	5	9	14	14	10	14	16	9	15	14	9	7	11	11	18	17	215
USSR/CIS	–	–	–	–	–	–	–	1	–	–	2	–	–	3	5	1	2	1	2	11	18	14	25	45	31	35	196
Czech Republic and Slovakia	–	–	–	–	–	–	–	–	–	2	1	–	4	13	9	13	8	6	11	5	8	21	9	17	15	18	160
Finland	1	–	–	–	–	1	3	2	3	2	–	4	12	5	9	10	4	10	6	7	3	9	6	8	9	8	122
Germany	–	–	–	–	–	–	–	–	–	2	–	–	2	–	1	2	1	1	2	–	–	2	1	–	3	1	18
Norway	–	–	–	–	–	–	–	–	–	–	–	–	–	–	–	–	–	–	–	2	–	–	2	1	–	–	5
Switzerland	–	–	–	–	–	–	–	1	–	–	–	–	–	–	–	–	–	–	–	–	–	–	1	–	2	1	5
Denmark	–	–	–	–	–	–	–	–	–	–	–	–	–	–	–	–	–	1	1	–	–	–	–	–	–	–	2
Scotland	–	–	–	–	–	–	–	–	–	–	–	–	–	–	–	–	–	–	1	–	–	–	–	–	–	–	1
Poland	–	–	–	–	–	–	–	–	–	–	–	–	–	–	–	–	–	–	–	–	–	–	–	1	–	–	1
Japan	–	–	–	–	–	–	–	–	–	–	–	–	–	–	–	–	–	–	–	–	–	–	–	1	–	–	1

Year	Total International Drafted	Total Players Drafted	International %
1969	1	84	1.2
1970	0	115	0
1971	0	117	0
1972	0	152	0
1973	0	168	0
1974	6	247	2.4
1975	6	217	2.8
1976	8	135	5.9
1977	5	185	2.7
1978	16	234	6.8
1979	6	126	4.8
1980	13	210	6.2
1981	32	211	15.2
1982	35	252	13.9
1983	34	242	14.0
1984	40	250	17.6
1985	31	252	12.3
1986	28	252	11.1
1987	38	252	15.1
1988	39	252	15.5
1989	38	252	15.1
1990	53	250	21.2
1991	55	264	20.8
1992	84	264	31.4
1993	78	286	27.3
1994	80	286	27.9

Note: Players drafted in the International category played outside North America in their draft year. European-born players drafted from the OHL, QMJHL, WHL or U.S. Colleges are not counted as International players. See Country of Origin, below.

Sweden

Club	'74	'75	'76	'77	'78	'79	'80	'81	'82	'83	'84	'85	'86	'87	'88	'89	'90	'91	'92	'93	'94	Total
Djurgarden Stockholm	1	1	1	–	1	2	–	1	2	1	–	1	2	–	1	1	2	1	1	–	–	19
Leksand	1	–	–	–	–	1	–	1	–	2	2	1	1	2	1	–	2	–	2	2	–	18
Farjestad Karlstad	–	–	2	2	1	2	1	1	2	–	–	1	–	–	1	1	2	1	–	–	–	17
AIK Solna	–	1	–	1	1	2	3	1	–	4	–	–	–	1	1	1	–	1	–	–	1	17
MoDo Hockey Ornskoldsvik	–	1	–	1	–	1	–	2	–	1	–	–	–	2	2	5	–	–	–	–	–	15
Brynas Gavle	1	–	1	1	1	1	–	1	2	–	4	–	–	–	–	–	–	–	–	–	–	13
Sodertalje	–	–	–	1	–	1	1	1	2	2	2	–	–	2	–	–	–	–	–	–	–	13
Vastra Frolunda Goteborg	–	–	–	–	–	–	2	1	–	1	1	–	1	1	–	1	–	–	–	–	3	10
Skelleftea	–	1	1	–	–	1	1	2	1	–	–	–	1	–	–	–	1	–	–	–	–	9
Vasteras	–	–	–	–	–	–	–	–	–	–	2	2	1	1	–	–	1	1	–	–	–	8
Rogle Angelholm	–	–	–	–	–	–	–	–	–	–	–	1	2	–	–	–	–	–	2	2	–	7
Lulea	–	–	–	–	–	–	–	–	–	–	1	1	1	–	–	–	1	1	–	–	–	6
Sundsvall Timra[1]	–	–	–	–	1	2	–	–	1	1	–	–	–	–	–	–	–	–	–	–	1	6
HV 71 Jonkoping	–	–	–	–	–	1	–	–	1	–	–	–	1	–	–	–	–	–	–	–	2	6
Bjorkloven Umea	–	–	–	–	2	1	–	1	–	1	–	–	–	–	–	–	–	–	–	–	–	5
Orebro	–	1	–	1	–	–	1	–	1	–	1	–	–	–	–	–	–	–	–	–	–	5
Nacka	–	–	–	–	–	–	–	–	–	–	–	1	–	–	1	–	2	–	–	–	–	4
Hammarby Stockholm	–	–	–	–	1	1	–	–	–	–	–	–	–	–	–	–	–	1	1	1	–	4
Malmo	–	–	–	–	–	–	1	–	–	–	–	1	–	–	1	–	–	1	–	–	–	4
Falun	–	–	–	–	–	1	–	–	–	–	1	–	–	–	1	–	–	–	–	–	–	3
Team Kiruna	–	–	1	–	1	–	–	1	–	–	–	–	–	–	–	–	–	–	–	–	–	3
Boden	1	–	–	–	–	–	–	–	–	–	–	–	–	–	–	–	–	–	–	–	1	3
Pitea	–	–	–	–	–	–	1	–	–	–	–	1	–	–	–	1	–	–	–	–	1	3
Mora	–	–	–	–	–	–	1	–	1	–	–	–	–	–	–	–	–	–	–	–	–	2
Troja	–	–	–	–	–	–	–	–	1	–	1	–	–	–	–	–	–	–	–	–	–	2
Ostersund	–	–	–	–	–	–	–	–	–	1	1	–	–	–	–	–	–	–	–	–	–	2
Almtuna	–	–	–	–	–	1	–	–	–	–	–	–	–	–	–	–	–	–	–	–	–	1
Danderyd Hockey	–	–	–	–	–	–	–	–	–	–	–	–	–	–	1	–	–	–	–	–	–	1
Fagersta	–	–	–	–	–	–	–	–	–	–	–	–	–	–	–	–	–	–	–	–	–	1
Huddinge	–	–	–	–	–	–	–	–	–	–	–	–	–	–	–	–	1	–	–	–	–	1
Karskoga	–	–	1	–	–	–	–	–	–	–	–	–	–	–	–	–	–	–	–	–	–	1
Stocksund	–	–	–	–	–	–	–	–	–	–	–	–	–	–	–	–	–	–	–	–	–	1
S/G Hockey 83 Gavle	–	–	–	–	–	–	–	–	1	–	–	–	–	–	–	–	–	–	–	–	–	1
Talje	–	–	–	–	–	–	–	–	–	–	–	1	–	–	–	–	–	–	–	–	–	1
Tunabro	1	–	–	–	–	–	–	–	–	–	–	–	–	–	–	–	–	–	–	–	–	1
Uppsala	–	–	–	–	–	–	–	–	–	–	–	–	–	–	–	–	1	–	–	–	–	1
Grums	–	–	–	–	–	–	–	–	–	–	–	–	–	–	–	–	–	–	–	–	1	1

Former club names: [1]—Timra

Russia/C.I.S.

Club	'74	'75	'76	'77	'78	'79	'80	'81	'82	'83	'84	'85	'86	'87	'88	'89	'90	'91	'92	'93	'94	Total
CSKA Moscow	–	–	–	–	1	–	–	–	1	4	–	1	1	1	5	8	3	4	7	3	5	44
Dynamo Moscow	–	–	–	–	–	–	–	–	–	–	–	–	2	3	4	7	10	2	1	–	–	29
Krylja Sovetov Moscow	–	–	–	–	–	–	–	–	–	–	–	1	1	2	4	3	1	5	–	–	–	17
Spartak Moscow	–	–	–	–	1	–	–	1	–	1	–	–	–	–	1	4	–	6	–	1	4	14
Traktor Chelyabinsk	–	–	–	–	–	–	–	–	–	–	–	–	2	–	–	2	7	1	–	–	–	12
Pardaugava Riga[1]	–	1	–	–	–	–	–	–	1	2	–	1	4	1	–	–	–	–	–	–	–	10
Sokol Kiev	–	–	–	–	–	–	1	–	–	–	1	–	1	2	3	1	–	–	–	–	–	9
Khimik Voskresensk	–	–	–	–	–	1	–	–	–	–	1	3	1	2	–	1	–	–	–	–	–	9
SKA St. Peterburg[2]	–	–	1	–	–	1	–	–	–	–	–	–	–	2	1	–	1	–	–	–	–	6
Dynamo-2 Moscow	–	–	–	–	–	–	–	–	–	–	–	–	–	–	2	1	2	–	–	–	–	5
Tivali Minsk[3]	–	–	–	–	–	–	–	–	–	–	1	–	–	2	–	1	–	–	–	–	–	4
Torpedo Yaroslavl	–	–	–	–	–	–	–	–	–	–	–	1	2	–	1	–	–	–	–	–	–	4
Salavat Yulayev Ufa	–	–	–	–	–	–	–	–	–	–	–	–	–	–	2	2	–	–	–	–	–	4
Torpedo Ust Kamenogorsk	–	–	–	–	–	–	–	–	–	–	–	–	–	–	–	1	1	2	–	–	–	4
Kristall Elektrostal	–	–	–	–	–	–	–	–	–	–	–	–	–	–	–	–	3	–	–	–	–	3
Lada Togliatti	–	–	–	–	–	–	–	–	–	–	–	–	–	–	1	2	–	–	–	–	–	3
Torpedo Nizhny Novgorod[4]	–	–	–	–	–	–	–	–	–	–	–	–	–	–	–	1	2	–	–	–	–	3
Avangard Omsk	–	–	–	–	–	–	–	–	–	–	–	–	–	–	–	–	–	–	3	–	–	3
Metallurg Cherepovets	–	–	–	–	–	–	–	–	–	–	–	–	–	–	–	1	1	–	–	–	–	2
Argus Moscow	–	–	–	–	–	–	–	–	–	–	–	–	–	–	–	–	–	1	–	–	–	1
Dizelist Penza	–	–	–	–	–	–	–	–	–	–	–	–	–	–	–	–	1	–	–	–	–	1
Dynamo Kharkov	–	–	–	–	–	–	–	–	–	–	–	–	–	–	1	–	–	–	–	–	–	1
Izhorets St. Peterburg	–	–	–	–	–	–	–	–	–	–	–	–	–	–	–	–	–	1	–	–	–	1
Khimik Novopolotsk	–	–	–	–	–	–	–	–	–	–	–	–	–	–	–	–	–	1	–	–	–	1
Kristall Saratov	–	–	–	–	–	–	–	–	–	–	–	–	–	–	–	–	–	1	–	–	–	1
Krylja Sovetov-2 Moscow	–	–	–	–	–	–	–	–	–	–	–	–	–	–	–	–	–	1	–	–	–	1
Itil Kazan	–	–	–	–	–	–	–	–	–	–	–	–	–	–	–	–	–	–	1	–	–	1
Molot Perm	–	–	–	–	–	–	–	–	–	–	–	–	–	–	–	–	–	–	1	–	–	1
Mechel Chelyabinsk	–	–	–	–	–	–	–	–	–	–	–	–	–	–	–	–	–	–	1	–	–	1
CSKA-2 Moscow	–	–	–	–	–	–	–	–	–	–	–	–	–	–	–	–	–	–	–	1	–	1

Former club names: [1]—Dynamo Riga, HC Riga, [2]—SKA Leningrad, [3]—Dynamo Minsk, [4]—Torpedo Gorky

1994 Entry Draft Analysis

Country of Origin

Country	Players Drafted
Canada	151
USA	48
Russia	30
Sweden	17
Czech Republic	16
Finland	7
Slovakia	4
Ukraine	4
Germany	2
Kazakhstan	1
Belarus	1
Estonia	1
England	1
Korea	1
Switzerland	1

Position

Position	Players Drafted
Defense	95
Center	68
Left Wing	55
Right Wing	38
Goaltender	30

Birth Year

Year	Players Drafted
1976	179
1975	73
1974	19
1973	4
1972	4
1971	3
1970	3
1966	1

Czech Republic and Slovakia

Club	'69	'70	'71	'72	'73	'74	'75	'76	'77	'78	'79	'80	'81	'82	'83	'84	'85	'86	'87	'88	'89	'90	'91	'92	'93	'94	Total
Dukla Jihlava	–	–	–	–	–	–	–	–	–	–	–	–	–	2	4	3	1	–	3	1	1	3	2	1	1	1	23
Chemopetrol Litvinov[1]	–	–	–	–	–	–	–	–	–	–	–	–	–	3	1	2	–	–	–	2	2	1	3	2	–	4	20
Sparta Praha	–	–	–	–	–	–	–	–	–	–	–	–	1	–	2	1	1	1	2	1	2	–	1	1	–	–	13
HC Ceske Budejovice[6]	–	–	–	–	–	–	–	–	–	–	–	–	–	2	1	1	–	2	1	2	–	1	–	1	–	2	11
HC Kladno[7]	–	–	–	–	–	–	–	–	2	1	–	1	–	1	–	–	1	–	–	1	2	–	1	–	1	2	11
Slovan Bratislava	–	–	–	–	–	1	1	–	2	–	1	1	1	–	1	–	–	–	–	–	–	–	–	–	–	3	11
Dukla Trencin	–	–	–	–	–	–	–	–	–	–	–	–	–	–	1	–	–	1	1	2	–	2	2	–	–	–	9
ZPS Zlin[2]	–	–	–	–	–	–	–	–	–	–	–	–	–	1	–	1	1	1	–	–	2	2	1	–	–	–	9
HC Kosice[3]	–	–	–	–	–	–	–	–	–	1	2	–	2	1	–	–	2	–	–	–	–	–	–	–	–	–	8
HC Vitkovice[8]	–	–	–	–	–	1	–	1	–	–	–	–	–	–	–	–	–	–	1	–	1	3	1	–	–	–	8
Zetor Brno	–	–	–	–	–	–	–	–	–	–	–	–	–	–	1	–	3	–	2	1	–	–	–	–	–	–	7
Skoda Plzen	–	–	–	–	–	–	–	–	–	–	–	–	–	–	1	–	1	1	–	3	–	1	–	–	–	–	7
HC Pardubice[4]	–	–	–	–	–	–	–	–	–	–	2	–	2	–	–	–	–	–	–	–	–	–	–	2	–	1	7
HC Olomouc[5]	–	–	–	–	–	–	–	–	–	–	–	–	–	–	–	–	–	–	1	–	–	2	–	1	–	–	4
AC Nitra	–	–	–	–	–	–	–	–	–	–	–	–	–	–	–	–	–	–	–	2	–	1	–	–	–	–	3
Slavia Praha	–	–	–	–	–	–	–	–	–	–	–	–	–	–	1	–	–	–	–	–	–	–	–	–	1	–	2
Ingstav Brno	–	–	–	–	–	–	–	–	–	–	–	–	–	–	1	–	–	–	–	–	–	–	–	–	–	–	1
Partizan Liptovsky Mikulas	–	–	–	–	–	–	–	–	–	–	–	–	–	–	–	–	–	–	–	–	1	–	–	–	–	–	1
VTJ Pisek	–	–	–	–	–	–	–	–	–	–	–	–	–	–	–	–	–	–	–	1	–	–	–	–	–	–	1
ZPA Presov	–	–	–	–	–	–	–	–	–	–	–	–	–	–	–	–	–	–	–	–	–	–	–	–	1	–	1
ZTK Zvolen	–	–	–	–	–	–	–	–	–	–	–	–	–	–	–	–	–	–	–	–	–	–	–	–	1	–	1
ZTS Martin	–	–	–	–	–	–	–	–	–	–	–	–	–	–	–	–	–	–	–	1	–	–	–	–	–	–	1
IS Banska Bystrica	–	–	–	–	–	–	–	–	–	–	–	–	–	–	–	–	–	–	–	–	–	–	–	–	1	–	1

Former club names: [1]–CHZ Litvinov, [2]–TJ Gottwaldov, TJ Zlin, [3]–VSZ Kosice, [4]–Tesla Pardubice, [5]–DS Olomouc, [6]–Motor Ceske Budejovice, [7]–Poldi Kladno, [8]–TJ Vitkovice

Finland

Club	'69	'70	'71	'72	'73	'74	'75	'76	'77	'78	'79	'80	'81	'82	'83	'84	'85	'86	'87	'88	'89	'90	'91	'92	'93	'94	Total
HIFK Helsinki	1	–	–	–	–	1	–	1	–	–	–	1	1	2	2	1	–	–	2	1	–	–	–	2	–	–	15
TPS Turku	–	–	–	–	–	–	–	–	–	–	1	6	–	–	1	1	–	–	1	–	1	–	–	3	2	–	14
Ilves Tampere	–	–	–	–	–	–	1	2	–	2	–	2	2	–	1	–	1	–	1	1	–	–	–	–	–	–	13
Jokerit Helsinki	–	–	–	–	–	–	–	–	–	2	1	–	–	1	–	–	1	1	–	1	1	3	–	–	1	–	12
Assat Pori	–	–	–	2	–	–	–	–	–	–	1	–	2	2	–	–	1	–	1	–	–	–	–	1	1	–	11
Karpat Oulu	–	–	–	–	–	–	–	–	–	1	–	1	–	1	1	2	2	–	–	–	–	1	1	–	–	–	9
Lukko Rauma	–	–	–	–	–	–	2	1	–	2	–	1	1	–	1	–	–	–	1	–	1	–	–	–	–	–	9
Tappara Tampere	–	–	–	1	–	–	–	–	–	–	2	–	–	4	–	1	–	1	–	–	–	–	–	–	–	–	9
Kiekko-Espoo	–	–	–	–	–	–	–	–	–	–	–	–	–	–	–	1	1	1	2	–	2	–	–	–	–	–	7
Reipas Lahti	–	–	–	–	–	–	–	–	–	–	–	–	1	1	1	–	–	–	–	–	–	2	–	1	–	–	6
KalPa Kuopio	–	–	–	–	–	–	–	–	–	–	–	–	–	–	–	–	1	–	–	–	–	–	1	2	–	–	4
HPK Hameenlinna	–	–	–	–	–	–	–	–	–	–	–	–	–	–	1	–	–	–	–	–	2	–	–	–	–	–	3
SaiPa Lappeenranta	–	–	–	–	–	–	–	1	–	–	–	–	–	–	1	–	–	–	–	–	–	–	–	–	–	–	2
Sapko Savonlinna	–	–	–	–	–	–	–	–	–	–	–	–	1	1	–	–	–	–	–	–	–	–	–	–	–	–	2
Sport Vaasa	–	–	–	–	–	–	–	–	–	–	–	–	–	–	–	–	1	–	1	–	–	–	–	–	–	–	2
GrIFK Kauniainen	–	–	–	–	–	–	–	–	–	–	–	–	–	–	–	–	–	–	–	–	–	–	1	–	–	–	1
JyP HT Jyvaskyla	–	–	–	–	–	–	–	–	–	–	–	–	–	–	–	–	1	–	–	–	–	–	–	–	–	–	1
Koo Koo Kouvola	–	–	–	–	–	–	–	–	–	–	–	–	–	–	–	–	–	–	–	1	–	–	–	–	–	1
S-Kiekko Seinajoki	–	–	–	–	–	–	–	–	–	–	–	–	–	–	–	1	–	–	–	–	–	–	–	–	–	–	1

Frantisek Musil, below, had played three years of Czechoslovakian hockey when he was chosen 38th overall by the Minnesota North Stars in the 1983 Entry Draft. Petri Skriko, right, was the first Finnish player drafted by the Vancouver Canucks, who selected him 157th overall in 1981.

First Round Draft Selections, 1994

1. FLORIDA • ED JOVANOVSKI • D
Despite the fact he didn't start playing hockey until he was eleven years old, Ed Jovanovski was named to the OHL First All-Rookie Team as well as the OHL Second All-Star Team in his first year of Major Junior competition. Selected second overall by Windsor Spitfires in the 1993 OHL Draft, Jovanovski collected 51 points in 1993-94. He is a solid body checker and a power-play specialist.

2. ANAHEIM • OLEG TVERDOVSKY • D
Tverdovsky is a highly skilled, offensive-defenseman with exceptional skating ability. Born in Donetsk, USSR in 1976, Tverdovsky was invited to Moscow at the age of 14 and became a regular with the Soviet Wings at 16. During the 1993-94 season, he registered 14 points in 46 games with the Soviet Wings. At the 1994 IIHF World Juniors, Tverdovsky led all Russian rearguards with six points in eight games.

3. OTTAWA • RADEK BONK • C
At 6'3", 215 pounds, Radek Bonk has the size needed to play as a power-forward in the NHL. In 1993-94, Bonk joined the IHL's Las Vegas Thunder, becoming the youngest European to ever play pro hockey in North America. In 76 games with the Thunder, Bonk compiled 42 goals and 45 assists and was named IHL rookie of the year. He collected 208 penalty minutes during the 1993-94 season.

4. EDMONTON • JASON BONSIGNORE • C
American-born Jason Bonsignore is a big centerman, whose style has been compared to Mario Lemieux. A smooth skater with excellent straightaway speed, Bonsignore notched 22 goals and 64 assists in 58 games with the OHL's Newmarket Royals and Niagara Falls Thunder. An unselfish playmaker noted for his finesse, Bonsignore is also an award winning bicycle racer and a collector of sports memorabilia.

5. HARTFORD • JEFF O'NEILL • C
O'Neill was selected first overall by the Guelph Storm in the 1992 OHL Draft and was named the OHL's Rookie of the Year in 1992-93. In two seasons of junior hockey, he has amassed 77 goals and 205 points while playing a sound defensive game. An excellent skater, stick handler and passer, O'Neill played at the 1993-94 CHL All-Star Game and finished third in league scoring with 126 points. He also won the OHL Top Prospect Award.

6. EDMONTON • RYAN SMYTH • LW
Smyth has impressed scouts with his character and work ethic. He can play a finesse game or be aggressive and has exceptional acceleration, agility and balance. In 1993-94, Smyth scored 22 powerplay goals for the WHL's Moose Jaw Warriors. He finished the year with 105 points and a 14-game scoring streak during the 1993-94 campaign, and was one of only 10 players in the WHL to score 50-or-more goals.

7. LOS ANGELES • JAMIE STORR • G
A stand up goaltender with excellent reflexes, Storr has improved his winning percentage in each of his three OHL seasons, rising from 11-16-1 in 1991-92 to 21-11-1 in 1993-94. The winner of the Best Goaltender Award at the 1994 World Juniors, Storr was also the 1993-94 OHL goaltender of the year and represented the Owen Sound Platers at the CHL All-Star Game. Storr plays with confidence and has a quick glove hand and good puck handling skills.

8. TAMPA BAY • JASON WIEMER • C
Jason Wiemer is a driving power forward who thrives as a goal scorer in heavy traffic. He is a tough competitor and styles his games after that of Mark Messier and Cam Neely. He netted 45 goals last season, including 17 powerplay goals, four short-handed markers and nine game winners. Wiemer is an all-around player with great desire, attitude and leadership qualities.

9. NY ISLANDERS • BRETT LINDROS • RW
Although he has sustained serious knee injuries, Brett Lindros has impressed scouts with his leadership qualities and toughness. Like his older brother Eric, Brett is a physical force on the ice. He is exceptionally strong on his skates, using his strength to create scoring opportunities for his teammates. Lindros played for Team Canada at the 1992-93 Izvestia Cup and also played for the Canadian National Team prior to the 1994 Olympics.

10. WASHINGTON • NOLAN BAUMGARTNER • D
Baumgartner is a coachable team player who combines scoring touch with sound defensive play. He tallied 55 points for the WHL's Kamloops Blazers during the 1993-94 season, with an impressive +/– rating of +62 in 69 games. Scouts are impressed with his toughness and excellent positional play. Baumgartner has been compared to rearguard Darryl Sydor of the Kings.

11. SAN JOSE • JEFF FRIESEN • C
A gifted goal scorer and puckhandler, Friesen led the WHL's Regina Pats in scoring with 51 goals and 67 assists in 66 games. A smooth and deceptively fast skater, Friesen has an excellent touch around the net. He utilizes a quick release on all of his shots, scoring often with accurate backhands. Friesen was named the WHL's and CHL's Rookie of the Year in 1992-93 and was a member of Team Canada at the 1994 World Junior Hockey Championships.

12. QUEBEC • WADE BELAK • D
Belak patterns his game after former defensive great Larry Robinson. In 1993-94, Belak played strong defense for the WHL's Saskatoon Blades. Scouting reports note his long stride, good acceleration, crisp outlet passes, low, hard shots from the point and disciplined, positional play. He is a punishing bodychecker and excellent at clearing traffic from in front of the net.

13. VANCOUVER • MATTIAS OHLUND • D
Ohlund is big, defensive rearguard who enjoyed great success in Swedish hockey last season. He uses his size and strength along the boards and in the corners and also clear forwards out from the crease and the slot. He won a silver medal at the 1994 World Juniors and scored three goals in three games at the Under-18 Four Nations tournament. Scouts note his powerful stride and accurate point shot.

14. CHICAGO • ETHAN MOREAU • LW
A veteran of three OHL seasons, Moreau has improved his scoring totals each year, climbing from 39 points in his rookie season of 1991-92 to lead the Niagara Falls Thunder with 98 points last season. He is a versatile power forward used on special teams. An exceptional student, Moreau was awarded The Bobby Smith Trophy as the OHL's Scholastic Player of the Year in 1993-94.

15. WASHINGTON • ALEXANDER KHARLAMOV • LW
The son of legendary Soviet star Valeri Kharlamov, Alexander earned his own place in Russian league competition. He is a creative and speedy winger, noted for his team play, good hands, excellent balance and quick shot. He finished the 1993-94 season with 14 points in 46 games for CSKA Moscow. Kharlamov excelled at the 1993-94 World Juniors, netting four goals in the tournament.

16. TORONTO • ERIC FICHAUD • G
Eric Fichaud is a workhorse goaltender who had a remarkable season with the QMJHL's Sagueneens de Chicoutimi in 1993-94. He led the QMJHL in games played (63), wins (37), saves (1,707), and minutes (3,493). After leading the Sagueneens to the Quebec League title in 1993-94, Fichaud was selected to the Memorial Cup All-Star Team and was named the tournament's top goaltender. Fichaud was also the unanimous winner of the QMJHL's Top Prospect Award.

17. BUFFALO • WAYNE PRIMEAU • C
The younger brother of Detroit star Keith Primeau, Wayne has improved his skill level each season. Selected fourth overall by the Owen Sound Platers in the 1992 OHL Draft, Primeau notched 37 points in his first season and improved to 75 points in 1993-94. In addition to his skills as a stick-handler and tenacious backchecker, Primeau is also a hard hitter.

18. MONTREAL • BRAD BROWN • D
A tough, stay-at-home defender, Brown's solid leadership skills aided the North Bay Centennials' drive to the OHL championship in 1993-94. He possesses a hard, low, accurate point shot, resulting in numerous tip-in opportunities and rebounds. He was an OHL First Team Rookie All-Star in 1991-92 and was voted the Leyden Division's best bodychecker in a 1994 OHL Coaches' Poll.

19. CALGARY • CHRIS DINGMAN • LW
At 6'3", 235 pounds, Chris Dingman loves to bang and crash his way to the net. He emulates Nordiques' forward Wendel Clark "because he plays hard and tough, hits consistently and can put the puck in the net." Dingman can complement any type of line combination. He plays on either wing and can work as a playmaker, cornerman or sniper. He is an all-round athlete, earning MVP honors in basketball and volleyball.

20. DALLAS • JASON BOTTERILL • LW
Botterill played hockey for the University of Michigan Wolverines in 1993-94, totalling 39 points in 36 games. He had a hat trick in his first college game and was named to the CCHA All-Rookie Team. He was a member of the gold medal winning 1994 Canadian National Junior Team. Scouting reports note his physical presence, his willingness to take a hit in front of the net and his unselfish playmaking skills.

21. BOSTON • EVGENI RYABCHIKOV • G
Ryabchikov played strongly in goal for Russia at the 1994 World Juniors, recording a goals-against-average of 2.43 in seven games. He plays for Molot Perm in the Russian Inter-State League and appeared in 28 games, registering a GAA of 3.66 in 1993-94. Possessing sharp instincts and a steady glove hand, Ryabchikov is well-suited to NHL hockey.

22. QUEBEC • JEFF KEALTY • D
Kealty is a mobile defenseman who has played four seasons at Catholic Memorial High School in Massachusetts. A smooth skating, two-way defender, Kealty is an above average stickhandler, passer and bodychecker. Scouts like his positive attitude and his ability to anticipate the flow of play. Kealty admires the playing style of Bruins star Ray Bourque.

23. DETROIT • YAN GOLUBOVSKY • D
Golubovsky exhibits all the tools necessary to become a top-notch NHL defenseman: size, mobility and quickness. After two seasons with Dynamo-2 in Moscow, he joined CSKA Moscow midway through the 1993-94 season. He is a skilled offensive performer and has earned accolades for his power play and penalty killing skills. He represented Russia at the Under-18 Pacific Cup Tournament in 1993.

24. PITTSBURGH • CHRIS WELLS • C
Wells is a 6'6", 215 pound two-way center. Scouts note his good touch around the net, his willingness to work hard and his leadership skills. He scored 30 goals in 1993-94 with the WHL's Seattle Thunderbirds. He is an aggressive forechecker, combining his long reach and exceptional view of the ice to set up a wide variety of scoring chances around the net.

25. NEW JERSEY • VADIM SHARIFIJANOV • RW
A grinding, hard-working winger, Sharifjanov is a crafty playmaker who collected four points for Russia at the 1994 World Juniors. A rookie with Salavat Yulayev Ufa in the Russian Inter-State League, Sharifjanov scored 10 goals in 46 games during the 1993-94 campaign. Scouts have noted his ability to stickhandle through traffic, his solid checking and his willingness to drive towards the net.

26. NY RANGERS • DAN CLOUTIER • G
Dan Cloutier is a stand-up netminder who thrives on competitive pressure. The first goalie selected in the 1992 OHL Draft, Cloutier joined the Sault Saint Marie Greyhounds, appearing in 12 games in his rookie season. In 1993-94, he played 55 games, compiling a 3.56 GAA. He has good puck handling skills, a quick glove hand and excellent anticipation of developing plays.

1994 Entry Draft

Transferred draft choice notation:

Example: Tor.-NYI represents a draft choice transferred from Toronto to New York Islanders.

Pick	Player	Claimed By	Amateur Club	Position
ROUND # 1				
1	JOVANOVSKI, Ed	Fla.	Windsor	D
2	TVERDOVSKY, Oleg	Ana.	Soviet Wings	D
3	BONK, Radek	Ott.	Las Vegas	C
4	BONSIGNORE, Jason	Wpg.-Edm.	Niagara Falls	C
5	O'NEILL, Jeff	Hfd.	Guelph	C
6	SMYTH, Ryan	Edm.	Moose Jaw	LW
7	STORR, Jamie	L.A.	Owen Sound	G
8	WIEMER, Jason	T.B.	Portland	LW
9	LINDROS, Brett	Que.-NYI	Kingston	RW
10	BAUMGARTNER, Nolan	Phi.-Que.-Tor.-Wsh.	Kamloops	D
11	FRIESEN, Jeff	S.J.	Regina	LW
12	BELAK, Wade	NYI-Que.	Saskatoon	D
13	OHLUND, Mattias	Van.	Pitea	D
14	MOREAU, Ethan	Chi.	Niagara Falls	LW
15	KHARLAMOV, Alexander	Wsh.	CSKA Moscow	C
16	FICHAUD, Eric	St.L.-Wsh.-Tor.	Chicoutimi	G
17	PRIMEAU, Wayne	Buf.	Owen Sound	C
18	BROWN, Brad	Mtl.	North Bay	D
19	DINGMAN, Chris	Cgy.	Brandon	LW
20	BOTTERILL, Jason	Dal.	U. of Michigan	LW
21	RYABCHIKOV, Evgeni	Bos.	Molot Perm	G
22	KEALTY, Jeffrey	Tor.-Que.	Catholic Memorial	D
23	GOLUBOVSKY, Yan	Det.	CSKA Jr. Moscow	D
24	WELLS, Chris	Pit.	Seattle	C
25	SHARIFIJANOV, Vadim	N.J.	Salavat Yulayev UFA	RW
26	CLOUTIER, Dan	NYR	Sault Ste. Marie	G
ROUND # 2				
27	WARRENER, Rhett	Fla.	Saskatoon	D
28	DAVIDSSON, Johan	Ana.	HV 71 Jonkoping	D
29	NECKAR, Stanislav	Ott.	HC Ceske Budejovice	D
30	QUINT, Deron	Wpg.	Seattle	D
31	PODOLLAN, Jason	Hfd.-Fla.	Spokane	C
32	WATT, Mike	Edm.	Stratford Jr. B	LW
33	JOHNSON, Matt	L.A.	Peterborough	LW
34	CLOUTIER, Colin	T.B.	Brandon	C
35	MARHA, Josef	Que.	Dukla Jihlava	C
36	JOHNSON, Ryan	Phi.-Fla.	Thunder Bay Jr. A	C
37	NIKOLOV, Angel	S.J.	Chemopetrol Litvinov	D
38	HOLLAND, Jason	NYI	Kamloops	D
39	GORDON, Robb	Van.	Powell River Jr. A	C
40	LEROUX, Jean-Yves	Chi.	Beauport	LW
41	CHERREY, Scott	Wsh.	North Bay	LW
42	SCATCHARD, Dave	St.L.-Van.	Portland	C
43	BROWN, Curtis	Buf.	Moose Jaw	C
44	THEODORE, Jose	Mtl.	St-Jean	G
45	RYABYKIN, Dmitri	Cgy.	Dynamo-2	D
46	JINMAN, Lee	Dal.	North Bay	C
47	GONEAU, Daniel	Bos.	Laval	LW
48	HAGGERTY, Sean	Tor.	Detroit	LW
49	DANDENAULT, Mathieu	Det.	Sherbrooke	RW
50	PARK, Richard	Pit.	Belleville	C
51	ELIAS, Patrik	N.J.	IHC-Kladno	LW
52	VERCIK, Rudolf	NYR	Slovan Bratislava	LW
ROUND # 3				
53	NEILSON, Corey	Fla.-Edm.	North Bay	D
54	MURRAY, Chris	Ana.-Mtl.	Kamloops	RW
55	EPANCHINTSEV, Vadim	Ott.-Ana.-T.B.	Spartak Moscow	C
56	ANNECK, Dorian	Wpg.	Victoria	C
57	BUTENSCHON, Sven	Hfd.-Pit.	Brandon	D
58	HANSEN, Tavis	Edm.-Wpg.	Tacoma	C
59	YACHMENEV, Vitali	L.A.	North Bay	RW
60	SYMES, Brad	T.B.-Edm.	Portland	D
61	BETY, Sebastien	Que.	Drummondville	D
62	ANISIMOV, Artem	Phi.	Itil Kazan	D
63	STRUDWICK, Jason	S.J.-NYI	Kamloops	D
64	MODIN, Fredrik	NYI-Tor.	Sundsvall Timra	LW
65	ALLAN, Chad	Van.	Saskatoon	D
66	YEGOROV, Alexei	Chi.-S.J.	SKA St. Petersburg	C
67	REICHERT, Craig	Wsh.-T.B.-Ana.	Red Deer	RW
68	ROY, Stephane	St.L.	Val D'Or	C
69	NDUR, Rumun	Buf.	Guelph	D
70	KIPRUSOFF, Marko	Mtl.	TPS Turku	D
71	SOURAY, Sheldon	Cgy.-N.J.	Tri-City	D
72	DRURY, Chris	Dal.-Que.	Fairfield Prep.	C
73	CROZIER, Greg	Bos.-Pit.	Lawrence Academy	LW
74	BELANGER, Martin	Tor.-Mtl.	Granby	D
75	GILLAM, Sean	Det.	Spokane	D
76	KRIVCHENKOV, Alexei	Pit.	CSKA Moscow	D
77	CLARK, Chris	N.J.-Cgy.	Springfield Jr. B	RW
78	SMITH, Adam	NYR	Tacoma	D

Players selected second through tenth in the 1994 NHL Entry Draft:
Top row, left to right: 2. Oleg Tverdovsky, D, Anaheim; 3. Radek Bonk, C, Ottawa.
Second row: 4. Jason Bonsignore, C, Edmonton; 5. Jeff O'Neill, C, Edmonton.
Third row: 6. Ryan Smyth, LW, Hartford; 7. Jamie Storr, G, Los Angeles.
Fourth row: 8. Jason Wiemer, LW, Tampa Bay; 9. Brett Lindros, RW, NY Islanders.
Bottom row: 10. Nolan Baumgartner, D, Washington.

ROUND # 4

#	Name	Team	Club	Pos
79	COPELAND, Adam	Fla.-Wpg.-Edm.	Burlington Jr. B	RW
80	BRISKE, Byron	Ana.	Red Deer	D
81	MASOTTA, Bryan	Ott.	Hotchkiss	G
82	CHEREDARYK, Steve	Wpg.	Medicine Hat	D
83	DOMENICHELLI, Hnat	Hfd.	Kamloops	C
84	NEMIROVSKY, David	Edm.-Fla.	Ottawa	RW
85	McLAREN, Steve	L.A.-Chi.	North Bay	D
86	KLEVAKIN, Dmitri	T.B.	Spartak Moscow	RW
87	HEJDUK, Milan	Que.	HC Pardubice	RW
88	MAGARRELL, Adam	Phi.	Brandon	D
89	VARADA, Vaclav	S.J.	HC Vitkovice	RW
90	LUKOWICH, Brad	NYI	Kamloops	D
91	DUTHIE, Ryan	Van.-T.B.-N.J.-Cgy.	Spokane	C
92	DUBINSKY, Mike	Chi.-Van.	Brandon	RW
93	HERR, Matthew	Wsh.	Hotchkiss	C
94	HARLTON, Tyler	St.L.	Vernon Jr. A	D
95	TARVAINEN, Jussi	Buf.-Edm.	KalPa Kuopio	C
96	KUKI, Arto	Mtl.	Kiekko-Espoo Jrs.	C
97	FINNSTROM, Johan	Cgy.	Rogle Angelholm	D
98	WRIGHT, Jamie	Dal.	Guelph	LW
99	NICKULAS, Eric	Bos.	Cushing Academy	C
100	KOROBOLIN, Alexander	Tor.-NYR	Mechel Chelyabinsk	D
101	VALLEE, Sebastien	Det.-Phi.	Victoriaville	LW
102	O'CONNOR, Thomas	Pit.	Springfield Jr. B	D
103	SKOREPA, Zdenek	N.J.	Chemopetrol Litvinov	LW
104	BLOUIN, Sylvain	NYR	Laval	D

ROUND # 5

#	Name	Team	Club	Pos
105	GERIS, Dave	Fla.	Windsor	D
106	TRNKA, Pavel	Ana.	Skoda Plzen	D
107	EKMAN, Nils	Ott.-N.J.-Cgy.	Hammarby Stockholm	RW
108	MILLS, Craig	Wpg.	Belleville	RW
109	RISIDORE, Ryan	Hfd.	Guelph	D
110	GASKINS, Jon	Edm.	Dubuque Jr. A	D
111	SCHMIDT, Chris	L.A.	Seattle	C
112	McARTHUR, Mark	T.B.-NYI	Guelph	G
113	TUZZOLINO, Tony	Que.	Michigan State	RW
114	DESCHENES, Frederic	Phi.-Det.	Granby	G
115	SWANSON, Brian	S.J.	Omaha Jr. A	C
116	O'CONNELL, Albert	NYI	St. Sebastian's	LW
117	DUBE, Yanick	Van.	Laval	C
118	DUPUIS, Marc	Chi.	Belleville	D
119	JEAN, Yanick	Wsh.	Chicoutimi	D
120	FRYLEN, Edvin	St.L.	Vasteras	D
121	KLIMENTJEV, Sergei	Buf.	Medicine Hat	D
122	DROLET, Jimmy	Mtl.	St-Hyacinthe	D
123	APPEL, Frank	Cgy.	Dusseldorf	D
124	TURCO, Marty	Dal.	Cambridge Jr. B	G
125	WRIGHT, Darren	Bos.	Prince Albert	D
126	DEYELL, Mark	Tor.	Saskatoon	C
127	BATTAGLIA, Doug	Det.	Brockville Jr. A	LW
128	JOHNSON, Clint	Pit.	Duluth East	LW
129	GOSSELIN, Christian	N.J.	St-Hyacinthe	D
130	ETHIER, Martin	NYR	Beauport	D

ROUND # 6

#	Name	Team	Club	Pos
131	GAFFNEY, Mike	Fla.-Ott.	St. John's H.S.	D
132	BATTAGLIA, Jon	Ana.	Caledon Jr. A	RW
133	ALFREDSSON, Daniel	Ott.	Vastra Frolunda	RW
134	SMART, Ryan	Wpg.-N.J.	Meadville	C
135	LITVINOV, Yuri	Hfd.-NYR	Soviet Wings	C
136	MARCHANT, Terry	Edm.	Niagara Jr. A	LW
137	JUDEN, Daniel	L.A.-T.B.	Governor Dummer	C
138	SALVADOR, Bryce	T.B.	Lethbridge	D
139	WINDSOR, Nicholas	Que.	Cornwall	D
140	SELIVANOV, Alexander	Phi.	Spartak Moscow	RW
141	KOROLYUK, Alexander	S.J.	Soviet Wings	RW
142	STEWART, Jason	NYI	Simley	D
143	VEZINA, Steve	Van.-Wpg.	Beauport	G
144	ENSON, Jim	Chi.	North Bay	C
145	MEKESHKIN, Dmitri	Wsh.	Avangard Omsk	D
146	KIBERMANIS, Chris	St.L.-Edm.-Wpg.	Red Deer	D
147	BENAZIC, Cal	Buf.	Medicine Hat	D
148	IRVING, Joel	Mtl.	Regina Midgets	D
149	HALTIA, Patrick	Cgy.	Grums	G
150	PETROCHININ, Yevgeny	Dal.	Spartak Moscow	D
151	ROY, Andre	Bos.	Chicoutimi	LW
152	WHITE, Kam	Tor.	Newmarket	D
153	AGARKOV, Pavel	Det.	Soviet Wings	RW
154	MOROZOV, Valentin	Pit.	CSKA Moscow	C
155	CARAVAGGIO, Luciano	N.J.	Michigan Tech	G
156	BROSSEAU, David	NYR	Shawinigan	C

ROUND # 7

#	Name	Team	Club	Pos
157	O'DETTE, Matt	Fla.	Kitchener	D
158	WELSING, Mark (Rocky)	Ana.	Wisconsin Jr. A	D
159	SPROULE, Doug	Ott.	Hotchkiss	LW
160	SHEPTAK, Curtis	Wpg.-Edm.	Olds Jr. A	LW
161	AUBIN, Serge	Hfd.-Pit.	Granby	C
162	SHULGA, Dmitri	Edm.	Tivali Minsk	RW
163	GAGNE, Luc	L.A.	Sudbury	RW
164	MAILLET, Chris	T.B.	Red Deer	D
165	ELFRING, Calvin	Que.	Powell River Jr. A	D
166	FORBES, Colin	Phi.	Sherwood Park Jr. A	LW
167	GORBACHEV, Sergei	S.J.	Dynamo Moscow	RW
168	PLOUFFE, Steve	NYI-Buf.	Granby	G
169	KUZNETSOV, Yuri	Van.	Avangard Omsk	C
170	PROSOTSKY, Tyler	Chi.	Tacoma	C
171	REJA, Daniel	Wsh.	London	C
172	VOPAT, Roman	St.L.	Chemopetrol Litvinov	C
173	HNIDY, Shane	Buf.	Prince Albert	D
174	REZANSOFF, Jessie	Mtl.	Regina	RW
175	KOHN, Ladislav	Cgy.	Swift Current	RW
176	WEBB, Steve	Dal.-Buf.	Peterborough	RW
177	SCHAEFER, Jeremy	Bos.	Medicine Hat	D
178	RAJAMAKI, Tommi	Tor.	Assat Pori Jrs.	D
179	WICKENHEISER, Chris	Det.-Edm.	Red Deer	G
180	PALMER, Drew	Pit.	Seattle	D
181	WILLIAMS, Jeff	N.J.	Guelph	C
182	LAZARENKO, Alexei	NYR	CSKA-2 Moscow	LW

ROUND # 8

#	Name	Team	Club	Pos
183	BOUDRIAS, Jasson	Fla.	Laval	C
184	ENGLEHART, John Brad	Ana.	Kimball Union	LW
185	GUINN, Rob	Ott.-Edm.	Newmarket	D
186	SAIFULLIN, Ramil	Wpg.	Avangard Omsk	C
187	BUCKLEY, Tom	Hfd.	St. Joseph	C
188	REID, Jason	Edm.	St. Andrew's	D
189	DALE, Andrew	L.A.	Sudbury	C
190	BARANOV, Alexei	T.B.	Dynamo-2 Moscow	D
191	BERTSCH, Jay	Que.	Spokane	RW
192	DIENER, Derek	Phi.	Lethbridge	D
193	LANDRY, Eric	S.J.	Guelph	RW
194	LOACH, Mike	NYI	Windsor	C
195	TRUMBLEY, Rob	Van.	Moose Jaw	C
196	JOSEPHSON, Mike	Chi.	Kamloops	LW
197	PATRICK, Chris	Wsh.	Kent	LW
198	NOBLE, Steve	St.L.	Stratford Jr. B	C
199	WESTERBY, Bob	Buf.	Kamloops	LW
200	STROM, Peter	Mtl.	Vastra Frolunda	LW
201	McCAMBRIDGE, Keith	Cgy.	Swift Current	D
202	GIROUX, Raymond	Dal.-Phi.	Powasson Jr.	D
203	HOGARDH, Peter	Bos.-NYI	Vastra Frolunda	LW
204	BUTLER, Rob	Tor.	Niagara Jr. A	LW
205	ELLIOT, Jason	Det.	Kimberley	G
206	ZELENKO, Boris	Pit.	CSKA Moscow	LW
207	BERTRAND, Eric	N.J.	Granby	LW
208	ANDERSON, Craig	NYR	Park Center	C

ROUND # 9

#	Name	Team	Club	Pos
209	YEREMEYEV, Vitali	Fla.-NYR	Torpedo Ust-Kamengorsk	G
210	CASSIVI, Frederic	Ana.-Ott.	St-Hyacinthe	G
211	DUPONT, Danny	Ott.	Laval	D
212	SMANGS, Henrik	Wpg.	Leksand Jrs.	G
213	HALFNIGHT, Ashlin	Hfd.	Harvard University	D
214	JABLONSKI, Jeremy	Edm.	Victoria	D
215	NEMECEK, Jan	L.A.	HC Ceske Budejovice	D
216	SMIRNOV, Yuri	T.B.	Spartak Moscow	C
217	THOMAS, Tim	Que.	U. of Vermont	G
218	HEDBERG, Johan	Phi.	Leksand	G
219	NABOKOV, Yevgeny	S.J.	Torpedo Ust-Kamengorsk	G
220	WALSH, Gord	NYI	Kingston	LW
221	MUCKALT, Bill	Van.	Kelowna Jr. A	C
222	JANDERA, Lubomir	Chi.	Chemopetrol Litvinov Jrs.	D
223	TUOHY, John	Wsh.	Kent	C
224	STEPHAN, Marc	St.L.	Tri-City	C
225	MILLAR, Craig	Buf.	Swift Current	D
226	VOKOUN, Tomas	Mtl.	HC Kladno	G
227	JONSSON, Jorgen	Cgy.	Rogle Angelholm	C
228	FLICHEL, Marty	Dal.	Tacoma	RW
229	GRAHAME, John	Bos.	Sioux City Jr. A	G
230	BALL, Matt	Tor.-Hfd.	Detroit	RW
231	MIKESCH, Jeff	Det.	Michigan Tech	C
232	GODBOUT, Jason	Pit.	Hill-Murray	D
233	SULLIVAN, Steve	N.J.	Sault Ste. Marie	C
234	BOULTON, Eric	NYR	Oshawa	LW

ROUND # 10

#	Name	Team	Club	Pos
235	LEHTERA, Tero	Fla.	Kiekko-Espoo	LW
236	MIETTINEN, Tommi	Ana.	KalPa Kuopio	C
237	MacKINNON, Stephen	Ott.	Cushing Academy	D
238	MADER, Mike	Wpg.	Loomis	D
239	REGAN, Brian	Hfd.	Westminster	G
240	PISA, Tomas	Edm.-S.J.	HC Pardubice Jrs.	RW
241	SHALOMAI, Sergei	L.A.	Spartak Moscow	LW
242	GERVAIS, Shawn	T.B.	Seattle	C
243	PITTMAN, Chris	Que.	Kitchener	LW
244	PAYETTE, Andre	Phi.	Sault Ste. Marie	C
245	DHADPHALE, Aniket	S.J.	Marouette	LW
246	DEWAELE, Kirk	NYI	Lethbridge	D
247	NASH, Tyson	Van.	Kamloops	LW
248	WEIBEL, Lars	Chi.	Lugaho	G
249	ZEDNIK, Richard	Wsh.	IS Banska Bystricia	RW
250	HARPER, Kevin	St.L.	Wexford Jr. A	D
251	POLAK, Mark	Buf.	Medicine Hat	C
252	ALDOUS, Chris	Mtl.	Northwood Prep.	D
253	PELUSO, Mike	Cgy.	Omaha Jr. A	C
254	ROY, Jimmy	Dal.	Thunder Bay Jr. A	C
255	SAVARY, Neil	Bos.	Hull	D
256	BEREZIN, Sergei	Tor.	Khimik Voskresensk	RW
257	HOLMSTROM, Tomas	Det.	Boden	LW
258	KAZAKEVICH, Mikhail	Pit.	Torpedo Yaroslavl	LW
259	SWANJORD, Scott	N.J.	Waterloo Jr. A	G
260	KROPAC, Radoslav	NYR	Slovan Bratislava	LW

ROUND # 11

#	Name	Team	Club	Pos
261	GUSTAFSSON, Per	Fla.	HV-71 Jonkoping	D
262	STEVENSON, Jeremy	Ana.	Sault Ste. Marie	LW
263	MARA, Rob	Ott.-Chi.	Belmont Hill	RW
264	ISSEL, Jason	Wpg.	Prince Albert	LW
265	NIMIGON, Steve	Hfd.	Niagara Falls	LW
266	BENYSEK, Ladislav	Edm.	HC Olomouc Jrs.	D
267	BUTT, Jamie	L.A.-NYR	Tacoma	LW
268	WHITE, Brian	T.B.	Arlington Catholic	D
269	HANSON, Mike	Que.-N.J.	Minot	C
270	LIPIANSKY, Jan	Phi.	Slovan Bratislava	RW
271	BEAUREGARD, David	S.J.	St-Hyacinthe	LW
272	TARNSTROM, Dick	NYI	AIK Solna	D
273	LONGPRE, Robert	Van.	Medicine Hat	C
274	TORMANEN, Antti	Chi.-Ott.	Jokerit Helsinki	RW
275	TERTYSHNY, Sergei	Wsh.	Traktor Chelyabinsk	D
276	FANKHOUSER, Scott	St.L.	Loomis	G
277	WRIGHT, Shayne	Buf.	Owen Sound	D
278	PARSONS, Ross	Mtl.	Regina	D
279	TORGAYEV, Pavel	Cgy.	TPS Turku	LW
280	SZYSKY, Chris	Dal.	Swift Current	LW
281	YAKHANOV, Andrei	Bos.	Salavat Yulayev UFA	D
282	NOLAN, Doug	Tor.	Catholic Memorial	LW
283	SUURSOO, Toivo	Det.	Soviet Wings	LW
284	LEITZA, Brian	Pit.	Sioux City Jr. A	G
285	LOW, Steven	N.J.-Que.	Sherbrooke	D
286	JOHNSSON, Kim	NYR	Malmo Jrs.	D

Draft Choices, 1993-69

1993

ROUND # 1

1 DAIGLE, Alexandre	Ott.	Victoriaville	C
2 PRONGER, Chris	S.J.-Hfd.	Peterborough	D
3 GRATTON, Chris	T.B.	Kingston	C
4 KARIYA, Paul	Ana.	University of Maine	LW
5 NIEDERMAYER, Rob	Fla.	Medicine Hat	C
6 KOZLOV, Viktor	Hfd.-S.J.	Dynamo Moscow	LW
7 ARNOTT, Jason	Edm.	Oshawa	C
8 SUNDSTROM, Niklas	NYR	MoDo	LW
9 HARVEY, Todd	Dal.	Detroit	C
10 THIBAULT, Jocelyn	Phi.-Que.	Sherbrooke	G
11 WITT, Brendan	St. L.-Wsh.	Seattle	D
12 JONSSON, Kenny	Buf.-Tor.	Rogle Angelholm	D
13 PEDERSON, Denis	N.J.	Prince Albert	C
14 DEADMARSH, Adam	NYI-Que.	Portland	C
15 LINDGREN, Mats	Wpg.	Skelleftea	C
16 STAJDUHAR, Nick	L.A.-Edm.	London	D
17 ALLISON, Jason	Wsh.	London	C
18 MATTSSON, Jesper	Cgy.	Malmo	C
19 WILSON, Landon	Tor.	Dubuque Jr. A	RW
20 WILSON, Mike	Van.	Sudbury	D
21 KOIVU, Saku	Mtl.	TPS Turku	C
22 ERIKSSON, Anders	Det.	MoDo	D
23 BERTUZZI, Todd	Que.-NYI	Guelph	C
24 LECOMPTE, Eric	Chi.	Hull	LW
25 ADAMS, Kevyn	Bos.	Miami-Ohio	C
26 BERGQVIST, Stefan	Pit.	Leksand	D

ROUND # 2

27 BICANEK, Radim	Ott.	Dukla Jihlava	D
28 DONOVAN, Shean	S.J.	Ottawa	RW
29 MOSS, Tyler	T.B.	Kingston	G
30 TSULYGIN, Nikolai	Ana.	Salavat Yulalev Ufa	D
31 LANGKOW, Scott	Fla.-Wpg.	Portland	G
32 PANDOLFO, Jay	Hfd.-N.J.	Boston University	LW
33 VYBORNY, David	Edm.	Sparta Praha	C
34 SOROCHAN, Lee	NYR	Lethbridge	D
35 LANGENBRUNNER, Jamie	Dal.	Cloquet	C
36 NIINIMAA, Janne	Phi.	Karpat Oulu	D
37 BETS, Maxim	St. L.	Spokane	LW
38 TSYGUROV, Denis	Buf.	Lada Togliatti	D
39 MORRISON, Brendan	N.J.	Penticton T-II Jr. A	C
40 McCABE, Bryan	NYI	Spokane	D
41 WEEKES, Kevin	Wpg.-Fla.	Owen Sound	G
42 TOPOROWSKI, Shayne	L.A.	Prince Albert	RW
43 BUDAYEV, Alexei	Wsh.-Wpg.	Kristall Elektrostal	C
44 ALLISON, Jamie	Cgy.	Detroit	D
45 KROUPA, Vlastimil	Tor.-Hfd.-S.J.	Chemopetrol Litvinov	D
46 GIRARD, Rick	Van.	Swift Current	C
47 FITZPATRICK, Rory	Mtl.	Sudbury	D
48 COLEMAN, Jonathan	Det.	Andover Academy	D
49 BUCKBERGER, Ashley	Que.	Swift Current	RW
50 MANLOW, Eric	Chi.	Kitchener	C
51 ALVEY, Matt	Bos.	Springfield Jr. B	RW
52 PITTIS, Domenic	Pit.	Lethbridge	C

1992

FIRST ROUND

Selection	Claimed By	Amateur Club	
1. HAMRLIK, Roman	T.B.	ZPS Zlin (Czech.)	D
2. YASHIN, Alexei	Ott.	Dynamo Moscow (CIS)	C
3. RATHJE, Mike	S.J.	Medicine Hat	D
4. WARRINER, Todd	Que.	Windsor	LW
5. KASPARAITIS, Darius	Tor.-NYI	Dynamo Moscow (CIS)	D
6. STILLMAN, Cory	Cgy.	Windsor	C
7. SITTLER, Ryan	Phi.	Nichols	LW
8. CONVERY, Brandon	NYI-Tor.	Sudbury	C
9. PETROVICKY, Robert	Hfd.	Dukla Trencin (Czech.)	C
10. NAZAROV, Andrei	Min.-S.J.	Dynamo Moscow	LW
11. COOPER, David	Buf.	Medicine Hat	D
12. KRIVOKRASOV, Sergei	Wpg.-Chi.	CSKA Moscow (CIS)	RW
13. HULBIG, Joe	Edm.	St. Sebastian's	LW
14. GONCHAR, Sergei	St.L.-Wsh.	Chelybinsk (CIS)	D
15. BOWEN, Jason	L.A.-Pit.-Phi.	Tri-City	LW
16. KVARTALNOV, Dmitri	Bos.	San Diego	LW
17. BAUTIN, Sergei	Chi.-Wpg.	Dynamo Moscow (CIS)	D
18. SMITH, Jason	N.J.	Regina	D
19. STRAKA, Martin	Pit.	Skoda Plzen (Czech.)	C
20. WILKIE, David	Mtl.	Kamloops	D
21. POLASEK, Libor	Van.	TJ Vitkovice (Czech.)	C
22. BOWEN, Curtis	Det.	Ottawa	LW
23. MARSHALL, Grant	Wsh.-Tor.	Ottawa	RW
24. FERRARO, Peter	NYR	Waterloo Jr. A	C

SECOND ROUND

25. PENNEY, Chad	Ott.	North Bay	LW
26. BANNISTER, Drew	T.B.	Sault-Ste-Marie	D
27. MIRANOV, Boris	S.J.-Chi.-Wpg.	CSKA Moscow (CIS)	D
28. BROUSSEAU, Paul	Que.	Hull	RW
29. GRONMAN, Toumas	Tor.-Que.	Tacoma	D
30. O'SULLIVAN, Chris	Cgy.	Catholic Memorial	D
31. METLYUK, Denis	Phi.	Lada Togliatti (CIS)	C
32. CAREY, Jim	NYI-Tor.-Wsh.	Catholic Memorial	G
33. BURE, Valeri	Hfd.-Mtl.	Spokane	LW
34. VARVIO, Jarkko	Min.	HPK (Finland)	RW
35. CIERNY, Jozef	Buf.	ZTK Zvolen (Czech.)	LW
36. SHANTZ, Jeff	Wpg.-Chi.	Regina	C
37. REICHEL, Martin	Edm.	Freiburg (Germany)	RW
38. KOROLEV, Igor	St.L.	Dynamo Moscow	RW
39. HOCKING, Justin	L.A.	Spokane	D
40. PECA, Mike	Bos.-Van.	Ottawa	C
41. KLIMOVICH, Sergei	Chi.	Dynamo Moscow	C
42. BRYLIN, Sergei	N.J.	CSKA Moscow (CIS)	C
43. HUSSEY, Marc	Pit.	Moose Jaw	D
44. CORPSE, Keli	Mtl.	Kingston	C
45. FOUNTAIN, Michael	Van.	Oshawa	G
46. McCARTY, Darren	Det.	Belleville	RW
47. NIKOLISHIN, Andrei	Wsh.-Hfd.	Dynamo Moscow	LW
48. NORSTROM, Mattias	NYR	AIK (Sweden)	D

1991

FIRST ROUND

Selection	Claimed By	Amateur Club	
1. LINDROS, Eric	Que.	Oshawa	C
2. FALLOON, Pat	S.J.	Spokane	RW
3. NIEDERMAYER, Scott	Tor.-N.J.	Kamloops	D
4. LACHANCE, Scott	NYI	Boston University	D
5. WARD, Aaron	Wpg.	U. of Michigan	D
6. FORSBERG, Peter	Phi.	MoDo (Sweden)	C
7. STOJANOV, Alex	Van.	Hamilton	RW
8. MATVICHUK, Richard	Min.	Saskatoon	D
9. POULIN, Patrick	Hfd.	St.-Hyacinthe	LW
10. LAPOINTE, Martin	Det.	Laval	RW
11. ROLSTON, Brian	N.J.	Detroit Comp. Jr. A	C
12. WRIGHT, Tyler	Edm.	Swift Current	C
13. BOUCHER, Phillipe	Buf.	Granby	D
14. PEAKE, Pat	Wsh.	Detroit	C
15. KOVALEV, Alexei	NYR	D'amo Moscow	RW
16. NASLUND, Markus	Pit.	MoDo	RW
17. BILODEAU, Brent	Mtl.	Seattle	D
18. MURRAY, Glen	Bos.	Sudbury	RW
19. SUNDBLAD, Niklas	Cgy.	AIK (Sweden)	RW
20. RUCINSKY, Martin	L.A.-Edm.	CHZ Litvinov (Czech.)	LW
21. HALVERSON, Trevor	St.L.-Wsh.	North Bay	LW
22. McAMMOND, Dean	Chi.	Prince Albert	C

SECOND ROUND

23. WHITNEY, Ray	S.J.	Spokane	C
24. CORBET, Rene	Que.	Drummondville	LW
25. LAVIGNE, Eric	Tor.-Que.-Wsh.	Hull	D
26. PALFFY, Zigmund	NYI	AC Nitra (Czech.)	LW
27. STAIOS, Steve	Wpg.-St.L.	Niagara Falls	D
28. CAMPBELL, Jim	Phi.-Mtl.	Northwood Prep	C
29. CULLIMORE, Jassen	Van.	Peterborough	D
30. OZOLINSH, Sandis	Min.-S.J.	Dynamo Riga (USSR)	D
31. HAMRLIK, Martin	Hfd.	TJ Zin (Czech.)	D
32. PUSHOR, Jamie	Det.	Lethbridge	D
33. HEXTALL, Donevan	N.J.	Prince Albert	LW
34. VERNER, Andrew	Edm.	Peterborough	G
35. DAWE, Jason	Buf.	Peterborough	LW
36. NELSON, Jeff	Wsh.	Prince Albert	C
37. WERENKA, Darcy	NYR	Lethbridge	D
38. FITZGERALD, Rusty	Pit.	Duluth East HS	C
39. POMICHTER, Michael	Mtl.-Chi.	Springfield Jr. B	C
40. STUMPEL, Jozef	Bos.	AC Nitra (Czech.)	RW
41. GROLEAU, Francois	Cgy.	Shawinigan	D
42. LEVEQUE, Guy	L.A.	Cornwall	C
43. DARBY, Craig	St.L.-Mtl.	Albany Academy	C
44. MATTHEWS, Jamie	Chi.	Sudbury	C

1990

FIRST ROUND

Selection	Claimed By	Amateur Club	
1. NOLAN, Owen	Que.	Cornwall	RW
2. NEDVED, Petr	Van.	Seattle	C
3. PRIMEAU, Keith	Det.	Niagara Falls	C
4. RICCI, Mike	Phi.	Peterborough	C
5. JAGR, Jaromir	Pit.	Poldi Kladno (Czech.)	LW
6. SCISSONS, Scott	NYI	Saskatoon	C
7. SYDOR, Darryl	L.A.	Kamloops	D
8. HATCHER, Derian	Min.	North Bay	D
9. SLANEY, John	Wsh.	Cornwall	D
10. BEREHOWSKY, Drake	Tor.	Kingston	D
11. KIDD, Trevor	N.J.-Cgy.	Brandon	G
12. STEVENSON, Turner	St.L.-Mtl.	Seattle	RW
13. STEWART, Michael	NYR	Michigan State	D
14. MAY, Brad	Wpg.-Buf.	Niagara Falls	LW
15. GREIG, Mark	Hfd.	Lethbridge	RW
16. DYKHUIS, Karl	Chi.	Hull	D
17. ALLISON, Scott	Edm.	Prince Albert	C
18. ANTOSKI, Shawn	Mtl.-St.L.-Van.	North Bay	LW
19. TKACHUK, Keith	Buf.-Wpg.	Malden Catholic	LW
20. BRODEUR, Martin	Cgy.-N.J.	St. Hyacinthe	G
21. SMOLINSKI, Bryan	Bos.	Michigan State	C

SECOND ROUND

22. HUGHES, Ryan	Que.	Cornell	C
23. SLEGR, Jiri	Van.	CHZ Litvinov (Czech.)	D
24. HARLOCK, David	Det.-Cgy.-N.J.	U. of Michigan	D
25. SIMON, Chris	Phi.	Ottawa	LW
26. PERREAULT, Nicolas P.	Pit.-Cgy.	Hawkesbury Jr. A	D
27. TAYLOR, Chris	NYI	London	C
28. SEMCHUK, Brandy	L.A.	Canadian National	RW
29. GOTZIAMAN, Chris	Min.-Cgy.-N.J.	Roseau	RW
30. PASMA, Rod	Wsh.	Cornwall	D
31. POTVIN, Felix	Tor.	Chicoutimi	G
32. VIITAKOSKI, Vesa	N.J.-Cgy.	SaiPa (Finland)	LW
33. JOHNSON, Craig	St.L.	Hill-Murray HS	C
34. WEIGHT, Doug	NYR	Lake Superior	C
35. MULLER, Mike	Wpg.	Wayzata	D
36. SANDERSON, Geoff	Hfd.	Swift Current	C
37. DROPPA, Ivan	Chi.	Partizan (Czech.)	D
38. LEGAULT, Alexandre	Edm.	Boston University	RW
39. KUWABARA, Ryan	Mtl.	Ottawa	RW
40. RENBERG, Mikael	Buf.-Phi.	Pitea (Sweden)	LW
41. BELZILE, Etienne	Cgy.	Cornell	D
42. SANDWITH, Terran	Bos.-Phi.	Tri-Cities	D

1989

FIRST ROUND

Selection	Claimed By	Amateur Club	
1. SUNDIN, Mats	Que.	Nacka (Sweden)	RW
2. CHYZOWSKI, Dave	NYI	Kamloops	LW
3. THORNTON, Scott	Tor.	Belleville	C
4. BARNES, Stu	Wpg.	Tri-Cities	C
5. GUERIN, Bill	N.J.	Springfield Jr. B	RW
6. BENNETT, Adam	Chi.	Sudbury	D
7. ZMOLEK, Doug	Min.	John Marshall	D
8. HERTER, Jason	Van.	U. of North Dakota	D
9. MARSHALL, Jason	St.L.	Vernon Jr. A	D
10. HOLIK, Robert	Hfd.	Dukla Jihlava (Czech.)	C
11. SILLINGER, Mike	Det.	Regina	C
12. PEARSON, Rob	Phi.-Tor.	Belleville	RW
13. VALLIS, Lindsay	NYR-Mtl.	Seattle	RW
14. HALLER, Kevin	Buf.	Regina	D
15. SOULES, Jason	Edm.	Niagara Falls	D
16. HEWARD, Jamie	Pit.	Regina	RW
17. STEVENSON, Shayne	Bos.	Kitchener	RW
18. MILLER, Jason	L.A.-Edm.-N.J.	Medicine Hat	C
19. KOLZIG, Olaf	Wsh.	Tri-Cities	G
20. RICE, Steven	Mtl.-NYR	Kitchener	RW
21. BANCROFT, Steve	Cgy.-Tor.	Belleville	D

SECOND ROUND

22. FOOTE, Adam	Que.	Sault Ste. Marie	D
23. GREEN, Travis	NYI	Spokane	C
24. MANDERVILLE, Kent	Tor.-Cgy.	Notre Dame Jr. A	LW
25. RATUSHNY, Dan	Wpg.	Cornell	D
26. SKALDE, Jarrod	N.J.	Oshawa	C
27. SPEER, Michael	Chi.	Guelph	D
28. CRAIG, Mike	Min.	Oshawa	RW
29. WOODWARD, Robert	Van.	Deerfield	LW
30. BRISEBOIS, Patrice	St.L.-Mtl.	Laval	D
31. CORRIVEAU, Rick	Hfd.-St.L.	London	D
32. BOUGHNER, Bob	Det.	Sault-Ste. Marie	D
33. JOHNSON, Greg	Phi.	Thunder Bay Jr. A	C
34. JUHLIN, Patrik	NYR-Phi.	Vasteras (Sweden)	LW
35. DAFOE, Byron	Buf.-Wsh.	Portland	D
36. BORGO, Richard	Edm.	Kitchener	G
37. LAUS, Paul	Pit.	Niagara Falls	D
38. PARSON, Mike	Bos.	Guelph	G
39. THOMPSON, Brent	L.A.	Medicine Hat	D
40. PROSOFSKY, Jason	Wsh.-NYR	Medicine Hat	RW
41. LAROUCHE, Steve	Mtl.	Trois-Rivieres	C
42. DRURY, Ted	Cgy.	Fairfield Prep	C

1988

FIRST ROUND

Selection	Claimed By	Amateur Club	
1. MODANO, Mike	Min.	Prince Albert	C
2. LINDEN, Trevor	Van.	Medicine Hat	RW
3. LESCHYSHYN, Curtis	Que.	Saskatoon	D
4. SHANNON, Darrin	Pit.	Windsor	LW
5. DORE, Daniel	NYR-Que.	Drummondville	RW
6. PEARSON, Scott	Tor.	Kingston	LW
7. GELINAS, Martin	L.A.	Hull	LW
8. ROENICK, Jeremy	Chi.	Thayer Academy	C
9. BRIND'AMOUR, Rod	St.L.	Notre Dame Jr. A	C
10. SELANNE, Teemu	Wpg.	Jokerit (Finland)	RW
11. GOVEDARIS, Chris	Hfd.	Toronto	LW
12. FOSTER, Corey	N.J.	Peterborough	D
13. SAVAGE, Joel	Buf.	Victoria	RW
14. BOIVIN, Claude	Phi.	Drummondville	LW
15. SAVAGE, Reginald	Wsh.	Victoriaville	C
16. CHEVELDAYOFF, Kevin	NYI	Brandon	D
17. KOCUR, Kory	Det.	Saskatoon	RW
18. CIMETTA, Robert	Bos.	Toronto	LW
19. LEROUX, Francois	Edm.	St. Jean	D
20. CHARRON, Eric	Mtl.	Trois-Rivieres	D
21. MUZZATTI, Jason	Cgy.	Michigan State	G

SECOND ROUND

22. MALLETTE, Troy	Min.-NYR	Sault Ste. Marie	C
23. CHRISTIAN, Jeff	Van.-N.J.	London	LW
24. FISET, Stephane	Que.	Victoriaville	G
25. MAJOR, Mark	Pit.	North Bay	D
26. DUVAL, Murray	NYR	Spokane	RW
27. DOMI, Tie	Tor.	Peterborough	RW
28. HOLDEN, Paul	L.A.	London	D
29. DOUCET, Wayne	Chi.-NYI	Hamilton	LW
30. PLAVSIC, Adrien	St.L.	U. of New Hampshire	D
31. ROMANIUK, Russell	Wpg.	St. Boniface Jr. A	LW
32. RICHTER, Barry	Hfd.	Culver Academy	D
33. ROHLIN, Leif	N.J.-Van.	Vasteras (Sweden)	D
34. ST. AMOUR, Martin	Buf.-Mtl.	Verdun	LW
35. MURRAY, Pat	Phi.	Michigan State	LW
36. TAYLOR, Tim	Wsh.	London	C
37. LEBRUN, Sean	NYI	New Westminster	LW
38. ANGLEHART, Serge	Det.	Drummondville	D
39. KOIVUNEN, Petro	Bos.-Edm.	Espoo (Finland)	C
40. GAETZ, Link	Edm.-Min.	Spokane	D
41. BARTLEY, Wade	Mtl.-St.L.-Wsh.	Dauphin Jr. A	D
42. HARKINS, Todd	Cgy.	Miami-Ohio	RW

1987

FIRST ROUND

Selection	Claimed By	Amateur Club	
1. TURGEON, Pierre	Buf.	Granby	C
2. SHANAHAN, Brendan	N.J.	London	C
3. WESLEY, Glen	Van.-Bos.	Portland	D
4. McBEAN, Wayne	Min.-L.A.	Medicine Hat	D
5. JOSEPH, Chris	Pit.	Seattle	D
6. ARCHIBALD, David	L.A.-Min.	Portland	C/LW
7. RICHARDSON, Luke	Tor.	Peterborough	D
8. WAITE, Jimmy	Chi.	Chicoutimi	G
9. FOGARTY, Bryan	Que.	Kingston	D
10. MORE, Jayson	NYR	New Westminster	D
11. RACINE, Yves	Det.	Longueuil	D
12. OSBORNE, Keith	St.L.	North Bay	RW
13. CHYNOWETH, Dean	NYI	Medicine Hat	D
14. QUINTAL, Stephane	Bos.	Granby	D
15. SAKIC, Joe	Wsh.-Que.	Swift Current	C
16. MARCHMENT, Bryan	Wpg.	Belleville	D
17. CASSELS, Andrew	Mtl.	Ottawa	C
18. HULL, Jody	Hfd.	Peterborough	RW
19. DEASLEY, Bryan	Cgy.	U. of Michigan	LW
20. RUMBLE, Darren	Phi.	Kitchener	D
21. SOBERLAK, Peter	Edm.	Swift Current	LW

SECOND ROUND

Selection	Claimed By	Amateur Club	
22. MILLER, Brad	Buf.	Regina	D
23. PERSSON, Rickard	N.J.	Ostersund (Sweden)	D
24. MURPHY, Rob	Van.	Laval	C
25. MATTEAU, Stephane	Min.-Cgy.	Hull	LW
26. TABARACCI, Richard	Pit.	Cornwall	G
27. FITZPATRICK, Mark	L.A.	Medicine Hat	G
28. MAROIS, Daniel	Tor.	Chicoutimi	RW
29. McGILL, Ryan	Chi.	Swift Current	D
30. HARDING, Jeff	Que.-Phi.	St. Michael's Jr. B	LW
31. LACROIX, Daniel	NYR	Granby	LW
32. KRUPPKE, Gordon	Det.	Prince Albert	D
33. LECLAIR, John	St.L.-Mtl.	Bellows Academy	D
34. HACKETT, Jeff	NYI	Oshawa	G
35. McCRADY, Scott	Bos.-Min.	Medicine Hat	D
36. BALLANTYNE, Jeff	Wsh.	Ottawa	D
37. ERICKSSON, Patrik	Wpg.	Brynas (Sweden)	C
38. DESJARDINS, Eric	Mtl.	Granby	D
39. BURT, Adam	Hfd.	North Bay	D
40. GRANT, Kevin	Cgy.	Kitchener	D
41. WILKIE, Bob	Phi.-Det.	Swift Current	D
42. WERENKA, Brad	Edm.	N. Michigan	D

1986

FIRST ROUND

Selection	Claimed By	Amateur Club	
1. MURPHY, Joe	Det.	Michigan State	C
2. CARSON, Jimmy	L.A.	Verdun	C
3. BRADY, Neil	N.J.	Medicine Hat	C
4. ZALAPSKI, Zarley	Pit.	Canadian National	D
5. ANDERSON, Shawn	Buf.	Canadian National	D
6. DAMPHOUSSE, Vincent	Tor.	Laval	LW
7. WOODLEY, Dan	Van.	Portland	C
8. ELYNUIK, Pat	Wpg.	Prince Albert	RW
9. LEETCH, Brian	NYR	Avon Old Farms HS	D
10. LEMIEUX, Jocelyn	St.L.	Laval	RW
11. YOUNG, Scott	Hfd.	Boston University	RW
12. BABE, Warren	Min.	Lethbridge	LW
13. JANNEY, Craig	Bos.	Boston College	C
14. SANIPASS, Everett	Chi.	Verdun	LW
15. PEDERSON, Mark	Mtl.	Medicine Hat	LW
16. PELAWA, George	Cgy.	Bemidji HS	RW
17. FITZGERALD, Tom	NYI	Austin Prep	C
18. McRAE, Ken	Que.	Sudbury	C
19. GREENLAW, Jeff	Wsh.	Canadian National	LW
20. HUFFMAN, Kerry	Phi.	Guelph	D
21. ISSEL, Kim	Edm.	Prince Albert	RW

SECOND ROUND

Selection	Claimed By	Amateur Club	
22. GRAVES, Adam	Det.	Windsor	C
23. SEPPO, Jukka	L.A.-Phi.	Sport (Finland)	LW
24. COPELAND, Todd	N.J.	Belmont Hill HS	D
25. CAPUANO, Dave	Pit.	Mt. St. Charles HS	C
26. BROWN, Greg	Buf.	St. Mark's	D
27. BRUNET, Benoit	Tor.-Mtl.	Hull	LW
28. HAWLEY, Kent	Van.-Phi.	Ottawa	C
29. NUMMINEN, Teppo	Wpg.	Tappara (Finland)	D
30. WILKINSON, Neil	NYR-Min.	Selkirk	D
31. POSMA, Mike	St.L.	Buffalo Jr. A	D
32. LaFORGE, Marc	Hfd.	Kingston	D
33. KOLSTAD, Dean	Min.	Prince Albert	D
34. TIRKKONEN, Pekka	Bos.	SaPKo (Finland)	C
35. KURZAWSKI, Mark	Chi.	Windsor	D
36. SHANNON, Darryl	Mtl.-Tor.	Windsor	D
37. GLYNN, Brian	Cgy.	Saskatoon	D
38. VASKE, Dennis	NYI	Armstrong HS	D
39. ROUTHIER, Jean-Marc	Que.	Hull	RW
40. SEFTEL, Steve	Wsh.	Kingston	LW
41. GUERARD, Stephane	Phi.-Que.	Shawinigan	D
42. NICHOLS, Jamie	Edm.	Portland	LW

1985

FIRST ROUND

Selection	Claimed By	Amateur Club	
1. CLARK, Wendel	Tor.	Saskatoon	D
2. SIMPSON, Craig	Pit.	Michigan State	C
3. WOLANIN, Craig	N.J.	Kitchener	D
4. SANDLAK, Jim	Van.	London	RW
5. MURZYN, Dana	Hfd.	Calgary	D
6. DALGARNO, Brad	Min.-NYI	Hamilton	RW
7. DAHLEN, Ulf	NYR	Ostersund (Sweden)	C
8. FEDYK, Brent	Det.	Regina	RW
9. DUNCANSON, Craig	L.A.	Sudbury	LW
10. GRATTON, Dan	Bos.-L.A.	Oshawa	C
11. MANSON, David	Chi.	Prince Albert	D
12. CHARBONNEAU, Jose	St.L.-Mtl.	Drummondville	RW
13. KING, Derek	NYI	Sault Ste. Marie	LW
14. JOHANSSON, Calle	Buf.	V. Frolunda (Sweden)	D
15. LATTA, Dave	Que.	Kitchener	LW
16. CHORSKE, Tom	Mtl.	Minneapolis SW HS	LW
17. BIOTTI, Chris	Cgy.	Belmont Hill HS	D
18. STEWART, Ryan	Wpg.	Kamloops	C
19. CORRIVEAU, Yvon	Wsh.	Toronto	LW
20. METCALFE, Scott	Edm.	Kingston	LW
21. SEABROOKE, Glen	Phi.	Peterborough	C

SECOND ROUND

Selection	Claimed By	Amateur Club	
22. SPANGLER, Ken	Tor.	Calgary	D
23. GIFFIN, Lee	Pit.	Oshawa	RW
24. BURKE, Sean	N.J.	Toronto	G
25. GAMBLE, Troy	Van.	Medicine Hat	G
26. WHITMORE, Kay	Hfd.	Peterborough	G
27. NIEUWENDYK, Joe	Min.-Cgy.	Cornell	C
28. RICHTER, Mike	NYR	Northwood Prep.	G
29. SHARPLES, Jeff	Det.	Kelowna	D
30. EDLUND, Par	L.A.	Bjorkloven (Sweden)	RW
31. COTE, Alain	Bos.	Quebec	D
32. WEINRICH, Eric	Chi.-N.J.	North Yarmouth	D
33. RICHARD, Todd	Mtl.	Armstrong HS	D
34. LAUER, Brad	NYI	Regina	RW
35. HOGUE, Benoit	Buf.	St-Jean	C
36. LAFRENIERE, Jason	Que.	Hamilton	C
37. RAGLAN, Herb	Mtl.-St.L.	Kingston	RW
38. WENAAS, Jeff	Cgy.	Medicine Hat	C
39. OHMAN, Roger	Wpg.	Leksand (Sweden)	D
40. DRUCE, John	Wsh.	Peterborough	RW
41. CARNELLEY, Todd	Edm.	Kamloops	D
42. RENDALL, Bruce	Phi.	Chatham	LW

1984

FIRST ROUND

Selection	Claimed By	Amateur Club	
1. LEMIEUX, Mario	Pit.	Laval	C
2. MULLER, Kirk	N.J.	Cdn-Nat.-Guelph	C
3. OLCZYK, Ed	L.A.-Chi.	U.S. National	RW
4. IAFRATE, Al	Tor.	U.S. National-Belleville	D
5. SVOBODA, Petr	Hfd.-Mtl.	CHZ (Czech.)	D
6. REDMOND, Craig	Chi.-L.A.	Canadian National	D
7. BURR, Shawn	Det.	Kitchener	C
8. CORSON, Shayne	St.L.-Mtl.	Brantford	C
9. BODGER, Doug	Wpg.-Pit.	Kamloops Jr. A	D
10. DAIGNEAULT, J.J.	Van.	Cdn. Nat.-Longueuil	D
11. COTE, Sylvain	Mtl.-Hfd.	Quebec	D
12. ROBERTS, Gary	Cgy.	Ottawa	LW
13. QUINN, David	Min.	Kent HS	D
14. CARKNER, Terry	NYR	Peterborough	D
15. STIENBURG, Trevor	Que.	Guelph	C
16. BELANGER, Roger	Phi.-Pit.	Kingston	D
17. HATCHER, Kevin	Wsh.	North Bay	D
18. ANDERSSON, Mikael	Buf.	V. Frolunda (Sweden)	C
19. PASIN, Dave	Bos.	Prince Albert	RW
20. MacPHERSON, Duncan	NYI	Saskatoon	D
21. ODELEIN, Selmar	Edm.	Regina	D

SECOND ROUND

Selection	Claimed By	Amateur Club	
22. SMYTH, Greg	Phi.	London	D
23. BILLINGTON, Craig	N.J.	Belleville	G
24. WILKS, Brian	L.A.	Kitchener	C
25. GILL, Todd	Tor.	Windsor	D
26. BENNING, Brian	Hfd.-St.L.	Portland	D
27. MELLANBY, Scott	Chi.-Phi.	Henry Carr Jr. B	RW
28. HOUDA, Doug	Det.	Calgary	D
29. RICHER, Stephane	St.L.-Mtl.	Granby	C
30. DOURIS, Peter	Wpg.	U. of New Hampshire	C
31. ROHLICEK, Jeff	Van.	Portland	LW
32. HRKAC, Anthony	Mtl.-St.L.	Orillia Jr. A	C
33. SABOURIN, Ken	Cgy.	Sault Ste. Marie	D
34. LEACH, Stephen	Min.-Wsh.	Matignon HS	RW
35. HELMINEN, Raimo	NYR	Ilves (Finland)	C
36. BROWN, Jeff	Que.	Sudbury	D
37. CHYCHRUN, Jeff	Phi.	Kingston	D
38. RANHEIM, Paul	Wsh.-Cgy.	Edina Hornets HS	C
39. TRAPP, Doug	Buf.	Regina	LW
40. PODLOSKI, Ray	Bos.	Portland	C
41. MELANSON, Bruce	NYI	Oshawa	RW
42. REAUGH, Daryl	Edm.	Kamloops Jr. A	G

1983

FIRST ROUND

Selection	Claimed By	Amateur Club	
1. LAWTON, Brian	Pit.-Min.	Mount St. Charles HS	C
2. TURGEON, Sylvain	Hfd.	Hull	C
3. LaFONTAINE, Pat	N.J.-NYI	Verdun	C
4. YZERMAN, Steve	Det.	Peterborough	C
5. BARRASSO, Tom	St.L.-Buf.	Acton-Boxboro HS	G
6. MacLEAN, John	L.A.-N.J.	Oshawa	RW
7. COURTNALL, Russ	Tor.	Victoria	C
8. McBAIN, Andrew	Wpg.	North Bay	RW
9. NEELY, Cam	Van.	Portland	RW
10. LACOMBE, Normand	Cgy.-Buf.	U. of New Hampshire	RW
11. CREIGHTON, Adam	Que.-Buf.	Ottawa	C
12. GAGNER, Dave	NYR	Brantford	C
13. QUINN, Dan	Buf.-Cgy.	Belleville	C
14. DOLLAS, Bobby	Wsh.-Wpg.	Laval	D
15. ERREY, Bob	Min.-Pit.	Peterborough	LW
16. DIDUCK, Gerald	NYI	Lethbridge	D
17. TURCOTTE, Alfie	Mtl.	Portland	C
18. CASSIDY, Bruce	Chi.	Ottawa	D
19. BEUKEBOOM, Jeff	Edm.	Sault Ste. Marie	D
20. JENSEN, David	Phi.-Hfd.	Lawrence	C
21. MARKWART, Nevin	Bos.	Regina	LW

SECOND ROUND

Selection	Claimed By	Amateur Club	
22. CHARLESWORTH, Todd	Pit.	Oshawa	D
23. SIREN, Ville	Hfd.	Ilves (Finland)	D
24. EVANS, Shawn	N.J.	Peterborough	D
25. LAMBERT, Lane	Det.	Saskatoon	RW
26. LEMIEUX, Claude	St.L.-Mtl.	Trois-Rivières	RW
27. MOMESSO, Sergio	L.A.-Mtl.	Shawinigan	C
28. JACKSON, Jeff	Tor.	Brantford	LW
29. BERRY, Brad	Wpg.	St. Albert	D
30. BRUCE, Dave	Van.	Kitchener	RW
31. TUCKER, John	Cgy.-Buf.	Kitchener	C
32. HEROUX, Yves	Que.	Chicoutimi	RW
33. HEATH, Randy	NYR	Portland	LW
34. HAJDU, Richard	Wsh.-Buf.	Kamloops Jr. A	LW
35. FRANCIS, Todd	Mtl.	Brantford	RW
36. PARKS, Malcolm	Min.	St. Albert	C
37. McKECHNEY, Garnet	NYI	Kitchener	RW
38. MUSIL, Frantisek	Mtl.-Min.	Tesla (Czech.)	D
39. PRESLEY, Wayne	Chi.	Kitchener	RW
40. GOLDEN, Mike	Edm.	Reading HS	C
41. ZEZEL, Peter	Phi.	Toronto	C
42. JOHNSTON, Greg	Bos.	Toronto	RW

1982

FIRST ROUND

Selection	Claimed By	Amateur Club	
1. KLUZAK, Gord	Col.-Bos.	Nanaimo	D
2. BELLOWS, Brian	Det.-Min.	Kitchener	RW
3. NYLUND, Gary	Tor.	Portland	D
4. SUTTER, Ron	Hfd.-Phi.	Lethbridge	C
5. STEVENS, Scott	L.A.-Wsh.	Kitchener	D
6. HOUSLEY, Phil	Wsh.-Buf.	S. St. Paul HS	D
7. YAREMCHUK, Ken	Chi.	Portland	C
8. TROTTIER, Rocky	St.L.-N.J.	Nanaimo	RW
9. CYR, Paul	Cgy.-Buf.	Victoria	LW
10. SUTTER, Rich	Pit.	Lethbridge	RW
11. PETIT, Michel	Van.	Sherbrooke	D
12. KYTE, Jim	Wpg.	Cornwall	D
13. SHAW, David	Que.	Kitchener	D
14. LAWLESS, Paul	Phi.-Hfd.	Windsor	LW
15. KONTOS, Chris	NYR	Toronto	C
16. ANDREYCHUK, Dave	Buf.	Oshawa	LW
17. CRAVEN, Murray	Min.-Det.	Medicine Hat	C
18. DANEYKO, Ken	Bos.-N.J.	Seattle	D
19. HEROUX, Alain	Mtl.	Chicoutimi	LW
20. PLAYFAIR, Jim	Edm.	Portland	D
21. FLATLEY, Pat	NYI	U. of Wisconsin	RW

SECOND ROUND

Selection	Claimed By	Amateur Club	
22. CURRAN, Brian	Col.-Bos.	Portland	D
23. COURTEAU, Yves	Det.	Laval	RW
24. LEEMAN, Gary	Tor.	Regina	D
25. IHNACAK, Peter	Hfd.-Tor.	Sparta (Czech.)	C
26. ANDERSON, Mike	L.A.-Buf.	N. St. Paul HS	C
27. HEIDT, Mike	Wsh.-L.A.	Calgary	D
28. BADEAU, Rene	St.L.-Chi.	Quebec	D
29. REIERSON, Dave	Cgy.	Prince Albert	D
30. JOHANSSON, Jens	Buf.	Pitea (Sweden)	D
31. GAUVREAU, Jocelyn	Pit.-Mtl.	Granby	D
32. CARLSON, Kent	Van.-Mtl.	St. Lawrence University	D
33. MALEY, David	Wpg.-Mtl.	Edina HS	C
34. GILLIS, Paul	Que.	Niagara Falls	C
35. PATERSON, Mark	Phi.-Hfd.	Ottawa	D
36. SANDSTROM, Tomas	NYR	Farjestads (Sweden)	RW
37. KROMM, Richard	Buf.-Cgy.	Portland	LW
38. HRYNEWICH, Tim	Min.-Pit.	Sudbury	LW
39. BYERS, yyndon	Bos.	Regina	RW
40. SANDELIN, Scott	Mtl.	Hibbing HS	D
41. GRAVES, Steve	Edm.	Sault Ste. Marie	C
42. SMITH, Vern	NYI	Lethbridge	D

1981

FIRST ROUND

Selection	Claimed By	Amateur Club	
1. HAWERCHUK, Dale	Wpg.	Cornwall	C
2. SMITH, Doug	Det.-L.A.	Ottawa	C
3. CARPENTER, Bobby	Col.-Wsh.	St. John's HS	C
4. FRANCIS, Ron	Hfd.	Sault Ste. Marie	C
5. CIRELLA, Joe	Wsh.-Col.	Oshawa	D
6. BENNING, Jim	Tor.	Portland	D
7. HUNTER, Mark	Pit.-Mtl.	Brantford	RW
8. FUHR, Grant	Edm.	Victoria	G
9. PATRICK, James	NYR	Prince Albert	D
10. BUTCHER, Garth	Van.	Regina	D
11. MOLLER, Randy	Que.	Lethbridge	D
12. TANTI, Tony	Chi.	Oshawa	RW
13. MEIGHAN, Ron	Min.	Niagara Falls	D
14. LEVEILLE, Normand	Bos.	Chicoutimi	LW
15. MacINNIS, Allan	Cgy.	Kitchener	D
16. SMITH, Steve	Phi.	Sault Ste. Marie	D
17. DUDACEK, Jiri	Buf.	Poldi Kladno (Czech.)	RW
18. DELORME, Gilbert	L.A.-Mtl.	Chicoutimi	D
19. INGMAN, Jan	Mtl.	Farjestad (Sweden)	LW
20. RUFF, Marty	St.L.	Lethbridge	D
21. BOUTILIER, Paul	NYI	Sherbrooke	D

SECOND ROUND

Selection	Claimed By	Amateur Club	
22. ARNIEL, Scott	Wpg.	Cornwall	LW
23. LOISELLE, Claude	Det.	Windsor	C
24. YAREMCHUK, Gary	Col.-Tor.	Portland	C
25. GRIFFIN, Kevin	Hfd.-Chi.	Portland	LW
26. CHERNOMAZ, Rich	Wsh.-Col.	Victoria	C
27. DONNELLY, Dave	Tor.-Min.	St. Albert	C
28. GATZOS, Steve	Pit.	Sault Ste. Marie	RW
29. STRUEBY, Todd	Edm.	Regina	LW
30. ERIXON, Jan	NYR	Skelleftea (Sweden)	RW
31. SANDS, Mike	Van.-Min.	Sudbury	G
32. ERIKSSON, Lars	Que.-Mtl.	Brynas (Sweden)	G
33. HIRSCH, Tom	Chi.-Min.	Patrick Henry HS	D
34. PREUSS, Dave	Min.	St. Thomas Academy	RW
35. DUFOUR, Luc	Bos.	Chicoutimi	RW
36. NORDIN, Hakan	Cgy.-St.L.	Farjestad (Sweden)	D
37. COSTELLO, Rich	Phi.	Natick HS	C
38. VIRTA, Hannu	Buf.	TPS (Finland)	D
39. KENNEDY, Dean	L.A.	Brandon	D
40. CHELIOS, Chris	Mtl.	Moose Jaw	D
41. WAHLSTEN, Jali	St.L.-Min.	TPS (Finland)	C
42. DINEEN, Gord	NYI	Sault Ste. Marie	D

1980

FIRST ROUND

Selection	Claimed By	Amateur Club	
1. WICKENHEISER, Doug	Col.-Mtl.	Regina	C
2. BABYCH, Dave	Wpg.	Portland	D
3. SAVARD, Denis	Que.-Chi.	Montreal	C
4. MURPHY, Larry	Det.-L.A.	Peterborough	D
5. VEITCH, Darren	Wsh.	Regina	D
6. COFFEY, Paul	Edm.	Kitchener	D
7. LANZ, Rick	Van.	Oshawa	D
8. ARTHUR, Fred	Hfd.	Cornwall	D
9. BULLARD, Mike	Pit.	Brantford	C
10. FOX, Jimmy	L.A.	Ottawa	RW
11. BLAISDELL, Mike	Tor.-Det.	Regina	RW
12. WILSON, Rik	St.L.	Kingston	D
13. CYR, Denis	Cgy.	Montreal	RW
14. MALONE, Jim	NYR	Toronto	C
15. DUPONT, Jerome	Chi.	Toronto	D
16. PALMER, Brad	Min.	Victoria	LW
17. SUTTER, Brent	NYI	Red Deer	C
18. PEDERSON, Barry	Bos.	Victoria	C
19. GAGNE, Paul	Mtl.-Col.	Windsor	LW
20. PATRICK, Steve	Buf.	Brandon	RW
21. STOTHERS, Mike	Phi.	Kingston	D

SECOND ROUND

Selection	Claimed By	Amateur Club	
22. WARD, Joe	Col.	Seattle	C
23. MANTHA, Moe	Wpg.	Toronto	D
24. ROCHEFORT, Normand	Que.	Quebec	D
25. MUNI, Craig	Det.-Tor.	Kingston	D
26. McGILL, Bob	Wsh.-Tor.	Victoria	D
27. NATTRESS, Ric	Edm.-Mtl.	Brantford	D
28. LUDZIK, Steve	Van.-Chi.	Niagara Falls	C
29. GALARNEAU, Michel	Hfd.	Hull	C
30. SOLHEIM, Ken	Pit.-Chi.	Medicine Hat	LW
31. CURTALE, Tony	L.A.-Cgy.	Brantford	D
32. LaVALLEE, Kevin	Tor.-Cgy.	Brantford	LW
33. TERRION, Greg	St.L.-L.A.	Brantford	LW
34. MORRISON, Dave	Cgy.-L.A.	Peterborough	RW
35. ALLISON, Mike	NYR	Sudbury	LW
36. DAWES, Len	Chi.	Victoria	D
37. BEAUPRE, Don	Min.	Sudbury	G
38. HRUDEY, Kelly	NYI	Medicine Hat	G
39. KONROYD, Steve	Cgy.	Oshawa	D
40. CHABOT, John	Mtl.	Hull	C
41. MOLLER, Mike	Buf.	Lethbridge	RW
42. FRASER, Jay	Phi.	Ottawa	LW

1979

FIRST ROUND

Selection	Claimed By	Amateur Club	
1. RAMAGE, Rob	Col.	London	D
2. TURNBULL, Perry	St.L.	Portland	C
3. FOLIGNO, Mike	Det.	Sudbury	RW
4. GARTNER, Mike	Wsh.	Niagara Falls	RW
5. VAIVE, Rick	Van.	Sherbrooke	RW
6. HARTSBURG, Craig	Min.	Sault St. Marie	D
7. BROWN, Keith	Chi.	Portland	D
8. BOURQUE, Raymond	L.A.-Bos.	Verdun	D
9. BOSCHMAN, Laurie	Tor.	Brandon	C
10. McCARTHY, Tom	Wsh.-Min.	Oshawa	LW
11. RAMSEY, Mike	Buf.	U. of Minnesota	D
12. REINHART, Paul	Atl.	Kitchener	D
13. SULLIMAN, Doug	NYR	Kitchener	RW
14. PROPP, Brian	Phi.	Brandon	LW
15. McCRIMMON, Brad	Bos.	Brandon	D
16. WELLS, Jay	Mtl.-L.A.	Kingston	D
17. SUTTER, Duane	NYI	Lethbridge	RW
18. ALLISON, Ray	Hfd.	Brandon	RW
19. MANN, Jimmy	Wpg.	Sherbrooke	RW
20. GOULET, Michel	Que.	Quebec	LW
21. LOWE, Kevin	Edm.	Quebec	D

SECOND ROUND

Selection	Claimed By	Amateur Club	
22. WESLEY, Blake	Col.-Phi.	Portland	D
23. PEROVICH, Mike	St.L.-Atl.	Brandon	D
24. RAUSSE, Errol	Det.-Wsh.	Seattle	LW
25. JONSSON, Tomas	Wsh.-NYI	MoDo AIK (Sweden)	D
26. ASHTON, Brent	Van.	Saskatoon	LW
27. GINGRAS, Gaston	Min.-Mtl.	Hamilton	D
28. TRIMPER, Tim	Chi.	Peterborough	LW
29. HOPKINS, Dean	L.A.	London	RW
30. HARDY, Mark	Tor.-L.A.	Montreal	D
31. MARSHALL, Paul	Wsh.-Pit.	Brantford	LW
32. RUFF, Lindy	Buf.	Lethbridge	D
33. RIGGIN, Pat	Atl.	London	G
34. HOSPODAR, Ed	NYR	Ottawa	D
35. LINDBERGH, Pelle	Phi.	AIK Solna (Sweden)	G
36. MORRISON, Doug	Bos.	Lethbridge	RW
37. NASLUND, Mats	Mtl.	Brynas IFK (Sweden)	LW
38. CARROLL, Billy	NYI	London	C
39. SMITH, Stuart	Hfd.	Peterborough	D
40. CHRISTIAN, Dave	Wpg.	U. of North Dakota	C
41. HUNTER, Dale	Que.	Sudbury	C
42. BROTEN, Neal	Min.	U. of Minnesota	C

1978

FIRST ROUND

Selection	Claimed By	Amateur Club	
1. SMITH, Bobby	Min.	Ottawa	C
2. WALTER, Ryan	Wsh.	Seattle	LW
3. BABYCH, Wayne	St.L.	Portland	RW
4. DERLAGO, Bill	Van.	Brandon	C
5. GILLIS, Mike	Col.	Kingston	LW
6. WILSON, Behn	Pit.-Phi.	Kingston	D
7. LINSEMAN, Ken	NYR-Phi.	Kingston	C
8. GEOFFRION, Danny	L.A.-Mtl.	Cornwall	RW
9. HUBER, Willie	Det.	Hamilton	D
10. HIGGINS, Tim	Chi.	Ottawa	RW
11. MARSH, Brad	Atl.	London	D
12. PETERSON, Brent	Tor.-Det.	Portland	C
13. PLAYFAIR, Larry	Buf.	Portland	D
14. LUCAS, Danny	Phi.	Sault Ste. Marie	RW
15. TAMBELLINI, Steve	NYI	Lethbridge	C
16. SECORD, Al	Bos.	Hamilton	LW
17. HUNTER, Dave	Mtl.	Sudbury	LW
18. COULIS, Tim	Wsh.	Hamilton	LW

SECOND ROUND

Selection	Claimed By	Amateur Club	
19. PAYNE, Steve	Min.	Ottawa	LW
20. MULVEY, Paul	Wsh.	Portland	RW
21. QUENNEVILLE, Joel	Tor.	Windsor	D
22. FRASER, Curt	Van.	Victoria	LW
23. MacKINNON, Paul	Wsh.	Peterborough	D
24. CHRISTOFF, Steve	Min.	U. of Minnesota	C
25. MEEKER, Mike	Pit.	Peterborough	RW
26. MALONEY, Don	NYR	Kitchener	LW
27. MALINOWSKI, Merlin	Col.	Medicine Hat	C
28. HICKS, Glenn	Det.	Flin Flon	LW
29. LECUYER, Doug	Chi.	Portland	LW
30. YAKIWCHUK, Dale	Mtl.	Portland	C
31. JENSEN, Al	Det.	Hamilton	G
32. McKEGNEY, Tony	Buf.	Kingston	LW
33. SIMURDA, Mike	Phi.	Kingston	RW
34. JOHNSTON, Randy	NYI	Peterborough	D
35. NICOLSON, Graeme	Bos.	Cornwall	D
36. CARTER, Ron	Mtl.	Sherbrooke	RW

1977

FIRST ROUND

Selection	Claimed By	Amateur Club	
1. McCOURT, Dale	Det.	St. Catharines	C
2. BECK, Barry	Col.	New Westminster	D
3. PICARD, Robert	Wsh.	Montreal	D
4. GILLIS, Jere	Van.	Sherbrooke	LW
5. CROMBEEN, Mike	Cle.	Kingston	RW
6. WILSON, Doug	Chi.	Ottawa	D
7. MAXWELL, Brad	Min.	New Westminster	D
8. DEBLOIS, Lucien	NYR	Sorel	C
9. CAMPBELL, Scott	St.L.	London	D
10. NAPIER, Mark	Atl.-Mtl.	Toronto	RW
11. ANDERSON, John	Tor.	Toronto	RW
12. JOHANSEN, Trevor	Pit.-Tor.	Toronto	D
13. DUGUAY, Ron	L.A.-NYR	Sudbury	C
14. SEILING, Ric	Buf.	St. Catharines	RW
15. BOSSY, Mike	NYI	Laval	RW
16. FOSTER, Dwight	Bos.	Kitchener	D
17. McCARTHY, Kevin	Phi.	Winnipeg	LW
18. DUPONT, Norm	Mtl.	Montreal	C

SECOND ROUND

Selection	Claimed By	Amateur Club	
19. SAVARD, Jean	Det.-Chi.	Quebec	C
20. ZAHARKO, Miles	Col.-Atl.	New Westminster	D
21. LOFTHOUSE, Mark	Wsh.	New Westminster	RW
22. BANDURA, Jeff	Van.	Portland	D
23. CHICOINE, Daniel	Cle.	Sherbrooke	RW
24. GLADNEY, Bob	Chi.-Tor.	Oshawa	D
25. SEMENKO, Dave	Min.	Brandon	LW
26. KEATING, Mike	NYR	St. Catharines	LW
27. LABATTE, Neil	St.L.	Toronto	D
28. LAURENCE, Don	Atl.	Kitchener	C
29. SAGANIUK, Rocky	Tor.	Lethbridge	RW
30. HAMILTON, Jim	Pit.	London	RW
31. HILL, Brian	L.A.-Atl.	Medicine Hat	RW
32. ARESHENKOFF, Ron	Buf.	Medicine Hat	C
33. TONELLI, John	NYI	Toronto	LW
34. PARRO, Dave	Bos.	Saskatoon	G
35. GORENCE, Tom	Phi.	U. of Minnesota	RW
36. LANGWAY, Rod	Mtl.	U. of New Hampshire	D

1976

FIRST ROUND

Selection	Claimed By	Amateur Club	
1. GREEN, Rick	K.C.-Wsh.	London	D
2. CHAPMAN, Blair	Pit.	Saskatoon	RW
3. SHARPLEY, Glen	Min.	Hull	C
4. WILLIAMS, Fred	Det.	Saskatoon	C
5. JOHANSSON, Bjorn	Cal.	Sweden	D
6. MURDOCH, Don	NYR	Medicine Hat	RW
7. FEDERKO, Bernie	St.L.	Saskatoon	C
8. SHAND, Dave	Van.-Atl.	Peterborough	D
9. CLOUTIER, Real	Chi.	Quebec	RW
10. PHILLIPOFF, Harold	Atl.	New Westminster	LW
11. GARDNER, Paul	Pit.-K.C.	Oshawa	C
12. LEE, Peter	Tor.-Mtl.	Ottawa	RW
13. SCHUTT, Rod	L.A.-Mtl.	Sudbury	LW
14. McKENDRY, Alex	NYI	Sudbury	LW
15. CARROLL, Greg	Buf.-Wsh.	Medicine Hat	C
16. PACHAL, Clayton	Bos.	New Westminster	C
17. SUZOR, Mark	Phi.	Kingston	D
18. BAKER, Bruce	Mtl.	Ottawa	RW

SECOND ROUND

Selection	Claimed By	Amateur Club	
19. MALONE, Greg	Wsh.-Pit.	Oshawa	C
20. SUTTER, Brian	K.C.-St.L.	Lethbridge	LW
21. CLIPPINGDALE, Steve	Min.-L.A.	New Westminster	LW
22. LARSON, Reed	Det.	U. of Minnesota	D
23. STENLUND, Vern	Cal.	London	C
24. FARRISH, Dave	NYR	Sudbury	D
25. SEMKRE, John	St.L.	Toronto	LW
26. MANNO, Bob	Van.	St. Catharines	D
27. McDILL, Jeff	Chi.	Victoria	RW
28. SIMPSON, Bobby	Atl.	Sherbrooke	LW
29. MARSH, Peter	Pit.	Sherbrooke	RW
30. CARLYLE, Randy	Tor.	Sudbury	D
31. ROBERTS, Jim	L.A.-Min.	Ottawa	LW
32. KASZYCKI, Mike	NYI	Sault Ste. Marie	C
33. KOWAL, Joe	Buf.	Hamilton	LW
34. GLOECKNER, Larry	Bos.	Victoria	D
35. CALLANDER, Drew	Phi.	Regina	C
36. MELROSE, Barry	Mtl.	Kamloops	D

1975

FIRST ROUND

Selection	Claimed By	Amateur Club	
1. BRIDGMAN, Mel	Wsh.-Phi.	Victoria	C
2. DEAN, Barry	K.C.	Medicine Hat	LW
3. KLASSEN, Ralph	Cal.	Saskatoon	C
4. MAXWELL, Brian	Min.	Medicine Hat	D
5. LAPOINTE, Rick	Det.	Victoria	D
6. ASHBY, Don	Tor.	Calgary	C
7. VAYDIK, Greg	Chi.	Medicine Hat	C
8. MULHERN, Richard	Atl.	Sherbrooke	D
9. SADLER, Robin	St.L.-Mtl.	Edmonton	D
10. BLIGHT, Rick	Van.	Brandon	RW
11. PRICE, Pat	NYI	Saskatoon	D
12. DILLON, Wayne	NYR	Toronto	C
13. LAXTON, Gord	Pit.	New Westminster	G
14. HALWARD, Doug	Bos.	Peterborough	D
15. MONDOU, Pierre	L.A.-Mtl.	Montreal	C
16. YOUNG, Tim	Mtl.-L.A.	Ottawa	C
17. SAUVE, Bob	Buf.	Laval	G
18. FORSYTH, Alex	Phi.-Wsh.	Kingston	C

SECOND ROUND

Selection	Claimed By	Amateur Club	
19. SCAMURRA, Peter	Wsh.	Peterborough	D
20. CAIRNS, Don	K.C.	Victoria	LW
21. MARUK, Dennis	Cal.	London	C
22. ENGBLOM, Brian	Min.-Mtl.	U. of Wisconsin	D
23. ROLLINS, Jerry	Det.	Winnipeg	D
24. JARVIS, Doug	Tor.	Peterborough	C
25. ARNDT, Daniel	Chi.	Saskatoon	LW
26. BOWNESS, Rick	Atl.	Montreal	RW
27. STANIOWSKI, Ed	St.L.	Regina	G
28. GASSOFF, Brad	Van.	Kamloops	D
29. SALVIAN, David	NYI	St. Catharines	RW
30. SOETAERT, Doug	NYR	Edmonton	G
31. ANDERSON, Russ	Pit.	U. of Minnesota	D
32. SMITH, Barry	Bos.	New Westminster	C
33. BUCYK, Terry	L.A.	Lethbridge	RW
34. GREENBANK, Kelvin	Mtl.	Winnipeg	RW
35. BREITENBACH, Ken	Buf.	St. Catharines	D
36. MASTERS, Jamie	Phi.-St.L.	Ottawa	D

1974

FIRST ROUND

Selection	Claimed By	Amateur Club	
1. JOLY, Greg	Wsh.	Regina	D
2. PAIEMENT, Wilfred	K.C.	St. Catharines	RW
3. HAMPTON, Rick	Cal.	St. Catharines	D
4. GILLIES, Clark	NYI	Regina	LW
5. CONNOR, Cam	Van.-Mtl.	Flin Flon	RW
6. HICKS, Doug	Min.	Flin Flon	D
7. RISEBROUGH, Doug	St.L.-Mtl.	Kitchener	C
8. LAROUCHE, Pierre	Pit.	Sorel	C
9. LOCHEAD, Bill	Det.	Oshawa	LW
10. CHARTRAW, Rick	Atl.-Mtl.	Kitchener	D
11. FOGOLIN, Lee	Buf.	Oshawa	D
12. TREMBLAY, Mario	L.A.-Mtl.	Montreal	RW
13. VALIQUETTE, Jack	Tor.	Sault Ste. Marie	C
14. MALONEY, Dave	NYR	Kitchener	D
15. McTAVISH, Gord	Mtl.	Sudbury	C
16. MULVEY, Grant	Chi.	Calgary	RW
17. CHIPPERFIELD, Ron	Phi.-Cal.	Brandon	C
18. LARWAY, Don	Bos.	Swift Current	RW

SECOND ROUND

Selection	Claimed By	Amateur Club	
19. MARSON, Mike	Wsh.	Sudbury	LW
20. BURDON, Glen	K.C.	Regina	C
21. AFFLECK, Bruce	Cal.	U. of Denver	D
22. TROTTIER, Bryan	NYI	Swift Current	C
23. SEDLBAUER, Ron	Van.	Kitchener	LW
24. NANTAIS, Rick	Min.	Quebec	LW
25. HOWE, Mark	St.L.-Bos.	Toronto	D
26. BOWNESS, Rick	Pit.-St.L.	New Westminster	D
27. COSSETTE, Jacques	Det.-Pit.	Sorel	RW
28. CHOUINARD, Guy	Atl.	Quebec	C
29. GARE, Danny	Buf.	Calgary	RW
30. MacGREGOR, Gary	L.A.-Mtl.	Cornwall	C
31. WILLIAMS, Dave	Tor.	Swift Current	LW
32. GRESCHNER, Ron	NYR	New Westminster	D
33. LUPIEN, Gilles	Mtl.	Montreal	D
34. DAIGLE, Alain	Chi.	Trois-Rivières	RW
35. McLEAN, Don	Phi.	Sudbury	D
36. STURGEON, Peter	Bos.	Kitchener	LW

1973

FIRST ROUND

Selection	Claimed By	Amateur Club	
1. POTVIN, Denis	NYI	Ottawa	D
2. LYSIAK, Tom	Cal.-Mtl.-Atl.	Medicine Hat	C
3. VERVERGAERT, Dennis	Van.	London	RW
4. McDONALD, Lanny	Tor.	Medicine Hat	RW
5. DAVIDSON, John	Atl.-Mtl.-St.L.	Calgary	G
6. SAVARD, Andre	L.A.-Bos.	Quebec	C
7. STOUGHTON, Blaine	Pit.	Flin Flon	RW
8. GAINEY, Bob	Mtl.	Peterborough	LW
9. DAILEY, Bob	Min.-Mtl.-Van.	Toronto	D
10. NEELEY, Bob	Phi.-Tor.	Peterborough	LW
11. RICHARDSON, Terry	Det.	New Westminster	G
12. TITANIC, Morris	Buf.	Sudbury	LW
13. ROTA, Darcy	Chi.	Edmonton	LW
14. MIDDLETON, Rick	NYR	Oshawa	RW
15. TURNBULL, Ian	Bos.-Tor.	Ottawa	D
16. MERCREDI, Vic	Mtl.-Atl.	New Westminster	C

SECOND ROUND

Selection	Claimed By	Amateur Club	
17. GOLDUP, Glen	NYI-Mtl.	Toronto	RW
18. DUNLOP, Blake	Cal.-Min.	Ottawa	C
19. BORDELEAU, Paulin	Van.	Toronto	RW
20. GOODENOUGH, Larry	Tor.-Phi.	London	D
21. VAIL, Eric	Atl.	Sudbury	LW
22. MARRIN, Peter	L.A.-Mtl.	Toronto	C
23. BIANCHIN, Wayne	Pit.	Flin Flon	LW
24. PESUT, George	St.L.	Saskatoon	D
25. ROGERS, John	Min.	Edmonton	RW
26. LEVINS, Brent	Phi.	Swift Current	
27. CAMPBELL, Colin	Det.-Pit.	Peterborough	D
28. LANDRY, Jean	Buf.	Quebec	D
29. THOMAS, Reg	Chi.	London	LW
30. HICKEY, Pat	NYR	Hamilton	LW
31. JONES, Jim	Bos.	Peterborough	RW
32. ANDRUFF, Ron	Mtl.	Flin Flon	C

1972

FIRST ROUND

Selection	Claimed By	Amateur Club	
1. HARRIS, Billy	NYI	Toronto	RW
2. RICHARD, Jacques	Atl.	Quebec	LW
3. LEVER, Don	Van.	Niagara Falls	C
4. SHUTT, Steve	L.A.-Mtl.	Toronto	LW
5. SCHOENFELD, Jim	Buf.	Niagara Falls	D
6. LAROCQUE, Michel	Cal.-Mtl.	Ottawa	G
7. BARBER, Bill	Phi.	Kitchener	LW
8. GARDNER, Dave	Pit.-Min.-Mtl.	Toronto	C
9. MERRICK, Wayne	St.L.	Ottawa	C
10. BLANCHARD, Albert	Det.-NYR	Kitchener	LW
11. FERGUSON, George	Tor.	Toronto	C
12. BYERS, Jerry	Min.	Kitchener	LW
13. RUSSELL, Phil	Chi.	Edmonton	D
14. VAN BOXMEER, John	Mtl.	Guelph	D
15. MacMILLAN, Bobby	NYR	St. Catharines	RW
16. BLOOM, Mike	Bos.	St. Catharines	LW

SECOND ROUND

Selection	Claimed By	Amateur Club	
17. HENNING Lorne	NYI	New Westminster	C
18. BIALOWAS, Dwight	Atl.	Regina	D
19. McSHEFFREY, Brian	Van.	Ottawa	RW
20. KOZAK, Don	L.A.	Edmonton	RW
21. SACHARUK, Larry	Buf.-NYR	Saskatoon	D
22. CASSIDY, Tom	Cal.	Kitchener	C
23. BLADON, Tom	Phi.	Edmonton	D
24. LYNCH, Jack	Pit.	Oshawa	D
25. CARRIERE, Larry	St.L.-Buf.	Loyola College	D
26. GUITE, Pierre	Det.	St. Catharines	LW
27. OSBURN, Randy	Tor.	London	LW
28. WEIR, Stan	Min.-Cal.	Medicine Hat	C
29. OGILVIE, Brian	Chi.	Edmonton	C
30. LUKOWICH, Bernie	Mtl.-Pit.	New Westminster	RW
31. VILLEMURE, Rene	NYR	Shawinigan	LW
32. ELDER, Wayne	Bos.	London	D

1971

FIRST ROUND

Selection	Claimed By	Amateur Club	
1. LAFLEUR, Guy	Cal.-Mtl.	Quebec	RW
2. DIONNE, Marcel	Det.	St. Catharines	C
3. GUEVREMONT, Jocelyn	Van.	Montreal	D
4. CARR, Gene	Pit.-St.L.	Flin Flon	C
5. MARTIN, Rick	Buf.	Montreal	LW
6. JONES, Ron	L.A.-Bos.	Edmonton	D
7. ARNASON, Chuck	Min.-Mtl.	Flin Flon	RW
8. WRIGHT, Larry	Phi.	Regina	C
9. PLANTE, Pierre	Tor.-Phi.	Drummondville	RW
10. VICKERS, Steve	St.L.-NYR	Toronto	LW
11. WILSON, Murray	Mtl.	Ottawa	LW
12. SPRING, Dan	Chi.	Edmonton	C
13. DURBANO, Steve	NYR	Toronto	D
14. O'REILLY, Terry	Bos.	Oshawa	RW

SECOND ROUND

Selection	Claimed By	Amateur Club	
15. BAIRD, Ken	Cal.	Flin Flon	D
16. BOUCHA, Henry	Det.	U.S. Nationals	C
17. LALONDE, Bobby	Van.	Montreal	C
18. McKENZIE, Brian	Pit.	St. Catharines	LW
19. RAMSAY, Craig	Buf.	Peterborough	LW
20. ROBINSON, Larry	L.A.-Mtl.	Kitchener	D
21. NORRISH, Rod	Min.	Regina	LW
22. KEHOE, Rick	Phi.-Tor.	Hamilton	RW
23. FORTIER, Dave	Tor.	St. Catharines	D
24. DEGUISE, Michel	St.L.-Mtl.	Sorel	G
25. FRENCH, Terry	Mtl.	Ottawa	C
26. KRYSKOW, Dave	Chi.	Edmonton	LW
27. WILLIAMS, Tom	NYR	Hamilton	LW
28. RIDLEY, Curt	Bos.	Portage	G

1970

FIRST ROUND

Selection	Claimed By	Amateur Club	
1. PERREAULT, Gilbert	Buf.	Montreal	C
2. TALLON, Dale	Van.	Toronto	D
3. LEACH, Reg	L.A.-Bos.	Flin Flon	LW
4. MacLEISH, Rick	Phi.-Bos.	Peterborough	C
5. MARTINIUK, Ray	Oak.-Mtl.	Flin Flon	G
6. LEFLEY, Chuck	Min.-Mtl.	Canadian Nationals	LW
7. POLIS, Greg	Pit.	Estevan	LW
8. SITTLER, Darryl	Tor.	London	C
9. PLUMB, Ron	Bos.	Peterborough	D
10. ODDLEIFSON, Chris	St.L.-Oak.	Winnipeg	C
11. GRATTON, Norm	Mtl.-NYR	Montreal	LW
12. LAJEUNESSE, Serge	Det.	Montreal	RW
13. STEWART, Bob	Bos.	Oshawa	D
14. MALONEY, Dan	Chi.	London	LW

SECOND ROUND

Selection	Claimed By	Amateur Club	
15. DEADMARSH, Butch	Buf.	Brandon	LW
16. HARGREAVES, Jim	Van.	Winnipeg	D
17. HARVEY, Fred	L.A.-Min.	Hamilton	RW
18. CLEMENT, Bill	Phi.	Ottawa	C
19. LAFRAMBOISE, Pete	Oak.	Ottawa	C
20. BARRETT, Fred	Min.	Toronto	D
21. STEWART, John	Pit.	Flin Flon	LW
22. THOMPSON, Errol	Tor.	Charlottetown	LW
23. KEOGAN, Murray	St.L.	U. of Minnesota	C
24. McDONOUGH, Al	Mtl.-L.A.	St. Catharines	RW
25. MURPHY, Mike	NYR	Toronto	RW
26. GUINDON, Bobby	Det.	Montreal	LW
27. BOUCHARD, Dan	Bos.	London	G
28. ARCHAMBAULT, Mike	Chi.	Drummondville	LW

1969

FIRST ROUND

Selection	Claimed By	Amateur Club	
1. HOULE, Rejean	Mtl.	Montreal	LW
2. TARDIF, Marc	Mtl.	Montreal	LW
3. TANNAHILL, Don	Min.-Bos.	Niagara Falls	LW
4. SPRING, Frank	Pit.-Bos.	Edmonton	RW
5. REDMOND, Dick	L.A.-Mtl.-Min.	St. Catharines	D
6. CURRIER, Bob	Phi.	Cornwall	C
7. FEATHERSTONE, Tony	Oak.	Peterborough	RW
8. DUPONT, André	St.L.-NYR	Montreal	D
9. MOSER, Ernie	Det.-Tor.	Estevan	RW
10. RUTHERFORD, Jim	Det.	Hamilton	G
11. BOLDIREV, Ivan	Bos.	Oshawa	C
12. JARRY, Pierre	NYR	Ottawa	LW
13. BORDELEAU, J.-P.	Chi.	Montreal	RW
14. O'BRIEN, Dennis	Min.	St. Catharines	D

SECOND ROUND

Selection	Claimed By	Amateur Club	
15. KESSELL, Rick	Pit.	Oshawa	C
16. HOGANSON, Dale	L.A.	Estevan	D
17. CLARKE, Bobby	Phi.	Flin Flon	C
18. STACKHOUSE, Ron	Oak.	Peterborough	D
19. LOWE, Mike	St.L.	Loyola College	
20. BRINDLEY, Doug	Tor.	Niagara Falls	C
21. GARWASIUK, Ron	Det.	Regina	LW
22. QUOQUOCHI, Art	Bos.	Montreal	
23. WILSON, Bert	NYR	London	LW
24. ROMANCHYCH, Larry	Chi.	Flin Flon	RW
25. GILBERT, Gilles	Min.	London	G
26. BRIERE, Michel	Pit.	Shawinigan Falls	C
27. BODDY, Greg	L.A.	Edmonton	D
28. BROSSART, Bill	Phi.	Estevan	D

NHL All-Stars

Active Players' All-Star Selection Records

	First Team Selections	Second Team Selections	Total
GOALTENDERS			
Patrick Roy	(3) 1988-89; 1989-90; 1991-92.	(2) 1987-88; 1990-91.	5
Tom Barrasso	(1) 1983-84.	(2) 1984-85; 1992-93.	3
Ed Belfour	(2) 1990-91; 1992-93.	(0)	2
Grant Fuhr	(1) 1987-88.	(1) 1981-82.	2
J.Vanbiesbrouck	(1) 1985-86.	(1) 1993-94.	2
Ron Hextall	(1) 1986-87.	(0)	1
Dominik Hasek	(1) 1993-94.	(0)	1
Mike Vernon	(0)	(1) 1988-89.	1
Daren Puppa	(0)	(1) 1989-90.	1
Kirk McLean	(0)	(1) 1991-92.	1
DEFENSEMEN			
Ray Bourque	(11) 1979-80; 1981-82; 1983-84; 1984-85; 1986-87; 1987-88; 1989-90; 1990-91; 1991-92; 1992-93; 1993-94.	(4) 1980-81; 1982-83; 1985-86; 1988-89.	15
Paul Coffey	(3) 1984-85; 1985-86; 1988-89.	(4) 1981-82; 1982-83; 1983-84; 1989-90.	7
Al MacInnis	(2) 1989-90; 1990-91.	(3) 1986-87; 1988-89; 1993-94.	5
Mark Howe	(3) 1982-83; 1985-86; 1986-87.	(0)	3
Chris Chelios	(2) 1988-89; 1992-93.	(1) 1990-91.	3
Scott Stevens	(2) 1987-88; 1993-94.	(1) 1991-92	3
Brian Leetch	(1) 1991-92.	(2) 1990-91; 1993-94.	3
Larry Murphy	(0)	(2) 1986-87; 1992-93.	2
Gary Suter	(0)	(1) 1987-88.	1
Brad McCrimmon	(0)	(1) 1987-88.	1
Phil Housley	(0)	(1) 1991-92	1
Al Iafrate	(0)	(1) 1992-93	1
CENTERS			
Wayne Gretzky	(8) 1980-81; 1981-82; 1982-83; 1983-84; 1984-85; 1985-86; 1986-87; 1990-91.	(5) 1979-80; 1987-88; 1988-89; 1989-90; 1993-94.	13
Mario Lemieux	(3) 1987-88; 1988-89; 1992-93.	(3) 1985-86; 1986-87; 1991-92.	6
Bryan Trottier	(2) 1977-78; 1978-79.	(2) 1981-82; 1983-84.	4
Mark Messier	(2) 1989-90; 1991-92.	(0)	2
Sergei Fedorov	(1) 1993-94.	(0)	1
Denis Savard	(0)	(1) 1982-83.	1
Dale Hawerchuk	(0)	(1) 1984-85.	1
Adam Oates	(0)	(1) 1990-91.	1
Pat LaFontaine	(0)	(1) 1992-93.	1
RIGHT WINGERS			
Jari Kurri	(2) 1984-85; 1986-87.	(3) 1983-84; 1985-86; 1988-89.	5
Cam Neely	(0)	(4) 1987-88; 1989-90; 1990-91; 1993-94.	4
Brett Hull	(3) 1989-90; 1990-91; 1991-92.	(0)	3
Joe Mullen	(1) 1988-89.	(0)	1
Teemu Selanne	(1) 1992-93.	(0)	1
Pavel Bure	(1) 1993-94.	(0)	1
Mark Recchi	(0)	(1) 1991-92.	1
Alexander Mogilny	(0)	(1) 1992-93.	1
LEFT WINGERS			
Luc Robitaille	(5) 1987-88; 1988-89; 1989-90; 1990-91; 1992-93.	(2) 1986-87; 1991-92.	7
Michel Goulet	(3) 1983-84; 1985-86; 1986-87.	(2) 1982-83; 1987-88.	5
Mark Messier	(2) 1981-82; 1982-83.	(1) 1983-84.	3
Kevin Stevens	(1) 1991-92.	(2) 1990-91; 1992-93.	3
Brendan Shanahan	(1) 1993-94.	(0)	1
Gerard Gallant	(0)	(1) 1988-89.	1
Brian Bellows	(0)	(1) 1989-90.	1
Adam Graves	(0)	(1) 1993-94.	1

Leading NHL All-Stars 1930-94

Player	Pos	Team	NHL Seasons	First Team Selections	Second Team Selections	Total Selections
Howe, Gordie	RW	Detroit	26	12	9	21
* Bourque, Ray	D	Boston	15	11	4	15
Richard, Maurice	RW	Montreal	18	8	6	14
* Gretzky, Wayne	C	Edm., L.A.	15	8	5	13
Hull, Bobby	LW	Chicago	16	10	2	12
Harvey, Doug	D	Mtl., NYR	19	10	1	11
Hall, Glenn	G	Chi., St.L.	18	7	4	11
Beliveau, Jean	C	Montreal	20	6	4	10
Seibert, Earl	D	NYR., Chi	15	4	6	10
Orr, Bobby	D	Boston	12	8	1	9
Lindsay, Ted	LW	Detroit	17	8	1	9
Mahovlich, Frank	LW	Tor., Det., Mtl.	18	3	6	9
Shore, Eddie	D	Boston	14	7	1	8
Mikita, Stan	C	Chicago	22	6	2	8
Kelly, Red	D	Detroit	20	6	2	8
Esposito, Phil	C	Boston	18	6	2	8
Pilote, Pierre	D	Chicago	14	5	3	8
Brimsek, Frank	G	Boston	10	2	6	8
Bossy, Mike	RW	NY Islanders	10	5	3	8
* Robitaille, Luc	LW	Los Angeles	8	5	2	7
Potvin, Denis	D	NY Islanders	15	5	2	7
Park, Brad	D	NYR, Bos.	17	5	2	7
* Coffey, Paul	D	Edm., Pit.	14	3	4	7
Plante, Jacques	G	Mtl-Tor	18	3	4	7
Gadsby, Bill	D	Chi., NYR, Det.	20	3	4	7
Sawchuk, Terry	G	Detroit	21	3	4	7
Durnan, Bill	G	Montreal	7	6	0	6
Lafleur, Guy	RW	Montreal	16	6	0	6
Dryden, Ken	G	Montreal	8	5	1	6
* Lemieux, Mario	C	Pittsburgh	10	3	3	6
Robinson, Larry	D	Montreal	20	3	3	6
Horton, Tim	D	Toronto	24	3	3	6
Salming, Borje	D	Toronto	17	1	5	6
Cowley, Bill	C	Boston	13	4	1	5
* Messier, Mark	LW/C	Edm., NYR	15	4	1	5
Jackson, Harvey	LW	Toronto	15	4	1	5
* Goulet, Michel	LW	Quebec	15	3	2	5
Conacher, Charlie	RW	Toronto	12	3	2	5
Stewart, Jack	D	Detroit	12	3	2	5
Lach, Elmer	C	Montreal	14	3	2	5
Quackenbush, Bill	D	Det., Bos.	14	3	2	5
Blake, Toe	LW	Montreal	15	3	2	5
Esposito, Tony	G	Chicago	16	3	2	5
* Roy, Patrick	G	Montreal	10	2	3	5
Reardon, Ken	D	Montreal	7	2	3	5
* Kurri, Jari	RW	Edmonton	13	2	3	5
Apps, Syl	C	Toronto	10	2	3	5
Giacomin, Ed	G	NY Rangers	13	2	3	5

* Active

Position Leaders in All-Star Selections

Position	Player	First Team	Second Team	Total
GOAL	Glenn Hall	7	4	11
	Frank Brimsek	2	6	8
	Jacques Plante	3	4	7
	Terry Sawchuk	3	4	7
	Bill Durnan	6	0	6
	Ken Dryden	5	1	6
DEFENSE	* Ray Bourque	11	4	15
	Doug Harvey	10	1	11
	Earl Seibert	4	6	10
	Bobby Orr	8	1	9
	Eddie Shore	7	1	8
	Red Kelly	6	2	8
	Pierre Pilote	5	3	8

Position	Player	First Team	Second Team	Total
LEFT WING	Bobby Hull	10	2	12
	Ted Lindsay	8	1	9
	Frank Mahovlich	3	6	9
	* Luc Robitaille	5	2	7
	Harvey Jackson	4	1	5
	* Michel Goulet	3	2	5
	Toe Blake	3	2	5
RIGHT WING	Gordie Howe	12	9	21
	Maurice Richard	8	6	14
	Mike Bossy	5	3	8
	Guy Lafleur	6	0	6
	Charlie Conacher	3	2	5
CENTER	* Wayne Gretzky	8	5	13
	Jean Beliveau	6	4	10
	Stan Mikita	6	2	8
	Phil Esposito	6	2	8
	* Mario Lemieux	3	3	6
	Bill Cowley	4	1	5
	Elmer Lach	3	2	5
	Syl Apps	2	3	5

* active player

All-Star Teams
1930-94

Voting for the NHL All-Star Team is conducted among the representatives of the Professional Hockey Writers' Association at the end of the season.

Following is a list of the First and Second All-Star Teams since their inception in 1930-31.

First Team		Second Team
1993-94		
Hasek, Dominik, Buf.	G	Vanbiesbrouck, John, Fla.
Bourque, Ray, Bos.	D	MacInnis, Al, Cgy.
Stevens, Scott, N.J.	D	Leetch, Brian, NYR
Fedorov, Sergei, Det.	C	Gretzky, Wayne, L.A.
Bure, Pavel, Van.	RW	Neely, Cam, Bos.
Shanahan, Brendan, St. L.	LW	Graves, Adam, NYR
1992-93		
Belfour, Ed, Chi.	G	Barrasso, Tom, Pit.
Chelios, Chris, Chi.	D	Murphy, Larry, Pit.
Bourque, Ray, Bos.	D	Iafrate, Al, Wsh.
Lemieux, Mario, Pit.	C	LaFontaine, Pat, Buf.
Selanne, Teemu, Wpg.	RW	Mogilny, Alexander, Buf.
Robitaille, Luc, L.A.	LW	Stevens, Kevin, Pit.
1991-92		
Roy, Patrick, Mtl.	G	McLean, Kirk, Van.
Leetch, Brian, NYR	D	Housley, Phil, Wpg.
Bourque, Ray, Bos.	D	Stevens, Scott, N.J.
Messier, Mark, NYR	C	Lemieux, Mario, Pit.
Hull, Brett, St. L.	RW	Recchi, Mark, Pit., Phi.
Stevens, Kevin, Pit.	LW	Robitaille, Luc, L.A.
1990-91		
Belfour, Ed, Chi.	G	Roy, Patrick, Mtl.
Bourque, Ray, Bos.	D	Chelios, Chris, Chi.
MacInnis, Al, Cgy.	D	Leetch, Brian, NYR
Gretzky, Wayne, L.A.	C	Oates, Adam, St. L.
Hull, Brett, St. L.	RW	Neely, Cam, Bos.
Robitaille, Luc, L.A.	LW	Stevens, Kevin, Pit.
1989-90		
Roy, Patrick, Mtl.	G	Puppa, Daren, Buf.
Bourque, Ray, Bos.	D	Coffey, Paul, Pit.
MacInnis, Al, Cgy.	D	Wilson, Doug, Chi.
Messier, Mark, Edm.	C	Gretzky, Wayne, L.A.
Hull, Brett, St. L.	RW	Neely, Cam, Bos.
Robitaille, Luc, L.A.	LW	Bellows, Brian, Min.
1988-89		
Roy, Patrick, Mtl.	G	Vernon, Mike, Cgy.
Chelios, Chris, Mtl.	D	MacInnis, Al, Cgy.
Coffey, Paul, Pit.	D	Bourque, Ray, Bos.
Lemieux, Mario, Pit.	C	Gretzky, Wayne, L.A.
Mullen, Joe, Cgy.	RW	Kurri, Jari, Edm.
Robitaille, Luc, L.A.	LW	Gallant, Gerard, Det.
1987-88		
Fuhr, Grant, Edm.	G	Roy, Patrick, Mtl.
Bourque, Ray, Bos.	D	Suter, Gary, Cgy.
Stevens, Scott, Wsh.	D	McCrimmon, Brad, Cgy.
Lemieux, Mario, Pit.	C	Gretzky, Wayne, Edm.
Loob, Hakan, Cgy.	RW	Neely, Cam, Bos.
Robitaille, Luc, L.A.	LW	Goulet, Michel, Que.
1986-87		
Hextall, Ron, Phi.	G	Liut, Mike, Hfd.
Bourque, Ray, Bos.	D	Murphy, Larry, Wsh.
Howe, Mark, Phi.	D	MacInnis, Al, Cgy.
Gretzky, Wayne, Edm.	C	Lemieux, Mario, Pit.
Kurri, Jari, Edm.	RW	Kerr, Tim, Phi.
Goulet, Michel, Que.	LW	Robitaille, Luc, L.A.

First Team		Second Team
1985-86		
Vanbiesbrouck, John, NYR	G	Froese, Bob, Phi.
Coffey, Paul, Edm.	D	Robinson, Larry, Mtl.
Howe, Mark, Phi.	D	Bourque, Ray, Bos.
Gretzky, Wayne, Edm.	C	Lemieux, Mario, Pit.
Bossy, Mike, NYI	RW	Kurri, Jari, Edm.
Goulet, Michel, Que.	LW	Naslund, Mats, Mtl.
1984-85		
Lindbergh, Pelle, Phi.	G	Barrasso, Tom, Buf.
Coffey, Paul, Edm.	D	Langway, Rod, Wsh.
Bourque, Ray, Bos.	D	Wilson, Doug, Chi.
Gretzky, Wayne, Edm.	C	Hawerchuk, Dale, Wpg.
Kurri, Jari, Edm.	RW	Bossy, Mike, NYI
Ogrodnick, John, Det.	LW	Tonelli, John, NYI

First Team		Second Team
1983-84		
Barrasso, Tom, Buf.	G	Riggin, Pat, Wsh.
Langway, Rod, Wsh.	D	Coffey, Paul, Edm.
Bourque, Ray, Bos.	D	Potvin, Denis, NYI
Gretzky, Wayne, Edm.	C	Trottier, Bryan, NYI
Bossy, Mike, NYI	RW	Kurri, Jari, Edm.
Goulet, Michel, Que.	LW	Messier, Mark, Edm.
1982-83		
Peeters, Pete, Bos.	G	Melanson, Roland, NYI
Howe, Mark, Phi.	D	Bourque, Ray, Bos.
Langway, Rod, Wsh.	D	Coffey, Paul, Edm.
Gretzky, Wayne, Edm.	C	Savard, Denis, Chi.
Bossy, Mike, NYI	RW	McDonald, Lanny, Cgy.
Messier, Mark, Edm.	LW	Goulet, Michel, Que.

Buffalo netminder Dominik Hasek earned First All-Star Team honors after allowing just 1.95 goals-against per game in 1993-94. Hasek's mark was the NHL's first sub-2.00 GAA since Bernie Parent managed the feat in 1973-74.

First Team		Second Team	First Team		Second Team	First Team		Second Team

1981-82

Smith, Bill, NYI	G	Fuhr, Grant, Edm.	
Wilson, Doug, Chi.	D	Coffey, Paul, Edm.	
Bourque, Ray, Bos.	D	Engblom, Brian, Mtl.	
Gretzky, Wayne, Edm.	C	Trottier, Bryan, NYI	
Bossy, Mike, NYI	RW	Middleton, Rick, Bos.	
Messier, Mark, Edm.	LW	Tonelli, John, NYI	

1980-81

Liut, Mike, St.L.	G	Lessard, Mario, L.A.
Potvin, Denis, NYI	D	Robinson, Larry, Mtl.
Carlyle, Randy, Pit.	D	Bourque, Ray, Bos.
Gretzky, Wayne, Edm.	C	Dionne, Marcel, L.A.
Bossy, Mike, NYI	RW	Taylor, Dave, L.A.
Simmer, Charlie, L.A.	LW	Barber, Bill, Phi.

1979-80

Esposito, Tony, Chi.	G	Edwards, Don, Buf.
Robinson, Larry, Mtl.	D	Salming, Borje, Tor.
Bourque, Ray, Bos.	D	Schoenfeld, Jim, Buf.
Dionne, Marcel, L.A.	C	Gretzky, Wayne, Edm.
Lafleur, Guy, Mtl.	RW	Gare, Danny, Buf.
Simmer, Charlie, L.A.	LW	Shutt, Steve, Mtl.

1978-79

Dryden, Ken, Mtl.	G	Resch, Glenn, NYI
Potvin, Denis, NYI	D	Salming, Borje, Tor.
Robinson, Larry, Mtl.	D	Savard, Serge, Mtl.
Trottier, Bryan, NYI	C	Dionne, Marcel, L.A.
Lafleur, Guy, Mtl.	RW	Bossy, Mike, NYI
Gillies, Clark, NYI	LW	Barber, Bill, Phi.

1977-78

Dryden, Ken, Mtl.	G	Edwards, Don, Buf.
Potvin, Denis, NYI	D	Robinson, Larry, Mtl.
Park, Brad, Bos.	D	Salming, Borje, Tor.
Trottier, Bryan, NYI	C	Sittler, Darryl, Tor.
Lafleur, Guy, Mtl.	RW	Bossy, Mike, NYI
Gillies, Clark, NYI	LW	Shutt, Steve, Mtl.

1976-77

Dryden, Ken, Mtl.	G	Vachon, Rogatien, L.A.
Robinson, Larry, Mtl.	D	Potvin, Denis, NYI
Salming, Borje, Tor.	D	Lapointe, Guy, Mtl.
Dionne, Marcel, L.A.	C	Perreault, Gilbert, Buf.
Lafleur, Guy, Mtl.	RW	McDonald, Lanny, Tor.
Shutt, Steve, Mtl.	LW	Martin, Richard, Buf.

1975-76

Dryden, Ken, Mtl.	G	Resch, Glenn, NYI
Potvin, Denis, NYI	D	Salming, Borje, Tor.
Park, Brad, Bos.	D	Lapointe, Guy, Mtl.
Clarke, Bobby, Phi.	C	Perreault, Gilbert, Buf.
Lafleur, Guy, Mtl.	RW	Leach, Reggie, Phi.
Barber, Bill, Phi.	LW	Martin, Richard, Buf.

1974-75

Parent, Bernie, Phi.	G	Vachon, Rogie, L.A.
Orr, Bobby, Bos.	D	Lapointe, Guy, Mtl.
Potvin, Denis, NYI	D	Salming, Borje, Tor.
Clarke, Bobby, Phi.	C	Esposito, Phil, Bos.
Lafleur, Guy, Mtl.	RW	Robert, René, Buf.
Martin, Richard, Buf.	LW	Vickers, Steve, NYR

1973-74

Parent, Bernie, Phi.	G	Esposito, Tony, Chi.
Orr, Bobby, Bos.	D	White, Bill, Chi.
Park, Brad, NYR	D	Ashbee, Barry, Phi.
Esposito, Phil, Bos.	C	Clarke, Bobby, Phi.
Hodge, Ken, Bos.	RW	Redmond, Mickey, Det.
Martin, Richard, Buf.	LW	Cashman, Wayne, Bos.

1972-73

Dryden, Ken, Mtl.	G	Esposito, Tony, Chi.
Orr, Bobby, Bos.	D	Park, Brad, NYR
Lapointe, Guy, Mtl.	D	White, Bill, Chi.
Esposito, Phil, Bos.	C	Clarke, Bobby, Phi.
Redmond, Mickey, Det.	RW	Cournoyer, Yvan, Mtl.
Mahovlich, Frank, Mtl.	LW	Hull, Dennis, Chi.

1971-72

Esposito, Tony, Chi.	G	Dryden, Ken, Mtl.
Orr, Bobby, Bos.	D	White, Bill, Chi.
Park, Brad, NYR	D	Stapleton, Pat, Chi.
Esposito, Phil, Bos.	C	Ratelle, Jean, NYR
Gilbert, Rod, NYR	RW	Cournoyer, Yvan, Mtl.
Hull, Bobby, Chi.	LW	Hadfield, Vic, NYR

1970-71

Giacomin, Ed, NYR	G	Plante, Jacques, Tor.
Orr, Bobby, Bos.	D	Park, Brad, NYR
Tremblay, J.C., Mtl.	D	Stapleton, Pat, Chi.
Esposito, Phil, Bos.	C	Keon, Dave, Tor.
Hodge, Ken, Bos.	RW	Cournoyer, Yvan, Mtl.
Bucyk, John, Bos.	LW	Hull, Bobby, Chi.

1969-70

Esposito, Tony, Chi.	G	Giacomin, Ed, NYR
Orr, Bobby, Bos.	D	Brewer, Carl, Det.
Park, Brad, NYR	D	Laperriere, Jacques, Mtl.
Esposito, Phil, Bos.	C	Mikita, Stan, Chi.
Howe, Gordie, Det.	RW	McKenzie, John, Bos.
Hull, Bobby, Chi.	LW	Mahovlich, Frank, Det.

1968-69

Hall, Glenn, St.L.	G	Giacomin, Ed, NYR
Orr, Bobby, Bos.	D	Green, Ted, Bos.
Horton, Tim, Tor.	D	Harris, Ted, Mtl.
Esposito, Phil, Bos.	C	Béliveau, Jean, Mtl.
Howe, Gordie, Det.	RW	Cournoyer, Yvan, Mtl.
Hull, Bobby, Chi.	LW	Mahovlich, Frank, Det.

1967-68

Worsley, Lorne, Mtl.	G	Giacomin, Ed, NYR
Orr, Bobby, Bos.	D	Tremblay, J.C., Mtl.
Horton, Tim, Tor.	D	Neilson, Jim, NYR
Mikita, Stan, Chi.	C	Esposito, Phil, Bos.
Howe, Gordie, Det.	RW	Gilbert, Rod, NYR
Hull, Bobby, Chi.	LW	Bucyk, John, Bos.

1966-67

Giacomin, Ed, NYR	G	Hall, Glenn, Chi.
Pilote, Pierre, Chi.	D	Horton, Tim, Tor.
Howell, Harry, NYR	D	Orr, Bobby, Bos.
Mikita, Stan, Chi.	C	Ullman, Norm, Det.
Wharram, Ken, Chi.	RW	Howe, Gordie, Det.
Hull, Bobby, Chi.	LW	Marshall, Don, NYR

1965-66

Hall, Glenn, Chi.	G	Worsley, Lorne, Mtl.
Laperriere, Jacques, Mtl.	D	Stanley, Allan, Tor.
Pilote, Pierre, Chi.	D	Stapleton, Pat, Chi.
Mikita, Stan, Chi.	C	Béliveau, Jean, Mtl.
Howe, Gordie, Det.	RW	Rousseau, Bobby, Mtl.
Hull, Bobby, Chi.	LW	Mahovlich, Frank, Tor.

1964-65

Crozier, Roger, Det.	G	Hodge, Charlie, Mtl.
Pilote, Pierre, Chi.	D	Gadsby, Bill, Det.
Laperriere, Jacques, Mtl.	D	Brewer, Carl, Tor.
Ullman, Norm, Det.	C	Mikita, Stan, Chi.
Provost, Claude, Mtl.	RW	Howe, Gordie, Det.
Hull, Bobby, Chi.	LW	Mahovlich, Frank, Tor.

1963-64

Hall, Glenn, Chi.	G	Hodge, Charlie, Mtl.
Pilote, Pierre, Chi.	D	Vasko, Elmer, Chi.
Horton, Tim, Tor.	D	Laperriere, Jacques, Mtl.
Mikita, Stan, Chi.	C	Béliveau, Jean, Mtl.
Wharram, Ken, Chi.	RW	Howe, Gordie, Det.
Hull, Bobby, Chi.	LW	Mahovlich, Frank, Tor.

1962-63

Hall, Glenn, Chi.	G	Sawchuk, Terry, Det.
Pilote, Pierre, Chi.	D	Horton, Tim, Tor.
Brewer, Carl, Tor.	D	Vasko, Elmer, Chi.
Mikita, Stan, Chi.	C	Richard, Henri, Mtl.
Howe, Gordie, Det.	RW	Bathgate, Andy, NYR
Mahovlich, Frank, Tor.	LW	Hull, Bobby, Chi.

1961-62

Plante, Jacques, Mtl.	G	Hall, Glenn, Chi.
Harvey, Doug, NYR	D	Brewer, Carl, Tor.
Talbot, Jean-Guy, Mtl.	D	Pilote, Pierre, Chi.
Mikita, Stan, Chi.	C	Keon, Dave, Tor.
Bathgate, Andy, NYR	RW	Howe, Gordie, Det.
Hull, Bobby, Chi.	LW	Mahovlich, Frank, Tor.

1960-61

Bower, Johnny, Tor.	G	Hall, Glenn, Chi.
Harvey, Doug, Mtl.	D	Stanley, Allan, Tor.
Pronovost, Marcel, Det.	D	Pilote, Pierre, Chi.
Béliveau, Jean, Mtl.	C	Richard, Henri, Mtl.
Geoffrion, Bernie, Mtl.	RW	Howe, Gordie, Det.
Mahovlich, Frank, Tor.	LW	Moore, Dickie, Mtl.

1959-60

Hall, Glenn, Chi.	G	Plante, Jacques, Mtl.
Harvey, Doug, Mtl.	D	Stanley, Allan, Tor.
Pronovost, Marcel, Det.	D	Pilote, Pierre, Chi.
Béliveau, Jean, Mtl.	C	Horvath, Bronco, Bos.
Howe, Gordie, Det.	RW	Geoffrion, Bernie, Mtl.
Hull, Bobby, Chi.	LW	Prentice, Dean, NYR

1958-59

Plante, Jacques, Mtl.	G	Sawchuk, Terry, Det.
Johnson, Tom, Mtl.	D	Pronovost, Marcel, Det.
Gadsby, Bill, NYR	D	Harvey, Doug, Mtl.
Béliveau, Jean, Mtl.	C	Richard, Henri, Mtl.
Bathgate, Andy, NYR	RW	Howe, Gordie, Det.
Moore, Dickie, Mtl.	LW	Delvecchio, Alex, Det.

First Team		Second Team

1957-58

First Team	Pos	Second Team
Hall, Glenn, Chi.	G	Plante, Jacques, Mtl.
Harvey, Doug, Mtl.	D	Flaman, Fern, Bos.
Gadsby, Bill, NYR	D	Pronovost, Marcel, Det.
Richard, Henri, Mtl.	C	Béliveau, Jean, Mtl.
Howe, Gordie, Det.	RW	Bathgate, Andy, NYR
Moore, Dickie, Mtl.	LW	Henry, Camille, NYR

1956-57

First Team	Pos	Second Team
Hall, Glenn, Det.	G	Plante, Jacques, Mtl.
Harvey, Doug, Mtl.	D	Flaman, Fern, Bos.
Kelly, Red, Det.	D	Gadsby, Bill, NYR
Béliveau, Jean, Mtl.	C	Litzenberger, Eddie, Chi.
Howe, Gordie, Det.	RW	Richard, Maurice, Mtl.
Lindsay, Ted, Det.	LW	Chevrefils, Real, Bos.

1955-56

First Team	Pos	Second Team
Plante, Jacques, Mtl.	G	Hall, Glenn, Det.
Harvey, Doug, Mtl.	D	Kelly, Red, Det.
Gadsby, Bill, NYR	D	Johnson, Tom, Mtl.
Béliveau, Jean, Mtl.	C	Sloan, Tod, Tor.
Richard, Maurice, Mtl.	RW	Howe, Gordie, Det.
Lindsay, Ted, Det.	LW	Olmstead, Bert, Mtl.

1954-55

First Team	Pos	Second Team
Lumley, Harry, Tor.	G	Sawchuk, Terry, Det.
Harvey, Doug, Mtl.	D	Goldham, Bob, Det.
Kelly, Red, Det.	D	Flaman, Fern, Bos.
Béliveau, Jean, Mtl.	C	Mosdell, Ken, Mtl.
Richard, Maurice, Mtl.	RW	Geoffrion, Bernie, Mtl.
Smith, Sid, Tor.	LW	Lewicki, Danny, NYR

1953-54

First Team	Pos	Second Team
Lumley, Harry, Tor.	G	Sawchuk, Terry, Det.
Kelly, Red, Det.	D	Gadsby, Bill, Chi.
Harvey, Doug, Mtl.	D	Horton, Tim, Tor.
Mosdell, Ken, Mtl.	C	Kennedy, Ted, Tor.
Howe, Gordie, Det.	RW	Richard, Maurice, Mtl.
Lindsay, Ted, Det.	LW	Sandford, Ed, Bos.

1952-53

First Team	Pos	Second Team
Sawchuk, Terry, Det.	G	McNeil, Gerry, Mtl.
Kelly, Red, Det.	D	Quackenbush, Bill, Bos.
Harvey, Doug, Mtl.	D	Gadsby, Bill, Chi.
Mackell, Fleming, Bos.	C	Delvecchio, Alex, Det.
Howe, Gordie, Det.	RW	Richard, Maurice, Mtl.
Lindsay, Ted, Det.	LW	Olmstead, Bert, Mtl.

1951-52

First Team	Pos	Second Team
Sawchuk, Terry, Det.	G	Henry, Jim, Bos.
Kelly, Red, Det.	D	Buller, Hy, NYR
Harvey, Doug, Mtl.	D	Thomson, Jim, Tor.
Lach, Elmer, Mtl.	C	Schmidt, Milt, Bos.
Howe, Gordie, Det.	RW	Richard, Maurice, Mtl.
Lindsay, Ted, Det.	LW	Smith, Sid, Tor.

1950-51

First Team	Pos	Second Team
Sawchuk, Terry, Det.	G	Rayner, Chuck, NYR
Kelly, Red, Det.	D	Thomson, Jim, Tor.
Quackenbush, Bill, Bos.	D	Reise, Leo, Det.
Schmidt, Milt, Bos.	C	Abel, Sid, Det.
	(tied)	Kennedy, Ted, Tor.
Howe, Gordie, Det.	RW	Richard, Maurice, Mtl.
Lindsay, Ted, Det.	LW	Smith, Sid, Tor.

1949-50

First Team	Pos	Second Team
Durnan, Bill, Mtl.	G	Rayner, Chuck, NYR
Mortson, Gus, Tor.	D	Reise, Leo, Det.
Reardon, Kenny, Mtl.	D	Kelly, Red, Det.
Abel, Sid, Det.	C	Kennedy, Ted, Tor.
Richard, Maurice, Mtl.	RW	Howe, Gordie, Det.
Lindsay, Ted, Det.	LW	Leswick, Tony, NYR

1948-49

First Team	Pos	Second Team
Durnan, Bill, Mtl.	G	Rayner, Chuck, NYR
Quackenbush, Bill, Det.	D	Harmon, Glen, Mtl.
Stewart, Jack, Det.	D	Reardon, Kenny, Mtl.
Abel, Sid, Det.	C	Bentley, Doug, Chi.
Richard, Maurice, Mtl.	RW	Howe, Gordie, Det.
Conacher, Roy, Chi.	LW	Lindsay, Ted, Det.

1947-48

First Team	Pos	Second Team
Broda, W. "Turk", Tor.	G	Brimsek, Frank, Bos.
Quackenbush, Bill, Det.	D	Reardon, Kenny, Mtl.
Stewart, Jack, Det.	D	Colville, Neil, NYR
Lach, Elmer, Mtl.	C	O'Connor, "Buddy", NYR
Richard, Maurice, Mtl.	RW	Poile, "Bud", Chi.
Lindsay, Ted, Det.	LW	Stewart, Gaye, Chi.

1946-47

First Team	Pos	Second Team
Durnan, Bill, Mtl.	G	Brimsek, Frank, Bos.
Reardon, Kenny, Mtl.	D	Stewart, Jack, Det.
Bouchard, Emile, Mtl.	D	Quackenbush, Bill, Det.
Schmidt, Milt, Bos.	C	Bentley, Max, Chi.
Richard, Maurice, Mtl.	RW	Bauer, Bobby, Bos.
Bentley, Doug, Chi.	LW	Dumart, Woody, Bos.

1945-46

First Team	Pos	Second Team
Durnan, Bill, Mtl.	G	Brimsek, Frank, Bos.
Crawford, Jack, Bos.	D	Reardon, Kenny, Mtl.
Bouchard, Emile, Mtl.	D	Stewart, Jack, Det.
Bentley, Max, Chi.	C	Lach, Elmer, Mtl.
Richard, Maurice, Mtl.	RW	Mosienko, Bill, Chi.
Stewart, Gaye, Tor.	LW	Blake, "Toe", Mtl.
Irvin, Dick, Mtl.	Coach	Gottselig, John, Chi.

1944-45

First Team	Pos	Second Team
Durnan, Bill, Mtl.	G	Karakas, Mike, Chi.
Bouchard, Emile, Mtl.	D	Harmon, Glen, Mtl.
Hollett, Bill, Det.	D	Pratt, "Babe", Tor.
Lach, Elmer, Mtl.	C	Cowley, Bill, Bos.
Richard, Maurice, Mtl.	RW	Mosienko, Bill, Chi.
Blake, "Toe", Mtl.	LW	Howe, Syd, Det.
Irvin, Dick, Mtl.	Coach	Adams, Jack, Det.

1943-44

First Team	Pos	Second Team
Durnan, Bill, Mtl.	G	Bibeault, Paul, Tor.
Seibert, Earl, Chi.	D	Bouchard, Emile, Mtl.
Pratt, "Babe", Tor.	D	Clapper, "Dit", Bos.
Cowley, Bill, Bos.	C	Lach, Elmer, Mtl.
Carr, Lorne, Tor.	RW	Richard, Maurice, Mtl.
Bentley, Doug, Chi.	LW	Cain, Herb, Bos.
Irvin, Dick, Mtl.	Coach	Day, "Hap", Tor.

1942-43

First Team	Pos	Second Team
Mowers, Johnny, Det.	G	Brimsek, Frank, Bos.
Seibert, Earl, Chi.	D	Crawford, Johnny, Bos.
Stewart, Jack, Det.	D	Hollett, Bill, Bos.
Cowley, Bill, Bos.	C	Apps, Syl, Tor.
Carr, Lorne, Tor.	RW	Hextall, Bryan, NYR
Bentley, Doug, Chi.	LW	Patrick, Lynn, NYR
Adams, Jack, Det.	Coach	Ross, Art, Bos.

1941-42

First Team	Pos	Second Team
Brimsek, Frank, Bos.	G	Broda, W. "Turk", Tor.
Seibert, Earl, Chi.	D	Egan, Pat, Bro.
Anderson, Tommy, Bro.	D	McDonald, Bucko, Tor.
Apps, Syl, Tor.	C	Watson, Phil, NYR
Hextall, Bryan, NYR	RW	Drillon, Gord, Tor.
Patrick, Lynn, NYR	LW	Abel, Sid, Det.
Boucher, Frank, NYR	Coach	Thompson, Paul, Chi.

1940-41

First Team	Pos	Second Team
Broda, W. "Turk", Tor.	G	Brimsek, Frank, Bos.
Clapper, "Dit", Bos.	D	Seibert, Earl, Chi.
Stanowski, Wally, Tor.	D	Heller, Ott, NYR
Cowley, Bill, Bos.	C	Apps, Syl, Tor.
Hextall, Bryan, NYR	RW	Bauer, Bobby, Bos.
Schriner, Dave, Tor.	LW	Dumart, Woody, Bos.
Weiland, "Cooney", Bos.	Coach	Irvin, Dick, Mtl.

1939-40

First Team	Pos	Second Team
Kerr, Dave, NYR	G	Brimsek, Frank, Bos.
Clapper, "Dit", Bos.	D	Coulter, Art, NYR
Goodfellow, Ebbie, Det.	D	Seibert, Earl, Chi.
Schmidt, Milt, Bos.	C	Colville, Neil, NYR
Hextall, Bryan, NYR	RW	Bauer, Bobby, Bos.
Blake, "Toe", Mtl.	LW	Dumart, Woody, Bos.
Thompson, Paul, Chi.	Coach	Boucher, Frank, NYR

1938-39

First Team	Pos	Second Team
Brimsek, Frank, Bos.	G	Robertson, Earl, NYA
Shore, Eddie, Bos.	D	Seibert, Earl, Chi.
Clapper, "Dit", Bos.	D	Coulter, Art, NYR
Apps, Syl, Tor.	C	Colville, Neil, NYR
Drillon, Gord, Tor.	RW	Bauer, Bobby, Bos.
Blake, "Toe", Mtl.	LW	Gottselig, Johnny, Chi.
Ross, Art, Bos.	Coach	Dutton, "Red", NYA

1937-38

First Team	Pos	Second Team
Thompson, "Tiny", Bos.	G	Kerr, Dave, NYR
Shore, Eddie, Bos.	D	Coulter, Art, NYR
Siebert, "Babe", Mtl.	D	Seibert, Eart, Chi.
Cowley, Bill, Bos.	C	Apps, Syl, Tor.
Dillon, Cecil, NYR	RW	Dillon, Cecil, NYR
Drillon, Gord, Tor.	(tied)	Drillon, Gord, Tor.
Thompson, Paul, Chi.	LW	Blake, Toe, Mtl.
Patrick, Lester, NYR	Coach	Ross, Art, Bos.

1936-37

First Team	Pos	Second Team
Smith, Norm, Det.	G	Cude, Wilf, Mtl.
Siebert, "Babe", Mtl.	D	Seibert, Earl, Chi.
Goodfellow, Ebbie, Det.	D	Conacher, Lionel, Mtl. M.
Barry, Marty, Det.	C	Chapman, Art, NYA
Aurie, Larry, Det.	RW	Dillon, Cecil, NYR
Jackson, Harvey, Tor.	LW	Schriner, Dave, NYA
Adams, Jack, Det.	Coach	Hart, Cecil, Mtl.

1935-36

First Team	Pos	Second Team
Thompson, "Tiny", Bos.	G	Cude, Wilf, Mtl.
Shore, Eddie, Bos.	D	Seibert, Earl, Chi.
Siebert, "Babe", Bos.	D	Goodfellow, Ebbie, Det.
Smith, "Hooley", Mtl. M.	C	Thoms, Bill, Tor.
Conacher, Charlie, Tor.	RW	Dillon, Cecil, NYR
Schriner, Dave, NYA	LW	Thompson, Paul, Chi.
Patrick, Lester, NYR	Coach	Gorman, T.P., Mtl. M.

1934-35

First Team	Pos	Second Team
Chabot, Lorne, Chi.	G	Thompson, "Tiny", Bos.
Shore, Eddie, Bos.	D	Wentworth, Cy, Mtl. M.
Seibert, Earl, NYR	D	Coulter, Art, Chi.
Boucher, Frank, NYR	C	Weiland, "Cooney", Det.
Conacher, Charlie, Tor.	RW	Clapper, "Dit", Bos.
Jackson, Harvey, Tor.	LW	Joliat, Aurel, Mtl.
Patrick, Lester, NYR	Coach	Irvin, Dick, Tor.

1933-34

First Team	Pos	Second Team
Gardiner, Charlie, Chi.	G	Worters, Roy, NYA
Clancy, "King", Tor.	D	Shore, Eddie, Bos.
Conacher, Lionel, Chi.	D	Johnson, "Ching", NYR
Boucher, Frank, NYR	C	Primeau, Joe, Tor.
Conacher, Charlie, Tor.	RW	Cook, Bill, NYR
Jackson, Harvey, Tor.	LW	Joliat, Aurel, Mtl.
Patrick, Lester, NYR	Coach	Irvin, Dick, Tor.

1932-33

First Team	Pos	Second Team
Roach, John Ross, Det.	G	Gardiner, Charlie, Chi.
Shore, Eddie, Bos.	D	Clancy, "King", Tor.
Johnson, "Ching", NYR	D	Conacher, Lionel, Mtl. M.
Boucher, Frank, NYR	C	Morenz, Howie, Mtl.
Cook, Bill, NYR	RW	Conacher, Charlie, Tor.
Northcott, "Baldy", Mtl M.	LW	Jackson, Harvey, Tor.
Patrick, Lester, NYR	Coach	Irvin, Dick, Tor.

1931-32

First Team	Pos	Second Team
Gardiner, Charlie, Chi.	G	Worters, Roy, NYA
Shore, Eddie, Bos.	D	Mantha, Sylvio, Mtl.
Johnson, "Ching", NYR	D	Clancy, "King", Tor.
Morenz, Howie, Mtl.	C	Smith, "Hooley", Mtl. M.
Cook, Bill, NYR	RW	Conacher, Charlie, Tor.
Jackson, Harvey, Tor.	LW	Joliat, Aurel, Mtl.
Patrick, Lester, NYR	Coach	Irvin, Dick, Tor.

1930-31

First Team	Pos	Second Team
Gardiner, Charlie, Chi.	G	Thompson, "Tiny", Bos.
Shore, Eddie, Bos.	D	Mantha, Sylvio, Mtl.
Clancy, "King", Tor.	D	Johnson, "Ching", NYR
Morenz, Howie, Mtl.	C	Boucher, Frank, NYR
Cook, Bill, NYR	RW	Clapper, "Dit", Bos.
Joliet, Aurel, Mtl.	LW	Cook, "Bun", NYR
Patrick, Lester, NYR	Coach	Irvin, Dick, Chi.

All-Star Game Results

Year	Venue	Score	Coaches	Attendance
1994	NY Rangers	Eastern 9, Western 8	Jacques Demers, Barry Melrose	18,200
1993	Montreal	Wales 16, Campbell 6	Scotty Bowman, Mike Keenan	17,137
1992	Philadelphia	Campbell 10, Wales 6	Bob Gainey, Scotty Bowman	17,380
1991	Chicago	Campbell 11, Wales 5	John Muckler, Mike Milbury	18,472
1990	Pittsburgh	Wales 12, Campbell 7	Pat Burns, Terry Crisp	16,236
1989	Edmonton	Campbell 9, Wales 5	Glen Sather, Terry O'Reilly	17,503
1988	St. Louis	Wales 6, Campbell 5 OT	Mike Keenan, Glen Sather	17,878
1986	Hartford	Wales 4, Campbell 3 OT	Mike Keenan, Glen Sather	15,100
1985	Calgary	Wales 6, Campbell 4	Al Arbour, Glen Sather	16,825
1984	New Jersey	Wales 7, Campbell 6	Al Arbour, Glen Sather	18,939
1983	NY Islanders	Campbell 9, Wales 3	Roger Neilson, Al Arbour	15,230
1982	Washington	Wales 4, Campbell 2	Al Arbour, Glen Sonmor	18,130
1981	Los Angeles	Campbell 4, Wales 1	Pat Quinn, Scotty Bowman	15,761
1980	Detroit	Wales 6, Campbell 3	Scotty Bowman, Al Arbour	21,002
1978	Buffalo	Wales 3, Campbell 2 OT	Scotty Bowman, Fred Shero	16,433
1977	Vancouver	Wales 4, Campbell 3	Scotty Bowman, Fred Shero	15,607
1976	Philadelphia	Wales 7, Campbell 5	Floyd Smith, Fred Shero	16,436
1975	Montreal	Wales 7, Campbell 1	Bep Guidolin, Fred Shero	16,080
1974	Chicago	West 6, East 4	Billy Reay, Scotty Bowman	16,426
1973	New York	East 5, West 4	Tom Johnson, Billy Reay	16,986
1972	Minnesota	East 3, West 2	Al MacNeil, Billy Reay	15,423
1971	Boston	West 2, East 1	Scotty Bowman, Harry Sinden	14,790
1970	St. Louis	East 4, West 1	Claude Ruel, Scotty Bowman	16,587
1969	Montreal	East 3, West 3	Toe Blake, Scotty Bowman	16,260
1968	Toronto	Toronto 4, All-Stars 3	Punch Imlach, Toe Blake	15,753
1967	Montreal	Montreal 3, All-Stars 0	Toe Blake, Sid Abel	14,284
1965	Montreal	All-Stars 5, Montreal 2	Billy Reay, Toe Blake	13,529
1964	Toronto	All-Stars 3, Toronto 2	Sid Abel, Punch Imlach	14,232
1963	Toronto	All-Stars 3, Toronto 3	Sid Abel, Punch Imlach	14,034
1962	Toronto	Toronto 4, All-Stars 1	Punch Imlach, Rudy Pilous	14,236
1961	Chicago	All-Stars 3, Chicago 1	Sid Abel, Rudy Pilous	14,534
1960	Montreal	All-Stars 2, Montreal 1	Punch Imlach, Toe Blake	13,949
1959	Montreal	Montreal 6, All-Stars 1	Toe Blake, Punch Imlach	13,818
1958	Montreal	Montreal 6, All-Stars 3	Toe Blake, Milt Schmidt	13,989
1957	Montreal	All-Stars 5, Montreal 3	Milt Schmidt, Toe Blake	13,003
1956	Montreal	All-Stars 1, Montreal 1	Jim Skinner, Toe Blake	13,095
1955	Detroit	Detroit 3, All-Stars 1	Jim Skinner, Dick Irvin	10,111
1954	Detroit	All-Stars 2, Detroit 2	King Clancy, Jim Skinner	10,689
1953	Montreal	All-Stars 3, Montreal 1	Lynn Patrick, Dick Irvin	14,153
1952	Detroit	1st team 1, 2nd team 1	Tommy Ivan, Dick Irvin	10,680
1951	Toronto	1st team 2, 2nd team 2	Joe Primeau, Hap Day	11,469
1950	Detroit	Detroit 7, All-Stars 1	Tommy Ivan, Lynn Patrick	9,166
1949	Toronto	All-Stars 3, Toronto 1	Tommy Ivan, Hap Day	13,541
1948	Chicago	All-Stars 3, Toronto 1	Tommy Ivan, Hap Day	12,794
1947	Toronto	All-Stars 4, Toronto 3	Dick Irvin, Hap Day	14,169

There was no All-Star contest during the calendar year of 1966 since the game was moved from the start of season to mid-season. In 1979, the Challenge Cup series between the Soviet Union and Team NHL replaced the All-Star Game. In 1987, Rendez-Vous '87, two games between the Soviet Union and Team NHL replaced the All-Star Game. Rendez-Vous '87 scores: game one, NHL All-Stars 4, Soviet Union 3; game two, Soviet Union 5, NHL All-Stars 3.

1993-94 All-Star Game Summary

January 22, 1994 at New York   Eastern 9, Western 8

PLAYERS ON ICE: **Western Conference** — Potvin, Irbe, Joseph, MacInnis, Blake, Kasatonov, Ozolinsh, Chelios, Coffey, Corson, Bure, Selanne, Andreychuk, Hull, Taylor, Shanahan, Nieuwendyk, Courtnall, Roenick, Fedorov, Gilmour, Gretzky

Eastern Conference — Roy, Richter, Vanbiesbrouck, Leetch, Galley, Stevens, Iafrate, Murphy, Bourque, Mullen, Recchi, Graves, Sanderson, Oates, Turgeon, Sakic, Bradley, Yashin, Kudelski, Messier, Lindros, Mogilny

GOALTENDERS				
	Western:	Potvin	20 minutes	3 goals against
		Irbe	20 minutes	2 goals against
		Joseph	19 minutes	4 goals against
	Eastern:	Roy	20 minutes	4 goals against
		Richter	20 minutes	2 goals against
		Vanbiesbrouck	20 minutes	2 goals against

SUMMARY

First Period

1. Western	Roenick	(Nieuwendyk, Blake)		7:31
2. Eastern	Kudelski	(Turgeon, Bourque)		9:46
3. Western	Fedorov	(Bure, Ozolinsh)		10:20
4. Eastern	Lindros			11:00
5. Western	Shanahan	(Gretzky, Hull)		13:21
6. Eastern	Yashin	(Sakic, Turgeon)		14:29
7. Western	Andreychuk	(MacInnis, Fedorov)		15:10

PENALTIES: None.

Second Period

8. Eastern	Stevens	(Oates, Sanderson)		10:37
9. Western	Coffey	(Andreychuk, Gilmour)		12:36
10. Western	Ozolinsh	(Taylor, Roenick)		14:39
11. Eastern	Messier	(Mullen, Graves)		15:05

PENALTIES: None.

Third Period

12. Western	Ozolinsh	(Bure)		:55
13. Eastern	Mullen	(Graves, Messier)		1:28
14. Western	Shanahan	(Gretzky, Chelios)		7:40
15. Eastern	Sakic	(Turgeon, Stevens)		10:41
16. Eastern	Kudelski	(Messier)		13:59
17. Eastern	Yashin	(Sakic, Turgeon)		16:18

PENALTIES: None.

SHOTS ON GOAL BY:

Western Conference	17	21	8	**46**
Eastern Conference	19	18	19	**56**

Attendance: 18,200

Referee: Bill McCreary   **Linesmen:** Gord Broseker, Pat Dapuzzo

NHL/UPPER DECK ALL-ROOKIE TEAM

Voting for the NHL/Upper Deck All-Rookie Team is conducted among the representatives of the Professional Hockey Writers' Association at the end of the season. The rookie all-star team was first selected for the 1982-83 season.

1993-94

Martin Brodeur, New Jersey	Goal
Chris Pronger, Hartford	Defense
Boris Mironov, Wpg., Edm.	Defense
Jason Arnott, Edmonton	Center
Mikael Renberg, Philadelphia	Right Wing
Oleg Petrov, Montreal	Left Wing

1991-92

Dominik Hasek, Chicago	Goal
Nicklas Lidstrom, Detroit	Defense
Vladimir Konstantinov, Detroit	Defense
Kevin Todd, New Jersey	Center
Tony Amonte, NY Rangers	Right Wing
Gilbert Dionne, Montreal	Left Wing

1989-90

Bob Essensa, Winnipeg	Goal
Brad Shaw, Hartford	Defense
Geoff Smith, Edmonton	Defense
Mike Modano, Minnesota	Center
Sergei Makarov, Calgary	Right Wing
Rod Brind'Amour, St. Louis	Left Wing

1992-93

Felix Potvin, Toronto	Goal
Vladimir Malakhov, NY Islanders	Defense
Scott Niedermayer, New Jersey	Defense
Eric Lindros, Philadelphia	Center
Teemu Selanne, Winnipeg	Right Wing
Joe Juneau, Boston	Left Wing

1990-91

Ed Belfour, Chicago	Goal
Eric Weinrich, New Jersey	Defense
Rob Blake, Los Angeles	Defense
Sergei Fedorov, Detroit	Center
Ken Hodge, Boston	Right Wing
Jaromir Jagr, Pittsburgh	Left Wing

1988-89

Peter Sidorkiewicz, Hartford	Goal
Brian Leetch, NY Rangers	Defense
Zarley Zalapski, Pittsburgh	Defense
Trevor Linden, Vancouver	Center
Tony Granato, NY Rangers	Right Wing
David Volek, NY Islanders	Left Wing

1987-88

Darren Pang, Chicago	Goal
Glen Wesley, Boston	Defense
Calle Johansson, Buffalo	Defense
Joe Nieuwendyk, Calgary	Center
Ray Sheppard, Buffalo	Right Wing
Iain Duncan, Winnipeg	Left Wing

1985-86

Patrick Roy, Montreal	Goal
Gary Suter, Calgary	Defense
Dana Murzyn, Hartford	Defense
Mike Ridley, NY Rangers	Center
Kjell Dahlin, Montreal	Right Wing
Wendel Clark, Toronto	Left Wing

1983-84

Tom Barrasso, Buffalo	Goal
Thomas Eriksson, Philadelphia	Defense
Jamie Macoun, Calgary	Defense
Steve Yzerman, Detroit	Center
Hakan Loob, Calgary	Right Wing
Sylvain Turgeon, Hartford	Left Wing

1986-87

Ron Hextall, Philadelphia	Goal
Steve Duchesne, Los Angeles	Defense
Brian Benning, St. Louis	Defense
Jimmy Carson, Los Angeles	Center
Jim Sandlak, Vancouver	Right Wing
Luc Robitaille, Los Angeles	Left Wing

1984-85

Steve Penney, Montreal	Goal
Chris Chelios, Montreal	Defense
Bruce Bell, Quebec	Defense
Mario Lemieux, Pittsburgh	Center
Tomas Sandstrom, NY Rangers	Right Wing
Warren Young, Pittsburgh	Left Wing

1982-83

Pelle Lindbergh, Philadelphia	Goal
Scott Stevens, Washington	Defense
Phil Housley, Buffalo	Defense
Dan Daoust, Montreal/Toronto	Center
Steve Larmer, Chicago	Right Wing
Mats Naslund, Montreal	Left Wing

All-Star Game Records 1947 through 1994

TEAM RECORDS

MOST GOALS, BOTH TEAMS, ONE GAME:
22 — Wales 16, Campbell 6, 1993 at Montreal
19 — Wales 12, Campbell 7, 1990 at Pittsburgh
17 — East 9, West 8, 1994 at NY Rangers
16 — Campbell 11, Wales 5, 1991 at Chicago
    — Campbell 10, Wales 6, 1992 at Philadelphia
14 — Campbell 9, Wales 5, 1989 at Edmonton
13 — Wales 7, Campbell 6, 1984 at New Jersey
12 — Wales 9, Campbell 3, 1983 at NY Islanders
    — Wales 7, Campbell 5, 1976 at Philadelphia

FEWEST GOALS, BOTH TEAMS, ONE GAME:
 2 — NHL All-Stars 1, Montreal Canadiens 1, 1956 at Montreal
    — First Team All-Stars 1, Second Team All-Stars 1, 1952 at Detroit
 3 — West 2, East 1, 1971 at Boston
    — Montreal Canadiens 3, NHL All-Stars 0, 1967 at Montreal
    — NHL All-Stars 2, Montreal Canadiens 1, 1960 at Montreal

MOST GOALS, ONE TEAM, ONE GAME:
16 — Wales 16, Campbell 6, 1993 at Montreal
12 — Wales 12, Campbell 7, 1990 at Pittsburgh
11 — Campbell 11, Wales 5, 1991 at Chicago
10 — Campbell 10, Wales 6, 1992 at Philadelphia
 9 — Campbell 9, Wales 3, 1983 at NY Islanders
    — Campbell 9, Wales 5, 1989 at Edmonton,
    — East 9, West 8, 1994 at NY Rangers
 8 — West 8, East 9, 1994 at NY Rangers

FEWEST GOALS, ONE TEAM, ONE GAME:
 0 — NHL All-Stars 0, Montreal Canadiens 3, 1967 at Montreal
 1 — 17 times (1981, 1975, 1971, 1970, 1962, 1961, 1960, 1959, both teams 1956, 1955, 1953, both teams 1952, 1950, 1949, 1948)

MOST SHOTS, BOTH TEAMS, ONE GAME (SINCE 1955):
102 — 1994 at NY Rangers — East 9 (56 shots),
    West 8 (46 shots)
90 — 1993 at Montreal — Wales 16 (49 shots),
    Campbell 6 (41 shots)
87 — 1990 at Pittsburgh — Wales 12 (45 shots),
    Campbell 7 (42 shots)
83 — 1992 at Philadelphia — Campbell 10 (42 shots),
    Wales 6 (41 shots)
82 — 1991 at Chicago — Campbell 11 (41 shots),
    Wales 5 (41 shots)

FEWEST SHOTS, BOTH TEAMS, ONE GAME (SINCE 1955):
52 — 1978 at Buffalo — Campbell 2 (12 shots)
    Wales 3 (40 shots)
53 — 1960 at Montreal — NHL All-Stars 2 (27 shots)
    Montreal Canadiens 1 (26 shots)
55 — 1956 at Montreal — NHL All-Stars 1 (28 shots)
    Montreal Canadiens 1 (27 shots)
    — 1971 at Boston — West 2 (28 shots)
    East 1 (27 shots)

MOST SHOTS, ONE TEAM, ONE GAME (SINCE 1955):
56 — 1994 at NY Rangers — East (9-8 vs. West)
49 — 1993 at Montreal — Wales (16-6 vs. Campbell)
46 — 1994 at NY Rangers — East (8-9 vs. West)
45 — 1990 at Pittsburgh — Wales (12-7 vs. Campbell)
44 — 1955 at Detroit — Detroit Red Wings (3-1 vs. NHL All-Stars)
    — 1970 at St. Louis — East (4-1 vs. West)
43 — 1981 at Los Angeles — Campbell (4-1 vs. Wales)

FEWEST SHOTS, ONE TEAM, ONE GAME (SINCE 1955):
12 — 1978 at Buffalo — Campbell (2-3 vs. Wales)
17 — 1970 at St. Louis — West (1-4 vs. East)
23 — 1961 at Chicago — Chicago Black Hawks (1-3 vs. NHL All-Stars)
24 — 1976 at Philadelphia — Campbell (5-7 vs. Wales)

MOST POWER-PLAY GOALS, BOTH TEAMS, ONE GAME (SINCE 1950):
 3 — 1953 at Montreal — NHL All-Stars 3 (2 power-play goals),
    Montreal Canadiens 1 (1 power-play goal)
    — 1954 at Detroit — NHL All-Stars 2 (1 power-play goal)
    Detroit Red Wings 2 (2 power-play goals)
    — 1958 at Montreal — NHL All-Stars 3 (1 power-play goal)
    Montreal Canadiens 6 (2 power-play goals)

FEWEST POWER-PLAY GOALS, BOTH TEAMS, ONE GAME (SINCE 1950):
 0 — 15 times (1952, 1959, 1960, 1967, 1968, 1969, 1972, 1973, 1976, 1980, 1981, 1984, 1985, 1992, 1994)

FASTEST TWO GOALS, BOTH TEAMS, FROM START OF GAME:
37 seconds — 1970 at St. Louis — Jacques Laperriere of East scored at 20 seconds and Dean Prentice of West scored at 37 seconds. Final score: East 4, West 1.
3:37 — 1993 at Montreal — Mike Gartner scored at 3:15 and at 3:37 for Wales. Final score: Wales 16, Campbell 6.
4:08 — 1963 at Toronto — Frank Mahovlich scored for Toronto Maple Leafs at 2:22 of first period and Henri Richard scored at 4:08 for NHL All-Stars. Final score: NHL All-Stars 3, Toronto Maple Leafs 3.

FASTEST TWO GOALS, BOTH TEAMS:
10 seconds — 1976 at Philadelphia — Dennis Ververgaert scored at 4:33 and at 4:43 of third period for Campbell. Final score: Wales 7, Campbell 5.
14 seconds — 1989 at Edmonton. Steve Yzerman and Gary Leeman scored at 17:21 and 17:35 of second period for Campbell. Final score: Campbell 9, Wales 5.
16 seconds — 1990 at Pittsburgh. Kirk Muller of Wales scored at 8:47 of second period and Al MacInnis of Campbell scored at 9:03. Final score: Wales 12, Campbell 7.

FASTEST THREE GOALS, BOTH TEAMS:
1:08 — 1993 at Montreal — all by Wales — Mike Gartner scored at 3:15 and at 3:37 of first period; Peter Bondra scored at 4:23. Final score: Wales 16, Campbell 6.
1:14 — 1994 at NY Rangers — Bob Kudelski scored at 9:46 of first period for East; Sergei Fedorov scored at 10:20 for West; Eric Lindros scored at 11:00 for East. Final score: East 9, West 8.
1:25 — 1992 at Philadelphia — Bryan Trottier scored at 4:03 of third period for Wales; Brian Bellows scored at 4:50 for Campbell; Alexander Mogilny scored at 5:28 for Wales. Final score: Campbell 10, Wales 6.

FASTEST FOUR GOALS, BOTH TEAMS:
3:29 — 1994 at NY Rangers — Jeremy Roenick scored at 7:31 of first period for West; Bob Kudelski scored at 9:46 for East; Sergei Fedorov scored at 10:20 for West; Eric Lindros scored at 11:00 for East. Final score: East 9, West 8.
3:35 — 1994 at NY Rangers — Bob Kudelski scored at 9:46 of first period for East; Sergei Fedorov scored at 10:20 for West; Eric Lindros scored at 11:00 for East; Brendan Shanahan scored at 13:21 for West. Final score: East 9, West 8.
3:40 — 1993 at Montreal — Pierre Turgeon scored at 15:51 of third period for Wales; Teemu Selanne scored at 17:03 for Campbell; Pavel Bure scored at 18:44 and 19:31 for Campbell. Final score: Wales 16, Campbell 6.

FASTEST TWO GOALS, ONE TEAM, FROM START OF GAME:
3:37 — 1993 at Montreal — Wales — Mike Gartner scored at 3:15 and at 3:37. Final socre: Wales 16, Campbell 6.
4:19 — 1980 at Detroit — Wales — Larry Robinson scored at 3:58 and Steve Payne scored at 4:19. Final score: Wales 6, Campbell 3.
4:33 — 1989 at Edmonton — Campbell — Jari Kurri scored at 1:07 and Wayne Gretzky scored at 4:33. Final score: Campbell 9, Wales 5.

FASTEST TWO GOALS, ONE TEAM:
10 seconds — 1976 at Philadelphia — Campbell — Dennis Ververgaert scored at 4:33 and at 4:43 of third period. Final score: Wales 7, Campbell 5.
14 seconds — 1989 at Edmonton — Campbell — Steve Yzerman and Gary Leeman scored at 17:21 and 17:35 of second period. Final score: Campbell 9, Wales 5.
17 seconds — 1993 at Montreal — Wales — Pierre Turgeon scored at 13:05 of first period and Mike Gartner scored at 13:22. Final score: Wales 16, Campbell 6.

FASTEST THREE GOALS, ONE TEAM:
1:08 — 1993 at Montreal — Wales — Mike Gartner scored at 3:15 and 3:37 of first period; Peter Bondra scored at 4:23. Final socre: Wales 16, Campbell 6.
1:32 — 1980 at Detroit — Wales — Ron Stackhouse scored at 11:40 of third period; Craig Hartsburg scored at 12:40; Reed Larson scored at 13:12. Final score: Wales 6, Campbell 3.
1:42 — 1993 at Montreal — Wales — Alexander Mogilny scored at 11:40 of first period; Pierre Turgeon scored at 13:05; Mike Gartner scored at 13:22. Final score: Wales 16, Campbell 6.

FASTEST FOUR GOALS, ONE TEAM:
4:19 — 1992 at Philadelphia — Campbell — Brian Bellows scored at 7:40 of second period, Jeremy Roenick scored at 8:13, Theoren Fleury scored at 11:06, Brett Hull scored at 11:59. Final score: Campbell 10, Wales 6.
4:26 — 1980 at Detroit — Wales — Ron Stackhouse scored at 11:40 of third period; Craig Hartsburg scored at 12:40; Reed Larson scored at 13:12; Real Cloutier scored at 16:06. Final score: Wales 6, Campbell 3.
5:34 — 1993 at Montreal — Campbell — Doug Gilmour scored at 13:57 of third period; Teemu Selanne scored at 17:03; Pavel Bure scored at 18:44 and 19:31. Final score: Wales 16, Campbell 6.

MOST GOALS, BOTH TEAMS, ONE PERIOD:
9 — 1990 at Pittsburgh — First Period — Wales (7), Campbell (2). Final score: Wales 12, Campbell 7.
8 — 1992 at Philadelphia — Second period — Campbell (6), Wales (2). Final score: Campbell 10, Wales 6.
    — 1993 at Montreal — Second period — Wales (6), Campbell (2). Final score: Wales 16, Campbell 6.
    — 1993 at Montreal — Third period — Wales (4), Campbell (4). Final score: Wales 16, Campbell 6.

MOST GOALS, ONE TEAM, ONE PERIOD:
7 — 1990 at Pittsburgh — First period — Wales. Final score: Wales 12, Campbell 7.
6 — 1983 at NY Islanders — Third period — Campbell.
Final score: Campbell 9, Wales 3.
— 1992 at Philadelphia — Second period — Campbell.
Final score: Campbell 10, Wales 6.
— 1993 at Montreal — First period — Wales.
Final score: Wales 16, Campbell 6.
— 1993 at Montreal — Second period — Wales.
Final score: Wales 16, Campbell 6.

MOST SHOTS, BOTH TEAMS, ONE PERIOD:
39 — 1994 at NY Rangers — Second period — West (21), East (18). Final score: East 9, West 8.
36 — 1990 at Pittsburgh — Third period — Campbell (22), Wales (14). Final score: Wales 12, Campbell 7.
— 1994 at NY Rangers — First period — East (19), West (17).
Final score: East 9, West 8.

MOST SHOTS, ONE TEAM, ONE PERIOD:
22 — 1990 at Pittsburgh — Third period — Campbell.
Final score: Wales 12, Campbell 7.
— 1991 at Chicago — Third Period — Wales.
Final score: Campbell 11, Wales 5.
— 1993 at Montreal — First period — Wales.
Final score: Wales 16, Campbell 6.
20 — 1970 at St. Louis — Third period — East. Final score: East 4, West 1.

FEWEST SHOTS, BOTH TEAMS, ONE PERIOD:
9 — 1971 at Boston — Third period — East (2), West (7). Final score: West 2, East 1.
— 1980 at Detroit — Second period — Campbell (4), Wales (5).
Final score: Wales 6, Campbell 3.
13 — 1982 at Washington — Third period — Campbell (6), Wales (7).
Final score: Wales 4, Campbell 2.
14 — 1978 at Buffalo — First period — Campbell (7), Wales (7).
Final score: Wales 3, Campbell 2.
— 1986 at Hartford — First period — Campbell (6), Wales (8).
Final score: Wales 4, Campbell 3.

FEWEST SHOTS, ONE TEAM, ONE PERIOD:
2 — 1971 at Boston   Third period   East
Final score: West 2, East 1
— 1978 at Buffalo   Second period   Campbell
Final score: Wales 3, Campbell 2.
3 — 1978 at Buffalo   Third period   Campbell
Final score: Wales 3, Campbell 2.
4 — 1955 at Detroit   First period   NHL All-Stars
Final score: Detroit Red Wings 3, NHL All-Stars 1
4 — 1980 at Detroit   Second period   Campbell
Final score: Wales 6, Campbell 3

Pierre Larouche (#28) slips the puck past Campbell Conference goaltender Murray Bannerman at the 17:14 mark of the first period to give the Wales Conference a commanding 5-0 lead in the 1984 All-Star Game. The Wales All-Stars held on to edge the Campbell Conference 7-6.

INDIVIDUAL RECORDS

Career

MOST GAMES PLAYED:
23 — **Gordie Howe** from 1948 through 1980
15 — Frank Mahovlich from 1959 through 1974
14 — Wayne Gretzky from 1980 through 1994
13 — Jean Beliveau from 1953 through 1969
— Alex Delvecchio from 1953 through 1967
— Doug Harvey from 1951 through 1969
— Maurice Richard from 1947 through 1959
— Ray Bourque from 1981 through 1994

MOST GOALS:
12 — **Wayne Gretzky** in 14GP
10 — Gordie Howe in 23GP
9 — Mario Lemieux in 6GP
8 — Frank Mahovlich in 15GP
7 — Maurice Richard in 13GP
6 — Mike Gartner in 6GP

MOST ASSISTS:
11 — **Ray Bourque** in 13GP
10 — Adam Oates in 4GP
— Joe Sakic in 5GP
9 — Gordie Howe in 23GP
— Larry Robinson in 10GP
7 — Doug Harvey in 13GP
— Guy Lafleur in 6GP
— Paul Coffey in 12GP
— Wayne Gretzky in 14GP

MOST POINTS:
19 — **Gordie Howe** (10G-9A in 23GP)
— Wayne Gretzky (12G-7A in 14GP)
15 — Mario Lemieux (9G-6A in 6GP)
13 — Frank Mahovlich (8G-5A in 15GP)
— Ray Bourque (2G-11A in 13GP)
11 — Adam Oates (1G-10A in 4GP)
10 — Bobby Hull (5G-5A in 12GP)
— Ted Lindsay (5G-5A in 11GP)
— Luc Robitaille (5G-5A in 6GP)
— Larry Robinson (1G-9A in 10GP)

MOST PENALTY MINUTES:
27 — **Gordie Howe** in 23GP
21 — Gus Mortson in 9GP
16 — Harry Howell in 7GP

MOST POWER-PLAY GOALS:
6 — **Gordie Howe** in 23GP
3 — Bobby Hull in 12GP
2 — Maurice Richard in 13GP

Game

MOST GOALS, ONE GAME:
4 — **Wayne Gretzky**, Campbell, 1983
— **Mario Lemieux**, Wales, 1990
— **Vince Damphousse**, Campbell, 1991
— **Mike Gartner**, Wales, 1993
3 — Ted Lindsay, Detroit Red Wings, 1950
— Mario Lemieux, Wales, 1988
— Pierre Turgeon, Wales, 1993
2 — Wally Hergesheimer, NHL All-Stars, 1953
— Earl Reibel, Detroit Red Wings, 1955
— Andy Bathgate, NHL All-Stars, 1958
— Maurice Richard, Montreal Canadiens, 1958
— Frank Mahovlich, Toronto Maple Leafs, 1963
— Gordie Howe, NHL All-Stars, 1965
— John Ferguson, Montreal Canadiens, 1967
— Frank Mahovlich, East All-Stars, 1969
— Greg Polis, West All-Stars, 1973
— Syl Apps, Wales, 1975
— Dennis Ververgaert, Campbell, 1976
— Richard Martin, Wales, 1977
— Lanny McDonald, Wales, 1977
— Mike Bossy, Wales, 1982
— Pierre Larouche, Wales, 1984
— Mario Lemieux, Wales 1985
— Brian Propp, Wales, 1986
— Luc Robitaille, Campbell, 1988
— Joe Mullen, Campbell, 1989
— Pierre Turgeon, Wales, 1990
— Kirk Muller, Wales, 1990
— Luc Robitaille, Campbell, 1990
— Pat LaFontaine, Wales, 1991
— Brett Hull, Campbell, 1992
— Theoren Fleury, Campbell, 1992
— Rick Tocchet, Wales, 1993
— Pavel Bure, Campbell, 1993
— Sandis Ozolinsh, West All-Stars, 1994
— Brendan Shanahan, West All-Stars, 1994
— Bob Kudelski, East All-Stars, 1994
— Alexei Yashin, East All-Stars, 1994

MOST ASSISTS, ONE GAME:
5 — Mats Naslund, Wales, 1988
4 — Ray Bourque, Wales, 1985
— Adam Oates, Campbell, 1991
— Adam Oates, Wales, 1993
— Mark Recchi, Wales, 1993
3 — Dickie Moore, Montreal Canadiens, 1958
— Doug Harvey, Montreal Canadiens, 1959
— Guy Lafleur, Wales, 1975
— Pete Mahovlich, Wales, 1976
— Mark Messier, Campbell, 1983
— Rick Vaive, Campbell, 1984
— Mark Johnson, Wales, 1984
— Don Maloney, Wales, 1984
— Mike Krushelnyski, Campbell, 1985
— Mario Lemieux, Wales, 1988
— Brett Hull, Campbell, 1990
— Luc Robitaille, Campbell, 1992
— Joe Sakic, Wales, 1993
— Pierre Turgeon, East All-Stars, 1994

MOST POINTS, ONE GAME:
6 — Mario Lemieux, Wales, 1988 (3G-3A)
5 — Mats Naslund, Wales, 1988 (5A)
— Adam Oates, Campbell, 1991 (1G-4A)
— Mike Gartner, Wales, 1993 (4G-1A)
— Mark Recchi, Wales, 1993 (1G-4A)
— Pierre Turgeon, Wales, 1993 (3G-2A)

MOST GOALS, ONE PERIOD:
4 — Wayne Gretzky, Campbell, Third period, 1983
3 — Mario Lemieux, Wales, First period, 1990
— Vince Damphousse, Campbell, Third period, 1991
— Mike Gartner, Wales, First period, 1993
2 — Ted Lindsay, Detroit Red Wings, First period, 1950
— Wally Hergesheimer, NHL All-Stars, First period, 1953
— Andy Bathgate, NHL All-Stars, Third period, 1958
— Frank Mahovlich, Toronto Maple Leafs, First period, 1963
— Dennis Ververgaert, Campbell, Third period, 1976
— Richard Martin, Wales, Third period, 1977
— Pierre Turgeon, Wales, First period, 1990
— Luc Robitaille, Campbell, Third period, 1990
— Theoren Fleury, Campbell, Second period, 1992
— Brett Hull, Campbell, Second period, 1992
— Rick Tocchet, Wales, Second period, 1993
— Pavel Bure, Campbell, Third period, 1993

MOST ASSISTS, ONE PERIOD:
4 — Adam Oates, Wales, First period, 1993
3 — Mark Messier, Campbell, Third period, 1983

MOST POINTS, ONE PERIOD:
4 — Wayne Gretzky, Campbell, Third period, 1983 (4G)
— Mike Gartner, Wales, First period, 1993 (3G-1A)
— Adam Oates, Wales, First period, 1993 (4A)
3 — Gordie Howe, NHL All-Stars, Second period, 1965 (1G-2A)
— Pete Mahovlich, Wales, First period, 1976 (1G-2A)
— Mark Messier, Campbell, Third period, 1983 (3A)
— Mario Lemieux, Wales, Second period, 1988 (1G-2A)
— Mario Lemieux, Wales, First period, 1990 (3G)
— Vince Damphousse, Campbell, Third period, 1991 (3G)
— Mark Recchi, Wales, Second period, 1993 (1G-2A)

FASTEST GOAL FROM START OF GAME:
19 seconds — Ted Lindsay, Detroit Red Wings, 1950
20 seconds — Jacques Laperriere, East All-Stars, 1970
21 seconds — Mario Lemieux, Wales, 1990
36 seconds — Chico Maki, West All-Stars, 1971
37 seconds — Dean Prentice, West All-Star, 1970

FASTEST GOAL FROM START OF A PERIOD:
19 seconds — Ted Lindsay, Detroit Red Wings, 1950 (first period)
— **Rick Tocchet**, Wales, 1993 (second period)
20 seconds — Jacques Laperriere, East, 1970 (first period)
21 seconds — Mario Lemieux, Wales, 1990 (first period)
26 seconds — Wayne Gretzky, Campbell, 1982 (second period)
28 seconds — Maurice Richard, NHL All-Stars, 1947 (third period)

FASTEST TWO GOALS (ONE PLAYER) FROM START OF GAME:
3:37 — Mike Gartner, Wales, 1993, at 3:15 and 3:37.
5:25 — Wally Hergesheimer, NHL All-Stars, 1953, at 4:06 and 5:25.
12:11 — Frank Mahovlich, Toronto, 1963, at 2:22 and 12:11.

FASTEST TWO GOALS (ONE PLAYER) FROM START OF A PERIOD:
3:37 — Mike Gartner, Wales, 1993, at 3:15 and 3:37 of first period.
4:43 — Dennis Ververgaert, Campbell, 1976, at 4:33 and 4:43 of third period.
4:57 — Rick Tocchet, Wales, 1993, at :19 and 4:57 of second period.

FASTEST TWO GOALS (ONE PLAYER):
10 seconds — Dennis Ververgaert, Campbell, 1976. Scored at 4:33 and 4:43 of third period.
22 seconds — Mike Gartner, Wales, 1993. Scored at 3:15 and 3:37 of first period.
47 seconds — Pavel Bure, Campbell, 1993. Scored at 18:44 and 19:31 of third period.

Goaltenders

MOST GAMES PLAYED:
13 — Glenn Hall from 1955-1969
11 — Terry Sawchuk from 1950-1968
8 — Jacques Plante from 1956-1970
6 — Tony Esposito from 1970-1980
— Ed Giacomin from 1967-1973
— Grant Fuhr from 1982-1989

MOST GOALS AGAINST:
22 — Glenn Hall in 13GP
21 — Mike Vernon in 5GP
19 — Terry Sawchuk in 11GP
18 — Jacques Plante in 8GP

**BEST GOALS-AGAINST-AVERAGE AMONG THOSE
WITH AT LEAST TWO GAMES PLAYED:**
0.68 — Gilles Villemure in 3GP
1.02 — Frank Brimsek in 2GP
1.59 — Johnny Bower in 4GP
1.64 — Lorne "Gump" Worsley in 4GP
1.98 — Gerry McNeil in 3GP
2.03 — Don Edwards in 2GP
2.44 — Terry Sawchuk in 11GP

MOST MINUTES PLAYED:
467 — Terry Sawchuk in 11GP
421 — Glenn Hall in 13GP
370 — Jacques Plante in 8GP
209 — Turk Broda in 4GP
182 — Ed Giacomin in 6GP
177 — Grant Fuhr in 6GP
165 — Tony Esposito in 6GP

Larry Robinson rides Clark Gillies into the boards during the 1978 All-Star Game, played before 16,433 fans in Buffalo. Hometown hero Gilbert Perreault scored at 3:55 of overtime to give the Wales Conference a 3-2 victory in the first NHL All-Star game to be decided in overtime.

Hockey Hall of Fame

Location: BCE Place, at the corner of Front and Yonge Streets in the heart of downtown Toronto. Easy access from all major highways running into Toronto. Close to TTC and Union Station.

Telephone: administration (416) 360-7735; information (416) 360-7765.

Spring/Summer Hours: Monday, Tuesday, Wednesday 9 a.m. to 6 p.m.; Thursday, Friday 9 a.m. to 9:30 p.m.; Saturday 9 a.m. to 6 p.m.; Sunday 10 a.m. to 6 p.m.

Fall/Winter Hours: Monday to Saturday 9 a.m. to 6 p.m.; Sunday 10 a.m. to 6 p.m. Closed Christmas and New Year's Day.

The Hockey Hall of Fame can be booked for private functions after hours

History: The Hockey Hall of Fame was established in 1943. Members were first honored in 1945. On August 26, 1961, the Hockey Hall of Fame opened its doors to the public in a building located on the grounds of the Canadian National Exhibition in Toronto. The Hockey Hall of Fame relocated to its new site at BCE place and welcomed the hockey world on June 18, 1993.

Honor Roll: There are 296 Honored Members in the Hockey Hall of Fame. 203 have been inducted as players, 80 as builders and 13 as Referees/Linesmen. In addition, there are 52 media honorees. Additional Honored Members will be inducted on November 15, 1994.

(Year of induction to the Hockey Hall of Fame is indicated in brackets after each Member's name.)

Founding Sponsors: Special thanks to Blockbuster Video, Bell Canada, Coca-Cola Canada, Household Finance, Ford of Canada, Imperial Oil, Molson Breweries, London Life, TSN/RDS and The Toronto Sun.

PLAYERS

Abel, Sidney Gerald (1969)
*Adams, John James "Jack" (1959)
Apps, Charles Joseph Sylvanus "Syl" (1961)
Armstrong, George Edward (1975)
*Bailey, Irvine Wallace "Ace" (1975)
*Bain, Donald H. "Dan" (1945)
*Baker, Hobart "Hobey" (1945)
Barber, William Charles "Bill" (1990)
*Barry, Martin J. "Marty" (1965)
Bathgate, Andrew James "Andy" (1978)
Beliveau, Jean Arthur (1972)
*Benedict, Clinton S. (1965)
*Bentley, Douglas Wagner (1964)
*Bentley, Maxwell H. L. (1966)
Blake, Hector "Toe" (1966)
Boivin, Leo Joseph (1986)
*Boon, Richard R. "Dickie" (1952)
Bossy, Michael (1991)
Bouchard, Emile Joseph "Butch" (1966)
*Boucher, Frank (1958)
*Boucher, George "Buck" (1960)
Bower, John William (1976)
*Bowie, Russell (1945)
Brimsek, Francis Charles (1966)
*Broadbent, Harry L. "Punch" (1962)
*Broda, Walter Edward "Turk" (1967)
Bucyk, John Paul (1981)
*Burch, Billy (1974)
*Cameron, Harold Hugh "Harry" (1962)
Cheevers, Gerald Michael "Gerry" (1985)
*Clancy, Francis Michael "King" (1958)
*Clapper, Aubrey "Dit" (1947)
Clarke, Robert "Bobby" (1987)
*Cleghorn, Sprague (1958)
*Colville, Neil MacNeil (1967)
*Conacher, Charles W. (1961)
*Connell, Alex (1958)
*Cook, William Osser (1952)
Coulter, Arthur Edmund (1974)
Cournoyer, Yvan Serge (1982)
*Cowley, William Mailes (1968)
*Crawford, Samuel Russell "Rusty" (1962)
*Darragh, John Proctor "Jack" (1962)
*Davidson, Allan M. "Scotty" (1950)
*Day, Clarence Henry "Hap" (1961)
Delvecchio, Alex (1977)
*Denneny, Cyril "Cy" (1959)
Dionne, Marcel (1992)
*Drillon, Gordon Arthur (1975)
*Drinkwater, Charles Graham (1950)
Dryden, Kenneth Wayne (1983)
Dumart, Woodrow "Woody" (1992)

*Dunderdale, Thomas (1974)
*Durnan, William Ronald (1964)
*Dutton, Mervyn A. "Red" (1958)
*Dye, Cecil Henry "Babe" (1970)
Esposito, Anthony James "Tony" (1988)
Esposito, Philip Anthony (1984)
*Farrell, Arthur F. (1965)
Flaman, Ferdinand Charles "Fern" (1990)
*Foyston, Frank (1958)
*Frederickson, Frank (1958)
Gadsby, William Alexander (1970)
Gainey, Bob (1992)
*Gardiner, Charles Robert "Chuck" (1945)
*Gardiner, Herbert Martin "Herb" (1958)
*Gardner, James Henry "Jimmy" (1962)
Geoffrion, Jos. A. Bernard "Boom Boom" (1972)
*Gerard, Eddie (1945)
Giacomin, Edward "Eddie" (1987)
Gilbert, Rodrigue Gabriel "Rod" (1982)
*Gilmour, Hamilton Livingstone "Billy" (1962)
*Goheen, Frank Xavier "Moose" (1952)
*Goodfellow, Ebenezer R. "Ebbie" (1963)
*Grant, Michael "Mike" (1950)
*Green, Wilfred "Shorty" (1962)
*Griffis, Silas Seth "Si" (1950)
*Hainsworth, George (1961)
Hall, Glenn Henry (1975)
*Hall, Joseph Henry (1961)
Harvey, Douglas Norman (1973)
*Hay, George (1958)
*Hern, William Milton "Riley" (1962)
*Hextall, Bryan Aldwyn (1969)
*Holmes, Harry "Hap" (1972)
*Hooper, Charles Thomas "Tom" (1962)
Horner, George Reginald "Red" (1965)
*Horton, Miles Gilbert "Tim" (1977)
Howe, Gordon (1972)
*Howe, Sydney Harris (1965)
Howell, Henry Vernon "Harry" (1979)
Hull, Robert Marvin (1983)
*Hutton, John Bower "Bouse" (1962)
*Hyland, Harry M. (1962)
*Irvin, James Dickenson "Dick" (1958)
*Johnson, Ernest "Moose" (1952)
*Johnson, Ivan "Ching" (1958)
Johnson, Thomas Christian (1970)
*Joliat, Aurel (1947)
*Keats, Gordon "Duke" (1958)
Kelly, Leonard Patrick "Red" (1969)
Kennedy, Theodore Samuel "Teeder" (1966)

Keon, David Michael (1986)
Lach, Elmer James (1966)
Lafleur, Guy Damien (1988)
*Lalonde, Edouard Charles "Newsy" (1950)
Laperriere, Jacques (1987)
Lapointe, Guy (1993)
Laprade, Edgar (1993)
*Laviolette, Jean Baptiste "Jack" (1962)
*Lehman, Hugh (1958)
Lemaire, Jacques Gerard (1984)
*LeSueur, Percy (1961)
*Lewis, Herbert A. (1989)
Lindsay, Robert Blake Theodore "Ted" (1966)
Lumley, Harry (1980)
*MacKay, Duncan "Mickey" (1952)
Mahovlich, Frank William (1981)
*Malone, Joseph "Joe" (1950)
*Mantha, Sylvio (1960)
*Marshall, John "Jack" (1965)
*Maxwell, Fred G. "Steamer" (1962)
McDonald, Lanny (1992)
*McGee, Frank (1945)
*McGimsie, William George "Billy" (1962)
*McNamara, George (1958)
Mikita, Stanley (1983)
Moore, Richard Winston (1974)
*Moran, Patrick Joseph "Paddy" (1958)
*Morenz, Howie (1945)
*Mosienko, William "Billy" (1965)
*Nighbor, Frank (1947)
*Noble, Edward Reginald "Reg" (1962)
*O'Connor, Herbert William "Buddy" (1988)
*Oliver, Harry (1967)
Olmstead, Murray Bert "Bert" (1985)
Orr, Robert Gordon (1979)
Parent, Bernard Marcel (1984)
Park, Douglas Bradford "Brad" (1988)
*Patrick, Joseph Lynn (1980)
*Patrick, Lester (1947)
Perreault, Gilbert (1990)
*Phillips, Tommy (1945)
Pilote, Joseph Albert Pierre Paul (1975)
*Pitre, Didier "Pit" (1962)
*Plante, Joseph Jacques Omer (1978)
Potvin, Denis (1991)
*Pratt, Walter "Babe" (1966)
*Primeau, A. Joseph (1963)
Pronovost, Joseph René Marcel (1978)
Pulford, Bob (1991)
*Pulford, Harvey (1945)
Quackenbush, Hubert George "Bill" (1976)

BUILDERS

*Adams, Charles Francis (1960)
*Adams, Weston W. (1972)
*Ahearn, Thomas Franklin "Frank" (1962)
*Ahearne, John Francis "Bunny" (1977)
*Allan, Sir Montagu (C.V.O.) (1945)
Allen, Keith (1992)
*Ballard, Harold Edwin (1977)
*Bauer, Father David (1989)
*Bickell, John Paris (1978)
Bowman, Scott (1991)
*Brown, George V. (1961)
*Brown, Walter A. (1962)
*Buckland, Frank (1975)
Butterfield, Jack Arlington (1980)
*Calder, Frank (1947)
*Campbell, Angus D. (1964)
*Campbell, Clarence Sutherland (1966)
*Cattarinich, Joseph (1977)
*Dandurand, Joseph Viateur "Leo" (1963)
Dilio, Francis Paul (1964)
*Dudley, George S. (1958)
*Dunn, James A. (1968)
Eagleson, Robert Alan (1989)
Francis, Emile (1982)
*Gibson, Dr. John L. "Jack" (1976)
*Gorman, Thomas Patrick "Tommy" (1963)
*Griffiths, Frank A. (1993)
*Hanley, William (1986)
*Hay, Charles (1974)
*Hendy, James C. (1968)
*Hewitt, Foster (1965)
*Hewitt, William Abraham (1947)
*Hume, Fred J. (1962)
*Imlach, George "Punch" (1984)
Ivan, Thomas N. (1974)
*Jennings, William M. (1975)
*Johnson, Bob (1992)
Juckes, Gordon W. (1979)
*Kilpatrick, Gen. John Reed (1960)
Knox, Seymour H. III (1993)
*Leader, George Alfred (1969)
LeBel, Robert (1970)
*Lockhart, Thomas F. (1965)
*Loicq, Paul (1961)
*Mariucci, John (1985)
Mathers, Frank (1992)
*McLaughlin, Major Frederic (1963)
Milford, John "Jake" (1984)
Molson, Hon. Hartland de Montarville (1973)
*Nelson, Francis (1947)
*Norris, Bruce A. (1969)
*Norris, Sr., James (1958)
*Norris, James Dougan (1962)
*Northey, William M. (1947)
*O'Brien, John Ambrose (1962)
Page, Fred (1993)
*Patrick, Frank (1958)
*Pickard, Allan W. (1958)
Pilous, Rudy (1985)
Poile, Norman "Bud" (1990)
Pollock, Samuel Patterson Smyth (1978)
*Raymond, Sen. Donat (1958)
*Robertson, John Ross (1947)
*Robinson, Claude C. (1947)
*Ross, Philip D. (1976)
*Selke, Frank J. (1960)
Sinden, Harry James (1983)
*Smith, Frank D. (1962)
*Smythe, Conn (1958)
Snider, Edward M. (1988)
*Stanley of Preston, Lord (G.C.B.) (1945)
*Sutherland, Cap. James T. (1947)
Tarasov, Anatoli V. (1974)
Turner, Lloyd (1958)
*Tutt, William Thayer (1978)
*Voss, Carl Potter (1974)
*Waghorn, Fred C. (1961)
*Wirtz, Arthur Michael (1971)
Wirtz, William W. "Bill" (1976)
Ziegler, John A. Jr. (1987)

REFEREES/LINESMEN

Armstrong, Neil (1991)
Ashley, John George (1981)
Chadwick, William L. (1964)
D'Amico, John (1993)
*Elliott, Chaucer (1961)
*Hayes, George William (1988)
*Hewitson, Robert W. (1963)
*Ion, Fred J. "Mickey" (1961)
Pavelich, Matt (1987)
*Rodden, Michael J. "Mike" (1962)
*Smeaton, J. Cooper (1961)
Storey, Roy Alvin "Red" (1967)
Udvari, Frank Joseph (1973)

*Deceased

*Rankin, Frank (1961)
Ratelle, Joseph Gilbert Yvan Jean "Jean" (1985)
Rayner, Claude Earl "Chuck" (1973)
Reardon, Kenneth Joseph (1966)
Richard, Joseph Henri (1979)
Richard, Joseph Henri Maurice "Rocket" (1961)
*Richardson, George Taylor (1950)
*Roberts, Gordon (1971)
*Ross, Arthur Howie (1945)
*Russel, Blair (1965)
*Russell, Ernest (1965)
*Ruttan, J.D. "Jack" (1962)
Savard, Serge A. (1986)
*Sawchuk, Terrance Gordon "Terry" (1971)
*Scanlan, Fred (1965)
Schmidt, Milton Conrad "Milt" (1961)
*Schriner, David "Sweeney" (1962)
*Seibert, Earl Walter (1963)
*Seibert, Oliver Levi (1961)
*Shore, Edward W. "Eddie" (1947)
Shutt, Stephen (1993)
*Siebert, Albert C. "Babe" (1964)
*Simpson, Harold Edward "Bullet Joe" (1962)
Sittler, Darryl Glen (1989)
*Smith, Alfred E. (1962)
Smith, Clint (1991)
*Smith, Reginald "Hooley" (1972)
*Smith, Thomas James (1973)
Smith, William John "Billy" (1993)
Stanley, Allan Herbert (1981)
*Stanley, Russell "Barney" (1962)
*Stewart, John Sherratt "Black Jack" (1964)
*Stewart, Nelson "Nels" (1962)
*Stuart, Bruce (1961)
*Stuart, Hod (1945)
*Taylor, Frederic "Cyclone" (O.B.E.) (1947)
*Thompson, Cecil R. "Tiny" (1959)
Tretiak, Vladislav (1989)
*Trihey, Col. Harry J. (1950)
Ullman, Norman Victor Alexander "Norm" (1982)
*Vezina, Georges (1945)
*Walker, John Phillip "Jack" (1960)
*Walsh, Martin "Marty" (1962)
*Watson, Harry E. (1962)
*Weiland, Ralph "Cooney" (1971)
*Westwick, Harry (1962)
*Whitcroft, Fred (1962)
*Wilson, Gordon Allan "Phat" (1962)
Worsley, Lorne John "Gump" (1980)
*Worters, Roy (1969)

Elmer Ferguson Memorial Award Winners

In recognition of distinguished members of the newspaper profession whose words have brought honor to journalism and to hockey. Selected by the Professional Hockey Writers' Association.

*Barton, Charlie, Buffalo-Courier Express
*Beauchamp, Jacques, Montreal Matin/Journal de Montreal
*Brennan, Bill, Detroit News
*Burchard, Jim, New York World Telegram
*Burnett, Red, Toronto Star
*Carroll, Dink, Montreal Gazette
Coleman, Jim, Southam Newspapers
*Damata, Ted, Chicago Tribune
Delano, Hugh, New York Post
Desjardins, Marcel, Montreal La Presse
Dulmage, Jack, Windsor Star
Dunnell, Milt, Toronto Star
*Ferguson, Elmer, Montreal Herald/Star
Fisher, Red, Montreal Star/Gazette
*Fitzgerald, Tom, Boston Globe
Frayne, Trent, Toronto Telegram/Globe and Mail/Sun
Gross, George, Toronto Telegram
Johnston, Dick, Buffalo News
*Laney, Al, New York Herald-Tribune
Larochelle, Claude, Le Soleil
L'Esperance, Zotique, Journal de Montreal, le Petit Journal
*Mayer, Charles, le Journal de Montréal, la Patrie
MacLeod, Rex, Toronto Globe and Mail
Monahan, Leo, Boston Herald
Moriarty, Tim, UPI/Newsday
*Nichols, Joe, New York Times
*O'Brien, Andy, Weekend Magazine
Orr, Frank, Toronto Star
Olan, Ben, New York Associated Press
*O'Meara, Basil, Montreal Star
Proudfoot, Jim, Toronto Star
Raymond, Bertrand, le Journal de Montréal
Rosa, Fran, Boston Globe
Strachan, Al, Globe and Mail
*Vipond, Jim, Toronto Globe and Mail
Walter, Lewis, Detroit Times
Young, Scott, Toronto Globe and Mail/Telegram

Foster Hewitt Memorial Award Winners

In recognition of members of the radio and television industry who made outstanding contributions to their profession and the game during their career in hockey broadcasting. Selected by the NHL Broadcasters' Association.

Cusick, Fred, Boston
*Gallivan, Danny, Montreal
*Hewitt, Foster, Toronto
Irvin, Dick, Montreal
*Kelly, Dan, St. Louis
Lecavelier, Rene, Montreal
Lynch, Budd, Detroit
Martyn, Bruce, Detroit
McDonald, Jiggs, NY Islanders
*McKnight, Wes, Toronto
Pettit, Lloyd, Chicago
Robson, Jim, Vancouver
Shaver, Al, Minnesota
*Smith, Doug, Montreal
Wilson, Bob, Boston

United States Hockey Hall of Fame

The United States Hockey Hall of Fame is located in Eveleth, Minnesota, 60 miles north of Duluth, on Highway 53. The facility is open Monday to Saturday 9 a.m. to 5 p.m. and Sundays 11 a.m to 5 p.m.; Adult $3.00; Seniors $2.00; Juniors 13-17 $1.50; and Children 6-12 $1.25; Children under 6 free. Group rates available.

The Hall was dedicated and opened on June 21, 1973, largely as the result of the work of D. Kelly Campbell, Chairman of the Eveleth Civic Association's Project H Committee. There are now 87 enshrinees consisting of 52 players, 19 coaches, 15 administrators, and one referee. New members are inducted annually in October and must have made a significant contribution toward hockey in the United States through the vehicle of their careers. Support for the Hall comes from sponsorship and membership programs, grants from the hockey community, and government agencies.

PLAYERS

*Abel, Clarence "Taffy"
*Baker, Hobart "Hobey"
Bartholome, Earl
Bessone, Peter
Blake, Robert
Brimsek, Frank
Cavanough, Joe
*Chaisson, Ray
Chase, John P.
Christian, Roger
Christian, William "Bill"
Cleary, Robert
Cleary, William
*Conroy, Anthony
Dahlstrom, Carl "Cully"
DesJardins, Victor
Desmond, Richard
*Dill, Robert
Everett, Doug
Ftorek, Robbie
*Garrison, John B.
Garrity, Jack
*Goheen, Frank "Moose"
Grant, Wally
Harding, Austin "Austie"
Iglehart, Stewart
Johnson, Virgil
Karakas, Mike
Kirrane, Jack
*Lane, Myles J.
Langevin, David R.
*Linder, Joseph
*LoPresti, Sam L.
*Mariucci, John
Matchefts, John
Mayasich, John
McCartan, Jack
Moe, William
*Moseley, Fred
*Murray, Hugh "Muzz" Sr.
*Nelson, Hubert "Hub"
Olson , Eddie
*Owen, Jr., George
*Palmer, Winthrop
Paradise, Robert
Purpur, Clifford "Fido"
Riley, William
*Romnes, Elwin "Doc"
Rondeau, Richard
*Williams, Thomas
*Winters, Frank "Coddy"
*Yackel, Ken

COACHES

*Almquist, Oscar
Bessone, Amo
Brooks, Herbert
Ceglarski, Len
*Fullerton, James
*Gordon, Malcolm K.
Harkness, Nevin D. "Ned"
Heyliger, Victor
Ikola, Willard
*Jeremiah, Edward J.
*Johnson, Bob
*Kelley, John "Snooks"
Kelley, John H. "Jack"
Pleban, John "Connie"
Riley, Jack
Ross, Larry
*Thompson, Clifford, R.
*Stewart, William
*Winsor, Alfred "Ralph"

ADMINISTRATORS

*Brown, George V.
*Brown, Walter A.
Bush, Walter
Clark, Donald
*Gibson, J.C. "Doc"
*Jennings, William M.
*Kahler, Nick
*Lockhart, Thomas F.
Marvin, Cal
Ridder, Robert
Schulz, Charles M.
Trumble, Harold
*Tutt, William Thayer
Wirtz, William W. "Bill"
*Wright, Lyle Z.

REFEREE

Chadwick, William

*Deceased

A collegiate star with the University of Minnesota, U.S. Hockey Hall of Fame inductee Herb Brooks later coached the Gophers to the NCAA championship in 1974, 1976 and 1979. He also guided the U.S. Olympic Hockey Team to a gold medal at the 1980 Winter Olympics in Lake Placid.

Results

CONFERENCE QUARTER-FINALS
(Best-of-seven series)

Eastern Conference

Series 'A'
Sun. Apr. 17	NY Islanders 0	at	NY Rangers 6
Mon. Apr. 18	NY Islanders 0	at	NY Rangers 6
Thu. Apr. 21	NY Rangers 5	at	NY Islanders 1
Sun. Apr. 24	NY Rangers 5	at	NY Islanders 2

NY Rangers won series 4-0

Series 'B'
Sun. Apr. 17	Washington 5	at	Pittsburgh 3
Tue. Apr. 19	Washington 1	at	Pittsburgh 2
Thu. Apr. 21	Pittsburgh 0	at	Washington 2
Sat. Apr. 23	Pittsburgh 1	at	Washington 4
Mon. Apr. 25	Washington 2	at	Pittsburgh 3
Wed. Apr. 27	Pittsburgh 3	at	Washington 6

Washington won series 4-2

Series 'C'
Sun. Apr. 17	Buffalo 2	at	New Jersey 0
Tue. Apr. 19	Buffalo 1	at	New Jersey 2
Thu. Apr. 21	New Jersey 2	at	Buffalo 1
Sat. Apr. 23	New Jersey 3	at	Buffalo 5
Mon. Apr. 25	Buffalo 3	at	New Jersey 5
Wed. Apr. 27	New Jersey 0	at	Buffalo 1 OT
Fri. Apr. 29	Buffalo 1	at	New Jersey 2

New Jersey won series 4-3

Series 'D'
Sat. Apr. 16	Montreal 2	at	Boston 3
Mon. Apr. 18	Montreal 3	at	Boston 2
Thu. Apr. 21	Boston 6	at	Montreal 3
Sat. Apr. 23	Boston 2	at	Montreal 5
Mon. Apr. 25	Montreal 2	at	Boston 1 OT
Wed. Apr. 27	Boston 3	at	Montreal 2
Fri. Apr. 29	Montreal 3	at	Boston 5

Boston won series 4-3

Western Conference

Series 'E'
Mon. Apr. 18	San Jose 5	at	Detroit 4
Wed. Apr. 20	San Jose 0	at	Detroit 4
Fri. Apr. 22	Detroit 3	at	San Jose 4
Sat. Apr. 23	Detroit 3	at	San Jose 4
Tue. Apr. 26	Detroit 4	at	San Jose 6
Thu. Apr. 28	San Jose 1	at	Detroit 7
Sat. Apr. 30	San Jose 3	at	Detroit 2

San Jose won series 4-3

Series 'F'
Mon. Apr. 18	Vancouver 5	at	Calgary 0
Wed. Apr. 20	Vancouver 5	at	Calgary 7
Fri. Apr. 22	Calgary 4	at	Vancouver 2
Sun. Apr. 24	Calgary 3	at	Vancouver 2
Tue. Apr. 26	Vancouver 2	at	Calgary 1 OT
Thu. Apr. 28	Calgary 2	at	Vancouver 3 OT
Sat. Apr. 30	Vancouver 4	at	Calgary 3 OT

Vancouver won series 4-3

Series 'G'
Mon. Apr. 18	Chicago 1	at	Toronto 5
Wed. Apr. 20	Chicago 0	at	Toronto 1 OT
Sat. Apr. 23	Toronto 4	at	Chicago 5
Sun. Apr. 24	Toronto 3	at	Chicago 4 OT
Tue. Apr. 26	Chicago 0	at	Toronto 1
Thu. Apr. 28	Toronto 1	at	Chicago 0

Toronto won series 4-2

Series 'H'
Sun. Apr. 17	St. Louis 3	at	Dallas 5
Wed. Apr. 20	St. Louis 2	at	Dallas 4
Fri. Apr. 22	Dallas 5	at	St. Louis 4 OT
Sun. Apr. 24	Dallas 2	at	St. Louis 1

Dallas won series 4-0

CONFERENCE SEMI-FINALS
(Best-of-seven series)

Eastern Conference

Series 'I'
Sun. May 1	Washington 3	at	NY Rangers 6
Tue. May 3	Washington 2	at	NY Rangers 5
Thu. May 5	NY Rangers 3	at	Washington 0
Sat. May 7	NY Rangers 2	at	Washington 4
Mon. May 9	Washington 3	at	NY Rangers 4

NY Rangers won series 4-1

Series 'J'
Sun. May 1	Boston 2	at	New Jersey 1
Tue. May 3	Boston 6	at	New Jersey 5 OT
Thu. May 5	New Jersey 4	at	Boston 2
Sat. May 7	New Jersey 5	at	Boston 4 OT
Mon. May 9	Boston 0	at	New Jersey 2
Wed. May 11	New Jersey 5	at	Boston 3

New Jersey won series 4-2

Western Conference

Series 'K'
Mon. May 2	San Jose 3	at	Toronto 2
Wed. May 4	San Jose 1	at	Toronto 5
Fri. May 6	Toronto 2	at	San Jose 5
Sun. May 8	Toronto 8	at	San Jose 3
Tue. May 10	Toronto 2	at	San Jose 5
Thu. May 12	San Jose 2	at	Toronto 3 OT
Sat. May 14	San Jose 2	at	Toronto 4

Toronto won series 4-3

Series 'L'
Mon. May 2	Vancouver 6	at	Dallas 4
Wed. May 4	Vancouver 3	at	Dallas 0
Fri. May 6	Dallas 4	at	Vancouver 3
Sun. May 8	Dallas 1	at	Vancouver 2 OT
Tue. May 10	Dallas 2	at	Vancouver 4

Vancouver won series 4-1

CONFERENCE FINALS
(Best-of-seven series)

Eastern Conference

Series 'M'
Sun. May 15	New Jersey 4	at	NY Rangers 3 OT
Tue. May 17	New Jersey 0	at	NY Rangers 4
Thu. May 19	NY Rangers 3	at	New Jersey 2 OT
Sat. May 21	NY Rangers 1	at	New Jersey 3
Mon. May 23	New Jersey 4	at	NY Rangers 1
Wed. May 25	NY Rangers 4	at	New Jersey 2
Fri. May 27	New Jersey 1	at	NY Rangers 2 OT

NY Rangers won series 4-3

Western Conference

Series 'N'
Mon. May 16	Vancouver 2	at	Toronto 3 OT
Wed. May 18	Vancouver 4	at	Toronto 3
Fri. May 20	Toronto 0	at	Vancouver 4
Sun. May 22	Toronto 2	at	Vancouver 2
Tue. May 24	Toronto 3	at	Vancouver 4 OT

Vancouver won series 4-1

1994 Stanley Cup Playoffs

Team Playoff Records

	GP	W	L	GF	GA	%
NY Rangers	23	16	7	81	50	.696
Vancouver	24	15	9	76	61	.625
New Jersey	20	11	9	52	49	.550
Toronto	18	9	9	50	47	.500
San Jose	14	7	7	42	53	.500
Boston	13	6	7	39	42	.462
Dallas	9	5	4	27	28	.556
Washington	11	5	6	32	32	.455
Detroit	7	3	4	27	21	.429
Buffalo	7	3	4	14	14	.429
Montreal	7	3	4	20	22	.429
Calgary	7	3	4	20	23	.429
Chicago	6	2	4	10	15	.333
Pittsburgh	6	2	4	12	20	.333
St. Louis	4	0	4	10	16	.000
NY Islanders	4	0	4	3	22	.000

STANLEY CUP CHAMPIONSHIP
(Best-of-seven series)

Series 'O'
Tue. May 31	Vancouver 3	at	NY Rangers 2 OT
Thu. June 2	Vancouver 1	at	NY Rangers 3
Sat. June 4	NY Rangers 5	at	Vancouver 1
Tue. June 7	NY Rangers 4	at	Vancouver 2
Thu. June 9	Vancouver 6	at	NY Rangers 3
Sat. June 11	NY Rangers 1	at	Vancouver 4
Tue. June 14	Vancouver 2	at	NY Rangers 3

NY Rangers won series 4-3

Individual Leaders

Abbreviations: * – rookie eligible for Calder Trophy; **A** – assists; **G** – goals; **GP** – Games Played; **OT** – overtime goals; **GW** – game-winning goals; **PIM** – penalties in minutes; **PP** – power play goals; **Pts** – points; **S** – shots on goal; **SH** – short-handed goals; **%** – percentage shots resulting in goals; **+/ – –** difference between Goals For (**GF**) scored when a player is on the ice with his team at even strength or short-handed and Goals Against (**GA**) scored when the same player is on the ice with his team at even strength or on a power play.

Playoff Scoring Leaders

Player	Team	GP	G	A	Pts	+/-	PIM	PP	SH	GW	OT	S	%
Brian Leetch	NY Rangers	23	11	23	34	19	6	4	0	4	0	88	12.5
Pavel Bure	Vancouver	24	16	15	31	8	40	3	0	2	1	101	15.8
Mark Messier	NY Rangers	23	12	18	30	14	33	2	1	4	0	75	16.0
Doug Gilmour	Toronto	18	6	22	28	3	42	5	0	1	0	31	19.4
Trevor Linden	Vancouver	24	12	13	25	3	18	5	1	1	1	67	17.9
Alexei Kovalev	NY Rangers	23	9	12	21	5	18	5	0	2	0	71	12.7
Geoff Courtnall	Vancouver	24	9	10	19	10	51	0	1	3	1	77	11.7
Sergei Zubov	NY Rangers	22	5	14	19	10	0	2	0	0	0	60	8.3
Claude Lemieux	New Jersey	20	7	11	18	4	44	0	0	2	0	50	14.0
Igor Larionov	San Jose	14	5	13	18	1 –	10	0	0	0	0	27	18.5
Dave Ellett	Toronto	18	3	15	18	1	31	3	0	0	0	33	9.1
Adam Graves	NY Rangers	23	10	7	17	12	24	3	0	0	0	93	10.8
Wendel Clark	Toronto	18	9	7	16	0	24	2	0	1	0	72	12.5
Steve Larmer	NY Rangers	23	9	7	16	8	14	3	0	0	0	54	16.7
John MacLean	New Jersey	20	6	10	16	2 –	22	2	0	1	0	65	9.2
Dmitri Mironov	Toronto	18	6	9	15	3 –	6	6	0	0	0	29	20.7
Jeff Brown	Vancouver	24	6	9	15	7	37	3	0	0	0	76	7.9
Cliff Ronning	Vancouver	24	5	10	15	2 –	16	2	0	2	0	69	7.2
Greg Adams	Vancouver	23	6	8	14	1	2	2	0	2	2	46	13.0
Bernie Nicholls	New Jersey	16	4	9	13	3	28	2	1	0	0	37	10.8
Murray Craven	Vancouver	22	4	9	13	10	18	0	0	1	0	38	10.5
Jyrki Lumme	Vancouver	24	2	11	13	8	16	2	0	1	0	53	3.8
Stephane Richer	New Jersey	20	7	5	12	2	6	3	0	2	2	72	9.7
Adam Oates	Boston	13	3	9	12	3 –	8	2	0	0	0	42	7.1

Playoff Defensemen Scoring Leaders

Player	Team	GP	G	A	Pts	+/-	PIM	PP	SH	GW	OT	S	%
Brian Leetch	NY Rangers	23	11	23	34	19	6	4	0	4	0	88	12.5
Sergei Zubov	NY Rangers	22	5	14	19	10	0	2	0	0	0	60	8.3
Dave Ellett	Toronto	18	3	15	18	1	31	3	0	0	0	33	9.1
Dmitri Mironov	Toronto	18	6	9	15	3 –	6	6	0	0	0	29	20.7
Jeff Brown	Vancouver	24	6	9	15	7	37	3	0	0	0	76	7.9
Jyrki Lumme	Vancouver	24	2	11	13	8	16	2	0	1	0	53	3.8
Scott Stevens	New Jersey	20	2	9	11	1 –	42	2	0	1	0	56	3.6
Ray Bourque	Boston	13	2	8	10	5 –	0	1	0	0	0	64	3.1
Sandis Ozolinsh	San Jose	14	0	10	10	3	8	0	0	0	0	23	.0
Paul Cavallini	Dallas	9	1	8	9	4 –	4	1	0	1	1	20	5.0
Sylvain Cote	Washington	9	1	8	9	3	6	0	0	0	0	30	3.3

GOALTENDING LEADERS

Goals Against Average

Goaltender	Team	GPI	Mins.	GA	Avg.
Dominik Hasek	Buffalo	7	484	13	1.61
*Martin Brodeur	New Jersey	17	1171	38	1.95
Mike Richter	NY Rangers	23	1417	49	2.07
Kirk McLean	Vancouver	24	1544	59	2.29
Felix Potvin	Toronto	18	1124	46	2.46

Wins

Goaltender	Team	GPI	Mins.	W	L
Mike Richter	NY Rangers	23	1417	16	7
Kirk McLean	Vancouver	24	1544	15	9
Felix Potvin	Toronto	18	1124	9	9
*Martin Brodeur	New Jersey	17	1171	8	9
Arturs Irbe	San Jose	14	806	7	7

Save Percentage

Goaltender	Team	GPI	Mins.	GA	SA	S%	W	L
Dominik Hasek	Buffalo	7	484	13	261	.950	3	4
Kirk McLean	Vancouver	24	1544	59	820	.928	15	9
*Martin Brodeur	New Jersey	17	1171	38	531	.928	8	9
Mike Richter	NY Rangers	23	1417	49	623	.921	16	7
Felix Potvin	Toronto	18	1124	46	520	.911	9	9

Shutouts

Goaltender	Team	GPI	Mins.	SO
Mike Richter	NY Rangers	23	1417	4
Kirk McLean	Vancouver	24	1544	4
Felix Potvin	Toronto	18	1124	3
Dominik Hasek	Buffalo	7	484	2

Goal Scoring

Name	Team	GP	G
Pavel Bure	Vancouver	24	16
Mark Messier	NY Rangers	23	12
Trevor Linden	Vancouver	24	12
Brian Leetch	NY Rangers	23	11
Adam Graves	NY Rangers	23	10
Wendel Clark	Toronto	18	9
Steve Larmer	NY Rangers	23	9
Alexei Kovalev	NY Rangers	23	9
Geoff Courtnall	Vancouver	24	9
Sergei Makarov	San Jose	14	8
Mike Modano	Dallas	9	7
Claude Lemieux	New Jersey	20	7
Stephane Richer	New Jersey	20	7

Assists

Name	Team	GP	A
Brian Leetch	NY Rangers	23	23
Doug Gilmour	Toronto	18	22
Mark Messier	NY Rangers	23	18
Dave Ellett	Toronto	18	15
Pavel Bure	Vancouver	24	15
Sergei Zubov	NY Rangers	22	14
Igor Larionov	San Jose	14	13
Trevor Linden	Vancouver	24	13
Alexei Kovalev	NY Rangers	23	12
Claude Lemieux	New Jersey	20	11
Jyrki Lumme	Vancouver	24	11

Power-play Goals

Name	Team	GP	PP
Dmitri Mironov	Toronto	18	6
Doug Gilmour	Toronto	18	5
Alexei Kovalev	NY Rangers	23	5

Game-winning Goals

Name	Team	GP	GW
Brian Leetch	NY Rangers	23	4
Mark Messier	NY Rangers	23	4
Mike Gartner	Toronto	18	3
Geoff Courtnall	Vancouver	24	3
Shawn Burr	Detroit	7	2
Theoren Fleury	Calgary	7	2

Short-handed Goals

Name	Team	GP	SH
Mark Osborne	Toronto	18	2
Kevin Miller	St. Louis	3	1
Kris Draper	Detroit	7	1
Nicklas Lidstrom	Detroit	7	1

Overtime Goals

Name	Team	GP	OT
Stephane Richer	New Jersey	20	2
Greg Adams	Vancouver	23	2
Stephane Matteau	NY Rangers	23	2
Jeremy Roenick	Chicago	6	1
Dave Hannan	Buffalo	7	1

Shots

Name	Team	GP	S
Pavel Bure	Vancouver	24	101
Adam Graves	NY Rangers	23	93
Brian Leetch	NY Rangers	23	88
Geoff Courtnall	Vancouver	24	77
Jeff Brown	Vancouver	24	76

Plus/Minus

Name	Team	GP	+/-
Brian Leetch	NY Rangers	23	19
Jeff Beukeboom	NY Rangers	22	17
Mark Messier	NY Rangers	23	14
Nathan Lafayette	Vancouver	20	13
Bret Hedican	Vancouver	24	13

First Goals

Name	Team	GP	FG
Dave Andreychuk	Toronto	21	5
Brett Hull	St. Louis	11	3
Pierre Turgeon	NY Islanders	11	3
Kirk Muller	Montreal	20	3

Team Statistics

TEAMS' HOME-AND-ROAD RECORD

	Home						Road					
	GP	W	L	GF	GA	%	GP	W	L	GF	GA	%
NYR	13	9	4	48	29	.692	10	7	3	33	21	.700
VAN	12	7	5	33	29	.583	12	8	4	43	32	.667
N.J.	10	5	5	24	23	.500	10	6	4	28	26	.600
TOR	9	7	2	27	15	.778	9	2	7	23	32	.222
S.J.	6	4	2	25	22	.667	8	3	5	17	31	.375
BOS	7	2	5	20	24	.286	6	4	2	19	18	.667
DAL	4	2	2	13	14	.500	5	3	2	14	14	.600
WSH	5	4	1	16	9	.800	6	1	5	16	23	.167
DET	4	2	2	17	9	.500	3	1	2	10	12	.333
BUF	3	2	1	7	5	.667	4	1	3	7	9	.250
MTL	3	1	2	10	11	.333	4	2	2	10	11	.500
CGY	4	1	3	11	16	.250	3	2	1	9	7	.667
CHI	3	2	1	9	8	.667	3	0	3	1	7	.000
PIT	3	2	1	8	8	.667	3	0	3	4	12	.000
STL	2	0	2	5	7	.000	2	0	2	5	9	.000
NYI	2	0	2	3	10	.000	2	0	2	0	12	.000
TOTAL	90	50	40	276	239	.556	90	40	50	239	276	.444

TEAMS' POWER-PLAY RECORD

Abbreviations: Adv-total advantages; **PPGF**-power play goals for; **%** arrived by dividing number of power-play goals by total advantages.

		Home						Road						Overall			
	Team	GP	ADV	PPGF	%	Team	GP	ADV	PPGF	%	Team	GP	ADV	PPGF	%		
1	MTL	3	10	4	40.0	TOR	9	30	11	36.7	TOR	18	74	22	29.7		
2	TOR	9	44	11	25.0	DAL	5	25	7	28.0	MTL	7	28	6	21.4		
3	DET	4	22	5	22.7	NYR	10	51	14	27.5	NYR	23	104	22	21.2		
4	CHI	3	14	3	21.4	STL	2	10	2	20.0	DAL	9	49	10	20.4		
5	BOS	7	33	7	21.2	VAN	12	53	9	17.0	BOS	13	54	10	18.5		
6	NYI	2	5	1	20.0	N.J.	10	36	6	16.7	N.J.	20	81	14	17.3		
7	S.J.	6	36	7	19.4	BOS	6	21	3	14.3	VAN	24	116	19	16.4		
8	N.J.	10	45	8	17.8	BUF	4	17	2	11.8	STL	4	20	3	15.0		
9	CGY	4	25	4	16.0	MTL	4	18	2	11.1	DET	7	35	5	14.3		
10	VAN	12	63	10	15.9	PIT	3	14	1	7.1	CHI	6	29	4	13.8		
11	NYR	13	53	8	15.1	CHI	3	15	1	6.7	S.J.	14	74	9	12.2		
12	WSH	5	23	3	13.0	WSH	6	32	2	6.3	CGY	7	44	5	11.4		
13	DAL	4	24	3	12.5	CGY	3	19	1	5.3	BUF	7	38	4	10.5		
14	STL	2	10	1	10.0	S.J.	8	38	2	5.3	WSH	11	55	5	9.1		
15	BUF	3	21	2	9.5	NYI	2	12	0	.0	PIT	6	27	2	7.4		
16	PIT	3	13	1	7.7	DET	3	13	0	.0	NYI	4	17	1	5.9		
	TOTAL	90	441	78	17.7		90	404	63	15.6		90	845	141	16.7		

TEAMS' PENALTY KILLING RECORD

Abbreviations: TSH – Total times short-handed; **PPGA** – power-play goals against; **%** arrived by dividing times short minus power-play goals against by times short.

		Home						Road						Overall			
	Team	GP	TSH	PPGA	%	Team	GP	TSH	PPGA	%	Team	GP	TSH	PPGA	%		
1	NYR	13	56	3	94.6	WSH	6	28	2	92.9	NYR	23	103	9	91.3		
2	PIT	3	17	1	94.1	CGY	3	19	2	89.5	PIT	6	30	3	90.0		
3	DET	4	22	2	90.9	NYR	10	47	6	87.2	WSH	11	52	6	88.5		
4	TOR	9	39	4	89.7	N.J.	10	47	6	87.2	N.J.	20	85	11	87.1		
5	N.J.	10	38	5	86.8	PIT	3	13	2	84.6	CGY	7	41	6	85.4		
6	BUF	3	13	2	84.6	DAL	5	25	4	84.0	TOR	18	86	13	84.9		
7	MTL	3	13	2	84.6	STL	2	12	2	83.3	DET	7	36	6	83.3		
8	VAN	12	55	9	83.6	CHI	3	18	3	83.3	DAL	9	41	7	82.9		
9	WSH	5	24	4	83.3	VAN	12	59	11	81.4	VAN	24	114	20	82.5		
10	BOS	7	29	5	82.8	TOR	9	47	9	80.9	BUF	7	32	6	81.3		
11	CGY	4	22	4	81.8	BUF	4	19	4	78.9	S.J.	14	61	13	78.7		
12	S.J.	6	22	4	81.8	NYI	2	14	3	78.6	BOS	13	51	11	78.4		
13	DAL	4	16	3	81.3	S.J.	8	39	9	76.9	MTL	7	31	7	77.4		
14	STL	2	11	4	63.6	BOS	6	22	6	72.7	STL	4	23	6	73.9		
15	NYI	2	13	5	61.5	MTL	4	18	5	72.2	CHI	6	32	9	71.9		
16	CHI	3	14	6	57.1	DET	3	14	4	71.4	NYI	4	27	8	70.4		
	TOTAL	90	404	63	84.4		90	441	78	82.3		90	845	141	83.3		

SHORT-HANDED GOALS

	For			Against	
Team	Games	Goals	Team	Games	Goals
TOR	18	4	BOS	13	0
WSH	11	3	WSH	11	0
DET	7	2	BUF	7	0
S.J.	14	2	NYI	4	0
NYR	23	2	STL	4	0
VAN	24	2	N.J.	20	1
STL	4	1	TOR	18	1
CGY	7	1	DAL	9	1
BOS	13	1	MTL	7	1
N.J.	20	1	DET	7	1
NYI	4	0	CGY	7	1
PIT	6	0	CHI	6	1
CHI	6	0	VAN	24	2
BUF	7	0	PIT	6	2
MTL	7	0	NYR	23	3
DAL	9	0	S.J.	14	5
TOTAL	90	19	**TOTAL**	90	19

TEAM PENALTIES

Abbreviations: GP – games played; **PEN** – total penalty minutes, including bench penalties; **BMI** – total bench penalty minutes; **AVG** – average penalty minutes per game.

Team	GP	PEN	BMI	AVG
BOS	13	168	2	12.9
DET	7	98	2	14.0
MTL	7	106	0	15.1
S.J.	14	224	6	16.0
NYR	23	379	2	16.5
DAL	9	149	4	16.6
VAN	24	436	0	18.2
CHI	6	121	2	20.2
STL	4	81	0	20.3
NYI	4	83	0	20.8
TOR	18	375	0	20.8
N.J.	20	421	4	21.1
BUF	7	157	0	22.4
PIT	6	140	2	23.3
WSH	11	256	0	23.3
CGY	7	173	8	24.7
TOTAL	90	3367	32	37.4

Both Mark Messier and teammate Brian Leetch scored four game-winning goals in the 1994 playoffs.

Stanley Cup Record Book

History: The Stanley Cup, the oldest trophy competed for by professional athletes in North America, was donated by Frederick Arthur, Lord Stanley of Preston and son of the Earl of Derby, in 1893. Lord Stanley purchased the trophy for 10 guineas ($50 at that time) for presentation to the amateur hockey champions of Canada. Since 1910, when the National Hockey Association took possession of the Stanley Cup, the trophy has been the symbol of professional hockey supremacy. It has been competed for only by NHL teams since 1926 and has been under the exclusive control of the NHL since 1946.

Stanley Cup Standings

1918-94
(ranked by Cup wins)

Teams	Cup Wins	Yrs.	Series	Wins	Losses	Games	Wins	Losses	Ties	Goals For	Goals Against	Winning %
Montreal	23*	69	130**	84	45	617	374	235	8	1921	1518	.613
Toronto	13	56	88	47	41	413	197	213	3	1080	1134	.481
Detroit	7	43	72	36	36	351	168	182	1	960	963	.480
Boston	5	55	96	46	50	466	226	234	6	1384	1386	.491
Edmonton	5	13	37	29	8	180	120	60	0	770	579	.667
NY Rangers	4	45	79	38	41	350	165	177	8	986	1004	.483
NY Islanders	4	17	43	30	13	218	128	90	0	748	650	.587
Chicago	3	49	83	37	46	374	170	199	5	1082	1203	.461
Philadelphia	2	20	43	25	18	223	116	107	0	715	688	.520
Pittsburgh	2	14	25	13	12	125	69	56	0	418	405	.552
Calgary***	1	20	30	12	18	145	66	79	0	487	531	.455
St. Louis	0	24	41	17	24	210	93	117	0	605	700	.443
Los Angeles	0	19	29	10	19	142	55	87	0	459	568	.387
Buffalo	0	19	29	10	19	138	61	77	0	435	462	.442
Dallas****	0	18	33	15	18	175	85	90	0	581	607	.486
Vancouver	0	14	22	8	14	107	48	59	0	327	360	.449
Washington	0	12	19	7	12	103	47	56	0	338	339	.456
Winnipeg	0	10	12	2	10	56	17	39	0	167	233	.304
Quebec	0	8	14	6	8	74	33	41	0	228	261	.446
Hartford	0	8	9	1	8	49	18	31	0	143	177	.367
New Jersey*****	0	7	11	4	7	67	31	36	0	199	219	.463
San Jose	0	1	2	1	1	14	7	7	0	42	53	.500

 * Montreal also won the Stanley Cup in 1916.
 ** 1919 final incomplete due to influenza epidemic.
 *** Includes totals of Atlanta 1972-80.
 **** Includes totals of Minnesota 1967-93.
***** Includes totals of Colorado 1976-82.

Stanley Cup Winners Prior to Formation of NHL in 1917

Season	Champions	Manager	Coach
1916-17	Seattle Metropolitans	Pete Muldoon	Pete Muldoon
1915-16	Montreal Canadiens	George Kennedy	George Kennedy
1914-15	Vancouver Millionaires	Frank Patrick	Frank Patrick
1913-14	Toronto Blueshirts	Jack Marshall	Scotty Davidson*
1912-13**	Quebec Bulldogs	M.J. Quinn	Joe Malone*
1911-12	Quebec Bulldogs	M.J. Quinn	C. Nolan*
1910-11	Ottawa Senators		Bruce Stuart*
1909-10	Montreal Wanderers	R. R. Boon	Pud Glass*
1908-09	Ottawa Senators		Bruce Stuart*
1907-08	Montreal Wanderers	R. R. Boon	Cecil Blachford
1906-07	Montreal Wanderers (March)	R. R. Boon	Cecil Blachford
1906-07	Kenora Thistles (January)	F.A. Hudson	Tommy Phillips*
1905-06	Montreal Wanderers		Cecil Blachford*
1904-05	Ottawa Silver Seven		A. T. Smith
1903-04	Ottawa Silver Seven		A. T. Smith
1902-03	Ottawa Silver Seven		A. T. Smith
1901-02	Montreal A.A.A.		C. McKerrow
1900-01	Winnipeg Victorias		D. H. Bain
1899-1900	Montreal Shamrocks		H.J. Trihey*
1898-99	Montreal Shamrocks		H.J. Trihey*
1897-98	Montreal Victorias		F. Richardson
1896-97	Montreal Victorias		Mike Grant*
1895-96	Montreal Victorias (December, 1896)		Mike Grant*
1895-96	Winnipeg Victorias (February)		J.C. G. Armytage
1894-95	Montreal Victorias		Mike Grant*
1893-94	Montreal A.A.A.		
1892-93	Montreal A.A.A.		

** Victoria defeated Quebec in challenge series. No official recognition.
 * In the early years the teams were frequently run by the Captain. *Indicates Captain

Stanley Cup Winners

Season	Champions	Manager	Coach
1993-94	New York Rangers	Neil Smith	Mike Keenan
1992-93	Montreal Canadiens	Serge Savard	Jacques Demers
1991-92	Pittsburgh Penguins	Craig Patrick	Scotty Bowman
1990-91	Pittsburgh Penguins	Craig Patrick	Bob Johnson
1989-90	Edmonton Oilers	Glen Sather	John Muckler
1988-89	Calgary Flames	Cliff Fletcher	Terry Crisp
1987-88	Edmonton Oilers	Glen Sather	Glen Sather
1986-87	Edmonton Oilers	Glen Sather	Glen Sather
1985-86	Montreal Canadiens	Serge Savard	Jean Perron
1984-85	Edmonton Oilers	Glen Sather	Glen Sather
1983-84	Edmonton Oilers	Glen Sather	Glen Sather
1982-83	New York Islanders	Bill Torrey	Al Arbour
1981-82	New York Islanders	Bill Torrey	Al Arbour
1980-81	New York Islanders	Bill Torrey	Al Arbour
1979-80	New York Islanders	Bill Torrey	Al Arbour
1978-79	Montreal Canadiens	Irving Grundman	Scotty Bowman
1977-78	Montreal Canadiens	Sam Pollock	Scotty Bowman
1976-77	Montreal Canadiens	Sam Pollock	Scotty Bowman
1975-76	Montreal Canadiens	Sam Pollock	Scotty Bowman
1974-75	Philadelphia Flyers	Keith Allen	Fred Shero
1973-74	Philadelphia Flyers	Keith Allen	Fred Shero
1972-73	Montreal Canadiens	Sam Pollock	Scotty Bowman
1971-72	Boston Bruins	Milt Schmidt	Tom Johnson
1970-71	Montreal Canadiens	Sam Pollock	Al MacNeil
1969-70	Boston Bruins	Milt Schmidt	Harry Sinden
1968-69	Montreal Canadiens	Sam Pollock	Claude Ruel
1967-68	Montreal Canadiens	Sam Pollock	Toe Blake
1966-67	Toronto Maple Leafs	Punch Imach	Punch Imlach
1965-66	Montreal Canadiens	Sam Pollock	Toe Blake
1964-65	Montreal Canadiens	Sam Pollock	Toe Blake
1963-64	Toronto Maple Leafs	Punch Imlach	Punch Imlach
1962-63	Toronto Maple Leafs	Punch Imlach	Punch Imlach
1961-62	Toronto Maple Leafs	Punch Imlach	Punch Imlach
1960-61	Chicago Black Hawks	Tommy Ivan	Rudy Pilous
1959-60	Montreal Canadiens	Frank Selke	Toe Blake
1958-59	Montreal Canadiens	Frank Selke	Toe Blake
1957-58	Montreal Canadiens	Frank Selke	Toe Blake
1956-57	Montreal Canadiens	Frank Selke	Toe Blake
1955-56	Montreal Canadiens	Frank Selke	Toe Blake
1954-55	Detroit Red Wings	Jack Adams	Jimmy Skinner
1953-54	Detroit Red Wings	Jack Adams	Tommy Ivan
1952-53	Montreal Canadiens	Frank Selke	Dick Irvin
1951-52	Detroit Red Wings	Jack Adams	Tommy Ivan
1950-51	Toronto Maple Leafs	Conn Smythe	Joe Primeau
1949-50	Detroit Red Wings	Jack Adams	Tommy Ivan
1948-49	Toronto Maple Leafs	Conn Smythe	Hap Day
1947-48	Toronto Maple Leafs	Conn Smythe	Hap Day
1946-47	Toronto Maple Leafs	Conn Smythe	Hap Day
1945-46	Montreal Canadiens	Tommy Gorman	Dick Irvin
1944-45	Toronto Maple Leafs	Conn Smythe	Hap Day
1943-44	Montreal Canadiens	Tommy Gorman	Dick Irvin
1942-43	Detroit Red Wings	Jack Adams	Jack Adams
1941-42	Toronto Maple Leafs	Conn Smythe	Hap Day
1940-41	Boston Bruins	Art Ross	Cooney Weiland
1939-40	New York Rangers	Lester Patrick	Frank Boucher
1938-39	Boston Bruins	Art Ross	Art Ross
1937-38	Chicago Black Hawks	Bill Stewart	Bill Stewart
1936-37	Detroit Red Wings	Jack Adams	Jack Adams
1935-36	Detroit Red Wings	Jack Adams	Jack Adams
1934-35	Montreal Maroons	Tommy Gorman	Tommy Gorman
1933-34	Chicago Black Hawks	Tommy Gorman	Tommy Gorman
1932-33	New York Rangers	Lester Patrick	Lester Patrick
1931-32	Toronto Maple Leafs	Conn Smythe	Dick Irvin
1930-31	Montreal Canadiens	Cecil Hart	Cecil Hart
1929-30	Montreal Canadiens	Cecil Hart	Cecil Hart
1928-29	Boston Bruins	Art Ross	Cy Denneny
1927-28	New York Rangers	Lester Patrick	Lester Patrick
1926-27	Ottawa Senators	Dave Gill	Dave Gill
1925-26	Montreal Maroons	Eddie Gerard	Eddie Gerard
1924-25	Victoria Cougars	Lester Patrick	Lester Patrick
1923-24	Montreal Canadiens	Leo Dandurand	Leo Dandurand
1922-23	Ottawa Senators	Tommy Gorman	Pete Green
1921-22	Toronto St. Pats	Charlie Querrie	Eddie Powers
1920-21	Ottawa Senators	Tommy Gorman	Pete Green
1919-20	Ottawa Senators	Tommy Gorman	Pete Green
1918-19	No decision*		
1917-18	Toronto Arenas	Charlie Querrie	Dick Carroll

* In the spring of 1919 the Montreal Canadiens travelled to Seattle to meet Seattle, PCHA champions. After five games had been played — teams were tied at 2 wins and 1 tie — the series was called off by the local Department of Health because of an influenza epidemic and the death from influenza of Montreal's Joe Hall.

Championship Trophies

PRINCE OF WALES TROPHY

Beginning with the 1993-94 season, the club which advances to the Stanley Cup Finals as the winner of the Eastern Conference Championship is presented with the Prince of Wales Trophy.

History: His Royal Highness, the Prince of Wales, donated the trophy to the National Hockey League in 1924. From 1927-28 through 1937-38, the award was presented to the team finishing first in the American Division of the NHL. From 1938-39, when the NHL reverted to one section, to 1966-67, it was presented to the team winning the NHL regular season championship. With expansion in 1967-68, it again became a divisional trophy, awarded to the regular season champions of the East Division through to the end of the 1973-74 season. Beginning in 1974-75, it was awarded to the regular-season winner of the conference bearing the name of the trophy. From 1981-82 to 1992-93 the trophy was presented to the playoff champion in the Wales Conference. Since 1993-94, the trophy has been presented to the playoff champion in the Eastern Conference.

1993-94 Winner: New York Rangers

The New York Rangers won their first Prince of Wales Trophy since 1941-42 on May 27, 1994 after defeating the New Jersey Devils 2-1 in game seven of the Eastern Conference Final series. Before defeating the Devils, the Rangers had series wins over the New York Islanders and the Washington Capitals.

PRINCE OF WALES TROPHY WINNERS

1993-94	**New York Rangers**	1958-59	Montreal Canadiens
1992-93	Montreal Canadiens	1957-58	Montreal Canadiens
1991-92	Pittsburgh Penguins	1956-57	Detroit Red Wings
1990-91	Pittsburgh Penguins	1955-56	Montreal Canadiens
1989-90	Boston Bruins	1954-55	Detroit Red Wings
1988-89	Montreal Canadiens	1953-54	Detroit Red Wings
1987-88	Boston Bruins	1952-53	Detroit Red Wings
1986-87	Philadelphia Flyers	1951-52	Detroit Red Wings
1985-86	Montreal Canadiens	1950-51	Detroit Red Wings
1984-85	Philadelphia Flyers	1949-50	Detroit Red Wings
1983-84	New York Islanders	1948-49	Detroit Red Wings
1982-83	New York Islanders	1947-48	Toronto Maple Leafs
1981-82	New York Islanders	1946-47	Montreal Canadiens
1980-81	Montreal Canadiens	1945-46	Montreal Canadiens
1979-80	Buffalo Sabres	1944-45	Montreal Canadiens
1978-79	Montreal Canadiens	1943-44	Montreal Canadiens
1977-78	Montreal Canadiens	1942-43	Detroit Red Wings
1976-77	Montreal Canadiens	1941-42	New York Rangers
1975-76	Montreal Canadiens	1940-41	Boston Bruins
1974-75	Buffalo Sabres	1939-40	Boston Bruins
1973-74	Boston Bruins	1938-39	Boston Bruins
1972-73	Montreal Canadiens	1937-38	Boston Bruins
1971-72	Boston Bruins	1936-37	Detroit Red Wings
1970-71	Boston Bruins	1935-36	Detroit Red Wings
1969-70	Chicago Blackhawks	1934-35	Boston Bruins
1968-69	Montreal Canadiens	1933-34	Detroit Red Wings
1967-68	Montreal Canadiens	1932-33	Boston Bruins
1966-67	Chicago Blackhawks	1931-32	New York Rangers
1965-66	Montreal Canadiens	1930-31	Boston Bruins
1964-65	Detroit Red Wings	1929-30	Boston Bruins
1963-64	Montreal Canadiens	1928-29	Boston Bruins
1962-63	Toronto Maple Leafs	1927-28	Boston Bruins
1961-62	Montreal Canadiens	1926-27	Ottawa Senators
1960-61	Montreal Canadiens	1925-26	Montreal Maroons
1959-60	Montreal Canadiens	1924-25	Montreal Canadiens
		1923-24	Montreal Canadiens

Prince of Wales Trophy

Clarence S. Campbell Bowl

Stanley Cup

CLARENCE S. CAMPBELL BOWL

Beginning with the 1993-94 season, the club which advances to the Stanley Cup Finals as the winner of the Western Conference Championship is presented with the Clarence S. Campbell Bowl.

History: Presented by the member clubs in 1968 for perpetual competition by the National Hockey League in recognition of the services of Clarence S. Campbell, President of the NHL from 1946 to 1977. From 1967-68 through 1973-74, the trophy was awarded to the regular season champions of the West Division. Beginning in 1974-75, it was awarded to the regular-season winner of the conference bearing the name of the trophy. From 1981-82 to 1992-93 the trophy was presented to the playoff champion in the Campbell Conference. Since 1993-94, the trophy has been presented to the playoff champion in the Western Conference. The trophy itself is a hallmark piece made of sterling silver and was crafted by a British silversmith in 1878.

1993-94 Winner: Vancouver Canucks

The Vancouver Canucks won their first Clarence Campbell Bowl since 1981-82 on May 24, 1994 after defeating the Toronto Maple Leafs 4-3 in game five of the Western Conference Final series. Before defeating the Maple Leafs, the Canucks had series wins over the Calgary Flames and the Dallas Stars.

CLARENCE S. CAMPBELL BOWL WINNERS

1993-94	**Vancouver Canucks**	1979-80	Philadelphia Flyers
1992-93	Los Angeles Kings	1978-79	New York Islanders
1991-92	Chicago Blackhawks	1977-78	New York Islanders
1990-91	Minnesota North Stars	1976-77	Philadelphia Flyers
1989-90	Edmonton Oilers	1975-76	Philadelphia Flyers
1988-89	Calgary Flames	1974-75	Philadelphia Flyers
1987-88	Edmonton Oilers	1973-74	Philadelphia Flyers
1986-87	Edmonton Oilers	1972-73	Chicago Blackhawks
1985-86	Calgary Flames	1971-72	Chicago Blackhawks
1984-85	Edmonton Oilers	1970-71	Chicago Blackhawks
1983-84	Edmonton Oilers	1969-70	St. Louis Blues
1982-83	Edmonton Oilers	1968-69	St. Louis Blues
1981-82	Vancouver Canucks	1967-68	Philadelphia Flyers
1980-81	New York Islanders		

Stanley Cup Winners:

Rosters and Final Series Scores

1993-94 — New York Rangers — Mark Messier (Captain), Brian Leetch, Kevin Lowe, Adam Graves, Steve Larmer, Glenn Anderson, Jeff Beukeboom, Greg Gilbert, Mike Hartman, Glenn Healy, Mike Hudson, Alexander Karpovtsev, Joe Kocur, Alexei Kovalev, Nick Kypreos, Doug Lidster, Stephane Matteau, Craig MacTavish, Sergei Nemchinov, Brian Noonan, Ed Olczyk, Mike Richter, Esa Tikkanen, Jay Wells, Sergei Zubov, Neil Smith (President, General Manager and Governor), Robert Gutkowski, Stanley Jaffe, Kenneth Munoz (Governors), Larry Pleau (Assistant General Manager), Mike Keenan (Head Coach), Colin Campbell (Associate Coach), Dick Todd (Assistant Coach), Matthew Loughren (Manager, Team Operations), Barry Watkins (Director, Communications), Christer Rockstrom, Tony Feltrin, Martin Madden, Herb Hammond, Darwin Bennett (Scouts), Dave Smith, Joe Murphy, Mike Folga, Bruce Lifrieri (Trainers).
Scores: May 31 at New York — Vancouver 3, NY Rangers 2; June 2 at New York — NY Rangers 3, Vancouver 1; June 4 at Vancouver — NY Rangers 5, Vancouver 1; June 7 at Vancouver — NY Rangers 4, Vancouver 2; June 9 at New York — Vancouver 6 at NY Rangers 3; June 11 at Vancouver — Vancouver 4, NY Rangers 1; June 14 at New York — NY Rangers 3, Vancouver 2.

1992-93 — Montreal Canadiens — Guy Carbonneau (Captain), Patrick Roy, Mike Keane, Eric Desjardins, Stephan Lebeau, Mathieu Schneider, Jean-Jacques Daigneault, Denis Savard, Lyle Odelein, Todd Ewen, Kirk Muller, John LeClair, Gilbert Dionne, Benoit Brunet, Patrice Brisebois, Paul Di Pietro, Andre Racicot, Donald Dufresne, Mario Roberge, Sean Hill, Ed Ronan, Kevin Haller, Vincent Damphousse, Brian Bellows, Gary Leeman, Rob Ramage, Ronald Corey (President), Serge Savard (Managing Director & Vice-President Hockey), Jacques Demers (Head Coach), Jacques Laperriere (Assistant Coach), Charles Thiffault (Assistant Coach), Francois Allaire (Goaltending Instructor), Jean Béliveau (Senior Vice-President, Corporate Affairs), Fred Steer (Vice-President, Finance & Adminstration), Aldo Giampaolo (Vice-President, Operations), Bernard Brisset (Vice-President, Marketing & Communications), André Boudrias (Assistant to the Managing Director & Director of Scouting), Jacques Lemaire (Assistant to the Managing Director), Gaeten Lefebvre (Athletic Trainer), John Shipman (Assistant to the Athletic Trainer), Eddy Palchak (Equipment Manager), Pierre Gervais (Assistant to the Equipment Manager), Robert Boulanger (Assistant to the Equipment Manager), Pierre Ouellete (Assistant to the Equipment Manager).
Scores: June 1 at Montreal — Los Angeles 4, Montreal 1; June 2 at Montreal — Montreal 3, Los Angeles 2; June 5 at Los Angeles — Montreal 4, Los Angeles 3; June 7 at Los Angeles — Montreal 3, Los Angeles 2; June 9 at Montreal — Montreal 4, Los Angeles 1.

1991-92 — Pittsburgh Penguins — Mario Lemieux (Captain), Ron Francis, Bryan Trottier, Kevin Stevens, Bob Errey, Phil Bourque, Troy Loney, Rick Tocchet, Joe Mullen, Jaromir Jagr, Jiri Hrdina, Shawn McEachern, Ulf Samuelsson, Kjell Samuelsson, Larry Murphy, Gord Roberts, Jim Paek, Paul Stanton, Tom Barrasso, Ken Wregget, Jay Caufield, Jamie Leach, Wendell Young, Grant Jennings, Peter Taglianetti, Jock Callander, Dave Michayluk, Mike Needham, Jeff Chychrun, Ken Priestlay, Jeff Daniels, Howard Baldwin (Owner and President), Morris Belzberg (Owner), Thomas Ruta (Owner), Donn Patton (Executive Vice President and Chief Financial Officer), Paul Martha (Executive Vice President and General Counsel), Craig Patrick (Executive Vice President and General Manager), Bob Johnson (Coach), Scotty Bowman (Director of Player Development and Coach), Barry Smith, Rick Kehoe, Pierre McGuire, Gilles Meloche, Rick Paterson (Assistant Coaches), Steve Latin (Equipment Manager), Skip Thayer (Trainer), John Welday (Strength and Conditioning Coach), Greg Malone, Les Binkley, Charlie Hodge, John Gill, Ralph Cox (Scouts).
Scores: May 26 at Pittsburgh — Pittsburgh 5, Chicago 4; May 28 at Pittsburgh — Pittsburgh 3, Chicago 1; May 30 at Chicago — Pittsburgh 1, Chicago 0; June 1 at Chicago — Pittsburgh 6, Chicago 5.

1990-91 — Pittsburgh Penguins — Mario Lemieux (Captain), Paul Coffey, Randy Hillier, Bob Errey, Tom Barrasso, Phil Bourque, Jay Caufield, Ron Francis, Randy Gilhen, Jiri Hrdina, Jaromir Jagr, Grant Jennings, Troy Loney, Joe Mullen, Larry Murphy, Jim Paek, Frank Pietrangelo, Barry Pederson, Mark Recchi, Gordie Roberts, Ulf Samuelsson, Paul Stanton, Kevin Stevens, Peter Taglianetti, Bryan Trottier, Scott Young, Wendell Young, Edward J. DeBartolo, Sr. (Owner), Marie D. DeBartolo York (President), Paul Martha (Vice-President & General Counsel), Craig Patrick (General Manager), Scotty Bowman (Director of Player Development & Recruitment), Bob Johnson (Coach), Rick Kehoe (Assistant Coach), Gilles Meloche (Goaltending Coach & Scout), Rick Paterson (Assistant Coach), Barry Smith (Assistant Coach), Steve Latin (Equipment Manager), Skip Thayer (Trainer), John Welday (Strength & Conditioning Coach), Greg Malone (Scout).
Scores: May 15 at Pittsburgh — Minnesota 5, Pittsburgh 4; May 17 at Pittsburgh — Pittsburgh 4, Minnesota 1; May 19 at Minnesota — Minnesota 3, Pittsburgh 1; May 21 at Minnesota — Pittsburgh 5, Minnesota 3; May 23 at Pittsburgh — Pittsburgh 6, Minnesota 4; May 25 at Minnesota — Pittsburgh 8, Minnesota 0.

1989-90 — Edmonton Oilers — Kevin Lowe, Steve Smith, Jeff Beukeboom, Mark Lamb, Joe Murphy, Glenn Anderson, Mark Messier, Adam Graves, Craig MacTavish, Kelly Buchberger, Jari Kurri, Craig Simpson, Martin Gelinas, Randy Gregg, Charlie Huddy, Geoff Smith, Reijo Ruotsalainen, Craig Muni, Bill Ranford, Dave Brown, Eldon Reddick, Petr Klima, Esa Tikkanen, Grant Fuhr, Peter Pocklington (Owner), Glen Sather (President/General Manager), John Muckler (Coach), Ted Green (Co-Coach), Ron Low (Ass't Coach), Bruce MacGregor (Ass't General Manager), Barry Fraser (Director of Player Personnel), John Blackwell (Director of Operations, AHL), Ace Bailey, Ed Chadwick, Lorne Davis, Harry Howell, Matti Vaisanen and Albert Reeves (Scouts), Bill Tuele (Director of Public Relations), Werner Baum (Controller), Dr. Gordon Cameron (Medical Chief of Staff), Dr. David Reid (Team Physician), Barrie Stafford (Athletic Trainer), Ken Lowe (Athletic Therapist), Stuart Poirier (Massage Therapist), Lyle Kulchisky (Ass't Trainer).
Scores: May 15 at Boston — Edmonton 3, Boston 2; May 18 at Boston — Edmonton 7, Boston 2; May 20 at Edmonton — Boston 2, Edmonton 1; May 22 at Edmonton — Edmonton 5, Boston 1; May 24 at Boston — Edmonton 4, Boston 1.

1988-89 — Calgary Flames — Mike Vernon, Rick Wamsley, Al MacInnis, Brad McCrimmon, Dana Murzyn, Ric Nattress, Joe Mullen, Lanny McDonald (Co-captain), Gary Roberts, Colin Patterson, Hakan Loob, Theoren Fleury, Jiri Hrdina, Tim Hunter (Ass't. captain), Gary Suter, Mark Hunter, Jim Peplinski (Co-captain), Joe Nieuwendyk, Brian MacLellan, Joel Otto, Jamie Macoun, Doug Gilmour, Rob Ramage. Norman Green, Harley Hotchkiss, Norman Kwong, Sonia Scurfield, B.J. Seaman, D.K. Seaman (Owners), Cliff Fletcher (President and General Manager), Al MacNeil (Ass't General Manager), Al Coates (Ass't to the President), Terry Crisp (Head Coach), Doug Risebrough, Tom Watt (Ass't Coaches), Glenn Hall (Goaltending Consultant), Jim Murray (Trainer), Bob Stewart (Equipment Manager), Al Murray (Ass't Trainer).
Scores: May 14 at Calgary — Calgary 3, Montreal 2; May 17 at Calgary — Montreal 4, Calgary 2; May 19 at Montreal — Montreal 4, Calgary 3; May 21 at Montreal — Calgary 4, Montreal 2; May 23 at Calgary — Calgary 3, Montreal 2; May 25 at Montreal — Calgary 4, Montreal 2.

1987-88 — Edmonton Oilers — Keith Acton, Glenn Anderson, Jeff Beukeboom, Geoff Courtnall, Grant Fuhr, Randy Gregg, Wayne Gretzky, Dave Hannan, Charlie Huddy, Mike Krushelnyski, Jari Kurri, Normand Lacombe, Kevin Lowe, Craig MacTavish, Kevin McClelland, Marty McSorley, Mark Messier, Craig Muni, Bill Ranford, Craig Simpson, Steve Smith, Esa Tikkanen, Peter Pocklington (Owner), Glen Sather (General Manager/Coach), John Muckler (Co-Coach), Ted Green (Ass't Coach), Bruce MacGregor (Ass't General Manager), Barry Fraser (Director of Player Personnel), Bill Tuele (Director of Public Relations), Dr. Gordon Cameron (Team Physician), Peter Millar (Athletic Therapist), Barrie Stafford (Trainer), Juergen Mers (Massage Therapist), Lyle Kulchisky (Ass't Trainer).
Scores: May 18 at Edmonton — Edmonton 2, Boston 1; May 20 at Edmonton — Edmonton 4, Boston 2; May 22 at Boston — Edmonton 6, Boston 3; May 24 at Boston — Boston 3, Edmonton 3 (suspended due to power failure); May 26 at Edmonton — Edmonton 6, Boston 3.

1986-87 — Edmonton Oilers — Glenn Anderson, Jeff Beukeboom, Kelly Buchberger, Paul Coffey, Grant Fuhr, Randy Gregg, Wayne Gretzky, Charlie Huddy, Dave Hunter, Mike Krushelnyski, Jari Kurri, Moe Lemay, Kevin Lowe, Craig MacTavish, Kevin McClelland, Marty McSorley, Mark Messier, Andy Moog, Craig Muni, Kent Nilsson, Jaroslav Pouzar, Reijo Ruotsalainen, Steve Smith, Esa Tikkanen, Peter Pocklington (Owner), Glen Sather (General Manager/Coach), John Muckler (Co-Coach), Ted Green (Ass't. Coach), Ron Low (Ass't. Coach), Bruce MacGregor (Ass't General Manager), Barry Fraser (Director of Player Personnel), Peter Millar (Athletic Therapist), Barrie Stafford (Trainer), Lyle Kulchisky (Ass't Trainer).
Scores: May 17 at Edmonton — Edmonton 4, Philadelphia 3; May 20 at Edmonton — Edmonton 3, Philadelphia 2; May 22 at Philadelphia — Philadelphia 5, Edmonton 3; May 24 at Philadelphia — Edmonton 4, Philadelphia 1; May 26 at Edmonton — Philadelphia 4, Edmonton 3; May 28 at Philadelphia — Philadelphia 3, Edmonton 2; May 31 at Edmonton — Edmonton 3, Philadelphia 1.

Bill Ranford was brilliant in leading the Edmonton Oilers to the Stanley Cup championship in 1989-90, leading all playoff goalies in wins (16) and games played (22) while recording a goals-against average of 2.53.

1985-86 — Montreal Canadiens — Bob Gainey, Doug Soetaert, Patrick Roy, Rick Green, David Maley, Ryan Walter, Serge Boisvert, Mario Tremblay, Bobby Smith, Craig Ludwig, Tom Kurvers, Kjell Dahlin, Larry Robinson, Guy Carbonneau, Chris Chelios, Petr Svoboda, Mats Naslund, Lucien DeBlois, Steve Rooney, Gaston Gingras, Mike Lalor, Chris Nilan, John Kordic, Claude Lemieux, Mike McPhee, Brian Skrudland, Stephane Richer, Ronald Corey (President), Serge Savard (General Manager), Jean Perron (Coach), Jacques Laperrière (Ass't. Coach), Jean Béliveau (Vice President), Francois-Xavier Seigneur (Vice President), Fred Steer (Vice President), Jacques Lemaire (Ass't. General Manager), André Boudrias (Ass't. General Manager), Claude Ruel, Yves Belanger (Athletic Therapist), Gaetan Lefebvre (Ass't. Athletic Therapist), Eddy Palchek (Trainer), Sylvain Toupin (Ass't. Trainer).
Scores: May 16 at Calgary — Calgary 5, Montreal 3; May 18 at Calgary — Montreal 3, Calgary 2; May 20 at Montreal — Montreal 5, Calgary 3; May 22 at Montreal — Montreal 1, Calgary 0; May 24 at Calgary — Montreal 4, Calgary 3.

1984-85 — Edmonton Oilers — Glenn Anderson, Bill Carroll, Paul Coffey, Lee Fogolin, Grant Fuhr, Randy Gregg, Wayne Gretzky, Charlie Huddy, Pat Hughes, Dave Hunter, Don Jackson, Mike Krushelnyski, Jari Kurri, Willy Lindstrom, Kevin Lowe, Dave Lumley, Kevin McClelland, Larry Melnyk, Mark Messier, Andy Moog, Mark Napier, Jaroslav Pouzar, Dave Semenko, Esa Tikkanen, Peter Pocklington (Owner), Glen Sather (General Manager/Coach), John Muckler (Ass't. Coach), Ted Green (Ass't. Coach), Bruce MacGregor (Ass't. General Manager), Barry Fraser (Director of Player Personnel/Chief Scout), Peter Millar (Athletic Therapist), Barrie Stafford, Lyle Kulchisky (Trainers)
Scores: May 21 at Philadelphia — Philadelphia 4, Edmonton 1; May 23 at Philadelphia — Edmonton 3, Philadelphia 1; May 25 at Edmonton — Edmonton 4, Philadelphia 3; May 28 at Edmonton — Edmonton 5, Philadelphia 3; May 30 at Edmonton — Edmonton 8, Philadelphia 3.

1983-84 — Edmonton Oilers — Glenn Anderson, Paul Coffey, Pat Conacher, Lee Fogolin, Grant Fuhr, Randy Gregg, Wayne Gretzky, Charlie Huddy, Pat Hughes, Dave Hunter, Don Jackson, Jari Kurri, Willy Lindstrom, Ken Linseman, Kevin Lowe, Dave Lumley, Kevin McClelland, Mark Messier, Andy Moog, Jaroslav Pouzar, Dave Semenko, Peter Pocklington (Owner), Glen Sather (General Manager/Coach), John Muckler (Ass't. Coach), Ted Green (Ass't. Coach), Bruce MacGregor (Ass't. General Manager), Barry Fraser (Director of Player Personnel/Chief Scout), Peter Millar (Athletic Therapist), Barrie Stafford (Trainer)
Scores: May 10 at New York — Edmonton 1, NY Islanders 0; May 12 at New York — NY Islanders 6, Edmonton 1; May 15 at Edmonton — Edmonton 7, NY Islanders 2; May 17 at Edmonton — Edmonton 7, NY Islanders 2; May 19 at Edmonton — Edmonton 5, NY Islanders 2.

1982-83 — New York Islanders — Mike Bossy, Bob Bourne, Paul Boutilier, Bill Carroll, Greg Gilbert, Clark Gillies, Butch Goring, Mats Hallin, Tomas Jonsson, Anders Kallur, Gord Lane, Dave Langevin, Mike McEwen, Roland Melanson, Wayne Merrick, Ken Morrow, Bob Nystrom, Stefan Persson, Denis Potvin, Bill Smith, Brent Sutter, Duane Sutter, John Tonelli, Bryan Trottier, Al Arbour (coach), Lorne Henning (ass't coach), Bill Torrey (general manager), Ron Waske, Jim Pickard (trainers)
Scores: May 10 at Edmonton — NY Islanders 2, Edmonton 0; May 12 at Edmonton — NY Islanders 6, Edmonton 3; May 14 at New York — NY Islanders 5, Edmonton 1; May 17 at New York — NY Islanders 4, Edmonton 2

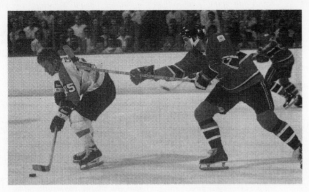

Terry Crisp (#15) and the Philadelphia Flyers surrendered their Stanley Cup title to the Montreal Canadiens in a four game sweep in the 1976 finals.

1981-82 — New York Islanders — Mike Bossy, Bob Bourne, Bill Carroll, Butch Goring, Greg Gilbert, Clark Gillies, Tomas Jonsson, Anders Kallur, Gord Lane, Dave Langevin, Hector Marini, Mike McEwen, Roland Melanson, Wayne Merrick, Ken Morrow, Bob Nystrom, Stefan Persson, Denis Potvin, Bill Smith, Brent Sutter, Duane Sutter, John Tonelli, Bryan Trottier, Al Arbour (coach), Lorne Henning (ass't coach), Bill Torrey (general manager), Ron Waske, Jim Pickard (trainers)
Scores: May 8 at New York — NY Islanders 6, Vancouver 5; May 11 at New York — NY Islanders 6, Vancouver 4; May 13 at Vancouver — NY Islanders 3, Vancouver 0; May 16 at Vancouver — NY Islanders 3, Vancouver 1

1980-81 — New York Islanders — Denis Potvin, Mike McEwen, Ken Morrow, Gord Lane, Bob Lorimer, Stefan Persson, Dave Langevin, Mike Bossy, Bryan Trottier, Butch Goring, Wayne Merrick, Clark Gillies, John Tonelli, Bob Nystrom, Bill Carroll, Bob Bourne, Hector Marini, Anders Kallur, Duane Sutter, Garry Howatt, Lorne Henning, Bill Smith, Roland Melanson, Al Arbour (coach), Bill Torrey (general manager), Ron Waske, Jim Pickard (trainers).
Scores: May 12 at New York — NY Islanders 6, Minnesota 3; May 14 at New York — NY Islanders 6, Minnesota 3; May 17 at Minnesota — NY Islanders 7, Minnesota 5; May 19 at Minnesota— Minnesota 4, NY Islanders 2; May 21 at New York — NY Islanders 5, Minnesota 1.

1979-80 — New York Islanders — Gord Lane, Jean Potvin, Bob Lorimer, Denis Potvin, Stefan Persson, Ken Morrow, Dave Langevin, Duane Sutter, Garry Howatt, Clark Gillies, Lorne Henning, Wayne Merrick, Bob Bourne, Steve Tambellini, Bryan Trottier, Mike Bossy, Bob Nystrom, John Tonelli, Anders Kallur, Butch Goring, Alex McKendry, Glenn Resch, Billy Smith, Al Arbour (coach), Bill Torrey (general manager), Ron Waske, Jim Pickard (trainers).
Scores: May 13 at Philadelphia — NY Islanders 4, Philadelphia 3; May 15 at Philadelphia — Philadelphia 8, NY Islanders 3; May 17 at New York — NY Islanders 6, Philadelphia 2; May 19 at New York — NY Islanders 5, Philadelphia 2; May 22 at Philadelphia — Philadelphia 6, NY Islanders 3; May 24 at New York — NY Islanders 5, Philadelphia 4.

1978-79 — Montreal Canadiens — Ken Dryden, Larry Robinson, Serge Savard, Guy Lapointe, Brian Engblom, Gilles Lupien, Rick Chartraw, Guy Lafleur, Steve Shutt, Jacques Lemaire, Yvan Cournoyer, Réjean Houle, Pierre Mondou, Bob Gainey, Doug Jarvis, Yvon Lambert, Doug Risebrough, Pierre Larouche, Mario Tremblay, Cam Connor, Pat Hughes, Rod Langway, Mark Napier, Michel Larocque, Richard Sévigny, Scotty Bowman (coach), Irving Grundman (managing director), Eddy Palchak, Pierre Meilleur (trainers).
Scores: May 13 at Montreal — NY Rangers 4, Montreal 1; May 15 at Montreal — Montreal 6, NY Rangers 2; May 17 at New York — Montreal 4, NY Rangers 1; May 19 at New York — Montreal 4, NY Rangers 3; May 21 at Montreal — Montreal 4, NY Rangers 1.

1977-78 — Montreal Canadiens — Ken Dryden, Larry Robinson, Serge Savard, Guy Lapointe, Bill Nyrop, Pierre Bouchard, Brian Engblom, Gilles Lupien, Rick Chartraw, Guy Lafleur, Steve Shutt, Jacques Lemaire, Yvan Cournoyer, Réjean Houle, Pierre Mondou, Bob Gainey, Doug Jarvis, Yvon Lambert, Doug Risebrough, Pierre Larouche, Mario Tremblay, Michel Larocque, Murray Wilson, Scotty Bowman (coach), Sam Pollock (general manager), Eddy Palchak, Pierre Meilleur (trainers).
Scores: May 13 at Montreal — Montreal 4, Boston 1; May 16 at Montreal — Montreal 3, Boston 2; May 18 at Boston — Boston 4, Montreal 0; May 21 at Boston — Boston 4, Montreal 3; May 23 at Montreal — Montreal 4, Boston 1; May 25 at Boston — Montreal 4, Boston 1.

1976-77 — Montreal Canadiens — Ken Dryden, Guy Lapointe, Larry Robinson, Serge Savard, Jimmy Roberts, Rick Chartraw, Bill Nyrop, Pierre Bouchard, Brian Engblom, Yvan Cournoyer, Guy Lafleur, Jacques Lemaire, Steve Shutt, Pete Mahovlich, Murray Wilson, Doug Jarvis, Yvon Lambert, Bob Gainey, Doug Risebrough, Mario Tremblay, Rejean Houle, Pierre Mondou, Mike Polich, Michel Larocque, Scotty Bowman (coach), Sam Pollock (general manager), Eddy Palchak, Pierre Meilleur (trainers).
Scores: May 7 at Montreal — Montreal 7, Boston 3; May 10 at Montreal — Montreal 3, Boston 0; May 12 at Boston — Montreal 4, Boston 2; May 14 at Boston — Montreal 2, Boston 1.

1975-76 — Montreal Canadiens — Ken Dryden, Serge Savard, Guy Lapointe, Larry Robinson, Bill Nyrop, Pierre Bouchard, Jim Roberts, Guy Lafleur, Steve Shutt, Pete Mahovlich, Yvan Cournoyer, Jacques Lemaire, Yvon Lambert, Bob Gainey, Doug Jarvis, Doug Risebrough, Murray Wilson, Mario Tremblay, Rick Chartraw, Michel Larocque, Scotty Bowman (coach), Sam Pollock (general manager), Eddy Palchak, Pierre Meilleur (trainers).
Scores: May 9 at Montreal — Montreal 4, Philadelphia 3; May 11 at Montreal — Montreal 2, Philadelphia 1; May 13 at Philadelphia — Montreal 3, Philadelphia 2; May 16 at Philadelphia — Montreal 5, Philadelphia 3.

1974-75 — Philadelphia Flyers — Bernie Parent, Wayne Stephenson, Ed Van Impe, Tom Bladon, André Dupont, Joe Watson, Jim Watson, Ted Harris, Larry Goodenough, Rick MacLeish, Bobby Clarke, Bill Barber, Reggie Leach, Gary Dornhoefer, Ross Lonsberry, Bob Kelly, Terry Crisp, Don Saleski, Dave Schultz, Orest Kindrachuk, Bill Clement, Fred Shero (coach), Keith Allen (general manager), Frank Lewis, Jim McKenzie (trainers).
Scores: May 15 at Philadelphia — Philadelphia 4, Buffalo 1; May 18 at Philadelphia — Philadelphia 2, Buffalo 1; May 20 at Buffalo — Buffalo 5, Philadelphia 4; May 22 at Buffalo — Buffalo 4, Philadelphia 2; May 25 at Philadelphia — Philadelphia 5, Buffalo 1; May 27 at Buffalo — Philadelphia 2, Buffalo 0.

1973-74 — Philadelphia Flyers — Bernie Parent, Ed Van Impe, Tom Bladon, André Dupont, Joe Watson, Jim Watson, Barry Ashbee, Bill Barber, Dave Schultz, Don Saleski, Gary Dornhoefer, Terry Crisp, Bobby Clarke, Simon Nolet, Ross Lonsberry, Rick MacLeish, Bill Flett, Orest Kindrachuk, Bill Clement, Bob Kelly, Bruce Cowick, Al MacAdam, Bobby Taylor, Fred Shero (coach), Keith Allen (general manager), Frank Lewis, Jim McKenzie (trainers).
Scores: May 7 at Boston — Boston 3, Philadelphia 2; May 9 at Boston — Philadelphia 3, Boston 2; May 12 at Philadelphia — Philadelphia 4, Boston 1; May 14 at Philadelphia — Philadelphia 4, Boston 2; May 16 at Boston — Boston 5, Philadelphia 1; May 19 at Philadelphia — Philadelphia 1, Boston 0.

1972-73 — Montreal Canadiens — Ken Dryden, Guy Lapointe, Serge Savard, Larry Robinson, Jacques Laperrière, Bob Murdoch, Pierre Bouchard, Jim Roberts, Yvan Cournoyer, Frank Mahovlich, Jacques Lemaire, Pete Mahovlich, Marc Tardif, Henri Richard, Réjean Houle, Guy Lafleur, Chuck Lefley, Claude Larose, Murray Wilson, Steve Shutt, Michel Plasse, Scotty Bowman (coach), Sam Pollock (general manager), Ed Palchak, Bob Williams (trainers).
Scores: April 29 at Montreal — Montreal 8, Chicago 3; May 1 at Montreal — Montreal 4, Chicago 1; May 3 at Chicago — Chicago 7, Montreal 4; May 6 at Chicago — Montreal 4, Chicago 0; May 8 at Montreal — Chicago 8, Montreal 7; May 10 at Chicago — Montreal 6, Chicago 4.

1971-72 — Boston Bruins — Gerry Cheevers, Ed Johnston, Bobby Orr, Ted Green, Carol Vadnais, Dallas Smith, Don Awrey, Phil Esposito, Ken Hodge, Mike Walton, Wayne Cashman, Garnet Bailey, Derek Sanderson, Fred Stanfield, Ed Westfall, John McKenzie, Don Marcotte, Garry Peters, Chris Hayes, Tom Johnson (coach), Milt Schmidt (general manager), Dan Canney, John Forristall (trainers).
Scores: April 30 at Boston — Boston 6, NY Rangers 5; May 2 at Boston — Boston 2, NY Rangers 1; May 4 at New York — NY Rangers 5, Boston 2; May 7 at New York — Boston 3, NY Rangers 2; May 9 at Boston — NY Rangers 3, Boston 2; May 11 at New York — Boston 3, NY Rangers 0.

1970-71 — Montreal Canadiens — Ken Dryden, Rogatien Vachon, Jacques Laperrière, Jean-Claude Tremblay, Guy Lapointe, Terry Harper, Pierre Bouchard, Jean Béliveau, Yvan Cournoyer, Réjean Houle, Claude Larose, Henri Richard, Phil Roberto, Pete Mahovlich, Leon Rochefort, John Ferguson, Bobby Sheehan, Jacques Lemaire, Frank Mahovlich, Bob Murdoch, Chuck Lefley, Al MacNeil (coach), Sam Pollock (general manager), Yvon Belanger, Ed Palchak (trainers).
Scores: May 4 at Chicago — Chicago 2, Montreal 1; May 6 at Chicago — Chicago 5, Montreal 3; May 9 at Montreal — Montreal 4, Chicago 2; May 11 at Montreal — Montreal 5, Chicago 2; May 13 at Chicago — Chicago 2, Montreal 0; May 16 at Montreal — Montreal 4, Chicago 3; May 18 at Chicago — Montreal 3, Chicago 2.

1969-70 — Boston Bruins — Gerry Cheevers, Ed Johnston, Bobby Orr, Rick Smith, Dallas Smith, Bill Speer, Gary Doak, Don Awrey, Phil Esposito, Ken Hodge, John Bucyk, Wayne Carleton, Wayne Cashman, Derek Sanderson, Fred Stanfield, Ed Westfall, John McKenzie, Jim Lorentz, Don Marcotte, Bill Lesuk, Dan Schock, Harry Sinden (coach), Milt Schmidt (general manager), Dan Canney, John Forristall (trainers).
Scores: May 3 at St. Louis — Boston 6, St. Louis 1; May 5 at St. Louis — Boston 6, St. Louis 2; May 7 at Boston — Boston 4, St. Louis 1; May 10 at Boston — Boston 4, St. Louis 3.

1968-69 — Montreal Canadiens — Lorne Worsley, Rogatien Vachon, Jacques Laperrière, Jean-Claude Tremblay, Ted Harris, Serge Savard, Terry Harper, Larry Hillman, Jean Béliveau, Ralph Backstrom, Dick Duff, Yvan Cournoyer, Claude Provost, Bobby Rousseau, Henri Richard, John Ferguson, Christian Bordeleau, Mickey Redmond, Jacques Lemaire, Lucien Grenier, Tony Esposito, Claude Ruel (coach), Sam Pollock (general manager), Larry Aubut, Eddy Palchak (trainers).
Scores: April 27 at Montreal — Montreal 3, St. Louis 1; April 29 at Montreal — Montreal 3, St. Louis 1; May 1 at St. Louis — Montreal 4, St. Louis 0; May 4 at St. Louis — Montreal 2, St. Louis 1.

1967-68 — Montreal Canadiens — Lorne Worsley, Rogatien Vachon, Jacques Laperrière, Jean-Claude Tremblay, Ted Harris, Serge Savard, Terry Harper, Carol Vadnais, Jean Béliveau, Gilles Tremblay, Ralph Backstrom, Dick Duff, Claude Larose, Yvan Cournoyer, Claude Provost, Bobby Rousseau, Henri Richard, John Ferguson, Danny Grant, Jacques Lemaire, Mickey Redmond, Toe Blake (coach), Sam Pollock (general manager), Larry Aubut, Eddy Palchak (trainers).
Scores: May 5 at St. Louis — Montreal 3, St. Louis 2; May 7 at St. Louis — Montreal 1, St. Louis 0; May 9 at Montreal — Montreal 4, St. Louis 3; May 11 at Montreal — Montreal 3, St. Louis 2.

1966-67 — Toronto Maple Leafs — Johnny Bower, Terry Sawchuk, Larry Hillman, Marcel Pronovost, Tim Horton, Bob Baun, Aut Erickson, Allan Stanley, Red Kelly, Ron Ellis, George Armstrong, Pete Stemkowski, Dave Keon, Mike Walton, Jim Pappin, Bob Pulford, Brian Conacher, Eddie Shack, Frank Mahovlich, Milan Marcetta, Larry Jeffrey, Bruce Gamble, Punch Imlach (manager-coach), Bob Haggart (trainer).
Scores: April 20 at Montreal — Toronto 2, Montreal 6; April 22 at Montreal — Toronto 3, Montreal 0; April 25 at Toronto — Toronto 3, Montreal 2; April 27 at Toronto — Toronto 2, Montreal 6; April 29 at Montreal — Toronto 4, Montreal 1; May 2 at Toronto — Toronto 3, Montreal 1.

1965-66 — Montreal Canadiens — Lorne Worsley, Charlie Hodge, Jean-Claude Tremblay, Ted Harris, Jean-Guy Talbot, Terry Harper, Jacques Laperrière, Noel Price, Jean Béliveau, Ralph Backstrom, Dick Duff, Gilles Tremblay, Claude Larose, Yvan Cournoyer, Claude Provost, Bobby Rousseau, Henri Richard, Dave Balon, John Ferguson, Leon Rochefort, Jim Roberts, Toe Blake (coch), Sam Pollock (general manager), Larry Aubut, Andy Galley (trainers).
Scores: April 24 at Montreal — Detroit 3, Montreal 2; April 26 at Montreal — Detroit 5, Montreal 2; April 28 at Detroit — Montreal 4, Detroit 2; May 1 at Detroit — Montreal 2, Detroit 1; May 3 at Montreal — Montreal 5, Detroit 1; May 5 at Detroit — Montreal 3, Detroit 2.

1964-65 — Montreal Canadiens — Lorne Worsley, Charlie Hodge, Jean-Claude Tremblay, Ted Harris, Jean-Guy Talbot, Terry Harper, Jean Gauthier, Noel Picard, Jean Béliveau, Ralph Backstrom, Dick Duff, Claude Larose, Yvan Cournoyer, Claude Provost, Bobby Rousseau, Henri Richard, John Ferguson, Red Berenson, Jim Roberts, Toe Blake (coach), Sam Pollock (general manager), Larry Aubut, Andy Galley (trainers).
Scores: April 17 at Montreal — Montreal 3, Chicago 2; April 20 at Montreal — Montreal 2, Chicago 0; April 22 at Chicago — Montreal 1, Chicago 3; April 25 at Chicago — Montreal 1, Chicago 5; April 7 at Montreal — Montreal 6, Chicago 0; April 29 at Chicago — Montreal 1, Chicago 2; May 1 at Montreal — Montreal 4, Chicago 0.

1963-64 — Toronto Maple Leafs — Johnny Bower, Carl Brewer, Tim Horton, Bob Baun, Allan Stanley, Larry Hillman, Al Arbour, Red Kelly, Gerry Ehman, Andy Bathgate, George Armstrong, Ron Stewart, Dave Keon, Billy Harris, Don McKenney, Jim Pappin, Bob Pulford, Eddie Shack, Frank Mahovlich, Eddie Litzenberger, Punch Imlach (manager-coach), Bob Haggart (trainer).
Scores April 11 at Toronto — Toronto 3, Detroit 2; April 14 at Toronto — Toronto 3, Detroit 4; April 16 at Detroit — Toronto 3, Detroit 4; April 18 at Detroit — Toronto 4, Detroit 2; April 21 at Toronto — Toronto 1, Detroit 2; April 23 at Detroit — Toronto 4, Detroit 3; April 25 at Toronto — Toronto 4, Detroit 0.

1962-63 — Toronto Maple Leafs — Johnny Bower, Don Simmons, Carl Brewer, Tim Horton, Kent Douglas, Allan Stanley, Bob Baun, Larry Hillman, Red Kelly, Dick Duff, George Armstrong, Bob Nevin, Ron Stewart, Dave Keon, Billy Harris, Bob Pulford, Eddie Shack, Ed Litzenberger, Frank Mahovlich, John MacMillan, Punch Imlach (manager-coach), Bob Haggart (trainer).
Scores: April 9 at Toronto — Toronto 4, Detroit 2; April 11 at Toronto — Toronto 4, Detroit 2; April 14 at Detroit — Toronto 3, Detroit 4; April 16 at Detroit — Toronto 4, Detroit 2; April 18 at Toronto — Toronto 3, Detroit 1.

1961-62 — Toronto Maple Leafs — Johnny Bower, Don Simmons, Carl Brewer, Tim Horton, Bob Baun, Allan Stanley, Al Arbour, Larry Hillman, Red Kelly, Dick Duff, George Armstrong, Frank Mahovlich, Bob Nevin, Ron Stewart, Bill Harris, Bert Olmstead, Bob Pulford, Eddie Shack, Dave Keon, Ed Litzenberger, John MacMillan, Punch Imlach (manager-coach), Bob Haggert (trainer).
Scores: April 10 at Toronto — Toronto 4, Chicago 1; April 12 at Toronto — Toronto 3, Chicago 2; April 15 at Chicago — Toronto 0, Chicago 3; April 17 at Chicago — Toronto 1, Chicago 4; April 19 at Toronto —Toronto 8, Chicago 4; April 22 at Chicago — Toronto 2, Chicago 1.

1960-61 — Chicago Black Hawks — Glenn Hall, Al Arbour, Pierre Pilote, Elmer Vasko, Jack Evans, Dollard St. Laurent, Reg Fleming, Tod Sloan, Ron Murphy, Eddie Litzenberger, Bill Hay, Bobby Hull, Ab McDonald, Eric Nesterenko, Ken Wharram, Earl Balfour, Stan Mikita, Murray Balfour, Chico Maki, Wayne Hicks, Tommy Ivan (manager), Rudy Pilous (coach), Nick Garen (trainer).
Scores: April 6 at Chicago — Chicago 3, Detroit 2; April 8 at Detroit — Detroit 3, Chicago 1; April 10 at Chicago — Chicago 3, Detroit 1; April 12 at Detroit — Detroit 2, Chicago 1; April 14 at Chicago — Chicago 6, Detroit 3; April 16 at Detroit — Chicago 5, Detroit 1.

1959-60 — Montreal Canadiens — Jacques Plante, Charlie Hodge, Doug Harvey, Tom Johnson, Bob Turner, Jean-Guy Talbot, Albert Langlois, Ralph Backstrom, Jean Béliveau, Marcel Bonin, Bernie Geoffrion, Phil Goyette, Bill Hicke, Don Marshall, Ab McDonald, Dickie Moore, André Pronovost, Claude Provost, Henri Richard, Maurice Richard, Frank Selke (manager), Toe Blake (coach), Larry Aubut (trainers).
Scores: April 7 at Montreal — Montreal 4, Toronto 2; April 9 at Montreal — Montreal 2, Toronto 1; April 12 at Toronto — Montreal 5, Toronto 2; April 14 at Toronto — Montreal 4, Toronto 0.

1958-59 — Montreal Canadiens — Jacques Plante, Charlie Hodge, Doug Harvey, Tom Johnson, Bob Turner, Jean-Guy Talbot, Albert Langlois, Bernie Geoffrion, Ralph Backstrom, Bill Hicke, Maurice Richard, Dickie Moore, Claude Provost, Ab McDonald, Henri Richard, Marcel Bonin, Phil Goyette, Don Marshall, Jean Béliveau, Frank Selke (manager), Toe Blake (coach), Hector Dubois, Larry Aubut (trainers).
Scores: April 9 at Montreal — Montreal 5, Toronto 3; April 11 at Montreal — Montreal 3, Toronto 1; April 14 at Toronto — Toronto 3, Montreal 2; April 16 at Toronto — Montreal 3, Toronto 2; April 18 at Montreal — Montreal 5, Toronto 3.

1957-58 — Montreal Canadiens — Jacques Plante, Gerry McNeil, Doug Harvey, Tom Johnson, Bob Turner, Dollard St-Laurent, Jean-Guy Talbot, Albert Langlois, Jean Béliveau, Bernie Geoffrion, Maurice Richard, Dickie Moore, Claude Provost, Floyd Curry, Bert Olmstead, Henri Richard, Marcel Bonin, Phil Goyette, Don Marshall, André Pronovost, Connie Broden, Frank Selke (manager), Toe Blake (coach), Hector Dubois, Larry Aubut (trainers).
Scores: April 8 at Montreal —Montreal 2, Boston 1; April 10 at Montreal — Boston 5, Montreal 2; April 13 at Boston — Montreal 3, Boston 0; April 15 at Boston — Boston 3, Montreal 1; April 17 at Montreal — Montreal 3, Boston 2; April 20 at Boston — Montreal 5, Boston 3.

Right: Frank Mahovlich, left, and Red Kelly combined to win 14 championships in their Hall-of-Fame careers. They are two of only four players to win multiple Stanley Cup titles with two-or-more teams. Below: Montreal Canadiens goaltender Gerry McNeil thwarts Detroit's Earl "Dutch" Reibel as Doug Harvey and Bernie Geoffrion look on during the 1954 Stanley Cup finals. The Red Wings went on to win the Stanley Cup with a seventh game overtime victory.

1956-57 — Montreal Canadiens — Jacques Plante, Gerry McNeil, Doug Harvey, Tom Johnson, Bob Turner, Dollard St. Laurent, Jean-Guy Talbot, Jean Béliveau, Bernie Geoffrion, Floyd Curry, Dickie Moore, Maurice Richard, Claude Provost, Bert Olmstead, Henri Richard, Phil Goyette, Don Marshall, André Pronovost, Connie Broden, Frank Selke (manager), Toe Blake (coach), Hector Dubois, Larry Aubut (trainers).
Scores: April 6, at Montreal — Montreal 5, Boston 1; April 9, at Montreal — Montreal 1, Boston 0; April 11, at Boston — Montreal 4, Boston 2; April 14, at Boston — Boston 2, Montreal 0; April 16, at Montreal — Montreal 5, Boston 1.

1955-56 — Montreal Canadiens — Jacques Plante, Doug Harvey, Emile Bouchard, Bob Turner, Tom Johnson, Jean-Guy Talbot, Dollard St. Laurent, Bernie Geoffrion, Bert Olmstead, Floyd Curry, Jackie Leclair, Maurice Richard, Dickie Moore, Henri Richard, Ken Mosdell, Don Marshall, Claude Provost, Frank Selke (manager), Toe Blake (coach), Hector Dubois (trainer).
Scores: March 31, at Montreal — Montreal 6, Detroit 4; April 3, at Montreal — Montreal 5, Detroit 1; April 5, at Detroit — Detroit 3, Montreal 1; April 8, at Detroit — Montreal 3, Detroit 0; April 10, at Montreal — Montreal 3, Detroit 1.

1954-55 — Detroit Red Wings — Terry Sawchuk, Red Kelly, Bob Goldham, Marcel Pronovost, Ben Woit, Jim Hay, Larry Hillman, Ted Lindsay, Tony Leswick, Gordie Howe, Alex Delvecchio, Marty Pavelich, Glen Skov, Earl Reibel, John Wilson, Bill Dineen, Vic Stasiuk, Marcel Bonin, Jack Adams (manager), Jimmy Skinner (coach), Carl Mattson (trainer).
Scores: April 3, at Detroit — Detroit 4, Montreal 2; April 5, at Detroit — Detroit 7, Montreal 1; April 7 at Montreal — Montreal 4, Detroit 2; April 9, at Montreal — Montreal 5, Detroit 3; April 10, at Detroit — Detroit 5, Montreal 1; April 12, at Montreal — Montreal 6, Detroit 3; April 14, at Detroit — Detroit 3, Montreal 1

1953-54 — Detroit Red Wings — Terry Sawchuk, Red Kelly, Bob Goldham, Ben Woit, Marcel Pronovost, Al Arbour, Keith Allen, Ted Lindsay, Tony Leswick, Gordie Howe, Marty Pavelich, Alex Delvecchio, Metro Prystai, Glen Skov, John Wilson, Bill Dineen, Jim Peters, Earl Reibel, Vic Stasiuk, Jack Adams (manager), Tommy Ivan (coach), Carl Mattson (trainer).
Scores: April 4, at Detroit — Detroit 3, Montreal 1; April 6, at Detroit — Montreal 3, Detroit 1; April 8, at Montreal — Detroit 5, Montreal 2; April 10, at Montreal — Detroit 2, Montreal 0; April 11, at Detroit — Montreal 1, Detroit 0; April 13, at Montreal — Montreal 4, Detroit 1; April 16, at Detroit — Detroit 2, Montreal 1.

1952-53 — Montreal Canadiens — Gerry McNeil, Jacques Plante, Doug Harvey, Emile Bouchard, Tom Johnson, Dollard St. Laurent, Bud MacPherson, Maurice Richard, Elmer Lach, Bert Olmstead, Bernie Geoffrion, Floyd Curry, Paul Masnick, Billy Reay, Dickie Moore, Ken Mosdell, Dick Gamble, Johnny McCormack, Lorne Davis, Calum McKay, Eddie Mazur, Frank Selke (manager), Dick Irvin (coach), Hector Dubois (trainer).
Scores: April 9, at Montreal — Montreal 4, Boston 2; April 11, at Montreal — Boston 4, Montreal 1; April 12, at Boston — Montreal 3, Boston 0; April 14, at Boston — Montreal 7, Boston 3; April 16, at Montreal — Montreal 1, Boston 0.

1951-52 — Detroit Red Wings — Terry Sawchuk, Bob Goldham, Ben Woit, Red Kelly, Leo Reise, Marcel Pronovost, Ted Lindsay, Tony Leswick, Gordie Howe, Metro Prystai, Marty Pavelich, Sid Abel, Glen Skov, Alex Delvecchio, John Wilson, Vic Stasiuk, Larry Zeidel, Jack Adams (manager), Carl Mattson (trainer).
Scores: April 10, at Montreal — Detroit 3, Montreal 1; April 12 at Montreal — Detroit 2, Montreal 1; April 13, at Detroit — Detroit 3, Montreal 0; April 15, at Detroit — Detroit 3, Montreal 0.

1950-51 — Toronto Maple Leafs — Turk Broda, Al Rollins, Jim Thomson, Gus Mortson, Bill Barilko, Bill Juzda, Fern Flaman, Hugh Bolton, Ted Kennedy, Sid Smith, Tod Sloan, Cal Gardner, Howie Meeker, Harry Watson, Max Bentley, Joe Klukay, Danny Lewicki, Ray Timgren, Fleming Mackell, Johnny McCormack, Bob Hassard, Conn Smythe (manager), Joe Primeau (coach), Tim Daly (trainer).
Scores: April 11, at Toronto — Toronto 3, Montreal 2; April 14, at Toronto — Montreal 3, Toronto 2; April 17, at Montreal — Toronto 2, Montreal 1; April 19, at Montreal — Toronto 3, Montreal 2; April 21, at Toronto — Toronto 3, Montreal 2.

1949-50 — Detroit Red Wings — Harry Lumley, Jack Stewart, Leo Reise, Clare Martin, Al Dewsbury, Lee Fogolin, Red Kelly, Gordie Howe, George Gee, Jimmy Peters, Marty Pavelich, Jim McFadden, Pete Babando, Max McNab, Gerry Couture, Joe Carveth, Steve Black, John Wilson, Larry Wilson, Jack Adams (manager), Tommy Ivan (coach), Carl Mattson (trainer).
Scores: April 11, at Detroit — Detroit 4, NY Rangers 1; April 13, at Toronto* — NY Rangers 3, Detroit 1; April 15, at Toronto — Detroit 4, NY Rangers 0; April 18, at Detroit — NY Rangers 4, Detroit 3; April 20, at Detroit — NY Rangers 2, Detroit 1; April 22, at Detroit — Detroit 5, NY Rangers 4; April 23, at Detroit — Detroit 4, NY Rangers 3.
* Ice was unavailable in Madison Square Garden and Rangers elected to play second and third games on Toronto ice.

1948-49 — Toronto Maple Leafs — Turk Broda, Jim Thomson, Gus Mortson, Bill Barilko, Garth Boesch, Bill Juzda, Ted Kennedy, Howie Meeker, Vic Lynn, Bill Ezinicki, Cal Gardner, Max Bentley, Joe Klukay, Sid Smith, Don Metz, Ray Timgren, Fleming Mackell, Harry Taylor, Bob Dawes, Tod Sloan, Conn Smythe (manager), Hap Day (coach), Tim Daly (trainer).
Scores: April 8, at Detroit — Toronto 3, Detroit 2; April 10, at Detroit — Toronto 3, Detroit 1; April 13, at Toronto — Toronto 3, Detroit 1; April 16, at Toronto — Toronto 3, Detroit 1.

1947-48 — Toronto Maple Leafs — Turk Broda, Jim Thomson, Wally Stanowski, Garth Boesch, Bill Barilko, Gus Mortson, Phil Samis, Syl Apps, Bill Ezinicki, Harry Watson, Ted Kennedy, Howie Meeker, Vic Lynn, Nick Metz, Max Bentley, Joe Klukay, Les Costello, Don Metz, Sid Smith, Conn Smythe (manager), Hap Day (coach), Tim Daly (trainer).
Scores: April 7, at Toronto — Toronto 5, Detroit 3; April 10, at Toronto — Toronto 4, Detroit 2; April 11, at Detroit — Toronto 2, Detroit 0; April 14, at Detroit — Toronto 7, Detroit 2.

In one of the most famous images in NHL history, Toronto defenceman "Bashing" Bill Barilko was just driven in from the blueline and deposited the Stanley Cup-winning goal past Montreal's Gerry McNeil in the 1951 finals.

1946-47 — Toronto Maple Leafs — Turk Broda, Garth Boesch, Gus Mortson, Jim Thomson, Wally Stanowski, Bill Barilko, Harry Watson, Bud Poile, Ted Kennedy, Syl Apps, Don Metz, Nick Metz, Bill Ezinicki, Vic Lynn, Howie Meeker, Gaye Stewart, Joe Klukay, Gus Bodnar, Bob Goldham, Conn Smythe (manager), Hap Day (coach), Tim Daly (trainer).
Scores: April 8, at Montreal — Montreal 6, Toronto 0; April 10, at Montreal — Toronto 4, Montreal 0; April 12, at Toronto — Toronto 4, Montreal 2; April 15, at Toronto — Toronto 2, Montreal 1; April 17, at Montreal — Montreal 3, Toronto 1; April 19, at Toronto — Toronto 2, Montreal 1.

1945-46 — Montreal Canadiens — Elmer Lach, Toe Blake, Maurice Richard, Bob Fillion, Dutch Hiller, Murph Chamberlain, Ken Mosdell, Buddy O'Connor, Glen Harmon, Jim Peters, Emile Bouchard, Bill Reay, Ken Reardon, Leo Lamoureux, Frank Eddolls, Gerry Plamondon, Bill Durnan, Tommy Gorman (manager), Dick Irvin (coach), Ernie Cook (trainer).
Scores: March 30, at Montreal — Montreal 4, Boston 3; April 2, at Montreal — Montreal 3, Boston 2; April 4, at Boston — Montreal 4, Boston 2; April 7, at Boston — Boston 3, Montreal 2; April 9, at Montreal — Montreal 6, Boston 3.

1944-45 — Toronto Maple Leafs — Don Metz, Frank McCool, Wally Stanowski, Reg Hamilton, Elwyn Morris, Johnny McCreedy, Tommy O'Neill, Ted Kennedy, Babe Pratt, Gus Bodnar, Art Jackson, Jack McLean, Mel Hill, Nick Metz, Bob Davidson, Dave Schriner, Lorne Carr, Conn Smythe (manager), Frank Selke (business manager), Hap Day (coach), Tim Daly (trainer).
Scores: April 6, at Detroit — Toronto 1, Detroit 0; April 8, at Detroit — Toronto 2, Detroit 0; April 12, at Toronto — Toronto 1, Detroit 0; April 14, at Toronto — Detroit 5, Toronto 3; April 19, at Detroit — Detroit 2, Toronto 0; April 21, at Toronto — Detroit 1, Toronto 0; April 22, at Detroit — Toronto 2, Detroit 1.

1943-44 — Montreal Canadiens — Toe Blake, Maurice Richard, Elmer Lach, Ray Getliffe, Murph Chamberlain, Phil Watson, Emile Bouchard, Glen Harmon, Buddy O'Connor, Jerry Heffernan, Mike McMahon, Leo Lamoureux, Fernand Majeau, Bob Fillion, Bill Durnan, Tommy Gorman (manager), Dick Irvin (coach), Ernie Cook (trainer).
Scores: April 4, at Montreal — Montreal 5, Chicago 1; April 6, at Chicago — Montreal 3, Chicago 1; April 9, at Chicago — Montreal 3, Chicago 2; April 13, at Montreal — Montreal 5, Chicago 4.

1942-43 — Detroit Red Wings — Jack Stewart, Jimmy Orlando, Sid Abel, Alex Motter, Harry Watson, Joe Carveth, Mud Bruneteau, Eddie Wares, Johnny Mowers, Cully Simon, Don Grosso, Carl Liscombe, Connie Brown, Syd Howe, Les Douglas, Hal Jackson, Joe Fisher, Jack Adams (manager), Ebbie Goodfellow (playing-coach), Honey Walker (trainer).
Scores: April 1, at Detroit — Detroit 6, Boston 2; April 4, at Detroit — Detroit 4, Boston 3; April 7, at Boston — Detroit 4, Boston 0; April 8, at Boston — Detroit 2, Boston 0.

1941-42 — Toronto Maple Leafs — Wally Stanowski, Syl Apps, Bob Goldham, Gord Drillon, Hank Goldup, Ernie Dickens, Dave Schriner, Bucko McDonald, Bob Davidson, Nick Metz, Bingo Kampman, Don Metz, Gaye Stewart, Turk Broda, Johnny McCreedy, Lorne Carr, Pete Langelle, Billy Taylor, Conn Smythe (manager), Hap Day (coach), Frank Selke (business manager), Tim Daly (trainer).
Scores: April 4, at Toronto — Detroit 3, Toronto 2; April 7, at Toronto — Detroit 4, Toronto 2; April 9, at Detroit — Detroit 5, Toronto 2; April 12, at Detroit — Toronto 4, Detroit 3; April 14, at Toronto — Toronto 9, Detroit 3; April 16, at Detroit — Toronto 3, Detroit 0; April 18, at Toronto — Toronto 3, Detroit 1.

1940-41 — Boston Bruins — Bill Cowley, Des Smith, Dit Clapper, Frank Brimsek, Flash Hollett, John Crawford, Bobby Bauer, Pat McCreavy, Herb Cain, Mel Hill, Milt Schmidt, Woody Dumart, Roy Conacher, Terry Reardon, Art Jackson, Eddie Wiseman, Art Ross (manager), Cooney Weiland (coach), Win Green (trainer).
Scores: April 6, at Boston — Detroit 2, Boston 3; April 8, at Boston — Detroit 1, Boston 2; April 10, at Detroit — Boston 4, Detroit 2; April 12, at Detroit — Boston 3, Detroit 1.

1939-40 — New York Rangers — Dave Kerr, Art Coulter, Ott Heller, Alex Shibicky, Mac Colville, Neil Colville, Phil Watson, Lynn Patrick, Clint Smith, Muzz Patrick, Babe Pratt, Bryan Hextall, Kilby Macdonald, Dutch Hiller, Alf Pike, Sanford Smith, Lester Patrick (manager), Frank Boucher (coach), Harry Westerby (trainer).
Scores: April 2, at New York — NY Rangers 2, Toronto 1; April 3, at New York — NY Rangers 6, Toronto 2; April 6, at Toronto — NY Rangers 1, Toronto 2; April 9, at Toronto — NY Rangers 0, Toronto 3; April 11, at Toronto — NY Rangers 2, Toronto 1; April 13, at Toronto — NY Rangers 3, Toronto 2.

1938-39 — Boston Bruins — Bobby Bauer, Mel Hill, Flash Hollett, Roy Conacher, Gord Pettinger, Milt Schmidt, Woody Dumart, Jack Crawford, Ray Getliffe, Frank Brimsek, Eddie Shore, Dit Clapper, Bill Cowley, Jack Portland, Red Hamill, Cooney Weiland, Art Ross (manager-coach), Win Green (trainer).
Scores: April 6, at Boston — Toronto 1, Boston 2; April 9, at Boston — Toronto 3, Boston 2; April 11, at Toronto — Toronto 1, Boston 3; April 13 at Toronto — Toronto 0, Boston 2; April 16, at Boston — Toronto 1, Boston 3.

1937-38 — Chicago Black Hawks — Art Wiebe, Carl Voss, Hal Jackson, Mike Karakas, Mush March, Jack Shill, Earl Seibert, Cully Dahlstrom, Alex Levinsky, Johnny Gottselig, Lou Trudel, Pete Palangio, Bill MacKenzie, Doc Romnes, Paul Thompson, Roger Jenkins, Alf Moore, Bert Connolly, Virgil Johnson, Paul Goodman, Bill Stewart (manager-coach), Eddie Froelich (trainer).
Scores: April 5, at Toronto — Chicago 3, Toronto 1; April 7, at Toronto — Chicago 1, Toronto 5; April 10 at Chicago — Chicago 2, Toronto 1; April 12, at Chicago — Chicago 4, Toronto 1.

1936-37 — Detroit Red Wings — Normie Smith, Pete Kelly, Larry Aurie, Herbie Lewis, Hec Kilrea, Mud Bruneteau, Syd Howe, Wally Kilrea, Jimmy Franks, Bucko McDonald, Gordon Pettinger, Ebbie Goodfellow, Johnny Gallagher, Scotty Bowman, Johnny Sorrell, Marty Barry, Earl Robertson, Johnny Sherf, Howard Mackie, Jack Adams (manager-coach), Honey Walker (trainer).
Scores: April 6, at New York — Detroit 1, NY Rangers 5; April 8, at Detroit — Detroit 4, NY Rangers 2; April 11, at Detroit — Detroit 0, NY Rangers 1; April 13, at Detroit — Detroit 1, NY Rangers 0; April 15, at Detroit — Detroit 3, NY Rangers 0.

1935-36 — Detroit Red Wings — Johnny Sorrell, Syd Howe, Marty Barry, Herbie Lewis, Mud Bruneteau, Wally Kilrea, Hec Kilrea, Gordon Pettinger, Bucko McDonald, Scotty Bowman, Pete Kelly, Doug Young, Ebbie Goodfellow, Normie Smith, Jack Adams (manager-coach), Honey Walker (trainer).
Scores: April 5, at Detroit — Detroit 3, Toronto 1; April 7, at Detroit — Detroit 9, Toronto 4; April 9, at Toronto — Detroit 3, Toronto 4; April 11, at Toronto — Detroit 3, Toronto 2.

1934-35 — Montreal Maroons — Marvin (Cy) Wentworth, Alex Connell, Toe Blake, Stew Evans, Earl Robinson, Bill Miller, Dave Trottier, Jimmy Ward, Larry Northcott, Hooley Smith, Russ Blinco, Allan Shields, Sammy McManus, Gus Marker, Bob Gracie, Herb Cain, Tommy Gorman (manager), Lionel Conacher (coach), Bill O'Brien (trainer).
Scores: April 4, at Toronto — Mtl. Maroons 3, Toronto 2; April 6, at Toronto — Mtl. Maroons 3, Toronto 1; April 9, at Montreal — Mtl. Maroons 4, Toronto 1.

1933-34 — Chicago Black Hawks — Taffy Abel, Lolo Couture, Lou Trudel, Lionel Conacher, Paul Thompson, Leroy Goldsworthy, Art Coulter, Roger Jenkins, Don McFayden, Tommy Cook, Doc Romnes, Johnny Gottselig, Mush March, Johnny Sheppard, Chuck Gardiner (captain), Bill Kendall, Tommy Gorman (manager-coach), Eddie Froelich (trainer).
Scores: April 3, at Detroit — Chicago 2, Detroit 1; April 5, at Detroit — Chicago 4, Detroit 1; April 8, at Chicago — Detroit 5, Chicago 2; April 10, at Chicago — Chicago 1, Detroit 0.

1932-33 — New York Rangers — Ching Johnson, Butch Keeling, Frank Boucher, Art Somers, Babe Siebert, Bun Cook, Andy Aitkenhead, Ott Heller, Ozzie Asmundson, Gord Pettinger, Doug Brennan, Cecil Dillon, Bill Cook (captain), Murray Murdoch, Earl Seibert, Lester Patrick (manager-coach), Harry Westerby (trainer).
Scores: April 4, at New York — NY Rangers 5, Toronto 1; April 8, at Toronto — NY Rangers 3, Toronto 1; April 11, at Toronto — Toronto 3, NY Rangers 2; April 13, at Toronto — NY Rangers 1, Toronto 0.

1931-32 — Toronto Maple Leafs — Charlie Conacher, Harvey Jackson, King Clancy, Andy Blair, Red Horner, Lorne Chabot, Alex Levinsky, Joe Primeau, Hal Darragh, Hal Cotton, Frank Finnigan, Hap Day, Ace Bailey, Bob Gracie, Fred Robertson, Earl Miller, Conn Smythe (manager), Dick Irvin (coach), Tim Daly (trainer).
Scores: April 5 at New York — Toronto 6, NY Rangers 4; April 7, at Boston* — Toronto 6, NY Rangers 2; April 9, at Toronto — Toronto 6, NY Rangers 4.
* Ice was unavailable in Madison Square Garden and Rangers elected to play the second game on neutral ice.

1930-31 — Montreal Canadiens — George Hainsworth, Wildor Larochelle, Marty Burke, Sylvio Mantha, Howie Morenz, Johnny Gagnon, Aurel Joliat, Armand Mondou, Pit Lepine, Albert Leduc, Georges Mantha, Art Lesieur, Nick Wasnie, Bert McCaffrey, Gus Rivers, Jean Pusie, Léo Dandurand (manager), Cecil Hart (coach), Ed Dufour (trainer).
Scores: April 3, at Chicago — Montreal 2, Chicago 1; April 5, at Chicago — Chicago 2, Montreal 1; April 9, at Montreal — Chicago 3, Montreal 2; April 11, at Montreal — Montreal 4, Chicago 2; April 14, at Montreal — Montreal 2, Chicago 0.

1929-30 — Montreal Canadiens — George Hainsworth, Marty Burke, Sylvio Mantha, Howie Morenz, Bert McCaffrey, Aurel Joliat, Albert Leduc, Pit Lepine, Wildor Larochelle, Nick Wasnie, Gerald Carson, Armand Mondou, Georges Mantha, Gus Rivers, Léo Dandurand (manager), Cecil Hart (coach), Ed Dufour (trainer).
Scores: April 1 at Boston — Montreal 3, Boston 0; April 3 at Montreal — Montreal 4, Boston 3.

1928-29 — Boston Bruins — Cecil (Tiny) Thompson, Eddie Shore, Lionel Hitchman, Perk Galbraith, Eric Pettinger, Frank Fredrickson, Mickey Mackay, Red Green, Dutch Gainor, Harry Oliver, Eddie Rodden, Dit Clapper, Cooney Weiland, Lloyd Klein, Cy Denneny, Bill Carson, George Owen, Myles Lane, Art Ross (manager-coach), Win Green (trainer).
Scores: March 28 at Boston — Boston 2, NY Rangers 0; March 29 at New York — Boston 2, NY Rangers 1.

1927-28 — New York Rangers — Lorne Chabot, Taffy Abel, Leon Bourgault, Ching Johnson, Bill Cook, Bun Cook, Frank Boucher, Billy Boyd, Murray Murdoch, Paul Thompson, Alex Gray, Joe Miller, Patsy Callighen, Lester Patrick (manager-coach), Harry Westerby (trainer).
Scores: April 5 at Montreal — Mtl. Maroons 2, NY Rangers 0; April 7 at Montreal — NY Rangers 2, Mtl. Maroons 1; April 10 at Montreal — Mtl. Maroons 2, NY Rangers 1; April 12 at Montreal — NY Rangers 1, Mtl. Maroons 0; April 14 at Montreal — NY Rangers 2, Mtl. Maroons 1.

1926-27 — Ottawa Senators — Alex Connell, King Clancy, George (Buck) Boucher, Ed Gorman, Frank Finnigan, Alex Smith, Hec Kilrea, Hooley Smith, Cy Denneny, Frank Nighbor, Jack Adams, Milt Halliday, Dave Gill (manager-coach).
Scores: April 7 at Boston — Ottawa 0, Boston 0; April 9 at Boston — Ottawa 3, Boston 1; April 11 at Ottawa — Boston 1, Ottawa 1; April 13 at Ottawa — Ottawa 3, Boston 1.

1925-26 — Montreal Maroons — Clint Benedict, Reg Noble, Frank Carson, Dunc Munro, Nels Stewart, Harry Broadbent, Babe Siebert, Dinny Dinsmore, Bill Phillips, Hobart (Hobie) Kitchen, Sammy Rothschield, Albert (Toots) Holway, Shorty Horne, Bern Brophy, Eddie Gerard (manager-coach), Bill O'Brien (trainer).
Scores: March 30 at Montreal — Mtl. Maroons 3, Victoria 0; April 1 at Montreal — Mtl. Maroons 3, Victoria 0; April 3 at Montreal — Victoria 3, Mtl. Maroons 2; April 6 at Montreal — Mtl. Maroons 2, Victoria 0.

The series in the spring of 1926 ended the annual playoffs between the champions of the East and the champions of the West. Since 1926-27 the annual playoffs in the National Hockey League have decided the Stanley Cup champions.

1924-25 — Victoria Cougars — Harry (Happy) Holmes, Clem Loughlin, Gordie Fraser, Frank Fredrickson, Jack Walker, Harold (Gizzy) Hart, Harold (Slim) Halderson, Frank Foyston, Wally Elmer, Harry Meeking, Jocko Anderson, Lester Patrick (manager-coach).
Scores: March 21 at Victoria — Victoria 5, Montreal 2; March 23 at Vancouver — Victoria 3, Montreal 1; March 27 at Victoria — Montreal 4, Victoria 2; March 30 at Victoria — Victoria 6, Montreal 1.

1923-24 — Montreal Canadiens — Georges Vezina, Sprague Cleghorn, Billy Couture, Howie Morenz, Aurel Joliat, Billy Boucher, Odie Cleghorn, Sylvio Mantha, Bobby Boucher, Billy Bell, Billy Cameron, Joe Malone, Charles Fortier, Leo Dandurand (manager-coach).
Scores: March 18 at Montreal — Montreal 3, Van. Maroons 2; March 20 at Montreal — Montreal 2, Van. Maroons 1. March 22 at Montreal — Montreal 6, Cgy. Tigers 1; March 25 at Ottawa* — Montreal 3, Cgy. Tigers 0.

* Game transferred to Ottawa to benefit from artificial ice surface.

1922-23 — Ottawa Senators — George (Buck) Boucher, Lionel Hitchman, Frank Nighbor, King Clancy, Harry Helman, Clint Benedict, Jack Darragh, Eddie Gerard, Cy Denneny, Harry Broadbent, Tommy Gorman (manager), Pete Green (coach), F. Dolan (trainer).
Scores: March 16 at Vancouver — Ottawa 1, Van. Maroons 0; March 19 at Vancouver — Van. Maroons 4, Ottawa 1; March 23 at Vancouver — Ottawa 3, Van. Maroons 2; March 26 at Vancouver — Ottawa 5, Van. Maroons 1; March 29 at Vancouver — Ottawa 2, Edm. Eskimos 1; March 31 at Vancouver — Ottawa 1, Edm. Eskimos 0.

*Toronto forward Robert "Red" Heron's backhander is handled by
New York Ranger goaltender Chuck Rayner during game two of the
1940 Stanley Cup Finals.*

1921-22 — Toronto St. Pats — Ted Stackhouse, Corb Denneny, Rod Smylie, Lloyd Andrews, John Ross Roach, Harry Cameron, Bill (Red) Stuart, Cecil (Babe) Dye, Ken Randall, Reg Noble, Eddie Gerard (borrowed for one game from Ottawa), Stan Jackson, Nolan Mitchell, Charlie Querrie (manager), Eddie Powers (coach).
Scores: March 17 at Toronto — Van. Millionaires 4, Toronto 3; March 20 at Toronto — Toronto 2, Van. Millionaires 1; March 23 at Toronto — Van. Millionaires 3, Toronto 0; March 25 at Toronto — Toronto 6, Van. Millionaires 0; March 28 at Toronto — Toronto 5, Van. Millionaires 1.

1920-21 — Ottawa Senators — Jack McKell, Jack Darragh, Morley Bruce, George (Buck) Boucher, Eddie Gerard, Clint Benedict, Sprague Cleghorn, Frank Nighbor, Harry Broadbent, Cy Denneny, Leth Graham, Tommy Gorman (manager),Pete Green (coach), F. Dolan (trainer).
Scores: March 21 at Vancouver — Van. Millionaires 2, Ottawa 1; March 24 at Vancouver — Ottawa 4, Van. Millionaires 3; March 28 at Vancouver — Ottawa 3, Van. Millionaires 2; March 31 at Vancouver — Van. Millionaires 3, Ottawa 2; April 4 at Vancouver — Ottawa 2, Van. Millionaires 1

1919-20 — Ottawa Senators — Jack McKell, Jack Darragh, Morley Bruce, Horrace Merrill, George (Buck) Boucher, Eddie Gerard, Clint Benedict, Sprague Cleghorn, Frank Nighbor, Harry Broadbent, Cy Denneny, Price, Tommy Gorman (manager), Pete Green (coach).
Scores: March 22 at Ottawa — Ottawa 3, Seattle 2; March 24 at Ottawa — Ottawa 3, Seattle 0; March 27 at Ottawa — Seattle 3, Ottawa 1; March 30 at Toronto* — Seattle 5, Ottawa 2; April 1 at Toronto* — Ottawa 6, Seattle 1.
* Games transferred to Toronto to benefit from artificial ice surface.

1918-19 — No decision, Series halted by Spanish influenza epidemic, illness of several players and death of Joe Hall of Montreal Canadiens from flu. Five games had been played when the series was halted, each team having won two and tied one. The results are shown:
Scores: March 19 at Seattle — Seattle 7, Montreal 0; March 22 at Seattle — Montreal 4, Seattle 2; March 24 at Seattle — Seattle 7, Montreal 2; March 26 at Seattle — Montreal 0, Seattle 0; March 30 at Seattle — Montreal 4, Seattle 3.

1917-18 — Toronto Arenas — Rusty Crawford, Harry Meeking, Ken Randall, Corb Denneny, Harry Cameron, Jack Adams, Alf Skinner, Harry Mummery, Harry (Happy) Holmes, Reg Noble, Sammy Hebert, Jack Marks, Jack Coughlin, Neville, Charlie Querrie (manager), Dick Carroll (coach), Frank Carroll (trainer).
Scores: March 20 at Toronto — Toronto 5, Van. Millionaires 3; March 23 at Toronto — Van. Millionaires 6, Toronto 4; March 26 at Toronto — Toronto 6, Van. Millionaires 3; March 28 at Toronto — Van. Millionaires 8, Toronto 1; March 30 at Toronto — Toronto 2, Van. Millionaires 1.

1916-17 — Seattle Metropolitans — Harry (Happy) Holmes, Ed Carpenter, Cully Wilson, Jack Walker, Bernie Morris, Frank Foyston, Roy Rickey, Jim Riley, Bobby Rowe (captain), Peter Muldoon (manager).
Scores: March 17 at Seattle — Montreal 8, Seattle 4; March 20 at Seattle — Seattle 6, Montreal 1; March 23 at Seattle — Seattle 4, Montreal 1; March 25 at Seattle — Seattle 9, Montreal 1.

1915-16 — Montreal Canadiens — Georges Vezina, Bert Corbeau, Jack Laviolette, Newsy Lalonde, Louis Berlinguette, Goldie Prodgers, Howard McNamara, Didier Pitre, Skene Ronan, Amos Arbour, Georges Poulin, Jacques Fournier, George Kennedy (manager).
Scores: March 20 at Montreal — Portland 2, Montreal 0; March 22 at Montreal — Montreal 2, Portland 1; March 25 at Montreal — Montreal 6, Portland 3; March 28 at Montreal — Portland 6, Montreal 5; March 30 at Montreal — Montreal 2, Portland 1.

1914-15 — Vancouver Millionaires — Kenny Mallen, Frank Nighbor, Fred (Cyclone) Taylor, Hughie Lehman, Lloyd Cook, Mickey MacKay, Barney Stanley, Jim Seaborn, Si Griffis (captain), Jean Matz, Frank Patrick (playing manager).
Scores: March 22 at Vancouver — Van. Millionaires 6, Ottawa 2; March 24 at Vancouver — Van. Millionaires 8, Ottawa 3; March 26 at Vancouver — Van. Millionaires 12, Ottawa 3.

1913-14 — Toronto Blueshirts — Con Corbeau, F. Roy McGiffen, Jack Walker, George McNamara, Cully Wilson, Frank Foyston, Harry Cameron, Harry (Happy) Holmes, Alan M. Davidson (captain), Harriston, Jack Marshall (playing-manager), Frank and Dick Carroll (trainers).
Scores: March 14 at Toronto — Toronto 5, Victoria 2; March 17 at Toronto — Toronto 6, Victoria 5; March 19 at Toronto — Toronto 2, Victoria 1.

1912-13 — Quebec Bulldogs — Joe Malone, Joe Hall, Paddy Moran, Harry Mummery, Tommy Smith, Jack Marks, Russell Crawford, Billy Creighton, Jeff Malone, Rocket Power, M.J. Quinn (manager), D. Beland (trainer).
Scores: March 8 at Quebec — Que. Bulldogs 14, Sydney 3; March 10 at Quebec — Que. Bulldogs 6, Sydney 2.

Victoria challenged Quebec but the Bulldogs refused to put the Stanley Cup in competition so the two teams played an exhibition series with Victoria winning two games to one by scores of 7-5, 3-6, 6-1. It was the first meeting between the Eastern champions and the Western champions. The following year, and until the Western Hockey League disbanded after the 1926 playoffs, the Cup went to the winner of the series between East and West.

1911-12 — Quebec Bulldogs — Goldie Prodgers, Joe Hall, Walter Rooney, Paddy Moran, Jack Marks, Jack McDonald, Eddie Oatman, George Leonard, Joe Malone (captain), C. Nolan (coach), M.J. Quinn (manager), D. Beland (trainer).
Scores: March 11 at Quebec — Que. Bulldogs 9, Moncton 3; March 13 at Quebec — Que. Bulldogs 8, Moncton 0.

Prior to 1912, teams could challenge the Stanley Cup champions for the title, thus there was more than one Championship Series played in most of the seasons between 1894 and 1911.

1910-11 — Ottawa Senators — Hamby Shore, Percy LeSueur, Jack Darragh, Bruce Stuart, Marty Walsh, Bruce Ridpath, Fred Lake, Albert (Dubby) Kerr, Alex Currie, Horace Gaul.
Scores: March 13 at Ottawa — Ottawa 7, Galt 4; March 16 at Ottawa — Ottawa 13, Port Arthur 4.

1909-10 — Montreal Wanderers — Cecil W. Blachford, Ernie (Moose) Johnson, Ernie Russell, Riley Hern, Harry Hyland, Jack Marshall, Frank (Pud) Glass (captain), Jimmy Gardner, R. R. Boon (manager).
Scores: March 12 at Montreal — Mtl. Wanderers 7, Berlin (Kitchener) 3.

1908-09 — Ottawa Senators — Fred Lake, Percy LeSueur, Fred (Cyclone) Taylor, H.L. (Billy) Gilmour, Albert Kerr, Edgar Dey, Marty Walsh, Bruce Stuart (captain).
Scores: Ottawa, as champions of the Eastern Canada Hockey Association took over the Stanley Cup in 1909 and, although a challenge was accepted by the Cup trustees from Winnipeg Shamrocks, games could not be arranged because of the lateness of the season. No other challenges were made in 1909. The following season — 1909-10 — however, the Senators accepted two challenges as defending Cup Champions. The first was against Galt in a two-game, total-goals series, and the second against Edmonton, also a two-game, total-goals series. Results: January 5 at Ottawa —Ottawa 12, Galt 3; January 7 at Ottawa — Ottawa 3, Galt 1. January 18 at Ottawa — Ottawa 8, Edm. Eskimos 4; January 20 at Ottawa — Ottawa 13, Edm. Eskimos 7.

1907-08 — Montreal Wanderers — Riley Hern, Art Ross, Walter Smaill, Frank (Pud) Glass, Bruce Stuart, Ernie Russell, Ernie (Moose) Johnson, Cecil Blachford (captain), Tom Hooper, Larry Gilmour, Ernie Liffiton, R.R. Boon (manager).
Scores: Wanderers accepted four challenges for the Cup: January 9 at Montreal — Mtl. Wanderers 9, Ott. Victorias 3; January 13 at Montreal — Mtl. Wanderers 13, Ott. Victorias 1; March 10 at Montreal — Mtl. Wanderers 11, Wpg. Maple Leafs 5; March 12 at Montreal — Mtl. Wanderers 9, Wpg. Maple Leafs 3; March 14 at Montreal — Mtl. Wanderers 6, Toronto (OPHL) 4. At start of following season, 1908-09, Wanderers were challenged by Edmonton. Results: December 28 at Montreal — Mtl. Wanderers 7, Edm. Eskimos 3; December 30 at Montreal — Edm. Eskimos 7, Mtl. Wanderers 6. Total goals: Mtl. Wanderers 13, Edm. Eskimos 10.

1906-07 — (March) **— Montreal Wanderers —** W. S. (Billy) Strachan, Riley Hern, Lester Patrick, Hod Stuart, Frank (Pud) Glass, Ernie Russell, Cecil Blachford (captain), Ernie (Moose) Johnson, Rod Kennedy, Jack Marshall, R.R. Boon (manager).
Scores: March 23 at Winnipeg — Mtl. Wanderers 7, Kenora 2; March 25 at Winnipeg — Kenora 6, Mtl. Wanderers 5. Total goals: Mtl. Wanderers 12, Kenora 8.

1906-07 — (January) **— Kenora Thistles —** Eddie Geroux, Art Ross, Si Griffis, Tom Hooper, Billy McGimsie, Roxy Beaudro, Tom Phillips.
Scores: January 17 at Montreal — Kenora 4, Mtl. Wanderers 2; Jan. 21 at Montreal — Kenora 8, Mtl. Wanderers 6.

1905-06 — (March) **— Montreal Wanderers —** Henri Menard, Billy Strachan, Rod Kennedy, Lester Patrick, Frank (Pud) Glass, Ernie Russell, Ernie (Moose) Johnson, Cecil Blachford (captain), Josh Arnold, R.R. Boon (manager).
Scores: March 14 at Montreal — Mtl. Wanderers 9, Ottawa 1; March 17 at Ottawa — Ottawa 9, Mtl. Wanderers 3. Total goals: Mtl. Wanderers 12, Ottawa 10. Wanderers accepted a challenge from New Glasgow, N.S., prior to the start of the 1906-07 season. Results: December 27 at Montreal — Mtl. Wanderers 10, New Glasgow 3; December 29 at Montreal — Mtl. Wanderers 7, New Glasgow 2.

1905-06 — (February) **— Ottawa Silver Seven —** Harvey Pulford (captain), Arthur Moore, Harry Westwick, Frank McGee, Alf Smith (playing coach), Billy Gilmour, Billy Hague, Percy LeSueur, Harry Smith, Tommy Smith, Dion, Ebbs.
Scores: February 27 at Ottawa — Ottawa 16, Queen's University 7; February 28 at Ottawa — Ottawa 12, Queen's University 7; March 6 at Ottawa — Ottawa 6, Smiths Falls 5; March 8 at Ottawa — Ottawa 8, Smiths Falls 2.

1904-05 — Ottawa Silver Seven — Dave Finnie, Harvey Pulford (captain), Arthur Moore, Harry Westwick, Frank McGee, Alf Smith (playing coach), Billy Gilmour, Frank White, Horace Gaul, Hamby Shore, Bones Allen.
Scores: January 13 at Ottawa — Ottawa 9, Dawson City 2; January 16 at Ottawa — Ottawa 23, Dawson City 2; March 7 at Ottawa — Rat Portage 9, Ottawa 3; March 9 at Ottawa — Ottawa 4, Rat Portage 2; March 11 at Ottawa — Ottawa 5, Rat Portage 4.

1903-04 — Ottawa Silver Seven — S.C. (Suddy) Gilmour, Arthur Moore, Frank McGee, J.B. (Bouse) Hutton, H.L. (Billy) Gilmour, Jim McGee, Harry Westwick, E. H. (Harvey) Pulford (captain), Scott, Alf Smith (playing coach).
Scores: December 30 at Ottawa — Ottawa 9, Wpg. Rowing Club 1; January 1 at Ottawa — Wpg. Rowing Club 6, Ottawa 2; January 4 at Ottawa — Ottawa 2, Wpg. Rowing Club 0. February 23 at Ottawa — Ottawa 6, Tor. Marlboros 3; February 25 at Ottawa — Ottawa 11, Tor. Marlboros 2; March 2 at Montreal — Ottawa 5, Mtl. Wanderers 5. Following the tie game, a new two-game series was ordered to be played in Ottawa but the Wanderers refused unless the tie game was replayed in Montreal. When no settlement could be reached, the series was abandoned and Ottawa retained the Cup and accepted a two-game challenge from Brandon. Results: (both games at Ottawa), March 9, Ottawa 6, Brandon 3; March 11, Ottawa 9, Brandon 3.

1902-03 — (March) **— Ottawa Silver Seven —** S.C. (Suddy) Gilmour, P.T. (Percy) Sims, J.B. (Bouse) Hutton, D.J. (Dave) Gilmour, H.L. (Billy) Gilmour, Harry Westwick, Frank McGee, F.H. Wood, A.A. Fraser, Charles D. Spittal, E.H. (Harvey) Pulford (captain), Arthur Moore, Alf Smith (coach.)
Scores: March 7 at Montreal — Ottawa 1, Mtl. Victorias 1; March 10 at Ottawa — Ottawa 8, Mtl. Victorias 0. Total goals: Ottawa 9, Mtl. Victorias 1; March 12 at Ottawa — Ottawa 6, Rat Portage 2; March 14 at Ottawa — Ottawa 4, Rat Portage 2.

1902-03 — (February) **— Montreal AAA —** Tom Hodge, R.R. (Dickie) Boon, W.C. (Billy) Nicholson, Tom Phillips, Art Hooper, W.J. (Billy) Bellingham, Charles A. Liffiton, Jack Marshall, Jim Gardner, Cecil Blachford, George Smith.
Scores: January 29 at Montreal — Mtl. AAA 8, Wpg. Victorias 1; January 31 at Montreal — Wpg. Victorias 2, Mtl. AAA 2; February 2 at Montreal — Wpg. Victorias 4, Mtl. AAA 2; February 4 at Montreal — Mtl. AAA 5, Wpg. Victorias 1.

1901-02 — (March) **— Montreal AAA —** Tom Hodge, R.R. (Dickie) Boon, William C. (Billy) Nicholson, Archie Hooper, W.J. (Billy) Bellingham, Charles A. Liffiton, Jack Marshall, Roland Elliott, Jim Gardner.
Scores: March 13 at Winnipeg — Wpg. Victorias 1, Mtl. AAA 0; March 15 at Winnipeg — Mtl. AAA 5, Wpg. Victorias 0; March 17 at Winnipeg — Mtl. AAA 2, Wpg. Victorias 1.

1901-02 — (January) **— Winnipeg Victorias —** Burke Wood, A.B. (Tony) Gingras, Charles W. Johnstone, R.M. (Rod) Flett, Magnus L. Flett, Dan Bain (captain), Fred Scanlon, F. Cadham, G. Brown.
Scores: January 21 at Winnipeg — Wpg. Victorias 5, Tor Wellingtons 3; January 23 at Winnipeg — Wpg. Victorias 5, Tor. Wellingtons 3.

1900-01 — Winnipeg Victorias — Burke Wood, Jack Marshall, A.B. (Tony) Gingras, Charles W. Johnstone, R.M. (Rod) Flett, Magnus L. Flett, Dan Bain (captain), G. Brown.
Scores: January 29 at Montreal — Wpg. Victorias 4, Mtl. Shamrocks 3; January 31 at Montreal — Wpg. Victorias 2, Mtl. Shamrocks 1.

1899-1900 — Montreal Shamrocks — Joe McKenna, Frank Tansey, Frank Wall, Art Farrell, Fred Scanlon, Harry Trihey (captain), Jack Brannen.
Scores: February 12 at Montreal — Mtl. Shamrocks 4, Wpg. Victorias 3; February 14 at Montreal — Wpg. Victorias 3, Mtl. Shamrocks 2; February 16 at Montreal — Mtl. Shamrocks 5, Wpg. Victorias 4; March 5 at Montreal — Mtl. Shamrocks 10, Halifax 2; March 7 at Montreal — Mtl. Shamrocks 11, Halifax 0.

1898-99 — (March) **— Montreal Shamrocks —** Jim McKenna, Frank Tansey, Frank Wall, Harry Trihey (captain), Art Farrell, Fred Scanlon, Jack Brannen, John Dobby, Charles Hoerner.
Scores: March 14 at Montreal — Mtl. Shamrocks 6, Queen's University 2.

1898-99 — (February) **— Montreal Victorias —** Gordon Lewis, Mike Grant, Graham Drinkwater, Cam Davidson, Bob McDougall, Ernie McLea, Frank Richardson, Jack Ewing, Russell Bowie, Douglas Acer, Fred McRobie.
Scores: February 15 at Montreal — Mtl. Victorias 2, Wpg. Victorias 1; February 18 at Montreal — Mtl. Victorias 3, Wpg. Victorias 2.

1897-98 — Montreal Victorias — Gordon Lewis, Hartland McDougall, Mike Grant, Graham Drinkwater, Cam Davidson, Bob McDougall, Ernie McLea, Frank Richardson (captain), Jack Ewing. The Victorias as champions of the Amateur Hockey Association, retained the Cup and were not called upon to defend it.

1896-97 — Montreal Victorias — Gordon Lewis, Harold Henderson, Mike Grant (captain), Cam Davidson, Graham Drinkwater, Robert McDougall, Ernie McLea, Shirley Davidson, Hartland McDougall, Jack Ewing, Percy Molson, David Gillilan, McLellan.
Scores: December 27 at Montreal — Mtl. Victorias 15, Ott. Capitals 2.

1895-96 — (December) **— Montreal Victorias —** Harold Henderson, Mike Grant (captain), Robert McDougall, Graham Drinkwater, Shirley Davidson, Ernie McLea, Robert Jones, Cam Davidson, David Gillilan, Stanley Willett.
Scores: December 30 at Winnipeg — Mtl. Victorias 6, Wpg. Victorias 5.

1895-96 — (February) **— Winnipeg Victorias —** G.H. Merritt, Rod Flett, Fred Higginbotham, Jack Armitage (captain), C.J. (Tote) Campbell, Dan Bain, Charles Johnstone, H. Howard.
Scores: February 14 at Montreal — Wpg. Victorias 2, Mtl. Victorias 0.

1894-95 — Montreal Victorias — Robert Jones, Harold Henderson, Mike Grant (captain), Shirley Davidson, Bob McDougall, Norman Rankin, Graham Drinkwater, Roland Elliot, William Pullan, Hartland McDougall, Jim Fenwick, A. McDougall.
Montreal Victorias, as champions of the Amateur Hockey Association, were prepared to defend the Stanley Cup. However, the Stanley Cup trustees had already accepted a challenge match between the 1894 champion Montreal AAA and Queen's University. It was declared that if Montreal AAA defeated Queen's University, Montreal Victorias would be declared Stanley Cup champions. If Queen's University won, the Cup would go to the university club. In a game played March 9, 1895, Montreal AAA defeated Queen's University 5-1. As a result, Montreal Victorias were awarded the Stanley Cup.

1893-94 — Montreal AAA — Herbert Collins, Allan Cameron, George James, Billy Barlow, Clare Mussen, Archie Hodgson, Haviland Routh, Alex Irving, James Stewart, A.C. (Toad) Wand, A. Kingan.
Scores: March 17 at Mtl. Victorias — Mtl. AAA 3, Mtl. Victorias 2; March 22 at Montreal — Mtl. AAA 3, Ott. Capitals 1.

1892-93 — Montreal AAA — Tom Paton, James Stewart, Allan Cameron, Haviland Routh, Archie Hodgson, Billy Barlow, A.B. Kingan, G.S. Lowe.
In accordance with the terms governing the presentation of the Stanley Cup, it was awarded for the first time to the Montreal AAA as champions of the Amateur Hockey Association in 1893. Once Montreal AAA had been declared holders of the Stanley Cup, any Canadian hockey team could challenge for the trophy.

All-Time NHL Playoff Formats

1917-18 — The regular-season was split into two halves. The winners of both halves faced each other in a two-game, total-goals series for the NHL championship and the right to meet the PCHA champion in the best-of-five Stanley Cup Finals.

1918-19 — Same as 1917-18, except that the Stanley Cup Finals was extended to a best-of-seven series.

1919-20 — Same as 1917-1918, except that Ottawa won both halves of the split regular-season schedule to earn an automatic berth into the best-of-five Stanley Cup Finals against the PCHA champions.

1921-22 — The top two teams at the conclusion of the regular-season faced each other in a two-game, total-goals series for the NHL championship. The NHL champion then moved on to play the winner of the PCHA-WCHL playoff series in the best-of-five Stanley Cup Finals.

1922-23 — The top two teams at the conclusion of the regular-season faced each other in a two-game, total-goals series for the NHL championship. The NHL champion then moved on to play the PCHA champion in the best-of-three Stanley Cup Semi-Finals, and the winner of the Semi-Finals played the WCHL champion, which had been given a bye, in the best-of-three Stanley Cup Finals.

1923-24 — The top two teams at the conclusion of the regular-season faced each other in a two-game, total-goals series for the NHL championship. The NHL champion then moved to play the loser of the PCHA-WCHL playoff (the winner of the PCHA-WCHL playoff earned a bye into the Stanley Cup Finals) in the best-of-three Stanley Cup Semi-Finals. The winner of this series met the PCHA-WCHL playoff winner in the best-of-three Stanley Cup Finals.

1924-25 — The first place team (Hamilton) at the conclusion of the regular-season was supposed to play the winner of a two-game, total goals series between the second (Toronto) and third (Montreal) place clubs. However, Hamilton refused to abide by this new format, demanding greater compensation than offered by the League. Thus, Toronto and Montreal played their two-game, total-goals series, and the winner (Montreal) earned the NHL title and then played the WCHL champion (Victoria) in the best-of-five Stanley Cup Finals.

1925-26 — The format which was intended for 1924-25 went into effect. The winner of the two-game, total-goals series between the second and third place teams squared off against the first place team in the two-game, total-goals NHL championship series. The NHL champion then moved on to play the WHL champion in the best-of-five Stanley Cup Finals.

After the 1925-26 season, the NHL was the only major professional hockey league still in existence and consequently took over sole control of the Stanley Cup competition.

1926-27 — The 10-team league was divided into two divisions — Canadian and American — of five teams apiece. In each division, the winner of the two-game, total-goals series between the second and third place teams faced the first place team in a two-game, total-goals series for the division title. The two division title winners then met in the best-of-five Stanley Cup Finals.

1928-29 — Both first place teams in the two divisions played each other in a best-of-five series. Both second place teams in the two divisions played each other in a two-game, total-goals series as did the two third place teams. The winners of these latter two series then played each other in a best-of-three series for the right to meet the winner of the series between the two first place clubs. This Stanley Cup Final was a best-of-three.

> Series A: First in Canadian Division versus first in American (best-of-five)
> Series B: Second in Canadian Division versus second in American (two-game, total-goals)
> Series C: Third in Canadian Division versus third in American (two-game, total-goals)
> Series D: Winner of Series B versus winner of Series C (best-of-three)
> Series E: Winner of Series A versus winner of Series D (best of three) for Stanley Cup

1931-32 — Same as 1928-29, except that Series D was changed to a two-game, total-goals format and Series E was changed to best of five.

1936-37 — Same as 1931-32, except that Series B, C, and D were each best-of-three.

1938-39 — With the NHL reduced to seven teams, the two-division system was replaced by one seven-team league. Based on final regular-season standings, the following playoff format was adopted:

> Series A: First versus Second (best-of-seven)
> Series B: Third versus Fourth (best-of-three)
> Series C: Fifth versus Sixth (best-of-three)
> Series D: Winner of Series B versus winner of Series C (best-of-three)
> Series E: Winner of Series A versus winner of Series D (best-of-seven)

1942-43 — With the NHL reduced to six teams (the "original six"), only the top four finishers qualified for playoff action. The best-of-seven Semi-Finals pitted Team #1 vs Team #3 and Team #2 vs Team #4. The winners of each Semi-Final series met in the best-of-seven Stanley Cup Finals.

1967-68 — When it doubled in size from 6 to 12 teams, the NHL once again was divided into two divisions — East and West — of six teams apiece. The top four clubs in each division qualified for the playoffs (all series were best-of-seven):

> Series A: Team #1 (East) vs Team #3 (East)
> Series B: Team #2 (East) vs Team #4 (East)
> Series C: Team #1 (West) vs Team #3 (West)
> Series D: Team #2 (West) vs Team #4 (West)
> Series E: Winner of Series A vs winner of Series B
> Series F: Winner of Series C vs winner of Series D
> Series G: Winner of Series E vs Winner of Series F

1970-71 — Same as 1967-68 except that Series E matched the winners of Series A and D, and Series F matched the winners of Series B and C.

1971-72 — Same as 1970-71, except that Series A and C matched Team #1 vs Team #4, and Series B and D matched Team #2 vs Team #3.

1974-75 — With the League now expanded to 18 teams in four divisions, a completely new playoff format was introduced. First, the #2 and #3 teams in each of the four divisions were pooled together in the Preliminary round. These eight (#2 and #3) clubs were ranked #1 to #8 based on regular-season record:

> Series A: Team #1 vs Team #8 (best-of-three)
> Series B: Team #2 vs Team #7 (best-of-three)
> Series C: Team #3 vs Team #6 (best-of-three)
> Series D: Team #4 vs Team #5 (best-of-three)

The winners of this Preliminary round then pooled together with the four division winners, which had received byes into this Quarter-Final round. These eight teams were again ranked #1 to #8 based on regular-season record:

> Series E: Team #1 vs Team #8 (best-of-seven)
> Series F: Team #2 vs Team #7 (best-of-seven)
> Series G: Team #3 vs Team #6 (best-of-seven)
> Series H: Team #4 vs Team #5 (best-of-seven)

The four Quarter-Finals winners, which moved on to the Semi-Finals, were then ranked #1 to #4 based on regular season record:

> Series I: Team #1 vs Team #4 (best-of-seven)
> Series J: Team #2 vs Team #3 (best-of-seven)
> Series K: Winner of Series I vs winner of Series J (best-of-seven)

1977-78 — Same as 1974-75, except that the Preliminary round consisted of the #2 teams in the four divisions and the next four teams based on regular-season record (not their standings within their divisions).

1979-80 — With the addition of four WHA franchises, the League expanded its playoff structure to include 16 of its 21 teams. The four first place teams in the four divisions automatically earned playoff berths. Among the 17 other clubs, the top 12, according to regular-season record, also earned berths. All 16 teams were then pooled together and ranked #1 to #16 based on regular-season record:

> Series A: Team #1 vs Team #16 (best-of-five)
> Series B: Team #2 vs Team #15 (best-of-five)
> Series C: Team #3 vs Team #14 (best-of-five)
> Series D: Team #4 vs Team #13 (best-of-five)
> Series E: Team #5 vs Team #12 (best-of-five)
> Series F: Team #6 vs Team #11 (best-of-five)
> Series G: Team #7 vs Team #10 (best-of-five)
> Series H: Team #8 vs Team # 9 (best-of-five)

The eight Preliminary round winners, ranked #1 to #8 based on regular-season record, moved on to the Quarter-Finals:

> Series I: Team #1 vs Team #8 (best-of-seven)
> Series J: Team #2 vs Team #7 (best-of-seven)
> Series K: Team #3 vs Team #6 (best-of-seven)
> Series L: Team #4 vs Team #5 (best-of-seven)

The eight Quarter-Finals winners, ranked #1 to #4 based on regular-season record, moved on to the semi-finals:

> Series M: Team #1 vs Team #4 (best-of-seven)
> Series N: Team #2 vs Team #3 (best-of-seven)
> Series O: Winner of Series M vs winner of Series N (best-of-seven)

1981-82 — The first four teams in each division earned playoff berths. In each division, the first-place team opposed the fourth-place team and the second-place team opposed the third-place team in a best-of-five Division Semi-Final series (DSF). In each division, the two winners of the DSF met in a best-of-seven Division Final series (DF). The two winners in each conference met in a best-of-seven Conference Final series (CF). In the Prince of Wales Conference, the Adams Division winner opposed the Patrick Division winner; in the Clarence Campbell Conference, the Smythe Division winner opposed the Norris Division winner. The two CF winners met in a best-of-seven Stanley Cup Final (F) series.

1986-87 — Division Semi-Final series changed from best-of-five to best-of-seven.

1993-94 — The NHL's playoff draw conference-based rather than division-based. At the conclusion of the regular season, the top eight teams in each of the Eastern and Western Conferences qualify for the playoffs. The teams that finish in first place in each of the League's divisions are seeded first and second in each conference's playoff draw and are assured of home ice advantage in the first two playoff rounds. The remaining teams are seeded based on their regular-season point totals. In each conference, the team seeded #1 plays #8; #2 vs. #7; #3 vs. #6; and #4 vs. #5. All series are best-of-seven with home ice rotating on a 2-2-1-1-1 basis, with the exception of matchups between Central and Pacific Division teams. These matchups will be played on a 2-3-2 basis to reduce travel. In a 2-3-2 series, the team with the most points will have its choice to start the series at home or on the road. The Eastern Conference champion will face the Western Conference champion in the Stanley Cup Final.

1994-95 — Same as 1993-94, except that in first, second or third-round playoff series involving Central and Pacific Division teams, the team with the better record has the choice of using either a 2-3-2 or a 2-2-1-1-1 format. In either case, the team with the better record opens at home. The format for the Stanley Cup Final remains 2-2-1-1-1.

The Toronto Maple Leafs collectively put their best foot forward to win three straight Stanley Cup championships from 1961-62 to 1963-64.

Team Records

1918-1994

MOST STANLEY CUP CHAMPIONSHIPS:
23 — Montreal Canadiens 1924-30-31-44-46-53-56-57-58-59-60-65-66-68-69-71-73-76-77-78-79-86-93
13 — Toronto Maple Leafs 1918-22-32-42-45-47-48-49-51-62-63-64-67
7 — Detroit Red Wings 1936-37-43-50-52-54-55

MOST FINAL SERIES APPEARANCES:
32 — Montreal Canadiens in 77-year history.
21 — Toronto Maple Leafs in 77-year history.
18 — Detroit Red Wings in 68-year history.

MOST YEARS IN PLAYOFFS:
69 — Montreal Canadiens in 77-year history.
56 — Toronto Maple Leafs in 77-year history.
55 — Boston Bruins in 70-year history.

MOST CONSECUTIVE STANLEY CUP CHAMPIONSHIPS:
5 — Montreal Canadiens (1956-57-58-59-60)
4 — Montreal Canadiens (1976-77-78-79)
— NY Islanders (1980-81-82-83)

MOST CONSECUTIVE FINAL SERIES APPEARANCES:
10 — Montreal Canadiens (1951-60, inclusive)
5 — Montreal Canadiens, (1965-69, inclusive)
— NY Islanders, (1980-84, inclusive)

MOST CONSECUTIVE PLAYOFF APPEARANCES:
27 — Boston Bruins (1968-94, inclusive)
25 — Chicago Blackhawks (1970-94, inclusive)
24 — Montreal Canadiens (1971-94, inclusive)
21 — Montreal Canadiens (1949-69, inclusive)
20 — Detroit Red Wings (1939-58, inclusive)

MOST GOALS BOTH TEAMS, ONE PLAYOFF SERIES:
69 — Edmonton Oilers, Chicago Blackhawks in 1985 CF. Edmonton won best-of-seven series 4-2, outscoring Chicago 44-25.
62 — Chicago Blackhawks, Minnesota North Stars in 1985 DF. Chicago won best-of-seven series 4-2, outscoring Minnesota 33-29.
61 — Los Angeles Kings, Calgary Flames in 1993 DSF. Los Angeles won best-of-seven series 4-2, outscoring Calgary 33-28.

MOST GOALS ONE TEAM, ONE PLAYOFF SERIES:
44 — Edmonton Oilers in 1985 CF. Edmonton won best-of-seven series 4-2, outscoring Chicago 44-25.
35 — Edmonton Oilers in 1983 DF. Edmonton won best-of-seven series 4-1, outscoring Calgary 35-13.

MOST GOALS, BOTH TEAMS, TWO-GAME SERIES:
17 — Toronto St. Patricks, Montreal Canadiens in 1918 NHL F. Toronto won two-game total goal series 10-7.
15 — Boston Bruins, Chicago Blackhawks in 1927 QF. Boston won two-game total goal series 10-5.
— Pittsburgh Penguins, St. Louis Blues in 1975 PR. Pittsburgh won best-of-three series 2-0, outscoring St. Louis 9-6.

MOST GOALS, ONE TEAM, TWO-GAME SERIES:
11 — Buffalo Sabres in 1977 PR. Buffalo won best-of-three series 2-0, outscoring Minnesota 11-3.
— Toronto Maple Leafs in 1978 PR. Toronto won best-of-three series 2-0, outscoring Los Angeles 11-3.
10 — Boston Bruins in 1927 QF. Boston won two-game total goal series 10-5.

MOST GOALS, BOTH TEAMS, THREE-GAME SERIES:
33 — Minnesota North Stars, Boston Bruins in 1981 PR. Minnesota won best-of-five series 3-0, outscoring Boston 20-13.
31 — Chicago Blackhawks, Detroit Red Wings in 1985 DSF. Chicago won best-of-five series 3-0, outscoring Detroit 23-8.
28 — Toronto Maple Leafs, NY Rangers in 1932 F. Toronto won best-of-five series 3-0, outscoring New York 18-10.

MOST GOALS, ONE TEAM, THREE-GAME SERIES:
23 — Chicago Blackhawks in 1985 DSF. Chicago won best-of-five series 3-0, outscoring Detroit 23-8.
20 — Minnesota North Stars in 1981 PR. Minnesota won best-of-five series 3-0, outscoring Boston 20-13.
— NY Islanders in 1981 PR. New York won best-of-five series 3-0, outscoring Toronto 20-4.

MOST GOALS, BOTH TEAMS, FOUR-GAME SERIES:
36 — Boston Bruins, St. Louis Blues in 1972 SF. Boston won best-of-seven series 4-0, outscoring St. Louis 28-8.
— **Edmonton Oilers, Chicago Blackhawks** in 1983 CF. Edmonton won best-of-seven series 4-0, outscoring Chicago 25-11.
— **Minnesota North Stars, Toronto Maple Leafs** in 1983 DSF. Minnesota won best-of-five series 3-1; teams tied in scoring 18-18.
35 — NY Rangers, Los Angeles Kings in 1981 PR. NY Rangers won best-of-five series 3-1, outscoring Los Angeles 23-12.

MOST GOALS, ONE TEAM, FOUR-GAME SERIES:
28 — Boston Bruins in 1972 SF. Boston won best-of-seven series 4-0, outscoring St. Louis 28-8.

MOST GOALS, BOTH TEAMS, FIVE-GAME SERIES:
52 — Edmonton Oilers, Los Angeles Kings in 1987 DSF. Edmonton won
best-of-seven series 4-1, outscoring Los Angeles 32-20.
50 — Los Angeles Kings, Edmonton Oilers in 1982 DSF. Los Angeles won best-of-five
series 3-2, outscoring Edmonton 27-23.
48 — Edmonton Oilers, Calgary Flames in 1983 DF. Edmonton won best-of-seven
series 4-1, outscoring Calgary 35-13.
— Calgary Flames, Los Angeles Kings in 1988 DSF. Calgary won best-of-seven
series 4-1, outscoring Los Angeles 30-18.

MOST GOALS, ONE TEAM, FIVE-GAME SERIES:
35 — Edmonton Oilers in 1983 DF. Edmonton won best-of-seven series 4-1,
outscoring Calgary 35-13.
32 — Edmonton Oilers in 1987 DSF. Edmonton won best-of-seven series 4-1,
outscoring Los Angeles 32-20.
28 — NY Rangers in 1979 QF. NY Rangers won best-of-seven series 4-1, outscoring
Philadelphia 28-8.
27 — Philadelphia Flyers in 1980 SF. Philadelphia won best-of-seven series 4-1,
outscoring Minnesota 27-14.
— Los Angeles Kings, in 1982 DSF. Los Angeles won best-of-five series 3-2,
outscoring Edmonton 27-23.

MOST GOALS, BOTH TEAMS, SIX-GAME SERIES:
69 — Edmonton Oilers, Chicago Blackhawks in 1985 CF. Edmonton won
best-of-seven series 4-2, outscoring Chicago 44-25.
62 — Chicago Blackhawks, Minnesota North Stars in 1985 DF. Chicago won
best-of-seven series 4-2, outscoring Minnesota 33-29.
61 — Los Angeles Kings, Calgary Flames in 1993 DSF. Los Angeles won best-of-seven
series 4-2, outscoring Calgary 33-28.

MOST GOALS, ONE TEAM, SIX-GAME SERIES:
44 — Edmonton Oilers in 1985 CF. Edmonton won best-of-seven series 4-2,
outscoring Chicago 44-25.
33 — Chicago Blackhawks in 1985 DF. Chicago won best-of-seven series 4-2,
outscoring Minnesota 33-29.
— Montreal Canadiens in 1973 F. Montreal won best-of-seven series 4-2,
outscoring Chicago 33-23.
— Los Angeles Kings in 1993 DSF. Los Angeles won best-of-seven series 4-2,
outscoring Calgary 33-28.

MOST GOALS, BOTH TEAMS, SEVEN-GAME SERIES:
60 — Edmonton Oilers, Calgary Flames in 1984 DF. Edmonton won best-of-seven
series 4-3, outscoring Calgary 33-27.

MOST GOALS, ONE TEAM, SEVEN-GAME SERIES:
33 — Philadelphia Flyers in 1976 QF. Philadelphia won best-of-seven series 4-3,
outscoring Toronto 33-23.
— **Boston Bruins** in 1983 DF. Boston won best-of-seven series 4-3, outscoring
Buffalo 33-23.
— **Edmonton Oilers** in 1984 DF. Edmonton won best-of-seven series 4-3,
outscoring Calgary 33-27.

FEWEST GOALS, BOTH TEAMS, TWO-GAME SERIES:
1 — NY Rangers, NY Americans, in 1929 SF. NY Rangers defeated NY Americans
1-0 in two-game, total-goal series.
— **Mtl. Maroons, Chicago Blackhawks** in 1935 SF. Mtl. Maroons defeated
Chicago 1-0 in two-game, total-goal series.

FEWEST GOALS, ONE TEAM, TWO-GAME SERIES:
0 — NY Americans in 1929 SF. Lost two-game total-goal series 1-0 against NY
Rangers.
— **Chicago Blackhawks** in 1935 SF. Lost two-game total-goal series 1-0 against
Mtl. Maroons.
— **Mtl. Maroons** in 1937 SF. Lost best-of-three series 2-0 to NY Rangers while
being outscored 5-0.
— **NY Americans** in 1939 QF. Lost best-of-three series 2-0 to Toronto while
being outscored 6-0.

FEWEST GOALS, BOTH TEAMS, THREE-GAME SERIES:
7 — Boston Bruins, Montreal Canadiens in 1929 SF. Boston won best-of-five
series 3-0, outscoring Montreal 5-2.
— **Detroit Red Wings, Mtl. Maroons** in 1936 SF. Detroit won best-of-five series
3-0, outscoring Mtl. Maroons 6-1.

FEWEST GOALS, ONE TEAM, THREE-GAME SERIES:
1 — Mtl. Maroons in 1936 SF. Lost best-of-five series 3-0 to Detroit and were
outscored 6-1.

FEWEST GOALS, BOTH TEAMS, FOUR-GAME SERIES:
9 — Toronto Maple Leafs, Boston Bruins in 1935 SF. Toronto won best-of-five
series 3-1, outscoring Boston 7-2.

FEWEST GOALS, ONE TEAM, FOUR-GAME SERIES:
2 — Boston Bruins in 1935 SF. Toronto won best-of-five series 3-1, outscoring
Boston 7-2.
— **Montreal Canadiens** in 1952 F. Detroit won best-of-seven series 4-0,
outscoring Montreal 11-2.

FEWEST GOALS, BOTH TEAMS, FIVE-GAME SERIES:
11 — NY Rangers, Mtl. Maroons in 1928 F. NY Rangers won best-of-five series
3-2, while outscored by Mtl. Maroons 6-5.

FEWEST GOALS, ONE TEAM, FIVE-GAME SERIES:
5 — NY Rangers in 1928 F. NY Rangers won best-of-five series 3-2, while
outscored by Mtl. Maroons 6-5.

FEWEST GOALS, BOTH TEAMS, SIX-GAME SERIES:
22 — Toronto Maple Leafs, Boston Bruins in 1951 SF. Toronto won best-of-seven
series 4-1 with 1 tie, outscoring Boston 17-5.

FEWEST GOALS, ONE TEAM, SIX-GAME SERIES:
5 — Boston Bruins in 1951 SF. Toronto won best-of-seven series 4-1 with 1 tie,
outscoring Boston 17-5.

FEWEST GOALS, BOTH TEAMS, SEVEN-GAME SERIES:
18 — Toronto Maple Leafs, Detroit Red Wings in 1945 F. Toronto won
best-of-seven series 4-3; teams tied in scoring 9-9.

FEWEST GOALS, ONE TEAM, SEVEN-GAME SERIES:
9 — Toronto Maple Leafs, in 1945 F. Toronto won best-of- seven series 4-3;
teams tied in scoring 9-9.
— **Detroit Red Wings,** in 1945 F. Toronto won best-of-seven series 4-3; teams
tied in scoring 9-9.

MOST GOALS, BOTH TEAMS, ONE GAME:
18 — Los Angeles Kings, Edmonton Oilers at Edmonton, April 7, 1982.
Los Angeles 10, Edmonton 8. Los Angeles won best-of-five DSF 3-2.
17 — Pittsburgh Penguins, Philadelphia Flyers at Pittsburgh, April 25, 1989.
Pittsburgh 10, Philadelphia 7. Philadelphia won best-of-seven DF 4-3.
16 — Edmonton Oilers, Los Angeles Kings at Edmonton, April 9, 1987.
Edmonton 13, Los Angeles 3. Edmonton won best-of-seven DSF 4-1.
— Los Angeles Kings, Calgary Flames at Los Angeles, April 10, 1990.
Los Angeles 12, Calgary 4. Los Angeles won best-of-seven DF 4-2.

MOST GOALS, ONE TEAM, ONE GAME:
13 — Edmonton Oilers at Edmonton, April 9, 1987. Edmonton 13, Los Angeles 3.
Edmonton won best-of-seven DSF 4-1.
12 — Los Angeles Kings at Los Angeles, April 10, 1990. Los Angeles 12, Calgary 4.
Los Angeles won best-of-seven DSF 4-2.
11 — Montreal Canadiens at Montreal, March 30, 1944. Montreal 11, Toronto 0.
Canadiens won best-of-seven SF 4-1.
— Edmonton Oilers at Edmonton May 4, 1985. Edmonton 11, Chicago 2.
Edmonton won best-of-seven CF 4-2.

MOST GOALS, BOTH TEAMS, ONE PERIOD:
9 — NY Rangers, Philadelphia Flyers, April 24, 1979, at Philadelphia, third
period. NY Rangers won 8-3 scoring six of nine third-period goals.
— **Los Angeles Kings, Calgary Flames** at Los Angeles, April 10, 1990, second
period. Los Angeles won game 12-4, scoring five of nine second-period goals.
8 — Chicago Blackhawks, Montreal Canadiens at Montreal, May 8, 1973, in the
second period. Chicago won 8-7 scoring five of eight second-period goals.
— Chicago Blackhawks, Edmonton Oilers at Chicago, May 12, 1985 in the first
period. Chicago won 8-6, scoring five of eight first-period goals.
— Edmonton Oilers, Winnipeg Jets at Edmonton, April 6, 1988 in the third period.
Edmonton won 7-4, scoring six of eight third period goals.
— Hartford Whalers, Montreal Canadiens at Hartford, April 10, 1988 in the third
period. Hartford won 7-5, scoring five of eight third period goals.

MOST GOALS, ONE TEAM, ONE PERIOD:
7 — Montreal Canadiens, March 30, 1944, at Montreal in third period, during
11-0 win against Toronto.

LONGEST OVERTIME:
116 Minutes, 30 Seconds — Detroit Red Wings, Mtl. Maroons at Montreal,
March 24, 25, 1936. Detroit 1, Mtl. Maroons 0. Mud Bruneteau scored,
assisted by Hec Kilrea, at 16:30 of sixth overtime period, or after 176 minutes,
30 seconds from start of game, which ended at 2:25 a.m. Detroit won
best-of-five SF 3-0.

SHORTEST OVERTIME:
9 Seconds — Montreal Canadiens, Calgary Flames, at Calgary, May 18,
1986. Montreal won 3-2 on Brian Skrudland's goal and captured the
best-of-seven F 4-1.
11 Seconds — NY Islanders, NY Rangers, at NY Rangers, April 11, 1975. NY
Islanders won 4-3 on Jean-Paul Parise's goal and captured the best-of-three PR
2-1.

MOST OVERTIME GAMES, ONE PLAYOFF YEAR:
28 — 1993. Of 85 games played, 28 went into overtime.
18 — 1994. Of 90 games played, 18 went into overtime.

FEWEST OVERTIME GAMES, ONE PLAYOFF YEAR:
0 — 1963. None of the 16 games went into overtime, the only year since 1926 that
no overtime was required in any playoff series.

MOST OVERTIME-GAME VICTORIES, ONE TEAM, ONE PLAYOFF YEAR:
10 — Montreal Canadiens, 1993. Two against Quebec in the DSF; three against
Buffalo in the DF; two against NY Islanders in the CF; and three against
Los Angeles in the F. Montreal played 20 games.
6 — NY Islanders, 1980. One against Los Angeles in the PR; two against Boston in
the QF; one against Buffalo in the SF; and two against Philadelphia in the F.
Islanders played 21 games.
— Vancouver Canucks, 1994. Three against Calgary in the CQF; one against
Dallas in the CSF; one against Toronto in the CF; and one against NY Rangers
in the F. Vancouver played 24 games.

MOST OVERTIME GAMES, FINAL SERIES:
5 — Toronto Maple Leafs,, Montreal Canadiens in 1951. Toronto defeated
Montreal 4-1 in best-of-seven series.

MOST OVERTIME GAMES, SEMI-FINAL SERIES:
4 — Toronto Maple Leafs, Boston Bruins in 1933. Toronto won best-of-five
series 3-2.
— **Boston Bruins, NY Rangers** in 1939. Boston won best-of-seven series 4-3.
— **St. Louis Blues, Minnesota North Stars** in 1968. St. Louis won best-of-seven
series 4-3.

MOST GAMES PLAYED BY ALL TEAMS, ONE PLAYOFF YEAR:
92 — 1991. There were 51 DSF, 24 DF, 11 CF and 6 F games.
90 — 1994. There were 48 CQF, 23 CSF, 12 CF and 7 F games.
87 — 1987. There were 44 DSF, 25 DF, 11 CF and 7 F games.

MOST GAMES PLAYED, ONE TEAM, ONE PLAYOFF YEAR:

26 — Philadelphia Flyers, 1987. Won DSF 4-2 against NY Rangers, DF 4-3 against NY Islanders, CF 4-2 against Montreal, and lost F 4-3 against Edmonton.

24 — Pittsburgh Penguins,1991. Won DSF 4-3 against New Jersey, DF 4-1 against Washington, CF 4-2 against Boston, and F 4-2 against Minnesota.

— Los Angeles Kings, 1993. Won DSF 4-2 against Calgary, DF 4-2 against Vancouver, CF 4-3 against Toronto, and lost F 4-1 against Montreal.

— Vancouver Canucks, 1994. Won CQF 4-3 against Calgary, CSF 4-1 against Dallas, CF 4-1 against Toronto, and lost F 4-3 against NY Rangers.

MOST ROAD VICTORIES, ONE TEAM, ONE PLAYOFF YEAR:

8 — NY Islanders, 1980. Won two at Los Angeles in PR; three at Boston in QF; two at Buffalo in SF; and one at Philadelphia in F series.

— **Philadelphia Flyers,** 1987. Won two at NY Rangers in DSF; two at NY Islanders in DF; three at Montreal in CF; and one at Edmonton in F series.

— **Edmonton Oilers,** 1990. Won one at Winnipeg in DSF; two at Los Angeles in DF; two at Chicago in CF and three at Boston in F series.

— **Pittsburgh Penguins,** 1992. Won two at Washington in DSF; two at NY Rangers in DF; two at Boston in CF; and two at Chicago in F series.

— **Vancouver Canucks,** 1994. Won three at Calgary in CQF; two at Dallas in CSF; one at Toronto in CF; and two at NY Rangers in F series.

MOST HOME VICTORIES, ONE TEAM, ONE PLAYOFF YEAR:

11 — Edmonton Oilers, 1988
10 — Edmonton Oilers, 1985 in 10 home-ice games.
— Montreal Canadiens, 1986
— Montreal Canadiens, 1993
9 — Philadelphia Flyers, 1974
— Philadelphia Flyers, 1980
— NY Islanders, 1981
— NY Islanders, 1983
— Edmonton Oilers, 1984
— Edmonton Oilers, 1987
— Calgary Flames, 1989
— Pittsburgh Penguins, 1991
— NY Rangers, 1994.

MOST ROAD VICTORIES, ALL TEAMS, ONE PLAYOFF YEAR:

46 — 1987. Of 87 games played, road teams won 46 (22 DSF, 14 DF, 8 CF and 2 Stanley Cup final).

MOST CONSECUTIVE PLAYOFF GAME VICTORIES:

14 — Pittsburgh Penguins. Streak started May 9, 1992, at Pittsburgh with a 5-4 in fourth game of a DF series against NY Rangers, won by Pittsburgh 4-2. Continued with a four-game sweep over Boston in the 1992 CF and a four-game win over Chicago in the 1992 F. Pittsburgh then won the first three games of the 1993 DSF versus New Jersey. New Jersey ended the streak April 25, 1993, at New Jersey with a 4-1 win.

12 — Edmonton Oilers. Streak began May 15, 1984 at Edmonton with a 7-2 win over NY Islanders in third game of F series, and ended May 9, 1985 when Chicago defeated Edmonton 5-2 at Chicago. Included in the streak were three wins over the NY Islanders, in 1984, three over Los Angeles, four over Winnipeg and two over Chicago, all in 1985.

11 — Montreal Canadiens. Streak began April 16, 1959, at Toronto with 3-2 win in fourth game of F series, won by Montreal 4-1, and ended March 23, 1961, when Chicago defeated Montreal 4-3 in second game of SF series. Included in streak were eight straight victories in 1960.

— Montreal Canadiens. Streak began April 28, 1968, at Montreal with 4-3 win in fifth game of SF series, won by Montreal 4-1, and ended April 17, 1969, at Boston when Boston defeated them 5-0 in third game of SF series. Included in the streak were four straight wins over St. Louis in the 1968 F and four straight wins over NY Rangers in a 1969 QF series.

— Boston Bruins. Streak began April 14, 1970, at Boston with 3-2 victory over NY Rangers in fifth game of a QF series, won by Boston 4-2. It continued with a four-game victory over Chicago in the 1970 SF and a four-game win over St. Louis in the 1970 F. Boston then won the first game of a 1971 QF series against Montreal. Montreal ended the streak April 8, 1971, at Boston with a 7-5 victory.

— Montreal Canadiens. Streak started May 6, 1976, at Montreal with 5-2 win in fifth game of a SF series against NY Islanders, won by Montreal 4-1. Continued with a four-game sweep over Philadelphia in the 1976 F and a four-game win against St. Louis in the 1977 QF. Montreal won the first two games of a 1977 SF series against the NY Islanders before NY Islanders ended the streak, April 2, 1977 at New York with a 5-3 victory.

— Chicago Blackhawks. Streak started April 24, 1992, at St. Louis with a 5-3 win in fourth game of a DSF series against St. Louis, won by Chicago 4-2. Continued with a four-game sweep over Detroit in the 1992 DF and a four-game win over Edmonton in the 1992 CF. Pittsburgh ended the streak May 26, 1992, at Pittsburgh with a 5-4 victory.

MOST CONSECUTIVE VICTORIES, ONE PLAYOFF YEAR:

11 — Chicago Blackhawks in 1992. Chicago won last three games of best-of-seven DSF against St. Louis to win series 4-2 and then defeated Detroit 4-0 in best-of-seven DF and Edmonton 4-0 in best-of-seven CF.

— **Pittsburgh Penguins** in 1992. Pittsburgh won last three games of best-of-seven DF against NY Rangers to win series 4-2 and then defeated Boston 4-0 in best-of-seven CF and Chicago 4-0 in best-of-seven F.

— **Montreal Canadiens** in 1993. Montreal won last for games of best-of-seven DSF against Quebec to win series 4-2, defeated Buffalo 4-0 in best-of-seven DF and won first three games of CF against NY Islanders.

Dirk Graham was Chicago's captain when the Blackhawks set an NHL record with 11 consecutive post-season victories during the 1991-92 playoffs.

LONGEST PLAYOFF LOSING STREAK:

16 Games — Chicago Blackhawks. Streak started in 1975 QF against Buffalo when Chicago lost last two games. Then Chicago lost four games to Montreal in 1976 QF; two games to NY Islanders in 1977 PR; four games to Boston in 1978 QF and four games to NY Islanders in 1979 QF. Streak ended on April 8, 1980 when Chicago defeated St. Louis 3-2 in the opening game of their 1980 PR series.

12 Games — Toronto Maple Leafs. Streak started on April 16, 1979 as Toronto lost four straight games in a QF series against Montreal. Continued with three-game PR defeats versus Philadelphia and NY Islanders in 1980 and 1981 respectively. Toronto failed to qualify for the 1982 playoffs and lost the first two games of a 1983 DSF against Minnesota. Toronto ended the streak with a 6-3 win against the North Stars on April 9, 1983.

10 Games — NY Rangers. Streak started in 1968 QF against Chicago when NY Rangers lost last four games and continued through 1969 (four straight losses to Montreal in QF) and 1970 (two straight losses to Boston in QF) before ending with a 4-3 win against Boston, at New York, April 11, 1970.

— Philadelphia Flyers. Streak started on April 18, 1968, the last game in the 1968 QF series against St. Louis, and continued through 1969 (four straight losses to St. Louis in QF), 1971 (four straight losses to Chicago in QF) and 1973 (opening game loss to Minnesota in QF) before ending with a 4-1 win against Minnesota, at Philadelphia, April 5, 1973.

— Chicago Blackhawks. Streak started on May 26, 1992 as Chicago lost four straight games in the F to Pittsburgh. Continued with four straight losses to St. Louis in 1993 DSF. Chicago lost the first two games of 1994 CQF to Toronto before ending the streak with a 5-4 win against Toronto on April 23, 1994.

MOST SHUTOUTS, ONE PLAYOFF YEAR, ALL TEAMS:

16 — 1994. Of 90 games played, NY Rangers and Vancouver had 4 each, Toronto had 3, Buffalo had 2, while Washington, Detroit and New Jersey had 1 each.

12 — 1992. Of 86 games played, Detroit, Edmonton and Vancouver had 2 each, while Boston, Buffalo, Chicago, Montreal, NY Rangers and Pittsburgh had 1 each.

FEWEST SHUTOUTS, ONE PLAYOFF YEAR, ALL TEAMS:

0 — 1959. 18 games played.

MOST SHUTOUTS, BOTH TEAMS, ONE SERIES:
5 — 1945 F, Toronto Maple Leafs, Detroit Red Wings. Toronto had 3 shutouts, Detroit 2. Toronto won best-of-seven series 4-3.
— 1950 SF, Toronto Maple Leafs, Detroit Red Wings. Toronto had 3 shutouts, Detroit 2. Detroit won best-of-seven series 4-3.

MOST PENALTIES, BOTH TEAMS, ONE SERIES:
219 — New Jersey Devils, Washington Capitals in 1988 DF won by New Jersey 4-3. New Jersey received 98 minors, 11 majors, 9 misconducts and 1 match penalty. Washington received 80 minors, 11 majors, 8 misconducts and 1 match penalty.

MOST PENALTY MINUTES, BOTH TEAMS, ONE SERIES:
656 — New Jersey Devils, Washington Capitals in 1988 DF won by New Jersey 4-3. New Jersey had 351 minutes; Washington 305.

MOST PENALTIES, ONE TEAM, ONE SERIES:
119 — New Jersey Devils in 1988 DF versus Washington. New Jersey received 98 minors, 11 majors, 9 misconducts and 1 match penalty.

MOST PENALTY MINUTES, ONE TEAM, ONE SERIES:
351 — New Jersey Devils in 1988 DF versus Washington. Series won by New Jersey 4-3.

MOST PENALTY MINUTES, BOTH TEAMS, ONE GAME:
298 Minutes — Detroit Red Wings, St. Louis Blues, at St. Louis, April 12, 1991. Detroit received 33 penalties for 152 minutes; St. Louis 33 penalties for 146 minutes. St. Louis won 6-1.
267 Minutes — NY Rangers, Los Angeles Kings, at Los Angeles, April 9, 1981. NY Rangers received 31 penalties for 142 minutes; Los Angeles 28 penalties for 125 minutes. Los Angeles won 5-4.

MOST PENALTIES, BOTH TEAMS, ONE GAME:
66 — Detroit Red Wings, St. Louis Blues, at St. Louis, April 12, 1991. Detroit received 33 penalties; St. Louis 33. St. Louis won 6-1.
62 — New Jersey Devils, Washington Capitals, at New Jersey, April 22, 1988. New Jersey received 32 penalties; Washington 30. New Jersey won 10-4.

MOST PENALTIES, ONE TEAM, ONE GAME:
33 — Detroit Red Wings, at St. Louis, April 12,1991. St. Louis won 6-1.
— St. Louis Blues, at St. Louis, April 12, 1991. St. Louis won 6-1.
32 — New Jersey Devils, at Washington, April 22,1988. New Jersey won 10-4.
31 — NY Rangers, at Los Angeles, April 9, 1981. Los Angeles won 5-4.
30 — Philadelphia Flyers, at Toronto, April 15, 1976. Toronto won 5-4.

MOST PENALTY MINUTES, ONE TEAM, ONE GAME:
152 — Detroit Red Wings, at St. Louis, April 12, 1991. St. Louis won 6-1.
146 — St. Louis Blues, at St. Louis, April 12, 1991. St. Louis won 6-1.
142 — NY Rangers, at Los Angeles, April 9, 1981. Los Angeles won 5-4.

Johnny Bower and Terry Sawchuk share a contented smile after leading the Toronto Maple Leafs to the Stanley Cup championship with a 3-1 victory over Montreal on May 2, 1967.

MOST PENALTIES, BOTH TEAMS, ONE PERIOD:
43 — NY Rangers, Los Angeles Kings, April 9, 1981, at Los Angeles, first period. NY Rangers had 24 penalties; Los Angeles 19. Los Angeles won 5-4.

MOST PENALTY MINUTES, BOTH TEAMS, ONE PERIOD:
248 — NY Islanders, Boston Bruins, April 17, 1980, first period, at Boston. Each team received 124 minutes. Islanders won 5-4.

MOST PENALTIES, ONE TEAM, ONE PERIOD: (AND) MOST PENALTY MINUTES, ONE TEAM, ONE PERIOD:
24 Penalties; 125 Minutes — NY Rangers, April 9, 1981, at Los Angeles, first period. Los Angeles won 5-4.

FEWEST PENALTIES, BOTH TEAMS, BEST-OF-SEVEN SERIES:
19 — Detroit Red Wings, Toronto Maple Leafs in 1945 F, won by Toronto 4-3. Detroit received 10 minors. Toronto 9 minors.

FEWEST PENALTIES, ONE TEAM, BEST-OF-SEVEN SERIES:
9 — Toronto Maple Leafs in 1945 F, won by Toronto 4-3 against Detroit.

MOST POWER-PLAY GOALS BY ALL TEAMS, ONE PLAYOFF YEAR:
199 — 1988 in 83 games.

MOST POWER-PLAY GOALS, ONE TEAM, ONE PLAYOFF YEAR:
35 — Minnesota North Stars, 1991 in 23 games.
32 — Edmonton Oilers, 1988 in 18 games.
31 — NY Islanders, 1981, in 18 games.

MOST POWER-PLAY GOALS, BOTH TEAMS, ONE SERIES:
21 — NY Islanders, Philadelphia Flyers in 1980 F, won by NY Islanders 4-2. NY Islanders had 15 and Flyers 6.
— NY Islanders, Edmonton Oilers in 1981 QF, won by NY Islanders 4-2. NY Islanders had 13 and Edmonton 8.
— Philadelphia Flyers, Pittsburgh Penguins in 1989 DF, won by Philadelphia 4-3. Philadelphia had 11 and Pittsburgh 10.
— Minnesota North Stars, Chicago Blackhawks in 1991 DSF, won by Minnesota 4-2. Minnesota had 15 and Chicago 6.
20 — Toronto Maple Leafs, Philadelphia Flyers in 1976 QF series won by Philadelphia 4-3. Toronto had 12 power-pay goals; Philadelphia 8.

MOST POWER-PLAY GOALS, ONE TEAM, ONE SERIES:
15 — NY Islanders in 1980 F against Philadelphia. NY Islanders won series 4-2.
— Minnesota North Stars in 1991 DSF against Chicago. Minnesota won series 4-2.
13 — NY Islanders in 1981 QF against Edmonton. NY Islanders won series 4-2.
— Calgary Flames in 1986 CF against St. Louis. Calgary won series 4-3.
12 — Toronto Maple Leafs in 1976 QF series won by Philadelphia 4-3.

MOST POWER-PLAY GOALS, BOTH TEAMS, ONE GAME:
8 — Minnesota North Stars, St. Louis Blues, April 24, 1991 at Minnesota. Minnesota had 4, St. Louis 4. Minnesota won 8-4.
7 — Minnesota North Stars, Edmonton Oilers, April 28, 1984 at Minnesota. Minnesota had 4, Edmonton 3. Edmonton won 8-5.
— Philadelphia Flyers, NY Rangers, April 13, 1985 at New York. Philadelphia had 4, NY Rangers 3. Philadelphia won 6-5.
— Edmonton Oilers, Chicago Blackhawks, May 14, 1985 at Edmonton. Chicago had 5, Edmonton 2. Edmonton won 10-5.
— Edmonton Oilers, Los Angeles Kings, April 9, 1987 at Edmonton. Edmonton had 5, Los Angeles 2. Edmonton won 13-3.
— Vancouver Canucks, Calgary Flames, April 9, 1989 at Vancouver. Vancouver had 4, Calgary 3. Vancouver won 5-3.

MOST POWER-PLAY GOALS, ONE TEAM, ONE GAME:
6 — Boston Bruins, April 2, 1969, at Boston against Toronto. Boston won 10-0.

MOST POWER-PLAY GOALS, BOTH TEAMS, ONE PERIOD:
5 — Minnesota North Stars, Edmonton Oilers, April 28, 1984, second period, at Minnesota. Minnesota had 4 and Edmonton 1. Edmonton won 8-5.
— Vancouver Canucks, Calgary Flames, April 9, 1989, third period at Vancouver. Vancouver had 3 and Calgary 2. Vancouver won 5-3.
— Minnesota North Stars, St. Louis Blues, April 24, 1991, second period, at Minnesota. Minnesota had 4 and St. Louis 1. Minnesota won 8-4.

MOST POWER-PLAY GOALS, ONE TEAM, ONE PERIOD:
4 — Toronto Maple Leafs, March 26, 1936, second period against Boston at Toronto. Toronto won 8-3.
— Minnesota North Stars, April 28, 1984, second period against Edmonton at Minnesota. Edmonton won 8-5.
— Boston Bruins, April 11, 1991, third period against Hartford at Boston. Boston won 6-1.
— Minnesota North Stars, April 24, 1991, second period against St. Louis at Minnesota. Minnesota won 8-4.

MOST SHORTHAND GOALS BY ALL TEAMS, ONE PLAYOFF YEAR:
33 — 1988, in 83 games.

MOST SHORTHAND GOALS, ONE TEAM, ONE PLAYOFF YEAR:
10 — Edmonton Oilers 1983, in 16 games.
9 — NY Islanders, 1981, in 19 games.
8 — Philadelphia Flyers, 1989, in 19 games.
7 — NY Islanders, 1980, in 21 games.
7 — Chicago Blackhawks, 1989, in 16 games.

MOST SHORTHAND GOALS, BOTH TEAMS, ONE SERIES:
7 — **Boston Bruins (4), NY Rangers (3),** in 1958 SF, won by Boston 4-2.
— **Edmonton Oilers (5), Calgary Flames (2),** in 1983 DF won by Edmonton 4-1.

MOST SHORTHAND GOALS, ONE TEAM, ONE SERIES:
5 — **Edmonton Oilers** in 1983 against Calgary in best-of-seven DF won by Edmonton 4-1.
— **NY Rangers** in 1979 against Philadelphia in best-of-seven QF, won by NY Rangers 4-1.
4 — Boston Bruins in 1958 against NY Rangers in best-of-seven SF series, won by Boston 4-2.
— Minnesota North Stars in 1981 against Calgary in best-of-seven SF, won by Minnesota 4-2.
— Chicago Blackhawks in 1989 against Detroit in best-of-seven DSF won by Chicago 4-2.
— Philadelphia Flyers in 1989 against Pittsburgh in best-of-seven DF won by Philadelphia 4-3.
— NY Rangers in 1992 against New Jersey in best-of-seven DSF won by NY Rangers 4-3.
— Detroit Red Wings in 1993 against Toronto in best-of-seven DSF won by Toronto 4-3.
— NY Islanders in 1993 against Pittsburgh in best-of-seven DF won by NY Islanders 4-3.
— Toronto Maple Leafs in 1994 against San Jose in best-of-seven CSF won by Toronto 4-3.

MOST SHORTHAND GOALS, BOTH TEAMS, ONE GAME:
4 — **NY Islanders, NY Rangers,** April 17, 1983 at NY Rangers. NY Islanders had 3 shorthand goals, NY Rangers 1. NY Rangers won 7-6.
— **Boston Bruins, Minnesota North Stars,** April 11, 1981, at Minnesota. Boston had 3 shorthand goals, Minnesota 1. Minnesota won 6-3.
— **San Jose Sharks, Toronto Maple Leafs,** May 8, 1994 at San Jose. Toronto had 3 shorthanded goals, San Jose 1. Toronto won 8-3.
3 — Toronto Maple Leafs, Detroit Red Wings, April 5, 1947, at Toronto. Toronto had 2 shorthand goals, Detroit 1. Toronto won 6-1.
— NY Rangers, Boston Bruins, April 1, 1958, at Boston. NY Rangers had 2 shorthand goals, Boston 1. NY Rangers won 5-2.
— Minnesota North Stars, Philadelphia Flyers, May 4, 1980, at Minnesota. Minnesota had 2 shorthand goals, Philadelphia 1. Philadelphia won 5-3.
— Edmonton Oilers, Winnipeg Jets, April 9, 1988 at Winnipeg. Winnipeg had 2 shorthand goals, Edmonton 1. Winnipeg won 6-4.
— New Jersey Devils, NY Islanders, April 14, 1988 at New Jersey. NY Islanders had 2 shorthand goals, New Jersey 1. New Jersey won 6-5.

MOST SHORTHAND GOALS, ONE TEAM, ONE GAME:
3 — **Boston Bruins,** April 11, 1981, at Minnesota. Minnesota won 6-3.
— **NY Islanders,** April 17, 1983, at NY Rangers. NY Rangers won 7-6.
— **Toronto Maple Leafs,** May 8, 1994, at San Jose. Toronto won 8-3.

MOST SHORTHAND GOALS, BOTH TEAMS, ONE PERIOD:
3 — **Toronto Maple Leafs, Detroit Red Wings,** April 5, 1947, at Toronto, first period. Toronto had 2 shorthand goals, Detroit 1. Toronto won 6-1.
— **Toronto Maple Leafs, San Jose Sharks,** May 8, 1994, at San Jose, third period. Toronto had 2 shorthanded goals, San Jose 1. Toronto won 8-3.

MOST SHORTHAND GOALS ONE TEAM, ONE PERIOD:
2 — **Toronto Maple Leafs,** April 5, 1947, at Toronto against Detroit, first period. Toronto won 6-1.
— **Toronto Maple Leafs,** April 13, 1965, at Toronto against Montreal, first period. Montreal won 4-3.
— **Boston Bruins,** April 20, 1969, at Boston against Montreal, first period. Boston won 3-2.
— **Boston Bruins,** April 8, 1970, at Boston against NY Rangers, second period. Boston won 8-2.
— **Boston Bruins,** April 30, 1972, at Boston against NY Rangers, first period. Boston won 6-5.
— **Chicago Blackhawks,** May 3, 1973, at Chicago against Montreal, first period. Chicago won 7-4.
— **Montreal Canadiens,** April 23, 1978, at Detroit, first period. Montreal won 8-0.
— **NY Islanders,** April 8, 1980, at New York against Los Angeles, second period. NY Islanders won 8-1.
— **Los Angeles Kings,** April 9, 1980, at NY Islanders, first period. Los Angeles won 6-3.
— **Boston Bruins,** April 13, 1980, at Pittsburgh, second period. Boston won 8-3.
— **Minnesota North Stars,** May 4, 1980, at Minnesota against Philadelphia, second period. Philadelphia won 5-3.
— **Boston Bruins,** April 11, 1981, at Minnesota, third period. Minnesota won 6-3.
— **NY Islanders,** May 12, 1981, at New York against Minnesota, first period. NY Islanders won 6-3.
— **Montreal Canadiens,** April 7, 1982, at Montreal against Quebec, third period. Montreal won 5-1.
— **Edmonton Oilers,** April 24, 1983, at Edmonton against Chicago, third period. Edmonton won 8-4.
— **Winnipeg Jets,** April 14, 1985, at Calgary, second period. Winnipeg won 5-3.
— **Boston Bruins,** April 6, 1988 at Boston against Buffalo, first period. Boston won 7-3.
— **NY Islanders,** April 14, 1988 at New Jersey, third period. New Jersey won 6-5.
— **Detroit Red Wings,** April 29, 1993 at Toronto, second period. Detroit won 7-3.
— **Toronto Maple Leafs,** May 8, 1994 at San Jose, third period. Toronto won 8-3.

Mark Osborne, below, of the Toronto Maple Leafs scored one of three shorthanded goals in the third period of a Conference Semi-Final game against the San Jose Sharks on May 8, 1994. Bobby LaLonde, right, scored two of Boston's record three shorthanded goals in a 6-3 loss to the Minnesota North Stars on March 11, 1981.

The Montreal Canadiens and the Calgary Flames combined to score four goals in 94 seconds in game one of the 1986 Stanley Cup finals. Joel Otto started the offensive onslaught by scoring a powerplay marker at 17:59 of the first period.

FASTEST TWO GOALS, BOTH TEAMS:

5 Seconds — Pittsburgh Penguins, Buffalo Sabres at Buffalo, April 14, 1979. Gilbert Perreault scored for Buffalo at 12:59 and Jim Hamilton for Pittsburgh at 13:04 of first period. Pittsburgh won 4-3 and best-of-three PR 2-1.

8 Seconds — Minnesota North Stars, St. Louis Blues at Minnesota, April 9, 1989. Bernie Federko scored for St. Louis at 2:28 of third period and Perry Berezan at 2:36 for Minnesota. Minnesota won 5-4. St. Louis won best-of-seven DSF 4-1.

9 Seconds — NY Islanders, Washington Capitals at Washington, April 10, 1986. Bryan Trottier scored for New York at 18:26 of second period and Scott Stevens at 18:35 for Washington. Washington won 5-2, and won best-of-five DSF 3-0.

10 Seconds — Washington Capitals, New Jersey Devils at New Jersey, April 5, 1990. Pat Conacher scored for New Jersey at 8:02 of second period and Dale Hunter at 8:12 for Washington. Washington won 5-4, and won best-of-seven DSF 4-2.

— Calgary Flames, Edmonton Oilers at Edmonton, April 8, 1991. Joe Nieuwendyk scored for Calgary at 2:03 of first period and Esa Tikkanen at 2:13 for Edmonton. Edmonton won 4-3, and won best-of-seven DSF 4-3.

FASTEST TWO GOALS, ONE TEAM:

5 Seconds — Detroit Red Wings at Detroit, April 11, 1965, against Chicago. Norm Ullman scored at 17:35 and 17:40, second period. Detroit won 4-2. Chicago won best-of-seven SF 4-3.

FASTEST THREE GOALS, BOTH TEAMS:

21 Seconds — Edmonton Oilers, Chicago Blackhawks at Edmonton, May 7, 1985. Behn Wilson scored for Chicago at 19:22 of third period, Jari Kurri at 19:36 and Glenn Anderson at 19:43 for Edmonton. Edmonton won 7-3 and best-of-seven CF 4-2.

30 Seconds — Chicago Blackhawks, Pittsburgh Penguins at Chicago, June 1, 1992. Dirk Graham scored for Chicago at 6:21 of first period, Kevin Stevens for Pittsburgh at 6:33 and Graham for Chicago at 6:51. Pittsburgh won 6-5 and best-of-seven F 4-0.

31 Seconds — Edmonton Oilers, Philadelphia Flyers at Edmonton, May 25, 1985. Wayne Gretzky scored for Edmonton at 1:10 and 1:25 of first period, Derrick Smith scored for Philadelphia at 1:41. Edmonton won 4-3 and best-of-seven F 4-1.

FASTEST THREE GOALS, ONE TEAM:

23 Seconds — Toronto Maple Leafs at Toronto, April 12, 1979, against Atlanta Flames. Darryl Sittler scored at 4:04 of first period and again at 4:16 and Ron Ellis at 4:27. Leafs won 7-4 and best-of-three PR 2-0.

38 Seconds — NY Rangers at New York, April 12, 1986. Jim Wiemer scored at 12:29 of third period, Bob Brooke at 12:43 and Ron Greschner at 13:07. NY Rangers won 5-2 and best-of-five DSF 3-2.

56 Seconds — Montreal Canadiens at Detroit, April 6, 1954. Dickie Moore scored at 15:03 of first period, Maurice Richard at 15:28 and again at 15:59. Montreal won 3-1. Detroit won best-of-seven F 4-3.

FASTEST FOUR GOALS, BOTH TEAMS:

1 Minute, 33 Seconds — Philadelphia Flyers, Toronto Maple Leafs at Philadelphia, April 20, 1976. Don Saleski of Philadelphia scored at 10:04 of second period; Bob Neely, Toronto, 10:42; Gary Dornhoefer, Philadelphia, 11:24; and Don Saleski, 11:37. Philadelphia won 7-1 and best-of-seven QF series 4-3.

1 minute, 34 seconds — Montreal Canadiens, Calgary Flames at Montreal, May 20, 1986. Joel Otto of Calgary scored at 17:59 of first period; Bobby Smith, Montreal, 18:25; Mats Naslund, Montreal, 19:17; and Bob Gainey, Montreal, 19:33. Montreal won 5-3 and best-of-seven F series 4-1.

1 Minute, 38 Seconds — Boston Bruins, Philadelphia Flyers at Philadelphia, April 26, 1977. Gregg Sheppard of Boston scored at 14:01 of second period; Mike Milbury, Boston, 15:01; Gary Dornhoefer, Philadelphia, 15:16; and Jean Ratelle, Boston, 15:39. Boston won 5-4 and best-of-seven SF series 4-0.

FASTEST FOUR GOALS, ONE TEAM:

2 Minutes, 35 Seconds — Montreal Canadiens at Montreal, March 30, 1944, against Toronto. Toe Blake scored at 7:58 of third period and again at 8:37; Maurice Richard, 9:17; Ray Getliffe, 10:33. Montreal won 11-0 and best-of-seven SF 4-1.

FASTEST FIVE GOALS, BOTH TEAMS:

3 Minutes, 6 Seconds — Chicago Blackhawks, Minnesota North Stars, at Chicago April 21, 1985. Keith Brown scored for Chicago at 1:12, second period; Ken Yaremchuk, Chicago, 1:27; Dino Ciccarelli, Minnesota, 2:48; Tony McKegney, Minnesota, 4:07; and Curt Fraser, Chicago, 4:18. Chicago won 6-2 and best-of-seven DF 4-2.

3 Minutes, 20 Seconds — Minnesota North Stars, Philadelphia Flyers, at Philadelphia, April 29, 1980. Paul Shmyr scored for Minnesota at 13:20, first period; Steve Christoff, Minnesota, 13:59; Ken Linseman, Philadelphia, 14:54; Tom Gorence, Philadelphia, 15:36; and Linseman, 16:40. Minnesota won 6-5. Philadelphia won best-of-seven SF 4-1.

4 Minutes, 19 Seconds — Toronto Maple Leafs, NY Rangers at Toronto, April 9, 1932. Ace Bailey scored for Toronto at 15:07, third period; Fred Cook, NY Rangers, 16:32; Bob Gracie, Toronto, 17:36; Frank Boucher, NY Rangers, 18:26 and again at 19:26. Toronto won 6-4 and best-of-five F 3-0.

FASTEST FIVE GOALS, ONE TEAM:

3 Minutes, 36 Seconds — Montreal Canadiens at Montreal, March 30, 1944, against Toronto. Toe Blake scored at 7:58 of third period and again at 8:37; Maurice Richard, 9:17; Ray Getliffe, 10:33; and Buddy O'Connor, 11:34. Canadiens won 11-0 and best-of-seven SF 4-1.

MOST THREE-OR-MORE GOAL GAMES BY ALL TEAMS, ONE PLAYOFF YEAR:

12 — 1983 in 66 games.
— 1988 in 83 games.
11 — 1985 in 70 games.
— 1992 in 86 games.

MOST THREE-OR-MORE GOAL GAMES, ONE TEAM, ONE PLAYOFF YEAR:

6 — Edmonton Oilers in 16 games, 1983.
— Edmonton Oilers in 18 games, 1985.

Individual Records

Career

MOST YEARS IN PLAYOFFS:
20 — Gordie Howe, Detroit, Hartford (1947-58 incl.; 60-61; 63-66 incl.; 70 & 80)
   — Larry Robinson, Montreal, Los Angeles (1973-92 incl.)
19 — Red Kelly, Detroit, Toronto
18 — Stan Mikita, Chicago
   — Henri Richard, Montreal

MOST CONSECUTIVE YEARS IN PLAYOFFS:
20 — Larry Robinson, Montreal, Los Angeles (1973-1992, inclusive).
17 — Brad Park, NY Rangers, Boston, Detroit (1969-1985, inclusive).
16 — Jean Beliveau, Montreal (1954-69, inclusive).

MOST PLAYOFF GAMES:
227 — Larry Robinson, Montreal, Los Angeles
221 — Bryan Trottier, NY Islanders, Pittsburgh
208 — Glenn Anderson, Edmonton, Toronto, NY Rangers
200 — Mark Messier, Edmonton, NY Rangers
192 — Kevin Lowe, Edmonton, NY Rangers

MOST POINTS IN PLAYOFFS (CAREER):
346 — Wayne Gretzky, Edmonton, Los Angeles, 110G, 236A
259 — Mark Messier, Edmonton, NY Rangers, 99G, 160A
222 — Jari Kurri, Edmonton, Los Angeles, 102G, 120A
207 — Glenn Anderson, Edmonton, Toronto, NY Rangers, 91G, 116A
184 — Bryan Trottier, NY Islanders, Pittsburgh 71G, 113A

MOST GOALS IN PLAYOFFS (CAREER):
110 — Wayne Gretzky, Edmonton, Los Angeles
102 — Jari Kurri, Edmonton, Los Angeles
99 — Mark Messier, Edmonton, NY Rangers
91 — Glenn Anderson, Edmonton, Toronto, NY Rangers
85 — Mike Bossy, NY Islanders

MOST ASSISTS IN PLAYOFFS (CAREER):
236 — Wayne Gretzky, Edmonton, Los Angeles
160 — Mark Messier, Edmonton, NY Rangers
120 — Jari Kurri, Edmonton, Los Angeles
116 — Larry Robinson, Montreal, Los Angeles
   — Glenn Anderson, Edmonton, Toronto, NY Rangers

MOST OVERTIME GOALS IN PLAYOFFS (CAREER):
6 — Maurice Richard, Montreal (1 in 1946; 3 in 1951; 1 in 1957; 1 in 1958.)
4 — Bob Nystrom, NY Islanders
   — Dale Hunter, Quebec, Washington
   — Glenn Anderson, Edmonton, Toronto
   — Wayne Gretzky, Edmonton, Los Angeles
   — Stephane Richer, Montreal, New Jersey
3 — Mel Hill, Boston
   — Rene Robert, Buffalo
   — Danny Gare, Buffalo
   — Jacques Lemaire, Montreal
   — Bobby Clarke, Philadelphia
   — Terry O'Reilly, Boston
   — Mike Bossy, NY Islanders
   — Steve Payne, Minnesota
   — Ken Morrow, NY Islanders
   — Lanny McDonald, Toronto, Calgary
   — Peter Stastny, Quebec
   — Dino Ciccarelli, Minnesota, Washington
   — Russ Courtnall, Montreal
   — Kirk Muller, Montreal
   — Greg Adams, Vancouver

MOST POWER-PLAY GOALS IN PLAYOFFS (CAREER):
35 — Mike Bossy, NY Islanders
30 — Wayne Gretzky, Edmonton, Los Angeles
27 — Denis Potvin, NY Islanders
26 — Jean Beliveau, Montreal
25 — Jari Kurri, Edmonton, Los Angeles
   — Mario Lemieux, Pittsburgh
24 — Bobby Smith, Minnesota, Montreal
23 — Glenn Anderson, Edmonton, Toronto, NY Rangers
   — Brian Propp, Philadelphia, Boston, Minnesota
   — Cam Neely, Vancouver, Boston

MOST SHORTHAND GOALS IN PLAYOFFS (CAREER):
14 — Mark Messier, Edmonton, NY Rangers
11 — Wayne Gretzky, Edmonton, Los Angeles
9 — Jari Kurri, Edmonton, Los Angeles
8 — Ed Westfall, Boston, NY Islanders
   — Hakan Loob, Calgary

MOST GAME-WINNING GOALS IN PLAYOFFS (CAREER):
21 — Wayne Gretzky, Edmonton, Los Angeles
18 — Maurice Richard, Montreal
17 — Mike Bossy, NY Islanders
16 — Glenn Anderson, Edmonton, Toronto, NY Rangers
15 — Jean Beliveau, Montreal
   — Yvan Cournoyer, Montreal

MOST THREE-OR-MORE-GOAL GAMES IN PLAYOFFS (CAREER):
8 — Wayne Gretzky, Edmonton. Six three-goal games; two four-goal games.
7 — Maurice Richard, Montreal. Four three-goal games; two four-goal games; one five-goal game.
   — Jari Kurri, Edmonton. Six three-goal games; one four-goal game.
5 — Mike Bossy, NY Islanders. Four three-goal games; one four-goal game.
   — Dino Ciccarelli, Minnesota, Washington, Detroit. Four three-goal games; one four-goal game.

MOST PENALTY MINUTES IN PLAYOFFS (CAREER):
613 — Dale Hunter, Quebec, Washington
541 — Chris Nilan, Montreal, NY Rangers, Boston
466 — Willi Plett, Atlanta, Calgary, Minnesota, Boston
455 — Dave Williams, Toronto, Vancouver, Los Angeles
412 — Dave Schultz, Philadelphia, Los Angeles, Buffalo

MOST SHUTOUTS IN PLAYOFFS (CAREER):
15 — Clint Benedict, Ottawa, Mtl. Maroons
14 — Jacques Plante, Montreal, St. Louis
13 — Turk Broda, Toronto
12 — Terry Sawchuk, Detroit, Toronto, Los Angeles

MOST PLAYOFF GAMES APPEARED IN BY A GOALTENDER (CAREER):
132 — Bill Smith, NY Islanders
119 — Grant Fuhr, Edmonton, Buffalo
115 — Glenn Hall, Detroit, Chicago, St. Louis
114 — Patrick Roy, Montreal
112 — Jacques Plante, Montreal, St. Louis, Toronto, Boston
   — Ken Dryden, Montreal
111 — Andy Moog, Edmonton, Boston, Dallas

MOST MINUTES PLAYED BY A GOALTENDER (CAREER):
7,645 — Billy Smith, NY Islanders
7,002 — Grant Fuhr, Edmonton, Buffalo
6,964 — Patrick Roy, Montreal
6,899 — Glenn Hall, Detroit, Chicago, St. Louis
6,846 — Ken Dryden, Montreal

Single Playoff Year

MOST POINTS, ONE PLAYOFF YEAR:
47 — Wayne Gretzky, Edmonton, in 1985. 17 goals, 30 assists in 18 games.
44 — Mario Lemieux, Pittsburgh, in 1991. 16 goals, 28 assists in 23 games.
43 — Wayne Gretzky, Edmonton, in 1988. 12 goals, 31 assists in 19 games.
40 — Wayne Gretzky, Los Angeles, in 1993. 15 goals, 25 assists in 24 games.
38 — Wayne Gretzky, Edmonton, in 1983. 12 goals, 26 assists in 16 games.
37 — Paul Coffey, Edmonton, in 1985. 12 goals, 25 assists in 18 games.
35 — Mike Bossy, NY Islanders, in 1981. 17 goals, 18 assists in 18 games.
   — Wayne Gretzky, Edmonton, in 1984. 13 goals, 22 assists in 19 games.
   — Mark Messier, Edmonton, in 1988. 11 goals, 23 assists in 19 games.
   — Doug Gilmour, Toronto, in 1993. 10 goals, 25 assists in 21 games.
34 — Wayne Gretzky, Edmonton, in 1987. 5 goals, 29 assists in 21 games.
   — Mark Recchi, Pittsburgh, in 1991. 10 goals, 24 assists in 24 games.
   — Mario Lemieux, Pittsburgh, in 1992. 16 goals, 18 assists in 15 games.
   — Brian Leetch, NY Rangers, in 1994. 11 goals, 23 assists in 23 games.

MOST POINTS BY A DEFENSEMAN, ONE PLAYOFF YEAR:
37 — Paul Coffey, Edmonton, in 1985. 12 goals, 25 assists in 18 games.
34 — Brian Leetch, NY Rangers, in 1994. 11 goals, 23 assists in 23 games.
31 — Al MacInnis, Calgary, in 1989. 7 goals, 24 assists in 18 games.
25 — Denis Potvin, NY Islanders, in 1981. 8 goals, 17 assists in 18 games.
   — Ray Bourque, Boston, in 1991. 7 goals, 18 assists in 19 games.

MOST POINTS BY A ROOKIE, ONE PLAYOFF YEAR:
21 — Dino Ciccarelli, Minnesota, in 1981. 14 goals, 7 assists in 19 games.
20 — Don Maloney, NY Rangers, in 1979. 7 goals, 13 assists in 18 games.

LONGEST CONSECUTIVE POINT-SCORING STREAK, ONE PLAYOFF YEAR:
18 games — Bryan Trottier, NY Islanders, 1981. 11 goals, 18 assists, 29 points.
17 games — Wayne Gretzky, Edmonton, 1988. 12 goals, 29 assists, 41 points.
   — Al MacInnis, Calgary, 1989. 7 goals, 19 assists, 24 points.

LONGEST CONSECUTIVE POINT-SCORING STREAK, MORE THAN ONE PLAYOFF YEAR:
27 games — Bryan Trottier, NY Islanders, 1980, 1981 and 1982. 7 games in 1980 (3 G, 5 A, 8 PTS), 18 games in 1981 (11 G, 18 A, 29 PTS), and two games in 1982 (2 G, 3 A, 5 PTS). Total points, 42.
19 games — Wayne Gretzky, Edmonton, Los Angeles 1988 and 1989. 17 games in 1988 (12 G, 29 A, 41 PTS with Edmonton), 2 games in 1989 (1 G, 2 A, 3 PTS with Los Angeles). Total points, 44.
18 games — Phil Esposito, Boston, 1970 and 1971. 13 G, 20 A, 33 PTS.

MOST GOALS, ONE PLAYOFF YEAR:
19 — Reggie Leach, Philadelphia, 1976. 16 games.
   — **Jari Kurri, Edmonton,** 1985. 18 games.
17 — Newsy Lalonde, Montreal, 1919. 10 games.
   — Mike Bossy, NY Islanders, 1981. 18 games.
   — Steve Payne, Minnesota, 1981. 19 games.
   — Mike Bossy, NY Islanders, 1982. 19 games.
   — Mike Bossy, NY Islanders, 1983. 19 games.
   — Wayne Gretzky, Edmonton, 1985. 18 games.
   — Kevin Stevens, Pittsburgh, 1991. 24 games.

MOST GOALS BY A DEFENSEMAN, ONE PLAYOFF YEAR:
12 — Paul Coffey, Edmonton, 1985. 18 games.
11 — Brian Leetch, NY Rangers, in 1994. 23 games.
9 — Bobby Orr, Boston, 1970. 14 games.
   — Brad Park, Boston, 1978. 15 games.
8 — Denis Potvin, NY Islanders, 1981. 18 games.
   — Raymond Bourque, Boston, 1983. 17 games.
   — Denis Potvin, NY Islanders, 1983. 20 games.
   — Paul Coffey, Edmonton, 1984. 19 games

MOST GOALS BY A ROOKIE, ONE PLAYOFF YEAR:
14 — Dino Ciccarelli, Minnesota, 1981. 19 games.
11 — Jeremy Roenick, Chicago, 1990. 20 games.
10 — Claude Lemieux, Montreal, 1986. 20 games.
9 — Pat Flatley, NY Islanders, 1984. 21 games.
8 — Steve Christoff, Minnesota, 1980. 14 games.
   — Brad Palmer, Minnesota, 1981. 19 games.
   — Mike Krushelnyski, Boston, 1983. 17 games.
   — Bob Joyce, Boston, 1988. 23 games.

MOST GAME-WINNING GOALS, ONE PLAYOFF YEAR:
5 — Mike Bossy, NY Islanders, 1983. 19 games.
   — **Jari Kurri, Edmonton,** 1987. 21 games.
   — **Bobby Smith, Minnesota,** 1991. 23 games.
   — **Mario Lemieux, Pittsburgh,** 1992. 15 games.

MOST OVERTIME GOALS, ONE PLAYOFF YEAR:
3 — Mel Hill, Boston, 1939. All against NY Rangers in best-of-seven SF, won by Boston 4-3.
   — **Maurice Richard, Montreal,** 1951. 2 against Detroit in best-of-seven SF, won by Montreal 4-2; 1 against Toronto best-of-seven F, won by Toronto 4-1.

MOST POWER-PLAY GOALS, ONE PLAYOFF YEAR:
9 — Mike Bossy, NY Islanders, 1981. 18 games against Toronto, Edmonton, NY Rangers and Minnesota.
   — **Cam Neely, Boston,** 1991. 19 games against Hartford, Montreal, Pittsburgh.
8 — Tim Kerr, Philadelphia, 1989. 19 games.
   — John Druce, Washington, 1990. 15 games
   — Brian Propp, Minnesota, 1991. 23 games.
   — Mario Lemieux, Pittsburgh, 1992. 15 games.
7 — Michel Goulet, Quebec, 1985. 17 games.
   — Mark Messier, Edmonton, 1988. 19 games.
   — Mario Lemieux, Pittsburgh, 1989. 11 games.
   — Brett Hull, St. Louis, 1990. 12 games.
   — Kevin Stevens, Pittsburgh, 1991. 24 games.

MOST SHORTHAND GOALS, ONE PLAYOFF YEAR:
3 — Derek Sanderson, Boston, 1969. 1 against Toronto in QF, won by Boston 4-0; 2 against Montreal in SF, won by Montreal, 4-2.
   — **Bill Barber, Philadelphia,** 1980. All against Minnesota in SF, won by Philadelphia 4-1.
   — **Lorne Henning, NY Islanders,** 1980. 1 against Boston in QF won by NY Islanders 4-1; 1 against Buffalo in SF, won by NY Islanders 4-2, 1 against Philadelphia in F, won by NY Islanders 4-2.
   — **Wayne Gretzky, Edmonton,** 1983. 2 against Winnipeg in DSF won by Edmonton 3-0; 1 against Calgary in DF, won by Edmonton 4-1.
   — **Wayne Presley, Chicago,** 1989. All against Detroit in DSF won by Chicago 4-2.

MOST THREE-OR-MORE GOAL GAMES, ONE PLAYOFF YEAR:
4 — Jari Kurri, Edmonton, 1985. 1 four-goal game, 3 three-goal games.
3 — Mark Messier, Edmonton, 1983. 3 three-goal games.
   — Mike Bossy, NY Islanders, 1983. 3 three-goal games.
2 — Newsy Lalonde, Montreal, 1919. 1 five-goal game, 1 four-goal game.
   — Maurice Richard, Montreal, 1944. 1 five-goal game; 1 three-goal game.
   — Doug Bentley, Chicago, 1944. 2 three-goal games.
   — Norm Ullman, Detroit, 1964. 2 three-goal games.
   — Phil Esposito, Boston, 1970. 2 three-goal games.
   — Pit Martin, Chicago, 1973. 2 three-goal games.
   — Rick MacLeish, Philadelphia, 1975. 2 three-goal games.
   — Lanny McDonald, Toronto, 1977. 1 three-goal game; 1 four-goal game.
   — Wayne Gretzky, Edmonton, 1981. 2 three-goal games.
   — Wayne Gretzky, Edmonton, 1983. 2 four-goal games.
   — Wayne Gretzky, Edmonton, 1985. 2 three-goal games.
   — Petr Klima, Detroit, 1988. 2 three-goal games.
   — Cam Neely, Boston, 1991. 2 three-goal games.

LONGEST CONSECUTIVE GOAL-SCORING STREAK, ONE PLAYOFF YEAR:
9 Games — Reggie Leach, Philadelphia, 1976. Streak started April 17 at Toronto and ended May 9 at Montreal. He scored one goal in each of seven games; two in one game; and five in another; a total of 14 goals.

MOST ASSISTS, ONE PLAYOFF YEAR:
31 — Wayne Gretzky, Edmonton, 1988. 19 games.
30 — Wayne Gretzky, Edmonton, 1985. 18 games.
29 — Wayne Gretzky, Edmonton, 1987. 21 games.
28 — Mario Lemieux, Pittsburgh, 1991. 23 games.
26 — Wayne Gretzky, Edmonton, 1983. 16 games.
25 — Paul Coffey, Edmonton, 1985. 18 games.
   — Wayne Gretzky, Los Angeles, 1993. 24 games.
   — Doug Gilmour, Toronto, 1993. 21 games.

MOST ASSISTS BY A DEFENSEMAN, ONE PLAYOFF YEAR:
25 — Paul Coffey, Edmonton, 1985. 18 games.
24 — Al MacInnis, Calgary, 1989. 22 games.
23 — Brian Leetch, NY Rangers, 1994. 23 games.
19 — Bobby Orr, Boston, 1972. 15 games.
18 — Ray Bourque, Boston, 1988. 23 games.
   — Ray Bourque, Boston, 1991. 19 games.
   — Larry Murphy, Pittsburgh, 1991. 23 games.

MOST MINUTES PLAYED BY A GOALTENDER, ONE PLAYOFF YEAR:
1,544 — Kirk McLean, Vancouver, 1994. 24 games.
1,540 — Ron Hextall, Philadelphia, 1987. 26 games.
1,477 — Mike Richter, NY Rangers, 1994. 23 games.
1,401 — Bill Ranford, Edmonton, 1990. 22 games.
1,381 — Mike Vernon, Calgary, 1989. 22 games.

MOST WINS BY A GOALTENDER, ONE PLAYOFF YEAR:
16 — Grant Fuhr, Edmonton, 1988. 19 games.
   — **Mike Vernon, Calgary,** 1989. 22 games.
   — **Bill Ranford, Edmonton,** 1990. 22 games
   — **Tom Barrasso, Pittsburgh,** 1992. 21 games.
   — **Patrick Roy, Montreal,** 1993. 20 games.
   — **Mike Richter, NY Rangers,** 1994. 23 games.
15 — Bill Smith, NY Islanders, 1980. 20 games.
   — Bill Smith, NY Islanders, 1982. 18 games.
   — Grant Fuhr, Edmonton, 1988. 18 games.
   — Patrick Roy, Montreal, 1986. 20 games.
   — Ron Hextall, Philadelphia, 1987. 26 games.
   — Kirk McLean, Vancouver, 1994. 24 games.

MOST CONSECUTIVE WINS BY A GOALTENDER, ONE PLAYOFF YEAR:
11 — Ed Belfour, Chicago, 1992. 3 wins against St. Louis in DSF, won by Chicago 4-2; 4 wins against Detroit in DF, won by Chicago 4-0; and 4 wins against Edmonton in CF, won by Chicago 4-0.
   — **Tom Barrasso, Pittsburgh,** 1992. 3 wins against NY Rangers in DF, won by Pittsburgh 4-2; 4 wins against Boston in CF, won by Pittsburgh 4-0; and 4 wins against Chicago in F, won by Pittsburgh 4-0.
   — **Patrick Roy, Montreal,** 1993. 4 wins against Quebec in DSF, won by Montreal 4-2; 4 wins against Buffalo in DF, won by Montreal 4-0; and 3 wins against NY Islanders in CF, won by Montreal 4-1.

MOST SHUTOUTS, ONE PLAYOFF YEAR:
4 — Clint Benedict, Mtl. Maroons, 1926. 8 games.
   — **Clint Benedict, Mtl. Maroons,** 1928. 9 games.
   — **Dave Kerr, NY Rangers,** 1937. 9 games.
   — **Frank McCool, Toronto,** 1945. 13 games.
   — **Terry Sawchuk, Detroit,** 1952. 8 games.
   — **Bernie Parent, Philadelphia,** 1975. 17 games.
   — **Ken Dryden, Montreal,** 1977. 14 games.
   — **Mike Richter, NY Rangers,** 1994. 23 games.
   — **Kirk McLean, Vancouver,** 1994. 24 games.

MOST CONSECUTIVE SHUTOUTS:
3 — Clint Benedict, Mtl. Maroons, 1926. Benedict shut out Ottawa 1-0, Mar. 27; he then shut out Victoria twice, 3-0, Mar. 30; 3-0, Apr. 1. Mtl. Maroons won NHL F vs. Ottawa 2 goals to 1 and won the best-of-five F vs. Victoria 3-1.
   — **Frank McCool, Toronto,** 1945. McCool shut out Detroit 1-0, April 6; 2-0, April 8; 1-0, April 12. Toronto won the best-of-seven F 4-3.

LONGEST SHUTOUT SEQUENCE:
248 Minutes, 32 Seconds — Norm Smith, Detroit, 1936. In best-of-five SF, Smith shut out Mtl. Maroons 1-0, March 24, in 116:30 overtime; shut out Maroons 3-0 in second game, March 26; and was scored against at 12:02 of first period, March 29, by Gus Marker. Detroit won SF 3-0.

Dave Keon, seen here being pursued by Philadelphia blueliner Ed Van Impe, scored all three goals in Toronto's 3-1 victory over Montreal in game seven of the 1964 semi-finals.

One-Series Records

MOST POINTS IN FINAL SERIES:
13 — Wayne Gretzky, Edmonton, in 1988, 4 games plus suspended game vs. Boston. 3 goals, 10 assists.
12 — Gordie Howe, Detroit, in 1955, 7 games vs. Montreal. 5 goals, 7 assists.
— Yvan Cournoyer, Montreal, in 1973, 6 games vs. Chicago. 6 goals, 6 assists.
— Jacques Lemaire, Montreal, in 1973, 6 games vs. Chicago. 3 goals, 9 assists.
— Mario Lemieux, Pittsburgh, in 1991, 5 games vs. Minnesota. 5 goals, 7 assists.

MOST GOALS IN FINAL SERIES:
9 — Babe Dye, Toronto, in 1922, 5 games vs. Van. Millionaires.
8 — Alf Skinner, Toronto, in 1918, 5 games vs. Van. Millionaires.
7 — Jean Beliveau, Montreal, in 1956, during 5 games vs. Detroit.
— Mike Bossy, NY Islanders, in 1982, during 4 games vs. Vancouver.
— Wayne Gretzky, Edmonton, in 1985, during 5 games vs. Philadelphia.

MOST ASSISTS IN FINAL SERIES:
10 — Wayne Gretzky, Edmonton, in 1988, 4 games plus suspended game vs. Boston.
9 — Jacques Lemaire, Montreal, in 1973, 6 games vs. Chicago.
— Wayne Gretzky, Edmonton, in 1987, 6 games vs. Philadelphia.
— Larry Murphy, Pittsburgh, in 1991, 6 games vs. Minnesota.

MOST POINTS IN ONE SERIES (OTHER THAN FINAL):
19 — Rick Middleton, Boston, in 1983 DF, 7 games vs. Buffalo. 5 goals, 14 assists.
18 — Wayne Gretzky, Edmonton, in 1985 CF, 6 games vs. Chicago. 4 goals, 14 assists.
17 — Mario Lemieux, Pittsburgh, in 1992 DSF, 6 games vs. Washington. 7 goals, 10 assists.
16 — Barry Pederson, Boston, in 1983 DF, 7 games vs. Buffalo. 7 goals, 9 assists.
— Doug Gilmour, Toronto, in 1994 CSF, 7 games vs. San Jose. 3 goals, 13 assists.
15 — Jari Kurri, Edmonton, in 1985 CF, 6 games vs. Chicago. 12 goals, 3 assists.
— Wayne Gretzky, Edmonton, in 1987 DSF, 5 games vs. Los Angeles. 2 goals, 13 assists.
— Tim Kerr, Philadelphia, in 1989 DF, 7 games vs. Pittsburgh. 10 goals, 5 assists.
— Mario Lemieux, Pittsburgh, in 1991 CF, 6 games vs. Boston. 6 goals, 9 assists.

MOST GOALS IN ONE SERIES (OTHER THAN FINAL):
12 — Jari Kurri, Edmonton, in 1985 CF, 6 games vs. Chicago.
11 — Newsy Lalonde, Montreal, in 1919 NHL F, 5 games vs. Ottawa.
10 — Tim Kerr, Philadelphia, in 1989 DF, 7 games vs. Pittsburgh.
9 — Reggie Leach, Philadelphia, in 1976 SF, 5 games vs. Boston.
— Bill Barber, Philadelphia, in 1980 SF, 5 games vs. Minnesota.
— Mike Bossy, NY Islanders, in 1983 CF, 6 games vs. Boston.
— Mario Lemieux, Pittsburgh, in 1989 DF, 7 games vs. Philadelphia.

MOST ASSISTS IN ONE SERIES (OTHER THAN FINAL):
14 — Rick Middleton, Boston, in 1983 DF, 7 games vs. Buffalo.
— **Wayne Gretzky, Edmonton,** in 1985 CF, 6 games vs. Chicago.
13 — Wayne Gretzky, Edmonton, in 1987 DSF, 5 games vs. Los Angeles.
— Doug Gilmour, Toronto, in 1994 CSF, 7 games vs. San Jose.
11 — Mark Messier, Edmonton, in 1989 DSF, 7 games vs. Los Angeles.
— Al MacInnis, Calgary, in 1984 DF, 7 games vs. Edmonton.
— Mike Ridley, Washington, in 1992 DSF, 7 games vs. Pittsburgh.
10 — Fleming Mackell, Boston, in 1958 SF, 6 games vs. NY Rangers.
— Stan Mikita, Chicago, in 1962 SF, 6 games vs. Montreal.
— Bob Bourne, NY Islanders, in 1983 DF, 6 games vs. NY Rangers.
— Wayne Gretzky, Edmonton, in 1988 DSF, 5 games vs. Winnipeg.
— Mario Lemieux, Pittsburgh, in 1992 DSF, 6 games vs. Washington.

MOST GAME-WINNING GOALS, ONE PLAYOFF SERIES:
4 — Mike Bossy, NY Islanders, 1983, CF vs. Boston, won by NY Islanders 4-2.

MOST OVERTIME GOALS, ONE PLAYOFF SERIES:
3 — Mel Hill, Boston, 1939, SF vs. NY Rangers, won by Boston 4-3. Hill scored at 59:25 overtime March 21 for a 2-1 win; at 8:24, March 23 for a 3-2 win; and at 48:00, April 2 for a 2-1 win.

MOST POWER-PLAY GOALS, ONE PLAYOFF SERIES:
6 — Chris Kontos, Los Angeles, 1989, DSF vs. Edmonton, won by Los Angeles 4-3.
5 — Andy Bathgate, Detroit, 1966, SF vs. Chicago, won by Detroit 4-2.
— Denis Potvin, NY Islanders, 1981, QF vs. Edmonton, won by NY Islanders 4-2.
— Ken Houston, Calgary, 1981, QF vs. Philadelphia, won by Calgary 4-3.
— Rick Vaive, Chicago, 1988, DSF vs. St. Louis, won by St. Louis 4-1.
— Tim Kerr, Philadelphia, 1989, DF vs. Pittsburgh, won by Philadelphia 4-3.
— Mario Lemieux, Pittsburgh, 1989, DF vs. Philadelphia, won by Philadelphia 4-3.
— John Druce, Washington, 1990, DF vs. NY Rangers won by Washington 4-1.
— Pat LaFontaine, Buffalo, 1992, DSF vs. Boston won by Boston 4-3.

MOST SHORTHAND GOALS, ONE PLAYOFF SERIES:
3 — Bill Barber, Philadelphia, 1980, SF vs. Minnesota, won by Philadelphia 4-1.
— **Wayne Presley, Chicago,** 1989, DSF vs. Detroit, won by Chicago 4-2.
2 — Mac Colville, NY Rangers, 1940, SF vs. Boston, won by NY Rangers 4-2.
— Jerry Toppazzini, Boston, 1958, SF vs. NY Rangers, won by Boston 4-2.
— Dave Keon, Toronto, 1963, F vs. Detroit, won by Toronto 4-1.
— Bob Pulford, Toronto, 1964, F vs. Detroit, won by Toronto 4-3.
— Serge Savard, Montreal, 1968, F vs. St. Louis, won by Montreal 4-0.
— Derek Sanderson, Boston, 1969, F vs. Montreal, won by Montreal 4-2.
— Bryan Trottier, NY Islanders, 1980, PR vs. Los Angeles, won by NY Islanders 3-1.
— Bobby Lalonde, Boston, 1981, PR vs. Minnesota, won by Minnesota 3-0.
— Butch Goring, NY Islanders, 1981, SF vs. NY Rangers, won by NY Islanders 4-0.
— Wayne Gretzky, Edmonton, 1983, DSF vs. Winnipeg, won by Edmonton 3-0.
— Mark Messier, Edmonton, 1983, DF vs. Calgary, won by Edmonton 4-1.
— Jari Kurri, Edmonton, 1983, CF vs. Chicago, won by Edmonton 4-0.
— Wayne Gretzky, Edmonton, 1985, DF vs. Winnipeg, won by Edmonton 4-0.
— Kevin Lowe, Edmonton, 1987, F vs. Philadelphia, won by Edmonton 4-3.
— Bob Gould, Washington, 1988, DSF vs. Philadelphia, won by Washington 4-3.
— Dave Poulin, Philadelphia, 1989, DF vs. Pittsburgh, won by Philadelphia 4-3.
— Russ Courtnall, Montreal, 1991, DF vs. Boston, won by Boston 4-3.
— Sergei Fedorov, Detroit, 1992 DSF vs. Minnesota, won by Detroit 4-3.
— Mark Messier, NY Rangers, 1992, DSF vs. New Jersey, won by NY Rangers 4-3.
— Tom Fitzgerald, NY Islanders, 1993, DF vs. Pittsburgh, won by NY Islanders 4-3.
— Mark Osbourne, Toronto, 1994, CSF vs. San Jose, won by Toronto 4-3.

MOST THREE-OR-MORE-GOAL GAMES, ONE PLAYOFF SERIES:
3 — Jari Kurri, Edmonton 1985, CF vs. Chicago won by Edmonton 4-2. Kurri scored 3 G May 7 at Edmonton in 7-3 win, 3 G May 14 in 10-5 win and 4 G May 16 at Chicago in 8-2 win.
2 — Doug Bentley, Chicago, 1944, SF vs. Detroit, won by Chicago 4-1. Bentley scored 3 G Mar. 28 at Chicago in 7-1 win and 3 G Mar. 30 at Detroit in 5-2 win.
— **Norm Ullman, Detroit,** 1964, SF vs. Chicago, won by Detroit 4-3. Ullman scored 3 G Mar. 29 at Chicago in 7-1 win and 3 G April 7 at Detroit in 7-2 win.
— **Mark Messier, Edmonton,** 1983, DF vs. Calgary won by Edmonton 4-1. Messier scored 4 G April 14 at Edmonton in 6-3 win and 3 G April 17 at Calgary in 10-2 win.
— **Mike Bossy, NY Islanders,** 1983, CF vs. Boston won by NY Islanders 4-2. Bossy scored 3 G May 3 at New York in 8-3 win and 4 G on May 7 at New York in 8-4 win.

Single Playoff Game Records

MOST POINTS, ONE GAME:
8 — Patrik Sundstrom, New Jersey, April 22, 1988 at New Jersey during 10-4 win over Washington. Sundstrom had 3 goals, 5 assists.
— **Mario Lemieux, Pittsburgh,** April 25, 1989 at Pittsburgh during 10-7 win over Philadelphia. Lemieux had 5 goals, 3 assists.
7 — Wayne Gretzky, Edmonton, April 17, 1983 at Calgary during 10-2 win. Gretzky had 4 goals, 3 assists.
— **Wayne Gretzky, Edmonton,** April 25,1985 at Winnipeg during 8-3 win. Gretzky had 3 goals, 4 assists.
— **Wayne Gretzky, Edmonton,** April 9, 1987, at Edmonton during 13-3 win over Los Angeles. Gretzky had 1 goal, 6 assists.
6 — Dickie Moore, Montreal, March 25, 1954, at Montreal during 8-1 win over Boston. Moore had 2 goals, 4 assists.
— **Phil Esposito, Boston,** April 2, 1969, at Boston during 10-0 win over Toronto. Esposito had 4 goals, 2 assists.
— **Darryl Sittler, Toronto,** April 22, 1976, at Toronto during 8-5 win over Philadelphia. Sittler had 5 goals, 1 assist.
— **Guy Lafleur, Montreal,** April 11, 1977, at Montreal during 7-2 victory vs. St. Louis. Lafleur had 3 goals, 3 assists.
— **Mikko Leinonen, NY Rangers,** April 8, 1982, at New York during 7-3 win over Philadelphia. Leinonen had 6 assists.
— **Paul Coffey, Edmonton,** May 14, 1985 at Edmonton during 10-5 win over Chicago. Coffey had 1 goal, 5 assists.
— **John Anderson, Hartford,** April 12, 1986 at Hartford during 9-4 win over Quebec. Anderson had 2 goals, 4 assists.
— **Mario Lemieux, Pittsburgh,** April 23, 1992 at Pittsburgh during 6-4 win over Washington. Lemieux had 3 goals, 3 assists.

MOST POINTS BY A DEFENSEMAN, ONE GAME:
6 — Paul Coffey, Edmonton, May 14, 1985 at Edmonton vs. Chicago. 1 goal, 5 assists. Edmonton won 10-5.
5 — Eddie Bush, Detroit, April 9, 1942, at Detroit vs. Toronto. 1 goal, 4 assists. Detroit won 5-2.
— **Bob Dailey, Philadelphia,** May 1, 1980, at Philadelphia vs. Minnesota. 1 goal, 4 assists. Philadelphia won 7-0.
— **Denis Potvin, NY Islanders,** April 17, 1981, at New York vs. Edmonton. 3 goals, 2 assists. NY Islanders won 6-3.
— **Risto Siltanen, Quebec,** April 14, 1987 at Hartford. 5 assists. Quebec won 7-5.

MOST GOALS, ONE GAME:
5 — Newsy Lalonde, Montreal, March 1, 1919, at Montreal. Final score: Montreal 6, Ottawa 3.
— **Maurice Richard, Montreal,** March 23, 1944, at Montreal. Final score: Montreal 5, Toronto 1.
— **Darryl Sittler, Toronto,** April 22, 1976, at Toronto. Final score: Toronto 8, Philadelphia 5.
— **Reggie Leach, Philadelphia,** May 6, 1976, at Philadelphia. Final score: Philadelphia 6, Boston 3.
— **Mario Lemieux, Pittsburgh,** April 25, 1989 at Pittsburgh. Final score: Pittsburgh 10, Philadelphia 7.

MOST GOALS BY A DEFENSEMAN, ONE GAME:
3 — Bobby Orr, Boston, April 11, 1971 at Montreal. Final score: Boston 5, Montreal 2.
— **Dick Redmond, Chicago,** April 4, 1973 at Chicago. Final score: Chicago 7, St. Louis 1.
— **Denis Potvin, NY Islanders,** April 17, 1981 at New York. Final score: NY Islanders 6, Edmonton 3.
— **Paul Reinhart, Calgary,** April 14, 1983 at Edmonton. Final score: Edmonton 6, Calgary 3.
— **Paul Reinhart, Calgary,** April 8, 1984 at Vancouver. Final score: Calgary 5, Vancouver 1.
— **Doug Halward, Vancouver,** April 7, 1984 at Vancouver. Final score: Vancouver 7, Calgary 0.
— **Al Iafrate, Washington,** April 26, 1993 at Washington. Final score: NY Islanders 4, Washington 6.
— **Eric Desjardins, Montreal,** June 3, 1993 at Montreal. Final score: Los Angeles 3, Montreal 3.
— **Gary Sutter, Chicago,** April 24, 1994, at Chicago. Final score: Chicago 4, Toronto 3.

MOST POWER-PLAY GOALS, ONE GAME:
3 — Syd Howe, Detroit, March 23, 1939, at Detroit vs. Montreal, Detroit won 7-3.
— **Sid Smith, Toronto,** April 10, 1949, at Detroit. Toronto won 3-1.
— **Phil Esposito, Boston,** April 2, 1969, at Boston vs. Toronto. Boston won 10-0.
— **John Bucyk, Boston,** April 21, 1974, at Boston vs. Chicago. Boston won 8-6.
— **Denis Potvin, NY Islanders,** April 17, 1981, at New York vs. Edmonton. NY Islanders won 6-3.
— **Tim Kerr, Philadelphia,** April 13, 1985, at NY Rangers. Philadelphia won 6-5.
— **Jari Kurri, Edmonton,** April 9, 1987, at Edmonton vs. Los Angeles. Edmonton won 13-3.
— **Mark Johnson, New Jersey,** April 22, 1988, at New Jersey vs. Washington. New Jersey won 10-4.
— **Dino Ciccarelli, Detroit,** April 29, 1993, at Toronto, in 7-3 win by Detroit.

MOST SHORTHAND GOALS, ONE GAME:
2 — Dave Keon, Toronto, April 18, 1963, at Toronto, in 3-1 win vs. Detroit.
— **Bryan Trottier, NY Islanders,** April 8, 1980 at New York, in 8-1 win vs. Los Angeles.
— **Bobby Lalonde, Boston,** April 11, 1981 at Minnesota, in 6-3 win by Minnesota.
— **Wayne Gretzky, Edmonton,** April 6, 1983, at Edmonton, in 6-3 win vs. Winnipeg.
— **Jari Kurri, Edmonton,** April 24, 1983, at Edmonton, in 8-3 win vs. Chicago.
— **Mark Messier, NY Rangers,** April 21, 1992, at New York, in 7-3 loss vs. New Jersey.
— **Tom Fitzgerald, NY Islanders,** May 8, 1993, at Long Island, in 6-5 win vs. Pittsburgh.

MOST ASSISTS, ONE GAME:
6 — Mikko Leinonen, NY Rangers, April 8, 1982, at New York. Final score: NY Rangers 7, Philadelphia 3.
— **Wayne Gretzky, Edmonton,** April 9, 1987, at Edmonton. Final score: Edmonton 13, Los Angeles 3.
5 — Toe Blake, Montreal, March 23, 1944, at Montreal. Final score: Montreal 5, Toronto 1.
— **Maurice Richard, Montreal,** March 27, 1956, at Montreal. Final score: Montreal 7, NY Rangers 0.
— **Bert Olmstead, Montreal,** March 30, 1957, at Montreal. Final score: Montreal 8, NY Rangers 3.
— **Don McKenney, Boston,** April 5, 1958, at Boston. Final score: Boston 8, NY Rangers 2.
— **Stan Mikita, Chicago,** April 4, 1973, at Chicago. Final score: Chicago 7, St. Louis 1.
— **Wayne Gretzky, Edmonton,** April 8, 1981, at Montreal. Final score: Edmonton 6, Montreal 3.
— **Paul Coffey, Edmonton,** May 14, 1985, at Edmonton. Final score: Edmonton 10, Chicago 5.
— **Doug Gilmour, St. Louis,** April 15, 1986, at Minnesota. Final score: St. Louis 6, Minnesota 3.
— **Risto Siltanen, Quebec,** April 14, 1987 at Hartford. Final score: Quebec 7, Hartford 5.
— **Patrik Sundstrom, New Jersey,** April 22, 1988, at New Jersey. Final score: New Jersey 10, Washington 4.

MOST PENALTY MINUTES, ONE GAME:
42 — Dave Schultz, Philadelphia, April 22, 1976, at Toronto. One minor, 2 majors, 1 10-minute misconduct and 2 game-misconducts. Final score: Toronto 8, Philadelphia 5.

MOST PENALTIES, ONE GAME:
8 — Forbes Kennedy, Toronto, April 2, 1969, at Boston. Four minors, 2 majors, 1 10-minute misconduct, 1 game misconduct. Final score: Boston 10, Toronto 0.
— **Kim Clackson, Pittsburgh,** April 14, 1980, at Boston. Five minors, 2 majors, 1 10-minute misconduct. Final score: Boston 6, Pittsburgh 2

MOST POINTS, ONE PERIOD:
4 — Maurice Richard, Montreal, March 29, 1945, at Montreal vs. Toronto. Third period, 3 goals, 1 assist. Final score: Montreal 10, Toronto 3.
— **Dickie Moore, Montreal,** March 25, 1954, at Montreal vs. Boston. First period, 2 goals, 2 assists. Final score: Montreal 8, Boston 1.
— **Barry Pederson, Boston,** April 8, 1982, at Boston vs. Buffalo. Second period, 3 goals, 1 assist. Final score: Boston 7, Buffalo 3.
— **Peter McNab, Boston,** April 11, 1982, at Buffalo. Second period, 1 goal, 3 assists. Final score: Boston 5, Buffalo 2.
— **Tim Kerr, Philadelphia,** April 13, 1985 at New York. Second period, 4 goals. Final score: Philadelphia 6, Rangers 5.
— **Ken Linseman, Boston,** April 14, 1985 at Boston vs. Montreal. Second period, 2 goals, 2 assists. Final score: Boston 7, Montreal 6.
— **Wayne Gretzky, Edmonton,** April 12, 1987, at Los Angeles. Third period, 1 goal, 3 assists. Final score: Edmonton 6, Los Angeles 3.
— **Glenn Anderson, Edmonton,** April 6, 1988, at Edmonton vs. Winnipeg. Third period, 3 goals, 1 assist. Final score: Edmonton 7, Winnipeg 4.
— **Mario Lemieux, Pittsburgh,** April 25, 1989, at Pittsburgh vs. Philadelphia. First period, 4 goals. Final score: Pittsburgh 10, Philadelphia 7.
— **Dave Gagner, Minnesota,** April 8, 1991, at Minnesota vs. Chicago. First period, 2 goals, 2 assists. Final score: Chicago 6, Minnesota 5.
— **Mario Lemieux, Pittsburgh,** April 23, 1992, at Pittsburgh vs. Washington. Second period, 2 goals, 2 assists. Final score: Pittsburgh 6, Washington 4.

MOST GOALS, ONE PERIOD:

4 — Tim Kerr, Philadelphia, April 13, 1985, at New York vs. NY Rangers, second period. Final score: Philadelphia 6, NY Rangers 5.

— Mario Lemieux, Pittsburgh, April 25, 1989, at Pittsburgh vs. Philadelphia, first period. Final score: Pittsburgh 10, Philadelphia 7.

3 — Harvey (Busher) Jackson, Toronto, April 5, 1932, at New York vs. NY Rangers, second period. Final score: Toronto 6, NY Rangers 4.

— Maurice Richard, Montreal, March 23, 1944, at Montreal vs. Toronto, second period. Final score: Montreal 5, Toronto 1.

— Maurice Richard, Montreal, March 29, 1945, at Montreal vs. Toronto, third period. Final score: Montreal 10, Toronto 3.

— Maurice Richard, Montreal, April 6, 1957 at Montreal vs. Boston, second period. Final score: Montreal 5, Boston 1.

— Ted Lindsay, Detroit, April 5, 1955, at Detroit vs. Montreal, second period. Final score: Detroit 7, Montreal 1.

— Red Berenson, St. Louis, April 15, 1969, at St. Louis vs. Los Angeles, second period. Final score: St. Louis 4, Los Angeles 0.

— Jacques Lemaire, Montreal, April 20, 1971, at Montreal vs. Minnesota, second period. Final score: Montreal 7, Minnesota 2.

— Rick MacLeish, Philadelphia, April 11, 1974, at Philadelphia vs. Atlanta, second period. Final score: Philadelphia 5, Atlanta 1.

— Tom Williams, Los Angeles, April 14, 1974, at Los Angeles vs. Chicago, third period. Final score: Los Angeles 5, Chicago 1.

— Darryl Sittler, Toronto, April 22, 1976, at Toronto vs. Philadelphia, second period. Final score: Toronto 8, Philadelphia 5.

— Reggie Leach, Philadelphia, May 6, 1976, at Philadelphia vs. Boston, second period. Final score: Philadelphia 6, Boston 3.

— Bobby Schmautz, Boston, April 11, 1977, at Boston vs. Los Angeles, first period. Final score: Boston 8, Los Angeles 3.

— George Ferguson, Toronto, April 11, 1978, at Toronto vs. Los Angeles, third period. Final score: Toronto 7, Los Angeles 3.

— Barry Pederson, Boston, April 8, 1982, at Boston vs. Buffalo, second period. Final score: Boston 7, Buffalo 3.

— Peter Stastny, Quebec, April 5, 1983, at Boston, first period. Final score: Boston 4, Quebec 3.

— Wayne Gretzky, Edmonton, April 6, 1983 at Edmonton, second period. Final score: Edmonton 6, Winnipeg 3.

— Mike Bossy, NY Islanders, May 7, 1983 at New York, second period. Final score: NY Islanders 8, Boston 4.

— Dave Andreychuk, Buffalo, April 14, 1985, at Buffalo vs. Quebec, third period. Final score: Buffalo 7, Quebec 4.

— Wayne Gretzky, Edmonton, May 25, 1985, at Edmonton vs. Philadelphia, first period. Final score: Edmonton 4, Philadelphia 3.

— Glenn Anderson, Edmonton, April 6, 1988, at Edmonton vs. Winnipeg, third period. Final score: Edmonton 7, Winnipeg 4.

— Tim Kerr, Philadelphia, April 19, 1989, at Pittsburgh vs. Penguins, first period. Final score: Philadelphia 4, Pittsburgh 2.

— Petr Klima, Edmonton, May 4, 1991, at Edmonton vs. Minnesota, first period. Final score: Edmonton 7, Minnesota 2.

— Dino Ciccarelli, Washington, April 25, 1992, at Pittsburgh, third period. Final score: Washington 7, Pittsburgh 2.

— Kevin Stevens, Pittsburgh, May 17, 1992, at Boston, first period. Final score: Pittsburgh 5, Boston 1.

— Dirk Graham, Chicago, June 1, 1992, at Chicago vs. Pittsburgh, first period. Final score: Pittsburgh 6, Chicago 5.

— Ray Ferraro, NY Islanders, April 26, 1993, at Washington, third period. Final score: Washington 6, NY Islanders 4.

— Mark Messier, NY Rangers, May 25, 1994, at New Jersey, third period. Final score: NY Rangers 4, New Jersey 2.

MOST POWER-PLAY GOALS, ONE PERIOD:

3 — Tim Kerr, Philadelphia, April 13, 1985 at New York, second period in 6-5 win vs. NY Rangers.

2 — Two power-play goals have been scored by one player in one period on 43 occasions. Charlie Conacher of Toronto was the first to score two power-play goals in one period, setting the mark on Mar. 26, 1936. Dmitri Mironov of Toronto is the most recent to equal this mark with two power-play goals in the second period at Toronto, May 18, 1994. Final score: Vancouver 4, Toronto 3.

MOST SHORTHAND GOALS, ONE PERIOD:

2 — Bryan Trottier, NY Islanders, April 8, 1980, second period at New York in 8-1 win vs. Los Angeles.

— Bobby Lalonde, Boston, April 11, 1981, third period at Minnesota in 6-3 win by Minnesota.

— Jari Kurri, Edmonton, April 24, 1983, third period at Edmonton in 8-4 win vs. Chicago.

MOST ASSISTS, ONE PERIOD:

3 — Three assists by one player in one period of a playoff game has been recorded on 59 occasions. Brian Leetch of the NY Rangers is the most recent to equal this mark with 3 assists in the first period at New York, May 9, 1994. Final score: NY Rangers 4, Washington 3.
Wayne Gretzky has had 3 assists in one period 5 times; Ray Bourque, 3 times; Toe Blake, Jean Beliveau, Doug Harvey and Bobby Orr, twice. Nick Metz of Toronto was the first player to be credited with 3 assists in one period of a playoff game Mar. 21, 1941 at Toronto vs. Detroit.

MOST PENALTIES, ONE PERIOD AND MOST PENALTY MINUTES, ONE PERIOD:

6 Penalties; 39 Minutes — Ed Hospodar, NY Rangers, April 9, 1981, at Los Angeles, first period. Two minors, 1 major, 1 10-minute misconduct, 2 game misconducts. Final score: Los Angeles 5, NY Rangers 4.

FASTEST TWO GOALS:

5 Seconds — Norm Ullman, Detroit, at Detroit, April 11, 1965, vs. Chicago and goaltender Glenn Hall. Ullman scored at 17:35 and 17:40 of second period. Detroit won 4-2.

FASTEST GOAL FROM START OF GAME:

6 Seconds — Don Kozak, Los Angeles, April 17, 1977, at Los Angeles vs. Boston and goaltender Gerry Cheevers. Los Angeles won 7-4.

7 Seconds — Bob Gainey, Montreal, May 5, 1977, at New York vs. NY Islanders and goaltender Glenn Resch. Montreal won 2-1.

— Terry Murray, Philadelphia, April 12, 1981, at Quebec vs. goaltender Dan Bouchard. Quebec won 4-3 in overtime.

8 Seconds — Stan Smyl, Vancouver, April 7, 1982, at Vancouver vs. Calgary and goaltender Pat Riggin. Vancouver won 5-3.

FASTEST GOAL FROM START OF PERIOD (OTHER THAN FIRST):

6 Seconds — Pelle Eklund, Phiadelphia, April 25, 1989, at Pittsburgh vs. goaltender Tom Barrasso, second period. Pittsburgh won 10-7.

9 Seconds — Bill Collins, Minnesota, April 9, 1968, at Minnesota vs. Los Angeles and goaltender Wayne Rutledge, third period. Minnesota won 7-5.

— Dave Balon, Minnesota, April 25, 1968, at St. Louis vs. goaltender Glenn Hall, third period. Minnesota won 5-1.

— Murray Oliver, Minnesota, April 8, 1971, at St. Louis vs. goaltender Ernie Wakely, third period. St. Louis won 4-2.

— Clark Gillies, NY Islanders, April 15, 1977, at Buffalo vs. goaltender Don Edwards, third period. NY Islanders won 4-3.

— Eric Vail, Atlanta, April 11, 1978, at Atlanta vs. Detroit and goaltender Ron Low, third period. Detroit won 5-3.

— Stan Smyl, Vancouver, April 10, 1979, at Philadelphia vs. goaltender Wayne Stephenson, third period. Vancouver won 3-2.

— Wayne Gretzky, Edmonton, April 6, 1983, at Edmonton vs. Winnipeg and goaltender Brian Hayward, second period. Edmonton won 6-3.

— Mark Messier, Edmonton, April 16, 1984, at Calgary vs. goaltender Don Edwards, third period. Edmonton won 5-3.

— Brian Skrudland, Montreal, May 18, 1986 at Calgary vs. Calgary and goaltender Mike Vernon, overtime. Montreal won 3-2.

FASTEST TWO GOALS FROM START OF GAME:

1 Minute, 8 Seconds — Dick Duff, Toronto, April 9, 1963 at Toronto vs. Detroit and goaltender Terry Sawchuk. Duff scored at 49 seconds and 1:08. Final score: Toronto 4, Detroit 2.

FASTEST TWO GOALS FROM START OF PERIOD:

35 Seconds — Pat LaFontaine, NY Islanders, May 19, 1984 at Edmonton vs. goaltender Andy Moog. LaFontaine scored at 13 and 35 seconds of third period. Final score: Edmonton 5, NY Islanders 2.

Early Playoff Records

1893-1918
Team Records

MOST GOALS, BOTH TEAMS, ONE GAME:

25 — Ottawa Silver Seven, Dawson City at Ottawa, Jan. 16, 1905. Ottawa 23, Dawson City 2. Ottawa won best-of-three series 2-0.

MOST GOALS, ONE TEAM, ONE GAME:

23 — Ottawa Silver Seven at Ottawa, Jan. 16, 1905. Ottawa defeated Dawson City 23-2.

MOST GOALS, BOTH TEAMS, BEST-OF-THREE SERIES:

42 — Ottawa Silver Seven, Queen's University at Ottawa, 1906. Ottawa defeated Queen's 16-7, Feb. 27, and 12-7, Feb. 28.

MOST GOALS, ONE TEAM, BEST-OF-THREE SERIES:

32 — Ottawa Silver Seven in 1905 at Ottawa. Defeated Dawson City 9-2, Jan. 13, and 23-2, Jan. 16.

MOST GOALS, BOTH TEAMS, BEST-OF-FIVE SERIES:

39 — Toronto Arenas, Vancouver Millionaires at Toronto, 1918. Toronto won 5-3, Mar. 20; 6-3, Mar. 26; 2-1, Mar. 30. Vancouver won 6-4, Mar. 23, and 8-1, Mar. 28. Toronto scored 18 goals; Vancouver 21.

MOST GOALS, ONE TEAM, BEST-OF-FIVE SERIES:

26 — Vancouver Millionaires in 1915 at Vancouver. Defeated Ottawa Senators 6-2, Mar. 22; 8-3, Mar. 24; and 12-3 Mar. 26.

Individual Records

MOST GOALS IN PLAYOFFS:

63 — Frank McGee, Ottawa Silver Seven, in 22 playoff games. Seven goals in four games, 1903; 21 goals in eight games, 1904; 18 goals in four games, 1905; 17 goals in six games, 1906.

MOST GOALS, ONE PLAYOFF SERIES:

15 — Frank McGee, Ottawa Silver Seven, in two games in 1905 at Ottawa. Scored one goal, Jan. 13, in 9-2 victory over Dawson City and 14 goals, Jan. 16, in 23-2 victory.

MOST GOALS, ONE PLAYOFF GAME:

14 — Frank McGee, Ottawa Silver Seven, Jan. 16, 1905 at Ottawa in 23-2 victory over Dawson City.

FASTEST THREE GOALS:

40 Seconds — Marty Walsh, Ottawa Senators, at Ottawa, March 16, 1911, at 3:00, 3:10, and 3:40 of third period. Ottawa defeated Port Arthur 13-4.

Brett Hull, left, has scored 52 goals in 72 playoff games. Brian Propp, below, has recorded 148 points in 13 years of post-season play.

All-Time Playoff Goal Leaders since 1918
(40 or more goals)

Player	Teams	Yrs.	GP	G
* Wayne Gretzky	Edm., L.A.	14	180	110
* Jari Kurri	Edm., L.A.	12	174	102
* Mark Messier	Edm., NYR	14	200	99
* Glenn Anderson	Edm., Tor., NYR	13	208	91
Mike Bossy	NY Islanders	10	129	85
Maurice Richard	Montreal	15	133	82
Jean Beliveau	Montreal	17	162	79
* Bryan Trottier	NYI, Pit.	17	221	71
Gordie Howe	Det., Hfd.	20	157	68
Yvan Cournoyer	Montreal	12	147	64
* Brian Propp	Phi., Bos., Min.	13	160	64
Bobby Smith	Min., Mtl.	13	184	64
Bobby Hull	Chi., Hfd.	14	119	62
Phil Esposito	Chi., Bos., NYR	15	130	61
Jacques Lemaire	Montreal	11	145	61
* Joe Mullen	St.L., Cgy., Pit.	13	130	60
Stan Mikita	Chicago	18	155	59
* Dino Ciccarelli	Min., Wsh., Det.	12	108	58
Guy Lafleur	Mtl., NYR	14	128	58
Bernie Geoffrion	Mtl., NYR	16	132	58
* Denis Savard	Chi., Mtl.	13	137	58
* Mario Lemieux	Pittsburgh	5	66	56
Denis Potvin	NY Islanders	14	185	56
* Cam Neely	Van., Bos.	8	88	55
* Esa Tikkanen	Edm., NYR	9	137	55
Rick MacLeish	Phi., Pit., Det.	11	114	54
* Steve Larmer	Chi., NYR	12	130	54
Bill Barber	Philadelphia	11	129	53
* Brett Hull	Cgy., St.L.	9	72	52
Frank Mahovlich	Tor., Det., Mtl.	14	137	51
Steve Shutt	Mtl., L.A.	12	99	50
Henri Richard	Montreal	18	180	49
* Doug Gilmour	St.L., Cgy., Tor.	10	123	48
Reggie Leach	Bos., Phi.	8	94	47
Ted Lindsay	Det., Chi.	16	133	47
Clark Gillies	NYI, Buf.	13	164	47
* Paul Coffey	Edm., Pit., L.A., Det.	12	137	47
* Stephane Richer	Mtl., N.J.	9	104	46
Dickie Moore	Mtl., Tor. St.L.	14	135	46
Rick Middleton	NYR, Bos.	12	114	45
Lanny McDonald	Tor., Cgy.	13	117	44
Ken Linseman	Phi., Edm., Bos.	11	113	43
Bobby Clarke	Philadelphia	13	136	42
* Brian Bellows	Min., Mtl.	10	105	41
John Bucyk	Det., Bos.	14	124	41
Tim Kerr	Phi., NYR	10	81	40
Peter McNab	Bos., Van.	10	107	40
Bob Bourne	NYI, L.A.	13	139	40
John Tonelli	NYI, Cgy., L.A.	12	172	40

* — Active player.

All-Time Playoff Assist Leaders since 1918
(60 or more assists)

Player	Teams	Yrs.	GP	A
* Wayne Gretzky	Edm., L.A.	14	180	236
* Mark Messier	Edm., NYR	14	200	160
* Jari Kurri	Edm., L.A.	12	174	120
* Glenn Anderson	Edm., Tor., NYR	13	208	116
Larry Robinson	Mtl., Pit.	20	227	116
* Bryan Trottier	NYI, Pit.	17	221	113
Denis Potvin	NY Islanders	14	185	108
* Paul Coffey	Edm., Pit., L.A., Det.	12	137	107
* Ray Bourque	Boston	15	152	103
* Doug Gilmour	St.L., Cgy., Tor.	10	123	98
Jean Beliveau	Montreal	17	162	97
Bobby Smith	Min., Mtl.	13	184	96
* Denis Savard	Chi., Mtl.	13	137	94
Gordie Howe	Det., Hfd.	20	157	92
Stan Mikita	Chicago	18	155	91
Brad Park	NYR, Bos., Det.	17	161	90
* Adam Oates	Det., St.L., Bos.	8	195	84
* Brian Propp	Phi., Bos., Min.	13	160	84
Henri Richard	Montreal	18	180	80
Jacques Lemaire	Montreal	11	145	78
* Al MacInnis	Calgary	10	95	77
Ken Linseman	Phi., Edm., Bos.	11	113	77
Bobby Clarke	Philadelphia	13	136	77
* Chris Chelios	Mtl., Chi.	11	132	77
Guy Lafleur	Mtl., NYR	14	128	76
Phil Esposito	Chi., Bos., NYR	15	130	76
Mike Bossy	NY Islanders	10	129	75
John Tonelli	NYI, Cgy., L.A.	13	172	75
* Craig Janney	Bos., St.L.	7	90	74
* Larry Murphy	L.A., Wsh., Min., Pit.	13	130	73
* Steve Larmer	Chi., NYR	12	130	73
* Peter Stastny	Que., N.J., St.L.	12	93	72
Gilbert Perreault	Buffalo	11	90	70
Alex Delvecchio	Detroit	14	121	69
Bobby Hull	Chi., Hfd.	14	119	67
Frank Mahovlich	Tor., Det., Mtl.	14	137	67
* Mario Lemieux	Pittsburgh	5	66	66
Bobby Orr	Boston	8	74	66
Bernie Federko	St. Louis	11	91	66
Jean Ratelle	NYR, Bos.	15	123	66
* Charlie Huddy	Edm., L.A.	12	167	66
Dickie Moore	Mtl., Tor., St.L.	14	135	64
Doug Harvey	Mtl., NYR, St.L.	15	137	64
Yvan Cournoyer	Montreal	12	147	63
John Bucyk	Det., Bos.	14	124	62
Doug Wilson	Chicago	12	95	61
* Brian Bellows	Min., Mtl.	10	105	60
* Dale Hunter	Que., Wsh.	14	133	60

All-Time Playoff Point Leaders since 1918
(100 or more points)

Player	Teams	Yrs.	GP	G	A	Pts.
* Wayne Gretzky	Edm., L.A.	14	180	110	236	346
* Mark Messier	Edm., NYR	14	200	99	160	259
* Jari Kurri	Edm., L.A.	12	174	102	120	222
* Glenn Anderson	Edm., Tor., NYR	13	208	91	116	207
* Bryan Trottier	NYI, Pit.	17	221	71	113	184
Jean Beliveau	Montreal	17	162	79	97	176
Denis Potvin	NY Islanders	14	185	56	108	164
Mike Bossy	NY Islanders	10	129	85	75	160
Gordie Howe	Det., Hfd.	20	157	68	92	160
Bobby Smith	Min., Mtl.	13	184	64	96	160
* Paul Coffey	Edm., Pit., L.A., Det.	12	137	47	107	154
* Denis Savard	Chi., Mtl.	13	137	58	94	152
Stan Mikita	Chicago	18	155	59	91	150
* Brian Propp	Phi., Bos., Min.	13	160	64	84	148
* Doug Gilmour	St.L., Cgy., Tor.	10	123	48	98	146
Larry Robinson	Mtl., L.A.	20	227	28	116	144
Jacques Lemaire	Montreal	11	145	61	78	139
Phil Esposito	Chi., Bos., NYR	15	130	61	76	137
* Ray Bourque	Boston	15	152	33	103	136
Guy Lafleur	Mtl, NYR	14	128	58	76	134
Bobby Hull	Chi., Hfd.	14	119	62	67	129
Henri Richard	Montreal	18	180	49	80	129
* Steve Larmer	Chi., NYR	12	130	54	73	127
Yvan Cournoyer	Montreal	12	147	64	63	127
Maurice Richard	Montreal	15	133	82	44	126
Brad Park	NYR, Bos., Det.	17	161	35	90	125
* Mario Lemieux	Pittsburgh	5	66	56	66	122
Ken Linseman	Phi., Edm., Bos.	11	113	43	77	120
Bobby Clarke	Philadelphia	13	136	42	77	119
Bernie Geoffrion	Mtl., NYR	16	132	58	60	118
Frank Mahovlich	Tor., Det., Mtl.	14	137	51	67	118
John Tonelli	NYI, Cgy., L.A.	13	172	40	75	115
* Adam Oates	Det., St.L., Bos.	8	95	29	84	113
Dickie Moore	Mtl., Tor., St.L.	14	135	46	64	110
Bill Barber	Philadelphia	11	129	53	55	108
Rick MacLeish	Phi., Pit., Det.	11	114	54	53	107
* Esa Tikkanen	Edm., NYR	9	137	55	50	105
* Peter Stastny	Que., N.J., St.L.	12	93	33	72	105
Alex Delvecchio	Detroit	14	121	35	69	104
Gilbert Perreault	Buffalo	11	90	33	70	103
John Bucyk	Det., Bos.	14	124	41	62	103
* Joe Mullen	St.L., Cgy., Pit.	13	130	60	43	103
* Al MacInnis	Cgy.	10	95	25	77	102
Bernie Federko	St. Louis	11	91	35	66	101
* Brian Bellows	Min., Mtl.	10	105	41	60	101
* Larry Murphy	L.A., Wsh., Min., Pit.	13	130	28	73	101
* Chris Chelios	Mtl., Chi.	11	132	24	77	101
Rick Middleton	NYR, Bos.	12	114	45	55	100

Three-or-more-Goal Games, Playoffs 1918 –1994

Player	Team	Date	City	Total Goals	Opposing Goaltender	Score	
Wayne Gretzky (8)	Edm.	Apr. 11/81	Edm.	3	Richard Sevigny	Edm. 6	Mtl. 2
		Apr. 19/81	Edm.	3	Billy Smith	Edm. 5	NYI 2
		Apr. 6/83	Edm.	4	Brian Hayward	Edm. 6	Wpg. 3
		Apr. 17/83	Cgy.	4	Rejean Lemelin	Edm. 10	Cgy. 2
		Apr. 25/85	Wpg.	3	Bryan Hayward (2) Marc Behrend (1)	Edm. 8	Wpg. 3
		May 25/85	Edm.	3	Pelle Lindbergh	Edm. 4	Phi. 3
		Apr. 24/86	Cgy.	3	Mike Vernon	Edm. 7	Cgy. 4
	L.A.	May 29/93	Tor.	3	Felix Potvin	L.A. 5	Tor. 4
Maurice Richard (7)	Mtl.	Mar. 23/44	Mtl.	5	Paul Bibeault	Mtl. 5	Tor. 1
		Apr. 7/44	Chi.	3	Mike Karakas	Mtl. 3	Chi. 1
		Mar. 29/45	Mtl.	4	Frank McCool	Mtl. 10	Tor. 3
		Apr. 14/53	Bos.	3	Gord Henry	Mtl. 7	Bos. 3
		Mar. 20/56	Mtl.	3	Lorne Worsley	Mtl. 7	NYR 1
		Apr. 6/57	Mtl.	4	Don Simmons	Mtl. 5	Bos. 1
		Apr. 1/58	Det.	3	Terry Sawchuk	Mtl. 4	Det. 3
Jari Kurri (7)	Edm.	Apr. 4/84	Edm.	3	Doug Soetaert (1) Mike Veisor (2)	Edm. 9	Wpg. 2
		Apr. 25/85	Wpg.	3	Bryan Hayward (2) Marc Behrend (1)	Edm. 8	Wpg. 3
		May 7/85	Edm.	3	Murray Bannerman	Edm. 7	Chi. 3
		May 14/85	Edm.	3	Murray Bannerman	Edm. 10	Chi. 5
		May 16/85	Chi.	4	Murray Bannerman	Edm. 8	Chi. 2
		Apr. 9/87	Edm.	4	Roland Melanson (2) Daren Eliot (2)	Edm. 13	L.A. 3
		May 18/90	Bos.	3	Andy Moog (2) Rejean Lemelin (1)	Edm. 7	Bos. 2
Mike Bossy (5)	NYI	Apr. 16/79	NYI	3	Tony Esposito	NYI 6	Chi. 2
		May 8/82	NYI	3	Richard Brodeur	NYI 6	Van. 5
		Apr. 10/83	Wsh.	3	Al Jensen	NYI 6	Wsh. 3
		May 3/83	NYI	3	Pete Peeters	NYI 8	Bos. 3
		May 7/83	NYI	4	Pete Peeters	NYI 8	Bos. 4
Dino Ciccarelli (5)	Min.	May 5/81	Min.	3	Pat Riggin	Min. 7	Cgy. 4
		Apr. 10/82	Min.	3	Murray Bannerman	Min. 7	Chi. 1
	Wsh.	Apr. 5/90	N.J.	3	Sean Burke	Wsh. 5	N.J. 4
		Apr. 25/92	Pit.	4	Tom Barrasso (1) Ken Wregget (3)	Wsh. 7	Pit. 2
	Det.	Apr. 29/93	Tor.	3	Felix Potvin (2) Daren Puppa (1)	Det. 7	Tor. 3
Phil Esposito (4)	Bos.	Apr. 2/69	Bos.	4	Bruce Gamble	Bos. 10	Tor. 0
		Apr. 8/70	Bos.	3	Ed Giacomin	Bos. 8	NYR 2
		Apr. 19/70	Chi.	3	Tony Esposito	Bos. 6	Chi. 3
		Apr. 8/75	Bos.	3	Tony Esposito (2) Michel Dumas (1)	Bos. 8	Chi. 2
Mark Messier (4)	Edm.	Apr. 14/83	Edm.	4	Rejean Lemelin	Edm. 6	Cgy. 3
		Apr. 17/83	Cgy.	3	Rejean Lemelin (1) Don Edwards (2)	Edm. 10	Cgy. 2
		Apr. 26/83	Edm.	3	Murray Bannerman	Edm. 8	Chi. 2
	NYR	May 25/94	N.J.	3	Martin Brodeur (2) ENG (1)	NYR 4	N.J. 2
Bernie Geoffrion (3)	Mtl.	Mar. 27/52	Mtl.	3	Jim Henry	Mtl. 4	Bos. 0
		Apr. 7/55	Mtl.	3	Terry Sawchuk	Mtl. 4	Det. 2
		Mar. 30/57	Mtl.	3	Lorne Worsley	Mtl. 8	NYR 3
Norm Ullman (3)	Det.	Mar. 29/64	Chi.	3	Glenn Hall	Det. 5	Chi. 4
		Apr. 7/64	Det.	3	Glenn Hall (2) Denis DeJordy (1)	Det. 7	Chi. 2
		Apr. 11/65	Det.	3	Glenn Hall	Det. 4	Chi. 2
John Bucyk (3)	Bos.	May 3/70	St. L.	3	Jacques Plante (1) Ernie Wakely (2)	Bos. 6	St. L. 1
		Apr. 20/72	Bos.	3	Jacques Caron (1) Ernie Wakely (2)	Bos. 10	St. L. 2
		Apr. 21/74	Bos.	3	Tony Esposito	Bos. 8	Chi. 6
Rick MacLeish (3)	Phil	Apr. 11/74	Phil	3	Phil Myre	Phi. 5	Atl. 1
		Apr. 13/75	Phil	3	Gord McRae	Phi. 6	Tor. 3
		May 13/75	Phil	3	Glenn Resch	Phi. 4	NYI 1
Denis Savard (3)	Chi.	Apr. 19/82	Chi.	3	Mike Liut	Chi. 7	StL. 4
		Apr. 10/86	Chi.	4	Ken Wregget	Tor. 6	Chi. 4
		Apr. 9/88	St. L.	3	Greg Millen	Chi. 6	St. L. 3
Tim Kerr (3)	Phi.	Apr. 13/85	NYR	4	Glen Hanlon	Phi. 6	NYR 5
		Apr. 20/87	Phi.	3	Kelly Hrudey	Phi. 4	NYI 2
		Apr. 19/89	Pit.	3	Tom Barrasso	Phi. 4	Pit. 2
Cam Neely (3)	Bos.	Apr. 9/87	Mtl.	3	Patrick Roy	Mtl. 4	Bos. 3
		Apr. 5/91	Bos.	3	Peter Sidorkiewicz	Bos. 4	Hfd. 3
		Apr. 25/91	Bos.	3	Patrick Roy	Bos. 4	Mtl. 1
Petr Klima (3)	Det.	Apr. 7/88	Tor.	3	Alan Bester (2) Ken Wregett (1)	Det. 6	Tor. 2
		Apr. 21/88	St. L.	3	Greg Millen	Det. 6	St. L. 0
	Edm.	May 4/91	Edm.	3	Jon Casey	Edm. 7	Min. 2
Esa Tikkanen (3)	Edm.	May 22/88	Edm.	3	Rejean Lemelin	Edm. 6	Bos. 3
		Apr. 16/91	Cgy.	3	Mike Vernon	Edm. 5	Cgy. 4
		Apr. 26/92	L.A.	3	Kelly Hrudey	Edm. 5	L.A. 2
Newsy Lalonde (2)	Mtl.	Mar. 1/19	Mtl.	5	Clint Benedict	Mtl. 6	Ott. 3
		Mar. 22/19	Sea.	4	Harry Holmes	Mtl. 4	Sea. 2
Howie Morenz (2)	Mtl.	Mar. 22/24	Mtl.	3	Charles Reid	Mtl. 6	Cgy.T. 1
		Mar. 27/25	Mtl.	3	Harry Holmes	Mtl. 4	Vic. 2
Toe Blake (2)	Mtl.	Mar. 22/38	Mtl.	3	Mike Karakas	Mtl. 6	Chi. 4
		Mar. 26/46	Chi.	3	Mike Karakas	Mtl. 7	Chi. 2
Doug Bentley (2)	Chi.	Mar. 28/44	Chi.	3	Connie Dion	Chi. 7	Det. 1
		Mar. 30/44	Det.	3	Connie Dion	Chi. 5	Det. 2
Ted Kennedy (2)	Tor.	Apr. 14/45	Tor.	3	Harry Lumley	Det. 5	Tor. 3
		Mar. 27/48	Tor.	4	Frank Brimsek	Tor. 5	Bos. 3
Bobby Hull (2)	Chi.	Apr. 7/63	Det.	3	Terry Sawchuk	Det. 7	Chi. 4
		Apr. 9/72	Pitt	3	Jim Rutherford	Chi. 6	Pit. 5
F. St. Marseille (2)	St. L.	Apr. 28/70	St. L.	3	Al Smith	St. L. 5	Pit. 0
		Apr. 6/72	Min.	3	Cesare Maniago	Min. 6	St. L. 5
Pit Martin (2)	Chi.	Apr. 4/73	Chi.	3	W. Stephenson	Chi. 7	St. L. 1
		May 10/73	Chi.	3	Ken Dryden	Mtl. 6	Chi. 4
Yvan Cournoyer (2)	Mtl.	Apr. 5/73	Mtl.	3	Dave Dryden	Mtl. 7	Buf. 3
		Apr. 11/74	Mtl.	3	Ed Giacomin	Mtl. 4	NYR 1
Guy Lafleur (2)	Mtl.	May 1/75	Mtl.	3	Roger Crozier (1) Gerry Desjardins (2)	Mtl. 7	Buf. 0
		Apr. 11/77	Mtl.	3	Ed Staniowski	Mtl. 7	St. L. 2
Lanny McDonald (2)	Tor.	Apr. 9/77	Pitt	3	Denis Herron	Tor. 5	Pit. 2
		Apr. 17/77	Tor.	4	W. Stephenson	Phi. 6	Tor. 5
Butch Goring (2)	L.A.	Apr. 9/77	L.A.	3	Phil Myre	L.A. 4	Atl. 2
	NYI	May 17/81	Min.	3	Gilles Meloche	NYI 7	Min. 5
Bryan Trottier (2)	NYI	Apr. 8/80	NYI	3	Doug Keans	NYI 8	L.A. 1
		Apr. 9/81	NYI	3	Michel Larocque	NYI 5	Tor. 1
Bill Barber (2)	Phil	May 4/80	Min.	4	Gilles Meloche	Phi. 5	Min. 3
		Apr. 9/81	Phil	3	Dan Bouchard	Phi. 8	Que. 5
Brian Propp (2)	Phi.	Apr. 22/81	Phi.	3	Pat Riggin	Phi. 9	Cgy. 4
		Apr. 21/85	Phi.	3	Billy Smith	Phi. 5	NYI 2
Paul Reinhart (2)	Cgy	Apr. 14/83	Edm.	3	Andy Moog	Edm. 6	Cgy. 3
		Apr. 8/84	Van	3	Richard Brodeur	Cgy. 5	Van. 1
Peter Stastny (2)	Que.	Apr. 5/83	Bos.	3	Pete Peeters	Bos. 4	Que. 3
		Apr. 11/87	Que.	3	Mike Liut (2) Steve Weeks (1)	Que. 5	Hfd. 1
Glenn Anderson (2)	Edm.	Apr. 26/83	Edm.	4	Murray Bannerman	Edm. 8	Chi. 2
		Apr. 6/88	Wpg.	3	Daniel Berthiaume	Edm. 7	Wpg. 4
Michel Goulet (2)	Que.	Apr. 23/85	Que.	3	Steve Penney	Que. 7	Mtl. 6
		Apr. 12/87	Que.	3	Mike Liut	Que. 4	Hfd. 1
Peter Zezel (2)	Phi.	Apr. 13/86	NYR	3	J. Vanbiesbrouck	Phi. 7	NYR 1
	St. L.	Apr. 11/89	St. L.	3	Jon Casey (2) Kari Takko (1)	St. L. 6	Min. 1
Steve Yzerman (2)	Det.	Apr. 6/89	Det.	3	Alain Chevrier	Chi. 5	Det. 4
		Apr. 4/91	St. L.	3	Vincent Riendeau (2) Pat Jablonski (1)	Det. 6	St. L. 3
Mario Lemieux (2)	Pit.	Apr. 25/89	Pit.	5	Ron Hextall	Pit. 10	Phi. 7
		Apr. 23/92	Pit.	3	Don Beaupre	Pit. 6	Wsh. 4
Mike Gartner (2)	NYR	Apr. 13/90	NYR	3	Mark Fitzpatrick (2) Glenn Healy (1)	NYR 6	NYI 5
		Apr. 27/92	NYR	3	Chris Terreri	NYR 8	N.J. 5
Geoff Courtnall (2)	Van.	Apr. 4/91	L.A.	3	Kelly Hrudey	Van. 6	L.A. 5
		Apr. 30/92	Van.	3	Rick Tabaracci	Van. 5	Win. 5
Harry Meeking	Tor.	Mar. 11/18	Tor.	3	Georges Vezina	Tor. 7	Mtl. 3
Alf Skinner	Tor.	Mar. 23/18	Tor.	3	Hugh Lehman	Van.M. 6	Tor. 4
Joe Malone	Mtl.	Feb. 23/19	Mtl.	3	Clint Benedict	Mtl. 8	Ott. 4
Odie Cleghorn	Mtl.	Feb. 27/19	Ott.	3	Clint Benedict	Mtl. 5	Ott. 3
Jack Darragh	Ott.	Apr. 1/20	Tor.	3	Harry Holmes	Ott. 6	Sea. 1
George Boucher	Ott.	Mar. 10/21	Ott.	3	Jake Forbes	Ott. 5	Tor. 0
Babe Dye	Tor.	Mar. 28/22	Tor.	4	Hugh Lehman	Tor. 5	Van.M.
Perk Galbraith	Bos.	Mar. 31/27	Bos.	3	Hugh Lehman	Bos. 4	Chi. 4
Busher Jackson	Tor.	Apr. 5/32	NYR	3	John Ross Roach	Tor. 6	NYR 4
Frank Boucher	NYR	Apr. 9/32	Tor.	3	Lorne Chabot	Tor. 6	NYR 4
Charlie Conacher	Tor.	Mar. 26/36	Tor.	3	Tiny Thompson	Tor. 8	Bos. 3
Syd Howe	Det.	Mar. 23/39	Det.	3	Claude Bourque	Det. 7	Mtl. 3
Bryan Hextall	NYR	Apr. 3/40	NYR	3	Turk Broda	NYR 6	Tor. 2
Joe Benoit	Mtl.	Mar. 22/41	Mtl.	3	Sam LoPresti	Mtl. 4	Chi. 3
Syl Apps	Tor.	Mar. 25/41	Tor.	3	Frank Brimsek	Tor. 7	Bos. 2
Jack McGill	Bos.	Mar. 29/42	Bos.	3	Johnny Mowers	Det. 6	Bos. 4
Don Metz	Tor.	Apr. 14/42	Tor.	3	Johnny Mowers	Tor. 9	Det. 3
Mud Bruneteau	Det.	Apr. 1/43	Det.	3	Frank Brimsek	Det. 6	Bos. 2
Don Grosso	Det.	Apr. 7/43	Bos.	3	Frank Brimsek	Det. 4	Bos. 0
Carl Liscombe	Det.	Apr. 3/45	Bos.	4	Paul Bibeault	Det. 5	Bos. 3
Billy Reay	Mtl.	Apr. 1/47	Bos.	4	Frank Brimsek	Mtl. 5	Bos. 1
Gerry Plamondon	Mtl.	Mar. 24/49	Det.	3	Harry Lumley	Mtl. 4	Det. 3
Sid Smith	Tor.	Apr. 10/49	Det.	3	Harry Lumley	Tor. 3	Det. 1
Pentti Lund	NYR	Apr. 2/50	NYR	3	Bill Durnan	NYR 4	Mtl. 1
Ted Lindsay	Det.	Apr. 5/55	Det.	4	Charlie Hodge (1) Jacques Plante (3)	Det. 7	Mtl. 1
Gordie Howe	Det.	Apr. 10/55	Det.	3	Jacques Plante	Det. 5	Mtl. 1
Phil Goyette	Mtl.	Mar. 25/58	Mtl.	3	Terry Sawchuk	Mtl. 8	Det. 1
Jerry Toppazzini	Bos.	Apr. 5/58	Bos.	3	Lorne Worsley	Bos. 8	NYR 2
Bob Pulford	Tor.	Apr. 19/62	Tor.	3	Glenn Hall	Tor. 8	Chi. 4
Dave Keon	Tor.	Apr. 9/64	Mtl.	3	Charlie Hodge	Tor. 3	Mtl. 1
Henri Richard	Mtl.	Apr. 20/67	Mtl.	3	Terry Sawchuk (2) Johnny Bower (1)	Mtl. 6	Tor. 2
Rosaire Paiement	Phi.	Apr. 13/68	Phi.	3	Glenn Hall (1) Seth Martin (2)	Phi. 6	St. L. 1
Jean Beliveau	Mtl.	Apr. 20/68	Mtl.	3	Denis DeJordy	Mtl. 4	Chi. 1
Red Berenson	St. L.	Apr. 15/69	St. L.	3	Gerry Desjardins	St. L. 4	L.A. 0
Ken Schinkel	Pit.	Apr. 11/70	Oak.	3	Gary Smith	Pit. 5	Oak. 2
Jim Pappin	Chi.	Apr. 11/71	Phi.	3	Bruce Gamble	Chi. 6	Phi. 2
Bobby Orr	Bos.	Apr. 11/71	Mtl.	3	Ken Dryden	Bos. 5	Mtl. 2
Jacques Lemaire	Mtl.	Apr. 20/71	Mtl.	3	Lorne Worsley	Mtl. 7	Min. 2
Vic Hadfield	NYR	Apr. 22/71	NYR	3	Tony Esposito	NYR 4	Chi. 1
Fred Stanfield	Bos.	Apr. 18/72	Bos.	3	Jacques Caron	Bos. 6	St. L. 1
Ken Hodge	Bos.	Apr. 30/72	Bos.	3	Ed Giacomin	Bos. 6	NYR 5
Steve Vickers	NYR	Apr. 10/73	Bos.	3	Ross Brooks (2) Ed Johnston (1)	NYR 6	Bos. 3
Dick Redmond	Chi.	Apr. 4/73	Chi.	3	Wayne Stephenson	Chi. 7	St. L. 1
Tom Williams	L.A.	Apr. 14/74	L.A.	3	Mike Veisor	L.A. 5	Chi. 1
Marcel Dionne	L.A.	Apr. 15/76	L.A.	3	Gilles Gilbert	L.A. 6	Bos. 4

Player	Team	Date	City	Total Goals	Opposing Goaltender	Score	
Don Saleski	Phi.	Apr. 20/76	Phil	3	Wayne Thomas	Phi. 7	Tor. 1
Darryl Sittler	Tor.	Apr. 22/76	Tor.	5	Bernie Parent	Tor. 8	Phi. 5
Reggie Leach	Phi.	May 6/76	Phi.	5	Gilles Gilbert	Phi. 6	Bos. 3
Jim Lorentz	Buf.	Apr. 7/77	Min.	3	Pete LoPresti (2)		
					Gary Smith (1)	Buf. 7	Min. 1
Bobby Schmautz	Bos.	Apr. 11/77	Bos.	3	Rogatien Vachon	Bos. 8	L.A. 3
Billy Harris	NYI	Apr. 23/77	Mtl.	3	Ken Dryden	Mtl. 4	NYI 3
George Ferguson	Tor.	Apr. 11/78	Tor.	3	Rogatien Vachon	Tor. 7	L.A. 3
Jean Ratelle	Bos.	May 3/79	Bos.	3	Ken Dryden	Bos. 4	Mtl. 3
Stan Jonathan	Bos.	May 8/79	Bos.	3	Ken Dryden	Bos. 5	Mtl. 2
Ron Duguay	NYR	Apr. 20/80	NYR	3	Pete Peeters	NYR 4	Phi. 2
Steve Shutt	Mtl.	Apr. 22/80	Mtl.	3	Gilles Meloche	Mtl. 6	Min. 2
Gilbert Perreault	Buf.	May 6/80	NYI	3	Billy Smith (2)		
					ENG (1)	Buf. 7	NYI 4
Paul Holmgren	Phi.	May 15/80	Phil	3	Billy Smith	Phi. 8	NYI 3
Steve Payne	Min.	Apr. 8/81	Bos.	3	Rogatien Vachon	Min. 5	Bos. 4
Denis Potvin	NYI	Apr. 17/81	NYI	3	Andy Moog	NYI 6	Edm. 3
Barry Pederson	Bos.	Apr. 8/82	Bos.	3	Don Edwards	Bos. 7	Buf. 3
Duane Sutter	NYI	Apr. 15/83	NYI	3	Glen Hanlon	NYI 5	NYR 0
Doug Halward	Van.	Apr. 7/84	Van.	3	Rejean Lemelin (2)		
					Don Edwards (1)	Van. 7	Cgy. 0
Jorgen Pettersson	St. L.	Apr. 8/84	Det.	3	Ed Mio	St. L. 3	Det. 2
Clark Gillies	NYI	May 12/84	NYI	3	Grant Fuhr	NYI 6	Edm. 1
Ken Linseman	Bos.	Apr. 14/85	Bos.	3	Steve Penney	Bos. 7	Mtl. 6
Dave Andreychuk	Buf.	Apr. 14/85	Buf.	3	Dan Bouchard	Que. 4	Buf. 7
Greg Paslawski	StL.	Apr. 15/86	Min.	3	Don Beaupre	St. L. 6	Min. 3
Doug Risebrough	Cgy.	May 4/86	Cgy.	3	Rick Wamsley	Cgy. 8	St. L. 2
Mike McPhee	Mtl.	Apr. 11/87	Bos.	3	Doug Keans	Mtl. 5	Bos. 4
John Ogrodnick	Que.	Apr. 14/87	Hfd.	3	Mike Liut	Que. 7	Hfd. 5
Pelle Eklund	Phi.	May 10/87	Mtl.	3	Patrick Roy (1)		
					Bryan Hayward (2)	Phi. 6	Mtl. 3
John Tucker	Buf.	Apr. 9/88	Bos.	4	Andy Moog	Buf. 6	Bos. 2
Tony Hrkac	St. L.	Apr. 10/88	St. L.	4	Darren Pang	St. L. 6	Chi. 5
Hakan Loob	Cgy.	Apr. 10/88	Cgy.	3	Glenn Healy	Cgy. 7	L.A. 3
Ed Olczyk	Tor.	Apr. 12/88	Tor.	3	Greg Stefan (2)		
					Glen Hanlon (1)	Tor. 6	Det. 5
Aaron Broten	N.J.	Apr. 20/88	N.J.	3	Pete Peeters	N.J. 5	Wsh. 2
Mark Johnson	N.J.	Apr. 22/88	Wsh.	4	Pete Peeters	N.J. 10	Wsh. 4
Patrik Sundstrom	N.J.	Apr. 22/88	Wsh.	3	Pete Peeters (2)		
					Clint Malarchuk (1)	N.J. 10	Wsh. 4
Bob Brooke	Min.	Apr. 5/89	St. L.	3	Greg Millen	St. L. 4	Min. 3
Chris Kontos	L.A.	Apr. 6/89	L.A.	3	Grant Fuhr	L.A. 5	Edm. 2
Wayne Presley	Chi.	Apr. 13/89	Chi.	3	Greg Stefan (1)		
					Glen Hanlon (2)	Chi. 7	Det. 1
Tony Granato	L.A.	Apr. 10/90	L.A.	3	Mike Vernon (1)		
					Rick Wamsley (2)	L.A. 12	Cgy. 4
Tomas Sandstrom	L.A.	Apr. 10/90	L.A.	3	Mike Vernon (1)		
					Rick Wamsley (2)	L.A. 12	Cgy. 4
Dave Taylor	L.A.	Apr. 10/90	L.A.	3	Mike Vernon (1)		
					Rick Wamsley (2)	L.A. 12	Cgy. 4
Bernie Nicholls	NYR	Apr. 19/90	NYR	3	Mike Liut	NYR 7	Wsh. 3
John Druce	Wsh.	Apr. 21/90	NYR	3	John Vanbiesbrouck	Wsh. 6	NYR 3
Adam Oates	St. L.	Apr. 12/91	St. L.	3	Tim Chevaldae	St. L. 6	Det. 1
Luc Robitaille	L.A.	Apr. 26/91	L.A.	3	Grant Fuhr	L.A. 5	Edm. 2
Ron Francis	Pit.	May. 9/92	Pit.	3	Mike Richter (2)		
					John V'brouck (1)	Pit. 5	NYR. 4
Dirk Graham	Chi.	June 1/92	Chi.	3	Tom Barrasso	Pit. 5	Chi. 2
Joe Murphy	Edm.	May 6/92	Edm.	3	Kirk McLean	Edm. 5	Van. 2
Ray Sheppard	Det.	Apr. 24/92	Min.	3	Jon Casey	Min. 5	Det. 2
Kevin Stevens	Pit.	May.21/92	Bos.	4	Andy Moog	Pit. 5	Bos. 2
Pavel Bure	Van.	Apr. 28/92	Wpg.	3	Rick Tabaracci	Van. 8	Wpg. 3
Brian Noonan	Chi.	Apr. 18/93	Chi.	3	Curtis Joseph	St. L. 4	Chi. 3
Dale Hunter	Wsh.	Apr. 20/93	Wsh.	3	Glenn Healy	NYI 5	Wsh. 4
Teemu Selanne	Wpg.	Apr. 23/93	Wpg.	3	Kirk McLean	Wpg. 5	Van. 4
Ray Ferraro	NYI	Apr. 26/93	Wsh.	4	Don Beaupre	Wsh. 6	NYI 4
Al Iafrate	Wsh.	Apr. 26/93	Wsh.	3	Glenn Healy (2)		
					Mark Fitzpatrick (1)	Wsh. 6	NYI 4
Paul Di Pietro	Mtl.	Apr. 28/93	Mtl.	3	Ron Hextall	Mtl. 6	Que. 2
Wendel Clark	Tor.	May 27/93	L.A.	3	Kelly Hrudey	L.A. 5	Tor. 4
Eric Desjardins	Mtl.	Jun. 3/93	Mtl.	3	Kelly Hrudey	Mtl. 3	L.A. 2
Tony Amonte	Chi.	Apr. 23/94	Chi.	4	Felix Potvin	Chi. 5	Tor. 4
Gary Suter	Chi.	Apr. 24/94	Chi.	3	Felix Potvin	Chi. 4	Tor. 3
Ulf Dahlen	S.J.	May 6/94	S.J.	3	Felix Potvin	S.J. 5	Tor. 2

Leading Playoff Scorers, 1918–1994

Season	Player and Club	Games Played	Goals	Assists	Points
1993-94	Brian Leetch, NY Rangers	23	11	23	34
1992-93	Wayne Gretzky, Los Angeles	24	15	25	40
1991-92	Mario Lemieux, Pittsburgh	15	16	18	34
1990-91	Mario Lemieux, Pittsburgh	23	16	28	44
1989-90	Craig Simpson, Edmonton	22	16	15	31
	Mark Messier, Edmonton	22	9	22	31
1988-89	Al MacInnis, Calgary	22	7	24	31
1987-88	Wayne Gretzky, Edmonton	19	12	31	43
1986-87	Wayne Gretzky, Edmonton	21	5	29	34
1985-86	Doug Gilmour, St. Louis	19	9	12	21
	Bernie Federko, St. Louis	19	7	14	21
1984-85	Wayne Gretzky, Edmonton	18	17	30	47
1983-84	Wayne Gretzky, Edmonton	19	13	22	35
1982-83	Wayne Gretzky, Edmonton	16	12	26	38
1981-82	Bryan Trottier, NY Islanders	19	6	23	29
1980-81	Mike Bossy, NY Islanders	18	17	18	35
1979-80	Bryan Trottier, NY Islanders	21	12	17	29
1978-79	Jacques Lemaire, Montreal	16	11	12	23
	Guy Lafleur, Montreal	16	10	13	23
1977-78	Guy Lafleur, Montreal	15	10	11	21
	Larry Robinson, Montreal	15	4	17	21
1976-77	Guy Lafleur, Montreal	14	9	17	26
1975-76	Reggie Leach, Philadelphia	16	19	5	24
1974-75	Rick MacLeish, Philadelphia	17	11	9	20
1973-74	Rick MacLeish, Philadelphia	17	13	9	22
1972-73	Yvan Cournoyer, Montreal	17	15	10	25
1971-72	Phil Esposito, Boston	15	9	15	24
	Bobby Orr, Boston	15	5	19	24
1970-71	Frank Mahovlich, Montreal	20	14	13	27
1969-70	Phil Esposito, Boston	14	13	14	27
1968-69	Phil Esposito, Boston	10	8	10	18
1967-68	Bill Goldsworthy, Minnesota	14	8	7	15
1966-67	Jim Pappin, Toronto	12	7	8	15
1965-66	Norm Ullman, Detroit	12	6	9	15
1964-65	Bobby Hull, Chicago	14	10	7	17
1963-64	Gordie Howe, Detroit	14	9	10	19
1962-63	Gordie Howe, Detroit	11	7	9	16
	Norm Ullman, Detroit	11	4	12	16
1961-62	Stan Mikita, Chicago	12	6	15	21
1960-61	Gordie Howe, Detroit	11	4	11	15
	Pierre Pilote, Chicago	12	3	12	15
1959-60	Henri Richard, Montreal	8	3	9	12
	Bernie Geoffrion, Montreal	8	2	10	12
1958-59	Dickie Moore, Montreal	11	5	12	17
1957-58	Fleming Mackell, Boston	12	5	14	19
1956-57	Bernie Geoffrion, Montreal	11	11	7	18
1955-56	Jean Béliveau, Montreal	10	12	7	19
1954-55	Gordie Howe, Detroit	11	9	11	20
1953-54	Dickie Moore, Montreal	11	5	8	13
1952-53	Ed Sandford, Boston	11	8	3	11
1951-52	Ted Lindsay, Detroit	8	5	2	7
	Floyd Curry, Montreal	11	4	3	7
	Metro Prystai, Detroit	8	2	5	7
	Gordie Howe, Detroit	8	2	5	7
1950-51	Maurice Richard, Montreal	11	9	4	13
	Max Bentley, Toronto	11	2	11	13
1949-50	Pentti Lund, NY Rangers	12	6	5	11
1948-49	Gordie Howe, Detroit	11	8	3	11
1947-48	Ted Kennedy, Toronto	9	8	6	14
1946-47	Maurice Richard, Montreal	10	6	5	11
1945-46	Elmer Lach, Montreal	9	5	12	17
1944-45	Joe Carveth, Detroit	14	5	6	11
1943-44	Toe Blake, Montreal	9	7	11	18
1942-43	Carl Liscombe, Detroit	10	6	8	14
1941-42	Don Grosso, Detroit	12	8	6	14
1940-41	Milt Schmidt, Boston	11	5	6	11
1939-40	Phil Watson, NY Rangers	12	3	6	9
	Neil Colville, NY Rangers	12	2	7	9
1938-39	Bill Cowley, Boston	12	3	11	14
1937-38	Johnny Gottselig, Chicago	10	5	3	8
1936-37	Marty Barry, Detroit	10	4	7	11
1935-36	Buzz Boll, Toronto	9	7	3	10
1934-35	Baldy Northcott, Mtl. Maroons	7	4	1	5
	Harvey Jackson, Toronto	7	3	2	5
	Marvin Wentworth, Mtl. Maroons	7	3	2	5
1933-34	Larry Aurie, Detroit	9	3	7	10
1932-33	Cecil Dillon, NY Rangers	8	8	2	10
1931-32	Frank Boucher, NY Rangers	7	3	6	9
1930-31	Cooney Weiland, Boston	5	6	3	9
1929-30	Marty Barry, Boston	6	3	3	6
	Cooney Weiland, Boston	6	1	5	6
1928-29	Andy Blair, Toronto	4	3	0	3
	Butch Keeling, NY Rangers	6	3	0	3
	Ace Bailey, Toronto	4	1	2	3
1927-28	Frank Boucher, NY Rangers	9	7	3	10
1926-27	Harry Oliver, Boston	8	4	2	6
	Perk Galbraith, Boston	8	3	3	6
	Frank Fredrickson, Boston	8	2	4	6
1925-26	Nels Stewart, Mtl. Maroons	8	6	3	9
1924-25	Howie Morenz, Montreal	6	7	1	8
1923-24	Howie Morenz, Montreal	6	7	2	9
1922-23	Punch Broadbent, Ottawa	8	6	1	7
1921-22	Babe Dye, Toronto	7	11	2	13
1920-21	Cy Denneny, Ottawa	7	4	2	6
1919-20	Frank Nighbor, Ottawa	5	6	1	7
	Jack Darragh, Ottawa	5	5	2	7
1918-19	Newsy Lalonde, Montreal	10	17	1	18
1917-18	Alf Skinner, Toronto	7	8	1	9

Overtime Games since 1918

Abbreviations: Teams/Cities: — **Atl.** - Atlanta; **Bos.** - Boston; **Buf.** - Buffalo; **Cgy.** - Calgary; **Cgy. T.** - Calgary Tigers (Western Canada Hockey League); **Chi.** - Chicago; **Col.** - Colorado; **Dal.** - Dallas; **Det.** - Detroit; **Edm.** - Edmonton; **Edm. E.** - Edmonton Eskimos (WCHL); **Hfd.** - Hartford; **K.C.** - Kansas City; **L.A.** - Los Angeles; **Min.** - Minnesota; **Mtl.** - Montreal; **Mtl.M.** - Montreal Maroons; **N.J.** - New Jersey; **NYA** - NY Americans; **NYI** - New York Islanders; **NYR** - New York Rangers; **Oak.** - Oakland; **Ott.** - Ottawa; **Phi.** - Philadelphia; **Pit.** - Pittsburgh; **Que.** - Quebec; **St. L.** - St. Louis; **Sea.** - Seattle Metropolitans (Pacific Coast Hockey Association); **S.J.** - San Jose; **Tor.** - Toronto; **Van.** - Vancouver; **Van. M** - Vancouver Millionaires (PCHA); **Vic.** - Victoria Cougars (WCHL); **Wpg.** - Winnipeg; **Wsh.** - Washington.

SERIES — **CF** - conference final; **CSF** - conference semi-final; **CQF** - conference quarter-final; **DF** - division final; **DSF** - division semi-final; **F** - final; **PR** - preliminary round; **QF** - quarter final; **SF** - semi-final.

Date	City	Series	Score		Scorer	Overtime	Series Winner
Mar. 26/19	Sea.	F	Mtl. 0	Sea. 0	no scorer	20:00	
Mar. 29/19	Sea.	F	Mtl. 4	Sea. 3	Odie Cleghorn	15:57	
Mar. 21/22	Tor.	F	Tor 2	Van.M. 1	Babe Dye	4:50	Tor.
Mar. 29/23	Van.	F	Ott. 2	Edm.E. 1	Cy Denneny	2:08	Ott.
Mar. 31/27	Mtl.	QF	Mtl. 1	Mtl. M. 0	Howie Morenz	12:05	Mtl.
Apr. 7/27	Bos.	F	Ott. 0	Bos. 0	no scorer	20:00	Ott.
Apr. 11/27	Ott.	F	Bos. 1	Ott. 1	no scorer	20:00	Ott.
Apr. 3/28	Mtl.	QF	Mtl. M. 1	Mtl. 0	Russ Oatman	8:20	Mtl. M.
Apr. 7/28	Mtl.	F	NYR 2	Mtl. M. 1	Frank Boucher	7:05	NYR
Mar. 21/29	NY	QF	NYR 1	NYA 0	Butch Keeling	29:50	NYR
Mar. 26/29	Tor.	SF	NYR 2	Tor. 1	Frank Boucher	2:03	NYR
Mar. 20/30	Mtl.	SF	Bos. 2	Mtl. M. 1	Harry Oliver	45:35	Bos.
Mar. 25/30	Bos.	SF	Mtl. M. 1	Bos. 0	Archie Wilcox	26:27	Bos.
Mar. 26/30	Mtl.	QF	Chi. 2	Mtl. 2	Howie Morenz (Mtl.)	51:43	Mtl.
Mar. 28/30	Mtl.	SF	Mtl. 2	NYR 1	Gus Rivers	68:52	Mtl.
Mar. 24/31	Bos.	SF	Bos. 5	Mtl. 4	Cooney Weiland	18:56	Mtl.
Mar. 26/31	Chi.	QF	Chi. 2	Tor. 1	Steward Adams	19:20	Chi.
Mar. 28/31	Mtl.	SF	Mtl. 4	Bos. 3	Georges Mantha	5:10	Mtl.
Apr. 1/31	Mtl.	SF	Mtl. 3	Bos. 2	Wildor Larochelle	19:00	Mtl.
Apr. 5/31	Chi.	F	Chi. 2	Mtl. 1	Johnny Gottselig	24:50	Mtl.
Apr. 9/31	Mtl.	F	Chi. 3	Mtl. 2	Cy Wentworth	53:50	Mtl.
Mar. 26/32	Mtl.	SF	NYR 4	Mtl. 3	Fred Cook	59:32	NYR
Apr. 2/32	Tor.	SF	Tor. 3	Mtl. M. 2	Bob Gracie	17:59	Tor.
Mar. 25/33	Bos.	SF	Bos. 2	Tor. 1	Marty Barry	14:14	Tor.
Mar. 28/33	Bos.	SF	Tor. 1	Bos. 0	Busher Jackson	15:03	Tor.
Mar. 30/33	Tor.	SF	Bos. 2	Tor. 1	Eddie Shore	4:23	Tor.
Apr. 3/33	Tor.	SF	Tor. 1	Bos. 0	Ken Doraty	104:46	Tor.
Apr. 13/33	Tor.	F	NYR 1	Tor. 0	Bill Cook	7:33	NYR
Mar. 22/34	Tor.	SF	Det. 2	Tor. 1	Herbie Lewis	1:33	Det.
Mar. 25/34	Chi.	QF	Chi. 1	Mtl. 1	Mush March (Chi)	11:05	Chi.
Apr. 3/34	Det.	F	Chi. 2	Det. 1	Paul Thompson	21:05	Chi.
Apr. 10/34	Chi.	F	Chi. 1	Det. 0	Mush March	30:05	Chi.
Mar. 23/35	Bos.	SF	Bos. 1	Tor. 0	Dit Clapper	33:26	Tor.
Mar. 26/35	Chi.	QF	Mtl. M. 1	Chi. 0	Baldy Northcott	4:02	Mtl. M.
Mar. 30/35	Tor.	SF	Tor. 2	Bos. 1	Pep Kelly	1:36	Tor.
Apr. 4/35	Tor.	F	Mtl. M. 3	Tor. 2	Dave Trottier	5:20	Mtl. M.
Mar. 24/36	Mtl.	SF	Det. 1	Mtl. M. 0	Mud Bruneteau	116:30	Det.
Apr. 9/36	Tor.	F	Tor. 4	Det. 3	Buzz Boll	0:31	Det.
Mar. 25/37	NY	QF	NYR 2	Tor. 1	Babe Pratt	13:05	NYR
Apr. 1/37	Mtl.	SF	Det. 2	Mtl. 1	Hec Kilrea	51:49	Det.
Mar. 22/38	NY	QF	NYA 2	NYR 1	Johnny Sorrell	21:25	NYA
Mar. 25/38	Tor.	SF	Tor. 1	Bos. 0	George Parsons	21:31	Tor.
Mar. 26/38	Mtl.	QF	Chi. 3	Mtl. 2	Paul Thompson	11:49	Chi.
Mar. 27/38	NY	QF	NYA 3	NYR 2	Lorne Carr	60:40	NYA
Mar. 29/38	Bos.	SF	Tor. 3	Bos. 2	Gord Drillon	10:04	Tor.
Mar. 31/38	Chi.	SF	Chi. 1	NYA 0	Cully Dahlstrom	33:01	Chi.
Mar. 21/39	NY	SF	Bos. 2	NYR 1	Mel Hill	59:25	Bos.
Mar. 23/39	Bos.	SF	Bos. 3	NYR 2	Mel Hill	8:24	Bos.
Mar. 26/39	Det.	QF	Det. 1	Mtl. 0	Marty Barry	7:47	Det.
Mar. 30/39	Bos.	SF	NYR 2	Bos. 1	Clint Smith	17:19	Bos.
Apr. 1/39	Tor.	SF	Tor. 5	Det. 4	Gord Drillon	5:42	Tor.
Apr. 2/39	Bos.	SF	Bos. 2	NYR 1	Mel Hill	48:00	Bos.
Apr. 9/39	Bos.	F	Tor. 3	Bos. 2	Doc Romnes	10:38	Bos.
Mar. 19/40	Det.	QF	Det. 2	NYA 1	Syd Howe	0:25	Det.
Mar. 19/40	Tor.	QF	Tor. 3	Chi. 2	Syl Apps	6:35	Tor.
Apr. 2/40	NY	F	NYR 2	Tor. 1	Alf Pike	15:30	NYR
Apr. 11/40	Tor.	F	NYR 2	Tor. 1	Muzz Patrick	31:43	NYR
Apr. 13/40	Tor.	F	NYR 3	Tor. 2	Bryan Hextall	2:07	NYR
Mar. 20/41	Det.	QF	Det. 2	NYR 1	Gus Giesebrecht	12:01	Det.
Mar. 22/41	Mtl.	QF	Mtl. 4	Chi. 3	Charlie Sands	34:04	Chi.
Mar. 29/41	Bos.	SF	Tor. 2	Bos. 1	Pete Langelle	17:31	Bos.
Mar. 30/41	Chi.	SF	Det. 2	Chi. 1	Gus Giesebrecht	9:15	Det.
Mar. 22/42	Chi.	QF	Bos. 2	Chi. 1	Des Smith	9:51	Bos.
Mar. 21/43	Bos.	SF	Bos. 5	Mtl. 4	Don Gallinger	12:30	Bos.
Mar. 23/43	Det.	SF	Tor. 3	Det. 2	Jack McLean	70:18	Det.
Mar. 25/43	Mtl.	SF	Bos. 3	Mtl. 2	Harvey Jackson	3:20	Bos.
Mar. 30/43	Tor.	SF	Det. 3	Tor. 2	Adam Brown	9:21	Det.
Mar. 30/43	Bos.	SF	Bos. 5	Mtl. 4	Ab DeMarco	3:41	Bos.
Apr. 13/44	Mtl.	F	Mtl. 5	Chi. 4	Toe Blake	9:12	Mtl.
Mar. 27/45	Tor.	SF	Tor. 4	Mtl. 3	Gus Bodnar	12:36	Tor.
Mar. 29/45	Det.	SF	Det. 3	Bos. 2	Mud Bruneteau	17:12	Det.
Apr. 21/45	Tor.	F	Det. 1	Tor. 0	Ed Bruneteau	14:16	Tor.
Mar. 28/46	Bos.	SF	Bos. 4	Det. 3	Don Gallinger	9:51	Bos.
Mar. 30/46	Mtl.	F	Mtl. 4	Bos. 3	Maurice Richard	9:08	Mtl.
Apr. 2/46	Mtl.	F	Mtl. 3	Bos. 2	Jim Peters	16:55	Mtl.
Apr. 7/46	Bos.	F	Bos. 3	Mtl. 2	Terry Reardon	15:13	Mtl.
Mar. 26/47	Tor.	SF	Tor. 3	Det. 2	Howie Meeker	3:05	Tor.
Mar. 27/47	Mtl.	SF	Mtl. 2	Bos. 1	Ken Mosdell	5:38	Mtl.
Apr. 3/47	Mtl.	SF	Mtl. 4	Bos. 3	John Quilty	36:40	Mtl.
Apr. 15/47	Tor.	F	Tor. 2	Mtl. 1	Syl Apps	16:36	Tor.
Mar. 24/48	Tor.	SF	Tor. 5	Bos. 4	Nick Metz	17:03	Tor.
Mar. 22/49	Det.	SF	Det. 2	Mtl. 1	Max McNab	44:52	Det.
Mar. 24/49	Det.	SF	Mtl. 4	Det. 3	Gerry Plamondon	2:59	Det.
Mar. 26/49	Tor.	SF	Bos. 5	Tor. 4	Woody Dumart	16:14	Tor.
Apr. 8/49	Det.	F	Tor. 3	Det. 2	Joe Klukay	17:31	Tor.
Apr. 4/50	Tor.	SF	Det. 2	Tor. 1	Leo Reise	20:38	Det.
Apr. 4/50	Mtl.	SF	Mtl. 3	NYR 2	Elmer Lach	15:19	Mtl.
Apr. 9/50	Det.	SF	Det. 1	Tor. 0	Leo Reise	8:39	Det.
Apr. 18/50	Det.	F	NYR 4	Det. 3	Don Raleigh	8:34	Det.
Apr. 20/50	Det.	F	NYR 2	Det. 1	Don Raleigh	1:38	Det.
Apr. 23/50	Det.	F	Det. 4	NYR 3	Pete Babando	28:31	Det.
Mar. 27/51	Det.	SF	Mtl. 3	Det. 2	Maurice Richard	61:09	Mtl.
Mar. 29/51	Det.	SF	Mtl. 1	Det. 0	Maurice Richard	42:20	Mtl.
Mar. 31/51	Tor.	SF	Bos. 1	Tor. 1	no scorer	20:00	Tor.
Apr. 11/51	Tor.	F	Tor. 3	Mtl. 2	Sid Smith	5:51	Tor.
Apr. 14/51	Tor.	F	Mtl. 3	Tor. 2	Maurice Richard	2:55	Tor.
Apr. 17/51	Mtl.	F	Tor. 2	Mtl. 1	Ted Kennedy	4:47	Tor.
Apr. 19/51	Mtl.	F	Tor. 3	Mtl. 2	Harry Watson	5:15	Tor.
Apr. 21/51	Tor.	F	Tor. 3	Mtl. 2	Bill Barilko	2:53	Tor.
Apr. 6/52	Bos.	SF	Mtl. 3	Bos. 2	Paul Masnick	27:49	Mtl.
Mar. 29/53	Bos.	SF	Bos. 2	Det. 1	Jack McIntyre	12:29	Bos.
Mar. 29/53	Chi.	SF	Chi. 2	Mtl. 1	Al Dewsbury	5:18	Mtl.
Apr. 16/53	Mtl.	F	Mtl. 1	Bos. 0	Elmer Lach	1:22	Mtl.
Apr. 1/54	Det.	SF	Det. 4	Tor. 3	Ted Lindsay	21:01	Det.
Apr. 11/54	Det.	F	Mtl. 1	Det. 0	Ken Mosdell	5:45	Det.
Apr. 16/54	Det.	F	Det. 2	Mtl. 1	Tony Leswick	4:29	Det.
Mar. 29/55	Bos.	SF	Mtl. 4	Bos. 3	Don Marshall	3:05	Mtl.
Mar. 24/56	Tor.	SF	Det. 5	Tor. 4	Ted Lindsay	4:22	Det.
Mar. 28/57	NY	SF	NYR 4	Mtl. 3	Andy Hebenton	13:38	Mtl.
Apr. 4/57	Mtl.	SF	Mtl. 4	NYR 3	Maurice Richard	1:11	Mtl.
Mar. 27/58	NY	SF	Bos. 4	NYR 3	Jerry Toppazzini	4:46	Bos.
Mar. 30/58	Det.	SF	Mtl. 2	Det. 1	André Pronovost	11:52	Mtl.
Apr. 17/58	Mtl.	F	Mtl. 3	Bos. 2	Maurice Richard	5:45	Mtl.
Mar. 28/59	Tor.	SF	Tor. 3	Bos. 2	Gerry Ehman	5:02	Tor.
Mar. 31/59	Tor.	SF	Tor. 3	Bos. 2	Frank Mahovlich	11:21	Tor.
Apr. 14/59	Tor.	F	Tor. 3	Mtl. 2	Dick Duff	10:06	Mtl.
Mar. 26/60	Mtl.	SF	Mtl. 4	Chi. 3	Doug Harvey	8:38	Mtl.
Mar. 27/60	Det.	SF	Tor. 5	Det. 4	Frank Mahovlich	43:00	Tor.
Mar. 29/60	Det.	SF	Det. 2	Tor. 1	Gerry Melnyk	1:54	Tor.
Mar. 22/61	Tor.	SF	Tor. 3	Det. 2	George Armstrong	24:51	Det.
Mar. 26/61	Chi.	SF	Chi. 2	Mtl. 1	Murray Balfour	52:12	Chi.
Apr. 5/62	Tor.	SF	Tor. 3	NYR 2	Red Kelly	24:23	Tor.
Apr. 2/64	Det.	SF	Chi. 3	Det. 2	Murray Balfour	8:21	Det.
Apr. 14/64	Tor.	F	Det. 4	Tor. 3	Larry Jeffrey	7:52	Tor.
Apr. 23/64	Det.	F	Tor. 4	Det. 3	Bobby Baun	1:43	Tor.
Apr. 6/65	Tor.	SF	Tor. 3	Mtl. 2	Dave Keon	4:17	Mtl.
Apr. 13/65	Tor.	SF	Mtl. 4	Tor. 3	Claude Provost	16:33	Mtl.
May 5/66	Det.	F	Mtl. 3	Det. 2	Henri Richard	2:20	Mtl.
Apr. 13/67	NY	SF	Mtl. 2	NYR 1	John Ferguson	6:28	Mtl.
Apr. 25/67	Tor.	F	Tor. 3	Mtl. 2	Bob Pulford	28:26	Tor.
Apr. 10/68	St. L.	QF	St. L. 3	Phi. 2	Larry Keenan	24:10	St. L.
Apr. 16/68	St. L.	QF	Phi. 2	St. L. 1	Don Blackburn	31:38	St. L.
Apr. 16/68	Min.	QF	Min. 4	L.A. 3	Milan Marcetta	9:11	Min.
Apr. 22/68	Min.	SF	Min. 3	St. L. 2	Parker MacDonald	3:41	St. L.
Apr. 27/68	St. L.	SF	St. L. 4	Min. 3	Gary Sabourin	1:32	St. L.
Apr. 28/68	Mtl.	SF	Mtl. 4	Chi. 3	Jacques Lemaire	2:14	Mtl.
Apr. 29/68	St. L.	SF	St. L. 3	Min. 2	Bill McCreary	17:27	St. L.
May 3/68	St. L.	SF	St. L. 2	Min. 1	Ron Schock	22:50	St. L.
May 5/68	St. L.	F	Mtl. 3	St. L. 2	Jacques Lemaire	1:41	Mtl.
May 9/68	Mtl.	F	Mtl. 4	St. L. 3	Bobby Rousseau	1:13	Mtl.
Apr. 2/69	Oak.	QF	L.A. 5	Oak. 4	Ted Irvine	0:19	L.A.
Apr. 10/69	Mtl.	SF	Mtl. 3	Bos. 2	Ralph Backstrom	0:42	Mtl.
Apr. 13/69	Mtl.	SF	Mtl. 4	Bos. 3	Mickey Redmond	4:55	Mtl.
Apr. 24/69	Bos.	SF	Mtl. 2	Bos. 1	Jean Béliveau	31:28	Mtl.
Apr. 12/70	Oak.	QF	Pit. 3	Oak. 2	Michel Briere	8:28	Pit.
May 10/70	Bos.	F	Bos. 4	St. L. 3	Bobby Orr	0:40	Bos.
Apr. 15/71	Tor.	QF	NYR 2	Tor. 1	Bob Nevin	9:07	NYR
Apr. 18/71	Chi.	SF	NYR 2	Chi. 1	Pete Stemkowski	1:37	Chi.
Apr. 27/71	Chi.	SF	Chi. 3	NYR 2	Bobby Hull	6:35	Chi.
Apr. 29/71	NY	SF	NYR 3	Chi. 2	Pete Stemkowski	41:29	Chi.
May 4/71	Chi.	F	Chi. 2	Mtl. 1	Jim Pappin	21:11	Mtl.
Apr. 6/72	Bos.	QF	Tor. 4	Bos. 3	Jim Harrison	2:58	Bos.
Apr. 6/72	Min.	QF	Min. 6	St. L. 5	Bill Goldsworthy	1:36	St. L.
Apr. 9/72	Pit.	QF	Chi. 6	Pit. 5	Pit Martin	0:12	Chi.
Apr. 16/72	Min.	QF	St. L. 2	Min. 1	Kevin O'Shea	10:07	St. L.
Apr. 1/73	Mtl.	QF	Buf. 3	Mtl. 2	René Robert	9:18	Mtl.
Apr. 10/73	Phi.	QF	Phi. 3	Min. 2	Gary Dornhoefer	8:35	Phi.
Apr. 14/73	Mtl.	SF	Phi. 5	Mtl. 4	Rick MacLeish	2:56	Mtl.
Apr. 17/73	Mtl.	SF	Mtl. 4	Phi. 3	Larry Robinson	6:45	Mtl.
Apr. 14/74	Tor.	QF	Bos. 4	Tor. 3	Ken Hodge	1:27	Bos.
Apr. 14/74	Atl.	QF	Phi. 4	Atl. 3	Dave Schultz	5:40	Phi.
Apr. 16/74	Mtl.	QF	NYR 3	Mtl. 2	Ron Harris	4:07	NYR
Apr. 23/74	Chi.	SF	Chi. 4	Bos. 3	Jim Pappin	3:48	Bos.
Apr. 28/74	NY	SF	NYR 2	Phi. 1	Rod Gilbert	4:20	Phi.
May 9/74	Bos.	F	Phi. 3	Bos. 2	Bobby Clarke	12:01	Phi.
Apr. 8/75	L.A.	PR	L.A. 3	Tor. 2	Mike Murphy	8:53	Tor.
Apr. 10/75	Tor.	PR	Tor. 3	L.A. 2	Blaine Stoughton	10:19	Tor.
Apr. 10/75	Chi.	PR	Chi. 4	Bos. 3	Ivan Boldirev	7:33	Chi.
Apr. 11/75	NY	PR	NYI 4	NYR 3	Jean-Paul Parise	0:11	NYI
Apr. 19/75	Tor.	QF	Phi. 4	Tor. 3	André Dupont	1:45	Phi.
Apr. 17/75	Chi.	QF	Chi. 5	Buf. 4	Stan Mikita	2:31	Buf.
Apr. 22/75	Mtl.	QF	Mtl. 5	Van. 4	Guy Lafleur	17:06	Mtl.
May 1/75	Phi.	SF	Phi. 5	NYI 4	Bobby Clarke	2:56	Phi.
May 7/75	NYI	SF	NYI 4	Phi. 3	Jude Drouin	1:53	Phi.
Apr. 27/75	Buf.	SF	Buf. 6	Mtl. 5	Danny Gare	4:42	Buf.
May 6/75	Buf.	SF	Buf. 5	Mtl. 4	René Robert	5:56	Buf.
May 20/75	Buf.	F	Buf. 5	Phi. 4	René Robert	18:29	Phi.
Apr. 8/76	Buf.	PR	Buf. 3	St. L. 2	Danny Gare	11:43	Buf.
Apr. 9/76	Buf.	PR	Buf. 2	St. L. 1	Don Luce	14:27	Buf.
Apr. 13/76	Bos.	QF	L.A. 3	Bos. 2	Butch Goring	0:27	Bos.
Apr. 13/76	Buf.	QF	Buf. 3	NYI 2	Danny Gare	14:04	NYI
Apr. 22/76	L.A.	QF	L.A. 4	Bos. 3	Butch Goring	18:28	Bos.
Apr. 29/76	Phi.	SF	Phi. 2	Bos. 1	Reggie Leach	13:38	Phi.
Apr. 15/77	Tor.	QF	Phi. 4	Tor. 3	Rick MacLeish	2:55	Phi.
Apr. 17/77	Tor.	QF	Phi. 6	Tor. 5	Reggie Leach	19:10	Phi.
Apr. 24/77	Phi.	SF	Bos. 4	Phi. 3	Rick Middleton	2:57	Bos.
Apr. 26/77	Phi.	SF	Bos. 5	Phi. 4	Terry O'Reilly	30:07	Bos.
May 3/77	Mtl.	SF	NYI 4	Mtl. 3	Billy Harris	3:58	Mtl.
May 14/77	Bos.	F	Mtl. 2	Bos. 1	Jacques Lemaire	4:32	Mtl.

Date	City	Series	Score		Scorer	Overtime	Series Winner
Apr. 11/78	Phi.	PR	Phi. 3	Col. 2	Mel Bridgman	0:23	Phi.
Apr. 13/78	NY	PR	NYR 4	Buf. 3	Don Murdoch	1:37	Buf.
Apr. 19/78	Bos.	QF	Bos. 4	Chi. 3	Terry O'Reilly	1:50	Bos.
Apr. 19/78	NYI	QF	NYI 3	Tor. 2	Mike Bossy	2:50	Tor.
Apr. 21/78	Chi.	QF	Bos. 4	Chi. 3	Peter McNab	10:17	Bos.
Apr. 25/78	NYI	QF	NYI 2	Tor. 1	Bob Nystrom	8:02	Tor.
Apr. 29/78	NYI	QF	Tor. 2	NYI 1	Lanny McDonald	4:13	Tor.
May 2/78	Bos.	SF	Bos. 3	Phi. 2	Rick Middleton	1:43	Bos.
May 16/78	Mtl.	F	Mtl. 3	Bos. 2	Guy Lafleur	13:09	Mtl.
May 21/78	Bos.	F	Bos. 4	Mtl. 3	Bobby Schmautz	6:22	Mtl.
Apr. 12/79	L.A.	PR	NYR 2	L.A. 1	Phil Esposito	6:11	NYR
Apr. 14/79	Buf.	PR	Pit. 4	Buf. 3	George Ferguson	0:47	Pit.
Apr. 16/79	Phi.	QF	Phi. 3	NYR 2	Ken Linseman	0:44	NYR
Apr. 18/79	NYI	QF	NYI 1	Chi. 0	Mike Bossy	2:31	NYI
Apr. 21/79	Tor.	QF	Mtl. 4	Tor. 3	Cam Connor	25:25	Mtl.
Apr. 22/79	Tor.	QF	Mtl. 5	Tor. 4	Larry Robinson	4:14	Mtl.
Apr. 28/79	NYI	SF	NYI 4	NYR 3	Denis Potvin	8:02	NYR
May 3/79	NY	SF	NYI 3	NYR 2	Bob Nystrom	3:40	NYR
May 3/79	Bos.	SF	Bos. 4	Mtl. 3	Jean Ratelle	3:46	Mtl.
May 10/79	Mtl.	SF	Mtl. 5	Bos. 4	Yvon Lambert	9:33	Mtl.
May 19/79	NY	F	Mtl. 4	NYR 3	Serge Savard	7:25	Mtl.
Apr. 8/80	NY	PR	NYR 2	Atl. 1	Steve Vickers	0:33	NYR
Apr. 8/80	Phi.	PR	Phi. 4	Edm. 3	Bobby Clarke	8:06	Phi.
Apr. 8/80	Chi.	PR	Chi. 3	St. L. 2	Doug Lecuyer	12:34	Chi.
Apr. 11/80	Hfd.	PR	Mtl. 4	Hfd. 3	Yvon Lambert	0:29	Mtl.
Apr. 11/80	Min.	PR	Min. 4	Tor. 3	Al MacAdam	0:32	Min.
Apr. 11/80	L.A.	PR	NYI 4	L.A. 3	Ken Morrow	6:55	NYI
Apr. 11/80	Edm.	PR	Phi. 3	Edm. 2	Ken Linseman	23:56	Phi.
Apr. 16/80	Bos.	QF	NYI 2	Bos. 1	Clark Gillies	1:02	NYI
Apr. 17/80	Bos.	QF	NYI 5	Bos. 4	Bob Bourne	1:24	NYI
Apr. 21/80	NYI	QF	Bos. 4	NYI 3	Terry O'Reilly	17:13	NYI
May 1/80	Buf.	SF	NYI 2	Buf. 1	Bob Nystrom	21:20	NYI
May 13/80	Phi.	F	NYI 4	Phi. 3	Denis Potvin	4:07	NYI
May 24/80	NYI	F	NYI 5	Phi. 4	Bob Nystrom	7:11	NYI
Apr. 8/81	Buf.	PR	Buf. 3	Van. 2	Alan Haworth	5:00	Buf.
Apr. 8/81	Bos.	PR	Min. 5	Bos. 4	Steve Payne	3:34	Min.
Apr. 11/81	Chi.	PR	Cgy. 5	Chi. 4	Willi Plett	35:17	Cgy.
Apr. 12/81	Que.	PR	Que. 4	Phi. 3	Dale Hunter	0:37	Phi.
Apr. 14/81	St. L.	PR	St. L. 4	Pit. 3	Mike Crombeen	25:16	St. L.
Apr. 16/81	Buf.	QF	Min. 4	Buf. 3	Steve Payne	0:22	Min.
Apr. 20/81	Min.	QF	Buf. 5	Min. 4	Craig Ramsay	16:32	Min.
Apr. 20/81	Edm.	QF	NYI 5	Edm. 4	Ken Morrow	5:41	NYI
Apr. 7/82	Min.	DSF	Chi. 3	Min. 2	Greg Fox	3:34	Chi.
Apr. 8/82	Edm.	DSF	Edm. 3	L.A. 2	Wayne Gretzky	6:20	L.A.
Apr. 8/82	Van.	DSF	Van. 2	Cgy. 1	Dave Williams	14:20	Van.
Apr. 10/82	Pit.	DSF	Pit. 2	NYI 1	Rick Kehoe	4:14	NYI
Apr. 10/82	L.A.	DSF	L.A. 6	Edm. 5	Daryl Evans	2:35	L.A.
Apr. 13/82	Mtl.	DSF	Que. 3	Mtl. 2	Dale Hunter	0:22	Que.
Apr. 13/82	NY	DSF	NYI 4	Pit. 3	John Tonelli	6:19	NYI
Apr. 16/82	Van.	DF	L.A. 3	Van. 2	Steve Bozek	4:33	Van.
Apr. 18/82	Que.	DF	Que. 3	Bos. 2	Wilf Paiement	11:44	Que.
Apr. 18/82	NY	DF	NYI 4	NYR 3	Bryan Trottier	3:00	NYI
Apr. 18/82	L.A.	DF	Van. 4	L.A. 3	Colin Campbell	1:23	Van.
Apr. 21/82	St. L.	DF	St. L. 3	Chi. 2	Bernie Federko	3:28	Chi.
Apr. 23/82	Que.	DF	Bos. 6	Que. 5	Peter McNab	10:54	Que.
Apr. 27/82	Chi.	CF	Van. 2	Chi. 1	Jim Nill	28:58	Van.
May 1/82	Que.	CF	NYI 5	Que. 4	Wayne Merrick	16:52	NYI
May 8/82	NYI	F	NYI 6	Van. 5	Mike Bossy	19:58	NYI
Apr. 5/83	Bos.	DSF	Bos. 4	Que. 3	Barry Pederson	1:46	Bos.
Apr. 6/83	Cgy.	DSF	Cgy. 4	Van. 3	Eddy Beers	12:27	Cgy.
Apr. 7/83	Min.	DSF	Min. 5	Tor. 4	Bobby Smith	5:03	Min.
Apr. 10/83	Tor.	DSF	Min. 5	Tor. 4	Dino Ciccarelli	8:05	Min.
Apr. 10/83	Van.	DSF	Cgy. 4	Van. 3	Greg Meredith	1:06	Cgy.
Apr. 18/83	Min.	DF	Chi. 4	Min. 3	Rich Preston	10:34	Chi.
Apr. 24/83	Bos.	DF	Bos. 3	Buf. 2	Brad Park	1:52	Bos.
Apr. 5/84	Edm.	DSF	Edm. 5	Wpg. 4	Randy Gregg	0:21	Edm.
Apr. 7/84	Det.	DSF	St. L. 4	Det. 3	Mark Reeds	37:07	St. L.
Apr. 8/84	Det.	DSF	St. L. 3	Det. 2	Jorgen Pettersson	2:42	St. L.
Apr. 10/84	NYI	DSF	NYI 3	NYR 2	Ken Morrow	8:56	NYI
Apr. 13/84	Min.	DF	St. L. 4	Min. 3	Doug Gilmour	16:16	Min.
Apr. 13/84	Edm.	DF	Cgy. 6	Edm. 5	Carey Wilson	3:42	Edm.
Apr. 13/84	NYI	DF	NYI 5	Wsh. 4	Anders Kallur	7:35	NYI
Apr. 16/84	Mtl.	DF	Que. 4	Mtl. 3	Bo Berglund	3:00	Mtl.
Apr. 20/84	Cgy.	DF	Cgy. 5	Edm. 4	Lanny McDonald	1:04	Edm.
Apr. 22/84	Min.	DF	Min. 4	St. L. 3	Steve Payne	6:00	Min.
Apr. 10/85	Phi.	DSF	Phi. 5	NYR 4	Mark Howe	8:01	Phi.

Tony Leswick's flip shot from the blueline at the 4:29 mark of overtime in game seven of the 1954 Stanley Cup Finals ticked off Montreal defenceman Doug Harvey's glove and went in, giving Detroit a 2-1 victory over the Canadiens.

Date	City	Series	Score	Scorer	Overtime	Series Winner
Apr. 10/85	Wsh.	DSF	Wsh. 4 NYI 3	Alan Haworth	2:28	NYI
Apr. 10/85	Edm.	DSF	L.A. 4 Edm. 3	Lee Fogolin	3:01	Edm.
Apr. 10/85	Wpg.	DSF	Wpg. 5 Cgy. 4	Brian Mullen	7:56	Wpg.
Apr. 11/85	Wsh.	DSF	Wsh. 2 NYI 1	Mike Gartner	21:23	NYI
Apr. 13/85	L.A.	DSF	L.A. 4 Edm. 3	Glenn Anderson	0:46	Edm.
Apr. 18/85	Mtl.	DF	Que. 2 Mtl. 1	Mark Kumpel	12:23	Que.
Apr. 23/85	Que.	DF	Que. 7 Mtl. 6	Dale Hunter	18:36	Que.
May 2/85	Mtl.	DF	Que. 3 Mtl. 2	Peter Stastny	2:22	Que.
Apr. 25/85	Min.	DF	Chi. 7 Min. 6	Darryl Sutter	21:57	Chi.
Apr. 28/85	Chi.	DF	Min. 5 Chi. 4	Dennis Maruk	1:14	Chi.
Apr. 30/85	Min.	DF	Chi. 6 Min. 5	Darryl Sutter	15:41	Chi.
May 5/85	Que.	CF	Que. 2 Phi. 1	Peter Stastny	6:20	Phi.
Apr. 9/86	Que.	DSF	Que. 2 Hfd. 1	Sylvain Turgeon	2:36	Hfd.
Apr. 12/86	Wpg.	DSF	Cgy. 4 Wpg. 3	Lanny McDonald	8:25	Cgy.
Apr. 17/86	Wsh.	DF	NYR 4 Wsh. 3	Brian MacLellan	1:16	NYR
Apr. 20/86	Edm.	DF	Edm. 6 Cgy. 5	Glenn Anderson	1:04	Cgy.
Apr. 23/86	Hfd.	DF	Hfd. 2 Mtl. 1	Kevin Dineen	1:07	Mtl.
Apr. 23/86	NYR	DF	NYR 6 Wsh. 5	Bob Brooke	2:40	NYR
Apr. 26/86	St L.	DF	St L. 4 Tor. 3	Mark Reeds	7:11	St L.
Apr. 29/86	Mtl.	DF	Mtl. 2 Hfd. 1	Claude Lemieux	5:55	Mtl.
May 5/86	NYR	CF	Mtl. 4 NYR 3	Claude Lemieux	9:41	Mtl.
May 12/86	St L.	CF	St L. 6 Cgy. 5	Doug Wickenheiser	7:30	Cgy.
May 18/86	Cgy.	F	Mtl. 3 Cgy. 2	Brian Skrudland	0:09	Mtl.
Apr. 8/87	Hfd.	DSF	Hfd. 3 Que. 2	Paul MacDermid	2:20	Que.
Apr. 9/87	Mtl.	DSF	Mtl. 4 Bos. 3	Mats Naslund	2:38	Mtl.
Apr. 9/87	St. L.	DSF	Tor. 3 St. L. 2	Rick Lanz	10:17	Tor.
Apr. 11/87	Wpg.	DSF	Cgy. 3 Wpg. 2	Mike Bullard	3:53	Wpg.
Apr. 11/87	Chi.	DSF	Det. 4 Chi. 3	Shawn Burr	4:51	Det.
Apr. 16/87	Que.	DSF	Que. 5 Hfd. 4	Peter Stastny	6:05	Que.
Apr. 18/87	Wsh.	DSF	NYI 3 Wsh. 2	Pat LaFontaine	68:47	NYI
Apr. 21/87	Edm.	DF	Edm. 3 Wpg. 2	Glenn Anderson	0:36	Edm.
Apr. 26/87	Que.	DF	Mtl. 3 Que. 2	Mats Naslund	5:30	Mtl.
Apr. 27/87	Tor.	DF	Tor. 3 Det. 2	Mike Allison	9:31	Det.
May 4/87	Phi.	CF	Phi. 4 Mtl. 3	Ilkka Sinislao	9:11	Phi.
May 20/87	Edm.	F	Edm. 3 Phi. 2	Jari Kurri	6:50	Edm.
Apr. 6/88	NYI	DSF	NYI 4 N.J. 3	Pat LaFontaine	6:11	N.J.
Apr. 10/88	Phi.	DSF	Phi. 5 Wsh. 4	Murray Craven	1:18	Wsh.
Apr. 10/88	N.J.	DSF	NYI 5 N.J. 4	Brent Sutter	15:07	N.J.
Apr. 10/88	Buf.	DSF	Buf. 6 Bos. 5	John Tucker	5:32	Bos.
Apr. 12/88	Det.	DSF	Tor. 6 Det. 5	Ed Olczyk	0:34	Det.
Apr. 16/88	Wsh.	DSF	Wsh. 5 Phi. 4	Dale Hunter	5:57	Wsh.
Apr. 21/88	Cgy.	DF	Edm. 4 Cgy. 3	Wayne Gretzky	7:54	Edm.
May 4/88	Bos.	CF	N.J. 3 Bos. 2	Doug Brown	17:46	Bos.
May 9/88	Det.	CF	Edm. 4 Det. 3	Jari Kurri	11:02	Edm.
Apr. 5/89	St. L.	DSF	St. L. 4 Min. 3	Brett Hull	11:55	St. L.
Apr. 5/89	Cgy.	DSF	Van. 4 Cgy. 3	Paul Reinhart	2:47	Cgy.
Apr. 6/89	St. L.	DSF	St. L. 4 Min. 3	Rick Meagher	5:30	St. L.
Apr. 6/89	Det.	DSF	Chi. 5 Det. 4	Duane Sutter	14:36	Chi.
Apr. 8/89	Hfd.	DSF	Mtl. 5 Hfd. 4	Stephane Richer	5:01	Mtl.
Apr. 8/89	Phi.	DSF	Wsh. 4 Phi. 3	Kelly Miller	0:51	Phi.
Apr. 9/89	Hfd.	DSF	Mtl. 4 Hfd. 3	Russ Courtnall	15:12	Mtl.
Apr. 15/89	Cgy.	DSF	Cgy. 4 Van. 3	Joel Otto	19:21	Cgy.
Apr. 18/89	Cgy.	DF	Cgy. 4 L.A. 3	Doug Gilmour	7:47	Cgy.
Apr. 19/89	Mtl.	DF	Mtl. 3 Bos. 2	Bobby Smith	12:24	Mtl.
Apr. 20/89	St. L.	DF	St. L. 5 Chi. 4	Tony Hrkac	33:49	Chi.
Apr. 21/89	Phi.	DF	Pit. 4 Phi. 3	Phil Bourque	12:08	Phi.
May 8/89	Chi.	CF	Cgy. 2 Chi. 1	Al MacInnis	15:05	Cgy.
May 9/89	Mtl.	CF	Phi. 2 Mtl. 1	Dave Poulin	5:02	Mtl.
May 19/89	Mtl.	F	Mtl. 4 Cgy. 3	Ryan Walter	38:08	Cgy.
Apr. 5/90	N.J.	DSF	Wsh. 5 N.J. 4	Dino Ciccarelli	5:34	Wsh.
Apr. 6/90	Edm.	DSF	Edm. 3 Wpg. 2	Mark Lamb	4:21	Edm.
Apr. 8/90	Tor.	DSF	St. L. 6 Tor. 5	Sergio Momesso	6:04	St. L.
Apr. 8/90	L.A.	DSF	L.A. 2 Cgy. 1	Tony Granato	8:37	L.A.
Apr. 9/90	Mtl.	DSF	Mtl. 2 Buf. 1	Brian Skrudland	12:35	Mtl.
Apr. 9/90	NYI	DSF	NYI 4 NYR 3	Brent Sutter	20:59	NYR
Apr. 10/90	Wpg.	DSF	Wpg. 4 Edm. 3	Dave Ellett	21:08	Edm.
Apr. 14/90	L.A.	DSF	L.A. 4 Cgy. 3	Mike Krushelnyski	23:14	L.A.
Apr. 15/90	Hfd.	DSF	Hfd. 3 Bos. 2	Kevin Dineen	12:30	Bos.
Apr. 21/90	Bos.	DF	Bos. 5 Mtl. 4	Garry Galley	3:42	Bos.
Apr. 24/90	L.A.	DF	Edm. 6 L.A. 5	Joe Murphy	4:42	Edm.
Apr. 25/90	Wsh.	DF	Wsh. 4 NYR 3	Rod Langway	0:34	Wsh.
Apr. 27/90	NYR	DF	Wsh. 2 NYR 1	John Druce	6:48	Wsh.
May 15/90	Bos.	F	Edm. 3 Bos. 2	Petr Klima	55:13	Edm.
Apr. 4/91	Chi.	DSF	Min. 4 Chi. 3	Brian Propp	4:14	Min.
Apr. 5/91	Pit.	DSF	Pit. 5 N.J. 4	Jaromir Jagr	8:52	Pit.
Apr. 6/91	L.A.	DSF	L.A. 3 Van. 2	Wayne Gretzky	11:08	L.A.
Apr. 8/91	Van.	DSF	Van. 2 L.A. 1	Cliff Ronning	3:12	L.A.
Apr. 11/91	NYR	DSF	Wsh. 5 NYR 4	Dino Ciccarelli	6:44	Wsh.
Apr. 11/91	Mtl.	DSF	Mtl. 4 Buf. 3	Russ Courtnall	5:56	Mtl.
Apr. 14/91	Edm.	DF	Cgy. 2 Edm. 1	Theo Fleury	4:40	Edm.
Apr. 16/91	Cgy.	DSF	Edm. 5 Cgy. 4	Esa Tikkanen	6:58	Edm.
Apr. 18/91	L.A.	DF	L.A. 4 Edm. 3	Luc Robitaille	2:13	Edm.
Apr. 19/91	Bos.	DF	Mtl. 4 Bos. 3	Stephane Richer	0:27	Bos.
Apr. 19/91	Pit.	DF	Pit. 7 Wsh. 6	Kevin Stevens	8:10	Pit.
Apr. 20/91	L.A.	DF	Edm. 4 L.A. 3	Petr Klima	24:48	Edm.
Apr. 22/91	Edm.	DF	Edm. 4 L.A. 3	Esa Tikkanen	20:48	Edm.
Apr. 27/91	Mtl.	DF	Mtl. 3 Bos. 2	Shayne Corson	17:47	Bos.
Apr. 28/91	Edm.	DF	Edm. 4 L.A. 3	Craig MacTavish	16:57	Edm.
May 3/91	Bos.	CF	Bos. 5 Pit. 4	Vladimir Ruzicka	8:14	Pit.
Apr. 21/92	Bos.	DSF	Bos. 3 Buf. 2	Adam Oates	11:24	Bos.
Apr. 22/92	Det.	DSF	Det. 5 Min. 4	Yves Racine	1:15	Det.
Apr. 22/92	St. L.	DSF	St. L. 5 Chi. 4	Brett Hull	23:33	Chi.
Apr. 25/92	Buf.	DSF	Bos. 5 Buf. 4	Ted Donato	2:08	Bos.
Apr. 28/92	Det.	DSF	Det. 1 Min. 0	Sergei Fedorov	16:13	Det.
Apr. 29/92	Hfd.	DSF	Hfd. 2 Mon. 1	Yvon Corriveau	0:24	Mtl.
May 1/92	Mtl.	DSF	Mtl. 3 Hfd. 2	Russ Courtnall	25:26	Mtl.
May 3/92	Van.	DF	Edm. 4 Van. 3	Joe Murphy	8:36	Edm.
May 5/92	Mtl.	DF	Bos. 3 Mtl. 2	Peter Douris	3:12	Bos.
May 7/92	Pit.	DF	NYR 6 Pit. 5	Kris King	1:29	Pit.
May 9/92	Pit.	DF	Pit. 5 NYR 4	Ron Francis	2:47	Pit.
May 17/92	Pit.	CF	Pit. 4 Bos. 3	Jaromir Jagr	9:44	Pit.
May 20/92	Edm.	CF	Chi. 4 Edm. 3	Jeremy Roenick	2:45	Chi.
Apr. 18/93	Bos.	DSF	Buf. 5 Bos. 4	Bob Sweeney	11:03	Buf.
Apr. 18/93	Que.	DSF	Que. 3 Mtl. 2	Scott Young	16:49	Mtl.
Apr. 20/93	Wsh.	DSF	NYI 5 Wsh. 4	Brian Mullen	34:50	NYI
Apr. 22/93	Mtl.	DSF	Mtl. 2 Que. 1	Vincent Damphousse	10:30	Mtl.
Apr. 22/93	Buf.	DSF	Buf. 4 Bos. 3	Yuri Khmylev	1:05	Buf.
Apr. 22/93	NYI	DSF	NYI 4 Wsh. 3	Ray Ferraro	4:46	NYI
Apr. 24/93	Buf.	DSF	Buf. 6 Bos. 5	Brad May	4:48	Buf.
Apr. 24/93	NYI	DSF	NYI 4 Wsh. 3	Ray Ferraro	25:40	NYI
Apr. 25/93	St. L.	DSF	St. L. 4 Chi. 3	Craig Janney	10:43	St. L.
Apr. 26/93	Que.	DSF	Mtl. 5 Que. 4	Kirk Muller	8:17	Mtl.
Apr. 27/93	Det.	DSF	Tor. 5 Det. 4	Mike Foligno	2:05	Tor.
Apr. 27/93	Van.	DSF	Wpg. 4 Van. 3	Teemu Selanne	6:18	Van.
Apr. 29/93	Wpg.	DSF	Van. 4 Wpg. 3	Greg Adams	4:30	Van.
May 1/93	Det.	DSF	Tor. 4 Det. 3	Nikolai Borschevsky	2:35	Tor.
May 3/93	Tor.	DF	Tor. 2 St. L. 1	Doug Gilmour	23:16	Tor.
May 4/93	Mtl.	DF	Mtl. 4 Buf. 3	Guy Carbonneau	2:50	Mtl.
May 5/93	Tor.	DF	St. L. 2 Tor. 1	Jeff Brown	23:03	Tor.
May 6/93	Buf.	DF	Mtl. 4 Buf. 3	Gilbert Dionne	8:28	Mtl.
May 8/93	Buf.	DF	Mtl. 4 Buf. 3	Kirk Muller	11:37	Mtl.
May 11/93	Van.	DF	L.A. 4 Van. 3	Gary Shuchuk	26:31	L.A.
May 14/93	Pit.	DF	NYI 4 Pit. 3	Dave Volek	5:16	NYI
May 18/93	Mtl.	CF	Mtl. 4 NYI 3	Stephan Lebeau	26:21	Mtl.
May 20/93	NYI	CF	Mtl. 2 NYI 1	Guy Carbonneau	12:34	Mtl.
May 25/93	Tor.	CF	Tor. 3 L.A. 2	Glenn Anderson	19:20	L.A.
May 27/93	L.A.	CF	L.A. 5 Tor. 4	Wayne Gretzky	1:41	L.A.
Jun. 3/93	Mtl.	F	Mtl. 3 L.A. 2	Eric Desjardins	0:51	Mtl.
Jun. 5/93	L.A.	F	Mtl. 4 L.A. 3	John LeClair	0:34	Mtl.
Jun. 7/93	L.A.	F	Mtl. 3 L.A. 2	John LeClair	14:37	Mtl.

Eric Desjardins became the first defenceman in NHL history to score three goals in a Stanley Cup Final series game on June 3, 1993. He completed his record-breaking hat-trick by scoring 51 seconds into overtime to give the Montreal Canadiens a 3-2 victory over the Los Angeles Kings in game two of the 1993 finals.

Date	City	Series	Score	Scorer	Overtime	Series Winner
Apr. 20/94	Tor.	CQF	Tor. 1 Chi. 0	Todd Gill	2:15	Tor.
Apr. 22/94	St. L.	CQF	Dal. 5 St. L. 4	Paul Cavallini	8:34	Dal.
Apr. 24/94	Chi.	CQF	Chi. 4 Tor. 3	Jeremy Roenick	1:23	Tor.
Apr. 25/94	Bos.	CQF	Mtl. 2 Bos. 1	Kirk Muller	17:18	Bos.
Apr. 26/94	Cgy.	CQF	Van. 2 Cgy. 1	Geoff Courtnall	7:15	Van.
Apr. 27/94	Buf.	CQF	Buf. 1 N.J. 0	Dave Hannan	65:43	N.J.
Apr. 28/94	Van.	CQF	Van. 3 Cgy. 2	Trevor Linden	16:43	Van.
Apr. 30/94	Cgy.	CQF	Van. 4 Cgy. 3	Pavel Bure	22:20	Van.
May 3/94	N.J.	CSF	Bos. 6 N.J. 5	Don Sweeney	9:08	N.J.
May 7/94	Bos.	CSF	N.J. 5 Bos. 4	Stephane Richer	14:19	N.J.
May 8/94	Van.	CSF	Van. 2 Dal. 1	Sergio Momesso	11:01	Van.
May 12/94	Tor.	CSF	Tor. 3 S.J. 2	Mike Gartner	8:53	Tor.
May 15/94	NYR	CF	NYR 4 N.J. 3	Stephane Richer	35:23	NYR
May 16/94	Tor.	CF	Tor. 3 Van. 2	Peter Zezel	16:55	Van.
May 19/94	N.J.	CF	NYR 3 N.J. 2	Stephane Matteau	26:13	NYR
May 24/94	Van.	CF	Van. 4 Tor. 3	Greg Adams	20:14	Van.
May 27/94	NYR	CF	NYR 2 N.J. 1	Stephane Matteau	24:24	NYR
May 31/94	NYR	F	Van. 3 NYR 2	Greg Adams	19:26	NYR

Jacques Demers, below, proudly raises the Stanley Cup after the Montreal Canadiens defeated the Los Angeles Kings in five games to win the 1993 championship. Demers-coached clubs have reached the playoffs eight times. Dick Irvin, Sr., right, is a Hall-of-Fame player who coached Chicago, Toronto, Montreal during a career behind the bench that spanned from 1930 to 1956. Irvin won four Stanley Cup championships

Stanley Cup
Coaching Records

Coaches listed in order of total games coached in playoffs. Minimum: 65 games.

Coach	Team	Years	Series	Series W	L	G	Games W	L	T	Cups	%
Bowman, Scott	St. Louis	4	10	6	4	52	26	26	0	0	.500
	Montreal	8	19	16	3	98	70	28	0	5	.714
	Buffalo	5	8	3	5	36	18	18	0	0	.500
	Pittsburgh	2	6	5	1	33	23	10	0	1	.696
	Detroit	1	1	0	1	7	3	4	0	0	.428
	Total	20	44	30	14	226	140	86	0	6	**.619**
Arbour, Al	St. Louis	1	2	1	1	11	4	7	0	0	.364
	NY Islanders	15	40	29	11	198	119	79	0	4	.601
	Total	16	42	30	12	209	123	86	0	4	**.589**
Irvin, Dick	Chicago	1	3	2	1	9	5	3	1	0	.611
	Toronto	9	20	12	8	66	33	32	1	1	.508
	Montreal	14	22	11	11	115	62	53	0	3	.539
	Total	24	45	25	20	190	100	88	2	4	**.532**
Keenan, Mike	Philadelphia	4	10	6	4	57	32	25	0	0	.561
	Chicago	4	11	7	4	60	33	27	0	0	.550
	NY Rangers	1	4	4	0	23	16	7	0	1	.695
	Total	9	25	17	8	140	81	59	0	1	**.578**
Sather, Glen	Edmonton	10	27	21	6	*126	89	37	0	4	**.706**
Blake, Toe	Montreal	13	23	18	5	119	82	37	0	8	**.689**
Reay, Billy	Chicago	12	22	10	12	117	57	60	0	0	**.487**
Shero, Fred	Philadelphia	6	16	12	4	83	48	35	0	2	.578
	NY Rangers	2	5	3	2	25	13	12	0	0	.520
	Total	8	21	15	6	108	61	47	0	2	**.565**
Adams, Jack	Detroit	15	27	15	12	105	52	52	1	3	**.500**
Demers, Jacques	St. Louis	3	6	3	3	33	16	17	0	0	.485
	Detroit	3	7	4	3	38	20	18	0	0	.526
	Montreal	2	5	4	1	27	19	8	0	1	.704
	Total	8	18	11	7	98	55	43	0	1	**.561**
Quinn, Pat	Philadelphia	3	8	5	3	39	22	17	0	0	.564
	Los Angeles	1	1	0	1	3	0	3	0	0	.000
	Vancouver	4	9	5	4	55	29	26	0	0	.527
	Total	8	18	10	8	97	51	46	0	0	**.525**
Burns, Pat	Montreal	4	10	6	4	56	30	26	0	0	.535
	Toronto	2	6	4	2	39	20	19	0	0	.512
	Total	6	16	10	6	95	50	45	0	0	**.526**
Francis, Emile	NY Rangers	9	14	5	9	75	34	41	0	0	.453
	St. Louis	3	4	1	3	18	6	12	0	0	.333
	Total	12	18	6	12	93	40	53	0	0	**.430**
Imlach, Punch	Toronto	11	17	10	7	92	44	48	0	4	**.478**
Day, Hap	Toronto	9	14	10	4	80	49	31	0	5	**.613**
Murray, Bryan	Washington	7	10	3	7	53	24	29	0	0	.452
	Detroit	3	4	1	3	25	10	15	0	0	.400
	Total	10	14	4	10	78	34	44	0	0	**.435**
Johnson, Bob	Calgary	5	10	5	5	52	25	27	0	0	.481
	Pittsburgh	1	4	4	0	24	16	8	0	1	.666
	Total	6	14	9	5	76	41	35	0	1	**.539**
Abel, Sid	Chicago	1	1	0	1	7	3	4	0	0	.429
	Detroit	8	12	4	8	69	29	40	0	0	.420
	Total	9	13	4	9	76	32	44	0	0	**.421**
Ross, Art	Boston	12	19	9	10	70	32	33	5	2	**.493**
Bergeron, Michel	Quebec	7	13	6	7	68	31	37	0	0	**.456**
Ivan, Tommy	Detroit	7	12	8	4	67	36	31	0	3	**.537**
Neilson, Roger	Toronto	2	5	3	2	19	8	11	0	0	.421
	Buffalo	1	2	1	1	8	4	4	0	0	.500
	Vancouver	2	5	3	2	21	12	9	0	0	.571
	NY Rangers	2	3	1	2	19	8	11	0	0	.421
	Total	7	15	8	7	67	32	35	0	0	**.473**
Pulford, Bob	Los Angeles	4	6	2	4	26	11	15	0	0	.423
	Chicago	5	9	4	5	41	17	24	0	0	.415
	Total	9	15	6	9	67	28	39	0	0	**.418**
Patrick, Lester	NY Rangers	12	24	14	10	65	31	26	8	2	**.538**

* Does not include suspended game, May 24, 1988.

Penalty Shots in Stanley Cup Playoff Games

Date	Player	Goaltender	Scored	Final Score				Series
Mar. 25/37	Lionel Conacher, Mtl. Maroons	Tiny Thompson, Boston	No	Mtl. M.	0	at Bos.	4	QF
Apr. 15/37	Alex Shibicky, NY Rangers	Earl Robertson, Detroit	No	NYR	0	at Det.	3	F
Apr. 13/44	Virgil Johnson, Chicago	Bill Durnan, Montreal	No	Chi.	4	at Mtl.	5*	F
Apr. 9/68	Wayne Connelly, Minnesota	Terry Sawchuk, Los Angeles	Yes	L.A.	5	at Min.	7	QF
Apr. 27/68	Jim Roberts, St. Louis	Cesare Maniago, Minnesota	No	St. L.	4	at Min.	3	SF
May 16/71	Frank Mahovlich, Montreal	Tony Esposito, Chicago	No	Chi.	3	at Mtl.	4	F
May 7/75	Bill Barber, Philadelphia	Glenn Resch, NY Islanders	No	Phi.	3	at NYI	4*	SF
Apr. 20/79	Mike Walton, Chicago	Glenn Resch, NY Islanders	No	NYI	4	at Chi.	0	QF
Apr. 9/81	Peter McNab, Boston	Don Beaupre, Minnesota	No	Min.	5	at Bos.	4*	PR
Apr. 17/81	Anders Hedberg, NY Rangers	Mike Liut, St. Louis	Yes	NYR	6	at St. L.	4	QF
Apr. 9/83	Denis Potvin, NY Islanders	Pat Riggin, Washington	No	NYI	6	at Wsh.	2	DSF
Apr. 28/84	Wayne Gretzky, Edmonton	Don Beaupre, Minnesota	Yes	Edm.	8	at Min.	5	CF
May 1/84	Mats Naslund, Montreal	Bill Smith, NY Islanders	No	Mtl.	1	at NYI	3	CF
Apr. 14/85	Bob Carpenter, Washington	Bill Smith, NY Islanders	No	Wsh.	4	at NYI.	6	DF
May 28/85	Ron Sutter, Philadelphia	Grant Fuhr, Edmonton	No	Phi.	3	at Edm.	5	F
May 30/85	Dave Poulin, Philadelphia	Grant Fuhr, Edmonton	No	Phi.	3	at Edm.	8	F
Apr. 9/88	John Tucker, Buffalo	Andy Moog, Boston	Yes	Bos.	2	at Buf.	6	DSF
Apr. 9/88	Petr Klima, Detroit	Allan Bester, Toronto	Yes	Det.	6	at Tor.	3	DSF
Apr. 8/89	Neal Broten, Minnesota	Greg Millen, St. Louis	Yes	St. L.	5	at Min.	3	DSF
Apr. 4/90	Al MacInnis, Calgary	Kelly Hrudey, Los Angeles	Yes	L.A.	5	at Cgy.	3	DSF
Apr. 5/90	Randy Wood, NY Islanders	Mike Richter, NY Rangers	No	NYI	1	at NYR	2	DSF
May 3/90	Kelly Miller, Washington	Andy Moog, Boston	No	Wsh.	3	at Bos.	5	CF
May 18/90	Petr Klima, Edmonton	Rejean Lemelin, Boston	No	Edm.	7	at Bos.	2	F
Apr. 6/91	Basil McRae, Minnesota	Ed Belfour, Chicago	Yes	Min.	2	at Chi.	5	DSF
Apr. 10/91	Steve Duchesne, Los Angeles	Kirk McLean, Vancouver	Yes	L.A.	6	at Van.	1	DSF
May 11/92	Jaromir Jagr, Pittsburgh	John Vanbiesbrouck, NYR	Yes	Pit.	3	at NYR	2	DF
May 13/92	Shawn McEachern, Pittsburgh	John Vanbiesbrouck, NYR	No	NYR	1	at Pit.	5	DF
June 7/94	Pavel Bure, Vancouver	Mike Richter, NYR	No	NYR	4	at Van.	2	F

* Game was decided in overtime, but shot taken during regulation time.

Buffalo's Dave Hannan ended the sixth longest playoff game in NHL history when he backhanded the puck past New Jersey's Martin Brodeur after 65 minutes and 43 seconds of overtime on April 27, 1994.

Ten Longest Overtime Games

Date	City	Series	Score				Scorer	Overtime	Series Winner
Mar. 24/36	Mtl.	SF	Det. 1	Mtl. M.	0		Mud Bruneteau	116:30	Det.
Apr. 3/33	Tor.	SF	Tor. 1	Bos.	0		Ken Doraty	104:46	Tor.
Mar. 23/43	Det.	SF	Tor. 3	Det.	2		Jack McLean	70:18	Det.
Mar. 28/30	Mtl.	SF	Mtl. 2	NYR	1		Gus Rivers	68:52	Mtl.
Apr. 18/87	Wsh.	DSF	NYI 3	Wsh.	2		Pat LaFontaine	68:47	NYI
Apr. 27/94	**Buf.**	**CQF**	**Buf. 1**	**N.J.**	**0**		**Dave Hannan**	**65:43**	**N.J.**
Mar. 27/51	Det.	SF	Mtl. 3	Det.	2		Maurice Richard	61:09	Mtl.
Mar. 27/38	NY	QF	NYA 3	NYR	2		Lorne Carr	60:40	NYA
Mar. 26/32	Mtl.	SF	NYR 4	Mtl.	3		Fred Cook	59:32	NYR
Mar. 21/39	NY	SF	Bos. 2	NYR	1		Mel Hill	59:25	Bos.

Overtime Record of Current Teams

(Listed by number of OT games played)

Team	Overall				Home				Last OT Game	Road				Last OT Game
	GP	W	L	T	GP	W	L	T		GP	W	L	T	
Montreal	115	66	47	2	53	35	17	1	Jun. 3/93	62	31	30	1	Apr. 25/94
Boston	92	36	53	3	43	20	22	1	May 9/94	49	16	31	2	May 3/94
Toronto	86	43	42	1	54	27	26	1	May 16/94	32	16	16	0	May 24/94
NY Rangers	56	26	30	0	24	10	14	0	May 31/94	32	16	16	0	May 19/94
Detroit	51	22	29	0	31	10	21	0	May 1/93	20	12	8	0	Apr. 28/92
Chicago	49	23	24	2	24	13	10	1	Apr. 24/94	25	10	14	1	Apr. 24/94
NY Islanders	38	29	9	0	17	14	3	0	May 20/93	21	15	6	0	May 18/93
Philadelphia	34	18	16	0	13	8	5	0	Apr. 21/89	21	10	11	0	May 9/89
St. Louis	32	19	13	0	16	13	3	0	Apr. 22/94	16	6	10	0	May 5/93
Los Angeles	30	12	18	0	16	8	8	0	Jun. 7/93	14	4	10	0	Jun. 3/93
* Dallas	28	12	16	0	14	5	9	0	Apr. 28/92	14	7	7	0	May 8/94
Edmonton	27	17	10	0	14	9	5	0	May 20/92	13	8	5	0	May 3/92
Buffalo	27	14	13	0	17	11	6	0	Apr. 27/94	10	3	7	0	May 4/93
** Calgary	27	11	16	0	11	4	7	0	Apr. 30/94	16	7	9	0	Apr. 28/94
Vancouver	24	12	12	0	10	5	5	0	May 24/94	14	7	7	0	May 31/94
Quebec	18	10	8	0	11	6	5	0	Apr. 26/93	7	4	3	0	Apr. 22/93
Washington	17	8	9	0	7	4	3	0	Apr. 20/93	10	4	6	0	Apr. 24/93
Pittsburgh	14	8	6	0	8	5	3	0	May 14/93	6	3	3	0	May 3/91
*** New Jersey	12	3	9	0	4	0	4	0	May 19/94	8	3	5	0	May 27/94
Hartford	11	5	6	0	7	4	3	0	Apr. 29/92	4	1	3	0	May 1/92
Winnipeg	9	4	5	0	5	2	3	0	Apr. 29/93	4	2	2	0	Apr. 27/93
San Jose	1	0	1	0	0	0	0	0		1	0	1	0	May 12/94

*Totals include those of Minnesota 1967-93.
**Totals include those of Atlanta 1972-80.
***Totals include those of Kansas City and Colorado 1974-82.

Glenn "Chico" Resch faced two playoff penalty shots in his career, stopping Bill Barber in 1975 and Mike Walton in 1979.

Key to Player and Goaltender Registers

Demographics: Position, shooting side (catching hand for goaltenders), height, weight, place and date of birth are found on first line. Draft information, if any, is located on second line.

Major Junior, NCAA, minor pro, senior European and NHL clubs form a permanent part of each player's data panel. If a player sees action with more than one club in any of the above categories, a separate line is included for each one.

High school, prep school, Tier II junior, European junior and U.S. junior listings are deleted if a player accumulates two or more years of Major Junior, NCAA or senior European experience.

Canadian and U.S. National Team statistics are also listed. Olympic Team participation is included as a separate line if a player joins an NHL club at the conclusion of the Games.

Some data is unavailable at press time. Readers are encouraged to contribute.
See page 5 for contact names and addresses.

Player's NHL organization as of August 19, 1994. This includes players under contract and/or on reserve lists. Free agents as of August 19, 1994 show a blank here.

The complete career data panel of players with NHL experience who announced their retirement before the start of the 1994-95 season are included in the 1994-95 Player Register. These newly-retired players also show a blank here.

Each NHL club's minor-pro affiliates are listed at the bottom of this page.

Footnotes are listed below player's year-by-year data and indicate league awards and all-star selections. Letter corresponding to footnote is placed beside the season in which awards or all-star selections were received.

PLAYER, JOHN SAMPLE   (PLAY-uhr)   **S.J.**
Center. Shoots left, 6'1", 200 lbs.   Born, Neepawa, Man., April 14, 1973.
(Pittsburgh's 3rd choice, 62nd overall in the 1991 Entry Draft).

| | | | Regular Season | | | | | Playoffs | | | | |
Season	Club	League	GP	G	A	TP	PIM	GP	G	A	TP	PIM
1989-90	Brandon	WHL	66	15	13	28	17	4	3	1	4	6
1990-91	Brandon	WHL	72	36	30	66	72	12	4	5	9	12
1991-92ab	Brandon	WHL	70	47	59	106	83	16	*16	8	*24	14
1992-93	**Pittsburgh**	**NHL**	10	1	2	3	6	....	....	....	....	....
	Cleveland	IHL	64	31	22	53	71	5	3	2	5	8
1993-94	**Montreal**	**NHL**	24	7	6	13	42	1	0	0	0	0
	Fredericton	AHL	47	41	31	72	106					
	NHL Totals		**34**	**8**	**8**	**16**	**48**	**1**	**0**	**0**	**0**	**0**

a WHL East Second All-Star Team (1992)
b Won Stafford Smythe Memorial Trophy (Memorial Cup MVP) (1992)
Traded to **Montreal** by **Pittsburgh** for Montreal's third round choice in 1995 Entry Draft, June 14, 1993. Signed as a free agent by **San Jose,** August 3, 1994.

All trades, free agent signings and other transactions involving NHL clubs are listed in chronological order. Players selected by NHL clubs after re-entering the NHL Entry Draft are noted here. NHL All-Star Game appearances are listed above trade notes.

Asterisk (*) indicates league leader in this statistical category.

NHL Clubs and Minor League Affiliates 1994-95

NHL CLUB	MINOR LEAGUE AFFILIATE
Anaheim	San Diego Gulls (IHL)
	Greensboro Monarchs (ECHL)
Boston	Providence Bruins (AHL)
	Charlotte Checkers (ECHL)
Buffalo	Rochester Americans (AHL)
Calgary	Saint John Flames (AHL)
	Brantford Smoke (ColHL)
Chicago	Indianapolis Ice (IHL)
	Columbus Chill (ECHL)
	Flint Generals (ColHL)
Dallas	Kalamazoo Wings (IHL)
	Dayton Bombers (ECHL)
Detroit	Adirondack Red Wings (AHL)
	Toledo Storm (ECHL)
	Detroit Falcons (ColHL)
Edmonton	Cape Breton Oilers (AHL)
	Wheeling Thunderbirds (ECHL)
Florida	Cincinnati Cyclones (IHL)
	Birmingham Bulls (ECHL)
Hartford	Springfield Falcons (AHL)
	Richmond Renegades (ECHL)
Los Angeles	Phoenix Roadrunners (IHL)
	Erie Panthers (ECHL)
Montreal	Fredericton Canadiens (AHL)
	Wheeling Thunderbirds (ECHL)
New Jersey	Albany River Rats (AHL)
	Raleigh IceCaps (ECHL)
	Flint Generals (ColHL)

NHL CLUB	MINOR LEAGUE AFFILIATE
NY Islanders	Denver Grizzlies (IHL)
	Tallahassee Tiger Sharks (ECHL)
NY Rangers	Binghamton Rangers (AHL)
	Erie Panthers (ECHL)
Ottawa	PEI Senators (AHL)
	Thunder Bay Senators (ColHL)
Philadelphia	Hershey Bears (AHL)
Pittsburgh	Cleveland Lumberjacks (IHL)
	Muskegon Fury (ColHL)
Quebec	Cornwall Aces (AHL)
St. Louis	Peoria Rivermen (IHL)
	Dayton Bombers (ECHL)
	London Blues (ColHL)
San Jose	Kansas City Blades (IHL)
	Roanoke Express (ECHL)
Tampa Bay	Atlanta Knights (IHL)
	Nashville Knights (ECHL)
Toronto	St. John's Maple Leafs (AHL)
	South Carolina Stingers (ECHL)
	Brantford Smoke (ColHL)
Vancouver	Syracuse Crunch (AHL)
	Columbus Chill (ColHL)
Washington	Portland Pirates (AHL)
	Hampton Road Admirals (ECHL)
Winnipeg	Springfield Falcons (AHL)

Pronunciation of Player's Name

United Press International phonetic style.

AY	long A as in mate
A	short A as in cat
AI	nasal A as on air
AH	short A as in father
AW	broad A as in talk
EE	long E as in meat
EH	short E as in get
UH	hollow E as in "the"
AY	French long E with acute accent as in Pathe
IH	middle E as in pretty
EW	EW dipthong as in few
IGH	long I as in time
EE	French long I as in machine
IH	short I as in pity
OH	long O as in note
AH	short O as in hot
AW	broad O as in fought
OO	long double OO as in fool
UH	short double O as in ouch
OW	OW dipthong as in how
EW	long U as in mule
OO	long U as in rule
U	middle U as in put
UH	short U as in shut or hurt
K	hard C as in cat
S	soft C as in cease
SH	soft CH as in machine
CH	hard CH or TCH as in catch
Z	hard S as in decrease
S	soft S as in sun
G	hard G as in gang
J	soft G as in general
ZH	soft J as in French version of Joliet

Late Additions to Player Register

BOUDRIAS, JASSON   FLA.

Center. Shoots right. 6', 200 lbs.   Born, Val D'or, Que., February 16, 1976.
(Florida's 8th choice, 183rd overall, in 1994 Entry Draft).

				Regular Season					Playoffs			
Season	Club	Lea	GP	G	A	TP	PIM	GP	G	A	TP	PIM
1993-94	Laval	QMJHL	61	17	25	42	62	21	5	9	14	10

GUSTAFFSON, PER   FLA.

Defense. Shoots left. 6'1", 187 lbs.   Born, Sweden, April 6, 1970.
(Florida's 10th choice, 261st overall, in 1994 Entry Draft).

				Regular Season					Playoffs			
Season	Club	Lea	GP	G	A	TP	PIM	GP	G	A	TP	PIM
1993-94	HV-71	Swe.	34	9	7	16	10	....	....	....	....	....

LEHTERA, TERO   FLA.

Left wing. Shoots right. 6'1", 185 lbs.   Born, Finland, April 21, 1972.
(Florida's 9th choice, 235th overall, in 1994 Entry Draft).

				Regular Season					Playoffs			
Season	Club	Lea	GP	G	A	TP	PIM	GP	G	A	TP	PIM
1993-94	Espoo	Fin.	48	19	27	46	2	....	....	....	....	....

LIPIANSKY, JAN   PHI.

Left wing. Shoots left. 6'2", 187 lbs.   Born, Bratislava, Czech., July 23, 1974.
(Philadelphia's 10th choice, 270th overall, in 1994 Entry Draft).

				Regular Season					Playoffs			
Season	Club	Lea	GP	G	A	TP	PIM	GP	G	A	TP	PIM
1993-94	Bratislava	Slovak	32	11	5	16	12	....	....	....	....	....

MAILLET, CHRIS   T.B.

Defense. Shoots left. 6'5", 188 lbs.   Born, Moncton, NB, January 28, 1976.
(Tampa Bay's 7th choice, 164th overall, in 1994 Entry Draft).

				Regular Season					Playoffs			
Season	Club	Lea	GP	G	A	TP	PIM	GP	G	A	TP	PIM
1993-94	Red Deer	WHL	52	0	0	0	102	1	0	0	0	5

McCAULEY, BILL   FLA.

Center. Shoots left. 6', 173 lbs.   Born, Detroit, MI, April 20, 1975.
(Florida's 6th choice, 83rd overall, in 1993 Entry Draft).

				Regular Season					Playoffs			
Season	Club	Lea	GP	G	A	TP	PIM	GP	G	A	TP	PIM
1992-93	Detroit	OHL	65	13	37	50	24	15	1	4	5	6
1993-94	Detroit	OHL	59	18	39	57	51	16	4	7	11	25

O'DETTE, MATT   FLA.

Defense. Shoots right. 6'4", 205 lbs.   Born, East York, Ont., November 9, 1975.
(Florida's 7th choice, 157th overall, in 1994 Entry Draft).

				Regular Season					Playoffs			
Season	Club	Lea	GP	G	A	TP	PIM	GP	G	A	TP	PIM
1993-94	Kitchener	OHL	46	1	3	4	107	....	....	....	....	....

SMITH, DAVID   NYR

Center. Shoots left. 6'1", 180 lbs.   Born, Arthur, Ont., November 21, 1968.

				Regular Season					Playoffs			
Season	Club	Lea	GP	G	A	TP	PIM	GP	G	A	TP	PIM
1993-94	Ft. Wayne	IHL	65	22	22	44	196	18	2	6	8	68

Signed as a free agent by **NY Rangers**, August, 1994.

SULLIVAN, STEVE   N.J.

Center. Shoots right. 5'9", 155 lbs.   Born, Timmins, Ont., July 6, 1974.
(New Jersey's 10th choice, 233rd overall, in 1994 Entry Draft).

				Regular Season					Playoffs			
Season	Club	Lea	GP	G	A	TP	PIM	GP	G	A	TP	PIM
1993-94	S.S. Marie	OHL	63	51	62	113	82	14	9	16	25	22

WILLIAMS, JEFF   N.J.

Center. Shoots left. 6', 175 lbs.   Born, Pointe-Claire, Que., February 11, 1976.
(New Jersey's 8th choice, 181st overall, in 1994 Entry Draft).

				Regular Season					Playoffs			
Season	Club	Lea	GP	G	A	TP	PIM	GP	G	A	TP	PIM
1993-94	Guelph	OHL	62	14	12	26	19	9	2	1	3	4

Trade Notes and Free Agent Signings

ANDERSSON, NICLAS signed as a free agent by NY Islanders, July 15, 1994.

BARRIE, LEN signed as a free agent by Pittsburgh, August 15, 1994.

BEERS, BOB signed as a free agent by NY Islanders, August 29, 1994.

CHABOT, FREDERIC signed as a free agent by Florida, August 11, 1994

CROWE, PHIL signed as a free agent by Philadelphia, July 19, 1994.

HOULDER, BILL traded to St. Louis by Anaheim for Jason Marshall, August 29, 1994.

MADILL, JEFF signed as a free agent by NY Islanders, August 25, 1994.

MARCHMENT, BRYAN acquired by Edmonton from Hartford as compensation for Hartford's signing of free agent Steven Rice, August 30, 1994.

MARSHALL, JASON traded to Anaheim by St. Louis for Bill Houlder, August 29, 1994

MILLER, JASON signed as a free agent by Detroit, August 26, 1994.

MILLER, KURTIS signed as a free agent by Detroit, August 10, 1994.

MOLLER, RANDY signed as a free agent by Florida, July 11, 1994.

OSBORNE, MARK signed as a free agent by NY Rangers, August, 1994.

PEDERSON, MARK signed as a free agent by Dallas, August 13, 1994.

PETIT, MICHEL signed as a free agent by Los Angeles, August, 1994.

TANCILL, CHRIS signed as a free agent by San Jose, August, 1994.

TWIST, TONY signed as a free agent by St. Louis, August 16, 1994.

WESLEY, GLEN traded to Hartford by Boston for Hartford's first round choices in 1995, 1996 and 1997 Entry Drafts, August 26, 1994.

WORTMAN, KEVIN signed as a free agent by San Jose, August, 1994.

CROWDER, TROY signed as a free agent by Los Angeles, September 1, 1994.

1994-95 Player Register

Note: The 1994-95 Player Register lists forwards and defensemen only. Goaltenders are listed separately. The Player Register lists every skater who appeared in an NHL game in the 1993-94 season, every skater drafted in the first six rounds of the 1993 and 1994 Entry Drafts, players on NHL Reserve Lists and other players. Trades and roster changes are current as of August 19, 1994.

Abbreviations: A – assists; **G** – goals; **GP** – games played; **Lea** – league; **PIM** – penalties in minutes; **TP** – total points; ***** – league-leading total.

Pronunciations courtesy of the NHL Broadcasters' Association and Igor Kuperman, Winnipeg Jets

Goaltender Register begins on page 423.

LEAGUES:

ACHL	Atlantic Coast Hockey League
AHL	American Hockey League
AJHL	Alberta Junior Hockey League
Alp.	Alpenliga
AUAA	Atlantic Universities Athletic Association
BCJHL	British Columbia Junior Hockey League
CCHA	Central Collegiate Hockey Association
CHL	Central Hockey League
CIAU	Canadian Interuniversity Athletic Union
COJHL	Central Ontario Junior Hockey League
ColHL	Colonial Hockey League
CWUAA	Canada West Universities Athletic Association
ECAC	Eastern Collegiate Athletic Association
ECHL	East Coast Hockey League
EJHL	Eastern Junior Hockey League
G.N.	Great Northern
GPAC	Great Plains Athletic Conference
H.E.	Hockey East
HS	High School
IHL	International Hockey League
Jr.	Junior
MJHA	(New York) Metropolitan Junior Hockey Association
MJHL	Manitoba Junior Hockey League
NAJHL	North American Junior Hockey League
NCAA	National Collegiate Athletic Association
NHL	**National Hockey League**
OHA	Ontario Hockey Association
OHL	Ontario Hockey League
OMJHL	Ontario Major Junior Hockey League
OPJHL	Ontario Provincial Junior Hockey League
OUAA	Ontario Universities Athletic Association
QJHL	Quebec Junior Hockey League
QMJHL	Quebec Major Junior Hockey League
SJHL	Saskatchewan Junior Hockey League
SOHL	Southern Ontario Hockey League
USHL	United States Hockey League (Junior)
WCHA	Western Collegiate Hockey Association
WHA	World Hockey Association
WHL	Western Hockey League

AALTO, ANTTI (AL-toh, AN-tee) ANA.

Center. Shoots left. 6'2", 185 lbs. Born, Lappeenranta, Finland, March 4, 1975.
Anaheim's 6th choice, 134th overall, in 1993 Entry Draft.

			Regular Season					Playoffs				
Season	Club	Lea	GP	G	A	TP	PIM	GP	G	A	TP	PIM
1991-92	SaiPa	Fin.2	20	6	6	12	20	....	....	....	....	....
1992-93	SaiPa	Fin.2	23	6	8	14	14	....	....	....	....	....
	TPS	Fin.	1	0	0	0	0	....	....	....	....	....
1993-94	TPS	Fin.	33	5	9	14	16	10	1	1	2	4

AALTONEN, PETRI (AL-tuh-nehn) QUE.

Center. Shoots left. 5'10", 185 lbs. Born, Tampere, Finland, May 31, 1970.
Quebec's 4th choice, 45th overall, in 1988 Entry Draft.

			Regular Season					Playoffs				
Season	Club	Lea	GP	G	A	TP	PIM	GP	G	A	TP	PIM
1986-87	HIFK	Fin. Jr.	30	8	5	13	24	4	0	0	0	0
1987-88	HIFK	Fin. Jr.	34	37	20	57	25	....	....	....	....	....
1988-89	HIFK	Fin.	2	0	0	0	0	....	....	....	....	....
1989-90	HIFK	Fin.	3	0	0	0	0	....	....	....	....	....
1990-91	HIFK	Fin.	43	6	9	15	12	3	1	1	2	0
1991-92	Tappara	Fin.	36	3	4	7	18	....	....	....	....	....
1992-93	Vantaa	Fin. 2	33	15	11	26	50	....	....	....	....	....
1993-94	Tappara	Fin.	25	2	4	6	12	....	....	....	....	....

ACTON, KEITH

Center. Shoots left. 5'8", 170 lbs. Born, Stouffville, Ont., April 15, 1958.
Montreal's 8th choice, 103rd overall, in 1978 Amateur Draft.

			Regular Season					Playoffs				
Season	Club	Lea	GP	G	A	TP	PIM	GP	G	A	TP	PIM
1976-77	Peterborough	OHA	65	52	69	121	93	4	1	4	5	6
1977-78	Peterborough	OHA	68	42	86	128	52	21	10	8	18	16
1978-79	Nova Scotia	AHL	79	15	26	41	22	10	4	2	6	4
1979-80	Montreal	NHL	2	0	1	1	0	....	....	....	....	....
a	Nova Scotia	AHL	75	45	53	98	38	6	1	2	3	8
1980-81	Montreal	NHL	61	15	24	39	74	2	0	0	0	6
1981-82	Montreal	NHL	78	36	52	88	88	5	0	4	4	16
1982-83	Montreal	NHL	78	24	26	50	63	3	0	0	0	0
1983-84	Montreal	NHL	9	3	7	10	4	....	....	....	....	....
	Minnesota	NHL	62	17	38	55	60	15	4	7	11	12
1984-85	Minnesota	NHL	78	20	38	58	90	9	4	4	8	6
1985-86	Minnesota	NHL	79	26	32	58	100	5	0	3	3	6
1986-87	Minnesota	NHL	78	16	29	45	56	....	....	....	....	....
1987-88	Minnesota	NHL	46	8	11	19	74	....	....	....	....	....
	Edmonton	NHL	26	3	6	9	21	7	2	0	2	16
1988-89	Edmonton	NHL	46	11	15	26	47	....	....	....	....	....
	Philadelphia	NHL	25	3	10	13	64	16	2	3	5	18
1989-90	Philadelphia	NHL	69	13	14	27	80	....	....	....	....	....
1990-91	Philadelphia	NHL	76	14	23	37	131	....	....	....	....	....
1991-92	Philadelphia	NHL	50	7	10	17	98	....	....	....	....	....
1992-93	Philadelphia	NHL	83	8	15	23	51	....	....	....	....	....
1993-94	Washington	NHL	6	0	0	0	21	....	....	....	....	....
	NY Islanders	NHL	71	2	7	9	50	4	0	0	0	8
	NHL Totals		**1023**	**226**	**358**	**584**	**1172**	**66**	**12**	**21**	**33**	**88**

a AHL Second All-Star Team (1980)
Played in NHL All-Star Game (1982)

Traded to **Minnesota** by **Montreal** with Mark Napier and Toronto's third round choice (previously acquired by Montreal — Minnesota selected Ken Hodge) in 1984 Entry Draft for Bobby Smith, October 28, 1983. Traded to **Edmonton** by **Minnesota** for Moe Mantha, January 22, 1988. Traded to **Philadelphia** by **Edmonton** with Edmonton's fifth round choice (Dimitri Yushkevich) in 1991 Entry Draft for Dave Brown, February 7, 1989. Traded to **Winnipeg** by **Philadelphia** with Pete Peeters for future considerations, September 28, 1989. Traded to **Philadelphia** by **Winnipeg** with Pete Peeters for Toronto's fifth round choice (previously acquired by Philadelphia — Winnipeg selected Juha Ylonen) in 1991 Entry Draft and the cancellation of future considerations owed Philadelphia from the trade of Shawn Cronin, October 3, 1989. Signed as a free agent by **Washington**, July 27, 1993. Claimed on waivers by **NY Islanders** from **Washington**, October 22, 1993.

ADAMS, GREG VAN.

Left wing. Shoots left. 6'3", 198 lbs. Born, Nelson, B.C.,, August 1, 1963.

			Regular Season					Playoffs				
Season	Club	Lea	GP	G	A	TP	PIM	GP	G	A	TP	PIM
1982-83	N. Arizona	NCAA	29	14	21	35	19	....	....	....	....	....
1983-84	N. Arizona	NCAA	26	44	29	73	24	....	....	....	....	....
1984-85	**New Jersey**	**NHL**	36	12	9	21	14	....	....	....	....	....
	Maine	AHL	41	15	20	35	12	11	3	4	7	0
1985-86	New Jersey	NHL	78	35	42	77	30	....	....	....	....	....
1986-87	New Jersey	NHL	72	20	27	47	19	....	....	....	....	....
1987-88	Vancouver	NHL	80	36	40	76	30	....	....	....	....	....
1988-89	Vancouver	NHL	61	19	14	33	24	7	2	3	5	2
1989-90	Vancouver	NHL	65	30	20	50	18	....	....	....	....	....
1990-91	Vancouver	NHL	55	21	24	45	10	5	0	0	0	2
1991-92	Vancouver	NHL	76	30	27	57	26	6	2	2	4	4
1992-93	Vancouver	NHL	53	25	31	56	14	12	7	6	13	6
1993-94	Vancouver	NHL	68	13	24	37	20	23	6	8	14	2
	NHL Totals		**644**	**241**	**258**	**499**	**205**	**53**	**15**	**19**	**34**	**16**

Played in NHL All-Star Game (1988)

Signed as a free agent by **New Jersey**, June 25, 1984. Traded to **Vancouver** by **New Jersey** with Kirk McLean for Patrik Sundstrom and Vancouver's fourth round choice (Matt Ruchty) in 1988 Entry Draft, September 10, 1987.

ADAMS, KEVYN BOS.

Center. Shoots right. 6'1", 182 lbs. Born, Washington, D.C., October 8, 1974.
(Boston's 1st choice, 25th overall, in 1993 Entry Draft).

			Regular Season					Playoffs				
Season	Club	Lea	GP	G	A	TP	PIM	GP	G	A	TP	PIM
1992-93	Miami-Ohio	CCHA	40	17	15	32	18	....	....	....	....	....
1993-94	Miami-Ohio	CCHA	36	15	28	43	24	....	....	....	....	....

AGARKOV, PAVEL (ah-GAHR-kohv) DET.

Right wing. Shoots left. 5'11", 167 lbs. Born, Moscow, USSR, April 23, 1975.
(Detroit's 6th choice, 153rd overall, in 1994 Entry Draft).

			Regular Season					Playoffs				
Season	Club	Lea	GP	G	A	TP	PIM	GP	G	A	TP	PIM
1993-94	Soviet Wings	CIS	27	2	0	2	12	....	....	....	....	....

AGNEW, JIM HFD.

Defense. Shoots left. 6'1", 190 lbs. Born, Hartney, Man., March 21, 1966.
(Vancouver's 10th choice, 157th overall, in 1984 Entry Draft).

			Regular Season					Playoffs				
Season	Club	Lea	GP	G	A	TP	PIM	GP	G	A	TP	PIM
1982-83	Brandon	WHL	14	1	1	2	9	....	....	....	....	....
1983-84	Brandon	WHL	71	6	17	23	107	12	0	1	1	39
1984-85	Brandon	WHL	19	3	15	18	82	....	....	....	....	....
	Portland	WHL	44	5	24	29	223	6	0	2	2	44
1985-86a	Portland	WHL	70	6	30	36	286	9	0	1	1	48
1986-87	Vancouver	NHL	4	0	0	0	0	....	....	....	....	....
	Fredericton	AHL	67	0	5	5	261	....	....	....	....	....
1987-88	Vancouver	NHL	10	0	1	1	16	....	....	....	....	....
	Fredericton	AHL	63	2	8	10	188	14	0	2	2	43
1988-89	Milwaukee	IHL	47	2	10	12	181	11	0	2	2	34
1989-90	Vancouver	NHL	7	0	0	0	36	....	....	....	....	....
b	Milwaukee	IHL	51	4	10	14	238	....	....	....	....	....
1990-91	Vancouver	NHL	20	0	0	0	81	....	....	....	....	....
	Milwaukee	IHL	3	0	0	0	33	....	....	....	....	....
1991-92	Vancouver	NHL	24	0	0	0	56	4	0	0	0	6
1992-93	Hartford	NHL	16	0	0	0	68	....	....	....	....	....
	Springfield	AHL	11	0	1	1	2	....	....	....	....	....
1993-94	Hartford	NHL				DID NOT PLAY						
	NHL Totals		**81**	**0**	**1**	**1**	**257**	**4**	**0**	**0**	**0**	**6**

a WHL West First All-Star Team (1986)
b IHL Second All-Star Team (1990)
Signed as a free agent by **Hartford**, July 8, 1992.

AHLUND, HAKAN　　　　　　　　　　　VAN.

Right wing. Shoots left. 6', 194 lbs.　Born, Orebro, Sweden, August 16, 1967.
(Vancouver's 8th choice, 151st overall, in 1985 Entry Draft).

			Regular Season					Playoffs			
Season	Club	Lea	GP	G	A	TP	PIM	GP	G	A	TP	PIM
1983-84	Orebro	Swe. 2	1	0	1	1	0	....	....	....	....	....
1984-85	Orebro	Swe. 2	25	2	6	8	10	....	....	....	....	....
1985-86	Orebro	Swe. 2	20	5	4	9	10	2	0	0	0	0
1986-87	Orebro	Swe. 2	27	16	9	25	6	6	0	3	3	6
1987-88	Orebro	Swe. 2	36	24	23	47	29	6	3	4	7	7
1988-89	Malmo	Swe. 2	35	20	27	47	44	....	....	....	....	....
1989-90	Malmo	Swe. 2	35	12	38	50	30	....	....	....	....	....
1990-91	Malmo	Swe.	29	9	18	27	46	2	0	0	0	0
1991-92	Malmo	Swe.	38	5	12	17	48	10	2	2	4	8
1992-93	Malmo	Swe.	33	5	10	15	30	6	2	1	3	6
1993-94	Malmo	Swe.	37	7	7	14	26	10	4	3	7	13

AHOLA, PETER　　　　　　　　　(AH-hoh-luh)

Defense. Shoots left. 6'3", 205 lbs.　Born, Espoo, Finland, May 14, 1968.

			Regular Season					Playoffs			
Season	Club	Lea	GP	G	A	TP	PIM	GP	G	A	TP	PIM
1989-90	Boston U.	H.E.	43	3	20	23	65	....	....	....	....	....
1990-91a	Boston U.	H.E.	39	12	24	36	88	....	....	....	....	....
1991-92	Los Angeles	NHL	71	7	12	19	101	6	0	0	0	2
	Phoenix	IHL	7	3	3	6	34	....	....	....	....	....
1992-93	Los Angeles	NHL	8	1	1	2	6	....	....	....	....	....
	Pittsburgh	NHL	22	0	1	1	14	....	....	....	....	....
	Cleveland	IHL	9	1	0	1	4	....	....	....	....	....
	San Jose	NHL	20	2	3	5	16	....	....	....	....	....
1993-94	Calgary	NHL	2	0	0	0	0	....	....	....	....	....
	Saint John	AHL	66	4	19	28	59	6	1	2	3	12
	NHL Totals		**123**	**10**	**17**	**27**	**137**	**6**	**0**	**0**	**0**	**2**

a NCAA East Second All-American Team (1991)
Signed as a free agent by **Los Angeles**, April 5, 1991. Traded to **Pittsburgh** by **Los Angeles** for Jeff Chychrun, November 6, 1992. Traded to **San Jose** by **Pittsburgh** for future considerations, February 26, 1993. Traded to **Tampa Bay** by **San Jose** for Dave Capuano, June 19, 1993. Traded to **Calgary** by **Tampa Bay** for cash, October 5, 1993.

AIVAZOFF, MICAH　　　　　(A-vuh-zahf, MIGH-kuh)　　DET.

Center. Shoots left. 6', 195 lbs.　Born, Powell River, B.C., May 4, 1969.
(Los Angeles' 6th choice, 109th overall, in 1988 Entry Draft).

			Regular Season					Playoffs			
Season	Club	Lea	GP	G	A	TP	PIM	GP	G	A	TP	PIM
1986-87	Victoria	WHL	72	18	39	57	112	5	1	0	1	2
1987-88	Victoria	WHL	69	26	57	83	79	8	3	4	7	14
1988-89	Victoria	WHL	70	35	65	100	136	8	5	7	12	2
1989-90	New Haven	AHL	77	20	39	59	71	....	....	....	....	....
1990-91	New Haven	AHL	79	11	29	40	84	....	....	....	....	....
1991-92	Adirondack	AHL	61	9	20	29	50	19	2	8	10	25
1992-93	Adirondack	AHL	79	32	53	85	100	11	8	6	14	10
1993-94	**Detroit**	**NHL**	**59**	**4**	**4**	**8**	**38**	....	....	....	....	....
	NHL Totals		**59**	**4**	**4**	**8**	**38**	....	....	....	....	....

Signed as a free agent by **Detroit**, March 18, 1993.

AKERSTROM, ROGER　　　　(OHK-uhr-struhm)　　VAN.

Defense. Shoots left. 5'11", 189 lbs.　Born, Lulea, Sweden, April 5, 1967.
(Vancouver's 8th choice, 170th overall, in 1988 Entry Draft).

			Regular Season					Playoffs			
Season	Club	Lea	GP	G	A	TP	PIM	GP	G	A	TP	PIM
1987-88	Lulea	Swe.	34	4	3	7	28	....	....	....	....	....
1988-89	Lulea	Swe.	38	6	12	18	32	....	....	....	....	....
1989-90	Lulea	Swe.	36	5	10	15	44	5	3	2	5	2
1990-91	Lulea	Swe.	37	2	10	12	38	5	0	1	1	6
1991-92	Vasteras	Swe.	39	3	9	12	20	....	....	....	....	....
1992-93	Vasteras	Swe.	37	13	13	26	36	3	0	0	0	6
1993-94	Vasteras	Swe.	36	5	4	9	37	4	2	1	3	4

ALATALO, MIKA　　　　　　　　　　WPG.

Left wing. Shoots left. 5'11", 185 lbs.　Born, Oulu, Finland, June 11, 1971.
(Winnipeg's 11th choice, 203rd overall, in 1990 Entry Draft).

			Regular Season					Playoffs			
Season	Club	Lea	GP	G	A	TP	PIM	GP	G	A	TP	PIM
1988-89	KooKoo	Fin.	34	8	6	14	10	....	....	....	....	....
1989-90	KooKoo	Fin.	41	3	5	8	22	....	....	....	....	....
1990-91	Lukko	Fin.	39	10	1	11	10	....	....	....	....	....
1991-92	Lukko	Fin.	43	20	17	37	32	2	0	0	0	0
1992-93	Lukko	Fin.	48	16	19	35	38	3	0	0	0	0
1993-94	Lukko	Fin.	45	19	15	34	77	9	2	2	4	4

ALBELIN, TOMMY　　　　　　(AL-buh-LEEN)　　N.J.

Defense. Shoots left. 6'1", 190 lbs.　Born, Stockholm, Sweden, May 21, 1964.
(Quebec's 7th choice, 152nd overall, in 1983 Entry Draft).

			Regular Season					Playoffs			
Season	Club	Lea	GP	G	A	TP	PIM	GP	G	A	TP	PIM
1982-83	Djurgarden	Swe.	19	2	5	7	4	6	1	0	1	2
1983-84	Djurgarden	Swe.	30	9	5	14	26	4	0	1	1	2
1984-85	Djurgarden	Swe.	32	9	8	17	22	8	2	1	3	4
1985-86	Djurgarden	Swe.	35	4	8	12	26	....	....	....	....	....
1986-87	Djurgarden	Swe.	33	7	5	12	49	2	0	0	0	4
1987-88	**Quebec**	**NHL**	**60**	**3**	**23**	**26**	**47**	....	....	....	....	....
1988-89	**Quebec**	**NHL**	**14**	**2**	**6**	**8**	**27**	....	....	....	....	....
	Halifax	AHL	8	2	5	7	4	....	....	....	....	....
	New Jersey	**NHL**	**46**	**7**	**24**	**31**	**40**	....	....	....	....	....
1989-90	**New Jersey**	**NHL**	**68**	**6**	**23**	**29**	**63**	....	....	....	....	....
1990-91	**New Jersey**	**NHL**	**47**	**2**	**12**	**14**	**44**	3	0	1	1	2
	Utica	AHL	14	4	2	6	10	....	....	....	....	....
1991-92	**New Jersey**	**NHL**	**19**	**0**	**4**	**4**	**4**	1	1	1	2	0
	Utica	AHL	11	4	6	10	4	....	....	....	....	....
1992-93	**New Jersey**	**NHL**	**36**	**1**	**5**	**6**	**14**	5	2	0	2	0
1993-94	**New Jersey**	**NHL**	**62**	**2**	**17**	**19**	**36**	20	2	5	7	14
	Albany	AHL	4	0	2	2	17	....	....	....	....	....
	NHL Totals		**352**	**23**	**112**	**135**	**275**	**29**	**5**	**7**	**12**	**16**

Traded to **New Jersey** by **Quebec** for New Jersey's fourth round choice (Niclas Andersson) in 1989 Entry Draft, December 12, 1988.

ALEXEYEV, ALEXANDER

Defense. Shoots left. 6', 216 lbs.　Born, Kiev, USSR, March 21, 1974.
(Winnipeg's 5th choice, 132nd overall, in 1992 Entry Draft).

			Regular Season					Playoffs			
Season	Club	Lea	GP	G	A	TP	PIM	GP	G	A	TP	PIM
1990-91	Sokol Kiev	USSR	5	0	0	0	2	....	....	....	....	....
1991-92	Sokol Kiev	CIS	1	5	6	22	....	....	....	....	....	....
1992-93	Tacoma	WHL	44	3	33	36	67	7	2	7	9	....
1993-94a	Tacoma	WHL	64	12	48	60	106	8	0	5	5	....

a WHL West Second All-Star Team (1994)

ALFREDSSON, DANIEL　　　(AHL-frehd-suhn)　　OTT.

Right wing. Shoots right. 5'11", 187 lbs.　Born, Grums, Sweden, December 11, 1972.
(Ottawa's 5th choice, 133rd overall, in 1994 Entry Draft).

			Regular Season					Playoffs			
Season	Club	Lea	GP	G	A	TP	PIM	GP	G	A	TP	PIM
1991-92	Molndal	Swe. 2	32	12	8	20	43	....	....	....	....	....
1992-93	V. Frolunda	Swe.	20	1	5	6	8	....	....	....	....	....
1993-94	V. Frolunda	Swe.	39	20	10	30	18	4	1	1	2	....

ALINC, JAN

Center. Shoots left. 6'2", 190 lbs.　Born, Most, Czech., May 27, 1972.
(Pittsburgh's 7th choice, 163rd overall, in 1992 Entry Draft).

			Regular Season					Playoffs			
Season	Club	Lea	GP	G	A	TP	PIM	GP	G	A	TP	PIM
1990-91	Litvinov	Czech.	7	1	1	2	....	....	....	....	....	....
1991-92	Litvinov	Czech.	45	21	16	37	24	....	....	....	....	....
1992-93	Litvinov	Czech.	36	16	13	29	....	....	....	....	....	....
1993-94	Litvinov	Czech.	36	16	25	41	....	4	1	4	5	....

ALLAN, CHAD　　　　　　　　　　VAN.

Defense. Shoots left. 6'1", 192 lbs.　Born, Saskatoon, Sask., July 12, 1976.
(Vancouver's 4th choice, 65th overall, in 1994 Entry Draft).

			Regular Season					Playoffs			
Season	Club	Lea	GP	G	A	TP	PIM	GP	G	A	TP	PIM
1991-92	Saskatoon	WHL	1	0	0	0	2	....	....	....	....	....
1992-93	Saskatoon	WHL	69	2	10	12	67	9	0	0	0	2
1993-94	Saskatoon	WHL	70	6	16	22	123	16	1	1	2	2

ALLISON, JAMIE　　　　　　　　　CGY.

Defense. Shoots left. 6'1", 190 lbs.　Born, Lindsay, Ont., May 13, 1975.
(Calgary's 2nd choice, 44th overall, in 1993 Entry Draft).

			Regular Season					Playoffs			
Season	Club	Lea	GP	G	A	TP	PIM	GP	G	A	TP	PIM
1991-92	Windsor	OHL	59	4	8	12	70	4	1	1	2	....
1992-93	Detroit	OHL	61	0	13	13	64	15	2	5	7	....
1993-94	Detroit	OHL	40	2	22	24	69	17	2	9	11	3

ALLISON, JASON　　　　　　　　　WSH

Center. Shoots right. 6'3", 200 lbs.　Born, North York, Ont., May 29, 1975.
(Washington's 2nd choice, 17th overall, in 1993 Entry Draft).

			Regular Season					Playoffs			
Season	Club	Lea	GP	G	A	TP	PIM	GP	G	A	TP	PIM
1991-92	London	OHL	65	11	19	30	15	7	0	0	0	0
1992-93	London	OHL	66	42	76	118	50	12	7	13	20	8
1993-94	**Washington**	**NHL**	**2**	**0**	**1**	**1**	**0**	....	....	....	....	....
abc	London	OHL	56	55	87	*142	68	5	2	13	15	13
	Portland	AHL	....	....	....	....	....	6	2	1	3	0
	NHL Totals		**2**	**0**	**1**	**1**	**0**	....	....	....	....	....

a OHL First All-Star Team (1994)
b Canadian Major Junior First All-Star Team (1994)
c Canadian Major Junior Player of the Year (1994)

ALLISON, SCOTT　　　　　　　　　EDM.

Center. Shoots left. 6'4", 194 lbs.　Born, St. Boniface, Man., April 22, 1972.
(Edmonton's 1st choice, 17th overall, in 1990 Entry Draft).

			Regular Season					Playoffs			
Season	Club	Lea	GP	G	A	TP	PIM	GP	G	A	TP	PIM
1988-89	Prince Albert	WHL	51	6	9	15	37	3	0	0	0	0
1989-90	Prince Albert	WHL	66	22	16	38	73	11	1	4	5	8
1990-91	Prince Albert	WHL	30	5	5	10	57	....	....	....	....	....
	Portland	WHL	44	5	17	22	105	....	....	....	....	....
1991-92	Moose Jaw	WHL	72	37	45	82	238	3	1	1	2	25
1992-93	Cape Breton	AHL	49	3	5	8	34	....	....	....	....	....
	Wheeling	ECHL	6	3	3	6	8	....	....	....	....	....
1993-94	Cape Breton	AHL	75	19	14	33	202	3	0	1	1	2

ALVEY, MATT　　　　　　　　　　BOS.

Right wing. Shoots right. 6'5", 195 lbs.　Born, Troy, NY, May 15, 1975.
(Boston's 2nd choice, 51st overall, in 1993 Entry Draft).

			Regular Season					Playoffs			
Season	Club	Lea	GP	G	A	TP	PIM	GP	G	A	TP	PIM
1992-93	Springfield	NEJHL	38	22	37	59	85	....	....	....	....	....
1993-94	Lake Superior	CCHA	41	6	8	14	16	....	....	....	....	....

AMBROZIAK, PETER　　　　　　　　BUF.

Left wing. Shoots left. 6', 206 lbs.　Born, Toronto, Ont., September 15, 1971.
(Buffalo's 4th choice, 72nd overall, in 1991 Entry Draft).

			Regular Season					Playoffs			
Season	Club	Lea	GP	G	A	TP	PIM	GP	G	A	TP	PIM
1990-91	Ottawa	OHL	62	30	32	62	56	17	15	9	24	24
1991-92	Ottawa	OHL	49	32	49	81	50	11	3	7	10	33
	Rochester	AHL	2	0	1	1	0	....	....	....	....	....
1992-93	Rochester	AHL	50	8	10	18	37	12	4	3	7	16
1993-94	Rochester	AHL	22	3	4	7	53	....	....	....	....	....

MONTE, TONY (eh-MAHN-tee) CHI.

ght wing. Shoots left. 6', 190 lbs. Born, Hingham, MA, August 2, 1970.
Y Rangers' 3rd choice, 68th overall, in 1988 Entry Draft).

			Regular Season					Playoffs				
eason	Club	Lea	GP	G	A	TP	PIM	GP	G	A	TP	PIM
989-90	Boston U.	H.E.	41	25	33	58	52	....	....	....	....	....
990-91ab	Boston U.	H.E.	38	31	37	68	82	....	....	....	....	....
	NY Rangers	NHL	....	....	....	....	....	2	0	2	2	2
991-92c	NY Rangers	NHL	79	35	34	69	55	13	3	6	9	2
992-93	NY Rangers	NHL	83	33	43	76	49	....	....	....	....	....
993-94	NY Rangers	NHL	72	16	22	38	31	....	....	....	....	....
	Chicago	NHL	7	1	3	4	6	6	4	2	6	4
	NHL Totals		241	85	102	187	141	21	7	10	17	8

Hockey East Second All-Star Team (1991)
NCAA Final Four All-Tournament Team (1991)
NHL/Upper Deck All-Rookie Team (1992)

raded to **Chicago** by **NY Rangers** with the rights to Matt Oates for Stephane Matteau and Brian oonan, March 21, 1994.

NDERSON, GLENN

ight wing. Shoots left. 6'1", 190 lbs. Born, Vancouver, B.C., October 2, 1960.
dmonton's 3rd choice, 69th overall, in 1979 Entry Draft).

			Regular Season					Playoffs				
eason	Club	Lea	GP	G	A	TP	PIM	GP	G	A	TP	PIM
978-79	U. of Denver	WCHA	40	26	29	55	58	....	....	....	....	....
979-80	Seattle	WHL	7	5	5	10	4	....	....	....	....	....
	Cdn. Olympic	....	49	21	21	42	46	....	....	....	....	....
980-81	Edmonton	NHL	58	30	23	53	24	9	5	7	12	12
981-82	Edmonton	NHL	80	38	67	105	71	5	2	5	7	8
982-83	Edmonton	NHL	72	48	56	104	70	16	10	10	20	32
983-84	Edmonton	NHL	80	54	45	99	65	19	6	11	17	33
984-85	Edmonton	NHL	80	42	39	81	69	18	10	16	26	38
985-86	Edmonton	NHL	72	54	48	102	90	10	8	3	11	14
986-87	Edmonton	NHL	80	35	38	73	65	21	14	13	27	59
987-88	Edmonton	NHL	80	38	50	88	58	19	9	16	25	49
988-89	Edmonton	NHL	79	16	48	64	93	7	1	2	3	8
989-90	Edmonton	NHL	73	34	38	72	107	22	10	12	22	20
990-91	Edmonton	NHL	74	24	31	55	59	18	6	7	13	41
991-92	Toronto	NHL	72	24	33	57	100	....	....	....	....	....
992-93	Toronto	NHL	76	22	43	65	117	21	7	11	18	31
993-94	Toronto	NHL	73	17	18	35	50	....	....	....	....	....
	NY Rangers	NHL	12	4	2	6	12	23	3	3	6	42
	NHL Totals		1061	480	579	1059	1050	208	91	116	207	387

layed in NHL All-Star Game (1984-86, 1988)

raded to **Toronto** by **Edmonton** with Grant Fuhr and Craig Berube for Vincent Damphousse, Peter ng, Scott Thornton, Luke Richardson, future considerations and cash, September 19, 1991. Traded o **NY Rangers** by **Toronto** with the rights to Scott Malone and Toronto's fourth round choice Alexander Korobolin) in 1994 Entry Draft for Mike Gartner, March 21, 1994.

ANDERSON, JOHN

Right wing. Shoots left. 5'11", 200 lbs. Born, Toronto, Ont., March 28, 1957.
Toronto's 1st choice, 11th overall, in 1977 Amateur Draft).

			Regular Season					Playoffs				
Season	Club	Lea	GP	G	A	TP	PIM	GP	G	A	TP	PIM
1973-74	Toronto	OMJHL	38	22	22	44	6	....	....	....	....	....
1974-75	Toronto	OMJHL	70	49	64	113	31	22	16	14	30	14
1975-76	Toronto	OHA	39	26	25	51	19	10	7	4	11	7
1976-77a	Toronto	OHA	64	57	62	119	42	6	3	5	8	0
1977-78	Toronto	NHL	17	1	2	3	2	2	0	0	0	0
	Dallas	CHL	55	22	23	45	6	13	*11	8	*19	2
1978-79	Toronto	NHL	71	15	11	26	10	6	0	2	2	0
1979-80	Toronto	NHL	74	25	28	53	22	3	1	1	2	0
1980-81	Toronto	NHL	75	17	26	43	31	2	0	0	0	0
1981-82	Toronto	NHL	69	31	26	57	30	....	....	....	....	....
1982-83	Toronto	NHL	80	31	49	80	24	4	2	4	6	0
1983-84	Toronto	NHL	73	37	31	68	22	....	....	....	....	....
1984-85	Toronto	NHL	75	32	31	63	27	....	....	....	....	....
1985-86	Quebec	NHL	65	21	28	49	26	....	....	....	....	....
	Hartford	NHL	14	8	17	25	2	10	5	8	13	0
1986-87	Hartford	NHL	76	31	44	75	19	6	1	2	3	0
1987-88	Hartford	NHL	63	17	32	49	20	....	....	....	....	....
1988-89	Hartford	NHL	62	16	24	40	28	4	0	1	1	2
1989-90	Binghamton	AHL	3	1	1	2	0	....	....	....	....	....
	Milano	Italy	9	7	9	16	18	....	....	....	....	....
1990-91	Fort Wayne	IHL	63	40	43	83	24	1	3	0	3	0
1991-92bcd	New Haven	AHL	68	41	54	95	24	4	0	4	4	0
1992-93	San Diego	IHL	65	34	46	80	18	11	5	6	11	4
1993-94	San Diego	IHL	72	24	24	48	32	4	1	1	2	8
	NHL Totals		814	282	349	631	263	37	9	18	27	2

a OHA First All-Star Team (1977)
b Won Fred Hunt Award (Sportsmanship - AHL) (1992)
c AHL First All-Star Team (1992)
d Won Les Cunningham Plaque (MVP - AHL) (1992)

Traded to **Quebec** by **Toronto** for Brad Maxwell, August 21, 1985. Traded to **Hartford** by **Quebec** for Risto Siltanen, March 8, 1986.

ANDERSON, SHAWN PHI.

Defense. Shoots left. 6'1", 200 lbs. Born, Montreal, Que., February 7, 1968.
(Buffalo's 1st choice, 5th overall, in 1986 Entry Draft).

			Regular Season					Playoffs				
Season	Club	Lea	GP	G	A	TP	PIM	GP	G	A	TP	PIM
1985-86	Maine	H.E.	16	5	8	13	22	....	....	....	....	....
	Cdn. Olympic	....	49	4	14	18	38	....	....	....	....	....
1986-87	Buffalo	NHL	41	2	11	13	23	....	....	....	....	....
	Rochester	AHL	15	2	5	7	11	....	....	....	....	....
1987-88	Buffalo	NHL	23	1	2	3	17	....	....	....	....	....
	Rochester	AHL	22	5	16	21	19	6	0	0	0	0
1988-89	Buffalo	NHL	33	2	10	12	18	5	0	1	1	4
	Rochester	AHL	31	5	14	19	24	....	....	....	....	....
1989-90	Buffalo	NHL	16	1	3	4	8	....	....	....	....	....
	Rochester	AHL	39	2	16	18	41	9	1	0	1	4
1990-91	Quebec	NHL	31	3	10	13	21	....	....	....	....	....
	Halifax	AHL	4	0	1	1	2	....	....	....	....	....
1991-92	Weiswasser	Ger.	38	7	15	22	83	....	....	....	....	....
1992-93	Washington	NHL	60	2	6	8	18	6	0	0	0	0
	Baltimore	AHL	10	1	5	6	8	....	....	....	....	....
1993-94	Washington	NHL	50	0	9	9	12	8	1	0	1	12
	NHL Totals		254	11	51	62	117	19	1	1	2	16

Traded to **Washington** by **Buffalo** for Bill Houlder, September 30, 1990. Claimed by **Quebec** in NHL Waiver Draft, October 1, 1990. Traded to **Winnipeg** by **Quebec** for Sergei Kharin, October 22, 1991. Traded to **Washington** by **Winnipeg** for future considerations, October 23, 1991. Signed as a free agent by **Philadelphia**, August 16, 1994.

ANDERSSON, ERIC L.A.

Right wing. Shoots left. 6'2", 187 lbs. Born, Stockholm, Sweden, August 19, 1971.
(Los Angeles' 5th choice, 112th overall, in 1990 Entry Draft).

			Regular Season					Playoffs				
Season	Club	Lea	GP	G	A	TP	PIM	GP	G	A	TP	PIM
1989-90	Danderyd	Swe.2	30	14	5	19	16	....	....	....	....	....
1990-91	AIK	Swe.	32	1	1	2	10	....	....	....	....	....
1991-92	AIK	Swe.	3	0	0	0	0	....	....	....	....	....
1992-93			DID NOT PLAY									
1993-94	U. of Denver	WCHA	38	10	20	30	26	....	....	....	....	....

ANDERSSON, MIKAEL (AN-duhr-suhn) T.B.

Left wing. Shoots left. 5'11", 185 lbs. Born, Malmo, Sweden, May 10, 1966.
(Buffalo's 1st choice, 18th overall, in 1984 Entry Draft).

			Regular Season					Playoffs				
Season	Club	Lea	GP	G	A	TP	PIM	GP	G	A	TP	PIM
1982-83	V. Frolunda	Swe.	1	1	0	1	0	....	....	....	....	....
1983-84	V. Frolunda	Swe.	18	0	3	3	6	....	....	....	....	....
1984-85	V. Frolunda	Swe. 2	30	16	11	27	18	6	3	2	5	2
1985-86	Buffalo	NHL	32	1	9	10	4	....	....	....	....	....
	Rochester	AHL	20	10	4	14	6	....	....	....	....	....
1986-87	Buffalo	NHL	16	0	3	3	0	....	....	....	....	....
	Rochester	AHL	42	6	20	26	14	9	1	2	3	2
1987-88	Buffalo	NHL	37	3	20	23	10	1	1	0	1	0
	Rochester	AHL	35	12	24	36	16	....	....	....	....	....
1988-89	Buffalo	NHL	14	0	1	1	4	....	....	....	....	....
	Rochester	AHL	56	18	33	51	12	....	....	....	....	....
1989-90	Hartford	NHL	50	13	24	37	6	5	0	3	3	2
1990-91	Hartford	NHL	41	4	7	11	8	....	....	....	....	....
	Springfield	AHL	26	7	22	29	10	18	*10	8	18	12
1991-92	Hartford	NHL	74	18	29	47	14	7	0	2	2	6
1992-93	Tampa Bay	NHL	77	16	11	27	14	....	....	....	....	....
1993-94	Tampa Bay	NHL	76	13	12	25	23	....	....	....	....	....
	NHL Totals		417	68	116	184	83	13	1	5	6	8

Claimed by **Hartford** in NHL Waiver Draft, October 2, 1989. Signed as a free agent by **Tampa Bay**, June 29, 1992.

ANDERSSON, NICLAS (AN-duhr-suhn)

Left wing. Shoots left. 5'9", 175 lbs. Born, Kungalv, Sweden, May 20, 1971.
(Quebec's 5th choice, 68th overall, in 1989 Entry Draft).

			Regular Season					Playoffs				
Season	Club	Lea	GP	G	A	TP	PIM	GP	G	A	TP	PIM
1987-88	V. Frolunda	Swe. 2	15	5	5	10	6	8	6	4	10	4
1988-89	V. Frolunda	Swe. 2	30	13	24	37	24	....	....	....	....	....
1989-90	V. Frolunda	Swe.	38	10	21	31	14	27	14	18	32	36
1990-91	V. Frolunda	Swe.	22	6	10	16	16	....	....	....	....	....
1991-92	Halifax	AHL	57	8	26	34	41	....	....	....	....	....
1992-93	Quebec	NHL	3	0	1	1	2	....	....	....	....	....
	Halifax	AHL	76	32	50	82	42	....	....	....	....	....
1993-94	Cornwall	AHL	42	18	34	52	8	....	....	....	....	....
	NHL Totals		3	0	1	1	2	....	....	....	....	....

ANDERSSON, PETER FLA.

Defense. Shoots left. 6', 196 lbs. Born, Orebro, Sweden, August 29, 1965.
(NY Rangers' 5th choice, 73rd overall, in 1983 Entry Draft).

			Regular Season					Playoffs				
Season	Club	Lea	GP	G	A	TP	PIM	GP	G	A	TP	PIM
1983-84	Farjestad	Swe.	36	4	7	11	22	....	....	....	....	....
1984-85	Farjestad	Swe.	35	5	12	17	24	....	....	....	....	....
1985-86	Farjestad	Swe.	34	6	10	16	18	....	....	....	....	....
1986-87	Farjestad	Swe.	32	9	8	17	32	....	....	....	....	....
1987-88	Farjestad	Swe.	38	14	20	34	44	....	....	....	....	....
1988-89	Farjestad	Swe.	33	6	17	23	44	....	....	....	....	....
1989-90	Malmo	Swe.	33	15	25	40	32	....	....	....	....	....
1990-91	Malmo	Swe.	34	9	17	26	26	....	....	....	....	....
1991-92	Malmo	Swe.	40	12	20	32	80	....	....	....	....	....
1992-93	NY Rangers	NHL	31	4	11	15	4	....	....	....	....	....
	Binghamton	AHL	27	11	22	33	16	....	....	....	....	....
1993-94	NY Rangers	NHL	8	1	1	2	2	....	....	....	....	....
	Florida	NHL	8	1	1	2	0	....	....	....	....	....
	NHL Totals		47	6	13	19	6	....	....	....	....	....

Traded to **Florida** by **NY Rangers** for Florida's ninth round choice (Vitali Yeremeyev) in 1994 Entry Draft, March 21, 1994.

ANDERSSON-JUNKKA, JONAS PIT.

Defense. Shoots right. 6'2", 170 lbs. Born, Kiruna, Sweden, May 4, 1975.
(Pittsburgh's 4th choice, 104th overall, in 1993 Entry Draft).

			Regular Season					Playoffs				
Season	Club	Lea	GP	G	A	TP	PIM	GP	G	A	TP	PIM
1991-92	Kiruna	Swe.2	1	0	0	0	0	....	....	....	....	....
1992-93	Kiruna	Swe.2	30	3	7	10	32	....	....	....	....	....
1993-94	Kiruna	Swe.2	32	6	10	16	84	....	....	....	....	....

ANDREWS, JEFF TOR.

Left wing. Shoots left. 6'4", 200 lbs. Born, Lindsay, Ont., May 10, 1975.
(Toronto's 5th choice, 175th overall, in 1993 Entry Draft).

			Regular Season					Playoffs				
Season	Club	Lea	GP	G	A	TP	PIM	GP	G	A	TP	PIM
1992-93	North Bay	OHL	65	5	11	16	27	5	1	2	3	6
1993-94	North Bay	OHL	36	11	8	19	42	....	....	....	....	....
	Oshawa	OHL	17	2	4	6	20	....	....	....	....	....

ANDREYCHUK, DAVE (AN-druh-chuhk) TOR.

Left wing. Shoots right. 6'3", 220 lbs. Born, Hamilton, Ont., September 29, 1963.
(Buffalo's 3rd choice, 16th overall, in 1982 Entry Draft).

			Regular Season					Playoffs				
Season	Club	Lea	GP	G	A	TP	PIM	GP	G	A	TP	PIM
1980-81	Oshawa	OHA	67	22	22	44	80	10	3	2	5	20
1981-82	Oshawa	OHL	67	57	43	100	71	3	1	4	5	16
1982-83	**Buffalo**	**NHL**	**43**	**14**	**23**	**37**	**16**	**4**	**1**	**0**	**1**	**4**
	Oshawa	OHL	14	8	24	32	6	....	....	....	....	....
1983-84	**Buffalo**	**NHL**	**78**	**38**	**42**	**80**	**42**	**2**	**0**	**1**	**1**	**2**
1984-85	**Buffalo**	**NHL**	**64**	**31**	**30**	**61**	**54**	**5**	**4**	**2**	**6**	**4**
1985-86	**Buffalo**	**NHL**	**80**	**36**	**51**	**87**	**61**	....	....	....	....	....
1986-87	**Buffalo**	**NHL**	**77**	**25**	**48**	**73**	**46**	....	....	....	....	....
1987-88	**Buffalo**	**NHL**	**80**	**30**	**48**	**78**	**112**	**6**	**2**	**4**	**6**	**0**
1988-89	**Buffalo**	**NHL**	**56**	**28**	**24**	**52**	**40**	**5**	**0**	**3**	**3**	**0**
1989-90	**Buffalo**	**NHL**	**73**	**40**	**42**	**82**	**42**	**6**	**2**	**5**	**7**	**2**
1990-91	**Buffalo**	**NHL**	**80**	**36**	**33**	**69**	**32**	**6**	**2**	**2**	**4**	**8**
1991-92	**Buffalo**	**NHL**	**80**	**41**	**50**	**91**	**71**	**7**	**1**	**3**	**4**	**12**
1992-93	**Buffalo**	**NHL**	**52**	**29**	**32**	**61**	**48**	....	....	....	....	....
	Toronto	**NHL**	**31**	**25**	**13**	**38**	**8**	**21**	**12**	**7**	**19**	**35**
1993-94	**Toronto**	**NHL**	**83**	**53**	**46**	**99**	**98**	**18**	**5**	**5**	**10**	**16**
	NHL Totals		**877**	**426**	**482**	**908**	**670**	**80**	**29**	**32**	**61**	**83**

Played in NHL All-Star Game (1990, 1994)

Traded to **Toronto** by **Buffalo** with Daren Puppa and Buffalo's first round choice (Kenny Jonsson) in 1993 Entry Draft for Grant Fuhr and future considerations, February 2, 1993.

ANDRIJEVSKI, ALEXANDER (an-dray-YEHV-skee)

Right wing. Shoots right. 6'5", 211 lbs. Born, Moscow, USSR, August 10, 1968.
(Chicago's 13th choice, 220th overall, in 1991 Entry Draft).

			Regular Season					Playoffs				
Season	Club	Lea	GP	G	A	TP	PIM	GP	G	A	TP	PIM
1990-91	Moscow D'amo	USSR	44	9	8	17	28	....	....	....	....	....
1991-92	Moscow D'amo	CIS	31	9	8	17	14	....	....	....	....	....
1992-93	**Chicago**	**NHL**	**1**	**0**	**0**	**0**	**0**	....	....	....	....	....
	Indianapolis	IHL	66	26	25	51	59	4	2	3	5	10
1993-94	Indianapolis	IHL	4	0	1	1	2	....	....	....	....	....
	Kalamazoo	IHL	57	6	22	28	58	1	0	0	0	2
	NHL Totals		**1**	**0**	**0**	**0**	**0**	....	....	....	....	....

ANDRUSAK, GREG (AN-druh-sak) PIT.

Defense. Shoots right. 6'1", 190 lbs. Born, Cranbrook, B.C., November 14, 1969.
(Pittsburgh's 5th choice, 88th overall, in 1988 Entry Draft).

			Regular Season					Playoffs				
Season	Club	Lea	GP	G	A	TP	PIM	GP	G	A	TP	PIM
1987-88	Minn.-Duluth	WCHA	37	4	5	9	42	....	....	....	....	....
1988-89	Minn.-Duluth	WCHA	35	4	8	12	74	....	....	....	....	....
	Cdn. Olympic	....	2	0	0	0	0	....	....	....	....	....
1989-90	Minn.-Duluth	WCHA	35	5	29	34	74	....	....	....	....	....
1990-91	Cdn. National	....	53	4	11	15	34	....	....	....	....	....
1991-92a	Minn.-Duluth	WCHA	36	7	27	34	125	....	....	....	....	....
1992-93	Cleveland	IHL	55	3	22	25	78	2	0	0	0	2
	Muskegon	ColHL	2	0	3	3	7	....	....	....	....	....
1993-94	**Pittsburgh**	**NHL**	**3**	**0**	**0**	**0**	**2**	....	....	....	....	....
	Cleveland	IHL	69	13	26	39	109	....	....	....	....	....
	NHL Totals		**3**	**0**	**0**	**0**	**2**	....	....	....	....	....

a WCHA First All-Star Team (1992)

ANGLEHART, SERGE DET.

Defense. Shoots right. 6'2", 190 lbs. Born, Hull, Que., April 18, 1970.
(Detroit's 2nd choice, 38th overall, in 1988 Entry Draft).

			Regular Season					Playoffs				
Season	Club	Lea	GP	G	A	TP	PIM	GP	G	A	TP	PIM
1987-88	Drummondville	QMJHL	44	1	8	9	122	17	0	3	3	19
1988-89	Drummondville	QMJHL	39	6	15	21	89	3	0	0	0	37
	Adirondack	AHL	....	....	....	....	....	2	0	0	0	0
1989-90	Laval	QMJHL	48	2	19	21	131	10	1	6	7	69
1990-91	Adirondack	AHL	52	3	8	11	113	....	....	....	....	....
1991-92	Adirondack	AHL	16	0	1	1	43	....	....	....	....	....
1992-93	Adirondack	AHL	3	0	0	0	4	....	....	....	....	....
	Fort Wayne	IHL	2	0	0	0	2	....	....	....	....	....
1993-94	Adirondack	AHL	31	0	2	2	87	....	....	....	....	....

ANISIMOV, ARTEM (ah-NIH-sih-mohv) PHI.

Defense. Shoots left. 6'1", 187 lbs. Born, Kazan, USSR, July 27, 1976.
(Philadelphia's 1st choice, 62nd overall, in 1994 Entry Draft).

			Regular Season					Playoffs				
Season	Club	Lea	GP	G	A	TP	PIM	GP	G	A	TP	PIM
1993-94	Itil Kazan	CIS	38	0	1	1	12	5	0	0	0	0

ANNECK, DORIAN WPG.

Center. Shoots left. 6'1", 183 lbs. Born, Winnipeg, Man., April 24, 1976.
(Winnipeg's 2nd choice, 56th overall, in 1994 Entry Draft).

			Regular Season					Playoffs				
Season	Club	Lea	GP	G	A	TP	PIM	GP	G	A	TP	PIM
1992-93	Victoria	WHL	63	5	6	11	19	....	....	....	....	....
1993-94	Victoria	WHL	71	26	53	79	30	....	....	....	....	....

ANTOSKI, SHAWN (an-TAW-skee) VAN.

Left wing. Shoots left. 6'4", 235 lbs. Born, Brantford, Ont., March 25, 1970.
(Vancouver's 2nd choice, 18th overall, in 1990 Entry Draft).

			Regular Season					Playoffs				
Season	Club	Lea	GP	G	A	TP	PIM	GP	G	A	TP	PIM
1987-88	North Bay	OHL	52	3	4	7	163	....	....	....	....	....
1988-89	North Bay	OHL	57	6	21	27	201	9	5	3	8	24
1989-90	North Bay	OHL	59	25	31	56	201	5	1	2	3	17
1990-91	**Vancouver**	**NHL**	**2**	**0**	**0**	**0**	**0**	....	....	....	....	....
	Milwaukee	IHL	62	17	7	24	330	5	1	2	3	10
1991-92	**Vancouver**	**NHL**	**4**	**0**	**0**	**0**	**29**	....	....	....	....	....
	Milwaukee	IHL	52	17	16	33	346	5	2	0	2	20
1992-93	**Vancouver**	**NHL**	**2**	**0**	**0**	**0**	**0**	....	....	....	....	....
	Hamilton	AHL	41	3	4	7	172	....	....	....	....	....
1993-94	**Vancouver**	**NHL**	**55**	**1**	**2**	**3**	**190**	**16**	**0**	**1**	**1**	**36**
	NHL Totals		**63**	**1**	**2**	**3**	**219**	**16**	**0**	**1**	**1**	**36**

APPEL, FRANK (AHP-pehl) CGY.

Defense. Shoots left. 6'4", 207 lbs. Born, Dusseldorf, West Germany, May 12, 1976.
(Calgary's 7th choice, 123rd overall, in 1994 Entry Draft).

			Regular Season					Playoffs				
Season	Club	Lea	GP	G	A	TP	PIM	GP	G	A	TP	PIM
1993-94	Dusseldorf	Ger.	4	0	0	0	4	....	....	....	....	....

ARCHIBALD, DAVE OT

Center/Left wing. Shoots left. 6'1", 210 lbs. Born, Chilliwack, B.C., April 14, 1969.
(Minnesota's 1st choice, 6th overall, in 1987 Entry Draft).

			Regular Season					Playoffs				
Season	Club	Lea	GP	G	A	TP	PIM	GP	G	A	TP	PIM
1984-85	Portland	WHL	47	7	11	18	10	3	0	2	2	[illegible]
1985-86	Portland	WHL	70	29	35	64	56	15	6	7	13	[illegible]
1986-87	Portland	WHL	65	50	57	107	40	20	10	18	28	[illegible]
1987-88	**Minnesota**	**NHL**	**78**	**13**	**20**	**33**	**26**	....	....	....	....	....
1988-89	**Minnesota**	**NHL**	**72**	**14**	**19**	**33**	**14**	**5**	**0**	**1**	**1**	[illegible]
1989-90	**Minnesota**	**NHL**	**12**	**1**	**5**	**6**	**6**	....	....	....	....	....
	NY Rangers	**NHL**	**19**	**2**	**3**	**5**	**6**	....	....	....	....	....
	Flint	IHL	41	14	38	52	16	4	3	2	5	[illegible]
1990-91	Cdn. National	....	29	19	12	31	20	....	....	....	....	....
1991-92	Cdn. National	....	58	20	43	63	62	....	....	....	....	....
	Cdn. Olympic	....	8	7	1	8	18	....	....	....	....	....
	Bolzano	....	5	4	3	7	16	7	8	5	13	[illegible]
1992-93	Binghamton	AHL	8	6	3	9	10	....	....	....	....	....
	Ottawa	**NHL**	**44**	**9**	**6**	**15**	**32**	....	....	....	....	....
1993-94	**Ottawa**	**NHL**	**33**	**10**	**8**	**18**	**14**	....	....	....	....	....
	NHL Totals		**258**	**49**	**61**	**110**	**98**	**5**	**0**	**1**	**1**	[illegible]

Traded to **NY Rangers** by **Minnesota** for Jayson More, November 1, 1989. Traded to **Ottawa** by **NY Rangers** for Ottawa's fifth round choice (later traded to Los Angeles — Los Angeles selected Frederick Beaubien) in 1993 Entry Draft, November 5, 1992.

ARMSTRONG, BILL BOS

Defense. Shoots left. 6'5", 220 lbs. Born, Richmond Hill, Ont., May 18, 1970.
(Philadelphia's 6th choice, 46th overall, in 1990 Entry Draft).

			Regular Season					Playoffs				
Season	Club	Lea	GP	G	A	TP	PIM	GP	G	A	TP	PIM
1987-88	Toronto	OHL	64	1	10	11	99	....	....	....	....	....
1988-89	Toronto	OHL	64	1	16	17	82	....	....	....	....	....
1989-90	Hamilton	OHL	18	0	2	2	38	....	....	....	....	....
	Niagara Falls	OHL	4	0	1	1	13	....	....	....	....	....
	Oshawa	OHL	41	2	8	10	115	17	0	7	7	[illegible]
1990-91	Hershey	AHL	56	1	9	10	117	....	....	....	....	....
1991-92	Hershey	AHL	80	2	14	16	159	3	0	0	0	[illegible]
1992-93	Hershey	AHL	80	2	10	12	205	....	....	....	....	....
1993-94	Providence	AHL	66	0	7	7	200	....	....	....	....	....

Signed as a free agent by **Boston**, July 22, 1993.

ARMSTRONG, BILL H. N.J

Center. Shoots left. 6'2", 195 lbs. Born, London, Ont., June 25, 1966.

			Regular Season					Playoffs				
Season	Club	Lea	GP	G	A	TP	PIM	GP	G	A	TP	PIM
1986-87	W. Michigan	CCHA	43	13	20	33	86	....	....	....	....	....
1987-88	W. Michigan	CCHA	41	22	17	39	88	....	....	....	....	....
1988-89	W. Michigan	CCHA	40	23	19	42	97	....	....	....	....	....
1989-90	Hershey	AHL	58	10	6	16	99	....	....	....	....	....
1990-91	**Philadelphia**	**NHL**	**1**	**0**	**1**	**1**	**0**	....	....	....	....	....
	Hershey	AHL	70	36	27	63	150	6	2	8	10	[illegible]
1991-92	Hershey	AHL	64	26	22	48	186	6	2	2	4	[illegible]
1992-93	Cincinnati	IHL	42	14	11	25	99	....	....	....	....	....
	Utica	AHL	32	18	21	39	60	....	....	....	....	....
1993-94	Albany	AHL	74	32	50	82	188	....	....	....	....	....
	NHL Totals		**1**	**0**	**1**	**1**	**0**	....	....	....	....	....

Signed as a free agent by **Philadelphia**, May 16, 1989. Signed as a free agent by **New Jersey**, March 21, 1993.

ARMSTRONG, CHRIS FLA

Defense. Shoots left. 6', 184 lbs. Born, Regina, Sask., June 26, 1975.
(Florida's 3rd choice, 57th overall, in 1993 Entry Draft).

			Regular Season					Playoffs				
Season	Club	Lea	GP	G	A	TP	PIM	GP	G	A	TP	PIM
1991-92	Moose Jaw	WHL	43	2	7	9	19	4	0	0	0	[illegible]
1992-93	Moose Jaw	WHL	67	9	35	44	104	....	....	....	....	....
1993-94ab	Moose Jaw	WHL	64	13	55	68	54	....	....	....	....	....
	Cincinnati	IHL	1	0	0	0	0	10	1	3	4	[illegible]

a WHL East First All-Star Team (1994)
b Canadian Major Junior Second All-Star Team (1994)

ARMSTRONG, DEREK NY

Center. Shoots right. 5'11", 180 lbs. Born, Ottawa, Ont., April 23, 1973.
(NY Islanders' 5th choice, 128th overall, in 1992 Entry Draft).

			Regular Season					Playoffs				
Season	Club	Lea	GP	G	A	TP	PIM	GP	G	A	TP	PIM
1991-92	Sudbury	OHL	66	31	54	85	22	9	2	2	4	[illegible]
1992-93	Sudbury	OHL	66	44	62	106	56	14	9	10	19	[illegible]
1993-94	**NY Islanders**	**NHL**	**1**	**0**	**0**	**0**	**0**	....	....	....	....	....
	Salt Lake	IHL	76	23	35	58	61	....	....	....	....	....
	NHL Totals		**1**	**0**	**0**	**0**	**0**	....	....	....	....	....

ARNIEL, SCOTT (ar-NEEL)

Left wing. Shoots left. 6'1", 188 lbs. Born, Kingston, Ont., September 17, 1962.
(Winnipeg's 2nd choice, 22nd overall, in 1981 Entry Draft).

			Regular Season					Playoffs				
Season	Club	Lea	GP	G	A	TP	PIM	GP	G	A	TP	PIM
1980-81	Cornwall	QJHL	68	52	71	123	102	19	14	19	33	24
1981-82	**Winnipeg**	**NHL**	**17**	**1**	**8**	**9**	**14**	**3**	**0**	**0**	**0**	**0**
	Cornwall	OHL	24	18	26	44	43	....	....	....	....	....
1982-83	**Winnipeg**	**NHL**	**75**	**13**	**5**	**18**	**46**	**2**	**0**	**0**	**0**	**0**
1983-84	**Winnipeg**	**NHL**	**80**	**21**	**35**	**56**	**68**	**2**	**0**	**0**	**0**	**5**
1984-85	**Winnipeg**	**NHL**	**79**	**22**	**22**	**44**	**81**	**8**	**1**	**2**	**3**	**9**
1985-86	**Winnipeg**	**NHL**	**80**	**18**	**25**	**43**	**40**	**3**	**0**	**0**	**0**	**12**
1986-87	**Buffalo**	**NHL**	**63**	**11**	**14**	**25**	**59**	....	....	....	....	....
1987-88	**Buffalo**	**NHL**	**73**	**17**	**23**	**40**	**61**	**6**	**0**	**1**	**1**	**5**
1988-89	**Buffalo**	**NHL**	**80**	**18**	**23**	**41**	**46**	**5**	**1**	**0**	**1**	**4**
1989-90	**Buffalo**	**NHL**	**79**	**18**	**14**	**32**	**77**	**5**	**1**	**0**	**1**	**4**
1990-91	**Winnipeg**	**NHL**	**75**	**5**	**17**	**22**	**87**	....	....	....	....	....
1991-92	**Boston**	**NHL**	**29**	**5**	**3**	**8**	**20**	....	....	....	....	....
	Maine	AHL	14	4	4	8	8	....	....	....	....	....
	New Haven	AHL	11	3	3	6	10	....	....	....	....	....
1992-93	San Diego	IHL	79	35	48	83	116	14	6	5	11	16
1993-94	San Diego	IHL	79	34	43	77	121	7	6	3	9	24
	NHL Totals		**730**	**149**	**189**	**338**	**599**	**34**	**3**	**3**	**6**	**39**

Traded to **Buffalo** by **Winnipeg** for Gilles Hamel, June 21, 1986. Traded to **Winnipeg** by **Buffalo** with Phil Housley, Jeff Parker and Buffalo's first round choice (Keith Tkachuk) in 1990 Entry Draft for Dale Hawerchuk, Winnipeg's first round choice (Brad May) in 1990 Entry Draft and future considerations, June 16, 1990. Traded to **Boston** by **Winnipeg** for future considerations, November 22, 1991.

RNOTT, JASON (AHR-nawt) EDM.

enter. Shoots right. 6'3", 195 lbs. Born, Collingwood, Ont., October 11, 1974.
dmonton's 1st choice, 7th overall, in 1993 Entry Draft).

			Regular Season					Playoffs				
eason	Club	Lea	GP	G	A	TP	PIM	GP	G	A	TP	PIM
991-92	Oshawa	OHL	57	9	15	24	12	....	....	....	....	....
992-93	Oshawa	OHL	56	41	57	98	74	13	9	9	18	20
993-94a	**Edmonton**	**NHL**	**78**	**33**	**35**	**68**	**104**	....	....	....	....	....
	NHL Totals		**78**	**33**	**35**	**68**	**104**	....	....	....	....	....

NHL/Upper Deck All-Rookie Team (1994)

SHTON, BRENT

eft wing. Shoots left. 6'1", 210 lbs. Born, Saskatoon, Sask., May 18, 1960.
/ancouver's 2nd choice, 26th overall, in 1979 Entry Draft).

			Regular Season					Playoffs				
eason	Club	Lea	GP	G	A	TP	PIM	GP	G	A	TP	PIM
977-78	Saskatoon	WHL	46	38	26	64	47	....	....	....	....	....
978-79	Saskatoon	WHL	62	64	55	119	80	11	14	4	18	5
979-80	**Vancouver**	**NHL**	**47**	**5**	**14**	**19**	**11**	**4**	**1**	**0**	**1**	**6**
980-81	**Vancouver**	**NHL**	**77**	**18**	**11**	**29**	**57**	**3**	**0**	**0**	**0**	**0**
981-82	**Colorado**	**NHL**	**80**	**24**	**36**	**60**	**26**	....	....	....	....	....
982-83	**New Jersey**	**NHL**	**76**	**14**	**19**	**33**	**47**	....	....	....	....	....
983-84	**Minnesota**	**NHL**	**68**	**7**	**10**	**17**	**54**	**12**	**1**	**2**	**3**	**22**
984-85	**Minnesota**	**NHL**	**29**	**4**	**7**	**11**	**15**	....	....	....	....	....
	Quebec	**NHL**	**49**	**27**	**24**	**51**	**38**	**18**	**6**	**4**	**10**	**13**
985-86	**Quebec**	**NHL**	**77**	**26**	**32**	**58**	**64**	**3**	**2**	**1**	**3**	**9**
986-87	**Quebec**	**NHL**	**46**	**25**	**19**	**44**	**17**	....	....	....	....	....
	Detroit	**NHL**	**35**	**15**	**16**	**31**	**22**	**16**	**4**	**9**	**13**	**6**
987-88	**Detroit**	**NHL**	**73**	**26**	**27**	**53**	**50**	**16**	**7**	**5**	**12**	**10**
988-89	**Winnipeg**	**NHL**	**75**	**31**	**37**	**68**	**36**	....	....	....	....	....
989-90	**Winnipeg**	**NHL**	**79**	**22**	**34**	**56**	**37**	**7**	**3**	**1**	**4**	**2**
990-91	**Winnipeg**	**NHL**	**61**	**12**	**24**	**36**	**58**	....	....	....	....	....
991-92	**Winnipeg**	**NHL**	**7**	**1**	**0**	**1**	**4**	....	....	....	....	....
	Boston	**NHL**	**61**	**17**	**22**	**39**	**47**	....	....	....	....	....
992-93	**Boston**	**NHL**	**26**	**2**	**2**	**4**	**11**	....	....	....	....	....
	Providence	AHL	11	4	8	12	10	....	....	....	....	....
	Calgary	**NHL**	**32**	**8**	**11**	**19**	**41**	**6**	**0**	**3**	**3**	**2**
993-94	Las Vegas	IHL	16	4	10	14	29	....	....	....	....	....
	NHL Totals		**998**	**284**	**345**	**629**	**635**	**85**	**24**	**25**	**49**	**70**

raded to **Winnipeg** by **Vancouver** with Vancouver's fourth round choice (Tom Martin) in the 1982 ntry Draft as compensation for Vancouver's signing of Ivan Hlinka, July 15, 1981. Traded to olorado by **Winnipeg** with Winnipeg's third round choice (Dave Kasper) in 1982 Entry Draft for ucien DeBlois, July 15, 1981. Traded to **Minnesota** by **New Jersey** for Dave Lewis, October 3, 983. Traded to **Quebec** by **Minnesota** with Brad Maxwell for Tony McKegney and Bo Berglund, ecember 14, 1984. Traded to **Detroit** by **Quebec** with Gilbert Delorme and Mark Kumpel for Basil AcRae, John Ogrodnick and Doug Shedden, January 17, 1987. Traded to **Winnipeg** by **Detroit** for aul MacLean, June 13, 1988. Traded to **Boston** by **Winnipeg** for Petri Skriko, October 29, 1991. raded to **Calgary** by **Boston** for C.J. Young, February 1, 1993.

STLEY, MARK BUF.

)efense. Shoots left. 5'11", 185 lbs. Born, Calgary, Alta., March 30, 1969.
Buffalo's 9th choice, 194th overall, in 1989 Entry Draft).

			Regular Season					Playoffs				
eason	Club	Lea	GP	G	A	TP	PIM	GP	G	A	TP	PIM
1988-89	Lake Superior	CCHA	42	3	12	15	26	....	....	....	....	....
1989-90	Lake Superior	CCHA	43	7	25	32	29	....	....	....	....	....
1990-91a	Lake Superior	CCHA	45	19	27	46	50	....	....	....	....	....
1991-92bcd	Lake Superior	CCHA	39	11	36	47	65	....	....	....	....	....
1992-93	Lugano	Switz.	30	10	12	22	57	....	....	....	....	....
	Cdn. National	....	22	4	14	18	14	....	....	....	....	....
1993-94	Cdn. National	....	13	4	8	12	6	....	....	....	....	....
	Cdn. Olympic	....	8	0	1	1	4	....	....	....	....	....
	Buffalo	**NHL**	**1**	**0**	**0**	**0**	**0**	....	....	....	....	....
	NHL Totals		**1**	**0**	**0**	**0**	**0**	....	....	....	....	....

a CCHA Second All-Star Team (1991)
b CCHA First All-Star Team (1992)
c NCAA West First All-American Team (1992)
d NCAA All-Tournament Team (1992)

AUCOIN, ADRIAN (oh-KWEHN) VAN.

Defense. Shoots right. 6'1", 194 lbs. Born, Ottawa, Ont., July 3, 1973.
(Vancouver's 7th choice, 117th overall, in 1992 Entry Draft).

			Regular Season					Playoffs				
Season	Club	Lea	GP	G	A	TP	PIM	GP	G	A	TP	PIM
1991-92	Boston U.	H.E.	32	2	10	12	60	....	....	....	....	....
1992-93	Cdn. National	....	41	9	1	20	67	....	....	....	....	....
1993-94	Cdn. National	....	59	5	12	17	80	....	....	....	....	....
	Cdn. Olympic	....	4	0	0	0	2	....	....	....	....	....
	Hamilton	AHL	13	1	2	3	19	4	0	2	2	6

AUDETTE, DONALD (aw-DEHT) BUF.

Right wing. Shoots right. 5'8", 175 lbs. Born, Laval, Que., September 23, 1969.
(Buffalo's 8th choice, 183rd overall, in 1989 Entry Draft).

			Regular Season					Playoffs				
Season	Club	Lea	GP	G	A	TP	PIM	GP	G	A	TP	PIM
1986-87	Laval	QMJHL	66	17	22	39	36	14	2	6	8	10
1987-88	Laval	QMJHL	63	48	61	109	56	14	7	12	19	20
1988-89a	Laval	QMJHL	70	76	85	161	123	17	17	12	29	43
1989-90bc	Rochester	AHL	70	42	46	88	78	15	9	8	17	29
	Buffalo	**NHL**	....	....	....	....	....	**2**	**0**	**0**	**0**	**0**
1990-91	**Buffalo**	**NHL**	**8**	**4**	**3**	**7**	**4**	....	....	....	....	....
	Rochester	AHL	5	4	0	4	2	....	....	....	....	....
1991-92	**Buffalo**	**NHL**	**63**	**31**	**17**	**48**	**75**	....	....	....	....	....
1992-93	**Buffalo**	**NHL**	**44**	**12**	**7**	**19**	**51**	**8**	**2**	**2**	**4**	**6**
	Rochester	AHL	6	8	4	12	10	....	....	....	....	....
1993-94	**Buffalo**	**NHL**	**77**	**29**	**30**	**59**	**41**	**7**	**0**	**1**	**1**	**6**
	NHL Totals		**192**	**76**	**57**	**133**	**171**	**17**	**2**	**3**	**5**	**12**

a QMJHL First All-Star Team (1989)
b AHL First All-Star Team (1990)
c Won Dudley "Red" Garret Memorial Trophy (Top Rookie - AHL) (1990)

AUGER, VINCENT QUE.

Center. Shoots left. 5'10", 175 lbs. Born, Quebec, Que., March 7, 1975.
(Quebec's 11th choice, 231st overall, in 1993 Entry Draft).

			Regular Season					Playoffs				
Season	Club	Lea	GP	G	A	TP	PIM	GP	G	A	TP	PIM
1992-93	Hawkesbury	Tier II	52	41	36	77	104	....	....	....	....	....
1993-94	Cornell	ECAC	29	11	13	24	33	....	....	....	....	....

AUGUSTA, PATRIK (ah-GOOS-tuh, pa-TREEK) TOR.

Right wing. Shoots left. 5'10", 170 lbs. Born, Jihlava, Czech., November 13, 1969.
(Toronto's 8th choice, 149th overall, in 1992 Entry Draft).

			Regular Season					Playoffs				
Season	Club	Lea	GP	G	A	TP	PIM	GP	G	A	TP	PIM
1988-89	Dukla Jihlava	Czech.	15	3	1	4	4	....	....	....	....	....
1989-90	Dukla Jihlava	Czech.	46	12	12	24	....	....	....	....	....	....
1990-91	Dukla Jihlava	Czech.	51	20	23	43	....	....	....	....	....	....
1991-92	Dukla Jihlava	Czech.	42	16	16	32	26	....	....	....	....	....
1992-93	St. John's	AHL	75	32	45	77	74	8	3	3	6	23
1993-94	**Toronto**	**NHL**	**2**	**0**	**0**	**0**	**0**	....	....	....	....	....
a	St. John's	AHL	77	*53	43	96	105	11	4	8	12	4
	NHL Totals		**2**	**0**	**0**	**0**	**0**	....	....	....	....	....

a AHL Second All-Star Team (1994)

BABARIKO, JEVGENI VAN.

Center. Shoots left. 6'1", 183 lbs. Born, Novgorod, USSR, March 3, 1974.
(Vancouver's 6th choice, 176th overall, in 1993 Entry Draft).

			Regular Season					Playoffs				
Season	Club	Lea	GP	G	A	TP	PIM	GP	G	A	TP	PIM
1991-92	Novgorod	CIS	14	5	0	5	2	....	....	....	....	....
1992-93	Novgorod	CIS	12	1	0	1	4	....	....	....	....	....
1993-94	Novgorod	CIS	44	3	5	8	12	....	....	....	....	....

BABYCH, DAVE (BAB-itch) VAN.

Defense. Shoots left. 6'2", 215 lbs. Born, Edmonton, Alta., May 23, 1961.
(Winnipeg's 1st choice, 2nd overall, in 1980 Entry Draft).

			Regular Season					Playoffs				
Season	Club	Lea	GP	G	A	TP	PIM	GP	G	A	TP	PIM
1978-79	Portland	WHL	67	20	59	79	63	25	7	22	29	22
1979-80a	Portland	WHL	50	22	60	82	71	8	1	10	11	2
1980-81	**Winnipeg**	**NHL**	**69**	**6**	**38**	**44**	**90**	....	....	....	....	....
1981-82	**Winnipeg**	**NHL**	**79**	**19**	**49**	**68**	**92**	**4**	**1**	**2**	**3**	**29**
1982-83	**Winnipeg**	**NHL**	**79**	**13**	**61**	**74**	**56**	**3**	**0**	**0**	**0**	**0**
1983-84	**Winnipeg**	**NHL**	**66**	**18**	**39**	**57**	**62**	**3**	**1**	**1**	**2**	**0**
1984-85	**Winnipeg**	**NHL**	**78**	**13**	**49**	**62**	**78**	**8**	**2**	**7**	**9**	**6**
1985-86	**Winnipeg**	**NHL**	**19**	**4**	**12**	**16**	**14**	....	....	....	....	....
	Hartford	**NHL**	**62**	**10**	**43**	**53**	**36**	**8**	**1**	**3**	**4**	**14**
1986-87	**Hartford**	**NHL**	**66**	**8**	**33**	**41**	**44**	**6**	**1**	**1**	**2**	**14**
1987-88	**Hartford**	**NHL**	**71**	**14**	**36**	**50**	**54**	**6**	**3**	**2**	**5**	**2**
1988-89	**Hartford**	**NHL**	**70**	**6**	**41**	**47**	**54**	**4**	**1**	**5**	**6**	**2**
1989-90	**Hartford**	**NHL**	**72**	**6**	**37**	**43**	**62**	**7**	**1**	**2**	**3**	**0**
1990-91	**Hartford**	**NHL**	**8**	**0**	**6**	**6**	**4**	....	....	....	....	....
1991-92	**Vancouver**	**NHL**	**75**	**5**	**24**	**29**	**63**	**13**	**2**	**6**	**8**	**10**
1992-93	**Vancouver**	**NHL**	**43**	**3**	**16**	**19**	**44**	**12**	**2**	**5**	**7**	**6**
1993-94	**Vancouver**	**NHL**	**73**	**4**	**28**	**32**	**52**	**24**	**3**	**5**	**8**	**12**
	NHL Totals		**930**	**129**	**512**	**641**	**805**	**98**	**18**	**39**	**57**	**95**

a WHL First All-Star Team (1980)

Played in NHL All-Star Game (1983, 1984)

Traded to **Hartford** by **Winnipeg** for Ray Neufeld, November 21, 1985. Claimed by **Minnesota** from **Hartford** in Expansion Draft, May 30, 1991. Traded to **Vancouver** by **Minnesota** for Tom Kurvers, June 22, 1991.

BACA, JERGUS

Defense. Shoots left. 6'2", 211 lbs. Born, Liptovsky Mikulas, Czech., January 4, 1965.
(Hartford's 6th choice, 141st overall, in 1990 Entry Draft).

			Regular Season					Playoffs				
Season	Club	Lea	GP	G	A	TP	PIM	GP	G	A	TP	PIM
1987-88	VSZ Kosice	Czech.	40	5	5	10	32	....	....	....	....	....
1988-89a	VSZ Kosice	Czech.	42	3	10	13	46	....	....	....	....	....
1989-90a	VSZ Kosice	Czech.	47	9	16	25	....	....	....	....	....	....
1990-91	**Hartford**	**NHL**	**9**	**0**	**2**	**2**	**14**	....	....	....	....	....
	Springfield	AHL	57	6	23	29	89	18	3	13	16	18
1991-92	**Hartford**	**NHL**	**1**	**0**	**0**	**0**	**0**	....	....	....	....	....
	Springfield	AHL	64	6	20	26	88	11	0	6	6	20
1992-93	Milwaukee	IHL	73	9	29	38	108	6	0	3	3	2
1993-94	Milwaukee	IHL	67	6	29	35	119	3	1	1	2	4
	NHL Totals		**10**	**0**	**2**	**2**	**14**	....	....	....	....	....

a Czechoslovakian National League First Team All-Star (1989, 1990)

BADDUKE, JOHN VAN.

Right wing. Shoots right. 6'2", 195 lbs. Born, Watson, Sask., June 21, 1972.

			Regular Season					Playoffs				
Season	Club	Lea	GP	G	A	TP	PIM	GP	G	A	TP	PIM
1988-89	Regina	WHL	8	0	0	0	4	....	....	....	....	....
1989-90	Victoria	WHL	49	1	2	3	138	....	....	....	....	....
1990-91	Victoria	WHL	66	8	9	17	305	....	....	....	....	....
1991-92	Portland	WHL	67	6	13	19	*335	6	1	1	2	42
1992-93	Portland	WHL	71	12	14	26	*367	16	3	4	7	57
1993-94	Hamilton	AHL	55	6	8	14	*356	4	0	1	1	18
	Columbus	ECHL	7	0	3	3	60	....	....	....	....	....
	Brantford	ColHL	1	1	0	1	2	....	....	....	....	....

Signed as a free agent by **Vancouver**, February 2, 1994.

BAKER, JAMIE S.J.

Center. Shoots left. 6', 190 lbs. Born, Ottawa, Ont., August 31, 1966.
(Quebec's 2nd choice, 8th overall, in 1988 Supplemental Draft).

			Regular Season					Playoffs				
Season	Club	Lea	GP	G	A	TP	PIM	GP	G	A	TP	PIM
1985-86	St. Lawrence	ECAC	31	9	16	25	52	....	....	....	....	....
1986-87	St. Lawrence	ECAC	32	8	24	32	59	....	....	....	....	....
1987-88	St. Lawrence	ECAC	34	26	24	50	38	....	....	....	....	....
1988-89	St. Lawrence	ECAC	13	11	16	27	16	....	....	....	....	....
1989-90	**Quebec**	**NHL**	**1**	**0**	**0**	**0**	**0**	....	....	....	....	....
	Halifax	AHL	74	17	43	60	47	6	0	0	0	7
1990-91	**Quebec**	**NHL**	**18**	**2**	**0**	**2**	**8**	....	....	....	....	....
	Halifax	AHL	50	14	22	36	85	....	....	....	....	....
1991-92	**Quebec**	**NHL**	**52**	**7**	**10**	**17**	**32**	....	....	....	....	....
	Halifax	AHL	9	5	0	5	12	....	....	....	....	....
1992-93	**Ottawa**	**NHL**	**76**	**19**	**29**	**48**	**54**	....	....	....	....	....
1993-94	**San Jose**	**NHL**	**65**	**12**	**5**	**17**	**38**	**14**	**3**	**2**	**5**	**30**
	NHL Totals		**212**	**40**	**44**	**84**	**132**	**14**	**3**	**2**	**5**	**30**

Signed as a free agent by **Ottawa**, September 2, 1992. Signed as a free agent by **San Jose**, September 11, 1993.

BAKULA, MARTIN — EDM.

Defense. Shoots left. 6'1", 190 lbs. Born, Kladno, Czech., June 23, 1970.
(Edmonton's 8th choice, 189th overall, in 1993 Entry Draft).

			Regular Season					Playoffs				
Season	Club	Lea	GP	G	A	TP	PIM	GP	G	A	TP	PIM
1987-88	Poldi Kladno	Czech.	30	0	1	1	4	....	....	....	....	....
1988-89	Poldi Kladno	Czech.	24	1	2	3	20	....	....	....	....	....
1989-90	Poldi Kladno	Czech.	17	0	1	1	....	....	....	....	....	....
1990-91			DID NOT PLAY									
1991-92	Alaska-Anch.	G.N.	28	5	14	19	24	....	....	....	....	....
1992-93	Alaska-Anch.	WCHA	35	9	15	24	62	....	....	....	....	....
1993-94	Cape Breton	AHL	71	6	22	28	65	4	0	1	1	0

BALKOVEC, MACO — CHI.

Defense. Shoots left. 6'2", 200 lbs. Born, New Westminster, B.C., January 17, 1971.
(Chicago's 5th choice, 110th overall, in 1991 Entry Draft).

			Regular Season					Playoffs				
Season	Club	Lea	GP	G	A	TP	PIM	GP	G	A	TP	PIM
1991-92	U. Wisconsin	WCHA	35	7	11	18	95	....	....	....	....	....
1992-93	U. Wisconsin	WCHA	16	1	9	10	16	....	....	....	....	....
1993-94	U. Wisconsin	WCHA	39	4	10	14	74	....	....	....	....	....

BANCROFT, STEVE — PIT.

Defense. Shoots left. 6'1", 214 lbs. Born, Toronto, Ont., October 6, 1970.
(Toronto's 3rd choice, 21st overall, in 1989 Entry Draft).

			Regular Season					Playoffs				
Season	Club	Lea	GP	G	A	TP	PIM	GP	G	A	TP	PIM
1987-88	Belleville	OHL	56	1	8	9	42	....	....	....	....	....
1988-89	Belleville	OHL	66	7	30	37	99	5	0	2	2	10
1989-90	Belleville	OHL	53	10	33	43	135	11	3	9	12	38
1990-91	Newmarket	AHL	9	0	3	3	22	....	....	....	....	....
	Maine	AHL	53	2	12	14	46	2	0	0	0	2
1991-92	Maine	AHL	26	1	3	4	45	....	....	....	....	....
	Indianapolis	IHL	36	8	23	31	49	....	....	....	....	....
1992-93	**Chicago**	**NHL**	**1**	**0**	**0**	**0**	**0**	....	....	....	....	....
	Indianapolis	IHL	53	10	35	45	138	....	....	....	....	....
	Moncton	AHL	21	3	13	16	16	5	0	0	0	16
1993-94	Cleveland	IHL	33	2	12	14	58	....	....	....	....	....
	NHL Totals		**1**	**0**	**0**	**0**	**0**	....	....	....	....	....

Traded to **Boston** by **Toronto** for Rob Cimetta, November 9, 1990. Traded to **Chicago** by **Boston** with Boston's eleventh round choice (later traded to Winnipeg — Winnipeg selected Russel Hewson) in 1993 Entry Draft for Chicago's eleventh round choice (Eugene Pavlov) in 1992 Entry Draft, January 9, 1992. Traded to **Winnipeg** by **Chicago** with future considerations for Troy Murray, February 21, 1993. Claimed by **Florida** from **Winnipeg** in Expansion Draft, June 24, 1993. Signed as a free agent by **Pittsburgh**, August 2, 1993.

BANHAM, FRANK

Right wing. Shoots right. 5'11", 175 lbs. Born, Calahoo, Alta., April 14, 1975.
(Washington's 4th choice, 147th overall, in 1993 Entry Draft).

			Regular Season					Playoffs				
Season	Club	Lea	GP	G	A	TP	PIM	GP	G	A	TP	PIM
1992-93	Saskatoon	WHL	71	29	33	62	55	9	2	7	9	8
1993-94	Saskatoon	WHL	65	28	39	67	99	16	8	11	19	36

BANKS, DARREN

Left wing. Shoots left. 6'2", 215 lbs. Born, Toronto, Ont., March 18, 1966.

			Regular Season					Playoffs				
Season	Club	Lea	GP	G	A	TP	PIM	GP	G	A	TP	PIM
1986-87	Brock	OUAA	24	5	3	8	82	....	....	....	....	....
1987-88	Brock	OUAA	26	10	11	21	110	....	....	....	....	....
1988-89	Brock	OUAA	26	19	14	33	88	....	....	....	....	....
1989-90	Salt Lake	IHL	6	0	0	0	11	1	0	0	0	10
	Fort Wayne	IHL	2	0	1	1	0	....	....	....	....	....
	Knoxville	ECHL	52	25	22	47	258	....	....	....	....	....
1990-91	Salt Lake	IHL	56	9	7	16	286	3	0	1	1	6
1991-92	Salt Lake	IHL	55	5	5	10	303	....	....	....	....	....
1992-93	**Boston**	**NHL**	**16**	**2**	**1**	**3**	**64**	....	....	....	....	....
	Providence	AHL	43	9	5	14	199	1	0	0	0	0
1993-94	**Boston**	**NHL**	**4**	**0**	**1**	**1**	**9**	....	....	....	....	....
	Providence	AHL	41	6	3	9	189	....	....	....	....	....
	NHL Totals		**20**	**2**	**2**	**4**	**73**	....	....	....	....	....

Signed as a free agent by **Calgary**, December 12, 1990. Signed as a free agent by **Boston**, July 16, 1992.

BANNISTER, DREW — T.B.

Defense. Shoots right. 6'1", 193 lbs. Born, Belleville, Ont., September 4, 1974.
(Tampa Bay's 2nd choice, 26th overall, in 1992 Entry Draft).

			Regular Season					Playoffs				
Season	Club	Lea	GP	G	A	TP	PIM	GP	G	A	TP	PIM
1990-91	S.S. Marie	OHL	41	2	8	10	51	4	0	0	0	0
1991-92	S.S. Marie	OHL	64	4	21	25	122	16	3	10	13	36
1992-93a	S.S. Marie	OHL	59	5	28	33	114	18	2	7	9	12
1993-94b	S.S. Marie	OHL	58	7	43	50	108	14	6	9	15	20

a Memorial Cup All-Star Team (1993)
b OHL Second All-Star Team (1994)

BARNABY, MATTHEW — BUF.

Left wing. Shoots left. 6', 170 lbs. Born, Ottawa, Ont., May 4, 1973.
(Buffalo's 5th choice, 83rd overall, in 1992 Entry Draft).

			Regular Season					Playoffs				
Season	Club	Lea	GP	G	A	TP	PIM	GP	G	A	TP	PIM
1990-91	Beauport	QMJHL	52	9	5	14	262	....	....	....	....	....
1991-92	Beauport	QMJHL	63	29	37	66	*476	....	....	....	....	....
1992-93	**Buffalo**	**NHL**	**2**	**1**	**0**	**1**	**10**	**1**	**0**	**1**	**1**	**4**
	Victoriaville	QMJHL	65	44	67	111	*448	6	2	4	6	44
1993-94	**Buffalo**	**NHL**	**35**	**2**	**4**	**6**	**106**	**3**	**0**	**0**	**0**	**17**
	Rochester	AHL	42	10	32	42	153	....	....	....	....	....
	NHL Totals		**37**	**3**	**4**	**7**	**116**	**4**	**0**	**1**	**1**	**21**

BARNES, STU — FLA

Center. Shoots right. 5'11", 180 lbs. Born, Edmonton, Alta., December 25, 1970.
(Winnipeg's 1st choice, 4th overall, in 1989 Entry Draft).

			Regular Season					Playoffs				
Season	Club	Lea	GP	G	A	TP	PIM	GP	G	A	TP	PI
1987-88	N. Westminster	WHL	71	37	64	101	88	5	2	3	5	
1988-89a	Tri-City	WHL	70	59	82	141	117	7	6	5	11	1
1989-90	Tri-City	WHL	63	52	92	144	165	7	1	5	6	2
1990-91	Cdn. National	....	53	22	27	49	68	....	....	....	....	..
1991-92	**Winnipeg**	**NHL**	**46**	**8**	**9**	**17**	**26**	....	....	....	....	..
	Moncton	AHL	30	13	19	32	10	11	3	9	12	
1992-93	**Winnipeg**	**NHL**	**38**	**12**	**10**	**22**	**10**	**6**	**1**	**3**	**4**	
	Moncton	AHL	42	23	31	54	58	....	....	....	....	..
1993-94	**Winnipeg**	**NHL**	**18**	**5**	**4**	**9**	**8**	....	....	....	....	..
	Florida	**NHL**	**59**	**18**	**20**	**38**	**30**	....	....	....	....	..
	NHL Totals		**161**	**43**	**43**	**86**	**74**	**6**	**1**	**3**	**4**	

a WHL West Second All-Star Team (1989)

Traded to **Florida** by **Winnipeg** with St. Louis' sixth round choice (previously acquired by Winnipeg — later traded to Edmonton — later traded to Winnipeg — Winnipeg selected Chris Kibermanis) for Randy Gilhen, November 25, 1993.

BARON, MURRAY — ST.L

Defense. Shoots left. 6'3", 215 lbs. Born, Prince George, B.C., June 1, 1967.
(Philadelphia's 7th choice, 167th overall, in 1986 Entry Draft).

			Regular Season					Playoffs				
Season	Club	Lea	GP	G	A	TP	PIM	GP	G	A	TP	PIM
1986-87	North Dakota	WCHA	41	4	10	14	62	....	....	....	....	..
1987-88	North Dakota	WCHA	41	1	10	11	95	....	....	....	....	..
1988-89	North Dakota	WCHA	40	2	6	8	92	....	....	....	....	..
	Hershey	AHL	9	0	3	3	8	....	....	....	....	..
1989-90	**Philadelphia**	**NHL**	**16**	**2**	**2**	**4**	**12**	....	....	....	....	..
	Hershey	AHL	50	0	10	10	101	....	....	....	....	..
1990-91	**Philadelphia**	**NHL**	**67**	**8**	**8**	**16**	**74**	....	....	....	....	..
	Hershey	AHL	6	2	3	5	0	....	....	....	....	..
1991-92	**St. Louis**	**NHL**	**67**	**3**	**8**	**11**	**94**	**2**	**0**	**0**	**0**	
1992-93	**St. Louis**	**NHL**	**53**	**2**	**2**	**4**	**59**	**11**	**0**	**0**	**0**	**1**
1993-94	**St. Louis**	**NHL**	**77**	**5**	**9**	**14**	**123**	**4**	**0**	**0**	**0**	**1**
	NHL Totals		**280**	**20**	**29**	**49**	**362**	**17**	**0**	**0**	**0**	**2**

Traded to **St. Louis** by **Philadelphia** with Ron Sutter for Dan Quinn and Rod Brind'Amour, September 22, 1991.

BARR, DAVE

Right wing. Shoots right. 6'1", 195 lbs. Born, Toronto, Ont., November 30, 1960.

			Regular Season					Playoffs				
Season	Club	Lea	GP	G	A	TP	PIM	GP	G	A	TP	PIM
1979-80	Lethbridge	WHL	60	16	38	54	47	....	....	....	....	..
1980-81	Lethbridge	WHL	72	26	62	88	106	....	....	....	....	..
1981-82	**Boston**	**NHL**	**2**	**0**	**0**	**0**	**0**	**5**	**1**	**0**	**1**	[illegible]
	Erie	AHL	76	18	48	66	29	....	....	....	....	..
1982-83	**Boston**	**NHL**	**10**	**1**	**1**	**2**	**7**	**10**	**0**	**0**	**0**	**2**
	Baltimore	AHL	72	27	51	78	67	....	....	....	....	..
1983-84	**NY Rangers**	**NHL**	**6**	**0**	**0**	**0**	**2**	....	....	....	....	..
	Tulsa	CHL	50	28	37	65	24	....	....	....	....	..
	St. Louis	**NHL**	**1**	**0**	**0**	**0**	**0**	....	....	....	....	..
1984-85	**St. Louis**	**NHL**	**75**	**16**	**18**	**34**	**32**	**2**	**0**	**0**	**0**	
1985-86	**St. Louis**	**NHL**	**72**	**13**	**38**	**51**	**70**	**11**	**1**	**1**	**2**	**14**
1986-87	**St. Louis**	**NHL**	**2**	**0**	**0**	**0**	**0**	....	....	....	....	..
	Hartford	**NHL**	**30**	**2**	**4**	**6**	**19**	....	....	....	....	..
	Detroit	**NHL**	**37**	**13**	**13**	**26**	**49**	**13**	**1**	**0**	**1**	**14**
1987-88	**Detroit**	**NHL**	**51**	**14**	**26**	**40**	**58**	**16**	**5**	**7**	**12**	**22**
1988-89	**Detroit**	**NHL**	**73**	**27**	**32**	**59**	**69**	**6**	**3**	**1**	**4**	**6**
1989-90	**Detroit**	**NHL**	**62**	**10**	**25**	**35**	**45**	....	....	....	....	..
	Adirondack	AHL	9	1	14	15	17	....	....	....	....	..
1990-91	**Detroit**	**NHL**	**70**	**18**	**22**	**40**	**55**	....	....	....	....	..
1991-92	**New Jersey**	**NHL**	**41**	**6**	**12**	**18**	**32**	....	....	....	....	..
	Utica	AHL	1	0	0	0	7	....	....	....	....	..
1992-93	**New Jersey**	**NHL**	**62**	**6**	**8**	**14**	**61**	**5**	**1**	**0**	**1**	**6**
1993-94	**Dallas**	**NHL**	**20**	**2**	**5**	**7**	**21**	**3**	**0**	**1**	**1**	**4**
	Kalamazoo	IHL	4	3	2	5	5	....	....	....	....	..
	NHL Totals		**614**	**128**	**204**	**332**	**520**	**71**	**12**	**10**	**22**	**70**

Signed as a free agent by **Boston**, September 28, 1981. Traded to **NY Rangers** by **Boston** for Dave Silk, October 5, 1983. Traded to **St. Louis** by **NY Rangers** with NY Rangers' third round choice (Alan Perry) in the 1984 Entry Draft for Larry Patey and Bob Brooke, March 5, 1984. Traded to **Hartford** by **St. Louis** for Tim Bothwell, October 21, 1986. Traded to **Detroit** by **Hartford** for Randy Ladouceur, January 12, 1987. Acquired by **New Jersey** from **Detroit** with Randy McKay as compensation for Detroit's signing of free agent Troy Crowder, September 9, 1991. Signed as a free agent by **Dallas**, August 28, 1993.

BARRAULT, DOUG — (buh-ROH) — FLA.

Right wing. Shoots right. 6'2", 205 lbs. Born, Golden, B.C., April 21, 1970.
(Minnesota's 8th choice, 155th overall, in 1990 Entry Draft).

			Regular Season					Playoffs				
Season	Club	Lea	GP	G	A	TP	PIM	GP	G	A	TP	PIM
1988-89	Lethbridge	WHL	57	14	13	27	34	....	....	....	....	....
1989-90	Lethbridge	WHL	54	14	16	30	36	19	7	3	10	0
1990-91a	Lethbridge	WHL	4	2	2	4	16	....	....	....	....	....
	Seattle	WHL	61	42	42	84	69	6	5	3	8	4
1991-92	Kalamazoo	IHL	60	5	14	19	26	....	....	....	....	....
1992-93	**Minnesota**	**NHL**	**2**	**0**	**0**	**0**	**2**	....	....	....	....	....
	Kalamazoo	IHL	78	32	34	66	74	....	....	....	....	....
1993-94	**Florida**	**NHL**	**2**	**0**	**0**	**0**	**0**	....	....	....	....	....
	Cincinnati	IHL	75	36	28	64	59	9	8	2	10	0
	NHL Totals		**4**	**0**	**0**	**0**	**2**	....	....	....	....	....

a WHL West Second All-Star Team (1991)

Claimed by **Florida** from **Dallas** in Expansion Draft, June 24, 1993.

BARRIE, LEN — PIT.

Center. Shoots left. 6', 200 lbs. Born, Kimberley, B.C., June 4, 1969.
(Edmonton's 7th choice, 124th overall, in 1988 Entry Draft).

			Regular Season					Playoffs				
Season	Club	Lea	GP	G	A	TP	PIM	GP	G	A	TP	PIM
1985-86	Calgary	WHL	32	3	0	3	18	....	....	....	....	....
1986-87	Calgary	WHL	34	13	13	26	81	....	....	....	....	....
	Victoria	WHL	34	7	6	13	92	5	0	1	1	15
1987-88	Victoria	WHL	70	37	49	86	192	8	2	0	2	29
1988-89	Victoria	WHL	67	39	48	87	157	7	5	2	7	23
1989-90	**Philadelphia**	**NHL**	**1**	**0**	**0**	**0**	**0**	....	....	....	....	....
a	Kamloops	WHL	70	*85	*100	*185	108	17	*14	23	*37	24
1990-91	Hershey	AHL	63	26	32	58	60	7	4	0	4	12
1991-92	Hershey	AHL	75	42	43	85	78	3	0	2	2	32
1992-93	**Philadelphia**	**NHL**	**8**	**2**	**2**	**4**	**9**	....	....	....	....	....
	Hershey	AHL	61	31	45	76	162	....	....	....	....	....
1993-94	**Florida**	**NHL**	**2**	**0**	**0**	**0**	**0**	....	....	....	....	....
b	Cincinnati	IHL	77	45	71	116	246	11	8	13	21	60
	NHL Totals		**11**	**2**	**2**	**4**	**9**	....	....	....	....	....

a WHL West First All-Star Team (1990)
b IHL Second All-Star Team (1994)

Signed as a free agent by **Philadelphia**, February 28, 1990. Signed as a free agent by **Florida**, July 20, 1993.

BARRIE, MIKE — BUF.

Center. Shoots right. 6'1", 170 lbs. Born, Kelowna, B.C., March 16, 1974.
(Buffalo's 6th choice, 194th overall, in 1993 Entry Draft).

			Regular Season					Playoffs				
Season	Club	Lea	GP	G	A	TP	PIM	GP	G	A	TP	PIM
1991-92	Victoria	WHL	54	15	15	30	165	....	....	....	....	....
1992-93	Victoria	WHL	70	31	39	70	244	....	....	....	....	....
1993-94	Red Deer	WHL	19	11	14	25	53	....	....	....	....	....
	Seattle	WHL	48	24	28	52	119	9	5	3	8	14
	Rochester	AHL	....	....	....	....	....	3	0	1	1	0

BARTELL, ADAM — QUE.

Defense. Shoots left. 6'1", 182 lbs. Born, Buffalo, NY, April 27, 1973.
(Quebec's 10th choice, 178th overall, in 1991 Entry Draft).

			Regular Season					Playoffs				
Season	Club	Lea	GP	G	A	TP	PIM	GP	G	A	TP	PIM
1991-92	RPI	ECAC	31	5	13	18	18	....	....	....	....	....
1992-93	RPI	ECAC	32	2	17	19	46	....	....	....	....	....
1993-94	RPI	ECAC	27	3	10	13	24	....	....	....	....	....

BARTELL, JOSH — PHI.

Defense. Shoots left. 6'3", 205 lbs. Born, Syracuse, NY, April 14, 1973.
(Philadelphia's 9th choice, 204th overall, in 1991 Entry Draft).

			Regular Season					Playoffs				
Season	Club	Lea	GP	G	A	TP	PIM	GP	G	A	TP	PIM
1992-93	Clarkson	ECAC	22	1	0	1	24	....	....	....	....	....
1993-94	Clarkson	ECAC	29	1	2	3	42	....	....	....	....	....

BASSEN, BOB — QUE.

Center. Shoots left. 5'10", 180 lbs. Born, Calgary, Alta., May 6, 1965.

			Regular Season					Playoffs				
Season	Club	Lea	GP	G	A	TP	PIM	GP	G	A	TP	PIM
1982-83	Medicine Hat	WHL	4	3	2	5	0	3	0	0	0	4
1983-84	Medicine Hat	WHL	72	29	29	58	93	14	5	11	16	12
1984-85a	Medicine Hat	WHL	65	32	50	82	143	10	2	8	10	39
1985-86	**NY Islanders**	**NHL**	**11**	**2**	**1**	**3**	**6**	**3**	**0**	**1**	**1**	**0**
	Springfield	AHL	54	13	21	34	111	....	....	....	....	....
1986-87	**NY Islanders**	**NHL**	**77**	**7**	**10**	**17**	**89**	**14**	**1**	**2**	**3**	**21**
1987-88	**NY Islanders**	**NHL**	**77**	**6**	**16**	**22**	**99**	**6**	**0**	**1**	**1**	**23**
1988-89	**NY Islanders**	**NHL**	**19**	**1**	**4**	**5**	**21**	....	....	....	....	....
	Chicago	**NHL**	**49**	**4**	**12**	**16**	**62**	**10**	**1**	**1**	**2**	**34**
1989-90	**Chicago**	**NHL**	**6**	**1**	**1**	**2**	**8**	**1**	**0**	**0**	**0**	**2**
b	Indianapolis	IHL	73	22	32	54	179	12	3	8	11	33
1990-91	**St. Louis**	**NHL**	**79**	**16**	**18**	**34**	**183**	**13**	**1**	**3**	**4**	**24**
1991-92	**St. Louis**	**NHL**	**79**	**7**	**25**	**32**	**167**	**6**	**0**	**2**	**2**	**4**
1992-93	**St. Louis**	**NHL**	**53**	**9**	**10**	**19**	**63**	**11**	**0**	**0**	**0**	**10**
1993-94	**St. Louis**	**NHL**	**46**	**2**	**7**	**9**	**44**	....	....	....	....	....
	Quebec	**NHL**	**37**	**11**	**8**	**19**	**55**	....	....	....	....	....
	NHL Totals		**533**	**66**	**112**	**178**	**797**	**64**	**3**	**10**	**13**	**118**

a WHL First All-Star Team (1985)
b IHL First All-Star Team (1990)

Signed as a free agent by **NY Islanders**, October 19, 1984. Traded to **Chicago** by **NY Islanders** with Steve Konroyd for Marc Bergevin and Gary Nylund, November 25, 1988. Claimed by **St. Louis** in NHL Waiver Draft, October 1, 1990. Traded to **Quebec** by **St. Louis** with Garth Butcher and Ron Sutter for Steve Duchesne and Denis Chasse, January 23, 1994.

BATES, SHAWN — BOS.

Center. Shoots right. 5'11", 160 lbs. Born, Melrose, MA, April 3, 1975.
(Boston's 4th choice, 103rd overall, in 1993 Entry Draft).

			Regular Season					Playoffs				
Season	Club	Lea	GP	G	A	TP	PIM	GP	G	A	TP	PIM
1992-93	Medford	HS	25	49	46	95	20	....	....	....	....	....
1993-94	Boston U.	H.E.	41	10	19	29	24	....	....	....	....	....

BATTAGLIA, DOUG — DET.

Left wing. Shoots left. 6'1", 185 lbs. Born, Newmarket, Ont., October 26, 1975.
(Detroit's 5th choice, 127th overall, in 1994 Entry Draft).

			Regular Season					Playoffs				
Season	Club	Lea	GP	G	A	TP	PIM	GP	G	A	TP	PIM
1992-93	Brockville	Jr. A	39	23	22	45	81	....	....	....	....	....
1993-94	Brockville	Jr. A	47	35	39	74	212	....	....	....	....	....

BATTAGLIA, JON — ANA.

Left wing. Shoots left. 6'2", 185 lbs. Born, Chicago, IL, December 13, 1975.
(Anaheim's 6th choice, 132nd overall, in 1994 Entry Draft).

			Regular Season					Playoffs				
Season	Club	Lea	GP	G	A	TP	PIM	GP	G	A	TP	PIM
1992-93	Illinois	Midget	60	42	42	84	68	....	....	....	....	....
1993-94	Caledon	Jr. A	44	15	33	48	104	....	....	....	....	....

BATTERS, JEFF — ST.L.

Defense. Shoots right. 6'2", 215 lbs. Born, Victoria, B.C., October 23, 1970.
(St. Louis' 7th choice, 135th overall, in 1989 Entry Draft).

			Regular Season					Playoffs				
Season	Club	Lea	GP	G	A	TP	PIM	GP	G	A	TP	PIM
1988-89	Alaska-Anch.	G.N.	33	8	14	22	123	....	....	....	....	....
1989-90	Alaska-Anch.	G.N.	34	6	9	15	102	....	....	....	....	....
1990-91	Alaska-Anch.	G.N.	39	16	14	30	90	....	....	....	....	....
1991-92	Alaska-Anch.	G.N.	33	6	16	22	84	....	....	....	....	....
1992-93	Peoria	IHL	74	5	18	23	113	4	0	0	0	10
1993-94	**St. Louis**	**NHL**	**6**	**0**	**0**	**0**	**7**	....	....	....	....	....
	Peoria	IHL	59	3	9	12	175	6	0	0	0	18
	NHL Totals		**6**	**0**	**0**	**0**	**7**	....	....	....	....	....

BATYRSHIN, RUSLAN — (ba-TEER-shihn)

Defense. Shoots left. 6'1", 180 lbs. Born, Moscow, USSR, February 19, 1975.
(Winnipeg's 4th choice, 79th overall, in 1993 Entry Draft).

			Regular Season					Playoffs				
Season	Club	Lea	GP	G	A	TP	PIM	GP	G	A	TP	PIM
1991-92	Mosc.D'amo-2	CIS 3	40	0	2	2	52	....	....	....	....	....
1992-93	Mosc.D'amo-2	CIS 2			UNAVAILABLE							
1993-94	Moscow D'amo	CIS	10	0	0	0	10	3	0	0	0	22

Rights traded to **Los Angeles** by **Winnipeg** with Winnipeg's second round choice in 1996 Entry Draft for Brent Thompson and future considerations, August 8, 1994.

BAUER, COLLIN

Defense. Shoots left. 6'1", 185 lbs. Born, Edmonton, Alta., September 6, 1970.
(Edmonton's 4th choice, 61st overall, in 1988 Entry Draft).

			Regular Season					Playoffs				
Season	Club	Lea	GP	G	A	TP	PIM	GP	G	A	TP	PIM
1986-87	Saskatoon	WHL	61	1	25	26	37	11	0	6	6	10
1987-88	Saskatoon	WHL	70	9	53	62	66	10	2	5	7	16
1988-89a	Saskatoon	WHL	61	17	62	79	71	8	1	8	9	8
1989-90	Saskatoon	WHL	29	4	25	29	49	10	1	8	9	14
1990-91	Cape Breton	AHL	40	4	14	18	18	4	1	1	2	4
1991-92	Cape Breton	AHL	55	7	15	22	36	3	0	0	0	7
1992-93	Kalamazoo	IHL	32	4	14	18	31	....	....	....	....	....
1993-94	Kalamazoo	IHL	66	3	19	22	56	5	0	1	1	6

a WHL East All-Star Team (1989)

Traded to **Minnesota** by **Edmonton** for future considerations, August 4, 1992.

BAUMGARTNER, KEN — TOR.

Left wing. Shoots left. 6'1", 205 lbs. Born, Flin Flon, Man., March 11, 1966.
(Buffalo's 12th choice, 245th overall, in 1985 Entry Draft).

			Regular Season					Playoffs				
Season	Club	Lea	GP	G	A	TP	PIM	GP	G	A	TP	PIM
1984-85	Prince Albert	WHL	60	3	9	12	252	13	1	3	4	89
1985-86	Prince Albert	WHL	70	4	23	27	277	20	3	9	12	112
1986-87	New Haven	AHL	13	0	3	3	99	6	0	0	0	60
1987-88	**Los Angeles**	**NHL**	**30**	**2**	**3**	**5**	**189**	**5**	**0**	**1**	**1**	**28**
	New Haven	AHL	48	1	5	6	181	....	....	....	....	....
1988-89	**Los Angeles**	**NHL**	**49**	**1**	**3**	**4**	**288**	**5**	**0**	**0**	**0**	**8**
	New Haven	AHL	10	1	3	4	26	....	....	....	....	....
1989-90	**Los Angeles**	**NHL**	**12**	**1**	**0**	**1**	**28**	....	....	....	....	....
	NY Islanders	**NHL**	**53**	**0**	**5**	**5**	**194**	**4**	**0**	**0**	**0**	**27**
1990-91	**NY Islanders**	**NHL**	**78**	**1**	**6**	**7**	**282**	....	....	....	....	....
1991-92	**NY Islanders**	**NHL**	**44**	**0**	**1**	**1**	**202**	....	....	....	....	....
	Toronto	**NHL**	**11**	**0**	**0**	**0**	**23**	....	....	....	....	....
1992-93	**Toronto**	**NHL**	**63**	**1**	**0**	**1**	**155**	**7**	**1**	**0**	**1**	**0**
1993-94	**Toronto**	**NHL**	**64**	**4**	**4**	**8**	**185**	**10**	**0**	**0**	**0**	**18**
	NHL Totals		**404**	**10**	**22**	**32**	**1546**	**31**	**1**	**1**	**2**	**81**

Traded to **Los Angeles** by **Buffalo** with Sean McKenna and Larry Playfair for Brian Engblom and Doug Smith, January 29, 1986. Traded to **NY Islanders** by **Los Angeles** with Hubie McDonough for Mikko Makela, November 29, 1989. Traded to **Toronto** by **NY Islanders** with Dave McLlwain for Daniel Marois and Claude Loiselle, March 10, 1992.

BAUMGARTNER, NOLAN — WSH.

Defense. Shoots right. 6'1", 187 lbs. Born, Calgary, Alta., March 23, 1976.
(Washington's 1st choice, 10th overall, in 1994 Entry Draft).

			Regular Season					Playoffs				
Season	Club	Lea	GP	G	A	TP	PIM	GP	G	A	TP	PIM
1992-93	Kamloops	WHL	43	0	5	5	30	11	1	1	2	0
1993-94a	Kamloops	WHL	69	13	42	55	109	19	3	14	17	33

a Memorial Cup All-Star Team (1994)

BAUTIN, SERGEI — (BOW-tin) — DET.

Defense. Shoots left. 6'3", 200 lbs. Born, Rogachev, USSR, March 11, 1967.
(Winnipeg's 1st choice, 17th overall, in 1992 Entry Draft).

			Regular Season					Playoffs				
Season	Club	Lea	GP	G	A	TP	PIM	GP	G	A	TP	PIM
1990-91	Moscow D'amo	USSR	33	2	0	2	28	....	....	....	....	....
1991-92	Moscow D'amo	CIS	37	1	3	4	88	....	....	....	....	....
1992-93	**Winnipeg**	**NHL**	**71**	**5**	**18**	**23**	**96**	**6**	**0**	**0**	**0**	**2**
1993-94	**Winnipeg**	**NHL**	**59**	**0**	**7**	**7**	**78**	....	....	....	....	....
	Detroit	**NHL**	**1**	**0**	**0**	**0**	**0**	....	....	....	....	....
	Adirondack	AHL	9	1	5	6	6	....	....	....	....	....
	NHL Totals		**131**	**5**	**25**	**30**	**174**	**6**	**0**	**0**	**0**	**2**

Traded to **Detroit** by **Winnipeg** with Bob Essensa for Tim Cheveldae and Dallas Drake, March 8, 1994.

BAVIS, MARK

Center. Shoots left. 6', 175 lbs. Born, Roslindale, MA, March 13, 1970.
(NY Rangers' 10th choice, 181st overall, in 1989 Entry Draft).

			Regular Season					Playoffs				
Season	Club	Lea	GP	G	A	TP	PIM	GP	G	A	TP	PIM
1989-90	Boston U.	H.E.	44	6	5	11	50	....	....	....	....	....
1990-91	Boston U.	H.E.	33	7	9	16	30	....	....	....	....	....
1991-92	Boston U.	H.E.	34	9	17	26	30	....	....	....	....	....
1992-93	Boston U.	H.E.	40	14	10	24	58	....	....	....	....	....
1993-94	Providence	AHL	12	2	5	7	18	....	....	....	....	....
	Fredericton	AHL	45	7	10	17	86	....	....	....	....	....

BAVIS, MICHAEL — BUF.

Right wing. Shoots right. 6', 180 lbs. Born, Roslindale, MA, March 13, 1970.
(Buffalo's 12th choice, 245th overall, in 1989 Entry Draft).

			Regular Season					Playoffs				
Season	Club	Lea	GP	G	A	TP	PIM	GP	G	A	TP	PIM
1989-90	Boston U.	H.E.	44	2	11	13	28	....	....	....	....	....
1990-91	Boston U.	H.E.	40	5	18	23	47	....	....	....	....	....
1991-92	Boston U.	H.E.	34	11	13	24	32	....	....	....	....	....
1992-93	Boston U.	H.E.	40	12	11	23	87	....	....	....	....	....
1993-94	Rochester	AHL	65	3	11	14	89	2	0	1	1	0

BAWA, ROBIN — (BAH-wah)

Right wing. Shoots right. 6'2", 214 lbs. Born, Chemainus, B.C., March 26, 1966.

			Regular Season					Playoffs				
Season	Club	Lea	GP	G	A	TP	PIM	GP	G	A	TP	PIM
1982-83	Kamloops	WHL	66	10	24	34	17	7	1	2	3	0
1983-84	Kamloops	WHL	64	16	28	44	40	13	4	2	6	4
1984-85	Kamloops	WHL	52	6	19	25	45	15	4	9	13	14
1985-86	Kamloops	WHL	63	29	43	72	78	16	5	13	18	4
1986-87a	Kamloops	WHL	62	57	56	113	91	13	6	7	13	22
1987-88	Fort Wayne	IHL	55	12	27	39	239	6	1	3	4	24
1988-89	Baltimore	AHL	75	23	24	47	205	....	....	....	....	....
1989-90	**Washington**	**NHL**	**5**	**1**	**0**	**1**	**6**	....	....	....	....	....
	Baltimore	AHL	61	7	18	25	189	11	1	2	3	49
1990-91	Fort Wayne	IHL	72	21	26	47	381	18	4	4	8	87
1991-92	**Vancouver**	**NHL**	**2**	**0**	**0**	**0**	**0**	**1**	**0**	**0**	**0**	**0**
	Milwaukee	IHL	70	27	14	41	238	5	2	2	4	8
1992-93	Hamilton	AHL	23	3	4	7	58	....	....	....	....	....
	San Jose	**NHL**	**42**	**5**	**0**	**5**	**47**	....	....	....	....	....
	Kansas City	IHL	5	2	0	2	20	....	....	....	....	....
1993-94	**Anaheim**	**NHL**	**12**	**0**	**1**	**1**	**7**	....	....	....	....	....
	San Diego	IHL	25	6	15	21	54	6	0	0	0	52
	NHL Totals		**61**	**6**	**1**	**7**	**60**	**1**	**0**	**0**	**0**	**0**

a WHL West All-Star Team (1987)

Signed as a free agent by **Washington**, May 22, 1987. Traded to **Vancouver** by **Washington** for cash, July 31, 1991. Traded to **San Jose** by **Vancouver** for Rick Lessard, December 15, 1992. Claimed by **Anaheim** from **San Jose** in Expansion Draft, June 24, 1993.

BEAUFAIT, MARK

Center. Shoots right. 5'9", 170 lbs. Born, Livonia, MI, May 13, 1970.
(San Jose's 2nd choice, 7th overall, in 1991 Supplemental Draft).

			Regular Season					Playoffs				
Season	Club	Lea	GP	G	A	TP	PIM	GP	G	A	TP	PIM
1988-89	N. Michigan	WCHA	11	2	1	3	2	....	....	....	....	....
1989-90	N. Michigan	WCHA	34	10	14	24	12	....	....	....	....	....
1990-91	N. Michigan	WCHA	47	19	30	49	18	....	....	....	....	....
1991-92	N. Michigan	WCHA	39	31	44	75	43	....	....	....	....	....
1992-93	**San Jose**	**NHL**	**5**	**1**	**0**	**1**	**0**	....	....	....	....	....
	Kansas City	IHL	66	19	40	59	22	9	1	1	2	8
1993-94	U.S. National	....	51	22	29	51	36	....	....	....	....	....
	U.S. Olympic	....	8	1	4	5	2	....	....	....	....	....
	Kansas City	IHL	21	12	9	21	18	....	....	....	....	....
	NHL Totals		**5**	**1**	**0**	**1**	**0**	....	....	....	....	....

BEAULIEU, COREY

Defense. Shoots left. 6'1", 210 lbs. Born, Winnipeg, Man., September 10, 1969.
(Hartford's 5th choice, 116th overall, in 1988 Entry Draft).

			Regular Season					Playoffs				
Season	Club	Lea	GP	G	A	TP	PIM	GP	G	A	TP	PIM
1985-86	Moose Jaw	WHL	68	3	1	4	111	13	1	1	2	13
1986-87	Moose Jaw	WHL	63	2	7	9	188	9	0	0	0	17
1987-88	Seattle	WHL	67	2	9	11	225	....	....	....	....	....
1988-89	Seattle	WHL	32	0	3	3	134	....	....	....	....	....
	Moose Jaw	WHL	29	3	17	20	91	7	1	2	3	16
1989-90	Binghamton	AHL	56	0	2	2	191	....	....	....	....	....
1990-91			DID NOT PLAY									
1991-92	Louisville	ECHL	8	1	5	6	60	....	....	....	....	....
	Springfield	AHL	52	0	0	0	157	2	0	0	0	2
1992-93	Springfield	AHL	68	1	5	6	201	4	0	0	1	21
1993-94	Springfield	AHL	69	0	8	8	257	3	0	0	0	12

BEDDOES, CLAYTON — BOS.

Center. Shoots left. 5'11", 190 lbs. Born, Bentley, Alta., November 10, 1970.

			Regular Season					Playoffs				
Season	Club	Lea	GP	G	A	TP	PIM	GP	G	A	TP	PIM
1990-91	Lake Superior	CCHA	45	14	28	42	26	....	....	....	....	....
1991-92	Lake Superior	CCHA	38	14	26	40	24	....	....	....	....	....
1992-93	Lake Superior	CCHA	43	18	40	58	30	....	....	....	....	....
1993-94ab	Lake Superior	CCHA	44	23	31	54	56	....	....	....	....	....

a CCHA Second All-Star Team (1994)
b NCAA West Second All-American Team (1994)

Signed as a free agent by **Boston**, June 2, 1994.

BEERS, BOB — NYI

Defense. Shoots right. 6'2", 200 lbs. Born, Pittsburgh, PA, May 20, 1967.
(Boston's 10th choice, 210th overall, in 1985 Entry Draft).

			Regular Season					Playoffs				
Season	Club	Lea	GP	G	A	TP	PIM	GP	G	A	TP	PIM
1985-86	N. Arizona	NCAA	28	11	39	50	96	....	....	....	....	....
1986-87	U. of Maine	H.E.	38	0	13	13	45	....	....	....	....	....
1987-88	U. of Maine	H.E.	41	3	11	14	72	....	....	....	....	....
1988-89ab	U. of Maine	H.E.	44	10	27	37	53	....	....	....	....	....
1989-90	**Boston**	**NHL**	**3**	**0**	**1**	**1**	**6**	**14**	**1**	**1**	**2**	**18**
	Maine	AHL	74	7	36	43	63	....	....	....	....	....
1990-91	**Boston**	**NHL**	**16**	**0**	**1**	**1**	**10**	**6**	**0**	**0**	**0**	**4**
	Maine	AHL	36	2	16	18	21	....	....	....	....	....
1991-92	**Boston**	**NHL**	**31**	**0**	**5**	**5**	**29**	**1**	**0**	**0**	**0**	**0**
	Maine	AHL	33	6	23	29	24	....	....	....	....	....
1992-93	Providence	AHL	6	1	2	3	10	....	....	....	....	....
	Tampa Bay	**NHL**	**64**	**12**	**24**	**36**	**70**	....	....	....	....	....
	Atlanta	IHL	1	0	0	0	0	....	....	....	....	....
1993-94	**Tampa Bay**	**NHL**	**16**	**1**	**5**	**6**	**12**	....	....	....	....	....
	Edmonton	**NHL**	**66**	**10**	**27**	**37**	**74**	....	....	....	....	....
	NHL Totals		**196**	**23**	**63**	**86**	**201**	**21**	**1**	**1**	**2**	**22**

a Hockey East Second All-Star Team (1989)
b NCAA East Second All-American Team (1989)

Traded to **Tampa Bay** by **Boston** for Stephane Richer, October 28, 1992. Traded to **Edmonton** by **Tampa Bay** for Chris Joseph, November 11, 1993.

BELAK, WADE — QUE

Defense. Shoots right. 6'4", 213 lbs. Born, Saskatoon, Sask., July 3, 1976.
(Quebec's 1st choice, 12th overall, in 1994 Entry Draft).

			Regular Season					Playoffs				
Season	Club	Lea	GP	G	A	TP	PIM	GP	G	A	TP	PIM
1992-93	N. Battleford	Midget	50	5	15	20	146	....	....	....	....	....
	Saskatoon	WHL	7	0	0	0	23	7	0	0	0	0
1993-94	Saskatoon	WHL	69	4	13	17	226	16	2	2	4	43

BELANGER, HUGO — CHI

Left wing. Shoots left. 6'1", 190 lbs. Born, St. Herbert, Que., May 28, 1970.
(Chicago's 6th choice, 163rd overall, in 1990 Entry Draft).

			Regular Season					Playoffs				
Season	Club	Lea	GP	G	A	TP	PIM	GP	G	A	TP	PIM
1989-90	Clarkson	ECAC	36	14	25	39	12	....	....	....	....	....
1990-91	Clarkson	ECAC	40	32	43	75	18	....	....	....	....	....
1991-92a	Clarkson	ECAC	32	18	31	49	26	....	....	....	....	....
1992-93	Clarkson	ECAC	31	17	23	40	36	....	....	....	....	....
1993-94	Indianapolis	IHL	75	23	15	38	8	....	....	....	....	....

a ECAC Second All-Star Team (1992)

BELANGER, JESSE — FLA.

Center. Shoots right. 6', 170 lbs. Born, St. Georges de Beauce, Que., June 15, 1969.

			Regular Season					Playoffs				
Season	Club	Lea	GP	G	A	TP	PIM	GP	G	A	TP	PIM
1987-88	Granby	QMJHL	69	33	43	76	10	5	3	3	6	0
1988-89	Granby	QMJHL	67	40	63	103	26	4	0	5	5	0
1989-90	Granby	QMJHL	67	53	54	107	53	....	....	....	....	....
1990-91	Fredericton	AHL	75	40	58	98	30	6	2	4	6	0
1991-92	**Montreal**	**NHL**	**4**	**0**	**0**	**0**	**0**	....	....	....	....	....
	Fredericton	AHL	65	30	41	71	26	7	3	3	6	2
1992-93	**Montreal**	**NHL**	**19**	**4**	**2**	**6**	**4**	**9**	**0**	**1**	**1**	**0**
	Fredericton	AHL	39	19	32	51	24	....	....	....	....	....
1993-94	**Florida**	**NHL**	**70**	**17**	**33**	**50**	**16**	....	....	....	....	....
	NHL Totals		**93**	**21**	**35**	**56**	**20**	**9**	**0**	**1**	**1**	**0**

Signed as a free agent by **Montreal**, October 3, 1990. Claimed by **Florida** from **Montreal** in Expansion Draft, June 24, 1993.

BELANGER, KEN — TOR.

Left wing. Shoots left. 6'4", 220 lbs. Born, Sault Ste. Marie, Ont., May 14, 1974.
(Hartford's 7th choice, 153rd overall, in 1992 Entry Draft).

			Regular Season					Playoffs				
Season	Club	Lea	GP	G	A	TP	PIM	GP	G	A	TP	PIM
1991-92	Ottawa	OHL	51	4	4	8	174	11	0	0	0	24
1992-93	Ottawa	OHL	34	6	12	18	139	....	....	....	....	....
	Guelph	OHL	29	10	14	24	86	5	2	1	3	14
1993-94	Guelph	OHL	55	11	22	33	185	9	2	3	5	30

Traded to **Toronto** by **Hartford** for Toronto's ninth round choice (Matt Ball) in 1994 Entry Draft, March 18, 1994.

BELANGER, MARTIN — MTL.

Defense. Shoots right. 6', 206 lbs. Born, Lasalle, Que., February 3, 1976.
(Montreal's 5th choice, 74th overall, in 1994 Entry Draft).

			Regular Season					Playoffs				
Season	Club	Lea	GP	G	A	TP	PIM	GP	G	A	TP	PIM
1992-93	Granby	QMJHL	49	2	19	21	24	....	....	....	....	....
1993-94	Granby	QMJHL	63	8	32	40	49	7	0	1	1	28

BELLOWS, BRIAN — MTL.

Left wing. Shoots right. 5'11", 209 lbs. Born, St. Catharines, Ont., September 1, 1964.
(Minnesota's 1st choice, 2nd overall, in 1982 Entry Draft).

			Regular Season					Playoffs				
Season	Club	Lea	GP	G	A	TP	PIM	GP	G	A	TP	PIM
1980-81	Kitchener	OHA	66	49	67	116	23	16	14	13	27	13
1981-82ab	Kitchener	OHL	47	45	52	97	23	15	16	13	29	11
1982-83	**Minnesota**	**NHL**	**78**	**35**	**30**	**65**	**27**	**9**	**5**	**4**	**9**	**18**
1983-84	**Minnesota**	**NHL**	**78**	**41**	**42**	**83**	**66**	**16**	**2**	**12**	**14**	**6**
1984-85	**Minnesota**	**NHL**	**78**	**26**	**36**	**62**	**72**	**9**	**2**	**4**	**6**	**9**
1985-86	**Minnesota**	**NHL**	**77**	**31**	**48**	**79**	**46**	**5**	**5**	**0**	**5**	**16**
1986-87	**Minnesota**	**NHL**	**65**	**26**	**27**	**53**	**34**	....	....	....	....	....
1987-88	**Minnesota**	**NHL**	**77**	**40**	**41**	**81**	**81**	....	....	....	....	....
1988-89	**Minnesota**	**NHL**	**60**	**23**	**27**	**50**	**55**	**5**	**2**	**3**	**5**	**8**
1989-90c	**Minnesota**	**NHL**	**80**	**55**	**44**	**99**	**72**	**7**	**4**	**3**	**7**	**10**
1990-91	**Minnesota**	**NHL**	**80**	**35**	**40**	**75**	**43**	**23**	**10**	**19**	**29**	**30**
1991-92	**Minnesota**	**NHL**	**80**	**30**	**45**	**75**	**41**	**7**	**4**	**4**	**8**	**14**
1992-93	**Montreal**	**NHL**	**82**	**40**	**48**	**88**	**44**	**18**	**6**	**9**	**15**	**18**
1993-94	**Montreal**	**NHL**	**77**	**33**	**38**	**71**	**36**	**6**	**1**	**2**	**3**	**2**
	NHL Totals		**912**	**415**	**466**	**881**	**617**	**105**	**41**	**60**	**101**	**131**

a OHL First All-Star Team (1982)
b Won George Parsons Trophy (Most Sportsmanlike Player, Memorial Cup Tournament) (1982)
c NHL Second All-Star Team (1990)

Played in NHL All-Star Game (1984, 1988, 1992)

Traded to **Montreal** by **Minnesota** for Russ Courtnall, August 31, 1992.

BENAZIC, CAL — BUF.

Defense. Shoots left. 6'3", 187 lbs. Born, Mackenzie, B.C., September 29, 1975.
(Buffalo's 5th choice, 147th overall, in 1994 Entry Draft).

			Regular Season					Playoffs				
Season	Club	Lea	GP	G	A	TP	PIM	GP	G	A	TP	PIM
1992-93	Surrey	Jr. A	60	5	37	40	210	....	....	....	....	....
1993-94	Medicine Hat	WHL	64	2	15	17	157	3	0	0	0	15

BENNETT, ADAM — EDM.

Defense. Shoots right. 6'4", 206 lbs. Born, Georgetown, Ont., March 30, 1971.
(Chicago's 1st choice, 6th overall, in 1989 Entry Draft).

			Regular Season					Playoffs				
Season	Club	Lea	GP	G	A	TP	PIM	GP	G	A	TP	PIM
1988-89	Sudbury	OHL	66	7	22	29	133	....	....	....	....	....
1989-90	Sudbury	OHL	65	18	43	61	116	7	1	2	3	23
1990-91a	Sudbury	OHL	54	21	29	50	123	5	1	2	3	11
	Indianapolis	IHL	3	0	1	1	12	2	0	0	0	0
1991-92	**Chicago**	**NHL**	**5**	**0**	**0**	**0**	**12**	....	....	....	....	....
	Indianapolis	IHL	59	4	10	14	89	....	....	....	....	....
1992-93	**Chicago**	**NHL**	**16**	**0**	**2**	**2**	**8**	....	....	....	....	....
	Indianapolis	IHL	39	8	16	24	69	2	0	0	0	2
1993-94	**Edmonton**	**NHL**	**48**	**3**	**6**	**9**	**49**	....	....	....	....	....
	Cape Breton	AHL	7	2	5	7	7	....	....	....	....	....
	NHL Totals		**69**	**3**	**8**	**11**	**69**	....	....	....	....	....

a OHL Second All-Star Team (1991)

Traded to **Edmonton** by **Chicago** for Kevin Todd, October 7, 1993.

BENNETT, RICK — HFD.

Left wing. Shoots left. 6'4", 215 lbs. Born, Springfield, MA, July 24, 1967.
(Minnesota's 4th choice, 54th overall, in 1986 Entry Draft).

			Regular Season					Playoffs				
Season	Club	Lea	GP	G	A	TP	PIM	GP	G	A	TP	PIM
1986-87	Providence	H.E.	32	15	12	27	34	....	....	....	....	....
1987-88	Providence	H.E.	33	9	16	25	70	....	....	....	....	....
1988-89a	Providence	H.E.	32	14	32	46	74	....	....	....	....	....
1989-90b	Providence	H.E.	31	12	24	36	74	....	....	....	....	....
	NY Rangers	**NHL**	**6**	**1**	**0**	**1**	**5**	....	....	....	....	....
1990-91	**NY Rangers**	**NHL**	**6**	**0**	**0**	**0**	**6**	....	....	....	....	....
	Binghamton	AHL	71	27	32	59	206	10	2	1	3	27
1991-92	**NY Rangers**	**NHL**	**3**	**0**	**1**	**1**	**2**	....	....	....	....	....
	Binghamton	AHL	69	19	23	42	112	11	0	1	1	23
1992-93	Binghamton	AHL	76	15	22	37	114	10	0	0	0	30
1993-94	Springfield	AHL	67	9	19	28	82	6	1	0	1	31
	NHL Totals		**15**	**1**	**1**	**2**	**13**	....	....	....	....	....

a NCAA East Second All-American Team (1989)
b Hockey East All-Star Team (1990)

Rights traded to **NY Rangers** by **Minnesota** with Brian Lawton and Igor Liba for Paul Jerrard, Mark Tinordi, the rights to Bret Barnett and Mike Sullivan, and Los Angeles' third round choice (previously acquired by NY Rangers — Minnesota selected Murray Garbutt) in 1989 Entry Draft, October 11, 1988. Signed as a free agent by **Hartford**, August 23, 1993.

BENNING, BRIAN — FLA.

Defense. Shoots left. 6', 195 lbs. Born, Edmonton, Alta., June 10, 1966.
(St. Louis' 1st choice, 26th overall, in 1984 Entry Draft).

			Regular Season					Playoffs				
Season	Club	Lea	GP	G	A	TP	PIM	GP	G	A	TP	PIM
1983-84	Portland	WHL	38	6	41	47	108	....	....	....	....	....
1984-85	**St. Louis**	**NHL**	**4**	**0**	**2**	**2**	**0**	....	....	....	....	....
	Kamloops	WHL	17	3	18	21	26	....	....	....	....	....
1985-86	Cdn. Olympic	....	60	6	13	19	43	....	....	....	....	....
	St. Louis	**NHL**	....	....	....	....	....	**6**	**1**	**2**	**3**	**13**
1986-87a	**St. Louis**	**NHL**	**78**	**13**	**36**	**49**	**110**	**6**	**0**	**4**	**4**	**9**
1987-88	**St. Louis**	**NHL**	**77**	**8**	**29**	**37**	**107**	**10**	**1**	**6**	**7**	**25**
1988-89	**St. Louis**	**NHL**	**66**	**8**	**26**	**34**	**102**	**7**	**1**	**1**	**2**	**11**
1989-90	**St. Louis**	**NHL**	**7**	**1**	**1**	**2**	**2**	....	....	....	....	....
	Los Angeles	**NHL**	**48**	**5**	**18**	**23**	**104**	**7**	**0**	**2**	**2**	**10**
1990-91	**Los Angeles**	**NHL**	**61**	**7**	**24**	**31**	**127**	**12**	**0**	**5**	**5**	**6**
1991-92	**Los Angeles**	**NHL**	**53**	**2**	**30**	**32**	**99**	....	....	....	....	....
	Philadelphia	**NHL**	**22**	**2**	**12**	**14**	**35**	....	....	....	....	....
1992-93	**Philadelphia**	**NHL**	**37**	**9**	**17**	**26**	**93**	....	....	....	....	....
	Edmonton	**NHL**	**18**	**1**	**7**	**8**	**59**	....	....	....	....	....
1993-94	**Florida**	**NHL**	**73**	**6**	**24**	**30**	**107**	....	....	....	....	....
	NHL Totals		**544**	**62**	**226**	**288**	**945**	**48**	**3**	**20**	**23**	**74**

a NHL All-Rookie Team (1987)

Traded to **Los Angeles** by **St Louis** for Los Angeles' third round choice (Kyle Reeves) in 1991 Entry Draft, November 10, 1989. Traded to **Pittsburgh** by **Los Angeles** with Jeff Chychrun and Los Angeles' first round choice (later traded to Philadelphia — Philadelphia selected Jason Bowen) in 1992 Entry Draft for Paul Coffey, February 19, 1992. Traded to **Philadelphia** by **Pittsburgh** with Mark Recchi and Los Angeles' first round choice (previously acquired by Pittsburgh — Philadelphia selected Jason Bowen) in 1992 Entry Draft for Rick Tocchet, Kjell Samuelsson, Ken Wregget and Philadelphia's third round choice (Dave Roche) in 1993 Entry Draft, February 19, 1992. Traded to **Edmonton** by **Philadelphia** for Greg Hawgood and Josef Beranek, January 16, 1993. Signed as a free agent by **Florida**, July 13, 1993.

BERANEK, JOSEF (buh-RAH-nehk, JOH-sehf) — PHI.

Left wing. Shoots left. 6'2", 185 lbs. Born, Litvinov, Czechoslovakia, October 25, 1969.
(Edmonton's 3rd choice, 78th overall, in 1989 Entry Draft).

			Regular Season					Playoffs				
Season	Club	Lea	GP	G	A	TP	PIM	GP	G	A	TP	PIM
1987-88	Litvinov	Czech.	14	7	4	11	12	....	....	....	....	....
1988-89	Litvinov	Czech.	32	18	10	28	47	....	....	....	....	....
1989-90	Dukla Trencin	Czech.	49	19	23	42	....	....	....	....	....	....
1990-91	Litvinov	Czech.	58	29	31	60	98	....	....	....	....	....
1991-92	**Edmonton**	**NHL**	**58**	**12**	**16**	**28**	**18**	**12**	**2**	**1**	**3**	**0**
1992-93	**Edmonton**	**NHL**	**26**	**2**	**6**	**8**	**28**	....	....	....	....	....
	Cape Breton	AHL	6	1	2	3	8	....	....	....	....	....
	Philadelphia	**NHL**	**40**	**13**	**12**	**25**	**50**	....	....	....	....	....
1993-94	**Philadelphia**	**NHL**	**80**	**28**	**21**	**49**	**85**	....	....	....	....	....
	NHL Totals		**204**	**55**	**55**	**110**	**181**	**12**	**2**	**1**	**3**	**0**

Traded to **Philadelphia** by **Edmonton** with Greg Hawgood for Brian Benning, January 16, 1993.

BEREHOWSKY, DRAKE (beh-reh-HOW-skee) — TOR.

Defense. Shoots right. 6'2", 211 lbs. Born, Toronto, Ont., January 3, 1972.
(Toronto's 1st choice, 10th overall, in 1990 Entry Draft).

			Regular Season					Playoffs				
Season	Club	Lea	GP	G	A	TP	PIM	GP	G	A	TP	PIM
1988-89	Kingston	OHL	63	7	39	46	85	....	....	....	....	....
1989-90	Kingston	OHL	9	3	11	14	28	....	....	....	....	....
1990-91	**Toronto**	**NHL**	**8**	**0**	**1**	**1**	**25**	....	....	....	....	....
	Kingston	OHL	13	5	13	18	38	....	....	....	....	....
	North Bay	OHL	26	7	23	30	51	10	2	7	9	21
1991-92	**Toronto**	**NHL**	**1**	**0**	**0**	**0**	**0**	....	....	....	....	....
ab	North Bay	OHL	62	19	63	82	147	21	7	24	31	22
	St. John's	AHL	....	....	....	....	....	6	0	5	5	21
1992-93	**Toronto**	**NHL**	**41**	**4**	**15**	**19**	**61**	....	....	....	....	....
	St. John's	AHL	28	10	17	27	38	....	....	....	....	....
1993-94	**Toronto**	**NHL**	**49**	**2**	**8**	**10**	**63**	....	....	....	....	....
	St. John's	AHL	18	3	12	15	40	....	....	....	....	....
	NHL Totals		**99**	**6**	**24**	**30**	**149**	....	....	....	....	....

a Canadian Major Junior Defenseman of the Year (1992)
b OHL First All-Star Team (1992)

BERG, BILL — TOR.

Left wing. Shoots left. 6'1", 205 lbs. Born, St. Catharines, Ont., October 21, 1967.
(NY Islanders' 3rd choice, 59th overall, in 1986 Entry Draft).

			Regular Season					Playoffs				
Season	Club	Lea	GP	G	A	TP	PIM	GP	G	A	TP	PIM
1985-86	Toronto	OHL	64	3	35	38	143	4	0	0	0	19
	Springfield	AHL	4	1	1	2	4	....	....	....	....	....
1986-87	Toronto	OHL	57	3	15	18	138	....	....	....	....	....
1987-88	Springfield	AHL	76	6	26	32	148	....	....	....	....	....
	Peoria	IHL	5	0	1	1	8	7	0	3	3	31
1988-89	**NY Islanders**	**NHL**	**7**	**1**	**2**	**3**	**10**	....	....	....	....	....
	Springfield	AHL	69	17	32	49	122	....	....	....	....	....
1989-90	Springfield	AHL	74	12	42	54	74	15	5	12	17	35
1990-91	**NY Islanders**	**NHL**	**78**	**9**	**14**	**23**	**67**	....	....	....	....	....
1991-92	**NY Islanders**	**NHL**	**47**	**5**	**9**	**14**	**28**	....	....	....	....	....
	Capital Dist.	AHL	3	0	2	2	16	....	....	....	....	....
1992-93	**NY Islanders**	**NHL**	**22**	**6**	**3**	**9**	**49**	....	....	....	....	....
	Toronto	**NHL**	**58**	**7**	**8**	**15**	**54**	**21**	**1**	**1**	**2**	**18**
1993-94	**Toronto**	**NHL**	**83**	**8**	**11**	**19**	**93**	**18**	**1**	**2**	**3**	**10**
	NHL Totals		**295**	**36**	**47**	**83**	**301**	**39**	**2**	**3**	**5**	**28**

Claimed on waivers by **Toronto** from **NY Islanders**, December 3, 1992.

BERGEVIN, MARC — T.B.

Defense. Shoots left. 6'1", 197 lbs. Born, Montreal, Que., August 11, 1965.
(Chicago's 3rd choice, 59th overall, in 1983 Entry Draft).

			Regular Season					Playoffs				
Season	Club	Lea	GP	G	A	TP	PIM	GP	G	A	TP	PIM
1982-83	Chicoutimi	QMJHL	64	3	27	30	113	....	....	....	....	....
1983-84	Chicoutimi	QMJHL	70	10	35	45	125	....	....	....	....	....
	Springfield	AHL	7	0	1	1	2	....	....	....	....	....
1984-85	**Chicago**	**NHL**	**60**	**0**	**6**	**6**	**54**	**6**	**0**	**3**	**3**	**2**
	Springfield	AHL	....	....	....	....	....	4	0	0	0	0
1985-86	**Chicago**	**NHL**	**71**	**7**	**7**	**14**	**60**	**3**	**0**	**0**	**0**	**0**
1986-87	**Chicago**	**NHL**	**66**	**4**	**10**	**14**	**66**	**3**	**1**	**0**	**1**	**2**
1987-88	**Chicago**	**NHL**	**58**	**1**	**6**	**7**	**85**	....	....	....	....	....
	Saginaw	IHL	10	2	7	9	20	....	....	....	....	....
1988-89	**Chicago**	**NHL**	**11**	**0**	**0**	**0**	**18**	....	....	....	....	....
	NY Islanders	**NHL**	**58**	**2**	**13**	**15**	**62**	....	....	....	....	....
1989-90	**NY Islanders**	**NHL**	**18**	**0**	**4**	**4**	**30**	....	....	....	....	....
	Springfield	AHL	47	7	16	23	66	17	2	11	13	16
1990-91	Capital Dist.	AHL	7	0	5	5	6	....	....	....	....	....
	Hartford	**NHL**	**4**	**0**	**0**	**0**	**4**	....	....	....	....	....
	Springfield	AHL	58	4	23	27	85	18	0	7	7	26
1991-92	**Hartford**	**NHL**	**75**	**7**	**17**	**24**	**64**	**5**	**0**	**0**	**0**	**2**
1992-93	**Tampa Bay**	**NHL**	**78**	**2**	**12**	**14**	**66**	....	....	....	....	....
1993-94	**Tampa Bay**	**NHL**	**83**	**1**	**15**	**16**	**87**	....	....	....	....	....
	NHL Totals		**582**	**24**	**90**	**114**	**596**	**17**	**1**	**3**	**4**	**6**

Traded to **NY Islanders** by **Chicago** with Gary Nylund for Steve Konroyd and Bob Bassen, November 25, 1988. Traded to **Hartford** by **NY Islanders** for Hartford's fifth round choice (Ryan Duthie) in 1992 Entry Draft, October 30, 1990. Signed as a free agent by **Tampa Bay**, July 9, 1992.

BERGLAND, TIM

Right wing. Shoots right. 6'3", 194 lbs. Born, Crookston, MN, January 11, 1965.
(Washington's 1st choice, 75th overall, in 1983 Entry Draft).

			Regular Season					Playoffs				
Season	Club	Lea	GP	G	A	TP	PIM	GP	G	A	TP	PIM
1983-84	U. Minnesota	WCHA	24	4	11	15	4	....	....	....	....	....
1984-85	U. Minnesota	WCHA	34	5	9	14	8	....	....	....	....	....
1985-86	U. Minnesota	WCHA	48	11	16	27	26	....	....	....	....	....
1986-87	U. Minnesota	WCHA	49	18	17	35	48	....	....	....	....	....
1987-88	Fort Wayne	IHL	13	2	1	3	9	....	....	....	....	....
	Binghamton	AHL	63	21	26	47	31	4	0	0	0	0
1988-89	Baltimore	AHL	78	24	29	53	39	....	....	....	....	....
1989-90	**Washington**	**NHL**	**32**	**2**	**5**	**7**	**31**	**15**	**1**	**1**	**2**	**10**
	Baltimore	AHL	47	12	19	31	55	....	....	....	....	....
1990-91	**Washington**	**NHL**	**47**	**5**	**9**	**14**	**21**	**11**	**1**	**1**	**2**	**12**
	Baltmore	AHL	15	8	9	17	16	....	....	....	....	....
1991-92	**Washington**	**NHL**	**22**	**1**	**4**	**5**	**2**	....	....	....	....	....
	Baltimore	AHL	11	6	10	16	5	....	....	....	....	....
1992-93	**Tampa Bay**	**NHL**	**27**	**3**	**3**	**6**	**11**	....	....	....	....	....
	Atlanta	IHL	49	18	21	39	26	9	3	3	6	10
1993-94	**Tampa Bay**	**NHL**	**51**	**6**	**5**	**11**	**6**	....	....	....	....	....
	Atlanta	IHL	19	6	7	13	6	....	....	....	....	....
	Washington	**NHL**	**3**	**0**	**0**	**0**	**4**	....	....	....	....	....
	NHL Totals		**182**	**17**	**26**	**43**	**75**	**26**	**2**	**2**	**4**	**22**

Claimed by **Tampa Bay** from **Washington** in Expansion Draft, June 18, 1992. Claimed on waivers by **Washington** from **Tampa Bay**, March 19, 1994.

BERGMAN, JAN (BURG-muhn) — VAN.

Defense. Shoots left. 5'11", 194 lbs. Born, Sodertalje, Sweden, August 7, 1969.
(Vancouver's 11th choice, 248th overall, in 1989 Entry Draft).

			Regular Season					Playoffs				
Season	Club	Lea	GP	G	A	TP	PIM	GP	G	A	TP	PIM
1988-89	Sodertalje	Swe.	34	2	4	6	14	....	....	....	....	....
1989-90	Sodertalje	Swe.	31	0	4	4	10	2	1	0	1	0
1990-91	Sodertalje	Swe.	40	4	4	8	16	2	0	0	0	0
1991-92	Sodertalje	Swe.	21	1	1	2	8	....	....	....	....	....
1992-93	Sodertalje	Swe. 2	24	6	4	10	8	....	....	....	....	....
1993-94	Sodertalje	Swe. 2	37	2	4	6	18	....	....	....	....	....

BERGQVIST, STEFAN — PIT.

Defense. Shoots left. 6'3", 216 lbs. Born, Leksand, Sweden, March 10, 1975.
(Pittsburgh's 1st choice, 26th overall, in 1993 Entry Draft).

			Regular Season					Playoffs				
Season	Club	Lea	GP	G	A	TP	PIM	GP	G	A	TP	PIM
1992-93	Leksand	Swe.	15	0	0	0	6	....	....	....	....	....
1993-94	Leksand	Swe.	6	0	0	0	0	....	....	....	....	....

BERMINGHAM, JIM

Center. Shoots left. 6'3", 201 lbs. Born, Montreal, Que., November 12, 1971.
(Detroit's 7th choice, 186th overall, in 1991 Entry Draft).

			Regular Season					Playoffs				
Season	Club	Lea	GP	G	A	TP	PIM	GP	G	A	TP	PIM
1990-91	Laval	QMJHL	67	21	39	60	109	13	4	8	12	17
1991-92	Laval	QMJHL	65	37	66	103	88	10	3	6	9	28
1992-93	Adirondack	AHL	21	0	2	2	8	....	....	....	....	....
	Toledo	ECHL	18	8	9	17	21	....	....	....	....	....
1993-94	Wheeling	ECHL	68	29	46	75	102	8	3	5	8	10

BERNARD, LOUIS — MTL.

Defense. Shoots right. 6'2", 205 lbs. Born, Victoriaville, Que., July 10, 1974.
(Montreal's 5th choice, 82nd overall, in 1992 Entry Draft).

			Regular Season					Playoffs				
Season	Club	Lea	GP	G	A	TP	PIM	GP	G	A	TP	PIM
1991-92	Drummondville	QMJHL	70	8	24	32	59	4	0	1	1	4
1992-93	Drummondville	QMJHL	68	8	38	46	78	10	0	4	4	14
1993-94	Sherbrooke	QMJHL	65	10	31	41	107	12	1	2	3	10

BERRY, BRAD

Defense. Shoots left. 6'2", 190 lbs. Born, Bashaw, Alta., April 1, 1965.
(Winnipeg's 3rd choice, 29th overall, in 1983 Entry Draft).

			Regular Season					Playoffs				
Season	Club	Lea	GP	G	A	TP	PIM	GP	G	A	TP	PIM
1983-84	North Dakota	WCHA	32	2	7	9	8	....	....	....	....	....
1984-85	North Dakota	WCHA	40	4	26	30	26	....	....	....	....	....
1985-86	North Dakota	WCHA	40	6	29	35	26	....	....	....	....	....
	Winnipeg	**NHL**	**13**	**1**	**0**	**1**	**10**	**3**	**0**	**0**	**0**	**0**
1986-87	**Winnipeg**	**NHL**	**52**	**2**	**8**	**10**	**60**	**7**	**0**	**1**	**1**	**14**
1987-88	**Winnipeg**	**NHL**	**48**	**0**	**6**	**6**	**75**	....	....	....	....	....
	Moncton	AHL	10	1	3	4	14	....	....	....	....	....
1988-89	**Winnipeg**	**NHL**	**38**	**0**	**9**	**9**	**45**	....	....	....	....	....
	Moncton	AHL	38	3	16	19	39	....	....	....	....	....
1989-90	**Winnipeg**	**NHL**	**12**	**1**	**2**	**3**	**6**	**1**	**0**	**0**	**0**	**0**
	Moncton	AHL	38	1	9	10	58	....	....	....	....	....
1990-91	Brynas	Swe.	38	3	1	4	38	....	....	....	....	....
1991-92	**Minnesota**	**NHL**	**7**	**0**	**0**	**0**	**6**	**2**	**0**	**0**	**0**	**2**
	Kalamazoo	IHL	65	5	18	23	90	5	2	0	2	6
1992-93	**Minnesota**	**NHL**	**63**	**0**	**3**	**3**	**109**	....	....	....	....	....
1993-94	**Dallas**	**NHL**	**8**	**0**	**0**	**0**	**12**	....	....	....	....	....
	Kalamazoo	IHL	45	3	19	22	91	1	0	0	0	0
	NHL Totals		**241**	**4**	**28**	**32**	**323**	**13**	**0**	**1**	**1**	**16**

Signed as a free agent by **Minnesota**, October 4, 1991.

BERTRAND, ERIC — N.J.

Left wing. Shoots left. 6'1", 195 lbs. Born, St. Ephrem, Que., April 16, 1975.
(New Jersey's 9th choice, 207th overall, in 1994 Entry Draft).

			Regular Season					Playoffs				
Season	Club	Lea	GP	G	A	TP	PIM	GP	G	A	TP	PIM
1992-93	Granby	QMJHL	64	10	15	25	82	....	....	....	....	....
1993-94	Granby	QMJHL	60	11	15	26	151	6	1	0	1	18

BERTUZZI, TODD — NYI

Center. Shoots left. 6'3", 227 lbs. Born, Sudbury, Ont., February 2, 1975.
(NY Islanders' 1st choice, 23rd overall, in 1993 Entry Draft).

			Regular Season					Playoffs				
Season	Club	Lea	GP	G	A	TP	PIM	GP	G	A	TP	PIM
1991-92	Guelph	OHL	47	7	14	21	145	....	....	....	....	....
1992-93	Guelph	OHL	59	27	32	59	164	5	2	2	4	6
1993-94	Guelph	OHL	61	28	54	82	165	9	2	6	8	30

BERUBE, CRAIG — (buh-ROO-bee) — WSH.

Left wing. Shoots left. 6'1", 205 lbs. Born, Calahoo, Alta., December 17, 1965.

			Regular Season					Playoffs				
Season	Club	Lea	GP	G	A	TP	PIM	GP	G	A	TP	PIM
1982-83	Kamloops	WHL	4	0	0	0	0	....	....	....	....	....
1983-84	N. Westminster	WHL	70	11	20	31	104	8	1	2	3	5
1984-85	N. Westminster	WHL	70	25	44	69	191	10	3	2	5	4
1985-86	Kamloops	WHL	32	17	14	31	119	....	....	....	....	....
	Medicine Hat	WHL	34	14	16	30	95	25	7	8	15	102
1986-87	**Philadelphia**	**NHL**	**7**	**0**	**0**	**0**	**57**	**5**	**0**	**0**	**0**	**17**
	Hershey	AHL	63	7	17	24	325	....	....	....	....	....
1987-88	**Philadelphia**	**NHL**	**27**	**3**	**2**	**5**	**108**	....	....	....	....	....
	Hershey	AHL	31	5	9	14	119	....	....	....	....	....
1988-89	**Philadelphia**	**NHL**	**53**	**1**	**1**	**2**	**199**	**16**	**0**	**0**	**0**	**56**
	Hershey	AHL	7	0	2	2	19	....	....	....	....	....
1989-90	**Philadelphia**	**NHL**	**74**	**4**	**14**	**18**	**291**	....	....	....	....	....
1990-91	**Philadelphia**	**NHL**	**74**	**8**	**9**	**17**	**293**	....	....	....	....	....
1991-92	**Toronto**	**NHL**	**40**	**5**	**7**	**12**	**109**	....	....	....	....	....
	Calgary	**NHL**	**36**	**1**	**4**	**5**	**155**	....	....	....	....	....
1992-93	**Calgary**	**NHL**	**77**	**4**	**8**	**12**	**209**	**6**	**0**	**1**	**1**	**21**
1993-94	**Washington**	**NHL**	**84**	**7**	**7**	**14**	**305**	**8**	**0**	**0**	**0**	**21**
	NHL Totals		**472**	**33**	**52**	**85**	**1726**	**35**	**0**	**1**	**1**	**115**

Signed as a free agent by **Philadelphia**, March 19, 1986. Traded to **Edmonton** by **Philadelphia** with Craig Fisher and Scott Mellanby for Dave Brown, Corey Foster and Jari Kurri, May 30, 1991. Traded to **Toronto** by **Edmonton** with Grant Fuhr and Glenn Anderson for Vincent Damphousse, Peter Ing, Scott Thornton, Luke Richardson, future considerations and cash, September 19, 1991. Traded to **Calgary** by **Toronto** with Alexander Godynyuk, Gary Leeman, Michel Petit and Jeff Reese for Doug Gilmour, Jamie Macoun, Ric Nattress, Rick Wamsley and Kent Manderville, January 2, 1992. Traded to **Washington** by **Calgary** for Washington's fifth round choice (Darryl Lafrance) in 1993 Entry Draft, June 26, 1993.

BES, JEFF — DAL

Center. Shoots left. 6', 186 lbs. Born, Tillsonburg, Ont., July 31, 1973.
(Minnesota's 2nd choice, 58th overall, in 1992 Entry Draft).

			Regular Season					Playoffs				
Season	Club	Lea	GP	G	A	TP	PIM	GP	G	A	TP	PIM
1990-91	Hamilton	OHL	66	23	47	70	53	4	1	4	5	[illegible]
1991-92	Guelph	OHL	62	40	62	102	123	....	....	....	....	....
1992-93	Guelph	OHL	59	48	67	115	128	5	3	5	8	[illegible]
	Kalamazoo	IHL	3	1	3	4	6	....	....	....	....	....
1993-94	Dayton	ECHL	2	2	0	2	12	....	....	....	....	....
	Kalamazoo	IHL	30	2	12	14	30	....	....	....	....	....

BETS, MAXIM — (BEHTS, MAKS-eem) — ANA

Left wing. Shoots left. 6'1", 185 lbs. Born, Chelyabinsk, USSR, January 31, 1974.
(St. Louis' 1st choice, 37th overall, in 1993 Entry Draft).

			Regular Season					Playoffs				
Season	Club	Lea	GP	G	A	TP	PIM	GP	G	A	TP	PIM
1991-92	Chelyabinsk	CIS	25	1	1	2	8	....	....	....	....	....
1992-93	Spokane	WHL	54	49	67	106	130	9	5	6	11	[illegible]
1993-94	Spokane	WHL	63	46	70	116	111	3	1	1	2	[illegible]
	Anaheim	**NHL**	**3**	**0**	**0**	**0**	**0**	....	....	....	....	....
	San Diego	IHL	....	....	....	....	....	9	0	2	2	[illegible]
	NHL Totals		**3**	**0**	**0**	**0**	**0**	....	....	....	....	....

Traded to **Anaheim** by **St. Louis** with St. Louis' sixth round choice in 1995 Entry Draft for Alexei Kasatonov, March 21, 1994.

BETY, SEBASTIEN — QUE

Defense. Shoots left. 6'2", 201 lbs. Born, St-Bernard Beauce, Que., May 6, 1976.
(Quebec's 4th choice, 61st overall, in 1994 Entry Draft).

			Regular Season					Playoffs				
Season	Club	Lea	GP	G	A	TP	PIM	GP	G	A	TP	PIM
1992-93	Drummondville	QMJHL	70	1	21	22	126	10	1	2	3	24
1993-94	Drummondville	QMJHL	67	3	8	11	164	10	0	0	0	17

BEUKEBOOM, JEFF — (BOO-kuh-BOOM) — NYR

Defense. Shoots right. 6'5", 225 lbs. Born, Ajax, Ont., March 28, 1965.
(Edmonton's 1st choice, 19th overall, in 1983 Entry Draft).

			Regular Season					Playoffs				
Season	Club	Lea	GP	G	A	TP	PIM	GP	G	A	TP	PIM
1982-83	S.S. Marie	OHL	70	0	25	25	143	16	1	4	5	46
1983-84	S.S. Marie	OHL	61	6	30	36	178	16	1	7	8	43
1984-85a	S.S. Marie	OHL	37	4	20	24	85	16	4	6	10	47
1985-86	Nova Scotia	AHL	77	9	20	29	175	....	....	....	....	....
	Edmonton	**NHL**	....	....	....	....	....	**1**	**0**	**0**	**0**	**4**
1986-87	**Edmonton**	**NHL**	**44**	**3**	**8**	**11**	**124**	....	....	....	....	....
	Nova Scotia	AHL	14	1	7	8	35	....	....	....	....	....
1987-88	**Edmonton**	**NHL**	**73**	**5**	**20**	**25**	**201**	**7**	**0**	**0**	**0**	**16**
1988-89	**Edmonton**	**NHL**	**36**	**0**	**5**	**5**	**94**	**1**	**0**	**0**	**0**	**2**
	Cape Breton	AHL	8	0	4	4	36	....	....	....	....	....
1989-90	**Edmonton**	**NHL**	**46**	**1**	**12**	**13**	**86**	**2**	**0**	**0**	**0**	**0**
1990-91	**Edmonton**	**NHL**	**67**	**3**	**7**	**10**	**150**	**18**	**1**	**3**	**4**	**28**
1991-92	**Edmonton**	**NHL**	**18**	**0**	**5**	**5**	**78**	....	....	....	....	....
	NY Rangers	**NHL**	**56**	**1**	**10**	**11**	**122**	**13**	**2**	**3**	**5**	**47**
1992-93	**NY Rangers**	**NHL**	**82**	**2**	**17**	**19**	**153**	....	....	....	....	....
1993-94	**NY Rangers**	**NHL**	**68**	**8**	**8**	**16**	**170**	**22**	**0**	**6**	**6**	**50**
	NHL Totals		**490**	**23**	**92**	**115**	**1178**	**64**	**3**	**12**	**15**	**147**

a OHL First All-Star Team (1985)

Traded to **NY Rangers** by **Edmonton** for David Shaw, November 12, 1991.

BIALOWAS, FRANK — TOR.

Defense. Shoots left. 5'11", 220 lbs. Born, Winnipeg, Man., September 25, 1970.

			Regular Season					Playoffs				
Season	Club	Lea	GP	G	A	TP	PIM	GP	G	A	TP	PIM
1991-92	Roanoke	ECHL	23	4	2	6	150	3	0	0	0	4
1992-93	Richmond	ECHL	60	3	18	21	261	1	0	0	0	2
1993-94	St. John's	AHL	69	2	8	10	352	7	0	3	3	25
	Toronto	**NHL**	**4**	**0**	**0**	**0**	**12**	....	....	....	....	....
	NHL Totals		**4**	**0**	**0**	**0**	**12**	....	....	....	....	....

Signed as a free agent by **Toronto**, March 20, 1994.

BICANEK, RADIM — (BEE-chah-nehk) — OTT.

Defense. Shoots left. 6'1", 195 lbs. Born, Uherske Hradiste, Czech., January 18, 1975.
(Ottawa's 2nd choice, 27th overall, in 1993 Entry Draft).

			Regular Season					Playoffs				
Season	Club	Lea	GP	G	A	TP	PIM	GP	G	A	TP	PIM
1992-93	Dukla Jihlava	Czech.	43	2	3	5	....	....	....	....	....	....
1993-94	Belleville	OHL	63	16	27	43	49	12	2	8	10	21

BIGGS, DON

Center. Shoots right. 5'8", 185 lbs. Born, Mississauga, Ont., April 7, 1965.
(Minnesota's 9th choice, 156th overall, in 1983 Entry Draft).

			Regular Season					Playoffs				
Season	Club	Lea	GP	G	A	TP	PIM	GP	G	A	TP	PIM
1982-83	Oshawa	OHL	70	22	53	75	145	16	3	6	9	17
1983-84	Oshawa	OHL	58	31	60	91	149	7	4	4	8	18
1984-85	**Minnesota**	**NHL**	**1**	**0**	**0**	**0**	**0**	....	....	....	....	....
	Springfield	AHL	6	0	3	3	0	2	1	0	1	0
	Oshawa	OHL	60	48	69	117	105	5	3	4	7	6
1985-86	Springfield	AHL	28	15	16	31	46	....	....	....	....	....
	Nova Scotia	AHL	47	6	23	29	36	....	....	....	....	....
1986-87	Nova Scotia	AHL	80	22	25	47	165	5	1	2	3	4
1987-88	Hershey	AHL	77	38	41	79	151	12	5	*11	*16	22
1988-89	Hershey	AHL	76	36	67	103	158	11	5	9	14	30
1989-90	**Philadelphia**	**NHL**	**11**	**2**	**0**	**2**	**8**	....	....	....	....	....
	Hershey	AHL	66	39	53	92	125	....	....	....	....	....
1990-91	Rochester	AHL	65	31	57	88	115	15	9	*14	*23	14
1991-92	Binghamton	AHL	74	32	50	82	122	11	3	7	10	8
1992-93abc	Binghamton	AHL	78	54	*84	*138	112	14	3	9	12	32
1993-94	Cincinnati	IHL	80	30	59	89	128	11	8	9	17	29
	NHL Totals		**12**	**2**	**0**	**2**	**8**	....	....	....	....	....

a Won Les Cunningham Plaque (MVP - AHL) (1993)
b Won John B. Sollenberger Trophy (Top Scorer - AHL) (1993)
c AHL First All-Star Team (1993)

Traded to **Edmonton** by **Minnesota** with Gord Sherven for Marc Habscheid, Don Barber and Emanuel Viveiros, December 20, 1985. Signed as a free agent by **Philadelphia**, July 17, 1987. Traded to **NY Rangers** by **Philadelphia** for future considerations, August 8, 1991.

LODEAU, BRENT (BIHL-uh-DOH) MTL.

efense. Shoots left. 6'4', 215 lbs. Born, Dallas, TX, March 27, 1973.
Montreal's 1st choice, 17th overall, in 1991 Entry Draft).

			Regular Season					Playoffs				
eason	Club	Lea	GP	G	A	TP	PIM	GP	G	A	TP	PIM
989-90	Seattle	WHL	68	14	29	43	170	13	3	5	8	31
990-91	Seattle	WHL	55	7	18	25	145	6	1	0	1	12
991-92a	Seattle	WHL	7	1	2	3	43	....	....	....	....	....
	Swift Current	WHL	56	10	47	57	118	8	2	3	5	11
992-93a	Swift Current	WHL	59	11	57	68	77	17	5	14	19	18
993-94	Fredericton	AHL	72	2	5	7	89	....	....	....	....	....

WHL East Second All-Star Team (1992, 1993)

LACK, JAMES

enter. Shoots left. 5'11", 185 lbs. Born, Regina, Sask., August 15, 1969.
artford's 4th choice, 94th overall, in 1989 Entry Draft).

			Regular Season					Playoffs				
eason	Club	Lea	GP	G	A	TP	PIM	GP	G	A	TP	PIM
987-88	Portland	WHL	72	30	50	80	50	....	....	....	....	....
988-89	Portland	WHL	71	45	51	96	57	19	13	6	19	28
989-90	**Hartford**	**NHL**	**1**	**0**	**0**	**0**	**0**	....	....	....	....	....
	Binghamton	AHL	80	37	35	72	34	....	....	....	....	....
990-91	**Hartford**	**NHL**	**1**	**0**	**0**	**0**	**0**	....	....	....	....	....
	Springfield	AHL	79	35	61	96	34	18	9	9	18	6
991-92	**Hartford**	**NHL**	**30**	**4**	**6**	**10**	**10**	....	....	....	....	....
	Springfield	AHL	47	15	25	40	33	10	3	2	5	18
992-93	**Minnesota**	**NHL**	**10**	**2**	**1**	**3**	**4**	....	....	....	....	....
	Kalamazoo	IHL	63	25	45	70	40	....	....	....	....	....
993-94	**Dallas**	**NHL**	**13**	**2**	**3**	**5**	**2**	....	....	....	....	....
	Buffalo	**NHL**	**2**	**0**	**0**	**0**	**0**	....	....	....	....	....
	Rochester	AHL	45	19	32	51	28	4	2	3	5	0
	NHL Totals		**57**	**8**	**10**	**18**	**16**	....	....	....	....	....

raded to **Minnesota** by **Hartford** for Mark Janssens, September 3, 1992. Traded to **Buffalo** by **allas** with Dallas' seventh round choice (Steve Webb) in 1994 Entry Draft for Gord Donnelly, ecember 15, 1993.

LACK, JAMIE PIT.

enter. Shoots left. 6', 185 lbs. Born, Calgary, Alta., April 4, 1972.

			Regular Season					Playoffs				
eason	Club	Lea	GP	G	A	TP	PIM	GP	G	A	TP	PIM
989-90	Portland	WHL	71	16	28	44	48	....	....	....	....	....
990-91	Portland	WHL	55	9	26	35	14	....	....	....	....	....
991-92	Tacoma	WHL	71	33	37	70	79	4	1	0	1	0
992-93a	Tacoma	WHL	69	42	61	103	53	7	7	15	22	2
993-94	Cleveland	IHL	71	12	16	28	36	....	....	....	....	....

WHL West Second All-Star Team (1993)

igned as a free agent by **Pittsburgh**, August 17, 1993.

LACK, RYAN

eft wing. Shoots left. 6'1", 180 lbs. Born, Guelph, Ont., October 25, 1973.
New Jersey's 6th choice, 114th overall, in 1992 Entry Draft).

			Regular Season					Playoffs				
eason	Club	Lea	GP	G	A	TP	PIM	GP	G	A	TP	PIM
990-91	Peterborough	OHL	59	7	16	23	41	4	0	1	1	0
991-92	Peterborough	OHL	66	18	33	51	57	7	1	1	2	11
992-93	Peterborough	OHL	66	30	41	71	43	20	7	4	11	28
993-94	London	OHL	60	36	58	94	50	5	5	8	13	8

LAKE, ROB L.A.

efense. Shoots right. 6'3", 215 lbs. Born, Simcoe, Ont., December 10, 1969.
.os Angeles' 4th choice, 70th overall, in 1988 Entry Draft).

			Regular Season					Playoffs				
eason	Club	Lea	GP	G	A	TP	PIM	GP	G	A	TP	PIM
987-88	Bowling Green	CCHA	43	5	8	13	88	....	....	....	....	....
988-89a	Bowling Green	CCHA	46	11	21	32	140	....	....	....	....	....
989-90bc	Bowling Green	CCHA	42	23	36	59	140	....	....	....	....	....
	Los Angeles	**NHL**	**4**	**0**	**0**	**0**	**4**	**8**	**1**	**3**	**4**	**4**
990-91d	**Los Angeles**	**NHL**	**75**	**12**	**34**	**46**	**125**	**12**	**1**	**4**	**5**	**26**
991-92	**Los Angeles**	**NHL**	**57**	**7**	**13**	**20**	**102**	**6**	**2**	**1**	**3**	**12**
992-93	**Los Angeles**	**NHL**	**76**	**16**	**43**	**59**	**152**	**23**	**4**	**6**	**10**	**46**
993-94	**Los Angeles**	**NHL**	**84**	**20**	**48**	**68**	**137**	....	....	....	....	....
	NHL Totals		**296**	**55**	**138**	**193**	**520**	**49**	**8**	**14**	**22**	**88**

CCHA Second All-Star Team (1989)
CCHA First All-Star Team (1990)
NCAA West First All-American Team (1990)
NHL/Upper Deck All-Rookie Team (1991)

layed in NHL All-Star Game (1994)

LOEMBERG, JEFF (BLOOM-buhrg)

efense. Shoots right. 6'2", 205 lbs. Born, Listowel, Ont., January 31, 1968.
NY Rangers' 5th choice, 93rd overall, in 1986 Entry Draft).

			Regular Season					Playoffs				
eason	Club	Lea	GP	G	A	TP	PIM	GP	G	A	TP	PIM
985-86	North Bay	OHL	60	2	11	13	76	8	1	2	3	9
986-87	North Bay	OHL	60	5	13	18	91	21	1	6	7	13
987-88	Colorado	IHL	5	0	0	0	0	11	1	0	1	8
	North Bay	OHL	46	9	26	35	60	4	1	4	5	2
988-89	**NY Rangers**	**NHL**	**9**	**0**	**0**	**0**	**0**	....	....	....	....	....
	Denver	IHL	64	7	22	29	55	1	0	0	0	0
989-90	**NY Rangers**	**NHL**	**28**	**3**	**3**	**6**	**25**	**7**	**0**	**3**	**3**	**5**
	Flint	IHL	41	7	14	21	24	....	....	....	....	....
990-91	**NY Rangers**	**NHL**	**3**	**0**	**2**	**2**	**0**	....	....	....	....	....
a	Binghamton	AHL	77	16	46	62	28	10	0	6	6	10
991-92	**NY Rangers**	**NHL**	**3**	**0**	**1**	**1**	**0**	....	....	....	....	....
	Binghamton	AHL	66	6	41	47	22	11	1	10	11	10
992-93	Cape Breton	AHL	76	6	45	51	34	16	5	10	15	10
993-94	Springfield	AHL	78	8	28	36	36	6	0	3	3	8
	NHL Totals		**43**	**3**	**6**	**9**	**25**	**7**	**0**	**3**	**3**	**5**

AHL Second All-Star Team (1991)

Claimed by **Tampa Bay** from **NY Rangers** in Expansion Draft, June 18, 1992. Traded to **Edmonton** by **Tampa Bay** for future considerations, September 25, 1992. Signed as a free agent by **Hartford**, August 9, 1993.

BLOMSTEN, ARTO (BLOOM-stehn) WPG.

Defense. Shoots left. 6'3", 210 lbs. Born, Vaasa, Finland, March 16, 1965.
(Winnipeg's 11th choice, 239th overall, in 1986 Entry Draft).

			Regular Season					Playoffs				
Season	Club	Lea	GP	G	A	TP	PIM	GP	G	A	TP	PIM
1983-84	Djurgarden	Swe.	3	0	0	0	4	....	....	....	....	....
1984-85	Djurgarden	Swe.	19	3	1	4	22	8	0	0	0	8
1985-86	Djurgarden	Swe.	8	0	3	3	6	....	....	....	....	....
1986-87	Djurgarden	Swe.	29	2	4	6	28	....	....	....	....	....
1987-88	Djurgarden	Swe.	39	12	6	18	36	2	1	0	1	0
1988-89	Djurgarden	Swe.	40	10	9	19	38	....	....	....	....	....
1989-90	Djurgarden	Swe.	36	5	21	26	28	8	0	1	1	6
1990-91	Djurgarden	Swe.	38	2	9	11	38	7	2	1	3	12
1991-92	Djurgarden	Swe.	39	6	8	14	34	10	2	0	2	8
1992-93	Djurgarden	Swe.	40	4	16	20	52	....	....	....	....	....
1993-94	**Winnipeg**	**NHL**	**18**	**0**	**2**	**2**	**6**	....	....	....	....	....
	Moncton	AHL	44	6	27	33	25	20	4	10	14	8
	NHL Totals		**18**	**0**	**2**	**2**	**6**	....	....	....	....	....

BLOUIN, SYLVAIN NYR

Defense. Shoots left. 6'2", 216 lbs. Born, Montreal, Que., May 21, 1974.
(NY Rangers' 5th choice, 104th overall, in 1994 Entry Draft).

			Regular Season					Playoffs				
Season	Club	Lea	GP	G	A	TP	PIM	GP	G	A	TP	PIM
1991-92	Laval	QMJHL	28	0	0	0	23	9	0	0	0	35
1992-93	Laval	QMJHL	68	0	10	10	373	13	1	0	1	*66
1993-94	Laval	QMJHL	62	18	22	40	*492	21	4	13	17	*177

BOBACK, MICHAEL WSH.

Center. Shoots right. 5'11", 180 lbs. Born, Mt. Clemens, MI, August 13, 1970.
(Washington's 12th choice, 198th overall, in 1990 Entry Draft).

			Regular Season					Playoffs				
Season	Club	Lea	GP	G	A	TP	PIM	GP	G	A	TP	PIM
1988-89	Providence	H.E.	38	21	27	48	26	....	....	....	....	....
1989-90a	Providence	H.E.	31	13	29	42	28	....	....	....	....	....
1990-91	Providence	H.E.	26	15	24	39	6	....	....	....	....	....
1991-92b	Providence	H.E.	36	24	*48	*72	34	....	....	....	....	....
1992-93	Baltimore	AHL	69	11	68	79	14	5	3	3	6	6
1993-94	Portland	AHL	68	16	43	59	50	17	10	17	*27	4

a Hockey East Second All-Star Team (1990)
b Hockey East First All-Star Team (1992)

BOBARIKO, YEVGENY (boh-bah-RIH-koh) VAN.

Center. Shoots left. 6'1", 196 lbs. Born, Gorky, USSR, March 3, 1974.
(Vancouver's 6th choice, 176th overall, in 1993 Entry Draft).

			Regular Season					Playoffs				
Season	Club	Lea	GP	G	A	TP	PIM	GP	G	A	TP	PIM
1991-92	Torpedo Nizhny	CIS	17	5	0	5	4	....	....	....	....	....
1992-93	Torpedo Nizhny	CIS	13	1	0	1	4	....	....	....	....	....
1993-94	Torpedo Nizhny	CIS	44	3	5	8	121	....	....	....	....	....

BODGER, DOUG BUF.

Defense. Shoots left. 6'2", 213 lbs. Born, Chemainus, B.C., June 18, 1966.
(Pittsburgh's 2nd choice, 9th overall, in 1984 Entry Draft).

			Regular Season					Playoffs				
Season	Club	Lea	GP	G	A	TP	PIM	GP	G	A	TP	PIM
1982-83a	Kamloops	WHL	72	26	66	92	98	7	0	5	5	2
1983-84	Kamloops	WHL	70	21	77	98	90	17	2	15	17	12
1984-85	**Pittsburgh**	**NHL**	**65**	**5**	**26**	**31**	**67**	....	....	....	....	....
1985-86	**Pittsburgh**	**NHL**	**79**	**4**	**33**	**37**	**63**	....	....	....	....	....
1986-87	**Pittsburgh**	**NHL**	**76**	**11**	**38**	**49**	**52**	....	....	....	....	....
1987-88	**Pittsburgh**	**NHL**	**69**	**14**	**31**	**45**	**103**	....	....	....	....	....
1988-89	**Pittsburgh**	**NHL**	**10**	**1**	**4**	**5**	**7**	....	....	....	....	....
	Buffalo	**NHL**	**61**	**7**	**40**	**47**	**52**	**5**	**1**	**1**	**2**	**11**
1989-90	**Buffalo**	**NHL**	**71**	**12**	**36**	**48**	**64**	**6**	**1**	**5**	**6**	**6**
1990-91	**Buffalo**	**NHL**	**58**	**5**	**23**	**28**	**54**	**4**	**0**	**1**	**1**	**0**
1991-92	**Buffalo**	**NHL**	**73**	**11**	**35**	**46**	**108**	**7**	**2**	**1**	**3**	**2**
1992-93	**Buffalo**	**NHL**	**81**	**9**	**45**	**54**	**87**	**8**	**2**	**3**	**5**	**0**
1993-94	**Buffalo**	**NHL**	**75**	**7**	**32**	**39**	**76**	**7**	**0**	**3**	**3**	**6**
	NHL Totals		**718**	**86**	**343**	**429**	**733**	**37**	**6**	**14**	**20**	**25**

a WHL Second All-Star Team (1983)

Traded to **Buffalo** by **Pittsburgh** wih Darrin Shannon for Tom Barrasso and Buffalo's third round choice (Joe Dziedzic) in 1990 Entry Draft, November 12, 1988.

BODKIN, RICK OTT.

Center. Shoots left. 6'4", 190 lbs. Born, Hamilton, Ont., March 30, 1975.
(Ottawa's 5th choice, 131st overall, in 1993 Entry Draft).

			Regular Season					Playoffs				
Season	Club	Lea	GP	G	A	TP	PIM	GP	G	A	TP	PIM
1992-93	Sudbury	OHL	50	4	4	8	17	11	0	0	0	0
1993-94	Sudbury	OHL	63	10	16	26	26	10	0	2	2	13

BODNARCHUK, MICHAEL BOS.

Right wing. Shoots right. 6'1", 175 lbs. Born, Bramalea, Ont., March 26, 1970.
(New Jersey's 6th choice, 64th overall, in 1990 Entry Draft).

			Regular Season					Playoffs				
Season	Club	Lea	GP	G	A	TP	PIM	GP	G	A	TP	PIM
1987-88	Kingston	OHL	68	12	20	32	12	....	....	....	....	....
1988-89	Kingston	OHL	63	22	38	60	30	....	....	....	....	....
1989-90a	Kingston	OHL	66	41	59	100	31	7	2	4	6	4
1990-91	Utica	AHL	69	23	32	55	28	....	....	....	....	....
1991-92	Utica	AHL	76	21	19	40	36	4	0	2	2	0
1992-93	Cincinnati	IHL	47	15	18	33	65	....	....	....	....	....
	Utica	AHL	21	6	10	16	4	4	2	0	2	4
1993-94	Albany	AHL	45	12	20	32	54	2	0	0	0	2
	Phoenix	IHL	8	3	1	4	6	....	....	....	....	....

a OHL Second All-Star Team (1990)

Signed as a free agent by **Boston**, June 30, 1994.

BOGUNIECKI, ERIC ST.L.

Center. Shoots right. 5'8", 192 lbs. Born, New Haven, CT, May 6, 1975.
(St. Louis' 6th choice, 193rd overall, in 1993 Entry Draft).

			Regular Season					Playoffs				
Season	Club	Lea	GP	G	A	TP	PIM	GP	G	A	TP	PIM
1992-93	Westminister	HS	24	30	24	54	55	....	....	....	....	....
1993-94	N. Hampshire	H.E.	40	17	16	33	66	....	....	....	....	....

BOH, AARON

Defense. Shoots left. 6'2", 185 lbs. Born, Lethbridge, Alta., April 4, 1974.
(Vancouver's 12th choice, 261st overall, in 1992 Entry Draft).

			Regular Season					Playoffs				
Season	Club	Lea	GP	G	A	TP	PIM	GP	G	A	TP	PIM
1991-92	Spokane	WHL	59	3	19	22	213	8	0	2	2	17
1992-93	Spokane	WHL	15	3	10	13	62	....	....	....	....	....
	Medicine Hat	WHL	58	6	21	27	173	10	0	4	4	27
1993-94	Medicine Hat	WHL	28	4	15	19	99	....	....	....	....	....
	Tri-City	WHL	27	3	7	10	97	....	....	....	....	....
	Columbus	ECHL	10	1	9	10	31	6	2	1	3	17

BOHONOS, LONNY (boh-HOH-nohz) VAN.

Right wing. Shoots right. 5'11", 190 lbs. Born, Winnipeg, Man., May 20, 1973.

			Regular Season					Playoffs				
Season	Club	Lea	GP	G	A	TP	PIM	GP	G	A	TP	PIM
1991-92	Moose Jaw	WHL	8	1	1	2	0	....	....	....	....	....
1992-93	Seattle	WHL	46	13	13	26	27	....	....	....	....	....
	Portland	WHL	27	20	17	37	16	15	8	13	21	19
1993-94ab	Portland	WHL	70	*62	*90	*152	80	10	8	11	19	13

a WHL West First All-Star Team (1994)
b Canadian Major Junior First All-Star Team (1994)

Signed as a free agent by **Vancouver**, May 31, 1994.

BOILEAU, PATRICK WSH.

Defense. Shoots right. 6', 184 lbs. Born, Montreal, Que., February 22, 1975.
(Washington's 3rd choice, 69th overall, in 1993 Entry Draft).

			Regular Season					Playoffs				
Season	Club	Lea	GP	G	A	TP	PIM	GP	G	A	TP	PIM
1991-92	Laval	Midget	42	9	36	45	94	....	....	....	....	....
1992-93	Laval	QMJHL	69	4	19	23	73	13	1	2	3	10
1993-94	Laval	QMJHL	64	13	57	70	56	21	1	7	8	24

BOIVIN, CLAUDE (BOY-vihn) OTT.

Left wing. Shoots left. 6'2", 200 lbs. Born, Ste. Foy, Que., March 1, 1970.
(Philadelphia's 1st choice, 14th overall, in 1988 Entry Draft).

			Regular Season					Playoffs				
Season	Club	Lea	GP	G	A	TP	PIM	GP	G	A	TP	PIM
1987-88	Drummondville	QMJHL	63	23	26	49	233	17	5	3	8	74
1988-89	Drummondville	QMJHL	63	20	36	56	218	4	0	2	2	27
1989-90	Laval	QMJHL	59	24	51	75	309	13	7	13	20	59
1990-91	Hershey	AHL	65	13	32	45	159	7	1	5	6	28
1991-92	**Philadelphia**	**NHL**	**58**	**5**	**13**	**18**	**187**	....	....	....	....	....
	Hershey	AHL	20	4	5	9	96	....	....	....	....	....
1992-93	**Philadelphia**	**NHL**	**30**	**5**	**4**	**9**	**76**	....	....	....	....	....
1993-94	**Philadelphia**	**NHL**	**26**	**1**	**1**	**2**	**57**	....	....	....	....	....
	Hershey	AHL	4	1	6	7	6	....	....	....	....	....
	Ottawa	**NHL**	**15**	**1**	**0**	**1**	**38**	....	....	....	....	....
	NHL Totals		**129**	**12**	**18**	**30**	**358**	....	....	....	....	....

Traded to **Ottawa** by **Philadelphia** with Kirk Daubenspeck for Mark Lamb, March 5, 1994.

BOMBARDIR, BRAD N.J.

Defense. Shoots left. 6'2", 190 lbs. Born, Powell River, B.C., May 5, 1972.
(New Jersey's 5th choice, 56th overall, in 1990 Entry Draft).

			Regular Season					Playoffs				
Season	Club	Lea	GP	G	A	TP	PIM	GP	G	A	TP	PIM
1990-91	North Dakota	WCHA	33	3	6	9	18	....	....	....	....	....
1991-92	North Dakota	WCHA	35	3	14	17	54	....	....	....	....	....
1992-93	North Dakota	WCHA	38	8	15	23	34	....	....	....	....	....
1993-94	North Dakota	WCHA	38	5	17	22	38	....	....	....	....	....

BONDRA, PETER WSH.

Right wing. Shoots left. 6', 200 lbs. Born, Lutsk, USSR, February 7, 1968.
(Washington's 9th choice, 156th overall, in 1990 Entry Draft).

			Regular Season					Playoffs				
Season	Club	Lea	GP	G	A	TP	PIM	GP	G	A	TP	PIM
1986-87	VSZ Kosice	Czech.	32	4	5	9	24	....	....	....	....	....
1987-88	VSZ Kosice	Czech.	45	27	11	38	20	....	....	....	....	....
1988-89	VSZ Kosice	Czech.	40	30	10	40	20	....	....	....	....	....
1989-90	VSZ Kosice	Czech.	49	36	19	55	....	....	....	....	....	....
1990-91	**Washington**	**NHL**	**54**	**12**	**16**	**28**	**47**	**4**	**0**	**1**	**1**	**2**
1991-92	**Washington**	**NHL**	**71**	**28**	**28**	**56**	**42**	**7**	**6**	**2**	**8**	**4**
1992-93	**Washington**	**NHL**	**83**	**37**	**48**	**85**	**70**	**6**	**0**	**6**	**6**	**0**
1993-94	**Washington**	**NHL**	**69**	**24**	**19**	**43**	**40**	**9**	**2**	**4**	**6**	**4**
	NHL Totals		**277**	**101**	**111**	**212**	**199**	**26**	**8**	**13**	**21**	**10**

Played in NHL All-Star Game (1993)

BONIN, BRIAN PIT.

Center. Shoots left. 5'10", 175 lbs. Born, White Bear Lake, MN, November 28, 1973.
(Pittsburgh's 9th choice, 211th overall, in 1992 Entry Draft).

			Regular Season					Playoffs				
Season	Club	Lea	GP	G	A	TP	PIM	GP	G	A	TP	PIM
1992-93	U. Minnesota	WCHA	38	10	18	28	10	....	....	....	....	....
1993-94	U. Minnesota	WCHA	42	24	20	44	14	....	....	....	....	....

BONK, RADEK (BOHNK) OTT.

Center. Shoots left. 6'3", 215 lbs. Born, Krnov, Czech., January 9, 1976.
(Ottawa's 1st choice, 3rd overall, in 1994 Entry Draft).

			Regular Season					Playoffs				
Season	Club	Lea	GP	G	A	TP	PIM	GP	G	A	TP	PIM
1992-93	ZPS Zlin	Czech.	30	5	5	10	10	....	....	....	....	....
1993-94a	Las Vegas	IHL	76	42	45	87	208	5	1	2	3	10

a Won Garry F. Longman Trophy (Top Rookie - IHL) (1994)

BONSIGNORE, JASON (bohn-SEE-nohr) EDM.

Center. Shoots right. 6'4", 208 lbs. Born, Rochester, NY, April 15, 1976.
(Edmonton's 1st choice, 4th overall, in 1994 Entry Draft).

			Regular Season					Playoffs				
Season	Club	Lea	GP	G	A	TP	PIM	GP	G	A	TP	PIM
1992-93	Newmarket	OHL	66	22	20	42	6	7	0	3	3	0
1993-94	Newmarket	OHL	17	7	17	24	22	....	....	....	....	....
	Niagara Falls	OHL	41	15	47	62	41	....	....	....	....	....

BORDELEAU, SEBASTIEN (BOHR-duh-loh) MTL

Center. Shoots right. 5'10", 176 lbs. Born, Vancouver, B.C., February 15, 1975.
(Montreal's 3rd choice, 73rd overall, in 1993 Entry Draft).

			Regular Season					Playoffs				
Season	Club	Lea	GP	G	A	TP	PIM	GP	G	A	TP	PIM
1991-92	Hull	QMJHL	62	26	32	58	91	5	0	3	3	[illegible]
1992-93	Hull	QMJHL	60	18	39	57	95	10	3	8	11	[illegible]
1993-94	Hull	QMJHL	60	26	57	83	147	17	6	14	20	[illegible]

BORSATO, LUCIANO (bohr-SAH-toh, LOO-chee-AH-noh) WPG

Center. Shoots right. 5'11", 190 lbs. Born, Richmond Hill, Ont., January 7, 1966.
(Winnipeg's 7th choice, 135th overall, in 1984 Entry Draft).

			Regular Season					Playoffs				
Season	Club	Lea	GP	G	A	TP	PIM	GP	G	A	TP	PIM
1984-85	Clarkson	ECAC	33	15	17	32	37	....	....	....	....	....
1985-86	Clarkson	ECAC	28	14	17	31	44	....	....	....	....	....
1986-87	Clarkson	ECAC	31	16	41	57	55	....	....	....	....	....
1987-88ab	Clarkson	ECAC	33	15	29	44	38	....	....	....	....	....
	Moncton	AHL	3	1	1	2	0	....	....	....	....	....
1988-89	Moncton	AHL	6	2	5	7	4	....	....	....	....	....
	Tappara	Fin.	44	31	36	67	69	7	0	3	3	[illegible]
1989-90	Moncton	AHL	1	1	0	1	0	....	....	....	....	....
1990-91	**Winnipeg**	**NHL**	**1**	**0**	**1**	**1**	**2**	....	....	....	....	....
	Moncton	AHL	41	14	24	38	40	9	3	7	10	[illegible]
1991-92	**Winnipeg**	**NHL**	**56**	**15**	**21**	**36**	**45**	**1**	**0**	**0**	**0**	[illegible]
	Moncton	AHL	14	2	7	9	39	....	....	....	....	....
1992-93	**Winnipeg**	**NHL**	**67**	**15**	**20**	**35**	**38**	**6**	**1**	**0**	**1**	[illegible]
1993-94	**Winnipeg**	**NHL**	**75**	**5**	**13**	**18**	**28**	....	....	....	....	....
	NHL Totals		**199**	**35**	**55**	**90**	**113**	**7**	**1**	**0**	**1**	[illegible]

a ECAC Second All-Star Team (1988)
b NCAA East Second All-American Team (1988)

BORSCHEVSKY, NIKOLAI (bohr-SHEHV-skee) TOR

Right wing. Shoots left. 5'9", 180 lbs. Born, Tomsk, USSR, January 12, 1965.
(Toronto's 3rd choice, 77th overall, in 1992 Entry Draft).

			Regular Season					Playoffs				
Season	Club	Lea	GP	G	A	TP	PIM	GP	G	A	TP	PIM
1983-84	Moscow D'amo	USSR	34	4	5	9	4	....	....	....	....	....
1984-85	Moscow D'amo	USSR	34	5	9	14	6	....	....	....	....	....
1985-86	Moscow D'amo	USSR	31	6	4	10	4	....	....	....	....	....
1986-87	Moscow D'amo	USSR	28	1	4	5	8	....	....	....	....	....
1987-88	Moscow D'amo	USSR	37	11	7	18	6	....	....	....	....	....
1988-89	Moscow D'amo	USSR	43	7	8	15	18	....	....	....	....	....
1989-90	Spartak	USSR	48	17	25	42	8	....	....	....	....	....
1990-91	Spartak	USSR	45	19	16	35	16	....	....	....	....	....
1991-92	Spartak	CIS	40	25	14	39	16	....	....	....	....	....
1992-93	**Toronto**	**NHL**	**78**	**34**	**40**	**74**	**28**	**16**	**2**	**7**	**9**	[illegible]
1993-94	**Toronto**	**NHL**	**45**	**14**	**20**	**34**	**10**	**15**	**2**	**2**	**4**	[illegible]
	NHL Totals		**123**	**48**	**60**	**108**	**38**	**31**	**4**	**9**	**13**	[illegible]

BOSTON, SCOTT

Defense. Shoots right. 6'2", 180 lbs. Born, Ottawa, Ont., July 13, 1971.

			Regular Season					Playoffs				
Season	Club	Lea	GP	G	A	TP	PIM	GP	G	A	TP	PIM
1990-91	Belleville	OHL	66	12	39	51	70	6	1	2	3	[illegible]
1991-92a	Belleville	OHL	65	13	71	84	89	5	0	6	6	[illegible]
1992-93	Atlanta	IHL	76	2	17	19	75	2	0	0	0	[illegible]
1993-94	Knoxville	ECHL	64	9	30	39	213	....	....	....	....	....
	Atlanta	IHL	7	0	0	0	2	....	....	....	....	....

a OHL First All-Star Team (1992)

Signed as a free agent by **Tampa Bay**, June 29, 1992.

BOTTERILL, JASON (BOH-tuhr-ihl) DAL

Left wing. Shoots left. 6'3", 205 lbs. Born, Edmonton, Alta., May 19, 1976.
(Dallas' 1st choice, 20th overall, in 1994 Entry Draft).

			Regular Season					Playoffs				
Season	Club	Lea	GP	G	A	TP	PIM	GP	G	A	TP	PIM
1992-93	St. Paul's	HS	22	22	26	48	....	....	....	....	....	....
1993-94	Michigan	CCHA	36	20	19	39	94	....	....	....	....	....

BOUCHARD, FRANCOIS T.B

Defense. Shoots right. 6', 185 lbs. Born, Brossard, Que., August 8, 1973.
(Tampa Bay's 1st choice, 8th overall, in 1994 Supplemental Draft).

			Regular Season					Playoffs				
Season	Club	Lea	GP	G	A	TP	PIM	GP	G	A	TP	PIM
1991-92	Northeastern	H.E.	34	4	9	13	28	....	....	....	....	....
1992-93	Northeastern	H.E.	26	4	6	10	20	....	....	....	....	....
1993-94a	Northeastern	H.E.	39	15	15	30	34	....	....	....	....	....

a Hockey East First All-Star Team (1994)

BOUCHARD, JOEL CGY

Defense. Shoots left. 6', 190 lbs. Born, Montreal, Que., January 23, 1974.
(Calgary's 7th choice, 129th overall, in 1992 Entry Draft).

			Regular Season					Playoffs				
Season	Club	Lea	GP	G	A	TP	PIM	GP	G	A	TP	PIM
1990-91	Longueuil	QMJHL	53	3	19	22	34	8	1	0	1	[illegible]
1991-92	Verdun	QMJHL	70	9	20	29	55	19	1	7	8	[illegible]
1992-93	Verdun	QMJHL	60	10	49	59	126	4	0	2	2	[illegible]
1993-94a	Verdun	QMJHL	60	15	55	70	62	4	1	0	1	[illegible]
	Saint John	AHL	1	0	0	0	0	2	0	0	0	[illegible]

a QMJHL First All-Star Team (1994)

BOUCHER, PHILIPPE BUF

Defense. Shoots right. 6'2", 189 lbs. Born, St. Apollinaire, Que., March 24, 1973.
(Buffalo's 1st choice, 13th overall, in 1991 Entry Draft).

			Regular Season					Playoffs				
Season	Club	Lea	GP	G	A	TP	PIM	GP	G	A	TP	PIM
1990-91ab	Granby	QMJHL	69	21	46	67	92	....	....	....	....	....
1991-92	Granby	QMJHL	49	22	37	59	47	....	....	....	....	....
b	Laval	QMJHL	16	7	11	18	36	10	5	6	11	[illegible]
1992-93	**Buffalo**	**NHL**	**18**	**0**	**4**	**4**	**14**	....	....	....	....	....
	Laval	QMJHL	16	12	15	27	37	13	6	15	21	[illegible]
	Rochester	AHL	5	4	3	7	8	3	0	1	1	[illegible]
1993-94	**Buffalo**	**NHL**	**38**	**6**	**8**	**14**	**29**	**7**	**1**	**1**	**2**	[illegible]
	Rochester	AHL	31	10	22	32	51	....	....	....	....	....
	NHL Totals		**56**	**6**	**12**	**18**	**43**	**7**	**1**	**1**	**2**	[illegible]

a Canadian Major Junior Rookie of the Year (1991)
b QMJHL Second All-Star Team (1991, 1992)

OUGHNER, BOB (BOOG-nuhr) FLA.

efense. Shoots right. 6', 201 lbs. Born, Windsor, Ont., March 8, 1971.
etroit's 2nd choice, 32nd overall, in 1989 Entry Draft).

			Regular Season					Playoffs				
ason	Club	Lea	GP	G	A	TP	PIM	GP	G	A	TP	PIM
88-89	S.S. Marie	OHL	64	6	15	21	182	....	....	....	....	....
89-90	S.S. Marie	OHL	49	7	23	30	122	....	....	....	....	....
90-91	S.S. Marie	OHL	64	13	33	46	156	14	2	9	11	35
91-92	Toledo	ECHL	28	3	10	13	79	5	2	0	2	15
	Adirondack	AHL	1	0	0	0	7	....	....	....	....	....
92-93	Adirondack	AHL	69	1	16	17	190	....	....	....	....	....
93-94	Adirondack	AHL	72	8	14	22	292	10	1	1	2	18

gned as a free agent by **Florida**, July 25, 1994.

OULIN, VLADISLAV PHI.

efense. Shoots left. 6'4", 196 lbs. Born, Penza, USSR, May 18, 1972.
hiladelphia's 5th choice, 103rd overall, in 1992 Entry Draft).

			Regular Season					Playoffs				
ason	Club	Lea	GP	G	A	TP	PIM	GP	G	A	TP	PIM
92-93	Moscow D'amo	CIS	32	2	1	3	55	....	....	....	....	....
93-94	Moscow D'amo	CIS	43	4	2	6	36	....	....	....	....	....

OURQUE, PHIL (BOHRK) OTT.

ft wing. Shoots left. 6'1", 196 lbs. Born, Chelmsford, MA, June 8, 1962.

			Regular Season					Playoffs				
ason	Club	Lea	GP	G	A	TP	PIM	GP	G	A	TP	PIM
80-81	Kingston	OHL	47	4	4	8	46	6	0	0	0	10
81-82	Kingston	OHL	67	11	40	51	111	4	0	0	0	0
82-83	Baltimore	AHL	65	1	15	16	93	....	....	....	....	....
83-84	**Pittsburgh**	**NHL**	**5**	**0**	**1**	**1**	**12**	....	....	....	....	....
	Baltimore	AHL	58	5	17	22	96	....	....	....	....	....
84-85	Baltimore	AHL	79	6	15	21	164	13	2	5	7	23
85-86	**Pittsburgh**	**NHL**	**4**	**0**	**0**	**0**	**2**	....	....	....	....	....
	Baltimore	AHL	74	8	18	26	226	....	....	....	....	....
86-87	**Pittsburgh**	**NHL**	**22**	**2**	**3**	**5**	**32**	....	....	....	....	....
	Baltimore	AHL	49	15	16	31	183	....	....	....	....	....
87-88	**Pittsburgh**	**NHL**	**21**	**4**	**12**	**16**	**20**	....	....	....	....	....
ab	Muskegon	IHL	52	16	36	52	66	6	1	2	3	16
88-89	**Pittsburgh**	**NHL**	**80**	**17**	**26**	**43**	**97**	**11**	**4**	**1**	**5**	**66**
89-90	**Pittsburgh**	**NHL**	**76**	**22**	**17**	**39**	**108**	....	....	....	....	....
90-91	**Pittsburgh**	**NHL**	**78**	**20**	**14**	**34**	**106**	**24**	**6**	**7**	**13**	**16**
91-92	**Pittsburgh**	**NHL**	**58**	**10**	**16**	**26**	**58**	**21**	**3**	**4**	**7**	**25**
92-93	**NY Rangers**	**NHL**	**55**	**6**	**14**	**20**	**39**	....	....	....	....	....
93-94	**NY Rangers**	**NHL**	**16**	**0**	**1**	**1**	**8**	....	....	....	....	....
	Ottawa	**NHL**	**11**	**2**	**3**	**5**	**0**	....	....	....	....	....
	NHL Totals		**426**	**83**	**107**	**190**	**482**	**56**	**13**	**12**	**25**	**107**

IHL First All-Star Team (1988)
Won Governor's Trophy (Outstanding Defenseman - IHL) (1988)

gned as a free agent by **Pittsburgh**, October 4, 1982. Signed as a free agent by **NY Rangers**, ugust 31, 1992. Traded to **Ottawa** by **NY Rangers** for future considerations, March 21, 1994.

OURQUE, RAY (BOHRK) BOS.

efense. Shoots left. 5'11", 215 lbs. Born, Montreal, Que., December 28, 1960.
oston's 1st choice, 8th overall, in 1979 Entry Draft).

			Regular Season					Playoffs				
eason	Club	Lea	GP	G	A	TP	PIM	GP	G	A	TP	PIM
976-77	Sorel	QJHL	69	12	36	48	61	....	....	....	....	....
977-78	Verdun	QJHL	72	22	57	79	90	4	2	1	3	0
978-79	Verdun	QJHL	63	22	71	93	44	11	3	16	19	18
979-80ab	**Boston**	**NHL**	**80**	**17**	**48**	**65**	**73**	**10**	**2**	**9**	**11**	**27**
980-81c	**Boston**	**NHL**	**67**	**27**	**29**	**56**	**96**	**3**	**0**	**1**	**1**	**2**
981-82b	**Boston**	**NHL**	**65**	**17**	**49**	**66**	**51**	**9**	**1**	**5**	**6**	**16**
982-83c	**Boston**	**NHL**	**65**	**22**	**51**	**73**	**20**	**17**	**8**	**15**	**23**	**10**
983-84b	**Boston**	**NHL**	**78**	**31**	**65**	**96**	**57**	**3**	**0**	**2**	**2**	**0**
984-85b	**Boston**	**NHL**	**73**	**20**	**66**	**86**	**53**	**5**	**0**	**3**	**3**	**4**
985-86c	**Boston**	**NHL**	**74**	**19**	**58**	**77**	**68**	**3**	**0**	**0**	**0**	**0**
986-87bd	**Boston**	**NHL**	**78**	**23**	**72**	**95**	**36**	**4**	**1**	**2**	**3**	**0**
987-88bd	**Boston**	**NHL**	**78**	**17**	**64**	**81**	**72**	**23**	**3**	**18**	**21**	**26**
988-89c	**Boston**	**NHL**	**60**	**18**	**43**	**61**	**52**	**10**	**0**	**4**	**4**	**6**
989-90bd	**Boston**	**NHL**	**76**	**19**	**65**	**84**	**50**	**17**	**5**	**12**	**17**	**16**
990-91bd	**Boston**	**NHL**	**76**	**21**	**73**	**94**	**75**	**19**	**7**	**18**	**25**	**12**
991-92be	**Boston**	**NHL**	**80**	**21**	**60**	**81**	**56**	**12**	**3**	**6**	**9**	**12**
992-93b	**Boston**	**NHL**	**78**	**19**	**63**	**82**	**40**	**4**	**1**	**0**	**1**	**2**
993-94bd	**Boston**	**NHL**	**72**	**20**	**71**	**91**	**58**	**13**	**2**	**8**	**10**	**0**
	NHL Totals		**1100**	**311**	**877**	**1188**	**857**	**152**	**33**	**103**	**136**	**133**

Won Calder Memorial Trophy (1980)
NHL First All-Star Team (1980, 1982, 1984, 1985, 1987, 1988, 1990, 1991, 1992, 1993, 1994)
NHL Second All-Star Team (1981, 1983, 1986, 1989)
Won James Norris Memorial Trophy (1987, 1988, 1990, 1991, 1994)
Won King Clancy Memorial Trophy (1992)

ayed in NHL All-Star Game (1981-86, 1988-94)

OUSQUET, DANY WSH.

enter. Shoots left. 5'11", 155 lbs. Born, Montreal, Que., April 3, 1973.
Vashington's 10th choice, 277th overall, in 1993 Entry Draft).

			Regular Season					Playoffs				
eason	Club	Lea	GP	G	A	TP	PIM	GP	G	A	TP	PIM
992-93	Penticton	BCJHL	21	24	18	42	31	....	....	....	....	....
993-94	Penticton	BCJHL	58	76	76	152	78	....	....	....	....	....

OWEN, CURTIS (BOW-ehn) DET.

eft wing. Shoots left. 6'1", 195 lbs. Born, Kenora, Ont., March 24, 1974.
Detroit's 1st choice, 22nd overall, in 1992 Entry Draft).

			Regular Season					Playoffs				
eason	Club	Lea	GP	G	A	TP	PIM	GP	G	A	TP	PIM
990-91	Ottawa	OHL	42	12	14	26	31	....	....	....	....	....
991-92	Ottawa	OHL	65	31	45	76	94	11	3	7	10	11
992-93	Ottawa	OHL	21	9	19	28	51	....	....	....	....	....
993-94	Ottawa	OHL	52	25	37	62	98	17	8	13	21	14

BOWEN, JASON (BOW-ehn) PHI.

Defense. Shoots left. 6'4", 215 lbs. Born, Port Alice, B.C., November 9, 1973.
(Philadelphia's 2nd choice, 15th overall, in 1992 Entry Draft).

			Regular Season					Playoffs				
Season	Club	Lea	GP	G	A	TP	PIM	GP	G	A	TP	PIM
1989-90	Tri-City	WHL	61	8	5	13	129	7	0	3	3	4
1990-91	Tri-City	WHL	60	7	13	20	252	6	2	2	4	18
1991-92	Tri-City	WHL	19	5	3	8	135	5	0	1	1	42
1992-93	**Philadelphia**	**NHL**	**7**	**1**	**0**	**1**	**2**	....	....	....	....	....
	Tri-City	WHL	62	10	12	22	219	3	1	1	2	18
1993-94	**Philadelphia**	**NHL**	**56**	**1**	**5**	**6**	**87**	....	....	....	....	....
	NHL Totals		**63**	**2**	**5**	**7**	**89**	....	....	....	....	....

BOYER, ZAC DAL.

Right wing. Shoots right. 6'1", 185 lbs. Born, Inuvik, N.W.T., October 25, 1971.
(Chicago's 4th choice, 88th overall, in 1991 Entry Draft).

			Regular Season					Playoffs				
Season	Club	Lea	GP	G	A	TP	PIM	GP	G	A	TP	PIM
1988-89	Kamloops	WHL	42	10	17	27	22	....	....	....	....	....
1989-90	Kamloops	WHL	71	24	47	71	163	17	4	4	8	8
1990-91	Kamloops	WHL	64	45	60	105	58	12	6	10	16	8
1991-92	Kamloops	WHL	70	40	69	109	90	17	9	*20	*29	16
1992-93	Indianapolis	IHL	59	7	14	21	26	....	....	....	....	....
1993-94	Indianapolis	IHL	54	13	12	25	67	....	....	....	....	....

BOZON, PHILIPPE (boh-ZOHN) ST.L.

Left wing. Shoots left. 5'10", 185 lbs. Born, Chamonix, France, November 30, 1966.

			Regular Season					Playoffs				
Season	Club	Lea	GP	G	A	TP	PIM	GP	G	A	TP	PIM
1984-85	St-Jean	QMJHL	67	32	50	82	82	5	0	5	5	4
1985-86a	St-Jean	QMJHL	65	59	52	111	72	10	10	6	16	16
	Peoria	IHL	....	....	....	....	....	5	1	0	1	0
1986-87	Peoria	IHL	28	4	11	15	17	....	....	....	....	....
	St-Jean	QMJHL	25	20	21	41	75	8	5	5	10	30
1987-88	Mont-Blanc	France	18	11	15	26	34	10	15	6	21	6
1988-89	Mont Blanc	France	18	11	18	29	18	11	11	17	28	38
1989-90	Grenoble	France	36	45	38	83	34	6	4	3	7	2
1990-91	Grenoble	France	26	22	16	38	16	10	7	8	15	8
1991-92	Chamonix	France	10	12	8	20	20	....	....	....	....	....
	St. Louis	**NHL**	**9**	**1**	**3**	**4**	**4**	**6**	**1**	**0**	**1**	**27**
1992-93	**St. Louis**	**NHL**	**54**	**6**	**6**	**12**	**55**	**9**	**1**	**0**	**1**	**0**
	Peoria	IHL	4	3	2	5	2	....	....	....	....	....
1993-94	**St. Louis**	**NHL**	**80**	**9**	**16**	**25**	**42**	**4**	**0**	**0**	**0**	**4**
	NHL Totals		**143**	**16**	**25**	**41**	**101**	**19**	**2**	**0**	**2**	**31**

a QMJHL Second All-Star Team (1986)

Signed as a free agent by **St. Louis**, September 29, 1985.

BRADLEY, BRIAN T.B.

Center. Shoots right. 5'10", 177 lbs. Born, Kitchener, Ont., January 21, 1965.
(Calgary's 2nd choice, 51st overall, in 1983 Entry Draft).

			Regular Season					Playoffs				
Season	Club	Lea	GP	G	A	TP	PIM	GP	G	A	TP	PIM
1982-83	London	OHL	67	37	82	119	37	3	1	0	1	0
1983-84	London	OHL	49	40	60	100	24	4	2	4	6	0
1984-85	London	OHL	32	27	49	76	22	8	5	10	15	4
1985-86	**Calgary**	**NHL**	**5**	**0**	**1**	**1**	**0**	**1**	**0**	**0**	**0**	**0**
	Moncton	AHL	59	23	42	65	40	10	6	9	15	4
1986-87	**Calgary**	**NHL**	**40**	**10**	**18**	**28**	**16**	....	....	....	....	....
	Moncton	AHL	20	12	16	28	8	....	....	....	....	....
1987-88	Cdn. National	....	47	18	19	37	42	....	....	....	....	....
	Cdn. Olympic	....	7	0	4	4	0	....	....	....	....	....
	Vancouver	**NHL**	**11**	**3**	**5**	**8**	**6**	....	....	....	....	....
1988-89	**Vancouver**	**NHL**	**71**	**18**	**27**	**45**	**42**	**7**	**3**	**4**	**7**	**10**
1989-90	**Vancouver**	**NHL**	**67**	**19**	**29**	**48**	**65**	....	....	....	....	....
1990-91	**Vancouver**	**NHL**	**44**	**11**	**20**	**31**	**42**	....	....	....	....	....
	Toronto	**NHL**	**26**	**0**	**11**	**11**	**20**	....	....	....	....	....
1991-92	**Toronto**	**NHL**	**59**	**10**	**21**	**31**	**48**	....	....	....	....	....
1992-93	**Tampa Bay**	**NHL**	**80**	**42**	**44**	**86**	**92**	....	....	....	....	....
1993-94	**Tampa Bay**	**NHL**	**78**	**24**	**40**	**64**	**56**	....	....	....	....	....
	NHL Totals		**481**	**137**	**216**	**353**	**387**	**8**	**3**	**4**	**7**	**10**

Played in NHL All-Star Game (1993, 1994)

Traded to **Vancouver** by **Calgary** with Peter Bakovic and Kevin Guy for Craig Coxe, March 6, 1988. Traded to **Toronto** by **Vancouver** for Tom Kurvers, January 12, 1991. Claimed by **Tampa Bay** from **Toronto** in Expansion Draft, June 18, 1992.

BRADLEY, E.J. PHI.

Center. Shoots left. 5'10", 182 lbs. Born, New Hyde Park, NY, January 2, 1975.
(Philadelphia's 9th choice, 226th overall, in 1993 Entry Draft).

			Regular Season					Playoffs				
Season	Club	Lea	GP	G	A	TP	PIM	GP	G	A	TP	PIM
1992-93	Tabor Aca.	HS	29	27	48	75	66	....	....	....	....	....
1993-94	Tabor Aca.	HS	48	33	37	70	....	....	....	....	....	....

BRADY, NEIL

Center. Shoots left. 6'2", 200 lbs. Born, Montreal, Que., April 12, 1968.
(New Jersey's 1st choice, 3rd overall, in 1986 Entry Draft).

			Regular Season					Playoffs				
Season	Club	Lea	GP	G	A	TP	PIM	GP	G	A	TP	PIM
1984-85	Calgary	Midget	37	25	50	75	75	....	....	....	....	....
	Medicine Hat	WHL	....	....	....	....	....	3	0	0	0	2
1985-86	Medicine Hat	WHL	72	21	60	81	104	21	9	11	20	23
1986-87	Medicine Hat	WHL	57	19	64	83	126	18	1	4	5	25
1987-88	Medicine Hat	WHL	61	16	35	51	110	15	0	3	3	19
1988-89	Utica	AHL	75	16	21	37	56	4	0	3	3	0
1989-90	**New Jersey**	**NHL**	**19**	**1**	**4**	**5**	**13**	....	....	....	....	....
	Utica	AHL	38	10	13	23	21	5	0	1	1	10
1990-91	**New Jersey**	**NHL**	**3**	**0**	**0**	**0**	**0**	....	....	....	....	....
	Utica	AHL	77	33	63	96	91	....	....	....	....	....
1991-92	**New Jersey**	**NHL**	**7**	**1**	**0**	**1**	**4**	....	....	....	....	....
	Utica	AHL	33	12	30	42	28	....	....	....	....	....
1992-93	**Ottawa**	**NHL**	**55**	**7**	**17**	**24**	**57**	....	....	....	....	....
	New Haven	AHL	8	6	3	9	2	....	....	....	....	....
1993-94	**Dallas**	**NHL**	**5**	**0**	**1**	**1**	**21**	....	....	....	....	....
	Kalamazoo	IHL	43	10	16	26	188	5	1	1	2	10
	NHL Totals		**89**	**9**	**22**	**31**	**95**	....	....	....	....	....

Traded to **Ottawa** by **New Jersey** for future considerations, September 3, 1992. Signed as a free agent by **Dallas**, December 3, 1993.

BRASHEAR, DONALD (bra-SHEER) MTL.

Left wing. Shoots left. 6'3", 214 lbs. Born, Bedford, IN, January 7, 1972.

			Regular Season					Playoffs				
Season	Club	Lea	GP	G	A	TP	PIM	GP	G	A	TP	PIM
1989-90	Longueuil	QMJHL	64	12	14	26	169	7	0	0	0	11
1990-91	Longueuil	QMJHL	68	12	26	38	195	8	0	3	3	33
1991-92	Verdun	QMJHL	65	18	24	42	283	18	4	2	6	98
1992-93	Fredericton	AHL	76	11	3	14	261	5	0	0	0	8
1993-94	**Montreal**	**NHL**	**14**	**2**	**2**	**4**	**34**	**2**	**0**	**0**	**0**	**0**
	Fredericton	AHL	62	38	28	66	250	....	....	....	....	....
	NHL Totals		**14**	**2**	**2**	**4**	**34**	**2**	**0**	**0**	**0**	**0**

Signed as a free agent by **Montreal**, July 28, 1992.

BREEN, GEORGE EDM.

Right wing. Shoots right. 6'2", 200 lbs. Born, Webster, MA, August 3, 1973.
(Edmonton's 4th choice, 56th overall, in 1991 Entry Draft).

			Regular Season					Playoffs				
Season	Club	Lea	GP	G	A	TP	PIM	GP	G	A	TP	PIM
1991-92	Providence	H.E.	36	8	4	12	24	....	....	....	....	....
1992-93	Providence	H.E.	31	11	7	18	45	....	....	....	....	....
1993-94	Providence	H.E.	32	8	14	22	22	....	....	....	....	....

BREKKE, BRENT QUE.

Defense. Shoots left. 6'1", 175 lbs. Born, Minot, ND, August 16, 1971.
(Quebec's 9th choice, 188th overall, in 1991 Entry Draft).

			Regular Season					Playoffs				
Season	Club	Lea	GP	G	A	TP	PIM	GP	G	A	TP	PIM
1990-91	W. Michigan	CCHA	38	1	8	9	57	....	....	....	....	....
1991-92	W. Michigan	CCHA	36	1	10	11	68	....	....	....	....	....
1992-93	W. Michigan	CCHA	38	3	2	5	42	....	....	....	....	....
1993-94	W. Michigan	CCHA	39	4	25	29	76	....	....	....	....	....

BRENNAN, RICHARD QUE.

Defense. Shoots right. 6'2", 200 lbs. Born, Schenectady, NY, November 26, 1972.
(Quebec's 3rd choice, 46th overall, in 1991 Entry Draft).

			Regular Season					Playoffs				
Season	Club	Lea	GP	G	A	TP	PIM	GP	G	A	TP	PIM
1991-92	Boston U.	H.E.	30	4	13	17	50	....	....	....	....	....
1992-93	Boston U.	H.E.	40	9	11	20	68	....	....	....	....	....
1993-94ab	Boston U.	H.E.	41	8	27	35	82	....	....	....	....	....

a Hockey East First All-Star Team (1994)
b NCAA East Second All-American Team (1994)

BRICKLEY, ANDY NYI

Left wing/Center. Shoots left. 5'11", 200 lbs. Born, Melrose, MA, August 9, 1961.
(Philadelphia's 10th choice, 210th overall, in 1980 Entry Draft).

			Regular Season					Playoffs				
Season	Club	Lea	GP	G	A	TP	PIM	GP	G	A	TP	PIM
1979-80	N. Hampshire	ECAC	27	15	17	32	8	....	....	....	....	....
1980-81	N. Hampshire	ECAC	31	27	25	52	16	....	....	....	....	....
1981-82ab	N. Hampshire	ECAC	35	26	27	53	6	....	....	....	....	....
1982-83	**Philadelphia**	**NHL**	**3**	**1**	**1**	**2**	**0**	....	....	....	....	....
c	Maine	AHL	76	29	54	83	10	17	9	5	14	0
1983-84	Springfield	AHL	7	1	5	6	2	....	....	....	....	....
	Pittsburgh	**NHL**	**50**	**18**	**20**	**38**	**9**	....	....	....	....	....
	Baltimore	AHL	4	0	5	5	2	....	....	....	....	....
1984-85	**Pittsburgh**	**NHL**	**45**	**7**	**15**	**22**	**10**	....	....	....	....	....
	Baltimore	AHL	31	13	14	27	8	15	*10	8	18	0
1985-86	Maine	AHL	60	26	34	60	20	5	0	4	4	0
1986-87	**New Jersey**	**NHL**	**51**	**11**	**12**	**23**	**8**	....	....	....	....	....
1987-88	**New Jersey**	**NHL**	**45**	**8**	**14**	**22**	**14**	**4**	**0**	**1**	**1**	**4**
	Utica	AHL	9	5	8	13	4	....	....	....	....	....
1988-89	**Boston**	**NHL**	**71**	**13**	**22**	**35**	**20**	**10**	**0**	**2**	**2**	**0**
1989-90	**Boston**	**NHL**	**43**	**12**	**28**	**40**	**8**	**2**	**0**	**0**	**0**	**0**
1990-91	**Boston**	**NHL**	**40**	**2**	**9**	**11**	**8**	....	....	....	....	....
	Maine	AHL	17	8	17	25	2	1	0	0	0	0
1991-92	**Boston**	**NHL**	**23**	**10**	**17**	**27**	**2**	....	....	....	....	....
	Maine	AHL	14	5	15	20	2	....	....	....	....	....
1992-93	**Winnipeg**	**NHL**	**12**	**0**	**2**	**2**	**2**	**1**	**1**	**1**	**2**	**0**
	Moncton	AHL	38	15	36	51	10	5	4	2	6	0
1993-94	**Winnipeg**	**NHL**	**2**	**0**	**0**	**0**	**0**	....	....	....	....	....
	Moncton	AHL	53	20	39	59	20	19	8	*19	*27	4
	NHL Totals		**385**	**82**	**140**	**222**	**81**	**17**	**1**	**4**	**5**	**4**

a ECAC First All-Star Team (1982)
b NCAA All-American Team (1982)
c AHL Second All-Star Team (1983)

Traded to **Pittsburgh** by **Philadelphia** with Mark Taylor, Ron Flockhart, Philadelphia's first round (Roger Belanger) and third round (later traded to Vancouver — Vancouver selected Mike Stevens) choices in 1984 Entry Draft for Rich Sutter and Pittsburgh's second round (Greg Smyth) and third round (David McLay) choices in 1984 Entry Draft, October 23, 1983. Signed as a free agent by **New Jersey**, July 8, 1986. Claimed by **Boston** in NHL Waiver Draft, October 3, 1988. Signed as a free agent by **Winnipeg**, November 11, 1992. Signed as a free agent by **NY Islanders**, July 27, 1994.

BRIERLEY, DAN NYR

Defense. Shoots left. 6'2", 185 lbs. Born, Nashua, NH, January 23, 1974.
(NY Rangers' 9th choice, 216th overall, in 1992 Entry Draft).

			Regular Season					Playoffs				
Season	Club	Lea	GP	G	A	TP	PIM	GP	G	A	TP	PIM
1992-93	Yale	ECAC	29	0	7	7	32	....	....	....	....	....
1993-94	Yale	ECAC	27	3	7	10	60	....	....	....	....	....

BRILL, JOHN

Right wing. Shoots left. 6'3", 180 lbs. Born, St. Paul, MN, December 3, 1970.
(Pittsburgh's 3rd choice, 58th overall, in 1989 Entry Draft).

			Regular Season					Playoffs				
Season	Club	Lea	GP	G	A	TP	PIM	GP	G	A	TP	PIM
1989-90	U. Minnesota	WCHA	34	2	8	10	22	....	....	....	....	....
1990-91	U. Minnesota	WCHA	44	6	13	19	36	....	....	....	....	....
1991-92	U. Minnesota	WCHA	35	7	9	16	46	....	....	....	....	....
1992-93	U. Minnesota	WCHA	41	12	13	25	64	....	....	....	....	....
1993-94	Dayton	ECHL	57	13	19	32	68	3	1	0	1	4
	Kalamazoo	IHL	3	0	0	0	0	....	....	....	....	....

BRIMANIS, ARIS PH

Defense. Shoots right. 6'3", 210 lbs. Born, Cleveland, OH, March 14, 1972.
(Philadelphia's 4th choice, 86th overall, in 1991 Entry Draft).

			Regular Season					Playoffs				
Season	Club	Lea	GP	G	A	TP	PIM	GP	G	A	TP	PIM
1990-91	Bowling Green	CCHA	38	3	6	9	42	....	....	....	....	....
1991-92	Bowling Green	CCHA	32	2	9	11	38	....	....	....	....	....
1992-93	Brandon	WHL	71	8	50	58	110	4	2	1	3	[illegible]
1993-94	**Philadelphia**	**NHL**	**1**	**0**	**0**	**0**	**0**	....	....	....	....	....
	Hershey	AHL	75	8	15	23	65	11	2	3	5	[illegible]
	NHL Totals		**1**	**0**	**0**	**0**	**0**	....	....	....	....	....

BRIND'AMOUR, ROD (BRIHND-uh-MOHR) PH

Center. Shoots left. 6'1", 202 lbs. Born, Ottawa, Ont., August 9, 1970.
(St. Louis' 1st choice, 9th overall, in 1988 Entry Draft).

			Regular Season					Playoffs				
Season	Club	Lea	GP	G	A	TP	PIM	GP	G	A	TP	PIM
1988-89	Michigan State	CCHA	42	27	32	59	63	....	....	....	....	....
	St. Louis	**NHL**	....	....	....	....	....	**5**	**2**	**0**	**2**	[illegible]
1989-90a	**St. Louis**	**NHL**	**79**	**26**	**35**	**61**	**46**	**12**	**5**	**8**	**13**	[illegible]
1990-91	**St. Louis**	**NHL**	**78**	**17**	**32**	**49**	**93**	**13**	**2**	**5**	**7**	[illegible]
1991-92	**Philadelphia**	**NHL**	**80**	**33**	**44**	**77**	**100**	....	....	....	....	....
1992-93	**Philadelphia**	**NHL**	**81**	**37**	**49**	**86**	**89**	....	....	....	....	....
1993-94	**Philadelphia**	**NHL**	**84**	**35**	**62**	**97**	**85**	....	....	....	....	....
	NHL Totals		**402**	**148**	**222**	**370**	**413**	**30**	**9**	**13**	**22**	[illegible]

a NHL All-Rookie Team (1990)

Played in NHL All-Star Game (1992)

Traded to **Philadelphia** by **St. Louis** with Dan Quinn for Ron Sutter and Murray Baron, September 22, 1991.

BRISEBOIS, PATRICE (BREES-bwah, pa-TREEZ) MTL

Defense. Shoots right. 6'2", 192 lbs. Born, Montreal, Que., January 27, 1971.
(Montreal's 2nd choice, 30th overall, in 1989 Entry Draft).

			Regular Season					Playoffs				
Season	Club	Lea	GP	G	A	TP	PIM	GP	G	A	TP	PIM
1987-88	Laval	QMJHL	48	10	34	44	95	6	0	2	2	[illegible]
1988-89	Laval	QMJHL	50	20	45	65	95	17	8	14	22	[illegible]
1989-90a	Laval	QMJHL	56	18	70	88	108	13	7	9	16	[illegible]
1990-91	**Montreal**	**NHL**	**10**	**0**	**2**	**2**	**4**	....	....	....	....	....
bcd	Drummondville	QMJHL	54	17	44	61	72	14	6	18	24	[illegible]
1991-92	**Montreal**	**NHL**	**26**	**2**	**8**	**10**	**20**	**11**	**2**	**4**	**6**	[illegible]
	Fredericton	AHL	53	12	27	39	51	....	....	....	....	....
1992-93	**Montreal**	**NHL**	**70**	**10**	**21**	**31**	**79**	**20**	**0**	**4**	**4**	[illegible]
1993-94	**Montreal**	**NHL**	**53**	**2**	**21**	**23**	**63**	**7**	**0**	**4**	**4**	[illegible]
	NHL Totals		**159**	**14**	**52**	**66**	**166**	**38**	**2**	**12**	**14**	[illegible]

a QMJHL Second All-Star Team (1990)
b Canadian Major Junior Defenseman of the Year (1991)
c QMJHL First All-Star Team (1991)
d Memorial Cup All-Star Team (1991)

BRISKE, BYRON ANA

Defense. Shoots right. 6'2", 194 lbs. Born, Humboldt, Sask., January 23, 1976.
(Anaheim's 4th choice, 80th overall, in 1994 Entry Draft).

			Regular Season					Playoffs				
Season	Club	Lea	GP	G	A	TP	PIM	GP	G	A	TP	PIM
1992-93	Victoria	WHL	66	1	10	11	110	....	....	....	....	....
1993-94	Red Deer	WHL	61	6	21	27	174	....	....	....	....	....

BROTEN, NEAL (BRAH-tuhn) DAL.

Center. Shoots left. 5'9", 170 lbs. Born, Roseau, MN, November 29, 1959.
(Minnesota's 3rd choice, 42nd overall, in 1979 Entry Draft).

			Regular Season					Playoffs				
Season	Club	Lea	GP	G	A	TP	PIM	GP	G	A	TP	PIM
1978-79	U. Minnesota	WCHA	40	21	50	71	18	....	....	....	....	....
1979-80	U.S. National	....	55	25	30	55	20	....	....	....	....	....
	U.S. Olympic	....	7	2	1	3	2	....	....	....	....	....
1980-81ab	U. Minnesota	WCHA	36	17	54	71	56	....	....	....	....	....
	Minnesota	**NHL**	**3**	**2**	**0**	**2**	**12**	**19**	**1**	**7**	**8**	**9**
1981-82	**Minnesota**	**NHL**	**73**	**38**	**60**	**98**	**42**	**4**	**0**	**2**	**2**	**0**
1982-83	**Minnesota**	**NHL**	**79**	**32**	**45**	**77**	**43**	**9**	**1**	**6**	**7**	**10**
1983-84	**Minnesota**	**NHL**	**76**	**28**	**61**	**89**	**43**	**16**	**5**	**5**	**10**	**4**
1984-85	**Minnesota**	**NHL**	**80**	**19**	**37**	**56**	**39**	**9**	**2**	**5**	**7**	**10**
1985-86	**Minnesota**	**NHL**	**80**	**29**	**76**	**105**	**47**	**5**	**3**	**2**	**5**	**2**
1986-87	**Minnesota**	**NHL**	**46**	**18**	**35**	**53**	**33**	....	....	....	....	....
1987-88	**Minnesota**	**NHL**	**54**	**9**	**30**	**39**	**32**	....	....	....	....	....
1988-89	**Minnesota**	**NHL**	**68**	**18**	**38**	**56**	**57**	**5**	**2**	**2**	**4**	**4**
1989-90	**Minnesota**	**NHL**	**80**	**23**	**62**	**85**	**45**	**7**	**2**	**2**	**4**	**18**
1990-91	**Minnesota**	**NHL**	**79**	**13**	**56**	**69**	**26**	**23**	**9**	**13**	**22**	**6**
1991-92	Preussen	Ger.	8	3	5	8	2	....	....	....	....	....
	Minnesota	**NHL**	**76**	**8**	**26**	**34**	**16**	**7**	**1**	**5**	**6**	**2**
1992-93	**Minnesota**	**NHL**	**82**	**12**	**21**	**33**	**22**	....	....	....	....	....
1993-94	**Dallas**	**NHL**	**79**	**17**	**35**	**52**	**62**	**9**	**2**	**1**	**3**	**6**
	NHL Totals		**955**	**266**	**582**	**848**	**519**	**113**	**28**	**50**	**78**	**71**

a WCHA First All-Star Team (1981)
b Won Hobey Baker Memorial Award (Top U.S. Collegiate Player) (1981)

Played in NHL All-Star Game (1983-86)

BROTEN, PAUL (BRAH-tuhn) DAL.

Right wing. Shoots right. 5'11", 188 lbs. Born, Roseau, MN, October 27, 1965.
(NY Rangers' 3rd choice, 77th overall, in 1984 Entry Draft).

			Regular Season					Playoffs				
Season	Club	Lea	GP	G	A	TP	PIM	GP	G	A	TP	PIM
1984-85	U. Minnesota	WCHA	44	8	8	16	26	....	....	....	....	....
1985-86	U. Minnesota	WCHA	38	6	16	22	24	....	....	....	....	....
1986-87	U. Minnesota	WCHA	48	17	22	39	52	....	....	....	....	....
1987-88	U. Minnesota	WCHA	38	18	21	39	42	....	....	....	....	....
1988-89	Denver	IHL	77	28	31	59	133	4	0	2	2	6
1989-90	**NY Rangers**	**NHL**	**32**	**5**	**3**	**8**	**26**	**6**	**1**	**1**	**2**	**2**
	Flint	IHL	28	17	9	26	55	....	....	....	....	....
1990-91	**NY Rangers**	**NHL**	**28**	**4**	**6**	**10**	**18**	**5**	**0**	**0**	**0**	**2**
	Binghamton	AHL	8	2	2	4	4	....	....	....	....	....
1991-92	**NY Rangers**	**NHL**	**74**	**13**	**15**	**28**	**102**	**13**	**1**	**2**	**3**	**10**
1992-93	**NY Rangers**	**NHL**	**60**	**5**	**9**	**14**	**48**	....	....	....	....	....
1993-94	**Dallas**	**NHL**	**64**	**12**	**12**	**24**	**30**	**9**	**1**	**1**	**2**	**2**
	NHL Totals		**258**	**39**	**45**	**84**	**224**	**33**	**3**	**4**	**7**	**16**

Claimed by **Dallas** from **NY Rangers** in NHL Waiver Draft, October 3, 1993.

ROUSSEAU, DAVID — NYR

enter. Shoots right. 6'2", 189 lbs. Born, Montreal, Que., January 16, 1976.
Y Rangers' 8th choice, 156th overall, in 1994 Entry Draft).

			Regular Season					Playoffs				
eason	Club	Lea	GP	G	A	TP	PIM	GP	G	A	TP	PIM
92-93	Shawinigan	QMJHL	56	5	4	9	28	....	....	....	....	....
93-94	Shawinigan	QMJHL	65	27	26	53	62	5	3	0	3	2

ROUSSEAU, PAUL — QUE.

ght wing. Shoots right. 6'2", 203 lbs. Born, Pierrefonds, Que., September 18, 1973.
uebec's 2nd choice, 28th overall, in 1992 Entry Draft).

			Regular Season					Playoffs				
eason	Club	Lea	GP	G	A	TP	PIM	GP	G	A	TP	PIM
89-90	Chicoutimi	QMJHL	57	17	24	41	32	7	0	3	3	0
90-91	Trois-Rivières	QMJHL	67	30	66	96	48	6	3	2	5	2
91-92	Hull	QMJHL	57	35	61	96	54	6	3	5	8	10
92-93	Hull	QMJHL	59	27	48	75	49	10	7	8	15	6
93-94	Cornwall	AHL	69	18	26	44	35	1	0	0	0	0

ROWN, BRAD — MTL.

efense. Shoots right. 6'3", 218 lbs. Born, Baie Verte, Nfld., December 27, 1975.
ontreal's 1st choice, 18th overall, in 1994 Entry Draft).

			Regular Season					Playoffs				
eason	Club	Lea	GP	G	A	TP	PIM	GP	G	A	TP	PIM
91-92	North Bay	OHL	49	2	9	11	170	18	0	6	6	43
92-93	North Bay	OHL	61	4	9	13	228	2	0	2	2	13
93-94	North Bay	OHL	66	8	24	32	196	18	3	12	15	33

ROWN, CURTIS — BUF.

enter. Shoots left. 6', 182 lbs. Born, Unity, Sask., February 12, 1976.
uffalo's 2nd choice, 43rd overall, in 1994 Entry Draft).

			Regular Season					Playoffs				
eason	Club	Lea	GP	G	A	TP	PIM	GP	G	A	TP	PIM
92-93	Moose Jaw	WHL	71	13	16	29	30	....	....	....	....	....
93-94	Moose Jaw	WHL	72	27	38	65	82	....	....	....	....	....

ROWN, DAVID — PHI.

ght wing. Shoots right. 6'5", 222 lbs. Born, Saskatoon, Sask., October 12, 1962.
hiladelphia's 7th choice, 140th overall, in 1982 Entry Draft).

			Regular Season					Playoffs				
eason	Club	Lea	GP	G	A	TP	PIM	GP	G	A	TP	PIM
980-81	Spokane	WHL	9	2	2	4	21	....	....	....	....	....
981-82	Saskatoon	WHL	62	11	33	44	344	5	1	0	1	4
982-83	**Philadelphia**	**NHL**	**2**	**0**	**0**	**0**	**5**	....	....	....	....	....
	Maine	AHL	71	8	6	14	*418	16	0	0	0	*107
983-84	**Philadelphia**	**NHL**	**19**	**1**	**5**	**6**	**98**	**2**	**0**	**0**	**0**	**12**
	Springfield	AHL	59	17	14	31	150	....	....	....	....	....
984-85	**Philadelphia**	**NHL**	**57**	**3**	**6**	**9**	**165**	**11**	**0**	**0**	**0**	**59**
985-86	**Philadelphia**	**NHL**	**76**	**10**	**7**	**17**	**277**	**5**	**0**	**0**	**0**	**16**
986-87	**Philadelphia**	**NHL**	**62**	**7**	**3**	**10**	**274**	**26**	**1**	**2**	**3**	**59**
987-88	**Philadelphia**	**NHL**	**47**	**12**	**5**	**17**	**114**	**7**	**1**	**0**	**1**	**27**
988-89	**Philadelphia**	**NHL**	**50**	**0**	**3**	**3**	**100**	....	....	....	....	....
	Edmonton	**NHL**	**22**	**0**	**2**	**2**	**56**	**7**	**0**	**0**	**0**	**6**
989-90	**Edmonton**	**NHL**	**60**	**0**	**6**	**6**	**145**	**3**	**0**	**0**	**0**	**0**
990-91	**Edmonton**	**NHL**	**58**	**3**	**4**	**7**	**160**	**16**	**0**	**1**	**1**	**30**
991-92	**Philadelphia**	**NHL**	**70**	**4**	**2**	**6**	**81**	....	....	....	....	....
992-93	**Philadelphia**	**NHL**	**70**	**0**	**2**	**2**	**78**	....	....	....	....	....
993-94	**Philadelphia**	**NHL**	**71**	**1**	**4**	**5**	**137**	....	....	....	....	....
	NHL Totals		**664**	**41**	**49**	**90**	**1690**	**77**	**2**	**3**	**5**	**209**

aded to **Edmonton** by **Philadelphia** for Keith Acton and Edmonton's fifth round choice (Dimitri ushkevich) in 1991 Entry Draft, February 7, 1989. Traded to **Philadelphia** by **Edmonton** with orey Foster and Jari Kurri for Craig Fisher, Scott Mellanby and Craig Berube, May 30, 1991.

ROWN, DOUG — PIT.

ght wing. Shoots right. 5'10", 185 lbs. Born, Southborough, MA, June 12, 1964.

			Regular Season					Playoffs				
eason	Club	Lea	GP	G	A	TP	PIM	GP	G	A	TP	PIM
982-83	Boston College	ECAC	22	9	8	17	0	....	....	....	....	....
983-84	Boston College	ECAC	38	11	10	21	6	....	....	....	....	....
984-85a	Boston College	H.E.	45	37	31	68	10	....	....	....	....	....
985-86a	Boston College	H.E.	38	16	40	56	16	....	....	....	....	....
986-87	**New Jersey**	**NHL**	**4**	**0**	**1**	**1**	**0**	....	....	....	....	....
	Maine	AHL	73	24	34	58	15	....	....	....	....	....
987-88	**New Jersey**	**NHL**	**70**	**14**	**11**	**25**	**20**	**19**	**5**	**1**	**6**	**6**
	Utica	AHL	2	0	2	2	2	....	....	....	....	....
988-89	**New Jersey**	**NHL**	**63**	**15**	**10**	**25**	**15**	....	....	....	....	....
	Utica	AHL	4	1	4	5	0	....	....	....	....	....
989-90	**New Jersey**	**NHL**	**69**	**14**	**20**	**34**	**16**	**6**	**0**	**1**	**1**	**2**
990-91	**New Jersey**	**NHL**	**58**	**14**	**16**	**30**	**4**	**7**	**2**	**2**	**4**	**2**
991-92	**New Jersey**	**NHL**	**71**	**11**	**17**	**28**	**27**	....	....	....	....	....
992-93	**New Jersey**	**NHL**	**15**	**0**	**5**	**5**	**2**	....	....	....	....	....
	Utica	AHL	25	11	17	28	8	....	....	....	....	....
993-94	**Pittsburgh**	**NHL**	**77**	**18**	**37**	**55**	**18**	**6**	**0**	**0**	**0**	**2**
	NHL Totals		**427**	**86**	**117**	**203**	**102**	**38**	**7**	**4**	**11**	**12**

Hockey East First All-Star Team (1985, 1986)

igned as a free agent by **New Jersey**, August 6, 1986. Signed as a free agent by **Pittsburgh**, eptember 28, 1993.

ROWN, GREG — PIT.

efense. Shoots right. 6', 185 lbs. Born, Hartford, CT, March 7, 1968.
uffalo's 2nd choice, 26th overall, in 1986 Entry Draft).

			Regular Season					Playoffs				
eason	Club	Lea	GP	G	A	TP	PIM	GP	G	A	TP	PIM
986-87	Boston College	H.E.	37	10	27	37	22	....	....	....	....	....
987-88	U.S. National	....	55	6	29	35	22	....	....	....	....	....
	U.S. Olympic	....	6	0	4	4	2	....	....	....	....	....
988-89abc	Boston College	H.E.	40	9	34	43	24	....	....	....	....	....
989-90abc	Boston College	H.E.	42	5	35	40	42	....	....	....	....	....
990-91	**Buffalo**	**NHL**	**39**	**1**	**2**	**3**	**35**	....	....	....	....	....
	Rochester	AHL	31	6	17	23	16	14	1	4	5	8
991-92	Rochester	AHL	56	8	30	38	25	16	1	5	6	4
	U.S. National	....	8	0	0	0	5	....	....	....	....	....
	U.S. Olympic	....	7	0	0	0	2	....	....	....	....	....
992-93	**Buffalo**	**NHL**	**10**	**0**	**1**	**1**	**6**	....	....	....	....	....
	Rochester	AHL	61	11	38	49	46	16	3	8	11	14
993-94	**Pittsburgh**	**NHL**	**36**	**3**	**8**	**11**	**28**	**6**	**0**	**1**	**1**	**4**
	San Diego	IHL	42	8	25	33	26	....	....	....	....	....
	NHL Totals		**85**	**4**	**11**	**15**	**69**	**6**	**0**	**1**	**1**	**4**

igned as a free agent by **Pittsburgh**, September 29, 1993.
Hockey East First All-Star Team (1989, 1990)
Hockey East Player of the Year (1989, 1990)
NCAA East First All-American Team (1989, 1990)

BROWN, JEFF — VAN.

Defense. Shoots right. 6'1", 204 lbs. Born, Ottawa, Ont., April 30, 1966.
(Quebec's 2nd choice, 36th overall, in 1984 Entry Draft).

			Regular Season					Playoffs				
Season	Club	Lea	GP	G	A	TP	PIM	GP	G	A	TP	PIM
1982-83	Sudbury	OHL	65	9	37	46	39	....	....	....	....	....
1983-84	Sudbury	OHL	68	17	60	77	39	....	....	....	....	....
1984-85	Sudbury	OHL	56	16	48	64	26	....	....	....	....	....
1985-86	**Quebec**	**NHL**	**8**	**3**	**2**	**5**	**6**	**1**	**0**	**0**	**0**	**0**
a	Sudbury	OHL	45	22	28	50	24	4	0	2	2	11
	Fredericton	AHL	....	....	....	....	....	1	0	1	1	0
1986-87	**Quebec**	**NHL**	**44**	**7**	**22**	**29**	**16**	**13**	**3**	**3**	**6**	**2**
	Fredericton	AHL	26	2	14	16	16	....	....	....	....	....
1987-88	**Quebec**	**NHL**	**78**	**16**	**36**	**52**	**64**	....	....	....	....	....
1988-89	**Quebec**	**NHL**	**78**	**21**	**47**	**68**	**62**	....	....	....	....	....
1989-90	**Quebec**	**NHL**	**29**	**6**	**10**	**16**	**18**	....	....	....	....	....
	St. Louis	**NHL**	**48**	**10**	**28**	**38**	**37**	**12**	**2**	**10**	**12**	**4**
1990-91	**St. Louis**	**NHL**	**67**	**12**	**47**	**59**	**39**	**13**	**3**	**9**	**12**	**6**
1991-92	**St. Louis**	**NHL**	**80**	**20**	**39**	**59**	**38**	**6**	**2**	**1**	**3**	**2**
1992-93	**St. Louis**	**NHL**	**71**	**25**	**53**	**78**	**58**	**11**	**3**	**8**	**11**	**6**
1993-94	**St. Louis**	**NHL**	**63**	**13**	**47**	**60**	**46**	....	....	....	....	....
	Vancouver	**NHL**	**11**	**1**	**5**	**6**	**10**	**24**	**6**	**9**	**15**	**37**
	NHL Totals		**577**	**134**	**336**	**470**	**394**	**80**	**19**	**40**	**59**	**57**

a OHL First All-Star Team (1986)

Traded to **St Louis** by **Quebec** for Tony Hrkac and Greg Millen, December 13, 1989. Traded to **Vancouver** by **St. Louis** with Bret Hedican and Nathan Lafayette for Craig Janney, March 21, 1994.

BROWN, KEITH — FLA.

Defense. Shoots right. 6'1", 192 lbs. Born, Corner Brook, Nfld., May 6, 1960.
(Chicago's 1st choice, 7th overall, in 1979 Entry Draft).

			Regular Season					Playoffs				
Season	Club	Lea	GP	G	A	TP	PIM	GP	G	A	TP	PIM
1977-78	Portland	WHL	72	11	53	64	51	8	0	3	3	2
1978-79a	Portland	WHL	70	11	85	96	75	25	3	*30	33	21
1979-80	**Chicago**	**NHL**	**76**	**2**	**18**	**20**	**27**	**6**	**0**	**0**	**0**	**4**
1980-81	**Chicago**	**NHL**	**80**	**9**	**34**	**43**	**80**	**3**	**0**	**2**	**2**	**2**
1981-82	**Chicago**	**NHL**	**33**	**4**	**20**	**24**	**26**	**4**	**0**	**2**	**2**	**5**
1982-83	**Chicago**	**NHL**	**50**	**4**	**27**	**31**	**20**	**7**	**0**	**0**	**0**	**11**
1983-84	**Chicago**	**NHL**	**74**	**10**	**25**	**35**	**94**	**5**	**0**	**1**	**1**	**10**
1984-85	**Chicago**	**NHL**	**56**	**1**	**22**	**23**	**55**	**11**	**2**	**7**	**9**	**31**
1985-86	**Chicago**	**NHL**	**70**	**11**	**29**	**40**	**87**	**3**	**0**	**1**	**1**	**9**
1986-87	**Chicago**	**NHL**	**73**	**4**	**23**	**27**	**86**	**4**	**0**	**1**	**1**	**6**
1987-88	**Chicago**	**NHL**	**24**	**3**	**6**	**9**	**45**	**5**	**0**	**2**	**2**	**10**
1988-89	**Chicago**	**NHL**	**74**	**2**	**16**	**18**	**84**	**13**	**1**	**3**	**4**	**25**
1989-90	**Chicago**	**NHL**	**67**	**5**	**20**	**25**	**87**	**18**	**0**	**4**	**4**	**43**
1990-91	**Chicago**	**NHL**	**45**	**1**	**10**	**11**	**55**	**6**	**1**	**0**	**1**	**8**
1991-92	**Chicago**	**NHL**	**57**	**6**	**10**	**16**	**69**	**14**	**0**	**8**	**8**	**18**
1992-93	**Chicago**	**NHL**	**33**	**2**	**6**	**8**	**39**	**4**	**0**	**1**	**1**	**2**
1993-94	**Florida**	**NHL**	**51**	**4**	**8**	**12**	**60**	....	....	....	....	....
	NHL Totals		**863**	**68**	**274**	**342**	**914**	**103**	**4**	**32**	**36**	**184**

a WHL First All-Star Team (1979)

Traded to **Florida** by **Chicago** for Darin Kimble, September 30, 1993.

BROWN, KEVIN — L.A.

Right wing. Shoots right. 6'1", 212 lbs. Born, Birmingham, England, May 11, 1974.
(Los Angeles' 3rd choice, 87th overall, in 1992 Entry Draft).

			Regular Season					Playoffs				
Season	Club	Lea	GP	G	A	TP	PIM	GP	G	A	TP	PIM
1991-92	Belleville	OHL	66	24	24	48	52	5	1	4	5	8
1992-93a	Belleville	OHL	6	2	5	7	4	....	....	....	....	....
	Detroit	OHL	56	48	86	134	76	15	10	18	28	18
1993-94bc	Detroit	OHL	57	54	81	135	85	17	14	*26	*40	28

a OHL Second All-Star Team (1993)
b OHL First All-Star Team (1994)
c Canadian Major Junior Second All-Star Team (1994)

BROWN, ROB — L.A.

Right wing. Shoots left. 5'11", 185 lbs. Born, Kingston, Ont., April 10, 1968.
(Pittsburgh's 4th choice, 67th overall, in 1986 Entry Draft).

			Regular Season					Playoffs				
Season	Club	Lea	GP	G	A	TP	PIM	GP	G	A	TP	PIM
1984-85	Kamloops	WHL	60	29	50	79	95	15	8	8	26	28
1985-86a	Kamloops	WHL	69	58	*115	*173	171	16	*18	*28	*46	14
1986-87ab	Kamloops	WHL	63	*76	*136	*212	101	5	6	5	11	6
1987-88	**Pittsburgh**	**NHL**	**51**	**24**	**20**	**44**	**56**	....	....	....	....	....
1988-89	**Pittsburgh**	**NHL**	**68**	**49**	**66**	**115**	**118**	**11**	**5**	**3**	**8**	**22**
1989-90	**Pittsburgh**	**NHL**	**80**	**33**	**47**	**80**	**102**	....	....	....	....	....
1990-91	**Pittsburgh**	**NHL**	**25**	**6**	**10**	**16**	**31**	....	....	....	....	....
	Hartford	**NHL**	**44**	**18**	**24**	**42**	**101**	**5**	**1**	**0**	**1**	**7**
1991-92	**Hartford**	**NHL**	**42**	**16**	**15**	**31**	**39**	....	....	....	....	....
	Chicago	**NHL**	**25**	**5**	**11**	**16**	**34**	**8**	**2**	**4**	**6**	**4**
1992-93	**Chicago**	**NHL**	**15**	**1**	**6**	**7**	**33**	....	....	....	....	....
	Indianapolis	IHL	19	14	19	33	32	2	0	1	1	2
1993-94	**Dallas**	**NHL**	**1**	**0**	**0**	**0**	**0**	....	....	....	....	....
cde	Kalamazoo	IHL	79	42	*113	*155	188	5	1	3	4	6
	NHL Totals		**351**	**152**	**199**	**351**	**514**	**24**	**8**	**7**	**15**	**33**

a WHL First All-Star Team (1986, 1987)
b Canadian Major Junior Player of the Year (1987)
c IHL First All-Star Team (1994)
d Won Leo P. Lamoureux Memorial Trophy (Top Scorer - IHL) (1994)
e Won James Gatschene Memorial Trophy (MVP - IHL) (1994)

Played in NHL All-Star Game (1989)

Traded to **Hartford** by **Pittsburgh** for Scott Young, December 21, 1990. Traded to **Chicago** by **Hartford** for Steve Konroyd, January 24, 1992. Signed as a free agent by **Dallas**, August 12, 1993. Signed as a free agent by **Los Angeles**, June 14, 1994.

BROWN, RYAN — T.B.

Defense. Shoots right. 6'3", 215 lbs. Born, Boyle, Alta., September 19, 1974.
(Tampa Bay's 5th choice, 107th overall, in 1993 Entry Draft).

			Regular Season					Playoffs				
Season	Club	Lea	GP	G	A	TP	PIM	GP	G	A	TP	PIM
1991-92	Seattle	WHL	60	1	1	2	230	14	0	2	2	38
1992-93	Seattle	WHL	19	0	1	1	70	....	....	....	....	....
	Swift Current	WHL	47	1	4	5	104	17	0	2	2	18
1993-94	Swift Current	WHL	72	2	10	12	173	7	0	0	0	6

BRUCE, DAVID — S.J.

Left wing. Shoots right. 5'11", 190 lbs. Born, Thunder Bay, Ont., October 7, 1964.
(Vancouver's 2nd choice, 30th overall, in 1983 Entry Draft).

			Regular Season					Playoffs				
Season	Club	Lea	GP	G	A	TP	PIM	GP	G	A	TP	PIM
1982-83	Kitchener	OHL	67	36	35	71	199	12	7	9	16	27
1983-84	Kitchener	OHL	62	52	40	92	203	10	5	8	13	20
1984-85	Fredericton	AHL	56	14	11	25	104	5	0	0	0	37
1985-86	**Vancouver**	**NHL**	**12**	**0**	**1**	**1**	**14**	**1**	**0**	**0**	**0**	**0**
	Fredericton	AHL	66	25	16	41	151	2	0	1	1	12
1986-87	**Vancouver**	**NHL**	**50**	**9**	**7**	**16**	**109**	....	....	....	....	....
	Fredericton	AHL	17	7	6	13	73	....	....	....	....	....
1987-88	**Vancouver**	**NHL**	**28**	**7**	**3**	**10**	**57**	....	....	....	....	....
	Fredericton	AHL	30	27	18	45	115	....	....	....	....	....
1988-89	**Vancouver**	**NHL**	**53**	**7**	**7**	**14**	**65**	....	....	....	....	....
1989-90a	Milwaukee	IHL	68	40	35	75	148	6	5	3	8	0
1990-91	**St. Louis**	**NHL**	**12**	**1**	**2**	**3**	**14**	**2**	**0**	**0**	**0**	**2**
ab	Peoria	IHL	60	*64	52	116	78	18	*18	11	*29	40
1991-92	**San Jose**	**NHL**	**60**	**22**	**16**	**38**	**46**	....	....	....	....	....
	Kansas City	IHL	7	5	5	10	6	....	....	....	....	....
1992-93	**San Jose**	**NHL**	**17**	**2**	**3**	**5**	**33**	....	....	....	....	....
1993-94	**San Jose**	**NHL**	**2**	**0**	**0**	**0**	**0**	....	....	....	....	....
	Kansas City	IHL	72	40	24	64	115	....	....	....	....	....
	NHL Totals		**234**	**48**	**39**	**87**	**338**	**3**	**0**	**0**	**0**	**2**

a IHL First All-Star Team (1990, 1991)
b Won James Gatschene Memorial Trophy (MVP - IHL) (1991)

Signed as a free agent by **St. Louis**, July 6, 1990. Claimed by **San Jose** from **St. Louis** in Expansion Draft, May 30, 1991.

BRULE, STEVE — N.J.

Center. Shoots right. 5'11", 184 lbs. Born, Montreal, Que., January 15, 1975.
(New Jersey's 6th choice, 143rd overall, in 1993 Entry Draft).

			Regular Season					Playoffs				
Season	Club	Lea	GP	G	A	TP	PIM	GP	G	A	TP	PIM
1992-93	St-Jean	QMJHL	70	33	47	80	46	4	0	0	0	9
1993-94	St-Jean	QMJHL	66	41	64	105	46	5	2	1	3	0

BRUNET, BENOIT — (broo-NAY, BEHN-wah) MTL.

Left wing. Shoots left. 5'11", 193 lbs. Born, Pointe-Claire, Que., August 24, 1968.
(Montreal's 2nd choice, 27th overall, in 1986 Entry Draft).

			Regular Season					Playoffs				
Season	Club	Lea	GP	G	A	TP	PIM	GP	G	A	TP	PIM
1985-86	Hull	QMJHL	71	33	37	70	81	....	....	....	....	....
1986-87a	Hull	QMJHL	60	43	67	110	105	6	7	5	12	8
1987-88	Hull	QMJHL	62	54	89	143	131	10	3	10	13	11
1988-89	**Montreal**	**NHL**	**2**	**0**	**1**	**1**	**0**	....	....	....	....	....
b	Sherbrooke	AHL	73	41	76	117	95	6	2	0	2	4
1989-90	Sherbrooke	AHL	72	32	35	67	82	12	8	7	15	20
1990-91	**Montreal**	**NHL**	**17**	**1**	**3**	**4**	**0**	....	....	....	....	....
	Fredericton	AHL	24	13	18	31	16	6	5	6	11	2
1991-92	**Montreal**	**NHL**	**18**	**4**	**6**	**10**	**14**	....	....	....	....	....
	Fredericton	AHL	6	7	9	16	27	....	....	....	....	....
1992-93	**Montreal**	**NHL**	**47**	**10**	**15**	**25**	**19**	**20**	**2**	**8**	**10**	**8**
1993-94	**Montreal**	**NHL**	**71**	**10**	**20**	**30**	**20**	**7**	**1**	**4**	**5**	**16**
	NHL Totals		**155**	**25**	**45**	**70**	**53**	**27**	**3**	**12**	**15**	**24**

a QMJHL Second All-Star Team (1987)
b AHL First All-Star Team (1989)

BRUNETTE, ANDREW

Left wing. Shoots left. 6', 212 lbs. Born, Sudbury, Ont., August 24, 1973.
(Washington's 6th choice, 174th overall, in 1993 Entry Draft).

			Regular Season					Playoffs				
Season	Club	Lea	GP	G	A	TP	PIM	GP	G	A	TP	PIM
1990-91	Owen Sound	OHL	63	15	20	35	15	....	....	....	....	....
1991-92	Owen Sound	OHL	66	51	47	98	42	5	5	0	5	8
1992-93ab	Owen Sound	OHL	66	*62	*100	*162	91	8	8	6	14	16
1993-94	Portland	AHL	23	9	11	20	10	2	0	1	1	0
	Hampton	ECHL	20	12	18	30	32	....	....	....	....	....

a OHL First All-Star Team (1993)
b Canadian Major Junior Second All-Star Team (1993)

BRYLIN, SERGEI — (BRIH-lin) N.J.

Center. Shoots left. 5'9", 176 lbs. Born, Moscow, USSR, January 13, 1974.
(New Jersey's 2nd choice, 42nd overall, in 1992 Entry Draft).

			Regular Season					Playoffs				
Season	Club	Lea	GP	G	A	TP	PIM	GP	G	A	TP	PIM
1991-92	CSKA	CIS	44	1	6	7	4	....	....	....	....	....
1992-93	CSKA	CIS	42	5	4	9	36	....	....	....	....	....
1993-94	CSKA	CIS	39	4	6	10	36	3	1	0	1	2
	Russian Pen's	IHL	13	4	5	9	18	....	....	....	....	....

BUCHANAN, JEFF — T.B.

Defense. Shoots right. 5'10", 165 lbs. Born, Swift Current, Sask., May 23, 1971.

			Regular Season					Playoffs				
Season	Club	Lea	GP	G	A	TP	PIM	GP	G	A	TP	PIM
1989-90	Saskatoon	WHL	66	7	12	19	96	9	0	2	2	2
1990-91	Saskatoon	WHL	69	10	26	36	123	....	....	....	....	....
1991-92	Saskatoon	WHL	72	17	37	54	145	22	10	14	24	39
1992-93	Atlanta	IHL	68	4	18	22	282	9	0	0	0	26
1993-94	Atlanta	IHL	76	5	24	29	253	14	0	1	1	20

Signed as a free agent by **Tampa Bay**, July 13, 1992.

BUCHBERGER, KELLY — (BUK-buhr-guhr) EDM.

Left wing. Shoots left. 6'2", 210 lbs. Born, Langenburg, Sask., December 2, 1966.
(Edmonton's 8th choice, 188th overall, in 1985 Entry Draft).

			Regular Season					Playoffs				
Season	Club	Lea	GP	G	A	TP	PIM	GP	G	A	TP	PIM
1984-85	Moose Jaw	WHL	51	12	17	29	114	....	....	....	....	....
1985-86	Moose Jaw	WHL	72	14	22	36	206	13	11	4	15	37
1986-87	Nova Scotia	AHL	70	12	20	32	257	5	0	1	1	23
	Edmonton	**NHL**	....	....	....	....	....	**3**	**0**	**1**	**1**	**5**
1987-88	**Edmonton**	**NHL**	**19**	**1**	**0**	**1**	**81**	....	....	....	....	....
	Nova Scotia	AHL	49	21	23	44	206	2	0	0	0	11
1988-89	**Edmonton**	**NHL**	**66**	**5**	**9**	**14**	**234**	....	....	....	....	....
1989-90	**Edmonton**	**NHL**	**55**	**2**	**6**	**8**	**168**	**19**	**0**	**5**	**5**	**13**
1990-91	**Edmonton**	**NHL**	**64**	**3**	**1**	**4**	**160**	**12**	**2**	**1**	**3**	**25**
1991-92	**Edmonton**	**NHL**	**79**	**20**	**24**	**44**	**157**	**16**	**1**	**4**	**5**	**32**
1992-93	**Edmonton**	**NHL**	**83**	**12**	**18**	**30**	**133**	....	....	....	....	....
1993-94	**Edmonton**	**NHL**	**84**	**3**	**18**	**21**	**199**	....	....	....	....	....
	NHL Totals		**450**	**46**	**76**	**122**	**1132**	**50**	**3**	**11**	**14**	**75**

BUCKBERGER, ASHLEY — QUE

Right wing. Shoots right. 6'2", 200 lbs. Born, Esterhazy, Sask., February 19, 1975.
(Quebec's 3rd choice, 49th overall, in 1993 Entry Draft).

			Regular Season					Playoffs				
Season	Club	Lea	GP	G	A	TP	PIM	GP	G	A	TP	PIM
1991-92	Swift Current	WHL	67	23	22	45	38	8	2	1	3	[illegible]
1992-93	Swift Current	WHL	72	23	44	67	41	17	6	7	13	[illegible]
1993-94	Swift Current	WHL	67	42	45	87	42	7	0	1	1	[illegible]

BUCKLEY, JEROME — HFD

Right wing. Shoots right. 6'2", 200 lbs. Born, Needham, MA, June 27, 1971.
(Boston's 3rd choice, 84th overall, in 1990 Entry Draft).

			Regular Season					Playoffs				
Season	Club	Lea	GP	G	A	TP	PIM	GP	G	A	TP	PIM
1991-92	Boston College	H.E.	30	2	0	2	46	....	....	....	....	....
1992-93	Boston College	H.E.	31	3	11	14	44	....	....	....	....	....
1993-94	Boston College	H.E.	36	13	10	23	74	....	....	....	....	....

BUCZKOWSKI, PAUL — CGY

Left wing. Shoots left. 5'11", 190 lbs. Born, Saskatoon, Sask., March 20, 1975.

			Regular Season					Playoffs				
Season	Club	Lea	GP	G	A	TP	PIM	GP	G	A	TP	PIM
1991-92	Saskatoon	WHL	45	9	16	25	37	....	....	....	....	....
1992-93	Saskatoon	WHL	72	22	43	65	57	9	1	5	6	8
1993-94	Saskatoon	WHL	71	30	48	78	71	16	3	6	9	2[illegible]

BUDAYEV, ALEXEI — WPG

Center. Shoots right. 6'2", 183 lbs. Born, Pavlov Posad, USSR, April 24, 1975.
(Winnipeg's 3rd choice, 43rd overall, in 1993 Entry Draft).

			Regular Season					Playoffs				
Season	Club	Lea	GP	G	A	TP	PIM	GP	G	A	TP	PIM
1992-93	Elektrostal	CIS 2				UNAVAILABLE						
1993-94	Elektrostal	CIS 2	46	6	5	11	26	....	....	....	....	....

BULJIN, VLADISLAV

Defense. Shoots left. 6'2", 196 lbs. Born, Penza, USSR, May 18, 1972.
(Philadelphia's 4th choice, 103rd overall, in 1992 Entry Draft).

			Regular Season					Playoffs				
Season	Club	Lea	GP	G	A	TP	PIM	GP	G	A	TP	PIM
1992-93	Moscow D'amo	CIS	32	2	1	3	55	....	....	....	....	....
1993-94	Moscow D'amo	CIS	43	4	2	6	36	7	0	1	1	16

BULLARD, MIKE — (BULL-ard)

Center. Shoots left. 6', 195 lbs. Born, Ottawa, Ont., March 10, 1961.
(Pittsburgh's 1st choice, 9th overall, in 1980 Entry Draft).

			Regular Season					Playoffs				
Season	Club	Lea	GP	G	A	TP	PIM	GP	G	A	TP	PIM
1978-79	Brantford	OHA	66	43	56	99	66	....	....	....	....	....
1979-80a	Brantford	OHA	66	66	84	150	86	11	10	6	16	29
1980-81	**Pittsburgh**	**NHL**	**15**	**1**	**2**	**3**	**19**	**4**	**3**	**3**	**6**	**0**
	Brantford	OHA	42	47	60	107	55	6	4	5	9	10
1981-82	**Pittsburgh**	**NHL**	**75**	**36**	**27**	**63**	**91**	**5**	**1**	**1**	**2**	**4**
1982-83	**Pittsburgh**	**NHL**	**57**	**22**	**22**	**44**	**60**	....	....	....	....	....
1983-84	**Pittsburgh**	**NHL**	**76**	**51**	**41**	**92**	**57**	....	....	....	....	....
1984-85	**Pittsburgh**	**NHL**	**68**	**32**	**31**	**63**	**75**	....	....	....	....	....
1985-86	**Pittsburgh**	**NHL**	**77**	**41**	**42**	**83**	**69**	....	....	....	....	....
1986-87	**Pittsburgh**	**NHL**	**14**	**2**	**10**	**12**	**17**	....	....	....	....	....
	Calgary	**NHL**	**57**	**28**	**26**	**54**	**34**	**6**	**4**	**3**	**7**	**2**
1987-88	**Calgary**	**NHL**	**79**	**48**	**55**	**103**	**68**	**6**	**0**	**2**	**2**	**6**
1988-89	**St. Louis**	**NHL**	**20**	**4**	**12**	**16**	**46**	....	....	....	....	....
	Philadelphia	**NHL**	**54**	**23**	**26**	**49**	**60**	**19**	**3**	**9**	**12**	**32**
1989-90	**Philadelphia**	**NHL**	**70**	**27**	**37**	**64**	**67**	....	....	....	....	....
1990-91	Ambri-Piotta	Switz.	36	36	33	69	....	5	6	4	10	....
1991-92	**Toronto**	**NHL**	**65**	**14**	**14**	**28**	**40**	....	....	....	....	....
1992-93	Rapperswil	Switz.2				UNAVAILABLE						
1993-94	Landshut	Ger.	44	37	26	63	45	....	....	....	....	....
	NHL Totals		**727**	**329**	**345**	**674**	**703**	**40**	**11**	**18**	**29**	**44**

a OHA Second All-Star Team (1980)

Traded to **Calgary** by **Pittsburgh** for Dan Quinn, November 12, 1986. Traded to **St. Louis** by **Calgary** with Craig Coxe and Tim Corkery for Mark Hunter, Doug Gilmour, Steve Bozek and Michael Dark, September 6, 1988. Traded to **Philadelphia** by **St. Louis** for Peter Zezel, November 29, 1988. Rights traded to **Toronto** by **Philadelphia** for Toronto's third round choice (Vaclav Prospal) in 1993 Entry Draft, July 29, 1991.

BURAKOVSKY, ROBERT — (boo-ruh-KAHV-skee)

Right wing. Shoots right. 5'10", 185 lbs. Born, Malmo, Sweden, November 24, 1966.
(NY Rangers' 11th choice, 217th overall, in 1985 Entry Draft).

			Regular Season					Playoffs				
Season	Club	Lea	GP	G	A	TP	PIM	GP	G	A	TP	PIM
1985-86	Leksand	Swe.	19	4	3	7	4	....	....	....	....	....
1986-87	Leksand	Swe.	36	21	15	36	26	....	....	....	....	....
1987-88	Leksand	Swe.	36	10	11	21	10	1	0	0	0	2
1988-89	Leksand	Swe.	40	23	20	43	44	10	6	7	13	4
1989-90	AIK	Swe.	37	27	29	56	32	3	0	2	2	12
1990-91	AIK	Swe.	30	8	15	23	26	....	....	....	....	....
1991-92	Malmo	Swe.	40	19	22	41	42	9	5	0	5	4
1992-93	Malmo	Swe.	32	8	10	18	40	6	4	4	8	9
1993-94	**Ottawa**	**NHL**	**23**	**2**	**3**	**5**	**6**	....	....	....	....	....
	PEI	AHL	52	29	38	67	28	....	....	....	....	....
	NHL Totals		**23**	**2**	**3**	**5**	**6**	....	....	....	....	....

Traded to **Ottawa** by **NY Rangers** for future considerations, May 7, 1993.

BURE, PAVEL — (boo-RAY) VAN.

Right wing. Shoots left. 5'10", 189 lbs. Born, Moscow, USSR, March 31, 1971.
(Vancouver's 4th choice, 113th overall, in 1989 Entry Draft).

			Regular Season					Playoffs				
Season	Club	Lea	GP	G	A	TP	PIM	GP	G	A	TP	PIM
1987-88	CSKA	USSR	5	1	1	2	0	....	....	....	....	....
1988-89a	CSKA	USSR	32	17	9	26	8	....	....	....	....	....
1989-90	CSKA	USSR	46	14	10	24	20	....	....	....	....	....
1990-91	CSKA	USSR	44	35	11	46	24	....	....	....	....	....
1991-92b	**Vancouver**	**NHL**	**65**	**34**	**26**	**60**	**30**	**13**	**6**	**4**	**10**	**14**
1992-93	**Vancouver**	**NHL**	**83**	**60**	**50**	**110**	**69**	**12**	**5**	**7**	**12**	**8**
1993-94c	**Vancouver**	**NHL**	**76**	***60**	**47**	**107**	**86**	**24**	***16**	**15**	**31**	**40**
	NHL Totals		**224**	**154**	**123**	**277**	**185**	**49**	**27**	**26**	**53**	**62**

a Named Soviet National League Rookie-of-the-Year (1989)
b Won Calder Memorial Trophy (1992)
c NHL First All-Star Team (1994)

Played in NHL All-Star Game (1993, 1994)

BURE, VALERI (boo-RAY) MTL.

Right wing. Shoots right. 5'11", 164 lbs. Born, Moscow, USSR, June 13, 1974.
(Montreal's 2nd choice, 33rd overall, in 1992 Entry Draft).

			Regular Season					Playoffs				
Season	Club	Lea	GP	G	A	TP	PIM	GP	G	A	TP	PIM
1990-91	CSKA	USSR	3	0	0	0	0					
1991-92	Spokane	WHL	53	27	22	49	78	10	11	6	17	10
1992-93a	Spokane	WHL	66	68	79	147	49	9	6	11	17	14
1993-94b	Spokane	WHL	59	40	62	102	48	3	5	3	8	2

a WHL West First All-Star Team (1993)
b WHL West Second All-Star Team (1994)

BUREAU, MARC (BEWR-oh) T.B.

Center. Shoots right. 6'1", 198 lbs. Born, Trois-Rivières, Que., May 19, 1966.

			Regular Season					Playoffs				
Season	Club	Lea	GP	G	A	TP	PIM	GP	G	A	TP	PIM
1983-84	Chicoutimi	QMJHL	56	6	16	22	14					
1984-85	Chicoutimi	QMJHL	41	30	25	55	15					
	Granby	QMJHL	27	20	45	65	14					
1985-86	Granby	QMJHL	19	6	17	23	36					
	Chicoutimi	QMJHL	44	30	45	75	33	9	3	7	10	10
1986-87	Longueuil	QMJHL	66	54	58	112	68	20	17	20	37	12
1987-88	Salt Lake	IHL	69	7	20	27	86	7	0	3	3	8
1988-89	Salt Lake	IHL	76	28	36	64	119	14	7	5	12	31
1989-90	**Calgary**	**NHL**	**5**	**0**	**0**	**0**	**4**					
a	Salt Lake	IHL	67	43	48	91	173	11	4	8	12	0
1990-91	**Calgary**	**NHL**	**5**	**0**	**0**	**0**	**2**					
a	Salt Lake	IHL	54	40	48	88	101					
	Minnesota	**NHL**	**9**	**0**	**6**	**6**	**4**	**23**	**3**	**2**	**5**	**20**
1991-92	**Minnesota**	**NHL**	**46**	**6**	**4**	**10**	**50**	**5**	**0**	**0**	**0**	**14**
	Kalamazoo	IHL	7	2	8	10	2					
1992-93	**Tampa Bay**	**NHL**	**63**	**10**	**21**	**31**	**111**					
1993-94	**Tampa Bay**	**NHL**	**75**	**8**	**7**	**15**	**30**					
	NHL Totals		**203**	**24**	**38**	**62**	**201**	**28**	**3**	**2**	**5**	**34**

a IHL Second All-Star Team (1990, 1991)

Signed as a free agent by **Calgary**, May 19, 1987. Traded to **Minnesota** by **Calgary** for Minnesota's third round choice (Sandy McCarthy) in 1991 Entry Draft, March 5, 1991. Claimed on waivers by **Tampa Bay** from **Minnesota**, October 16, 1992.

BURKETT, MICHAEL

Left wing. Shoots left. 6'3", 180 lbs. Born, Toronto, Ont., March 15, 1972.
(Minnesota's 8th choice, 174th overall, in 1991 Entry Draft).

			Regular Season					Playoffs				
Season	Club	Lea	GP	G	A	TP	PIM	GP	G	A	TP	PIM
1990-91	Michigan State	CCHA	35	3	6	9	14					
1991-92	Michigan State	CCHA	33	7	5	12	42					
1992-93	Michigan State	CCHA	39	2	10	12	28					
	Cdn. National	....	2	1	2	3	0					
1993-94	Michigan State	CCHA	41	7	7	14	48					

BURMAN, MICHAEL

Defense. Shoots left. ', lbs. Born, North Bay, Ont., April 1, 1974.
(Montreal's 8th choice, 188th overall, in 1992 Entry Draft).

			Regular Season					Playoffs				
Season	Club	Lea	GP	G	A	TP	PIM	GP	G	A	TP	PIM
1990-91	North Bay	OHL	57	1	18	19	30	10	0	1	1	4
1991-92	North Bay	OHL	63	3	22	25	64	21	3	12	15	21
1992-93	North Bay	OHL	64	10	37	47	59	5	1	3	4	2
1993-94	North Bay	OHL	61	13	50	63	46	18	2	20	22	22

BURR, SHAWN DET.

Left wing/Center. Shoots left. 6'1", 195 lbs. Born, Sarnia, Ont., July 1, 1966.
(Detroit's 1st choice, 7th overall, in 1984 Entry Draft).

			Regular Season					Playoffs				
Season	Club	Lea	GP	G	A	TP	PIM	GP	G	A	TP	PIM
1983-84	Kitchener	OHL	68	41	44	85	50	16	5	12	17	22
1984-85	**Detroit**	**NHL**	**9**	**0**	**0**	**0**	**2**					
	Adirondack	AHL	4	0	0	0	2					
	Kitchener	OHL	48	24	42	66	50	4	3	3	6	2
1985-86	**Detroit**	**NHL**	**5**	**1**	**0**	**1**	**4**					
	Adirondack	AHL	3	2	2	4	2	17	5	7	12	32
a	Kitchener	OHL	59	60	67	127	104	5	2	3	5	8
1986-87	**Detroit**	**NHL**	**80**	**22**	**25**	**47**	**107**	**16**	**7**	**2**	**9**	**20**
1987-88	**Detroit**	**NHL**	**78**	**17**	**23**	**40**	**97**	**9**	**3**	**1**	**4**	**14**
1988-89	**Detroit**	**NHL**	**79**	**19**	**27**	**46**	**78**	**6**	**1**	**2**	**3**	**6**
1989-90	**Detroit**	**NHL**	**76**	**24**	**32**	**56**	**82**					
	Adirondack	AHL	3	4	2	6	2					
1990-91	**Detroit**	**NHL**	**80**	**20**	**30**	**50**	**112**	**7**	**0**	**4**	**4**	**15**
1991-92	**Detroit**	**NHL**	**79**	**19**	**32**	**51**	**118**	**11**	**1**	**5**	**6**	**10**
1992-93	**Detroit**	**NHL**	**80**	**10**	**25**	**35**	**74**	**7**	**2**	**1**	**3**	**2**
1993-94	**Detroit**	**NHL**	**51**	**10**	**12**	**22**	**31**	**7**	**2**	**0**	**2**	**6**
	NHL Totals		**617**	**142**	**206**	**348**	**705**	**63**	**16**	**15**	**31**	**73**

a OHL Second All-Star Team (1986)

BURRIDGE, RANDY WSH.

Left wing. Shoots left. 5'9", 185 lbs. Born, Fort Erie, Ont., January 7, 1966.
(Boston's 7th choice, 157th overall, in 1985 Entry Draft).

			Regular Season					Playoffs				
Season	Club	Lea	GP	G	A	TP	PIM	GP	G	A	TP	PIM
1983-84	Peterborough	OHL	55	6	7	13	44	8	3	2	5	7
1984-85	Peterborough	OHL	66	49	57	106	88	17	9	16	25	18
1985-86	**Boston**	**NHL**	**52**	**17**	**25**	**42**	**28**	**3**	**0**	**4**	**4**	**12**
	Peterborough	OHL	17	15	11	26	23	3	1	3	4	2
	Moncton	AHL	....	....	....	....	....	3	0	2	2	2
1986-87	**Boston**	**NHL**	**23**	**1**	**4**	**5**	**16**	**2**	**1**	**0**	**1**	**2**
	Moncton	AHL	47	26	41	67	139	3	1	2	3	30
1987-88	**Boston**	**NHL**	**79**	**27**	**28**	**55**	**105**	**23**	**2**	**10**	**12**	**16**
1988-89	**Boston**	**NHL**	**80**	**31**	**30**	**61**	**39**	**10**	**5**	**2**	**7**	**6**
1989-90	**Boston**	**NHL**	**63**	**17**	**15**	**32**	**47**	**21**	**4**	**11**	**15**	**14**
1990-91	**Boston**	**NHL**	**62**	**15**	**13**	**28**	**40**	**19**	**0**	**3**	**3**	**39**
1991-92	**Washington**	**NHL**	**66**	**23**	**44**	**67**	**50**	**2**	**0**	**1**	**1**	**0**
1992-93	**Washington**	**NHL**	**4**	**0**	**0**	**0**	**0**	**4**	**1**	**0**	**1**	**0**
	Baltimore	AHL	2	0	1	1	2					
1993-94	**Washington**	**NHL**	**78**	**25**	**17**	**42**	**73**	**11**	**0**	**2**	**2**	**12**
	NHL Totals		**507**	**156**	**176**	**332**	**398**	**95**	**13**	**33**	**46**	**101**

Played in NHL All-Star Game (1992)

Traded to **Washington** by **Boston** for Stephen Leach, June 21, 1991.

BURT, ADAM HFD.

Defense. Shoots left. 6', 190 lbs. Born, Detroit, MI, January 15, 1969.
(Hartford's 2nd choice, 39th overall, in 1987 Entry Draft).

			Regular Season					Playoffs				
Season	Club	Lea	GP	G	A	TP	PIM	GP	G	A	TP	PIM
1985-86	North Bay	OHL	49	0	11	11	81	10	0	0	0	24
1986-87	North Bay	OHL	57	4	27	31	138	24	1	6	7	68
1987-88	Binghamton	AHL	....	....	....	....	....	2	1	1	2	0
a	North Bay	OHL	66	17	53	70	176	2	0	3	3	6
1988-89	**Hartford**	**NHL**	**5**	**0**	**0**	**0**	**6**					
	Binghamton	AHL	5	0	2	2	13					
	North Bay	OHL	23	4	11	15	45	12	2	12	14	12
1989-90	**Hartford**	**NHL**	**63**	**4**	**8**	**12**	**105**	**2**	**0**	**0**	**0**	**0**
1990-91	**Hartford**	**NHL**	**42**	**2**	**7**	**9**	**63**					
	Springfield	AHL	9	1	3	4	22					
1991-92	**Hartford**	**NHL**	**66**	**9**	**15**	**24**	**93**	**2**	**0**	**0**	**0**	**0**
1992-93	**Hartford**	**NHL**	**65**	**6**	**14**	**20**	**116**					
1993-94	**Hartford**	**NHL**	**63**	**1**	**17**	**18**	**75**					
	NHL Totals		**304**	**22**	**61**	**83**	**458**	**4**	**0**	**0**	**0**	**0**

a OHL Second All-Star Team (1988)

BUSCHAN, ANDREI S.J.

Defense. Shoots left. 6'2", 200 lbs. Born, Kiev, USSR, August 21, 1970.
(San Jose's 6th choice, 106th overall, in 1993 Entry Draft).

			Regular Season					Playoffs				
Season	Club	Lea	GP	G	A	TP	PIM	GP	G	A	TP	PIM
1988-89	Kharkov	USSR	2	0	0	0	0					
1989-90	Kharkov	USSR	21	0	0	0	10					
1990-91	Kharkov	USSR 2	62	0	3	3	14					
1991-92	Kharkov	CIS 2			UNAVAILABLE							
1992-93	Sokol Kiev	CIS	41	8	5	13	16	3	0	0	0	4
1993-94	Kansas City	IHL	60	5	13	18	68					

BUSKAS, ROD

Defense. Shoots right. 6'1", 206 lbs. Born, Wetaskiwin, Alta., January 7, 1961.
(Pittsburgh's 5th choice, 112th overall, in 1981 Entry Draft).

			Regular Season					Playoffs				
Season	Club	Lea	GP	G	A	TP	PIM	GP	G	A	TP	PIM
1978-79	Billings	WHL	1	0	0	0	0					
	Medicine Hat	WHL	34	1	12	13	60					
1979-80	Medicine Hat	WHL	72	7	40	47	284					
1980-81	Medicine Hat	WHL	72	14	46	60	164	5	1	1	2	8
1981-82	Erie	AHL	69	1	18	19	78					
1982-83	**Pittsburgh**	**NHL**	**41**	**2**	**2**	**4**	**102**					
	Baltimore	AHL	31	2	8	10	45					
1983-84	**Pittsburgh**	**NHL**	**47**	**2**	**4**	**6**	**60**					
	Baltimore	AHL	33	2	12	14	100	10	1	3	4	22
1984-85	**Pittsburgh**	**NHL**	**69**	**2**	**7**	**9**	**191**					
1985-86	**Pittsburgh**	**NHL**	**72**	**2**	**7**	**9**	**159**					
1986-87	**Pittsburgh**	**NHL**	**68**	**3**	**15**	**18**	**123**					
1987-88	**Pittsburgh**	**NHL**	**76**	**4**	**8**	**12**	**206**					
1988-89	**Pittsburgh**	**NHL**	**52**	**1**	**5**	**6**	**105**	**10**	**0**	**0**	**0**	**23**
1989-90	**Vancouver**	**NHL**	**17**	**0**	**3**	**3**	**36**					
	Pittsburgh	**NHL**	**6**	**0**	**0**	**0**	**13**					
1990-91	**Los Angeles**	**NHL**	**57**	**3**	**8**	**11**	**182**	**2**	**0**	**2**	**2**	**22**
1991-92	**Los Angeles**	**NHL**	**5**	**0**	**0**	**0**	**11**					
	Chicago	**NHL**	**42**	**0**	**4**	**4**	**80**	**6**	**0**	**1**	**1**	**0**
1992-93	**Chicago**	**NHL**	**4**	**0**	**0**	**0**	**26**					
	Indianapolis	IHL	15	0	3	3	40					
	Salt Lake	IHL	31	0	2	2	52					
1993-94	Las Vegas	IHL	69	2	9	11	131	5	0	2	2	2
	NHL Totals		**556**	**19**	**63**	**82**	**1294**	**18**	**0**	**3**	**3**	**45**

Traded to **Vancouver** by **Pittsburgh** for Vancouver's sixth round choice (Ian Moran) in 1990 Entry Draft, October 24, 1989. Traded to **Pittsburgh** by **Vancouver** with Barry Pederson and Tony Tanti for Dave Capuano, Andrew McBain and Dan Quinn, January 8, 1990. Claimed by **Los Angeles** in NHL Waiver Draft, October 1, 1990. Traded to **Chicago** by **Los Angeles** for Chris Norton and future considerations, October 28, 1991.

BUSSEY, FRAN PIT.

Center. Shoots left. 6'3", 190 lbs. Born, Duluth, MN, July 9, 1974.
(Pittsburgh's 8th choice, 187th overall, in 1992 Entry Draft).

			Regular Season					Playoffs				
Season	Club	Lea	GP	G	A	TP	PIM	GP	G	A	TP	PIM
1992-93	Duluth East	HS	24	18	20	38	14					
1993-94	U. of Wisconsin	WCHA				DID NOT PLAY						

BUTCHER, GARTH TOR.

Defense. Shoots right. 6', 204 lbs. Born, Regina, Sask., January 8, 1963.
(Vancouver's 1st choice, 10th overall, in 1981 Entry Draft).

			Regular Season					Playoffs				
Season	Club	Lea	GP	G	A	TP	PIM	GP	G	A	TP	PIM
1979-80	Regina	WHL	13	0	4	4	20					
1980-81a	Regina	WHL	69	9	77	86	230	11	5	17	22	60
1981-82	**Vancouver**	**NHL**	**5**	**0**	**0**	**0**	**9**	**1**	**0**	**0**	**0**	**0**
a	Regina	WHL	65	24	68	92	318	19	3	17	20	95
1982-83	**Vancouver**	**NHL**	**55**	**1**	**13**	**14**	**104**	**3**	**1**	**0**	**1**	**2**
1983-84	**Vancouver**	**NHL**	**28**	**2**	**0**	**2**	**34**					
	Fredericton	AHL	25	4	13	17	43	6	0	2	2	19
1984-85	**Vancouver**	**NHL**	**75**	**3**	**9**	**12**	**152**					
	Fredericton	AHL	3	1	0	1	11					
1985-86	**Vancouver**	**NHL**	**70**	**4**	**7**	**11**	**188**	**3**	**0**	**0**	**0**	**0**
1986-87	**Vancouver**	**NHL**	**70**	**5**	**15**	**20**	**207**					
1987-88	**Vancouver**	**NHL**	**80**	**6**	**17**	**23**	**285**					
1988-89	**Vancouver**	**NHL**	**78**	**0**	**20**	**20**	**227**	**7**	**1**	**1**	**2**	**22**
1989-90	**Vancouver**	**NHL**	**80**	**6**	**14**	**20**	**205**					
1990-91	**Vancouver**	**NHL**	**69**	**6**	**12**	**18**	**257**					
	St. Louis	**NHL**	**13**	**0**	**4**	**4**	**32**	**13**	**2**	**1**	**3**	**54**
1991-92	**St. Louis**	**NHL**	**68**	**5**	**15**	**20**	**189**	**5**	**1**	**2**	**3**	**16**
1992-93	**St. Louis**	**NHL**	**84**	**5**	**10**	**15**	**211**	**11**	**1**	**1**	**2**	**20**
1993-94	**St. Louis**	**NHL**	**43**	**1**	**6**	**7**	**76**					
	Quebec	**NHL**	**34**	**3**	**9**	**12**	**67**					
	NHL Totals		**852**	**47**	**151**	**198**	**2243**	**43**	**6**	**5**	**11**	**114**

a WHL First All-Star Team (1981, 1982)

Played in NHL All-Star Game (1993)

Traded to **St. Louis** by **Vancouver** with Dan Quinn for Geoff Courtnall, Robert Dirk, Sergio Momesso, Cliff Ronning and St Louis' fifth round choice (Brian Loney) in 1992 Entry Draft, March 5, 1991. Traded to **Quebec** by **St. Louis** with Ron Sutter and Bob Bassen for Steve Duchesne and Denis Chasse, January 23, 1994. Traded to **Toronto** by **Quebec** with Mats Sundin, Todd Warriner and Philadelphia's first round choice (previously acquired by Quebec — later traded to Washington — Washington selected Nolan Baumgartner) in 1994 Entry Draft for Wendel Clark, Sylvain Lefebvre, Landon Wilson and Toronto's first round choice (Jeffrey Kealty) in 1994 Entry Draft, June 28, 1994.

BUTENSCHON, SVEN (BUH-tehn-shohn) PIT.

Defense. Shoots left. 6'5", 201 lbs. Born, Itzehoe, West Germany, March 22, 1976.
(Pittsburgh's 3rd choice, 57th overall, in 1994 Entry Draft).

			Regular Season					Playoffs				
Season	Club	Lea	GP	G	A	TP	PIM	GP	G	A	TP	PIM
1992-93	Eastman	Midget	35	14	22	36	101	....	....	....	....	....
1993-94	Brandon	WHL	70	3	19	22	51	4	0	0	0	6

BUTSAYEV, VYACHESLAV (boot-SIGH-yehf) S.J.

Center. Shoots left. 6'2", 200 lbs. Born, Togliatti, USSR, June 13, 1970.
(Philadelphia's 10th choice, 109th overall, in 1990 Entry Draft).

			Regular Season					Playoffs				
Season	Club	Lea	GP	G	A	TP	PIM	GP	G	A	TP	PIM
1989-90	CSKA	USSR	48	14	4	18	30	....	....	....	....	....
1990-91	CSKA	USSR	46	14	9	23	32	....	....	....	....	....
1991-92	CSKA	CIS	36	12	13	25	26	....	....	....	....	....
1992-93	CSKA	CIS	5	3	4	7	6	....	....	....	....	....
	Philadelphia	**NHL**	**52**	**2**	**14**	**16**	**61**	....	....	....	....	....
	Hershey	AHL	24	8	10	18	51	....	....	....	....	....
1993-94	**Philadelphia**	**NHL**	**47**	**12**	**9**	**21**	**58**	....	....	....	....	....
	San Jose	**NHL**	**12**	**0**	**2**	**2**	**10**	....	....	....	....	....
	NHL Totals		**111**	**14**	**25**	**39**	**129**	....	....	....	....	....

Traded to **San Jose** by **Philadelphia** for Rob Zettler, February 1, 1994.

BUTZ, ROB TOR.

Left wing. Shoots left. 6'3", 195 lbs. Born, Dewberry, Alta., February 24, 1975.

			Regular Season					Playoffs				
Season	Club	Lea	GP	G	A	TP	PIM	GP	G	A	TP	PIM
1992-93	Victoria	WHL	67	7	11	18	64	....	....	....	....	....
1993-94	Victoria	WHL	72	24	24	48	161	....	....	....	....	....
	St. John's	AHL	5	0	0	0	26	....	....	....	....	....

Signed as a free agent by **Toronto**, April 1, 1993.

BYAKIN, ILYA EDM.

Defense. Shoots left. 5'9", 185 lbs. Born, Sverdlovsk, USSR, February 2, 1963.
(Edmonton's 11th choice, 267th overall, in 1993 Entry Draft).

			Regular Season					Playoffs				
Season	Club	Lea	GP	G	A	TP	PIM	GP	G	A	TP	PIM
1983-84	Spartak	USSR	44	9	12	21	26	....	....	....	....	....
1984-85	Spartak	USSR	46	7	11	18	56	....	....	....	....	....
1985-86	Spartak	USSR	34	8	7	15	41	....	....	....	....	....
1986-87						DID NOT PLAY						
1987-88	Sverdlovsk	USSR	30	10	10	20	37	....	....	....	....	....
1988-89	Sverdlovsk	USSR	40	11	9	20	53	....	....	....	....	....
1989-90	Sverdlovsk	USSR	27	14	7	21	20	....	....	....	....	....
1990-91	CSKA	USSR	29	4	7	11	20	....	....	....	....	....
1991-92	Rapperswil	Switz.2	36	27	40	67	36	....	....	....	....	....
1992-93	Landshut	Ger.	44	12	19	31	43	6	5	6	11	6
1993-94	**Edmonton**	**NHL**	**44**	**8**	**20**	**28**	**30**	....	....	....	....	....
	Cape Breton	AHL	12	2	9	11	8	....	....	....	....	....
	NHL Totals		**44**	**8**	**20**	**28**	**30**	....	....	....	....	....

BYERS, LYNDON

Right wing. Shoots right. 6'1", 200 lbs. Born, Nipawin, Sask., February 29, 1964.
(Boston's 3rd choice, 39th overall, in 1982 Entry Draft).

			Regular Season					Playoffs				
Season	Club	Lea	GP	G	A	TP	PIM	GP	G	A	TP	PIM
1981-82	Regina	WHL	57	18	25	43	169	20	5	6	11	48
1982-83	Regina	WHL	70	32	38	70	153	5	1	1	2	16
1983-84	**Boston**	**NHL**	**10**	**2**	**4**	**6**	**32**	....	....	....	....	....
	Regina	WHL	58	32	57	89	154	23	17	18	35	78
1984-85	**Boston**	**NHL**	**33**	**3**	**8**	**11**	**41**	....	....	....	....	....
	Hershey	AHL	27	4	6	10	55	....	....	....	....	....
1985-86	**Boston**	**NHL**	**5**	**0**	**2**	**2**	**9**	....	....	....	....	....
	Moncton	AHL	14	2	4	6	26	....	....	....	....	....
	Milwaukee	IHL	8	0	2	2	22	....	....	....	....	....
1986-87	**Boston**	**NHL**	**18**	**2**	**3**	**5**	**53**	**1**	**0**	**0**	**0**	**0**
	Moncton	AHL	27	5	5	10	63	....	....	....	....	....
1987-88	**Boston**	**NHL**	**53**	**10**	**14**	**24**	**236**	**11**	**1**	**2**	**3**	**62**
	Maine	AHL	2	0	1	1	18	....	....	....	....	....
1988-89	**Boston**	**NHL**	**49**	**0**	**4**	**4**	**218**	**2**	**0**	**0**	**0**	**0**
	Maine	AHL	4	1	3	4	2	....	....	....	....	....
1989-90	**Boston**	**NHL**	**43**	**4**	**4**	**8**	**159**	**17**	**1**	**0**	**1**	**12**
1990-91	**Boston**	**NHL**	**19**	**2**	**2**	**4**	**82**	**1**	**0**	**0**	**0**	**10**
1991-92	**Boston**	**NHL**	**31**	**1**	**1**	**2**	**129**	**5**	**0**	**0**	**0**	**12**
	Maine	AHL	11	5	4	9	47	....	....	....	....	....
1992-93	**San Jose**	**NHL**	**18**	**4**	**1**	**5**	**122**	....	....	....	....	....
	Kansas City	IHL	4	1	1	2	22	....	....	....	....	....
	San Diego	IHL	9	0	3	3	35	....	....	....	....	....
1993-94	Las Vegas	IHL	31	3	5	8	176	1	0	0	0	4
	NHL Totals		**279**	**28**	**43**	**71**	**1081**	**37**	**2**	**2**	**4**	**96**

Signed as a free agent by **San Jose**, November 7, 1992.

BYKOV, VIACHESLAV (BIH-kahf) QUE.

Center. Shoots left. 5'8", 175 lbs. Born, Chelyabinsk, USSR, July 24, 1960.
(Quebec's 11th choice, 169th overall, in 1989 Entry Draft).

			Regular Season					Playoffs				
Season	Club	Lea	GP	G	A	TP	PIM	GP	G	A	TP	PIM
1979-80	Chelyabinsk	USSR	3	2	0	2	0	....	....	....	....	....
1980-81	Chelyabinsk	USSR	48	26	16	42	4	....	....	....	....	....
1981-82	Chelyabinsk	USSR	44	20	16	36	14	....	....	....	....	....
1982-83	CSKA	USSR	44	22	22	44	10	....	....	....	....	....
1983-84	CSKA	USSR	44	22	11	33	12	....	....	....	....	....
1984-85	CSKA	USSR	36	21	14	35	4	....	....	....	....	....
1985-86	CSKA	USSR	36	10	10	20	6	....	....	....	....	....
1986-87	CSKA	USSR	40	18	15	33	10	....	....	....	....	....
1987-88	CSKA	USSR	47	17	30	47	26	....	....	....	....	....
1988-89	CSKA	USSR	40	16	20	36	10	....	....	....	....	....
1989-90	CSKA	USSR	48	21	16	37	12	....	....	....	....	....
1990-91	Fribourg	Switz.	36	35	49	84	....	8	8	14	22	....
1991-92	Fribourg	Switz.	34	38	47	85	24	14	4	14	18	10
1992-93	Fribourg	Switz.	35	25	50	75	14	....	....	....	....	....
1993-94	Fribourg	Switz.	36	30	44	74	6	11	11	20	31	2

BYLSMA, DAN L.A.

Left wing. Shoots left. 6'2", 205 lbs. Born, Grand Rapids, MI, September 19, 1970.
(Winnipeg's 7th choice, 109th overall, in 1989 Entry Draft).

			Regular Season					Playoffs				
Season	Club	Lea	GP	G	A	TP	PIM	GP	G	A	TP	PIM
1988-89	Bowling Green	CCHA	32	3	7	10	10	....	....	....	....	....
1989-90	Bowling Green	CCHA	44	13	17	30	30	....	....	....	....	....
1990-91	Bowling Green	CCHA	40	9	12	21	48	....	....	....	....	....
1991-92	Bowling Green	CCHA	34	11	14	25	24	....	....	....	....	....
1992-93	Rochester	AHL	2	0	1	1	0	....	....	....	....	....
1993-94	Greensboro	ECHL	25	14	16	30	52	....	....	....	....	....
	Albany	AHL	3	0	1	1	2	....	....	....	....	....
	Moncton	AHL	50	12	16	28	25	21	3	4	7	31

Signed as a free agent by **Los Angeles**, July 7, 1994.

BYRAM, SHAWN

Left wing. Shoots left. 6'2", 204 lbs. Born, Neepawa, Man., September 12, 1968.
(NY Islanders' 4th choice, 80th overall, in 1986 Entry Draft).

			Regular Season					Playoffs				
Season	Club	Lea	GP	G	A	TP	PIM	GP	G	A	TP	PIM
1985-86	Regina	WHL	46	7	6	13	45	9	0	1	1	11
1986-87	Prince Albert	WHL	67	19	21	40	147	7	1	1	2	10
1987-88	Prince Albert	WHL	61	23	28	51	178	10	5	2	7	27
1988-89	Springfield	AHL	45	5	11	16	195	....	....	....	....	....
	Indianapolis	IHL	1	0	0	0	2	....	....	....	....	....
1989-90	Springfield	AHL	31	4	4	8	30	....	....	....	....	....
1990-91	Capital Dist.	AHL	62	28	35	63	162	....	....	....	....	....
1991-92	**Chicago**	**NHL**	**1**	**0**	**0**	**0**	**0**	....	....	....	....	....
	Indianapolis	IHL	69	18	21	39	154	....	....	....	....	....
1992-93	Indianapolis	IHL	41	2	13	15	123	....	....	....	....	....
1993-94	Indianapolis	IHL	77	23	24	47	170	....	....	....	....	....
	NHL Totals		**1**	**0**	**0**	**0**	**0**	....	....	....	....	....

Signed as a free agent by **Chicago**, August 2, 1991.

CABANA, CHAD FLA.

Left wing. Shoots left. 6'1", 200 lbs. Born, Bonnyville, Alta., October 1, 1974.
(Florida's 11th choice, 213th overall, in 1993 Entry Draft).

			Regular Season					Playoffs				
Season	Club	Lea	GP	G	A	TP	PIM	GP	G	A	TP	PIM
1991-92	Tri-City	WHL	57	5	8	13	145	4	0	1	1	21
1992-93	Tri-City	WHL	68	19	23	42	104	4	1	0	1	10
1993-94	Tri-City	WHL	67	27	33	60	201	4	2	0	2	24

CAIRNS, ERIC NYR

Defense. Shoots left. 6'5", 217 lbs. Born, Oakville, Ont., June 27, 1974.
(NY Rangers' 3rd choice, 72nd overall, in 1992 Entry Draft).

			Regular Season					Playoffs				
Season	Club	Lea	GP	G	A	TP	PIM	GP	G	A	TP	PIM
1991-92	Detroit	OHL	64	1	11	12	232	7	0	0	0	31
1992-93	Detroit	OHL	64	3	13	16	194	15	0	3	3	24
1993-94	Detroit	OHL	59	7	35	42	204	17	0	4	4	46

CALLAHAN, BRIAN

Center. Shoots left. 6'1", 190 lbs. Born, Melrose, MA, July 13, 1974.
(Pittsburgh's 10th choice, 235th overall, in 1992 Entry Draft).

			Regular Season					Playoffs				
Season	Club	Lea	GP	G	A	TP	PIM	GP	G	A	TP	PIM
1992-93	Belmont Hill	HS	15	19	16	35	16	....	....	....	....	....
1993-94	Boston College	H.E.	36	11	11	22	58	....	....	....	....	....

CALLAHAN, GREGORY WSH.

Defense. Shoots left. 6'3", 200 lbs. Born, Chestnut Hill, MA, April 25, 1973.
(Washington's 9th choice, 239th overall, in 1992 Entry Draft).

			Regular Season					Playoffs				
Season	Club	Lea	GP	G	A	TP	PIM	GP	G	A	TP	PIM
1992-93	Boston College	H.E.	38	1	4	5	49	....	....	....	....	....
1993-94	Boston College	H.E.	24	3	2	5	65	....	....	....	....	....

CALLANDER, JOHN (JOCK)

Right wing. Shoots right. 6'1", 188 lbs. Born, Regina, Sask., April 23, 1961.

			Regular Season					Playoffs				
Season	Club	Lea	GP	G	A	TP	PIM	GP	G	A	TP	PIM
1979-80	Regina	WHL	39	9	11	20	25	18	8	5	13	0
1980-81	Regina	WHL	72	67	86	153	37	11	6	7	13	14
1981-82	Regina	WHL	71	79	111	*190	59	20	13	*26	39	37
1982-83	Salt Lake	CHL	68	20	27	47	26	6	0	1	1	9
1983-84	Montana	CHL	72	27	32	59	69	....	....	....	....	....
	Toledo	IHL	2	0	0	0	0	....	....	....	....	....
1984-85	Muskegon	IHL	82	39	68	107	86	17	13	*21	*34	33
1985-86a	Muskegon	IHL	82	39	72	111	121	14	*12	11	*23	12
1986-87bcd	Muskegon	IHL	82	54	82	*136	110	15	13	7	20	23
1987-88	**Pittsburgh**	**NHL**	**41**	**11**	**16**	**27**	**45**	....	....	....	....	....
	Muskegon	IHL	31	20	36	56	49	6	2	3	5	25
1988-89	**Pittsburgh**	**NHL**	**30**	**6**	**5**	**11**	**20**	**10**	**2**	**5**	**7**	**10**
	Muskegon	IHL	48	25	39	64	40	7	5	5	10	30
1989-90	**Pittsburgh**	**NHL**	**30**	**4**	**7**	**11**	**49**	....	....	....	....	....
	Muskegon	IHL	46	29	49	78	118	15	6	*14	20	54
1990-91	Muskegon	IHL	30	14	20	34	102	....	....	....	....	....
1991-92b	Muskegon	IHL	81	42	70	112	160	10	4	10	14	13
	Pittsburgh	**NHL**	....	....	....	....	....	**12**	**1**	**3**	**4**	**2**
1992-93	**Tampa Bay**	**NHL**	**8**	**1**	**1**	**2**	**2**	....	....	....	....	....
	Atlanta	IHL	69	34	50	84	172	9	*7	5	12	25
1993-94	Cleveland	IHL	81	31	70	101	126	....	....	....	....	....
	NHL Totals		**109**	**22**	**29**	**51**	**116**	**22**	**3**	**8**	**11**	**12**

a IHL Playoff MVP (1986)
b IHL First All-Star Team (1987, 1992)
c Shared James Gatschene Memorial Trophy (MVP - IHL) with Jeff Pyle (1987)
d Shared Leo P. Lamoureux Memorial Trophy (Top Scorer - IHL) with Jeff Pyle (1987)

Signed as a free agent by **St. Louis**, September 28, 1981. Signed as a free agent by **Pittsburgh**, July 31, 1987. Signed as a free agent by **Tampa Bay**, July 29, 1992.

CALOUN, JAN (CHAH-loon) S.J.

Right wing. Shoots right. 5'10", 175 lbs. Born, Usti-Nad-Labem, Czech., December 20, 1972.
(San Jose's 4th choice, 75th overall, in 1992 Entry Draft).

			Regular Season					Playoffs				
Season	Club	Lea	GP	G	A	TP	PIM	GP	G	A	TP	PIM
1990-91	Litvinov	Czech.	50	28	19	47	12	....	....	....	....	....
1991-92	Litvinov	Czech.	46	39	13	52	24	....	....	....	....	....
1992-93	Litvinov	Czech.	47	45	22	67	....	....	....	....	....	....
1993-94	Litvinov	Czech.	38	25	17	42	....	4	2	2	4	0

CAMPBELL, EDDY — NYR

Defense. Shoots left. 6'2", 212 lbs. Born, Worcester, MA, November 26, 1974.
(NY Rangers' 9th choice, 190th overall, in 1993 Entry Draft).

			Regular Season					Playoffs				
Season	Club	Lea	GP	G	A	TP	PIM	GP	G	A	TP	PIM
1992-93	Omaha	US Jr.	42	9	19	28	160	....	....	....	....	....
1993-94	Lowell	H.E.	40	8	16	24	114	....	....	....	....	....

CAMPBELL, JIM — MTL.

Center. Shoots right. 6'1", 175 lbs. Born, Worcester, MA, April 3, 1973.
(Montreal's 2nd choice, 28th overall, in 1991 Entry Draft).

			Regular Season					Playoffs				
Season	Club	Lea	GP	G	A	TP	PIM	GP	G	A	TP	PIM
1991-92	Hull	QMJHL	64	41	44	85	51	6	7	3	10	8
1992-93	Hull	QMJHL	50	42	29	71	66	8	11	4	15	43
1993-94	U.S. National	....	56	24	33	57	59	....	....	....	....	....
	U.S. Olympic	....	8	0	0	0	6	....	....	....	....	....
	Fredericton	AHL	19	6	17	23	6	....	....	....	....	....

CAMPEAU, CHRISTIAN — T.B.

Right wing. Shoots right. 5'10", 178 lbs. Born, Verdun, Que., June 2, 1971.

			Regular Season					Playoffs				
Season	Club	Lea	GP	G	A	TP	PIM	GP	G	A	TP	PIM
1990-91	Granby	QMJHL	69	16	27	43	128	....	....	....	....	....
1991-92	Rouen	France	16	3	5	8	12	....	....	....	....	....
1992-93	Atlanta	IHL	66	3	5	8	40	3	0	0	0	2
1993-94	Atlanta	IHL	65	8	9	17	74	14	1	0	1	2

Signed as a free agent by **Tampa Bay**, July 10, 1992.

CANAVAN, ROBERT — NYI

Left wing. Shoots left. 5'11", 180 lbs. Born, Boston, MA, February 4, 1973.
(NY Islanders' 10th choice, 202nd overall, in 1991 Entry Draft).

			Regular Season					Playoffs				
Season	Club	Lea	GP	G	A	TP	PIM	GP	G	A	TP	PIM
1991-92	Boston College	H.E.	30	7	4	11	28	....	....	....	....	....
1992-93	Boston College	H.E.	30	8	8	16	30	....	....	....	....	....
1993-94	Boston College	H.E.	30	7	14	21	28	....	....	....	....	....

CAPUANO, DAVE — (KAP-yew-AN-oh)

Left wing. Shoots left. 6'2", 190 lbs. Born, Warwick, RI, July 27, 1968.
(Pittsburgh's 2nd choice, 25th overall, in 1986 Entry Draft).

			Regular Season					Playoffs				
Season	Club	Lea	GP	G	A	TP	PIM	GP	G	A	TP	PIM
1986-87	U. of Maine	H.E.	38	18	41	59	14	....	....	....	....	....
1987-88abc	U. of Maine	H.E.	42	*34	*51	*85	51	....	....	....	....	....
1988-89ac	U. of Maine	H.E.	41	37	30	67	38	....	....	....	....	....
1989-90	**Pittsburgh**	**NHL**	**6**	**0**	**0**	**0**	**2**	....	....	....	....	....
	Muskegon	IHL	27	15	15	30	22	....	....	....	....	....
	Vancouver	**NHL**	**27**	**3**	**5**	**8**	**10**	....	....	....	....	....
	Milwaukee	IHL	2	0	4	4	0	6	1	5	6	0
1990-91	**Vancouver**	**NHL**	**61**	**13**	**31**	**44**	**42**	**6**	**1**	**1**	**2**	**5**
1991-92	Milwaukee	IHL	9	2	6	8	8	....	....	....	....	....
1992-93	Hamilton	AHL	4	0	1	1	0	....	....	....	....	....
	Tampa Bay	**NHL**	**6**	**1**	**1**	**2**	**2**	....	....	....	....	....
	Atlanta	IHL	58	19	40	59	50	8	2	2	4	9
1993-94	**San Jose**	**NHL**	**4**	**0**	**1**	**1**	**0**	....	....	....	....	....
	Providence	AHL	51	24	29	53	64	....	....	....	....	....
	NHL Totals		**104**	**17**	**38**	**55**	**56**	**6**	**1**	**1**	**2**	**5**

a NCAA East First All-American Team (1988, 1989)
b NCAA All-Tournament Team (1988)
c Hockey East First All-Star Team (1988, 1989)

Traded to **Vancouver** by **Pittsburgh** with Andrew McBain and Dan Quinn for Rod Buskas, Barry Pederson and Tony Tanti, January 8, 1990. Traded to **Tampa Bay** by **Vancouver** with Vancouver's fourth round choice (later traded to New Jersey — later traded to Calgary — Calgary selected Ryan Duthie) in 1994 Entry Draft for Anatoli Semenov, November 3, 1992. Traded to **San Jose** by **Tampa Bay** for Peter Ahola, June 19, 1993. Traded to **Boston** by **San Jose** for cash, November 5, 1993.

CAPUANO, DEAN — BOS.

Defense. Shoots right. 6'1", 175 lbs. Born, Providence, RI, November 3, 1971.
(Boston's 10th choice, 210th overall, in 1990 Entry Draft).

			Regular Season					Playoffs				
Season	Club	Lea	GP	G	A	TP	PIM	GP	G	A	TP	PIM
1990-91	Providence	H.E.	19	3	5	8	6	....	....	....	....	....
1991-92	Providence	H.E.	3	0	0	0	0	....	....	....	....	....
1992-93	Merrimack	H.E.			DID NOT PLAY							
1993-94	Merrimack	H.E.	19	0	6	6	20	....	....	....	....	....

CARBONNEAU, GUY — (KAR-buhn-oh, GEE) ST.L.

Center. Shoots right. 5'11", 184 lbs. Born, Sept-Iles, Que., March 18, 1960.
(Montreal's 4th choice, 44th overall, in 1979 Entry Draft).

			Regular Season					Playoffs				
Season	Club	Lea	GP	G	A	TP	PIM	GP	G	A	TP	PIM
1976-77	Chicoutimi	QJHL	59	9	20	29	8	4	1	0	1	0
1977-78	Chicoutimi	QJHL	70	28	55	83	60	....	....	....	....	....
1978-79	Chicoutimi	QJHL	72	62	79	141	47	4	2	1	3	4
1979-80	Chicoutimi	QJHL	72	72	110	182	66	12	9	15	24	28
	Nova Scotia	AHL	....	....	....	....	....	2	1	1	2	2
1980-81	**Montreal**	**NHL**	**2**	**0**	**1**	**1**	**0**	....	....	....	....	....
	Nova Scotia	AHL	78	35	53	88	87	6	1	3	4	9
1981-82	Nova Scotia	AHL	77	27	67	94	124	9	2	7	9	8
1982-83	**Montreal**	**NHL**	**77**	**18**	**29**	**47**	**68**	**3**	**0**	**0**	**0**	**2**
1983-84	**Montreal**	**NHL**	**78**	**24**	**30**	**54**	**75**	**15**	**4**	**3**	**7**	**12**
1984-85	**Montreal**	**NHL**	**79**	**23**	**34**	**57**	**43**	**12**	**4**	**3**	**7**	**8**
1985-86	**Montreal**	**NHL**	**80**	**20**	**36**	**56**	**57**	**20**	**7**	**5**	**12**	**35**
1986-87	**Montreal**	**NHL**	**79**	**18**	**27**	**45**	**68**	**17**	**3**	**8**	**11**	**20**
1987-88a	**Montreal**	**NHL**	**80**	**17**	**21**	**38**	**61**	**11**	**0**	**4**	**4**	**2**
1988-89a	**Montreal**	**NHL**	**79**	**26**	**30**	**56**	**44**	**21**	**4**	**5**	**9**	**10**
1989-90	**Montreal**	**NHL**	**68**	**19**	**36**	**55**	**37**	**11**	**2**	**3**	**5**	**6**
1990-91	**Montreal**	**NHL**	**78**	**20**	**24**	**44**	**63**	**13**	**1**	**5**	**6**	**10**
1991-92a	**Montreal**	**NHL**	**72**	**18**	**21**	**39**	**39**	**11**	**1**	**1**	**2**	**6**
1992-93	**Montreal**	**NHL**	**61**	**4**	**13**	**17**	**20**	**20**	**3**	**3**	**6**	**10**
1993-94	**Montreal**	**NHL**	**79**	**14**	**24**	**38**	**48**	**7**	**1**	**3**	**4**	**4**
	NHL Totals		**912**	**221**	**326**	**547**	**623**	**161**	**30**	**43**	**73**	**125**

a Won Frank J. Selke Trophy (1988, 1989, 1992)

Traded to **St. Louis** by **Montreal** for Jim Montgomery, August 19, 1994.

CARKNER, TERRY — DET.

Defense. Shoots left. 6'3", 210 lbs. Born, Smiths Falls, Ont., March 7, 1966.
(NY Rangers' 1st choice, 14th overall, in 1984 Entry Draft).

			Regular Season					Playoffs				
Season	Club	Lea	GP	G	A	TP	PIM	GP	G	A	TP	PIM
1983-84	Peterborough	OHL	58	4	19	23	77	8	0	6	6	13
1984-85a	Peterborough	OHL	64	14	47	61	125	17	2	10	12	11
1985-86b	Peterborough	OHL	54	12	32	44	106	16	1	7	8	17
1986-87	**NY Rangers**	**NHL**	**52**	**2**	**13**	**15**	**118**	**1**	**0**	**0**	**0**	**0**
	New Haven	AHL	12	2	6	8	56	3	1	0	1	0
1987-88	**Quebec**	**NHL**	**63**	**3**	**24**	**27**	**159**	....	....	....	....	....
1988-89	**Philadelphia**	**NHL**	**78**	**11**	**32**	**43**	**149**	**19**	**1**	**5**	**6**	**28**
1989-90	**Philadelphia**	**NHL**	**63**	**4**	**18**	**22**	**169**	....	....	....	....	....
1990-91	**Philadelphia**	**NHL**	**79**	**7**	**25**	**32**	**204**	....	....	....	....	....
1991-92	**Philadelphia**	**NHL**	**73**	**4**	**12**	**16**	**195**	....	....	....	....	....
1992-93	**Philadelphia**	**NHL**	**83**	**3**	**16**	**19**	**150**	....	....	....	....	....
1993-94	**Detroit**	**NHL**	**68**	**1**	**6**	**7**	**130**	**7**	**0**	**0**	**0**	**4**
	NHL Totals		**559**	**35**	**146**	**181**	**1274**	**27**	**1**	**5**	**6**	**32**

a OHL Second All-Star Team (1985)
b OHL First All-Star Team (1986)

Traded to **Quebec** by **NY Rangers** with Jeff Jackson for John Ogrodnick and David Shaw, September 30, 1987. Traded to **Philadelphia** by **Quebec** for Greg Smyth and Philadelphia's third round choice (John Tanner) in the 1989 Entry Draft, July 25, 1988. Traded to **Detroit** by **Philadelphia** for Yves Racine and Detroit's fourth round choice (Sebastien Vallee) in 1994 Entry Draft, October 5, 1993.

CARNBACK, PATRIK — (KAHRN-buhk) ANA.

Center. Shoots left. 6', 187 lbs. Born, Goteborg, Sweden, February 1, 1968.
(Montreal's 7th choice, 125th overall, in 1988 Entry Draft).

			Regular Season					Playoffs				
Season	Club	Lea	GP	G	A	TP	PIM	GP	G	A	TP	PIM
1986-87	V. Frolunda	Swe.2	28	3	1	4	4	....	....	....	....	....
1987-88	V. Frolunda	Swe.2	33	16	19	35	24	11	4	5	9	8
1988-89	V. Frolunda	Swe.2	53	39	36	75	52	....	....	....	....	....
1989-90	V. Frolunda	Swe.	40	26	27	53	34	....	....	....	....	....
1990-91	V. Frolunda	Swe.	22	10	9	19	46	28	15	24	39	24
1991-92	V. Frolunda	Swe.	33	17	22	39	32	3	1	5	6	20
1992-93	**Montreal**	**NHL**	**6**	**0**	**0**	**0**	**2**	....	....	....	....	....
	Fredericton	AHL	45	20	37	57	45	5	0	3	3	14
1993-94	**Anaheim**	**NHL**	**73**	**12**	**11**	**23**	**54**	....	....	....	....	....
	NHL Totals		**79**	**12**	**11**	**23**	**56**	....	....	....	....	....

Traded to **Anaheim** by **Montreal** with Todd Ewen for Anaheim's third round choice (Chris Murray) in 1994 Entry Draft, August 10, 1993.

CARNEY, KEITH E. — CHI.

Defense. Shoots left. 6'2", 205 lbs. Born, Providence, RI, February 3, 1970.
(Buffalo's 3rd choice, 76th overall, in 1988 Entry Draft).

			Regular Season					Playoffs				
Season	Club	Lea	GP	G	A	TP	PIM	GP	G	A	TP	PIM
1988-89	U. of Maine	H.E.	40	4	22	26	24	....	....	....	....	....
1989-90ab	U. of Maine	H.E.	41	3	41	44	43	....	....	....	....	....
1990-91cd	U. of Maine	H.E.	40	7	49	56	38	....	....	....	....	....
1991-92	U.S. National	....	49	2	17	19	16	....	....	....	....	....
	Buffalo	**NHL**	**14**	**1**	**2**	**3**	**18**	**7**	**0**	**3**	**3**	**0**
	Rochester	AHL	24	1	10	11	2	2	0	2	2	0
1992-93	**Buffalo**	**NHL**	**30**	**2**	**4**	**6**	**55**	**8**	**0**	**3**	**3**	**6**
	Rochester	AHL	41	5	21	26	32	....	....	....	....	....
1993-94	**Buffalo**	**NHL**	**7**	**1**	**3**	**4**	**4**	....	....	....	....	....
	Chicago	**NHL**	**30**	**3**	**5**	**8**	**35**	**6**	**0**	**1**	**1**	**4**
	Indianapolis	IHL	28	0	14	14	20	....	....	....	....	....
	NHL Totals		**81**	**7**	**14**	**21**	**112**	**21**	**0**	**7**	**7**	**10**

a Hockey East Second All-Star Team (1990)
b NCAA East Second All-American Team (1990)
c Hockey East First All-Star Team (1991)
d NCAA East First All-American Team (1991)

Traded to **Chicago** by **Buffalo** with contingent draft choices for Craig Muni and contingent draft choices, October 27, 1993.

CARPENTER, BOB — N.J.

Center. Shoots left. 6', 200 lbs. Born, Beverly, MA, July 13, 1963.
(Washington's 1st choice, 3rd overall, in 1981 Entry Draft).

			Regular Season					Playoffs				
Season	Club	Lea	GP	G	A	TP	PIM	GP	G	A	TP	PIM
1980-81	St. John's	HS	18	14	24	38	....	....	....	....	....	....
1981-82	**Washington**	**NHL**	**80**	**32**	**35**	**67**	**69**	....	....	....	....	....
1982-83	**Washington**	**NHL**	**80**	**32**	**37**	**69**	**64**	**4**	**1**	**0**	**1**	**2**
1983-84	**Washington**	**NHL**	**80**	**28**	**40**	**68**	**51**	**8**	**2**	**1**	**3**	**25**
1984-85	**Washington**	**NHL**	**80**	**53**	**42**	**95**	**87**	**5**	**1**	**4**	**5**	**8**
1985-86	**Washington**	**NHL**	**80**	**27**	**29**	**56**	**105**	**9**	**5**	**4**	**9**	**12**
1986-87	**Washington**	**NHL**	**22**	**5**	**7**	**12**	**21**	....	....	....	....	....
	NY Rangers	**NHL**	**28**	**2**	**8**	**10**	**20**	....	....	....	....	....
	Los Angeles	**NHL**	**10**	**2**	**3**	**5**	**6**	**5**	**1**	**2**	**3**	**2**
1987-88	**Los Angeles**	**NHL**	**71**	**19**	**33**	**52**	**84**	**5**	**1**	**1**	**2**	**0**
1988-89	**Los Angeles**	**NHL**	**39**	**11**	**15**	**26**	**16**	....	....	....	....	....
	Boston	**NHL**	**18**	**5**	**9**	**14**	**10**	**8**	**1**	**1**	**2**	**4**
1989-90	**Boston**	**NHL**	**80**	**25**	**31**	**56**	**97**	**21**	**4**	**6**	**10**	**39**
1990-91	**Boston**	**NHL**	**29**	**8**	**8**	**16**	**22**	**1**	**0**	**1**	**1**	**2**
1991-92	**Boston**	**NHL**	**60**	**25**	**23**	**48**	**46**	**8**	**0**	**1**	**1**	**6**
1992-93	**Washington**	**NHL**	**68**	**11**	**17**	**28**	**65**	**6**	**1**	**4**	**5**	**6**
1993-94	**New Jersey**	**NHL**	**76**	**10**	**23**	**33**	**51**	**20**	**1**	**7**	**8**	**20**
	NHL Totals		**901**	**295**	**360**	**655**	**814**	**100**	**18**	**32**	**50**	**126**

Played in NHL All-Star Game (1985)

Traded to **NY Rangers** by **Washington** with Washington's second round choice (Jason Prosofsky) in 1989 Entry Draft for Bob Crawford, Kelly Miller and Mike Ridley, January 1, 1987. Traded to **Los Angeles** by **NY Rangers** with Tom Laidlaw for Jeff Crossman, Marcel Dionne and Los Angeles' third round choice (later traded to Minnesota — Minnesota selected Murray Garbutt) in 1989 Entry Draft. Traded to **Boston** by **Los Angeles** for Steve Kasper, January 23, 1989. Signed as a free agent by **Washington**, June 30, 1992. Signed as a free agent by **New Jersey**, September 30, 1993.

CARPER, BRANDON — CGY.

Defense. Shoots left. 6'2", 200 lbs. Born, Highland Park, IL, April 2, 1972.
(Calgary's 9th choice, 198th overall, in 1992 Entry Draft).

			Regular Season					Playoffs				
Season	Club	Lea	GP	G	A	TP	PIM	GP	G	A	TP	PIM
1991-92	Bowling Green	CCHA	34	2	16	18	44	....	....	....	....	....
1992-93	Bowling Green	CCHA	41	7	20	27	72	....	....	....	....	....
1993-94	Bowling Green	CCHA	36	3	9	12	62	....	....	....	....	....

CARSON, JIMMY — HFD.

Center. Shoots right. 6'1", 200 lbs. Born, Southfield, MI, July 20, 1968.
(Los Angeles' 1st choice, 2nd overall, in 1986 Entry Draft).

			Regular Season					Playoffs				
Season	Club	Lea	GP	G	A	TP	PIM	GP	G	A	TP	PIM
1984-85	Verdun	QMJHL	68	44	72	116	12	14	9	17	26	12
1985-86a	Verdun	QMJHL	69	70	83	153	46	5	2	6	8	0
1986-87b	**Los Angeles**	**NHL**	**80**	**37**	**42**	**79**	**22**	**5**	**1**	**2**	**3**	**6**
1987-88	**Los Angeles**	**NHL**	**80**	**55**	**52**	**107**	**45**	**5**	**5**	**3**	**8**	**4**
1988-89	**Edmonton**	**NHL**	**80**	**49**	**51**	**100**	**36**	**7**	**2**	**1**	**3**	**6**
1989-90	**Edmonton**	**NHL**	**4**	**1**	**2**	**3**	**0**	....	....	....	....	....
	Detroit	**NHL**	**44**	**20**	**16**	**36**	**8**	....	....	....	....	....
1990-91	**Detroit**	**NHL**	**64**	**21**	**25**	**46**	**28**	**7**	**2**	**1**	**3**	**4**
1991-92	**Detroit**	**NHL**	**80**	**34**	**35**	**69**	**30**	**11**	**2**	**3**	**5**	**0**
1992-93	**Detroit**	**NHL**	**52**	**25**	**26**	**51**	**18**	....	....	....	....	....
	Los Angeles	**NHL**	**34**	**12**	**10**	**22**	**14**	**18**	**5**	**4**	**9**	**2**
1993-94	**Los Angeles**	**NHL**	**25**	**4**	**7**	**11**	**2**	....	....	....	....	....
	Vancouver	**NHL**	**34**	**7**	**10**	**17**	**22**	**2**	**0**	**1**	**1**	**0**
	NHL Totals		**577**	**265**	**276**	**541**	**225**	**55**	**17**	**15**	**32**	**22**

a QMJHL Second All-Star Team (1986)
b Named to NHL All-Rookie Team (1987)

Played in NHL All-Star Game (1989)

Traded to **Edmonton** by **Los Angeles** with Martin Gelinas, Los Angeles' first round choices in 1989 (later traded to New Jersey — New Jersey selected Jason Miller), 1991 (Martin Rucinsky) and 1993 (Nick Stajduhar) Entry Drafts and cash for Wayne Gretzky, Mike Krushelnyski and Marty McSorley, August 9, 1988. Traded to **Detroit** by **Edmonton** with Kevin McClelland and Edmonton's fifth round choice (later traded to Montreal — Montreal selected Brad Layzell) in 1991 Entry Draft for Petr Klima, Joe Murphy, Adam Graves and Jeff Sharples, November 2, 1989. Traded to **Los Angeles** by **Detroit** with Marc Potvin and Gary Shuchuk for Paul Coffey, Sylvain Couturier and Jim Hiller, January 29, 1993. Traded to **Vancouver** by **Los Angeles** for Dixon Ward and a conditional draft choice in 1995 Entry Draft, January 8, 1994. Signed as a free agent by **Hartford**, July 15, 1994.

CARTER, ANSON — QUE.

Center. Shoots right. 6'1", 175 lbs. Born, Toronto, Ont., June 6, 1974.
(Quebec's 10th choice, 220th overall, in 1992 Entry Draft).

			Regular Season					Playoffs				
Season	Club	Lea	GP	G	A	TP	PIM	GP	G	A	TP	PIM
1992-93	Michigan State	CCHA	34	15	7	22	20	....	....	....	....	....
1993-94a	Michigan State	CCHA	39	30	24	54	36	....	....	....	....	....

a CCHA First All-Star Team (1994)

CARTER, JOHN

Left wing. Shoots left. 5'10", 181 lbs. Born, Winchester, MA, May 3, 1963.

			Regular Season					Playoffs				
Season	Club	Lea	GP	G	A	TP	PIM	GP	G	A	TP	PIM
1982-83	RPI	ECAC	29	16	22	38	33	....	....	....	....	....
1983-84	RPI	ECAC	38	35	39	74	52	....	....	....	....	....
1984-85	RPI	ECAC	37	43	29	72	52	....	....	....	....	....
1985-86	RPI	ECAC	27	23	18	41	68	....	....	....	....	....
	Boston	**NHL**	**3**	**0**	**0**	**0**	**0**	....	....	....	....	....
1986-87	**Boston**	**NHL**	**8**	**0**	**1**	**1**	**0**	....	....	....	....	....
	Moncton	AHL	58	25	30	55	60	6	2	3	5	5
1987-88	**Boston**	**NHL**	**4**	**0**	**1**	**1**	**2**	....	....	....	....	....
	Maine	AHL	76	38	38	76	145	10	4	4	8	44
1988-89	**Boston**	**NHL**	**44**	**12**	**10**	**22**	**24**	**10**	**1**	**2**	**3**	**6**
	Maine	AHL	24	13	6	19	12	....	....	....	....	....
1989-90	**Boston**	**NHL**	**76**	**17**	**22**	**39**	**26**	**21**	**6**	**3**	**9**	**45**
	Maine	AHL	2	2	2	4	2	....	....	....	....	....
1990-91	**Boston**	**NHL**	**50**	**4**	**7**	**11**	**68**	....	....	....	....	....
	Maine	AHL	16	5	9	14	16	1	0	0	0	10
1991-92	**San Jose**	**NHL**	**4**	**0**	**0**	**0**	**0**	....	....	....	....	....
	Kansas City	IHL	42	11	15	26	116	15	6	9	15	18
1992-93	**San Jose**	**NHL**	**55**	**7**	**9**	**16**	**81**	....	....	....	....	....
	Kansas City	IHL	9	4	2	6	14	....	....	....	....	....
1993-94	Providence	AHL	47	11	5	16	82	....	....	....	....	....
	NHL Totals		**244**	**40**	**50**	**90**	**201**	**31**	**7**	**5**	**12**	**51**

Signed as a free agent by **Boston**, May 3, 1986. Signed as a free agent by **San Jose**, August 22, 1991.

CARUSO, BRIAN — CGY.

Left wing. Shoots left. 6'2", 225 lbs. Born, Thunder Bay, Ont., September 20, 1972.
(Calgary's 4th choice, 63rd overall, in 1991 Entry Draft).

			Regular Season					Playoffs				
Season	Club	Lea	GP	G	A	TP	PIM	GP	G	A	TP	PIM
1990-91	Minn.-Duluth	WCHA	31	5	6	11	24	....	....	....	....	....
1991-92	Minn.-Duluth	WCHA	29	2	3	5	34	....	....	....	....	....
1992-93	Minn. Duluth	WCHA	40	12	13	25	24	....	....	....	....	....
	Cdn. National	....	2	0	0	0	2	....	....	....	....	....
1993-94	Minn.-Duluth	WCHA	37	11	10	21	61	....	....	....	....	....

CASSELMAN, MIKE — DET.

Center. Shoots left. 5'11", 190 lbs. Born, Morrisburg, Ont., August 23, 1968.
(Detroit's 1st choice, 3rd overall, in 1990 Supplemental Draft).

			Regular Season					Playoffs				
Season	Club	Lea	GP	G	A	TP	PIM	GP	G	A	TP	PIM
1987-88	Clarkson	ECAC	24	4	1	5	....	....	....	....	....	....
1988-89	Clarkson	ECAC	31	3	14	17	....	....	....	....	....	....
1989-90	Clarkson	ECAC	34	22	21	43	69	....	....	....	....	....
1990-91	Clarkson	ECAC	40	19	35	54	44	....	....	....	....	....
1991-92a	Toledo	ECHL	61	39	60	99	83	5	0	1	1	6
	Adirondack	AHL	1	0	0	0	0	....	....	....	....	....
1992-93	Adirondack	AHL	60	12	19	31	27	8	3	3	6	0
	Toledo	ECHL	3	0	1	1	2	....	....	....	....	....
1993-94	Adirondack	AHL	77	17	38	55	34	12	2	4	6	10

a ECHL Second All-Star Team (1992)

CASSELS, ANDREW — (KAS-uhls) HFD.

Center. Shoots left. 6', 192 lbs. Born, Bramalea, Ont., July 23, 1969.
(Montreal's 1st choice, 17th overall, in 1987 Entry Draft).

			Regular Season					Playoffs				
Season	Club	Lea	GP	G	A	TP	PIM	GP	G	A	TP	PIM
1986-87	Ottawa	OHL	66	26	66	92	28	11	5	9	14	7
1987-88a	Ottawa	OHL	61	48	*103	*151	39	16	8	*24	*32	13
1988-89a	Ottawa	OHL	56	37	97	134	66	12	5	10	15	10
1989-90	**Montreal**	**NHL**	**6**	**2**	**0**	**2**	**2**	....	....	....	....	....
	Sherbrooke	AHL	55	22	45	67	25	12	2	11	13	6
1990-91	**Montreal**	**NHL**	**54**	**6**	**19**	**25**	**20**	**8**	**0**	**2**	**2**	**2**
1991-92	**Hartford**	**NHL**	**67**	**11**	**30**	**41**	**18**	**7**	**2**	**4**	**6**	**6**
1992-93	**Hartford**	**NHL**	**84**	**21**	**64**	**85**	**62**	....	....	....	....	....
1993-94	**Hartford**	**NHL**	**79**	**16**	**42**	**58**	**37**	....	....	....	....	....
	NHL Totals		**290**	**56**	**155**	**211**	**139**	**15**	**2**	**6**	**8**	**8**

a OHL First All-Star Team (1988,1989)

Traded to **Hartford** by **Montreal** for Hartford's second round choice (Valeri Bure) in 1992 Entry Draft, September 17, 1991.

CAUFIELD, JAY

Right wing. Shoots right. 6'4", 237 lbs. Born, Philadelphia, PA, July 17, 1960.

			Regular Season					Playoffs				
Season	Club	Lea	GP	G	A	TP	PIM	GP	G	A	TP	PIM
1984-85	North Dakota	WCHA	1	0	0	0	0	....	....	....	....	....
1985-86	Toledo	IHL	30	5	4	9	54	....	....	....	....	....
	New Haven	AHL	40	2	3	5	40	1	0	0	0	0
1986-87	**NY Rangers**	**NHL**	**13**	**2**	**1**	**3**	**45**	**3**	**0**	**0**	**0**	**12**
	Flint	IHL	12	4	3	7	59	....	....	....	....	....
	New Haven	AHL	13	0	0	0	43	....	....	....	....	....
1987-88	**Minnesota**	**NHL**	**1**	**0**	**0**	**0**	**0**	....	....	....	....	....
	Kalamazoo	IHL	65	5	10	15	273	6	0	1	1	47
1988-89	**Pittsburgh**	**NHL**	**58**	**1**	**4**	**5**	**285**	**9**	**0**	**0**	**0**	**28**
1989-90	**Pittsburgh**	**NHL**	**37**	**1**	**2**	**3**	**123**	....	....	....	....	....
1990-91	**Pittsburgh**	**NHL**	**23**	**1**	**1**	**2**	**71**	....	....	....	....	....
	Muskegon	IHL	3	1	0	1	18	....	....	....	....	....
1991-92	**Pittsburgh**	**NHL**	**50**	**0**	**0**	**0**	**175**	**5**	**0**	**0**	**0**	**2**
1992-93	**Pittsburgh**	**NHL**	**26**	**0**	**0**	**0**	**60**	....	....	....	....	....
1993-94	Kalamazoo	IHL	45	2	3	5	176	4	0	0	0	18
	NHL Totals		**208**	**5**	**8**	**13**	**759**	**17**	**0**	**0**	**0**	**42**

Signed as a free agent by **NY Rangers**, October 8, 1985. Traded to **Minnesota** by **NY Rangers** with Dave Gagne for Jari Gronstrand and Paul Boutilier, October 8, 1987. Claimed by **Pittsburgh** in NHL Waiver Draft, October 3, 1988.

CAVALLINI, GINO

Left wing. Shoots left. 6'1", 215 lbs. Born, Toronto, Ont., November 24, 1962.

			Regular Season					Playoffs				
Season	Club	Lea	GP	G	A	TP	PIM	GP	G	A	TP	PIM
1982-83	Bowling Green	CCHA	40	8	16	24	52	....	....	....	....	....
1983-84	Bowling Green	CCHA	43	25	23	48	16	....	....	....	....	....
1984-85	**Calgary**	**NHL**	**27**	**6**	**10**	**16**	**14**	**3**	**0**	**0**	**0**	**4**
	Moncton	AHL	51	29	19	48	28	....	....	....	....	....
1985-86	**Calgary**	**NHL**	**27**	**7**	**7**	**14**	**26**	....	....	....	....	....
	Moncton	AHL	4	3	2	5	7	....	....	....	....	....
	St. Louis	**NHL**	**30**	**6**	**5**	**11**	**36**	**17**	**4**	**5**	**9**	**10**
1986-87	**St. Louis**	**NHL**	**80**	**18**	**26**	**44**	**54**	**6**	**3**	**1**	**4**	**2**
1987-88	**St. Louis**	**NHL**	**64**	**15**	**17**	**32**	**62**	**10**	**5**	**5**	**10**	**19**
1988-89	**St. Louis**	**NHL**	**74**	**20**	**23**	**43**	**79**	**9**	**0**	**2**	**2**	**17**
1989-90	**St. Louis**	**NHL**	**80**	**15**	**15**	**30**	**77**	**12**	**1**	**3**	**4**	**12**
1990-91	**St. Louis**	**NHL**	**78**	**8**	**27**	**35**	**81**	**13**	**1**	**3**	**4**	**2**
1991-92	**St. Louis**	**NHL**	**48**	**9**	**7**	**16**	**40**	....	....	....	....	....
	Quebec	**NHL**	**18**	**1**	**7**	**8**	**4**	....	....	....	....	....
1992-93	**Quebec**	**NHL**	**67**	**9**	**15**	**24**	**34**	**4**	**0**	**0**	**0**	**0**
1993-94	Milwaukee	IHL	78	43	35	78	64	4	3	4	7	6
	NHL Totals		**593**	**114**	**159**	**273**	**507**	**74**	**14**	**19**	**33**	**66**

Signed as a free agent by **Calgary**, May 16, 1984. Traded to **St. Louis** by **Calgary** with Eddy Beers and Charles Bourgeois for Joe Mullen, Terry Johnson and Rik Wilson, February 1, 1986. Claimed on waivers by **Quebec** from **St. Louis**, February 27, 1992.

CAVALLINI, PAUL — DAL.

Defense. Shoots left. 6'1", 210 lbs. Born, Toronto, Ont., October 13, 1965.
(Washington's 9th choice, 205th overall, in 1984 Entry Draft).

			Regular Season					Playoffs				
Season	Club	Lea	GP	G	A	TP	PIM	GP	G	A	TP	PIM
1984-85	Providence	H.E.	37	4	10	14	52	....	....	....	....	....
1985-86	Cdn. Olympic	....	52	1	11	12	95	....	....	....	....	....
	Binghamton	AHL	15	3	4	7	20	6	0	2	2	56
1986-87	**Washington**	**NHL**	**6**	**0**	**2**	**2**	**8**	....	....	....	....	....
	Binghamton	AHL	66	12	24	36	188	13	2	7	9	35
1987-88	**Washington**	**NHL**	**24**	**2**	**3**	**5**	**66**	....	....	....	....	....
	St. Louis	**NHL**	**48**	**4**	**7**	**11**	**86**	**10**	**1**	**6**	**7**	**26**
1988-89	**St. Louis**	**NHL**	**65**	**4**	**20**	**24**	**128**	**10**	**2**	**2**	**4**	**14**
1989-90a	**St. Louis**	**NHL**	**80**	**8**	**39**	**47**	**106**	**12**	**2**	**3**	**5**	**20**
1990-91	**St. Louis**	**NHL**	**67**	**10**	**25**	**35**	**89**	**13**	**2**	**3**	**5**	**20**
1991-92	**St. Louis**	**NHL**	**66**	**10**	**25**	**35**	**95**	**4**	**0**	**1**	**1**	**6**
1992-93	**St. Louis**	**NHL**	**11**	**1**	**4**	**5**	**10**	....	....	....	....	....
	Washington	**NHL**	**71**	**5**	**8**	**13**	**46**	**6**	**0**	**2**	**2**	**18**
1993-94	**Dallas**	**NHL**	**74**	**11**	**33**	**44**	**82**	**9**	**1**	**8**	**9**	**4**
	NHL Totals		**512**	**55**	**166**	**221**	**716**	**64**	**8**	**25**	**33**	**108**

a Won Alka-Seltzer Plus Award (1990)

Played in NHL All-Star Game (1990)

Traded to **St. Louis** by **Washington** for Montreal's second round choice (previously acquired by St. Louis — Washington selected Wade Bartley) in 1988 Entry Draft, December 11, 1987. Traded to **Washington** by **St. Louis** for Kevin Miller, November 2, 1992. Traded to **Dallas** by **Washington** for future considerations (Enrico Ciccone, June 25, 1993), June 20, 1993.

CHABOT, JOHN (shuh-BAHT)

Center. Shoots left. 6'2", 200 lbs. Born, Summerside, P.E.I., May 18, 1962.
(Montreal's 3rd choice, 40th overall, in 1980 Entry Draft).

			Regular Season					Playoffs				
Season	Club	Lea	GP	G	A	TP	PIM	GP	G	A	TP	PIM
1979-80	Hull	QMJHL	68	26	57	83	28	4	1	2	3	0
1980-81	Hull	QMJHL	70	27	62	89	24					
	Nova Scotia	AHL	1	0	0	0	0	2	0	0	0	0
1981-82a	Sherbrooke	QMJHL	62	34	*109	143	42	19	6	26	32	6
1982-83	Nova Scotia	AHL	76	16	73	89	19	7	1	3	4	0
1983-84	**Montreal**	**NHL**	**56**	**18**	**25**	**43**	**13**	**11**	**1**	**4**	**5**	**0**
1984-85	**Montreal**	**NHL**	**10**	**1**	**6**	**7**	**2**					
	Pittsburgh	**NHL**	**67**	**8**	**45**	**53**	**12**					
1985-86	**Pittsburgh**	**NHL**	**77**	**14**	**31**	**45**	**6**					
1986-87	**Pittsburgh**	**NHL**	**72**	**14**	**22**	**36**	**8**					
1987-88	**Detroit**	**NHL**	**78**	**13**	**44**	**57**	**10**	**16**	**4**	**15**	**19**	**2**
1988-89	**Detroit**	**NHL**	**52**	**2**	**10**	**12**	**6**	**6**	**1**	**1**	**2**	**0**
	Adirondack	AHL	8	3	12	15	0					
1989-90	**Detroit**	**NHL**	**69**	**9**	**40**	**49**	**24**					
1990-91	**Detroit**	**NHL**	**27**	**5**	**5**	**10**	**4**					
	Adirondack	AHL	27	11	30	41	4	2	0	1	1	0
1991-92	Milano	Italy	18	10	36	46	4	12	3	13	16	2
1992-93	Preussen Berlin	Ger.	20	10	17	27	14					
1993-94	Preussen Berlin	Ger.	32	9	29	38	27					
	NHL Totals		**508**	**84**	**228**	**312**	**85**	**33**	**6**	**20**	**26**	**2**

a QMJHL First All-Star Team (1982)

Traded to **Pittsburgh** by **Montreal** for Ron Flockhart, November 9, 1984. Signed as a free agent by **Detroit**, June 25, 1987.

CHALIFOUX, DENIS (SHAL-ih-foo)

Center. Shoots right. 5'8", 165 lbs. Born, Laval, Que., February 28, 1971.
(Hartford's 11th choice, 246th overall, in 1990 Entry Draft).

			Regular Season					Playoffs				
Season	Club	Lea	GP	G	A	TP	PIM	GP	G	A	TP	PIM
1989-90	Laval	QMJHL	70	41	68	109	32	14	*14	14	*28	14
1990-91a	Laval	QMJHL	67	38	79	117	77	4	1	1	2	4
1991-92	Springfield	AHL	66	17	20	37	26	4	1	0	1	4
1992-93	Springfield	AHL	64	17	27	44	22	15	5	8	13	14
1993-94	Springfield	AHL	44	14	38	52	24					

a QMJHL Second All-Star Team (1991)

CHAMBERS, SHAWN T.B.

Defense. Shoots left. 6'2", 200 lbs. Born, Royal Oaks, MI, October 11, 1966.
(Minnesota's 1st choice, 4th overall, in 1987 Supplemental Draft).

			Regular Season					Playoffs				
Season	Club	Lea	GP	G	A	TP	PIM	GP	G	A	TP	PIM
1985-86	Alaska-Fair.	G.N.	25	15	21	36	34					
1986-87	Alaska-Fair.	G.N.	28	8	29	37	84					
	Seattle	WHL	28	8	25	33	58					
	Fort Wayne	IHL	12	2	6	8	0	10	1	4	5	5
1987-88	**Minnesota**	**NHL**	**19**	**1**	**7**	**8**	**21**					
	Kalamazoo	IHL	19	1	6	7	22					
1988-89	**Minnesota**	**NHL**	**72**	**5**	**19**	**24**	**80**	**3**	**0**	**2**	**2**	**0**
1989-90	**Minnesota**	**NHL**	**78**	**8**	**18**	**26**	**81**	**7**	**2**	**1**	**3**	**10**
1990-91	**Minnesota**	**NHL**	**29**	**1**	**3**	**4**	**24**	**23**	**0**	**7**	**7**	**16**
	Kalamazoo	IHL	3	1	1	2	0					
1991-92	**Washington**	**NHL**	**2**	**0**	**0**	**0**	**2**					
	Baltimore	AHL	5	2	3	5	9					
1992-93	**Tampa Bay**	**NHL**	**55**	**10**	**29**	**39**	**36**					
	Atlanta	IHL	6	0	2	2	18					
1993-94	**Tampa Bay**	**NHL**	**66**	**11**	**23**	**34**	**23**					
	NHL Totals		**321**	**36**	**99**	**135**	**267**	**33**	**2**	**10**	**12**	**26**

Traded to **Washington** by **Minnesota** for Steve Maltais and Trent Klatt, June 21, 1991. Claimed by **Tampa Bay** from **Washington** in Expansion Draft, June 18, 1992.

CHAPMAN, BRIAN

Defense. Shoots left. 6', 195 lbs. Born, Brockville, Ont., February 10, 1968.
(Hartford's 3rd choice, 74th overall, in 1986 Entry Draft).

			Regular Season					Playoffs				
Season	Club	Lea	GP	G	A	TP	PIM	GP	G	A	TP	PIM
1985-86	Belleville	OHL	66	6	31	37	168	24	2	6	8	54
1986-87	Belleville	OHL	54	4	32	36	142	6	1	1	2	10
1987-88	Belleville	OHL	63	11	57	68	180	6	1	4	5	13
1988-89	Binghamton	AHL	71	5	25	30	216					
1989-90	Binghamton	AHL	68	2	15	17	180					
1990-91	**Hartford**	**NHL**	**3**	**0**	**0**	**0**	**29**					
	Springfield	AHL	60	4	23	27	200	18	1	4	5	62
1991-92	Springfield	AHL	73	3	26	29	245	10	2	2	4	25
1992-93	Springfield	AHL	72	17	34	51	212	15	2	5	7	43
1993-94	Phoenix	IHL	78	6	35	41	280					
	NHL Totals		**3**	**0**	**0**	**0**	**29**					

Signed as a free agent by **Los Angeles**, July 16, 1993.

CHARBONNEAU, JOSE (SHAHR-buh-noh, JOH-see) VAN.

Right wing. Shoots right. 6', 195 lbs. Born, Ferme-Neuve, Que., November 21, 1966.
(Montreal's 1st choice, 12th overall, in 1985 Entry Draft).

			Regular Season					Playoffs				
Season	Club	Lea	GP	G	A	TP	PIM	GP	G	A	TP	PIM
1983-84	Drummondville	QMJHL	65	31	59	90	110					
1984-85	Drummondville	QMJHL	46	34	40	74	91	12	5	10	15	20
1985-86	Drummondville	QMJHL	57	44	45	89	158	23	16	20	36	40
1986-87	Sherbrooke	AHL	72	14	27	41	94	16	5	12	17	17
1987-88	**Montreal**	**NHL**	**16**	**0**	**2**	**2**	**6**	**8**	**0**	**0**	**0**	**4**
	Sherbrooke	AHL	55	30	35	65	108					
1988-89	**Montreal**	**NHL**	**9**	**1**	**3**	**4**	**6**					
	Sherbrooke	AHL	33	13	15	28	95					
	Vancouver	**NHL**	**13**	**0**	**1**	**1**	**6**					
	Milwaukee	IHL	13	8	5	13	46	10	3	2	5	23
1989-90	Milwaukee	IHL	65	23	38	61	137	5	0	1	1	8
1990-91	Cdn. National	....	56	22	29	51	54					
1991-92						DID NOT PLAY						
1992-93						DID NOT PLAY						
1993-94	**Vancouver**	**NHL**	**30**	**7**	**7**	**14**	**49**	**3**	**1**	**0**	**1**	**4**
	Hamilton	AHL	7	3	2	5	8					
	NHL Totals		**68**	**8**	**13**	**21**	**67**	**11**	**1**	**0**	**1**	**8**

Traded to **Vancouver** by **Montreal** for Dan Woodley, January 25, 1989. Signed as a free agent by **Vancouver**, October 3, 1993.

CHARLAND, CARL NYI

Left wing. Shoots left. 5'11", 180 lbs. Born, Chicoutimi, Que., May 13, 1975.
(NY Islanders' 11th choice, 274th overall, in 1993 Entry Draft).

			Regular Season					Playoffs				
Season	Club	Lea	GP	G	A	TP	PIM	GP	G	A	TP	PIM
1992-93	Hull	QMJHL	70	8	12	20	122	10	1	0	1	36
1993-94	Hull	QMJHL	65	15	19	34	223	19	3	3	6	38

CHARRON, ERIC T.B.

Defense. Shoots left. 6'3", 192 lbs. Born, Verdun, Que., January 14, 1970.
(Montreal's 1st choice, 20th overall, in 1988 Entry Draft).

			Regular Season					Playoffs				
Season	Club	Lea	GP	G	A	TP	PIM	GP	G	A	TP	PIM
1987-88	Trois-Rivières	QMJHL	67	3	13	16	135					
1988-89	Trois-Rivières	QMJHL	38	2	16	18	111					
	Verdun	QMJHL	28	2	15	17	66					
	Sherbrooke	AHL	1	0	0	0	0					
1989-90	St-Hyacinthe	QMJHL	68	13	38	51	152	11	3	4	7	67
	Sherbrooke	AHL	....	....	....	....	....	2	0	0	0	0
1990-91	Fredericton	AHL	71	1	11	12	108	2	1	0	1	29
1991-92	Fredericton	AHL	59	2	11	13	98	6	1	0	1	4
1992-93	**Montreal**	**NHL**	**3**	**0**	**0**	**0**	**2**					
	Fredericton	AHL	54	3	13	16	93					
	Atlanta	IHL	11	0	2	2	12	3	0	1	1	6
1993-94	**Tampa Bay**	**NHL**	**4**	**0**	**0**	**0**	**2**					
	Atlanta	IHL	66	5	18	23	144	14	1	4	5	28
	NHL Totals		**7**	**0**	**0**	**0**	**4**					

Traded to **Tampa Bay** by **Montreal** with Alain Cote and future considerations (Donald Dufresne, June 18, 1993) for Rob Ramage, March 20, 1993.

CHARTIER, SCOTT (SHAR-tee-yayr) ANA.

Defense. Shoots right. 6'1", 200 lbs. Born, St. Lazare, Man., January 19, 1972.

			Regular Season					Playoffs				
Season	Club	Lea	GP	G	A	TP	PIM	GP	G	A	TP	PIM
1992-93	W. Michigan	CCHA	38	6	23	29	84					
1993-94	San Diego	IHL	49	2	6	8	84	4	0	0	0	6

Signed as a free agent by **Anaheim**, July 30, 1993.

CHASE, DON MTL.

Center. Shoots right. 5'11", 190 lbs. Born, Springfield, MA, March 17, 1974.
(Montreal's 7th choice, 116th overall, in 1992 Entry Draft).

			Regular Season					Playoffs				
Season	Club	Lea	GP	G	A	TP	PIM	GP	G	A	TP	PIM
1992-93	Boston College	H.E.	38	7	5	12	48					
1993-94	Boston College	H.E.	35	14	13	27	58					

CHASE, KELLY ST.L.

Right wing. Shoots right. 5'11", 195 lbs. Born, Porcupine Plain, Sask., October 25, 1967.

			Regular Season					Playoffs				
Season	Club	Lea	GP	G	A	TP	PIM	GP	G	A	TP	PIM
1985-86	Saskatoon	WHL	57	7	18	25	172	10	3	4	7	37
1986-87	Saskatoon	WHL	68	17	29	46	285	11	2	8	10	37
1987-88	Saskatoon	WHL	70	21	34	55	*343	9	3	5	8	32
1988-89	Peoria	IHL	38	14	7	21	278					
1989-90	**St. Louis**	**NHL**	**43**	**1**	**3**	**4**	**244**	**9**	**1**	**0**	**1**	**46**
	Peoria	IHL	10	1	2	3	76					
1990-91	**St. Louis**	**NHL**	**2**	**1**	**0**	**1**	**15**	**6**	**0**	**0**	**0**	**18**
	Peoria	IHL	61	20	34	54	406	10	4	3	7	61
1991-92	**St. Louis**	**NHL**	**46**	**1**	**2**	**3**	**264**	**1**	**0**	**0**	**0**	**7**
1992-93	**St. Louis**	**NHL**	**49**	**2**	**5**	**7**	**204**					
1993-94	**St. Louis**	**NHL**	**68**	**2**	**5**	**7**	**278**	**4**	**0**	**1**	**1**	**6**
	NHL Totals		**208**	**7**	**15**	**22**	**1005**	**20**	**1**	**1**	**2**	**77**

Signed as a free agent by **St. Louis**, February 23, 1988.

CHASSE, DENIS (shah-SAY) ST.L.

Right wing. Shoots right. 6'2", 190 lbs. Born, Montreal, Que., February 7, 1970.

			Regular Season					Playoffs				
Season	Club	Lea	GP	G	A	TP	PIM	GP	G	A	TP	PIM
1987-88	St-Jean	QMJHL	13	0	1	1	2	1	0	0	0	0
1988-89	Verdun	QMJHL	38	12	12	24	61					
	Drummondville	QMJHL	30	15	16	31	77	3	0	2	2	28
1989-90	Drummondville	QMJHL	34	14	29	43	85					
	Chicoutimi	QMJHL	33	19	27	46	105	7	7	4	11	50
1990-91	Drummondville	QMJHL	62	47	54	101	246	13	9	11	20	56
1991-92	Halifax	AHL	73	26	35	61	254					
1992-93	Halifax	AHL	75	35	41	76	242					
1993-94	Cornwall	AHL	48	27	39	66	194					
	St. Louis	**NHL**	**3**	**0**	**1**	**1**	**15**	**4**	**0**	**1**	**1**	**6**
	NHL Totals		**3**	**0**	**1**	**1**	**15**	**4**	**0**	**1**	**1**	**6**

Signed as a free agent by **Quebec**, May 14, 1991. Traded to **St. Louis** by **Quebec** with Steve Duchesne for Garth Butcher, Ron Sutter and Bob Bassen, January 23, 1994.

CHEBATOR, BOB TOR.

Left wing. Shoots left. 6', 190 lbs. Born, Arlington, MA, December 1, 1970.
(Toronto's 9th choice, 199th overall, in 1990 Entry Draft).

			Regular Season					Playoffs				
Season	Club	Lea	GP	G	A	TP	PIM	GP	G	A	TP	PIM
1990-91	N. Hampshire	H.E.	33	4	2	6	14					
1991-92	N. Hampshire	H.E.	36	5	6	11	24					
1992-93	N. Hampshire	H.E.	38	3	10	13	68					
1993-94	N. Hampshire	H.E.	40	4	8	12	50					

CHECCO, NICHOLAS QUE.

Center. Shoots left. 5'11", 185 lbs. Born, Minneapolis, MN, November 18, 1974.
(Quebec's 7th choice, 137th overall, in 1993 Entry Draft).

			Regular Season					Playoffs				
Season	Club	Lea	GP	G	A	TP	PIM	GP	G	A	TP	PIM
1992-93	Bloom'ton-Jeff.	HS	26	22	23	45	18					
1993-94	U. Minnesota	WCHA	41	7	5	12	28					

CHELIOS, CHRIS (CHELL-EE-ohs) CHI.

Defense. Shoots right. 6'1", 186 lbs. Born, Chicago, IL, January 25, 1962.
(Montreal's 5th choice, 40th overall, in 1981 Entry Draft).

			Regular Season					Playoffs				
Season	Club	Lea	GP	G	A	TP	PIM	GP	G	A	TP	PIM
1981-82	U. Wisconsin	WCHA	43	6	43	49	50	....	....	....	....	....
1982-83ab	U. Wisconsin	WCHA	26	9	17	26	50	....	....	....	....	....
1983-84	U.S. National	....	60	14	35	49	58	....	....	....	....	....
	U.S. Olympic	....	6	0	4	4	8	....	....	....	....	....
	Montreal	NHL	12	0	2	2	12	15	1	9	10	17
1984-85c	Montreal	NHL	74	9	55	64	87	9	2	8	10	17
1985-86	Montreal	NHL	41	8	26	34	67	20	2	9	11	49
1986-87	Montreal	NHL	71	11	33	44	124	17	4	9	13	38
1987-88	Montreal	NHL	71	20	41	61	172	11	3	1	4	29
1988-89de	Montreal	NHL	80	15	58	73	185	21	4	15	19	28
1989-90	Montreal	NHL	53	9	22	31	136	5	0	1	1	8
1990-91f	Chicago	NHL	77	12	52	64	192	6	1	7	8	46
1991-92	Chicago	NHL	80	9	47	56	245	18	6	15	21	37
1992-93de	Chicago	NHL	84	15	58	73	282	4	0	2	2	14
1993-94	Chicago	NHL	76	16	44	60	212	6	1	1	2	8
	NHL Totals		719	124	438	562	1714	132	24	77	101	291

a WCHA Second All-Star Team (1983)
b NCAA All-Tournament Team (1983)
c NHL All-Rookie Team (1985)
d NHL First All-Star Team (1989, 1993)
e Won Norris Trophy (1989, 1993)
f NHL Second All-Star Team (1991)

Played in NHL All-Star Game (1985, 1990-94)

Traded to **Chicago** by **Montreal** with Montreal's second round choice (Michael Pomichter) in 1991 Entry Draft for Denis Savard, June 29, 1990.

CHERBATURKIN, VLADIMIR NYI

Defense. Shoots left. 6'2", 189 lbs. Born, Tyumen, USSR, April 23, 1975.
(NY Islanders' 3rd choice, 66th overall, in 1993 Entry Draft).

			Regular Season					Playoffs				
Season	Club	Lea	GP	G	A	TP	PIM	GP	G	A	TP	PIM
1992-93	Elektrostal	CIS 2				UNAVAILABLE						
1993-94	Elektrostal	CIS 2	42	4	4	8	38	....	....	....	....	....

CHERBAYEV, ALEXANDER (chuhr-BIGH-ehv) S.J.

Left wing. Shoots left. 6'1", 190 lbs. Born, Voskresensk, USSR, August 13, 1973.
(San Jose's 3rd choice, 51st overall, in 1992 Entry Draft).

			Regular Season					Playoffs				
Season	Club	Lea	GP	G	A	TP	PIM	GP	G	A	TP	PIM
1990-91	Khimik	USSR	16	2	2	4	0	....	....	....	....	....
1991-92	Khimik	CIS	38	3	3	6	14	....	....	....	....	....
1992-93	Khimik	CIS	33	18	9	27	74	2	1	0	1	0
1993-94	Kansas City	IHL	43	17	15	32	100	....	....	....	....	....

CHEREDARYK, STEVE WPG.

Defense. Shoots left. 6'2", 197 lbs. Born, Calgary, Alta., November 20, 1975.
(Winnipeg's 4th choice, 82nd overall, in 1994 Entry Draft).

			Regular Season					Playoffs				
Season	Club	Lea	GP	G	A	TP	PIM	GP	G	A	TP	PIM
1987-88	Dynamo Riga	USSR	51	7	9	16	28	....	....	....	....	....
1988-89	Dynamo Riga	USSR	43	2	4	6	23	....	....	....	....	....
1992-93	Medicine Hat	WHL	67	1	9	10	88	10	0	1	1	16
1993-94	Medicine Hat	WHL	72	3	35	38	151	3	0	1	1	9

CHERNOMAZ, RICH (CHUHR-noh-mas)

Right wing. Shoots right. 5'8", 185 lbs. Born, Selkirk, Man., September 1, 1963.
(Colorado's 2nd choice, 26th overall, in 1981 Entry Draft).

			Regular Season					Playoffs				
Season	Club	Lea	GP	G	A	TP	PIM	GP	G	A	TP	PIM
1980-81	Victoria	WHL	72	49	64	113	92	15	11	15	26	38
1981-82	Colorado	NHL	2	0	0	0	0	....	....	....	....	....
	Victoria	WHL	49	36	62	98	69	4	1	2	3	13
1982-83a	Victoria	WHL	64	71	53	124	113	12	10	5	15	18
1983-84	New Jersey	NHL	7	2	1	3	2	....	....	....	....	....
	Maine	AHL	69	17	29	46	39	2	0	1	1	0
1984-85	New Jersey	NHL	3	0	2	2	2	....	....	....	....	....
	Maine	AHL	64	17	34	51	64	10	2	2	4	4
1985-86	Maine	AHL	78	21	28	49	82	5	0	0	0	2
1986-87	New Jersey	NHL	25	6	4	10	8	....	....	....	....	....
	Maine	AHL	58	35	27	62	65	....	....	....	....	....
1987-88	Calgary	NHL	2	1	0	1	0	....	....	....	....	....
b	Salt Lake	IHL	73	48	47	95	122	18	4	14	18	30
1988-89	Calgary	NHL	1	0	0	0	0	....	....	....	....	....
	Salt Lake	IHL	81	33	68	101	122	14	7	5	12	47
1989-90	Salt Lake	IHL	65	39	35	74	170	11	6	6	12	32
1990-91b	Salt Lake	IHL	81	39	58	97	213	4	3	1	4	8
1991-92	Calgary	NHL	11	0	0	0	6	....	....	....	....	....
	Salt Lake	IHL	66	20	40	60	201	5	1	2	3	10
1992-93	Salt Lake	IHL	76	26	48	74	172	....	....	....	....	....
1993-94cd	St. John's	AHL	78	45	65	110	199	11	5	11	16	18
	NHL Totals		51	9	7	16	18	....	....	....	....	....

a WHL First All-Star Team (1983)
b IHL Second All-Star Team (1988, 1991)
c AHL First All-Star Team (1994)
d Won Les Cunningham Plaque (MVP - AHL) (1994)

Signed as a free agent by **Calgary**, August 4, 1987. Signed as a free agent by **Toronto**, August 3, 1993.

CHERREY, SCOTT WSH.

Left wing. Shoots left. 6'1", 199 lbs. Born, Drayton, Ont., May 27, 1976.
(Washington's 3rd choice, 41st overall, in 1994 Entry Draft).

			Regular Season					Playoffs				
Season	Club	Lea	GP	G	A	TP	PIM	GP	G	A	TP	PIM
1992-93	Listowel	Jr. B	46	17	10	27	63	....	....	....	....	....
1993-94	North Bay	OHL	63	15	26	41	45	18	5	3	8	10

CHERVYAKOV, DENIS (CHAIR-vuh-kahf) BOS

Defense. Shoots left. 6', 185 lbs. Born, Leningrad, USSR, April 20, 1970.
(Boston's 9th choice, 256th overall, in 1992 Entry Draft).

			Regular Season					Playoffs				
Season	Club	Lea	GP	G	A	TP	PIM	GP	G	A	TP	PIM
1990-91	Leningrad	USSR	28	2	1	3	40	....	....	....	....	....
1991-92	Riga	CIS	14	0	1	1	12	....	....	....	....	....
1992-93	Boston	NHL	2	0	0	0	2	....	....	....	....	....
	Providence	AHL	48	4	12	16	99	....	....	....	....	....
	Atlanta	IHL	1	0	0	0	0	....	....	....	....	....
1993-94	Providence	AHL	58	2	16	18	128	....	....	....	....	....
	NHL Totals		2	0	0	0	2	....	....	....	....	....

CHEVELDAYOFF, KEVIN (sheh-vehl-DAY-ahf)

Defense. Shoots right. 6', 202 lbs. Born, Saskatoon, Sask., February 4, 1970.
(NY Islanders' 1st choice, 16th overall, in 1988 Entry Draft).

			Regular Season					Playoffs				
Season	Club	Lea	GP	G	A	TP	PIM	GP	G	A	TP	PIM
1986-87	Brandon	WHL	70	0	16	16	259	....	....	....	....	....
1987-88	Brandon	WHL	71	3	29	32	265	4	0	2	2	20
1988-89	Brandon	WHL	40	4	12	16	135	....	....	....	....	....
1989-90	Brandon	WHL	33	5	12	17	56	....	....	....	....	....
	Springfield	AHL	4	0	0	0	0	....	....	....	....	....
1990-91	Capital Dist.	AHL	76	0	14	14	203	....	....	....	....	....
1991-92	Capital Dist.	AHL	44	0	4	4	110	7	0	0	0	22
1992-93	Capital Dist.	AHL	79	3	8	11	113	4	0	1	1	8
1993-94	Salt Lake	IHL	73	0	4	4	216	....	....	....	....	....

CHIASSON, STEVE (CHAY-sahn) CGY.

Defense. Shoots left. 6'1", 205 lbs. Born, Barrie, Ont., April 14, 1967.
(Detroit's 3rd choice, 50th overall, in 1985 Entry Draft).

			Regular Season					Playoffs				
Season	Club	Lea	GP	G	A	TP	PIM	GP	G	A	TP	PIM
1984-85	Guelph	OHL	61	8	22	30	139	....	....	....	....	....
1985-86	Guelph	OHL	54	12	30	42	126	18	10	10	20	37
1986-87	Detroit	NHL	45	1	4	5	73	2	0	0	0	19
1987-88	Detroit	NHL	29	2	9	11	57	9	2	2	4	31
	Adirondack	AHL	23	6	11	17	58	....	....	....	....	....
1988-89	Detroit	NHL	65	12	35	47	149	5	2	1	3	6
1989-90	Detroit	NHL	67	14	28	42	114	....	....	....	....	....
1990-91	Detroit	NHL	42	3	17	20	80	5	3	1	4	19
1991-92	Detroit	NHL	62	10	24	34	136	11	1	5	6	12
1992-93	Detroit	NHL	79	12	50	62	155	7	2	2	4	19
1993-94	Detroit	NHL	82	13	33	46	122	7	2	3	5	2
	NHL Totals		471	67	200	267	886	46	12	14	26	108

Played in NHL All-Star Game (1993)

Traded to **Calgary** by **Detroit** for Mike Vernon, June 29, 1994.

CHIBIREV, IGOR (CHEE-bihr-ehv) HFD.

Center. Shoots left. 6', 180 lbs. Born, Kiev, USSR, April 19, 1968.
(Hartford's 8th choice, 266th overall, in 1993 Entry Draft).

			Regular Season					Playoffs				
Season	Club	Lea	GP	G	A	TP	PIM	GP	G	A	TP	PIM
1987-88	CSKA	USSR	29	5	1	6	8	....	....	....	....	....
1988-89	CSKA	USSR	34	7	9	16	16	....	....	....	....	....
1989-90	CSKA	USSR	46	8	2	10	12	....	....	....	....	....
1990-91	CSKA	USSR	40	10	9	19	4	....	....	....	....	....
1991-92	CSKA	CIS	38	21	17	38	46	....	....	....	....	....
1992-93	Fort Wayne	IHL	60	33	36	69	2	12	*7	13	20	2
1993-94	Hartford	NHL	37	4	11	15	2	....	....	....	....	....
	Springfield	AHL	36	28	23	51	4	....	....	....	....	....
	NHL Totals		37	4	11	15	2	....	....	....	....	....

CHINAKOV, VITALI (chih-NAH-khov)

Center. Shoots left. 5'11", 183 lbs. Born, Perm, USSR, January 15, 1972.
(NY Rangers' 10th choice, 235th overall, in 1991 Entry Draft).

			Regular Season					Playoffs				
Season	Club	Lea	GP	G	A	TP	PIM	GP	G	A	TP	PIM
1990-91	Torpedo Yaro.	USSR	21	1	2	3	10	....	....	....	....	....
1991-92	Torpedo Yaro.	CIS	18	4	1	5	4	....	....	....	....	....
1992-93	Torpedo Yaro.	CIS	3	0	0	0	0	....	....	....	....	....
	Molot Perm	CIS	20	2	4	6	12	....	....	....	....	....
1993-94	Molot Perm	CIS	45	14	10	24	....	....	....	....	....	....

CHITARONI, TERRY TOR.

Center. Shoots right. 5'11", 200 lbs. Born, Haileybury, Ont., December 9, 1972.
(Toronto's 2nd choice, 69th overall, in 1991 Entry Draft).

			Regular Season					Playoffs				
Season	Club	Lea	GP	G	A	TP	PIM	GP	G	A	TP	PIM
1988-89	Sudbury	OHL	58	17	23	40	103	....	....	....	....	....
1989-90	Sudbury	OHL	65	21	47	68	173	7	4	1	5	15
1990-91	Sudbury	OHL	61	28	43	71	162	5	1	1	2	18
1991-92	Sudbury	OHL	51	31	47	78	119	11	7	5	12	39
	St. John's	AHL	....	....	....	....	....	2	0	1	1	5
1992-93	St. John's	AHL	30	4	7	11	107	....	....	....	....	....
	Baltimore	AHL	16	2	1	3	14	....	....	....	....	....
1993-94	St. John's	AHL	19	2	2	4	43	....	....	....	....	....

CHORSKE, TOM (CHOHR-skee) N.J.

Right wing. Shoots right. 6'1", 205 lbs. Born, Minneapolis, MN, September 18, 1966.
(Montreal's 2nd choice, 16th overall, in 1985 Entry Draft).

			Regular Season					Playoffs				
Season	Club	Lea	GP	G	A	TP	PIM	GP	G	A	TP	PIM
1985-86	U. Minnesota	WCHA	39	6	4	10	16	....	....	....	....	....
1986-87	U. Minnesota	WCHA	47	20	22	42	20	....	....	....	....	....
1987-88	U.S. National	....	36	9	16	25	24	....	....	....	....	....
1988-89a	U. Minnesota	WCHA	37	25	24	49	28	....	....	....	....	....
1989-90	Montreal	NHL	14	3	1	4	2	....	....	....	....	....
	Sherbrooke	AHL	59	22	24	46	54	12	4	4	8	8
1990-91	Montreal	NHL	57	9	11	20	32	....	....	....	....	....
1991-92	New Jersey	NHL	76	19	17	36	32	7	0	3	3	4
1992-93	New Jersey	NHL	50	7	12	19	25	1	0	0	0	0
	Utica	AHL	6	1	4	5	2	....	....	....	....	....
1993-94	New Jersey	NHL	76	21	20	41	32	20	4	3	7	0
	NHL Totals		273	59	61	120	123	28	4	6	10	4

a WCHA First All-Star Team (1989)

Traded to **New Jersey** by **Montreal** with Stephane Richer for Kirk Muller and Roland Melanson, September 20, 1991.

HRISTIAN, DAVE

ght wing. Shoots right. 5'11", 175 lbs. Born, Warroad, MN, May 12, 1959.
Vinnipeg's 2nd choice, 40th overall, in 1979 Entry Draft).

			Regular Season					Playoffs				
eason	Club	Lea	GP	G	A	TP	PIM	GP	G	A	TP	PIM
977-78	North Dakota	WCHA	38	8	16	24	14	....	....	....	....	....
978-79	North Dakota	WCHA	40	22	24	46	22	....	....	....	....	....
979-80	U.S. National	....	59	10	20	30	26	....	....	....	....	....
	U.S. Olympic	....	7	0	8	8	6	....	....	....	....	....
	Winnipeg	**NHL**	**15**	**8**	**10**	**18**	**2**	....	....	....	....	....
980-81	**Winnipeg**	**NHL**	**80**	**28**	**43**	**71**	**22**	....	....	....	....	....
981-82	**Winnipeg**	**NHL**	**80**	**25**	**51**	**76**	**28**	**4**	**0**	**1**	**1**	**2**
982-83	**Winnipeg**	**NHL**	**55**	**18**	**26**	**44**	**23**	**3**	**0**	**0**	**0**	**0**
983-84	**Washington**	**NHL**	**80**	**29**	**52**	**81**	**28**	**8**	**5**	**4**	**9**	**5**
984-85	**Washington**	**NHL**	**80**	**26**	**43**	**69**	**14**	**5**	**1**	**1**	**2**	**0**
985-86	**Washington**	**NHL**	**80**	**41**	**42**	**83**	**15**	**9**	**4**	**4**	**8**	**0**
986-87	**Washington**	**NHL**	**76**	**23**	**27**	**50**	**8**	**7**	**1**	**3**	**4**	**6**
987-88	**Washington**	**NHL**	**80**	**37**	**21**	**58**	**26**	**14**	**5**	**6**	**11**	**6**
988-89	**Washington**	**NHL**	**80**	**34**	**31**	**65**	**12**	**6**	**1**	**1**	**2**	**0**
989-90	**Washington**	**NHL**	**28**	**3**	**8**	**11**	**4**	....	....	....	....	....
	Boston	**NHL**	**50**	**12**	**17**	**29**	**8**	**21**	**4**	**1**	**5**	**4**
990-91	**Boston**	**NHL**	**78**	**32**	**21**	**53**	**41**	**19**	**8**	**4**	**12**	**4**
991-92	**St. Louis**	**NHL**	**78**	**20**	**24**	**44**	**41**	**4**	**3**	**0**	**3**	**0**
992-93	**Chicago**	**NHL**	**60**	**4**	**14**	**18**	**12**	**1**	**0**	**0**	**0**	**0**
993-94	**Chicago**	**NHL**	**9**	**0**	**3**	**3**	**0**	**1**	**0**	**0**	**0**	**0**
	Indianapolis	IHL	40	8	18	26	6	....	....	....	....	....
	NHL Totals		**1009**	**340**	**433**	**773**	**284**	**102**	**32**	**25**	**57**	**27**

layed in NHL All-Star Game (1991)

Traded to **Washington** by **Winnipeg** for Washington's first round choice (Bob Dollas) in the 1983 Entry Draft, June 8, 1983. Traded to **Boston** by **Washington** for Bob Joyce, December 13, 1989. Acquired by **St. Louis** from **Boston** with Boston's third round choice (Vitali Prokhorov) in 1992 Entry Draft and Boston's seventh round choice (Lance Burns) in 1992 Entry Draft as compensation for Boston's free agent signings of Glen Featherstone and Dave Thomlinson, July 30, 1991. Claimed by **Chicago** from **St. Louis** in NHL Waiver Draft, October 4, 1992.

CHRISTIAN, JEFF — PIT.

Left wing. Shoots left. 6'1", 195 lbs. Born, Burlington, Ont., July 30, 1970.
(New Jersey's 2nd choice, 23rd overall, in 1988 Entry Draft).

			Regular Season					Playoffs				
Season	Club	Lea	GP	G	A	TP	PIM	GP	G	A	TP	PIM
1987-88	London	OHL	64	15	29	44	154	9	1	5	6	27
1988-89	London	OHL	60	27	30	57	221	20	3	4	7	56
1989-90	London	OHL	18	14	7	21	64	....	....	....	....	....
	Owen Sound	OHL	37	19	26	45	145	10	6	7	13	43
1990-91	Utica	AHL	80	24	42	66	165	....	....	....	....	....
1991-92	**New Jersey**	**NHL**	**2**	**0**	**0**	**0**	**2**	....	....	....	....	....
	Utica	AHL	76	27	24	51	198	4	0	0	0	16
1992-93	Utica	AHL	22	4	6	10	39	....	....	....	....	....
	Hamilton	AHL	11	2	5	7	35	....	....	....	....	....
	Cincinnati	IHL	36	5	12	17	113	....	....	....	....	....
1993-94	Albany	AHL	76	34	43	77	227	5	1	2	3	19
	NHL Totals		**2**	**0**	**0**	**0**	**2**	....	....	....	....	....

Signed as a free agent by **Pittsburgh**, August 2, 1994.

CHURLA, SHANE — DAL.

Right wing. Shoots right. 6'1", 200 lbs. Born, Fernie, B.C., June 24, 1965.
(Hartford's 4th choice, 110th overall, in 1985 Entry Draft).

			Regular Season					Playoffs				
Season	Club	Lea	GP	G	A	TP	PIM	GP	G	A	TP	PIM
1983-84	Medicine Hat	WHL	48	3	7	10	115	14	1	5	6	41
1984-85	Medicine Hat	WHL	70	14	20	34	370	9	1	0	1	55
1985-86	Binghamton	AHL	52	4	10	14	306	3	0	0	0	22
1986-87	**Hartford**	**NHL**	**20**	**0**	**1**	**1**	**78**	**2**	**0**	**0**	**0**	**42**
	Binghamton	AHL	24	1	5	6	249	....	....	....	....	....
1987-88	**Hartford**	**NHL**	**2**	**0**	**0**	**0**	**14**	....	....	....	....	....
	Binghamton	AHL	25	5	8	13	168	....	....	....	....	....
	Calgary	**NHL**	**29**	**1**	**5**	**6**	**132**	**7**	**0**	**1**	**1**	**17**
1988-89	**Calgary**	**NHL**	**5**	**0**	**0**	**0**	**25**	....	....	....	....	....
	Salt Lake	IHL	32	3	13	16	278	....	....	....	....	....
	Minnesota	**NHL**	**13**	**1**	**0**	**1**	**54**	....	....	....	....	....
1989-90	**Minnesota**	**NHL**	**53**	**2**	**3**	**5**	**292**	**7**	**0**	**0**	**0**	**44**
1990-91	**Minnesota**	**NHL**	**40**	**2**	**2**	**4**	**286**	**22**	**2**	**1**	**3**	**90**
1991-92	**Minnesota**	**NHL**	**57**	**4**	**1**	**5**	**278**	....	....	....	....	....
1992-93	**Minnesota**	**NHL**	**73**	**5**	**16**	**21**	**286**	....	....	....	....	....
1993-94	**Dallas**	**NHL**	**69**	**6**	**7**	**13**	**333**	**9**	**1**	**3**	**4**	**35**
	NHL Totals		**361**	**21**	**35**	**56**	**1778**	**47**	**3**	**5**	**8**	**228**

Traded to **Calgary** by **Hartford** with Dana Murzyn for Neil Sheehy, Carey Wilson, and the rights to Lane MacDonald, January 3, 1988. Traded to **Minnesota** by **Calgary** with Perry Berezan for Brian MacLellan and Minnesota's fourth round choice (Robert Reichel) in 1989 Entry Draft, March 4, 1989. Claimed by **San Jose** from **Minnesota** in Dispersal Draft, May 30, 1991. Traded to **Minnesota** by **San Jose** for Kelly Kisio, June 3, 1991.

CHYCHRUN, JEFF (CHIHK-ruhn) — HFD.

Defense. Shoots right. 6'4", 215 lbs. Born, LaSalle, Que., May 3, 1966.
(Philadelphia's 3rd choice, 37th overall, in 1984 Entry Draft).

			Regular Season					Playoffs				
Season	Club	Lea	GP	G	A	TP	PIM	GP	G	A	TP	PIM
1983-84	Kingston	OHL	63	1	13	14	137	....	....	....	....	....
1984-85	Kingston	OHL	58	4	10	14	206	....	....	....	....	....
1985-86	Kingston	OHL	61	4	21	25	127	10	2	1	3	17
	Hershey	AHL	....	....	....	....	....	4	0	1	1	9
	Kalamazoo	IHL	....	....	....	....	....	3	1	0	1	0
1986-87	**Philadelphia**	**NHL**	**1**	**0**	**0**	**0**	**4**	....	....	....	....	....
	Hershey	AHL	74	1	17	18	239	4	0	0	0	10
1987-88	**Philadelphia**	**NHL**	**3**	**0**	**0**	**0**	**4**	....	....	....	....	....
	Hershey	AHL	55	0	5	5	210	12	0	2	2	44
1988-89	**Philadelphia**	**NHL**	**80**	**1**	**4**	**5**	**245**	**19**	**0**	**2**	**2**	**65**
1989-90	**Philadelphia**	**NHL**	**79**	**2**	**7**	**9**	**250**	....	....	....	....	....
1990-91	**Philadelphia**	**NHL**	**36**	**0**	**6**	**6**	**105**	....	....	....	....	....
1991-92	**Los Angeles**	**NHL**	**26**	**0**	**3**	**3**	**76**	....	....	....	....	....
	Phoenix	IHL	3	0	0	0	6	....	....	....	....	....
	Pittsburgh	**NHL**	**17**	**0**	**1**	**1**	**35**	....	....	....	....	....
1992-93	**Pittsburgh**	**NHL**	**1**	**0**	**0**	**0**	**2**	....	....	....	....	....
	Los Angeles	**NHL**	**17**	**0**	**1**	**1**	**23**	....	....	....	....	....
	Phoenix	IHL	11	2	0	2	44	....	....	....	....	....
1993-94	**Edmonton**	**NHL**	**2**	**0**	**0**	**0**	**0**	....	....	....	....	....
	Cape Breton	AHL	41	2	16	18	111	....	....	....	....	....
	NHL Totals		**262**	**3**	**22**	**25**	**744**	**19**	**0**	**2**	**2**	**65**

Traded to **Los Angeles** by **Philadelphia** with Jari Kurri for Steve Duchesne, Steve Kasper and Los Angeles' fourth round choice (Aris Brimanis) in 1991 Entry Draft, May 30, 1991. Traded to **Pittsburgh** by **Los Angeles** with Brian Benning and Los Angeles' first round choice (later traded to Philadelphia — Philadelphia selected Jason Bowen) in 1992 Entry Draft, for Paul Coffey, February 19, 1992. Traded to **Los Angeles** by **Pittsburgh** for Peter Ahola, November 6, 1992. Traded to **Edmonton** by **Los Angeles** for a conditional draft choice in 1995 Entry Draft, November 2, 1993. Signed as a free agent by **Hartford**, May 27, 1994.

CHYNOWETH, DEAN (shih-NOWTH) — NYI

Defense. Shoots right. 6'2", 190 lbs. Born, Calgary, Alta., October 30, 1968.
(NY Islanders' 1st choice, 13th overall, in 1987 Entry Draft).

			Regular Season					Playoffs				
Season	Club	Lea	GP	G	A	TP	PIM	GP	G	A	TP	PIM
1985-86	Medicine Hat	WHL	69	3	12	15	208	17	3	2	5	52
1986-87	Medicine Hat	WHL	67	3	18	21	285	13	4	2	6	28
1987-88	Medicine Hat	WHL	64	1	21	22	274	16	0	6	6	*87
1988-89	**NY Islanders**	**NHL**	**6**	**0**	**0**	**0**	**48**	....	....	....	....	....
1989-90	**NY Islanders**	**NHL**	**20**	**0**	**2**	**2**	**39**	....	....	....	....	....
	Springfield	AHL	40	0	7	7	98	17	0	4	4	36
1990-91	**NY Islanders**	**NHL**	**25**	**1**	**1**	**2**	**59**	....	....	....	....	....
	Capital Dist.	AHL	44	1	5	6	176	....	....	....	....	....
1991-92	**NY Islanders**	**NHL**	**11**	**1**	**0**	**1**	**23**	....	....	....	....	....
	Capital Dist.	AHL	43	4	6	10	164	6	1	1	2	39
1992-93	Capital Dist.	AHL	52	3	10	13	197	4	0	1	1	9
1993-94	**NY Islanders**	**NHL**	**39**	**0**	**4**	**4**	**122**	**2**	**0**	**0**	**0**	**2**
	Salt Lake	IHL	5	0	1	1	33	....	....	....	....	....
	NHL Totals		**101**	**2**	**7**	**9**	**291**	**2**	**0**	**0**	**0**	**2**

CHYZOWSKI, DAVID (chih-ZOW-skee) — NYI

Left wing. Shoots left. 6'1", 190 lbs. Born, Edmonton, Alta., July 11, 1971.
(NY Islanders' 1st choice, 2nd overall, in 1989 Entry Draft).

			Regular Season					Playoffs				
Season	Club	Lea	GP	G	A	TP	PIM	GP	G	A	TP	PIM
1987-88	Kamloops	WHL	66	16	17	33	117	18	2	4	6	26
1988-89a	Kamloops	WHL	68	56	48	104	139	16	15	13	28	32
1989-90	**NY Islanders**	**NHL**	**34**	**8**	**6**	**14**	**45**	....	....	....	....	....
	Springfield	AHL	4	0	0	0	7	....	....	....	....	....
	Kamloops	WHL	4	5	2	7	17	17	11	6	17	46
1990-91	**NY Islanders**	**NHL**	**56**	**5**	**9**	**14**	**61**	....	....	....	....	....
	Capital Dist.	AHL	7	3	6	9	22	....	....	....	....	....
1991-92	**NY Islanders**	**NHL**	**12**	**1**	**1**	**2**	**17**	....	....	....	....	....
	Capital Dist.	AHL	55	15	18	33	121	6	1	1	2	23
1992-93	Capital Dist.	AHL	66	15	21	36	177	3	2	0	2	0
1993-94	**NY Islanders**	**NHL**	**3**	**1**	**0**	**1**	**4**	**2**	**0**	**0**	**0**	**0**
	Salt Lake	IHL	66	27	13	40	151	....	....	....	....	....
	NHL Totals		**105**	**15**	**16**	**31**	**127**	**2**	**0**	**0**	**0**	**0**

a WHL West All-Star Team (1989)

CIAVAGLIA, PETER

Center. Shoots left. 5'10", 173 lbs. Born, Albany, NY, July 15, 1969.
(Calgary's 8th choice, 145th overall, in 1987 Entry Draft).

			Regular Season					Playoffs				
Season	Club	Lea	GP	G	A	TP	PIM	GP	G	A	TP	PIM
1987-88	Harvard	ECAC	30	10	23	33	16	....	....	....	....	....
1988-89a	Harvard	ECAC	34	15	48	63	36	....	....	....	....	....
1989-90	Harvard	ECAC	28	17	18	35	22	....	....	....	....	....
1990-91ab	Harvard	ECAC	27	24	*38	*62	2	....	....	....	....	....
1991-92	**Buffalo**	**NHL**	**2**	**0**	**0**	**0**	**0**	....	....	....	....	....
	Rochester	AHL	77	37	61	98	16	6	2	5	7	6
1992-93	**Buffalo**	**NHL**	**3**	**0**	**0**	**0**	**0**	....	....	....	....	....
	Rochester	AHL	64	35	67	102	32	17	9	16	25	12
1993-94	Leksand	Swe.	39	14	18	32	34	....	....	....	....	....
	U.S. National	....	18	2	9	11	6	....	....	....	....	....
	U.S. Olympic	....	8	2	4	6	0	....	....	....	....	....
	NHL Totals		**5**	**0**	**0**	**0**	**0**	....	....	....	....	....

a ECAC Second All-Star Team (1989, 1991)
b NCAA East Second All-American Team (1991)

Signed as a free agent by **Buffalo**, August 30, 1991.

CICCARELLI, DINO
(sih-sih-REHL-ee) DET.

Right wing. Shoots right. 5'10", 185 lbs.   Born, Sarnia, Ont., February 8, 1960.

				Regular Season					Playoffs			
Season	Club	Lea	GP	G	A	TP	PIM	GP	G	A	TP	PIM
1977-78a	London	OHA	68	72	70	142	49	9	6	10	16	6
1978-79	London	OHA	30	8	11	19	35	7	3	5	8	0
1979-80	London	OHA	62	50	53	103	72	5	2	6	8	15
1980-81	**Minnesota**	**NHL**	32	18	12	30	29	19	14	7	21	25
	Oklahoma City	CHL	48	32	25	57	45					
1981-82	Minnesota	NHL	76	55	51	106	138	4	3	1	4	2
1982-83	Minnesota	NHL	77	37	38	75	94	9	4	6	10	11
1983-84	Minnesota	NHL	79	38	33	71	58	16	4	5	9	27
1984-85	Minnesota	NHL	51	15	17	32	41	9	3	3	6	8
1985-86	Minnesota	NHL	75	44	45	89	51	5	0	1	1	6
1986-87	Minnesota	NHL	80	52	51	103	88	....	....	....	....	....
1987-88	Minnesota	NHL	67	41	45	86	79	....	....	....	....	....
1988-89	Minnesota	NHL	65	32	27	59	64	....	....	....	....	....
	Washington	NHL	11	12	3	15	12	6	3	3	6	12
1989-90	Washington	NHL	80	41	38	79	122	8	8	3	11	6
1990-91	Washington	NHL	54	21	18	39	66	11	5	4	9	22
1991-92	Washington	NHL	78	38	38	76	78	7	5	4	9	14
1992-93	Detroit	NHL	82	41	56	97	81	7	4	2	6	16
1993-94	Detroit	NHL	66	28	29	57	73	7	5	2	7	14
	NHL Totals		**973**	**513**	**501**	**1014**	**1074**	**108**	**58**	**41**	**99**	**163**

a   OHA Second All-Star Team (1978)
Played in NHL All-Star Game (1982, 1983, 1989)
Signed as a free agent by **Minnesota**, September 28, 1979. Traded to **Washington** by **Minnesota** with Bob Rouse for Mike Gartner and Larry Murphy, March 7, 1989. Traded to **Detroit** by **Washington** for Kevin Miller, June 20, 1992.

CICCONE, ENRICO
(CHIH-koh-nee) T.B.

Defense. Shoots left. 6'4", 200 lbs.   Born, Montreal, Que., April 10, 1970.
(Minnesota's 5th choice, 92nd overall, in 1990 Entry Draft).

				Regular Season					Playoffs			
Season	Club	Lea	GP	G	A	TP	PIM	GP	G	A	TP	PIM
1987-88	Shawinigan	QMJHL	61	2	12	14	324	....	....	....	....	....
1988-89	Shawinigan	QMJHL	34	7	11	18	132	....	....	....	....	....
	Trois-Rivières	QMJHL	24	0	7	7	153	....	....	....	....	....
1989-90	Trois-Rivières	QMJHL	40	4	24	28	227	3	0	0	0	15
1990-91	Kalamazoo	IHL	57	4	9	13	384	4	0	1	1	32
1991-92	**Minnesota**	**NHL**	11	0	0	0	48	....	....	....	....	....
	Kalamazoo	IHL	53	4	16	20	406	10	0	1	1	58
1992-93	Minnesota	NHL	31	0	1	1	115	....	....	....	....	....
	Kalamazoo	IHL	13	1	3	4	50	....	....	....	....	....
	Hamilton	AHL	6	1	3	4	44	....	....	....	....	....
1993-94	Washington	NHL	46	1	1	2	174	....	....	....	....	....
	Portland	AHL	6	0	0	0	27	....	....	....	....	....
	Tampa Bay	**NHL**	11	0	1	1	52	....	....	....	....	....
	NHL Totals		**99**	**1**	**3**	**4**	**389**	....	....	....	....	....

Traded to **Washington** by **Dallas** to complete June 20, 1993 trade which sent Paul Cavallini to Dallas for future considerations, June 25, 1993. Traded to **Tampa Bay** by **Washington** with Washington's third round choice (later traded to Anaheim — Anaheim selected Craig Reichert) in 1994 Entry Draft and the return of future draft choices transferred in the Pat Elynuik trade for Joe Reekie, March 21, 1994.

CICHOCKI, CHRIS
(chih-HAH-kee)

Right wing. Shoots right. 5'11", 185 lbs.   Born, Detroit, MI, September 17, 1963.

				Regular Season					Playoffs			
Season	Club	Lea	GP	G	A	TP	PIM	GP	G	A	TP	PIM
1982-83	Michigan Tech	CCHA	36	12	10	22	10	....	....	....	....	....
1983-84	Michigan Tech	CCHA	40	25	20	45	36	....	....	....	....	....
1984-85	Michigan Tech	CCHA	40	30	24	54	14	....	....	....	....	....
1985-86	**Detroit**	**NHL**	59	10	11	21	21	....	....	....	....	....
	Adirondack	AHL	9	4	4	8	6	....	....	....	....	....
1986-87	**Detroit**	**NHL**	2	0	0	0	2	....	....	....	....	....
	Adirondack	AHL	55	31	34	65	27	....	....	....	....	....
	Maine	AHL	7	2	2	4	0	....	....	....	....	....
1987-88	**New Jersey**	**NHL**	5	1	0	1	2	....	....	....	....	....
	Utica	AHL	69	36	30	66	66	....	....	....	....	....
1988-89	**New Jersey**	**NHL**	2	0	1	1	2	....	....	....	....	....
	Utica	AHL	59	32	31	63	50	5	0	1	1	2
1989-90	Utica	AHL	11	3	1	4	10	....	....	....	....	....
	Binghamton	AHL	60	21	26	47	22	....	....	....	....	....
1990-91	Binghamton	AHL	80	35	30	65	70	9	0	4	4	2
1991-92	Binghamton	AHL	75	28	29	57	132	6	5	4	9	4
1992-93	Binghamton	AHL	65	23	29	52	78	9	3	2	5	25
1993-94	Cincinnati	IHL	69	22	20	42	101	11	2	2	4	12
	NHL Totals		**68**	**11**	**12**	**23**	**27**	....	....	....	....	....

Signed as a free agent by **Detroit**, June 28, 1985. Traded to **New Jersey** by **Detroit** with Detroit's third round choice (later traded to Buffalo – Buffalo selected Andrew MacVicar) in 1987 Entry Draft for Mel Bridgman, March 9, 1987. Traded to **Hartford** by **New Jersey** for Jim Thomson, October 31, 1989. Signed as a free agent by **NY Rangers**, September 6, 1990.

CIERNY, JOZEF
(chee-ER-nee) EDM.

Left wing. Shoots left. 6'2", 185 lbs.   Born, Zvolen, Czech., May 13, 1974.
(Buffalo's 2nd choice, 35th overall, in 1992 Entry Draft).

				Regular Season					Playoffs			
Season	Club	Lea	GP	G	A	TP	PIM	GP	G	A	TP	PIM
1991-92	ZTK Zvolen	Czech.2	26	10	3	13	8	....	....	....	....	....
1992-93	Rochester	AHL	54	27	27	54	36	....	....	....	....	....
1993-94	**Edmonton**	**NHL**	1	0	0	0	0	....	....	....	....	....
	Cape Breton	AHL	73	30	27	57	88	4	1	1	2	4
	NHL Totals		**1**	**0**	**0**	**0**	**0**	....	....	....	....	....

Traded to **Edmonton** by **Buffalo** with Buffalo's fourth round choice (Jussi Tarvainen) in 1994 Entry Draft for Craig Simpson, September 1, 1993.

CIGER, ZDENO
(SEE-gur) EDM.

Left wing. Shoots left. 6'1", 190 lbs.   Born, Martin, Czech., October 19, 1969.
(New Jersey's 3rd choice, 54th overall, in 1988 Entry Draft).

				Regular Season					Playoffs			
Season	Club	Lea	GP	G	A	TP	PIM	GP	G	A	TP	PIM
1987-88	Dukla Trencin	Czech.	8	3	4	7	2	....	....	....	....	....
1988-89	Dukla Trencin	Czech.	43	18	13	31	18	....	....	....	....	....
1989-90	Dukla Trencin	Czech.	53	18	28	46		....	....	....	....	....
1990-91	**New Jersey**	**NHL**	45	8	17	25	8	6	0	2	2	
	Utica	AHL	8	5	4	9	2	....	....	....	....	....
1991-92	**New Jersey**	**NHL**	20	6	5	11	10	7	2	4	6	
1992-93	New Jersey	NHL	27	4	8	12	2	....	....	....	....	....
	Edmonton	NHL	37	9	15	24	6	....	....	....	....	....
1993-94	Edmonton	NHL	84	22	35	57	8	....	....	....	....	....
	NHL Totals		**213**	**49**	**80**	**129**	**34**	**13**	**2**	**6**	**8**	

Traded to **Edmonton** by **New Jersey** with Kevin Todd for Bernie Nicholls, January 13, 1993.

CIMELLARO, TONY
(sih-mih-LAIR-oh)

Center. Shoots left. 5'11", 180 lbs.   Born, Kingston, Ont., June 14, 1971.

				Regular Season					Playoffs			
Season	Club	Lea	GP	G	A	TP	PIM	GP	G	A	TP	PIM
1990-91	Kingston	OHL	64	26	25	51	42	....	....	....	....	....
1991-92	Belleville	OHL	48	39	44	83	51	5	6	4	10	10
1992-93	**Ottawa**	**NHL**	2	0	0	0	0	....	....	....	....	....
	New Haven	AHL	76	18	16	34	73	....	....	....	....	....
1993-94	PEI	AHL	19	1	0	1	30	....	....	....	....	....
	Asiago	Italy	16	16	11	27	13	....	....	....	....	....
	NHL Totals		**2**	**0**	**0**	**0**	**0**	....	....	....	....	....

Signed as a free agent by **Ottawa**, July 30, 1992.

CIMETTA, ROBERT
(sih-MEH-tuh) CHI.

Left/Right wing. Shoots left. 6', 190 lbs.   Born, Toronto, Ont., February 15, 1970.
(Boston's 1st choice, 18th overall, in 1988 Entry Draft).

				Regular Season					Playoffs			
Season	Club	Lea	GP	G	A	TP	PIM	GP	G	A	TP	PIM
1986-87	Toronto	OHL	66	21	35	56	65	....	....	....	....	....
1987-88	Toronto	OHL	64	34	42	76	90	4	2	2	4	7
1988-89	**Boston**	**NHL**	7	2	0	2	0	1	0	0	0	15
a	Toronto	OHL	58	*55	47	102	89	6	3	3	6	0
1989-90	**Boston**	**NHL**	47	8	9	17	33	....	....	....	....	....
	Maine	AHL	9	3	2	5	13	....	....	....	....	....
1990-91	**Toronto**	**NHL**	25	2	4	6	21	....	....	....	....	....
	Newmarket	AHL	29	16	18	34	24	....	....	....	....	....
1991-92	**Toronto**	**NHL**	24	4	3	7	12	....	....	....	....	....
	St. John's	AHL	19	4	13	17	23	10	3	7	10	24
1992-93	St. John's	AHL	76	28	57	85	125	9	2	10	12	32
1993-94	Indianapolis	IHL	79	26	54	80	178	....	....	....	....	....
	NHL Totals		**103**	**16**	**16**	**32**	**66**	**1**	**0**	**0**	**0**	**15**

a   OHL First All-Star Team (1989)
Traded to **Toronto** by **Boston** for Steve Bancroft, November 9, 1990. Signed as a free agent by **Chicago**, September 8, 1993.

CIRELLA, JOE
(suh-REHL-uh) FLA.

Defense. Shoots right. 6'3", 210 lbs.   Born, Hamilton, Ont., May 9, 1963.
(Colorado's 1st choice, 5th overall, in 1981 Entry Draft).

				Regular Season					Playoffs			
Season	Club	Lea	GP	G	A	TP	PIM	GP	G	A	TP	PIM
1980-81	Oshawa	OHA	56	5	31	36	220	11	0	2	2	41
1981-82	**Colorado**	**NHL**	65	7	12	19	52	....	....	....	....	....
	Oshawa	OHL	3	0	1	1	0	11	7	10	17	32
1982-83	**New Jersey**	**NHL**	2	0	1	1	4	....	....	....	....	....
a	Oshawa	OHL	56	13	55	68	110	17	4	16	20	37
1983-84	New Jersey	NHL	79	11	33	44	137	....	....	....	....	....
1984-85	New Jersey	NHL	66	6	18	24	141	....	....	....	....	....
1985-86	New Jersey	NHL	66	6	23	29	147	....	....	....	....	....
1986-87	New Jersey	NHL	65	9	22	31	111	....	....	....	....	....
1987-88	New Jersey	NHL	80	8	31	39	191	19	0	7	7	49
1988-89	New Jersey	NHL	80	3	19	22	155	....	....	....	....	....
1989-90	Quebec	NHL	56	4	14	18	67	....	....	....	....	....
1990-91	Quebec	NHL	39	2	10	12	59	....	....	....	....	....
	NY Rangers	NHL	19	1	0	1	52	6	0	2	2	26
1991-92	NY Rangers	NHL	67	3	12	15	121	13	0	4	4	23
1992-93	NY Rangers	NHL	55	3	6	9	85	....	....	....	....	....
1993-94	Florida	NHL	63	1	9	10	99	....	....	....	....	....
	NHL Totals		**802**	**64**	**210**	**274**	**1421**	**38**	**0**	**13**	**13**	**98**

a   OHL First All-Star Team (1983)
Played in NHL All-Star Game (1984)
Traded to **Quebec** by **New Jersey** with Claude Loiselle and New Jersey's eighth round choice (Alexander Karpovtsev) in 1990 Entry Draft for Walt Poddubny and Quebec's fourth round choice (Mike Bodnarchuk) in 1990 Entry Draft, June 17, 1989. Traded to **NY Rangers** by **Quebec** for Aaron Miller and NY Rangers' fifth round choice (Bill Lindsay) in 1991 Entry Draft, January 17, 1991. Claimed by **Florida** from **NY Rangers** in Expansion Draft, June 24, 1993.

CIRONE, JASON
(suh-ROHN) FLA.

Center. Shoots left. 5'9", 185 lbs.   Born, Toronto, Ont., February 21, 1971.
(Winnipeg's 3rd choice, 46th overall, in 1989 Entry Draft).

				Regular Season					Playoffs			
Season	Club	Lea	GP	G	A	TP	PIM	GP	G	A	TP	PIM
1987-88	Cornwall	OHL	53	12	11	23	41	11	1	2	3	4
1988-89	Cornwall	OHL	64	39	44	83	67	17	19	8	27	14
1989-90	Cornwall	OHL	32	22	41	63	56	6	4	2	6	14
1990-91	Windsor	OHL	40	31	29	60	66	11	9	8	17	14
1991-92	**Winnipeg**	**NHL**	3	0	0	0	2	....	....	....	....	....
	Moncton	AHL	64	32	27	59	124	10	1	1	2	8
1992-93	Asiago	Alp.	25	24	14	38	36	....	....	....	....	....
	Asiago	Italy	16	6	5	11	18	2	1	5	6	18
1993-94	Cincinnati	IHL	26	4	2	6	61	....	....	....	....	....
	Birmingham	ECHL	11	3	3	6	45	10	8	8	16	*67
	NHL Totals		**3**	**0**	**0**	**0**	**2**	....	....	....	....	....

Traded to **Florida** by **Winnipeg** for Dave Tomlinson, August 3, 1993.

CLARK, CHRIS
CGY.

Right wing. Shoots right. 6', 190 lbs.   Born, Manchester, CT, March 8, 1976.
(Calgary's 3rd choice, 77th overall, in 1994 Entry Draft).

				Regular Season					Playoffs			
Season	Club	Lea	GP	G	A	TP	PIM	GP	G	A	TP	PIM
1992-93	Springfield	Jr. B	43	17	60	77	120	....	....	....	....	....
1993-94	Springfield	Jr. B	35	31	26	57	185	....	....	....	....	....

LARK, JASON — VAN.

enter. Shoots left. 6'1", 185 lbs. Born, Belmont, Ont., May 6, 1972.
/ancouver's 8th choice, 141st overall, in 1992 Entry Draft).

			Regular Season					Playoffs				
eason	Club	Lea	GP	G	A	TP	PIM	GP	G	A	TP	PIM
992-93	Bowling Green	CCHA	40	10	17	27	42	....	....	....	....	....
993-94	Bowling Green	CCHA	37	10	18	28	39	....	....	....	....	....

LARK, KERRY

ight wing. Shoots right. 6'1", 190 lbs. Born, Kelvington, Sask., August 21, 1968.
Y Islanders' 12th choice, 206th overall, in 1986 Entry Draft).

			Regular Season					Playoffs				
eason	Club	Lea	GP	G	A	TP	PIM	GP	G	A	TP	PIM
985-86	Regina	WHL	23	4	4	8	58	....	....	....	....	....
	Saskatoon	WHL	39	5	8	13	104	13	2	2	4	33
986-87	Saskatoon	WHL	54	12	10	22	229	8	0	1	1	23
987-88	Saskatoon	WHL	67	15	11	26	241	10	2	2	4	16
988-89	Springfield	AHL	63	7	7	14	264	....	....	....	....	....
	Indianapolis	IHL	3	0	1	1	12	....	....	....	....	....
989-90	Springfield	AHL	21	0	1	1	73	....	....	....	....	....
	Phoenix	IHL	38	4	8	12	262	....	....	....	....	....
990-91	Salt Lake	IHL	62	14	14	28	372	4	1	1	2	12
991-92	Salt Lake	IHL	74	12	14	26	266	5	1	0	1	34
992-93	Salt Lake	IHL	64	14	15	29	255	....	....	....	....	....
993-94	Portland	AHL	55	9	5	14	309	5	0	0	0	26

igned as a free agent by **Calgary**, July 23, 1990.

LARK, WENDEL — QUE.

.eft wing. Shoots left. 5'11", 194 lbs. Born, Kelvington, Sask., October 25, 1966.
Toronto's 1st choice, 1st overall, in 1985 Entry Draft).

			Regular Season					Playoffs				
eason	Club	Lea	GP	G	A	TP	PIM	GP	G	A	TP	PIM
1983-84	Saskatoon	WHL	72	23	45	68	225	....	....	....	....	....
1984-85a	Saskatoon	WHL	64	32	55	87	253	3	3	3	6	7
1985-86b	**Toronto**	**NHL**	**66**	**34**	**11**	**45**	**227**	**10**	**5**	**1**	**6**	**47**
1986-87	**Toronto**	**NHL**	**80**	**37**	**23**	**60**	**271**	**13**	**6**	**5**	**11**	**38**
1987-88	**Toronto**	**NHL**	**28**	**12**	**11**	**23**	**80**	....	....	....	....	....
1988-89	**Toronto**	**NHL**	**15**	**7**	**4**	**11**	**66**	....	....	....	....	....
1989-90	**Toronto**	**NHL**	**38**	**18**	**8**	**26**	**116**	**5**	**1**	**1**	**2**	**19**
1990-91	**Toronto**	**NHL**	**63**	**18**	**16**	**34**	**152**	....	....	....	....	....
1991-92	**Toronto**	**NHL**	**43**	**19**	**21**	**40**	**123**	....	....	....	....	....
1992-93	**Toronto**	**NHL**	**66**	**17**	**22**	**39**	**193**	**21**	**10**	**10**	**20**	**51**
1993-94	**Toronto**	**NHL**	**64**	**46**	**30**	**76**	**115**	**18**	**9**	**7**	**16**	**24**
	NHL Totals		**463**	**208**	**146**	**354**	**1343**	**67**	**31**	**24**	**55**	**179**

a WHL East First All-Star Team (1985)
b NHL All-Rookie Team (1986)

Played in NHL All-Star Game (1986)

Traded to **Quebec** by **Toronto** with Sylvain Lefebvre, Landon Wilson and Toronto's first round choice (Jeffrey Kealty) in 1994 Entry Draft for Mats Sundin, Garth Butcher, Todd Warriner and Philadelphia's first round choice (previously acquired by Quebec — later traded to Washington — Washington selected Nolan Baumgartner) in 1994 Entry Draft, June 28, 1994.

CLARKE, WAYNE — TOR.

Right wing. Shoots right. 6'1", 187 lbs. Born, Sterling, Ont., August 30, 1972.
(Toronto's 9th choice, 197th overall, in 1992 Entry Draft).

			Regular Season					Playoffs				
Season	Club	Lea	GP	G	A	TP	PIM	GP	G	A	TP	PIM
1991-92	RPI	ECAC	33	12	17	29	28	....	....	....	....	....
1992-93	RPI	ECAC	32	13	16	29	23	....	....	....	....	....
1993-94	RPI	ECAC	30	22	13	35	18	....	....	....	....	....

CLIFFORD, BRIAN — PIT.

Center. Shoots right. 6', 185 lbs. Born, Buffalo, NY, June 18, 1973.
(Pittsburgh's 6th choice, 126th overall, in 1991 Entry Draft).

			Regular Season					Playoffs				
Season	Club	Lea	GP	G	A	TP	PIM	GP	G	A	TP	PIM
1992-93	Michigan State	CCHA	34	15	7	22	20	....	....	....	....	....
1993-94	Michigan State	CCHA	35	6	4	10	22	....	....	....	....	....

CLOUTIER, COLIN — T.B.

Center. Shoots left. 6'3", 224 lbs. Born, Winnipeg, Man., January 27, 1976.
(Tampa Bay's 2nd choice, 34th overall, in 1994 Entry Draft).

			Regular Season					Playoffs				
Season	Club	Lea	GP	G	A	TP	PIM	GP	G	A	TP	PIM
1992-93	Brandon	WHL	60	11	15	26	138	4	0	0	0	18
1993-94	Brandon	WHL	30	10	13	23	102	11	2	5	7	23

CLOUTIER, SYLVAIN (kloo-CHAY) — DET.

Center. Shoots left. 6', 195 lbs. Born, Mont-Laurier, Que., February 13, 1974.
(Detroit's 3rd choice, 70th overall, in 1992 Entry Draft).

			Regular Season					Playoffs				
Season	Club	Lea	GP	G	A	TP	PIM	GP	G	A	TP	PIM
1991-92	Guelph	OHL	62	35	31	66	74	....	....	....	....	....
1992-93	Guelph	OHL	44	26	29	55	78	5	0	5	5	14
1993-94	Guelph	OHL	66	45	71	116	127	9	7	9	16	32
	Adirondack	AHL	2	0	2	2	2	....	....	....	....	....

COFFEY, PAUL — DET.

Defense. Shoots left. 6', 190 lbs. Born, Weston, Ont., June 1, 1961.
(Edmonton's 1st choice, 6th overall, in the 1980 Draft).

			Regular Season					Playoffs				
Season	Club	Lea	GP	G	A	TP	PIM	GP	G	A	TP	PIM
1978-79	S.S. Marie	OHA	68	17	72	89	103	....	....	....	....	....
1979-80a	S.S. Marie	OHA	23	10	21	31	63	....	....	....	....	....
	Kitchener	OHA	52	19	52	71	130	....	....	....	....	....
1980-81	**Edmonton**	**NHL**	**74**	**9**	**23**	**32**	**130**	**9**	**4**	**3**	**7**	**22**
1981-82b	**Edmonton**	**NHL**	**80**	**29**	**60**	**89**	**106**	**5**	**1**	**1**	**2**	**6**
1982-83b	**Edmonton**	**NHL**	**80**	**29**	**67**	**96**	**87**	**16**	**7**	**7**	**14**	**14**
1983-84b	**Edmonton**	**NHL**	**80**	**40**	**86**	**126**	**104**	**19**	**8**	**14**	**22**	**21**
1984-85cd	**Edmonton**	**NHL**	**80**	**37**	**84**	**121**	**97**	**18**	**12**	**25**	**37**	**44**
1985-86cd	**Edmonton**	**NHL**	**79**	**48**	**90**	**138**	**120**	**10**	**1**	**9**	**10**	**30**
1986-87	**Edmonton**	**NHL**	**59**	**17**	**50**	**67**	**49**	**17**	**3**	**8**	**11**	**30**
1987-88	**Pittsburgh**	**NHL**	**46**	**15**	**52**	**67**	**93**	....	....	....	....	....
1988-89d	**Pittsburgh**	**NHL**	**75**	**30**	**83**	**113**	**195**	**11**	**2**	**13**	**15**	**31**
1989-90b	**Pittsburgh**	**NHL**	**80**	**29**	**74**	**103**	**95**	....	....	....	....	....
1990-91	**Pittsburgh**	**NHL**	**76**	**24**	**69**	**93**	**128**	**12**	**2**	**9**	**11**	**6**
1991-92	**Pittsburgh**	**NHL**	**54**	**10**	**54**	**64**	**62**	....	....	....	....	....
	Los Angeles	**NHL**	**10**	**1**	**4**	**5**	**25**	**6**	**4**	**3**	**7**	**2**
1992-93	**Los Angeles**	**NHL**	**50**	**8**	**49**	**57**	**50**	....	....	....	....	....
	Detroit	**NHL**	**30**	**4**	**26**	**30**	**27**	**7**	**2**	**9**	**11**	**2**
1993-94	**Detroit**	**NHL**	**80**	**14**	**63**	**77**	**106**	**7**	**1**	**6**	**7**	**8**
	NHL Totals		**1033**	**344**	**934**	**1278**	**1474**	**137**	**47**	**107**	**154**	**216**

a OHA Second All-Star Team (1980)
b NHL Second All-Star Team (1982, 1983, 1984, 1990)
c Won James Norris Memorial Trophy (1985, 1986)
d NHL First All-Star Team (1985, 1986, 1989)

Played in NHL All-Star Game (1982-86, 1988-94)

Traded to **Pittsburgh** by **Edmonton** with Dave Hunter and Wayne Van Dorp for Craig Simpson, Dave Hannan, Moe Mantha and Chris Joseph, November 24, 1987. Traded to **Los Angeles** by **Pittsburgh** for Brian Benning, Jeff Chychrun and Los Angeles' first round choice (later traded to Philadelphia — Philadelphia selected Jason Bowen) in 1992 Entry Draft, February 19, 1992. Traded to **Detroit** by **Los Angeles** with Sylvain Couturier and Jim Hiller for Jimmy Carson, Marc Potvin and Gary Shuchuk, January 29, 1993.

COLE, DANTON — T.B.

Center/Right wing. Shoots right. 5'11", 185 lbs. Born, Pontiac, MI, January 10, 1967.
(Winnipeg's 6th choice, 123rd overall, in 1985 Entry Draft).

			Regular Season					Playoffs				
Season	Club	Lea	GP	G	A	TP	PIM	GP	G	A	TP	PIM
1985-86	Michigan State	CCHA	43	11	10	21	22	....	....	....	....	....
1986-87	Michigan State	CCHA	44	9	15	24	16	....	....	....	....	....
1987-88	Michigan State	CCHA	46	20	36	56	38	....	....	....	....	....
1988-89	Michigan State	CCHA	47	29	33	62	46	....	....	....	....	....
1989-90	**Winnipeg**	**NHL**	**2**	**1**	**1**	**2**	**0**	....	....	....	....	....
	Moncton	AHL	80	31	42	73	18	....	....	....	....	....
1990-91	**Winnipeg**	**NHL**	**66**	**13**	**11**	**24**	**24**	....	....	....	....	....
	Moncton	AHL	3	1	1	2	0	....	....	....	....	....
1991-92	**Winnipeg**	**NHL**	**52**	**7**	**5**	**12**	**32**	....	....	....	....	....
1992-93	**Tampa Bay**	**NHL**	**67**	**12**	**15**	**27**	**23**	....	....	....	....	....
	Atlanta	IHL	1	1	0	1	2	....	....	....	....	....
1993-94	**Tampa Bay**	**NHL**	**81**	**20**	**23**	**43**	**32**	....	....	....	....	....
	NHL Totals		**268**	**53**	**55**	**108**	**111**	....	....	....	....	....

Traded to **Tampa Bay** by **Winnipeg** for future considerations, June 19, 1992.

COLEMAN, JONATHAN — DET.

Defense. Shoots right. 6'1", 190 lbs. Born, Boston, MA, March 9, 1975.
(Detroit's 2nd choice, 48th overall, in 1993 Entry Draft).

			Regular Season					Playoffs				
Season	Club	Lea	GP	G	A	TP	PIM	GP	G	A	TP	PIM
1992-93	Andover	HS	23	14	33	47	0	....	....	....	....	....
1993-94	Boston U.	H.E.	29	1	14	15	26	....	....	....	....	....

CONACHER, PAT (KAH-nuh-kuhr) — L.A.

Left wing. Shoots left. 5'9", 190 lbs. Born, Edmonton, Alta., May 1, 1959.
(NY Rangers' 3rd choice, 76th overall, in 1979 Entry Draft).

			Regular Season					Playoffs				
Season	Club	Lea	GP	G	A	TP	PIM	GP	G	A	TP	PIM
1977-78	Billings	WHL	72	31	44	75	105	20	15	14	29	22
1978-79	Billings	WHL	39	25	37	62	50	....	....	....	....	....
	Saskatoon	WHL	33	15	32	47	37	....	....	....	....	....
1979-80	**NY Rangers**	**NHL**	**17**	**0**	**5**	**5**	**4**	**3**	**0**	**1**	**1**	**2**
	New Haven	AHL	53	11	14	25	43	7	1	1	2	4
1980-81						DID NOT PLAY						
1981-82	Springfield	AHL	77	23	22	45	38	....	....	....	....	....
1982-83	**NY Rangers**	**NHL**	**5**	**0**	**1**	**1**	**4**	....	....	....	....	....
	Tulsa	CHL	63	29	28	57	44	....	....	....	....	....
1983-84	**Edmonton**	**NHL**	**45**	**2**	**8**	**10**	**31**	**3**	**1**	**0**	**1**	**2**
	Moncton	AHL	28	7	16	23	30	....	....	....	....	....
1984-85	Nova Scotia	AHL	68	20	45	65	44	6	3	2	5	0
1985-86	**New Jersey**	**NHL**	**2**	**0**	**2**	**2**	**2**	....	....	....	....	....
	Maine	AHL	69	15	30	45	83	5	1	1	2	11
1986-87	Maine	AHL	56	12	14	26	47	....	....	....	....	....
1987-88	**New Jersey**	**NHL**	**24**	**2**	**5**	**7**	**12**	**17**	**2**	**2**	**4**	**14**
	Utica	AHL	47	14	33	47	32	....	....	....	....	....
1988-89	**New Jersey**	**NHL**	**55**	**7**	**5**	**12**	**14**	....	....	....	....	....
1989-90	**New Jersey**	**NHL**	**19**	**3**	**3**	**6**	**4**	**5**	**1**	**0**	**1**	**10**
	Utica	AHL	57	13	36	49	53	....	....	....	....	....
1990-91	**New Jersey**	**NHL**	**49**	**5**	**11**	**16**	**27**	**7**	**0**	**2**	**2**	**2**
	Utica	AHL	4	0	1	1	6	....	....	....	....	....
1991-92	**New Jersey**	**NHL**	**44**	**7**	**3**	**10**	**16**	**7**	**1**	**1**	**2**	**4**
1992-93	**Los Angeles**	**NHL**	**81**	**9**	**8**	**17**	**20**	**24**	**6**	**4**	**10**	**6**
1993-94	**Los Angeles**	**NHL**	**77**	**15**	**13**	**28**	**71**	....	....	....	....	....
	NHL Totals		**418**	**50**	**64**	**114**	**205**	**66**	**11**	**10**	**21**	**40**

Signed as a free agent by **Edmonton**, October 4, 1983. Signed as a free agent by **New Jersey**, August 14, 1985. Traded to **Los Angeles** by **New Jersey** for future considerations, September 3, 1992.

CONLAN, WAYNE — ST.L.

Center. Shoots right. 5'10", 180 lbs. Born, New Haven, CT, January 9, 1972.
(St. Louis' 5th choice, 138th overall, in 1990 Entry Draft).

			Regular Season					Playoffs				
Season	Club	Lea	GP	G	A	TP	PIM	GP	G	A	TP	PIM
1991-92	U. of Maine	H.E.	22	8	1	9	10	....	....	....	....	....
1992-93	U. of Maine	H.E.	3	0	3	3	0	....	....	....	....	....
1993-94	U. of Maine	H.E.	29	7	9	16	28	....	....	....	....	....

CONN, ROB — CHI.

Left/Right wing. Shoots right. 6'2", 200 lbs. Born, Calgary, Alta., September 3, 1968.

			Regular Season					Playoffs				
Season	Club	Lea	GP	G	A	TP	PIM	GP	G	A	TP	PIM
1988-89	Alaska-Anch.	G.N.	33	21	17	38	46	....	....	....	....	....
1989-90	Alaska-Anch.	G.N.	34	27	21	48	46	....	....	....	....	....
1990-91	Alaska-Anch.	G.N.	43	28	32	60	53	....	....	....	....	....
1991-92	**Chicago**	**NHL**	**2**	**0**	**0**	**0**	**2**	....	....	....	....	....
	Indianapolis	IHL	72	19	16	35	100	....	....	....	....	....
1992-93	Indianapolis	IHL	75	13	14	27	81	5	0	1	1	6
1993-94	Indianapolis	IHL	51	16	11	27	46	....	....	....	....	....
	NHL Totals		**2**	**0**	**0**	**0**	**2**	....	....	....	....	....

Signed as a free agent by **Chicago**, July 31, 1991.

CONNOLLY, JEFF — VAN.

Center. Shoots right. 6', 185 lbs. Born, Worcester, MA, February 1, 1974.
(Vancouver's 4th choice, 69th overall, in 1992 Entry Draft).

			Regular Season					Playoffs				
Season	Club	Lea	GP	G	A	TP	PIM	GP	G	A	TP	PIM
1992-93	St. Sebastien's	HS	24	17	34	51	....	....	....	....	....	....
1993-94	Boston College	H.E.	22	8	10	18	20	....	....	....	....	....

CONROY, AL

Center. Shoots right. 5'8", 170 lbs. Born, Calgary, Alta., January 17, 1966.

			Regular Season					Playoffs				
Season	Club	Lea	GP	G	A	TP	PIM	GP	G	A	TP	PIM
1986-87	Rapperswill	Switz.	36	30	32	62	0	....	....	....	....	....
	Rochester	AHL	13	4	4	8	40	13	1	3	4	50
1987-88	Varese	Italy	36	25	39	64	....	....	....	....	....	....
	Adirondack	AHL	13	5	8	13	20	11	1	3	4	41
1988-89	Dortmund	W. Ger.	46	53	78	131	....	....	....	....	....	....
1989-90	Adirondack	AHL	77	23	33	56	147	....	....	....	....	....
1990-91	Adirondack	AHL	80	26	39	65	172	....	....	....	....	....
1991-92	**Philadelphia**	**NHL**	**31**	**2**	**9**	**11**	**74**	....	....	....	....	....
	Hershey	AHL	47	17	28	45	90	6	4	2	6	12
1992-93	**Philadelphia**	**NHL**	**21**	**3**	**2**	**5**	**17**	....	....	....	....	....
	Hershey	AHL	60	28	32	60	130	....	....	....	....	....
1993-94	**Philadelphia**	**NHL**	**62**	**4**	**3**	**7**	**65**	....	....	....	....	....
	NHL Totals		**114**	**9**	**14**	**23**	**156**	....	....	....	....	....

Signed as a free agent by **Detroit**, August 16, 1989. Signed as a free agent by **Philadelphia**, August 21, 1991.

CONROY, CRAIG — MTL.

Center. Shoots right. 6'2", 190 lbs. Born, Potsdam, NY, September 4, 1971.
(Montreal's 7th choice, 123rd overall, in 1990 Entry Draft).

			Regular Season					Playoffs				
Season	Club	Lea	GP	G	A	TP	PIM	GP	G	A	TP	PIM
1990-91	Clarkson	ECAC	40	8	21	29	24	....	....	....	....	....
1991-92	Clarkson	ECAC	31	19	17	36	36	....	....	....	....	....
1992-93	Clarkson	ECAC	35	10	23	33	26	....	....	....	....	....
1993-94abc	Clarkson	ECAC	34	26	*40	*66	46	....	....	....	....	....

a ECAC First All-Star Team (1994)
b NCAA East First All-American Team (1994)
c NCAA Final Four All-Tournament Team (1994)

CONVERY, BRANDON — TOR.

Center. Shoots right. 6'1", 182 lbs. Born, Kingston, Ont., February 4, 1974.
(Toronto's 1st choice, 8th overall, in 1992 Entry Draft).

			Regular Season					Playoffs				
Season	Club	Lea	GP	G	A	TP	PIM	GP	G	A	TP	PIM
1990-91	Sudbury	OHL	56	26	22	48	18	5	1	1	2	2
1991-92	Sudbury	OHL	44	40	26	66	44	5	3	2	5	4
1992-93	Sudbury	OHL	7	7	9	16	6	....	....	....	....	....
	Niagara Falls	OHL	51	38	39	77	24	4	1	3	4	4
	St. John's	AHL	3	0	0	0	0	5	0	1	1	0
1993-94	Niagara Falls	OHL	29	24	29	53	30	....	....	....	....	....
	Belleville	OHL	23	16	19	35	22	12	4	10	14	13
	St. John's	AHL	....	....	....	....	....	1	0	0	0	0

COOPER, DAVID — BUF.

Defense. Shoots left. 6'2", 204 lbs. Born, Ottawa, Ont., November 2, 1973.
(Buffalo's 1st choice, 11th overall, in 1992 Entry Draft).

			Regular Season					Playoffs				
Season	Club	Lea	GP	G	A	TP	PIM	GP	G	A	TP	PIM
1989-90	Medicine Hat	WHL	61	4	11	15	65	3	0	2	2	2
1990-91	Medicine Hat	WHL	64	12	31	43	66	11	1	3	4	23
1991-92a	Medicine Hat	WHL	72	17	47	64	176	4	1	4	5	8
1992-93	Medicine Hat	WHL	63	15	50	65	88	10	2	2	4	32
	Rochester	AHL	....	....	....	....	....	2	0	0	0	2
1993-94	Rochester	AHL	68	10	25	35	82	4	1	1	2	2

a WHL East First All-Star Team (1992)

COPELAND, ADAM — EDM.

Right wing. Shoots right. 6'1", 185 lbs. Born, St. Catharines, Ont., June 5, 1976.
(Edmonton's 6th choice, 79th overall, in 1994 Entry Draft).

			Regular Season					Playoffs				
Season	Club	Lea	GP	G	A	TP	PIM	GP	G	A	TP	PIM
1992-93	Burlington	Jr. A	44	18	14	32	21	....	....	....	....	....
1993-94	Burlington	Jr. A	39	28	44	72	55	....	....	....	....	....

COPELAND, TODD — BUF.

Defense. Shoots left. 6'2", 210 lbs. Born, Ridgewood, NJ, May 18, 1967.
(New Jersey's 2nd choice, 24th overall, in 1986 Entry Draft).

			Regular Season					Playoffs				
Season	Club	Lea	GP	G	A	TP	PIM	GP	G	A	TP	PIM
1986-87	U. of Michigan	CCHA	34	2	11	13	59	....	....	....	....	....
1987-88	U. of Michigan	CCHA	41	3	10	13	58	....	....	....	....	....
1988-89	U. of Michigan	CCHA	39	5	14	19	102	....	....	....	....	....
1989-90	U. of Michigan	CCHA	34	6	16	22	62	....	....	....	....	....
1990-91	Utica	AHL	79	6	24	30	53	....	....	....	....	....
1991-92	Utica	AHL	80	4	23	27	98	4	2	2	4	2
1992-93	Utica	AHL	16	3	2	5	10	....	....	....	....	....
	Moncton	AHL	16	1	4	5	16	5	1	3	4	2
1993-94	Moncton	AHL	80	4	17	21	158	19	0	1	1	54

Signed as a free agent by **Winnipeg**, September 17, 1993. Signed as a free agent by **Buffalo**, July 7, 1994.

CORBET, RENE — QUE

Left wing. Shoots left. 6', 187 lbs. Born, Victoriaville, Que., June 25, 1973.
(Quebec's 2nd choice, 24th overall, in 1991 Entry Draft).

			Regular Season					Playoffs				
Season	Club	Lea	GP	G	A	TP	PIM	GP	G	A	TP	PIM
1990-91	Drummondville	QMJHL	45	25	40	65	34	14	11	6	17	15
1991-92	Drummondville	QMJHL	56	46	50	96	90	4	1	2	3	17
1992-93ab	Drummondville	QMJHL	63	*79	69	*148	143	10	7	13	20	16
1993-94	**Quebec**	**NHL**	**9**	**1**	**1**	**2**	**0**	....	....	....	....	....
c	Cornwall	AHL	68	37	40	77	56	13	7	2	9	18
	NHL Totals		**9**	**1**	**1**	**2**	**0**	....	....	....	....	....

a QMJHL First All-Star Team (1993)
b Canadian Major Junior First All-Star Team (1993)
c Won Dudley "Red" Garrett Memorial Trophy (Top Rookie - AHL) (1994)

CORKUM, BOB — ANA.

Center. Shoots right. 6'2", 212 lbs. Born, Salisbury, MA, December 18, 1967.
(Buffalo's 3rd choice, 47th overall, in 1986 Entry Draft).

			Regular Season					Playoffs				
Season	Club	Lea	GP	G	A	TP	PIM	GP	G	A	TP	PIM
1985-86	U. of Maine	H.E.	39	7	26	33	53	....	....	....	....	....
1986-87	U. of Maine	H.E.	35	18	11	29	24	....	....	....	....	....
1987-88	U. of Maine	H.E.	40	14	18	32	64	....	....	....	....	....
1988-89	U. of Maine	H.E.	45	17	31	48	64	....	....	....	....	....
1989-90	**Buffalo**	**NHL**	**8**	**2**	**0**	**2**	**4**	**5**	**1**	**0**	**1**	**4**
	Rochester	AHL	43	8	11	19	45	12	2	5	7	16
1990-91	Rochester	AHL	69	13	21	34	77	15	4	4	8	4
1991-92	**Buffalo**	**NHL**	**20**	**2**	**4**	**6**	**21**	**4**	**1**	**0**	**1**	**0**
	Rochester	AHL	52	16	12	28	47	8	0	6	6	8
1992-93	**Buffalo**	**NHL**	**68**	**6**	**4**	**10**	**38**	**5**	**0**	**0**	**0**	**2**
1993-94	**Anaheim**	**NHL**	**76**	**23**	**28**	**51**	**18**	....	....	....	....	....
	NHL Totals		**172**	**33**	**36**	**69**	**81**	**14**	**2**	**0**	**2**	**6**

Claimed by **Anaheim** from **Buffalo** in Expansion Draft, June 24, 1993.

CORPSE, KELI — (KOHRPS, KAL-ee) — MTL.

Center. Shoots left. 5'11", 176 lbs. Born, London, Ont., May 14, 1974.
(Montreal's 3rd choice, 44th overall, in 1992 Entry Draft).

			Regular Season					Playoffs				
Season	Club	Lea	GP	G	A	TP	PIM	GP	G	A	TP	PIM
1990-91	Kingston	OHL	58	18	33	51	34	....	....	....	....	....
1991-92	Kingston	OHL	65	31	52	83	20	....	....	....	....	....
1992-93	Kingston	OHL	54	32	75	107	45	16	9	*20	29	10
1993-94a	Kingston	OHL	63	42	84	126	55	6	1	7	8	2

a OHL Second All-Star Team (1994)

CORRIVEAU, YVON — (KOHR-ih-voh, IGH-vihn) — HFD.

Left wing. Shoots left. 6'1", 195 lbs. Born, Welland, Ont., February 8, 1967.
(Washington's 1st choice, 19th overall, in 1985 Entry Draft).

			Regular Season					Playoffs				
Season	Club	Lea	GP	G	A	TP	PIM	GP	G	A	TP	PIM
1984-85	Toronto	OHL	59	23	28	51	65	3	0	0	0	5
1985-86	**Washington**	**NHL**	**2**	**0**	**0**	**0**	**0**	**4**	**0**	**3**	**3**	**2**
	Toronto	OHL	59	54	36	90	75	4	1	1	2	0
1986-87	**Washington**	**NHL**	**17**	**1**	**1**	**2**	**24**	....	....	....	....	....
	Toronto	OHL	23	14	19	33	23	....	....	....	....	....
	Binghamton	AHL	7	0	0	0	2	8	0	1	1	0
1987-88	**Washington**	**NHL**	**44**	**10**	**9**	**19**	**84**	**13**	**1**	**2**	**3**	**30**
	Binghamton	AHL	35	15	14	29	64	....	....	....	....	....
1988-89	**Washington**	**NHL**	**33**	**3**	**2**	**5**	**62**	**1**	**0**	**0**	**0**	**0**
	Baltimore	AHL	33	16	23	39	65	....	....	....	....	....
1989-90	**Washington**	**NHL**	**50**	**9**	**6**	**15**	**50**	....	....	....	....	....
	Hartford	**NHL**	**13**	**4**	**1**	**5**	**22**	**4**	**1**	**0**	**1**	**0**
1990-91	**Hartford**	**NHL**	**23**	**1**	**1**	**2**	**18**	....	....	....	....	....
	Springfield	AHL	44	17	25	42	10	18	*10	6	16	31
1991-92	**Hartford**	**NHL**	**38**	**12**	**8**	**20**	**36**	**7**	**3**	**2**	**5**	**18**
	Springfield	AHL	39	26	15	41	40	....	....	....	....	....
1992-93	**San Jose**	**NHL**	**20**	**3**	**7**	**10**	**0**	....	....	....	....	....
	Hartford	**NHL**	**37**	**5**	**5**	**10**	**14**	....	....	....	....	....
1993-94	**Hartford**	**NHL**	**3**	**0**	**0**	**0**	**0**	....	....	....	....	....
	Springfield	AHL	71	42	39	81	53	6	7	3	10	20
	NHL Totals		**280**	**48**	**40**	**88**	**310**	**29**	**5**	**7**	**12**	**50**

Traded to **Hartford** by **Washington** for Mike Liut, March 6, 1990. Traded to **Washington** by **Hartford** to complete June 15, 1992 deal in which Mark Hunter and future considerations were traded to Washington for Nick Kypreos, August 20, 1992. Claimed on waivers by **San Jose** from **Washington**, October 4, 1992. Traded to **Hartford** by **San Jose** to complete October 9, 1992 trade in which Michel Picard was traded to San Jose for future considerations, January 21, 1993.

CORSON, SHAYNE — EDM.

Left wing. Shoots left. 6'1", 200 lbs. Born, Midland, Ont., August 13, 1966.
(Montreal's 2nd choice, 8th overall, in 1984 Entry Draft).

			Regular Season					Playoffs				
Season	Club	Lea	GP	G	A	TP	PIM	GP	G	A	TP	PIM
1983-84	Brantford	OHL	66	25	46	71	165	6	4	1	5	26
1984-85	Hamilton	OHL	54	27	63	90	154	11	3	7	10	19
1985-86	**Montreal**	**NHL**	**3**	**0**	**0**	**0**	**2**	....	....	....	....	....
	Hamilton	OHL	47	41	57	98	153	....	....	....	....	....
1986-87	**Montreal**	**NHL**	**55**	**12**	**11**	**23**	**144**	**17**	**6**	**5**	**11**	**30**
1987-88	**Montreal**	**NHL**	**71**	**12**	**27**	**39**	**152**	**3**	**1**	**0**	**1**	**12**
1988-89	**Montreal**	**NHL**	**80**	**26**	**24**	**50**	**193**	**21**	**4**	**5**	**9**	**65**
1989-90	**Montreal**	**NHL**	**76**	**31**	**44**	**75**	**144**	**11**	**2**	**8**	**10**	**20**
1990-91	**Montreal**	**NHL**	**71**	**23**	**24**	**47**	**138**	**13**	**9**	**6**	**15**	**36**
1991-92	**Montreal**	**NHL**	**64**	**17**	**36**	**53**	**118**	**10**	**2**	**5**	**7**	**15**
1992-93	**Edmonton**	**NHL**	**80**	**16**	**31**	**47**	**209**	....	....	....	....	....
1993-94	**Edmonton**	**NHL**	**64**	**25**	**29**	**54**	**118**	....	....	....	....	....
	NHL Totals		**564**	**162**	**226**	**388**	**1218**	**75**	**24**	**29**	**53**	**178**

Played in NHL All-Star Game (1990, 1994)

Traded to **Edmonton** by **Montreal** with Brent Gilchrist and Vladimir Vujtek for Vincent Damphousse and Edmonton's fourth round choice (Adam Wiesel) in 1993 Entry Draft, August 27, 1992.

OTE, ALAIN (koh-TAY) QUE.

efense. Shoots right. 6', 207 lbs. Born, Montmagny, Que., April 14, 1967.
3oston's 1st choice, 31st overall, in 1985 Entry Draft).

			Regular Season					Playoffs				
eason	Club	Lea	GP	G	A	TP	PIM	GP	G	A	TP	PIM
983-84	Quebec	QMJHL	60	3	17	20	40	5	1	3	4	8
984-85	Quebec	QMJHL	68	9	25	34	173	4	0	1	1	12
985-86	**Boston**	**NHL**	**32**	**0**	**6**	**6**	**14**	....	....	....	....	....
	Granby	QMJHL	22	4	12	16	48	....	....	....	....	....
986-87	**Boston**	**NHL**	**3**	**0**	**0**	**0**	**0**	....	....	....	....	....
	Granby	QMJHL	43	7	24	31	185	4	0	3	3	2
987-88	**Boston**	**NHL**	**2**	**0**	**0**	**0**	**0**	....	....	....	....	....
	Maine	AHL	69	9	34	43	108	9	2	4	6	19
988-89	**Boston**	**NHL**	**31**	**2**	**3**	**5**	**51**	....	....	....	....	....
	Maine	AHL	37	5	16	21	111	....	....	....	....	....
989-90	**Washington**	**NHL**	**2**	**0**	**0**	**0**	**7**	....	....	....	....	....
	Baltimore	AHL	57	5	19	24	161	3	0	0	0	9
990-91	**Montreal**	**NHL**	**28**	**0**	**6**	**6**	**26**	**11**	**0**	**2**	**2**	**26**
	Fredericton	AHL	49	8	19	27	110	....	....	....	....	....
991-92	**Montreal**	**NHL**	**13**	**0**	**3**	**3**	**22**	....	....	....	....	....
	Fredericton	AHL	20	1	10	11	24	7	0	1	1	4
992-93	Fredericton	AHL	61	10	17	27	83	....	....	....	....	....
	Tampa Bay	**NHL**	**2**	**0**	**0**	**0**	**0**	....	....	....	....	....
	Atlanta	IHL	8	1	0	1	0	1	0	0	0	0
993-94	**Quebec**	**NHL**	**6**	**0**	**0**	**0**	**4**	....	....	....	....	....
	Cornwall	AHL	67	10	34	44	80	13	0	2	2	10
	NHL Totals		**119**	**2**	**18**	**20**	**124**	**11**	**0**	**2**	**2**	**26**

raded to **Washington** by **Boston** for Bob Gould, September 28, 1989. Traded to **Montreal** by **Vashington** for Marc Deschamps, June 22, 1990. Traded to **Tampa Bay** by **Montreal** with Eric Charron and future considerations (Donald Dufresne, June 18, 1993) for Rob Ramage, March 20, 1993. Signed as a free agent by **Quebec**, July 2, 1993.

COTE, SYLVAIN (KOH-tay) WSH.

Defense. Shoots right. 5'11", 185 lbs. Born, Quebec City, Que., January 19, 1966.
(Hartford's 1st choice, 11th overall, in 1984 Entry Draft).

			Regular Season					Playoffs				
Season	Club	Lea	GP	G	A	TP	PIM	GP	G	A	TP	PIM
1982-83	Quebec	QMJHL	66	10	24	34	50	....	....	....	....	....
1983-84	Quebec	QMJHL	66	15	50	65	89	5	1	1	2	0
1984-85	**Hartford**	**NHL**	**67**	**3**	**9**	**12**	**17**	....	....	....	....	....
1985-86	**Hartford**	**NHL**	**2**	**0**	**0**	**0**	**0**	....	....	....	....	....
a	Hull	QMJHL	26	10	33	43	14	13	6	*28	34	22
	Binghamton	AHL	12	2	4	6	0	....	....	....	....	....
1986-87	**Hartford**	**NHL**	**67**	**2**	**8**	**10**	**20**	**2**	**0**	**2**	**2**	**2**
1987-88	**Hartford**	**NHL**	**67**	**7**	**21**	**28**	**30**	**6**	**1**	**1**	**2**	**4**
1988-89	**Hartford**	**NHL**	**78**	**8**	**9**	**17**	**49**	**3**	**0**	**1**	**1**	**4**
1989-90	**Hartford**	**NHL**	**28**	**4**	**2**	**6**	**14**	....	....	....	....	....
1990-91	**Hartford**	**NHL**	**73**	**7**	**12**	**19**	**17**	**6**	**0**	**2**	**2**	**2**
1991-92	**Washington**	**NHL**	**78**	**11**	**29**	**40**	**31**	**7**	**1**	**2**	**3**	**4**
1992-93	**Washington**	**NHL**	**77**	**21**	**29**	**50**	**34**	**6**	**1**	**1**	**2**	**4**
1993-94	**Washington**	**NHL**	**84**	**16**	**35**	**51**	**66**	**9**	**1**	**8**	**9**	**6**
	NHL Totals		**621**	**79**	**154**	**233**	**278**	**39**	**4**	**17**	**21**	**26**

a QMJHL First All-Star Team (1986).

Traded to **Washington** by **Hartford** for Washington's second round choice (Andrei Nikolishin) in 1992 Entry Draft, September 8, 1991.

COURTENAY, EDWARD S.J.

Right wing. Shoots right. 6'4", 215 lbs. Born, Verdun, Que., February 2, 1968.

			Regular Season					Playoffs				
Season	Club	Lea	GP	G	A	TP	PIM	GP	G	A	TP	PIM
1987-88	Granby	QMJHL	54	37	34	71	19	5	1	1	2	2
1988-89	Granby	QMJHL	68	59	55	114	68	4	1	1	2	22
	Kalamazoo	IHL	1	0	0	0	0	1	0	0	0	2
1989-90	Kalamazoo	IHL	57	25	28	53	16	3	0	0	0	0
1990-91	Kalamazoo	IHL	76	35	36	71	37	8	2	3	5	12
1991-92	**San Jose**	**NHL**	**5**	**0**	**0**	**0**	**0**	....	....	....	....	....
	Kansas City	IHL	36	14	12	26	46	15	8	9	17	15
1992-93	**San Jose**	**NHL**	**39**	**7**	**13**	**20**	**10**	....	....	....	....	....
	Kansas City	IHL	32	15	12	27	25	....	....	....	....	....
1993-94	Kansas City	IHL	62	27	21	48	60	....	....	....	....	....
	NHL Totals		**44**	**7**	**13**	**20**	**10**	....	....	....	....	....

Signed as a free agent by **Minnesota**, October 1, 1989. Claimed by **San Jose** from **Minnesota** in Dispersal Draft, May 30, 1991.

COURTNALL, GEOFF VAN.

Left wing. Shoots left. 6'1", 195 lbs. Born, Duncan, B.C., August 18, 1962.

			Regular Season					Playoffs				
Season	Club	Lea	GP	G	A	TP	PIM	GP	G	A	TP	PIM
1980-81	Victoria	WHL	11	3	4	7	6	15	2	1	3	7
1981-82	Victoria	WHL	72	35	57	90	100	4	1	0	1	2
1982-83	Victoria	WHL	71	41	73	114	186	12	6	7	13	42
1983-84	**Boston**	**NHL**	**4**	**0**	**0**	**0**	**0**	....	....	....	....	....
	Hershey	AHL	74	14	12	26	51	....	....	....	....	....
1984-85	**Boston**	**NHL**	**64**	**12**	**16**	**28**	**82**	**5**	**0**	**2**	**2**	**7**
	Hershey	AHL	9	8	4	12	4	....	....	....	....	....
1985-86	**Boston**	**NHL**	**64**	**21**	**16**	**37**	**61**	**3**	**0**	**0**	**0**	**2**
	Moncton	AHL	12	8	8	16	6	....	....	....	....	....
1986-87	**Boston**	**NHL**	**65**	**13**	**23**	**36**	**117**	**1**	**0**	**0**	**0**	**0**
1987-88	**Boston**	**NHL**	**62**	**32**	**26**	**58**	**108**	....	....	....	....	....
	Edmonton	**NHL**	**12**	**4**	**4**	**8**	**15**	**19**	**0**	**3**	**3**	**23**
1988-89	**Washington**	**NHL**	**79**	**42**	**38**	**80**	**112**	**6**	**2**	**5**	**7**	**12**
1989-90	**Washington**	**NHL**	**80**	**35**	**39**	**74**	**104**	**15**	**4**	**9**	**13**	**32**
1990-91	**St. Louis**	**NHL**	**66**	**27**	**30**	**57**	**56**	....	....	....	....	....
	Vancouver	**NHL**	**11**	**6**	**2**	**8**	**8**	**6**	**3**	**5**	**8**	**4**
1991-92	**Vancouver**	**NHL**	**70**	**23**	**34**	**57**	**116**	**12**	**6**	**8**	**14**	**20**
1992-93	**Vancouver**	**NHL**	**84**	**31**	**46**	**77**	**167**	**12**	**4**	**10**	**14**	**12**
1993-94	**Vancouver**	**NHL**	**82**	**26**	**44**	**70**	**123**	**24**	**9**	**10**	**19**	**51**
	NHL Totals		**743**	**272**	**318**	**590**	**1069**	**103**	**28**	**52**	**80**	**163**

Signed as a free agent by **Boston**, July 6, 1983. Traded to **Edmonton** by **Boston** with Bill Ranford and future considerations for Andy Moog, March 8, 1988. Rights traded to **Washington** by **Edmonton** for Greg C. Adams, July 22, 1988. Traded to **St. Louis** by **Washington** for Peter Zezel and Mike Lalor, July 13, 1990. Traded to **Vancouver** by **St. Louis** with Robert Dirk, Sergio Momesso, Cliff Ronning and St. Louis' fifth round choice (Brian Loney) in 1992 Entry Draft for Dan Quinn and Garth Butcher, March 5, 1991.

COURTNALL, RUSS DAL.

Right wing. Shoots right. 5'11", 185 lbs. Born, Duncan, B.C., June 2, 1965.
(Toronto's 1st choice, 7th overall, in 1983 Entry Draft).

			Regular Season					Playoffs				
Season	Club	Lea	GP	G	A	TP	PIM	GP	G	A	TP	PIM
1982-83	Victoria	WHL	60	36	61	97	33	12	11	7	18	6
1983-84	Victoria	WHL	32	29	37	66	63	....	....	....	....	....
	Cdn. National	....	16	4	7	11	10	....	....	....	....	....
	Cdn. Olympic	....	7	1	3	4	2	....	....	....	....	....
	Toronto	**NHL**	**14**	**3**	**9**	**12**	**6**	....	....	....	....	....
1984-85	**Toronto**	**NHL**	**69**	**12**	**10**	**22**	**44**	....	....	....	....	....
1985-86	**Toronto**	**NHL**	**73**	**22**	**38**	**60**	**52**	**10**	**3**	**6**	**9**	**8**
1986-87	**Toronto**	**NHL**	**79**	**29**	**44**	**73**	**90**	**13**	**3**	**4**	**7**	**11**
1987-88	**Toronto**	**NHL**	**65**	**23**	**26**	**49**	**47**	**6**	**2**	**1**	**3**	**0**
1988-89	**Toronto**	**NHL**	**9**	**1**	**1**	**2**	**4**	....	....	....	....	....
	Montreal	**NHL**	**64**	**22**	**17**	**39**	**15**	**21**	**8**	**5**	**13**	**18**
1989-90	**Montreal**	**NHL**	**80**	**27**	**32**	**59**	**27**	**11**	**5**	**1**	**6**	**10**
1990-91	**Montreal**	**NHL**	**79**	**26**	**50**	**76**	**29**	**13**	**8**	**3**	**11**	**7**
1991-92	**Montreal**	**NHL**	**27**	**7**	**14**	**21**	**6**	**10**	**1**	**1**	**2**	**4**
1992-93	**Minnesota**	**NHL**	**84**	**36**	**43**	**79**	**49**	....	....	....	....	....
1993-94	**Dallas**	**NHL**	**84**	**23**	**57**	**80**	**59**	**9**	**1**	**8**	**9**	**0**
	NHL Totals		**727**	**231**	**341**	**572**	**428**	**93**	**31**	**29**	**60**	**58**

Played in NHL All-Star Game (1994)

Traded to **Montreal** by **Toronto** for John Kordic and Montreal's sixth round choice (Michael Doers) in 1989 Entry Draft, November 7, 1988. Traded to **Minnesota** by **Montreal** for Brian Bellows, August 31, 1992.

COURVILLE, LARRY WPG.

Left wing. Shoots left. 6'1", 180 lbs. Born, Timmins, Ont., April 2, 1975.
(Winnipeg's 6th choice, 119th overall, in 1993 Entry Draft).

			Regular Season					Playoffs				
Season	Club	Lea	GP	G	A	TP	PIM	GP	G	A	TP	PIM
1991-92	Cornwall	OHL	60	8	12	20	80	6	0	0	0	8
1992-93	Newmarket	OHL	64	21	18	39	181	7	0	6	6	14
1993-94	Newmarket	OHL	39	20	19	39	134	....	....	....	....	....
	Moncton	AHL	8	2	0	2	37	10	2	2	4	27

COUTURIER, SYLVAIN (koo-TOOR-ee-yah, SIHL-vay)

Center. Shoots left. 6'2", 205 lbs. Born, Greenfield Park, Que., April 23, 1968.
(Los Angeles' 3rd choice, 65th overall, in 1986 Entry Draft).

			Regular Season					Playoffs				
Season	Club	Lea	GP	G	A	TP	PIM	GP	G	A	TP	PIM
1985-86	Laval	QMJHL	68	21	37	58	64	14	1	7	8	28
1986-87	Laval	QMJHL	67	39	51	90	77	13	12	14	26	19
1987-88	Laval	QMJHL	67	70	67	137	115	....	....	....	....	....
1988-89	**Los Angeles**	**NHL**	**16**	**1**	**3**	**4**	**2**	....	....	....	....	....
	New Haven	AHL	44	18	20	38	33	10	2	2	4	11
1989-90	New Haven	AHL	50	9	8	17	47	....	....	....	....	....
1990-91	**Los Angeles**	**NHL**	**3**	**0**	**1**	**1**	**0**	....	....	....	....	....
	Phoenix	IHL	66	50	37	87	49	10	8	2	10	10
1991-92	**Los Angeles**	**NHL**	**14**	**3**	**1**	**4**	**2**	....	....	....	....	....
	Phoenix	IHL	39	19	20	39	68	....	....	....	....	....
1992-93	Phoenix	IHL	38	23	16	39	63	....	....	....	....	....
	Adirondack	AHL	29	17	17	34	12	11	3	5	8	10
	Fort Wayne	IHL	....	....	....	....	....	4	2	3	5	2
1993-94	Milwaukee	IHL	80	41	51	92	123	4	1	2	3	2
	NHL Totals		**33**	**4**	**5**	**9**	**4**	....	....	....	....	....

Traded to **Detroit** by **Los Angeles** with Paul Coffey and Jim Hiller for Jimmy Carson, Marc Potvin and Gary Shuchuk, January 29, 1993.

COWIE, ROB L.A.

Defense. Shoots left. 6', 195 lbs. Born, Toronto, Ont., November 3, 1967.

			Regular Season					Playoffs				
Season	Club	Lea	GP	G	A	TP	PIM	GP	G	A	TP	PIM
1987-88	Northeastern	H.E.	36	7	8	15	38	....	....	....	....	....
1988-89a	Northeastern	H.E.	36	7	34	41	60	....	....	....	....	....
1989-90bc	Northeastern	H.E.	34	14	31	45	54	....	....	....	....	....
1990-91a	Northeastern	H.E.	33	18	23	41	56	....	....	....	....	....
1991-92	Moncton	AHL	64	11	30	41	89	5	1	1	2	0
1992-93	Moncton	AHL	67	12	20	32	91	5	3	5	8	2
1993-94d	Springfield	AHL	78	17	57	74	124	6	3	6	9	4

a Hockey East Second All-Star Team (1989,1991)
b Hockey East First All-Star Team (1990)
c NCAA East First All-American Team (1990)
d AHL Second All-Star Team (1994)

Signed as a free agent by **Winnipeg**, July 4, 1991. Signed as a free agent by **Hartford**, August 9, 1993. Signed as a free agent by **Los Angeles**, July 8,1994.

CRAIG, MIKE TOR.

Right wing. Shoots right. 6'1", 185 lbs. Born, St. Mary, Ont., June 6, 1971.
(Minnesota's 2nd choice, 28th overall, in 1989 Entry Draft).

			Regular Season					Playoffs				
Season	Club	Lea	GP	G	A	TP	PIM	GP	G	A	TP	PIM
1987-88	Oshawa	OHL	61	6	10	16	39	7	7	0	1	11
1988-89	Oshawa	OHL	63	36	36	72	34	6	3	1	4	6
1989-90	Oshawa	OHL	43	36	40	76	85	17	10	16	26	46
1990-91	**Minnesota**	**NHL**	**39**	**8**	**4**	**12**	**32**	**10**	**1**	**1**	**2**	**20**
1991-92	**Minnesota**	**NHL**	**67**	**15**	**16**	**31**	**155**	**4**	**1**	**0**	**1**	**7**
1992-93	**Minnesota**	**NHL**	**70**	**15**	**23**	**38**	**106**	....	....	....	....	....
1993-94	**Dallas**	**NHL**	**72**	**13**	**24**	**37**	**139**	**4**	**0**	**0**	**0**	**2**
	NHL Totals		**248**	**51**	**67**	**118**	**432**	**18**	**2**	**1**	**3**	**29**

Signed as a free agent by **Toronto**, July 29, 1994.

CRAIGWELL, DALE S.J.

Center. Shoots left. 5'11", 180 lbs. Born, Toronto, Ont., April 24, 1971.
(San Jose's 11th choice, 199th overall, in 1991 Entry Draft).

			Regular Season					Playoffs				
Season	Club	Lea	GP	G	A	TP	PIM	GP	G	A	TP	PIM
1988-89	Oshawa	OHL	55	9	14	23	15	....	....	....	....	....
1989-90	Oshawa	OHL	64	22	41	63	39	17	7	7	14	11
1990-91	Oshawa	OHL	56	27	68	95	34	16	7	16	23	9
1991-92	**San Jose**	**NHL**	**32**	**5**	**11**	**16**	**8**	....	....	....	....	....
	Kansas City	IHL	48	6	19	25	29	12	4	7	11	4
1992-93	**San Jose**	**NHL**	**8**	**3**	**1**	**4**	**4**	....	....	....	....	....
	Kansas City	IHL	60	15	38	53	24	12	*7	5	12	2
1993-94	**San Jose**	**NHL**	**58**	**3**	**6**	**9**	**16**	....	....	....	....	....
	Kansas City	IHL	5	3	1	4	0	....	....	....	....	....
	NHL Totals		**98**	**11**	**18**	**29**	**28**	....	....	....	....	....

CRAVEN, MURRAY — VAN.

Left wing. Shoots left. 6'2", 185 lbs. Born, Medicine Hat, Alta., July 20, 1964.
(Detroit's 1st choice, 17th overall, in 1982 Entry Draft).

			Regular Season					Playoffs				
Season	Club	Lea	GP	G	A	TP	PIM	GP	G	A	TP	PIM
1980-81	Medicine Hat	WHL	69	5	10	15	18	5	0	0	0	2
1981-82	Medicine Hat	WHL	72	35	46	81	49	....	....	....	....	....
1982-83	**Detroit**	**NHL**	**31**	**4**	**7**	**11**	**6**	....	....	....	....	....
	Medicine Hat	WHL	28	17	29	46	35	....	....	....	....	....
1983-84	**Detroit**	**NHL**	**15**	**0**	**4**	**4**	**6**	....	....	....	....	....
	Medicine Hat	WHL	48	38	56	94	53	4	5	3	8	4
1984-85	**Philadelphia**	**NHL**	**80**	**26**	**35**	**61**	**30**	**19**	**4**	**6**	**10**	**11**
1985-86	**Philadelphia**	**NHL**	**78**	**21**	**33**	**54**	**34**	**5**	**0**	**3**	**3**	**4**
1986-87	**Philadelphia**	**NHL**	**77**	**19**	**30**	**49**	**38**	**12**	**3**	**1**	**4**	**9**
1987-88	**Philadelphia**	**NHL**	**72**	**30**	**46**	**76**	**58**	**7**	**2**	**5**	**7**	**4**
1988-89	**Philadelphia**	**NHL**	**51**	**9**	**28**	**37**	**52**	**1**	**0**	**0**	**0**	**0**
1989-90	**Philadelphia**	**NHL**	**76**	**25**	**50**	**75**	**42**	....	....	....	....	....
1990-91	**Philadelphia**	**NHL**	**77**	**19**	**47**	**66**	**53**	....	....	....	....	....
1991-92	**Philadelphia**	**NHL**	**12**	**3**	**3**	**6**	**8**	....	....	....	....	....
	Hartford	**NHL**	**61**	**24**	**30**	**54**	**38**	**7**	**3**	**3**	**6**	**6**
1992-93	**Hartford**	**NHL**	**67**	**25**	**42**	**67**	**20**	....	....	....	....	....
	Vancouver	**NHL**	**10**	**0**	**10**	**10**	**12**	**12**	**4**	**6**	**10**	**4**
1993-94	**Vancouver**	**NHL**	**78**	**15**	**40**	**55**	**30**	**22**	**4**	**9**	**13**	**18**
	NHL Totals		**785**	**220**	**405**	**625**	**427**	**85**	**20**	**33**	**53**	**56**

Traded to **Philadelphia** by **Detroit** with Joe Paterson for Darryl Sittler, October 10, 1984. Traded to **Hartford** by **Philadelphia** with Philadelphia's fourth round choice (Kevin Smyth) in 1992 Entry Draft for Kevin Dineen, November 13, 1991. Traded to **Vancouver** by **Hartford** with Vancouver's fifth round choice (previously acquired by Hartford — Vancouver selected Scott Walker) in 1993 Entry Draft for Robert Kron, Vancouver's third round choice (Marek Malik) in 1993 Entry Draft and future considerations (Jim Sandlak, May 17, 1993), March 22, 1993.

CREIGHTON, ADAM — (KRAY-ton) — T.B.

Center. Shoots left. 6'5", 210 lbs. Born, Burlington, Ont., June 2, 1965.
(Buffalo's 3rd choice, 11th overall, in 1983 Entry Draft).

			Regular Season					Playoffs				
Season	Club	Lea	GP	G	A	TP	PIM	GP	G	A	TP	PIM
1981-82	Ottawa	OHL	60	15	27	42	73	17	7	1	8	40
1982-83	Ottawa	OHL	68	44	46	90	88	9	0	2	2	12
1983-84	**Buffalo**	**NHL**	**7**	**2**	**2**	**4**	**4**	....	....	....	....	....
	Ottawa	OHL	56	42	49	91	79	13	16	11	27	28
1984-85	**Buffalo**	**NHL**	**30**	**2**	**8**	**10**	**33**	....	....	....	....	....
	Rochester	AHL	6	5	3	8	2	5	2	1	3	20
	Ottawa	OHL	10	4	14	18	23	5	6	2	8	11
1985-86	**Buffalo**	**NHL**	**19**	**1**	**1**	**2**	**2**	....	....	....	....	....
	Rochester	AHL	32	17	21	38	27	....	....	....	....	....
1986-87	**Buffalo**	**NHL**	**56**	**18**	**22**	**40**	**26**	....	....	....	....	....
1987-88	**Buffalo**	**NHL**	**36**	**10**	**17**	**27**	**87**	....	....	....	....	....
1988-89	**Buffalo**	**NHL**	**24**	**7**	**10**	**17**	**44**	....	....	....	....	....
	Chicago	**NHL**	**43**	**15**	**14**	**29**	**92**	**15**	**5**	**6**	**11**	**44**
1989-90	**Chicago**	**NHL**	**80**	**34**	**36**	**70**	**224**	**20**	**3**	**6**	**9**	**59**
1990-91	**Chicago**	**NHL**	**72**	**22**	**29**	**51**	**135**	**6**	**0**	**1**	**1**	**10**
1991-92	**Chicago**	**NHL**	**11**	**6**	**6**	**12**	**16**	....	....	....	....	....
	NY Islanders	**NHL**	**66**	**15**	**9**	**24**	**102**	....	....	....	....	....
1992-93	**Tampa Bay**	**NHL**	**83**	**19**	**20**	**39**	**110**	....	....	....	....	....
1993-94	**Tampa Bay**	**NHL**	**53**	**10**	**10**	**20**	**37**	....	....	....	....	....
	NHL Totals		**580**	**161**	**184**	**345**	**912**	**41**	**8**	**13**	**21**	**113**

Traded to **Chicago** by **Buffalo** for Rick Vaive, December 26, 1988. Traded to **NY Islanders** by **Chicago** with Steve Thomas for Brent Sutter and Brad Lauer, October 25, 1991. Claimed by **Tampa Bay** from **NY Islanders** in NHL Waiver Draft, October 4, 1992.

CREURER, TROY — VAN.

Defense. Shoots left. 6'1", 185 lbs. Born, Weyburn, Sask., May 2, 1975.
(Vancouver's 5th choice, 158th overall, in 1993 Entry Draft).

			Regular Season					Playoffs				
Season	Club	Lea	GP	G	A	TP	PIM	GP	G	A	TP	PIM
1992-93	Notre Dame	SJHL	62	6	21	27	71	....	....	....	....	....
1993-94	St. Lawrence	ECAC	31	5	10	15	22	....	....	....	....	....

CRONAN, EARL — MTL.

Left wing. Shoots left. 6'1", 195 lbs. Born, Warwick, RI, January 2, 1973.
(Montreal's 11th choice, 212th overall, in 1992 Entry Draft).

			Regular Season					Playoffs				
Season	Club	Lea	GP	G	A	TP	PIM	GP	G	A	TP	PIM
1992-93	Colgate	ECAC	33	8	9	17	40	....	....	....	....	....
1993-94	Colgate	ECAC	32	14	17	31	80	....	....	....	....	....

CRONIN, SHAWN — S.J.

Defense. Shoots left. 6'2", 225 lbs. Born, Joliet, IL, August 20, 1963.

			Regular Season					Playoffs				
Season	Club	Lea	GP	G	A	TP	PIM	GP	G	A	TP	PIM
1983-84	Ill.-Chicago	CCHA	32	0	4	4	41	....	....	....	....	....
1984-85	Ill.-Chicago	CCHA	31	2	6	8	52	....	....	....	....	....
1985-86	Ill.-Chicago	CCHA	35	3	8	11	70	....	....	....	....	....
1986-87	Salt Lake	IHL	53	8	16	24	118	....	....	....	....	....
	Binghamton	AHL	12	0	1	1	60	10	0	0	0	41
1987-88	Binghamton	AHL	65	3	8	11	212	4	0	0	0	15
1988-89	**Washington**	**NHL**	**1**	**0**	**0**	**0**	**0**	....	....	....	....	....
	Baltimore	AHL	75	3	9	12	267	....	....	....	....	....
1989-90	**Winnipeg**	**NHL**	**61**	**0**	**4**	**4**	**243**	**5**	**0**	**0**	**0**	**7**
1990-91	**Winnipeg**	**NHL**	**67**	**1**	**5**	**6**	**189**	....	....	....	....	....
1991-92	**Winnipeg**	**NHL**	**65**	**0**	**4**	**4**	**271**	**4**	**0**	**0**	**0**	**6**
1992-93	**Philadelphia**	**NHL**	**35**	**2**	**1**	**3**	**37**	....	....	....	....	....
	Hershey	AHL	7	0	1	1	12	....	....	....	....	....
1993-94	**San Jose**	**NHL**	**34**	**0**	**2**	**2**	**76**	**14**	**1**	**0**	**1**	**20**
	NHL Totals		**263**	**3**	**16**	**19**	**816**	**23**	**1**	**0**	**1**	**33**

Signed as a free agent by **Hartford**, March, 1986. Signed as a free agent by **Washington**, June 6, 1988. Signed as a free agent by **Philadelphia**, June 12, 1989. Traded to **Winnipeg** by **Philadelphia** for future considerations (Keith Acton and Pete Peeters were traded to Philadelphia for Toronto's fifth round choice (previously acquired by Philadelphia — Winnipeg selected Juha Ylonen), October 3, 1989), July 21, 1989. Traded to **Quebec** by **Winnipeg** for Dan Lambert, August 25, 1992. Claimed by **Philadelphia** from **Quebec** in NHL Waiver Draft, October 4, 1992. Traded to **San Jose** by **Philadelphia** for cash, August 5, 1993.

CROSS, CORY — T.B.

Defense. Shoots left. 6'5", 212 lbs. Born, Lloydminster, Alta., January 3, 1971.
(Tampa Bay's 1st choice, 1st overall, in 1992 Supplemental Draft).

			Regular Season					Playoffs				
Season	Club	Lea	GP	G	A	TP	PIM	GP	G	A	TP	PIM
1989-90	U. of Alberta	CWUAA				UNAVAILABLE						
1990-91	U. of Alberta	CWUAA				UNAVAILABLE						
1991-92	U. of Alberta	CWUAA	41	4	11	15	82	....	....	....	....	....
1992-93	U. of Alberta	CWUAA	43	11	28	39	105	....	....	....	....	....
	Atlanta	IHL	7	0	1	1	2	4	0	0	0	[illegible]
1993-94	**Tampa Bay**	**NHL**	**5**	**0**	**0**	**0**	**6**	....	....	....	....	....
	Atlanta	IHL	70	4	14	18	72	9	1	2	3	1[illegible]
	NHL Totals		**5**	**0**	**0**	**0**	**6**	....	....	....	....	....

CROSSMAN, DOUG

Defense. Shoots left. 6'2", 190 lbs. Born, Peterborough, Ont., June 30, 1960.
(Chicago's 6th choice, 112th overall, in 1979 Entry Draft).

			Regular Season					Playoffs				
Season	Club	Lea	GP	G	A	TP	PIM	GP	G	A	TP	PIM
1977-78	Ottawa	OHA	65	4	17	21	17	....	....	....	....	....
1978-79	Ottawa	OHA	67	12	51	63	65	4	1	3	4	0
1979-80	Ottawa	OHA	66	20	96	116	48	11	7	6	13	19
1980-81	**Chicago**	**NHL**	**9**	**0**	**2**	**2**	**2**	....	....	....	....	....
	New Brunswick	AHL	70	13	43	56	90	13	5	6	11	36
1981-82	**Chicago**	**NHL**	**70**	**12**	**28**	**40**	**24**	**11**	**0**	**3**	**3**	**4**
1982-83	**Chicago**	**NHL**	**80**	**13**	**40**	**53**	**46**	**13**	**3**	**7**	**10**	**6**
1983-84	**Philadelphia**	**NHL**	**78**	**7**	**28**	**35**	**63**	**3**	**0**	**0**	**0**	**0**
1984-85	**Philadelphia**	**NHL**	**80**	**4**	**33**	**37**	**65**	**19**	**4**	**6**	**10**	**38**
1985-86	**Philadelphia**	**NHL**	**80**	**6**	**37**	**43**	**55**	**5**	**0**	**1**	**1**	**4**
1986-87	**Philadelphia**	**NHL**	**78**	**9**	**31**	**40**	**29**	**26**	**4**	**14**	**18**	**31**
1987-88	**Philadelphia**	**NHL**	**76**	**9**	**29**	**38**	**43**	**7**	**1**	**1**	**2**	**8**
1988-89	**Los Angeles**	**NHL**	**74**	**10**	**15**	**25**	**53**	**2**	**0**	**1**	**1**	**2**
	New Haven	AHL	3	0	0	0	0	....	....	....	....	....
1989-90	**NY Islanders**	**NHL**	**80**	**15**	**44**	**59**	**54**	**5**	**0**	**1**	**1**	**6**
1990-91	**NY Islanders**	**NHL**	**16**	**1**	**6**	**7**	**12**	....	....	....	....	....
	Hartford	**NHL**	**41**	**4**	**19**	**23**	**19**	....	....	....	....	....
	Detroit	**NHL**	**17**	**3**	**4**	**7**	**17**	**6**	**0**	**5**	**5**	**6**
1991-92	**Detroit**	**NHL**	**26**	**0**	**8**	**8**	**14**	....	....	....	....	....
1992-93	**Tampa Bay**	**NHL**	**40**	**8**	**21**	**29**	**18**	....	....	....	....	....
	St. Louis	**NHL**	**19**	**2**	**7**	**9**	**10**	....	....	....	....	....
1993-94	**St. Louis**	**NHL**	**50**	**2**	**7**	**9**	**10**	....	....	....	....	....
	Peoria	IHL	8	3	5	8	0	....	....	....	....	....
	NHL Totals		**914**	**105**	**359**	**464**	**534**	**97**	**12**	**39**	**51**	**105**

Traded to **Philadelphia** by **Chicago** with Chicago's second round choice (Scott Mellanby) in 1984 Entry Draft for Behn Wilson, June 8, 1983. Traded to **Los Angeles** by **Philadelphia** for Jay Wells, September 29, 1988. Traded to **NY Islanders** by **Los Angeles** to complete February 22, 1989, transaction in which Mark Fitzpatrick, Wayne McBean and future considerations were traded to **NY Islanders** by **Los Angeles** for Kelly Hrudey, May 23, 1989. Traded to **Hartford** by **NY Islanders** for Ray Ferraro, November 13, 1990. Traded to **Detroit** by **Hartford** for Doug Houda, February 20, 1991. Traded to **Quebec** by **Detroit** with Dennis Vial for cash, June 15, 1992. Claimed by **Tampa Bay** from **Quebec** in Expansion Draft, June 18, 1992. Traded to **St. Louis** by **Tampa Bay** with Basil McRae and Tampa Bay's fourth round choice in 1996 Entry Draft for Jason Ruff and future considerations, January 28, 1993.

CROWE, PHILIP

Left wing. Shoots left. 6'2", 220 lbs. Born, Nanton, Alta., April 14, 1970.

			Regular Season					Playoffs				
Season	Club	Lea	GP	G	A	TP	PIM	GP	G	A	TP	PIM
1991-92	Adirondack	AHL	6	1	0	1	29	....	....	....	....	....
	Columbus	ECHL	32	4	7	11	145	....	....	....	....	....
1992-93	Phoenix	IHL	53	3	3	6	190	....	....	....	....	....
1993-94	Phoenix	IHL	7	0	1	1	26	....	....	....	....	....
	Los Angeles	**NHL**	**31**	**0**	**2**	**2**	**77**	....	....	....	....	....
	NHL Totals		**31**	**0**	**2**	**2**	**77**	....	....	....	....	....

Signed as a free agent by **Los Angeles**, November 8, 1993.

CROWLEY, TED — HFD.

Defense. Shoots right. 6'2", 188 lbs. Born, Concord, MA, May 3, 1970.
(Toronto's 4th choice, 69th overall, in 1988 Entry Draft).

			Regular Season					Playoffs				
Season	Club	Lea	GP	G	A	TP	PIM	GP	G	A	TP	PIM
1989-90	Boston College	H.E.	39	7	24	31	34	....	....	....	....	....
1990-91ab	Boston College	H.E.	39	12	24	36	61	....	....	....	....	....
1991-92	U.S. National	....	42	6	7	13	65	....	....	....	....	....
	St. John's	AHL	29	5	4	9	33	10	3	1	4	11
1992-93	St. John's	AHL	79	19	38	57	41	9	2	2	4	4
1993-94	U.S. National	....	48	9	13	22	80	....	....	....	....	....
	U.S. Olympic	....	8	0	2	2	8	....	....	....	....	....
	Hartford	**NHL**	**21**	**1**	**2**	**3**	**10**	....	....	....	....	....
	NHL Totals		**21**	**1**	**2**	**3**	**10**	....	....	....	....	....

a Hockey East First All-Star Team (1991)
b NCAA East Second All-American Team (1991)

Traded to **Hartford** by **Toronto** for Mark Greig and Hartford's sixth round choice (later traded to NY Rangers — NY Rangers selected Yuri Litvinov) in 1994 Entry Draft, January 25, 1994.

CROZIER, GREG — PIT.

Left wing. Shoots left. 6'4", 200 lbs. Born, Calgary, Alta., July 6, 1976.
(Pittsburgh's 4th choice, 73rd overall, in 1994 Entry Draft).

			Regular Season					Playoffs				
Season	Club	Lea	GP	G	A	TP	PIM	GP	G	A	TP	PIM
1992-93	Lawrence	HS	21	22	13	35	9	....	....	....	....	....
1993-94	Lawrence	HS	18	22	26	48	12	....	....	....	....	....

CULL, TRENT — TOR.

Defense. Shoots left. 6'3", 210 lbs. Born, Brampton, Ont., September 27, 1973.

			Regular Season					Playoffs				
Season	Club	Lea	GP	G	A	TP	PIM	GP	G	A	TP	PIM
1989-90	Owen Sound	OHL	57	0	5	5	53	12	0	2	2	11
1990-91	Owen Sound	OHL	24	1	2	3	19	....	....	....	....	....
	Windsor	OHL	33	1	6	7	34	11	0	0	0	8
1991-92	Windsor	OHL	32	0	6	6	66	....	....	....	....	....
	Kingston	OHL	18	0	0	0	31	....	....	....	....	....
1992-93	Kingston	OHL	60	11	28	39	144	16	2	8	10	37
1993-94	Kingston	OHL	50	2	30	32	147	6	0	1	1	6

Signed as a free agent by **Toronto**, June 4, 1994.

CULLEN, JOHN — PIT.

Center. Shoots right. 5'10", 180 lbs. Born, Puslinch, Ont., August 2, 1964.
(Buffalo's 2nd choice, 10th overall, in 1986 Supplemental Draft).

			Regular Season					Playoffs				
Season	Club	Lea	GP	G	A	TP	PIM	GP	G	A	TP	PIM
1983-84	Boston U.	ECAC	40	23	33	56	28	....	....	....	....	....
1984-85a	Boston U.	H.E.	41	27	32	59	46	....	....	....	....	....
1985-86ab	Boston U.	H.E.	43	25	49	74	54	....	....	....	....	....
1986-87c	Boston U.	H.E.	36	23	29	52	35	....	....	....	....	....
1987-88defg	Flint	IHL	81	48	*109	*157	113	16	11	*15	26	16
1988-89	**Pittsburgh**	**NHL**	**79**	**12**	**37**	**49**	**112**	**11**	**3**	**6**	**9**	**28**
1989-90	**Pittsburgh**	**NHL**	**72**	**32**	**60**	**92**	**138**	....	....	....	....	....
1990-91	**Pittsburgh**	**NHL**	**65**	**31**	**63**	**94**	**83**	....	....	....	....	....
	Hartford	**NHL**	**13**	**8**	**8**	**16**	**18**	**6**	**2**	**7**	**9**	**10**
1991-92	**Hartford**	**NHL**	**77**	**26**	**51**	**77**	**141**	**7**	**2**	**1**	**3**	**12**
1992-93	**Hartford**	**NHL**	**19**	**5**	**4**	**9**	**58**	....	....	....	....	....
	Toronto	**NHL**	**47**	**13**	**28**	**41**	**53**	**12**	**2**	**3**	**5**	**0**
1993-94	**Toronto**	**NHL**	**53**	**13**	**17**	**30**	**67**	**3**	**0**	**0**	**0**	**0**
	NHL Totals		**425**	**140**	**268**	**408**	**670**	**39**	**9**	**17**	**26**	**50**

a Hockey East First All-Star Team (1985, 1986)
b NCAA East Second All-American Team (1986)
c Hockey East Second All-Star Team (1987)
d IHL First All-Star Team (1988)
e Won James Gatschene Memorial Trophy (MVP - IHL) (1988)
f Shared Garry F. Longman Memorial Trophy (Top Rookie - IHL) with Ed Belfour (1988)
g Won Leo P. Lamoureux Memorial Trophy (Top Scorer - IHL) (1988)

Played in NHL All-Star Game (1991, 1992)

Signed as a free agent by **Pittsburgh**, June 21, 1988. Traded to **Hartford** by **Pittsburgh** with Jeff Parker and Zarley Zalapski for Ron Francis, Grant Jennings and Ulf Samuelsson, March 4, 1991. Traded to **Toronto** by **Hartford** for future considerations, November 24, 1992. Signed as a free agent by **Pittsburgh**, August 3, 1994.

CULLEN, THOMAS — N.J.

Defense. Shoots left. 6'1", 205 lbs. Born, Mississauga, Ont., July 14, 1975.
(New Jersey's 8th choice, 195th overall, in 1993 Entry Draft).

			Regular Season					Playoffs				
Season	Club	Lea	GP	G	A	TP	PIM	GP	G	A	TP	PIM
1992-93	Wexford	Jr. A	43	6	11	17	76	....	....	....	....	....
1993-94	St. Lawrence	ECAC	23	1	3	4	32	....	....	....	....	....

CULLIMORE, JASSEN — VAN.

Defense. Shoots left. 6'5", 225 lbs. Born, Simcoe, Ont., December 4, 1972.
(Vancouver's 2nd choice, 29th overall, in 1991 Entry Draft).

			Regular Season					Playoffs				
Season	Club	Lea	GP	G	A	TP	PIM	GP	G	A	TP	PIM
1989-90	Peterborough	OHL	59	2	6	8	61	11	0	2	2	8
1990-91	Peterborough	OHL	62	8	16	24	74	4	1	0	1	7
1991-92a	Peterborough	OHL	54	9	37	46	65	10	3	6	9	8
1992-93	Hamilton	AHL	56	5	7	12	60	....	....	....	....	....
1993-94	Hamilton	AHL	71	8	20	28	86	3	0	1	1	2

a OHL Second All-Star Team (1992)

CUMMINS, JIM — T.B.

Right wing. Shoots right. 6'2", 203 lbs. Born, Dearborn, MI, May 17, 1970.
(NY Rangers' 5th choice, 67th overall, in 1989 Entry Draft).

			Regular Season					Playoffs				
Season	Club	Lea	GP	G	A	TP	PIM	GP	G	A	TP	PIM
1988-89	Michigan State	CCHA	30	3	8	11	98	....	....	....	....	....
1989-90	Michigan State	CCHA	41	8	7	15	94	....	....	....	....	....
1990-91	Michigan State	CCHA	34	9	6	15	110	....	....	....	....	....
1991-92	**Detroit**	**NHL**	**1**	**0**	**0**	**0**	**7**	....	....	....	....	....
	Adirondack	AHL	65	7	13	20	338	5	0	0	0	19
1992-93	**Detroit**	**NHL**	**7**	**1**	**1**	**2**	**58**	....	....	....	....	....
	Adirondack	AHL	43	16	4	20	179	9	3	1	4	4
1993-94	**Philadelphia**	**NHL**	**22**	**1**	**2**	**3**	**71**	....	....	....	....	....
	Hershey	AHL	17	6	6	12	70	....	....	....	....	....
	Tampa Bay	**NHL**	**4**	**0**	**0**	**0**	**13**	....	....	....	....	....
	Atlanta	IHL	7	4	5	9	14	13	1	2	3	90
	NHL Totals		**34**	**2**	**3**	**5**	**149**	....	....	....	....	....

Traded to **Detroit** by **NY Rangers** with Kevin Miller and Dennis Vial for Joey Kocur and Per Djoos, March 5, 1991. Traded to **Philadelphia** by **Detroit** with Philadelphia's fourth round choice (previously acquired by Detroit — later traded to Boston — Boston selected Charles Paquette) in 1993 Entry Draft for Greg Johnson and Philadelphia's fifth round choice (Frederic Deschenes) in 1994 Entry Draft, June 20, 1993. Traded to **Tampa Bay** by **Philadelphia** with Philadelphia's fourth round choice in 1995 Entry Draft for Rob DiMaio, March 18, 1994.

CUNNEYWORTH, RANDY — OTT.

Left wing. Shoots left. 6', 180 lbs. Born, Etobicoke, Ont., May 10, 1961.
(Buffalo's 9th choice, 167th overall, in 1980 Entry Draft).

			Regular Season					Playoffs				
Season	Club	Lea	GP	G	A	TP	PIM	GP	G	A	TP	PIM
1979-80	Ottawa	OHA	63	16	25	41	145	11	0	1	1	13
1980-81	**Buffalo**	**NHL**	**1**	**0**	**0**	**0**	**2**	....	....	....	....	....
	Rochester	AHL	1	0	1	1	2	....	....	....	....	....
	Ottawa	OHA	67	54	74	128	240	15	5	8	13	35
1981-82	**Buffalo**	**NHL**	**20**	**2**	**4**	**6**	**47**	....	....	....	....	....
	Rochester	AHL	57	12	15	27	86	9	4	0	4	30
1982-83	Rochester	AHL	78	23	33	56	111	16	4	4	8	35
1983-84	Rochester	AHL	54	18	17	35	85	17	5	5	10	55
1984-85	Rochester	AHL	72	30	38	68	148	5	2	1	3	16
1985-86	**Pittsburgh**	**NHL**	**75**	**15**	**30**	**45**	**74**	....	....	....	....	....
1986-87	**Pittsburgh**	**NHL**	**79**	**26**	**27**	**53**	**142**	....	....	....	....	....
1987-88	**Pittsburgh**	**NHL**	**71**	**35**	**39**	**74**	**141**	....	....	....	....	....
1988-89	**Pittsburgh**	**NHL**	**70**	**25**	**19**	**44**	**156**	**11**	**3**	**5**	**8**	**26**
1989-90	**Winnipeg**	**NHL**	**28**	**5**	**6**	**11**	**34**	....	....	....	....	....
	Hartford	**NHL**	**43**	**9**	**9**	**18**	**41**	**4**	**0**	**0**	**0**	**2**
1990-91	**Hartford**	**NHL**	**32**	**9**	**5**	**14**	**49**	**1**	**0**	**0**	**0**	**0**
	Springfield	AHL	2	0	0	0	5	....	....	....	....	....
1991-92	**Hartford**	**NHL**	**39**	**7**	**10**	**17**	**71**	**7**	**3**	**0**	**3**	**9**
1992-93	**Hartford**	**NHL**	**39**	**5**	**4**	**9**	**63**	....	....	....	....	....
1993-94	**Hartford**	**NHL**	**63**	**9**	**8**	**17**	**87**	....	....	....	....	....
	Chicago	**NHL**	**16**	**4**	**3**	**7**	**13**	**6**	**0**	**0**	**0**	**8**
	NHL Totals		**576**	**151**	**164**	**315**	**920**	**29**	**6**	**5**	**11**	**45**

Traded to **Pittsburgh** by **Buffalo** with Mike Moller for Pat Hughes, October 4, 1985. Traded to **Winnipeg** by **Pittsburgh** with Rick Tabaracci and Dave McLlwain for Jim Kyte, Andrew McBain and Randy Gilhen, June 17, 1989. Traded to **Hartford** by **Winnipeg** for Paul MacDermid, December 13, 1989. Traded to **Chicago** by **Hartford** with Gary Suter and a future draft choice for Frantisek Kucera and Jocelyn Lemieux, March 11, 1994. Signed as a free agent by **Ottawa**, July 15, 1994.

CURRAN, BRIAN

Defense. Shoots left. 6'5", 220 lbs. Born, Toronto, Ont., November 5, 1963.
(Boston's 2nd choice, 22nd overall, in 1982 Entry Draft).

			Regular Season					Playoffs				
Season	Club	Lea	GP	G	A	TP	PIM	GP	G	A	TP	PIM
1980-81	Portland	WHL	59	2	28	30	275	7	0	1	1	13
1981-82	Portland	WHL	51	2	16	18	132	14	1	7	8	63
1982-83	Portland	WHL	56	1	30	31	187	14	1	3	4	57
1983-84	**Boston**	**NHL**	**16**	**1**	**1**	**2**	**57**	**3**	**0**	**0**	**0**	**7**
	Hershey	AHL	23	0	2	2	94	....	....	....	....	....
1984-85	**Boston**	**NHL**	**56**	**0**	**1**	**1**	**158**	....	....	....	....	....
	Hershey	AHL	4	0	0	0	19	....	....	....	....	....
1985-86	**Boston**	**NHL**	**43**	**2**	**5**	**7**	**192**	**2**	**0**	**0**	**0**	**4**
1986-87	**NY Islanders**	**NHL**	**68**	**0**	**10**	**10**	**356**	**8**	**0**	**0**	**0**	**51**
1987-88	**NY Islanders**	**NHL**	**22**	**0**	**1**	**1**	**68**	....	....	....	....	....
	Springfield	AHL	8	1	0	1	43	....	....	....	....	....
	Toronto	**NHL**	**7**	**0**	**1**	**1**	**19**	**6**	**0**	**0**	**0**	**41**
1988-89	**Toronto**	**NHL**	**47**	**1**	**4**	**5**	**185**	....	....	....	....	....
1989-90	**Toronto**	**NHL**	**72**	**2**	**9**	**11**	**301**	**5**	**0**	**1**	**1**	**19**
1990-91	**Toronto**	**NHL**	**4**	**0**	**0**	**0**	**7**	....	....	....	....	....
	Newmarket	AHL	6	0	1	1	32	....	....	....	....	....
	Buffalo	**NHL**	**17**	**0**	**1**	**1**	**43**	....	....	....	....	....
	Rochester	AHL	10	0	0	0	36	....	....	....	....	....
1991-92	**Buffalo**	**NHL**	**3**	**0**	**0**	**0**	**14**	....	....	....	....	....
	Rochester	AHL	36	0	3	3	122	....	....	....	....	....
1992-93	Cape Breton	AHL	61	2	24	26	223	12	0	3	3	12
1993-94	**Washington**	**NHL**	**26**	**1**	**0**	**1**	**61**	....	....	....	....	....
	Portland	AHL	46	1	6	7	247	15	0	1	1	59
	NHL Totals		**381**	**7**	**33**	**40**	**1461**	**24**	**0**	**1**	**1**	**122**

Signed as a free agent by **NY Islanders**, August 29, 1987. Traded to **Toronto** by **NY Islanders** for Toronto's sixth round choice (Pavel Gross) in 1988 Entry Draft, March 8, 1988. Traded to **Buffalo** by **Toronto** with Lou Franceschetti for Mike Foligno and Buffalo's eighth round choice (Thomas Kucharcik) in 1991 Entry Draft, December 17, 1990. Signed as a free agent by **Edmonton**, October 27, 1992. Signed as a free agent by **Washington**, October 21, 1993.

CURRIE, DAN

Left wing. Shoots left. 6'2", 195 lbs. Born, Burlington, Ont., March 15, 1968.
(Edmonton's 4th choice, 84th overall, in 1986 Entry Draft).

			Regular Season					Playoffs				
Season	Club	Lea	GP	G	A	TP	PIM	GP	G	A	TP	PIM
1985-86	S.S. Marie	OHL	66	21	24	45	37	....	....	....	....	....
1986-87	S.S. Marie	OHL	66	31	52	83	53	4	2	1	3	2
1987-88	Nova Scotia	AHL	3	4	2	6	0	5	4	3	7	0
	S.S. Marie	OHL	57	50	59	109	53	6	3	9	12	4
1988-89	Cape Breton	AHL	77	29	36	65	29	....	....	....	....	....
1989-90	Cape Breton	AHL	77	36	40	76	28	6	4	4	8	0
1990-91	**Edmonton**	**NHL**	**5**	**0**	**0**	**0**	**0**	....	....	....	....	....
	Cape Breton	AHL	71	47	45	92	51	4	3	1	4	8
1991-92	**Edmonton**	**NHL**	**7**	**1**	**0**	**1**	**0**	....	....	....	....	....
a	Cape Breton	AHL	66	*50	42	92	39	5	4	5	9	4
1992-93	**Edmonton**	**NHL**	**5**	**0**	**0**	**0**	**4**	....	....	....	....	....
	Cape Breton	AHL	75	57	41	98	73	16	7	4	11	29
1993-94	**Los Angeles**	**NHL**	**5**	**1**	**1**	**2**	**0**	....	....	....	....	....
	Phoenix	IHL	74	37	49	86	96	....	....	....	....	....
	NHL Totals		**22**	**2**	**1**	**3**	**4**	....	....	....	....	....

a AHL Second All-Star Team (1992)
b AHL First All-Star Team (1993)

Signed as a free agent by **Los Angeles**, July 16, 1993.

CZERKAWSKI, MARIUSZ — (chehr-KAWV-skee) BOS.

Right wing. Shoots right. 6', 195 lbs. Born, Radomsko, Poland, April 13, 1972.
(Boston's 5th choice, 106th overall, in 1991 Entry Draft).

			Regular Season					Playoffs				
Season	Club	Lea	GP	G	A	TP	PIM	GP	G	A	TP	PIM
1990-91	GKS Tychy	Poland	24	25	15	40	....	....	....	....	....	....
1991-92	Djurgarden	Swe.	39	8	5	13	4	3	0	0	0	2
1992-93	Hammarby	Swe.2	32	39	30	69	74	....	....	....	....	....
1993-94	Djurgarden	Swe.	39	13	21	34	20	6	3	1	4	2
	Boston	**NHL**	**4**	**2**	**1**	**3**	**0**	**13**	**3**	**3**	**6**	**4**
	NHL Totals		**4**	**2**	**1**	**3**	**0**	**13**	**3**	**3**	**6**	**4**

DAGENAIS, MIKE — (DA-shuh-NAY) PIT.

Defense. Shoots left. 6'3", 200 lbs. Born, Gloucester, Ont., July 22, 1969.
(Chicago's 4th choice, 60th overall, in 1987 Entry Draft).

			Regular Season					Playoffs				
Season	Club	Lea	GP	G	A	TP	PIM	GP	G	A	TP	PIM
1985-86	Peterborough	OHL	45	1	3	4	40	....	....	....	....	....
1986-87	Peterborough	OHL	56	1	17	18	66	12	4	1	5	20
1987-88	Peterborough	OHL	66	11	23	34	125	12	1	1	2	31
1988-89	Peterborough	OHL	62	14	23	37	122	13	3	3	6	12
1989-90	Peterborough	OHL	44	14	26	40	74	12	4	1	5	18
1990-91	Indianapolis	IHL	76	13	14	27	115	4	0	0	0	4
1991-92	Halifax	AHL	69	11	21	32	143	....	....	....	....	....
1992-93	Cincinnati	IHL	69	14	22	36	128	....	....	....	....	....
1993-94	Cleveland	IHL	65	8	18	26	120	....	....	....	....	....

Signed as a free agent by **Pittsburgh**, August 26, 1993.

DAHL, KEVIN — (DAHL) CGY.

Defense. Shoots right. 5'11", 190 lbs. Born, Regina, Sask., December 30, 1968.
(Montreal's 12th choice, 230th overall, in 1988 Entry Draft).

			Regular Season					Playoffs				
Season	Club	Lea	GP	G	A	TP	PIM	GP	G	A	TP	PIM
1986-87	Bowling Green	CCHA	32	2	6	8	54	....	....	....	....	....
1987-88	Bowling Green	CCHA	44	2	23	25	78	....	....	....	....	....
1988-89	Bowling Green	CCHA	46	9	26	35	51	....	....	....	....	....
1989-90	Bowling Green	CCHA	43	8	22	30	74	....	....	....	....	....
1990-91	Fredericton	AHL	32	1	15	16	45	9	0	1	1	11
	Winston-Salem	ECHL	36	7	17	24	58	....	....	....	....	....
1991-92	Cdn. National	....	45	2	15	17	44	....	....	....	....	....
	Cdn. Olympic	....	8	2	0	2	6	....	....	....	....	....
	Salt Lake	IHL	13	0	2	2	12	5	0	0	0	13
1992-93	**Calgary**	**NHL**	**61**	**2**	**9**	**11**	**56**	**6**	**0**	**2**	**2**	**8**
1993-94	**Calgary**	**NHL**	**33**	**0**	**3**	**3**	**23**	**6**	**0**	**0**	**0**	**4**
	Saint John	AHL	2	0	0	0	0	....	....	....	....	....
	NHL Totals		**94**	**2**	**12**	**14**	**79**	**12**	**0**	**2**	**2**	**12**

Signed as a free agent by **Calgary**, July 27, 1991.

DAHLEN, ULF (DAH-lehn) S.J.

Right wing. Shoots left. 6'2", 195 lbs. Born, Ostersund, Sweden, January 12, 1967.
(NY Rangers' 1st choice, 7th overall, in 1985 Entry Draft).

			Regular Season					Playoffs				
Season	Club	Lea	GP	G	A	TP	PIM	GP	G	A	TP	PIM
1983-84	Ostersund	Swe.2	36	15	11	26	10	....	....	....	....	....
1984-85	Ostersund	Swe.2	36	33	26	59	20	....	....	....	....	....
1985-86	Bjorkloven	Swe.	22	4	3	7	8	....	....	....	....	....
1986-87	Bjorkloven	Swe.	31	9	12	21	20	6	6	2	8	4
1987-88	**NY Rangers**	**NHL**	**70**	**29**	**23**	**52**	**26**	....	....	....	....	....
	Colorado	IHL	2	2	2	4	0	....	....	....	....	....
1988-89	**NY Rangers**	**NHL**	**56**	**24**	**19**	**43**	**50**	**4**	**0**	**0**	**0**	**0**
1989-90	**NY Rangers**	**NHL**	**63**	**18**	**18**	**36**	**30**	....	....	....	....	....
	Minnesota	**NHL**	**13**	**2**	**4**	**6**	**0**	**7**	**1**	**4**	**5**	**2**
1990-91	**Minnesota**	**NHL**	**66**	**21**	**18**	**39**	**6**	**15**	**2**	**6**	**8**	**4**
1991-92	**Minnesota**	**NHL**	**79**	**36**	**30**	**66**	**10**	**7**	**0**	**3**	**3**	**2**
1992-93	**Minnesota**	**NHL**	**83**	**35**	**39**	**74**	**6**	....	....	....	....	....
1993-94	**Dallas**	**NHL**	**65**	**19**	**38**	**57**	**10**	....	....	....	....	....
	San Jose	**NHL**	**13**	**6**	**6**	**12**	**0**	**14**	**6**	**2**	**8**	**0**
	NHL Totals		**508**	**190**	**195**	**385**	**138**	**47**	**9**	**15**	**24**	**8**

Traded to **Minnesota** by **NY Rangers** with Los Angeles' fourth round choice (previously acquired by NY Rangers — Minnesota selected Cal McGowan) in 1990 Entry Draft and future considerations for Mike Gartner, March 6, 1990. Traded to **San Jose** by **Dallas** with a future draft choice for Doug Zmolek and Mike Lalor, March 19, 1994.

DAHLQUIST, CHRIS (DAHL-kwist) OTT.

Defense. Shoots left. 6'1", 195 lbs. Born, Fridley, MN, December 14, 1962.

			Regular Season					Playoffs				
Season	Club	Lea	GP	G	A	TP	PIM	GP	G	A	TP	PIM
1981-82	Lake Superior	CCHA	39	4	10	14	62	....	....	....	....	....
1982-83	Lake Superior	CCHA	35	0	12	12	63	....	....	....	....	....
1983-84	Lake Superior	CCHA	40	4	19	23	76	....	....	....	....	....
1984-85	Lake Superior	CCHA	32	4	10	14	18	....	....	....	....	....
1985-86	**Pittsburgh**	**NHL**	**5**	**1**	**2**	**3**	**2**	....	....	....	....	....
	Baltimore	AHL	65	4	21	25	64	....	....	....	....	....
1986-87	**Pittsburgh**	**NHL**	**19**	**0**	**1**	**1**	**20**	....	....	....	....	....
	Baltimore	AHL	51	1	16	17	50	....	....	....	....	....
1987-88	**Pittsburgh**	**NHL**	**44**	**3**	**6**	**9**	**69**	....	....	....	....	....
1988-89	**Pittsburgh**	**NHL**	**43**	**1**	**5**	**6**	**42**	**2**	**0**	**0**	**0**	**0**
	Muskegon	IHL	10	3	6	9	14	....	....	....	....	....
1989-90	**Pittsburgh**	**NHL**	**62**	**4**	**10**	**14**	**56**	....	....	....	....	....
	Muskegon	IHL	6	1	1	2	8	....	....	....	....	....
1990-91	**Pittsburgh**	**NHL**	**22**	**1**	**2**	**3**	**30**	....	....	....	....	....
	Minnesota	**NHL**	**42**	**2**	**6**	**8**	**33**	**23**	**1**	**6**	**7**	**20**
1991-92	**Minnesota**	**NHL**	**74**	**1**	**13**	**14**	**68**	**7**	**0**	**0**	**0**	**6**
1992-93	**Calgary**	**NHL**	**74**	**3**	**7**	**10**	**66**	**6**	**3**	**1**	**4**	**4**
1993-94	**Calgary**	**NHL**	**77**	**1**	**11**	**12**	**52**	**1**	**0**	**0**	**0**	**0**
	NHL Totals		**462**	**17**	**63**	**80**	**438**	**39**	**4**	**7**	**11**	**30**

Signed as a free agent by **Pittsburgh**, May 7, 1985. Traded to **Minnesota** by **Pittsburgh** with Jim Johnson for Larry Murphy and Peter Taglianetti, December 11, 1990. Claimed by **Calgary** from **Minnesota** in NHL Waiver Draft, October 4, 1992. Signed as a free agent by **Ottawa**, July 4, 1994.

DAIGLE, ALEXANDRE (DAYG) OTT.

Center. Shoots left. 6', 185 lbs. Born, Montreal, Que., February 7, 1975.
(Ottawa's 1st choice, 1st overall, in 1993 Entry Draft).

			Regular Season					Playoffs				
Season	Club	Lea	GP	G	A	TP	PIM	GP	G	A	TP	PIM
1991-92ab	Victoriaville	QMJHL	66	35	75	110	63	....	....	....	....	....
1992-93c	Victoriaville	QMJHL	53	45	92	137	85	6	5	6	11	4
1993-94	**Ottawa**	**NHL**	**84**	**20**	**31**	**51**	**40**	....	....	....	....	....
	NHL Totals		**84**	**20**	**31**	**51**	**40**	....	....	....	....	....

a QMJHL Second All-Star Team (1992)
b Canadian Major Junior Rookie of the Year (1992)
c QMJHL First All-Star Team (1993)

DAIGNEAULT, JEAN-JACQUES (J.J.) (DAYN-yoh) MTL.

Defense. Shoots left. 5'11", 199 lbs. Born, Montreal, Que., October 12, 1965.
(Vancouver's 1st choice, 10th overall, in 1984 Entry Draft).

			Regular Season					Playoffs				
Season	Club	Lea	GP	G	A	TP	PIM	GP	G	A	TP	PIM
1981-82	Laval	QMJHL	64	4	25	29	41	18	1	3	4	2
1982-83a	Longueuil	QMJHL	70	26	58	84	58	15	4	11	15	35
1983-84	Cdn. National	....	62	6	15	21	40	....	....	....	....	....
	Cdn. Olympic	....	7	1	1	2	0	....	....	....	....	....
	Longueuil	QMJHL	10	2	11	13	6	14	3	13	16	30
1984-85	**Vancouver**	**NHL**	**67**	**4**	**23**	**27**	**69**	....	....	....	....	....
1985-86	**Vancouver**	**NHL**	**64**	**5**	**23**	**28**	**45**	**3**	**0**	**2**	**2**	**0**
1986-87	**Philadelphia**	**NHL**	**77**	**6**	**16**	**22**	**56**	**9**	**1**	**0**	**1**	**0**
1987-88	**Philadelphia**	**NHL**	**28**	**2**	**2**	**4**	**12**	....	....	....	....	....
	Hershey	AHL	10	1	5	6	8	....	....	....	....	....
1988-89	Hershey	AHL	12	0	10	10	13	....	....	....	....	....
	Sherbrooke	AHL	63	10	33	43	48	6	1	3	4	2
1989-90	**Montreal**	**NHL**	**36**	**2**	**10**	**12**	**14**	**9**	**0**	**0**	**0**	**2**
	Sherbrooke	AHL	28	8	19	27	18	....	....	....	....	....
1990-91	**Montreal**	**NHL**	**51**	**3**	**16**	**19**	**31**	**5**	**0**	**1**	**1**	**0**
1991-92	**Montreal**	**NHL**	**79**	**4**	**14**	**18**	**36**	**11**	**0**	**3**	**3**	**4**
1992-93	**Montreal**	**NHL**	**66**	**8**	**10**	**18**	**25**	**20**	**1**	**3**	**4**	**2**
1993-94	**Montreal**	**NHL**	**68**	**2**	**12**	**14**	**73**	**7**	**0**	**1**	**1**	**12**
	NHL Totals		**536**	**36**	**126**	**162**	**361**	**64**	**2**	**10**	**12**	**20**

a QMJHL First All-Star Team (1983)

Traded to **Philadelphia** by **Vancouver** with Vancouver's second round choice (Kent Hawley) in 1986 Entry Draft for Dave Richter, Rich Sutter and Vancouver's third round choice (previously acquired by Philadelphia — Vancouver selected Don Gibson) in 1986 Entry Draft, June 6, 1986. Traded to **Montreal** by **Philadelphia** for Scott Sandelin, November 7, 1988.

DALE, ANDREW L.A.

Center. Shoots left. 6'1", 196 lbs. Born, Sudbury, Ont., February 16, 1976.
(Los Angeles' 6th choice, 189th overall, in 1994 Entry Draft).

			Regular Season					Playoffs				
Season	Club	Lea	GP	G	A	TP	PIM	GP	G	A	TP	PIM
1993-94	Sudbury	OHL	53	8	13	21	21	9	0	3	3	4

DALGARNO, BRAD NYI

Right wing. Shoots right. 6'3", 215 lbs. Born, Vancouver, B.C., August 11, 1967.
(NY Islanders' 1st choice, 6th overall, in 1985 Entry Draft).

			Regular Season					Playoffs				
Season	Club	Lea	GP	G	A	TP	PIM	GP	G	A	TP	PIM
1984-85	Hamilton	OHA	66	23	30	53	86	....	....	....	....	....
1985-86	**NY Islanders**	**NHL**	**2**	**1**	**0**	**1**	**0**	....	....	....	....	....
	Hamilton	OHL	54	22	43	65	79	....	....	....	....	....
1986-87	Hamilton	OHL	60	27	32	59	100	....	....	....	....	....
	NY Islanders	**NHL**	....	....	....	....	....	**1**	**0**	**1**	**1**	**0**
1987-88	**NY Islanders**	**NHL**	**38**	**2**	**8**	**10**	**58**	**4**	**0**	**0**	**0**	**19**
	Springfield	AHL	39	13	11	24	76	....	....	....	....	....
1988-89	**NY Islanders**	**NHL**	**55**	**11**	**10**	**21**	**86**	....	....	....	....	....
1989-90						DID NOT PLAY						
1990-91	**NY Islanders**	**NHL**	**41**	**3**	**12**	**15**	**24**	....	....	....	....	....
	Capital Dist.	AHL	27	6	14	20	26	....	....	....	....	....
1991-92	**NY Islanders**	**NHL**	**15**	**2**	**1**	**3**	**12**	....	....	....	....	....
	Capital Dist.	AHL	14	7	8	15	34	....	....	....	....	....
1992-93	**NY Islanders**	**NHL**	**57**	**15**	**17**	**32**	**62**	**18**	**2**	**2**	**4**	**14**
	Capital Dist.	AHL	19	10	4	14	16	....	....	....	....	....
1993-94	**NY Islanders**	**NHL**	**73**	**11**	**19**	**30**	**62**	**4**	**0**	**1**	**1**	**4**
	NHL Totals		**281**	**45**	**67**	**112**	**304**	**27**	**2**	**4**	**6**	**37**

DAL GRANDE, DAVID NYR

Defense. Shoots left. 6'5", 195 lbs. Born, Ottawa, Ont., July 8, 1974.
(NY Rangers' 6th choice, 144th overall, in 1992 Entry Draft).

			Regular Season					Playoffs				
Season	Club	Lea	GP	G	A	TP	PIM	GP	G	A	TP	PIM
1992-93	Notre Dame	CCHA	22	1	1	2	10	....	....	....	....	....
1993-94	Notre Dame	CCHA	32	2	4	6	20	....	....	....	....	....

DAMEWORTH, CHAD EDM.

Defense. Shoots left. 6'2", 200 lbs. Born, Marquette, MI, July 6, 1972.
(Edmonton's 1st choice, 6th overall, in 1994 Supplemental Draft).

			Regular Season					Playoffs				
Season	Club	Lea	GP	G	A	TP	PIM	GP	G	A	TP	PIM
1991-92	N. Michigan	WCHA	13	0	2	2	8	....	....	....	....	....
1992-93	N. Michigan	WCHA	29	0	2	2	22	....	....	....	....	....
1993-94	N. Michigan	WCHA	36	0	4	4	26	....	....	....	....	....

DAMPHOUSSE, VINCENT (DAHM-fooz) MTL.

Left wing. Shoots left. 6'1", 199 lbs. Born, Montreal, Que., December 17, 1967.
(Toronto's 1st choice, 6th overall, in 1986 Entry Draft).

			Regular Season					Playoffs				
Season	Club	Lea	GP	G	A	TP	PIM	GP	G	A	TP	PIM
1983-84	Laval	QMJHL	66	29	36	65	25	....	....	....	....	....
1984-85	Laval	QMJHL	68	35	68	103	62	....	....	....	....	....
1985-86a	Laval	QMJHL	69	45	110	155	70	14	9	27	36	12
1986-87	**Toronto**	**NHL**	**80**	**21**	**25**	**46**	**26**	**12**	**1**	**5**	**6**	**8**
1987-88	**Toronto**	**NHL**	**75**	**12**	**36**	**48**	**40**	**6**	**0**	**1**	**1**	**10**
1988-89	**Toronto**	**NHL**	**80**	**26**	**42**	**68**	**75**	....	....	....	....	....
1989-90	**Toronto**	**NHL**	**80**	**33**	**61**	**94**	**56**	**5**	**0**	**2**	**2**	**2**
1990-91	**Toronto**	**NHL**	**79**	**26**	**47**	**73**	**65**	....	....	....	....	....
1991-92	**Edmonton**	**NHL**	**80**	**38**	**51**	**89**	**53**	**16**	**6**	**8**	**14**	**8**
1992-93	**Montreal**	**NHL**	**84**	**39**	**58**	**97**	**98**	**20**	**11**	**12**	**23**	**16**
1993-94	**Montreal**	**NHL**	**84**	**40**	**51**	**91**	**75**	**7**	**1**	**2**	**3**	**8**
	NHL Totals		**642**	**235**	**371**	**606**	**488**	**66**	**19**	**30**	**49**	**52**

a QMJHL Second All-Star Team (1986)

Played in NHL All-Star Game (1991, 1992)

Traded to **Edmonton** by **Toronto** with Peter Ing, Scott Thornton, Luke Richardson, future considerations and cash for Grant Fuhr, Glenn Anderson and Craig Berube, September 19, 1991. Traded to **Montreal** by **Edmonton** with Edmonton's fourth round choice (Adam Wiesel) in 1993 Entry Draft for Shayne Corson, Brent Gilchrist and Vladimir Vujtek, August 27, 1992.

DANDENAULT, ERIC

Left wing. Shoots right. 6', 193 lbs. Born, Sherbrooke, Que., March 10, 1970.

			Regular Season					Playoffs				
Season	Club	Lea	GP	G	A	TP	PIM	GP	G	A	TP	PIM
1990-91	Drummondville	QMJHL	67	14	33	47	215	14	5	6	11	84
1991-92	Hershey	AHL	69	6	13	19	149	3	0	0	0	4
1992-93	Hershey	AHL	72	20	19	39	118	....	....	....	....	....
1993-94	Hershey	AHL	14	2	1	3	49	....	....	....	....	....
	Johnstown	ECHL	2	1	1	2	6	....	....	....	....	....

Signed as a free agent by **Philadelphia**, December 4, 1991.

DANDENAULT, MATHIEU DET.

Right wing. Shoots right. 6', 174 lbs. Born, Sherbrooke, Que., February 3, 1976.
(Detroit's 2nd choice, 49th overall, in 1994 Entry Draft).

			Regular Season					Playoffs				
Season	Club	Lea	GP	G	A	TP	PIM	GP	G	A	TP	PIM
1992-93	Gloucester	Jr. A	52	14	28	42	75	....	....	....	....	....
1993-94	Sherbrooke	QMJHL	67	17	36	53	67	12	4	10	14	12

DANEYKO, KEN (DAN-ee-KOH) N.J.

Defense. Shoots left. 6', 210 lbs. Born, Windsor, Ont., April 17, 1964.
(New Jersey's 2nd choice, 18th overall, in 1982 Entry Draft).

			Regular Season					Playoffs				
Season	Club	Lea	GP	G	A	TP	PIM	GP	G	A	TP	PIM
1980-81	Spokane	WHL	62	6	13	19	40	4	0	0	0	6
1981-82	Spokane	WHL	26	1	11	12	147	....	....	....	....	....
	Seattle	WHL	38	1	22	23	151	14	1	9	10	49
1982-83	Seattle	WHL	69	17	43	60	150	4	1	3	4	14
1983-84	**New Jersey**	**NHL**	**11**	**1**	**4**	**5**	**17**	....	....	....	....	....
	Kamloops	WHL	19	6	28	34	52	17	4	9	13	28
1984-85	**New Jersey**	**NHL**	**1**	**0**	**0**	**0**	**10**	....	....	....	....	....
	Maine	AHL	80	4	9	13	206	11	1	3	4	36
1985-86	**New Jersey**	**NHL**	**44**	**0**	**10**	**10**	**100**	....	....	....	....	....
	Maine	AHL	21	3	2	5	75	....	....	....	....	....
1986-87	**New Jersey**	**NHL**	**79**	**2**	**12**	**14**	**183**	....	....	....	....	....
1987-88	**New Jersey**	**NHL**	**80**	**5**	**7**	**12**	**239**	**20**	**1**	**6**	**7**	**83**
1988-89	**New Jersey**	**NHL**	**80**	**5**	**5**	**10**	**283**	....	....	....	....	....
1989-90	**New Jersey**	**NHL**	**74**	**6**	**15**	**21**	**216**	**6**	**2**	**0**	**2**	**21**
1990-91	**New Jersey**	**NHL**	**80**	**4**	**16**	**20**	**249**	**7**	**0**	**1**	**1**	**10**
1991-92	**New Jersey**	**NHL**	**80**	**1**	**7**	**8**	**170**	**7**	**0**	**3**	**3**	**16**
1992-93	**New Jersey**	**NHL**	**84**	**2**	**11**	**13**	**236**	**5**	**0**	**0**	**0**	**8**
1993-94	**New Jersey**	**NHL**	**78**	**1**	**9**	**10**	**176**	**20**	**0**	**1**	**1**	**45**
	NHL Totals		**691**	**27**	**96**	**123**	**1879**	**65**	**3**	**11**	**14**	**183**

DANIELS, JEFF — FLA.

Left wing. Shoots left. 6'1", 200 lbs. Born, Oshawa, Ont., June 24, 1968.
(Pittsburgh's 6th choice, 109th overall, in 1986 Entry Draft).

			Regular Season					Playoffs				
Season	**Club**	**Lea**	**GP**	**G**	**A**	**TP**	**PIM**	**GP**	**G**	**A**	**TP**	**PIM**
1984-85	Oshawa	OHL	59	7	11	18	16	....	....	....	....	....
1985-86	Oshawa	OHL	62	13	19	32	23	6	0	1	1	0
1986-87	Oshawa	OHL	54	14	9	23	22	15	3	2	5	5
1987-88	Oshawa	OHL	64	29	39	68	59	4	2	3	5	0
1988-89	Muskegon	IHL	58	21	21	42	58	11	3	5	8	11
1989-90	Muskegon	IHL	80	30	47	77	39	6	1	1	2	7
1990-91	**Pittsburgh**	**NHL**	**11**	**0**	**2**	**2**	**2**	....	....	....	....	....
	Muskegon	IHL	62	23	29	52	18	5	1	3	4	2
1991-92	**Pittsburgh**	**NHL**	**2**	**0**	**0**	**0**	**0**	....	....	....	....	....
	Muskegon	IHL	44	19	16	35	38	10	5	4	9	9
1992-93	**Pittsburgh**	**NHL**	**58**	**5**	**4**	**9**	**14**	**12**	**3**	**2**	**5**	**0**
	Cleveland	IHL	3	2	1	3	0	....	....	....	....	....
1993-94	**Pittsburgh**	**NHL**	**63**	**3**	**5**	**8**	**20**	....	....	....	....	....
	Florida	**NHL**	**7**	**0**	**0**	**0**	**0**	....	....	....	....	....
	NHL Totals		**141**	**8**	**11**	**19**	**36**	**12**	**3**	**2**	**5**	**0**

Traded to **Florida** by **Pittsburgh** for Greg Hawgood, March 19, 1994.

DANIELS, KIMBI

Center. Shoots right. 5'10", 175 lbs. Born, Brandon, Man., January 19, 1972.
(Philadelphia's 5th choice, 44th overall, in 1990 Entry Draft).

			Regular Season					Playoffs				
Season	**Club**	**Lea**	**GP**	**G**	**A**	**TP**	**PIM**	**GP**	**G**	**A**	**TP**	**PIM**
1988-89	Swift Current	WHL	68	30	31	61	48	12	6	6	12	12
1989-90	Swift Current	WHL	69	43	51	94	84	4	1	3	4	10
1990-91	**Philadelphia**	**NHL**	**2**	**0**	**1**	**1**	**0**	....	....	....	....	....
	Swift Current	WHL	69	54	64	118	68	3	4	2	6	6
1991-92	**Philadelphia**	**NHL**	**25**	**1**	**1**	**2**	**4**	....	....	....	....	....
	Seattle	WHL	19	7	14	21	133	15	5	10	15	27
1992-93	Tri-City	WHL	9	9	12	21	12	3	0	1	1	8
1993-94	Salt Lake	IHL	25	6	9	15	8	....	....	....	....	....
	Detroit	ColHL	23	11	28	39	42	....	....	....	....	....
	NHL Totals		**27**	**1**	**2**	**3**	**4**	....	....	....	....	....

DANIELS, SCOTT — HFD.

Left wing. Shoots left. 6'3", 200 lbs. Born, Prince Albert, Sask., September 19, 1969.
(Hartford's 6th choice, 136th overall, in 1989 Entry Draft).

			Regular Season					Playoffs				
Season	**Club**	**Lea**	**GP**	**G**	**A**	**TP**	**PIM**	**GP**	**G**	**A**	**TP**	**PIM**
1986-87	Kamloops	WHL	43	6	4	10	68	....	....	....	....	....
	N. Westminster	WHL	19	4	7	11	30	....	....	....	....	....
1987-88	N. Westminster	WHL	37	6	11	17	157	....	....	....	....	....
	Regina	WHL	19	2	3	5	83	....	....	....	....	....
1988-89	Regina	WHL	64	21	26	47	241	....	....	....	....	....
1989-90	Regina	WHL	52	28	31	59	171	....	....	....	....	....
1990-91	Springfield	AHL	40	2	6	8	121	....	....	....	....	....
	Louisville	ECHL	9	5	3	8	34	1	0	2	2	0
1991-92	Springfield	AHL	54	7	15	22	213	10	0	0	0	32
1992-93	**Hartford**	**NHL**	**1**	**0**	**0**	**0**	**19**	....	....	....	....	....
	Springfield	AHL	60	11	12	23	181	12	2	7	9	12
1993-94	Springfield	AHL	52	9	11	20	185	6	0	1	1	53
	NHL Totals		**1**	**0**	**0**	**0**	**19**	....	....	....	....	....

DANYLUK, CAM — VAN.

Left wing. Shoots left. 6'4", 215 lbs. Born, Andrew, Alta., September 6, 1972.

			Regular Season					Playoffs				
Season	**Club**	**Lea**	**GP**	**G**	**A**	**TP**	**PIM**	**GP**	**G**	**A**	**TP**	**PIM**
1991-92	Spokana	WHL	6	0	4	4	37	....	....	....	....	....
	Brandon	WHL	5	3	0	3	16	....	....	....	....	....
	Medicine Hat	WHL	52	27	26	53	158	4	0	2	2	6
1992-93	Medicine Hat	WHL	57	29	19	48	214	10	9	5	14	29
1993-94	Hamilton	AHL	60	11	12	23	159	2	1	0	1	0

Signed as a free agent by **Vancouver**, April 21, 1993.

DARBY, CRAIG — MTL.

Center. Shoots right. 6'3", 180 lbs. Born, Oneida, NY, September 26, 1972.
(Montreal's 3rd choice, 43rd overall, in 1991 Entry Draft).

			Regular Season					Playoffs				
Season	**Club**	**Lea**	**GP**	**G**	**A**	**TP**	**PIM**	**GP**	**G**	**A**	**TP**	**PIM**
1991-92	Providence	H.E.	35	17	24	41	47	....	....	....	....	....
1992-93	Providence	H.E.	35	11	21	32	62	....	....	....	....	....
1993-94	Fredericton	AHL	66	23	33	56	51	....	....	....	....	....

DARLING, DION — MTL.

Defense. Shoots left. 6'3", 205 lbs. Born, Edmonton, Alta., October 22, 1974.
(Montreal's 7th choice, 125th overall, in 1993 Entry Draft).

			Regular Season					Playoffs				
Season	**Club**	**Lea**	**GP**	**G**	**A**	**TP**	**PIM**	**GP**	**G**	**A**	**TP**	**PIM**
1991-92	St. Albert	AJHL	29	5	15	20	101	....	....	....	....	....
1992-93	Spokane	WHL	69	1	4	5	168	9	0	1	1	14
1993-94	Spokane	WHL	45	1	8	9	190	....	....	....	....	....
	Moose Jaw	WHL	23	4	6	10	96	....	....	....	....	....
	Wheeling	ECHL	3	0	1	1	7	9	0	1	1	14

DAVIDSSON, JOHAN (DAH-vihd-suhn) — ANA.

Center. Shoots right. 5'11", 170 lbs. Born, Jonkoping, Sweden, January 6, 1976.
(Anaheim's 2nd choice, 28th overall, in 1994 Entry Draft).

			Regular Season					Playoffs				
Season	**Club**	**Lea**	**GP**	**G**	**A**	**TP**	**PIM**	**GP**	**G**	**A**	**TP**	**PIM**
1992-93	HV-71	Swe.	8	1	0	1	0	....	....	....	....	....
1993-94	HV-71	Swe.	38	2	5	7	4	....	....	....	....	....

DAVYDOV, EVGENY (dah-VEE-dohv, yev-GEHN-ee) — OTT.

Left wing. Shoots right. 6', 200 lbs. Born, Chelyabinsk, USSR, May 27, 1967.
(Winnipeg's 14th choice, 235th overall, in 1989 Entry Draft).

			Regular Season					Playoffs				
Season	**Club**	**Lea**	**GP**	**G**	**A**	**TP**	**PIM**	**GP**	**G**	**A**	**TP**	**PIM**
1984-85	Chelyabinsk	USSR	5	1	0	1	2	....	....	....	....	....
1985-86	Chelyabinsk	USSR	39	11	5	16	22	....	....	....	....	....
1986-87	CSKA	USSR	32	11	2	13	8	....	....	....	....	....
1987-88	CSKA	USSR	44	16	7	23	18	....	....	....	....	....
1988-89	CSKA	USSR	35	9	7	16	4	....	....	....	....	....
1989-90	CSKA	USSR	44	17	6	23	16	....	....	....	....	....
1990-91	CSKA	USSR	44	10	10	20	26	....	....	....	....	....
1991-92	CSKA	CIS	27	13	12	25	14	....	....	....	....	....
	Winnipeg	**NHL**	**12**	**4**	**3**	**7**	**8**	**7**	**2**	**2**	**4**	**2**
1992-93	**Winnipeg**	**NHL**	**79**	**28**	**21**	**49**	**66**	**4**	**0**	**0**	**0**	**0**
1993-94	**Florida**	**NHL**	**21**	**2**	**6**	**8**	**8**	....	....	....	....	....
	Ottawa	**NHL**	**40**	**5**	**7**	**12**	**38**	....	....	....	....	....
	NHL Totals		**152**	**39**	**37**	**76**	**120**	**11**	**2**	**2**	**4**	**2**

Traded to **Florida** by **Winnipeg** for Florida's fourth round choice (later traded to Edmonton — Edmonton selected Adam Copeland) in 1994 Entry Draft, September 30, 1993. Traded to **Ottawa** by **Florida** with Scott Levins and future draft choices for Bob Kudelski, January 6, 1994.

DAWE, JASON (DAW) — BUF.

Left wing. Shoots left. 5'10", 195 lbs. Born, North York, Ont., May 29, 1973.
(Buffalo's 2nd choice, 35th overall, in 1991 Entry Draft).

			Regular Season					Playoffs				
Season	**Club**	**Lea**	**GP**	**G**	**A**	**TP**	**PIM**	**GP**	**G**	**A**	**TP**	**PIM**
1989-90	Peterborough	OHL	50	15	18	33	19	12	4	7	11	4
1990-91	Peterborough	OHL	66	43	27	70	43	4	3	1	4	0
1991-92	Peterborough	OHL	66	53	55	108	55	4	5	0	5	0
1992-93ab	Peterborough	OHL	59	58	68	126	80	21	18	33	51	18
	Rochester	AHL	....	....	....	....	....	3	1	0	1	0
1993-94	**Buffalo**	**NHL**	**32**	**6**	**7**	**13**	**12**	**6**	**0**	**1**	**1**	**6**
	Rochester	AHL	48	22	14	36	44	....	....	....	....	....
	NHL Totals		**32**	**6**	**7**	**13**	**12**	**6**	**0**	**1**	**1**	**6**

a OHL First All-Star Team (1993)
b Canadian Major Junior Second All-Star Team (1993)

DAY, JOE — NYI

Left wing. Shoots left. 5'11", 180 lbs. Born, Chicago, IL, May 11, 1968.
(Hartford's 8th choice, 186th overall, in 1987 Entry Draft).

			Regular Season					Playoffs				
Season	**Club**	**Lea**	**GP**	**G**	**A**	**TP**	**PIM**	**GP**	**G**	**A**	**TP**	**PIM**
1986-87	St. Lawrence	ECAC	33	9	11	20	25	....	....	....	....	....
1987-88	St. Lawrence	ECAC	30	21	16	37	36	....	....	....	....	....
1988-89	St. Lawrence	ECAC	36	21	27	48	44	....	....	....	....	....
1989-90a	St. Lawrence	ECAC	32	19	26	45	30	....	....	....	....	....
1990-91	Springfield	AHL	75	24	29	53	82	18	5	5	10	27
1991-92	**Hartford**	**NHL**	**24**	**0**	**3**	**3**	**10**	....	....	....	....	....
	Springfield	AHL	50	33	25	58	92	....	....	....	....	....
1992-93	**Hartford**	**NHL**	**24**	**1**	**7**	**8**	**47**	....	....	....	....	....
	Springfield	AHL	33	15	20	35	118	15	0	8	8	40
1993-94	**NY Islanders**	**NHL**	**24**	**0**	**0**	**0**	**30**	....	....	....	....	....
	Salt Lake	IHL	33	16	10	26	153	....	....	....	....	....
	NHL Totals		**72**	**1**	**10**	**11**	**87**	....	....	....	....	....

a ECAC Second All-Star Team (1990)

Signed as a free agent by **NY Islanders**, August 24, 1993.

DAZE, ERIC — CHI.

Left wing. Shoots left. 6'4", 202 lbs. Born, Montreal, Que., July 2, 1975.
(Chicago's 5th choice, 90th overall, in 1993 Entry Draft).

			Regular Season					Playoffs				
Season	**Club**	**Lea**	**GP**	**G**	**A**	**TP**	**PIM**	**GP**	**G**	**A**	**TP**	**PIM**
1992-93	Beauport	QMJHL	68	19	36	55	24	....	....	....	....	....
1993-94a	Beauport	QMJHL	66	59	48	107	31	15	16	8	24	2

a QMJHL First All-Star Team (1994)

DEADMARSH, ADAM — QUE.

Center. Shoots right. 6', 195 lbs. Born, Trail, B.C., May 10, 1975.
(Quebec's 2nd choice, 14th overall, in 1993 Entry Draft).

			Regular Season					Playoffs				
Season	**Club**	**Lea**	**GP**	**G**	**A**	**TP**	**PIM**	**GP**	**G**	**A**	**TP**	**PIM**
1991-92	Portland	WHL	68	30	30	60	81	6	3	3	6	13
1992-93	Portland	WHL	58	33	36	69	126	16	7	8	15	29
1993-94	Portland	WHL	65	43	56	99	212	....	....	....	....	....

DEAN, KEVIN — N.J.

Defense. Shoots left. 6'2", 195 lbs. Born, Madison, WI, April 1, 1969.
(New Jersey's 4th choice, 86th overall, in 1987 Entry Draft).

			Regular Season					Playoffs				
Season	**Club**	**Lea**	**GP**	**G**	**A**	**TP**	**PIM**	**GP**	**G**	**A**	**TP**	**PIM**
1987-88	N. Hampshire	H.E.	27	1	6	7	34	....	....	....	....	....
1988-89	N. Hampshire	H.E.	34	1	12	13	28	....	....	....	....	....
1989-90	N. Hampshire	H.E.	39	2	6	8	42	....	....	....	....	....
1990-91	N. Hampshire	H.E.	31	10	12	22	22	....	....	....	....	....
	Utica	AHL	7	0	1	1	2	....	....	....	....	....
1991-92	Utica	AHL	23	0	3	3	6	....	....	....	....	....
	Cincinnati	ECHL	30	3	22	25	43	9	1	6	7	8
1992-93	Cincinnati	IHL	13	2	1	3	15	....	....	....	....	....
	Utica	AHL	57	2	16	18	76	5	1	0	1	8
1993-94	Albany	AHL	70	9	33	42	92	5	0	2	2	7

DEAZELEY, MARK — WPG.

Left wing. Shoots left. 6'4", 240 lbs. Born, North York, Ont., April 8, 1972.

			Regular Season					Playoffs				
Season	**Club**	**Lea**	**GP**	**G**	**A**	**TP**	**PIM**	**GP**	**G**	**A**	**TP**	**PIM**
1989-90	Oshawa	OHL	27	3	1	4	56	....	....	....	....	....
1990-91	Oshawa	OHL	65	17	19	36	149	16	1	2	3	38
1991-92	Oshawa	OHL	66	19	21	40	215	7	0	0	0	16
1992-93	Toledo	ECHL	63	27	18	45	263	15	8	6	14	66
1993-94	Toledo	ECHL	57	41	36	77	231	14	*16	10	*26	37
	Fort Wayne	IHL	1	0	0	0	2	....	....	....	....	....

Signed as a free agent by **Winnipeg**, June 17, 1994.

DEBRUSK, LOUIE (dah-BRUHSK)

Left wing. Shoots left. 6'2", 215 lbs. Born, Cambridge, Ont., March 19, 1971.
(NY Rangers' 4th choice, 49th overall, in 1989 Entry Draft).

			Regular Season					Playoffs				
Season	Club	Lea	GP	G	A	TP	PIM	GP	G	A	TP	PIM
1988-89	London	OHL	59	11	11	22	149	19	1	1	2	43
1989-90	London	OHL	61	21	19	40	198	6	2	2	4	24
1990-91	London	OHL	61	31	33	64	*223	7	2	2	4	14
	Binghamton	AHL	2	0	0	0	7	2	0	0	0	9
1991-92	**Edmonton**	**NHL**	**25**	**2**	**1**	**3**	**124**	....	....	....	....	....
	Cape Breton	AHL	28	2	2	4	73	....	....	....	....	....
1992-93	**Edmonton**	**NHL**	**51**	**8**	**2**	**10**	**205**	....	....	....	....	....
1993-94	**Edmonton**	**NHL**	**48**	**4**	**6**	**10**	**185**	....	....	....	....	....
	Cape Breton	AHL	5	3	1	4	58	....	....	....	....	....
	NHL Totals		**124**	**14**	**9**	**23**	**514**	....	....	....	....	....

Traded to **Edmonton** by **NY Rangers** with Bernie Nicholls and Steven Rice for Mark Messier and future considerations, October 4, 1991.

DEMITRA, PAVOL (deh-MIHT-rah) OTT.

Left wing. Shoots left. 6', 189 lbs. Born, Dubnica, Czech., November 29, 1974.
(Ottawa's 9th choice, 227th overall, in 1993 Entry Draft).

			Regular Season					Playoffs				
Season	Club	Lea	GP	G	A	TP	PIM	GP	G	A	TP	PIM
1991-92	Spartak Dubnica	Czech. 2	28	13	10	23	12	....	....	....	....	....
1992-93	Dukla Trencin	Czech.	46	10	18	28	....	....	....	....	....	....
	CAPEH Dubnica	Czech. 2	4	3	0	3	....	....	....	....	....	....
1993-94	**Ottawa**	**NHL**	**12**	**1**	**1**	**2**	**4**	....	....	....	....	....
	P.E.I.	AHL	41	18	23	41	8	....	....	....	....	....
	NHL Totals		**12**	**1**	**1**	**2**	**4**	....	....	....	....	....

DEMPSEY, NATHAN TOR.

Defense. Shoots left. 6', 170 lbs. Born, Spruce Grove, Alta., July 14, 1974.
(Toronto's 11th choice, 148th overall, in 1992 Entry Draft).

			Regular Season					Playoffs				
Season	Club	Lea	GP	G	A	TP	PIM	GP	G	A	TP	PIM
1991-92	Regina	WHL	70	4	22	26	72	....	....	....	....	....
1992-93	Regina	WHL	72	12	29	41	95	13	3	8	11	14
	St. John's	AHL	....	....	....	....	....	2	0	0	0	0
1993-94a	Regina	WHL	56	14	36	50	100	4	0	0	0	4

a WHL East Second All-Star Team (1994)

DEPALMA, LARRY

Left wing. Shoots left. 6', 195 lbs. Born, Trenton, MI, October 27, 1965.

			Regular Season					Playoffs				
Season	Club	Lea	GP	G	A	TP	PIM	GP	G	A	TP	PIM
1984-85	N. Westminster	WHL	65	14	16	30	87	10	1	1	2	25
1985-86	Saskatoon	WHL	65	61	51	112	232	13	7	9	16	58
	Minnesota	**NHL**	**1**	**0**	**0**	**0**	**0**	....	....	....	....	....
1986-87	**Minnesota**	**NHL**	**56**	**9**	**6**	**15**	**219**	....	....	....	....	....
	Springfield	AHL	9	2	2	4	82	....	....	....	....	....
1987-88	**Minnesota**	**NHL**	**7**	**1**	**1**	**2**	**15**	....	....	....	....	....
	Baltimore	AHL	16	8	10	18	121	....	....	....	....	....
	Kalamazoo	IHL	22	6	11	17	215	....	....	....	....	....
1988-89	**Minnesota**	**NHL**	**43**	**5**	**7**	**12**	**102**	**2**	**0**	**0**	**0**	**6**
1989-90	Kalamazoo	IHL	36	7	14	21	218	4	1	1	2	32
1990-91	**Minnesota**	**NHL**	**14**	**3**	**0**	**3**	**26**	....	....	....	....	....
	Kalamazoo	IHL	55	27	32	59	160	11	5	4	9	25
1991-92	Kansas City	IHL	62	28	29	57	188	15	7	*13	20	34
1992-93	**San Jose**	**NHL**	**20**	**2**	**6**	**8**	**41**	....	....	....	....	....
	Kansas City	IHL	30	11	11	22	83	10	1	4	5	20
1993-94	Atlanta	IHL	21	10	10	20	109	....	....	....	....	....
	Salt Lake	IHL	34	4	12	16	125	....	....	....	....	....
	Pittsburgh	**NHL**	**7**	**1**	**0**	**1**	**5**	**1**	**0**	**0**	**0**	**0**
	Cleveland	IHL	9	4	1	5	49	....	....	....	....	....
	NHL Totals		**148**	**21**	**20**	**41**	**408**	**3**	**0**	**0**	**0**	**6**

Signed as a free agent by **Minnesota**, May 12, 1986. Signed as a free agent by **San Jose**, August 30, 1991. Signed as a free agent by **NY Islanders**, November 29, 1993. Claimed on waivers by **Pittsburgh** from **NY Islanders**, March 9, 1994.

DE RUITER, CHRIS TOR.

Right wing. Shoots right. 6'2", 190 lbs. Born, Kingston, Ont., February 27, 1974.
(Toronto's 6th choice, 106th overall, in 1992 Entry Draft).

			Regular Season					Playoffs				
Season	Club	Lea	GP	G	A	TP	PIM	GP	G	A	TP	PIM
1992-93	Clarkson	ECAC	32	2	5	7	40	....	....	....	....	....
1993-94	Clarkson	ECAC	33	4	10	14	42	....	....	....	....	....

DESANTIS, MARK ANA.

Defense. Shoots right. 6', 205 lbs. Born, Brampton, Ont., January 12, 1972.

			Regular Season					Playoffs				
Season	Club	Lea	GP	G	A	TP	PIM	GP	G	A	TP	PIM
1989-90	Cornwall	OHL	59	3	17	20	79	6	0	2	2	13
1990-91	Cornwall	OHL	41	7	15	22	78	....	....	....	....	....
1991-92	Cornwall	OHL	66	10	45	55	105	6	1	2	3	7
1992-93a	Newmarket	OHL	66	19	70	89	131	7	3	11	14	14
1993-94	San Diego	IHL	54	5	10	15	95	....	....	....	....	....

a OHL First All-Star Team (1993)

Signed as a free agent by **Anaheim**, August 2, 1993.

DESJARDINS, ERIC (deh-ZHAHR-dai) MTL.

Defense. Shoots right. 6'1", 200 lbs. Born, Rouyn, Que., June 14, 1969.
(Montreal's 3rd choice, 38th overall, in 1987 Entry Draft).

			Regular Season					Playoffs				
Season	Club	Lea	GP	G	A	TP	PIM	GP	G	A	TP	PIM
1986-87a	Granby	QMJHL	66	14	24	38	178	8	3	2	5	10
1987-88	Sherbrooke	AHL	3	0	0	0	6	4	0	2	2	2
b	Granby	QMJHL	62	18	49	67	138	5	0	3	3	10
1988-89	**Montreal**	**NHL**	**36**	**2**	**12**	**14**	**26**	**14**	**1**	**1**	**2**	**6**
1989-90	**Montreal**	**NHL**	**55**	**3**	**13**	**16**	**51**	**6**	**0**	**0**	**0**	**10**
1990-91	**Montreal**	**NHL**	**62**	**7**	**18**	**25**	**27**	**13**	**1**	**4**	**5**	**8**
1991-92	**Montreal**	**NHL**	**77**	**6**	**32**	**38**	**50**	**11**	**3**	**3**	**6**	**4**
1992-93	**Montreal**	**NHL**	**82**	**13**	**32**	**45**	**98**	**20**	**4**	**10**	**14**	**23**
1993-94	**Montreal**	**NHL**	**84**	**12**	**23**	**35**	**97**	**7**	**0**	**2**	**2**	**4**
	NHL Totals		**396**	**43**	**130**	**173**	**349**	**71**	**9**	**20**	**29**	**55**

a QMJHL Second All-Star Team (1987)
b QMJHL First All-Star Team (1988)

Played in NHL All-Star Game (1992)

DEULING, JARRETT NY

Left wing. Shoots left. 5'11", 194 lbs. Born, Vernon, B.C., March 4, 1974.
(NY Islanders' 2nd choice, 56th overall, in 1992 Entry Draft).

			Regular Season					Playoffs				
Season	Club	Lea	GP	G	A	TP	PIM	GP	G	A	TP	PIM
1990-91	Kamloops	WHL	48	4	12	16	43	12	5	2	7	[illegible]
1991-92	Kamloops	WHL	68	28	26	54	79	17	10	6	16	1[illegible]
1992-93	Kamloops	WHL	68	31	32	63	93	13	6	7	13	1[illegible]
1993-94	Kamloops	WHL	70	44	59	103	171	18	*13	8	21	4[illegible]

DE VRIES, GREG EDM

Defense. Shoots left. 6'3", 218 lbs. Born, Sundridge, Ont., January 4, 1973.

			Regular Season					Playoffs				
Season	Club	Lea	GP	G	A	TP	PIM	GP	G	A	TP	PIM
1991-92	Bowling Green	CCHA	24	0	3	3	20	....	....	....	....	....
1992-93	Niagara Falls	OHL	62	3	23	26	86	4	0	1	1	[illegible]
1993-94	Niagara Falls	OHL	64	5	40	45	135	....	....	....	....	....
	Cape Breton	AHL	9	0	0	0	11	1	0	0	0	[illegible]

Signed as a free agent by **Edmonton**, March 20, 1994.

DEYELL, MARK TOR.

Center. Shoots right. 5'11", 170 lbs. Born, Winnipeg, Man., March 26, 1976.
(Toronto's 4th choice, 126th overall, in 1994 Entry Draft).

			Regular Season					Playoffs				
Season	Club	Lea	GP	G	A	TP	PIM	GP	G	A	TP	PIM
1992-93	Winnipeg	Midget	35	46	56	102	125	....	....	....	....	....
1993-94	Saskatoon	WHL	66	17	36	53	52	16	5	2	7	20

DIDUCK, GERALD (DIH-duhk) VAN.

Defense. Shoots right. 6'2", 207 lbs. Born, Edmonton, Alta., April 6, 1965.
(NY Islanders' 2nd choice, 16th overall, in 1983 Entry Draft).

			Regular Season					Playoffs				
Season	Club	Lea	GP	G	A	TP	PIM	GP	G	A	TP	PIM
1981-82	Lethbridge	WHL	71	1	15	16	81	12	0	3	3	27
1982-83	Lethbridge	WHL	67	8	16	24	151	20	3	12	15	49
1983-84	Lethbridge	WHL	65	10	24	34	133	5	1	4	5	27
	Indianapolis	IHL	....	....	....	....	....	10	1	6	7	19
1984-85	**NY Islanders**	**NHL**	**65**	**2**	**8**	**10**	**80**	....	....	....	....	....
1985-86	**NY Islanders**	**NHL**	**10**	**1**	**2**	**3**	**2**	....	....	....	....	....
	Springfield	AHL	61	6	14	20	173	....	....	....	....	....
1986-87	**NY Islanders**	**NHL**	**30**	**2**	**3**	**5**	**67**	**14**	**0**	**1**	**1**	**35**
	Springfield	AHL	45	6	8	14	120	....	....	....	....	....
1987-88	**NY Islanders**	**NHL**	**68**	**7**	**12**	**19**	**113**	**6**	**1**	**0**	**1**	**42**
1988-89	**NY Islanders**	**NHL**	**65**	**11**	**21**	**32**	**155**	....	....	....	....	....
1989-90	**NY Islanders**	**NHL**	**76**	**3**	**17**	**20**	**163**	**5**	**0**	**0**	**0**	**12**
1990-91	**Montreal**	**NHL**	**32**	**1**	**2**	**3**	**39**	....	....	....	....	....
	Vancouver	**NHL**	**31**	**3**	**7**	**10**	**66**	**6**	**1**	**0**	**1**	**11**
1991-92	**Vancouver**	**NHL**	**77**	**6**	**21**	**27**	**229**	**5**	**0**	**0**	**0**	**10**
1992-93	**Vancouver**	**NHL**	**80**	**6**	**14**	**20**	**171**	**12**	**4**	**2**	**6**	**12**
1993-94	**Vancouver**	**NHL**	**55**	**1**	**10**	**11**	**72**	**24**	**1**	**7**	**8**	**22**
	NHL Totals		**589**	**43**	**117**	**160**	**1157**	**72**	**7**	**10**	**17**	**144**

Traded to **Montreal** by **NY Islanders** for Craig Ludwig, September 4, 1990. Traded to **Vancouver** by **Montreal** for Vancouver's fourth round choice (Vladimir Vujtek) in 1991 Entry Draft, January 12, 1991.

DILLABOUGH, TRAVIS L.A.

Center. Shoots left. 6', 175 lbs. Born, Peterborough, Ont., June 20, 1975.
(Los Angeles' 9th choice, 198th overall, in 1993 Entry Draft).

			Regular Season					Playoffs				
Season	Club	Lea	GP	G	A	TP	PIM	GP	G	A	TP	PIM
1992-93	Presov	Slavic Jr.	20	6	9	15	0	....	....	....	....	....
1993-94	Providence	H.E.	33	4	8	12	42	....	....	....	....	....

DIMAIO, ROB (duh-MIGH-oh) PHI.

Center. Shoots right. 5'10", 190 lbs. Born, Calgary, Alta., February 19, 1968.
(NY Islanders' 6th choice, 118th overall, in 1987 Entry Draft).

			Regular Season					Playoffs				
Season	Club	Lea	GP	G	A	TP	PIM	GP	G	A	TP	PIM
1986-87	Medicine Hat	WHL	70	27	43	70	130	20	7	11	18	46
1987-88	Medicine Hat	WHL	54	47	43	90	120	14	12	19	*31	59
1988-89	**NY Islanders**	**NHL**	**16**	**1**	**0**	**1**	**30**	....	....	....	....	....
	Springfield	AHL	40	13	18	31	67	....	....	....	....	....
1989-90	**NY Islanders**	**NHL**	**7**	**0**	**0**	**0**	**2**	**1**	**1**	**0**	**1**	**4**
	Springfield	AHL	54	25	27	52	69	16	4	7	11	45
1990-91	**NY Islanders**	**NHL**	**1**	**0**	**0**	**0**	**0**	....	....	....	....	....
	Capital Dist.	AHL	12	3	4	7	22	....	....	....	....	....
1991-92	**NY Islanders**	**NHL**	**50**	**5**	**2**	**7**	**43**	....	....	....	....	....
1992-93	**Tampa Bay**	**NHL**	**54**	**9**	**15**	**24**	**62**	....	....	....	....	....
1993-94	**Tampa Bay**	**NHL**	**39**	**8**	**7**	**15**	**40**	....	....	....	....	....
	Philadelphia	**NHL**	**14**	**3**	**5**	**8**	**6**	....	....	....	....	....
	NHL Totals		**181**	**26**	**29**	**55**	**183**	**1**	**1**	**0**	**1**	**4**

Claimed by **Tampa Bay** from **NY Islanders** in Expansion Draft, June 18, 1992. Traded to **Philadelphia** by **Tampa Bay** for Jim Cummins and Philadelphia's fourth round choice in 1995 Entry Draft, March 18, 1994.

DINEEN, GORD — NYI

Defense. Shoots right. 6', 195 lbs. Born, Quebec City, Que., September 21, 1962.
(NY Islanders' 2nd choice, 42nd overall, in 1981 Entry Draft).

			Regular Season					Playoffs				
Season	Club	Lea	GP	G	A	TP	PIM	GP	G	A	TP	PIM
1980-81	S.S. Marie	OHA	68	4	26	30	158	19	1	7	8	58
1981-82	S.S. Marie	OHL	68	9	45	54	185	13	1	2	3	52
1982-83	NY Islanders	NHL	2	0	0	0	4	....	....	....	....	....
abc	Indianapolis	CHL	73	10	47	57	78	13	2	10	12	29
1983-84	NY Islanders	NHL	43	1	11	12	32	9	1	1	2	28
	Indianapolis	CHL	26	4	13	17	63	....	....	....	....	....
1984-85	NY Islanders	NHL	48	1	12	13	89	10	0	0	0	26
	Springfield	AHL	25	1	8	9	46	....	....	....	....	....
1985-86	NY Islanders	NHL	57	1	8	9	81	3	0	0	0	2
	Springfield	AHL	11	2	3	5	20	....	....	....	....	....
1986-87	NY Islanders	NHL	71	4	10	14	110	7	0	4	4	4
1987-88	NY Islanders	NHL	57	4	12	16	62	....	....	....	....	....
	Minnesota	NHL	13	1	1	2	21	....	....	....	....	....
1988-89	Minnesota	NHL	2	0	1	1	2	....	....	....	....	....
	Kalamazoo	IHL	25	2	6	8	49	....	....	....	....	....
	Pittsburgh	NHL	38	1	2	3	42	11	0	2	2	8
1989-90	Pittsburgh	NHL	69	1	8	9	125	....	....	....	....	....
1990-91	Pittsburgh	NHL	9	0	0	0	4	....	....	....	....	....
	Muskegon	IHL	40	1	14	15	57	5	0	2	2	0
1991-92	Pittsburgh	NHL	1	0	0	0	0	....	....	....	....	....
d	Muskegon	IHL	79	8	37	45	83	14	2	4	6	33
1992-93	Ottawa	NHL	32	2	4	6	30	....	....	....	....	....
	San Diego	IHL	41	6	23	29	36	....	....	....	....	....
1993-94	Ottawa	NHL	77	0	21	21	89	....	....	....	....	....
	San Diego	IHL	3	0	0	0	2	....	....	....	....	....
	NHL Totals		519	16	90	106	691	40	1	7	8	68

a CHL First All-Star Team (1983)
b Won Bob Gassoff Trophy (Most Improved Defenseman - CHL) (1983)
c Won Bobby Orr Trophy (Top Defenseman - CHL) (1983)
d IHL First All-Star Team (1992)

Traded to **Minnesota** by **NY Islanders** for Chris Pryor and future considerations, March 8, 1988. Traded to **Pittsburgh** by **Minnesota** with Scott Bjugstad for Ville Siren and Steve Gotaas, December 17, 1988. Signed as a free agent by **Ottawa**, August 31, 1992. Signed as a free agent by **NY Islanders**, July 26, 1994.

DINEEN, KEVIN — PHI.

Right wing. Shoots right. 5'11", 190 lbs. Born, Quebec City, Que., October 28, 1963.
(Hartford's 3rd choice, 56th overall, in 1982 Entry Draft).

			Regular Season					Playoffs				
Season	Club	Lea	GP	G	A	TP	PIM	GP	G	A	TP	PIM
1981-82	U. of Denver	WCHA	26	10	10	20	70	....	....	....	....	....
1982-83	U. of Denver	WCHA	36	16	13	29	108	....	....	....	....	....
1983-84	Cdn. National	....	52	5	11	16	2	....	....	....	....	....
	Cdn Olympic	....	7	0	0	0	0	....	....	....	....	....
1984-85	Hartford	NHL	57	25	16	41	120	....	....	....	....	....
	Binghamton	AHL	25	15	8	23	41	....	....	....	....	....
1985-86	Hartford	NHL	57	33	35	68	124	10	6	7	13	18
1986-87	Hartford	NHL	78	40	39	79	110	6	2	1	3	31
1987-88	Hartford	NHL	74	25	25	50	217	6	4	4	8	8
1988-89	Hartford	NHL	79	45	44	89	167	4	1	0	1	10
1989-90	Hartford	NHL	67	25	41	66	164	6	3	2	5	18
1990-91a	Hartford	NHL	61	17	30	47	104	6	1	0	1	16
1991-92	Hartford	NHL	16	4	2	6	23	....	....	....	....	....
	Philadelphia	NHL	64	26	30	56	130	....	....	....	....	....
1992-93	Philadelphia	NHL	83	35	28	63	201	....	....	....	....	....
1993-94	Philadelphia	NHL	71	19	23	42	113	....	....	....	....	....
	NHL Totals		707	294	313	607	1473	38	17	14	31	101

a Won Bud Light/NHL Man of the Year Award (1991)

Played in NHL All-Star Game (1988, 1989)

Traded to **Philadelphia** by **Hartford** for Murray Craven and Philadelphia's fourth round choice (Kevin Smyth) in 1992 Entry Draft, November 13, 1991.

DINGMAN, CHRIS — CGY.

Left wing. Shoots left. 6'3", 231 lbs. Born, Edmonton, Alta., July 6, 1976.
(Calgary's 1st choice, 19th overall, in 1994 Entry Draft).

			Regular Season					Playoffs				
Season	Club	Lea	GP	G	A	TP	PIM	GP	G	A	TP	PIM
1992-93	Brandon	WHL	50	10	17	27	64	4	0	0	0	0
1993-94	Brandon	WHL	45	21	20	41	77	13	1	7	8	39

DIONNE, GILBERT (dee-AHN, ZHIHL-bair) — MTL.

Left wing. Shoots left. 6', 194 lbs. Born, Drummondville, Que., September 19, 1970.
(Montreal's 5th choice, 81st overall, in 1990 Entry Draft).

			Regular Season					Playoffs				
Season	Club	Lea	GP	G	A	TP	PIM	GP	G	A	TP	PIM
1988-89	Kitchener	OHL	66	11	33	44	13	5	1	1	2	4
1989-90	Kitchener	OHL	64	48	57	105	85	17	13	10	23	22
1990-91	Montreal	NHL	2	0	0	0	0	....	....	....	....	....
	Fredericton	AHL	77	40	47	87	62	9	6	5	11	8
1991-92a	Montreal	NHL	39	21	13	34	10	11	3	4	7	10
	Fredericton	AHL	29	19	27	46	20	....	....	....	....	....
1992-93	Montreal	NHL	75	20	28	48	63	20	6	6	12	20
	Fredericton	AHL	3	4	3	7	0	....	....	....	....	....
1993-94	Montreal	NHL	74	19	26	45	31	5	1	2	3	0
	NHL Totals		190	60	67	127	104	36	10	12	22	30

a NHL/Upper Deck All-Rookie Team (1992)

DI PIETRO, PAUL (dee-pee-AY-troh) — MTL.

Center. Shoots right. 5'9", 181 lbs. Born, Sault Ste. Marie, Ont., September 8, 1970.
(Montreal's 6th choice, 102nd overall, in 1990 Entry Draft).

			Regular Season					Playoffs				
Season	Club	Lea	GP	G	A	TP	PIM	GP	G	A	TP	PIM
1986-87	Sudbury	OHL	49	5	11	16	13	....	....	....	....	....
1987-88	Sudbury	OHL	63	25	42	67	27	....	....	....	....	....
1988-89	Sudbury	OHL	57	31	48	79	27	....	....	....	....	....
1989-90	Sudbury	OHL	66	56	63	119	57	7	3	6	9	7
1990-91	Fredericton	AHL	78	39	31	70	38	9	5	6	11	2
1991-92	Montreal	NHL	33	4	6	10	25	....	....	....	....	....
	Fredericton	AHL	43	26	31	57	52	7	3	4	7	8
1992-93	Montreal	NHL	29	4	13	17	14	17	8	5	13	8
	Fredericton	AHL	26	8	16	24	16	....	....	....	....	....
1993-94	Montreal	NHL	70	13	20	33	37	7	2	4	6	2
	NHL Totals		132	21	39	60	76	24	10	9	19	10

DIRK, ROBERT — ANA.

Defense. Shoots left. 6'4", 218 lbs. Born, Regina, Sask., August 20, 1966.
(St. Louis' 4th choice, 53rd overall, in 1984 Entry Draft).

			Regular Season					Playoffs				
Season	Club	Lea	GP	G	A	TP	PIM	GP	G	A	TP	PIM
1982-83	Regina	WHL	1	0	0	0	0	....	....	....	....	....
1983-84	Regina	WHL	62	2	10	12	64	23	1	12	13	24
1984-85	Regina	WHL	69	10	34	44	97	8	0	0	0	4
1985-86	Regina	WHL	72	19	60	79	140	10	3	5	8	8
1986-87	Peoria	IHL	76	5	17	22	155	....	....	....	....	....
1987-88	St. Louis	NHL	7	0	1	1	16	6	0	1	1	2
	Peoria	IHL	54	4	21	25	126	....	....	....	....	....
1988-89	St. Louis	NHL	9	0	1	1	11	....	....	....	....	....
	Peoria	IHL	22	0	2	2	54	....	....	....	....	....
1989-90	St. Louis	NHL	37	1	1	2	128	3	0	0	0	0
	Peoria	IHL	24	1	2	3	79	....	....	....	....	....
1990-91	St. Louis	NHL	41	1	3	4	100	....	....	....	....	....
	Peoria	IHL	3	0	0	0	2	....	....	....	....	....
	Vancouver	NHL	11	1	0	1	20	6	0	0	0	13
1991-92	Vancouver	NHL	72	2	7	9	126	13	0	0	0	20
1992-93	Vancouver	NHL	69	4	8	12	150	9	0	0	0	6
1993-94	Vancouver	NHL	65	2	3	5	105	....	....	....	....	....
	Chicago	NHL	6	0	0	0	26	2	0	0	0	15
	NHL Totals		317	11	24	35	682	39	0	1	1	56

Traded to **Vancouver** by **St. Louis** with Geoff Courtnall, Sergio Momesso, Cliff Ronning and St. Louis' fifth round choice (Brian Loney) in 1992 Entry Draft for Dan Quinn and Garth Butcher, March 5, 1991. Traded to **Chicago** by **Vancouver** for Chicago's fourth round choice (Mike Dubinsky) in 1994 Entry Draft, March 21, 1994. Traded to **Anaheim** by **Chicago** for Tampa Bay's fourth round choice (previously acquired by Anaheim) in 1995 Entry Draft, July 12, 1994.

DISHER, JASON — OTT.

Defense. Shoots left. 6'2", 208 lbs. Born, Windsor, Ont., May 28, 1975.
(Ottawa's 7th choice, 183rd overall, in 1993 Entry Draft).

			Regular Season					Playoffs				
Season	Club	Lea	GP	G	A	TP	PIM	GP	G	A	TP	PIM
1992-93	Kingston	OHL	46	2	4	6	100	14	0	1	1	18
1993-94	Kingston	OHL	62	4	12	16	170	4	0	0	0	5

DOBBIN, BRIAN

Right wing. Shoots right. 5'11", 205 lbs. Born, Petrolia, Ont., August 18, 1966.
(Philadelphia's 7th choice, 100th overall, in 1984 Entry Draft).

			Regular Season					Playoffs				
Season	Club	Lea	GP	G	A	TP	PIM	GP	G	A	TP	PIM
1982-83	Kingston	OHL	69	16	39	55	35	....	....	....	....	....
1983-84	London	OHL	70	30	40	70	70	....	....	....	....	....
1984-85	London	OHL	53	42	57	99	63	8	7	4	11	2
1985-86	London	OHL	59	38	55	93	113	5	2	1	3	9
	Hershey	AHL	2	1	0	1	0	18	5	5	10	21
1986-87	Philadelphia	NHL	12	2	1	3	14	....	....	....	....	....
	Hershey	AHL	52	26	35	61	66	5	4	2	6	15
1987-88	Philadelphia	NHL	21	3	5	8	6	....	....	....	....	....
	Hershey	AHL	54	36	47	83	58	12	7	8	15	15
1988-89	Philadelphia	NHL	14	0	1	1	8	2	0	0	0	17
a	Hershey	AHL	59	43	48	91	61	11	7	6	13	12
1989-90	Philadelphia	NHL	9	1	1	2	11	....	....	....	....	....
b	Hershey	AHL	68	38	47	85	58	....	....	....	....	....
1990-91	Hershey	AHL	80	35	43	78	82	7	1	2	3	7
1991-92	New Haven	AHL	33	16	21	37	20	....	....	....	....	....
	Boston	NHL	7	1	0	1	22	....	....	....	....	....
	Maine	AHL	33	21	15	36	14	....	....	....	....	....
1992-93	Milwaukee	IHL	80	39	45	84	50	6	4	3	7	6
1993-94c	Milwaukee	IHL	81	48	53	101	73	4	1	0	1	4
	NHL Totals		63	7	8	15	61	2	0	0	0	17

a AHL First All-Star Team (1989)
b AHL Second All-Star Team (1990)
c IHL Second All-Star Team (1994)

Traded to **Boston** by **Philadelphia** with Gord Murphy, Philadelphia's third round choice (Sergei Zholtok) in 1992 Entry Draft and Philadelphia's fourth round choice (Charles Paquette) in 1993 Entry Draft for Garry Galley, Wes Walz and Boston's third round choice (Milos Holan) in 1993 Entry Draft, January 2, 1992.

DOERS, MICHAEL

Right wing. Shoots right. 6', 175 lbs. Born, Madison, WI, June 17, 1971.
(Toronto's 7th choice, 125th overall, in 1989 Entry Draft).

			Regular Season					Playoffs				
Season	Club	Lea	GP	G	A	TP	PIM	GP	G	A	TP	PIM
1991-92	U. Wisconsin	WCHA	37	3	3	6	18	....	....	....	....	....
1992-93	U. Wisconsin	WCHA	40	4	5	9	30	....	....	....	....	....
1993-94	U. Wisconsin	WCHA	41	4	8	12	39	....	....	....	....	....

DOLLAS, BOBBY — ANA.

Defense. Shoots left. 6'2", 212 lbs. Born, Montreal, Que., January 31, 1965.
(Winnipeg's 2nd choice, 14th overall, in 1983 Entry Draft).

			Regular Season					Playoffs				
Season	Club	Lea	GP	G	A	TP	PIM	GP	G	A	TP	PIM
1982-83a	Laval	QMJHL	63	16	45	61	144	11	5	5	10	23
1983-84	Winnipeg	NHL	1	0	0	0	0	....	....	....	....	....
	Laval	QMJHL	54	12	33	45	80	14	1	8	9	23
1984-85	Winnipeg	NHL	9	0	0	0	0	....	....	....	....	....
	Sherbrooke	AHL	8	1	3	4	4	17	3	6	9	17
1985-86	Winnipeg	NHL	46	0	5	5	66	3	0	0	0	2
	Sherbrooke	AHL	25	4	7	11	29	....	....	....	....	....
1986-87	Sherbrooke	AHL	75	6	18	24	87	16	2	4	6	13
1987-88	Quebec	NHL	9	0	0	0	2	....	....	....	....	....
	Moncton	AHL	26	4	10	14	20	....	....	....	....	....
	Fredericton	AHL	33	4	8	12	27	15	2	2	4	24
1988-89	Quebec	NHL	16	0	3	3	16	....	....	....	....	....
	Halifax	AHL	57	5	19	24	65	4	1	0	1	14
1989-90	Cdn. National	....	68	8	29	37	60	....	....	....	....	....
1990-91	Detroit	NHL	56	3	5	8	20	7	1	0	1	13
1991-92	Detroit	NHL	27	3	1	4	20	2	0	1	1	0
	Adirondack	AHL	19	1	6	7	33	18	7	4	11	22
1992-93	Detroit	NHL	6	0	0	0	2	....	....	....	....	....
c	Adirondack	AHL	64	7	36	43	54	11	3	8	11	8
1993-94	Anaheim	NHL	77	9	11	20	55	....	....	....	....	....
	NHL Totals		247	15	25	40	181	12	1	1	2	15

a QMJHL Second All-Star Team (1983)
b Won Eddie Shore Plaque (Outstanding Defenseman - AHL) (1993)
c AHL Second All-Star Team (1993)

Traded to **Quebec** by **Winnipeg** for Stu Kulak, December 17, 1987. Signed as a free agent by **Detroit**, October 18, 1990. Claimed by **Anaheim** from **Detroit** in Expansion Draft, June 24, 1993.

DOMENICHELLI, HNAT — HFD.

Center/Left wing. Shoots left. 5'11", 173 lbs. Born, Edmonton, Alta., February 17, 1976.
(Hartford's 2nd choice, 83rd overall, in 1994 Entry Draft).

			Regular Season					Playoffs				
Season	Club	Lea	GP	G	A	TP	PIM	GP	G	A	TP	PIM
1992-93	Kamloops	WHL	45	12	8	20	15	11	1	1	2	2
1993-94	Kamloops	WHL	69	27	40	67	31	19	10	12	22	0

DOMI, TIE — (DOH-mee) WPG.

Right wing. Shoots right. 5'10", 200 lbs. Born, Windsor, Ont., November 1, 1969.
(Toronto's 2nd choice, 27th overall, in 1988 Entry Draft).

			Regular Season					Playoffs				
Season	Club	Lea	GP	G	A	TP	PIM	GP	G	A	TP	PIM
1986-87	Peterborough	OHL	18	1	1	2	79	....	....	....	....	....
1987-88	Peterborough	OHL	60	22	21	43	292	12	3	9	12	24
1988-89	Peterborough	OHL	43	14	16	30	175	17	10	9	19	70
1989-90	**Toronto**	**NHL**	**2**	**0**	**0**	**0**	**42**	....	....	....	....	....
	Newmarket	AHL	57	14	11	25	285	....	....	....	....	....
1990-91	**NY Rangers**	**NHL**	**28**	**1**	**0**	**1**	**185**	....	....	....	....	....
	Binghamton	AHL	25	11	6	17	219	7	3	2	5	16
1991-92	**NY Rangers**	**NHL**	**42**	**2**	**4**	**6**	**246**	**6**	**1**	**1**	**2**	**32**
1992-93	**NY Rangers**	**NHL**	**12**	**2**	**0**	**2**	**95**	....	....	....	....	....
	Winnipeg	**NHL**	**49**	**3**	**10**	**13**	**249**	**6**	**1**	**0**	**1**	**23**
1993-94	**Winnipeg**	**NHL**	**81**	**8**	**11**	**19**	***347**	....	....	....	....	....
	NHL Totals		**214**	**16**	**25**	**41**	**1164**	**12**	**2**	**1**	**3**	**55**

Traded to **NY Rangers** by **Toronto** with Mark LaForest for Greg Johnston, June 28, 1990. Traded to **Winnipeg** by **NY Rangers** with Kris King for Ed Olczyk, December 28, 1992.

DONATELLI, CLARK

Left wing. Shoots left. 5'10", 180 lbs. Born, Providence, RI, November 22, 1967.
(NY Rangers' 4th choice, 98th overall, in 1984 Entry Draft).

			Regular Season					Playoffs				
Season	Club	Lea	GP	G	A	TP	PIM	GP	G	A	TP	PIM
1984-85	Boston U.	H.E.	40	17	18	35	46	....	....	....	....	....
1985-86ab	Boston U.	H.E.	43	28	34	62	30	....	....	....	....	....
1986-87	Boston U.	H.E.	37	15	23	38	46	....	....	....	....	....
1987-88	U.S. National	....	50	11	27	38	26	....	....	....	....	....
	U.S. Olympic	....	6	2	1	3	5	....	....	....	....	....
1988-89					DID NOT PLAY							
1989-90	**Minnesota**	**NHL**	**25**	**3**	**3**	**6**	**17**	....	....	....	....	....
	Kalamazoo	IHL	27	8	9	17	47	4	0	2	2	12
1990-91	San Diego	IHL	46	17	10	27	45	....	....	....	....	....
1991-92	U.S. National	....	42	13	25	38	50	....	....	....	....	....
	U.S. Olympic	....	8	2	1	3	6	....	....	....	....	....
	Boston	**NHL**	**10**	**0**	**1**	**1**	**22**	**2**	**0**	**0**	**0**	**0**
1992-93	Providence	AHL	57	12	14	26	40	4	2	1	3	2
1993-94	San Diego	IHL	50	11	32	43	54	9	0	1	1	23
	NHL Totals		**35**	**3**	**4**	**7**	**39**	**2**	**0**	**0**	**0**	**0**

a NCAA East Second All-American Team (1986)
b Hockey East Second All-Star Team (1986)

Traded to **Edmonton** by **NY Rangers** with Ville Kentala, Reijo Ruotsalainen and Jim Wiemer for Mike Golden, Don Jackson and Miloslav Horava, October 2, 1986. Signed as a free agent by **Minnesota**, June 20, 1989. Signed as a free agent by **Boston**, March 10, 1992.

DONATO, TED — (duh-NAH-toh) BOS.

Left wing. Shoots left. 5'10", 180 lbs. Born, Dedham, MA, April 28, 1969.
(Boston's 6th choice, 98th overall, in 1987 Entry Draft).

			Regular Season					Playoffs				
Season	Club	Lea	GP	G	A	TP	PIM	GP	G	A	TP	PIM
1987-88	Harvard	ECAC	28	12	14	26	24	....	....	....	....	....
1988-89	Harvard	ECAC	34	14	37	51	30	....	....	....	....	....
1989-90	Harvard	ECAC	16	5	6	11	34	....	....	....	....	....
1990-91a	Harvard	ECAC	27	19	*37	56	26	....	....	....	....	....
1991-92	U.S. National	....	52	11	22	33	24	....	....	....	....	....
	U.S. Olympic	....	8	4	3	7	8	....	....	....	....	....
	Boston	**NHL**	**10**	**1**	**2**	**3**	**8**	**15**	**3**	**4**	**7**	**4**
1992-93	**Boston**	**NHL**	**82**	**15**	**20**	**35**	**61**	**4**	**0**	**1**	**1**	....
1993-94	**Boston**	**NHL**	**84**	**22**	**32**	**54**	**59**	**13**	**4**	**2**	**6**	**10**
	NHL Totals		**176**	**38**	**54**	**92**	**128**	**32**	**7**	**7**	**14**	**14**

a ECAC First All-Star Team (1991)

DONNELLY, GORD — DAL.

Defense. Shoots right. 6'1", 202 lbs. Born, Montreal, Que., April 5, 1962.
(St. Louis' 3rd choice, 62nd overall, in 1981 Entry Draft).

			Regular Season					Playoffs				
Season	Club	Lea	GP	G	A	TP	PIM	GP	G	A	TP	PIM
1980-81	Sherbrooke	QMJHL	67	15	23	38	252	14	1	2	3	35
1981-82	Sherbrooke	QMJHL	60	8	41	49	250	22	2	7	9	106
1982-83	Salt Lake	CHL	67	3	12	15	222	6	1	1	2	8
1983-84	**Quebec**	**NHL**	**38**	**0**	**5**	**5**	**60**	....	....	....	....	....
	Fredericton	AHL	30	2	3	5	146	7	1	1	2	43
1984-85	**Quebec**	**NHL**	**22**	**0**	**0**	**0**	**33**	....	....	....	....	....
	Fredericton	AHL	42	1	5	6	134	6	0	1	1	25
1985-86	**Quebec**	**NHL**	**36**	**2**	**2**	**4**	**85**	**1**	**0**	**0**	**0**	**0**
	Fredericton	AHL	38	3	5	8	103	5	0	0	0	33
1986-87	**Quebec**	**NHL**	**38**	**0**	**2**	**2**	**143**	**13**	**0**	**0**	**0**	**53**
1987-88	**Quebec**	**NHL**	**63**	**4**	**3**	**7**	**301**	....	....	....	....	....
1988-89	**Quebec**	**NHL**	**16**	**4**	**0**	**4**	**46**	....	....	....	....	....
	Winnipeg	**NHL**	**57**	**6**	**10**	**16**	**228**	....	....	....	....	....
1989-90	**Winnipeg**	**NHL**	**55**	**3**	**3**	**6**	**222**	**6**	**0**	**1**	**1**	**8**
1990-91	**Winnipeg**	**NHL**	**57**	**3**	**4**	**7**	**265**	....	....	....	....	....
1991-92	**Winnipeg**	**NHL**	**4**	**0**	**0**	**0**	**11**	....	....	....	....	....
	Buffalo	**NHL**	**67**	**2**	**3**	**5**	**305**	**6**	**0**	**1**	**1**	**0**
1992-93	**Buffalo**	**NHL**	**60**	**3**	**8**	**11**	**221**	....	....	....	....	....
1993-94	**Buffalo**	**NHL**	**7**	**0**	**0**	**0**	**31**	....	....	....	....	....
	Dallas	**NHL**	**18**	**0**	**1**	**1**	**66**	....	....	....	....	....
	NHL Totals		**538**	**27**	**41**	**68**	**2017**	**26**	**0**	**2**	**2**	**61**

Rights transferred to **Quebec** by **St. Louis** with rights to Claude Julien when St. Louis signed Jacques Demers as coach, August 19, 1983. Traded to **Winnipeg** by **Quebec** for Mario Marois, December 6, 1988. Traded to **Buffalo** by **Winnipeg** with Dave McLlwain, Winnipeg's fifth round choice (Yuri Khmylev) in 1992 Entry Draft and future considerations for Darrin Shannon, Mike Hartman and Dean Kennedy, October 11, 1991. Traded to **Dallas** by **Buffalo** for James Black and Dallas' seventh round choice (Steve Webb) in 1994 Entry Draft, December 15, 1993.

DONNELLY, MIKE — L.A.

Left wing. Shoots left. 5'11", 185 lbs. Born, Detroit, MI, October 10, 1963.

			Regular Season					Playoffs				
Season	Club	Lea	GP	G	A	TP	PIM	GP	G	A	TP	PIM
1982-83	Michigan State	CCHA	24	7	13	20	8	....	....	....	....	....
1983-84	Michigan State	CCHA	44	18	14	32	40	....	....	....	....	....
1984-85	Michigan State	CCHA	44	26	21	47	48	....	....	....	....	....
1985-86ab	Michigan State	CCHA	44	*59	38	97	65	....	....	....	....	....
1986-87	**NY Rangers**	**NHL**	**5**	**1**	**1**	**2**	**0**	....	....	....	....	....
	New Haven	AHL	58	27	34	61	52	7	2	0	2	[illegible]
1987-88	**NY Rangers**	**NHL**	**17**	**2**	**2**	**4**	**8**	....	....	....	....	....
	Colorado	IHL	8	7	11	18	15	....	....	....	....	....
	Buffalo	**NHL**	**40**	**6**	**8**	**14**	**44**	....	....	....	....	....
1988-89	**Buffalo**	**NHL**	**22**	**4**	**6**	**10**	**10**	....	....	....	....	....
	Rochester	AHL	53	32	37	69	53	....	....	....	....	....
1989-90	**Buffalo**	**NHL**	**12**	**1**	**2**	**3**	**8**	....	....	....	....	....
	Rochester	AHL	68	43	55	98	71	16	*12	7	19	[illegible]
1990-91	**Los Angeles**	**NHL**	**53**	**7**	**5**	**12**	**41**	**12**	**5**	**4**	**9**	[illegible]
	New Haven	AHL	18	10	6	16	2	....	....	....	....	....
1991-92	**Los Angeles**	**NHL**	**80**	**29**	**16**	**45**	**20**	**6**	**1**	**0**	**1**	[illegible]
1992-93	**Los Angeles**	**NHL**	**84**	**29**	**40**	**69**	**45**	**24**	**6**	**7**	**13**	[illegible]
1993-94	**Los Angeles**	**NHL**	**81**	**21**	**21**	**42**	**34**	....	....	....	....	....
	NHL Totals		**394**	**100**	**101**	**201**	**210**	**42**	**12**	**11**	**23**	[illegible]

a CCHA First All-Star Team (1986)
b NCAA West First All-American Team (1986)

Signed as a free agent by **NY Rangers**, August 15, 1986. Traded to **Buffalo** by **NY Rangers** with Rangers' fifth round choice (Alexander Mogilny) in 1988 Entry Draft for Paul Cyr and Buffalo's tenth round choice (Eric Fenton) in 1988 Entry Draft, December 31, 1987. Traded to **Los Angeles** by **Buffalo** for Mikko Makela, September 30, 1990.

DONOVAN, SHEAN — S.J.

Right wing. Shoots right. 6'2", 190 lbs. Born, Timmins, Ont., January 22, 1975.
(San Jose's 2nd choice, 28th overall, in 1993 Entry Draft).

			Regular Season					Playoffs				
Season	Club	Lea	GP	G	A	TP	PIM	GP	G	A	TP	PIM
1991-92	Ottawa	OHL	58	11	8	19	14	11	1	0	1	[illegible]
1992-93	Ottawa	OHL	66	29	23	52	33	....	....	....	....	....
1993-94	Ottawa	OHL	62	35	49	84	63	17	10	11	21	[illegible]

DOPITA, JIRI — BOS.

Center. Shoots left. 6'3", 202 lbs. Born, Sumperk, Czech., December 2, 1968.
(Boston's 4th choice, 133rd overall, in 1992 Entry Draft).

			Regular Season					Playoffs				
Season	Club	Lea	GP	G	A	TP	PIM	GP	G	A	TP	PIM
1989-90	Dukla Jihlava	Czech.	5	1	2	3	....	....	....	....	....	....
1990-91	Olomouc	Czech.	42	11	13	24	26	....	....	....	....	....
1991-92	Olomouc	Czech.	41	25	24	49	28	....	....	....	....	....
1992-93	Olomouc	Czech.	28	12	17	29	....	....	....	....	....	....
	Eisbaren Berlin	Ger.	11	7	8	15	49	....	....	....	....	....
1993-94	Eisbaren Berlin	Ger.	42	23	21	44	52	....	....	....	....	....

DOURIS, PETER — (DOOR-ihs) ANA.

Right wing. Shoots right. 6'1", 195 lbs. Born, Toronto, Ont., February 19, 1966.
(Winnipeg's 1st choice, 30th overall, in 1984 Entry Draft).

			Regular Season					Playoffs				
Season	Club	Lea	GP	G	A	TP	PIM	GP	G	A	TP	PIM
1983-84	N. Hampshire	ECAC	37	19	15	34	14	....	....	....	....	....
1984-85	N. Hampshire	H.E.	42	27	24	51	34	....	....	....	....	....
1985-86	**Winnipeg**	**NHL**	**11**	**0**	**0**	**0**	**0**	....	....	....	....	....
	Cdn. Olympic	....	33	16	7	23	18	....	....	....	....	....
1986-87	**Winnipeg**	**NHL**	**6**	**0**	**0**	**0**	**0**	....	....	....	....	....
	Sherbrooke	AHL	62	14	28	42	24	17	7	*15	*22	16
1987-88	**Winnipeg**	**NHL**	**4**	**0**	**2**	**2**	**0**	**1**	**0**	**0**	**0**	**0**
	Moncton	AHL	73	42	37	79	53	....	....	....	....	....
1988-89	Peoria	IHL	81	28	41	69	32	4	1	2	3	0
1989-90	**Boston**	**NHL**	**36**	**5**	**6**	**11**	**15**	**8**	**0**	**1**	**1**	**8**
	Maine	AHL	38	17	20	37	14	....	....	....	....	....
1990-91	**Boston**	**NHL**	**39**	**5**	**2**	**7**	**9**	**7**	**0**	**1**	**1**	**6**
	Maine	AHL	35	16	15	31	9	2	3	0	3	2
1991-92	**Boston**	**NHL**	**54**	**10**	**13**	**23**	**10**	**7**	**2**	**3**	**5**	**0**
	Maine	AHL	12	4	3	7	2	....	....	....	....	....
1992-93	**Boston**	**NHL**	**19**	**4**	**4**	**8**	**4**	**4**	**1**	**0**	**1**	**0**
	Providence	AHL	50	29	26	55	12	....	....	....	....	....
1993-94	**Anaheim**	**NHL**	**74**	**12**	**22**	**34**	**21**	....	....	....	....	....
	NHL Totals		**243**	**36**	**49**	**85**	**59**	**27**	**3**	**5**	**8**	**14**

Traded to **St. Louis** by **Winnipeg** for Kent Carlson and St. Louis' twelfth round choice (Sergei Kharin) in 1989 Entry Draft and St. Louis' fourth round choice (Scott Levins) in 1990 Entry Draft, September 29, 1988. Signed as a free agent by **Boston**, June 27, 1989. Signed as a free agent by **Anaheim**, July 22, 1993.

DOWD, JIM — N.J.

Center. Shoots right. 6'1", 190 lbs. Born, Brick, NJ, December 25, 1968.
(New Jersey's 7th choice, 149th overall, in 1987 Entry Draft).

			Regular Season					Playoffs				
Season	Club	Lea	GP	G	A	TP	PIM	GP	G	A	TP	PIM
1987-88	Lake Superior	CCHA	45	18	27	45	16	....	....	....	....	....
1988-89	Lake Superior	CCHA	46	24	35	59	40	....	....	....	....	....
1989-90ab	Lake Superior	CCHA	46	25	*67	92	30	....	....	....	....	....
1990-91cd	Lake Superior	CCHA	44	24	*54	*78	53	....	....	....	....	....
1991-92	**New Jersey**	**NHL**	**1**	**0**	**0**	**0**	**0**	....	....	....	....	....
	Utica	AHL	78	17	42	59	47	4	2	2	4	4
1992-93	**New Jersey**	**NHL**	**1**	**0**	**0**	**0**	**0**	....	....	....	....	....
	Utica	AHL	78	27	45	72	62	5	1	7	8	10
1993-94	**New Jersey**	**NHL**	**15**	**5**	**10**	**15**	**0**	**19**	**2**	**6**	**8**	**8**
	Albany	AHL	58	26	37	63	76	....	....	....	....	....
	NHL Totals		**17**	**5**	**10**	**15**	**0**	**19**	**2**	**6**	**8**	**8**

a CCHA Second All-Star Team (1990)
b NCAA West Second All-American Team (1990)
c CCHA First All-Star Team (1991)
d NCAA West First All-American Team (1991)

DOWNEY, BRIAN — OTT.

Left wing. Shoots left. 6'1", 188 lbs. Born, Manotick Station, Ont., June 30, 1968.

			Regular Season					Playoffs				
Season	Club	Lea	GP	G	A	TP	PIM	GP	G	A	TP	PIM
1989-90	U. of Maine	H.E.	32	11	15	26	8	....	....	....	....	....
1990-91	U. of Maine	H.E.	43	29	34	63	20	....	....	....	....	....
1991-92	U. of Maine	H.E.	37	19	32	51	29	....	....	....	....	....
1992-93	New Haven	AHL	6	0	2	2	0	....	....	....	....	....
	Thunder Bay	ColHL	43	17	31	48	14	11	4	5	9	14
1993-94	Thunder Bay	ColHL	61	30	51	81	17	9	3	11	14	2

Signed as a free agent by **Ottawa**, July 30, 1992.

DOYLE, TREVOR — FLA.

Defense. Shoots right. 6'3", 204 lbs. Born, Ottawa, Ont., January 1, 1974.
(Florida's 9th choice, 161st overall, in 1993 Entry Draft).

			Regular Season					Playoffs				
Season	Club	Lea	GP	G	A	TP	PIM	GP	G	A	TP	PIM
1991-92	Kingston	OHL	26	0	1	1	19	....	....	....	....	....
	Nepean/Smith Falls	Jr. A	34	5	13	18	64	....	....	....	....	....
1992-93	Kingston	OHL	62	1	8	9	148	16	2	3	5	25
1993-94	Kingston	OHL	53	2	12	14	246	3	0	0	0	4

DOYON, MARIO (doh-YAWN)

Defense. Shoots right. 6', 174 lbs. Born, Quebec City, Que., August 27, 1968.
(Chicago's 5th choice, 119th overall, in 1986 Entry Draft).

			Regular Season					Playoffs				
Season	Club	Lea	GP	G	A	TP	PIM	GP	G	A	TP	PIM
1985-86	Drummondville	QMJHL	71	5	14	19	129	23	5	4	9	32
1986-87	Drummondville	QMJHL	65	18	47	65	150	8	1	3	4	30
1987-88	Drummondville	QMJHL	68	23	54	77	233	17	3	14	17	46
1988-89	**Chicago**	**NHL**	**7**	**1**	**1**	**2**	**6**	....	....	....	....	....
	Saginaw	IHL	71	16	32	48	69	6	0	0	0	8
1989-90	Indianapolis	IHL	66	9	25	34	50	....	....	....	....	....
	Quebec	**NHL**	**9**	**2**	**3**	**5**	**6**	....	....	....	....	....
	Halifax	AHL	5	1	2	3	0	6	1	3	4	2
1990-91	**Quebec**	**NHL**	**12**	**0**	**0**	**0**	**4**	....	....	....	....	....
	Halifax	AHL	59	14	23	37	58	....	....	....	....	....
1991-92	Halifax	AHL	9	0	0	0	22	....	....	....	....	....
	New Haven	AHL	64	11	29	40	44	5	1	1	2	2
1992-93	Halifax	AHL	79	5	31	36	73	....	....	....	....	....
1993-94	Fredericton	AHL	56	12	21	33	44	....	....	....	....	....
	Kansas City	IHL	5	0	3	3	0	....	....	....	....	....
	NHL Totals		**28**	**3**	**4**	**7**	**16**	....	....	....	....	....

Traded to **Quebec** by **Chicago** with Everett Sanipass and Dan Vincelette for Greg Millen, Michel Goulet and Quebec's sixth round choice (Kevin St. Jacques) in 1991 Entry Draft, March 5, 1990.

DRAKE, DALLAS — WPG.

Center. Shoots left. 6', 180 lbs. Born, Trail, B.C., February 4, 1969.
(Detroit's 6th choice, 116th overall, in 1989 Entry Draft).

			Regular Season					Playoffs				
Season	Club	Lea	GP	G	A	TP	PIM	GP	G	A	TP	PIM
1988-89	N. Michigan	WCHA	38	17	22	39	22	....	....	....	....	....
1989-90	N. Michigan	WCHA	46	13	24	37	42	....	....	....	....	....
1990-91	N. Michigan	WCHA	44	22	36	58	89	....	....	....	....	....
1991-92ab	N. Michigan	WCHA	38	*39	41	*80	46	....	....	....	....	....
1992-93	**Detroit**	**NHL**	**72**	**18**	**26**	**44**	**93**	**7**	**3**	**3**	**6**	**6**
1993-94	**Detroit**	**NHL**	**47**	**10**	**22**	**32**	**37**	....	....	....	....	....
	Adirondack	AHL	1	2	0	2	0	....	....	....	....	....
	Winnipeg	**NHL**	**15**	**3**	**5**	**8**	**12**	....	....	....	....	....
	NHL Totals		**134**	**31**	**53**	**84**	**142**	**7**	**3**	**3**	**6**	**6**

a WCHA First All-Star Team (1992)
b NCAA West First All-American Team (1992)

Traded to **Winnipeg** by **Detroit** with Tim Cheveldae for Bob Essensa and Sergei Bautin, March 8, 1994.

DRAPER, KRIS — DET.

Center. Shoots left. 5'11", 185 lbs. Born, Toronto, Ont., May 24, 1971.
(Winnipeg's 4th choice, 62nd overall, in 1989 Entry Draft).

			Regular Season					Playoffs				
Season	Club	Lea	GP	G	A	TP	PIM	GP	G	A	TP	PIM
1988-89	Cdn. National	....	60	11	15	26	16	....	....	....	....	....
1989-90	Cdn. National	....	61	12	22	34	44	....	....	....	....	....
1990-91	**Winnipeg**	**NHL**	**3**	**1**	**0**	**1**	**5**	....	....	....	....	....
	Ottawa	OHL	39	19	42	61	35	17	8	11	19	20
	Moncton	AHL	7	2	1	3	2	....	....	....	....	....
1991-92	**Winnipeg**	**NHL**	**10**	**2**	**0**	**2**	**2**	**2**	**0**	**0**	**0**	**0**
	Moncton	AHL	61	11	18	29	113	4	0	1	1	6
1992-93	**Winnipeg**	**NHL**	**7**	**0**	**0**	**0**	**2**	....	....	....	....	....
	Moncton	AHL	67	12	23	35	40	5	2	2	4	18
1993-94	**Detroit**	**NHL**	**39**	**5**	**8**	**13**	**31**	**7**	**2**	**2**	**4**	**4**
	Adirondack	AHL	46	20	23	43	49	....	....	....	....	....
	NHL Totals		**59**	**8**	**8**	**16**	**40**	**9**	**2**	**2**	**4**	**4**

Traded to **Detroit** by **Winnipeg** for future considerations, June 30, 1993.

DRIVER, BRUCE — N.J.

Defense. Shoots left. 6', 185 lbs. Born, Toronto, Ont., April 29, 1962.
(Colorado's 6th choice, 108th overall, in 1981 Entry Draft).

			Regular Season					Playoffs				
Season	Club	Lea	GP	G	A	TP	PIM	GP	G	A	TP	PIM
1980-81	U. Wisconsin	WCHA	42	5	15	20	42	....	....	....	....	....
1981-82ab	U. Wisconsin	WCHA	46	7	37	44	84	....	....	....	....	....
1982-83c	U. Wisconsin	WCHA	49	19	42	61	100	....	....	....	....	....
1983-84	Cdn. National	....	52	8	15	23	22	....	....	....	....	....
	Cdn. Olympic	....	7	3	1	4	10	....	....	....	....	....
	New Jersey	**NHL**	**4**	**0**	**2**	**2**	**0**	....	....	....	....	....
	Maine	AHL	12	2	6	8	15	16	0	10	10	8
1984-85	**New Jersey**	**NHL**	**67**	**9**	**23**	**32**	**36**	....	....	....	....	....
1985-86	**New Jersey**	**NHL**	**40**	**3**	**15**	**18**	**32**	....	....	....	....	....
	Maine	AHL	15	4	7	11	16	....	....	....	....	....
1986-87	**New Jersey**	**NHL**	**74**	**6**	**28**	**34**	**36**	....	....	....	....	....
1987-88	**New Jersey**	**NHL**	**74**	**15**	**40**	**55**	**68**	**20**	**3**	**7**	**10**	**14**
1988-89	**New Jersey**	**NHL**	**27**	**1**	**15**	**16**	**24**	....	....	....	....	....
1989-90	**New Jersey**	**NHL**	**75**	**7**	**46**	**53**	**63**	**6**	**1**	**5**	**6**	**6**
1990-91	**New Jersey**	**NHL**	**73**	**9**	**36**	**45**	**62**	**7**	**1**	**2**	**3**	**12**
1991-92	**New Jersey**	**NHL**	**78**	**7**	**35**	**42**	**66**	**7**	**0**	**4**	**4**	**2**
1992-93	**New Jersey**	**NHL**	**83**	**14**	**40**	**54**	**66**	**5**	**1**	**3**	**4**	**4**
1993-94	**New Jersey**	**NHL**	**66**	**8**	**24**	**32**	**63**	**20**	**3**	**5**	**8**	**12**
	NHL Totals		**661**	**79**	**304**	**383**	**516**	**65**	**9**	**26**	**35**	**50**

a WCHA First All-Star Team (1982)
b NCAA All-Tournament Team (1982)
c WCHA Second All-Star Team (1983)

DROLET, JIMMY — MTL.

Defense. Shoots left. 6', 168 lbs. Born, Vanier, Que., February 19, 1976.
(Montreal's 7th choice, 122nd overall, in 1994 Entry Draft).

			Regular Season					Playoffs				
Season	Club	Lea	GP	G	A	TP	PIM	GP	G	A	TP	PIM
1992-93	Ste-Foy	Midget	42	13	33	46	130	....	....	....	....	....
1993-94	St-Hyacinthe	QMJHL	72	10	46	56	93	7	1	7	8	10

DROPPA, IVAN — CHI.

Defense. Shoots left. 6'2", 209 lbs. Born, Liptovsky Mikulas, Czech., February 1, 1972.
(Chicago's 2nd choice, 37th overall, in 1990 Entry Draft).

			Regular Season					Playoffs				
Season	Club	Lea	GP	G	A	TP	PIM	GP	G	A	TP	PIM
1990-91	VSZ Kosice	Czech.	54	1	7	8	12	....	....	....	....	....
1991-92	VSZ Kosice	Czech.	43	4	9	13	24	....	....	....	....	....
1992-93	Indianapolis	IHL	77	14	29	43	92	5	0	1	1	2
1993-94	**Chicago**	**NHL**	**12**	**0**	**1**	**1**	**12**	....	....	....	....	....
	Indianapolis	IHL	55	9	10	19	71	....	....	....	....	....
	NHL Totals		**12**	**0**	**1**	**1**	**12**	....	....	....	....	....

DRUCE, JOHN — L.A.

Right wing. Shoots right. 6'2", 195 lbs. Born, Peterborough, Ont., February 23, 1966.
(Washington's 2nd choice, 40th overall, in 1985 Entry Draft).

			Regular Season					Playoffs				
Season	Club	Lea	GP	G	A	TP	PIM	GP	G	A	TP	PIM
1984-85	Peterborough	OHL	54	12	14	26	90	17	6	2	8	21
1985-86	Peterborough	OHL	49	22	24	46	84	16	0	5	5	34
1986-87	Binghamton	AHL	77	13	9	22	131	12	0	3	3	28
1987-88	Binghamton	AHL	68	32	29	61	82	1	0	0	0	0
1988-89	**Washington**	**NHL**	**48**	**8**	**7**	**15**	**62**	**1**	**0**	**0**	**0**	**0**
	Baltimore	AHL	16	2	11	13	10	....	....	....	....	....
1989-90	**Washington**	**NHL**	**45**	**8**	**3**	**11**	**52**	**15**	**14**	**3**	**17**	**23**
	Baltimore	AHL	26	15	16	31	38	....	....	....	....	....
1990-91	**Washington**	**NHL**	**80**	**22**	**36**	**58**	**46**	**11**	**1**	**1**	**2**	**7**
1991-92	**Washington**	**NHL**	**67**	**19**	**18**	**37**	**39**	**7**	**1**	**0**	**1**	**2**
1992-93	**Winnipeg**	**NHL**	**50**	**6**	**14**	**20**	**37**	**2**	**0**	**0**	**0**	**0**
1993-94	**Los Angeles**	**NHL**	**55**	**14**	**17**	**31**	**50**	....	....	....	....	....
	Phoenix	IHL	8	5	6	11	9	....	....	....	....	....
	NHL Totals		**345**	**77**	**95**	**172**	**286**	**36**	**16**	**4**	**20**	**32**

Traded to **Winnipeg** by **Washington** with Toronto's fourth round choice (previously acquired by Washington — later traded to Detroit — Detroit selected John Jakopin) in 1993 Entry Draft for Pat Elynuik, October 1, 1992. Signed as a free agent by Los Angeles, August 2, 1993.

DRULIA, STAN

Right wing. Shoots right. 5'11", 190 lbs. Born, Elmira, NY, January 5, 1968.
(Pittsburgh's 11th choice, 214th overall, in 1986 Entry Draft).

			Regular Season					Playoffs				
Season	Club	Lea	GP	G	A	TP	PIM	GP	G	A	TP	PIM
1985-86	Belleville	OHL	66	43	36	79	73	....	....	....	....	....
1986-87	Hamilton	OHL	55	27	51	78	26	....	....	....	....	....
1987-88	Hamilton	OHL	65	52	69	121	44	14	8	16	24	12
1988-89	Maine	AHL	3	1	1	2	0	....	....	....	....	....
a	Niagara Falls	OHL	47	52	93	145	59	17	11	*26	37	18
1989-90	Phoenix	IHL	16	6	3	9	2	....	....	....	....	....
	Cape Breton	AHL	31	5	7	12	2	....	....	....	....	....
1990-91bc	Knoxville	ECHL	64	*63	77	*140	39	3	3	2	5	4
1991-92d	New Haven	AHL	77	49	53	102	46	5	2	4	6	4
1992-93	**Tampa Bay**	**NHL**	**24**	**2**	**1**	**3**	**10**	....	....	....	....	....
	Atlanta	IHL	47	28	26	54	38	3	2	3	5	4
1993-94ef	Atlanta	IHL	79	54	60	114	70	14	13	12	25	8
	NHL Totals		**24**	**2**	**1**	**3**	**10**	....	....	....	....	....

a OHL First All-Star Team (1989)
b MVP - ECHL (1991)
c ECHL First All-Star Team (1991)
d AHL Second All-Star Team (1992)
e IHL First All-Star Team (1994)
f Won "Bud" Poile Trophy (Playoff MVP - IHL) (1994)

Signed as a free agent by **Edmonton**, February 24, 1989. Signed as a free agent by **Tampa Bay**, September 1, 1992.

DRURY, CHRIS — QUE.

Center. Shoots right. 5'10", 180 lbs. Born, Trumbull, CT, August 20, 1976.
(Quebec's 5th choice, 72nd overall, in 1994 Entry Draft).

			Regular Season					Playoffs				
Season	Club	Lea	GP	G	A	TP	PIM	GP	G	A	TP	PIM
1992-93	Fairfield Prep.	HS	24	25	32	57	15	....	....	....	....	....
1993-94	Fairfield Prep.	HS	24	37	18	55	....	....	....	....	....	....

DRURY, TED (DROO-ree) — HFD.

Center. Shoots left. 6', 185 lbs. Born, Boston, MA, September 13, 1971.
(Calgary's 2nd choice, 42nd overall, in 1989 Entry Draft).

			Regular Season					Playoffs				
Season	Club	Lea	GP	G	A	TP	PIM	GP	G	A	TP	PIM
1989-90	Harvard	ECAC	17	9	13	22	10	....	....	....	....	....
1990-91	Harvard	ECAC	25	18	18	36	22	....	....	....	....	....
1991-92	U.S. National	....	53	11	23	34	30	....	....	....	....	....
	U.S. Olympic	....	7	1	1	2	0	....	....	....	....	....
1992-93ab	Harvard	ECAC	31	22	*41	*63	28	....	....	....	....	....
1993-94	**Calgary**	**NHL**	**34**	**5**	**7**	**12**	**26**	....	....	....	....	....
	U.S. National	....	11	1	4	5	11	....	....	....	....	....
	U.S. Olympic	....	7	1	2	3	2	....	....	....	....	....
	Hartford	**NHL**	**16**	**1**	**5**	**6**	**10**	....	....	....	....	....
	NHL Totals		**50**	**6**	**12**	**18**	**36**	....	....	....	....	....

a ECAC First All-Star Team (1993)
b NCAA East First All-America Team (1993)

Traded to **Hartford** by **Calgary** with Gary Suter and Paul Ranheim for James Patrick, Zarley Zalapski and Michael Nylander, March 10, 1994.

DUBE, YANNICK — VAN.

Center. Shoots right. 5'9", 170 lbs. Born, Gaspé, Que., June 14, 1974.
(Vancouver's 6th choice, 117th overall, in 1994 Entry Draft).

			Regular Season					Playoffs				
Season	Club	Lea	GP	G	A	TP	PIM	GP	G	A	TP	PIM
1991-92	Laval	QMJHL	65	14	19	33	8	10	0	2	2	2
1992-92	Laval	QMJHL	68	45	38	83	25	13	6	7	13	6
1993-94abcd	Laval	QMJHL	64	*66	75	*141	30	21	12	18	30	8

a QMJHL First All-Star Team (1994)
b Canadian Major Junior Second All-Star Team (1994)
c Canadian Major Junior Most Sportsmanlike Player of the Year (1994)
d Won George Parsons Trophy (Memorial Cup Most Sportsmanlike Player) (1994)

DUBERMAN, JUSTIN — PIT.

Right wing. Shoots right. 6'1", 185 lbs. Born, New Haven, CT, March 23, 1970.
(Montreal's 11th choice, 230th overall, in 1989 Entry Draft).

			Regular Season					Playoffs				
Season	Club	Lea	GP	G	A	TP	PIM	GP	G	A	TP	PIM
1988-89	North Dakota	WCHA	33	3	1	4	30	....	....	....	....	....
1989-90	North Dakota	WCHA	42	10	9	19	50	....	....	....	....	....
1990-91	North Dakota	WCHA	42	19	18	37	68	....	....	....	....	....
1991-92	North Dakota	WCHA	39	17	27	44	90	....	....	....	....	....
1992-93	Cleveland	IHL	77	29	42	71	69	4	0	0	0	12
1993-94	**Pittsburgh**	**NHL**	**4**	**0**	**0**	**0**	**0**	....	....	....	....	....
	Cleveland	IHL	59	9	13	22	63	....	....	....	....	....
	NHL Totals		**4**	**0**	**0**	**0**	**0**	....	....	....	....	....

Signed as a free agent by **Pittsburgh**, November 2, 1992.

DUBINSKY, MIKE — VAN.

Right wing. Shoots right. 6'2", 185 lbs. Born, Sherwood Park, Alta., June 28, 1976.
(Vancouver's 5th choice, 92nd overall, in 1994 Entry Draft).

			Regular Season					Playoffs				
Season	Club	Lea	GP	G	A	TP	PIM	GP	G	A	TP	PIM
1992-93	Brandon	WHL	64	10	25	35	44	3	0	0	0	0
1993-94	Brandon	WHL	20	9	13	22	23	....	....	....	....	....

DUBINSKY, STEVE — CHI.

Center. Shoots left. 6', 190 lbs. Born, Montreal, Que., July 9, 1970.
(Chicago's 9th choice, 226th overall, in 1990 Entry Draft).

			Regular Season					Playoffs				
Season	Club	Lea	GP	G	A	TP	PIM	GP	G	A	TP	PIM
1989-90	Clarkson	ECAC	35	7	10	17	24	....	....	....	....	....
1990-91	Clarkson	ECAC	39	13	23	36	26	....	....	....	....	....
1991-92	Clarkson	ECAC	32	20	31	51	40	....	....	....	....	....
1992-93	Clarkson	ECAC	35	18	26	44	58	....	....	....	....	....
1993-94	**Chicago**	**NHL**	**27**	**2**	**6**	**8**	**16**	**6**	**0**	**0**	**0**	**10**
	Indianapolis	IHL	54	15	25	40	63	....	....	....	....	....
	NHL Totals		**27**	**2**	**6**	**8**	**16**	**6**	**0**	**0**	**0**	**10**

DUBOIS, ERIC — T.B.

Defense. Shoots right. 6', 195 lbs. Born, Montreal, Que., May 9, 1970.
(Quebec's 6th choice, 76th overall, in 1989 Entry Draft).

			Regular Season					Playoffs				
Season	Club	Lea	GP	G	A	TP	PIM	GP	G	A	TP	PIM
1986-87	Laval	QMJHL	61	1	17	18	29	....	....	....	....	....
1987-88	Laval	QMJHL	69	8	32	40	132	14	1	7	8	12
1988-89	Laval	QMJHL	68	15	44	59	126	17	1	11	12	55
1989-90	Laval	QMJHL	66	9	36	45	153	13	3	8	11	29
1990-91	Laval	QMJHL	57	15	45	60	122	13	3	5	8	29
1991-92	Halifax	AHL	14	0	0	0	8	....	....	....	....	....
	New Haven	AHL	1	0	0	0	2	....	....	....	....	....
	Greensboro	ECHL	36	7	17	24	62	11	4	4	8	40
1992-93	Oklahoma City	CHL	25	5	20	25	70	....	....	....	....	....
	Atlanta	IHL	43	3	9	12	44	9	0	0	0	10
1993-94	Atlanta	IHL	80	13	26	39	174	14	0	7	7	48

Signed as a free agent by **Tampa Bay**, June 2, 1993.

DUCHESNE, ALEXANDRE (doo-SHAYN) — MTL.

Left wing. Shoots left. 6', 212 lbs. Born, Val d'Or, Que., January 4, 1974.
(Montreal's 11th choice, 229th overall, in 1993 Entry Draft).

			Regular Season					Playoffs				
Season	Club	Lea	GP	G	A	TP	PIM	GP	G	A	TP	PIM
1991-92	Drummondville	QMJHL	67	6	11	17	51	3	0	0	0	0
1992-93	Drummondville	QMJHL	61	18	26	44	157	10	8	6	14	13
1993-94	Drummondville	QMJHL	53	38	36	74	109	7	3	0	3	8

DUCHESNE, GAETAN (doo-SHAYN) — S.J.

Left wing. Shoots left. 5'11", 200 lbs. Born, Les Saulles, Que., July 11, 1962.
(Washington's 8th choice, 152nd overall, in 1981 Entry Draft).

			Regular Season					Playoffs				
Season	Club	Lea	GP	G	A	TP	PIM	GP	G	A	TP	PIM
1979-80	Quebec	QJHL	46	9	28	37	22	5	0	2	2	9
1980-81	Quebec	QJHL	72	27	45	72	63	7	1	4	5	6
1981-82	**Washington**	**NHL**	**74**	**9**	**14**	**23**	**46**	....	....	....	....	....
1982-83	**Washington**	**NHL**	**77**	**18**	**19**	**37**	**52**	**4**	**1**	**1**	**2**	**4**
	Hershey	AHL	1	1	0	1	0	....	....	....	....	....
1983-84	**Washington**	**NHL**	**79**	**17**	**19**	**36**	**29**	**8**	**2**	**1**	**3**	**2**
1984-85	**Washington**	**NHL**	**67**	**15**	**23**	**38**	**32**	**5**	**0**	**1**	**1**	**7**
1985-86	**Washington**	**NHL**	**80**	**11**	**28**	**39**	**39**	**9**	**4**	**3**	**7**	**12**
1986-87	**Washington**	**NHL**	**74**	**17**	**35**	**52**	**53**	**7**	**3**	**0**	**3**	**14**
1987-88	**Quebec**	**NHL**	**80**	**24**	**23**	**47**	**83**	....	....	....	....	....
1988-89	**Quebec**	**NHL**	**70**	**8**	**21**	**29**	**56**	....	....	....	....	....
1989-90	**Minnesota**	**NHL**	**72**	**12**	**8**	**20**	**33**	**7**	**0**	**0**	**0**	**6**
1990-91	**Minnesota**	**NHL**	**68**	**9**	**9**	**18**	**18**	**23**	**2**	**3**	**5**	**34**
1991-92	**Minnesota**	**NHL**	**73**	**8**	**15**	**23**	**102**	**7**	**1**	**0**	**1**	**6**
1992-93	**Minnesota**	**NHL**	**84**	**16**	**13**	**29**	**30**	....	....	....	....	....
1993-94	**San Jose**	**NHL**	**84**	**12**	**18**	**30**	**28**	**14**	**1**	**4**	**5**	**12**
	NHL Totals		**982**	**176**	**245**	**421**	**601**	**84**	**14**	**13**	**27**	**97**

Traded to **Quebec** by **Washington** with Alan Haworth and Washington's first round choice (Joe Sakic) in 1987 Entry Draft for Clint Malarchuk and Dale Hunter, June 13, 1987. Traded to **Minnesota** by **Quebec** for Kevin Kaminski, June 19, 1989. Traded to **San Jose** by **Dallas** for San Jose's sixth round choice (later traded back to San Jose — San Jose selected Petri Varis) in 1993 Entry Draft, June 20, 1993.

DUCHESNE, STEVE (doo-SHAYN) — ST.L

Defense. Shoots left. 5'11", 195 lbs. Born, Sept-Iles, Que., June 30, 1965.

			Regular Season					Playoffs				
Season	Club	Lea	GP	G	A	TP	PIM	GP	G	A	TP	PIM
1983-84	Drummondville	QMJHL	67	1	34	35	79	....	....	....	....	....
1984-85a	Drummondville	QMJHL	65	22	54	76	94	5	4	7	11	8
1985-86	New Haven	AHL	75	14	35	49	76	5	0	2	2	9
1986-87b	**Los Angeles**	**NHL**	**75**	**13**	**25**	**38**	**74**	**5**	**2**	**2**	**4**	**4**
1987-88	**Los Angeles**	**NHL**	**71**	**16**	**39**	**55**	**109**	**5**	**1**	**3**	**4**	**14**
1988-89	**Los Angeles**	**NHL**	**79**	**25**	**50**	**75**	**92**	**11**	**4**	**4**	**8**	**12**
1989-90	**Los Angeles**	**NHL**	**79**	**20**	**42**	**62**	**36**	**10**	**2**	**9**	**11**	**6**
1990-91	**Los Angeles**	**NHL**	**78**	**21**	**41**	**62**	**66**	**12**	**4**	**8**	**12**	**8**
1991-92	**Philadelphia**	**NHL**	**78**	**18**	**38**	**56**	**86**	....	....	....	....	....
1992-93	**Quebec**	**NHL**	**82**	**20**	**62**	**82**	**57**	**6**	**0**	**5**	**5**	**6**
1993-94	**St. Louis**	**NHL**	**36**	**12**	**19**	**31**	**14**	**4**	**0**	**2**	**2**	**2**
	NHL Totals		**578**	**145**	**316**	**461**	**534**	**53**	**13**	**33**	**46**	**52**

a QMJHL First All-Star Team (1985)
b NHL All-Rookie Team (1987)

Played in NHL All-Star Game (1989, 1990, 1993)

Signed as a free agent by **Los Angeles,** October 1, 1984. Traded to **Philadelphia** by **Los Angeles** with Steve Kasper and Los Angeles' fourth round choice (Aris Brimanis) in 1991 Entry Draft for Jari Kurri and Jeff Chychrun, May 30, 1991. Traded to **Quebec** by **Philadelphia** with Peter Forsberg, Kerry Huffman, Mike Ricci, Ron Hextall, Chris Simon, Philadelphia's first choice in the 1993 (Jocelyn Thibault) and 1994 (later traded to Toronto — later traded to Wahington — Washington selected Nolan Baumgartner) Entry Drafts and cash for Eric Lindros, June 30, 1992. Traded to **St. Louis** by **Quebec** with Denis Chasse for Garth Butcher, Ron Sutter and Bob Bassen, January 23, 1994.

DUFRESNE, DONALD (doo-FRAYN, DOH-nal) — L.A.

Defense. Shoots right. 6'1", 206 lbs. Born, Quebec City, Que., April 10, 1967.
(Montreal's 8th choice, 117th overall, in 1985 Entry Draft).

			Regular Season					Playoffs				
Season	Club	Lea	GP	G	A	TP	PIM	GP	G	A	TP	PIM
1983-84	Trois-Rivières	QMJHL	67	7	12	19	97	....	....	....	....	....
1984-85	Trois-Rivières	QMJHL	65	5	30	35	112	7	1	3	4	12
1985-86a	Trois-Rivières	QMJHL	63	8	32	40	160	1	0	0	0	0
1986-87a	Trois-Rivières	QMJHL	51	5	21	26	79	....	....	....	....	....
	Longueuil	QMJHL	16	0	8	8	18	20	1	8	9	38
1987-88	Sherbrooke	AHL	47	1	8	9	107	6	1	0	1	34
1988-89	**Montreal**	**NHL**	**13**	**0**	**1**	**1**	**43**	**6**	**1**	**1**	**2**	**4**
	Sherbrooke	AHL	47	0	12	12	170	....	....	....	....	....
1989-90	**Montreal**	**NHL**	**18**	**0**	**4**	**4**	**23**	**10**	**0**	**1**	**1**	**18**
	Sherbrooke	AHL	38	2	11	13	104	....	....	....	....	....
1990-91	**Montreal**	**NHL**	**53**	**2**	**13**	**15**	**55**	**10**	**0**	**1**	**1**	**21**
	Fredericton	AHL	10	1	4	5	35	1	0	0	0	0
1991-92	**Montreal**	**NHL**	**3**	**0**	**0**	**0**	**2**	....	....	....	....	....
	Fredericton	AHL	31	8	12	20	60	7	0	0	0	10
1992-93	**Montreal**	**NHL**	**32**	**1**	**2**	**3**	**32**	**2**	**0**	**0**	**0**	**0**
1993-94	**Tampa Bay**	**NHL**	**51**	**2**	**6**	**8**	**48**	....	....	....	....	....
	Los Angeles	**NHL**	**9**	**0**	**0**	**0**	**10**	....	....	....	....	....
	NHL Totals		**179**	**5**	**26**	**31**	**213**	**28**	**1**	**3**	**4**	**43**

a QMJHL Second All-Star Team (1986, 1987)

Traded to **Tampa Bay** by **Montreal** to complete March 20, 1993 trade in which Rob Ramage was traded to Montreal for Eric Charron, Alain Cote and future considerations, June 20, 1993. Traded to **Los Angeles** by **Tampa Bay** for Los Angeles' sixth round choice (Daniel Juden) in 1994 Entry Draft, March 19, 1994.

DUNCAN, BRETT — T.B.

Defense. Shoots right. 6', 208 lbs. Born, Kitchener, Ont., February 15, 1973.
(Tampa Bay's 10th choice, 237th overall, in 1993 Entry Draft).

			Regular Season					Playoffs				
Season	Club	Lea	GP	G	A	TP	PIM	GP	G	A	TP	PIM
1991-92	Seattle	WHL	....	....	....	....	....	6	0	0	0	33
1992-93	Seattle	WHL	64	0	12	12	343	5	0	1	1	33
1993-94	Seattle	WHL	66	5	10	15	283	9	0	3	3	18

DUNCANSON, CRAIG — NYR

Left wing. Shoots left. 6', 190 lbs. Born, Sudbury, Ont., March 17, 1967.
(Los Angeles' 1st choice, 9th overall, in 1985 Entry Draft).

			Regular Season					Playoffs				
Season	Club	Lea	GP	G	A	TP	PIM	GP	G	A	TP	PIM
1983-84	Sudbury	OHL	62	38	38	76	176	....	....	....	....	....
1984-85	Sudbury	OHL	53	35	28	63	129	....	....	....	....	....
1985-86	**Los Angeles**	**NHL**	**2**	**0**	**1**	**1**	**0**	....	....	....	....	....
	Sudbury	OHL	21	12	17	29	55	....	....	....	....	....
	Cornwall	OHL	40	31	50	81	135	6	4	7	11	2
	New Haven	AHL	....	....	....	....	....	2	0	0	0	5
1986-87	**Los Angeles**	**NHL**	**2**	**0**	**0**	**0**	**24**	....	....	....	....	....
	Cornwall	OHL	52	22	45	67	88	5	4	3	7	20
1987-88	**Los Angeles**	**NHL**	**9**	**0**	**0**	**0**	**12**	....	....	....	....	....
	New Haven	AHL	57	15	25	40	170	....	....	....	....	....
1988-89	**Los Angeles**	**NHL**	**5**	**0**	**0**	**0**	**0**	....	....	....	....	....
	New Haven	AHL	69	25	39	64	200	17	4	8	12	60
1989-90	**Los Angeles**	**NHL**	**10**	**3**	**2**	**5**	**9**	....	....	....	....	....
	New Haven	AHL	51	17	30	47	152	....	....	....	....	....
1990-91	**Winnipeg**	**NHL**	**7**	**2**	**0**	**2**	**16**	....	....	....	....	....
	Moncton	AHL	58	16	34	50	107	9	3	11	14	31
1991-92	Baltimore	AHL	46	20	26	46	98	....	....	....	....	....
	Moncton	AHL	19	12	9	21	6	11	6	4	10	10
1992-93	**NY Rangers**	**NHL**	**3**	**0**	**1**	**1**	**0**	....	....	....	....	....
	Binghamton	AHL	69	35	59	94	126	14	7	5	12	9
1993-94	Binghamton	AHL	70	25	44	69	83	....	....	....	....	....
	NHL Totals		**38**	**5**	**4**	**9**	**61**	....	....	....	....	....

Traded to **Minnesota** by **Los Angeles** for Daniel Berthiaume, September 6, 1990. Traded to **Winnipeg** by **Minnesota** for Brian Hunt, September 6, 1990. Traded to **Washington** by **Winnipeg** with Brent Hughes and Simon Wheeldon for Bob Joyce, Tyler Larter and Kent Paynter, May 21, 1991. Signed as a free agent by **NY Rangers**, September 4, 1992.

DUPAUL, COSMO — OTT.

Center. Shoots left. 6', 186 lbs. Born, Pointe-Claire, Que., April 11, 1975.
(Ottawa's 4th choice, 91st overall, in 1993 Entry Draft).

			Regular Season					Playoffs				
Season	Club	Lea	GP	G	A	TP	PIM	GP	G	A	TP	PIM
1992-93	Victoriaville	QMJHL	67	23	35	58	16	6	1	3	4	2
1993-94	Victoriaville	QMJHL	66	26	46	72	32	5	2	2	4	6

DUPRE, YANICK (doo-PRAY, YAH-nihk) PHI.

Left wing. Shoots left. 6', 189 lbs. Born, Montreal, Que., November 20, 1972.
(Philadelphia's 2nd choice, 50th overall, in 1991 Entry Draft).

			Regular Season					Playoffs				
Season	Club	Lea	GP	G	A	TP	PIM	GP	G	A	TP	PIM
1989-90	Chicoutimi	QMJHL	24	5	9	14	27	....	....	....	....	....
	Drummondville	QMJHL	29	10	10	20	42	....	....	....	....	....
1990-91	Drummondville	QMJHL	58	29	38	67	87	11	8	5	13	33
1991-92	**Philadelphia**	**NHL**	**1**	**0**	**0**	**0**	**0**	....	....	....	....	....
	Drummondville	QMJHL	28	19	17	36	48	....	....	....	....	....
	Verdun	QMJHL	12	7	14	21	21	19	9	9	18	20
1992-93	Hershey	AHL	63	13	24	37	22	....	....	....	....	....
1993-94	Hershey	AHL	51	22	20	42	42	8	1	3	4	2
	NHL Totals		**1**	**0**	**0**	**0**	**0**	....	....	....	....	....

DUPUIS, MARC CHI.

Defense. Shoots left. 5'11", 176 lbs. Born, Cornwall, Ont., April 22, 1976.
(Chicago's 4th choice, 118th overall, in 1994 Entry Draft).

			Regular Season					Playoffs				
Season	Club	Lea	GP	G	A	TP	PIM	GP	G	A	TP	PIM
1992-93	Belleville	OHL	64	2	10	12	34	7	0	5	5	10
1993-94	Belleville	OHL	66	7	25	32	37	12	2	3	5	6

DUTHIE, RYAN CGY.

Center. Shoots right. 5'10", 180 lbs. Born, Red Deer, Alta., September 2, 1974.
(NY Islanders' 4th choice, 105th overall, in 1992 Entry Draft).

			Regular Season					Playoffs				
Season	Club	Lea	GP	G	A	TP	PIM	GP	G	A	TP	PIM
1991-92	Spokane	WHL	67	23	37	60	119	10	5	10	15	18
1992-93	Spokane	WHL	60	26	58	84	122	9	7	2	9	8
1993-94a	Spokane	WHL	71	57	69	126	111	3	3	5	8	11

a WHL West First All-Star Team (1994)

Re-entered NHL Entry Draft. **Calgary's** 4th choice, 91st overall in 1994 Entry Draft.

DYCK, PAUL PIT.

Defense. Shoots left. 6'1", 192 lbs. Born, Steinbach, Man., April 20, 1971.
(Pittsburgh's 11th choice, 236th overall, in 1991 Entry Draft).

			Regular Season					Playoffs				
Season	Club	Lea	GP	G	A	TP	PIM	GP	G	A	TP	PIM
1990-91	Moose Jaw	WHL	72	12	41	53	63	8	0	7	7	17
1991-92	Muskegon	IHL	73	6	21	27	40	14	1	3	4	4
1992-93	Cleveland	IHL	69	6	21	27	69	1	0	0	0	0
1993-94	Cleveland	IHL	60	1	10	11	57	....	....	....	....	....

DYKHUIS, KARL (DIGH-kowz) CHI.

Defense. Shoots left. 6'3", 195 lbs. Born, Sept-Iles, Que., July 8, 1972.
(Chicago's 1st choice, 16th overall, in 1990 Entry Draft).

			Regular Season					Playoffs				
Season	Club	Lea	GP	G	A	TP	PIM	GP	G	A	TP	PIM
1988-89	Hull	QMJHL	63	2	29	31	59	9	1	9	10	6
1989-90a	Hull	QMJHL	69	10	46	56	119	11	2	5	7	2
1990-91	Cdn. National	....	37	2	9	11	16	....	....	....	....	....
	Longueuil	QMJHL	3	1	4	4	6	8	2	5	7	6
1991-92	**Chicago**	**NHL**	**6**	**1**	**3**	**4**	**4**	....	....	....	....	....
	Verdun	QMJHL	29	5	19	24	55	17	0	12	12	14
1992-93	**Chicago**	**NHL**	**12**	**0**	**5**	**5**	**0**	....	....	....	....	....
	Indianapolis	IHL	59	5	18	23	76	5	1	1	2	8
1993-94	Indianapolis	IHL	73	7	25	32	132	....	....	....	....	....
	NHL Totals		**18**	**1**	**8**	**9**	**4**	....	....	....	....	....

a QMJHL First All-Star Team (1990)

DZIEDZIC, JOE PIT.

Left wing. Shoots left. 6'3", 200 lbs. Born, Minneapolis, MN, December 18, 1971.
(Pittsburgh's 2nd choice, 61st overall, in 1990 Entry Draft).

			Regular Season					Playoffs				
Season	Club	Lea	GP	G	A	TP	PIM	GP	G	A	TP	PIM
1990-91	U. Minnesota	WCHA	20	6	4	10	26	....	....	....	....	....
1991-92	U. Minnesota	WCHA	34	8	9	17	68	....	....	....	....	....
1992-93	U. Minnesota	WCHA	41	11	14	25	62	....	....	....	....	....
1993-94	U. Minnesota	WCHA	18	7	10	17	48	....	....	....	....	....

EAGLES, MIKE WPG.

Center/Left wing. Shoots left. 5'10", 190 lbs. Born, Sussex, N.B., March 7, 1963.
(Quebec's 5th choice, 116th overall, in 1981 Entry Draft).

			Regular Season					Playoffs				
Season	Club	Lea	GP	G	A	TP	PIM	GP	G	A	TP	PIM
1980-81	Kitchener	OHA	56	11	27	38	64	18	4	2	6	36
1981-82	Kitchener	OHL	62	26	40	66	148	15	3	11	14	27
1982-83	**Quebec**	**NHL**	**2**	**0**	**0**	**0**	**2**	....	....	....	....	....
	Kitchener	OHL	58	26	36	62	133	12	5	7	12	27
1983-84	Fredericton	AHL	68	13	29	42	85	4	0	0	0	5
1984-85	Fredericton	AHL	36	4	20	24	80	3	0	0	0	2
1985-86	**Quebec**	**NHL**	**73**	**11**	**12**	**23**	**49**	**3**	**0**	**0**	**0**	**2**
1986-87	**Quebec**	**NHL**	**73**	**13**	**19**	**32**	**55**	**4**	**1**	**0**	**1**	**10**
1987-88	**Quebec**	**NHL**	**76**	**10**	**10**	**20**	**74**	....	....	....	....	....
1988-89	**Chicago**	**NHL**	**47**	**5**	**11**	**16**	**44**	....	....	....	....	....
1989-90	**Chicago**	**NHL**	**23**	**1**	**2**	**3**	**34**	....	....	....	....	....
	Indianapolis	IHL	24	11	13	24	47	13	*10	10	20	34
1990-91	**Winnipeg**	**NHL**	**44**	**0**	**9**	**9**	**79**	....	....	....	....	....
	Indianapolis	IHL	25	15	14	29	47	....	....	....	....	....
1991-92	**Winnipeg**	**NHL**	**65**	**7**	**10**	**17**	**118**	**7**	**0**	**0**	**0**	**8**
1992-93	**Winnipeg**	**NHL**	**84**	**8**	**18**	**26**	**131**	**5**	**0**	**1**	**1**	**6**
1993-94	**Winnipeg**	**NHL**	**73**	**4**	**8**	**12**	**96**	....	....	....	....	....
	NHL Totals		**560**	**59**	**99**	**158**	**682**	**19**	**1**	**1**	**2**	**26**

Traded to **Chicago** by **Quebec** for Bob Mason, July 5, 1988. Traded to **Winnipeg** by **Chicago** for Winnipeg's fourth round choice (Igor Kravchuk) in 1991 Entry Draft, December 14, 1990.

EAKINS, DALLAS (EE-kins) FLA.

Defense. Shoots left. 6'2", 195 lbs. Born, Dade City, FL, February 27, 1967.
(Washington's 11th choice, 208th overall, in 1985 Entry Draft).

			Regular Season					Playoffs				
Season	Club	Lea	GP	G	A	TP	PIM	GP	G	A	TP	PIM
1984-85	Peterborough	OHL	48	0	8	8	96	7	0	0	0	18
1985-86	Peterborough	OHL	60	6	16	22	134	16	0	1	1	30
1986-87	Peterborough	OHL	54	3	11	14	145	12	1	4	5	37
1987-88	Peterborough	OHL	64	11	27	38	129	12	3	12	15	16
1988-89	Baltimore	AHL	62	0	10	10	139	....	....	....	....	....
1989-90	Moncton	AHL	75	2	11	13	189	....	....	....	....	....
1990-91	Moncton	AHL	75	1	12	13	132	9	0	1	1	44
1991-92	Moncton	AHL	67	3	13	16	136	11	2	1	3	16
1992-93	**Winnipeg**	**NHL**	**14**	**0**	**2**	**2**	**38**	....	....	....	....	....
	Moncton	AHL	55	4	6	10	132	....	....	....	....	....
1993-94	**Florida**	**NHL**	**1**	**0**	**0**	**0**	**0**	....	....	....	....	....
	Cincinnati	IHL	80	1	18	19	143	8	0	1	1	41
	NHL Totals		**15**	**0**	**2**	**2**	**38**	....	....	....	....	....

Signed as a free agent by **Winnipeg**, October 17, 1989. Signed as a free agent by **Florida**, July 8, 1993.

EASTWOOD, MIKE TOR.

Center. Shoots right. 6'3", 205 lbs. Born, Ottawa, Ont., July 1, 1967.
(Toronto's 5th choice, 91st overall, in 1987 Entry Draft).

			Regular Season					Playoffs				
Season	Club	Lea	GP	G	A	TP	PIM	GP	G	A	TP	PIM
1987-88	W. Michigan	CCHA	42	5	8	13	14	....	....	....	....	....
1988-89	W. Michigan	CCHA	40	10	13	23	87	....	....	....	....	....
1989-90	W. Michigan	CCHA	40	25	27	52	36	....	....	....	....	....
1990-91a	W. Michigan	CCHA	42	29	32	61	84	....	....	....	....	....
1991-92	**Toronto**	**NHL**	**9**	**0**	**2**	**2**	**4**	....	....	....	....	....
	St. John's	AHL	61	18	25	43	28	16	9	10	19	16
1992-93	**Toronto**	**NHL**	**12**	**1**	**6**	**7**	**21**	**10**	**1**	**2**	**3**	**8**
	St. John's	AHL	60	24	35	59	32	....	....	....	....	....
1993-94	**Toronto**	**NHL**	**54**	**8**	**10**	**18**	**28**	**18**	**3**	**2**	**5**	**12**
	NHL Totals		**75**	**9**	**18**	**27**	**53**	**28**	**4**	**4**	**8**	**20**

a CCHA Second All-Star Team (1991)

EGELAND, ALLAN T.B.

Center. Shoots left. 6', 184 lbs. Born, Lethbridge, Alta., January 31, 1973.
(Tampa Bay's 3rd choice, 55th overall, in 1993 Entry Draft).

			Regular Season					Playoffs				
Season	Club	Lea	GP	G	A	TP	PIM	GP	G	A	TP	PIM
1990-91	Lethbridge	WHL	67	2	16	18	57	9	0	0	0	0
1991-92	Tacoma	WHL	72	35	39	74	135	4	0	1	1	18
1992-93a	Tacoma	WHL	71	56	57	113	119	7	9	7	16	18
1993-94b	Tacoma	WHL	70	47	76	123	204	8	5	3	8	26

a WHL West First All-Star Team (1993)
b WHL West Second All-Star Team (1994)

EGELAND, TRACY (EHG-luhnd) PHI.

Left wing. Shoots right. 6'1", 197 lbs. Born, Lethbridge, Alta., August 20, 1970.
(Chicago's 5th choice, 132nd overall, in 1989 Entry Draft).

			Regular Season					Playoffs				
Season	Club	Lea	GP	G	A	TP	PIM	GP	G	A	TP	PIM
1986-87	Swift Current	WHL	48	3	2	5	20	....	....	....	....	....
1987-88	Swift Current	WHL	63	10	22	32	34	....	....	....	....	....
1988-89	Medicine Hat	WHL	42	11	12	23	64	....	....	....	....	....
	Prince Albert	WHL	24	17	10	27	24	4	0	1	1	13
1989-90	Prince Albert	WHL	61	39	26	65	160	13	7	10	17	26
1990-91	Indianapolis	IHL	79	17	22	39	205	7	2	1	3	21
1991-92	Indianapolis	IHL	66	20	11	31	214	....	....	....	....	....
1992-93	Indianapolis	IHL	43	11	14	25	122	....	....	....	....	....
1993-94	Hershey	AHL	57	7	11	18	266	4	0	0	0	2

Signed as a free agent by **Philadelphia**, August 4, 1993.

EISENHUT, NEIL (IGHS-ihn-huht) CGY.

Center. Shoots left. 6'1", 190 lbs. Born, Osoyoos, B.C., February 9, 1967.
(Vancouver's 11th choice, 238th overall, in 1987 Entry Draft).

			Regular Season					Playoffs				
Season	Club	Lea	GP	G	A	TP	PIM	GP	G	A	TP	PIM
1987-88	North Dakota	WCHA	42	12	20	32	14	....	....	....	....	....
1988-89	North Dakota	WCHA	41	22	16	38	20	....	....	....	....	....
1989-90	North Dakota	WCHA	45	22	32	54	46	....	....	....	....	....
1990-91	North Dakota	WCHA	20	9	15	24	10	....	....	....	....	....
1991-92	Milwaukee	IHL	76	13	23	36	26	2	1	2	3	0
1992-93	Hamilton	AHL	72	22	40	62	41	....	....	....	....	....
1993-94	**Vancouver**	**NHL**	**13**	**1**	**3**	**4**	**21**	....	....	....	....	....
	Hamilton	AHL	60	17	36	53	30	4	1	4	5	0
	NHL Totals		**13**	**1**	**3**	**4**	**21**	....	....	....	....	....

Signed as a free agent by **Calgary**, June 16, 1994.

EKLUND, PER-ERIK (PELLE) (EHK-luhnd) DAL.

Center. Shoots left. 5'10", 175 lbs. Born, Stockholm, Sweden, March 22, 1963.
(Philadelphia's 7th choice, 167th overall, in 1983 Entry Draft).

			Regular Season					Playoffs				
Season	Club	Lea	GP	G	A	TP	PIM	GP	G	A	TP	PIM
1981-82	AIK	Swe.	23	2	3	5	2	....	....	....	....	....
1982-83	AIK	Swe.	34	13	17	30	14	3	1	4	5	2
1983-84	AIK	Swe.	35	9	18	27	24	6	6	7	13	2
1984-85	AIK	Swe.	35	16	33	49	10	....	....	....	....	....
1985-86	**Philadelphia**	**NHL**	**70**	**15**	**51**	**66**	**12**	**5**	**0**	**2**	**2**	**0**
1986-87	**Philadelphia**	**NHL**	**72**	**14**	**41**	**55**	**2**	**26**	**7**	**20**	**27**	**2**
1987-88	**Philadelphia**	**NHL**	**71**	**10**	**32**	**42**	**12**	**7**	**0**	**3**	**3**	**0**
1988-89	**Philadelphia**	**NHL**	**79**	**18**	**51**	**69**	**23**	**19**	**3**	**8**	**11**	**2**
1989-90	**Philadelphia**	**NHL**	**70**	**23**	**39**	**62**	**16**	....	....	....	....	....
1990-91	**Philadelphia**	**NHL**	**73**	**19**	**50**	**69**	**14**	....	....	....	....	....
1991-92	**Philadelphia**	**NHL**	**51**	**7**	**16**	**23**	**4**	....	....	....	....	....
1992-93	**Philadelphia**	**NHL**	**55**	**11**	**38**	**49**	**16**	....	....	....	....	....
1993-94	**Philadelphia**	**NHL**	**48**	**1**	**16**	**17**	**8**	....	....	....	....	....
	Dallas	**NHL**	**5**	**2**	**1**	**3**	**2**	**9**	**0**	**3**	**3**	**4**
	NHL Totals		**594**	**120**	**335**	**455**	**109**	**66**	**10**	**36**	**46**	**8**

Traded to **Dallas** by **Philadelphia** for Dallas' eighth round choice (Raymond Giroux) in 1994 Entry Draft, March 21, 1994.

EKMAN, NILS (EHK-mahn) CGY.

Left wing. Shoots left. 5'11", 167 lbs. Born, Stockholm, Sweden, March 11, 1976.
(Calgary's 6th choice, 107th overall, in 1994 Entry Draft).

			Regular Season					Playoffs				
Season	Club	Lea	GP	G	A	TP	PIM	GP	G	A	TP	PIM
1993-94	Hammarby	Swe.	18	7	2	9	4	....	....	....	....	....

ELIAS, PATRIK (EH-lih-ahsh) N.J.

Left wing. Shoots left. 6', 176 lbs. Born, Trebic, Czech., April 13, 1976.
(New Jersey's 2nd choice, 51st overall, in 1994 Entry Draft).

			Regular Season					Playoffs				
Season	Club	Lea	GP	G	A	TP	PIM	GP	G	A	TP	PIM
1992-93	Kladno	Czech.	2	0	0	0	....	....	....	....	....	....
1993-94	Kladno	Czech.	15	1	2	3	....	11	2	2	4	....

ELICK, MICKEY NYR

Defense. Shoots left. 6'1", 180 lbs. Born, Calgary, Alta., March 17, 1974.
(NY Rangers' 8th choice, 192nd overall, in 1992 Entry Draft).

			Regular Season					Playoffs				
Season	Club	Lea	GP	G	A	TP	PIM	GP	G	A	TP	PIM
1992-93	U. Wisconsin	WCHA	33	1	6	7	24	....	....	....	....	....
1993-94	U. Wisconsin	WCHA	42	7	12	19	54	....	....	....	....	....

ELIK, TODD (EHL-ihk) S.J.

Center. Shoots left. 6'2", 195 lbs. Born, Brampton, Ont., April 15, 1966.

			Regular Season					Playoffs				
Season	Club	Lea	GP	G	A	TP	PIM	GP	G	A	TP	PIM
1984-85	Kingston	OHL	34	14	11	25	6	....	....	....	....	....
	North Bay	OHL	23	4	6	10	2	4	2	0	2	0
1985-86	North Bay	OHL	40	12	34	46	20	10	7	6	13	0
1986-87	U. of Regina	CWUAA	27	26	34	60	137	....	....	....	....	....
1987-88	Colorado	IHL	81	44	56	100	83	12	8	12	20	9
1988-89	Denver	IHL	28	20	15	35	22	....	....	....	....	....
	New Haven	AHL	43	11	25	36	31	17	10	12	22	44
1989-90	**Los Angeles**	**NHL**	**48**	**10**	**23**	**33**	**41**	**10**	**3**	**9**	**12**	**10**
	New Haven	AHL	32	20	23	43	42	....	....	....	....	....
1990-91	**Los Angeles**	**NHL**	**74**	**21**	**37**	**58**	**58**	**12**	**2**	**7**	**9**	**6**
1991-92	**Minnesota**	**NHL**	**62**	**14**	**32**	**46**	**125**	**5**	**1**	**1**	**2**	**2**
1992-93	**Minnesota**	**NHL**	**46**	**13**	**18**	**31**	**48**	....	....	....	....	....
	Edmonton	**NHL**	**14**	**1**	**9**	**10**	**8**	....	....	....	....	....
1993-94	**Edmonton**	**NHL**	**4**	**0**	**0**	**0**	**6**	....	....	....	....	....
	San Jose	**NHL**	**75**	**25**	**41**	**66**	**89**	**14**	**5**	**5**	**10**	**12**
	NHL Totals		**323**	**84**	**160**	**244**	**375**	**41**	**11**	**22**	**33**	**30**

Signed as a free agent by **NY Rangers**, February 26, 1988. Traded to **Los Angeles** by **NY Rangers** with Igor Liba, Michael Boyce and future considerations for Dean Kennedy and Denis Larocque, December 12, 1988. Traded to **Minnesota** by **Los Angeles** for Randy Gilhen, Charlie Huddy, Jim Thomson and NY Rangers' fourth round choice (previously acquired by Minnesota — Los Angeles selected Alexei Zhitnik) in 1991 Entry Draft, June 22, 1991. Traded to **Edmonton** by **Minnesota** for Brent Gilchrist, March 5, 1993. Claimed on waivers by **San Jose** from **Edmonton**, October 26, 1993.

ELLETT, DAVE TOR.

Defense. Shoots left. 6'2", 200 lbs. Born, Cleveland, OH, March 30, 1964.
(Winnipeg's 3rd choice, 75th overall, in 1982 Entry Draft).

			Regular Season					Playoffs				
Season	Club	Lea	GP	G	A	TP	PIM	GP	G	A	TP	PIM
1982-83	Bowling Green	CCHA	40	4	13	17	34	....	....	....	....	....
1983-84ab	Bowling Green	CCHA	43	15	39	54	96	....	....	....	....	....
1984-85	**Winnipeg**	**NHL**	**80**	**11**	**27**	**38**	**85**	**8**	**1**	**5**	**6**	**4**
1985-86	**Winnipeg**	**NHL**	**80**	**15**	**31**	**46**	**96**	**3**	**0**	**1**	**1**	**0**
1986-87	**Winnipeg**	**NHL**	**78**	**13**	**31**	**44**	**53**	**10**	**0**	**8**	**8**	**2**
1987-88	**Winnipeg**	**NHL**	**68**	**13**	**45**	**58**	**106**	**5**	**1**	**2**	**3**	**10**
1988-89	**Winnipeg**	**NHL**	**75**	**22**	**34**	**56**	**62**	....	....	....	....	....
1989-90	**Winnipeg**	**NHL**	**77**	**17**	**29**	**46**	**96**	**7**	**2**	**0**	**2**	**6**
1990-91	**Winnipeg**	**NHL**	**17**	**4**	**7**	**11**	**6**	....	....	....	....	....
	Toronto	**NHL**	**60**	**8**	**30**	**38**	**69**	....	....	....	....	....
1991-92	**Toronto**	**NHL**	**79**	**18**	**33**	**51**	**95**	....	....	....	....	....
1992-93	**Toronto**	**NHL**	**70**	**6**	**34**	**40**	**46**	**21**	**4**	**8**	**12**	**8**
1993-94	**Toronto**	**NHL**	**68**	**7**	**36**	**43**	**42**	**18**	**3**	**15**	**18**	**31**
	NHL Totals		**752**	**134**	**337**	**471**	**756**	**72**	**11**	**39**	**50**	**61**

a CCHA Second All-Star Team (1984)
b Named to NCAA All-Tournament Team (1984)

Played in NHL All-Star Game (1989, 1992)

Traded to **Toronto** by **Winnipeg** with Paul Fenton for Ed Olczyk and Mark Osborne, November 10, 1990.

ELVENAS, STEFAN CHI.

Left wing. Shoots left. 6'1", 183 lbs. Born, Lund, Sweden, March 30, 1970.
(Chicago's 3rd choice, 71st overall, in 1988 Entry Draft).

			Regular Season					Playoffs				
Season	Club	Lea	GP	G	A	TP	PIM	GP	G	A	TP	PIM
1987-88	Rogle	Swe.2	36	21	17	38	30	2	0	0	0	2
1988-89	Rogle	Swe.2				UNAVAILABLE						
1989-90	Rogle	Swe.2	35	18	25	43	56	....	....	....	....	....
1990-91	Rogle	Swe.2	18	14	6	20	10	....	....	....	....	....
1991-92	Rogle	Swe.2	35	31	19	50	10	....	....	....	....	....
1992-93	Rogle	Swe.	40	18	14	32	18	....	....	....	....	....
1993-94	Rogle	Swe.	40	15	17	32	36	3	2	0	2	2

ELYNUIK, PAT (EL-ih-NYUK) OTT.

Right wing. Shoots right. 6', 185 lbs. Born, Foam Lake, Sask., October 30, 1967.
(Winnipeg's 1st choice, 8th overall, in 1986 Entry Draft).

			Regular Season					Playoffs				
Season	Club	Lea	GP	G	A	TP	PIM	GP	G	A	TP	PIM
1984-85	Prince Albert	WHL	70	23	20	43	54	13	9	3	12	7
1985-86a	Prince Albert	WHL	68	53	53	106	62	20	7	9	16	17
1986-87a	Prince Albert	WHL	64	51	62	113	40	8	5	5	10	12
1987-88	**Winnipeg**	**NHL**	**13**	**1**	**3**	**4**	**12**	....	....	....	....	....
	Moncton	AHL	30	11	18	29	35	....	....	....	....	....
1988-89	**Winnipeg**	**NHL**	**56**	**26**	**25**	**51**	**29**	....	....	....	....	....
	Moncton	AHL	7	8	2	10	2	....	....	....	....	....
1989-90	**Winnipeg**	**NHL**	**80**	**32**	**42**	**74**	**83**	**7**	**2**	**4**	**6**	**2**
1990-91	**Winnipeg**	**NHL**	**80**	**31**	**34**	**65**	**73**	....	....	....	....	....
1991-92	**Winnipeg**	**NHL**	**60**	**25**	**25**	**50**	**65**	**7**	**2**	**2**	**4**	**4**
1992-93	**Washington**	**NHL**	**80**	**22**	**35**	**57**	**66**	**6**	**2**	**3**	**5**	**19**
1993-94	**Washington**	**NHL**	**4**	**1**	**1**	**2**	**0**	....	....	....	....	....
	Tampa Bay	**NHL**	**63**	**12**	**14**	**26**	**64**	....	....	....	....	....
	NHL Totals		**436**	**150**	**179**	**329**	**392**	**20**	**6**	**9**	**15**	**25**

a WHL East All-Star Team (1986, 1987)

Traded to **Washington** by **Winnipeg** for John Druce and Toronto's fourth round choice (previously acquired by Washington — later traded to Detroit — Detroit selected John Jakopin) in 1993 Entry Draft, October 1, 1992. Signed as a free agent by **Ottawa**, June 22, 1994. Traded to **Tampa Bay** by **Washington** for future draft choices, October 22, 1993. Signed as a free agent by **Ottawa**, June 21, 1994.

EMERSON, NELSON WPG.

Center. Shoots right. 5'11", 175 lbs. Born, Hamilton, Ont., August 17, 1967.
(St. Louis' 2nd choice, 44th overall, in 1985 Entry Draft).

			Regular Season					Playoffs				
Season	Club	Lea	GP	G	A	TP	PIM	GP	G	A	TP	PIM
1986-87	Bowling Green	CCHA	45	26	35	61	28	....	....	....	....	....
1987-88ab	Bowling Green	CCHA	45	34	49	83	54	....	....	....	....	....
1988-89c	Bowling Green	CCHA	44	22	46	68	46	....	....	....	....	....
1989-90bd	Bowling Green	CCHA	44	30	52	82	42	....	....	....	....	....
	Peoria	IHL	3	1	1	2	0	....	....	....	....	....
1990-91	**St. Louis**	**NHL**	**4**	**0**	**3**	**3**	**2**	....	....	....	....	....
ef	Peoria	IHL	73	36	79	115	91	17	9	12	21	16
1991-92	**St. Louis**	**NHL**	**79**	**23**	**36**	**59**	**66**	**6**	**3**	**3**	**6**	**21**
1992-93	**St. Louis**	**NHL**	**82**	**22**	**51**	**73**	**62**	**11**	**1**	**6**	**7**	**6**
1993-94	**Winnipeg**	**NHL**	**83**	**33**	**41**	**74**	**80**	....	....	....	....	....
	NHL Totals		**248**	**78**	**131**	**209**	**210**	**17**	**4**	**9**	**13**	**27**

a NCAA West Second All-American Team (1988)
b CCHA First All-Star Team (1988, 1990)
c CCHA Second All-Star Team (1989)
d NCAA West First All-American Team (1990)
e IHL First All-Star Team (1991)
f Won Garry F. Longman Memorial Trophy (Top Rookie - IHL) (1991)

Traded to **Winnipeg** by **St. Louis** with Stephane Quintal for Phil Housley, September 24, 1993.

EMMA, DAVID N.J.

Center. Shoots left. 5'11", 180 lbs. Born, Cranston, RI, January 14, 1969.
(New Jersey's 6th choice, 110th overall, in 1989 Entry Draft).

			Regular Season					Playoffs				
Season	Club	Lea	GP	G	A	TP	PIM	GP	G	A	TP	PIM
1987-88	Boston College	H.E.	30	19	16	35	30	....	....	....	....	....
1988-89	Boston College	H.E.	36	20	31	51	36	....	....	....	....	....
1989-90ab	Boston College	H.E.	42	38	34	*72	46	....	....	....	....	....
1990-91abcd	Boston College	H.E.	39	*35	46	*81	44	....	....	....	....	....
1991-92	U.S. National	....	55	15	16	31	32	....	....	....	....	....
	U.S. Olympic	....	6	0	1	1	6	....	....	....	....	....
	Utica	AHL	15	4	7	11	12	4	1	1	2	2
1992-93	**New Jersey**	**NHL**	**2**	**0**	**0**	**0**	**0**	....	....	....	....	....
	Utica	AHL	61	21	40	61	47	5	2	1	3	6
1993-94	**New Jersey**	**NHL**	**15**	**5**	**5**	**10**	**2**	....	....	....	....	....
	Albany	AHL	56	26	29	55	53	5	1	2	3	8
	NHL Totals		**17**	**5**	**5**	**10**	**2**	....	....	....	....	....

a Hockey East First All-Star Team (1990, 1991)
b NCAA East First All-American Team (1990, 1991)
c Hockey East Player of the Year (1991)
d Won Hobey Baker Memorial Award (Top U.S. Collegiate Player) (1991)

EMMONS, GARY

Center. Shoots right. 6', 185 lbs. Born, Winnipeg, Man., December 30, 1963.
(NY Rangers' 1st choice, 14th overall, in 1986 Supplemental Draft).

			Regular Season					Playoffs				
Season	Club	Lea	GP	G	A	TP	PIM	GP	G	A	TP	PIM
1983-84	N. Michigan	CCHA	40	28	21	49	42	....	....	....	....	....
1984-85	N. Michigan	CCHA	40	25	28	53	22	....	....	....	....	....
1985-86	N. Michigan	CCHA	36	45	30	75	34	....	....	....	....	....
1986-87	N. Michigan	CCHA	35	32	34	66	59	....	....	....	....	....
1987-88	Milwaukee	IHL	13	3	4	7	4	....	....	....	....	....
	Nova Scotia	AHL	59	18	27	45	22	....	....	....	....	....
1988-89	Cdn. National	....	49	16	26	42	42	....	....	....	....	....
1989-90	Kalamazoo	IHL	81	41	59	100	38	8	2	7	9	2
1990-91	Kalamazoo	IHL	62	25	33	58	26	11	5	8	13	6
1991-92	Kansas City	IHL	80	29	54	83	60	15	6	13	19	8
1992-93	Kansas City	IHL	80	37	44	81	80	12	*7	6	13	8
1993-94	**San Jose**	**NHL**	**3**	**1**	**0**	**1**	**0**	....	....	....	....	....
	Kansas City	IHL	63	20	49	69	28	....	....	....	....	....
	NHL Totals		**3**	**1**	**0**	**1**	**0**	....	....	....	....	....

Signed as a free agent by **Edmonton**, July 27, 1987. Signed as a free agent by **Minnesota**, July 11, 1989. Signed as a free agent by **San Jose**, October 19, 1993.

EMMONS, JOHN CGY.

Center. Shoots left. 6', 185 lbs. Born, San Jose, CA, August 17, 1974.
(Calgary's 7th choice, 122nd overall, in 1993 Entry Draft).

			Regular Season					Playoffs				
Season	Club	Lea	GP	G	A	TP	PIM	GP	G	A	TP	PIM
1992-93	Yale	ECAC	28	3	5	8	66	....	....	....	....	....
1993-94	Yale	ECAC	25	5	12	17	66	....	....	....	....	....

ENGA, RICHARD NYI

Center. Shoots right. 5'10", 156 lbs. Born, Bitburg, Germany, February 15, 1972.
(NY Islanders' 9th choice, 195th overall, in 1990 Entry Draft).

			Regular Season					Playoffs				
Season	Club	Lea	GP	G	A	TP	PIM	GP	G	A	TP	PIM
1991-92	Colorado	WCHA	40	11	16	27	18	....	....	....	....	....
1992-93	Colorado	WCHA	36	12	19	31	16	....	....	....	....	....
1993-94	Colorado	WCHA	39	15	23	38	49	....	....	....	....	....

NGLUND, PATRIK — PHI.

eft wing. Shoots left. 6', 185 lbs. Born, Stockholm, Sweden, June 3, 1970.
Philadelphia's 11th choice, 151st overall, in 1990 Entry Draft).

			Regular Season					Playoffs				
eason	Club	Lea	GP	G	A	TP	PIM	GP	G	A	TP	PIM
988-89	AIK	Swe.	19	2	3	5	6	....	....	....	....	....
989-90	AIK	Swe.	31	11	7	18	2	3	0	0	0	12
990-91	AIK	Swe.	40	9	6	15	6	....	....	....	....	....
991-92	AIK	Swe.	39	8	5	13	8	3	0	0	0	0
992-93	AIK	Swe.	22	3	1	4	8	....	....	....	....	....
993-94	AIK	Swe.	35	14	25	39	18	....	....	....	....	....

NSOM, JIM — CHI.

enter. Shoots left. 6'3", 191 lbs. Born, Oshawa, Ont., August 24, 1976.
Chicago's 5th choice, 144th overall, in 1994 Entry Draft).

			Regular Season					Playoffs				
eason	Club	Lea	GP	G	A	TP	PIM	GP	G	A	TP	PIM
992-93	North Bay	OHL	65	7	17	24	70	5	1	0	1	7
993-94	North Bay	OHL	44	16	20	36	67	16	4	5	9	6

PANCHINTSEV, VADIM — (yeh-pahn-CHIHN-tsehv) T.B.

enter. Shoots left. 5'9", 165 lbs. Born, Orsk, USSR, March 16, 1976.
Tampa Bay's 3rd choice, 55th overall, in 1994 Entry Draft).

			Regular Season					Playoffs				
eason	Club	Lea	GP	G	A	TP	PIM	GP	G	A	TP	PIM
993-94	Spartak	CIS	46	6	5	11	16	3	0	1	1	0

RICKSON, BRYAN

ight wing. Shoots right. 5'9", 175 lbs. Born, Roseau, MN, March 7, 1960.

			Regular Season					Playoffs				
eason	Club	Lea	GP	G	A	TP	PIM	GP	G	A	TP	PIM
1981-82	U. Minnesota	WCHA	35	25	20	45	20	....	....	....	....	....
1982-83	U. Minnesota	WCHA	42	35	47	82	34	....	....	....	....	....
	Hershey	AHL	1	0	1	1	0	3	3	0	3	0
1983-84	**Washington**	**NHL**	**45**	**12**	**17**	**29**	**16**	**8**	**2**	**3**	**5**	**7**
	Hershey	AHL	31	16	12	28	11	....	....	....	....	....
1984-85	**Washington**	**NHL**	**57**	**15**	**13**	**28**	**23**	....	....	....	....	....
	Binghamton	AHL	13	6	11	17	8	....	....	....	....	....
1985-86	**Los Angeles**	**NHL**	**55**	**20**	**23**	**43**	**36**	....	....	....	....	....
	Binghamton	AHL	7	5	3	8	2	....	....	....	....	....
	New Haven	AHL	14	8	3	11	11	....	....	....	....	....
1986-87	**Los Angeles**	**NHL**	**68**	**20**	**30**	**50**	**26**	**3**	**1**	**1**	**2**	**0**
1987-88	**Los Angeles**	**NHL**	**42**	**6**	**15**	**21**	**20**	....	....	....	....	....
	New Haven	AHL	3	0	0	0	0	....	....	....	....	....
	Pittsburgh	**NHL**	**11**	**1**	**4**	**5**	**0**	....	....	....	....	....
1988-89					DID NOT PLAY							
1989-90	Moncton	AHL	13	4	7	11	4	....	....	....	....	....
1990-91	**Winnipeg**	**NHL**	**6**	**0**	**7**	**7**	**0**	....	....	....	....	....
	Moncton	AHL	36	18	14	32	16	9	9	2	11	6
1991-92	**Winnipeg**	**NHL**	**10**	**2**	**4**	**6**	**0**	....	....	....	....	....
1992-93	**Winnipeg**	**NHL**	**41**	**4**	**12**	**16**	**14**	**3**	**0**	**0**	**0**	**0**
	Moncton	AHL	2	1	1	2	4	....	....	....	....	....
1993-94	**Winnipeg**	**NHL**	**16**	**0**	**0**	**0**	**6**	....	....	....	....	....
	Moncton	AHL	3	0	1	1	2	....	....	....	....	....
	NHL Totals		**351**	**80**	**125**	**205**	**141**	**14**	**3**	**4**	**7**	**7**

Signed as a free agent by **Washington**, April 5, 1983. Traded to **Los Angeles** by **Washington** for Bruce Shoebottom, October 31, 1985. Traded to **Pittsburgh** by **Los Angeles** for Chris Kontos and Pittsburgh's sixth round draft choice (Micah Aivazoff) in 1988 Entry Draft, February 5, 1988. Signed as a free agent by **Winnipeg**, March 2, 1990.

ERIKSSON, ANDERS — DET.

Defense. Shoots left. 6'3", 218 lbs. Born, Bollnas, Sweden, January 9, 1975.
(Detroit's 1st choice, 22nd overall, in 1993 Entry Draft).

			Regular Season					Playoffs				
Season	Club	Lea	GP	G	A	TP	PIM	GP	G	A	TP	PIM
1992-93	MoDo	Swe.	20	0	2	2	2	1	0	0	0	0
1993-94	MoDo	Swe.	38	2	8	10	42	11	0	0	0	8

ERIKSSON, NIKLAS — (AIR-ihk-suhn) PHI.

Center. Shoots left. 5'10", 183 lbs. Born, Vastervik, Sweden, February 17, 1969.
(Philadelphia's 4th choice, 117th overall, in 1989 Entry Draft).

			Regular Season					Playoffs				
Season	Club	Lea	GP	G	A	TP	PIM	GP	G	A	TP	PIM
1987-88	Leksand	Swe.	16	1	8	9	4	2	0	0	0	0
1988-89	Leksand	Swe.	33	18	12	30	22	....	....	....	....	....
1989-90	Leksand	Swe.	40	18	16	34	16	3	0	2	2	2
1990-91	Leksand	Swe.	8	2	2	4	2	....	....	....	....	....
1991-92	Leksand	Swe.	22	10	7	17	16	....	....	....	....	....
1992-93	Leksand	Swe.	37	6	19	25	28	2	0	1	1	2
1993-94	Leksand	Swe.	33	10	25	35	34	4	1	2	3	2

ERIKSSON, TOMAZ — (AIR-ihk-suhn) PHI.

Left wing. Shoots left. 6', 194 lbs. Born, Stockholm, Sweden, March 23, 1967.
(Philadelphia's 4th choice, 83rd overall, in 1987 Entry Draft).

			Regular Season					Playoffs				
Season	Club	Lea	GP	G	A	TP	PIM	GP	G	A	TP	PIM
1986-87	Djurgarden	Swe.	20	7	4	11	14	2	2	0	2	0
1987-88	Djurgarden	Swe.	26	4	5	9	16	....	....	....	....	....
1988-89	Djurgarden	Swe.	4	0	0	0	0	....	....	....	....	....
1989-90	Sodertalje	Swe.	39	14	10	24	26	2	1	1	2	2
1990-91	Sodertalje	Swe.	26	12	14	26	26	2	0	0	0	2
1991-92	Sodertalje	Swe.	22	3	6	9	14	....	....	....	....	....
1992-93	Sodertalje	Swe. 2	27	16	18	34	66	....	....	....	....	....
1993-94	Huddinge	Swe. 2	34	5	13	18	36	....	....	....	....	....

ERREY, BOB — (AIRY) S.J.

Left wing. Shoots left. 5'10", 185 lbs. Born, Montreal, Que., September 21, 1964.
(Pittsburgh's 1st choice, 15th overall, in 1983 Entry Draft).

			Regular Season					Playoffs				
Season	Club	Lea	GP	G	A	TP	PIM	GP	G	A	TP	PIM
1981-82	Peterborough	OHL	68	29	31	60	39	9	3	1	4	9
1982-83a	Peterborough	OHL	67	53	47	100	74	4	1	3	4	7
1983-84	**Pittsburgh**	**NHL**	**65**	**9**	**13**	**22**	**29**	....	....	....	....	....
1984-85	**Pittsburgh**	**NHL**	**16**	**0**	**2**	**2**	**7**	....	....	....	....	....
	Baltimore	AHL	59	17	24	41	14	8	3	4	7	11
1985-86	**Pittsburgh**	**NHL**	**37**	**11**	**6**	**17**	**8**	....	....	....	....	....
	Baltimore	AHL	18	8	7	15	28	....	....	....	....	....
1986-87	**Pittsburgh**	**NHL**	**72**	**16**	**18**	**34**	**46**	....	....	....	....	....
1987-88	**Pittsburgh**	**NHL**	**17**	**3**	**6**	**9**	**18**	....	....	....	....	....
1988-89	**Pittsburgh**	**NHL**	**76**	**26**	**32**	**58**	**124**	**11**	**1**	**2**	**3**	**12**
1989-90	**Pittsburgh**	**NHL**	**78**	**20**	**19**	**39**	**109**	....	....	....	....	....
1990-91	**Pittsburgh**	**NHL**	**79**	**20**	**22**	**42**	**115**	**24**	**5**	**2**	**7**	**29**
1991-92	**Pittsburgh**	**NHL**	**78**	**19**	**16**	**35**	**119**	**14**	**3**	**0**	**3**	**10**
1992-93	**Pittsburgh**	**NHL**	**54**	**8**	**6**	**14**	**76**	....	....	....	....	....
	Buffalo	**NHL**	**8**	**1**	**3**	**4**	**4**	**4**	**0**	**1**	**1**	**10**
1993-94	**San Jose**	**NHL**	**64**	**12**	**18**	**30**	**126**	**14**	**3**	**2**	**5**	**10**
	NHL Totals		**644**	**145**	**161**	**306**	**781**	**67**	**12**	**7**	**19**	**71**

a OHL First All-Star Team (1983)

Traded to **Buffalo** by **Pittsburgh** for Mike Ramsey, March 22, 1993. Signed as a free agent by **San Jose**, August 17, 1993.

ESAU, LEONARD — CGY.

Defense. Shoots right. 6'3", 190 lbs. Born, Meadow Lake, Sask., June 3, 1968.
(Toronto's 5th choice, 86th overall, in 1988 Entry Draft).

			Regular Season					Playoffs				
Season	Club	Lea	GP	G	A	TP	PIM	GP	G	A	TP	PIM
1988-89	St. Cloud	NCAA	35	12	27	39	69	....	....	....	....	....
1989-90	St. Cloud	NCAA	29	8	11	19	83	....	....	....	....	....
1990-91	Newmarket	AHL	76	4	14	18	28	....	....	....	....	....
1991-92	**Toronto**	**NHL**	**2**	**0**	**0**	**0**	**0**	....	....	....	....	....
	St. John's	AHL	78	9	29	38	68	13	0	2	2	14
1992-93	**Quebec**	**NHL**	**4**	**0**	**1**	**1**	**2**	....	....	....	....	....
	Halifax	AHL	75	11	31	42	79	....	....	....	....	....
1993-94	**Calgary**	**NHL**	**6**	**0**	**3**	**3**	**7**	....	....	....	....	....
	Saint John	AHL	75	12	36	48	129	7	2	2	4	6
	NHL Totals		**12**	**0**	**4**	**4**	**9**	....	....	....	....	....

Traded to **Quebec** by **Toronto** for Ken McRae, July 21, 1992. Signed as a free agent by **Calgary**, September 6, 1993.

ESBJORS, JOACIM — HFD.

Defense. Shoots left. 6'1", 194 lbs. Born, Goteborg, Sweden, July 4, 1970.
(Hartford's 11th choice, 249th overall, in 1992 Entry Draft).

			Regular Season					Playoffs				
Season	Club	Lea	GP	G	A	TP	PIM	GP	G	A	TP	PIM
1989-90	V. Frolunda	Swe.	24	0	4	4	23	....	....	....	....	....
1990-91	V. Frolunda	Swe.	22	1	5	6	16	....	....	....	....	....
1991-92	V. Frolunda	Swe.	40	9	9	18	22	3	1	0	1	2
1992-93	V. Frolunda	Swe.	20	1	6	7	26	....	....	....	....	....
1993-94	V. Frolunda	Swe.	38	4	7	11	44	4	0	0	0	2

ETHIER, MARTIN — NYR

Defense. Shoots right. 6'1", 178 lbs. Born, Ste-Eustache, Que., September 3, 1976.
(NY Rangers' 6th choice, 130th overall, in 1994 Entry Draft).

			Regular Season					Playoffs				
Season	Club	Lea	GP	G	A	TP	PIM	GP	G	A	TP	PIM
1992-93	Laval	Midget	42	3	22	25	44	....	....	....	....	....
1993-94	Beauport	QMJHL	61	4	19	23	53	15	0	3	3	32

EVANS, DOUG

Left wing. Shoots left. 5'9", 185 lbs. Born, Peterborough, Ont., June 2, 1963.

			Regular Season					Playoffs				
Season	Club	Lea	GP	G	A	TP	PIM	GP	G	A	TP	PIM
1981-82	Peterborough	OHL	56	17	49	66	176	9	0	2	2	41
1982-83	Peterborough	OHL	65	31	55	86	165	4	0	3	3	23
1983-84	Peterborough	OHL	61	45	79	124	98	8	4	12	16	26
1984-85	Peoria	IHL	81	36	61	97	189	20	18	14	32	*88
1985-86	**St. Louis**	**NHL**	**13**	**1**	**0**	**1**	**2**	....	....	....	....	....
a	Peoria	IHL	60	46	51	97	179	10	4	6	10	32
1986-87	**St. Louis**	**NHL**	**53**	**3**	**13**	**16**	**91**	**5**	**0**	**0**	**0**	**10**
	Peoria	IHL	18	10	15	25	39	....	....	....	....	....
1987-88	**St. Louis**	**NHL**	**41**	**5**	**7**	**12**	**49**	**2**	**0**	**0**	**0**	**0**
	Peoria	IHL	11	4	16	20	64	....	....	....	....	....
1988-89	**St. Louis**	**NHL**	**53**	**7**	**12**	**19**	**81**	**7**	**1**	**2**	**3**	**16**
1989-90	**St. Louis**	**NHL**	**3**	**0**	**0**	**0**	**0**	....	....	....	....	....
	Peoria	IHL	42	19	28	47	128	....	....	....	....	....
	Winnipeg	**NHL**	**27**	**10**	**8**	**18**	**33**	**7**	**2**	**2**	**4**	**10**
1990-91	**Winnipeg**	**NHL**	**70**	**7**	**27**	**34**	**108**	....	....	....	....	....
1991-92	**Winnipeg**	**NHL**	**30**	**7**	**7**	**14**	**68**	**1**	**0**	**0**	**0**	**2**
	Moncton	AHL	10	7	8	15	10	....	....	....	....	....
	Peoria	IHL	16	5	14	19	38	....	....	....	....	....
1992-93	**Philadelphia**	**NHL**	**65**	**8**	**13**	**21**	**70**	....	....	....	....	....
1993-94	Peoria	IHL	76	27	63	90	108	6	2	6	8	10
	NHL Totals		**355**	**48**	**87**	**135**	**502**	**22**	**3**	**4**	**7**	**38**

a IHL First All-Star Team (1986)

Signed as a free agent by **St. Louis**, June 10, 1985. Traded to **Winnipeg** by **St. Louis** for Ron Wilson, January 22, 1990. Traded to **Boston** by **Winnipeg** for Daniel Berthiaume, June 10, 1992. Claimed by **Philadelphia** from **Boston** in NHL Waiver Draft, October 4, 1992.

EVANS, KEVIN

Left wing. Shoots left. 5'9", 185 lbs. Born, Peterborough, Ont., July 10, 1965.

			Regular Season					Playoffs				
Season	Club	Lea	GP	G	A	TP	PIM	GP	G	A	TP	PIM
1984-85	London	OHL	52	3	7	10	148	....	....	....	....	....
1985-86	Victoria	WHL	66	16	39	55	441	....	....	....	....	....
	Kalamazoo	IHL	11	3	5	8	97	6	3	0	3	56
1986-87	Kalamazoo	IHL	73	19	31	50	*648	3	1	0	1	24
1987-88	Kalamazoo	IHL	54	9	28	37	404	5	1	1	2	46
1988-89	Kalamazoo	IHL	50	22	34	56	326	....	....	....	....	....
1989-90	Kalamazoo	IHL	76	30	54	84	346	10	8	4	12	86
1990-91	**Minnesota**	**NHL**	**4**	**0**	**0**	**0**	**19**	....	....	....	....	....
	Kalamazoo	IHL	16	10	12	22	70	....	....	....	....	....
1991-92	**San Jose**	**NHL**	**5**	**0**	**1**	**1**	**25**	....	....	....	....	....
	Kansas City	IHL	66	10	39	49	342	14	2	*13	15	70
1992-93	Kalamazoo	IHL	49	7	24	31	283	....	....	....	....	....
1993-94	Peoria	IHL	67	10	29	39	254	4	0	0	0	6
	NHL Totals		**9**	**0**	**1**	**1**	**44**	....	....	....	....	....

Signed as a free agent by **Minnesota**, August 8, 1988. Claimed by **San Jose** from **Minnesota** in Dispersal Draft, May 30, 1991. Signed as a free agent by **Minnesota**, July 20, 1992.

EVASON, DEAN (EH-vih-suhn) DAL.

Center. Shoots right. 5'10", 180 lbs. Born, Flin Flon, Man., August 22, 1964.
(Washington's 3rd choice, 89th overall, in 1982 Entry Draft).

			Regular Season					Playoffs				
Season	Club	Lea	GP	G	A	TP	PIM	GP	G	A	TP	PIM
1980-81	Spokane	WHL	3	1	1	2	0	....	....	....	....	....
1981-82	Spokane	WHL	26	8	14	22	65	....	....	....	....	....
	Kamloops	WHL	44	21	55	76	47	4	2	1	3	0
1982-83	Kamloops	WHL	70	71	93	164	102	7	5	7	12	18
1983-84	**Washington**	**NHL**	**2**	**0**	**0**	**0**	**2**	....	....	....	....	....
a	Kamloops	WHL	57	49	88	137	89	17	*21	20	41	33
1984-85	**Washington**	**NHL**	**15**	**3**	**4**	**7**	**2**	....	....	....	....	....
	Hartford	**NHL**	**2**	**0**	**0**	**0**	**0**	....	....	....	....	....
	Binghamton	AHL	65	27	49	76	38	8	3	5	8	9
1985-86	**Hartford**	**NHL**	**55**	**20**	**28**	**48**	**65**	**10**	**1**	**4**	**5**	**10**
	Binghamton	AHL	26	9	17	26	29	....	....	....	....	....
1986-87	**Hartford**	**NHL**	**80**	**22**	**37**	**59**	**67**	**5**	**3**	**2**	**5**	**35**
1987-88	**Hartford**	**NHL**	**77**	**10**	**18**	**28**	**115**	**6**	**1**	**1**	**2**	**2**
1988-89	**Hartford**	**NHL**	**67**	**11**	**17**	**28**	**60**	**4**	**1**	**2**	**3**	**10**
1989-90	**Hartford**	**NHL**	**78**	**18**	**25**	**43**	**138**	**7**	**2**	**2**	**4**	**22**
1990-91	**Hartford**	**NHL**	**75**	**6**	**23**	**29**	**170**	**6**	**0**	**4**	**4**	**29**
1991-92	**San Jose**	**NHL**	**74**	**11**	**15**	**26**	**99**	....	....	....	....	....
1992-93	**San Jose**	**NHL**	**84**	**12**	**19**	**31**	**132**	....	....	....	....	....
1993-94	**Dallas**	**NHL**	**80**	**11**	**33**	**44**	**66**	**9**	**0**	**2**	**2**	**12**
	NHL Totals		**689**	**124**	**219**	**343**	**916**	**47**	**8**	**17**	**25**	**120**

a WHL First All-Star Team, West Division (1984)

Traded to **Hartford** by **Washington** with Peter Sidorkiewicz for David Jensen, March 12, 1985. Traded to **San Jose** by **Hartford** for Dan Keczmer, October 2, 1991. Traded to **Dallas** by **San Jose** for San Jose's sixth round choice (previously acquired by Dallas — San Jose selected Petri Varis) in 1993 Entry Draft, June 26, 1993.

EWEN, DEAN (YOO-ihn) ANA.

Left wing. Shoots left. 6'2", 225 lbs. Born, St. Albert, Alta., February 28, 1969.
(NY Islanders' 3rd choice, 55th overall, in 1987 Entry Draft).

			Regular Season					Playoffs				
Season	Club	Lea	GP	G	A	TP	PIM	GP	G	A	TP	PIM
1988-89	Spokane	WHL	5	0	0	0	5	....	....	....	....	....
	Seattle	WHL	56	22	30	52	254	....	....	....	....	....
1989-90	Springfield	AHL	34	0	7	7	....	....	....	....	....	....
1990-91	Capital Dist.	AHL	DID NOT PLAY									
1991-92	Capital Dist.	AHL	41	5	8	13	106	....	....	....	....	....
1992-93			DID NOT PLAY – INJURED									
1993-94	San Diego	IHL	19	0	3	3	45	3	1	0	1	8

Signed as a free agent by **Anaheim**, January 25, 1994.

EWEN, TODD (YOO-ihn) ANA.

Right wing. Shoots right. 6'2", 220 lbs. Born, Saskatoon, Sask., March 22, 1966.
(Edmonton's 9th choice, 168th overall, in 1984 Entry Draft).

			Regular Season					Playoffs				
Season	Club	Lea	GP	G	A	TP	PIM	GP	G	A	TP	PIM
1982-83	Kamloops	WHL	3	0	0	0	2	2	0	0	0	0
1983-84	N. Westminster	WHL	68	11	13	24	176	7	2	1	3	15
1984-85	N. Westminster	WHL	56	11	20	31	304	10	1	8	9	60
1985-86	N. Westminster	WHL	60	28	24	52	289	....	....	....	....	....
	Maine	AHL	....	....	....	....	....	3	0	0	0	7
1986-87	**St. Louis**	**NHL**	**23**	**2**	**0**	**2**	**84**	**4**	**0**	**0**	**0**	**23**
	Peoria	IHL	16	3	3	6	110	....	....	....	....	....
1987-88	**St. Louis**	**NHL**	**64**	**4**	**2**	**6**	**227**	**6**	**0**	**0**	**0**	**21**
1988-89	**St. Louis**	**NHL**	**34**	**4**	**5**	**9**	**171**	**2**	**0**	**0**	**0**	**21**
1989-90	**St. Louis**	**NHL**	**3**	**0**	**0**	**0**	**11**	....	....	....	....	....
	Peoria	IHL	2	0	0	0	12	....	....	....	....	....
	Montreal	**NHL**	**41**	**4**	**6**	**10**	**158**	**10**	**0**	**0**	**0**	**4**
1990-91	**Montreal**	**NHL**	**28**	**3**	**2**	**5**	**128**	....	....	....	....	....
1991-92	**Montreal**	**NHL**	**46**	**1**	**2**	**3**	**130**	**3**	**0**	**0**	**0**	**18**
1992-93	**Montreal**	**NHL**	**75**	**5**	**9**	**14**	**193**	**1**	**0**	**0**	**0**	**0**
1993-94	**Anaheim**	**NHL**	**76**	**9**	**9**	**18**	**272**	....	....	....	....	....
	NHL Totals		**390**	**32**	**35**	**67**	**1374**	**26**	**0**	**0**	**0**	**87**

Traded to **St. Louis** by **Edmonton** for Shawn Evans, October 15, 1986. Traded to **Montreal** by **St. Louis** for future considerations, December 12, 1989. Traded to **Anaheim** by **Montreal** with Patrik Carnback for Anaheim's third round choice (Chris Murray) in 1994 Entry Draft, August 10, 1993.

FAIR, QUINN L.A.

Defense. Shoots right. 6'1", 210 lbs. Born, Campbell River, B.C., May 23, 1973.
(Los Angeles' 1st choice, 74th overall, in 1994 Supplemental Draft).

			Regular Season					Playoffs				
Season	Club	Lea	GP	G	A	TP	PIM	GP	G	A	TP	PIM
1992-93	Kent State	CCHA	37	6	6	12	77	....	....	....	....	....
1993-94	Kent State	CCHA	39	11	13	24	92	....	....	....	....	....

FAIRCHILD, KELLY L.A.

Center. Shoots left. 5'11", 180 lbs. Born, Hibbing, MN, April 9, 1973.
(Los Angeles' 7th choice, 152nd overall, in 1991 Entry Draft).

			Regular Season					Playoffs				
Season	Club	Lea	GP	G	A	TP	PIM	GP	G	A	TP	PIM
1991-92	U. Wisconsin	WCHA	37	11	10	21	45	....	....	....	....	....
1992-93	U. Wisconsin	WCHA	42	25	29	54	54	....	....	....	....	....
1993-94a	U. Wisconsin	WCHA	42	20	44	*64	81	....	....	....	....	....

a WCHA First All-Star Team (1994)

FALLOON, PAT (fah-LOON) S.J.

Right wing. Shoots right. 5'11", 198 lbs. Born, Foxwarren, Man., September 22, 1972.
(San Jose's 1st choice, 2nd overall, in 1991 Entry Draft).

			Regular Season					Playoffs				
Season	Club	Lea	GP	G	A	TP	PIM	GP	G	A	TP	PIM
1988-89	Spokane	WHL	72	22	56	78	41	....	....	....	....	....
1989-90	Spokane	WHL	71	60	64	124	48	6	5	8	13	[illegible]
1990-91abcd	Spokane	WHL	61	64	74	138	33	15	10	14	24	[illegible]
1991-92	**San Jose**	**NHL**	**79**	**25**	**34**	**59**	**16**	....	....	....	....	....
1992-93	**San Jose**	**NHL**	**41**	**14**	**14**	**28**	**12**	....	....	....	....	....
1993-94	**San Jose**	**NHL**	**83**	**22**	**31**	**53**	**18**	**14**	**1**	**2**	**3**	[illegible]
	NHL Totals		**203**	**61**	**79**	**140**	**46**	**14**	**1**	**2**	**3**	[illegible]

a WHL West First All-Star Team (1991)
b Canadian Major Junior Most Sportsmanlike Player of the Year (1991)
c Memorial Cup All-Star Team (1991)
d Won Stafford Smythe Memorial Trophy (Memorial Cup MVP) (1991)

FARRELL, BRIAN PIT

Center. Shoots left. 5'11", 190 lbs. Born, West Hartford, CT, April 16, 1972.
(Pittsburgh's 4th choice, 89th overall, in 1990 Entry Draft).

			Regular Season					Playoffs				
Season	Club	Lea	GP	G	A	TP	PIM	GP	G	A	TP	PIM
1990-91	Harvard	ECAC	28	3	8	11	16	....	....	....	....	....
1991-92	Harvard	ECAC	9	5	3	8	6	....	....	....	....	....
1992-93	Harvard	ECAC	31	10	23	33	33	....	....	....	....	....
1993-94a	Harvard	ECAC	33	*29	14	43	47	....	....	....	....	....

a ECAC First All-Star Team (1994)

FAUST, ANDRE PHI

Center. Shoots left. 5'11", 191 lbs. Born, Joliette, Que., October 7, 1969.
(New Jersey's 8th choice, 173rd overall, in 1989 Entry Draft).

			Regular Season					Playoffs				
Season	Club	Lea	GP	G	A	TP	PIM	GP	G	A	TP	PIM
1988-89	Princeton	ECAC	27	15	24	39	28	....	....	....	....	....
1989-90a	Princeton	ECAC	22	9	28	37	20	....	....	....	....	....
1990-91	Princeton	ECAC	26	15	22	37	51	....	....	....	....	....
1991-92a	Princeton	ECAC	27	14	21	35	38	....	....	....	....	....
1992-93	**Philadelphia**	**NHL**	**10**	**2**	**2**	**4**	**4**	....	....	....	....	....
	Hershey	AHL	62	26	25	51	71	....	....	....	....	....
1993-94	**Philadelphia**	**NHL**	**37**	**8**	**5**	**13**	**10**	....	....	....	....	....
	Hershey	AHL	13	6	7	13	10	10	4	3	7	26
	NHL Totals		**47**	**10**	**7**	**17**	**14**	....	....	....	....	....

a ECAC Second All-Star Team (1990, 1992)

Signed as a free agent by **Philadelphia**, October 5, 1992.

FEARNS, KENT HFD.

Defense. Shoots left. 6', 180 lbs. Born, Langley, B.C., September 13, 1972.
(Hartford's 1st choice, 6th overall, in 1993 Supplemental Draft).

			Regular Season					Playoffs				
Season	Club	Lea	GP	G	A	TP	PIM	GP	G	A	TP	PIM
1991-92	Colorado	WCHA	41	10	27	37	48	....	....	....	....	....
1992-93	Colorado	WCHA	33	7	15	22	76	....	....	....	....	....
1993-94a	Colorado	WCHA	39	11	19	30	62	....	....	....	....	....

a WCHA Second All-Star Team (1994)

FEATHERSTONE, GLEN NYR

Defense. Shoots left. 6'4", 215 lbs. Born, Toronto, Ont., July 8, 1968.
(St. Louis' 4th choice, 73rd overall, in 1986 Entry Draft).

			Regular Season					Playoffs				
Season	Club	Lea	GP	G	A	TP	PIM	GP	G	A	TP	PIM
1985-86	Windsor	OHL	49	0	6	6	135	14	1	1	2	23
1986-87	Windsor	OHL	47	6	11	17	154	14	2	6	8	19
1987-88	Windsor	OHL	53	7	27	34	201	12	6	9	15	47
1988-89	**St. Louis**	**NHL**	**18**	**0**	**2**	**2**	**22**	**6**	**0**	**0**	**0**	**0**
	Peoria	IHL	37	5	19	24	97	....	....	....	....	....
1989-90	**St. Louis**	**NHL**	**58**	**0**	**12**	**12**	**145**	**12**	**0**	**2**	**2**	**47**
	Peoria	IHL	15	1	4	5	43	....	....	....	....	....
1990-91	**St. Louis**	**NHL**	**68**	**5**	**15**	**20**	**204**	**9**	**0**	**0**	**0**	**31**
1991-92	**Boston**	**NHL**	**7**	**1**	**0**	**1**	**20**	....	....	....	....	....
1992-93	**Boston**	**NHL**	**34**	**5**	**5**	**10**	**102**	....	....	....	....	....
	Providence	AHL	8	3	4	7	60	....	....	....	....	....
1993-94	**Boston**	**NHL**	**58**	**1**	**8**	**9**	**152**	**1**	**0**	**0**	**0**	**0**
	NHL Totals		**243**	**12**	**42**	**54**	**645**	**28**	**0**	**2**	**2**	**78**

Signed as a free agent by **Boston**, July 25, 1991. Traded to **NY Rangers**, by **Boston** for Daniel Lacroix, August 19, 1994.

FEDOROV, SERGEI (FEH-duh-rahf) DET.

Center. Shoots left. 6'1", 200 lbs. Born, Pskov, USSR, December 13, 1969.
(Detroit's 4th choice, 74th overall, in 1989 Entry Draft).

			Regular Season					Playoffs				
Season	Club	Lea	GP	G	A	TP	PIM	GP	G	A	TP	PIM
1986-87	CSKA	USSR	29	6	6	12	12	....	....	....	....	....
1987-88	CSKA	USSR	48	7	9	16	20	....	....	....	....	....
1988-89	CSKA	USSR	44	9	8	17	35	....	....	....	....	....
1989-90	CSKA	USSR	48	19	10	29	22	....	....	....	....	....
1990-91a	**Detroit**	**NHL**	**77**	**31**	**48**	**79**	**66**	**7**	**1**	**5**	**6**	**4**
1991-92	**Detroit**	**NHL**	**80**	**32**	**54**	**86**	**72**	**11**	**5**	**5**	**10**	**8**
1992-93	**Detroit**	**NHL**	**73**	**34**	**53**	**87**	**72**	**7**	**3**	**6**	**9**	**23**
1993-94bcde	**Detroit**	**NHL**	**82**	**56**	**64**	**120**	**34**	**7**	**1**	**7**	**8**	**6**
	NHL Totals		**312**	**153**	**219**	**372**	**244**	**32**	**10**	**23**	**33**	**41**

a NHL/Upper Deck All-Rookie Team (1991)
b NHL First All-Star Team (1994)
c Won Frank J. Selke Trophy (1994)
d Won Lester B. Pearson Award (1994)
e Won Hart Trophy (1994)

Played in NHL All-Star Game (1992, 1994)

EDOTOV, ANATOLI (FEH-duh-tahf, AN-uh-TOH-lee) ANA.

efense. Shoots left. 5'11", 178 lbs. Born, Saratov, USSR, May 11, 1966.
Anaheim's 10th choice, 238th overall, in 1993 Entry Draft).

			Regular Season					Playoffs				
eason	Club	Lea	GP	G	A	TP	PIM	GP	G	A	TP	PIM
985-86	Moscow D'amo	USSR	35	0	2	2	10	....	....	....	....	....
986-87	Moscow D'amo	USSR	18	3	2	5	12	....	....	....	....	....
987-88	Moscow D'amo	USSR	48	2	3	5	38	....	....	....	....	....
988-89	Moscow D'amo	USSR	40	2	1	3	24	....	....	....	....	....
989-90	Moscow D'amo	USSR	41	2	4	6	22	....	....	....	....	....
990-91					DID NOT PLAY							
991-92	Moscow D'amo	CIS	11	1	0	1	8	....	....	....	....	....
992-93	**Winnipeg**	**NHL**	**1**	**0**	**2**	**2**	**0**	....	....	....	....	....
	Moncton	AHL	76	10	37	47	99	2	0	0	0	0
993-94	**Anaheim**	**NHL**	**3**	**0**	**0**	**0**	**0**	....	....	....	....	....
	San Diego	IHL	66	14	12	26	42	8	0	1	1	6
	NHL Totals		**4**	**0**	**2**	**2**	**0**	....	....	....	....	....

EDYK, BRENT (FEH-dihk) PHI.

eft wing. Shoots right. 6', 195 lbs. Born, Yorkton, Sask., March 8, 1967.
Detroit's 1st choice, 8th overall, in 1985 Entry Draft).

			Regular Season					Playoffs				
eason	Club	Lea	GP	G	A	TP	PIM	GP	G	A	TP	PIM
983-84	Regina	WHL	63	15	28	43	30	23	8	7	15	6
984-85	Regina	WHL	66	35	35	70	48	8	5	4	9	0
985-86	Regina	WHL	50	43	34	77	47	5	0	1	1	0
986-87	Regina	WHL	12	9	6	15	9	....	....	....	....	....
	Seattle	WHL	13	5	11	16	9	....	....	....	....	....
	Portland	WHL	11	5	4	9	6	14	5	6	11	0
987-88	**Detroit**	**NHL**	**2**	**0**	**1**	**1**	**2**	....	....	....	....	....
	Adirondack	AHL	34	9	11	20	22	5	0	2	2	6
988-89	**Detroit**	**NHL**	**5**	**2**	**0**	**2**	**0**	....	....	....	....	....
	Adirondack	AHL	66	40	28	68	33	15	7	8	15	23
989-90	**Detroit**	**NHL**	**27**	**1**	**4**	**5**	**6**	....	....	....	....	....
	Adirondack	AHL	33	14	15	29	24	6	2	1	3	4
990-91	**Detroit**	**NHL**	**67**	**16**	**19**	**35**	**38**	**6**	**1**	**0**	**1**	**2**
991-92	**Detroit**	**NHL**	**61**	**5**	**8**	**13**	**42**	**1**	**0**	**0**	**0**	**2**
	Adirondack	AHL	1	0	2	2	0	....	....	....	....	....
992-93	**Philadelphia**	**NHL**	**74**	**21**	**38**	**59**	**48**	....	....	....	....	....
993-94	**Philadelphia**	**NHL**	**72**	**20**	**18**	**38**	**74**	....	....	....	....	....
	NHL Totals		**308**	**65**	**88**	**153**	**210**	**7**	**1**	**0**	**1**	**4**

raded to **Philadelphia** by **Detroit** for Philadelphia's fourth round choice (later traded to Boston — oston selected Charles Paquette) in 1993 Entry Draft, October 1, 1992.

ELSNER, DENNY ST.L.

eft wing. Shoots left. 6', 195 lbs. Born, Warren, MI, April 29, 1970.
St. Louis' 3rd choice, 55th overall, in 1989 Entry Draft).

			Regular Season					Playoffs				
eason	Club	Lea	GP	G	A	TP	PIM	GP	G	A	TP	PIM
988-89	U. of Michigan	CCHA	39	30	19	49	22	....	....	....	....	....
989-90	U. of Michigan	CCHA	33	27	16	43	24	....	....	....	....	....
990-91ab	U. of Michigan	CCHA	46	*40	35	75	58	....	....	....	....	....
991-92ac	U. of Michigan	CCHA	44	42	52	94	46	....	....	....	....	....
	St. Louis	**NHL**	**3**	**0**	**1**	**1**	**0**	**1**	**0**	**0**	**0**	**0**
992-93	**St. Louis**	**NHL**	**6**	**0**	**3**	**3**	**2**	**9**	**2**	**3**	**5**	**2**
	Peoria	IHL	29	14	21	35	8	....	....	....	....	....
993-94	**St. Louis**	**NHL**	**6**	**1**	**0**	**1**	**2**	....	....	....	....	....
	Peoria	IHL	6	8	3	11	14	....	....	....	....	....
	NHL Totals		**15**	**1**	**4**	**5**	**4**	**10**	**2**	**3**	**5**	**2**

CCHA First All-Star Team (1991, 1992)
NCAA West Second All-American Team (1991)
NCAA West First All-American Team (1992)

ERGUSON, CRAIG MTL.

Right wing. Shoots left. 6', 185 lbs. Born, Castro Valley, CA, April 8, 1970.
Montreal's 7th choice, 146th overall, in 1989 Entry Draft).

			Regular Season					Playoffs				
eason	Club	Lea	GP	G	A	TP	PIM	GP	G	A	TP	PIM
988-89	Yale	ECAC	24	11	6	17	20	....	....	....	....	....
989-90	Yale	ECAC	28	6	13	19	36	....	....	....	....	....
990-91	Yale	ECAC	29	11	10	21	34	....	....	....	....	....
991-92	Yale	ECAC	27	9	16	25	26	....	....	....	....	....
992-93	Fredericton	AHL	55	15	13	28	20	5	0	1	1	2
	Wheeling	ECHL	9	6	5	11	24	....	....	....	....	....
993-94	**Montreal**	**NHL**	**2**	**0**	**1**	**1**	**0**	....	....	....	....	....
	Fredericton	AHL	57	29	32	61	60	....	....	....	....	....
	NHL Totals		**2**	**0**	**1**	**1**	**0**	....	....	....	....	....

FERGUSON, KYLE TOR.

Right wing. Shoots right. 6'3", 215 lbs. Born, Toronto, Ont., August 12, 1973.
Toronto's 7th choice, 253rd overall, in 1993 Entry Draft).

			Regular Season					Playoffs				
Season	Club	Lea	GP	G	A	TP	PIM	GP	G	A	TP	PIM
1992-93	Michigan Tech	WCHA	31	9	5	14	74	....	....	....	....	....
1993-94	Michigan Tech	WCHA	36	4	5	9	63	....	....	....	....	....

FERGUSON, SCOTT EDM.

Defense. Shoots left. 6'1", 195 lbs. Born, Camrose, Alta., January 6, 1973.

			Regular Season					Playoffs				
Season	Club	Lea	GP	G	A	TP	PIM	GP	G	A	TP	PIM
1990-91	Kamloops	WHL	4	0	0	0	0	....	....	....	....	....
1991-92	Kamloops	WHL	62	4	10	14	138	12	0	2	2	21
1992-93	Kamloops	WHL	71	4	19	23	206	13	0	2	2	24
1993-94a	Kamloops	WHL	68	5	49	54	180	19	5	11	16	48

a WHL West Second All-Star Team (1994)

Signed as a free agent by **Edmonton**, June 2, 1994.

FERNER, MARK ANA.

Defense. Shoots left. 6', 193 lbs. Born, Regina, Sask., September 5, 1965.
(Buffalo's 12th choice, 194th overall, in 1983 Entry Draft).

			Regular Season					Playoffs				
Season	Club	Lea	GP	G	A	TP	PIM	GP	G	A	TP	PIM
1982-83	Kamloops	WHL	69	6	15	21	81	7	0	0	0	7
1983-84	Kamloops	WHL	72	9	30	39	169	14	1	8	9	20
1984-85a	Kamloops	WHL	69	15	39	54	91	15	4	9	13	21
1985-86	Rochester	AHL	63	3	14	17	87	....	....	....	....	....
1986-87	**Buffalo**	**NHL**	**13**	**0**	**3**	**3**	**9**	....	....	....	....	....
	Rochester	AHL	54	0	12	12	157	....	....	....	....	....
1987-88	Rochester	AHL	69	1	25	26	165	7	1	4	5	31
1988-89	**Buffalo**	**NHL**	**2**	**0**	**0**	**0**	**2**	....	....	....	....	....
	Rochester	AHL	55	0	18	18	97	....	....	....	....	....
1989-90	**Washington**	**NHL**	**2**	**0**	**0**	**0**	**0**	....	....	....	....	....
	Baltimore	AHL	74	7	28	35	76	11	1	2	3	21
1990-91	**Washington**	**NHL**	**7**	**0**	**1**	**1**	**4**	....	....	....	....	....
b	Baltimore	AHL	61	14	40	54	38	6	1	4	5	24
1991-92	Baltimore	AHL	57	7	38	45	67	....	....	....	....	....
	St. John's	AHL	15	1	8	9	6	14	2	14	16	38
1992-93	New Haven	AHL	34	5	7	12	69	....	....	....	....	....
	San Diego	IHL	26	0	15	15	34	11	1	2	3	8
1993-94	**Anaheim**	**NHL**	**50**	**3**	**5**	**8**	**30**	....	....	....	....	....
	NHL Totals		**74**	**3**	**9**	**12**	**45**	....	....	....	....	....

a WHL West First All-Star Team (1985)
b AHL Second All-Star Team (1991)

Traded to **Washington** by **Buffalo** for Scott McCrory, June 1, 1989. Traded to **Toronto** by **Washington** for future considerations, February 27, 1992. Signed as a free agent by **Ottawa**, August 6, 1992. Claimed by **Anaheim** from **Ottawa** in Expansion Draft, June 24, 1993.

FERRARO, CHRIS NYR

Right wing. Shoots right. 5'10", 175 lbs. Born, Port Jefferson, NY, January 24, 1973.
(NY Rangers' 4th choice, 85th overall, in 1992 Entry Draft).

			Regular Season					Playoffs				
Season	Club	Lea	GP	G	A	TP	PIM	GP	G	A	TP	PIM
1992-93	U. of Maine	H.E.	39	25	26	51	46	....	....	....	....	....
1993-94	U. of Maine	H.E.	4	0	1	1	8	....	....	....	....	....
	U.S. National	....	48	8	34	42	58	....	....	....	....	....

FERRARO, PETER NYR

Center. Shoots right. 5'10", 175 lbs. Born, Port Jefferson, NY, January 24, 1973.
(NY Rangers' 1st choice, 24th overall, in 1992 Entry Draft).

			Regular Season					Playoffs				
Season	Club	Lea	GP	G	A	TP	PIM	GP	G	A	TP	PIM
1992-93	U. of Maine	H.E.	36	18	32	50	106	....	....	....	....	....
1993-94	U. of Maine	H.E.	4	3	6	9	16	....	....	....	....	....
	U.S. National	....	60	30	34	64	87	....	....	....	....	....
	U.S. Olympic	....	8	6	0	6	6	....	....	....	....	....

FERRARO, RAY NYI

Center. Shoots left. 5'10", 185 lbs. Born, Trail, B.C., August 23, 1964.
(Hartford's 5th choice, 88th overall, in 1982 Entry Draft).

			Regular Season					Playoffs				
Season	Club	Lea	GP	G	A	TP	PIM	GP	G	A	TP	PIM
1982-83	Portland	WHL	50	41	49	90	39	14	14	10	24	13
1983-84ab	Brandon	WHL	72	*108	84	*192	84	11	13	15	28	20
1984-85	**Hartford**	**NHL**	**44**	**11**	**17**	**28**	**40**	....	....	....	....	....
	Binghamton	AHL	37	20	13	33	29	....	....	....	....	....
1985-86	**Hartford**	**NHL**	**76**	**30**	**47**	**77**	**57**	**10**	**3**	**6**	**9**	**4**
1986-87	**Hartford**	**NHL**	**80**	**27**	**32**	**59**	**42**	**6**	**1**	**1**	**2**	**8**
1987-88	**Hartford**	**NHL**	**68**	**21**	**29**	**50**	**81**	**6**	**1**	**1**	**2**	**6**
1988-89	**Hartford**	**NHL**	**80**	**41**	**35**	**76**	**86**	**4**	**2**	**0**	**2**	**4**
1989-90	**Hartford**	**NHL**	**79**	**25**	**29**	**54**	**109**	**7**	**0**	**3**	**3**	**2**
1990-91	**Hartford**	**NHL**	**15**	**2**	**5**	**7**	**18**	....	....	....	....	....
	NY Islanders	**NHL**	**61**	**19**	**16**	**35**	**52**	....	....	....	....	....
1991-92	**NY Islanders**	**NHL**	**80**	**40**	**40**	**80**	**92**	....	....	....	....	....
1992-93	**NY Islanders**	**NHL**	**46**	**14**	**13**	**27**	**40**	**18**	**13**	**7**	**20**	**18**
	Capital Dist.	AHL	1	0	2	2	2	....	....	....	....	....
1993-94	**NY Islanders**	**NHL**	**82**	**21**	**32**	**53**	**83**	**4**	**1**	**0**	**1**	**6**
	NHL Totals		**711**	**251**	**295**	**546**	**700**	**55**	**21**	**18**	**39**	**48**

a WHL First All-Star Team (1984)
b WHL Most Valuable Player (1984)

Played in NHL All-Star Game (1992)

Traded to **NY Islanders** by **Hartford** for Doug Crossman, November 13, 1990.

FETISOV, VIACHESLAV (feh-TEE-sahf) N.J.

Defense. Shoots left. 6'1", 220 lbs. Born, Moscow, USSR, April 20, 1958.
(New Jersey's 6th choice, 150th overall, in 1983 Entry Draft).

			Regular Season					Playoffs				
Season	Club	Lea	GP	G	A	TP	PIM	GP	G	A	TP	PIM
1974-75	CSKA	USSR	1	0	0	0	0	....	....	....	....	....
1976-77	CSKA	USSR	28	3	4	7	14	....	....	....	....	....
1977-78a	CSKA	USSR	35	9	18	27	46	....	....	....	....	....
1978-79	CSKA	USSR	29	10	19	29	40	....	....	....	....	....
1979-80	CSKA	USSR	37	10	14	24	46	....	....	....	....	....
1980-81	CSKA	USSR	48	13	16	29	44	....	....	....	....	....
1981-82ac	CSKA	USSR	46	15	26	41	20	....	....	....	....	....
1982-83a	CSKA	USSR	43	6	17	23	46	....	....	....	....	....
1983-84ab	CSKA	USSR	44	19	30	49	38	....	....	....	....	....
1984-85a	CSKA	USSR	20	13	12	25	6	....	....	....	....	....
1985-86abc	CSKA	USSR	40	15	19	34	12	....	....	....	....	....
1986-87ab	CSKA	USSR	39	13	20	33	18	....	....	....	....	....
1987-88ab	CSKA	USSR	46	18	17	35	26	....	....	....	....	....
1988-89	CSKA	USSR	23	9	8	17	18	....	....	....	....	....
1989-90	**New Jersey**	**NHL**	**72**	**8**	**34**	**42**	**52**	**6**	**0**	**2**	**2**	**10**
1990-91	**New Jersey**	**NHL**	**67**	**3**	**16**	**19**	**62**	**7**	**0**	**0**	**0**	**17**
	Utica	AHL	1	1	1	2	0	....	....	....	....	....
1991-92	**New Jersey**	**NHL**	**70**	**3**	**23**	**26**	**108**	**6**	**0**	**3**	**3**	**8**
1992-93	**New Jersey**	**NHL**	**76**	**4**	**23**	**27**	**158**	**5**	**0**	**2**	**2**	**4**
1993-94	**New Jersey**	**NHL**	**52**	**1**	**14**	**15**	**30**	**14**	**1**	**0**	**1**	**8**
	NHL Totals		**337**	**19**	**110**	**129**	**410**	**38**	**1**	**7**	**8**	**47**

a Soviet National League All-Star Team (1979, 1980, 1982-88)
b Leningradskaya-Pravda Trophy-Top Scoring Defenseman (1984, 1986-88)
c Soviet Player of the Year (1982, 1986, 1988)

FIEBELKORN, JED — ST.L.

Right wing. Shoots right. 6'3", 220 lbs. Born, Minneapolis, MN, September 1, 1972.
(St. Louis' 9th choice, 197th overall, in 1991 Entry Draft).

			Regular Season					Playoffs				
Season	Club	Lea	GP	G	A	TP	PIM	GP	G	A	TP	PIM
1991-92	U. Minnesota	WCHA	7	0	0	0	10	....	....	....	....	....
1992-93	U. Minnesota	WCHA	34	8	5	13	42	....	....	....	....	....
1993-94	U. Minnesota	WCHA	39	5	6	11	65	....	....	....	....	....

FILATOV, ANATOLI (fih-LAH-tohv) — S.J.

Right wing. Shoots right. 5'10", 195 lbs. Born, Kamenogorsk, USSR, April 28, 1975.
(San Jose's 9th choice, 158th overall, in 1993 Entry Draft).

			Regular Season					Playoffs				
Season	Club	Lea	GP	G	A	TP	PIM	GP	G	A	TP	PIM
1992-93	Ust-Kamenogorsk	CIS	17	4	0	4	14	....	....	....	....	....
1993-94	Ust-Kamenogorsk	CIS	20	3	3	6	22	....	....	....	....	....

FILIMONOV, DMITRI (fih-lih-MAHN-ahf) — OTT.

Defense. Shoots right. 6'4", 220 lbs. Born, Perm, USSR, October 14, 1971.
(Winnipeg's 2nd choice, 49th overall, in 1991 Entry Draft).

			Regular Season					Playoffs				
Season	Club	Lea	GP	G	A	TP	PIM	GP	G	A	TP	PIM
1990-91	Moscow D'amo	USSR	45	4	6	10	12	....	....	....	....	....
1991-92	Moscow D'amo	CIS	38	3	2	5	12	....	....	....	....	....
1992-93	Moscow D'amo	CIS	42	2	3	5	30	10	1	2	3	2
1993-94	**Ottawa**	**NHL**	**30**	**1**	**4**	**5**	**18**	....	....	....	....	....
	PEI	AHL	48	10	16	26	14	....	....	....	....	....
	NHL Totals		**30**	**1**	**4**	**5**	**18**	....	....	....	....	....

Rights traded to **Ottawa** by **Winnipeg** for Ottawa's fourth round choice (Ruslam Batyrshin) in 1993 Entry Draft, March 14, 1993.

FILIPEK, DARYL — VAN.

Defense. Shoots left. 6'2", 200 lbs. Born, Acton, Ont., November 13, 1970.
(Vancouver's 6th choice, 128th overall, in 1990 Entry Draft).

			Regular Season					Playoffs				
Season	Club	Lea	GP	G	A	TP	PIM	GP	G	A	TP	PIM
1989-90	Ferris State	CCHA	38	4	20	24	44	....	....	....	....	....
1990-91	Ferris State	CCHA	39	6	11	17	68	....	....	....	....	....
1991-92	Ferris State	CCHA	30	4	6	10	28	....	....	....	....	....
1992-93	Ferris State	CCHA	41	12	12	24	62	....	....	....	....	....
1993-94	Hamilton	AHL	68	5	17	22	27	1	1	0	1	0

FINLEY, JEFF — PHI.

Defense. Shoots left. 6'2", 204 lbs. Born, Edmonton, Alta., April 14, 1967.
(NY Islanders' 4th choice, 55th overall, in 1985 Entry Draft).

			Regular Season					Playoffs				
Season	Club	Lea	GP	G	A	TP	PIM	GP	G	A	TP	PIM
1983-84	Portland	WHL	5	0	0	0	5	5	0	1	1	4
1984-85	Portland	WHL	69	6	44	50	57	6	1	2	3	2
1985-86	Portland	WHL	70	11	59	70	83	15	1	7	8	16
1986-87	Portland	WHL	72	13	53	66	113	20	1	*21	22	27
1987-88	**NY Islanders**	**NHL**	**10**	**0**	**5**	**5**	**15**	**1**	**0**	**0**	**0**	**2**
	Springfield	AHL	52	5	18	23	50	....	....	....	....	....
1988-89	**NY Islanders**	**NHL**	**4**	**0**	**0**	**0**	**6**	....	....	....	....	....
	Springfield	AHL	65	3	16	19	55	....	....	....	....	....
1989-90	**NY Islanders**	**NHL**	**11**	**0**	**1**	**1**	**0**	**5**	**0**	**2**	**2**	**2**
	Springfield	AHL	57	1	15	16	41	13	1	4	5	23
1990-91	**NY Islanders**	**NHL**	**11**	**0**	**0**	**0**	**4**	....	....	....	....	....
	Capital Dist.	AHL	67	10	34	44	34	....	....	....	....	....
1991-92	**NY Islanders**	**NHL**	**51**	**1**	**10**	**11**	**26**	....	....	....	....	....
	Capital Dist.	AHL	20	1	9	10	6	....	....	....	....	....
1992-93	Capital Dist.	AHL	61	6	29	35	34	4	0	1	1	0
1993-94	**Philadelphia**	**NHL**	**55**	**1**	**8**	**9**	**24**	....	....	....	....	....
	NHL Totals		**142**	**2**	**24**	**26**	**75**	**6**	**0**	**2**	**2**	**4**

Traded to **Ottawa** by **NY Islanders** for Chris Luongo, June 30, 1993. Signed as a free agent by **Philadelphia**, July 30, 1993.

FINN, SHANNON — PHI.

Defense. Shoots left. 6'2", 190 lbs. Born, Brampton, Ont., January 25, 1972.
(Philadelphia's 1st choice, 10th overall, in 1993 Supplemental Draft).

			Regular Season					Playoffs				
Season	Club	Lea	GP	G	A	TP	PIM	GP	G	A	TP	PIM
1991-92	Ill.-Chicago	CCHA	36	6	14	20	80	....	....	....	....	....
1992-93	Ill.-Chicago	CCHA	36	6	13	19	48	....	....	....	....	....
1993-94	Ill.-Chicago	CCHA	39	5	22	27	42	....	....	....	....	....

FINN, STEVEN — QUE.

Defense. Shoots left. 6', 191 lbs. Born, Laval, Que., August 20, 1966.
(Quebec's 3rd choice, 57th overall, in 1984 Entry Draft).

			Regular Season					Playoffs				
Season	Club	Lea	GP	G	A	TP	PIM	GP	G	A	TP	PIM
1982-83	Laval	QMJHL	69	7	30	37	108	6	0	2	2	6
1983-84	Laval	QMJHL	68	7	39	46	159	14	1	6	7	27
1984-85a	Laval	QMJHL	61	20	33	53	169	....	....	....	....	....
	Fredericton	AHL	4	0	0	0	14	6	1	1	2	4
1985-86	**Quebec**	**NHL**	**17**	**0**	**1**	**1**	**28**	....	....	....	....	....
	Laval	QMJHL	29	4	15	19	111	14	6	16	22	57
1986-87	**Quebec**	**NHL**	**36**	**2**	**5**	**7**	**40**	**13**	**0**	**2**	**2**	**29**
	Fredericton	AHL	38	7	19	26	73	....	....	....	....	....
1987-88	**Quebec**	**NHL**	**75**	**3**	**7**	**10**	**198**	....	....	....	....	....
1988-89	**Quebec**	**NHL**	**77**	**2**	**6**	**8**	**235**	....	....	....	....	....
1989-90	**Quebec**	**NHL**	**64**	**3**	**9**	**12**	**208**	....	....	....	....	....
1990-91	**Quebec**	**NHL**	**71**	**6**	**13**	**19**	**228**	....	....	....	....	....
1991-92	**Quebec**	**NHL**	**65**	**4**	**7**	**11**	**194**	....	....	....	....	....
1992-93	**Quebec**	**NHL**	**80**	**5**	**9**	**14**	**160**	**6**	**0**	**1**	**1**	**8**
1993-94	**Quebec**	**NHL**	**80**	**4**	**13**	**17**	**159**	....	....	....	....	....
	NHL Totals		**565**	**29**	**70**	**99**	**1450**	**19**	**0**	**3**	**3**	**37**

a QMJHL Second All-Star Team (1985)

FINNSTROM, JOHAN (FIHN-struhm) — CGY.

Defense. Shoots left. 6'3", 205 lbs. Born, Broby, Sweden, March 27, 1976.
(Calgary's 5th choice, 97th overall, in 1994 Entry Draft).

			Regular Season					Playoffs				
Season	Club	Lea	GP	G	A	TP	PIM	GP	G	A	TP	PIM
1993-94	Rogle	Swe.	7	1	1	2	2	....	....	....	....	....

FIORENTINO, PETER — NYR

Defense. Shoots right. 6'1", 205 lbs. Born, Niagara Falls, Ont., December 22, 1968.
(NY Rangers' 11th choice, 215th overall, in 1988 Entry Draft).

			Regular Season					Playoffs				
Season	Club	Lea	GP	G	A	TP	PIM	GP	G	A	TP	PIM
1985-86	S.S. Marie	OHL	58	1	6	7	87	....	....	....	....	....
1986-87	S.S. Marie	OHL	64	1	12	13	187	....	....	....	....	....
1987-88	S.S. Marie	OHL	65	5	27	32	252	6	2	2	4	21
1988-89	S.S. Marie	OHL	55	5	24	29	220	....	....	....	....	....
	Denver	IHL	10	0	0	0	39	4	0	0	0	24
1989-90	Flint	IHL	64	2	7	9	302	....	....	....	....	....
1990-91	Binghamton	AHL	55	2	11	13	361	1	0	0	0	0
1991-92	**NY Rangers**	**NHL**	**1**	**0**	**0**	**0**	**0**	....	....	....	....	....
	Binghamton	AHL	70	2	11	13	340	5	0	1	1	24
1992-93	Binghamton	AHL	64	9	5	14	286	13	0	3	3	22
1993-94	Binghamton	AHL	68	7	15	22	220	....	....	....	....	....
	NHL Totals		**1**	**0**	**0**	**0**	**0**	....	....	....	....	....

FISHER, CRAIG — CHI.

Center. Shoots left. 6'3", 180 lbs. Born, Oshawa, Ont., June 30, 1970.
(Philadelphia's 3rd choice, 56th overall, in 1988 Entry Draft).

			Regular Season					Playoffs				
Season	Club	Lea	GP	G	A	TP	PIM	GP	G	A	TP	PIM
1988-89	Miami-Ohio	CCHA	37	22	20	42	37	....	....	....	....	....
1989-90a	Miami-Ohio	CCHA	39	37	29	66	38	....	....	....	....	....
	Philadelphia	**NHL**	**2**	**0**	**0**	**0**	**0**	....	....	....	....	....
1990-91	**Philadelphia**	**NHL**	**2**	**0**	**0**	**0**	**0**	....	....	....	....	....
	Hershey	AHL	77	43	36	79	46	7	5	3	8	2
1991-92	Cape Breton	AHL	60	20	25	45	28	1	0	0	0	0
1992-93	Cape Breton	AHL	75	32	29	61	74	1	0	0	0	2
1993-94	Cape Breton	AHL	16	5	5	10	11	....	....	....	....	....
	Winnipeg	**NHL**	**4**	**0**	**0**	**0**	**2**	....	....	....	....	....
	Moncton	AHL	46	26	35	61	36	21	11	11	22	28
	NHL Totals		**8**	**0**	**0**	**0**	**2**	....	....	....	....	....

a CCHA First All-Star Team (1990)

Traded to **Edmonton** by **Philadelphia** with Scott Mellanby and Craig Berube for Dave Brown, Corey Foster and Jari Kurri, May 30, 1991. Traded to **Winnipeg** by **Edmonton** for cash, December 9, 1993. Signed as a free agent by **Chicago**, June 9, 1994.

FITZGERALD, RUSTY — PIT.

Center. Shoots left. 6'1", 190 lbs. Born, Minneapolis, MN, October 4, 1972.
(Pittsburgh's 2nd choice, 38th overall, in 1991 Entry Draft).

			Regular Season					Playoffs				
Season	Club	Lea	GP	G	A	TP	PIM	GP	G	A	TP	PIM
1991-92	Minn.-Duluth	WCHA	37	9	11	20	40	....	....	....	....	....
1992-93	Minn.-Duluth	WCHA	39	24	23	47	48	....	....	....	....	....
1993-94	Minn.-Duluth	WCHA	37	11	25	36	59	....	....	....	....	....

FITZGERALD, TOM — FLA.

Right wing/Center. Shoots right. 6'1", 195 lbs. Born, Melrose, MA, August 28, 1968.
(NY Islanders' 1st choice, 17th overall, in 1986 Entry Draft).

			Regular Season					Playoffs				
Season	Club	Lea	GP	G	A	TP	PIM	GP	G	A	TP	PIM
1986-87	Providence	H.E.	27	8	14	22	22	....	....	....	....	....
1987-88	Providence	H.E.	36	19	15	34	50	....	....	....	....	....
1988-89	**NY Islanders**	**NHL**	**23**	**3**	**5**	**8**	**10**	....	....	....	....	....
	Springfield	AHL	61	24	18	42	43	....	....	....	....	....
1989-90	**NY Islanders**	**NHL**	**19**	**2**	**5**	**7**	**4**	**4**	**1**	**0**	**1**	**4**
	Springfield	AHL	53	30	23	53	32	14	2	9	11	13
1990-91	**NY Islanders**	**NHL**	**41**	**5**	**5**	**10**	**24**	....	....	....	....	....
	Capital Dist.	AHL	27	7	7	14	50	....	....	....	....	....
1991-92	**NY Islanders**	**NHL**	**45**	**6**	**11**	**17**	**28**	....	....	....	....	....
	Capital Dist.	AHL	4	1	1	2	4	....	....	....	....	....
1992-93	**NY Islanders**	**NHL**	**77**	**9**	**18**	**27**	**34**	**18**	**2**	**5**	**7**	**18**
1993-94	**Florida**	**NHL**	**83**	**18**	**14**	**32**	**54**	....	....	....	....	....
	NHL Totals		**288**	**43**	**58**	**101**	**154**	**22**	**3**	**5**	**8**	**22**

Claimed by **Florida** from **NY Islanders** in Expansion Draft, June 24, 1993.

FITZPATRICK, RORY — MTL.

Defense. Shoots right. 6'1", 195 lbs. Born, Rochester, NY, January 11, 1975.
(Montreal's 2nd choice, 47th overall, in 1993 Entry Draft).

			Regular Season					Playoffs				
Season	Club	Lea	GP	G	A	TP	PIM	GP	G	A	TP	PIM
1992-93	Sudbury	OHL	58	4	20	24	68	14	0	0	0	17
1993-94	Sudbury	OHL	65	12	34	46	112	10	2	5	7	10

FLATLEY, PAT (FLAT-lee) — NYI

Right wing. Shoots right. 6'2", 197 lbs. Born, Toronto, Ont., October 3, 1963.
(NY Islanders' 1st choice, 21st overall, in 1982 Entry Draft).

			Regular Season					Playoffs				
Season	Club	Lea	GP	G	A	TP	PIM	GP	G	A	TP	PIM
1981-82	U. Wisconsin	WCHA	17	10	9	19	40	....	....	....	....	....
1982-83ab	U. Wisconsin	WCHA	26	17	24	41	48	....	....	....	....	....
1983-84	Cdn. National	....	57	33	17	50	136	....	....	....	....	....
	Cdn. Olympic	....	7	3	3	6	70	....	....	....	....	....
	NY Islanders	**NHL**	**16**	**2**	**7**	**9**	**6**	**21**	**9**	**6**	**15**	**14**
1984-85	**NY Islanders**	**NHL**	**78**	**20**	**31**	**51**	**106**	**4**	**1**	**0**	**1**	**6**
1985-86	**NY Islanders**	**NHL**	**73**	**18**	**34**	**52**	**66**	**3**	**0**	**0**	**0**	**21**
1986-87	**NY Islanders**	**NHL**	**63**	**16**	**35**	**51**	**81**	**11**	**3**	**2**	**5**	**6**
1987-88	**NY Islanders**	**NHL**	**40**	**9**	**15**	**24**	**28**	....	....	....	....	....
1988-89	**NY Islanders**	**NHL**	**41**	**10**	**15**	**25**	**31**	....	....	....	....	....
	Springfield	AHL	2	1	1	2	2	....	....	....	....	....
1989-90	**NY Islanders**	**NHL**	**62**	**17**	**32**	**49**	**101**	**5**	**3**	**0**	**3**	**2**
1990-91	**NY Islanders**	**NHL**	**56**	**20**	**25**	**45**	**74**	....	....	....	....	....
1991-92	**NY Islanders**	**NHL**	**38**	**8**	**28**	**36**	**31**	....	....	....	....	....
1992-93	**NY Islanders**	**NHL**	**80**	**13**	**47**	**60**	**63**	**15**	**2**	**7**	**9**	**12**
1993-94	**NY Islanders**	**NHL**	**64**	**12**	**30**	**42**	**40**	....	....	....	....	....
	NHL Totals		**611**	**145**	**299**	**444**	**627**	**59**	**18**	**15**	**33**	**61**

a WCHA First All-Star Team (1983)
b Named to NCAA All-Tournament Team (1983)

LEMING, GERRY — MTL.

eft wing. Shoots left. 6'5", 240 lbs. Born, Montreal, Que., October 16, 1967.

			Regular Season					Playoffs				
eason	Club	Lea	GP	G	A	TP	PIM	GP	G	A	TP	PIM
990-91	U.P.E.I.	AUAA			UNAVAILABLE							
991-92	Charlottetown	Sr.			UNAVAILABLE							
	Fredericton	AHL	37	4	6	10	133	1	0	0	0	7
992-93	Fredericton	AHL	64	9	17	26	262	5	1	2	3	14
993-94	**Montreal**	**NHL**	**5**	**0**	**0**	**0**	**25**	....	....	....	....	....
	Fredericton	AHL	46	6	16	22	188	....	....	....	....	....
	NHL Totals		**5**	**0**	**0**	**0**	**25**	....	....	....	....	....

gned as a free agent by **Montreal**, February 17, 1992.

LEURY, THEOREN — (FLUH-ree, THAIR-ihn) CGY.

ght wing. Shoots right. 5'6", 160 lbs. Born, Oxbow, Sask., June 29, 1968.
algary's 9th choice, 166th overall, in 1987 Entry Draft).

			Regular Season					Playoffs				
eason	Club	Lea	GP	G	A	TP	PIM	GP	G	A	TP	PIM
984-85	Moose Jaw	WHL	71	29	46	75	82	....	....	....	....	....
985-86	Moose Jaw	WHL	72	43	65	108	124	....	....	....	....	....
986-87	Moose Jaw	WHL	66	61	68	129	110	9	7	9	16	34
987-88	Moose Jaw	WHL	65	68	92	*160	235	....	....	....	....	....
	Salt Lake	IHL	2	3	4	7	7	8	11	5	16	16
988-89	**Calgary**	**NHL**	**36**	**14**	**20**	**34**	**46**	**22**	**5**	**6**	**11**	**24**
	Salt Lake	IHL	40	37	37	74	81	....	....	....	....	....
989-90	**Calgary**	**NHL**	**80**	**31**	**35**	**66**	**157**	**6**	**2**	**3**	**5**	**10**
990-91a	**Calgary**	**NHL**	**79**	**51**	**53**	**104**	**136**	**7**	**2**	**5**	**7**	**14**
991-92	**Calgary**	**NHL**	**80**	**33**	**40**	**73**	**133**	....	....	....	....	....
992-93	**Calgary**	**NHL**	**83**	**34**	**66**	**100**	**88**	**6**	**5**	**7**	**12**	**27**
993-94	**Calgary**	**NHL**	**83**	**40**	**45**	**85**	**186**	**7**	**6**	**4**	**10**	**5**
	NHL Totals		**441**	**203**	**259**	**462**	**746**	**48**	**20**	**25**	**45**	**80**

Co-winner of Alka-Seltzer Plus Award with Marty McSorley (1991)
layed in NHL All-Star Game (1991, 1992)

LINTON, ERIC — OTT.

eft wing. Shoots left. 6'2", 200 lbs. Born, William Lake, B.C., February 2, 1972.
Ottawa's 1st choice, 1st overall, in 1993 Supplemental Draft).

			Regular Season					Playoffs				
eason	Club	Lea	GP	G	A	TP	PIM	GP	G	A	TP	PIM
991-92	N. Hampshire	H.E.	36	6	4	10	10	....	....	....	....	....
992-93	N. Hampshire	H.E.	37	18	18	36	14	....	....	....	....	....
993-94	N. Hampshire	H.E.	40	16	25	41	36	....	....	....	....	....

LOMENHOFT, STEVE

enter. Shoots right. 6', 215 lbs. Born, Riverwoods, IL, May 4, 1971.
Ottawa's 1st choice, 2nd overall, in 1992 Supplemental Draft).

			Regular Season					Playoffs				
eason	Club	Lea	GP	G	A	TP	PIM	GP	G	A	TP	PIM
989-90	Harvard	ECAC	28	5	5	10	22	....	....	....	....	....
990-91	Harvard	ECAC	29	12	14	26	48	....	....	....	....	....
991-92	Harvard	ECAC	27	14	17	31	30	....	....	....	....	....
992-93	Harvard	ECAC	31	11	25	36	60	....	....	....	....	....
	New Haven	AHL	2	0	1	1	0	....	....	....	....	....
993-94	Knoxville	ECHL	64	38	55	93	52	3	1	2	3	0
	Atlanta	IHL	4	0	0	0	0	....	....	....	....	....

OGARTY, BRYAN — MTL.

efense. Shoots left. 6'2", 206 lbs. Born, Brantford, Ont., June 11, 1969.
Quebec's 1st choice, 9th overall, in 1987 Entry Draft).

			Regular Season					Playoffs				
eason	Club	Lea	GP	G	A	TP	PIM	GP	G	A	TP	PIM
985-86	Kingston	OHL	47	2	19	21	14	10	1	3	4	4
986-87a	Kingston	OHL	56	20	50	70	46	12	2	3	5	5
987-88	Kingston	OHL	48	11	36	47	50	....	....	....	....	....
988-89abc	Niagara Falls	OHL	60	47	*108	*155	88	17	10	22	32	36
989-90	**Quebec**	**NHL**	**45**	**4**	**10**	**14**	**31**	....	....	....	....	....
	Halifax	AHL	22	5	14	19	6	6	2	4	6	0
990-91	**Quebec**	**NHL**	**45**	**9**	**22**	**31**	**24**	....	....	....	....	....
	Halifax	AHL	5	0	2	2	0	....	....	....	....	....
991-92	**Quebec**	**NHL**	**20**	**3**	**12**	**15**	**16**	....	....	....	....	....
	Halifax	AHL	2	0	0	0	2	....	....	....	....	....
	New Haven	AHL	4	0	1	1	6	....	....	....	....	....
	Muskegon	IHL	8	2	4	6	30	....	....	....	....	....
992-93	**Pittsburgh**	**NHL**	**12**	**0**	**4**	**4**	**4**	....	....	....	....	....
	Cleveland	IHL	15	2	5	7	8	3	0	1	1	17
993-94	Atlanta	IHL	8	1	5	6	4	....	....	....	....	....
	Las Vegas	IHL	33	3	16	19	38	....	....	....	....	....
	Kansas City	IHL	3	2	1	3	2	....	....	....	....	....
	Montreal	**NHL**	**13**	**1**	**2**	**3**	**10**	....	....	....	....	....
	NHL Totals		**135**	**17**	**50**	**67**	**85**	....	....	....	....	....

OHL First All-Star Team (1987, 1989)
Canadian Major Junior Player of the Year (1989)
Canadian Major Junior Defenseman of the Year (1989)

raded to **Pittsburgh** by **Quebec** for Scott Young, March 10, 1992. Signed as a free agent by **ampa Bay**, September 28, 1993. Signed as a free agent by **Montreal**, February 25, 1994.

FOLIGNO, MIKE — (foh-LEE-noh) FLA.

Right wing. Shoots right. 6'2", 195 lbs. Born, Sudbury, Ont., January 29, 1959.
(Detroit's 1st choice, 3rd overall, in 1979 Entry Draft).

			Regular Season					Playoffs				
Season	Club	Lea	GP	G	A	TP	PIM	GP	G	A	TP	PIM
1975-76	Sudbury	OHA	57	22	14	36	45	....	....	....	....	....
1976-77	Sudbury	OHA	66	31	44	75	62	....	....	....	....	....
1977-78	Sudbury	OHA	67	47	39	86	112	....	....	....	....	....
1978-79a	Sudbury	OHA	68	65	85	*150	98	10	5	5	10	14
1979-80	**Detroit**	**NHL**	**80**	**36**	**35**	**71**	**109**	....	....	....	....	....
1980-81	**Detroit**	**NHL**	**80**	**28**	**35**	**63**	**210**	....	....	....	....	....
1981-82	**Detroit**	**NHL**	**26**	**13**	**13**	**26**	**28**	....	....	....	....	....
	Buffalo	**NHL**	**56**	**20**	**31**	**51**	**149**	**4**	**2**	**0**	**2**	**9**
1982-83	**Buffalo**	**NHL**	**66**	**22**	**25**	**47**	**135**	**10**	**2**	**3**	**5**	**39**
1983-84	**Buffalo**	**NHL**	**70**	**32**	**31**	**63**	**151**	**3**	**2**	**1**	**3**	**19**
1984-85	**Buffalo**	**NHL**	**77**	**27**	**29**	**56**	**154**	**5**	**1**	**3**	**4**	**12**
1985-86	**Buffalo**	**NHL**	**79**	**41**	**39**	**80**	**168**	....	....	....	....	....
1986-87	**Buffalo**	**NHL**	**75**	**30**	**29**	**59**	**176**	....	....	....	....	....
1987-88	**Buffalo**	**NHL**	**74**	**29**	**28**	**57**	**220**	**6**	**3**	**2**	**5**	**31**
1988-89	**Buffalo**	**NHL**	**75**	**27**	**22**	**49**	**156**	**5**	**3**	**1**	**4**	**21**
1989-90	**Buffalo**	**NHL**	**61**	**15**	**25**	**40**	**99**	**6**	**0**	**1**	**1**	**12**
1990-91	**Buffalo**	**NHL**	**31**	**4**	**5**	**9**	**42**	....	....	....	....	....
	Toronto	**NHL**	**37**	**8**	**7**	**15**	**65**	....	....	....	....	....
1991-92	**Toronto**	**NHL**	**33**	**6**	**8**	**14**	**50**	....	....	....	....	....
1992-93	**Toronto**	**NHL**	**55**	**13**	**5**	**18**	**84**	**18**	**2**	**6**	**8**	**42**
1993-94	**Toronto**	**NHL**	**4**	**0**	**0**	**0**	**4**	....	....	....	....	....
	Florida	**NHL**	**39**	**4**	**5**	**9**	**49**	....	....	....	....	....
	NHL Totals		**1018**	**355**	**372**	**727**	**2049**	**57**	**15**	**17**	**32**	**185**

a OHL First All-Star Team (1979)

Traded to **Buffalo** by **Detroit** with Dale McCourt and Brent Peterson for Danny Gare, Jim Schoenfeld and Derek Smith, December 2, 1981. Traded to **Toronto** by **Buffalo** with Buffalo's eighth round choice (Thomas Kucharcik) in 1991 Entry Draft for Brian Curran and Lou Franceschetti, December 17, 1990. Traded to **Florida** by **Toronto** for cash, November 5, 1993.

FOOTE, ADAM — QUE.

Defense. Shoots right. 6'1", 202 lbs. Born, Toronto, Ont., July 10, 1971.
(Quebec's 2nd choice, 22nd overall, in 1989 Entry Draft).

			Regular Season					Playoffs				
Season	Club	Lea	GP	G	A	TP	PIM	GP	G	A	TP	PIM
1988-89	S.S. Marie	OHL	66	7	32	39	120	....	....	....	....	....
1989-90	S.S. Marie	OHL	61	12	43	55	199	....	....	....	....	....
1990-91a	S.S. Marie	OHL	59	18	51	69	93	14	5	12	17	28
1991-92	**Quebec**	**NHL**	**46**	**2**	**5**	**7**	**44**	....	....	....	....	....
	Halifax	AHL	6	0	1	1	2	....	....	....	....	....
1992-93	**Quebec**	**NHL**	**81**	**4**	**12**	**16**	**168**	**6**	**0**	**1**	**1**	**2**
1993-94	**Quebec**	**NHL**	**45**	**2**	**6**	**8**	**67**	....	....	....	....	....
	NHL Totals		**172**	**8**	**23**	**31**	**279**	**6**	**0**	**1**	**1**	**2**

a OHL First All-Star Team (1991)

FORSBERG, PETER — (FOHRS-buhrg) QUE.

Center. Shoots left. 6', 190 lbs. Born, Ornskoldsvik, Sweden, July 20, 1973.
(Philadelphia's 1st choice, 6th overall, in 1991 Entry Draft).

			Regular Season					Playoffs				
Season	Club	Lea	GP	G	A	TP	PIM	GP	G	A	TP	PIM
1990-91	MoDo	Swe.	23	7	10	17	22	....	....	....	....	....
1991-92	MoDo	Swe.	39	9	18	27	78	....	....	....	....	....
1992-93	MoDo	Swe.	39	23	24	47	92	3	4	1	5	0
1993-94	MoDo	Swe.	39	18	26	44	82	11	9	7	16	14

Traded to **Quebec** by **Philadelphia** with Steve Duchesne, Kerry Huffman, Mike Ricci, Ron Hextall, Chris Simon, Philadelphia's first choice in the 1993 (Jocelyn Thibault) and 1994 (later traded to Toronto — later traded to Washington — Washington selected Nolan Baumgartner) Entry Drafts and cash for Eric Lindros, June 30, 1992.

FORTIER, MARC — (FOHRT-yay)

Center. Shoots right. 6', 192 lbs. Born, Windsor, Que., February 26, 1966.

			Regular Season					Playoffs				
Season	Club	Lea	GP	G	A	TP	PIM	GP	G	A	TP	PIM
1983-84	Chicoutimi	QMJHL	67	16	30	46	51	....	....	....	....	....
1984-85	Chicoutimi	QMJHL	68	35	63	98	114	14	8	4	12	16
1985-86	Chicoutimi	QMJHL	71	47	86	133	49	9	2	14	16	12
1986-87	Chicoutimi	QMJHL	65	66	135	201	39	19	11	40	51	20
1987-88	**Quebec**	**NHL**	**27**	**4**	**10**	**14**	**12**	....	....	....	....	....
	Fredericton	AHL	50	26	36	62	48	....	....	....	....	....
1988-89	**Quebec**	**NHL**	**57**	**20**	**19**	**39**	**45**	....	....	....	....	....
	Halifax	AHL	16	11	11	22	14	....	....	....	....	....
1989-90	**Quebec**	**NHL**	**59**	**13**	**17**	**30**	**28**	....	....	....	....	....
	Halifax	AHL	15	5	6	11	6	....	....	....	....	....
1990-91	**Quebec**	**NHL**	**14**	**0**	**4**	**4**	**6**	....	....	....	....	....
	Halifax	AHL	58	24	32	56	85	....	....	....	....	....
1991-92	**Quebec**	**NHL**	**39**	**5**	**9**	**14**	**33**	....	....	....	....	....
	Halifax	AHL	16	9	16	25	44	....	....	....	....	....
1992-93	**Ottawa**	**NHL**	**10**	**0**	**1**	**1**	**6**	....	....	....	....	....
	New Haven	AHL	16	9	15	24	42	....	....	....	....	....
	Los Angeles	**NHL**	**6**	**0**	**0**	**0**	**5**	....	....	....	....	....
	Phoenix	IHL	17	4	9	13	34	....	....	....	....	....
1993-94	Phoenix	IHL	81	39	61	100	96	....	....	....	....	....
	NHL Totals		**212**	**42**	**60**	**102**	**135**	....	....	....	....	....

Signed as a free agent by **Quebec**, February 3, 1987. Signed as a free agent by **Ottawa**, October 1, 1992. Traded to **Los Angeles** by **Ottawa** with Jim Thomson for Bob Kudelski and Shawn McCosh, December 19, 1992.

FORTIER, SEBASTIEN — MTL.

Left wing. Shoots left. 6', 198 lbs. Born, Greenfield Park, Que., October 12, 1973.

			Regular Season					Playoffs				
Season	Club	Lea	GP	G	A	TP	PIM	GP	G	A	TP	PIM
1991-92	Granby	QMJHL	62	14	31	45	65	....	....	....	....	....
1992-93	Sherbrooke	QMJHL	38	10	20	30	33	14	1	6	7	21
1993-94	Fredericton	AHL	4	0	3	3	11	....	....	....	....	....
	Wheeling	ECHL	62	6	22	28	36	....	....	....	....	....

Signed as a free agent by **Montreal**, September 18, 1992.

FOSTER, COREY — OTT.

Defense. Shoots left. 6'3", 204 lbs. Born, Ottawa, Ont., October 27, 1969.
(New Jersey's 1st choice, 12th overall, in 1988 Entry Draft).

			Regular Season					Playoffs				
Season	**Club**	**Lea**	**GP**	**G**	**A**	**TP**	**PIM**	**GP**	**G**	**A**	**TP**	**PIM**
1986-87	Peterborough	OHL	30	3	4	7	4	1	0	0	0	0
1987-88	Peterborough	OHL	66	13	31	44	58	11	5	9	14	13
1988-89	**New Jersey**	**NHL**	**2**	**0**	**0**	**0**	**0**	....	....	....	....	....
	Peterborough	OHL	55	14	42	56	42	17	1	17	18	12
1989-90	Cape Breton	AHL	54	7	17	24	32	1	0	0	0	0
1990-91	Cape Breton	AHL	67	14	11	25	51	4	2	4	6	4
1991-92	**Philadelphia**	**NHL**	**25**	**3**	**4**	**7**	**20**	....	....	....	....	....
	Hershey	AHL	19	5	9	14	26	6	1	1	2	5
1992-93	Hershey	AHL	80	9	25	34	102	....	....	....	....	....
1993-94	Hershey	AHL	66	21	37	58	96	9	2	5	7	10
	NHL Totals		**27**	**3**	**4**	**7**	**20**	....	....	....	....	....

Traded to **Edmonton** by **New Jersey** for Edmonton's first round choice (Jason Miller) in 1989 Entry Draft, June 17, 1989. Traded to **Philadelphia** by **Edmonton** with Dave Brown and Jari Kurri for Craig Fisher, Scott Mellanby and Craig Berube, May 30, 1991. Signed as a free agent by **Ottawa**, June 20, 1994.

FOSTER, STEPHEN — BOS.

Defense. Shoots right. 6'3", 210 lbs. Born, Brockton, MA, March 21, 1971.
(Boston's 6th choice, 122nd overall, in 1989 Entry Draft).

			Regular Season					Playoffs				
Season	**Club**	**Lea**	**GP**	**G**	**A**	**TP**	**PIM**	**GP**	**G**	**A**	**TP**	**PIM**
1989-90	Boston U.	H.E.	28	0	8	8	26	....	....	....	....	....
1990-91	Boston U.	H.E.				DID NOT PLAY						
1991-92	Boston U.	H.E.	12	0	4	4	12	....	....	....	....	....
1992-93	Boston U.	H.E.	34	2	6	8	42	....	....	....	....	....
1993-94	Boston U.	H.E.	10	1	4	5	26	....	....	....	....	....

FRANCIS, RON — PIT.

Center. Shoots left. 6'2", 200 lbs. Born, Sault Ste. Marie, Ont., March 1, 1963.
(Hartford's 1st choice, 4th overall, in 1981 Entry Draft).

			Regular Season					Playoffs				
Season	**Club**	**Lea**	**GP**	**G**	**A**	**TP**	**PIM**	**GP**	**G**	**A**	**TP**	**PIM**
1980-81	S.S. Marie	OHA	64	26	43	69	33	19	7	8	15	34
1981-82	**Hartford**	**NHL**	**59**	**25**	**43**	**68**	**51**	....	....	....	....	....
	S.S. Marie	OHL	25	18	30	48	46	....	....	....	....	....
1982-83	**Hartford**	**NHL**	**79**	**31**	**59**	**90**	**60**	....	....	....	....	....
1983-84	**Hartford**	**NHL**	**72**	**23**	**60**	**83**	**45**	....	....	....	....	....
1984-85	**Hartford**	**NHL**	**80**	**24**	**57**	**81**	**66**	....	....	....	....	....
1985-86	**Hartford**	**NHL**	**53**	**24**	**53**	**77**	**24**	**10**	**1**	**2**	**3**	**4**
1986-87	**Hartford**	**NHL**	**75**	**30**	**63**	**93**	**45**	**6**	**2**	**2**	**4**	**6**
1987-88	**Hartford**	**NHL**	**80**	**25**	**50**	**75**	**87**	**6**	**2**	**5**	**7**	**2**
1988-89	**Hartford**	**NHL**	**69**	**29**	**48**	**77**	**36**	**4**	**0**	**2**	**2**	**0**
1989-90	**Hartford**	**NHL**	**80**	**32**	**69**	**101**	**73**	**7**	**3**	**3**	**6**	**8**
1990-91	**Hartford**	**NHL**	**67**	**21**	**55**	**76**	**51**	....	....	....	....	....
	Pittsburgh	**NHL**	**14**	**2**	**9**	**11**	**21**	**24**	**7**	**10**	**17**	**24**
1991-92	**Pittsburgh**	**NHL**	**70**	**21**	**33**	**54**	**30**	**21**	**8**	***19**	**27**	**6**
1992-93	**Pittsburgh**	**NHL**	**84**	**24**	**76**	**100**	**68**	**12**	**6**	**11**	**17**	**19**
1993-94	**Pittsburgh**	**NHL**	**82**	**27**	**66**	**93**	**62**	**6**	**0**	**2**	**2**	**6**
	NHL Totals		**964**	**338**	**741**	**1079**	**719**	**96**	**29**	**56**	**85**	**75**

Played in NHL All-Star Game (1983, 1985, 1990)

Traded to **Pittsburgh** by **Hartford** with Grant Jennings and Ulf Samuelsson for John Cullen, Jeff Parker and Zarley Zalapski, March 4, 1991.

FRASER, IAIN — QUE.

Center. Shoots left. 5'10", 175 lbs. Born, Scarborough, Ont., August 10, 1969.
(NY Islanders' 12th choice, 233rd overall, in 1989 Entry Draft).

			Regular Season					Playoffs				
Season	**Club**	**Lea**	**GP**	**G**	**A**	**TP**	**PIM**	**GP**	**G**	**A**	**TP**	**PIM**
1986-87	Oshawa	OHL	5	1	2	3	0	....	....	....	....	....
1987-88	Oshawa	OHL	16	4	4	8	22	6	2	3	5	2
1988-89	Oshawa	OHL	62	33	57	90	87	6	2	8	10	12
1989-90ab	Oshawa	OHL	56	40	65	105	75	17	10	*22	32	8
1990-91	Capital Dist.	AHL	32	5	13	18	16	....	....	....	....	....
	Richmond	ECHL	3	1	1	2	0	....	....	....	....	....
1991-92	Capital Dist.	AHL	45	9	11	20	24	....	....	....	....	....
1992-93	**NY Islanders**	**NHL**	**7**	**2**	**2**	**4**	**2**	....	....	....	....	....
c	Capital Dist.	AHL	74	41	69	110	16	4	0	1	1	0
1993-94	**Quebec**	**NHL**	**60**	**17**	**20**	**37**	**23**	....	....	....	....	....
	NHL Totals		**67**	**19**	**22**	**41**	**25**	....	....	....	....	....

a Memorial Cup All-Star Team (1990)
b Won Stafford Smythe Memorial Trophy (Memorial Cup MVP) (1990)
c AHL Second All-Star Team (1993)

Signed as a free agent by **Quebec**, August 3, 1993.

FRASER, SCOTT — MTL.

Center. Shoots right. 6'1", 200 lbs. Born, Moncton, N.B., May 3, 1972.
(Montreal's 12th choice, 193rd overall, in 1991 Entry Draft).

			Regular Season					Playoffs				
Season	**Club**	**Lea**	**GP**	**G**	**A**	**TP**	**PIM**	**GP**	**G**	**A**	**TP**	**PIM**
1990-91	Dartmouth	ECAC	24	10	10	20	30	....	....	....	....	....
1991-92	Dartmouth	ECAC	24	11	7	18	60	....	....	....	....	....
1992-93	Cdn. National	....	5	1	0	1	0	....	....	....	....	....
a	Dartmouth	ECAC	26	21	23	44	13	....	....	....	....	....
1993-94	Dartmouth	ECAC	24	17	13	30	34	....	....	....	....	....
	Cdn. National	....	4	0	1	1	4	....	....	....	....	....

a ECAC Second All-Star Team (1993)

FREDERICK, JOSEPH — DET.

Right wing. Shoots right. 6'1", 190 lbs. Born, St. Hubert, Que., August 6, 1969.
(Detroit's 13th choice, 242nd overall, in 1989 Entry Draft).

			Regular Season					Playoffs				
Season	**Club**	**Lea**	**GP**	**G**	**A**	**TP**	**PIM**	**GP**	**G**	**A**	**TP**	**PIM**
1990-91	N. Michigan	WCHA	40	9	11	20	77	....	....	....	....	....
1991-92	N. Michigan	WCHA	36	23	8	31	100	....	....	....	....	....
1992-93a	N. Michigan	WCHA	29	28	20	48	100	....	....	....	....	....
	Adirondack	AHL	5	0	1	1	2	8	0	0	0	6
1993-94	Adirondack	AHL	68	28	30	58	130	12	11	4	15	22

a WCHA Second All-Star Team (1993)

FREDERICK, TROY

Center. Shoots left. 6'5", 225 lbs. Born, Virden, Man., April 4, 1969.

			Regular Season					Playoffs				
Season	**Club**	**Lea**	**GP**	**G**	**A**	**TP**	**PIM**	**GP**	**G**	**A**	**TP**	**PIM**
1987-88	Brandon	WHL	66	15	13	28	17	4	3	1	4	[illegible]
1988-89	Brandon	WHL	72	26	30	56	72	....	....	....	....	....
1989-90	Brandon	WHL	70	27	29	56	133	....	....	....	....	....
1990-91	Kansas City	IHL	39	2	3	5	79	....	....	....	....	....
	Knoxville	ECHL	4	0	3	3	71	....	....	....	....	....
1991-92	Kansas City	IHL	13	0	3	3	29	....	....	....	....	....
1992-93	Kansas City	IHL	16	0	1	1	27	....	....	....	....	....
1993-94	Kansas City	IHL	21	0	3	3	55	....	....	....	....	....
	Fort Worth	CHL	10	3	7	10	2	....	....	....	....	....

Signed as a free agent by **San Jose**, September 3, 1991.

FREER, MARK — (FRIHR)

Center. Shoots left. 5'10", 180 lbs. Born, Peterborough, Ont., July 14, 1968.

			Regular Season					Playoffs				
Season	**Club**	**Lea**	**GP**	**G**	**A**	**TP**	**PIM**	**GP**	**G**	**A**	**TP**	**PIM**
1985-86	Peterborough	OHL	65	16	28	44	24	14	3	4	7	[illegible]
1986-87	**Philadelphia**	**NHL**	**1**	**0**	**1**	**1**	**0**	....	....	....	....	....
	Peterborough	OHL	65	39	43	82	44	12	2	6	8	[illegible]
1987-88	**Philadelphia**	**NHL**	**1**	**0**	**0**	**0**	**0**	....	....	....	....	....
	Peterborough	OHL	63	38	70	108	63	12	5	12	17	[illegible]
1988-89	**Philadelphia**	**NHL**	**5**	**0**	**1**	**1**	**0**	....	....	....	....	....
	Hershey	AHL	75	30	49	79	77	12	4	6	10	[illegible]
1989-90	**Philadelphia**	**NHL**	**2**	**0**	**0**	**0**	**0**	....	....	....	....	....
	Hershey	AHL	65	28	36	64	31	....	....	....	....	....
1990-91	Hershey	AHL	77	18	44	62	45	7	1	3	4	[illegible]
1991-92	**Philadelphia**	**NHL**	**50**	**6**	**7**	**13**	**18**	....	....	....	....	....
	Hershey	AHL	31	13	11	24	38	6	0	3	3	[illegible]
1992-93	**Ottawa**	**NHL**	**63**	**10**	**14**	**24**	**39**	....	....	....	....	....
1993-94	**Calgary**	**NHL**	**2**	**0**	**0**	**0**	**4**	....	....	....	....	....
	Saint John	AHL	77	33	53	86	45	7	2	4	6	[illegible]
	NHL Totals		**124**	**16**	**23**	**39**	**61**	....	....	....	....	....

Signed as a free agent by **Philadelphia**, October 7, 1986. Claimed by **Ottawa** from **Philadelphia** in Expansion Draft, June 18, 1992. Signed as a free agent by **Calgary**, August 10, 1993.

FRENETTE, DEREK

Left wing. Shoots left. 6'1", 205 lbs. Born, Montreal, Que., July 13, 1971.
(St. Louis' 6th choice, 124th overall, in 1989 Entry Draft).

			Regular Season					Playoffs				
Season	**Club**	**Lea**	**GP**	**G**	**A**	**TP**	**PIM**	**GP**	**G**	**A**	**TP**	**PIM**
1988-89	Ferris State	CCHA	25	3	4	7	17	....	....	....	....	....
1989-90	Ferris State	CCHA	28	1	4	5	48	....	....	....	....	....
1990-91	Hull	QMJHL	66	27	42	69	72	6	4	3	7	12
	Peoria	IHL	....	....	....	....	....	6	0	0	0	0
1991-92	Peoria	IHL	46	2	11	13	51	10	0	3	3	4
1992-93	Peoria	IHL	73	18	19	37	44	4	1	2	3	2
1993-94	Peoria	IHL	55	5	7	12	35	3	1	2	3	6

FRIEDMAN, DOUG — QUE.

Left wing. Shoots left. 6'1", 189 lbs. Born, Cape Elizabeth, ME, September 1, 1971.
(Quebec's 11th choice, 222nd overall, in 1991 Entry Draft).

			Regular Season					Playoffs				
Season	**Club**	**Lea**	**GP**	**G**	**A**	**TP**	**PIM**	**GP**	**G**	**A**	**TP**	**PIM**
1990-91	Boston U.	H.E.	36	6	6	12	37	....	....	....	....	....
1991-92	Boston U.	H.E.	34	11	8	19	42	....	....	....	....	....
1992-93	Boston U.	H.E.	38	17	24	41	62	....	....	....	....	....
1993-94	Boston U.	H.E.	41	9	23	32	110	....	....	....	....	....

FRIESEN, JEFF — S.J.

Center. Shoots left. 6', 185 lbs. Born, Meadow Lake, Sask., August 5, 1976.
(San Jose's 1st choice, 11th overall, in 1994 Entry Draft).

			Regular Season					Playoffs				
Season	**Club**	**Lea**	**GP**	**G**	**A**	**TP**	**PIM**	**GP**	**G**	**A**	**TP**	**PIM**
1991-92	Regina	WHL	4	3	1	4	2	....	....	....	....	....
1992-93	Regina	WHL	70	45	38	83	23	13	7	10	17	8
1993-94	Regina	WHL	66	51	67	118	48	4	3	2	5	2

FRYLEN, EDVIN — (FRYUH-lehn) ST.L.

Defense. Shoots left. 6', 211 lbs. Born, Jarfalla, Sweden, December 23, 1975.
(St. Louis' 3rd choice, 120th overall, in 1994 Entry Draft).

			Regular Season					Playoffs				
Season	**Club**	**Lea**	**GP**	**G**	**A**	**TP**	**PIM**	**GP**	**G**	**A**	**TP**	**PIM**
1991-92	Vasteras	Swe.	2	0	0	0	0	....	....	....	....	....
1992-93	Vasteras	Swe.	29	0	2	2	14	3	0	0	0	0
1993-94	Vasteras	Swe.	32	1	0	1	26	....	....	....	....	....

GAETZ, LINK — (GAYTZ) EDM.

Defense. Shoots left. 6'3", 215 lbs. Born, Vancouver, B.C., October 2, 1968.
(Minnesota's 2nd choice, 40th overall, in 1988 Entry Draft).

			Regular Season					Playoffs				
Season	**Club**	**Lea**	**GP**	**G**	**A**	**TP**	**PIM**	**GP**	**G**	**A**	**TP**	**PIM**
1986-87	N. Westminster	WHL	44	2	7	9	52	....	....	....	....	....
1987-88	Spokane	WHL	59	9	20	29	313	10	2	2	4	70
1988-89	**Minnesota**	**NHL**	**12**	**0**	**2**	**2**	**53**	....	....	....	....	....
	Kalamazoo	IHL	37	3	4	7	192	5	0	0	0	56
1989-90	**Minnesota**	**NHL**	**5**	**0**	**0**	**0**	**33**	....	....	....	....	....
	Kalamazoo	IHL	61	5	16	21	318	9	2	2	4	59
1990-91	Kalamazoo	IHL	9	0	1	1	44	....	....	....	....	....
	Kansas City	IHL	18	1	10	11	178	....	....	....	....	....
1991-92	**San Jose**	**NHL**	**48**	**6**	**6**	**12**	**326**	....	....	....	....	....
1992-93	Nashville	ECHL	3	1	0	1	10	....	....	....	....	....
	Kansas City	IHL	2	0	0	0	14	....	....	....	....	....
1993-94	Cape Breton	AHL	21	0	1	1	140	....	....	....	....	....
	Nashville	ECHL	24	1	1	2	261	....	....	....	....	....
	NHL Totals		**65**	**6**	**8**	**14**	**412**	....	....	....	....	....

Claimed by **San Jose** from **Minnesota** in Dispersal Draft, May 30, 1991. Traded to **Edmonton** by **San Jose** for Edmonton's tenth round choice (Tomas Pisa) in 1994 Entry Draft, September 10, 1993.

GAFFNEY, MIKE — OTT.

Defense. Shoots right. 6'1", 202 lbs. Born, Worchester, MA, June 19, 1976.
(Ottawa's 4th choice, 131st overall, in 1994 Entry Draft).

			Regular Season					Playoffs				
Season	**Club**	**Lea**	**GP**	**G**	**A**	**TP**	**PIM**	**GP**	**G**	**A**	**TP**	**PIM**
1992-93	St. John's	HS	24	6	19	25	10	....	....	....	....	....
1993-94	St. John's	HS	20	6	16	22	....	....	....	....	....	....

AGE, JODY — BUF.

ght wing. Shoots right. 6', 190 lbs. Born, Toronto, Ont., November 29, 1959.
etroit's 2nd choice, 45th overall, in 1979 Entry Draft).

			Regular Season					Playoffs				
ason	Club	Lea	GP	G	A	TP	PIM	GP	G	A	TP	PIM
77-78	Hamilton	OHA	32	15	18	33	19	....	....	....	....	....
	Kitchener	OHA	36	17	27	44	21	9	4	3	7	4
78-79	Kitchener	OHA	58	46	43	89	40	10	1	2	3	6
79-80	Adirondack	AHL	63	25	21	46	15	5	2	1	3	0
80-81	Detroit	NHL	16	2	2	4	22	....	....	....	....	....
	Adirondack	AHL	59	17	31	48	44	17	9	6	15	12
81-82	Detroit	NHL	31	9	10	19	2	....	....	....	....	....
	Adirondack	AHL	47	21	20	41	21	....	....	....	....	....
82-83	Adirondack	AHL	65	23	30	53	33	6	1	5	6	8
83-84	Detroit	NHL	3	0	0	0	0	....	....	....	....	....
	Adirondack	AHL	73	40	32	72	32	6	3	4	7	2
84-85	Adirondack	AHL	78	27	33	60	55	....	....	....	....	....
85-86	Buffalo	NHL	7	3	2	5	0	....	....	....	....	....
a	Rochester	AHL	73	42	57	99	56	....	....	....	....	....
86-87	Rochester	AHL	70	26	39	65	60	17	*14	5	19	24
87-88	Buffalo	NHL	2	0	0	0	0	....	....	....	....	....
ab	Rochester	AHL	76	*60	44	104	46	5	2	5	7	10
88-89	Rochester	AHL	65	31	38	69	60	....	....	....	....	....
89-90	Rochester	AHL	75	45	38	83	42	17	4	6	10	12
90-91a	Rochester	AHL	73	42	43	85	34	15	6	10	16	14
91-92	Buffalo	NHL	9	0	1	1	2	....	....	....	....	....
	Rochester	AHL	67	40	40	80	54	16	5	9	14	10
92-93	Rochester	AHL	71	40	40	80	76	9	5	8	13	2
93-94	Rochester	AHL	44	18	21	39	57	....	....	....	....	....
	NHL Totals		68	14	15	29	26	....	....	....	....	....

AHL First All-Star Team (1986, 1988, 1991)
Won Les Cunningham Plaque (MVP - AHL) (1988)

gned as a free agent by **Buffalo**, July 31, 1985.

AGNE, LUC — L.A.

ght wing. Shoots right. 6'1", 190 lbs. Born, Sturgeon Falls, Ont., May 4, 1976.
os Angeles' 5th choice, 163rd overall, in 1994 Entry Draft).

			Regular Season					Playoffs				
eason	Club	Lea	GP	G	A	TP	PIM	GP	G	A	TP	PIM
993-94	Sudbury	OHL	11	3	1	4	2	....	....	....	....	....
	Newmarket	OHL	19	1	2	3	17	....	....	....	....	....

AGNER, DAVE (GAH-nyay) — DAL.

enter. Shoots left. 5'10", 180 lbs. Born, Chatham, Ont., December 11, 1964.
Y Rangers' 1st choice, 12th overall, in 1983 Entry Draft).

			Regular Season					Playoffs				
eason	Club	Lea	GP	G	A	TP	PIM	GP	G	A	TP	PIM
981-82	Brantford	OHL	68	30	46	76	31	11	3	6	9	6
982-83a	Brantford	OHL	70	55	66	121	57	8	5	5	10	4
983-84	Cdn. National	....	50	19	18	37	26	....	....	....	....	....
	Cdn. Olympic	....	7	5	2	7	6	....	....	....	....	....
	Brantford	OHL	12	7	13	20	4	6	0	4	4	6
984-85	NY Rangers	NHL	38	6	6	12	16	....	....	....	....	....
	New Haven	AHL	38	13	20	33	23	....	....	....	....	....
985-86	NY Rangers	NHL	32	4	6	10	19	....	....	....	....	....
	New Haven	AHL	16	10	11	21	11	4	1	2	3	2
986-87	NY Rangers	NHL	10	1	4	5	12	....	....	....	....	....
	New Haven	AHL	56	22	41	63	50	7	1	5	6	18
987-88	Minnesota	NHL	51	8	11	19	55	....	....	....	....	....
	Kalamazoo	IHL	14	16	10	26	26	....	....	....	....	....
988-89	Minnesota	NHL	75	35	43	78	104	....	....	....	....	....
	Kalamazoo	IHL	1	0	1	1	4	....	....	....	....	....
989-90	Minnesota	NHL	79	40	38	78	54	7	2	3	5	16
990-91	Minnesota	NHL	73	40	42	82	114	23	12	15	27	28
991-92	Minnesota	NHL	78	31	40	71	107	7	2	4	6	8
992-93	Minnesota	NHL	84	33	43	76	143	....	....	....	....	....
993-94	Dallas	NHL	76	32	29	61	83	9	5	1	6	2
	NHL Totals		596	230	262	492	707	46	21	23	44	54

OHL Second All-Star Team (1983)

layed in NHL All-Star Game (1991)

raded to **Minnesota** by **NY Rangers** with Jay Caulfield for Jari Gronstrand and Paul Boutilier, ctober 8, 1987.

ALANOV, MAXIM — NYR

efense. Shoots left. 6'1", 167 lbs. Born, Krasnoyarsk, USSR, March 13, 1974.
Y Rangers' 3rd choice, 61st overall, in 1993 Entry Draft).

			Regular Season					Playoffs				
eason	Club	Lea	GP	G	A	TP	PIM	GP	G	A	TP	PIM
992-93	Togliatti	CIS	41	4	2	6	12	10	1	1	2	12
993-94	Togliatti	CIS	7	1	0	1	4	12	1	0	1	8

ALLANT, GERARD (guh-LANT) — T.B.

eft wing. Shoots left. 5'10", 190 lbs. Born, Summerside, P.E.I., September 2, 1963.
etroit's 4th choice, 107th overall, in 1981 Entry Draft).

			Regular Season					Playoffs				
eason	Club	Lea	GP	G	A	TP	PIM	GP	G	A	TP	PIM
980-81	Sherbrooke	QMJHL	68	41	59	100	265	14	6	13	19	46
981-82	Sherbrooke	QMJHL	58	34	58	92	260	22	14	24	38	84
982-83	St-Jean	QMJHL	33	28	25	53	139	....	....	....	....	....
	Verdun	QMJHL	29	26	49	75	105	15	14	19	33	84
983-84	Adirondack	AHL	77	31	33	64	195	7	1	3	4	34
984-85	Detroit	NHL	32	6	12	18	66	3	0	0	0	11
	Adirondack	AHL	46	18	29	47	131	....	....	....	....	....
985-86	Detroit	NHL	52	20	19	39	106	....	....	....	....	....
986-87	Detroit	NHL	80	38	34	72	216	16	8	6	14	43
987-88	Detroit	NHL	73	34	39	73	242	16	6	9	15	55
988-89a	Detroit	NHL	76	39	54	93	230	6	1	2	3	40
989-90	Detroit	NHL	69	36	44	80	254	....	....	....	....	....
990-91	Detroit	NHL	45	10	16	26	111	....	....	....	....	....
991-92	Detroit	NHL	69	14	22	36	187	11	2	2	4	25
992-93	Detroit	NHL	67	10	20	30	188	6	1	2	3	4
993-94	Tampa Bay	NHL	51	4	9	13	74	....	....	....	....	....
	NHL Totals		614	211	269	480	1674	58	18	21	39	178

NHL Second All-Star Team (1989).

igned as a free agent by **Tampa Bay**, July 21, 1993.

GALLEY, GARRY — PHI.

Defense. Shoots left. 6', 204 lbs. Born, Montreal, Que., April 16, 1963.
(Los Angeles' 4th choice, 100th overall, in 1983 Entry Draft).

			Regular Season					Playoffs				
Season	Club	Lea	GP	G	A	TP	PIM	GP	G	A	TP	PIM
1981-82	Bowling Green	CCHA	42	3	36	39	48	....	....	....	....	....
1982-83	Bowling Green	CCHA	40	17	29	46	40	....	....	....	....	....
1983-84ab	Bowling Green	CCHA	44	15	52	67	61	....	....	....	....	....
1984-85	Los Angeles	NHL	78	8	30	38	82	3	1	0	1	2
1985-86	Los Angeles	NHL	49	9	13	22	46	....	....	....	....	....
	New Haven	AHL	4	2	6	8	6	....	....	....	....	....
1986-87	Los Angeles	NHL	30	5	11	16	57	....	....	....	....	....
	Washington	NHL	18	1	10	11	10	2	0	0	0	0
1987-88	Washington	NHL	58	7	23	30	44	13	2	4	6	13
1988-89	Boston	NHL	78	8	21	29	80	9	0	1	1	33
1989-90	Boston	NHL	71	8	27	35	75	21	3	3	6	34
1990-91	Boston	NHL	70	6	21	27	84	16	1	5	6	17
1991-92	Boston	NHL	38	2	12	14	83	....	....	....	....	....
	Philadelphia	NHL	39	3	15	18	34	....	....	....	....	....
1992-93	Philadelphia	NHL	83	13	49	62	115	....	....	....	....	....
1993-94	Philadelphia	NHL	81	10	60	70	91	....	....	....	....	....
	NHL Totals		693	80	292	372	801	64	7	13	20	99

a CCHA First All-Star Team (1984)
b NCAA All-American (1984)

Played in NHL All-Star Game (1991, 1994)

Traded to **Washington** by **Los Angeles** for Al Jensen, February 14, 1987. Signed as a free agent by **Boston**, July 8, 1988. Traded to **Philadelphia** by **Boston** with Wes Walz and Boston's third round choice (Milos Holan) in 1993 Entry Draft for Gord Murphy, Brian Dobbin, Philadelphia's third round choice (Sergei Zholtok) in 1992 Entry Draft and Philadelphia's fourth round choice (Charles Paquette) in 1993 Entry Draft, January 2, 1992.

GARANIN, YEVGENY — WPG.

Center. Shoots left. 6'4", 191 lbs. Born, Voskresensk, USSR, August 3, 1973.
(Winnipeg's 9th choice, 228th overall, in 1992 Entry Draft).

			Regular Season					Playoffs				
Season	Club	Lea	GP	G	A	TP	PIM	GP	G	A	TP	PIM
1991-92	Khimik	CIS	1	1	0	1	0	....	....	....	....	....
1992-93	Khimik	CIS	34	5	4	9	10	1	0	0	0	2
1993-94	Khimik	CIS	46	6	4	10	12	3	0	0	0	0

GARDINER, BRUCE — OTT.

Center. Shoots right. 6'1", 185 lbs. Born, Barrie, Ont., February 11, 1971.
(St. Louis' 6th choice, 131st overall, in 1991 Entry Draft).

			Regular Season					Playoffs				
Season	Club	Lea	GP	G	A	TP	PIM	GP	G	A	TP	PIM
1990-91	Colgate	ECAC	27	4	9	13	72	....	....	....	....	....
1991-92	Colgate	ECAC	23	7	8	15	77	....	....	....	....	....
1992-93	Colgate	ECAC	33	17	12	29	64	....	....	....	....	....
1993-94a	Colgate	ECAC	33	23	23	46	68	....	....	....	....	....
	Peoria	IHL	3	0	0	0	0	....	....	....	....	....

a ECAC Second All-Star Team (1994)

Signed as a free agent by **Ottawa**, June 14, 1994.

GARPENLOV, JOHAN (GAHR-pehn-LAHV, YOH-hahn) — S.J.

Left wing. Shoots left. 5'11", 185 lbs. Born, Stockholm, Sweden, March 21, 1968.
(Detroit's 5th choice, 85th overall, in 1986 Entry Draft).

			Regular Season					Playoffs				
Season	Club	Lea	GP	G	A	TP	PIM	GP	G	A	TP	PIM
1986-87	Djurgarden	Swe.	29	5	8	13	22	2	0	0	0	0
1987-88	Djurgarden	Swe.	30	7	10	17	12	3	1	3	4	4
1988-89	Djurgarden	Swe.	36	12	19	31	20	8	3	4	7	10
1989-90	Djurgarden	Swe.	39	20	13	33	35	8	2	4	6	4
1990-91	Detroit	NHL	71	18	22	40	18	6	0	1	1	4
1991-92	Detroit	NHL	16	1	1	2	4	....	....	....	....	....
	Adirondack	AHL	9	3	3	6	6	....	....	....	....	....
	San Jose	NHL	12	5	6	11	4	....	....	....	....	....
1992-93	San Jose	NHL	79	22	44	66	56	....	....	....	....	....
1993-94	San Jose	NHL	80	18	35	53	28	14	4	6	10	6
	NHL Totals		258	64	108	172	110	20	4	7	11	10

Traded to **San Jose** by **Detroit** for Bob McGill and Vancouver's eighth round choice (previously acquired by Detroit — San Jose selected C.J. Denomme) in 1992 Entry Draft, March 9, 1992.

GARTNER, MIKE — TOR.

Right wing. Shoots right. 6', 190 lbs. Born, Ottawa, Ont., October 29, 1959.
(Washington's 1st choice, 4th overall, in 1979 Entry Draft).

			Regular Season					Playoffs				
Season	Club	Lea	GP	G	A	TP	PIM	GP	G	A	TP	PIM
1976-77	Niagara Falls	OHA	62	33	42	75	125	....	....	....	....	....
1977-78a	Niagara Falls	OHA	64	41	49	90	56	....	....	....	....	....
1978-79	Cincinnati	WHA	78	27	25	52	123	3	0	2	2	2
1979-80	Washington	NHL	77	36	32	68	66	....	....	....	....	....
1980-81	Washington	NHL	80	48	46	94	100	....	....	....	....	....
1981-82	Washington	NHL	80	35	45	80	121	....	....	....	....	....
1982-83	Washington	NHL	73	38	38	76	54	4	0	0	0	4
1983-84	Washington	NHL	80	40	45	85	90	8	3	7	10	16
1984-85	Washington	NHL	80	50	52	102	71	5	4	3	7	9
1985-86	Washington	NHL	74	35	40	75	63	9	2	10	12	4
1986-87	Washington	NHL	78	41	32	73	61	7	4	3	7	14
1987-88	Washington	NHL	80	48	33	81	73	14	3	4	7	14
1988-89	Washington	NHL	56	26	29	55	71	....	....	....	....	....
	Minnesota	NHL	13	7	7	14	2	5	0	0	0	6
1989-90	Minnesota	NHL	67	34	36	70	32	....	....	....	....	....
	NY Rangers	NHL	12	11	5	16	6	10	5	3	8	12
1990-91	NY Rangers	NHL	79	49	20	69	53	6	1	1	2	0
1991-92	NY Rangers	NHL	76	40	41	81	55	13	8	8	16	4
1992-93	NY Rangers	NHL	84	45	23	68	59	....	....	....	....	....
1993-94	NY Rangers	NHL	71	28	24	52	58	....	....	....	....	....
	Toronto	NHL	10	6	6	12	4	18	5	6	11	14
	NHL Totals		1170	617	554	1171	1039	99	35	45	80	97

a OHA First All-Star Team (1978)

Played in NHL All-Star Game (1980, 1985, 1986, 1988, 1990, 1993)

Traded to **Minnesota** by **Washington** with Larry Murphy for Dino Ciccarelli and Bob Rouse, March 7, 1989. Traded to **NY Rangers** by **Minnesota** for Ulf Dahlen, Los Angeles' fourth round choice (previously acquired by NY Rangers — Minnesota selected Cal McGowan) in 1990 Entry Draft and future considerations, March 6, 1990. Traded to **Toronto** by **NY Rangers** for Glenn Anderson, the rights to Scott Malone and Toronto's fourth round choice (Alexander Korobolin) in 1994 Entry Draft, March 21, 1994.

GASKINS, JON — EDM.

Defense. Shoots left. 6'3", 205 lbs. Born, Dallas, TX, January 11, 1976.
(Edmonton's 8th choice, 110th overall, in 1994 Entry Draft).

			Regular Season					Playoffs				
Season	Club	Lea	GP	G	A	TP	PIM	GP	G	A	TP	PIM
1992-93	Dubuque	USHL	25	6	9	15	20	....	....	....	....	....
1993-94	Dubuque	USHL	30	6	13	19	52	....	....	....	....	....

GAUDREAU, ROB — (GUH-droh) S.J.

Right wing. Shoots right. 5'11", 185 lbs. Born, Lincoln, RI, January 20, 1970.
(Pittsburgh's 8th choice, 172nd overall, in 1988 Entry Draft).

			Regular Season					Playoffs				
Season	Club	Lea	GP	G	A	TP	PIM	GP	G	A	TP	PIM
1988-89	Providence	H.E.	42	28	29	57	32	....	....	....	....	....
1989-90	Providence	H.E.	32	20	18	38	12	....	....	....	....	....
1990-91a	Providence	H.E.	36	34	27	61	20	....	....	....	....	....
1991-92bc	Providence	H.E.	21	34	55	22		....	....	....	....	....
1992-93	**San Jose**	**NHL**	**59**	**23**	**20**	**43**	**18**	....	....	....	....	....
	Kansas City	IHL	19	8	6	14	6	....	....	....	....	....
1993-94	**San Jose**	**NHL**	**84**	**15**	**20**	**35**	**28**	**14**	**2**	**0**	**2**	**0**
	NHL Totals		**143**	**38**	**40**	**78**	**46**	**14**	**2**	**0**	**2**	**0**

a Hockey East Second All-Star Team (1991)
b NCAA East Second All-American Team (1992)
c Hockey East First All-Star Team (1992)

Rights traded to **Minnesota** by **Pittsburgh** for Richard Zemlak, November 1, 1988. Claimed by **San Jose** from **Minnesota** in Dispersal Draft, May 30, 1991.

GAUL, MICHAEL — L.A.

Defense. Shoots right. 6'1", 197 lbs. Born, Lachine, Que., April 22, 1973.
(Los Angeles' 12th choice, 262nd overall, in 1991 Entry Draft).

			Regular Season					Playoffs				
Season	Club	Lea	GP	G	A	TP	PIM	GP	G	A	TP	PIM
1990-91	St. Lawrence	ECAC	31	1	3	4	46	....	....	....	....	....
1991-92	Laval	QMJHL	50	6	38	44	44	10	0	2	2	20
1992-93a	Laval	QMJHL	57	16	57	73	66	13	3	10	13	10
1993-94	Laval	QMJHL	22	10	17	27	24	21	5	15	20	14

a Memorial Cup All-Star Team (1993)

GAUTHIER, DANIEL — CHI.

Left wing. Shoots left. 6'1", 190 lbs. Born, Charlemagne, Que., May 17, 1970.
(Pittsburgh's 3rd choice, 62nd overall, in 1988 Entry Draft).

			Regular Season					Playoffs				
Season	Club	Lea	GP	G	A	TP	PIM	GP	G	A	TP	PIM
1986-87	Longueuil	QMJHL	64	23	22	45	23	18	4	5	9	15
1987-88	Victoriaville	QMJHL	66	43	47	90	53	5	2	1	3	0
1988-89	Victoriaville	QMJHL	64	41	75	116	84	16	12	17	29	30
1989-90	Victoriaville	QMJHL	62	45	69	114	32	16	8	*19	27	16
1990-91	Albany	IHL	1	1	0	1	0	....	....	....	....	....
ab	Knoxville	ECHL	61	41	*93	134	40	2	0	4	4	4
1991-92	Muskegon	IHL	68	19	18	37	28	9	3	6	9	8
1992-93	Cleveland	IHL	80	40	66	106	88	4	2	2	4	14
1993-94	Cincinnati	IHL	74	30	34	64	101	10	2	3	5	14

a ECHL First All-Star Team (1991)
b ECHL Rookie of the Year (1991)

Signed as a free agent by **Florida**, July 14, 1993. Signed as a free agent by **Chicago**, June 14, 1994.

GAVEY, AARON — T.B.

Center. Shoots left. 6'1", 170 lbs. Born, Sudbury, Ont., February 22, 1974.
(Tampa Bay's 4th choice, 74th overall, in 1992 Entry Draft).

			Regular Season					Playoffs				
Season	Club	Lea	GP	G	A	TP	PIM	GP	G	A	TP	PIM
1991-92	S.S. Marie	OHL	48	7	11	18	27	19	5	1	6	10
1992-93	S.S. Marie	OHL	62	45	39	84	116	18	5	9	14	36
1993-94	S.S. Marie	OHL	60	42	60	102	116	14	11	10	21	22

GEARY, DEREK — BOS.

Right wing. Shoots right. 6'3", 180 lbs. Born, Gloucester, MA, February 18, 1970.
(Boston's 5th choice, 123rd overall, in 1988 Entry Draft).

			Regular Season					Playoffs				
Season	Club	Lea	GP	G	A	TP	PIM	GP	G	A	TP	PIM
1991-92	Dartmouth	ECAC	26	7	6	13	30	....	....	....	....	....
1992-93	Dartmouth	ECAC	27	7	8	15	4	....	....	....	....	....
1993-94	Dartmouth	ECAC	26	3	6	9	16	....	....	....	....	....

GELINAS, MARTIN — (ZHEHL-in-nuh, MAHR-ta) VAN.

Left wing. Shoots left. 5'11", 195 lbs. Born, Shawinigan, Que., June 5, 1970.
(Los Angeles' 1st choice, 7th overall, in 1988 Entry Draft).

			Regular Season					Playoffs				
Season	Club	Lea	GP	G	A	TP	PIM	GP	G	A	TP	PIM
1987-88	Hull	QMJHL	65	63	68	131	74	17	15	18	33	32
1988-89	**Edmonton**	**NHL**	**6**	**1**	**2**	**3**	**0**	....	....	....	....	....
	Hull	QMJHL	41	38	39	77	31	9	5	4	9	14
1989-90	**Edmonton**	**NHL**	**46**	**17**	**8**	**25**	**30**	**20**	**2**	**3**	**5**	**6**
1990-91	**Edmonton**	**NHL**	**73**	**20**	**20**	**40**	**34**	**18**	**3**	**6**	**9**	**25**
1991-92	**Edmonton**	**NHL**	**68**	**11**	**18**	**29**	**62**	**15**	**1**	**3**	**4**	**10**
1992-93	**Edmonton**	**NHL**	**65**	**11**	**12**	**23**	**30**	....	....	....	....	....
1993-94	**Quebec**	**NHL**	**31**	**6**	**6**	**12**	**8**	....	....	....	....	....
	Vancouver	**NHL**	**33**	**8**	**8**	**16**	**26**	**24**	**5**	**4**	**9**	**14**
	NHL Totals		**322**	**74**	**74**	**148**	**190**	**77**	**11**	**16**	**27**	**55**

Traded to **Edmonton** by **Los Angeles** with Jimmy Carson and Los Angeles' first round choices in 1989, (acquired by New Jersey — New Jersey selected Jason Miller), 1991 (Martin Rucinsky) and 1993 (Nick Stajduhar) Entry Drafts and cash for Wayne Gretzky, Mike Krushelnyski and Marty McSorley, August 9, 1988. Traded to **Quebec** by **Edmonton** with Edmonton's sixth round choice (Nicholas Checco) in 1993 Entry Draft for Scott Pearson, June 20, 1993. Claimed on waivers by **Vancouver** from **Quebec**, January 15, 1994.

GENDRON, MARTIN — WSH.

Right wing. Shoots right. 5'8", 182 lbs. Born, Valleyfield, Que., February 15, 1974.
(Washington's 4th choice, 71st overall, in 1992 Entry Draft).

			Regular Season					Playoffs				
Season	Club	Lea	GP	G	A	TP	PIM	GP	G	A	TP	PIM
1990-91	St-Hyacinthe	QMJHL	55	34	23	57	33	4	1	2	3	
1991-92a	St-Hyacinthe	QMJHL	69	*71	66	137	45	6	7	4	11	
1992-93bc	St-Hyacinthe	QMJHL	63	73	61	134	44	....	....	....	....	....
	Baltimore	AHL	10	1	2	3	2	3	0	0	0	
1993-94	Cdn. National	....	19	4	5	9	2	....	....	....	....	....
	Hull	QMJHL	37	39	36	75	18	20	*21	17	38	

a QMJHL First All-Star Team (1992)
b QMJHL Second All-Star Team (1993)
c Canadian Major Junior First All-Star Team (1993)

GERIS, DAVE — FLA.

Defense. Shoots left. 6'5", 221 lbs. Born, North Bay, Ont., June 7, 1976.
(Florida's 6th choice, 105th overall, in 1994 Entry Draft).

			Regular Season					Playoffs				
Season	Club	Lea	GP	G	A	TP	PIM	GP	G	A	TP	PIM
1992-93	Toronto R.W.	Midget	42	7	13	20	96	....	....	....	....	....
1993-94	Windsor	OHL	63	0	6	6	121	3	0	0	0	

GERNANDER, KEN — NYR

Center. Shoots left. 5'10", 175 lbs. Born, Coleraine, MN, June 30, 1969.
(Winnipeg's 4th choice, 96th overall, in 1987 Entry Draft).

			Regular Season					Playoffs				
Season	Club	Lea	GP	G	A	TP	PIM	GP	G	A	TP	PIM
1987-88	U. Minnesota	WCHA	44	14	14	28	14	....	....	....	....	....
1988-89	U. Minnesota	WCHA	44	9	11	20	2	....	....	....	....	....
1989-90	U. Minnesota	WCHA	44	32	17	49	24	....	....	....	....	....
1990-91	U. Minnesota	WCHA	44	23	20	43	24	....	....	....	....	....
1991-92	Fort Wayne	IHL	13	7	6	13	2	....	....	....	....	....
	Moncton	AHL	43	8	18	26	9	8	1	1	2	
1992-93	Moncton	AHL	71	18	29	47	20	5	1	4	5	
1993-94	Moncton	AHL	71	22	25	47	12	19	6	1	7	

GIBSON, STEVE — EDM.

Left wing. Shoots left. 6', 204 lbs. Born, Listowel, Ont., October 10, 1972.
(Edmonton's 7th choice, 157th overall, in 1992 Entry Draft).

			Regular Season					Playoffs				
Season	Club	Lea	GP	G	A	TP	PIM	GP	G	A	TP	PIM
1990-91	Windsor	OHL	62	15	18	33	37	11	1	3	4	
1991-92	Windsor	OHL	63	49	40	89	41	7	4	1	5	
1992-93	Windsor	OHL	60	48	52	100	49	....	....	....	....	....
	Johnstown	ECHL	3	0	1	1	2	....	....	....	....	....
1993-94	Cape Breton	AHL	3	0	0	0	2	....	....	....	....	....
	Wheeling	ECHL	55	29	30	59	47	9	1	3	4	

GILBERT, GREG — NYR

Left wing. Shoots left. 6'1", 191 lbs. Born, Mississauga, Ont., January 22, 1962.
(NY Islanders' 5th choice, 80th overall, in 1980 Entry Draft).

			Regular Season					Playoffs				
Season	Club	Lea	GP	G	A	TP	PIM	GP	G	A	TP	PIM
1979-80	Toronto	OHA	68	10	11	21	35	....	....	....	....	....
1980-81	Toronto	OHA	64	30	37	67	73	5	2	6	8	16
1981-82	**NY Islanders**	**NHL**	**1**	**0**	**1**	**0**	**1**	**0**	**4**	**1**	**1**	**2**
	Toronto	OHL	65	41	67	108	119	10	4	12	16	23
1982-83	**NY Islanders**	**NHL**	**45**	**8**	**11**	**19**	**30**	**10**	**1**	**0**	**1**	**14**
	Indianapolis	CHL	24	11	16	27	23	....	....	....	....	....
1983-84	**NY Islanders**	**NHL**	**79**	**31**	**35**	**66**	**59**	**21**	**5**	**7**	**12**	
1984-85	**NY Islanders**	**NHL**	**58**	**13**	**25**	**38**	**36**	....	....	....	....	....
1985-86	**NY Islanders**	**NHL**	**60**	**9**	**19**	**28**	**82**	**2**	**0**	**0**	**0**	
	Springfield	AHL	2	0	0	0	2	....	....	....	....	....
1986-87	**NY Islanders**	**NHL**	**51**	**6**	**7**	**13**	**26**	**10**	**2**	**2**	**4**	
1987-88	**NY Islanders**	**NHL**	**76**	**17**	**28**	**45**	**46**	**4**	**0**	**0**	**0**	
1988-89	**NY Islanders**	**NHL**	**55**	**8**	**13**	**21**	**45**	....	....	....	....	....
	Chicago	**NHL**	**4**	**0**	**0**	**0**	**0**	**15**	**1**	**5**	**6**	**20**
1989-90	**Chicago**	**NHL**	**70**	**12**	**25**	**37**	**54**	**19**	**5**	**8**	**13**	**34**
1990-91	**Chicago**	**NHL**	**72**	**10**	**15**	**25**	**58**	**5**	**0**	**1**	**1**	**2**
1991-92	**Chicago**	**NHL**	**50**	**7**	**5**	**12**	**35**	**10**	**1**	**3**	**4**	**16**
1992-93	**Chicago**	**NHL**	**77**	**13**	**19**	**32**	**57**	**3**	**0**	**0**	**0**	
1993-94	**NY Rangers**	**NHL**	**76**	**4**	**11**	**15**	**29**	**23**	**1**	**3**	**4**	
	NHL Totals		**774**	**139**	**213**	**352**	**557**	**126**	**17**	**30**	**47**	**156**

Traded to **Chicago** by **NY Islanders** for Chicago's fifth round choice (Steve Young) in 1989 Entry Draft, March 7, 1989. Signed as a free agent by **NY Rangers**, July 29, 1993.

GILCHRIST, BRENT — DAL.

Left wing. Shoots left. 5'11", 181 lbs. Born, Moose Jaw, Sask., April 3, 1967.
(Montreal's 6th choice, 79th overall, in 1985 Entry Draft).

			Regular Season					Playoffs				
Season	Club	Lea	GP	G	A	TP	PIM	GP	G	A	TP	PIM
1983-84	Kelowna	WHL	69	16	11	27	16	....	....	....	....	....
1984-85	Kelowna	WHL	51	35	38	73	58	6	5	2	7	8
1985-86	Spokane	WHL	52	45	45	90	57	9	6	7	13	19
1986-87	Spokane	WHL	46	45	55	100	71	5	2	7	9	6
	Sherbrooke	AHL	....	....	....	....	....	10	2	7	9	4
1987-88	Sherbrooke	AHL	77	26	48	74	83	6	1	3	4	6
1988-89	**Montreal**	**NHL**	**49**	**8**	**16**	**24**	**16**	**9**	**1**	**1**	**2**	
	Sherbrooke	AHL	7	6	5	11	7	....	....	....	....	....
1989-90	**Montreal**	**NHL**	**57**	**9**	**15**	**24**	**28**	**8**	**2**	**0**	**2**	
1990-91	**Montreal**	**NHL**	**51**	**6**	**9**	**15**	**10**	**13**	**5**	**3**	**8**	
1991-92	**Montreal**	**NHL**	**79**	**23**	**27**	**50**	**57**	**11**	**2**	**4**	**6**	
1992-93	**Edmonton**	**NHL**	**60**	**10**	**10**	**20**	**47**	....	....	....	....	....
	Minnesota	**NHL**	**8**	**0**	**1**	**1**	**2**	....	....	....	....	....
1993-94	**Dallas**	**NHL**	**76**	**17**	**14**	**31**	**31**	**9**	**3**	**1**	**4**	
	NHL Totals		**380**	**73**	**92**	**165**	**191**	**50**	**13**	**9**	**22**	**26**

Traded to **Edmonton** by **Montreal** with Shayne Corson and Vladimir Vujtek for Vincent Damphousse and Edmonton's fourth round choice (Adam Wiesel) in 1993 Entry Draft, August 27, 1992. Traded to **Minnesota** by **Edmonton** for Todd Elik, March 5, 1993.

GILHEN, RANDY (GIHL-uhn) WPG.

Center. Shoots left. 6', 190 lbs. Born, Zweibrucken, W. Germany, June 13, 1963.
(Hartford's 6th choice, 109th overall, in 1982 Entry Draft).

			Regular Season					Playoffs				
Season	Club	Lea	GP	G	A	TP	PIM	GP	G	A	TP	PIM
1980-81	Saskatoon	WHL	68	10	5	15	154	....	....	....	....	....
1981-82	Saskatoon	WHL	25	15	9	24	45	....	....	....	....	....
	Winnipeg	WHL	36	26	28	54	42	....	....	....	....	....
1982-83	**Hartford**	**NHL**	**2**	**0**	**1**	**1**	**0**	....	....	....	....	....
	Winnipeg	WHL	71	57	44	101	84	3	2	2	4	0
1983-84	Binghamton	AHL	73	8	12	20	72	....	....	....	....	....
1984-85	Salt Lake	IHL	57	20	20	40	28	....	....	....	....	....
	Binghamton	AHL	18	3	3	6	9	8	4	1	5	16
1985-86	Fort Wayne	IHL	82	44	40	84	48	15	10	8	18	6
1986-87	**Winnipeg**	**NHL**	**2**	**0**	**0**	**0**	**0**	....	....	....	....	....
	Sherbrooke	AHL	75	36	29	65	44	17	7	13	20	10
1987-88	**Winnipeg**	**NHL**	**13**	**3**	**2**	**5**	**15**	**4**	**1**	**0**	**1**	**10**
	Moncton	AHL	68	40	47	87	51	....	....	....	....	....
1988-89	**Winnipeg**	**NHL**	**64**	**5**	**3**	**8**	**38**	....	....	....	....	....
1989-90	**Pittsburgh**	**NHL**	**61**	**5**	**11**	**16**	**54**	....	....	....	....	....
1990-91	**Pittsburgh**	**NHL**	**72**	**15**	**10**	**25**	**51**	**16**	**1**	**0**	**1**	**14**
1991-92	**Los Angeles**	**NHL**	**33**	**3**	**6**	**9**	**14**	....	....	....	....	....
	NY Rangers	**NHL**	**40**	**7**	**7**	**14**	**14**	**13**	**1**	**2**	**3**	**2**
1992-93	**NY Rangers**	**NHL**	**33**	**3**	**2**	**5**	**8**	....	....	....	....	....
	Tampa Bay	**NHL**	**11**	**0**	**2**	**2**	**6**	....	....	....	....	....
1993-94	**Florida**	**NHL**	**20**	**4**	**4**	**8**	**16**	....	....	....	....	....
	Winnipeg	**NHL**	**40**	**3**	**3**	**6**	**34**	....	....	....	....	....
	NHL Totals		**391**	**48**	**51**	**99**	**250**	**33**	**3**	**2**	**5**	**26**

Signed as a free agent by **Winnipeg**, November 8, 1985. Traded to **Pittsburgh** by **Winnipeg** with Jim Kyte and Andrew McBain for Randy Cunneyworth, Rick Tabaracci and Dave McLlwain, June 17, 1989. Claimed by **Minnesota** from **Pittsburgh** in Expansion Draft, May 30, 1991. Traded to **Los Angeles** by **Minnesota** with Charlie Huddy, Jim Thomson and NY Rangers' fourth round choice (previously acquired by Minnesota — Los Angeles selected Alexei Zhitnik) in 1991 Entry Draft for Todd Elik, June 22, 1991. Traded to **NY Rangers** by **Los Angeles** for Corey Millen, December 23, 1991. Traded to **Tampa Bay** by **NY Rangers** for Mike Hartman, March 22, 1993. Claimed by **Florida** from **Tampa Bay** in Expansion Draft, June 24, 1993. Traded to **Winnipeg** by **Florida** for Stu Barnes and St. Louis' sixth round choice (previously acquired by Winnipeg — later traded to Edmonton — later traded to Winnipeg — Winnipeg selected Chris Kibermanis), November 25, 1993.

GILL, HAL BOS.

Defense. Shoots left. 6'6", 200 lbs. Born, Concord, MA, April 6, 1975.
(Boston's 8th choice, 207th overall, in 1993 Entry Draft).

			Regular Season					Playoffs				
Season	Club	Lea	GP	G	A	TP	PIM	GP	G	A	TP	PIM
1992-93	Nashoba	HS	20	25	25	50	....	....	....	....	....	....
1993-94	Providence	NCAA	31	1	2	3	26	....	....	....	....	....

GILL, TODD (GIHL) TOR.

Defense. Shoots left. 6', 185 lbs. Born, Brockville, Ont., November 9, 1965.
(Toronto's 2nd choice, 25th overall, in 1984 Entry Draft).

			Regular Season					Playoffs				
Season	Club	Lea	GP	G	A	TP	PIM	GP	G	A	TP	PIM
1982-83	Windsor	OHL	70	12	24	36	108	3	0	0	0	11
1983-84	Windsor	OHL	68	9	48	57	184	3	1	1	2	10
1984-85	**Toronto**	**NHL**	**10**	**1**	**0**	**1**	**13**	....	....	....	....	....
	Windsor	OHL	53	17	40	57	148	4	0	1	1	14
1985-86	**Toronto**	**NHL**	**15**	**1**	**2**	**3**	**28**	**1**	**0**	**0**	**0**	**0**
	St. Catharines	AHL	58	8	25	33	90	10	1	6	7	17
1986-87	**Toronto**	**NHL**	**61**	**4**	**27**	**31**	**92**	**13**	**2**	**2**	**4**	**42**
	Newmarket	AHL	11	1	8	9	33	....	....	....	....	....
1987-88	**Toronto**	**NHL**	**65**	**8**	**17**	**25**	**131**	**6**	**1**	**3**	**4**	**20**
	Newmarket	AHL	2	0	1	1	2	....	....	....	....	....
1988-89	**Toronto**	**NHL**	**59**	**11**	**14**	**25**	**72**	....	....	....	....	....
1989-90	**Toronto**	**NHL**	**48**	**1**	**14**	**15**	**92**	**5**	**0**	**3**	**3**	**16**
1990-91	**Toronto**	**NHL**	**72**	**2**	**22**	**24**	**113**	....	....	....	....	....
1991-92	**Toronto**	**NHL**	**74**	**2**	**15**	**17**	**91**	....	....	....	....	....
1992-93	**Toronto**	**NHL**	**69**	**11**	**32**	**43**	**66**	**21**	**1**	**10**	**11**	**26**
1993-94	**Toronto**	**NHL**	**45**	**4**	**24**	**28**	**44**	**18**	**1**	**5**	**6**	**37**
	NHL Totals		**518**	**45**	**167**	**212**	**742**	**64**	**5**	**23**	**28**	**141**

GILLAM, SEAN DET.

Defense. Shoots right. 6'2", 187 lbs. Born, Lethbridge, Alta., May 7, 1976.
(Detroit's 3rd choice, 75th overall, in 1994 Entry Draft).

			Regular Season					Playoffs				
Season	Club	Lea	GP	G	A	TP	PIM	GP	G	A	TP	PIM
1992-93	Spokane	WHL	70	6	27	33	121	10	0	2	2	10
1993-94	Spokane	WHL	70	7	17	24	106	3	0	0	0	6

GILLINGHAM, TODD

Left wing. Shoots left. 6'2", 200 lbs. Born, Labrador City, Nfld., January 31, 1970.

			Regular Season					Playoffs				
Season	Club	Lea	GP	G	A	TP	PIM	GP	G	A	TP	PIM
1988-89	Verdun	QMJHL	67	16	25	41	253	....	....	....	....	....
1989-90	Trois-Rivières	QMJHL	62	22	36	58	349	6	3	1	4	72
1990-91a	Trois-Rivières	QMJHL	66	46	102	148	353	6	2	4	6	40
1991-92	St. John's	AHL	66	12	35	47	306	16	4	7	11	80
	Salt Lake	IHL	1	0	0	0	2	....	....	....	....	....
1992-93	Salt Lake	IHL	75	12	21	33	267	....	....	....	....	....
1993-94	St. John's	AHL	59	20	25	45	260	10	0	2	2	12

a QMJHL First All-Star Team (1991)

Signed as a free agent by **Calgary**, May 1, 1991. Traded to **Toronto** by **Calgary** for cash, January 15, 1992. Traded to **Calgary** by **Toronto** for cash, June 2, 1992. Traded to **Toronto** by **Calgary** with Paul Holden for Brad Miller and Jeff Perry, September 2, 1993.

GILMOUR, DOUG TOR.

Center. Shoots left. 5'11", 172 lbs. Born, Kingston, Ont., June 25, 1963.
(St. Louis' 4th choice, 134th overall, in 1982 Entry Draft).

			Regular Season					Playoffs				
Season	Club	Lea	GP	G	A	TP	PIM	GP	G	A	TP	PIM
1981-82	Cornwall	OHL	67	46	73	119	42	5	6	9	15	2
1982-83a	Cornwall	OHL	68	70	*107	*177	62	8	8	10	18	16
1983-84	**St. Louis**	**NHL**	**80**	**25**	**28**	**53**	**57**	**11**	**2**	**9**	**11**	**10**
1984-85	**St. Louis**	**NHL**	**78**	**21**	**36**	**57**	**49**	**3**	**1**	**1**	**2**	**2**
1985-86	**St. Louis**	**NHL**	**74**	**25**	**28**	**53**	**41**	**19**	**9**	**12**	***21**	**25**
1986-87	**St. Louis**	**NHL**	**80**	**42**	**63**	**105**	**58**	**6**	**2**	**2**	**4**	**16**
1987-88	**St. Louis**	**NHL**	**72**	**36**	**50**	**86**	**59**	**10**	**3**	**14**	**17**	**18**
1988-89	**Calgary**	**NHL**	**72**	**26**	**59**	**85**	**44**	**22**	**11**	**11**	**22**	**20**
1989-90	**Calgary**	**NHL**	**78**	**24**	**67**	**91**	**54**	**6**	**3**	**1**	**4**	**8**
1990-91	**Calgary**	**NHL**	**78**	**20**	**61**	**81**	**144**	**7**	**1**	**1**	**2**	**0**
1991-92	**Calgary**	**NHL**	**38**	**11**	**27**	**38**	**46**	....	....	....	....	....
	Toronto	**NHL**	**40**	**15**	**34**	**49**	**32**	....	....	....	....	....
1992-93b	**Toronto**	**NHL**	**83**	**32**	**95**	**127**	**100**	**21**	**10**	***25**	**35**	**30**
1993-94	**Toronto**	**NHL**	**83**	**27**	**84**	**111**	**105**	**18**	**6**	**22**	**28**	**42**
	NHL Totals		**856**	**304**	**632**	**936**	**789**	**123**	**48**	**98**	**146**	**171**

a OHL First All-Star Team (1983)
b Won Frank J. Selke Trophy (1993)

Played in NHL All-Star Game (1993, 1994)

Traded to **Calgary** by **St. Louis** with Mark Hunter, Steve Bozek and Michael Dark for Mike Bullard, Craig Coxe and Tim Corkery, September 6, 1988. Traded to **Toronto** by **Calgary** with Jamie Macoun, Ric Nattress, Kent Manderville and Rick Wamsley for Gary Leeman, Alexander Godynyuk, Jeff Reese, Michel Petit and Craig Berube, January 2, 1992.

GIRARD, RICK VAN.

Center. Shoots left. 5'11", 175 lbs. Born, Edmonton, Alta., May 1, 1974.
(Vancouver's 2nd choice, 46th overall, in 1993 Entry Draft).

			Regular Season					Playoffs				
Season	Club	Lea	GP	G	A	TP	PIM	GP	G	A	TP	PIM
1991-92	Swift Current	WHL	45	14	17	31	6	8	2	0	2	2
1992-93ab	Swift Current	WHL	72	71	70	141	25	17	9	17	26	10
1993-94a	Swift Current	WHL	58	40	49	89	43	7	1	8	9	6
	Hamilton	AHL	1	1	1	2	0	....	....	....	....	....

a WHL East First All-Star Team (1993, 1994)
b Canadian Major Junior Sportsmanlike Player of the Year (1993)

GLADNEY, JASON

Defense. Shoots left. 6'1", 190 lbs. Born, Toronto, Ont., January 26, 1974.
(Washington's 8th choice, 225th overall, in 1993 Entry Draft).

			Regular Season					Playoffs				
Season	Club	Lea	GP	G	A	TP	PIM	GP	G	A	TP	PIM
1991-92	Kitchener	OHL	62	2	18	20	54	14	1	1	2	14
1992-93	Kitchener	OHL	64	16	55	71	82	7	2	11	13	14
1993-94	Kitchener	OHL	61	18	74	92	96	5	1	8	9	10
	Portland	AHL	2	0	0	0	0	2	0	0	0	0

GLYNN, BRIAN (GLIHN) VAN.

Defense. Shoots left. 6'4", 220 lbs. Born, Iserlohn, West Germany, November 23, 1967.
(Calgary's 2nd choice, 37th overall, in 1986 Entry Draft).

			Regular Season					Playoffs				
Season	Club	Lea	GP	G	A	TP	PIM	GP	G	A	TP	PIM
1984-85	Saskatoon	WHL	12	1	0	1	2	3	0	0	0	0
1985-86	Saskatoon	WHL	66	7	25	32	131	13	0	3	3	30
1986-87	Saskatoon	WHL	44	2	26	28	163	11	1	3	4	19
1987-88	**Calgary**	**NHL**	**67**	**5**	**14**	**19**	**87**	**1**	**0**	**0**	**0**	**0**
1988-89	**Calgary**	**NHL**	**9**	**0**	**1**	**1**	**19**	....	....	....	....	....
	Salt Lake	IHL	31	3	10	13	105	14	3	7	10	31
1989-90	**Calgary**	**NHL**	**1**	**0**	**0**	**0**	**0**	....	....	....	....	....
ab	Salt Lake	IHL	80	17	44	61	164	....	....	....	....	....
1990-91	Salt Lake	IHL	8	1	3	4	18	....	....	....	....	....
	Minnesota	**NHL**	**66**	**8**	**11**	**19**	**83**	**23**	**2**	**6**	**8**	**18**
1991-92	**Minnesota**	**NHL**	**37**	**2**	**12**	**14**	**24**	....	....	....	....	....
	Edmonton	**NHL**	**25**	**2**	**6**	**8**	**6**	**16**	**4**	**1**	**5**	**12**
1992-93	**Edmonton**	**NHL**	**64**	**4**	**12**	**16**	**60**	....	....	....	....	....
1993-94	**Ottawa**	**NHL**	**48**	**2**	**13**	**15**	**41**	....	....	....	....	....
	Vancouver	**NHL**	**16**	**0**	**0**	**0**	**12**	**17**	**0**	**3**	**3**	**10**
	NHL Totals		**333**	**23**	**69**	**92**	**332**	**57**	**6**	**10**	**16**	**40**

a IHL First All-Star Team (1990)
b Won Governors' Trophy (Outstanding Defenseman - IHL) (1990)

Traded to **Minnesota** by **Calgary** for Frantisek Musil, October 26, 1990. Traded to **Edmonton** by **Minnesota** for David Shaw, January 21, 1992. Traded to **Ottawa** by **Edmonton** for Ottawa's eighth round choice (Rob Quinn) in 1994 Entry Draft, September 15, 1993. Claimed on waivers by **Vancouver** from **Ottawa**, February 5, 1994.

GODBOUT, DANIEL TOR.

Defense. Shoots left. 6'2", 195 lbs. Born, Grand Falls, N.B., March 20, 1975.

			Regular Season					Playoffs				
Season	Club	Lea	GP	G	A	TP	PIM	GP	G	A	TP	PIM
1991-92	Belleville	OHL	60	1	8	9	44	5	0	1	1	5
1992-93	Belleville	OHL	65	2	17	19	66	7	0	1	1	4
1993-94	Belleville	OHL	66	0	15	15	45	12	0	1	1	10

Signed as a free agent by **Toronto**, 1993.

GODYNYUK, ALEXANDER (goh-dih-NYOOK) HFD.

Defense. Shoots left. 6', 207 lbs. Born, Kiev, USSR, January 27, 1970.
(Toronto's 5th choice, 115th overall, in 1990 Entry Draft).

			Regular Season					Playoffs				
Season	Club	Lea	GP	G	A	TP	PIM	GP	G	A	TP	PIM
1986-87	Sokol Kiev	USSR	9	0	1	1	2	....	....	....	....	....
1987-88	Sokol Kiev	USSR	2	0	0	0	2	....	....	....	....	....
1988-89	Sokol Kiev	USSR	30	3	3	6	12	....	....	....	....	....
1989-90	Sokol Kiev	USSR	37	3	2	5	31	....	....	....	....	....
1990-91	Sokol Kiev	USSR	19	3	1	4	20	....	....	....	....	....
	Toronto	**NHL**	**18**	**0**	**3**	**3**	**16**	....	....	....	....	....
	Newmarket	AHL	11	0	1	1	29	....	....	....	....	....
1991-92	**Toronto**	**NHL**	**31**	**3**	**6**	**9**	**59**	....	....	....	....	....
	Calgary	**NHL**	**6**	**0**	**1**	**1**	**4**	....	....	....	....	....
	Salt Lake	IHL	17	2	1	3	24	....	....	....	....	....
1992-93	**Calgary**	**NHL**	**27**	**3**	**4**	**7**	**19**	....	....	....	....	....
1993-94	**Florida**	**NHL**	**26**	**0**	**10**	**10**	**35**	....	....	....	....	....
	Hartford	**NHL**	**43**	**3**	**9**	**12**	**40**	....	....	....	....	....
	NHL Totals		**151**	**9**	**33**	**42**	**173**	....	....	....	....	....

Traded to **Calgary** by **Toronto** with Craig Berube, Gary Leeman, Michel Petit and Jeff Reese for Doug Gilmour, Jamie Macoun, Ric Nattress, Rick Wamsley and Kent Manderville, January 2, 1992. Claimed by **Florida** from **Calgary** in Expansion Draft, June 24, 1993. Traded to **Hartford** by **Florida** for Jim McKenzie, December 16, 1993.

GOLDEN, RYAN — BOS.

Center. Shoots left. 6'3", 197 lbs. Born, Boston, MA, October 15, 1974.
(Boston's 7th choice, 181st overall, in 1993 Entry Draft).

			Regular Season					Playoffs				
Season	Club	Lea	GP	G	A	TP	PIM	GP	G	A	TP	PIM
1992-93	Reading	HS	18	19	15	34	....	....	....	....	....	....
1993-94	Lowell	HE	14	0	3	3	12	....	....	....	....	....

GOLUBOVSKY, YAN (goh-luh-BOHV-skee) — DET.

Defense. Shoots right. 6'3", 183 lbs. Born, Novosibirsk, USSR, March 9, 1976.
(Detroit's 1st choice, 23rd overall, in 1994 Entry Draft).

			Regular Season					Playoffs				
Season	Club	Lea	GP	G	A	TP	PIM	GP	G	A	TP	PIM
1993-94	Mosc. D'amo 2	CIS 3				UNAVAILABLE						

GONCHAR, SERGEI (gohn-CHAR) — WSH.

Defense. Shoots left. 6'2", 212 lbs. Born, Chelyabinsk, USSR, April 13, 1974.
(Washington's 1st choice, 14th overall, in 1992 Entry Draft).

			Regular Season					Playoffs				
Season	Club	Lea	GP	G	A	TP	PIM	GP	G	A	TP	PIM
1991-92	Chelyabinsk	CIS	31	1	0	1	6	....	....	....	....	....
1992-93	Moscow D'amo	CIS	31	1	3	4	70	10	0	0	0	12
1993-94	Moscow D'amo	CIS	44	4	5	9	36	10	0	3	3	14
	Portland	AHL	....	....	....	....	....	2	0	0	0	0

GONEAU, DANIEL — BOS.

Left wing. Shoots left. 6'1", 196 lbs. Born, Montreal, Que., January 16, 1976.
(Boston's 2nd choice, 47th overall, in 1994 Entry Draft).

			Regular Season					Playoffs				
Season	Club	Lea	GP	G	A	TP	PIM	GP	G	A	TP	PIM
1992-93	Laval	QMJHL	62	16	25	41	44	13	0	4	4	4
1993-94	Laval	QMJHL	68	29	57	86	81	19	8	21	29	45

GORDIOUK, VIKTOR (gohr-dee-YOOK) — BUF.

Left wing. Shoots right. 5'10", 176 lbs. Born, Odintsovo, USSR, April 11, 1970.
(Buffalo's 6th choice, 142nd overall, in 1990 Entry Draft).

			Regular Season					Playoffs				
Season	Club	Lea	GP	G	A	TP	PIM	GP	G	A	TP	PIM
1986-87	Soviet Wings	USSR	2	0	0	0	0	....	....	....	....	....
1987-88	Soviet Wings	USSR	26	2	2	4	6	....	....	....	....	....
1988-89	Soviet Wings	USSR	41	5	1	6	10	....	....	....	....	....
1989-90	Soviet Wings	USSR	48	11	4	15	24	....	....	....	....	....
1990-91	Soviet Wings	USSR	46	12	10	22	22	....	....	....	....	....
1991-92	Soviet Wings	CIS	42	16	7	23	24	....	....	....	....	....
1992-93	**Buffalo**	**NHL**	**16**	**3**	**6**	**9**	**0**	....	....	....	....	....
	Rochester	AHL	35	11	14	25	8	17	9	9	18	4
1993-94	Rochester	AHL	74	28	39	67	26	4	3	0	3	2
	NHL Totals		**16**	**3**	**6**	**9**	**0**	....	....	....	....	....

GORDON, ROBB — VAN.

Center. Shoots right. 5'11", 170 lbs. Born, Murrayville, B.C., January 13, 1976.
(Vancouver's 2nd choice, 39th overall, in 1994 Entry Draft).

			Regular Season					Playoffs				
Season	Club	Lea	GP	G	A	TP	PIM	GP	G	A	TP	PIM
1992-93	Powell River	BCJHL	60	55	38	93	76	....	....	....	....	....
1993-94	Powell River	BCJHL	60	69	89	158	141	....	....	....	....	....

GORENKO, DMITRI (goh-REHN-koh) — HFD.

Left wing. Shoots left. 6', 165 lbs. Born, Barnaul, USSR, February 13, 1975.
(Hartford's 6th choice, 214th overall, in 1993 Entry Draft).

			Regular Season					Playoffs				
Season	Club	Lea	GP	G	A	TP	PIM	GP	G	A	TP	PIM
1991-92	CSKA	CIS	14	0	1	1	6	....	....	....	....	....
1992-93	CSKA	CIS	42	3	0	3	20	....	....	....	....	....
1993-94	CSKA	CIS	40	5	1	6	28	3	1	0	1	2

GOSSELIN, CHRISTIAN — N.J.

Defense. Shoots left. 6'4", 205 lbs. Born, St. Redempteur, Que., August 21, 1976.
(New Jersey's 5th choice, 129th overall, in 1994 Entry Draft).

			Regular Season					Playoffs				
Season	Club	Lea	GP	G	A	TP	PIM	GP	G	A	TP	PIM
1993-94	St-Hyacinthe	QMJHL	12	3	2	5	16	....	....	....	....	....

GOTZIAMAN, CHRIS

Right wing. Shoots right. 6'3", 200 lbs. Born, Roseau, MN, November 29, 1971.
(New Jersey's 3rd choice, 29th overall, in 1990 Entry Draft).

			Regular Season					Playoffs				
Season	Club	Lea	GP	G	A	TP	PIM	GP	G	A	TP	PIM
1990-91	North Dakota	WCHA	40	11	8	19	26	....	....	....	....	....
1991-92	North Dakota	WCHA	38	9	6	15	47	....	....	....	....	....
1992-93	North Dakota	WCHA	35	10	10	20	50	....	....	....	....	....
1993-94	North Dakota	WCHA	33	8	4	12	29	....	....	....	....	....
	Albany	AHL	3	1	1	2	0	....	....	....	....	....

GOULET, MICHEL (goo-LAY) — CHI.

Left wing. Shoots left. 6'1", 195 lbs. Born, Peribonka, Que., April 21, 1960.
(Quebec's 1st choice, 20th overall, in 1979 Entry Draft).

			Regular Season					Playoffs				
Season	Club	Lea	GP	G	A	TP	PIM	GP	G	A	TP	PIM
1976-77	Quebec	QJHL	37	17	18	35	9	14	3	8	11	19
1977-78	Quebec	QJHL	72	73	62	135	109	1	0	1	1	0
1978-79	Birmingham	WHA	78	28	30	58	65	....	....	....	....	....
1979-80	**Quebec**	**NHL**	**77**	**22**	**32**	**54**	**48**	....	....	....	....	....
1980-81	**Quebec**	**NHL**	**76**	**32**	**39**	**71**	**45**	**4**	**3**	**4**	**7**	**7**
1981-82	**Quebec**	**NHL**	**80**	**42**	**42**	**84**	**48**	**16**	**8**	**5**	**13**	**6**
1982-83a	**Quebec**	**NHL**	**80**	**57**	**48**	**105**	**51**	**4**	**0**	**0**	**0**	**6**
1983-84b	**Quebec**	**NHL**	**75**	**56**	**65**	**121**	**76**	**9**	**2**	**4**	**6**	**17**
1984-85	**Quebec**	**NHL**	**69**	**55**	**40**	**95**	**55**	**17**	**11**	**10**	**21**	**17**
1985-86b	**Quebec**	**NHL**	**75**	**53**	**51**	**104**	**64**	**3**	**1**	**2**	**3**	**10**
1986-87b	**Quebec**	**NHL**	**75**	**49**	**47**	**96**	**61**	**13**	**9**	**5**	**14**	**35**
1987-88a	**Quebec**	**NHL**	**80**	**48**	**58**	**106**	**56**	....	....	....	....	....
1988-89	**Quebec**	**NHL**	**69**	**26**	**38**	**64**	**67**	....	....	....	....	....
1989-90	**Quebec**	**NHL**	**57**	**16**	**29**	**45**	**42**	....	....	....	....	....
	Chicago	**NHL**	**8**	**4**	**1**	**5**	**9**	**14**	**2**	**4**	**6**	**6**
1990-91	**Chicago**	**NHL**	**74**	**27**	**38**	**65**	**65**	....	....	....	....	....
1991-92	**Chicago**	**NHL**	**75**	**22**	**41**	**63**	**69**	**9**	**3**	**4**	**7**	**6**
1992-93	**Chicago**	**NHL**	**63**	**23**	**21**	**44**	**43**	**3**	**0**	**1**	**1**	**0**
1993-94	**Chicago**	**NHL**	**56**	**16**	**14**	**30**	**26**	....	....	....	....	....
	NHL Totals		**1089**	**548**	**604**	**1152**	**825**	**92**	**39**	**39**	**78**	**110**

a NHL Second All-Star Team (1983, 1988)
b NHL First All-Star Team (1984, 1986, 1987)

Played in NHL All-Star Game (1983-86, 1988)

Traded to **Chicago** by **Quebec** with Greg Millen and Quebec's sixth round choice (Kevin St. Jacques) in 1991 Entry Draft for Mario Doyon, Everett Sanipass and Dan Vincelette, March 5, 1990.

GOVEDARIS, CHRIS (goh-va-DAIR-us)

Left wing. Shoots left. 6', 200 lbs. Born, Toronto, Ont., February 2, 1970.
(Hartford's 1st choice, 11th overall, in 1988 Entry Draft).

			Regular Season					Playoffs				
Season	Club	Lea	GP	G	A	TP	PIM	GP	G	A	TP	PIM
1986-87	Toronto	OHL	64	36	28	64	148	....	....	....	....	....
1987-88	Toronto	OHL	62	42	38	80	118	4	2	1	3	10
1988-89	Toronto	OHL	49	41	38	79	117	6	2	3	5	0
1989-90	**Hartford**	**NHL**	**12**	**0**	**1**	**1**	**6**	**2**	**0**	**0**	**0**	**2**
	Binghamton	AHL	14	3	3	6	4	....	....	....	....	....
	Hamilton	OHL	23	11	21	32	53	....	....	....	....	....
1990-91	**Hartford**	**NHL**	**14**	**1**	**3**	**4**	**4**	....	....	....	....	....
	Springfield	AHL	56	26	36	62	133	9	2	5	7	36
1991-92	Springfield	AHL	43	14	25	39	55	11	3	2	5	25
1992-93	**Hartford**	**NHL**	**7**	**1**	**0**	**1**	**0**	....	....	....	....	....
	Springfield	AHL	65	31	24	55	58	15	7	4	11	18
1993-94	**Toronto**	**NHL**	**12**	**2**	**2**	**4**	**14**	**2**	**0**	**0**	**0**	**0**
	St. John's	AHL	62	35	35	70	76	11	6	5	11	22
	NHL Totals		**45**	**4**	**6**	**10**	**24**	**4**	**0**	**0**	**0**	**2**

Signed as a free agent by **Toronto**, September 16, 1993.

GRACHEV, VLADIMIR — NYI

Left wing. Shoots left. 6', 178 lbs. Born, Moscow, USSR, January 28, 1973.
(NY Islanders' 6th choice, 152nd overall, in 1992 Entry Draft).

			Regular Season					Playoffs				
Season	Club	Lea	GP	G	A	TP	PIM	GP	G	A	TP	PIM
1991-92	Mosc. D'amo 2	CIS 3	62	13	3	16	26	....	....	....	....	....
1992-93	Moscow D'amo	CIS	33	2	1	3	26	7	0	0	0	2
1993-94	Moscow D'amo	CIS	36	4	3	7	10	6	0	0	0	4

GRAHAM, DIRK — CHI.

Left/Right wing. Shoots right. 5'11", 198 lbs. Born, Regina, Sask., July 29, 1959.
(Vancouver's 5th choice, 89th overall, in 1979 Entry Draft).

			Regular Season					Playoffs				
Season	Club	Lea	GP	G	A	TP	PIM	GP	G	A	TP	PIM
1975-76	Regina	WCHL	2	0	0	0	0	6	1	1	2	5
1976-77	Regina	WCHL	65	37	28	65	66	....	....	....	....	....
1977-78	Regina	WCHL	72	49	61	110	87	13	15	19	34	37
1978-79	Regina	WHL	71	48	60	108	252	....	....	....	....	....
1979-80	Dallas	CHL	62	17	15	32	96	....	....	....	....	....
1980-81	Fort Wayne	IHL	6	1	2	3	12	....	....	....	....	....
a	Toledo	IHL	61	40	45	85	88	....	....	....	....	....
1981-82	Toledo	IHL	72	49	56	105	68	13	10	11	*21	8
1982-83b	Toledo	IHL	78	70	55	125	88	11	13	7	*20	30
1983-84	**Minnesota**	**NHL**	**6**	**1**	**1**	**2**	**0**	**1**	**0**	**0**	**0**	**2**
c	Salt Lake	CHL	57	37	57	94	72	5	3	8	11	2
1984-85	**Minnesota**	**NHL**	**36**	**12**	**11**	**23**	**23**	**9**	**0**	**4**	**4**	**7**
	Springfield	AHL	37	20	28	48	41	....	....	....	....	....
1985-86	**Minnesota**	**NHL**	**80**	**22**	**33**	**55**	**87**	**5**	**3**	**1**	**4**	**2**
1986-87	**Minnesota**	**NHL**	**76**	**25**	**29**	**54**	**142**	....	....	....	....	....
1987-88	**Minnesota**	**NHL**	**28**	**7**	**5**	**12**	**39**	....	....	....	....	....
	Chicago	**NHL**	**42**	**17**	**19**	**36**	**32**	**4**	**1**	**2**	**3**	**4**
1988-89	**Chicago**	**NHL**	**80**	**33**	**45**	**78**	**89**	**16**	**2**	**4**	**6**	**38**
1989-90	**Chicago**	**NHL**	**73**	**22**	**32**	**54**	**102**	**5**	**1**	**5**	**6**	**2**
1990-91d	**Chicago**	**NHL**	**80**	**24**	**21**	**45**	**88**	**6**	**1**	**2**	**3**	**17**
1991-92	**Chicago**	**NHL**	**80**	**17**	**30**	**47**	**89**	**18**	**7**	**5**	**12**	**8**
1992-93	**Chicago**	**NHL**	**84**	**20**	**17**	**37**	**139**	**4**	**0**	**0**	**0**	**0**
1993-94	**Chicago**	**NHL**	**67**	**15**	**18**	**33**	**45**	**6**	**0**	**1**	**1**	**4**
	NHL Totals		**732**	**215**	**261**	**476**	**875**	**74**	**15**	**24**	**39**	**84**

a IHL Second All-Star Team (1981)
b IHL First All-Star Team (1983)
c CHL First All-Star Team (1984)
d Won Frank J. Selke Trophy (1991)

Signed as a free agent by **Minnesota**, August 17, 1983. Traded to **Chicago** by **Minnesota** for Curt Fraser, January 4, 1988.

GRANATO, TONY — L.A.

Left wing. Shoots right. 5'10", 185 lbs. Born, Downers Grove, IL, July 25, 1964.
(NY Rangers' 5th choice, 120th overall, in 1982 Entry Draft).

			Regular Season						Playoffs				
Season	Club	Lea	GP	G	A	TP	PIM	GP	G	A	TP	PIM
1983-84	U. Wisconsin	WCHA	35	14	17	31	48	....	....	....	....	....
1984-85	U. Wisconsin	WCHA	42	33	34	67	94	....	....	....	....	....
1985-86	U. Wisconsin	WCHA	33	25	24	49	36	....	....	....	....	....
1986-87ab	U. Wisconsin	WCHA	42	28	45	73	64	....	....	....	....	....
1987-88	U.S. National	....	49	40	31	71	55	....	....	....	....	....
	U.S. Olympic	....	6	1	7	8	4	....	....	....	....	....
	Colorado	IHL	22	13	14	27	36	8	9	4	13	16
1988-89c	NY Rangers	NHL	78	36	27	63	140	4	1	1	2	21
1989-90	NY Rangers	NHL	37	7	18	25	77	....	....	....	....	....
	Los Angeles	NHL	19	5	6	11	45	10	5	4	9	12
1990-91	Los Angeles	NHL	68	30	34	64	154	12	1	4	5	28
1991-92	Los Angeles	NHL	80	39	29	68	187	6	1	5	6	10
1992-93	Los Angeles	NHL	81	37	45	82	171	24	6	11	17	50
1993-94	Los Angeles	NHL	50	7	14	21	150	....	....	....	....	....
	NHL Totals		413	161	173	334	924	56	14	25	39	121

a WCHA Second All-Star Team (1987)
b NCAA West Second All-American Team (1987)
c NHL All-Rookie Team (1989)
Traded to **Los Angeles** by **NY Rangers** with Tomas Sandstrom for Bernie Nicholls, January 20, 1990.

GRATTON, CHRIS — T.B.

Center. Shoots left. 6'3", 202 lbs. Born, Brantford, Ont., July 5, 1975.
(Tampa Bay's 1st choice, 3rd overall, in 1993 Entry Draft).

			Regular Season						Playoffs				
Season	Club	Lea	GP	G	A	TP	PIM	GP	G	A	TP	PIM
1991-92	Kingston	OHL	62	27	39	66	37	....	....	....	....	....
1992-93	Kingston	OHL	58	55	54	109	125	16	11	18	29	42
1993-94	**Tampa Bay**	**NHL**	84	13	29	42	123	....	....	....	....	....
	NHL Totals		84	13	29	42	123					

GRAVELLE, DAN

Center. Shoots left. 5'11", 190 lbs. Born, Montreal, Que., March 10, 1970.
(Chicago's 1st choice, 28th overall, in 1991 Supplemental Draft).

			Regular Season						Playoffs				
Season	Club	Lea	GP	G	A	TP	PIM	GP	G	A	TP	PIM
1989-90	Merrimack	H.E.	10	2	1	3	13	....	....	....	....	....
1990-91	Merrimack	H.E.	32	18	21	39	22	....	....	....	....	....
1991-92	Merrimack	H.E.	34	23	28	51	40	....	....	....	....	....
1992-93	Merrimack	H.E.	36	18	24	42	59	....	....	....	....	....
1993-94ab	Greensboro	ECHL	58	38	66	104	73	8	3	3	6	14
	Indianapolis	IHL	9	1	1	2	0	....	....	....	....	....

a ECHL Second All-Star Team (1994)
b ECHL Rookie of the Year (1994)

GRAVES, ADAM — NYR

Center. Shoots left. 6', 207 lbs. Born, Toronto, Ont., April 12, 1968.
(Detroit's 2nd choice, 22nd overall, in 1986 Entry Draft).

			Regular Season						Playoffs				
Season	Club	Lea	GP	G	A	TP	PIM	GP	G	A	TP	PIM
1985-86	Windsor	OHL	62	27	37	64	35	16	5	11	16	10
1986-87	Windsor	OHL	66	45	55	100	70	14	9	8	17	32
	Adirondack	AHL	....	....	....	....	....	5	0	1	1	0
1987-88	**Detroit**	**NHL**	9	0	1	1	8	....	....	....	....	....
	Windsor	OHL	37	28	32	60	107	12	14	18	*32	16
1988-89	**Detroit**	**NHL**	56	7	5	12	60	5	0	0	0	4
	Adirondack	AHL	14	10	11	21	28	14	11	7	18	17
1989-90	**Detroit**	**NHL**	13	0	1	1	13	....	....	....	....	....
	Edmonton	**NHL**	63	9	12	21	123	22	5	6	11	17
1990-91	**Edmonton**	**NHL**	76	7	18	25	127	18	2	4	6	22
1991-92	**NY Rangers**	**NHL**	80	26	33	59	139	10	5	3	8	22
1992-93	**NY Rangers**	**NHL**	84	36	29	65	148	....	....	....	....	....
1993-94ab	**NY Rangers**	**NHL**	84	52	27	79	127	23	10	7	17	24
	NHL Totals		465	137	126	263	745	78	22	20	42	89

a NHL Second All-Star Team (1994)
b Won King Clancy Memorial Trophy (1994)

Played in NHL All-Star Game (1994)

Traded to **Edmonton** by **Detroit** with Petr Klima, Joe Murphy and Jeff Sharples for Jimmy Carson, Kevin McClelland and Edmonton's fifth round choice (later traded to Montreal — Montreal selected Brad Layzell) in 1991 Entry Draft, November 2, 1989. Signed as a free agent by **NY Rangers**, September 3, 1991.

GREEN, TRAVIS — NYI

Center. Shoots right. 6'2", 200 lbs. Born, Castlegar, B.C., December 20, 1970.
(NY Islanders' 2nd choice, 23rd overall, in 1989 Entry Draft).

			Regular Season						Playoffs				
Season	Club	Lea	GP	G	A	TP	PIM	GP	G	A	TP	PIM
1986-87	Spokane	WHL	64	8	17	25	27	3	0	0	0	0
1987-88	Spokane	WHL	72	33	54	87	42	15	10	10	20	13
1988-89	Spokane	WHL	75	51	51	102	79	....	....	....	....	....
1989-90	Spokane	WHL	50	45	44	89	80	....	....	....	....	....
	Medicine Hat	WHL	25	15	24	39	19	3	0	0	0	2
1990-91	Capital Dist.	AHL	73	21	34	55	26	....	....	....	....	....
1991-92	Capital Dist.	AHL	71	23	27	50	10	7	0	4	4	21
1992-93	**NY Islanders**	**NHL**	61	7	18	25	43	12	3	1	4	6
	Capital Dist.	AHL	20	12	11	23	39	....	....	....	....	....
1993-94	**NY Islanders**	**NHL**	83	18	22	40	44	4	0	0	0	2
	NHL Totals		144	25	40	65	87	16	3	1	4	8

GREENLAW, JEFF — FLA.

Left wing. Shoots left. 6'1", 230 lbs. Born, Toronto, Ont., February 28, 1968.
(Washington's 1st choice, 19th overall, in 1986 Entry Draft).

			Regular Season						Playoffs				
Season	Club	Lea	GP	G	A	TP	PIM	GP	G	A	TP	PIM
1985-86	Cdn. National	....	57	3	16	19	81	....	....	....	....	....
1986-87	**Washington**	**NHL**	22	0	3	3	44	....	....	....	....	....
	Binghamton	AHL	4	0	2	2	0	....	....	....	....	....
1987-88	Binghamton	AHL	56	8	7	15	142	1	0	0	0	2
	Washington	**NHL**	....	....	....	....	....	1	0	0	0	19
1988-89	Baltimore	AHL	55	12	15	27	115	....	....	....	....	....
1989-90	Baltimore	AHL	10	3	2	5	26	7	1	0	1	13
1990-91	**Washington**	**NHL**	10	2	0	2	10	1	0	0	0	2
	Baltimore	AHL	50	17	17	34	93	3	1	1	2	2
1991-92	**Washington**	**NHL**	5	0	1	1	34	....	....	....	....	....
	Baltimore	AHL	37	6	8	14	57	....	....	....	....	....
1992-93	**Washington**	**NHL**	16	1	1	2	18	....	....	....	....	....
	Baltimore	AHL	49	12	14	26	66	7	3	1	4	0
1993-94	**Florida**	**NHL**	4	0	1	1	2	....	....	....	....	....
	Cincinnati	IHL	55	14	15	29	85	11	2	2	4	28
	NHL Totals		57	3	6	9	108	2	0	0	0	21

Signed as a free agent by **Florida**, July 14, 1993.

GREIG, MARK — (GREG) CGY.

Right wing. Shoots right. 5'11", 190 lbs. Born, High River, Alta., January 25, 1970.
(Hartford's 1st choice, 15th overall, in 1990 Entry Draft).

			Regular Season						Playoffs				
Season	Club	Lea	GP	G	A	TP	PIM	GP	G	A	TP	PIM
1987-88	Lethbridge	WHL	65	9	18	27	38	....	....	....	....	....
1988-89	Lethbridge	WHL	71	36	72	108	113	8	5	5	10	16
1989-90a	Lethbridge	WHL	65	55	80	135	149	18	11	21	32	35
1990-91	**Hartford**	**NHL**	4	0	0	0	0	....	....	....	....	....
	Springfield	AHL	73	32	55	87	73	17	2	6	8	22
1991-92	**Hartford**	**NHL**	17	0	5	5	6	....	....	....	....	....
	Springfield	AHL	50	20	27	47	38	9	1	1	2	20
1992-93	**Hartford**	**NHL**	22	1	7	8	27	....	....	....	....	....
	Springfield	AHL	55	20	38	58	86	....	....	....	....	....
1993-94	**Hartford**	**NHL**	31	4	5	9	31	....	....	....	....	....
	Springfield	AHL	4	0	4	4	21	....	....	....	....	....
	Toronto	**NHL**	13	2	2	4	10	....	....	....	....	....
	St. John's	AHL	9	4	6	10	0	11	4	2	6	26
	NHL Totals		87	7	19	26	74					

a WHL East First All-Star Team (1990)
Traded to **Toronto** by **Hartford** with Hartford's sixth round choice (later traded to NY Rangers — NY Rangers selected Yuri Litvinov) in 1994 Entry Draft for Ted Crowley, January 25, 1994. Signed as a free agent by **Calgary**, August 9, 1994.

GRENIER, DAVID — MTL.

Left wing. Shoots left. 6'2", 195 lbs. Born, Montreal, Que., February 5, 1975.

			Regular Season						Playoffs				
Season	Club	Lea	GP	G	A	TP	PIM	GP	G	A	TP	PIM
1992-93	Shawinigan	QMJHL	63	1	4	5	120	....	....	....	....	....
1993-94	Shawinigan	QMJHL	67	13	37	40	115	5	1	1	2	8

Signed as a free agent by **Montreal**, September 14, 1993.

GRETZKY, BRENT — (GRETZ-kee) T.B.

Center. Shoots left. 5'10", 160 lbs. Born, Brantford, Ont., February 20, 1972.
(Tampa Bay's 3rd choice, 49th overall, in 1992 Entry Draft).

			Regular Season						Playoffs				
Season	Club	Lea	GP	G	A	TP	PIM	GP	G	A	TP	PIM
1989-90	Belleville	OHL	66	15	32	47	30	11	0	0	0	0
1990-91	Belleville	OHL	66	26	56	82	25	6	3	3	6	2
1991-92	Belleville	OHL	62	43	78	121	37	....	....	....	....	....
1992-93	Atlanta	IHL	77	20	34	54	84	9	3	2	5	8
1993-94	**Tampa Bay**	**NHL**	10	1	2	3	2	....	....	....	....	....
	Atlanta	IHL	54	17	23	40	30	14	1	1	2	2
	NHL Totals		10	1	2	3	2					

GRETZKY, WAYNE (GRETZ-kee) L.A.

Center. Shoots left. 6', 180 lbs. Born, Brantford, Ont., January 26, 1961.

Season	Club	Lea	Regular Season GP	G	A	TP	PIM	Playoffs GP	G	A	TP	PIM
1976-77	Peterborough	OHA	3	0	3	3	0	....	....	....	....	....
1977-78a	S.S. Marie	OHA	64	70	112	182	14	13	6	20	26	0
1978-79	Indianapolis	WHA	8	3	3	6	0	....	....	....	....	....
bc	Edmonton	WHA	72	43	61	104	19	13	*10	10	*20	2
1979-80def	**Edmonton**	**NHL**	**79**	**51**	***86**	***137**	**21**	**3**	**2**	**1**	**3**	**0**
1980-81 dghij	**Edmonton**	**NHL**	**80**	**55**	***109**	***164**	**28**	**9**	**7**	**14**	**21**	**4**
1981-82 dghijklp	**Edmonton**	**NHL**	**80**	***92**	***120**	***212**	**26**	**5**	**5**	**7**	**12**	**8**
1982-83 dghilmn	**Edmonton**	**NHL**	**80**	***71**	***125**	***196**	**59**	**16**	**12**	***26**	***38**	**4**
1983-84 dghlp	**Edmonton**	**NHL**	**74**	***87**	***118**	***205**	**39**	**19**	**13**	***22**	***35**	**12**
1984-85 dghilmnopq	**Edmonton**	**NHL**	**80**	***73**	***135**	***208**	**52**	**18**	**17**	***30**	***47**	**4**
1985-86 dghijq	**Edmonton**	**NHL**	**80**	**52**	***163**	***215**	**46**	**10**	**8**	**11**	**19**	**2**
1986-87 dghlpq	**Edmonton**	**NHL**	**79**	***62**	***121**	***183**	**28**	**21**	**5**	***29**	***34**	**6**
1987-88fmo	**Edmonton**	**NHL**	**64**	**40**	***109**	**149**	**24**	**19**	**12**	***31**	***43**	**16**
1988-89dfr	**Los Angeles**	**NHL**	**78**	**54**	***114**	**168**	**26**	**11**	**5**	**17**	**22**	**0**
1989-90fh	**Los Angeles**	**NHL**	**73**	**40**	***102**	***142**	**42**	**7**	**3**	**7**	**10**	**0**
1990-91egh	**Los Angeles**	**NHL**	**78**	**41**	***122**	***163**	**16**	**12**	**4**	**11**	**15**	**2**
1991-92e	**Los Angeles**	**NHL**	**74**	**31**	***90**	**121**	**34**	**6**	**2**	**5**	**7**	**2**
1992-93	**Los Angeles**	**NHL**	**45**	**16**	**49**	**65**	**6**	**24**	***15**	***25**	***40**	**4**
1993-94efh	**Los Angeles**	**NHL**	**81**	**38**	***92**	***130**	**20**	....	....	....	....	....
	NHL Totals		**1125**	***803**	***1655**	***2458**	**467**	**180**	***110**	***236**	***346**	**64**

a OHA Second All-Star Team (1978)
b WHA Second All-Star Team (1979)
c Named WHA's Rookie of the Year (1979)
d Won Hart Trophy (1980, 1981, 1982, 1983, 1984, 1985, 1986, 1987, 1989)
e Won Lady Byng Trophy (1980, 1991, 1992, 1994)
f NHL Second All-Star Team (1980, 1988, 1989, 1990, 1994)
g NHL First All-Star Team (1981, 1982, 1983, 1984, 1985, 1986, 1987, 1991)
h Won Art Ross Trophy (1981, 1982, 1983, 1984, 1985, 1986, 1987, 1990, 1991, 1994)
i NHL record for assists in regular season (1981, 1982, 1983, 1985, 1986)
j NHL record for points in regular season (1981, 1982, 1986)
k NHL record for goals in regular season (1982)
l Won Lester B. Pearson Award (1982, 1983, 1984, 1985, 1987)
m NHL record for assists in one playoff year (1983, 1985, 1988)
n NHL record for points in one playoff year (1983, 1985)
o Won Conn Smythe Trophy (1985, 1988)
p NHL Plus/Minus Leader (1982, 1984, 1985, 1987)
q Selected Chrysler-Dodge/NHL Performer of the Year (1985, 1986, 1987)
r Won Dodge Performance of the Year Award (1989)

Played in NHL All-Star Game (1980-1986, 1988-94)

Reclaimed by **Edmonton** as an under-age junior prior to Expansion Draft, June 9, 1979. Claimed as priority selection by **Edmonton**, June 9, 1979. Traded to **Los Angeles** by **Edmonton** with Mike Krushelnyski and Marty McSorley for Jimmy Carson, Martin Gelinas, Los Angeles' first round choices in 1989 (acquired by New Jersey — New Jersey selected Jason Miller), 1991 (Martin Rucinsky) and 1993 (Nick Stajduhar) Entry Drafts and cash, August 9, 1988.

GRIER, MICHAEL ST.L.

Right wing. Shoots right. 6'1", 215 lbs. Born, Detroit, MI, January 5, 1975.
(St. Louis' 7th choice, 219th overall, in 1993 Entry Draft).

Season	Club	Lea	Regular Season GP	G	A	TP	PIM	Playoffs GP	G	A	TP	PIM
1992-93	St. Sebastian's	HS	22	16	27	43	32	....	....	....	....	....
1993-94	Boston U.	H.E.	39	9	9	18	56	....	....	....	....	....

GRIEVE, BRENT CHI.

Left wing. Shoots left. 6'1", 202 lbs. Born, Oshawa, Ont., May 9, 1969.
(NY Islanders' 4th choice, 65th overall, in 1989 Entry Draft).

Season	Club	Lea	Regular Season GP	G	A	TP	PIM	Playoffs GP	G	A	TP	PIM
1986-87	Oshawa	OHL	60	9	19	28	102	24	3	8	11	22
1987-88	Oshawa	OHL	55	19	20	39	122	7	0	1	1	8
1988-89	Oshawa	OHL	49	34	33	67	105	6	4	3	7	4
1989-90	Oshawa	OHL	62	46	47	93	125	17	10	10	20	26
1990-91	Capital Dist.	AHL	61	14	13	27	80	....	....	....	....	....
	Kansas City	IHL	5	2	2	4	2	....	....	....	....	....
1991-92	Capital Dist.	AHL	74	34	32	66	84	7	3	1	4	16
1992-93	Capital Dist.	AHL	79	34	28	62	122	4	1	1	2	10
1993-94	**NY Islanders**	**NHL**	**3**	**0**	**0**	**0**	**7**	....	....	....	....	....
	Salt Lake	IHL	22	9	5	14	30	....	....	....	....	....
	Edmonton	**NHL**	**24**	**13**	**5**	**18**	**14**	....	....	....	....	....
	Cape Breton	AHL	20	10	11	21	14	4	2	4	6	16
	NHL Totals		**27**	**13**	**5**	**18**	**21**	....	....	....	....	....

Traded to **Edmonton**, by **NY Islanders** for Marc Laforge, December 15, 1993. Signed as a free agent by **Chicago**, July 7, 1994.

GRILLO, DEAN S.J.

Right wing. Shoots right. 6'2", 210 lbs. Born, Bemidji, MN, December 8, 1972.
(San Jose's 9th choice, 155th overall, in 1991 Entry Draft).

Season	Club	Lea	Regular Season GP	G	A	TP	PIM	Playoffs GP	G	A	TP	PIM
1992-93	North Dakota	WCHA	29	7	4	11	14	....	....	....	....	....
1993-94	North Dakota	WCHA	38	11	14	25	14	....	....	....	....	....

GRIMES, JAKE OTT.

Center. Shoots left. 6'1", 196 lbs. Born, Montreal, Que., September 13, 1972.
(Ottawa's 10th choice, 217th overall, in 1992 Entry Draft).

Season	Club	Lea	Regular Season GP	G	A	TP	PIM	Playoffs GP	G	A	TP	PIM
1990-91	Belleville	OHL	66	31	41	72	16	6	2	0	2	0
1991-92	Belleville	OHL	66	44	69	113	18	5	4	0	4	0
1992-93	New Haven	AHL	76	18	20	38	30	....	....	....	....	....
1993-94	Thunder Bay	ColHL	10	7	5	12	6	....	....	....	....	....
	PEI	AHL	42	12	13	25	24	....	....	....	....	....

GRIMSON, STU ANA.

Left wing. Shoots left. 6'5", 227 lbs. Born, Kamloops, B.C., May 20, 1965.
(Calgary's 8th choice, 143rd overall, in 1985 Entry Draft).

Season	Club	Lea	Regular Season GP	G	A	TP	PIM	Playoffs GP	G	A	TP	PIM
1982-83	Regina	WHL	48	0	1	1	105	5	0	0	0	14
1983-84	Regina	WHL	63	8	8	16	131	21	0	1	1	29
1984-85	Regina	WHL	71	24	32	56	248	8	1	2	3	14
1985-86	U. Manitoba	CWUAA	12	7	4	11	113	3	1	1	2	20
1986-87	U. Manitoba	CWUAA	29	8	8	16	67	14	4	2	6	28
1987-88	Salt Lake	IHL	38	9	5	14	268	....	....	....	....	....
1988-89	**Calgary**	**NHL**	**1**	**0**	**0**	**0**	**5**	....	....	....	....	....
	Salt Lake	IHL	72	9	18	27	397	14	2	3	5	86
1989-90	**Calgary**	**NHL**	**3**	**0**	**0**	**0**	**17**	....	....	....	....	....
	Salt Lake	IHL	62	8	8	16	319	4	0	0	0	8
1990-91	**Chicago**	**NHL**	**35**	**0**	**1**	**1**	**183**	**5**	**0**	**0**	**0**	**46**
1991-92	**Chicago**	**NHL**	**54**	**2**	**2**	**4**	**234**	**14**	**0**	**1**	**1**	**10**
	Indianapolis	IHL	5	1	1	2	17	....	....	....	....	....
1992-93	**Chicago**	**NHL**	**78**	**1**	**1**	**2**	**193**	**2**	**0**	**0**	**0**	**4**
1993-94	**Anaheim**	**NHL**	**77**	**1**	**5**	**6**	**199**	....	....	....	....	....
	NHL Totals		**248**	**4**	**9**	**13**	**831**	**21**	**0**	**1**	**1**	**60**

Claimed by **Chicago** on conditional waivers, October 1, 1990. Claimed by **Anaheim** from **Chicago** in Expansion Draft, June 24, 1993.

GROLEAU, FRANCOIS CGY.

Defense. Shoots left. 6', 200 lbs. Born, Longueuil, Que., January 23, 1973.
(Calgary's 2nd choice, 41st overall, in 1991 Entry Draft).

Season	Club	Lea	Regular Season GP	G	A	TP	PIM	Playoffs GP	G	A	TP	PIM
1989-90a	Shawinigan	QMJHL	65	11	54	65	80	6	0	1	1	12
1990-91	Shawinigan	QMJHL	70	9	60	69	70	6	0	3	3	2
1991-92b	Shawinigan	QMJHL	65	8	70	78	74	10	5	15	20	8
1992-93	St-Jean	QMJHL	48	7	38	45	66	4	0	1	1	14
1993-94	Saint John	AHL	73	8	14	22	49	7	0	1	1	2

a QMJHL Second All-Star Team (1990)
b QMJHL First All-Star Team (1992)

GRONMAN, TUOMAS (GROHN-mahn) QUE.

Defense. Shoots right. 6'3", 198 lbs. Born, Viitasaari, Finland, March 22, 1974.
(Quebec's 3rd choice, 29th overall, in 1992 Entry Draft).

Season	Club	Lea	Regular Season GP	G	A	TP	PIM	Playoffs GP	G	A	TP	PIM
1991-92	Tacoma	WHL	61	5	18	23	102	4	0	1	1	2
1992-93	Lukko	Fin.	45	2	11	13	46	3	1	0	1	2
1993-94	Lukko	Fin.	44	4	12	16	60	9	0	1	1	14

GRONVALL, JANNE (GROHN-vahl, YAH-neh) TOR.

Defense. Shoots left. 6'3", 195 lbs. Born, Rauma, Finland, July 17, 1973.
(Toronto's 5th choice, 101st overall, in 1992 Entry Draft).

Season	Club	Lea	Regular Season GP	G	A	TP	PIM	Playoffs GP	G	A	TP	PIM
1989-90	Lukko	Fin.	5	0	0	0	0	....	....	....	....	....
1990-91	Lukko	Fin.	40	2	8	10	30	....	....	....	....	....
1991-92	Lukko	Fin.	42	2	6	8	40	2	0	0	0	2
1992-93	Tappara	Fin.	46	1	7	8	54	....	....	....	....	....
1993-94	Tappara	Fin.	47	2	9	11	54	10	0	4	4	31
	St. John's	AHL	....	....	....	....	....	9	0	0	0	2

GROSEK, MICHAL WPG.

Left wing. Shoots right. 6'2", 180 lbs. Born, Vyskov, Czech., June 1, 1975.
(Winnipeg's 7th choice, 145th overall, in 1993 Entry Draft).

Season	Club	Lea	Regular Season GP	G	A	TP	PIM	Playoffs GP	G	A	TP	PIM
1992-93	ZPS Zlin	Czech.	17	1	3	4	....	....	....	....	....	....
1993-94	**Winnipeg**	**NHL**	**3**	**1**	**0**	**1**	**0**	....	....	....	....	....
	Tacoma	WHL	30	25	20	45	106	7	2	2	4	30
	Moncton	AHL	20	1	2	3	47	2	0	0	0	0
	NHL Totals		**3**	**1**	**0**	**1**	**0**	....	....	....	....	....

GROSS, PAVEL (GROHSS) NYI

Right wing. Shoots right. 6'3", 195 lbs. Born, Ustin Ogroh, Czech., May 11, 1968.
(NY Islanders' 7th choice, 111th overall, in 1988 Entry Draft).

Season	Club	Lea	Regular Season GP	G	A	TP	PIM	Playoffs GP	G	A	TP	PIM
1987-88	Sparta Praha	Czech.	29	4	6	10	10	....	....	....	....	....
1988-89	Sparta Praha	Czech.	39	13	9	22	22	....	....	....	....	....
1989-90	Sparta Praha	Czech.	36	10	9	19	....	....	....	....	....	....
1990-91	Freiburg	Ger.	32	11	24	35	66	....	....	....	....	....
1991-92	Freiburg	Ger.	43	15	22	37	59	....	....	....	....	....
1992-93	Freiburg	Ger.	41	11	20	31	62	8	5	5	10	6
1993-94	Mannheim	Ger.	42	14	24	38	30	3	0	0	0	16

GRUBA, TONY

Right wing. Shoots right. 6', 205 lbs. Born, St. Paul, MN, August 23, 1972.
(Detroit's 8th choice, 171st overall, in 1990 Entry Draft).

Season	Club	Lea	Regular Season GP	G	A	TP	PIM	Playoffs GP	G	A	TP	PIM
1990-91	St. Cloud St.	WCHA	29	1	5	6	34	....	....	....	....	....
1991-92	St. Cloud St.	WCHA	37	14	22	36	76	....	....	....	....	....
1992-93	St. Cloud St.	WCHA	35	15	27	42	79	....	....	....	....	....
1993-94	St. Cloud St.	WCHA	38	10	17	27	106	....	....	....	....	....
	Adirondack	AHL	1	1	0	1	0	....	....	....	....	....

GRUDEN, JOHN BOS.

Defense. Shoots left. 6', 189 lbs. Born, Hastings, MN, April 6, 1970.
(Boston's 7th choice, 168th overall, in 1990 Entry Draft).

Season	Club	Lea	Regular Season GP	G	A	TP	PIM	Playoffs GP	G	A	TP	PIM
1990-91	Ferris State	CCHA	37	4	11	15	27	....	....	....	....	....
1991-92	Ferris State	CCHA	37	9	14	23	24	....	....	....	....	....
1992-93	Ferris State	CCHA	41	16	14	30	58	....	....	....	....	....
1993-94ab	Ferris State	CCHA	38	11	25	36	52	....	....	....	....	....
	Boston	**NHL**	**7**	**0**	**1**	**1**	**2**	....	....	....	....	....
	NHL Totals		**7**	**0**	**1**	**1**	**2**	....	....	....	....	....

a CCHA First All-Star Team (1994)
b NCAA West First All-American Team (1994)

GRUHL, SCOTT (GROOL)

Left wing. Shoots left. 5'11", 185 lbs. Born, Port Colborne, Ont., September 13, 1959.

			Regular Season					Playoffs				
Season	Club	Lea	GP	G	A	TP	PIM	GP	G	A	TP	PIM
1978-79	Sudbury	OHA	68	35	49	94	78	10	5	7	12	15
1979-80	Binghamton	AHL	4	1	0	1	0	....	....	....	....	....
a	Saginaw	IHL	75	53	40	93	100	7	2	6	8	16
1980-81	Houston	CHL	4	0	0	0	0	....	....	....	....	....
	Saginaw	IHL	77	56	34	90	87	13	*11	8	*19	12
1981-82	**Los Angeles**	**NHL**	**7**	**2**	**1**	**3**	**2**	....	....	....	....	....
	New Haven	AHL	73	28	41	69	107	4	0	4	4	2
1982-83	**Los Angeles**	**NHL**	**7**	**0**	**2**	**2**	**4**	....	....	....	....	....
	New Haven	AHL	68	25	38	63	114	12	3	3	6	22
1983-84b	Muskegon	IHL	56	40	56	96	46	....	....	....	....	....
1984-85bc	Muskegon	IHL	82	62	64	126	102	17	7	16	23	25
1985-86a	Muskegon	IHL	82	*59	50	109	178	14	7	*13	20	22
1986-87	Muskegon	IHL	67	34	39	73	157	15	5	7	12	54
1987-88	**Pittsburgh**	**NHL**	**6**	**1**	**0**	**1**	**0**	....	....	....	....	....
	Muskegon	IHL	55	28	47	75	115	6	5	1	6	12
1988-89	Muskegon	IHL	79	37	55	92	163	14	8	11	19	37
1989-90	Muskegon	IHL	80	41	51	92	206	15	8	6	14	26
1990-91	Fort Wayne	IHL	59	23	47	70	109	19	4	6	10	39
1991-92a	Fort Wayne	IHL	78	44	61	105	196	6	2	2	4	48
1992-93	Fort Wayne	IHL	73	34	47	81	290	12	4	11	15	14
1993-94	Milwaukee	IHL	28	6	9	15	102	....	....	....	....	....
	Kalamazoo	IHL	30	15	12	27	85	5	1	4	5	26
	NHL Totals		**20**	**3**	**3**	**6**	**6**	....	....	....	....	....

a IHL Second All-Star Team (1980, 1986, 1992)
b IHL First All-Star Team (1984, 1985)
c Won James Gatschene Memorial Trophy (MVP - IHL) (1985)

Signed as a free agent by **Los Angeles**, October 11, 1979. Signed as a free agent by **Pittsburgh**, December 14, 1987.

GUERARD, DANIEL — OTT.

Right wing. Shoots right. 6'4", 215 lbs. Born, LaSalle, Que., April 9, 1974.
(Ottawa's 5th choice, 98th overall, in 1992 Entry Draft).

			Regular Season					Playoffs				
Season	Club	Lea	GP	G	A	TP	PIM	GP	G	A	TP	PIM
1991-92	Victoriaville	QMJHL	31	5	16	21	66	....	....	....	....	....
1992-93	Verdun	QMJHL	58	31	26	57	131	4	1	1	2	17
	New Haven	AHL	2	2	1	3	0	....	....	....	....	....
1993-94	Verdun	QMJHL	53	31	34	65	169	4	3	1	4	4
	PEI	AHL	3	0	0	0	17	....	....	....	....	....

GUERIN, BILL (GAIR-ihn) — N.J.

Right wing. Shoots right. 6'2", 200 lbs. Born, Wilbraham, MA, November 9, 1970.
(New Jersey's 1st choice, 5th overall, in 1989 Entry Draft).

			Regular Season					Playoffs				
Season	Club	Lea	GP	G	A	TP	PIM	GP	G	A	TP	PIM
1989-90	Boston College	H.E.	39	14	11	25	54	....	....	....	....	....
1990-91	Boston College	H.E.	38	26	19	45	102	....	....	....	....	....
	U.S. National	....	46	12	15	27	67	....	....	....	....	....
1991-92	**New Jersey**	**NHL**	**5**	**0**	**1**	**1**	**9**	**6**	**3**	**0**	**3**	**4**
	Utica	AHL	22	13	10	23	6	4	1	3	4	14
1992-93	**New Jersey**	**NHL**	**65**	**14**	**20**	**34**	**63**	**5**	**1**	**1**	**2**	**4**
	Utica	AHL	18	10	7	17	47	....	....	....	....	....
1993-94	**New Jersey**	**NHL**	**81**	**25**	**19**	**44**	**101**	**17**	**2**	**1**	**3**	**35**
	NHL Totals		**151**	**39**	**40**	**79**	**173**	**28**	**6**	**2**	**8**	**43**

GUILLET, ROBERT — MTL.

Right wing. Shoots right. 5'11", 189 lbs. Born, Montreal, Que., February 22, 1972.
(Montreal's 4th choice, 60th overall, in 1990 Entry Draft).

			Regular Season					Playoffs				
Season	Club	Lea	GP	G	A	TP	PIM	GP	G	A	TP	PIM
1989-90	Longueuil	QMJHL	69	32	40	72	132	7	2	1	3	15
1990-91a	Longueuil	QMJHL	69	55	32	87	96	8	4	7	11	27
1991-92b	Verdun	QMJHL	67	56	62	118	104	19	*14	11	*25	26
1992-93	Fredericton	AHL	42	16	15	31	38	1	0	0	0	0
	Wheeling	ECHL	15	16	14	30	8	....	....	....	....	....
1993-94	Fredericton	AHL	78	38	40	78	48	....	....	....	....	....

a QMJHL First All-Star Team (1991)
b QMJHL Second All-Star Team (1992)

GUIRESTANTE, JOHN — N.J.

Right wing. Shoots right. 6'2", 172 lbs. Born, Toronto, Ont., May 11, 1975.
(New Jersey's 5th choice, 110th overall, in 1993 Entry Draft).

			Regular Season					Playoffs				
Season	Club	Lea	GP	G	A	TP	PIM	GP	G	A	TP	PIM
1992-93	London	OHL	32	7	12	19	13	4	0	0	0	0
1993-94	London	OHL	29	3	12	15	29	....	....	....	....	....
	North Bay	OHL	13	1	1	2	7	....	....	....	....	....

GUNKO, YURI

Defense. Shoots left. 6'1", 187 lbs. Born, Kiev, USSR, February 28, 1972.
(St. Louis' 11th choice, 230th overall, in 1992 Entry Draft).

			Regular Season					Playoffs				
Season	Club	Lea	GP	G	A	TP	PIM	GP	G	A	TP	PIM
1990-91	Sokol Kiev	USSR	14	0	0	0	8	....	....	....	....	....
1991-92	Sokol Kiev	CIS	22	1	0	1	16	....	....	....	....	....
1992-93	Sokol Kiev	CIS	40	2	3	5	28	....	....	....	....	....
1993-94	Sokol Kiev	CIS	42	0	8	8	28	....	....	....	....	....

GUOLLA, STEPHEN — OTT.

Left wing. Shoots left. 6', 180 lbs. Born, Scarborough, Ont., March 15, 1973.
(Ottawa's 1st choice, 3rd overall, in 1994 Supplemental Draft).

			Regular Season					Playoffs				
Season	Club	Lea	GP	G	A	TP	PIM	GP	G	A	TP	PIM
1991-92	Michigan State	CCHA	33	4	9	13	8	....	....	....	....	....
1992-93	Michigan State	CCHA	39	19	35	54	6	....	....	....	....	....
1993-94ab	Michigan State	CCHA	41	23	46	69	16	....	....	....	....	....

a CCHA Second All-Star Team (1994)
b NCAA West Second All-American Team (1994)

GUSAROV, ALEXEI (goo-SAH-rahf) — QUE.

Defense. Shoots left. 6'3", 185 lbs. Born, Leningrad, USSR, July 8, 1964.
(Quebec's 11th choice, 213th overall, in 1988 Entry Draft).

			Regular Season					Playoffs				
Season	Club	Lea	GP	G	A	TP	PIM	GP	G	A	TP	PIM
1981-82	SKA Leningrad	USSR	20	1	2	3	16	....	....	....	....	....
1982-83	SKA Leningrad	USSR	42	2	1	3	32	....	....	....	....	....
1983-84	SKA Leningrad	USSR	43	2	3	5	32	....	....	....	....	....
1984-85	CSKA	USSR	36	3	2	5	26	....	....	....	....	....
1985-86	CSKA	USSR	40	3	5	8	30	....	....	....	....	....
1986-87	CSKA	USSR	38	4	7	11	24	....	....	....	....	....
1987-88	CSKA	USSR	39	3	2	5	28	....	....	....	....	....
1988-89	CSKA	USSR	42	5	4	9	37	....	....	....	....	....
1989-90	CSKA	USSR	42	4	7	11	42	....	....	....	....	....
1990-91	CSKA	USSR	15	0	0	0	12	....	....	....	....	....
	Quebec	**NHL**	**36**	**3**	**9**	**12**	**12**	....	....	....	....	....
	Halifax	AHL	2	0	3	3	2	....	....	....	....	....
1991-92	**Quebec**	**NHL**	**68**	**5**	**18**	**23**	**22**	....	....	....	....	....
	Halifax	AHL	3	0	0	0	0	....	....	....	....	....
1992-93	**Quebec**	**NHL**	**79**	**8**	**22**	**30**	**57**	**5**	**0**	**1**	**1**	**0**
1993-94	**Quebec**	**NHL**	**76**	**5**	**20**	**25**	**38**	....	....	....	....	....
	NHL Totals		**259**	**21**	**69**	**90**	**129**	**5**	**0**	**1**	**1**	**0**

GUSMANOV, RAVIL — WPG.

Left wing. Shoots left. 6'3", 185 lbs. Born, Naberezhnye Chelny, USSR, July 25, 1972.
(Winnipeg's 5th choice, 93rd overall, in 1993 Entry Draft).

			Regular Season					Playoffs				
Season	Club	Lea	GP	G	A	TP	PIM	GP	G	A	TP	PIM
1990-91	Chelyabinsk	USSR	15	0	0	0	10	....	....	....	....	....
1991-92	Chelyabinsk	CIS	38	4	4	8	20	....	....	....	....	....
1992-93	Chelyabinsk	CIS	39	15	8	23	30	....	....	....	....	....
1993-94	Chelyabinsk	CIS	43	18	9	27	51	....	....	....	....	....

GUY, KEVAN (GIGH) — NYI

Defense. Shoots right. 6'3", 202 lbs. Born, Edmonton, Alta., July 16, 1965.
(Calgary's 5th choice, 71st overall, in 1983 Entry Draft).

			Regular Season					Playoffs				
Season	Club	Lea	GP	G	A	TP	PIM	GP	G	A	TP	PIM
1982-83	Medicine Hat	WHL	69	7	20	27	89	5	0	3	3	16
1983-84	Medicine Hat	WHL	72	15	42	57	117	14	3	4	7	14
1984-85	Medicine Hat	WHL	31	7	17	24	46	10	1	2	3	2
1985-86	Moncton	AHL	73	4	20	24	56	10	0	2	2	6
1986-87	**Calgary**	**NHL**	**24**	**0**	**4**	**4**	**19**	**4**	**0**	**1**	**1**	**23**
	Moncton	AHL	46	2	10	12	38	....	....	....	....	....
1987-88	**Calgary**	**NHL**	**11**	**0**	**3**	**3**	**8**	....	....	....	....	....
	Salt Lake	IHL	61	6	30	36	51	19	1	6	7	26
1988-89	**Vancouver**	**NHL**	**45**	**2**	**2**	**4**	**34**	**1**	**0**	**0**	**0**	**0**
1989-90	**Vancouver**	**NHL**	**30**	**2**	**5**	**7**	**32**	....	....	....	....	....
	Milwaukee	IHL	29	2	11	13	33	....	....	....	....	....
1990-91	**Vancouver**	**NHL**	**39**	**1**	**6**	**7**	**39**	....	....	....	....	....
	Calgary	**NHL**	**4**	**0**	**0**	**0**	**4**	....	....	....	....	....
1991-92	**Calgary**	**NHL**	**3**	**0**	**0**	**0**	**2**	....	....	....	....	....
	Salt Lake	IHL	60	3	14	17	89	5	0	1	1	4
1992-93	Salt Lake	IHL	33	1	9	10	50	....	....	....	....	....
1993-94	Salt Lake	IHL	62	4	17	21	45	....	....	....	....	....
	NHL Totals		**156**	**5**	**20**	**25**	**138**	**5**	**0**	**1**	**1**	**23**

Traded to **Vancouver** by **Calgary** with Brian Bradley and Peter Bakovic for Craig Coxe, March 6, 1988. Traded to **Calgary** by **Vancouver** with Ron Stern and future considerations, March 5, 1991. Signed as a free agent by **NY Islanders**, September 18, 1993.

GUZIOR, RUSS — MTL.

Center. Shoots right. 5'10", 165 lbs. Born, Chicago, IL, January 12, 1974.
(Montreal's 13th choice, 281st overall, in 1993 Entry Draft).

			Regular Season					Playoffs				
Season	Club	Lea	GP	G	A	TP	PIM	GP	G	A	TP	PIM
1992-93	Culver Academy	HS	37	34	38	72	20	....	....	....	....	....
1993-94	Providence	H.E.	34	9	13	22	8	....	....	....	....	....

HAAS, DAVID (HAHS)

Left wing. Shoots left. 6'2", 200 lbs. Born, Toronto, Ont., June 23, 1968.
(Edmonton's 5th choice, 105th overall, in 1986 Entry Draft).

			Regular Season					Playoffs				
Season	Club	Lea	GP	G	A	TP	PIM	GP	G	A	TP	PIM
1985-86	London	OHL	62	4	13	17	91	5	0	1	1	0
1986-87	London	OHL	5	1	0	1	5	....	....	....	....	....
	Kitchener	OHL	4	0	1	1	4	....	....	....	....	....
	Belleville	OHL	55	10	13	23	86	6	3	0	3	13
1987-88a	Windsor	OHL	63	60	47	107	246	11	9	11	20	50
1988-89	Cape Breton	AHL	61	9	9	18	325	....	....	....	....	....
1989-90	Cape Breton	AHL	53	6	12	18	230	4	2	2	4	15
1990-91	**Edmonton**	**NHL**	**5**	**1**	**0**	**1**	**0**	....	....	....	....	....
	Cape Breton	AHL	60	24	23	47	137	3	0	2	2	12
1991-92	Cape Breton	AHL	16	3	7	10	32	....	....	....	....	....
	New Haven	AHL	50	13	23	36	97	5	3	0	3	13
1992-93	Cape Breton	AHL	73	22	56	78	121	16	11	13	24	36
1993-94	**Calgary**	**NHL**	**2**	**1**	**1**	**2**	**7**	....	....	....	....	....
	Saint John	AHL	37	11	17	28	108	....	....	....	....	....
	Phoenix	IHL	11	7	4	11	43	....	....	....	....	....
	NHL Totals		**7**	**2**	**1**	**3**	**7**	....	....	....	....	....

a OHL Second All-Star Team (1988)

Signed as a free agent by **Calgary**, August 10, 1993.

HAGGERTY, RYAN — EDM.

Center. Shoots left. 6'1", 185 lbs. Born, Rye, NY, May 2, 1973.
(Edmonton's 6th choice, 93rd overall, in 1991 Entry Draft).

			Regular Season					Playoffs				
Season	Club	Lea	GP	G	A	TP	PIM	GP	G	A	TP	PIM
1991-92	Boston College	H.E.	34	12	5	17	16	....	....	....	....	....
1992-93	Boston College	H.E.	32	6	5	11	12	....	....	....	....	....
1993-94	Boston College	H.E.	36	17	23	40	16	....	....	....	....	....

HAGGERTY, SEAN — TOR.

Left wing. Shoots left. 6'1", 186 lbs. Born, Rye, NY, February 11, 1976.
(Toronto's 2nd choice, 48th overall, in 1994 Entry Draft).

			Regular Season					Playoffs				
Season	Club	Lea	GP	G	A	TP	PIM	GP	G	A	TP	PIM
1992-93	Boston	Jr. B	72	70	92	162	....	....	....	....	....	....
1993-94	Detroit	OHL	60	31	32	63	21	17	9	10	19	11

HAKANSSON, JONAS — PHI.

Left wing. Shoots right. 6'1", 202 lbs. Born, Malmo, Sweden, January 4, 1974.
(Philadelphia's 8th choice, 199th overall, in 1992 Entry Draft).

			Regular Season					Playoffs				
Season	Club	Lea	GP	G	A	TP	PIM	GP	G	A	TP	PIM
1990-91	Malmo	Swe.	8	0	0	0	0	1	0	0	0	0
1991-92	Malmo Jrs.	Swe.			UNAVAILABLE							
1992-93	Malmo	Swe.	11	0	0	0	0	....	....	....	....	....
1993-94	Pantern	Swe. 2	26	9	5	14	20	....	....	....	....	....

HAKANSSON, MIKAEL — TOR.

Center. Shoots left. 6'1", 196 lbs. Born, Stockholm, Sweden, May 31, 1974.
(Toronto's 7th choice, 125th overall, in 1992 Entry Draft).

			Regular Season					Playoffs				
Season	Club	Lea	GP	G	A	TP	PIM	GP	G	A	TP	PIM
1990-91	Nacka	Swe.2	27	2	5	7	6	....	....	....	....	....
1991-92	Nacka	Swe.2	29	3	15	18	24	....	....	....	....	....
1992-93	Djurgarden	Swe.	40	0	1	1	6	3	0	0	0	0
1993-94	Djurgarden	Swe.	37	3	3	6	12	4	0	0	0	0

HAKSTOL, DAVID

Defense. Shoots right. 6'1", 200 lbs. Born, Warbery, Alta., July 30, 1968.

			Regular Season					Playoffs				
Season	Club	Lea	GP	G	A	TP	PIM	GP	G	A	TP	PIM
1989-90	North Dakota	WCHA	44	4	16	20	76	....	....	....	....	....
1990-91	North Dakota	WCHA	42	3	9	12	63	....	....	....	....	....
1991-92	Indianapolis	IHL	35	1	6	7	30	....	....	....	....	....
1992-93	Indianapolis	IHL	54	1	3	4	82	....	....	....	....	....
1993-94	Indianapolis	IHL	79	5	12	17	150	....	....	....	....	....

Signed as a free agent by **Chicago**, January 25, 1992.

HALKIDIS, BOB (hal-KEE-dihs) — DET.

Defense. Shoots left. 5'11", 205 lbs. Born, Toronto, Ont., March 5, 1966.
(Buffalo's 4th choice, 81st overall, in 1984 Entry Draft).

			Regular Season					Playoffs				
Season	Club	Lea	GP	G	A	TP	PIM	GP	G	A	TP	PIM
1983-84	London	OHL	51	9	22	31	123	8	0	2	2	27
1984-85a	London	OHL	62	14	50	64	154	8	3	6	9	22
	Buffalo	**NHL**	....	....	....	....	....	**4**	**0**	**0**	**0**	**19**
1985-86	**Buffalo**	**NHL**	**37**	**1**	**9**	**10**	**115**	....	....	....	....	....
1986-87	**Buffalo**	**NHL**	**6**	**1**	**1**	**2**	**19**	....	....	....	....	....
	Rochester	AHL	59	1	8	9	144	8	0	0	0	43
1987-88	**Buffalo**	**NHL**	**30**	**0**	**3**	**3**	**115**	**4**	**0**	**0**	**0**	**22**
	Rochester	AHL	15	2	5	7	50	....	....	....	....	....
1988-89	**Buffalo**	**NHL**	**16**	**0**	**1**	**1**	**66**	....	....	....	....	....
	Rochester	AHL	16	0	6	6	64	....	....	....	....	....
1989-90	Rochester	AHL	18	1	13	14	70	....	....	....	....	....
	Los Angeles	**NHL**	**20**	**0**	**4**	**4**	**56**	....	....	....	....	....
	New Haven	AHL	30	3	17	20	67	....	....	....	....	....
1990-91	**Los Angeles**	**NHL**	**34**	**1**	**3**	**4**	**133**	**3**	**0**	**0**	**0**	**0**
	New Haven	AHL	7	1	3	4	10	....	....	....	....	....
	Phoenix	IHL	4	1	5	6	6	....	....	....	....	....
1991-92	**Toronto**	**NHL**	**46**	**3**	**3**	**6**	**145**	....	....	....	....	....
1992-93	St. John's	AHL	29	2	13	15	61	....	....	....	....	....
	Milwaukee	IHL	26	0	9	9	79	5	0	1	1	27
1993-94	**Detroit**	**NHL**	**28**	**1**	**4**	**5**	**93**	**1**	**0**	**0**	**0**	**2**
	Adirondack	AHL	15	0	6	6	46	....	....	....	....	....
	NHL Totals		**217**	**7**	**28**	**35**	**742**	**12**	**0**	**0**	**0**	**43**

a OHL First All-Star Team (1985)

Traded to **Los Angeles** by **Buffalo** with future considerations for Dale DeGray and future considerations, November 24, 1989. Signed as a free agent by **Toronto**, July 24, 1991. Signed as a free agent by **Detroit**, September 2, 1993.

HALKO, STEVEN — HFD.

Defense. Shoots right. 6'1", 183 lbs. Born, Etobicoke, Ont., March 8, 1974.
(Hartford's 10th choice, 225th overall, in 1992 Entry Draft).

			Regular Season					Playoffs				
Season	Club	Lea	GP	G	A	TP	PIM	GP	G	A	TP	PIM
1992-93	U. of Michigan	CCHA	39	1	12	13	12	....	....	....	....	....
1993-94	U. of Michigan	CCHA	41	2	13	15	32	....	....	....	....	....

HALL, TODD — HFD.

Defense. Shoots left. 6'1", 212 lbs. Born, Hamden, CT, January 22, 1973.
(Hartford's 3rd choice, 53rd overall, in 1991 Entry Draft).

			Regular Season					Playoffs				
Season	Club	Lea	GP	G	A	TP	PIM	GP	G	A	TP	PIM
1991-92	Boston College	H.E.	33	2	10	12	14	....	....	....	....	....
1992-93	Boston College	H.E.	34	2	10	12	22	....	....	....	....	....
1993-94	N. Hampshire	H.E.			DID NOT PLAY							

HALLER, KEVIN (HAHL-ehr) — PHI.

Defense. Shoots left. 6'2", 183 lbs. Born, Trochu, Alta., December 5, 1970.
(Buffalo's 1st choice, 14th overall, in 1989 Entry Draft).

			Regular Season					Playoffs				
Season	Club	Lea	GP	G	A	TP	PIM	GP	G	A	TP	PIM
1988-89	Regina	WHL	72	10	31	41	99	....	....	....	....	....
1989-90	**Buffalo**	**NHL**	**2**	**0**	**0**	**0**	**0**	....	....	....	....	....
a	Regina	WHL	58	16	37	53	93	11	2	9	11	16
1990-91	**Buffalo**	**NHL**	**21**	**1**	**8**	**9**	**20**	**6**	**1**	**4**	**5**	**10**
	Rochester	AHL	52	2	8	10	53	10	2	1	3	6
1991-92	**Buffalo**	**NHL**	**58**	**6**	**15**	**21**	**75**	....	....	....	....	....
	Rochester	AHL	4	0	0	0	18	....	....	....	....	....
	Montreal	**NHL**	**8**	**2**	**2**	**4**	**17**	**9**	**0**	**0**	**0**	**6**
1992-93	**Montreal**	**NHL**	**73**	**11**	**14**	**25**	**117**	**17**	**1**	**6**	**7**	**16**
1993-94	**Montreal**	**NHL**	**68**	**4**	**9**	**13**	**118**	**7**	**1**	**1**	**2**	**19**
	NHL Totals		**230**	**24**	**48**	**72**	**347**	**39**	**3**	**11**	**14**	**51**

a WHL East First All-Star Team (1990)

Traded to **Montreal** by **Buffalo** for Petr Svoboda, March 10, 1992. Traded to **Philadelphia** by **Montreal** for Yves Racine, June 29, 1994.

HALVERSON, TREVOR

Left wing. Shoots left. 6'1", 195 lbs. Born, White River, Ont., April 6, 1971.
(Washington's 2nd choice, 21st overall, in 1991 Entry Draft).

			Regular Season					Playoffs				
Season	Club	Lea	GP	G	A	TP	PIM	GP	G	A	TP	PIM
1989-90	North Bay	OHL	54	22	20	42	172	2	2	1	3	2
1990-91a	North Bay	OHL	64	59	36	95	128	10	3	6	9	4
1991-92	Baltimore	AHL	74	10	11	21	181	....	....	....	....	....
1992-93	Baltimore	AHL	67	19	21	40	170	2	1	0	1	0
	Hampton Rds.	ECHL	9	7	5	12	6	....	....	....	....	....
1993-94	San Diego	IHL	58	4	9	13	115	....	....	....	....	....
	Milwaukee	IHL	4	1	0	1	8	2	0	0	0	17

a OHL First All-Star Team (1991)

Claimed by **Anaheim** from **Washington** in Expansion Draft, June 24, 1993.

HAMMOND, KEN — BOS.

Defense. Shoots left. 6'1", 190 lbs. Born, Port Credit, Ont., August 22, 1963.
(Los Angeles' 8th choice, 152nd overall, in 1983 Entry Draft).

			Regular Season					Playoffs				
Season	Club	Lea	GP	G	A	TP	PIM	GP	G	A	TP	PIM
1982-83	RPI	ECAC	28	17	26	43	8	....	....	....	....	....
1983-84	RPI	ECAC	34	5	11	16	72	....	....	....	....	....
1984-85	**Los Angeles**	**NHL**	**3**	**1**	**0**	**1**	**0**	**3**	**0**	**0**	**0**	**4**
ab	RPI	ECAC	38	11	28	39	90	....	....	....	....	....
1985-86	**Los Angeles**	**NHL**	**3**	**0**	**1**	**1**	**2**	....	....	....	....	....
	New Haven	AHL	67	4	12	16	96	4	0	0	0	7
1986-87	**Los Angeles**	**NHL**	**10**	**0**	**2**	**2**	**11**	....	....	....	....	....
	New Haven	AHL	66	1	15	16	76	6	0	1	1	21
1987-88	**Los Angeles**	**NHL**	**46**	**7**	**9**	**16**	**69**	**2**	**0**	**0**	**0**	**4**
	New Haven	AHL	26	3	8	11	27	....	....	....	....	....
1988-89	**Edmonton**	**NHL**	**5**	**0**	**1**	**1**	**8**	....	....	....	....	....
	NY Rangers	**NHL**	**3**	**0**	**0**	**0**	**0**	....	....	....	....	....
	Denver	IHL	38	5	18	23	24	....	....	....	....	....
	Toronto	**NHL**	**14**	**0**	**2**	**2**	**12**	....	....	....	....	....
1989-90	Newmarket	AHL	75	9	45	54	106	....	....	....	....	....
1990-91	**Boston**	**NHL**	**1**	**1**	**0**	**1**	**2**	**8**	**0**	**0**	**0**	**10**
	Maine	AHL	80	10	41	51	159	2	0	1	1	16
1991-92	**San Jose**	**NHL**	**46**	**5**	**10**	**15**	**82**	....	....	....	....	....
	Vancouver	**NHL**	....	....	....	....	....	**2**	**0**	**0**	**0**	**6**
1992-93	**Ottawa**	**NHL**	**62**	**4**	**4**	**8**	**104**	....	....	....	....	....
	New Haven	AHL	4	0	1	1	4	....	....	....	....	....
1993-94	Providence	AHL	65	12	45	57	100	....	....	....	....	....
	NHL Totals		**193**	**18**	**29**	**47**	**290**	**15**	**0**	**0**	**0**	**24**

a ECAC First All-Star Team (1985)
b NCAA East All-American Team (1985)

Claimed by **Edmonton** in NHL Waiver Draft, October 3, 1988. Claimed on waivers by **NY Rangers** from **Edmonton**, November 1, 1988. Traded to **Toronto** by **NY Rangers** for Chris McRae, February 21, 1989. Traded to **Boston** by **Toronto** for cash, August 20, 1990. Signed as a free agent by **San Jose**, August 9, 1991. Traded to **Vancouver** by **San Jose** for Vancouver's eighth round choice (later traded to Detroit — Detroit selected C.J. Denomme) in 1992 Entry Draft, March 9, 1992. Claimed by **Ottawa** from **Vancouver** in Expansion Draft, June 18, 1992.

HAMR, RADEK (HAM-uhr, RA-dehk) — OTT.

Defense. Shoots left. 5'11", 175 lbs. Born, Usti-Nad-Labem, Czech., June 15, 1974.
(Ottawa's 4th choice, 73rd overall, in 1992 Entry Draft).

			Regular Season					Playoffs				
Season	Club	Lea	GP	G	A	TP	PIM	GP	G	A	TP	PIM
1991-92	Sparta Praha	Czech.	3	0	0	0	....	....	....	....	....	....
1992-93	**Ottawa**	**NHL**	**4**	**0**	**0**	**0**	**0**	....	....	....	....	....
	New Haven	AHL	59	4	21	25	18	....	....	....	....	....
1993-94	**Ottawa**	**NHL**	**7**	**0**	**0**	**0**	**0**	....	....	....	....	....
	PEI	AHL	69	10	26	36	44	....	....	....	....	....
	NHL Totals		**11**	**0**	**0**	**0**	**0**	....	....	....	....	....

HAMRLIK, MARTIN (HAHM-reh-lik) — ST.L.

Defense. Shoots right. 5'11", 185 lbs. Born, Gottwaldov, Czech., May 6, 1973.
(Hartford's 2nd choice, 31st overall, in 1991 Entry Draft).

			Regular Season					Playoffs				
Season	Club	Lea	GP	G	A	TP	PIM	GP	G	A	TP	PIM
1989-90	TJ Zlin	Czech.	11	2	0	2	....	....	....	....	....	....
1990-91	TJ Zlin	Czech.	50	8	14	22	44	....	....	....	....	....
1991-92	ZPS Zlin	Czech.	4	0	2	2	23	....	....	....	....	....
1992-93	Ottawa	OHL	26	4	11	15	41	....	....	....	....	....
	Springfield	AHL	8	1	3	4	16	....	....	....	....	....
1993-94	Springfield	AHL	1	0	0	0	0	....	....	....	....	....
	Peoria	IHL	47	1	11	12	61	6	0	1	1	2

Traded to **St. Louis** by **Hartford** for cash, November 12, 1993.

HAMRLIK, ROMAN (HAHM-reh-lik) — T.B.

Defense. Shoots left. 6'2", 202 lbs. Born, Gottwaldov, Czech., April 12, 1974.
(Tampa Bay's 1st choice, 1st overall, in 1992 Entry Draft).

			Regular Season					Playoffs				
Season	Club	Lea	GP	G	A	TP	PIM	GP	G	A	TP	PIM
1990-91	TJ Zlin	Czech.	14	2	2	4	18	....	....	....	....	....
1991-92	ZPS Zlin	Czech.	34	5	5	10	50	....	....	....	....	....
1992-93	**Tampa Bay**	**NHL**	**67**	**6**	**15**	**21**	**71**	....	....	....	....	....
	Atlanta	IHL	2	1	1	2	2	....	....	....	....	....
1993-94	**Tampa Bay**	**NHL**	**64**	**3**	**18**	**21**	**135**	....	....	....	....	....
	NHL Totals		**131**	**9**	**33**	**42**	**206**	....	....	....	....	....

HANKINSON, BEN — N.J.

Right wing. Shoots right. 6'2", 210 lbs. Born, Edina, MN, May 1, 1969.
(New Jersey's 5th choice, 107th overall, in 1987 Entry Draft).

			Regular Season					Playoffs				
Season	Club	Lea	GP	G	A	TP	PIM	GP	G	A	TP	PIM
1987-88	U. Minnesota	WCHA	24	4	7	11	36	....	....	....	....	....
1988-89	U. Minnesota	WCHA	43	7	11	18	115	....	....	....	....	....
1989-90a	U. Minnesota	WCHA	46	25	41	66	34	....	....	....	....	....
1990-91	U. Minnesota	WCHA	43	19	21	40	133	....	....	....	....	....
1991-92	Utica	AHL	77	17	16	33	186	4	3	1	4	2
1992-93	**New Jersey**	**NHL**	**4**	**2**	**1**	**3**	**9**	....	....	....	....	....
	Utica	AHL	75	35	27	62	145	5	2	2	4	6
1993-94	**New Jersey**	**NHL**	**13**	**1**	**0**	**1**	**23**	**2**	**1**	**0**	**1**	**4**
	Albany	AHL	29	9	14	23	80	5	3	1	4	6
	NHL Totals		**17**	**3**	**1**	**4**	**32**	**2**	**1**	**0**	**1**	**4**

a WCHA First All-Star Team (1990)

HANNAN, DAVE — BUF.

Center. Shoots left. 5'10", 185 lbs. Born, Sudbury, Ont., November 26, 1961.
(Pittsburgh's 9th choice, 196th overall, in 1981 Entry Draft).

			Regular Season					Playoffs				
Season	Club	Lea	GP	G	A	TP	PIM	GP	G	A	TP	PIM
1979-80	S.S. Marie	OHA	28	11	10	21	31	....	....	....	....	....
	Brantford	OHA	25	5	10	15	26	....	....	....	....	....
1980-81	Brantford	OHA	56	46	35	81	155	6	2	4	6	20
1981-82	**Pittsburgh**	**NHL**	**1**	**0**	**0**	**0**	**0**	....	....	....	....	....
	Erie	AHL	76	33	37	70	129	....	....	....	....	....
1982-83	**Pittsburgh**	**NHL**	**74**	**11**	**22**	**33**	**127**	....	....	....	....	....
	Baltimore	AHL	5	2	2	4	13	....	....	....	....	....
1983-84	**Pittsburgh**	**NHL**	**24**	**2**	**3**	**5**	**33**	....	....	....	....	....
	Baltimore	AHL	47	18	24	42	98	10	2	6	8	27
1984-85	**Pittsburgh**	**NHL**	**30**	**6**	**7**	**13**	**43**	....	....	....	....	....
	Baltimore	AHL	49	20	25	45	91	....	....	....	....	....
1985-86	**Pittsburgh**	**NHL**	**75**	**17**	**18**	**35**	**91**	....	....	....	....	....
1986-87	**Pittsburgh**	**NHL**	**58**	**10**	**15**	**25**	**56**	....	....	....	....	....
1987-88	**Pittsburgh**	**NHL**	**21**	**4**	**3**	**7**	**23**	....	....	....	....	....
	Edmonton	**NHL**	**51**	**9**	**11**	**20**	**43**	**12**	**1**	**1**	**2**	**8**
1988-89	**Pittsburgh**	**NHL**	**72**	**10**	**20**	**30**	**157**	**8**	**0**	**1**	**1**	**4**
1989-90	**Toronto**	**NHL**	**39**	**6**	**9**	**15**	**55**	**3**	**1**	**0**	**1**	**4**
1990-91	**Toronto**	**NHL**	**74**	**11**	**23**	**34**	**82**	....	....	....	....	....
1991-92	**Toronto**	**NHL**	**35**	**2**	**2**	**4**	**16**	....	....	....	....	....
	Cdn. National	....	3	0	0	0	2	....	....	....	....	....
	Cdn. Olympic	....	8	3	5	8	8	....	....	....	....	....
	Buffalo	**NHL**	**12**	**2**	**4**	**6**	**48**	**7**	**2**	**0**	**2**	**2**
1992-93	**Buffalo**	**NHL**	**55**	**5**	**15**	**20**	**43**	**8**	**1**	**1**	**2**	**18**
1993-94	**Buffalo**	**NHL**	**83**	**6**	**15**	**21**	**53**	**7**	**1**	**0**	**1**	**6**
	NHL Totals		**704**	**101**	**167**	**268**	**870**	**45**	**6**	**3**	**9**	**42**

Traded to **Edmonton** by **Pittsburgh** with Craig Simpson, Moe Mantha and Chris Joseph for Paul Coffey, Dave Hunter and Wayne Van Dorp, November 24, 1987. Claimed by **Pittsburgh** in NHL Waiver Draft, October 3, 1988. Claimed by **Toronto** in NHL Waiver Draft, October 2, 1989. Traded to **Buffalo** by **Toronto** for Minnesota's fifth round choice (previously acquired by Buffalo — Toronto selected Chris Deruiter) in 1992 Entry Draft, March 10, 1992.

HANSEN, TAVIS — WPG.

Center. Shoots right. 6'1", 180 lbs. Born, Prince Albert, Sask., June 17, 1975.
(Winnipeg's 3rd choice, 58th overall, in 1994 Entry Draft).

			Regular Season					Playoffs				
Season	Club	Lea	GP	G	A	TP	PIM	GP	G	A	TP	PIM
1992-93	Shellbrook	Midget	42	42	53	105	107	....	....	....	....	....
1993-94	Tacoma	WHL	71	23	31	54	122	8	1	3	4	17

HANSON, GREG — PHI.

Defense. Shoots left. 6'3", 215 lbs. Born, Bloomington, MN, September 4, 1971.
(Philadelphia's 13th choice, 193rd overall, in 1990 Entry Draft).

			Regular Season					Playoffs				
Season	Club	Lea	GP	G	A	TP	PIM	GP	G	A	TP	PIM
1992-93	Minn.-Duluth	WCHA	15	0	2	2	12	....	....	....	....	....
1993-94	Minn.-Duluth	WCHA	27	3	6	9	40	....	....	....	....	....

HANSSON, ROGER — VAN.

Right wing. Shoots left. 6'1", 170 lbs. Born, Angelholm, Sweden, April 29, 1969.
(Vancouver's 10th choice, 213th overall, in 1987 Entry Draft).

			Regular Season					Playoffs				
Season	Club	Lea	GP	G	A	TP	PIM	GP	G	A	TP	PIM
1987-88	Rogle	Swe.	36	31	18	49	10	....	....	....	....	....
1988-89	Rogle	Swe.	36	32	18	50	....	....	....	....	....	....
1989-90	Rogle	Swe.	32	22	18	40	18	....	....	....	....	....
1990-91	Rogle	Swe.	31	27	27	54	25	....	....	....	....	....
1991-92	Malmo	Swe.	36	12	13	25	10	....	....	....	....	....
1992-93	Malmo	Swe.	32	9	8	17	10	....	....	....	....	....
1993-94	Malmo	Swe.	39	12	12	24	30	....	....	....	....	....

HARBERTS, TIMOTHY — PIT.

Center. Shoots right. 6'1", 185 lbs. Born, Edina, MN, May 20, 1975.
(Pittsburgh's 9th choice, 234th overall, in 1993 Entry Draft).

			Regular Season					Playoffs				
Season	Club	Lea	GP	G	A	TP	PIM	GP	G	A	TP	PIM
1992-93	Wayzata	HS	23	24	18	42	22	....	....	....	....	....
1993-94	Notre Dame	CCHA	36	10	12	22	19	....	....	....	....	....

HARDING, MIKE — HFD.

Right wing. Shoots right. 6'4", 221 lbs. Born, Edsow, Alta., February 24, 1971.
(Hartford's 6th choice, 119th overall, in 1991 Entry Draft).

			Regular Season					Playoffs				
Season	Club	Lea	GP	G	A	TP	PIM	GP	G	A	TP	PIM
1991-92	N. Michigan	WCHA	28	6	8	14	46	....	....	....	....	....
1992-93	N. Michigan	WCHA	39	17	18	35	66	....	....	....	....	....
1993-94a	N. Michigan	WCHA	38	24	25	49	66	....	....	....	....	....

a WCHA Second All-Star Team (1994)

HARDY, MARK

Defense. Shoots left. 5'11", 195 lbs. Born, Semaden, Switz., February 1, 1959.
(Los Angeles' 3rd choice, 30th overall, in 1979 Entry Draft).

			Regular Season					Playoffs				
Season	Club	Lea	GP	G	A	TP	PIM	GP	G	A	TP	PIM
1977-78	Montreal	QJHL	72	25	57	82	150	13	3	10	13	22
1978-79	Montreal	QJHL	67	18	52	70	117	11	5	8	13	40
1979-80	Binghamton	AHL	56	3	13	16	32	....	....	....	....	....
	Los Angeles	**NHL**	**15**	**0**	**1**	**1**	**10**	**4**	**1**	**1**	**2**	**9**
1980-81	**Los Angeles**	**NHL**	**77**	**5**	**20**	**25**	**77**	**4**	**1**	**2**	**3**	**4**
1981-82	**Los Angeles**	**NHL**	**77**	**6**	**39**	**45**	**130**	**10**	**1**	**2**	**3**	**9**
1982-83	**Los Angeles**	**NHL**	**74**	**5**	**34**	**39**	**101**	....	....	....	....	....
1983-84	**Los Angeles**	**NHL**	**79**	**8**	**41**	**49**	**122**	....	....	....	....	....
1984-85	**Los Angeles**	**NHL**	**78**	**14**	**39**	**53**	**97**	**3**	**0**	**1**	**1**	**2**
1985-86	**Los Angeles**	**NHL**	**55**	**6**	**21**	**27**	**71**	....	....	....	....	....
1986-87	**Los Angeles**	**NHL**	**73**	**3**	**27**	**30**	**120**	**5**	**1**	**2**	**3**	**10**
1987-88	**Los Angeles**	**NHL**	**61**	**6**	**22**	**28**	**99**	....	....	....	....	....
	NY Rangers	**NHL**	**19**	**2**	**2**	**4**	**31**	....	....	....	....	....
1988-89	**Minnesota**	**NHL**	**15**	**2**	**4**	**6**	**26**	....	....	....	....	....
	NY Rangers	**NHL**	**45**	**2**	**12**	**14**	**45**	**4**	**0**	**1**	**1**	**31**
1989-90	**NY Rangers**	**NHL**	**54**	**0**	**15**	**15**	**94**	**3**	**0**	**1**	**1**	**2**
1990-91	**NY Rangers**	**NHL**	**70**	**1**	**5**	**6**	**89**	**6**	**0**	**1**	**1**	**30**
1991-92	**NY Rangers**	**NHL**	**52**	**1**	**8**	**9**	**65**	**13**	**0**	**3**	**3**	**31**
1992-93	**NY Rangers**	**NHL**	**44**	**1**	**10**	**11**	**85**	....	....	....	....	....
	Los Angeles	**NHL**	**11**	**0**	**3**	**3**	**4**	**15**	**1**	**2**	**3**	**30**
1993-94	**Los Angeles**	**NHL**	**16**	**0**	**3**	**3**	**27**	....	....	....	....	....
	Phoenix	IHL	54	5	3	8	48	....	....	....	....	....
	NHL Totals		**915**	**62**	**306**	**368**	**1293**	**67**	**5**	**16**	**21**	**158**

Traded to **NY Rangers** by **Los Angeles** for Ron Duguay, February 23, 1988. Traded to **Minnesota** by **NY Rangers** for future considerations (Louie Debrusk) June 13, 1988. Traded to **NY Rangers** by **Minnesota** for Larry Bernard and NY Rangers' fifth round choice (Rhys Hollyman) in 1989 Entry Draft, December 9, 1988. Traded to **Los Angeles** by **NY Rangers** with Ottawa's fifth round choice (previously acquired by NY Rangers — Los Angeles selected Frederick Beaubien) in 1993 Entry Draft for John McIntyre, March 22, 1993.

HARKINS, BRETT

Left wing. Shoots left. 6'1", 170 lbs. Born, North Ridgeville, OH, July 2, 1970.
(NY Islanders' 9th choice, 133rd overall, in 1989 Entry Draft).

			Regular Season					Playoffs				
Season	Club	Lea	GP	G	A	TP	PIM	GP	G	A	TP	PIM
1989-90	Bowling Green	CCHA	41	11	43	54	45	....	....	....	....	....
1990-91	Bowling Green	CCHA	40	22	38	60	30	....	....	....	....	....
1991-92	Bowling Green	CCHA	34	8	39	47	32	....	....	....	....	....
1992-93	Bowling Green	CCHA	35	19	28	47	28	....	....	....	....	....
1993-94	Adirondack	AHL	80	22	47	69	23	10	1	5	6	4

HARKINS, TODD — HFD.

Center. Shoots right. 6'3", 210 lbs. Born, Cleveland, OH, October 8, 1968.
(Calgary's 2nd choice, 42nd overall, in 1988 Entry Draft).

			Regular Season					Playoffs				
Season	Club	Lea	GP	G	A	TP	PIM	GP	G	A	TP	PIM
1987-88	Miami-Ohio	CCHA	34	9	7	16	133	....	....	....	....	....
1988-89	Miami-Ohio	CCHA	36	8	7	15	77	....	....	....	....	....
1989-90	Miami-Ohio	CCHA	40	27	17	44	78	....	....	....	....	....
1990-91	Salt Lake	IHL	79	15	27	42	113	3	0	0	0	0
1991-92	**Calgary**	**NHL**	**5**	**0**	**0**	**0**	**7**	....	....	....	....	....
	Salt Lake	IHL	72	32	30	62	67	5	1	1	2	6
1992-93	**Calgary**	**NHL**	**15**	**2**	**3**	**5**	**22**	....	....	....	....	....
	Salt Lake	IHL	53	13	21	34	90	....	....	....	....	....
1993-94	Saint John	AHL	38	13	9	22	64	....	....	....	....	....
	Hartford	**NHL**	**28**	**1**	**0**	**1**	**49**	....	....	....	....	....
	Springfield	AHL	1	0	3	3	0	....	....	....	....	....
	NHL Totals		**48**	**3**	**3**	**6**	**78**	....	....	....	....	....

Traded to **Hartford** by **Calgary** for Scott Morrow, January 24, 1994.

HARLOCK, DAVID — TOR.

Defense. Shoots left. 6'2", 195 lbs. Born, Toronto, Ont., March 16, 1971.
(New Jersey's 2nd choice, 24th overall, in 1990 Entry Draft).

			Regular Season					Playoffs				
Season	Club	Lea	GP	G	A	TP	PIM	GP	G	A	TP	PIM
1989-90	U. of Michigan	CCHA	42	2	13	15	44	....	....	....	....	....
1990-91	U. of Michigan	CCHA	39	2	8	10	70	....	....	....	....	....
1991-92	U. of Michigan	CCHA	44	1	6	7	80	....	....	....	....	....
1992-93	Cdn. National	....	4	0	0	0	2	....	....	....	....	....
	U. of Michigan	CCHA	38	3	9	12	58	....	....	....	....	....
1993-94	Cdn. National	....	41	0	3	3	28	....	....	....	....	....
	Cdn. Olympic	....	8	0	0	0	8	....	....	....	....	....
	Toronto	**NHL**	**6**	**0**	**0**	**0**	**0**	....	....	....	....	....
	St. John's	AHL	10	0	3	3	2	9	0	0	0	6
	NHL Totals		**6**	**0**	**0**	**0**	**0**	....	....	....	....	....

Signed as a free agent by **Toronto**, August 20, 1993.

HARLTON, TYLER — ST.L.

Defense. Shoots left. 6'3", 201 lbs. Born, Pense, Sask., January 11, 1976.
(St. Louis' 2nd choice, 94th overall, in 1994 Entry Draft).

			Regular Season					Playoffs				
Season	Club	Lea	GP	G	A	TP	PIM	GP	G	A	TP	PIM
1993-94	Vernon	Jr. A	60	3	18	21	102	....	....	....	....	....

HARPER, KELLY — CGY.

Center. Shoots right. 6'2", 180 lbs. Born, Sudbury, Ont., May 9, 1972.
(Calgary's 8th choice, 151st overall, in 1991 Entry Draft).

			Regular Season					Playoffs				
Season	Club	Lea	GP	G	A	TP	PIM	GP	G	A	TP	PIM
1990-91	Michigan State	CCHA	34	1	8	9	21	....	....	....	....	....
1991-92	Michigan State	CCHA	33	4	4	8	2	....	....	....	....	....
1992-93	Michigan State	CCHA	39	11	20	31	20	....	....	....	....	....
1993-94	Michigan State	CCHA	41	14	18	32	26	....	....	....	....	....

HARTJE, TOD (HAHRT-jee)

Center. Shoots left. 6'1", 190 lbs. Born, Anoka, MN, February 27, 1968.
(Winnipeg's 7th choice, 142nd overall, in 1987 Entry Draft).

			Regular Season					Playoffs				
Season	Club	Lea	GP	G	A	TP	PIM	GP	G	A	TP	PIM
1986-87	Harvard	ECAC	32	3	9	12	36	....	....	....	....	....
1987-88	Harvard	ECAC	32	5	17	22	40	....	....	....	....	....
1988-89	Harvard	ECAC	33	4	17	21	40	....	....	....	....	....
1989-90	Harvard	ECAC	28	6	10	16	29	....	....	....	....	....
1990-91	Sokol Kiev	USSR	32	2	4	6	18	....	....	....	....	....
	Fort Wayne	IHL	1	1	0	1	2	....	....	....	....	....
1991-92	Moncton	AHL	38	9	9	18	35	....	....	....	....	....
1992-93	Moncton	AHL	29	3	7	10	2	....	....	....	....	....
	Fort Wayne	IHL	5	1	2	3	6	....	....	....	....	....
	Providence	AHL	29	2	14	16	32	4	1	0	1	20
1993-94	Providence	AHL	80	22	27	49	157	....	....	....	....	....

HARTMAN, MIKE NYR

Left wing. Shoots left. 6', 190 lbs. Born, Detroit, MI, February 7, 1967.
(Buffalo's 8th choice, 131st overall, in 1986 Entry Draft).

			Regular Season					Playoffs				
Season	Club	Lea	GP	G	A	TP	PIM	GP	G	A	TP	PIM
1984-85	Belleville	OHL	49	13	12	25	119	....	....	....	....	....
1985-86	Belleville	OHL	4	2	1	3	5	....	....	....	....	....
	North Bay	OHL	53	19	16	35	205	10	2	4	6	34
1986-87	Buffalo	NHL	17	3	3	6	69	....	....	....	....	....
	North Bay	OHL	32	15	24	39	144	19	7	8	15	88
1987-88	Buffalo	NHL	18	3	1	4	90	6	0	0	0	35
	Rochester	AHL	57	13	14	27	283	4	1	0	1	22
1988-89	Buffalo	NHL	70	8	9	17	316	5	0	0	0	34
1989-90	Buffalo	NHL	60	11	10	21	211	6	0	0	0	18
1990-91	Buffalo	NHL	60	9	3	12	204	2	0	0	0	17
1991-92	Winnipeg	NHL	75	4	4	8	264	2	0	0	0	2
1992-93	Tampa Bay	NHL	58	4	4	8	154	....	....	....	....	....
	NY Rangers	NHL	3	0	0	0	6	....	....	....	....	....
1993-94	NY Rangers	NHL	35	1	1	2	70	....	....	....	....	....
	NHL Totals		396	43	35	78	1384	21	0	0	0	106

Traded to **Winnipeg** by **Buffalo** with Darrin Shannon and Dean Kennedy for Dave McLlwain, Gord Donnelly, Winnipeg's fifth round choice (Yuri Khmylev) in 1992 Entry Draft and future considerations, October 11, 1991. Claimed by **Tampa Bay** from **Winnipeg** in Expansion Draft, June 18, 1992. Traded to **NY Rangers** by **Tampa Bay** for Randy Gilhen, March 22, 1993.

HARVEY, TODD DAL.

Center. Shoots right. 5'11", 190 lbs. Born, Hamilton, Ont., February 17, 1975.
(Dallas' 1st choice, 9th overall, in 1993 Entry Draft).

			Regular Season					Playoffs				
Season	Club	Lea	GP	G	A	TP	PIM	GP	G	A	TP	PIM
1991-92	Detroit	OHL	58	21	43	64	141	7	3	5	8	30
1992-93	Detroit	OHL	55	50	50	100	83	15	9	12	21	39
1993-94	Detroit	OHL	49	34	51	85	75	17	10	12	22	26

HASSELBLAD, PETER CGY.

Defense. Shoots left. 6'5", 220 lbs. Born, Orebro, Swe., April 20, 1966.
(Calgary's 12th choice, 229th overall, in 1987 Entry Draft).

			Regular Season					Playoffs				
Season	Club	Lea	GP	G	A	TP	PIM	GP	G	A	TP	PIM
1989-90	Farjestad	Swe.	36	3	6	9	51	10	1	2	3	12
1990-91	Farjestad	Swe.	40	0	7	7	56	8	0	0	0	16
1991-92	Team Boro	Swe.2	27	2	12	14	52	....	....	....	....	....
1992-93	Malmo	Swe.	39	4	9	13	52	6	0	0	0	6
1993-94	Malmo	Swe.	37	3	7	10	50	11	0	0	0	6

HATCHER, DERIAN DAL.

Defense. Shoots left. 6'5", 225 lbs. Born, Sterling Heights, MI, June 4, 1972.
(Minnesota's 1st choice, 8th overall, in 1990 Entry Draft).

			Regular Season					Playoffs				
Season	Club	Lea	GP	G	A	TP	PIM	GP	G	A	TP	PIM
1989-90	North Bay	OHL	64	14	38	52	81	5	2	3	5	8
1990-91	North Bay	OHL	64	13	49	62	163	10	2	10	12	28
1991-92	Minnesota	NHL	43	8	4	12	88	5	0	2	2	8
1992-93	Minnesota	NHL	67	4	15	19	178	....	....	....	....	....
	Kalamazoo	IHL	2	1	2	3	21	....	....	....	....	....
1993-94	Dallas	NHL	83	12	19	31	211	9	0	2	2	14
	NHL Totals		193	24	38	62	477	14	0	4	4	22

HATCHER, KEVIN WSH.

Defense. Shoots right. 6'4", 225 lbs. Born, Detroit, MI, September 9, 1966.
(Washington's 1st choice, 17th overall, in 1984 Entry Draft).

			Regular Season					Playoffs				
Season	Club	Lea	GP	G	A	TP	PIM	GP	G	A	TP	PIM
1983-84	North Bay	OHL	67	10	39	49	61	4	2	2	4	11
1984-85	Washington	NHL	2	1	0	1	0	1	0	0	0	0
a	North Bay	OHL	58	26	37	63	75	8	3	8	11	9
1985-86	Washington	NHL	79	9	10	19	119	9	1	1	2	19
1986-87	Washington	NHL	78	8	16	24	144	7	1	0	1	20
1987-88	Washington	NHL	71	14	27	41	137	14	5	7	12	55
1988-89	Washington	NHL	62	13	27	40	101	6	1	4	5	20
1989-90	Washington	NHL	80	13	41	54	102	11	0	8	8	32
1990-91	Washington	NHL	79	24	50	74	69	11	3	3	6	8
1991-92	Washington	NHL	79	17	37	54	105	7	2	4	6	19
1992-93	Washington	NHL	83	34	45	79	114	6	0	1	1	14
1993-94	Washington	NHL	72	16	24	40	108	11	3	4	7	37
	NHL Totals		685	149	277	426	999	83	16	32	48	224

a OHL Second All-Star Team (1985)

Played in NHL All-Star Game (1990, 1991, 1992)

HAUER, BRETT VAN.

Defense. Shoots right. 6'2", 200 lbs. Born, Richfield, MN, July 11, 1971.
(Vancouver's 3rd choice, 71st overall, in 1989 Entry Draft).

			Regular Season					Playoffs				
Season	Club	Lea	GP	G	A	TP	PIM	GP	G	A	TP	PIM
1989-90	Minn.-Duluth	WCHA	37	2	6	8	44	....	....	....	....	....
1990-91	Minn.-Duluth	WCHA	30	1	7	8	54	....	....	....	....	....
1991-92	Minn.-Duluth	WCHA	33	8	14	22	40	....	....	....	....	....
1992-93ab	Minn. Duluth	WCHA	40	10	46	56	52	....	....	....	....	....
1993-94	U.S. National	....	57	6	14	20	88	....	....	....	....	....
	U.S. Olympic	....	8	0	0	0	10	....	....	....	....	....
	Las Vegas	IHL	21	0	7	7	8	1	0	0	0	0

a WCHA First All-Star Team (1993)
b NCAA West First All-American Team (1993)

HAWERCHUK, DALE (HOW-uhr-CHUHK) BUF.

Center. Shoots left. 5'11", 190 lbs. Born, Toronto, Ont., April 4, 1963.
(Winnipeg's 1st choice, 1st overall, in 1981 Entry Draft).

			Regular Season					Playoffs				
Season	Club	Lea	GP	G	A	TP	PIM	GP	G	A	TP	PIM
1979-80	Cornwall	QJHL	72	37	66	103	21	18	20	25	45	0
1980-81ab	Cornwall	QJHL	72	81	102	183	69	19	15	20	35	8
1981-82c	Winnipeg	NHL	80	45	58	103	47	4	1	7	8	5
1982-83	Winnipeg	NHL	79	40	51	91	31	3	1	4	5	8
1983-84	Winnipeg	NHL	80	37	65	102	73	3	1	1	2	0
1984-85d	Winnipeg	NHL	80	53	77	130	74	3	2	1	3	4
1985-86	Winnipeg	NHL	80	46	59	105	44	3	0	3	3	0
1986-87	Winnipeg	NHL	80	47	53	100	52	10	5	8	13	4
1987-88	Winnipeg	NHL	80	44	77	121	59	5	3	4	7	16
1988-89	Winnipeg	NHL	75	41	55	96	28	....	....	....	....	....
1989-90	Winnipeg	NHL	79	26	55	81	60	7	3	5	8	2
1990-91	Buffalo	NHL	80	31	58	89	32	6	2	4	6	10
1991-92	Buffalo	NHL	77	23	75	98	27	7	2	5	7	0
1992-93	Buffalo	NHL	81	16	80	96	52	8	5	9	14	2
1993-94	Buffalo	NHL	81	35	51	86	91	7	0	7	7	4
	NHL Totals		1032	484	814	1298	670	66	25	58	83	55

a QMJHL First All-Star Team (1981)
b Canadian Major Junior Player of the Year (1981)
c Won Calder Memorial Trophy (1982)
d NHL Second All-Star Team (1985)

Played in NHL All-Star Game (1982, 1985, 1986, 1988)

Traded to **Buffalo** by **Winnipeg** with Winnipeg's first round choice (Brad May in 1990 Entry Draft and future considerations for Phil Housley, Scott Arniel, Jeff Parker and Buffalo's first round choice (Keith Tkachuk) in 1990 Entry Draft, June 16, 1990.

HAWGOOD, GREG (HAW-guhd) PIT.

Defense. Shoots left. 5'10", 190 lbs. Born, Edmonton, Alta., August 10, 1968.
(Boston's 9th choice, 202nd overall, in 1986 Entry Draft).

			Regular Season					Playoffs				
Season	Club	Lea	GP	G	A	TP	PIM	GP	G	A	TP	PIM
1983-84	Kamloops	WHL	49	10	23	33	39	....	....	....	....	....
1984-85	Kamloops	WHL	66	25	40	65	72	....	....	....	....	....
1985-86a	Kamloops	WHL	71	34	85	119	86	16	9	22	31	16
1986-87a	Kamloops	WHL	61	30	93	123	139	....	....	....	....	....
1987-88	Boston	NHL	1	0	0	0	0	3	1	0	1	0
ab	Kamloops	WHL	63	48	85	133	142	16	10	16	26	33
1988-89	Boston	NHL	56	16	24	40	84	10	0	2	2	2
	Maine	AHL	21	2	9	11	41	....	....	....	....	....
1989-90	Boston	NHL	77	11	27	38	76	15	1	3	4	12
1990-91	Asiago	Italy	2	3	0	3	9	....	....	....	....	....
	Edmonton	NHL	6	0	1	1	6	....	....	....	....	....
	Maine	AHL	5	0	1	1	13	....	....	....	....	....
	Cape Breton	AHL	55	10	32	42	73	4	0	3	3	23
1991-92	Edmonton	NHL	20	2	11	13	22	13	0	3	3	23
cd	Cape Breton	AHL	56	20	55	75	26	3	2	2	4	0
1992-93	Edmonton	NHL	29	5	13	18	35	....	....	....	....	....
	Philadelphia	NHL	40	6	22	28	39	....	....	....	....	....
1993-94	Philadelphia	NHL	19	3	12	15	19	....	....	....	....	....
	Florida	NHL	33	2	14	16	9	....	....	....	....	....
	Pittsburgh	NHL	12	1	2	3	8	1	0	0	0	0
	NHL Totals		293	46	126	172	298	42	2	8	10	37

a WHL West All-Star Team (1986, 1987, 1988)
b Canadian Major Junior Defenseman of the Year (1988)
c AHL First All-Star Team (1992)
d Won Eddie Shore Plaque (Outstanding Defenseman - AHL) (1992)

Traded to **Edmonton** by **Boston** for Vladimir Ruzicka, October 22, 1990. Traded to **Philadelphia** by **Edmonton** with Josef Beranek for Brian Benning, January 16, 1993. Traded to **Florida** by **Philadelphia** for cash, November 30, 1993. Traded to **Pittsburgh** by **Florida** for Jeff Daniels, March 19, 1994.

HAWKINS, TODD PIT.

Left/Right wing. Shoots right. 6'1", 195 lbs. Born, Kingston, Ont., August 2, 1966.
(Vancouver's 10th choice, 217th overall, in 1986 Entry Draft).

			Regular Season					Playoffs				
Season	Club	Lea	GP	G	A	TP	PIM	GP	G	A	TP	PIM
1984-85	Belleville	OHL	58	7	16	23	117	12	1	0	1	10
1985-86	Belleville	OHL	60	14	13	27	172	24	9	7	16	60
1986-87	Belleville	OHL	60	47	40	87	187	6	3	5	8	16
1987-88	Flint	IHL	50	13	13	26	337	16	3	5	8	*174
	Fredericton	AHL	2	0	4	4	11	....	....	....	....	....
1988-89	Vancouver	NHL	4	0	0	0	9	....	....	....	....	....
	Milwaukee	IHL	63	12	14	26	307	9	1	0	1	33
1989-90	Vancouver	NHL	4	0	0	0	6	....	....	....	....	....
	Milwaukee	IHL	61	23	17	40	273	5	4	1	5	19
1990-91	Newmarket	AHL	22	2	5	7	66	....	....	....	....	....
	Milwaukee	IHL	39	9	11	20	134	....	....	....	....	....
1991-92	Toronto	NHL	2	0	0	0	0	....	....	....	....	....
	St. John's	AHL	66	30	27	57	139	7	1	0	1	10
1992-93	St. John's	AHL	72	21	41	62	103	9	1	3	4	10
1993-94	Cleveland	IHL	76	19	14	33	115	....	....	....	....	....
	NHL Totals		10	0	0	0	15	....	....	....	....	....

Traded to **Toronto** by **Vancouver** for Brian Blad, January 22, 1991. Signed as a free agent by **Pittsburgh**, August 20, 1993.

HAYWARD, RICK

Defense. Shoots left. 6', 200 lbs. Born, Toledo, OH, February 25, 1966.
(Montreal's 9th choice, 162nd overall, in 1986 Entry Draft).

			Regular Season					Playoffs				
Season	Club	Lea	GP	G	A	TP	PIM	GP	G	A	TP	PIM
1984-85	Hull	QMJHL	56	7	27	34	367	....	....	....	....	....
1985-86	Hull	QMJHL	59	3	40	43	354	15	2	11	13	98
1986-87	Sherbrooke	AHL	46	2	3	5	153	3	0	1	1	15
1987-88	Saginaw	IHL	24	3	4	7	129	....	....	....	....	....
	Salt Lake	IHL	17	1	3	4	124	13	0	1	1	*120
1988-89	Salt Lake	IHL	72	4	20	24	313	....	....	....	....	....
1989-90	Salt Lake	IHL	58	5	13	18	419	....	....	....	....	....
1990-91	Phoenix	IHL	60	9	13	22	369	7	1	2	3	44
	Los Angeles	NHL	4	0	0	0	5	....	....	....	....	....
1991-92	Capital Dist.	AHL	27	3	8	11	139	7	0	0	0	58
1992-93	Moncton	AHL	47	1	3	4	231	....	....	....	....	....
	Capital Dist.	AHL	19	0	1	1	80	4	1	1	2	27
1993-94	Cincinnati	IHL	61	2	6	8	302	8	0	1	1	*99
	NHL Totals		4	0	0	0	5	....	....	....	....	....

Traded to **Calgary** by **Montreal** for Martin Nicoletti, February 20, 1988. Signed as a free agent by **Los Angeles**, December 10, 1990. Signed as a free agent by **NY Islanders**, July 25, 1991. Signed as a free agent by **Florida**, September 7, 1993.

HEALEY, PAUL — PHI.

Right wing. Shoots right. 6'2", 185 lbs. Born, Edmonton, Alta., March 20, 1975.
(Philadelphia's 7th choice, 192nd overall, in 1993 Entry Draft).

			Regular Season					Playoffs				
Season	Club	Lea	GP	G	A	TP	PIM	GP	G	A	TP	PIM
1992-93	Prince Albert	WHL	72	12	20	32	66	....	....	....	....	....
1993-94	Prince Albert	WHL	63	23	26	49	70	....	....	....	....	....

HEAPHY, SHAWN

Center. Shoots left. 5'8", 180 lbs. Born, Sudbury, Ont., November 27, 1968.
(Calgary's 1st choice, 26th overall, in 1989 Supplemental Draft).

			Regular Season					Playoffs				
Season	Club	Lea	GP	G	A	TP	PIM	GP	G	A	TP	PIM
1987-88	Michigan State	CCHA	44	19	24	43	48	....	....	....	....	....
1988-89	Michigan State	CCHA	47	26	17	43	80	....	....	....	....	....
1989-90	Michigan State	CCHA	45	28	31	59	54	....	....	....	....	....
1990-91	Michigan State	CCHA	39	30	19	49	57	....	....	....	....	....
	Salt Lake	IHL	....	....	....	....	....	1	0	0	0	0
1991-92	Salt Lake	IHL	76	41	36	77	85	5	2	2	4	2
1992-93	**Calgary**	**NHL**	**1**	**0**	**0**	**0**	**0**	....	....	....	....	....
	Salt Lake	IHL	78	29	36	65	63	....	....	....	....	....
1993-94	Brunico	Alp.	28	20	19	39	42	....	....	....	....	....
	Brunico	Italy	11	10	8	18	15	....	....	....	....	....
	Las Vegas	IHL	37	10	5	15	45	5	0	0	0	6
	NHL Totals		**1**	**0**	**0**	**0**	**0**	....	....	....	....	....

HEDICAN, BRET — VAN.

Defense. Shoots left. 6'2", 195 lbs. Born, St. Paul, MN, August 10, 1970.
(St. Louis' 10th choice, 198th overall, in 1988 Entry Draft).

			Regular Season					Playoffs				
Season	Club	Lea	GP	G	A	TP	PIM	GP	G	A	TP	PIM
1988-89	St. Cloud	NCAA	28	5	3	8	28	....	....	....	....	....
1989-90	St. Cloud	NCAA	36	4	17	21	37	....	....	....	....	....
1990-91a	St. Cloud	WCHA	41	21	26	47	26	....	....	....	....	....
1991-92	U.S. National	....	54	1	8	9	59	....	....	....	....	....
	U.S. Olympic	....	8	0	0	0	4	....	....	....	....	....
	St. Louis	**NHL**	**4**	**1**	**0**	**1**	**0**	**5**	**0**	**0**	**0**	**0**
1992-93	**St. Louis**	**NHL**	**42**	**0**	**8**	**8**	**30**	**10**	**0**	**0**	**0**	**14**
	Peoria	IHL	19	0	8	8	10	....	....	....	....	....
1993-94	**St. Louis**	**NHL**	**61**	**0**	**11**	**11**	**64**	....	....	....	....	....
	Vancouver	**NHL**	**8**	**0**	**1**	**1**	**0**	**24**	**1**	**6**	**7**	**16**
	NHL Totals		**115**	**1**	**20**	**21**	**94**	**39**	**1**	**6**	**7**	**30**

a WCHA First All-Star Team (1991)

Traded to **Vancouver** by **St. Louis** with Jeff Brown and Nathan Lafayette for Craig Janney, March 21, 1994.

HEDLUND, TODD — NYR

Right wing. Shoots right. 6'1", 177 lbs. Born, Roseau, MN, August 20, 1971.
(NY Rangers' 10th choice, 160th overall, in 1990 Entry Draft).

			Regular Season					Playoffs				
Season	Club	Lea	GP	G	A	TP	PIM	GP	G	A	TP	PIM
1991-92	U. Wisconsin	WCHA	5	0	1	1	2	....	....	....	....	....
1992-93	U. Wisconsin	WCHA	8	0	0	0	0	....	....	....	....	....
1993-94					DID NOT PLAY							

HEHR, JASON — N.J.

Defense. Shoots left. 6'1", 193 lbs. Born, Medicine Hat, Alta., February 8, 1971.
(New Jersey's 12th choice, 253rd overall, in 1991 Entry Draft).

			Regular Season					Playoffs				
Season	Club	Lea	GP	G	A	TP	PIM	GP	G	A	TP	PIM
1991-92	N. Michigan	WCHA	40	8	17	25	38	....	....	....	....	....
1992-93	N. Michigan	WCHA	43	8	27	35	40	....	....	....	....	....
1993-94	N. Michigan	WCHA	39	11	26	37	56	....	....	....	....	....

HEINZE, STEPHEN (HIGHNS) — BOS.

Right wing. Shoots right. 5'11", 192 lbs. Born, Lawrence, MA, January 30, 1970.
(Boston's 2nd choice, 60th overall, in 1988 Entry Draft).

			Regular Season					Playoffs				
Season	Club	Lea	GP	G	A	TP	PIM	GP	G	A	TP	PIM
1988-89	Boston College	H.E.	36	26	23	49	26	....	....	....	....	....
1989-90ab	Boston College	H.E.	40	27	36	63	41	....	....	....	....	....
1990-91	Boston College	H.E.	35	21	26	47	35	....	....	....	....	....
1991-92	U.S. National	....	49	18	15	33	38	....	....	....	....	....
	U.S. Olympic	....	8	1	3	4	8	....	....	....	....	....
	Boston	**NHL**	**14**	**3**	**4**	**7**	**6**	**7**	**0**	**3**	**3**	**17**
1992-93	**Boston**	**NHL**	**73**	**18**	**13**	**31**	**24**	**4**	**1**	**1**	**2**	**2**
1993-94	**Boston**	**NHL**	**77**	**10**	**11**	**21**	**32**	**13**	**2**	**3**	**5**	**7**
	NHL Totals		**164**	**31**	**28**	**59**	**62**	**24**	**3**	**7**	**10**	**26**

a Hockey East First All-Star Team (1990)
b NCAA East First All-American Team (1990)

HEJDUK, MILAN (HEHI-duhk) — QUE.

Right wing. Shoots right. 5'11", 163 lbs. Born, Usti-nad-Labem, Czech., February 14, 1976.
(Quebec's 6th choice, 87th overall, in 1994 Entry Draft).

			Regular Season					Playoffs				
Season	Club	Lea	GP	G	A	TP	PIM	GP	G	A	TP	PIM
1993-94	Pardubice	Czech.	22	6	3	9	....	10	5	1	6	....

HELENIUS, SAMI — CGY.

Defense. Shoots left. 6'5", 225 lbs. Born, Finland, January 22, 1974.
(Calgary's 5th choice, 102nd overall, in 1992 Entry Draft).

			Regular Season					Playoffs				
Season	Club	Lea	GP	G	A	TP	PIM	GP	G	A	TP	PIM
1992-93	Jokerit	Fin.	1	0	0	0	0	....	....	....	....	....
1993-94	Reipas	Fin.	37	2	3	5	46	....	....	....	....	....

HELMER, BRYAN — N.J.

Defense. Shoots right. 6'1", 190 lbs. Born, Sault Ste. Marie, Ont., July 15, 1972.

			Regular Season					Playoffs				
Season	Club	Lea	GP	G	A	TP	PIM	GP	G	A	TP	PIM
1992-93	Wellington	Jr.A	57	25	62	87	62	....	....	....	....	....
1993-94	Albany	AHL	65	4	19	23	79	5	0	0	0	9

Signed as a free agent by **New Jersey**, July 10, 1994.

HEMENWAY, KEN — PHI.

Defense. Shoots right. 6'1", 175 lbs. Born, Boston, MA, August 1, 1975.
(Philadelphia's 11th choice, 270th overall, in 1993 Entry Draft).

			Regular Season					Playoffs				
Season	Club	Lea	GP	G	A	TP	PIM	GP	G	A	TP	PIM
1992-93	Alaska AS	USAHL	45	18	48	66	35	....	....	....	....	....
1993-94	Omaha	USHL	31	2	22	24	26	14	1	7	8	16

HENDRICKSON, DANIEL — WSH.

Right wing. Shoots right. 5'10", 180 lbs. Born, Minneapolis, MN, December 26, 1974.
(Washington's 5th choice, 173rd overall, in 1993 Entry Draft).

			Regular Season					Playoffs				
Season	Club	Lea	GP	G	A	TP	PIM	GP	G	A	TP	PIM
1992-93	St. Paul	USJHL	44	29	31	60	74	....	....	....	....	....
1993-94	U. Minnesota	WCHA	39	3	2	5	60	....	....	....	....	....

HENDRICKSON, DARBY — TOR.

Center. Shoots left. 6', 185 lbs. Born, Richfield, MN, August 28, 1972.
(Toronto's 3rd choice, 73rd overall, in 1990 Entry Draft).

			Regular Season					Playoffs				
Season	Club	Lea	GP	G	A	TP	PIM	GP	G	A	TP	PIM
1991-92	U. Minnesota	WCHA	41	25	28	53	61	....	....	....	....	....
1992-93	U. Minnesota	WCHA	31	12	15	27	35	....	....	....	....	....
1993-94	U.S. National	....	59	12	16	28	30	....	....	....	....	....
	U.S. Olympic	....	8	0	0	0	6	....	....	....	....	....
	St. John's	AHL	6	4	1	5	4	3	1	1	2	0
	Toronto	**NHL**	....	....	....	....	....	**2**	**0**	**0**	**0**	**0**
	NHL Totals		**0**	**0**	**0**	**0**	**0**	**2**	**0**	**0**	**0**	**0**

HENDRY, JOHN — DET.

Left wing. Shoots left. 6'1", 180 lbs. Born, Mississauga, Ont., May 15, 1970.
(Detroit's 11th choice, 234th overall, in 1990 Entry Draft).

			Regular Season					Playoffs				
Season	Club	Lea	GP	G	A	TP	PIM	GP	G	A	TP	PIM
1989-90	Lake Superior	CCHA	41	4	7	11	30	....	....	....	....	....
1990-91	Lake Superior	CCHA	44	7	10	17	42	....	....	....	....	....
1991-92	Lake Superior	CCHA	39	12	8	20	53	....	....	....	....	....
1992-93	Lake Superior	CCHA	37	13	20	33	46	....	....	....	....	....
1993-94	Toledo	ECHL	68	23	31	54	107	14	9	6	15	26

HENRICH, ED

Defense. Shoots left. 6'2", 185 lbs. Born, Buffalo, NY, February 2, 1971.
(Montreal's 10th choice, 209th overall, in 1989 Entry Draft).

			Regular Season					Playoffs				
Season	Club	Lea	GP	G	A	TP	PIM	GP	G	A	TP	PIM
1990-91	Clarkson	ECAC	37	4	23	27	22	....	....	....	....	....
1991-92	Clarkson	ECAC	28	2	11	13	22	....	....	....	....	....
1992-93	Clarkson	ECAC	35	0	11	11	30	....	....	....	....	....
1993-94	Clarkson	ECAC	34	3	11	14	26	....	....	....	....	....

HERBERS, IAN — EDM.

Defense. Shoots left. 6'4", 225 lbs. Born, Jasper, Alta., July 18, 1967.
(Buffalo's 11th choice, 190th overall, in 1987 Entry Draft).

			Regular Season					Playoffs				
Season	Club	Lea	GP	G	A	TP	PIM	GP	G	A	TP	PIM
1984-85	Kelowna	WHL	68	3	14	17	120	6	0	1	1	9
1985-86	Spokane	WHL	29	1	6	7	85	....	....	....	....	....
	Lethbridge	WHL	32	1	4	5	109	10	1	0	1	37
1986-87	Swift Current	WHL	72	5	8	13	230	4	1	1	2	12
1987-88	Swift Current	WHL	56	5	14	19	238	4	0	2	2	4
1988-89	U. of Alberta	CWUAA	47	4	22	26	137	....	....	....	....	....
1989-90a	U. of Alberta	CWUAA	45	5	31	36	83	....	....	....	....	....
1990-91bc	U. of Alberta	CWUAA	45	6	24	30	87	....	....	....	....	....
1991-92bcde	U. of Alberta	CWUAA	43	14	34	48	86	....	....	....	....	....
1992-93	Cape Breton	AHL	77	7	15	22	129	10	0	1	1	16
1993-94	**Edmonton**	**NHL**	**22**	**0**	**2**	**2**	**32**	....	....	....	....	....
	Cape Breton	AHL	53	7	16	23	122	5	0	3	3	12
	NHL Totals		**22**	**0**	**2**	**2**	**32**	....	....	....	....	....

a CWUAA Second All-Star Team (1990)
b CWUAA First All-Star Team (1991, 1992)
c CIAU All-Canadian Team (1991, 1992)
d Mervyn "Red" Dutton Trophy (CWUAA Outstanding Defenseman) (1992)
e CWUAA Student-Athlete-of-the-Year (1992)

Signed as a free agent by **Edmonton**, September 9, 1992.

HEROUX, YVES (hair-OO, EEV)

Right wing. Shoots right. 5'11", 185 lbs. Born, Terrebonne, Que., April 27, 1965.
(Quebec's 1st choice, 32nd overall, in 1983 Entry Draft).

			Regular Season					Playoffs				
Season	Club	Lea	GP	G	A	TP	PIM	GP	G	A	TP	PIM
1982-83	Chicoutimi	QMJHL	70	41	40	81	44	5	0	4	4	8
1983-84	Chicoutimi	QMJHL	56	28	25	53	67	....	....	....	....	....
	Fredericton	AHL	4	0	0	0	0	....	....	....	....	....
1984-85	Chicoutimi	QMJHL	66	42	54	96	123	14	5	8	13	16
1985-86	Fredericton	AHL	31	12	10	22	42	2	0	1	1	7
	Muskegon	IHL	42	14	8	22	41	....	....	....	....	....
1986-87	**Quebec**	**NHL**	**1**	**0**	**0**	**0**	**0**	....	....	....	....	....
	Fredericton	AHL	37	8	6	14	13	....	....	....	....	....
	Muskegon	IHL	25	6	8	14	31	2	0	0	0	0
1987-88	Baltimore	AHL	5	0	2	2	2	....	....	....	....	....
1988-89	Flint	IHL	82	43	42	85	98	....	....	....	....	....
1989-90	Peoria	IHL	14	3	2	5	42	5	2	2	4	0
1990-91	Albany	IHL	45	22	18	40	46	....	....	....	....	....
	Peoria	IHL	33	16	8	24	26	17	4	4	8	16
1991-92	Peoria	IHL	80	41	36	77	72	8	5	1	6	6
1992-93	Kalamazoo	IHL	80	38	30	68	86	....	....	....	....	....
1993-94	Kalamazoo	IHL	3	0	2	2	4	....	....	....	....	....
	Indianapolis	IHL	74	28	30	58	113	....	....	....	....	....
	NHL Totals		**1**	**0**	**0**	**0**	**0**	....	....	....	....	....

Signed as a free agent by **St. Louis**, March 13, 1990. Signed as a free agent by **Minnesota**, August 10, 1992.

HERPERGER, CHRIS   PHI.

Left wing. Shoots left. 6', 190 lbs.   Born, Esterhazy, Sask., February 24, 1974.
(Philadelphia's 10th choice, 223rd overall, in 1992 Entry Draft).

			Regular Season						Playoffs			
Season	Club	Lea	GP	G	A	TP	PIM	GP	G	A	TP	PIM
1990-91	Swift Current	WHL	10	0	1	1	5	....	....	....	....	....
1991-92	Swift Current	WHL	72	14	19	33	44	8	0	1	1	9
1992-93	Swift Current	WHL	20	9	7	16	31	....	....	....	....	....
	Seattle	WHL	46	20	11	31	30	5	1	1	2	6
1993-94	Seattle	WHL	71	44	51	95	110	9	12	10	22	12

HERR, MATT   WSH.

Center. Shoots left. 6'1", 180 lbs.   Born, Hackensack, NJ, May 26, 1976.
(Washington's 4th choice, 93rd overall, in 1994 Entry Draft).

			Regular Season						Playoffs			
Season	Club	Lea	GP	G	A	TP	PIM	GP	G	A	TP	PIM
1992-93	Hotchkiss	HS	24	48	30	78	....	....	....	....	....	....
1993-94	Hotchkiss	HS	24	28	19	47	....	....	....	....	....	....

HERTER, JASON   DAL.

Defense. Shoots right. 6'1", 190 lbs.   Born, Hafford, Sask., October 2, 1970.
(Vancouver's 1st choice, 8th overall, in 1989 Entry Draft).

			Regular Season						Playoffs			
Season	Club	Lea	GP	G	A	TP	PIM	GP	G	A	TP	PIM
1988-89	North Dakota	WCHA	41	8	24	32	62	....	....	....	....	....
1989-90a	North Dakota	WCHA	38	11	39	50	40	....	....	....	....	....
1990-91a	North Dakota	WCHA	39	11	26	37	52	....	....	....	....	....
1991-92	Milwaukee	IHL	56	7	18	25	34	1	0	0	0	2
1992-93	Hamilton	AHL	70	7	16	23	68	....	....	....	....	....
1993-94	Kalamazoo	IHL	68	14	28	42	92	5	3	0	3	14

a WCHA Second All-Star Team (1990, 1991)
Signed as a free agent by **Dallas**, August 6, 1993.

HEWARD, JAMIE

Right wing. Shoots right. 6'2", 183 lbs.   Born, Regina, Sask., March 30, 1971.
(Pittsburgh's 1st choice, 16th overall, in 1989 Entry Draft).

			Regular Season						Playoffs			
Season	Club	Lea	GP	G	A	TP	PIM	GP	G	A	TP	PIM
1987-88	Regina	WHL	68	10	17	27	17	4	1	1	2	2
1988-89	Regina	WHL	52	31	28	59	29	....	....	....	....	....
1989-90	Regina	WHL	72	14	44	58	42	11	2	2	4	10
1990-91a	Regina	WHL	71	23	61	84	41	8	2	9	11	6
1991-92	Muskegon	IHL	54	6	21	27	37	14	1	4	5	4
1992-93	Cleveland	IHL	58	9	18	27	64	....	....	....	....	....
1993-94	Cleveland	IHL	73	8	16	24	72	....	....	....	....	....

a WHL East First All-Star Team (1991)

HEWSON, RUSSELL   WPG.

Left wing. Shoots left. 6'5", 191 lbs.   Born, Provost, Alta., January 12, 1975.
(Winnipeg's 13th choice, 285th overall, in 1993 Entry Draft).

			Regular Season						Playoffs			
Season	Club	Lea	GP	G	A	TP	PIM	GP	G	A	TP	PIM
1992-93	Swift Current	WHL	70	6	20	26	39	17	2	4	6	4
1993-94	Swift Current	WHL	48	15	25	40	31	....	....	....	....	....
	Regina	WHL	22	8	12	20	24	4	1	2	3	2

HEXTALL, DONEVAN   N.J.

Center. Shoots left. 6'2", 190 lbs.   Born, Wolseley, Sask., February 24, 1972.
(New Jersey's 3rd choice, 33rd overall, in 1991 Entry Draft).

			Regular Season						Playoffs			
Season	Club	Lea	GP	G	A	TP	PIM	GP	G	A	TP	PIM
1989-90	Weyburn	SJHL	63	23	45	68	127	....	....	....	....	....
	Prince Albert	WHL	7	1	2	3	4	....	....	....	....	....
1990-91	Prince Albert	WHL	70	30	59	89	55	3	1	3	4	0
1991-92a	Prince Albert	WHL	71	33	71	104	105	10	3	6	9	10
1992-93	Cdn. National	....	6	0	1	1	4	....	....	....	....	....
	Utica	AHL	51	11	11	22	12	2	1	0	1	0
1993-94	Albany	AHL	4	1	0	1	0	....	....	....	....	....
	Raleigh	ECHL	61	13	49	62	55	13	1	8	9	18

a WHL East Second All-Star Team (1992)

HILL, KILEY   T.B.

Left wing. Shoots left. 6'3", 205 lbs.   Born, Sudbury, Ont., January 2, 1975.
(Tampa Bay's 6th choice, 133rd overall, in 1993 Entry Draft).

			Regular Season						Playoffs			
Season	Club	Lea	GP	G	A	TP	PIM	GP	G	A	TP	PIM
1991-92	S.S. Marie	OHL	32	4	3	7	28	5	1	0	1	0
1992-93	S.S. Marie	OHL	49	6	8	14	76	1	0	0	0	2
1993-94	S.S. Marie	OHL	7	2	3	5	13	....	....	....	....	....
	Newmarket	OHL	52	7	15	22	58	....	....	....	....	....

HILL, SEAN   (HIHL, SHAWN)   OTT.

Defense. Shoots right. 6', 195 lbs.   Born, Duluth, MN, February 14, 1970.
(Montreal's 9th choice, 167th overall, in 1988 Entry Draft).

			Regular Season						Playoffs			
Season	Club	Lea	GP	G	A	TP	PIM	GP	G	A	TP	PIM
1988-89	U. Wisconsin	WCHA	45	2	23	25	69	....	....	....	....	....
1989-90a	U. Wisconsin	WCHA	42	14	39	53	78	....	....	....	....	....
1990-91ab	U. Wisconsin	WCHA	37	19	32	51	122	....	....	....	....	....
	Montreal	**NHL**	....	....	....	....	....	1	0	0	0	0
	Fredericton	AHL	....	....	....	....	....	3	0	2	2	2
1991-92	Fredericton	AHL	42	7	20	27	65	7	1	3	4	6
	U.S. National	....	12	4	3	7	16	....	....	....	....	....
	U.S. Olympic	....	8	2	0	2	6	....	....	....	....	....
	Montreal	**NHL**	....	....	....	....	....	4	1	0	1	2
1992-93	**Montreal**	**NHL**	31	2	6	8	54	3	0	0	0	4
	Fredericton	AHL	6	1	3	4	10	....	....	....	....	....
1993-94	**Anaheim**	**NHL**	68	7	20	27	78	....	....	....	....	....
	NHL Totals		**99**	**9**	**26**	**35**	**132**	**8**	**1**	**0**	**1**	**6**

a WCHA Second All-Star Team (1990, 1991)
b NCAA West Second All-American Team (1991)
Claimed by **Anaheim** from **Montreal** in Expansion Draft, June 24, 1993. Traded to **Ottawa** by **Anaheim** with Anaheim's ninth round choice (Frederic Cassivi) in 1994 Entry Draft for Ottawa's third round choice (later traded to Tampa Bay — Tampa Bay selected Vadim Epanchintsev) in 1994 Entry Draft, June 29, 1994.

HILLER, JIM   NYR

Right wing. Shoots right. 6', 190 lbs.   Born, Port Alberni, B.C., May 15, 1969.
(Los Angeles' 10th choice, 207th overall, in 1989 Entry Draft).

			Regular Season						Playoffs			
Season	Club	Lea	GP	G	A	TP	PIM	GP	G	A	TP	PIM
1989-90	N. Michigan	WCHA	39	23	33	56	52	....	....	....	....	....
1990-91	N. Michigan	WCHA	43	22	41	63	59	....	....	....	....	....
1991-92ab	N. Michigan	WCHA	39	28	52	80	115	....	....	....	....	....
1992-93	**Los Angeles**	**NHL**	40	6	6	12	90	....	....	....	....	....
	Phoenix	IHL	3	0	2	2	2	....	....	....	....	....
	Detroit	**NHL**	21	2	6	8	19	2	0	0	0	4
1993-94	**NY Rangers**	**NHL**	2	0	0	0	7	....	....	....	....	....
	Binghamton	AHL	67	27	34	61	61	....	....	....	....	....
	NHL Totals		**63**	**8**	**12**	**20**	**116**	**2**	**0**	**0**	**0**	**4**

a NCAA West Second All-American Team (1992)
b WCHA Second All-Star Team (1992)
Traded to **Detroit** by **Los Angeles** with Paul Coffey and Sylvain Couturier for Jimmy Carson, Marc Potvin and Gary Shuchuk, January 29, 1993. Claimed on waivers by **NY Rangers** from **Detroit**, October 12, 1993.

HILLMAN, JOHN   QUE.

Center. Shoots left. 6'1", 200 lbs.   Born, Fridley, MN, October 10, 1974.
(Quebec's 13th choice, 283rd overall, in 1983 Entry Draft).

			Regular Season						Playoffs			
Season	Club	Lea	GP	G	A	TP	PIM	GP	G	A	TP	PIM
1984-85	SaPKo	Fin.2	21	3	5	8	0	6	6	0	6	0
1985-86	SaPKo	Fin.2	40	14	13	27	12	....	....	....	....	....
1986-87	SaPKo	Fin.2	40	15	21	36	10	....	....	....	....	....
1992-93	St. Paul	Jr. A	30	11	8	19	86	....	....	....	....	....
1993-94	U. Minnesota	WCHA	20	0	0	0	8	....	....	....	....	....

HILTON, KEVIN   DET.

Center. Shoots left. 5'11", 170 lbs.   Born, Trenton, MI, January 5, 1975.
(Detroit's 3rd choice, 74th overall, in 1993 Entry Draft).

			Regular Season						Playoffs			
Season	Club	Lea	GP	G	A	TP	PIM	GP	G	A	TP	PIM
1992-93	U. of Michigan	CCHA	36	16	15	31	8	....	....	....	....	....
1993-94	U. of Michigan	CCHA	39	11	12	23	16	....	....	....	....	....

HINKS, ROD   NYI

Center. Shoots left. 5'10", 185 lbs.   Born, Etobicoke, Ont., April 11, 1973.
(NY Islanders' 8th choice, 196th overall, in 1993 Entry Draft).

			Regular Season						Playoffs			
Season	Club	Lea	GP	G	A	TP	PIM	GP	G	A	TP	PIM
1990-91	Sudbury	OHL	50	2	9	11	28	....	....	....	....	....
1991-92	Sudbury	OHL	66	35	21	56	62	11	2	3	5	6
1992-93	Sudbury	OHL	64	47	57	104	100	14	7	10	17	30
1993-94	Sudbury	OHL	12	6	14	20	14	....	....	....	....	....
	Owen Sound	OHL	50	40	44	84	79	9	5	4	9	19

HLUSHKO, TODD   (huh-LUSH-koh)   CGY.

Center. Shoots left. 5'11", 195 lbs.   Born, Toronto, Ont., February 7, 1970.
(Washington's 14th choice, 240th overall, in 1989 Entry Draft).

			Regular Season						Playoffs			
Season	Club	Lea	GP	G	A	TP	PIM	GP	G	A	TP	PIM
1988-89	Guelph	OHL	66	28	18	46	71	7	5	3	8	18
1989-90	Owen Sound	OHL	25	9	17	26	31	....	....	....	....	....
	London	OHL	40	27	17	44	39	6	2	4	6	10
1990-91	Baltimore	AHL	66	9	14	23	55	....	....	....	....	....
1991-92	Baltimore	AHL	74	16	35	51	113	....	....	....	....	....
1992-93	Cdn. National	....	58	22	26	48	10	....	....	....	....	....
1993-94	Cdn. National	....	55	22	6	28	61	....	....	....	....	....
	Cdn. Olympic	....	8	5	0	5	6	....	....	....	....	....
	Philadelphia	**NHL**	2	1	0	1	0	....	....	....	....	....
	Hershey	AHL	9	6	0	6	4	6	2	1	3	4
	NHL Totals		**2**	**1**	**0**	**1**	**0**					

Signed as a free agent by **Philadelphia**, March 7, 1994. Signed as a free agent by **Calgary**, June 17, 1994.

HOCKING, JUSTIN   L.A.

Defense. Shoots right. 6'4", 205 lbs.   Born, Stettler, Alta., January 9, 1974.
(Los Angeles' 1st choice, 39th overall, in 1992 Entry Draft).

			Regular Season						Playoffs			
Season	Club	Lea	GP	G	A	TP	PIM	GP	G	A	TP	PIM
1991-92	Spokane	WHL	71	4	6	10	309	10	0	3	3	28
1992-93	Spokane	WHL	16	0	1	1	75	....	....	....	....	....
	Medicine Hat	WHL	54	1	9	10	119	10	0	1	1	13
1993-94	**Los Angeles**	**NHL**	1	0	0	0	0	....	....	....	....	....
a	Medicine Hat	WHL	68	7	26	33	236	3	0	0	0	6
	Phoenix	IHL	3	0	0	0	15	....	....	....	....	....
	NHL Totals		**1**	**0**	**0**	**0**	**0**					

a WHL East Second All-Star Team (1994)

HODGE, DAN   BOS.

Defense. Shoots right. 6'3", 205 lbs.   Born, Melrose, MA, September 18, 1971.
(Boston's 8th choice, 194th overall, in 1991 Entry Draft).

			Regular Season						Playoffs			
Season	Club	Lea	GP	G	A	TP	PIM	GP	G	A	TP	PIM
1990-91	Merrimack	H.E.	11	2	3	5	4	....	....	....	....	....
1991-92	Omaha	USHL	45	5	18	23	89	....	....	....	....	....
1992-93	Merrimack	H.E.	36	3	17	20	30	....	....	....	....	....
1993-94	Merrimack	H.E.	37	9	22	31	72	....	....	....	....	....

HODGE, KEN

Center/Right wing. Shoots left. 6'1", 200 lbs. Born, Windsor, Ont., April 13, 1966.
(Minnesota's 2nd choice, 46th overall, in 1984 Entry Draft).

			Regular Season					Playoffs				
Season	Club	Lea	GP	G	A	TP	PIM	GP	G	A	TP	PIM
1984-85	Boston College	H.E.	41	20	44	64	28	....	....	....	....	....
1985-86	Boston College	H.E.	21	11	17	28	16	....	....	....	....	....
1986-87	Boston College	H.E.	37	29	33	62	30	....	....	....	....	....
1987-88	Kalamazoo	IHL	70	15	35	50	24	....	....	....	....	....
1988-89	**Minnesota**	**NHL**	**5**	**1**	**1**	**2**	**0**	....	....	....	....	....
	Kalamazoo	IHL	72	26	45	71	34	6	1	5	6	16
1989-90	Kalamazoo	IHL	68	33	53	86	19	10	5	13	18	2
1990-91a	**Boston**	**NHL**	**70**	**30**	**29**	**59**	**20**	**15**	**4**	**6**	**10**	**6**
	Maine	AHL	8	7	10	17	2	....	....	....	....	....
1991-92	**Boston**	**NHL**	**42**	**6**	**11**	**17**	**10**	....	....	....	....	....
	Maine	AHL	19	6	11	17	4	....	....	....	....	....
1992-93	**Tampa Bay**	**NHL**	**25**	**2**	**7**	**9**	**2**	....	....	....	....	....
	Atlanta	IHL	16	10	17	27	0	....	....	....	....	....
	San Diego	IHL	30	11	24	35	16	14	4	6	10	6
1993-94	Binghamton	AHL	79	22	56	78	51	....	....	....	....	....
	NHL Totals		**142**	**39**	**48**	**87**	**32**	**15**	**4**	**6**	**10**	**6**

a NHL/Upper Deck All-Rookie Team (1991)

Traded to **Boston** by **Minnesota** for Boston's fourth round choice (Jere Lehtinen) in 1992 Entry Draft, August 21, 1990. Traded to **Tampa Bay** by **Boston** with Matt Hervey for Darin Kimble and future considerations, September 4, 1992. Signed as a free agent by **NY Rangers**, September 2, 1993.

HOGAN, TIM — CHI.

Defense. Shoots right. 6'2", 180 lbs. Born, Oshawa, Ont., January 7, 1974.
(Chicago's 5th choice, 113th overall, in 1992 Entry Draft).

			Regular Season					Playoffs				
Season	Club	Lea	GP	G	A	TP	PIM	GP	G	A	TP	PIM
1991-92	U. of Michigan	CCHA	34	2	8	10	34	....	....	....	....	....
1992-93	U. of Michigan	CCHA	22	4	1	5	24	....	....	....	....	....
1993-94	U. of Michigan	CCHA	37	2	10	12	36	....	....	....	....	....

HOGLUND, JONAS — CGY.

Right wing. Shoots right. 6'3", 200 lbs. Born, Hammaro, Sweden, August 29, 1972.
(Calgary's 11th choice, 222nd overall, in 1992 Entry Draft).

			Regular Season					Playoffs				
Season	Club	Lea	GP	G	A	TP	PIM	GP	G	A	TP	PIM
1988-89	Farjestad	Swe.	1	0	0	0	0	....	....	....	....	....
1989-90	Farjestad	Swe.	1	0	0	0	0	....	....	....	....	....
1990-91	Farjestad	Swe.	40	5	5	10	4	8	1	0	1	0
1991-92	Farjestad	Swe.	40	14	11	25	6	6	2	4	6	2
1992-93	Farjestad	Swe.	40	13	13	26	14	3	1	0	1	0
1993-94	Farjestad	Swe.	22	7	2	9	10	....	....	....	....	....

HOGUE, BENOIT (HOHG)

Center. Shoots left. 5'10", 190 lbs. Born, Repentigny, Que., October 28, 1966.
(Buffalo's 2nd choice, 35th overall, in 1985 Entry Draft).

			Regular Season					Playoffs				
Season	Club	Lea	GP	G	A	TP	PIM	GP	G	A	TP	PIM
1983-84	St-Jean	QMJHL	59	14	11	25	42	....	....	....	....	....
1984-85	St-Jean	QMJHL	63	46	44	90	92	....	....	....	....	....
1985-86	St-Jean	QMJHL	65	54	54	108	115	9	6	4	10	26
1986-87	Rochester	AHL	52	14	20	34	52	12	5	4	9	8
1987-88	**Buffalo**	**NHL**	**3**	**1**	**1**	**2**	**0**	....	....	....	....	....
	Rochester	AHL	62	24	31	55	141	7	6	1	7	46
1988-89	**Buffalo**	**NHL**	**69**	**14**	**30**	**44**	**120**	**5**	**0**	**0**	**0**	**17**
1989-90	**Buffalo**	**NHL**	**45**	**11**	**7**	**18**	**79**	**3**	**0**	**0**	**0**	**10**
1990-91	**Buffalo**	**NHL**	**76**	**19**	**28**	**47**	**76**	**5**	**3**	**1**	**4**	**10**
1991-92	**Buffalo**	**NHL**	**3**	**0**	**1**	**1**	**0**	....	....	....	....	....
	NY Islanders	**NHL**	**72**	**30**	**45**	**75**	**67**	....	....	....	....	....
1992-93	**NY Islanders**	**NHL**	**70**	**33**	**42**	**75**	**108**	**18**	**6**	**6**	**12**	**31**
1993-94	**NY Islanders**	**NHL**	**83**	**36**	**33**	**69**	**73**	**4**	**0**	**1**	**1**	**4**
	NHL Totals		**421**	**144**	**187**	**331**	**523**	**35**	**9**	**8**	**17**	**72**

Traded to **NY Islanders** by **Buffalo** with Pierre Turgeon, Uwe Krupp and Dave McLlwain for Pat Lafontaine, Randy Hillier, Randy Wood and NY Islanders' fourth round choice (Dean Melanson) in 1992 Entry Draft, October 25, 1991.

HOLAN, MILOS — PHI.

Defense. Shoots left. 5'11", 196 lbs. Born, Bilovec, Czech., April 22, 1971.
(Philadelphia's 3rd choice, 77th overall, in 1993 Entry Draft).

			Regular Season					Playoffs				
Season	Club	Lea	GP	G	A	TP	PIM	GP	G	A	TP	PIM
1988-89	TJ Vitkovice	Czech.	7	0	0	0	0	....	....	....	....	....
1989-90	TJ Vitkovice	Czech.	50	8	8	16	....	....	....	....	....	....
1990-91	Dukla Trencin	Czech.	53	6	13	19	....	....	....	....	....	....
1991-92	Dukla Trencin	Czech.	51	13	22	35	32	....	....	....	....	....
1992-93a	TJ Vitkovice	Czech.	53	35	33	68	....	....	....	....	....	....
1993-94	**Philadelphia**	**NHL**	**8**	**1**	**1**	**2**	**4**	....	....	....	....	....
	Hershey	AHL	27	7	22	29	16	....	....	....	....	....
	NHL Totals		**8**	**1**	**1**	**2**	**4**	....	....	....	....	....

a Czechoslovakian Player of the Year (1993)

HOLDEMAN, TOM — EDM.

Right wing. Shoots right. 6'2", 205 lbs. Born, Columbus, IN, November 8, 1970.
(Edmonton's 1st choice, 18th overall, in 1991 Supplemental Draft).

			Regular Season					Playoffs				
Season	Club	Lea	GP	G	A	TP	PIM	GP	G	A	TP	PIM
1989-90	Miami-Ohio	CCHA	28	3	1	4	8	....	....	....	....	....
1990-91	Miami-Ohio	CCHA	28	2	2	4	42	....	....	....	....	....
1991-92	W. Michigan	CCHA				DID NOT PLAY						
1992-93	Wheeling	ECHL	2	0	1	1	2	....	....	....	....	....
1993-94	S. Carolina	ECHL	6	4	1	5	2	....	....	....	....	....
	Roanoke	ECHL	14	1	2	3	12	....	....	....	....	....

HOLDEN, PAUL

Defense. Shoots left. 6'3", 210 lbs. Born, Kitchener, Ont., March 15, 1970.
(Los Angeles' 2nd choice, 28th overall, in 1988 Entry Draft).

			Regular Season					Playoffs				
Season	Club	Lea	GP	G	A	TP	PIM	GP	G	A	TP	PIM
1987-88	London	OHL	65	8	12	20	87	12	1	1	2	10
1988-89	London	OHL	54	11	21	32	90	20	1	3	4	17
1989-90a	London	OHL	61	11	31	42	78	6	1	1	2	7
	New Haven	AHL	2	1	1	2	2	....	....	....	....	....
1990-91	New Haven	AHL	59	2	8	10	23	....	....	....	....	....
1991-92	Phoenix	IHL	47	3	3	6	63	....	....	....	....	....
1992-93	Phoenix	IHL	3	0	0	0	6	....	....	....	....	....
	Salt Lake	IHL	63	5	8	13	86	....	....	....	....	....
1993-94	St. John's	AHL	75	6	14	20	101	11	0	4	4	18

a OHL Second All-Star Team (1990)

Traded to **Calgary** by **Los Angeles** for Kevin Grant, October 16, 1992. Traded to **Toronto** by **Calgary** with Todd Gillingham for Brad Miller and Jeff Perry, September 2, 1993.

HOLIK, BOBBY (HOH-leek) — N.J.

Left wing. Shoots right. 6'3", 220 lbs. Born, Jihlava, Czech., January 1, 1971.
(Hartford's 1st choice, 10th overall, in 1989 Entry Draft).

			Regular Season					Playoffs				
Season	Club	Lea	GP	G	A	TP	PIM	GP	G	A	TP	PIM
1987-88	Dukla Jihlava	Czech.	31	5	9	14	16	....	....	....	....	....
1988-89	Dukla Jihlava	Czech.	24	7	10	17	32	....	....	....	....	....
1989-90	Dukla Jihlava	Czech.	42	15	26	41	....					
1990-91	**Hartford**	**NHL**	**78**	**21**	**22**	**43**	**113**	**6**	**0**	**0**	**0**	**7**
1991-92	**Hartford**	**NHL**	**76**	**21**	**24**	**45**	**44**	**7**	**0**	**1**	**1**	**6**
1992-93	**New Jersey**	**NHL**	**61**	**20**	**19**	**39**	**76**	**5**	**1**	**1**	**2**	**6**
	Utica	AHL	1	0	0	0	2	....	....	....	....	....
1993-94	**New Jersey**	**NHL**	**70**	**13**	**20**	**33**	**72**	**20**	**0**	**3**	**3**	**6**
	NHL Totals		**285**	**75**	**85**	**160**	**305**	**38**	**1**	**5**	**6**	**25**

Traded to **New Jersey** by **Hartford** with Hartford's second round choice (Jay Pandolfo) in 1993 Entry Draft and future considerations for Sean Burke and Eric Weinrich, August 28, 1992.

HOLLAND, DENNIS — BOS.

Center. Shoots left. 5'10", 165 lbs. Born, Vernon, B.C., January 30, 1969.
(Detroit's 4th choice, 52nd overall, in 1987 Entry Draft).

			Regular Season					Playoffs				
Season	Club	Lea	GP	G	A	TP	PIM	GP	G	A	TP	PIM
1986-87	Portland	WHL	72	36	77	113	96	20	7	14	21	20
1987-88a	Portland	WHL	67	58	86	144	115	....	....	....	....	....
1988-89a	Portland	WHL	69	*82	85	*167	120	19	15	*22	37	18
1989-90	Adirondack	AHL	78	19	34	53	53	6	1	1	2	10
1990-91	San Diego	IHL	45	25	30	55	129	....	....	....	....	....
	Adirondack	AHL	28	8	7	15	31	2	0	0	0	4
1991-92	Fort Wayne	IHL	6	2	4	6	21	....	....	....	....	....
	Salt Lake	IHL	73	20	25	45	102	4	0	2	2	2
1992-93	Cincinnati	IHL	71	23	47	70	140	....	....	....	....	....
1993-94	Providence	AHL	61	10	26	36	44	....	....	....	....	....

a WHL West All-Star Team (1988, 1989)

Traded to **Calgary** by **Detroit** for future considerations, October 21, 1991. Signed as a free agent by **Boston**, August 30, 1993.

HOLLAND, JASON — NYI

Defense. Shoots right. 6'2", 190 lbs. Born, Morinville, Alta., April 30, 1976.
(NY Islanders' 2nd choice, 38th overall, in 1994 Entry Draft).

			Regular Season					Playoffs				
Season	Club	Lea	GP	G	A	TP	PIM	GP	G	A	TP	PIM
1992-93	St. Albert	Midget	31	11	25	36	36	....	....	....	....	....
1993-94	Kamloops	WHL	59	14	15	29	80	18	2	3	5	4

HOLLINGER, TERRY — ST.L.

Defense. Shoots left. 6'1", 200 lbs. Born, Regina, Sask., February 24, 1971.
(St. Louis' 7th choice, 153rd overall, in 1991 Entry Draft).

			Regular Season					Playoffs				
Season	Club	Lea	GP	G	A	TP	PIM	GP	G	A	TP	PIM
1990-91	Regina	WHL	8	1	6	7	6	....	....	....	....	....
	Lethbridge	WHL	62	9	32	41	113	16	3	14	17	22
1991-92	Lethbridge	WHL	65	23	62	85	155	5	1	2	3	13
	Peoria	IHL	1	0	2	2	0	5	0	1	1	0
1992-93	Peoria	IHL	72	2	28	30	67	4	1	1	2	0
1993-94	**St. Louis**	**NHL**	**2**	**0**	**0**	**0**	**0**	....	....	....	....	....
	Peoria	IHL	78	12	31	43	96	6	0	3	3	31
	NHL Totals		**2**	**0**	**0**	**0**	**0**	....	....	....	....	....

HOLLIS, SCOTT

Right wing. Shoots right. 5'11", 183 lbs. Born, Kingston, Ont., September 18, 1972.
(Vancouver's 7th choice, 165th overall, in 1992 Entry Draft).

			Regular Season					Playoffs				
Season	Club	Lea	GP	G	A	TP	PIM	GP	G	A	TP	PIM
1990-91	Oshawa	OHL	66	24	33	57	91	16	5	3	8	20
1991-92a	Oshawa	OHL	66	47	54	101	183	7	7	3	10	8
1992-93	Oshawa	OHL	62	49	53	102	148	13	8	15	23	22
1993-94	Las Vegas	IHL	23	3	1	4	65	....	....	....	....	....
	Knoxville	ECHL	28	20	16	36	99	3	3	1	4	8

a OHL Second All-Star Team (1992)

HOLT, TODD — S.J.

Right wing. Shoots right. 5'7", 155 lbs. Born, Estevan, Sask., January 20, 1973.
(San Jose's 10th choice, 184th overall, in 1993 Entry Draft).

			Regular Season					Playoffs				
Season	Club	Lea	GP	G	A	TP	PIM	GP	G	A	TP	PIM
1989-90	Swift Current	WHL	63	26	22	48	29	4	1	0	1	2
1990-91	Swift Current	WHL	69	47	27	74	72	3	1	0	1	0
1991-92	Swift Current	WHL	66	47	54	101	155	8	4	5	9	10
1992-93	Swift Current	WHL	67	56	57	113	90	16	10	12	22	18
1993-94	Swift Current	WHL	56	40	47	87	59	7	11	7	18	8

HOLZINGER, BRIAN — BUF.

Center. Shoots right. 5'11", 180 lbs. Born, Parma, OH, October 10, 1972.
(Buffalo's 7th choice, 124th overall, in 1991 Entry Draft).

			Regular Season					Playoffs				
Season	Club	Lea	GP	G	A	TP	PIM	GP	G	A	TP	PIM
1991-92	Bowling Green	CCHA	30	14	8	22	36	....	....	....	....	....
1992-93a	Bowling Green	CCHA	41	31	26	57	44	....	....	....	....	....
1993-94	Bowling Green	CCHA	38	22	15	37	24	....	....	....	....	....

a CCHA Second All-Star Team (1993)

HOOPER, DALE

Defense. Shoots left. 6'2", 190 lbs. Born, Winchester, MA, November 28, 1972.
(Montreal's 15th choice, 259th overall, in 1991 Entry Draft).

			Regular Season					Playoffs				
Season	Club	Lea	GP	G	A	TP	PIM	GP	G	A	TP	PIM
1993-94	U. Mass.	NCAA	14	1	9	10	18	....	....	....	....	....

HOOVER, RON

Center. Shoots left. 6'1", 185 lbs. Born, Oakville, Ont., October 28, 1966.
(Hartford's 7th choice, 158th overall, in 1986 Entry Draft).

			Regular Season					Playoffs				
Season	Club	Lea	GP	G	A	TP	PIM	GP	G	A	TP	PIM
1985-86	W. Michigan	CCHA	43	10	23	33	36	....	....	....	....	....
1986-87	W. Michigan	CCHA	34	7	10	17	22	....	....	....	....	....
1987-88a	W. Michigan	CCHA	42	39	23	62	40	....	....	....	....	....
1988-89	W. Michigan	CCHA	42	32	27	59	66	....	....	....	....	....
1989-90	**Boston**	**NHL**	**2**	**0**	**0**	**0**	**0**	....	....	....	....	....
	Maine	AHL	75	28	26	54	57	....	....	....	....	....
1990-91	**Boston**	**NHL**	**15**	**4**	**0**	**4**	**31**	**8**	**0**	**0**	**0**	**18**
	Maine	AHL	62	28	16	44	40	....	....	....	....	....
1991-92	**St. Louis**	**NHL**	**1**	**0**	**0**	**0**	**0**	....	....	....	....	....
	Peoria	IHL	71	27	34	61	30	10	4	4	8	4
1992-93	Peoria	IHL	58	17	13	30	28	4	1	1	2	2
1993-94	Peoria	IHL	80	26	24	50	89	6	0	1	1	10
	NHL Totals		**18**	**4**	**0**	**4**	**31**	**8**	**0**	**0**	**0**	**18**

a CCHA Second All-Star Team (1988)

Signed as a free agent by **Boston**, September 1, 1989. Signed as a free agent by **St. Louis**, July 23, 1991.

HORACEK, TONY (HOHR-uh-chehk) CHI.

Left wing. Shoots left. 6'4", 210 lbs. Born, Vancouver, B.C., February 3, 1967.
(Philadelphia's 8th choice, 147th overall, in 1985 Entry Draft).

			Regular Season					Playoffs				
Season	Club	Lea	GP	G	A	TP	PIM	GP	G	A	TP	PIM
1984-85	Kelowna	WHL	67	9	18	27	114	6	0	1	1	11
1985-86	Spokane	WHL	64	19	28	47	129	9	4	5	9	29
1986-87	Spokane	WHL	64	23	37	60	177	5	1	3	4	18
	Hershey	AHL	....	....	....	....	....	1	0	0	0	0
1987-88	Hershey	AHL	1	0	0	0	0	....	....	....	....	....
	Spokane	WHL	24	17	23	40	63	....	....	....	....	....
	Kamloops	WHL	26	14	17	31	51	18	6	4	10	73
1988-89	Hershey	AHL	10	0	0	0	38	....	....	....	....	....
	Indianapolis	IHL	43	11	13	24	138	....	....	....	....	....
1989-90	**Philadelphia**	**NHL**	**48**	**5**	**5**	**10**	**117**	....	....	....	....	....
	Hershey	AHL	12	0	5	5	25	....	....	....	....	....
1990-91	**Philadelphia**	**NHL**	**34**	**3**	**6**	**9**	**49**	....	....	....	....	....
	Hershey	AHL	19	5	3	8	35	4	2	0	2	14
1991-92	**Philadelphia**	**NHL**	**34**	**1**	**3**	**4**	**51**	....	....	....	....	....
	Chicago	**NHL**	**12**	**1**	**4**	**5**	**21**	**2**	**1**	**0**	**1**	**2**
1992-93	Indianapolis	IHL	6	1	1	2	28	5	3	2	5	18
1993-94	**Chicago**	**NHL**	**7**	**0**	**0**	**0**	**53**	....	....	....	....	....
	Indianapolis	IHL	29	6	7	13	63	....	....	....	....	....
	NHL Totals		**135**	**10**	**18**	**28**	**291**	**2**	**1**	**0**	**1**	**2**

Traded to **Chicago** by **Philadelphia** for Ryan McGill, February 7, 1992.

HOUDA, DOUG (HOO-duh) BUF.

Defense. Shoots right. 6'2", 190 lbs. Born, Blairmore, Alta., June 3, 1966.
(Detroit's 2nd choice, 28th overall, in 1984 Entry Draft).

			Regular Season					Playoffs				
Season	Club	Lea	GP	G	A	TP	PIM	GP	G	A	TP	PIM
1982-83	Calgary	WHL	71	5	23	28	99	16	1	3	4	44
1983-84	Calgary	WHL	69	6	30	36	195	4	0	0	0	7
1984-85a	Calgary	WHL	65	20	54	74	182	8	3	4	7	29
1985-86	**Detroit**	**NHL**	**6**	**0**	**0**	**0**	**4**	....	....	....	....	....
	Calgary	WHL	16	4	10	14	60	....	....	....	....	....
	Medicine Hat	WHL	35	9	23	32	80	25	4	19	23	64
1986-87	Adirondack	AHL	77	6	23	29	142	11	1	8	9	50
1987-88	**Detroit**	**NHL**	**11**	**1**	**1**	**2**	**10**	....	....	....	....	....
b	Adirondack	AHL	71	10	32	42	169	11	0	3	3	44
1988-89	**Detroit**	**NHL**	**57**	**2**	**11**	**13**	**67**	**6**	**0**	**1**	**1**	**0**
	Adirondack	AHL	7	0	3	3	8	....	....	....	....	....
1989-90	**Detroit**	**NHL**	**73**	**2**	**9**	**11**	**127**	....	....	....	....	....
1990-91	**Detroit**	**NHL**	**22**	**0**	**4**	**4**	**43**	....	....	....	....	....
	Adirondack	AHL	38	9	17	26	67	....	....	....	....	....
	Hartford	**NHL**	**19**	**1**	**2**	**3**	**41**	**6**	**0**	**0**	**0**	**8**
1991-92	**Hartford**	**NHL**	**56**	**3**	**6**	**9**	**125**	**6**	**0**	**2**	**2**	**13**
1992-93	**Hartford**	**NHL**	**60**	**2**	**6**	**8**	**167**	....	....	....	....	....
1993-94	**Hartford**	**NHL**	**7**	**0**	**0**	**0**	**23**	....	....	....	....	....
	Los Angeles	**NHL**	**54**	**2**	**6**	**8**	**165**	....	....	....	....	....
	NHL Totals		**365**	**13**	**45**	**58**	**772**	**18**	**0**	**3**	**3**	**21**

a WHL East Second All-Star Team (1985)
b AHL First All-Star Team (1988)

Traded to **Hartford** by **Detroit** for DougCrossman, February 20, 1991. Traded to **Los Angeles** by **Hartford** for Marc Potvin, November 3, 1993. Traded to **Buffalo** by **Los Angeles** for Sean O'Donnell, July 26, 1994.

HOUGH, MIKE (HUHF) FLA.

Left wing. Shoots left. 6'1", 192 lbs. Born, Montreal, Que., February 6, 1963.
(Quebec's 7th choice, 181st overall, in 1982 Entry Draft).

			Regular Season					Playoffs				
Season	Club	Lea	GP	G	A	TP	PIM	GP	G	A	TP	PIM
1981-82	Kitchener	OHL	58	14	24	38	172	14	4	1	5	16
1982-83	Kitchener	OHL	61	17	27	44	156	12	5	4	9	30
1983-84	Fredericton	AHL	69	11	16	27	142	1	0	0	0	7
1984-85	Fredericton	AHL	76	21	27	48	49	6	1	1	2	2
1985-86	Fredericton	AHL	74	21	33	54	68	6	0	3	3	8
1986-87	**Quebec**	**NHL**	**56**	**6**	**8**	**14**	**79**	**9**	**0**	**3**	**3**	**26**
	Fredericton	AHL	10	1	3	4	20	....	....	....	....	....
1987-88	**Quebec**	**NHL**	**17**	**3**	**2**	**5**	**2**	....	....	....	....	....
	Fredericton	AHL	46	16	25	41	133	15	4	8	12	55
1988-89	**Quebec**	**NHL**	**46**	**9**	**10**	**19**	**39**	....	....	....	....	....
	Halifax	AHL	22	11	10	21	87	....	....	....	....	....
1989-90	**Quebec**	**NHL**	**43**	**13**	**13**	**26**	**84**	....	....	....	....	....
1990-91	**Quebec**	**NHL**	**63**	**13**	**20**	**33**	**111**	....	....	....	....	....
1991-92	**Quebec**	**NHL**	**61**	**16**	**22**	**38**	**77**	....	....	....	....	....
1992-93	**Quebec**	**NHL**	**77**	**8**	**22**	**30**	**69**	**6**	**0**	**1**	**1**	**2**
1993-94	**Florida**	**NHL**	**78**	**6**	**23**	**29**	**62**	....	....	....	....	....
	NHL Totals		**441**	**74**	**120**	**194**	**523**	**15**	**0**	**4**	**4**	**28**

Traded to **Washington** by **Quebec** for Reggie Savage and Paul MacDermid, June 20, 1993. Claimed by **Florida** from **Washington** in Expansion Draft, June 24, 1993.

HOULDER, BILL (HOHL-duhr) ANA.

Defense. Shoots left. 6'3", 218 lbs. Born, Thunder Bay, Ont., March 11, 1967.
(Washington's 4th choice, 82nd overall, in 1985 Entry Draft).

			Regular Season					Playoffs				
Season	Club	Lea	GP	G	A	TP	PIM	GP	G	A	TP	PIM
1984-85	North Bay	OHL	66	4	20	24	37	8	0	0	0	2
1985-86	North Bay	OHL	59	5	30	35	97	10	1	6	7	12
1986-87	North Bay	OHL	62	17	51	68	68	22	4	19	23	20
1987-88	**Washington**	**NHL**	**30**	**1**	**2**	**3**	**10**	....	....	....	....	....
	Fort Wayne	IHL	43	10	14	24	32	....	....	....	....	....
1988-89	**Washington**	**NHL**	**8**	**0**	**3**	**3**	**4**	....	....	....	....	....
	Baltimore	AHL	65	10	36	46	50	....	....	....	....	....
1989-90	**Washington**	**NHL**	**41**	**1**	**11**	**12**	**28**	....	....	....	....	....
	Baltimore	AHL	26	3	7	10	12	7	0	2	2	2
1990-91	**Buffalo**	**NHL**	**7**	**0**	**2**	**2**	**4**	....	....	....	....	....
a	Rochester	AHL	69	13	53	66	28	15	5	13	18	4
1991-92	**Buffalo**	**NHL**	**10**	**1**	**0**	**1**	**8**	....	....	....	....	....
	Rochester	AHL	42	8	26	34	16	16	5	6	11	4
1992-93	**Buffalo**	**NHL**	**15**	**3**	**5**	**8**	**6**	**8**	**0**	**2**	**2**	**4**
bc	San Diego	IHL	64	24	48	72	39	....	....	....	....	....
1993-94	**Anaheim**	**NHL**	**80**	**14**	**25**	**39**	**40**	....	....	....	....	....
	NHL Totals		**191**	**20**	**48**	**68**	**100**	**8**	**0**	**2**	**2**	**4**

a AHL First All-Star Team (1991)
b Won Governor's Trophy (Outstanding Defenseman - IHL) (1993)
c IHL First All-Star Team (1993)

Traded to **Buffalo** by **Washington** for Shawn Anderson, September 30, 1990. Claimed by **Anaheim** from **Buffalo** in Expansion Draft, June 24, 1993.

HOULE, JEAN-FRANCOIS MTL.

Left wing. Shoots left. 5'9", 175 lbs. Born, Charlesbourg, Que., January 14, 1975.
(Montreal's 5th choice, 99th overall, in 1993 Entry Draft).

			Regular Season					Playoffs				
Season	Club	Lea	GP	G	A	TP	PIM	GP	G	A	TP	PIM
1992-93	Northwood	HS	28	37	45	82	0	....	....	....	....	....
1993-94	Clarkson	ECAC	34	6	19	25	20	....	....	....	....	....

HOUSE, BOBBY CHI.

Right wing. Shoots right. 6'1", 200 lbs. Born, Whitehorse, Yukon, January 7, 1973.
(Chicago's 4th choice, 66th overall, in 1991 Entry Draft).

			Regular Season					Playoffs				
Season	Club	Lea	GP	G	A	TP	PIM	GP	G	A	TP	PIM
1989-90	Spokane	WHL	64	18	16	34	74	5	0	0	0	6
1990-91	Spokane	WHL	38	11	19	30	63	....	....	....	....	....
	Brandon	WHL	23	18	7	25	14	....	....	....	....	....
1991-92	Brandon	WHL	71	35	42	77	133	....	....	....	....	....
1992-93a	Brandon	WHL	61	57	39	96	87	4	2	2	4	0
1993-94	Indianapolis	IHL	42	10	8	18	51	....	....	....	....	....
	Flint	ColHL	4	3	3	6	0	....	....	....	....	....

a WHL East Second All-Star Team (1993)

HOUSLEY, PHIL (HOWZ-lee) CGY.

Defense. Shoots left. 5'10", 185 lbs. Born, St. Paul, MN, March 9, 1964.
(Buffalo's 1st choice, 6th overall, in 1982 Entry Draft).

			Regular Season					Playoffs				
Season	Club	Lea	GP	G	A	TP	PIM	GP	G	A	TP	PIM
1981-82	South St. Paul	HS	22	31	34	65	18	....	....	....	....	....
1982-83a	**Buffalo**	**NHL**	**77**	**19**	**47**	**66**	**39**	**10**	**3**	**4**	**7**	**2**
1983-84	**Buffalo**	**NHL**	**75**	**31**	**46**	**77**	**33**	**3**	**0**	**0**	**0**	**6**
1984-85	**Buffalo**	**NHL**	**73**	**16**	**53**	**69**	**28**	**5**	**3**	**2**	**5**	**2**
1985-86	**Buffalo**	**NHL**	**79**	**15**	**47**	**62**	**54**	....	....	....	....	....
1986-87	**Buffalo**	**NHL**	**78**	**21**	**46**	**67**	**57**	....	....	....	....	....
1987-88	**Buffalo**	**NHL**	**74**	**29**	**37**	**66**	**96**	**6**	**2**	**4**	**6**	**6**
1988-89	**Buffalo**	**NHL**	**72**	**26**	**44**	**70**	**47**	**5**	**1**	**3**	**4**	**2**
1989-90	**Buffalo**	**NHL**	**80**	**21**	**60**	**81**	**32**	**6**	**1**	**4**	**5**	**4**
1990-91	**Winnipeg**	**NHL**	**78**	**23**	**53**	**76**	**24**	....	....	....	....	....
1991-92b	**Winnipeg**	**NHL**	**74**	**23**	**63**	**86**	**92**	**7**	**1**	**4**	**5**	**0**
1992-93	**Winnipeg**	**NHL**	**80**	**18**	**79**	**97**	**52**	**6**	**0**	**7**	**7**	**2**
1993-94	**St. Louis**	**NHL**	**26**	**7**	**15**	**22**	**12**	**4**	**2**	**1**	**3**	**4**
	NHL Totals		**866**	**249**	**590**	**839**	**566**	**52**	**13**	**29**	**42**	**28**

a NHL All-Rookie Team (1983)
b NHL Second All-Star Team (1992)

Played in NHL All-Star Game (1984, 1989-93)

Traded to **Winnipeg** by **Buffalo** with Scott Arniel, Jeff Parker and Buffalo's first round choice (Keith Tkachuk) in 1990 Entry Draft for Dale Hawerchuk, Winnipeg's first round choice (Brad May) in 1990 Entry Draft and future considerations, June 16, 1990. Traded to **St. Louis** by **Winnipeg** for Nelson Emerson and Stephane Quintal, September 24, 1993. Traded to **Calgary** by **St. Louis** with St. Louis' second round choice in 1996 Entry Draft and second round choice in 1997 Entry Draft for Al MacInnis and Calgary's fourth round choice in 1997 Entry Draft, July 4, 1994.

HOWALD, PATRICK (HOH-wahld)

Left wing. Shoots left. 6', 185 lbs. Born, Bern, Switzerland, December 26, 1969.
(Los Angeles' 12th choice, 276th overall, in 1993 Entry Draft).

			Regular Season					Playoffs				
Season	Club	Lea	GP	G	A	TP	PIM	GP	G	A	TP	PIM
1986-87	Bern	Switz.	....	....	....	....	....	....	....	....	....	....
1987-88	Bern	Switz.	....	....	....	....	....	....	....	....	....	....
1988-89	Bern	Switz.	....	....	....	....	....	....	....	....	....	....
1989-90	Bern	Switz.	....	....	....	....	....	....	....	....	....	....
1990-91	Bern	Switz.	36	18	15	33	....	10	7	7	14	....
1991-92	Bern	Switz.	36	20	11	31	....	11	7	6	13	....
1992-93	Lugano	Switz.	36	15	9	24	50	9	6	1	7	10
1993-94	Lugano	Switz.	36	10	13	23	24	9	1	2	3	2

HOWE, MARK — DET.

Defense. Shoots left. 5'11", 185 lbs. Born, Detroit, MI, May 28, 1955.
(Boston's 2nd choice, 25th overall, in 1974 Amateur Draft).

			Regular Season					Playoffs				
Season	**Club**	**Lea**	**GP**	**G**	**A**	**TP**	**PIM**	**GP**	**G**	**A**	**TP**	**PIM**
1972-73	Toronto	OMJHL	60	38	66	104	27	....	....	....	....	....
1973-74ab	Houston	WHA	76	38	41	79	20	14	9	10	19	4
1974-75	Houston	WHA	74	36	40	76	30	13	*10	12	*22	0
1975-76	Houston	WHA	72	39	37	76	38	17	6	10	16	18
1976-77a	Houston	WHA	57	23	52	75	46	10	4	10	14	2
1977-78	New England	WHA	70	30	61	91	32	14	8	7	15	18
1978-79c	New England	WHA	77	42	65	107	32	6	4	2	6	6
1979-80	**Hartford**	**NHL**	**74**	**24**	**56**	**80**	**20**	**3**	**1**	**2**	**3**	**2**
1980-81	**Hartford**	**NHL**	**63**	**19**	**46**	**65**	**54**	....	....	....	....	....
1981-82	**Hartford**	**NHL**	**76**	**8**	**45**	**53**	**18**	....	....	....	....	....
1982-83d	**Philadelphia**	**NHL**	**76**	**20**	**47**	**67**	**18**	**3**	**0**	**2**	**2**	**4**
1983-84	**Philadelphia**	**NHL**	**71**	**19**	**34**	**53**	**44**	**3**	**0**	**0**	**0**	**2**
1984-85	**Philadelphia**	**NHL**	**73**	**18**	**39**	**57**	**31**	**19**	**3**	**8**	**11**	**6**
1985-86de	**Philadelphia**	**NHL**	**77**	**24**	**58**	**82**	**36**	**5**	**0**	**4**	**4**	**0**
1986-87d	**Philadelphia**	**NHL**	**69**	**15**	**43**	**58**	**37**	**26**	**2**	**10**	**12**	**4**
1987-88	**Philadelphia**	**NHL**	**75**	**19**	**43**	**62**	**62**	**7**	**3**	**6**	**9**	**4**
1988-89	**Philadelphia**	**NHL**	**52**	**9**	**29**	**38**	**45**	**19**	**0**	**15**	**15**	**10**
1989-90	**Philadelphia**	**NHL**	**40**	**7**	**21**	**28**	**24**	....	....	....	....	....
1990-91	**Philadelphia**	**NHL**	**19**	**0**	**10**	**10**	**8**	....	....	....	....	....
1991-92	**Philadelphia**	**NHL**	**42**	**7**	**18**	**25**	**18**	....	....	....	....	....
1992-93	**Detroit**	**NHL**	**60**	**3**	**31**	**34**	**22**	**7**	**1**	**3**	**4**	**2**
1993-94	**Detroit**	**NHL**	**44**	**4**	**20**	**24**	**8**	**6**	**0**	**1**	**1**	**0**
	NHL Totals		**911**	**196**	**540**	**736**	**445**	**98**	**10**	**51**	**61**	**34**

a WHA Second All-Star Team (1974, 1977)
b Named WHA's Rookie of the Year (1974)
c WHA First All-Star Team (1979)
d NHL First All-Star Team (1983, 1986, 1987)
e NHL Plus/Minus Leader (1986)

Played in NHL All-Star Game (1981, 1983, 1986, 1988)

Reclaimed by **Boston** from **Hartford** prior to Expansion Draft, June 9, 1979. Claimed as priority selection by **Hartford**, June 9, 1979. Traded to **Philadelphia** by **Hartford** with Hartford's third round choice (Derrick Smith) in 1983 Entry Draft for Ken Linseman, Greg Adams and Philadelphia's first (David Jensen) and third round choices (Leif Karlsson) in the 1983 Entry Draft, August 19, 1982. Signed as a free agent by **Detroit**, July 7, 1992.

HRKAC, TONY (HUHR-kuhz) — ST.L.

Center. Shoots left. 5'11", 170 lbs. Born, Thunder Bay, Ont., July 7, 1966.
(St. Louis' 2nd choice, 32nd overall, in 1984 Entry Draft).

			Regular Season					Playoffs				
Season	**Club**	**Lea**	**GP**	**G**	**A**	**TP**	**PIM**	**GP**	**G**	**A**	**TP**	**PIM**
1984-85	North Dakota	WCHA	36	18	36	54	16	....	....	....	....	....
1985-86	Cdn. National	....	62	19	30	49	36	....	....	....	....	....
1986-87abcd	North Dakota	WCHA	48	46	79	125	48	....	....	....	....	....
	St. Louis	**NHL**	....	....	....	....	....	**3**	**0**	**0**	**0**	**0**
1987-88	**St. Louis**	**NHL**	**67**	**11**	**37**	**48**	**22**	**10**	**6**	**1**	**7**	**4**
1988-89	**St. Louis**	**NHL**	**70**	**17**	**28**	**45**	**8**	**4**	**1**	**1**	**2**	**0**
1989-90	**St. Louis**	**NHL**	**28**	**5**	**12**	**17**	**8**	....	....	....	....	....
	Quebec	**NHL**	**22**	**4**	**8**	**12**	**2**	....	....	....	....	....
	Halifax	AHL	20	12	21	33	4	6	5	9	14	4
1990-91	**Quebec**	**NHL**	**70**	**16**	**32**	**48**	**16**	....	....	....	....	....
	Halifax	AHL	3	4	1	5	2	....	....	....	....	....
1991-92	**San Jose**	**NHL**	**22**	**2**	**10**	**12**	**4**	....	....	....	....	....
	Chicago	**NHL**	**18**	**1**	**2**	**3**	**6**	**3**	**0**	**0**	**0**	**2**
1992-93efg	Indianapolis	IHL	80	45	*87	*132	70	5	0	2	2	2
1993-94	**St. Louis**	**NHL**	**36**	**6**	**5**	**11**	**8**	**4**	**0**	**0**	**0**	**0**
	Peoria	IHL	45	30	51	81	25	1	1	2	3	0
	NHL Totals		**333**	**62**	**134**	**196**	**74**	**24**	**7**	**2**	**9**	**6**

a WCHA First All-Star Team (1987)
b NCAA West First All-American Team (1987)
c NCAA All-Tournament Team, Tournament MVP (1987)
d Won 1987 Hobey Baker Memorial Award (Top U.S. Collegiate Player) (1987)
e Won James Gatschene Memorial Trophy (MVP - IHL) (1993)
f Won Leo P. Lamoureux Trophy (Leading Scorer - IHL) (1993)
g IHL First All-Star Team (1993)

Traded to **Quebec** by **St. Louis** with Greg Millen for Jeff Brown, December 13, 1989. Traded to **San Jose** by **Quebec** for Greg Paslawski, May 31, 1991. Traded to **Chicago** by **San Jose** for future considerations, February 7, 1992. Signed as a free agent by **St. Louis**, July 30, 1993.

HUARD, BILL (HYOO-ahrd) — OTT.

Left wing. Shoots left. 6'1", 215 lbs. Born, Welland, Ont., June 24, 1967.

			Regular Season					Playoffs				
Season	**Club**	**Lea**	**GP**	**G**	**A**	**TP**	**PIM**	**GP**	**G**	**A**	**TP**	**PIM**
1986-87	Peterborough	OHL	61	14	11	25	61	12	5	2	7	19
1987-88	Peterborough	OHL	66	28	33	61	132	12	7	8	15	33
1988-89	Carolina	ECHL	40	27	21	48	177	10	7	2	9	70
1989-90	Utica	AHL	27	1	7	8	67	5	0	1	1	33
	Nashville	ECHL	34	24	27	51	212	....	....	....	....	....
1990-91	Utica	AHL	72	11	16	27	359	....	....	....	....	....
1991-92	Utica	AHL	62	9	11	20	233	4	1	1	2	4
1992-93	**Boston**	**NHL**	**2**	**0**	**0**	**0**	**0**	....	....	....	....	....
	Providence	AHL	72	18	19	37	302	6	3	0	3	9
1993-94	**Ottawa**	**NHL**	**63**	**2**	**2**	**4**	**162**	....	....	....	....	....
	NHL Totals		**65**	**2**	**2**	**4**	**162**	....	....	....	....	....

Signed as a free agent by **New Jersey**, October 1, 1989. Signed as a free agent by **Boston**, December 4, 1992. Signed as a free agent by **Ottawa**, June 30, 1993.

HUDDY, CHARLIE (HUH-dee) — L.A.

Defense. Shoots left. 6', 210 lbs. Born, Oshawa, Ont., June 2, 1959.

			Regular Season					Playoffs				
Season	**Club**	**Lea**	**GP**	**G**	**A**	**TP**	**PIM**	**GP**	**G**	**A**	**TP**	**PIM**
1977-78	Oshawa	OHA	59	17	18	35	81	6	2	1	3	10
1978-79	Oshawa	OHA	64	20	38	58	108	5	3	4	7	12
1979-80	Houston	CHL	79	14	34	48	46	6	1	0	1	2
1980-81	**Edmonton**	**NHL**	**12**	**2**	**5**	**7**	**6**	....	....	....	....	....
	Wichita	CHL	47	8	36	44	71	17	3	11	14	10
1981-82	**Edmonton**	**NHL**	**41**	**4**	**11**	**15**	**46**	**5**	**1**	**2**	**3**	**14**
	Wichita	CHL	32	7	19	26	51	....	....	....	....	....
1982-83a	**Edmonton**	**NHL**	**76**	**20**	**37**	**57**	**58**	**15**	**1**	**6**	**7**	**10**
1983-84	**Edmonton**	**NHL**	**75**	**8**	**34**	**42**	**43**	**12**	**1**	**9**	**10**	**8**
1984-85	**Edmonton**	**NHL**	**80**	**7**	**44**	**51**	**46**	**18**	**3**	**17**	**20**	**17**
1985-86	**Edmonton**	**NHL**	**76**	**6**	**35**	**41**	**55**	**7**	**0**	**2**	**2**	**0**
1986-87	**Edmonton**	**NHL**	**58**	**4**	**15**	**19**	**35**	**21**	**1**	**7**	**8**	**21**
1987-88	**Edmonton**	**NHL**	**77**	**13**	**28**	**41**	**71**	**13**	**4**	**5**	**9**	**10**
1988-89	**Edmonton**	**NHL**	**76**	**11**	**33**	**44**	**52**	**7**	**2**	**0**	**2**	**4**
1989-90	**Edmonton**	**NHL**	**70**	**1**	**23**	**24**	**56**	**22**	**0**	**6**	**6**	**11**
1990-91	**Edmonton**	**NHL**	**53**	**5**	**22**	**27**	**32**	**18**	**3**	**7**	**10**	**10**
1991-92	**Los Angeles**	**NHL**	**56**	**4**	**19**	**23**	**43**	**6**	**1**	**1**	**2**	**10**
1992-93	**Los Angeles**	**NHL**	**82**	**2**	**25**	**27**	**64**	**23**	**1**	**4**	**5**	**12**
1993-94	**Los Angeles**	**NHL**	**79**	**5**	**13**	**18**	**71**	....	....	....	....	....
	NHL Totals		**911**	**92**	**344**	**436**	**678**	**167**	**18**	**66**	**84**	**127**

a NHL Plus/Minus Leader (1983)

Signed as a free agent by **Edmonton**, September 14, 1979. Claimed by **Minnesota** from **Edmonton** in Expansion Draft, May 30, 1991. Traded to **Los Angeles** by **Minnesota** with Randy Gilhen, Jim Thomson and NY Rangers' fourth round choice (previously acquired by Minnesota — Los Angeles selected Alexei Zhitnik) in 1991 Entry Draft for Todd Elik, June 22, 1991.

HUDSON, MIKE — NYR

Center/Left wing. Shoots left. 6'1", 205 lbs. Born, Guelph, Ont., February 6, 1967.
(Chicago's 6th choice, 140th overall, in 1986 Entry Draft).

			Regular Season					Playoffs				
Season	**Club**	**Lea**	**GP**	**G**	**A**	**TP**	**PIM**	**GP**	**G**	**A**	**TP**	**PIM**
1984-85	Hamilton	OHL	50	10	12	22	13	....	....	....	....	....
1985-86	Hamilton	OHL	7	3	2	5	4	....	....	....	....	....
	Sudbury	OHL	59	35	42	77	20	4	2	5	7	7
1986-87	Sudbury	OHL	63	40	57	97	18	....	....	....	....	....
1987-88	Saginaw	IHL	75	18	30	48	44	10	2	3	5	20
1988-89	**Chicago**	**NHL**	**41**	**7**	**16**	**23**	**20**	**10**	**1**	**2**	**3**	**18**
	Saginaw	IHL	30	15	17	32	10	....	....	....	....	....
1989-90	**Chicago**	**NHL**	**49**	**9**	**12**	**21**	**56**	**4**	**0**	**0**	**0**	**2**
1990-91	**Chicago**	**NHL**	**55**	**7**	**9**	**16**	**62**	**6**	**0**	**2**	**2**	**8**
	Indianapolis	IHL	3	1	2	3	0	....	....	....	....	....
1991-92	**Chicago**	**NHL**	**76**	**14**	**15**	**29**	**92**	**16**	**3**	**5**	**8**	**26**
1992-93	**Chicago**	**NHL**	**36**	**1**	**6**	**7**	**44**	....	....	....	....	....
	Edmonton	**NHL**	**5**	**0**	**1**	**1**	**2**	....	....	....	....	....
1993-94	**NY Rangers**	**NHL**	**48**	**4**	**7**	**11**	**47**	....	....	....	....	....
	NHL Totals		**310**	**42**	**66**	**108**	**323**	**36**	**4**	**9**	**13**	**54**

Traded to **Edmonton** by **Chicago** for Craig Muni, March 22, 1993. Claimed by **NY Rangers** from **Edmonton** in NHL Waiver Draft, October 3, 1993.

HUFFMAN, KERRY — OTT.

Defense. Shoots left. 6'2", 200 lbs. Born, Peterborough, Ont., January 3, 1968.
(Philadelphia's 1st choice, 20th overall, in 1986 Entry Draft).

			Regular Season					Playoffs				
Season	**Club**	**Lea**	**GP**	**G**	**A**	**TP**	**PIM**	**GP**	**G**	**A**	**TP**	**PIM**
1985-86	Guelph	OHL	56	3	24	27	35	20	1	10	11	10
1986-87	**Philadelphia**	**NHL**	**9**	**0**	**0**	**0**	**2**	....	....	....	....	....
	Hershey	AHL	3	0	1	1	0	4	0	0	0	0
a	Guelph	OHL	44	4	31	35	20	5	0	2	2	8
1987-88	**Philadelphia**	**NHL**	**52**	**6**	**17**	**23**	**34**	**2**	**0**	**0**	**0**	**0**
1988-89	**Philadelphia**	**NHL**	**29**	**0**	**11**	**11**	**31**	....	....	....	....	....
	Hershey	AHL	29	2	13	15	16	....	....	....	....	....
1989-90	**Philadelphia**	**NHL**	**43**	**1**	**12**	**13**	**34**	....	....	....	....	....
1990-91	**Philadelphia**	**NHL**	**10**	**1**	**2**	**3**	**10**	....	....	....	....	....
	Hershey	AHL	45	5	29	34	20	7	1	2	3	0
1991-92	**Philadelphia**	**NHL**	**60**	**14**	**18**	**32**	**41**	....	....	....	....	....
1992-93	**Quebec**	**NHL**	**52**	**4**	**18**	**22**	**54**	**3**	**0**	**0**	**0**	**0**
1993-94	**Quebec**	**NHL**	**28**	**0**	**6**	**6**	**28**	....	....	....	....	....
	Ottawa	**NHL**	**34**	**4**	**8**	**12**	**12**	....	....	....	....	....
	NHL Totals		**317**	**30**	**92**	**122**	**246**	**5**	**0**	**0**	**0**	**0**

a Won George Parsons Trophy (Memorial Cup Most Sportsmanlike Player) (1986)
b OHL First All-Star Team (1987)

Traded to **Quebec** by **Philadelphia** with Peter Forsberg, Steve Duchesne, Mike Ricci, Ron Hextall, Chris Simon, Philadelphia's first choice in the 1993 (Jocelyn Thibault) and 1994 (later traded to Toronto — later traded to Wahington — Wahington selected Nolan Baumgartner) — Entry Drafts and cash for Eric Lindros, June 30, 1992. Claimed on waivers by **Ottawa** from **Quebec**, January 15, 1994.

HUGHES, BRENT — BOS.

Left wing. Shoots left. 5'11", 195 lbs. Born, New Westminster, B.C., April 5, 1966.

			Regular Season					Playoffs				
Season	**Club**	**Lea**	**GP**	**G**	**A**	**TP**	**PIM**	**GP**	**G**	**A**	**TP**	**PIM**
1983-84	N. Westminster	WHL	67	21	18	39	133	9	2	2	4	27
1984-85	N. Westminster	WHL	64	25	32	57	135	11	2	1	3	37
1985-86	N. Westminster	WHL	71	28	52	80	180	....	....	....	....	....
1986-87	N. Westminster	WHL	8	5	4	9	22	....	....	....	....	....
	Victoria	WHL	61	38	61	99	146	5	4	1	5	8
1987-88	Moncton	AHL	73	13	19	32	206	....	....	....	....	....
1988-89	**Winnipeg**	**NHL**	**28**	**3**	**2**	**5**	**82**	....	....	....	....	....
	Moncton	AHL	54	34	34	68	286	10	9	4	13	40
1989-90	**Winnipeg**	**NHL**	**11**	**1**	**2**	**3**	**33**	....	....	....	....	....
	Moncton	AHL	65	31	29	60	277	....	....	....	....	....
1990-91	Moncton	AHL	63	21	22	43	144	3	0	0	0	7
1991-92	Baltimore	AHL	55	25	29	54	190	....	....	....	....	....
	Boston	**NHL**	**8**	**1**	**1**	**2**	**38**	**10**	**2**	**0**	**2**	**20**
	Maine	AHL	12	6	4	10	34	....	....	....	....	....
1992-93	**Boston**	**NHL**	**62**	**5**	**4**	**9**	**191**	**1**	**0**	**0**	**0**	**2**
1993-94	**Boston**	**NHL**	**77**	**13**	**11**	**24**	**143**	**13**	**2**	**1**	**3**	**27**
	Providence	AHL	6	2	5	7	4	....	....	....	....	....
	NHL Totals		**186**	**23**	**20**	**43**	**487**	**24**	**4**	**1**	**5**	**49**

Signed as a free agent by **Winnipeg**, June 13, 1988. Traded to **Washington** by **Winnipeg** with Craig Duncanson and Simon Wheeldon for Bob Joyce, Tyler Larter and Kent Paynter, May 21, 1991. Traded to **Boston** by **Washington** with future considerations for John Byce and Dennis Smith, February 24, 1992.

HUGHES, RYAN — QUE.

Center. Shoots left. 6'2", 196 lbs. Born, Montreal, Que., January 17, 1972.
(Quebec's 2nd choice, 22nd overall, in 1990 Entry Draft).

			Regular Season					Playoffs				
Season	Club	Lea	GP	G	A	TP	PIM	GP	G	A	TP	PIM
1989-90	Cornell	ECAC	27	7	16	23	35	....	....	....	....	....
1990-91	Cornell	ECAC	32	18	34	52	28	....	....	....	....	....
1991-92	Cornell	ECAC	27	8	13	21	36	....	....	....	....	....
1992-93	Cornell	ECAC	26	8	14	22	30	....	....	....	....	....
1993-94	Cornwall	AHL	54	17	12	29	24	13	2	4	6	6

HULBIG, JOE — EDM.

Left wing. Shoots left. 6'3", 212 lbs. Born, Norwood, MA, September 29, 1973.
(Edmonton's 1st choice, 13th overall, in 1992 Entry Draft).

			Regular Season					Playoffs				
Season	Club	Lea	GP	G	A	TP	PIM	GP	G	A	TP	PIM
1992-93	Providence	H.E.	26	3	13	16	22	....	....	....	....	....
1993-94	Providence	H.E.	28	6	4	10	36	....	....	....	....	....

HULETT, DEAN

Right wing. Shoots right. 6'6", 210 lbs. Born, San Juan, Puerto Rico, July 25, 1971.
(Los Angeles' 7th choice, 154th overall, in 1990 Entry Draft).

			Regular Season					Playoffs				
Season	Club	Lea	GP	G	A	TP	PIM	GP	G	A	TP	PIM
1989-90	Lake Superior	CCHA	13	1	4	5	18	....	....	....	....	....
1990-91	Lake Superior	CCHA	36	5	8	13	52	....	....	....	....	....
1991-92	Lake Superior	CCHA	33	10	12	22	56	....	....	....	....	....
1992-93	Lake Superior	CCHA	42	12	27	39	71	....	....	....	....	....
1993-94	Phoenix	IHL	43	8	7	15	76	....	....	....	....	....

HULL, BRETT — ST.L.

Right wing. Shoots right. 5'10", 201 lbs. Born, Belleville, Ont., August 9, 1964.
(Calgary's 6th choice, 117th overall, in 1984 Entry Draft).

			Regular Season					Playoffs				
Season	Club	Lea	GP	G	A	TP	PIM	GP	G	A	TP	PIM
1984-85	Minn.-Duluth	WCHA	48	32	28	60	24	....	....	....	....	....
1985-86a	Minn.-Duluth	WCHA	42	52	32	84	46	....	....	....	....	....
	Calgary	**NHL**	**....**	**....**	**....**	**....**	**....**	**2**	**0**	**0**	**0**	**0**
1986-87	**Calgary**	**NHL**	**5**	**1**	**0**	**1**	**0**	**4**	**2**	**1**	**3**	**0**
bc	Moncton	AHL	67	50	42	92	16	3	2	2	4	2
1987-88	**Calgary**	**NHL**	**52**	**26**	**24**	**50**	**12**	....	....	....	....	....
	St. Louis	**NHL**	**13**	**6**	**8**	**14**	**4**	**10**	**7**	**2**	**9**	**4**
1988-89	**St. Louis**	**NHL**	**78**	**41**	**43**	**84**	**33**	**10**	**5**	**5**	**10**	**6**
1989-90def	**St. Louis**	**NHL**	**80**	***72**	**41**	**113**	**24**	**12**	**13**	**8**	**21**	**17**
1990-91 dfghi	**St. Louis**	**NHL**	**78**	***86**	**45**	**131**	**22**	**13**	**11**	**8**	**19**	**4**
1991-92d	**St. Louis**	**NHL**	**73**	***70**	**39**	**109**	**48**	**6**	**4**	**4**	**8**	**4**
1992-93	**St. Louis**	**NHL**	**80**	**54**	**47**	**101**	**41**	**11**	**8**	**5**	**13**	**2**
1993-94	**St. Louis**	**NHL**	**81**	**57**	**40**	**97**	**38**	**4**	**2**	**1**	**3**	**0**
	NHL Totals		**540**	**413**	**287**	**700**	**222**	**72**	**52**	**34**	**86**	**37**

a WCHA First All-Star Team (1986)
b AHL First All-Star Team (1987)
c Won Dudley "Red" Garrett Memorial Trophy (Top Rookie - AHL) (1987)
d NHL First All-Star Team (1990, 1991, 1992)
e Won Lady Byng Trophy (1990)
f Won Dodge Ram Tough Award (1990, 1991)
g Won Hart Memorial Trophy (1991)
h Won Lester B. Pearson Award (1991)
i Won ProSet/NHL Player of the Year Award (1991)

Played in NHL All-Star Game (1989, 1990, 1992-1994)

Traded to **St. Louis** by **Calgary** with Steve Bozek for Rob Ramage and Rick Wamsley, March 7, 1988.

HULL, JODY — FLA.

Right wing. Shoots right. 6'2", 200 lbs. Born, Cambridge, Ont., February 2, 1969.
(Hartford's 1st choice, 18th overall, in 1987 Entry Draft).

			Regular Season					Playoffs				
Season	Club	Lea	GP	G	A	TP	PIM	GP	G	A	TP	PIM
1985-86	Peterborough	OHL	61	20	22	42	29	16	1	5	6	4
1986-87	Peterborough	OHL	49	18	34	52	22	12	4	9	13	14
1987-88a	Peterborough	OHL	60	50	44	94	33	12	10	8	18	8
1988-89	**Hartford**	**NHL**	**60**	**16**	**18**	**34**	**10**	**1**	**0**	**0**	**0**	**2**
1989-90	**Hartford**	**NHL**	**38**	**7**	**10**	**17**	**21**	**5**	**0**	**1**	**1**	**2**
	Binghamton	AHL	21	7	10	17	6	....	....	....	....	....
1990-91	**NY Rangers**	**NHL**	**47**	**5**	**8**	**13**	**10**	....	....	....	....	....
1991-92	**NY Rangers**	**NHL**	**3**	**0**	**0**	**0**	**2**	....	....	....	....	....
	Binghamton	AHL	69	34	31	65	28	11	5	2	7	4
1992-93	**Ottawa**	**NHL**	**69**	**13**	**21**	**34**	**14**	....	....	....	....	....
1993-94	**Florida**	**NHL**	**69**	**13**	**13**	**26**	**8**	....	....	....	....	....
	NHL Totals		**286**	**54**	**70**	**124**	**65**	**6**	**0**	**1**	**1**	**4**

a OHL Second All-Star Team (1988)

Traded to **NY Rangers** by **Hartford** for Carey Wilson and NY Rangers' third round choice (Mikael Nylander) in the 1991 Entry Draft, July 9, 1990. Traded to **Ottawa** by **NY Rangers** for future considerations, July 28, 1992. Signed as a free agent by **Florida**, August 10, 1993.

HULSE, CALE — N.J.

Defense. Shoots right. 6'3", 210 lbs. Born, Edmonton, Alta., November 10, 1973.
(New Jersey's 3rd choice, 66th overall, in 1992 Entry Draft).

			Regular Season					Playoffs				
Season	Club	Lea	GP	G	A	TP	PIM	GP	G	A	TP	PIM
1991-92	Portland	WHL	70	4	18	22	250	6	0	2	2	27
1992-93	Portland	WHL	72	10	26	36	284	16	4	4	8	65
1993-94	Albany	AHL	79	7	14	21	186	5	0	3	3	11

HUMENIUK, SCOTT

Defense. Shoots right. 6', 190 lbs. Born, Saskatoon, Sask., September 10, 1969.

			Regular Season					Playoffs				
Season	Club	Lea	GP	G	A	TP	PIM	GP	G	A	TP	PIM
1986-87	Spokane	WHL	10	0	2	2	2	1	0	0	0	0
1987-88	Spokane	WHL	58	6	20	26	154	8	1	0	1	19
1988-89	Moose Jaw	WHL	56	18	39	57	159	7	5	0	5	32
1989-90a	Moose Jaw	WHL	71	23	47	70	141	....	....	....	....	....
	Binghamton	AHL	4	0	1	1	11	....	....	....	....	....
1990-91	Springfield	AHL	57	6	17	23	69	14	2	2	4	18
1991-92	Springfield	AHL	28	2	3	5	27	....	....	....	....	....
	Louisville	ECHL	26	7	21	28	93	13	1	11	12	33
1992-93	Springfield	AHL	16	0	3	3	28	14	1	3	4	8
	Louisville	ECHL	36	14	31	45	117	....	....	....	....	....
1993-94	Springfield	AHL	71	15	42	57	91	6	0	3	3	8

a WHL East Second All-Star Team (1990)

Signed as a free agent by **Hartford**, March 23, 1990.

HUNT, CURTIS

Defense. Shoots left. 6', 195 lbs. Born, North Battleford, Sask., January 28, 1967.
(Vancouver's 9th choice, 172nd overall, in 1985 Entry Draft).

			Regular Season					Playoffs				
Season	Club	Lea	GP	G	A	TP	PIM	GP	G	A	TP	PIM
1984-85	Prince Albert	WHL	64	2	13	15	61	13	0	3	3	24
1985-86	Prince Albert	WHL	72	5	29	34	108	18	2	8	10	28
1986-87	Prince Albert	WHL	47	6	31	37	101	8	1	3	4	4
1987-88	Flint	IHL	76	4	17	21	181	2	0	0	0	16
	Fredericton	AHL	1	0	0	0	2	....	....	....	....	....
1988-89	Milwaukee	IHL	65	3	17	20	226	11	1	2	3	43
1989-90	Milwaukee	IHL	69	8	25	33	237	3	0	1	1	4
1990-91	Albany	IHL	45	2	12	14	122	....	....	....	....	....
	Milwaukee	IHL	27	1	5	6	85	6	0	1	1	10
1991-92	St. John's	AHL	52	5	18	23	106	12	1	5	6	36
1992-93	St. John's	AHL	48	4	19	23	148	7	0	3	3	6
1993-94	St. John's	AHL	72	3	13	16	175	6	0	0	0	16

Signed as a free agent by **Toronto**, July 19, 1991.

HUNT, GORDON

Center. Shoots left. 6'5", 200 lbs. Born, Greenwich, CT, July 15, 1975.
(Detroit's 12th choice, 282nd overall, in 1993 Entry Draft).

			Regular Season					Playoffs				
Season	Club	Lea	GP	G	A	TP	PIM	GP	G	A	TP	PIM
1992-93	Detroit Comp.	USHL	....	....	....	....	....	....	....	....	....	....
1993-94	Ferris State	CCHA	37	2	3	5	42	....	....	....	....	....

HUNTER, DALE — WSH.

Center. Shoots left. 5'10", 198 lbs. Born, Petrolia, Ont., July 31, 1960.
(Quebec's 2nd choice, 41st overall, in 1979 Entry Draft).

			Regular Season					Playoffs				
Season	Club	Lea	GP	G	A	TP	PIM	GP	G	A	TP	PIM
1977-78	Kitchener	OHA	68	22	42	64	115	....	....	....	....	....
1978-79	Sudbury	OHA	59	42	68	110	188	10	4	12	16	47
1979-80	Sudbury	OHA	61	34	51	85	189	9	6	9	15	45
1980-81	**Quebec**	**NHL**	**80**	**19**	**44**	**63**	**226**	**5**	**4**	**2**	**6**	**34**
1981-82	**Quebec**	**NHL**	**80**	**22**	**50**	**72**	**272**	**16**	**3**	**7**	**10**	**52**
1982-83	**Quebec**	**NHL**	**80**	**17**	**46**	**63**	**206**	**4**	**2**	**1**	**3**	**24**
1983-84	**Quebec**	**NHL**	**77**	**24**	**55**	**79**	**232**	**9**	**2**	**3**	**5**	**41**
1984-85	**Quebec**	**NHL**	**80**	**20**	**52**	**72**	**209**	**17**	**4**	**6**	**10**	***97**
1985-86	**Quebec**	**NHL**	**80**	**28**	**42**	**70**	**265**	**3**	**0**	**0**	**0**	**15**
1986-87	**Quebec**	**NHL**	**46**	**10**	**29**	**39**	**135**	**13**	**1**	**7**	**8**	**56**
1987-88	**Washington**	**NHL**	**79**	**22**	**37**	**59**	**240**	**14**	**7**	**5**	**12**	**98**
1988-89	**Washington**	**NHL**	**80**	**20**	**37**	**57**	**219**	**6**	**0**	**4**	**4**	**29**
1989-90	**Washington**	**NHL**	**80**	**23**	**39**	**62**	**233**	**15**	**4**	**8**	**12**	**61**
1990-91	**Washington**	**NHL**	**76**	**16**	**30**	**46**	**234**	**11**	**1**	**9**	**10**	**41**
1991-92	**Washington**	**NHL**	**80**	**28**	**50**	**78**	**205**	**7**	**1**	**4**	**5**	**16**
1992-93	**Washington**	**NHL**	**84**	**20**	**59**	**79**	**198**	**6**	**7**	**1**	**8**	**35**
1993-94	**Washington**	**NHL**	**52**	**9**	**29**	**38**	**131**	**7**	**0**	**3**	**3**	**14**
	NHL Totals		**1054**	**278**	**599**	**877**	**3005**	**133**	**36**	**60**	**96**	**613**

Traded to **Washington** by **Quebec** with Clint Malarchuk for Gaetan Duchesne, Alan Haworth, and Washington's first round choice (Joe Sakic) in 1987 Entry Draft, June 13, 1987.

HUNTER, TIM — VAN.

Right wing. Shoots right. 6'2", 202 lbs. Born, Calgary, Alta., September 10, 1960.
(Atlanta's 4th choice, 54th overall, in 1979 Entry Draft).

			Regular Season					Playoffs				
Season	Club	Lea	GP	G	A	TP	PIM	GP	G	A	TP	PIM
1979-80	Seattle	WHL	72	14	53	67	311	12	1	2	3	41
1980-81	Birmingham	CHL	58	3	5	8	*236	....	....	....	....	....
	Nova Scotia	AHL	17	0	0	0	62	6	0	1	1	45
1981-82	**Calgary**	**NHL**	**2**	**0**	**0**	**0**	**9**	....	....	....	....	....
	Oklahoma City	CHL	55	4	12	16	222	....	....	....	....	....
1982-83	**Calgary**	**NHL**	**16**	**1**	**0**	**1**	**54**	**9**	**1**	**0**	**1**	***70**
	Colorado	CHL	46	5	12	17	225	....	....	....	....	....
1983-84	**Calgary**	**NHL**	**43**	**4**	**4**	**8**	**130**	**7**	**0**	**0**	**0**	**21**
1984-85	**Calgary**	**NHL**	**71**	**11**	**11**	**22**	**259**	**4**	**0**	**0**	**0**	**24**
1985-86	**Calgary**	**NHL**	**66**	**8**	**7**	**15**	**291**	**19**	**0**	**3**	**3**	**108**
1986-87	**Calgary**	**NHL**	**73**	**6**	**15**	**21**	***361**	**6**	**0**	**0**	**0**	**51**
1987-88	**Calgary**	**NHL**	**68**	**8**	**5**	**13**	**337**	**9**	**4**	**0**	**4**	**32**
1988-89	**Calgary**	**NHL**	**75**	**3**	**9**	**12**	***375**	**19**	**0**	**4**	**4**	**32**
1989-90	**Calgary**	**NHL**	**67**	**2**	**3**	**5**	**279**	**6**	**0**	**0**	**0**	**4**
1990-91	**Calgary**	**NHL**	**34**	**5**	**2**	**7**	**143**	**7**	**0**	**0**	**0**	**10**
1991-92	**Calgary**	**NHL**	**30**	**1**	**3**	**4**	**167**	....	....	....	....	....
1992-93	**Quebec**	**NHL**	**48**	**5**	**3**	**8**	**94**	....	....	....	....	....
	Vancouver	**NHL**	**26**	**0**	**4**	**4**	**99**	**11**	**0**	**0**	**0**	**26**
1993-94	**Vancouver**	**NHL**	**56**	**3**	**4**	**7**	**171**	**24**	**0**	**0**	**0**	**26**
	NHL Totals		**675**	**57**	**70**	**127**	**2769**	**121**	**5**	**7**	**12**	**404**

Claimed by **Tampa Bay** from **Calgary** in Expansion Draft, June 18, 1992. Traded to **Quebec** by **Tampa Bay** for future considerations (Martin Simard, September 14, 1992), June 19, 1992. Claimed on waivers by **Vancouver** from **Quebec**, February 12, 1993.

HURLBUT, MIKE — QUE.

Defense. Shoots left. 6'2", 200 lbs. Born, Massena, NY, October 7, 1966.
(NY Rangers' 1st choice, 5th overall, in 1988 Supplemental Draft).

			Regular Season					Playoffs				
Season	Club	Lea	GP	G	A	TP	PIM	GP	G	A	TP	PIM
1985-86	St. Lawrence	ECAC	25	2	10	12	40	....	....	....	....	....
1986-87	St. Lawrence	ECAC	35	8	15	23	44	....	....	....	....	....
1987-88	St. Lawrence	ECAC	38	6	12	18	18	....	....	....	....	....
1988-89ab	St. Lawrence	ECAC	36	8	25	33	30	....	....	....	....	....
	Denver	IHL	8	0	2	2	13	4	1	2	3	2
1989-90	Flint	IHL	74	3	34	37	38	3	0	1	1	2
1990-91	San Diego	IHL	2	1	0	1	0	....	....	....	....	....
	Binghamton	AHL	33	2	11	13	27	3	0	1	1	0
1991-92	Binghamton	AHL	79	16	39	55	64	11	2	7	9	8
1992-93	**NY Rangers**	**NHL**	**23**	**1**	**8**	**9**	**16**	....	....	....	....	....
	Binghamton	AHL	45	11	25	36	46	14	2	5	7	12
1993-94	**Quebec**	**NHL**	**1**	**0**	**0**	**0**	**0**	....	....	....	....	....
	Cornwall	AHL	77	13	33	46	100	13	3	7	10	12
	NHL Totals		**24**	**1**	**8**	**9**	**16**	....	....	....	....	....

a ECAC First All-Star Team (1989)
b NCAA East First All-American Team (1989)

Traded to **Quebec** by **NY Rangers** for Alexander Karpovtsev, September 7, 1993.

HUSCROFT, JAMIE

Defense. Shoots right. 6'2", 200 lbs. Born, Creston, B.C., January 9, 1967.
(New Jersey's 9th choice, 171st overall, in 1985 Entry Draft).

			Regular Season					Playoffs				
Season	Club	Lea	GP	G	A	TP	PIM	GP	G	A	TP	PIM
1983-84	Seattle	WHL	63	0	12	12	77	5	0	0	0	15
1984-85	Seattle	WHL	69	3	13	16	273	....	....	....	....	....
1985-86	Seattle	WHL	66	6	20	26	394	5	0	1	1	18
1986-87	Seattle	WHL	21	1	18	19	99	....	....	....	....	....
	Medicine Hat	WHL	35	4	21	25	170	20	0	3	3	*125
1987-88	Utica	AHL	71	5	7	12	316	....	....	....	....	....
	Flint	IHL	3	1	0	1	2	16	0	1	1	110
1988-89	**New Jersey**	**NHL**	**15**	**0**	**2**	**2**	**51**	....	....	....	....	....
	Utica	AHL	41	2	10	12	215	5	0	0	0	40
1989-90	**New Jersey**	**NHL**	**42**	**2**	**3**	**5**	**149**	**5**	**0**	**0**	**0**	**16**
	Utica	AHL	22	3	6	9	122	....	....	....	....	....
1990-91	**New Jersey**	**NHL**	**8**	**0**	**1**	**1**	**27**	**3**	**0**	**0**	**0**	**6**
	Utica	AHL	59	3	15	18	339	....	....	....	....	....
1991-92	Utica	AHL	50	4	7	11	224	....	....	....	....	....
1992-93	Providence	AHL	69	2	15	17	257	2	0	1	1	6
1993-94	**Boston**	**NHL**	**36**	**0**	**1**	**1**	**144**	**4**	**0**	**0**	**0**	**9**
	Providence	AHL	32	1	10	11	157	....	....	....	....	....
	NHL Totals		**101**	**2**	**7**	**9**	**371**	**12**	**0**	**0**	**0**	**31**

Signed as a free agent by **Boston**, July 23, 1992.

HUSKA, RYAN — CHI.

Left wing. Shoots left. 6'2", 194 lbs. Born, Cranbrook, B.C., July 2, 1975.
(Chicago's 4th choice, 76th overall, in 1993 Entry Draft).

			Regular Season					Playoffs				
Season	Club	Lea	GP	G	A	TP	PIM	GP	G	A	TP	PIM
1991-92	Kamloops	WHL	44	4	5	9	23	6	0	1	1	0
1992-93	Kamloops	WHL	68	17	15	32	50	13	2	6	8	4
1993-94	Kamloops	WHL	69	23	31	54	66	19	9	5	14	23

HUSSEY, MARC

Defense. Shoots right. 6'4", 182 lbs. Born, Chatham, N.B., January 22, 1974.
(Pittsburgh's 2nd choice, 43rd overall, in 1992 Entry Draft).

			Regular Season					Playoffs				
Season	Club	Lea	GP	G	A	TP	PIM	GP	G	A	TP	PIM
1990-91	Moose Jaw	WHL	68	5	8	13	67	8	2	2	4	7
1991-92	Moose Jaw	WHL	72	7	27	34	203	4	1	1	2	0
1992-93	Moose Jaw	WHL	68	12	28	40	121	....	....	....	....	....
1993-94	Moose Jaw	WHL	17	4	5	9	33	....	....	....	....	....
	Tri-City	WHL	16	3	6	9	26	....	....	....	....	....
	Medicine Hat	WHL	41	6	24	30	90	3	0	1	1	4

HUURA, PASI (HOO-rah) — PIT.

Defense. Shoots left. 6'4", 220 lbs. Born, Tampere, Fin., March 23, 1966.
(Pittsburgh's 12th choice, 258th overall, in 1991 Entry Draft).

			Regular Season					Playoffs				
Season	Club	Lea	GP	G	A	TP	PIM	GP	G	A	TP	PIM
1987-88	Ilves	Fin.	8	1	0	1	2	....	....	....	....	....
1988-89	Ilves	Fin.	35	3	5	8	22	....	....	....	....	....
1989-90	Ilves	Fin.	41	1	4	5	48	9	1	0	1	17
1990-91	Ilves	Fin.	39	2	6	8	50	....	....	....	....	....
1991-92	Lukko	Fin.	44	1	5	6	40	2	0	0	0	2
1992-93	Lukko	Fin.	48	6	6	12	38	3	0	0	0	4
1993-94	Lukko	Fin.	27	1	2	3	24	8	1	0	1	4

HYMOVITZ, DAVID — CHI.

Left wing. Shoots left. 5'11", 170 lbs. Born, Boston, MA, May 30, 1974.
(Chicago's 9th choice, 209th overall, in 1992 Entry Draft).

			Regular Season					Playoffs				
Season	Club	Lea	GP	G	A	TP	PIM	GP	G	A	TP	PIM
1992-93	Boston College	H.E.	37	7	6	13	6	....	....	....	....	....
1993-94	Boston College	H.E.	36	18	14	32	18	....	....	....	....	....

HYNES, GORD

Defense. Shoots left. 6'1", 170 lbs. Born, Montreal, Que., July 22, 1966.
(Boston's 5th choice, 115th overall, in 1985 Entry Draft).

			Regular Season					Playoffs				
Season	Club	Lea	GP	G	A	TP	PIM	GP	G	A	TP	PIM
1983-84	Medicine Hat	WHL	72	5	14	19	39	14	0	0	0	0
1984-85	Medicine Hat	WHL	70	18	45	63	61	10	6	9	15	17
1985-86	Medicine Hat	WHL	58	22	39	61	45	25	8	15	23	32
1986-87	Moncton	AHL	69	2	19	21	21	4	0	0	0	2
1987-88	Maine	AHL	69	5	30	35	65	7	1	3	4	4
1988-89	Cdn. National	....	61	8	38	46	44	....	....	....	....	....
1989-90	Cdn. National	....	12	3	1	4	4	....	....	....	....	....
	Varese	Italy	29	13	36	49	16	3	3	3	6	0
1990-91	Cdn. National	....	57	12	30	42	62	....	....	....	....	....
1991-92	Cdn. National	....	48	12	22	34	50	....	....	....	....	....
	Cdn. Olympic	....	8	3	3	6	6	....	....	....	....	....
	Boston	**NHL**	**15**	**0**	**5**	**5**	**6**	**12**	**1**	**2**	**3**	**6**
1992-93	**Philadelphia**	**NHL**	**37**	**3**	**4**	**7**	**16**	....	....	....	....	....
	Hershey	AHL	9	1	3	4	4	....	....	....	....	....
1993-94	Cincinnati	IHL	80	15	43	58	50	11	2	6	8	24
	NHL Totals		**52**	**3**	**9**	**12**	**22**	**12**	**1**	**2**	**3**	**6**

Signed as a free agent by **Philadelphia**, August 25, 1992. Claimed by **Florida** from **Philadelphia** in Expansion Draft, June 24, 1993.

IAFRATE, AL (IGH-uh-FRAY-tee) — BOS.

Defense. Shoots left. 6'3", 235 lbs. Born, Dearborn, MI, March 21, 1966.
(Toronto's 1st choice, 4th overall, in 1984 Entry Draft).

			Regular Season					Playoffs				
Season	Club	Lea	GP	G	A	TP	PIM	GP	G	A	TP	PIM
1983-84a	U.S. National	....	55	4	17	21	26	....	....	....	....	....
	U.S. Olympic	....	6	0	0	0	2	....	....	....	....	....
	Belleville	OHL	10	2	4	6	2	3	0	1	1	5
1984-85	**Toronto**	**NHL**	**68**	**5**	**16**	**21**	**51**	....	....	....	....	....
1985-86	**Toronto**	**NHL**	**65**	**8**	**25**	**33**	**40**	**10**	**0**	**3**	**3**	**4**
1986-87	**Toronto**	**NHL**	**80**	**9**	**21**	**30**	**55**	**13**	**1**	**3**	**4**	**11**
1987-88	**Toronto**	**NHL**	**77**	**22**	**30**	**52**	**80**	**6**	**3**	**4**	**7**	**6**
1988-89	**Toronto**	**NHL**	**65**	**13**	**20**	**33**	**72**	....	....	....	....	....
1989-90	**Toronto**	**NHL**	**75**	**21**	**42**	**63**	**135**	....	....	....	....	....
1990-91	**Toronto**	**NHL**	**42**	**3**	**15**	**18**	**113**	....	....	....	....	....
	Washington	**NHL**	**30**	**6**	**8**	**14**	**124**	**10**	**1**	**3**	**4**	**22**
1991-92	**Washington**	**NHL**	**78**	**17**	**34**	**51**	**180**	**7**	**4**	**2**	**6**	**14**
1992-93a	**Washington**	**NHL**	**81**	**25**	**41**	**66**	**169**	**6**	**6**	**0**	**6**	**4**
1993-94	**Washington**	**NHL**	**67**	**10**	**35**	**45**	**143**	....	....	....	....	....
	Boston	**NHL**	**12**	**5**	**8**	**13**	**20**	**13**	**3**	**1**	**4**	**6**
	NHL Totals		**740**	**144**	**295**	**439**	**1182**	**65**	**18**	**16**	**34**	**67**

a NHL Second All-Star Team (1993)

Played in NHL All-Star Game (1988, 1990, 1993, 1994)

Traded to **Washington** by **Toronto** for Peter Zezel and Bob Rouse, January 16, 1991. Traded to **Boston** by **Washington** for Joe Juneau, March 21, 1994.

IGNATJEV, VIKTOR

Defense. Shoots left. 6'3", 220 lbs. Born, Riga, Latvia, April 26, 1970.
(San Jose's 11th choice, 243rd overall, in 1992 Entry Draft).

			Regular Season					Playoffs				
Season	Club	Lea	GP	G	A	TP	PIM	GP	G	A	TP	PIM
1989-90	Riga	USSR	40	0	0	0	26	....	....	....	....	....
1990-91	Riga	USSR	10	0	0	0	2	....	....	....	....	....
1991-92	Riga	CIS	22	4	5	9	22	....	....	....	....	....
1992-93	Kansas City	IHL	64	5	16	21	68	4	1	2	3	24
1993-94	Kansas City	IHL	67	1	24	25	123	....	....	....	....	....

IMES, CHRIS (IGHMS) — FLA.

Defense. Shoots right. 5'11", 195 lbs. Born, South Paris, ME, August 27, 1972.
(Florida's 1st choice, 4th overall, in 1993 Supplemental Draft).

			Regular Season					Playoffs				
Season	Club	Lea	GP	G	A	TP	PIM	GP	G	A	TP	PIM
1990-91	U. of Maine	H.E.	37	6	8	14	16	....	....	....	....	....
1991-92	U. of Maine	H.E.	31	4	19	23	22	....	....	....	....	....
1992-93abc	U. of Maine	H.E.	45	12	23	35	24	....	....	....	....	....
1993-94	U.S. National	....	58	6	10	16	12	....	....	....	....	....
	U.S. Olympic	....	8	0	0	0	2	....	....	....	....	....

a Hockey East First All-Star Team (1993)
b NCAA East First All-American Team (1993)
c NCAA Final Four All-Tournament Team (1993)

INTRANUOVO, RALPH (ihn-trah-NOO-voh) — EDM.

Center. Shoots left. 5'8", 185 lbs. Born, East York, Ont., December 11, 1973.
(Edmonton's 5th choice, 96th overall, in 1992 Entry Draft).

			Regular Season					Playoffs				
Season	Club	Lea	GP	G	A	TP	PIM	GP	G	A	TP	PIM
1990-91	S.S. Marie	OHL	63	25	42	67	22	14	7	13	20	17
1991-92	S.S. Marie	OHL	65	50	63	113	44	18	10	14	24	12
1992-93ab	S.S. Marie	OHL	54	31	47	78	61	18	10	16	26	30
1993-94	Cape Breton	AHL	66	21	31	52	39	4	1	1	2	3	2

a Won Stafford Smythe Memorial Trophy (Memorial Cup Tournament MVP) (1993)
b Memorial Cup All-Star Team (1993)

IRVING, JOEL — MTL.

Center. Shoots right. 6'3", 190 lbs. Born, Lumsden, Sask., January 2, 1976.
(Montreal's 8th choice, 148th overall, in 1994 Entry Draft).

			Regular Season					Playoffs				
Season	Club	Lea	GP	G	A	TP	PIM	GP	G	A	TP	PIM
1992-93	Regina	Midget	36	13	23	36	36	....	....	....	....	....
1993-94	Regina	Midget	32	16	46	62	22	....	....	....	....	....

JACKSON, DANE — VAN.

Right wing. Shoots right. 6'1", 200 lbs. Born, Castlegar, B.C., May 17, 1970.
(Vancouver's 3rd choice, 44th overall, in 1988 Entry Draft).

			Regular Season					Playoffs				
Season	Club	Lea	GP	G	A	TP	PIM	GP	G	A	TP	PIM
1988-89	North Dakota	WCHA	30	4	5	9	33	....	....	....	....	....
1989-90	North Dakota	WCHA	44	15	11	26	56	....	....	....	....	....
1990-91	North Dakota	WCHA	37	17	9	26	79	....	....	....	....	....
1991-92	North Dakota	WCHA	39	23	19	42	81	....	....	....	....	....
1992-93	Hamilton	AHL	68	23	20	43	59	....	....	....	....	....
1993-94	**Vancouver**	**NHL**	**12**	**5**	**1**	**6**	**9**	....	....	....	....	....
	Hamilton	AHL	60	25	35	60	75	4	2	2	4	16
	NHL Totals		**12**	**5**	**1**	**6**	**9**	....	....	....	....	....

JAGR, JAROMIR (YAH-guhr) — PIT.

Right wing. Shoots left. 6'2", 208 lbs. Born, Kladno, Czech., February 15, 1972.
(Pittsburgh's 1st choice, 5th overall, in 1990 Entry Draft).

			Regular Season					Playoffs				
Season	Club	Lea	GP	G	A	TP	PIM	GP	G	A	TP	PIM
1988-89	Kladno	Czech.	39	8	10	18	4	....	....	....	....	....
1989-90	Kladno	Czech.	51	30	29	59	....	....	....	....	....	....
1990-91a	**Pittsburgh**	**NHL**	**80**	**27**	**30**	**57**	**42**	**24**	**3**	**10**	**13**	**6**
1991-92	**Pittsburgh**	**NHL**	**70**	**32**	**37**	**69**	**34**	**21**	**11**	**13**	**24**	**6**
1992-93	**Pittsburgh**	**NHL**	**81**	**34**	**60**	**94**	**61**	**12**	**5**	**4**	**9**	**23**
1993-94	**Pittsburgh**	**NHL**	**80**	**32**	**67**	**99**	**61**	**6**	**2**	**4**	**6**	**16**
	NHL Totals		**311**	**125**	**194**	**319**	**198**	**63**	**21**	**31**	**52**	**51**

a NHL/Upper Deck All-Rookie Team (1991)

Played in NHL All-Star Game (1992, 1993)

JAKOPIN, JOHN — DET.

Defense. Shoots right. 6'5", 220 lbs. Born, Toronto, Ont., May 16, 1975.
(Detroit's 4th choice, 97th overall, in 1993 Entry Draft).

			Regular Season					Playoffs				
Season	Club	Lea	GP	G	A	TP	PIM	GP	G	A	TP	PIM
1992-93	St. Michael's	Jr. A	45	9	21	30	42	....	....	....	....	....
1993-94	Merrimack	H.E.	36	2	8	10	64	....	....	....	....	....

JANDERA, LUBOMIR — CHI.

Defense. Shoots left. 5'11", 180 lbs. Born, Chomutov, Czech., April 21, 1976.
(Chicago's 9th choice, 222nd overall, in 1994 Entry Draft).

			Regular Season					Playoffs				
Season	Club	Lea	GP	G	A	TP	PIM	GP	G	A	TP	PIM
1993-94	Litvinov	Cz. Jrs.	UNAVAILABLE									

JANNEY, CRAIG — ST.L.

Center. Shoots left. 6'1", 190 lbs. Born, Hartford, CT, September 26, 1967.
(Boston's 1st choice, 13th overall, in 1986 Entry Draft).

			Regular Season					Playoffs				
Season	Club	Lea	GP	G	A	TP	PIM	GP	G	A	TP	PIM
1985-86	Boston College	H.E.	34	13	14	27	8	....	....	....	....	....
1986-87ab	Boston College	H.E.	37	26	55	81	6	....	....	....	....	....
1987-88	U.S. National	....	52	26	44	70	6	....	....	....	....	....
	U.S. Olympic	....	5	3	1	4	2	....	....	....	....	....
	Boston	**NHL**	**15**	**7**	**9**	**16**	**0**	**23**	**6**	**10**	**16**	**11**
1988-89	**Boston**	**NHL**	**62**	**16**	**46**	**62**	**12**	**10**	**4**	**9**	**13**	**21**
1989-90	**Boston**	**NHL**	**55**	**24**	**38**	**62**	**4**	**18**	**3**	**19**	**22**	**2**
1990-91	**Boston**	**NHL**	**77**	**26**	**66**	**92**	**8**	**18**	**4**	**18**	**22**	**11**
1991-92	**Boston**	**NHL**	**53**	**12**	**39**	**51**	**20**	....	....	....	....	....
	St. Louis	**NHL**	**25**	**6**	**30**	**36**	**2**	**6**	**0**	**6**	**6**	**0**
1992-93	**St. Louis**	**NHL**	**84**	**24**	**82**	**106**	**12**	**11**	**2**	**9**	**11**	**0**
1993-94	**St. Louis**	**NHL**	**69**	**16**	**68**	**84**	**24**	**4**	**1**	**3**	**4**	**0**
	NHL Totals		**440**	**131**	**378**	**509**	**82**	**90**	**20**	**74**	**94**	**45**

a Hockey East First All-Star Team (1987)
b NCAA East First All-American Team (1987)

Traded to **St. Louis** by **Boston** with Stephane Quintal for Adam Oates, February 7, 1992. Acquired by **Vancouver** from **St. Louis** with St. Louis' second round choice (Scott Cherrey) in 1994 Entry Draft as compensation for St. Louis' signing of free agent Petr Nedved, March 14, 1994. Traded to **St. Louis** by **Vancouver** for Jeff Brown, Bret Hedican and Nathan Lafayette, March 21, 1994.

JANSSENS, MARK — HFD.

Center. Shoots left. 6'3", 216 lbs. Born, Surrey, B.C., May 19, 1968.
(NY Rangers' 4th choice, 72nd overall, in 1986 Entry Draft).

			Regular Season					Playoffs				
Season	Club	Lea	GP	G	A	TP	PIM	GP	G	A	TP	PIM
1984-85	Regina	WHL	70	8	22	30	51	....	....	....	....	....
1985-86	Regina	WHL	71	25	38	63	146	9	0	2	2	17
1986-87	Regina	WHL	68	24	38	62	209	3	0	1	1	14
1987-88	**NY Rangers**	**NHL**	**1**	**0**	**0**	**0**	**0**	....	....	....	....	....
	Colorado	IHL	6	2	2	4	24	12	3	2	5	20
	Regina	WHL	71	39	51	90	202	4	3	4	7	6
1988-89	**NY Rangers**	**NHL**	**5**	**0**	**0**	**0**	**0**	....	....	....	....	....
	Denver	IHL	38	19	19	38	104	4	3	0	3	18
1989-90	**NY Rangers**	**NHL**	**80**	**5**	**8**	**13**	**161**	**9**	**2**	**1**	**3**	**10**
1990-91	**NY Rangers**	**NHL**	**67**	**9**	**7**	**16**	**172**	**6**	**3**	**0**	**3**	**6**
1991-92	**NY Rangers**	**NHL**	**4**	**0**	**0**	**0**	**5**	....	....	....	....	....
	Binghamton	AHL	55	10	23	33	109	....	....	....	....	....
	Minnesota	**NHL**	**3**	**0**	**0**	**0**	**0**	....	....	....	....	....
	Kalamazoo	IHL	2	0	0	0	2	11	1	2	3	22
1992-93	**Hartford**	**NHL**	**76**	**12**	**17**	**29**	**237**	....	....	....	....	....
1993-94	**Hartford**	**NHL**	**84**	**2**	**10**	**12**	**137**	....	....	....	....	....
	NHL Totals		**320**	**28**	**42**	**70**	**712**	**15**	**5**	**1**	**6**	**16**

Traded to **Minnesota** by **NY Rangers** for Mario Thyer and Minnesota's third round choice (Maxim Galanov) in 1993 Entry Draft, March 10, 1992. Traded to **Hartford** by **Minnesota** for James Black, September 3, 1992.

JANTUNEN, MARKO (YAHN-tuh-nen) — CGY.

Center. Shoots left. 5'10", 185 lbs. Born, Lahti, Finland, February 14, 1971.
(Calgary's 12th choice, 239th overall, in 1991 Entry Draft).

			Regular Season					Playoffs				
Season	Club	Lea	GP	G	A	TP	PIM	GP	G	A	TP	PIM
1990-91	Reipas	Fin.	39	9	20	29	20	....	....	....	....	....
1991-92	Reipas	Fin.	42	10	14	24	46	....	....	....	....	....
1992-93	KalPa	Fin.	48	21	27	48	63	....	....	....	....	....
1993-94	TPS	Fin.	48	29	29	58	22	11	2	6	8	12

JAY, BOB

Defense. Shoots right. 5'11", 190 lbs. Born, Burlington, MA, November 18, 1965.

			Regular Season					Playoffs				
Season	Club	Lea	GP	G	A	TP	PIM	GP	G	A	TP	PIM
1990-91	Fort Wayne	IHL	40	1	8	9	24	14	0	3	3	16
1991-92	Fort Wayne	IHL	76	1	19	20	119	7	0	2	2	4
1992-93	Fort Wayne	IHL	78	5	21	26	100	8	0	2	2	14
1993-94	**Los Angeles**	**NHL**	**3**	**0**	**1**	**1**	**0**	....	....	....	....	....
	Phoenix	IHL	65	7	15	22	54	....	....	....	....	....
	NHL Totals		**3**	**0**	**1**	**1**	**0**	....	....	....	....	....

Signed as a free agent by **Los Angeles**, July 16, 1993.

JEAN, YANICK — WSH.

Defense. Shoots left. 6'1", 198 lbs. Born, Alma, Que., November 26, 1975.
(Washington's 5th choice, 119th overall, in 1994 Entry Draft).

			Regular Season					Playoffs				
Season	Club	Lea	GP	G	A	TP	PIM	GP	G	A	TP	PIM
1992-93	Chicoutimi	QMJHL	50	2	2	4	40	3	0	0	0	0
1993-94	Chicoutimi	QMJHL	65	11	30	41	177	27	8	12	20	82

JENNINGS, GRANT — PIT

Defense. Shoots left. 6'3", 210 lbs. Born, Hudson Bay, Sask., May 5, 1965.

			Regular Season					Playoffs				
Season	Club	Lea	GP	G	A	TP	PIM	GP	G	A	TP	PIM
1983-84	Saskatoon	WHL	64	5	13	18	102	....	....	....	....	....
1984-85	Saskatoon	WHL	47	10	24	34	134	2	1	0	1	2
1985-86	Binghamton	AHL	51	0	4	4	109	....	....	....	....	....
1986-87	Fort Wayne	IHL	3	0	0	0	0	....	....	....	....	....
	Binghamton	AHL	47	1	5	6	125	13	0	2	2	17
1987-88	**Washington**	**NHL**	....	....	....	....	....	**1**	**0**	**0**	**0**	**0**
	Binghamton	AHL	56	2	12	14	195	3	1	0	1	15
1988-89	**Hartford**	**NHL**	**55**	**3**	**10**	**13**	**159**	**4**	**1**	**0**	**1**	**17**
	Binghamton	AHL	2	0	0	0	2	....	....	....	....	....
1989-90	**Hartford**	**NHL**	**64**	**3**	**6**	**9**	**171**	**7**	**0**	**0**	**0**	**13**
1990-91	**Hartford**	**NHL**	**44**	**1**	**4**	**5**	**82**	....	....	....	....	....
	Pittsburgh	**NHL**	**13**	**1**	**3**	**4**	**26**	**13**	**1**	**1**	**2**	**16**
1991-92	**Pittsburgh**	**NHL**	**53**	**4**	**5**	**9**	**104**	**10**	**0**	**0**	**0**	**12**
1992-93	**Pittsburgh**	**NHL**	**58**	**0**	**5**	**5**	**65**	**12**	**0**	**0**	**0**	**8**
1993-94	**Pittsburgh**	**NHL**	**61**	**2**	**4**	**6**	**126**	**3**	**0**	**0**	**0**	**2**
	NHL Totals		**348**	**14**	**37**	**51**	**733**	**50**	**2**	**1**	**3**	**68**

Signed as a free agent by **Washington**, June 25, 1985. Traded to **Hartford** by **Washington** with Ed Kastelic for Mike Millar and Neil Sheehy, July 6, 1988. Traded to **Pittsburgh** by **Hartford** with Ron Francis and Ulf Samuelsson for John Cullen, Jeff Parker and Zarley Zalapski, March 4, 1991.

JENNINGS, JASON

Right wing. Shoots right. 5'11", 185 lbs. Born, Vancouver, B.C., March 16, 1971.
(Winnipeg's 9th choice, 225th overall, in 1991 Entry Draft).

			Regular Season					Playoffs				
Season	Club	Lea	GP	G	A	TP	PIM	GP	G	A	TP	PIM
1989-90	W. Michigan	CCHA	28	3	1	4	50	....	....	....	....	....
1990-91	W. Michigan	CCHA	42	10	19	29	50	....	....	....	....	....
1991-92	W. Michigan	CCHA	35	8	9	17	52	....	....	....	....	....
1992-93	W. Michigan	CCHA	37	11	9	20	36	....	....	....	....	....
1993-94	Raleigh	ECHL	2	0	0	0	4	....	....	....	....	....
	Johnstown	ECHL	44	19	26	45	38	3	0	1	1	0

JENSEN, CHRIS

Right wing. Shoots right. 5'11", 180 lbs. Born, Fort St. John, B.C., October 28, 1963.
(NY Rangers' 4th choice, 78th overall, in 1982 Entry Draft).

			Regular Season					Playoffs				
Season	Club	Lea	GP	G	A	TP	PIM	GP	G	A	TP	PIM
1982-83	North Dakota	WCHA	13	3	3	6	28	....	....	....	....	....
1983-84	North Dakota	WCHA	44	24	25	49	100	....	....	....	....	....
1984-85	North Dakota	WCHA	40	25	27	52	80	....	....	....	....	....
1985-86	North Dakota	WCHA	34	25	40	65	53	....	....	....	....	....
	NY Rangers	**NHL**	**9**	**1**	**3**	**4**	**0**	....	....	....	....	....
1986-87	**NY Rangers**	**NHL**	**37**	**6**	**7**	**13**	**21**	....	....	....	....	....
	New Haven	AHL	14	4	9	13	41	....	....	....	....	....
1987-88	**NY Rangers**	**NHL**	**7**	**0**	**1**	**1**	**2**	....	....	....	....	....
	Colorado	IHL	43	10	23	33	68	10	3	7	10	8
1988-89	Hershey	AHL	45	27	31	58	66	10	4	5	9	29
1989-90	**Philadelphia**	**NHL**	**1**	**0**	**0**	**0**	**2**	....	....	....	....	....
	Hershey	AHL	43	16	26	42	101	....	....	....	....	....
1990-91	**Philadelphia**	**NHL**	**18**	**2**	**1**	**3**	**2**	....	....	....	....	....
	Hershey	AHL	50	26	20	46	83	6	2	2	4	10
1991-92	**Philadelphia**	**NHL**	**2**	**0**	**0**	**0**	**0**	....	....	....	....	....
	Hershey	AHL	71	38	33	71	134	6	0	1	1	2
1992-93	Hershey	AHL	74	33	47	80	95	....	....	....	....	....
1993-94	Portland	AHL	56	33	28	61	52	16	6	10	16	22
	NHL Totals		**74**	**9**	**12**	**21**	**27**	....	....	....	....	....

Traded to **Philadelphia** by **NY Rangers** for Michael Boyce, September 28, 1988.

JICKLING, MIKE — QUE.

Center. Shoots right. 5'11", 191 lbs. Born, Eckville, Alta., January 5, 1973.
(Quebec's 8th choice, 172nd overall, in 1992 Entry Draft).

			Regular Season					Playoffs				
Season	Club	Lea	GP	G	A	TP	PIM	GP	G	A	TP	PIM
1990-91	Spokane	WHL	71	10	27	37	67	15	5	1	6	6
1991-92	Spokane	WHL	69	30	44	74	92	10	7	6	13	20
1992-93	Medicine Hat	WHL	62	22	39	61	97	10	3	3	6	6
1993-94	U. of Alberta	CWUAA	28	7	16	23	69	....	....	....	....	....

JINMAN, LEE — DAL.

Center. Shoots right. 5'10", 155 lbs. Born, Toronto, Ont., January 10, 1976.
(Dallas' 2nd choice, 46th overall, in 1994 Entry Draft).

			Regular Season					Playoffs				
Season	Club	Lea	GP	G	A	TP	PIM	GP	G	A	TP	PIM
1992-93	Wexford	Midget	42	37	53	90	14	....	....	....	....	....
1993-94	North Bay	OHL	66	31	66	97	33	18	*18	19	37	8

JIRANEK, MARTIN (jih-RA-nihk)

Center. Shoots left. 5'11", 170 lbs. Born, Bashaw, Alta., October 3, 1969.
(Washington's 1st choice, 14th overall, in 1990 Supplemental Draft).

			Regular Season					Playoffs				
Season	Club	Lea	GP	G	A	TP	PIM	GP	G	A	TP	PIM
1988-89	Bowling Green	CCHA	41	9	18	27	36	....	....	....	....	....
1989-90	Bowling Green	CCHA	41	13	21	34	38	....	....	....	....	....
1990-91	Bowling Green	CCHA	39	31	23	54	33	....	....	....	....	....
1991-92a	Bowling Green	CCHA	34	25	28	53	46	....	....	....	....	....
	Baltimore	AHL	8	2	8	10	0	....	....	....	....	....
1992-93	Baltimore	AHL	64	18	26	44	39	7	1	2	3	23
1993-94	Portland	AHL	73	15	37	52	75	13	2	4	6	2

a CCHA Second All-Star Team (1992)

JOHANSSON, ANDREAS — NYI

Center. Shoots left. 5'10", 198 lbs. Born, Hofors, Sweden, May 19, 1973.
(NY Islanders' 7th choice, 136th overall, in 1991 Entry Draft).

			Regular Season					Playoffs				
Season	Club	Lea	GP	G	A	TP	PIM	GP	G	A	TP	PIM
1990-91	Falun	Swe. 2	31	12	10	22	38	....	....	....	....	....
1991-92	Farjestad	Swe.	30	3	1	4	10	6	0	0	0	4
1992-93	Farjestad	Swe.	38	4	7	11	38	2	0	0	0	0
1993-94	Farjestad	Swe.	20	3	6	9	6	....	....	....	....	....

OHANSSON, CALLE (yo-HAHN-sehn, KAL-ee) WSH.

)efense. Shoots left. 5'11", 205 lbs. Born, Goteborg, Sweden, February 14, 1967.
3uffalo's 1st choice, 14th overall, in 1985 Entry Draft).

			Regular Season					Playoffs				
eason	Club	Lea	GP	G	A	TP	PIM	GP	G	A	TP	PIM
983-84	V. Frolunda	Swe.	28	4	4	8	10	....	....	....	....	....
984-85	V. Frolunda	Swe.2	25	8	13	21	16	6	1	2	3	4
985-86	Bjorkloven	Swe.	17	1	2	3	4	....	....	....	....	....
986-87	Bjorkloven	Swe.	30	2	13	15	20	6	1	3	4	6
1987-88a	**Buffalo**	**NHL**	**71**	**4**	**38**	**42**	**37**	**6**	**0**	**1**	**1**	**0**
1988-89	**Buffalo**	**NHL**	**47**	**2**	**11**	**13**	**33**	....	....	....	....	....
	Washington	**NHL**	**12**	**1**	**7**	**8**	**4**	**6**	**1**	**2**	**3**	**0**
1989-90	**Washington**	**NHL**	**70**	**8**	**31**	**39**	**25**	**15**	**1**	**6**	**7**	**4**
1990-91	**Washington**	**NHL**	**80**	**11**	**41**	**52**	**23**	**10**	**2**	**7**	**9**	**8**
1991-92	**Washington**	**NHL**	**80**	**14**	**42**	**56**	**49**	**7**	**0**	**5**	**5**	**4**
1992-93	**Washington**	**NHL**	**77**	**7**	**38**	**45**	**56**	**6**	**0**	**5**	**5**	**4**
1993-94	**Washington**	**NHL**	**84**	**9**	**33**	**42**	**59**	**6**	**1**	**3**	**4**	**4**
	NHL Totals		**521**	**56**	**241**	**297**	**286**	**56**	**5**	**29**	**34**	**24**

a NHL All-Rookie Team (1988)
Traded to **Washington** by **Buffalo** with Buffalo's second round choice (Byron Dafoe) in 1989 Entry Draft for Clint Malarchuk, Grant Ledyard and Washington's sixth round choice (Brian Holzinger) in 1991 Entry Draft, March 7, 1989.

JOHANSSON, DANIEL (YOOH-hahn-suhn) NYI

Defense. Shoots right. 5'11", 180 lbs. Born, Glimakra, Sweden, September 10, 1974.
(NY Islanders' 9th choice, 222nd overall, in 1993 Entry Draft).

			Regular Season					Playoffs				
Season	Club	Lea	GP	G	A	TP	PIM	GP	G	A	TP	PIM
1991-92	Rogle	Swe. 2	33	4	9	13	30	....	....	....	....	....
1992-93	Rogle	Swe.	28	2	4	6	20	....	....	....	....	....
1993-94	Rogle	Swe.	37	5	10	15	34	3	0	0	0	0

JOHANSSON, MATHIAS

Center. Shoots left. 6'2", 190 lbs. Born, Oskarshamn, Sweden, February 22, 1974.
(Calgary's 3rd choice, 54th overall, in 1992 Entry Draft).

			Regular Season					Playoffs				
Season	Club	Lea	GP	G	A	TP	PIM	GP	G	A	TP	PIM
1990-91	Farjestad	Swe.	3	0	0	0	0	....	....	....	....	....
1991-92	Farjestad	Swe.	16	0	0	0	2	1	0	0	0	0
1992-93	Farjestad	Swe.	11	2	1	3	4	3	0	0	0	0
1993-94	Farjestad	Swe.	16	2	1	3	4	....	....	....	....	....

JOHANSSON, MIKAEL QUE.

Center. Shoots left. 5'10", 183 lbs. Born, Stockholm, Sweden, June 12, 1966.
(Quebec's 7th choice, 134th overall, in 1991 Entry Draft).

			Regular Season					Playoffs				
Season	Club	Lea	GP	G	A	TP	PIM	GP	G	A	TP	PIM
1986-87	Djurgarden	Swe.	32	9	16	25	8	....	....	....	....	....
1987-88	Djurgarden	Swe.	38	11	22	33	10	3	1	1	2	0
1988-89	Djurgarden	Swe.	29	6	15	21	10	....	....	....	....	....
1989-90	Djurgarden	Swe.	37	14	20	34	12	8	5	4	9	0
1990-91	Djurgarden	Swe.	39	13	27	40	21	7	2	7	9	0
1991-92	Djurgarden	Swe.	30	15	21	36	12	9	1	5	6	4
1992-93	Kloten	Switz.	36	18	30	48	2	....	....	....	....	....
1993-94	Kloten	Switz.	36	22	29	51	24	12	9	14	23	8

JOHANSSON, ROGER (yo-HAHN-suhn) CGY.

Defense. Shoots left. 6'1", 190 lbs. Born, Ljungby, Sweden, April 17, 1967.
(Calgary's 5th choice, 80th overall, in 1985 Entry Draft).

			Regular Season					Playoffs				
Season	Club	Lea	GP	G	A	TP	PIM	GP	G	A	TP	PIM
1983-84	Troja	Swe.2	11	2	2	4	12	....	....	....	....	....
1984-85	Troja	Swe.2	30	1	6	7	20	9	0	4	4	8
1985-86	Troja	Swe.2	32	5	16	21	42	....	....	....	....	....
1986-87	Farjestad	Swe.	31	6	11	17	20	7	1	1	2	8
1987-88	Farjestad	Swe.	24	3	11	14	20	9	1	6	7	12
1988-89	Farjestad	Swe.	40	5	15	20	38	....	....	....	....	....
1989-90	**Calgary**	**NHL**	**35**	**0**	**5**	**5**	**48**	....	....	....	....	....
1990-91	**Calgary**	**NHL**	**38**	**4**	**13**	**17**	**47**	....	....	....	....	....
1991-92	Leksand	Swe.	22	3	9	12	42	....	....	....	....	....
1992-93	**Calgary**	**NHL**	**77**	**4**	**16**	**20**	**62**	**5**	**0**	**1**	**1**	**2**
1993-94	Leksand	Swe.	38	6	15	21	56	....	....	....	....	....
	NHL Totals		**150**	**8**	**34**	**42**	**157**	**5**	**0**	**1**	**1**	**2**

JOHNSON, CLINT PIT.

Left wing. Shoots left. 6'2", 200 lbs. Born, Duluth, MN, April 7, 1976.
(Pittsburgh's 7th choice, 128th overall, in 1994 Entry Draft).

			Regular Season					Playoffs				
Season	Club	Lea	GP	G	A	TP	PIM	GP	G	A	TP	PIM
1992-93	Duluth E.	HS	23	15	14	29	24	....	....	....	....	....
1993-94	Duluth E.	HS	28	30	31	61	....	....	....	....	....	....

JOHNSON, CRAIG ST.L.

Left wing/Center. Shoots left. 6'2", 197 lbs. Born, St. Paul, MN, March 18, 1972.
(St. Louis' 1st choice, 33rd overall, in 1990 Entry Draft).

			Regular Season					Playoffs				
Season	Club	Lea	GP	G	A	TP	PIM	GP	G	A	TP	PIM
1990-91	U. Minnesota	WCHA	33	13	18	31	34	....	....	....	....	....
1991-92	U. Minnesota	WCHA	41	17	38	55	66	....	....	....	....	....
1992-93	U. Minnesota	WCHA	42	22	24	46	70	....	....	....	....	....
1993-94	U.S. National	....	54	25	26	51	64	....	....	....	....	....
	U.S. Olympic	....	8	0	4	4	4	....	....	....	....	....

JOHNSON, ERIC VAN.

Right wing. Shoots right. 6'1", 200 lbs. Born, Plymouth, MN, December 31, 1972.
(Vancouver's 8th choice, 161st overall, in 1991 Entry Draft).

			Regular Season					Playoffs				
Season	Club	Lea	GP	G	A	TP	PIM	GP	G	A	TP	PIM
1991-92	St. Cloud	WCHA	20	0	2	2	8	....	....	....	....	....
1992-93	St. Cloud	WCHA	33	3	7	10	6	....	....	....	....	....
1993-94	St. Cloud	WCHA	33	9	21	30	16	....	....	....	....	....

JOHNSON, GREG DET.

Center. Shoots left. 5'10", 185 lbs. Born, Thunder Bay, Ont., March 16, 1971.
(Philadelphia's 1st choice, 33rd overall, in 1989 Entry Draft).

			Regular Season					Playoffs				
Season	Club	Lea	GP	G	A	TP	PIM	GP	G	A	TP	PIM
1989-90	North Dakota	WCHA	44	17	38	55	11	....	....	....	....	....
1990-91ab	North Dakota	WCHA	38	18	*61	79	6	....	....	....	....	....
1991-92ac	North Dakota	WCHA	39	20	*54	74	8	....	....	....	....	....
1992-93ab	North Dakota	WCHA	34	19	45	64	18	....	....	....	....	....
	Cdn. National	....	23	6	14	20	2	....	....	....	....	....
1993-94	**Detroit**	**NHL**	**52**	**6**	**11**	**17**	**22**	**7**	**2**	**2**	**4**	**2**
	Cdn. National	....	6	2	6	8	4	....	....	....	....	....
	Cdn. Olympic	....	8	0	3	3	0	....	....	....	....	....
	Adirondack	AHL	3	2	4	6	0	4	0	4	4	2
	NHL Totals		**52**	**6**	**11**	**17**	**22**	**7**	**2**	**2**	**4**	**2**

a WCHA First All-Star Team (1991, 1993)
b NCAA West First All-American Team (1991, 1993)
c NCAA West Second All-American Team (1992)

Traded to **Detroit** by **Philadelphia** with Philadelphia's fifth round choice (Frederic Deschenes) in 1994 Entry Draft for Jim Cummins and Philadelphia's fourth round choice (previously acquired by Detroit — later traded to Boston — Boston selected Charles Paquette) in 1993 Entry Draft, June 20, 1993.

JOHNSON, JIM WSH.

Defense. Shoots left. 6'1", 190 lbs. Born, New Hope, MN, August 9, 1962.

			Regular Season					Playoffs				
Season	Club	Lea	GP	G	A	TP	PIM	GP	G	A	TP	PIM
1981-82	Minn.-Duluth	WCHA	40	0	10	10	62	....	....	....	....	....
1982-83	Minn.-Duluth	WCHA	44	3	18	21	118	....	....	....	....	....
1983-84	Minn.-Duluth	WCHA	43	3	13	16	116	....	....	....	....	....
1984-85	Minn.-Duluth	WCHA	47	7	29	36	49	....	....	....	....	....
1985-86	**Pittsburgh**	**NHL**	**80**	**3**	**26**	**29**	**115**	....	....	....	....	....
1986-87	**Pittsburgh**	**NHL**	**80**	**5**	**25**	**30**	**116**	....	....	....	....	....
1987-88	**Pittsburgh**	**NHL**	**55**	**1**	**12**	**13**	**87**	....	....	....	....	....
1988-89	**Pittsburgh**	**NHL**	**76**	**2**	**14**	**16**	**163**	**11**	**0**	**5**	**5**	**44**
1989-90	**Pittsburgh**	**NHL**	**75**	**3**	**13**	**16**	**154**	....	....	....	....	....
1990-91	**Pittsburgh**	**NHL**	**24**	**0**	**5**	**5**	**23**	....	....	....	....	....
	Minnesota	**NHL**	**44**	**1**	**9**	**10**	**100**	**14**	**0**	**1**	**1**	**52**
1991-92	**Minnesota**	**NHL**	**71**	**4**	**10**	**14**	**102**	**7**	**1**	**3**	**4**	**18**
1992-93	**Minnesota**	**NHL**	**79**	**3**	**20**	**23**	**105**	....	....	....	....	....
1993-94	**Dallas**	**NHL**	**53**	**0**	**7**	**7**	**51**	....	....	....	....	....
	Washington	**NHL**	**8**	**0**	**0**	**0**	**12**	....	....	....	....	....
	NHL Totals		**645**	**22**	**141**	**163**	**1028**	**32**	**1**	**9**	**10**	**114**

Signed as a free agent by **Pittsburgh**, June 9, 1985. Traded to **Minnesota** by **Pittsburgh** with Chris Dahlquist for Larry Murphy and Peter Taglianetti, December 11, 1990. Traded to **Washington** by **Dallas** for Alan May and Washington's seventh round choice in 1995 Entry Draft, March 21, 1994.

JOHNSON, MATT L.A.

Left wing. Shoots left. 6'5", 223 lbs. Born, Welland, Ont., November 23, 1975.
(Los Angeles' 2nd choice, 33rd overall, in 1994 Entry Draft).

			Regular Season					Playoffs				
Season	Club	Lea	GP	G	A	TP	PIM	GP	G	A	TP	PIM
1992-93	Peterborough	OHL	66	8	17	25	211	16	1	1	2	56
1993-94	Peterborough	OHL	50	13	24	37	233	....	....	....	....	....

JOHNSON, MICHAEL

Defense. Shoots left. 6'3", 175 lbs. Born, Halifax, N.S., May 29, 1974.
(Minnesota's 4th choice, 130th overall, in 1992 Entry Draft).

			Regular Season					Playoffs				
Season	Club	Lea	GP	G	A	TP	PIM	GP	G	A	TP	PIM
1991-92	Ottawa	OHL	63	1	8	9	49	11	1	0	1	14
1992-93	Ottawa	OHL	66	7	10	17	139	....	....	....	....	....
1993-94	Ottawa	OHL	65	12	17	29	102	17	4	6	10	10

JOHNSON, RYAN FLA.

Center. Shoots left. 6'2", 180 lbs. Born, Thunder Bay, Ont., June 14, 1976.
(Florida's 4th choice, 36th overall, in 1994 Entry Draft).

			Regular Season					Playoffs				
Season	Club	Lea	GP	G	A	TP	PIM	GP	G	A	TP	PIM
1992-93	Thunder Bay	Midget	60	25	33	58	....	....	....	....	....	....
1993-94	Thunder Bay	USHL	48	14	36	50	28	....	....	....	....	....

JOMPHE, JEAN-FRANCOIS (zhohm-PHEE) ANA.

Center. Shoots left. 6'1", 193 lbs. Born, Harve' St. Pierre, Que., December 28, 1972.

			Regular Season					Playoffs				
Season	Club	Lea	GP	G	A	TP	PIM	GP	G	A	TP	PIM
1990-91	Shawinigan	QMJHL	42	17	22	39	14	6	2	1	3	2
1991-92	Shawinigan	QMJHL	44	28	33	61	69	10	6	10	16	10
1992-93	Sherbrooke	QMJHL	60	43	43	86	86	15	10	13	23	18
1993-94	San Diego	IHL	29	2	3	5	12	....	....	....	....	....
	Greensboro	ECHL	25	9	9	18	41	1	1	0	1	0

Signed as a free agent by **Anaheim**, September 7, 1993

JONES, KEITH WSH.

Right wing. Shoots left. 6'2", 190 lbs. Born, Brantford, Ont., November 8, 1968.
(Washington's 7th choice, 141st overall, in 1988 Entry Draft).

			Regular Season					Playoffs				
Season	Club	Lea	GP	G	A	TP	PIM	GP	G	A	TP	PIM
1988-89	W. Michigan	CCHA	37	9	12	21	51	....	....	....	....	....
1989-90	W. Michigan	CCHA	40	19	18	37	82	....	....	....	....	....
1990-91	W. Michigan	CCHA	41	30	19	49	106	....	....	....	....	....
1991-92a	W. Michigan	CCHA	35	25	31	56	77	....	....	....	....	....
	Baltimore	AHL	6	2	4	6	0	....	....	....	....	....
1992-93	**Washington**	**NHL**	**71**	**12**	**14**	**26**	**124**	**6**	**0**	**0**	**0**	**10**
	Baltimore	AHL	8	7	3	10	4	....	....	....	....	....
1993-94	**Washington**	**NHL**	**68**	**16**	**19**	**35**	**149**	**11**	**0**	**1**	**1**	**36**
	Portland	AHL	6	5	7	12	4	....	....	....	....	....
	NHL Totals		**139**	**28**	**33**	**61**	**273**	**17**	**0**	**1**	**1**	**46**

a CCHA First All-Star Team (1992)

JONSSON, HANS (YOOHN-suhn) PIT.

Defense. Shoots left. 6'1", 183 lbs. Born, Jarved, Sweden, August 2, 1973.
(Pittsburgh's 11th choice, 286th overall, in 1993 Entry Draft).

			Regular Season					Playoffs				
Season	Club	Lea	GP	G	A	TP	PIM	GP	G	A	TP	PIM
1991-92	MoDo	Swe.	6	0	1	1	4	....	....	....	....	....
1992-93	MoDo	Swe.	40	2	2	4	24	3	0	1	1	2
1993-94	MoDo	Swe.	23	4	1	5	18	10	0	1	1	12

JONSSON, JORGEN — CGY.

Left wing. Shoots left. 6', 185 lbs. Born, Angelholm, Sweden, September 29, 1972.
(Calgary's 11th choice, 227th overall, in 1994 Entry Draft).

			Regular Season					Playoffs				
Season	Club	Lea	GP	G	A	TP	PIM	GP	G	A	TP	PIM
1992-93	Rogle	Swe.	40	17	11	28	28	....	....	....	....	....
1993-94	Rogle	Swe.	40	17	14	31	46	....	....	....	....	....

JONSSON, KENNY — (YAHN-suhn) TOR.

Defense. Shoots left. 6'3", 195 lbs. Born, Angelholm, Sweden, October 6, 1974.
(Toronto's 1st choice, 12th overall, in 1993 Entry Draft).

			Regular Season					Playoffs				
Season	Club	Lea	GP	G	A	TP	PIM	GP	G	A	TP	PIM
1991-92	Rogle	Swe. 2	30	4	11	15	24	....	....	....	....	....
1992-93a	Rogle	Swe.	39	3	10	13	42	....	....	....	....	....
1993-94	Rogle	Swe.	36	4	13	17	40	3	1	1	2	2

a Swedish Rookie of the Year (1993)

JOSEPH, CHRIS — T.B.

Defense. Shoots right. 6'2", 210 lbs. Born, Burnaby, B.C., September 10, 1969.
(Pittsburgh's 1st choice, 5th overall, in 1987 Entry Draft).

			Regular Season					Playoffs				
Season	Club	Lea	GP	G	A	TP	PIM	GP	G	A	TP	PIM
1985-86	Seattle	WHL	72	4	8	12	50	5	0	3	3	12
1986-87	Seattle	WHL	67	13	45	58	155	....	....	....	....	....
1987-88	**Pittsburgh**	**NHL**	**17**	**0**	**4**	**4**	**12**	....	....	....	....	....
	Seattle	WHL	23	5	14	19	49	....	....	....	....	....
	Edmonton	**NHL**	**7**	**0**	**4**	**4**	**6**	....	....	....	....	....
	Nova Scotia	AHL	8	0	2	2	8	4	0	0	0	9
1988-89	**Edmonton**	**NHL**	**44**	**4**	**5**	**9**	**54**	....	....	....	....	....
	Cape Breton	AHL	5	1	1	2	18	....	....	....	....	....
1989-90	**Edmonton**	**NHL**	**4**	**0**	**2**	**2**	**2**	....	....	....	....	....
	Cape Breton	AHL	61	10	20	30	69	6	2	1	3	4
1990-91	**Edmonton**	**NHL**	**49**	**5**	**17**	**22**	**59**	....	....	....	....	....
1991-92	**Edmonton**	**NHL**	**7**	**0**	**0**	**0**	**8**	**5**	**1**	**3**	**4**	**2**
	Cape Breton	AHL	63	14	29	43	72	5	0	2	2	8
1992-93	**Edmonton**	**NHL**	**33**	**2**	**10**	**12**	**48**	....	....	....	....	....
1993-94	**Edmonton**	**NHL**	**10**	**1**	**1**	**2**	**28**	....	....	....	....	....
	Tampa Bay	**NHL**	**66**	**10**	**19**	**29**	**108**	....	....	....	....	....
	NHL Totals		**237**	**22**	**62**	**84**	**325**	**5**	**1**	**3**	**4**	**2**

Traded to **Edmonton** by **Pittsburgh** with Craig Simpson, Dave Hannan and Moe Mantha for Paul Coffey, Dave Hunter and Wayne Van Dorp, November 24, 1987. Traded to **Tampa Bay** by **Edmonton** for Bob Beers, November 11, 1993.

JOSEPHSON, MIKE — CHI.

Left wing. Shoots left. 5'11", 195 lbs. Born, Vancouver, B.C., April 6, 1976.
(Chicago's 8th choice, 196th overall, in 1994 Entry Draft).

			Regular Season					Playoffs				
Season	Club	Lea	GP	G	A	TP	PIM	GP	G	A	TP	PIM
1992-93	Kamloops	WHL	46	5	9	14	60	10	0	2	2	4
1993-94	Kamloops	WHL	48	11	12	23	114	19	1	10	11	8

JOUBERT, JACQUES — DAL.

Forward. Shoots left. 6'1", 191 lbs. Born, South Bend, IN, March 23, 1971.
(Dallas' 1st choice, 9th overall, in 1993 Supplemental Draft).

			Regular Season					Playoffs				
Season	Club	Lea	GP	G	A	TP	PIM	GP	G	A	TP	PIM
1992-93	Boston U.	H.E.	40	17	18	35	54	....	....	....	....	....
1993-94ab	Boston U.	H.E.	41	20	24	44	82	....	....	....	....	....

a Hockey East First All-Star Team (1994)
b NCAA East Second All-American Team (1994)

JOVANOVSKI, ED — (joh-van-OHV-skee) FLA.

Defense. Shoots left. 6'2", 205 lbs. Born, Windsor, Ont., June 26, 1976.
(Florida's 1st choice, 1st overall, in 1994 Entry Draft).

			Regular Season					Playoffs				
Season	Club	Lea	GP	G	A	TP	PIM	GP	G	A	TP	PIM
1992-93	Windsor	Jr. B	48	7	46	53	88	....	....	....	....	....
1993-94a	Windsor	OHL	62	15	36	51	221	4	0	0	0	15

a OHL Second All-Star Team (1994)

JOYCE, BOB

Left wing. Shoots left. 6', 195 lbs. Born, St. John, N.B., July 11, 1966.
(Boston's 4th choice, 82nd overall, in 1984 Entry Draft).

			Regular Season					Playoffs				
Season	Club	Lea	GP	G	A	TP	PIM	GP	G	A	TP	PIM
1984-85	North Dakota	WCHA	41	18	16	34	10	....	....	....	....	....
1985-86	North Dakota	WCHA	38	31	28	59	40	....	....	....	....	....
1986-87abc	North Dakota	WCHA	48	52	37	89	42	....	....	....	....	....
1987-88	Cdn. National	....	46	12	10	22	28	....	....	....	....	....
	Cdn. Olympic	....	4	1	0	1	0	....	....	....	....	....
	Boston	**NHL**	**15**	**7**	**5**	**12**	**10**	**23**	**8**	**6**	**14**	**18**
1988-89	**Boston**	**NHL**	**77**	**18**	**31**	**49**	**46**	**9**	**5**	**2**	**7**	**2**
1989-90	**Boston**	**NHL**	**23**	**1**	**2**	**3**	**22**	....	....	....	....	....
	Washington	**NHL**	**24**	**5**	**8**	**13**	**4**	**14**	**2**	**1**	**3**	**9**
1990-91	**Washington**	**NHL**	**17**	**3**	**3**	**6**	**8**	....	....	....	....	....
	Baltimore	AHL	36	10	8	18	14	6	1	0	1	4
1991-92	**Winnipeg**	**NHL**	**1**	**0**	**0**	**0**	**0**	....	....	....	....	....
	Moncton	AHL	66	19	29	48	51	10	0	5	5	9
1992-93	**Winnipeg**	**NHL**	**1**	**0**	**0**	**0**	**0**	....	....	....	....	....
	Moncton	AHL	75	25	32	57	52	5	0	0	0	2
1993-94	Las Vegas	IHL	63	15	18	33	45	5	2	1	3	8
	NHL Totals		**158**	**34**	**49**	**83**	**90**	**46**	**15**	**9**	**24**	**29**

a WCHA First All-Star Team (1987)
b NCAA West First All-American Team (1987)
c Named to NCAA All-Tournament Team (1987)

Traded to **Washington** by **Boston** for Dave Christian, December 13, 1989. Traded to **Winnipeg** by **Washington** with Tyler Larter and Kent Paynter for Craig Duncanson, Brent Hughes and Simon Wheeldon, May 21, 1991.

JOYCE, DUANE

Defense. Shoots right. 6'2", 203 lbs. Born, Pembroke, MA, May 5, 1965.

			Regular Season					Playoffs				
Season	Club	Lea	GP	G	A	TP	PIM	GP	G	A	TP	PIM
1989-90	Kalamazoo	IHL	2	0	0	0	2	....	....	....	....	....
	Fort Wayne	IHL	66	10	26	36	53	....	....	....	....	....
	Muskegon	IHL	13	3	10	13	8	12	3	7	10	13
1990-91	Kalamazoo	IHL	80	12	32	44	53	11	0	3	3	6
1991-92	Kansas City	IHL	80	12	32	44	62	15	6	11	17	8
1992-93	Kansas City	IHL	75	15	25	40	30	12	1	2	3	6
1993-94	Kansas City	IHL	43	9	23	32	40	....	....	....	....	....
	Dallas	**NHL**	**3**	**0**	**0**	**0**	**0**	....	....	....	....	....
	NHL Totals		**3**	**0**	**0**	**0**	**0**	....	....	....	....	....

Signed as a free agent by **San Jose**, August 13, 1991. Signed as free agent by **Dallas**, December 3, 1993.

JUDEN, DANIEL — T.B.

Right wing. Shoots right. 6'3", 190 lbs. Born, Beverly, MA, April 17, 1976.
(Tampa Bay's 5th choice, 137th overall, in 1994 Entry Draft).

			Regular Season					Playoffs				
Season	Club	Lea	GP	G	A	TP	PIM	GP	G	A	TP	PIM
1992-93	Gov. Dummer	HS	25	14	15	29	2	....	....	....	....	....
1993-94	Gov. Dummer	HS	30	20	28	48	8	....	....	....	....	....

JUDSON, RICK

Left wing. Shoots left. 5'11", 180 lbs. Born, Toledo, OH, August 13, 1969.
(Detroit's 11th choice, 204th overall, in 1989 Entry Draft).

			Regular Season					Playoffs				
Season	Club	Lea	GP	G	A	TP	PIM	GP	G	A	TP	PIM
1988-89	Ill.-Chicago	CCHA	42	14	20	34	20	....	....	....	....	....
1989-90	Ill.-Chicago	CCHA	38	19	22	41	18	....	....	....	....	....
1990-91	Ill.-Chicago	CCHA	38	24	26	50	12	....	....	....	....	....
1991-92	Ill.-Chicago	CCHA	35	17	19	36	26	....	....	....	....	....
	Toledo	ECHL	2	1	0	1	2	....	....	....	....	....
1992-93	Adirondack	AHL	7	3	0	3	0	....	....	....	....	....
	Toledo	ECHL	56	23	28	51	39	16	7	16	23	10
1993-94	Adirondack	AHL	2	1	0	1	0	....	....	....	....	....
a	Toledo	ECHL	61	39	49	88	16	14	5	13	18	6

a ECHL Second All-Star Team (1994)

JUHLIN, PATRIK — (ew-LEEN) PHI.

Left wing. Shoots left. 6', 194 lbs. Born, Huddinge, Sweden, April 24, 1970.
(Philadelphia's 2nd choice, 34th overall, in 1989 Entry Draft).

			Regular Season					Playoffs				
Season	Club	Lea	GP	G	A	TP	PIM	GP	G	A	TP	PIM
1988-89	Vasteras	Swe. 2	30	29	13	42	....	....	....	....	....	....
1989-90	Vasteras	Swe.	35	10	13	23	18	2	0	0	0	0
1990-91	Vasteras	Swe.	40	13	9	22	24	4	3	1	4	0
1991-92	Vasteras	Swe.	39	15	12	27	40	....	....	....	....	....
1992-93	Vasteras	Swe.	34	14	12	26	22	3	0	1	1	2
1993-94	Vasteras	Swe.	40	15	16	31	20	4	1	1	2	2

JUNEAU, JOE — (ZHOO-noh, ZHOH-ay) WSH.

Center/Left Wing. Shoots right. 6', 195 lbs. Born, Pont-Rouge, Que., January 5, 1968.
(Boston's 3rd choice, 81st overall, in 1988 Entry Draft).

			Regular Season					Playoffs				
Season	Club	Lea	GP	G	A	TP	PIM	GP	G	A	TP	PIM
1987-88	RPI	ECAC	31	16	29	45	18	....	....	....	....	....
1988-89	RPI	ECAC	30	12	23	35	40	....	....	....	....	....
1989-90a	RPI	ECAC	34	18	*52	*70	31	....	....	....	....	....
1990-91bc	RPI	ECAC	29	23	40	63	68	....	....	....	....	....
	Cdn. National	....	7	2	3	5	0	....	....	....	....	....
1991-92	Cdn. National	....	60	20	49	69	35	....	....	....	....	....
	Cdn. Olympic	....	8	6	9	15	4	....	....	....	....	....
	Boston	**NHL**	**14**	**5**	**14**	**19**	**4**	**15**	**4**	**8**	**12**	**21**
1992-93d	**Boston**	**NHL**	**84**	**32**	**70**	**102**	**33**	**4**	**2**	**4**	**6**	**6**
1993-94	**Boston**	**NHL**	**63**	**14**	**58**	**72**	**35**	....	....	....	....	....
	Washington	**NHL**	**11**	**5**	**8**	**13**	**6**	**11**	**4**	**5**	**9**	**6**
	NHL Totals		**172**	**56**	**150**	**206**	**78**	**30**	**10**	**17**	**27**	**33**

a NCAA East First All-American Team (1990)
b ECAC Second All-Star Team (1991)
c NCAA East Second All-American Team (1991)
d NHL/Upper Deck All-Rookie Team (1993)

Traded to **Washington** by **Boston** for Al Iafrate, March 21, 1994.

JUNKER, STEVE — NYI

Left wing. Shoots left. 6', 184 lbs. Born, Castlegar, B.C., June 26, 1972.
(NY Islanders' 5th choice, 92nd overall, in 1991 Entry Draft).

			Regular Season					Playoffs				
Season	Club	Lea	GP	G	A	TP	PIM	GP	G	A	TP	PIM
1990-91	Spokane	WHL	71	39	38	77	86	15	5	13	18	6
1991-92	Spokane	WHL	58	28	32	60	110	10	6	7	13	18
1992-93	Capital Dist.	AHL	79	16	31	47	20	4	0	0	0	0
	NY Islanders	**NHL**	....	....	....	....	....	**3**	**0**	**1**	**1**	**0**
1993-94	**NY Islanders**	**NHL**	**5**	**0**	**0**	**0**	**0**	....	....	....	....	....
	Salt Lake	IHL	71	9	14	23	36	....	....	....	....	....
	NHL Totals		**5**	**0**	**0**	**0**	**0**	**3**	**0**	**1**	**1**	**0**

KACIR, MARIAN — T.B.

Right wing. Shoots left. 6'1", 183 lbs. Born, Hodonin, Czech., September 29, 1974.
(Tampa Bay's 4th choice, 81st overall, in 1993 Entry Draft).

			Regular Season					Playoffs				
Season	Club	Lea	GP	G	A	TP	PIM	GP	G	A	TP	PIM
1992-93	Owen Sound	OHL	56	20	36	56	8	8	3	5	8	4
1993-94	Owen Sound	OHL	66	23	64	87	26	9	5	4	9	2

AMENSKY, VALERI (kah-MEHN-skee) QUE.

eft wing. Shoots right. 6'2", 198 lbs. Born, Voskresensk, USSR, April 18, 1966.
uebec's 8th choice, 129th overall, in 1988 Entry Draft).

			Regular Season					Playoffs				
eason	Club	Lea	GP	G	A	TP	PIM	GP	G	A	TP	PIM
982-83	Khimik	USSR	5	0	0	0	0					
983-84	Khimik	USSR	20	2	2	4	6					
984-85	Khimik	USSR	45	9	3	12	24					
985-86	CSKA	USSR	40	15	9	24	8					
986-87	CSKA	USSR	37	13	8	21	16					
987-88	CSKA	USSR	51	26	20	46	40					
988-89	CSKA	USSR	40	18	10	28	30					
989-90	CSKA	USSR	45	19	18	37	40					
990-91	CSKA	USSR	46	20	26	46	66					
991-92	Quebec	NHL	23	7	14	21	14					
992-93	Quebec	NHL	32	15	22	37	14	6	0	1	1	6
993-94	Quebec	NHL	76	28	37	65	42					
	NHL Totals		131	50	73	123	70	6	0	1	1	6

AMINSKI, KEVIN (kah-MIN-skee) WSH.

enter. Shoots left. 5'9", 170 lbs. Born, Churchbridge, Sask., March 13, 1969.
Minnesota's 3rd choice, 48th overall, in 1987 Entry Draft).

			Regular Season					Playoffs				
eason	Club	Lea	GP	G	A	TP	PIM	GP	G	A	TP	PIM
986-87	Saskatoon	WHL	67	26	44	70	325	11	5	6	11	45
987-88	Saskatoon	WHL	55	38	61	99	247	10	5	7	12	37
988-89	Minnesota	NHL	1	0	0	0	0					
	Saskatoon	WHL	52	25	43	68	199	8	4	9	13	25
989-90	Quebec	NHL	1	0	0	0	0					
	Halifax	AHL	19	3	4	7	128	2	0	0	0	5
990-91	Halifax	AHL	7	1	0	1	44					
	Fort Wayne	IHL	56	9	15	24	*455	19	4	2	6	*169
991-92	Quebec	NHL	5	0	0	0	45					
	Halifax	AHL	63	18	27	45	329					
992-93	Halifax	AHL	79	27	37	64	*345					
993-94	Washington	NHL	13	0	5	5	87					
	Portland	AHL	39	10	22	32	263	16	4	5	9	*91
	NHL Totals		20	0	5	5	132					

raded to **Quebec** by **Minnesota** for Gaetan Duchesne, June 19, 1989. Traded to **Washington** by **Quebec** for Mark Matier, June 15, 1993.

KAMINSKY, YAN (kah-MEHN-skee) NYI

Right wing. Shoots left. 6'1", 176 lbs. Born, Penza, USSR, July 28, 1971.
(Winnipeg's 4th choice, 99th overall, in 1991 Entry Draft).

			Regular Season					Playoffs				
Season	Club	Lea	GP	G	A	TP	PIM	GP	G	A	TP	PIM
1989-90	Moscow D'amo	USSR	6	1	0	1	4					
1990-91	Moscow D'amo	USSR	25	10	5	15	2					
1991-92	Moscow D'amo	CIS	42	9	7	16	22					
1992-93	Moscow D'amo	CIS	39	15	14	29	12	10	2	5	7	8
1993-94	Winnipeg	NHL	1	0	0	0	0					
	NY Islanders	NHL	23	2	1	3	4	2	0	0	0	4
	NHL Totals		24	2	1	3	4	2	0	0	0	4

Traded to **NY Islanders** by **Winnipeg** for Wayne McBean, February 1, 1994.

KARABIN, LADISLAV (kar-ah-BIN) PIT.

Left wing. Shoots left. 6'1", 189 lbs. Born, Spisska Nova Ves, Czech., February 16, 1970.
(Pittsburgh's 11th choice, 173rd overall, in 1990 Entry Draft).

			Regular Season					Playoffs				
Season	Club	Lea	GP	G	A	TP	PIM	GP	G	A	TP	PIM
1988-89	Bratislava	Czech.	31	7	2	9	10					
1989-90	Bratislava	Czech.2			UNAVAILABLE							
1990-91	Bratislava	Czech.	49	21	7	28	57					
1991-92	Bratislava	Czech.	27	4	8	12	10					
1992-93	Bratislava	Czech.	39	21	23	44						
1993-94	Pittsburgh	NHL	9	0	0	0	2					
	Cleveland	IHL	58	13	26	39	48					
	NHL Totals		9	0	0	0	2					

KARALAHTI, JERE L.A.

Defense. Shoots right. 6'2", 185 lbs. Born, Helsinki, Finland, March 25, 1975.
(Los Angeles' 7th choice, 146th overall, in 1993 Entry Draft).

			Regular Season					Playoffs				
Season	Club	Lea	GP	G	A	TP	PIM	GP	G	A	TP	PIM
1992-93	HIFK	Fin. Jr.	30	2	13	15	49					
1993-94	HIFK	Fin.	46	1	10	11	36	3	0	0	0	6

KARAMNOV, VITALI (kuh-RAHM-nov) ST.L.

Left wing. Shoots left. 6'2", 185 lbs. Born, Moscow, USSR, July 6, 1968.
(St. Louis' 2nd choice, 62nd overall, in 1992 Entry Draft).

			Regular Season					Playoffs				
Season	Club	Lea	GP	G	A	TP	PIM	GP	G	A	TP	PIM
1986-87	Moscow D'amo	USSR	4	0	0	0	0					
1987-88	Moscow D'amo	USSR	2	0	1	1	0					
1988-89	D'amo Kharkov	USSR	23	4	1	5	19					
1989-90	Torpedo Yaro.	USSR	47	6	7	13	32					
1990-91	Torpedo Yaro.	USSR	45	14	7	21	30					
1991-92	Moscow D'amo	CIS	40	13	19	32	25					
1992-93	St. Louis	NHL	7	0	1	1	0					
	Peoria	IHL	23	8	12	20	47					
1993-94	St. Louis	NHL	59	9	12	21	51					
	Peoria	IHL	3	0	1	1	2	1	0	1	1	0
	NHL Totals		66	9	13	22	51					

KARIYA, PAUL (kah-REE-ah) ANA.

Left wing. Shoots left. 5'11", 175 lbs. Born, Vancouver, B.C., October 16, 1974.
(Anaheim's 1st choice, 4th overall, in 1993 Entry Draft).

			Regular Season					Playoffs				
Season	Club	Lea	GP	G	A	TP	PIM	GP	G	A	TP	PIM
1992-93abcd	U. of Maine	H.E.	36	24	*69	*93	12					
1993-94	U. of Maine	H.E.	12	8	16	24	4					
	Cdn. National	....	23	7	34	41	2					
	Cdn. Olympic	....	8	3	4	7	2					

a Hockey East First All-Star Team (1993)
b NCAA East First All-American Team (1993)
c NCAA Final Four All-Tournament Team (1993)
d Won Hobey Baker Memorial Award (Top U.S. Collegiate Player) (1993)

KARLSSON, ANDREAS CGY.

Center. Shoots left. 6'2", 180 lbs. Born, Leksand, Sweden, August 19, 1975.
(Calgary's 8th choice, 148th overall, in 1993 Entry Draft).

			Regular Season					Playoffs				
Season	Club	Lea	GP	G	A	TP	PIM	GP	G	A	TP	PIM
1992-93	Leksand	Swe.	13	0	0	0	6					
1993-94	Leksand	Swe.	21	0	0	0	10	3	0	0	0	0

KARPA, DAVE QUE.

Defense. Shoots right. 6'1", 202 lbs. Born, Regina, Sask., May 7, 1971.
(Quebec's 4th choice, 68th overall, in 1991 Entry Draft).

			Regular Season					Playoffs				
Season	Club	Lea	GP	G	A	TP	PIM	GP	G	A	TP	PIM
1990-91	Ferris State	CCHA	41	6	19	25	109					
1991-92	Ferris State	CCHA	34	7	12	19	124					
	Quebec	NHL	4	0	0	0	14					
	Halifax	AHL	2	0	0	0	4					
1992-93	Quebec	NHL	12	0	1	1	13	3	0	0	0	0
	Halifax	AHL	71	4	27	31	167					
1993-94	Quebec	NHL	60	5	12	17	148					
	Cornwall	AHL	1	0	0	0	0	12	2	2	4	27
	NHL Totals		76	5	13	18	175	3	0	0	0	0

KARPOV, VALERI (KAHR-pahf) ANA.

Right wing. Shoots left. 5'10", 176 lbs. Born, Chelyabinsk, USSR, August 5, 1971.
(Anaheim's 3rd choice, 56th overall, in 1993 Entry Draft).

			Regular Season					Playoffs				
Season	Club	Lea	GP	G	A	TP	PIM	GP	G	A	TP	PIM
1988-89	Chelyabinsk	USSR	5	0	0	0	0					
1989-90	Chelyabinsk	USSR	24	1	2	3	6					
1990-91	Chelyabinsk	USSR	25	8	4	12	15					
1991-92	Chelyabinsk	CIS	44	16	10	26	34					
1992-93	CSKA	CIS	9	2	6	8	0					
a	Chelyabinsk	CIS	29	10	15	25	6	8	0	1	1	10
1993-94	Chelyabinsk	CIS	32	13	16	29	....	6	2	5	7	2

a CIS All-Star Team (1993)

KARPOVTSEV, ALEXANDER (kar-POHV-tzehv) NYR

Defense. Shoots right. 6'1", 205 lbs. Born, Moscow, USSR, April 7, 1970.
(Quebec's 7th choice, 158th overall, in 1990 Entry Draft).

			Regular Season					Playoffs				
Season	Club	Lea	GP	G	A	TP	PIM	GP	G	A	TP	PIM
1987-88	Moscow D'amo	USSR	2	0	1	1	10					
1989-90	Moscow D'amo	USSR	35	1	1	2	27					
1990-91	Moscow D'amo	USSR	40	0	5	5	15					
1991-92	Moscow D'amo	CIS	35	4	2	6	26					
1992-93	Moscow D'amo	CIS	36	3	11	14	100	7	2	1	3	0
1993-94	NY Rangers	NHL	67	3	15	18	58	17	0	4	4	12
	NHL Totals		67	3	15	18	58	17	0	4	4	12

Traded to **NY Rangers** by **Quebec** for Mike Hurlbut, September 7, 1993.

KARPOVTSEV, ANDREI (kar-POHV-tzehv)

Left wing. Shoots left. 6'2", 211 lbs. Born, Moscow, USSR, February 25, 1974.
(Winnipeg's 11th choice, 252nd overall, in 1992 Entry Draft).

			Regular Season					Playoffs				
Season	Club	Lea	GP	G	A	TP	PIM	GP	G	A	TP	PIM
1991-92	Mosc. D'amo 2	CIS 3	33	4	0	4	39					
1992-93	Mosc. D'amo 2	CIS 2	40	15	12	27	96					
1993-94	Mosc. D'amo 2	CIS 3				UNAVAILABLE						
	Dayton	ECHL	3	0	0	0	4					

KASATONOV, ALEXEI (kah-sah-TOH-nahf) BOS.

Defense. Shoots left. 6'1", 215 lbs. Born, Leningrad, USSR, October 14, 1959.
(New Jersey's 10th choice, 225th overall, in 1983 Entry Draft).

			Regular Season					Playoffs				
Season	Club	Lea	GP	G	A	TP	PIM	GP	G	A	TP	PIM
1976-77	SKA Leningrad	USSR	7	0	0	0	0					
1977-78	SKA Leningrad	USSR	35	4	7	11	15					
1978-79	CSKA	USSR	40	5	14	19	30					
1979-80a	CSKA	USSR	37	5	8	13	26					
1980-81a	CSKA	USSR	47	10	12	22	38					
1981-82a	CSKA	USSR	46	12	27	39	45					
1982-83a	CSKA	USSR	44	12	19	31	37					
1983-84a	CSKA	USSR	39	12	24	36	20					
1984-85a	CSKA	USSR	40	18	18	36	26					
1985-86a	CSKA	USSR	40	6	17	23	27					
1986-87a	CSKA	USSR	40	13	17	30	16					
1987-88a	CSKA	USSR	43	8	12	20	8					
1988-89	CSKA	USSR	41	8	14	22	8					
1989-90	CSKA	USSR	30	6	7	13	16					
	New Jersey	NHL	39	6	15	21	16	6	0	3	3	14
	Utica	AHL	3	0	2	2	7					
1990-91	New Jersey	NHL	78	10	31	41	76	7	1	3	4	10
1991-92	New Jersey	NHL	76	12	28	40	70	7	1	1	2	12
1992-93	New Jersey	NHL	64	3	14	17	57	4	0	0	0	0
1993-94	Anaheim	NHL	55	4	18	22	43					
	St. Louis	NHL	8	0	2	2	19	4	2	0	2	2
	NHL Totals		320	35	108	143	281	28	4	7	11	38

a Soviet National League All-Star Team (1980-88)

Played in NHL All-Star Game (1994)

Claimed by **Anaheim** from **New Jersey** in Expansion Draft, June 24, 1993. Traded to **St. Louis** by **Anaheim** for Maxim Bets and St. Louis' sixth round choice in 1995 Entry Draft, March 21, 1994. Signed as a free agent by **Boston**, June 22, 1994.

KASPARAITIS, DARIUS (KAZ-puhr-IGH-tihz) NYI

Defense. Shoots left. 5'11", 187 lbs. Born, Elektrenai, USSR, October 16, 1972.
(NY Islanders' 1st choice, 5th overall, in 1992 Entry Draft).

			Regular Season					Playoffs				
Season	Club	Lea	GP	G	A	TP	PIM	GP	G	A	TP	PIM
1988-89	Moscow D'amo	USSR	3	0	0	0	0					
1989-90	Moscow D'amo	USSR	1	0	0	0	0					
1990-91	Moscow D'amo	USSR	17	0	1	1	10					
1991-92	Moscow D'amo	CIS	31	2	10	12	14					
1992-93	Moscow D'amo	CIS	7	1	3	4	8					
	NY Islanders	NHL	79	4	17	21	166	18	0	5	5	31
1993-94	NY Islanders	NHL	76	1	10	11	142	4	0	0	0	8
	NHL Totals		155	5	27	32	308	22	0	5	5	39

KEALTY, JEFF — QUE.

Defense. Shoots left. 6'4", 175 lbs.　Born, Boston, MA, April 9, 1976.
(Quebec's 2nd choice, 22nd overall, in 1994 Entry Draft).

Season	Club	Lea	GP	G	A	TP	PIM	GP	G	A	TP	PIM
				Regular Season					Playoffs			
1992-93	Catholic Mem.	HS	24	3	22	25	10	....	....	....	....	....
1993-94	Catholic Mem.	HS	25	10	22	32	....	....	....	....	....	....

KEANE, MIKE — MTL.

Right wing. Shoots right. 5'10", 180 lbs.　Born, Winnipeg, Man., May 29, 1967.

Season	Club	Lea	GP	G	A	TP	PIM	GP	G	A	TP	PIM
				Regular Season					Playoffs			
1984-85	Moose Jaw	WHL	65	17	26	43	141	....	....	....	....	....
1985-86	Moose Jaw	WHL	67	34	49	83	162	13	6	8	14	9
1986-87	Moose Jaw	WHL	53	25	45	70	107	9	3	9	12	11
	Sherbrooke	AHL	....	....	....	....	....	9	2	4	6	16
1987-88	Sherbrooke	AHL	78	25	43	68	70	6	1	1	2	18
1988-89	**Montreal**	**NHL**	**69**	**16**	**19**	**35**	**69**	21	4	3	7	17
1989-90	**Montreal**	**NHL**	**74**	**9**	**15**	**24**	**78**	11	0	1	1	8
1990-91	**Montreal**	**NHL**	**73**	**13**	**23**	**36**	**50**	12	3	2	5	6
1991-92	**Montreal**	**NHL**	**67**	**11**	**30**	**41**	**64**	8	1	1	2	16
1992-93	**Montreal**	**NHL**	**77**	**15**	**45**	**60**	**95**	19	2	13	15	6
1993-94	**Montreal**	**NHL**	**80**	**16**	**30**	**46**	**119**	6	3	1	4	4
	NHL Totals		**440**	**80**	**162**	**242**	**475**	**77**	**13**	**21**	**34**	**57**

Signed as a free agent by **Montreal**, September 25, 1985.

KECZMER, DAN — CGY.

Defense. Shoots left. 6'1", 190 lbs.　Born, Mt. Clemens, MI, May 25, 1968.
(Minnesota's 11th choice, 201st overall, in 1986 Entry Draft).

Season	Club	Lea	GP	G	A	TP	PIM	GP	G	A	TP	PIM
				Regular Season					Playoffs			
1986-87	Lake Superior	CCHA	38	3	5	8	26	....	....	....	....	....
1987-88	Lake Superior	CCHA	41	2	15	17	34	....	....	....	....	....
1988-89	Lake Superior	CCHA	46	3	26	29	68	....	....	....	....	....
1989-90a	Lake Superior	CCHA	43	13	23	36	48	....	....	....	....	....
1990-91	**Minnesota**	**NHL**	**9**	**0**	**1**	**1**	**6**	....	....	....	....	....
	Kalamazoo	IHL	60	4	20	24	60	9	1	2	3	10
1991-92	U.S. National	....	51	3	11	14	56	....	....	....	....	....
	Hartford	**NHL**	**1**	**0**	**0**	**0**	**0**	....	....	....	....	....
	Springfield	AHL	18	3	4	7	10	4	0	0	0	6
1992-93	**Hartford**	**NHL**	**23**	**4**	**4**	**8**	**28**	....	....	....	....	....
	Springfield	AHL	37	4	13	14	38	12	0	4	4	14
1993-94	**Hartford**	**NHL**	**12**	**0**	**1**	**1**	**12**	....	....	....	....	....
	Springfield	AHL	7	0	1	1	4	....	....	....	....	....
	Calgary	**NHL**	**57**	**1**	**20**	**21**	**48**	3	0	0	0	4
	NHL Totals		**102**	**5**	**26**	**31**	**94**	**3**	**0**	**0**	**0**	**4**

a CCHA Second All-Star Team (1990)

Claimed by **San Jose** from **Minnesota** in Dispersal Draft, May 30, 1991. Traded to **Hartford** by **San Jose** for Dean Evason, October 2, 1991. Traded to **Calgary** by **Hartford** for Jeff Reese, November 19, 1993.

KEKALAINEN, JARMO — (kee-kuh-LAY-nehn, YAHR-moh)

Left wing. Shoots left. 6', 190 lbs.　Born, Tampere, Finland, July 3, 1966.

Season	Club	Lea	GP	G	A	TP	PIM	GP	G	A	TP	PIM
				Regular Season					Playoffs			
1985-86	Ilves	Fin.	29	6	6	12	8	....	....	....	....	....
1986-87	Ilves	Fin.	42	3	4	7	4	....	....	....	....	....
1987-88	Clarkson	ECAC	32	7	11	18	38	....	....	....	....	....
1988-89	Clarkson	ECAC	31	19	25	44	47	....	....	....	....	....
1989-90	**Boston**	**NHL**	**11**	**2**	**2**	**4**	**8**	....	....	....	....	....
	Maine	AHL	18	5	11	16	6	....	....	....	....	....
1990-91	**Boston**	**NHL**	**16**	**2**	**1**	**3**	**6**	....	....	....	....	....
	Maine	AHL	11	2	4	6	4	1	0	1	1	0
1991-92	KalPa	Fin.	24	2	8	10	24	....	....	....	....	....
1992-93	Tappara	Fin.	47	15	12	27	34	....	....	....	....	....
1993-94	**Ottawa**	**NHL**	**28**	**1**	**5**	**6**	**14**	....	....	....	....	....
	PEI	AHL	18	6	6	12	18	....	....	....	....	....
	NHL Totals		**55**	**5**	**8**	**13**	**28**					

Signed as a free agent by **Boston**, May 3, 1989. Signed as a free agent by **Ottawa**, August 13, 1993.

KELLEHER, CHRIS — PIT.

Defense. Shoots left. 6'1", 215 lbs.　Born, Cambridge, MA, March 23, 1975.
(Pittsburgh's 5th choice, 130th overall, in 1993 Entry Draft).

Season	Club	Lea	GP	G	A	TP	PIM	GP	G	A	TP	PIM
				Regular Season					Playoffs			
1992-93	St. Sebastien's	HS	25	8	30	38	16	....	....	....	....	....
1993-94	St. Sebastien's	HS	24	10	21	31	....	....	....	....	....	....

KELLEY, JONATHAN — TOR.

Center. Shoots right. 6'1", 180 lbs.　Born, Brighton, MA, June 25, 1973.
(Toronto's 12th choice, 223rd overall, in 1991 Entry Draft).

Season	Club	Lea	GP	G	A	TP	PIM	GP	G	A	TP	PIM
				Regular Season					Playoffs			
1992-93	Princeton	ECAC	23	4	3	7	34	....	....	....	....	....
1993-94	Princeton	ECAC	28	6	13	19	41	....	....	....	....	....

KELLOGG, BOB — CHI.

Defense. Shoots left. 6'4", 210 lbs.　Born, Springfield, MA, February 16, 1971.
(Chicago's 3rd choice, 48th overall, in 1989 Entry Draft).

Season	Club	Lea	GP	G	A	TP	PIM	GP	G	A	TP	PIM
				Regular Season					Playoffs			
1989-90	Northeastern	H.E.	36	3	12	15	30	....	....	....	....	....
1990-91	Northeastern	H.E.	2	0	0	0	6	....	....	....	....	....
1991-92	Northeastern	H.E.	27	2	3	5	34	....	....	....	....	....
1992-93	Northeastern	H.E.	35	5	15	20	44	....	....	....	....	....
1993-94	Indianapolis	IHL	68	6	13	19	63	....	....	....	....	....

KELMAN, TODD — ST.L.

Defense. Shoots left. 6'1", 190 lbs.　Born, Calgary, Alta., January 5, 1975.
(St. Louis' 4th choice, 141st overall, in 1993 Entry Draft).

Season	Club	Lea	GP	G	A	TP	PIM	GP	G	A	TP	PIM
				Regular Season					Playoffs			
1992-93	Vernon	BCJHL	48	16	30	46	54	....	....	....	....	....
1993-94	Bowling Green	CCHA	18	0	2	2	12	....	....	....	....	....

KEMPER, ANDREW

Defense. Shoots right. 6'2", 186 lbs.　Born, Montreal, Que., April 7, 1974.
(Tampa Bay's 9th choice, 193rd overall, in 1992 Entry Draft).

Season	Club	Lea	GP	G	A	TP	PIM	GP	G	A	TP	PIM
				Regular Season					Playoffs			
1991-92	Seattle	WHL	68	2	9	11	90	1	0	0	0	0
1992-93	Seattle	WHL	30	1	3	4	34	....	....	....	....	....
	Saskatoon	WHL	24	0	3	3	41	9	1	1	2	2
1993-94	Saskatoon	WHL	71	7	25	32	144	16	0	1	1	2

KENADY, CHRISTOPHER — ST.L.

Right wing. Shoots right. 6'2", 195 lbs.　Born, Mound, MN, April 10, 1973.
(St. Louis' 8th choice, 175th overall, in 1991 Entry Draft).

Season	Club	Lea	GP	G	A	TP	PIM	GP	G	A	TP	PIM
				Regular Season					Playoffs			
1991-92	U. of Denver	WCHA	36	8	5	13	56	....	....	....	....	....
1992-93	U. of Denver	WCHA	38	8	16	24	95	....	....	....	....	....
1993-94	U. of Denver	WCHA	37	14	11	25	125	....	....	....	....	....

KENNEDY, DEAN — WPG.

Defense. Shoots right. 6'2", 208 lbs.　Born, Redvers, Sask., January 18, 1963.
(Los Angeles' 2nd choice, 39th overall, in 1981 Entry Draft).

Season	Club	Lea	GP	G	A	TP	PIM	GP	G	A	TP	PIM
				Regular Season					Playoffs			
1980-81	Brandon	WHL	71	3	29	32	157	5	0	2	2	7
1981-82	Brandon	WHL	49	5	38	43	103	....	....	....	....	....
1982-83	**Los Angeles**	**NHL**	**55**	**0**	**12**	**12**	**97**	....	....	....	....	....
	Brandon	WHL	14	2	15	17	22	....	....	....	....	....
	Saskatoon	WHL						4	0	3	3	0
1983-84	**Los Angeles**	**NHL**	**37**	**1**	**5**	**6**	**50**	....	....	....	....	....
	New Haven	AHL	26	1	7	8	23	....	....	....	....	....
1984-85	New Haven	AHL	76	3	14	17	104	....	....	....	....	....
1985-86	**Los Angeles**	**NHL**	**78**	**2**	**10**	**12**	**132**	....	....	....	....	....
1986-87	**Los Angeles**	**NHL**	**66**	**6**	**14**	**20**	**91**	5	0	2	2	10
1987-88	**Los Angeles**	**NHL**	**58**	**1**	**11**	**12**	**158**	4	0	1	1	10
1988-89	**NY Rangers**	**NHL**	**16**	**0**	**1**	**1**	**40**	....	....	....	....	....
	Los Angeles	**NHL**	**51**	**3**	**10**	**13**	**63**	11	0	2	2	8
1989-90	**Buffalo**	**NHL**	**80**	**2**	**12**	**14**	**53**	6	1	1	2	12
1990-91	**Buffalo**	**NHL**	**64**	**4**	**8**	**12**	**119**	2	0	1	1	17
1991-92	**Winnipeg**	**NHL**	**18**	**1**	**5**	**6**	**21**	2	0	0	0	0
1992-93	**Winnipeg**	**NHL**	**78**	**1**	**7**	**8**	**105**	6	0	0	0	2
1993-94	**Winnipeg**	**NHL**	**76**	**2**	**8**	**10**	**164**	....	....	....	....	....
	NHL Totals		**677**	**24**	**102**	**126**	**1093**	**36**	**1**	**7**	**8**	**59**

Traded to **NY Rangers** by **Los Angeles** with Denis Larocque for Igor Liba, Michael Boyce, Todd Elik and future considerations, December 12, 1988. Traded to **Los Angeles** by **NY Rangers** for Los Angeles' fourth round choice – later traded to Minnesota (Cal McGowan) – in 1990 Entry Draft, February 3, 1989. Traded to **Buffalo** by **Los Angeles** for Buffalo's fourth round choice (Keith Redmond) in 1991 Entry Draft, October 4, 1989. Traded to **Winnipeg** by **Buffalo** with Darrin Shannon and Mike Hartman for Dave McLlwain, Gord Donnelly, Winnipeg's fifth round choice (Yuri Khmylev) in 1992 Entry Draft and future considerations, October 11, 1991.

KENNEDY, MIKE — DAL.

Center. Shoots right. 6'1", 170 lbs.　Born, Vancouver, B.C., April 13, 1972.
(Minnesota's 5th choice, 97th overall, in 1991 Entry Draft).

Season	Club	Lea	GP	G	A	TP	PIM	GP	G	A	TP	PIM
				Regular Season					Playoffs			
1989-90	U.B.C.	CIAU	9	5	7	12	0	....	....	....	....	....
1990-91	U.B.C.	CIAU	28	17	17	34	18	....	....	....	....	....
1991-92a	Seattle	WHL	71	42	47	89	134	15	11	6	17	20
1992-93	Kalamazoo	IHL	77	21	30	51	39	....	....	....	....	....
1993-94	Kalamazoo	IHL	63	20	18	38	42	3	1	2	3	2

a WHL West Second All-Star Team (1992)

KENNEDY, SHELDON — WPG.

Right wing. Shoots right. 5'10", 175 lbs.　Born, Elkhorn, Man., June 15, 1969.
(Detroit's 5th choice, 80th overall, in 1988 Entry Draft).

Season	Club	Lea	GP	G	A	TP	PIM	GP	G	A	TP	PIM
				Regular Season					Playoffs			
1986-87	Swift Current	WHL	49	23	41	64	43	4	0	3	3	4
1987-88	Swift Current	WHL	59	53	64	117	45	10	8	9	17	12
1988-89a	Swift Current	WHL	51	58	48	106	92	12	9	15	24	22
1989-90	**Detroit**	**NHL**	**20**	**2**	**7**	**9**	**10**	....	....	....	....	....
	Adirondack	AHL	26	11	15	26	35	....	....	....	....	....
1990-91	**Detroit**	**NHL**	**7**	**1**	**0**	**1**	**12**	....	....	....	....	....
	Adirondack	AHL	11	1	3	4	8	....	....	....	....	....
1991-92	**Detroit**	**NHL**	**27**	**3**	**8**	**11**	**24**	....	....	....	....	....
	Adirondack	AHL	46	25	24	49	56	16	5	9	14	12
1992-93	**Detroit**	**NHL**	**68**	**19**	**11**	**30**	**46**	7	1	1	2	2
1993-94	**Detroit**	**NHL**	**61**	**6**	**7**	**13**	**30**	7	1	2	3	0
	NHL Totals		**183**	**31**	**33**	**64**	**122**	**14**	**2**	**3**	**5**	**2**

a Memorial Cup All-Star Team (1989)

Traded to **Winnipeg** by **Detroit** for Winnipeg's third round choice in 1995 Entry Draft, May 25, 1994.

KENNEY, JAY — OTT.

Defense. Shoots left. 6'2", 190 lbs.　Born, New York, NY, September 21, 1973.
(Ottawa's 8th choice, 169th overall, in 1992 Entry Draft).

Season	Club	Lea	GP	G	A	TP	PIM	GP	G	A	TP	PIM
				Regular Season					Playoffs			
1992-93	Providence	H.E.	24	1	8	9	10	....	....	....	....	....
1993-94	Providence	H.E.	21	2	7	9	8	....	....	....	....	....

KENNY, ROB — NYR

Left wing. Shoots left. 6'1", 205 lbs.　Born, New York, NY, September 19, 1968.

Season	Club	Lea	GP	G	A	TP	PIM	GP	G	A	TP	PIM
				Regular Season					Playoffs			
1989-90	Northeastern	H.E.	32	2	7	9	29	....	....	....	....	....
1990-91	Northeastern	H.E.	29	6	11	17	40	....	....	....	....	....
1991-92	Northeastern	H.E.	34	19	14	33	44	....	....	....	....	....
1992-93	Binghamton	AHL	66	12	11	23	56	8	2	4	6	8
1993-94	Binghamton	AHL	63	27	14	41	90	....	....	....	....	....

Signed as a free agent by **NY Rangers**, August 24, 1992.

KERCH, ALEXANDER (KUHRCH) EDM.

Left wing. Shoots right. 5'10", 190 lbs. Born, Arkhangelsk, USSR, March 16, 1967.
(Edmonton's 5th choice, 60th overall, in 1993 Entry Draft).

			Regular Season					Playoffs				
Season	Club	Lea	GP	G	A	TP	PIM	GP	G	A	TP	PIM
1984-85	Riga	USSR	8	0	0	0	6	....	....	....	....	....
1985-86	Riga	USSR	23	5	2	7	16	....	....	....	....	....
1986-87	Riga	USSR	26	5	4	9	10	....	....	....	....	....
1987-88	Riga	USSR	50	14	4	18	28	....	....	....	....	....
1988-89	Riga	USSR	39	6	7	13	41	....	....	....	....	....
1989-90	Riga	USSR	46	9	11	20	22	....	....	....	....	....
1990-91	Riga	USSR	46	16	17	33	46	....	....	....	....	....
1991-92	Riga	CIS	27	7	9	16	20	....	....	....	....	....
1992-93	Riga	CIS	42	23	14	37	28	2	1	2	3	2
1993-94	**Edmonton**	**NHL**	**5**	**0**	**0**	**0**	**2**	....	....	....	....	....
	Cape Breton	AHL	57	24	38	62	16	4	1	1	2	2
	NHL Totals		**5**	**0**	**0**	**0**	**2**	....	....	....	....	....

KESA, DANNY (KEH-suh) VAN.

Right wing. Shoots right. 6', 198 lbs. Born, Vancouver, B.C., November 23, 1971.
(Vancouver's 5th choice, 95th overall, in 1991 Entry Draft).

			Regular Season					Playoffs				
Season	Club	Lea	GP	G	A	TP	PIM	GP	G	A	TP	PIM
1990-91	Prince Albert	WHL	69	30	23	53	116	3	1	1	2	0
1991-92	Prince Albert	WHL	62	46	51	97	201	10	9	10	19	27
1992-93	Hamilton	AHL	62	16	24	40	76	....	....	....	....	....
1993-94	**Vancouver**	**NHL**	**19**	**2**	**4**	**6**	**18**	....	....	....	....	....
	Hamilton	AHL	53	37	33	70	33	4	1	4	5	4
	NHL Totals		**19**	**2**	**4**	**6**	**18**	....	....	....	....	....

KESKINEN, ESA (KEHS-kee-nehn) CGY.

Center. Shoots right. 5'9", 195 lbs. Born, Ylojarvi, Finland, February 3, 1965.
(Calgary's 6th choice, 101st overall, in 1985 Entry Draft).

			Regular Season					Playoffs				
Season	Club	Lea	GP	G	A	TP	PIM	GP	G	A	TP	PIM
1982-83	FoPS	Fin.2	15	5	14	19	8	4	4	6	10	0
1983-84	TPS	Fin.	31	10	25	35	0	6	0	0	0	0
1984-85	TPS	Fin.	35	11	22	33	66	10	2	3	5	0
1985-86	TPS	Fin.	36	18	28	46	4	7	2	0	2	0
1986-87	TPS	Fin.	46	25	36	61	4	5	1	1	2	0
1987-88	TPS	Fin.	44	14	55	69	14	....	....	....	....	....
1988-89	Lukko	Fin.	41	24	46	70	12	....	....	....	....	....
1989-90	Lukko	Fin.	44	25	26	51	16	....	....	....	....	....
1990-91	Lukko	Fin.	44	17	51	68	14	....	....	....	....	....
1991-92	TPS	Fin.	44	24	45	69	12	3	1	1	2	0
1992-93	TPS	Fin.	46	16	43	59	12	12	1	6	7	4
1993-94	TPS	Fin.	47	23	47	70	28	11	5	4	9	4

KHARLAMOV, ALEXANDER (khahr-LAH-mohv) WSH.

Center. Shoots left. 5'11", 183 lbs. Born, Moscow, USSR, September 23, 1975.
(Washington's 2nd choice, 15th overall, in 1994 Entry Draft).

			Regular Season					Playoffs				
Season	Club	Lea	GP	G	A	TP	PIM	GP	G	A	TP	PIM
1992-93	CSKA	CIS	42	8	4	12	12	....	....	....	....	....
1993-94	CSKA	CIS	46	7	7	14	26	3	1	0	1	2

KHMYLEV, YURI (kheh-meh-LUHV) BUF.

Left wing. Shoots right. 6'1", 189 lbs. Born, Moscow, USSR, August 9, 1964.
(Buffalo's 7th choice, 108th overall, in 1992 Entry Draft).

			Regular Season					Playoffs				
Season	Club	Lea	GP	G	A	TP	PIM	GP	G	A	TP	PIM
1981-82	Soviet Wings	USSR	8	2	2	4	2	....	....	....	....	....
1982-83	Soviet Wings	USSR	51	9	7	16	14	....	....	....	....	....
1983-84	Soviet Wings	USSR	43	7	8	15	10	....	....	....	....	....
1984-85	Soviet Wings	USSR	30	11	4	15	24	....	....	....	....	....
1985-86	Soviet Wings	USSR	40	24	9	33	22	....	....	....	....	....
1986-87	Soviet Wings	USSR	40	15	15	30	48	....	....	....	....	....
1987-88	Soviet Wings	USSR	48	21	8	29	46	....	....	....	....	....
1988-89	Soviet Wings	USSR	44	16	18	34	38	....	....	....	....	....
1989-90	Soviet Wings	USSR	44	14	13	27	30	....	....	....	....	....
1990-91	Soviet Wings	USSR	45	25	14	39	26	....	....	....	....	....
1991-92	Soviet Wings	CIS	42	19	17	36	20	....	....	....	....	....
1992-93	**Buffalo**	**NHL**	**68**	**20**	**19**	**39**	**28**	**8**	**4**	**3**	**7**	**4**
1993-94	**Buffalo**	**NHL**	**72**	**27**	**31**	**58**	**49**	**7**	**3**	**1**	**4**	**8**
	NHL Totals		**140**	**47**	**50**	**97**	**77**	**15**	**7**	**4**	**11**	**12**

KHOMOUTOV, ANDREI (hoh-moo-TAHF) QUE.

Right wing. Shoots left. 5'10", 176 lbs. Born, Yaroslavl, USSR, April 21, 1961.
(Quebec's 12th choice, 190th overall, in 1989 Entry Draft).

			Regular Season					Playoffs				
Season	Club	Lea	GP	G	A	TP	PIM	GP	G	A	TP	PIM
1979-80	CSKA	USSR	4	0	0	0	0	....	....	....	....	....
1980-81	CSKA	USSR	43	23	18	41	4	....	....	....	....	....
1981-82	CSKA	USSR	44	17	13	30	12	....	....	....	....	....
1982-83	CSKA	USSR	44	21	17	38	6	....	....	....	....	....
1983-84	CSKA	USSR	39	17	9	26	14	....	....	....	....	....
1984-85	CSKA	USSR	37	21	13	34	18	....	....	....	....	....
1985-86	CSKA	USSR	38	14	15	29	10	....	....	....	....	....
1986-87	CSKA	USSR	33	15	18	33	22	....	....	....	....	....
1987-88	CSKA	USSR	48	29	14	43	22	....	....	....	....	....
1988-89	CSKA	USSR	44	19	16	35	14	....	....	....	....	....
1989-90a	CSKA	USSR	47	21	14	35	16	....	....	....	....	....
1990-91	Fribourg	Switz.	36	39	43	82	....	8	13	12	25	....
1991-92	Fribourg	Switz.	35	31	43	74	34	14	10	12	22	6
1992-93	Fribourg	Switz.	27	23	36	59	14	....	....	....	....	....
1993-94	Fribourg	Switz.	35	39	34	73	12	11	12	14	26	6

a Soviet Player of the Year (1990)

KHRISTICH, DIMITRI (KRIH-stihch) WSH.

Left wing/Center. Shoots right. 6'2", 195 lbs. Born, Kiev, USSR, July 23, 1969.
(Washington's 6th choice, 120th overall, in 1988 Entry Draft).

			Regular Season					Playoffs				
Season	Club	Lea	GP	G	A	TP	PIM	GP	G	A	TP	PIM
1985-86	Sokol Kiev	USSR	4	0	0	0	0	....	....	....	....	....
1986-87	Sokol Kiev	USSR	20	3	0	3	4	....	....	....	....	....
1987-88	Sokol Kiev	USSR	37	9	1	10	18	....	....	....	....	....
1988-89	Sokol Kiev	USSR	42	17	10	27	15	....	....	....	....	....
1989-90	Sokol Kiev	USSR	47	14	22	36	32	....	....	....	....	....
1990-91	Sokol Kiev	USSR	28	10	12	22	20	....	....	....	....	....
	Washington	**NHL**	**40**	**13**	**14**	**27**	**21**	**11**	**1**	**3**	**4**	**6**
	Baltimore	AHL	3	0	0	0	0	....	....	....	....	....
1991-92	**Washington**	**NHL**	**80**	**36**	**37**	**73**	**35**	**7**	**3**	**2**	**5**	**15**
1992-93	**Washington**	**NHL**	**64**	**31**	**35**	**66**	**28**	**6**	**2**	**5**	**7**	**2**
1993-94	**Washington**	**NHL**	**83**	**29**	**29**	**58**	**73**	**11**	**2**	**3**	**5**	**10**
	NHL Totals		**267**	**109**	**115**	**224**	**157**	**35**	**8**	**13**	**21**	**33**

KIBERMANIS, CHRIS WPG.

Defense. Shoots right. 6'5", 184 lbs. Born, Calgary, Alta., March 24, 1976.
(Winnipeg's 7th choice, 146th overall, in 1994 Entry Draft).

			Regular Season					Playoffs				
Season	Club	Lea	GP	G	A	TP	PIM	GP	G	A	TP	PIM
1992-93	Leduc	Midget	28	2	9	11	37	....	....	....	....	....
1993-94	Red Deer	WHL	49	1	5	6	57	4	0	0	0	7

KIENASS, TORSTEN BOS.

Defense. Shoots left. 5'11", 180 lbs. Born, Berlin, East Germany, February 23, 1971.
(Boston's 11th choice, 260th overall, in 1991 Entry Draft).

			Regular Season					Playoffs				
Season	Club	Lea	GP	G	A	TP	PIM	GP	G	A	TP	PIM
1990-91	Dynamo Berlin	Ger.	27	1	1	2	19	7	1	0	1	4
1991-92	Dynamo Berlin	Ger. 2	45	8	6	14	33	....	....	....	....	....
1992-93	Ratingen	Ger.	44	3	12	15	16	3	0	0	0	2
1993-94	Dusseldorf	Ger.	44	0	18	18	12	12	3	2	5	12

KIMBLE, DARIN CHI.

Right wing. Shoots right. 6'2", 210 lbs. Born, Lucky Lake, Sask., November 22, 1968.
(Quebec's 5th choice, 66th overall, in 1988 Entry Draft).

			Regular Season					Playoffs				
Season	Club	Lea	GP	G	A	TP	PIM	GP	G	A	TP	PIM
1985-86	Calgary	WHL	37	14	8	22	93	....	....	....	....	....
	N. Westminster	WHL	11	1	1	2	22	....	....	....	....	....
	Brandon	WHL	15	1	6	7	39	....	....	....	....	....
1986-87	Prince Albert	WHL	68	17	13	30	190	....	....	....	....	....
1987-88	Prince Albert	WHL	67	35	36	71	307	10	3	2	5	4
1988-89	**Quebec**	**NHL**	**26**	**3**	**1**	**4**	**154**	....	....	....	....	....
	Halifax	AHL	39	8	6	14	188	....	....	....	....	....
1989-90	**Quebec**	**NHL**	**44**	**5**	**5**	**10**	**185**	....	....	....	....	....
	Halifax	AHL	18	6	6	12	37	6	1	1	2	61
1990-91	**Quebec**	**NHL**	**35**	**2**	**5**	**7**	**114**	....	....	....	....	....
	Halifax	AHL	7	1	4	5	20	....	....	....	....	....
	St. Louis	**NHL**	**26**	**1**	**1**	**2**	**128**	**13**	**0**	**0**	**0**	**38**
1991-92	**St. Louis**	**NHL**	**46**	**1**	**3**	**4**	**166**	**5**	**0**	**0**	**0**	**7**
1992-93	**Boston**	**NHL**	**55**	**7**	**3**	**10**	**177**	**4**	**0**	**0**	**0**	**2**
	Providence	AHL	12	1	4	5	34	....	....	....	....	....
1993-94	**Chicago**	**NHL**	**65**	**4**	**2**	**6**	**133**	**1**	**0**	**0**	**0**	**5**
	NHL Totals		**297**	**23**	**20**	**43**	**1057**	**23**	**0**	**0**	**0**	**52**

Traded to **St. Louis** by **Quebec** for Herb Raglan, Tony Twist and Andy Rymsha, February 4, 1991. Traded to **Tampa Bay** by **St. Louis** with Pat Jablonski and Steve Tuttle for future considerations, June 19, 1992. Traded to **Boston** by **Tampa Bay** with future considerations for Ken Hodge and Matt Hervey, September 4, 1992. Signed as a free agent by **Florida**, July 9, 1993. Traded to **Chicago** by **Florida** for Keith Brown, September 30, 1993.

KING, DEREK NYI

Left wing. Shoots left. 6'1", 203 lbs. Born, Hamilton, Ont., February 11, 1967.
(NY Islanders' 2nd choice, 13th overall, in 1985 Entry Draft).

			Regular Season					Playoffs				
Season	Club	Lea	GP	G	A	TP	PIM	GP	G	A	TP	PIM
1984-85	S.S. Marie	OHL	63	35	38	73	106	16	3	13	16	11
1985-86	S.S. Marie	OHL	25	12	17	29	33	....	....	....	....	....
	Oshawa	OHL	19	8	13	21	15	6	3	2	5	13
1986-87	**NY Islanders**	**NHL**	**2**	**0**	**0**	**0**	**0**	....	....	....	....	....
a	Oshawa	OHL	57	53	53	106	74	17	14	10	24	40
1987-88	**NY Islanders**	**NHL**	**55**	**12**	**24**	**36**	**30**	**5**	**0**	**2**	**2**	**2**
	Springfield	AHL	10	7	6	13	6	....	....	....	....	....
1988-89	**NY Islanders**	**NHL**	**60**	**14**	**29**	**43**	**14**	....	....	....	....	....
	Springfield	AHL	4	4	0	4	0	....	....	....	....	....
1989-90	**NY Islanders**	**NHL**	**46**	**13**	**27**	**40**	**20**	**4**	**0**	**0**	**0**	**4**
	Springfield	AHL	21	11	12	23	33	....	....	....	....	....
1990-91	**NY Islanders**	**NHL**	**66**	**19**	**26**	**45**	**44**	....	....	....	....	....
1991-92	**NY Islanders**	**NHL**	**80**	**40**	**38**	**78**	**46**	....	....	....	....	....
1992-93	**NY Islanders**	**NHL**	**77**	**38**	**38**	**76**	**47**	**18**	**3**	**11**	**14**	**14**
1993-94	**NY Islanders**	**NHL**	**78**	**30**	**40**	**70**	**59**	**4**	**0**	**1**	**1**	**0**
	NHL Totals		**464**	**166**	**222**	**388**	**260**	**31**	**3**	**14**	**17**	**20**

a OHL First All-Star Team (1987)

KING, KRIS WPG.

Left wing. Shoots left. 5'11", 208 lbs. Born, Bracebridge, Ont., February 18, 1966.
(Washington's 4th choice, 80th overall, in 1984 Entry Draft).

			Regular Season					Playoffs				
Season	Club	Lea	GP	G	A	TP	PIM	GP	G	A	TP	PIM
1983-84	Peterborough	OHL	62	13	18	31	168	8	3	3	6	14
1984-85	Peterborough	OHL	61	18	35	53	222	16	2	8	10	28
1985-86	Peterborough	OHL	58	19	40	59	254	8	4	0	4	21
1986-87	Binghamton	AHL	7	0	0	0	18	....	....	....	....	....
	Peterborough	OHL	46	23	33	56	160	12	5	8	13	41
1987-88	**Detroit**	**NHL**	**3**	**1**	**0**	**1**	**2**	....	....	....	....	....
	Adirondack	AHL	76	21	32	53	337	10	4	4	8	53
1988-89	**Detroit**	**NHL**	**55**	**2**	**3**	**5**	**168**	**2**	**0**	**0**	**0**	**2**
1989-90	**NY Rangers**	**NHL**	**68**	**6**	**7**	**13**	**286**	**10**	**0**	**1**	**1**	**38**
1990-91	**NY Rangers**	**NHL**	**72**	**11**	**14**	**25**	**154**	**6**	**2**	**0**	**2**	**36**
1991-92	**NY Rangers**	**NHL**	**79**	**10**	**9**	**19**	**224**	**13**	**4**	**1**	**5**	**14**
1992-93	**NY Rangers**	**NHL**	**30**	**0**	**3**	**3**	**67**	....	....	....	....	....
	Winnipeg	**NHL**	**48**	**8**	**8**	**16**	**136**	**6**	**1**	**1**	**2**	**4**
1993-94	**Winnipeg**	**NHL**	**83**	**4**	**8**	**12**	**205**	....	....	....	....	....
	NHL Totals		**438**	**42**	**52**	**94**	**1242**	**37**	**7**	**3**	**10**	**94**

Signed as a free agent by **Detroit**, March 23, 1987. Traded to **NY Rangers** by **Detroit** for Chris McRae and Detroit's fifth round choice (previously acquired by NY Rangers — Detroit selected Tony Burns) in 1990 Entry Draft, September 7, 1989. Traded to **Winnipeg** by **NY Rangers** with Tie Domi for Ed Olczyk, December 28, 1992.

KING, STEVEN — ANA.

Right wing. Shoots right. 6', 195 lbs. Born, Greenwich, RI, July 22, 1969.
(NY Rangers' 1st choice, 21st overall, in 1991 Supplemental Draft).

			Regular Season					Playoffs				
Season	Club	Lea	GP	G	A	TP	PIM	GP	G	A	TP	PIM
1989-90	Brown	ECAC	27	19	8	27	53	....	....	....	....	....
1990-91	Brown	ECAC	27	19	15	34	76	....	....	....	....	....
1991-92	Binghamton	AHL	66	27	15	42	56	10	2	0	2	14
1992-93	**NY Rangers**	**NHL**	**24**	**7**	**5**	**12**	**16**	....	....	....	....	....
	Binghamton	AHL	53	35	33	68	100	14	7	9	16	26
1993-94	**Anaheim**	**NHL**	**36**	**8**	**3**	**11**	**44**	....	....	....	....	....
	NHL Totals		**60**	**15**	**8**	**23**	**60**	....	....	....	....	....

Claimed by **Anaheim** from **NY Rangers** in Expansion Draft, June 24, 1993.

KINNEAR, GEORDIE — N.J.

Defense. Shoots left. 6'1", 200 lbs. Born, Simcoe, Ont., July 9, 1973.
(New Jersey's 7th choice, 162nd overall, in 1992 Entry Draft).

			Regular Season					Playoffs				
Season	Club	Lea	GP	G	A	TP	PIM	GP	G	A	TP	PIM
1990-91	Peterborough	OHL	37	1	0	1	76	2	0	0	0	10
1991-92	Peterborough	OHL	63	5	16	21	195	10	0	2	2	36
1992-93	Peterborough	OHL	58	6	22	28	161	19	1	5	6	43
1993-94	Albany	AHL	59	3	12	15	197	5	0	0	0	21

KIPRUSOFF, MARKO (KIHP-ruh-sohf) — MTL.

Defense. Shoots right. 6', 194 lbs. Born, Turku, Finland, June 6, 1972.
(Montreal's 4th choice, 70th overall, in 1994 Entry Draft).

			Regular Season					Playoffs				
Season	Club	Lea	GP	G	A	TP	PIM	GP	G	A	TP	PIM
1990-91	TPS	Fin.	3	0	0	0	0	....	....	....	....	....
1991-92	TPS	Fin.	23	0	2	2	0	....	....	....	....	....
	HPK	Fin.	3	0	0	0	0	....	....	....	....	....
1992-93	TPS	Fin.	43	3	7	10	14	12	2	3	5	6
1993-94	TPS	Fin.	48	5	19	24	8	11	0	6	6	4

KIRTON, SCOTT — CHI.

Right wing. Shoots right. 6'4", 215 lbs. Born, Penetanguishene, Ont., October 4, 1971.
(Chicago's 7th choice, 154th overall, in 1991 Entry Draft).

			Regular Season					Playoffs				
Season	Club	Lea	GP	G	A	TP	PIM	GP	G	A	TP	PIM
1991-92	North Dakota	WCHA	37	5	6	11	68	....	....	....	....	....
1992-93	North Dakota	WCHA	30	4	16	20	100	....	....	....	....	....
1993-94	North Dakota	WCHA	37	3	6	9	49	....	....	....	....	....

KISIO, KELLY — CGY.

Center. Shoots right. 5'10", 185 lbs. Born, Peace River, Alta., September 18, 1959.

			Regular Season					Playoffs				
Season	Club	Lea	GP	G	A	TP	PIM	GP	G	A	TP	PIM
1978-79	Calgary	WHL	70	60	61	121	73	....	....	....	....	....
1979-80	Calgary	WHL	71	65	73	138	64	....	....	....	....	....
1980-81	Adirondack	AHL	41	10	14	24	43	....	....	....	....	....
	Kalamazoo	IHL	31	27	16	43	48	8	7	7	14	13
1981-82	Dallas	CHL	78	*62	39	101	59	16	*12	*17	*29	38
1982-83	Davos	Switz.	40	49	38	87	....	....	....	....	....	....
	Detroit	**NHL**	**15**	**4**	**3**	**7**	**0**	....	....	....	....	....
1983-84	**Detroit**	**NHL**	**70**	**23**	**37**	**60**	**34**	**4**	**1**	**0**	**1**	**4**
1984-85	**Detroit**	**NHL**	**75**	**20**	**41**	**61**	**56**	**3**	**0**	**2**	**2**	**2**
1985-86	**Detroit**	**NHL**	**76**	**21**	**48**	**69**	**85**	....	....	....	....	....
1986-87	**NY Rangers**	**NHL**	**70**	**24**	**40**	**64**	**73**	**4**	**0**	**1**	**1**	**2**
1987-88	**NY Rangers**	**NHL**	**77**	**23**	**55**	**78**	**88**	....	....	....	....	....
1988-89	**NY Rangers**	**NHL**	**70**	**26**	**36**	**62**	**91**	**4**	**0**	**0**	**0**	**9**
1989-90	**NY Rangers**	**NHL**	**68**	**22**	**44**	**66**	**105**	**10**	**2**	**8**	**10**	**8**
1990-91	**NY Rangers**	**NHL**	**51**	**15**	**20**	**35**	**58**	....	....	....	....	....
1991-92	**San Jose**	**NHL**	**48**	**11**	**26**	**37**	**54**	....	....	....	....	....
1992-93	**San Jose**	**NHL**	**78**	**26**	**52**	**78**	**90**	....	....	....	....	....
1993-94	**Calgary**	**NHL**	**51**	**7**	**23**	**30**	**28**	**7**	**0**	**2**	**2**	**8**
	NHL Totals		**749**	**222**	**425**	**647**	**762**	**32**	**3**	**13**	**16**	**33**

Played in NHL All-Star Game (1993)

Signed as a free agent by **Detroit**, May 2, 1983. Traded to **NY Rangers** by **Detroit** with Lane Lambert and Jim Leavins for Glen Hanlon and New York's third round choices in 1987 (Dennis Holland) and 1988 (Guy Dupuis) Entry Drafts, July 29, 1986. Claimed by **Minnesota** from **NY Rangers** in Expansion Draft, May 30, 1991. Traded to **San Jose** by **Minnesota** for Shane Churla, June 3, 1991. Signed as a free agent by **Calgary**, August 18, 1993.

KITCHING, GARY — EDM.

Center. Shoots left. 6'2", 190 lbs. Born, Thunder Bay, Ont., January 9, 1971.
(Edmonton's 8th choice, 166th overall, in 1991 Entry Draft).

			Regular Season					Playoffs				
Season	Club	Lea	GP	G	A	TP	PIM	GP	G	A	TP	PIM
1991-92	Ferris State	CCHA	36	7	9	16	52	....	....	....	....	....
1992-93	Ferris State	CCHA	28	8	19	27	62	....	....	....	....	....
1993-94	Ferris State	CCHA	18	4	5	9	18	....	....	....	....	....

KIVI, KARRI — VAN.

Defense. Shoots left. 6', 180 lbs. Born, Turku, Finland, January 1, 1970.
(Vancouver's 11th choice, 233rd overall, in 1990 Entry Draft).

			Regular Season					Playoffs				
Season	Club	Lea	GP	G	A	TP	PIM	GP	G	A	TP	PIM
1988-89	Ilves	Fin.	39	5	7	12	10	5	0	0	0	0
1989-90	Ilves	Fin.	43	6	15	21	14	8	1	4	5	2
1990-91	Ilves	Fin.	43	2	9	11	18	....	....	....	....	....
1991-92	TPS	Fin.	33	3	1	4	14	3	0	0	0	0
1992-93	Kiekko-67	Fin. 2	11	2	7	9	4	....	....	....	....	....
	Assat	Fin.	34	2	11	13	16	8	1	2	3	0
1993-94	Assat	Fin.	48	1	12	13	49	5	1	2	3	0

KLATT, TRENT — DAL

Right wing. Shoots right. 6'1", 205 lbs. Born, Robbinsdale, MN, January 30, 1971.
(Washington's 5th choice, 82nd overall, in 1989 Entry Draft).

			Regular Season					Playoffs				
Season	Club	Lea	GP	G	A	TP	PIM	GP	G	A	TP	PIM
1989-90	U. Minnesota	WCHA	38	22	14	36	16	....	....	....	....	....
1990-91	U. Minnesota	WCHA	39	16	28	44	58	....	....	....	....	....
1991-92	U. Minnesota	WCHA	41	27	36	63	76	....	....	....	....	....
	Minnesota	**NHL**	**1**	**0**	**0**	**0**	**0**	**6**	**0**	**0**	**0**	**2**
1992-93	**Minnesota**	**NHL**	**47**	**4**	**19**	**23**	**38**	....	....	....	....	....
	Kalamazoo	IHL	31	8	11	19	18	....	....	....	....	....
1993-94	**Dallas**	**NHL**	**61**	**14**	**24**	**38**	**30**	**9**	**2**	**1**	**3**	**4**
	Kalamazoo	IHL	6	3	2	5	4	....	....	....	....	....
	NHL Totals		**109**	**18**	**43**	**61**	**68**	**15**	**2**	**1**	**3**	**6**

Traded to **Minnesota** by **Washington** with Steve Maltais for Shawn Chambers, June 21, 1991.

KLEE, KEN — WSH

Defense. Shoots right. 6'1", 200 lbs. Born, Indianapolis, IN, April 24, 1971.
(Washington's 11th choice, 177th overall, in 1990 Entry Draft).

			Regular Season					Playoffs				
Season	Club	Lea	GP	G	A	TP	PIM	GP	G	A	TP	PIM
1989-90	Bowling Green	CCHA	39	0	5	5	52	....	....	....	....	....
1990-91	Bowling Green	CCHA	37	7	28	35	50	....	....	....	....	....
1991-92	Bowling Green	CCHA	10	0	1	1	14	....	....	....	....	....
1992-93	Baltimore	AHL	77	4	14	18	93	7	0	1	1	15
1993-94	Portland	AHL	65	2	9	11	87	17	1	2	3	14

KLEMM, JON — QUE.

Defense. Shoots right. 6'3", 200 lbs. Born, Cranbrook, B.C., January 8, 1970.

			Regular Season					Playoffs				
Season	Club	Lea	GP	G	A	TP	PIM	GP	G	A	TP	PIM
1988-89	Seattle	WHL	2	1	1	2	0	....	....	....	....	....
	Spokane	WHL	66	6	34	40	42	....	....	....	....	....
1989-90	Spokane	WHL	66	3	28	31	100	6	1	1	2	5
1990-91	Spokane	WHL	72	7	58	65	65	15	3	6	9	8
1991-92	**Quebec**	**NHL**	**4**	**0**	**1**	**1**	**0**	....	....	....	....	....
	Halifax	AHL	70	6	13	19	40	....	....	....	....	....
1992-93	Halifax	AHL	80	3	20	23	32	....	....	....	....	....
1993-94	**Quebec**	**NHL**	**7**	**0**	**0**	**0**	**4**	....	....	....	....	....
	Cornwall	AHL	66	4	26	30	78	13	1	2	3	6
	NHL Totals		**11**	**0**	**1**	**1**	**4**	....	....	....	....	....

Signed as a free agent by **Quebec**, May 14, 1991.

KLEVAKIN, DMITRI (kleh-VAH-kihn) — T.B.

Right wing. Shoots left. 5'11", 163 lbs. Born, Angarsk, USSR, February 20, 1976.
(Tampa Bay's 4th choice, 86th overall, in 1994 Entry Draft).

			Regular Season					Playoffs				
Season	Club	Lea	GP	G	A	TP	PIM	GP	G	A	TP	PIM
1992-93	Spartak	CIS	8	1	1	2	0	....	....	....	....	....
1993-94	Spartak	CIS	42	6	3	9	6	4	1	0	1	0

KLIMA, PETR (KLEE-muh) — T.B.

Right/Left wing. Shoots right. 6', 190 lbs. Born, Chomutov, Czech., December 23, 1964.
(Detroit's 5th choice, 86th overall, in 1983 Entry Draft).

			Regular Season					Playoffs				
Season	Club	Lea	GP	G	A	TP	PIM	GP	G	A	TP	PIM
1981-82	Litvinov	Czech.	18	7	3	10	8	....	....	....	....	....
1982-83	Litvinov	Czech.	44	19	17	36	74	....	....	....	....	....
1983-84	Dukla Jihlava	Czech.	41	20	16	36	46	....	....	....	....	....
1984-85	Dukla Jihlava	Czech.	35	23	22	45	76	....	....	....	....	....
1985-86	**Detroit**	**NHL**	**74**	**32**	**24**	**56**	**16**	....	....	....	....	....
1986-87	**Detroit**	**NHL**	**77**	**30**	**23**	**53**	**42**	**13**	**1**	**2**	**3**	**4**
1987-88	**Detroit**	**NHL**	**78**	**37**	**25**	**62**	**46**	**12**	**10**	**8**	**18**	**10**
1988-89	**Detroit**	**NHL**	**51**	**25**	**16**	**41**	**44**	**6**	**2**	**4**	**6**	**19**
	Adirondack	AHL	5	5	1	6	4	....	....	....	....	....
1989-90	**Detroit**	**NHL**	**13**	**5**	**5**	**10**	**6**	....	....	....	....	....
	Edmonton	**NHL**	**63**	**25**	**28**	**53**	**66**	**21**	**5**	**0**	**5**	**8**
1990-91	**Edmonton**	**NHL**	**70**	**40**	**28**	**68**	**113**	**18**	**7**	**6**	**13**	**16**
1991-92	**Edmonton**	**NHL**	**57**	**21**	**13**	**34**	**52**	**15**	**1**	**4**	**5**	**8**
1992-93	**Edmonton**	**NHL**	**68**	**32**	**16**	**48**	**100**	....	....	....	....	....
1993-94	**Tampa Bay**	**NHL**	**75**	**28**	**27**	**55**	**76**	....	....	....	....	....
	NHL Totals		**626**	**275**	**205**	**480**	**561**	**85**	**26**	**24**	**50**	**65**

Traded to **Edmonton** by **Detroit** with Joe Murphy, Adam Graves and Jeff Sharples for Jimmy Carson, Kevin McClelland and Edmonton's fifth round choice (later traded to Montreal — Montreal selected Brad Layzell) in 1991 Entry Draft, November 2, 1989. Traded to **Tampa Bay** by **Edmonton** for Tampa Bay's third round choice (Brad Symes) in 1994 Entry Draft, June 16, 1993.

KLIMENTIEV, SERGEI (klih-MEHN-tyehv) — BUF.

Defense. Shoots left. 5'11", 200 lbs. Born, Kiev, USSR, April 5, 1975.
(Buffalo's 4th choice, 121st overall, in 1994 Entry Draft).

			Regular Season					Playoffs				
Season	Club	Lea	GP	G	A	TP	PIM	GP	G	A	TP	PIM
1991-92	SVSM Kiev	CIS 3	42	4	15	19	....	....	....	....	....	....
1992-93	Sokol Kiev	CIS	3	0	0	0	4	1	0	0	0	0
1993-94	Medicine Hat	WHL	72	16	26	42	165	3	0	0	0	4

KLIMOVICH, SERGEI (klee-MOH-vich) — CHI.

Center. Shoots right. 6'3", 189 lbs. Born, Novosibirsk, USSR, March 8, 1974.
(Chicago's 3rd choice, 41st overall, in 1992 Entry Draft).

			Regular Season					Playoffs				
Season	Club	Lea	GP	G	A	TP	PIM	GP	G	A	TP	PIM
1991-92	Moscow D'amo	CIS	3	0	0	0	0	....	....	....	....	....
1992-93	Moscow D'amo	CIS	30	4	1	5	14	10	1	0	1	2
1993-94	Moscow D'amo	CIS	39	7	4	11	14	12	2	3	5	6

KLIMT, TOMAS — NYI

Center. Shoots left. 6'1", 183 lbs. Born, Plzen, Czech., December 26, 1973.
(NY Islanders' 3rd choice, 104th overall, in 1992 Entry Draft).

			Regular Season					Playoffs				
Season	Club	Lea	GP	G	A	TP	PIM	GP	G	A	TP	PIM
1991-92	Skoda Plzen	Czech.	40	3	6	9	4	....	....	....	....	....
1992-93	Skoda Plzen	Czech.	34	3	8	11	....	....	....	....	....	....
1993-94	Skoda Plzen	Czech.	29	5	3	8	0	....	....	....	....	....

KLIPPENSTEIN, WADE — QUE.

Left wing. Shoots left. 6'3", 219 lbs. Born, Boissevain, Man., May 9, 1970.
(Quebec's 11th choice, 232nd overall, in 1990 Entry Draft).

			Regular Season					Playoffs				
Season	Club	Lea	GP	G	A	TP	PIM	GP	G	A	TP	PIM
1989-90	Alaska-Fair.	G.N.	37	17	14	31	....	....	....	....	....	....
1990-91	Alaska-Fair.	G.N.	35	22	11	33	32	....	....	....	....	....
1991-92	Alaska-Fair.	G.N.	33	12	13	25	108	....	....	....	....	....
1992-93	Alaska-Fair.	CCHA	36	29	22	51	48	....	....	....	....	....
1993-94	Cornwall	AHL	27	2	3	5	4	....	....	....	....	....
	Greensboro	ECHL	4	0	0	0	0	....	....	....	....	....

KNIPSCHEER, FRED (kuh-NIHP-sheer) — BOS.

Center. Shoots left. 5'11", 185 lbs. Born, Ft. Wayne, IN, September 3, 1969.

			Regular Season					Playoffs				
Season	Club	Lea	GP	G	A	TP	PIM	GP	G	A	TP	PIM
1990-91	St. Cloud	WCHA	40	9	10	19	57	....	....	....	....	....
1991-92	St. Cloud	WCHA	33	15	17	32	48	....	....	....	....	....
1992-93ab	St. Cloud	WCHA	36	34	26	60	68	....	....	....	....	....
1993-94	**Boston**	**NHL**	**11**	**3**	**2**	**5**	**14**	**12**	**2**	**1**	**3**	**6**
	Providence	AHL	62	26	13	39	50	....	....	....	....	....
	NHL Totals		**11**	**3**	**2**	**5**	**14**	**12**	**2**	**1**	**3**	**6**

a WCHA First All-Star Team (1993)
b NCAA West Second All-American Team (1993)

Signed as a free agent by **Boston**, April 30, 1993.

KNUBLE, MICHAEL — DET.

Right wing. Shoots right. 6'3", 208 lbs. Born, Toronto, Ont., July 4, 1972.
(Detroit's 4th choice, 76th overall, in 1991 Entry Draft).

			Regular Season					Playoffs				
Season	Club	Lea	GP	G	A	TP	PIM	GP	G	A	TP	PIM
1991-92	U. of Michigan	CCHA	43	7	8	15	48	....	....	....	....	....
1992-93	U. of Michigan	CCHA	39	26	16	42	57	....	....	....	....	....
1993-94a	U. of Michigan	CCHA	41	32	26	58	71	....	....	....	....	....

a CCHA Second All-Star Team (1994)

KNUTSEN, ESPEN — HFD.

Center. Shoots left. 5'11", 172 lbs. Born, Oslo, Norway, January 12, 1972.
(Hartford's 9th choice, 204th overall, in 1990 Entry Draft).

			Regular Season					Playoffs				
Season	Club	Lea	GP	G	A	TP	PIM	GP	G	A	TP	PIM
1989-90	Valerengen	Nor.	34	22	26	48	....	....	....	....	....	....
1990-91	Valerengen	Nor.	31	30	24	54	42	5	3	4	7	....
1991-92	Valerengen	Nor.	30	28	26	54	37	8	7	8	15	....
1992-93	Valerengen	Nor.	13	11	13	24	4	....	....	....	....	....
1993-94	Valerengen	Nor.	38	32	26	58	20	....	....	....	....	....

KOCH, PAUL — QUE.

Defense. Shoots left. 6'3", 205 lbs. Born, St. Paul, MN, June 30, 1971.
(Quebec's 12th choice, 200th overall, in 1991 Entry Draft).

			Regular Season					Playoffs				
Season	Club	Lea	GP	G	A	TP	PIM	GP	G	A	TP	PIM
1991-92	U. of Denver	WCHA	36	4	13	17	48	....	....	....	....	....
1992-93	U. of Denver	WCHA	37	0	9	9	111	....	....	....	....	....
1993-94	U. of Denver	WCHA	17	2	2	4	22	....	....	....	....	....

KOCUR, JOEY (KOH-suhr) — NYR

Right wing. Shoots right. 6', 205 lbs. Born, Calgary, Alta., December 21, 1964.
(Detroit's 6th choice, 88th overall, in 1983 Entry Draft).

			Regular Season					Playoffs				
Season	Club	Lea	GP	G	A	TP	PIM	GP	G	A	TP	PIM
1982-83	Saskatoon	WHL	62	23	17	40	289	6	2	3	5	25
1983-84	Saskatoon	WHL	69	40	41	81	258	....	....	....	....	....
	Adirondack	AHL	....	....	....	....	....	5	0	0	0	20
1984-85	**Detroit**	**NHL**	**17**	**1**	**0**	**1**	**64**	**3**	**1**	**0**	**1**	**5**
	Adirondack	AHL	47	12	7	19	171	....	....	....	....	....
1985-86	**Detroit**	**NHL**	**59**	**9**	**6**	**15**	***377**	....	....	....	....	....
	Adirondack	AHL	9	6	2	8	34	....	....	....	....	....
1986-87	**Detroit**	**NHL**	**77**	**9**	**9**	**18**	**276**	**16**	**2**	**3**	**5**	**71**
1987-88	**Detroit**	**NHL**	**63**	**7**	**7**	**14**	**263**	**10**	**0**	**1**	**1**	**13**
1988-89	**Detroit**	**NHL**	**60**	**9**	**9**	**18**	**213**	**3**	**0**	**1**	**1**	**6**
1989-90	**Detroit**	**NHL**	**71**	**16**	**20**	**36**	**268**	....	....	....	....	....
1990-91	**Detroit**	**NHL**	**52**	**5**	**4**	**9**	**253**	....	....	....	....	....
	NY Rangers	**NHL**	**5**	**0**	**0**	**0**	**36**	**6**	**0**	**2**	**2**	**21**
1991-92	**NY Rangers**	**NHL**	**51**	**7**	**4**	**11**	**121**	**12**	**1**	**1**	**2**	**38**
1992-93	**NY Rangers**	**NHL**	**65**	**3**	**6**	**9**	**131**	....	....	....	....	....
1993-94	**NY Rangers**	**NHL**	**71**	**2**	**1**	**3**	**129**	**20**	**1**	**1**	**2**	**17**
	NHL Totals		**591**	**68**	**66**	**134**	**2131**	**70**	**5**	**9**	**14**	**171**

Traded to **NY Rangers** by **Detroit** with Per Djoos for Kevin Miller, Jim Cummins and Dennis Vial, March 5, 1991.

KOHN, LADISLAV — CGY.

Right wing. Shoots left. 5'10", 175 lbs. Born, Uherske Hradiste, Czech., March 4, 1975.
(Calgary's 9th choice, 175th overall, in 1994 Entry Draft).

			Regular Season					Playoffs				
Season	Club	Lea	GP	G	A	TP	PIM	GP	G	A	TP	PIM
1993-94	Brandon	WHL	2	0	0	0	0	....	....	....	....	....
	Swift Current	WHL	69	33	35	68	68	7	5	4	9	8

KOIVU, SAKU (KOY-voo, SA-koo) — MTL.

Center. Shoots left. 5'9", 165 lbs. Born, Turku, Finland, November 23, 1974.
(Montreal's 1st choice, 21st overall, in 1993 Entry Draft).

			Regular Season					Playoffs				
Season	Club	Lea	GP	G	A	TP	PIM	GP	G	A	TP	PIM
1992-93	TPS	Fin.	46	3	7	10	28	11	3	2	5	2
1993-94	TPS	Fin.	47	23	30	53	42	11	4	8	12	16

KOIVUNEN, PETRO — EDM.

Right wing. Shoots right. 6', 183 lbs. Born, Espoo, Finland, May 30, 1970.
(Edmonton's 2nd choice, 39th overall, in 1988 Entry Draft).

			Regular Season					Playoffs				
Season	Club	Lea	GP	G	A	TP	PIM	GP	G	A	TP	PIM
1988-89	Espoo	Fin.2	39	32	37	69	42	....	....	....	....	....
1989-90	Espoo	Fin.2	39	24	35	59	28	....	....	....	....	....
1990-91	HIFK	Fin.	39	8	15	23	20	3	0	1	1	4
1991-92	HIFK	Fin.	41	11	3	14	0	8	0	0	0	2
1992-93	Kiekko-Espoo	Fin.	47	12	13	25	24	....	....	....	....	....
1993-94	Kiekko-Espoo	Fin.	47	21	23	44	16	....	....	....	....	....

KOLESAR, MARK — TOR.

Left wing. Shoots right. 6'1", 188 lbs. Born, Brampton, Ont., January 23, 1973.

			Regular Season					Playoffs				
Season	Club	Lea	GP	G	A	TP	PIM	GP	G	A	TP	PIM
1991-92	Brandon	WHL	56	6	7	13	36	....	....	....	....	....
1992-93	Brandon	WHL	68	27	33	60	110	4	0	0	0	4
1993-94	Brandon	WHL	59	29	37	66	131	14	8	3	11	48

Signed as a free agent by **Toronto**, May 24, 1994.

KOLSTAD, DEAN

Defense. Shoots left. 6'6", 220 lbs. Born, Edmonton, Alta., June 16, 1968.
(Minnesota's 3rd choice, 33rd overall, in 1986 Entry Draft).

			Regular Season					Playoffs				
Season	Club	Lea	GP	G	A	TP	PIM	GP	G	A	TP	PIM
1985-86	N. Westminster	WHL	13	0	0	0	16	....	....	....	....	....
	Prince Albert	WHL	54	2	15	17	80	20	5	3	8	26
1986-87	Prince Albert	WHL	72	17	37	54	112	8	1	5	6	8
1987-88	Prince Albert	WHL	72	14	37	51	121	10	0	9	9	20
1988-89	**Minnesota**	**NHL**	**25**	**1**	**5**	**6**	**42**	....	....	....	....	....
	Kalamazoo	IHL	51	10	23	33	91	6	1	0	1	23
1989-90a	Kalamazoo	IHL	77	10	40	50	172	10	3	4	7	14
1990-91	**Minnesota**	**NHL**	**5**	**0**	**0**	**0**	**15**	....	....	....	....	....
	Kalamazoo	IHL	33	4	8	12	50	9	1	6	7	4
1991-92	Kansas City	IHL	74	9	20	29	83	15	3	6	9	8
1992-93	**San Jose**	**NHL**	**10**	**0**	**2**	**2**	**12**	....	....	....	....	....
	Kansas City	IHL	63	9	21	30	79	3	0	0	0	2
1993-94	Binghamton	AHL	68	7	26	33	92	....	....	....	....	....
	NHL Totals		**40**	**1**	**7**	**8**	**69**	....	....	....	....	....

a IHL Second All-Star Team (1990)

Claimed by **San Jose** from **Minnesota** in Dispersal Draft, May 30, 1991. Signed as a free agent by **NY Rangers**, September 1, 1993.

KOMAROV, PAVEL (koh-mah-ROHV) — NYR

Defense. Shoots left. 6'2", 183 lbs. Born, Gorky, USSR, February 28, 1974.
(NY Rangers' 12th choice, 261st overall, in 1993 Entry Draft).

			Regular Season					Playoffs				
Season	Club	Lea	GP	G	A	TP	PIM	GP	G	A	TP	PIM
1991-92	Nizhny Novg.	CIS	10	0	1	1	0	....	....	....	....	....
1992-93	Nizhny Novg.	CIS	28	0	0	0	25	....	....	....	....	....
1993-94	Nizhny Novg.	CIS	18	1	0	1	20	1	0	0	0	2
	Binghamton	AHL	1	1	0	1	2	....	....	....	....	....

KONDRASHKIN, SERGEI (kohn-DRAHSH-kihn) — NYR

Right wing. Shoots left. 6', 192 lbs. Born, USSR, April 2, 1975.
(NY Rangers' 7th choice, 162nd overall, in 1993 Entry Draft).

			Regular Season					Playoffs				
Season	Club	Lea	GP	G	A	TP	PIM	GP	G	A	TP	PIM
1992-93	Cherepovets	CIS	41	7	3	10	8	....	....	....	....	....
1993-94	Cherepovets	CIS	41	7	2	9	26	....	....	....	....	....

KONOWALCHUK, BRIAN

Center. Shoots left. 5'11", 180 lbs. Born, Prince Albert, Sask., October 14, 1971.
(San Jose's 1st choice, 3rd overall, in 1992 Supplemental Draft).

			Regular Season					Playoffs				
Season	Club	Lea	GP	G	A	TP	PIM	GP	G	A	TP	PIM
1990-91	U. of Denver	WCHA	38	8	19	27	40	....	....	....	....	....
1991-92	U. of Denver	WCHA	33	8	17	25	53	....	....	....	....	....
1992-93	U. of Denver	WCHA	37	12	20	32	59	....	....	....	....	....
1993-94	U. of Denver	WCHA	34	9	15	24	26	....	....	....	....	....

KONOWALCHUK, STEVE (kahn-uh-WAHL-chuhk) — WSH.

Center. Shoots left. 6', 180 lbs. Born, Salt Lake City, UT, November 11, 1972.
(Washington's 5th choice, 58th overall, in 1991 Entry Draft).

			Regular Season					Playoffs				
Season	Club	Lea	GP	G	A	TP	PIM	GP	G	A	TP	PIM
1990-91	Portland	WHL	72	43	49	92	78	....	....	....	....	....
1991-92	**Washington**	**NHL**	**1**	**0**	**0**	**0**	**0**	....	....	....	....	....
	Baltimore	AHL	3	1	1	2	0	....	....	....	....	....
a	Portland	WHL	64	51	53	104	95	6	3	6	9	12
1992-93	**Washington**	**NHL**	**36**	**4**	**7**	**11**	**16**	**2**	**0**	**1**	**1**	**0**
	Baltimore	AHL	37	18	28	46	74	....	....	....	....	....
1993-94	**Washington**	**NHL**	**62**	**12**	**14**	**26**	**33**	**11**	**0**	**1**	**1**	**10**
	Portland	AHL	8	11	4	15	4	....	....	....	....	....
	NHL Totals		**99**	**16**	**21**	**37**	**49**	**13**	**0**	**2**	**2**	**10**

a WHL West First All-Star Team (1992)

KONROYD, STEVE (KON-royd) OTT.

Defense. Shoots left. 6'1", 195 lbs. Born, Scarborough, Ont., February 10, 1961.
(Atlanta's 4th choice, 39th overall, in 1980 Entry Draft).

			Regular Season					Playoffs				
Season	Club	Lea	GP	G	A	TP	PIM	GP	G	A	TP	PIM
1979-80	Oshawa	OHA	62	11	23	34	133	7	0	2	2	14
1980-81	Calgary	NHL	4	0	0	0	4					
a	Oshawa	OHA	59	19	47	68	232	11	3	11	14	35
1981-82	Calgary	NHL	63	3	14	17	78	3	0	0	0	12
	Oklahoma City	CHL	14	2	3	5	15					
1982-83	Calgary	NHL	79	4	13	17	73	9	2	1	3	18
1983-84	Calgary	NHL	80	1	13	14	94	8	1	2	3	8
1984-85	Calgary	NHL	64	3	23	26	73	4	1	4	5	2
1985-86	Calgary	NHL	59	7	20	27	64					
	NY Islanders	NHL	14	0	5	5	16	3	0	0	0	6
1986-87	NY Islanders	NHL	72	5	16	21	70	14	1	4	5	10
1987-88	NY Islanders	NHL	62	2	15	17	99	6	1	0	1	4
1988-89	NY Islanders	NHL	21	1	5	6	2					
	Chicago	NHL	57	5	7	12	40	16	2	0	2	10
1989-90	Chicago	NHL	75	3	14	17	34	20	1	3	4	19
1990-91	Chicago	NHL	70	0	12	12	40	6	1	0	1	8
1991-92	Chicago	NHL	49	2	14	16	65					
	Hartford	NHL	33	2	10	12	32	7	0	1	1	2
1992-93	Hartford	NHL	59	3	11	14	63					
	Detroit	NHL	6	0	1	1	4	1	0	0	0	0
1993-94	Detroit	NHL	19	0	0	0	10					
	Ottawa	NHL	8	0	2	2	2					
	NHL Totals		894	41	195	236	863	97	10	15	25	99

a OHA Second All-Star Team (1981)

Traded to **NY Islanders** by **Calgary** with Richard Kromm for John Tonelli, March 11, 1986. Traded to **Chicago** by **NY Islanders** with Bob Bassen for Marc Bergevin and Gary Nylund, November 25, 1988. Traded to **Hartford** by **Chicago** for Rob Brown, January 24, 1992. Traded to **Detroit** by **Hartford** for Detroit's sixth round choice (later traded back to Detroit — Detroit selected Tim Spitzig) in 1993 Entry Draft, March 22, 1993. Traded to **Ottawa** by **Detroit** for Daniel Berthiaume, March 21, 1994.

KONSTANTINOV, VLADIMIR (kohn-stahn-TEE-nahf) DET.

Defense. Shoots right. 5'11", 190 lbs. Born, Murmansk, USSR, March 19, 1967.
(Detroit's 12th choice, 221st overall, in 1989 Entry Draft).

			Regular Season					Playoffs				
Season	Club	Lea	GP	G	A	TP	PIM	GP	G	A	TP	PIM
1984-85	CSKA	USSR	40	1	4	5	10					
1985-86	CSKA	USSR	26	4	3	7	12					
1986-87	CSKA	USSR	35	2	2	4	19					
1987-88	CSKA	USSR	50	3	6	9	32					
1988-89	CSKA	USSR	37	7	8	15	20					
1989-90	CSKA	USSR	47	14	14	28	44					
1990-91	CSKA	USSR	45	5	12	17	42					
1991-92a	Detroit	NHL	79	8	26	34	172	11	0	1	1	16
1992-93	Detroit	NHL	82	5	17	22	137	7	0	1	1	8
1993-94	Detroit	NHL	80	12	21	33	138	7	0	2	2	4
	NHL Totals		241	25	64	89	447	25	0	4	4	28

a NHL/Upper Deck All-Rookie Team (1992)

KONTOS, CHRIS (KONN-tohs)

Left wing/Center. Shoots left. 6'1", 195 lbs. Born, Toronto, Ont., December 10, 1963.
(NY Rangers' 1st choice, 15th overall, in 1982 Entry Draft).

			Regular Season					Playoffs				
Season	Club	Lea	GP	G	A	TP	PIM	GP	G	A	TP	PIM
1980-81	Sudbury	OHA	57	17	27	44	36					
1981-82	Sudbury	OHL	12	6	6	12	18					
	Toronto	OHL	59	36	56	92	68	10	7	9	16	2
1982-83	NY Rangers	NHL	44	8	7	15	33					
	Toronto	OHL	28	21	33	54	23					
1983-84	NY Rangers	NHL	6	0	1	1	8					
	Tulsa	CHL	21	5	13	18	8					
1984-85	NY Rangers	NHL	28	4	8	12	24					
	New Haven	AHL	48	19	24	43	30					
1985-86	Ilves	Fin.	36	16	15	31	30					
	New Haven	AHL	21	8	15	23	12	5	4	2	6	4
1986-87	Pittsburgh	NHL	31	8	9	17	6					
	New Haven	AHL	36	14	17	31	29					
1987-88	Pittsburgh	NHL	36	1	7	8	12					
	Muskegon	IHL	10	3	6	9	8					
	Los Angeles	NHL	6	2	10	12	2	4	1	0	1	4
	New Haven	AHL	16	8	16	24	4					
1988-89	EHC Kloten	Swiss	36	33	22	55		6	6	2	8	
	Los Angeles	NHL	7	2	1	3	2	11	9	0	9	8
1989-90	Los Angeles	NHL	6	2	2	4	4	5	1	0	1	0
	New Haven	AHL	42	10	20	30	25					
1990-91	Phoenix	IHL	69	26	36	62	19	11	9	12	21	0
1991-92	Cdn. National	....	25	10	10	20	16					
1992-93	Tampa Bay	NHL	66	27	24	51	12					
1993-94	Cdn. National	....	35	16	16	32	12					
	Cdn. Olympic	....	8	3	1	4	2					
	NHL Totals		230	54	69	123	103	20	11	0	11	12

Traded to **Pittsburgh** by **NY Rangers** for Ron Duguay, January 21, 1987. Traded to **Los Angeles** by **Pittsburgh** with Pittsburgh's sixth round choice (Micah Aivazoff) in 1988 Entry Draft for Bryan Erickson, February 5, 1988. Signed as a free agent by **Tampa Bay**, July 21, 1992.

KONTSEK, ROMAN (KON-chek) WSH.

Right wing. Shoots left. 5'11", 183 lbs. Born, Zilina, Czech., June 11, 1970.
(Washington's 8th choice, 135th overall, in 1990 Entry Draft).

			Regular Season					Playoffs				
Season	Club	Lea	GP	G	A	TP	PIM	GP	G	A	TP	PIM
1988-89	Dukla Trencin	Czech.	21	4	8	12	12					
1989-90	Dukla Trencin	Czech.	21	8	7	15						
1990-91	Dukla Trencin	Czech.	54	15	23	38	24					
1991-92	Dukla Trencin	Czech.	35	5	6	11	12					
1992-93	Dukla Trencin	Czech.	49	12	23	35						
1993-94	Dukla Trencin	Slovak	29	22	24	46	14					

KORDIC, DAN PHI.

Defense. Shoots left. 6'5", 220 lbs. Born, Edmonton, Alta., April 18, 1971.
(Philadelphia's 9th choice, 88th overall, in 1990 Entry Draft).

			Regular Season					Playoffs				
Season	Club	Lea	GP	G	A	TP	PIM	GP	G	A	TP	PIM
1987-88	Medicine Hat	WHL	63	1	5	6	75					
1988-89	Medicine Hat	WHL	70	1	13	14	190					
1989-90	Medicine Hat	WHL	59	4	12	16	182	3	0	0	0	9
1990-91	Medicine Hat	WHL	67	8	15	23	150	12	2	6	8	42
1991-92	Philadelphia	NHL	46	1	3	4	126					
1992-93	Hershey	AHL	14	0	2	2	17					
1993-94	Philadelphia	NHL	4	0	0	0	5					
	Hershey	AHL	64	0	4	4	164	11	0	3	3	26
	NHL Totals		50	1	3	4	131					

KOROBOLIN, ALEXANDER (koh-roh-BOH-lihn) NYR

Defense. Shoots left. 6'2", 189 lbs. Born, Chelyabinsk, USSR, March 12, 1976.
(NY Rangers' 4th choice, 100th overall, in 1994 Entry Draft).

			Regular Season					Playoffs				
Season	Club	Lea	GP	G	A	TP	PIM	GP	G	A	TP	PIM
1993-94	Chelyabinsk	CIS	32	0	0	0	30					

KOROLEV, IGOR (koh-roh-LEHV) ST.L.

Right wing. Shoots left. 6'1", 187 lbs. Born, Moscow, USSR, September 6, 1970.
(St. Louis' 1st choice, 38th overall, in 1992 Entry Draft).

			Regular Season					Playoffs				
Season	Club	Lea	GP	G	A	TP	PIM	GP	G	A	TP	PIM
1988-89	Moscow D'amo	USSR	1	0	0	0	2					
1989-90	Moscow D'amo	USSR	17	3	2	5	2					
1990-91	Moscow D'amo	USSR	38	12	4	16	12					
1991-92	Moscow D'amo	CIS	39	15	12	27	16					
1992-93	Moscow D'amo	CIS	5	1	2	3	4					
	St. Louis	NHL	74	4	23	27	20	3	0	0	0	0
1993-94	St. Louis	NHL	73	6	10	16	40	2	0	0	0	0
	NHL Totals		147	10	33	43	60	5	0	0	0	0

KOROLYUK, ALEXANDER (koh-roh-LYUHK) S.J.

Right wing. Shoots left. 5'9", 170 lbs. Born, Moscow, USSR, January 15, 1976.
(San Jose's 6th choice, 141st overall, in 1994 Entry Draft).

			Regular Season					Playoffs				
Season	Club	Lea	GP	G	A	TP	PIM	GP	G	A	TP	PIM
1993-94	Soviet Wings	CIS	22	4	4	8	20	3	1	0	1	4

KOROTKOV, KONSTANTIN (KOH-raht-kohv) HFD.

Center. Shoots left. 5'9", 174 lbs. Born, Moscow, USSR, January 25, 1972.
(Hartford's 8th choice, 177th overall, in 1992 Entry Draft).

			Regular Season					Playoffs				
Season	Club	Lea	GP	G	A	TP	PIM	GP	G	A	TP	PIM
1987-88	Spartak	USSR	1	0	0	0	0					
1988-89	Spartak	USSR	3	0	0	0	0					
1989-90	Spartak	USSR	31	2	3	5	2					
1990-91	Spartak	USSR	34	3	3	6	11					
1991-92	Spartak	CIS	35	4	1	5	46					
1992-93	Spartak	CIS	39	5	6	11	32	3	0	2	2	4
1993-94	Spartak	CIS	36	4	14	18	30	6	2	1	3	12

KOVALENKO, ANDREI QUE.

Right wing. Shoots left. 5'10", 200 lbs. Born, Balakovo, USSR, June 7, 1970.
(Quebec's 6th choice, 148th overall, in 1990 Entry Draft).

			Regular Season					Playoffs				
Season	Club	Lea	GP	G	A	TP	PIM	GP	G	A	TP	PIM
1988-89	CSKA	USSR	10	1	0	1	0					
1989-90	CSKA	USSR	48	8	5	13	20					
1990-91	CSKA	USSR	45	13	8	21	26					
1991-92	CSKA	CIS	44	19	13	32	32					
1992-93	CSKA	CIS	3	3	1	4	4					
	Quebec	NHL	81	27	41	68	57	4	1	0	1	2
1993-94	Quebec	NHL	58	16	17	33	46					
	NHL Totals		139	43	58	101	103	4	1	0	1	2

KOVALEV, ALEXEI NYR

Right wing. Shoots left. 6', 200 lbs. Born, Togliatti, USSR, February 24, 1973.
(NY Rangers' 1st choice, 15th overall, in 1991 Entry Draft).

			Regular Season					Playoffs				
Season	Club	Lea	GP	G	A	TP	PIM	GP	G	A	TP	PIM
1989-90	Moscow D'amo	USSR	1	0	0	0	0					
1990-91	Moscow D'amo	USSR	18	1	2	3	4					
1991-92	Moscow D'amo	CIS	33	16	9	25	20					
1992-93	NY Rangers	NHL	65	20	18	38	79					
	Binghamton	AHL	13	13	11	24	35	9	3	5	8	14
1993-94	NY Rangers	NHL	76	23	33	56	154	23	9	12	21	18
	NHL Totals		141	43	51	94	233	23	9	12	21	18

KOWALSKY, RICK

Right wing. Shoots right. 6', 184 lbs. Born, Simcoe, Ont., March 20, 1972.
(Buffalo's 10th choice, 227th overall, in 1992 Entry Draft).

			Regular Season					Playoffs				
Season	Club	Lea	GP	G	A	TP	PIM	GP	G	A	TP	PIM
1990-91	S.S. Marie	OHL	46	5	9	14	59	13	4	4	8	17
1991-92	S.S. Marie	OHL	66	25	44	39	119	19	6	10	16	39
1992-93	S.S. Marie	OHL	54	23	47	70	58	10	7	6	13	30
1993-94	Cornwall	AHL	65	9	8	17	86					

KOZEL, VITALY (KOH-zehl) ANA.

Center. Shoots left. 6'3", 193 lbs. Born, Minsk, USSR, May 26, 1975.
(Anaheim's 9th choice, 212th overall, in 1993 Entry Draft).

			Regular Season					Playoffs				
Season	Club	Lea	GP	G	A	TP	PIM	GP	G	A	TP	PIM
1992-93	Khimik	CIS 2				UNAVAILABLE						
1993-94	Beauport	QMJHL	58	2	10	12	51	11	3	1	4	2

KOZLOV, VIKTOR (KAHS-lahf) S.J.

Left wing. Shoots right. 6'5", 225 lbs. Born, Togliatti, USSR, February 14, 1975.
(San Jose's 1st choice, 6th overall, in 1993 Entry Draft).

			Regular Season					Playoffs				
Season	Club	Lea	GP	G	A	TP	PIM	GP	G	A	TP	PIM
1990-91	Togliatti	USSR 2	2	2	0	2	0					
1991-92	Togliatti	CIS	3	0	0	0	0					
1992-93	Moscow D'amo	CIS	30	6	5	11	4	10	3	0	3	0
1993-94	Moscow D'amo	CIS	42	16	9	25	14	7	3	2	5	0

KOZLOV, VYACHESLAV (KAHS-lahf, VYACH-ih-slav) DET.

Center. Shoots left. 5'10", 180 lbs. Born, Voskresensk, USSR, May 3, 1972.
(Detroit's 2nd choice, 45th overall, in 1990 Entry Draft).

			Regular Season					Playoffs				
Season	Club	Lea	GP	G	A	TP	PIM	GP	G	A	TP	PIM
1987-88	Khimik	USSR	2	0	0	0	0					
1988-89	Khimik	USSR	14	0	1	1	2					
1989-90	Khimik	USSR	45	14	12	26	38					
1990-91	Khimik	USSR	45	11	13	24	46					
1991-92	CSKA	CIS	11	6	5	11	12					
	Detroit	**NHL**	**7**	**0**	**2**	**2**	**2**					
1992-93	**Detroit**	**NHL**	**17**	**4**	**1**	**5**	**14**	**4**	**0**	**2**	**2**	**2**
	Adirondack	AHL	45	23	36	59	54	4	1	1	2	4
1993-94	**Detroit**	**NHL**	**77**	**34**	**39**	**73**	**50**	**7**	**2**	**5**	**7**	**12**
	Adirondack	AHL	3	0	1	1	15					
	NHL Totals		**101**	**38**	**42**	**80**	**66**	**11**	**2**	**7**	**9**	**14**

KRALL, JUSTIN DET.

Defense. Shoots left. 6'2", 170 lbs. Born, Toledo, OH, February 20, 1974.
(Detroit's 8th choice, 183rd overall, in 1992 Entry Draft).

			Regular Season					Playoffs				
Season	Club	Lea	GP	G	A	TP	PIM	GP	G	A	TP	PIM
1992-93	Miami-Ohio	CCHA	39	5	6	11	26					
1993-94	Miami-Ohio	CCHA	38	1	4	6	32					

KRAMER, BRADY MTL.

Center. Shoots left. 6'2", 170 lbs. Born, Philadelphia, PA, June 13, 1973.
(Montreal's 10th choice, 149th overall, in 1991 Entry Draft).

			Regular Season					Playoffs				
Season	Club	Lea	GP	G	A	TP	PIM	GP	G	A	TP	PIM
1991-92	Providence	H.E.	36	11	10	21	47					
1992-93	Providence	H.E.	32	14	14	28	52					
1993-94	Providence	H.E.	36	12	26	38	50					

KRAVCHUK, IGOR (krahv-CHOOK)

Defense. Shoots left. 6'1", 200 lbs. Born, Ufa, USSR, September 13, 1966.
(Chicago's 5th choice, 71st overall, in 1991 Entry Draft).

			Regular Season					Playoffs				
Season	Club	Lea	GP	G	A	TP	PIM	GP	G	A	TP	PIM
1982-83	Yulayev	USSR	10	0	0	0	0					
	Yulayev	USSR 2										
1984-85	Yulayev	USSR 2	50	3	2	5	22					
1985-86	Yulayev	USSR	21	2	2	4	6					
1986-87	Yulayev	USSR	22	0	1	1	8					
1987-88	CSKA	USSR	48	1	8	9	12					
1988-89	CSKA	USSR	22	3	3	6	2					
1989-90	CSKA	USSR	48	1	3	4	16					
1990-91	CSKA	USSR	41	6	5	11	16					
1991-92	CSKA	CIS	30	3	8	11	6					
	Chicago	**NHL**	**18**	**1**	**8**	**9**	**4**	**18**	**2**	**6**	**8**	**8**
1992-93	**Chicago**	**NHL**	**38**	**6**	**9**	**15**	**30**					
	Edmonton	**NHL**	**17**	**4**	**8**	**12**	**2**					
1993-94	**Edmonton**	**NHL**	**81**	**12**	**38**	**50**	**16**					
	NHL Totals		**154**	**23**	**63**	**86**	**52**	**18**	**2**	**6**	**8**	**8**

Traded to **Edmonton** by **Chicago** with Dean McAmmond for Joe Murphy, February 24, 1993.

KRAVETS, MIKHAIL

Right wing. Shoots left. 5'10", 195 lbs. Born, Leningrad, USSR, November 12, 1963.
(San Jose's 13th choice, 243rd overall, in 1991 Entry Draft).

			Regular Season					Playoffs				
Season	Club	Lea	GP	G	A	TP	PIM	GP	G	A	TP	PIM
1985-86	SKA Leningrad	USSR	38	14	7	21	20					
1986-87	SKA Leningrad	USSR	36	16	11	27	37					
1987-88	SKA Leningrad	USSR	44	9	5	14	36					
1988-89	SKA Leningrad	USSR	43	8	18	26	20					
1989-90	SKA Leningrad	USSR	30	10	14	24	36					
1990-91	SKA Leningrad	USSR	25	8	8	16	28					
1991-92	**San Jose**	**NHL**	**1**	**0**	**0**	**0**	**0**					
	Kansas City	IHL	74	10	32	42	172	15	6	8	14	12
1992-93	**San Jose**	**NHL**	**1**	**0**	**0**	**0**	**0**					
	Kansas City	IHL	71	19	49	68	153	10	2	5	7	55
1993-94	Kansas City	IHL	63	14	44	58	171					
	NHL Totals		**2**	**0**	**0**	**0**	**0**					

KRECHIN, VLADIMIR PHI.

Left wing. Shoots left. 5'11", 190 lbs. Born, Chelyabinsk, USSR, March 23, 1975.
(Philadelphia's 4th choice, 114th overall, in 1993 Entry Draft).

			Regular Season					Playoffs				
Season	Club	Lea	GP	G	A	TP	PIM	GP	G	A	TP	PIM
1992-93	Chelyabinsk	CIS	1	0	0	0	0					
1993-94	Windsor	OHL	45	13	12	25	27	4	2	1	3	0

KRISS, AARON S.J.

Defense. Shoots left. 6'2", 185 lbs. Born, Parma, OH, September 17, 1972.
(San Jose's 11th choice, 221st overall, in 1991 Entry Draft).

			Regular Season					Playoffs				
Season	Club	Lea	GP	G	A	TP	PIM	GP	G	A	TP	PIM
1991-92	Lowell	H.E.	29	1	4	5	22					
1992-93	Lowell	H.E.	25	3	5	8	10					
1993-94	Lowell	H.E.	34	5	10	15	48					

KRIVCHENKOV, ALEXEI (krihv-chehn-KOHV) PIT.

Defense. Shoots left. 6', 185 lbs. Born, Novosibirsk, USSR, June 11, 1974.
(Pittsburgh's 5th choice, 76th overall, in 1994 Entry Draft).

			Regular Season					Playoffs				
Season	Club	Lea	GP	G	A	TP	PIM	GP	G	A	TP	PIM
1993-94	Sibir Novosibirsk	CIS 2	37	1	3	4	48					
	CSKA	CIS	4	0	0	0	2	3	0	0	0	0

KRIVOKRASOV, SERGEI (krih-vuh-KRA-sahf) CHI.

Right wing. Shoots left. 5'10", 174 lbs. Born, Angarsk, USSR, April 15, 1974.
(Chicago's 1st choice, 12th overall, in 1992 Entry Draft).

			Regular Season					Playoffs				
Season	Club	Lea	GP	G	A	TP	PIM	GP	G	A	TP	PIM
1990-91	CSKA	USSR	41	4	0	4	8					
1991-92	CSKA	CIS	42	10	8	18	35					
1992-93	**Chicago**	**NHL**	**4**	**0**	**0**	**0**	**2**					
	Indianapolis	IHL	78	36	33	69	157	5	3	1	4	2
1993-94	**Chicago**	**NHL**	**9**	**1**	**0**	**1**	**4**					
	Indianapolis	IHL	53	19	26	45	145					
	NHL Totals		**13**	**1**	**0**	**1**	**6**					

KRON, ROBERT (KROHN) HFD.

Left wing. Shoots left. 5'10", 180 lbs. Born, Brno, Czech., February 27, 1967.
(Vancouver's 5th choice, 88th overall, in 1985 Entry Draft).

			Regular Season					Playoffs				
Season	Club	Lea	GP	G	A	TP	PIM	GP	G	A	TP	PIM
1983-84	Ingstav Brno	Czech.2	3	0	1	1	0					
1984-85	Zetor Brno	Czech.	40	6	8	14	6					
1985-86	Zetor Brno	Czech.	44	5	6	11	....					
1986-87	Zetor Brno	Czech.	34	18	11	29	10					
1987-88	Zetor Brno	Czech.	44	14	7	21	30					
1988-89	Dukla Trencin	Czech.	43	28	19	47	26					
1989-90	Dukla Trencin	Czech.	39	22	22	44	....					
1990-91	**Vancouver**	**NHL**	**76**	**12**	**20**	**32**	**21**					
1991-92	**Vancouver**	**NHL**	**36**	**2**	**2**	**4**	**2**	**11**	**1**	**2**	**3**	**2**
1992-93	**Vancouver**	**NHL**	**32**	**10**	**11**	**21**	**14**					
	Hartford	**NHL**	**13**	**4**	**2**	**6**	**4**					
1993-94	**Hartford**	**NHL**	**77**	**24**	**26**	**50**	**8**					
	NHL Totals		**234**	**52**	**61**	**113**	**49**	**11**	**1**	**2**	**3**	**2**

Traded to **Hartford** by **Vancouver** with Vancouver's third round choice (Marek Malik) in 1993 Entry Draft and future considerations (Jim Sandlak, May 17, 1993) for Murray Craven and Vancouver's fifth round choice (previously acquired by Hartford — Vancouver selected Scott Walker) in 1993 Entry Draft, March 22, 1993.

KROUPA, VLASTIMIL (KROO-pah, VLAS-tuh-meel) S.J.

Defense. Shoots left. 6'2", 185 lbs. Born, Most, Czech., April 27, 1975.
(San Jose's 3rd choice, 45th overall, in 1993 Entry Draft).

			Regular Season					Playoffs				
Season	Club	Lea	GP	G	A	TP	PIM	GP	G	A	TP	PIM
1992-93	Litvinov	Czech.	9	0	1	1	....					
1993-94	**San Jose**	**NHL**	**27**	**1**	**3**	**4**	**20**	**14**	**1**	**2**	**3**	**21**
	Kansas City	IHL	39	3	12	15	12					
	NHL Totals		**27**	**1**	**3**	**4**	**20**	**14**	**1**	**2**	**3**	**21**

KRUPP, UWE (KROOP, OO-VAY) QUE.

Defense. Shoots right. 6'6", 235 lbs. Born, Cologne, West Germany, June 24, 1965.
(Buffalo's 13th choice, 214th overall, in 1983 Entry Draft).

			Regular Season					Playoffs				
Season	Club	Lea	GP	G	A	TP	PIM	GP	G	A	TP	PIM
1982-83	Koln	W.Ger.	11	0	0	0	0					
1983-84	Koln	W.Ger.	26	0	4	4	22					
1984-85	Koln	W.Ger.	39	11	8	19	36					
1985-86	Koln	W.Ger.	45	10	21	31	83					
1986-87	**Buffalo**	**NHL**	**26**	**1**	**4**	**5**	**23**					
	Rochester	AHL	42	3	19	22	50	17	1	11	12	16
1987-88	**Buffalo**	**NHL**	**75**	**2**	**9**	**11**	**151**	**6**	**0**	**0**	**0**	**15**
1988-89	**Buffalo**	**NHL**	**70**	**5**	**13**	**18**	**55**	**5**	**0**	**1**	**1**	**4**
1989-90	**Buffalo**	**NHL**	**74**	**3**	**20**	**23**	**85**	**6**	**0**	**0**	**0**	**4**
1990-91	**Buffalo**	**NHL**	**74**	**12**	**32**	**44**	**66**	**6**	**1**	**1**	**2**	**6**
1991-92	**Buffalo**	**NHL**	**8**	**2**	**0**	**2**	**6**					
	NY Islanders	**NHL**	**59**	**6**	**29**	**35**	**43**					
1992-93	**NY Islanders**	**NHL**	**80**	**9**	**29**	**38**	**67**	**18**	**1**	**5**	**6**	**12**
1993-94	**NY Islanders**	**NHL**	**41**	**7**	**14**	**21**	**30**	**4**	**0**	**1**	**1**	**4**
	NHL Totals		**507**	**47**	**150**	**197**	**526**	**45**	**2**	**8**	**10**	**45**

Played in NHL All-Star Game (1991)

Traded to **NY Islanders** by **Buffalo** with Pierre Turgeon, Benoit Hogue and Dave McLlwain for Pat Lafontaine, Randy Hillier, Randy Wood and NY Islanders' fourth round choice (Dean Melanson) in 1992 Entry Draft, October 25, 1991. Traded to **Quebec** by **NY Islanders** with NY Islanders' first round choice (Wade Belak) in 1994 Entry Draft for Ron Sutter and Quebec's first round choice (Brett Lindros) in 1994 Entry Draft, June 28, 1994.

KRUPPKE, GORD (KRUHP-kee) DET.

Defense. Shoots right. 6'1", 215 lbs. Born, Slave Lake, Alta., April 2, 1969.
(Detroit's 2nd choice, 32nd overall, in 1987 Entry Draft).

			Regular Season					Playoffs				
Season	Club	Lea	GP	G	A	TP	PIM	GP	G	A	TP	PIM
1985-86	Prince Albert	WHL	62	1	8	9	81	20	4	4	8	22
1986-87	Prince Albert	WHL	49	2	10	12	129	8	0	0	0	9
1987-88	Prince Albert	WHL	54	8	8	16	113	10	0	0	0	46
1988-89	Prince Albert	WHL	62	6	26	32	254	3	0	0	0	11
1989-90	Adirondack	AHL	59	2	12	14	103					
1990-91	**Detroit**	**NHL**	**4**	**0**	**0**	**0**	**0**					
	Adirondack	AHL	45	1	8	9	153					
1991-92	Adirondack	AHL	65	3	9	12	208	16	0	1	1	52
1992-93	**Detroit**	**NHL**	**10**	**0**	**0**	**0**	**20**					
	Adirondack	AHL	41	2	12	14	197	9	1	2	3	20
1993-94	**Detroit**	**NHL**	**9**	**0**	**0**	**0**	**12**					
	Adirondack	AHL	54	2	9	11	210	12	1	3	4	32
	NHL Totals		**23**	**0**	**0**	**0**	**32**					

KRUSE, PAUL CGY.

Left wing. Shoots left. 6', 202 lbs. Born, Merritt, B.C., March 15, 1970.
(Calgary's 6th choice, 83rd overall, in 1990 Entry Draft).

			Regular Season					Playoffs				
Season	Club	Lea	GP	G	A	TP	PIM	GP	G	A	TP	PIM
1988-89	Kamloops	WHL	68	8	15	23	209					
1989-90	Kamloops	WHL	67	22	23	45	291	17	3	5	8	79
1990-91	**Calgary**	**NHL**	**1**	**0**	**0**	**0**	**7**					
	Salt Lake	IHL	83	24	20	44	313	4	1	1	2	4
1991-92	**Calgary**	**NHL**	**16**	**3**	**1**	**4**	**65**					
	Salt Lake	IHL	57	14	15	29	267	5	1	2	3	19
1992-93	**Calgary**	**NHL**	**27**	**2**	**3**	**5**	**41**					
	Salt Lake	IHL	35	1	4	5	206					
1993-94	**Calgary**	**NHL**	**68**	**3**	**8**	**11**	**185**	**7**	**0**	**0**	**0**	**14**
	NHL Totals		**112**	**8**	**12**	**20**	**298**	**7**	**0**	**0**	**0**	**14**

KRUSHELNYSKI, MIKE (KROO-shuhl-NIH-skee) DET.

Left wing/Center. Shoots left. 6'2", 200 lbs. Born, Montreal, Que., April 27, 1960.
(Boston's 7th choice, 120th overall, in 1979 Entry Draft).

			Regular Season					Playoffs				
Season	Club	Lea	GP	G	A	TP	PIM	GP	G	A	TP	PIM
1978-79	Montreal	QJHL	46	15	29	44	42	11	3	4	7	8
1979-80	Montreal	QJHL	72	39	60	99	78	6	2	3	5	2
1980-81	Springfield	AHL	80	25	28	53	47	7	1	1	2	29
1981-82	**Boston**	**NHL**	**17**	**3**	**3**	**6**	**2**	**1**	**0**	**0**	**0**	**2**
	Erie	AHL	62	31	52	83	44	....	....	....	....	....
1982-83	**Boston**	**NHL**	**79**	**23**	**42**	**65**	**43**	**17**	**8**	**6**	**14**	**12**
1983-84	**Boston**	**NHL**	**66**	**25**	**20**	**45**	**55**	**2**	**0**	**0**	**0**	**0**
1984-85	**Edmonton**	**NHL**	**80**	**43**	**45**	**88**	**60**	**18**	**5**	**8**	**13**	**22**
1985-86	**Edmonton**	**NHL**	**54**	**16**	**24**	**40**	**22**	**10**	**4**	**5**	**9**	**16**
1986-87	**Edmonton**	**NHL**	**80**	**16**	**35**	**51**	**67**	**21**	**3**	**4**	**7**	**18**
1987-88	**Edmonton**	**NHL**	**76**	**20**	**27**	**47**	**64**	**19**	**4**	**6**	**10**	**12**
1988-89	**Los Angeles**	**NHL**	**78**	**26**	**36**	**62**	**110**	**11**	**1**	**4**	**5**	**4**
1989-90	**Los Angeles**	**NHL**	**63**	**16**	**25**	**41**	**50**	**10**	**1**	**3**	**4**	**12**
1990-91	**Los Angeles**	**NHL**	**15**	**1**	**5**	**6**	**10**	....	....	....	....	....
	Toronto	**NHL**	**59**	**17**	**22**	**39**	**48**	....	....	....	....	....
1991-92	**Toronto**	**NHL**	**72**	**9**	**15**	**24**	**72**	....	....	....	....	....
1992-93	**Toronto**	**NHL**	**84**	**19**	**20**	**39**	**62**	**16**	**3**	**7**	**10**	**8**
1993-94	**Toronto**	**NHL**	**54**	**5**	**6**	**11**	**28**	**6**	**0**	**0**	**0**	**0**
	NHL Totals		**877**	**239**	**325**	**564**	**693**	**131**	**29**	**43**	**72**	**106**

Played in NHL All-Star Game (1985)

Traded to **Edmonton** by **Boston** for Ken Linseman, June 21, 1984. Traded to **Los Angeles** by **Edmonton** with Wayne Gretzky and Marty McSorley for Jimmy Carson, Martin Gelinas, Los Angeles' first round choices in 1989 (acquired by New Jersey — New Jersey selected Jason Miller), 1991 (Martin Rucinsky) and 1993 (Nick Stajduhar) Entry Drafts and cash, August 9, 1988. Traded to **Toronto** by **Los Angeles** for John McIntyre, November 9, 1990. Signed as a free agent by **Detroit**, August 1, 1994.

KRYGIER, TODD (KREE-guhr) WSH.

Left wing. Shoots left. 5'11", 180 lbs. Born, Chicago Heights, MI, October 12, 1965.
(Hartford's 1st choice, 16th overall, in 1988 Supplemental Draft).

			Regular Season					Playoffs				
Season	Club	Lea	GP	G	A	TP	PIM	GP	G	A	TP	PIM
1984-85	U. Connecticut	NCAA	14	14	11	25	12	....	....	....	....	....
1985-86	U. Connecticut	NCAA	32	29	27	56	46	....	....	....	....	....
1986-87	U. Connecticut	NCAA	28	24	24	48	44	....	....	....	....	....
1987-88	U. Connecticut	NCAA	27	32	39	71	28	....	....	....	....	....
	New Haven	AHL	13	1	5	6	34	....	....	....	....	....
1988-89	Binghamton	AHL	76	26	42	68	77	....	....	....	....	....
1989-90	**Hartford**	**NHL**	**58**	**18**	**12**	**30**	**52**	**7**	**2**	**1**	**3**	**4**
	Binghamton	AHL	12	1	9	10	16	....	....	....	....	....
1990-91	**Hartford**	**NHL**	**72**	**13**	**17**	**30**	**95**	**6**	**0**	**2**	**2**	**0**
1991-92	**Washington**	**NHL**	**67**	**13**	**17**	**30**	**107**	**5**	**2**	**1**	**3**	**4**
1992-93	**Washington**	**NHL**	**77**	**11**	**12**	**23**	**60**	**6**	**1**	**1**	**2**	**4**
1993-94	**Washington**	**NHL**	**66**	**12**	**18**	**30**	**60**	**5**	**2**	**0**	**2**	**10**
	NHL Totals		**340**	**67**	**76**	**143**	**374**	**29**	**7**	**5**	**12**	**22**

Traded to **Washington** by **Hartford** for future considerations (Washington's fourth round choice — later traded to Calgary — Calgary selected Jason Smith in 1993 Entry Draft), October 3, 1991.

KRYS, MARK

Defense. Shoots right. 6', 185 lbs. Born, Timmins, Ont., May 29, 1969.
(Boston's 6th choice, 165th overall, in 1988 Entry Draft).

			Regular Season					Playoffs				
Season	Club	Lea	GP	G	A	TP	PIM	GP	G	A	TP	PIM
1987-88	Boston U.	H.E.	34	0	6	6	40	....	....	....	....	....
1988-89	Boston U.	H.E.	35	0	7	7	54	....	....	....	....	....
1989-90	Boston U.	H.E.	30	0	4	4	34	....	....	....	....	....
1990-91	Boston U.	H.E.	36	1	9	10	18	....	....	....	....	....
1991-92	Maine	AHL	28	1	2	3	18	....	....	....	....	....
	Johnstown	ECHL	43	8	12	20	73	....	....	....	....	....
1992-93	Providence	AHL	34	1	10	11	36	6	0	0	0	2
	Johnstown	ECHL	25	4	14	18	18	....	....	....	....	....
	Cincinnati	IHL	3	0	1	1	2	....	....	....	....	....
1993-94	Providence	AHL	23	1	2	3	32	....	....	....	....	....
	Rochester	AHL	58	2	13	15	77	4	0	1	1	6

Traded to **Buffalo** by **Boston** for cash, December 2, 1993.

KUCERA, FRANTISEK (koo-CHAIR-uh) HFD.

Defense. Shoots right. 6'2", 205 lbs. Born, Prague, Czech., February 3, 1968.
(Chicago's 3rd choice, 77th overall, in 1986 Entry Draft).

			Regular Season					Playoffs				
Season	Club	Lea	GP	G	A	TP	PIM	GP	G	A	TP	PIM
1985-86	Sparta Praha	Czech.	15	0	0	0	....	....	....	....	....	....
1986-87	Sparta Praha	Czech.	40	5	2	7	14	....	....	....	....	....
1987-88	Sparta Praha	Czech.	46	7	2	9	30	....	....	....	....	....
1988-89	Dukla Jihlava	Czech.	45	10	9	19	28	....	....	....	....	....
1989-90	Dukla Jihlava	Czech.	43	9	10	19	....	....	....	....	....	....
1990-91	**Chicago**	**NHL**	**40**	**2**	**12**	**14**	**32**	....	....	....	....	....
	Indianapolis	IHL	35	8	19	27	23	7	0	1	1	15
1991-92	**Chicago**	**NHL**	**61**	**3**	**10**	**13**	**36**	**6**	**0**	**0**	**0**	**0**
	Indianapolis	IHL	7	1	2	3	4	....	....	....	....	....
1992-93	**Chicago**	**NHL**	**71**	**5**	**14**	**19**	**59**	....	....	....	....	....
1993-94	**Chicago**	**NHL**	**60**	**4**	**13**	**17**	**34**	....	....	....	....	....
	Hartford	**NHL**	**16**	**1**	**3**	**4**	**14**	....	....	....	....	....
	NHL Totals		**248**	**15**	**52**	**67**	**175**	**6**	**0**	**0**	**0**	**0**

Traded to **Hartford** by **Chicago** with Jocelyn Lemieux for Gary Suter, Randy Cunneyworth and a future draft choice, March 11, 1994.

KUCERA, JIRI (kuh-CHEH-rah) PIT.

Center. Shoots left. 5'11", 180 lbs. Born, Plzen, Czech., March 28, 1966.
(Pittsburgh's 8th choice, 152nd overall, in 1987 Entry Draft).

			Regular Season					Playoffs				
Season	Club	Lea	GP	G	A	TP	PIM	GP	G	A	TP	PIM
1986-87	Dukla Jihlava	Czech.	43	13	12	25	18	....	....	....	....	....
1987-88	Skoda Plzen	Czech.	41	21	24	45	22	....	....	....	....	....
1988-89	Skoda Plzen	Czech.	40	20	15	35	22	....	....	....	....	....
1989-90	Skoda Plzen	Czech.	47	13	24	37	....	....	....	....	....	....
1990-91	Tappara	Fin.	44	23	34	57	26	3	0	2	2	4
1991-92	Tappara	Fin.	44	22	20	42	8	....	....	....	....	....
1992-93	Tappara	Fin.	48	22	32	54	20	....	....	....	....	....
1993-94	Tappara	Fin.	47	16	26	42	37	10	7	5	12	4

KUCHARCIK, TOMAS (koo-HAHR-chihk) TOR.

Center. Shoots left. 6'2", 200 lbs. Born, Vlasim, Czech., May 10, 1970.
(Toronto's 11th choice, 167th overall, in 1991 Entry Draft).

			Regular Season					Playoffs				
Season	Club	Lea	GP	G	A	TP	PIM	GP	G	A	TP	PIM
1990-91	Dukla Jihlava	Czech.	30	10	6	16	6	....	....	....	....	....
1991-92	Dukla Jihlava	Czech.	45	16	23	39	24	....	....	....	....	....
1992-93	Dukla Jihlava	Czech.	39	17	20	37	....	....	....	....	....	....
1993-94	Skoda Plzen	Czech.	32	10	10	20	0	....	....	....	....	....

KUDASHOV, ALEXEI (koo-dah-SHOV) TOR.

Center. Shoots right. 6', 183 lbs. Born, Elektrostal, USSR, July 21, 1971.
(Toronto's 3rd choice, 102nd overall, in 1991 Entry Draft).

			Regular Season					Playoffs				
Season	Club	Lea	GP	G	A	TP	PIM	GP	G	A	TP	PIM
1989-90	Soviet Wings	USSR	45	0	5	5	14	....	....	....	....	....
1990-91	Soviet Wings	USSR	45	9	5	14	10	....	....	....	....	....
1991-92	Soviet Wings	CIS	42	9	16	25	14	....	....	....	....	....
1992-93	Soviet Wings	CIS	41	8	20	28	24	7	1	3	4	4
1993-94	Soviet Wings	CIS	1	2	0	2	0	....	....	....	....	....
	Toronto	**NHL**	**25**	**1**	**0**	**1**	**4**	....	....	....	....	....
	Rus. Olympic	....	8	1	2	3	4	....	....	....	....	....
	St. John's	AHL	27	7	15	22	21	....	....	....	....	....
	NHL Totals		**25**	**1**	**0**	**1**	**4**	....	....	....	....	....

KUDELSKI, BOB FLA.

Right wing. Shoots right. 6'1", 200 lbs. Born, Springfield, MA, March 3, 1964.
(Los Angeles' 1st choice, 2nd overall, in 1986 Supplemental Draft).

			Regular Season					Playoffs				
Season	Club	Lea	GP	G	A	TP	PIM	GP	G	A	TP	PIM
1983-84	Yale	ECAC	21	14	12	26	12	....	....	....	....	....
1984-85	Yale	ECAC	32	21	23	44	38	....	....	....	....	....
1985-86	Yale	ECAC	31	18	23	41	48	....	....	....	....	....
1986-87a	Yale	ECAC	30	25	22	47	34	....	....	....	....	....
1987-88	**Los Angeles**	**NHL**	**26**	**0**	**1**	**1**	**8**	....	....	....	....	....
	New Haven	AHL	50	15	19	34	41	....	....	....	....	....
1988-89	**Los Angeles**	**NHL**	**14**	**1**	**3**	**4**	**17**	....	....	....	....	....
	New Haven	AHL	60	32	19	51	43	17	8	5	13	12
1989-90	**Los Angeles**	**NHL**	**62**	**23**	**13**	**36**	**49**	**8**	**1**	**2**	**3**	**2**
1990-91	**Los Angeles**	**NHL**	**72**	**23**	**13**	**36**	**46**	**8**	**3**	**2**	**5**	**2**
1991-92	**Los Angeles**	**NHL**	**80**	**22**	**21**	**43**	**42**	**6**	**0**	**0**	**0**	**0**
1992-93	**Los Angeles**	**NHL**	**15**	**3**	**3**	**6**	**8**	....	....	....	....	....
	Ottawa	**NHL**	**48**	**21**	**14**	**35**	**22**	....	....	....	....	....
1993-94	**Ottawa**	**NHL**	**42**	**26**	**15**	**41**	**14**	....	....	....	....	....
	Florida	**NHL**	**44**	**14**	**15**	**29**	**10**	....	....	....	....	....
	NHL Totals		**403**	**133**	**98**	**231**	**216**	**22**	**4**	**4**	**8**	**4**

a ECAC First All-Star Team (1987)

Played in NHL All-Star Game (1994)

Traded to **Ottawa** by **Los Angeles** with Shawn McCosh for Marc Fortier and Jim Thomson, December 19, 1992. Traded to **Florida** by **Ottawa** for Evgeny Davydov, Scott Levins and future draft choices, January 6, 1994.

KUDINOV, ANDREI (kuh-DIH-nohv) NYR

Center. Shoots left. 6', 185 lbs. Born, Chelyabinsk, USSR, June 28, 1970.
(NY Rangers' 11th choice, 242nd overall, in 1993 Entry Draft).

			Regular Season					Playoffs				
Season	Club	Lea	GP	G	A	TP	PIM	GP	G	A	TP	PIM
1990-91	Chelyabinsk	USSR	24	2	3	5	20	....	....	....	....	....
1991-92	Chelyabinsk	CIS	44	12	8	20	56	....	....	....	....	....
1992-93	Chelyabinsk	CIS	41	13	23	36	50	8	0	1	1	6
1993-94	Chelyabinsk	CIS	6	0	3	3	4	....	....	....	....	....
	Binghamton	AHL	25	3	3	6	6	....	....	....	....	....

KUKI, ARTO (KUH-kee) MTL.

Center. Shoots left. 6'3", 205 lbs. Born, Espoo, Finland, February 22, 1976.
(Montreal's 6th choice, 96th overall, in 1994 Entry Draft).

			Regular Season					Playoffs				
Season	Club	Lea	GP	G	A	TP	PIM	GP	G	A	TP	PIM
1993-94	Espoo	Fin. Jr.	26	1	10	11	28	....	....	....	....	....

KUNTOS, JIRI (KOON-tohsh) BUF.

Defense. Shoots left. 5'11", 207 lbs. Born, Vlasim, Czech., December 11, 1971.
(Buffalo's 9th choice, 162nd overall, in 1991 Entry Draft).

			Regular Season					Playoffs				
Season	Club	Lea	GP	G	A	TP	PIM	GP	G	A	TP	PIM
1990-91	Dukla Jihlava	Czech.	15	3	1	4	....	....	....	....	....	....
1991-92	Dukla Jihlava	Czech.	45	2	8	10	49	....	....	....	....	....
1992-93	Dukla Jihlava	Czech.	35	4	2	6	....	....	....	....	....	....
1993-94	Olomouc	Czech.	43	3	6	9	0	12	1	0	1	0

KURRI, JARI (KUHR-ree, YAH-ree) L.A.

Right wing. Shoots right. 6'1", 195 lbs. Born, Helsinki, Finland, May 18, 1960.
(Edmonton's 3rd choice, 69th overall, in 1980 Entry Draft).

			Regular Season					Playoffs				
Season	**Club**	**Lea**	**GP**	**G**	**A**	**TP**	**PIM**	**GP**	**G**	**A**	**TP**	**PIM**
1977-78	Jokerit	Fin.	29	2	9	11	12	....	....	....	....	....
1978-79	Jokerit	Fin.	33	16	14	30	12	....	....	....	....	....
1979-80	Jokerit	Fin.	33	23	16	39	22	6	7	2	9	13
1980-81	**Edmonton**	**NHL**	**75**	**32**	**43**	**75**	**40**	**9**	**5**	**7**	**12**	**4**
1981-82	**Edmonton**	**NHL**	**71**	**32**	**54**	**86**	**32**	**5**	**2**	**5**	**7**	**10**
1982-83	**Edmonton**	**NHL**	**80**	**45**	**59**	**104**	**22**	**16**	**8**	**15**	**23**	**8**
1983-84a	**Edmonton**	**NHL**	**64**	**52**	**61**	**113**	**14**	**19**	***14**	**14**	**28**	**13**
1984-85bc	**Edmonton**	**NHL**	**73**	**71**	**64**	**135**	**30**	**18**	***19**	**12**	**31**	**6**
1985-86a	**Edmonton**	**NHL**	**78**	***68**	**63**	**131**	**22**	**10**	**2**	**10**	**12**	**4**
1986-87c	**Edmonton**	**NHL**	**79**	**54**	**54**	**108**	**41**	**21**	***15**	**10**	**25**	**20**
1987-88	**Edmonton**	**NHL**	**80**	**43**	**53**	**96**	**30**	**19**	***14**	**17**	**31**	**12**
1988-89a	**Edmonton**	**NHL**	**76**	**44**	**58**	**102**	**69**	**7**	**3**	**5**	**8**	**6**
1989-90	**Edmonton**	**NHL**	**78**	**33**	**60**	**93**	**48**	**22**	**10**	**15**	**25**	**18**
1990-91	Milan Devils	Italy	30	27	48	75	6	10	10	12	22	2
1991-92	**Los Angeles**	**NHL**	**73**	**23**	**37**	**60**	**24**	**4**	**1**	**2**	**3**	**4**
1992-93	**Los Angeles**	**NHL**	**82**	**27**	**60**	**87**	**38**	**24**	**9**	**8**	**17**	**12**
1993-94	**Los Angeles**	**NHL**	**81**	**31**	**46**	**77**	**48**	....	....	....	....	....
	NHL Totals		**990**	**555**	**712**	**1267**	**458**	**174**	**102**	**120**	**222**	**117**

a NHL Second All-Star Team (1984, 1986, 1989)
b Won Lady Byng Memorial Trophy (1985)
c NHL First All-Star Team (1985, 1987)

Played in NHL All-Star Game (1983, 1985, 1986, 1988-90, 1993)

Traded to **Philadelphia** by **Edmonton** with Dave Brown and Corey Foster for Craig Fisher, Scott Mellanby and Craig Berube, May 30, 1991. Traded to **Los Angeles** by **Philadelphia** with Jeff Chychrun for Steve Duchesne, Steve Kasper and Los Angeles' fourth round choice (Aris Brimanis) in 1991 Entry Draft, May 30, 1991.

KURVERS, TOM ANA.

Defense. Shoots left. 6'2", 195 lbs. Born, Minneapolis, MN, September 14, 1962.
(Montreal's 10th choice, 145th overall, in 1981 Entry Draft).

			Regular Season					Playoffs				
Season	**Club**	**Lea**	**GP**	**G**	**A**	**TP**	**PIM**	**GP**	**G**	**A**	**TP**	**PIM**
1980-81	Minn.-Duluth	WCHA	39	6	24	30	48	....	....	....	....	....
1981-82	Minn.-Duluth	WCHA	37	11	31	42	18	....	....	....	....	....
1982-83	Minn.-Duluth	WCHA	26	4	23	27	24	....	....	....	....	....
1983-84ab	Minn.-Duluth	WCHA	43	18	58	76	46	....	....	....	....	....
1984-85	**Montreal**	**NHL**	**75**	**10**	**35**	**45**	**30**	**12**	**0**	**6**	**6**	**6**
1985-86	**Montreal**	**NHL**	**62**	**7**	**23**	**30**	**36**	....	....	....	....	....
1986-87	**Montreal**	**NHL**	**1**	**0**	**0**	**0**	**0**	....	....	....	....	....
	Buffalo	**NHL**	**55**	**6**	**17**	**23**	**22**	....	....	....	....	....
1987-88	**New Jersey**	**NHL**	**56**	**5**	**29**	**34**	**46**	**19**	**6**	**9**	**15**	**38**
1988-89	**New Jersey**	**NHL**	**74**	**16**	**50**	**66**	**38**	....	....	....	....	....
1989-90	**New Jersey**	**NHL**	**1**	**0**	**0**	**0**	**0**	....	....	....	....	....
	Toronto	**NHL**	**70**	**15**	**37**	**52**	**29**	**5**	**0**	**3**	**3**	**4**
1990-91	**Toronto**	**NHL**	**19**	**0**	**3**	**3**	**8**	....	....	....	....	....
	Vancouver	**NHL**	**32**	**4**	**23**	**27**	**20**	**6**	**2**	**2**	**4**	**12**
1991-92	**NY Islanders**	**NHL**	**74**	**9**	**47**	**56**	**30**	....	....	....	....	....
1992-93	**NY Islanders**	**NHL**	**52**	**8**	**30**	**38**	**38**	**12**	**0**	**2**	**2**	**6**
	Capital Dist.	AHL	7	3	4	7	8	....	....	....	....	....
1993-94	**NY Islanders**	**NHL**	**66**	**9**	**31**	**40**	**47**	**3**	**0**	**0**	**0**	**2**
	NHL Totals		**637**	**89**	**325**	**414**	**344**	**57**	**8**	**22**	**30**	**68**

a WCHA First All-Star Team (1984)
b Won Hobey Baker Memorial Award (Top U.S. Collegiate Player) (1984)

Traded to **Buffalo** by **Montreal** for Buffalo's second round choice (Martin St. Amour) in 1988 Entry Draft, November 18, 1986. Traded to **New Jersey** by **Buffalo** for Detroit's third round choice (previously acquired by New Jersey — Buffalo selected Andrew MacVicar) in 1987 Entry Draft, June 13, 1987. Traded to **Toronto** by **New Jersey** for Toronto's first round choice (Scott Niedermayer) in 1991 Entry Draft, October 16, 1989. Traded to **Vancouver** by **Toronto** for Brian Bradley, January 12, 1991. Traded to **Minnesota** by **Vancouver** for Dave Babych, June 22, 1991. Traded to **NY Islanders** by **Minnesota** for Craig Ludwig, June 22, 1991. Traded to **Anaheim** by **NY Islanders** for Troy Loney, June 29, 1994.

KUSHNER, DALE CGY.

Right wing. Shoots left. 6'1", 195 lbs. Born, Terrace, B.C., June 13, 1966.

			Regular Season					Playoffs				
Season	**Club**	**Lea**	**GP**	**G**	**A**	**TP**	**PIM**	**GP**	**G**	**A**	**TP**	**PIM**
1983-84	Prince Albert	WHL	1	2	0	2	5	....	....	....	....	....
1984-85	Prince Albert	WHL	2	0	0	0	2	....	....	....	....	....
	Moose Jaw	WHL	17	5	2	7	23	....	....	....	....	....
	Medicine Hat	WHL	48	23	17	40	173	10	3	3	6	18
1985-86	Medicine Hat	WHL	66	25	19	44	218	25	0	5	5	114
1986-87	Medicine Hat	WHL	63	34	34	68	250	20	8	13	21	57
1987-88	Springfield	AHL	68	13	23	36	201	....	....	....	....	....
1988-89	Springfield	AHL	45	5	8	13	132	....	....	....	....	....
1989-90	**NY Islanders**	**NHL**	**2**	**0**	**0**	**0**	**2**	....	....	....	....	....
	Springfield	AHL	45	14	11	25	163	7	2	3	5	61
1990-91	**Philadelphia**	**NHL**	**63**	**7**	**11**	**18**	**195**	....	....	....	....	....
	Hershey	AHL	5	3	4	7	14	....	....	....	....	....
1991-92	**Philadelphia**	**NHL**	**19**	**3**	**2**	**5**	**18**	....	....	....	....	....
	Hershey	AHL	46	9	7	16	98	6	0	2	2	23
1992-93	Hershey	AHL	26	1	7	8	98	....	....	....	....	....
	Capital Dist.	AHL	7	0	1	1	29	2	1	0	1	29
1993-94	Saint John	AHL	73	20	17	37	199	7	2	1	3	28
	NHL Totals		**84**	**10**	**13**	**23**	**215**	....	....	....	....	....

Signed as a free agent by **NY Islanders**, April 7, 1987. Signed as a free agent by **Philadelphia**, July 31, 1990. Signed as a free agent by **Calgary**, August 10, 1993.

KUWABARA, RYAN (koo-wah-BAH-ruh)

Right wing. Shoots right. 6', 205 lbs. Born, Hamilton, Ont., March 23, 1972.
(Montreal's 2nd choice, 39th overall, in 1990 Entry Draft).

			Regular Season					Playoffs				
Season	**Club**	**Lea**	**GP**	**G**	**A**	**TP**	**PIM**	**GP**	**G**	**A**	**TP**	**PIM**
1989-90	Ottawa	OHL	66	30	38	68	62	4	0	0	0	0
1990-91	Ottawa	OHL	64	34	38	72	67	17	12	15	27	25
1991-92	Ottawa	OHL	66	43	57	100	84	10	6	5	11	9
1992-93	Fredericton	AHL	10	0	2	2	4	....	....	....	....	....
	Wheeling	ECHL	18	7	13	20	22	16	5	8	13	40
1993-94	Fredericton	AHL	44	13	8	21	51	....	....	....	....	....

KVARTALNOV, DMITRI (kvahr-TAHL-nov)

Left wing. Shoots left. 5'11", 180 lbs. Born, Voskresensk, USSR, March 25, 1966.
(Boston's 1st choice, 16th overall, in 1992 Entry Draft).

			Regular Season					Playoffs				
Season	**Club**	**Lea**	**GP**	**G**	**A**	**TP**	**PIM**	**GP**	**G**	**A**	**TP**	**PIM**
1982-83	Khimik	USSR	7	0	0	0	0	....	....	....	....	....
1983-84	Khimik	USSR	2	0	0	0	0	....	....	....	....	....
1984-85	SKA Kalinen	USSR 2				UNAVAILABLE						
1985-86	SKA Kalinen	USSR 2				UNAVAILABLE						
1986-87	Khimik	USSR	40	11	6	17	28	....	....	....	....	....
1987-88	Khimik	USSR	43	16	11	27	16	....	....	....	....	....
1988-89	Khimik	USSR	44	20	12	32	18	....	....	....	....	....
1989-90	Khimik	USSR	46	25	28	53	33	....	....	....	....	....
1990-91	Khimik	USSR	42	12	10	22	18	....	....	....	....	....
1991-92abcd	San Diego	IHL	77	*60	58	*118	16	4	2	0	2	2
1992-93	Khimik	CIS	3	0	0	0	0	....	....	....	....	....
	Boston	**NHL**	**73**	**30**	**42**	**72**	**16**	**4**	**0**	**0**	**0**	**0**
1993-94	**Boston**	**NHL**	**39**	**12**	**7**	**19**	**10**	....	....	....	....	....
	Providence	AHL	23	13	13	26	8	....	....	....	....	....
	NHL Totals		**112**	**42**	**49**	**91**	**26**	**4**	**0**	**0**	**0**	**0**

a Won James Gatschene Memorial Trophy (MVP - IHL) 1992
b Won Leo P. Lamoureaux Memorial Trophy (Top Scorer - IHL) 1992
c Won Garry F. Longman Memorial Trophy (Top Rookie - IHL) 1992
d IHL First All-Star Team (1992)

KYPREOS, NICK (KIH-pree-ohz) NYR

Left wing. Shoots left. 6', 205 lbs. Born, Toronto, Ont., June 4, 1966.

			Regular Season					Playoffs				
Season	**Club**	**Lea**	**GP**	**G**	**A**	**TP**	**PIM**	**GP**	**G**	**A**	**TP**	**PIM**
1983-84	North Bay	OHL	51	12	11	23	36	4	3	2	5	9
1984-85	North Bay	OHL	64	41	36	77	71	8	2	2	4	15
1985-86a	North Bay	OHL	64	62	35	97	112	....	....	....	....	....
1986-87	Hershey	AHL	10	0	1	1	4	....	....	....	....	....
b	North Bay	OHL	46	49	41	90	54	24	11	5	16	78
1987-88	Hershey	AHL	71	24	20	44	101	12	0	2	2	17
1988-89	Hershey	AHL	28	12	15	27	19	12	4	5	9	11
1989-90	**Washington**	**NHL**	**31**	**5**	**4**	**9**	**82**	**7**	**1**	**0**	**1**	**15**
	Baltimore	AHL	14	6	5	11	6	7	4	1	5	17
1990-91	**Washington**	**NHL**	**79**	**9**	**9**	**18**	**196**	**9**	**0**	**1**	**1**	**38**
1991-92	**Washington**	**NHL**	**65**	**4**	**6**	**10**	**206**	....	....	....	....	....
1992-93	**Hartford**	**NHL**	**75**	**17**	**10**	**27**	**325**	....	....	....	....	....
1993-94	**Hartford**	**NHL**	**10**	**0**	**0**	**0**	**37**	....	....	....	....	....
	NY Rangers	**NHL**	**46**	**3**	**5**	**8**	**102**	**3**	**0**	**0**	**0**	**2**
	NHL Totals		**306**	**38**	**34**	**72**	**948**	**19**	**1**	**1**	**2**	**55**

a OHL First All-Star Team (1986)
b OHL Second All-Star Team (1987)

Signed as a free agent by **Philadelphia,** September 30, 1984. Claimed by **Washington** in NHL Waiver Draft, October 2, 1989. Traded to **Hartford** by **Washington** for Mark Hunter and future considerations (Yvon Corriveau, August 20, 1992), June 15, 1992. Traded to **NY Rangers** by **Hartford** with Steve Larmer, Barry Richter and Hartford's sixth round choice (Yuri Litvinov) in 1994 Entry Draft for Darren Turcotte and James Patrick, November 2, 1993.

KYTE, JIM (KITE)

Defense. Shoots left. 6'5", 210 lbs. Born, Ottawa, Ont., March 21, 1964.
(Winnipeg's 1st choice, 12th overall, in 1982 Entry Draft).

			Regular Season					Playoffs				
Season	**Club**	**Lea**	**GP**	**G**	**A**	**TP**	**PIM**	**GP**	**G**	**A**	**TP**	**PIM**
1981-82	Cornwall	OHL	52	4	13	17	148	5	0	0	0	10
1982-83	**Winnipeg**	**NHL**	**2**	**0**	**0**	**0**	**0**	....	....	....	....	....
	Cornwall	OHL	65	6	30	36	195	8	0	2	2	24
1983-84	**Winnipeg**	**NHL**	**58**	**1**	**2**	**3**	**55**	**3**	**0**	**0**	**0**	**11**
1984-85	**Winnipeg**	**NHL**	**71**	**0**	**3**	**3**	**111**	**8**	**0**	**0**	**0**	**14**
1985-86	**Winnipeg**	**NHL**	**71**	**1**	**3**	**4**	**126**	**3**	**0**	**0**	**0**	**12**
1986-87	**Winnipeg**	**NHL**	**72**	**5**	**5**	**10**	**162**	**10**	**0**	**4**	**4**	**36**
1987-88	**Winnipeg**	**NHL**	**51**	**1**	**3**	**4**	**128**	....	....	....	....	....
1988-89	**Winnipeg**	**NHL**	**74**	**3**	**9**	**12**	**190**	....	....	....	....	....
1989-90	**Pittsburgh**	**NHL**	**56**	**3**	**1**	**4**	**125**	....	....	....	....	....
1990-91	**Pittsburgh**	**NHL**	**1**	**0**	**0**	**0**	**2**	....	....	....	....	....
	Muskegon	IHL	25	2	5	7	157	....	....	....	....	....
	Calgary	**NHL**	**42**	**0**	**9**	**9**	**153**	**7**	**0**	**0**	**0**	**7**
1991-92	**Calgary**	**NHL**	**21**	**0**	**1**	**1**	**107**	....	....	....	....	....
	Salt Lake	IHL	6	0	1	1	9	....	....	....	....	....
1992-93	**Ottawa**	**NHL**	**4**	**0**	**1**	**1**	**4**	....	....	....	....	....
	New Haven	AHL	63	6	18	24	163	....	....	....	....	....
1993-94	Las Vegas	IHL	75	2	16	18	246	4	0	1	1	51
	NHL Totals		**523**	**14**	**37**	**51**	**1163**	**31**	**0**	**4**	**4**	**80**

Traded to **Pittsburgh** by **Winnipeg** with Andrew McBain and Randy Gilhen for Randy Cunneyworth, Rick Tabaracci and Dave McLlwain, June 17, 1989. Traded to **Calgary** by **Pittsburgh** for Jiri Hrdina, December 13, 1990. Signed as a free agent by **Ottawa**, September 10, 1992.

LACHANCE, BOB ST.L.

Right wing. Shoots right. 5'11", 180 lbs. Born, Northampton, MA, February 1, 1974.
(St. Louis' 5th choice, 134th overall, in 1992 Entry Draft).

			Regular Season					Playoffs				
Season	**Club**	**Lea**	**GP**	**G**	**A**	**TP**	**PIM**	**GP**	**G**	**A**	**TP**	**PIM**
1992-93	Boston U.	H.E.	33	4	10	14	24	....	....	....	....	....
1993-94	Boston U.	H.E.	32	13	19	32	42	....	....	....	....	....

LACHANCE, SCOTT NYI

Defense. Shoots left. 6'1", 197 lbs. Born, Charlottesville, VA, October 22, 1972.
(NY Islanders' 1st choice, 4th overall, in 1991 Entry Draft).

			Regular Season					Playoffs				
Season	**Club**	**Lea**	**GP**	**G**	**A**	**TP**	**PIM**	**GP**	**G**	**A**	**TP**	**PIM**
1990-91	Boston U.	H.E.	31	5	19	24	48	....	....	....	....	....
1991-92	U.S. National	....	36	1	10	11	34	....	....	....	....	....
	U.S. Olympic	....	8	0	1	1	6	....	....	....	....	....
	NY Islanders	**NHL**	**17**	**1**	**4**	**5**	**9**	....	....	....	....	....
1992-93	**NY Islanders**	**NHL**	**75**	**7**	**17**	**24**	**67**	....	....	....	....	....
1993-94	**NY Islanders**	**NHL**	**74**	**3**	**11**	**14**	**70**	**3**	**0**	**0**	**0**	**0**
	NHL Totals		**166**	**11**	**32**	**43**	**146**	**3**	**0**	**0**	**0**	**0**

LACROIX, DANIEL (luh-KWAH) BOS.

Left wing. Shoots left. 6'2", 188 lbs. Born, Montreal, Que., March 11, 1969.
(NY Rangers' 2nd choice, 31st overall, in 1987 Entry Draft).

			Regular Season					Playoffs				
Season	Club	Lea	GP	G	A	TP	PIM	GP	G	A	TP	PIM
1986-87	Granby	QMJHL	54	9	16	25	311	8	1	2	3	22
1987-88	Granby	QMJHL	58	24	50	74	468	5	0	4	4	12
1988-89	Granby	QMJHL	70	45	49	94	320	4	1	1	2	57
	Denver	IHL	2	0	1	1	0	2	0	1	1	0
1989-90	Flint	IHL	61	12	16	28	128	4	2	0	2	24
1990-91	Binghamton	AHL	54	7	12	19	237	5	1	0	4	24
1991-92	Binghamton	AHL	52	12	20	32	149	11	2	4	6	28
1992-93	Binghamton	AHL	73	21	22	43	255	....	....	....	....	....
1993-94	**NY Rangers**	**NHL**	**4**	**0**	**0**	**0**	**0**	....	....	....	....	....
	Binghamton	AHL	59	20	23	43	278	....	....	....	....	....
	NHL Totals		**4**	**0**	**0**	**0**	**0**	....	....	....	....	....

Traded to **Boston** by **NY Rangers** for Glen Featherstone, August 19, 1994.

LACROIX, ERIC TOR.

Left wing. Shoots left. 6'1", 200 lbs. Born, Montreal, Que., July 15, 1971.
(Toronto's 6th choice, 136th overall, in 1990 Entry Draft).

			Regular Season					Playoffs				
Season	Club	Lea	GP	G	A	TP	PIM	GP	G	A	TP	PIM
1990-91	St. Lawrence	ECAC	35	13	11	24	35	....	....	....	....	....
1991-92	St. Lawrence	ECAC	34	11	20	31	40	....	....	....	....	....
1992-93	St. John's	AHL	76	15	19	34	59	9	5	3	8	4
1993-94	**Toronto**	**NHL**	**3**	**0**	**0**	**0**	**2**	**2**	**0**	**0**	**0**	**0**
	St. John's	AHL	59	17	22	39	69	11	5	3	8	6
	NHL Totals		**3**	**0**	**0**	**0**	**2**	**2**	**0**	**0**	**0**	**0**

LADOUCEUR, RANDY (LAD-uh-SOOR) ANA.

Defense. Shoots left. 6'2", 220 lbs. Born, Brockville, Ont., June 30, 1960.

			Regular Season					Playoffs				
Season	Club	Lea	GP	G	A	TP	PIM	GP	G	A	TP	PIM
1978-79	Brantford	OHA	64	3	17	20	141	....	....	....	....	....
1979-80	Brantford	OHA	37	6	15	21	125	8	0	5	5	18
1980-81	Kalamazoo	IHL	80	7	30	37	52	8	1	3	4	10
1981-82	Adirondack	AHL	78	4	28	32	78	5	1	1	2	6
1982-83	**Detroit**	**NHL**	**27**	**0**	**4**	**4**	**16**	....	....	....	....	....
	Adirondack	AHL	48	11	21	32	54	....	....	....	....	....
1983-84	**Detroit**	**NHL**	**71**	**3**	**17**	**20**	**58**	**4**	**1**	**0**	**1**	**6**
	Adirondack	AHL	11	3	5	8	12	....	....	....	....	....
1984-85	**Detroit**	**NHL**	**80**	**3**	**27**	**30**	**108**	**3**	**1**	**0**	**1**	**0**
1985-86	**Detroit**	**NHL**	**78**	**5**	**13**	**18**	**196**	....	....	....	....	....
1986-87	**Detroit**	**NHL**	**34**	**3**	**6**	**9**	**70**	....	....	....	....	....
	Hartford	**NHL**	**36**	**2**	**3**	**5**	**51**	**6**	**0**	**2**	**2**	**12**
1987-88	**Hartford**	**NHL**	**67**	**1**	**7**	**8**	**91**	**6**	**1**	**1**	**2**	**4**
1988-89	**Hartford**	**NHL**	**75**	**2**	**5**	**7**	**95**	**1**	**0**	**0**	**0**	**10**
1989-90	**Hartford**	**NHL**	**71**	**3**	**12**	**15**	**126**	**7**	**1**	**0**	**1**	**10**
1990-91	**Hartford**	**NHL**	**67**	**1**	**3**	**4**	**118**	**6**	**1**	**4**	**5**	**6**
1991-92	**Hartford**	**NHL**	**74**	**1**	**9**	**10**	**127**	**7**	**0**	**1**	**1**	**11**
1992-93	**Hartford**	**NHL**	**62**	**2**	**4**	**6**	**109**	....	....	....	....	....
1993-94	**Anaheim**	**NHL**	**81**	**1**	**9**	**10**	**74**	....	....	....	....	....
	NHL Totals		**823**	**27**	**119**	**146**	**1239**	**40**	**5**	**8**	**13**	**59**

Signed as a free agent by **Detroit**, November 1, 1979. Traded to **Hartford** by **Detroit** for Dave Barr, January 12, 1987. Claimed by **Anaheim** from **Hartford** in Expansion Draft, June 24, 1993.

La FAYETTE, NATHAN (LAH-fay-eht) VAN.

Center. Shoots right. 6'1", 194 lbs. Born, New Westminster, B.C., February 17, 1973.
(St. Louis' 3rd choice, 65th overall, in 1991 Entry Draft).

			Regular Season					Playoffs				
Season	Club	Lea	GP	G	A	TP	PIM	GP	G	A	TP	PIM
1989-90	Kingston	OHL	53	6	8	14	14	7	0	1	1	0
1990-91	Kingston	OHL	35	13	13	26	10	....	....	....	....	....
	Cornwall	OHL	28	16	22	38	25	....	....	....	....	....
1991-92a	Cornwall	OHL	66	28	45	73	26	6	2	5	7	15
1992-93	Newmarket	OHL	58	49	38	87	26	7	4	5	9	19
1993-94	**St. Louis**	**NHL**	**38**	**2**	**3**	**5**	**14**	....	....	....	....	....
	Peoria	IHL	27	13	11	24	20	....	....	....	....	....
	Vancouver	**NHL**	**11**	**1**	**1**	**2**	**4**	**20**	**2**	**7**	**9**	**4**
	NHL Totals		**49**	**3**	**4**	**7**	**18**	**20**	**2**	**7**	**9**	**4**

a Canadian Major Junior Scholastic Player of the Year (1992)

Traded to **Vancouver** by **St. Louis** with Jeff Brown and Bret Hedican for Craig Janney, March 21, 1994.

LaFONTAINE, PAT (luh-FAHN-tayn) BUF.

Center. Shoots right. 5'10", 177 lbs. Born, St. Louis, MO, February 22, 1965.
(NY Islanders' 1st choice, 3rd overall, in 1983 Entry Draft).

			Regular Season					Playoffs				
Season	Club	Lea	GP	G	A	TP	PIM	GP	G	A	TP	PIM
1982-83ab	Verdun	QMJHL	70	*104	*130	*234	10	15	11	*24	*35	4
1983-84	U.S. National	....	58	56	55	111	22	....	....	....	....	....
	U.S. Olympic	....	6	5	5	10	0	....	....	....	....	....
	NY Islanders	**NHL**	**15**	**13**	**6**	**19**	**6**	**16**	**3**	**6**	**9**	**8**
1984-85	**NY Islanders**	**NHL**	**67**	**19**	**35**	**54**	**32**	**9**	**1**	**2**	**3**	**4**
1985-86	**NY Islanders**	**NHL**	**65**	**30**	**23**	**53**	**43**	**3**	**1**	**0**	**1**	**0**
1986-87	**NY Islanders**	**NHL**	**80**	**38**	**32**	**70**	**70**	**14**	**5**	**7**	**12**	**10**
1987-88	**NY Islanders**	**NHL**	**75**	**47**	**45**	**92**	**52**	**6**	**4**	**5**	**9**	**8**
1988-89	**NY Islanders**	**NHL**	**79**	**45**	**43**	**88**	**26**	....	....	....	....	....
1989-90c	**NY Islanders**	**NHL**	**74**	**54**	**51**	**105**	**38**	**2**	**0**	**1**	**1**	**0**
1990-91	**NY Islanders**	**NHL**	**75**	**41**	**44**	**85**	**42**	....	....	....	....	....
1991-92	**Buffalo**	**NHL**	**57**	**46**	**47**	**93**	**98**	**7**	**8**	**3**	**11**	**4**
1992-93d	**Buffalo**	**NHL**	**84**	**53**	**95**	**148**	**63**	**7**	**2**	**10**	**12**	**0**
1993-94	**Buffalo**	**NHL**	**16**	**5**	**13**	**18**	**2**	....	....	....	....	....
	NHL Totals		**687**	**391**	**434**	**825**	**472**	**64**	**24**	**34**	**58**	**34**

a QMJHL First All-Star Team (1983)
b Canadian Major Junior Player of the Year (1983)
c Won Dodge Performer of the Year Award (1990)
d NHL Second All-Star Team (1993)

Played in NHL All-Star Game (1988-91, 1993)

Traded to **Buffalo** by **NY Islanders** with Randy Hillier, Randy Wood and NY Islanders' fourth round choice (Dean Melanson) in 1992 Entry Draft for Pierre Turgeon, Uwe Krupp, Benoit Hogue and Dave McLlwain, October 25, 1991.

LAFORGE, MARC

Left wing. Shoots left. 6'2", 210 lbs. Born, Sudbury, Ont., January 3, 1968.
(Hartford's 2nd choice, 32nd overall, in 1986 Entry Draft).

			Regular Season					Playoffs				
Season	Club	Lea	GP	G	A	TP	PIM	GP	G	A	TP	PIM
1984-85	Kingston	OHL	57	1	5	6	214	....	....	....	....	....
1985-86	Kingston	OHL	60	1	13	14	248	10	0	1	1	30
1986-87	Binghamton	AHL	....	....	....	....	....	4	0	0	0	7
	Kingston	OHL	53	2	10	12	224	12	1	0	1	79
1987-88	Sudbury	OHL	14	0	2	2	68	....	....	....	....	....
1988-89	Binghamton	AHL	38	2	2	4	179	....	....	....	....	....
	Indianapolis	IHL	14	0	2	2	138	....	....	....	....	....
1989-90	**Hartford**	**NHL**	**9**	**0**	**0**	**0**	**43**	....	....	....	....	....
	Binghamton	AHL	25	2	6	8	111	....	....	....	....	....
	Cape Breton	AHL	3	0	1	1	24	3	0	0	0	27
1990-91	Cape Breton	AHL	49	1	7	8	217	....	....	....	....	....
1991-92	Cape Breton	AHL	59	0	14	14	341	4	0	0	0	24
1992-93	Cape Breton	AHL	77	1	12	13	208	15	1	2	3	*78
1993-94	**Edmonton**	**NHL**	**5**	**0**	**0**	**0**	**21**	....	....	....	....	....
	Cape Breton	AHL	14	0	0	0	91	....	....	....	....	....
	Salt Lake	IHL	43	0	2	2	242	....	....	....	....	....
	NHL Totals		**14**	**0**	**0**	**0**	**64**	....	....	....	....	....

Traded to **Edmonton** by **Hartford** for the rights to Cam Brauer, March 6, 1990. Traded to **NY Islanders** by **Edmonton** for Brent Grieve, December 15, 1993.

LAFRANCE, DARRYL CGY.

Center. Shoots right. 5'11", 175 lbs. Born, Sudbury, Ont., March 20, 1974.
(Calgary's 6th choice, 121st overall, in 1993 Entry Draft).

			Regular Season					Playoffs				
Season	Club	Lea	GP	G	A	TP	PIM	GP	G	A	TP	PIM
1991-92	Oshawa	OHL	48	12	20	32	24	7	0	1	1	2
1992-93	Oshawa	OHL	66	35	51	86	24	13	8	8	16	0
1993-94	Oshawa	OHL	61	45	61	106	17	5	1	9	10	0

LAFRENIERE, JASON (LAH-frehn-YAIR)

Center. Shoots right. 5'11", 185 lbs. Born, St. Catharines, Ont., December 6, 1966.
(Quebec's 2nd choice, 36th overall, in 1985 Entry Draft).

			Regular Season					Playoffs				
Season	Club	Lea	GP	G	A	TP	PIM	GP	G	A	TP	PIM
1983-84	Brantford	OHL	70	24	57	81	4	6	2	4	6	2
1984-85	Hamilton	OHL	59	26	69	95	10	17	12	16	28	0
1985-86	Hamilton	OHL	14	12	10	22	2	....	....	....	....	....
a	Belleville	OHL	48	37	73	110	2	23	10	*22	*32	6
1986-87	**Quebec**	**NHL**	**56**	**13**	**15**	**28**	**8**	**12**	**1**	**5**	**6**	**2**
	Fredericton	AHL	11	3	11	14	0	....	....	....	....	....
1987-88	**Quebec**	**NHL**	**40**	**10**	**19**	**29**	**4**	....	....	....	....	....
	Fredericton	AHL	32	12	19	31	38	....	....	....	....	....
1988-89	**NY Rangers**	**NHL**	**38**	**8**	**16**	**24**	**6**	**3**	**0**	**0**	**0**	**17**
	Denver	IHL	24	10	19	29	17	....	....	....	....	....
1989-90	Flint	IHL	41	9	25	34	34	....	....	....	....	....
	Phoenix	IHL	14	4	9	13	0	....	....	....	....	....
1990-91	Cdn. National	....	59	26	33	59	50	....	....	....	....	....
1991-92	Landshut	Ger.	23	7	22	29	16	....	....	....	....	....
	San Diego	IHL	5	1	2	3	2	....	....	....	....	....
1992-93	**Tampa Bay**	**NHL**	**11**	**3**	**3**	**6**	**4**	....	....	....	....	....
	Atlanta	IHL	63	23	47	70	34	9	3	4	7	22
1993-94	**Tampa Bay**	**NHL**	**1**	**0**	**0**	**0**	**0**	....	....	....	....	....
	Milwaukee	IHL	52	14	47	61	16	....	....	....	....	....
	NHL Totals		**146**	**34**	**53**	**87**	**22**	**15**	**1**	**5**	**6**	**19**

a OHL First All-Star Team (1986)

Traded to **NY Rangers** by **Quebec** with Normand Rochefort for Bruce Bell, Jari Gronstrand, Walt Poddubny and NY Rangers' fourth round choice (Eric Dubois) in 1989 Entry Draft, August 1, 1988. Signed as a free agent by **Tampa Bay**, July 29, 1992.

LALOR, MIKE (LAH-luhr) DAL.

Defense. Shoots left. 6', 200 lbs. Born, Buffalo, NY, March 8, 1963.

			Regular Season					Playoffs				
Season	Club	Lea	GP	G	A	TP	PIM	GP	G	A	TP	PIM
1981-82	Brantford	OHL	64	3	13	16	114	11	0	6	6	11
1982-83	Brantford	OHL	65	10	30	40	113	8	1	3	4	20
1983-84	Nova Scotia	AHL	67	5	11	16	80	12	0	2	2	13
1984-85	Sherbrooke	AHL	79	9	23	32	114	17	3	5	8	36
1985-86	**Montreal**	**NHL**	**62**	**3**	**5**	**8**	**56**	**17**	**1**	**2**	**3**	**29**
1986-87	**Montreal**	**NHL**	**57**	**0**	**10**	**10**	**47**	**13**	**2**	**1**	**3**	**29**
1987-88	**Montreal**	**NHL**	**66**	**1**	**10**	**11**	**113**	**11**	**0**	**0**	**0**	**11**
1988-89	**Montreal**	**NHL**	**12**	**1**	**4**	**5**	**15**	....	....	....	....	....
	St. Louis	**NHL**	**36**	**1**	**14**	**15**	**54**	**10**	**1**	**1**	**2**	**14**
1989-90	**St. Louis**	**NHL**	**78**	**0**	**16**	**16**	**81**	**12**	**0**	**2**	**2**	**31**
1990-91	**Washington**	**NHL**	**68**	**1**	**5**	**6**	**61**	**10**	**1**	**2**	**3**	**22**
1991-92	**Washington**	**NHL**	**64**	**5**	**7**	**12**	**64**	....	....	....	....	....
	Winnipeg	**NHL**	**15**	**2**	**3**	**5**	**14**	**7**	**0**	**0**	**0**	**19**
1992-93	**Winnipeg**	**NHL**	**64**	**1**	**8**	**9**	**76**	**4**	**0**	**2**	**2**	**4**
1993-94	**San Jose**	**NHL**	**23**	**0**	**2**	**2**	**8**	....	....	....	....	....
	Dallas	**NHL**	**12**	**0**	**1**	**1**	**6**	**5**	**0**	**0**	**0**	**6**
	NHL Totals		**557**	**15**	**85**	**100**	**595**	**89**	**5**	**10**	**15**	**165**

Signed as a free agent by **Montreal**, September, 1983. Traded to **St. Louis** by **Montreal** with Montreal's first round choice (later traded to Vancouver — Vancouver selected Shawn Antoski) in 1990 Entry Draft for St. Louis' first round choice (Turner Stevenson) in 1990 Entry Draft, January 16, 1989. Traded to **Washington** by **St. Louis** with Peter Zezel for Geoff Courtnall, July 13, 1990. Traded to **Winnipeg** by **Washington** for Paul MacDermid, March 2, 1992. Signed as a free agent by **San Jose**, August 13, 1993. Traded to **Dallas** by **San Jose** with Doug Zmolek for Ulf Dahlen and a future draft choice, March 19, 1994.

LAMB, MARK — PHI.

Center. Shoots left. 5'9", 180 lbs. Born, Ponteix, Sask., August 3, 1964.
(Calgary's 5th choice, 72nd overall, in 1982 Entry Draft).

			Regular Season					Playoffs				
Season	Club	Lea	GP	G	A	TP	PIM	GP	G	A	TP	PIM
1981-82	Billings	WHL	72	45	56	101	46	5	4	6	10	4
1982-83	Nanaimo	WHL	30	14	37	51	16	....	....	....	....	....
	Medicine Hat	WHL	46	22	43	65	33	5	3	2	5	4
	Colorado	CHL	....	....	....	....	....	6	0	2	2	0
1983-84a	Medicine Hat	WHL	72	59	77	136	30	14	12	11	23	6
1984-85	Moncton	AHL	80	23	49	72	53	....	....	....	....	....
1985-86	**Calgary**	**NHL**	**1**	**0**	**0**	**0**	**0**	....	....	....	....	....
	Moncton	AHL	79	26	50	76	51	10	2	6	8	17
1986-87	**Detroit**	**NHL**	**22**	**2**	**1**	**3**	**8**	**11**	**0**	**0**	**0**	**11**
	Adirondack	AHL	49	14	36	50	45	....	....	....	....	....
1987-88	**Edmonton**	**NHL**	**2**	**0**	**0**	**0**	**0**	....	....	....	....	....
	Nova Scotia	AHL	69	27	61	88	45	5	0	5	5	6
1988-89	**Edmonton**	**NHL**	**20**	**2**	**8**	**10**	**14**	**6**	**0**	**2**	**2**	**8**
	Cape Breton	AHL	54	33	49	82	29	....	....	....	....	....
1989-90	**Edmonton**	**NHL**	**58**	**12**	**16**	**28**	**42**	**22**	**6**	**11**	**17**	**2**
1990-91	**Edmonton**	**NHL**	**37**	**4**	**8**	**12**	**25**	**15**	**0**	**5**	**5**	**20**
1991-92	**Edmonton**	**NHL**	**59**	**6**	**22**	**28**	**46**	**16**	**1**	**1**	**2**	**10**
1992-93	**Ottawa**	**NHL**	**71**	**7**	**19**	**26**	**64**	....	....	....	....	....
1993-94	**Ottawa**	**NHL**	**66**	**11**	**18**	**29**	**56**	....	....	....	....	....
	Philadelphia	**NHL**	**19**	**1**	**6**	**7**	**16**	....	....	....	....	....
	NHL Totals		**355**	**45**	**98**	**143**	**271**	**70**	**7**	**19**	**26**	**51**

a WHL East First All-Star Team (1984)

Signed as a free agent by **Detroit**, July 28, 1986. Claimed by **Edmonton** in NHL Waiver Draft, October 5, 1987. Claimed by **Ottawa** from **Edmonton** in Expansion Draft, June 18, 1992. Traded to **Philadelphia** by **Ottawa** for Claude Boivin and Kirk Daubenspeck, March 5, 1994.

LAMBERT, DAN

Defense. Shoots left. 5'8", 177 lbs. Born, St. Boniface, Man., January 12, 1970.
(Quebec's 8th choice, 106th overall, in 1989 Entry Draft).

			Regular Season					Playoffs				
Season	Club	Lea	GP	G	A	TP	PIM	GP	G	A	TP	PIM
1986-87	Swift Current	WHL	68	13	53	66	95	4	1	1	2	9
1987-88	Swift Current	WHL	69	20	63	83	120	10	2	10	12	45
1988-89ab	Swift Current	WHL	57	25	77	102	158	12	9	19	28	12
1989-90a	Swift Current	WHL	50	17	51	68	119	4	2	3	5	12
1990-91	**Quebec**	**NHL**	**1**	**0**	**0**	**0**	**0**	....	....	....	....	....
	Halifax	AHL	30	7	13	20	20	....	....	....	....	....
	Fort Wayne	IHL	49	10	27	37	65	19	4	10	14	20
1991-92	**Quebec**	**NHL**	**28**	**6**	**9**	**15**	**22**	....	....	....	....	....
	Halifax	AHL	47	3	28	31	33	....	....	....	....	....
1992-93	Moncton	AHL	73	11	30	41	100	5	1	2	3	2
1993-94	HIFK	Fin.	13	1	2	3	8	....	....	....	....	....
	Fort Wayne	IHL	62	10	27	37	138	18	3	12	15	20
	NHL Totals		**29**	**6**	**9**	**15**	**22**	....	....	....	....	....

a WHL East First All-Star Team (1989, 1990)
b Memorial Cup All-Star Team (1989)

Traded to **Winnipeg** by **Quebec** for Shawn Cronin, August 25, 1992.

LAMBERT, DENNY — ANA.

Left wing. Shoots left. 5'11", 200 lbs. Born, Wawa, Ont., January 7, 1970.

			Regular Season					Playoffs				
Season	Club	Lea	GP	G	A	TP	PIM	GP	G	A	TP	PIM
1988-89	S.S. Marie	OHL	61	14	15	29	2032	....	....	....	....	....
1989-90	S.S. Marie	OHL	61	23	29	52	276	....	....	....	....	....
1990-91	S.S. Marie	OHL	59	28	39	67	169	14	7	9	16	48
1991-92	San Diego	IHL	71	17	14	31	229	3	0	0	0	10
	St. Thomas	ColHL	5	2	6	8	9	....	....	....	....	....
1992-93	San Diego	IHL	56	18	12	30	277	14	1	1	2	44
1993-94	San Diego	IHL	79	13	14	27	314	6	1	0	1	55

Signed as a free agent by **Anaheim**, August 16, 1993.

LAMMENS, HANK

Defense. Shoots left. 6'2", 210 lbs. Born, Brockville, Ont., February 21, 1966.
(NY Islanders' 10th choice, 160th overall, in 1985 Entry Draft).

			Regular Season					Playoffs				
Season	Club	Lea	GP	G	A	TP	PIM	GP	G	A	TP	PIM
1984-85	St. Lawrence	ECAC	21	17	9	26	16	....	....	....	....	....
1985-86	St. Lawrence	ECAC	30	3	14	17	60	....	....	....	....	....
1986-87ab	St. Lawrence	ECAC	35	6	13	19	92	....	....	....	....	....
1987-88a	St. Lawrence	ECAC	32	3	6	9	64	....	....	....	....	....
1988-89	Springfield	AHL	69	1	13	14	55	....	....	....	....	....
1989-90	Springfield	AHL	43	0	6	6	27	....	....	....	....	....
1990-91	Capital Dist.	AHL	32	0	5	5	14	....	....	....	....	....
	Kansas City	IHL	17	0	1	1	27	....	....	....	....	....
1992-93	Cdn. National	....	75	8	22	30	75	....	....	....	....	....
1993-94	**Ottawa**	**NHL**	**27**	**1**	**2**	**3**	**22**	....	....	....	....	....
	PEI	AHL	50	2	9	11	32	....	....	....	....	....
	NHL Totals		**27**	**1**	**2**	**3**	**22**	....	....	....	....	....

a ECAC Second All-Star Team (1987, 1988)
b NCAA East Second All-American Team (1987)

Signed as a free agent by **Ottawa**, June 25, 1993.

LANG, BILL — DAL.

Center. Shoots right. 5'10", 181 lbs. Born, Newmarket, Ont., July 16, 1973.
(Dallas' 9th choice, 249th overall, in 1993 Entry Draft).

			Regular Season					Playoffs				
Season	Club	Lea	GP	G	A	TP	PIM	GP	G	A	TP	PIM
1990-91	North Bay	OHL	65	14	23	37	82	9	0	1	1	18
1991-92	North Bay	OHL	62	24	37	61	101	21	5	8	13	38
1992-93	North Bay	OHL	64	45	50	95	112	5	4	3	7	9
1993-94	North Bay	OHL	58	22	51	73	118	18	9	12	21	43

LANG, ROBERT — (LUHNG) — L.A.

Center. Shoots right. 6'2", 189 lbs. Born, Teplice, Czech., December 19, 1970.
(Los Angeles' 6th choice, 133rd overall, in 1990 Entry Draft).

			Regular Season					Playoffs				
Season	Club	Lea	GP	G	A	TP	PIM	GP	G	A	TP	PIM
1988-89	Litvinov	Czech.	7	3	2	5	0	....	....	....	....	....
1989-90	Litvinov	Czech.	39	11	10	21	....	....	....	....	....	....
1990-91	Litvinov	Czech.	56	26	26	52	38	....	....	....	....	....
1991-92	Litvinov	Czech.	43	12	31	43	34	....	....	....	....	....
1992-93	**Los Angeles**	**NHL**	**11**	**0**	**5**	**5**	**2**	....	....	....	....	....
	Phoenix	IHL	38	9	21	30	20	....	....	....	....	....
1993-94	**Los Angeles**	**NHL**	**32**	**9**	**10**	**19**	**10**	....	....	....	....	....
	Phoenix	IHL	44	11	24	35	34	....	....	....	....	....
	NHL Totals		**43**	**9**	**15**	**24**	**12**	....	....	....	....	....

LANGDON, DARREN — NYR

Left wing. Shoots left. 6'1", 200 lbs. Born, Deer Lake, Nfld., January 8, 1971.

			Regular Season					Playoffs				
Season	Club	Lea	GP	G	A	TP	PIM	GP	G	A	TP	PIM
1991-92	Summerside	MJHL	44	34	49	83	441	....	....	....	....	....
1992-93	Binghamton	AHL	18	3	4	7	115	8	0	1	1	14
	Dayton	ECHL	54	23	22	45	429	3	0	1	1	40
1993-94	Binghamton	AHL	54	2	7	9	327	....	....	....	....	....

Signed as a free agent by **NY Rangers**, August 16, 1993.

LANGENBRUNNER, JAMIE — DAL.

Center. Shoots right. 5'11", 180 lbs. Born, Duluth, MN, July 24, 1975.
(Dallas' 2nd choice, 35th overall, in 1993 Entry Draft).

			Regular Season					Playoffs				
Season	Club	Lea	GP	G	A	TP	PIM	GP	G	A	TP	PIM
1992-93	Cloquet	HS	27	27	62	89	18	....	....	....	....	....
1993-94	Peterborough	OHL	62	33	58	91	53	7	4	6	10	2

LANIEL, MARC

Defense. Shoots left. 6'1", 194 lbs. Born, Oshawa, Ont., January 16, 1968.
(New Jersey's 4th choice, 62nd overall, in 1986 Entry Draft).

			Regular Season					Playoffs				
Season	Club	Lea	GP	G	A	TP	PIM	GP	G	A	TP	PIM
1985-86	Oshawa	OHL	66	9	25	34	27	6	2	3	5	6
1986-87	Oshawa	OHL	63	14	31	45	42	26	3	13	16	20
1987-88	Oshawa	OHL	41	8	32	40	56	7	2	2	4	4
	Utica	AHL	2	0	0	0	....	....	....	....	....	....
1988-89	Utica	AHL	80	6	28	34	43	5	0	1	1	2
1989-90	Utica	AHL	20	0	0	0	25	....	....	....	....	....
	Phoenix	IHL	26	3	15	18	10	....	....	....	....	....
1990-91	Utica	AHL	57	6	9	15	45	....	....	....	....	....
1991-92	San Diego	AHL	10	0	2	2	16	....	....	....	....	....
	Winston-Salem	ECHL	57	15	36	51	90	....	....	....	....	....
1992-93	Cincinnati	IHL	13	1	9	10	2	....	....	....	....	....
	Birmingham	ECHL	21	5	9	14	26	....	....	....	....	....
	Fredericton	AHL	7	0	1	1	6	5	0	2	2	23
1993-94	Fredericton	AHL	79	6	41	47	76	....	....	....	....	....

Signed as a free agent by **Montreal**, May 3, 1993.

LANK, JEFF — MTL.

Defense. Shoots left. 6'3", 185 lbs. Born, Indian Head, Sask., March 1, 1975.
(Montreal's 6th choice, 113th overall, in 1993 Entry Draft).

			Regular Season					Playoffs				
Season	Club	Lea	GP	G	A	TP	PIM	GP	G	A	TP	PIM
1991-92	Prince Albert	WHL	56	2	8	10	26	9	0	0	0	2
1992-93	Prince Albert	WHL	63	1	11	12	60	....	....	....	....	....
1993-94	Prince Albert	WHL	72	9	38	47	62	....	....	....	....	....

LAPERRIERE, DANIEL — (luh-PAIR-ee-YAIR) — ST.L.

Defense. Shoots left. 6'1", 195 lbs. Born, Laval, Que., March 28, 1969.
(St. Louis' 4th choice, 93rd overall, in 1989 Entry Draft).

			Regular Season					Playoffs				
Season	Club	Lea	GP	G	A	TP	PIM	GP	G	A	TP	PIM
1988-89	St. Lawrence	ECAC	28	0	7	7	10	....	....	....	....	....
1989-90	St. Lawrence	ECAC	31	6	19	25	16	....	....	....	....	....
1990-91a	St. Lawrence	ECAC	34	7	31	38	18	....	....	....	....	....
1991-92bc	St. Lawrence	ECAC	32	8	*45	53	36	....	....	....	....	....
1992-93	**St. Louis**	**NHL**	**5**	**0**	**1**	**1**	**0**	....	....	....	....	....
	Peoria	IHL	54	4	20	24	28	....	....	....	....	....
1993-94	**St. Louis**	**NHL**	**20**	**1**	**3**	**4**	**8**	....	....	....	....	....
	Peoria	IHL	56	10	37	47	16	6	0	2	2	2
	NHL Totals		**25**	**1**	**4**	**5**	**8**	....	....	....	....	....

a ECAC Second All-Star Team (1991)
b ECAC First All-Star Team (1992)
c NCAA East First All-American Team (1992)

LAPERRIERE, IAN — (luh-PAIR-ee-YAIR, EE-ihn) — ST.L.

Center. Shoots right. 6', 191 lbs. Born, Montreal, Que., January 19, 1974.
(St. Louis' 6th choice, 158th overall, in 1992 Entry Draft).

			Regular Season					Playoffs				
Season	Club	Lea	GP	G	A	TP	PIM	GP	G	A	TP	PIM
1990-91	Drummondville	QMJHL	65	19	29	48	117	14	2	9	11	48
1991-92	Drummondville	QMJHL	70	28	49	77	160	4	2	2	4	9
1992-93a	Drummondville	QMJHL	60	44	*96	140	188	10	6	13	19	20
1993-94	**St. Louis**	**NHL**	**1**	**0**	**0**	**0**	**0**	....	....	....	....	....
	Drummondville	QMJHL	62	41	72	113	150	9	4	6	10	35
	Peoria	IHL	....	....	....	....	....	5	1	3	4	2
	NHL Totals		**1**	**0**	**0**	**0**	**0**	....	....	....	....	....

a QMJHL Second All-Star Team (1993)

LAPIN, MIKHAIL — (LAH-pihn) — TOR.

Defense. Shoots left. 6'2", 190 lbs. Born, Moscow, USSR, May 12, 1975.
(Toronto's 8th choice, 279th overall, in 1993 Entry Draft).

			Regular Season					Playoffs				
Season	Club	Lea	GP	G	A	TP	PIM	GP	G	A	TP	PIM
1992-93	W. Michigan	CCHA	30	0	3	3	58	....	....	....	....	....
1993-94	W. Michigan	CCHA	35	6	9	15	68	....	....	....	....	....

LAPOINTE, CLAUDE (luh-PWAH, KLOHD) QUE.

Center. Shoots left. 5'9", 181 lbs. Born, Lachine, Que., October 11, 1968.
(Quebec's 12th choice, 234th overall, in 1988 Entry Draft).

			Regular Season					Playoffs				
Season	Club	Lea	GP	G	A	TP	PIM	GP	G	A	TP	PIM
1986-87	Trois-Rivières	QMJHL	70	47	57	104	123	....	....	....	....	....
1987-88	Laval	QMJHL	69	37	83	120	143	13	2	17	19	53
1988-89	Laval	QMJHL	63	32	72	104	158	17	5	14	19	66
1989-90	Halifax	AHL	63	18	19	37	51	6	1	1	2	34
1990-91	**Quebec**	**NHL**	**13**	**2**	**2**	**4**	**4**	....	....	....	....	....
	Halifax	AHL	43	17	17	34	46	....	....	....	....	....
1991-92	**Quebec**	**NHL**	**78**	**13**	**20**	**33**	**86**	....	....	....	....	....
1992-93	**Quebec**	**NHL**	**74**	**10**	**26**	**36**	**98**	**6**	**2**	**4**	**6**	**8**
1993-94	**Quebec**	**NHL**	**59**	**11**	**17**	**28**	**70**	....	....	....	....	....
	NHL Totals		**224**	**36**	**65**	**101**	**258**	**6**	**2**	**4**	**6**	**8**

LAPOINTE, MARTIN (luh-POYNT, MAHR-tai) DET.

Right wing. Shoots right. 5'11", 200 lbs. Born, Lachine, Que., September 12, 1973.
(Detroit's 1st choice, 10th overall, in 1991 Entry Draft).

			Regular Season					Playoffs				
Season	Club	Lea	GP	G	A	TP	PIM	GP	G	A	TP	PIM
1989-90a	Laval	QMJHL	65	42	54	96	77	14	8	17	25	54
1990-91b	Laval	QMJHL	64	44	54	98	66	13	7	14	21	26
1991-92	**Detroit**	**NHL**	**4**	**0**	**1**	**1**	**5**	**3**	**0**	**1**	**1**	**4**
	Laval	QMJHL	31	25	30	55	84	10	4	10	14	32
	Adirondack	AHL	....	....	....	....	....	8	2	2	4	4
1992-93	**Detroit**	**NHL**	**3**	**0**	**0**	**0**	**0**	....	....	....	....	....
ac	Laval	QMJHL	35	38	51	89	41	13	*13	*17	*30	22
	Adirondack	AHL	8	1	2	3	9	....	....	....	....	....
1993-94	**Detroit**	**NHL**	**50**	**8**	**8**	**16**	**55**	**4**	**0**	**0**	**0**	**6**
	Adirondack	AHL	28	25	21	46	47	4	1	1	2	8
	NHL Totals		**57**	**8**	**9**	**17**	**60**	**7**	**0**	**1**	**1**	**10**

a QMJHL First All-Star Team (1990, 1993)
b QMJHL Second All-Star Team (1991)
c Memorial Cup All-Star Team (1993)

LAPORTE, ALEXANDRE T.B.

Defense. Shoots right. 6'3", 210 lbs. Born, Cowansville, Que., May 1, 1975.
(Tampa Bay's 9th choice, 211th overall, in 1993 Entry Draft).

			Regular Season					Playoffs				
Season	Club	Lea	GP	G	A	TP	PIM	GP	G	A	TP	PIM
1991-92	Victoriaville	QMJHL	44	1	4	5	43	....	....	....	....	....
1992-93	Victoriaville	QMJHL	56	1	3	4	30	6	0	0	0	2
1993-94	Victoriaville	QMJHL	56	3	9	12	68	5	1	0	1	2

LARIONOV, IGOR (LAIR-ee-AH-nohv) S.J.

Center. Shoots left. 5'9", 170 lbs. Born, Voskresensk, USSR, December 3, 1960.
(Vancouver's 11th choice, 214th overall, in 1985 Entry Draft).

			Regular Season					Playoffs				
Season	Club	Lea	GP	G	A	TP	PIM	GP	G	A	TP	PIM
1977-78	Khimik	USSR	6	3	0	3	4	....	....	....	....	....
1978-79	Khimik	USSR	32	3	4	7	12	....	....	....	....	....
1979-80	Khimik	USSR	42	11	7	18	24	....	....	....	....	....
1980-81	Khimik	USSR	43	22	23	45	36	....	....	....	....	....
1981-82	CSKA	USSR	46	31	22	53	6	....	....	....	....	....
1982-83a	CSKA	USSR	44	20	19	39	20	....	....	....	....	....
1983-84	CSKA	USSR	43	15	26	41	30	....	....	....	....	....
1984-85	CSKA	USSR	40	18	28	46	20	....	....	....	....	....
1985-86a	CSKA	USSR	40	21	31	52	33	....	....	....	....	....
1986-87a	CSKA	USSR	39	20	26	46	34	....	....	....	....	....
1987-88ab	CSKA	USSR	51	25	32	57	54	....	....	....	....	....
1988-89	CSKA	USSR	31	15	12	27	22	....	....	....	....	....
1989-90	**Vancouver**	**NHL**	**74**	**17**	**27**	**44**	**20**	....	....	....	....	....
1990-91	**Vancouver**	**NHL**	**64**	**13**	**21**	**34**	**14**	**6**	**1**	**0**	**1**	**6**
1991-92	**Vancouver**	**NHL**	**72**	**21**	**44**	**65**	**54**	**13**	**3**	**7**	**10**	**4**
1992-93	Lugano	Switz.	24	10	19	29	44	....	....	....	....	....
1993-94	**San Jose**	**NHL**	**60**	**18**	**38**	**56**	**40**	**14**	**5**	**13**	**18**	**10**
	NHL Totals		**270**	**69**	**130**	**199**	**128**	**33**	**9**	**20**	**29**	**20**

a Soviet National League All-Star (1983, 1985-88)
b Soviet Player of the Year (1988)

Claimed by **San Jose** from **Vancouver** in NHL Waiver Draft, October 4, 1992.

LARKIN, MIKE CHI.

Defense. Shoots right. 6'1", 180 lbs. Born, Boston, MA, March 15, 1973.
(Chicago's 11th choice, 242nd overall, in 1991 Entry Draft).

			Regular Season					Playoffs				
Season	Club	Lea	GP	G	A	TP	PIM	GP	G	A	TP	PIM
1991-92	U. of Vermont	ECAC	14	2	2	4	14	....	....	....	....	....
1992-93	U. of Vermont	ECAC	28	0	2	2	66	....	....	....	....	....
1993-94	U. of Vermont	ECAC	32	4	3	7	72	....	....	....	....	....

LARMER, STEVE NYR

Right wing. Shoots left. 5'11", 185 lbs. Born, Peterborough, Ont., June 16, 1961.
(Chicago's 11th choice, 120th overall, in 1980 Entry Draft).

			Regular Season					Playoffs				
Season	Club	Lea	GP	G	A	TP	PIM	GP	G	A	TP	PIM
1977-78	Peterborough	OHA	62	24	17	41	51	18	5	7	12	27
1978-79	Niagara Falls	OHA	66	37	47	84	108	....	....	....	....	....
1979-80	Niagara Falls	OHA	67	45	69	114	71	10	5	9	14	15
1980-81	**Chicago**	**NHL**	**4**	**0**	**1**	**1**	**0**	....	....	....	....	....
a	Niagara Falls	OHA	61	55	78	133	73	12	13	8	21	24
1981-82	**Chicago**	**NHL**	**3**	**0**	**0**	**0**	**0**	....	....	....	....	....
b	New Brunswick	AHL	74	38	44	82	46	15	6	6	12	0
1982-83cd	**Chicago**	**NHL**	**80**	**43**	**47**	**90**	**28**	**11**	**5**	**7**	**12**	**8**
1983-84	**Chicago**	**NHL**	**80**	**35**	**40**	**75**	**34**	**5**	**2**	**2**	**4**	**7**
1984-85	**Chicago**	**NHL**	**80**	**46**	**40**	**86**	**16**	**15**	**9**	**13**	**22**	**14**
1985-86	**Chicago**	**NHL**	**80**	**31**	**45**	**76**	**47**	**3**	**0**	**3**	**3**	**4**
1986-87	**Chicago**	**NHL**	**80**	**28**	**56**	**84**	**22**	**4**	**0**	**0**	**0**	**2**
1987-88	**Chicago**	**NHL**	**80**	**41**	**48**	**89**	**42**	**5**	**1**	**6**	**7**	**0**
1988-89	**Chicago**	**NHL**	**80**	**43**	**44**	**87**	**54**	**16**	**8**	**9**	**17**	**22**
1989-90	**Chicago**	**NHL**	**80**	**31**	**59**	**90**	**40**	**20**	**7**	**15**	**22**	**2**
1990-91	**Chicago**	**NHL**	**80**	**44**	**57**	**101**	**79**	**6**	**5**	**1**	**6**	**4**
1991-92	**Chicago**	**NHL**	**80**	**29**	**45**	**74**	**65**	**18**	**8**	**7**	**15**	**6**
1992-93	**Chicago**	**NHL**	**84**	**35**	**35**	**70**	**48**	**4**	**0**	**3**	**3**	**0**
1993-94	**NY Rangers**	**NHL**	**68**	**21**	**39**	**60**	**41**	**23**	**9**	**7**	**16**	**14**
	NHL Totals		**959**	**427**	**556**	**983**	**516**	**130**	**54**	**73**	**127**	**83**

a OHA Second All-Star Team (1981)
b AHL Second All-Star Team (1982)
c Won Calder Trophy (1983)
d NHL All-Rookie Team (1983)

Played in NHL All-Star Game (1990, 1991)

Traded to **Hartford** by **Chicago** with Bryan Marchment for Eric Weinrich and Patrick Poulin, November 2, 1993. Traded to **NY Rangers** by **Hartford** with Nick Kypreos, Barry Richter and Hartford's sixth round choice (Yuri Litvinov) in 1994 Entry Draft for Darren Turcotte and James Patrick, November 2, 1993.

LAROCQUE, STEPHANE NYI

Right wing. Shoots right. 6'1", 214 lbs. Born, Hull, Que., July 24, 1974.
(NY Islanders' 10th choice, 248th overall, in 1993 Entry Draft).

			Regular Season					Playoffs				
Season	Club	Lea	GP	G	A	TP	PIM	GP	G	A	TP	PIM
1991-92	Victoriaville	QMJHL	50	8	10	18	77	....	....	....	....	....
1992-93	Sherbrooke	QMJHL	70	44	42	86	129	14	5	9	14	35
1993-94	Drummondville	QMJHL	59	37	51	88	113	10	3	8	11	17

LAROSE, BENOIT DET.

Defense. Shoots left. 6', 200 lbs. Born, Ottawa, Ont., May 31, 1973.
(Detroit's 5th choice, 100th overall, in 1993 Entry Draft).

			Regular Season					Playoffs				
Season	Club	Lea	GP	G	A	TP	PIM	GP	G	A	TP	PIM
1991-92a	Laval	QMJHL	70	11	53	64	171	10	5	6	11	20
1992-93b	Laval	QMJHL	63	16	62	78	218	8	1	6	7	10
1993-94	Shawinigan	QMJHL	61	2	21	23	120	5	0	1	1	21

a QMJHL Second All-Star Team (1992)
b QMJHL First All-Star Team (1993)

LAROSE, GUY (luh-ROHS)

Center. Shoots left. 5'9", 180 lbs. Born, Hull, Que., August 31, 1967.
(Buffalo's 11th choice, 224th overall, in 1985 Entry Draft).

			Regular Season					Playoffs				
Season	Club	Lea	GP	G	A	TP	PIM	GP	G	A	TP	PIM
1984-85	Guelph	OHL	58	30	30	60	63	....	....	....	....	....
1985-86	Guelph	OHL	37	12	36	48	55	....	....	....	....	....
	Ottawa	OHL	28	19	25	44	63	....	....	....	....	....
1986-87	Ottawa	OHL	66	28	49	77	77	11	2	8	10	27
1987-88	Moncton	AHL	77	22	31	53	127	....	....	....	....	....
1988-89	**Winnipeg**	**NHL**	**3**	**0**	**1**	**1**	**6**	....	....	....	....	....
	Moncton	AHL	72	32	27	59	176	10	4	4	8	37
1989-90	Moncton	AHL	79	44	26	70	232	....	....	....	....	....
1990-91	**Winnipeg**	**NHL**	**7**	**0**	**0**	**0**	**8**	....	....	....	....	....
	Moncton	AHL	35	14	10	24	60	....	....	....	....	....
	Binghamton	AHL	34	21	15	36	48	10	8	5	13	37
1991-92	Binghamton	AHL	30	10	11	21	36	....	....	....	....	....
	Toronto	**NHL**	**34**	**9**	**5**	**14**	**27**	....	....	....	....	....
	St. John's	AHL	15	7	7	14	26	....	....	....	....	....
1992-93	**Toronto**	**NHL**	**9**	**0**	**0**	**0**	**8**	....	....	....	....	....
	St. John's	AHL	5	0	1	1	8	9	5	2	7	6
1993-94	**Toronto**	**NHL**	**10**	**1**	**2**	**3**	**10**	....	....	....	....	....
	St. John's	AHL	23	13	16	29	41	....	....	....	....	....
	Calgary	**NHL**	**7**	**0**	**1**	**1**	**4**	....	....	....	....	....
	Saint John	AHL	15	11	11	22	20	7	3	2	5	22
	NHL Totals		**70**	**10**	**9**	**19**	**63**	....	....	....	....	....

Signed as a free agent by **Winnipeg**, July 16, 1987. Traded to **NY Rangers** by **Winnipeg** for Rudy Poeschek, January 22, 1991. Traded to **Toronto** by **NY Rangers** for Mike Stevens, December 26, 1991. Claimed on waivers by **Calgary** from **Toronto**, January 1, 1994.

LAROUCHE, STEVE

Center. Shoots right. 6', 180 lbs. Born, Rouyn, Que., April 14, 1971.
(Montreal's 3rd choice, 41st overall, in 1989 Entry Draft).

			Regular Season					Playoffs				
Season	Club	Lea	GP	G	A	TP	PIM	GP	G	A	TP	PIM
1987-88	Trois-Rivières	QMJHL	66	11	29	40	25	....	....	....	....	....
1988-89	Trois-Rivières	QMJHL	70	51	102	153	53	4	4	2	6	6
1989-90a	Trois-Rivières	QMJHL	60	55	90	145	40	7	3	5	8	8
1990-91	Chicoutimi	QMJHL	45	35	41	76	64	17	*13	*20	*33	20
1991-92	Fredericton	AHL	74	21	35	56	41	7	1	0	1	0
1992-93	Fredericton	AHL	77	27	65	92	52	5	2	5	7	6
1993-94	Atlanta	IHL	80	43	53	96	73	14	*16	10	*26	16

a QMJHL Second All-Star Team (1990)

LARSON, BRETT DET.

Defense. Shoots right. 6', 175 lbs. Born, Duluth, MN, August 20, 1972.
(Detroit's 10th choice, 213th overall, in 1990 Entry Draft).

			Regular Season					Playoffs				
Season	Club	Lea	GP	G	A	TP	PIM	GP	G	A	TP	PIM
1991-92	Minn.-Duluth	WCHA	26	2	1	3	20	....	....	....	....	....
1992-93	Minn.-Duluth	WCHA	32	2	3	5	8	....	....	....	....	....
1993-94	Minn.-Duluth	WCHA	38	14	14	28	40	....	....	....	....	....

LAUER, BRAD (LAU-er)

Left wing. Shoots left. 6', 195 lbs. Born, Humboldt, Sask., October 27, 1966.
(NY Islanders' 3rd choice, 34th overall, in 1985 Entry Draft).

			Regular Season					Playoffs				
Season	Club	Lea	GP	G	A	TP	PIM	GP	G	A	TP	PIM
1983-84	Regina	WHL	60	5	7	12	51	16	0	1	1	24
1984-85	Regina	WHL	72	33	46	79	57	8	6	6	12	9
1985-86	Regina	WHL	57	36	38	74	69	10	4	5	9	2
1986-87	**NY Islanders**	**NHL**	**61**	**7**	**14**	**21**	**65**	**6**	**2**	**0**	**2**	**4**
1987-88	**NY Islanders**	**NHL**	**69**	**17**	**18**	**35**	**67**	**5**	**3**	**1**	**4**	**4**
1988-89	**NY Islanders**	**NHL**	**14**	**3**	**2**	**5**	**2**	....	....	....	....	....
	Springfield	AHL	8	1	5	6	0	....	....	....	....	....
1989-90	**NY Islanders**	**NHL**	**63**	**6**	**18**	**24**	**19**	**4**	**0**	**2**	**2**	**10**
	Springfield	AHL	7	4	2	6	0	....	....	....	....	....
1990-91	**NY Islanders**	**NHL**	**44**	**4**	**8**	**12**	**45**	....	....	....	....	....
	Capital Dist.	AHL	11	5	11	16	14	....	....	....	....	....
1991-92	**NY Islanders**	**NHL**	**8**	**1**	**0**	**1**	**2**	....	....	....	....	....
	Chicago	**NHL**	**6**	**0**	**0**	**0**	**4**	**7**	**1**	**1**	**2**	**2**
	Indianapolis	IHL	57	24	30	54	46	....	....	....	....	....
1992-93	**Chicago**	**NHL**	**7**	**0**	**1**	**1**	**2**	....	....	....	....	....
	Indianapolis	IHL	62	*50	41	91	80	5	3	1	4	6
1993-94	**Ottawa**	**NHL**	**30**	**2**	**5**	**7**	**6**	....	....	....	....	....
	Las Vegas	IHL	32	21	21	42	30	4	1	0	1	2
	NHL Totals		**302**	**40**	**66**	**106**	**212**	**22**	**6**	**4**	**10**	**20**

a IHL First All-Star Team (1993)

Traded to **Chicago** by **NY Islanders** with Brent Sutter for Adam Creighton and Steve Thomas, October 25, 1991. Signed as a free agent by **Ottawa**, January 3, 1994.

LAUKKANEN, JANNE (LOW-kah-nehn) QUE.

Defense. Shoots left. 6', 180 lbs. Born, Lahti, Finland, March 19, 1970.
(Quebec's 8th choice, 156th overall, in 1991 Entry Draft).

			Regular Season					Playoffs				
Season	Club	Lea	GP	G	A	TP	PIM	GP	G	A	TP	PIM
1990-91	Reipas	Fin.	44	8	14	22	56	....	....	....	....	....
1991-92	HPK	Fin.	43	5	14	19	62	....	....	....	....	....
1992-93	HPK	Fin.	47	8	21	29	76	12	1	4	5	10
1993-94	HPK	Fin.	48	5	24	29	46	....	....	....	....	....

LAUS, PAUL (LOWZ) FLA.

Defense. Shoots right. 6'1", 212 lbs. Born, Beamsville, Ont., September 26, 1970.
(Pittsburgh's 2nd choice, 37th overall, in 1989 Entry Draft).

			Regular Season					Playoffs				
Season	Club	Lea	GP	G	A	TP	PIM	GP	G	A	TP	PIM
1987-88	Hamilton	OHL	56	1	9	10	171	14	0	0	0	28
1988-89	Niagara Falls	OHL	49	1	10	11	225	15	0	5	5	56
1989-90	Niagara Falls	OHL	60	13	35	48	231	16	6	16	22	71
1990-91	Albany	IHL	7	0	0	0	7	....	....	....	....	....
	Knoxville	ECHL	20	6	12	18	83	....	....	....	....	....
	Muskegon	IHL	35	3	4	7	103	4	0	0	0	13
1991-92	Muskegon	IHL	75	0	21	21	248	14	2	5	7	70
1992-93	Cleveland	IHL	76	8	18	26	427	4	1	0	1	27
1993-94	**Florida**	**NHL**	**39**	**2**	**0**	**2**	**109**	....	....	....	....	....
	NHL Totals		**39**	**2**	**0**	**2**	**109**	....	....	....	....	....

Claimed by **Florida** from **Pittsburgh** in Expansion Draft, June 24, 1993.

LAVIGNE, ERIC (luh-VEEN) L.A.

Defense. Shoots left. 6'3", 195 lbs. Born, Victoriaville, Que., November 4, 1972.
(Washington's 3rd choice, 25th overall, in 1991 Entry Draft).

			Regular Season					Playoffs				
Season	Club	Lea	GP	G	A	TP	PIM	GP	G	A	TP	PIM
1989-90	Hull	QMJHL	69	7	11	18	203	11	0	0	0	32
1990-91	Hull	QMJHL	66	11	11	22	153	4	0	1	1	16
1991-92	Hull	QMJHL	46	4	17	21	101	6	0	0	0	32
1992-93	Hull	QMJHL	59	7	20	27	221	10	2	4	6	47
1993-94	Phoenix	IHL	62	3	11	14	168	....	....	....	....	....

Signed as a free agent by **Los Angeles**, October 13, 1993.

LAVIOLETTE, PETER (LAH-vee-oh-LEHT)

Defense. Shoots left. 6'2", 200 lbs. Born, Norwood, MA, December 7, 1964.

			Regular Season					Playoffs				
Season	Club	Lea	GP	G	A	TP	PIM	GP	G	A	TP	PIM
1985-86	Westfield State	NCAA	19	12	8	20	44	....	....	....	....	....
1986-87	Indianapolis	IHL	72	10	20	30	146	....	....	....	....	....
1987-88	U.S. National	....	54	4	20	24	82	....	....	....	....	....
	U.S. Olympic	....	5	0	2	2	4	....	....	....	....	....
	Colorado	IHL	19	2	5	7	27	9	3	5	8	7
1988-89	**NY Rangers**	**NHL**	**12**	**0**	**0**	**0**	**6**	....	....	....	....	....
	Denver	IHL	57	6	19	25	120	3	0	0	0	4
1989-90	Flint	IHL	62	6	18	24	82	4	0	0	0	4
1990-91	Binghamton	AHL	65	12	24	36	72	10	2	7	9	30
1991-92	Binghamton	AHL	50	4	10	14	50	11	2	7	9	9
1992-93	Providence	AHL	74	13	42	55	64	6	0	4	4	10
1993-94	U.S. National	....	56	10	25	35	63	....	....	....	....	....
	U.S. Olympic	....	8	1	0	1	6	....	....	....	....	....
	San Diego	IHL	17	3	4	7	20	9	3	0	3	6
	NHL Totals		**12**	**0**	**0**	**0**	**6**	....	....	....	....	....

Signed as a free agent by **NY Rangers**, August 12, 1987.

LAVOIE, DOMINIC

Defense. Shoots right. 6'2", 205 lbs. Born, Montreal, Que., November 21, 1967.

			Regular Season					Playoffs				
Season	Club	Lea	GP	G	A	TP	PIM	GP	G	A	TP	PIM
1985-86	St-Jean	QMJHL	70	12	37	49	99	10	2	3	5	20
1986-87	St-Jean	QMJHL	64	12	42	54	97	8	2	7	9	2
1987-88	Peoria	IHL	65	7	26	33	54	7	2	2	4	8
1988-89	**St. Louis**	**NHL**	**1**	**0**	**0**	**0**	**0**	....	....	....	....	....
	Peoria	IHL	69	11	31	42	98	4	0	0	0	4
1989-90	**St. Louis**	**NHL**	**13**	**1**	**1**	**2**	**16**	....	....	....	....	....
	Peoria	IHL	58	19	23	42	32	5	2	2	4	16
1990-91	**St. Louis**	**NHL**	**6**	**1**	**2**	**3**	**2**	....	....	....	....	....
a	Peoria	IHL	46	15	25	40	72	16	5	7	12	22
1991-92	**St. Louis**	**NHL**	**6**	**0**	**1**	**1**	**10**	....	....	....	....	....
b	Peoria	IHL	58	20	32	52	87	10	3	4	7	12
1992-93	**Ottawa**	**NHL**	**2**	**0**	**1**	**1**	**0**	....	....	....	....	....
	New Haven	AHL	14	2	7	9	14	....	....	....	....	....
	Boston	**NHL**	**2**	**0**	**0**	**0**	**2**	....	....	....	....	....
	Providence	AHL	53	16	27	43	62	6	1	2	3	24
1993-94	**Los Angeles**	**NHL**	**8**	**3**	**3**	**6**	**2**	....	....	....	....	....
	Phoenix	IHL	58	20	33	53	70	....	....	....	....	....
	San Diego	IHL	9	2	2	4	12	8	1	0	1	20
	NHL Totals		**38**	**5**	**8**	**13**	**32**	....	....	....	....	....

a IHL First All-Star Team (1991)
b IHL Second All-Star Team (1992)

Signed as a free agent by **St. Louis**, September 22, 1986. Claimed by **Ottawa** from **St. Louis** in Expansion Draft, June 18, 1992. Claimed on waivers by **Boston** from **Ottawa**, November 20, 1992. Signed as a free agent by **Los Angeles**, July 16, 1993.

LAWRENCE, MARK DAL.

Right wing. Shoots right. 6'4", 212 lbs. Born, Burlington, Ont., January 27, 1972.
(Minnesota's 6th choice, 118th overall, in 1991 Entry Draft).

			Regular Season					Playoffs				
Season	Club	Lea	GP	G	A	TP	PIM	GP	G	A	TP	PIM
1988-89	Niagara Falls	OHL	63	9	27	36	142	....	....	....	....	....
1989-90	Niagara Falls	OHL	54	15	18	33	123	16	2	5	7	42
1990-91	Detroit	OHL	66	27	38	65	53	....	....	....	....	....
1991-92	Detroit	OHL	28	19	26	45	54	....	....	....	....	....
	North Bay	OHL	24	13	14	27	21	21	*23	12	35	36
1992-93	Dayton	ECHL	20	8	14	22	46	....	....	....	....	....
	Kalamazoo	IHL	57	22	13	35	47	....	....	....	....	....
1993-94	Kalamazoo	IHL	64	17	20	37	90	....	....	....	....	....

LAYZELL, BRAD

Defense. Shoots left. 6'3", 200 lbs. Born, Beaconsfield, Que., March 15, 1972.
(Montreal's 5th choice, 100th overall, in 1991 Entry Draft).

			Regular Season					Playoffs				
Season	Club	Lea	GP	G	A	TP	PIM	GP	G	A	TP	PIM
1990-91	RPI	ECAC	24	1	2	3	28	....	....	....	....	....
1991-92	RPI	ECAC	31	1	8	9	46	....	....	....	....	....
1992-93a	RPI	ECAC	35	5	24	29	40	....	....	....	....	....
1993-94	RPI	ECAC	30	2	20	22	54	....	....	....	....	....

a ECAC Second All-Star Team (1993)

LAZARO, JEFF

Left wing. Shoots left. 5'10", 180 lbs. Born, Waltham, MA, March 21, 1968.

			Regular Season					Playoffs				
Season	Club	Lea	GP	G	A	TP	PIM	GP	G	A	TP	PIM
1986-87	N. Hampshire	H.E.	38	7	14	21	38	....	....	....	....	....
1987-88	N. Hampshire	H.E.	30	4	13	17	48	....	....	....	....	....
1988-89	N. Hampshire	H.E.	31	8	14	22	38	....	....	....	....	....
1989-90	N. Hampshire	H.E.	39	16	19	35	34	....	....	....	....	....
1990-91	**Boston**	**NHL**	**49**	**5**	**13**	**18**	**67**	**19**	**3**	**2**	**5**	**30**
	Maine	AHL	26	8	11	19	18	....	....	....	....	....
1991-92	**Boston**	**NHL**	**27**	**3**	**6**	**9**	**31**	**9**	**0**	**1**	**1**	**2**
	Maine	AHL	21	8	4	12	32	....	....	....	....	....
1992-93	**Ottawa**	**NHL**	**26**	**6**	**4**	**10**	**16**	....	....	....	....	....
	New Haven	AHL	27	12	13	25	49	....	....	....	....	....
1993-94	U.S. National	....	43	18	25	43	57	....	....	....	....	....
	U.S. Olympic	....	8	2	2	4	4	....	....	....	....	....
	Providence	AHL	16	3	4	7	26	....	....	....	....	....
	NHL Totals		**102**	**14**	**23**	**37**	**114**	**28**	**3**	**3**	**6**	**32**

Signed as a free agent by **Boston**, September 26, 1990. Claimed by **Ottawa** from **Boston** in Expansion Draft, June 18, 1992.

LEACH, JAMIE FLA.

Right wing. Shoots right. 6'1", 205 lbs. Born, Winnipeg, Man., August 25, 1969.
(Pittsburgh's 3rd choice, 47th overall, in 1987 Entry Draft).

			Regular Season					Playoffs				
Season	Club	Lea	GP	G	A	TP	PIM	GP	G	A	TP	PIM
1985-86	N. Westminster	WHL	58	8	7	15	20	....	....	....	....	....
1986-87	Hamilton	OHL	64	12	19	31	67	....	....	....	....	....
1987-88	Hamilton	OHL	64	24	19	43	79	14	6	7	13	12
1988-89	Niagara Falls	OHL	58	45	62	107	47	17	9	11	20	25
1989-90	**Pittsburgh**	**NHL**	**10**	**0**	**3**	**3**	**0**	....	....	....	....	....
	Muskegon	IHL	72	22	36	58	39	15	9	4	13	14
1990-91	**Pittsburgh**	**NHL**	**7**	**2**	**0**	**2**	**0**	....	....	....	....	....
	Muskegon	IHL	43	33	22	55	26	....	....	....	....	....
1991-92	**Pittsburgh**	**NHL**	**38**	**5**	**4**	**9**	**8**	....	....	....	....	....
	Muskegon	IHL	3	1	1	2	2	....	....	....	....	....
1992-93	**Pittsburgh**	**NHL**	**5**	**0**	**0**	**0**	**2**	....	....	....	....	....
	Cleveland	IHL	9	5	3	8	2	4	1	2	3	0
	Hartford	**NHL**	**19**	**3**	**2**	**5**	**2**	....	....	....	....	....
	Springfield	AHL	29	13	15	28	33	....	....	....	....	....
1993-94	**Florida**	**NHL**	**2**	**1**	**0**	**1**	**0**	....	....	....	....	....
	Cincinnati	IHL	74	15	19	34	64	11	1	0	1	4
	NHL Totals		**81**	**11**	**9**	**20**	**12**	....	....	....	....	....

Claimed on waivers by **Hartford** from **Pittsburgh**, November 21, 1992. Signed as a free agent by **Florida**, August 31, 1993.

LEACH, STEPHEN — BOS.

Right wing. Shoots right. 5'11", 197 lbs. Born, Cambridge, MA, January 16, 1966.
(Washington's 2nd choice, 34th overall, in 1984 Entry Draft).

			Regular Season					Playoffs				
Season	Club	Lea	GP	G	A	TP	PIM	GP	G	A	TP	PIM
1984-85	N. Hampshire	H.E.	41	12	25	37	53	....	....	....	....	....
1985-86	**Washington**	**NHL**	**11**	**1**	**1**	**2**	**2**	**6**	**0**	**1**	**1**	**0**
	N. Hampshire	H.E.	25	22	6	28	30	....	....	....	....	....
1986-87	**Washington**	**NHL**	**15**	**1**	**0**	**1**	**6**	....	....	....	....	....
	Binghamton	AHL	54	18	21	39	39	13	3	1	4	6
1987-88	**Washington**	**NHL**	**8**	**1**	**1**	**2**	**17**	**9**	**2**	**1**	**3**	**0**
	U.S. National	....	49	26	20	46	30	....	....	....	....	....
	U.S. Olympic	....	6	1	2	3	0	....	....	....	....	....
1988-89	**Washington**	**NHL**	**74**	**11**	**19**	**30**	**94**	**6**	**1**	**0**	**1**	**12**
1989-90	**Washington**	**NHL**	**70**	**18**	**14**	**32**	**104**	**14**	**2**	**2**	**4**	**8**
1990-91	**Washington**	**NHL**	**68**	**11**	**19**	**30**	**99**	**9**	**1**	**2**	**3**	**8**
1991-92	**Boston**	**NHL**	**78**	**31**	**29**	**60**	**147**	**15**	**4**	**0**	**4**	**10**
1992-93	**Boston**	**NHL**	**79**	**26**	**25**	**51**	**126**	**4**	**1**	**1**	**2**	**2**
1993-94	**Boston**	**NHL**	**42**	**5**	**10**	**15**	**74**	**5**	**0**	**1**	**1**	**2**
	NHL Totals		**445**	**105**	**118**	**223**	**669**	**68**	**11**	**8**	**19**	**42**

Traded to **Boston** by **Washington** for Randy Burridge, June 21, 1991.

LEBEAU, PATRICK — (leh-BOH) FLA.

Left wing. Shoots left. 5'10", 172 lbs. Born, St. Jerome, Que., March 17, 1970.
(Montreal's 8th choice, 167th overall, in 1989 Entry Draft).

			Regular Season					Playoffs				
Season	Club	Lea	GP	G	A	TP	PIM	GP	G	A	TP	PIM
1986-87	Shawinigan	QMJHL	66	26	52	78	90	13	2	6	8	17
1987-88	Shawinigan	QMJHL	53	43	56	99	116	11	3	9	12	16
1988-89	Shawinigan	QMJHL	17	19	17	36	18	....	....	....	....	....
	St-Jean	QMJHL	49	43	70	113	71	4	4	3	7	6
1989-90a	Victoriaville	QMJHL	72	68	*106	*174	109	16	7	15	22	12
1990-91	**Montreal**	**NHL**	**2**	**1**	**1**	**2**	**0**	....	....	....	....	....
bc	Fredericton	AHL	69	50	51	101	32	9	4	7	11	8
1991-92	Fredericton	AHL	55	33	38	71	48	7	4	5	9	10
	Cdn. National	....	7	4	1	5	6	....	....	....	....	....
	Cdn. Olympic	....	8	1	3	4	4	....	....	....	....	....
1992-93	**Calgary**	**NHL**	**1**	**0**	**0**	**0**	**0**	....	....	....	....	....
	Salt Lake	IHL	75	40	60	100	65	....	....	....	....	....
1993-94	**Florida**	**NHL**	**4**	**1**	**1**	**2**	**4**	....	....	....	....	....
	Cincinnati	IHL	74	47	42	89	90	11	4	8	12	14
	NHL Totals		**7**	**2**	**2**	**4**	**4**	....	....	....	....	....

a QMJHL First All-Star Team (1990)
b AHL Second All-Star Team (1991)
c Won Dudley "Red" Garrett Memorial Trophy (Top Rookie - AHL) (1991)

Traded to **Calgary** by **Montreal** for future considerations, October 5, 1992. Signed as a free agent by **Florida**, July 26, 1993.

LEBEAU, STEPHAN — (leh-BOH) ANA.

Center. Shoots right. 5'10", 173 lbs. Born, St. Jerome, Que., February 28, 1968.

			Regular Season					Playoffs				
Season	Club	Lea	GP	G	A	TP	PIM	GP	G	A	TP	PIM
1984-85	Shawinigan	QMJHL	66	41	38	79	18	9	4	5	9	4
1985-86	Shawinigan	QMJHL	72	69	77	146	22	5	4	2	6	4
1986-87a	Shawinigan	QMJHL	65	77	90	167	60	14	9	20	29	20
1987-88a	Shawinigan	QMJHL	67	*94	94	188	66	11	17	9	26	10
	Sherbrooke	AHL	....	....	....	....	....	1	0	1	1	0
1988-89	**Montreal**	**NHL**	**1**	**0**	**1**	**1**	**2**	....	....	....	....	....
bcde	Sherbrooke	AHL	78	*70	64	*134	47	6	1	4	5	8
1989-90	**Montreal**	**NHL**	**57**	**15**	**20**	**35**	**11**	**2**	**3**	**0**	**3**	**0**
1990-91	**Montreal**	**NHL**	**73**	**22**	**31**	**53**	**24**	**7**	**2**	**1**	**3**	**2**
1991-92	**Montreal**	**NHL**	**77**	**27**	**31**	**58**	**14**	**8**	**1**	**3**	**4**	**4**
1992-93	**Montreal**	**NHL**	**71**	**31**	**49**	**80**	**20**	**13**	**3**	**3**	**6**	**6**
1993-94	**Montreal**	**NHL**	**34**	**9**	**7**	**16**	**8**	....	....	....	....	....
	Anaheim	**NHL**	**22**	**6**	**4**	**10**	**14**	....	....	....	....	....
	NHL Totals		**335**	**110**	**143**	**253**	**93**	**30**	**9**	**7**	**16**	**12**

a QMJHL Second All-Star Team (1987, 1988)
b AHL First All-Star Team (1989)
c Won Dudley "Red" Garrett Memorial Trophy (Top Rookie - AHL) (1989)
d Won John B. Sollenberger Trophy (Top Scorer - AHL) (1989)
e Won Les Cunningham Plaque (MVP - AHL) (1989)

Signed as a free agent by **Montreal**, September 27, 1986. Traded to **Anaheim** by **Montreal** for Ron Tugnutt, February 20, 1994.

LEBLANC, JOHN — (leh-BLAHNK) WPG.

Right wing. Shoots left. 6'1", 190 lbs. Born, Campbellton, N.B., January 21, 1964.

			Regular Season					Playoffs				
Season	Club	Lea	GP	G	A	TP	PIM	GP	G	A	TP	PIM
1983-84	Hull	QMJHL	69	39	35	74	32	....	....	....	....	....
1984-85	New Brunswick	AUAA	24	25	34	59	32	....	....	....	....	....
1985-86a	New Brunswick	AUAA	24	38	28	66	35	....	....	....	....	....
1986-87	**Vancouver**	**NHL**	**2**	**1**	**0**	**1**	**0**	....	....	....	....	....
	Fredericton	AHL	75	40	30	70	27	....	....	....	....	....
1987-88	**Vancouver**	**NHL**	**41**	**12**	**10**	**22**	**18**	....	....	....	....	....
	Fredericton	AHL	35	26	25	51	54	15	6	7	13	34
1988-89	Milwaukee	IHL	61	39	31	70	42	....	....	....	....	....
	Edmonton	**NHL**	**2**	**1**	**0**	**1**	**0**	**1**	**0**	**0**	**0**	**0**
	Cape Breton	AHL	3	4	0	4	0	....	....	....	....	....
1989-90	Cape Breton	AHL	77	*54	34	88	50	6	4	0	4	4
1990-91			DID NOT PLAY									
1991-92	**Winnipeg**	**NHL**	**16**	**6**	**1**	**7**	**6**	....	....	....	....	....
	Moncton	AHL	56	31	22	53	24	10	3	2	5	8
1992-93	**Winnipeg**	**NHL**	**3**	**0**	**0**	**0**	**2**	....	....	....	....	....
	Moncton	AHL	77	48	40	88	29	5	2	1	3	6
1993-94	**Winnipeg**	**NHL**	**17**	**6**	**2**	**8**	**2**	....	....	....	....	....
	Moncton	AHL	41	25	26	51	38	20	3	6	9	6
	NHL Totals		**81**	**26**	**13**	**39**	**28**	**1**	**0**	**0**	**0**	**0**

a Canadian University Player of the Year (1986)

Signed as a free agent by **Vancouver**, April 12, 1986. Traded to **Edmonton** by **Vancouver** with Vancouver's fifth round choice (Peter White) in 1989 Entry Draft for Doug Smith and Gregory C. Adams, March 7, 1989. Traded to **Winnipeg** by **Edmonton** with Edmonton's tenth round choice (Teemu Numminen) in 1992 Entry Draft for Winnipeg's fifth round choice (Ryan Haggerty) in 1991 Entry Draft, June 12, 1991.

LeBOUTILLIER, PETER — NYI

Right wing. Shoots right. 6'1", 198 lbs. Born, Neepawa, Man., January 11, 1975.
(NY Islanders' 6th choice, 144th overall, in 1993 Entry Draft).

			Regular Season					Playoffs				
Season	Club	Lea	GP	G	A	TP	PIM	GP	G	A	TP	PIM
1992-93	Red Deer	WHL	67	8	26	34	284	2	0	1	1	5
1993-94	Red Deer	WHL	66	19	20	39	300	2	0	1	1	4

LECLAIR, JOHN — MTL.

Center. Shoots left. 6'2", 219 lbs. Born, St. Albans, VT, July 5, 1969.
(Montreal's 2nd choice, 33rd overall, in 1987 Entry Draft).

			Regular Season					Playoffs				
Season	Club	Lea	GP	G	A	TP	PIM	GP	G	A	TP	PIM
1987-88	U. of Vermont	ECAC	31	12	22	34	62	....	....	....	....	....
1988-89	U. of Vermont	ECAC	18	9	12	21	40	....	....	....	....	....
1989-90	U. of Vermont	ECAC	10	10	6	16	38	....	....	....	....	....
1990-91a	U. of Vermont	ECAC	33	25	20	45	58	....	....	....	....	....
	Montreal	**NHL**	**10**	**2**	**5**	**7**	**2**	**3**	**0**	**0**	**0**	**0**
1991-92	**Montreal**	**NHL**	**59**	**8**	**11**	**19**	**14**	**8**	**1**	**1**	**2**	**4**
	Fredericton	AHL	8	7	7	14	10	2	0	0	0	4
1992-93	**Montreal**	**NHL**	**72**	**19**	**25**	**44**	**33**	**20**	**4**	**6**	**10**	**14**
1993-94	**Montreal**	**NHL**	**74**	**19**	**24**	**43**	**32**	**7**	**2**	**1**	**3**	**8**
	NHL Totals		**215**	**48**	**65**	**113**	**81**	**38**	**7**	**8**	**15**	**26**

a ECAC Second All-Star Team (1991)

LECOMPTE, ERIC — CHI.

Left wing. Shoots left. 6'4", 190 lbs. Born, Montreal, Que., April 4, 1975.
(Chicago's 1st choice, 24th overall, in 1993 Entry Draft).

			Regular Season					Playoffs				
Season	Club	Lea	GP	G	A	TP	PIM	GP	G	A	TP	PIM
1991-92	Hull	QMJHL	60	16	17	33	138	6	1	0	1	4
1992-93	Hull	QMJHL	66	33	38	71	149	10	4	4	8	52
1993-94	Hull	QMJHL	62	39	49	88	171	20	10	10	20	68

LEDYARD, GRANT — DAL.

Defense. Shoots left. 6'2", 195 lbs. Born, Winnipeg, Man., November 19, 1961.

			Regular Season					Playoffs				
Season	Club	Lea	GP	G	A	TP	PIM	GP	G	A	TP	PIM
1980-81	Saskatoon	WHL	71	9	28	37	148	....	....	....	....	....
1981-82	Fort Garry	MJHL	63	25	45	70	150	....	....	....	....	....
1982-83	Tulsa	CHL	80	13	29	42	115	....	....	....	....	....
1983-84a	Tulsa	CHL	58	9	17	26	71	9	5	4	9	10
1984-85	**NY Rangers**	**NHL**	**42**	**8**	**12**	**20**	**53**	**3**	**0**	**2**	**2**	**4**
	New Haven	AHL	36	6	20	26	18	....	....	....	....	....
1985-86	**NY Rangers**	**NHL**	**27**	**2**	**9**	**11**	**20**	....	....	....	....	....
	Los Angeles	**NHL**	**52**	**7**	**18**	**25**	**78**	....	....	....	....	....
1986-87	**Los Angeles**	**NHL**	**67**	**14**	**23**	**37**	**93**	**5**	**0**	**0**	**0**	**10**
1987-88	**Los Angeles**	**NHL**	**23**	**1**	**7**	**8**	**52**	....	....	....	....	....
	New Haven	AHL	3	2	1	3	4	....	....	....	....	....
	Washington	**NHL**	**21**	**4**	**3**	**7**	**14**	**14**	**1**	**0**	**1**	**30**
1988-89	**Washington**	**NHL**	**61**	**3**	**11**	**14**	**43**	....	....	....	....	....
	Buffalo	**NHL**	**13**	**1**	**5**	**6**	**8**	**5**	**1**	**2**	**3**	**2**
1989-90	**Buffalo**	**NHL**	**67**	**2**	**13**	**15**	**37**	....	....	....	....	....
1990-91	**Buffalo**	**NHL**	**60**	**8**	**23**	**31**	**46**	**6**	**3**	**3**	**6**	**10**
1991-92	**Buffalo**	**NHL**	**50**	**5**	**16**	**21**	**45**	....	....	....	....	....
1992-93	**Buffalo**	**NHL**	**50**	**2**	**14**	**16**	**45**	**8**	**0**	**0**	**0**	**8**
	Rochester	AHL	5	0	2	2	8	....	....	....	....	....
1993-94	**Dallas**	**NHL**	**84**	**9**	**37**	**46**	**42**	**9**	**1**	**2**	**3**	**6**
	NHL Totals		**617**	**66**	**191**	**257**	**576**	**50**	**6**	**9**	**15**	**70**

a Won Bob Gassoff Trophy (CHL's Most Improved Defenseman) (1984)

Signed as a free agent by **NY Rangers**, July 7, 1982. Traded to **Los Angeles** by **NY Rangers** with Roland Melanson for Los Angeles' fourth round choice (Mike Sullivan) in 1987 Entry Draft and Brian MacLellan, December 7, 1985. Traded to **Washington** by **Los Angeles** for Craig Laughlin, February 9, 1988. Traded to **Buffalo** by **Washington** with Clint Malarchuk and Washington's sixth round choice (Brian Holzinger) in 1991 Entry Draft for Calle Johansson and Buffalo's second round choice (Byron Dafoe) in 1989 Entry Draft, March 7, 1989. Signed as a free agent by **Dallas**, August 12, 1993.

LEEMAN, GARY — MTL.

Right wing. Shoots right. 5'11", 175 lbs. Born, Toronto, Ont., February 19, 1964.
(Toronto's 2nd choice, 24th overall, in 1982 Entry Draft).

			Regular Season					Playoffs				
Season	Club	Lea	GP	G	A	TP	PIM	GP	G	A	TP	PIM
1981-82	Regina	WHL	72	19	41	60	112	3	2	2	4	0
1982-83a	Regina	WHL	63	24	62	86	88	5	1	5	6	4
	Toronto	**NHL**	....	....	....	....	....	**2**	**0**	**0**	**0**	**0**
1983-84	**Toronto**	**NHL**	**52**	**4**	**8**	**12**	**31**	....	....	....	....	....
1984-85	**Toronto**	**NHL**	**53**	**5**	**26**	**31**	**72**	....	....	....	....	....
	St. Catharines	AHL	7	2	2	4	11	....	....	....	....	....
1985-86	**Toronto**	**NHL**	**53**	**9**	**23**	**32**	**20**	**10**	**2**	**10**	**12**	**2**
	St. Catharines	AHL	25	15	13	28	6	....	....	....	....	....
1986-87	**Toronto**	**NHL**	**80**	**21**	**31**	**52**	**66**	**5**	**0**	**1**	**1**	**14**
1987-88	**Toronto**	**NHL**	**80**	**30**	**31**	**61**	**62**	**2**	**2**	**0**	**2**	**2**
1988-89	**Toronto**	**NHL**	**61**	**32**	**43**	**75**	**66**	....	....	....	....	....
1989-90	**Toronto**	**NHL**	**80**	**51**	**44**	**95**	**63**	**5**	**3**	**3**	**6**	**16**
1990-91	**Toronto**	**NHL**	**52**	**17**	**12**	**29**	**39**	....	....	....	....	....
1991-92	**Toronto**	**NHL**	**34**	**7**	**13**	**20**	**44**	....	....	....	....	....
	Calgary	**NHL**	**29**	**2**	**7**	**9**	**27**	....	....	....	....	....
1992-93	**Calgary**	**NHL**	**30**	**9**	**5**	**14**	**10**	....	....	....	....	....
	Montreal	**NHL**	**20**	**6**	**12**	**18**	**14**	**11**	**1**	**2**	**3**	**2**
1993-94	**Montreal**	**NHL**	**31**	**4**	**11**	**15**	**17**	**1**	**0**	**0**	**0**	**0**
	Fredericton	AHL	23	18	8	26	16	....	....	....	....	....
	NHL Totals		**655**	**197**	**266**	**463**	**531**	**36**	**8**	**16**	**24**	**36**

a WHL First All-Star Team (1983)

Played in NHL All-Star Game (1989)

Traded to **Calgary** by **Toronto** with Craig Berube, Alexander Godynyuk, Michel Petit and Jeff Reese for Doug Gilmour, Jamie Macoun, Ric Nattress, Rick Wamsley and Kent Manderville, January 2, 1992. Traded to **Montreal** by **Calgary** for Brian Skrudland, January 28, 1993.

EETCH, BRIAN NYR

Defense. Shoots left. 5'11", 195 lbs.   Born, Corpus Christi, TX, March 3, 1968.
NY Rangers' 1st choice, 9th overall, in 1986 Entry Draft.

			Regular Season						Playoffs			
Season	Club	Lea	GP	G	A	TP	PIM	GP	G	A	TP	PIM
1986-87ab	Boston College	H.E.	37	9	38	47	10	....	....	....	....	....
1987-88	U.S. National	....	50	13	61	74	38	....	....	....	....	....
	U.S. Olympic	....	6	1	5	6	4	....	....	....	....	....
	NY Rangers	NHL	17	2	12	14	0	....	....	....	....	....
1988-89cd	NY Rangers	NHL	68	23	48	71	50	4	3	2	5	2
1989-90	NY Rangers	NHL	72	11	45	56	26	....	....	....	....	....
1990-91e	NY Rangers	NHL	80	16	72	88	42	6	1	3	4	0
1991-92fg	NY Rangers	NHL	80	22	80	102	26	13	4	11	15	4
1992-93	NY Rangers	NHL	36	6	30	36	26	....	....	....	....	....
1993-94eh	NY Rangers	NHL	84	23	56	79	67	23	11	*23	*34	6
	NHL Totals		437	103	343	446	237	46	19	39	58	12

a Hockey East First All-Star Team (1987)
b NCAA East First All-American Team (1987)
c NHL All-Rookie Team (1989)
d Won Calder Memorial Trophy (1989)
e NHL Second All-Star Team (1991, 1994)
f Won James Norris Memorial Trophy (1992)
g NHL First All-Star Team (1992)
h Won Conn Smythe Trophy (1994)

Played in NHL All-Star Game (1990-92, 1994)

EFEBVRE, SYLVAIN (luh-FAYV) QUE.

Defense. Shoots left. 6'2", 205 lbs.   Born, Richmond, Que., October 14, 1967.

			Regular Season						Playoffs			
Season	Club	Lea	GP	G	A	TP	PIM	GP	G	A	TP	PIM
1984-85	Laval	QMJHL	66	7	5	12	31	....	....	....	....	....
1985-86	Laval	QMJHL	71	8	17	25	48	14	1	0	1	25
1986-87	Laval	QMJHL	70	10	36	46	44	15	1	6	7	12
1987-88	Sherbrooke	AHL	79	3	24	27	73	6	2	3	5	4
1988-89a	Sherbrooke	AHL	77	15	32	47	119	6	1	3	4	4
1989-90	Montreal	NHL	68	3	10	13	61	6	0	0	0	2
1990-91	Montreal	NHL	63	5	18	23	30	11	1	0	1	6
1991-92	Montreal	NHL	69	3	14	17	91	2	0	0	0	2
1992-93	Toronto	NHL	81	2	12	14	90	21	3	3	6	20
1993-94	Toronto	NHL	84	2	9	11	79	18	0	3	3	16
	NHL Totals		365	15	63	78	351	58	4	6	10	46

a AHL Second All-Star Team (1989)

Signed as a free agent by **Montreal**, September 24, 1986. Traded to **Toronto** by **Montreal** for Toronto's third round choice (Martin Belanger) in 1994 Entry Draft, August 20, 1992. Traded to **Quebec** by **Toronto** with Wendel Clark, Landon Wilson and Toronto's first round choice (Jeffrey Kealty) in 1994 Entry Draft for Mats Sundin, Garth Butcher, Todd Warriner and Philadelphia's first round choice (previously acquired by Quebec — later traded to Washington — Washington selected Nolan Baumgartner) in 1994 Entry Draft, June 28, 1994.

LEGG, MIKE N.J.

Right wing. Shoots right. 5'11", 165 lbs.   Born, London, Ont., May 25, 1975.
(New Jersey's 11th choice, 273rd overall, in 1993 Entry Draft).

			Regular Season						Playoffs			
Season	Club	Lea	GP	G	A	TP	PIM	GP	G	A	TP	PIM
1992-93	London	Jr. B	52	49	55	104	32	....	....	....	....	....
1993-94	U. of Michigan	CCHA	37	10	13	23	20	....	....	....	....	....

LEHOUX, GUY (leh-HOO)

Defense. Shoots left. 5'11", 205 lbs.   Born, Disraeli, Que., October 19, 1971.
(Toronto's 9th choice, 179th overall, in 1991 Entry Draft).

			Regular Season						Playoffs			
Season	Club	Lea	GP	G	A	TP	PIM	GP	G	A	TP	PIM
1989-90	Drummondville	QMJHL	66	4	17	21	178	....	....	....	....	....
1990-91	Drummondville	QMJHL	63	8	26	34	107	14	1	7	8	24
1991-92	St. John's	AHL	67	1	7	8	134	....	....	....	....	....
1992-93	St. John's	AHL	42	3	2	5	89	....	....	....	....	....
	Brantford	ColHL	13	0	5	5	28	4	0	1	1	15
1993-94	St. John's	AHL	71	2	8	10	217	9	1	1	2	8

LEHTINEN, JERE (lehkh-TIH-nehn) DAL.

Right wing. Shoots right. 6', 185 lbs.   Born, Espoo, Finland, June 24, 1973.
(Minnesota's 3rd choice, 88th overall, in 1992 Entry Draft).

			Regular Season						Playoffs			
Season	Club	Lea	GP	G	A	TP	PIM	GP	G	A	TP	PIM
1990-91	Espoo	Fin.2	32	15	9	24	12	....	....	....	....	....
1991-92	Espoo	Fin.2	43	32	17	49	6	....	....	....	....	....
1992-93	Kiekko-Espoo	Fin.	45	13	14	27	6	....	....	....	....	....
1993-94	TPS	Fin.	42	19	20	39	6	11	11	2	13	2

LEMIEUX, CLAUDE (lehm-YOO) N.J.

Right wing. Shoots right. 6'1", 215 lbs.   Born, Buckingham, Que., July 16, 1965.
(Montreal's 2nd choice, 26th overall, in 1983 Entry Draft).

			Regular Season						Playoffs			
Season	Club	Lea	GP	G	A	TP	PIM	GP	G	A	TP	PIM
1982-83	Trois-Rivières	QMJHL	62	28	38	66	187	4	1	0	1	30
1983-84	Montreal	NHL	8	1	1	2	12	....	....	....	....	....
	Verdun	QMJHL	51	41	45	86	225	9	8	12	20	63
	Nova Scotia	AHL	....	....	....	....	....	2	1	0	1	0
1984-85	Montreal	NHL	1	0	1	1	7	....	....	....	....	....
	Verdun	QMJHL	52	58	66	124	152	14	23	17	40	38
1985-86	Montreal	NHL	10	1	2	3	22	20	10	6	16	68
	Sherbrooke	AHL	58	21	32	53	145	....	....	....	....	....
1986-87	Montreal	NHL	76	27	26	53	156	17	4	9	13	41
1987-88	Montreal	NHL	78	31	30	61	137	11	3	2	5	20
1988-89	Montreal	NHL	69	29	22	51	136	18	4	3	7	58
1989-90	Montreal	NHL	39	8	10	18	106	11	1	3	4	38
1990-91	New Jersey	NHL	78	30	17	47	105	7	4	0	4	34
1991-92	New Jersey	NHL	74	41	27	68	109	7	4	3	7	26
1992-93	New Jersey	NHL	77	30	51	81	155	5	2	0	2	19
1993-94	New Jersey	NHL	79	18	26	44	86	20	7	11	18	44
	NHL Totals		589	216	213	429	1031	116	39	37	76	348

a QMJHL First All-Star Team (1985)
Traded to **New Jersey** by **Montreal** for Sylvain Turgeon, September 4, 1990.

LEMIEUX, JOCELYN (lehm-YOO) HFD.

Right wing. Shoots left. 5'10", 200 lbs.   Born, Mont-Laurier, Que., November 18, 1967.
(St. Louis' 1st choice, 10th overall, in 1986 Entry Draft).

			Regular Season						Playoffs			
Season	Club	Lea	GP	G	A	TP	PIM	GP	G	A	TP	PIM
1984-85	Laval	QMJHL	68	13	19	32	92	....	....	....	....	....
1985-86a	Laval	QMJHL	71	57	68	125	131	14	9	15	24	37
1986-87	St. Louis	NHL	53	10	8	18	94	5	0	1	1	6
1987-88	St. Louis	NHL	23	1	0	1	42	5	0	0	0	15
	Peoria	IHL	8	0	5	5	35	....	....	....	....	....
1988-89	Montreal	NHL	1	0	1	1	0	....	....	....	....	....
	Sherbrooke	AHL	73	25	28	53	134	4	3	1	4	6
1989-90	Montreal	NHL	34	4	2	6	61	....	....	....	....	....
	Chicago	NHL	39	10	11	21	47	18	1	8	9	28
1990-91	Chicago	NHL	67	6	7	13	119	4	0	0	0	0
1991-92	Chicago	NHL	78	6	10	16	80	18	3	1	4	33
1992-93	Chicago	NHL	81	10	21	31	111	4	1	0	1	2
1993-94	Chicago	NHL	66	12	8	20	63	....	....	....	....	....
	Hartford	NHL	16	6	1	7	19	....	....	....	....	....
	NHL Totals		458	65	69	134	636	54	5	10	15	84

a QMJHL First All-Star Team (1986)

Traded to **Montreal** by **St. Louis** with Darrell May and St. Louis' second round choice (Patrice Brisebois) in the 1989 Entry Draft for Sergio Momesso and Vincent Riendeau, August 9, 1988. Traded to **Chicago** by **Montreal** for Chicago's third round choice (Charles Poulin) in 1990 Entry Draft, January 5, 1990. Traded to **Hartford** by **Chicago** with Frantisek Kucera for Gary Suter, Randy Cunneyworth and a future draft choice, March 11, 1994.

LEMIEUX, MARIO (lehm-YOO) PIT.

Center. Shoots right. 6'4", 210 lbs.   Born, Montreal, Que., October 5, 1965.
(Pittsburgh's 1st choice, 1st overall, in 1984 Entry Draft).

			Regular Season						Playoffs			
Season	Club	Lea	GP	G	A	TP	PIM	GP	G	A	TP	PIM
1981-82	Laval	QMJHL	64	30	66	96	22	18	5	9	14	31
1982-83a	Laval	QMJHL	66	84	100	184	76	12	14	18	32	18
1983-84bc	Laval	QMJHL	70	*133	*149	*282	92	14	*29	*23	*52	29
1984-85de	Pittsburgh	NHL	73	43	57	100	54	....	....	....	....	....
1985-86fg	Pittsburgh	NHL	79	48	93	141	43	....	....	....	....	....
1986-87f	Pittsburgh	NHL	63	54	53	107	57	....	....	....	....	....
1987-88												
ghijkl	Pittsburgh	NHL	77	*70	98	*168	92	....	....	....	....	....
1988-89ijlm	Pittsburgh	NHL	76	*85	*114	*199	100	11	12	7	19	16
1989-90	Pittsburgh	NHL	59	45	78	123	78	....	....	....	....	....
1990-91n	Pittsburgh	NHL	26	19	26	45	30	23	16	*28	*44	16
1991-92fino	Pittsburgh	NHL	64	44	87	*131	94	15	*16	18	*34	2
1992-93												
ghijpq	Pittsburgh	NHL	60	69	91	*160	38	11	8	10	18	10
1993-94	Pittsburgh	NHL	22	17	20	37	32	6	4	3	7	2
	NHL Totals		599	494	717	1211	618	66	56	66	122	46

a QMJHL Second All-Star Team (1983)
b QMJHL First All-Star Team (1984)
c Canadian Major Junior Player of the Year (1984)
d Won Calder Memorial Trophy (1985)
e NHL All-Rookie Team (1985)
f NHL Second All-Star Team (1986, 1987, 1992)
g Won Lester B. Pearson Award (1986, 1988, 1993)
h Won Hart Trophy (1988, 1993)
i Won Art Ross Trophy (1988, 1989, 1992, 1993)
j NHL First All-Star Team (1988, 1989, 1993)
k Won Dodge Performance of the Year Award (1988)
l Won Dodge Performer of the Year Award (1988, 1989)
m Won Dodge Ram Tough Award (1988)
n Won Conn Smythe Trophy (1991, 1992)
o Won ProSet/NHL Player of the Year Award (1992)
p Won Bill Masterton Memorial Trophy (1993)
q Won Alka-Seltzer Plus Award (1993)
Played in NHL All-Star Game (1985, 1986, 1988-90, 1992)

LEPAGE, MARTIN

Defense. Shoots left. 6'1", 185 lbs.   Born, Longueuil, Que., February 26, 1974.
(Quebec's 7th choice, 148th overall, in 1992 Entry Draft).

			Regular Season						Playoffs			
Season	Club	Lea	GP	G	A	TP	PIM	GP	G	A	TP	PIM
1990-91	Hull	QMJHL	60	0	8	8	48	6	0	1	1	6
1991-92	Hull	QMJHL	69	2	10	12	71	6	0	0	0	4
1992-93	Shawinigan	QMJHL	61	7	26	33	133	....	....	....	....	....
1993-94	Shawinigan	QMJHL	66	6	28	34	119	5	0	1	1	21

LEPLER, PAUL MTL.

Defense. Shoots left. 6'3", 185 lbs.   Born, Granite Falls, MN, November 26, 1972.
(Montreal's 14th choice, 237th overall, in 1991 Entry Draft).

			Regular Season						Playoffs			
Season	Club	Lea	GP	G	A	TP	PIM	GP	G	A	TP	PIM
1992-93	St. Cloud St.	WCHA	26	2	4	6	16	....	....	....	....	....
1993-94	St. Cloud St.	WCHA	35	1	4	5	48	....	....	....	....	....

LEROUX, FRANCOIS OTT.

Defense. Shoots left. 6'6", 225 lbs.   Born, Ste.-Adele, Que., April 18, 1970.
(Edmonton's 1st choice, 19th overall, in 1988 Entry Draft).

			Regular Season						Playoffs			
Season	Club	Lea	GP	G	A	TP	PIM	GP	G	A	TP	PIM
1987-88	St-Jean	QMJHL	58	3	8	11	143	7	2	0	2	21
1988-89	Edmonton	NHL	2	0	0	0	0	....	....	....	....	....
	St-Jean	QMJHL	57	8	34	42	185	....	....	....	....	....
1989-90	Edmonton	NHL	3	0	1	1	0	....	....	....	....	....
	Victoriaville	QMJHL	54	4	33	37	169	....	....	....	....	....
1990-91	Edmonton	NHL	1	0	2	2	0	....	....	....	....	....
	Cape Breton	AHL	71	2	7	9	124	4	0	1	1	19
1991-92	Edmonton	NHL	4	0	0	0	7	....	....	....	....	....
	Cape Breton	AHL	61	7	22	29	114	5	0	0	0	8
1992-93	Edmonton	NHL	1	0	0	0	4	....	....	....	....	....
	Cape Breton	AHL	55	10	24	34	139	16	0	5	5	29
1993-94	Ottawa	NHL	23	0	1	1	70	....	....	....	....	....
	PEI	AHL	25	4	6	10	52	....	....	....	....	....
	NHL Totals		34	0	4	4	81					

Claimed on waivers by **Ottawa** from **Edmonton**, October 6, 1993.

LEROUX, JEAN-YVES — CHI.

Left wing. Shoots left. 6'2", 193 lbs. Born, Montreal, Que., June 24, 1976.
(Chicago's 2nd choice, 40th overall, in 1994 Entry Draft).

			Regular Season					Playoffs				
Season	Club	Lea	GP	G	A	TP	PIM	GP	G	A	TP	PIM
1988-89	Minsk Dynamo	USSR	26	17	4	21	6	....	....	....	....	....
1992-93	Beauport	QMJHL	62	20	25	45	33	....	....	....	....	....
1993-94a	Beauport	QMJHL	45	14	25	39	43	15	7	6	13	33

a QMJHL Second All-Star Team (1994)

LESCHYSHYN, CURTIS (luh-SIH-shuhn) — QUE.

Defense. Shoots left. 6'1", 205 lbs. Born, Thompson, Man., September 21, 1969.
(Quebec's 1st choice, 3rd overall, in 1988 Entry Draft).

			Regular Season					Playoffs				
Season	Club	Lea	GP	G	A	TP	PIM	GP	G	A	TP	PIM
1986-87	Saskatoon	WHL	70	14	26	40	107	11	1	5	6	14
1987-88	Saskatoon	WHL	56	14	41	55	86	10	2	5	7	16
1988-89	Quebec	NHL	71	4	9	13	71	....	....	....	....	....
1989-90	Quebec	NHL	68	2	6	8	44	....	....	....	....	....
1990-91	Quebec	NHL	55	3	7	10	49	....	....	....	....	....
1991-92	Quebec	NHL	42	5	12	17	42	....	....	....	....	....
	Halifax	AHL	6	0	2	2	4	....	....	....	....	....
1992-93	Quebec	NHL	82	9	23	32	61	6	1	1	2	6
1993-94	Quebec	NHL	72	5	17	22	65	....	....	....	....	....
	NHL Totals		390	28	74	102	332	6	1	1	2	6

LESLIE, LEE J. — S.J.

Left wing. Shoots left. 6'4", 190 lbs. Born, Prince George, B.C., August 15, 1972.
(St. Louis' 4th choice, 86th overall, in 1992 Entry Draft).

			Regular Season					Playoffs				
Season	Club	Lea	GP	G	A	TP	PIM	GP	G	A	TP	PIM
1989-90	Prince Albert	WHL	62	14	16	30	13	14	2	3	5	4
1990-91	Prince Albert	WHL	72	29	42	71	68	3	0	0	0	5
1991-92	Prince Albert	WHL	72	52	48	100	70	10	6	6	12	12
1992-93	Peoria	IHL	72	22	24	46	46	4	0	3	3	2
1993-94	Kansas City	IHL	43	8	7	15	21	....	....	....	....	....

Signed as a free agent by **San Jose**, June 21, 1993.

LESSARD, RICK

Defense. Shoots left. 6'2", 206 lbs. Born, Timmins, Ont., January 9, 1968.
(Calgary's 6th choice, 142nd overall, in 1986 Entry Draft).

			Regular Season					Playoffs				
Season	Club	Lea	GP	G	A	TP	PIM	GP	G	A	TP	PIM
1985-86	Ottawa	OHL	64	1	20	21	231	....	....	....	....	....
1986-87	Ottawa	OHL	66	5	36	41	188	11	1	7	8	30
1987-88	Ottawa	OHL	58	5	34	39	210	16	1	0	1	31
1988-89	Calgary	NHL	6	0	1	1	2	....	....	....	....	....
a	Salt Lake	IHL	76	10	42	52	239	14	1	6	7	35
1989-90	Salt Lake	IHL	66	3	18	21	169	10	1	2	3	64
1990-91	Calgary	NHL	1	0	1	1	0	....	....	....	....	....
	Salt Lake	IHL	80	8	27	35	272	4	0	1	1	12
1991-92	San Jose	NHL	8	0	2	2	16	....	....	....	....	....
	Kansas City	IHL	46	3	16	19	117	3	0	0	0	2
1992-93	Kansas City	IHL	1	0	0	0	0	....	....	....	....	....
	Providence	AHL	6	0	0	0	6	....	....	....	....	....
	Hamilton	AHL	52	0	17	17	151	....	....	....	....	....
1993-94	S. Carolina	ECHL	5	1	0	1	10	....	....	....	....	....
	Salt Lake	IHL	31	1	2	3	110	....	....	....	....	....
	Rochester	AHL	8	1	2	3	2	4	0	0	0	2
	NHL Totals		15	0	4	4	18	....	....	....	....	....

a IHL First All-Star Team (1989)

Claimed by **San Jose** from **Calgary** in Expansion Draft, May 30, 1991. Traded to **Vancouver** by **San Jose** for Robin Bawa, December 15, 1992.

LETANG, ALAN — MTL.

Defense. Shoots left. 6', 183 lbs. Born, Renfrew, Ont., September 4, 1975.
(Montreal's 10th choice, 203rd overall, in 1993 Entry Draft).

			Regular Season					Playoffs				
Season	Club	Lea	GP	G	A	TP	PIM	GP	G	A	TP	PIM
1987-88	Lulea	Swe.	16	7	2	9	2	....	....	....	....	....
1992-93	Newmarket	OHL	66	1	25	26	14	6	0	3	3	2
1993-94	Newmarket	OHL	58	3	21	24	30	....	....	....	....	....

LEVEQUE, GUY — L.A.

Center. Shoots right. 5'11", 180 lbs. Born, Kingston, Ont., December 28, 1972.
(Los Angeles' 1st choice, 42nd overall, in 1991 Entry Draft).

			Regular Season					Playoffs				
Season	Club	Lea	GP	G	A	TP	PIM	GP	G	A	TP	PIM
1989-90	Cornwall	OHL	62	10	15	25	30	3	0	0	0	4
1990-91	Cornwall	OHL	66	41	56	97	34	....	....	....	....	....
1991-92	Cornwall	OHL	37	23	36	59	40	6	3	5	8	2
1992-93	Los Angeles	NHL	12	2	1	3	19	....	....	....	....	....
	Phoenix	IHL	56	27	30	57	71	....	....	....	....	....
1993-94	Los Angeles	NHL	5	0	1	1	2	....	....	....	....	....
	Phoenix	IHL	39	10	16	26	47	....	....	....	....	....
	NHL Totals		17	2	2	4	21	....	....	....	....	....

LEVINS, SCOTT — OTT.

Center/Right wing. Shoots right. 6'4", 210 lbs. Born, Spokane, WA, January 30, 1970.
(Winnipeg's 4th choice, 75th overall, in 1990 Entry Draft).

			Regular Season					Playoffs				
Season	Club	Lea	GP	G	A	TP	PIM	GP	G	A	TP	PIM
1989-90a	Tri-Cities	WHL	71	25	37	62	132	6	2	3	5	18
1990-91	Moncton	AHL	74	12	26	38	133	4	0	0	0	4
1991-92	Moncton	AHL	69	15	18	33	271	11	3	4	7	30
1992-93	Winnipeg	NHL	9	0	1	1	18	....	....	....	....	....
	Moncton	AHL	54	22	26	48	158	5	1	3	4	14
1993-94	Florida	NHL	29	5	6	11	69	....	....	....	....	....
	Ottawa	NHL	33	3	5	8	93	....	....	....	....	....
	NHL Totals		71	8	12	20	180	....	....	....	....	....

a WHL West Second All-Star Team (1990)

Claimed by **Florida** from **Winnipeg** in Expansion Draft, June 24, 1993. Traded to **Ottawa** by **Florida** with Evgeny Davydov and future draft choices for Bob Kudelski, January 6, 1994.

LIDSTER, DOUG — ST.L.

Defense. Shoots right. 6'1", 200 lbs. Born, Kamloops, B.C., October 18, 1960.
(Vancouver's 6th choice, 133rd overall, in 1980 Entry Draft).

			Regular Season					Playoffs				
Season	Club	Lea	GP	G	A	TP	PIM	GP	G	A	TP	PIM
1977-78	Seattle	WHL	2	0	0	0	0	....	....	....	....	....
1978-79	Kamloops	BCJHL	59	36	47	83	50	....	....	....	....	....
1979-80	Colorado	WCHA	39	18	25	43	52	....	....	....	....	....
1980-81	Colorado	WCHA	36	10	30	40	54	....	....	....	....	....
1981-82	Colorado	WCHA	36	13	22	35	32	....	....	....	....	....
1982-83	Colorado	WCHA	34	15	41	56	30	....	....	....	....	....
1983-84	Cdn. National	....	59	6	20	26	28	....	....	....	....	....
	Cdn. Olympic	....	7	0	2	2	2	....	....	....	....	....
	Vancouver	NHL	8	0	0	0	4	2	0	1	1	0
1984-85	Vancouver	NHL	78	6	24	30	55	....	....	....	....	....
1985-86	Vancouver	NHL	78	12	16	28	56	3	0	1	1	2
1986-87	Vancouver	NHL	80	12	51	63	40	....	....	....	....	....
1987-88	Vancouver	NHL	64	4	32	36	105	....	....	....	....	....
1988-89	Vancouver	NHL	63	5	17	22	78	7	1	1	2	9
1989-90	Vancouver	NHL	80	8	28	36	36	....	....	....	....	....
1990-91	Vancouver	NHL	78	6	32	38	77	6	0	2	2	6
1991-92	Vancouver	NHL	66	6	23	29	39	11	1	2	3	11
1992-93	Vancouver	NHL	71	6	19	25	36	12	0	3	3	8
1993-94	NY Rangers	NHL	34	0	2	2	33	9	2	0	2	10
	NHL Totals		700	65	244	309	559	50	4	10	14	46

Traded to **NY Rangers** by **Vancouver** to complete June 20, 1993 trade which sent John Vanbiesbrouck to Vancouver for future considerations, June 25, 1993. Traded to **St. Louis** by **NY Rangers** with Esa Tikkanen for Petr Nedved, July 24, 1994.

LIDSTROM, NICKLAS (LID-struhm) — DET.

Defense. Shoots left. 6'2", 185 lbs. Born, Vasteras, Sweden, April 28, 1970.
(Detroit's 3rd choice, 53rd overall, in 1989 Entry Draft).

			Regular Season					Playoffs				
Season	Club	Lea	GP	G	A	TP	PIM	GP	G	A	TP	PIM
1987-88	Vasteras	Swe.2	3	0	0	0	....	....	....	....	....	....
1988-89	Vasteras	Swe.	19	0	2	2	4	....	....	....	....	....
1989-90	Vasteras	Swe.	39	8	8	16	14	2	0	1	1	2
1990-91	Vasteras	Swe.	38	4	19	23	2	4	0	0	0	4
1991-92a	Detroit	NHL	80	11	49	60	22	11	1	2	3	0
1992-93	Detroit	NHL	84	7	34	41	28	7	1	0	1	0
1993-94	Detroit	NHL	84	10	46	56	26	7	3	2	5	0
	NHL Totals		248	28	129	157	76	25	5	4	9	0

a NHL/Upper Deck All-Rookie Team (1992)

LIEVERS, BRETT — NYR

Center. Shoots right. 6', 170 lbs. Born, Syracuse, NY, June 18, 1971.
(NY Rangers' 13th choice, 223rd overall, in 1990 Entry Draft).

			Regular Season					Playoffs				
Season	Club	Lea	GP	G	A	TP	PIM	GP	G	A	TP	PIM
1990-91	St. Cloud St.	WCHA	40	14	18	32	4	....	....	....	....	....
1991-92	St. Cloud St.	WCHA	16	2	10	12	2	....	....	....	....	....
1992-93	St. Cloud St.	WCHA				DID NOT PLAY						
1993-94	St. Cloud St.	WCHA	32	16	16	32	2	....	....	....	....	....

LILLEY, JOHN — ANA.

Right wing. Shoots right. 5'9", 170 lbs. Born, Wakefield, MA, August 3, 1972.
(Winnipeg's 8th choice, 140th overall, in 1990 Entry Draft).

			Regular Season					Playoffs				
Season	Club	Lea	GP	G	A	TP	PIM	GP	G	A	TP	PIM
1991-92	Boston U.	H.E.	23	9	9	18	43	....	....	....	....	....
1992-93	Boston U.	H.E.	4	0	1	1	13	....	....	....	....	....
	Seattle	WHL	45	22	28	50	55	5	1	3	4	9
1993-94	U.S. National	....	58	27	23	50	117	....	....	....	....	....
	U.S. Olympic	....	8	3	1	4	4	....	....	....	....	....
	Anaheim	NHL	13	1	6	7	8	....	....	....	....	....
	San Diego	IHL	2	2	1	3	0	....	....	....	....	....
	NHL Totals		13	1	6	7	8	....	....	....	....	....

Signed as a free agent by **Anaheim**, March 9, 1994.

LIND, JUHA — DAL.

Center. Shoots left. 5'11", 172 lbs. Born, Helsinki, Finland, January 2, 1974.
(Minnesota's 6th choice, 178th overall, in 1992 Entry Draft).

			Regular Season					Playoffs				
Season	Club	Lea	GP	G	A	TP	PIM	GP	G	A	TP	PIM
1991-92	Jokerit Jrs.	Fin.	28	16	24	40	10	....	....	....	....	....
1992-93	Vantaa	Fin. 2	25	8	12	20	8	....	....	....	....	....
	Jokerit	Fin.	6	0	0	0	2	1	0	0	0	0
1993-94	Jokerit	Fin.	47	17	11	28	37	11	2	5	7	4

LINDBERG, CHRIS

Left wing. Shoots left. 6'1", 190 lbs. Born, Fort Frances, Ont., April 16, 1967.

			Regular Season					Playoffs				
Season	Club	Lea	GP	G	A	TP	PIM	GP	G	A	TP	PIM
1987-88	Minn.-Duluth	WCHA	35	12	10	22	36	....	....	....	....	....
1988-89	Minn.-Duluth	WCHA	36	15	18	33	51	....	....	....	....	....
1989-90	Binghamton	AHL	32	4	4	8	36	....	....	....	....	....
	Virginia	ECHL	26	11	23	34	27	4	0	3	3	2
1990-91	Cdn. National	....	55	25	31	56	53	....	....	....	....	....
	Springfield	AHL	1	0	0	0	2	1	0	0	0	0
1991-92	Cdn. National	....	56	33	35	68	63	....	....	....	....	....
	Cdn. Olympic	....	8	1	4	5	4	....	....	....	....	....
	Calgary	NHL	17	2	5	7	17	....	....	....	....	....
1992-93	Calgary	NHL	62	9	12	21	18	2	0	1	1	2
1993-94	Quebec	NHL	37	6	8	14	12	....	....	....	....	....
	Cornwall	AHL	23	14	13	27	28	13	11	3	14	10
	NHL Totals		116	17	25	42	47	2	0	1	1	2

Signed as a free agent by **Hartford**, March 17, 1989. Signed as a free agent by **Calgary**, August 2, 1991. Claimed by **Ottawa** from **Calgary** in Expansion Draft, June 18, 1992. Traded to **Calgary** by **Ottawa** for Mark Osiecki, June 22, 1992. Signed as a free agent by **Quebec**, September 9, 1993.

LINDEN, JAMIE   FLA.

Right wing. Shoots right. 6'3", 185 lbs.   Born, Medicine Hat, Alta., July 19, 1972.

				Regular Season					Playoffs			
Season	Club	Lea	GP	G	A	TP	PIM	GP	G	A	TP	PIM
1990-91	Prince Albert	WHL	64	9	12	21	114	3	0	0	0	0
1991-92	Prince Albert	WHL	4	2	1	3	8	....	....	....	....	....
	Spokane	WHL	60	7	10	17	302	10	0	0	0	69
1992-93	Medicine Hat	WHL	65	12	10	22	205	10	1	6	7	15
1993-94	Cincinnati	IHL	47	1	5	6	55	2	0	0	0	2
	Birmingham	ECHL	16	3	7	10	38	....	....	....	....	....

Signed as a free agent by **Florida**, October 4, 1993.

LINDEN, TREVOR   VAN.

Center/Right wing. Shoots right. 6'4", 210 lbs.   Born, Medicine Hat, Alta., April 11, 1970.
(Vancouver's 1st choice, 2nd overall, in 1988 Entry Draft).

				Regular Season					Playoffs			
Season	Club	Lea	GP	G	A	TP	PIM	GP	G	A	TP	PIM
1986-87	Medicine Hat	WHL	72	14	22	36	59	20	5	4	9	17
1987-88	Medicine Hat	WHL	67	46	64	110	76	16	*13	12	25	19
1988-89a	**Vancouver**	**NHL**	80	30	29	59	41	7	3	4	7	8
1989-90	**Vancouver**	**NHL**	73	21	30	51	43	....	....	....	....	....
1990-91	**Vancouver**	**NHL**	80	33	37	70	65	6	0	7	7	2
1991-92	**Vancouver**	**NHL**	80	31	44	75	101	13	4	8	12	6
1992-93	**Vancouver**	**NHL**	84	33	39	72	64	12	5	8	13	16
1993-94	**Vancouver**	**NHL**	84	32	29	61	73	24	12	13	25	18
	NHL Totals		**481**	**180**	**208**	**388**	**387**	**62**	**24**	**40**	**64**	**50**

a   NHL All-Rookie Team (1989)
Played in NHL All-Star Game (1991, 1992)

LINDGREN, MATS   EDM.

Center. Shoots left. 6'1", 187 lbs.   Born, Skelleftea, Sweden, October 1, 1974.
(Winnipeg's 1st choice, 15th overall, in 1993 Entry Draft).

				Regular Season					Playoffs			
Season	Club	Lea	GP	G	A	TP	PIM	GP	G	A	TP	PIM
1991-92	Skelleftea	Swe. 2	29	14	8	22	14	....	....	....	....	....
1992-93	Skelleftea	Swe. 2	32	20	14	34	18	....	....	....	....	....
1993-94	Farjestad	Swe.	22	11	6	17	26	....	....	....	....	....

Traded to **Edmonton** by **Winnipeg** with Boris Mironov, Winnipeg's first round choice (Jason Bonsignore) in 1994 Entry Draft and Florida's fourth round choice (previously acquired by Winnipeg — Edmonton selected Adam Copeland) in 1994 Entry Draft for Dave Manson and St. Louis' sixth round choice (previously acquired by Edmonton — Winnipeg selected Chris Kibermanis) in 1994 Entry Draft, March 15, 1994.

LINDQVIST, FREDRIK   N.J.

Center. Shoots left. 5'11", 176 lbs.   Born, Sodertalje, Sweden, June 21, 1973.
(New Jersey's 4th choice, 55th overall, in 1991 Entry Draft).

				Regular Season					Playoffs			
Season	Club	Lea	GP	G	A	TP	PIM	GP	G	A	TP	PIM
1989-90	Huddinge	Swe. 2	2	0	0	0	0	....	....	....	....	....
1990-91	Djurgarden	Swe.	28	6	4	10	0	7	1	0	1	2
1991-92	Djurgarden	Swe.	39	9	6	15	14	10	1	1	2	2
1992-93	Djurgarden	Swe.	39	9	11	20	8	4	1	2	3	2
1993-94	Djurgarden	Swe.	25	5	8	13	8	6	2	1	3	2

LINDROS, BRETT   (LIHND-rahz)   NYI

Right wing. Shoots right. 6'4", 215 lbs.   Born, London, Ont., December 2, 1975.
(NY Islanders' 1st choice, 9th overall, in 1994 Entry Draft).

				Regular Season					Playoffs			
Season	Club	Lea	GP	G	A	TP	PIM	GP	G	A	TP	PIM
1992-93	Kingston	OHL	31	11	11	22	162	....	....	....	....	....
1993-94	Cdn. National		44	7	7	14	118	....	....	....	....	....
	Kingston	OHL	15	4	6	10	94	3	0	0	0	18

LINDROS, ERIC   (LIHND-rahz)   PHI.

Center. Shoots right. 6'4", 229 lbs.   Born, London, Ont., February 28, 1973.
(Quebec's 1st choice, 1st overall, in 1991 Entry Draft).

				Regular Season					Playoffs			
Season	Club	Lea	GP	G	A	TP	PIM	GP	G	A	TP	PIM
1989-90	Det. Compuware	USHL	14	23	29	52	123	....	....	....	....	....
a	Oshawa	OHL	25	17	19	36	61	17	18	18	36	76
1990-91bc	Oshawa	OHL	57	*71	78	*149	189	16	*18	20	*38	*93
1991-92	Oshawa	OHL	13	9	22	31	54	....	....	....	....	....
	Cdn. National		24	19	16	35	34	....	....	....	....	....
	Cdn. Olympic		8	5	6	11	6	....	....	....	....	....
1992-93d	**Philadelphia**	**NHL**	61	41	34	75	147	....	....	....	....	....
1993-94	**Philadelphia**	**NHL**	65	44	53	97	103	....	....	....	....	....
	NHL Totals		**126**	**85**	**87**	**172**	**250**					

a   Memorial Cup All-Star Team (1990)
b   OHL First All-Star Team (1991)
c   Canadian Major Junior Player of the Year (1991)
d   NHL/Upper Deck All-Rookie Team (1993)
Played in NHL All-Star Game (1994)

Traded to **Philadelphia** by **Quebec** for Peter Forsberg, Steve Duchesne, Kerry Huffman, Mike Ricci, Ron Hextall, Chris Simon, Philadelphia's first choice in the 1993 (Jocelyn Thibault) and 1994 (later traded to Toronto — later traded to Washington — Washington selected Nolan Baumgartner) Entry Drafts and cash, June 30, 1992.

LINDSAY, BILL   FLA.

Left wing. Shoots left. 5'11", 185 lbs.   Born, Big Fork, MT, May 17, 1971.
(Quebec's 6th choice, 103rd overall, in 1991 Entry Draft).

				Regular Season					Playoffs			
Season	Club	Lea	GP	G	A	TP	PIM	GP	G	A	TP	PIM
1990-91	Tri-Cities	WHL	63	46	47	93	151	5	3	6	9	10
1991-92	**Quebec**	**NHL**	23	2	4	6	14	....	....	....	....	....
a	Tri-Cities	WHL	42	34	59	93	111	3	2	3	5	16
1992-93	**Quebec**	**NHL**	44	4	9	13	16	....	....	....	....	....
	Halifax	AHL	20	11	13	24	18	....	....	....	....	....
1993-94	**Florida**	**NHL**	84	6	6	12	97	....	....	....	....	....
	NHL Totals		**151**	**12**	**19**	**31**	**127**					

a   WHL West Second All-Star Team (1992)
Claimed by **Florida** from **Quebec** in Expansion Draft, June 24, 1993.

LING, DAVID   QUE.

Right wing. Shoots right. 5'9", 185 lbs.   Born, Halifax, N.S., January 9, 1975.
(Quebec's 9th choice, 179th overall, in 1993 Entry Draft).

				Regular Season					Playoffs			
Season	Club	Lea	GP	G	A	TP	PIM	GP	G	A	TP	PIM
1992-93	Kingston	OHL	64	17	46	63	275	16	3	12	15	*72
1993-94	Kingston	OHL	61	37	40	77	*254	6	4	2	6	16

LIPUMA, CHRIS   T.B.

Defense. Shoots left. 6', 183 lbs.   Born, Bridgeview, IL, March 23, 1971.

				Regular Season					Playoffs			
Season	Club	Lea	GP	G	A	TP	PIM	GP	G	A	TP	PIM
1990-91	Kitchener	OHL	61	6	30	36	145	4	0	1	1	4
1991-92	Kitchener	OHL	61	13	59	72	115	14	4	9	13	34
1992-93	**Tampa Bay**	**NHL**	15	0	5	5	34	....	....	....	....	....
	Atlanta	IHL	66	4	14	18	379	9	1	1	2	35
1993-94	**Tampa Bay**	**NHL**	27	0	4	4	77	....	....	....	....	....
	Atlanta	IHL	42	2	10	12	254	11	1	1	2	28
	NHL Totals		**42**	**0**	**9**	**9**	**111**					

Signed as a free agent by **Tampa Bay**, June 29, 1992.

LITVINOV, YURI   (liht-VIH-nohv)   NYR

Center. Shoots right. 5'10", 176 lbs.   Born, Donetsk, USSR, April 11, 1976.
(NY Rangers' 7th choice, 135th overall, in 1994 Entry Draft).

				Regular Season					Playoffs			
Season	Club	Lea	GP	G	A	TP	PIM	GP	G	A	TP	PIM
1993-94	Soviet Wings	CIS	42	5	6	11	34	....	....	....	....	....

LOACH, LONNIE   NYI

Left wing. Shoots left. 5'10", 181 lbs.   Born, New Liskeard, Ont., April 14, 1968.
(Chicago's 4th choice, 98th overall, in 1986 Entry Draft).

				Regular Season					Playoffs			
Season	Club	Lea	GP	G	A	TP	PIM	GP	G	A	TP	PIM
1985-86	Guelph	OHL	65	41	42	83	63	20	7	8	15	16
1986-87	Guelph	OHL	56	31	24	55	42	5	2	1	3	2
1987-88	Guelph	OHL	66	43	49	92	75	....	....	....	....	....
1988-89	Flint	IHL	41	22	26	48	30	....	....	....	....	....
	Saginaw	IHL	32	7	6	13	27	....	....	....	....	....
1989-90	Indianapolis	IHL	3	0	0	0	0	....	....	....	....	....
	Fort Wayne	IHL	54	15	33	48	40	5	4	2	6	15
1990-91ab	Fort Wayne	IHL	81	55	76	*131	45	19	5	11	16	13
1991-92	Adirondack	AHL	67	37	49	86	69	19	*13	4	17	10
1992-93	**Ottawa**	**NHL**	3	0	0	0	0	....	....	....	....	....
	Los Angeles	NHL	50	10	13	23	27	1	0	0	0	0
	Phoenix	IHL	4	2	3	5	10	....	....	....	....	....
1993-94	**Anaheim**	**NHL**	3	0	0	0	2	....	....	....	....	....
	San Diego	IHL	74	42	49	91	65	9	4	10	14	6
	NHL Totals		**56**	**10**	**13**	**23**	**29**	**1**	**0**	**0**	**0**	**0**

a   IHL Second All-Star Team (1991)
b   Won Leo P. Lamoureux Trophy (Leading Scorer - IHL) (1991)
Signed as a free agent by **Detroit**, June 7, 1991. Claimed by **Ottawa** from **Detroit** in Expansion Draft, June 18, 1992. Claimed on waivers by **Los Angeles** from **Ottawa**, October 21, 1992. Claimed by **Anaheim** from **Los Angeles** in Expansion Draft, June 24, 1993.

LOACH, MIKE   NYI

Center. Shoots right. 6'1", 181 lbs.   Born, New Liskeard, Ont., September 8, 1976.
(NY Islanders' 8th choice, 194th overall, in 1994 Draft).

				Regular Season					Playoffs			
Season	Club	Lea	GP	G	A	TP	PIM	GP	G	A	TP	PIM
1993-94	Windsor	OHL	47	12	13	25	86	4	0	0	0	9

LOEWEN, DARCY   (LOH-wihn)

Left wing. Shoots left. 5'10", 185 lbs.   Born, Calgary, Alta., February 26, 1969.
(Buffalo's 2nd choice, 55th overall, in 1988 Entry Draft).

				Regular Season					Playoffs			
Season	Club	Lea	GP	G	A	TP	PIM	GP	G	A	TP	PIM
1986-87	Spokane	WHL	68	15	25	40	129	5	0	0	0	16
1987-88	Spokane	WHL	72	30	44	74	231	15	7	5	12	54
1988-89	Spokane	WHL	60	31	27	58	194	....	....	....	....	....
	Cdn. National		2	0	0	0	0	....	....	....	....	....
1989-90	**Buffalo**	**NHL**	4	0	0	0	4	....	....	....	....	....
	Rochester	AHL	50	7	11	18	193	5	1	0	1	6
1990-91	**Buffalo**	**NHL**	6	0	0	0	8	....	....	....	....	....
	Rochester	AHL	71	13	15	28	130	15	1	5	6	14
1991-92	**Buffalo**	**NHL**	2	0	0	0	2	....	....	....	....	....
	Rochester	AHL	73	11	20	31	193	4	0	1	1	8
1992-93	**Ottawa**	**NHL**	79	4	5	9	145	....	....	....	....	....
1993-94	**Ottawa**	**NHL**	44	0	3	3	52	....	....	....	....	....
	NHL Totals		**135**	**4**	**8**	**12**	**211**					

Claimed by **Ottawa** from **Buffalo** in Expansion Draft, June 18, 1992.

LOISELLE, CLAUDE (lwah-ZEHL) NYI

Center. Shoots left. 5'11", 195 lbs. Born, Ottawa, Ont., May 29, 1963.
(Detroit's 1st choice, 23rd overall, in 1981 Entry Draft).

			Regular Season					Playoffs				
Season	Club	Lea	GP	G	A	TP	PIM	GP	G	A	TP	PIM
1980-81	Windsor	OHA	68	38	56	94	103	11	3	3	6	40
1981-82	**Detroit**	**NHL**	**4**	**1**	**0**	**1**	**2**	....	....	....	....	....
	Windsor	OHL	68	36	73	109	192	9	2	10	12	42
1982-83	**Detroit**	**NHL**	**18**	**2**	**0**	**2**	**15**	....	....	....	....	....
	Adirondack	AHL	6	1	7	8	0	6	2	4	6	0
1983-84	**Detroit**	**NHL**	**28**	**4**	**6**	**10**	**32**	....	....	....	....	....
	Adirondack	AHL	29	13	16	29	59	....	....	....	....	....
1984-85	**Detroit**	**NHL**	**30**	**8**	**1**	**9**	**45**	**3**	**0**	**2**	**2**	**0**
	Adirondack	AHL	47	22	29	51	24	....	....	....	....	....
1985-86	**Detroit**	**NHL**	**48**	**7**	**15**	**22**	**142**	....	....	....	....	....
	Adirondack	AHL	21	15	11	26	32	16	5	10	15	38
1986-87	**New Jersey**	**NHL**	**75**	**16**	**24**	**40**	**137**	....	....	....	....	....
1987-88	**New Jersey**	**NHL**	**68**	**17**	**18**	**35**	**121**	**20**	**4**	**6**	**10**	**50**
1988-89	**New Jersey**	**NHL**	**74**	**7**	**14**	**21**	**209**	....	....	....	....	....
1989-90	**Quebec**	**NHL**	**72**	**11**	**14**	**25**	**104**	....	....	....	....	....
1990-91	**Quebec**	**NHL**	**59**	**5**	**10**	**15**	**86**	....	....	....	....	....
	Toronto	**NHL**	**7**	**1**	**1**	**2**	**2**	....	....	....	....	....
1991-92	**Toronto**	**NHL**	**64**	**6**	**9**	**15**	**102**	....	....	....	....	....
	NY Islanders	**NHL**	**11**	**1**	**1**	**2**	**13**	....	....	....	....	....
1992-93	**NY Islanders**	**NHL**	**41**	**5**	**3**	**8**	**90**	**18**	**0**	**3**	**3**	**10**
1993-94	**NY Islanders**	**NHL**	**17**	**1**	**1**	**2**	**49**	....	....	....	....	....
	NHL Totals		**616**	**92**	**117**	**209**	**1149**	**41**	**4**	**11**	**15**	**60**

Traded to **New Jersey** by **Detroit** for Tim Higgins, June 25, 1986. Traded to **Quebec** by **New Jersey** with Joe Cirella and New Jersey's eighth round choice (Alexander Karpovtsev) in 1990 Entry Draft for Walt Poddubny and Quebec's fourth round choice (Mike Bodnarchuk) in 1990 Entry Draft, June 17, 1989. Claimed on waivers by **Toronto**, March 5, 1991. Traded to **NY Islanders** by **Toronto** with Daniel Marois for Ken Baumgartner and Dave McLlwain, March 10, 1992.

LOMAKIN, ANDREI FLA.

Right wing. Shoots left. 5'10", 175 lbs. Born, Voskresensk, USSR, April 3, 1964.
(Philadelphia's 7th choice, 138th overall, in 1991 Entry Draft).

			Regular Season					Playoffs				
Season	Club	Lea	GP	G	A	TP	PIM	GP	G	A	TP	PIM
1981-82	Khimik	USSR	8	1	1	2	2	....	....	....	....	....
1982-83	Khimik	USSR	56	15	8	23	32	....	....	....	....	....
1983-84	Khimik	USSR	44	10	8	18	26	....	....	....	....	....
1984-85	Khimik	USSR	52	13	10	23	24	....	....	....	....	....
1985-86						DID NOT PLAY						
1986-87	Moscow D'amo	USSR	40	15	14	29	30	....	....	....	....	....
1987-88	Moscow D'amo	USSR	45	10	15	25	24	....	....	....	....	....
1988-89	Moscow D'amo	USSR	44	9	16	25	22	....	....	....	....	....
1989-90	Moscow D'amo	USSR	48	11	15	26	36	....	....	....	....	....
1990-91	Moscow D'amo	USSR	45	16	17	33	22	....	....	....	....	....
1991-92	Moscow D'amo	CIS	2	1	3	4	2	....	....	....	....	....
	Philadelphia	**NHL**	**57**	**14**	**16**	**30**	**26**	....	....	....	....	....
1992-93	**Philadelphia**	**NHL**	**51**	**8**	**12**	**20**	**34**	....	....	....	....	....
1993-94	**Florida**	**NHL**	**76**	**19**	**28**	**47**	**26**	....	....	....	....	....
	NHL Totals		**184**	**41**	**56**	**97**	**86**	....	....	....	....	....

Claimed by **Florida** from **Philadelphia** in Expansion Draft, June 24, 1993.

LOMBARDI, STEPHEN BOS.

Left wing. Shoots left. 6'1", 180 lbs. Born, South Easton, MA, April 14, 1973.
(Boston's 10th choice, 238th overall, in 1991 Entry Draft).

			Regular Season					Playoffs				
Season	Club	Lea	GP	G	A	TP	PIM	GP	G	A	TP	PIM
1991-92	Yale	ECAC	14	2	3	5	2	....	....	....	....	....
1992-93	Yale	ECAC	27	1	6	7	14	....	....	....	....	....
1993-94	Yale	ECAC	20	4	2	6	16	....	....	....	....	....

LONEY, BRIAN VAN.

Right wing. Shoots right. 6'2", 200 lbs. Born, Winnipeg, Man., August 9, 1972.
(Vancouver's 6th choice, 110th overall, in 1992 Entry Draft).

			Regular Season					Playoffs				
Season	Club	Lea	GP	G	A	TP	PIM	GP	G	A	TP	PIM
1991-92	Ohio State	CCHA	37	21	34	55	109	....	....	....	....	....
1992-93	Red Deer	WHL	66	39	36	75	147	4	1	1	2	19
	Cdn. National	....	1	0	1	1	0	....	....	....	....	....
	Hamilton	AHL	3	0	2	2	0	....	....	....	....	....
1993-94	Hamilton	AHL	67	18	16	34	76	4	0	0	0	8

LONEY, TROY (LOH-nee) NYI

Left wing. Shoots left. 6'3", 209 lbs. Born, Bow Island, Alta., September 21, 1963.
(Pittsburgh's 3rd choice, 52nd overall, in 1982 Entry Draft).

			Regular Season					Playoffs				
Season	Club	Lea	GP	G	A	TP	PIM	GP	G	A	TP	PIM
1980-81	Lethbridge	WHL	71	18	13	31	100	9	2	2	5	14
1981-82	Lethbridge	WHL	71	26	33	59	152	12	3	3	6	10
1982-83	Lethbridge	WHL	72	33	34	67	156	20	10	7	17	43
1983-84	**Pittsburgh**	**NHL**	**13**	**0**	**0**	**0**	**9**	....	....	....	....	....
	Baltimore	AHL	63	18	13	31	147	10	0	2	2	19
1984-85	**Pittsburgh**	**NHL**	**46**	**10**	**8**	**18**	**59**	....	....	....	....	....
	Baltimore	AHL	15	4	2	6	25	....	....	....	....	....
1985-86	**Pittsburgh**	**NHL**	**47**	**3**	**9**	**12**	**95**	....	....	....	....	....
	Baltimore	AHL	33	12	11	23	84	....	....	....	....	....
1986-87	**Pittsburgh**	**NHL**	**23**	**8**	**7**	**15**	**22**	....	....	....	....	....
	Baltimore	AHL	40	13	14	27	134	....	....	....	....	....
1987-88	**Pittsburgh**	**NHL**	**65**	**5**	**13**	**18**	**151**	....	....	....	....	....
1988-89	**Pittsburgh**	**NHL**	**69**	**10**	**6**	**16**	**165**	**11**	**1**	**3**	**4**	**24**
1989-90	**Pittsburgh**	**NHL**	**67**	**11**	**16**	**27**	**168**	....	....	....	....	....
1990-91	**Pittsburgh**	**NHL**	**44**	**7**	**9**	**16**	**85**	**24**	**2**	**2**	**4**	**41**
	Muskegon	IHL	2	0	0	0	5	....	....	....	....	....
1991-92	**Pittsburgh**	**NHL**	**76**	**10**	**16**	**26**	**127**	**21**	**4**	**5**	**9**	**32**
1992-93	**Pittsburgh**	**NHL**	**82**	**5**	**16**	**21**	**99**	**10**	**1**	**4**	**5**	**0**
1993-94	**Anaheim**	**NHL**	**62**	**13**	**6**	**19**	**88**	....	....	....	....	....
	NHL Totals		**594**	**82**	**106**	**188**	**1068**	**66**	**8**	**14**	**22**	**97**

Claimed by **Anaheim** from **Pittsburgh** in Expansion Draft, June 24, 1993. Traded to **NY Islanders** by **Anaheim** for Tom Kurvers, June 29, 1994.

LONGO, CHRIS WSH.

Right wing. Shoots right. 5'10", 180 lbs. Born, Belleville, Ont., January 5, 1972.
(Washington's 3rd choice, 51st overall, in 1990 Entry Draft).

			Regular Season					Playoffs				
Season	Club	Lea	GP	G	A	TP	PIM	GP	G	A	TP	PIM
1989-90	Peterborough	OHL	66	33	41	74	48	11	2	3	5	14
1990-91	Peterborough	OHL	64	30	38	68	68	4	1	0	1	0
1991-92	Peterborough	OHL	25	5	14	19	16	10	5	6	11	16
1992-93	Baltimore	AHL	74	7	18	25	52	7	0	1	1	0
1993-94	Portland	AHL	69	6	19	25	69	17	2	4	6	11

LONSINGER, BRYAN

Defense. Shoots right. 6'2", 210 lbs. Born, Caldwell, NY, July 21, 1972.
(NY Rangers' 9th choice, 139th overall, in 1990 Entry Draft).

			Regular Season					Playoffs				
Season	Club	Lea	GP	G	A	TP	PIM	GP	G	A	TP	PIM
1991-92	Harvard	ECAC	19	1	5	6	4	....	....	....	....	....
1992-93	Harvard	ECAC	31	2	9	11	6	....	....	....	....	....
1993-94	Harvard	ECAC	33	1	5	6	14	....	....	....	....	....

LOWE, KEVIN (LOH) NYR

Defense. Shoots left. 6'2", 195 lbs. Born, Lachute, Que., April 15, 1959.
(Edmonton's 1st choice, 21st overall, in 1979 Entry Draft).

			Regular Season					Playoffs				
Season	Club	Lea	GP	G	A	TP	PIM	GP	G	A	TP	PIM
1977-78	Quebec	QJHL	64	13	52	65	86	4	1	2	3	6
1978-79a	Quebec	QJHL	68	26	60	86	120	6	1	7	8	36
1979-80	**Edmonton**	**NHL**	**64**	**2**	**19**	**21**	**70**	**3**	**0**	**1**	**1**	**0**
1980-81	**Edmonton**	**NHL**	**79**	**10**	**24**	**34**	**94**	**9**	**0**	**2**	**2**	**11**
1981-82	**Edmonton**	**NHL**	**80**	**9**	**31**	**40**	**63**	**5**	**0**	**3**	**3**	**0**
1982-83	**Edmonton**	**NHL**	**80**	**6**	**34**	**40**	**43**	**16**	**1**	**8**	**9**	**10**
1983-84	**Edmonton**	**NHL**	**80**	**4**	**42**	**46**	**59**	**19**	**3**	**7**	**10**	**16**
1984-85	**Edmonton**	**NHL**	**80**	**4**	**21**	**25**	**104**	**16**	**0**	**5**	**5**	**8**
1985-86	**Edmonton**	**NHL**	**74**	**2**	**16**	**18**	**90**	**10**	**1**	**3**	**4**	**15**
1986-87	**Edmonton**	**NHL**	**77**	**8**	**29**	**37**	**94**	**21**	**2**	**4**	**6**	**22**
1987-88	**Edmonton**	**NHL**	**70**	**9**	**15**	**24**	**89**	**19**	**0**	**2**	**2**	**26**
1988-89	**Edmonton**	**NHL**	**76**	**7**	**18**	**25**	**98**	**7**	**1**	**2**	**3**	**4**
1989-90bc	**Edmonton**	**NHL**	**78**	**7**	**26**	**33**	**140**	**20**	**0**	**2**	**2**	**10**
1990-91	**Edmonton**	**NHL**	**73**	**3**	**13**	**16**	**113**	**14**	**1**	**1**	**2**	**14**
1991-92	**Edmonton**	**NHL**	**55**	**2**	**8**	**10**	**107**	**11**	**0**	**3**	**3**	**16**
1992-93	**NY Rangers**	**NHL**	**49**	**3**	**12**	**15**	**58**	....	....	....	....	....
1993-94	**NY Rangers**	**NHL**	**71**	**5**	**14**	**19**	**70**	**22**	**1**	**0**	**1**	**20**
	NHL Totals		**1086**	**81**	**322**	**403**	**1292**	**192**	**10**	**43**	**53**	**172**

a QMJHL Second All-Star Team (1979)
b Won Bud Man of the Year Award (1990)
c Won King Clancy Memorial Trophy (1990)

Played in NHL All-Star Game (1984-86, 1988-90, 1993)

Traded to **NY Rangers** by **Edmonton** for Roman Oksyuta and NY Rangers' third round choice (Alexander Kerch) in 1993 Entry Draft, December 11, 1992.

LOWRY, DAVE FLA.

Left wing. Shoots left. 6'1", 195 lbs. Born, Sudbury, Ont., February 14, 1965.
(Vancouver's 6th choice, 110th overall, in 1983 Entry Draft).

			Regular Season					Playoffs				
Season	Club	Lea	GP	G	A	TP	PIM	GP	G	A	TP	PIM
1982-83	London	OHL	42	11	16	27	48	3	0	0	0	14
1983-84	London	OHL	66	29	47	76	125	8	6	6	12	41
1984-85a	London	OHL	61	60	60	120	94	8	6	5	11	10
1985-86	**Vancouver**	**NHL**	**73**	**10**	**8**	**18**	**143**	**3**	**0**	**0**	**0**	**0**
1986-87	**Vancouver**	**NHL**	**70**	**8**	**10**	**18**	**176**	....	....	....	....	....
1987-88	**Vancouver**	**NHL**	**22**	**1**	**3**	**4**	**38**	....	....	....	....	....
	Fredericton	AHL	46	18	27	45	59	14	7	3	10	72
1988-89	**St. Louis**	**NHL**	**21**	**3**	**3**	**6**	**11**	**10**	**0**	**5**	**5**	**4**
	Peoria	IHL	58	31	35	66	45	....	....	....	....	....
1989-90	**St. Louis**	**NHL**	**78**	**19**	**6**	**25**	**75**	**12**	**2**	**1**	**3**	**39**
1990-91	**St. Louis**	**NHL**	**79**	**19**	**21**	**40**	**168**	**13**	**1**	**4**	**5**	**35**
1991-92	**St. Louis**	**NHL**	**75**	**7**	**13**	**20**	**77**	**6**	**0**	**1**	**1**	**20**
1992-93	**St. Louis**	**NHL**	**58**	**5**	**8**	**13**	**101**	**11**	**2**	**0**	**2**	**14**
1993-94	**Florida**	**NHL**	**80**	**15**	**22**	**37**	**64**	....	....	....	....	....
	NHL Totals		**556**	**87**	**94**	**181**	**853**	**55**	**5**	**11**	**16**	**112**

a OHL First All-Star Team (1985)

Traded to **St. Louis** by **Vancouver** for Ernie Vargas, September 29, 1988. Claimed by **Florida** from **St. Louis** in Expansion Draft, June 24, 1993.

LUDWIG, CRAIG DAL.

Defense. Shoots left. 6'3", 222 lbs. Born, Rhinelander, WI, March 15, 1961.
(Montreal's 5th choice, 61st overall, in 1980 Entry Draft).

			Regular Season					Playoffs				
Season	Club	Lea	GP	G	A	TP	PIM	GP	G	A	TP	PIM
1979-80	North Dakota	WCHA	33	1	8	9	32	....	....	....	....	....
1980-81	North Dakota	WCHA	34	4	8	12	48	....	....	....	....	....
1981-82	North Dakota	WCHA	37	4	17	21	42	....	....	....	....	....
1982-83	**Montreal**	**NHL**	**80**	**0**	**25**	**25**	**59**	**3**	**0**	**0**	**0**	**2**
1983-84	**Montreal**	**NHL**	**80**	**7**	**18**	**25**	**52**	**15**	**0**	**3**	**3**	**23**
1984-85	**Montreal**	**NHL**	**72**	**5**	**14**	**19**	**90**	**12**	**0**	**2**	**2**	**6**
1985-86	**Montreal**	**NHL**	**69**	**2**	**4**	**6**	**63**	**20**	**0**	**1**	**1**	**48**
1986-87	**Montreal**	**NHL**	**75**	**4**	**12**	**16**	**105**	**17**	**2**	**3**	**5**	**30**
1987-88	**Montreal**	**NHL**	**74**	**4**	**10**	**14**	**69**	**11**	**1**	**1**	**2**	**6**
1988-89	**Montreal**	**NHL**	**74**	**3**	**13**	**16**	**73**	**21**	**0**	**2**	**2**	**24**
1989-90	**Montreal**	**NHL**	**73**	**1**	**15**	**16**	**108**	**11**	**0**	**1**	**1**	**16**
1990-91	**NY Islanders**	**NHL**	**75**	**1**	**8**	**9**	**77**	....	....	....	....	....
1991-92	**Minnesota**	**NHL**	**73**	**2**	**9**	**11**	**54**	**7**	**0**	**1**	**1**	**19**
1992-93	**Minnesota**	**NHL**	**78**	**1**	**10**	**11**	**153**	....	....	....	....	....
1993-94	**Dallas**	**NHL**	**84**	**1**	**13**	**14**	**123**	**9**	**0**	**3**	**3**	**8**
	NHL Totals		**907**	**31**	**151**	**182**	**1026**	**126**	**3**	**17**	**20**	**182**

Traded to **NY Islanders** by **Montreal** for Gerald Diduck, September 4, 1990. Traded to **Minnesota** by **NY Islanders** for Tom Kurvers, June 22, 1991.

LUHNING, WARREN NYI

Right wing. Shoots right. 6'2", 185 lbs. Born, Edmonton, Alta., July 3, 1975.
(NY Islanders' 4th choice, 92nd overall, in 1993 Entry Draft).

			Regular Season					Playoffs				
Season	Club	Lea	GP	G	A	TP	PIM	GP	G	A	TP	PIM
1992-93	Cgy. Royals	AJHL	46	18	25	43	287	....	....	....	....	....
1993-94	U. of Michigan	CCHA	38	13	6	19	83	....	....	....	....	....

LUKOWICH, BRAD — NYI

Defense. Shoots left. 6'1", 170 lbs. Born, Cranbrook, B.C., August 12, 1976.
(NY Islanders' 4th choice, 90th overall, in 1994 Entry Draft).

			Regular Season					Playoffs				
Season	Club	Lea	GP	G	A	TP	PIM	GP	G	A	TP	PIM
1992-93	Kamloops	WHL	1	0	0	0	0	....	....	....	....	....
1993-94	Kamloops	WHL	42	5	11	16	166	16	0	1	1	35

LUMME, JYRKI (LOO-mee, YUHR-kee) — VAN.

Defense. Shoots left. 6'1", 205 lbs. Born, Tampere, Finland, July 16, 1966.
(Montreal's 3rd choice, 57th overall, in 1986 Entry Draft).

			Regular Season					Playoffs				
Season	Club	Lea	GP	G	A	TP	PIM	GP	G	A	TP	PIM
1984-85	KooVee	Fin. 3	30	6	4	10	44	....	....	....	....	....
1985-86	Ilves	Fin.	31	1	4	5	4	....	....	....	....	....
1986-87	Ilves	Fin.	43	12	12	24	52	4	0	1	1	2
1987-88	Ilves	Fin.	43	8	22	30	75	....	....	....	....	....
1988-89	**Montreal**	**NHL**	**21**	**1**	**3**	**4**	**10**	....	....	....	....	....
	Sherbrooke	AHL	26	4	11	15	10	6	1	3	4	4
1989-90	**Montreal**	**NHL**	**54**	**1**	**19**	**20**	**41**	....	....	....	....	....
	Vancouver	**NHL**	**11**	**3**	**7**	**10**	**8**	....	....	....	....	....
1990-91	**Vancouver**	**NHL**	**80**	**5**	**27**	**32**	**59**	**6**	**2**	**3**	**5**	**0**
1991-92	**Vancouver**	**NHL**	**75**	**12**	**32**	**44**	**65**	**13**	**2**	**3**	**5**	**4**
1992-93	**Vancouver**	**NHL**	**74**	**8**	**36**	**44**	**55**	**12**	**0**	**5**	**5**	**6**
1993-94	**Vancouver**	**NHL**	**83**	**13**	**42**	**55**	**50**	**24**	**2**	**11**	**13**	**16**
	NHL Totals		**398**	**43**	**166**	**209**	**288**	**55**	**6**	**22**	**28**	**26**

Traded to **Vancouver** by **Montreal** for St. Louis' second round choice (previously acquired by Vancouver — Montreal selected Craig Darby) in 1991 Entry Draft, March 6, 1990.

LUONGO, CHRIS (loo-WAHN-goh) — NYI

Defense. Shoots right. 6', 180 lbs. Born, Detroit, MI, March 17, 1967.
(Detroit's 5th choice, 92nd overall, in 1985 Entry Draft).

			Regular Season					Playoffs				
Season	Club	Lea	GP	G	A	TP	PIM	GP	G	A	TP	PIM
1985-86	Michigan State	CCHA	38	1	5	6	29	....	....	....	....	....
1986-87a	Michigan State	CCHA	27	4	16	20	38	....	....	....	....	....
1987-88	Michigan State	CCHA	45	3	15	18	49	....	....	....	....	....
1988-89b	Michigan State	CCHA	47	4	21	25	42	....	....	....	....	....
1989-90	Adirondack	AHL	53	9	14	23	37	3	0	0	0	0
	Phoenix	IHL	23	5	9	14	41	....	....	....	....	....
1990-91	**Detroit**	**NHL**	**4**	**0**	**1**	**1**	**4**	....	....	....	....	....
	Adirondack	AHL	76	14	25	39	71	2	0	0	0	7
1991-92	Adirondack	AHL	80	6	20	26	60	19	3	5	8	10
1992-93	**Ottawa**	**NHL**	**76**	**3**	**9**	**12**	**68**	....	....	....	....	....
	New Haven	AHL	7	0	2	2	2	....	....	....	....	....
1993-94	**NY Islanders**	**NHL**	**17**	**1**	**3**	**4**	**13**	....	....	....	....	....
	Salt Lake	IHL	51	9	31	40	54	....	....	....	....	....
	NHL Totals		**97**	**4**	**13**	**17**	**85**	....	....	....	....	....

a Named to NCAA All-Tournament Team (1987)
b CCHA Second All-Star Team (1989)

Signed as a free agent by **Ottawa**, September 9, 1992. Traded to **NY Islanders** by **Ottawa** for Jeff Finley, June 30, 1993.

MacDERMID, PAUL — QUE.

Right wing. Shoots right. 6'1", 205 lbs. Born, Chesley, Ont., April 14, 1963.
(Hartford's 2nd choice, 61st overall, in 1981 Entry Draft).

			Regular Season					Playoffs				
Season	Club	Lea	GP	G	A	TP	PIM	GP	G	A	TP	PIM
1980-81	Windsor	OHA	68	15	17	32	106	....	....	....	....	....
1981-82	**Hartford**	**NHL**	**3**	**1**	**0**	**1**	**2**	....	....	....	....	....
	Windsor	OHL	65	26	45	71	179	9	6	4	10	17
1982-83	**Hartford**	**NHL**	**7**	**0**	**0**	**0**	**2**	....	....	....	....	....
	Windsor	OHL	42	35	45	80	9	....	....	....	....	....
1983-84	**Hartford**	**NHL**	**3**	**0**	**1**	**1**	**0**	....	....	....	....	....
	Binghamton	AHL	70	31	30	61	130	....	....	....	....	....
1984-85	**Hartford**	**NHL**	**31**	**4**	**7**	**11**	**29**	....	....	....	....	....
	Binghamton	AHL	48	9	31	40	87	....	....	....	....	....
1985-86	**Hartford**	**NHL**	**74**	**13**	**10**	**23**	**160**	**10**	**2**	**1**	**3**	**20**
1986-87	**Hartford**	**NHL**	**72**	**7**	**11**	**18**	**202**	**6**	**2**	**1**	**3**	**34**
1987-88	**Hartford**	**NHL**	**80**	**20**	**15**	**35**	**139**	**6**	**0**	**5**	**5**	**14**
1988-89	**Hartford**	**NHL**	**74**	**17**	**27**	**44**	**141**	**4**	**1**	**1**	**2**	**16**
1989-90	**Hartford**	**NHL**	**29**	**6**	**12**	**18**	**69**	....	....	....	....	....
	Winnipeg	**NHL**	**44**	**7**	**10**	**17**	**100**	**7**	**0**	**2**	**2**	**8**
1990-91	**Winnipeg**	**NHL**	**69**	**15**	**21**	**36**	**128**	....	....	....	....	....
1991-92	**Winnipeg**	**NHL**	**59**	**10**	**11**	**21**	**151**	....	....	....	....	....
	Washington	**NHL**	**15**	**2**	**5**	**7**	**43**	**7**	**0**	**1**	**1**	**22**
1992-93	**Washington**	**NHL**	**72**	**9**	**8**	**17**	**80**	....	....	....	....	....
1993-94	**Quebec**	**NHL**	**44**	**2**	**3**	**5**	**35**	....	....	....	....	....
	NHL Totals		**676**	**113**	**141**	**254**	**1281**	**40**	**5**	**11**	**16**	**114**

Traded to **Winnipeg** by **Hartford** for Randy Cunneyworth, December 13, 1989. Traded to **Washington** by **Winnipeg** for Mike Lalor, March 2, 1992. Traded to **Quebec** by **Washington** with Reggie Savage for Mike Hough, June 20, 1993.

MacDONALD, DOUG — BUF.

Left wing. Shoots left. 6', 192 lbs. Born, Assiniboia, Sask., February 8, 1969.
(Buffalo's 3rd choice, 77th overall, in 1989 Entry Draft).

			Regular Season					Playoffs				
Season	Club	Lea	GP	G	A	TP	PIM	GP	G	A	TP	PIM
1988-89	U. Wisconsin	WCHA	44	23	25	48	50	....	....	....	....	....
1989-90	U. Wisconsin	WCHA	44	16	35	51	52	....	....	....	....	....
1990-91	U. Wisconsin	WCHA	31	20	26	46	50	....	....	....	....	....
1991-92	U. Wisconsin	WCHA	29	14	25	39	58	....	....	....	....	....
1992-93	**Buffalo**	**NHL**	**5**	**1**	**0**	**1**	**2**	....	....	....	....	....
	Rochester	AHL	64	25	33	58	58	7	0	2	2	4
1993-94	**Buffalo**	**NHL**	**4**	**0**	**0**	**0**	**0**	....	....	....	....	....
	Rochester	AHL	63	25	19	44	46	4	1	1	2	8
	NHL Totals		**9**	**1**	**0**	**1**	**2**	....	....	....	....	....

MacDONALD, GARETT — PHI.

Defense. Shoots left. 6', 183 lbs. Born, Burnaby, B.C., January 12, 1971.
(Philadelphia's 1st choice, 7th overall, in 1992 Supplemental Draft).

			Regular Season					Playoffs				
Season	Club	Lea	GP	G	A	TP	PIM	GP	G	A	TP	PIM
1990-91	N. Michigan	WCHA	41	2	8	10	56	....	....	....	....	....
1991-92	N. Michigan	WCHA	34	0	5	5	39	....	....	....	....	....
1992-93	N. Michigan	WCHA	39	4	12	16	68	....	....	....	....	....
1993-94	N. Michigan	WCHA	35	2	14	16	90	....	....	....	....	....

MacDONALD, JASON — DET.

Right wing. Shoots right. 6', 195 lbs. Born, Charlottetown, P.E.I., April 1, 1974.
(Detroit's 5th choice, 142nd overall, in 1992 Entry Draft).

			Regular Season					Playoffs				
Season	Club	Lea	GP	G	A	TP	PIM	GP	G	A	TP	PIM
1990-91	North Bay	OHL	57	12	15	27	126	10	3	3	6	15
1991-92	North Bay	OHL	17	5	8	13	50	....	....	....	....	....
	Owen Sound	OHL	42	17	19	36	129	5	0	3	3	16
1992-93	Owen Sound	OHL	56	46	43	89	197	8	6	5	11	28
1993-94a	Owen Sound	OHL	66	55	61	116	177	9	7	11	18	36

a OHL Second All-Star Team (1994)

MacDONALD, KEVIN

Defense. Shoots left. 6', 200 lbs. Born, Prescott, Ont., February 24, 1966.

			Regular Season					Playoffs				
Season	Club	Lea	GP	G	A	TP	PIM	GP	G	A	TP	PIM
1988-89	Muskegon	IHL	64	2	13	15	190	11	2	3	5	22
1989-90	New Haven	AHL	27	0	1	1	111	....	....	....	....	....
	Phoenix	IHL	30	1	5	6	201	....	....	....	....	....
1990-91	Phoenix	IHL	74	1	9	10	327	11	0	1	1	22
1991-92	Phoenix	IHL	76	7	14	21	304	....	....	....	....	....
1992-93	Phoenix	IHL	6	0	1	1	23	....	....	....	....	....
	Ft. Wayne	IHL	65	4	9	13	283	11	0	0	0	21
1993-94	Ft. Wayne	IHL	29	0	3	3	140	....	....	....	....	....
	Ottawa	**NHL**	**1**	**0**	**0**	**0**	**2**	....	....	....	....	....
	P.E.I.	AHL	40	2	4	6	245	....	....	....	....	....
	NHL Totals		**1**	**0**	**0**	**0**	**2**	....	....	....	....	....

Signed as a free agent by **Los Angeles**, July, 1990. Signed as a free agent by **Ottawa**, December 22, 1993.

MacDONALD, TOM — T.B.

Center. Shoots left. 5'11", 190 lbs. Born, Toronto, Ont., April 14, 1974.
(Tampa Bay's 11th choice, 241st overall, in 1992 Entry Draft).

			Regular Season					Playoffs				
Season	Club	Lea	GP	G	A	TP	PIM	GP	G	A	TP	PIM
1990-91	S.S. Marie	OHL	41	3	6	9	71	6	0	1	1	19
1991-92	S.S. Marie	OHL	52	11	15	26	139	19	3	7	10	31
1992-93	S.S. Marie	OHL	50	13	24	37	134	18	5	9	14	62
1993-94	S.S. Marie	OHL	55	34	36	70	175	14	3	7	10	38

MACHANIC, COREY — NYR

Defense. Shoots right. 6'3", 197 lbs. Born, Rome, NY, September 26, 1972.
(NY Rangers' 5th choice, 96th overall, in 1991 Entry Draft).

			Regular Season					Playoffs				
Season	Club	Lea	GP	G	A	TP	PIM	GP	G	A	TP	PIM
1990-91	U. of Vermont	ECAC	31	0	8	8	30	....	....	....	....	....
1991-92	U. of Vermont	ECAC	30	3	8	11	24	....	....	....	....	....
1992-93	U. of Vermont	ECAC	31	1	4	5	16	....	....	....	....	....
1993-94	U. of Vermont	ECAC	29	2	6	8	24	....	....	....	....	....

MacINNIS, AL — ST.L.

Defense. Shoots right. 6'2", 196 lbs. Born, Inverness, N.S., July 11, 1963.
(Calgary's 1st choice, 15th overall, in 1981 Entry Draft).

			Regular Season					Playoffs				
Season	Club	Lea	GP	G	A	TP	PIM	GP	G	A	TP	PIM
1980-81	Kitchener	OHA	47	11	28	39	59	18	4	12	16	20
1981-82	**Calgary**	**NHL**	**2**	**0**	**0**	**0**	**0**	....	....	....	....	....
a	Kitchener	OHL	59	25	50	75	145	15	5	10	15	44
1982-83	**Calgary**	**NHL**	**14**	**1**	**3**	**4**	**9**	....	....	....	....	....
a	Kitchener	OHL	51	38	46	84	67	8	3	8	11	9
1983-84	**Calgary**	**NHL**	**51**	**11**	**34**	**45**	**42**	**11**	**2**	**12**	**14**	**13**
	Colorado	CHL	19	5	14	19	22	....	....	....	....	....
1984-85	**Calgary**	**NHL**	**67**	**14**	**52**	**66**	**75**	**4**	**1**	**2**	**3**	**8**
1985-86	**Calgary**	**NHL**	**77**	**11**	**57**	**68**	**76**	**21**	**4**	***15**	**19**	**30**
1986-87b	**Calgary**	**NHL**	**79**	**20**	**56**	**76**	**97**	**4**	**1**	**0**	**1**	**0**
1987-88	**Calgary**	**NHL**	**80**	**25**	**58**	**83**	**114**	**7**	**3**	**6**	**9**	**18**
1988-89bc	**Calgary**	**NHL**	**79**	**16**	**58**	**74**	**126**	**22**	**7**	***24**	***31**	**46**
1989-90d	**Calgary**	**NHL**	**79**	**28**	**62**	**90**	**82**	**6**	**2**	**3**	**5**	**8**
1990-91d	**Calgary**	**NHL**	**78**	**28**	**75**	**103**	**90**	**7**	**2**	**3**	**5**	**8**
1991-92	**Calgary**	**NHL**	**72**	**20**	**57**	**77**	**83**	....	....	....	....	....
1992-93	**Calgary**	**NHL**	**50**	**11**	**43**	**54**	**61**	**6**	**1**	**6**	**7**	**10**
1993-94b	**Calgary**	**NHL**	**75**	**28**	**54**	**82**	**95**	**7**	**2**	**6**	**8**	**12**
	NHL Totals		**803**	**213**	**609**	**822**	**950**	**95**	**25**	**77**	**102**	**153**

a OHL First All-Star Team (1982, 1983)
b NHL Second All-Star Team (1987, 1989, 1994)
c Won Conn Smythe Trophy (1989)
d NHL First All-Star Team (1990, 1991)

Played in NHL All-Star Game (1985, 1988, 1990-92, 1994)

Traded to **St. Louis** by **Calgary** with Calgary's fourth round choice in 1997 Entry Draft for Phil Housley, St. Louis' second round choice in 1996 Entry Draft and second round choice in 1997 Entry Draft, July 4, 1994.

MacINTYRE, ANDY — CHI.

Left wing. Shoots left. 6'1", 190 lbs. Born, Thunder Bay, Ont., April 16, 1974.
(Chicago's 4th choice, 89th overall, in 1992 Entry Draft).

			Regular Season					Playoffs				
Season	Club	Lea	GP	G	A	TP	PIM	GP	G	A	TP	PIM
1990-91	Seattle	WHL	71	16	13	29	52	4	0	0	0	2
1991-92	Seattle	WHL	12	6	2	8	18	....	....	....	....	....
	Saskatoon	WHL	55	22	13	35	66	22	10	2	12	17
1992-93	Saskatoon	WHL	72	35	29	64	82	9	3	2	5	2
1993-94a	Saskatoon	WHL	72	54	35	89	58	16	6	6	12	16

a WHL East Second All-Star Team (1994)

MACIVER, NORM (mac-IGH-ver) OTT.

Defense. Shoots left. 5'11", 180 lbs. Born, Thunder Bay, Ont., September 8, 1964.

			Regular Season					Playoffs				
Season	Club	Lea	GP	G	A	TP	PIM	GP	G	A	TP	PIM
1982-83	Minn.-Duluth	WCHA	45	1	26	27	40	6	0	2	2	2
1983-84a	Minn.-Duluth	WCHA	31	13	28	41	28	8	1	10	11	8
1984-85bc	Minn.-Duluth	WCHA	47	14	47	61	63	10	3	3	6	6
1985-86bc	Minn.-Duluth	WCHA	42	11	51	62	36	4	2	3	5	2
1986-87	**NY Rangers**	**NHL**	**3**	**0**	**1**	**1**	**0**	....	....	....	....	....
	New Haven	AHL	71	6	30	36	73	7	0	0	0	9
1987-88	**NY Rangers**	**NHL**	**37**	**9**	**15**	**24**	**14**	....	....	....	....	....
	Colorado	IHL	27	6	20	26	22	....	....	....	....	....
1988-89	**NY Rangers**	**NHL**	**26**	**0**	**10**	**10**	**14**	....	....	....	....	....
	Hartford	**NHL**	**37**	**1**	**22**	**23**	**24**	**1**	**0**	**0**	**0**	**2**
1989-90	Binghamton	AHL	2	0	0	0	0	....	....	....	....	....
	Edmonton	**NHL**	**1**	**0**	**0**	**0**	**0**	....	....	....	....	....
	Cape Breton	AHL	68	13	37	50	55	6	0	7	7	10
1990-91	**Edmonton**	**NHL**	**21**	**2**	**5**	**7**	**14**	**18**	**0**	**4**	**4**	**8**
de	Cape Breton	AHL	56	13	46	59	60	....	....	....	....	....
1991-92	**Edmonton**	**NHL**	**57**	**6**	**34**	**40**	**38**	**13**	**1**	**2**	**3**	**10**
1992-93	**Ottawa**	**NHL**	**80**	**17**	**46**	**63**	**84**	....	....	....	....	....
1993-94	**Ottawa**	**NHL**	**53**	**3**	**20**	**23**	**26**	....	....	....	....	....
	NHL Totals		**315**	**38**	**153**	**191**	**214**	**32**	**1**	**6**	**7**	**20**

a WCHA Second All-Star Team (1984)
b WCHA First All-Star Team (1985, 1986)
c NCAA West First All-Star Team (1985, 1986)
d AHL First All-Star Team (1991)
e Won Eddie Shore Plaque (Outstanding Defenseman - AHL) (1991)

Signed as a free agent by **NY Rangers**, September 8, 1986. Traded to **Hartford** by **NY Rangers** with Brian Lawton and Don Maloney for Carey Wilson and Hartford's fifth round choice (Lubos Rob) in 1990 Entry Draft, December 26, 1988. Traded to **Edmonton** by **Hartford** for Jim Ennis, October 10, 1989. Claimed by **Ottawa** from **Edmonton** in NHL Waiver Draft, October 4, 1992.

MACKEY, DAVID

Left wing. Shoots left. 6'4", 205 lbs. Born, Richmond, B.C., July 24, 1966.
(Chicago's 12th choice, 224th overall, in 1984 Entry Draft).

			Regular Season					Playoffs				
Season	Club	Lea	GP	G	A	TP	PIM	GP	G	A	TP	PIM
1982-83	Victoria	WHL	69	16	16	32	53	12	11	1	2	4
1983-84	Victoria	WHL	69	15	15	30	97	....	....	....	....	....
1984-85	Victoria	WHL	16	5	6	11	45	....	....	....	....	....
	Portland	WHL	56	28	32	60	122	6	2	1	3	13
1985-86	Kamloops	WHL	9	3	4	7	13	....	....	....	....	....
	Medicine Hat	WHL	60	25	32	57	167	25	6	3	9	72
1986-87	Saginaw	IHL	81	26	49	75	173	10	5	6	11	22
1987-88	**Chicago**	**NHL**	**23**	**1**	**3**	**4**	**71**	....	....	....	....	....
	Saginaw	IHL	62	29	22	51	211	10	3	7	10	44
1988-89	**Chicago**	**NHL**	**23**	**1**	**2**	**3**	**78**	....	....	....	....	....
	Saginaw	IHL	57	22	23	45	223	....	....	....	....	....
1989-90	**Minnesota**	**NHL**	**16**	**2**	**0**	**2**	**28**	....	....	....	....	....
1990-91	Milwaukee	IHL	82	28	30	58	226	6	7	2	9	6
1991-92	**St. Louis**	**NHL**	**19**	**1**	**0**	**1**	**49**	**1**	**0**	**0**	**0**	**0**
	Peoria	IHL	35	20	17	37	90	....	....	....	....	....
1992-93	**St. Louis**	**NHL**	**15**	**1**	**4**	**5**	**23**	....	....	....	....	....
	Peoria	IHL	42	24	22	46	112	4	1	0	1	22
1993-94	**St. Louis**	**NHL**	**30**	**2**	**3**	**5**	**56**	**2**	**0**	**0**	**0**	**2**
	Peoria	IHL	49	14	21	35	132	....	....	....	....	....
	NHL Totals		**126**	**8**	**12**	**20**	**305**	**3**	**0**	**0**	**0**	**2**

Claimed by **Minnesota** in NHL Waiver Draft, October 2, 1989. Traded to **Vancouver** by **Minnesota** for future considerations, September 7, 1990. Signed as a free agent by **St. Louis**, August 7, 1991.

MACKEY, JAMES BOS.

Defense. Shoots right. 6'4", 225 lbs. Born, Saratoga Springs, NY, January 20, 1972.
(Boston's 6th choice, 147th overall, in 1990 Entry Draft).

			Regular Season					Playoffs				
Season	Club	Lea	GP	G	A	TP	PIM	GP	G	A	TP	PIM
1990-91	Yale	ECAC	18	0	1	1	12	....	....	....	....	....
1991-92	Yale	ECAC	27	1	7	8	44	....	....	....	....	....
1992-93	Yale	ECAC	31	1	4	5	52	....	....	....	....	....
1993-94	Yale	ECAC	26	1	5	6	46	....	....	....	....	....

MacLEAN, JOHN N.J.

Right wing. Shoots right. 6', 200 lbs. Born, Oshawa, Ont., November 20, 1964.
(New Jersey's 1st choice, 6th overall, in 1983 Entry Draft).

			Regular Season					Playoffs				
Season	Club	Lea	GP	G	A	TP	PIM	GP	G	A	TP	PIM
1981-82	Oshawa	OHL	67	17	22	39	197	12	3	6	9	63
1982-83	Oshawa	OHL	66	47	51	98	138	17	*18	20	*38	35
1983-84	**New Jersey**	**NHL**	**23**	**1**	**0**	**1**	**10**	....	....	....	....	....
	Oshawa	OHL	30	23	36	59	58	7	2	5	7	18
1984-85	**New Jersey**	**NHL**	**61**	**13**	**20**	**33**	**44**	....	....	....	....	....
1985-86	**New Jersey**	**NHL**	**74**	**21**	**36**	**57**	**112**	....	....	....	....	....
1986-87	**New Jersey**	**NHL**	**80**	**31**	**36**	**67**	**120**	....	....	....	....	....
1987-88	**New Jersey**	**NHL**	**76**	**23**	**16**	**39**	**147**	**20**	**7**	**11**	**18**	**60**
1988-89	**New Jersey**	**NHL**	**74**	**42**	**45**	**87**	**122**	....	....	....	....	....
1989-90	**New Jersey**	**NHL**	**80**	**41**	**38**	**79**	**80**	**6**	**4**	**1**	**5**	**12**
1990-91	**New Jersey**	**NHL**	**78**	**45**	**33**	**78**	**150**	**7**	**5**	**3**	**8**	**20**
1991-92			DID NOT PLAY – INJURED									
1992-93	**New Jersey**	**NHL**	**80**	**24**	**24**	**48**	**102**	**5**	**0**	**1**	**1**	**10**
1993-94	**New Jersey**	**NHL**	**80**	**37**	**33**	**70**	**95**	**20**	**6**	**10**	**16**	**22**
	NHL Totals		**706**	**278**	**281**	**559**	**982**	**58**	**22**	**26**	**48**	**124**

Played in NHL All-Star Game (1989, 1991)

MacLEOD, PAT

Defense. Shoots left. 5'11", 190 lbs. Born, Melfort, Sask., June 15, 1969.
(Minnesota's 5th choice, 87th overall, in 1989 Entry Draft).

			Regular Season					Playoffs				
Season	Club	Lea	GP	G	A	TP	PIM	GP	G	A	TP	PIM
1987-88	Kamloops	WHL	50	13	33	46	27	18	2	7	9	6
1988-89	Kamloops	WHL	37	11	34	45	14	15	7	18	25	24
1989-90	Kalamazoo	IHL	82	9	38	47	27	10	1	6	7	2
1990-91	**Minnesota**	**NHL**	**1**	**0**	**1**	**1**	**0**	....	....	....	....	....
	Kalamazoo	IHL	59	10	30	40	16	11	1	2	3	5
1991-92	**San Jose**	**NHL**	**37**	**5**	**11**	**16**	**4**	....	....	....	....	....
	Kansas City	IHL	45	9	21	30	19	11	1	4	5	4
1992-93	**San Jose**	**NHL**	**13**	**0**	**1**	**1**	**10**	....	....	....	....	....
	Kansas City	IHL	18	8	8	16	14	10	2	4	6	7
1993-94a	Milwaukee	IHL	73	21	52	73	18	3	1	2	3	0
	NHL Totals		**51**	**5**	**13**	**18**	**14**	....	....	....	....	....

a IHL First All-Star Team (1994)

Claimed by **San Jose** from **Minnesota** in Dispersal Draft, May 30, 1991.

MACOUN, JAMIE (muh-KOW-uhn) TOR.

Defense. Shoots left. 6'2", 200 lbs. Born, Newmarket, Ont., August 17, 1961.

			Regular Season					Playoffs				
Season	Club	Lea	GP	G	A	TP	PIM	GP	G	A	TP	PIM
1980-81	Ohio State	CCHA	38	9	20	29	83	....	....	....	....	....
1981-82	Ohio State	CCHA	25	2	18	20	89	....	....	....	....	....
1982-83	Ohio State	CCHA	19	6	21	27	54	....	....	....	....	....
	Calgary	**NHL**	**22**	**1**	**4**	**5**	**25**	**9**	**0**	**2**	**2**	**8**
1983-84a	**Calgary**	**NHL**	**72**	**9**	**23**	**32**	**97**	**11**	**1**	**0**	**1**	**0**
1984-85	**Calgary**	**NHL**	**70**	**9**	**30**	**39**	**67**	**4**	**1**	**0**	**1**	**4**
1985-86	**Calgary**	**NHL**	**77**	**11**	**21**	**32**	**81**	**22**	**1**	**6**	**7**	**23**
1986-87	**Calgary**	**NHL**	**79**	**7**	**33**	**40**	**111**	**3**	**0**	**1**	**1**	**8**
1987-88			DID NOT PLAY – INJURED									
1988-89	**Calgary**	**NHL**	**72**	**8**	**19**	**27**	**76**	**22**	**3**	**6**	**9**	**30**
1989-90	**Calgary**	**NHL**	**78**	**8**	**27**	**35**	**70**	**6**	**0**	**3**	**3**	**10**
1990-91	**Calgary**	**NHL**	**79**	**7**	**15**	**22**	**84**	**7**	**0**	**1**	**1**	**4**
1991-92	**Calgary**	**NHL**	**37**	**2**	**12**	**14**	**53**	....	....	....	....	....
	Toronto	**NHL**	**39**	**3**	**13**	**16**	**18**	....	....	....	....	....
1992-93	**Toronto**	**NHL**	**77**	**4**	**15**	**19**	**55**	**21**	**0**	**6**	**6**	**36**
1993-94	**Toronto**	**NHL**	**82**	**3**	**27**	**30**	**115**	**18**	**1**	**1**	**2**	**12**
	NHL Totals		**784**	**72**	**239**	**311**	**852**	**123**	**7**	**26**	**33**	**135**

a NHL All-Rookie Team (1984)

Signed as a free agent by **Calgary**, January 30, 1983. Traded to **Toronto** by **Calgary** with Doug Gilmour, Ric Natress, Kent Manderville and Rick Wamsley for Gary Leeman, Alexander Godynyuk, Jeff Reese, Michel Petit and Craig Berube, January 2, 1992.

MacPHERSON, BILLY JO (B.J.) HFD.

Left wing. Shoots left. 6'2", 200 lbs. Born, Toronto, Ont., September 23, 1973.
(Washington's 10th choice, 263rd overall, in 1992 Entry Draft).

			Regular Season					Playoffs				
Season	Club	Lea	GP	G	A	TP	PIM	GP	G	A	TP	PIM
1990-91	Oshawa	OHL	57	8	16	24	77	16	3	1	4	25
1991-92	Oshawa	OHL	60	20	32	52	108	7	2	5	7	27
1992-93	Oshawa	OHL	57	42	55	97	112	13	7	14	21	30
1993-94	North Bay	OHL	59	42	65	107	112	18	11	20	31	24

MacTAVISH, CRAIG PHI.

Center. Shoots left. 6'1", 195 lbs. Born, London, Ont., August 15, 1958.
(Boston's 9th choice, 153rd overall, in 1978 Amateur Draft).

			Regular Season					Playoffs				
Season	Club	Lea	GP	G	A	TP	PIM	GP	G	A	TP	PIM
1978-79	Lowell	ECAC	....	....	....	....	....	....	....	....	....	....
1979-80	**Boston**	**NHL**	**46**	**11**	**17**	**28**	**8**	**10**	**2**	**3**	**5**	**7**
	Binghamton	AHL	34	17	15	32	29	....	....	....	....	....
1980-81	**Boston**	**NHL**	**24**	**3**	**5**	**8**	**13**	....	....	....	....	....
	Springfield	AHL	53	19	24	43	81	7	5	4	9	8
1981-82	**Boston**	**NHL**	**2**	**0**	**1**	**1**	**0**	....	....	....	....	....
	Erie	AHL	72	23	32	55	37	....	....	....	....	....
1982-83	**Boston**	**NHL**	**75**	**10**	**20**	**30**	**18**	**17**	**3**	**1**	**4**	**18**
1983-84	**Boston**	**NHL**	**70**	**20**	**23**	**43**	**35**	**1**	**0**	**0**	**0**	**0**
1984-85			DID NOT PLAY									
1985-86	**Edmonton**	**NHL**	**74**	**23**	**24**	**47**	**70**	**10**	**4**	**4**	**8**	**11**
1986-87	**Edmonton**	**NHL**	**79**	**20**	**19**	**39**	**55**	**21**	**1**	**9**	**10**	**16**
1987-88	**Edmonton**	**NHL**	**80**	**15**	**17**	**32**	**47**	**19**	**0**	**1**	**1**	**31**
1988-89	**Edmonton**	**NHL**	**80**	**21**	**31**	**52**	**55**	**7**	**0**	**1**	**1**	**8**
1989-90	**Edmonton**	**NHL**	**80**	**21**	**22**	**43**	**89**	**22**	**2**	**6**	**8**	**29**
1990-91	**Edmonton**	**NHL**	**80**	**17**	**15**	**32**	**76**	**18**	**3**	**3**	**6**	**20**
1991-92	**Edmonton**	**NHL**	**80**	**12**	**18**	**30**	**98**	**16**	**3**	**0**	**3**	**28**
1992-93	**Edmonton**	**NHL**	**82**	**10**	**20**	**30**	**110**	....	....	....	....	....
1993-94	**Edmonton**	**NHL**	**66**	**16**	**10**	**26**	**80**	....	....	....	....	....
	NY Rangers	**NHL**	**12**	**4**	**2**	**6**	**11**	**23**	**1**	**4**	**5**	**22**
	NHL Totals		**930**	**203**	**244**	**447**	**765**	**164**	**19**	**32**	**51**	**190**

Signed as a free agent by **Edmonton,** February 1, 1985. Traded to **NY Rangers** by **Edmonton** for Todd Marchant, March 21, 1994. Signed as a free agent by **Philadelphia**, July 6, 1994.

MADILL, JEFF (muh-DILL)

Right wing. Shoots left. 5'11", 195 lbs. Born, Oshawa, Ont., June 21, 1965.
(New Jersey's 2nd choice, 7th overall, in 1987 Supplemental Draft).

			Regular Season					Playoffs				
Season	Club	Lea	GP	G	A	TP	PIM	GP	G	A	TP	PIM
1984-85	Ohio State	CCHA	12	5	6	11	18	....	....	....	....	....
1985-86	Ohio State	CCHA	41	32	25	57	65	....	....	....	....	....
1986-87	Ohio State	CCHA	43	38	32	70	139	....	....	....	....	....
1987-88	Utica	AHL	58	18	15	33	127	....	....	....	....	....
1988-89	Utica	AHL	69	23	25	48	225	4	1	0	1	35
1989-90	Utica	AHL	74	43	26	69	233	4	1	2	3	33
1990-91	**New Jersey**	**NHL**	**14**	**4**	**0**	**4**	**46**	**7**	**0**	**2**	**2**	**8**
a	Utica	AHL	54	42	35	77	151	....	....	....	....	....
1991-92	Kansas City	IHL	62	32	20	52	167	6	2	2	4	30
1992-93	Cincinnati	IHL	58	36	17	53	175	....	....	....	....	....
	Milwaukee	IHL	23	13	6	19	53	4	3	0	3	9
1993-94	Atlanta	IHL	80	42	44	86	186	14	4	2	6	33
	NHL Totals		**14**	**4**	**0**	**4**	**46**	**7**	**0**	**2**	**2**	**8**

a AHL Second All-Star Team (1991)
b IHL Second All-Star Team (1993)

Claimed by **San Jose** from **New Jersey** in Expansion Draft, May 30, 1991.

MAGARRELL, ADAM PHI.

Defense. Shoots left. 6'3", 178 lbs. Born, Winnipeg, Man., February 1, 1976.
(Philadelphia's 2nd choice, 88th overall, in 1994 Entry Draft).

			Regular Season					Playoffs				
Season	Club	Lea	GP	G	A	TP	PIM	GP	G	A	TP	PIM
1988-89	Sokol Kiev	USSR	2	0	0	0	0	....	....	....	....	....
1989-90	Sokol Kiev	USSR	39	2	3	5	6	....	....	....	....	....
1992-93	Brandon	WHL	8	0	0	0	0	....	....	....	....	....
1993-94	Brandon	WHL	40	2	1	3	69	13	0	2	2	32

MAGNUSSON, STEVEN CGY.

Center. Shoots left. 5'11", 180 lbs. Born, Coon Rapids, MN, November 15, 1972.
(Calgary's 5th choice, 85th overall, in 1991 Entry Draft).

			Regular Season					Playoffs				
Season	Club	Lea	GP	G	A	TP	PIM	GP	G	A	TP	PIM
1991-92	U. Minnesota	WCHA	38	9	21	30	54	....	....	....	....	....
1992-93	U. Minnesota	WCHA	21	1	10	11	22	....	....	....	....	....
1993-94	U. Minnesota	WCHA	16	2	12	14	16	....	....	....	....	....

MAGUIRE, DEREK — MTL.

Defense. Shoots right. 6', 185 lbs. Born, Delbarton, NJ, December 9, 1971.
(Montreal's 10th choice, 186th overall, in 1990 Entry Draft).

			Regular Season					Playoffs				
Season	Club	Lea	GP	G	A	TP	PIM	GP	G	A	TP	PIM
1990-91	Harvard	ECAC	25	3	14	17	12	....	....	....	....	....
1991-92	Harvard	ECAC	25	1	16	17	16	....	....	....	....	....
1992-93	Harvard	ECAC	16	3	9	12	10	....	....	....	....	....
1993-94abc	Harvard	ECAC	31	6	32	38	14	....	....	....	....	....

a ECAC Second All-Star Team (1994)
b NCAA East Second All-American Team (1994)
c NCAA Final Four All-Tournament Team (1994)

MAHER, JIM — L.A.

Defense. Shoots left. 6'1", 210 lbs. Born, Warren, MI, June 30, 1970.
(Los Angeles' 2nd choice, 81st overall, in 1989 Entry Draft).

			Regular Season					Playoffs				
Season	Club	Lea	GP	G	A	TP	PIM	GP	G	A	TP	PIM
1988-89	Ill.-Chicago	CCHA	31	1	5	6	40	....	....	....	....	....
1989-90	Ill.-Chicago	CCHA	38	4	12	16	64	....	....	....	....	....
1990-91	Ill.-Chicago	CCHA	37	6	8	14	49	....	....	....	....	....
1991-92	Ill.-Chicago	CCHA	34	5	9	14	52	....	....	....	....	....
	Phoenix	IHL	9	0	3	3	21	....	....	....	....	....
1992-93	Phoenix	IHL	47	5	13	18	72	....	....	....	....	....
	Muskegon	ColHL	2	1	0	1	2	....	....	....	....	....
1993-94	Phoenix	IHL	46	2	8	10	45	....	....	....	....	....
	Rochester	AHL	5	1	0	1	0	....	....	....	....	....

MAJIC, XAVIER — MTL.

Center. Shoots left. 6', 190 lbs. Born, Fernie, B.C., March 10, 1973.
(Vancouver's 12th choice, 249th overall, in 1991 Entry Draft).

			Regular Season					Playoffs				
Season	Club	Lea	GP	G	A	TP	PIM	GP	G	A	TP	PIM
1990-91	RPI	ECAC	31	4	10	14	26	....	....	....	....	....
1991-92	RPI	ECAC	32	13	19	32	48	....	....	....	....	....
1992-93	RPI	ECAC	35	16	26	42	18	....	....	....	....	....
1993-94	RPI	ECAC	30	9	15	24	36	....	....	....	....	....

Signed as a free agent by **Montreal**, April 22, 1994.

MAJOR, MARK

Left wing. Shoots left. 6'3", 223 lbs. Born, Toronto, Ont., March 20, 1970.
(Pittsburgh's 2nd choice, 25th overall, in 1988 Entry Draft).

			Regular Season					Playoffs				
Season	Club	Lea	GP	G	A	TP	PIM	GP	G	A	TP	PIM
1987-88	North Bay	OHL	57	16	17	33	272	4	0	2	2	8
1988-89	North Bay	OHL	11	3	2	5	58	....	....	....	....	....
	Kingston	OHL	53	22	29	51	193	....	....	....	....	....
1989-90	Kingston	OHL	62	29	32	61	168	6	3	3	6	12
1990-91	Muskegon	IHL	60	8	10	18	160	5	0	0	0	0
1991-92	Muskegon	IHL	80	13	18	31	302	12	1	3	4	29
1992-93	Cleveland	IHL	82	13	15	28	155	3	0	0	0	0
1993-94	Providence	AHL	61	17	9	26	176	....	....	....	....	....

Signed as a free agent by **Boston**, July 22, 1993.

MAKAROV, SERGEI (muh-KAH-rov) — S.J.

Right wing. Shoots left. 5'11", 185 lbs. Born, Chelyabinsk, USSR, June 19, 1958.
(Calgary's 14th choice, 231st overall, in 1983 Entry Draft).

			Regular Season					Playoffs				
Season	Club	Lea	GP	G	A	TP	PIM	GP	G	A	TP	PIM
1976-77	Chelyabinsk	USSR	11	1	0	1	4	....	....	....	....	....
1977-78	Chelyabinsk	USSR	36	18	13	31	10	....	....	....	....	....
1978-79a	CSKA	USSR	44	18	21	39	12	....	....	....	....	....
1979-80bc	CSKA	USSR	44	29	39	68	16	....	....	....	....	....
1980-81ab	CSKA	USSR	49	42	37	79	22	....	....	....	....	....
1981-82ab	CSKA	USSR	46	32	43	75	18	....	....	....	....	....
1982-83a	CSKA	USSR	30	25	17	42	6	....	....	....	....	....
1983-84ab	CSKA	USSR	44	36	37	73	28	....	....	....	....	....
1984-85abc	CSKA	USSR	40	26	39	65	28	....	....	....	....	....
1985-86ab	CSKA	USSR	40	30	32	62	28	....	....	....	....	....
1986-87ab	CSKA	USSR	40	21	32	53	26	....	....	....	....	....
1987-88ab	CSKA	USSR	51	23	45	68	50	....	....	....	....	....
1988-89bc	CSKA	USSR	44	21	33	54	42	....	....	....	....	....
1989-90de	**Calgary**	**NHL**	**80**	**24**	**62**	**86**	**55**	**6**	**0**	**6**	**6**	**0**
1990-91	**Calgary**	**NHL**	**78**	**30**	**49**	**79**	**44**	**3**	**1**	**0**	**1**	**0**
1991-92	**Calgary**	**NHL**	**68**	**22**	**48**	**70**	**60**	....	....	....	....	....
1992-93	**Calgary**	**NHL**	**71**	**18**	**39**	**57**	**40**	....	....	....	....	....
1993-94	**San Jose**	**NHL**	**80**	**30**	**38**	**68**	**78**	**14**	**8**	**2**	**10**	**4**
	NHL Totals		**377**	**124**	**236**	**360**	**277**	**23**	**9**	**8**	**17**	**4**

a Soviet National League All-Star (1981-88)
b Izvestia Trophy - leading scorer (1980-82, 1984-89)
c Soviet Player of the Year (1980, 1985, 1989)
d NHL All-Rookie Team (1990)
e Won Calder Memorial Trophy (1990)

Traded to **Hartford** by **Calgary** for future considerations (Washington's fourth round choice — previously acquired by Hartford — Calgary selected Jason Smith — in 1993 Entry Draft, June 26, 1993), June 20, 1993. Traded to **San Jose** by **Hartford** with Hartford's first (Viktor Kozlov) and third (Ville Peltonen) round choices in 1993 Entry Draft and Toronto's second round choice (previously acquired by Hartford — San Jose selected Vlastimil Kroupa) in 1993 Entry Draft for San Jose's first round choice (Chris Pronger) in 1993 Entry Draft, June 26, 1993.

MAKELA, MIKKO (MAK-uh-luh, MEE-koh) — BOS.

Left wing. Shoots left. 6'1", 194 lbs. Born, Tampere, Finland, February 28, 1965.
(NY Islanders' 5th choice, 65th overall, in 1983 Entry Draft).

			Regular Season					Playoffs				
Season	Club	Lea	GP	G	A	TP	PIM	GP	G	A	TP	PIM
1983-84	Ilves	Fin.	35	17	11	28	26	2	0	1	1	0
1984-85a	Ilves	Fin.	36	34	25	59	24	9	4	7	11	10
1985-86	**NY Islanders**	**NHL**	**58**	**16**	**20**	**36**	**28**	....	....	....	....	....
	Springfield	AHL	2	1	1	2	0	....	....	....	....	....
1986-87	**NY Islanders**	**NHL**	**80**	**24**	**33**	**57**	**24**	**11**	**2**	**4**	**6**	**8**
1987-88	**NY Islanders**	**NHL**	**73**	**36**	**40**	**76**	**22**	**6**	**1**	**4**	**5**	**6**
1988-89	**NY Islanders**	**NHL**	**76**	**17**	**28**	**45**	**22**	....	....	....	....	....
1989-90	**NY Islanders**	**NHL**	**20**	**2**	**3**	**5**	**2**	....	....	....	....	....
	Los Angeles	**NHL**	**45**	**7**	**14**	**21**	**16**	**1**	**0**	**0**	**0**	**0**
1990-91	**Buffalo**	**NHL**	**60**	**15**	**7**	**22**	**25**	....	....	....	....	....
1991-92	TPS	Fin.	44	25	45	*70	38	3	2	3	5	0
1992-93	TPS	Fin.	38	17	27	44	22	11	4	8	12	0
1993-94	Malmo	Swe.	37	15	21	36	20	....	....	....	....	....
	NHL Totals		**412**	**117**	**145**	**262**	**139**	**18**	**3**	**8**	**11**	**14**

a Finnish League First All-Star Team (1985)

Traded to **Los Angeles** by **NY Islanders** for Ken Baumgartner and Hubie McDonough, November 29, 1989. Traded to **Buffalo** by **Los Angeles** for Mike Donnelly, September 30, 1990. Signed as a free agent by **Boston**, July 18, 1994.

MALAKHOV, VLADIMIR (mah-LAH-kahf) — NYI

Defense. Shoots left. 6'2", 207 lbs. Born, Sverdlovsk, USSR, August 30, 1968.
(NY Islanders' 12th choice, 191st overall, in 1989 Entry Draft).

			Regular Season					Playoffs				
Season	Club	Lea	GP	G	A	TP	PIM	GP	G	A	TP	PIM
1986-87	Spartak	USSR	22	0	1	1	12	....	....	....	....	....
1987-88	Spartak	USSR	28	2	2	4	26	....	....	....	....	....
1988-89	CSKA	USSR	34	6	2	8	16	....	....	....	....	....
1989-90	CSKA	USSR	48	2	10	12	34	....	....	....	....	....
1990-91	CSKA	USSR	46	5	13	18	22	....	....	....	....	....
1991-92	CSKA	CIS	40	1	9	10	12	....	....	....	....	....
1992-93a	**NY Islanders**	**NHL**	**64**	**14**	**38**	**52**	**59**	**17**	**3**	**6**	**9**	**12**
	Capital Dist.	AHL	3	2	1	3	11	....	....	....	....	....
1993-94	**NY Islanders**	**NHL**	**76**	**10**	**47**	**57**	**80**	**4**	**0**	**0**	**0**	**6**
	NHL Totals		**140**	**24**	**85**	**109**	**139**	**21**	**3**	**6**	**9**	**18**

a NHL/Upper Deck All-Rookie Team (1993)

MALEY, DAVID (MAY-lee)

Left wing. Shoots left. 6'2", 195 lbs. Born, Beaver Dam, WI, April 24, 1963.
(Montreal's 4th choice, 33rd overall, in 1982 Entry Draft).

			Regular Season					Playoffs				
Season	Club	Lea	GP	G	A	TP	PIM	GP	G	A	TP	PIM
1982-83	U. Wisconsin	WCHA	47	17	23	40	24	....	....	....	....	....
1983-84	U. Wisconsin	WCHA	38	10	28	38	56	....	....	....	....	....
1984-85	U. Wisconsin	WCHA	38	19	9	28	86	....	....	....	....	....
1985-86	U. Wisconsin	WCHA	42	20	40	60	135	....	....	....	....	....
	Montreal	**NHL**	**3**	**0**	**0**	**0**	**0**	**7**	**1**	**3**	**4**	**2**
1986-87	**Montreal**	**NHL**	**48**	**6**	**12**	**18**	**55**	....	....	....	....	....
	Sherbrooke	AHL	11	1	5	6	25	12	7	7	14	10
1987-88	**New Jersey**	**NHL**	**44**	**4**	**2**	**6**	**65**	**20**	**3**	**1**	**4**	**80**
	Utica	AHL	9	5	3	8	40	....	....	....	....	....
1988-89	**New Jersey**	**NHL**	**68**	**5**	**6**	**11**	**249**	....	....	....	....	....
1989-90	**New Jersey**	**NHL**	**67**	**8**	**17**	**25**	**160**	**6**	**0**	**0**	**0**	**25**
1990-91	**New Jersey**	**NHL**	**64**	**8**	**14**	**22**	**151**	....	....	....	....	....
1991-92	**New Jersey**	**NHL**	**37**	**7**	**11**	**18**	**58**	....	....	....	....	....
	Edmonton	**NHL**	**23**	**3**	**6**	**9**	**46**	**10**	**1**	**1**	**2**	**4**
1992-93	**Edmonton**	**NHL**	**13**	**1**	**1**	**2**	**29**	....	....	....	....	....
	San Jose	**NHL**	**43**	**1**	**6**	**7**	**126**	....	....	....	....	....
1993-94	**San Jose**	**NHL**	**19**	**0**	**0**	**0**	**30**	....	....	....	....	....
	NY Islanders	**NHL**	**37**	**0**	**6**	**6**	**74**	**3**	**0**	**0**	**0**	**0**
	NHL Totals		**466**	**43**	**81**	**124**	**1043**	**46**	**5**	**5**	**10**	**111**

Traded to **New Jersey** by **Montreal** for New Jersey's third round choice (Mathieu Schneider) in 1987 Entry Draft, June 13, 1987. Traded to **Edmonton** by **New Jersey** for Troy Mallette, January 12, 1992. Claimed on waivers by **San Jose** from **Edmonton**, January 1, 1993. Traded to **NY Islanders** by **San Jose** for cash, January 23, 1994.

MALGUNAS, STEWART (mal-GOO-nuhs) — PHI.

Defense. Shoots left. 6', 200 lbs. Born, Prince George, B.C., April 21, 1970.
(Detroit's 3rd choice, 66th overall, in 1990 Entry Draft).

			Regular Season					Playoffs				
Season	Club	Lea	GP	G	A	TP	PIM	GP	G	A	TP	PIM
1987-88	N. Westminster	WHL	6	0	0	0	0	....	....	....	....	....
1988-89	Seattle	WHL	72	11	41	52	51	....	....	....	....	....
1989-90a	Seattle	WHL	63	15	48	63	116	....	....	....	....	....
1990-91	Adirondack	AHL	78	5	19	24	70	2	0	0	0	4
1991-92	Adirondack	AHL	69	4	28	32	82	18	2	6	8	28
1992-93	Adirondack	AHL	45	3	12	15	39	11	3	3	6	8
1993-94	**Philadelphia**	**NHL**	**67**	**1**	**3**	**4**	**86**	....	....	....	....	....
	NHL Totals		**67**	**1**	**3**	**4**	**86**	....	....	....	....	....

a WHL West First All-Star Team (1990)

Traded to **Philadelphia** by **Detroit** for future considerations, September 9, 1993.

MALIK, MAREK (MAW-leck) — HFD.

Defense. Shoots left. 6'5", 185 lbs. Born, Ostrava, Czech., June 24, 1975.
(Hartford's 2nd choice, 72nd overall, in 1993 Entry Draft).

			Regular Season					Playoffs				
Season	Club	Lea	GP	G	A	TP	PIM	GP	G	A	TP	PIM
1992-93	TJ Vitkovice Jr.	Czech.	20	5	10	15	16	....	....	....	....	....
1993-94	TJ Vitkovice	Czech.	38	3	3	6	0	3	0	1	1	0

MALKOC, DEAN — N.J.

Defense. Shoots left. 6'3", 200 lbs. Born, Vancouver, B.C., January 26, 1970.
(New Jersey's 7th choice, 95th overall, in 1990 Entry Draft).

			Regular Season					Playoffs				
Season	Club	Lea	GP	G	A	TP	PIM	GP	G	A	TP	PIM
1989-90	Kamloops	WHL	48	3	18	21	209	17	0	3	3	56
1990-91	Kamloops	WHL	8	1	4	5	47	....	....	....	....	....
	Swift Current	WHL	56	10	23	33	248	3	0	2	2	5
	Utica	AHL	1	0	0	0	0	....	....	....	....	....
1991-92	Utica	AHL	66	1	11	12	274	4	0	2	2	6
1992-93	Utica	AHL	73	5	19	24	255	5	0	1	1	8
1993-94	Albany	AHL	79	0	9	9	296	5	0	0	0	21

MALLETTE, TROY

(muh-LEHT)　　OTT.

Left wing. Shoots left. 6'2", 210 lbs.　Born, Sudbury, Ont., February 25, 1970.
(NY Rangers' 1st choice, 22nd overall, in 1988 Entry Draft).

			Regular Season					Playoffs				
Season	Club	Lea	GP	G	A	TP	PIM	GP	G	A	TP	PIM
1986-87	S.S. Marie	OHL	65	20	25	45	157	4	0	2	2	12
1987-88	S.S. Marie	OHL	62	18	30	48	186	6	1	3	4	12
1988-89	S.S. Marie	OHL	64	39	37	76	172	....	....	....	....	....
1989-90	**NY Rangers**	**NHL**	**79**	**13**	**16**	**29**	**305**	**10**	**2**	**2**	**4**	**81**
1990-91	**NY Rangers**	**NHL**	**71**	**12**	**10**	**22**	**252**	**5**	**0**	**0**	**0**	**18**
1991-92	**Edmonton**	**NHL**	**15**	**1**	**3**	**4**	**36**	....	....	....	....	....
	New Jersey	**NHL**	**17**	**3**	**4**	**7**	**43**	....	....	....	....	....
1992-93	**New Jersey**	**NHL**	**34**	**4**	**3**	**7**	**56**	....	....	....	....	....
	Utica	AHL	5	3	3	6	17	....	....	....	....	....
1993-94	**Ottawa**	**NHL**	**82**	**7**	**16**	**23**	**166**	....	....	....	....	....
	NHL Totals		**298**	**40**	**52**	**92**	**858**	**15**	**2**	**2**	**4**	**99**

Acquired by **Edmonton** from **NY Rangers** as compensation for NY Rangers' signing of free agent Adam Graves, September 12, 1991. Traded to **New Jersey** by **Edmonton** for David Maley, January 12, 1992. Traded to **Ottawa** by **New Jersey** with Craig Billington and New Jersey's fourth round choice (Cosmo Dupaul) in 1993 Entry Draft for Peter Sidorkiewicz and future considerations (Mike Peluso, June 26, 1993), June 20, 1993.

MALLGRAVE, MATTHEW

TOR.

Right wing. Shoots right. 6', 180 lbs.　Born, Washington, D.C., May 3, 1970.
(Toronto's 6th choice, 132nd overall, in 1988 Entry Draft).

			Regular Season					Playoffs				
Season	Club	Lea	GP	G	A	TP	PIM	GP	G	A	TP	PIM
1989-90	Harvard	ECAC	26	3	3	6	33	....	....	....	....	....
1990-91	Harvard	ECAC	25	5	14	19	14	....	....	....	....	....
1991-92	Harvard	ECAC	27	12	15	27	20	....	....	....	....	....
1992-93	Harvard	ECAC	31	*27	13	40	36	....	....	....	....	....
1993-94	St. John's	AHL	15	2	4	6	16	....	....	....	....	....
	S. Carolina	ECHL	4	1	0	1	6	....	....	....	....	....

MALONE, SCOTT

NYR

Defense. Shoots left. 6', 180 lbs.　Born, Boston, MA, January 16, 1971.
(Toronto's 10th choice, 220th overall, in 1990 Entry Draft).

			Regular Season					Playoffs				
Season	Club	Lea	GP	G	A	TP	PIM	GP	G	A	TP	PIM
1991-92	N. Hampshire	H.E.	27	0	4	4	52	....	....	....	....	....
1992-93	N. Hampshire	H.E.	36	5	6	11	96	....	....	....	....	....
1993-94a	N. Hampshire	H.E.	40	14	6	20	*162	....	....	....	....	....

a　Hockey East Second All-Star Team (1994)

Rights traded to **NY Rangers** by **Toronto** with Glenn Anderson and Toronto's fourth round choice (Alexander Korobolin) in 1994 Entry Draft for Mike Gartner, March 21, 1994.

MALTAIS, STEVE

(MAHL-tay)

Left wing. Shoots left. 6'2", 205 lbs.　Born, Arvida, Que., January 25, 1969.
(Washington's 2nd choice, 57th overall, in 1987 Entry Draft).

			Regular Season					Playoffs				
Season	Club	Lea	GP	G	A	TP	PIM	GP	G	A	TP	PIM
1986-87	Cornwall	OHL	65	32	12	44	29	5	0	0	0	2
1987-88	Cornwall	OHL	59	39	46	85	30	11	9	6	15	33
1988-89	Cornwall	OHL	58	53	70	123	67	18	14	16	30	16
	Fort Wayne	IHL	....	....	....	....	....	4	2	1	3	0
1989-90	**Washington**	**NHL**	**8**	**0**	**0**	**0**	**2**	**1**	**0**	**0**	**0**	**0**
	Baltimore	AHL	67	29	37	66	54	12	6	10	16	6
1990-91	**Washington**	**NHL**	**7**	**0**	**0**	**0**	**2**	....	....	....	....	....
	Baltimore	AHL	73	36	43	79	97	6	1	4	5	10
1991-92	**Minnesota**	**NHL**	**12**	**2**	**1**	**3**	**2**	....	....	....	....	....
	Kalamazoo	IHL	48	25	31	56	51	....	....	....	....	....
	Halifax	AHL	10	3	3	6	0	....	....	....	....	....
1992-93	**Tampa Bay**	**NHL**	**63**	**7**	**13**	**20**	**35**	....	....	....	....	....
	Atlanta	IHL	16	14	10	24	22	....	....	....	....	....
1993-94	**Detroit**	**NHL**	**4**	**0**	**1**	**1**	**0**	....	....	....	....	....
	Adirondack	AHL	73	35	49	84	79	12	5	11	16	14
	NHL Totals		**94**	**9**	**15**	**24**	**41**	**1**	**0**	**0**	**0**	**0**

Traded to **Minnesota** by **Washington** with Trent Klatt for Shawn Chambers, June 21, 1991. Traded to **Quebec** by **Minnesota** for Kip Miller, March 8, 1992. Claimed by **Tampa Bay** from **Quebec** in Expansion Draft, June 18, 1992. Traded to **Detroit** by **Tampa Bay** for Dennis Vial, June 8, 1993.

MALTBY, KIRK

EDM.

Right wing. Shoots right. 6', 180 lbs.　Born, Guelph, Ont., December 22, 1972.
(Edmonton's 4th choice, 65th overall, in 1992 Entry Draft).

			Regular Season					Playoffs				
Season	Club	Lea	GP	G	A	TP	PIM	GP	G	A	TP	PIM
1989-90	Owen Sound	OHL	61	12	15	27	90	12	1	6	7	15
1990-91	Owen Sound	OHL	66	34	32	66	100	....	....	....	....	....
1991-92	Owen Sound	OHL	66	50	41	91	99	5	3	3	6	18
1992-93	Cape Breton	AHL	73	22	23	45	130	16	3	3	6	45
1993-94	**Edmonton**	**NHL**	**68**	**11**	**8**	**19**	**74**	....	....	....	....	....
	NHL Totals		**68**	**11**	**8**	**19**	**74**	....	....	....	....	....

MANDERVILLE, KENT

TOR.

Left wing. Shoots left. 6'3", 207 lbs.　Born, Edmonton, Alta., April 12, 1971.
(Calgary's 1st choice, 24th overall, in 1989 Entry Draft).

			Regular Season					Playoffs				
Season	Club	Lea	GP	G	A	TP	PIM	GP	G	A	TP	PIM
1989-90	Cornell	ECAC	26	11	15	26	28	....	....	....	....	....
1990-91	Cornell	ECAC	28	17	14	31	60	....	....	....	....	....
	Cdn. National	....	3	1	2	3	0	....	....	....	....	....
1991-92	Cdn. National	....	63	16	23	39	75	....	....	....	....	....
	Cdn. Olympic	....	8	1	2	3	0	....	....	....	....	....
	Toronto	**NHL**	**15**	**0**	**4**	**4**	**0**	....	....	....	....	....
	St. John's	AHL	....	....	....	....	....	12	5	9	14	14
1992-93	**Toronto**	**NHL**	**18**	**1**	**1**	**2**	**17**	**18**	**1**	**0**	**1**	**8**
	St. John's	AHL	56	19	28	47	86	2	0	2	2	0
1993-94	**Toronto**	**NHL**	**67**	**7**	**9**	**16**	**63**	**12**	**1**	**0**	**1**	**4**
	NHL Totals		**100**	**8**	**14**	**22**	**80**	**30**	**2**	**0**	**2**	**12**

Traded to **Toronto** by **Calgary** with Doug Gilmour, Jamie Macoun, Rick Wamsley and Ric Nattress for Gary Leeman, Alexander Godynyuk, Jeff Reese, Michel Petit and Craig Berube, January 2, 1992.

MANELUK, MIKE

ANA.

Left wing. Shoots right. 5'11", 188 lbs.　Born, Winnipeg, Man., October 1, 1973.

			Regular Season					Playoffs				
Season	Club	Lea	GP	G	A	TP	PIM	GP	G	A	TP	PIM
1991-92	Brandon	WHL	68	23	30	53	102	....	....	....	....	....
1992-93	Brandon	WHL	72	36	51	87	75	4	2	1	3	2
1993-94	Brandon	WHL	63	50	47	97	112	13	11	3	14	23

Signed as a free agent by **Anaheim**, January 28, 1994.

MANLOW, ERIC

CHI.

Center. Shoots left. 6', 190 lbs.　Born, Belleville, Ont., April 7, 1975.
(Chicago's 2nd choice, 50th overall, in 1993 Entry Draft).

			Regular Season					Playoffs				
Season	Club	Lea	GP	G	A	TP	PIM	GP	G	A	TP	PIM
1991-92	Kitchener	OHL	59	26	21	47	31	14	2	5	7	10
1992-93	Kitchener	OHL	53	12	20	32	17	4	0	1	1	2
1993-94	Kitchener	OHL	49	28	32	60	25	3	0	1	1	4

MANSON, DAVE

WPG.

Defense. Shoots left. 6'2", 202 lbs.　Born, Prince Albert, Sask., January 27, 1967.
(Chicago's 1st choice, 11th overall, in 1985 Entry Draft).

			Regular Season					Playoffs				
Season	Club	Lea	GP	G	A	TP	PIM	GP	G	A	TP	PIM
1983-84	Prince Albert	WHL	70	2	7	9	233	5	0	0	0	4
1984-85	Prince Albert	WHL	72	8	30	38	247	13	1	0	1	34
1985-86	Prince Albert	WHL	70	14	34	48	177	20	1	8	9	63
1986-87	**Chicago**	**NHL**	**63**	**1**	**8**	**9**	**146**	**3**	**0**	**0**	**0**	**10**
1987-88	**Chicago**	**NHL**	**54**	**1**	**6**	**7**	**185**	**5**	**0**	**0**	**0**	**27**
	Saginaw	IHL	6	0	3	3	37	....	....	....	....	....
1988-89	**Chicago**	**NHL**	**79**	**18**	**36**	**54**	**352**	**16**	**0**	**8**	**8**	**84**
1989-90	**Chicago**	**NHL**	**59**	**5**	**23**	**28**	**301**	**20**	**2**	**4**	**6**	**46**
1990-91	**Chicago**	**NHL**	**75**	**14**	**15**	**29**	**191**	**6**	**0**	**1**	**1**	**36**
1991-92	**Edmonton**	**NHL**	**79**	**15**	**32**	**47**	**220**	**16**	**3**	**9**	**12**	**44**
1992-93	**Edmonton**	**NHL**	**83**	**15**	**30**	**45**	**210**	....	....	....	....	....
1993-94	**Edmonton**	**NHL**	**57**	**3**	**13**	**16**	**140**	....	....	....	....	....
	Winnipeg	**NHL**	**13**	**1**	**4**	**5**	**51**	....	....	....	....	....
	NHL Totals		**562**	**73**	**167**	**240**	**1796**	**66**	**5**	**22**	**27**	**247**

Played in NHL All-Star Game (1989, 1993)

Traded to **Edmonton** by **Chicago** with Chicago's third round choice (Kirk Maltby) in 1992 Entry Draft for Steve Smith, October 2, 1991. Traded to **Winnipeg** by **Edmonton** with St. Louis' sixth round choice (previously acquired by Edmonton — Winnipeg selected Chris Kibermanis) in 1994 Entry Draft for Boris Mironov, Mats Lindgren, Winnipeg's first round choice (Jason Bonsignore) in 1994 Entry Draft and Florida's fourth round choice (previously acquired by Winnipeg — Edmonton selected Adam Copeland) in 1994 Entry Draft, March 15, 1994.

MARA, ROB

CHI.

Right wing. Shoots right. 6'1", 175 lbs.　Born, Boston, MA, September 25, 1975.
(Chicago's 11th choice, 263rd overall, in 1994 Entry Draft).

			Regular Season					Playoffs				
Season	Club	Lea	GP	G	A	TP	PIM	GP	G	A	TP	PIM
1993-94	Belmont Hill	HS	28	18	28	46	....	....	....	....	....	....

MARCHANT, TERRY

EDM.

Left wing. Shoots left. 6'2", 205 lbs.　Born, Buffalo, NY, February 24, 1976.
(Edmonton's 9th choice, 136th overall, in 1994 Entry Draft).

			Regular Season					Playoffs				
Season	Club	Lea	GP	G	A	TP	PIM	GP	G	A	TP	PIM
1992-93	Buffalo	Midget	30	33	38	71	24	....	....	....	....	....
1993-94	Niagara	NAJHL	42	27	40	67	43	....	....	....	....	....

MARCHANT, TODD

EDM.

Center. Shoots left. 6', 190 lbs.　Born, Buffalo, NY, August 12, 1973.
(NY Rangers' 8th choice, 164th overall, in 1993 Entry Draft).

			Regular Season					Playoffs				
Season	Club	Lea	GP	G	A	TP	PIM	GP	G	A	TP	PIM
1991-92	Clarkson	ECAC	32	20	12	32	32	....	....	....	....	....
1992-93a	Clarkson	ECAC	33	18	28	46	38	....	....	....	....	....
1993-94	U.S. National	....	59	28	39	67	48	....	....	....	....	....
	U.S. Olympic	....	8	1	1	2	6	....	....	....	....	....
	NY Rangers	**NHL**	**1**	**0**	**0**	**0**	**0**	....	....	....	....	....
	Edmonton	**NHL**	**3**	**0**	**1**	**1**	**2**	....	....	....	....	....
	Cape Breton	AHL	3	1	4	5	2	5	1	1	2	0
	NHL Totals		**4**	**0**	**1**	**1**	**2**	....	....	....	....	....

a　ECAC Second All-Star Team (1993)

Traded to **Edmonton** by **NY Rangers** for Craig MacTavish, March 21, 1994.

MARCHMENT, BRYAN

HFD.

Defense. Shoots left. 6'1", 198 lbs.　Born, Scarborough, Ont., May 1, 1969.
(Winnipeg's 1st choice, 16th overall, in 1987 Entry Draft).

			Regular Season					Playoffs				
Season	Club	Lea	GP	G	A	TP	PIM	GP	G	A	TP	PIM
1985-86	Belleville	OHL	57	5	15	20	225	21	0	7	7	83
1986-87	Belleville	OHL	52	6	38	44	238	6	0	4	4	17
1987-88	Belleville	OHL	56	7	51	58	200	6	1	3	4	19
1988-89	**Winnipeg**	**NHL**	**2**	**0**	**0**	**0**	**2**	....	....	....	....	....
a	Belleville	OHL	43	14	36	50	118	5	0	1	1	12
1989-90	**Winnipeg**	**NHL**	**7**	**0**	**2**	**2**	**28**	....	....	....	....	....
	Moncton	AHL	56	4	19	23	217	....	....	....	....	....
1990-91	**Winnipeg**	**NHL**	**28**	**2**	**2**	**4**	**91**	....	....	....	....	....
	Moncton	AHL	33	2	11	13	101	....	....	....	....	....
1991-92	**Chicago**	**NHL**	**58**	**5**	**10**	**15**	**168**	**16**	**1**	**0**	**1**	**36**
1992-93	**Chicago**	**NHL**	**78**	**5**	**15**	**20**	**313**	**4**	**0**	**0**	**0**	**12**
1993-94	**Chicago**	**NHL**	**13**	**1**	**4**	**5**	**42**	....	....	....	....	....
	Hartford	**NHL**	**42**	**3**	**7**	**10**	**124**	....	....	....	....	....
	NHL Totals		**228**	**16**	**40**	**56**	**768**	**20**	**1**	**0**	**1**	**48**

a　OHL Second All-Star Team (1989)

Traded to **Chicago** by **Winnipeg** with Chris Norton for Troy Murray and Warren Rychel, July 22, 1991. Traded to **Hartford** by **Chicago** with Steve Larmer for Eric Weinrich and Patrick Poulin, November 2, 1993.

MARHA, JOSEF

(MAHR-hah)　　QUE.

Center. Shoots left. 6', 176 lbs.　Born, Havlickuv Brod, Czech., June 2, 1976.
(Quebec's 3rd choice, 35th overall, in 1994 Entry Draft).

			Regular Season					Playoffs				
Season	Club	Lea	GP	G	A	TP	PIM	GP	G	A	TP	PIM
1992-93	Dukla Jihlava	Czech.	7	2	2	4	....	....	....	....	....	....
1993-94	Dukla Jihlava	Czech.	41	7	2	9	....	3	0	1	1	....

MARINUCCI, CHRIS   NYI

Center. Shoots left. 6', 175 lbs.   Born, Grand Rapids, MN, December 29, 1971.
(NY Islanders' 4th choice, 90th overall, in 1990 Entry Draft).

				Regular Season					Playoffs			
Season	Club	Lea	GP	G	A	TP	PIM	GP	G	A	TP	PIM
1990-91	Minn.-Duluth	WCHA	36	6	10	16	20	....	....	....	....	....
1991-92	Minn.-Duluth	WCHA	37	6	13	19	41	....	....	....	....	....
1992-93a	Minn.-Duluth	WCHA	40	35	42	77	52	....	....	....	....	....
1993-94bcd	Minn.-Duluth	WCHA	38	*30	31	61	65	....	....	....	....	....

a WCHA Second All-Star Team (1993)
b WCHA First All-Star Team (1994)
c NCAA West First All-American Team (1994)
d Won Hobey Baker Memorial Award (Top U.S. Collegiate Player) (1994)

MARK, GORDON   EDM.

Defense. Shoots right. 6'4", 218 lbs.   Born, Edmonton, Alta., September 10, 1964.
(New Jersey's 4th choice, 108th overall, in 1983 Entry Draft).

				Regular Season					Playoffs			
Season	Club	Lea	GP	G	A	TP	PIM	GP	G	A	TP	PIM
1982-83	Kamloops	WHL	71	12	20	32	135	7	1	1	2	8
1983-84	Kamloops	WHL	67	12	30	42	202	17	2	6	8	27
1984-85	Kamloops	WHL	32	11	23	34	68	7	1	2	3	10
1985-86	Maine	AHL	77	9	13	22	134	5	0	1	1	9
1986-87	**New Jersey**	**NHL**	**36**	**3**	**5**	**8**	**82**	....	....	....	....	....
	Maine	AHL	29	4	10	14	66	....	....	....	....	....
1987-88	**New Jersey**	**NHL**	**19**	**0**	**2**	**2**	**27**	....	....	....	....	....
	Utica	AHL	50	5	21	26	96	....	....	....	....	....
1988-89	Stony Plain	Sr.				UNAVAILABLE						
1989-90	Stony Plain	Sr.				UNAVAILABLE						
1990-91	Stony Plain	Sr.				UNAVAILABLE						
1991-92	Stony Plain	Sr.				UNAVAILABLE						
1992-93	Cape Breton	AHL	60	3	21	24	78	16	1	7	8	20
1993-94	Cape Breton	AHL	49	11	20	31	116	....	....	....	....	....
	Edmonton	**NHL**	**12**	**0**	**1**	**1**	**43**	....	....	....	....	....
	NHL Totals		**67**	**3**	**8**	**11**	**152**	....	....	....	....	....

Signed as a free agent by **Edmonton**, February 1, 1994.

MAROIS, DANIEL

Right wing. Shoots right. 6', 190 lbs.   Born, Montreal, Que., October 3, 1968.
(Toronto's 2nd choice, 28th overall, in 1987 Entry Draft).

				Regular Season					Playoffs			
Season	Club	Lea	GP	G	A	TP	PIM	GP	G	A	TP	PIM
1985-86	Verdun	QMJHL	58	42	35	77	110	5	4	2	6	6
1986-87	Chicoutimi	QMJHL	40	22	26	48	143	16	7	14	21	25
1987-88	Verdun	QMJHL	67	52	36	88	153	....	....	....	....	....
	Newmarket	AHL	8	4	4	8	4	....	....	....	....	....
	Toronto	**NHL**	....	....	....	....	....	3	1	0	1	0
1988-89	**Toronto**	**NHL**	**76**	**31**	**23**	**54**	**76**	....	....	....	....	....
1989-90	**Toronto**	**NHL**	**68**	**39**	**37**	**76**	**82**	5	2	2	4	12
1990-91	**Toronto**	**NHL**	**78**	**21**	**9**	**30**	**112**	....	....	....	....	....
1991-92	**Toronto**	**NHL**	**63**	**15**	**11**	**26**	**76**	....	....	....	....	....
	NY Islanders	**NHL**	**12**	**2**	**5**	**7**	**18**	....	....	....	....	....
1992-93	**NY Islanders**	**NHL**	**28**	**2**	**5**	**7**	**35**	....	....	....	....	....
	Capital Dist.	AHL	4	2	0	2	0	....	....	....	....	....
1993-94	**Boston**	**NHL**	**22**	**7**	**3**	**10**	**18**	11	0	1	1	16
	Providence	AHL	6	1	2	3	6	....	....	....	....	....
	NHL Totals		**347**	**117**	**93**	**210**	**417**	**19**	**3**	**3**	**6**	**28**

Traded to **NY Islanders** by **Toronto** with Claude Loiselle for Ken Baumgartner and Dave McLlwain, March 10, 1992. Traded to **Boston** by **NY Islanders** for Boston's eighth round choice (Peter Hogardh) in 1994 Entry Draft, March 18, 1993.

MARSHALL, BOBBY   CGY.

Defense. Shoots left. 6'1", 190 lbs.   Born, North York, Ont., April 11, 1972.
(Calgary's 6th choice, 129th overall, in 1991 Entry Draft).

				Regular Season					Playoffs			
Season	Club	Lea	GP	G	A	TP	PIM	GP	G	A	TP	PIM
1990-91	Miami-Ohio	CCHA	37	3	15	18	44	....	....	....	....	....
1991-92	Miami-Ohio	CCHA	40	5	20	25	48	....	....	....	....	....
1992-93ab	Miami-Ohio	CCHA	40	2	43	45	40	....	....	....	....	....
1993-94a	Miami-Ohio	CCHA	38	3	24	27	76	....	....	....	....	....

a CCHA Second All-Star Team (1993, 1994)
b NCAA West Second All-American Team (1993)

MARSHALL, GRANT   DAL.

Right wing. Shoots right. 6'1", 185 lbs.   Born, Mississauga, Ont., June 9, 1973.
(Toronto's 2nd choice, 23rd overall, in 1992 Entry Draft).

				Regular Season					Playoffs			
Season	Club	Lea	GP	G	A	TP	PIM	GP	G	A	TP	PIM
1990-91	Ottawa	OHL	26	6	11	17	25	1	0	0	0	0
1991-92	Ottawa	OHL	61	32	51	83	132	11	6	11	17	11
1992-93	Ottawa	OHL	30	14	29	43	83	....	....	....	....	....
	Newmarket	OHL	31	11	25	36	89	7	4	7	11	20
	St. John's	AHL	2	0	0	0	0	2	0	0	0	2
1993-94	St. John's	AHL	67	11	29	40	155	11	1	5	6	17

Acquired by **Dallas** from **Toronto** with Peter Zezel as compensation for Toronto's signing of free agent Mike Craig, August 10, 1994.

MARSHALL, JASON   ST.L.

Defense. Shoots right. 6'2", 195 lbs.   Born, Cranbrook, B.C., February 22, 1971.
(St. Louis' 1st choice, 9th overall, in 1989 Entry Draft).

				Regular Season					Playoffs			
Season	Club	Lea	GP	G	A	TP	PIM	GP	G	A	TP	PIM
1989-90	Cdn. National	....	72	1	11	12	57	....	....	....	....	....
1990-91	Tri-Cities	WHL	59	10	34	44	236	7	1	2	3	20
	Peoria	IHL	....	....	....	....	....	18	0	1	1	48
1991-92	**St. Louis**	**NHL**	**2**	**1**	**0**	**1**	**4**	....	....	....	....	....
	Peoria	IHL	78	4	18	22	178	10	0	1	1	16
1992-93	Peoria	IHL	77	4	16	20	229	4	0	0	0	20
1993-94	Cdn. National	....	41	3	10	13	60	....	....	....	....	....
	Peoria	IHL	20	1	1	2	72	3	2	0	2	2
	NHL Totals		**2**	**1**	**0**	**1**	**4**	....	....	....	....	....

MARTIN, CRAIG   DET.

Right wing. Shoots right. 6'2", 215 lbs.   Born, Amherst, N.S., January 21, 1971.
(Winnipeg's 6th choice, 98th overall, in 1990 Entry Draft).

				Regular Season					Playoffs			
Season	Club	Lea	GP	G	A	TP	PIM	GP	G	A	TP	PIM
1989-90	Hull	QMJHL	66	14	31	45	299	11	2	1	3	65
1990-91	Hull	QMJHL	18	5	6	11	87	....	....	....	....	....
	St-Hyacinthe	QMJHL	36	8	9	17	166	....	....	....	....	....
1991-92	Moncton	AHL	11	1	1	2	70	....	....	....	....	....
	Fort Wayne	IHL	24	0	0	0	115	....	....	....	....	....
1992-93	Moncton	AHL	64	5	13	18	198	5	0	1	1	22
1993-94	Adirondack	AHL	76	15	24	39	297	12	2	2	4	63

Signed as a free agent by **Detroit**, July 28, 1993.

MARTIN, JUSTIN   L.A.

Right wing. Shoots right. 6'3", 210 lbs.   Born, Syracuse, NY, May 1, 1975.
(Los Angeles' 8th choice, 172nd overall, in 1993 Entry Draft).

				Regular Season					Playoffs			
Season	Club	Lea	GP	G	A	TP	PIM	GP	G	A	TP	PIM
1992-93	Essex Junction	HS	43	13	28	41	35	....	....	....	....	....
1993-94	Taft Prep.	HS	20	16	10	26	26	....	....	....	....	....

MARTIN, MATT   TOR.

Defense. Shoots left. 6'3", 190 lbs.   Born, Hamden, CT, April 30, 1971.
(Toronto's 4th choice, 66th overall, in 1989 Entry Draft).

				Regular Season					Playoffs			
Season	Club	Lea	GP	G	A	TP	PIM	GP	G	A	TP	PIM
1990-91	U. of Maine	H.E.	35	3	12	15	48	....	....	....	....	....
1991-92	U. of Maine	H.E.	30	4	14	18	46	....	....	....	....	....
1992-93	U. of Maine	H.E.	44	6	26	32	88	....	....	....	....	....
	St. John's	AHL	2	0	0	0	2	9	1	5	6	4
1993-94	U.S. National	....	39	7	8	15	127	....	....	....	....	....
	U.S. Olympic	....	8	0	2	2	8	....	....	....	....	....
	Toronto	**NHL**	**12**	**0**	**1**	**1**	**6**	....	....	....	....	....
	St. John's	AHL	12	1	5	6	9	11	1	5	6	33
	NHL Totals		**12**	**0**	**1**	**1**	**6**	....	....	....	....	....

MARTINI, DARCY   EDM.

Defense. Shoots left. 6'4", 220 lbs.   Born, Castlegar, B.C., January 30, 1969.
(Edmonton's 8th choice, 162nd overall, in 1989 Entry Draft).

				Regular Season					Playoffs			
Season	Club	Lea	GP	G	A	TP	PIM	GP	G	A	TP	PIM
1988-89	Michigan Tech	WCHA	35	1	2	3	103	....	....	....	....	....
1989-90	Michigan Tech	WCHA	36	3	6	9	151	....	....	....	....	....
1990-91	Michigan Tech	WCHA	34	10	13	23	*184	....	....	....	....	....
1991-92	Michigan Tech	WCHA	17	5	13	18	58	....	....	....	....	....
1992-93	Cape Breton	AHL	47	1	6	7	36	2	0	1	1	0
	Wheeling	ECHL	6	0	2	2	2	....	....	....	....	....
1993-94	**Edmonton**	**NHL**	**2**	**0**	**0**	**0**	**0**	....	....	....	....	....
	Cape Breton	AHL	65	18	38	56	131	5	1	3	4	26
	NHL Totals		**2**	**0**	**0**	**0**	**0**	....	....	....	....	....

MARTINS, STEVE   HFD.

Center. Shoots left. 5'9", 175 lbs.   Born, Gatineau, Que., April 13, 1972.
(Hartford's 1st choice, 5th overall, in 1994 Supplemental Draft).

				Regular Season					Playoffs			
Season	Club	Lea	GP	G	A	TP	PIM	GP	G	A	TP	PIM
1991-92	Harvard	ECAC	20	13	14	27	26	....	....	....	....	....
1992-93	Harvard	ECAC	18	6	8	14	40	....	....	....	....	....
1993-94abc	Harvard	ECAC	32	25	35	60	*93	....	....	....	....	....

a ECAC First All-Star Team (1994)
b NCAA East First All-American Team (1994)
c NCAA Final Four All-Tournament Team (1994)

MASTAD, MILT   (MIHZ-tahd)   BOS.

Defense. Shoots left. 6'3", 205 lbs.   Born, Regina, Sask., March 5, 1975.
(Boston's 6th choice, 155th overall, in 1993 Entry Draft).

				Regular Season					Playoffs			
Season	Club	Lea	GP	G	A	TP	PIM	GP	G	A	TP	PIM
1992-93	Seattle	WHL	60	1	1	2	123	5	0	1	1	14
1993-94	Seattle	WHL	29	1	3	4	59	....	....	....	....	....
	Moose Jaw	WHL	41	2	8	10	74	....	....	....	....	....

MATHIESON, JIM

Defense. Shoots left. 6'1", 209 lbs.   Born, Kindersley, Sask., January 24, 1970.
(Washington's 3rd choice, 59th overall, in 1989 Entry Draft).

				Regular Season					Playoffs			
Season	Club	Lea	GP	G	A	TP	PIM	GP	G	A	TP	PIM
1986-87	Regina	WHL	40	0	9	9	40	3	0	1	1	2
1987-88	Regina	WHL	72	3	12	15	115	4	0	2	2	4
1988-89	Regina	WHL	62	5	22	27	151	....	....	....	....	....
1989-90	**Washington**	**NHL**	**2**	**0**	**0**	**0**	**4**	....	....	....	....	....
	Regina	WHL	67	1	26	27	158	11	0	7	7	16
	Baltimore	AHL	....	....	....	....	....	3	0	0	0	4
1990-91	Baltimore	AHL	65	3	5	8	168	4	1	0	1	6
1991-92	Baltimore	AHL	74	2	9	11	206	....	....	....	....	....
1992-93	Baltimore	AHL	46	3	5	8	88	3	0	1	1	23
1993-94	Portland	AHL	43	0	7	7	89	12	0	1	1	36
	NHL Totals		**2**	**0**	**0**	**0**	**4**	....	....	....	....	....

MATIER, MARK   QUE.

Defense. Shoots left. 6'1", 209 lbs.   Born, St. Catharines, Ont., December 14, 1973.
(Washington's 6th choice, 167th overall, in 1992 Entry Draft).

				Regular Season					Playoffs			
Season	Club	Lea	GP	G	A	TP	PIM	GP	G	A	TP	PIM
1991-92	S.S. Marie	OHL	46	0	5	5	15	19	3	5	8	14
1992-93	S.S. Marie	OHL	64	7	27	34	89	18	1	4	5	13
1993-94	Cornwall	AHL	67	1	16	17	100	3	0	0	0	4

Traded to **Quebec** by **Washington** for Kevin Kaminski, June 15, 1993.

MATTE, CHRISTIAN — QUE.

Right wing. Shoots right. 5'11", 166 lbs. Born, Hull, Que., January 20, 1975.
(Quebec's 8th choice, 153rd overall, in 1993 Entry Draft).

			Regular Season					Playoffs				
Season	Club	Lea	GP	G	A	TP	PIM	GP	G	A	TP	PIM
1992-93	Granby	QMJHL	68	17	36	53	59	....	....	....	....	....
1993-94a	Granby	QMJHL	59	50	47	97	103	7	5	5	10	12
	Cornwall	AHL	1	0	0	0	0	....	....	....	....	....

a QMJHL Second All-Star Team (1994)

MATTEAU, STEPHANE (mah-TOH) — NYR

Left wing. Shoots left. 6'3", 200 lbs. Born, Rouyn-Noranda, Que., September 2, 1969.
(Calgary's 2nd choice, 25th overall, in 1987 Entry Draft).

			Regular Season					Playoffs				
Season	Club	Lea	GP	G	A	TP	PIM	GP	G	A	TP	PIM
1985-86	Hull	QMJHL	60	6	8	14	19	4	0	0	0	0
1986-87	Hull	QMJHL	69	27	48	75	113	8	3	7	10	8
1987-88	Hull	QMJHL	57	17	40	57	179	18	5	14	19	94
1988-89	Hull	QMJHL	59	44	45	89	202	9	8	6	14	30
	Salt Lake	IHL	....	....	....	....	....	9	0	4	4	13
1989-90	Salt Lake	IHL	81	23	35	58	130	10	6	3	9	38
1990-91	**Calgary**	**NHL**	**78**	**15**	**19**	**34**	**93**	**5**	**0**	**1**	**1**	**0**
1991-92	**Calgary**	**NHL**	**4**	**1**	**0**	**1**	**19**	....	....	....	....	....
	Chicago	**NHL**	**20**	**5**	**8**	**13**	**45**	**18**	**4**	**6**	**10**	**24**
1992-93	**Chicago**	**NHL**	**79**	**15**	**18**	**33**	**98**	**3**	**0**	**1**	**1**	**2**
1993-94	**Chicago**	**NHL**	**65**	**15**	**16**	**31**	**55**	....	....	....	....	....
	NY Rangers	**NHL**	**12**	**4**	**3**	**7**	**2**	**23**	**6**	**3**	**9**	**20**
	NHL Totals		**258**	**55**	**64**	**119**	**312**	**49**	**10**	**11**	**21**	**46**

Traded to **Chicago** by **Calgary** for Trent Yawney, December 16, 1991. Traded to **NY Rangers** by **Chicago** with Brian Noonan for Tony Amonte and the rights to Matt Oates, March 21, 1994.

MATTHEWS, JAMIE — S.J.

Center. Shoots right. 6'1", 215 lbs. Born, Amherst, N.S., May 25, 1973.
(Chicago's 3rd choice, 44th overall, in 1991 Entry Draft).

			Regular Season					Playoffs				
Season	Club	Lea	GP	G	A	TP	PIM	GP	G	A	TP	PIM
1989-90	Sudbury	OHL	60	16	17	33	25	7	1	0	1	4
1990-91	Sudbury	OHL	66	14	38	52	41	5	3	5	8	8
1991-92	Sudbury	OHL	64	26	69	95	30	11	2	11	13	4
1992-93	Sudbury	OHL	65	30	62	92	65	14	7	17	24	22
1993-94	Sudbury	OHL	46	34	63	97	24	10	6	6	12	4

Re-entered NHL Entry Draft. **San Jose's** 13th choice, 262nd overall in 1993 Entry Draft.

MATTSSON, JESPER — CGY.

Center. Shoots right. 6', 180 lbs. Born, Malmo, Sweden, May 13, 1975.
(Calgary's 1st choice, 18th overall, in 1993 Entry Draft).

			Regular Season					Playoffs				
Season	Club	Lea	GP	G	A	TP	PIM	GP	G	A	TP	PIM
1991-92	Malmo	Swe.	24	0	1	1	2	....	....	....	....	....
1992-93	Malmo	Swe.	40	9	8	17	14	5	0	0	0	0
1993-94	Malmo	Swe.	9	1	2	3	2	9	1	2	3	2

MATVICHUK, RICHARD (MAT-vih-chuhk) — DAL.

Defense. Shoots left. 6'2", 190 lbs. Born, Edmonton, Alta., February 5, 1973.
(Minnesota's 1st choice, 8th overall, in 1991 Entry Draft).

			Regular Season					Playoffs				
Season	Club	Lea	GP	G	A	TP	PIM	GP	G	A	TP	PIM
1989-90	Saskatoon	WHL	56	8	24	32	126	10	2	8	10	16
1990-91	Saskatoon	WHL	68	13	36	49	117	....	....	....	....	....
1991-92a	Saskatoon	WHL	58	14	40	54	126	....	....	....	....	....
1992-93	**Minnesota**	**NHL**	**53**	**2**	**3**	**5**	**26**	....	....	....	....	....
	Kalamazoo	IHL	3	0	1	1	6	....	....	....	....	....
1993-94	**Dallas**	**NHL**	**25**	**0**	**3**	**3**	**22**	**7**	**1**	**1**	**2**	**12**
	Kalamazoo	IHL	43	8	17	25	84	....	....	....	....	....
	NHL Totals		**78**	**2**	**6**	**8**	**48**	**7**	**1**	**1**	**2**	**12**

a WHL East First All-Star Team (1992)

MAXWELL, DENNIS

Center. Shoots left. 6', 188 lbs. Born, Dauphin, Man., June 4, 1974.
(Tampa Bay's 8th choice, 170th overall, in 1992 Entry Draft).

			Regular Season					Playoffs				
Season	Club	Lea	GP	G	A	TP	PIM	GP	G	A	TP	PIM
1991-92	Niagara Falls	OHL	66	19	26	45	139	17	4	9	13	32
1992-93	Niagara Falls	OHL	12	5	9	14	21	....	....	....	....	....
	Sudbury	OHL	52	15	24	39	116	14	3	4	7	42
1993-94	Niagara Falls	OHL	17	2	14	16	41	....	....	....	....	....
	Newmarket	OHL	41	12	24	36	113	....	....	....	....	....

MAY, ALAN — DAL.

Right wing. Shoots right. 6'1", 200 lbs. Born, Swan Hills, Alta., January 14, 1965.

			Regular Season					Playoffs				
Season	Club	Lea	GP	G	A	TP	PIM	GP	G	A	TP	PIM
1985-86	Medicine Hat	WHL	6	1	0	1	25	....	....	....	....	....
	N. Westminster	WHL	32	8	9	17	81	....	....	....	....	....
1986-87	Springfield	AHL	4	0	2	2	11	....	....	....	....	....
	Carolina	ACHL	42	23	14	37	310	5	2	2	4	57
1987-88	**Boston**	**NHL**	**3**	**0**	**0**	**0**	**15**	....	....	....	....	....
	Maine	AHL	61	14	11	25	257	....	....	....	....	....
	Nova Scotia	AHL	13	4	1	5	54	4	0	0	0	51
1988-89	**Edmonton**	**NHL**	**3**	**1**	**0**	**1**	**7**	....	....	....	....	....
	Cape Breton	AHL	50	12	13	25	214	....	....	....	....	....
	New Haven	AHL	12	2	8	10	99	16	6	3	9	*105
1989-90	**Washington**	**NHL**	**77**	**7**	**10**	**17**	**339**	**15**	**0**	**0**	**0**	**37**
1990-91	**Washington**	**NHL**	**67**	**4**	**6**	**10**	**264**	**11**	**1**	**1**	**2**	**37**
1991-92	**Washington**	**NHL**	**75**	**6**	**9**	**15**	**221**	**7**	**0**	**0**	**0**	**0**
1992-93	**Washington**	**NHL**	**83**	**6**	**10**	**16**	**268**	**6**	**0**	**1**	**1**	**6**
1993-94	**Washington**	**NHL**	**43**	**4**	**7**	**11**	**97**	....	....	....	....	....
	Dallas	**NHL**	**8**	**1**	**0**	**1**	**18**	**1**	**0**	**0**	**0**	**0**
	NHL Totals		**359**	**29**	**42**	**71**	**1229**	**40**	**1**	**2**	**3**	**80**

Signed as a free agent by **Boston**, October 30, 1987. Traded to **Edmonton** by **Boston** for Moe Lemay, March 8, 1988. Traded to **Los Angeles** by **Edmonton** with Jim Wiemer for Brian Wilks and John English, March 7, 1989. Traded to **Washington** by **Los Angeles** for Washington's fifth round choice (Thomas Newman) in 1989 Entry Draft, June 17, 1989. Traded to **Dallas** by **Washington** with Washington's seventh round choice in 1995 Entry Draft for Jim Johnson, March 21, 1994.

MAY, BRAD — BUF.

Left wing. Shoots left. 6'1", 210 lbs. Born, Toronto, Ont., November 29, 1971.
(Buffalo's 1st choice, 14th overall, in 1990 Entry Draft).

			Regular Season					Playoffs				
Season	Club	Lea	GP	G	A	TP	PIM	GP	G	A	TP	PIM
1988-89	Niagara Falls	OHL	65	8	14	22	304	17	0	1	1	55
1989-90a	Niagara Falls	OHL	61	32	58	90	223	16	9	13	22	64
1990-91a	Niagara Falls	OHL	34	37	32	69	93	14	11	14	25	53
1991-92	**Buffalo**	**NHL**	**69**	**11**	**6**	**17**	**309**	**7**	**1**	**4**	**5**	**2**
1992-93	**Buffalo**	**NHL**	**82**	**13**	**13**	**26**	**242**	**8**	**1**	**1**	**2**	**14**
1993-94	**Buffalo**	**NHL**	**84**	**18**	**27**	**45**	**171**	**7**	**0**	**2**	**2**	**9**
	NHL Totals		**235**	**42**	**46**	**88**	**722**	**22**	**2**	**7**	**9**	**25**

a OHL Second All-Star Team (1990, 1991)

MAYER, DEREK — OTT.

Defense. Shoots right. 6', 200 lbs. Born, Rossland, B.C., May 21, 1967.
(Detroit's 3rd choice, 43rd overall, in 1986 Entry Draft).

			Regular Season					Playoffs				
Season	Club	Lea	GP	G	A	TP	PIM	GP	G	A	TP	PIM
1985-86	Denver	WCHA	44	2	7	9	42	....	....	....	....	....
1986-87	Denver	WCHA	38	5	17	22	87	....	....	....	....	....
1987-88	Denver	WCHA	34	5	16	21	82	....	....	....	....	....
1988-89	Cdn. National	....	58	3	13	16	81	....	....	....	....	....
1989-90	Adirondack	AHL	62	4	26	30	56	5	0	6	6	4
1990-91	San Diego	IHL	31	9	24	33	31	....	....	....	....	....
	Adirondack	AHL	21	4	9	13	20	2	0	1	1	0
1991-92	Adirondack	AHL	25	4	11	15	31	....	....	....	....	....
	San Diego	IHL	30	7	16	23	47	4	0	0	0	20
1992-93	Cdn. National	....	64	12	28	40	108	....	....	....	....	....
1993-94	Cdn. National	....	49	4	15	19	61	....	....	....	....	....
	Cdn. Olympic	....	8	1	2	3	18	....	....	....	....	....
	Ottawa	**NHL**	**17**	**2**	**2**	**4**	**8**	....	....	....	....	....
	NHL Totals		**17**	**2**	**2**	**4**	**8**	....	....	....	....	....

Signed as a free agent by **Ottawa**, March 4, 1994.

MAYERS, JAMAL — ST.L.

Center. Shoots right. 6', 190 lbs. Born, Toronto, Ont., October 24, 1974.
(St. Louis' 3rd choice, 89th overall, in 1993 Entry Draft).

			Regular Season					Playoffs				
Season	Club	Lea	GP	G	A	TP	PIM	GP	G	A	TP	PIM
1992-93	W. Michigan	CCHA	38	8	17	25	26	....	....	....	....	....
1993-94	W. Michigan	CCHA	40	17	32	49	40	....	....	....	....	....

MAZUR, JAY

Center/Right wing. Shoots right. 6'2", 205 lbs. Born, Hamilton, Ont., January 22, 1965.
(Vancouver's 12th choice, 230th overall, in 1983 Entry Draft).

			Regular Season					Playoffs				
Season	Club	Lea	GP	G	A	TP	PIM	GP	G	A	TP	PIM
1983-84	Maine	H.E.	34	14	9	23	14	....	....	....	....	....
1984-85	Maine	H.E.	31	0	6	6	20	....	....	....	....	....
1985-86	Maine	H.E.	34	5	7	12	18	....	....	....	....	....
1986-87	Maine	H.E.	39	16	10	26	61	....	....	....	....	....
1987-88	Flint	IHL	39	17	11	28	28	....	....	....	....	....
	Fredericton	AHL	31	14	6	20	28	15	4	2	6	38
1988-89	**Vancouver**	**NHL**	**1**	**0**	**0**	**0**	**0**	....	....	....	....	....
	Milwaukee	IHL	73	33	31	64	86	11	6	5	11	2
1989-90	**Vancouver**	**NHL**	**5**	**0**	**0**	**0**	**4**	....	....	....	....	....
	Milwaukee	IHL	70	20	27	47	63	6	3	0	3	6
1990-91	**Vancouver**	**NHL**	**36**	**11**	**7**	**18**	**14**	**6**	**0**	**1**	**1**	**8**
	Milwaukee	IHL	7	2	3	5	21	....	....	....	....	....
1991-92	**Vancouver**	**NHL**	**5**	**0**	**0**	**0**	**2**	....	....	....	....	....
	Milwaukee	IHL	56	17	20	37	49	5	2	3	5	0
1992-93	Hamilton	AHL	59	21	17	38	30	....	....	....	....	....
1993-94	Hamilton	AHL	78	40	55	95	40	4	2	2	4	4
	NHL Totals		**47**	**11**	**7**	**18**	**20**	**6**	**0**	**1**	**1**	**8**

McALPINE, CHRIS — N.J.

Defense. Shoots right. 6', 190 lbs. Born, Roseville, MN, December 1, 1971.
(New Jersey's 10th choice, 137th overall, in 1990 Entry Draft).

			Regular Season					Playoffs				
Season	Club	Lea	GP	G	A	TP	PIM	GP	G	A	TP	PIM
1990-91	U. Minnesota	WCHA	38	7	9	16	112	....	....	....	....	....
1991-92	U. Minnesota	WCHA	39	3	9	12	126	....	....	....	....	....
1992-93	U. Minnesota	WCHA	41	14	9	23	82	....	....	....	....	....
1993-94ab	U. Minnesota	WCHA	36	12	18	30	121	....	....	....	....	....

a WCHA First All-Star Team (1994)
b NCAA West Second All-American Team (1994)

McAMMOND, DEAN — EDM.

Center. Shoots left. 5'11", 185 lbs. Born, Grande Cache, Alta., June 15, 1973
(Chicago's 1st choice, 22nd overall, in 1991 Entry Draft).

			Regular Season					Playoffs				
Season	Club	Lea	GP	G	A	TP	PIM	GP	G	A	TP	PIM
1989-90	Prince Albert	WHL	53	11	11	22	49	14	2	3	5	18
1990-91	Prince Albert	WHL	71	33	35	68	108	2	0	1	1	6
1991-92	**Chicago**	**NHL**	**5**	**0**	**2**	**2**	**0**	**3**	**0**	**0**	**0**	**2**
	Prince Albert	WHL	63	37	54	91	189	10	12	11	23	26
1992-93	Prince Albert	WHL	30	19	29	48	44	....	....	....	....	....
	Swift Current	WHL	18	10	13	23	24	17	*16	19	35	20
1993-94	**Edmonton**	**NHL**	**45**	**6**	**21**	**27**	**16**	....	....	....	....	....
	Cape Breton	AHL	28	9	12	21	38	....	....	....	....	....
	NHL Totals		**50**	**6**	**23**	**29**	**16**	**3**	**0**	**0**	**0**	**2**

Traded to **Edmonton** by **Chicago** with Igor Kravchuk for Joe Murphy, February 24, 1993.

McBAIN, ANDREW

Right wing. Shoots right. 6'1", 205 lbs. Born, Scarborough, Ont., January 18, 1965.
(Winnipeg's 1st choice, 8th overall, in 1983 Entry Draft).

			Regular Season					Playoffs				
Season	Club	Lea	GP	G	A	TP	PIM	GP	G	A	TP	PIM
1981-82	Niagara Falls	OHL	68	19	25	44	35	5	0	3	3	4
1982-83a	North Bay	OHL	67	33	87	120	61	8	2	6	8	17
1983-84	Winnipeg	NHL	78	11	19	30	37	3	2	0	2	0
1984-85	Winnipeg	NHL	77	7	15	22	45	7	1	0	1	0
1985-86	Winnipeg	NHL	28	3	3	6	17	....				
1986-87	Winnipeg	NHL	71	11	21	32	106	9	0	2	2	10
1987-88	Winnipeg	NHL	74	32	31	63	145	5	2	5	7	29
1988-89	Winnipeg	NHL	80	37	40	77	71	....				
1989-90	Pittsburgh	NHL	41	5	9	14	51	....				
	Vancouver	NHL	26	4	5	9	22	....				
1990-91	Vancouver	NHL	13	0	5	5	32	....				
	Milwaukee	IHL	47	27	24	51	69	6	2	5	7	12
1991-92	Vancouver	NHL	6	1	0	1	0	....				
	Milwaukee	IHL	65	24	54	78	132	5	1	2	3	10
1992-93	Ottawa	NHL	59	7	16	23	43	....				
	New Haven	AHL	1	0	1	1	4	....				
1993-94	Ottawa	NHL	55	11	8	19	64	....				
	PEI	AHL	26	6	10	16	102	....				
	NHL Totals		608	129	172	301	633	24	5	7	12	39

a OHL Second All-Star Team (1983)

Traded to **Pittsburgh** by **Winnipeg** with Jim Kyte and Randy Gilhen for Randy Cunneyworth, Rick Tabaracci and Dave McLlwain, June 17, 1989. Traded to **Vancouver** by **Pittsburgh** with Dave Capuano and Dan Quinn for Rod Buskas, Barry Pederson and Tony Tanti, January 8, 1990. Signed as a free agent by **Ottawa**, July 30, 1992.

McBAIN, JASON — HFD.

Defense. Shoots left. 6'2", 178 lbs. Born, Ilion, NY, April 12, 1974.
(Hartford's 5th choice, 81st overall, in 1992 Entry Draft).

			Regular Season					Playoffs				
Season	Club	Lea	GP	G	A	TP	PIM	GP	G	A	TP	PIM
1990-91	Lethbridge	WHL	52	2	7	9	39	1	0	0	0	0
1991-92	Lethbridge	WHL	13	0	1	1	12	....				
	Portland	WHL	54	9	23	32	95	6	1	0	1	13
1992-93	Portland	WHL	71	9	35	44	76	16	2	12	14	14
1993-94	Portland	WHL	63	15	51	66	86	....				

McBEAN, WAYNE — WPG.

Defense. Shoots left. 6'2", 185 lbs. Born, Calgary, Alta., February 21, 1969.
(Los Angeles' 1st choice, 4th overall, in 1987 Entry Draft).

			Regular Season					Playoffs				
Season	Club	Lea	GP	G	A	TP	PIM	GP	G	A	TP	PIM
1985-86	Medicine Hat	WHL	67	1	14	15	73	25	1	5	6	36
1986-87a	Medicine Hat	WHL	71	12	41	53	163	20	2	8	10	40
1987-88	Los Angeles	NHL	27	0	1	1	26	....				
	Medicine Hat	WHL	30	15	30	45	48	16	6	17	23	50
1988-89	Los Angeles	NHL	33	0	5	5	23	....				
	New Haven	AHL	7	1	1	2	2	....				
	NY Islanders	NHL	19	0	1	1	12	....				
1989-90	NY Islanders	NHL	5	0	1	1	2	2	1	1	2	0
	Springfield	AHL	58	6	33	39	48	17	4	11	15	31
1990-91	NY Islanders	NHL	52	5	14	19	47	....				
	Capital Dist.	AHL	22	9	9	18	19	....				
1991-92	NY Islanders	NHL	25	2	4	6	18	....				
1992-93	Capital Dist.	AHL	20	1	9	10	35	3	0	1	1	9
1993-94	NY Islanders	NHL	19	1	4	5	16	....				
	Salt Lake	IHL	5	0	6	6	2	....				
	Winnipeg	NHL	31	2	9	11	24	....				
	NHL Totals		211	10	39	49	168	2	1	1	2	0

a WHL East All-Star Team (1987)

Traded to **NY Islanders** by **Los Angeles** with Mark Fitzpatrick and future considerations (Doug Crossman, May 23, 1989) for Kelly Hrudey, February 22, 1989. Traded to **Winnipeg** by **NY Islanders** for Yan Kaminsky, February 1, 1994.

McCABE, BRYAN — NYI

Defense. Shoots left. 6'1", 200 lbs. Born, St. Catharines, Ont., June 8, 1975.
(NY Islanders' 2nd choice, 40th overall, in 1993 Entry Draft).

			Regular Season					Playoffs				
Season	Club	Lea	GP	G	A	TP	PIM	GP	G	A	TP	PIM
1991-92	Medicine Hat	WHL	68	6	24	30	157	4	0	0	0	6
1992-93	Medicine Hat	WHL	14	0	13	13	83	....				
a	Spokane	WHL	46	3	44	47	134	6	1	5	6	28
1993-94	Spokane	WHL	64	22	62	84	218	3	0	4	4	4

a WHL West Second All-Star Team (1993)

McCABE, SCOTT — N.J.

Defense. Shoots left. 6'4", 189 lbs. Born, St. Clair Shores, MI, May 28, 1974.
(New Jersey's 4th choice, 94th overall, in 1992 Entry Draft).

			Regular Season					Playoffs				
Season	Club	Lea	GP	G	A	TP	PIM	GP	G	A	TP	PIM
1992-93	Lake Superior	CCHA	DID NOT PLAY									
1993-94	Lake Superior	CCHA	18	3	5	8	14	....				

McCAMBRIDGE, KEITH — CGY.

Defense. Shoots left. 6'2", 205 lbs. Born, Thompson, Man., February 1, 1974.
(Calgary's 10th choice, 201st overall, in 1994 Entry Draft).

			Regular Season					Playoffs				
Season	Club	Lea	GP	G	A	TP	PIM	GP	G	A	TP	PIM
1991-92	Swift Current	WHL	72	1	4	5	84	8	0	0	0	2
1992-93	Swift Current	WHL	70	0	6	6	87	17	0	1	1	27
1993-94	Swift Current	WHL	71	0	10	10	179	7	0	0	0	4

McCANN, SEAN — FLA.

Defense. Shoots right. 6', 195 lbs. Born, North York, Ont., September 18, 1971.
(Florida's 1st choice, 1st overall, in 1994 Supplemental Draft).

			Regular Season					Playoffs				
Season	Club	Lea	GP	G	A	TP	PIM	GP	G	A	TP	PIM
1990-91	Harvard	ECAC	28	2	9	11	88	....				
1991-92	Harvard	ECAC	27	4	10	14	51	....				
1992-93	Harvard	ECAC	31	4	5	9	38	....				
1993-94abcd	Harvard	ECAC	33	22	17	39	82	....				

a ECAC First All-Star Team (1994)
b NCAA East First All-American Team (1994)
c NCAA Final Four All-Tournament Team (1994)
d NCAA Final Four Tournament Most Valuable Player (1994)

McCARTHY, BRIAN — BUF.

Center. Shoots left. 6'2", 190 lbs. Born, Salem, MA, December 6, 1971.
(Buffalo's 2nd choice, 82nd overall, in 1990 Entry Draft).

			Regular Season					Playoffs				
Season	Club	Lea	GP	G	A	TP	PIM	GP	G	A	TP	PIM
1990-91	Providence	H.E.	33	7	6	13	33	....				
1991-92			DID NOT PLAY									
1992-93	St. Lawrence	ECAC	18	7	5	12	44	....				
1993-94	St. Lawrence	ECAC	29	12	15	27	32	....				

McCARTHY, SANDY — CGY.

Right wing. Shoots right. 6'3", 225 lbs. Born, Toronto, Ont., June 15, 1972.
(Calgary's 3rd choice, 52nd overall, in 1991 Entry Draft).

			Regular Season					Playoffs				
Season	Club	Lea	GP	G	A	TP	PIM	GP	G	A	TP	PIM
1989-90	Laval	QMJHL	65	10	11	21	269	14	3	3	6	60
1990-91	Laval	QMJHL	68	21	19	40	297	13	6	5	11	67
1991-92	Laval	QMJHL	62	39	51	90	326	8	4	5	9	81
1992-93	Salt Lake	IHL	77	18	20	38	220	....				
1993-94	Calgary	NHL	79	5	5	10	173	7	0	0	0	34
	NHL Totals		79	5	5	10	173	7	0	0	0	34

McCARTY, DARREN — DET.

Right wing. Shoots right. 6'1", 210 lbs. Born, Burnaby, B.C., April 1, 1972.
(Detroit's 2nd choice, 46th overall, in 1992 Entry Draft).

			Regular Season					Playoffs				
Season	Club	Lea	GP	G	A	TP	PIM	GP	G	A	TP	PIM
1990-91	Belleville	OHL	60	30	37	67	151	6	2	2	4	13
1991-92a	Belleville	OHL	65	*55	72	127	177	5	1	4	5	13
1992-93	Adirondack	AHL	73	17	19	36	278	11	0	1	1	33
1993-94	Detroit	NHL	67	9	17	26	181	7	2	2	4	8
	NHL Totals		67	9	17	26	181	7	2	2	4	8

a OHL First All-Star Team (1992)

McCLEARY, TRENT — OTT.

Right wing. Shoots right. 6', 180 lbs. Born, Swift Current, Sask., October 10, 1972.

			Regular Season					Playoffs				
Season	Club	Lea	GP	G	A	TP	PIM	GP	G	A	TP	PIM
1991-92	Swift Current	WHL	72	23	22	45	240	8	1	2	3	16
1992-93	Swift Current	WHL	63	17	33	50	138	17	5	4	9	16
	New Haven	AHL	2	1	0	1	6	....				
1993-94	P.E.I.	AHL	4	0	0	0	6	....				
	Thunder Bay	ColHL	51	23	17	40	123	9	2	11	13	15

Signed as a free agent by **Ottawa**, October 9, 1992.

McCLELLAND, KEVIN — BUF.

Right wing. Shoots right. 6'2", 205 lbs. Born, Oshawa, Ont., July 4, 1962.
(Hartford's 4th choice, 71st overall, in 1980 Entry Draft).

			Regular Season					Playoffs				
Season	Club	Lea	GP	G	A	TP	PIM	GP	G	A	TP	PIM
1980-81	Niagara Falls	OHA	68	36	72	108	186	12	8	13	21	42
1981-82	Pittsburgh	NHL	10	1	4	5	4	5	1	1	2	5
	Niagara Falls	OHL	46	36	47	83	184	....				
1982-83	Pittsburgh	NHL	38	5	4	9	73	....				
1983-84	Pittsburgh	NHL	24	2	4	6	62	....				
	Baltimore	AHL	3	1	1	2	0	....				
	Edmonton	NHL	52	8	20	28	127	18	4	6	10	42
1984-85	Edmonton	NHL	62	8	15	23	205	18	1	3	4	75
1985-86	Edmonton	NHL	79	11	25	36	266	10	1	0	1	32
1986-87	Edmonton	NHL	72	12	13	25	238	21	2	3	5	43
1987-88	Edmonton	NHL	74	10	6	16	281	19	2	3	5	68
1988-89	Edmonton	NHL	79	6	14	20	161	7	0	2	2	16
1989-90	Edmonton	NHL	10	1	1	2	13	....				
	Detroit	NHL	61	4	5	9	183	....				
1990-91	Detroit	NHL	3	0	0	0	7	....				
	Adirondack	AHL	27	5	14	19	125	....				
1991-92	Toronto	NHL	18	0	1	1	33	....				
	St. John's	AHL	34	7	15	22	199	5	0	1	1	9
1992-93	St. John's	AHL	55	7	20	27	221	1	0	0	0	7
1993-94	Winnipeg	NHL	6	0	0	0	19	....				
	Moncton	AHL	39	3	5	8	233	1	0	0	0	2
	NHL Totals		588	68	112	180	1672	98	11	18	29	281

Traded to **Pittsburgh** by **Hartford** with Pat Boutette as compensation for Hartford's signing of free agent goaltender Greg Millen, June 29, 1981. Traded to **Edmonton** by **Pittsburgh** with Pittsburgh's sixth round choice (Emanuel Viveiros) in 1984 Entry Draft for Tom Roulston, December 5, 1983. Traded to **Detroit** by **Edmonton** with Jimmy Carson and Edmonton's fifth round choice (later traded to Montreal — Montreal selected Brad Layzell) in 1991 Entry Draft for Petr Klima, Joe Murphy, Adam Graves and Jeff Sharples, November 2, 1989. Signed as a free agent by **Toronto**, September 2, 1991. Traded to **Winnipeg** by **Toronto** for cash, August 12, 1993. Traded to **Buffalo** by **Winnipeg** for future considerations, July 8, 1994.

McCOSH, SHAWN — NYR

Center. Shoots right. 6', 188 lbs. Born, Oshawa, Ont., June 5, 1969.
(Detroit's 5th choice, 95th overall, in 1989 Entry Draft).

			Regular Season					Playoffs				
Season	Club	Lea	GP	G	A	TP	PIM	GP	G	A	TP	PIM
1986-87	Hamilton	OHL	50	11	17	28	49	6	1	0	1	2
1987-88	Hamilton	OHL	64	17	36	53	96	14	6	8	14	14
1988-89	Niagara Falls	OHL	56	41	62	103	75	14	4	13	17	23
1989-90	Niagara Falls	OHL	9	6	10	16	24	....				
	Hamilton	OHL	39	24	28	52	65	....				
1990-91	New Haven	AHL	66	16	21	37	104	....				
1991-92	Los Angeles	NHL	4	0	0	0	4	....				
	Phoenix	IHL	71	21	32	53	118	....				
	New Haven	AHL	....					5	0	1	1	0
1992-93	New Haven	AHL	46	22	32	54	54	....				
	Phoenix	IHL	22	9	8	17	36	....				
1993-94	Binghamton	AHL	75	31	44	75	68	....				
	NHL Totals		4	0	0	0	4	....				

Traded to **Los Angeles** by **Detroit** for Los Angeles' eighth round choice (Justin Krall) in 1992 Entry Draft, August 15, 1990. Traded to **Ottawa** by **Los Angeles** with Bob Kudelski for Marc Fortier and Jim Thomson, December 19, 1992. Signed as a free agent by **NY Rangers**, July 30, 1993.

McCOSH, SHAYNE — HFD.

Defense. Shoots left. 6', 183 lbs. Born, Oshawa, Ont., January 27, 1974.

			Regular Season					Playoffs				
Season	Club	Lea	GP	G	A	TP	PIM	GP	G	A	TP	PIM
1990-91	Kitchener	OHL	62	3	22	25	26	6	0	1	1	4
1991-92	Kitchener	OHL	62	7	36	43	46	14	1	2	3	28
1992-93	Kitchener	OHL	32	7	25	32	43	....	....	....	....	....
	Windsor	OHL	36	5	35	40	38	....	....	....	....	....
1993-94	Windsor	OHL	34	3	21	24	46	....	....	....	....	....
	Detroit	OHL	25	3	18	21	33	17	3	8	11	24

Signed as a free agent by **Hartford**, October 5, 1992.

McCRIMMON, BRAD — HFD.

Defense. Shoots left. 5'11", 197 lbs. Born, Dodsland, Sask., March 29, 1959.
(Boston's 2nd choice, 15th overall, in 1979 Entry Draft).

			Regular Season					Playoffs				
Season	Club	Lea	GP	G	A	TP	PIM	GP	G	A	TP	PIM
1977-78a	Brandon	WHL	65	19	78	97	245	8	2	11	13	20
1978-79a	Brandon	WHL	66	24	74	98	139	22	9	19	28	34
1979-80	**Boston**	**NHL**	**72**	**5**	**11**	**16**	**94**	**10**	**1**	**1**	**2**	**28**
1980-81	**Boston**	**NHL**	**78**	**11**	**18**	**29**	**148**	**3**	**0**	**1**	**1**	**2**
1981-82	**Boston**	**NHL**	**78**	**1**	**8**	**9**	**83**	**2**	**0**	**0**	**0**	**2**
1982-83	**Philadelphia**	**NHL**	**79**	**4**	**21**	**25**	**61**	**3**	**0**	**0**	**0**	**4**
1983-84	**Philadelphia**	**NHL**	**71**	**0**	**24**	**24**	**76**	**1**	**0**	**0**	**0**	**4**
1984-85	**Philadelphia**	**NHL**	**66**	**8**	**35**	**43**	**81**	**11**	**2**	**1**	**3**	**15**
1985-86	**Philadelphia**	**NHL**	**80**	**13**	**43**	**56**	**85**	**5**	**2**	**0**	**2**	**2**
1986-87	**Philadelphia**	**NHL**	**71**	**10**	**29**	**39**	**52**	**26**	**3**	**5**	**8**	**30**
1987-88bc	**Calgary**	**NHL**	**80**	**7**	**35**	**42**	**98**	**9**	**2**	**3**	**5**	**22**
1988-89	**Calgary**	**NHL**	**72**	**5**	**17**	**22**	**96**	**22**	**0**	**3**	**3**	**30**
1989-90	**Calgary**	**NHL**	**79**	**4**	**15**	**19**	**78**	**6**	**0**	**2**	**2**	**8**
1990-91	**Detroit**	**NHL**	**64**	**0**	**13**	**13**	**81**	**7**	**1**	**1**	**2**	**21**
1991-92	**Detroit**	**NHL**	**79**	**7**	**22**	**29**	**118**	**11**	**0**	**1**	**1**	**8**
1992-93	**Detroit**	**NHL**	**60**	**1**	**14**	**15**	**71**	....	....	....	....	....
1993-94	**Hartford**	**NHL**	**65**	**1**	**5**	**6**	**72**	....	....	....	....	....
	NHL Totals		**1094**	**77**	**310**	**387**	**1294**	**116**	**11**	**18**	**29**	**176**

a WHL First All-Star Team (1978, 1979)
b NHL Second All-Star Team (1988)
c NHL Plus/Minus Leader (1988)

Played in NHL All-Star Game (1988)

Traded to **Philadelphia** by **Boston** for Pete Peeters, June 9, 1982. Traded to **Calgary** by **Philadelphia** for Calgary's third round choice (Dominic Roussel) in 1988 Entry Draft and first round choice (later traded to Toronto — Toronto selected Steve Bancroft) in 1989 Entry Draft, August 26, 1987. Traded to **Detroit** by **Calgary** for Detroit's second round choice (later traded to New Jersey — New Jersey selected David Harlock) in 1990 Entry Draft, June 15, 1990. Traded to **Hartford** by **Detroit** for Detroit's sixth round choice (previously acquired by Hartford — Detroit selected Tim Spitzig) in 1993 Entry Draft, June 1, 1993.

McDONOUGH, HUBIE

Center. Shoots left. 5'9", 180 lbs. Born, Manchester, NH, July 8, 1963.

			Regular Season					Playoffs				
Season	Club	Lea	GP	G	A	TP	PIM	GP	G	A	TP	PIM
1986-87	Flint	IHL	82	27	52	79	59	6	3	2	5	0
1987-88	New Haven	AHL	78	30	29	59	43	....	....	....	....	....
1988-89	**Los Angeles**	**NHL**	**4**	**0**	**1**	**1**	**0**	....	....	....	....	....
	New Haven	AHL	74	37	55	92	41	17	10	*21	*31	6
1989-90	**Los Angeles**	**NHL**	**22**	**3**	**4**	**7**	**10**	....	....	....	....	....
	NY Islanders	**NHL**	**54**	**18**	**11**	**29**	**26**	**5**	**1**	**0**	**1**	**4**
1990-91	**NY Islanders**	**NHL**	**52**	**6**	**6**	**12**	**10**	....	....	....	....	....
	Capital Dist.	AHL	17	9	9	18	4	....	....	....	....	....
1991-92	**NY Islanders**	**NHL**	**33**	**7**	**2**	**9**	**15**	....	....	....	....	....
	Capital Dist.	AHL	21	11	18	29	14	....	....	....	....	....
1992-93	**San Jose**	**NHL**	**30**	**6**	**2**	**8**	**6**	....	....	....	....	....
	San Diego	IHL	48	26	49	75	26	14	4	7	11	6
1993-94	San Diego	IHL	69	31	48	79	61	8	0	7	7	6
	NHL Totals		**195**	**40**	**26**	**66**	**67**	**5**	**1**	**0**	**1**	**4**

a IHL Second All-Star Team (1993)

Signed as a free agent by **Los Angeles**, April 18, 1988. Traded to **NY Islanders** by **Los Angeles** with Ken Baumgartner for Mikko Makela, November 29, 1989. Traded to **San Jose** by **NY Islanders** for cash, August 28, 1992.

McDOUGALL, BILL

Center. Shoots right. 6', 185 lbs. Born, Mississauga, Ont., August 10, 1966.

			Regular Season					Playoffs				
Season	Club	Lea	GP	G	A	TP	PIM	GP	G	A	TP	PIM
1988-89	Pt. Basques	Sr.	26	20	41	61	129	....	....	....	....	....
1989-90abc	Erie	ECHL	57	80	68	148	226	7	5	5	10	20
	Adirondack	AHL	11	10	7	17	4	2	1	1	2	2
1990-91	**Detroit**	**NHL**	**2**	**0**	**1**	**1**	**0**	**1**	**0**	**0**	**0**	**0**
	Adirondack	AHL	71	47	52	99	192	2	1	2	3	2
1991-92	Adirondack	AHL	45	28	24	52	112	....	....	....	....	....
	Cape Breton	AHL	22	8	18	26	36	4	0	1	1	8
1992-93	**Edmonton**	**NHL**	**4**	**2**	**1**	**3**	**4**	....	....	....	....	....
d	Cape Breton	AHL	71	42	46	88	16	16	*26	*26	*52	30
1993-94	**Tampa Bay**	**NHL**	**22**	**3**	**3**	**6**	**8**	....	....	....	....	....
	Atlanta	IHL	48	17	30	47	141	14	12	7	19	30
	NHL Totals		**28**	**5**	**5**	**10**	**12**	**1**	**0**	**0**	**0**	**0**

a ECHL Most Valuable Player (1990)
b ECHL Rookie of the Year (1990)
c ECHL First Team All-Star (1990)
d Won Jack A. Butterfield Trophy (AHL Playoff MVP) (1993)

Signed as a free agent by **Detroit**, January 9, 1990. Traded to **Edmonton** by **Detroit** for Max Middendorf, February 22, 1992. Signed as a free agent by **Tampa Bay**, August 13, 1993.

McEACHERN, SHAWN (muh-GEH-kruhn) — PIT.

Center. Shoots left. 5'11", 195 lbs. Born, Waltham, MA, February 28, 1969.
(Pittsburgh's 6th choice, 110th overall, in 1987 Entry Draft).

			Regular Season					Playoffs				
Season	Club	Lea	GP	G	A	TP	PIM	GP	G	A	TP	PIM
1988-89	Boston U.	H.E.	36	20	28	48	32	....	....	....	....	....
1989-90a	Boston U.	H.E.	43	25	31	56	78	....	....	....	....	....
1990-91bc	Boston U.	H.E.	41	34	48	82	43	....	....	....	....	....
1991-92	U.S. National	....	57	26	23	49	38	....	....	....	....	....
	U.S. Olympic	....	8	1	0	1	10	....	....	....	....	....
	Pittsburgh	**NHL**	**15**	**0**	**4**	**4**	**0**	**19**	**2**	**7**	**9**	**4**
1992-93	**Pittsburgh**	**NHL**	**84**	**28**	**33**	**61**	**46**	**12**	**3**	**2**	**5**	**10**
1993-94	**Los Angeles**	**NHL**	**49**	**8**	**13**	**21**	**24**	....	....	....	....	....
	Pittsburgh	**NHL**	**27**	**12**	**9**	**21**	**10**	**6**	**1**	**0**	**1**	**2**
	NHL Totals		**175**	**48**	**59**	**107**	**80**	**37**	**6**	**9**	**15**	**16**

a Hockey East Second All-Star Team (1990)
b Hockey East First All-Star Team (1991)
c NCAA East First All-American Team (1991)

Traded to **Los Angeles** by **Pittsburgh** for Marty McSorley, August 27, 1993. Traded to **Pittsburgh** by **Los Angeles** with Tomas Sandstrom for Marty McSorley and Jim Paek, February 16, 1994.

McGHAN, MIKE — CHI.

Left wing. Shoots left. 6'1", 177 lbs. Born, Prince Albert, Alta., July 11, 1975.
(Chicago's 11th choice, 258th overall, in 1993 Entry Draft).

			Regular Season					Playoffs				
Season	Club	Lea	GP	G	A	TP	PIM	GP	G	A	TP	PIM
1991-92	Prince Albert	WHL	2	0	0	0	2	....	....	....	....	....
1992-93	Prince Albert	WHL	69	11	9	20	143	....	....	....	....	....
1993-94	Prince Albert	WHL	51	9	22	31	142	....	....	....	....	....

McGILL, BOB

Defense. Shoots right. 6'1", 193 lbs. Born, Edmonton, Alta., April 27, 1962.
(Toronto's 2nd choice, 26th overall, in 1980 Entry Draft).

			Regular Season					Playoffs				
Season	Club	Lea	GP	G	A	TP	PIM	GP	G	A	TP	PIM
1979-80	Victoria	WHL	70	3	18	21	230	15	0	5	5	64
1980-81	Victoria	WHL	66	5	36	41	295	11	1	5	6	67
1981-82	**Toronto**	**NHL**	**68**	**1**	**10**	**11**	**263**	....	....	....	....	....
1982-83	**Toronto**	**NHL**	**30**	**0**	**0**	**0**	**146**	....	....	....	....	....
	St. Catharines	AHL	32	2	5	7	95	....	....	....	....	....
1983-84	**Toronto**	**NHL**	**11**	**0**	**2**	**2**	**51**	....	....	....	....	....
	St. Catharines	AHL	55	1	15	16	217	6	0	0	0	26
1984-85	**Toronto**	**NHL**	**72**	**0**	**5**	**5**	**250**	....	....	....	....	....
1985-86	**Toronto**	**NHL**	**61**	**1**	**4**	**5**	**141**	**9**	**0**	**0**	**0**	**35**
1986-87	**Toronto**	**NHL**	**56**	**1**	**4**	**5**	**103**	**3**	**0**	**0**	**0**	**0**
1987-88	**Chicago**	**NHL**	**67**	**4**	**7**	**11**	**131**	**3**	**0**	**0**	**0**	**2**
1988-89	**Chicago**	**NHL**	**68**	**0**	**4**	**4**	**155**	**16**	**0**	**0**	**0**	**33**
1989-90	**Chicago**	**NHL**	**69**	**2**	**10**	**12**	**204**	**5**	**0**	**0**	**0**	**2**
1990-91	**Chicago**	**NHL**	**77**	**4**	**5**	**9**	**151**	**5**	**0**	**0**	**0**	**2**
1991-92	**San Jose**	**NHL**	**62**	**3**	**1**	**4**	**70**	....	....	....	....	....
	Detroit	**NHL**	**12**	**0**	**0**	**0**	**21**	**8**	**0**	**0**	**0**	**14**
1992-93	**Toronto**	**NHL**	**19**	**1**	**0**	**1**	**34**	....	....	....	....	....
1993-94	**NY Islanders**	**NHL**	**3**	**0**	**0**	**0**	**5**	....	....	....	....	....
	Hartford	**NHL**	**30**	**0**	**3**	**3**	**41**	....	....	....	....	....
	Springfield	AHL	5	0	0	0	24	....	....	....	....	....
	NHL Totals		**705**	**17**	**55**	**72**	**1766**	**49**	**0**	**0**	**0**	**88**

Traded to **Chicago** by **Toronto** with Steve Thomas and Rick Vaive for Al Secord and Ed Olczyk, September 3, 1987. Claimed by **San Jose** from **Chicago** in Expansion Draft, May 30, 1991. Traded to **Detroit** by **San Jose** with Vancouver's eighth round choice (previously acquired by San Jose — Detroit selected C.J. Denomme) in 1992 Entry Draft for Johan Garpenlov, March 10, 1992. Claimed by **Tampa Bay** from **Detroit** in Expansion Draft, June 18, 1992. Claimed on waivers by **Toronto** from **Tampa Bay**, September 9, 1992. Signed as a free agent by **NY Islanders**, September 7, 1993. Claimed on waivers by **Hartford** from **NY Islanders**, November 3, 1993.

McGILL, RYAN — PHI.

Defense. Shoots right. 6'2", 210 lbs. Born, Prince Albert, Sask., February 28, 1969.
(Chicago's 2nd choice, 29th overall, in 1987 Entry Draft).

			Regular Season					Playoffs				
Season	Club	Lea	GP	G	A	TP	PIM	GP	G	A	TP	PIM
1985-86	Lethbridge	WHL	64	5	10	15	171	10	0	1	1	9
1986-87	Swift Current	WHL	72	12	36	48	226	4	1	0	1	9
1987-88	Medicine Hat	WHL	67	5	30	35	224	15	7	3	10	47
1988-89	Medicine Hat	WHL	57	26	45	71	172	3	0	2	2	15
	Saginaw	IHL	8	2	0	2	12	6	0	0	0	42
1989-90	Indianapolis	IHL	77	11	17	28	215	14	2	2	4	29
1990-91	Halifax	AHL	7	0	4	4	6	....	....	....	....	....
a	Indianapolis	IHL	63	11	40	51	200	....	....	....	....	....
1991-92	**Chicago**	**NHL**	**9**	**0**	**2**	**2**	**20**	....	....	....	....	....
	Indianapolis	IHL	40	7	19	26	170	....	....	....	....	....
	Hershey	AHL	17	3	5	8	67	6	1	1	2	4
1992-93	**Philadelphia**	**NHL**	**72**	**3**	**10**	**13**	**238**	....	....	....	....	....
	Hershey	AHL	4	0	2	2	26	....	....	....	....	....
1993-94	**Philadelphia**	**NHL**	**50**	**1**	**3**	**4**	**112**	....	....	....	....	....
	NHL Totals		**131**	**4**	**15**	**19**	**370**	....	....	....	....	....

a IHL Second All-Star Team (1991)

Traded to **Quebec** by **Chicago** with Mike McNeil for Paul Gillis and Dan Vincelette, March 5, 1991. Traded to **Chicago** by **Quebec** for Mike Dagenais, September 27, 1991. Traded to **Philadelphia** by **Chicago** for Tony Horacek, February 7, 1992.

McGILLIS, DANIEL — DET.

Defense. Shoots left. 6'2", 220 lbs. Born, Hawkesbury, Ont., July 1, 1972.
(Detroit's 10th choice, 238th overall, in 1992 Entry Draft).

			Regular Season					Playoffs				
Season	Club	Lea	GP	G	A	TP	PIM	GP	G	A	TP	PIM
1992-93	Northeastern	H.E.	35	5	12	17	42	....	....	....	....	....
1993-94	Northeastern	H.E.	38	4	25	29	82	....	....	....	....	....

McGOWAN, CAL — DAL.

Center. Shoots left. 6'1", 185 lbs. Born, Sydney, N.S., June 19, 1970.
(Minnesota's 3rd choice, 70th overall, in 1990 Entry Draft).

			Regular Season					Playoffs				
Season	Club	Lea	GP	G	A	TP	PIM	GP	G	A	TP	PIM
1988-89	Kamloops	WHL	72	21	31	52	44	....	....	....	....	....
1989-90	Kamloops	WHL	71	33	45	78	76	17	4	5	9	42
1990-91a	Kamloops	WHL	71	58	81	139	147	12	7	7	14	24
1991-92	Kalamazoo	IHL	77	13	30	43	62	1	0	0	0	2
1992-93	Kalamazoo	IHL	78	18	42	60	62	....	....	....	....	....
1993-94	Kalamazoo	IHL	49	9	18	27	48	4	0	0	0	2

a WHL West First All-Star Team (1991)

McHUGH, MIKE

Left wing. Shoots left. 5'10", 190 lbs. Born, Bowdoin, MA, August 16, 1965.
(Minnesota's 1st choice, 1st overall, in 1988 Supplemental Draft).

			Regular Season					Playoffs				
Season	Club	Lea	GP	G	A	TP	PIM	GP	G	A	TP	PIM
1984-85	U. of Maine	H.E.	25	9	8	17	9	....	....	....	....	....
1985-86	U. of Maine	H.E.	38	9	10	19	24	....	....	....	....	....
1986-87	U. of Maine	H.E.	42	21	29	50	40	....	....	....	....	....
1987-88	U. of Maine	H.E.	44	29	37	66	90	....	....	....	....	....
1988-89	**Minnesota**	**NHL**	**3**	**0**	**0**	**0**	**2**	....	....	....	....	....
	Kalamazoo	IHL	70	17	29	46	89	6	3	1	4	17
1989-90	**Minnesota**	**NHL**	**3**	**0**	**0**	**0**	**0**	....	....	....	....	....
	Kalamazoo	IHL	73	14	17	31	96	10	0	6	6	16
1990-91	**Minnesota**	**NHL**	**6**	**0**	**0**	**0**	**0**	....	....	....	....	....
	Kalamazoo	IHL	69	27	38	65	82	11	3	8	11	6
1991-92	**San Jose**	**NHL**	**8**	**1**	**0**	**1**	**14**	....	....	....	....	....
	Springfield	AHL	70	23	31	54	51	11	4	7	11	25
1992-93	Springfield	AHL	67	19	27	46	111	11	5	2	7	12
1993-94	Hershey	AHL	80	27	43	70	58	11	9	3	12	14
	NHL Totals		**20**	**1**	**0**	**1**	**16**	....	....	....	....	....

Claimed by **San Jose** from **Minnesota** in Dispersal Draft, May 30, 1991. Traded to **Hartford** by **San Jose** for Paul Fenton, October 18, 1991.

McINNIS, MARTY — NYI

Center. Shoots right. 6', 185 lbs. Born, Hingham, MA., June 2, 1970.
(NY Islanders' 10th choice, 163rd overall, in 1988 Entry Draft).

			Regular Season					Playoffs				
Season	Club	Lea	GP	G	A	TP	PIM	GP	G	A	TP	PIM
1988-89	Boston College	H.E.	39	13	19	32	8	....	....	....	....	....
1989-90	Boston College	H.E.	41	24	29	53	43	....	....	....	....	....
1990-91	Boston College	H.E.	38	21	36	57	40	....	....	....	....	....
1991-92	U.S. National	....	54	15	19	34	20	....	....	....	....	....
	U.S. Olympic	....	8	6	2	8	4	....	....	....	....	....
	NY Islanders	**NHL**	**15**	**3**	**5**	**8**	**0**	....	....	....	....	....
1992-93	**NY Islanders**	**NHL**	**56**	**10**	**20**	**30**	**24**	**3**	**0**	**1**	**1**	**0**
	Capital Dist.	AHL	10	4	12	16	2	....	....	....	....	....
1993-94	**NY Islanders**	**NHL**	**81**	**25**	**31**	**56**	**24**	**4**	**0**	**0**	**0**	**0**
	NHL Totals		**152**	**38**	**56**	**94**	**48**	**7**	**0**	**1**	**1**	**0**

McINTYRE, IAN

Defense. Shoots left. 6', 187 lbs. Born, Montreal, Que., February 12, 1974.
(Quebec's 5th choice, 76th overall, in 1992 Entry Draft).

			Regular Season					Playoffs				
Season	Club	Lea	GP	G	A	TP	PIM	GP	G	A	TP	PIM
1991-92	Beauport	QMJHL	63	29	32	61	250	....	....	....	....	....
1992-93	Beauport	QMJHL	44	14	18	32	115	....	....	....	....	....
1993-94	Beauport	QMJHL	71	23	53	76	129	12	3	11	14	27

McINTYRE, JOHN — VAN.

Center. Shoots left. 6'1", 190 lbs. Born, Ravenswood, Ont., April 29, 1969.
(Toronto's 3rd choice, 49th overall, in 1987 Entry Draft).

			Regular Season					Playoffs				
Season	Club	Lea	GP	G	A	TP	PIM	GP	G	A	TP	PIM
1985-86	Guelph	OHL	30	4	6	10	25	20	1	5	6	31
1986-87	Guelph	OHL	47	8	22	30	95	....	....	....	....	....
1987-88	Guelph	OHL	39	24	18	42	109	....	....	....	....	....
1988-89	Guelph	OHL	52	30	26	56	129	7	5	4	9	25
	Newmarket	AHL	3	0	2	2	7	5	1	1	2	20
1989-90	**Toronto**	**NHL**	**59**	**5**	**12**	**17**	**117**	**2**	**0**	**0**	**0**	**2**
	Newmarket	AHL	6	2	2	4	12	....	....	....	....	....
1990-91	**Toronto**	**NHL**	**13**	**0**	**3**	**3**	**25**	....	....	....	....	....
	Los Angeles	**NHL**	**56**	**8**	**5**	**13**	**115**	**12**	**0**	**1**	**1**	**24**
1991-92	**Los Angeles**	**NHL**	**73**	**5**	**19**	**24**	**100**	**6**	**0**	**4**	**4**	**12**
1992-93	**Los Angeles**	**NHL**	**49**	**2**	**5**	**7**	**80**	....	....	....	....	....
	NY Rangers	**NHL**	**11**	**1**	**0**	**1**	**4**	....	....	....	....	....
1993-94	**Vancouver**	**NHL**	**62**	**3**	**6**	**9**	**38**	**24**	**0**	**1**	**1**	**16**
	NHL Totals		**323**	**24**	**50**	**74**	**479**	**44**	**0**	**6**	**6**	**54**

Traded to **Los Angeles** by **Toronto** for Mike Krushelnyski, November 9, 1990. Traded to **NY Rangers** by **Los Angeles** for Mark Hardy and Ottawa's fifth round choice (previously acquired by NY Rangers — Los Angeles selected Frederick Beaubien) in 1993 Entry Draft, March 22, 1993. Claimed by **Vancouver** from **NY Rangers** in NHL Waiver Draft, October 3, 1993.

McINTYRE, ROBB — TOR.

Left wing. Shoots left. 6'1", 190 lbs. Born, Royal Oak, MI, April 27, 1972.
(Toronto's 10th choice, 164th overall, in 1991 Entry Draft).

			Regular Season					Playoffs				
Season	Club	Lea	GP	G	A	TP	PIM	GP	G	A	TP	PIM
1991-92	Ferris State	CCHA	32	4	3	7	48	....	....	....	....	....
1992-93	Ferris State	CCHA	32	10	9	19	76	....	....	....	....	....
1993-94	Ferris State	CCHA	32	6	17	23	84	....	....	....	....	....

McKAY, RANDY — N.J.

Right wing. Shoots right. 6'1", 205 lbs. Born, Montreal, Que., January 25, 1967.
(Detroit's 6th choice, 113th overall, in 1985 Entry Draft).

			Regular Season					Playoffs				
Season	Club	Lea	GP	G	A	TP	PIM	GP	G	A	TP	PIM
1984-85	Michigan Tech	WCHA	25	4	5	9	32	....	....	....	....	....
1985-86	Michigan Tech	WCHA	40	12	22	34	46	....	....	....	....	....
1986-87	Michigan Tech	WCHA	39	5	11	16	46	....	....	....	....	....
1987-88	Michigan Tech	WCHA	41	17	24	41	70	....	....	....	....	....
	Adirondack	AHL	10	0	3	3	12	6	0	4	4	0
1988-89	**Detroit**	**NHL**	**3**	**0**	**0**	**0**	**0**	**2**	**0**	**0**	**0**	**2**
	Adirondack	AHL	58	29	34	63	170	14	4	7	11	60
1989-90	**Detroit**	**NHL**	**33**	**3**	**6**	**9**	**51**	....	....	....	....	....
	Adirondack	AHL	36	16	23	39	99	6	3	0	3	35
1990-91	**Detroit**	**NHL**	**47**	**1**	**7**	**8**	**183**	**5**	**0**	**1**	**1**	**41**
1991-92	**New Jersey**	**NHL**	**80**	**17**	**16**	**33**	**246**	**7**	**1**	**3**	**4**	**10**
1992-93	**New Jersey**	**NHL**	**73**	**11**	**11**	**22**	**206**	**5**	**0**	**0**	**0**	**16**
1993-94	**New Jersey**	**NHL**	**78**	**12**	**15**	**27**	**244**	**20**	**1**	**2**	**3**	**24**
	NHL Totals		**314**	**44**	**55**	**99**	**930**	**39**	**2**	**6**	**8**	**93**

Acquired by **New Jersey** from **Detroit** with Dave Barr as compensation for Detroit's signing of free agent Troy Crowder, September 9, 1991.

McKAY, SCOTT — ANA.

Center. Shoots right. 5'11", 200 lbs. Born, Burlington, Ont., January 26, 1972.

			Regular Season					Playoffs				
Season	Club	Lea	GP	G	A	TP	PIM	GP	G	A	TP	PIM
1989-90	London	OHL	59	20	29	49	37	5	1	1	2	12
1990-91	London	OHL	62	29	40	69	29	7	4	2	6	6
1991-92	London	OHL	64	30	45	75	97	10	3	8	11	8
1992-93	London	OHL	63	38	57	95	49	12	1	14	15	6
1993-94	**Anaheim**	**NHL**	**1**	**0**	**0**	**0**	**0**	....	....	....	....	....
	San Diego	IHL	58	10	6	16	35	9	2	5	7	6
	NHL Totals		**1**	**0**	**0**	**0**	**0**	....	....	....	....	....

Signed as a free agent by **Anaheim**, August 2, 1993.

McKEE, MIKE — QUE.

Left wing. Shoots right. 6'3", 203 lbs. Born, Toronto, Ont., June 18, 1969.
(Quebec's 1st choice, 1st overall, in 1990 Supplemental Draft).

			Regular Season					Playoffs				
Season	Club	Lea	GP	G	A	TP	PIM	GP	G	A	TP	PIM
1988-89	Princeton	ECAC	16	2	1	3	14	....	....	....	....	....
1989-90a	Princeton	ECAC	26	7	18	25	18	....	....	....	....	....
1990-91	Princeton	ECAC	15	1	4	5	16	....	....	....	....	....
1991-92	Princeton	ECAC	27	12	17	29	34	....	....	....	....	....
1992-93	Halifax	AHL	32	6	7	13	25	....	....	....	....	....
	Greensboro	ECHL	7	1	3	4	6	....	....	....	....	....
1993-94	**Quebec**	**NHL**	**48**	**3**	**12**	**15**	**41**	....	....	....	....	....
	Cornwall	AHL	24	6	14	20	18	10	0	3	3	4
	NHL Totals		**48**	**3**	**12**	**15**	**41**	....	....	....	....	....

a ECAC Second All-Star Team (1990)

McKENZIE, JIM — PIT.

Left wing/Defense. Shoots left. 6'3", 205 lbs. Born, Gull Lake, Sask., November 3, 1969.
(Hartford's 3rd choice, 73rd overall, in 1989 Entry Draft).

			Regular Season					Playoffs				
Season	Club	Lea	GP	G	A	TP	PIM	GP	G	A	TP	PIM
1985-86	Moose Jaw	WHL	3	0	2	2	0	....	....	....	....	....
1986-87	Moose Jaw	WHL	65	5	3	8	125	9	0	0	0	7
1987-88	Moose Jaw	WHL	62	1	17	18	134	....	....	....	....	....
1988-89	Victoria	WHL	67	15	27	42	176	8	1	4	5	30
1989-90	**Hartford**	**NHL**	**5**	**0**	**0**	**0**	**4**	....	....	....	....	....
	Binghamton	AHL	56	4	12	16	149	....	....	....	....	....
1990-91	**Hartford**	**NHL**	**41**	**4**	**3**	**7**	**108**	**6**	**0**	**0**	**0**	**8**
	Springfield	AHL	24	3	4	7	102	....	....	....	....	....
1991-92	**Hartford**	**NHL**	**67**	**5**	**1**	**6**	**87**	....	....	....	....	....
1992-93	**Hartford**	**NHL**	**64**	**3**	**6**	**9**	**202**	....	....	....	....	....
1993-94	**Hartford**	**NHL**	**26**	**1**	**2**	**3**	**67**	....	....	....	....	....
	Dallas	**NHL**	**34**	**2**	**3**	**5**	**63**	....	....	....	....	....
	Pittsburgh	**NHL**	**11**	**0**	**0**	**0**	**16**	**3**	**0**	**0**	**0**	**0**
	NHL Totals		**248**	**15**	**15**	**30**	**547**	**9**	**0**	**0**	**0**	**8**

Traded to **Florida** by **Hartford** for Alexander Godynyuk, December 16, 1993. Traded to **Dallas** by **Florida** for Dallas' fourth round choice in 1995 Entry Draft, December 16, 1993. Traded to **Pittsburgh** by **Dallas** for Mike Needham, March 21, 1994.

McKIM, ANDREW

Center. Shoots right. 5'8", 175 lbs. Born, St. John, N.B., July 6, 1970.

			Regular Season					Playoffs				
Season	Club	Lea	GP	G	A	TP	PIM	GP	G	A	TP	PIM
1988-89	Verdun	QMJHL	68	50	56	106	36	....	....	....	....	....
1989-90a	Hull	QMJHL	70	66	84	130	44	11	8	10	18	8
1990-91	Salt Lake	IHL	74	30	30	60	48	4	0	2	2	6
1991-92	St. John's	AHL	79	43	50	93	79	16	11	12	23	4
1992-93	**Boston**	**NHL**	**7**	**1**	**3**	**4**	**0**	....	....	....	....	....
	Providence	AHL	61	23	46	69	64	6	2	2	4	0
1993-94	**Boston**	**NHL**	**29**	**0**	**1**	**1**	**4**	....	....	....	....	....
	Providence	AHL	46	13	24	37	49	....	....	....	....	....
	NHL Totals		**36**	**1**	**4**	**5**	**4**	....	....	....	....	....

a QMJHL First All-Star Team (1990)

Signed as a free agent by **Calgary**, October 5, 1990. Signed as a free agent by **Boston**, July 23, 1992.

McLAREN, STEVE — CHI.

Defense. Shoots left. 6', 194 lbs. Born, Owen Sound, Ont., February 3, 1975.
(Chicago's 3rd choice, 85th overall, in 1994 Entry Draft).

			Regular Season					Playoffs				
Season	Club	Lea	GP	G	A	TP	PIM	GP	G	A	TP	PIM
1992-93	North Bay	Midget	30	15	18	33	110	....	....	....	....	....
1993-94	North Bay	OHL	55	2	15	17	130	18	0	3	3	50

McLAUGHLIN, MICHAEL — NYR

Left wing. Shoots left. 6'1", 175 lbs. Born, Longmeadow, MA, March 29, 1970.
(Buffalo's 7th choice, 118th overall, in 1988 Entry Draft).

			Regular Season					Playoffs				
Season	Club	Lea	GP	G	A	TP	PIM	GP	G	A	TP	PIM
1988-89	U. of Vermont	ECAC	32	5	6	11	12	....	....	....	....	....
1989-90	U. of Vermont	ECAC	29	11	12	23	37	....	....	....	....	....
1990-91	U. of Vermont	ECAC	32	12	14	26	34	....	....	....	....	....
1991-92	U. of Vermont	ECAC	30	9	9	18	34	....	....	....	....	....
1992-93	Rochester	AHL	71	19	35	54	27	16	4	2	6	8
1993-94	Binghamton	AHL	56	11	13	24	33	....	....	....	....	....

Signed as a free agent by **NY Rangers**, August 17, 1993.

McLAUGHLIN, PETER — PIT.

Defense. Shoots left. 6'3", 190 lbs. Born, Norwood, MA, June 29, 1973.
(Pittsburgh's 8th choice, 170th overall, in 1991 Entry Draft).

			Regular Season					Playoffs				
Season	Club	Lea	GP	G	A	TP	PIM	GP	G	A	TP	PIM
1992-93	Harvard	ECAC	31	2	6	8	28	....	....	....	....	....
1993-94	Harvard	ECAC	33	0	7	7	32	....	....	....	....	....

McLEAN, JEFF

Center. Shoots left. 5'10", 190 lbs. Born, Port Moody, B.C., October 6, 1969.
(San Jose's 1st choice, 1st overall, in 1991 Supplemental Draft).

			Regular Season					Playoffs				
Season	Club	Lea	GP	G	A	TP	PIM	GP	G	A	TP	PIM
1989-90	North Dakota	WCHA	45	10	16	26	42					
1990-91	North Dakota	WCHA	42	19	26	45	22					
1991-92	North Dakota	WCHA	38	27	43	70	40					
1992-93	Kansas City	IHL	60	21	23	44	45	10	3	1	4	2
1993-94	**San Jose**	**NHL**	**6**	**1**	**0**	**1**	**0**					
	Kansas City	IHL	69	27	30	57	44					
	NHL Totals		**6**	**1**	**0**	**1**	**0**					

McLLWAIN, DAVE

(MA-kuhl-WAYN) **OTT.**

Center/Right wing. Shoots left. 6', 185 lbs. Born, Seaforth, Ont., January 9, 1967.
(Pittsburgh's 9th choice, 172nd overall, in 1986 Entry Draft).

			Regular Season					Playoffs				
Season	Club	Lea	GP	G	A	TP	PIM	GP	G	A	TP	PIM
1984-85	Kitchener	OHL	61	13	21	34	29					
1985-86	Kitchener	OHL	13	7	7	14	12					
	North Bay	OHL	51	30	28	58	25	10	4	4	8	2
1986-87a	North Bay	OHL	60	46	73	119	35	24	7	18	25	40
1987-88	**Pittsburgh**	**NHL**	**66**	**11**	**8**	**19**	**40**					
	Muskegon	IHL	9	4	6	10	23	6	2	3	5	8
1988-89	**Pittsburgh**	**NHL**	**24**	**1**	**2**	**3**	**4**	**3**	**0**	**1**	**1**	**0**
	Muskegon	IHL	46	37	35	72	51	7	8	2	10	6
1989-90	**Winnipeg**	**NHL**	**80**	**25**	**26**	**51**	**60**	**7**	**0**	**1**	**1**	**2**
1990-91	**Winnipeg**	**NHL**	**60**	**14**	**11**	**25**	**46**					
1991-92	**Winnipeg**	**NHL**	**3**	**1**	**1**	**2**	**2**					
	Buffalo	**NHL**	**5**	**0**	**0**	**0**	**2**					
	NY Islanders	**NHL**	**54**	**8**	**15**	**23**	**28**					
	Toronto	**NHL**	**11**	**1**	**2**	**3**	**4**					
1992-93	**Toronto**	**NHL**	**66**	**14**	**4**	**18**	**30**	**4**	**0**	**0**	**0**	**0**
1993-94	**Ottawa**	**NHL**	**66**	**17**	**26**	**43**	**48**					
	NHL Totals		**435**	**92**	**95**	**187**	**264**	**14**	**0**	**2**	**2**	**2**

a OHL Second All-Star Team (1987)

Traded to **Winnipeg** by **Pittsburgh** with Randy Cunneyworth and Rick Tabaracci for Jim Kyte, Andrew McBain and Randy Gilhen, June 17, 1989. Traded to **Buffalo** by **Winnipeg** with Gord Donnelly, Winnipeg's fifth round choice (Yuri Khmylev) in 1992 Entry Draft and future considerations for Darrin Shannon, Mike Hartman and Dean Kennedy, October 11, 1991. Traded to **NY Islanders** by **Buffalo** with Pierre Turgeon, Uwe Krupp and Benoit Hogue for Pat Lafontaine, Randy Hillier, Randy Wood and NY Islanders' fourth round choice (Dean Melanson) in 1992 Entry Draft, October 25, 1991. Traded to **Toronto** by **NY Islanders** with Ken Baumgartner for Daniel Marois and Claude Loiselle, March 10, 1992. Claimed by **Ottawa** from **Toronto** in NHL Waiver Draft, October 3, 1993.

McMORRAN, LARRY

PIT.

Center. Shoots right. 6'3", 193 lbs. Born, Toronto, Ont., May 16, 1975.
(Pittsburgh's 8th choice, 208th overall, in 1993 Entry Draft).

			Regular Season					Playoffs				
Season	Club	Lea	GP	G	A	TP	PIM	GP	G	A	TP	PIM
1992-93	Seattle	WHL	54	9	1	10	25	3	0	0	0	0
1993-94	Seattle	WHL	12	2	3	5	11					
	Lethbridge	WHL	23	2	0	2	4	3	0	0	0	0

McMURTRY, CHRIS

TOR.

Defense. Shoots left. 6'4", 190 lbs. Born, Hamilton, Ont., July 13, 1974.

			Regular Season					Playoffs				
Season	Club	Lea	GP	G	A	TP	PIM	GP	G	A	TP	PIM
1991-92	Guelph	OHL	55	2	9	11	56					
1992-93	Guelph	OHL	57	1	10	11	38	1	0	0	0	2
1993-94	Guelph	OHL	3	0	1	1	0					
	Sudbury	OHL	40	3	2	5	41					

Signed as a free agent by **Toronto**, October 5, 1992.

McNEILL, MICHAEL

Right wing. Shoots left. 6'1", 195 lbs. Born, Winona, MN, July 22, 1966.
(St. Louis' 1st choice, 14th overall, in 1988 Supplemental Draft).

			Regular Season					Playoffs				
Season	Club	Lea	GP	G	A	TP	PIM	GP	G	A	TP	PIM
1984-85	Notre Dame	NCAA	28	16	26	42	12					
1985-86	Notre Dame	NCAA	34	18	29	47	32					
1986-87	Notre Dame	NCAA	30	21	16	37	24					
1987-88	Notre Dame	NCAA	32	28	44	72	12					
1988-89	Moncton	AHL	1	0	0	0	0					
	Fort Wayne	IHL	75	27	35	62	12	11	1	5	6	2
1989-90a	Indianapolis	IHL	74	17	24	41	10	14	6	4	10	21
1990-91	**Chicago**	**NHL**	**23**	**2**	**2**	**4**	**6**					
	Indianapolis	IHL	33	16	9	25	19					
	Quebec	**NHL**	**14**	**2**	**5**	**7**	**4**					
1991-92	**Quebec**	**NHL**	**26**	**1**	**4**	**5**	**8**					
	Halifax	AHL	30	10	8	18	20					
1992-93	Milwaukee	IHL	75	17	17	34	34	6	2	0	2	0
1993-94	Milwaukee	IHL	78	21	25	46	40	4	0	1	1	6
	NHL Totals		**63**	**5**	**11**	**16**	**18**					

a Won N.R. Poile Trophy (Playoff MVP - IHL) (1990)

Signed as a free agent by **Chicago**, September, 1989. Traded to **Quebec** by **Chicago** with Ryan McGill for Paul Gillis and Dan Vincelette, March 5, 1991.

McPHEE, MIKE

DAL.

Left wing. Shoots left. 6'1", 203 lbs. Born, Sydney, N.S., July 14, 1960.
(Montreal's 8th choice, 124th overall, in 1980 Entry Draft).

			Regular Season					Playoffs				
Season	Club	Lea	GP	G	A	TP	PIM	GP	G	A	TP	PIM
1980-81	RPI	ECAC	29	28	18	46	22					
1981-82	RPI	ECAC	6	0	3	3	4					
1982-83	Nova Scotia	AHL	42	10	15	25	29	7	1	1	2	14
1983-84	**Montreal**	**NHL**	**14**	**5**	**2**	**7**	**41**	**15**	**1**	**0**	**1**	**31**
	Nova Scotia	AHL	67	22	33	55	101					
1984-85	**Montreal**	**NHL**	**70**	**17**	**22**	**39**	**120**	**12**	**4**	**1**	**5**	**32**
1985-86	**Montreal**	**NHL**	**70**	**19**	**21**	**40**	**69**	**20**	**3**	**4**	**7**	**45**
1986-87	**Montreal**	**NHL**	**79**	**18**	**21**	**39**	**58**	**17**	**7**	**2**	**9**	**13**
1987-88	**Montreal**	**NHL**	**77**	**23**	**20**	**43**	**53**	**11**	**4**	**3**	**7**	**8**
1988-89	**Montreal**	**NHL**	**73**	**19**	**22**	**41**	**74**	**20**	**4**	**7**	**11**	**30**
1989-90	**Montreal**	**NHL**	**56**	**23**	**18**	**41**	**47**	**9**	**1**	**1**	**2**	**16**
1990-91	**Montreal**	**NHL**	**64**	**22**	**21**	**43**	**56**	**13**	**1**	**7**	**8**	**12**
1991-92	**Montreal**	**NHL**	**78**	**16**	**15**	**31**	**63**	**8**	**1**	**1**	**2**	**4**
1992-93	**Minnesota**	**NHL**	**84**	**18**	**22**	**40**	**44**					
1993-94	**Dallas**	**NHL**	**79**	**20**	**15**	**35**	**36**	**9**	**2**	**1**	**3**	**2**
	NHL Totals		**744**	**200**	**199**	**399**	**661**	**134**	**28**	**27**	**55**	**193**

Played in NHL All-Star Game (1989)

Traded to **Minnesota** by **Montreal** for Minnesota's fifth round choice (Jeff Lank) in 1993 Entry Draft, August 14, 1992.

McRAE, BASIL

(muh-KRAY, BA-zihl) **ST.L.**

Left wing. Shoots left. 6'2", 205 lbs. Born, Beaverton, Ont., January 5, 1961.
(Quebec's 3rd choice, 87th overall, in 1980 Entry Draft).

			Regular Season					Playoffs				
Season	Club	Lea	GP	G	A	TP	PIM	GP	G	A	TP	PIM
1979-80	London	OHA	67	24	36	60	116	5	0	0	0	18
1980-81	London	OHA	65	29	23	52	266					
1981-82	**Quebec**	**NHL**	**20**	**4**	**3**	**7**	**69**	**9**	**1**	**0**	**1**	**34**
	Fredericton	AHL	47	11	15	26	175					
1982-83	**Quebec**	**NHL**	**22**	**1**	**1**	**2**	**59**					
	Fredericton	AHL	53	22	19	41	146	12	1	5	6	75
1983-84	**Toronto**	**NHL**	**3**	**0**	**0**	**0**	**19**					
	St. Catharines	AHL	78	14	25	39	187	6	0	0	0	40
1984-85	**Toronto**	**NHL**	**1**	**0**	**0**	**0**	**0**					
	St. Catharines	AHL	72	30	25	55	186					
1985-86	**Detroit**	**NHL**	**4**	**0**	**0**	**0**	**5**					
	Adirondack	AHL	69	22	30	52	259	17	5	4	9	101
1986-87	**Detroit**	**NHL**	**36**	**2**	**2**	**4**	**193**					
	Quebec	**NHL**	**33**	**9**	**5**	**14**	**149**	**13**	**3**	**1**	**4**	***99**
1987-88	**Minnesota**	**NHL**	**80**	**5**	**11**	**16**	**382**					
1988-89	**Minnesota**	**NHL**	**78**	**12**	**19**	**31**	**365**	**5**	**0**	**0**	**0**	**58**
1989-90	**Minnesota**	**NHL**	**66**	**9**	**17**	**26**	***351**	**7**	**1**	**0**	**1**	**24**
1990-91	**Minnesota**	**NHL**	**40**	**1**	**3**	**4**	**224**	**22**	**1**	**1**	**2**	***94**
1991-92	**Minnesota**	**NHL**	**59**	**5**	**8**	**13**	**245**					
1992-93	**Tampa Bay**	**NHL**	**14**	**2**	**3**	**5**	**71**					
	St. Louis	**NHL**	**33**	**1**	**3**	**4**	**98**	**11**	**0**	**1**	**1**	**24**
1993-94	**St. Louis**	**NHL**	**40**	**1**	**2**	**3**	**103**	**2**	**0**	**0**	**0**	**12**
	NHL Totals		**529**	**52**	**77**	**129**	**2333**	**69**	**6**	**3**	**9**	**345**

Traded to **Toronto** by **Quebec** for Richard Turmel, August 12, 1983. Signed as a free agent by **Detroit**, July 17, 1985. Traded to **Quebec** by **Detroit** with John Ogrodnick and Doug Shedden for Brent Ashton, Gilbert Delorme and Mark Kumpel, January 17, 1987. Signed as a free agent by **Minnesota**, June 29, 1987. Claimed by **Tampa Bay** from **Minnesota** in Expansion Draft, June 18, 1992. Traded to **St. Louis** by **Tampa Bay** with Doug Crossman and Tampa Bay's fourth round choice in 1996 Entry Draft for Jason Ruff and future considerations, January 28, 1993.

McRAE, KEN

TOR.

Center. Shoots right. 6'1", 195 lbs. Born, Winchester, Ont., April 23, 1968.
(Quebec's 1st choice, 18th overall, in 1986 Entry Draft).

			Regular Season					Playoffs				
Season	Club	Lea	GP	G	A	TP	PIM	GP	G	A	TP	PIM
1985-86	Sudbury	OHL	66	25	49	74	127	4	2	1	3	12
1986-87	Sudbury	OHL	21	12	15	27	40					
	Hamilton	OHL	20	7	12	19	25	7	1	1	2	12
1987-88	**Quebec**	**NHL**	**1**	**0**	**0**	**0**	**0**					
	Hamilton	OHL	62	30	55	85	158	14	13	9	22	35
	Fredericton	AHL						3	0	0	0	8
1988-89	**Quebec**	**NHL**	**37**	**6**	**11**	**17**	**68**					
	Halifax	AHL	41	20	21	41	87					
1989-90	**Quebec**	**NHL**	**66**	**7**	**8**	**15**	**191**					
1990-91	**Quebec**	**NHL**	**12**	**0**	**0**	**0**	**36**					
	Halifax	AHL	60	10	36	46	193					
1991-92	**Quebec**	**NHL**	**10**	**0**	**1**	**1**	**31**					
	Halifax	AHL	52	30	41	71	184					
1992-93	**Toronto**	**NHL**	**2**	**0**	**0**	**0**	**2**					
	St. John's	AHL	64	30	44	74	135	9	6	6	12	27
1993-94	**Toronto**	**NHL**	**9**	**1**	**1**	**2**	**36**	**6**	**0**	**0**	**0**	**4**
	St. John's	AHL	65	23	41	64	200					
	NHL Totals		**137**	**14**	**21**	**35**	**364**	**6**	**0**	**0**	**0**	**4**

Traded to **Toronto** by **Quebec** for Len Esau, July 21, 1992.

McREYNOLDS, BRIAN

L.A.

Center. Shoots left. 6'1", 192 lbs. Born, Penetanguishene, Ont., January 5, 1965.
(NY Rangers' 6th choice, 112th overall, in 1985 Entry Draft).

			Regular Season					Playoffs				
Season	Club	Lea	GP	G	A	TP	PIM	GP	G	A	TP	PIM
1985-86	Michigan State	CCHA	45	14	24	38	78					
1986-87	Michigan State	CCHA	45	16	24	40	68					
1987-88	Michigan State	CCHA	43	10	24	34	50					
1988-89	Cdn. National	....	58	5	25	30	59					
1989-90	**Winnipeg**	**NHL**	**9**	**0**	**2**	**2**	**4**					
	Moncton	AHL	72	18	41	59	87					
1990-91	**NY Rangers**	**NHL**	**1**	**0**	**0**	**0**	**0**					
	Binghamton	AHL	77	30	42	72	74	10	0	4	4	6
1991-92	Binghamton	AHL	48	19	28	47	22	7	2	2	4	12
1992-93	Binghamton	AHL	79	30	70	100	88	14	3	10	13	18
1993-94	**Los Angeles**	**NHL**	**20**	**1**	**3**	**4**	**4**					
	Phoenix	IHL	51	14	33	47	65					
	NHL Totals		**30**	**1**	**5**	**6**	**8**					

Signed as a free agent by **Winnipeg**, June 20, 1989. Traded to **NY Rangers** by **Winnipeg** for Simon Wheeldon, July 10, 1990. Signed as a free agent by **Los Angeles**, July 29, 1993.

McSORLEY, MARTY — L.A.

Defense. Shoots right. 6'1", 235 lbs. Born, Hamilton, Ont., May 18, 1963.

			Regular Season					Playoffs				
Season	Club	Lea	GP	G	A	TP	PIM	GP	G	A	TP	PIM
1981-82	Belleville	OHL	58	6	13	19	234	....	....	....	....	....
1982-83	Belleville	OHL	70	10	41	51	183	4	0	0	0	7
	Baltimore	AHL	2	0	0	0	22	....	....	....	....	....
1983-84	**Pittsburgh**	**NHL**	**72**	**2**	**7**	**9**	**224**	....	....	....	....	....
1984-85	**Pittsburgh**	**NHL**	**15**	**0**	**0**	**0**	**15**	....	....	....	....	....
	Baltimore	AHL	58	6	24	30	154	14	0	7	7	47
1985-86	**Edmonton**	**NHL**	**59**	**11**	**12**	**23**	**265**	**8**	**0**	**2**	**2**	**50**
	Nova Scotia	AHL	9	2	4	6	34	....	....	....	....	....
1986-87	**Edmonton**	**NHL**	**41**	**2**	**4**	**6**	**159**	**21**	**4**	**3**	**7**	**65**
	Nova Scotia	AHL	7	2	2	4	48	....	....	....	....	....
1987-88	**Edmonton**	**NHL**	**60**	**9**	**17**	**26**	**223**	**16**	**0**	**3**	**3**	**67**
1988-89	**Los Angeles**	**NHL**	**66**	**10**	**17**	**27**	**350**	**11**	**0**	**2**	**2**	**33**
1989-90	**Los Angeles**	**NHL**	**75**	**15**	**21**	**36**	**322**	**10**	**1**	**3**	**4**	**18**
1990-91a	**Los Angeles**	**NHL**	**61**	**7**	**32**	**39**	**221**	**12**	**0**	**0**	**0**	**58**
1991-92	**Los Angeles**	**NHL**	**71**	**7**	**22**	**29**	**268**	**6**	**1**	**0**	**1**	**21**
1992-93	**Los Angeles**	**NHL**	**81**	**15**	**26**	**41**	***399**	**24**	**4**	**6**	**10**	***60**
1993-94	**Pittsburgh**	**NHL**	**47**	**3**	**18**	**21**	**139**	....	....	....	....	....
	Los Angeles	**NHL**	**18**	**4**	**6**	**10**	**55**	....	....	....	....	....
	NHL Totals		**666**	**85**	**182**	**267**	**2640**	**108**	**10**	**19**	**29**	**372**

a Co-winner of Alka-Seltzer Plus Award with Theoren Fleury (1991)

Signed as a free agent by **Pittsburgh**, July 30, 1982. Traded to **Edmonton** by **Pittsburgh** with Tim Hrynewich and future considerations (Craig Muni, October 6, 1986) for Gilles Meloche, September 12, 1985. Traded to **Los Angeles** by **Edmonton** with Wayne Gretzky and Mike Krushelnyski for Jimmy Carson, Martin Gelinas, Los Angeles' first round choices in 1989 (acquired by New Jersey — New Jersey selected Jason Miller), 1991 (Martin Rucinsky) and 1993 (Nick Stajduhar) Entry Drafts and cash, August 9, 1988. Traded to **Pittsburgh** by **Los Angeles**, for Shawn McEachern, August 27, 1993. Traded to **Los Angeles** by **Pittsburgh** with Jim Paek for Tomas Sandstrom and Shawn McEachern, February 16, 1994.

McSWEEN, DON — ANA.

Defense. Shoots left. 5'11", 197 lbs. Born, Detroit, MI, June 9, 1964.
(Buffalo's 10th choice, 154th overall, in 1983 Entry Draft).

			Regular Season					Playoffs				
Season	Club	Lea	GP	G	A	TP	PIM	GP	G	A	TP	PIM
1983-84	Michigan State	CCHA	46	10	26	36	30	....	....	....	....	....
1984-85	Michigan State	CCHA	44	2	23	25	52	....	....	....	....	....
1985-86a	Michigan State	CCHA	45	9	29	38	18	....	....	....	....	....
1986-87abc	Michigan State	CCHA	45	7	23	30	34	....	....	....	....	....
1987-88	**Buffalo**	**NHL**	**5**	**0**	**1**	**1**	**6**	....	....	....	....	....
	Rochester	AHL	63	9	29	38	108	6	0	1	1	15
1988-89	Rochester	AHL	66	7	22	29	45	....	....	....	....	....
1989-90	**Buffalo**	**NHL**	**4**	**0**	**0**	**0**	**6**	....	....	....	....	....
d	Rochester	AHL	70	16	43	59	43	17	3	10	13	12
1990-91	Rochester	AHL	74	7	44	51	57	15	2	5	7	8
1991-92	Rochester	AHL	75	6	32	38	60	16	5	6	11	18
1992-93	San Diego	IHL	80	15	40	55	85	14	1	2	3	10
1993-94	San Diego	IHL	38	5	13	18	36	....	....	....	....	....
	Anaheim	**NHL**	**32**	**3**	**9**	**12**	**39**	....	....	....	....	....
	NHL Totals		**41**	**3**	**10**	**13**	**51**	....	....	....	....	....

a CCHA First All-Star Team (1986, 1987)
b NCAA West Second All-American Team (1987)
c NCAA Final Four All-Tournament Team (1987)
d AHL First All-Star Team (1990)

Signed as a free agent by **Anaheim**, January 12, 1994.

MEKESHKIN, DMITRI — (meh-KEHSH-kihn) WSH.

Defense. Shoots left. 6'1", 174 lbs. Born, Izhevsk, USSR, January 29, 1976.
(Washington's 6th choice, 145th overall, in 1994 Entry Draft).

			Regular Season					Playoffs				
Season	Club	Lea	GP	G	A	TP	PIM	GP	G	A	TP	PIM
1993-94	Avangard Omsk	CIS	21	0	0	0	14	3	0	0	0	2

MELANSON, DEAN — (meh-LAHN-suhn) BUF.

Defense. Shoots right. 5'11", 211 lbs. Born, Antigonish, N.S., November 19, 1973.
(Buffalo's 4th choice, 80th overall, in 1992 Entry Draft).

			Regular Season					Playoffs				
Season	Club	Lea	GP	G	A	TP	PIM	GP	G	A	TP	PIM
1990-91	St-Hyacinthe	QMJHL	69	10	17	27	110	4	0	1	1	2
1991-92	St-Hyacinthe	QMJHL	42	8	19	27	158	6	1	2	3	25
1992-93	Rochester	AHL	8	0	1	1	6	14	1	6	7	18
	St. Hyacinthe	QMJHL	57	13	29	42	253	....	....	....	....	....
1993-94	Rochester	AHL	80	1	21	22	138	4	0	1	1	2

MELANSON, ROBERT — (meh-LAHN-suhn) PIT.

Defense. Shoots left. 6'1", 202 lbs. Born, Antigonish, N.S., March 5, 1971.
(Pittsburgh's 5th choice, 104th overall, in 1991 Entry Draft).

			Regular Season					Playoffs				
Season	Club	Lea	GP	G	A	TP	PIM	GP	G	A	TP	PIM
1990-91	Hull	QMJHL	66	1	8	9	210	6	0	1	1	34
1991-92	Knoxville	ECHL	49	0	11	11	186	....	....	....	....	....
	Muskegon	IHL	7	0	2	2	2	1	0	0	0	0
1992-93	Cleveland	IHL	27	0	5	5	123	1	0	0	0	0
	Muskegon	ColHL	23	0	7	7	108	7	0	0	0	11
1993-94	Rochester	AHL	13	0	1	1	24	....	....	....	....	....
	Muskegon	ColHL	44	2	8	10	184	3	1	1	2	6

MELLANBY, SCOTT — FLA.

Right wing. Shoots right. 6'1", 205 lbs. Born, Montreal, Que., June 11, 1966.
(Philadelphia's 2nd choice, 27th overall, in 1984 Entry Draft).

			Regular Season					Playoffs				
Season	Club	Lea	GP	G	A	TP	PIM	GP	G	A	TP	PIM
1984-85	U. Wisconsin	WCHA	40	14	24	38	60	....	....	....	....	....
1985-86	U. Wisconsin	WCHA	32	21	23	44	89	....	....	....	....	....
	Philadelphia	**NHL**	**2**	**0**	**0**	**0**	**0**	....	....	....	....	....
1986-87	**Philadelphia**	**NHL**	**71**	**11**	**21**	**32**	**94**	**24**	**5**	**5**	**10**	**46**
1987-88	**Philadelphia**	**NHL**	**75**	**25**	**26**	**51**	**185**	**7**	**0**	**1**	**1**	**16**
1988-89	**Philadelphia**	**NHL**	**76**	**21**	**29**	**50**	**183**	**19**	**4**	**5**	**9**	**28**
1989-90	**Philadelphia**	**NHL**	**57**	**6**	**17**	**23**	**77**	....	....	....	....	....
1990-91	**Philadelphia**	**NHL**	**74**	**20**	**21**	**41**	**155**	....	....	....	....	....
1991-92	**Edmonton**	**NHL**	**80**	**23**	**27**	**50**	**197**	**16**	**2**	**1**	**3**	**29**
1992-93	**Edmonton**	**NHL**	**69**	**15**	**17**	**32**	**147**	....	....	....	....	....
1993-94	**Florida**	**NHL**	**80**	**30**	**30**	**60**	**149**	....	....	....	....	....
	NHL Totals		**584**	**151**	**188**	**339**	**1187**	**66**	**11**	**12**	**23**	**119**

Traded to **Edmonton** by **Philadelphia** with Craig Fisher and Craig Berube for Dave Brown, Corey Foster and Jari Kurri, May 30, 1991. Claimed by **Florida** from **Edmonton** in Expansion Draft, June 24, 1993.

MESSIER, JOBY — (MEHS-see-ay) NYR

Defense. Shoots right. 6', 200 lbs. Born, Regina, Sask., March 2, 1970.
(NY Rangers' 7th choice, 118th overall, in 1989 Entry Draft).

			Regular Season					Playoffs				
Season	Club	Lea	GP	G	A	TP	PIM	GP	G	A	TP	PIM
1988-89	Michigan State	CCHA	39	2	10	12	66	....	....	....	....	....
1989-90	Michigan State	CCHA	42	1	11	12	58	....	....	....	....	....
1990-91	Michigan State	CCHA	39	5	11	16	71	....	....	....	....	....
1991-92ab	Michigan State	CCHA	41	13	15	28	81	....	....	....	....	....
1992-93	**NY Rangers**	**NHL**	**11**	**0**	**0**	**0**	**6**	....	....	....	....	....
	Binghamton	AHL	60	5	16	21	63	14	1	1	2	6
1993-94	**NY Rangers**	**NHL**	**4**	**0**	**2**	**2**	**0**	....	....	....	....	....
	Binghamton	AHL	42	6	14	20	58	....	....	....	....	....
	NHL Totals		**15**	**0**	**2**	**2**	**6**	....	....	....	....	....

a CCHA First All-Star Team (1992)
b NCAA West First All-American Team (1992)

MESSIER, MARK — (MEHS-see-ay) NYR

Center. Shoots left. 6'1", 205 lbs. Born, Edmonton, Alta., January 18, 1961.
(Edmonton's 2nd choice, 48th overall, in 1979 Entry Draft).

			Regular Season					Playoffs				
Season	Club	Lea	GP	G	A	TP	PIM	GP	G	A	TP	PIM
1977-78	Portland	WHL	....	....	....	....	....	7	4	1	5	2
1978-79	Indianapolis	WHA	5	0	0	0	0	....	....	....	....	....
	Cincinnati	WHA	47	1	10	11	58	....	....	....	....	....
1979-80	**Edmonton**	**NHL**	**75**	**12**	**21**	**33**	**120**	**3**	**1**	**2**	**3**	**2**
	Houston	CHL	4	0	3	3	4	....	....	....	....	....
1980-81	**Edmonton**	**NHL**	**72**	**23**	**40**	**63**	**102**	**9**	**2**	**5**	**7**	**13**
1981-82a	**Edmonton**	**NHL**	**78**	**50**	**38**	**88**	**119**	**5**	**1**	**2**	**3**	**8**
1982-83a	**Edmonton**	**NHL**	**77**	**48**	**58**	**106**	**72**	**15**	**15**	**6**	**21**	**14**
1983-84bc	**Edmonton**	**NHL**	**73**	**37**	**64**	**101**	**165**	**19**	**8**	**18**	**26**	**19**
1984-85	**Edmonton**	**NHL**	**55**	**23**	**31**	**54**	**57**	**18**	**12**	**13**	**25**	**12**
1985-86	**Edmonton**	**NHL**	**63**	**35**	**49**	**84**	**68**	**10**	**4**	**6**	**10**	**18**
1986-87	**Edmonton**	**NHL**	**77**	**37**	**70**	**107**	**73**	**21**	**12**	**16**	**28**	**16**
1987-88	**Edmonton**	**NHL**	**77**	**37**	**74**	**111**	**103**	**19**	**11**	**23**	**34**	**29**
1988-89	**Edmonton**	**NHL**	**72**	**33**	**61**	**94**	**130**	**7**	**1**	**11**	**12**	**8**
1989-90ade	**Edmonton**	**NHL**	**79**	**45**	**84**	**129**	**79**	**22**	**9**	***22**	**31**	**20**
1990-91	**Edmonton**	**NHL**	**53**	**12**	**52**	**64**	**34**	**18**	**4**	**11**	**15**	**16**
1991-92ade	**NY Rangers**	**NHL**	**79**	**35**	**72**	**107**	**76**	**11**	**7**	**7**	**14**	**6**
1992-93	**NY Rangers**	**NHL**	**75**	**25**	**66**	**91**	**72**	....	....	....	....	....
1993-94	**NY Rangers**	**NHL**	**76**	**26**	**58**	**84**	**76**	**23**	**12**	**18**	**30**	**33**
	NHL Totals		**1081**	**478**	**838**	**1316**	**1346**	**200**	**99**	**160**	**259**	**214**

a NHL First All-Star Team (1982, 1983, 1990, 1992)
b NHL Second All-Star Team (1984)
c Won Conn Smythe Trophy (1984)
d Won Hart Trophy (1990, 1992)
e Won Lester B. Pearson Award (1990, 1992)

Played in NHL All-Star Game (1982-86, 1988-92, 1994)

Traded to **NY Rangers** by **Edmonton** with future considerations for Bernie Nicholls, Steven Rice and Louie DeBrusk, October 4, 1991.

METLYUK, DENIS — (MEHT-lee-ook) PHI.

Center. Shoots left. 6', 183 lbs. Born, Togliatti, USSR, January 30, 1972.
(Philadelphia's 3rd choice, 31st overall, in 1992 Entry Draft).

			Regular Season					Playoffs				
Season	Club	Lea	GP	G	A	TP	PIM	GP	G	A	TP	PIM
1990-91	Togliatti	USSR 2	25	5	6	11	8	....	....	....	....	....
1991-92	Togliatti	CIS	26	0	1	1	6	....	....	....	....	....
1992-93	Togliatti	CIS	39	7	12	19	20	10	0	1	1	2
1993-94	Hershey	AHL	73	8	13	21	46	11	4	2	6	4

MICHAYLUK, DAVE — (muh-KIGH-luhk)

Left wing. Shoots left. 5'10", 189 lbs. Born, Wakaw, Sask., May 18, 1962.
(Philadelphia's 5th choice, 65th overall, in 1981 Entry Draft).

			Regular Season					Playoffs				
Season	Club	Lea	GP	G	A	TP	PIM	GP	G	A	TP	PIM
1980-81	Regina	WHL	72	62	71	133	39	11	5	12	17	8
1981-82	**Philadelphia**	**NHL**	**1**	**0**	**0**	**0**	**0**	....	....	....	....	....
a	Regina	WHL	72	62	111	172	128	12	16	24	*40	23
1982-83	**Philadelphia**	**NHL**	**13**	**2**	**6**	**8**	**8**	....	....	....	....	....
	Maine	AHL	69	32	40	72	16	8	0	2	2	0
1983-84	Springfield	AHL	79	18	44	62	37	4	0	0	0	2
1984-85	Hershey	AHL	3	0	2	2	2	....	....	....	....	....
b	Kalamazoo	IHL	82	*66	33	99	49	11	7	7	14	0
1985-86	Nova Scotia	AHL	3	0	1	1	0	....	....	....	....	....
	Muskegon	IHL	77	52	52	104	73	14	6	9	15	12
1986-87c	Muskegon	IHL	82	47	53	100	29	15	2	14	16	8
1987-88c	Muskegon	IHL	81	*56	81	137	46	6	2	0	2	18
1988-89cdef	Muskegon	IHL	80	50	72	*122	84	13	*9	12	*21	24
1989-90c	Muskegon	IHL	79	*51	51	102	80	15	8	*14	22	10
1990-91	Muskegon	IHL	83	40	62	102	16	5	2	2	4	4
1991-92b	Muskegon	IHL	82	39	63	102	154	13	9	8	17	4
	Pittsburgh	**NHL**	....	....	....	....	....	**7**	**1**	**1**	**2**	**0**
1992-93c	Cleveland	IHL	82	47	65	112	104	4	1	2	3	4
1993-94	Cleveland	IHL	81	48	51	99	92	....	....	....	....	....
	NHL Totals		**14**	**2**	**6**	**8**	**8**	**7**	**1**	**1**	**2**	**0**

a WHL Second All-Star Team (1982)
b IHL Second All-Star Team (1985, 1992)
c IHL First All-Star Team (1987, 1988, 1989, 1990, 1993)
d IHL Playoff MVP (1989)
e Won James Gatschene Memorial Trophy (MVP - IHL) (1989)
f Won Leo P. Lamoureux Memorial Trophy (Top Scorer - IHL) (1989)

Signed as a free agent by **Pittsburgh**, May 24, 1989.

MIDDENDORF, MAX

Right wing. Shoots right. 6'4", 210 lbs. Born, Syracuse, NY, August 18, 1967.
(Quebec's 3rd choice, 57th overall, in 1985 Entry Draft).

			Regular Season					Playoffs				
Season	Club	Lea	GP	G	A	TP	PIM	GP	G	A	TP	PIM
1984-85	Sudbury	OHL	63	16	28	44	106	....	....	....	....	....
1985-86	Sudbury	OHL	61	40	42	82	71	4	4	2	6	11
1986-87	**Quebec**	**NHL**	**6**	**1**	**4**	**5**	**4**	....	....	....	....	....
	Sudbury	OHL	31	31	29	60	7	....	....	....	....	....
	Kitchener	OHL	17	7	15	22	6	4	2	5	7	5
1987-88	**Quebec**	**NHL**	**1**	**0**	**0**	**0**	**0**	....	....	....	....	....
	Fredericton	AHL	38	11	13	24	57	12	4	4	8	18
1988-89	Halifax	AHL	72	41	39	80	85	4	1	2	3	6
1989-90	**Quebec**	**NHL**	**3**	**0**	**0**	**0**	**0**	....	....	....	....	....
	Halifax	AHL	48	20	17	37	60	....	....	....	....	....
1990-91	**Edmonton**	**NHL**	**3**	**1**	**0**	**1**	**2**	....	....	....	....	....
	Fort Wayne	IHL	15	9	11	20	12	....	....	....	....	....
	Cape Breton	AHL	44	14	21	35	82	4	0	1	1	6
1991-92	Cape Breton	AHL	51	20	19	39	108	....	....	....	....	....
	Adirondack	AHL	6	3	5	8	12	5	0	1	1	16
1992-93	Fort Wayne	IHL	24	9	13	22	58	....	....	....	....	....
	San Diego	IHL	30	15	11	26	25	8	1	2	3	8
1993-94	Fort Wayne	IHL	36	16	20	36	43	9	1	2	3	24
	NHL Totals		**13**	**2**	**4**	**6**	**6**	....	....	....	....	....

Traded to **Edmonton** by **Quebec** for Edmonton's ninth round choice (Brent Brekke) in 1991 Entry Draft, November 10, 1990. Traded to **Detroit** by **Edmonton** for Bill McDougall, February 22, 1992.

MIEHM, KEVIN (MEE-yuhm) ST.L.

Centre. Shoots left. 6'2", 200 lbs. Born, Kitchener, Ont., September 10, 1969.
(St. Louis' 2nd choice, 54th overall, in 1987 Entry Draft).

			Regular Season					Playoffs				
Season	Club	Lea	GP	G	A	TP	PIM	GP	G	A	TP	PIM
1986-87	Oshawa	OHL	61	12	27	39	19	26	1	8	9	12
1987-88	Oshawa	OHL	52	16	36	52	30	7	2	5	7	0
1988-89	Oshawa	OHL	63	43	79	122	19	6	6	6	12	0
	Peoria	IHL	3	1	1	2	0	4	0	2	2	0
1989-90	Peoria	IHL	76	23	38	61	20	3	0	0	0	4
1990-91	Peoria	IHL	73	25	39	64	14	16	5	7	12	2
1991-92	Peoria	IHL	66	21	53	74	22	10	3	4	7	2
1992-93	**St. Louis**	**NHL**	**8**	**1**	**3**	**4**	**4**	**2**	**0**	**1**	**1**	**0**
	Peoria	IHL	30	12	33	45	13	4	0	1	1	2
1993-94	**St. Louis**	**NHL**	**14**	**0**	**1**	**1**	**4**	....	....	....	....	....
	Peoria	IHL	11	2	3	5	0	4	1	0	1	0
	NHL Totals		**22**	**1**	**4**	**5**	**8**	**2**	**0**	**1**	**1**	**0**

MIKULCHIK, OLEG (mih-KOOL-chihk, OH-lehg) WPG.

Defense. Shoots right. 6'2", 200 lbs. Born, Minsk, USSR, June 27, 1964.

			Regular Season					Playoffs				
Season	Club	Lea	GP	G	A	TP	PIM	GP	G	A	TP	PIM
1983-84	Moscow D'amo	USSR	17	0	0	0	6	....	....	....	....	....
1984-85	Moscow D'amo	USSR	30	1	3	4	26	....	....	....	....	....
1985-86	Moscow D'amo	USSR	40	0	1	1	36	....	....	....	....	....
1986-87	Moscow D'amo	USSR	39	5	3	8	34	....	....	....	....	....
1987-88	Moscow D'amo	USSR	48	7	8	15	63	....	....	....	....	....
1988-89	Moscow D'amo	USSR	43	4	7	11	52	....	....	....	....	....
1989-90	Moscow D'amo	USSR	32	1	3	4	31	....	....	....	....	....
1990-91	Moscow D'amo	USSR	36	2	6	8	40	....	....	....	....	....
1991-92	Khimik	CIS	15	3	2	5	20	....	....	....	....	....
	New Haven	AHL	30	3	3	6	63	4	1	3	4	6
1992-93	Moncton	AHL	75	6	20	26	159	5	0	0	0	4
1993-94	**Winnipeg**	**NHL**	**4**	**0**	**1**	**1**	**17**	....	....	....	....	....
	Moncton	AHL	67	9	38	47	121	21	2	10	12	18
	NHL Totals		**4**	**0**	**1**	**1**	**17**	....	....	....	....	....

Signed as a free agent by **Winnipeg**, July 26, 1993.

MILLEN, COREY N.J.

Center. Shoots right. 5'7", 170 lbs. Born, Cloquet, MN, March 30, 1964.
(NY Rangers' 3rd choice, 57th overall, in 1982 Entry Draft).

			Regular Season					Playoffs				
Season	Club	Lea	GP	G	A	TP	PIM	GP	G	A	TP	PIM
1982-83	U. Minnesota	WCHA	21	14	15	29	18	....	....	....	....	....
1983-84	U.S. National	....	45	15	11	26	10	....	....	....	....	....
	U.S. Olympic	....	6	0	0	0	2	....	....	....	....	....
1984-85	U. Minnesota	WCHA	38	28	36	64	60	....	....	....	....	....
1985-86ab	U. Minnesota	WCHA	48	41	42	83	64	....	....	....	....	....
1986-87bc	U. Minnesota	WCHA	42	36	29	65	62	....	....	....	....	....
1987-88	U.S. National	....	47	41	43	84	26	....	....	....	....	....
	U.S. Olympic	....	6	6	5	11	4	....	....	....	....	....
1988-89	Ambri	Switz.	36	32	22	54	18	6	4	3	7	0
1989-90	**NY Rangers**	**NHL**	**4**	**0**	**0**	**0**	**2**	....	....	....	....	....
	Flint	IHL	11	4	5	9	2	....	....	....	....	....
1990-91	**NY Rangers**	**NHL**	**4**	**3**	**1**	**4**	**0**	**6**	**1**	**2**	**3**	**0**
	Binghamton	AHL	40	19	37	56	68	6	0	7	7	6
1991-92	**NY Rangers**	**NHL**	**11**	**1**	**4**	**5**	**10**	....	....	....	....	....
	Binghamton	AHL	15	8	7	15	44	....	....	....	....	....
	Los Angeles	**NHL**	**46**	**20**	**21**	**41**	**44**	**6**	**0**	**1**	**1**	**6**
1992-93	**Los Angeles**	**NHL**	**42**	**23**	**16**	**39**	**42**	**23**	**2**	**4**	**6**	**12**
1993-94	**New Jersey**	**NHL**	**78**	**20**	**30**	**50**	**52**	**7**	**1**	**0**	**1**	**2**
	NHL Totals		**185**	**67**	**72**	**139**	**150**	**42**	**4**	**7**	**11**	**20**

a NCAA West Second All-American Team (1986)
b WCHA Second All-Star Team (1986, 1987)
c NCAA Final Four All-Tournament Team (1987)

Traded to **Los Angeles** by **NY Rangers** for Randy Gilhen, December 23, 1991. Traded to **New Jersey** by **Los Angeles** for New Jersey's fifth round choice (Jason Saal) in 1993 Entry Draft, June 26, 1993.

MILLER, AARON QUE.

Defense. Shoots right. 6'3", 197 lbs. Born, Buffalo, NY, August 11, 1971.
(NY Rangers' 6th choice, 88th overall, in 1989 Entry Draft).

			Regular Season					Playoffs				
Season	Club	Lea	GP	G	A	TP	PIM	GP	G	A	TP	PIM
1989-90	U. of Vermont	ECAC	31	1	15	16	24	....	....	....	....	....
1990-91	U. of Vermont	ECAC	30	3	7	10	22	....	....	....	....	....
1991-92	U. of Vermont	ECAC	31	3	16	19	28	....	....	....	....	....
1992-93ab	U. of Vermont	ECAC	30	4	13	17	16	....	....	....	....	....
1993-94	**Quebec**	**NHL**	**1**	**0**	**0**	**0**	**0**	....	....	....	....	....
	Cornwall	AHL	64	4	10	14	49	8	0	2	2	10
	NHL Totals		**1**	**0**	**0**	**0**	**0**	....	....	....	....	....

a ECAC First All-Star Team (1993)
b NCAA East Second All-American Team (1993)

Traded to **Quebec** by **NY Rangers** with NY Rangers' fifth round choice (Bill Lindsay) in 1991 Entry Draft for Joe Cirella, January 17, 1991.

MILLER, ANDREW DET.

Right wing. Shoots right. 5'11", 200 lbs. Born, North York, Ont., January 20, 1971.
(Detroit's 10th choice, 252nd overall, in 1991 Entry Draft).

			Regular Season					Playoffs				
Season	Club	Lea	GP	G	A	TP	PIM	GP	G	A	TP	PIM
1991-92	Miami-Ohio	CCHA	40	9	16	25	34	....	....	....	....	....
1992-93	Miami-Ohio	CCHA	25	5	5	10	8	....	....	....	....	....
1993-94	Miami-Ohio	CCHA	37	12	13	25	14	....	....	....	....	....

MILLER, BRAD

Defense. Shoots left. 6'4", 220 lbs. Born, Edmonton, Alta., July 23, 1969.
(Buffalo's 2nd choice, 22nd overall, in 1987 Entry Draft).

			Regular Season					Playoffs				
Season	Club	Lea	GP	G	A	TP	PIM	GP	G	A	TP	PIM
1985-86	Regina	WHL	71	2	14	16	99	10	1	1	2	4
1986-87	Regina	WHL	67	10	38	48	154	3	0	0	0	6
1987-88	Rochester	AHL	3	0	0	0	4	2	0	0	0	2
	Regina	WHL	61	9	34	43	148	4	1	1	2	12
1988-89	**Buffalo**	**NHL**	**7**	**0**	**0**	**0**	**6**	....	....	....	....	....
	Regina	WHL	34	8	18	26	95	....	....	....	....	....
	Rochester	AHL	3	0	0	0	4	....	....	....	....	....
1989-90	**Buffalo**	**NHL**	**1**	**0**	**0**	**0**	**0**	....	....	....	....	....
	Rochester	AHL	60	2	10	12	273	8	1	0	1	52
1990-91	**Buffalo**	**NHL**	**13**	**0**	**0**	**0**	**67**	....	....	....	....	....
	Rochester	AHL	49	0	9	9	248	12	0	4	4	67
1991-92	**Buffalo**	**NHL**	**42**	**1**	**4**	**5**	**192**	....	....	....	....	....
	Rochester	AHL	27	0	4	4	113	11	0	0	0	61
1992-93	**Ottawa**	**NHL**	**11**	**0**	**0**	**0**	**42**	....	....	....	....	....
	New Haven	AHL	41	1	9	10	138	....	....	....	....	....
	St. John's	AHL	20	0	3	3	61	8	0	2	2	10
1993-94	**Calgary**	**NHL**	**8**	**0**	**1**	**1**	**14**	....	....	....	....	....
	Saint John	AHL	36	3	12	15	174	6	1	0	1	21
	NHL Totals		**82**	**1**	**5**	**6**	**321**	....	....	....	....	....

Claimed by **Ottawa** from **Buffalo** in Expansion Draft, June 18, 1992. Traded to **Toronto** by **Ottawa** for Toronto's ninth round choice (Pavol Demitra) in 1993 Entry Draft, February 25, 1993. Traded to **Calgary** by **Toronto** with Jeff Perry for Todd Gillingham and Paul Holden, September 2, 1993.

MILLER, COLIN T.B.

Center. Shoots right. 6', 188 lbs. Born, Grimsby, Ont., August 21, 1971.

			Regular Season					Playoffs				
Season	Club	Lea	GP	G	A	TP	PIM	GP	G	A	TP	PIM
1990-91	S.S. Marie	OHL	62	26	60	86	35	14	4	18	22	17
1991-92ab	S.S. Marie	OHL	66	37	73	110	52	19	10	23	33	18
1992-93	Atlanta	IHL	76	20	39	59	52	9	2	4	6	22
1993-94	Atlanta	IHL	80	13	32	45	48	3	2	3	5	0

a Memorial Cup All-Star Team (1992)
b Won George Parsons Trophy (Memorial Cup Most Sportsmanlike Player) (1992)

Signed as a free agent by **Tampa Bay**, June 29, 1992.

MILLER, JASON DET.

Left wing. Shoots left. 6'1", 190 lbs. Born, Edmonton, Alta., March 1, 1971.
(New Jersey's 2nd choice, 18th overall, in 1989 Entry Draft).

			Regular Season					Playoffs				
Season	Club	Lea	GP	G	A	TP	PIM	GP	G	A	TP	PIM
1987-88	Medicine Hat	WHL	71	11	18	29	28	15	0	1	1	2
1988-89	Medicine Hat	WHL	72	51	55	106	44	3	1	2	3	2
1989-90	Medicine Hat	WHL	66	43	56	99	40	3	3	2	5	0
1990-91	**New Jersey**	**NHL**	**1**	**0**	**0**	**0**	**0**	....	....	....	....	....
a	Medicine Hat	WHL	66	60	76	136	31	12	9	10	19	8
1991-92	**New Jersey**	**NHL**	**3**	**0**	**0**	**0**	**0**	....	....	....	....	....
	Utica	AHL	71	23	32	55	31	4	1	3	4	0
1992-93	**New Jersey**	**NHL**	**2**	**0**	**0**	**0**	**0**	....	....	....	....	....
	Utica	AHL	72	28	42	70	43	5	4	4	8	2
1993-94	Albany	AHL	77	22	53	75	65	5	1	1	2	4
	NHL Totals		**6**	**0**	**0**	**0**	**0**	....	....	....	....	....

a WHL East Second All-Star Team (1991)

MILLER, KELLY WSH.

Left wing. Shoots left. 5'11", 197 lbs. Born, Lansing, MI, March 3, 1963.
(NY Rangers' 9th choice, 183rd overall, in 1982 Entry Draft).

			Regular Season					Playoffs				
Season	Club	Lea	GP	G	A	TP	PIM	GP	G	A	TP	PIM
1981-82	Michigan State	CCHA	38	11	18	29	17	....	....	....	....	....
1982-83	Michigan State	CCHA	36	16	19	35	12	....	....	....	....	....
1983-84	Michigan State	CCHA	46	28	21	49	12	....	....	....	....	....
1984-85ab	Michigan State	CCHA	43	27	23	50	21	....	....	....	....	....
	NY Rangers	**NHL**	**5**	**0**	**2**	**2**	**2**	**3**	**0**	**0**	**0**	**2**
1985-86	**NY Rangers**	**NHL**	**74**	**13**	**20**	**33**	**52**	**16**	**3**	**4**	**7**	**4**
1986-87	**NY Rangers**	**NHL**	**38**	**6**	**14**	**20**	**22**	....	....	....	....	....
	Washington	**NHL**	**39**	**10**	**12**	**22**	**26**	**7**	**2**	**2**	**4**	**0**
1987-88	**Washington**	**NHL**	**80**	**9**	**23**	**32**	**35**	**14**	**4**	**4**	**8**	**10**
1988-89	**Washington**	**NHL**	**78**	**19**	**21**	**40**	**45**	**6**	**1**	**0**	**1**	**2**
1989-90	**Washington**	**NHL**	**80**	**18**	**22**	**40**	**49**	**15**	**3**	**5**	**8**	**23**
1990-91	**Washington**	**NHL**	**80**	**24**	**26**	**50**	**29**	**11**	**4**	**2**	**6**	**6**
1991-92	**Washington**	**NHL**	**78**	**14**	**38**	**52**	**49**	**7**	**1**	**2**	**3**	**4**
1992-93	**Washington**	**NHL**	**84**	**18**	**27**	**45**	**32**	**6**	**0**	**3**	**3**	**2**
1993-94	**Washington**	**NHL**	**84**	**14**	**25**	**39**	**32**	**11**	**2**	**7**	**9**	**0**
	NHL Totals		**720**	**145**	**230**	**375**	**373**	**96**	**20**	**29**	**49**	**53**

a CCHA First All-Star Team (1985)
b Named to NCAA All-American Team (1985)

Traded to **Washington** by **NY Rangers** with Bob Crawford and Mike Ridley for Bob Carpenter and Washington's second round choice (Jason Prosofsky) in 1989 Entry Draft, January 1, 1987.

MILLER, KEVIN — ST.L.

Center. Shoots right. 5'11", 190 lbs. Born, Lansing, MI, September 2, 1965.
(NY Rangers' 10th choice, 202nd overall, in 1984 Entry Draft).

			Regular Season					Playoffs				
Season	Club	Lea	GP	G	A	TP	PIM	GP	G	A	TP	PIM
1984-85	Michigan State	CCHA	44	11	29	40	84	....	....	....	....	....
1985-86	Michigan State	CCHA	45	19	52	71	112	....	....	....	....	....
1986-87	Michigan State	CCHA	42	25	56	81	63	....	....	....	....	....
1987-88	Michigan State	CCHA	9	6	3	9	18	....	....	....	....	....
	U.S. National	....	48	31	32	63	33	....	....	....	....	....
	U.S. Olympic	....	5	1	3	4	4	....	....	....	....	....
1988-89	**NY Rangers**	**NHL**	**24**	**3**	**5**	**8**	**2**	....	....	....	....	....
	Denver	IHL	55	29	47	76	19	4	2	1	3	2
1989-90	**NY Rangers**	**NHL**	**16**	**0**	**5**	**5**	**2**	**1**	**0**	**0**	**0**	**0**
	Flint	IHL	48	19	23	42	41	....	....	....	....	....
1990-91	**NY Rangers**	**NHL**	**63**	**17**	**27**	**44**	**63**	....	....	....	....	....
	Detroit	**NHL**	**11**	**5**	**2**	**7**	**4**	**7**	**3**	**2**	**5**	**20**
1991-92	**Detroit**	**NHL**	**80**	**20**	**26**	**46**	**53**	**9**	**0**	**2**	**2**	**4**
1992-93	**Washington**	**NHL**	**10**	**0**	**3**	**3**	**35**	....	....	....	....	....
	St. Louis	**NHL**	**72**	**24**	**22**	**46**	**65**	**10**	**0**	**3**	**3**	**11**
1993-94	**St. Louis**	**NHL**	**75**	**23**	**25**	**48**	**83**	**3**	**1**	**0**	**1**	**4**
	NHL Totals		**351**	**92**	**115**	**207**	**307**	**30**	**4**	**7**	**11**	**39**

Traded to **Detroit** by **NY Rangers** with Jim Cummins and Dennis Vial for Joey Kocur and Per Djoos, March 5, 1991. Traded to **Washington** by **Detroit** for Dino Ciccarelli, June 20, 1992. Traded to **St. Louis** by **Washington** for Paul Cavallini, November 2, 1992.

MILLER, KIP — NYI

Center. Shoots left. 5'10", 190 lbs. Born, Lansing, MI, June 11, 1969.
(Quebec's 4th choice, 72nd overall, in 1987 Entry Draft).

			Regular Season					Playoffs				
Season	Club	Lea	GP	G	A	TP	PIM	GP	G	A	TP	PIM
1986-87	Michigan State	CCHA	41	20	19	39	92	....	....	....	....	....
1987-88	Michigan State	CCHA	39	16	25	41	51	....	....	....	....	....
1988-89ab	Michigan State	CCHA	47	32	45	77	94	....	....	....	....	....
1989-90abc	Michigan State	CCHA	45	*48	53	*101	60	....	....	....	....	....
1990-91	**Quebec**	**NHL**	**13**	**4**	**3**	**7**	**7**	....	....	....	....	....
	Halifax	AHL	66	36	33	69	40	....	....	....	....	....
1991-92	**Quebec**	**NHL**	**36**	**5**	**10**	**15**	**12**	....	....	....	....	....
	Halifax	AHL	24	9	17	26	8	....	....	....	....	....
	Minnesota	**NHL**	**3**	**1**	**2**	**3**	**2**	....	....	....	....	....
	Kalamazoo	IHL	6	1	8	9	4	12	3	9	12	12
1992-93	Kalamazoo	IHL	61	17	39	56	59	....	....	....	....	....
1993-94	**San Jose**	**NHL**	**11**	**2**	**2**	**4**	**6**	....	....	....	....	....
	Kansas City	IHL	71	38	54	92	51	....	....	....	....	....
	NHL Totals		**63**	**12**	**17**	**29**	**27**	....	....	....	....	....

a CCHA First All-Star Team (1989, 1990)
b NCAA West First All-American Team (1989, 1990)
c Won Hobey Baker Memorial Award (Top U.S. Collegiate Player) (1990)

Traded to **Minnesota** by **Quebec** for Steve Maltais, March 8, 1992. Signed as a free agent by **San Jose**, August 10, 1993. Signed as a free agent by **NY Islanders**, July 7, 1994.

MILLER, KRIS

Defense. Shoots left. 6', 200 lbs. Born, Bemidji, MN, March 30, 1969.
(Montreal's 6th choice, 80th overall, in 1987 Entry Draft).

			Regular Season					Playoffs				
Season	Club	Lea	GP	G	A	TP	PIM	GP	G	A	TP	PIM
1987-88	Minn.-Duluth	WCHA	32	1	6	7	30	....	....	....	....	....
1988-89	Minn.-Duluth	WCHA	39	2	10	12	37	....	....	....	....	....
1989-90	Minn.-Duluth	WCHA	39	2	11	13	59	....	....	....	....	....
1990-91	Minn.-Duluth	WCHA	40	6	22	28	24	....	....	....	....	....
1991-92	Phoenix	IHL	16	1	2	3	17	....	....	....	....	....
	Utica	AHL	1	0	0	0	0	....	....	....	....	....
	Raleigh	ECHL	42	12	27	39	78	4	2	3	5	8
1992-93	Raleigh	ECHL	30	8	24	32	62	....	....	....	....	....
	Salt Lake	IHL	45	4	21	25	45	....	....	....	....	....
1993-94	Saint John	AHL	58	2	17	19	38	....	....	....	....	....

Signed as a free agent by **Calgary**, December 27, 1993.

MILLER, KURTIS — DET.

Left wing. Shoots left. 5'11", 190 lbs. Born, Bemidji, MN, June 1, 1970.
(St. Louis' 4th choice, 117th overall, in 1990 Entry Draft).

			Regular Season					Playoffs				
Season	Club	Lea	GP	G	A	TP	PIM	GP	G	A	TP	PIM
1990-91	Lake Superior	CCHA	45	10	12	22	48	....	....	....	....	....
1991-92	Lake Superior	CCHA	15	6	7	13	32	....	....	....	....	....
1992-93	Lake Superior	CCHA	26	9	14	23	24	....	....	....	....	....
1993-94	Lake Superior	CCHA	40	19	23	42	58	....	....	....	....	....

MILLS, CRAIG — WPG.

Right wing. Shoots right. 5'11", 174 lbs. Born, Toronto, Ont., August 27, 1976.
(Winnipeg's 5th choice, 108th overall, in 1994 Entry Draft).

			Regular Season					Playoffs				
Season	Club	Lea	GP	G	A	TP	PIM	GP	G	A	TP	PIM
1992-93	St. Michael's	Jr. A	44	8	12	20	51	....	....	....	....	....
1993-94	Belleville	OHL	63	15	18	33	88	12	2	1	3	11

MIRONOV, BORIS — (mih-RAH-nahf) — EDM.

Defense. Shoots right. 6'3", 196 lbs. Born, Moscow, USSR, March 21, 1972.
(Winnipeg's 2nd choice, 27th overall, in 1992 Entry Draft).

			Regular Season					Playoffs				
Season	Club	Lea	GP	G	A	TP	PIM	GP	G	A	TP	PIM
1988-89	CSKA	USSR	1	0	0	0	0	....	....	....	....	....
1989-90	CSKA	USSR	7	0	0	0	0	....	....	....	....	....
1990-91	CSKA	USSR	36	1	5	6	16	....	....	....	....	....
1991-92	CSKA	CIS	36	2	1	3	22	....	....	....	....	....
1992-93	CSKA	CIS	19	0	5	5	20	....	....	....	....	....
1993-94a	**Winnipeg**	**NHL**	**65**	**7**	**22**	**29**	**96**	....	....	....	....	....
	Edmonton	**NHL**	**14**	**0**	**2**	**2**	**14**	....	....	....	....	....
	NHL Totals		**79**	**7**	**24**	**31**	**110**	....	....	....	....	....

a NHL/Upper Deck All-Rookie Team (1994)

Traded to **Edmonton** by **Winnipeg** with Mats Lindgren, Winnipeg's first round choice (Jason Bonsignore) in 1994 Entry Draft and Florida's fourth round choice (previously acquired by Winnipeg — Edmonton selected Adam Copeland) in 1994 Entry Draft for Dave Manson and St. Louis' sixth round choice (previously acquired by Edmonton — Winnipeg selected Chris Kibermanis) in 1994 Entry Draft, March 15, 1994.

MIRONOV, DMITRI — (mih-RAWN-ohv) — TOR.

Defense. Shoots right. 6'2", 214 lbs. Born, Moscow, USSR, December 25, 1965.
(Toronto's 9th choice, 160th overall, in 1991 Entry Draft).

			Regular Season					Playoffs				
Season	Club	Lea	GP	G	A	TP	PIM	GP	G	A	TP	PIM
1985-86	CSKA	USSR	9	0	1	1	8	....	....	....	....	....
1986-87	CSKA	USSR	20	1	3	4	10	....	....	....	....	....
1987-88	Soviet Wings	USSR	44	12	6	18	30	....	....	....	....	....
1988-89	Soviet Wings	USSR	44	5	6	11	44	....	....	....	....	....
1989-90	Soviet Wings	USSR	45	4	11	15	34	....	....	....	....	....
1990-91	Soviet Wings	USSR	45	16	12	28	22	....	....	....	....	....
1991-92	Soviet Wings	CIS	35	15	16	31	62	....	....	....	....	....
	Toronto	**NHL**	**7**	**1**	**0**	**1**	**0**	....	....	....	....	....
1992-93	**Toronto**	**NHL**	**59**	**7**	**24**	**31**	**40**	**14**	**1**	**2**	**3**	**2**
1993-94	**Toronto**	**NHL**	**76**	**9**	**27**	**36**	**78**	**18**	**6**	**9**	**15**	**6**
	NHL Totals		**142**	**17**	**51**	**68**	**118**	**32**	**7**	**11**	**18**	**8**

MITCHELL, JEFF — L.A.

Center/Right wing. Shoots right. 6'1", 175 lbs. Born, Wayne, MI, May 16, 1975.
(Los Angeles' 2nd choice, 68th overall, in 1993 Entry Draft).

			Regular Season					Playoffs				
Season	Club	Lea	GP	G	A	TP	PIM	GP	G	A	TP	PIM
1992-93	Detroit	OHL	62	10	15	25	100	15	3	3	6	16
1993-94	Detroit	OHL	59	25	18	43	99	17	3	5	8	22

MITCHELL, ROY

Defense. Shoots right. 6'1", 199 lbs. Born, Edmonton, Alta., March 14, 1969.
(Montreal's 9th choice, 188th overall, in 1989 Entry Draft).

			Regular Season					Playoffs				
Season	Club	Lea	GP	G	A	TP	PIM	GP	G	A	TP	PIM
1986-87	Portland	WHL	68	7	32	39	103	20	0	3	3	23
1987-88	Portland	WHL	72	5	42	47	219	....	....	....	....	....
1988-89	Portland	WHL	72	9	34	43	177	19	1	8	9	38
1989-90	Sherbrooke	AHL	77	5	12	17	98	12	0	2	2	31
1990-91	Fredericton	AHL	71	2	15	17	137	9	0	1	1	11
1991-92	Kalamazoo	IHL	69	3	26	29	102	11	1	4	5	18
1992-93	**Minnesota**	**NHL**	**3**	**0**	**0**	**0**	**0**	....	....	....	....	....
	Kalamazoo	IHL	79	7	25	32	119	....	....	....	....	....
1993-94	Kalamazoo	IHL	13	0	4	4	21	....	....	....	....	....
	Binghamton	AHL	11	1	3	4	18	....	....	....	....	....
	Albany	AHL	42	3	12	15	43	3	0	0	0	0
	NHL Totals		**3**	**0**	**0**	**0**	**0**	....	....	....	....	....

Signed as a free agent by **Minnesota**, July 25, 1991. Traded to **New Jersey** by **Dallas** with Reid Simpson for future considerations, March 21, 1994.

MODANO, MIKE — DAL.

Center. Shoots left. 6'3", 190 lbs. Born, Livonia, MI, June 7, 1970.
(Minnesota's 1st choice, 1st overall, in 1988 Entry Draft).

			Regular Season					Playoffs				
Season	Club	Lea	GP	G	A	TP	PIM	GP	G	A	TP	PIM
1986-87	Prince Albert	WHL	70	32	30	62	96	8	1	4	5	4
1987-88	Prince Albert	WHL	65	47	80	127	80	9	7	11	18	18
1988-89a	Prince Albert	WHL	41	39	66	105	74	....	....	....	....	....
	Minnesota	**NHL**	....	....	....	....	....	**2**	**0**	**0**	**0**	**0**
1989-90b	**Minnesota**	**NHL**	**80**	**29**	**46**	**75**	**63**	**7**	**1**	**1**	**2**	**12**
1990-91	**Minnesota**	**NHL**	**79**	**28**	**36**	**64**	**65**	**23**	**8**	**12**	**20**	**16**
1991-92	**Minnesota**	**NHL**	**76**	**33**	**44**	**77**	**46**	**7**	**3**	**2**	**5**	**4**
1992-93	**Minnesota**	**NHL**	**82**	**33**	**60**	**93**	**83**	....	....	....	....	....
1993-94	**Dallas**	**NHL**	**76**	**50**	**43**	**93**	**54**	**9**	**7**	**3**	**10**	**16**
	NHL Totals		**393**	**173**	**229**	**402**	**311**	**48**	**19**	**18**	**37**	**48**

a WHL East All-Star Team (1989)
b NHL All-Rookie Team (1990)

Played in NHL All-Star Game (1993)

MODIN, FREDRIK — (muh-DEEN) — TOR.

Left wing. Shoots left. 6'3", 202 lbs. Born, Sundsvall, Sweden, October 8, 1974.
(Toronto's 3rd choice, 64th overall, in 1994 Entry Draft).

			Regular Season					Playoffs				
Season	Club	Lea	GP	G	A	TP	PIM	GP	G	A	TP	PIM
1991-92	Sundsvall	Swe. 2	11	1	0	1	0	....	....	....	....	....
1992-93	Sundsvall	Swe. 2	30	5	7	12	12	....	....	....	....	....
1993-94	Sundsvall	Swe. 2	30	16	15	31	36	....	....	....	....	....

MODRY, JAROSLAV — (MOHD-ree) — N.J.

Defense. Shoots left. 6'2", 195 lbs. Born, Ceske-Budejovice, Czech., February 27, 1971.
(New Jersey's 11th choice, 179th overall, in 1990 Entry Draft).

			Regular Season					Playoffs				
Season	Club	Lea	GP	G	A	TP	PIM	GP	G	A	TP	PIM
1987-88	Budejovice	Czech.	3	0	0	0	0	....	....	....	....	....
1988-89	Budejovice	Czech.	28	0	1	1	8	....	....	....	....	....
1989-90	Budejovice	Czech.	41	2	2	4		....	....	....	....	....
1990-91	Dukla Trencin	Czech.	33	1	9	10	6	....	....	....	....	....
1991-92	Dukla Trencin	Czech.	18	0	4	4	6	....	....	....	....	....
	Budejovice	Czech.2	14	4	10	14	....	....	....	....	....	....
1992-93	Utica	AHL	80	7	35	42	62	5	0	2	2	2
1993-94	**New Jersey**	**NHL**	**41**	**2**	**15**	**17**	**18**	....	....	....	....	....
	Albany	AHL	19	1	5	6	25	....	....	....	....	....
	NHL Totals		**41**	**2**	**15**	**17**	**18**	....	....	....	....	....

MOGER, SANDY — BOS.

Center. Shoots right. 6'3", 215 lbs. Born, 100 Mile House, B.C., March 21, 1969.
(Vancouver's 7th choice, 176th overall, in 1989 Entry Draft).

			Regular Season					Playoffs				
Season	Club	Lea	GP	G	A	TP	PIM	GP	G	A	TP	PIM
1988-89	Lake Superior	CCHA	21	3	5	8	26	....	....	....	....	....
1989-90	Lake Superior	CCHA	46	17	15	32	76	....	....	....	....	....
1990-91	Lake Superior	CCHA	45	27	21	48	*172	....	....	....	....	....
1991-92a	Lake Superior	CCHA	38	24	24	48	93	....	....	....	....	....
1992-93	Hamilton	AHL	78	23	26	49	57	....	....	....	....	....
1993-94	Hamilton	AHL	29	9	8	17	41	....	....	....	....	....

a CCHA Second All-Star Team (1992)

MOGILNY, ALEXANDER (moh-GIHL-nee) BUF.

Right wing. Shoots left. 5'11", 187 lbs. Born, Khabarovsk, USSR, February 18, 1969.
(Buffalo's 4th choice, 89th overall, in 1988 Entry Draft).

			Regular Season					Playoffs				
Season	Club	Lea	GP	G	A	TP	PIM	GP	G	A	TP	PIM
1986-87	CSKA	USSR	28	15	1	16	4	....	....	....	....	....
1987-88	CSKA	USSR	39	12	8	20	14	....	....	....	....	....
1988-89	CSKA	USSR	31	11	11	22	24	....	....	....	....	....
1989-90	**Buffalo**	NHL	65	15	28	43	16	4	0	1	1	2
1990-91	**Buffalo**	NHL	62	30	34	64	16	6	0	6	6	2
1991-92	**Buffalo**	NHL	67	39	45	84	73	2	0	2	2	0
1992-93a	**Buffalo**	NHL	77	*76	51	127	40	7	7	3	10	6
1993-94	**Buffalo**	NHL	66	32	47	79	22	7	4	2	6	6
	NHL Totals		337	192	205	397	167	26	11	14	25	16

a NHL Second All-Star Team (1993)

Played in NHL All-Star Game (1992-1994)

MOLLER, RANDY FLA.

Defense. Shoots right. 6'2", 207 lbs. Born, Red Deer, Alta., August 23, 1963.
(Quebec's 1st choice, 11th overall, in 1981 Entry Draft).

			Regular Season					Playoffs				
Season	Club	Lea	GP	G	A	TP	PIM	GP	G	A	TP	PIM
1980-81	Lethbridge	WHL	46	4	21	25	176	9	0	4	4	24
1981-82a	Lethbridge	WHL	60	20	55	75	249	12	4	6	10	65
	Quebec	NHL	....	....	....	....	....	1	0	0	0	0
1982-83	**Quebec**	NHL	75	2	12	14	145	4	1	0	1	4
1983-84	**Quebec**	NHL	74	4	14	18	147	9	1	0	1	45
1984-85	**Quebec**	NHL	79	7	22	29	120	18	2	2	4	40
1985-86	**Quebec**	NHL	69	5	18	23	141	3	0	0	0	26
1986-87	**Quebec**	NHL	71	5	9	14	144	13	1	4	5	23
1987-88	**Quebec**	NHL	66	3	22	25	169	....	....	....	....	....
1988-89	**Quebec**	NHL	74	7	22	29	136	....	....	....	....	....
1989-90	**NY Rangers**	NHL	60	1	12	13	139	10	1	6	7	32
1990-91	**NY Rangers**	NHL	61	4	19	23	161	6	0	2	2	11
1991-92	**NY Rangers**	NHL	43	2	7	9	78	....	....	....	....	....
	Binghamton	AHL	3	0	1	1	0	....	....	....	....	....
	Buffalo	NHL	13	1	2	3	59	7	0	0	0	8
1992-93	**Buffalo**	NHL	35	2	7	9	83	....	....	....	....	....
	Rochester	AHL	3	1	0	1	10	....	....	....	....	....
1993-94	**Buffalo**	NHL	78	2	11	13	154	7	0	2	2	8
	NHL Totals		798	45	177	222	1676	78	6	16	22	197

a WHL Second All-Star Team (1982)

Traded to **NY Rangers** by **Quebec** for Michel Petit, October 5, 1989. Traded to **Buffalo** by **NY Rangers** for Jay Wells, March 9, 1992.

MOMESSO, SERGIO (moh-MESS-oh) VAN.

Left wing. Shoots left. 6'3", 215 lbs. Born, Montreal, Que., September 4, 1965.
(Montreal's 3rd choice, 27th overall, in 1983 Entry Draft).

			Regular Season					Playoffs				
Season	Club	Lea	GP	G	A	TP	PIM	GP	G	A	TP	PIM
1982-83	Shawinigan	QMJHL	70	27	42	69	93	10	5	4	9	55
1983-84	**Montreal**	NHL	1	0	0	0	0	....	....	....	....	....
	Shawinigan	QMJHL	68	42	88	130	235	6	4	4	8	13
	Nova Scotia	AHL	....	....	....	....	....	8	0	2	2	4
1984-85a	Shawinigan	QMJHL	64	56	90	146	216	8	7	8	15	17
1985-86	**Montreal**	NHL	24	8	7	15	46	....	....	....	....	....
1986-87	**Montreal**	NHL	59	14	17	31	96	11	1	3	4	31
	Sherbrooke	AHL	6	1	6	7	10	....	....	....	....	....
1987-88	**Montreal**	NHL	53	7	14	21	101	6	0	2	2	16
1988-89	**St. Louis**	NHL	53	9	17	26	139	10	2	5	7	24
1989-90	**St. Louis**	NHL	79	24	32	56	199	12	3	2	5	63
1990-91	**St. Louis**	NHL	59	10	18	28	131	....	....	....	....	....
	Vancouver	NHL	11	6	2	8	43	6	0	3	3	25
1991-92	**Vancouver**	NHL	58	20	23	43	198	13	0	5	5	30
1992-93	**Vancouver**	NHL	84	18	20	38	200	12	3	0	3	30
1993-94	**Vancouver**	NHL	68	14	13	27	149	24	3	4	7	56
	NHL Totals		549	130	163	293	1302	94	12	24	36	275

a QMJHL First All-Star Team (1985)

Traded to **St. Louis** by **Montreal** with Vincent Riendeau for Jocelyn Lemieux, Darrell May and St. Louis' second round choice (Patrice Brisebois) in the 1989 Entry Draft, August 9, 1988. Traded to **Vancouver** by **St. Louis** with Geoff Courtnall, Robert Dirk, Cliff Ronning and St. Louis' fifth round choice (Brian Loney) in 1992 Entry Draft for Dan Quinn and Garth Butcher, March 5, 1991.

MONGEAU, MICHEL (MOHN-zhoh)

Center. Shoots left. 5'9", 190 lbs. Born, Montreal, Que., February 9, 1965.

			Regular Season					Playoffs				
Season	Club	Lea	GP	G	A	TP	PIM	GP	G	A	TP	PIM
1983-84	Laval	QMJHL	60	45	49	94	30	....	....	....	....	....
1984-85	Laval	QMJHL	67	60	84	144	56	....	....	....	....	....
1985-86	Laval	QMJHL	72	71	109	180	45	....	....	....	....	....
1986-87	Saginaw	IHL	76	42	53	95	34	10	3	6	9	6
1987-88	France	....	30	31	21	52	....	....	....	....	....	....
1988-89	Flint	IHL	82	41	76	117	57	....	....	....	....	....
1989-90	**St. Louis**	NHL	7	1	5	6	2	2	0	1	1	0
abc	Peoria	IHL	73	39	*78	*117	53	5	3	4	7	6
1990-91	**St. Louis**	NHL	7	1	1	2	0	....	....	....	....	....
de	Peoria	IHL	73	41	65	106	114	19	10	*16	26	32
1991-92	**St. Louis**	NHL	36	3	12	15	6	....	....	....	....	....
	Peoria	IHL	32	21	34	55	77	10	5	14	19	8
1992-93	**Tampa Bay**	NHL	4	1	1	2	2	....	....	....	....	....
	Milwaukee	IHL	45	24	41	65	69	4	1	4	5	4
	Halifax	AHL	22	13	18	31	10	....	....	....	....	....
1993-94	Cornwall	AHL	7	3	11	14	4	....	....	....	....	....
	Peoria	IHL	52	29	36	65	50	....	....	....	....	....
	NHL Totals		54	6	19	25	10	2	0	1	1	0

a IHL First All-Star Team (1990)
b Won James Gatschene Memorial Trophy (MVP - IHL) (1990)
c Won Leo P. Lamoureux Memorial Trophy (Top Scorer - IHL) (1990)
d IHL Second All-Star Team (1991)
e Won N.R. Poile Trophy (Playoff MVP - IHL) (1991)

Signed as a free agent by **St. Louis**, August 21, 1989. Claimed by **Tampa Bay** from **St. Louis** in Expansion Draft, June 18, 1992. Traded to **Quebec** by **Tampa Bay** with Martin Simard and Steve Tuttle for Herb Raglan, February 12, 1993.

MONTGOMERY, JIM MTL.

Center. Shoots right. 5'10", 180 lbs. Born, Montreal, Que., June 30, 1969.

			Regular Season					Playoffs				
Season	Club	Lea	GP	G	A	TP	PIM	GP	G	A	TP	PIM
1989-90	U. of Maine	H.E.	45	26	34	60	35	....	....	....	....	....
1990-91	U. of Maine	H.E.	43	24	*57	81	44	....	....	....	....	....
1991-92a	U. of Maine	H.E.	37	21	44	65	46	....	....	....	....	....
1992-93bcde	U. of Maine	H.E.	45	32	63	95	40	....	....	....	....	....
1993-94	**St. Louis**	NHL	67	6	14	20	44	....	....	....	....	....
	Peoria	IHL	12	7	8	15	10	....	....	....	....	....
	NHL Totals		67	6	14	20	44	....	....	....	....	....

a Hockey East Second All-Star Team (1992)
b Hockey East First All-Star Team (1993)
c NCAA East Second All-American Team (1993)
d NCAA Final Four All-Tournament Team (1993)
e NCAA Final Four Tournament Most Valuable Player (1993)

Signed as a free agent by **St. Louis**, June 2, 1993. Traded to **Montreal** by **St. Louis** for Guy Carbonneau, August 19, 1994.

MONTREUIL, ERIC FLA.

Center. Shoots left. 6'1", 170 lbs. Born, Verdun, Que., May 18, 1975.
(Florida's 13th choice, 265th overall, in 1993 Draft).

			Regular Season					Playoffs				
Season	Club	Lea	GP	G	A	TP	PIM	GP	G	A	TP	PIM
1992-93	Chicoutimi	QMJHL	70	19	13	32	98	4	0	1	1	2
1993-94	Beauport	QMJHL	67	31	40	71	122	15	4	8	12	39

MOORE, BARRIE BUF.

Left wing. Shoots left. 6', 195 lbs. Born, London, Ont., May 22, 1975.
(Buffalo's 7th choice, 220th overall, in 1993 Entry Draft).

			Regular Season					Playoffs				
Season	Club	Lea	GP	G	A	TP	PIM	GP	G	A	TP	PIM
1991-92	Sudbury	OHL	62	15	38	53	57	11	0	7	7	12
1992-93	Sudbury	OHL	57	13	26	39	71	14	4	3	7	19
1993-94	Sudbury	OHL	65	36	49	85	69	10	3	5	8	14

MORAN, IAN PIT.

Defense. Shoots right. 5'11", 180 lbs. Born, Cleveland, OH, August 24, 1972.
(Pittsburgh's 6th choice, 107th overall, in 1990 Entry Draft).

			Regular Season					Playoffs				
Season	Club	Lea	GP	G	A	TP	PIM	GP	G	A	TP	PIM
1991-92	Boston College	H.E.	30	2	16	18	44	....	....	....	....	....
1992-93	Boston College	H.E.	31	8	12	20	32	....	....	....	....	....
1993-94	U.S. National	....	50	8	15	23	69	....	....	....	....	....
	Cleveland	IHL	33	5	13	18	39	....	....	....	....	....

MORE, JAYSON S.J.

Defense. Shoots right. 6'1", 200 lbs. Born, Souris, Man., January 12, 1969.
(NY Rangers' 1st choice, 10th overall, in 1987 Entry Draft).

			Regular Season					Playoffs				
Season	Club	Lea	GP	G	A	TP	PIM	GP	G	A	TP	PIM
1984-85	Lethbridge	WHL	71	3	9	12	101	4	1	0	1	7
1985-86	Lethbridge	WHL	61	7	18	25	155	9	0	2	2	36
1986-87	Brandon	WHL	21	4	6	10	62	....	....	....	....	....
	N. Westminster	WHL	43	4	23	27	155	....	....	....	....	....
1987-88a	N. Westminster	WHL	70	13	47	60	270	5	0	2	2	26
1988-89	**NY Rangers**	NHL	1	0	0	0	0	....	....	....	....	....
	Denver	IHL	62	7	15	22	138	3	0	1	1	26
1989-90	Flint	IHL	9	1	5	6	41	....	....	....	....	....
	Minnesota	NHL	5	0	0	0	16	....	....	....	....	....
	Kalamazoo	IHL	64	9	25	34	316	10	0	3	3	13
1990-91	Kalamazoo	IHL	10	0	5	5	46	....	....	....	....	....
	Fredericton	AHL	57	7	17	24	152	9	1	1	2	34
1991-92	**San Jose**	NHL	46	4	13	17	85	....	....	....	....	....
	Kansas City	IHL	2	0	2	2	4	....	....	....	....	....
1992-93	**San Jose**	NHL	73	5	6	11	179	....	....	....	....	....
1993-94	**San Jose**	NHL	49	1	6	7	63	13	0	2	2	32
	Kansas City	IHL	2	1	0	1	25	....	....	....	....	....
	NHL Totals		174	10	25	35	343	13	0	2	2	32

a WHL All-Star Team (1988)

Traded to **Minnesota** by **NY Rangers** for Dave Archibald, November 1, 1989. Traded to **Montreal** by **Minnesota** for Brian Hayward, November 7, 1990. Claimed by **San Jose** from **Montreal** in Expansion Draft, May 30, 1991.

MOREAU, ETHAN CHI.

Left wing. Shoots left. 6'2", 205 lbs. Born, Huntsville, Ont., September 22, 1975.
(Chicago's 1st choice, 14th overall, in 1994 Entry Draft).

			Regular Season					Playoffs				
Season	Club	Lea	GP	G	A	TP	PIM	GP	G	A	TP	PIM
1991-92	Niagara Falls	OHL	62	20	35	55	39	17	4	6	10	4
1992-93	Niagara Falls	OHL	65	32	41	73	69	4	0	3	3	4
1993-94	Niagara Falls	OHL	59	44	54	98	100	....	....	....	....	....

MORIN, STEPHANE (moh-RAI) VAN.

Center. Shoots left. 6', 174 lbs. Born, Montreal, Que., March 27, 1969.
(Quebec's 3rd choice, 43rd overall, in 1989 Entry Draft).

			Regular Season					Playoffs				
Season	Club	Lea	GP	G	A	TP	PIM	GP	G	A	TP	PIM
1986-87	Shawinigan	QMJHL	65	9	14	23	28	....	....	....	....	....
1987-88	Chicoutimi	QMJHL	68	38	45	83	18	6	3	8	11	2
1988-89a	Chicoutimi	QMJHL	70	77	*109	*186	71	....	....	....	....	....
1989-90	**Quebec**	NHL	6	0	2	2	2	....	....	....	....	....
	Halifax	AHL	65	28	32	60	60	6	3	4	7	6
1990-91	**Quebec**	NHL	48	13	27	40	30	....	....	....	....	....
	Halifax	AHL	17	8	14	22	18	....	....	....	....	....
1991-92	**Quebec**	NHL	30	2	8	10	14	....	....	....	....	....
	Halifax	AHL	30	17	13	30	29	....	....	....	....	....
1992-93	**Vancouver**	NHL	1	0	1	1	0	....	....	....	....	....
	Hamilton	AHL	70	31	54	85	49	....	....	....	....	....
1993-94	**Vancouver**	NHL	5	1	1	2	6	....	....	....	....	....
b	Hamilton	AHL	69	38	71	109	48	4	3	2	5	4
	NHL Totals		90	16	39	55	52	....	....	....	....	....

a QMJHL First All-Star Team (1989)
b AHL Second All-Star Team (1994)

Signed as a free agent by **Vancouver**, October 5, 1992.

MOROZOV, VALENTIN (moh-ROH-zohv) PIT.

Center. Shoots left. 5'11", 176 lbs. Born, Moscow, USSR, June 1, 1975.
(Pittsburgh's 8th choice, 154th overall, in 1994 Entry Draft).

			Regular Season					Playoffs				
Season	Club	Lea	GP	G	A	TP	PIM	GP	G	A	TP	PIM
1992-93	CSKA	CIS	17	0	0	0	6	....	....	....	....	....
1993-94	CSKA	CIS	18	4	1	5	8	3	0	1	1	0

MORRIS, JON

Center. Shoots right. 6', 175 lbs. Born, Lowell, MA, May 6, 1966.
(New Jersey's 5th choice, 86th overall, in 1984 Entry Draft).

			Regular Season					Playoffs				
Season	Club	Lea	GP	G	A	TP	PIM	GP	G	A	TP	PIM
1984-85	Lowell	H.E.	42	29	31	60	16	....	....	....	....	....
1985-86	Lowell	H.E.	39	25	31	56	52	....	....	....	....	....
1986-87ab	Lowell	H.E.	35	28	33	61	48	....	....	....	....	....
1987-88	Lowell	H.E.	37	15	39	54	39	....	....	....	....	....
1988-89	**New Jersey**	**NHL**	**4**	**0**	**2**	**2**	**0**	....	....	....	....	....
1989-90	**New Jersey**	**NHL**	**20**	**6**	**7**	**13**	**8**	**6**	**1**	**3**	**4**	**23**
	Utica	AHL	49	27	37	64	6	....	....	....	....	....
1990-91	**New Jersey**	**NHL**	**53**	**9**	**19**	**28**	**27**	**5**	**0**	**4**	**4**	**2**
	Utica	AHL	6	4	2	6	5	....	....	....	....	....
1991-92	**New Jersey**	**NHL**	**7**	**1**	**2**	**3**	**6**	....	....	....	....	....
	Utica	AHL	7	1	4	5	0	....	....	....	....	....
1992-93	**New Jersey**	**NHL**	**2**	**0**	**0**	**0**	**0**	....	....	....	....	....
	Utica	AHL	31	16	24	40	28	....	....	....	....	....
	Cincinnati	IHL	18	7	19	26	24	....	....	....	....	....
	San Jose	**NHL**	**13**	**0**	**3**	**3**	**6**	....	....	....	....	....
1993-94	Kansas City	IHL	3	0	3	3	2	....	....	....	....	....
	Boston	**NHL**	**4**	**0**	**0**	**0**	**0**	....	....	....	....	....
	Providence	AHL	67	22	44	66	20	....	....	....	....	....
	NHL Totals		**103**	**16**	**33**	**49**	**47**	**11**	**1**	**7**	**8**	**25**

a Hockey East First All-Star Team (1987)
b NCAA East Second All-American Team (1987)

Claimed on waivers by **San Jose** from **New Jersey**, March 13, 1993. Traded to **Boston** by **San Jose** for cash, October 28, 1993.

MORRIS, KEITH

Center. Shoots left. 6'1", 185 lbs. Born, Winnipeg, Man., April 24, 1971.
(Winnipeg's 13th choice, 245th overall, in 1990 Entry Draft).

			Regular Season					Playoffs				
Season	Club	Lea	GP	G	A	TP	PIM	GP	G	A	TP	PIM
1989-90	Alaska-Anch.	G.N.	28	10	18	28	14	....	....	....	....	....
1990-91	Alaska-Anch.	G.N.	25	11	11	22	36	....	....	....	....	....
1991-92	Alaska-Anch.	G.N.	35	24	26	50	18	....	....	....	....	....
1992-93	Cdn. National	....	53	7	16	23	27	....	....	....	....	....
1993-94	Alaska-Anch.	WCHA	36	16	18	34	66	....	....	....	....	....

MORRISON, BRENDAN N.J.

Center. Shoots left. 5'11", 170 lbs. Born, N. Vancouver, B.C., August 12, 1975.
(New Jersey's 3rd choice, 39th overall, in 1993 Entry Draft).

			Regular Season					Playoffs				
Season	Club	Lea	GP	G	A	TP	PIM	GP	G	A	TP	PIM
1992-93	Penticton	BCJHL	56	35	59	94	45	....	....	....	....	....
1993-94	U. of Michigan	CCHA	38	20	28	48	24	....	....	....	....	....

MORROW, SCOTT CGY.

Left wing. Shoots left. 6'1", 185 lbs. Born, Chicago, IL, June 18, 1969.
(Hartford's 4th choice, 95th overall, in 1988 Entry Draft).

			Regular Season					Playoffs				
Season	Club	Lea	GP	G	A	TP	PIM	GP	G	A	TP	PIM
1988-89	N. Hampshire	H.E.	19	6	7	13	14	....	....	....	....	....
1989-90	N. Hampshire	H.E.	29	10	11	21	35	....	....	....	....	....
1990-91	N. Hampshire	H.E.	31	11	11	22	52	....	....	....	....	....
1991-92a	N. Hampshire	H.E.	35	30	23	53	65	....	....	....	....	....
	Springfield	AHL	2	0	1	1	0	5	0	0	0	9
1992-93	Springfield	AHL	70	22	29	51	80	15	6	9	15	21
1993-94	Springfield	AHL	30	12	15	27	28	....	....	....	....	....
	Saint John	AHL	8	2	2	4	0	7	2	1	3	10

a Hockey East Second All-Star Team (1992)

Traded to **Calgary** by **Hartford** for Todd Harkins, January 24, 1994.

MOSER, JAY BOS.

Defense. Shoots left. 6'2", 170 lbs. Born, Cottage Grove, MN, December 26, 1972.
(Boston's 7th choice, 172nd overall, in 1991 Entry Draft).

			Regular Season					Playoffs				
Season	Club	Lea	GP	G	A	TP	PIM	GP	G	A	TP	PIM
1991-92	St. Cloud	WCHA	35	3	9	12	40	....	....	....	....	....
1992-93	St. Cloud	WCHA	33	2	9	11	77	....	....	....	....	....
1993-94					DID NOT PLAY							

MOTKOV, DMITRI (moht-KOHV) DET.

Defense. Shoots left. 6'3", 191 lbs. Born, Moscow, USSR, February 23, 1971.
(Detroit's 5th choice, 98th overall, in 1991 Entry Draft).

			Regular Season					Playoffs				
Season	Club	Lea	GP	G	A	TP	PIM	GP	G	A	TP	PIM
1989-90	CSKA	USSR	30	0	1	1	20	....	....	....	....	....
1990-91	CSKA	USSR	32	0	2	2	14	....	....	....	....	....
1991-92	CSKA	CIS	44	1	3	4	59	....	....	....	....	....
1992-93	Adirondack	AHL	41	3	7	10	30	....	....	....	....	....
1993-94	Adirondack	AHL	70	2	14	16	124	8	0	2	2	23

MROZIK, RICK DAL.

Defense. Shoots left. 6'2", 185 lbs. Born, Duluth, MN, January 2, 1975.
(Dallas' 4th choice, 136th overall, in 1993 Entry Draft).

			Regular Season					Playoffs				
Season	Club	Lea	GP	G	A	TP	PIM	GP	G	A	TP	PIM
1992-93	Cloquet	HS	28	9	38	47	12	....	....	....	....	....
1993-94	Minn.-Duluth	WCHA	38	2	9	11	38	....	....	....	....	....

MUELLER, BRIAN HFD.

Defense. Shoots left. 5'11", 200 lbs. Born, Liverpool, NY, June 2, 1972.
(Hartford's 7th choice, 141st overall, in 1991 Entry Draft).

			Regular Season					Playoffs				
Season	Club	Lea	GP	G	A	TP	PIM	GP	G	A	TP	PIM
1991-92	Clarkson	ECAC	28	4	13	17	30	....	....	....	....	....
1992-93	Clarkson	ECAC	32	6	23	29	12	....	....	....	....	....
1993-94ab	Clarkson	ECAC	34	17	39	56	60	....	....	....	....	....

a ECAC First All-Star Team (1994)
b NCAA East First All-American Team (1994)

MULHERN, RYAN CGY.

Center. Shoots right. 6'1", 180 lbs. Born, Philadelphia, PA, January 11, 1973.
(Calgary's 8th choice, 174th overall, in 1992 Entry Draft).

			Regular Season					Playoffs				
Season	Club	Lea	GP	G	A	TP	PIM	GP	G	A	TP	PIM
1992-93	Brown	ECAC	31	15	9	24	46	....	....	....	....	....
1993-94	Brown	ECAC	27	18	17	35	48	....	....	....	....	....

MULLEN, BRIAN NYI

Right wing. Shoots left. 5'10", 180 lbs. Born, New York, NY, March 16, 1962.
(Winnipeg's 7th choice, 128th overall, in 1980 Entry Draft).

			Regular Season					Playoffs				
Season	Club	Lea	GP	G	A	TP	PIM	GP	G	A	TP	PIM
1980-81	U. Wisconsin	WCHA	38	11	13	24	28	....	....	....	....	....
1981-82	U. Wisconsin	WCHA	33	20	17	37	10	....	....	....	....	....
1982-83	**Winnipeg**	**NHL**	**80**	**24**	**26**	**50**	**14**	**3**	**1**	**0**	**1**	**0**
1983-84	**Winnipeg**	**NHL**	**75**	**21**	**41**	**62**	**28**	**3**	**0**	**3**	**3**	**6**
1984-85	**Winnipeg**	**NHL**	**69**	**32**	**39**	**71**	**32**	**8**	**1**	**2**	**3**	**4**
1985-86	**Winnipeg**	**NHL**	**79**	**28**	**34**	**62**	**38**	**3**	**1**	**2**	**3**	**6**
1986-87	**Winnipeg**	**NHL**	**69**	**19**	**32**	**51**	**20**	**9**	**4**	**2**	**6**	**0**
1987-88	**NY Rangers**	**NHL**	**74**	**25**	**29**	**54**	**42**	....	....	....	....	....
1988-89	**NY Rangers**	**NHL**	**78**	**29**	**35**	**64**	**60**	**3**	**0**	**1**	**1**	**4**
1989-90	**NY Rangers**	**NHL**	**76**	**27**	**41**	**68**	**42**	**10**	**2**	**2**	**4**	**8**
1990-91	**NY Rangers**	**NHL**	**79**	**19**	**43**	**62**	**44**	**5**	**0**	**2**	**2**	**0**
1991-92	**San Jose**	**NHL**	**72**	**18**	**28**	**46**	**66**	....	....	....	....	....
1992-93	**NY Islanders**	**NHL**	**81**	**18**	**14**	**32**	**28**	**18**	**3**	**4**	**7**	**2**
1993-94	**NY Islanders**	**NHL**				DID NOT PLAY						
	NHL Totals		**832**	**260**	**362**	**622**	**414**	**62**	**12**	**18**	**30**	**30**

Played in NHL All-Star Game (1989)

Traded to **NY Rangers** by **Winnipeg** with Winnipeg's tenth round choice (Brett Barnett) in 1987 Entry Draft for NY Rangers' fifth round choice (Benoit Lebeau) in 1988 Entry Draft and NY Rangers' third round choice (later traded to St. Louis — St. Louis selected Denny Felsner) in 1989 Entry Draft, June 8, 1987. Traded to **San Jose** by **NY Rangers** with future considerations for Tim Kerr, May 30, 1991. Traded to **NY Islanders** by **San Jose** for the rights to Marcus Thuresson, August 24, 1992.

MULLEN, JOE PIT.

Right wing. Shoots right. 5'9", 180 lbs. Born, New York, NY, February 26, 1957.

			Regular Season					Playoffs				
Season	Club	Lea	GP	G	A	TP	PIM	GP	G	A	TP	PIM
1977-78a	Boston College	ECAC	34	34	34	68	12	....	....	....	....	....
1978-79a	Boston College	ECAC	25	32	24	56	8	....	....	....	....	....
1979-80bc	Salt Lake	CHL	75	40	32	72	21	13	*9	11	20	0
	St. Louis	**NHL**	....	....	....	....	....	**1**	**0**	**0**	**0**	**0**
1980-81de	Salt Lake	CHL	80	59	58	*117	8	17	11	9	20	0
1981-82	**St. Louis**	**NHL**	**45**	**25**	**34**	**59**	**4**	**10**	**7**	**11**	**18**	**4**
	Salt Lake	CHL	27	21	27	48	12	....	....	....	....	....
1982-83	**St. Louis**	**NHL**	**49**	**17**	**30**	**47**	**6**	....	....	....	....	....
1983-84	**St. Louis**	**NHL**	**80**	**41**	**44**	**85**	**19**	**6**	**2**	**0**	**2**	**0**
1984-85	**St. Louis**	**NHL**	**79**	**40**	**52**	**92**	**6**	**3**	**0**	**0**	**0**	**0**
1985-86	**St. Louis**	**NHL**	**48**	**28**	**24**	**52**	**10**	....	....	....	....	....
	Calgary	**NHL**	**29**	**16**	**22**	**38**	**11**	**21**	***12**	**7**	**19**	**4**
1986-87f	**Calgary**	**NHL**	**79**	**47**	**40**	**87**	**14**	**6**	**2**	**1**	**3**	**0**
1987-88	**Calgary**	**NHL**	**80**	**40**	**44**	**84**	**30**	**7**	**2**	**4**	**6**	**10**
1988-89fgh	**Calgary**	**NHL**	**79**	**51**	**59**	**110**	**16**	**21**	***16**	**8**	**24**	**4**
1989-90	**Calgary**	**NHL**	**78**	**36**	**33**	**69**	**24**	**6**	**3**	**0**	**3**	**0**
1990-91	**Pittsburgh**	**NHL**	**47**	**17**	**22**	**39**	**6**	**22**	**8**	**9**	**17**	**4**
1991-92	**Pittsburgh**	**NHL**	**77**	**42**	**45**	**87**	**30**	**9**	**3**	**1**	**4**	**4**
1992-93	**Pittsburgh**	**NHL**	**72**	**33**	**37**	**70**	**14**	**12**	**4**	**2**	**6**	**6**
1993-94	**Pittsburgh**	**NHL**	**84**	**38**	**32**	**70**	**41**	**6**	**1**	**0**	**1**	**2**
	NHL Totals		**926**	**471**	**518**	**989**	**231**	**130**	**60**	**43**	**103**	**38**

a ECAC First All-Star Team (1978, 1979)
b CHL Second All-Star Team (1980)
c Won Ken McKenzie Trophy (Top Rookie - CHL) (1980)
d CHL First All-Star Team (1981)
e Won Tommy Ivan Trophy (Most Valuable Player - CHL) (1981)
f Won Lady Byng Trophy (1987, 1989)
g NHL First All-Star Team (1989)
h NHL Plus/Minus Leader (1989)

Played in NHL All-Star Game (1989, 1990, 1994)

Signed as a free agent by **St. Louis,** August 16, 1979. Traded to **Calgary** by **St. Louis** with Terry Johnson and Rik Wilson for Ed Beers, Charles Bourgeois and Gino Cavallini, February 1, 1986. Traded to **Pittsburgh** by **Calgary** for Pittsburgh's second round choice (Nicolas Perreault) in 1990 Entry Draft, June 16, 1990.

MULLER, KIRK MTL.

Left wing. Shoots left. 6', 205 lbs. Born, Kingston, Ont., February 8, 1966.
(New Jersey's 1st choice, 2nd overall, in 1984 Entry Draft).

			Regular Season					Playoffs				
Season	Club	Lea	GP	G	A	TP	PIM	GP	G	A	TP	PIM
1981-82	Kingston	OHL	67	12	39	51	27	4	5	1	6	4
1982-83	Guelph	OHL	66	52	60	112	41	....	....	....	....	....
1983-84	Cdn. National	....	21	4	3	7	6	....	....	....	....	....
	Cdn. Olympic	....	6	2	1	3	0	....	....	....	....	....
	Guelph	OHL	49	31	63	94	27	....	....	....	....	....
1984-85	**New Jersey**	**NHL**	**80**	**17**	**37**	**54**	**69**	....	....	....	....	....
1985-86	**New Jersey**	**NHL**	**77**	**25**	**41**	**66**	**45**	....	....	....	....	....
1986-87	**New Jersey**	**NHL**	**79**	**26**	**50**	**76**	**75**	....	....	....	....	....
1987-88	**New Jersey**	**NHL**	**80**	**37**	**57**	**94**	**114**	**20**	**4**	**8**	**12**	**37**
1988-89	**New Jersey**	**NHL**	**80**	**31**	**43**	**74**	**119**	....	....	....	....	....
1989-90	**New Jersey**	**NHL**	**80**	**30**	**56**	**86**	**74**	**6**	**1**	**3**	**4**	**11**
1990-91	**New Jersey**	**NHL**	**80**	**19**	**51**	**70**	**76**	**7**	**0**	**2**	**2**	**10**
1991-92	**Montreal**	**NHL**	**78**	**36**	**41**	**77**	**86**	**11**	**4**	**3**	**7**	**31**
1992-93	**Montreal**	**NHL**	**80**	**37**	**57**	**94**	**77**	**20**	**10**	**7**	**17**	**18**
1993-94	**Montreal**	**NHL**	**76**	**23**	**34**	**57**	**96**	**7**	**6**	**2**	**8**	**4**
	NHL Totals		**790**	**281**	**467**	**748**	**831**	**71**	**25**	**25**	**50**	**111**

Played in NHL All-Star Game (1985, 1986, 1988, 1990, 1992, 1993)

Traded to **Montreal** by **New Jersey** with Roland Melanson for Stephane Richer and Tom Chorske, September 20, 1991.

MULLER, MIKE — WPG.

Defense. Shoots left. 6'2", 205 lbs. Born, Fairview, MN, September 18, 1971.
(Winnipeg's 2nd choice, 35th overall, in 1990 Entry Draft).

			Regular Season					Playoffs				
Season	Club	Lea	GP	G	A	TP	PIM	GP	G	A	TP	PIM
1990-91	U. Minnesota	WCHA	33	4	4	8	44	....	....	....	....	....
1991-92	U. Minnesota	WCHA	41	4	12	16	52	....	....	....	....	....
1992-93	Moscow D'amo	CIS	11	1	0	1	8	....	....	....	....	....
1993-94	Moncton	AHL	61	2	14	16	88	....	....	....	....	....

MULLIN, KORY — TOR.

Defense. Shoots left. 6'2", 200 lbs. Born, Lethbridge, Alta., May 24, 1975.

			Regular Season					Playoffs				
Season	Club	Lea	GP	G	A	TP	PIM	GP	G	A	TP	PIM
1991-92	Tri-City	WHL	49	2	5	7	82	5	1	0	1	6
1992-93	Tri-City	WHL	68	2	10	12	95	4	0	0	0	11
1993-94	Tri-City	WHL	6	0	5	5	11	....	....	....	....	....
	Tacoma	WHL	59	3	11	14	86	8	0	0	0	0

Signed as a free agent by **Toronto**, September 23, 1993.

MUNI, CRAIG (MYOO-ne) — BUF.

Defense. Shoots left. 6'3", 208 lbs. Born, Toronto, Ont., July 19, 1962.
(Toronto's 1st choice, 25th overall, in 1980 Entry Draft).

			Regular Season					Playoffs				
Season	Club	Lea	GP	G	A	TP	PIM	GP	G	A	TP	PIM
1980-81	Kingston	OHA	38	2	14	16	65	....	....	....	....	....
	Windsor	OHA	25	5	11	16	41	11	1	4	5	14
	New Brunswick	AHL	....	....	....	....	....	2	0	1	1	10
1981-82	**Toronto**	**NHL**	**3**	**0**	**0**	**0**	**2**	....	....	....	....	....
	Windsor	OHL	49	5	32	37	92	9	2	3	5	16
	Cincinnati	CHL	....	....	....	....	....	3	0	2	2	2
1982-83	**Toronto**	**NHL**	**2**	**0**	**1**	**1**	**0**	....	....	....	....	....
	St. Catharines	AHL	64	6	32	38	52	....	....	....	....	....
1983-84	St. Catharines	AHL	64	4	16	20	79	7	0	1	1	0
1984-85	**Toronto**	**NHL**	**8**	**0**	**0**	**0**	**0**	....	....	....	....	....
	St. Catharines	AHL	68	7	17	24	54	....	....	....	....	....
1985-86	**Toronto**	**NHL**	**6**	**0**	**1**	**1**	**4**	....	....	....	....	....
	St. Catharines	AHL	73	3	34	37	91	13	0	5	5	16
1986-87	**Edmonton**	**NHL**	**79**	**7**	**22**	**29**	**85**	**14**	**0**	**2**	**2**	**17**
1987-88	**Edmonton**	**NHL**	**72**	**4**	**15**	**19**	**77**	**19**	**0**	**4**	**4**	**31**
1988-89	**Edmonton**	**NHL**	**69**	**5**	**13**	**18**	**71**	**7**	**0**	**3**	**3**	**8**
1989-90	**Edmonton**	**NHL**	**71**	**5**	**12**	**17**	**81**	**22**	**0**	**3**	**3**	**16**
1990-91	**Edmonton**	**NHL**	**76**	**1**	**9**	**10**	**77**	**18**	**0**	**3**	**3**	**20**
1991-92	**Edmonton**	**NHL**	**54**	**2**	**5**	**7**	**34**	**3**	**0**	**0**	**0**	**2**
1992-93	**Edmonton**	**NHL**	**72**	**0**	**11**	**11**	**67**	....	....	....	....	....
	Chicago	**NHL**	**9**	**0**	**0**	**0**	**8**	**4**	**0**	**0**	**0**	**2**
1993-94	**Chicago**	**NHL**	**9**	**0**	**4**	**4**	**4**	....	....	....	....	....
	Buffalo	**NHL**	**73**	**2**	**8**	**10**	**62**	**7**	**0**	**0**	**0**	**4**
	NHL Totals		**603**	**26**	**101**	**127**	**572**	**94**	**0**	**15**	**15**	**100**

Signed as a free agent by **Edmonton,** August 18, 1986. Sold to **Buffalo** by **Edmonton**, October 2, 1986. Traded to **Pittsburgh** by **Buffalo** for future considerations, October 3, 1986. Traded to **Edmonton** by **Pittsburgh** to complete September 11, 1985 trade which sent Gilles Meloche to Pittsburgh for Tim Hrynewich, Marty McSorley and future considerations, October 6, 1986. Traded to **Chicago** by **Edmonton** for Mike Hudson, March 22, 1993. Traded to **Buffalo** by **Chicago** with contingent draft choices for Keith Carney and contingent draft choices, October 27, 1993.

MURANO, ERIC

Center. Shoots right. 6', 200 lbs. Born, Montreal, Que., May 4, 1967.
(Vancouver's 4th choice, 91st overall, in 1986 Entry Draft).

			Regular Season					Playoffs				
Season	Club	Lea	GP	G	A	TP	PIM	GP	G	A	TP	PIM
1986-87	U. of Denver	WCHA	31	5	7	12	12	....	....	....	....	....
1987-88	U. of Denver	WCHA	37	8	13	21	26	....	....	....	....	....
1988-89	U. of Denver	WCHA	42	13	16	29	52	....	....	....	....	....
1989-90a	U. of Denver	WCHA	42	33	35	68	52	....	....	....	....	....
	Cdn. National	....	6	1	0	1	4	....	....	....	....	....
1990-91	Milwaukee	IHL	63	32	35	67	63	3	0	1	1	4
1991-92	Milwaukee	IHL	80	35	48	83	61	5	3	4	7	0
1992-93	Hamilton	AHL	42	25	24	49	10	....	....	....	....	....
	Baltimore	AHL	32	16	14	30	10	7	7	5	12	6
1993-94	Binghamton	AHL	75	35	37	72	36	....	....	....	....	....

a WCHA Second All-Star Team (1990)

Traded to **Washington** by **Vancouver** for Tim Taylor, January 29, 1993. Signed as a free agent by **NY Rangers**, August 24, 1993.

MURPHY, BURKE — CGY.

Left wing. Shoots left. 6', 180 lbs. Born, Gloucester, Ont., June 5, 1973.
(Calgary's 11th choice, 278th overall, in 1993 Entry Draft).

			Regular Season					Playoffs				
Season	Club	Lea	GP	G	A	TP	PIM	GP	G	A	TP	PIM
1992-93	St. Lawrence	ECAC	32	19	10	29	32	....	....	....	....	....
1993-94	St. Lawrence	ECAC	30	20	17	37	42	....	....	....	....	....

MURPHY, GORD — FLA.

Defense. Shoots right. 6'2", 195 lbs. Born, Willowdale, Ont., March 23, 1967.
(Philadelphia's 10th choice, 189th overall, in 1985 Entry Draft).

			Regular Season					Playoffs				
Season	Club	Lea	GP	G	A	TP	PIM	GP	G	A	TP	PIM
1984-85	Oshawa	OHL	59	3	12	15	25	....	....	....	....	....
1985-86	Oshawa	OHL	64	7	15	22	56	6	1	1	2	6
1986-87	Oshawa	OHL	56	7	30	37	95	24	6	16	22	22
1987-88	Hershey	AHL	62	8	20	28	44	12	0	8	8	12
1988-89	**Philadelphia**	**NHL**	**75**	**4**	**31**	**35**	**68**	**19**	**2**	**7**	**9**	**13**
1989-90	**Philadelphia**	**NHL**	**75**	**14**	**27**	**41**	**95**	....	....	....	....	....
1990-91	**Philadelphia**	**NHL**	**80**	**11**	**31**	**42**	**58**	....	....	....	....	....
1991-92	**Philadelphia**	**NHL**	**31**	**2**	**8**	**10**	**33**	....	....	....	....	....
	Boston	**NHL**	**42**	**3**	**6**	**9**	**51**	**15**	**1**	**0**	**1**	**12**
1992-93	**Boston**	**NHL**	**49**	**5**	**12**	**17**	**62**	....	....	....	....	....
	Providence	AHL	2	1	3	4	2	....	....	....	....	....
1993-94	**Florida**	**NHL**	**84**	**14**	**29**	**43**	**71**	....	....	....	....	....
	NHL Totals		**436**	**53**	**144**	**197**	**438**	**34**	**3**	**7**	**10**	**25**

Traded to **Boston** by **Philadelphia** with Brian Dobbin, Philadelphia's third round choice (Sergei Zholtok) in 1992 Entry Draft and Philadelphia's fourth round choice (Charles Paquette) in 1993 Entry Draft, for Garry Galley, Wes Walz and Boston's third round choice (Milos Holan) in 1993 Entry Draft, January 2, 1992. Traded to **Dallas** by **Boston** for future considerations (Jon Casey traded to Boston for Andy Moog, June 25, 1993), June 20, 1993. Claimed by **Florida** from **Dallas** in Expansion Draft, June 24, 1993.

MURPHY, JOE — CHI.

Right wing. Shoots left. 6'1", 190 lbs. Born, London, Ont., October 16, 1967.
(Detroit's 1st choice, 1st overall, in 1986 Entry Draft).

			Regular Season					Playoffs				
Season	Club	Lea	GP	G	A	TP	PIM	GP	G	A	TP	PIM
1985-86	Cdn. National	....	8	3	3	6	2	....	....	....	....	....
	Michigan State	CCHA	35	24	37	61	50	....	....	....	....	....
1986-87	**Detroit**	**NHL**	**5**	**0**	**1**	**1**	**2**	....	....	....	....	....
	Adirondack	AHL	71	21	38	59	61	10	2	1	3	33
1987-88	**Detroit**	**NHL**	**50**	**10**	**9**	**19**	**37**	**8**	**0**	**1**	**1**	**6**
	Adirondack	AHL	6	5	6	11	4	....	....	....	....	....
1988-89	**Detroit**	**NHL**	**26**	**1**	**7**	**8**	**28**	....	....	....	....	....
	Adirondack	AHL	47	31	35	66	66	16	6	11	17	17
1989-90	**Detroit**	**NHL**	**9**	**3**	**1**	**4**	**4**	....	....	....	....	....
	Edmonton	**NHL**	**62**	**7**	**18**	**25**	**56**	**22**	**6**	**8**	**14**	**16**
1990-91	**Edmonton**	**NHL**	**80**	**27**	**35**	**62**	**35**	**15**	**2**	**5**	**7**	**14**
1991-92	**Edmonton**	**NHL**	**80**	**35**	**47**	**82**	**52**	**16**	**8**	**16**	**24**	**12**
1992-93	**Chicago**	**NHL**	**19**	**7**	**10**	**17**	**18**	**4**	**0**	**0**	**0**	**8**
1993-94	**Chicago**	**NHL**	**81**	**31**	**39**	**70**	**111**	**6**	**1**	**3**	**4**	**25**
	NHL Totals		**412**	**121**	**167**	**288**	**343**	**71**	**17**	**33**	**50**	**81**

Traded to **Edmonton** by **Detroit** with Petr Klima, Adam Graves and Jeff Sharples for Jimmy Carson, Kevin McClelland and Edmonton's fifth round choice (later traded to Montreal — Montreal selected Brad Layzell) in 1991 Entry Draft, November 2, 1989. Traded to **Chicago** by **Edmonton** for Igor Kravchuk and Dean McAmmond, February 24, 1993.

MURPHY, LARRY — PIT.

Defense. Shoots right. 6'2", 210 lbs. Born, Scarborough, Ont., March 8, 1961.
(Los Angeles' 1st choice, 4th overall, in 1980 Entry Draft).

			Regular Season					Playoffs				
Season	Club	Lea	GP	G	A	TP	PIM	GP	G	A	TP	PIM
1978-79	Peterborough	OHA	66	6	21	27	82	19	1	9	10	42
1979-80a	Peterborough	OHA	68	21	68	89	88	14	4	13	17	20
1980-81	**Los Angeles**	**NHL**	**80**	**16**	**60**	**76**	**79**	**4**	**3**	**0**	**3**	**2**
1981-82	**Los Angeles**	**NHL**	**79**	**22**	**44**	**66**	**95**	**10**	**2**	**8**	**10**	**12**
1982-83	**Los Angeles**	**NHL**	**77**	**14**	**48**	**62**	**81**	....	....	....	....	....
1983-84	**Los Angeles**	**NHL**	**6**	**0**	**3**	**3**	**0**	....	....	....	....	....
	Washington	**NHL**	**72**	**13**	**33**	**46**	**50**	**8**	**0**	**3**	**3**	**6**
1984-85	**Washington**	**NHL**	**79**	**13**	**42**	**55**	**51**	**5**	**2**	**3**	**5**	**0**
1985-86	**Washington**	**NHL**	**78**	**21**	**44**	**65**	**50**	**9**	**1**	**5**	**6**	**6**
1986-87b	**Washington**	**NHL**	**80**	**23**	**58**	**81**	**39**	**7**	**2**	**2**	**4**	**6**
1987-88	**Washington**	**NHL**	**79**	**8**	**53**	**61**	**72**	**13**	**4**	**4**	**8**	**33**
1988-89	**Washington**	**NHL**	**65**	**7**	**29**	**36**	**70**	....	....	....	....	....
	Minnesota	**NHL**	**13**	**4**	**6**	**10**	**12**	**5**	**0**	**2**	**2**	**8**
1989-90	**Minnesota**	**NHL**	**77**	**10**	**58**	**68**	**44**	**7**	**1**	**2**	**3**	**31**
1990-91	**Minnesota**	**NHL**	**31**	**4**	**11**	**15**	**38**	....	....	....	....	....
	Pittsburgh	**NHL**	**44**	**5**	**23**	**28**	**30**	**23**	**5**	**18**	**23**	**44**
1991-92	**Pittsburgh**	**NHL**	**77**	**21**	**56**	**77**	**48**	**21**	**6**	**10**	**16**	**19**
1992-93b	**Pittsburgh**	**NHL**	**83**	**22**	**63**	**85**	**73**	**12**	**2**	**11**	**13**	**10**
1993-94	**Pittsburgh**	**NHL**	**84**	**17**	**56**	**73**	**44**	**6**	**0**	**5**	**5**	**0**
	NHL Totals		**1104**	**220**	**687**	**907**	**876**	**130**	**28**	**73**	**101**	**177**

a OHA First All-Star Team (1980)
b NHL Second All-Star Team (1987, 1993)

Played in NHL All-Star Game (1994)

Traded to **Washington** by **Los Angeles** for Ken Houston and Brian Engblom, October 18, 1983. Traded to **Minnesota** by **Washington** with Mike Gartner for Dino Ciccarelli and Bob Rouse, March 7, 1989. Traded to **Pittsburgh** by **Minnesota** with Peter Taglianetti for Chris Dahlquist and Jim Johnson, December 11, 1990.

MURPHY, ROB — L.A.

Center. Shoots left. 6'3", 205 lbs. Born, Hull, Que., April 7, 1969.
(Vancouver's 1st choice, 24th overall, in 1987 Entry Draft).

			Regular Season					Playoffs				
Season	Club	Lea	GP	G	A	TP	PIM	GP	G	A	TP	PIM
1986-87	Laval	QMJHL	70	35	54	89	86	14	3	4	7	15
1987-88	**Vancouver**	**NHL**	**5**	**0**	**0**	**0**	**2**	....	....	....	....	....
	Laval	QMJHL	26	11	25	36	82	....	....	....	....	....
	Drummondville	QMJHL	33	16	28	44	41	17	4	15	19	45
1988-89	**Vancouver**	**NHL**	**8**	**0**	**1**	**1**	**2**	....	....	....	....	....
	Milwaukee	IHL	8	4	2	6	4	11	3	5	8	34
	Drummondville	QMJHL	26	13	25	38	16	4	1	3	4	20
1989-90	**Vancouver**	**NHL**	**12**	**1**	**1**	**2**	**0**	....	....	....	....	....
a	Milwaukee	IHL	64	24	47	71	87	6	2	6	8	12
1990-91	**Vancouver**	**NHL**	**42**	**5**	**1**	**6**	**90**	**4**	**0**	**0**	**0**	**2**
	Milwaukee	IHL	23	1	7	8	48	....	....	....	....	....
1991-92	**Vancouver**	**NHL**	**6**	**0**	**1**	**1**	**6**	....	....	....	....	....
	Milwaukee	IHL	73	26	38	64	141	5	0	3	3	2
1992-93	**Ottawa**	**NHL**	**44**	**3**	**7**	**10**	**30**	....	....	....	....	....
	New Haven	AHL	26	8	12	20	28	....	....	....	....	....
1993-94	**Los Angeles**	**NHL**	**8**	**0**	**1**	**1**	**22**	....	....	....	....	....
	Phoenix	IHL	72	23	34	57	101	....	....	....	....	....
	NHL Totals		**125**	**9**	**12**	**21**	**152**	**4**	**0**	**0**	**0**	**2**

a Won Garry F. Longman Memorial Trophy (Top Rookie - IHL) (1990)

Claimed by **Ottawa** from **Vancouver** in Expansion Draft, June 18, 1992. Signed as a free agent by **Los Angeles**, August 2, 1993.

MURRAY, ADRIAN — WPG.

Defense. Shoots left. 6'3", 216 lbs. Born, Ajax, Ont., September 4, 1975.
(Winnipeg's 9th choice, 197th overall, in 1993 Entry Draft).

			Regular Season					Playoffs				
Season	Club	Lea	GP	G	A	TP	PIM	GP	G	A	TP	PIM
1992-93	Newmarket	OHL	51	0	1	1	34	7	0	0	0	0
1993-94	Newmarket	OHL	9	0	2	2	11	....	....	....	....	....
	Peterborough	OHL	54	2	11	13	96	7	0	3	3	6

MURRAY, CHRIS — MTL.

Right wing. Shoots right. 6'2", 214 lbs. Born, Port Hardy, B.C., October 25, 1974.
(Montreal's 3rd choice, 54th overall, in 1994 Entry Draft).

			Regular Season					Playoffs				
Season	Club	Lea	GP	G	A	TP	PIM	GP	G	A	TP	PIM
1991-92	Kamloops	WHL	33	1	1	2	218	5	0	0	0	10
1992-93	Kamloops	WHL	62	6	10	16	217	13	0	4	4	34
1993-94	Kamloops	WHL	59	14	16	30	260	15	4	2	6	*107

MURRAY, GLEN   BOS.

Right wing. Shoots right. 6'2", 213 lbs.   Born, Halifax, N.S., November 1, 1972.
(Boston's 1st choice, 18th overall, in 1991 Entry Draft).

			Regular Season					Playoffs			
Season	Club	Lea	GP	G	A	TP	PIM	GP	G	A	TP	PIM
1989-90	Sudbury	OHL	62	8	28	36	17	7	0	0	0	4
1990-91	Sudbury	OHL	66	27	38	65	82	5	8	4	12	10
1991-92	**Boston**	**NHL**	**5**	**3**	**1**	**4**	**0**	**15**	**4**	**2**	**6**	**10**
	Sudbury	OHL	54	37	47	84	93	11	7	4	11	18
1992-93	**Boston**	**NHL**	**27**	**3**	**4**	**7**	**8**	....	....	....	....	....
	Providence	AHL	48	30	26	56	42	6	1	4	5	4
1993-94	**Boston**	**NHL**	**81**	**18**	**13**	**31**	**48**	**13**	**4**	**5**	**9**	**14**
	NHL Totals		**113**	**24**	**18**	**42**	**56**	**28**	**8**	**7**	**15**	**24**

MURRAY, MARTY   CGY.

Center. Shoots left. 5'9", 170 lbs.   Born, Deloraine, Man., February 16, 1975.
(Calgary's 5th choice, 96th overall, in 1993 Entry Draft).

			Regular Season					Playoffs			
Season	Club	Lea	GP	G	A	TP	PIM	GP	G	A	TP	PIM
1991-92	Brandon	WHL	68	20	36	56	22	....	....	....	....	....
1992-93	Brandon	WHL	67	29	15	94	50	4	1	3	4	0
1993-94ab	Brandon	WHL	64	43	71	114	33	14	6	14	20	14

a   WHL East First All-Star Team (1994)
b   Canadian Major Junior Second All-Star Team (1994)

MURRAY, MICHAEL   CGY.

Right wing. Shoots right. 6'1", 200 lbs.   Born, Cumberland, RI, April 18, 1971.
(Calgary's 10th choice, 188th overall, in 1990 Entry Draft).

			Regular Season					Playoffs			
Season	Club	Lea	GP	G	A	TP	PIM	GP	G	A	TP	PIM
1990-91	Lowell	H.E.	30	5	8	13	18	....	....	....	....	....
1991-92	Lowell	H.E.	31	22	15	37	40	....	....	....	....	....
1992-93a	Lowell	H.E.	39	23	33	56	78	....	....	....	....	....
1993-94	Lowell	H.E.	35	17	11	28	92	....	....	....	....	....

a   Hockey East Second All-Star Team (1993)

MURRAY, RAYMOND (REM)   L.A.

Left wing. Shoots left. 6'1", 183 lbs.   Born, Stratford, Ont., October 9, 1972.
(Los Angeles' 5th choice, 135th overall, in 1992 Entry Draft).

			Regular Season					Playoffs			
Season	Club	Lea	GP	G	A	TP	PIM	GP	G	A	TP	PIM
1991-92	Michigan State	CCHA	41	12	36	48	16	....	....	....	....	....
1992-93	Michigan State	CCHA	40	22	35	57	24	....	....	....	....	....
1993-94	Michigan State	CCHA	41	16	38	54	18	....	....	....	....	....

MURRAY, ROB   WPG.

Center. Shoots right. 6'1", 180 lbs.   Born, Toronto, Ont., April 4, 1967.
(Washington's 3rd choice, 61st overall, in 1985 Entry Draft).

			Regular Season					Playoffs			
Season	Club	Lea	GP	G	A	TP	PIM	GP	G	A	TP	PIM
1984-85	Peterborough	OHL	63	12	9	21	155	17	2	7	9	45
1985-86	Peterborough	OHL	52	14	18	32	125	16	1	2	3	50
1986-87	Peterborough	OHL	62	17	37	54	204	3	1	4	5	8
1987-88	Fort Wayne	IHL	80	12	21	33	139	6	0	2	2	16
1988-89	Baltimore	AHL	80	11	23	34	235	....	....	....	....	....
1989-90	**Washington**	**NHL**	**41**	**2**	**7**	**9**	**58**	**9**	**0**	**0**	**0**	**18**
	Baltimore	AHL	23	5	4	9	63	....	....	....	....	....
1990-91	**Washington**	**NHL**	**17**	**0**	**3**	**3**	**19**	....	....	....	....	....
	Baltimore	AHL	48	6	20	26	177	4	0	0	0	12
1991-92	**Winnipeg**	**NHL**	**9**	**0**	**1**	**1**	**18**	....	....	....	....	....
	Moncton	AHL	60	16	15	31	247	8	0	1	1	56
1992-93	**Winnipeg**	**NHL**	**10**	**1**	**0**	**1**	**6**	....	....	....	....	....
	Moncton	AHL	56	16	21	37	147	3	0	0	0	6
1993-94	**Winnipeg**	**NHL**	**6**	**0**	**0**	**0**	**2**	....	....	....	....	....
	Moncton	AHL	69	25	32	57	280	21	2	3	5	60
	NHL Totals		**83**	**3**	**11**	**14**	**103**	**9**	**0**	**0**	**0**	**18**

Claimed by **Minnesota** from **Washington** in Expansion Draft, May 30, 1991. Traded to **Winnipeg** by **Minnesota** with future considerations for Winnipeg's seventh round choice (Geoff Finch) in 1991 Entry Draft and future considerations, May 31, 1991.

MURRAY, TROY   OTT.

Center. Shoots right. 6'1", 195 lbs.   Born, Calgary, Alta., July 31, 1962.
(Chicago's 6th choice, 57th overall, in 1980 Entry Draft).

			Regular Season					Playoffs			
Season	Club	Lea	GP	G	A	TP	PIM	GP	G	A	TP	PIM
1980-81a	North Dakota	WCHA	38	33	45	78	28	....	....	....	....	....
1981-82a	North Dakota	WCHA	26	13	17	30	62	....	....	....	....	....
	Chicago	**NHL**	**1**	**0**	**0**	**0**	**0**	**7**	**1**	**0**	**1**	**5**
1982-83	**Chicago**	**NHL**	**54**	**8**	**8**	**16**	**27**	**2**	**0**	**0**	**0**	**0**
1983-84	**Chicago**	**NHL**	**61**	**15**	**15**	**30**	**45**	**5**	**1**	**0**	**1**	**7**
1984-85	**Chicago**	**NHL**	**80**	**26**	**40**	**66**	**82**	**15**	**5**	**14**	**19**	**24**
1985-86b	**Chicago**	**NHL**	**80**	**45**	**54**	**99**	**94**	**2**	**0**	**0**	**0**	**2**
1986-87	**Chicago**	**NHL**	**77**	**28**	**43**	**71**	**59**	**4**	**0**	**0**	**0**	**5**
1987-88	**Chicago**	**NHL**	**79**	**22**	**36**	**58**	**96**	**5**	**1**	**0**	**1**	**8**
1988-89	**Chicago**	**NHL**	**79**	**21**	**30**	**51**	**113**	**16**	**3**	**6**	**9**	**25**
1989-90	**Chicago**	**NHL**	**68**	**17**	**38**	**55**	**86**	**20**	**4**	**4**	**8**	**2**
1990-91	**Chicago**	**NHL**	**75**	**14**	**23**	**37**	**74**	**6**	**0**	**1**	**1**	**12**
1991-92	**Winnipeg**	**NHL**	**74**	**17**	**30**	**47**	**69**	**7**	**0**	**0**	**0**	**2**
1992-93	**Winnipeg**	**NHL**	**29**	**3**	**4**	**7**	**34**	....	....	....	....	....
	Chicago	**NHL**	**22**	**1**	**3**	**4**	**25**	**4**	**0**	**0**	**0**	**2**
1993-94	**Chicago**	**NHL**	**12**	**0**	**1**	**1**	**6**	....	....	....	....	....
	Indianapolis	IHL	8	3	3	6	12	....	....	....	....	....
	Ottawa	**NHL**	**15**	**2**	**3**	**5**	**4**	....	....	....	....	....
	NHL Totals		**806**	**219**	**328**	**547**	**814**	**93**	**15**	**25**	**40**	**94**

a   WCHA Second All-Star Team (1981, 1982)
b   Won Frank J. Selke Memorial Trophy (1986)

Traded to **Winnipeg** by **Chicago** with Warren Rychel for Bryan Marchment and Chris Norton, July 22, 1991. Traded to **Chicago** by **Winnipeg** for Steve Bancroft and future considerations, February 21, 1993. Traded to **Ottawa** by **Chicago** with Chicago's eleventh round choice (Antti Tormanen) in 1994 Entry Draft for Ottawa's eleventh round choice (Rob Mara) in 1994 Entry Draft, March 11, 1994.

MURZYN, DANA   (MUHR-zihn)   VAN.

Defense. Shoots left. 6'2", 200 lbs.   Born, Calgary, Alta., December 9, 1966.
(Hartford's 1st choice, 5th overall, in 1985 Entry Draft).

			Regular Season					Playoffs			
Season	Club	Lea	GP	G	A	TP	PIM	GP	G	A	TP	PIM
1983-84	Calgary	WHL	65	11	20	31	135	2	0	0	0	10
1984-85a	Calgary	WHL	72	32	60	92	233	8	1	11	12	16
1985-86b	**Hartford**	**NHL**	**78**	**3**	**23**	**26**	**125**	**4**	**0**	**0**	**0**	**10**
1986-87	**Hartford**	**NHL**	**74**	**9**	**19**	**28**	**95**	**6**	**2**	**1**	**3**	**29**
1987-88	**Hartford**	**NHL**	**33**	**1**	**6**	**7**	**45**	....	....	....	....	....
	Calgary	**NHL**	**41**	**6**	**5**	**11**	**94**	**5**	**2**	**0**	**2**	**13**
1988-89	**Calgary**	**NHL**	**63**	**3**	**19**	**22**	**142**	**21**	**0**	**3**	**3**	**20**
1989-90	**Calgary**	**NHL**	**78**	**7**	**13**	**20**	**140**	**6**	**2**	**2**	**4**	**2**
1990-91	**Calgary**	**NHL**	**19**	**0**	**2**	**2**	**30**	....	....	....	....	....
	Vancouver	**NHL**	**10**	**1**	**0**	**1**	**8**	**6**	**0**	**1**	**1**	**8**
1991-92	**Vancouver**	**NHL**	**70**	**3**	**11**	**14**	**147**	**1**	**0**	**0**	**0**	**15**
1992-93	**Vancouver**	**NHL**	**79**	**5**	**11**	**16**	**196**	**12**	**3**	**2**	**5**	**18**
1993-94	**Vancouver**	**NHL**	**80**	**6**	**14**	**20**	**109**	**7**	**0**	**0**	**0**	**4**
	NHL Totals		**625**	**44**	**123**	**167**	**1131**	**68**	**9**	**9**	**18**	**119**

a   WHL East First All-Star Team, (1985)
b   NHL All-Rookie Team (1986)

Traded to **Calgary** by **Hartford** with Shane Churla for Neil Sheehy, Carey Wilson and the rights to Lane MacDonald, January 3, 1988. Traded to **Vancouver** by **Calgary** for Ron Stern, Kevan Guy and future considerations, March 5, 1991.

MUSIL, FRANK   (moo-SIHL)   CGY.

Defense. Shoots left. 6'3", 215 lbs.   Born, Pardubice, Czech., December 17, 1964.
(Minnesota's 3rd choice, 38th overall, in 1983 Entry Draft).

			Regular Season					Playoffs			
Season	Club	Lea	GP	G	A	TP	PIM	GP	G	A	TP	PIM
1980-81	Pardubice	Czech.	2	0	0	0	0	....	....	....	....	....
1981-82	Pardubice	Czech.	35	1	3	4	34	....	....	....	....	....
1982-83	Pardubice	Czech.	33	1	2	3	44	....	....	....	....	....
1983-84	Pardubice	Czech.	37	4	8	12	72	....	....	....	....	....
1984-85	Dukla Jihlava	Czech.	44	4	6	10	76	....	....	....	....	....
1985-86	Dukla Jihlava	Czech.	34	4	7	11	42	....	....	....	....	....
1986-87	**Minnesota**	**NHL**	**72**	**2**	**9**	**11**	**148**	....	....	....	....	....
1987-88	**Minnesota**	**NHL**	**80**	**9**	**8**	**17**	**213**	....	....	....	....	....
1988-89	**Minnesota**	**NHL**	**55**	**1**	**19**	**20**	**54**	**5**	**1**	**1**	**2**	**4**
1989-90	**Minnesota**	**NHL**	**56**	**2**	**8**	**10**	**109**	**4**	**0**	**0**	**0**	**14**
1990-91	**Minnesota**	**NHL**	**8**	**0**	**2**	**2**	**23**	....	....	....	....	....
	Calgary	**NHL**	**67**	**7**	**14**	**21**	**160**	**7**	**0**	**0**	**0**	**10**
1991-92	**Calgary**	**NHL**	**78**	**4**	**8**	**12**	**103**	....	....	....	....	....
1992-93	**Calgary**	**NHL**	**80**	**6**	**10**	**16**	**131**	**6**	**1**	**1**	**2**	**7**
1993-94	**Calgary**	**NHL**	**75**	**1**	**8**	**9**	**50**	**7**	**0**	**1**	**1**	**4**
	NHL Totals		**571**	**32**	**86**	**118**	**991**	**29**	**2**	**3**	**5**	**39**

Traded to **Calgary** by **Minnesota** for Brian Glynn, October 26, 1990.

MYHRES, BRANTT   T.B.

Left wing. Shoots right. 6'3", 200 lbs.   Born, Edmonton, Alta., March 18, 1974.
(Tampa Bay's 6th choice, 122nd overall, in 1992 Entry Draft).

			Regular Season					Playoffs			
Season	Club	Lea	GP	G	A	TP	PIM	GP	G	A	TP	PIM
1990-91	Portland	WHL	59	2	7	9	125	....	....	....	....	....
1991-92	Portland	WHL	4	0	2	2	22	....	....	....	....	....
	Lethbridge	WHL	53	4	11	15	359	5	0	0	0	36
1992-93	Lethbridge	WHL	64	13	35	48	277	3	0	0	0	11
1993-94	Lethbridge	WHL	34	10	21	31	103	....	....	....	....	....
	Spokane	WHL	27	10	22	32	139	3	1	4	5	7
	Atlanta	IHL	2	0	0	0	17	....	....	....	....	....

MYRVOLD, ANDERS   QUE.

Defense. Shoots left. 6'1", 178 lbs.   Born, Lorenskog, Norway, August 12, 1975.
(Quebec's 6th choice, 127th overall, in 1993 Entry Draft).

			Regular Season					Playoffs			
Season	Club	Lea	GP	G	A	TP	PIM	GP	G	A	TP	PIM
1992-93	Farjestad	Swe.	2	0	0	0	0	....	....	....	....	....
1993-94	Grum	Swe. 2	24	1	0	1	59	....	....	....	....	....

NAMESTNIKOV, YEVGENY   (nah-MEST-nih-kov, yev-GAIN-ee)   VAN.

Defense. Shoots right. 5'11", 190 lbs.   Born, Arzamis-Ig, USSR, October 9, 1971.
(Vancouver's 6th choice, 117th overall, in 1991 Entry Draft).

			Regular Season					Playoffs			
Season	Club	Lea	GP	G	A	TP	PIM	GP	G	A	TP	PIM
1988-89	Torpedo Gorky	USSR	2	0	0	0	2	....	....	....	....	....
1989-90	Torpedo Gorky	USSR	23	0	0	0	25	....	....	....	....	....
1990-91	Torpedo Niz.	USSR	42	1	2	3	49	....	....	....	....	....
1991-92	CSKA	CIS	42	1	1	2	47	....	....	....	....	....
1992-93	CSKA	CIS	42	5	5	10	68	....	....	....	....	....
1993-94	**Vancouver**	**NHL**	**17**	**0**	**5**	**5**	**10**	....	....	....	....	....
	NHL Totals		**17**	**0**	**5**	**5**	**10**					

NASLUND, MARKUS   (NAZ-luhnd)   PIT.

Right wing. Shoots left. 6', 186 lbs.   Born, Ornskoldsvik, Sweden, July 30, 1973.
(Pittsburgh's 1st choice, 16th overall, in 1991 Entry Draft).

			Regular Season					Playoffs			
Season	Club	Lea	GP	G	A	TP	PIM	GP	G	A	TP	PIM
1990-91	MoDo	Swe.	32	10	9	19	14	....	....	....	....	....
1991-92	MoDo	Swe.	39	22	18	40	54	....	....	....	....	....
1992-93	MoDo	Swe.	39	22	17	39	67	3	3	2	5	0
1993-94	**Pittsburgh**	**NHL**	**71**	**4**	**7**	**11**	**27**	....	....	....	....	....
	Cleveland	IHL	5	1	6	7	4	....	....	....	....	....
	NHL Totals		**71**	**4**	**7**	**11**	**27**					

NASREDDINE, ALAIN   (NAS-ruh-deen, AL-ay)   FLA.

Defense. Shoots left. 6'1", 201 lbs.   Born, Montreal, Que., July 10, 1975.
(Florida's 8th choice, 135th overall, in 1993 Entry Draft).

			Regular Season					Playoffs			
Season	Club	Lea	GP	G	A	TP	PIM	GP	G	A	TP	PIM
1991-92	Drummondville	QMJHL	61	1	9	10	78	4	0	0	0	17
1992-93	Drummondville	QMJHL	64	0	14	14	137	10	0	1	1	36
1993-94	Chicoutimi	QMJHL	60	3	24	27	218	26	2	10	12	118

NAUMENKO, NICHOLAS   ST.L.

Defense. Shoots right. 5'11", 180 lbs.   Born, Chicago, IL, July 7, 1974.
(St. Louis' 9th choice, 182nd overall, in 1992 Entry Draft).

			Regular Season					Playoffs			
Season	Club	Lea	GP	G	A	TP	PIM	GP	G	A	TP	PIM
1992-93	North Dakota	WCHA	38	10	24	34	26	....	....	....	....	....
1993-94	North Dakota	WCHA	32	4	22	26	22	....	....	....	....	....

NAUSS, RYAN (NOWZ) T.B.

Left wing. Shoots left. 6'5", 196 lbs. Born, Toronto, Ont., January 19, 1975.
(Tampa Bay's 8th choice, 185th overall, in 1993 Entry Draft).

			Regular Season					Playoffs				
Season	Club	Lea	GP	G	A	TP	PIM	GP	G	A	TP	PIM
1992-93	Peterborough	OHL	27	2	2	4	15	1	0	0	0	0
1993-94	Peterborough	OHL	61	2	6	8	34	7	0	0	0	0

NAZAROV, ANDREI (nah-ZAH-rohv) S.J.

Left wing. Shoots right. 6'5", 230 lbs. Born, Chelyabinsk, USSR, May 22, 1974.
(San Jose's 2nd choice, 10th overall, in 1992 Entry Draft).

			Regular Season					Playoffs				
Season	Club	Lea	GP	G	A	TP	PIM	GP	G	A	TP	PIM
1991-92	Moscow D'amo	CIS	2	1	0	1	2	....	....	....	....	....
1992-93	Moscow D'amo	CIS	42	8	2	10	79	10	1	1	2	8
1993-94	Moscow D'amo	CIS	6	2	2	4	0	....	....	....	....	....
	San Jose	**NHL**	**1**	**0**	**0**	**0**	**0**	....	....	....	....	....
	Kansas City	IHL	71	15	18	33	64	....	....	....	....	....
	NHL Totals		**1**	**0**	**0**	**0**	**0**	....	....	....	....	....

NDUR, RUMAN (nih-DOOR, ROO-muhn) BUF.

Defense. Shoots left. 6'2", 200 lbs. Born, Zaria, Nigeria, July 7, 1975.
(Buffalo's 3rd choice, 69th overall, in 1994 Entry Draft).

			Regular Season					Playoffs				
Season	Club	Lea	GP	G	A	TP	PIM	GP	G	A	TP	PIM
1992-93	Guelph	OHL	22	1	3	4	30	4	0	1	1	4
1993-94	Guelph	OHL	61	6	33	39	176	9	4	1	5	24

NEATON, PAT PIT.

Defense. Shoots left. 6', 180 lbs. Born, Redford, MI, May 21, 1971.
(Pittsburgh's 9th choice, 145th overall, in 1990 Entry Draft).

			Regular Season					Playoffs				
Season	Club	Lea	GP	G	A	TP	PIM	GP	G	A	TP	PIM
1989-90	U. of Michigan	CCHA	42	3	23	26	36	....	....	....	....	....
1990-91a	U. of Michigan	CCHA	44	15	28	43	78	....	....	....	....	....
1991-92	U. of Michigan	CCHA	43	10	20	30	62	....	....	....	....	....
1992-93b	U. of Michigan	CCHA	38	10	18	28	37	....	....	....	....	....
1993-94	**Pittsburgh**	**NHL**	**9**	**1**	**1**	**2**	**12**	....	....	....	....	....
	Cleveland	IHL	71	8	24	32	78	....	....	....	....	....
	NHL Totals		**9**	**1**	**1**	**2**	**12**	....	....	....	....	....

a CCHA Second All-Star Team (1991)
b CCHA First All-Star Team (1993)

NECKAR, STANISLAV (NEHTS-kahrzh) OTT.

Defense. Shoots left. 6'1", 196 lbs. Born, Ceske Budejovice, Czech., December 22, 1975.
(Ottawa's 2nd choice, 29th overall, in 1994 Entry Draft).

			Regular Season					Playoffs				
Season	Club	Lea	GP	G	A	TP	PIM	GP	G	A	TP	PIM
1992-93	Budejovice	Czech.	42	2	9	11	12	....	....	....	....	....
1993-94	Budejovice	Czech.	12	3	2	5	2	3	0	0	0	....

NEDOMA, MILAN (neh-DOH-mah) BUF.

Defense. Shoots left. 5'10", 180 lbs. Born, Brno, Czech., March 29, 1972.
(Buffalo's 7th choice, 166th overall, in 1990 Entry Draft).

			Regular Season					Playoffs				
Season	Club	Lea	GP	G	A	TP	PIM	GP	G	A	TP	PIM
1989-90	Zetor Brno	Czech.	35	1	4	5	....	....	....	....	....	....
1990-91	Zetor Brno	Czech.2				UNAVAILABLE						
1991-92	Dukla Trencin	Czech.	47	4	5	9	22	....	....	....	....	....
1992-93	Dukla Trencin	Czech.	43	10	16	26	....	....	....	....	....	....
1993-94	Stadion	Czech.	37	11	7	18	0	....	....	....	....	....

NEDVED, PETR (NEHD-VEHD) NYR

Center. Shoots left. 6'3", 185 lbs. Born, Liberec, Czech., December 9, 1971.
(Vancouver's 1st choice, 2nd overall, in 1990 Entry Draft).

			Regular Season					Playoffs				
Season	Club	Lea	GP	G	A	TP	PIM	GP	G	A	TP	PIM
1988-89	Litvinov	Czech.Jrs.	20	32	19	51	12	....	....	....	....	....
1989-90a	Seattle	WHL	71	65	80	145	80	11	4	9	13	2
1990-91	**Vancouver**	**NHL**	**61**	**10**	**6**	**16**	**20**	**6**	**0**	**1**	**1**	**0**
1991-92	**Vancouver**	**NHL**	**77**	**15**	**22**	**37**	**36**	**10**	**1**	**4**	**5**	**16**
1992-93	**Vancouver**	**NHL**	**84**	**38**	**33**	**71**	**96**	**12**	**2**	**3**	**5**	**2**
1993-94	Cdn. National	....	17	19	12	31	16	....	....	....	....	....
	Cdn. Olympic	....	8	5	1	6	6	....	....	....	....	....
	St. Louis	**NHL**	**19**	**6**	**14**	**20**	**8**	**4**	**0**	**1**	**1**	**4**
	NHL Totals		**241**	**69**	**75**	**144**	**160**	**32**	**3**	**9**	**12**	**22**

a Canadian Major Junior Rookie of the Year (1990)

Signed as a free agent by **St. Louis**, March 5, 1994. Traded to **NY Rangers** by **St. Louis** for Esa Tikkanen and Doug Lidster, July 24, 1994.

NEDVED, ZDENEK (NEHD-VEHD) TOR.

Right wing. Shoots left. 6', 180 lbs. Born, Lany, Czech., March 3, 1975.
(Toronto's 3rd choice, 123rd overall, in 1993 Entry Draft).

			Regular Season					Playoffs				
Season	Club	Lea	GP	G	A	TP	PIM	GP	G	A	TP	PIM
1991-92	Kladno	Czech.	19	15	12	27	22	....	....	....	....	....
1992-93	Sudbury	OHL	18	3	9	12	6	....	....	....	....	....
1993-94	Sudbury	OHL	60	50	50	100	42	10	7	8	15	10

NEEDHAM, MIKE DAL.

Right wing. Shoots right. 5'10", 185 lbs. Born, Calgary, Alta., April 4, 1970.
(Pittsburgh's 7th choice, 126th overall, in 1989 Entry Draft).

			Regular Season					Playoffs				
Season	Club	Lea	GP	G	A	TP	PIM	GP	G	A	TP	PIM
1986-87	Kamloops	WHL	3	1	2	3	0	11	2	1	3	5
1987-88	Kamloops	WHL	64	31	33	64	93	5	0	1	1	5
1988-89	Kamloops	WHL	49	24	27	51	55	16	2	9	11	13
1989-90a	Kamloops	WHL	60	59	66	125	75	17	11	13	24	10
1990-91	Muskegon	IHL	65	14	31	45	17	5	2	2	4	5
1991-92	Muskegon	IHL	80	41	37	78	83	8	4	4	8	6
	Pittsburgh	**NHL**	....	....	....	....	....	**5**	**1**	**0**	**1**	**2**
1992-93	**Pittsburgh**	**NHL**	**56**	**8**	**5**	**13**	**14**	**9**	**1**	**0**	**1**	**2**
	Cleveland	IHL	1	2	0	2	0	....	....	....	....	....
1993-94	**Pittsburgh**	**NHL**	**25**	**1**	**0**	**1**	**2**	....	....	....	....	....
	Cleveland	IHL	6	4	3	7	7	....	....	....	....	....
	Dallas	**NHL**	**5**	**0**	**0**	**0**	**0**	....	....	....	....	....
	NHL Totals		**86**	**9**	**5**	**14**	**16**	**14**	**2**	**0**	**2**	**4**

a WHL West First All-Star Team (1990)

Traded to **Dallas** by **Pittsburgh** for Jim McKenzie, March 21, 1994.

NEELY, CAM BOS.

Right wing. Shoots right. 6'1", 217 lbs. Born, Comox, B.C., June 6, 1965.
(Vancouver's 1st choice, 9th overall, in 1983 Entry Draft).

			Regular Season					Playoffs				
Season	Club	Lea	GP	G	A	TP	PIM	GP	G	A	TP	PIM
1982-83	Portland	WHL	72	56	64	120	130	14	9	11	20	17
1983-84	**Vancouver**	**NHL**	**56**	**16**	**15**	**31**	**57**	**4**	**2**	**0**	**2**	**2**
	Portland	WHL	19	8	18	26	29	....	....	....	....	....
1984-85	**Vancouver**	**NHL**	**72**	**21**	**18**	**39**	**137**	....	....	....	....	....
1985-86	**Vancouver**	**NHL**	**73**	**14**	**20**	**34**	**126**	**3**	**0**	**0**	**0**	**6**
1986-87	**Boston**	**NHL**	**75**	**36**	**36**	**72**	**143**	**4**	**5**	**1**	**6**	**8**
1987-88a	**Boston**	**NHL**	**69**	**42**	**27**	**69**	**175**	**23**	**9**	**8**	**17**	**51**
1988-89	**Boston**	**NHL**	**74**	**37**	**38**	**75**	**190**	**10**	**7**	**2**	**9**	**8**
1989-90a	**Boston**	**NHL**	**76**	**55**	**37**	**92**	**117**	**21**	**12**	**16**	**28**	**51**
1990-91a	**Boston**	**NHL**	**69**	**51**	**40**	**91**	**98**	**19**	**16**	**4**	**20**	**36**
1991-92	**Boston**	**NHL**	**9**	**9**	**3**	**12**	**16**	....	....	....	....	....
1992-93	**Boston**	**NHL**	**13**	**11**	**7**	**18**	**25**	**4**	**4**	**1**	**5**	**4**
1993-94ab	**Boston**	**NHL**	**49**	**50**	**24**	**74**	**54**	....	....	....	....	....
	NHL Totals		**635**	**342**	**265**	**607**	**1138**	**88**	**55**	**32**	**87**	**166**

a NHL Second All-Star Team (1988, 1990, 1991, 1994)
b Won Bill Masterton Memorial Trophy (1994)

Played in NHL All-Star Game (1988-91)

Traded to **Boston** by **Vancouver** with Vancouver's first round choice (Glen Wesley) in 1987 Entry Draft for Barry Pederson, June 6, 1986.

NEILSON, COREY EDM.

Defense. Shoots right. 6'5", 207 lbs. Born, Oromocto, N.B., August 22, 1976.
(Edmonton's 4th choice, 53rd overall, in 1994 Entry Draft).

			Regular Season					Playoffs				
Season	Club	Lea	GP	G	A	TP	PIM	GP	G	A	TP	PIM
1992-93	Fredericton	Midget	43	12	32	44	54	....	....	....	....	....
1993-94	North Bay	OHL	62	3	35	38	46	18	1	5	6	10

NELSON, JEFF WSH.

Center. Shoots left. 6', 180 lbs. Born, Prince Albert, Sask., December 18, 1972.
(Washington's 4th choice, 36th overall, in 1991 Entry Draft).

			Regular Season					Playoffs				
Season	Club	Lea	GP	G	A	TP	PIM	GP	G	A	TP	PIM
1989-90	Prince Albert	WHL	72	28	69	97	79	14	2	11	13	10
1990-91a	Prince Albert	WHL	72	46	74	120	58	3	1	1	2	4
1991-92a	Prince Albert	WHL	64	48	65	113	84	9	7	14	21	18
1992-93	Baltimore	AHL	72	14	38	52	12	7	1	3	4	2
1993-94	Portland	AHL	80	34	73	107	92	17	10	5	15	20

a WHL East Second All-Star Team (1991, 1992)

NELSON, TODD WSH.

Defense. Shoots left. 6', 201 lbs. Born, Prince Albert, Sask., May 11, 1969.
(Pittsburgh's 4th choice, 79th overall, in 1989 Entry Draft).

			Regular Season					Playoffs				
Season	Club	Lea	GP	G	A	TP	PIM	GP	G	A	TP	PIM
1985-86	Prince Albert	WHL	4	0	0	0	0	....	....	....	....	....
1986-87	Prince Albert	WHL	35	1	6	7	10	4	0	0	0	0
1987-88	Prince Albert	WHL	72	3	21	24	59	10	3	2	5	4
1988-89a	Prince Albert	WHL	72	14	45	59	72	4	1	3	4	4
1989-90a	Prince Albert	WHL	69	13	42	55	88	14	3	12	15	12
1990-91	Muskegon	IHL	79	4	20	24	32	3	0	0	0	4
1991-92	**Pittsburgh**	**NHL**	**1**	**0**	**0**	**0**	**0**	....	....	....	....	....
	Muskegon	IHL	80	6	35	41	46	14	1	11	12	4
1992-93	Cleveland	IHL	76	7	35	42	115	4	0	2	2	4
1993-94	**Washington**	**NHL**	**2**	**1**	**0**	**1**	**2**	**4**	**0**	**0**	**0**	**0**
	Portland	AHL	80	11	34	45	69	11	0	6	6	6
	NHL Totals		**3**	**1**	**0**	**1**	**2**	**4**	**0**	**0**	**0**	**0**

a WHL East Second All-Star Team (1989, 1990)

Signed as a free agent by **Washington**, August 15, 1993.

NEMCHINOV, SERGEI (nehm-CHEE-nahf, SAIR-gay) NYR

Center. Shoots left. 6', 201 lbs. Born, Moscow, USSR, January 14, 1964.
(NY Rangers' 14th choice, 244th overall, in 1990 Entry Draft).

			Regular Season					Playoffs				
Season	Club	Lea	GP	G	A	TP	PIM	GP	G	A	TP	PIM
1981-82	Soviet Wings	USSR	15	1	0	1	0	....	....	....	....	....
1982-83	CSKA	USSR	11	0	0	0	2	....	....	....	....	....
1983-84	CSKA	USSR	20	6	5	11	4	....	....	....	....	....
1984-85	CSKA	USSR	31	2	4	6	4	....	....	....	....	....
1985-86	Soviet Wings	USSR	39	7	12	19	28	....	....	....	....	....
1986-87	Soviet Wings	USSR	40	13	9	22	24	....	....	....	....	....
1987-88	Soviet Wings	USSR	48	17	11	28	26	....	....	....	....	....
1988-89	Soviet Wings	USSR	43	15	14	29	28	....	....	....	....	....
1989-90	Soviet Wings	USSR	48	17	16	33	34	....	....	....	....	....
1990-91	Soviet Wings	USSR	46	21	24	45	30	....	....	....	....	....
1991-92	**NY Rangers**	**NHL**	**73**	**30**	**28**	**58**	**15**	**13**	**1**	**4**	**5**	**8**
1992-93	**NY Rangers**	**NHL**	**81**	**23**	**31**	**54**	**34**	....	....	....	....	....
1993-94	**NY Rangers**	**NHL**	**76**	**22**	**27**	**49**	**36**	**23**	**2**	**5**	**7**	**6**
	NHL Totals		**230**	**75**	**86**	**161**	**85**	**36**	**3**	**9**	**12**	**14**

NEMECEK, JAN — L.A.

Defense. Shoots right. 6'1", 194 lbs. Born, Pisek, Czech., February 14, 1976.
(Los Angeles' 7th choice, 215th overall, in 1994 Entry Draft).

			Regular Season					Playoffs				
Season	Club	Lea	GP	G	A	TP	PIM	GP	G	A	TP	PIM
1992-93	Budejovice	Czech.	15	0	0	0	....	....	....	....	....	....
1993-94	Budejovice	Czech.	16	0	1	1	16	....	....	....	....	....

NEMIROVSKY, DAVID — FLA.

Right wing. Shoots right. 6'2", 176 lbs. Born, Toronto, Ont., August 1, 1976.
(Florida's 5th choice, 84th overall, in 1994 Entry Draft).

			Regular Season					Playoffs				
Season	Club	Lea	GP	G	A	TP	PIM	GP	G	A	TP	PIM
1992-93	North York	Jr. A	40	19	23	42	27	....	....	....	....	....
1993-94	Ottawa	OHL	64	21	31	52	18	17	10	10	20	2

NICHOL, SCOTT — BUF.

Center. Shoots right. 5'9", 175 lbs. Born, Calgary, Alta., December 31, 1974.
(Buffalo's 9th choice, 272nd overall, in 1993 Entry Draft).

			Regular Season					Playoffs				
Season	Club	Lea	GP	G	A	TP	PIM	GP	G	A	TP	PIM
1992-93	Portland	WHL	67	31	33	64	146	16	8	8	16	41
1993-94	Portland	WHL	65	40	53	93	144	....	....	....	....	....

NICHOLLS, BERNIE — (NICK-els) — CHI.

Center. Shoots right. 6'1", 185 lbs. Born, Haliburton, Ont., June 24, 1961.
(Los Angeles' 6th choice, 73rd overall, in 1980 Entry Draft).

			Regular Season					Playoffs				
Season	Club	Lea	GP	G	A	TP	PIM	GP	G	A	TP	PIM
1979-80	Kingston	OHA	68	36	43	79	85	3	1	0	1	10
1980-81	Kingston	OHA	65	63	89	152	109	14	8	10	18	17
1981-82	**Los Angeles**	**NHL**	**22**	**14**	**18**	**32**	**27**	**10**	**4**	**0**	**4**	**23**
	New Haven	AHL	55	41	30	71	31	....	....	....	....	....
1982-83	**Los Angeles**	**NHL**	**71**	**28**	**22**	**50**	**124**	....	....	....	....	....
1983-84	**Los Angeles**	**NHL**	**78**	**41**	**54**	**95**	**83**	....	....	....	....	....
1984-85	**Los Angeles**	**NHL**	**80**	**46**	**54**	**100**	**76**	**3**	**1**	**1**	**2**	**9**
1985-86	**Los Angeles**	**NHL**	**80**	**36**	**61**	**97**	**78**	....	....	....	....	....
1986-87	**Los Angeles**	**NHL**	**80**	**33**	**48**	**81**	**101**	**5**	**2**	**5**	**7**	**6**
1987-88	**Los Angeles**	**NHL**	**65**	**32**	**46**	**78**	**114**	**5**	**2**	**6**	**8**	**11**
1988-89a	**Los Angeles**	**NHL**	**79**	**70**	**80**	**150**	**96**	**11**	**7**	**9**	**16**	**12**
1989-90	**Los Angeles**	**NHL**	**47**	**27**	**48**	**75**	**66**	....	....	....	....	....
	NY Rangers	**NHL**	**32**	**12**	**25**	**37**	**20**	**10**	**7**	**5**	**12**	**16**
1990-91	**NY Rangers**	**NHL**	**71**	**25**	**48**	**73**	**96**	**5**	**4**	**3**	**7**	**8**
1991-92	**NY Rangers**	**NHL**	**1**	**0**	**0**	**0**	**0**	....	....	....	....	....
	Edmonton	**NHL**	**49**	**20**	**29**	**49**	**60**	**16**	**8**	**11**	**19**	**25**
1992-93	**Edmonton**	**NHL**	**46**	**8**	**32**	**40**	**40**	....	....	....	....	....
	New Jersey	**NHL**	**23**	**5**	**15**	**20**	**40**	**5**	**0**	**0**	**0**	**6**
1993-94	**New Jersey**	**NHL**	**61**	**19**	**27**	**46**	**86**	**16**	**4**	**9**	**13**	**28**
	NHL Totals		**885**	**416**	**607**	**1023**	**1107**	**86**	**39**	**49**	**88**	**144**

a NHL Second All-Star Team (1989)

Played in NHL All-Star Game (1984, 1989, 1990)

Traded to **NY Rangers** by **Los Angeles** for Tomas Sandstrom and Tony Granato, January 20, 1990. Traded to **Edmonton** by **NY Rangers** with Steven Rice and Louie DeBrusk for Mark Messier and future considerations, October 4, 1991. Traded to **New Jersey** by **Edmonton** for Zdeno Ciger and Kevin Todd, January 13, 1993. Signed as a free agent by **Chicago**, July 14, 1994.

NICKULAS, ERIC — BOS.

Center. Shoots right. 5'11", 190 lbs. Born, Cape Cod, MA, March 25, 1975.
(Boston's 3rd choice, 99th overall, in 1994 Entry Draft).

			Regular Season					Playoffs				
Season	Club	Lea	GP	G	A	TP	PIM	GP	G	A	TP	PIM
1992-93	Tabor Acad.	HS	28	25	25	50	....	....	....	....	....	....
1993-94	Cushing	HS	25	46	36	82	....	....	....	....	....	....

NIECKAR, BARRY — (NIGH-kahr)

Left wing. Shoots left. 6'3", 200 lbs. Born, Rama, Sask., December 16, 1967.

			Regular Season					Playoffs				
Season	Club	Lea	GP	G	A	TP	PIM	GP	G	A	TP	PIM
1991-92	Phoenix	IHL	5	0	0	0	9	....	....	....	....	....
	Raleigh	ECHL	46	10	18	28	229	4	4	0	4	22
1992-93	**Hartford**	**NHL**	**2**	**0**	**0**	**0**	**2**	....	....	....	....	....
	Springfield	AHL	21	2	4	6	65	6	1	0	1	14
1993-94	Springfield	AHL	30	0	2	2	67	....	....	....	....	....
	Raleigh	ECHL	18	4	6	10	126	15	5	7	12	51
	NHL Totals		**2**	**0**	**0**	**0**	**2**	....	....	....	....	....

Signed as a free agent by **Hartford**, September 25, 1992.

NIEDERMAYER, ROB — (nee-duhr-MIGH-uhr) — FLA.

Center. Shoots left. 6'2", 200 lbs. Born, Cassiar, B.C., December 28, 1974.
(Florida's 1st choice, 5th overall, in 1993 Entry Draft).

			Regular Season					Playoffs				
Season	Club	Lea	GP	G	A	TP	PIM	GP	G	A	TP	PIM
1990-91	Medicine Hat	WHL	71	24	26	50	8	12	3	7	10	2
1991-92	Medicine Hat	WHL	71	32	46	78	77	4	2	3	5	2
1992-93a	Medicine Hat	WHL	52	43	34	77	67	....	....	....	....	....
1993-94	**Florida**	**NHL**	**65**	**9**	**17**	**26**	**51**	....	....	....	....	....
	NHL Totals		**65**	**9**	**17**	**26**	**51**	....	....	....	....	....

a WHL East First All-Star Team (1993)

NIEDERMAYER, SCOTT — (NEE-duhr-MIGH-uhr) — N.J.

Defense. Shoots left. 6', 200 lbs. Born, Edmonton, Alta., August 31, 1973.
(New Jersey's 1st choice, 3rd overall, in 1991 Entry Draft).

			Regular Season					Playoffs				
Season	Club	Lea	GP	G	A	TP	PIM	GP	G	A	TP	PIM
1989-90	Kamloops	WHL	64	14	55	69	64	17	2	14	16	35
1990-91ab	Kamloops	WHL	57	26	56	82	52	....	....	....	....	....
1991-92	**New Jersey**	**NHL**	**4**	**0**	**1**	**1**	**2**	....	....	....	....	....
acd	Kamloops	WHL	35	7	32	39	61	17	9	14	23	28
1992-93e	**New Jersey**	**NHL**	**80**	**11**	**29**	**40**	**47**	**5**	**0**	**3**	**3**	**2**
1993-94	**New Jersey**	**NHL**	**81**	**10**	**36**	**46**	**42**	**20**	**2**	**2**	**4**	**8**
	NHL Totals		**165**	**21**	**66**	**87**	**91**	**25**	**2**	**5**	**7**	**10**

a WHL West First All-Star Team (1991, 1992)
b Canadian Major Junior Scholastic Player of the Year (1991)
c Memorial Cup All-Star Team (1992)
d Won Stafford Smythe Memorial Trophy (Memorial Cup MVP) (1992)
e NHL/Upper Deck All-Rookie Team (1993)

NIELSEN, JEFF — NYR

Right wing. Shoots right. 6', 170 lbs. Born, Grand Rapids, MN, September 20, 1971.
(NY Rangers' 4th choice, 69th overall, in 1990 Entry Draft).

			Regular Season					Playoffs				
Season	Club	Lea	GP	G	A	TP	PIM	GP	G	A	TP	PIM
1990-91	U. Minnesota	WCHA	45	11	14	25	50	....	....	....	....	....
1991-92	U. Minnesota	WCHA	41	14	14	28	70	....	....	....	....	....
1992-93	U. Minnesota	WCHA	42	21	20	41	80	....	....	....	....	....
1993-94a	U. Minnesota	WCHA	41	29	16	45	94	....	....	....	....	....

a WCHA Second All-Star Team (1994)

NIELSEN, KIRK — PHI.

Right wing. Shoots right. 6'1", 190 lbs. Born, Grand Rapids, MN, October 19, 1973.
(Philadelphia's 1st choice, 10th overall, in 1994 Supplemental Draft).

			Regular Season					Playoffs				
Season	Club	Lea	GP	G	A	TP	PIM	GP	G	A	TP	PIM
1992-93	Harvard	ECAC	30	2	2	4	38	....	....	....	....	....
1993-94	Harvard	ECAC	32	6	9	15	41	....	....	....	....	....

NIEUWENDYK, JOE — (NOO-ihn-DIGHK) — CGY.

Center. Shoots left. 6'1", 195 lbs. Born, Oshawa, Ont., September 10, 1966.
(Calgary's 2nd choice, 27th overall, in 1985 Entry Draft).

			Regular Season					Playoffs				
Season	Club	Lea	GP	G	A	TP	PIM	GP	G	A	TP	PIM
1984-85	Cornell	ECAC	23	18	21	39	20	....	....	....	....	....
1985-86ab	Cornell	ECAC	21	21	21	42	45	....	....	....	....	....
1986-87ab	Cornell	ECAC	23	26	26	52	26	....	....	....	....	....
	Calgary	**NHL**	**9**	**5**	**1**	**6**	**0**	**6**	**2**	**2**	**4**	**0**
1987-88cde	**Calgary**	**NHL**	**75**	**51**	**41**	**92**	**23**	**8**	**3**	**4**	**7**	**2**
1988-89	**Calgary**	**NHL**	**77**	**51**	**31**	**82**	**40**	**22**	**10**	**4**	**14**	**10**
1989-90	**Calgary**	**NHL**	**79**	**45**	**50**	**95**	**40**	**6**	**4**	**6**	**10**	**4**
1990-91	**Calgary**	**NHL**	**79**	**45**	**40**	**85**	**36**	**7**	**4**	**1**	**5**	**10**
1991-92	**Calgary**	**NHL**	**69**	**22**	**34**	**56**	**55**	....	....	....	....	....
1992-93	**Calgary**	**NHL**	**79**	**38**	**37**	**75**	**52**	**6**	**3**	**6**	**9**	**10**
1993-94	**Calgary**	**NHL**	**64**	**36**	**39**	**75**	**51**	**6**	**2**	**2**	**4**	**0**
	NHL Totals		**531**	**293**	**273**	**566**	**297**	**61**	**28**	**25**	**53**	**36**

a NCAA East First All-American Team (1986, 1987)
b ECAC First All-Star Team (1986, 1987)
c Won Calder Memorial Trophy (1988)
d NHL All-Rookie Team (1988)
e Won Dodge Ram Tough Award (1988)

Played in NHL All-Star Game (1988-90, 1994)

NIINIMAA, JANNE — PHI.

Defense. Shoots left. 6'1", 196 lbs. Born, Raahe, Finland, May 22, 1975.
(Philadelphia's 1st choice, 36th overall, in 1993 Entry Draft).

			Regular Season					Playoffs				
Season	Club	Lea	GP	G	A	TP	PIM	GP	G	A	TP	PIM
1991-92	Karpat	Fin.2	41	2	11	13	49	....	....	....	....	....
1992-93	Karpat	Fin.2	29	2	3	5	14	....	....	....	....	....
1993-94	Jokerit	Fin.	45	3	8	11	24	12	1	1	2	4

NIKOLIC, ALEX

Left wing. Shoots left. 6'1", 200 lbs. Born, Sudbury, Ont., March 1, 1970.
(Calgary's 8th choice, 147th overall, in 1989 Entry Draft).

			Regular Season					Playoffs				
Season	Club	Lea	GP	G	A	TP	PIM	GP	G	A	TP	PIM
1988-89	Cornell	ECAC	13	0	3	3	31	....	....	....	....	....
1989-90	Cornell	ECAC	28	6	9	15	54	....	....	....	....	....
1990-91	Cornell	ECAC	15	4	3	7	16	....	....	....	....	....
1991-92	Cornell	ECAC	26	5	9	14	60	....	....	....	....	....
1992-93	Salt Lake	IHL	37	4	4	8	133	....	....	....	....	....
1993-94	Saint John	AHL	57	6	13	19	285	....	....	....	....	....

NIKOLISHIN, ANDREI — (nee-koh-LEE-shin) — HFD.

Left wing. Shoots left. 5'11", 180 lbs. Born, Vorkuta, USSR, March 25, 1973.
(Hartford's 2nd choice, 47th overall, in 1992 Entry Draft).

			Regular Season					Playoffs				
Season	Club	Lea	GP	G	A	TP	PIM	GP	G	A	TP	PIM
1990-91	Moscow D'amo	USSR	2	0	0	0	0	....	....	....	....	....
1991-92	Moscow D'amo	CIS	18	1	0	1	4	....	....	....	....	....
1992-93	Moscow D'amo	CIS	42	5	7	12	30	10	2	1	3	8
1993-94	Moscow D'amo	CIS	41	8	12	20	30	9	1	3	4	4

NIKOLOV, ANGEL — (NIH-koh-lohv) — S.J.

Defense. Shoots left. 6'1", 176 lbs. Born, Most, Czech., November 18, 1975.
(San Jose's 2nd choice, 37th overall, in 1994 Entry Draft).

			Regular Season					Playoffs				
Season	Club	Lea	GP	G	A	TP	PIM	GP	G	A	TP	PIM
1993-94	Litvinov	Czech.	10	2	2	4	....	3	0	0	0	....

NILSSON, FREDRIK — (NEEL-suhn) — S.J.

Center. Shoots left. 6'1", 200 lbs. Born, Stockholm, Sweden, April 16, 1971.
(San Jose's 7th choice, 111th overall, in 1991 Entry Draft).

			Regular Season					Playoffs				
Season	Club	Lea	GP	G	A	TP	PIM	GP	G	A	TP	PIM
1988-89	Vasteras	Swe.	1	0	0	0	0	....	....	....	....	....
1989-90	Vasteras	Swe.	23	1	1	2	4	1	0	0	0	0
1990-91	Vasteras	Swe.	35	13	7	20	20	4	0	1	1	2
1991-92	Vasteras	Swe.	40	5	14	19	40	....	....	....	....	....
1992-93	Vasteras	Swe.	40	14	15	29	69	1	1	1	2	0
1993-94	Kansas City	IHL	13	2	7	9	2	....	....	....	....	....

NOLAN, OWEN — QUE.

Right wing. Shoots right. 6'1", 201 lbs. Born, Belfast, Ireland, September 22, 1971.
(Quebec's 1st choice, 1st overall, in 1990 Entry Draft).

			Regular Season					Playoffs				
Season	Club	Lea	GP	G	A	TP	PIM	GP	G	A	TP	PIM
1988-89	Cornwall	OHL	62	34	25	59	213	18	5	11	16	41
1989-90a	Cornwall	OHL	58	51	59	110	240	6	7	5	12	26
1990-91	**Quebec**	**NHL**	**59**	**3**	**10**	**13**	**109**	....	....	....	....	....
	Halifax	AHL	6	4	4	8	11	....	....	....	....	....
1991-92	**Quebec**	**NHL**	**75**	**42**	**31**	**73**	**183**	....	....	....	....	....
1992-93	**Quebec**	**NHL**	**73**	**36**	**41**	**77**	**185**	**5**	**1**	**0**	**1**	**2**
1993-94	**Quebec**	**NHL**	**6**	**2**	**2**	**4**	**8**	....	....	....	....	....
	NHL Totals		**213**	**83**	**84**	**167**	**485**	**5**	**1**	**0**	**1**	**2**

a OHL First All-Star Team (1990)

Played in NHL All-Star Game (1992)

NOONAN, BRIAN — NYR

Right wing. Shoots right. 6'1", 200 lbs. Born, Boston, MA, May 29, 1965.
(Chicago's 10th choice, 179th overall, in 1983 Entry Draft).

			Regular Season					Playoffs				
Season	Club	Lea	GP	G	A	TP	PIM	GP	G	A	TP	PIM
1984-85	N. Westminster	WHL	72	50	66	116	76	11	8	7	15	4
1985-86	Nova Scotia	AHL	2	0	0	0	0	....	....	....	....	....
	Saginaw	IHL	76	39	39	78	69	11	6	3	9	6
1986-87	Nova Scotia	AHL	70	25	26	51	30	5	3	1	4	4
1987-88	**Chicago**	**NHL**	**77**	**10**	**20**	**30**	**44**	**3**	**0**	**0**	**0**	**4**
1988-89	**Chicago**	**NHL**	**45**	**4**	**12**	**16**	**28**	**1**	**0**	**0**	**0**	**0**
	Saginaw	IHL	19	18	13	31	36	1	0	0	0	0
1989-90	**Chicago**	**NHL**	**8**	**0**	**2**	**2**	**6**	....	....	....	....	....
a	Indianapolis	IHL	56	40	36	76	85	14	6	9	15	20
1990-91	**Chicago**	**NHL**	**7**	**0**	**4**	**4**	**2**	....	....	....	....	....
b	Indianapolis	IHL	59	38	53	91	67	7	6	4	10	18
1991-92	**Chicago**	**NHL**	**65**	**19**	**12**	**31**	**81**	**18**	**6**	**9**	**15**	**30**
1992-93	**Chicago**	**NHL**	**63**	**16**	**14**	**30**	**82**	**4**	**3**	**0**	**3**	**4**
1993-94	**Chicago**	**NHL**	**64**	**14**	**21**	**35**	**57**	....	....	....	....	....
	NY Rangers	**NHL**	**12**	**4**	**2**	**6**	**12**	**22**	**4**	**7**	**11**	**17**
	NHL Totals		**341**	**67**	**87**	**154**	**312**	**48**	**13**	**16**	**29**	**55**

a IHL Second All-Star Team (1990)
b IHL First All-Star Team (1991)

Traded to **NY Rangers** by **Chicago** with Stephane Matteau for Tony Amonte and the rights to Matt Oates, March 21, 1994.

NORRIS, CLAYTON — PHI.

Right wing. Shoots right. 6'2", 205 lbs. Born, Edmonton, Alta., March 8, 1972.
(Philadelphia's 6th choice, 116th overall, in 1991 Entry Draft).

			Regular Season					Playoffs				
Season	Club	Lea	GP	G	A	TP	PIM	GP	G	A	TP	PIM
1990-91	Medicine Hat	WHL	71	26	27	53	165	12	5	4	9	41
1991-92a	Medicine Hat	WHL	69	26	39	65	300	2	0	0	0	9
1992-93	Medicine Hat	WHL	41	21	16	37	128	10	3	2	5	14
	Hershey	AHL	4	0	0	0	5	....	....	....	....	....
	Roanoke	ECHL	4	0	0	0	0	....	....	....	....	....
1993-94	Hershey	AHL	62	8	10	18	217	10	1	0	1	18

a WHL East Second All-Star Team (1992)

NORRIS, DWAYNE — QUE.

Right wing. Shoots right. 5'10", 175 lbs. Born, St. John's, Nfld., January 8, 1970.
(Quebec's 5th choice, 127th overall, in 1990 Entry Draft).

			Regular Season					Playoffs				
Season	Club	Lea	GP	G	A	TP	PIM	GP	G	A	TP	PIM
1988-89	Michigan State	CCHA	40	16	21	37	32	....	....	....	....	....
1989-90	Michigan State	CCHA	33	18	25	43	30	....	....	....	....	....
1990-91	Michigan State	CCHA	40	26	25	51	60	....	....	....	....	....
1991-92ab	Michigan State	CCHA	41	40	38	78	58	....	....	....	....	....
1992-93	Halifax	AHL	50	25	28	53	62	....	....	....	....	....
1993-94	Cdn. National	....	48	18	14	32	22	....	....	....	....	....
	Cdn. Olympic	....	8	2	2	4	4	....	....	....	....	....
	Quebec	**NHL**	**4**	**1**	**1**	**2**	**4**	....	....	....	....	....
	Cornwall	AHL	9	2	9	11	0	13	7	4	11	17
	NHL Totals		**4**	**1**	**1**	**2**	**4**	....	....	....	....	....

a CCHA First All-Star Team (1992)
b NCAA West First All-American Team (1992)

NORSTROM, MATTIAS — NYR

Defense. Shoots left. 6'1", 205 lbs. Born, Mora, Sweden, January 2, 1972.
(NY Rangers' 2nd choice, 48th overall, in 1992 Entry Draft).

			Regular Season					Playoffs				
Season	Club	Lea	GP	G	A	TP	PIM	GP	G	A	TP	PIM
1991-92	AIK	Swe.	39	4	3	7	28	3	0	2	2	2
1992-93	AIK	Swe.	22	0	1	1	16	....	....	....	....	....
1993-94	**NY Rangers**	**NHL**	**9**	**0**	**2**	**2**	**6**	....	....	....	....	....
	Binghamton	AHL	55	1	9	10	70	....	....	....	....	....
	NHL Totals		**9**	**0**	**2**	**2**	**6**	....	....	....	....	....

NORTON, BRAD — EDM.

Defense. Shoots left. 6'4", 225 lbs. Born, Cambridge, MA, February 13, 1975.
(Edmonton's 9th choice, 215th overall, in 1993 Entry Draft).

			Regular Season					Playoffs				
Season	Club	Lea	GP	G	A	TP	PIM	GP	G	A	TP	PIM
1992-93	Cushing	HS	31	10	26	36	....	....	....	....	....	....
1993-94	Cushing	HS				UNAVAILABLE						

NORTON, JEFF — S.J.

Defense. Shoots left. 6'2", 190 lbs. Born, Acton, MA, November 25, 1965.
(NY Islanders' 3rd choice, 62nd overall, in 1984 Entry Draft).

			Regular Season					Playoffs				
Season	Club	Lea	GP	G	A	TP	PIM	GP	G	A	TP	PIM
1984-85	U. of Michigan	CCHA	37	8	16	24	103	....	....	....	....	....
1985-86	U. of Michigan	CCHA	37	15	30	45	99	....	....	....	....	....
1986-87a	U. of Michigan	CCHA	39	12	36	48	92	....	....	....	....	....
1987-88	U.S. National	....	54	7	22	29	52	....	....	....	....	....
	U.S. Olympic	....	6	0	4	4	4	....	....	....	....	....
	NY Islanders	**NHL**	**15**	**1**	**6**	**7**	**14**	**3**	**0**	**2**	**2**	**13**
1988-89	**NY Islanders**	**NHL**	**69**	**1**	**30**	**31**	**74**	....	....	....	....	....
1989-90	**NY Islanders**	**NHL**	**60**	**4**	**49**	**53**	**65**	**4**	**1**	**3**	**4**	**17**
1990-91	**NY Islanders**	**NHL**	**44**	**3**	**25**	**28**	**16**	....	....	....	....	....
1991-92	**NY Islanders**	**NHL**	**28**	**1**	**18**	**19**	**18**	....	....	....	....	....
1992-93	**NY Islanders**	**NHL**	**66**	**12**	**38**	**50**	**45**	**10**	**1**	**1**	**2**	**4**
1993-94	**San Jose**	**NHL**	**64**	**7**	**33**	**40**	**36**	**14**	**1**	**5**	**6**	**20**
	NHL Totals		**346**	**29**	**199**	**228**	**268**	**31**	**3**	**11**	**14**	**54**

a CCHA Second All-Star Team (1987)

Traded to **San Jose** by **NY Islanders** for San Jose's third round choice (Jason Strudwick) in 1994 Entry Draft, June 20, 1993.

NORTON, STEVE

Defense. Shoots left. 6'3", 210 lbs. Born, Mississauga, Ont., February 29, 1972.
(Boston's 9th choice, 216th overall, in 1991 Entry Draft).

			Regular Season					Playoffs				
Season	Club	Lea	GP	G	A	TP	PIM	GP	G	A	TP	PIM
1990-91	Michigan State	CCHA	39	1	4	5	42	....	....	....	....	....
1991-92	Michigan State	CCHA	41	0	6	6	36	....	....	....	....	....
1992-93	Michigan State	CCHA	40	2	9	11	58	....	....	....	....	....
1993-94	Michigan State	CCHA	23	0	3	3	36	....	....	....	....	....

NORWOOD, LEE

Defense. Shoots left. 6'1", 198 lbs. Born, Oakland, CA, February 2, 1960.
(Quebec's 3rd choice, 62nd overall, in 1979 Entry Draft).

			Regular Season					Playoffs				
Season	Club	Lea	GP	G	A	TP	PIM	GP	G	A	TP	PIM
1978-79	Oshawa	OHA	61	23	38	61	171	5	2	2	4	17
1979-80	Oshawa	OHA	60	13	39	52	143	6	2	7	9	15
1980-81	**Quebec**	**NHL**	**11**	**1**	**1**	**2**	**9**	**3**	**0**	**0**	**0**	**2**
	Hershey	AHL	52	11	32	43	78	8	0	4	4	14
1981-82	**Quebec**	**NHL**	**2**	**0**	**0**	**0**	**2**	....	....	....	....	....
	Fredericton	AHL	29	6	13	19	74	....	....	....	....	....
	Washington	**NHL**	**26**	**7**	**10**	**17**	**125**	....	....	....	....	....
1982-83	**Washington**	**NHL**	**8**	**0**	**1**	**1**	**14**	....	....	....	....	....
	Hershey	AHL	67	12	36	48	90	5	0	1	1	2
1983-84	St. Catharines	AHL	75	13	46	59	91	7	0	5	5	31
1984-85ab	Peoria	IHL	80	17	60	77	229	18	1	11	12	62
1985-86	**St. Louis**	**NHL**	**71**	**5**	**24**	**29**	**134**	**19**	**2**	**7**	**9**	**64**
1986-87	**Detroit**	**NHL**	**57**	**6**	**21**	**27**	**163**	**16**	**1**	**6**	**7**	**31**
	Adirondack	AHL	3	0	3	3	0	....	....	....	....	....
1987-88	**Detroit**	**NHL**	**51**	**9**	**22**	**31**	**131**	**16**	**2**	**6**	**8**	**40**
1988-89	**Detroit**	**NHL**	**66**	**10**	**32**	**42**	**100**	**6**	**1**	**2**	**3**	**16**
1989-90	**Detroit**	**NHL**	**64**	**8**	**14**	**22**	**95**	....	....	....	....	....
1990-91	**Detroit**	**NHL**	**21**	**3**	**7**	**10**	**50**	....	....	....	....	....
	New Jersey	**NHL**	**28**	**3**	**2**	**5**	**87**	**4**	**0**	**0**	**0**	**18**
1991-92	**Hartford**	**NHL**	**6**	**0**	**0**	**0**	**16**	....	....	....	....	....
	St. Louis	**NHL**	**44**	**3**	**11**	**14**	**94**	**1**	**0**	**1**	**1**	**0**
1992-93	**St. Louis**	**NHL**	**32**	**3**	**7**	**10**	**63**	....	....	....	....	....
1993-94	**Calgary**	**NHL**	**16**	**0**	**1**	**1**	**16**	....	....	....	....	....
	San Diego	IHL	4	0	0	0	0	8	0	1	1	11
	NHL Totals		**503**	**58**	**153**	**211**	**1099**	**65**	**6**	**22**	**28**	**171**

a Won Governors' Trophy (Top Defenseman - IHL) (1985)
b IHL First All-Star Team (1985)

Traded to **Washington** by **Quebec** for Tim Tookey and Washington's seventh round choice (Daniel Poudrier) in 1982 Entry Draft, February 1, 1982. Traded to **Toronto** by **Washington** for Dave Shand, October 6, 1983. Signed as a free agent by **St. Louis**, August 13, 1985. Traded to **Detroit** by **St. Louis** for Larry Trader, August 7, 1986. Traded to **New Jersey** by **Detroit** with Detroit's fourth round choice (Scott McCabe) in 1992 Entry Draft for Paul Ysebaert, November 27, 1990. Traded to **Hartford** by **New Jersey** for Hartford's fifth round choice (John Guirestante) in 1993 Entry Draft, October 3, 1991. Traded to **St. Louis** by **Hartford** for St. Louis' fifth round choice (Nolan Pratt) in 1993 Entry Draft, November 13, 1991. Signed as a free agent by **Calgary**, October 22, 1993.

NUMMINEN, TEEMU — (NOO-mih-nehn)

Center. Shoots left. 6'3", 194 lbs. Born, Tampere, Finland, December 23, 1973.
(Winnipeg's 10th choice, 229th overall, in 1992 Entry Draft).

			Regular Season					Playoffs				
Season	Club	Lea	GP	G	A	TP	PIM	GP	G	A	TP	PIM
1992-93	Tappara	Fin.	7	0	0	0	0	....	....	....	....	....
1993-94	Tappara	Fin.	41	1	2	3	4	5	0	0	0	0

NUMMINEN, TEPPO — (NOO-mih-nehn, TEH-poh) WPG.

Defense. Shoots right. 6'1", 190 lbs. Born, Tampere, Finland, July 3, 1968.
(Winnipeg's 2nd choice, 29th overall, in 1986 Entry Draft).

			Regular Season					Playoffs				
Season	Club	Lea	GP	G	A	TP	PIM	GP	G	A	TP	PIM
1985-86	Tappara	Fin.	31	2	4	6	6	8	0	0	0	0
1986-87	Tappara	Fin.	44	9	9	18	16	9	4	1	5	4
1987-88	Tappara	Fin.	40	10	10	20	29	10	6	6	12	6
1988-89	**Winnipeg**	**NHL**	**69**	**1**	**14**	**15**	**36**	....	....	....	....	....
1989-90	**Winnipeg**	**NHL**	**79**	**11**	**32**	**43**	**20**	**7**	**1**	**2**	**3**	**10**
1990-91	**Winnipeg**	**NHL**	**80**	**8**	**25**	**33**	**28**	....	....	....	....	....
1991-92	**Winnipeg**	**NHL**	**80**	**5**	**34**	**39**	**32**	**7**	**0**	**0**	**0**	**0**
1992-93	**Winnipeg**	**NHL**	**66**	**7**	**30**	**37**	**33**	**6**	**1**	**1**	**2**	**2**
1993-94	**Winnipeg**	**NHL**	**57**	**5**	**18**	**23**	**28**	....	....	....	....	....
	NHL Totals		**431**	**37**	**153**	**190**	**177**	**20**	**2**	**3**	**5**	**12**

NUUTINEN, SAMI — EDM.

Defense. Shoots left. 6'1", 189 lbs. Born, Espoo, Finland, June 11, 1971.
(Edmonton's 11th choice, 248th overall, in 1990 Entry Draft).

			Regular Season					Playoffs				
Season	Club	Lea	GP	G	A	TP	PIM	GP	G	A	TP	PIM
1988-89	Espoo	Fin. 2	39	18	10	28	46	....	....	....	....	....
1989-90	Espoo	Fin. 2	40	8	15	23		....	....	....	....	....
1990-91	K-Kissat	Fin. 2	3	1	0	1	0	....	....	....	....	....
	HIFK	Fin.	27	1	3	4	6	3	0	0	0	0
1991-92	HIFK	Fin.	44	5	6	11	10	9	0	1	1	4
1992-93	Kiekko-Espoo	Fin.	48	7	11	18	59	....	....	....	....	....
1993-94	Kiekko-Espoo	Fin.	46	9	15	24	36	....	....	....	....	....

NYLANDER, MICHAEL — (NEE-lan-duhr) CGY.

Center. Shoots left. 5'11", 190 lbs. Born, Stockholm, Sweden, October 3, 1972.
(Hartford's 4th choice, 59th overall, in 1991 Entry Draft).

			Regular Season					Playoffs				
Season	Club	Lea	GP	G	A	TP	PIM	GP	G	A	TP	PIM
1989-90	Huddinge	Swe. 2	31	7	15	22	4	....	....	....	....	....
1990-91	Huddinge	Swe. 2	33	14	20	34	10	....	....	....	....	....
1991-92	AIK	Swe.	40	11	17	28	30	3	1	4	5	4
1992-93	**Hartford**	**NHL**	**59**	**11**	**22**	**33**	**36**	....	....	....	....	....
	Springfield	AHL	....	....	....	....	....	3	3	3	6	2
1993-94	**Hartford**	**NHL**	**58**	**11**	**33**	**44**	**24**	....	....	....	....	....
	Springfield	AHL	4	0	9	9	0	....	....	....	....	....
	Calgary	**NHL**	**15**	**2**	**9**	**11**	**6**	**3**	**0**	**0**	**0**	**0**
	NHL Totals		**132**	**24**	**64**	**88**	**66**	**3**	**0**	**0**	**0**	**0**

Traded to **Calgary** by **Hartford** with James Patrick and Zarley Zalapski for Gary Suter, Paul Ranheim and Ted Drury, March 10, 1994.

OATES, ADAM — BOS.

Center. Shoots right. 5'11", 185 lbs. Born, Weston, Ont., August 27, 1962.

			Regular Season					Playoffs				
Season	Club	Lea	GP	G	A	TP	PIM	GP	G	A	TP	PIM
1982-83	RPI	ECAC	22	9	33	42	8	....	....	....	....	....
1983-84	RPI	ECAC	38	26	57	83	15	....	....	....	....	....
1984-85ab	RPI	ECAC	38	31	60	91	29	....	....	....	....	....
1985-86	**Detroit**	**NHL**	**38**	**9**	**11**	**20**	**10**	....	....	....	....	....
	Adirondack	AHL	34	18	28	46	4	17	7	14	21	4
1986-87	**Detroit**	**NHL**	**76**	**15**	**32**	**47**	**21**	**16**	**4**	**7**	**11**	**6**
1987-88	**Detroit**	**NHL**	**63**	**14**	**40**	**54**	**20**	**16**	**8**	**12**	**20**	**6**
1988-89	**Detroit**	**NHL**	**69**	**16**	**62**	**78**	**14**	**6**	**0**	**8**	**8**	**2**
1989-90	**St. Louis**	**NHL**	**80**	**23**	**79**	**102**	**30**	**12**	**2**	**12**	**14**	**4**
1990-91c	**St. Louis**	**NHL**	**61**	**25**	**90**	**115**	**29**	**13**	**7**	**13**	**20**	**10**
1991-92	**St. Louis**	**NHL**	**54**	**10**	**59**	**69**	**12**	....	....	....	....	....
	Boston	**NHL**	**26**	**10**	**20**	**30**	**10**	**15**	**5**	**14**	**19**	**4**
1992-93	**Boston**	**NHL**	**84**	**45**	***97**	**142**	**32**	**4**	**0**	**9**	**9**	**4**
1993-94	**Boston**	**NHL**	**77**	**32**	**80**	**112**	**45**	**13**	**3**	**9**	**12**	**8**
	NHL Totals		**628**	**199**	**570**	**769**	**223**	**95**	**29**	**84**	**113**	**44**

a ECAC First All-Star Team (1985)
b NCAA East First All-American Team (1985)
c NHL Second All-Star Team (1991)

Played in NHL All-Star Game (1991-94)

Signed as a free agent by **Detroit**, June 28, 1985. Traded to **St. Louis** by **Detroit** with Paul MacLean for Bernie Federko and Tony McKegney, June 15, 1989. Traded to **Boston** by **St. Louis** for Craig Janney and Stephane Quintal, February 7, 1992.

OATES, MATT — CHI.

Left wing. Shoots left. 6'3", 208 lbs. Born, Evanston, IL, December 20, 1972.
(NY Rangers' 7th choice, 168th overall, in 1992 Entry Draft).

			Regular Season					Playoffs				
Season	Club	Lea	GP	G	A	TP	PIM	GP	G	A	TP	PIM
1991-92	Miami-Ohio	CCHA	40	8	13	21	23	....	....	....	....	....
1992-93	Miami-Ohio	CCHA	38	11	14	25	82	....	....	....	....	....
1993-94	Miami-Ohio	CCHA	33	14	12	26	60	....	....	....	....	....

Rights traded to **Chicago** by **NY Rangers** with Tony Amonte for Stephane Matteau and Brian Noonan, March 21, 1994.

O'BRIEN, JAMES

Defense. Shoots left. 6', 190 lbs. Born, Stoney Creek, Ont., May 8, 1970.
(Calgary's 1st choice, 6th overall, in 1992 Supplemental Draft).

			Regular Season					Playoffs				
Season	Club	Lea	GP	G	A	TP	PIM	GP	G	A	TP	PIM
1989-90	Brown	ECAC	29	3	12	15	78	....	....	....	....	....
1990-91	Brown	ECAC	25	3	8	11	50	....	....	....	....	....
1991-92	Brown	ECAC	28	3	11	14	61	....	....	....	....	....
1992-93	Brown	ECAC	26	5	10	15	60	....	....	....	....	....
1993-94	Saint John	AHL	52	6	11	17	41	4	0	0	0	0

O'CONNELL, ALBERT — NYI

Left wing. Shoots left. 6', 188 lbs. Born, Cambridge, MA, May 20, 1976.
(NY Islanders' 6th choice, 116th overall, in 1994 Entry Draft).

			Regular Season					Playoffs				
Season	Club	Lea	GP	G	A	TP	PIM	GP	G	A	TP	PIM
1992-93	St. Sebastian's	HS	23	7	15	22	15	....	....	....	....	....
1993-94	St. Sebastian's	HS	24	16	23	39	26	....	....	....	....	....

O'CONNOR, MYLES — ANA.

Defense. Shoots left. 5'11", 190 lbs. Born, Calgary, Alta., April 2, 1967.
(New Jersey's 4th choice, 45th overall, in 1985 Entry Draft).

			Regular Season					Playoffs				
Season	Club	Lea	GP	G	A	TP	PIM	GP	G	A	TP	PIM
1985-86	U. of Michigan	CCHA	37	6	19	25	73	....	....	....	....	....
	Cdn. National	....	8	0	0	0	0	....	....	....	....	....
1986-87	U. of Michigan	CCHA	39	15	39	54	111	....	....	....	....	....
1987-88	U. of Michigan	CCHA	40	9	25	34	78	....	....	....	....	....
1988-89ab	U. of Michigan	CCHA	40	3	31	34	91	....	....	....	....	....
	Utica	AHL	1	0	0	0	0	....	....	....	....	....
1989-90	Utica	AHL	76	14	33	47	124	5	1	2	3	26
1990-91	**New Jersey**	**NHL**	**22**	**3**	**1**	**4**	**41**	....	....	....	....	....
	Utica	AHL	33	6	17	23	62	....	....	....	....	....
1991-92	**New Jersey**	**NHL**	**9**	**0**	**2**	**2**	**13**	....	....	....	....	....
	Utica	AHL	66	9	39	48	184	....	....	....	....	....
1992-93	**New Jersey**	**NHL**	**7**	**0**	**0**	**0**	**9**	....	....	....	....	....
	Utica	AHL	9	1	5	6	10	....	....	....	....	....
1993-94	**Anaheim**	**NHL**	**5**	**0**	**1**	**1**	**6**	....	....	....	....	....
	San Diego	IHL	39	1	13	14	117	9	1	4	5	83
	NHL Totals		**43**	**3**	**4**	**7**	**69**	....	....	....	....	....

a CCHA First All-Star Team (1989)
b NCAA West First All-American Team (1989)

Signed as a free agent by **Anaheim**, July 22, 1993.

O'CONNOR, THOMAS — PIT.

Defense. Shoots left. 6'2", 190 lbs. Born, Springfield, MA, January 9, 1976.
(Pittsburgh's 6th choice, 102nd overall, in 1994 Entry Draft).

			Regular Season					Playoffs				
Season	Club	Lea	GP	G	A	TP	PIM	GP	G	A	TP	PIM
1992-93	Springfield	Jr. B	42	11	19	30	40	....	....	....	....	....
1993-94	Springfield	NEJHL	36	4	15	19	73	....	....	....	....	....

ODELEIN, LYLE — (OH-duh-LIGHN) — MTL.

Defense. Shoots right. 5'10", 206 lbs. Born, Quill Lake, Sask., July 21, 1968.
(Montreal's 8th choice, 141st overall, in 1986 Entry Draft).

			Regular Season					Playoffs				
Season	Club	Lea	GP	G	A	TP	PIM	GP	G	A	TP	PIM
1985-86	Moose Jaw	WHL	67	9	37	46	117	13	1	6	7	34
1986-87	Moose Jaw	WHL	59	9	50	59	70	9	2	5	7	26
1987-88	Moose Jaw	WHL	63	15	43	58	166	....	....	....	....	....
1988-89	Sherbrooke	AHL	33	3	4	7	120	3	0	2	2	5
	Peoria	IHL	36	2	8	10	116	....	....	....	....	....
1989-90	**Montreal**	**NHL**	**8**	**0**	**2**	**2**	**33**	....	....	....	....	....
	Sherbrooke	AHL	68	7	24	31	265	12	6	5	11	79
1990-91	**Montreal**	**NHL**	**52**	**0**	**2**	**2**	**259**	**12**	**0**	**0**	**0**	**54**
1991-92	**Montreal**	**NHL**	**71**	**1**	**7**	**8**	**212**	**7**	**0**	**0**	**0**	**11**
1992-93	**Montreal**	**NHL**	**83**	**2**	**14**	**16**	**205**	**20**	**1**	**5**	**6**	**30**
1993-94	**Montreal**	**NHL**	**79**	**11**	**29**	**40**	**276**	**7**	**0**	**0**	**0**	**17**
	NHL Totals		**293**	**14**	**54**	**68**	**985**	**46**	**1**	**5**	**6**	**112**

ODGERS, JEFF — S.J.

Right wing. Shoots right. 6', 195 lbs. Born, Spy Hill, Sask., May 31, 1969.

			Regular Season					Playoffs				
Season	Club	Lea	GP	G	A	TP	PIM	GP	G	A	TP	PIM
1988-89	Brandon	WHL	71	31	29	60	277	....	....	....	....	....
1989-90	Brandon	WHL	64	37	28	65	209	....	....	....	....	....
1990-91	Kansas City	IHL	77	12	19	31	318	....	....	....	....	....
1991-92	**San Jose**	**NHL**	**61**	**7**	**4**	**11**	**217**	....	....	....	....	....
	Kansas City	IHL	12	2	2	4	56	4	2	1	3	0
1992-93	**San Jose**	**NHL**	**66**	**12**	**15**	**27**	**253**	....	....	....	....	....
1993-94	**San Jose**	**NHL**	**81**	**13**	**8**	**21**	**222**	**11**	**0**	**0**	**0**	**11**
	NHL Totals		**208**	**32**	**27**	**59**	**692**	**11**	**0**	**0**	**0**	**11**

Signed as a free agent by **San Jose**, September 3, 1991.

ODJICK, GINO — (OH-jihk) — VAN.

Left wing. Shoots left. 6'3", 210 lbs. Born, Maniwaki, Que., September 7, 1970.
(Vancouver's 5th choice, 86th overall, in 1990 Entry Draft).

			Regular Season					Playoffs				
Season	Club	Lea	GP	G	A	TP	PIM	GP	G	A	TP	PIM
1988-89	Laval	QMJHL	50	9	15	24	278	16	0	9	9	129
1989-90	Laval	QMJHL	51	12	26	38	280	....	....	....	....	....
1990-91	**Vancouver**	**NHL**	**45**	**7**	**1**	**8**	**296**	**6**	**0**	**0**	**0**	**18**
	Milwaukee	IHL	17	7	3	10	102	....	....	....	....	....
1991-92	**Vancouver**	**NHL**	**65**	**4**	**6**	**10**	**348**	**4**	**0**	**0**	**0**	**6**
1992-93	**Vancouver**	**NHL**	**75**	**4**	**13**	**17**	**370**	**1**	**0**	**0**	**0**	**0**
1993-94	**Vancouver**	**NHL**	**76**	**16**	**13**	**29**	**271**	**10**	**0**	**0**	**0**	**18**
	NHL Totals		**261**	**31**	**33**	**64**	**1285**	**21**	**0**	**0**	**0**	**42**

O'DONNELL, SEAN — L.A.

Defense. Shoots left. 6'2", 224 lbs. Born, Ottawa, Ont., October 13, 1971.
(Buffalo's 6th choice, 123rd overall, in 1991 Entry Draft).

			Regular Season					Playoffs				
Season	Club	Lea	GP	G	A	TP	PIM	GP	G	A	TP	PIM
1990-91	Sudbury	OHL	66	8	23	31	114	5	1	4	5	10
1991-92	Rochester	AHL	73	4	9	13	193	16	1	2	3	21
1992-93	Rochester	AHL	74	3	18	21	203	17	1	6	7	38
1993-94	Rochester	AHL	64	2	10	12	242	4	0	1	1	21

Traded to **Los Angeles** by **Buffalo** for Doug Houda, July 26, 1994.

ODUYA, FREDRIK — S.J.

Defense. Shoots left. 6'2", 185 lbs. Born, Stockholm, Sweden, May 31, 1975.
(San Jose's 8th choice, 154th overall, in 1993 Entry Draft).

			Regular Season					Playoffs				
Season	Club	Lea	GP	G	A	TP	PIM	GP	G	A	TP	PIM
1992-93	Guelph	OHL	23	2	4	6	29	....	....	....	....	....
	Ottawa	OHL	17	0	3	3	70	....	....	....	....	....
1993-94	Ottawa	OHL	51	11	12	23	181	17	0	3	3	22

OHLUND, MATTIAS — (EH-luhnd) — VAN.

Defense. Shoots left. 6'3", 209 lbs. Born, Pitea, Sweden, September 9, 1976.
(Vancouver's 1st choice, 13th overall, in 1994 Entry Draft).

			Regular Season					Playoffs				
Season	Club	Lea	GP	G	A	TP	PIM	GP	G	A	TP	PIM
1992-93	Pitea	Swe. 2	22	0	6	6	16	....	....	....	....	....
1993-94	Pitea	Swe. 2	28	7	10	17	62	....	....	....	....	....

OKSIUTA, ROMAN — (ohk-SEW-tah) — EDM.

Right wing. Shoots left. 6'3", 229 lbs. Born, Murmansk, USSR, August 21, 1970.
(NY Rangers' 11th choice, 202nd overall, in 1989 Entry Draft).

			Regular Season					Playoffs				
Season	Club	Lea	GP	G	A	TP	PIM	GP	G	A	TP	PIM
1987-88	Khimik	USSR	11	1	0	1	4	....	....	....	....	....
1988-89	Khimik	USSR	34	13	3	16	14	....	....	....	....	....
1989-90	Khimik	USSR	37	13	6	19	16	....	....	....	....	....
1990-91	Khimik	USSR	41	12	8	20	24	....	....	....	....	....
1991-92	Khimik	CIS	42	24	20	44	28	....	....	....	....	....
1992-93	Khimik	CIS	20	11	2	13	42	....	....	....	....	....
	Cape Breton	AHL	43	26	25	51	22	16	9	19	28	12
1993-94	**Edmonton**	**NHL**	**10**	**1**	**2**	**3**	**4**	....	....	....	....	....
	Cape Breton	AHL	47	31	22	53	90	4	2	2	4	22
	NHL Totals		**10**	**1**	**2**	**3**	**4**	....	....	....	....	....

Traded to **Edmonton** by **NY Rangers** with NY Rangers' third round choice (Alexander Kerch) in 1993 Entry Draft for Kevin Lowe, December 11, 1992.

OKTYABREV, ARTUR — VAN.

Defense. Shoots left. 5'11", 183 lbs. Born, Irkutsk, USSR, November 26, 1973.
(Winnipeg's 6th choice, 155th overall, in 1992 Entry Draft).

			Regular Season					Playoffs				
Season	Club	Lea	GP	G	A	TP	PIM	GP	G	A	TP	PIM
1991-92	CSKA	CIS	38	1	2	3	19	....	....	....	....	....
1992-93	CSKA	CIS	41	0	5	5	44	....	....	....	....	....
1993-94	CSKA	CIS	45	1	1	2	46	3	0	0	0	4
	Russian Pen's	IHL	10	0	2	2	12	....	....	....	....	....

Traded to **Vancouver** by **Winnipeg** for Vancouver's sixth round choice (Steve Vezina) in 1994 Entry Draft, June 29, 1994.

OLAUSSON, FREDRIK — (OHL-ah-suhn) — EDM.

Defense. Shoots right. 6'2", 195 lbs. Born, Dadesjo, Sweden, October 5, 1966.
(Winnipeg's 4th choice, 81st overall, in 1985 Entry Draft).

			Regular Season					Playoffs				
Season	Club	Lea	GP	G	A	TP	PIM	GP	G	A	TP	PIM
1982-83	Nybro	Swe. 2	31	4	4	8	12	....	....	....	....	....
1983-84	Nybro	Swe. 2	28	8	14	22	32	....	....	....	....	....
1984-85	Farjestad	Swe.	29	5	12	17	22	3	1	0	1	0
1985-86	Farjestad	Swe.	33	4	12	16	22	8	3	2	5	6
1986-87	**Winnipeg**	**NHL**	**72**	**7**	**29**	**36**	**24**	**10**	**2**	**3**	**5**	**4**
1987-88	**Winnipeg**	**NHL**	**38**	**5**	**10**	**15**	**18**	**5**	**1**	**1**	**2**	**0**
1988-89	**Winnipeg**	**NHL**	**75**	**15**	**47**	**62**	**32**	....	....	....	....	....
1989-90	**Winnipeg**	**NHL**	**77**	**9**	**46**	**55**	**32**	**7**	**0**	**2**	**2**	**2**
1990-91	**Winnipeg**	**NHL**	**71**	**12**	**29**	**41**	**24**	....	....	....	....	....
1991-92	**Winnipeg**	**NHL**	**77**	**20**	**42**	**62**	**34**	**7**	**1**	**5**	**6**	**4**
1992-93	**Winnipeg**	**NHL**	**68**	**16**	**41**	**57**	**22**	**6**	**0**	**2**	**2**	**2**
1993-94	**Winnipeg**	**NHL**	**18**	**2**	**5**	**7**	**10**	....	....	....	....	....
	Edmonton	**NHL**	**55**	**9**	**19**	**28**	**20**	....	....	....	....	....
	NHL Totals		**551**	**95**	**268**	**363**	**216**	**35**	**4**	**13**	**17**	**12**

Traded to **Edmonton** by **Winnipeg** with Winnipeg's seventh round choice (Curtis Sheptak) in 1994 Entry Draft for Edmonton's third round choice (Tavis Hansen) in 1994 Entry Draft, December 6, 1993.

OLCZYK, EDDIE (OHL-chehk) NYR

Center. Shoots left. 6'1", 205 lbs. Born, Chicago, IL, August 16, 1966.
(Chicago's 1st choice, 3rd overall, in 1984 Entry Draft).

			Regular Season					Playoffs				
Season	Club	Lea	GP	G	A	TP	PIM	GP	G	A	TP	PIM
1983-84	U.S. National	....	62	21	47	68	36	....	....	....	....	....
1984-85	**Chicago**	**NHL**	**70**	**20**	**30**	**50**	**67**	**15**	**6**	**5**	**11**	**11**
1985-86	**Chicago**	**NHL**	**79**	**29**	**50**	**79**	**47**	**3**	**0**	**0**	**0**	**0**
1986-87	**Chicago**	**NHL**	**79**	**16**	**35**	**51**	**119**	**4**	**1**	**1**	**2**	**4**
1987-88	**Toronto**	**NHL**	**80**	**42**	**33**	**75**	**55**	**6**	**5**	**4**	**9**	**2**
1988-89	**Toronto**	**NHL**	**80**	**38**	**52**	**90**	**75**	....	....	....	....	....
1989-90	**Toronto**	**NHL**	**79**	**32**	**56**	**88**	**78**	**5**	**1**	**2**	**3**	**14**
1990-91	**Toronto**	**NHL**	**18**	**4**	**10**	**14**	**13**	....	....	....	....	....
	Winnipeg	**NHL**	**61**	**26**	**31**	**57**	**69**	....	....	....	....	....
1991-92	**Winnipeg**	**NHL**	**64**	**32**	**33**	**65**	**67**	**6**	**2**	**1**	**3**	**4**
1992-93	**Winnipeg**	**NHL**	**25**	**8**	**12**	**20**	**26**	....	....	....	....	....
	NY Rangers	**NHL**	**46**	**13**	**16**	**29**	**26**	....	....	....	....	....
1993-94	**NY Rangers**	**NHL**	**37**	**3**	**5**	**8**	**28**	**1**	**0**	**0**	**0**	**0**
	NHL Totals		**718**	**263**	**363**	**626**	**670**	**40**	**15**	**13**	**28**	**35**

Traded to **Toronto** by **Chicago** with Al Secord for Rick Vaive, Steve Thomas and Bob McGill, September 3, 1987. Traded to **Winnipeg** by **Toronto** with Mark Osborne for Dave Ellett and Paul Fenton, November 10, 1990. Traded to **NY Rangers** by **Winnipeg** for Kris King and Tie Domi, December 28, 1992.

OLIVER, DAVID EDM.

Right wing. Shoots right. 5'11", 185 lbs. Born, Sechelt, B.C., April 17, 1971.
(Edmonton's 7th choice, 144th overall, in 1991 Entry Draft).

			Regular Season					Playoffs				
Season	Club	Lea	GP	G	A	TP	PIM	GP	G	A	TP	PIM
1990-91	U. of Michigan	CCHA	27	13	11	24	34	....	....	....	....	....
1991-92	U. of Michigan	CCHA	44	31	27	58	32	....	....	....	....	....
1992-93a	U. of Michigan	CCHA	40	35	20	55	18	....	....	....	....	....
1993-94bc	U. of Michigan	CCHA	41	28	40	68	16	....	....	....	....	....

a CCHA Second All-Star Team (1993)
b CCHA First All-Star Team (1994)
c NCAA West First All-American Team (1994)

OLIWA, KRZYSZTOF (oh-LEE-vuh, KHRIH-stahf) N.J.

Left wing. Shoots left. 6'5", 220 lbs. Born, Tychy, Poland, April 12, 1973.
(New Jersey's 4th choice, 65th overall, in 1993 Entry Draft).

			Regular Season					Playoffs				
Season	Club	Lea	GP	G	A	TP	PIM	GP	G	A	TP	PIM
1991-92	GKS Tychy	Poland	10	3	7	10	6	....	....	....	....	....
1992-93	Welland	Jr.B	30	13	21	34	127	....	....	....	....	....
1993-94	Albany	AHL	33	2	4	6	151	....	....	....	....	....
	Raleigh	ECHL	15	0	2	2	65	9	0	0	0	35

OLSEN, DARRYL

Defense. Shoots left. 6', 180 lbs. Born, Calgary, Alta., October 7, 1966.
(Calgary's 10th choice, 185th overall, in 1985 Entry Draft).

			Regular Season					Playoffs				
Season	Club	Lea	GP	G	A	TP	PIM	GP	G	A	TP	PIM
1985-86	N. Michigan	WCHA	37	5	20	25	46	....	....	....	....	....
1986-87	N. Michigan	WCHA	37	5	20	25	96	....	....	....	....	....
1987-88	N. Michigan	WCHA	35	11	20	31	59	....	....	....	....	....
1988-89	Cdn. National	....	3	1	0	1	4	....	....	....	....	....
ab	N. Michigan	WCHA	45	16	26	42	88	....	....	....	....	....
1989-90	Salt Lake	IHL	72	16	50	66	90	11	3	6	9	2
1990-91	Salt Lake	IHL	76	15	40	55	89	4	1	5	6	2
1991-92	**Calgary**	**NHL**	**1**	**0**	**0**	**0**	**0**	....	....	....	....	....
	Salt Lake	IHL	59	7	33	40	80	5	2	1	3	4
1992-93	Providence	AHL	50	7	27	34	38	....	....	....	....	....
	San Diego	IHL	21	2	8	10	26	10	1	3	4	30
1993-94	Salt Lake	IHL	73	17	32	49	97	....	....	....	....	....
	NHL Totals		**1**	**0**	**0**	**0**	**0**	....	....	....	....	....

a NCAA West Second All-American Team (1989)
b WCHA First All-Star Team (1989)

Signed as a free agent by **Boston**, July 23, 1992.

OLSSON, CHRISTER (OOL-suhn) ST.L.

Defense. Shoots left. 5'11", 187 lbs. Born, Arboga, Sweden, July 24, 1970.
(St. Louis' 10th choice, 275th overall, in 1993 Entry Draft).

			Regular Season					Playoffs				
Season	Club	Lea	GP	G	A	TP	PIM	GP	G	A	TP	PIM
1991-92	Mora	Swe. 2	36	6	10	16	38	....	....	....	....	....
1992-93	Brynas	Swe.	22	4	4	8	18	....	....	....	....	....
1993-94	Brynas	Swe.	38	7	3	10	50	7	0	3	3	6

OLSSON, MATTIAS L.A.

Defense. Shoots right. 6'1", 191 lbs. Born, Karlstad, Sweden, April 1, 1971.
(Los Angeles' 10th choice, 218th overall, in 1991 Entry Draft).

			Regular Season					Playoffs				
Season	Club	Lea	GP	G	A	TP	PIM	GP	G	A	TP	PIM
1988-89	Farjestad	Swe.	4	1	1	2	2	....	....	....	....	....
1989-90	Farjestad	Swe.	33	2	8	10	18	10	0	2	2	2
1990-91	Farjestad	Swe.	36	3	7	10	22	8	0	0	0	8
1991-92	Farjestad	Swe.	40	5	11	16	28	6	0	0	0	4
1992-93	Farjestad	Swe.	35	6	6	12	26	3	0	1	1	0
1993-94	Farjestad	Swe.	21	1	7	8	10	....	....	....	....	....

OLYMPIJEV, SERGEI

Left wing. Shoots left. 6'1", 189 lbs. Born, Minsk, USSR, January 12, 1975.
(NY Rangers' 4th choice, 86th overall, in 1993 Entry Draft).

			Regular Season					Playoffs				
Season	Club	Lea	GP	G	A	TP	PIM	GP	G	A	TP	PIM
1991-92	Lipetsk	CIS 3	20	0	0	0	2	....	....	....	....	....
1992-93	Minsk Dynamo	CIS	6	1	0	1	2	....	....	....	....	....
1993-94	Ottawa	OHL	20	3	5	8	4	....	....	....	....	....
	Kitchener	OHL	21	6	5	11	24	5	0	0	0	0

O'NEILL, JEFF HFD.

Center. Shoots right. 6'1", 183 lbs. Born, Richmond Hill, Ont., February 23, 1976.
(Hartford's 1st choice, 5th overall, in 1994 Entry Draft).

			Regular Season					Playoffs				
Season	Club	Lea	GP	G	A	TP	PIM	GP	G	A	TP	PIM
1992-93	Guelph	OHL	65	32	47	79	88	5	2	2	4	6
1993-94	Guelph	OHL	66	45	81	126	95	9	2	11	13	31

O'ROURKE, STEVE

Right wing. Shoots right. 6', 190 lbs. Born, Calgary, Alta., September 11, 1974.
(NY Islanders' 7th choice, 159th overall, in 1992 Entry Draft).

			Regular Season					Playoffs				
Season	Club	Lea	GP	G	A	TP	PIM	GP	G	A	TP	PIM
1991-92	Tri-City	WHL	42	3	9	12	45	2	0	1	1	2
1992-93	Tri-City	WHL	61	3	17	20	104	3	0	2	2	2
1993-94	Moose Jaw	WHL	12	0	3	3	11	....	....	....	....	....

OSADCHY, ALEXANDER (oh-SAHD-chee) S.J.

Defense. Shoots right. 5'11", 190 lbs. Born, Kharkov, USSR, July 19, 1975.
(San Jose's 5th choice, 80th overall, in 1993 Entry Draft).

			Regular Season					Playoffs				
Season	Club	Lea	GP	G	A	TP	PIM	GP	G	A	TP	PIM
1992-93	CSKA	CIS	37	0	1	1	60	....	....	....	....	....
1993-94	CSKA	CIS	46	5	2	7	33	3	0	0	0	0

OSBORNE, MARK (AWS-born)

Left wing. Shoots left. 6'2", 205 lbs. Born, Toronto, Ont., August 13, 1961.
(Detroit's 2nd choice, 46th overall, in 1980 Entry Draft).

			Regular Season					Playoffs				
Season	Club	Lea	GP	G	A	TP	PIM	GP	G	A	TP	PIM
1979-80	Niagara Falls	OHA	52	10	33	43	104	10	2	1	3	23
1980-81	Niagara Falls	OHA	54	39	41	80	140	12	11	10	21	20
	Adirondack	AHL	....	....	....	....	....	13	2	3	5	2
1981-82	**Detroit**	**NHL**	**80**	**26**	**41**	**67**	**61**	....	....	....	....	....
1982-83	**Detroit**	**NHL**	**80**	**19**	**24**	**43**	**83**	....	....	....	....	....
1983-84	**NY Rangers**	**NHL**	**73**	**23**	**28**	**51**	**88**	**5**	**0**	**1**	**1**	**7**
1984-85	**NY Rangers**	**NHL**	**23**	**4**	**4**	**8**	**33**	**3**	**0**	**0**	**0**	**4**
1985-86	**NY Rangers**	**NHL**	**62**	**16**	**24**	**40**	**80**	**15**	**2**	**3**	**5**	**26**
1986-87	**NY Rangers**	**NHL**	**58**	**17**	**15**	**32**	**101**	....	....	....	....	....
	Toronto	**NHL**	**16**	**5**	**10**	**15**	**12**	**9**	**1**	**3**	**4**	**6**
1987-88	**Toronto**	**NHL**	**79**	**23**	**37**	**60**	**102**	**6**	**1**	**3**	**4**	**16**
1988-89	**Toronto**	**NHL**	**75**	**16**	**30**	**46**	**112**	....	....	....	....	....
1989-90	**Toronto**	**NHL**	**78**	**23**	**50**	**73**	**91**	**5**	**2**	**3**	**5**	**12**
1990-91	**Toronto**	**NHL**	**18**	**3**	**3**	**6**	**4**	....	....	....	....	....
	Winnipeg	**NHL**	**37**	**8**	**8**	**16**	**59**	....	....	....	....	....
1991-92	**Winnipeg**	**NHL**	**43**	**4**	**12**	**16**	**65**	....	....	....	....	....
	Toronto	**NHL**	**11**	**3**	**1**	**4**	**8**	....	....	....	....	....
1992-93	**Toronto**	**NHL**	**76**	**12**	**14**	**26**	**89**	**19**	**1**	**1**	**2**	**16**
1993-94	**Toronto**	**NHL**	**73**	**9**	**15**	**24**	**145**	**18**	**4**	**2**	**6**	**52**
	NHL Totals		**882**	**211**	**316**	**527**	**1133**	**80**	**11**	**16**	**27**	**139**

Traded to **NY Rangers** by **Detroit** with Willie Huber and Mike Blaisdell for Ron Duguay, Eddie Mio and Eddie Johnstone, June 13, 1983. Traded to **Toronto** by **NY Rangers** for Jeff Jackson and Toronto's third round choice (Rod Zamuner) in 1989 Entry Draft, March 5, 1987. Traded to **Winnipeg** by **Toronto** with Ed Olcyk for Dave Ellett and Paul Fenton, November 10, 1990. Traded to **Toronto** by **Winnipeg** for Lucien Deblois, March 10, 1992.

OSIECKI, MARK

Defense. Shoots right. 6'2", 200 lbs. Born, St. Paul, MN, July 23, 1968.
(Calgary's 10th choice, 187th overall, in 1987 Entry Draft).

			Regular Season					Playoffs				
Season	Club	Lea	GP	G	A	TP	PIM	GP	G	A	TP	PIM
1986-87	U. Wisconsin	WCHA	8	0	1	1	4	....	....	....	....	....
1987-88	U. Wisconsin	WCHA	18	0	1	1	22	....	....	....	....	....
1988-89	U. Wisconsin	WCHA	44	1	3	4	56	....	....	....	....	....
1989-90a	U. Wisconsin	WCHA	46	5	38	43	78	....	....	....	....	....
1990-91	Salt Lake	IHL	75	1	24	25	36	4	2	0	2	2
1991-92	**Calgary**	**NHL**	**50**	**2**	**7**	**9**	**24**	....	....	....	....	....
	Salt Lake	IHL	1	0	0	0	0	....	....	....	....	....
1992-93	**Ottawa**	**NHL**	**34**	**0**	**4**	**4**	**12**	....	....	....	....	....
	New Haven	AHL	4	0	1	1	0	....	....	....	....	....
	Winnipeg	**NHL**	**4**	**1**	**0**	**1**	**2**	....	....	....	....	....
	Minnesota	**NHL**	**5**	**0**	**0**	**0**	**5**	....	....	....	....	....
1993-94	Kalamazoo	IHL	65	4	14	18	45	5	0	0	0	5
	NHL Totals		**93**	**3**	**11**	**14**	**43**	....	....	....	....	....

a NCAA All-Tournament Team (1990)

Traded to **Ottawa** by **Calgary** for Chris Lindberg, June 22, 1992. Claimed on waivers by **Winnipeg** from **Ottawa**, February 20, 1993. Traded to **Minnesota** by **Winnipeg** with Winnipeg's tenth round choice (Bill Lang) in 1993 Entry Draft for Minnesota's ninth round choice (Vladimir Potatov) in 1993 Entry Draft, March 20, 1993.

OSMAK, COREY HFD.

Center. Shoots left. 5'11", 173 lbs. Born, Edmonton, Alta., August 20, 1970.
(Hartford's 8th choice, 183rd overall, in 1990 Entry Draft).

			Regular Season					Playoffs				
Season	Club	Lea	GP	G	A	TP	PIM	GP	G	A	TP	PIM
1990-91	Minn.-Duluth	WCHA	22	3	0	3	34	....	....	....	....	....
1991-92	Minn.-Duluth	WCHA	26	1	4	5	58	....	....	....	....	....
1992-93	Minn.-Duluth	WCHA	39	11	15	26	86	....	....	....	....	....
1993-94	Minn.-Duluth	WCHA	34	11	7	18	78	....	....	....	....	....

O'SULLIVAN, CHRIS CGY.

Defense. Shoots left. 6'2", 185 lbs. Born, Dorchester, MA, May 15, 1974.
(Calgary's 2nd choice, 30th overall, in 1992 Entry Draft).

			Regular Season					Playoffs				
Season	Club	Lea	GP	G	A	TP	PIM	GP	G	A	TP	PIM
1992-93	Boston U.	H.E.	5	0	2	2	4	....	....	....	....	....
1993-94	Boston U.	H.E.	32	5	18	23	25	....	....	....	....	....

O'SULLIVAN, KEVIN MTL.

Defense. Shoots left. 6', 197 lbs. Born, Dorchester, MA, November 13, 1970.
(NY Islanders' 7th choice, 99th overall, in 1989 Entry Draft).

			Regular Season					Playoffs				
Season	Club	Lea	GP	G	A	TP	PIM	GP	G	A	TP	PIM
1989-90	Boston U.	H.E.	43	0	6	6	42	....	....	....	....	....
1990-91	Boston U.	H.E.	37	4	7	11	50	....	....	....	....	....
1991-92a	Boston U.	H.E.	32	3	18	21	62	....	....	....	....	....
1992-93b	Boston U.	H.E.	40	5	20	25	78	....	....	....	....	....
1993-94	Fredericton	AHL	62	2	11	13	73	....	....	....	....	....

a Hockey East Second All-Star Team (1992)
b Hockey East First All-Star Team (1993)

Signed as a free agent by **Montreal**, September 15, 1993.

OTEVREL, JAROSLAV (oh-TEHV-rehl)

Left wing. Shoots left. 6'3", 215 lbs. Born, Gottwaldov, Czech., September 16, 1968.
(San Jose's 8th choice, 133rd overall, in 1991 Entry Draft).

Season	Club	Lea	Regular Season GP	G	A	TP	PIM	Playoffs GP	G	A	TP	PIM
1987-88	TJ Gottwaldov	Czech.	32	4	7	11	18	....	....	....	....	....
1988-89	TJ Gottwaldov	Czech.	40	14	6	20	37	....	....	....	....	....
1989-90	Dukla Trencin	Czech.	43	7	10	17	20	....	....	....	....	....
1990-91	TJ Zlin	Czech.	49	24	26	50	105	....	....	....	....	....
1991-92	ZPS Zlin	Czech.	40	14	15	29	44	....	....	....	....	....
1992-93	**San Jose**	**NHL**	**7**	**0**	**2**	**2**	**0**	....	....	....	....	....
	Kansas City	IHL	62	17	27	44	58	6	1	4	5	4
1993-94	**San Jose**	**NHL**	**9**	**3**	**2**	**5**	**2**	....	....	....	....	....
	Kansas City	IHL	62	20	33	53	46	....	....	....	....	....
	NHL Totals		**16**	**3**	**4**	**7**	**2**	....	....	....	....	....

OTTO, JOEL — CGY.

Center. Shoots right. 6'4", 220 lbs. Born, Elk River, MN, October 29, 1961.

Season	Club	Lea	Regular Season GP	G	A	TP	PIM	Playoffs GP	G	A	TP	PIM
1980-81	Bemidji State	NCAA	23	5	11	16	10	....	....	....	....	....
1981-82	Bemidji State	NCAA	31	19	33	52	24	....	....	....	....	....
1982-83	Bemidji State	NCAA	37	33	28	61	68	....	....	....	....	....
1983-84	Bemidji State	NCAA	31	32	43	75	32	....	....	....	....	....
1984-85	**Calgary**	**NHL**	**17**	**4**	**8**	**12**	**30**	**3**	**2**	**1**	**3**	**10**
	Moncton	AHL	56	27	36	63	89	....	....	....	....	....
1985-86	**Calgary**	**NHL**	**79**	**25**	**34**	**59**	**188**	**22**	**5**	**10**	**15**	**80**
1986-87	**Calgary**	**NHL**	**68**	**19**	**31**	**50**	**185**	**2**	**0**	**2**	**2**	**6**
1987-88	**Calgary**	**NHL**	**62**	**13**	**39**	**52**	**194**	**9**	**3**	**2**	**5**	**26**
1988-89	**Calgary**	**NHL**	**72**	**23**	**30**	**53**	**213**	**22**	**6**	**13**	**19**	**46**
1989-90	**Calgary**	**NHL**	**75**	**13**	**20**	**33**	**116**	**6**	**2**	**2**	**4**	**2**
1990-91	**Calgary**	**NHL**	**76**	**19**	**20**	**39**	**183**	**7**	**1**	**2**	**3**	**8**
1991-92	**Calgary**	**NHL**	**78**	**13**	**21**	**34**	**161**	....	....	....	....	....
1992-93	**Calgary**	**NHL**	**75**	**19**	**33**	**52**	**150**	**6**	**4**	**2**	**6**	**4**
1993-94	**Calgary**	**NHL**	**81**	**11**	**12**	**23**	**92**	**3**	**0**	**1**	**1**	**4**
	NHL Totals		**683**	**159**	**248**	**407**	**1512**	**80**	**23**	**35**	**58**	**186**

Signed as a free agent by **Calgary,** September 11, 1984.

OZOLINSH, SANDIS (OH-zoh-LIHNCH, SAN-dihz) S.J.

Defense. Shoots left. 6'1", 195 lbs. Born, Riga, Latvia, August 3, 1972.
(San Jose's 3rd choice, 30th overall, in 1991 Entry Draft).

Season	Club	Lea	Regular Season GP	G	A	TP	PIM	Playoffs GP	G	A	TP	PIM
1990-91	Riga	USSR	44	0	3	3	51	....	....	....	....	....
1991-92	Riga	CIS	30	6	0	6	42	....	....	....	....	....
	Kansas City	IHL	34	6	9	15	20	15	2	5	7	22
1992-93	**San Jose**	**NHL**	**37**	**7**	**16**	**23**	**40**	....	....	....	....	....
1993-94	**San Jose**	**NHL**	**81**	**26**	**38**	**64**	**24**	**14**	**0**	**10**	**10**	**8**
	NHL Totals		**118**	**33**	**54**	**87**	**64**	**14**	**0**	**10**	**10**	**8**

Played in NHL All-Star Game (1994)

PADEN, KEVIN — EDM.

Center/Left wing. Shoots left. 6'3", 175 lbs. Born, Woodhaven, MI, February 12, 1975.
(Edmonton's 4th choice, 59th overall, in 1993 Entry Draft).

Season	Club	Lea	Regular Season GP	G	A	TP	PIM	Playoffs GP	G	A	TP	PIM
1992-93	Detroit	OHL	54	14	9	23	41	15	1	1	2	2
1993-94	Detroit	OHL	38	10	19	29	54	....	....	....	....	....
	Windsor	OHL	24	8	11	19	30	4	0	1	1	4

PAEK, JIM (PAK) OTT.

Defense. Shoots left. 6'1", 195 lbs. Born, Seoul, South Korea, April 7, 1967.
(Pittsburgh's 9th choice, 170th overall, in 1985 Entry Draft).

Season	Club	Lea	Regular Season GP	G	A	TP	PIM	Playoffs GP	G	A	TP	PIM
1984-85	Oshawa	OHL	54	2	13	15	57	5	1	0	1	9
1985-86	Oshawa	OHL	64	5	21	26	122	6	0	1	1	9
1986-87	Oshawa	OHL	57	5	17	22	75	26	1	14	15	43
1987-88	Muskegon	IHL	82	7	52	59	141	6	0	0	0	29
1988-89	Muskegon	IHL	80	3	54	57	96	14	1	10	11	24
1989-90	Muskegon	IHL	81	9	41	50	115	15	1	10	11	41
1990-91	Cdn. National	....	48	2	12	14	24	....	....	....	....	....
	Pittsburgh	**NHL**	**3**	**0**	**0**	**0**	**9**	**8**	**1**	**0**	**1**	**2**
1991-92	**Pittsburgh**	**NHL**	**49**	**1**	**7**	**8**	**36**	**19**	**0**	**4**	**4**	**6**
1992-93	**Pittsburgh**	**NHL**	**77**	**3**	**15**	**18**	**64**	....	....	....	....	....
1993-94	**Pittsburgh**	**NHL**	**41**	**0**	**4**	**4**	**8**	....	....	....	....	....
	Los Angeles	**NHL**	**18**	**1**	**1**	**2**	**10**	....	....	....	....	....
	NHL Totals		**188**	**5**	**27**	**32**	**127**	**27**	**1**	**4**	**5**	**8**

Traded to **Los Angeles** by **Pittsburgh** with Marty McSorley for Tomas Sandstrom and Shawn McEachern, February 16, 1994. Traded to **Ottawa** by **Los Angeles** for future considerations, June 26, 1994.

PALFFY, ZIGMUND (PAHL-fee) NYI

Left wing. Shoots left. 5'10", 169 lbs. Born, Skalica, Czech., May 5, 1972.
(NY Islanders' 2nd choice, 26th overall, in 1991 Entry Draft).

Season	Club	Lea	Regular Season GP	G	A	TP	PIM	Playoffs GP	G	A	TP	PIM
1990-91	Nitra	Czech.	50	34	16	50	18	....	....	....	....	....
1991-92	Dukla Trencin	Czech.	45	41	33	74	36	....	....	....	....	....
1992-93	Dukla Trencin	Czech.	43	38	41	79	....	....	....	....	....	....
1993-94	**NY Islanders**	**NHL**	**5**	**0**	**0**	**0**	**0**	....	....	....	....	....
	Salt Lake	IHL	57	25	32	57	83	....	....	....	....	....
	NHL Totals		**5**	**0**	**0**	**0**	**0**	....	....	....	....	....

PANDOLFO, JAY — N.J.

Left wing. Shoots left. 6'1", 195 lbs. Born, Winchester, MA, December 27, 1974.
(New Jersey's 2nd choice, 32nd overall, in 1993 Entry Draft).

Season	Club	Lea	Regular Season GP	G	A	TP	PIM	Playoffs GP	G	A	TP	PIM
1992-93	Boston U.	H.E.	37	16	22	38	16	....	....	....	....	....
1993-94	Boston U.	H.E.	37	17	25	42	27	....	....	....	....	....

PANKEWICZ, GREG — OTT.

Right wing. Shoots right. 6', 185 lbs. Born, Drayton Valley, Alta., October 6, 1970.

Season	Club	Lea	Regular Season GP	G	A	TP	PIM	Playoffs GP	G	A	TP	PIM
1989-90	Regina	WHL	63	14	24	38	136	10	1	3	4	19
1990-91	Regina	WHL	72	39	41	80	134	8	4	7	11	12
1991-92	Knoxville	ECHL	59	41	39	80	214	....	....	....	....	....
1992-93	New Haven	AHL	62	23	20	43	163	....	....	....	....	....
1993-94	**Ottawa**	**NHL**	**3**	**0**	**0**	**0**	**2**	....	....	....	....	....
	PEI	AHL	69	33	29	62	241	....	....	....	....	....
	NHL Totals		**3**	**0**	**0**	**0**	**2**	....	....	....	....	....

Signed as a free agent by **Ottawa**, May 27, 1993.

PANTELEEV, GRIGORI (pan-teh-LAY-ehv) BOS.

Left wing. Shoots left. 5'9", 190 lbs. Born, Gastello, USSR, November 13, 1972.
(Boston's 5th choice, 136th overall, in 1992 Entry Draft).

Season	Club	Lea	Regular Season GP	G	A	TP	PIM	Playoffs GP	G	A	TP	PIM
1990-91	Riga	USSR	23	4	1	5	4	....	....	....	....	....
1991-92	Riga	CIS	26	4	8	12	4	....	....	....	....	....
1992-93	**Boston**	**NHL**	**39**	**8**	**6**	**14**	**12**	....	....	....	....	....
	Providence	AHL	39	17	30	47	22	3	0	0	0	10
1993-94	**Boston**	**NHL**	**10**	**0**	**0**	**0**	**0**	....	....	....	....	....
	Providence	AHL	55	24	26	50	20	....	....	....	....	....
	NHL Totals		**49**	**8**	**6**	**14**	**12**	....	....	....	....	....

PAQUETTE, CHARLES — BOS.

Defense. Shoots left. 6'1", 193 lbs. Born, Lachute, Que., June 17, 1975.
(Boston's 3rd choice, 88th overall, in 1993 Entry Draft).

Season	Club	Lea	Regular Season GP	G	A	TP	PIM	Playoffs GP	G	A	TP	PIM
1991-92	Trois-Rivieres	QMJHL	60	1	7	8	101	6	0	0	0	2
1992-93	Sherbrooke	QMJHL	54	2	5	7	104	15	0	0	0	33
1993-94	Sherbrooke	QMJHL	63	5	14	19	165	8	0	2	2	15

PAQUIN, PATRICE — PHI.

Left wing. Shoots left. 6'2", 192 lbs. Born, St. Jerome, Que., June 26, 1974.
(Philadelphia's 11th choice, 247th overall, in 1992 Entry Draft).

Season	Club	Lea	Regular Season GP	G	A	TP	PIM	Playoffs GP	G	A	TP	PIM
1991-92	Beauport	QMJHL	60	10	15	25	169	....	....	....	....	....
1992-93	Beauport	QMJHL	59	17	23	40	271	....	....	....	....	....
1993-94	Beauport	QMJHL	45	22	24	46	188	15	1	7	8	39

PARK, RICHARD — PIT.

Center. Shoots right. 5'11", 176 lbs. Born, Seoul, S. Korea, May 27, 1976.
(Pittsburgh's 2nd choice, 50th overall, in 1994 Entry Draft).

Season	Club	Lea	Regular Season GP	G	A	TP	PIM	Playoffs GP	G	A	TP	PIM
1992-93	Belleville	OHL	66	23	38	61	38	5	0	0	0	14
1993-94	Belleville	OHL	59	27	49	76	70	12	3	5	8	18

PARKS, GREG

Center. Shoots right. 5'9", 180 lbs. Born, Edmonton, Alta., March 25, 1967.

Season	Club	Lea	Regular Season GP	G	A	TP	PIM	Playoffs GP	G	A	TP	PIM
1985-86	Bowling Green	CCHA	41	16	26	42	43	....	....	....	....	....
1986-87	Bowling Green	CCHA	45	23	27	50	52	....	....	....	....	....
1987-88	Bowling Green	CCHA	45	30	44	74	84	....	....	....	....	....
1988-89a	Bowling Green	CCHA	47	32	42	74	98	....	....	....	....	....
1989-90	Springfield	AHL	49	22	32	54	30	18	9	*13	*22	22
	Johnstown	ECHL	8	5	9	14	7	....	....	....	....	....
1990-91	**NY Islanders**	**NHL**	**20**	**1**	**2**	**3**	**4**	....	....	....	....	....
	Capital Dist.	AHL	48	32	43	75	67	....	....	....	....	....
1991-92	**NY Islanders**	**NHL**	**1**	**0**	**0**	**0**	**2**	....	....	....	....	....
	Capital Dist.	AHL	70	36	57	93	84	7	5	8	13	4
1992-93	Leksand	Swe.	39	21	19	40	66	1	0	0	0	4
	Cdn. National	....	9	2	2	4	4	....	....	....	....	....
	NY Islanders	**NHL**	**2**	**0**	**0**	**0**	**0**	**2**	**0**	**0**	**0**	**0**
1993-94	Leksand	Swe.	39	21	18	39	44	....	....	....	....	....
	Cdn. National	....	13	1	1	2	112	....	....	....	....	....
	Cdn. Olympic	....	8	1	2	3	10	....	....	....	....	....
	NHL Totals		**23**	**1**	**2**	**3**	**6**	**2**	**0**	**0**	**0**	**0**

a NCAA West First All-Star Team (1989)

Signed as a free agent by **NY Islanders**, August 13, 1990.

PARROTT, JEFF — QUE.

Defense. Shoots right. 6'1", 195 lbs. Born, The Pas, Man., April 6, 1971.
(Quebec's 4th choice, 106th overall, in 1990 Entry Draft).

Season	Club	Lea	Regular Season GP	G	A	TP	PIM	Playoffs GP	G	A	TP	PIM
1989-90	Minn.-Duluth	WCHA	35	1	5	6	60	....	....	....	....	....
1990-91	Minn.-Duluth	WCHA	39	2	8	10	65	....	....	....	....	....
1991-92	Minn.-Duluth	WCHA	33	1	8	9	78	....	....	....	....	....
1992-93	Minn. Duluth	WCHA	39	4	13	17	116	....	....	....	....	....
1993-94	Cornwall	AHL	52	4	11	15	37	....	....	....	....	....

PARSON, STEVE — OTT.

Left wing. Shoots left. 6', 180 lbs. Born, Elmira, Ont., March 14, 1973.

Season	Club	Lea	Regular Season GP	G	A	TP	PIM	Playoffs GP	G	A	TP	PIM
1989-90	Owen Sound	OHL	58	13	12	25	51	12	1	0	1	14
1990-91	Owen Sound	OHL	63	23	31	54	34	....	....	....	....	....
1991-92	Owen Sound	OHL	27	10	17	27	19	....	....	....	....	....
	Kingston	OHL	39	18	20	38	24	....	....	....	....	....
1992-93	Kingston	OHL	66	28	55	83	62	16	11	11	22	18
1993-94	Kingston	OHL	64	35	63	98	70	2	0	3	3	0

Signed as a free agent by **Ottawa**, June 9, 1994.

PASLAWSKI, GREG (pas-LAW-skee)

Right wing. Shoots right. 5'11", 190 lbs. Born, Kindersley, Sask., August 25, 1961.

			Regular Season					Playoffs				
Season	Club	Lea	GP	G	A	TP	PIM	GP	G	A	TP	PIM
1980-81	Prince Albert	SJHL	59	55	60	115	106	....	....	....	....	....
1981-82	Nova Scotia	AHL	43	15	11	26	31	....	....	....	....	....
1982-83	Nova Scotia	AHL	75	46	42	88	32	6	1	3	4	8
1983-84	Montreal	NHL	26	1	4	5	4	....	....	....	....	....
	St. Louis	NHL	34	8	6	14	17	9	1	0	1	2
1984-85	St. Louis	NHL	72	22	20	42	21	3	0	0	0	2
1985-86	St. Louis	NHL	56	22	11	33	18	17	10	7	17	13
1986-87	St. Louis	NHL	76	29	35	64	27	6	1	1	2	4
1987-88	St. Louis	NHL	17	2	1	3	4	3	1	1	2	2
1988-89	St. Louis	NHL	75	26	26	52	18	9	2	1	3	2
1989-90	Winnipeg	NHL	71	18	30	48	14	7	1	3	4	0
1990-91	Winnipeg	NHL	43	9	10	19	10	....	....	....	....	....
	Buffalo	NHL	12	2	1	3	4	....	....	....	....	....
1991-92	Quebec	NHL	80	28	17	45	18	....	....	....	....	....
1992-93	Philadelphia	NHL	60	14	19	33	12	....	....	....	....	....
	Calgary	NHL	13	4	5	9	0	6	3	0	3	0
1993-94	Calgary	NHL	15	2	0	2	2	....	....	....	....	....
	Peoria	IHL	29	16	16	32	12	6	3	3	6	0
	NHL Totals		650	187	185	372	169	60	19	13	32	25

Signed as a free agent by **Montreal**, October 5, 1981. Traded to **St. Louis** by **Montreal** with Gilbert Delorme and Doug Wickenheiser for Perry Turnbull, December 21, 1983. Traded to **Winnipeg** by **St. Louis** with St. Louis' third round choice (Kris Draper) in 1989 Entry Draft for Winnipeg's third round choice (Denny Felsner) in 1989 Entry Draft and second round choice (Steve Staios) in 1991 Entry Draft, June 17, 1989. Traded to **Buffalo** by **Winnipeg** for future considerations, February 4, 1991. Claimed by **San Jose** from **Buffalo** in Expansion Draft, May 30, 1991. Traded to **Quebec** by **San Jose** for Tony Hrkac, May 31, 1991. Signed as a free agent by **Philadelphia**, August 25, 1992. Traded to **Calgary** by **Philadelphia** for Calgary's ninth round choice (E.J. Bradley) in 1993 Entry Draft, March 18, 1993.

PATRICK, JAMES — CGY.

Defense. Shoots right. 6'2", 198 lbs. Born, Winnipeg, Man., June 14, 1963.
(NY Rangers' 1st choice, 9th overall, in 1981 Entry Draft).

			Regular Season					Playoffs				
Season	Club	Lea	GP	G	A	TP	PIM	GP	G	A	TP	PIM
1981-82ab	North Dakota	WCHA	42	5	24	29	26	....	....	....	....	....
1982-83cd	North Dakota	WCHA	36	12	36	48	29	....	....	....	....	....
1983-84	Cdn. National	....	63	7	24	31	52	....	....	....	....	....
	Cdn. Olympic	....	7	0	3	3	4	....	....	....	....	....
	NY Rangers	NHL	12	1	7	8	2	5	0	3	3	2
1984-85	NY Rangers	NHL	75	8	28	36	71	3	0	0	0	4
1985-86	NY Rangers	NHL	75	14	29	43	88	16	1	5	6	34
1986-87	NY Rangers	NHL	78	10	45	55	62	6	1	2	3	2
1987-88	NY Rangers	NHL	70	17	45	62	52	....	....	....	....	....
1988-89	NY Rangers	NHL	68	11	36	47	41	4	0	1	1	2
1989-90	NY Rangers	NHL	73	14	43	57	50	10	3	8	11	0
1990-91	NY Rangers	NHL	74	10	49	59	58	6	0	0	0	6
1991-92	NY Rangers	NHL	80	14	57	71	54	13	0	7	7	12
1992-93	NY Rangers	NHL	60	5	21	26	61	....	....	....	....	....
1993-94	NY Rangers	NHL	6	0	3	3	2	....	....	....	....	....
	Hartford	NHL	47	8	20	28	32	....	....	....	....	....
	Calgary	NHL	15	2	2	4	6	7	0	1	1	6
	NHL Totals		733	114	385	499	579	70	5	27	32	68

a WCHA Second All-Star Team (1982)
b NCAA Final Four All-Tournament Team (1982)
c WCHA First All-Star Team (1983)
d NCAA West All-American Team (1983)

Traded to **Hartford** by **NY Rangers** with Darren Turcotte for Steve Larmer, Nick Kypreos, Barry Richter and Hartford's sixth round choice (Yuri Litvinov) in 1994 Entry Draft, November 2, 1993. Traded to **Calgary** by **Hartford** with Zarley Zalapski and Michael Nylander for Gary Suter, Paul Ranheim and Ted Drury, March 10, 1994.

PATTERSON, ED — PIT.

Right wing. Shoots right. 6'2", 213 lbs. Born, Delta, B.C., November 14, 1972.
(Pittsburgh's 7th choice, 148th overall, in 1991 Entry Draft).

			Regular Season					Playoffs				
Season	Club	Lea	GP	G	A	TP	PIM	GP	G	A	TP	PIM
1990-91	Swift Current	WHL	7	2	7	9	0	....	....	....	....	....
	Kamloops	WHL	55	14	33	47	134	5	0	0	0	7
1991-92	Kamloops	WHL	38	19	25	44	120	1	0	0	0	0
1992-93	Cleveland	IHL	63	4	16	20	131	3	1	1	2	2
1993-94	Pittsburgh	NHL	27	3	1	4	10	....	....	....	....	....
	Cleveland	IHL	55	21	32	53	73	....	....	....	....	....
	NHL Totals		27	3	1	4	10	....	....	....	....	....

PAYNTER, KENT

Defense. Shoots left. 6', 183 lbs. Born, Summerside, P.E.I., April 17, 1965.
(Chicago's 9th choice, 159th overall, in 1983 Entry Draft).

			Regular Season					Playoffs				
Season	Club	Lea	GP	G	A	TP	PIM	GP	G	A	TP	PIM
1982-83	Kitchener	OHL	65	4	11	15	97	12	1	0	1	20
1983-84	Kitchener	OHL	65	9	27	36	94	16	4	9	13	18
1984-85	Kitchener	OHL	58	7	28	35	93	4	2	1	3	4
1985-86	Nova Scotia	AHL	23	1	2	3	36	....	....	....	....	....
	Saginaw	IHL	4	0	1	1	2	....	....	....	....	....
1986-87	Nova Scotia	AHL	66	2	6	8	57	2	0	0	0	0
1987-88	Chicago	NHL	2	0	0	0	2	....	....	....	....	....
	Saginaw	IHL	74	8	20	28	141	10	0	1	1	30
1988-89	Chicago	NHL	1	0	0	0	2	....	....	....	....	....
	Saginaw	IHL	69	12	14	26	148	6	2	2	4	17
1989-90	Washington	NHL	13	1	2	3	18	3	0	0	0	10
	Baltimore	AHL	60	7	20	27	110	11	5	6	1	34
1990-91	Washington	NHL	1	0	0	0	15	1	0	0	0	0
	Baltimore	AHL	43	10	17	27	64	6	2	1	3	8
1991-92	Winnipeg	NHL	5	0	0	0	4	....	....	....	....	....
	Moncton	AHL	62	3	30	33	71	11	2	6	8	25
1992-93	Ottawa	NHL	6	0	0	0	20	....	....	....	....	....
	New Haven	AHL	48	7	17	24	81	....	....	....	....	....
1993-94	Ottawa	NHL	9	0	1	1	8	....	....	....	....	....
	PEI	AHL	63	6	20	26	125	....	....	....	....	....
	NHL Totals		37	1	3	4	69	4	0	0	0	10

Signed as a free agent by **Washington**, August 21, 1989. Traded to **Winnipeg** by **Washington** with Tyler Larter and Bob Joyce for Craig Duncanson, Brent Hughes and Simon Wheeldon, May 21, 1991. Claimed by **Ottawa** from **Winnipeg** in Expansion Draft, June 18, 1992.

PEACOCK, SHANE

Defense. Shoots right. 5'10", 198 lbs. Born, Winterburn, Alta., July 7, 1973.
(Pittsburgh's 3rd choice, 60th overall, in 1991 Entry Draft).

			Regular Season					Playoffs				
Season	Club	Lea	GP	G	A	TP	PIM	GP	G	A	TP	PIM
1989-90	Lethbridge	WHL	65	7	23	30	60	19	2	8	10	42
1990-91	Lethbridge	WHL	69	12	50	62	102	16	1	14	15	26
1991-92	Lethbridge	WHL	67	35	45	80	217	5	2	5	7	2
1992-93	Lethbridge	WHL	65	27	75	102	100	4	4	3	7	2
1993-94	Lethbridge	WHL	70	27	65	92	92	9	3	9	12	6

PEAKE, PAT — WSH.

Center. Shoots right. 6', 195 lbs. Born, Rochester, MI, May 28, 1973.
(Washington's 1st choice, 14th overall, in 1991 Entry Draft).

			Regular Season					Playoffs				
Season	Club	Lea	GP	G	A	TP	PIM	GP	G	A	TP	PIM
1990-91	Detroit	OHL	63	39	51	90	54	....	....	....	....	....
1991-92	Detroit	OHL	53	41	52	93	44	7	8	9	17	10
	Baltimore	AHL	3	1	0	1	4	....	....	....	....	....
1992-93abc	Detroit	OHL	46	58	78	136	64	2	1	3	4	2
1993-94	Washington	NHL	49	11	18	29	39	8	0	1	1	8
	Portland	AHL	4	0	5	5	2	....	....	....	....	....
	NHL Totals		49	11	18	29	39	8	0	1	1	8

a Canadian Major Junior Player of the Year (1993)
b Canadian Major Junior First All-Star Team (1993)
c OHL First All-Star Team (1993)

PEARCE, RANDY

Left wing. Shoots left. 5'11", 203 lbs. Born, Kitchener, Ont., February 23, 1970.
(Washington's 4th choice, 72nd overall, in 1990 Entry Draft).

			Regular Season					Playoffs				
Season	Club	Lea	GP	G	A	TP	PIM	GP	G	A	TP	PIM
1988-89	Kitchener	OHL	64	23	21	44	87	5	0	1	1	6
1989-90	Kitchener	OHL	62	31	34	65	139	17	8	15	23	42
1990-91			DID NOT PLAY – INJURED									
1991-92	Hampton Rds.	ECHL	55	32	46	78	134	11	5	9	14	56
	Baltimore	AHL	12	2	2	4	8	....	....	....	....	....
1992-93	Baltimore	AHL	42	12	5	17	46	....	....	....	....	....
	Hampton Rds.	ECHL	16	10	14	24	53	....	....	....	....	....
1993-94	Portland	AHL	80	32	36	68	97	17	1	4	5	36

PEARSON, ROB — WSH.

Right wing. Shoots right. 6'3", 198 lbs. Born, Oshawa, Ont., March 8, 1971.
(Toronto's 2nd choice, 12th overall, in 1989 Entry Draft).

			Regular Season					Playoffs				
Season	Club	Lea	GP	G	A	TP	PIM	GP	G	A	TP	PIM
1988-89	Belleville	OHL	26	8	12	20	51	....	....	....	....	....
1989-90	Belleville	OHL	58	48	40	88	174	11	5	5	10	26
1990-91	Belleville	OHL	10	6	3	9	27	....	....	....	....	....
a	Oshawa	OHL	41	57	52	109	76	16	16	17	33	39
	Newmarket	AHL	3	0	0	0	29	....	....	....	....	....
1991-92	Toronto	NHL	47	14	10	24	58	....	....	....	....	....
	St. John's	AHL	27	15	14	29	107	13	5	4	9	40
1992-93	Toronto	NHL	78	23	14	37	211	14	2	2	4	31
1993-94	Toronto	NHL	67	12	18	30	189	14	1	0	1	32
	NHL Totals		192	49	42	91	458	28	3	2	5	63

a OHL First All-Star Team (1991)

Traded to **Washington** by **Toronto** with Philadelphia's first round choice (previously acquired by Toronto — Washington selected Nolan Baumgartner) in 1994 Entry Draft for Mike Ridley and St. Louis' first round choice (previously acquired by Washington — Toronto selected Eric Fichaud) in 1994 Entry Draft, June 28, 1994.

PEARSON, SCOTT — EDM.

Left wing. Shoots left. 6'1", 205 lbs. Born, Cornwall, Ont., December 19, 1969.
(Toronto's 1st choice, 6th overall, in 1988 Entry Draft).

			Regular Season					Playoffs				
Season	Club	Lea	GP	G	A	TP	PIM	GP	G	A	TP	PIM
1986-87	Kingston	OHL	62	30	24	54	101	9	3	3	6	42
1987-88	Kingston	OHL	46	26	32	58	117	....	....	....	....	....
1988-89	Toronto	NHL	9	0	1	1	2	....	....	....	....	....
	Kingston	OHL	13	9	8	17	34	....	....	....	....	....
	Niagara Falls	OHL	32	26	34	60	90	17	14	10	24	53
1989-90	Toronto	NHL	41	5	10	15	90	2	2	0	2	10
	Newmarket	AHL	18	12	11	23	64	....	....	....	....	....
1990-91	Toronto	NHL	12	0	0	0	20	....	....	....	....	....
	Quebec	NHL	35	11	4	15	86	....	....	....	....	....
	Halifax	AHL	24	12	15	27	44	....	....	....	....	....
1991-92	Quebec	NHL	10	1	2	3	14	....	....	....	....	....
	Halifax	AHL	5	2	1	3	4	....	....	....	....	....
1992-93	Quebec	NHL	41	13	1	14	95	3	0	0	0	0
	Halifax	AHL	5	3	1	4	25	....	....	....	....	....
1993-94	Edmonton	NHL	72	19	18	37	165	....	....	....	....	....
	NHL Totals		220	49	36	85	472	5	2	0	2	10

Traded to **Quebec** by **Toronto** with Toronto's second round choices in 1991 (later traded to Washington — Washington selected Eric Lavigne) and 1992 (Tuomas Gronman) Entry Drafts for Aaron Broten, Lucien Deblois and Michel Petit, November 17, 1990. Traded to **Edmonton** by **Quebec** for Martin Gelinas and Edmonton's sixth round choice (Nicholas Checco) in 1993 Entry Draft, June 20, 1993.

PECA, MICHAEL (PEH-kuh) — VAN.

Right wing. Shoots right. 5'11", 180 lbs. Born, Toronto, Ont., March 26, 1974.
(Vancouver's 2nd choice, 40th overall, in 1992 Entry Draft).

			Regular Season					Playoffs				
Season	Club	Lea	GP	G	A	TP	PIM	GP	G	A	TP	PIM
1990-91	Sudbury	OHL	62	14	27	41	24	5	1	0	1	7
1991-92	Sudbury	OHL	39	16	34	50	61	....	....	....	....	....
	Ottawa	OHL	27	8	17	25	32	11	6	10	16	6
1992-93	Ottawa	OHL	55	38	64	102	80	....	....	....	....	....
	Hamilton	AHL	9	6	3	9	11	....	....	....	....	....
1993-94	Vancouver	NHL	4	0	0	0	2	....	....	....	....	....
	Ottawa	OHL	55	50	63	113	101	17	7	22	29	30
	NHL Totals		4	0	0	0	2	....	....	....	....	....

PEDERSEN, ALLEN — HFD.

Defense. Shoots left. 6'3", 210 lbs. Born, Fort Saskatchewan, Alta., January 13, 1965.
(Boston's 5th choice, 105th overall, in 1983 Entry Draft).

			Regular Season					Playoffs				
Season	Club	Lea	GP	G	A	TP	PIM	GP	G	A	TP	PIM
1982-83	Medicine Hat	WHL	63	3	10	13	49	5	0	0	0	7
1983-84	Medicine Hat	WHL	44	0	11	11	47	14	0	2	2	24
1984-85	Medicine Hat	WHL	72	6	16	22	66	10	0	0	0	9
1985-86	Moncton	AHL	59	1	8	9	39	3	0	0	0	0
1986-87	**Boston**	**NHL**	**79**	**1**	**11**	**12**	**71**	**4**	**0**	**0**	**0**	**4**
1987-88	**Boston**	**NHL**	**78**	**0**	**6**	**6**	**90**	**21**	**0**	**0**	**0**	**34**
1988-89	**Boston**	**NHL**	**51**	**0**	**6**	**6**	**69**	**10**	**0**	**0**	**0**	**2**
1989-90	**Boston**	**NHL**	**68**	**1**	**2**	**3**	**71**	**21**	**0**	**0**	**0**	**41**
1990-91	**Boston**	**NHL**	**57**	**2**	**6**	**8**	**107**	**8**	**0**	**0**	**0**	**10**
	Maine	AHL	15	0	6	6	18	2	0	1	1	2
1991-92	**Minnesota**	**NHL**	**29**	**0**	**1**	**1**	**10**	....	....	....	....	....
1992-93	**Hartford**	**NHL**	**59**	**1**	**4**	**5**	**60**	....	....	....	....	....
1993-94	**Hartford**	**NHL**	**7**	**0**	**0**	**0**	**9**	....	....	....	....	....
	Springfield	AHL	45	2	4	6	28	3	0	1	1	6
	NHL Totals		**428**	**5**	**36**	**41**	**487**	**64**	**0**	**0**	**0**	**91**

Claimed by **Minnesota** from **Boston** in Expansion Draft, May 30, 1991. Traded to **Hartford** by **Minnesota** for Hartford's sixth round choice (Rick Mrozik) in 1993 Entry Draft, June 15, 1992.

PEDERSON, DENIS — N.J.

Center. Shoots right. 6'2", 190 lbs. Born, Prince Albert, Sask., September 10, 1975.
(New Jersey's 1st choice, 13th overall, in 1993 Entry Draft).

			Regular Season					Playoffs				
Season	Club	Lea	GP	G	A	TP	PIM	GP	G	A	TP	PIM
1991-92	Prince Albert	Midget	21	33	25	58	40	....	....	....	....	....
	Prince Albert	WHL	10	0	0	0	6	7	0	1	1	13
1992-93	Prince Albert	WHL	72	33	40	73	134	....	....	....	....	....
1993-94a	Prince Albert	WHL	71	53	45	98	157	....	....	....	....	....

a WHL East Second All-Star Team (1994)

PEDERSON, MARK — DET.

Left wing. Shoots left. 6'2", 196 lbs. Born, Prelate, Sask., January 14, 1968.
(Montreal's 1st choice, 15th overall, in 1986 Entry Draft).

			Regular Season					Playoffs				
Season	Club	Lea	GP	G	A	TP	PIM	GP	G	A	TP	PIM
1984-85	Medicine Hat	WHL	71	42	40	82	63	10	3	2	5	0
1985-86	Medicine Hat	WHL	72	46	60	106	46	25	12	6	18	25
1986-87a	Medicine Hat	WHL	69	56	46	102	58	20	*19	7	26	14
1987-88	Medicine Hat	WHL	62	53	58	111	55	16	*13	6	19	16
1988-89	Sherbrooke	AHL	75	43	38	81	53	6	7	5	12	4
1989-90	**Montreal**	**NHL**	**9**	**0**	**2**	**2**	**2**	**2**	**0**	**0**	**0**	**0**
b	Sherbrooke	AHL	72	53	42	95	60	11	10	8	18	19
1990-91	**Montreal**	**NHL**	**47**	**8**	**15**	**23**	**18**	....	....	....	....	....
	Philadelphia	**NHL**	**12**	**2**	**1**	**3**	**5**	....	....	....	....	....
1991-92	**Philadelphia**	**NHL**	**58**	**15**	**25**	**40**	**22**	....	....	....	....	....
1992-93	**Philadelphia**	**NHL**	**14**	**3**	**4**	**7**	**6**	....	....	....	....	....
	San Jose	**NHL**	**27**	**7**	**3**	**10**	**22**	....	....	....	....	....
1993-94	**Detroit**	**NHL**	**2**	**0**	**0**	**0**	**2**	....	....	....	....	....
b	Adirondack	AHL	62	52	45	97	37	12	4	7	11	10
	NHL Totals		**169**	**35**	**50**	**85**	**77**	**2**	**0**	**0**	**0**	**0**

a WHL East All-Star Team (1987)
b AHL First All-Star Team (1990, 1994)

Traded to **Philadelphia** by **Montreal** for Philadelphia's second round choice (Jim Campbell) in 1991 Entry Draft, March 5, 1991. Traded to **San Jose** by **Philadelphia** with future considerations for Dave Snuggerud, December 19, 1992. Signed as a free agent by **Detroit**, August 23, 1993.

PEDERSON, TOM — S.J.

Defense. Shoots right. 5'9", 175 lbs. Born, Bloomington, MN, January 14, 1970.
(Minnesota's 12th choice, 217th overall, in 1989 Entry Draft).

			Regular Season					Playoffs				
Season	Club	Lea	GP	G	A	TP	PIM	GP	G	A	TP	PIM
1988-89	U. Minnesota	WCHA	36	4	20	24	40	....	....	....	....	....
1989-90	U. Minnesota	WCHA	43	8	30	38	58	....	....	....	....	....
1990-91	U. Minnesota	WCHA	36	12	20	32	46	....	....	....	....	....
1991-92	U.S. National	....	44	3	11	14	41	....	....	....	....	....
	Kansas City	IHL	20	6	9	15	16	13	1	6	7	14
1992-93	**San Jose**	**NHL**	**44**	**7**	**13**	**20**	**31**	....	....	....	....	....
	Kansas City	IHL	26	6	15	21	10	12	1	6	7	2
1993-94	**San Jose**	**NHL**	**74**	**6**	**19**	**25**	**31**	**14**	**1**	**6**	**7**	**2**
	Kansas City	IHL	7	3	1	4	0	....	....	....	....	....
	NHL Totals		**118**	**13**	**32**	**45**	**62**	**14**	**1**	**6**	**7**	**2**

Claimed by **San Jose** from **Minnesota** in Dispersal Draft, May 30, 1991.

PELLERIN, BRIAN

Right wing. Shoots right. 5'10", 185 lbs. Born, Hinton, Alta., February 20, 1970.

			Regular Season					Playoffs				
Season	Club	Lea	GP	G	A	TP	PIM	GP	G	A	TP	PIM
1987-88	Prince Albert	WHL	62	6	2	8	113	10	0	0	0	17
1988-89	Prince Albert	WHL	60	17	16	33	216	3	0	1	1	27
1989-90	Prince Albert	WHL	53	6	15	21	175	10	1	3	4	26
1990-91a	Prince Albert	WHL	68	46	42	88	223	3	0	0	0	12
1991-92	Peoria	IHL	70	7	16	23	231	10	1	2	3	49
1992-93	Peoria	IHL	78	15	25	40	204	4	1	1	2	8
1993-94	Peoria	IHL	79	14	24	38	225	5	0	0	0	16

a WHL East First All-Star Team (1991)

Signed as a free agent by **St. Louis**, May 31, 1991.

PELLERIN, SCOTT (PEHL-ih-rihn) — N.J.

Left wing. Shoots left. 5'11", 180 lbs. Born, Shediac, N.B., January 9, 1970.
(New Jersey's 4th choice, 47th overall, in 1989 Entry Draft).

			Regular Season					Playoffs				
Season	Club	Lea	GP	G	A	TP	PIM	GP	G	A	TP	PIM
1988-89	U. of Maine	H.E.	45	29	33	62	92	....	....	....	....	....
1989-90	U. of Maine	H.E.	42	22	34	56	68	....	....	....	....	....
1990-91	U. of Maine	H.E.	43	23	25	48	60	....	....	....	....	....
1991-92abc	U. of Maine	H.E.	37	*32	25	57	54	....	....	....	....	....
	Utica	AHL	....	....	....	....	....	3	1	0	1	0
1992-93	**New Jersey**	**NHL**	**45**	**10**	**11**	**21**	**41**	....	....	....	....	....
	Utica	AHL	27	15	18	33	33	2	0	1	1	0
1993-94	**New Jersey**	**NHL**	**1**	**0**	**0**	**0**	**2**	....	....	....	....	....
	Albany	AHL	73	28	46	74	84	5	2	1	3	11
	NHL Totals		**46**	**10**	**11**	**21**	**43**	....	....	....	....	....

a Won Hobey Baker Memorial Award (Top U.S. Collegiate Player) (1992)
b Hockey East First All-Star Team (1992)
c NCAA East First All-American Team (1992)

PELTONEN, VILLE (PEHL-TOH-ner) — S.J.

Left wing. Shoots left. 5'11", 172 lbs. Born, Vantaa, Finland, May 24, 1973.
(San Jose's 4th choice, 58th overall, in 1993 Entry Draft).

			Regular Season					Playoffs				
Season	Club	Lea	GP	G	A	TP	PIM	GP	G	A	TP	PIM
1991-92	HIFK	Fin.	6	0	0	0	0	....	....	....	....	....
1992-93	HIFK	Fin.	46	13	24	37	16	4	0	2	2	2
1993-94	HIFK	Fin.	43	16	22	38	14	3	0	0	0	2

PELUSO, MIKE — N.J.

Left wing. Shoots left. 6'4", 220 lbs. Born, Pengilly, MN, November 8, 1965.
(New Jersey's 10th choice, 190th overall, in 1984 Entry Draft).

			Regular Season					Playoffs				
Season	Club	Lea	GP	G	A	TP	PIM	GP	G	A	TP	PIM
1985-86	Alaska-Anch.	G.N.	32	2	11	13	59	....	....	....	....	....
1986-87	Alaska-Anch.	G.N.	30	5	21	26	68	....	....	....	....	....
1987-88	Alaska-Anch.	G.N.	35	4	33	37	76	....	....	....	....	....
1988-89	Alaska-Anch.	G.N.	33	10	27	37	75	....	....	....	....	....
1989-90	**Chicago**	**NHL**	**2**	**0**	**0**	**0**	**15**	....	....	....	....	....
	Indianapolis	IHL	75	7	10	17	279	14	0	1	1	58
1990-91	**Chicago**	**NHL**	**53**	**6**	**1**	**7**	**320**	**3**	**0**	**0**	**0**	**2**
	Indianapolis	IHL	6	2	1	3	21	5	0	2	2	40
1991-92	**Chicago**	**NHL**	**63**	**6**	**3**	**9**	***408**	**17**	**1**	**2**	**3**	**8**
	Indianapolis	IHL	4	0	1	1	15	....	....	....	....	....
1992-93	**Ottawa**	**NHL**	**81**	**15**	**10**	**25**	**318**	....	....	....	....	....
1993-94	**New Jersey**	**NHL**	**69**	**4**	**16**	**20**	**238**	**17**	**1**	**0**	**1**	***64**
	NHL Totals		**268**	**31**	**30**	**61**	**1299**	**37**	**2**	**2**	**4**	**74**

Signed as a free agent by **Chicago**, September 7, 1989. Claimed by **Ottawa** from **Chicago** in Expansion Draft, June 18, 1992. Traded to **New Jersey** by **Ottawa** to complete June 20, 1993 trade which sent Craig Billington, Troy Mallette and New Jersey's fourth round choice (Cosmo Dupaul) in 1993 Entry Draft to Ottawa for Peter Sidorkiewicz and future considerations, June 26, 1993.

PENNEY, CHAD — OTT.

Left wing. Shoots left. 6', 195 lbs. Born, Labrador City, Nfld., September 18, 1973.
(Ottawa's 2nd choice, 25th overall, in 1992 Entry Draft).

			Regular Season					Playoffs				
Season	Club	Lea	GP	G	A	TP	PIM	GP	G	A	TP	PIM
1990-91	North Bay	OHL	66	33	34	67	56	10	2	6	8	12
1991-92	North Bay	OHL	57	25	27	52	90	21	13	17	30	9
1992-93	North Bay	OHL	18	8	7	15	19	....	....	....	....	....
a	S.S. Marie	OHL	48	29	44	73	67	18	7	10	17	18
1993-94	**Ottawa**	**NHL**	**3**	**0**	**0**	**0**	**2**	....	....	....	....	....
	PEI	AHL	73	20	30	50	66	....	....	....	....	....
	NHL Totals		**3**	**0**	**0**	**0**	**2**	....	....	....	....	....

a Memorial Cup All-Star Team (1993)

PENNEY, DAVID — ANA.

Left wing. Shoots left. 6'1", 175 lbs. Born, Easton, MA, May 16, 1974.
(Anaheim's 11th choice, 264th overall, in 1993 Entry Draft).

			Regular Season					Playoffs				
Season	Club	Lea	GP	G	A	TP	PIM	GP	G	A	TP	PIM
1993-94	Northeastern	H.E.	36	5	9	14	18	....	....	....	....	....

PERREAULT, NICOLAS P. (puh-ROH) — CGY.

Defense. Shoots left. 6'3", 200 lbs. Born, Loretteville, Que., April 24, 1972.
(Calgary's 2nd choice, 26th overall, in 1990 Entry Draft).

			Regular Season					Playoffs				
Season	Club	Lea	GP	G	A	TP	PIM	GP	G	A	TP	PIM
1990-91	Michigan State	CCHA	34	1	7	8	32	....	....	....	....	....
1991-92	Michigan State	CCHA	41	11	11	22	75	....	....	....	....	....
1992-93	Michigan State	CCHA	38	7	6	13	90	....	....	....	....	....
1993-94	Michigan State	CCHA	40	6	10	16	109	....	....	....	....	....

PERREAULT, YANIC (puh-ROH, YAH-nihk) — L.A.

Center. Shoots left. 5'11", 182 lbs. Born, Sherbrooke, Que., April 4, 1971.
(Toronto's 1st choice, 47th overall, in 1991 Entry Draft).

			Regular Season					Playoffs				
Season	Club	Lea	GP	G	A	TP	PIM	GP	G	A	TP	PIM
1988-89	Trois-Rivières	QMJHL	70	53	55	108	48	....	....	....	....	....
1989-90	Trois-Rivières	QMJHL	63	51	63	114	75	7	6	5	11	19
1990-91a	Trois-Rivières	QMJHL	67	*87	98	*185	103	6	4	7	11	6
1991-92	St. John's	AHL	62	38	38	76	19	16	7	8	15	4
1992-93	St. John's	AHL	79	49	46	95	56	9	4	5	9	2
1993-94	**Toronto**	**NHL**	**13**	**3**	**3**	**6**	**0**	....	....	....	....	....
	St. John's	AHL	62	45	60	105	38	11	*12	6	18	14
	NHL Totals		**13**	**3**	**3**	**6**	**0**	....	....	....	....	....

a QMJHL First All-Star Team (1991)

Traded to **Los Angeles** by **Toronto** for a conditional draft choice in 1996 Entry Draft, July 11, 1994.

PERRY, JEFF — CGY.

Left wing. Shoots left. 6', 195 lbs. Born, Sarnia, Ont., April 12, 1971.
(Toronto's 6th choice, 113th overall, in 1991 Entry Draft).

			Regular Season					Playoffs				
Season	Club	Lea	GP	G	A	TP	PIM	GP	G	A	TP	PIM
1990-91	Owen Sound	OHL	60	31	49	80	83	....	....	....	....	....
1991-92	Owen Sound	OHL	7	0	5	5	8	....	....	....	....	....
	St. John's	AHL	6	0	1	1	4	....	....	....	....	....
	Raleigh	ECHL	8	2	2	4	18	4	0	1	1	11
1992-93	St. John's	AHL	13	1	1	2	22	....	....	....	....	....
	Brantford	ColHL	23	1	13	24	36	14	8	7	15	27
1993-94	Saint John	AHL	42	8	3	11	97	4	0	0	0	4

Traded to **Calgary** by **Toronto** with Brad Miller for Todd Gillingham and Paul Holden, September 2, 1993.

PERSSON, RICKARD — N.J.

Defense. Shoots left. 6'1", 205 lbs. Born, Ostersund, Sweden, August 24, 1969.
(New Jersey's 2nd choice, 23rd overall, in 1987 Entry Draft).

			Regular Season					Playoffs				
Season	Club	Lea	GP	G	A	TP	PIM	GP	G	A	TP	PIM
1985-86	Ostersund	Swe. 2	24	2	2	4	16	....	....	....	....	....
1986-87	Ostersund	Swe. 2	31	10	11	21	28	....	....	....	....	....
1987-88	Leksand	Swe.	31	2	0	2	8	2	0	1	1	2
1988-89	Leksand	Swe.	33	2	4	6	28	9	0	1	1	6
1989-90	Leksand	Swe.	43	9	10	19	62	3	0	0	0	6
1990-91	Leksand	Swe.	37	6	9	15	42	....	....	....	....	....
1991-92	Leksand	Swe.	21	0	7	7	28	....	....	....	....	....
1992-93	Leksand	Swe.	36	7	15	22	63	2	0	2	2	0
1993-94	Malmo	Swe.	40	11	9	20	38	11	2	0	2	12

PETERS, ROB — HFD.

Defense. Shoots left. 6'6", 205 lbs. Born, North Tonowanda, NY, May 15, 1972.
(Hartford's 12th choice, 251st overall, in 1991 Entry Draft).

			Regular Season					Playoffs				
Season	Club	Lea	GP	G	A	TP	PIM	GP	G	A	TP	PIM
1990-91	Ohio State	CCHA	33	0	1	1	65	....	....	....	....	....
1991-92	Ohio State	CCHA	28	3	7	10	53	....	....	....	....	....
1992-93	Ohio State	CCHA	35	2	9	11	72	....	....	....	....	....
1993-94	Ohio State	CCHA	28	1	4	5	59	....	....	....	....	....

PETERSON, BRENT — T.B.

Left wing. Shoots left. 6'3", 195 lbs. Born, Calgary, Alta., July 20, 1972.
(Tampa Bay's 1st choice, 3rd overall, in 1993 Supplemental Draft).

			Regular Season					Playoffs				
Season	Club	Lea	GP	G	A	TP	PIM	GP	G	A	TP	PIM
1991-92	Michigan Tech	WCHA	39	11	9	20	18	....	....	....	....	....
1992-93	Michigan Tech	WCHA	37	24	18	42	32	....	....	....	....	....
1993-94	Michigan Tech	WCHA	43	25	21	46	30	....	....	....	....	....

PETERSON, COREY — DAL.

Defense. Shoots left. 6'2", 205 lbs. Born, Minneapolis, MN, June 10, 1975.
(Dallas' 10th choice, 269th overall, in 1993 Entry Draft).

			Regular Season					Playoffs				
Season	Club	Lea	GP	G	A	TP	PIM	GP	G	A	TP	PIM
1992-93	Jefferson	HS	28	11	13	24	42	....	....	....	....	....
1993-94	Madison	USHL	41	2	9	11	89	....	....	....	....	....

PETERSON, ERIK — CHI.

Center. Shoots left. 6', 185 lbs. Born, Boston, MA, March 31, 1972.
(Chicago's 8th choice, 205th overall, in 1990 Entry Draft).

			Regular Season					Playoffs				
Season	Club	Lea	GP	G	A	TP	PIM	GP	G	A	TP	PIM
1990-91	Providence	H.E.	34	8	4	12	12	....	....	....	....	....
1991-92	Providence	H.E.	32	9	5	14	26	....	....	....	....	....
1992-93	Providence	H.E.	34	7	14	21	28	....	....	....	....	....
1993-94	Providence	H.E.	34	5	5	10	44	....	....	....	....	....

PETERSON, KYLE — DAL.

Center. Shoots left. 6'3", 195 lbs. Born, Calgary, Alta., April 17, 1974.
(Minnesota's 5th choice, 154th overall, in 1992 Entry Draft).

			Regular Season					Playoffs				
Season	Club	Lea	GP	G	A	TP	PIM	GP	G	A	TP	PIM
1992-93	Thunder Bay	USHL	24	8	23	31	22	....	....	....	....	....
1993-94	Michigan Tech	WCHA	45	5	9	14	82	....	....	....	....	....

PETERSON, MATT — ANA.

Defense. Shoots left. 6'1", 190 lbs. Born, Maple Grove, MN, February 15, 1975.
(Anaheim's 7th choice, 160th overall, in 1993 Entry Draft).

			Regular Season					Playoffs				
Season	Club	Lea	GP	G	A	TP	PIM	GP	G	A	TP	PIM
1992-93	Osseo	US	4	13	17	20	....	....	....	....	....	....
1993-94	U. Wisconsin	WCHA				DID NOT PLAY						

PETIT, MICHEL — (puh-TEE) L.A.

Defense. Shoots right. 6'1", 205 lbs. Born, St. Malo, Que., February 12, 1964.
(Vancouver's 1st choice, 11th overall, in 1982 Entry Draft).

			Regular Season					Playoffs				
Season	Club	Lea	GP	G	A	TP	PIM	GP	G	A	TP	PIM
1981-82a	Sherbrooke	QMJHL	63	10	39	49	106	22	5	20	25	24
1982-83	**Vancouver**	**NHL**	**2**	**0**	**0**	**0**	**0**	....	....	....	....	....
a	St-Jean	QMJHL	62	19	67	86	196	3	0	0	0	35
1983-84	Cdn. National	....	19	3	10	13	58	....	....	....	....	....
	Vancouver	**NHL**	**44**	**6**	**9**	**15**	**53**	**1**	**0**	**0**	**0**	**0**
1984-85	**Vancouver**	**NHL**	**69**	**5**	**26**	**31**	**127**	....	....	....	....	....
1985-86	**Vancouver**	**NHL**	**32**	**1**	**6**	**7**	**27**	....	....	....	....	....
	Fredericton	AHL	25	0	13	13	79	....	....	....	....	....
1986-87	**Vancouver**	**NHL**	**69**	**12**	**13**	**25**	**131**	....	....	....	....	....
1987-88	**Vancouver**	**NHL**	**10**	**0**	**3**	**3**	**35**	....	....	....	....	....
	NY Rangers	**NHL**	**64**	**9**	**24**	**33**	**223**	....	....	....	....	....
1988-89	**NY Rangers**	**NHL**	**69**	**8**	**25**	**33**	**154**	**4**	**0**	**2**	**2**	**27**
1989-90	**Quebec**	**NHL**	**63**	**12**	**24**	**36**	**215**	....	....	....	....	....
1990-91	**Quebec**	**NHL**	**19**	**4**	**7**	**11**	**47**	....	....	....	....	....
	Toronto	**NHL**	**54**	**9**	**19**	**28**	**132**	....	....	....	....	....
1991-92	**Toronto**	**NHL**	**34**	**1**	**13**	**14**	**85**	....	....	....	....	....
	Calgary	**NHL**	**36**	**3**	**10**	**13**	**79**	....	....	....	....	....
1992-93	**Calgary**	**NHL**	**35**	**3**	**9**	**12**	**54**	....	....	....	....	....
1993-94	**Calgary**	**NHL**	**63**	**2**	**21**	**23**	**110**	....	....	....	....	....
	NHL Totals		**663**	**75**	**209**	**284**	**1472**	**5**	**0**	**2**	**2**	**27**

a QMJHL First All-Star Team (1982, 1983)

Traded to **NY Rangers** by **Vancouver** for Willie Huber and Larry Melnyk, November 4, 1987. Traded to **Quebec** by **NY Rangers** for Randy Moller, October 5, 1989. Traded to **Toronto** by **Quebec** with Aaron Broten and Lucien Deblois for Scott Pearson and Toronto's second round choices in 1991 (later traded to Washington — Washington selected Eric Lavigne) and 1992 (Tuomas Gronman) Entry Drafts, November 17, 1990. Traded to **Calgary** by **Toronto** with Craig Berube, Alexander Godynyuk, Gary Leeman and Jeff Reese for Doug Gilmour, Jamie Macoun, Ric Nattress, Rick Wamsley and Kent Manderville, January 2, 1992.

PETRENKO, SERGEI — BUF.

Left wing. Shoots left. 6', 176 lbs. Born, Kharkov, USSR, September 10, 1968.
(Buffalo's 5th choice, 168th overall, in 1993 Entry Draft).

			Regular Season					Playoffs				
Season	Club	Lea	GP	G	A	TP	PIM	GP	G	A	TP	PIM
1987-88	Moscow D'amo	USSR	31	2	5	7	4	....	....	....	....	....
1988-89	Moscow D'amo	USSR	23	4	6	10	6	....	....	....	....	....
1989-90	Moscow D'amo	USSR	33	5	4	9	8	....	....	....	....	....
1990-91	Moscow D'amo	USSR	43	14	13	27	10	....	....	....	....	....
1991-92	Moscow D'amo	CIS	31	9	10	19	10	....	....	....	....	....
1992-93	Moscow D'amo	CIS	36	12	12	24	10	10	4	5	9	6
1993-94	**Buffalo**	**NHL**	**14**	**0**	**4**	**4**	**0**	....	....	....	....	....
	Rochester	AHL	38	16	15	31	8	....	....	....	....	....
	NHL Totals		**14**	**0**	**4**	**4**	**0**	....	....	....	....	....

PETROCHININ, YEVGENY — (peht-roh-CHIH-nihn) DAL.

Defense. Shoots left. 5'9", 165 lbs. Born, Murmansk, USSR, February 7, 1976.
(Dallas' 5th choice, 150th overall, in 1994 Entry Draft).

			Regular Season					Playoffs				
Season	Club	Lea	GP	G	A	TP	PIM	GP	G	A	TP	PIM
1993-94	Spartak	CIS	2	0	0	0	0	....	....	....	....	....

PETROV, OLEG — (PEH-trahf) MTL.

Right wing. Shoots left. 5'9", 166 lbs. Born, Moscow, USSR, April 18, 1971.
(Montreal's 6th choice, 127th overall, in 1991 Entry Draft).

			Regular Season					Playoffs				
Season	Club	Lea	GP	G	A	TP	PIM	GP	G	A	TP	PIM
1989-90	CSKA	USSR	30	4	7	11	4	....	....	....	....	....
1990-91	CSKA	USSR	43	7	4	11	8	....	....	....	....	....
1991-92	CSKA	CIS	42	10	16	26	8	....	....	....	....	....
1992-93	**Montreal**	**NHL**	**9**	**2**	**1**	**3**	**10**	**1**	**0**	**0**	**0**	**0**
	Fredericton	AHL	55	26	29	55	36	5	4	1	5	0
1993-94a	**Montreal**	**NHL**	**55**	**12**	**15**	**27**	**2**	**2**	**0**	**0**	**0**	**0**
	Fredericton	AHL	23	8	20	28	18	....	....	....	....	....
	NHL Totals		**64**	**14**	**16**	**30**	**12**	**3**	**0**	**0**	**0**	**0**

a NHL/Upper Deck All-Rookie Team (1994)

PETROV, SERGEI — (PEH-trahf) CHI.

Left wing. Shoots left. 5'11", 185 lbs. Born, Leningrad, USSR, January 22, 1975.
(Chicago's 9th choice, 206th overall, in 1993 Entry Draft).

			Regular Season					Playoffs				
Season	Club	Lea	GP	G	A	TP	PIM	GP	G	A	TP	PIM
1992-93	Cloquet	HS	28	37	32	69	....	....	....	....	....	....
1993-94	Minn.-Duluth	WCHA	28	2	4	6	26	....	....	....	....	....

PETROVICKY, ROBERT — (PEHT-roh-VEETS-kee) HFD.

Center. Shoots left. 5'11", 172 lbs. Born, Kosice, Czech., October 26, 1973.
(Hartford's 1st choice, 9th overall, in 1992 Entry Draft).

			Regular Season					Playoffs				
Season	Club	Lea	GP	G	A	TP	PIM	GP	G	A	TP	PIM
1990-91	Dukla Trencin	Czech.	33	9	14	23	12	....	....	....	....	....
1991-92	Dukla Trencin	Czech.	46	25	36	61	28	....	....	....	....	....
1992-93	**Hartford**	**NHL**	**42**	**3**	**6**	**9**	**45**	....	....	....	....	....
	Springfield	AHL	16	5	3	8	39	15	5	6	11	14
1993-94	**Hartford**	**NHL**	**33**	**6**	**5**	**11**	**39**	....	....	....	....	....
	Springfield	AHL	30	16	8	24	39	4	0	2	2	4
	NHL Totals		**75**	**9**	**11**	**20**	**84**	....	....	....	....	....

PHILPOTT, ETHAN — BUF.

Right wing. Shoots right. 6'4", 230 lbs. Born, Rochester, MN, February 11, 1975.
(Buffalo's 2nd choice, 64th overall, in 1993 Entry Draft).

			Regular Season					Playoffs				
Season	Club	Lea	GP	G	A	TP	PIM	GP	G	A	TP	PIM
1992-93	Andover	HS	18	17	19	36	22	....	....	....	....	....
1993-94	Harvard	ECAC	3	1	0	1	8	....	....	....	....	....

PICARD, MICHEL — OTT.

Left wing. Shoots left. 5'11", 190 lbs. Born, Beauport, Que., November 7, 1969.
(Hartford's 8th choice, 178th overall, in 1989 Entry Draft).

			Regular Season					Playoffs				
Season	Club	Lea	GP	G	A	TP	PIM	GP	G	A	TP	PIM
1986-87	Trois-Rivières	QMJHL	66	33	35	68	53	....	....	....	....	....
1987-88	Trois-Rivières	QMJHL	69	40	55	95	71	....	....	....	....	....
1988-89	Trois-Rivières	QMJHL	66	59	81	140	170	4	1	3	4	2
1989-90	Binghamton	AHL	67	16	24	40	98	....	....	....	....	....
1990-91	**Hartford**	**NHL**	**5**	**1**	**0**	**1**	**2**	....	....	....	....	....
a	Springfield	AHL	77	*56	40	96	61	18	8	13	21	18
1991-92	**Hartford**	**NHL**	**25**	**3**	**5**	**8**	**6**	....	....	....	....	....
	Springfield	AHL	40	21	17	38	44	11	2	0	2	34
1992-93	**San Jose**	**NHL**	**25**	**4**	**0**	**4**	**24**	....	....	....	....	....
	Kansas City	IHL	33	7	10	17	51	12	3	2	5	20
1993-94b	Portland	AHL	61	41	44	85	99	17	11	10	21	22
	NHL Totals		**55**	**8**	**5**	**13**	**32**	....	....	....	....	....

a AHL First All-Star Team (1991)
b AHL Second All-Star Team (1994)

Traded to **San Jose** by **Hartford** for future considerations (Yvon Corriveau, January 21, 1993), October 9, 1992. Signed as a free agent by **Ottawa**, June 16, 1994.

PIERCE, BILL

Center. Shoots left. 6'1", 190 lbs. Born, Woburn, MA, October 6, 1974.
(Quebec's 4th choice, 75th overall, in 1993 Entry Draft).

			Regular Season					Playoffs				
Season	Club	Lea	GP	G	A	TP	PIM	GP	G	A	TP	PIM
1992-93	Lawrence	HS	20	12	26	38	22	....	....	....	....	....
1993-94	Boston U.	H.E.	31	4	4	8	28	....	....	....	....	....

PILON, RICHARD — (PEE-lahn) NYI

Defense. Shoots left. 6', 202 lbs. Born, Saskatoon, Sask., April 30, 1968.
(NY Islanders' 9th choice, 143rd overall, in 1986 Entry Draft).

			Regular Season					Playoffs				
Season	Club	Lea	GP	G	A	TP	PIM	GP	G	A	TP	PIM
1986-87	Prince Albert	WHL	68	4	21	25	192	7	1	6	7	17
1987-88	Prince Albert	WHL	65	13	34	47	177	9	0	6	6	38
1988-89	**NY Islanders**	**NHL**	**62**	**0**	**14**	**14**	**242**	....	....	....	....	....
1989-90	**NY Islanders**	**NHL**	**14**	**0**	**2**	**2**	**31**	....	....	....	....	....
1990-91	**NY Islanders**	**NHL**	**60**	**1**	**4**	**5**	**126**	....	....	....	....	....
1991-92	**NY Islanders**	**NHL**	**65**	**1**	**6**	**7**	**183**	....	....	....	....	....
1992-93	**NY Islanders**	**NHL**	**44**	**1**	**3**	**4**	**164**	**15**	**0**	**0**	**0**	**50**
	Capital Dist.	AHL	6	0	1	1	8	....	....	....	....	....
1993-94	**NY Islanders**	**NHL**	**28**	**1**	**4**	**5**	**75**	....	....	....	....	....
	Salt Lake	IHL	2	0	0	0	8	....	....	....	....	....
	NHL Totals		**273**	**4**	**33**	**37**	**821**	**15**	**0**	**0**	**0**	**50**

PION, RICHARD

Right wing. Shoots right. 5'10", 180 lbs. Born, Oxnard, CA., July 20, 1965.

			Regular Season					Playoffs				
Season	Club	Lea	GP	G	A	TP	PIM	GP	G	A	TP	PIM
1985-86	Merrimack	NCAA	14	9	13	22	10	....	....	....	....	....
1986-87	Merrimack	NCAA	37	31	33	64	46	....	....	....	....	....
1987-88	Merrimack	NCAA	40	35	40	75	58	4	3	3	6	....
1988-89	Merrimack	NCAA	34	28	42	70	34	....	....	....	....	....
1989-90	Peoria	IHL	69	10	21	31	58	5	0	0	0	0
1990-91	Peoria	IHL	76	14	24	38	113	17	3	5	8	36
1991-92	Peoria	IHL	82	21	50	71	173	9	3	1	4	30
1992-93	Peoria	IHL	74	20	35	55	119	3	2	1	3	8
1993-94	Peoria	IHL	73	13	32	45	96	6	2	1	3	8

Signed as a free agent by **St. Louis**, August 21, 1989.

PITLICK, LANCE — OTT.

Defense. Shoots right. 6', 190 lbs. Born, Minneapolis, MN, November 5, 1967.
(Minnesota's 10th choice, 108th overall, in 1986 Entry Draft).

			Regular Season					Playoffs				
Season	Club	Lea	GP	G	A	TP	PIM	GP	G	A	TP	PIM
1986-87	U. Minnesota	WCHA	45	0	9	9	88	....	....	....	....	....
1987-88	U. Minnesota	WCHA	38	3	9	12	76	....	....	....	....	....
1988-89	U. Minnesota	WCHA	47	4	9	13	95	....	....	....	....	....
1989-90	U. Minnestoa	WCHA	14	3	2	5	26	....	....	....	....	....
1990-91	Hershey	AHL	64	6	15	21	75	3	0	0	0	9
1991-92	U.S. National	....	19	0	1	1	38	....	....	....	....	....
	Hershey	AHL	4	0	0	0	6	3	0	0	0	4
1992-93	Hershey	AHL	53	5	10	15	77	....	....	....	....	....
1993-94	Hershey	AHL	58	4	13	17	93	11	1	0	1	11

Signed as a free agent by **Philadelphia**, September 5, 1990. Signed as a free agent by **Ottawa**, June 22, 1994.

PITTIS, DOMENIC — PIT.

Center. Shoots left. 5'11", 180 lbs. Born, Calgary, Alta., October 1, 1974.
(Pittsburgh's 2nd choice, 52nd overall, in 1993 Entry Draft).

			Regular Season					Playoffs				
Season	Club	Lea	GP	G	A	TP	PIM	GP	G	A	TP	PIM
1991-92	Lethbridge	WHL	65	6	17	23	48	5	0	2	2	4
1992-93	Lethbridge	WHL	66	46	73	119	69	4	3	3	6	8
1993-94a	Lethbridge	WHL	72	58	69	127	93	8	4	11	15	16

a WHL East Second All-Star Team (1994)

PIVETZ, MARK — QUE.

Defense. Shoots left. 6'3", 205 lbs. Born, Edmonton, Alta., December 9, 1973.
(Quebec's 12th choice, 257th overall, in 1993 Entry Draft).

			Regular Season					Playoffs				
Season	Club	Lea	GP	G	A	TP	PIM	GP	G	A	TP	PIM
1992-93	Saskatchewan	SJHL	62	13	32	45	60	....	....	....	....	....
1993-94	North Dakota	WCHA	36	2	5	7	96	....	....	....	....	....

PIVONKA, MICHAL — (pih-VAHN-kuh) WSH.

Center. Shoots left. 6'2", 198 lbs. Born, Kladno, USSR, January 28, 1966.
(Washington's 3rd choice, 59th overall, in 1984 Entry Draft).

			Regular Season					Playoffs				
Season	Club	Lea	GP	G	A	TP	PIM	GP	G	A	TP	PIM
1984-85	Dukla Jihlava	Czech.	33	8	11	19	18	....	....	....	....	....
1985-86	Dukla Jihlava	Czech.	42	5	13	18	18	....	....	....	....	....
1986-87	**Washington**	**NHL**	73	18	25	43	41	7	1	1	2	2
1987-88	**Washington**	**NHL**	71	11	23	34	28	14	4	9	13	4
1988-89	**Washington**	**NHL**	52	8	19	27	30	6	3	1	4	10
	Baltimore	AHL	31	12	24	36	19	....	....	....	....	....
1989-90	**Washington**	**NHL**	77	25	39	64	54	11	0	2	2	6
1990-91	**Washington**	**NHL**	79	20	50	70	34	11	2	3	5	8
1991-92	**Washington**	**NHL**	80	23	57	80	47	7	1	5	6	13
1992-93	**Washington**	**NHL**	69	21	53	74	66	6	0	2	2	0
1993-94	**Washington**	**NHL**	82	14	36	50	38	7	4	4	8	4
	NHL Totals		**583**	**140**	**302**	**442**	**338**	**69**	**15**	**27**	**42**	**47**

PLANTE, DAN — NYI

Right wing. Shoots right. 5'11", 198 lbs. Born, St. Louis, MO, October 5, 1971.
(NY Islanders' 3rd choice, 48th overall, in 1990 Entry Draft).

			Regular Season					Playoffs				
Season	Club	Lea	GP	G	A	TP	PIM	GP	G	A	TP	PIM
1990-91	U. Wisconsin	WCHA	33	1	2	3	54	....	....	....	....	....
1991-92	U. Wisconsin	WCHA	36	13	13	26	107	....	....	....	....	....
1992-93	U. Wisconsin	WCHA	42	26	31	57	142	....	....	....	....	....
1993-94	**NY Islanders**	**NHL**	12	0	1	1	4	1	1	0	1	2
	Salt Lake	IHL	66	7	17	24	148	....	....	....	....	....
	NHL Totals		**12**	**0**	**1**	**1**	**4**	**1**	**1**	**0**	**1**	**2**

PLANTE, DEREK — (PLAHNT) BUF.

Center. Shoots left. 5'11", 180 lbs. Born, Cloquet, MN, January 17, 1971.
(Buffalo's 7th choice, 161st overall, in 1989 Entry Draft).

			Regular Season					Playoffs				
Season	Club	Lea	GP	G	A	TP	PIM	GP	G	A	TP	PIM
1989-90	Minn.-Duluth	WCHA	28	10	11	21	12	....	....	....	....	....
1990-91	Minn.-Duluth	WCHA	36	23	20	43	6	....	....	....	....	....
1991-92a	Minn.-Duluth	WCHA	37	27	36	63	28	....	....	....	....	....
1992-93bc	Minn.-Duluth	WCHA	37	*36	*56	*92	30	....	....	....	....	....
1993-94	**Buffalo**	**NHL**	77	21	35	56	24	7	1	0	1	0
	U.S. National	....	2	0	1	1	0	....	....	....	....	....
	NHL Totals		**77**	**21**	**35**	**56**	**24**	**7**	**1**	**0**	**1**	**0**

a WCHA Second All-Star Team (1992)
b WCHA First All-Star Team (1993)
c NCAA West First All-American Team (1993)

PLAVSIC, ADRIEN — (PLAV-sihk)

Defense. Shoots left. 6'1", 200 lbs. Born, Montreal, Que., January 13, 1970.
(St. Louis' 2nd choice, 30th overall, in 1988 Entry Draft).

			Regular Season					Playoffs				
Season	Club	Lea	GP	G	A	TP	PIM	GP	G	A	TP	PIM
1987-88	N. Hampshire	H.E.	30	5	6	11	45	....	....	....	....	....
1988-89	Cdn. National	....	62	5	10	15	25	....	....	....	....	....
1989-90	**St. Louis**	**NHL**	4	0	1	1	2	....	....	....	....	....
	Peoria	IHL	51	7	14	21	87	....	....	....	....	....
	Vancouver	**NHL**	11	3	2	5	8	....	....	....	....	....
	Milwaukee	IHL	3	1	2	3	14	6	1	3	4	6
1990-91	**Vancouver**	**NHL**	48	2	10	12	62	....	....	....	....	....
1991-92	Cdn. National	....	38	6	8	14	29	....	....	....	....	....
	Cdn. Olympic	....	8	0	2	2	0	....	....	....	....	....
	Vancouver	**NHL**	16	1	9	10	14	13	1	7	8	4
1992-93	**Vancouver**	**NHL**	57	6	21	27	53	....	....	....	....	....
1993-94	**Vancouver**	**NHL**	47	1	9	10	6	....	....	....	....	....
	Hamilton	AHL	2	0	0	0	0	....	....	....	....	....
	NHL Totals		**183**	**13**	**52**	**65**	**145**	**13**	**1**	**7**	**8**	**4**

Traded to **Vancouver** by **St. Louis** with Montreal's first round choice (previously acquired by St. Louis — Vancouver selected Shawn Antoski) in 1990 Entry Draft and St. Louis' second round choice (later traded to Montreal — Montreal selected Craig Darby) in 1991 Entry Draft for Rich Sutter, Harold Snepsts and St. Louis' second round choice (previously acquired by Vancouver — St. Louis selected Craig Johnson) in 1990 Entry Draft, March 6, 1990.

PODEIN, SHJON — (poh-DEEN, SHAWN) PHI.

Center. Shoots left. 6'2", 200 lbs. Born, Rochester, MN, March 5, 1968.
(Edmonton's 9th choice, 166th overall, in 1988 Entry Draft).

			Regular Season					Playoffs				
Season	Club	Lea	GP	G	A	TP	PIM	GP	G	A	TP	PIM
1987-88	Minn.-Duluth	WCHA	30	4	4	8	48	....	....	....	....	....
1988-89	Minn.-Duluth	WCHA	36	7	5	12	46	....	....	....	....	....
1989-90	Minn.-Duluth	WCHA	35	21	18	39	36	....	....	....	....	....
1990-91	Cape Breton	AHL	63	14	15	29	65	4	0	0	0	5
1991-92	Cape Breton	AHL	80	30	24	54	46	5	3	1	4	2
1992-93	**Edmonton**	**NHL**	40	13	6	19	25	....	....	....	....	....
	Cape Breton	AHL	38	18	21	39	32	9	2	2	4	29
1993-94	**Edmonton**	**NHL**	28	3	5	8	8	....	....	....	....	....
	Cape Breton	AHL	5	4	4	8	4	....	....	....	....	....
	NHL Totals		**68**	**16**	**11**	**27**	**33**					

Signed as a free agent by **Philadelphia**, July 27, 1994.

PODOLLAN, JASON — FLA.

Right wing. Shoots right. 6'1", 181 lbs. Born, Vernon, B.C., February 18, 1976.
(Florida's 3rd choice, 31st overall, in 1994 Entry Draft).

			Regular Season					Playoffs				
Season	Club	Lea	GP	G	A	TP	PIM	GP	G	A	TP	PIM
1992-93	Spokane	WHL	72	36	33	69	108	10	4	4	8	14
1993-94	Spokane	WHL	69	29	37	66	108	3	3	0	3	2

POESCHEK, RUDY — (POH-shehk) T.B.

Right wing/Defense. Shoots right. 6'2", 210 lbs. Born, Kamloops, B.C., September 29, 1966.
(NY Rangers' 12th choice, 238th overall, in 1985 Entry Draft).

			Regular Season					Playoffs				
Season	Club	Lea	GP	G	A	TP	PIM	GP	G	A	TP	PIM
1983-84	Kamloops	WHL	47	3	9	12	93	8	0	2	2	7
1984-85	Kamloops	WHL	34	6	7	13	100	15	0	3	3	56
1985-86	Kamloops	WHL	32	3	13	16	92	16	3	7	10	40
1986-87	Kamloops	WHL	54	13	18	31	153	15	2	4	6	37
1987-88	**NY Rangers**	**NHL**	1	0	0	0	2	....	....	....	....	....
	Colorado	IHL	82	7	31	38	210	12	2	2	4	31
1988-89	**NY Rangers**	**NHL**	52	0	2	2	199	....	....	....	....	....
	Colorado	IHL	2	0	0	0	6	....	....	....	....	....
1989-90	**NY Rangers**	**NHL**	15	0	0	0	55	....	....	....	....	....
	Flint	IHL	38	8	13	21	109	4	0	0	0	16
1990-91	Binghamton	AHL	38	1	3	4	162	....	....	....	....	....
	Winnipeg	**NHL**	1	0	0	0	5	....	....	....	....	....
	Moncton	AHL	23	2	4	6	67	9	1	1	2	41
1991-92	**Winnipeg**	**NHL**	4	0	0	0	17	....	....	....	....	....
	Moncton	AHL	63	4	18	22	170	11	0	2	2	48
1992-93	St. John's	AHL	78	7	24	31	189	9	0	4	4	13
1993-94	**Tampa Bay**	**NHL**	71	3	6	9	118	....	....	....	....	....
	NHL Totals		**144**	**3**	**8**	**11**	**396**					

Traded to **Winnipeg** by **NY Rangers** for Guy Larose, January 22, 1991. Signed as a free agent by **Toronto**, July 8, 1992. Signed as a free agent by **Tampa Bay**, August 10, 1993.

POIRIER, JOEL — WSH.

Left wing. Shoots left. 6'1", 190 lbs. Born, Richmond Hill, Ont., January 15, 1975.
(Washington's 7th choice, 199th overall, in 1993 Entry Draft).

			Regular Season					Playoffs				
Season	Club	Lea	GP	G	A	TP	PIM	GP	G	A	TP	PIM
1992-93	Sudbury	OHL	64	18	15	33	94	14	0	2	2	8
1993-94	Sudbury	OHL	28	17	5	22	44	....	....	....	....	....
	Windsor	OHL	13	6	8	14	20	....	....	....	....	....

POLASEK, LIBOR — (poh-LAH-shehk) VAN.

Center. Shoots right. 6'3", 220 lbs. Born, Vitkovice, Czech., April 22, 1974.
(Vancouver's 1st choice, 21st overall, in 1992 Entry Draft).

			Regular Season					Playoffs				
Season	Club	Lea	GP	G	A	TP	PIM	GP	G	A	TP	PIM
1991-92	TJ Vitkovice	Czech.	17	2	2	4	4	....	....	....	....	....
1992-93	Hamilton	AHL	60	7	12	19	34	....	....	....	....	....
1993-94	Hamilton	AHL	76	11	12	23	40	3	0	0	0	0

POLISTCHUK, SERGEI — (poh-leh-SCHUHK) OTT.

Defense. Shoots left. 6'2", 200 lbs. Born, Moscow, USSR, January 11, 1975.
(Ottawa's 6th choice, 157th overall, in 1993 Entry Draft).

			Regular Season					Playoffs				
Season	Club	Lea	GP	G	A	TP	PIM	GP	G	A	TP	PIM
1992-93	Soviet Wings	CIS 2			UNAVAILABLE			....	....	....	....	....
1993-94	Shawinigan	QMJHL	52	1	5	6	100	5	0	0	0	10

POMICHTER, MICHAEL — CHI.

Center. Shoots left. 6'1", 222 lbs. Born, New Haven, CT, September 10, 1973.
(Chicago's 2nd choice, 39th overall, in 1991 Entry Draft).

			Regular Season					Playoffs				
Season	Club	Lea	GP	G	A	TP	PIM	GP	G	A	TP	PIM
1991-92	Boston U.	H.E.	34	11	27	38	14	....	....	....	....	....
1992-93	Boston U.	H.E.	30	16	14	30	23	....	....	....	....	....
1993-94a	Boston U.	H.E.	40	*28	26	54	37	....	....	....	....	....

a NCAA East First All-American Team (1994)

POPE, BRENT — EDM.

Defense. Shoots right. 6'3", 214 lbs. Born, Hamilton, Ont., February 20, 1973.

			Regular Season					Playoffs				
Season	Club	Lea	GP	G	A	TP	PIM	GP	G	A	TP	PIM
1989-90	Peterborough	OHL	31	0	7	7	14	....	....	....	....	....
1990-91	Peterborough	OHL	29	3	11	14	15	....	....	....	....	....
	Hamilton	OHL	29	1	6	7	30	....	....	....	....	....
1991-92	Guelph	OHL	65	10	38	48	108	....	....	....	....	....
1992-93	Guelph	OHL	34	10	14	24	40	....	....	....	....	....
	Ottawa	OHL	26	5	8	13	18	....	....	....	....	....
	Wheeling	ECHL	....	....	....	....	....	2	0	0	0	6
1993-94	Wheeling	ECHL	63	8	19	27	230	9	0	2	2	32

Signed as a free agent by **Edmonton**, January 28, 1993.

POPOVIC, PETER — MTL.

Defense. Shoots right. 6'5", 241 lbs. Born, Koping, Sweden, February 10, 1968.
(Montreal's 5th choice, 93rd overall, in 1988 Entry Draft).

			Regular Season					Playoffs				
Season	Club	Lea	GP	G	A	TP	PIM	GP	G	A	TP	PIM
1986-87	Vasteras	Swe. 2	24	1	2	3	10	....	....	....	....	....
1987-88	Vasteras	Swe. 2	28	3	17	20	16	....	....	....	....	....
1988-89	Vasteras	Swe.	22	1	4	5	32	....	....	....	....	....
1989-90	Vasteras	Swe.	30	2	10	12	24	2	0	1	1	2
1990-91	Vasteras	Swe.	40	3	2	5	62	4	0	0	0	4
1991-92	Vasteras	Swe.	34	7	10	17	30	....	....	....	....	....
1992-93	Vasteras	Swe.	39	6	12	18	46	3	0	1	1	2
1993-94	**Montreal**	**NHL**	**47**	**2**	**12**	**14**	**26**	**6**	**0**	**1**	**1**	**0**
	NHL Totals		**47**	**2**	**12**	**14**	**26**	**6**	**0**	**1**	**1**	**0**

PORKKA, TONI

Defense. Shoots right. 6'2", 190 lbs. Born, Rauma, Finland, February 4, 1970.
(Philadelphia's 12th choice, 172nd overall, in 1990 Entry Draft).

			Regular Season					Playoffs				
Season	Club	Lea	GP	G	A	TP	PIM	GP	G	A	TP	PIM
1988-89	Lukko	Fin.	44	2	2	4	18	....	....	....	....	....
1989-90	Lukko	Fin.	41	0	3	3	18	....	....	....	....	....
1990-91	Lukko	Fin.	34	2	2	4	8	....	....	....	....	....
1991-92	Hershey	AHL	64	3	5	8	34	....	....	....	....	....
1992-93	Hershey	AHL	49	6	13	19	22	....	....	....	....	....
1993-94	Hershey	AHL	51	6	7	13	43	10	0	1	1	8

POTAICHUK, ANDREI — CGY.

Right wing. Shoots left. 5'10", 195 lbs. Born, Temirtau, USSR, August 18, 1970.
(Calgary's 12th choice, 246th overall, in 1992 Entry Draft).

			Regular Season					Playoffs				
Season	Club	Lea	GP	G	A	TP	PIM	GP	G	A	TP	PIM
1987-88	Soviet Wings	USSR	11	1	0	1	0	....	....	....	....	....
1988-89	Soviet Wings	USSR	22	2	1	3	6	....	....	....	....	....
1989-90	Soviet Wings	USSR	46	8	8	16	22	....	....	....	....	....
1990-91	Soviet Wings	USSR	34	8	6	14	12	....	....	....	....	....
1991-92	Soviet Wings	CIS	41	16	7	23	34	....	....	....	....	....
1992-93	Soviet Wings	CIS	42	17	12	29	54	7	4	2	6	4
1993-94	Soviet Wings	CIS	43	13	22	35	20	3	1	0	1	2

POTAPOV, VLADIMIR (poh-TAH-pohv)

Right wing. Shoots left. 6'2", 187 lbs. Born, Murmansk, USSR, June 21, 1975.
(Winnipeg's 10th choice, 217th overall, in 1993 Entry Draft).

			Regular Season					Playoffs				
Season	Club	Lea	GP	G	A	TP	PIM	GP	G	A	TP	PIM
1992-93	Elektrostal	CIS 2				UNAVAILABLE						
1993-94	Elektrostal	CIS 2	41	3	3	6	4	....	....	....	....	....

POTOMSKI, BARRY — L.A.

Left wing. Shoots left. 6'2", 215 lbs. Born, Windsor, Ont., November 24, 1972.

			Regular Season					Playoffs				
Season	Club	Lea	GP	G	A	TP	PIM	GP	G	A	TP	PIM
1990-91	London	OHL	65	14	17	31	202	7	0	2	2	10
1991-92	London	OHL	61	19	32	51	224	10	5	1	6	22
1992-93	Erie	ECHL	5	1	1	2	31	....	....	....	....	....
	Toledo	ECHL	43	5	18	23	184	14	5	2	7	73
1993-94	Toledo	ECHL	13	9	4	13	81	....	....	....	....	....
	Adirondack	AHL	50	9	5	14	224	11	1	1	2	44

Signed as a free agent by **Los Angeles**, July 7, 1994.

POTVIN, MARC (POT-vahn) — HFD.

Right wing. Shoots right. 6'1", 200 lbs. Born, Ottawa, Ont., January 29, 1967.
(Detroit's 9th choice, 169th overall, in 1986 Entry Draft).

			Regular Season					Playoffs				
Season	Club	Lea	GP	G	A	TP	PIM	GP	G	A	TP	PIM
1986-87	Bowling Green	CCHA	43	5	15	20	74	....	....	....	....	....
1987-88	Bowling Green	CCHA	45	15	21	36	80	....	....	....	....	....
1988-89	Bowling Green	CCHA	46	23	12	35	63	....	....	....	....	....
1989-90	Bowling Green	CCHA	40	19	17	36	72	....	....	....	....	....
	Adirondack	AHL	5	2	1	3	9	4	0	1	1	23
1990-91	**Detroit**	**NHL**	**9**	**0**	**0**	**0**	**55**	**6**	**0**	**0**	**0**	**32**
	Adirondack	AHL	63	9	13	22	*365	....	....	....	....	....
1991-92	**Detroit**	**NHL**	**5**	**1**	**0**	**1**	**52**	**1**	**0**	**0**	**0**	**0**
	Adirondack	AHL	51	13	16	29	314	19	5	4	9	57
1992-93	Adirondack	AHL	37	8	12	20	109	....	....	....	....	....
	Los Angeles	**NHL**	**20**	**0**	**1**	**1**	**61**	**1**	**0**	**0**	**0**	**0**
1993-94	**Los Angeles**	**NHL**	**3**	**0**	**0**	**0**	**26**	....	....	....	....	....
	Hartford	**NHL**	**51**	**2**	**3**	**5**	**246**	....	....	....	....	....
	NHL Totals		**88**	**3**	**4**	**7**	**440**	**8**	**0**	**0**	**0**	**32**

Traded to **Los Angeles** by **Detroit** with Jimmy Carson and Gary Shuchuk for Paul Coffey, Sylvain Couturier and Jim Hiller, January 29, 1993. Traded to **Hartford** by **Los Angeles** for Doug Houda, November 3, 1993. Signed as a free agent by **Boston**, June 29, 1994.

POULIN, CHARLES (POO-lai)

Center. Shoots left. 6', 172 lbs. Born, St. Jean d'Iberville, Que., July 27, 1972.
(Montreal's 3rd choice, 58th overall, in 1990 Entry Draft).

			Regular Season					Playoffs				
Season	Club	Lea	GP	G	A	TP	PIM	GP	G	A	TP	PIM
1989-90	St-Hyacinthe	QMJHL	65	39	45	84	132	11	5	8	13	47
1990-91	St-Hyacinthe	QMJHL	64	25	46	71	166	4	1	1	2	6
1991-92ab	St-Hyacinthe	QMJHL	68	38	*97	135	113	6	2	2	4	20
1992-93	Fredericton	AHL	58	12	19	31	99	1	0	0	0	0
1993-94	Fredericton	AHL	35	9	15	24	70	....	....	....	....	....

a QMJHL First All-Star Team (1992)
b Canadian Major Junior Player of the Year (1992)

POULIN, DAVE (POO-lihn) — WSH.

Center. Shoots left. 5'11", 190 lbs. Born, Timmins, Ont., December 17, 1958.

			Regular Season					Playoffs				
Season	Club	Lea	GP	G	A	TP	PIM	GP	G	A	TP	PIM
1978-79	Notre Dame	WCHA	37	28	31	59	32	....	....	....	....	....
1979-80	Notre Dame	WCHA	24	19	24	43	46	....	....	....	....	....
1980-81	Notre Dame	WCHA	35	13	22	35	53	....	....	....	....	....
1981-82a	Notre Dame	CCHA	39	29	30	59	44	....	....	....	....	....
1982-83	Rogle	Swe.	32	35	27	62	64	....	....	....	....	....
	Philadelphia	**NHL**	**2**	**2**	**0**	**2**	**2**	**3**	**1**	**3**	**4**	**9**
	Maine	AHL	16	7	9	16	2	....	....	....	....	....
1983-84	**Philadelphia**	**NHL**	**73**	**31**	**45**	**76**	**47**	**3**	**0**	**0**	**0**	**2**
1984-85	**Philadelphia**	**NHL**	**73**	**30**	**44**	**74**	**59**	**11**	**3**	**5**	**8**	**6**
1985-86	**Philadelphia**	**NHL**	**79**	**27**	**42**	**69**	**49**	**5**	**2**	**0**	**2**	**2**
1986-87b	**Philadelphia**	**NHL**	**75**	**25**	**45**	**70**	**53**	**15**	**3**	**3**	**6**	**14**
1987-88	**Philadelphia**	**NHL**	**68**	**19**	**32**	**51**	**32**	**7**	**2**	**6**	**8**	**4**
1988-89	**Philadelphia**	**NHL**	**69**	**18**	**17**	**35**	**49**	**19**	**6**	**5**	**11**	**16**
1989-90	**Philadelphia**	**NHL**	**28**	**9**	**8**	**17**	**12**	....	....	....	....	....
	Boston	**NHL**	**32**	**6**	**19**	**25**	**12**	**18**	**8**	**5**	**13**	**8**
1990-91	**Boston**	**NHL**	**31**	**8**	**12**	**20**	**25**	**16**	**0**	**9**	**9**	**20**
1991-92	**Boston**	**NHL**	**18**	**4**	**4**	**8**	**18**	**15**	**3**	**3**	**6**	**22**
1992-93c	**Boston**	**NHL**	**84**	**16**	**33**	**49**	**62**	**4**	**1**	**1**	**2**	**10**
1993-94	**Washington**	**NHL**	**63**	**6**	**19**	**25**	**52**	**11**	**2**	**2**	**4**	**19**
	NHL Totals		**695**	**201**	**320**	**521**	**472**	**127**	**31**	**42**	**73**	**132**

a CCHA Second All-Star Team (1982)
b Won Frank J. Selke Trophy (1987)
c Won King Clancy Memorial Trophy (1993)

Played in NHL All-Star Game (1986, 1988)

Signed as a free agent by **Philadelphia**, March 8, 1983. Traded to **Boston** by **Philadelphia** for Ken Linseman, January 16, 1990. Signed as a free agent by **Washington**, August 3, 1993.

POULIN, PATRICK (poo-LIHN) — CHI.

Left wing. Shoots left. 6'1", 208 lbs. Born, Vanier, Que., April 23, 1973.
(Hartford's 1st choice, 9th overall, in 1991 Entry Draft).

			Regular Season					Playoffs				
Season	Club	Lea	GP	G	A	TP	PIM	GP	G	A	TP	PIM
1989-90	St-Hyacinthe	QMJHL	60	25	26	51	55	12	1	9	10	5
1990-91	St-Hyacinthe	QMJHL	56	32	38	70	82	4	0	2	2	23
1991-92	**Hartford**	**NHL**	**1**	**0**	**0**	**0**	**2**	**7**	**2**	**1**	**3**	**0**
a	St-Hyacinthe	QMJHL	56	52	86	*138	58	5	2	2	4	4
	Springfield	AHL	....	....	....	....	....	1	0	0	0	0
1992-93	**Hartford**	**NHL**	**81**	**20**	**31**	**51**	**37**	....	....	....	....	....
1993-94	**Hartford**	**NHL**	**9**	**2**	**1**	**3**	**11**	....	....	....	....	....
	Chicago	**NHL**	**58**	**12**	**13**	**25**	**40**	**4**	**0**	**0**	**0**	**0**
	NHL Totals		**149**	**34**	**45**	**79**	**90**	**11**	**2**	**1**	**3**	**0**

a QMJHL First All-Star Team (1992)

Traded to **Chicago** by **Hartford** with Eric Weinrich for Steve Larmer and Bryan Marchment, November 2, 1993.

POZZO, KEVIN

Defense. Shoots right. 6'1", 176 lbs. Born, Calgary, Alta., October 11, 1974.
(Buffalo's 4th choice, 142nd overall, in 1993 Entry Draft).

			Regular Season					Playoffs				
Season	Club	Lea	GP	G	A	TP	PIM	GP	G	A	TP	PIM
1992-93	Moose Jaw	WHL	72	10	29	39	95	....	....	....	....	....
1993-94	Moose Jaw	WHL	40	7	20	27	71	....	....	....	....	....
	Spokane	WHL	17	3	7	10	23	3	0	1	1	4

PRATT, JONATHAN

Center. Shoots left. 6'1", 195 lbs. Born, Danvers, MA, September 25, 1970.
(Minnesota's 9th choice, 154th overall, in 1989 Entry Draft).

			Regular Season					Playoffs				
Season	Club	Lea	GP	G	A	TP	PIM	GP	G	A	TP	PIM
1990-91	Boston U.	H.E.	16	3	1	4	26	....	....	....	....	....
1991-92	Boston U.	H.E.	29	8	4	12	42	....	....	....	....	....
1992-93	Boston U.	H.E.	31	9	8	17	70	....	....	....	....	....
1993-94	Boston U.	H.E.	32	11	8	19	66	....	....	....	....	....

PRATT, NOLAN — HFD.

Defense. Shoots left. 6'2", 190 lbs. Born, Fort McMurray, Alta., August 14, 1975.
(Hartford's 4th choice, 115th overall, in 1993 Entry Draft).

			Regular Season					Playoffs				
Season	Club	Lea	GP	G	A	TP	PIM	GP	G	A	TP	PIM
1991-92	Portland	WHL	22	2	9	11	13	6	1	3	4	12
1992-93	Portland	WHL	70	4	19	23	97	16	2	7	9	31
1993-94	Portland	WHL	72	4	32	36	105	....	....	....	....	....

PRESLEY, WAYNE — BUF.

Right wing. Shoots right. 5'11", 180 lbs. Born, Dearborn, MI, March 23, 1965.
(Chicago's 2nd choice, 39th overall, in 1983 Entry Draft).

			Regular Season					Playoffs				
Season	Club	Lea	GP	G	A	TP	PIM	GP	G	A	TP	PIM
1982-83	Kitchener	OHL	70	39	48	87	99	12	1	4	5	9
1983-84a	Kitchener	OHL	70	63	76	139	156	16	12	16	28	38
1984-85	**Chicago**	**NHL**	**3**	**0**	**1**	**1**	**0**	....	....	....	....	....
	Kitchener	OHL	31	25	21	46	77	....	....	....	....	....
	S.S. Marie	OHL	11	5	9	14	14	16	13	9	22	13
1985-86	**Chicago**	**NHL**	**38**	**7**	**8**	**15**	**38**	**3**	**0**	**0**	**0**	**0**
	Nova Scotia	AHL	29	6	9	15	22	....	....	....	....	....
1986-87	**Chicago**	**NHL**	**80**	**32**	**29**	**61**	**114**	**4**	**1**	**0**	**1**	**9**
1987-88	**Chicago**	**NHL**	**42**	**12**	**10**	**22**	**52**	**5**	**0**	**0**	**0**	**4**
1988-89	**Chicago**	**NHL**	**72**	**21**	**19**	**40**	**100**	**14**	**7**	**5**	**12**	**18**
1989-90	**Chicago**	**NHL**	**49**	**6**	**7**	**13**	**69**	**19**	**9**	**6**	**15**	**29**
1990-91	**Chicago**	**NHL**	**71**	**15**	**19**	**34**	**122**	**6**	**0**	**1**	**1**	**38**
1991-92	**San Jose**	**NHL**	**47**	**8**	**14**	**22**	**76**	....	....	....	....	....
	Buffalo	**NHL**	**12**	**2**	**2**	**4**	**57**	**7**	**3**	**3**	**6**	**14**
1992-93	**Buffalo**	**NHL**	**79**	**15**	**17**	**32**	**96**	**8**	**1**	**0**	**1**	**6**
1993-94	**Buffalo**	**NHL**	**65**	**17**	**8**	**25**	**103**	**7**	**2**	**1**	**3**	**14**
	NHL Totals		**558**	**135**	**134**	**269**	**827**	**73**	**23**	**16**	**39**	**132**

a OHL First All-Star Team (1984)

Traded to **San Jose** by **Chicago** for San Jose's third round choice (Bogdan Savenko) in 1993 Entry Draft, September 20, 1991. Traded to **Buffalo** by **San Jose** for Dave Snuggerud, March 9, 1992.

PRIESTLAY, KEN

Center. Shoots left. 5'10", 190 lbs. Born, Richmond, B.C., August 24, 1967.
(Buffalo's 5th choice, 98th overall, in 1985 Entry Draft).

			Regular Season					Playoffs				
Season	Club	Lea	GP	G	A	TP	PIM	GP	G	A	TP	PIM
1983-84	Victoria	WHL	55	10	18	28	31	....	....	....	....	....
1984-85	Victoria	WHL	50	25	37	62	48	....	....	....	....	....
1985-86	Victoria	WHL	72	73	72	145	45	....	....	....	....	....
	Rochester	AHL	4	0	2	2	0	....	....	....	....	....
1986-87	**Buffalo**	**NHL**	**34**	**11**	**6**	**17**	**8**	....	....	....	....	....
	Victoria	WHL	33	43	39	82	37	....	....	....	....	....
	Rochester	AHL	....	....	....	....	....	8	3	2	5	4
1987-88	**Buffalo**	**NHL**	**33**	**5**	**12**	**17**	**35**	**6**	**0**	**0**	**0**	**11**
	Rochester	AHL	43	27	24	51	47	....	....	....	....	....
1988-89	**Buffalo**	**NHL**	**15**	**2**	**0**	**2**	**2**	**3**	**0**	**0**	**0**	**2**
	Rochester	AHL	64	56	37	93	60	....	....	....	....	....
1989-90	**Buffalo**	**NHL**	**35**	**7**	**7**	**14**	**14**	**5**	**0**	**0**	**0**	**8**
	Rochester	AHL	40	19	39	58	46	....	....	....	....	....
1990-91	Cdn. National		40	20	26	46	34	....	....	....	....	....
	Pittsburgh	**NHL**	**2**	**0**	**1**	**1**	**0**	....	....	....	....	....
1991-92	**Pittsburgh**	**NHL**	**49**	**2**	**8**	**10**	**4**	....	....	....	....	....
	Muskegon	IHL	13	4	11	15	6	13	5	11	16	10
1992-93	Cleveland	IHL	66	33	36	69	72	4	2	1	3	4
1993-94	Kalamazoo	IHL	25	9	5	14	34	5	2	1	3	2
	NHL Totals		**168**	**27**	**34**	**61**	**63**	**14**	**0**	**0**	**0**	**21**

Traded to **Pittsburgh** by **Buffalo** for Tony Tanti, March 5, 1991.

PRIMEAU, KEITH — DET.

Center. Shoots left. 6'4", 210 lbs. Born, Toronto, Ont., November 24, 1971.
(Detroit's 1st choice, 3rd overall, in 1990 Entry Draft).

			Regular Season					Playoffs				
Season	Club	Lea	GP	G	A	TP	PIM	GP	G	A	TP	PIM
1987-88	Hamilton	OHL	47	6	6	12	69	....	....	....	....	....
1988-89	Niagara Falls	OHL	48	20	35	55	56	17	9	16	25	12
1989-90a	Niagara Falls	OHL	65	*57	70	*127	97	16	*16	17	*33	49
1990-91	**Detroit**	**NHL**	**58**	**3**	**12**	**15**	**106**	**5**	**1**	**1**	**2**	**25**
	Adirondack	AHL	6	3	5	8	8	....	....	....	....	....
1991-92	**Detroit**	**NHL**	**35**	**6**	**10**	**16**	**83**	**11**	**0**	**0**	**0**	**14**
	Adirondack	AHL	42	21	24	45	89	9	1	7	8	27
1992-93	**Detroit**	**NHL**	**73**	**15**	**17**	**32**	**152**	**7**	**0**	**2**	**2**	**26**
1993-94	**Detroit**	**NHL**	**78**	**31**	**42**	**73**	**173**	**7**	**0**	**2**	**2**	**6**
	NHL Totals		**244**	**55**	**81**	**136**	**514**	**30**	**1**	**5**	**6**	**71**

a OHL Second All-Star Team (1990)

PRIMEAU, WAYNE — BUF.

Center. Shoots left. 6'3", 193 lbs. Born, Scarborough, Ont., June 4, 1976.
(Buffalo's 1st choice, 17th overall, in 1994 Entry Draft).

			Regular Season					Playoffs				
Season	Club	Lea	GP	G	A	TP	PIM	GP	G	A	TP	PIM
1986-87	Skelleftea	Swe.	33	2	4	6	16	....	....	....	....	....
1987-88	Skelleftea	Swe.	16	1	4	5	8	....	....	....	....	....
1991-92	Brynas	Swe.	40	7	9	16	22	5	....	....	....	2
1992-93	Owen Sound	OHL	66	10	27	37	108	8	1	4	5	0
1993-94	Owen Sound	OHL	65	25	50	75	75	9	1	6	7	8

PROBERT, BOB (PROH-buhrt) — CHI.

Right wing. Shoots left. 6'3", 225 lbs. Born, Windsor, Ont., June 5, 1965.
(Detroit's 3rd choice, 46th overall, in 1983 Entry Draft).

			Regular Season					Playoffs				
Season	Club	Lea	GP	G	A	TP	PIM	GP	G	A	TP	PIM
1982-83	Brantford	OHL	51	12	16	28	133	8	2	2	4	23
1983-84	Brantford	OHL	65	35	38	73	189	6	0	3	3	16
1984-85	S.S. Marie	OHL	44	20	52	72	172	....	....	....	....	....
	Hamilton	OHL	4	0	1	1	21	....	....	....	....	....
1985-86	**Detroit**	**NHL**	**44**	**8**	**13**	**21**	**186**	....	....	....	....	....
	Adirondack	AHL	32	12	15	27	152	10	2	3	5	68
1986-87	**Detroit**	**NHL**	**63**	**13**	**11**	**24**	**221**	**16**	**3**	**4**	**7**	**63**
	Adirondack	AHL	7	1	4	5	15	....	....	....	....	....
1987-88	**Detroit**	**NHL**	**74**	**29**	**33**	**62**	***398**	**16**	**8**	**13**	**21**	**51**
1988-89	**Detroit**	**NHL**	**25**	**4**	**2**	**6**	**106**	....	....	....	....	....
1989-90	**Detroit**	**NHL**	**4**	**3**	**0**	**3**	**21**	....	....	....	....	....
1990-91	**Detroit**	**NHL**	**55**	**16**	**23**	**39**	**315**	**6**	**1**	**2**	**3**	**50**
1991-92	**Detroit**	**NHL**	**63**	**20**	**24**	**44**	**276**	**11**	**1**	**6**	**7**	**28**
1992-93	**Detroit**	**NHL**	**80**	**14**	**29**	**43**	**292**	**7**	**0**	**3**	**3**	**10**
1993-94	**Detroit**	**NHL**	**66**	**7**	**10**	**17**	**275**	**7**	**1**	**1**	**2**	**8**
	NHL Totals		**474**	**114**	**145**	**259**	**2090**	**63**	**14**	**29**	**43**	**210**

Played in NHL All-Star Game (1988)

Signed as a free agent by **Chicago**, July 23, 1994.

PROCHAZKA, LIBOR (proh-HAHZ-kah) — ST.L.

Defense. Shoots right. 6', 185 lbs. Born, Vlasim, Czech., April 25, 1974.
(St. Louis' 8th choice, 245th overall, in 1993 Entry Draft).

			Regular Season					Playoffs				
Season	Club	Lea	GP	G	A	TP	PIM	GP	G	A	TP	PIM
1991-92	Poldi Kladno	Czech.	7	0	0	0	0	....	....	....	....	....
1992-93	Poldi Kladno	Czech.	34	2	2	4	....	....	....	....	....	....
1993-94	Poldi Kladno	Czech.	41	4	7	11	....	8	0	3	3	....

PROCHAZKA, MARTIN (pro-HAHS-kah) — TOR.

Center. Shoots right. 5'11", 180 lbs. Born, Slany, Czech., March 3, 1972.
(Toronto's 8th choice, 135th overall, in 1991 Entry Draft).

			Regular Season					Playoffs				
Season	Club	Lea	GP	G	A	TP	PIM	GP	G	A	TP	PIM
1989-90	Kladno	Czech.	49	18	12	30	....	....	....	....	....	....
1990-91	Kladno	Czech.	50	19	10	29	21	....	....	....	....	....
1991-92	Dukla Jihlava	Czech.	44	18	11	29	2	....	....	....	....	....
1992-93	Kladno	Czech.	46	26	12	38	....	....	....	....	....	....
1993-94	Kladno	Czech.	43	24	16	40	0	2	2	0	2	....

PROKHOROV, VITALI (PROH-kohr-ohv) — ST.L.

Left wing. Shoots left. 5'9", 185 lbs. Born, Moscow, USSR, December 25, 1966.
(St. Louis' 3rd choice, 64th overall, in 1992 Entry Draft).

			Regular Season					Playoffs				
Season	Club	Lea	GP	G	A	TP	PIM	GP	G	A	TP	PIM
1983-84	Spartak	USSR	5	0	0	0	0	....	....	....	....	....
1984-85	Spartak	USSR	31	1	1	2	10	....	....	....	....	....
1985-86	Spartak	USSR	29	3	9	12	4	....	....	....	....	....
1986-87	Spartak	USSR	27	1	6	7	2	....	....	....	....	....
1987-88	Spartak	USSR	19	5	0	5	4	....	....	....	....	....
1988-89	Spartak	USSR	37	11	5	16	10	....	....	....	....	....
1989-90	Spartak	USSR	43	13	8	21	35	....	....	....	....	....
1990-91	Spartak	USSR	43	21	10	31	29	....	....	....	....	....
1991-92	Spartak	CIS	38	13	19	32	68	....	....	....	....	....
1992-93	**St. Louis**	**NHL**	**26**	**4**	**1**	**5**	**15**	....	....	....	....	....
1993-94	**St. Louis**	**NHL**	**55**	**15**	**10**	**25**	**20**	**4**	**0**	**0**	**0**	**0**
	Peoria	IHL	19	13	10	23	16	....	....	....	....	....
	NHL Totals		**81**	**19**	**11**	**30**	**35**	**4**	**0**	**0**	**0**	**0**

PROKOPEC, MIKE — CHI.

Right wing. Shoots right. 6'2", 190 lbs. Born, Toronto, Ont., May 17, 1974.
(Chicago's 7th choice, 161st overall, in 1992 Entry Draft).

			Regular Season					Playoffs				
Season	Club	Lea	GP	G	A	TP	PIM	GP	G	A	TP	PIM
1991-92	Cornwall	OHL	59	12	15	27	75	6	0	0	0	0
1992-93	Newmarket	OHL	40	6	14	20	70	....	....	....	....	....
	Guelph	OHL	28	10	14	24	27	5	1	0	1	14
1993-94	Guelph	OHL	66	52	58	110	93	9	12	4	16	17

PRONGER, CHRIS — HFD.

Defense. Shoots left. 6'5", 190 lbs. Born, Dryden, Ont., October 10, 1974.
(Hartford's 1st choice, 2nd overall, in 1993 Entry Draft).

			Regular Season					Playoffs				
Season	Club	Lea	GP	G	A	TP	PIM	GP	G	A	TP	PIM
1991-92	Peterborough	OHL	63	17	45	62	90	10	1	8	9	28
1992-93ab	Peterborough	OHL	61	15	62	77	108	21	15	25	40	51
1993-94c	**Hartford**	**NHL**	**81**	**5**	**25**	**30**	**113**	....	....	....	....	....
	NHL Totals		**81**	**5**	**25**	**30**	**113**	....	....	....	....	....

a OHL First All-Star Team (1993)
b Canadian Major Junior First All-Star Team (1993)
c NHL/Upper Deck All-Rookie Team (1994)

PRONGER, SEAN

Center. Shoots left. 6'2", 205 lbs. Born, Dryden, Ont., November 30, 1972.
(Vancouver's 3rd choice, 51st overall, in 1991 Entry Draft).

			Regular Season					Playoffs				
Season	Club	Lea	GP	G	A	TP	PIM	GP	G	A	TP	PIM
1990-91	Bowling Green	CCHA	40	3	7	10	30	....	....	....	....	....
1991-92	Bowling Green	CCHA	34	9	7	16	28	....	....	....	....	....
1992-93	Bowling Green	CCHA	39	23	23	46	35	....	....	....	....	....
1993-94	Bowling Green	CCHA	38	17	17	34	38	....	....	....	....	....

PROPP, BRIAN

Left wing. Shoots left. 5'10", 195 lbs. Born, Lanigan, Sask., February 15, 1959.
(Philadelphia's 1st choice, 14th overall, in 1979 Entry Draft).

			Regular Season					Playoffs				
Season	Club	Lea	GP	G	A	TP	PIM	GP	G	A	TP	PIM
1976-77	Brandon	WHL	72	55	80	135	47	16	*14	12	26	5
1977-78a	Brandon	WHL	70	70	*112	*182	200	8	7	6	13	12
1978-79a	Brandon	WHL	71	*94	*100	*194	127	22	15	23	*38	40
1979-80	**Philadelphia**	**NHL**	**80**	**34**	**41**	**75**	**54**	**19**	**5**	**10**	**15**	**29**
1980-81	**Philadelphia**	**NHL**	**79**	**26**	**40**	**66**	**110**	**12**	**6**	**6**	**12**	**32**
1981-82	**Philadelphia**	**NHL**	**80**	**44**	**47**	**91**	**117**	**4**	**2**	**2**	**4**	**4**
1982-83	**Philadelphia**	**NHL**	**80**	**40**	**42**	**82**	**72**	**3**	**1**	**2**	**3**	**8**
1983-84	**Philadelphia**	**NHL**	**79**	**39**	**53**	**92**	**37**	**3**	**0**	**1**	**1**	**6**
1984-85	**Philadelphia**	**NHL**	**76**	**43**	**54**	**97**	**43**	**19**	**8**	**10**	**18**	**6**
1985-86	**Philadelphia**	**NHL**	**72**	**40**	**57**	**97**	**47**	**5**	**0**	**2**	**2**	**4**
1986-87	**Philadelphia**	**NHL**	**53**	**31**	**36**	**67**	**45**	**26**	**12**	**16**	**28**	**10**
1987-88	**Philadelphia**	**NHL**	**74**	**27**	**49**	**76**	**76**	**7**	**4**	**2**	**6**	**8**
1988-89	**Philadelphia**	**NHL**	**77**	**32**	**46**	**78**	**37**	**18**	**14**	**9**	**23**	**14**
1989-90	**Philadelphia**	**NHL**	**40**	**13**	**15**	**28**	**31**	....	....	....	....	....
	Boston	**NHL**	**14**	**3**	**9**	**12**	**10**	**20**	**4**	**9**	**13**	**2**
1990-91	**Minnesota**	**NHL**	**79**	**26**	**47**	**73**	**58**	**23**	**8**	**15**	**23**	**28**
1991-92	**Minnesota**	**NHL**	**51**	**12**	**23**	**35**	**49**	**1**	**0**	**0**	**0**	**0**
1992-93	**Minnesota**	**NHL**	**17**	**3**	**3**	**6**	**0**	....	....	....	....	....
	Lugano	Switz.	24	21	6	27	32	....	....	....	....	....
	Cdn. National	....	3	3	1	4	2	....	....	....	....	....
1993-94	**Hartford**	**NHL**	**65**	**12**	**17**	**29**	**44**	....	....	....	....	....
	NHL Totals		**1016**	**425**	**579**	**1004**	**830**	**160**	**64**	**84**	**148**	**151**

a WHL First All-Star Team (1978, 1979)

Played in NHL All-Star Game (1980, 1982, 1984, 1986, 1990)

Traded to **Boston** by **Philadelphia** for Boston's second round choice (Terran Sandwith) in 1990 Entry Draft, March 2, 1990. Signed as a free agent by **Minnesota**, July 25, 1990. Signed as a free agent by **Hartford**, October 4, 1993.

PROSOFSKY, TYLER — CHI.

Center. Shoots left. 5'11", 175 lbs. Born, Saskatoon, Sask., February 19, 1976.
(Chicago's 7th choice, 170th overall, in 1994 Entry Draft).

			Regular Season					Playoffs				
Season	Club	Lea	GP	G	A	TP	PIM	GP	G	A	TP	PIM
1992-93	Tacoma	WHL	62	10	9	19	79	7	0	0	0	5
1993-94	Tacoma	WHL	70	20	22	42	132	8	1	1	2	23

PROSPAL, VACLAV — PHI.

Center. Shoots left. 6'2", 173 lbs. Born, Ceske-Budejovice, Czech., February 17, 1975.
(Philadelphia's 2nd choice, 71st overall, in 1993 Entry Draft).

			Regular Season					Playoffs				
Season	Club	Lea	GP	G	A	TP	PIM	GP	G	A	TP	PIM
1992-93	Budejovice Jrs.	Czech.	32	26	31	57	24	....	....	....	....	....
1993-94	Hershey	AHL	55	14	21	35	38	2	0	0	0	2

PROULX, CHRISTIAN (PROO) MTL.

Defense. Shoots left. 6'1", 190 lbs. Born, Sherbrooke, Que., December 10, 1973.
(Montreal's 7th choice, 164th overall, in 1992 Entry Draft).

			Regular Season					Playoffs				
Season	Club	Lea	GP	G	A	TP	PIM	GP	G	A	TP	PIM
1990-91	St-Jean	QMJHL	67	1	8	9	73	....	....	....	....	....
1991-92	St-Jean	QMJHL	68	1	17	18	180	....	....	....	....	....
1992-93	St-Jean	QMJHL	70	3	34	37	147	4	0	0	0	12
	Fredericton	AHL	2	1	0	1	2	4	0	0	0	0
1993-94	**Montreal**	**NHL**	**7**	**1**	**2**	**3**	**20**	....	....	....	....	....
	Fredericton	AHL	70	2	12	14	183	....	....	....	....	....
	NHL Totals		**7**	**1**	**2**	**3**	**20**	....	....	....	....	....

PROVENCHER, JIMMY N.J.

Right wing. Shoots right. 6'3", 200 lbs. Born, Kitchener, Ont., March 22, 1975.
(New Jersey's 10th choice, 247th overall, in 1993 Entry Draft).

			Regular Season					Playoffs				
Season	Club	Lea	GP	G	A	TP	PIM	GP	G	A	TP	PIM
1992-93	St-Jean	QMJHL	45	7	12	19	16	4	0	0	0	8
1993-94	St-Jean	QMJHL	64	33	29	62	82	5	1	1	2	6

PRPIC, JOEL BOS.

Center. Shoots left. 6'6", 200 lbs. Born, Sudbury, Ont., September 25, 1974.
(Boston's 9th choice, 233rd overall, in 1993 Entry Draft).

			Regular Season					Playoffs				
Season	Club	Lea	GP	G	A	TP	PIM	GP	G	A	TP	PIM
1992-93	Waterloo	Jr. B	45	17	43	60	160	....	....	....	....	....
1993-94	St. Lawrence	ECAC	31	2	4	6	90	....	....	....	....	....

PRPIC, TONY (PUHR-pihk) MTL.

Right wing. Shoots right. 6'4", 207 lbs. Born, Euclid, OH, June 16, 1973.
(Montreal's 8th choice, 105th overall, in 1991 Entry Draft).

			Regular Season					Playoffs				
Season	Club	Lea	GP	G	A	TP	PIM	GP	G	A	TP	PIM
1992-93	Tri-City	WHL	63	16	17	33	119	3	1	0	1	0
1993-94	Fredericton	AHL	13	1	2	3	7	....	....	....	....	....
	Wheeling	ECHL	40	17	16	33	39	8	3	3	6	15

PULLOLA, TOMMI (PUHL-loh-lah) CHI.

Center. Shoots left. 6'5", 202 lbs. Born, Vaasa, Finland, May 18, 1971.
(Chicago's 4th choice, 111th overall, in 1989 Entry Draft).

			Regular Season					Playoffs				
Season	Club	Lea	GP	G	A	TP	PIM	GP	G	A	TP	PIM
1988-89	Sport	Fin. 2	40	11	13	24	....	....	....	....	....	....
1989-90	Lukko	Fin.	40	7	9	16	8	....	....	....	....	....
1990-91	Lukko	Fin.	42	17	17	34	40	....	....	....	....	....
1991-92	Lukko	Fin.	44	15	9	24	36	2	1	0	1	2
1992-93	Lukko	Fin.	25	3	7	10	14	....	....	....	....	....
1993-94	Lukko	Fin.	1	0	0	0	0	....	....	....	....	....
	Tuto	Fin.	36	13	29	42	69	....	....	....	....	....

PUSHOR, JAMIE DET.

Defense. Shoots right. 6'3", 205 lbs. Born, Lethbridge, Alta., February 11, 1973.
(Detroit's 2nd choice, 32nd overall, in 1991 Entry Draft).

			Regular Season					Playoffs				
Season	Club	Lea	GP	G	A	TP	PIM	GP	G	A	TP	PIM
1989-90	Lethbridge	WHL	10	0	2	2	2	....	....	....	....	....
1990-91	Lethbridge	WHL	71	1	13	14	193	....	....	....	....	....
1991-92	Lethbridge	WHL	49	2	15	17	232	5	0	0	0	33
1992-93	Lethbridge	WHL	72	6	22	28	200	4	0	1	1	9
1993-94	Adirondack	AHL	73	1	17	18	124	12	0	0	0	22

PYSZ, PATRIK CHI.

Center. Shoots left. 5'11", 187 lbs. Born, Novy Targ, Poland, January 15, 1975.
(Chicago's 6th choice, 102nd overall, in 1993 Entry Draft).

			Regular Season					Playoffs				
Season	Club	Lea	GP	G	A	TP	PIM	GP	G	A	TP	PIM
1992-93	Augsburg	Ger. 2	36	7	5	12	12	8	2	1	3	0
1993-94	Augsburg	Aut.	41	7	20	27	....	9	5	5	10	8

QUINN, DAN

Center. Shoots left. 5'11", 182 lbs. Born, Ottawa, Ont., June 1, 1965.
(Calgary's 1st choice, 13th overall, in 1983 Entry Draft).

			Regular Season					Playoffs				
Season	Club	Lea	GP	G	A	TP	PIM	GP	G	A	TP	PIM
1981-82	Belleville	OHL	67	19	32	51	41	....	....	....	....	....
1982-83	Belleville	OHL	70	59	88	147	27	4	2	6	8	2
1983-84	**Calgary**	**NHL**	**54**	**19**	**33**	**52**	**20**	**8**	**3**	**5**	**8**	**4**
	Belleville	OHL	24	23	36	59	12	....	....	....	....	....
1984-85	**Calgary**	**NHL**	**74**	**20**	**38**	**58**	**22**	**3**	**0**	**0**	**0**	**0**
1985-86	**Calgary**	**NHL**	**78**	**30**	**42**	**72**	**44**	**18**	**8**	**7**	**15**	**10**
1986-87	**Calgary**	**NHL**	**16**	**3**	**6**	**9**	**14**	....	....	....	....	....
	Pittsburgh	**NHL**	**64**	**28**	**43**	**71**	**40**	....	....	....	....	....
1987-88	**Pittsburgh**	**NHL**	**70**	**40**	**39**	**79**	**50**	....	....	....	....	....
1988-89	**Pittsburgh**	**NHL**	**79**	**34**	**60**	**94**	**102**	**11**	**6**	**3**	**9**	**10**
1989-90	**Pittsburgh**	**NHL**	**41**	**9**	**20**	**29**	**22**	....	....	....	....	....
	Vancouver	**NHL**	**37**	**16**	**18**	**34**	**27**	....	....	....	....	....
1990-91	**Vancouver**	**NHL**	**64**	**18**	**31**	**49**	**46**	....	....	....	....	....
	St. Louis	**NHL**	**14**	**4**	**7**	**11**	**20**	**13**	**4**	**7**	**11**	**32**
1991-92	**Philadelphia**	**NHL**	**67**	**11**	**26**	**37**	**26**	....	....	....	....	....
1992-93	**Minnesota**	**NHL**	**11**	**0**	**4**	**4**	**6**	....	....	....	....	....
1993-94	**Ottawa**	**NHL**	**13**	**7**	**0**	**7**	**6**	....	....	....	....	....
	NHL Totals		**682**	**239**	**367**	**606**	**445**	**53**	**21**	**22**	**43**	**56**

Traded to **Pittsburgh** by **Calgary** for Mike Bullard, November 12, 1986. Traded to **Vancouver** by **Pittsburgh** with Dave Capuano and Andrew McBain for Rod Buskas, Barry Pederson and Tony Tanti, January 8, 1990. Traded to **St. Louis** by **Vancouver** with Garth Butcher for Geoff Courtnall, Robert Dirk, Sergio Momesso, Cliff Ronning and St. Louis' fifth round choice (Brian Loney) in 1992 Entry Draft, March 5, 1991. Traded to **Philadelphia** by **St. Louis** with Rod Brind'Amour for Ron Sutter and Murray Baron, September 22, 1991. Signed as a free agent by **Minnesota**, October 4, 1992. Signed as a free agent by **Ottawa**, March 15, 1994.

QUINNEY, KEN (KWIH-nee)

Right wing. Shoots right. 5'10", 186 lbs. Born, New Westminster, B.C., May 23, 1965.
(Quebec's 9th choice, 203rd overall, in 1984 Entry Draft).

			Regular Season					Playoffs				
Season	Club	Lea	GP	G	A	TP	PIM	GP	G	A	TP	PIM
1981-82	Calgary	WHL	63	11	17	28	55	2	0	0	0	15
1982-83	Calgary	WHL	71	26	25	51	71	16	6	1	7	46
1983-84	Calgary	WHL	71	64	54	118	38	4	5	2	7	0
1984-85a	Calgary	WHL	56	47	67	114	65	7	6	4	10	15
1985-86	Fredericton	AHL	61	11	26	37	34	6	2	2	4	9
1986-87	**Quebec**	**NHL**	**25**	**2**	**7**	**9**	**16**	....	....	....	....	....
	Fredericton	AHL	48	14	27	41	20	....	....	....	....	....
1987-88	**Quebec**	**NHL**	**15**	**2**	**2**	**4**	**5**	....	....	....	....	....
	Fredericton	AHL	58	37	39	76	39	13	3	5	8	35
1988-89	Halifax	AHL	72	41	49	90	65	4	3	0	3	0
1989-90	Halifax	AHL	44	9	16	25	63	2	0	0	0	2
1990-91	**Quebec**	**NHL**	**19**	**3**	**4**	**7**	**2**	....	....	....	....	....
	Halifax	AHL	44	20	20	40	76	....	....	....	....	....
1991-92	Adirondack	AHL	63	31	29	60	33	19	7	12	19	9
1992-93	Adirondack	AHL	63	32	34	66	15	10	2	9	11	9
1993-94b	Las Vegas	IHL	79	*55	53	108	52	5	3	3	6	2
	NHL Totals		**59**	**7**	**13**	**20**	**23**	....	....	....	....	....

a WHL East First All-Star Team (1985)
b IHL First All-Star Team (1994)

Signed as a free agent by **Detroit**, August 12, 1991.

QUINT, DERON WPG.

Defense. Shoots left. 6'1", 182 lbs. Born, Durham, NH, March 12, 1976.
(Winnipeg's 1st choice, 30th overall, in 1994 Entry Draft).

			Regular Season					Playoffs				
Season	Club	Lea	GP	G	A	TP	PIM	GP	G	A	TP	PIM
1992-93	Tabor Acad.	HS	28	16	26	42	12	1	0	2	2	0
1993-94	Seattle	WHL	63	15	29	44	47	9	4	12	16	8

QUINTAL, STEPHANE (KAYN-tahl) WPG.

Defense. Shoots right. 6'3", 215 lbs. Born, Boucherville, Que., October 22, 1968.
(Boston's 2nd choice, 14th overall, in 1987 Entry Draft).

			Regular Season					Playoffs				
Season	Club	Lea	GP	G	A	TP	PIM	GP	G	A	TP	PIM
1985-86	Granby	QMJHL	67	2	17	19	144	....	....	....	....	....
1986-87a	Granby	QMJHL	67	13	41	54	178	8	0	9	9	10
1987-88	Hull	QMJHL	38	13	23	36	138	19	7	12	19	30
1988-89	**Boston**	**NHL**	**26**	**0**	**1**	**1**	**29**	....	....	....	....	....
	Maine	AHL	16	4	10	14	28	....	....	....	....	....
1989-90	**Boston**	**NHL**	**38**	**2**	**2**	**4**	**22**	....	....	....	....	....
	Maine	AHL	37	4	16	20	27	....	....	....	....	....
1990-91	**Boston**	**NHL**	**45**	**2**	**6**	**8**	**89**	**3**	**0**	**1**	**1**	**7**
	Maine	AHL	23	1	5	6	30	....	....	....	....	....
1991-92	**Boston**	**NHL**	**49**	**4**	**10**	**14**	**77**	....	....	....	....	....
	St. Louis	**NHL**	**26**	**0**	**6**	**6**	**32**	**4**	**1**	**2**	**3**	**6**
1992-93	**St. Louis**	**NHL**	**75**	**1**	**10**	**11**	**100**	**9**	**0**	**0**	**0**	**8**
1993-94	**Winnipeg**	**NHL**	**81**	**8**	**18**	**26**	**119**	....	....	....	....	....
	NHL Totals		**340**	**17**	**53**	**70**	**468**	**16**	**1**	**3**	**4**	**21**

a QMJHL First All-Star Team (1987)

Traded to **St. Louis** by **Boston** with Craig Janney for Adam Oates, February 7, 1992. Traded to **Winnipeg** by **St. Louis** with Nelson Emerson for Phil Housley, September 24, 1993.

QUINTIN, JEAN-FRANCOIS S.J.

Left wing. Shoots left. 6', 187 lbs. Born, St. Jean, Que., May 28, 1969.
(Minnesota's 4th choice, 75th overall, in 1989 Entry Draft).

			Regular Season					Playoffs				
Season	Club	Lea	GP	G	A	TP	PIM	GP	G	A	TP	PIM
1987-88	Shawinigan	QMJHL	70	28	70	98	143	11	5	8	13	26
1988-89	Shawinigan	QMJHL	69	52	100	152	105	10	9	15	24	16
1989-90	Kalamazoo	IHL	68	20	18	38	38	10	8	4	12	14
1990-91	Kalamazoo	IHL	78	31	43	74	64	9	1	5	6	11
1991-92	**San Jose**	**NHL**	**8**	**3**	**0**	**3**	**0**	....	....	....	....	....
	Kansas City	IHL	21	4	6	10	29	13	2	10	12	29
1992-93	**San Jose**	**NHL**	**14**	**2**	**5**	**7**	**4**	....	....	....	....	....
	Kansas City	IHL	64	20	29	49	169	11	2	1	3	16
1993-94	Kansas City	IHL	41	14	19	33	117	....	....	....	....	....
	NHL Totals		**22**	**5**	**5**	**10**	**4**	....	....	....	....	....

Claimed by **San Jose** from **Minnesota** in Dispersal Draft, May 30, 1991.

RABY, MATHIEU T.B.

Defense. Shoots right. 6'2", 204 lbs. Born, Hull, Que., January 19, 1975.
(Tampa Bay's 7th choice, 159th overall, in 1993 Entry Draft).

			Regular Season					Playoffs				
Season	Club	Lea	GP	G	A	TP	PIM	GP	G	A	TP	PIM
1992-93	Victoriaville	QMJHL	53	2	2	4	103	2	0	0	0	0
1993-94	Victoriaville	QMJHL	67	3	7	10	264	5	0	0	0	22

RACINE, YVES (ruh-SEEN, EEV) MTL.

Defense. Shoots left. 6', 200 lbs. Born, Matane, Que., February 7, 1969.
(Detroit's 1st choice, 11th overall, in 1987 Entry Draft).

			Regular Season					Playoffs				
Season	Club	Lea	GP	G	A	TP	PIM	GP	G	A	TP	PIM
1986-87	Longueuil	QMJHL	70	7	43	50	50	20	3	11	14	14
1987-88	Adirondack	AHL	....	....	....	....	....	9	4	2	6	2
a	Victoriaville	QMJHL	69	10	84	94	150	5	0	0	0	13
1988-89a	Victoriaville	QMJHL	63	23	85	108	95	16	3	*30	*33	41
	Adirondack	AHL	....	....	....	....	....	2	1	1	2	0
1989-90	**Detroit**	**NHL**	**28**	**4**	**9**	**13**	**23**	....	....	....	....	....
	Adirondack	AHL	46	8	27	35	31	....	....	....	....	....
1990-91	**Detroit**	**NHL**	**62**	**7**	**40**	**47**	**33**	**7**	**2**	**0**	**2**	**0**
	Adirondack	AHL	16	3	9	12	10	....	....	....	....	....
1991-92	**Detroit**	**NHL**	**61**	**2**	**22**	**24**	**94**	**11**	**2**	**1**	**3**	**10**
1992-93	**Detroit**	**NHL**	**80**	**9**	**31**	**40**	**80**	**7**	**1**	**3**	**4**	**27**
1993-94	**Philadelphia**	**NHL**	**67**	**9**	**43**	**52**	**48**	....	....	....	....	....
	NHL Totals		**298**	**31**	**145**	**176**	**278**	**25**	**5**	**4**	**9**	**37**

a QMJHL First-All Star Team (1988, 1989)

Traded to **Philadelphia** by **Detroit** with Detroit's fourth round choice (Sebastien Vallee) in 1994 Entry Draft for Terry Carkner, October 5, 1993. Traded to **Montreal** by **Philadelphia** for Kevin Haller, June 29, 1994.

RAGLAN, HERB

Right wing. Shoots right. 6', 205 lbs. Born, Peterborough, Ont., August 5, 1967.
(St. Louis' 1st choice, 37th overall, in 1985 Entry Draft).

			Regular Season					Playoffs				
Season	Club	Lea	GP	G	A	TP	PIM	GP	G	A	TP	PIM
1984-85	Peterborough	OHL	58	20	22	42	166	....	....	....	....	....
1985-86	**St. Louis**	**NHL**	**7**	**0**	**0**	**0**	**5**	**10**	**1**	**1**	**2**	**24**
	Kingston	OHL	28	10	9	19	88	10	5	2	7	30
1986-87	**St. Louis**	**NHL**	**62**	**6**	**10**	**16**	**159**	**4**	**0**	**0**	**0**	**2**
1987-88	**St. Louis**	**NHL**	**73**	**10**	**15**	**25**	**190**	**10**	**1**	**3**	**4**	**11**
1988-89	**St. Louis**	**NHL**	**50**	**7**	**10**	**17**	**144**	**8**	**1**	**2**	**3**	**13**
1989-90	**St. Louis**	**NHL**	**11**	**0**	**1**	**1**	**21**	....	....	....	....	....
1990-91	**St. Louis**	**NHL**	**32**	**3**	**3**	**6**	**52**	....	....	....	....	....
	Quebec	**NHL**	**15**	**1**	**3**	**4**	**30**	....	....	....	....	....
1991-92	**Quebec**	**NHL**	**62**	**6**	**14**	**20**	**120**	....	....	....	....	....
1992-93	Halifax	AHL	28	3	9	12	83	....	....	....	....	....
	Tampa Bay	**NHL**	**2**	**0**	**0**	**0**	**2**	....	....	....	....	....
	Atlanta	IHL	24	4	10	14	139	9	3	3	6	32
1993-94	**Ottawa**	**NHL**	**29**	**0**	**0**	**0**	**52**	....	....	....	....	....
	Kalamazoo	IHL	29	6	11	17	112	5	0	0	0	32
	NHL Totals		**343**	**33**	**56**	**89**	**775**	**32**	**3**	**6**	**9**	**50**

Traded to **Quebec** by **St. Louis** with Tony Twist and Andy Rymsha for Darin Kimble, February 4, 1991. Traded to **Tampa Bay** by **Quebec** for Martin Simard, Steve Tuttle and Michel Mongeau, February 12, 1993.

RAGNARSSON, MARCUS — S.J.

Defense. Shoots left. 6'1", 200 lbs. Born, Ostervala, Sweden, August 13, 1971.
(San Jose's 5th choice, 99th overall, in 1992 Entry Draft).

			Regular Season					Playoffs				
Season	Club	Lea	GP	G	A	TP	PIM	GP	G	A	TP	PIM
1989-90	Djurgarden	Swe.	13	0	2	2	0	1	0	0	0	0
1990-91	Djurgarden	Swe.	35	4	1	5	12	7	0	0	0	6
1991-92	Djurgarden	Swe.	40	8	5	13	14	10	0	1	1	4
1992-93	Djurgarden	Swe.	35	3	3	6	53	6	0	3	3	8
1993-94	Djurgarden	Swe.	19	0	4	4	24	....	....	....	....	....

RAITANEN, RAULI — WPG.

Center. Shoots left. 6'2", 187 lbs. Born, Pori, Finland, January 14, 1970.
(Winnipeg's 10th choice, 182nd overall, in 1990 Entry Draft).

			Regular Season					Playoffs				
Season	Club	Lea	GP	G	A	TP	PIM	GP	G	A	TP	PIM
1987-88	Assat	Fin.	18	1	5	6	2	....	....	....	....	....
1988-89	Assat	Fin.	40	21	17	38	18	....	....	....	....	....
1989-90	Assat	Fin. 2	41	17	44	61	20	....	....	....	....	....
1990-91	Assat	Fin.	43	6	16	22	14	....	....	....	....	....
1991-92	Assat	Fin.	41	12	22	34	34	8	1	5	6	2
1992-93	Assat	Fin.	43	15	20	35	28	8	0	4	4	6
1993-94	Assat	Fin.	48	15	25	40	50	5	1	1	2	4

RAJNOHA, PAVEL — CGY.

Defense. Shoots right. 6', 185 lbs. Born, Gottwaldov, Czech., February 23, 1974.
(Calgary's 8th choice, 150th overall, in 1992 Entry Draft).

			Regular Season					Playoffs				
Season	Club	Lea	GP	G	A	TP	PIM	GP	G	A	TP	PIM
1990-91	TJ Zlin	Czech.	6	0	0	0	4	....	....	....	....	....
1991-92	ZPS Zlin	Czech.	24	0	1	1	4	....	....	....	....	....
1992-93	ZPS Zlin	Czech.	26	2	1	3		....	....	....	....	....
1993-94	ZPS Zlin	Czech.	28	2	1	3	0	3	0	4	4	....

RAMAGE, ROB — (RAM-ihj)

Defense. Shoots right. 6'2", 200 lbs. Born, Byron, Ont., January 11, 1959.
(Colorado's 1st choice, 1st overall, in 1979 Entry Draft).

			Regular Season					Playoffs				
Season	Club	Lea	GP	G	A	TP	PIM	GP	G	A	TP	PIM
1975-76	London	OHA	65	12	31	43	113	5	0	1	1	11
1976-77	London	OHA	65	15	58	73	177	20	3	11	14	55
1977-78a	London	OHA	59	17	48	65	162	11	4	5	9	29
1978-79	Birmingham	WHA	80	12	36	48	165	....	....	....	....	....
1979-80	**Colorado**	**NHL**	**75**	**8**	**20**	**28**	**135**	....	....	....	....	....
1980-81	**Colorado**	**NHL**	**79**	**20**	**42**	**62**	**193**	....	....	....	....	....
1981-82	**Colorado**	**NHL**	**80**	**13**	**29**	**42**	**201**	....	....	....	....	....
1982-83	**St. Louis**	**NHL**	**78**	**16**	**35**	**51**	**193**	**4**	**0**	**3**	**3**	**22**
1983-84	**St. Louis**	**NHL**	**80**	**15**	**45**	**60**	**121**	**11**	**1**	**8**	**9**	**32**
1984-85	**St. Louis**	**NHL**	**80**	**7**	**31**	**38**	**178**	**3**	**1**	**3**	**4**	**6**
1985-86	**St. Louis**	**NHL**	**77**	**10**	**56**	**66**	**171**	**19**	**1**	**10**	**11**	**66**
1986-87	**St. Louis**	**NHL**	**59**	**11**	**28**	**39**	**108**	**6**	**2**	**2**	**4**	**21**
1987-88	**St. Louis**	**NHL**	**67**	**8**	**34**	**42**	**127**	....	....	....	....	....
	Calgary	**NHL**	**12**	**1**	**6**	**7**	**37**	**9**	**1**	**3**	**4**	**21**
1988-89	**Calgary**	**NHL**	**68**	**3**	**13**	**16**	**156**	**20**	**1**	**11**	**12**	**26**
1989-90	**Toronto**	**NHL**	**80**	**8**	**41**	**49**	**202**	**5**	**1**	**2**	**3**	**20**
1990-91	**Toronto**	**NHL**	**80**	**10**	**25**	**35**	**173**	....	....	....	....	....
1991-92	**Minnesota**	**NHL**	**34**	**4**	**5**	**9**	**69**	....	....	....	....	....
1992-93	**Tampa Bay**	**NHL**	**66**	**5**	**12**	**17**	**138**	....	....	....	....	....
	Montreal	**NHL**	**8**	**0**	**1**	**1**	**8**	**7**	**0**	**0**	**0**	**4**
1993-94	**Montreal**	**NHL**	**6**	**0**	**1**	**1**	**2**	....	....	....	....	....
	Philadelphia	**NHL**	**15**	**0**	**1**	**1**	**14**	....	....	....	....	....
	NHL Totals		**1044**	**139**	**425**	**564**	**2226**	**84**	**8**	**42**	**50**	**218**

a OHA First All-Star Team (1978)

Played in NHL All-Star Game (1981, 1984, 1986, 1988)

Traded to **St. Louis** by **New Jersey** for St. Louis' first round choice (Rocky Trottier) in 1982 Entry Draft and first round choice (John MacLean) in 1983 Entry Draft, June 9, 1982. Traded to **Calgary** by **St. Louis** with Rick Wamsley for Brett Hull and Steve Bozek, March 7, 1988. Traded to **Toronto** by **Calgary** for Toronto's second round choice (Kent Manderville) in 1989 Entry Draft, June 16, 1989. Claimed by **Minnesota** from **Toronto** in Expansion Draft, May 30, 1991. Claimed by **Tampa Bay** from **Minnesota** in Expansion Draft, June 18, 1992. Traded to **Montreal** by **Tampa Bay** for Eric Charron, Alain Cote and future considerations (Donald Dufresne, June 18, 1993), March 20, 1993. Traded to **Philadelphia** by **Montreal** for cash, November 28, 1993.

RAMSEY, MIKE — DET.

Defense. Shoots left. 6'3", 195 lbs. Born, Minneapolis, MN, December 3, 1960.
(Buffalo's 1st choice, 11th overall, in 1979 Entry Draft).

			Regular Season					Playoffs				
Season	Club	Lea	GP	G	A	TP	PIM	GP	G	A	TP	PIM
1978-79	U. Minnesota	WCHA	26	6	11	17	30	....	....	....	....	....
1979-80	U.S. National	....	56	11	22	33	55	....	....	....	....	....
	U.S. Olympic	....	7	0	2	2	8	....	....	....	....	....
	Buffalo	**NHL**	**13**	**1**	**6**	**7**	**6**	**13**	**1**	**2**	**3**	**12**
1980-81	**Buffalo**	**NHL**	**72**	**3**	**14**	**17**	**56**	**8**	**0**	**3**	**3**	**20**
1981-82	**Buffalo**	**NHL**	**80**	**7**	**23**	**30**	**56**	**4**	**1**	**1**	**2**	**14**
1982-83	**Buffalo**	**NHL**	**77**	**8**	**30**	**38**	**55**	**10**	**4**	**4**	**8**	**15**
1983-84	**Buffalo**	**NHL**	**72**	**9**	**22**	**31**	**82**	**3**	**0**	**1**	**1**	**6**
1984-85	**Buffalo**	**NHL**	**79**	**8**	**22**	**30**	**102**	**5**	**0**	**1**	**1**	**23**
1985-86	**Buffalo**	**NHL**	**76**	**7**	**21**	**28**	**117**	....	....	....	....	....
1986-87	**Buffalo**	**NHL**	**80**	**8**	**31**	**39**	**109**	....	....	....	....	....
1987-88	**Buffalo**	**NHL**	**63**	**5**	**16**	**21**	**77**	**6**	**0**	**3**	**3**	**29**
1988-89	**Buffalo**	**NHL**	**56**	**2**	**14**	**16**	**84**	**5**	**1**	**0**	**1**	**11**
1989-90	**Buffalo**	**NHL**	**73**	**4**	**21**	**25**	**47**	**6**	**0**	**1**	**1**	**8**
1990-91	**Buffalo**	**NHL**	**71**	**6**	**14**	**20**	**46**	**5**	**1**	**0**	**1**	**12**
1991-92	**Buffalo**	**NHL**	**66**	**3**	**14**	**17**	**67**	**7**	**0**	**2**	**2**	**8**
1992-93	**Buffalo**	**NHL**	**33**	**2**	**8**	**10**	**20**	....	....	....	....	....
	Pittsburgh	**NHL**	**12**	**1**	**2**	**3**	**8**	**12**	**0**	**6**	**6**	**4**
1993-94	**Pittsburgh**	**NHL**	**65**	**2**	**2**	**4**	**22**	**1**	**0**	**0**	**0**	**0**
	NHL Totals		**988**	**76**	**260**	**336**	**954**	**85**	**8**	**24**	**32**	**162**

Played in NHL All-Star Game (1982, 1983, 1985, 1986)

Traded to **Pittsburgh** by **Buffalo** for Bob Errey, March 22, 1993. Signed as a free agent by **Detroit**, August 3, 1994.

RANHEIM, PAUL — HFD.

Left wing. Shoots right. 6', 195 lbs. Born, St. Louis, MO, January 25, 1966.
(Calgary's 3rd choice, 38th overall, in 1984 Entry Draft).

			Regular Season					Playoffs				
Season	Club	Lea	GP	G	A	TP	PIM	GP	G	A	TP	PIM
1984-85	U. Wisconsin	WCHA	42	11	11	22	40	....	....	....	....	....
1985-86	U. Wisconsin	WCHA	33	17	17	34	34	....	....	....	....	....
1986-87a	U. Wisconsin	WCHA	42	24	35	59	54	....	....	....	....	....
1987-88bc	U. Wisconsin	WCHA	44	36	26	62	63	....	....	....	....	....
1988-89	**Calgary**	**NHL**	**5**	**0**	**0**	**0**	**0**	....	....	....	....	....
def	Salt Lake	IHL	75	*68	29	97	16	14	5	5	10	8
1989-90	**Calgary**	**NHL**	**80**	**26**	**28**	**54**	**23**	**6**	**1**	**3**	**4**	**2**
1990-91	**Calgary**	**NHL**	**39**	**14**	**16**	**30**	**4**	**7**	**2**	**2**	**4**	**0**
1991-92	**Calgary**	**NHL**	**80**	**23**	**20**	**43**	**32**	....	....	....	....	....
1992-93	**Calgary**	**NHL**	**83**	**21**	**22**	**43**	**26**	**6**	**0**	**1**	**1**	**0**
1993-94	**Calgary**	**NHL**	**67**	**10**	**14**	**24**	**20**	....	....	....	....	....
	Hartford	**NHL**	**15**	**0**	**3**	**3**	**2**	....	....	....	....	....
	NHL Totals		**369**	**94**	**103**	**197**	**107**	**19**	**3**	**6**	**9**	**2**

a WCHA Second All-Star Team (1987)
b NCAA West First All-American Team (1988)
c WCHA First All-Star Team (1988)
d IHL Second All-Star Team (1989)
e Won Garry F. Longman Memorial Trophy (Top Rookie - IHL) (1989)
f Won Ken McKenzie Trophy (Outstanding U.S.-born Rookie - IHL) (1989)

Traded to **Hartford** by **Calgary** with Gary Suter and Ted Drury for James Patrick, Zarley Zalapski and Michael Nylander, March 10, 1994.

RAPPANA, KEVIN — ST.L.

Defense. Shoots right. 6'2", 182 lbs. Born, Duluth, MN, January 24, 1973.
(St. Louis' 11th choice, 241st overall, in 1991 Entry Draft).

			Regular Season					Playoffs				
Season	Club	Lea	GP	G	A	TP	PIM	GP	G	A	TP	PIM
1992-93	North Dakota	WCHA	12	0	0	0	0	....	....	....	....	....
1993-94	North Dakota	WCHA	28	0	2	2	63	....	....	....	....	....

RATHJE, MIKE — (RATH-jee) — S.J.

Defense. Shoots left. 6'6", 220 lbs. Born, Mannville, Alta., May 11, 1974.
(San Jose's 1st choice, 3rd overall, in 1992 Entry Draft).

			Regular Season					Playoffs				
Season	Club	Lea	GP	G	A	TP	PIM	GP	G	A	TP	PIM
1990-91	Medicine Hat	WHL	64	1	16	17	28	12	0	4	4	2
1991-92a	Medicine Hat	WHL	67	11	23	34	109	4	0	1	1	2
1992-93a	Medicine Hat	WHL	57	12	37	49	103	10	3	3	6	12
	Kansas City	IHL	....	....	....	....	....	5	0	0	0	12
1993-94	**San Jose**	**NHL**	**47**	**1**	**9**	**10**	**59**	**1**	**0**	**0**	**0**	**0**
	Kansas City	IHL	6	0	2	2	0	....	....	....	....	....
	NHL Totals		**47**	**1**	**9**	**10**	**59**	**1**	**0**	**0**	**0**	**0**

a WHL East Second All-Star Team (1992, 1993)

RATUSHNY, DAN — (rah-TOOSH-nee)

Defense. Shoots right. 6'1", 205 lbs. Born, Nepean, Ont., October 29, 1970.
(Winnipeg's 2nd choice, 25th overall, in 1989 Entry Draft).

			Regular Season					Playoffs				
Season	Club	Lea	GP	G	A	TP	PIM	GP	G	A	TP	PIM
1988-89	Cornell	ECAC	28	2	13	15	50	....	....	....	....	....
1989-90ab	Cornell	ECAC	26	5	14	19	54	....	....	....	....	....
1990-91ac	Cornell	ECAC	26	7	24	31	52	....	....	....	....	....
	Cdn. National	....	12	0	1	1	6	....	....	....	....	....
1991-92	Cdn. National	....	58	5	13	18	50	....	....	....	....	....
	Cdn. Olympic	....	8	0	0	0	4	....	....	....	....	....
1992-93	Fort Wayne	IHL	63	6	19	25	48	....	....	....	....	....
	Vancouver	**NHL**	**1**	**0**	**1**	**1**	**2**	....	....	....	....	....
1993-94	Hamilton	AHL	62	8	31	39	22	4	0	0	0	4
	NHL Totals		**1**	**0**	**1**	**1**	**2**	....	....	....	....	....

a ECAC First All-Star Team (1990, 1991)
b NCAA East Second All-American Team (1990)
c NCAA East First All-American Team (1991)

Traded to **Vancouver** by **Winnipeg** for Vancouver's ninth round choice (Harijs Vitolinsh) in 1993 Entry Draft, March 22, 1993.

RAY, ROB — BUF.

Left wing. Shoots left. 6', 203 lbs. Born, Belleville, Ont., June 8, 1968.
(Buffalo's 5th choice, 97th overall, in 1988 Entry Draft).

			Regular Season					Playoffs				
Season	Club	Lea	GP	G	A	TP	PIM	GP	G	A	TP	PIM
1985-86	Cornwall	OHL	53	6	13	19	253	6	0	0	0	26
1986-87	Cornwall	OHL	46	17	20	37	158	5	1	1	2	16
1987-88	Cornwall	OHL	61	11	41	52	179	11	2	3	5	33
1988-89	Rochester	AHL	74	11	18	29	*446	....	....	....	....	....
1989-90	**Buffalo**	**NHL**	**27**	**2**	**1**	**3**	**99**	....	....	....	....	....
	Rochester	AHL	43	2	13	15	335	17	1	3	4	115
1990-91	**Buffalo**	**NHL**	**66**	**8**	**8**	**16**	***350**	**6**	**1**	**1**	**2**	**56**
	Rochester	AHL	8	1	1	2	15	....	....	....	....	....
1991-92	**Buffalo**	**NHL**	**63**	**5**	**3**	**8**	**354**	**7**	**0**	**0**	**0**	**2**
1992-93	**Buffalo**	**NHL**	**68**	**3**	**2**	**5**	**211**	....	....	....	....	....
1993-94	**Buffalo**	**NHL**	**82**	**3**	**4**	**7**	**274**	**7**	**1**	**0**	**1**	**43**
	NHL Totals		**306**	**21**	**18**	**39**	**1288**	**20**	**2**	**1**	**3**	**101**

RECCHI, MARK (REH-kee) — PHI.

Right wing. Shoots left. 5'10", 185 lbs. Born, Kamloops, B.C., February 1, 1968.
(Pittsburgh's 4th choice, 67th overall, in 1988 Entry Draft).

			Regular Season					Playoffs				
Season	Club	Lea	GP	G	A	TP	PIM	GP	G	A	TP	PIM
1985-86	N. Westminster	WHL	72	21	40	61	55	....	....	....	....	....
1986-87	Kamloops	WHL	40	26	50	76	63	13	3	16	19	17
1987-88a	Kamloops	WHL	62	61	*93	154	75	17	10	*21	*31	18
1988-89	**Pittsburgh**	**NHL**	**15**	**1**	**1**	**2**	**0**	....	....	....	....	....
b	Muskegon	IHL	63	50	49	99	86	14	7	*14	*21	28
1989-90	**Pittsburgh**	**NHL**	**74**	**30**	**37**	**67**	**44**	....	....	....	....	....
	Muskegon	IHL	4	7	4	11	2	....	....	....	....	....
1990-91	**Pittsburgh**	**NHL**	**78**	**40**	**73**	**113**	**48**	**24**	**10**	**24**	**34**	**33**
1991-92	**Pittsburgh**	**NHL**	**58**	**33**	**37**	**70**	**78**	....	....	....	....	....
c	**Philadelphia**	**NHL**	**22**	**10**	**17**	**27**	**18**	....	....	....	....	....
1992-93	**Philadelphia**	**NHL**	**84**	**53**	**70**	**123**	**95**	....	....	....	....	....
1993-94	**Philadelphia**	**NHL**	**84**	**40**	**67**	**107**	**46**	....	....	....	....	....
	NHL Totals		**415**	**207**	**302**	**509**	**329**	**24**	**10**	**24**	**34**	**33**

a WHL West All-Star Team (1988)
b IHL Second All-Star Team (1989)
c NHL Second All-Star Team (1992)

Played in NHL All-Star Game (1991, 1993, 1994)

Traded to **Philadelphia** by **Pittsburgh** with Brian Benning and Los Angeles' first round choice (previously acquired by Pittsburgh — Philadelphia selected Jason Bowen) in 1992 Entry Draft for Rick Tocchet, Kjell Samuelsson, Ken Wregget and Philadelphia's third round choice (Dave Roche) in 1993 Entry Draft, February 19, 1992.

REDMOND, KEITH — L.A.

Left wing. Shoots left. 6'3", 205 lbs. Born, Richmond Hill, Ont., October 25, 1972.
(Los Angeles' 4th choice, 79th overall, in 1991 Entry Draft).

			Regular Season					Playoffs				
Season	Club	Lea	GP	G	A	TP	PIM	GP	G	A	TP	PIM
1990-91	Bowling Green	CCHA	35	1	3	4	72	....	....	....	....	....
1991-92	Bowling Green	CCHA	8	0	0	0	14	....	....	....	....	....
	Belleville	OHL	16	1	7	8	52	....	....	....	....	....
	Detroit	OHL	25	6	12	18	61	7	1	3	4	49
1992-93	Phoenix	IHL	53	6	10	16	285	....	....	....	....	....
	Muskegon	ColHL	4	1	0	1	46	....	....	....	....	....
1993-94	**Los Angeles**	**NHL**	**12**	**1**	**0**	**1**	**20**	....	....	....	....	....
	Phoenix	IHL	43	8	10	18	196	....	....	....	....	....
	NHL Totals		**12**	**1**	**0**	**1**	**20**	....	....	....	....	....

REEKIE, JOE — WSH.

Defense. Shoots left. 6'3", 215 lbs. Born, Victoria, B.C., February 22, 1965.
(Hartford's 8th choice, 124th overall in 1983 Entry Draft)

			Regular Season					Playoffs				
Season	Club	Lea	GP	G	A	TP	PIM	GP	G	A	TP	PIM
1982-83	North Bay	OHL	59	2	9	11	49	8	0	1	1	11
1983-84	North Bay	OHL	9	1	0	1	18	....	....	....	....	....
	Cornwall	OHL	53	6	27	33	166	3	0	0	0	4
1984-85	Cornwall	OHL	65	19	63	82	134	9	4	13	17	18
1985-86	**Buffalo**	**NHL**	**3**	**0**	**0**	**0**	**14**	....	....	....	....	....
	Rochester	AHL	77	3	25	28	178	....	....	....	....	....
1986-87	**Buffalo**	**NHL**	**56**	**1**	**8**	**9**	**82**	....	....	....	....	....
	Rochester	AHL	22	0	6	6	52	....	....	....	....	....
1987-88	**Buffalo**	**NHL**	**30**	**1**	**4**	**5**	**68**	**2**	**0**	**0**	**0**	**4**
1988-89	**Buffalo**	**NHL**	**15**	**1**	**3**	**4**	**26**	....	....	....	....	....
	Rochester	AHL	21	1	2	3	56	....	....	....	....	....
1989-90	**NY Islanders**	**NHL**	**31**	**1**	**8**	**9**	**43**	....	....	....	....	....
	Springfield	AHL	15	1	4	5	24	....	....	....	....	....
1990-91	**NY Islanders**	**NHL**	**66**	**3**	**16**	**19**	**96**	....	....	....	....	....
	Capital Dist.	AHL	2	1	0	1	0	....	....	....	....	....
1991-92	**NY Islanders**	**NHL**	**54**	**4**	**12**	**16**	**85**	....	....	....	....	....
	Capital Dist.	AHL	3	2	2	4	2	....	....	....	....	....
1992-93	**Tampa Bay**	**NHL**	**42**	**2**	**11**	**13**	**69**	....	....	....	....	....
1993-94	**Tampa Bay**	**NHL**	**73**	**1**	**11**	**12**	**127**	....	....	....	....	....
	Washington	**NHL**	**12**	**0**	**5**	**5**	**29**	**11**	**2**	**1**	**3**	**29**
	NHL Totals		**382**	**14**	**78**	**92**	**639**	**13**	**2**	**1**	**3**	**33**

Re-entered NHL Entry Draft. **Buffalo's** 6th choice, 119th overall, in 1985 Entry Draft.

Traded to **NY Islanders** by **Buffalo** for NY Islanders' sixth round choice (Bill Pye) in 1989 Entry Draft, June 17, 1989. Claimed by **Tampa Bay** from **NY Islanders** in Expansion Draft, June 18, 1992. Traded to **Washington** by **Tampa Bay** for Enrico Ciccone, Washington's third round choice (later traded to Anaheim — Anaheim selected Craig Reichert) in 1994 Entry Draft and the return of future draft choices transferred in the Pat Elynuik trade, March 21, 1994.

REEVES, KYLE

Right wing. Shoots right. 5'11", 190 lbs. Born, Stonewall, Man., May 12, 1971.
(St. Louis' 2nd choice, 64th overall, in 1991 Entry Draft).

			Regular Season					Playoffs				
Season	Club	Lea	GP	G	A	TP	PIM	GP	G	A	TP	PIM
1988-89	Swift Current	WHL	2	1	1	2	2	....	....	....	....	....
1989-90	Tri-City	WHL	67	67	36	103	94	7	2	1	3	8
1990-91a	Tri-City	WHL	63	*89	40	129	146	3	1	3	4	10
1991-92	Peoria	IHL	60	12	7	19	92	....	....	....	....	....
1992-93	Peoria	IHL	50	17	14	31	83	3	0	2	2	2
1993-94	Peoria	IHL	3	0	1	1	2	....	....	....	....	....
	Toledo	ECHL	33	12	13	25	75	....	....	....	....	....

a WHL West Second All-Star Team (1991)

REGNIER, CURT (REHN-yay) — N.J.

Left wing. Shoots left. 6'2", 220 lbs. Born, Prince Albert, Sask., January 24, 1972.
(New Jersey's 6th choice, 121st overall, in 1991 Entry Draft).

			Regular Season					Playoffs				
Season	Club	Lea	GP	G	A	TP	PIM	GP	G	A	TP	PIM
1990-91	Prince Albert	WHL	69	20	39	59	40	3	2	2	4	6
1991-92	Prince Albert	WHL	58	30	42	72	98	10	1	9	10	2
1992-93	Utica	AHL	37	6	4	10	21	2	0	1	1	0
1993-94	Albany	AHL	34	12	20	32	4	....	....	....	....	....
	Raleigh	ECHL	7	6	5	11	10	16	6	9	15	6

REICHEL, MARTIN (RIGH-khul) — EDM.

Right wing. Shoots left. 6'1", 183 lbs. Born, Most, Czech., November 7, 1973.
(Edmonton's 2nd choice, 37th overall, in 1992 Entry Draft).

			Regular Season					Playoffs				
Season	Club	Lea	GP	G	A	TP	PIM	GP	G	A	TP	PIM
1990-91	Freiburg	Ger.	23	7	8	15	19	....	....	....	....	....
1991-92	Freiburg	Ger.	27	15	16	31	8	4	1	1	2	4
1992-93	Freiburg	Ger.	37	13	9	22	27	9	4	4	8	11
1993-94	Rosenheim	Ger.	20	5	15	20	6	....	....	....	....	....

REICHEL, ROBERT (RIGH-khul) — CGY.

Center. Shoots left. 5'10", 185 lbs. Born, Litvinov, Czech., June 25, 1971.
(Calgary's 5th choice, 70th overall, in 1989 Entry Draft).

			Regular Season					Playoffs				
Season	Club	Lea	GP	G	A	TP	PIM	GP	G	A	TP	PIM
1987-88	Litvinov	Czech.	36	17	10	27	8	....	....	....	....	....
1988-89	Litvinov	Czech.	44	23	25	48	32	....	....	....	....	....
1989-90	Litvinov	Czech.	52	*49	34	*83	....	....	....	....	....	....
1990-91	**Calgary**	**NHL**	**66**	**19**	**22**	**41**	**22**	**6**	**1**	**1**	**2**	**0**
1991-92	**Calgary**	**NHL**	**77**	**20**	**34**	**54**	**32**	....	....	....	....	....
1992-93	**Calgary**	**NHL**	**80**	**40**	**48**	**88**	**54**	**6**	**2**	**4**	**6**	**2**
1993-94	**Calgary**	**NHL**	**84**	**40**	**53**	**93**	**58**	**7**	**0**	**5**	**5**	**0**
	NHL Totals		**307**	**119**	**157**	**276**	**166**	**19**	**3**	**10**	**13**	**2**

REICHERT, CRAIG — ANA.

Right wing. Shoots right. 6'1", 196 lbs. Born, Winnipeg, Man., May 11, 1974.
(Anaheim's 3rd choice, 67th overall, in 1994 Entry Draft).

			Regular Season					Playoffs				
Season	Club	Lea	GP	G	A	TP	PIM	GP	G	A	TP	PIM
1991-92	Spokane	WHL	68	13	20	33	86	4	1	0	1	4
1992-93	Red Deer	WHL	66	32	33	65	62	4	3	1	4	2
1993-94	Red Deer	WHL	72	52	67	119	153	4	2	2	4	8

REID, DAVID — BOS.

Left wing. Shoots left. 6'1", 217 lbs. Born, Toronto, Ont., May 15, 1964.
(Boston's 4th choice, 60th overall, in 1982 Entry Draft).

			Regular Season					Playoffs				
Season	Club	Lea	GP	G	A	TP	PIM	GP	G	A	TP	PIM
1981-82	Peterborough	OHL	68	10	32	42	41	9	2	3	5	11
1982-83	Peterborough	OHL	70	23	34	57	33	4	3	1	4	0
1983-84	**Boston**	**NHL**	**8**	**1**	**0**	**1**	**2**	....	....	....	....	....
	Peterborough	OHL	60	33	64	97	12	....	....	....	....	....
1984-85	**Boston**	**NHL**	**35**	**14**	**13**	**27**	**27**	**5**	**1**	**0**	**1**	**0**
	Hershey	AHL	43	10	14	24	6	....	....	....	....	....
1985-86	**Boston**	**NHL**	**37**	**10**	**10**	**20**	**10**	....	....	....	....	....
	Moncton	AHL	26	14	18	32	4	....	....	....	....	....
1986-87	**Boston**	**NHL**	**12**	**3**	**3**	**6**	**0**	**2**	**0**	**0**	**0**	**0**
	Moncton	AHL	40	12	22	34	23	5	0	1	1	0
1987-88	**Boston**	**NHL**	**3**	**0**	**0**	**0**	**0**	....	....	....	....	....
	Maine	AHL	63	21	37	58	40	10	6	7	13	0
1988-89	**Toronto**	**NHL**	**77**	**9**	**21**	**30**	**22**	....	....	....	....	....
1989-90	**Toronto**	**NHL**	**70**	**9**	**19**	**28**	**9**	**3**	**0**	**0**	**0**	**0**
1990-91	**Toronto**	**NHL**	**69**	**15**	**13**	**28**	**18**	....	....	....	....	....
1991-92	**Boston**	**NHL**	**43**	**7**	**7**	**14**	**27**	**15**	**2**	**5**	**7**	**4**
	Maine	AHL	12	1	5	6	4	....	....	....	....	....
1992-93	**Boston**	**NHL**	**65**	**20**	**16**	**36**	**10**	....	....	....	....	....
1993-94	**Boston**	**NHL**	**83**	**6**	**17**	**23**	**25**	**13**	**2**	**1**	**3**	**2**
	NHL Totals		**502**	**94**	**119**	**213**	**150**	**38**	**5**	**6**	**11**	**6**

Signed as a free agent by **Toronto**, June 23, 1988. Signed as a free agent by **Boston**, December 1, 1991.

REID, JARRETT — HFD.

Center. Shoots right. 5'10", 180 lbs. Born, Sault Ste. Marie, Ont., March 10, 1973.
(Hartford's 6th choice, 143rd overall, in 1992 Entry Draft).

			Regular Season					Playoffs				
Season	Club	Lea	GP	G	A	TP	PIM	GP	G	A	TP	PIM
1990-91	S.S. Marie	OHL	63	37	29	66	18	14	5	12	17	14
1991-92	S.S. Marie	OHL	61	53	40	93	67	19	5	13	18	17
1992-93	S.S. Marie	OHL	64	36	60	96	28	18	*19	16	*35	20
1993-94	Belleville	OHL	25	15	23	38	16	12	5	7	12	6
	Springfield	AHL	6	2	0	2	2	....	....	....	....	....
	Raleigh	ECHL	10	3	6	9	8	....	....	....	....	....

REID, SHAWN — NYR

Defense. Shoots left. 6', 195 lbs. Born, Toronto, Ont., September 21, 1970.

			Regular Season					Playoffs				
Season	Club	Lea	GP	G	A	TP	PIM	GP	G	A	TP	PIM
1990-91	Colorado	WCHA	38	10	8	18	36	....	....	....	....	....
1991-92	Colorado	WCHA	41	12	22	34	64	....	....	....	....	....
1992-93	Colorado	WCHA	32	3	11	14	54	....	....	....	....	....
1993-94ab	Colorado	WCHA	39	7	20	27	25	....	....	....	....	....

a WCHA First All-Star Team (1994)
b NCAA West First All-American Team (1994)

Signed as a free agent by **NY Rangers**, July 6, 1994.

REIMANN, DANIEL — N.J.

Defense. Shoots left. 6'1", 190 lbs. Born, Fridley, MN, December 17, 1972.
(New Jersey's 9th choice, 187th overall, in 1991 Entry Draft).

			Regular Season					Playoffs				
Season	Club	Lea	GP	G	A	TP	PIM	GP	G	A	TP	PIM
1992-93	St. Cloud St.	WCHA	36	5	2	7	58	....	....	....	....	....
1993-94	St. Cloud St.	WCHA	36	1	10	11	61	....	....	....	....	....

REIRDEN, TODD — N.J.

Defense. Shoots left. 6'4", 175 lbs. Born, Arlington Heights, IL, June 25, 1971.
(New Jersey's 14th choice, 242nd overall, in 1990 Entry Draft).

			Regular Season					Playoffs				
Season	Club	Lea	GP	G	A	TP	PIM	GP	G	A	TP	PIM
1990-91	Bowling Green	CCHA	28	1	5	6	22	....	....	....	....	....
1991-92	Bowling Green	CCHA	33	8	7	15	34	....	....	....	....	....
1992-93	Bowling Green	CCHA	41	8	17	25	48	....	....	....	....	....
1993-94	Bowling Green	CCHA	38	7	23	30	56	....	....	....	....	....

RENBERG, MIKAEL (REHN-buhrg) — PHI.

Right wing. Shoots left. 6'1", 218 lbs. Born, Pitea, Sweden, May 5, 1972.
(Philadelphia's 3rd choice, 40th overall, in 1990 Entry Draft).

			Regular Season					Playoffs				
Season	Club	Lea	GP	G	A	TP	PIM	GP	G	A	TP	PIM
1988-89	Pitea	Swe. 2	12	6	3	9	....	....	....	....	....	....
1989-90	Pitea	Swe. 2	29	15	19	34	....	....	....	....	....	....
1990-91	Lulea	Swe.	29	11	6	17	12	5	1	1	2	4
1991-92	Lulea	Swe.	38	8	15	23	20	2	0	0	0	0
1992-93	Lulea	Swe.	39	19	13	32	61	11	4	4	8	4
1993-94a	**Philadelphia**	**NHL**	**83**	**38**	**44**	**82**	**36**	....	....	....	....	....
	NHL Totals		**83**	**38**	**44**	**82**	**36**	....	....	....	....	....

a NHL/Upper Deck All-Rookie Team (1994)

RHEAUME, PASCAL (ray-OHM) — N.J.

Center. Shoots left. 6'1", 185 lbs. Born, Quebec, Que., June 21, 1973.

			Regular Season					Playoffs				
Season	Club	Lea	GP	G	A	TP	PIM	GP	G	A	TP	PIM
1991-92	Trois Rivières	QMJHL	65	17	20	37	84	14	5	4	9	23
1992-93	Sherbrooke	QMJHL	65	28	34	62	88	14	6	5	11	31
1993-94	Albany	AHL	55	17	18	35	43	5	0	1	1	0

Signed as a free agent by **New Jersey**, October 1, 1992.

RIABYKIN, DMITRI (ryah-BEE-kihn) — CGY.

Defense. Shoots right. 6'1", 185 lbs. Born, Moscow, USSR, March 24, 1976.
(Calgary's 2nd choice, 45th overall, in 1994 Entry Draft).

			Regular Season					Playoffs				
Season	Club	Lea	GP	G	A	TP	PIM	GP	G	A	TP	PIM
1993-94	Mosc. D'amo 2	CIS 3				UNAVAILABLE						

RICCI, MIKE (REE-CHEE) — QUE.

Center. Shoots left. 6', 190 lbs. Born, Scarborough, Ont., October 27, 1971.
(Philadelphia's 1st choice, 4th overall, in 1990 Entry Draft).

			Regular Season					Playoffs				
Season	Club	Lea	GP	G	A	TP	PIM	GP	G	A	TP	PIM
1987-88	Peterborough	OHL	41	24	37	61	20	....	....	....	....	....
1988-89a	Peterborough	OHL	60	54	52	106	43	17	19	16	35	18
1989-90bc	Peterborough	OHL	60	52	64	116	39	12	5	7	12	26
1990-91	**Philadelphia**	**NHL**	**68**	**21**	**20**	**41**	**64**	....	....	....	....	....
1991-92	**Philadelphia**	**NHL**	**78**	**20**	**36**	**56**	**93**	....	....	....	....	....
1992-93	**Quebec**	**NHL**	**77**	**27**	**51**	**78**	**123**	**6**	**0**	**6**	**6**	**8**
1993-94	**Quebec**	**NHL**	**83**	**30**	**21**	**51**	**113**	....	....	....	....	....
	NHL Totals		**306**	**98**	**128**	**226**	**393**	**6**	**0**	**6**	**6**	**8**

a OHL Second All-Star Team (1989)
b Canadian Major Junior Player of the Year (1990)
c OHL First All-Star Team (1990)

Traded to **Quebec** by **Philadelphia** with Peter Forsberg, Steve Duchesne, Kerry Huffman, Ron Hextall, Chris Simon, Philadelphia's first choice in the 1993 (Jocelyn Thibault) and 1994 (later traded to Toronto — later traded to Washington — Washington selected Nolan Baumgartner) Entry Drafts and cash for Eric Lindros, June 30, 1992.

RICCIARDI, JEFF — CHI.

Defense. Shoots left. 5'10", 203 lbs. Born, Thunder Bay, Ont., June 22, 1971.
(Winnipeg's 8th choice, 159th overall, in 1991 Entry Draft).

			Regular Season					Playoffs				
Season	Club	Lea	GP	G	A	TP	PIM	GP	G	A	TP	PIM
1990-91	Ottawa	OHL	54	12	40	52	172	17	1	11	12	61
1991-92a	Ottawa	OHL	61	15	41	56	220	11	3	8	11	45
1992-93	Providence	AHL	3	0	0	0	0	....	....	....	....	....
	Johnstown	ECHL	61	7	29	36	248	5	2	2	4	6
1993-94	Indianapolis	IHL	75	3	20	23	307	....	....	....	....	....

a OHL Second All-Star Team (1992)

Traded to **Boston** by **Winnipeg** for future considerations, September 8, 1992. Signed as a free agent by **Chicago**, July 28, 1993.

RICE, STEVEN — HFD.

Right wing. Shoots right. 6', 215 lbs. Born, Kitchener, Ont., May 26, 1971.
(NY Rangers' 1st choice, 20th overall, in 1989 Entry Draft).

			Regular Season					Playoffs				
Season	Club	Lea	GP	G	A	TP	PIM	GP	G	A	TP	PIM
1987-88	Kitchener	OHL	59	11	14	25	43	4	0	1	1	0
1988-89	Kitchener	OHL	64	36	30	66	42	5	2	1	3	8
1989-90a	Kitchener	OHL	58	39	37	76	102	16	4	8	12	24
1990-91	**NY Rangers**	**NHL**	**11**	**1**	**1**	**2**	**4**	**2**	**2**	**1**	**3**	**6**
	Binghamton	AHL	8	4	1	5	12	5	2	0	2	2
b	Kitchener	OHL	29	30	30	60	43	6	5	6	11	2
1991-92	**Edmonton**	**NHL**	**3**	**0**	**0**	**0**	**2**	....	....	....	....	....
	Cape Breton	AHL	45	32	20	52	38	5	4	4	8	10
1992-93	**Edmonton**	**NHL**	**28**	**2**	**5**	**7**	**28**	....	....	....	....	....
c	Cape Breton	AHL	51	34	28	62	63	14	4	6	10	22
1993-94	**Edmonton**	**NHL**	**63**	**17**	**15**	**32**	**36**	....	....	....	....	....
	NHL Totals		**105**	**20**	**21**	**41**	**70**	**2**	**2**	**1**	**3**	**6**

a Memorial Cup All-Star Team (1990)
b OHL Second All-Star Team (1991)
c AHL Second All-Star Team (1993)

Traded to **Edmonton** by **NY Rangers** with Bernie Nicholls and Louie DeBrusk for Mark Messier and future considerations, October 4, 1991. Signed as a free agent by **Hartford**, August 18, 1994.

RICHARDS, TODD

Defense. Shoots right. 6', 194 lbs. Born, Robindale, MN, October 20, 1966.
(Montreal's 3rd choice, 33rd overall, in 1985 Entry Draft).

			Regular Season					Playoffs				
Season	Club	Lea	GP	G	A	TP	PIM	GP	G	A	TP	PIM
1985-86	U. Minnesota	WCHA	38	6	23	29	38	....	....	....	....	....
1986-87	U. Minnesota	WCHA	49	8	43	51	70	....	....	....	....	....
1987-88a	U. Minnesota	WCHA	34	10	30	40	26	....	....	....	....	....
1988-89abc	U. Minnesota	WCHA	46	6	32	38	60	....	....	....	....	....
1989-90	Sherbrooke	AHL	71	6	18	24	73	5	1	2	3	6
1990-91	Fredericton	AHL	3	0	1	1	2	....	....	....	....	....
	Hartford	**NHL**	**2**	**0**	**4**	**4**	**2**	**6**	**0**	**0**	**0**	**2**
	Springfield	AHL	71	10	41	51	62	14	2	8	10	2
1991-92	**Hartford**	**NHL**	**6**	**0**	**0**	**0**	**2**	**5**	**0**	**3**	**3**	**4**
	Springfield	AHL	43	6	23	29	33	11	0	3	3	2
1992-93	Springfield	AHL	78	13	42	55	53	9	1	5	6	2
1993-94d	Las Vegas	IHL	80	11	35	46	122	5	1	4	5	18
	NHL Totals		**8**	**0**	**4**	**4**	**4**	**11**	**0**	**3**	**3**	**6**

a WCHA Second All-Star Team (1988, 1989)
b NCAA West Second All-American Team (1989)
c NCAA All-Tournament Team (1989)
d IHL Second All-Star Team (1994)

Traded to **Hartford** by **Montreal** for future considerations, October 11, 1990.

RICHARDS, TRAVIS — DAL.

Defense. Shoots left. 6'1", 185 lbs. Born, Crystal, MN, March 22, 1970.
(Minnesota's 6th choice, 169th overall, in 1988 Entry Draft).

			Regular Season					Playoffs				
Season	Club	Lea	GP	G	A	TP	PIM	GP	G	A	TP	PIM
1989-90	U. Minnesota	WCHA	45	4	24	28	38	....	....	....	....	....
1990-91	U. Minnesota	WCHA	45	9	25	34	28	....	....	....	....	....
1991-92a	U. Minnesota	WCHA	41	10	22	32	65	....	....	....	....	....
1992-93a	U. Minnesota	WCHA	42	12	26	38	52	....	....	....	....	....
1993-94	U.S. National	....	51	1	11	12	38	....	....	....	....	....
	U.S. Olympic	....	8	0	0	0	2	....	....	....	....	....
	Kalamazoo	IHL	19	2	10	12	20	4	1	1	2	0

a WCHA Second All-Star Team (1992, 1993)

RICHARDSON, LUKE

Defense. Shoots left. 6'4", 210 lbs. Born, Ottawa, Ont., March 26, 1969.
(Toronto's 1st choice, 7th overall, in 1987 Entry Draft).

			Regular Season					Playoffs				
Season	Club	Lea	GP	G	A	TP	PIM	GP	G	A	TP	PIM
1985-86	Peterborough	OHL	63	6	18	24	57	16	2	1	3	50
1986-87	Peterborough	OHL	59	13	32	45	70	12	0	5	5	24
1987-88	**Toronto**	**NHL**	**78**	**4**	**6**	**10**	**90**	**2**	**0**	**0**	**0**	**0**
1988-89	**Toronto**	**NHL**	**55**	**2**	**7**	**9**	**106**	....	....	....	....	....
1989-90	**Toronto**	**NHL**	**67**	**4**	**14**	**18**	**122**	**5**	**0**	**0**	**0**	**22**
1990-91	**Toronto**	**NHL**	**78**	**1**	**9**	**10**	**238**	....	....	....	....	....
1991-92	**Edmonton**	**NHL**	**75**	**2**	**19**	**21**	**118**	**16**	**0**	**5**	**5**	**45**
1992-93	**Edmonton**	**NHL**	**82**	**3**	**10**	**13**	**142**	....	....	....	....	....
1993-94	**Edmonton**	**NHL**	**69**	**2**	**6**	**8**	**131**	....	....	....	....	....
	NHL Totals		**504**	**18**	**71**	**89**	**947**	**23**	**0**	**5**	**5**	**67**

Traded to **Edmonton** by **Toronto** with Vincent Damphousse, Peter Ing, Scott Thornton, future considerations and cash for Grant Fuhr, Glenn Anderson and Craig Berube, September 19, 1991.

RICHER, STEPHANE J. G. (REE-shay) — FLA.

Defense. Shoots right. 5'11", 190 lbs. Born, Hull, Que., April 28, 1966.

			Regular Season					Playoffs				
Season	Club	Lea	GP	G	A	TP	PIM	GP	G	A	TP	PIM
1986-87	Hull	QMJHL	33	6	22	28	74	8	3	4	7	17
1987-88	Baltimore	AHL	22	0	3	3	6	....	....	....	....	....
	Sherbrooke	AHL	41	4	7	11	46	5	1	0	1	10
1988-89	Sherbrooke	AHL	70	7	26	33	158	6	1	2	3	18
1989-90	Sherbrooke	AHL	60	10	12	22	85	12	4	9	13	16
1990-91	New Haven	AHL	3	0	1	1	0	....	....	....	....	....
	Phoenix	IHL	67	11	38	49	48	11	4	6	10	6
1991-92a	Fredericton	AHL	80	17	47	64	74	7	0	5	5	18
1992-93	**Tampa Bay**	**NHL**	**3**	**0**	**0**	**0**	**0**	....	....	....	....	....
	Atlanta	IHL	3	0	4	4	4	....	....	....	....	....
	Boston	**NHL**	**21**	**1**	**4**	**5**	**18**	**3**	**0**	**0**	**0**	**0**
	Providence	AHL	53	8	20	28	60	....	....	....	....	....
1993-94	**Florida**	**NHL**	**2**	**0**	**1**	**1**	**0**	....	....	....	....	....
b	Cincinnati	IHL	66	9	55	64	80	11	2	9	11	26
	NHL Totals		**26**	**1**	**5**	**6**	**18**	**3**	**0**	**0**	**0**	**0**

a AHL Second All-Star Team (1992)
b IHL Second All-Star Team (1994)

Signed as a free agent by **Montreal**, January 9, 1988. Signed as a free agent by **Los Angeles**, July 11, 1990. Signed as a free agent by **Tampa Bay**, July 29, 1992. Traded to **Boston** by **Tampa Bay** for Bob Beers, October 28, 1992. Claimed by **Florida** from **Boston** in Expansion Draft, June 24, 1993.

RICHER, STEPHANE J. J. (REE-shay) — N.J.

Right wing. Shoots right. 6'2", 215 lbs. Born, Ripon, Que., June 7, 1966.
(Montreal's 3rd choice, 29th overall, in 1984 Entry Draft).

			Regular Season					Playoffs				
Season	Club	Lea	GP	G	A	TP	PIM	GP	G	A	TP	PIM
1983-84a	Granby	QMJHL	67	39	37	76	58	3	1	1	2	4
1984-85	Granby	QMJHL	30	30	27	57	31	....	....	....	....	....
b	Chicoutimi	QMJHL	27	31	32	63	40	12	13	13	26	25
	Montreal	**NHL**	**1**	**0**	**0**	**0**	**0**	....	....	....	....	....
	Sherbrooke	AHL	....	....	....	....	....	9	6	3	9	10
1985-86	**Montreal**	**NHL**	**65**	**21**	**16**	**37**	**50**	**16**	**4**	**1**	**5**	**23**
1986-87	**Montreal**	**NHL**	**57**	**20**	**19**	**39**	**80**	**5**	**3**	**2**	**5**	**0**
	Sherbrooke	AHL	12	10	4	14	11	....	....	....	....	....
1987-88	**Montreal**	**NHL**	**72**	**50**	**28**	**78**	**72**	**8**	**7**	**5**	**12**	**6**
1988-89	**Montreal**	**NHL**	**68**	**25**	**35**	**60**	**61**	**21**	**6**	**5**	**11**	**14**
1989-90	**Montreal**	**NHL**	**75**	**51**	**40**	**91**	**46**	**9**	**7**	**3**	**10**	**2**
1990-91	**Montreal**	**NHL**	**75**	**31**	**30**	**61**	**53**	**13**	**9**	**5**	**14**	**6**
1991-92	**New Jersey**	**NHL**	**74**	**29**	**35**	**64**	**25**	**7**	**1**	**2**	**3**	**0**
1992-93	**New Jersey**	**NHL**	**78**	**38**	**35**	**73**	**44**	**5**	**2**	**2**	**4**	**2**
1993-94	**New Jersey**	**NHL**	**80**	**36**	**36**	**72**	**16**	**20**	**7**	**5**	**12**	**2**
	NHL Totals		**645**	**301**	**274**	**575**	**447**	**104**	**46**	**30**	**76**	**55**

a QMJHL Rookie of the Year (1984)
b QMJHL Second All-Star Team (1985)

Played in NHL All-Star Game (1990)

Traded to **New Jersey** by **Montreal** with Tom Chorske for Kirk Muller and Roland Melanson, September 20, 1991.

RICHTER, BARRY — NYR

Defense. Shoots left. 6'2", 203 lbs. Born, Madison, WI, September 11, 1970.
(Hartford's 2nd choice, 32nd overall, in 1988 Entry Draft).

			Regular Season					Playoffs				
Season	Club	Lea	GP	G	A	TP	PIM	GP	G	A	TP	PIM
1989-90	U. Wisconsin	WCHA	42	13	23	36	36	....	....	....	....	....
1990-91	U. Wisconsin	WCHA	43	15	20	35	42	....	....	....	....	....
1991-92a	U. Wisconsin	WCHA	39	10	25	35	62	....	....	....	....	....
1992-93bc	U. Wisconsin	WCHA	42	14	32	46	74	....	....	....	....	....
1993-94	U.S. National	....	56	7	16	23	50	....	....	....	....	....
	U.S. Olympic	....	8	0	3	3	4	....	....	....	....	....
	Binghamton	AHL	21	0	9	9	12	....	....	....	....	....

a NCAA All-Tournament Team (1992)
b WCHA First All-Star Team (1993)
c NCAA West First All-American Team (1993)

Traded to **NY Rangers** by **Hartford** with Steve Larmer, Nick Kypreos and Hartford's sixth round choice (Yuri Litvinov) in 1994 Entry Draft for Darren Turcotte and James Patrick, November 2, 1993.

RIDLEY, MIKE — TOR.

Center. Shoots left. 6', 195 lbs. Born, Winnipeg, Man., July 8, 1963.

			Regular Season					Playoffs				
Season	Club	Lea	GP	G	A	TP	PIM	GP	G	A	TP	PIM
1983-84a	U. of Manitoba	GPAC	46	39	41	80	....	....	....	....	....	....
1984-85b	U. of Manitoba	GPAC	30	29	38	67	48	....	....	....	....	....
1985-86c	**NY Rangers**	**NHL**	**80**	**22**	**43**	**65**	**69**	**16**	**6**	**8**	**14**	**26**
1986-87	**NY Rangers**	**NHL**	**38**	**16**	**20**	**36**	**20**	....	....	....	....	....
	Washington	**NHL**	**40**	**15**	**19**	**34**	**20**	**7**	**2**	**1**	**3**	**6**
1987-88	**Washington**	**NHL**	**70**	**28**	**31**	**59**	**22**	**14**	**6**	**5**	**11**	**10**
1988-89	**Washington**	**NHL**	**80**	**41**	**48**	**89**	**49**	**6**	**0**	**5**	**5**	**2**
1989-90	**Washington**	**NHL**	**74**	**30**	**43**	**73**	**27**	**14**	**3**	**4**	**7**	**8**
1990-91	**Washington**	**NHL**	**79**	**23**	**48**	**71**	**26**	**11**	**3**	**4**	**7**	**8**
1991-92	**Washington**	**NHL**	**80**	**29**	**40**	**69**	**38**	**7**	**0**	**11**	**11**	**0**
1992-93	**Washington**	**NHL**	**84**	**26**	**56**	**82**	**44**	**6**	**1**	**5**	**6**	**0**
1993-94	**Washington**	**NHL**	**81**	**26**	**44**	**70**	**24**	**11**	**4**	**6**	**10**	**6**
	NHL Totals		**706**	**256**	**392**	**648**	**339**	**92**	**25**	**49**	**74**	**66**

a Canadian University Player of the Year; CIAU All-Canadian, GPAC MVP and First All-Star Team (1984)
b CIAU All-Canadian, GPAC First All-Star Team (1985)
c NHL All-Rookie Team (1986)

Played in NHL All-Star Game (1989)

Signed as a free agent by **NY Rangers**, September 26, 1985. Traded to **Washington** by **NY Rangers** with Bob Crawford and Kelly Miller for Bob Carpenter and Washington's second round choice (Jason Prosofsky) in 1989 Entry Draft, January 1, 1987. Traded to **Toronto** by **Washington** with St. Louis' first round choice (previously acquired by Washington — Toronto selected Eric Fichaud) in 1994 Entry Draft for Rob Pearson and Philadelphia's first round choice (previously acquired by Toronto — Washington selected Nolan Baumgartner) in 1994 Entry Draft, June 28, 1994.

RIEHL, KEVIN — N.J.

Center. Shoots left. 5'8", 160 lbs. Born, Leader, Sask., March 11, 1971.
(New Jersey's 11th choice, 231st overall, in 1991 Entry Draft).

			Regular Season					Playoffs				
Season	Club	Lea	GP	G	A	TP	PIM	GP	G	A	TP	PIM
1990-91	Medicine Hat	WHL	72	66	50	116	43	....	....	....	....	....
1991-92	Medicine Hat	WHL	69	*65	50	115	125	4	2	2	4	4
1992-93	Utica	AHL	3	0	0	0	2	....	....	....	....	....
	Cincinnati	IHL	3	0	2	2	0	....	....	....	....	....
	Birmingham	ECHL	34	23	18	41	36	....	....	....	....	....
1993-94	Albany	AHL	1	0	0	0	0	....	....	....	....	....
	Raleigh	ECHL	21	11	14	25	35	....	....	....	....	....

RISIDORE, RYAN — HFD.

Defense. Shoots left. 6'4", 192 lbs. Born, Hamilton, Ont., April 4, 1976.
(Hartford's 3rd choice, 109th overall, in 1994 Entry Draft).

			Regular Season					Playoffs				
Season	Club	Lea	GP	G	A	TP	PIM	GP	G	A	TP	PIM
1992-93	Hamilton	Jr. B	41	2	11	13	61	....	....	....	....	....
1993-94	Guelph	OHL	51	2	9	11	39	9	0	0	0	12

RIVERS, JAMIE — ST.L.

Defense. Shoots left. 6', 180 lbs. Born, Ottawa, Ont., March 16, 1975.
(St. Louis' 2nd choice, 63rd overall, in 1993 Entry Draft).

			Regular Season					Playoffs				
Season	Club	Lea	GP	G	A	TP	PIM	GP	G	A	TP	PIM
1991-92	Sudbury	OHL	55	3	13	16	20	8	0	0	0	0
1992-93	Sudbury	OHL	62	12	43	55	20	14	7	19	26	4
1993-94ab	Sudbury	OHL	65	32	*89	121	58	10	1	9	10	14

a OHL First All-Star Team (1994)
b Canadian Major Junior Second All-Star Team (1994)

RIVERS, SHAWN

Defense. Shoots left. 5'10", 185 lbs. Born, Ottawa, Ont., January 30, 1971.

			Regular Season					Playoffs				
Season	Club	Lea	GP	G	A	TP	PIM	GP	G	A	TP	PIM
1988-89	St. Lawrence	ECAC	36	3	23	26	20	....	....	....	....	....
1989-90	St. Lawrence	ECAC	26	3	14	17	29	....	....	....	....	....
1990-91	Sudbury	OHL	66	18	33	51	43	5	2	7	9	0
1991-92	Sudbury	OHL	64	26	54	80	34	11	0	4	4	10
1992-93	**Tampa Bay**	**NHL**	**4**	**0**	**2**	**2**	**2**	....	....	....	....	....
	Atlanta	IHL	78	9	34	43	101	9	1	3	4	8
1993-94	Atlanta	IHL	76	6	30	36	88	12	1	4	5	21
	NHL Totals		**4**	**0**	**2**	**2**	**2**	....	....	....	....	....

Signed as a free agent by **Tampa Bay**, June 29, 1992.

RIVET, CRAIG — MTL.

Defense. Shoots right. 6'2", 178 lbs. Born, North Bay, Ont., September 13, 1974.
(Montreal's 4th choice, 68th overall, in 1992 Entry Draft).

			Regular Season					Playoffs				
Season	Club	Lea	GP	G	A	TP	PIM	GP	G	A	TP	PIM
1991-92	Kingston	OHL	66	5	21	26	97	....	....	....	....	....
1992-93	Kingston	OHL	64	19	55	74	117	16	5	7	12	39
1993-94	Kingston	OHL	61	12	52	64	100	6	0	3	3	6
	Fredericton	AHL	4	0	2	2	2	....	....	....	....	....

ROACH, GARY — NYR

Defense. Shoots left. 6'1", 180 lbs. Born, Sault Ste. Marie, Ont., February 4, 1975.
(NY Rangers' 5th choice, 112th overall, in 1993 Entry Draft).

			Regular Season					Playoffs				
Season	Club	Lea	GP	G	A	TP	PIM	GP	G	A	TP	PIM
1991-92	S.S. Marie	OHL	41	2	9	11	6	9	0	0	0	0
1992-93	S.S. Marie	OHL	65	4	27	31	31	18	0	8	8	4
1993-94	S.S. Marie	OHL	45	5	35	40	28	14	1	17	18	16

ROB, LUBOS — NYR

Center. Shoots left. 5'11", 183 lbs. Born, Budejovice, Czech., August 5, 1970.
(NY Rangers' 7th choice, 99th overall, in 1990 Entry Draft).

			Regular Season					Playoffs				
Season	Club	Lea	GP	G	A	TP	PIM	GP	G	A	TP	PIM
1989-90	Budejovice	Czech.	42	16	24	40	....	....	....	....	....	....
1990-91						UNAVAILABLE						
1991-92						UNAVAILABLE						
1992-93	Budejovice	Czech.	40	23	21	44	....	....	....	....	....	....
1993-94	Budejovice	Czech.	33	14	20	34	0	3	0	2	2	....

ROBERGE, MARIO (roh-BAIRZH) — MTL.

Left wing. Shoots left. 5'11", 193 lbs. Born, Quebec City, Que., January 25, 1964.

			Regular Season					Playoffs				
Season	Club	Lea	GP	G	A	TP	PIM	GP	G	A	TP	PIM
1987-88	Pt. Basques	Sr.	35	25	64	89	152	....	....	....	....	....
1988-89	Sherbrooke	AHL	58	4	9	13	249	6	0	2	2	8
1989-90	Sherbrooke	AHL	73	13	27	40	247	12	5	2	7	53
1990-91	**Montreal**	**NHL**	**5**	**0**	**0**	**0**	**21**	**12**	**0**	**0**	**0**	**24**
	Fredericton	AHL	68	12	27	39	*365	2	0	2	2	5
1991-92	**Montreal**	**NHL**	**20**	**2**	**1**	**3**	**62**	....	....	....	....	....
	Fredericton	AHL	6	1	2	3	20	7	0	2	2	20
1992-93	**Montreal**	**NHL**	**50**	**4**	**4**	**8**	**142**	**3**	**0**	**0**	**0**	**0**
1993-94	**Montreal**	**NHL**	**28**	**1**	**2**	**3**	**55**	....	....	....	....	....
	NHL Totals		**103**	**7**	**7**	**14**	**280**	**15**	**0**	**0**	**0**	**24**

Signed as a free agent by **Montreal**, October 5, 1988.

ROBERTS, DAVID — ST.L.

Left wing. Shoots left. 6', 185 lbs. Born, Alameda, CA, May 28, 1970.
(St. Louis' 5th choice, 114th overall, in 1989 Entry Draft).

			Regular Season					Playoffs				
Season	Club	Lea	GP	G	A	TP	PIM	GP	G	A	TP	PIM
1989-90	U. of Michigan	CCHA	42	21	32	53	46	....	....	....	....	....
1990-91ab	U. of Michigan	CCHA	43	40	35	75	58	....	....	....	....	....
1991-92	U. of Michigan	CCHA	44	16	42	58	68	....	....	....	....	....
1992-93a	U. of Michigan	CCHA	40	27	38	65	40	....	....	....	....	....
1993-94	U.S. National	....	49	17	28	45	68	....	....	....	....	....
	U.S. Olympic	....	8	1	5	6	4	....	....	....	....	....
	St. Louis	**NHL**	**1**	**0**	**0**	**0**	**2**	**3**	**0**	**0**	**0**	**12**
	Peoria	IHL	10	4	6	10	4	....	....	....	....	....
	NHL Totals		**1**	**0**	**0**	**0**	**2**	**3**	**0**	**0**	**0**	**12**

a CCHA Second All-Star Team (1991, 1993)
b NCAA West Second All-American Team (1991)

ROBERTS, GARY — CGY.

Left wing. Shoots left. 6'1", 190 lbs. Born, North York, Ont., May 23, 1966.
(Calgary's 1st choice, 12th overall, in 1984 Entry Draft).

			Regular Season					Playoffs				
Season	Club	Lea	GP	G	A	TP	PIM	GP	G	A	TP	PIM
1982-83	Ottawa	OHL	53	12	8	20	83	5	1	0	1	19
1983-84	Ottawa	OHL	48	27	30	57	144	13	10	7	17	62
1984-85	Moncton	AHL	7	4	2	6	7	....	....	....	....	....
a	Ottawa	OHL	59	44	62	106	186	5	2	8	10	10
1985-86	Ottawa	OHL	24	26	25	51	83	....	....	....	....	....
a	Guelph	OHL	23	18	15	33	65	20	18	13	31	43
1986-87	**Calgary**	**NHL**	**32**	**5**	**10**	**15**	**85**	**2**	**0**	**0**	**0**	**4**
	Moncton	AHL	38	20	18	38	72	....	....	....	....	....
1987-88	**Calgary**	**NHL**	**74**	**13**	**15**	**28**	**282**	**9**	**2**	**3**	**5**	**29**
1988-89	**Calgary**	**NHL**	**71**	**22**	**16**	**38**	**250**	**22**	**5**	**7**	**12**	**57**
1989-90	**Calgary**	**NHL**	**78**	**39**	**33**	**72**	**222**	**6**	**2**	**5**	**7**	**41**
1990-91	**Calgary**	**NHL**	**80**	**22**	**31**	**53**	**252**	**7**	**1**	**3**	**4**	**18**
1991-92	**Calgary**	**NHL**	**76**	**53**	**37**	**90**	**207**	....	....	....	....	....
1992-93	**Calgary**	**NHL**	**58**	**38**	**41**	**79**	**172**	**5**	**1**	**6**	**7**	**43**
1993-94	**Calgary**	**NHL**	**73**	**41**	**43**	**84**	**145**	**7**	**2**	**6**	**8**	**24**
	NHL Totals		**542**	**233**	**226**	**459**	**1615**	**58**	**13**	**30**	**43**	**216**

a OHL Second All-Star Team (1985, 1986)

Played in NHL All-Star Game (1992, 1993)

ROBERTS, GORDIE

Defense. Shoots left. 6'1", 195 lbs. Born, Detroit, MI, October 2, 1957.
(Montreal's 7th choice, 54th overall, in 1977 Amateur Draft).

			Regular Season					Playoffs				
Season	**Club**	**Lea**	**GP**	**G**	**A**	**TP**	**PIM**	**GP**	**G**	**A**	**TP**	**PIM**
1974-75	Victoria	WHL	53	19	45	64	145	12	1	9	10	42
1975-76	New England	WHA	77	3	19	22	102	17	2	9	11	36
1976-77	New England	WHA	77	13	33	46	169	5	2	2	4	6
1977-78	New England	WHA	78	15	46	61	118	14	0	5	5	29
1978-79	New England	WHA	79	11	46	57	113	10	0	4	4	10
1979-80	**Hartford**	**NHL**	**80**	**8**	**28**	**36**	**89**	**3**	**1**	**1**	**2**	**2**
1980-81	**Hartford**	**NHL**	**27**	**2**	**11**	**13**	**81**	....	....	....	....	....
	Minnesota	**NHL**	**50**	**6**	**31**	**37**	**94**	**19**	**1**	**5**	**6**	**17**
1981-82	**Minnesota**	**NHL**	**79**	**4**	**30**	**34**	**119**	**4**	**0**	**3**	**3**	**27**
1982-83	**Minnesota**	**NHL**	**80**	**3**	**41**	**44**	**103**	**9**	**1**	**5**	**6**	**14**
1983-84	**Minnesota**	**NHL**	**77**	**8**	**45**	**53**	**132**	**15**	**3**	**7**	**10**	**23**
1984-85	**Minnesota**	**NHL**	**78**	**6**	**36**	**42**	**112**	**9**	**1**	**6**	**7**	**6**
1985-86	**Minnesota**	**NHL**	**76**	**2**	**21**	**23**	**101**	**5**	**0**	**4**	**4**	**8**
1986-87	**Minnesota**	**NHL**	**67**	**3**	**10**	**13**	**68**	....	....	....	....	....
1987-88	**Minnesota**	**NHL**	**48**	**1**	**10**	**11**	**103**	....	....	....	....	....
	Philadelphia	**NHL**	**11**	**1**	**2**	**3**	**15**	....	....	....	....	....
	St. Louis	**NHL**	**11**	**1**	**3**	**4**	**25**	**10**	**1**	**2**	**3**	**33**
1988-89	**St. Louis**	**NHL**	**77**	**2**	**24**	**26**	**90**	**10**	**1**	**7**	**8**	**8**
1989-90	**St. Louis**	**NHL**	**75**	**3**	**14**	**17**	**140**	**10**	**0**	**2**	**2**	**26**
1990-91	**St. Louis**	**NHL**	**3**	**0**	**1**	**1**	**8**	....	....	....	....	....
	Peoria	IHL	6	0	8	8	4	....	....	....	....	....
	Pittsburgh	**NHL**	**61**	**3**	**12**	**15**	**70**	**24**	**1**	**2**	**3**	**63**
1991-92	**Pittsburgh**	**NHL**	**73**	**2**	**22**	**24**	**87**	**19**	**0**	**2**	**2**	**32**
1992-93	**Boston**	**NHL**	**65**	**5**	**12**	**17**	**105**	**4**	**0**	**0**	**0**	**6**
1993-94	**Boston**	**NHL**	**59**	**1**	**6**	**7**	**40**	**12**	**0**	**1**	**1**	**8**
	NHL Totals		**1097**	**61**	**359**	**420**	**1582**	**153**	**10**	**47**	**57**	**273**

Claimed by **Hartford** from **Montreal** in 1979 Expansion Draft, June 22, 1979. Traded to **Minnesota** by **Hartford** for Mike Fidler, December 16, 1980. Traded to **Philadelphia** by **Minnesota** for future considerations, February 8, 1988. Traded to **St. Louis** by **Philadelphia** for future considerations, March 8, 1988. Traded to **Pittsburgh** by **St. Louis** for Pittsburgh's eleventh round choice (Wade Salzman) in 1992 Entry Draft, October 27, 1990. Signed as a free agent by **Boston**, July 23, 1992.

ROBERTSSON, BERT (ROH-behrt-suhn) VAN.

Defense. Shoots left. 6'2", 198 lbs. Born, Sodertalje, Sweden, June 30, 1974.
(Vancouver's 8th choice, 254th overall, in 1993 Entry Draft).

			Regular Season					Playoffs				
Season	**Club**	**Lea**	**GP**	**G**	**A**	**TP**	**PIM**	**GP**	**G**	**A**	**TP**	**PIM**
1992-93	Sodertalje	Swe. 2	23	2	1	3	24	....	....	....	....	....
1993-94	Sodertalje	Swe. 2	28	0	1	1	12	....	....	....	....	....

ROBINSON, ROB

Defense. Shoots left. 6'1", 214 lbs. Born, St. Catharines, Ont., April 19, 1967.
(St. Louis' 6th choice, 117th overall, in 1987 Entry Draft).

			Regular Season					Playoffs				
Season	**Club**	**Lea**	**GP**	**G**	**A**	**TP**	**PIM**	**GP**	**G**	**A**	**TP**	**PIM**
1985-86	Miami-Ohio	CCHA	38	1	9	10	24	....	....	....	....	....
1986-87	Miami-Ohio	CCHA	33	3	5	8	32	....	....	....	....	....
1987-88	Miami-Ohio	CCHA	35	1	3	4	56	....	....	....	....	....
1988-89	Miami-Ohio	CCHA	30	3	4	7	42	....	....	....	....	....
	Peoria	IHL	11	2	0	2	6	....	....	....	....	....
1989-90	Peoria	IHL	60	2	11	13	72	5	0	1	1	10
1990-91a	Peoria	IHL	79	2	21	23	42	19	0	6	6	8
1991-92	**St. Louis**	**NHL**	**22**	**0**	**1**	**1**	**8**	....	....	....	....	....
	Peoria	IHL	35	1	10	11	29	10	0	2	2	12
1992-93	Peoria	IHL	34	0	4	4	38	....	....	....	....	....
1993-94	Kalamazoo	IHL	67	3	12	15	32	5	0	0	0	2
	NHL Totals		**22**	**0**	**1**	**1**	**8**	....	....	....	....	....

a IHL Second All-Star Team (1991)

Traded to **Tampa Bay** by **St. Louis** for future considerations, June 19, 1992.

ROBITAILLE, LUC (ROH-buh-tigh) PIT.

Left wing. Shoots left. 6'1", 195 lbs. Born, Montreal, Que., February 17, 1966.
(Los Angeles' 9th choice, 171st overall, in 1984 Entry Draft).

			Regular Season					Playoffs				
Season	**Club**	**Lea**	**GP**	**G**	**A**	**TP**	**PIM**	**GP**	**G**	**A**	**TP**	**PIM**
1983-84	Hull	QMJHL	70	32	53	85	48	....	....	....	....	....
1984-85a	Hull	QMJHL	64	55	94	149	115	5	4	2	6	27
1985-86bc	Hull	QMJHL	63	68	123	191	91	15	17	27	44	28
1986-87def	**Los Angeles**	**NHL**	**79**	**45**	**39**	**84**	**28**	**5**	**1**	**4**	**5**	**2**
1987-88g	**Los Angeles**	**NHL**	**80**	**53**	**58**	**111**	**82**	**5**	**2**	**5**	**7**	**18**
1988-89g	**Los Angeles**	**NHL**	**78**	**46**	**52**	**98**	**65**	**11**	**2**	**6**	**8**	**10**
1989-90g	**Los Angeles**	**NHL**	**80**	**52**	**49**	**101**	**38**	**10**	**5**	**5**	**10**	**10**
1990-91g	**Los Angeles**	**NHL**	**76**	**45**	**46**	**91**	**68**	**12**	**12**	**4**	**16**	**22**
1991-92f	**Los Angeles**	**NHL**	**80**	**44**	**63**	**107**	**95**	**6**	**3**	**4**	**7**	**12**
1992-93g	**Los Angeles**	**NHL**	**84**	**63**	**62**	**125**	**100**	**24**	**9**	**13**	**22**	**28**
1993-94	**Los Angeles**	**NHL**	**83**	**44**	**42**	**86**	**86**	....	....	....	....	....
	NHL Totals		**640**	**392**	**411**	**803**	**562**	**73**	**34**	**41**	**75**	**102**

a QMJHL Second All-Star Team (1985)
b QMJHL First All-Star Team (1986)
c Canadian Major Junior Player of the Year (1986)
d NHL All-Rookie Team (1987)
e Won Calder Memorial Trophy (1987)
f NHL Second All-Star Team (1987, 1992)
g NHL First All-Star Team (1988, 1989, 1990, 1991, 1993)

Played in NHL All-Star Game (1988-93)

Traded to **Pittsburgh** by **Los Angeles** for Rick Tocchet and Pittsburgh's second round choice in 1995 Entry Draft, July 29, 1994.

ROCHE, DAVE PIT.

Center. Shoots left. 6'4", 224 lbs. Born, Lindsay, Ont., June 13, 1975.
(Pittsburgh's 3rd choice, 62nd overall, in 1993 Entry Draft).

			Regular Season					Playoffs				
Season	**Club**	**Lea**	**GP**	**G**	**A**	**TP**	**PIM**	**GP**	**G**	**A**	**TP**	**PIM**
1991-92	Peterborough	OHL	62	10	17	27	134	10	0	0	0	34
1992-93	Peterborough	OHL	56	40	60	100	105	21	14	15	29	42
1993-94	Peterborough	OHL	34	15	22	37	127	....	....	....	....	....
	Windsor	OHL	29	14	20	34	73	4	1	1	2	15

ROCHEFORT, NORMAND

Defense. Shoots left. 6'1", 214 lbs. Born, Trois-Rivières, Que., January 28, 1961.
(Quebec's 1st choice, 24th overall, in 1980 Entry Draft).

			Regular Season					Playoffs				
Season	**Club**	**Lea**	**GP**	**G**	**A**	**TP**	**PIM**	**GP**	**G**	**A**	**TP**	**PIM**
1978-79	Trois-Rivières	QJHL	72	17	57	74	30	13	3	11	14	17
1979-80	Trois-Rivières	QJHL	20	5	25	30	22	....	....	....	....	....
a	Quebec	QJHL	52	8	39	47	68	5	1	3	4	8
1980-81	**Quebec**	**NHL**	**56**	**3**	**7**	**10**	**51**	**5**	**0**	**0**	**0**	**4**
	Quebec	QJHL	9	2	6	8	14	....	....	....	....	....
1981-82	**Quebec**	**NHL**	**72**	**4**	**14**	**18**	**115**	**16**	**0**	**2**	**2**	**10**
1982-83	**Quebec**	**NHL**	**62**	**6**	**17**	**23**	**40**	**1**	**0**	**0**	**0**	**2**
1983-84	**Quebec**	**NHL**	**75**	**2**	**22**	**24**	**47**	**6**	**1**	**0**	**1**	**6**
1984-85	**Quebec**	**NHL**	**73**	**3**	**21**	**24**	**74**	**18**	**2**	**1**	**3**	**8**
1985-86	**Quebec**	**NHL**	**26**	**5**	**4**	**9**	**30**	....	....	....	....	....
1986-87	**Quebec**	**NHL**	**70**	**6**	**9**	**15**	**46**	**13**	**2**	**1**	**3**	**26**
1987-88	**Quebec**	**NHL**	**46**	**3**	**10**	**13**	**49**	....	....	....	....	....
1988-89	**NY Rangers**	**NHL**	**11**	**1**	**5**	**6**	**18**	....	....	....	....	....
1989-90	**NY Rangers**	**NHL**	**31**	**3**	**1**	**4**	**24**	**10**	**2**	**1**	**3**	**26**
	Flint	IHL	7	0	32	5	4	....	....	....	....	....
1990-91	**NY Rangers**	**NHL**	**44**	**3**	**7**	**10**	**35**	....	....	....	....	....
1991-92	**NY Rangers**	**NHL**	**26**	**0**	**2**	**2**	**31**	....	....	....	....	....
1992-93	Eisbaren	Ger.	17	4	2	6	21	....	....	....	....	....
1993-94	**Tampa Bay**	**NHL**	**6**	**0**	**0**	**0**	**10**	....	....	....	....	....
	Atlanta	IHL	65	5	7	12	43	13	0	2	2	6
	NHL Totals		**598**	**39**	**119**	**158**	**570**	**69**	**7**	**5**	**12**	**82**

a QMJHL Second All-Star Team (1980)

Traded to **NY Rangers** by **Quebec** with Jason Lafreniere for Bruce Bell, Jari Gronstrand, Walt Poddubny and NY Rangers' fourth round draft choice (Eric Dubois) in 1989 Entry Draft, August 1, 1988. Signed as a free agent by **Tampa Bay**, September 27, 1993.

RODERICK, JOHN

Defense. Shoots left. 6'2", 195 lbs. Born, Cambridge, MA, February 25, 1971.
(St. Louis' 9th choice, 177th overall, in 1989 Entry Draft).

			Regular Season					Playoffs				
Season	**Club**	**Lea**	**GP**	**G**	**A**	**TP**	**PIM**	**GP**	**G**	**A**	**TP**	**PIM**
1989-90	St. Lawrence	ECAC	16	0	1	1	20	....	....	....	....	....
1990-91	St. Lawrence	ECAC	21	0	2	2	20	....	....	....	....	....
1991-92	St. Lawrence	ECAC	28	1	1	2	40	....	....	....	....	....
1992-93	St. Lawrence	ECAC	27	2	2	4	40	....	....	....	....	....
1993-94	Peoria	IHL	13	0	0	0	10	....	....	....	....	....
	Dayton	ECHL	26	2	1	3	46	....	....	....	....	....
	Huntsville	ECHL	8	1	0	1	22	3	1	0	1	10

ROENICK, JEREMY (ROH-nihk) CHI.

Center. Shoots right. 6', 170 lbs. Born, Boston, MA, January 17, 1970.
(Chicago's 1st choice, 8th overall, in 1988 Entry Draft).

			Regular Season					Playoffs				
Season	**Club**	**Lea**	**GP**	**G**	**A**	**TP**	**PIM**	**GP**	**G**	**A**	**TP**	**PIM**
1988-89a	Hull	QMJHL	28	34	36	70	14	....	....	....	....	....
	U.S. Jr. Nat'l.	....	11	8	8	16	0	....	....	....	....	....
	Chicago	**NHL**	**20**	**9**	**9**	**18**	**4**	**10**	**1**	**3**	**4**	**7**
1989-90	**Chicago**	**NHL**	**78**	**26**	**40**	**66**	**54**	**20**	**11**	**7**	**18**	**8**
1990-91	**Chicago**	**NHL**	**79**	**41**	**53**	**94**	**80**	**6**	**3**	**5**	**8**	**4**
1991-92	**Chicago**	**NHL**	**80**	**53**	**50**	**103**	**98**	**18**	**12**	**10**	**22**	**12**
1992-93	**Chicago**	**NHL**	**84**	**50**	**57**	**107**	**86**	**4**	**1**	**2**	**3**	**2**
1993-94	**Chicago**	**NHL**	**84**	**46**	**61**	**107**	**125**	**6**	**1**	**6**	**7**	**2**
	NHL Totals		**425**	**225**	**270**	**495**	**447**	**64**	**29**	**33**	**62**	**35**

a QMJHL Second All-Star Team (1989)

Played in NHL All-Star Game (1991-94)

ROENICK, TREVOR HFD.

Right wing. Shoots right. 6'1", 200 lbs. Born, Derby, CT, October 7, 1974.
(Hartford's 3rd choice, 84th overall, in 1993 Entry Draft).

			Regular Season					Playoffs				
Season	**Club**	**Lea**	**GP**	**G**	**A**	**TP**	**PIM**	**GP**	**G**	**A**	**TP**	**PIM**
1992-93	Jr. Bruins	NEJHL	58	61	48	109	94	....	....	....	....	....
1993-94	U. of Maine	H.E.	32	4	3	7	18	....	....	....	....	....

ROHLIN, LEIF (roh-LEEN) VAN.

Defense. Shoots left. 6'1", 198 lbs. Born, Vasteras, Sweden, February 26, 1968.
(Vancouver's 2nd choice, 33rd overall, in 1988 Entry Draft).

			Regular Season					Playoffs				
Season	**Club**	**Lea**	**GP**	**G**	**A**	**TP**	**PIM**	**GP**	**G**	**A**	**TP**	**PIM**
1986-87	Vasteras	Swe. 2	27	2	5	7	12	12	0	2	2	8
1987-88	Vasteras	Swe. 2	30	2	15	17	46	7	0	4	4	8
1988-89	Vasteras	Swe.	22	3	7	10	18	....	....	....	....	....
1989-90	Vasteras	Swe.	32	3	6	9	40	2	0	0	0	2
1990-91	Vasteras	Swe.	40	4	10	14	46	4	0	1	1	8
1991-92	Vasteras	Swe.	39	4	6	10	52	....	....	....	....	....
1992-93	Vasteras	Swe.	37	5	7	12	24	2	0	0	0	0
1993-94	Vasteras	Swe.	40	6	14	20	26	4	0	1	1	6

ROHLOFF, JON BOS.

Defense. Shoots right. 5'11", 220 lbs. Born, Mankato, MN, October 3, 1969.
(Boston's 7th choice, 186th overall, in 1988 Entry Draft).

			Regular Season					Playoffs				
Season	**Club**	**Lea**	**GP**	**G**	**A**	**TP**	**PIM**	**GP**	**G**	**A**	**TP**	**PIM**
1988-89	Minn.-Duluth	WCHA	39	1	2	3	44	....	....	....	....	....
1989-90	Minn.-Duluth	WCHA	5	0	1	1	6	....	....	....	....	....
1990-91	Minn.-Duluth	WCHA	32	6	11	17	38	....	....	....	....	....
1991-92	Minn.-Duluth	WCHA	27	9	9	18	48	....	....	....	....	....
1992-93a	Minn.-Duluth	WCHA	36	15	20	35	87	....	....	....	....	....
1993-94	Providence	AHL	55	12	23	35	59	....	....	....	....	....

a WCHA Second All-Star Team (1993)

ROHR, STEPHEN

Center. Shoots right. 6'3", 200 lbs. Born, Flint, MI, March 22, 1972.
(Montreal's 8th choice, 144th overall, in 1990 Entry Draft).

			Regular Season					Playoffs				
Season	**Club**	**Lea**	**GP**	**G**	**A**	**TP**	**PIM**	**GP**	**G**	**A**	**TP**	**PIM**
1990-91	Miami-Ohio	CCHA	26	6	6	12	8	....	....	....	....	....
1991-92	Miami-Ohio	CCHA	21	1	3	4	26	....	....	....	....	....
1992-93	Miami-Ohio	CCHA	27	9	8	17	20	....	....	....	....	....
1993-94	Miami-Ohio	CCHA	36	1	10	11	20	....	....	....	....	....

ROLAND, LAYNE

Right wing. Shoots right. 6'1", 215 lbs.   Born, Vernon, B.C., February 6, 1974.
(Chicago's 8th choice, 185th overall, in 1992 Entry Draft).

			Regular Season					Playoffs				
Season	Club	Lea	GP	G	A	TP	PIM	GP	G	A	TP	PIM
1990-91	Portland	WHL	60	10	12	22	56	....	....	....	....	....
1991-92	Portland	WHL	67	28	31	59	80	6	3	2	5	10
1992-93	Portland	WHL	69	41	36	77	99	15	6	9	15	16
1993-94	Portland	WHL	72	50	46	96	89	....	....	....	....	....

ROLSTON, BRIAN   N.J.

Center. Shoots left. 6'2", 185 lbs.   Born, Flint, MI, February 21, 1973.
(New Jersey's 2nd choice, 11th overall, in 1991 Entry Draft).

			Regular Season					Playoffs				
Season	Club	Lea	GP	G	A	TP	PIM	GP	G	A	TP	PIM
1991-92a	Lake Superior	CCHA	37	14	23	37	14	....	....	....	....	....
1992-93abc	Lake Superior	CCHA	39	33	31	64	20	....	....	....	....	....
1993-94	U.S. National	....	41	20	28	48	36	....	....	....	....	....
	U.S. Olympic	....	8	7	0	7	8	....	....	....	....	....
	Albany	AHL	17	5	5	10	8	5	1	2	3	0

a NCAA Final Four All-Tournament Team (1992, 1993)
b CCHA First All-Star Team (1993)
c NCAA West Second All-American Team (1993)

ROMANIUK, RUSSELL   (ROH-muh-NUHK)   WPG.

Left wing. Shoots left. 6', 195 lbs.   Born, Winnipeg, Man., June 9, 1970.
(Winnipeg's 2nd choice, 31st overall, in 1988 Entry Draft).

			Regular Season					Playoffs				
Season	Club	Lea	GP	G	A	TP	PIM	GP	G	A	TP	PIM
1988-89	North Dakota	WCHA	39	17	14	31	32	....	....	....	....	....
	Cdn. National	....	3	1	0	1	0	....	....	....	....	....
1989-90	North Dakota	WCHA	45	36	15	51	54	....	....	....	....	....
1990-91a	North Dakota	WCHA	39	40	28	68	30	....	....	....	....	....
1991-92	Winnipeg	NHL	27	3	5	8	18	....	....	....	....	....
	Moncton	AHL	45	16	15	31	25	10	5	4	9	19
1992-93	Winnipeg	NHL	28	3	1	4	22	1	0	0	0	0
	Moncton	AHL	28	18	8	26	40	5	0	4	4	2
	Fort Wayne	IHL	4	2	0	2	7	....	....	....	....	....
1993-94	Cdn. National	....	34	8	9	17	17	....	....	....	....	....
	Winnipeg	NHL	24	4	8	12	6	....	....	....	....	....
	Moncton	AHL	18	16	8	24	24	17	2	6	8	30
	NHL Totals		79	10	14	24	46	1	0	0	0	0

a WCHA First All-Star Team (1991)

ROMFO, JEFF   DAL.

Center. Shoots left. 6', 185 lbs.   Born, St. Paul, MN, February 9, 1974.
(Minnesota's 10th choice, 226th overall, in 1992 Entry Draft).

			Regular Season					Playoffs				
Season	Club	Lea	GP	G	A	TP	PIM	GP	G	A	TP	PIM
1992-93	Minn.-Duluth	WCHA	38	4	4	8	8	....	....	....	....	....
1993-94	Minn.-Duluth	WCHA	38	7	4	11	16	....	....	....	....	....

RONAN, EDWARD (ED)   MTL.

Right wing. Shoots right. 6', 197 lbs.   Born, Quincy, MA, March 21, 1968.
(Montreal's 13th choice, 227th overall, in 1987 Entry Draft).

			Regular Season					Playoffs				
Season	Club	Lea	GP	G	A	TP	PIM	GP	G	A	TP	PIM
1987-88	Boston U.	H.E.	31	2	5	7	20	....	....	....	....	....
1988-89	Boston U.	H.E.	36	4	11	15	34	....	....	....	....	....
1989-90	Boston U.	H.E.	44	17	23	40	50	....	....	....	....	....
1990-91	Boston U.	H.E.	41	16	19	35	38	....	....	....	....	....
1991-92	Montreal	NHL	3	0	0	0	0	....	....	....	....	....
	Fredericton	AHL	78	25	34	59	82	7	5	1	6	6
1992-93	Montreal	NHL	53	5	7	12	20	14	2	3	5	10
	Fredericton	AHL	16	10	5	15	15	5	2	4	6	6
1993-94	Montreal	NHL	61	6	8	14	42	7	1	0	1	0
	NHL Totals		117	11	15	26	62	21	3	3	6	10

RONNING, CLIFF   VAN.

Center. Shoots left. 5'8", 170 lbs.   Born, Burnaby, B.C., October 1, 1965.
(St. Louis' 9th choice, 134th overall, in 1984 Entry Draft).

			Regular Season					Playoffs				
Season	Club	Lea	GP	G	A	TP	PIM	GP	G	A	TP	PIM
1983-84	N. Westminster	WHL	71	69	67	136	10	9	8	13	21	10
1984-85a	N. Westminster	WHL	70	*89	108	*197	20	11	10	14	24	4
1985-86	Cdn. National	....	71	55	63	118	53	....	....	....	....	....
	St. Louis	NHL	....	....	....	....	....	5	1	1	2	2
1986-87	St. Louis	NHL	42	11	14	25	6	4	0	1	1	0
	Cdn. National	....	26	16	16	32	12	....	....	....	....	....
1987-88	St. Louis	NHL	26	5	8	13	12	....	....	....	....	....
1988-89	St. Louis	NHL	64	24	31	55	18	7	1	3	4	0
	Peoria	IHL	12	11	20	31	8	....	....	....	....	....
1989-90	Asiago	Italy	36	67	49	116	25	6	7	12	19	4
1990-91	St. Louis	NHL	48	14	18	32	10	....	....	....	....	....
	Vancouver	NHL	11	6	6	12	0	6	6	3	9	12
1991-92	Vancouver	NHL	80	24	47	71	42	13	8	5	13	6
1992-93	Vancouver	NHL	79	29	56	85	30	12	2	9	11	6
1993-94	Vancouver	NHL	76	25	43	68	42	24	5	10	15	16
	NHL Totals		426	138	223	361	160	71	23	32	55	42

a WHL First All-Star Team (1985)

Traded to **Vancouver** by **St. Louis** with Geoff Courtnall, Robert Dirk, Sergio Momesso and St. Louis' fifth round choice (Brian Loney) in 1992 Entry Draft for Dan Quinn and Garth Butcher, March 5, 1991.

ROUSE, BOB   DET.

Defense. Shoots right. 6'1", 210 lbs.   Born, Surrey, B.C., June 18, 1964.
(Minnesota's 3rd choice, 80th overall, in 1982 Entry Draft).

			Regular Season					Playoffs				
Season	Club	Lea	GP	G	A	TP	PIM	GP	G	A	TP	PIM
1980-81	Billings	WHL	70	0	13	13	116	5	0	0	0	2
1981-82	Billings	WHL	71	7	22	29	209	5	0	2	2	10
1982-83	Nanaimo	WHL	29	7	20	27	86	....	....	....	....	....
	Lethbridge	WHL	42	8	30	38	82	20	2	13	15	55
1983-84	Minnesota	NHL	1	0	0	0	0	....	....	....	....	....
a	Lethbridge	WHL	71	18	42	60	101	5	0	1	1	28
1984-85	Minnesota	NHL	63	2	9	11	113	....	....	....	....	....
	Springfield	AHL	8	0	3	3	6	....	....	....	....	....
1985-86	Minnesota	NHL	75	1	14	15	151	3	0	0	0	0
1986-87	Minnesota	NHL	72	2	10	12	179	....	....	....	....	....
1987-88	Minnesota	NHL	74	0	12	12	168	....	....	....	....	....
1988-89	Minnesota	NHL	66	4	13	17	124	....	....	....	....	....
	Washington	NHL	13	0	2	2	36	6	2	0	2	4
1989-90	Washington	NHL	70	4	16	20	123	15	2	3	5	47
1990-91	Washington	NHL	47	5	15	20	65	....	....	....	....	....
	Toronto	NHL	13	2	4	6	10	....	....	....	....	....
1991-92	Toronto	NHL	79	3	19	22	97	....	....	....	....	....
1992-93	Toronto	NHL	82	3	11	14	130	21	3	8	11	29
1993-94	Toronto	NHL	63	5	11	16	101	18	0	3	3	29
	NHL Totals		718	31	136	167	1297	63	7	14	21	109

a WHL East First All-Star Team (1984)

Traded to **Washington** by **Minnesota** with Dino Ciccarelli for Mike Gartner and Larry Murphy, March 7, 1989. Traded to **Toronto** by **Washington** with Peter Zezel for Al Iafrate, January 16, 1991. Signed as a free agent by **Detroit**, August 5, 1994.

ROWLAND, CHRIS   OTT.

Right wing. Shoots right. 6'1", 188 lbs.   Born, Calgary, Alta., March 30, 1971.

			Regular Season					Playoffs				
Season	Club	Lea	GP	G	A	TP	PIM	GP	G	A	TP	PIM
1990-91	Portland	WHL	67	15	24	39	163	....	....	....	....	....
1991-92	Portland	WHL	70	34	31	65	246	6	2	4	6	28
1992-93	New Haven	AHL	34	4	4	8	65	....	....	....	....	....
	Thunder Bay	Col.	22	5	3	8	65	....	....	....	....	....
1993-94	ColHL	AHL	40	6	2	8	122	....	....	....	....	....
	Thunder Bay	ColHL	14	4	6	10	13	9	3	2	5	31

Signed as a free agent by **Ottawa**, July 30, 1992.

ROY, ANDRE   BOS.

Left wing. Shoots left. 6'3", 178 lbs.   Born, Port Chester, NY, February 8, 1975.
(Boston's 5th choice, 151st overall, in 1994 Entry Draft).

			Regular Season					Playoffs				
Season	Club	Lea	GP	G	A	TP	PIM	GP	G	A	TP	PIM
1993-94	Chicoutimi	QMJHL	65	10	21	31	277	25	3	6	9	94

ROY, JEAN-YVES   (WAH)   NYR

Right wing. Shoots left. 5'10", 185 lbs.   Born, Rosemere, Que., February 17, 1969.

			Regular Season					Playoffs				
Season	Club	Lea	GP	G	A	TP	PIM	GP	G	A	TP	PIM
1989-90a	U. of Maine	H.E.	46	*39	26	65	52	....	....	....	....	....
1990-91bcd	U. of Maine	H.E.	43	37	45	82	62	....	....	....	....	....
1991-92ce	U. of Maine	H.E.	35	32	24	56	62	....	....	....	....	....
1992-93	Binghamton	AHL	49	13	15	28	21	14	5	2	7	4
	Cdn. National	....	23	9	6	15	35	....	....	....	....	....
1993-94	Binghamton	AHL	65	41	24	65	33	....	....	....	....	....
	Cdn. National	....	6	3	2	5	2	....	....	....	....	....
	Cdn. Olympic	....	8	1	0	1	0	....	....	....	....	....

a NCAA East Second All-American Team (1990)
b Hockey East First All-Star Team (1991)
c NCAA East First All-American Team (1991, 1992)
d NCAA Final Four All-Tournament Team (1991)
e Hockey East Second All-Star Team (1992)

Signed as a free agent by **NY Rangers**, July 20, 1992.

ROY, SIMON   (WAH)

Defense. Shoots left. 6'1", 180 lbs.   Born, Montreal, Que., June 14, 1974.
(Edmonton's 3rd choice, 61st overall, in 1992 Entry Draft).

			Regular Season					Playoffs				
Season	Club	Lea	GP	G	A	TP	PIM	GP	G	A	TP	PIM
1991-92	Shawinigan	QMJHL	63	3	24	27	24	10	1	4	5	9
1992-93	Shawinigan	QMJHL	68	5	34	39	56	....	....	....	....	....
1993-94	Shawinigan	QMJHL	64	10	46	56	30	5	1	4	5	6

ROY, STEPHANE   (WAH)   ST.L.

Center. Shoots left. 5'10", 173 lbs.   Born, Ste-Martine, Que., January 26, 1976.
(St. Louis' 1st choice, 68th overall, in 1994 Entry Draft).

			Regular Season					Playoffs				
Season	Club	Lea	GP	G	A	TP	PIM	GP	G	A	TP	PIM
1992-93	Lac St-Louis	Midget	42	38	27	65	34	....	....	....	....	....
1993-94	Val D'or	QMJHL	72	25	28	53	116	....	....	....	....	....

RUBACHUK, BRAD

Center. Shoots left. 5'11", 185 lbs.   Born, Winnipeg, Man., June 11, 1970.
(Buffalo's 11th choice, 250th overall, in 1990 Entry Draft).

			Regular Season					Playoffs				
Season	Club	Lea	GP	G	A	TP	PIM	GP	G	A	TP	PIM
1988-89	Lethbridge	WHL	66	19	13	32	161	6	3	1	4	25
1989-90	Lethbridge	WHL	67	37	36	73	179	16	3	7	10	51
1990-91	Lethbridge	WHL	70	64	68	132	237	16	*14	14	28	55
1991-92	Rochester	AHL	70	18	16	34	201	13	4	0	4	19
1992-93	Rochester	AHL	61	10	15	25	218	12	3	1	4	63
1993-94	Rochester	AHL	65	18	18	36	246	4	1	1	2	10

RUCCHIN, STEVE   ANA.

Center. Shoots left. 6'3", 210 lbs.   Born, London, Ont., July 4, 1971.
(Anaheim's 1st choice, 2nd overall, in 1994 Supplemental Draft).

			Regular Season					Playoffs				
Season	Club	Lea	GP	G	A	TP	PIM	GP	G	A	TP	PIM
1990-91	Western Ont.	OUAA	34	13	16	29	14	....	....	....	....	....
1991-92	Western Ont.	OUAA	37	28	34	62	36	....	....	....	....	....
1992-93	Western Ont.	OUAA	34	22	26	48	16	....	....	....	....	....
1993-94	Western Ont.	OUAA	35	30	23	53	30	....	....	....	....	....

RUCHTY, MATTHEW (RUHK-tee) N.J.

Left wing. Shoots left. 6'1", 210 lbs. Born, Kitchener, Ont., November 27, 1969.
(New Jersey's 4th choice, 65th overall, in 1988 Entry Draft).

			Regular Season					Playoffs				
Season	Club	Lea	GP	G	A	TP	PIM	GP	G	A	TP	PIM
1987-88	Bowling Green	CCHA	41	6	15	21	78	....	....	....	....	....
1988-89	Bowling Green	CCHA	43	11	21	32	110	....	....	....	....	....
1989-90	Bowling Green	CCHA	42	28	21	49	135	....	....	....	....	....
1990-91	Bowling Green	CCHA	38	13	18	31	147	....	....	....	....	....
1991-92	Utica	AHL	73	9	14	23	250	4	0	0	0	25
1992-93	Utica	AHL	74	4	14	18	253	4	0	2	2	15
1993-94	Albany	AHL	68	11	11	22	303	5	0	1	1	18

RUCINSKY, MARTIN (roo-SHIHN-skee) QUE.

Left wing. Shoots left. 6', 178 lbs. Born, Most, Czech., March 11, 1971.
(Edmonton's 2nd choice, 20th overall, in 1991 Entry Draft).

			Regular Season					Playoffs				
Season	Club	Lea	GP	G	A	TP	PIM	GP	G	A	TP	PIM
1988-89	Litvinov	Czech.	3	1	0	1	2	....	....	....	....	....
1989-90	Litvinov	Czech.	47	17	9	26	....	....	....	....	....	....
1990-91	Litvinov	Czech.	56	24	20	44	69	....	....	....	....	....
1991-92	**Edmonton**	**NHL**	**2**	**0**	**0**	**0**	**0**	....	....	....	....	....
	Cape Breton	AHL	35	11	12	23	34	....	....	....	....	....
	Quebec	**NHL**	**4**	**1**	**1**	**2**	**2**	....	....	....	....	....
	Halifax	AHL	7	1	1	2	6	....	....	....	....	....
1992-93	**Quebec**	**NHL**	**77**	**18**	**30**	**48**	**51**	**6**	**1**	**1**	**2**	**4**
1993-94	**Quebec**	**NHL**	**60**	**9**	**23**	**32**	**58**	....	....	....	....	....
	NHL Totals		**143**	**28**	**54**	**82**	**111**	**6**	**1**	**1**	**2**	**4**

Traded to **Quebec** by **Edmonton** for Ron Tugnutt and Brad Zavisha, March 10, 1992.

RUFF, JASON T.B.

Left wing. Shoots left. 6'2", 192 lbs. Born, Kelowna, B.C., January 27, 1970.
(St Louis' 3rd choice, 96th overall, in 1990 Entry Draft).

			Regular Season					Playoffs				
Season	Club	Lea	GP	G	A	TP	PIM	GP	G	A	TP	PIM
1989-90	Lethbridge	WHL	72	55	64	119	114	19	9	10	19	18
1990-91a	Lethbridge	WHL	66	61	75	136	154	16	12	17	29	18
	Peoria	IHL	....	....	....	....	....	5	0	0	0	2
1991-92	Peoria	IHL	67	27	45	72	148	10	7	7	14	19
1992-93	**St. Louis**	**NHL**	**7**	**2**	**1**	**3**	**8**	....	....	....	....	....
	Peoria	IHL	40	22	21	43	81	....	....	....	....	....
	Tampa Bay	**NHL**	**1**	**0**	**0**	**0**	**0**	....	....	....	....	....
	Atlanta	IHL	26	11	14	25	90	7	2	1	3	26
1993-94	**Tampa Bay**	**NHL**	**6**	**1**	**2**	**3**	**2**	....	....	....	....	....
	Atlanta	IHL	71	24	25	49	122	14	6	*17	23	41
	NHL Totals		**14**	**3**	**3**	**6**	**10**	....	....	....	....	....

a WHL East First All-Star Team (1991)

Traded to **Tampa Bay** by **St. Louis** with future considerations for Doug Crossman, Basil McRae and Tampa Bay's fourth round choice in 1996 Entry Draft, January 28, 1993.

RUHLY, DAVID MTL.

Left wing. Shoots left. 6'1", 167 lbs. Born, Baldwin, WI, January 23, 1974.
(Montreal's 9th choice, 177th overall, in 1993 Entry Draft).

			Regular Season					Playoffs				
Season	Club	Lea	GP	G	A	TP	PIM	GP	G	A	TP	PIM
1992-93	Culver Mill Ac.	US	38	17	24	41	46	....	....	....	....	....
1993-94	Providence	H.E.	21	2	8	10	26	....	....	....	....	....

RUMBLE, DARREN OTT.

Defense. Shoots left. 6'1", 200 lbs. Born, Barrie, Ont., January 23, 1969.
(Philadelphia's 1st choice, 20th overall, in 1987 Entry Draft).

			Regular Season					Playoffs				
Season	Club	Lea	GP	G	A	TP	PIM	GP	G	A	TP	PIM
1986-87	Kitchener	OHL	64	11	32	43	44	4	0	1	1	9
1987-88	Kitchener	OHL	55	15	50	65	64	....	....	....	....	....
1988-89	Kitchener	OHL	46	11	28	39	25	5	1	0	1	2
1989-90	Hershey	AHL	57	2	13	15	31	....	....	....	....	....
1990-91	**Philadelphia**	**NHL**	**3**	**1**	**0**	**1**	**0**	....	....	....	....	....
	Hershey	AHL	73	6	35	41	48	3	0	5	5	2
1991-92	Hershey	AHL	79	12	54	66	118	6	0	3	3	2
1992-93	**Ottawa**	**NHL**	**69**	**3**	**13**	**16**	**61**	....	....	....	....	....
	New Haven	AHL	2	1	0	1	0	....	....	....	....	....
1993-94	**Ottawa**	**NHL**	**70**	**6**	**9**	**15**	**116**	....	....	....	....	....
	PEI	AHL	3	2	0	2	0	....	....	....	....	....
	NHL Totals		**142**	**10**	**22**	**32**	**177**	....	....	....	....	....

Claimed by **Ottawa** from **Philadelphia** in Expansion Draft, June 18, 1992.

RUSHFORTH, PAUL BUF.

Center. Shoots right. 6', 189 lbs. Born, Prince George, B.C., April 22, 1974.
(Buffalo's 8th choice, 131st overall, in 1992 Entry Draft).

			Regular Season					Playoffs				
Season	Club	Lea	GP	G	A	TP	PIM	GP	G	A	TP	PIM
1991-92	North Bay	OHL	65	8	11	19	24	19	0	2	2	6
1992-93	North Bay	OHL	21	4	10	14	24	....	....	....	....	....
	Belleville	OHL	36	21	19	40	38	7	7	2	9	4
1993-94	Belleville	OHL	63	28	35	63	109	12	6	3	9	8

RUSHIN, JOHN NYR

Center. Shoots right. 6'5", 201 lbs. Born, Edina, MN, September 12, 1972.
(NY Rangers' 7th choice, 147th overall, in 1991 Entry Draft).

			Regular Season					Playoffs				
Season	Club	Lea	GP	G	A	TP	PIM	GP	G	A	TP	PIM
1991-92	Notre Dame	NCAA	17	8	2	10	30	....	....	....	....	....
1992-93	Notre Dame	CCHA	36	1	4	5	46	....	....	....	....	....
1993-94	Notre Dame	CCHA	36	3	6	9	60	....	....	....	....	....

RUSK, MIKE CHI.

Defense. Shoots left. 6'1", 175 lbs. Born, Milton, Ont., April 26, 1975.
(Chicago's 10th choice, 232nd overall, in 1993 Entry Draft).

			Regular Season					Playoffs				
Season	Club	Lea	GP	G	A	TP	PIM	GP	G	A	TP	PIM
1986-87	TJ Gottwaldov	Czech.	36	3	3	6	12	....	....	....	....	....
1992-93	Guelph	OHL	62	3	15	18	67	5	0	1	1	8
1993-94	Guelph	OHL	48	8	26	34	59	9	2	9	11	12

RUSSELL, CAM CHI.

Defense. Shoots left. 6'4", 174 lbs. Born, Halifax, N.S., January 12, 1969.
(Chicago's 3rd choice, 50th overall, in 1987 Entry Draft).

			Regular Season					Playoffs				
Season	Club	Lea	GP	G	A	TP	PIM	GP	G	A	TP	PIM
1985-86	Hull	QMJHL	56	3	4	7	24	15	0	2	2	4
1986-87	Hull	QMJHL	66	3	16	19	119	8	0	1	1	16
1987-88	Hull	QMJHL	53	9	18	27	141	19	2	5	7	39
1988-89	Hull	QMJHL	66	8	32	40	109	9	2	6	8	6
1989-90	**Chicago**	**NHL**	**19**	**0**	**1**	**1**	**27**	**1**	**0**	**0**	**0**	**0**
	Indianapolis	IHL	46	3	15	18	114	9	0	1	1	24
1990-91	**Chicago**	**NHL**	**3**	**0**	**0**	**0**	**5**	**1**	**0**	**0**	**0**	**0**
	Indianapolis	IHL	53	5	9	14	125	6	0	2	2	30
1991-92	**Chicago**	**NHL**	**19**	**0**	**0**	**0**	**34**	**12**	**0**	**2**	**2**	**2**
	Indianapolis	IHL	41	4	9	13	78	....	....	....	....	....
1992-93	**Chicago**	**NHL**	**67**	**2**	**4**	**6**	**151**	**4**	**0**	**0**	**0**	**0**
1993-94	**Chicago**	**NHL**	**67**	**1**	**7**	**8**	**200**	....	....	....	....	....
	NHL Totals		**175**	**3**	**12**	**15**	**417**	**18**	**0**	**2**	**2**	**2**

RUUTTU, CHRISTIAN (ROO-TOO) CHI.

Center. Shoots left. 5'11", 194 lbs. Born, Lappeenranta, Finland, February 20, 1964.
(Buffalo's 9th choice, 134th overall, in 1983 Entry Draft).

			Regular Season					Playoffs				
Season	Club	Lea	GP	G	A	TP	PIM	GP	G	A	TP	PIM
1982-83	Assat	Fin.	36	15	18	33	34	....	....	....	....	....
1983-84	Assat	Fin.	37	18	42	60	72	9	2	5	7	12
1984-85	Assat	Fin.	32	14	32	46	34	8	1	6	7	8
1985-86	HIFK	Fin.	36	16	38	54	47	10	3	6	9	8
1986-87	**Buffalo**	**NHL**	**76**	**22**	**43**	**65**	**62**	....	....	....	....	....
1987-88	**Buffalo**	**NHL**	**73**	**26**	**45**	**71**	**85**	**6**	**2**	**5**	**7**	**4**
1988-89	**Buffalo**	**NHL**	**67**	**14**	**46**	**60**	**98**	**2**	**0**	**0**	**0**	**2**
1989-90	**Buffalo**	**NHL**	**75**	**19**	**41**	**60**	**66**	**6**	**0**	**0**	**0**	**4**
1990-91	**Buffalo**	**NHL**	**77**	**16**	**34**	**50**	**96**	**6**	**1**	**3**	**4**	**29**
1991-92	**Buffalo**	**NHL**	**70**	**4**	**21**	**25**	**76**	**3**	**0**	**0**	**0**	**6**
1992-93	**Chicago**	**NHL**	**84**	**17**	**37**	**54**	**134**	**4**	**0**	**0**	**0**	**2**
1993-94	**Chicago**	**NHL**	**54**	**9**	**20**	**29**	**68**	**6**	**0**	**0**	**0**	**2**
	NHL Totals		**576**	**127**	**287**	**414**	**685**	**33**	**3**	**8**	**11**	**49**

Played in NHL All-Star Game (1988)

Traded to **Winnipeg** by **Buffalo** with future considerations for Stephane Beauregard, June 15, 1992. Traded to **Chicago** by **Winnipeg** for Stephane Beauregard, August 10, 1992.

RUZICKA, VLADIMIR (roo-ZEECH-kuh)

Center. Shoots left. 6'3", 215 lbs. Born, Most, Czech., June 6, 1963.
(Toronto's 5th choice, 73rd overall, in 1982 Entry Draft).

			Regular Season					Playoffs				
Season	Club	Lea	GP	G	A	TP	PIM	GP	G	A	TP	PIM
1979-80	Litvinov	Czech.	9	1	1	2	0	....	....	....	....	....
1980-81	Litvinov	Czech.	41	12	13	25	10	....	....	....	....	....
1981-82	Litvinov	Czech.	44	27	22	49	50	....	....	....	....	....
1982-83	Litvinov	Czech.	43	22	24	46	40	....	....	....	....	....
1983-84	Litvinov	Czech.	44	31	23	54	50	....	....	....	....	....
1984-85	Litvinov	Czech.	41	38	22	60	29	....	....	....	....	....
1985-86	Litvinov	Czech.	43	41	32	73	....	....	....	....	....	....
1986-87	Litvinov	Czech.	39	29	21	50	46	....	....	....	....	....
1987-88	Dukla Trencin	Czech.	44	38	27	65	70	....	....	....	....	....
1988-89	Dukla Trencin	Czech.	45	46	38	84	42	....	....	....	....	....
1989-90	Litvinov	Czech.	32	21	23	44	....	....	....	....	....	....
	Edmonton	**NHL**	**25**	**11**	**6**	**17**	**10**	....	....	....	....	....
1990-91	**Boston**	**NHL**	**29**	**8**	**8**	**16**	**19**	**17**	**2**	**11**	**13**	**0**
1991-92	**Boston**	**NHL**	**77**	**39**	**36**	**75**	**48**	**13**	**2**	**3**	**5**	**2**
1992-93	**Boston**	**NHL**	**60**	**19**	**22**	**41**	**38**	....	....	....	....	....
1993-94	**Ottawa**	**NHL**	**42**	**5**	**13**	**18**	**14**	....	....	....	....	....
	NHL Totals		**233**	**82**	**85**	**167**	**129**	**30**	**4**	**14**	**18**	**2**

Traded to **Edmonton** by **Toronto** for Edmonton's fourth round choice (Greg Walters) in 1990 Entry Draft, December 21, 1989. Traded to **Boston** by **Edmonton** for Greg Hawgood, October 22, 1990. Signed as a free agent by **Ottawa**, August 12, 1993.

RYCHEL, WARREN (RIGH-kuhl) L.A.

Left wing. Shoots left. 6', 202 lbs. Born, Tecumseh, Ont., May 12, 1967.

			Regular Season					Playoffs				
Season	Club	Lea	GP	G	A	TP	PIM	GP	G	A	TP	PIM
1984-85	Sudbury	OHL	35	5	8	13	74	....	....	....	....	....
	Guelph	OHL	29	1	3	4	48	....	....	....	....	....
1985-86	Guelph	OHL	38	14	5	19	119	....	....	....	....	....
	Ottawa	OHL	29	11	18	29	54	....	....	....	....	....
1986-87	Ottawa	OHL	28	11	7	18	57	....	....	....	....	....
	Kitchener	OHL	21	5	5	10	39	4	0	0	0	9
1987-88	Peoria	IHL	7	2	1	3	7	....	....	....	....	....
	Saginaw	IHL	51	2	7	9	113	1	0	0	0	0
1988-89	**Chicago**	**NHL**	**2**	**0**	**0**	**0**	**17**	....	....	....	....	....
	Saginaw	IHL	50	15	14	29	226	6	0	0	0	51
1989-90	Indianapolis	IHL	77	23	16	39	374	14	1	3	4	64
1990-91	Indianapolis	IHL	68	33	30	63	338	5	2	1	3	30
	Chicago	**NHL**	....	....	....	....	....	**3**	**1**	**3**	**4**	**2**
1991-92	Moncton	AHL	36	14	15	29	211	....	....	....	....	....
	Kalamazoo	IHL	45	15	20	35	165	8	0	3	3	51
1992-93	**Los Angeles**	**NHL**	**70**	**6**	**7**	**13**	**314**	**23**	**6**	**7**	**13**	**39**
1993-94	**Los Angeles**	**NHL**	**80**	**10**	**9**	**19**	**322**	....	....	....	....	....
	NHL Totals		**152**	**16**	**16**	**32**	**653**	**26**	**7**	**10**	**17**	**41**

Signed as a free agent by **Chicago**, September 19, 1986. Traded to **Winnipeg** by **Chicago** with Troy Murray for Bryan Marchment and Chris Norton, July 22, 1991. Traded to **Minnesota** by **Winnipeg** for Tony Joseph, December 30, 1991. Signed as a free agent by **Los Angeles**, October 1, 1992.

RYDMARK, DANIEL (REWD-mahrk) L.A.

Center. Shoots left. 5'10", 180 lbs. Born, Vasteras, Sweden, February 23, 1970.
(Los Angeles' 5th choice, 123rd overall, in 1989 Entry Draft).

			Regular Season					Playoffs				
Season	Club	Lea	GP	G	A	TP	PIM	GP	G	A	TP	PIM
1986-87	Farjestad	Swe.	4	0	1	1	0	....	....	....	....	....
1987-88	Farjestad	Swe.	28	2	1	3	10	5	0	0	0	2
1988-89	Farjestad	Swe.	35	9	9	18	24	....	....	....	....	....
1989-90	Farjestad	Swe.	35	9	12	21	20	5	0	0	0	4
1990-91	Malmo	Swe.	39	14	13	27	34	1	0	0	0	0
1991-92	Malmo	Swe.	30	17	15	32	56	7	0	3	3	6
1992-93	Malmo	Swe.	39	18	13	31	70	6	5	4	9	8
1993-94	Malmo	Swe.	38	14	18	32	48	11	3	7	10	18

SABOURIN, KEN

Defense. Shoots left. 6'3", 205 lbs. Born, Scarborough, Ont., April 28, 1966.
(Calgary's 2nd choice, 33rd overall, in 1984 Entry Draft).

			Regular Season					Playoffs				
Season	Club	Lea	GP	G	A	TP	PIM	GP	G	A	TP	PIM
1982-83	S.S. Marie	OHL	58	0	8	8	90	10	0	0	0	14
1983-84	S.S. Marie	OHL	63	7	14	21	157	9	0	1	1	25
1984-85	S.S. Marie	OHL	63	5	19	24	139	16	1	4	5	10
1985-86	Moncton	AHL	3	0	0	0	0	6	0	1	1	2
	S.S. Marie	OHL	25	1	5	6	77	....	....	....	....	....
	Cornwall	OHL	37	3	12	15	94	6	1	2	3	6
1986-87	Moncton	AHL	75	1	10	11	166	6	0	1	1	27
1987-88	Salt Lake	IHL	71	2	8	10	186	16	1	6	7	57
1988-89	**Calgary**	**NHL**	**6**	**0**	**1**	**1**	**26**	**1**	**0**	**0**	**0**	**0**
	Salt Lake	IHL	74	2	18	20	197	11	0	1	1	26
1989-90	**Calgary**	**NHL**	**5**	**0**	**0**	**0**	**10**	....	....	....	....	....
	Salt Lake	IHL	76	5	19	24	336	11	0	2	2	40
1990-91	**Calgary**	**NHL**	**16**	**1**	**3**	**4**	**36**	....	....	....	....	....
	Salt Lake	IHL	28	2	15	17	77	....	....	....	....	....
	Washington	**NHL**	**28**	**1**	**4**	**5**	**81**	**11**	**0**	**0**	**0**	**34**
1991-92	**Washington**	**NHL**	**19**	**0**	**0**	**0**	**48**	....	....	....	....	....
	Baltimore	AHL	30	3	8	11	106	....	....	....	....	....
1992-93	Baltimore	AHL	30	5	14	19	68	....	....	....	....	....
	Salt Lake	IHL	52	2	11	13	140	....	....	....	....	....
1993-94	Milwaukee	IHL	81	6	13	19	279	4	0	0	0	10
	NHL Totals		**74**	**2**	**8**	**10**	**201**	**12**	**0**	**0**	**0**	**34**

Traded to **Washington** by **Calgary** for Paul Fenton, January 24, 1991. Traded to **Calgary** by **Washington** for future considerations, December 16, 1992.

SACCO, DAVID (SAK-oh) TOR.

Right wing. Shoots right. 6', 190 lbs. Born, Malden, MA, July 31, 1970.
(Toronto's 9th choice, 195th overall, in 1988 Entry Draft).

			Regular Season					Playoffs				
Season	Club	Lea	GP	G	A	TP	PIM	GP	G	A	TP	PIM
1988-89	Boston U.	H.E.	35	14	29	43	40	....	....	....	....	....
1989-90	Boston U.	H.E.	3	0	4	4	2	....	....	....	....	....
1990-91	Boston U.	H.E.	40	21	40	61	24	....	....	....	....	....
1991-92ab	Boston U.	H.E.	34	13	32	45	30	....	....	....	....	....
1992-93ab	Boston U.	H.E.	40	25	37	62	86	....	....	....	....	....
1993-94	U.S. National	....	32	8	20	28	88	....	....	....	....	....
	U.S. Olympic	....	8	3	5	8	12	....	....	....	....	....
	Toronto	**NHL**	**4**	**1**	**1**	**2**	**4**	....	....	....	....	....
	St. John's	AHL	5	3	1	4	2	....	....	....	....	....
	NHL Totals		**4**	**1**	**1**	**2**	**4**	....	....	....	....	....

a NCAA East First All-American Team (1992, 1993)
b Hockey East First All-Star Team (1992, 1993)

SACCO, JOE (SAK-oh) ANA.

Left wing. Shoots right. 6'1", 195 lbs. Born, Medford, MA, February 4, 1969.
(Toronto's 4th choice, 71st overall, in 1987 Entry Draft).

			Regular Season					Playoffs				
Season	Club	Lea	GP	G	A	TP	PIM	GP	G	A	TP	PIM
1987-88	Boston U.	H.E.	34	16	20	36	40	....	....	....	....	....
1988-89	Boston U.	H.E.	33	21	19	40	66	....	....	....	....	....
1989-90	Boston U.	H.E.	44	28	24	52	70	....	....	....	....	....
1990-91	**Toronto**	**NHL**	**20**	**0**	**5**	**5**	**2**	....	....	....	....	....
	Newmarket	AHL	49	18	17	35	24	....	....	....	....	....
1991-92	U.S. National	....	50	11	26	37	61	....	....	....	....	....
	U.S. Olympic	....	8	0	2	2	0	....	....	....	....	....
	Toronto	**NHL**	**17**	**7**	**4**	**11**	**4**	....	....	....	....	....
	St. John's	AHL	....	....	....	....	....	1	1	1	2	0
1992-93	**Toronto**	**NHL**	**23**	**4**	**4**	**8**	**8**	....	....	....	....	....
	St. John's	AHL	37	14	16	30	45	7	6	4	10	2
1993-94	**Anaheim**	**NHL**	**84**	**19**	**18**	**37**	**61**	....	....	....	....	....
	NHL Totals		**144**	**30**	**31**	**61**	**75**	....	....	....	....	....

Claimed by **Anaheim** from **Toronto** in Expansion Draft, June 24, 1993.

SAFARIK, RICHARD BUF.

Right wing. Shoots left. 6'3", 194 lbs. Born, Nova Zamky, Czech., February 26, 1975.
(Buffalo's 3rd choice, 116th overall, in 1993 Entry Draft).

			Regular Season					Playoffs				
Season	Club	Lea	GP	G	A	TP	PIM	GP	G	A	TP	PIM
1991-92	Nitra	Czech.2	2	0	0	0	0	....	....	....	....	....
1992-93	Nitra	Czech.2	16	0	0	0	2	....	....	....	....	....
1993-94	Hull	QMJHL	65	7	14	21	24	19	1	3	4	2

SAILYNOJA, KEIJO (sayl-yeh-NOY-ah) EDM.

Left wing. Shoots left. 6'2", 187 lbs. Born, Vantaa, Finland, February 17, 1970.
(Edmonton's 6th choice, 122nd overall, in 1990 Entry Draft).

			Regular Season					Playoffs				
Season	Club	Lea	GP	G	A	TP	PIM	GP	G	A	TP	PIM
1989-90	Jokerit	Fin.	41	15	13	28	14	....	....	....	....	....
1990-91	Jokerit	Fin.	44	21	25	46	14	....	....	....	....	....
1991-92	Jokerit	Fin.	42	21	25	46	14	10	5	6	11	2
1992-93	Jokerit	Fin.	47	29	13	42	14	3	1	1	2	0
1993-94	Jokerit	Fin.	37	11	8	19	43	12	2	0	2	6

ST. AMOUR, MARTIN

Left wing. Shoots left. 6'3", 194 lbs. Born, Montreal, Que., January 30, 1970.
(Montreal's 2nd choice, 34th overall, in 1988 Entry Draft).

			Regular Season					Playoffs				
Season	Club	Lea	GP	G	A	TP	PIM	GP	G	A	TP	PIM
1987-88	Verdun	QMJHL	61	20	50	70	111	....	....	....	....	....
1988-89	Verdun	QMJHL	28	19	17	36	87	....	....	....	....	....
	Trois-Rivières	QMJHL	26	8	21	29	69	4	1	2	3	0
1989-90	Trois-Rivières	QMJHL	60	57	79	136	162	7	7	9	16	19
	Sherbrooke	AHL	....	....	....	....	....	1	0	0	0	0
1990-91	Fredericton	AHL	45	13	16	29	51	1	0	0	0	0
1991-92	Cincinnati	ECHL	60	44	44	88	183	9	4	9	13	18
1992-93	**Ottawa**	**NHL**	**1**	**0**	**0**	**0**	**2**	....	....	....	....	....
	New Haven	AHL	71	21	39	60	78	....	....	....	....	....
1993-94	PEI	AHL	37	13	12	25	65	....	....	....	....	....
	Providence	AHL	12	0	3	3	22	....	....	....	....	....
	NHL Totals		**1**	**0**	**0**	**0**	**2**	....	....	....	....	....

Signed as a free agent by **Ottawa**, July 16, 1992.

ST. CYR, GERRY OTT.

Left wing. Shoots right. 6'1", 188 lbs. Born, North Vancouver, B.C., August 18, 1971.

			Regular Season					Playoffs				
Season	Club	Lea	GP	G	A	TP	PIM	GP	G	A	TP	PIM
1991-92	Victoria	WHL	70	38	55	93	407	....	....	....	....	....
1992-93	New Haven	AHL	40	5	5	10	195	....	....	....	....	....
1993-94a	Thunder Bay	ColHL	62	50	63	113	265	9	4	4	8	23

a ColHL Second All-Star Team (1994)

Signed as a free agent by **Ottawa**, July 30, 1992.

ST. JACQUES, KEVIN CHI.

Left wing. Shoots right. 5'11", 190 lbs. Born, Edmonton, Alta., February 25, 1971.
(Chicago's 6th choice, 112th overall, in 1991 Entry Draft).

			Regular Season					Playoffs				
Season	Club	Lea	GP	G	A	TP	PIM	GP	G	A	TP	PIM
1990-91a	Lethbridge	WHL	72	45	63	108	64	16	13	10	23	20
1991-92b	Lethbridge	WHL	71	*65	75	140	159	3	2	2	4	2
1992-93	Indianapolis	IHL	71	10	21	31	93	4	0	0	0	0
1993-94	Indianapolis	IHL	49	5	23	28	91	....	....	....	....	....
	Flint	ColHL	10	5	13	18	2	10	4	14	18	19

a WHL East Second All-Star Team (1991)
b WHL East First All-Star Team (1992)

ST. PIERRE, DAVID CGY.

Center. Shoots right. 6', 185 lbs. Born, Montreal, Que., March 22, 1972.
(Calgary's 9th choice, 173rd overall, in 1991 Entry Draft).

			Regular Season					Playoffs				
Season	Club	Lea	GP	G	A	TP	PIM	GP	G	A	TP	PIM
1990-91	Longueuil	QMJHL	66	34	45	79	51	8	4	4	8	8
1991-92	Verdun	QMJHL	69	40	55	95	98	15	3	6	9	15
1992-93	Salt Lake	IHL	35	7	8	15	18	....	....	....	....	....
1993-94	Saint John	AHL	77	19	30	49	42	5	0	2	2	0

SAKIC, JOE (SAK-ihk) QUE.

Center. Shoots left. 5'11", 185 lbs. Born, Burnaby, B.C., July 7, 1969.
(Quebec's 2nd choice, 15th overall, in 1987 Entry Draft).

			Regular Season					Playoffs				
Season	Club	Lea	GP	G	A	TP	PIM	GP	G	A	TP	PIM
1986-87	Swift Current	WHL	72	60	73	133	31	4	0	1	1	0
1987-88ab	Swift Current	WHL	64	*78	82	*160	64	10	11	13	24	12
1988-89	**Quebec**	**NHL**	**70**	**23**	**39**	**62**	**24**	....	....	....	....	....
1989-90	**Quebec**	**NHL**	**80**	**39**	**63**	**102**	**27**	....	....	....	....	....
1990-91	**Quebec**	**NHL**	**80**	**48**	**61**	**109**	**24**	....	....	....	....	....
1991-92	**Quebec**	**NHL**	**69**	**29**	**65**	**94**	**20**	....	....	....	....	....
1992-93	**Quebec**	**NHL**	**78**	**48**	**57**	**105**	**40**	**6**	**3**	**3**	**6**	**2**
1993-94	**Quebec**	**NHL**	**84**	**28**	**64**	**92**	**18**	....	....	....	....	....
	NHL Totals		**461**	**215**	**349**	**564**	**153**	**6**	**3**	**3**	**6**	**2**

a Canadian Major Junior Player of the Year (1988)
b WHL East All-Star Team (1988)

Played in NHL All-Star Game (1990-94)

SALLE, JOHAN PHI.

Defense. Shoots left. 6'1", 200 lbs. Born, Lindloven, Sweden, February 21, 1967.
(Philadelphia's 9th choice, 161st overall, in 1988 Entry Draft).

			Regular Season					Playoffs				
Season	Club	Lea	GP	G	A	TP	PIM	GP	G	A	TP	PIM
1987-88	Orebro	Swe. 2	36	9	4	13	48	8	1	1	2	14
1988-89	Malmo	Swe. 2	32	10	15	25	60	....	....	....	....	....
1989-90	Malmo	Swe. 2	32	12	16	28	98	....	....	....	....	....
1990-91	Malmo	Swe.	38	4	5	9	34	2	0	0	0	12
1991-92	Malmo	Swe.	29	2	5	7	62	10	2	0	2	12
1992-93	Malmo	Swe.	30	3	2	5	38	6	0	0	0	8
1993-94	Malmo	Swe.	24	3	2	6	26	11	1	0	1	12

SALVADOR, BRYCE T.B.

Defense. Shoots left. 6'2", 194 lbs. Born, Brandon, Man., February 11, 1976.
(Tampa Bay's 6th choice, 138th overall, in 1994 Entry Draft).

			Regular Season					Playoffs				
Season	Club	Lea	GP	G	A	TP	PIM	GP	G	A	TP	PIM
1992-93	Lethbridge	WHL	64	1	4	5	29	4	0	0	0	0
1993-94	Lethbridge	WHL	61	4	14	18	36	9	0	1	1	2

SAMUELSSON, KJELL (SAM-yuhl-suhn, SHEHL) PIT.

Defense. Shoots right. 6'6", 235 lbs. Born, Tingsryd, Sweden, October 18, 1958.
(NY Rangers' 5th choice, 119th overall, in 1984 Entry Draft).

			Regular Season					Playoffs				
Season	Club	Lea	GP	G	A	TP	PIM	GP	G	A	TP	PIM
1977-78	Tingsryd	Swe. 2	20	3	0	3	41	....	....	....	....	....
1978-79	Tingsryd	Swe. 2	24	3	4	7	67	....	....	....	....	....
1979-80	Tingsryd	Swe. 2	26	5	4	9	45	....	....	....	....	....
1980-81	Tingsryd	Swe. 2	35	6	7	13	61	2	0	1	1	14
1981-82	Tingsryd	Swe. 2	33	11	14	25	68	3	0	2	2	2
1982-83	Tingsryd	Swe. 2	32	11	6	17	57	....	....	....	....	....
1983-84	Leksand	Swe.	36	6	6	12	59	....	....	....	....	....
1984-85	Leksand	Swe.	35	9	5	14	34	....	....	....	....	....
1985-86	**NY Rangers**	**NHL**	**9**	**0**	**0**	**0**	**10**	**9**	**0**	**1**	**1**	**8**
	New Haven	AHL	56	6	21	27	87	3	0	0	0	10
1986-87	**NY Rangers**	**NHL**	**30**	**2**	**6**	**8**	**50**	....	....	....	....	....
	Philadelphia	**NHL**	**46**	**1**	**6**	**7**	**86**	**26**	**0**	**4**	**4**	**25**
1987-88	**Philadelphia**	**NHL**	**74**	**6**	**24**	**30**	**184**	**7**	**2**	**5**	**7**	**23**
1988-89	**Philadelphia**	**NHL**	**69**	**3**	**14**	**17**	**140**	**19**	**1**	**3**	**4**	**24**
1989-90	**Philadelphia**	**NHL**	**66**	**5**	**17**	**22**	**91**	....	....	....	....	....
1990-91	**Philadelphia**	**NHL**	**78**	**9**	**19**	**28**	**82**	....	....	....	....	....
1991-92	**Philadelphia**	**NHL**	**54**	**4**	**9**	**13**	**76**	....	....	....	....	....
	Pittsburgh	**NHL**	**20**	**1**	**2**	**3**	**34**	**15**	**0**	**3**	**3**	**12**
1992-93	**Pittsburgh**	**NHL**	**63**	**3**	**6**	**9**	**106**	**12**	**0**	**3**	**3**	**2**
1993-94	**Pittsburgh**	**NHL**	**59**	**5**	**8**	**13**	**118**	**6**	**0**	**0**	**0**	**26**
	NHL Totals		**568**	**39**	**111**	**150**	**977**	**94**	**3**	**19**	**22**	**120**

Played in NHL All-Star Game (1988)

Traded to **Philadelphia** by **NY Rangers** with NY Rangers' second round choice (Patrik Juhlin) in 1989 Entry Draft for Bob Froese, December 18, 1986. Traded to **Pittsburgh** by **Philadelphia** with Rick Tocchet, Ken Wregget and Philadelphia's third round choice (Dave Roche) in 1993 Entry Draft for Mark Recchi, Brian Benning and Los Angeles' first round choice (previously acquired by Pittsburgh — Philadelphia selected Jason Bowen) in 1992 Entry Draft, February 19, 1992.

SAMUELSSON, ULF (SAM-yuhl-suhn, UHLF) PIT.

Defense. Shoots left. 6'1", 195 lbs. Born, Fagersta, Sweden, March 26, 1964.
(Hartford's 4th choice, 67th overall, in 1982 Entry Draft).

			Regular Season					Playoffs				
Season	Club	Lea	GP	G	A	TP	PIM	GP	G	A	TP	PIM
1981-82	Leksand	Swe.	31	3	1	4	40	....	....	....	....	....
1982-83	Leksand	Swe.	33	9	6	15	72	....	....	....	....	....
1983-84	Leksand	Swe.	36	5	11	16	53	....	....	....	....	....
1984-85	Hartford	NHL	41	2	6	8	83	....	....	....	....	....
	Binghamton	AHL	36	5	11	16	92	....	....	....	....	....
1985-86	Hartford	NHL	80	5	19	24	174	10	1	2	3	38
1986-87	Hartford	NHL	78	2	31	33	162	5	0	1	1	41
1987-88	Hartford	NHL	76	8	33	41	159	5	0	0	0	8
1988-89	Hartford	NHL	71	9	26	35	181	4	0	2	2	4
1989-90	Hartford	NHL	55	2	11	13	177	7	1	0	1	2
1990-91	Hartford	NHL	62	3	18	21	174	....	....	....	....	....
	Pittsburgh	NHL	14	1	4	5	37	20	3	2	5	34
1991-92	Pittsburgh	NHL	62	1	14	15	206	21	0	2	2	39
1992-93	Pittsburgh	NHL	77	3	26	29	249	12	1	5	6	24
1993-94	Pittsburgh	NHL	80	5	24	29	199	6	0	1	1	18
	NHL Totals		696	41	212	253	1801	90	6	15	21	208

Traded to **Pittsburgh** by **Hartford** with Ron Francis and Grant Jennings for John Cullen, Jeff Parker and Zarley Zalapski, March 4, 1991.

SANDERSON, GEOFF HFD.

Center. Shoots left. 6', 185 lbs. Born, Hay River, N.W.T., February 1, 1972.
(Hartford's 2nd choice, 36th overall, in 1990 Entry Draft).

			Regular Season					Playoffs				
Season	Club	Lea	GP	G	A	TP	PIM	GP	G	A	TP	PIM
1988-89	Swift Current	WHL	58	17	11	28	16	12	3	5	8	6
1989-90	Swift Current	WHL	70	32	62	94	56	4	1	4	5	8
1990-91	Hartford	NHL	2	1	0	1	0	3	0	0	0	0
	Swift Current	WHL	70	62	50	112	57	3	1	2	3	4
	Springfield	AHL	....	....	....	....	....	1	0	0	0	2
1991-92	Hartford	NHL	64	13	18	31	18	7	0	1	1	2
1992-93	Hartford	NHL	82	46	43	89	28	....	....	....	....	....
1993-94	Hartford	NHL	82	41	26	67	42	....	....	....	....	....
	NHL Totals		230	101	87	188	88	10	0	1	1	2

Played in NHL All-Star Game (1994)

SANDLAK, JIM HFD.

Right wing. Shoots right. 6'4", 219 lbs. Born, Kitchener, Ont., December 12, 1966.
(Vancouver's 1st choice, 4th overall, in 1985 Entry Draft).

			Regular Season					Playoffs				
Season	Club	Lea	GP	G	A	TP	PIM	GP	G	A	TP	PIM
1983-84	London	OHL	68	23	18	41	143	8	1	11	12	13
1984-85	London	OHL	58	40	24	64	128	8	3	2	5	14
1985-86	Vancouver	NHL	23	1	3	4	10	3	0	1	1	0
	London	OHL	16	8	14	22	38	5	2	3	5	24
1986-87a	Vancouver	NHL	78	15	21	36	66	....	....	....	....	....
1987-88	Vancouver	NHL	49	16	15	31	81	....	....	....	....	....
	Fredericton	AHL	24	10	15	25	47	....	....	....	....	....
1988-89	Vancouver	NHL	72	20	20	40	99	6	1	1	2	2
1989-90	Vancouver	NHL	70	15	8	23	104	....	....	....	....	....
1990-91	Vancouver	NHL	59	7	6	13	125	....	....	....	....	....
1991-92	Vancouver	NHL	66	16	24	40	176	13	4	6	10	22
1992-93	Vancouver	NHL	59	10	18	28	122	6	2	2	4	4
1993-94	Hartford	NHL	27	6	2	8	32	....	....	....	....	....
	NHL Totals		503	106	117	223	815	28	7	10	17	28

a NHL All-Rookie Team (1987)

Traded to **Hartford** by **Vancouver** to complete March 22, 1993 deal which sent Murray Craven to Vancouver by Hartford with Vancouver's fifth round choice (previously acquired by Hartford — Vancouver selected Scott Walker) in 1993 Entry Draft for Robert Kron, Vancouver's third round choice (Marek Malik) in 1993 Entry Draft and future considerations, May 17, 1993.

SANDSTROM, TOMAS (SAND-struhm)

Right wing. Shoots left. 6'2", 200 lbs. Born, Jakobstad, Finland, September 4, 1964.
(NY Rangers' 2nd choice, 36th overall, in 1982 Entry Draft).

			Regular Season					Playoffs				
Season	Club	Lea	GP	G	A	TP	PIM	GP	G	A	TP	PIM
1981-82	Fagersta	Swe. 2	32	28	11	39	74	....	....	....	....	....
1982-83	Brynas	Swe.	36	23	14	37	50	....	....	....	....	....
1983-84	Brynas	Swe.	34	19	10	29	81	....	....	....	....	....
1984-85a	NY Rangers	NHL	74	29	29	58	51	3	0	2	2	0
1985-86	NY Rangers	NHL	73	25	29	54	109	16	4	6	10	20
1986-87	NY Rangers	NHL	64	40	34	74	60	6	1	2	3	20
1987-88	NY Rangers	NHL	69	28	40	68	95	....	....	....	....	....
1988-89	NY Rangers	NHL	79	32	56	88	148	4	3	2	5	12
1989-90	NY Rangers	NHL	48	19	19	38	100	....	....	....	....	....
	Los Angeles	NHL	28	13	20	33	28	10	5	4	9	19
1990-91	Los Angeles	NHL	68	45	44	89	106	10	4	4	8	14
1991-92	Los Angeles	NHL	49	17	22	39	70	6	0	3	3	8
1992-93	Los Angeles	NHL	39	25	27	52	57	24	8	17	25	12
1993-94	Los Angeles	NHL	51	17	24	41	59	....	....	....	....	....
	Pittsburgh	NHL	27	6	11	17	24	6	0	0	0	4
	NHL Totals		669	296	355	651	907	85	25	40	65	109

a NHL All-Rookie Team (1985)

Played in NHL All-Star Game (1988, 1991)

Traded to **Los Angeles** by **NY Rangers** with Tony Granato for Bernie Nicholls, January 20, 1990. Traded to **Pittsburgh** by **Los Angeles** with Shawn McEachern for Marty McSorley and Jim Paek, February 16, 1994.

SANDWITH, TERRAN PHI.

Defense. Shoots left. 6'4", 210 lbs. Born, Edmonton, Alta., April 17, 1972.
(Philadelphia's 4th choice, 42nd overall, in 1990 Entry Draft).

			Regular Season					Playoffs				
Season	Club	Lea	GP	G	A	TP	PIM	GP	G	A	TP	PIM
1988-89	Tri-City	WHL	31	0	0	0	29	6	0	0	0	4
1989-90	Tri-City	WHL	70	4	14	18	92	7	0	2	2	14
1990-91	Tri-City	WHL	46	5	17	22	132	7	1	0	1	14
1991-92	Brandon	WHL	41	6	14	20	145	....	....	....	....	....
	Saskatoon	WHL	18	2	5	7	53	18	2	1	3	28
1992-93	Hershey	AHL	61	1	12	13	140	....	....	....	....	....
1993-94	Hershey	AHL	62	3	5	8	169	2	0	1	1	4

SAPOZHNIKOV, ANDREI (sa-PAWZH-nik-kawv) BOS.

Defense. Shoots left. 6'1", 185 lbs. Born, Chelyabinsk, USSR, June 15, 1971.
(Boston's 5th choice, 129th overall, in 1993 Entry Draft).

			Regular Season					Playoffs				
Season	Club	Lea	GP	G	A	TP	PIM	GP	G	A	TP	PIM
1990-91	Chelyabinsk	USSR	28	0	0	0	14	....	....	....	....	....
1991-92	Chelyabinsk	CIS	43	3	4	7	22	....	....	....	....	....
1992-93	Chelyabinsk	CIS	40	2	7	9	30	8	0	1	1	6
1993-94	Chelyabinsk	CIS	40	4	8	12	34	6	0	0	0	0

SARAULT, YVES MTL.

Left wing. Shoots left. 6'1", 170 lbs. Born, Valleyfield, Que., December 23, 1972.
(Montreal's 3rd choice, 61st overall, in 1991 Entry Draft).

			Regular Season					Playoffs				
Season	Club	Lea	GP	G	A	TP	PIM	GP	G	A	TP	PIM
1989-90	Victoriaville	QMJHL	70	12	28	40	140	16	0	3	3	26
1990-91	St-Jean	QMJHL	56	22	24	46	113	....	....	....	....	....
1991-92a	St-Jean	QMJHL	50	28	38	66	96	....	....	....	....	....
a	Trois-Rivières	QMJHL	18	15	14	29	12	15	10	10	20	18
1992-93	Fredericton	AHL	59	14	17	31	41	3	0	1	1	2
	Wheeling	ECHL	2	1	3	4	0	....	....	....	....	....
1993-94	Fredericton	AHL	60	13	14	27	72	....	....	....	....	....

a QMJHL Second All-Star Team (1992)

SATAN, MIROSLAV (shuh-TEEN) EDM.

Center. Shoots left. 6'1", 180 lbs. Born, Topolcany, Czech., October 22, 1974.
(Edmonton's 6th choice, 111th overall, in 1993 Entry Draft).

			Regular Season					Playoffs				
Season	Club	Lea	GP	G	A	TP	PIM	GP	G	A	TP	PIM
1991-92	Topocalny	Czech.2	9	2	1	3	6	....	....	....	....	....
1992-93	Dukla Trencin	Czech.	38	11	6	17	....	....	....	....	....	....
1993-94	Dukla Trencin	Slovak	30	32	16	48	16	....	....	....	....	....

SAVAGE, BRIAN MTL.

Center. Shoots left. 6'2", 191 lbs. Born, Sudbury, Ont., February 24, 1971.
(Montreal's 8th choice, 171st overall, in 1991 Entry Draft).

			Regular Season					Playoffs				
Season	Club	Lea	GP	G	A	TP	PIM	GP	G	A	TP	PIM
1990-91	Miami-Ohio	CCHA	28	5	6	11	26	....	....	....	....	....
1991-92	Miami-Ohio	CCHA	40	24	16	40	43	....	....	....	....	....
1992-93ab	Miami-Ohio	CCHA	38	*37	21	58	44	....	....	....	....	....
	Cdn. National	....	9	3	0	3	12	....	....	....	....	....
1993-94	Cdn. National	....	51	20	26	46	38	....	....	....	....	....
	Cdn. Olympic	....	8	2	2	4	6	....	....	....	....	....
	Montreal	NHL	3	1	0	1	0	3	0	2	2	0
	Fredericton	AHL	17	12	15	27	4	....	....	....	....	....
	NHL Totals		3	1	0	1	0	3	0	2	2	0

a CCHA First All-Star Team (1993)
b NCAA West Second All-American Team (1993)

SAVAGE, REGGIE QUE.

Center. Shoots left. 5'10", 192 lbs. Born, Montreal, Que., May 1, 1970.
(Washington's 1st choice, 15th overall, in 1988 Entry Draft).

			Regular Season					Playoffs				
Season	Club	Lea	GP	G	A	TP	PIM	GP	G	A	TP	PIM
1987-88	Victoriaville	QMJHL	68	68	54	122	77	5	2	3	5	8
1988-89	Victoriaville	QMJHL	54	58	55	113	178	16	15	13	28	52
1989-90	Victoriaville	QMJHL	63	51	43	94	79	16	13	10	23	40
1990-91	Washington	NHL	1	0	0	0	0	....	....	....	....	....
	Baltimore	AHL	62	32	29	61	10	6	1	1	2	6
1991-92	Baltimore	AHL	77	42	28	70	51	....	....	....	....	....
1992-93	Washington	NHL	16	2	3	5	12	....	....	....	....	....
	Baltimore	AHL	40	37	18	55	28	....	....	....	....	....
1993-94	Quebec	NHL	17	3	4	7	16	....	....	....	....	....
	Cornwall	AHL	33	21	13	34	56	....	....	....	....	....
	NHL Totals		34	5	7	12	28	....	....	....	....	....

Traded to **Quebec** by **Washington** with Paul MacDermid for Mike Hough, June 20, 1993.

SAVARD, DENIS (sa-VARH, den-NEE) T.B.

Center. Shoots right. 5'10", 175 lbs. Born, Pointe Gatineau, Que., February 4, 1961.
(Chicago's 1st choice, 3rd overall, in 1980 Entry Draft).

			Regular Season					Playoffs				
Season	Club	Lea	GP	G	A	TP	PIM	GP	G	A	TP	PIM
1978-79	Montreal	QJHL	70	46	*112	158	88	11	5	6	11	46
1979-80a	Montreal	QJHL	72	63	118	181	93	10	7	16	23	8
1980-81	Chicago	NHL	76	28	47	75	47	3	0	0	0	0
1981-82	Chicago	NHL	80	32	87	119	82	15	11	7	18	52
1982-83b	Chicago	NHL	78	35	86	121	99	13	8	9	17	22
1983-84	Chicago	NHL	75	37	57	94	71	5	1	3	4	9
1984-85	Chicago	NHL	79	38	67	105	56	15	9	20	29	20
1985-86	Chicago	NHL	80	47	69	116	111	3	4	1	5	6
1986-87	Chicago	NHL	70	40	50	90	108	4	1	0	1	12
1987-88	Chicago	NHL	80	44	87	131	95	5	4	3	7	17
1988-89	Chicago	NHL	58	23	59	82	110	16	8	11	19	10
1989-90	Chicago	NHL	60	27	53	80	56	20	7	15	22	41
1990-91	Montreal	NHL	70	28	31	59	52	13	2	11	13	35
1991-92	Montreal	NHL	77	28	42	70	73	11	3	9	12	8
1992-93	Montreal	NHL	63	16	34	50	90	14	0	5	5	4
1993-94	Tampa Bay	NHL	74	18	28	46	106	....	....	....	....	....
	NHL Totals		1020	441	797	1238	1156	137	58	94	152	236

a QMJHL First All-Star Team (1980)
b NHL Second All-Star Team (1983)

Played in NHL All-Star Game (1982-84, 1986, 1988, 1991)

Traded to **Montreal** by **Chicago** for Chris Chelios and Montreal's second round choice (Michael Pomichter) in 1991 Entry Draft, June 29, 1990. Signed as a free agent by **Tampa Bay**, July 29, 1993.

SAVENKO, BOGDAN CHI.

Right wing. Shoots right. 6'1", 192 lbs. Born, Kiev, USSR, November 20, 1974.
(Chicago's 3rd choice, 54th overall, in 1993 Entry Draft).

			Regular Season					Playoffs				
Season	Club	Lea	GP	G	A	TP	PIM	GP	G	A	TP	PIM
1990-91	SVSM Kiev	USSR 2	40	30	18	48	24	....	....	....	....	....
1991-92	Sokol Kiev	CIS	25	3	1	4	4	....	....	....	....	....
1992-93	Niagara Falls	OHL	51	29	19	48	15	2	1	0	1	2
1993-94	Niagara Falls	OHL	62	42	49	91	22	....	....	....	....	....

SAVOIE, CLAUDE — OTT.

Right wing. Shoots right. 5'11", 200 lbs. Born, Montreal, Que., March 12, 1973.
(Ottawa's 9th choice, 194th overall, in 1992 Entry Draft).

			Regular Season					Playoffs				
Season	Club	Lea	GP	G	A	TP	PIM	GP	G	A	TP	PIM
1990-91	Victoriaville	QMJHL	61	20	22	42	101	....	....	....	....	....
1991-92	Victoriaville	QMJHL	69	39	40	79	140	....	....	....	....	....
1992-93	Victoriaville	QMJHL	67	70	61	131	113	6	4	5	9	6
	New Haven	AHL	2	1	1	2	0	....	....	....	....	....
1993-94	PEI	AHL	77	13	15	28	118	....	....	....	....	....

SCATCHARD, DAVE — VAN.

Center. Shoots right. 6'2", 185 lbs. Born, Hinton, Alta., February 20, 1976.
(Vancouver's 3rd choice, 42nd overall, in 1994 Entry Draft).

			Regular Season					Playoffs				
Season	Club	Lea	GP	G	A	TP	PIM	GP	G	A	TP	PIM
1992-93	Kimberley	Jr. A	51	20	23	43	61	....	....	....	....	....
1993-94	Portland	WHL	47	9	11	20	46	....	....	....	....	....

SCHLEGEL, BRAD — (shlay-GUHL)

Defense. Shoots right. 5'10", 188 lbs. Born, Kitchener, Ont., July 22, 1968.
(Washington's 8th choice, 144th overall, in 1988 Entry Draft).

			Regular Season					Playoffs				
Season	Club	Lea	GP	G	A	TP	PIM	GP	G	A	TP	PIM
1986-87	London	OHL	65	4	23	27	24	....	....	....	....	....
1987-88a	London	OHL	66	13	63	76	49	12	8	17	25	6
1988-89	Cdn. National	....	60	2	22	24	30	....	....	....	....	....
1989-90	Cdn. National	....	72	7	25	32	44	....	....	....	....	....
1990-91	Cdn. National	....	59	8	20	28	64	....	....	....	....	....
1991-92	Cdn. National	....	61	3	18	21	84	....	....	....	....	....
	Cdn. Olympic	....	8	1	2	3	4	....	....	....	....	....
	Washington	**NHL**	**15**	**0**	**1**	**1**	**0**	**7**	**0**	**1**	**1**	**2**
	Baltimore	AHL	2	0	1	1	0	....	....	....	....	....
1992-93	**Washington**	**NHL**	**7**	**0**	**1**	**1**	**6**	....	....	....	....	....
	Baltimore	AHL	61	3	20	23	40	7	0	5	5	6
1993-94	**Calgary**	**NHL**	**26**	**1**	**6**	**7**	**4**	....	....	....	....	....
	Cdn. National	....	4	0	0	0	2	....	....	....	....	....
	Cdn. Olympic	....	8	0	0	0	6	....	....	....	....	....
	Saint John	AHL	21	2	8	10	6	7	0	1	1	6
	NHL Totals		**48**	**1**	**8**	**9**	**10**	**7**	**0**	**1**	**1**	**2**

a OHL Second All-Star Team (1988)

Traded to **Calgary** by **Washington** for Calgary's seventh round choice (Andrew Brunette) in 1993 Entry Draft, June 26, 1993.

SCHMIDT, CHRIS — L.A.

Center. Shoots left. 6'3", 193 lbs. Born, Beaverlodge, Alta., March 1, 1976.
(Los Angeles' 4th choice, 111th overall, in 1994 Entry Draft).

			Regular Season					Playoffs				
Season	Club	Lea	GP	G	A	TP	PIM	GP	G	A	TP	PIM
1992-93	Seattle	WHL	61	6	7	13	17	5	0	1	1	0
1993-94	Seattle	WHL	68	7	17	24	26	9	3	1	4	2

SCHMIDT, COLIN — EDM.

Center. Shoots left. 5'11", 185 lbs. Born, Regina, Sask., February 3, 1974.
(Edmonton's 9th choice, 190th overall, in 1992 Entry Draft).

			Regular Season					Playoffs				
Season	Club	Lea	GP	G	A	TP	PIM	GP	G	A	TP	PIM
1992-93	Colorado	WCHA	27	8	13	21	26	....	....	....	....	....
1993-94	Colorado	WCHA	38	14	22	36	49	....	....	....	....	....

SCHNEIDER, ANDY — OTT.

Left wing. Shoots left. 5'9", 170 lbs. Born, Edmonton, Alta., March 29, 1972.

			Regular Season					Playoffs				
Season	Club	Lea	GP	G	A	TP	PIM	GP	G	A	TP	PIM
1990-91	Swift Current	WHL	69	12	74	86	103	3	0	0	0	2
1991-92	Swift Current	WHL	63	44	60	104	120	8	4	9	13	8
1992-93a	Swift Current	WHL	38	19	66	85	78	17	13	*26	*39	40
	New Haven	AHL	19	2	2	4	13	....	....	....	....	....
1993-94	**Ottawa**	**NHL**	**10**	**0**	**0**	**0**	**15**	....	....	....	....	....
	PEI	AHL	61	15	46	61	119	....	....	....	....	....
	NHL Totals		**10**	**0**	**0**	**0**	**15**	....	....	....	....	....

a WHL East Second All-Star Team (1993)

Signed as a free agent by **Ottawa**, October 9, 1992.

SCHNEIDER, MATHIEU — MTL.

Defense. Shoots left. 5'11", 189 lbs. Born, New York, NY, June 12, 1969.
(Montreal's 4th choice, 44th overall, in 1987 Entry Draft).

			Regular Season					Playoffs				
Season	Club	Lea	GP	G	A	TP	PIM	GP	G	A	TP	PIM
1986-87	Cornwall	OHL	63	7	29	36	75	5	0	0	0	22
1987-88	**Montreal**	**NHL**	**4**	**0**	**0**	**0**	**2**	....	....	....	....	....
a	Cornwall	OHL	48	21	40	61	83	11	2	6	8	14
	Sherbrooke	AHL	....	....	....	....	....	3	0	3	3	12
1988-89	Cornwall	OHL	59	16	57	73	96	18	7	20	27	30
1989-90	**Montreal**	**NHL**	**44**	**7**	**14**	**21**	**25**	**9**	**1**	**3**	**4**	**31**
	Sherbrooke	AHL	28	6	13	19	20	....	....	....	....	....
1990-91	**Montreal**	**NHL**	**69**	**10**	**20**	**30**	**63**	**13**	**2**	**7**	**9**	**18**
1991-92	**Montreal**	**NHL**	**78**	**8**	**24**	**32**	**72**	**10**	**1**	**4**	**5**	**6**
1992-93	**Montreal**	**NHL**	**60**	**13**	**31**	**44**	**91**	**11**	**1**	**2**	**3**	**16**
1993-94	**Montreal**	**NHL**	**75**	**20**	**32**	**52**	**62**	**1**	**0**	**0**	**0**	**0**
	NHL Totals		**330**	**58**	**121**	**179**	**315**	**44**	**5**	**16**	**21**	**71**

a OHL First All-Star Team (1988)

SCHRINER, MARTY

Center. Shoots left. 5'11", 175 lbs. Born, Port Huron, MI, May 20, 1972.
(NY Islanders' 12th choice, 246th overall, in 1991 Entry Draft).

			Regular Season					Playoffs				
Season	Club	Lea	GP	G	A	TP	PIM	GP	G	A	TP	PIM
1990-91	North Dakota	WCHA	40	6	11	17	90	....	....	....	....	....
1991-92	North Dakota	WCHA	32	10	12	22	112	....	....	....	....	....
1992-93	North Dakota	WCHA	36	8	19	27	*156	....	....	....	....	....
1993-94	North Dakota	WCHA	37	11	22	33	129	....	....	....	....	....

SCHULTE, PAXTON — QUE.

Left wing. Shoots left. 6'2", 217 lbs. Born, Ionaway, Alta., July 16, 1972.
(Quebec's 7th choice, 124th overall, in 1992 Entry Draft).

			Regular Season					Playoffs				
Season	Club	Lea	GP	G	A	TP	PIM	GP	G	A	TP	PIM
1990-91	North Dakota	WCHA	38	2	4	6	32	....	....	....	....	....
1991-92	Spokane	WHL	70	42	42	84	222	10	2	8	10	48
1992-93	Spokane	WHL	45	38	35	73	142	10	5	6	11	12
1993-94	**Quebec**	**NHL**	**1**	**0**	**0**	**0**	**2**	....	....	....	....	....
	Cornwall	AHL	56	15	15	30	102	....	....	....	....	....
	NHL Totals		**1**	**0**	**0**	**0**	**2**	....	....	....	....	....

SCHUWERK, RICK — OTT.

Defense. Shoots right. 6'1", 212 lbs. Born, Hingham, MA, March 22, 1973.
(Ottawa's 10th choice, 235th overall, in 1993 Entry Draft).

			Regular Season					Playoffs				
Season	Club	Lea	GP	G	A	TP	PIM	GP	G	A	TP	PIM
1986-87	V. Frolunda	Swe. 2	25	23	10	33	10	2	1	2	3	....
1992-93	Canterbury	....	34	10	26	36	38	....	....	....	....	....
1993-94	Northeastern	H.E.	37	2	5	7	6	....	....	....	....	....

SCISSONS, SCOTT — (SIH-shuhns) — NYI

Center. Shoots left. 6'1", 201 lbs. Born, Saskatoon, Sask., October 29, 1971.
(NY Islanders' 1st choice, 6th overall, in 1990 Entry Draft).

			Regular Season					Playoffs				
Season	Club	Lea	GP	G	A	TP	PIM	GP	G	A	TP	PIM
1988-89	Saskatoon	WHL	71	30	56	86	65	7	0	4	4	16
1989-90	Saskatoon	WHL	61	40	47	87	81	10	3	8	11	6
1990-91	**NY Islanders**	**NHL**	**1**	**0**	**0**	**0**	**0**	....	....	....	....	....
	Saskatoon	WHL	57	24	53	77	61	....	....	....	....	....
1991-92	Cdn. National	....	27	4	8	12	23	....	....	....	....	....
1992-93	Capital Dist.	AHL	43	14	30	44	33	4	0	0	0	0
	NY Islanders	**NHL**	....	....	....	....	....	**1**	**0**	**0**	**0**	**0**
1993-94	**NY Islanders**	**NHL**	**1**	**0**	**0**	**0**	**0**	....	....	....	....	....
	Salt Lake	IHL	72	10	26	36	123	....	....	....	....	....
	NHL Totals		**2**	**0**	**0**	**0**	**0**	**1**	**0**	**0**	**0**	**0**

SCOTT, BLAIR — QUE.

Defense. Shoots left. 6', 202 lbs. Born, Winnipeg, Man., February 25, 1972.

			Regular Season					Playoffs				
Season	Club	Lea	GP	G	A	TP	PIM	GP	G	A	TP	PIM
1990-91	Belleville	OHL	45	2	7	9	79	6	0	2	2	10
1991-92	Belleville	OHL	41	3	15	18	83	....	....	....	....	....
	Detroit	OHL	28	1	16	17	68	7	0	3	3	23
1992-93	Detroit	OHL	64	11	67	78	100	15	3	14	17	27
1993-94	Cornwall	OHL	19	1	2	3	13	....	....	....	....	....

Signed as a free agent by **Quebec**, July 6, 1993.

SCREMIN, CLAUDIO

Defense. Shoots right. 6'2", 205 lbs. Born, Burnaby, B.C., May 28, 1968.
(Washington's 12th choice, 204th overall, in 1988 Entry Draft).

			Regular Season					Playoffs				
Season	Club	Lea	GP	G	A	TP	PIM	GP	G	A	TP	PIM
1986-87	U. of Maine	H.E.	15	0	1	1	2	....	....	....	....	....
1987-88	U. of Maine	H.E.	44	6	18	24	22	....	....	....	....	....
1988-89	U. of Maine	H.E.	45	5	24	29	42	....	....	....	....	....
1989-90	U. of Maine	H.E.	45	4	26	30	14	....	....	....	....	....
1990-91	Kansas City	IHL	77	7	14	21	60	....	....	....	....	....
1991-92	**San Jose**	**NHL**	**13**	**0**	**0**	**0**	**25**	....	....	....	....	....
	Kansas City	IHL	70	5	23	28	44	15	1	6	7	14
1992-93	**San Jose**	**NHL**	**4**	**0**	**1**	**1**	**4**	....	....	....	....	....
	Kansas City	IHL	75	10	22	32	93	12	0	5	5	18
1993-94	Varese	Alp.	28	10	12	22	20	....	....	....	....	....
	Varese	Italy	7	2	4	6	11	....	....	....	....	....
	Kansas City	IHL	38	7	17	24	39	....	....	....	....	....
	NHL Totals		**17**	**0**	**1**	**1**	**29**	....	....	....	....	....

Traded to **Minnesota** by **Washington** for Don Beaupre, November 1, 1988. Signed as a free agent by **San Jose**, September 3, 1991.

SEGUIN, BRETT — L.A.

Center. Shoots left. 5'9", 185 lbs. Born, Rochester, NY, February 20, 1972.
(Los Angeles' 6th choice, 130th overall, in 1991 Entry Draft).

			Regular Season					Playoffs				
Season	Club	Lea	GP	G	A	TP	PIM	GP	G	A	TP	PIM
1989-90	Ottawa	OHL	63	28	*80	108	30	....	....	....	....	....
1990-91	Ottawa	OHL	63	24	*87	111	85	17	10	*25	35	21
1991-92	Ottawa	OHL	64	34	*100	134	70	11	8	10	18	16
1992-93	Phoenix	IHL	16	2	7	9	8	....	....	....	....	....
	Muskegon	ColHL	49	24	40	64	48	7	6	8	14	20
1993-94	Fort Wayne	IHL	6	0	0	0	4	....	....	....	....	....
	Muskegon	ColHL	46	24	50	74	105	3	1	3	4	8

SEHER, KURT

Defense. Shoots left. 6'1", 180 lbs. Born, Lethbridge, Alta., April 15, 1973.
(Boston's 8th choice, 184th overall, in 1992 Entry Draft).

			Regular Season					Playoffs				
Season	Club	Lea	GP	G	A	TP	PIM	GP	G	A	TP	PIM
1990-91	Swift Current	WHL	59	4	26	30	63	2	0	0	0	0
1991-92	Seattle	WHL	60	15	23	38	128	15	3	12	15	32
1992-93	Seattle	WHL	69	9	20	29	125	5	0	3	3	10
	Providence	AHL	2	0	0	0	2	3	0	0	0	2
1993-94	Providence	AHL	8	0	0	0	8	....	....	....	....	....
	Charlotte	ECHL	51	6	21	27	54	3	0	0	0	2

SELANNE, TEEMU (SEH-lahn-nay, TEE-moo) WPG.

Right wing. Shoots right. 6', 200 lbs. Born, Helsinki, Finland, July 3, 1970.
(Winnipeg's 1st choice, 10th overall, in 1988 Entry Draft).

			Regular Season					Playoffs				
Season	Club	Lea	GP	G	A	TP	PIM	GP	G	A	TP	PIM
1987-88	Jokerit	Fin. Jr.	33	43	23	66	18	5	4	3	7	2
	Jokerit	Fin. 2	5	1	1	2	0	....	....	....	....	....
1988-89	Jokerit	Fin. 2	34	35	33	68	12	5	7	3	10	4
1989-90	Jokerit	Fin.	11	4	8	12	0	....	....	....	....	....
1990-91	Jokerit	Fin.	42	33	25	58	12	....	....	....	....	....
1991-92	Jokerit	Fin.	44	*39	23	62	20	10	10	7	17	18
1992-93abc	**Winnipeg**	**NHL**	**84**	***76**	**56**	**132**	**45**	**6**	**4**	**2**	**6**	**2**
1993-94	**Winnipeg**	**NHL**	**51**	**25**	**29**	**54**	**22**	....	....	....	....	....
	NHL Totals		**135**	**101**	**85**	**186**	**67**	**6**	**4**	**2**	**6**	**2**

a Won Calder Memorial Trophy (1993)
b NHL First All-Star Team (1993)
c NHL/Upper Deck All-Rookie Team (1993)
Played in NHL All-Star Game (1993, 1994)

SELIVANOV, ALEXANDER (seh-lih-VAH-nohv) PHI.

Right wing. Shoots left. 6'1", 187 lbs. Born, Moscow, USSR, March 23, 1971.
(Philadelphia's 4th choice, 140th overall, in 1994 Entry Draft).

			Regular Season					Playoffs				
Season	Club	Lea	GP	G	A	TP	PIM	GP	G	A	TP	PIM
1988-89	Spartak	USSR	1	0	0	0	0	....	....	....	....	....
1989-90	Spartak	USSR	4	0	0	0	0	....	....	....	....	....
1990-91	Spartak	USSR	21	3	1	4	6	....	....	....	....	....
1991-92	Spartak	CIS	31	6	7	13	16	....	....	....	....	....
1992-93	Spartak	CIS	42	12	19	31	66	3	2	0	2	2
1993-94	Spartak	CIS	45	30	11	41	50	6	5	1	6	2

SELMSER, SEAN PIT.

Left wing. Shoots left. 6'1", 180 lbs. Born, Calgary, Alta., November 10, 1974.
(Pittsburgh's 7th choice, 182nd overall, in 1993 Entry Draft).

			Regular Season					Playoffs				
Season	Club	Lea	GP	G	A	TP	PIM	GP	G	A	TP	PIM
1992-93	Red Deer	WHL	70	13	27	40	216	4	0	0	0	10
1993-94	Red Deer	WHL	71	25	25	50	201	4	1	0	1	14

SEMAK, ALEXANDER (seh-MAHK) N.J.

Center. Shoots right. 5'10", 180 lbs. Born, Ufa, USSR, February 11, 1966.
(New Jersey's 12th choice, 207th overall, in 1988 Entry Draft).

			Regular Season					Playoffs				
Season	Club	Lea	GP	G	A	TP	PIM	GP	G	A	TP	PIM
1982-83	Yulayev	USSR	13	2	1	3	4	....	....	....	....	....
1983-84	Yulayev	USSR 2			UNAVAILABLE							
1984-85	Yulayev	USSR 2	47	19	17	36	64	....	....	....	....	....
1985-86	Yulayev	USSR	22	9	7	16	22	....	....	....	....	....
1986-87	Moscow D'amo	USSR	40	20	8	28	32	....	....	....	....	....
1987-88	Moscow D'amo	USSR	47	21	14	35	40	....	....	....	....	....
1988-89	Moscow D'amo	USSR	44	18	10	28	22	....	....	....	....	....
1989-90	Moscow D'amo	USSR	43	23	11	34	33	....	....	....	....	....
1990-91	Moscow D'amo	USSR	46	17	21	38	48	....	....	....	....	....
1991-92	Moscow D'amo	CIS	26	10	13	23	26	....	....	....	....	....
	New Jersey	**NHL**	**25**	**5**	**6**	**11**	**0**	**1**	**0**	**0**	**0**	**0**
	Utica	AHL	7	3	2	5	0	....	....	....	....	....
1992-93	**New Jersey**	**NHL**	**82**	**37**	**42**	**79**	**70**	**5**	**1**	**1**	**2**	**0**
1993-94	**New Jersey**	**NHL**	**54**	**12**	**17**	**29**	**22**	**2**	**0**	**0**	**0**	**0**
	NHL Totals		**161**	**54**	**65**	**119**	**92**	**8**	**1**	**1**	**2**	**0**

SEMCHUK, BRANDY

Right wing. Shoots right. 6'1", 185 lbs. Born, Calgary, Alta., September 22, 1971.
(Los Angeles' 2nd choice, 28th overall, in 1990 Entry Draft).

			Regular Season					Playoffs				
Season	Club	Lea	GP	G	A	TP	PIM	GP	G	A	TP	PIM
1988-89	Cdn. National	....	42	11	11	22	60	....	....	....	....	....
1989-90	Cdn. National	....	55	10	15	25	40	....	....	....	....	....
1990-91	Lethbridge	WHL	14	9	8	17	10	15	8	5	13	18
	New Haven	AHL	21	1	4	5	6	....	....	....	....	....
1991-92	Phoenix	IHL	15	1	5	6	6	....	....	....	....	....
	Raleigh	ECHL	5	1	2	3	16	2	1	0	1	4
1992-93	**Los Angeles**	**NHL**	**1**	**0**	**0**	**0**	**2**	....	....	....	....	....
	Phoenix	IHL	56	13	12	25	58	....	....	....	....	....
1993-94	Erie	ECHL	44	17	15	32	37	....	....	....	....	....
	Phoenix	IHL	2	0	0	0	6	....	....	....	....	....
	NHL Totals		**1**	**0**	**0**	**0**	**2**	....	....	....	....	....

SEMENOV, ANATOLI (seh-MEH-nahf) ANA.

Center/Left wing. Shoots left. 6'2", 190 lbs. Born, Moscow, USSR, March 5, 1962.
(Edmonton's 5th choice, 120th overall, in 1989 Entry Draft).

			Regular Season					Playoffs				
Season	Club	Lea	GP	G	A	TP	PIM	GP	G	A	TP	PIM
1979-80	Moscow D'amo	USSR	8	3	0	3	2	....	....	....	....	....
1980-81	Moscow D'amo	USSR	47	18	14	32	18	....	....	....	....	....
1981-82	Moscow D'amo	USSR	44	12	14	26	28	....	....	....	....	....
1982-83	Moscow D'amo	USSR	44	22	18	40	26	....	....	....	....	....
1983-84	Moscow D'amo	USSR	19	10	5	15	14	....	....	....	....	....
1984-85	Moscow D'amo	USSR	30	17	12	29	32	....	....	....	....	....
1985-86	Moscow D'amo	USSR	32	18	17	35	19	....	....	....	....	....
1986-87	Moscow D'amo	USSR	40	15	29	44	32	....	....	....	....	....
1987-88	Moscow D'amo	USSR	32	17	8	25	22	....	....	....	....	....
1988-89	Moscow D'amo	USSR	31	9	12	21	24	....	....	....	....	....
1989-90	Moscow D'amo	USSR	48	13	20	33	16	....	....	....	....	....
	Edmonton	**NHL**	....	....	....	....	....	**2**	**0**	**0**	**0**	**0**
1990-91	**Edmonton**	**NHL**	**57**	**15**	**16**	**31**	**26**	**12**	**5**	**5**	**10**	**6**
1991-92	**Edmonton**	**NHL**	**59**	**20**	**22**	**42**	**16**	**8**	**1**	**1**	**2**	**6**
1992-93	**Tampa Bay**	**NHL**	**13**	**2**	**3**	**5**	**4**	....	....	....	....	....
	Vancouver	**NHL**	**62**	**10**	**34**	**44**	**28**	**12**	**1**	**3**	**4**	**0**
1993-94	**Anaheim**	**NHL**	**49**	**11**	**19**	**30**	**12**	....	....	....	....	....
	NHL Totals		**240**	**58**	**94**	**152**	**86**	**34**	**7**	**9**	**16**	**12**

Claimed by **Tampa Bay** from **Edmonton** in Expansion Draft, June 18, 1992. Traded to **Vancouver** by **Tampa Bay** for Dave Capuano and Vancouver's fourth round choice (later traded to New Jersey — later traded to Calgary — Calgary selected Ryan Duthie) in 1994 Entry Draft, November 3, 1992. Claimed by **Anaheim** from **Vancouver** in Expansion Draft, June 24, 1993.

SEPPO, JUKKA (SEHP-poh) PHI.

Center. Shoots left. 6'2", 198 lbs. Born, Vaasa, Finland, January 22, 1968.
(Philadelphia's 2nd choice, 23rd overall, in 1986 Entry Draft).

			Regular Season					Playoffs				
Season	Club	Lea	GP	G	A	TP	PIM	GP	G	A	TP	PIM
1986-87	Tappara	Fin.	39	11	16	27	50	9	1	4	5	14
1987-88	Sport	Fin. 2	42	28	37	65	78	....	....	....	....	....
1988-89	HIFK	Fin.	35	7	13	20	28	2	2	1	3	2
1989-90	HIFK	Fin.	39	15	27	42	50	....	....	....	....	....
1990-91	HIFK	Fin.	35	17	22	39	81	1	1	0	1	0
1991-92	HIFK	Fin.	43	16	31	47	53	7	2	4	6	33
1992-93	HIFK	Fin.	45	16	17	33	52	4	0	1	1	2
1993-94	HPK	Fin.	39	10	12	22	56	....	....	....	....	....

SEROWIK, JEFF (sair-OH-wihk) BOS.

Defense. Shoots right. 6'1", 210 lbs. Born, Manchester, NH, January 10, 1967.
(Toronto's 5th choice, 85th overall, in 1985 Entry Draft).

			Regular Season					Playoffs				
Season	Club	Lea	GP	G	A	TP	PIM	GP	G	A	TP	PIM
1986-87	Providence	H.E.	33	3	8	11	22	....	....	....	....	....
1987-88	Providence	H.E.	33	3	9	12	44	....	....	....	....	....
1988-89	Providence	H.E.	35	3	14	17	48	....	....	....	....	....
1989-90a	Providence	H.E.	35	6	19	25	34	....	....	....	....	....
1990-91	**Toronto**	**NHL**	**1**	**0**	**0**	**0**	**0**	....	....	....	....	....
	Newmarket	AHL	60	8	15	23	45	....	....	....	....	....
1991-92	St. John's	AHL	78	11	34	45	60	16	4	9	13	22
1992-93b	St. John's	AHL	77	19	35	54	92	9	1	5	6	8
1993-94	Cincinnati	IHL	79	6	21	27	98	7	0	1	1	8
	NHL Totals		**1**	**0**	**0**	**0**	**0**	....	....	....	....	....

a Hockey East Second All-Star Team (1990)
b AHL Second All-Star Team (1993)
Signed as a free agent by **Florida**, July 20, 1993. Signed as a free agent by **Boston**, June 29, 1994.

SEVERYN, BRENT

Defense. Shoots left. 6'2", 210 lbs. Born, Vegreville, Alta., February 22, 1966.

			Regular Season					Playoffs				
Season	Club	Lea	GP	G	A	TP	PIM	GP	G	A	TP	PIM
1983-84	Seattle	WHL	72	14	22	36	49	....	....	....	....	....
1984-85	Seattle	WHL	38	8	32	40	54	....	....	....	....	....
	Brandon	WHL	26	7	16	23	57	....	....	....	....	....
1985-86	Seattle	WHL	33	11	20	31	164	....	....	....	....	....
	Saskatoon	WHL	9	1	4	5	38	....	....	....	....	....
1986-87	U. of Alberta	CWUAA				UNAVAILABLE						
1987-88	U. of Alberta	CWUAA	46	21	29	50	178	....	....	....	....	....
1988-89	Halifax	AHL	47	2	12	14	141	....	....	....	....	....
1989-90	**Quebec**	**NHL**	**35**	**0**	**2**	**2**	**42**	....	....	....	....	....
	Halifax	AHL	43	6	9	15	105	6	1	2	3	49
1990-91	Halifax	AHL	50	7	26	33	202	....	....	....	....	....
1991-92	Utica	AHL	80	11	33	44	211	4	0	1	1	4
1992-93a	Utica	AHL	77	20	32	52	240	5	0	0	0	35
1993-94	**Florida**	**NHL**	**67**	**4**	**7**	**11**	**156**	....	....	....	....	....
	NHL Totals		**102**	**4**	**9**	**13**	**198**	....	....	....	....	....

a AHL First All-Star Team (1993)
Signed as a free agent by **Quebec**, July 15, 1988. Traded to **New Jersey** by **Quebec** for Dave Marcinyshyn, June 3, 1991. Traded to **Winnipeg** by **New Jersey** for Winnipeg's sixth round choice (Ryan Smart) in 1994 Entry Draft, September 30, 1993. Traded to **Florida** by **Winnipeg** for Milan Tichy, October 3, 1993.

SEVIGNY, PIERRE (seh-VIH-nee) MTL.

Left wing. Shoots left. 6', 189 lbs. Born, Trois-Rivières, Que., September 8, 1971.
(Montreal's 4th choice, 51st overall, in 1989 Entry Draft).

			Regular Season					Playoffs				
Season	Club	Lea	GP	G	A	TP	PIM	GP	G	A	TP	PIM
1988-89	Verdun	QMJHL	67	27	43	70	88	....	....	....	....	....
1989-90a	St-Hyacinthe	QMJHL	67	47	72	119	205	12	8	8	16	42
1990-91a	St-Hyacinthe	QMJHL	60	36	46	82	203	....	....	....	....	....
1991-92	Fredericton	AHL	74	22	37	59	145	7	1	1	2	26
1992-93	Fredericton	AHL	80	36	40	76	113	5	1	1	2	2
1993-94	**Montreal**	**NHL**	**43**	**4**	**5**	**9**	**42**	**3**	**0**	**1**	**1**	**0**
	NHL Totals		**43**	**4**	**5**	**9**	**42**	**3**	**0**	**1**	**1**	**0**

a QMJHL Second All-Star Team (1990, 1991)

SHALOMAI, SERGEI L.A.

Left wing. Shoots left. 5'6", 147 lbs. Born, Moscow, USSR, June 12, 1976.
(Los Angeles' 8th choice, 241st overall, in 1994 Entry Draft).

			Regular Season					Playoffs				
Season	Club	Lea	GP	G	A	TP	PIM	GP	G	A	TP	PIM
1992-93	Spartak	CIS	4	1	0	1	0	....	....	....	....	....
1993-94	Spartak	CIS	43	8	7	15	10	....	....	....	....	....

SHANAHAN, BRENDAN ST.L.

Left wing. Shoots right. 6'3", 215 lbs. Born, Mimico, Ont., January 23, 1969.
(New Jersey's 1st choice, 2nd overall, in 1987 Entry Draft).

			Regular Season					Playoffs				
Season	Club	Lea	GP	G	A	TP	PIM	GP	G	A	TP	PIM
1985-86	London	OHL	59	28	34	62	70	5	5	5	10	5
1986-87	London	OHL	56	39	53	92	92	....	....	....	....	....
1987-88	**New Jersey**	**NHL**	**65**	**7**	**19**	**26**	**131**	**12**	**2**	**1**	**3**	**44**
1988-89	**New Jersey**	**NHL**	**68**	**22**	**28**	**50**	**115**	....	....	....	....	....
1989-90	**New Jersey**	**NHL**	**73**	**30**	**42**	**72**	**137**	**6**	**3**	**3**	**6**	**20**
1990-91	**New Jersey**	**NHL**	**75**	**29**	**37**	**66**	**141**	**7**	**3**	**5**	**8**	**12**
1991-92	**St. Louis**	**NHL**	**80**	**33**	**36**	**69**	**171**	**6**	**2**	**3**	**5**	**14**
1992-93	**St. Louis**	**NHL**	**71**	**51**	**43**	**94**	**174**	**11**	**4**	**3**	**7**	**18**
1993-94a	**St. Louis**	**NHL**	**81**	**52**	**50**	**102**	**211**	**4**	**2**	**5**	**7**	**4**
	NHL Totals		**513**	**224**	**255**	**479**	**1080**	**46**	**16**	**20**	**36**	**112**

a NHL First All-Star Team (1994)
Played in NHL All-Star Game (1994)
Signed as a free agent by **St. Louis**, July 25, 1991.

SHANAHAN, RYAN

Right wing. Shoots right. 6', 161 lbs. Born, Buffalo, NY, April 3, 1975.
(Detroit's 10th choice, 230th overall, in 1993 Entry Draft).

			Regular Season					Playoffs				
Season	Club	Lea	GP	G	A	TP	PIM	GP	G	A	TP	PIM
1992-93	Sudbury	OHL	60	7	10	17	65	14	2	2	4	12
1993-94	Sudbury	OHL	58	9	20	29	118	10	2	0	2	15

SHANK, DANIEL

Right wing. Shoots right. 5'10", 190 lbs. Born, Montreal, Que., May 12, 1967.

			Regular Season					Playoffs				
Season	**Club**	**Lea**	**GP**	**G**	**A**	**TP**	**PIM**	**GP**	**G**	**A**	**TP**	**PIM**
1985-86	Shawinigan	QMJHL	51	34	38	72	184	....	....	....	....	....
1986-87	Hull	QMJHL	46	26	43	69	325	....	....	....	....	....
1987-88	Hull	QMJHL	42	23	34	57	274	5	3	2	5	16
1988-89	Adirondack	AHL	42	5	20	25	113	17	11	8	19	102
1989-90	**Detroit**	**NHL**	**57**	**11**	**13**	**24**	**143**	....	....	....	....	....
	Adirondack	AHL	14	8	8	16	36	....	....	....	....	....
1990-91	**Detroit**	**NHL**	**7**	**0**	**1**	**1**	**14**	....	....	....	....	....
	Adirondack	AHL	60	26	49	75	278	....	....	....	....	....
1991-92	Adirondack	AHL	27	13	21	34	112	....	....	....	....	....
	Hartford	**NHL**	**13**	**2**	**0**	**2**	**18**	**5**	**0**	**0**	**0**	**22**
	Springfield	AHL	31	9	19	28	83	8	8	0	8	48
1992-93a	San Diego	IHL	77	39	53	92	*495	14	5	10	15	*131
1993-94	San Diego	IHL	63	27	36	63	273	....	....	....	....	....
	Phoenix	IHL	7	4	6	10	26	....	....	....	....	....
	NHL Totals		**77**	**13**	**14**	**27**	**175**	**5**	**0**	**0**	**0**	**22**

a IHL First All-Star Team (1993)

Signed as a free agent by **Detroit**, May 26, 1989. Traded to **Hartford** by **Detroit** for Chris Tancill, December 18, 1991.

SHANNON, DARRIN — WPG.

Left wing. Shoots left. 6'2", 210 lbs. Born, Barrie, Ont., December 8, 1969.
(Pittsburgh's 1st choice, 4th overall, in 1988 Entry Draft).

			Regular Season					Playoffs				
Season	**Club**	**Lea**	**GP**	**G**	**A**	**TP**	**PIM**	**GP**	**G**	**A**	**TP**	**PIM**
1986-87	Windsor	OHL	60	16	67	83	116	14	4	6	10	8
1987-88	Windsor	OHL	43	33	41	74	49	12	6	12	18	9
1988-89	**Buffalo**	**NHL**	**3**	**0**	**0**	**0**	**0**	**2**	**0**	**0**	**0**	**0**
	Windsor	OHL	54	33	48	81	47	4	1	6	7	2
1989-90	**Buffalo**	**NHL**	**17**	**2**	**7**	**9**	**4**	**6**	**0**	**1**	**1**	**4**
	Rochester	AHL	50	20	23	43	25	9	4	1	5	2
1990-91	**Buffalo**	**NHL**	**34**	**8**	**6**	**14**	**12**	**6**	**1**	**2**	**3**	**4**
	Rochester	AHL	49	26	34	60	56	10	3	5	8	22
1991-92	**Buffalo**	**NHL**	**1**	**0**	**1**	**1**	**0**	....	....	....	....	....
	Winnipeg	**NHL**	**68**	**13**	**26**	**39**	**41**	**7**	**0**	**1**	**1**	**10**
1992-93	**Winnipeg**	**NHL**	**84**	**20**	**40**	**60**	**91**	**6**	**2**	**4**	**6**	**6**
1993-94	**Winnipeg**	**NHL**	**77**	**21**	**37**	**58**	**87**	....	....	....	....	....
	NHL Totals		**284**	**64**	**117**	**181**	**235**	**27**	**3**	**8**	**11**	**24**

Traded to **Buffalo** by **Pittsburgh** with Doug Bodger for Tom Barrasso and Buffalo's third round choice (Joe Dziedzic) in 1990 Entry Draft, November 12, 1988. Traded to **Winnipeg** by **Buffalo** with Mike Hartman and Dean Kennedy for Dave McLlwain, Gord Donnelly, Winnipeg's fifth round choice (Yuri Khmylev) in 1992 Entry Draft and future considerations, October 11, 1991.

SHANNON, DARRYL — WPG.

Defense. Shoots left. 6'2", 200 lbs. Born, Barrie, Ont., June 21, 1968.
(Toronto's 2nd choice, 36th overall, in 1986 Entry Draft).

			Regular Season					Playoffs				
Season	**Club**	**Lea**	**GP**	**G**	**A**	**TP**	**PIM**	**GP**	**G**	**A**	**TP**	**PIM**
1985-86	Windsor	OHL	57	6	21	27	52	16	5	6	11	22
1986-87a	Windsor	OHL	64	23	27	50	83	14	4	8	12	18
1987-88b	Windsor	OHL	60	16	67	83	116	12	3	8	11	17
1988-89	**Toronto**	**NHL**	**14**	**1**	**3**	**4**	**6**	....	....	....	....	....
	Newmarket	AHL	61	5	24	29	37	5	0	3	3	10
1989-90	**Toronto**	**NHL**	**10**	**0**	**1**	**1**	**12**	....	....	....	....	....
	Newmarket	AHL	47	4	15	19	58	....	....	....	....	....
1990-91	**Toronto**	**NHL**	**10**	**0**	**1**	**1**	**0**	....	....	....	....	....
	Newmarket	AHL	47	2	14	16	51	....	....	....	....	....
1991-92	**Toronto**	**NHL**	**48**	**2**	**8**	**10**	**23**	....	....	....	....	....
1992-93	**Toronto**	**NHL**	**16**	**0**	**0**	**0**	**11**	....	....	....	....	....
	St. John's	AHL	7	1	1	2	4	....	....	....	....	....
1993-94	**Winnipeg**	**NHL**	**20**	**0**	**4**	**4**	**18**	....	....	....	....	....
	Moncton	AHL	37	1	10	11	62	20	1	7	8	32
	NHL Totals		**118**	**3**	**17**	**20**	**70**	....	....	....	....	....

a OHL Second All-Star Team (1987)
b OHL First All-Star Team (1988)

Signed as a free agent by **Winnipeg**, June 30, 1993.

SHANTZ, JEFF — CHI.

Center. Shoots right. 6', 184 lbs. Born, Duchess, Alta., October 10, 1973.
(Chicago's 2nd choice, 36th overall, in 1992 Entry Draft).

			Regular Season					Playoffs				
Season	**Club**	**Lea**	**GP**	**G**	**A**	**TP**	**PIM**	**GP**	**G**	**A**	**TP**	**PIM**
1990-91	Regina	WHL	69	16	21	37	22	8	2	2	4	2
1991-92	Regina	WHL	72	39	50	89	75	....	....	....	....	....
1992-93a	Regina	WHL	64	29	54	83	75	13	2	12	14	14
1993-94	**Chicago**	**NHL**	**52**	**3**	**13**	**16**	**30**	**6**	**0**	**0**	**0**	**6**
	Indianapolis	IHL	19	5	9	14	20	....	....	....	....	....
	NHL Totals		**52**	**3**	**13**	**16**	**30**	**6**	**0**	**0**	**0**	**6**

a WHL East First All-Star Team (1993)

SHARIFIJANOV, VADIM (shah-rih-FYAH-nohv) — N.J.

Right wing. Shoots left. 5'11", 210 lbs. Born, Ufa, USSR, December 23, 1975.
(New Jersey's 1st choice, 25th overall, in 1994 Entry Draft).

			Regular Season					Playoffs				
Season	**Club**	**Lea**	**GP**	**G**	**A**	**TP**	**PIM**	**GP**	**G**	**A**	**TP**	**PIM**
1992-93	Ufa Salavat	CIS	37	6	4	10	16	2	1	0	1	0
1993-94	Ufa Salavat	CIS	46	10	6	16	36	5	3	0	3	4

SHARPLES, JEFF

Defense. Shoots left. 6'1", 195 lbs. Born, Terrace, B.C., July 28, 1967.
(Detroit's 2nd choice, 29th overall, in 1985 Entry Draft).

			Regular Season					Playoffs				
Season	**Club**	**Lea**	**GP**	**G**	**A**	**TP**	**PIM**	**GP**	**G**	**A**	**TP**	**PIM**
1983-84	Kelowna	WHL	72	9	24	33	51	....	....	....	....	....
1984-85a	Kelowna	WHL	72	12	41	53	90	6	0	1	1	6
1985-86	Spokane	WHL	3	0	0	0	4	....	....	....	....	....
	Portland	WHL	19	2	6	8	44	15	2	6	8	6
1986-87	**Detroit**	**NHL**	**3**	**0**	**1**	**1**	**2**	**2**	**0**	**0**	**0**	**2**
	Portland	WHL	44	25	35	60	92	20	7	15	22	23
1987-88	**Detroit**	**NHL**	**56**	**10**	**25**	**35**	**42**	**4**	**0**	**3**	**3**	**4**
	Adirondack	AHL	4	2	1	3	4	....	....	....	....	....
1988-89	**Detroit**	**NHL**	**46**	**4**	**9**	**13**	**26**	**1**	**0**	**0**	**0**	**0**
	Adirondack	AHL	10	0	4	4	8	....	....	....	....	....
1989-90	Adirondack	AHL	9	2	5	7	6	....	....	....	....	....
	Cape Breton	AHL	38	4	13	17	28	....	....	....	....	....
	Utica	AHL	13	2	5	7	19	5	1	2	3	15
1990-91	Utica	AHL	64	16	29	45	42	....	....	....	....	....
1991-92	Capital Dist.	AHL	31	3	12	15	18	7	6	5	11	4
1992-93	Kansas City	IHL	39	5	21	26	43	8	0	0	0	6
1993-94	Las Vegas	IHL	68	18	32	50	68	5	2	1	3	6
	NHL Totals		**105**	**14**	**35**	**49**	**70**	**7**	**0**	**3**	**3**	**6**

a WHL West Second All-Star Team (1985)

Traded to **Edmonton** by **Detroit** with Petr Klima, Joe Murphy and Adam Graves for Jimmy Carson, Kevin McClelland and Edmonton's fifth round choice (later traded to Montreal — Montreal selected Brad Layzell) in 1991 Entry Draft, November 2, 1989. Traded to **New Jersey** by **Edmonton** for Reijo Ruotsalainen, March 6, 1990.

SHAW, BRAD — OTT.

Defense. Shoots right. 6', 190 lbs. Born, Cambridge, Ont., April 28, 1964.
(Detroit's 5th choice, 86th overall, in 1982 Entry Draft).

			Regular Season					Playoffs				
Season	**Club**	**Lea**	**GP**	**G**	**A**	**TP**	**PIM**	**GP**	**G**	**A**	**TP**	**PIM**
1981-82	Ottawa	OHL	68	13	59	72	24	15	1	13	14	4
1982-83	Ottawa	OHL	63	12	66	78	24	9	2	9	11	4
1983-84a	Ottawa	OHL	68	11	71	82	75	13	2	*27	29	9
1984-85	Binghamton	AHL	24	1	10	11	4	8	1	8	9	6
	Salt Lake	IHL	44	3	29	32	25	....	....	....	....	....
1985-86	**Hartford**	**NHL**	**8**	**0**	**2**	**2**	**4**	....	....	....	....	....
	Binghamton	AHL	64	10	44	54	33	5	0	2	2	6
1986-87	**Hartford**	**NHL**	**2**	**0**	**0**	**0**	**0**	....	....	....	....	....
bc	Binghamton	AHL	77	9	30	39	43	12	1	8	9	2
1987-88	**Hartford**	**NHL**	**1**	**0**	**0**	**0**	**0**	....	....	....	....	....
b	Binghamton	AHL	73	12	50	62	50	4	0	5	5	4
1988-89	Verese	Italy	35	10	30	40	44	11	4	8	12	13
	Cdn. National	....	4	1	0	1	2	....	....	....	....	....
	Hartford	**NHL**	**3**	**1**	**0**	**1**	**0**	**3**	**1**	**0**	**1**	**0**
1989-90d	**Hartford**	**NHL**	**64**	**3**	**32**	**35**	**30**	**7**	**2**	**5**	**7**	**0**
1990-91	**Hartford**	**NHL**	**72**	**4**	**28**	**32**	**29**	**6**	**1**	**2**	**3**	**2**
1991-92	**Hartford**	**NHL**	**62**	**3**	**22**	**25**	**44**	**3**	**0**	**1**	**1**	**4**
1992-93	**Ottawa**	**NHL**	**81**	**7**	**34**	**41**	**34**	....	....	....	....	....
1993-94	**Ottawa**	**NHL**	**66**	**4**	**19**	**23**	**59**	....	....	....	....	....
	NHL Totals		**359**	**22**	**137**	**159**	**200**	**19**	**4**	**8**	**12**	**6**

a OHL First All-Star Team (1984)
b AHL First All-Star Team (1987, 1988)
c Won Eddie Shore Plaque (Outstanding Defenseman - AHL) (1987)
d NHL All-Rookie Team (1990)

Rights traded to **Hartford** by **Detroit** for Hartford's eighth round choice (Urban Nordin) in 1984 Entry Draft, May 29, 1984. Traded to **New Jersey** by **Hartford** for cash, June 13, 1992. Claimed by **Ottawa** from **New Jersey** in Expansion Draft, June 18, 1992.

SHAW, DAVID — BOS.

Defense. Shoots right. 6'2", 205 lbs. Born, St. Thomas, Ont., May 25, 1964.
(Quebec's 1st choice, 13th overall, in 1982 Entry Draft).

			Regular Season					Playoffs				
Season	**Club**	**Lea**	**GP**	**G**	**A**	**TP**	**PIM**	**GP**	**G**	**A**	**TP**	**PIM**
1981-82	Kitchener	OHL	68	6	25	31	94	15	2	2	4	51
1982-83	**Quebec**	**NHL**	**2**	**0**	**0**	**0**	**0**	....	....	....	....	....
	Kitchener	OHL	57	18	56	74	78	12	2	10	12	18
1983-84	**Quebec**	**NHL**	**3**	**0**	**0**	**0**	**0**	....	....	....	....	....
a	Kitchener	OHL	58	14	34	48	73	16	4	9	13	12
1984-85	**Quebec**	**NHL**	**14**	**0**	**0**	**0**	**11**	....	....	....	....	....
	Fredericton	AHL	48	7	6	13	73	2	0	0	0	7
1985-86	**Quebec**	**NHL**	**73**	**7**	**19**	**26**	**78**	....	....	....	....	....
1986-87	**Quebec**	**NHL**	**75**	**0**	**19**	**19**	**69**	....	....	....	....	....
1987-88	**NY Rangers**	**NHL**	**68**	**7**	**25**	**32**	**100**	....	....	....	....	....
1988-89	**NY Rangers**	**NHL**	**63**	**6**	**11**	**17**	**88**	**4**	**0**	**2**	**2**	**30**
1989-90	**NY Rangers**	**NHL**	**22**	**2**	**10**	**12**	**22**	....	....	....	....	....
1990-91	**NY Rangers**	**NHL**	**77**	**2**	**10**	**12**	**89**	**6**	**0**	**0**	**0**	**11**
1991-92	**NY Rangers**	**NHL**	**10**	**0**	**1**	**1**	**15**	....	....	....	....	....
	Edmonton	**NHL**	**12**	**1**	**1**	**2**	**8**	....	....	....	....	....
	Minnesota	**NHL**	**37**	**0**	**7**	**7**	**49**	**7**	**2**	**2**	**4**	**10**
1992-93	**Boston**	**NHL**	**77**	**10**	**14**	**24**	**108**	**4**	**0**	**1**	**1**	**6**
1993-94	**Boston**	**NHL**	**55**	**1**	**9**	**10**	**85**	**13**	**1**	**2**	**3**	**16**
	NHL Totals		**588**	**36**	**126**	**162**	**722**	**34**	**3**	**7**	**10**	**73**

a OHL First All-Star Team (1984)

Traded to **NY Rangers** by **Quebec** with John Ogrodnick for Jeff Jackson and Terry Carkner, September 30, 1987. Traded to **Edmonton** by **NY Rangers** for Jeff Beukeboom, November 12, 1991. Traded to **Minnesota** by **Edmonton** for Brian Glynn, January 21, 1992. Traded to **Boston** by **Minnesota** for future considerations, September 2, 1992.

SHEPPARD, RAY — DET.

Right wing. Shoots right. 6'1", 195 lbs. Born, Pembroke, Ont., May 27, 1966.
(Buffalo's 3rd choice, 60th overall, in 1984 Entry Draft).

			Regular Season					Playoffs				
Season	Club	Lea	GP	G	A	TP	PIM	GP	G	A	TP	PIM
1983-84	Cornwall	OHL	68	44	36	80	69	....	....	....	....	....
1984-85	Cornwall	OHL	49	25	33	58	51	9	2	12	14	4
1985-86a	Cornwall	OHL	63	*81	61	*142	25	6	7	4	11	0
1986-87	Rochester	AHL	55	18	13	31	11	15	12	3	15	2
1987-88b	**Buffalo**	**NHL**	**74**	**38**	**27**	**65**	**14**	**6**	**1**	**1**	**2**	**2**
1988-89	**Buffalo**	**NHL**	**67**	**22**	**21**	**43**	**15**	**1**	**0**	**1**	**1**	**0**
1989-90	**Buffalo**	**NHL**	**18**	**4**	**2**	**6**	**0**	....	....	....	....	....
	Rochester	AHL	5	3	5	8	2	17	8	7	15	9
1990-91	**NY Rangers**	**NHL**	**59**	**24**	**23**	**47**	**21**	....	....	....	....	....
1991-92	**Detroit**	**NHL**	**74**	**36**	**26**	**62**	**27**	**11**	**6**	**2**	**8**	**4**
1992-93	**Detroit**	**NHL**	**70**	**32**	**34**	**66**	**29**	**7**	**2**	**3**	**5**	**0**
1993-94	**Detroit**	**NHL**	**82**	**52**	**41**	**93**	**26**	**7**	**2**	**1**	**3**	**4**
	NHL Totals		**444**	**208**	**174**	**382**	**132**	**32**	**11**	**8**	**19**	**10**

a OHL First All-Star Team (1986)
b NHL All-Rookie Team (1988)

Traded to **NY Rangers** by **Buffalo** for cash and future considerations, July 9, 1990. Signed as a free agent by **Detroit**, August 5, 1991.

SHEVALIER, JEFF — L.A.

Left wing. Shoots left. 5'11", 185 lbs. Born, Mississauga, Ont., March 14, 1974.
(Los Angeles' 4th choice, 111th overall, in 1992 Entry Draft).

			Regular Season					Playoffs				
Season	Club	Lea	GP	G	A	TP	PIM	GP	G	A	TP	PIM
1991-92	North Bay	OHL	64	28	29	57	26	21	5	11	16	25
1992-93	North Bay	OHL	62	59	54	113	46	2	1	2	3	4
1993-94a	North Bay	OHL	64	52	49	101	52	17	8	14	22	18

a OHL First All-Star Team (1994)

SHIER, ANDREW

Center. Shoots right. 5'11", 165 lbs. Born, Lansing, MI, August 15, 1971.
(NY Islanders' 11th choice, 237th overall, in 1990 Entry Draft).

			Regular Season					Playoffs				
Season	Club	Lea	GP	G	A	TP	PIM	GP	G	A	TP	PIM
1990-91	U. Wisconsin	WCHA	20	4	9	13	28	....	....	....	....	....
1991-92	U. Wisconsin	WCHA	39	10	25	35	60	....	....	....	....	....
1992-93	U. Wisconsin	WCHA	41	22	36	58	87	....	....	....	....	....
1993-94a	U. Wisconsin	WCHA	42	17	*45	62	76	....	....	....	....	....

a WCHA Second All-Star Team (1994)

SHIM, KYUIN

Right wing. Shoots right. 6'2", 190 lbs. Born, Edmonton, Alta., April 5, 1974.
(Edmonton's 8th choice, 181st overall, in 1992 Entry Draft).

			Regular Season					Playoffs				
Season	Club	Lea	GP	G	A	TP	PIM	GP	G	A	TP	PIM
1992-93	N. Michigan	WCHA	20	4	2	6	6	....	....	....	....	....
	Tri-City	WHL	2	0	1	1	6	....	....	....	....	....
1993-94	Tri-City	WHL	42	10	12	22	33	....	....	....	....	....
	Medicine Hat	WHL	14	6	4	10	2	3	0	0	0	0

SHUCHUK, GARY — (SHOO-chuhk) L.A.

Right wing. Shoots right. 5'10", 185 lbs. Born, Edmonton, Alta., February 17, 1967.
(Detroit's 1st choice, 22nd overall, in 1988 Supplemental Draft).

			Regular Season					Playoffs				
Season	Club	Lea	GP	G	A	TP	PIM	GP	G	A	TP	PIM
1986-87	U. Wisconsin	WCHA	42	19	11	30	72	....	....	....	....	....
1987-88	U. Wisconsin	WCHA	44	7	22	29	70	....	....	....	....	....
1988-89	U. Wisconsin	WCHA	46	18	19	37	102	....	....	....	....	....
1989-90ab	U. Wisconsin	WCHA	45	*41	39	*80	70	....	....	....	....	....
1990-91	**Detroit**	**NHL**	**6**	**1**	**2**	**3**	**6**	**3**	**0**	**0**	**0**	**0**
	Adirondack	AHL	59	23	24	47	32	....	....	....	....	....
1991-92	Adirondack	AHL	79	32	48	80	48	19	4	9	13	18
1992-93	Adirondack	AHL	47	24	53	77	66	....	....	....	....	....
	Los Angeles	**NHL**	**25**	**2**	**4**	**6**	**16**	**17**	**2**	**2**	**4**	**12**
1993-94	**Los Angeles**	**NHL**	**56**	**3**	**4**	**7**	**30**	....	....	....	....	....
	NHL Totals		**87**	**6**	**10**	**16**	**52**	**20**	**2**	**2**	**4**	**12**

a WCHA First All-Star Team (1990)
b NCAA West First All-American Team (1990)

Traded to **Los Angeles** by **Detroit** with Jimmy Carson and Marc Potvin for Paul Coffey, Sylvain Couturier and Jim Hiller, January 29, 1993.

SILLINGER, MIKE — DET.

Center. Shoots right. 5'10", 190 lbs. Born, Regina, Sask., June 29, 1971.
(Detroit's 1st choice, 11th overall, in 1989 Entry Draft).

			Regular Season					Playoffs				
Season	Club	Lea	GP	G	A	TP	PIM	GP	G	A	TP	PIM
1987-88	Regina	WHL	67	18	25	43	17	4	2	2	4	0
1988-89	Regina	WHL	72	53	78	131	52	....	....	....	....	....
1989-90a	Regina	WHL	70	57	72	129	41	11	12	10	22	2
	Adirondack	AHL	....	....	....	....	....	1	0	0	0	0
1990-91	**Detroit**	**NHL**	**3**	**0**	**1**	**1**	**0**	**3**	**0**	**1**	**1**	**0**
b	Regina	WHL	57	50	66	116	42	8	6	9	15	4
1991-92	Adirondack	AHL	64	25	41	66	26	15	9	*19	*28	12
	Detroit	**NHL**	....	....	....	....	....	**8**	**2**	**2**	**4**	**2**
1992-93	**Detroit**	**NHL**	**51**	**4**	**17**	**21**	**16**	....	....	....	....	....
	Adirondack	AHL	15	10	20	30	31	11	5	13	18	10
1993-94	**Detroit**	**NHL**	**62**	**8**	**21**	**29**	**10**	....	....	....	....	....
	NHL Totals		**116**	**12**	**39**	**51**	**26**	**11**	**2**	**3**	**5**	**2**

a WHL East Second All-Star Team (1990)
b WHL East First All-Star Team (1991)

SILVERMAN, ANDREW — NYR

Defense. Shoots left. 6'3", 210 lbs. Born, Beverly, MA, August 23, 1972.
(NY Rangers' 11th choice, 181st overall, in 1990 Entry Draft).

			Regular Season					Playoffs				
Season	Club	Lea	GP	G	A	TP	PIM	GP	G	A	TP	PIM
1991-92	U. of Maine	H.E.	30	2	9	11	18	....	....	....	....	....
1992-93	U. of Maine	H.E.	37	1	7	8	56	....	....	....	....	....
1993-94	U. of Maine	H.E.	35	0	3	3	80	....	....	....	....	....

SIMARD, MARTIN

Right wing. Shoots right. 6'1", 215 lbs. Born, Montreal, Que., June 25, 1966.

			Regular Season					Playoffs				
Season	Club	Lea	GP	G	A	TP	PIM	GP	G	A	TP	PIM
1984-85	Granby	QMJHL	58	22	31	53	78	8	3	7	10	21
1985-86	Granby	QMJHL	54	32	28	60	129	....	....	....	....	....
	Hull	QMJHL	14	8	8	16	55	14	8	19	27	19
1986-87	Granby	QMJHL	41	30	47	77	105	8	3	7	10	21
1987-88	Salt Lake	IHL	82	8	23	31	281	19	6	3	9	100
1988-89	Salt Lake	IHL	71	13	15	28	221	14	4	0	4	45
1989-90	Salt Lake	IHL	59	22	23	45	151	11	5	8	13	12
1990-91	**Calgary**	**NHL**	**16**	**0**	**2**	**2**	**53**	....	....	....	....	....
	Salt Lake	IHL	54	24	25	49	113	4	3	0	3	20
1991-92	**Calgary**	**NHL**	**21**	**1**	**3**	**4**	**119**	....	....	....	....	....
	Salt Lake	IHL	11	3	7	10	51	....	....	....	....	....
	Halifax	AHL	10	5	3	8	26	....	....	....	....	....
1992-93	**Tampa Bay**	**NHL**	**7**	**0**	**0**	**0**	**11**	....	....	....	....	....
	Atlanta	IHL	19	5	5	10	77	....	....	....	....	....
	Halifax	AHL	13	3	4	7	17	....	....	....	....	....
1993-94	Cornwall	AHL	57	10	10	20	152	7	3	1	4	7
	NHL Totals		**44**	**1**	**5**	**6**	**183**	....	....	....	....	....

Signed as a free agent by **Calgary**, May 19, 1987. Traded to **Quebec** by **Calgary** for Greg Smyth, March 10, 1992. Traded to **Tampa Bay** by **Quebec** to complete June 19, 1992 trade which sent Tim Hunter to Quebec for future considerations, September 14, 1992. Traded to **Quebec** by **Tampa Bay** with Steve Tuttle and Michel Mongeau for Herb Raglan, February 12, 1993.

SIMON, CHRIS — QUE.

Left wing. Shoots left. 6'3", 219 lbs. Born, Wawa, Ont., January 30, 1972.
(Philadelphia's 2nd choice, 25th overall, in 1990 Entry Draft).

			Regular Season					Playoffs				
Season	Club	Lea	GP	G	A	TP	PIM	GP	G	A	TP	PIM
1988-89	Ottawa	OHL	36	4	2	6	31	....	....	....	....	....
1989-90	Ottawa	OHL	57	36	38	74	146	3	2	1	3	4
1990-91	Ottawa	OHL	20	16	6	22	69	17	5	9	14	59
1991-92	Ottawa	OHL	2	1	1	2	24	....	....	....	....	....
	S.S. Marie	OHL	31	19	25	44	143	11	5	8	13	49
1992-93	**Quebec**	**NHL**	**16**	**1**	**1**	**2**	**67**	**5**	**0**	**0**	**0**	**26**
	Halifax	AHL	36	12	6	18	131	....	....	....	....	....
1993-94	**Quebec**	**NHL**	**37**	**4**	**4**	**8**	**132**	....	....	....	....	....
	NHL Totals		**53**	**5**	**5**	**10**	**199**	**5**	**0**	**0**	**0**	**26**

Traded to **Quebec** by **Philadelphia** with Peter Forsberg, Steve Duchesne, Kerry Huffman, Mike Ricci, Ron Hextall, Philadelphia's first round choice in the 1993 (Jocelyn Thibault) and 1994 (later traded to Toronto — later traded to Washington — Washington selected Nolan Baumgartner) Entry Drafts and cash for Eric Lindros, June 30, 1992.

SIMON, DARCY

Defense. Shoots right. 6'1", 200 lbs. Born, North Battleford, Sask., January 21, 1970.

			Regular Season					Playoffs				
Season	Club	Lea	GP	G	A	TP	PIM	GP	G	A	TP	PIM
1987-88	Seattle	WHL	67	5	9	14	226	....	....	....	....	....
1988-89	Seattle	WHL	62	3	15	18	208	....	....	....	....	....
1989-90	Seattle	WHL	63	5	13	18	285	13	1	2	3	79
1990-91	Fredericton	AHL	29	0	3	3	183	9	2	0	2	45
1991-92	Fredericton	AHL	58	9	11	20	308	4	0	0	0	13
1992-93	Fredericton	AHL	57	2	7	9	257	2	0	0	0	6
	Wheeling	ECHL	3	0	1	1	26	....	....	....	....	....
1993-94	PEI	AHL	45	1	5	6	263	....	....	....	....	....

Signed as a free agent by **Montreal**, October 3, 1990. Signed as a free agent by **Ottawa**, August 24, 1993.

SIMON, JASON — NYI

Left wing. Shoots left. 6'1", 190 lbs. Born, Sarnia, Ont., March 21, 1969.
(New Jersey's 9th choice, 215th overall, in 1989 Entry Draft).

			Regular Season					Playoffs				
Season	Club	Lea	GP	G	A	TP	PIM	GP	G	A	TP	PIM
1986-87	London	OHL	33	1	2	3	33	....	....	....	....	....
	Sudbury	OHL	26	2	3	5	50	....	....	....	....	....
1987-88	Sudbury	OHL	26	5	7	12	35	....	....	....	....	....
	Hamilton	OHL	29	5	13	18	124	11	0	2	2	15
1988-89	Windsor	OHL	62	23	39	62	193	4	1	4	5	13
1989-90	Utica	AHL	16	3	4	7	28	2	0	0	0	12
	Nashville	ECHL	13	4	3	7	81	5	1	3	4	17
1990-91	Utica	AHL	50	2	12	14	189	....	....	....	....	....
	Johnstown	ECHL	22	11	9	20	55	....	....	....	....	....
1991-92	Utica	AHL	1	0	0	0	12	....	....	....	....	....
	San Diego	IHL	13	1	4	5	45	3	0	1	1	9
1992-93	Detroit	ColHL	11	7	13	20	38	....	....	....	....	....
	Flint	ColHL	44	17	32	49	202	....	....	....	....	....
1993-94	**NY Islanders**	**NHL**	**4**	**0**	**0**	**0**	**34**	....	....	....	....	....
	Salt Lake	IHL	50	7	7	14	*323	....	....	....	....	....
	Detroit	ColHL	13	9	16	25	87	....	....	....	....	....
	NHL Totals		**4**	**0**	**0**	**0**	**34**	....	....	....	....	....

Signed as a free agent by **NY Islanders**, January 6, 1994.

SIMON, TODD — BUF.

Center. Shoots right. 5'10", 188 lbs. Born, Toronto, Ont., April 21, 1972.
(Buffalo's 9th choice, 203rd overall, in 1992 Entry Draft).

			Regular Season					Playoffs				
Season	Club	Lea	GP	G	A	TP	PIM	GP	G	A	TP	PIM
1990-91	Niagara Falls	OHL	65	51	74	125	35	14	7	8	15	12
1991-92a	Niagara Falls	OHL	66	53	93	*146	72	17	17	24	*41	36
1992-93	Rochester	AHL	67	27	66	93	54	12	3	14	17	15
1993-94	**Buffalo**	**NHL**	**15**	**0**	**1**	**1**	**0**	**5**	**1**	**0**	**1**	**0**
	Rochester	AHL	55	33	52	85	79	....	....	....	....	....
	NHL Totals		**15**	**0**	**1**	**1**	**0**	**5**	**1**	**0**	**1**	**0**

a OHL First All-Star Team (1992)

SIMONOV, SERGEI — TOR.

Defense. Shoots left. 6'3", 194 lbs. Born, Saratov, USSR, May 20, 1974.
(Toronto's 11th choice, 221st overall, in 1992 Entry Draft).

			Regular Season					Playoffs				
Season	Club	Lea	GP	G	A	TP	PIM	GP	G	A	TP	PIM
1992-93	Saratov	CIS	40	0	2	2	34	....	....	....	....	....
1993-94	CSKA	CIS	28	0	0	0	6	....	....	....	....	....

SIMONTON, REID — QUE.

Defense. Shoots right. 6'2", 195 lbs. Born, Calgary, Alta., March 1, 1973.
(Quebec's 1st choice, 9th overall, in 1994 Supplemental Draft).

			Regular Season					Playoffs				
Season	Club	Lea	GP	G	A	TP	PIM	GP	G	A	TP	PIM
1992-93	Union	ECAC	25	7	5	12	78	....	....	....	....	....
1993-94	Union	ECAC	30	4	20	24	76	....	....	....	....	....

SIMPSON, CRAIG — BUF.

Left wing. Shoots right. 6'2", 195 lbs. Born, London, Ont., February 15, 1967.
(Pittsburgh's 1st choice, 2nd overall, in 1985 Entry Draft).

			Regular Season					Playoffs				
Season	Club	Lea	GP	G	A	TP	PIM	GP	G	A	TP	PIM
1983-84	Michigan State	CCHA	46	14	43	57	38	....	....	....	....	....
1984-85ab	Michigan State	CCHA	42	31	53	84	33	....	....	....	....	....
1985-86	**Pittsburgh**	**NHL**	**76**	**11**	**17**	**28**	**49**	....	....	....	....	....
1986-87	**Pittsburgh**	**NHL**	**72**	**26**	**25**	**51**	**57**	....	....	....	....	....
1987-88	**Pittsburgh**	**NHL**	**21**	**13**	**13**	**26**	**34**	....	....	....	....	....
	Edmonton	**NHL**	**59**	**43**	**21**	**64**	**43**	**19**	**13**	**6**	**19**	**26**
1988-89	**Edmonton**	**NHL**	**66**	**35**	**41**	**76**	**80**	**7**	**2**	**0**	**2**	**10**
1989-90	**Edmonton**	**NHL**	**80**	**29**	**32**	**61**	**180**	**22**	***16**	**15**	***31**	**8**
1990-91	**Edmonton**	**NHL**	**75**	**30**	**27**	**57**	**66**	**18**	**5**	**11**	**16**	**12**
1991-92	**Edmonton**	**NHL**	**79**	**24**	**37**	**61**	**80**	**1**	**0**	**0**	**0**	**0**
1992-93	**Edmonton**	**NHL**	**60**	**24**	**22**	**46**	**36**	....	....	....	....	....
1993-94	**Buffalo**	**NHL**	**22**	**8**	**8**	**16**	**8**	....	....	....	....	....
	NHL Totals		**610**	**243**	**243**	**486**	**633**	**67**	**36**	**32**	**68**	**56**

a CCHA First All-Star Team (1985)
b NCAA West First All-American Team (1985)

Traded to **Edmonton** by **Pittsburgh** with Dave Hannan, Moe Mantha and Chris Joseph for Paul Coffey, Dave Hunter and Wayne Van Dorp, November 24, 1987. Traded to **Buffalo** by **Edmonton** for Jozef Cierny and Buffalo's fourth round choice (Jussi Tarvainen) in 1994 Entry Draft, September 1, 1993.

SIMPSON, GEOFF — BOS.

Defense. Shoots right. 6'1", 180 lbs. Born, Victoria, B.C., March 6, 1969.
(Boston's 10th choice, 206th overall, in 1989 Entry Draft).

			Regular Season					Playoffs				
Season	Club	Lea	GP	G	A	TP	PIM	GP	G	A	TP	PIM
1989-90	N. Michigan	WCHA	39	4	19	23	40	....	....	....	....	....
1990-91	N. Michigan	WCHA	44	2	15	17	27	....	....	....	....	....
1991-92	N. Michigan	WCHA	25	1	3	4	20	....	....	....	....	....
1992-93	N. Michigan	WCHA	43	8	14	22	18	....	....	....	....	....
1993-94	Charlotte	ECHL	7	1	0	1	7	....	....	....	....	....
	Huntington	ECHL	60	16	28	44	77	....	....	....	....	....

SIMPSON, REID

Left wing. Shoots left. 6'1", 211 lbs. Born, Flin Flon, Man., May 21, 1969.
(Philadelphia's 3rd choice, 72nd overall, in 1989 Entry Draft).

			Regular Season					Playoffs				
Season	Club	Lea	GP	G	A	TP	PIM	GP	G	A	TP	PIM
1987-88	Prince Albert	WHL	72	13	14	27	164	10	1	0	1	43
1988-89	Prince Albert	WHL	59	26	29	55	264	4	2	1	3	30
1989-90	Prince Albert	WHL	29	15	17	32	121	14	4	7	11	34
	Hershey	AHL	28	2	2	4	175	....	....	....	....	....
1990-91	Hershey	AHL	54	9	15	24	183	1	0	0	0	0
1991-92	**Philadelphia**	**NHL**	**1**	**0**	**0**	**0**	**0**	....	....	....	....	....
	Hershey	AHL	60	11	7	18	145	....	....	....	....	....
1992-93	**Minnesota**	**NHL**	**1**	**0**	**0**	**0**	**5**	....	....	....	....	....
	Kalamazoo	IHL	45	5	5	10	193	....	....	....	....	....
1993-94	Kalamazoo	IHL	5	0	0	0	16	....	....	....	....	....
	Albany	AHL	37	9	5	14	135	5	1	1	2	18
	NHL Totals		**2**	**0**	**0**	**0**	**5**	....	....	....	....	....

Signed as a free agent by **Minnesota**, December 14, 1992. Traded to **New Jersey** by **Dallas** with Roy Mitchell for future considerations, March 21, 1994.

SIMPSON, TODD — CGY.

Defense. Shoots left. 6'3", 215 lbs. Born, Edmonton, Alta., May 28, 1973.

			Regular Season					Playoffs				
Season	Club	Lea	GP	G	A	TP	PIM	GP	G	A	TP	PIM
1992-93	Tri-City	WHL	69	5	18	23	196	4	0	0	0	13
1993-94	Tri-City	WHL	12	2	3	5	32	....	....	....	....	....
	Saskatoon	WHL	51	7	19	26	175	16	0	1	1	29

Signed as free agent by **Calgary**, July 6, 1994.

SINCLAIR, AL — OTT.

Defense. Shoots right. 6'3", 210 lbs. Born, Mississauga, Ont., April 3, 1973.
(Ottawa's 6th choice, 121st overall, in 1992 Entry Draft).

			Regular Season					Playoffs				
Season	Club	Lea	GP	G	A	TP	PIM	GP	G	A	TP	PIM
1991-92	U. of Michigan	CCHA	22	0	4	4	40	....	....	....	....	....
1992-93	U. of Michigan	CCHA	20	0	3	3	26	....	....	....	....	....
1993-94	U. of Michigan	CCHA	18	0	4	4	14	....	....	....	....	....

SITTLER, RYAN — PHI.

Left wing. Shoots left. 6'2", 185 lbs. Born, London, Ont., January 28, 1974.
(Philadelphia's 1st choice, 7th overall, in 1992 Entry Draft).

			Regular Season					Playoffs				
Season	Club	Lea	GP	G	A	TP	PIM	GP	G	A	TP	PIM
1992-93	U. of Michigan	CCHA	35	9	24	33	43	....	....	....	....	....
1993-94	U. of Michigan	CCHA	26	9	9	18	14	....	....	....	....	....

SJODIN, TOMMY — (SHOH-deen) QUE.

Defense. Shoots right. 5'11", 190 lbs. Born, Timra, Sweden, August 13, 1965.
(Minnesota's 10th choice, 237th overall, in 1985 Entry Draft).

			Regular Season					Playoffs				
Season	Club	Lea	GP	G	A	TP	PIM	GP	G	A	TP	PIM
1983-84	Timra	Swe. 2	16	4	4	8	6	6	0	....	....	4
1984-85	Timra	Swe. 2	23	8	11	19	14	....	....	....	....	....
1985-86	Timra	Swe. 2	32	13	12	25	40	....	....	....	....	....
1986-87	Brynas	Swe.	29	0	4	4	24	....	....	....	....	....
1987-88	Brynas	Swe.	40	6	9	15	28	....	....	....	....	....
1988-89	Brynas	Swe.	40	8	11	19	52	5	1	0	1	6
1989-90	Brynas	Swe.	40	14	14	28	46	5	0	0	0	2
1990-91	Brynas	Swe.	38	12	17	29	77	2	0	1	1	2
1991-92	Brynas	Swe.	40	6	16	22	46	5	0	3	3	4
1992-93	**Minnesota**	**NHL**	**77**	**7**	**29**	**36**	**30**	....	....	....	....	....
1993-94	**Dallas**	**NHL**	**7**	**0**	**2**	**2**	**4**	....	....	....	....	....
	Kalamazoo	IHL	38	12	32	44	22	....	....	....	....	....
	Quebec	**NHL**	**22**	**1**	**9**	**10**	**18**	....	....	....	....	....
	NHL Totals		**106**	**8**	**40**	**48**	**52**	....	....	....	....	....

Traded to **Quebec** by **Dallas** with Dallas' third round choice (Chris Drury) in 1994 Entry Draft for the rights to Emanuel Fernandez, February 13, 1994.

SKALDE, JARROD — (SKAHL-dee)

Center. Shoots left. 6', 170 lbs. Born, Niagara Falls, Ont., February 26, 1971.
(New Jersey's 3rd choice, 26th overall, in 1989 Entry Draft).

			Regular Season					Playoffs				
Season	Club	Lea	GP	G	A	TP	PIM	GP	G	A	TP	PIM
1987-88	Oshawa	OHL	60	12	16	28	24	7	2	1	3	2
1988-89	Oshawa	OHL	65	38	38	76	36	6	1	5	6	2
1989-90	Oshawa	OHL	62	40	52	92	66	17	10	7	17	6
1990-91	**New Jersey**	**NHL**	**1**	**0**	**1**	**1**	**0**	....	....	....	....	....
	Utica	AHL	3	3	2	5	0	....	....	....	....	....
	Oshawa	OHL	15	8	14	22	14	....	....	....	....	....
a	Belleville	OHL	40	30	52	82	21	6	9	6	15	10
1991-92	**New Jersey**	**NHL**	**15**	**2**	**4**	**6**	**4**	....	....	....	....	....
	Utica	AHL	62	20	20	40	56	4	3	1	4	8
1992-93	**New Jersey**	**NHL**	**11**	**0**	**2**	**2**	**4**	....	....	....	....	....
	Utica	AHL	59	21	39	60	76	5	0	2	2	19
	Cincinnati	IHL	4	1	2	3	4	....	....	....	....	....
1993-94	**Anaheim**	**NHL**	**20**	**5**	**4**	**9**	**10**	....	....	....	....	....
	San Diego	IHL	57	25	38	63	79	9	3	12	15	10
	NHL Totals		**47**	**7**	**11**	**18**	**18**	....	....	....	....	....

a OHL Second All-Star Team (1991)

Claimed by **Anaheim** from **New Jersey** in Expansion Draft, June 24, 1993.

SKOREPA, ZDENEK — (SKOHR-zheh-pah) N.J.

Right wing. Shoots left. 6', 187 lbs. Born, Duchcov, Czech., August 10, 1976.
(New Jersey's 4th choice, 103rd overall, in 1994 Entry Draft).

			Regular Season					Playoffs				
Season	Club	Lea	GP	G	A	TP	PIM	GP	G	A	TP	PIM
1993-94	Litvinov	Czech.	20	4	7	11	....	4	0	0	0	....

SKRUDLAND, BRIAN — (SKROOD-luhnd) FLA.

Center. Shoots left. 6', 196 lbs. Born, Peace River, Alta., July 31, 1963.

			Regular Season					Playoffs				
Season	Club	Lea	GP	G	A	TP	PIM	GP	G	A	TP	PIM
1980-81	Saskatoon	WHL	66	15	27	42	97	....	....	....	....	....
1981-82	Saskatoon	WHL	71	27	29	56	135	5	0	1	1	2
1982-83	Saskatoon	WHL	71	35	59	94	42	6	1	3	4	19
1983-84	Nova Scotia	AHL	56	13	12	25	55	12	2	8	10	14
1984-85a	Sherbrooke	AHL	70	22	28	50	109	17	9	8	17	23
1985-86	**Montreal**	**NHL**	**65**	**9**	**13**	**22**	**57**	**20**	**2**	**4**	**6**	**76**
1986-87	**Montreal**	**NHL**	**79**	**11**	**17**	**28**	**107**	**14**	**1**	**5**	**6**	**29**
1987-88	**Montreal**	**NHL**	**79**	**12**	**24**	**36**	**112**	**11**	**1**	**5**	**6**	**24**
1988-89	**Montreal**	**NHL**	**71**	**12**	**29**	**41**	**84**	**21**	**3**	**7**	**10**	**40**
1989-90	**Montreal**	**NHL**	**59**	**11**	**31**	**42**	**56**	**11**	**3**	**5**	**8**	**30**
1990-91	**Montreal**	**NHL**	**57**	**15**	**19**	**34**	**85**	**13**	**3**	**10**	**13**	**42**
1991-92	**Montreal**	**NHL**	**42**	**3**	**3**	**6**	**36**	**11**	**1**	**1**	**2**	**20**
1992-93	**Montreal**	**NHL**	**23**	**5**	**3**	**8**	**55**	....	....	....	....	....
	Calgary	**NHL**	**16**	**2**	**4**	**6**	**10**	**6**	**0**	**3**	**3**	**12**
1993-94	**Florida**	**NHL**	**79**	**15**	**25**	**40**	**136**	....	....	....	....	....
	NHL Totals		**570**	**95**	**168**	**263**	**738**	**107**	**14**	**40**	**54**	**273**

a Won Jack Butterfield Trophy (Playoff MVP - AHL) (1985)

Signed as a free agent by **Montreal**, September 13, 1983. Traded to **Calgary** by **Montreal** for Gary Leeman, January 28, 1993. Claimed by **Florida** from **Calgary** in Expansion Draft, June 24, 1993.

SKRYPEC, GERRY — CHI.

Defense. Shoots left. 6', 190 lbs. Born, Kitchener, Ont., June 21, 1974.
(Chicago's 6th choice, 137th overall, in 1992 Entry Draft).

			Regular Season					Playoffs				
Season	Club	Lea	GP	G	A	TP	PIM	GP	G	A	TP	PIM
1990-91	Ottawa	OHL	62	2	7	9	53	17	0	4	4	2
1991-92	Ottawa	OHL	65	6	21	27	105	5	0	1	1	8
1992-93	Ottawa	OHL	20	1	3	4	20	....	....	....	....	....
	Newmarket	OHL	19	1	6	7	24	7	1	0	1	20
1993-94	Newmarket	OHL	17	0	10	10	59	....	....	....	....	....
	Niagara Falls	OHL	16	0	8	8	41	....	....	....	....	....
	Detroit	OHL	21	1	5	6	48	17	0	2	2	36

SKUTA, VITEZSLAV — (SHKUH-tah) DET.

Defense. Shoots left. 6'4", 205 lbs. Born, Ostrava, Czech., July 17, 1974.
(Detroit's 9th choice, 204th overall, in 1993 Entry Draft).

			Regular Season					Playoffs				
Season	Club	Lea	GP	G	A	TP	PIM	GP	G	A	TP	PIM
1992-93	TJ Vitkovice	Czech.	34	1	2	3	....	....	....	....	....	....
1993-94	TJ Vitkovice	Czech.	34	1	4	5	....	4	0	3	3	....

SLANEY, JOHN — WSH.

Defense. Shoots left. 6', 185 lbs. Born, St. John's, Nfld., February 7, 1972.
(Washington's 1st choice, 9th overall, in 1990 Entry Draft).

			Regular Season					Playoffs				
Season	Club	Lea	GP	G	A	TP	PIM	GP	G	A	TP	PIM
1988-89	Cornwall	OHL	66	16	43	59	23	18	8	16	24	10
1989-90ab	Cornwall	OHL	64	38	59	97	68	6	0	8	8	11
1990-91c	Cornwall	OHL	34	21	25	46	28	....	....	....	....	....
1991-92	Cornwall	OHL	34	19	41	60	43	6	3	8	11	0
	Baltimore	AHL	6	2	4	6	0	....	....	....	....	....
1992-93	Baltimore	AHL	79	20	46	66	60	7	0	7	7	8
1993-94	**Washington**	**NHL**	**47**	**7**	**9**	**16**	**27**	**11**	**1**	**1**	**2**	**2**
	Portland	AHL	29	14	13	27	17	....	....	....	....	....
	NHL Totals		**47**	**7**	**9**	**16**	**27**	**11**	**1**	**1**	**2**	**2**

a OHL First All-Star Team (1990)
b Canadian Major Junior Defenseman of the Year (1990)
c OHL Second All-Star Team (1991)

SLEGR, JIRI — (SLAY-guhr, YOO-ree) VAN.

Defense. Shoots left. 6'1", 205 lbs. Born, Jihlava, Czech., May 30, 1971.
(Vancouver's 3rd choice, 23rd overall, in 1990 Entry Draft).

			Regular Season					Playoffs				
Season	Club	Lea	GP	G	A	TP	PIM	GP	G	A	TP	PIM
1987-88	Litvinov	Czech.	4	1	1	2	0	....	....	....	....	....
1988-89	Litvinov	Czech.	8	0	0	0	4	....	....	....	....	....
1989-90	Litvinov	Czech.	51	4	15	19	....	....	....	....	....	....
1990-91	Litvinov	Czech.	47	11	36	47	26	....	....	....	....	....
1991-92	Litvinov	Czech.	42	9	23	32	38	....	....	....	....	....
1992-93	**Vancouver**	**NHL**	**41**	**4**	**22**	**26**	**109**	**5**	**0**	**3**	**3**	**4**
	Hamilton	AHL	21	4	14	18	42	....	....	....	....	....
1993-94	**Vancouver**	**NHL**	**78**	**5**	**33**	**38**	**86**	....	....	....	....	....
	NHL Totals		**119**	**9**	**55**	**64**	**195**	**5**	**0**	**3**	**3**	**4**

SMART, JASON — CGY.

Center. Shoots left. 6'4", 212 lbs. Born, Prince George, B.C., January 23, 1970.
(Pittsburgh's 13th choice, 247th overall, in 1989 Entry Draft).

			Regular Season					Playoffs				
Season	Club	Lea	GP	G	A	TP	PIM	GP	G	A	TP	PIM
1986-87	Prince Albert	WHL	57	9	22	31	62	8	3	3	6	8
1987-88	Prince Albert	WHL	72	16	29	45	77	10	1	2	3	11
1988-89	Prince Albert	WHL	12	1	3	4	31	....	....	....	....	....
	Saskatoon	WHL	36	6	17	23	33	8	1	6	7	16
1989-90	Saskatoon	WHL	66	27	48	75	187	10	1	5	6	19
1990-91	Albany	IHL	15	4	2	6	28	....	....	....	....	....
	Muskegon	IHL	36	12	27	39	55	5	0	3	3	11
1991-92	Muskegon	IHL	45	10	14	24	49	....	....	....	....	....
1992-93	Cleveland	IHL	78	12	36	48	151	3	0	0	0	6
1993-94	Columbus	ECHL	63	29	50	79	141	6	3	4	7	10

SMART, RYAN — N.J.

Center. Shoots right. 6', 175 lbs. Born, Meadville, PA, September 22, 1975.
(New Jersey's 6th choice, 134th overall, in 1994 Entry Draft).

			Regular Season					Playoffs				
Season	Club	Lea	GP	G	A	TP	PIM	GP	G	A	TP	PIM
1993-94	Meadville	HS	46	59	57	116	....					

SMEHLIK, RICHARD — (SHMEH-lihk) BUF.

Defense. Shoots left. 6'3", 208 lbs. Born, Ostrava, Czech., January 23, 1970.
(Buffalo's 3rd choice, 97th overall, in 1990 Entry Draft).

			Regular Season					Playoffs				
Season	Club	Lea	GP	G	A	TP	PIM	GP	G	A	TP	PIM
1988-89	TJ Vitkovice	Czech.	38	2	5	7	12	....	....	....	....	....
1989-90	TJ Vitkovice	Czech.	51	5	4	9	....	....	....	....	....	....
1990-91	Dukla Jihlava	Czech.	58	4	3	7	22	....	....	....	....	....
1991-92	TJ Vitkovice	Czech.	47	9	10	19	42	....	....	....	....	....
1992-93	**Buffalo**	**NHL**	**80**	**4**	**27**	**31**	**59**	**8**	**0**	**4**	**4**	**2**
1993-94	**Buffalo**	**NHL**	**84**	**14**	**27**	**41**	**69**	**7**	**0**	**2**	**2**	**10**
	NHL Totals		**164**	**18**	**54**	**72**	**128**	**15**	**0**	**6**	**6**	**12**

SMELNITSKI, MAXIM — (smehl-NIHTS-kee) NYR

Right wing. Shoots left. 6'1", 200 lbs. Born, Chelyabinsk, USSR, March 24, 1974.
(NY Rangers' 13th choice, 268th overall, in 1993 Entry Draft).

			Regular Season					Playoffs				
Season	Club	Lea	GP	G	A	TP	PIM	GP	G	A	TP	PIM
1992-93	Chelyabinsk	CIS	35	0	1	1	7	2	0	0	0	0
1993-94	Chelyabinsk	CIS	23	4	0	4	4	3	0	0	0	0

SMITH, ADAM — NYR

Defense. Shoots left. 6', 190 lbs. Born, Digby, N.S., May 24, 1976.
(NY Rangers' 3rd choice, 78th overall, in 1994 Entry Draft).

			Regular Season					Playoffs				
Season	Club	Lea	GP	G	A	TP	PIM	GP	G	A	TP	PIM
1992-93	Tacoma	WHL	67	0	12	12	43	7	0	1	1	4
1993-94	Tacoma	WHL	66	4	19	23	119	8	0	0	0	10

SMITH, DERRICK

Left wing. Shoots left. 6'2", 215 lbs. Born, Scarborough, Ont., January 22, 1965.
(Philadelphia's 2nd choice, 44th overall, in 1983 Entry Draft).

			Regular Season					Playoffs				
Season	Club	Lea	GP	G	A	TP	PIM	GP	G	A	TP	PIM
1982-83	Peterborough	OHL	70	16	19	35	47	....	....	....	....	....
1983-84	Peterborough	OHL	70	30	36	66	31	8	4	4	8	7
1984-85	**Philadelphia**	**NHL**	**77**	**17**	**22**	**39**	**31**	**19**	**2**	**5**	**7**	**16**
1985-86	**Philadelphia**	**NHL**	**69**	**6**	**6**	**12**	**57**	**4**	**0**	**0**	**0**	**10**
1986-87	**Philadelphia**	**NHL**	**71**	**11**	**21**	**32**	**34**	**26**	**6**	**4**	**10**	**26**
1987-88	**Philadelphia**	**NHL**	**76**	**16**	**8**	**24**	**104**	**7**	**0**	**0**	**0**	**6**
1988-89	**Philadelphia**	**NHL**	**74**	**16**	**14**	**30**	**43**	**19**	**5**	**2**	**7**	**12**
1989-90	**Philadelphia**	**NHL**	**55**	**3**	**6**	**9**	**32**	....	....	....	....	....
1990-91	**Philadelphia**	**NHL**	**72**	**11**	**10**	**21**	**37**	....	....	....	....	....
1991-92	**Minnesota**	**NHL**	**33**	**2**	**4**	**6**	**33**	**7**	**1**	**0**	**1**	**9**
	Kalamazoo	IHL	6	1	5	6	4	....	....	....	....	....
1992-93	**Minnesota**	**NHL**	**9**	**0**	**1**	**1**	**2**	....	....	....	....	....
	Kalamazoo	IHL	52	22	13	35	43	....	....	....	....	....
1993-94	**Dallas**	**NHL**	**1**	**0**	**0**	**0**	**0**	....	....	....	....	....
a	Kalamazoo	IHL	77	44	37	81	90	5	0	0	0	18
	NHL Totals		**537**	**82**	**92**	**174**	**373**	**82**	**14**	**11**	**25**	**79**

a IHL Second All-Star Team (1994)

Claimed on waivers by **Minnesota**, October 26, 1991.

SMITH, GEOFF

Defense. Shoots left. 6'3", 200 lbs. Born, Edmonton, Alta., March 7, 1969.
(Edmonton's 3rd choice, 63rd overall, in 1987 Entry Draft).

			Regular Season					Playoffs				
Season	Club	Lea	GP	G	A	TP	PIM	GP	G	A	TP	PIM
1987-88	North Dakota	WCHA	42	4	12	16	34	....	....	....	....	....
1988-89	North Dakota	WCHA	9	0	1	1	8	....	....	....	....	....
	Kamloops	WHL	32	4	31	35	29	6	1	3	4	12
1989-90a	**Edmonton**	**NHL**	**74**	**4**	**11**	**15**	**52**	**3**	**0**	**0**	**0**	**0**
1990-91	**Edmonton**	**NHL**	**59**	**1**	**12**	**13**	**55**	**4**	**0**	**0**	**0**	**0**
1991-92	**Edmonton**	**NHL**	**74**	**2**	**16**	**18**	**43**	**5**	**0**	**1**	**1**	**6**
1992-93	**Edmonton**	**NHL**	**78**	**4**	**14**	**18**	**30**	....	....	....	....	....
1993-94	**Edmonton**	**NHL**	**21**	**0**	**3**	**3**	**12**	....	....	....	....	....
	Florida	**NHL**	**56**	**1**	**5**	**6**	**38**	....	....	....	....	....
	NHL Totals		**362**	**12**	**61**	**73**	**230**	**12**	**0**	**1**	**1**	**6**

a NHL All-Rookie Team (1990)

Traded to **Florida** by **Edmonton** with Edmonton's fourth round choice (David Nemirovsky) in 1994 Entry Draft for Florida's third round choice (Corey Neilson) in 1994 Entry Draft and St. Louis' sixth round choice (previously acquired by Florida — later traded to Winnipeg — Winnipeg selected Chris Kibermanis) in 1994 Entry Draft, December 6, 1993.

SMITH, JASON — N.J.

Defense. Shoots right. 6'3", 185 lbs. Born, Calgary, Alta., November 2, 1973.
(New Jersey's 1st choice, 18th overall, in 1992 Entry Draft).

			Regular Season					Playoffs				
Season	Club	Lea	GP	G	A	TP	PIM	GP	G	A	TP	PIM
1990-91	Regina	WHL	2	0	0	0	7	4	0	0	0	2
1991-92	Regina	WHL	62	9	29	38	168	....	....	....	....	....
1992-93a	Regina	WHL	64	14	52	66	175	13	4	8	12	39
	Utica	AHL	....	....	....	....	....	1	0	0	0	2
1993-94	**New Jersey**	**NHL**	**41**	**0**	**5**	**5**	**43**	**6**	**0**	**0**	**0**	**7**
	Albany	AHL	20	6	3	9	31	....	....	....	....	....
	NHL Totals		**41**	**0**	**5**	**5**	**43**	**6**	**0**	**0**	**0**	**7**

a Canadian Major Junior First All-Star Team (1993).

SMITH, JASON — CGY.

Defense. Shoots left. 6'4", 210 lbs. Born, Calgary, Alta., November 19, 1974.
(Calgary's 4th choice, 95th overall, in 1993 Entry Draft).

			Regular Season					Playoffs				
Season	Club	Lea	GP	G	A	TP	PIM	GP	G	A	TP	PIM
1992-93	Princeton	ECAC	28	5	4	9	94	....	....	....	....	....
1993-94	Princeton	ECAC	16	1	4	5	56	....	....	....	....	....

SMITH, MIKE

Defense. Shoots left. 6', 185 lbs. Born, Winnipeg, Man., January 17, 1971.
(Buffalo's 13th choice, 255th overall, in 1991 Entry Draft).

			Regular Season					Playoffs				
Season	Club	Lea	GP	G	A	TP	PIM	GP	G	A	TP	PIM
1989-90	Lake Superior	CCHA	41	4	10	14	6	....	....	....	....	....
1990-91	Lake Superior	CCHA	43	5	29	34	30	....	....	....	....	....
1991-92	Lake Superior	CCHA	39	6	16	22	28	....	....	....	....	....
1992-93abc	Lake Superior	CCHA	42	5	25	30	42	....	....	....	....	....
	Rochester	AHL	2	0	1	1	0	....	....	....	....	....
1993-94	Roanoke	ECHL	67	5	57	62	32	2	0	0	0	0

a CCHA Second All-Star Team (1993)
b NCAA West Second All-American Team (1993)
c NCAA Final Four All-Tournament Team (1993)

SMITH, RYAN

Defense. Shoots left. 6'2", 200 lbs. Born, Lethbridge, Alta., June 28, 1974.
(San Jose's 8th choice, 171st overall, in 1992 Entry Draft).

			Regular Season					Playoffs				
Season	Club	Lea	GP	G	A	TP	PIM	GP	G	A	TP	PIM
1990-91	Lethbridge	AJHL	34	8	19	27	103	....	....	....	....	....
1991-92	Brandon	WHL	71	7	24	31	48	....	....	....	....	....
1992-93	Brandon	WHL	71	9	38	47	103	4	0	1	1	4
1993-94	Lethbridge	WHL	63	5	31	36	131	....	....	....	....	....

SMITH, STEVE — CHI.

Defense. Shoots left. 6'4", 215 lbs. Born, Glasgow, Scotland, April 30, 1963.
(Edmonton's 5th choice, 111th overall, in 1981 Entry Draft).

			Regular Season					Playoffs				
Season	Club	Lea	GP	G	A	TP	PIM	GP	G	A	TP	PIM
1980-81	London	OHA	62	4	12	16	141	....	....	....	....	....
1981-82	London	OHL	58	10	36	46	207	4	1	2	3	13
1982-83	Moncton	AHL	2	0	0	0	0	....	....	....	....	....
	London	OHL	50	6	35	41	133	3	1	0	1	10
1983-84	Moncton	AHL	64	1	8	9	176	....	....	....	....	....
1984-85	**Edmonton**	**NHL**	**2**	**0**	**0**	**0**	**2**	....	....	....	....	....
	Nova Scotia	AHL	68	2	28	30	161	5	0	3	3	40
1985-86	**Edmonton**	**NHL**	**55**	**4**	**20**	**24**	**166**	**6**	**0**	**1**	**1**	**14**
	Nova Scotia	AHL	4	0	2	2	11	....	....	....	....	....
1986-87	**Edmonton**	**NHL**	**62**	**7**	**15**	**22**	**165**	**15**	**1**	**3**	**4**	**45**
1987-88	**Edmonton**	**NHL**	**79**	**12**	**43**	**55**	**286**	**19**	**1**	**11**	**12**	**55**
1988-89	**Edmonton**	**NHL**	**35**	**3**	**19**	**22**	**97**	**7**	**2**	**2**	**4**	**20**
1989-90	**Edmonton**	**NHL**	**75**	**7**	**34**	**41**	**171**	**22**	**5**	**10**	**15**	**37**
1990-91	**Edmonton**	**NHL**	**77**	**13**	**41**	**54**	**193**	**18**	**1**	**2**	**3**	**45**
1991-92	**Chicago**	**NHL**	**76**	**9**	**21**	**30**	**304**	**18**	**1**	**11**	**12**	**16**
1992-93	**Chicago**	**NHL**	**78**	**10**	**47**	**57**	**214**	**4**	**0**	**0**	**0**	**10**
1993-94	**Chicago**	**NHL**	**57**	**5**	**22**	**27**	**174**	....	....	....	....	....
	NHL Totals		**596**	**70**	**262**	**332**	**1772**	**109**	**11**	**40**	**51**	**242**

Played in NHL All-Star Game (1991)

Traded to **Chicago** by **Edmonton** for Dave Manson and Chicago's third round choice (Kirk Maltby) in 1992 Entry Draft, October 2, 1991.

SMOLINSKI, BRYAN — BOS.

Center. Shoots right. 6'1", 200 lbs. Born, Toledo, OH, December 27, 1971.
(Boston's 1st choice, 21st overall, in 1990 Entry Draft).

			Regular Season					Playoffs				
Season	Club	Lea	GP	G	A	TP	PIM	GP	G	A	TP	PIM
1989-90	Michigan State	CCHA	35	9	13	22	34	....	....	....	....	....
1990-91	Michigan State	CCHA	35	9	12	21	24	....	....	....	....	....
1991-92	Michigan State	CCHA	41	28	33	61	55	....	....	....	....	....
1992-93ab	Michigan State	CCHA	40	31	37	*68	93	....	....	....	....	....
	Boston	**NHL**	**9**	**1**	**3**	**4**	**0**	**4**	**1**	**0**	**1**	**2**
1993-94	**Boston**	**NHL**	**83**	**31**	**20**	**51**	**82**	**13**	**5**	**4**	**9**	**4**
	NHL Totals		**92**	**32**	**23**	**55**	**82**	**17**	**6**	**4**	**10**	**6**

a CCHA First All-Star Team (1993)
b NCAA West First All-American Team (1993)

SMYTH, BRAD (SMIHTH) FLA.

Right wing. Shoots right. 6', 200 lbs. Born, Ottawa, Ont., March 13, 1973.

			Regular Season					Playoffs				
Season	Club	Lea	GP	G	A	TP	PIM	GP	G	A	TP	PIM
1990-91	London	OHL	29	2	6	8	22	....	....	....	....	....
1991-92	London	OHL	58	17	18	35	93	10	2	0	2	8
1992-93	London	OHL	66	54	55	109	118	12	7	8	15	25
1993-94	Cincinnati	IHL	30	7	3	10	54	....	....	....	....	....
	Birmingham	ECHL	29	26	30	56	38	10	8	8	16	....

Signed as a free agent by **Florida**, October 4, 1993.

SMYTH, GREG (SMIHTH) CHI.

Defense. Shoots right. 6'3", 212 lbs. Born, Oakville, Ont., April 23, 1966.
(Philadelphia's 1st choice, 22nd overall, in 1984 Entry Draft).

			Regular Season					Playoffs				
Season	Club	Lea	GP	G	A	TP	PIM	GP	G	A	TP	PIM
1983-84	London	OHL	64	4	21	25	252	6	1	0	1	24
1984-85	London	OHL	47	7	16	23	188	8	2	2	4	27
1985-86	Hershey	AHL	2	0	1	1	5	8	0	0	0	60
a	London	OHL	46	12	42	54	199	4	1	2	3	28
1986-87	**Philadelphia**	**NHL**	**1**	**0**	**0**	**0**	**0**	**1**	**0**	**0**	**0**	**2**
	Hershey	AHL	35	0	2	2	158	2	0	0	0	19
1987-88	**Philadelphia**	**NHL**	**48**	**1**	**6**	**7**	**192**	**5**	**0**	**0**	**0**	**38**
	Hershey	AHL	21	0	10	10	102	....	....	....	....	....
1988-89	**Quebec**	**NHL**	**10**	**0**	**1**	**1**	**70**	....	....	....	....	....
	Halifax	AHL	43	3	9	12	310	4	0	1	1	35
1989-90	**Quebec**	**NHL**	**13**	**0**	**0**	**0**	**57**	....	....	....	....	....
	Halifax	AHL	49	5	14	19	235	6	1	0	1	52
1990-91	**Quebec**	**NHL**	**1**	**0**	**0**	**0**	**0**	....	....	....	....	....
	Halifax	AHL	56	6	23	29	340	....	....	....	....	....
1991-92	**Quebec**	**NHL**	**29**	**0**	**2**	**2**	**138**	....	....	....	....	....
	Halifax	AHL	9	1	3	4	35	....	....	....	....	....
	Calgary	**NHL**	**7**	**1**	**1**	**2**	**15**	....	....	....	....	....
1992-93	**Calgary**	**NHL**	**35**	**1**	**2**	**3**	**95**	....	....	....	....	....
	Salt Lake	IHL	5	0	1	1	31	....	....	....	....	....
1993-94	**Florida**	**NHL**	**12**	**1**	**0**	**1**	**37**	....	....	....	....	....
	Toronto	**NHL**	**11**	**0**	**1**	**1**	**38**	....	....	....	....	....
	Chicago	**NHL**	**38**	**0**	**0**	**0**	**108**	**6**	**0**	**0**	**0**	**0**
	NHL Totals		**205**	**4**	**13**	**17**	**750**	**12**	**0**	**0**	**0**	**40**

a OHL Second All-Star Team (1986)

Traded to **Quebec** by **Philadelphia** with Philadelphia's third round choice (John Tanner) in the 1989 Entry Draft for Terry Carkner, July 25, 1988. Traded to **Calgary** by **Quebec** for Martin Simard, March 10, 1992. Signed as a free agent by **Florida**, August 10, 1993. Traded to **Toronto** by **Florida** for cash, December 7, 1993. Claimed on waivers by **Chicago** from **Toronto**, January 8, 1994.

SMYTH, KEVIN (SMIHTH) HFD.

Left wing. Shoots left. 6'2", 217 lbs. Born, Banff, Alta., November 22, 1973.
(Hartford's 4th choice, 79th overall, in 1992 Entry Draft).

			Regular Season					Playoffs				
Season	Club	Lea	GP	G	A	TP	PIM	GP	G	A	TP	PIM
1990-91	Moose Jaw	WHL	66	30	45	75	96	6	1	1	2	0
1991-92	Moose Jaw	WHL	71	30	55	85	114	4	1	3	4	6
1992-93	Moose Jaw	WHL	64	44	38	82	111	....	....	....	....	....
1993-94	**Hartford**	**NHL**	**21**	**3**	**2**	**5**	**10**	....	....	....	....	....
	Springfield	AHL	42	22	27	49	72	6	4	5	9	0
	NHL Totals		**21**	**3**	**2**	**5**	**10**	....	....	....	....	....

SMYTH, RYAN EDM.

Left wing. Shoots left. 6'1", 185 lbs. Born, Banff, Alta., February 21, 1976.
(Edmonton's 2nd choice, 6th overall, in 1994 Entry Draft).

			Regular Season					Playoffs				
Season	Club	Lea	GP	G	A	TP	PIM	GP	G	A	TP	PIM
1991-92	Moose Jaw	WHL	2	0	0	0	0	....	....	....	....	....
1992-93	Moose Jaw	WHL	64	19	14	33	59	....	....	....	....	....
1993-94	Moose Jaw	WHL	72	50	55	105	88	....	....	....	....	....

SNELL, CHRIS TOR.

Defense. Shoots left. 5'11", 200 lbs. Born, Regina, Sask., May 12, 1971.
(Buffalo's 8th choice, 145th overall, in 1991 Entry Draft).

			Regular Season					Playoffs				
Season	Club	Lea	GP	G	A	TP	PIM	GP	G	A	TP	PIM
1989-90a	Ottawa	OHL	63	18	62	80	36	3	2	4	6	4
1990-91	Ottawa	OHL	54	23	59	82	58	17	3	14	17	8
1991-92	Rochester	AHL	65	5	27	32	66	10	2	1	3	6
1992-93	Rochester	AHL	76	14	57	71	83	17	5	8	13	39
1993-94	**Toronto**	**NHL**	**2**	**0**	**0**	**0**	**2**	....	....	....	....	....
bc	St. John's	AHL	75	22	74	96	92	11	1	15	16	10
	NHL Totals		**2**	**0**	**0**	**0**	**2**	....	....	....	....	....

a OHL First All-Star Team (1990)
b AHL First All-Star Team (1994)
c Won Eddie Shore Plaque (Top Defenseman - AHL) (1994)

Signed as a free agent by **Toronto**, August 3, 1993.

SOCHA, GARY

Center. Shoots left. 6'4", 190 lbs. Born, North Attleboro, MA, December 30, 1969.
(Calgary's 3rd choice, 84th overall, in 1988 Entry Draft).

			Regular Season					Playoffs				
Season	Club	Lea	GP	G	A	TP	PIM	GP	G	A	TP	PIM
1989-90	Providence	H.E.	25	2	2	4	8	....	....	....	....	....
1990-91	Providence	H.E.	35	15	13	28	20	....	....	....	....	....
1991-92	Providence	H.E.	26	11	14	25	34	....	....	....	....	....
1992-93	Providence	H.E.	33	13	15	28	22	....	....	....	....	....
	Salt Lake	IHL	4	0	0	0	0	....	....	....	....	....
1993-94	Saint John	AHL	3	0	1	1	0	....	....	....	....	....
	S. Carolina	ECHL	64	23	37	60	60	....	....	....	....	....

SOROCHAN, LEE NYR

Defense. Shoots left. 5'11", 208 lbs. Born, Edmonton, Alta., September 9, 1975.
(NY Rangers' 2nd choice, 34th overall, in 1993 Entry Draft).

			Regular Season					Playoffs				
Season	Club	Lea	GP	G	A	TP	PIM	GP	G	A	TP	PIM
1991-92	Lethbridge	WHL	67	2	9	11	105	5	0	2	2	6
1992-93	Lethbridge	WHL	69	8	32	40	208	4	0	1	1	12
1993-94	Lethbridge	WHL	46	5	27	32	123	9	4	3	7	16

SOROKIN, SERGEI (suh-ROH-kihn, SAIR-gay)

Defense. Shoots left. 5'11", 187 lbs. Born, Dzerzhinsk, USSR, October 2, 1969.
(Winnipeg's 10th choice, 247th overall, in 1991 Entry Draft).

			Regular Season					Playoffs				
Season	Club	Lea	GP	G	A	TP	PIM	GP	G	A	TP	PIM
1985-86	Torpedo Gorky	USSR	3	0	0	0	0	....	....	....	....	....
1986-87	Torpedo Gorky	USSR	34	0	0	0	22	....	....	....	....	....
1987-88	Torpedo Gorky	USSR	19	2	0	2	20	....	....	....	....	....
1988-89	Torpedo Gorky	USSR	25	1	1	2	29	....	....	....	....	....
1989-90	Moscow D'amo	USSR	10	0	2	2	2	....	....	....	....	....
1990-91	Moscow D'amo	USSR	41	4	5	9	20	....	....	....	....	....
1991-92	Moscow D'amo	CIS	42	7	11	18	34	....	....	....	....	....
1992-93	Moscow D'amo	CIS	38	12	8	20	20	10	1	0	1	6
1993-94	Moscow D'amo	CIS	9	1	3	4	4	....	....	....	....	....
	Moncton	AHL	11	2	8	10	4	....	....	....	....	....

SOULLIERE, STEPHANE L.A.

Left wing. Shoots left. 5'11", 180 lbs. Born, Greenfield Park, Que., May 30, 1975.

			Regular Season					Playoffs				
Season	Club	Lea	GP	G	A	TP	PIM	GP	G	A	TP	PIM
1992-93	Oshawa	OHL	65	11	7	18	77	13	1	0	1	19
1993-94	Oshawa	OHL	63	25	24	49	120	5	0	1	1	12

Signed as a free agent by **Los Angeles**, July 1, 1994.

SOURAY, SHELDON N.J.

Defense. Shoots left. 6'2", 210 lbs. Born, Elk Point, Alta., July 13, 1976.
(New Jersey's 3rd choice, 71st overall, in 1994 Entry Draft).

			Regular Season					Playoffs				
Season	Club	Lea	GP	G	A	TP	PIM	GP	G	A	TP	PIM
1992-93	Ft. Sask.	Jr. A	35	0	12	12	125	....	....	....	....	....
1993-94	Tri-City	WHL	42	3	6	9	122	....	....	....	....	....

SPEER, MICHAEL

Defense. Shoots left. 6'2", 202 lbs. Born, Toronto, Ont., March 26, 1971.
(Chicago's 2nd choice, 27th overall, in 1989 Entry Draft).

			Regular Season					Playoffs				
Season	Club	Lea	GP	G	A	TP	PIM	GP	G	A	TP	PIM
1987-88	Guelph	OHL	53	4	10	14	60	....	....	....	....	....
1988-89	Guelph	OHL	65	9	31	40	185	7	2	4	6	23
1989-90	Owen Sound	OHL	61	18	39	57	176	12	3	7	10	21
1990-91	Owen Sound	OHL	32	13	19	32	86	....	....	....	....	....
	Windsor	OHL	25	8	28	36	40	11	2	7	9	15
	Indianapolis	IHL	1	0	1	1	0	1	0	0	0	5
1991-92	Indianapolis	IHL	54	0	6	6	67	....	....	....	....	....
1992-93	Indianapolis	IHL	38	1	1	2	109	5	1	0	1	26
1993-94	Indianapolis	IHL	64	7	11	18	146	....	....	....	....	....

SPITZIG, TIM DET.

Right wing. Shoots right. 6', 195 lbs. Born, Goderich, Ont., April 15, 1974.
(Detroit's 7th choice, 152nd overall, in 1993 Entry Draft).

			Regular Season					Playoffs				
Season	Club	Lea	GP	G	A	TP	PIM	GP	G	A	TP	PIM
1991-92	Kitchener	OHL	62	8	13	21	89	4	0	0	0	2
1992-93	Kitchener	OHL	66	40	39	79	127	7	5	4	9	14
1993-94	Kitchener	OHL	62	48	38	86	111	5	7	2	9	8

STAGG, BRIAN

Right wing. Shoots right. 6'2", 177 lbs. Born, North Bay, Ont., May 23, 1974.
(Washington's 9th choice, 215th overall, in 1992 Entry Draft).

			Regular Season					Playoffs				
Season	Club	Lea	GP	G	A	TP	PIM	GP	G	A	TP	PIM
1991-92	Kingston	OHL	65	17	14	31	23	....	....	....	....	....
1992-93	Kingston	OHL	20	4	5	9	17	....	....	....	....	....
	Belleville	OHL	9	1	0	1	2	....	....	....	....	....
	North Bay	OHL	42	16	13	29	27	5	2	0	2	0
1993-94	North Bay	OHL	....	....	....	....	....	5	1	0	1	4

STAIOS, STEVE ST.L.

Defense. Shoots right. 6', 185 lbs. Born, Hamilton, Ont., July 28, 1973.
(St. Louis' 1st choice, 27th overall, in 1991 Entry Draft).

			Regular Season					Playoffs				
Season	Club	Lea	GP	G	A	TP	PIM	GP	G	A	TP	PIM
1990-91	Niagara Falls	OHL	66	17	29	46	115	12	2	3	5	10
1991-92	Niagara Falls	OHL	65	11	42	53	122	17	7	8	15	27
1992-93	Niagara Falls	OHL	12	4	14	18	30	....	....	....	....	....
	Sudbury	OHL	53	13	44	57	67	11	5	6	11	22
1993-94	Peoria	IHL	38	3	9	12	42	....	....	....	....	....

STAJDUHAR, NICK (STAD-joo-hahr) EDM.

Defense. Shoots left. 6'2", 195 lbs. Born, Kitchener, Ont., December 6, 1974.
(Edmonton's 2nd choice, 16th overall, in 1993 Entry Draft).

			Regular Season					Playoffs				
Season	Club	Lea	GP	G	A	TP	PIM	GP	G	A	TP	PIM
1990-91	London	OHL	66	3	12	15	51	7	0	0	0	2
1991-92	London	OHL	66	6	15	21	62	10	1	4	5	10
1992-93	London	OHL	49	15	45	60	58	12	4	11	15	10
1993-94a	London	OHL	52	34	52	86	58	5	0	2	2	8

a OHL First All-Star Team (1994)

STANTON, PAUL

Defense. Shoots right. 6'1", 195 lbs. Born, Boston, MA, June 22, 1967.
(Pittsburgh's 8th choice, 149th overall, in 1985 Entry Draft).

			Regular Season					Playoffs				
Season	Club	Lea	GP	G	A	TP	PIM	GP	G	A	TP	PIM
1985-86	U. Wisconsin	WCHA	36	4	6	10	16	....	....	....	....	....
1986-87	U. Wisconsin	WCHA	41	5	17	22	70	....	....	....	....	....
1987-88ab	U. Wisconsin	WCHA	45	9	38	47	98	....	....	....	....	....
1988-89c	U. Wisconsin	WCHA	45	7	29	36	126	....	....	....	....	....
1989-90	Muskegon	IHL	77	5	27	32	61	15	2	4	6	21
1990-91	**Pittsburgh**	**NHL**	**75**	**5**	**18**	**23**	**40**	**22**	**1**	**2**	**3**	**24**
1991-92	**Pittsburgh**	**NHL**	**54**	**2**	**8**	**10**	**62**	**21**	**1**	**7**	**8**	**42**
1992-93	**Pittsburgh**	**NHL**	**77**	**4**	**12**	**16**	**97**	**1**	**0**	**1**	**1**	**0**
1993-94	**Boston**	**NHL**	**71**	**3**	**7**	**10**	**54**	....	....	....	....	....
	NHL Totals		**277**	**14**	**45**	**59**	**253**	**44**	**2**	**10**	**12**	**66**

a NCAA West First All-American Team (1988)
b WCHA Second All-Star Team (1988)
c WCHA First All-Star Team (1989)

Traded to **Boston** by **Pittsburgh** for Boston's third round choice (Greg Crozier) in 1994 Entry Draft, October 8, 1993.

STAPLES, JEFF — PHI.

Defense. Shoots left. 6'2", 207 lbs. Born, Kitimat, B.C., March 4, 1975.
(Philadelphia's 10th choice, 244th overall, in 1993 Entry Draft).

			Regular Season					Playoffs				
Season	Club	Lea	GP	G	A	TP	PIM	GP	G	A	TP	PIM
1991-92	Brandon	WHL	3	0	0	0	0	....	....	....	....	....
1992-93	Brandon	WHL	40	0	5	5	114	4	0	1	1	4
1993-94	Brandon	WHL	37	0	7	7	126	....	....	....	....	....

STAPLETON, MIKE

Center. Shoots right. 5'10", 183 lbs. Born, Sarnia, Ont., May 5, 1966.
(Chicago's 7th choice, 132nd overall, in 1984 Entry Draft).

			Regular Season					Playoffs				
Season	Club	Lea	GP	G	A	TP	PIM	GP	G	A	TP	PIM
1983-84	Cornwall	OHL	70	24	45	69	94	3	1	2	3	4
1984-85	Cornwall	OHL	56	41	44	85	68	9	2	4	6	23
1985-86	Cornwall	OHL	56	39	64	103	74	6	2	3	5	2
1986-87	**Chicago**	**NHL**	**39**	**3**	**6**	**9**	**6**	**4**	**0**	**0**	**0**	**2**
	Cdn. National	....	21	2	4	6	4	....	....	....	....	....
1987-88	**Chicago**	**NHL**	**53**	**2**	**9**	**11**	**59**	....	....	....	....	....
	Saginaw	IHL	31	11	19	30	52	10	5	6	11	10
1988-89	**Chicago**	**NHL**	**7**	**0**	**1**	**1**	**7**	....	....	....	....	....
	Saginaw	IHL	69	21	47	68	162	6	1	3	4	4
1989-90	Indianapolis	IHL	16	5	10	15	6	13	9	10	19	38
1990-91	**Chicago**	**NHL**	**7**	**0**	**1**	**1**	**2**	....	....	....	....	....
	Indianapolis	IHL	75	29	52	81	76	7	1	4	5	0
1991-92	**Chicago**	**NHL**	**19**	**4**	**4**	**8**	**8**	....	....	....	....	....
	Indianapolis	IHL	59	18	40	58	65	....	....	....	....	....
1992-93	**Pittsburgh**	**NHL**	**78**	**4**	**9**	**13**	**10**	**4**	**0**	**0**	**0**	**0**
1993-94	**Pittsburgh**	**NHL**	**58**	**7**	**4**	**11**	**18**	....	....	....	....	....
	Edmonton	**NHL**	**23**	**5**	**9**	**14**	**28**	....	....	....	....	....
	NHL Totals		**284**	**25**	**43**	**68**	**138**	**8**	**0**	**0**	**0**	**2**

Signed as a free agent by **Pittsburgh**, September 30, 1992. Claimed on waivers by **Edmonton** from **Pittsburgh**, February 19, 1994.

STAROSTENKO, DMITRI — (stahr-oh-STEN-koh) NYR

Right wing. Shoots left. 6', 185 lbs. Born, Minsk, USSR, March 18, 1973.
(NY Rangers' 5th choice, 120th overall, in 1992 Entry Draft).

			Regular Season					Playoffs				
Season	Club	Lea	GP	G	A	TP	PIM	GP	G	A	TP	PIM
1989-90	D'amo Minsk	USSR	7	0	0	0	2	....	....	....	....	....
1990-91	CSKA	USSR	20	2	1	3	4	....	....	....	....	....
1991-92	CSKA	CIS	32	3	1	4	12	....	....	....	....	....
1992-93	CSKA	CIS	42	15	12	27	22	....	....	....	....	....
1993-94	CSKA	CIS	1	0	1	1	0	....	....	....	....	....
	Binghamton	AHL	41	12	9	21	10	....	....	....	....	....

STASHENKOV, ILJA — (stah-shehn-KOHV) WPG.

Defense. Shoots left. 5'11", 178 lbs. Born, Moscow, USSR, August 26, 1974.
(Winnipeg's 11th choice, 223rd overall, in 1993 Entry Draft).

			Regular Season					Playoffs				
Season	Club	Lea	GP	G	A	TP	PIM	GP	G	A	TP	PIM
1991-92	Soviet Wings	CIS	7	0	0	0	2	....	....	....	....	....
1992-93	Soviet Wings	CIS	42	0	0	0	22	1	0	0	0	0
1993-94	Soviet Wings	CIS	46	3	0	3	10	....	....	....	....	....

STASIUK, JEREMY — DAL.

Right wing. Shoots right. 5'11", 189 lbs. Born, Saskatoon, Sask., December 26, 1974.
(Dallas' 6th choice, 165th overall, in 1993 Entry Draft).

			Regular Season					Playoffs				
Season	Club	Lea	GP	G	A	TP	PIM	GP	G	A	TP	PIM
1991-92	Spokane	WHL	2	0	0	0	0	....	....	....	....	....
1992-93	Spokane	WHL	63	14	23	37	111	10	3	5	8	15
1993-94	Spokane	WHL	59	12	25	37	84	....	....	....	....	....

STASTNY, PETER — (STAHST-nee) ST.L.

Center. Shoots left. 6'1", 200 lbs. Born, Bratislava, Czech., September 18, 1956.

			Regular Season					Playoffs				
Season	Club	Lea	GP	G	A	TP	PIM	GP	G	A	TP	PIM
1973-74	Bratislava	Czech.				UNAVAILABLE						
1974-75	Bratislava	Czech.				UNAVAILABLE						
1975-76	Bratislava	Czech.	32	19	9	28	....	....	....	....	....	....
1976-77	Bratislava	Czech.	44	25	27	52	....	....	....	....	....	....
1977-78	Bratislava	Czech.	42	29	24	53	28	....	....	....	....	....
1978-79	Bratislava	Czech.	39	32	23	55	21	....	....	....	....	....
1979-80a	Bratislava	Czech.	41	26	26	52	58	....	....	....	....	....
1980-81bcd	**Quebec**	**NHL**	**77**	**39**	**70**	**109**	**37**	**5**	**2**	**8**	**10**	**7**
1981-82	**Quebec**	**NHL**	**80**	**46**	**93**	**139**	**91**	**12**	**7**	**11**	**18**	**10**
1982-83	**Quebec**	**NHL**	**75**	**47**	**77**	**124**	**78**	**4**	**3**	**2**	**5**	**10**
1983-84	**Quebec**	**NHL**	**80**	**46**	**73**	**119**	**73**	**9**	**2**	**7**	**9**	**31**
1984-85	**Quebec**	**NHL**	**75**	**32**	**68**	**100**	**95**	**18**	**4**	**19**	**23**	**24**
1985-86	**Quebec**	**NHL**	**76**	**41**	**81**	**122**	**60**	**3**	**0**	**1**	**1**	**2**
1986-87	**Quebec**	**NHL**	**64**	**24**	**53**	**77**	**43**	**13**	**6**	**9**	**15**	**12**
1987-88	**Quebec**	**NHL**	**76**	**46**	**65**	**111**	**69**	....	....	....	....	....
1988-89	**Quebec**	**NHL**	**72**	**35**	**50**	**85**	**117**	....	....	....	....	....
1989-90	**Quebec**	**NHL**	**62**	**24**	**38**	**62**	**24**	....	....	....	....	....
	New Jersey	**NHL**	**12**	**5**	**6**	**11**	**16**	**6**	**3**	**2**	**5**	**2**
1990-91	**New Jersey**	**NHL**	**77**	**18**	**42**	**60**	**53**	**7**	**3**	**4**	**7**	**2**
1991-92	**New Jersey**	**NHL**	**66**	**24**	**38**	**62**	**42**	**7**	**3**	**7**	**10**	**19**
1992-93	**New Jersey**	**NHL**	**62**	**17**	**23**	**40**	**22**	**5**	**0**	**2**	**2**	**2**
1993-94	Bratislava	Slovak	4	0	4	4	0	....	....	....	....	....
	Slov. Olympic	....	8	5	4	9	9	....	....	....	....	....
	St. Louis	**NHL**	**17**	**5**	**11**	**16**	**4**	**4**	**0**	**0**	**0**	**2**
	NHL Totals		**971**	**449**	**788**	**1237**	**824**	**93**	**33**	**72**	**105**	**123**

a Czechoslovakian League Player of the Year (1980)
b Won Calder Memorial Trophy (1981)
c NHL record for assists by a rookie (1981)
d NHL record for points by a rookie (1981)

Played in NHL All-Star Game (1981, 1982-84, 1986, 1988)

Signed as a free agent by **Quebec**, August 26, 1980. Traded to **New Jersey** by **Quebec** for Craig Wolanin and future considerations (Randy Velischek, August 13, 1990), March 6, 1990. Signed as a free agent by **St. Louis**, March 9, 1994.

STEEN, THOMAS — (STEEN) WPG.

Center. Shoots left. 5'11", 190 lbs. Born, Grums, Sweden, June 8, 1960.
(Winnipeg's 5th choice, 103rd overall, in 1979 Entry Draft).

			Regular Season					Playoffs				
Season	Club	Lea	GP	G	A	TP	PIM	GP	G	A	TP	PIM
1976-77	Leksand	Swe.	2	1	1	2	2	....	....	....	....	....
1977-78	Leksand	Swe.	35	5	6	11	30	....	....	....	....	....
1978-79	Leksand	Swe.	23	13	4	17	35	2	0	0	0	0
1979-80	Leksand	Swe.	18	7	7	14	14	2	0	0	0	6
1980-81	Farjestad	Swe.	32	16	23	39	30	7	4	2	6	8
1981-82	**Winnipeg**	**NHL**	**73**	**15**	**29**	**44**	**42**	**4**	**0**	**4**	**4**	**2**
1982-83	**Winnipeg**	**NHL**	**75**	**26**	**33**	**59**	**60**	**3**	**0**	**2**	**2**	**0**
1983-84	**Winnipeg**	**NHL**	**78**	**20**	**45**	**65**	**69**	**3**	**0**	**1**	**1**	**9**
1984-85	**Winnipeg**	**NHL**	**79**	**30**	**54**	**84**	**80**	**8**	**2**	**3**	**5**	**17**
1985-86	**Winnipeg**	**NHL**	**78**	**17**	**47**	**64**	**76**	**3**	**1**	**1**	**2**	**4**
1986-87	**Winnipeg**	**NHL**	**75**	**17**	**33**	**50**	**59**	**10**	**3**	**4**	**7**	**8**
1987-88	**Winnipeg**	**NHL**	**76**	**16**	**38**	**54**	**53**	**5**	**1**	**5**	**6**	**2**
1988-89	**Winnipeg**	**NHL**	**80**	**27**	**61**	**88**	**80**	....	....	....	....	....
1989-90	**Winnipeg**	**NHL**	**53**	**18**	**48**	**66**	**35**	**7**	**2**	**5**	**7**	**16**
1990-91	**Winnipeg**	**NHL**	**58**	**19**	**48**	**67**	**49**	....	....	....	....	....
1991-92	**Winnipeg**	**NHL**	**38**	**13**	**25**	**38**	**29**	**7**	**2**	**4**	**6**	**2**
1992-93	**Winnipeg**	**NHL**	**80**	**22**	**50**	**72**	**75**	**6**	**1**	**3**	**4**	**2**
1993-94	**Winnipeg**	**NHL**	**76**	**19**	**32**	**51**	**32**	....	....	....	....	....
	NHL Totals		**919**	**259**	**543**	**802**	**739**	**56**	**12**	**32**	**44**	**62**

STEINER, ONDREJ — BUF.

Center. Shoots left. 6'1", 176 lbs. Born, Plzen, Czech., February 12, 1974.
(Buffalo's 3rd choice, 59th overall, in 1992 Entry Draft).

			Regular Season					Playoffs				
Season	Club	Lea	GP	G	A	TP	PIM	GP	G	A	TP	PIM
1991-92	Skoda Plzen	Czech.	4	0	1	1	0	....	....	....	....	....
1992-93	Skoda Plzen	Czech.	29	1	7	8	....	....	....	....	....	....
1993-94	Skoda Plzen	Czech.	31	3	6	9	0	....	....	....	....	....

STERN, RONNIE — CGY.

Right wing. Shoots right. 6', 195 lbs. Born, Ste. Agathe, Que., January 11, 1967.
(Vancouver's 3rd choice, 70th overall, in 1986 Entry Draft).

			Regular Season					Playoffs				
Season	Club	Lea	GP	G	A	TP	PIM	GP	G	A	TP	PIM
1984-85	Longueuil	QMJHL	67	6	14	20	176	....	....	....	....	....
1985-86	Longueuil	QMJHL	70	39	33	72	317	....	....	....	....	....
1986-87	Longueuil	QMJHL	56	32	39	71	266	19	11	9	20	55
1987-88	**Vancouver**	**NHL**	**15**	**0**	**0**	**0**	**52**	....	....	....	....	....
	Fredericton	AHL	2	1	0	1	4	....	....	....	....	....
	Flint	IHL	55	14	19	33	294	16	8	8	16	94
1988-89	**Vancouver**	**NHL**	**17**	**1**	**0**	**1**	**49**	**3**	**0**	**1**	**1**	**17**
	Milwaukee	IHL	45	19	23	42	280	5	1	0	1	11
1989-90	**Vancouver**	**NHL**	**34**	**2**	**3**	**5**	**208**	....	....	....	....	....
	Milwaukee	IHL	26	8	9	17	165	....	....	....	....	....
1990-91	**Vancouver**	**NHL**	**31**	**2**	**3**	**5**	**171**	....	....	....	....	....
	Milwaukee	IHL	7	2	2	4	81	....	....	....	....	....
	Calgary	**NHL**	**13**	**1**	**3**	**4**	**69**	**7**	**1**	**3**	**4**	**14**
1991-92	**Calgary**	**NHL**	**72**	**13**	**9**	**22**	**338**	....	....	....	....	....
1992-93	**Calgary**	**NHL**	**70**	**10**	**15**	**25**	**207**	**6**	**0**	**0**	**0**	**43**
1993-94	**Calgary**	**NHL**	**71**	**9**	**20**	**29**	**243**	**7**	**2**	**0**	**2**	**12**
	NHL Totals		**323**	**38**	**53**	**91**	**1337**	**23**	**3**	**4**	**7**	**86**

Traded to **Calgary** by **Vancouver** with Kevan Guy for Dana Murzyn, March 5, 1991.

STEVENS, JOHN — HFD.

Defense. Shoots left. 6'1", 195 lbs. Born, Campbellton, N.B., May 4, 1966.
(Philadelphia's 5th choice, 47th overall, in 1984 Entry Draft).

			Regular Season					Playoffs				
Season	Club	Lea	GP	G	A	TP	PIM	GP	G	A	TP	PIM
1983-84	Oshawa	OHL	70	1	10	11	71	7	0	1	1	6
1984-85	Oshawa	OHL	44	2	10	12	61	5	0	2	2	4
	Hershey	AHL	3	0	0	0	0	....	....	....	....	....
1985-86	Oshawa	OHL	65	1	7	8	146	6	0	2	2	14
	Kalamazoo	IHL	6	0	1	1	8	6	0	3	3	9
1986-87	**Philadelphia**	**NHL**	**6**	**0**	**2**	**2**	**14**	....	....	....	....	....
	Hershey	AHL	63	1	15	16	131	3	0	0	0	7
1987-88	**Philadelphia**	**NHL**	**3**	**0**	**0**	**0**	**0**	....	....	....	....	....
	Hershey	AHL	59	1	15	16	108	....	....	....	....	....
1988-89	Hershey	AHL	78	3	13	16	129	12	1	1	2	29
1989-90	Hershey	AHL	79	3	10	13	193	....	....	....	....	....
1990-91	**Hartford**	**NHL**	**14**	**0**	**1**	**1**	**11**	....	....	....	....	....
	Springfield	AHL	65	0	12	12	139	18	0	6	6	35
1991-92	**Hartford**	**NHL**	**21**	**0**	**4**	**4**	**19**	....	....	....	....	....
	Springfield	AHL	45	1	12	13	73	11	1	3	4	27
1992-93	Springfield	AHL	74	1	19	20	111	15	0	1	1	18
1993-94	**Hartford**	**NHL**	**9**	**0**	**3**	**3**	**4**	....	....	....	....	....
	Springfield	AHL	71	3	9	12	85	3	0	0	0	0
	NHL Totals		**53**	**0**	**10**	**10**	**48**	....	....	....	....	....

Signed as a free agent by **Hartford**, July 30, 1990.

STEVENS, KEVIN — PIT.

Left wing. Shoots left. 6'3", 217 lbs. Born, Brockton, MA, April 15, 1965.
(Los Angeles' 6th choice, 108th overall, in 1983 Entry Draft).

			Regular Season					Playoffs				
Season	Club	Lea	GP	G	A	TP	PIM	GP	G	A	TP	PIM
1983-84	Boston College	ECAC	37	6	14	20	36	....	....	....	....	....
1984-85	Boston College	H.E.	40	13	23	36	36	....	....	....	....	....
1985-86	Boston College	H.E.	42	17	27	44	56	....	....	....	....	....
1986-87ab	Boston College	H.E.	39	35	35	70	54	....	....	....	....	....
1987-88	U.S. National	....	44	22	23	45	52	....	....	....	....	....
	U.S. Olympic	....	5	1	3	4	2	....	....	....	....	....
	Pittsburgh	**NHL**	**16**	**5**	**2**	**7**	**8**	....	....	....	....	....
1988-89	**Pittsburgh**	**NHL**	**24**	**12**	**3**	**15**	**19**	**11**	**3**	**7**	**10**	**16**
	Muskegon	IHL	45	24	41	65	113	....	....	....	....	....
1989-90	**Pittsburgh**	**NHL**	**76**	**29**	**41**	**70**	**171**	....	....	....	....	....
1990-91c	**Pittsburgh**	**NHL**	**80**	**40**	**46**	**86**	**133**	**24**	***17**	**16**	**33**	**53**
1991-92d	**Pittsburgh**	**NHL**	**80**	**54**	**69**	**123**	**254**	**21**	**13**	**15**	**28**	**28**
1992-93c	**Pittsburgh**	**NHL**	**72**	**55**	**56**	**111**	**177**	**12**	**5**	**11**	**16**	**22**
1993-94	**Pittsburgh**	**NHL**	**83**	**41**	**47**	**88**	**155**	**6**	**1**	**1**	**2**	**10**
	NHL Totals		**431**	**236**	**264**	**500**	**917**	**74**	**39**	**50**	**89**	**129**

a Hockey East First All-Star Team (1987)
b NCAA East Second All-American Team (1987)
c NHL Second All-Star Team (1991, 1993)
d NHL First All-Star Team (1992)

Played in NHL All-Star Game (1991-93)

Rights traded to **Pittsburgh** by **Los Angeles** for Anders Hakansson, September 9, 1983.

STEVENS, MIKE

Left wing. Shoots left. 6', 202 lbs. Born, Kitchener, Ont., December 30, 1965.
(Vancouver's 5th choice, 58th overall, in 1984 Entry Draft).

			Regular Season					Playoffs				
Season	Club	Lea	GP	G	A	TP	PIM	GP	G	A	TP	PIM
1982-83	Kitchener	OHL	13	0	4	4	16	12	0	1	1	9
1983-84	Kitchener	OHL	66	19	21	40	109	16	10	7	17	40
1984-85	**Vancouver**	**NHL**	**6**	**0**	**3**	**3**	**6**	....	....	....	....	....
	Kitchener	OHL	37	17	18	35	121	4	1	1	2	8
1985-86	Fredericton	AHL	79	12	19	31	208	6	1	1	2	35
1986-87	Fredericton	AHL	71	7	18	25	258	....	....	....	....	....
1987-88	**Boston**	**NHL**	**7**	**0**	**1**	**1**	**9**	....	....	....	....	....
	Maine	AHL	63	30	25	55	265	7	1	2	3	37
1988-89	**NY Islanders**	**NHL**	**9**	**1**	**0**	**1**	**14**	....	....	....	....	....
	Springfield	AHL	42	17	13	30	120	....	....	....	....	....
1989-90	Springfield	AHL	28	12	10	22	75	....	....	....	....	....
	Toronto	**NHL**	**1**	**0**	**0**	**0**	**0**	....	....	....	....	....
	Newmarket	AHL	46	16	28	44	86	....	....	....	....	....
1990-91	Newmarket	AHL	68	24	23	47	229	....	....	....	....	....
1991-92	St. John's	AHL	30	13	11	24	65	....	....	....	....	....
	Binghamton	AHL	44	15	15	30	87	11	7	6	13	45
1992-93	Binghamton	AHL	68	31	61	92	230	14	5	5	10	63
1993-94	Saint John	AHL	79	20	37	57	293	6	1	3	4	34
	NHL Totals		**23**	**1**	**4**	**5**	**29**	....	....	....	....	....

Traded to **Boston** by **Vancouver** for cash, October 6, 1987. Signed as a free agent by **NY Islanders**, August 20, 1988. Traded to **Toronto** by **NY Islanders** with Gilles Thibaudeau for Jack Capuano, Paul Gagne and Derek Laxdal, December 20, 1989. Traded to **NY Rangers** by **Toronto** for Guy Larose, December 26, 1991. Signed as a free agent by **Calgary**, August 10, 1993.

STEVENS, RANDY — WPG.

Right wing. Shoots right. 6', 190 lbs. Born, Sault Ste. Marie, MI, August 9, 1973.
(Winnipeg's 1st choice, 4th overall, in 1994 Supplemental Draft).

			Regular Season					Playoffs				
Season	Club	Lea	GP	G	A	TP	PIM	GP	G	A	TP	PIM
1991-92	Michigan Tech	WCHA	28	1	3	4	16	....	....	....	....	....
1992-93	Michigan Tech	WCHA	37	12	12	24	28	....	....	....	....	....
1993-94	Michigan Tech	WCHA	42	21	12	33	42	....	....	....	....	....

STEVENS, ROD — VAN.

Center. Shoots left. 5'10", 175 lbs. Born, Fort St. John, B.C., April 5, 1974.

			Regular Season					Playoffs				
Season	Club	Lea	GP	G	A	TP	PIM	GP	G	A	TP	PIM
1991-92	Kamloops	WHL	57	8	13	21	20	15	2	2	4	0
1992-93	Kamloops	WHL	68	26	28	54	42	13	9	2	11	4
1993-94a	Kamloops	WHL	62	51	58	109	31	19	9	12	21	10

a Memorial Cup All-Star Team (1994)

Signed as a free agent by **Vancouver**, October 4, 1993.

STEVENS, SCOTT — N.J.

Defense. Shoots left. 6'2", 210 lbs. Born, Kitchener, Ont., April 1, 1964.
(Washington's 1st choice, 5th overall, in 1982 Entry Draft).

			Regular Season					Playoffs				
Season	Club	Lea	GP	G	A	TP	PIM	GP	G	A	TP	PIM
1980-81	Kitchener	OPJHL	39	7	33	40	82	....	....	....	....	....
	Kitchener	OHA	1	0	0	0	0	....	....	....	....	....
1981-82	Kitchener	OHL	68	6	36	42	158	15	1	10	11	71
1982-83a	**Washington**	**NHL**	**77**	**9**	**16**	**25**	**195**	**4**	**1**	**0**	**1**	**26**
1983-84	**Washington**	**NHL**	**78**	**13**	**32**	**45**	**201**	**8**	**1**	**8**	**9**	**21**
1984-85	**Washington**	**NHL**	**80**	**21**	**44**	**65**	**221**	**5**	**0**	**1**	**1**	**20**
1985-86	**Washington**	**NHL**	**73**	**15**	**38**	**53**	**165**	**9**	**3**	**8**	**11**	**12**
1986-87	**Washington**	**NHL**	**77**	**10**	**51**	**61**	**283**	**7**	**0**	**5**	**5**	**19**
1987-88b	**Washington**	**NHL**	**80**	**12**	**60**	**72**	**184**	**13**	**1**	**11**	**12**	**46**
1988-89	**Washington**	**NHL**	**80**	**7**	**61**	**68**	**225**	**6**	**1**	**4**	**5**	**11**
1989-90	**Washington**	**NHL**	**56**	**11**	**29**	**40**	**154**	**15**	**2**	**7**	**9**	**25**
1990-91	**St. Louis**	**NHL**	**78**	**5**	**44**	**49**	**150**	**13**	**0**	**3**	**3**	**36**
1991-92c	**New Jersey**	**NHL**	**68**	**17**	**42**	**59**	**124**	**7**	**2**	**1**	**3**	**29**
1992-93	**New Jersey**	**NHL**	**81**	**12**	**45**	**57**	**120**	**5**	**2**	**2**	**4**	**10**
1993-94bd	**New Jersey**	**NHL**	**83**	**18**	**60**	**78**	**112**	**20**	**2**	**9**	**11**	**42**
	NHL Totals		**911**	**150**	**522**	**672**	**2134**	**112**	**15**	**59**	**74**	**297**

a NHL All-Rookie Team (1983)
b NHL First All-Star Team (1988, 1994)
c NHL Second All-Star Team (1992)
d Won Alka-Seltzer Plus Award (1994)

Played in NHL All-Star Game (1985, 1989, 1991-94)

Signed as a free agent by **St. Louis**, July 16, 1990. Acquired by **New Jersey** from **St. Louis** as compensation for St. Louis' signing of free agent Brendan Shanahan, September 3, 1991.

STEVENSON, JEREMY — ANA.

Left wing. Shoots left. 6'1", 208 lbs. Born, San Bernadino, CA, July 28, 1974.
(Winnipeg's 3rd choice, 60th overall, in 1992 Entry Draft).

			Regular Season					Playoffs				
Season	Club	Lea	GP	G	A	TP	PIM	GP	G	A	TP	PIM
1990-91	Cornwall	OHL	58	13	20	33	124	....	....	....	....	....
1991-92	Cornwall	OHL	63	15	23	38	176	6	3	1	4	4
1992-93	Newmarket	OHL	54	28	28	56	144	5	5	1	6	28
1993-94	Newmarket	OHL	9	2	4	6	27	....	....	....	....	....
	S.S. Marie	OHL	48	18	19	37	183	14	1	1	2	23

STEVENSON, TURNER — MTL.

Right wing. Shoots right. 6'3", 200 lbs. Born, Prince George, B.C., May 18, 1972.
(Montreal's 1st choice, 12th overall, in 1990 Entry Draft).

			Regular Season					Playoffs				
Season	Club	Lea	GP	G	A	TP	PIM	GP	G	A	TP	PIM
1989-90	Seattle	WHL	62	29	32	61	276	....	....	....	....	....
1990-91	Seattle	WHL	57	36	27	63	222	6	1	5	6	15
	Fredericton	AHL	....	....	....	....	....	4	0	0	0	5
1991-92ab	Seattle	WHL	58	20	32	52	264	15	9	3	12	55
1992-93	**Montreal**	**NHL**	**1**	**0**	**0**	**0**	**0**	....	....	....	....	....
	Fredericton	AHL	79	25	34	59	102	5	2	3	5	11
1993-94	**Montreal**	**NHL**	**2**	**0**	**0**	**0**	**2**	**3**	**0**	**2**	**2**	**0**
	Fredericton	AHL	66	19	28	47	155	....	....	....	....	....
	NHL Totals		**3**	**0**	**0**	**0**	**2**	**3**	**0**	**2**	**2**	**0**

a WHL West First All-Star Team (1992)
b Memorial Cup All-Star Team (1992)

STEWART, CAMERON — BOS.

Left wing. Shoots left. 5'11", 196 lbs. Born, Kitchener, Ont., September 18, 1971.
(Boston's 2nd choice, 63rd overall, in 1990 Entry Draft).

			Regular Season					Playoffs				
Season	Club	Lea	GP	G	A	TP	PIM	GP	G	A	TP	PIM
1990-91	U. of Michigan	CCHA	44	8	24	32	122	....	....	....	....	....
1991-92	U. of Michigan	CCHA	44	13	15	28	106	....	....	....	....	....
1992-93	U. of Michigan	CCHA	39	20	39	59	69	....	....	....	....	....
1993-94	**Boston**	**NHL**	**57**	**3**	**6**	**9**	**66**	**8**	**0**	**3**	**3**	**7**
	Providence	AHL	14	3	2	5	5	....	....	....	....	....
	NHL Totals		**57**	**3**	**6**	**9**	**66**	**8**	**0**	**3**	**3**	**7**

STEWART, DAVE

Defense. Shoots right. 5'11", 195 lbs. Born, Norwood, Ont., January 11, 1972.

			Regular Season					Playoffs				
Season	Club	Lea	GP	G	A	TP	PIM	GP	G	A	TP	PIM
1990-91	Kingston	OHL	64	10	41	51	127	....	....	....	....	....
1991-92	Kingston	OHL	65	15	45	60	143	....	....	....	....	....
	Toledo	ECHL	3	0	2	2	2	....	....	....	....	....
1992-93	Phoenix	IHL	32	0	3	3	53	....	....	....	....	....
	Muskegon	ColHL	17	3	11	14	35	2	0	0	0	0
1993-94	Phoenix	IHL	25	2	3	5	53	....	....	....	....	....
	Flint	ColHL	8	1	14	15	8	10	1	10	11	39

Signed as a free agent by **Los Angeles**, August 3, 1992.

STEWART, JASON — NYI

Defense. Shoots right. 5'11", 185 lbs. Born, St. Paul, MN, April 30, 1976.
(NY Islanders' 7th choice, 142nd overall, in 1994 Entry Draft).

			Regular Season					Playoffs				
Season	Club	Lea	GP	G	A	TP	PIM	GP	G	A	TP	PIM
1992-93	Simley	HS	23	19	15	34	20	....	....	....	....	....
1993-94	Simley	HS	23	15	15	30	32	....	....	....	....	....

STEWART, MICHAEL — NYR

Defense. Shoots left. 6'2", 210 lbs. Born, Calgary, Alta., May 30, 1972.
(NY Rangers' 1st choice, 13th overall, in 1990 Entry Draft).

			Regular Season					Playoffs				
Season	Club	Lea	GP	G	A	TP	PIM	GP	G	A	TP	PIM
1989-90	Michigan State	CCHA	40	2	6	8	39	....	....	....	....	....
1990-91	Michigan State	CCHA	37	3	12	15	58	....	....	....	....	....
1991-92	Michigan State	CCHA	8	1	3	4	6	....	....	....	....	....
1992-93	Binghamton	AHL	68	2	10	12	71	1	0	0	0	0
1993-94	Binghamton	AHL	79	8	42	50	75	....	....	....	....	....

STICKNEY, BRETT

Center. Shoots left. 6'5", 205 lbs. Born, Hanover, NH, May 26, 1972.
(Chicago's 6th choice, 121st overall, in 1990 Entry Draft).

			Regular Season					Playoffs				
Season	Club	Lea	GP	G	A	TP	PIM	GP	G	A	TP	PIM
1991-92	Boston College	H.E.	29	1	2	3	10	....	....	....	....	....
1992-93	Boston College	H.E.	21	2	4	6	10	....	....	....	....	....
1993-94	Flint	ColHL	40	4	9	13	22	....	....	....	....	....

STIENBURG, TREVOR (STIGHN-buhrg)

Right wing. Shoots right. 6'1", 200 lbs. Born, Kingston, Ont., May 13, 1966.
(Quebec's 1st choice, 15th overall, in 1984 Entry Draft).

			Regular Season					Playoffs				
Season	Club	Lea	GP	G	A	TP	PIM	GP	G	A	TP	PIM
1983-84	Guelph	OHL	65	33	18	51	104	....	....	....	....	....
1984-85	Guelph	OHL	18	7	12	19	38	....	....	....	....	....
	London	OHL	22	9	11	20	45	8	1	3	4	22
1985-86	**Quebec**	**NHL**	**2**	**1**	**0**	**1**	**0**	**1**	**0**	**0**	**0**	**0**
	London	OHL	31	12	18	30	88	5	0	0	0	20
1986-87	**Quebec**	**NHL**	**6**	**1**	**0**	**1**	**12**	....	....	....	....	....
	Fredericton	AHL	48	14	12	26	123	....	....	....	....	....
1987-88	**Quebec**	**NHL**	**8**	**0**	**1**	**1**	**24**	....	....	....	....	....
	Fredericton	AHL	55	12	24	36	279	13	3	3	6	115
1988-89	**Quebec**	**NHL**	**55**	**6**	**3**	**9**	**125**	....	....	....	....	....
1989-90	Halifax	AHL	11	3	3	6	36	....	....	....	....	....
1990-91	Halifax	AHL	41	16	7	23	190	....	....	....	....	....
1991-92	New Haven	AHL	66	17	22	39	201	1	0	0	0	2
1992-93	Springfield	AHL	65	14	20	34	244	10	0	0	0	31
1993-94	Springfield	AHL	47	4	10	14	134	....	....	....	....	....
	NHL Totals		**71**	**8**	**4**	**12**	**161**	**1**	**0**	**0**	**0**	**0**

Signed as a free agent by **Hartford**, July 21, 1992.

STILLMAN, CORY — CGY.

Center. Shoots left. 6', 180 lbs. Born, Peterborough, Ont., December 20, 1973.
(Calgary's 1st choice, 6th overall, in 1992 Entry Draft).

			Regular Season					Playoffs				
Season	Club	Lea	GP	G	A	TP	PIM	GP	G	A	TP	PIM
1990-91	Windsor	OHL	64	31	70	101	31	11	3	6	9	8
1991-92	Windsor	OHL	53	29	61	90	59	7	2	4	6	8
1992-93	Peterborough	OHL	61	25	55	80	55	18	3	8	11	18
	Cdn. National	....	1	0	0	0	0	....	....	....	....	....
1993-94	Saint John	AHL	79	35	48	83	52	7	2	4	6	16

STIVER, DAN

Right wing. Shoots right. 6', 185 lbs. Born, Chicoutimi, Que., September 14, 1971.
(Toronto's 7th choice, 157th overall, in 1990 Entry Draft).

			Regular Season					Playoffs				
Season	Club	Lea	GP	G	A	TP	PIM	GP	G	A	TP	PIM
1989-90	U. of Michigan	CCHA	40	9	10	19	6	....	....	....	....	....
1990-91	U. of Michigan	CCHA	41	14	15	29	26	....	....	....	....	....
1991-92	U. of Michigan	CCHA	41	8	8	16	8	....	....	....	....	....
1992-93	U. of Michigan	CCHA	36	23	20	43	22	....	....	....	....	....
1993-94	St. John's	AHL	57	11	18	29	39	....	....	....	....	....
	Springfield	AHL	9	1	6	7	0	6	0	1	1	2

STOJANOV, ALEK (STOY-uh-nahf) VAN.

Right wing. Shoots left. 6'4", 220 lbs. Born, Windsor, Ont., April 25, 1973.
(Vancouver's 1st choice, 7th overall, in 1991 Entry Draft).

			Regular Season					Playoffs				
Season	Club	Lea	GP	G	A	TP	PIM	GP	G	A	TP	PIM
1989-90	Hamilton	OHL	37	4	4	8	91					
1990-91	Hamilton	OHL	62	25	20	45	181	4	1	1	2	14
1991-92	Guelph	OHL	33	12	15	27	91					
1992-93	Guelph	OHL	36	27	28	55	62					
	Newmarket	OHL	14	9	7	16	26	7	1	3	4	26
	Hamilton	AHL	4	4	0	4	0					
1993-94	Hamilton	AHL	4	0	1	1	5					

STOLK, DARREN (STOHLK) BOS.

Defense. Shoots left. 6'4", 210 lbs. Born, Tabler, Alta., July 22, 1968.
(Pittsburgh's 11th choice, 235th overall, in 1988 Entry Draft).

			Regular Season					Playoffs				
Season	Club	Lea	GP	G	A	TP	PIM	GP	G	A	TP	PIM
1986-87	Brandon	WHL	71	3	9	12	60					
1987-88	Lethbridge	WHL	60	3	10	13	79					
1988-89	Medicine Hat	WHL	65	8	31	39	141	3	0	0	0	2
1989-90	Muskegon	IHL	65	3	3	6	59	6	1	0	1	2
1990-91	Kansas City	IHL	23	2	10	12	36					
	Muskegon	IHL	47	2	8	10	40					
1991-92	Salt Lake	IHL	65	2	8	10	68	5	0	0	0	2
1992-93	Salt Lake	IHL	64	4	5	9	65					
1993-94	Providence	AHL	57	4	10	14	56					

Signed as a free agent by **Calgary**, August 1, 1991. Signed as a free agent by **Boston**, July 13, 1993.

STORM, JIM HFD.

Left wing. Shoots left. 6'2", 200 lbs. Born, Milford, MI, February 5, 1971.
(Hartford's 5th choice, 75th overall, in 1991 Entry Draft).

			Regular Season					Playoffs				
Season	Club	Lea	GP	G	A	TP	PIM	GP	G	A	TP	PIM
1990-91	Michigan Tech	WCHA	36	16	18	34	46					
1991-92	Michigan Tech	WCHA	39	25	33	58	12					
1992-93	Michigan Tech	WCHA	33	22	32	54	30					
1993-94	**Hartford**	**NHL**	**68**	**6**	**10**	**16**	**27**					
	NHL Totals		**68**	**6**	**10**	**16**	**27**					

STRACHAN, WAYNE NYR

Right wing. Shoots right. 5'10", 185 lbs. Born, Fort Frances, Ont., December 12, 1972.
(NY Rangers' 1st choice, 8th overall, in 1993 Supplemental Draft).

			Regular Season					Playoffs				
Season	Club	Lea	GP	G	A	TP	PIM	GP	G	A	TP	PIM
1991-92	Lake Superior	CCHA	42	12	18	30	35					
1992-93	Lake Superior	CCHA	38	20	21	41	28					
1993-94	Lake Superior	CCHA	45	24	23	47	74					

STRAKA, MARTIN (STRAH-kuh) PIT.

Center. Shoots left. 5'10", 178 lbs. Born, Plzen, Czech., September 3, 1972.
(Pittsburgh's 1st choice, 19th overall, in 1992 Entry Draft).

			Regular Season					Playoffs				
Season	Club	Lea	GP	G	A	TP	PIM	GP	G	A	TP	PIM
1989-90	Skoda Plzen	Czech.	1	0	3	3	....					
1990-91	Skoda Plzen	Czech.	47	7	24	31	6					
1991-92	Skoda Plzen	Czech.	50	27	28	55	20					
1992-93	**Pittsburgh**	**NHL**	**42**	**3**	**13**	**16**	**29**	**11**	**2**	**1**	**3**	**2**
	Cleveland	IHL	4	4	3	7	0					
1993-94	**Pittsburgh**	**NHL**	**84**	**30**	**34**	**64**	**24**	**6**	**1**	**0**	**1**	**2**
	NHL Totals		**126**	**33**	**47**	**80**	**53**	**17**	**3**	**1**	**4**	**4**

STRAUB, BRIAN

Defense. Shoots left. 6'2", 195 lbs. Born, Bozeman, MT, July 2, 1968.

			Regular Season					Playoffs				
Season	Club	Lea	GP	G	A	TP	PIM	GP	G	A	TP	PIM
1989-90	U. of Maine	H.E.	43	7	14	21	18					
1990-91	U. of Maine	H.E.	42	6	25	31	14					
1991-92	San Diego	IHL	43	3	16	19	75					
	Kalamazoo	IHL	29	2	12	14	45	11	0	5	5	6
1992-93	Kalamazoo	IHL	75	6	14	20	101					
1993-94	Moncton	AHL	76	8	24	32	107	20	1	9	10	25

Signed as a free agent by **Minnesota**, August 19, 1992.

STRBAK, MARTIN (SHTEHR-bahk) L.A.

Defense. Shoots left. 6'3", 198 lbs. Born, Presov, Czech., January 15, 1975.
(Los Angeles' 10th choice, 224th overall, in 1993 Entry Draft).

			Regular Season					Playoffs				
Season	Club	Lea	GP	G	A	TP	PIM	GP	G	A	TP	PIM
1992-93	ZPA Presov	Czech. 2	1	0	0	0	....					
1993-94	Notre Dame	SJHL	54	8	18	26	157					

STRUCH, DAVID CGY.

Center. Shoots left. 5'10", 180 lbs. Born, Flin Flon, Man., February 11, 1971.
(Calgary's 10th choice, 195th overall, in 1991 Entry Draft).

			Regular Season					Playoffs				
Season	Club	Lea	GP	G	A	TP	PIM	GP	G	A	TP	PIM
1990-91	Saskatoon	WHL	72	45	57	102	69					
1991-92	Saskatoon	WHL	47	29	26	55	34	22	8	15	23	26
	Salt Lake	IHL	12	4	1	5	8					
1992-93	Salt Lake	IHL	78	20	22	42	73					
1993-94	**Calgary**	**NHL**	**4**	**0**	**0**	**0**	**4**					
	Saint John	AHL	58	18	25	43	87	7	0	1	1	4
	NHL Totals		**4**	**0**	**0**	**0**	**4**					

STRUDWICK, JASON NYI

Defense. Shoots left. 6'3", 210 lbs. Born, Edmonton, Alta., July 17, 1975.
(NY Islanders' 3rd choice, 63rd overall, in 1994 Entry Draft).

			Regular Season					Playoffs				
Season	Club	Lea	GP	G	A	TP	PIM	GP	G	A	TP	PIM
1992-93	Edmonton	Midget	33	8	20	28	135					
1993-94	Kamloops	WHL	61	6	8	14	118	19	0	4	4	24

STUMPEL, JOZEF (STUM-puhl) BOS.

Center. Shoots right. 6'1", 208 lbs. Born, Nitra, Czech., June 20, 1972.
(Boston's 2nd choice, 40th overall, in 1991 Entry Draft).

			Regular Season					Playoffs				
Season	Club	Lea	GP	G	A	TP	PIM	GP	G	A	TP	PIM
1989-90	Nitra	Czech. 2	38	12	11	23	....					
1990-91	Nitra	Czech.	49	23	22	45	14					
1991-92	Koln	Ger.	37	20	19	39	35					
	Boston	**NHL**	**4**	**1**	**0**	**1**	**0**					
1992-93	**Boston**	**NHL**	**13**	**1**	**3**	**4**	**4**					
	Providence	AHL	56	31	61	92	26	6	4	4	8	0
1993-94	**Boston**	**NHL**	**59**	**8**	**15**	**23**	**14**	**13**	**1**	**7**	**8**	**4**
	Providence	AHL	17	5	12	17	4					
	NHL Totals		**76**	**10**	**18**	**28**	**18**	**13**	**1**	**7**	**8**	**4**

SULLIVAN, BRIAN

Right wing. Shoots right. 6'4", 195 lbs. Born, South Windsor, CT, April 23, 1969.
(New Jersey's 3rd choice, 65th overall, in 1987 Entry Draft).

			Regular Season					Playoffs				
Season	Club	Lea	GP	G	A	TP	PIM	GP	G	A	TP	PIM
1987-88	Northeastern	H.E.	37	20	12	32	18					
1988-89	Northeastern	H.E.	34	13	14	27	65					
1989-90	Northeastern	H.E.	34	24	21	45	72					
1990-91	Northeastern	H.E.	32	17	23	40	75					
1991-92	Utica	AHL	70	23	24	47	58	4	0	4	4	6
1992-93	**New Jersey**	**NHL**	**2**	**0**	**1**	**1**	**0**					
	Utica	AHL	75	30	27	57	88	5	0	0	0	12
1993-94	Albany	AHL	77	31	30	61	140	5	1	1	2	18
	NHL Totals		**2**	**0**	**1**	**1**	**0**					

SULLIVAN, MICHAEL (MIKE)

Center. Shoots left. 6'1", 190 lbs. Born, Woburn, MA, October 16, 1973.
(Detroit's 4th choice, 118th overall, in 1992 Entry Draft).

			Regular Season					Playoffs				
Season	Club	Lea	GP	G	A	TP	PIM	GP	G	A	TP	PIM
1992-93	N. Hampshire	H.E.	36	5	5	10	12					
1993-94	N. Hampshire	H.E.	40	13	14	27	30					

SULLIVAN, MIKE CGY.

Center. Shoots left. 6'2", 190 lbs. Born, Marshfield, MA, February 27, 1968.
(NY Rangers' 4th choice, 69th overall, in 1987 Entry Draft).

			Regular Season					Playoffs				
Season	Club	Lea	GP	G	A	TP	PIM	GP	G	A	TP	PIM
1986-87	Boston U.	H.E.	37	13	18	31	18					
1987-88	Boston U.	H.E.	30	18	22	40	30					
1988-89	Boston U.	H.E.	36	19	17	36	30					
1989-90	Boston U.	H.E.	38	11	20	31	26					
1990-91	San Diego	IHL	74	12	23	35	27					
1991-92	**San Jose**	**NHL**	**64**	**8**	**11**	**19**	**15**					
	Kansas City	IHL	10	2	8	10	8					
1992-93	**San Jose**	**NHL**	**81**	**6**	**8**	**14**	**30**					
1993-94	**San Jose**	**NHL**	**26**	**2**	**2**	**4**	**4**					
	Kansas City	IHL	6	3	3	6	0					
	Calgary	**NHL**	**19**	**2**	**3**	**5**	**6**	**7**	**1**	**1**	**2**	**8**
	Saint John	AHL	5	2	0	2	4					
	NHL Totals		**190**	**18**	**24**	**42**	**55**	**7**	**1**	**1**	**2**	**8**

Rights traded to **Minnesota** by **NY Rangers** with Paul Jerrard, the rights to Bret Barnett, and Los Angeles' third round choice (previously acquired by NY Rangers — Minnesota selected Murray Garbutt) in 1989 Entry Draft for Brian Lawton, Igor Liba and the rights to Eric Bennett, October 11, 1988. Signed as a free agent by **San Jose**, August 9, 1991. Claimed on waivers by **Calgary** from **San Jose**, January 6, 1994.

SUNDBLAD, NIKLAS CGY.

Right wing. Shoots right. 6'1", 200 lbs. Born, Stockholm, Sweden, January 3, 1973.
(Calgary's 1st choice, 19th overall, in 1991 Entry Draft).

			Regular Season					Playoffs				
Season	Club	Lea	GP	G	A	TP	PIM	GP	G	A	TP	PIM
1990-91	AIK	Swe.	39	1	3	4	14					
1991-92	AIK	Swe.	33	9	2	11	20	3	3	1	4	0
1992-93	AIK	Swe.	22	5	4	9	56					
1993-94	Saint John	AHL	76	13	19	32	75	4	1	1	2	2

SUNDIN, MATS (SUHN-deen) TOR.

Center/Right wing. Shoots right. 6'4", 204 lbs. Born, Bromma, Sweden, February 13, 1971.
(Quebec's 1st choice, 1st overall, in 1989 Entry Draft).

			Regular Season					Playoffs				
Season	Club	Lea	GP	G	A	TP	PIM	GP	G	A	TP	PIM
1988-89	Nacka	Swe. 2	25	10	8	18	18					
1989-90	Djurgarden	Swe.	34	10	8	18	16	8	7	0	7	4
1990-91	**Quebec**	**NHL**	**80**	**23**	**36**	**59**	**58**					
1991-92	**Quebec**	**NHL**	**80**	**33**	**43**	**76**	**103**					
1992-93	**Quebec**	**NHL**	**80**	**47**	**67**	**114**	**96**	**6**	**3**	**1**	**4**	**6**
1993-94	**Quebec**	**NHL**	**84**	**32**	**53**	**85**	**60**					
	NHL Totals		**324**	**135**	**199**	**334**	**317**	**6**	**3**	**1**	**4**	**6**

Traded to **Toronto** by **Quebec** with Garth Butcher, Todd Warriner and Philadelphia's first round choice (previously acquired by Quebec — later traded to Washington — Washington selected Nolan Baumgartner) in 1994 Entry Draft for Wendel Clark, Sylvain Lefebvre, Landon Wilson and Toronto's first round choice (Jeffrey Kealty) in 1994 Entry Draft, June 28, 1994.

SUNDSTROM, NIKLAS NYR

Left wing. Shoots left. 6', 183 lbs. Born, Ornskoldsvik, Sweden, June 6, 1975.
(NY Rangers' 1st choice, 8th overall, in 1993 Entry Draft).

			Regular Season					Playoffs				
Season	Club	Lea	GP	G	A	TP	PIM	GP	G	A	TP	PIM
1991-92	MoDo	Swe.	9	1	3	4	0					
1992-93	MoDo	Swe.	40	7	11	18	18	3	0	0	0	0
1993-94	MoDo	Swe.	37	7	12	19	28	11	4	3	7	2

SUTER, GARY (SOO-tuhr) CHI.

Defense. Shoots left. 6', 190 lbs. Born, Madison, WI, June 24, 1964.
(Calgary's 9th choice, 180th overall, in 1984 Entry Draft).

			Regular Season					Playoffs				
Season	Club	Lea	GP	G	A	TP	PIM	GP	G	A	TP	PIM
1983-84	U. Wisconsin	WCHA	35	4	18	22	32	....	....	....	....	....
1984-85	U. Wisconsin	WCHA	39	12	39	51	110	....	....	....	....	....
1985-86ab	**Calgary**	**NHL**	80	18	50	68	141	10	2	8	10	8
1986-87	**Calgary**	**NHL**	68	9	40	49	70	6	0	3	3	10
1987-88c	**Calgary**	**NHL**	75	21	70	91	124	9	1	9	10	6
1988-89	**Calgary**	**NHL**	63	13	49	62	78	5	0	3	3	10
1989-90	**Calgary**	**NHL**	76	16	60	76	97	6	0	1	1	14
1990-91	**Calgary**	**NHL**	79	12	58	70	102	7	1	6	7	12
1991-92	**Calgary**	**NHL**	70	12	43	55	128	....	....	....	....	....
1992-93	**Calgary**	**NHL**	81	23	58	81	112	6	2	3	5	8
1993-94	**Calgary**	**NHL**	25	4	9	13	20	....	....	....	....	....
	Chicago	**NHL**	16	2	3	5	18	6	3	2	5	6
	NHL Totals		633	130	440	570	890	55	9	35	44	74

a Won Calder Memorial Trophy (1986)
b NHL All-Rookie Team (1986)
c NHL Second All-Star Team (1988)

Played in NHL All-Star Game (1986, 1988, 1989, 1991)

Traded to **Hartford** by **Calgary** with Paul Ranheim and Ted Drury for James Patrick, Zarley Zalapski and Michael Nylander, March 10, 1994. Traded to **Chicago** by **Hartford** with Randy Cunneyworth and a future draft choice for Frantisek Kucera and Jocelyn Lemieux, March 11, 1994.

SUTTER, BRENT (SUH-tuhr) CHI.

Center. Shoots right. 5'11", 180 lbs. Born, Viking, Alta., June 10, 1962.
(NY Islanders' 1st choice, 17th overall, in 1980 Entry Draft).

			Regular Season					Playoffs				
Season	Club	Lea	GP	G	A	TP	PIM	GP	G	A	TP	PIM
1979-80	Red Deer	AJHL	59	70	101	171	....	....	....	....	....	....
	Lethbridge	WHL	5	1	0	1	2	....	....	....	....	....
1980-81	**NY Islanders**	**NHL**	3	2	2	4	0	....	....	....	....	....
	Lethbridge	WHL	68	54	54	108	116	9	6	4	10	51
1981-82	**NY Islanders**	**NHL**	43	21	22	43	114	19	2	6	8	36
	Lethbridge	WHL	34	46	33	79	162	....	....	....	....	....
1982-83	**NY Islanders**	**NHL**	80	21	19	40	128	20	10	11	21	26
1983-84	**NY Islanders**	**NHL**	69	34	15	49	69	20	4	10	14	18
1984-85	**NY Islanders**	**NHL**	72	42	60	102	51	10	3	3	6	14
1985-86	**NY Islanders**	**NHL**	61	24	31	55	74	3	0	1	1	2
1986-87	**NY Islanders**	**NHL**	69	27	36	63	73	5	1	0	1	4
1987-88	**NY Islanders**	**NHL**	70	29	31	60	55	6	2	1	3	18
1988-89	**NY Islanders**	**NHL**	77	29	34	63	77	....	....	....	....	....
1989-90	**NY Islanders**	**NHL**	67	33	35	68	65	5	2	3	5	2
1990-91	**NY Islanders**	**NHL**	75	21	32	53	49	....	....	....	....	....
1991-92	**NY Islanders**	**NHL**	8	4	6	10	6	....	....	....	....	....
	Chicago	**NHL**	61	18	32	50	30	18	3	5	8	22
1992-93	**Chicago**	**NHL**	65	20	34	54	67	4	1	1	2	4
1993-94	**Chicago**	**NHL**	73	9	29	38	43	6	0	0	0	2
	NHL Totals		893	334	418	752	901	116	28	41	69	148

Played in NHL All-Star Game (1985)

Traded to **Chicago** by **NY Islanders** with Brad Lauer for Adam Creighton and Steve Thomas, October 25, 1991.

SUTTER, RICH (SUH-tuhr) CHI.

Right wing. Shoots right. 5'11", 188 lbs. Born, Viking, Alta., December 2, 1963.
(Pittsburgh's 1st choice, 10th overall, in 1982 Entry Draft).

			Regular Season					Playoffs				
Season	Club	Lea	GP	G	A	TP	PIM	GP	G	A	TP	PIM
1980-81	Lethbridge	WHL	72	23	18	41	255	9	3	1	4	35
1981-82	Lethbridge	WHL	57	38	31	69	263	12	3	3	6	55
1982-83	**Pittsburgh**	**NHL**	4	0	0	0	0	....	....	....	....	....
	Lethbridge	WHL	64	37	30	67	200	17	14	9	23	43
1983-84	**Pittsburgh**	**NHL**	5	0	0	0	0	....	....	....	....	....
	Baltimore	AHL	2	0	1	1	0	....	....	....	....	....
	Philadelphia	**NHL**	70	16	12	28	93	3	0	0	0	15
1984-85	**Philadelphia**	**NHL**	56	6	10	16	89	11	3	0	3	10
	Hershey	AHL	13	3	7	10	14	....	....	....	....	....
1985-86	**Philadelphia**	**NHL**	78	14	25	39	199	5	2	0	2	19
1986-87	**Vancouver**	**NHL**	74	20	22	42	113	....	....	....	....	....
1987-88	**Vancouver**	**NHL**	80	15	15	30	165	....	....	....	....	....
1988-89	**Vancouver**	**NHL**	75	17	15	32	122	7	2	1	3	12
1989-90	**Vancouver**	**NHL**	62	9	9	18	133	....	....	....	....	....
	St. Louis	**NHL**	12	2	0	2	22	12	2	1	3	39
1990-91	**St. Louis**	**NHL**	77	16	11	27	122	13	4	2	6	16
1991-92	**St. Louis**	**NHL**	77	9	16	25	107	6	0	0	0	8
1992-93	**St. Louis**	**NHL**	84	13	14	27	100	11	0	1	1	10
1993-94	**Chicago**	**NHL**	83	12	14	26	108	6	0	0	0	2
	NHL Totals		837	149	163	312	1373	74	13	5	18	131

Traded to **Philadelphia** by **Pittsburgh** with Pittsburgh's second round (Greg Smyth) and third round (David McLay) choices in 1984 Entry Draft for Andy Brickley, Mark Taylor, Ron Flockhart, Philadelphia's first round (Roger Belanger) and third round (later traded to Vancouver — Vancouver selected Mike Stevens) choices in 1984 Entry Draft, October 23, 1983. Traded to **Vancouver** by **Philadelphia**, with Dave Richter and Vancouver's third round choice (previously acquired by Philadelphia — Vancouver selected Don Gibson) in 1986 Entry Draft for J.J. Daigneault and Vancouver's second round choice (Kent Hawley) in 1986 Entry Draft, June 6, 1986. Traded to **St Louis** by **Vancouver** with Harold Snepsts and St. Louis' second round choice (previously acquired by Vancouver — St. Louis selected Craig Johnson) in 1990 Entry Draft for Adrien Plavsic, Montreal's first round choice (previously acquired by St. Louis — Vancouver selected Shawn Antoski) in 1990 Entry Draft and St. Louis' second round choice (later traded to Montreal — Montreal selected Craig Darby) in 1991 Entry Draft, March 6, 1990. Claimed by **Chicago** from **St. Louis** in NHL Waiver Draft, October 3, 1993.

SUTTER, RON (SUH-tuhr) NYI

Center. Shoots right. 6', 180 lbs. Born, Viking, Alta., December 2, 1963.
(Philadelphia's 1st choice, 4th overall, in 1982 Entry Draft).

			Regular Season					Playoffs				
Season	Club	Lea	GP	G	A	TP	PIM	GP	G	A	TP	PIM
1980-81	Lethbridge	WHL	72	13	32	45	152	9	2	5	7	29
1981-82	Lethbridge	WHL	59	38	54	92	207	12	6	5	11	28
1982-83	**Philadelphia**	**NHL**	10	1	1	2	9	....	....	....	....	....
	Lethbridge	WHL	58	35	48	83	98	20	*22	*19	*41	45
1983-84	**Philadelphia**	**NHL**	79	19	32	51	101	3	0	0	0	22
1984-85	**Philadelphia**	**NHL**	73	16	29	45	94	19	4	8	12	28
1985-86	**Philadelphia**	**NHL**	75	18	42	60	159	5	0	2	2	10
1986-87	**Philadelphia**	**NHL**	39	10	17	27	69	16	1	7	8	12
1987-88	**Philadelphia**	**NHL**	69	8	25	33	146	7	0	1	1	26
1988-89	**Philadelphia**	**NHL**	55	26	22	48	80	19	1	9	10	51
1989-90	**Philadelphia**	**NHL**	75	22	26	48	104	....	....	....	....	....
1990-91	**Philadelphia**	**NHL**	80	17	28	45	92	....	....	....	....	....
1991-92	**St. Louis**	**NHL**	68	19	27	46	91	6	1	3	4	8
1992-93	**St. Louis**	**NHL**	59	12	15	27	99	....	....	....	....	....
1993-94	**St. Louis**	**NHL**	36	6	12	18	46	....	....	....	....	....
	Quebec	**NHL**	37	9	13	22	44	....	....	....	....	....
	NHL Totals		755	183	289	472	1134	75	7	30	37	157

Traded to **St. Louis** by **Philadelphia** with Murray Baron for Dan Quinn and Rod Brind'Amour, September 22, 1991. Traded to **Quebec** by **St. Louis** with Garth Butcher and Bob Bassen for Steve Duchesne and Denis Chasse, January 23, 1994. Traded to **NY Islanders** by **Quebec** with Quebec's first round choice (Brett Lindros) in 1994 Entry Draft for Uwe Krupp and **NY Islanders'** first round choice (Wade Belak) in 1994 Entry Draft, June 28, 1994.

SUTTON, KEN BUF.

Defense. Shoots left. 6', 198 lbs. Born, Edmonton, Alta., November 5, 1969.
(Buffalo's 4th choice, 98th overall, in 1989 Entry Draft).

			Regular Season					Playoffs				
Season	Club	Lea	GP	G	A	TP	PIM	GP	G	A	TP	PIM
1988-89a	Saskatoon	WHL	71	22	31	53	104	8	2	5	7	12
1989-90	Rochester	AHL	57	5	14	19	83	11	1	6	7	15
1990-91	**Buffalo**	**NHL**	15	3	6	9	13	6	0	1	1	2
	Rochester	AHL	62	7	24	31	65	3	1	1	2	14
1991-92	**Buffalo**	**NHL**	64	2	18	20	71	7	0	2	2	4
1992-93	**Buffalo**	**NHL**	63	8	14	22	30	8	3	1	4	8
1993-94	**Buffalo**	**NHL**	78	4	20	24	71	4	0	0	0	2
	NHL Totals		220	17	58	75	185	25	3	4	7	16

a Memorial Cup All-Star Team (1989)

SVARTVADET, PER DAL.

Center. Shoots left. 6'1", 180 lbs. Born, Solleftea, Sweden, May 17, 1975.
(Dallas' 5th choice, 139th overall, in 1993 Entry Draft).

			Regular Season					Playoffs				
Season	Club	Lea	GP	G	A	TP	PIM	GP	G	A	TP	PIM
1992-93	MoDo	Swe.	2	0	0	0	0	....	....	....	....	....
1993-94	MoDo	Swe.	36	2	1	3	4	11	0	0	0	6

SVEHLA, ROBERT (SCHVE-khlah) CGY.

Defense. Shoots right. 6', 190 lbs. Born, Martin, Czech., January 2, 1969.
(Calgary's 4th choice, 78th overall, in 1992 Entry Draft).

			Regular Season					Playoffs				
Season	Club	Lea	GP	G	A	TP	PIM	GP	G	A	TP	PIM
1989-90	Dukla Trencin	Czech.	29	4	3	7	....	....	....	....	....	....
1990-91	Dukla Trencin	Czech.	52	16	9	25	62	....	....	....	....	....
1991-92	Dukla Trencin	Czech.	51	23	28	51	74	....	....	....	....	....
1992-93	Malmo	Swe.	40	19	10	29	86	6	0	1	1	14
1993-94	Malmo	Swe.	37	14	25	39	127	10	5	1	6	23

SVENSSON, MAGNUS (SVEHN-suhn) CGY.

Defense. Shoots left. 5'11", 180 lbs. Born, Tranas, Sweden, March 1, 1963.
(Calgary's 13th choice, 250th overall, in 1987 Entry Draft).

			Regular Season					Playoffs				
Season	Club	Lea	GP	G	A	TP	PIM	GP	G	A	TP	PIM
1983-84	Leksand	Swe.	35	3	8	11	20	....	....	....	....	....
1984-85	Leksand	Swe.	35	8	7	15	22	....	....	....	....	....
1985-86	Leksand	Swe.	36	6	9	15	62	....	....	....	....	....
1986-87	Leksand	Swe.	33	8	16	24	42	....	....	....	....	....
1987-88	Leksand	Swe.	40	12	11	23	20	3	0	0	0	8
1988-89	Leksand	Swe.	39	15	22	37	40	9	3	5	8	8
1989-90	Leksand	Swe.	26	11	12	23	60	1	0	0	0	0
1990-91	Lugano	Switz.	33	16	20	36	....	11	3	2	5	....
1991-92	Leksand	Swe.	22	4	10	14	32	....	....	....	....	....
1992-93	Leksand	Swe.	37	10	17	27	36	2	0	2	2	0
1993-94	Leksand	Swe.	39	13	16	29	22	4	3	1	4	0

SVOBODA, PETR (svah-BOH-duh) BUF.

Defense. Shoots left. 6'1", 174 lbs. Born, Most, Czech., February 14, 1966.
(Montreal's 1st choice, 5th overall, in 1984 Entry Draft).

			Regular Season					Playoffs				
Season	Club	Lea	GP	G	A	TP	PIM	GP	G	A	TP	PIM
1982-83	Litvinov	Czech.	4	0	0	0	2	....	....	....	....	....
1983-84	Litvinov	Czech.	18	3	1	4	20	....	....	....	....	....
1984-85	**Montreal**	**NHL**	73	4	27	31	65	7	1	1	2	12
1985-86	**Montreal**	**NHL**	73	1	18	19	93	8	0	0	0	21
1986-87	**Montreal**	**NHL**	70	5	17	22	63	14	0	5	5	10
1987-88	**Montreal**	**NHL**	69	7	22	29	149	10	0	5	5	12
1988-89	**Montreal**	**NHL**	71	8	37	45	147	21	1	11	12	16
1989-90	**Montreal**	**NHL**	60	5	31	36	98	10	0	5	5	7
1990-91	**Montreal**	**NHL**	60	4	22	26	52	2	0	1	1	2
1991-92	**Montreal**	**NHL**	58	5	16	21	94	....	....	....	....	....
	Buffalo	**NHL**	13	1	6	7	52	7	1	4	5	6
1992-93	**Buffalo**	**NHL**	40	2	24	26	59	....	....	....	....	....
1993-94	**Buffalo**	**NHL**	60	2	14	16	89	3	0	0	0	4
	NHL Totals		647	44	234	278	961	82	3	32	35	90

Traded to **Buffalo** by **Montreal** for Kevin Haller, March 10, 1992.

SWANSON, BRIAN S.J.

Center. Shoots left. 5'10", 180 lbs. Born, Anchorage, AK, March 24, 1976.
(San Jose's 5th choice, 115th overall, in 1994 Entry Draft).

			Regular Season					Playoffs				
Season	Club	Lea	GP	G	A	TP	PIM	GP	G	A	TP	PIM
1992-93	Anchorage	Midget	45	40	50	90	12	....	....	....	....	....
1993-94	Omaha	USHL	47	38	42	80	40	....	....	....	....	....

SWEENEY, BOB — BUF.

Center/Right wing. Shoots right. 6'3", 200 lbs. Born, Concord, MA, January 25, 1964.
(Boston's 6th choice, 123rd overall, in 1982 Entry Draft).

			Regular Season					Playoffs				
Season	Club	Lea	GP	G	A	TP	PIM	GP	G	A	TP	PIM
1982-83	Boston College	ECAC	30	17	11	28	10	....	....	....	....	....
1983-84	Boston College	ECAC	23	14	7	21	10	....	....	....	....	....
1984-85a	Boston College	ECAC	44	32	32	64	43	....	....	....	....	....
1985-86	Boston College	H.E.	41	15	24	39	52	....	....	....	....	....
1986-87	**Boston**	**NHL**	**14**	**2**	**4**	**6**	**21**	**3**	**0**	**0**	**0**	**0**
	Moncton	AHL	58	29	26	55	81	4	0	2	2	13
1987-88	**Boston**	**NHL**	**80**	**22**	**23**	**45**	**73**	**23**	**6**	**8**	**14**	**66**
1988-89	**Boston**	**NHL**	**75**	**14**	**14**	**28**	**99**	**10**	**2**	**4**	**6**	**19**
1989-90	**Boston**	**NHL**	**70**	**22**	**24**	**46**	**93**	**20**	**0**	**2**	**2**	**30**
1990-91	**Boston**	**NHL**	**80**	**15**	**33**	**48**	**115**	**17**	**4**	**2**	**6**	**45**
1991-92	**Boston**	**NHL**	**63**	**6**	**14**	**20**	**103**	**14**	**1**	**0**	**1**	**25**
	Maine	AHL	1	1	0	1	0	....	....	....	....	....
1992-93	**Buffalo**	**NHL**	**80**	**21**	**26**	**47**	**118**	**8**	**2**	**2**	**4**	**8**
1993-94	**Buffalo**	**NHL**	**60**	**11**	**14**	**25**	**94**	**1**	**0**	**0**	**0**	**0**
	NHL Totals		**522**	**113**	**152**	**265**	**716**	**96**	**15**	**18**	**33**	**193**

a ECAC Second Team All-Star (1985)

Claimed on waivers by **Buffalo** from **Boston**, October 9, 1992.

SWEENEY, DON — BOS.

Defense. Shoots left. 5'10", 188 lbs. Born, St. Stephen, N.B., August 17, 1966.
(Boston's 8th choice, 166th overall, in 1984 Entry Draft).

			Regular Season					Playoffs				
Season	Club	Lea	GP	G	A	TP	PIM	GP	G	A	TP	PIM
1984-85	Harvard	ECAC	29	3	7	10	30	....	....	....	....	....
1985-86	Harvard	ECAC	31	4	5	9	12	....	....	....	....	....
1986-87	Harvard	ECAC	34	7	4	11	22	....	....	....	....	....
1987-88ab	Harvard	ECAC	30	6	23	29	37	....	....	....	....	....
	Maine	AHL	....	....	....	....	....	6	1	3	4	0
1988-89	**Boston**	**NHL**	**36**	**3**	**5**	**8**	**20**	....	....	....	....	....
	Maine	AHL	42	8	17	25	24	....	....	....	....	....
1989-90	**Boston**	**NHL**	**58**	**3**	**5**	**8**	**58**	**21**	**1**	**5**	**6**	**18**
	Maine	AHL	11	0	8	8	8	....	....	....	....	....
1990-91	**Boston**	**NHL**	**77**	**8**	**13**	**21**	**67**	**19**	**3**	**0**	**3**	**25**
1991-92	**Boston**	**NHL**	**75**	**3**	**11**	**14**	**74**	**15**	**0**	**0**	**0**	**10**
1992-93	**Boston**	**NHL**	**84**	**7**	**27**	**34**	**68**	**4**	**0**	**0**	**0**	**4**
1993-94	**Boston**	**NHL**	**75**	**6**	**15**	**21**	**50**	**12**	**2**	**1**	**3**	**4**
	NHL Totals		**405**	**30**	**76**	**106**	**337**	**71**	**6**	**6**	**12**	**61**

a NCAA East All-American Team (1988)
b ECAC First All-Star Team (1988)

SWEENEY, TIM — ANA.

Left wing. Shoots left. 5'11", 185 lbs. Born, Boston, MA, April 12, 1967.
(Calgary's 7th choice, 122nd overall, in 1985 Entry Draft).

			Regular Season					Playoffs				
Season	Club	Lea	GP	G	A	TP	PIM	GP	G	A	TP	PIM
1985-86	Boston College	H.E.	32	8	4	12	8	....	....	....	....	....
1986-87	Boston College	H.E.	38	31	18	49	28	....	....	....	....	....
1987-88	Boston College	H.E.	18	9	11	20	18	....	....	....	....	....
1988-89ab	Boston College	H.E.	39	29	44	73	26	....	....	....	....	....
1989-90cd	Salt Lake	IHL	81	46	51	97	32	11	5	4	9	4
1990-91	**Calgary**	**NHL**	**42**	**7**	**9**	**16**	**8**	....	....	....	....	....
	Salt Lake	IHL	31	19	16	35	8	4	3	3	6	0
1991-92	U.S. National	....	21	9	11	20	10	....	....	....	....	....
	U.S. Olympic	....	8	3	4	7	6	....	....	....	....	....
	Calgary	**NHL**	**11**	**1**	**2**	**3**	**4**	....	....	....	....	....
1992-93	**Boston**	**NHL**	**14**	**1**	**7**	**8**	**6**	**3**	**0**	**0**	**0**	**0**
e	Providence	AHL	60	41	55	96	32	3	2	2	4	0
1993-94	**Anaheim**	**NHL**	**78**	**16**	**27**	**43**	**49**	....	....	....	....	....
	NHL Totals		**145**	**25**	**45**	**70**	**67**	**3**	**0**	**0**	**0**	**0**

a Hockey East First All-Star Team (1989)
b NCAA East Second All-American Team (1989)
c IHL Second All-Star Team (1990)
d Won Ken McKenzie Trophy (Outstanding U.S.-born rookie - IHL) (1990)
e AHL Second All-Star Team (1993)

Signed as a free agent by **Boston**, September 16, 1992. Claimed by **Anaheim** from **Boston** in Expansion Draft, June 24, 1993.

SWINSON, WES — HFD.

Defense. Shoots left. 6'2", 183 lbs. Born, Peterborough, Ont., May 26, 1975.
(Hartford's 7th choice, 240th overall, in 1993 Entry Draft).

			Regular Season					Playoffs				
Season	Club	Lea	GP	G	A	TP	PIM	GP	G	A	TP	PIM
1992-93	Kitchener	OHL	61	0	16	16	103	6	0	2	2	14
1993-94	Kitchener	OHL	64	26	46	72	111	5	2	6	8	18

SYCHRA, MARTIN — MTL.

Center. Shoots left. 6'1", 180 lbs. Born, Brno, Czech., June 19, 1974.
(Montreal's 8th choice, 140th overall, in 1992 Entry Draft).

			Regular Season					Playoffs				
Season	Club	Lea	GP	G	A	TP	PIM	GP	G	A	TP	PIM
1991-92	Zetor Brno	Czech.	14	2	2	4	2	....	....	....	....	....
1992-93	Dukla Trencin	Czech.	4	0	1	1	....	....	....	....	....	....
	Dukla Jihlava	Czech.	14	1	2	3	....	....	....	....	....	....
1993-94	Kingston	OHL	59	29	32	61	32	6	0	3	3	7

SYDOR, DARRYL (sih-DOHR) — L.A.

Defense. Shoots left. 6', 205 lbs. Born, Edmonton, Alta., May 13, 1972.
(Los Angeles' 1st choice, 7th overall, in 1990 Entry Draft).

			Regular Season					Playoffs				
Season	Club	Lea	GP	G	A	TP	PIM	GP	G	A	TP	PIM
1988-89	Kamloops	WHL	65	12	14	26	86	15	1	4	5	19
1989-90a	Kamloops	WHL	67	29	66	95	129	17	2	9	11	28
1990-91a	Kamloops	WHL	66	27	78	105	88	12	3	*22	25	10
1991-92	**Los Angeles**	**NHL**	**18**	**1**	**5**	**6**	**22**	....	....	....	....	....
a	Kamloops	WHL	29	9	39	48	43	17	3	15	18	18
1992-93	**Los Angeles**	**NHL**	**80**	**6**	**23**	**29**	**63**	**24**	**3**	**8**	**11**	**16**
1993-94	**Los Angeles**	**NHL**	**84**	**8**	**27**	**35**	**94**	....	....	....	....	....
	NHL Totals		**182**	**15**	**55**	**70**	**179**	**24**	**3**	**8**	**11**	**16**

a WHL West First All-Star Team (1990, 1991, 1992)

SYKORA, MICHAL (SEE-koh-ra) — S.J.

Defense. Shoots left. 6'5", 225 lbs. Born, Pardubice, Czech., July 5, 1973.
(San Jose's 6th choice, 123rd overall, in 1992 Entry Draft).

			Regular Season					Playoffs				
Season	Club	Lea	GP	G	A	TP	PIM	GP	G	A	TP	PIM
1990-91	Pardubice	Czech.	2	0	0	0	....	....	....	....	....	....
1991-92	Tacoma	WHL	61	13	23	36	66	4	0	2	2	2
1992-93a	Tacoma	WHL	70	23	50	73	73	7	4	8	12	2
1993-94	**San Jose**	**NHL**	**22**	**1**	**4**	**5**	**14**	....	....	....	....	....
	Kansas City	IHL	47	5	11	16	30	....	....	....	....	....
	NHL Totals		**22**	**1**	**4**	**5**	**14**	....	....	....	....	....

a WHL West First All-Star Team (1993)

SYLVESTER, DEAN — S.J.

Right wing. Shoots right. 6'2", 185 lbs. Born, Hanson, MA, December 30, 1972.
(San Jose's 1st choice, 2nd overall, in 1993 Supplemental Draft).

			Regular Season					Playoffs				
Season	Club	Lea	GP	G	A	TP	PIM	GP	G	A	TP	PIM
1991-92	Kent State	CCHA	31	7	21	28	....	....	....	....	....	....
1992-93	Kent State	CCHA	38	33	20	53	28	....	....	....	....	....
1993-94	Kent State	CCHA	39	22	24	46	28	....	....	....	....	....

SYLVESTER, DEREK — CGY.

Right wing. Shoots right. 6'2", 215 lbs. Born, Columbus, OH, May 15, 1975.
(Calgary's 9th choice, 200th overall, in 1993 Entry Draft).

			Regular Season					Playoffs				
Season	Club	Lea	GP	G	A	TP	PIM	GP	G	A	TP	PIM
1992-93	Niagara Falls	OHL	23	3	3	6	27	2	0	0	0	4
1993-94	Niagara Falls	OHL	61	4	15	19	83	....	....	....	....	....

SYMES, BRAD — EDM.

Defense. Shoots left. 6'2", 210 lbs. Born, Edmonton, Alta., April 26, 1976.
(Edmonton's 5th choice, 60th overall, in 1994 Entry Draft).

			Regular Season					Playoffs				
Season	Club	Lea	GP	G	A	TP	PIM	GP	G	A	TP	PIM
1992-93	Portland	WHL	68	4	2	6	107	16	0	1	1	7
1993-94	Portland	WHL	71	7	15	22	170	....	....	....	....	....

SZOKE, MARK — T.B.

Left wing. Shoots left. 5'9", 176 lbs. Born, High Level, Alta., August 12, 1974.
(Tampa Bay's 11th choice, 263rd overall, in 1993 Entry Draft).

			Regular Season					Playoffs				
Season	Club	Lea	GP	G	A	TP	PIM	GP	G	A	TP	PIM
1992-93	Lethbridge	WHL	71	55	44	99	152	4	3	1	4	8
1993-94	Lethbridge	WHL	72	42	48	90	151	9	2	8	10	8

TAGLIANETTI, PETER (TAG-lee-uh-NEH-tee) — PIT.

Defense. Shoots left. 6'2", 200 lbs. Born, Framingham, MA, August 15, 1963.
(Winnipeg's 4th choice, 43rd overall, in 1983 Entry Draft).

			Regular Season					Playoffs				
Season	Club	Lea	GP	G	A	TP	PIM	GP	G	A	TP	PIM
1981-82	Providence	ECAC	2	0	0	0	2	....	....	....	....	....
1982-83	Providence	ECAC	43	4	17	21	68	....	....	....	....	....
1983-84	Providence	ECAC	30	4	25	29	68	....	....	....	....	....
1984-85	**Winnipeg**	**NHL**	**1**	**0**	**0**	**0**	**0**	**1**	**0**	**0**	**0**	**0**
a	Providence	H.E.	35	6	18	24	32	....	....	....	....	....
1985-86	**Winnipeg**	**NHL**	**18**	**0**	**0**	**0**	**48**	**3**	**0**	**0**	**0**	**2**
	Sherbrooke	AHL	24	1	18	9	75	....	....	....	....	....
1986-87	**Winnipeg**	**NHL**	**3**	**0**	**0**	**0**	**12**	....	....	....	....	....
	Sherbrooke	AHL	54	5	14	19	104	10	2	5	7	25
1987-88	**Winnipeg**	**NHL**	**70**	**6**	**17**	**23**	**182**	**5**	**1**	**1**	**2**	**12**
1988-89	**Winnipeg**	**NHL**	**66**	**1**	**14**	**15**	**226**	....	....	....	....	....
1989-90	**Winnipeg**	**NHL**	**49**	**3**	**6**	**9**	**136**	**5**	**0**	**0**	**0**	**6**
	Moncton	AHL	3	0	2	2	2	....	....	....	....	....
1990-91	**Minnesota**	**NHL**	**16**	**0**	**1**	**1**	**14**	....	....	....	....	....
	Pittsburgh	**NHL**	**39**	**3**	**8**	**11**	**93**	**19**	**0**	**3**	**3**	**49**
1991-92	**Pittsburgh**	**NHL**	**44**	**1**	**3**	**4**	**57**	....	....	....	....	....
1992-93	**Tampa Bay**	**NHL**	**61**	**1**	**8**	**9**	**150**	....	....	....	....	....
	Pittsburgh	**NHL**	**11**	**1**	**4**	**5**	**34**	**11**	**1**	**2**	**3**	**16**
1993-94	**Pittsburgh**	**NHL**	**60**	**2**	**12**	**14**	**142**	**5**	**0**	**2**	**2**	**16**
	NHL Totals		**438**	**18**	**73**	**91**	**1094**	**49**	**2**	**8**	**10**	**101**

a Hockey East First All-Star Team (1985)

Traded to **Minnesota** by **Winnipeg** for future considerations, September 30, 1990. Traded to **Pittsburgh** by **Minnesota** with Larry Murphy for Chris Dahlquist and Jim Johnson, December 11, 1990. Claimed by **Tampa Bay** from **Pittsburgh** in Expansion Draft, June 18, 1992. Traded to **Pittsburgh** by **Tampa Bay** for Pittsburgh's third round choice (later traded to Florida — Florida selected Steve Washburn) in 1993 Entry Draft, March 22, 1993.

TALLAIRE, SEAN — VAN.

Right wing. Shoots right. 5'10", 185 lbs. Born, Steinbach, MN, October 3, 1973.
(Vancouver's 7th choice, 202nd overall, in 1993 Entry Draft).

			Regular Season					Playoffs				
Season	Club	Lea	GP	G	A	TP	PIM	GP	G	A	TP	PIM
1992-93	Lake Superior	CCHA	43	26	26	52	26	....	....	....	....	....
1993-94	Lake Superior	CCHA	45	23	32	55	22	....	....	....	....	....

TAMER, CHRIS — PIT.

Defense. Shoots left. 6'2", 185 lbs. Born, Dearborn, MI, November 17, 1970.
(Pittsburgh's 3rd choice, 68th overall, in 1990 Entry Draft).

			Regular Season					Playoffs				
Season	Club	Lea	GP	G	A	TP	PIM	GP	G	A	TP	PIM
1989-90	U. of Michigan	CCHA	42	2	7	9	147	....	....	....	....	....
1990-91	U. of Michigan	CCHA	45	8	19	27	130	....	....	....	....	....
1991-92	U. of Michigan	CCHA	43	4	15	19	125	....	....	....	....	....
1992-93	U. of Michigan	CCHA	39	5	18	23	113	....	....	....	....	....
1993-94	**Pittsburgh**	**NHL**	**12**	**0**	**0**	**0**	**9**	**5**	**0**	**0**	**0**	**2**
	Cleveland	IHL	53	1	2	3	160	....	....	....	....	....
	NHL Totals		**12**	**0**	**0**	**0**	**9**	**5**	**0**	**0**	**0**	**2**

TAMMINEN, JOE — PIT.

Center. Shoots left. 6'2", 187 lbs. Born, Virginia, MN, January 23, 1973.
(Pittsburgh's 4th choice, 82nd overall, in 1991 Entry Draft).

			Regular Season					Playoffs				
Season	Club	Lea	GP	G	A	TP	PIM	GP	G	A	TP	PIM
1991-92	Minn.-Duluth	WCHA	23	1	3	4	12	....	....	....	....	....
1992-93	Minn.-Duluth	WCHA	39	4	6	10	42	....	....	....	....	....
1993-94	Minn.-Duluth	WCHA	19	2	4	6	22	....	....	....	....	....

TANCILL, CHRIS (TAN-sihl) DAL.

Center. Shoots left. 5'10", 185 lbs. Born, Livonia, MI, February 7, 1968.
(Hartford's 1st choice, 15th overall, in 1989 Supplemental Draft).

			Regular Season					Playoffs				
Season	Club	Lea	GP	G	A	TP	PIM	GP	G	A	TP	PIM
1986-87	U. Wisconsin	WCHA	40	9	23	32	26	....	....	....	....	....
1987-88	U. Wisconsin	WCHA	44	13	14	27	48	....	....	....	....	....
1988-89	U. Wisconsin	WCHA	44	20	23	43	50	....	....	....	....	....
1989-90a	U. Wisconsin	WCHA	45	39	32	71	44	....	....	....	....	....
1990-91	**Hartford**	**NHL**	**9**	**1**	**1**	**2**	**4**	....	....	....	....	....
	Springfield	AHL	72	37	35	72	46	17	8	4	12	32
1991-92	**Hartford**	**NHL**	**10**	**0**	**0**	**0**	**2**	....	....	....	....	....
b	Springfield	AHL	17	12	7	19	20	....	....	....	....	....
	Detroit	**NHL**	**1**	**0**	**0**	**0**	**0**	....	....	....	....	....
	Adirondack	AHL	50	36	34	70	42	19	7	9	16	31
1992-93	**Detroit**	**NHL**	**4**	**1**	**0**	**1**	**2**	....	....	....	....	....
b	Adirondack	AHL	68	*59	43	102	62	10	7	7	14	10
1993-94	**Dallas**	**NHL**	**12**	**1**	**3**	**4**	**8**	....	....	....	....	....
	Kalamazoo	IHL	60	41	54	95	55	5	0	2	2	8
	NHL Totals		**36**	**3**	**4**	**7**	**16**	....	....	....	....	....

a NCAA All-Tournament Team, Tournament MVP (1990)
b AHL First All-Star Team (1992, 1993)

Traded to **Detroit** by **Hartford** for Daniel Shank, December 18, 1991. Signed as a free agent by **Dallas**, August 28, 1993.

TANGUAY, MARTIN T.B.

Center. Shoots left. 5'11", 185 lbs. Born, Ste-Julie, Que., January 12, 1973.
(Tampa Bay's 6th choice, 122nd overall, in 1992 Entry Draft).

			Regular Season					Playoffs				
Season	Club	Lea	GP	G	A	TP	PIM	GP	G	A	TP	PIM
1989-90	Longueuil	QMJHL	69	11	16	27	35	7	1	4	5	9
1990-91	Longueuil	QMJHL	69	27	34	61	14	8	3	4	7	6
1991-92	Verdun	QMJHL	67	41	50	91	117	19	8	13	21	32
1992-93	St-Jean	QMJHL	72	53	58	111	78	4	1	2	3	21
1993-94	Knoxville	ECHL	17	7	19	26	13	....	....	....	....	....
	Atlanta	IHL	58	7	15	22	28	9	2	1	3	8

TANTI, TONY (TAN-tee)

Right wing. Shoots left. 5'9", 180 lbs. Born, Toronto, Ont., September 7, 1963.
(Chicago's 1st choice, 12th overall, in 1981 Entry Draft).

			Regular Season					Playoffs				
Season	Club	Lea	GP	G	A	TP	PIM	GP	G	A	TP	PIM
1980-81a	Oshawa	OHA	67	81	69	150	197	11	7	8	15	41
1981-82	**Chicago**	**NHL**	**2**	**0**	**0**	**0**	**0**	....	....	....	....	....
b	Oshawa	OHL	57	62	64	126	138	12	14	12	26	15
1982-83	**Chicago**	**NHL**	**1**	**1**	**0**	**1**	**0**	....	....	....	....	....
	Oshawa	OHL	30	34	28	62	35	....	....	....	....	....
	Vancouver	**NHL**	**39**	**8**	**8**	**16**	**16**	**4**	**0**	**1**	**1**	**0**
1983-84	**Vancouver**	**NHL**	**79**	**45**	**41**	**86**	**50**	**4**	**1**	**2**	**3**	**0**
1984-85	**Vancouver**	**NHL**	**68**	**39**	**20**	**59**	**45**	....	....	....	....	....
1985-86	**Vancouver**	**NHL**	**77**	**39**	**33**	**72**	**85**	**3**	**0**	**1**	**1**	**11**
1986-87	**Vancouver**	**NHL**	**77**	**41**	**38**	**79**	**84**	....	....	....	....	....
1987-88	**Vancouver**	**NHL**	**73**	**40**	**37**	**77**	**90**	....	....	....	....	....
1988-89	**Vancouver**	**NHL**	**77**	**24**	**25**	**49**	**69**	**7**	**0**	**5**	**5**	**4**
1989-90	**Vancouver**	**NHL**	**41**	**14**	**18**	**32**	**50**	....	....	....	....	....
	Pittsburgh	**NHL**	**37**	**14**	**18**	**32**	**22**	....	....	....	....	....
1990-91	**Pittsburgh**	**NHL**	**46**	**6**	**12**	**18**	**44**	....	....	....	....	....
	Buffalo	**NHL**	**10**	**1**	**7**	**8**	**6**	**5**	**2**	**0**	**2**	**8**
1991-92	**Buffalo**	**NHL**	**70**	**15**	**16**	**31**	**100**	**7**	**0**	**3**	**3**	**4**
1992-93	Preussen Berlin	Ger.	34	14	17	31	73	....	....	....	....	....
1993-94	Preussen Berlin	Ger.	41	13	19	32	44	....	....	....	....	....
	NHL Totals		**697**	**287**	**273**	**560**	**661**	**30**	**3**	**12**	**15**	**27**

a OHA First All-Star Team (1981)
b OHL Second All-Star Team (1982)

Played in NHL All-Star Game (1986)

Traded to **Vancouver** by **Chicago** for Curt Fraser, January 6, 1983. Traded to **Pittsburgh** by **Vancouver** with Rod Buskas and Barry Pederson for Dave Capuano, Andrew McBain and Dan Quinn, January 8, 1990. Traded to **Buffalo** by **Pittsburgh** for Ken Priestlay, March 5, 1991.

TARDIF, MARC T.B.

Left wing. Shoots left. 6'1", 199 lbs. Born, Montreal, Que., January 6, 1973.
(Tampa Bay's 10th choice, 218th overall, in 1992 Entry Draft).

			Regular Season					Playoffs				
Season	Club	Lea	GP	G	A	TP	PIM	GP	G	A	TP	PIM
1990-91	Shawinigan	QMJHL	66	11	26	37	174	6	0	2	2	38
1991-92	Shawinigan	QMJHL	55	25	34	59	214	10	0	8	8	57
1992-93	Sherbrooke	QMJHL	63	21	46	67	249	14	4	8	12	55
1993-94	Atlanta	IHL	65	9	13	22	154	....	....	....	....	....

TARDIF, PATRICE ST.L.

Center. Shoots left. 6'2", 185 lbs. Born, Thetford Mines, Que., October 30, 1970.
(St. Louis' 2nd choice, 54th overall, in 1990 Entry Draft).

			Regular Season					Playoffs				
Season	Club	Lea	GP	G	A	TP	PIM	GP	G	A	TP	PIM
1990-91	U. of Maine	H.E.	36	13	12	25	18	....	....	....	....	....
1991-92	U. of Maine	H.E.	31	18	20	38	14	....	....	....	....	....
1992-93	U. of Maine	H.E.	45	23	25	48	22	....	....	....	....	....
1993-94	U. of Maine	H.E.	34	18	15	33	42	....	....	....	....	....
	Peoria	IHL	11	4	4	8	21	4	2	0	2	4

TARVAINEN, JUSSI (tahr-VAHI-nehn) EDM.

Center. Shoots right. 6'2", 185 lbs. Born, Lahti, Finland, May 31, 1976.
(Edmonton's 7th choice, 95th overall, in 1994 Entry Draft).

			Regular Season					Playoffs				
Season	Club	Lea	GP	G	A	TP	PIM	GP	G	A	TP	PIM
1992-93	KalPa	Fin. Jr.	17	3	6	9	35	....	....	....	....	....
1993-94	KalPa	Fin.	42	3	4	7	20	....	....	....	....	....

TATARINOV, MIKHAIL (tah-TAH-ree-nahf)

Defense. Shoots left. 5'10", 195 lbs. Born, Angarsk, USSR, July 16, 1966.
(Washington's 10th choice, 225th overall, in 1984 Entry Draft).

			Regular Season					Playoffs				
Season	Club	Lea	GP	G	A	TP	PIM	GP	G	A	TP	PIM
1983-84	Sokol Kiev	USSR	38	7	3	10	46	....	....	....	....	....
1984-85	Sokol Kiev	USSR	34	3	6	9	54	....	....	....	....	....
1985-86	Sokol Kiev	USSR	37	7	5	12	41	....	....	....	....	....
1986-87	Moscow D'amo	USSR	40	10	8	18	43	....	....	....	....	....
1987-88	Moscow D'amo	USSR	30	2	2	4	8	....	....	....	....	....
1988-89	Moscow D'amo	USSR	4	1	0	1	2	....	....	....	....	....
1989-90	Moscow D'amo	USSR	44	11	10	21	34	....	....	....	....	....
1990-91	Moscow D'amo	USSR	11	5	4	9	6	....	....	....	....	....
	Washington	**NHL**	**65**	**8**	**15**	**23**	**82**	....	....	....	....	....
1991-92	**Quebec**	**NHL**	**66**	**11**	**27**	**38**	**72**	....	....	....	....	....
1992-93	**Quebec**	**NHL**	**28**	**2**	**6**	**8**	**28**	....	....	....	....	....
1993-94	**Boston**	**NHL**	**2**	**0**	**0**	**0**	**2**	....	....	....	....	....
	Providence	AHL	3	0	3	3	0	....	....	....	....	....
	NHL Totals		**161**	**21**	**48**	**69**	**184**	....	....	....	....	....

Traded to **Quebec** by **Washington** for Toronto's second round choice (previously acquired by Quebec – Washington selected Eric Lavigne) in 1991 Entry Draft, June 22, 1991. Signed as a free agent by **Boston**, July 30, 1993.

TAYLOR, CHRIS NYI

Center. Shoots left. 6', 185 lbs. Born, Stratford, Ont., March 6, 1972.
(NY Islanders' 2nd choice, 27th overall, in 1990 Entry Draft).

			Regular Season					Playoffs				
Season	Club	Lea	GP	G	A	TP	PIM	GP	G	A	TP	PIM
1988-89	London	OHL	62	7	16	23	52	15	0	2	2	15
1989-90	London	OHL	66	45	60	105	60	6	3	2	5	6
1990-91	London	OHL	65	50	78	128	50	7	4	8	12	6
1991-92	London	OHL	66	48	74	122	57	10	8	16	24	9
1992-93	Capital Dist.	AHL	77	19	43	62	32	4	0	1	1	2
1993-94	Salt Lake	IHL	79	21	20	41	38	....	....	....	....	....
	Raleigh	ECHL	2	0	0	0	0	....	....	....	....	....

TAYLOR, DAVE

Right wing. Shoots right. 6', 190 lbs. Born, Levack, Ont., December 4, 1955.
(Los Angeles' 14th choice, 210th overall, in 1975 Amateur Draft).

			Regular Season					Playoffs				
Season	Club	Lea	GP	G	A	TP	PIM	GP	G	A	TP	PIM
1976-77	Clarkson	ECAC	34	41	67	108	....	....	....	....	....	....
	Fort Worth	CHL	7	2	4	6	6	....	....	....	....	....
1977-78	**Los Angeles**	**NHL**	**64**	**22**	**21**	**43**	**47**	**2**	**0**	**0**	**0**	**5**
1978-79	**Los Angeles**	**NHL**	**78**	**43**	**48**	**91**	**124**	**2**	**0**	**0**	**0**	**2**
1979-80	**Los Angeles**	**NHL**	**61**	**37**	**53**	**90**	**72**	**4**	**2**	**1**	**3**	**4**
1980-81a	**Los Angeles**	**NHL**	**72**	**47**	**65**	**112**	**130**	**4**	**2**	**2**	**4**	**10**
1981-82	**Los Angeles**	**NHL**	**78**	**39**	**67**	**106**	**130**	**10**	**4**	**6**	**10**	**20**
1982-83	**Los Angeles**	**NHL**	**46**	**21**	**37**	**58**	**76**	....	....	....	....	....
1983-84	**Los Angeles**	**NHL**	**63**	**20**	**49**	**69**	**91**	....	....	....	....	....
1984-85	**Los Angeles**	**NHL**	**79**	**41**	**51**	**92**	**132**	**3**	**2**	**2**	**4**	**8**
1985-86	**Los Angeles**	**NHL**	**76**	**33**	**38**	**71**	**110**	....	....	....	....	....
1986-87	**Los Angeles**	**NHL**	**67**	**18**	**44**	**62**	**84**	**5**	**2**	**3**	**5**	**6**
1987-88	**Los Angeles**	**NHL**	**68**	**26**	**41**	**67**	**129**	**5**	**3**	**3**	**6**	**6**
1988-89	**Los Angeles**	**NHL**	**70**	**26**	**37**	**63**	**80**	**11**	**1**	**5**	**6**	**19**
1989-90	**Los Angeles**	**NHL**	**58**	**15**	**26**	**41**	**96**	**6**	**4**	**4**	**8**	**2**
1990-91bc	**Los Angeles**	**NHL**	**73**	**23**	**30**	**53**	**148**	**12**	**2**	**1**	**3**	**12**
1991-92	**Los Angeles**	**NHL**	**77**	**10**	**19**	**29**	**63**	**6**	**1**	**1**	**2**	**20**
1992-93	**Los Angeles**	**NHL**	**48**	**6**	**9**	**15**	**49**	**22**	**3**	**5**	**8**	**31**
1993-94	**Los Angeles**	**NHL**	**33**	**4**	**3**	**7**	**28**	....	....	....	....	....
	NHL Totals		**1111**	**431**	**638**	**1069**	**1589**	**92**	**26**	**33**	**59**	**145**

a NHL Second All-Star Team (1981)
b Won Bill Masterton Memorial Trophy (1991)
c Won King Clancy Memorial Trophy (1991)

Played in NHL All-Star Game (1981, 1982, 1986, 1994)

TAYLOR, TIM DET.

Center. Shoots left. 6'1", 188 lbs. Born, Stratford, Ont., February 6, 1969.
(Washington's 2nd choice, 36th overall, in 1988 Entry Draft).

			Regular Season					Playoffs				
Season	Club	Lea	GP	G	A	TP	PIM	GP	G	A	TP	PIM
1986-87	London	OHL	34	7	9	16	11	....	....	....	....	....
1987-88	London	OHL	64	46	50	96	66	12	9	9	18	26
1988-89	London	OHL	61	34	80	114	93	21	*21	25	*46	58
1989-90	Baltimore	AHL	79	31	36	67	124	9	2	2	4	13
1990-91	Baltimore	AHL	79	25	42	67	75	5	0	1	1	4
1991-92	Baltimore	AHL	65	9	18	27	131	....	....	....	....	....
1992-93	Baltimore	AHL	41	15	16	31	49	....	....	....	....	....
	Hamilton	AHL	36	15	22	37	37	....	....	....	....	....
1993-94	**Detroit**	**NHL**	**1**	**1**	**0**	**1**	**0**	....	....	....	....	....
ab	Adirondack	AHL	79	36	*81	*117	86	12	2	10	12	12
	NHL Totals		**1**	**1**	**0**	**1**	**0**	....	....	....	....	....

a AHL First All-Star Team (1994)
b Won John B. Sollenberger Trophy (Top Scorer - AHL) (1994)

Traded to **Vancouver** by **Washington** for Eric Murano, January 29, 1993. Signed as a free agent by **Detroit**, July 28, 1993.

TEPPER, STEPHEN

Right wing. Shoots right. 6'4", 215 lbs. Born, Santa Ana, CA, March 10, 1969.
(Chicago's 7th choice, 134th overall, in 1987 Entry Draft).

			Regular Season					Playoffs				
Season	Club	Lea	GP	G	A	TP	PIM	GP	G	A	TP	PIM
1988-89	U. of Maine	H.E.	26	3	9	12	32	....	....	....	....	....
1989-90	U. of Maine	H.E.	41	10	6	16	68	....	....	....	....	....
1990-91	U. of Maine	H.E.	38	6	11	17	58	....	....	....	....	....
1991-92	U. of Maine	H.E.	16	0	3	3	20	....	....	....	....	....
1992-93	**Chicago**	**NHL**	**1**	**0**	**0**	**0**	**0**	....	....	....	....	....
	Indianapolis	IHL	12	0	1	1	40	....	....	....	....	....
	Kansas City	IHL	32	4	10	14	51	4	0	1	1	6
1993-94	Fort Worth	CHL	25	23	11	34	54	....	....	....	....	....
	Roanoke	ECHL	9	2	2	4	33	....	....	....	....	....
	Kansas City	IHL	23	1	3	4	52	....	....	....	....	....
	NHL Totals		**1**	**0**	**0**	**0**	**0**	....	....	....	....	....

TERTYSHNY, SERGEI — WSH.

Defense. Shoots left. 6', 187 lbs. Born, Chelyabinsk, USSR, June 3, 1970.
(Washington's 11th choice, 275th overall, in 1994 Entry Draft).

			Regular Season					Playoffs				
Season	Club	Lea	GP	G	A	TP	PIM	GP	G	A	TP	PIM
1987-88	Chelyabinsk	USSR	19	0	0	0	4	....	....	....	....	....
1988-89	SKA Sverdlovsk	USSR 2			UNAVAILABLE							
1989-90	SKA Leningrad	USSR	4	0	0	0	0	....	....	....	....	....
1990-91	SKA Leningrad	USSR	28	2	2	4	12	....	....	....	....	....
1991-92	Chelyabinsk	CIS	44	4	2	6	20	....	....	....	....	....
1992-93	Chelyabinsk	CIS	41	8	3	11	10	8	2	0	2	4
1993-94	Chelyabinsk	CIS	37	8	8	16	22	6	0	1	1	0

THERIEN, CHRIS (TEH-ree-ehn) — PHI.

Defense. Shoots left. 6'3", 230 lbs. Born, Ottawa, Ont., December 14, 1971.
(Philadelphia's 7th choice, 47th overall, in 1990 Entry Draft).

			Regular Season					Playoffs				
Season	Club	Lea	GP	G	A	TP	PIM	GP	G	A	TP	PIM
1990-91	Providence	H.E.	36	4	18	22	36	....	....	....	....	....
1991-92	Providence	H.E.	36	16	25	41	38	....	....	....	....	....
1992-93a	Providence	H.E.	33	8	11	19	52	....	....	....	....	....
	Cdn. National	....	8	1	4	5	8	....	....	....	....	....
1993-94	Cdn. National	....	59	7	15	22	46	....	....	....	....	....
	Cdn. Olympic	....	4	0	0	0	4	....	....	....	....	....
	Hershey	AHL	6	0	0	0	2	....	....	....	....	....

a Hockey East Second All-Star Team (1993)

THIESSEN, TRAVIS — CHI.

Defense. Shoots left. 6'3", 203 lbs. Born, North Battleford, Sask., July 11, 1972.
(Pittsburgh's 3rd choice, 67th overall, in 1992 Entry Draft).

			Regular Season					Playoffs				
Season	Club	Lea	GP	G	A	TP	PIM	GP	G	A	TP	PIM
1990-91	Moose Jaw	WHL	69	4	14	18	80	8	0	0	0	10
1991-92	Moose Jaw	WHL	72	9	50	59	112	4	0	2	2	8
1992-93	Cleveland	IHL	64	3	7	10	69	4	0	0	0	16
1993-94	Cleveland	IHL	74	2	13	15	75	....	....	....	....	....

Signed as a free agent by **Chicago**, June 9, 1994.

THOMAS, SCOTT — BUF.

Right wing. Shoots right. 6'2", 195 lbs. Born, Buffalo, NY, January 18, 1970.
(Buffalo's 2nd choice, 56th overall, in 1989 Entry Draft).

			Regular Season					Playoffs				
Season	Club	Lea	GP	G	A	TP	PIM	GP	G	A	TP	PIM
1989-90	Clarkson	ECAC	34	19	13	32	95	....	....	....	....	....
1990-91	Clarkson	ECAC	40	28	14	42	89	....	....	....	....	....
1991-92	Clarkson	ECAC	29	22	20	42	57	....	....	....	....	....
	Rochester	AHL	....	....	....	....	....	9	0	1	1	17
1992-93	**Buffalo**	**NHL**	**7**	**1**	**1**	**2**	**15**	....	....	....	....	....
	Rochester	AHL	65	32	27	59	38	17	8	5	13	6
1993-94	**Buffalo**	**NHL**	**32**	**2**	**2**	**4**	**8**	....	....	....	....	....
	Rochester	AHL	11	4	5	9	0	....	....	....	....	....
	NHL Totals		**39**	**3**	**3**	**6**	**23**	....	....	....	....	....

THOMAS, STEVE — NYI

Left wing. Shoots left. 5'11", 185 lbs. Born, Stockport, England, July 15, 1963.

			Regular Season					Playoffs				
Season	Club	Lea	GP	G	A	TP	PIM	GP	G	A	TP	PIM
1983-84	Toronto	OHL	70	51	54	105	77	....	....	....	....	....
1984-85	**Toronto**	**NHL**	**18**	**1**	**1**	**2**	**2**	....	....	....	....	....
ab	St. Catharines	AHL	64	42	48	90	56	....	....	....	....	....
1985-86	**Toronto**	**NHL**	**65**	**20**	**37**	**57**	**36**	**10**	**6**	**8**	**14**	**9**
	St. Catharines	AHL	19	18	14	32	35	....	....	....	....	....
1986-87	**Toronto**	**NHL**	**78**	**35**	**27**	**62**	**114**	**13**	**2**	**3**	**5**	**13**
1987-88	**Chicago**	**NHL**	**30**	**13**	**13**	**26**	**40**	**3**	**1**	**2**	**3**	**6**
1988-89	**Chicago**	**NHL**	**45**	**21**	**19**	**40**	**69**	**12**	**3**	**5**	**8**	**10**
1989-90	**Chicago**	**NHL**	**76**	**40**	**30**	**70**	**91**	**20**	**7**	**6**	**13**	**33**
1990-91	**Chicago**	**NHL**	**69**	**19**	**35**	**54**	**129**	**6**	**1**	**2**	**3**	**15**
1991-92	**Chicago**	**NHL**	**11**	**2**	**6**	**8**	**26**	....	....	....	....	....
	NY Islanders	**NHL**	**71**	**28**	**42**	**70**	**71**	....	....	....	....	....
1992-93	**NY Islanders**	**NHL**	**79**	**37**	**50**	**87**	**111**	**18**	**9**	**8**	**17**	**37**
1993-94	**NY Islanders**	**NHL**	**78**	**42**	**33**	**75**	**139**	**4**	**1**	**0**	**1**	**8**
	NHL Totals		**620**	**258**	**293**	**551**	**828**	**86**	**30**	**34**	**64**	**131**

a AHL Rookie of the Year (1985)
b AHL First All-Star Team (1985)

Signed as a free agent by **Toronto**, May 12, 1984. Traded to **Chicago** by **Toronto** with Rick Vaive and Bob McGill for Al Secord and Ed Olczyk, September 3, 1987. Traded to **NY Islanders** by **Chicago** with Adam Creighton for Brent Sutter and Brad Lauer, October 25, 1991.

THOMLINSON, DAVE — L.A.

Left wing. Shoots left. 6'1", 196 lbs. Born, Edmonton, Alta., October 22, 1966.
(Toronto's 3rd choice, 43rd overall, in 1985 Entry Draft).

			Regular Season					Playoffs				
Season	Club	Lea	GP	G	A	TP	PIM	GP	G	A	TP	PIM
1984-85	Brandon	WHL	26	13	14	27	70	....	....	....	....	....
1985-86	Brandon	WHL	53	25	20	45	116	....	....	....	....	....
1986-87	Brandon	WHL	2	0	1	1	9	....	....	....	....	....
	Moose Jaw	WHL	70	44	36	80	117	9	7	3	10	19
1987-88	Peoria	IHL	74	27	30	57	56	7	4	3	7	11
1988-89	Peoria	IHL	64	27	29	56	154	3	0	1	1	8
1989-90	**St. Louis**	**NHL**	**19**	**1**	**2**	**3**	**12**	....	....	....	....	....
	Peoria	IHL	59	27	40	67	87	5	1	1	2	15
1990-91	**St. Louis**	**NHL**	**3**	**0**	**0**	**0**	**0**	**9**	**3**	**1**	**4**	**4**
	Peoria	IHL	80	53	54	107	107	11	6	7	13	28
1991-92	**Boston**	**NHL**	**12**	**0**	**1**	**1**	**17**	....	....	....	....	....
	Maine	AHL	25	9	11	20	36	....	....	....	....	....
1992-93	Binghamton	AHL	54	25	35	60	61	12	2	5	7	8
1993-94	**Los Angeles**	**NHL**	**7**	**0**	**0**	**0**	**21**	....	....	....	....	....
	Phoenix	IHL	39	10	15	25	70	....	....	....	....	....
	NHL Totals		**41**	**1**	**3**	**4**	**50**	**9**	**3**	**1**	**4**	**4**

Signed as a free agent by **St. Louis**, June 4, 1987. Signed as a free agent by **Boston**, July 30, 1991. Signed as a free agent by **NY Rangers**, September 4, 1992. Signed as a free agent by **Los Angeles**, July 22, 1993.

THOMPSON, BRENT

Defense. Shoots left. 6'2", 200 lbs. Born, Calgary, Alta., January 9, 1971.
(Los Angeles' 1st choice, 39th overall, in 1989 Entry Draft).

			Regular Season					Playoffs				
Season	Club	Lea	GP	G	A	TP	PIM	GP	G	A	TP	PIM
1988-89	Medicine Hat	WHL	72	3	10	13	160	3	0	0	0	2
1989-90	Medicine Hat	WHL	68	10	35	45	167	3	0	1	1	14
1990-91a	Medicine Hat	WHL	51	5	40	45	87	12	1	7	8	16
	Phoenix	IHL	....	....	....	....	....	4	0	1	1	6
1991-92	**Los Angeles**	**NHL**	**27**	**0**	**5**	**5**	**89**	**4**	**0**	**0**	**0**	**4**
	Phoenix	IHL	42	4	13	17	139	....	....	....	....	....
1992-93	**Los Angeles**	**NHL**	**30**	**0**	**4**	**4**	**76**	....	....	....	....	....
	Phoenix	IHL	22	0	5	5	112	....	....	....	....	....
1993-94	**Los Angeles**	**NHL**	**24**	**1**	**0**	**1**	**81**	....	....	....	....	....
	Phoenix	IHL	26	1	11	12	118	....	....	....	....	....
	NHL Totals		**81**	**1**	**9**	**10**	**246**	**4**	**0**	**0**	**0**	**4**

a WHL East Second All-Star Team (1991)

Traded to **Winnipeg** by **Los Angeles** with future considerations for the rights to Ruslan Batyrshin and Winnipeg's second round choice in 1996 Entry Draft, August 8, 1994.

THOMPSON, BRIANE — FLA.

Defense. Shoots left. 6'3", 205 lbs. Born, Peterborough, Ont., April 17, 1974.
(Florida's 10th choice, 187th overall, in 1993 Draft).

			Regular Season					Playoffs				
Season	Club	Lea	GP	G	A	TP	PIM	GP	G	A	TP	PIM
1991-92	S.S. Marie	OHL	46	0	4	4	17	6	0	0	0	4
1992-93	S.S. Marie	OHL	63	2	21	23	57	22	0	6	6	41
1993-94	S.S. Marie	OHL	60	5	36	41	136	14	0	3	3	27

THOMPSON, PAT — ANA.

Defense. Shoots right. 6'2", 190 lbs. Born, Halifax County, N.S., January 16, 1972.
(Anaheim's 1st choice, 5th overall, in 1993 Supplemental Draft).

			Regular Season					Playoffs				
Season	Club	Lea	GP	G	A	TP	PIM	GP	G	A	TP	PIM
1991-92	Brown	ECAC	15	1	0	1	6	....	....	....	....	....
1992-93	Brown	ECAC	30	1	7	8	16	....	....	....	....	....
1993-94	Brown	ECAC	32	3	4	7	36	....	....	....	....	....

THOMSON, JIM — ANA.

Right wing. Shoots right. 6'1", 220 lbs. Born, Edmonton, Alta., December 30, 1965.
(Washington's 8th choice, 185th overall, in 1984 Entry Draft).

			Regular Season					Playoffs				
Season	Club	Lea	GP	G	A	TP	PIM	GP	G	A	TP	PIM
1983-84	Toronto	OHL	60	10	18	28	68	9	1	0	1	26
1984-85	Toronto	OHL	63	23	28	51	122	5	3	1	4	25
	Binghamton	AHL	4	0	0	0	2	....	....	....	....	....
1985-86	Binghamton	AHL	59	15	9	24	195	....	....	....	....	....
1986-87	**Washington**	**NHL**	**10**	**0**	**0**	**0**	**35**	....	....	....	....	....
	Binghamton	AHL	57	13	10	23	360	10	0	1	1	40
1987-88	Binghamton	AHL	25	8	9	17	64	4	1	2	3	7
1988-89	**Washington**	**NHL**	**14**	**2**	**0**	**2**	**53**	....	....	....	....	....
	Baltimore	AHL	41	25	16	41	129	....	....	....	....	....
	Hartford	**NHL**	**5**	**0**	**0**	**0**	**14**	....	....	....	....	....
1989-90	Binghamton	AHL	8	1	2	3	30	....	....	....	....	....
	New Jersey	**NHL**	**3**	**0**	**0**	**0**	**31**	....	....	....	....	....
	Utica	AHL	60	20	23	43	124	4	1	0	1	19
1990-91	**Los Angeles**	**NHL**	**8**	**1**	**0**	**1**	**19**	....	....	....	....	....
	New Haven	AHL	27	5	8	13	121	....	....	....	....	....
1991-92	**Los Angeles**	**NHL**	**45**	**1**	**2**	**3**	**162**	....	....	....	....	....
	Phoenix	IHL	2	1	0	1	0	....	....	....	....	....
1992-93	**Ottawa**	**NHL**	**15**	**0**	**1**	**1**	**41**	....	....	....	....	....
	Los Angeles	**NHL**	**9**	**0**	**0**	**0**	**56**	**1**	**0**	**0**	**0**	**0**
	Phoenix	IHL	14	4	5	9	44	....	....	....	....	....
1993-94	**Anaheim**	**NHL**	**6**	**0**	**0**	**0**	**5**	....	....	....	....	....
	NHL Totals		**115**	**4**	**3**	**7**	**416**	**1**	**0**	**0**	**0**	**0**

Traded to **Hartford** by **Washington** for Scot Kleinendorst, March 6, 1989. Traded to **New Jersey** by **Hartford** for Chris Cichocki, October 31, 1989. Signed as a free agent by **Los Angeles**, July 2, 1990. Claimed by **Minnesota** from **Los Angeles** in Expansion Draft, May 30, 1991. Traded to **Los Angeles** by **Minnesota** with Randy Gilhen, Charlie Huddy and NY Rangers' fourth round choice (previously acquired by Minnesota - Alexei Zhitnik) in 1991 Entry Draft for Todd Elik, June 22, 1991. Claimed by **Ottawa** from **Los Angeles** in Expansion Draft, June 18, 1992. Traded to **Los Angeles** by **Ottawa** with Marc Fortier for Bob Kudelski and Shawn McCosh, December 19, 1992. Claimed by **Anaheim** from **Los Angeles** in Expansion Draft, June 24, 1993.

THORNTON, SCOTT

Center. Shoots left. 6'2", 200 lbs. Born, London, Ont., January 9, 1971.
(Toronto's 1st choice, 3rd overall, in 1989 Entry Draft).

			Regular Season					Playoffs				
Season	Club	Lea	GP	G	A	TP	PIM	GP	G	A	TP	PIM
1987-88	Belleville	OHL	62	11	19	30	54	6	0	1	1	2
1988-89	Belleville	OHL	59	28	34	62	103	5	1	1	2	6
1989-90	Belleville	OHL	47	21	28	49	91	11	2	10	12	15
1990-91	**Toronto**	**NHL**	**33**	**1**	**3**	**4**	**30**	....	....	....	....	....
	Newmarket	AHL	5	1	0	1	4	....	....	....	....	....
	Belleville	OHL	3	2	1	3	2	6	0	7	7	14
1991-92	**Edmonton**	**NHL**	**15**	**0**	**1**	**1**	**43**	**1**	**0**	**0**	**0**	**0**
	Cape Breton	AHL	49	9	14	23	40	5	1	0	1	8
1992-93	**Edmonton**	**NHL**	**9**	**0**	**1**	**1**	**0**	....	....	....	....	....
	Cape Breton	AHL	58	23	27	50	102	16	1	2	3	35
1993-94	**Edmonton**	**NHL**	**61**	**4**	**7**	**11**	**104**	....	....	....	....	....
	Cape Breton	AHL	2	1	1	2	31	....	....	....	....	....
	NHL Totals		**118**	**5**	**12**	**17**	**177**	**1**	**0**	**0**	**0**	**0**

Traded to **Edmonton** by **Toronto** with Vincent Damphousse, Peter Ing, Luke Richardson, future considerations and cash for Grant Fuhr, Glenn Anderson and Craig Berube, September 19, 1991.

THURESSON, MARCUS — S.J.

Center. Shoots left. 6'1", 180 lbs. Born, Jon Koping, Sweden, May 31, 1971.
(NY Islanders' 11th choice, 224th overall, in 1991 Entry Draft).

			Regular Season					Playoffs				
Season	Club	Lea	GP	G	A	TP	PIM	GP	G	A	TP	PIM
1989-90	Leksand	Swe.	28	8	7	15	18	3	2	0	2	12
1990-91	Leksand	Swe.	22	3	2	5	20	....	....	....	....	....
1991-92	Leksand	Swe.	21	2	4	6	22	....	....	....	....	....
1992-93	Leksand	Swe.	31	6	10	16	22	2	2	0	2	2
1993-94	Leksand	Swe.	32	3	4	7	28	4	0	1	1	0

Rights traded to **San Jose** by **NY Islanders** for Brian Mullen, August 24, 1992.

TICHY, MILAN (TEE-CHEE, MEE-lahn) NYI

Defense. Shoots left. 6'3", 198 lbs. Born, Plzen, Czech., September 22, 1969.
(Chicago's 6th choice, 153rd overall, in 1989 Entry Draft).

			Regular Season					Playoffs				
Season	Club	Lea	GP	G	A	TP	PIM	GP	G	A	TP	PIM
1987-88	Skoda Plzen	Czech.	30	1	3	4	20	....	....	....	....	....
1988-89	Skoda Plzen	Czech.	36	1	12	13	44	....	....	....	....	....
1989-90	Dukla Trencin	Czech.	51	14	8	22	....	....	....	....	....	....
1990-91	Dukla Trencin	Czech.	41	9	12	21	72	....	....	....	....	....
1991-92	Indianapolis	IHL	49	6	23	29	28	....	....	....	....	....
1992-93	**Chicago**	**NHL**	**13**	**0**	**1**	**1**	**30**	....	....	....	....	....
	Indianapolis	IHL	49	7	32	39	62	4	0	5	5	14
1993-94	Moncton	AHL	48	1	20	21	103	20	3	3	6	12
	NHL Totals		**13**	**0**	**1**	**1**	**30**	....	....	....	....	....

Claimed by **Florida** from **Chicago** in Expansion Draft, June 24, 1993. Traded to **Winnipeg** by **Florida** for Brent Severyn, October 3, 1993. Signed as a free agent by **NY Islanders**, August 2, 1994.

TIILIKAINEN, JUKKA L.A.

Left wing. Shoots left. 6', 180 lbs. Born, Espoo, Finland, April 4, 1974.
(Los Angeles' 8th choice, 255th overall, in 1992 Entry Draft).

			Regular Season					Playoffs				
Season	Club	Lea	GP	G	A	TP	PIM	GP	G	A	TP	PIM
1991-92	Kiekko	Fin.2	1	0	0	0	0	....	....	....	....	....
1992-93	Vantaa	Fin.2	18	7	3	10	10	....	....	....	....	....
	Kiekko	Fin.	5	0	0	0	4	....	....	....	....	....
1993-94	Kiekko-Espoo	Fin.	33	2	4	6	12	....	....	....	....	....

TIKKANEN, ESA (TEE-kuh-nehn, EHZ-uh) ST.L.

Left wing. Shoots left. 6'1", 200 lbs. Born, Helsinki, Finland, January 25, 1965.
(Edmonton's 4th choice, 80th overall, in 1983 Entry Draft).

			Regular Season					Playoffs				
Season	Club	Lea	GP	G	A	TP	PIM	GP	G	A	TP	PIM
1981-82	Regina	SJHL	59	38	37	75	216	....	....	....	....	....
	Regina	WHL	2	0	0	0	0	....	....	....	....	....
1982-83	HIFK	Fin. Jr.	30	34	31	65	104	4	4	3	7	10
	HIFK	Fin.	....	....	....	....	....	1	0	0	0	2
1983-84	HIFK	Fin. Jr.	6	5	9	14	13	4	4	3	7	8
	HIFK	Fin.	36	19	11	30	30	2	0	0	0	0
1984-85	HIFK	Fin.	36	21	33	54	42	....	....	....	....	....
	Edmonton	**NHL**	....	....	....	....	....	**3**	**0**	**0**	**0**	**2**
1985-86	**Edmonton**	**NHL**	**35**	**7**	**6**	**13**	**28**	**8**	**3**	**2**	**5**	**7**
	Nova Scotia	AHL	15	4	8	12	17	....	....	....	....	....
1986-87	**Edmonton**	**NHL**	**76**	**34**	**44**	**78**	**120**	**21**	**7**	**2**	**9**	**22**
1987-88	**Edmonton**	**NHL**	**80**	**23**	**51**	**74**	**153**	**19**	**10**	**17**	**27**	**72**
1988-89	**Edmonton**	**NHL**	**67**	**31**	**47**	**78**	**92**	**7**	**1**	**3**	**4**	**12**
1989-90	**Edmonton**	**NHL**	**79**	**30**	**33**	**63**	**161**	**22**	**13**	**11**	**24**	**26**
1990-91	**Edmonton**	**NHL**	**79**	**27**	**42**	**69**	**85**	**18**	**12**	**8**	**20**	**24**
1991-92	**Edmonton**	**NHL**	**40**	**12**	**16**	**28**	**44**	**16**	**5**	**3**	**8**	**8**
1992-93	**Edmonton**	**NHL**	**66**	**14**	**19**	**33**	**76**	....	....	....	....	....
	NY Rangers	**NHL**	**15**	**2**	**5**	**7**	**18**	....	....	....	....	....
1993-94	**NY Rangers**	**NHL**	**83**	**22**	**32**	**54**	**114**	**23**	**4**	**4**	**8**	**34**
	NHL Totals		**620**	**202**	**295**	**497**	**891**	**137**	**55**	**50**	**105**	**207**

Traded to **NY Rangers** by **Edmonton** for Doug Weight, March 17, 1993. Traded to **St. Louis** by **NY Rangers** with Doug Lidster for Petr Nedved, July 24, 1994.

TILEY, BRAD (TIGH-lee) HFD.

Defense. Shoots left. 6'1", 185 lbs. Born, Markdale, Ont., July 5, 1971.
(Boston's 4th choice, 84th overall, in 1991 Entry Draft).

			Regular Season					Playoffs				
Season	Club	Lea	GP	G	A	TP	PIM	GP	G	A	TP	PIM
1988-89	S.S. Marie	OHL	50	4	11	15	31	....	....	....	....	....
1989-90	S.S. Marie	OHL	66	9	32	41	47	....	....	....	....	....
1990-91a	S.S. Marie	OHL	66	11	55	66	29	14	4	15	19	12
1991-92	Maine	AHL	62	7	22	29	36	....	....	....	....	....
1992-93	Phoenix	IHL	46	11	27	38	35	....	....	....	....	....
	Binghamton	AHL	26	6	10	16	19	8	0	1	1	2
1993-94	Binghamton	AHL	29	6	10	16	6	....	....	....	....	....
	Phoenix	IHL	35	8	15	23	21	....	....	....	....	....

a Memorial Cup All-Star Team (1991)

Signed as a free agent by **NY Rangers**, September 4, 1992. Traded to **Los Angeles** by **NY Rangers** for Los Angeles' eleventh round choice (Jamie Butt) in 1994 Entry Draft, January 28, 1994.

TILLEY, TOM ST.L.

Defense. Shoots right. 6', 190 lbs. Born, Trenton, Ont., March 28, 1965.
(St. Louis' 13th choice, 196th overall, in 1984 Entry Draft).

			Regular Season					Playoffs				
Season	Club	Lea	GP	G	A	TP	PIM	GP	G	A	TP	PIM
1984-85	Michigan State	CCHA	37	1	5	6	58	....	....	....	....	....
1985-86	Michigan State	CCHA	42	9	25	34	48	....	....	....	....	....
1986-87	Michigan State	CCHA	42	7	14	21	48	....	....	....	....	....
1987-88a	Michigan State	CCHA	46	8	18	26	44	....	....	....	....	....
1988-89	**St. Louis**	**NHL**	**70**	**1**	**22**	**23**	**47**	**10**	**1**	**2**	**3**	**17**
1989-90	**St. Louis**	**NHL**	**34**	**0**	**5**	**5**	**6**	....	....	....	....	....
	Peoria	IHL	22	1	8	9	13	....	....	....	....	....
1990-91	**St. Louis**	**NHL**	**22**	**2**	**4**	**6**	**4**	....	....	....	....	....
b	Peoria	IHL	48	7	38	45	53	13	2	9	11	25
1991-92	Milan Devils	Italy	18	7	13	20	12	12	5	12	17	10
1992-93	Milan Devils	Alp.	32	5	17	22	21	....	....	....	....	....
	Milan Devils	Italy	14	8	3	11	2	8	1	5	6	4
1993-94	**St. Louis**	**NHL**	**48**	**1**	**7**	**8**	**32**	**4**	**0**	**1**	**1**	**2**
	NHL Totals		**174**	**4**	**38**	**42**	**89**	**14**	**1**	**3**	**4**	**19**

a CCHA First All-Star Team (1988)
b IHL Second All-Star Team (1991)

TILTGEN, DEAN

Center. Shoots left. 5'11", 175 lbs. Born, Ponoka, Alta., February 3, 1974.
(Buffalo's 8th choice, 179th overall, in 1992 Entry Draft).

			Regular Season					Playoffs				
Season	Club	Lea	GP	G	A	TP	PIM	GP	G	A	TP	PIM
1990-91	Tri-City	WHL	53	5	6	11	11	2	0	0	0	2
1991-92	Tri-City	WHL	69	29	34	63	43	5	2	0	2	6
1992-93	Red Deer	WHL	72	50	61	111	33	4	1	2	3	0
1993-94	Victoria	WHL	29	9	14	23	24	....	....	....	....	....
	Tri-City	WHL	35	8	15	23	26	4	1	1	2	12

TIMANDER, MATTIAS BOS.

Defense. Shoots left. 6'1", 194 lbs. Born, Solleftea, Sweden, April 16, 1974.
(Boston's 7th choice, 208th overall, in 1992 Entry Draft).

			Regular Season					Playoffs				
Season	Club	Lea	GP	G	A	TP	PIM	GP	G	A	TP	PIM
1992-93	MoDo	Swe.	1	0	0	0	0	....	....	....	....	....
1993-94	MoDo	Swe.	23	2	2	4	6	11	2	0	2	10

TIMONEN, KIMMO (TIH-moh-nehn) L.A.

Defense. Shoots left. 5'10", 180 lbs. Born, Kuopio, Finland, March 18, 1975.
(Los Angeles' 11th choice, 250th overall, in 1993 Entry Draft).

			Regular Season					Playoffs				
Season	Club	Lea	GP	G	A	TP	PIM	GP	G	A	TP	PIM
1991-92	KalPa	Fin.	5	0	0	0	0	....	....	....	....	....
1992-93	KalPa	Fin.	33	0	2	2	4	....	....	....	....	....
1993-94	KalPa	Fin.	46	6	7	13	55	....	....	....	....	....

TINORDI, MARK DAL.

Defense. Shoots left. 6'4", 205 lbs. Born, Red Deer, Alta., May 9, 1966.

			Regular Season					Playoffs				
Season	Club	Lea	GP	G	A	TP	PIM	GP	G	A	TP	PIM
1982-83	Lethbridge	WHL	64	0	4	4	50	20	1	1	2	6
1983-84	Lethbridge	WHL	72	5	14	19	53	5	0	1	1	7
1984-85	Lethbridge	WHL	58	10	15	25	134	4	0	2	2	12
1985-86	Lethbridge	WHL	58	8	30	38	139	8	1	3	4	15
1986-87	Calgary	WHL	61	29	37	66	148	....	....	....	....	....
	New Haven	AHL	2	0	0	0	2	2	0	0	0	0
1987-88	**NY Rangers**	**NHL**	**24**	**1**	**2**	**3**	**50**	....	....	....	....	....
	Colorado	IHL	41	8	19	27	150	11	1	5	6	31
1988-89	**Minnesota**	**NHL**	**47**	**2**	**3**	**5**	**107**	**5**	**0**	**0**	**0**	**0**
	Kalamazoo	IHL	10	0	0	0	35	....	....	....	....	....
1989-90	**Minnesota**	**NHL**	**66**	**3**	**7**	**10**	**240**	**7**	**0**	**1**	**1**	**16**
1990-91	**Minnesota**	**NHL**	**69**	**5**	**27**	**32**	**189**	**23**	**5**	**6**	**11**	**78**
1991-92	**Minnesota**	**NHL**	**63**	**4**	**24**	**28**	**179**	**7**	**1**	**2**	**3**	**11**
1992-93	**Minnesota**	**NHL**	**69**	**15**	**27**	**42**	**157**	....	....	....	....	....
1993-94	**Dallas**	**NHL**	**61**	**6**	**18**	**24**	**143**	....	....	....	....	....
	NHL Totals		**399**	**36**	**108**	**144**	**1065**	**42**	**6**	**9**	**15**	**105**

Played in NHL All-Star Game (1992)

Signed as a free agent by **NY Rangers**, January 4, 1987. Traded to **Minnesota** by **NY Rangers** with Paul Jerrard, the rights to Bret Barnett and Mike Sullivan, and Los Angeles' third round choice (previously acquired by NY Rangers — Minnesota selected Murray Garbutt) in 1989 Entry Draft for Brian Lawton, Igor Liba and the rights to Eric Bennett, October 11, 1988.

TIPPETT, DAVE (TIHP-iht)

Left wing. Shoots left. 5'10", 180 lbs. Born, Moosomin, Sask., August 25, 1961.

			Regular Season					Playoffs				
Season	Club	Lea	GP	G	A	TP	PIM	GP	G	A	TP	PIM
1981-82	North Dakota	WCHA	43	13	28	41	20	....	....	....	....	....
1982-83	North Dakota	WCHA	36	15	31	46	24	....	....	....	....	....
1983-84	Cdn. National	....	66	14	19	33	24	....	....	....	....	....
	Cdn. Olympic	....	7	1	1	2	2	....	....	....	....	....
	Hartford	**NHL**	**17**	**4**	**2**	**6**	**2**	....	....	....	....	....
1984-85	**Hartford**	**NHL**	**80**	**7**	**12**	**19**	**12**	....	....	....	....	....
1985-86	**Hartford**	**NHL**	**80**	**14**	**20**	**34**	**18**	**10**	**2**	**2**	**4**	**4**
1986-87	**Hartford**	**NHL**	**80**	**9**	**22**	**31**	**42**	**6**	**0**	**2**	**2**	**4**
1987-88	**Hartford**	**NHL**	**80**	**16**	**21**	**37**	**32**	**6**	**0**	**0**	**0**	**2**
1988-89	**Hartford**	**NHL**	**80**	**17**	**24**	**41**	**45**	**4**	**0**	**1**	**1**	**0**
1989-90	**Hartford**	**NHL**	**66**	**8**	**19**	**27**	**32**	**7**	**1**	**3**	**4**	**2**
1990-91	**Washington**	**NHL**	**61**	**6**	**9**	**15**	**24**	**10**	**2**	**3**	**5**	**8**
1991-92	**Washington**	**NHL**	**30**	**2**	**10**	**12**	**16**	**7**	**0**	**1**	**1**	**0**
	Cdn. National	....	1	0	0	0	4	....	....	....	....	....
	Cdn. Olympic	....	7	1	2	3	10	....	....	....	....	....
1992-93	**Pittsburgh**	**NHL**	**74**	**6**	**19**	**25**	**56**	**12**	**1**	**4**	**5**	**14**
1993-94	**Philadelphia**	**NHL**	**73**	**4**	**11**	**15**	**38**	....	....	....	....	....
	NHL Totals		**721**	**93**	**169**	**262**	**317**	**62**	**6**	**16**	**22**	**34**

Signed as a free agent by **Hartford**, February 29, 1984. Traded to **Washington** by **Hartford** for Washington's sixth round choice (Jarret Reid) in 1992 Entry Draft, September 30, 1990. Signed as a free agent by **Pittsburgh**, August 25, 1992. Signed as a free agent by **Philadelphia**, August 30, 1993.

TITOV, GERMAN (TEE-tahf, GUHR-mihn) CGY.

Center. Shoots left. 6'1", 190 lbs. Born, Moscow, USSR, October 16, 1965.
(Calgary's 10th choice, 252nd overall, in 1993 Entry Draft).

			Regular Season					Playoffs				
Season	Club	Lea	GP	G	A	TP	PIM	GP	G	A	TP	PIM
1982-83	Khimik	USSR	16	0	2	2	4	....	....	....	....	....
1983-84						DID NOT PLAY						
1984-85						DID NOT PLAY						
1985-86						DID NOT PLAY						
1986-87	Khimik	USSR	23	1	0	1	10	....	....	....	....	....
1987-88	Khimik	USSR	39	6	5	11	10	....	....	....	....	....
1988-89	Khimik	USSR	44	10	3	13	24	....	....	....	....	....
1989-90	Khimik	USSR	44	6	14	20	19	....	....	....	....	....
1990-91	Khimik	USSR	45	13	11	24	28	....	....	....	....	....
1991-92	Khimik	CIS	42	18	13	31	35	....	....	....	....	....
1992-93	TPS	Fin.	47	25	19	44	49	12	5	12	17	10
1993-94	**Calgary**	**NHL**	**76**	**27**	**18**	**45**	**28**	**7**	**2**	**1**	**3**	**4**
	NHL Totals		**76**	**27**	**18**	**45**	**28**	**7**	**2**	**1**	**3**	**4**

TJALLDEN, MIKAEL FLA.

Defense. Shoots left. 6'2", 194 lbs. Born, Ornskoldsvik, Sweden, February 16, 1975.
(Florida's 4th choice, 67th overall, in 1993 Entry Draft).

			Regular Season					Playoffs				
Season	Club	Lea	GP	G	A	TP	PIM	GP	G	A	TP	PIM
1992-93	MoDo Jrs.	Swe.				UNAVAILABLE						
1993-94	Sundsvall-Timra	Swe. 2	24	4	5	9	32	....	....	....	....	....

TKACHUK, KEITH (kuh-CHUK) WPG.

Left wing. Shoots left. 6'2", 210 lbs. Born, Melrose, MA, March 28, 1972.
(Winnipeg's 1st choice, 19th overall, in 1990 Entry Draft).

			Regular Season					Playoffs				
Season	Club	Lea	GP	G	A	TP	PIM	GP	G	A	TP	PIM
1990-91	Boston U.	H.E.	36	17	23	40	70	....	....	....	....	....
1991-92	U.S. National	....	45	10	10	20	141	....	....	....	....	....
	U.S. Olympic	....	8	1	1	2	12	....	....	....	....	....
	Winnipeg	**NHL**	**17**	**3**	**5**	**8**	**28**	**7**	**3**	**0**	**3**	**30**
1992-93	**Winnipeg**	**NHL**	**83**	**28**	**23**	**51**	**201**	**6**	**4**	**0**	**4**	**14**
1993-94	**Winnipeg**	**NHL**	**84**	**41**	**40**	**81**	**255**	....	....	....	....	....
	NHL Totals		**184**	**72**	**68**	**140**	**484**	**13**	**7**	**0**	**7**	**44**

OCCHET, RICK (TAH-keht) L.A.

ght wing. Shoots right. 6', 205 lbs. Born, Scarborough, Ont., April 9, 1964.
hiladelphia's 5th choice, 121st overall, in 1983 Entry Draft).

			Regular Season					Playoffs				
eason	Club	Lea	GP	G	A	TP	PIM	GP	G	A	TP	PIM
981-82	S.S. Marie	OHL	59	7	15	22	184	11	1	1	2	28
982-83	S.S. Marie	OHL	66	32	34	66	146	16	4	13	17	67
983-84	S.S. Marie	OHL	64	44	64	108	209	16	*22	14	*36	41
984-85	**Philadelphia**	**NHL**	**75**	**14**	**25**	**39**	**181**	**19**	**3**	**4**	**7**	**72**
985-86	**Philadelphia**	**NHL**	**69**	**14**	**21**	**35**	**284**	**5**	**1**	**2**	**3**	**26**
986-87	**Philadelphia**	**NHL**	**69**	**21**	**26**	**47**	**288**	**26**	**11**	**10**	**21**	**72**
987-88	**Philadelphia**	**NHL**	**65**	**31**	**33**	**64**	**301**	**5**	**1**	**4**	**5**	**55**
988-89	**Philadelphia**	**NHL**	**66**	**45**	**36**	**81**	**183**	**16**	**6**	**6**	**12**	**69**
989-90	**Philadelphia**	**NHL**	**75**	**37**	**59**	**96**	**196**	....	....	....	....	....
990-91	**Philadelphia**	**NHL**	**70**	**40**	**31**	**71**	**150**	....	....	....	....	....
991-92	**Philadelphia**	**NHL**	**42**	**13**	**16**	**29**	**102**	....	....	....	....	....
	Pittsburgh	**NHL**	**19**	**14**	**16**	**30**	**49**	**14**	**6**	**13**	**19**	**24**
992-93	**Pittsburgh**	**NHL**	**80**	**48**	**61**	**109**	**252**	**12**	**7**	**6**	**13**	**24**
993-94	**Pittsburgh**	**NHL**	**51**	**14**	**26**	**40**	**134**	**6**	**2**	**3**	**5**	**20**
	NHL Totals		**681**	**291**	**350**	**641**	**2120**	**103**	**37**	**48**	**85**	**362**

layed in NHL All-Star Game (1989-91, 1993)

raded to **Pittsburgh** by **Philadelphia** with Kjell Samuelsson, Ken Wregget and Philadelphia's third ound choice (Dave Roche) in 1993 Entry Draft for Mark Recchi, Brian Benning and Los Angeles' first ound choice (previously acquired by Pittsburgh — Philadelphia selected Jason Bowen) in 1992 Entry raft, February 19, 1992 Traded to **Los Angeles** by **Pittsburgh** with Pittsburgh's second round hoice in 1995 Entry Draft for Luc Robitaille, July 29, 1994.

OCHER, RYAN QUE.

efense. Shoots right. 6'2", 194 lbs. Born, Hamilton, Ont., June 14, 1975.
Quebec's 5th choice, 101st overall, in 1993 Entry Draft).

			Regular Season					Playoffs				
eason	Club	Lea	GP	G	A	TP	PIM	GP	G	A	TP	PIM
1991-92	Niagara Falls	OHL	58	4	8	12	53	16	0	0	0	2
1992-93	Niagara Falls	OHL	59	6	17	23	68	4	0	0	0	4
1993-94	Niagara Falls	OHL	13	5	6	11	30	....	....	....	....	....
	Newmarket	OHL	48	7	19	26	71	....	....	....	....	....

ODD, KEVIN L.A.

Center. Shoots left. 5'10", 180 lbs. Born, Winnipeg, Man., May 4, 1968.
New Jersey's 7th choice, 129th overall, in 1986 Entry Draft).

			Regular Season					Playoffs				
Season	Club	Lea	GP	G	A	TP	PIM	GP	G	A	TP	PIM
1985-86	Prince Albert	WHL	55	14	25	39	19	20	7	6	13	29
1986-87	Prince Albert	WHL	71	39	46	85	92	8	2	5	7	17
1987-88	Prince Albert	WHL	72	49	72	121	83	10	8	11	19	27
1988-89	**New Jersey**	**NHL**	**1**	**0**	**0**	**0**	**0**	....	....	....	....	....
	Utica	AHL	78	26	45	71	62	4	2	0	2	6
1989-90	Utica	AHL	71	18	36	54	72	5	2	4	6	2
1990-91	**New Jersey**	**NHL**	**1**	**0**	**0**	**0**	**0**	**1**	**0**	**0**	**0**	**6**
abc	Utica	AHL	75	37	*81	*118	75	....	....	....	....	....
1991-92d	**New Jersey**	**NHL**	**80**	**21**	**42**	**63**	**69**	**7**	**3**	**2**	**5**	**8**
1992-93	**New Jersey**	**NHL**	**30**	**5**	**5**	**10**	**16**	....	....	....	....	....
	Utica	AHL	2	2	1	3	0	....	....	....	....	....
	Edmonton	**NHL**	**25**	**4**	**9**	**13**	**10**	....	....	....	....	....
1993-94	**Chicago**	**NHL**	**35**	**5**	**6**	**11**	**16**	....	....	....	....	....
	Los Angeles	**NHL**	**12**	**3**	**8**	**11**	**8**	....	....	....	....	....
	NHL Totals		**184**	**38**	**70**	**108**	**119**	**8**	**3**	**2**	**5**	**14**

a AHL First All-Star Team (1991)
b Won Les Cunningham Plaque (MVP - AHL) (1991)
c Won John B. Sollenberger Trophy (Leading Scorer - AHL) (1991)
d NHL/Upper Deck All-Rookie Team (1992)

Traded to **Edmonton** by **New Jersey** with Zdeno Ciger for Bernie Nicholls, January 13, 1993. Traded to **Chicago** by **Edmonton** for Adam Bennett, October 7, 1993. Traded to **Los Angeles** by **Chicago** for Los Angeles' fourth round choice (Steve McLaren) in 1994 Entry Draft, March 21, 1994.

TOK, CHRIS PIT.

Defense. Shoots left. 6'1", 185 lbs. Born, Grand Rapids, MN, March 19, 1973.
(Pittsburgh's 10th choice, 214th overall, in 1991 Entry Draft).

			Regular Season					Playoffs				
Season	Club	Lea	GP	G	A	TP	PIM	GP	G	A	TP	PIM
1991-92	U. Wisconsin	WCHA	19	0	2	2	8	....	....	....	....	....
1992-93	U. Wisconsin	WCHA	41	3	12	15	68	....	....	....	....	....
1993-94	U. Wisconsin	WCHA	41	2	5	7	97	....	....	....	....	....

TOMBERLIN, JUSTIN TOR.

Center. Shoots left. 6'1", 195 lbs. Born, Grand Rapids, MN, November 15, 1970.
(Toronto's 11th choice, 192nd overall, in 1989 Entry Draft).

			Regular Season					Playoffs				
Season	Club	Lea	GP	G	A	TP	PIM	GP	G	A	TP	PIM
1989-90	U. of Maine	H.E.	35	10	7	17	6	....	....	....	....	....
1990-91	U. of Maine	H.E.	26	8	5	13	10	....	....	....	....	....
1991-92						DID NOT PLAY						
1992-93	U. of Maine	H.E.	34	13	9	22	22	....	....	....	....	....
1993-94	U. of Maine	H.E.	32	11	17	28	10	....	....	....	....	....

TOMILIN, VITALI N.J.

Left wing. Shoots left. 6', 183 lbs. Born, Elektrostal, USSR, January 15, 1974.
(New Jersey's 4th choice, 90th overall, in 1992 Entry Draft).

			Regular Season					Playoffs				
Season	Club	Lea	GP	G	A	TP	PIM	GP	G	A	TP	PIM
1990-91	Soviet Wings	USSR	1	0	0	0	0	....	....	....	....	....
1991-92	Soviet Wings	CIS	34	1	1	2	6	....	....	....	....	....
1992-93	Soviet Wings	CIS	28	0	1	1	14	2	0	0	0	0
1993-94	Soviet Wings	CIS	44	5	4	9	62	3	0	0	0	0

TOMLAK, MIKE

Center/Left wing. Shoots left. 6'3", 205 lbs. Born, Thunder Bay, Ont., October 17, 1964.
(Toronto's 10th choice, 208th overall, in 1983 Entry Draft).

			Regular Season					Playoffs				
Season	Club	Lea	GP	G	A	TP	PIM	GP	G	A	TP	PIM
1982-83	Cornwall	OHL	70	18	49	67	26	....	....	....	....	....
1983-84	Cornwall	OHL	64	24	64	88	21	....	....	....	....	....
1984-85	Cornwall	OHL	66	30	70	100	9	....	....	....	....	....
1985-86	Western Ont.	OUAA	38	28	20	48	45	....	....	....	....	....
1986-87	Western Ont.	OUAA	38	16	30	46	10	....	....	....	....	....
1987-88	Western Ont.	OUAA	39	24	52	76	....	....	....	....	....	....
1988-89	Western Ont.	OUAA	35	16	34	50	....	....	....	....	....	....
1989-90	**Hartford**	**NHL**	**70**	**7**	**14**	**21**	**48**	**7**	**0**	**1**	**1**	**2**
1990-91	**Hartford**	**NHL**	**64**	**8**	**8**	**16**	**55**	**3**	**0**	**0**	**0**	**2**
	Springfield	AHL	15	4	9	13	15	....	....	....	....	....
1991-92	**Hartford**	**NHL**	**6**	**0**	**0**	**0**	**0**	....	....	....	....	....
	Springfield	AHL	39	16	21	37	24	....	....	....	....	....
1992-93	Springfield	AHL	38	16	21	37	56	5	1	1	2	2
1993-94	**Hartford**	**NHL**	**1**	**0**	**0**	**0**	**0**	....	....	....	....	....
	Springfield	AHL	79	44	56	100	53	4	2	5	7	4
	NHL Totals		**141**	**15**	**22**	**37**	**103**	**10**	**0**	**1**	**1**	**4**

Signed as a free agent by **Hartford**, November 14, 1988.

TOMLINSON, DAVE FLA.

Center. Shoots left. 5'11", 177 lbs. Born, North Vancouver, B.C., May 8, 1969.
(Toronto's 1st choice, 3rd overall, in 1989 Supplemental Draft).

			Regular Season					Playoffs				
Season	Club	Lea	GP	G	A	TP	PIM	GP	G	A	TP	PIM
1987-88	Boston U.	H.E.	34	16	20	36	28	....	....	....	....	....
1988-89	Boston U.	H.E.	34	16	30	46	40	....	....	....	....	....
1989-90	Boston U.	H.E.	43	15	22	37	53	....	....	....	....	....
1990-91	Boston U.	H.E.	41	30	30	60	55	....	....	....	....	....
1991-92	**Toronto**	**NHL**	**3**	**0**	**0**	**0**	**2**	....	....	....	....	....
	St. John's	AHL	75	23	34	57	75	12	4	5	9	6
1992-93	**Toronto**	**NHL**	**3**	**0**	**0**	**0**	**2**	....	....	....	....	....
	St. John's	AHL	70	36	48	84	115	9	1	4	5	8
1993-94	**Winnipeg**	**NHL**	**31**	**1**	**3**	**4**	**24**	....	....	....	....	....
	Moncton	AHL	39	23	23	46	38	20	6	6	12	24
	NHL Totals		**37**	**1**	**3**	**4**	**28**	....	....	....	....	....

Traded to **Florida** by **Toronto** for cash, July 30, 1993. Traded to **Winnipeg** by **Florida** for Jason Cirone, August 3, 1993. Signed as a free agent by **Florida**, June 23, 1994.

TOMPKINS, DAN CGY.

Left wing. Shoots left. 6'2", 205 lbs. Born, MN, January 31, 1975.
(Calgary's 3rd choice, 70th overall, in 1993 Entry Draft).

			Regular Season					Playoffs				
Season	Club	Lea	GP	G	A	TP	PIM	GP	G	A	TP	PIM
1992-93	Omaha	USHL	43	16	34	50	48	....	....	....	....	....
1993-94	U. Wisconsin	WCHA	18	1	0	1	31	....	....	....	....	....

TOMS, JEFF T.B.

Left wing. Shoots left. 6'3", 180 lbs. Born, Swift Current, Sask., June 4, 1974.
(New Jersey's 9th choice, 210th overall, in 1992 Entry Draft).

			Regular Season					Playoffs				
Season	Club	Lea	GP	G	A	TP	PIM	GP	G	A	TP	PIM
1991-92	S.S. Marie	OHL	36	9	5	14	0	16	0	1	1	2
1992-93	S.S. Marie	OHL	59	16	23	39	20	16	4	4	8	7
1993-94	S.S. Marie	OHL	64	52	45	97	19	14	11	4	15	2

Traded to **Tampa Bay** by **New Jersey** for Vancouver's fourth round choice (previously acquired by Tampa Bay — later traded to Calgary — Calgary selected Ryan Duthie) in 1994 Entry Draft, May 31, 1994.

TOOKEY, TIM

Center. Shoots left. 5'11", 185 lbs. Born, Edmonton, Alta., August 29, 1960.
(Washington's 4th choice, 88th overall, in 1979 Entry Draft).

			Regular Season					Playoffs				
Season	Club	Lea	GP	G	A	TP	PIM	GP	G	A	TP	PIM
1977-78	Portland	WHL	72	16	15	31	55	8	2	2	4	5
1978-79	Portland	WHL	56	33	47	80	55	25	6	14	20	6
1979-80	Portland	WHL	70	58	83	141	55	8	2	5	7	4
1980-81	**Washington**	**NHL**	**29**	**10**	**13**	**23**	**18**	....	....	....	....	....
	Hershey	AHL	47	20	38	58	129	....	....	....	....	....
1981-82	**Washington**	**NHL**	**28**	**8**	**8**	**16**	**35**	....	....	....	....	....
	Hershey	AHL	14	4	9	13	10	....	....	....	....	....
	Fredericton	AHL	16	6	10	16	16	....	....	....	....	....
1982-83	**Quebec**	**NHL**	**12**	**1**	**6**	**7**	**4**	....	....	....	....	....
	Fredericton	AHL	53	24	43	67	24	9	5	4	9	0
1983-84	**Pittsburgh**	**NHL**	**8**	**0**	**2**	**2**	**2**	....	....	....	....	....
	Baltimore	AHL	58	16	28	44	25	8	1	1	2	2
1984-85	Baltimore	AHL	74	25	43	68	74	15	8	10	18	13
1985-86ab	Hershey	AHL	69	35	*62	97	66	18	*11	8	19	10
1986-87	**Philadelphia**	**NHL**	**2**	**0**	**0**	**0**	**0**	**10**	**1**	**3**	**4**	**2**
cde	Hershey	AHL	80	51	*73	*124	45	5	5	4	9	0
1987-88	**Los Angeles**	**NHL**	**20**	**1**	**6**	**7**	**8**	....	....	....	....	....
	New Haven	AHL	11	6	7	13	2	....	....	....	....	....
1988-89	**Los Angeles**	**NHL**	**7**	**2**	**1**	**3**	**4**	....	....	....	....	....
	New Haven	AHL	33	11	18	29	30	....	....	....	....	....
	Muskegon	IHL	18	7	14	21	7	8	2	9	11	4
1989-90	Hershey	AHL	42	18	22	40	28	....	....	....	....	....
1990-91	Hershey	AHL	51	17	42	59	43	5	0	5	5	0
1991-92a	Hershey	AHL	80	36	69	105	63	6	4	2	6	4
1992-93f	Hershey	AHL	80	38	70	108	63	....	....	....	....	....
1993-94	Hershey	AHL	66	32	57	89	43	11	4	9	13	8
	NHL Totals		**106**	**22**	**36**	**58**	**71**	**10**	**1**	**3**	**4**	**2**

a AHL Second All-Star Team (1986, 1992)
b Won Jack Butterfield Trophy (Playoff MVP - AHL) (1986)
c AHL First All-Star Team (1987)
d Won Les Cunningham Plaque (MVP - AHL) (1987)
e Won John B. Sollenberger Trophy (Top Scorer - AHL) (1987)
f Won Fred T. Hunt Memorial Trophy (Most Sportsmanlike Player - AHL) (1993)

Traded to **Quebec** by **Washington** with Washington's seventh round choice (later traded to Calgary — Calgary traded Daniel Poudrier) in 1982 Entry Draft for Lee Norwood and Quebec's sixth round choice (Mats Kilstrom) in 1982 Entry Draft, February 1, 1982. Signed as a free agent by **Pittsburgh**, September 12, 1983. Signed as a free agent by **Philadelphia**, July 23, 1985. Claimed by **Los Angeles** in NHL Waiver Draft, October 5, 1987. Traded to **Pittsburgh** by **Los Angeles** for Patrick Mayer, March 7, 1989. Signed as a free agent by **Philadelphia**, June 30, 1989.

TOPOROWSKI, KERRY (toh-poh-ROW-skee) CHI.

Defense. Shoots right. 6'2", 213 lbs. Born, Paddockwood, Sask., April 9, 1971.
(San Jose's 5th choice, 67th overall, in 1991 Entry Draft).

			Regular Season					Playoffs				
Season	Club	Lea	GP	G	A	TP	PIM	GP	G	A	TP	PIM
1989-90	Spokane	WHL	65	1	13	14	384	6	0	0	0	37
1990-91	Spokane	WHL	65	11	16	27	*505	15	2	2	4	*108
1991-92	Indianapolis	IHL	18	1	2	3	206	....	....	....	....	....
1992-93	Indianapolis	IHL	17	0	0	0	57	....	....	....	....	....
1993-94	Indianapolis	IHL	32	1	4	5	126	....	....	....	....	....
	Las Vegas	IHL	13	1	0	1	129	2	0	0	0	31

Traded to **Chicago** by **San Jose** with San Jose's second round choice (later traded to Winnipeg — Winnipeg selected Boris Mironov) in 1992 Entry Draft for Doug Wilson, September 6, 1991.

TOPOROWSKI, SHAYNE (toh-poh-ROW-skee) L.A.

Right wing. Shoots right. 6'2", 215 lbs. Born, Paddockwood, Sask., August 6, 1975.
(Los Angeles' 1st choice, 42nd overall, in 1993 Entry Draft).

			Regular Season					Playoffs				
Season	Club	Lea	GP	G	A	TP	PIM	GP	G	A	TP	PIM
1991-92	Prince Albert	WHL	6	2	0	2	2	7	2	1	3	6
1992-93	Prince Albert	WHL	72	25	32	57	235	....	....	....	....	....
1993-94	Prince Albert	WHL	68	37	45	82	183	....	....	....	....	....

TOROPCHENKO, LEONID (tohr-ahp-CHEHN-koh, LEE-oh-NEED) PIT.

Center. Shoots right. 6'4", 220 lbs. Born, Moscow, USSR, August 28, 1968.
(Pittsburgh's 10th choice, 260th overall, in 1993 Entry Draft).

			Regular Season					Playoffs				
Season	Club	Lea	GP	G	A	TP	PIM	GP	G	A	TP	PIM
1987-88	SKA Leningrad	USSR	6	2	0	2	0	....	....	....	....	....
1988-89	SKA Leningrad	USSR	33	7	4	11	11	....	....	....	....	....
1989-90	Khimik	USSR	42	6	2	8	24	....	....	....	....	....
1990-91	Khimik	USSR	46	6	4	10	24	....	....	....	....	....
1991-92	Khimik	CIS	42	14	4	18	34	....	....	....	....	....
1992-93	Springfield	AHL	71	31	30	61	59	13	4	4	8	8
1993-94	Cleveland	IHL	59	13	20	33	36	....	....	....	....	....

TOWNSHEND, GRAEME (TOWN-SEHND, GRAY-ihm)

Right wing. Shoots right. 6'2", 225 lbs. Born, Kingston, Jamaica, October 2, 1965.

			Regular Season					Playoffs				
Season	Club	Lea	GP	G	A	TP	PIM	GP	G	A	TP	PIM
1985-86	RPI	ECAC	29	1	7	8	52	....	....	....	....	....
1986-87	RPI	ECAC	29	6	1	7	50	....	....	....	....	....
1987-88	RPI	ECAC	32	6	14	20	64	....	....	....	....	....
1988-89	Maine	AHL	5	2	1	3	11	....	....	....	....	....
	RPI	ECAC	31	6	16	22	50	....	....	....	....	....
1989-90	**Boston**	**NHL**	**4**	**0**	**0**	**0**	**7**	....	....	....	....	....
	Maine	AHL	64	15	13	28	162	....	....	....	....	....
1990-91	**Boston**	**NHL**	**18**	**2**	**5**	**7**	**12**	....	....	....	....	....
	Maine	AHL	46	16	10	26	119	2	2	0	2	4
1991-92	**NY Islanders**	**NHL**	**7**	**1**	**2**	**3**	**0**	....	....	....	....	....
	Capital Dist.	AHL	61	14	23	37	94	4	0	2	2	0
1992-93	**NY Islanders**	**NHL**	**2**	**0**	**0**	**0**	**0**	....	....	....	....	....
	Capital Dist.	AHL	67	29	21	50	45	2	0	0	0	0
1993-94	**Ottawa**	**NHL**	**14**	**0**	**0**	**0**	**9**	....	....	....	....	....
	PEI	AHL	56	16	13	29	107	....	....	....	....	....
	NHL Totals		**45**	**3**	**7**	**10**	**28**	....	....	....	....	....

Signed as a free agent by **Boston**, May 12, 1989. Signed as a free agent by **NY Islanders**, September 3, 1991. Signed as a free agent by **Ottawa**, August 24, 1993.

TRAVERSE, PATRICK OTT.

Defense. Shoots left. 6'3", 200 lbs. Born, Montreal, Que., March 14, 1974.
(Ottawa's 3rd choice, 50th overall, in 1992 Entry Draft).

			Regular Season					Playoffs				
Season	Club	Lea	GP	G	A	TP	PIM	GP	G	A	TP	PIM
1991-92	Shawinigan	QMJHL	59	3	11	14	12	10	0	0	0	4
1992-93	St-Jean	QMJHL	68	6	30	36	24	4	0	1	1	2
	New Haven	AHL	2	0	0	0	2	....	....	....	....	....
1993-94	St-Jean	QMJHL	66	15	37	52	30	5	0	4	4	4
	PEI	AHL	3	0	1	1	2	....	....	....	....	....

TREBIL, DANIEL N.J.

Defense. Shoots right. 6'3", 185 lbs. Born, Edina, MN, April 10, 1974.
(New Jersey's 7th choice, 138th overall, in 1992 Entry Draft).

			Regular Season					Playoffs				
Season	Club	Lea	GP	G	A	TP	PIM	GP	G	A	TP	PIM
1992-93	U. Minnesota	WCHA	36	2	11	13	16	....	....	....	....	....
1993-94	U. Minnesota	WCHA	42	1	21	22	24	....	....	....	....	....

TRNKA, PAVEL (tehrn-KAH) ANA.

Defense. Shoots left. 6'3", 187 lbs. Born, Plzen, Czech., July 27, 1976.
(Anaheim's 5th choice, 106th overall, in 1994 Entry Draft).

			Regular Season					Playoffs				
Season	Club	Lea	GP	G	A	TP	PIM	GP	G	A	TP	PIM
1993-94	Skoda Plzen	Czech.	12	0	1	1	....	....	....	....	....	....

TROTTIER, BRYAN (TRAH-chay)

Center. Shoots left. 5'11", 195 lbs. Born, Val Marie, Sask., July 17, 1956.
(NY Islanders' 2nd choice, 22nd overall, in 1974 Amateur Draft).

			Regular Season					Playoffs				
Season	Club	Lea	GP	G	A	TP	PIM	GP	G	A	TP	PIM
1972-73	Swift Current	WHL	67	16	29	45	10	....	....	....	....	..
1973-74	Swift Current	WHL	68	41	71	112	76	13	7	8	15	[illegible]
1974-75a	Lethbridge	WHL	67	46	*98	144	103	6	2	5	7	1[illegible]
1975-76b	**NY Islanders**	**NHL**	**80**	**32**	**63**	**95**	**21**	**13**	**1**	**7**	**8**	[illegible]
1976-77	**NY Islanders**	**NHL**	**76**	**30**	**42**	**72**	**34**	**12**	**2**	**8**	**10**	[illegible]
1977-78c	**NY Islanders**	**NHL**	**77**	**46**	***77**	**123**	**46**	**7**	**0**	**3**	**3**	[illegible]
1978-79cdef	**NY Islanders**	**NHL**	**76**	**47**	***87**	***134**	**50**	**10**	**2**	**4**	**6**	**1[illegible]**
1979-80g	**NY Islanders**	**NHL**	**78**	**42**	**62**	**104**	**68**	**21**	***12**	**17**	***29**	**1[illegible]**
1980-81	**NY Islanders**	**NHL**	**73**	**31**	**72**	**103**	**74**	***18**	**11**	***18**	**29**	**3[illegible]**
1981-82h	**NY Islanders**	**NHL**	**80**	**50**	**79**	**129**	**88**	**19**	**6**	***23**	***29**	**4[illegible]**
1982-83	**NY Islanders**	**NHL**	**80**	**34**	**55**	**89**	**68**	**17**	**8**	**12**	**20**	**1[illegible]**
1983-84h	**NY Islanders**	**NHL**	**68**	**40**	**71**	**111**	**59**	**21**	**8**	**6**	**14**	**4[illegible]**
1984-85	**NY Islanders**	**NHL**	**68**	**28**	**31**	**59**	**47**	**10**	**4**	**2**	**6**	[illegible]
1985-86	**NY Islanders**	**NHL**	**78**	**37**	**59**	**96**	**72**	**3**	**1**	**1**	**2**	[illegible]
1986-87	**NY Islanders**	**NHL**	**80**	**23**	**64**	**87**	**50**	**14**	**8**	**5**	**13**	**1[illegible]**
1987-88i	**NY Islanders**	**NHL**	**77**	**30**	**52**	**82**	**48**	**6**	**0**	**0**	**0**	**1[illegible]**
1988-89j	**NY Islanders**	**NHL**	**73**	**17**	**28**	**45**	**44**	....	....	....	....	..
1989-90	**NY Islanders**	**NHL**	**59**	**13**	**11**	**24**	**29**	**4**	**1**	**0**	**1**	[illegible]
1990-91	**Pittsburgh**	**NHL**	**52**	**9**	**19**	**28**	**24**	**23**	**3**	**4**	**7**	**4[illegible]**
1991-92	**Pittsburgh**	**NHL**	**63**	**11**	**18**	**29**	**54**	**21**	**4**	**3**	**7**	[illegible]
1992-93						DID NOT PLAY						
1993-94	**Pittsburgh**	**NHL**	**41**	**4**	**11**	**15**	**36**	**2**	**0**	**0**	**0**	[illegible]
	NHL Totals		**1279**	**524**	**901**	**1425**	**912**	**221**	**71**	**113**	**184**	**27[illegible]**

a WHL First All-Star Team (1975)
b Won Calder Memorial Trophy (1976)
c NHL First All-Star Team (1978, 1979)
d Won Art Ross Trophy (1979)
e Won Hart Trophy (1979)
f NHL Plus/Minus Leader (1979)
g Won Conn Smythe Trophy (1980)
h NHL Second All-Star Team (1982, 1984)
i Named Budweiser/NHL Man of the Year (1988)
j Won King Clancy Memorial Trophy (1989)

Played in NHL All-Star Game (1976, 1978, 1980, 1982, 1983, 1985, 1986, 1992)

Signed as a free agent by **Pittsburgh**, July 20, 1990. Signed as a free agent by **Pittsburgh**, June 22, 1993.

TSULYGIN, NIKOLAI (tsoo-LEE-gihn) ANA.

Defense. Shoots right. 6'3", 196 lbs. Born, Ufa, USSR, June 29, 1975.
(Anaheim's 2nd choice, 30th overall, in 1993 Entry Draft).

			Regular Season					Playoffs				
Season	Club	Lea	GP	G	A	TP	PIM	GP	G	A	TP	PIM
1992-93	Yulayev	CIS	42	5	4	9	21	2	0	0	0	0
1993-94	Yulayev	CIS	43	0	14	14	24	5	0	1	1	0

TSYGUROV, DENIS (tsih-GOO-rawv) BUF.

Defense. Shoots left. 6'3", 198 lbs. Born, Chelyabinsk, USSR, February 26, 1971.
(Buffalo's 1st choice, 38th overall, in 1993 Entry Draft).

			Regular Season					Playoffs				
Season	Club	Lea	GP	G	A	TP	PIM	GP	G	A	TP	PIM
1988-89	Chelyabinsk	USSR	8	0	0	0	2	....	....	....	....	....
1989-90	Chelyabinsk	USSR	27	0	1	1	18	....	....	....	....	....
1990-91	Chelyabinsk	USSR	26	0	1	1	16	....	....	....	....	....
1991-92	Togliatti	CIS	29	3	2	5	6	....	....	....	....	....
1992-93a	Togliatti	CIS	37	7	13	20	29	10	1	1	2	6
1993-94	**Buffalo**	**NHL**	**8**	**0**	**0**	**0**	**8**	....	....	....	....	....
	Rochester	AHL	24	1	10	11	10	1	0	1	1	0
	NHL Totals		**8**	**0**	**0**	**0**	**8**	....	....	....	....	....

a CIS All-Star Team (1993)

TUCKER, CHRIS CHI.

Center. Shoots left. 5'11", 183 lbs. Born, White Plains, NY, February 9, 1972.
(Chicago's 3rd choice, 79th overall, in 1990 Entry Draft).

			Regular Season					Playoffs				
Season	Club	Lea	GP	G	A	TP	PIM	GP	G	A	TP	PIM
1990-91	U. Wisconsin	WCHA	35	5	6	11	6	....	....	....	....	....
1991-92	U. Wisconsin	WCHA	34	12	8	20	23	....	....	....	....	....
1992-93	U. Wisconsin	WCHA	40	10	9	19	12	....	....	....	....	....
1993-94	U. Wisconsin	WCHA	42	9	19	28	32	....	....	....	....	....

TUCKER, DARCY MTL.

Center. Shoots left. 5'10", 163 lbs. Born, Castor, Alta., March 15, 1975.
(Montreal's 8th choice, 151st overall, in 1993 Entry Draft).

			Regular Season					Playoffs				
Season	Club	Lea	GP	G	A	TP	PIM	GP	G	A	TP	PIM
1991-92	Kamloops	WHL	26	3	10	13	32	9	0	1	1	16
1992-93	Kamloops	WHL	67	31	58	89	155	13	7	6	13	34
1993-94abcd	Kamloops	WHL	66	52	88	140	143	19	9	*18	*27	43

a WHL West First All-Star Team (1994)
b Canadian Major Junior First All-Star Team (1994)
c Memorial Cup All-Star Team (1994)
d Won Stafford Smythe Memorial Trophy (Memorial Cup Tournament MVP) (1994)

TUCKER, JOHN — T.B.

Center. Shoots right. 6', 200 lbs. Born, Windsor, Ont., September 29, 1964.
(Buffalo's 4th choice, 31st overall, in 1983 Entry Draft).

			Regular Season					Playoffs				
Season	Club	Lea	GP	G	A	TP	PIM	GP	G	A	TP	PIM
1981-82	Kitchener	OHL	67	16	32	48	32	15	2	3	5	2
1982-83	Kitchener	OHL	70	60	80	140	33	11	5	9	14	10
1983-84	**Buffalo**	**NHL**	**21**	**12**	**4**	**16**	**4**	**3**	**1**	**0**	**1**	**0**
a	Kitchener	OHL	39	40	60	100	25	12	12	18	30	8
1984-85	**Buffalo**	**NHL**	**64**	**22**	**27**	**49**	**21**	**5**	**1**	**5**	**6**	**0**
1985-86	**Buffalo**	**NHL**	**75**	**31**	**34**	**65**	**39**	....	....	....	....	....
1986-87	**Buffalo**	**NHL**	**54**	**17**	**34**	**51**	**21**	....	....	....	....	....
1987-88	**Buffalo**	**NHL**	**45**	**19**	**19**	**38**	**20**	**6**	**7**	**3**	**10**	**18**
1988-89	**Buffalo**	**NHL**	**60**	**13**	**31**	**44**	**31**	**3**	**0**	**3**	**3**	**0**
1989-90	**Buffalo**	**NHL**	**8**	**1**	**2**	**3**	**2**	....	....	....	....	....
	Washington	**NHL**	**38**	**9**	**19**	**28**	**10**	**12**	**1**	**7**	**8**	**4**
1990-91	**Buffalo**	**NHL**	**18**	**1**	**3**	**4**	**4**	....	....	....	....	....
	NY Islanders	**NHL**	**20**	**3**	**4**	**7**	**4**	....	....	....	....	....
1991-92	Asiago	Italy	18	16	21	37	6	11	7	13	20	15
1992-93	**Tampa Bay**	**NHL**	**78**	**17**	**39**	**56**	**69**	....	....	....	....	....
1993-94	**Tampa Bay**	**NHL**	**66**	**17**	**23**	**40**	**28**	....	....	....	....	....
	NHL Totals		**547**	**162**	**239**	**401**	**253**	**29**	**10**	**18**	**28**	**22**

a OHL First All-Star Team (1984)

Traded to **Washington** by **Buffalo** for future considerations, January 5, 1990. Traded to **Buffalo** by **Washington** for cash, July 3, 1990. Traded to **NY Islanders** by **Buffalo** for future considerations, January 21, 1991. Signed as a free agent by **Tampa Bay**, August 5, 1992.

TUCKER, TRAVIS

Defense. Shoots right. 6'4", 205 lbs. Born, Hartford, CT, March 15, 1971.
(Detroit's 9th choice, 192nd overall, in 1990 Entry Draft).

			Regular Season					Playoffs				
Season	Club	Lea	GP	G	A	TP	PIM	GP	G	A	TP	PIM
1990-91	Lowell	H.E.	22	0	0	0	40	....	....	....	....	....
1991-92	Lowell	H.E.	32	1	7	8	77	....	....	....	....	....
1992-93	Lowell	H.E.	31	2	9	11	90	....	....	....	....	....
1993-94	Lowell	H.E.	30	1	6	7	83	....	....	....	....	....

TULLY, BRENT — VAN.

Defense. Shoots right. 6'3", 195 lbs. Born, Peterborough, Ont., March 26, 1974.
(Vancouver's 5th choice, 93rd overall, in 1992 Entry Draft).

			Regular Season					Playoffs				
Season	Club	Lea	GP	G	A	TP	PIM	GP	G	A	TP	PIM
1990-91	Peterborough	OHL	45	3	5	8	35	2	0	0	0	0
1991-92	Peterborough	OHL	65	9	23	32	65	10	0	0	0	2
1992-93a	Peterborough	OHL	59	15	45	60	81	21	8	24	32	32
1993-94	Peterborough	OHL	37	17	26	43	81	7	5	3	8	12
	Cdn. National	....	1	0	1	1	0	....	....	....	....	....
	Hamilton	AHL	1	0	0	0	0	1	1	0	1	0

a OHL Second All-Star Team (1993)

TUOMAINEN, MARKO — EDM.

Right wing. Shoots right. 6'2", 190 lbs. Born, Kuopio, Finland, April 25, 1972.
(Edmonton's 10th choice, 205th overall, in 1992 Entry Draft).

			Regular Season					Playoffs				
Season	Club	Lea	GP	G	A	TP	PIM	GP	G	A	TP	PIM
1989-90	KalPa	Fin.	5	0	0	0	0	....	....	....	....	....
1990-91	KalPa	Fin.	30	2	1	3	2	8	0	0	0	6
1991-92	Clarkson	ECAC	28	11	12	23	32	....	....	....	....	....
1992-93a	Clarkson	ECAC	35	25	30	55	26	....	....	....	....	....
1993-94	Clarkson	ECAC	34	23	29	52	60	....	....	....	....	....

a ECAC First All-Star Team (1993)

TURCOTTE, DARREN — HFD.

Center. Shoots left. 6', 178 lbs. Born, Boston, MA, March 2, 1968.
(NY Rangers' 6th choice, 114th overall, in 1986 Entry Draft).

			Regular Season					Playoffs				
Season	Club	Lea	GP	G	A	TP	PIM	GP	G	A	TP	PIM
1984-85	North Bay	OHL	62	33	32	65	28	....	....	....	....	....
1985-86	North Bay	OHL	62	35	37	72	35	10	3	4	7	8
1986-87	North Bay	OHL	55	30	48	78	20	18	12	8	20	6
1987-88	North Bay	OHL	32	30	33	63	16	4	3	0	3	4
	Colorado	IHL	8	4	3	7	9	6	2	6	8	8
1988-89	**NY Rangers**	**NHL**	**20**	**7**	**3**	**10**	**4**	**1**	**0**	**0**	**0**	**0**
	Denver	IHL	40	21	28	49	32	....	....	....	....	....
1989-90	**NY Rangers**	**NHL**	**76**	**32**	**34**	**66**	**32**	**10**	**1**	**6**	**7**	**4**
1990-91	**NY Rangers**	**NHL**	**74**	**26**	**41**	**67**	**37**	**6**	**1**	**2**	**3**	**0**
1991-92	**NY Rangers**	**NHL**	**71**	**30**	**23**	**53**	**57**	**8**	**4**	**0**	**4**	**6**
1992-93	**NY Rangers**	**NHL**	**71**	**25**	**28**	**53**	**40**	....	....	....	....	....
1993-94	**NY Rangers**	**NHL**	**13**	**2**	**4**	**6**	**13**	....	....	....	....	....
	Hartford	**NHL**	**19**	**2**	**11**	**13**	**4**	....	....	....	....	....
	NHL Totals		**344**	**124**	**144**	**268**	**187**	**25**	**6**	**8**	**14**	**10**

Played in NHL All-Star Game (1991)

Traded to **Hartford** by **NY Rangers** with James Patrick for Steve Larmer, Nick Kypreos, Barry Richter and Hartford's sixth round choice (Yuri Litvinov) in 1994 Entry Draft, November 2, 1993.

TURGEON, PIERRE — (TUHR-zhaw) — NYI

Center. Shoots left. 6'1", 202 lbs. Born, Rouyn, Que., August 29, 1969.
(Buffalo's 1st choice, 1st overall, in 1987 Entry Draft).

			Regular Season					Playoffs				
Season	Club	Lea	GP	G	A	TP	PIM	GP	G	A	TP	PIM
1985-86	Granby	QMJHL	69	47	67	114	31	....	....	....	....	....
1986-87	Granby	QMJHL	58	69	85	154	8	7	9	6	15	15
1987-88	**Buffalo**	**NHL**	**76**	**14**	**28**	**42**	**34**	**6**	**4**	**3**	**7**	**4**
1988-89	**Buffalo**	**NHL**	**80**	**34**	**54**	**88**	**26**	**5**	**3**	**5**	**8**	**2**
1989-90	**Buffalo**	**NHL**	**80**	**40**	**66**	**106**	**29**	**6**	**2**	**4**	**6**	**2**
1990-91	**Buffalo**	**NHL**	**78**	**32**	**47**	**79**	**26**	**6**	**3**	**1**	**4**	**6**
1991-92	**Buffalo**	**NHL**	**8**	**2**	**6**	**8**	**4**	....	....	....	....	....
	NY Islanders	**NHL**	**69**	**38**	**49**	**87**	**16**	....	....	....	....	....
1992-93a	**NY Islanders**	**NHL**	**83**	**58**	**74**	**132**	**26**	**11**	**6**	**7**	**13**	**0**
1993-94	**NY Islanders**	**NHL**	**69**	**38**	**56**	**94**	**18**	**4**	**0**	**1**	**1**	**0**
	NHL Totals		**543**	**256**	**380**	**636**	**179**	**38**	**18**	**21**	**39**	**14**

a Won Lady Byng Memorial Trophy (1993)

Played in NHL All-Star Game (1990, 1993, 1994)

Traded to **NY Islanders** by **Buffalo** with Uwe Krupp, Benoit Hogue and Dave McLlwain for Pat Lafontaine, Randy Hillier, Randy Wood and NY Islanders' fourth round choice (Dean Melanson) in 1992 Entry Draft, October 25, 1991.

TURGEON, SYLVAIN — (TUHR-zhaw) — OTT.

Left wing. Shoots left. 6', 200 lbs. Born, Noranda, Que., January 17, 1965.
(Hartford's 1st choice, 2nd overall, in 1983 Entry Draft).

			Regular Season					Playoffs				
Season	Club	Lea	GP	G	A	TP	PIM	GP	G	A	TP	PIM
1981-82	Hull	QMJHL	57	33	40	73	78	14	11	11	22	16
1982-83a	Hull	QMJHL	67	54	109	163	103	7	8	7	15	10
1983-84b	**Hartford**	**NHL**	**76**	**40**	**32**	**72**	**55**	....	....	....	....	....
1984-85	**Hartford**	**NHL**	**64**	**31**	**31**	**62**	**67**	....	....	....	....	....
1985-86	**Hartford**	**NHL**	**76**	**45**	**34**	**79**	**88**	**9**	**2**	**3**	**5**	**4**
1986-87	**Hartford**	**NHL**	**41**	**23**	**13**	**36**	**45**	**6**	**1**	**2**	**3**	**4**
1987-88	**Hartford**	**NHL**	**71**	**23**	**26**	**49**	**71**	**6**	**0**	**0**	**0**	**4**
1988-89	**Hartford**	**NHL**	**42**	**16**	**14**	**30**	**40**	**4**	**0**	**2**	**2**	**4**
1989-90	**New Jersey**	**NHL**	**72**	**30**	**17**	**47**	**81**	**1**	**0**	**0**	**0**	**0**
1990-91	**Montreal**	**NHL**	**19**	**5**	**7**	**12**	**20**	**5**	**0**	**0**	**0**	**2**
1991-92	**Montreal**	**NHL**	**56**	**9**	**11**	**20**	**39**	**5**	**1**	**0**	**1**	**4**
1992-93	**Ottawa**	**NHL**	**72**	**25**	**18**	**43**	**104**	....	....	....	....	....
1993-94	**Ottawa**	**NHL**	**47**	**11**	**15**	**26**	**52**	....	....	....	....	....
	NHL Totals		**636**	**258**	**218**	**476**	**662**	**36**	**4**	**7**	**11**	**22**

a QMJHL First All-Star Team (1983)
b NHL All-Rookie Team (1984)

Played in NHL All-Star Game (1986)

Traded to **New Jersey** by **Hartford** for Pat Verbeek, June 17, 1989. Traded to **Montreal** by **New Jersey** for Claude Lemieux, September 4, 1990. Claimed by **Ottawa** from **Montreal** in Expansion Draft, June 18, 1992.

TURNER, BART — DET.

Left wing. Shoots left. 6'3", 200 lbs. Born, Beaverton, OR, January 11, 1972.
(Detroit's 9th choice, 230th overall, in 1991 Entry Draft).

			Regular Season					Playoffs				
Season	Club	Lea	GP	G	A	TP	PIM	GP	G	A	TP	PIM
1990-91	Michigan State	CCHA	21	3	1	4	4	....	....	....	....	....
1991-92	Michigan State	CCHA	41	8	7	15	36	....	....	....	....	....
1992-93	Michigan State	CCHA	39	5	9	14	53	....	....	....	....	....
1993-94	Michigan State	CCHA	41	5	11	16	40	....	....	....	....	....

TURNER, BRAD

Defense. Shoots right. 6'2", 205 lbs. Born, Winnipeg, Man., May 25, 1968.
(Minnesota's 6th choice, 58th overall, in 1986 Entry Draft).

			Regular Season					Playoffs				
Season	Club	Lea	GP	G	A	TP	PIM	GP	G	A	TP	PIM
1986-87	U. of Michigan	CCHA	40	3	10	13	40	....	....	....	....	....
1987-88	U. of Michigan	CCHA	39	3	11	14	52	....	....	....	....	....
1988-89	U. of Michigan	CCHA	33	3	8	11	38	....	....	....	....	....
1989-90	U. of Michigan	CCHA	32	8	9	17	34	....	....	....	....	....
1990-91	Capital Dist.	AHL	31	1	2	3	8	....	....	....	....	....
	Richmond	ECHL	40	16	25	41	31	....	....	....	....	....
1991-92	**NY Islanders**	**NHL**	**3**	**0**	**0**	**0**	**0**	....	....	....	....	....
	Capital Dist.	AHL	35	3	6	9	17	....	....	....	....	....
	New Haven	AHL	32	6	11	17	58	....	....	....	....	....
1992-93	Capital Dist.	AHL	65	8	11	19	71	3	0	0	0	2
1993-94	Cdn. National	....	30	6	9	15	21	....	....	....	....	....
	Cornwall	AHL	29	3	13	16	19	4	1	1	2	4
	NHL Totals		**3**	**0**	**0**	**0**	**0**	....	....	....	....	....

Signed as a free agent by **NY Islanders**, June 4, 1991.

TUTTLE, STEVE

Right wing. Shoots right. 6'1", 197 lbs. Born, Vancouver, B.C., January 5, 1966.
(St. Louis' 8th choice, 113th overall, in 1984 Entry Draft).

			Regular Season					Playoffs				
Season	Club	Lea	GP	G	A	TP	PIM	GP	G	A	TP	PIM
1984-85	U. Wisconsin	WCHA	28	3	4	7	0	....	....	....	....	....
1985-86	U. Wisconsin	WCHA	32	2	10	12	2	....	....	....	....	....
1986-87	U. Wisconsin	WCHA	42	31	21	52	14	....	....	....	....	....
1987-88ab	U. Wisconsin	WCHA	45	27	39	66	18	....	....	....	....	....
1988-89	**St. Louis**	**NHL**	**53**	**13**	**12**	**25**	**6**	**6**	**1**	**2**	**3**	**0**
1989-90	**St. Louis**	**NHL**	**71**	**12**	**10**	**22**	**4**	**5**	**0**	**1**	**1**	**2**
1990-91	**St. Louis**	**NHL**	**20**	**3**	**6**	**9**	**2**	**6**	**0**	**3**	**3**	**0**
	Peoria	IHL	42	24	32	56	8	....	....	....	....	....
1991-92c	Peoria	IHL	71	43	46	89	22	10	4	8	12	4
1992-93	Milwaukee	IHL	51	27	34	61	12	4	0	2	2	2
	Halifax	AHL	22	11	17	28	2	....	....	....	....	....
1993-94	Milwaukee	IHL	78	27	44	71	34	4	0	2	2	4
	NHL Totals		**144**	**28**	**28**	**56**	**12**	**17**	**1**	**6**	**7**	**2**

a NCAA West Second All-American Team (1988)
b WCHA Second All-Star Team (1988)
c IHL First All-Star Team (1992)

Traded to **Tampa Bay** by **St. Louis** with Pat Jablonski and Darin Kimble for future considerations, June 19, 1992. Traded to **Quebec** by **Tampa Bay** with Martin Simard and Michel Mongeau for Herb Raglan, February 12, 1993.

TUZZOLINO, TONY — QUE.

Right wing. Shoots right. 6'2", 180 lbs. Born, Buffalo, NY, October 9, 1975.
(Quebec's 7th choice, 113th overall, in 1994 Entry Draft).

			Regular Season					Playoffs				
Season	Club	Lea	GP	G	A	TP	PIM	GP	G	A	TP	PIM
1992-93	Niagara	NAJHL	50	36	41	77	134	....	....	....	....	....
1993-94	Michigan State	CCHA	35	4	3	7	46	....	....	....	....	....

TVERDOVSKY, OLEG — (tvehr-DOHV-skee) — ANA.

Defense. Shoots left. 6', 183 lbs. Born, Donetsk, USSR, May 18, 1976.
(Anaheim's 1st choice, 2nd overall, in 1994 Entry Draft).

			Regular Season					Playoffs				
Season	Club	Lea	GP	G	A	TP	PIM	GP	G	A	TP	PIM
1992-93	Soviet Wings	CIS	21	0	1	1	6	6	0	0	0	0
1993-94	Soviet Wings	CIS	46	4	10	14	22	3	1	0	1	2

TWIST, TONY

Left wing/Defense. Shoots left. 6', 208 lbs. Born, Sherwood Park, Alta., May 9, 1968.
(St. Louis' 9th choice, 177th overall, in 1988 Entry Draft).

			Regular Season					Playoffs				
Season	Club	Lea	GP	G	A	TP	PIM	GP	G	A	TP	PIM
1987-88	Saskatoon	WHL	55	1	8	9	226	10	1	1	2	6
1988-89	Peoria	IHL	67	3	8	11	312	....	....	....	....	....
1989-90	**St. Louis**	**NHL**	**28**	**0**	**0**	**0**	**124**	....	....	....	....	....
	Peoria	IHL	36	1	5	6	200	5	0	1	1	8
1990-91	Peoria	IHL	38	2	10	12	244	....	....	....	....	....
	Quebec	**NHL**	**24**	**0**	**0**	**0**	**104**	....	....	....	....	....
1991-92	**Quebec**	**NHL**	**44**	**0**	**1**	**1**	**164**	....	....	....	....	....
1992-93	**Quebec**	**NHL**	**34**	**0**	**2**	**2**	**64**	....	....	....	....	....
1993-94	**Quebec**	**NHL**	**49**	**0**	**4**	**4**	**101**	....	....	....	....	....
	NHL Totals		**179**	**0**	**7**	**7**	**557**	....	....	....	....	....

Traded to **Quebec** by **St. Louis** with Herb Raglan and Andy Rymsha for Darin Kimble, February 4, 1991.

ULANOV, IGOR (oo-LAH-nahf, EE-gohr) WPG.

Defense. Shoots left. 6'2", 205 lbs. Born, Krasnokamsk, USSR, October 1, 1969.
(Winnipeg's 8th choice, 203rd overall, in 1991 Entry Draft).

			Regular Season					Playoffs				
Season	Club	Lea	GP	G	A	TP	PIM	GP	G	A	TP	PIM
1990-91	Khimik	USSR	41	2	2	4	52	....	....	....	....	....
1991-92	Khimik	CIS	27	1	4	5	24	....	....	....	....	....
	Winnipeg	**NHL**	**27**	**2**	**9**	**11**	**67**	**7**	**0**	**0**	**0**	**39**
	Moncton	AHL	3	0	1	1	16	....	....	....	....	....
1992-93	**Winnipeg**	**NHL**	**56**	**2**	**14**	**16**	**124**	**4**	**0**	**0**	**0**	**4**
	Moncton	AHL	9	1	3	4	26	....	....	....	....	....
	Fort Wayne	IHL	3	0	1	1	29	....	....	....	....	....
1993-94	**Winnipeg**	**NHL**	**74**	**0**	**17**	**17**	**165**	....	....	....	....	....
	NHL Totals		**157**	**4**	**40**	**44**	**356**	**11**	**0**	**0**	**0**	**43**

USTORF, STEFAN WSH.

Center. Shoots left. 5'11", 190 lbs. Born, Kaufbeuren, Germany, January 3, 1974.
(Washington's 3rd choice, 53rd overall, in 1992 Entry Draft).

			Regular Season					Playoffs				
Season	Club	Lea	GP	G	A	TP	PIM	GP	G	A	TP	PIM
1991-92	Kaufbeuren	Ger.	41	2	22	24	46	5	2	7	9	6
1992-93	Kaufbeuren	Ger.	37	14	18	32	32	3	1	0	1	10
1993-94	Kaufbeuren	Ger.	38	10	20	30	21	3	0	0	0	4

UVAYEV, VYACHESLAV (oo-VIH-ev)

Defense. Shoots left. 5'11", 189 lbs. Born, Moscow, USSR, April 15, 1966.
(NY Rangers' 9th choice, 191st overall, in 1991 Entry Draft).

			Regular Season					Playoffs				
Season	Club	Lea	GP	G	A	TP	PIM	GP	G	A	TP	PIM
1988-89	Torpedo Yaro.	USSR	22	0	1	1	14	....	....	....	....	....
1989-90	Torpedo Yaro.	USSR	48	4	8	12	64	....	....	....	....	....
1990-91	Spartak	USSR	45	1	10	11	44	....	....	....	....	....
1991-92	Spartak	CIS	42	0	7	7	12	....	....	....	....	....
1992-93	Spartak	CIS	40	3	9	12	30	3	0	0	0	2
1993-94	Asiago	Alp.	28	1	11	12	24	....	....	....	....	....
	Asiago	Italy	20	4	8	12	25	....	....	....	....	....

VACHON, NICK

Center. Shoots left. 5'10", 190 lbs. Born, Montreal, Que., July 20, 1972.
(Toronto's 11th choice, 241st overall, in 1990 Entry Draft).

			Regular Season					Playoffs				
Season	Club	Lea	GP	G	A	TP	PIM	GP	G	A	TP	PIM
1990-91	Boston U.	H.E.	8	0	1	1	4	....	....	....	....	....
1991-92	Boston U.	H.E.	16	6	7	13	10	....	....	....	....	....
	Portland	WHL	25	9	19	28	46	6	0	3	3	14
1992-93	Portland	WHL	66	33	58	91	100	16	11	7	18	34
1993-94	Atlanta	IHL	3	1	1	2	0	....	....	....	....	....
	Knoxville	ECHL	61	29	57	86	139	3	0	0	0	2

VALICEVIC, ROBERT NYI

Right wing. Shoots right. 6'2", 197 lbs. Born, Detroit, MI, January 6, 1971.
(NY Islanders' 6th choice, 114th overall, in 1991 Entry Draft).

			Regular Season					Playoffs				
Season	Club	Lea	GP	G	A	TP	PIM	GP	G	A	TP	PIM
1991-92	Lake Superior	CCHA	32	8	4	12	12	....	....	....	....	....
1992-93	Lake Superior	CCHA	43	21	20	41	28	....	....	....	....	....
1993-94	Lake Superior	CCHA	45	18	20	38	46	....	....	....	....	....

VALILA, MIKA PIT.

Center. Shoots left. 6', 187 lbs. Born, Sodertalje, Sweden, February 20, 1970.
(Pittsburgh's 7th choice, 130th overall, in 1990 Entry Draft).

			Regular Season					Playoffs				
Season	Club	Lea	GP	G	A	TP	PIM	GP	G	A	TP	PIM
1988-89	Tappara	Fin.	14	2	5	7	8	3	1	0	1	2
1989-90	Tappara	Fin.	44	8	16	24	16	7	2	2	4	4
1990-91	Tappara	Fin.	41	10	9	19	16	3	0	1	1	0
1991-92	Jokerit	Fin.	30	4	3	7	4	8	1	1	2	2
1992-93	Lukko	Fin.	48	8	10	18	24	3	0	0	0	0
1993-94	Lukko	Fin.	45	7	7	14	18	9	0	0	0	8

VALK, GARRY (VAHLK) ANA.

Left wing. Shoots left. 6'1", 205 lbs. Born, Edmonton, Alta., November 27, 1967.
(Vancouver's 5th choice, 108th overall, in 1987 Entry Draft).

			Regular Season					Playoffs				
Season	Club	Lea	GP	G	A	TP	PIM	GP	G	A	TP	PIM
1987-88	North Dakota	WCHA	38	23	12	35	64	....	....	....	....	....
1988-89	North Dakota	WCHA	40	14	17	31	71	....	....	....	....	....
1989-90	North Dakota	WCHA	43	22	17	39	92	....	....	....	....	....
1990-91	**Vancouver**	**NHL**	**59**	**10**	**11**	**21**	**67**	**5**	**0**	**0**	**0**	**20**
	Milwaukee	IHL	10	12	4	16	13	3	0	0	0	2
1991-92	**Vancouver**	**NHL**	**65**	**8**	**17**	**25**	**56**	**4**	**0**	**0**	**0**	**5**
1992-93	**Vancouver**	**NHL**	**48**	**6**	**7**	**13**	**77**	**7**	**0**	**1**	**1**	**12**
	Hamilton	AHL	7	3	6	9	6	....	....	....	....	....
1993-94	**Anaheim**	**NHL**	**78**	**18**	**27**	**45**	**100**	....	....	....	....	....
	NHL Totals		**250**	**42**	**62**	**104**	**300**	**16**	**0**	**1**	**1**	**37**

Claimed by **Anaheim** from **Vancouver** in NHL Waiver Draft, October 3, 1993.

VALLEE, SEBASTIEN PHI.

Left wing. Shoots left. 6'4", 180 lbs. Born, Thetford Mines, Que., January 2, 1976.
(Philadelphia's 3rd choice, 101st overall, in 1994 Entry Draft).

			Regular Season					Playoffs				
Season	Club	Lea	GP	G	A	TP	PIM	GP	G	A	TP	PIM
1992-93	Beauce	Midget	30	20	15	35	10	....	....	....	....	....
1993-94	Victoriaville	QMJHL	72	17	22	39	22	1	0	0	0	0

VALLIS, LINDSAY

Defense. Shoots right. 6'3", 207 lbs. Born, Winnipeg, Man., January 12, 1971.
(Montreal's 1st choice, 13th overall, in 1989 Entry Draft).

			Regular Season					Playoffs				
Season	Club	Lea	GP	G	A	TP	PIM	GP	G	A	TP	PIM
1987-88	Seattle	WHL	68	31	45	76	65	....	....	....	....	....
1988-89	Seattle	WHL	63	21	32	53	48	....	....	....	....	....
1989-90	Seattle	WHL	65	34	43	77	68	13	6	5	11	14
1990-91	Seattle	WHL	72	41	38	79	119	6	1	3	4	17
	Fredericton	AHL	....	....	....	....	....	7	0	0	0	6
1991-92	Fredericton	AHL	71	10	19	29	84	4	0	1	1	7
1992-93	Fredericton	AHL	65	18	16	34	38	5	0	2	2	10
1993-94	**Montreal**	**NHL**	**1**	**0**	**0**	**0**	**0**	....	....	....	....	....
	Fredericton	AHL	75	9	30	39	103	....	....	....	....	....
	NHL Totals		**1**	**0**	**0**	**0**	**0**	....	....	....	....	....

VAN ALLEN, SHAUN ANA.

Center. Shoots left. 6'1", 200 lbs. Born, Shaunavon, Sask., August 29, 1967.
(Edmonton's 5th choice, 105th overall, in 1987 Entry Draft).

			Regular Season					Playoffs				
Season	Club	Lea	GP	G	A	TP	PIM	GP	G	A	TP	PIM
1984-85	Swift Current	WHL	61	12	20	32	136	....	....	....	....	....
1985-86	Saskatoon	WHL	55	12	11	23	43	13	4	8	12	28
1986-87	Saskatoon	WHL	72	38	59	97	116	11	4	6	10	24
1987-88	Milwaukee	IHL	40	14	28	42	34	....	....	....	....	....
	Nova Scotia	AHL	19	4	10	14	17	4	1	1	2	4
1988-89	Cape Breton	AHL	76	32	42	74	81	....	....	....	....	....
1989-90	Cape Breton	AHL	61	25	44	69	83	4	0	2	2	8
1990-91	**Edmonton**	**NHL**	**2**	**0**	**0**	**0**	**0**	....	....	....	....	....
a	Cape Breton	AHL	76	25	75	100	182	4	0	1	1	8
1991-92bc	Cape Breton	AHL	77	29	*84	*113	80	5	3	7	10	14
1992-93	**Edmonton**	**NHL**	**21**	**1**	**4**	**5**	**6**	....	....	....	....	....
	Cape Breton	AHL	43	14	62	76	68	15	8	9	17	18
1993-94	**Anaheim**	**NHL**	**80**	**8**	**25**	**33**	**64**	....	....	....	....	....
	NHL Totals		**103**	**9**	**29**	**38**	**70**	....	....	....	....	....

a AHL Second All-Star Team (1991)
b Won John B. Sollenberger Trophy (Top Scorer - AHL) (1992)
c AHL First All-Star Team (1992)

Signed as a free agent by **Anaheim**, July 22, 1993.

VANDENBUSSCHE, RYAN TOR.

Right wing. Shoots right. 5'11", 187 lbs. Born, Simcoe, Ont., February 28, 1973.
(Toronto's 8th choice, 173rd overall, in 1992 Entry Draft).

			Regular Season					Playoffs				
Season	Club	Lea	GP	G	A	TP	PIM	GP	G	A	TP	PIM
1990-91	Cornwall	OHL	49	3	8	11	139	....	....	....	....	....
1991-92	Cornwall	OHL	61	13	15	28	232	6	0	2	2	9
1992-93	Newmarket	OHL	30	15	12	27	161	....	....	....	....	....
	Guelph	OHL	29	3	14	17	99	5	1	3	4	13
	St. John's	AHL	1	0	0	0	0	....	....	....	....	....
1993-94	St. John's	AHL	44	4	10	14	124	....	....	....	....	....
	Springfield	AHL	9	1	2	3	29	5	0	0	0	16

VAN IMPE, DARREN NYI

Defense. Shoots left. 6', 195 lbs. Born, Saskatoon, Sask., May 18, 1973.
(NY Islanders' 7th choice, 170th overall, in 1993 Entry Draft).

			Regular Season					Playoffs				
Season	Club	Lea	GP	G	A	TP	PIM	GP	G	A	TP	PIM
1992-93a	Red Deer	WHL	54	23	47	70	118	4	2	5	7	16
1993-94a	Red Deer	WHL	58	20	64	84	125	4	2	4	6	6

a WHL First All-Star Team (1993, 1994)

VARADA, VACLAV (VAH-rah-dah) S.J.

Right wing. Shoots left. 6', 198 lbs. Born, Vseyin, Czech., April 26, 1976.
(San Jose's 4th choice, 89th overall, in 1994 Entry Draft).

			Regular Season					Playoffs				
Season	Club	Lea	GP	G	A	TP	PIM	GP	G	A	TP	PIM
1992-93	Vitkovice	Czech.	1	0	0	0	....	....	....	....	....	....
1993-94	Vitkovice	Czech.	24	6	7	13	....	5	1	1	2	....

VARGA, JOHN WSH.

Left wing. Shoots left. 5'9", 172 lbs. Born, Chicago, IL, January 31, 1974.
(Washington's 5th choice, 119th overall, in 1992 Entry Draft).

			Regular Season					Playoffs				
Season	Club	Lea	GP	G	A	TP	PIM	GP	G	A	TP	PIM
1991-92	Tacoma	WHL	72	25	34	59	93	4	1	2	3	0
1992-93	Tacoma	WHL	61	32	32	64	63	7	1	1	2	8
1993-94a	Tacoma	WHL	65	60	62	122	122	8	2	8	10	14

a WHL West Second All-Star Team (1994)

VARIS, PETRI S.J.

Left wing. Shoots left. 6'1", 200 lbs. Born, Varkaus, Finland, May 13, 1969.
(San Jose's 7th choice, 132nd overall, in 1993 Entry Draft).

			Regular Season					Playoffs				
Season	Club	Lea	GP	G	A	TP	PIM	GP	G	A	TP	PIM
1990-91	KooKoo	Fin.2	44	20	31	51	42	....	....	....	....	....
1991-92a	Assat	Fin.	36	13	23	36	24	....	....	....	....	....
1992-93	Assat	Fin.	46	14	35	49	42	8	2	2	4	12
1993-94	Jokerit	Fin.	31	14	15	29	16	11	3	4	7	6

a Finnish Rookie of the Year (1992)

VARVIO, JARKKO (VAHR-vee-oh, YAHR-koh) DAL.

Right wing. Shoots right. 5'9", 175 lbs. Born, Tampere, Finland, April 28, 1972.
(Minnesota's 1st choice, 34th overall, in 1992 Entry Draft).

			Regular Season					Playoffs				
Season	Club	Lea	GP	G	A	TP	PIM	GP	G	A	TP	PIM
1989-90	Ilves	Fin.	1	0	0	0	0	....	....	....	....	....
1990-91	Ilves	Fin.	37	10	7	17	6	....	....	....	....	....
1991-92	HPK	Fin.	41	25	9	34	6	....	....	....	....	....
1992-93	HPK	Fin.	40	29	19	48	16	12	3	2	5	8
1993-94	**Dallas**	**NHL**	**8**	**2**	**3**	**5**	**4**	....	....	....	....	....
	Kalamazoo	IHL	58	29	16	45	18	1	0	0	0	0
	NHL Totals		**8**	**2**	**3**	**5**	**4**	....	....	....	....	....

VASILEVSKII, ALEXANDER (vah-sih-LEHV-skee) ST.L.

Right wing. Shoots left. 5'11", 190 lbs. Born, Kiev, USSR, January 8, 1975.
(St. Louis' 9th choice, 271st overall, in 1993 Entry Draft).

			Regular Season					Playoffs				
Season	Club	Lea	GP	G	A	TP	PIM	GP	G	A	TP	PIM
1992-93	Victoria	WHL	71	27	25	52	52	....	....	....	....	....
1993-94	Victoria	WHL	69	34	51	85	78	....	....	....	....	....

VASILJEV, ANDREI

Left wing. Shoots right. 5'9", 180 lbs. Born, Voskresensk, USSR, March 30, 1972.
(NY Islanders' 11th choice, 248th overall, in 1992 Entry Draft).

			Regular Season					Playoffs				
Season	Club	Lea	GP	G	A	TP	PIM	GP	G	A	TP	PIM
1991-92	CSKA	CIS	28	7	2	9	2	....	....	....	....	....
1992-93	Khimik	CIS	34	4	8	12	20	....	....	....	....	....
1993-94	CSKA	CIS	46	17	6	23	8	3	1	0	1	0

VASKE, DENNIS (VAS-kee) NYI

Defense. Shoots left. 6'2", 210 lbs. Born, Rockford, IL, October 11, 1967.
(NY Islanders' 2nd choice, 38th overall, in 1986 Entry Draft).

			Regular Season					Playoffs				
Season	Club	Lea	GP	G	A	TP	PIM	GP	G	A	TP	PIM
1986-87	Minn.-Duluth	WCHA	33	0	2	2	40	....	....	....	....	....
1987-88	Minn.-Duluth	WCHA	39	1	6	7	90	....	....	....	....	....
1988-89	Minn.-Duluth	WCHA	37	9	19	28	86	....	....	....	....	....
1989-90	Minn.-Duluth	WCHA	37	5	24	29	72	....	....	....	....	....
1990-91	**NY Islanders**	**NHL**	**5**	**0**	**0**	**0**	**2**	....	....	....	....	....
	Capital Dist.	AHL	67	10	10	20	65	....	....	....	....	....
1991-92	**NY Islanders**	**NHL**	**39**	**0**	**1**	**1**	**5**	....	....	....	....	....
	Capital Dist.	AHL	31	1	11	12	59	....	....	....	....	....
1992-93	**NY Islanders**	**NHL**	**27**	**1**	**5**	**6**	**32**	**18**	**0**	**6**	**6**	**14**
	Capital Dist.	AHL	42	4	15	19	70	....	....	....	....	....
1993-94	**NY Islanders**	**NHL**	**65**	**2**	**11**	**13**	**76**	**4**	**0**	**1**	**1**	**2**
	NHL Totals		**136**	**3**	**17**	**20**	**115**	**22**	**0**	**7**	**7**	**16**

VAUHKONEN, JONNI CHI.

Left wing. Shoots left. 6'2", 189 lbs. Born, Suonenjoki, Finland, January 1, 1975.
(Chicago's 7th choice, 128th overall, in 1993 Entry Draft).

			Regular Season					Playoffs				
Season	Club	Lea	GP	G	A	TP	PIM	GP	G	A	TP	PIM
1992-93	Reipas	Fin.	41	8	5	13	63	....	....	....	....	....
1993-94	Reipas	Fin.	33	2	3	5	22	....	....	....	....	....

VEILLEUX, ERIC QUE.

Center. Shoots left. 5'7", 148 lbs. Born, Quebec, Que., February 20, 1972.

			Regular Season					Playoffs				
Season	Club	Lea	GP	G	A	TP	PIM	GP	G	A	TP	PIM
1991-92	Laval	QMJHL	60	31	40	71	87	10	3	5	8	27
1992-93	Laval	QMJHL	70	55	70	125	100	13	9	11	20	19
1993-94	Cornwall	AHL	77	8	19	27	69	13	1	7	8	20

Signed as a free agent by **Quebec**, October 6, 1993.

VELISCHEK, RANDY (VEHL-ih-shehk)

Defense. Shoots left. 6', 200 lbs. Born, Montreal, Que., February 10, 1962.
(Minneota's 3rd choice, 53rd overall, in 1980 Entry Draft).

			Regular Season					Playoffs				
Season	Club	Lea	GP	G	A	TP	PIM	GP	G	A	TP	PIM
1979-80	Providence	ECAC	31	5	5	10	20	....	....	....	....	....
1980-81	Providence	ECAC	33	3	12	15	26	....	....	....	....	....
1981-82a	Providence	ECAC	33	1	14	15	38	....	....	....	....	....
1982-83b	Providence	ECAC	41	18	34	52	50	....	....	....	....	....
	Minnesota	**NHL**	**3**	**0**	**0**	**0**	**2**	**9**	**0**	**0**	**0**	**0**
1983-84	**Minnesota**	**NHL**	**33**	**2**	**2**	**4**	**10**	**1**	**0**	**0**	**0**	**0**
	Salt Lake	CHL	43	7	21	28	54	5	0	3	3	2
1984-85	**Minnesota**	**NHL**	**52**	**4**	**9**	**13**	**26**	**9**	**2**	**3**	**5**	**8**
	Springfield	AHL	26	2	7	9	22	....	....	....	....	....
1985-86	**New Jersey**	**NHL**	**47**	**2**	**7**	**9**	**39**	....	....	....	....	....
	Maine	AHL	21	0	4	4	4	....	....	....	....	....
1986-87	**New Jersey**	**NHL**	**64**	**2**	**16**	**18**	**52**	....	....	....	....	....
1987-88	**New Jersey**	**NHL**	**51**	**3**	**9**	**12**	**66**	**19**	**0**	**2**	**2**	**20**
1988-89	**New Jersey**	**NHL**	**80**	**4**	**14**	**18**	**70**	....	....	....	....	....
1989-90	**New Jersey**	**NHL**	**62**	**0**	**6**	**6**	**72**	**6**	**0**	**0**	**0**	**4**
1990-91	**Quebec**	**NHL**	**79**	**2**	**10**	**12**	**42**	....	....	....	....	....
1991-92	**Quebec**	**NHL**	**38**	**2**	**3**	**5**	**22**	....	....	....	....	....
	Halifax	AHL	16	3	6	9	0	....	....	....	....	....
1992-93	Halifax	AHL	49	6	16	22	18	....	....	....	....	....
1993-94	Cornwall	AHL	18	1	6	7	17	....	....	....	....	....
	Milwaukee	IHL	53	7	11	18	28	4	0	0	0	2
	NHL Totals		**509**	**21**	**76**	**97**	**401**	**44**	**2**	**5**	**7**	**32**

a ECAC Second All-Star Team (1982)
b ECAC First All-Star Team (1983)

Claimed by **New Jersey** from **Minnesota** in NHL Waiver Draft, October 7, 1985. Traded to **Quebec** by **New Jersey** to complete March 6, 1990 trade which sent Peter Stastny to New Jersey for Craig Wolanin and future considerations, August 13, 1990.

VERBEEK, PAT (vuhr-BEEK) HFD.

Right/Left wing. Shoots right. 5'9", 190 lbs. Born, Sarnia, Ont., May 24, 1964.
(New Jersey's 3rd choice, 43rd overall, in 1982 Entry Draft).

			Regular Season					Playoffs				
Season	Club	Lea	GP	G	A	TP	PIM	GP	G	A	TP	PIM
1981-82	Sudbury	OHL	66	37	51	88	180	....	....	....	....	....
1982-83	**New Jersey**	**NHL**	**6**	**3**	**2**	**5**	**8**	....	....	....	....	....
	Sudbury	OHL	61	40	67	107	184	....	....	....	....	....
1983-84	**New Jersey**	**NHL**	**79**	**20**	**27**	**47**	**158**	....	....	....	....	....
1984-85	**New Jersey**	**NHL**	**78**	**15**	**18**	**33**	**162**	....	....	....	....	....
1985-86	**New Jersey**	**NHL**	**76**	**25**	**28**	**53**	**79**	....	....	....	....	....
1986-87	**New Jersey**	**NHL**	**74**	**35**	**24**	**59**	**120**	....	....	....	....	....
1987-88	**New Jersey**	**NHL**	**73**	**46**	**31**	**77**	**227**	**20**	**4**	**8**	**12**	**51**
1988-89	**New Jersey**	**NHL**	**77**	**26**	**21**	**47**	**189**	....	....	....	....	....
1989-90	**Hartford**	**NHL**	**80**	**44**	**45**	**89**	**228**	**7**	**2**	**2**	**4**	**26**
1990-91	**Hartford**	**NHL**	**80**	**43**	**39**	**82**	**246**	**6**	**3**	**2**	**5**	**40**
1991-92	**Hartford**	**NHL**	**76**	**22**	**35**	**57**	**243**	**7**	**0**	**2**	**2**	**12**
1992-93	**Hartford**	**NHL**	**84**	**39**	**43**	**82**	**197**	....	....	....	....	....
1993-94	**Hartford**	**NHL**	**84**	**37**	**38**	**75**	**177**	....	....	....	....	....
	NHL Totals		**867**	**355**	**351**	**706**	**2034**	**40**	**9**	**14**	**23**	**129**

Played in NHL All-Star Game (1991)

Traded to **Hartford** by **New Jersey** for Sylvain Turgeon, June 17, 1989.

VERCIK, RUDOLF (VEHR-chihk) NYR

Left wing. Shoots left. 6'1", 189 lbs. Born, Bratislava, Czech., March 19, 1976.
(NY Rangers' 2nd choice, 52nd overall, in 1994 Entry Draft).

			Regular Season					Playoffs				
Season	Club	Lea	GP	G	A	TP	PIM	GP	G	A	TP	PIM
1993-94	Bratislava	Slov.	17	1	4	5	14	....	....	....	....	....

VERMETTE, MARK

Right wing. Shoots right. 6'1", 203 lbs. Born, Cochenour, Ont., October 3, 1967.
(Quebec's 8th choice, 134th overall, in 1986 Entry Draft).

			Regular Season					Playoffs				
Season	Club	Lea	GP	G	A	TP	PIM	GP	G	A	TP	PIM
1985-86	Lake Superior	CCHA	32	1	4	5	7	....	....	....	....	....
1986-87	Lake Superior	CCHA	38	19	17	36	59	....	....	....	....	....
1987-88ab	Lake Superior	CCHA	46	*45	30	75	154	....	....	....	....	....
1988-89	**Quebec**	**NHL**	**12**	**0**	**4**	**4**	**7**	....	....	....	....	....
	Halifax	AHL	52	12	16	28	30	1	0	0	0	0
1989-90	**Quebec**	**NHL**	**11**	**1**	**5**	**6**	**8**	....	....	....	....	....
	Halifax	AHL	47	20	17	37	44	6	1	5	6	6
1990-91	**Quebec**	**NHL**	**34**	**3**	**4**	**7**	**10**	....	....	....	....	....
	Halifax	AHL	46	26	22	48	37	....	....	....	....	....
1991-92	**Quebec**	**NHL**	**10**	**1**	**0**	**1**	**8**	....	....	....	....	....
	Halifax	AHL	44	21	18	39	39	....	....	....	....	....
1992-93	Halifax	AHL	67	42	37	79	32	....	....	....	....	....
1993-94	Las Vegas	IHL	77	22	38	60	61	4	0	0	0	2
	NHL Totals		**67**	**5**	**13**	**18**	**33**	....	....	....	....	....

a NCAA West All-American Team (1988)
b CCHA First All-Star Team (1988)

VESEY, JIM

Center/Right wing. Shoots right. 6'1", 202 lbs. Born, Columbus, MA, October 29, 1965.
(St. Louis' 11th choice, 155th overall, in 1984 Entry Draft).

			Regular Season					Playoffs				
Season	Club	Lea	GP	G	A	TP	PIM	GP	G	A	TP	PIM
1984-85	Merrimack	NCAA	33	19	11	30	28	....	....	....	....	....
1985-86	Merrimack	NCAA	32	29	32	61	67	....	....	....	....	....
1986-87	Merrimack	NCAA	35	22	36	58	57	....	....	....	....	....
1987-88	Merrimack	NCAA	33	33	50	83	....	....	....	....	....	....
1988-89	**St. Louis**	**NHL**	**5**	**1**	**1**	**2**	**7**	....	....	....	....	....
a	Peoria	IHL	76	47	46	93	137	4	1	2	3	6
1989-90	**St. Louis**	**NHL**	**6**	**0**	**1**	**1**	**0**	....	....	....	....	....
	Peoria	IHL	60	47	44	91	75	5	1	3	4	21
1990-91	Peoria	IHL	58	32	41	73	69	19	4	14	18	26
1991-92	**Boston**	**NHL**	**4**	**0**	**0**	**0**	**0**	....	....	....	....	....
	Maine	AHL	10	6	7	13	13	....	....	....	....	....
1992-93	Providence	AHL	71	38	39	77	42	6	2	5	7	4
1993-94	Phoenix	IHL	60	20	30	50	75	....	....	....	....	....
	NHL Totals		**15**	**1**	**2**	**3**	**7**	....	....	....	....	....

a IHL First All-Star Team (1989)

Traded to **Winnipeg** by **St. Louis** to complete February 28, 1991 trade which sent Tom Draper to St. Louis for future considerations, May 24, 1991. Traded to **Boston** by **Winnipeg** for future considerations, June 20, 1991.

VIAL, DENNIS (vee-AL) OTT.

Defense. Shoots left. 6'2", 218 lbs. Born, Sault Ste. Marie, Ont., April 10, 1969.
(NY Rangers' 5th choice, 110th overall, in 1988 Entry Draft).

			Regular Season					Playoffs				
Season	Club	Lea	GP	G	A	TP	PIM	GP	G	A	TP	PIM
1985-86	Hamilton	OHL	31	1	1	2	66	....	....	....	....	....
1986-87	Hamilton	OHL	53	1	8	9	194	8	0	0	0	8
1987-88	Hamilton	OHL	52	3	17	20	229	13	2	2	4	49
1988-89	Niagara Falls	OHL	50	10	27	37	227	15	1	7	8	44
1989-90	Flint	IHL	79	6	29	35	351	4	0	0	0	10
1990-91	**NY Rangers**	**NHL**	**21**	**0**	**0**	**0**	**61**	....	....	....	....	....
	Binghamton	AHL	40	2	7	9	250	....	....	....	....	....
	Detroit	**NHL**	**9**	**0**	**0**	**0**	**16**	....	....	....	....	....
1991-92	**Detroit**	**NHL**	**27**	**1**	**0**	**1**	**72**	....	....	....	....	....
	Adirondack	AHL	20	2	4	6	107	17	1	3	4	43
1992-93	**Detroit**	**NHL**	**9**	**0**	**1**	**1**	**20**	....	....	....	....	....
	Adirondack	AHL	30	2	11	13	177	11	1	1	2	14
1993-94	**Ottawa**	**NHL**	**55**	**2**	**5**	**7**	**214**	....	....	....	....	....
	NHL Totals		**121**	**3**	**6**	**9**	**383**	....	....	....	....	....

Traded to **Detroit** by **NY Rangers** with Kevin Miller and Jim Cummins for Joey Kocur and Per Djoos, March 5, 1991. Traded to **Quebec** by **Detroit** with Doug Crossman for cash, June 15, 1992. Traded to **Detroit** by **Quebec** for cash, September 9, 1992. Traded to **Tampa Bay** by **Detroit** for Steve Maltais, June 8, 1993. Claimed by **Anaheim** from **Tampa Bay** in Expansion Draft, June 24, 1993. Claimed by **Ottawa** from **Anaheim** in Phase II of Expansion Draft, June 25, 1993.

VIITAKOSKI, VESA — CGY.

Left wing. Shoots left. 6'3", 215 lbs. Born, Lappeenranta, Finland, February 13, 1971.
(Calgary's 3rd choice, 32nd overall, in 1990 Entry Draft).

			Regular Season					Playoffs				
Season	Club	Lea	GP	G	A	TP	PIM	GP	G	A	TP	PIM
1988-89	SaiPa	Fin.	11	4	1	5	6					
1989-90	SaiPa	Fin.	44	24	10	34	8					
1990-91	Tappara	Fin.	41	17	23	40	14	3	2	0	2	4
1991-92	Tappara	Fin.	44	19	19	38	39					
1992-93	Tappara	Fin.	48	27	27	54	28					
1993-94	**Calgary**	**NHL**	**8**	**1**	**2**	**3**	**0**					
	Saint John	AHL	67	28	39	67	24	5	1	2	3	2
	NHL Totals		**8**	**1**	**2**	**3**	**0**					

VILGRAIN, CLAUDE — PHI.

Right wing. Shoots right. 6'1", 205 lbs. Born, Port-au-Prince, Haiti, March 1, 1963.
(Detroit's 6th choice, 107th overall, in 1982 Entry Draft).

			Regular Season					Playoffs				
Season	Club	Lea	GP	G	A	TP	PIM	GP	G	A	TP	PIM
1983-84	U. of Moncton	AUAA	20	11	20	31	8					
1984-85	U. of Moncton	AUAA	24	35	28	63	20					
1985-86	U. of Moncton	AUAA	19	17	20	37	25					
1986-87	Cdn. National	....	78	28	42	70	38					
1987-88	Cdn. National	....	61	21	20	41	41					
	Cdn. Olympic	....	6	0	0	0	0					
	Vancouver	**NHL**	**6**	**1**	**1**	**2**	**0**					
1988-89	Milwaukee	IHL	23	9	13	22	26					
	Utica	AHL	55	23	30	53	41	5	0	2	2	2
1989-90	**New Jersey**	**NHL**	**6**	**1**	**2**	**3**	**4**	**4**	**0**	**0**	**0**	**0**
	Utica	AHL	73	37	52	89	32					
1990-91	Utica	AHL	59	32	46	78	26					
1991-92	**New Jersey**	**NHL**	**71**	**19**	**27**	**46**	**74**	**7**	**1**	**1**	**2**	**17**
1992-93	**New Jersey**	**NHL**	**4**	**0**	**2**	**2**	**0**					
	Utica	AHL	22	6	8	14	4	5	0	1	1	0
	Cincinnati	IHL	57	19	26	45	22					
1993-94	**Philadelphia**	**NHL**	**2**	**0**	**0**	**0**	**0**					
	Hershey	AHL	76	30	53	83	45	11	1	6	7	2
	NHL Totals		**89**	**21**	**32**	**53**	**78**	**11**	**1**	**1**	**2**	**17**

Signed as a free agent by **Vancouver**, June 18, 1987. Traded to **New Jersey** by **Vancouver** for Tim Lenardon, March 7, 1989. Signed as a free agent by **Philadelphia**, August 3, 1993.

VINCENT, PAUL — TOR.

Center. Shoots left. 6'4", 200 lbs. Born, Utica, NY, January 4, 1975.
(Toronto's 4th choice, 149th overall, in 1993 Entry Draft).

			Regular Season					Playoffs				
Season	Club	Lea	GP	G	A	TP	PIM	GP	G	A	TP	PIM
1992-93	Cushing	HS	25	30	32	62	62					
1993-94	Seattle	WHL	66	27	26	53	57	8	1	3	4	8

VISHEAU, MARK — (VEE-SHOO) — WPG.

Defense. Shoots right. 6'4", 200 lbs. Born, Burlington, Ont., June 27, 1973.
(Winnipeg's 4th choice, 84th overall, in 1992 Entry Draft).

			Regular Season					Playoffs				
Season	Club	Lea	GP	G	A	TP	PIM	GP	G	A	TP	PIM
1990-91	London	OHL	59	4	11	15	40	7	0	1	1	6
1991-92	London	OHL	66	5	31	36	104	10	0	4	4	27
1992-93	London	OHL	62	8	52	60	88	12	0	5	5	26
1993-94	**Winnipeg**	**NHL**	**1**	**0**	**0**	**0**	**0**					
	Moncton	AHL	48	4	5	9	58					
	NHL Totals		**1**	**0**	**0**	**0**	**0**					

VITOLINSH, HARIJS — (VEE-toh-LIHNSH, HAIR-ihz) — WPG.

Center. Shoots left. 6'3", 212 lbs. Born, Riga, Latvia, April 30, 1968.
(Montreal's 10th choice, 188th overall, in 1988 Entry Draft).

			Regular Season					Playoffs				
Season	Club	Lea	GP	G	A	TP	PIM	GP	G	A	TP	PIM
1986-87	Dynamo Riga	USSR	17	1	1	2	8					
1987-88	Dynamo Riga	USSR	30	3	3	6	24					
1988-89	Dynamo Riga	USSR	36	3	2	5	16					
1989-90	Dynamo Riga	USSR	45	7	6	13	18					
1990-91	Dynamo Riga	USSR	46	12	19	31	22					
1991-92	Riga	CIS	30	12	5	17	10					
1992-93	Chur	Switz.	17	12	6	18	23					
	Thunder Bay	Col.	8	6	7	13	12					
	New Haven	AHL	7	6	3	9	4					
1993-94	**Winnipeg**	**NHL**	**8**	**0**	**0**	**0**	**4**					
	Moncton	AHL	70	28	34	62	41	20	1	3	4	4
	NHL Totals		**8**	**0**	**0**	**0**	**4**					

Re-entered NHL Entry Draft. **Winnipeg's** 12th choice, 228th overall in 1993 Entry Draft.

VLASAK, TOMAS — L.A.

Center. Shoots right. 5'10", 175 lbs. Born, Prague, Czech., February 1, 1975.
(Los Angeles' 6th choice, 120th overall, in 1993 Entry Draft).

			Regular Season					Playoffs				
Season	Club	Lea	GP	G	A	TP	PIM	GP	G	A	TP	PIM
1992-93	Slavia Praha	Czech.2	31	17	6	23	....					
1993-94	Litvinov	Czech.	41	16	11	27	0	4	0	1	1	....

VOLEK, DAVID — (VOH-lehk)

Left/Right wing. Shoots left. 6', 185 lbs. Born, Prague, Czech., June 18, 1966.
(NY Islanders' 11th choice, 208th overall, in 1984 Entry Draft).

			Regular Season					Playoffs				
Season	Club	Lea	GP	G	A	TP	PIM	GP	G	A	TP	PIM
1984-85	Sparta Praha	Czech.	32	5	5	10	14					
1985-86	Sparta Praha	Czech.	35	10	7	17	....					
1986-87	Sparta Praha	Czech.	39	27	25	52	38					
1987-88	Sparta Praha	Czech.	42	29	18	47	58					
1988-89a	**NY Islanders**	**NHL**	**77**	**25**	**34**	**59**	**24**					
1989-90	**NY Islanders**	**NHL**	**80**	**17**	**22**	**39**	**41**	**5**	**1**	**4**	**5**	**0**
1990-91	**NY Islanders**	**NHL**	**77**	**22**	**34**	**56**	**57**					
1991-92	**NY Islanders**	**NHL**	**74**	**18**	**42**	**60**	**35**					
1992-93	**NY Islanders**	**NHL**	**56**	**8**	**13**	**21**	**34**	**10**	**4**	**1**	**5**	**2**
1993-94	**NY Islanders**	**NHL**	**32**	**5**	**9**	**14**	**10**					
	NHL Totals		**396**	**95**	**154**	**249**	**201**	**15**	**5**	**5**	**10**	**2**

a NHL All-Rookie Team (1989)

VOLKOV, MIKHAIL — (VOHL-kahf) — BUF.

Right wing. Shoots left. 5'10", 174 lbs. Born, Voronezh, USSR, March 9, 1972.
(Buffalo's 12th choice, 233rd overall, in 1991 Entry Draft).

			Regular Season					Playoffs				
Season	Club	Lea	GP	G	A	TP	PIM	GP	G	A	TP	PIM
1989-90	Soviet Wings	USSR	24	0	2	2	4					
1990-91	Soviet Wings	USSR	40	8	4	12	8					
1991-92	Soviet Wings	CIS	37	3	6	9	16					
1992-93	Soviet Wings	CIS	33	9	6	15	11	5	0	1	1	2
1993-94	Rochester	AHL	62	12	26	38	28	4	0	2	2	2

VOLOGJANINOV, IVAN — (voh-log-ZHAHN-ih-nahf, ee-VAHN) — HFD.

Right wing. Shoots left. 5'10", 174 lbs. Born, Ukhta, USSR, March 9, 1972.
(Winnipeg's 12th choice, 254th overall, in 1992 Entry Draft).

			Regular Season					Playoffs				
Season	Club	Lea	GP	G	A	TP	PIM	GP	G	A	TP	PIM
1990-91	Sokol Kiev	CIS	3	0	1	1	0					
1991-92	Sokol Kiev	CIS	23	2	2	4	4					
1992-93	Lethbridge	WHL	71	48	60	108	12	4	1	2	3	2
1993-94	Lethbridge	WHL	65	37	53	90	28	9	3	7	10	2

VON STEFENELLI, PHILIP

Defense. Shoots left. 6'1", 200 lbs. Born, Vancouver, B.C., April 10, 1969.
(Vancouver's 5th choice, 122nd overall, in 1988 Entry Draft).

			Regular Season					Playoffs				
Season	Club	Lea	GP	G	A	TP	PIM	GP	G	A	TP	PIM
1987-88	Boston U.	H.E.	34	3	13	16	38					
1988-89	Boston U.	H.E.	33	2	6	8	34					
1989-90	Boston U.	H.E.	44	8	20	28	40					
1990-91	Boston U.	H.E.	41	7	23	30	32					
1991-92	Milwaukee	IHL	80	2	34	36	40	5	1	2	3	2
1992-93	Hamilton	AHL	78	11	20	31	75					
1993-94	Hamilton	AHL	80	10	31	41	89	4	1	0	1	2

VOPAT, JAN — (VOH-paht) — HFD.

Defense. Shoots left. 6', 198 lbs. Born, Most, Czech., March 22, 1973.
(Hartford's 3rd choice, 57th overall, in 1992 Entry Draft).

			Regular Season					Playoffs				
Season	Club	Lea	GP	G	A	TP	PIM	GP	G	A	TP	PIM
1990-91	Litvinov	Czech.	25	1	4	5	4					
1991-92	Litvinov	Czech.	46	4	2	6	16					
1992-93	Litvinov	Czech.	45	12	10	22	....					
1993-94	Litvinov	Czech.	41	9	19	28	0	4	1	1	2	....

VOROBIEV, VLADIMIR

Left wing. Shoots right. 5'11", 185 lbs. Born, Cherepovets, USSR, October 2, 1972.
(NY Rangers' 10th choice, 240th overall, in 1992 Entry Draft).

			Regular Season					Playoffs				
Season	Club	Lea	GP	G	A	TP	PIM	GP	G	A	TP	PIM
1992-93	Cherepovets	CIS	42	18	5	23	18					
1993-94	Moscow D'amo	CIS	11	3	1	4	2					

VUJTEK, VLADIMIR — (VYOO-tehk) — EDM.

Left wing. Shoots left. 6'1", 190 lbs. Born, Ostrava, Czech., February 17, 1972.
(Montreal's 4th choice, 73rd overall, in 1991 Entry Draft).

			Regular Season					Playoffs				
Season	Club	Lea	GP	G	A	TP	PIM	GP	G	A	TP	PIM
1988-89	TJ Vitkovice	Czech.	3	0	1	1	0					
1989-90	TJ Vitkovice	Czech.	29	7	7	14	....					
1990-91	TJ Vitkovice	Czech.	26	7	4	11	....					
	Tri-City	WHL	37	26	18	44	25	7	2	3	5	4
1991-92	**Montreal**	**NHL**	**2**	**0**	**0**	**0**	**0**					
a	Tri-City	WHL	53	41	61	102	114					
1992-93	**Edmonton**	**NHL**	**30**	**1**	**10**	**11**	**8**					
	Cape Breton	AHL	20	10	9	19	14	1	0	0	0	0
1993-94	**Edmonton**	**NHL**	**40**	**4**	**15**	**19**	**14**					
	NHL Totals		**72**	**5**	**25**	**30**	**22**					

a WHL West First All-Star Team (1992)

Traded to **Edmonton** by **Montreal** with Shayne Corson and Brent Gilchrist for Vincent Damphousse and Edmonton's fourth round choice (Adam Wiesel) in 1993 Entry Draft, August 27, 1992.

VUKONICH, MICHAEL

Center. Shoots left. 6'1", 190 lbs. Born, Duluth, MN, May 11, 1968.
(Los Angeles' 4th choice, 90th overall, in 1987 Entry Draft).

			Regular Season					Playoffs				
Season	Club	Lea	GP	G	A	TP	PIM	GP	G	A	TP	PIM
1987-88	Harvard	ECAC	32	9	14	23	24					
1988-89	Harvard	ECAC	27	11	8	19	12					
1989-90a	Harvard	ECAC	27	22	29	51	18					
1990-91b	Harvard	ECAC	27	*31	23	54	28					
1991-92	Phoenix	IHL	68	17	11	28	21					
1992-93	Phoenix	IHL	70	25	15	40	27					
1993-94	Phoenix	IHL	22	4	6	10	8					
	Binghamton	AHL	3	1	0	1	0					
	Flint	ColHL	8	7	8	15	12	10	7	7	14	12

a ECAC First All-Star Team (1990)
b ECAC Second All-Star Team (1991)

VUKOTA, MICK — (vuh-KOH-tuh) — NYI

Right wing. Shoots right. 6'2", 195 lbs. Born, Saskatoon, Sask., September 14, 1966.

			Regular Season					Playoffs				
Season	Club	Lea	GP	G	A	TP	PIM	GP	G	A	TP	PIM
1983-84	Winnipeg	WHL	3	1	1	2	10					
1984-85	Kelowna	WHL	66	10	6	16	247					
1985-86	Spokane	WHL	64	19	14	33	369	9	6	4	10	68
1986-87	Spokane	WHL	61	25	28	53	*337	4	0	0	0	40
1987-88	**NY Islanders**	**NHL**	**17**	**1**	**0**	**1**	**82**	**2**	**0**	**0**	**0**	**23**
	Springfield	AHL	52	7	9	16	375					
1988-89	**NY Islanders**	**NHL**	**48**	**2**	**2**	**4**	**237**					
	Springfield	AHL	3	1	0	1	33					
1989-90	**NY Islanders**	**NHL**	**76**	**4**	**8**	**12**	**290**	**1**	**0**	**0**	**0**	**17**
1990-91	**NY Islanders**	**NHL**	**60**	**2**	**4**	**6**	**238**					
	Capital Dist.	AHL	2	0	0	0	9					
1991-92	**NY Islanders**	**NHL**	**74**	**0**	**6**	**6**	**293**					
1992-93	**NY Islanders**	**NHL**	**74**	**2**	**5**	**7**	**216**	**15**	**0**	**0**	**0**	**16**
1993-94	**NY Islanders**	**NHL**	**72**	**3**	**1**	**4**	**237**	**4**	**0**	**0**	**0**	**17**
	NHL Totals		**421**	**14**	**26**	**40**	**1593**	**22**	**0**	**0**	**0**	**73**

Signed as a free agent by **NY Islanders**, March 2, 1987.

VYBORNY, DAVID (vigh-BOHR-nee) EDM.

Center. Shoots left. 5'10", 174 lbs. Born, Jihlava, Czech., January 22, 1975.
(Edmonton's 3rd choice, 33rd overall, in 1993 Entry Draft).

			Regular Season					Playoffs				
Season	Club	Lea	GP	G	A	TP	PIM	GP	G	A	TP	PIM
1990-91	Sparta Praha	Czech.	3	0	0	0	0	....	....	....	....	....
1991-92a	Sparta Praha	Czech.	32	6	9	15	2	....	....	....	....	....
1992-93	Sparta Praha	Czech.	52	20	24	44	....	....	....	....	....	....
1993-94	Sparta Praha	Czech.	44	15	20	35	0	6	4	7	11	0

a Czech. Rookie of the Year (1992)

WAINWRIGHT, DAVID NYI

Defense. Shoots left. 6', 193 lbs. Born, Boston, MA, January 17, 1974.
(NY Islanders' 10th choice, 224th overall, in 1992 Entry Draft).

			Regular Season					Playoffs				
Season	Club	Lea	GP	G	A	TP	PIM	GP	G	A	TP	PIM
1991-92	Thayer Academy	HS	25	4	25	29	0	....	....	....	....	....
1992-93					UNAVAILABLE							
1993-94	Boston College	H.E.	36	2	1	3	38	....	....	....	....	....

WALBY, STEFFON TOR.

Right wing. Shoots right. 6'1", 190 lbs. Born, Madison, WI, November 22, 1972.

			Regular Season					Playoffs				
Season	Club	Lea	GP	G	A	TP	PIM	GP	G	A	TP	PIM
1992-93	Kelowna	BCJHL	59	53	68	121	76	....	....	....	....	....
1993-94	St. John's	AHL	63	15	22	37	79	2	0	0	0	2

Signed as a free agent by **Toronto**, August 20, 1993.

WALKER, SCOTT VAN.

Defense. Shoots right. 5'9", 180 lbs. Born, Montreal, Que., July 19, 1973.
(Vancouver's 4th choice, 124th overall, in 1993 Entry Draft).

			Regular Season					Playoffs				
Season	Club	Lea	GP	G	A	TP	PIM	GP	G	A	TP	PIM
1991-92	Owen Sound	OHL	53	7	31	38	128	5	0	7	7	8
1992-93a	Owen Sound	OHL	57	23	68	91	110	8	1	5	6	16
	Cdn. National	....	2	3	0	3	0	....	....	....	....	....
1993-94	Hamilton	AHL	77	10	29	39	272	4	0	1	1	25

a OHL Second All-Star Team (1993)

WALZ, WES (WAHLS) CGY.

Center. Shoots right. 5'10", 185 lbs. Born, Calgary, Alta., May 15, 1970.
(Boston's 3rd choice, 57th overall, in 1989 Entry Draft).

			Regular Season					Playoffs				
Season	Club	Lea	GP	G	A	TP	PIM	GP	G	A	TP	PIM
1988-89	Lethbridge	WHL	63	29	75	104	32	8	1	5	6	6
1989-90	**Boston**	**NHL**	**2**	**1**	**1**	**2**	**0**	....	....	....	....	....
a	Lethbridge	WHL	56	54	86	140	69	19	13	*24	*37	33
1990-91	**Boston**	**NHL**	**56**	**8**	**8**	**16**	**32**	**2**	**0**	**0**	**0**	**0**
	Maine	AHL	20	8	12	20	19	2	0	0	0	21
1991-92	**Boston**	**NHL**	**15**	**0**	**3**	**3**	**12**	....	....	....	....	....
	Maine	AHL	21	13	11	24	38	....	....	....	....	....
	Philadelphia	**NHL**	**2**	**1**	**0**	**1**	**0**	....	....	....	....	....
	Hershey	AHL	41	13	28	41	37	6	1	2	3	0
1992-93	Hershey	AHL	78	35	45	80	106	....	....	....	....	....
1993-94	**Calgary**	**NHL**	**53**	**11**	**27**	**38**	**16**	**6**	**3**	**0**	**3**	**2**
	Saint John	AHL	15	6	6	12	14	....	....	....	....	....
	NHL Totals		**128**	**21**	**39**	**60**	**60**	**8**	**3**	**0**	**3**	**2**

a WHL East First All-Star Team (1990)

Traded to **Philadelphia** by **Boston** with Garry Galley and Boston's third round choice (Milos Holan) in 1993 Entry Draft for Gord Murphy, Brian Dobbin, Philadelphia's third round choice (Sergei Zholtok) in 1992 Entry Draft and Philadelphia's fourth round choice (Charles Paquette) in 1993 Entry Draft, January 2, 1992. Signed as a free agent by **Calgary**, August 26, 1993.

WARD, AARON DET.

Defense. Shoots right. 6'2", 200 lbs. Born, Windsor, Ont., January 17, 1973.
(Winnipeg's 1st choice, 5th overall, in 1991 Entry Draft).

			Regular Season					Playoffs				
Season	Club	Lea	GP	G	A	TP	PIM	GP	G	A	TP	PIM
1990-91	U. of Michigan	CCHA	46	8	11	19	126	....	....	....	....	....
1991-92	U. of Michigan	CCHA	42	7	12	19	64	....	....	....	....	....
1992-93	U. of Michigan	CCHA	30	5	8	13	73	....	....	....	....	....
	Cdn. National	....	4	0	0	0	8	....	....	....	....	....
1993-94	**Detroit**	**NHL**	**5**	**1**	**0**	**1**	**4**	....	....	....	....	....
	Adirondack	AHL	58	4	12	16	87	9	2	6	8	6
	NHL Totals		**5**	**1**	**0**	**1**	**4**	....	....	....	....	....

Traded to **Detroit** by **Winnipeg** with Toronto's fourth round choice (previously acquired by Winnipeg — later traded to Detroit — Detroit selected John Jakopin) in 1993 Entry Draft for Paul Ysebaert and future considerations (Alan Kerr, June 18, 1993), June 11, 1993.

WARD, DIXON L.A.

Right wing. Shoots right. 6', 200 lbs. Born, Leduc, Alta., September 23, 1968.
(Vancouver's 6th choice, 128th overall, in 1988 Entry Draft).

			Regular Season					Playoffs				
Season	Club	Lea	GP	G	A	TP	PIM	GP	G	A	TP	PIM
1988-89	North Dakota	WCHA	37	8	9	17	26	....	....	....	....	....
1989-90	North Dakota	WCHA	45	35	34	69	44	....	....	....	....	....
1990-91a	North Dakota	WCHA	43	34	35	69	84	....	....	....	....	....
1991-92a	North Dakota	WCHA	38	33	31	64	90	....	....	....	....	....
1992-93	**Vancouver**	**NHL**	**70**	**22**	**30**	**52**	**82**	**9**	**2**	**3**	**5**	**0**
1993-94	**Vancouver**	**NHL**	**33**	**6**	**1**	**7**	**37**	....	....	....	....	....
	Los Angeles	**NHL**	**34**	**6**	**2**	**8**	**45**	....	....	....	....	....
	NHL Totals		**137**	**34**	**33**	**67**	**164**	**9**	**2**	**3**	**5**	**0**

a WCHA Second All-Star Team (1991, 1992)

Traded to **Los Angeles** by **Vancouver** with a conditional draft choice in 1995 Entry Draft for Jimmy Carson, January 8, 1994.

WARD, ED QUE.

Right wing. Shoots right. 6'3", 205 lbs. Born, Edmonton, Alta., November 10, 1969.
(Quebec's 7th choice, 108th overall, in 1988 Entry Draft).

			Regular Season					Playoffs				
Season	Club	Lea	GP	G	A	TP	PIM	GP	G	A	TP	PIM
1987-88	N. Michigan	WCHA	25	0	2	2	40	....	....	....	....	....
1988-89	N. Michigan	WCHA	42	5	15	20	36	....	....	....	....	....
1989-90	N. Michigan	WCHA	39	5	11	16	77	....	....	....	....	....
1990-91	N. Michigan	WCHA	46	13	18	31	109	....	....	....	....	....
1991-92	Greensboro	ECHL	12	4	8	12	21	....	....	....	....	....
	Halifax	AHL	51	7	11	18	65	....	....	....	....	....
1992-93	Halifax	AHL	70	13	19	32	56	....	....	....	....	....
1993-94	**Quebec**	**NHL**	**7**	**1**	**0**	**1**	**5**	....	....	....	....	....
	Cornwall	AHL	60	12	30	42	65	12	1	3	4	14
	NHL Totals		**7**	**1**	**0**	**1**	**5**	....	....	....	....	....

WARRENER, RHETT FLA.

Defense. Shoots left. 6'1", 209 lbs. Born, Shaunavon, Sask., January 27, 1976.
(Florida's 2nd choice, 27th overall, in 1994 Entry Draft).

			Regular Season					Playoffs				
Season	Club	Lea	GP	G	A	TP	PIM	GP	G	A	TP	PIM
1991-92	Saskatoon	WHL	2	0	0	0	0	....	....	....	....	....
1992-93	Saskatoon	WHL	68	2	17	19	100	9	0	0	0	14
1993-94	Saskatoon	WHL	61	7	19	26	131	16	0	5	5	33

WARRINER, TODD TOR.

Left wing. Shoots left. 6'1", 182 lbs. Born, Blenheim, Ont., January 3, 1974.
(Quebec's 1st choice, 4th overall, in 1992 Entry Draft).

			Regular Season					Playoffs				
Season	Club	Lea	GP	G	A	TP	PIM	GP	G	A	TP	PIM
1990-91	Windsor	OHL	57	36	28	64	26	11	5	6	11	12
1991-92a	Windsor	OHL	50	41	41	82	64	7	5	4	9	6
1992-93	Windsor	OHL	23	13	21	34	29	....	....	....	....	....
	Kitchener	OHL	32	19	24	43	35	7	5	14	19	14
1993-94	Cdn. National	....	50	11	20	31	33	....	....	....	....	....
	Cdn. Olympic	....	4	1	1	2	0	....	....	....	....	....
	Kitchener	OHL	....	....	....	....	....	1	0	1	1	0
	Cornwall	AHL	....	....	....	....	....	10	1	4	5	4

a OHL First All-Star Team (1992)

Traded to **Toronto** by **Quebec** with Mats Sundin, Garth Butcher and Philadelphia's first round choice (previously acquired by Quebec — later traded to Washington — Washington selected Nolan Baumgartner) in 1994 Entry Draft for Wendel Clark, Sylvain Lefebvre, Landon Wilson and Toronto's first round choice (Jeffrey Kealty) in 1994 Entry Draft, June 28, 1994.

WASHBURN, STEVE FLA.

Center. Shoots left. 6'2", 185 lbs. Born, Ottawa, Ont., April 10, 1975.
(Florida's 5th choice, 78th overall, in 1993 Entry Draft).

			Regular Season					Playoffs				
Season	Club	Lea	GP	G	A	TP	PIM	GP	G	A	TP	PIM
1991-92	Ottawa	OHL	59	5	17	22	10	11	2	3	5	4
1992-93	Ottawa	OHL	66	20	38	58	54	....	....	....	....	....
1993-94	Ottawa	OHL	65	30	50	80	88	17	7	16	23	10

WASLEY, CHARLIE QUE.

Defense. Shoots left. 6'2", 173 lbs. Born, Minneapolis, MN, April 4, 1974.
(Quebec's 6th choice, 100th overall, in 1992 Entry Draft).

			Regular Season					Playoffs				
Season	Club	Lea	GP	G	A	TP	PIM	GP	G	A	TP	PIM
1992-93	U. Minnesota	WCHA	35	2	5	7	42	....	....	....	....	....
1993-94	U. Minnesota	WCHA	36	1	14	15	29	....	....	....	....	....

WATT, MIKE EDM.

Left wing. Shoots left. 6'2", 210 lbs. Born, Seaforth, Ont., March 31, 1976.
(Edmonton's 3rd choice, 32nd overall, in 1994 Entry Draft).

			Regular Season					Playoffs				
Season	Club	Lea	GP	G	A	TP	PIM	GP	G	A	TP	PIM
1992-93	Stratford	Jr. B	45	20	35	55	100	....	....	....	....	....
1993-94	Stratford	Jr. B	48	34	34	68	165	....	....	....	....	....

WATTERS, TIM L.A.

Defense. Shoots left. 5'11", 185 lbs. Born, Kamloops, B.C., July 25, 1959.
(Winnipeg's 6th choice, 124th overall, in 1979 Entry Draft).

			Regular Season					Playoffs				
Season	Club	Lea	GP	G	A	TP	PIM	GP	G	A	TP	PIM
1978-79	Michigan Tech	WCHA	38	6	21	27	48	....	....	....	....	....
1979-80	Cdn. National	....	56	8	21	29	43	....	....	....	....	....
	Cdn. Olympic	....	6	1	1	2	0	....	....	....	....	....
1980-81ab	Michigan Tech	WCHA	43	12	38	50	36	....	....	....	....	....
1981-82	Tulsa	CHL	5	1	2	3	0	....	....	....	....	....
	Winnipeg	**NHL**	**69**	**2**	**22**	**24**	**97**	**4**	**0**	**1**	**1**	**8**
1982-83	**Winnipeg**	**NHL**	**77**	**5**	**18**	**23**	**98**	**3**	**0**	**0**	**0**	**2**
1983-84	**Winnipeg**	**NHL**	**74**	**3**	**20**	**23**	**169**	**3**	**1**	**0**	**1**	**2**
1984-85	**Winnipeg**	**NHL**	**63**	**2**	**20**	**22**	**74**	**8**	**0**	**1**	**1**	**16**
1985-86	**Winnipeg**	**NHL**	**56**	**6**	**8**	**14**	**97**	....	....	....	....	....
1986-87	**Winnipeg**	**NHL**	**63**	**3**	**13**	**16**	**119**	**10**	**0**	**0**	**0**	**21**
1987-88	Cdn. National	....	8	0	1	1	2	....	....	....	....	....
	Cdn. Olympic	....	2	0	2	2	0	....	....	....	....	....
	Winnipeg	**NHL**	**36**	**0**	**0**	**0**	**106**	**4**	**0**	**0**	**0**	**4**
1988-89	**Los Angeles**	**NHL**	**76**	**3**	**18**	**21**	**168**	**11**	**0**	**1**	**1**	**6**
1989-90	**Los Angeles**	**NHL**	**62**	**1**	**10**	**11**	**92**	**4**	**0**	**0**	**0**	**6**
1990-91	**Los Angeles**	**NHL**	**45**	**0**	**4**	**4**	**92**	**7**	**0**	**0**	**0**	**12**
1991-92	**Los Angeles**	**NHL**	**37**	**0**	**7**	**7**	**92**	**6**	**0**	**0**	**0**	**8**
	Phoenix	IHL	5	0	3	3	6	....	....	....	....	....
1992-93	**Los Angeles**	**NHL**	**22**	**0**	**2**	**2**	**18**	**22**	**0**	**2**	**2**	**30**
	Phoenix	IHL	31	3	3	6	43	....	....	....	....	....
1993-94	**Los Angeles**	**NHL**	**60**	**1**	**9**	**10**	**67**	....	....	....	....	....
	NHL Totals		**740**	**26**	**151**	**177**	**1289**	**82**	**1**	**5**	**6**	**115**

a WCHA First All-Star Team (1981)
b Named to NCAA All-Tournament Team (1981)

Signed as a free agent by **Los Angeles**, June 27, 1988.

WEIGHT, DOUG (WAYT) EDM.

Center. Shoots left. 5'11", 191 lbs. Born, Warren, MI, January 21, 1971.
(NY Rangers' 2nd choice, 34th overall, in 1990 Entry Draft).

			Regular Season					Playoffs				
Season	Club	Lea	GP	G	A	TP	PIM	GP	G	A	TP	PIM
1989-90	Lake Superior	CCHA	46	21	48	69	44	....	....	....	....	....
1990-91ab	Lake Superior	CCHA	42	29	46	75	86	....	....	....	....	....
	NY Rangers	NHL	....	....	....	....	....	1	0	0	0	0
1991-92	NY Rangers	NHL	53	8	22	30	23	7	2	2	4	0
	Binghamton	AHL	9	3	14	17	2	4	1	4	5	6
1992-93	NY Rangers	NHL	65	15	25	40	55	....	....	....	....	....
	Edmonton	NHL	13	2	6	8	10	....	....	....	....	....
1993-94	Edmonton	NHL	84	24	50	74	47	....	....	....	....	....
	NHL Totals		215	49	103	152	135	8	2	2	4	0

a CCHA First All-Star Team (1991)
b NCAA West Second All-American Team (1991)

Traded to **Edmonton** by **NY Rangers** for Esa Tikkanen, March 17, 1993.

WEINRICH, ERIC (WIGHN-rihc) CHI.

Defense. Shoots left. 6'1", 210 lbs. Born, Roanoke, VA, December 19, 1966.
(New Jersey's 3rd choice, 32nd overall, in 1985 Entry Draft).

			Regular Season					Playoffs				
Season	Club	Lea	GP	G	A	TP	PIM	GP	G	A	TP	PIM
1985-86	U. of Maine	H.E.	34	0	15	15	26	....	....	....	....	....
1986-87ab	U. of Maine	H.E.	41	12	32	44	59	....	....	....	....	....
1987-88	U. of Maine	H.E.	8	4	7	11	22	....	....	....	....	....
	U.S. National	....	38	3	9	12	24	....	....	....	....	....
	U.S. Olympic	....	3	0	0	0	0	....	....	....	....	....
1988-89	New Jersey	NHL	2	0	0	0	0	....	....	....	....	....
	Utica	AHL	80	17	27	44	70	5	0	1	1	4
1989-90	New Jersey	NHL	19	2	7	9	11	6	1	3	4	17
cd	Utica	AHL	57	12	48	60	38	....	....	....	....	....
1990-91e	New Jersey	NHL	76	4	34	38	48	7	1	2	3	6
1991-92	New Jersey	NHL	76	7	25	32	55	7	0	2	2	4
1992-93	Hartford	NHL	79	7	29	36	76	....	....	....	....	....
1993-94	Hartford	NHL	8	1	1	2	2	....	....	....	....	....
	Chicago	NHL	54	3	23	26	31	6	0	2	2	6
	NHL Totals		314	24	119	143	223	26	2	9	11	33

a Hockey East First All-Star Team (1987)
b NCAA East Second All-American Team (1987)
c AHL First All-Star Team (1990)
d Won Eddie Shore Plaque (Outstanding Defenseman - AHL) (1990)
e NHL/Upper Deck All-Rookie Team (1991)

Traded to **Hartford** by **New Jersey** with Sean Burke for Bobby Holik, Hartford's second round choice (Jay Pandolfo) in 1993 Entry Draft and future considerations, August 28, 1992. Traded to **Chicago** by **Hartford** with Patrick Poulin for Steve Larmer and Bryan Marchment, November 2, 1993.

WEINRICH, JASON NYR

Defense. Shoots right. 6'2", 189 lbs. Born, Lewiston, ME, February 13, 1972.
(NY Rangers' 8th choice, 118th overall, in 1990 Entry Draft).

			Regular Season					Playoffs				
Season	Club	Lea	GP	G	A	TP	PIM	GP	G	A	TP	PIM
1990-91	U. of Maine	H.E.	14	1	1	2	4	....	....	....	....	....
1991-92	U. of Maine	H.E.	36	1	15	16	18	....	....	....	....	....
1992-93	U. of Maine	H.E.	38	1	8	9	42	....	....	....	....	....
1993-94	U. of Maine	H.E.	18	3	4	7	30	....	....	....	....	....

WELLS, CHRIS PIT.

Center. Shoots left. 6'6", 215 lbs. Born, Calgary, Alta., November 12, 1975.
(Pittsburgh's 1st choice, 24th overall, in 1994 Entry Draft).

			Regular Season					Playoffs				
Season	Club	Lea	GP	G	A	TP	PIM	GP	G	A	TP	PIM
1991-92	Seattle	WHL	64	13	8	21	80	11	0	0	0	15
1992-93	Seattle	WHL	63	18	37	55	111	5	2	3	5	4
1993-94	Seattle	WHL	69	30	44	74	150	9	6	5	11	23

WELLS, JAY NYR

Defense. Shoots left. 6'1", 210 lbs. Born, Paris, Ont., May 18, 1959.
(Los Angeles' 1st choice, 16th overall, in 1979 Entry Draft).

			Regular Season					Playoffs				
Season	Club	Lea	GP	G	A	TP	PIM	GP	G	A	TP	PIM
1977-78	Kingston	OHA	68	9	13	22	195	5	1	2	3	6
1978-79a	Kingston	OHA	48	6	21	27	100	11	2	7	9	29
1979-80	Los Angeles	NHL	43	0	0	0	113	4	0	0	0	11
	Binghamton	AHL	28	0	6	6	48	....	....	....	....	....
1980-81	Los Angeles	NHL	72	5	13	18	155	4	0	0	0	27
1981-82	Los Angeles	NHL	60	1	8	9	145	10	1	3	4	41
1982-83	Los Angeles	NHL	69	3	12	15	167	....	....	....	....	....
1983-84	Los Angeles	NHL	69	3	18	21	141	....	....	....	....	....
1984-85	Los Angeles	NHL	77	2	9	11	185	3	0	1	1	0
1985-86	Los Angeles	NHL	79	11	31	42	226	....	....	....	....	....
1986-87	Los Angeles	NHL	77	7	29	36	155	5	1	2	3	10
1987-88	Los Angeles	NHL	58	2	23	25	159	5	1	2	3	21
1988-89	Philadelphia	NHL	67	2	19	21	184	18	0	2	2	51
1989-90	Philadelphia	NHL	59	3	16	19	129	....	....	....	....	....
	Buffalo	NHL	1	0	1	1	0	6	0	0	0	12
1990-91	Buffalo	NHL	43	1	2	3	86	1	0	1	1	0
1991-92	Buffalo	NHL	41	2	9	11	157	....	....	....	....	....
	NY Rangers	NHL	11	0	0	0	24	13	0	2	2	10
1992-93	NY Rangers	NHL	53	1	9	10	107	....	....	....	....	....
1993-94	NY Rangers	NHL	79	2	7	9	110	23	0	0	0	20
	NHL Totals		958	45	206	251	2243	92	3	13	16	203

a OHA First All-Star Team (1979)

Traded to **Philadelphia** by **Los Angeles** for Doug Crossman, September 29, 1988. Traded to **Buffalo** by **Philadelphia** with Philadelphia's fourth round choice (Peter Ambroziak) in 1991 Entry Draft for Kevin Maguire and Buffalo's second round choice (Mikael Renberg) in 1990 Entry Draft, March 5, 1990. Traded to **NY Rangers** by **Buffalo** for Randy Moller, March 9, 1992.

WERENKA, BRAD (wuh-REHN-kuh) QUE.

Defense. Shoots left. 6'2", 205 lbs. Born, Two Hills, Alta., February 12, 1969.
(Edmonton's 2nd choice, 42nd overall, in 1987 Entry Draft).

			Regular Season					Playoffs				
Season	Club	Lea	GP	G	A	TP	PIM	GP	G	A	TP	PIM
1986-87	N. Michigan	WCHA	30	4	4	8	35	....	....	....	....	....
1987-88	N. Michigan	WCHA	34	7	23	30	26	....	....	....	....	....
1988-89	N. Michigan	WCHA	28	7	13	20	16	....	....	....	....	....
1989-90	N. Michigan	WCHA	8	2	5	7	8	....	....	....	....	....
1990-91abc	N. Michigan	WCHA	47	20	43	63	36	....	....	....	....	....
1991-92	Cape Breton	AHL	66	6	21	27	95	5	0	3	3	6
1992-93	Edmonton	NHL	27	5	3	8	24	....	....	....	....	....
	Cdn. National	....	18	3	7	10	10	....	....	....	....	....
	Cape Breton	AHL	4	1	1	2	4	16	4	17	21	12
1993-94	Edmonton	NHL	15	0	4	4	14	....	....	....	....	....
	Cape Breton	AHL	25	6	17	23	19	....	....	....	....	....
	Cdn. Olympic	....	8	2	2	4	8	....	....	....	....	....
	Quebec	NHL	11	0	7	7	8	....	....	....	....	....
	Cornwall	AHL	....	....	....	....	....	12	2	10	12	22
	NHL Totals		53	5	14	19	46	....	....	....	....	....

a WCHA First All-Star Team (1991)
b NCAA West First All-American Team (1991)
c NCAA Final Four All-Tournament Team (1991)

Traded to **Quebec** by **Edmonton** for Steve Passmore, March 21, 1994.

WERENKA, DARCY NYR

Defense. Shoots right. 6'1", 210 lbs. Born, Edmonton, Alta., May 13, 1973.
(NY Rangers' 2nd choice, 37th overall, in 1991 Entry Draft).

			Regular Season					Playoffs				
Season	Club	Lea	GP	G	A	TP	PIM	GP	G	A	TP	PIM
1990-91	Lethbridge	WHL	72	13	37	50	39	16	1	7	8	4
1991-92	Lethbridge	WHL	69	17	58	75	56	5	2	1	3	0
1992-93	Lethbridge	WHL	19	4	17	21	12	....	....	....	....	....
	Brandon	WHL	36	4	25	29	19	3	0	0	0	2
	Binghamton	AHL	3	0	1	1	2	3	0	0	0	0
1993-94	Binghamton	AHL	53	5	22	27	10	....	....	....	....	....

WERNBLOM, MAGNUS L.A.

Right wing. Shoots left. 6', 187 lbs. Born, Kramfors, Sweden, February 3, 1973.
(Los Angeles' 6th choice, 207th overall, in 1992 Entry Draft).

			Regular Season					Playoffs				
Season	Club	Lea	GP	G	A	TP	PIM	GP	G	A	TP	PIM
1990-91	MoDo	Swe.	16	4	2	6	8	....	....	....	....	....
1991-92	MoDo	Swe.	35	7	6	13	50	....	....	....	....	....
1992-93	MoDo	Swe.	37	8	3	11	36	3	0	0	0	0
1993-94	MoDo	Swe.	39	14	9	23	46	11	2	3	5	12

WESLEY, GLEN

Defense. Shoots left. 6'1", 201 lbs. Born, Red Deer, Alta., October 2, 1968.
(Boston's 1st choice, 3rd overall, in 1987 Entry Draft).

			Regular Season					Playoffs				
Season	Club	Lea	GP	G	A	TP	PIM	GP	G	A	TP	PIM
1983-84	Portland	WHL	3	1	2	3	0	....	....	....	....	....
1984-85	Portland	WHL	67	16	52	68	76	6	1	6	7	8
1985-86a	Portland	WHL	69	16	75	91	96	15	3	11	14	29
1986-87a	Portland	WHL	63	16	46	62	72	20	8	18	26	27
1987-88b	Boston	NHL	79	7	30	37	69	23	6	8	14	22
1988-89	Boston	NHL	77	19	35	54	61	10	0	2	2	4
1989-90	Boston	NHL	78	9	27	36	48	21	2	6	8	36
1990-91	Boston	NHL	80	11	32	43	78	19	2	9	11	19
1991-92	Boston	NHL	78	9	37	46	54	15	2	4	6	16
1992-93	Boston	NHL	64	8	25	33	47	4	0	0	0	0
1993-94	Boston	NHL	81	14	44	58	64	13	3	3	6	12
	NHL Totals		537	77	230	307	421	105	15	32	47	109

a WHL West All-Star Team (1986, 1987)
b NHL All-Rookie Team (1988)

Played in NHL All-Star Game (1989)

WETHERILL, DARREN BOS.

Defense. Shoots left. 6', 180 lbs. Born, Regina, Sask., January 28, 1970.
(Boston's 8th choice, 189th overall, in 1990 Entry Draft).

			Regular Season					Playoffs				
Season	Club	Lea	GP	G	A	TP	PIM	GP	G	A	TP	PIM
1990-91	Lake Superior	CCHA	26	0	6	6	14	....	....	....	....	....
1991-92	Lake Superior	CCHA	27	1	4	5	42	....	....	....	....	....
1992-93	Lake Superior	CCHA	43	2	10	12	64	....	....	....	....	....
1993-94	Lake Superior	CCHA	44	1	8	9	92	....	....	....	....	....

WHITE, KAM TOR.

Defense. Shoots left. 6'3", 195 lbs. Born, Chicago, IL, February 13, 1976.
(Toronto's 5th choice, 152nd overall, in 1994 Entry Draft).

			Regular Season					Playoffs				
Season	Club	Lea	GP	G	A	TP	PIM	GP	G	A	TP	PIM
1992-93	Newmarket	OHL	8	0	0	0	8	....	....	....	....	....
1993-94	Newmarket	OHL	44	0	5	5	125	....	....	....	....	....

WHITE, PETER EDM.

Left wing. Shoots left. 5'11", 200 lbs. Born, Montreal, Que., March 15, 1969.
(Edmonton's 4th choice, 92nd overall, in 1989 Entry Draft).

			Regular Season					Playoffs				
Season	Club	Lea	GP	G	A	TP	PIM	GP	G	A	TP	PIM
1988-89	Michigan State	CCHA	46	20	33	53	17	....	....	....	....	....
1989-90	Michigan State	CCHA	45	22	40	62	6	....	....	....	....	....
1990-91	Michigan State	CCHA	37	7	31	38	28	....	....	....	....	....
1991-92	Michigan State	CCHA	41	26	49	75	32	....	....	....	....	....
1992-93	Cape Breton	AHL	64	12	28	40	10	16	3	3	6	12
1993-94	Edmonton	NHL	26	3	5	8	2	....	....	....	....	....
	Cape Breton	AHL	45	21	49	70	12	5	2	3	5	2
	NHL Totals		26	3	5	8	2	....	....	....	....	....

WHITE, SCOTT

Defense. Shoots right. 6'1", 195 lbs. Born, Ormstown, Que., March 15, 1968.
(Quebec's 6th choice, 117th overall, in 1986 Entry Draft).

			Regular Season					Playoffs				
Season	Club	Lea	GP	G	A	TP	PIM	GP	G	A	TP	PIM
1985-86	Michigan Tech.	WCHA	40	3	15	18	58	....	....	....	....	....
1986-87	Michigan Tech.	WCHA	36	4	15	19	58	....	....	....	....	....
1987-88	Michigan Tech.	WCHA	40	7	25	32	32	....	....	....	....	....
1988-89	Michigan Tech.	WCHA	38	6	18	24	38	....	....	....	....	....
1989-90	Bergen	Nor.	29	10	21	31	76	....	....	....	....	....
	Greensboro	ECHL	30	9	13	22	67	11	4	10	14	24
1990-91	Kansas City	IHL	18	3	2	5	37	....	....	....	....	....
	Kalamazoo	IHL	6	0	1	1	8	....	....	....	....	....
	Greensboro	ECHL	42	8	29	37	93	13	2	11	13	10
1991-92ab	Greensboro	ECHL	57	21	63	84	204	8	1	6	7	12
	Fort Wayne	IHL	....	....	....	....	....	1	0	0	0	2
1992-93	New Haven	AHL	80	10	44	54	72	....	....	....	....	....
1993-94	PEI	AHL	15	1	4	5	6	....	....	....	....	....
	Salt Lake	IHL	15	0	3	3	8	....	....	....	....	....
	Greensboro	ECHL	27	3	21	24	65	8	1	5	6	8

a ECHL Best Defenseman (1992)
b ECHL First All-Star Team (1992)

Signed as a free agent by **Ottawa**, August 4, 1992.

WHITE, TOM — CHI.

Center. Shoots left. 6'1", 185 lbs. Born, Chicago, IL, August 25, 1975.

			Regular Season					Playoffs				
Season	Club	Lea	GP	G	A	TP	PIM	GP	G	A	TP	PIM
1992-93	Westminister	HS	22	14	13	27	22	....	....	....	....	....
1993-94	Miami	CCHA	31	1	6	7	26	....	....	....	....	....

WHITNEY, RAY — S.J.

Center. Shoots right. 5'9", 160 lbs. Born, Fort Saskatchewan, Alta., May 8, 1972.
(San Jose's 2nd choice, 23rd overall, in 1991 Entry Draft).

			Regular Season					Playoffs				
Season	Club	Lea	GP	G	A	TP	PIM	GP	G	A	TP	PIM
1988-89	Spokane	WHL	71	17	33	50	16	....	....	....	....	....
1989-90	Spokane	WHL	71	57	56	113	50	6	3	4	7	6
1990-91abc	Spokane	WHL	72	67	118	*185	36	15	13	18	*31	12
1991-92	Koln	Ger.	10	3	6	9	4	....	....	....	....	....
	San Diego	IHL	63	36	54	90	12	4	0	0	0	0
	San Jose	**NHL**	**2**	**0**	**3**	**3**	**0**	....	....	....	....	....
1992-93	**San Jose**	**NHL**	**26**	**4**	**6**	**10**	**4**	....	....	....	....	....
	Kansas City	IHL	46	20	33	53	14	12	5	7	12	2
1993-94	**San Jose**	**NHL**	**61**	**14**	**26**	**40**	**14**	**14**	**0**	**4**	**4**	**8**
	NHL Totals		**89**	**18**	**35**	**53**	**18**	**14**	**0**	**4**	**4**	**8**

a WHL West First All-Star Team (1991)
b Memorial Cup All-Star Team (1991)
c Won George Parsons Trophy (Memorial Cup Most Sportsmanlike Player) (1991)

WHYTE, SEAN

Right wing. Shoots right. 6', 198 lbs. Born, Sudbury, Ont., May 4, 1970.
(Los Angeles' 7th choice, 165th overall, in 1989 Entry Draft).

			Regular Season					Playoffs				
Season	Club	Lea	GP	G	A	TP	PIM	GP	G	A	TP	PIM
1986-87	Guelph	OHL	41	1	3	4	13	....	....	....	....	....
1987-88	Guelph	OHL	62	6	22	28	71	....	....	....	....	....
1988-89	Guelph	OHL	53	20	44	64	57	....	....	....	....	....
1989-90	Owen Sound	OHL	54	23	30	53	90	3	0	1	1	10
1990-91	Phoenix	IHL	60	18	17	35	61	4	1	0	1	2
1991-92	**Los Angeles**	**NHL**	**3**	**0**	**0**	**0**	**0**	....	....	....	....	....
	Phoenix	IHL	72	24	30	54	113	....	....	....	....	....
1992-93	**Los Angeles**	**NHL**	**18**	**0**	**2**	**2**	**12**	....	....	....	....	....
	Phoenix	IHL	51	11	35	46	65	....	....	....	....	....
1993-94	Tulsa	CHL	50	42	29	71	93	....	....	....	....	....
	Cornwall	AHL	18	6	9	15	16	9	1	2	3	2
	NHL Totals		**21**	**0**	**2**	**2**	**12**	....	....	....	....	....

WIDMER, JASON — NYI

Defense. Shoots left. 6', 205 lbs. Born, Calgary, Alta., August 1, 1973.
(NY Islanders' 8th choice, 176th overall, in 1992 Entry Draft).

			Regular Season					Playoffs				
Season	Club	Lea	GP	G	A	TP	PIM	GP	G	A	TP	PIM
1990-91	Lethbridge	WHL	58	2	12	14	55	16	0	1	1	12
1991-92	Lethbridge	WHL	40	2	19	21	181	5	0	4	4	9
1992-93	Lethbridge	WHL	55	3	15	18	140	4	0	3	3	2
	Capital Dist.	AHL	4	0	0	0	2	....	....	....	....	....
1993-94	Lethbridge	WHL	64	11	31	42	191	9	3	5	8	34

WIEMER, JASON — T.B.

Center. Shoots left. 6'1", 215 lbs. Born, Kimberley, B.C., April 14, 1976.
(Tampa Bay's 1st choice, 8th overall, in 1994 Entry Draft).

			Regular Season					Playoffs				
Season	Club	Lea	GP	G	A	TP	PIM	GP	G	A	TP	PIM
1991-92	Portland	WHL	2	0	1	1	0	....	....	....	....	....
1992-93	Portland	WHL	68	18	34	52	159	16	7	3	10	27
1993-94	Portland	WHL	72	45	51	96	236	....	....	....	....	....

WIEMER, JIM — (WEE-muhr)

Defense. Shoots left. 6'4", 216 lbs. Born, Sudbury, Ont., January 9, 1961.
(Buffalo's 5th choice, 83rd overall, in 1980 Entry Draft).

			Regular Season					Playoffs				
Season	Club	Lea	GP	G	A	TP	PIM	GP	G	A	TP	PIM
1978-79	Peterborough	OHA	61	15	12	27	50	18	4	4	8	15
1979-80	Peterborough	OHA	53	17	32	49	63	14	6	9	15	19
1980-81	Peterborough	OHA	65	41	54	95	102	5	1	2	3	15
1981-82	Rochester	AHL	74	19	26	45	57	9	0	4	4	2
1982-83	Rochester	AHL	74	15	44	59	43	15	5	15	20	22
	Buffalo	**NHL**	....	....	....	....	....	**1**	**0**	**0**	**0**	**0**
1983-84	**Buffalo**	**NHL**	**64**	**5**	**15**	**20**	**48**	....	....	....	....	....
	Rochester	AHL	12	4	11	15	11	18	3	13	16	20
1984-85	**Buffalo**	**NHL**	**10**	**3**	**2**	**5**	**4**	....	....	....	....	....
	Rochester	AHL	13	1	9	10	24	....	....	....	....	....
	NY Rangers	**NHL**	**22**	**4**	**3**	**7**	**30**	**1**	**0**	**0**	**0**	**0**
	New Haven	AHL	33	9	27	36	39	....	....	....	....	....
1985-86	**NY Rangers**	**NHL**	**7**	**3**	**0**	**3**	**2**	**8**	**1**	**0**	**1**	**6**
ab	New Haven	AHL	73	24	49	73	108	....	....	....	....	....
1986-87	New Haven	AHL	6	0	7	7	6	....	....	....	....	....
	Nova Scotia	AHL	59	9	25	34	72	5	0	4	4	2
1987-88	**Edmonton**	**NHL**	**12**	**1**	**2**	**3**	**15**	**2**	**0**	**0**	**0**	**2**
	Nova Scotia	AHL	57	11	32	43	99	5	1	1	2	14
1988-89	Cape Breton	AHL	51	12	29	41	80	....	....	....	....	....
	Los Angeles	**NHL**	**9**	**2**	**3**	**5**	**20**	**10**	**2**	**1**	**3**	**19**
	New Haven	AHL	3	1	1	2	2	7	2	3	5	2
1989-90	**Boston**	**NHL**	**61**	**5**	**14**	**19**	**63**	**8**	**0**	**1**	**1**	**4**
	Maine	AHL	6	3	4	7	27	....	....	....	....	....
1990-91	**Boston**	**NHL**	**61**	**4**	**19**	**23**	**62**	**16**	**1**	**3**	**4**	**14**
1991-92	**Boston**	**NHL**	**47**	**1**	**8**	**9**	**84**	**15**	**1**	**3**	**4**	**14**
	Maine	AHL	3	0	1	1	4	....	....	....	....	....
1992-93	**Boston**	**NHL**	**28**	**1**	**6**	**7**	**48**	**1**	**0**	**0**	**0**	**4**
	Providence	AHL	4	2	1	3	2	....	....	....	....	....
1993-94	**Boston**	**NHL**	**4**	**0**	**0**	**0**	**2**	....	....	....	....	....
	Providence	AHL	35	5	12	17	81	....	....	....	....	....
	NHL Totals		**325**	**29**	**72**	**101**	**378**	**62**	**5**	**8**	**13**	**63**

a AHL First All-Star Team (1986)
b Won Eddie Shore Plaque (Outstanding Defenseman - AHL) (1986)

Traded to **NY Rangers** by **Buffalo** with Steve Patrick for Dave Maloney and Chris Renaud, December 6, 1984. Traded to **Edmonton** by **NY Rangers** with Reijo Ruotsalainen, Clark Donatelli and Ville Kentala for Don Jackson, Mike Golden, Miloslav Horvava and future considerations, October 23, 1986. Traded to **Los Angeles** by **Edmonton** with Alan May for Brian Wilks and John English, March 7, 1989. Signed as a free agent by **Boston**, July 6, 1989.

WIESEL, ADAM — MTL.

Defense. Shoots right. 6'3", 205 lbs. Born, Holyoke, MA, January 25, 1975.
(Montreal's 4th choice, 85th overall, in 1993 Entry Draft).

			Regular Season					Playoffs				
Season	Club	Lea	GP	G	A	TP	PIM	GP	G	A	TP	PIM
1992-93	Springfield	Jr. B	41	11	20	31	34	....	....	....	....	....
1993-94	Clarkson	ECAC	33	3	7	10	26	....	....	....	....	....

WILKIE, BOB — PHI.

Defense. Shoots right. 6'2", 215 lbs. Born, Calgary, Alta., February 11, 1969.
(Detroit's 3rd choice, 41st overall, in 1987 Entry Draft).

			Regular Season					Playoffs				
Season	Club	Lea	GP	G	A	TP	PIM	GP	G	A	TP	PIM
1985-86	Calgary	WHL	63	8	19	27	56	....	....	....	....	....
1986-87	Swift Current	WHL	65	12	38	50	50	4	1	3	4	2
1987-88	Swift Current	WHL	67	12	68	80	124	10	4	12	16	8
1988-89	Swift Current	WHL	62	18	67	85	89	12	1	11	12	47
1989-90	Adirondack	AHL	58	5	33	38	64	6	1	4	5	2
1990-91	**Detroit**	**NHL**	**8**	**1**	**2**	**3**	**2**	....	....	....	....	....
	Adirondack	AHL	43	6	18	24	71	2	1	0	1	2
1991-92	Adirondack	AHL	7	1	4	5	6	16	2	5	7	12
1992-93	Adirondack	AHL	14	0	5	5	20	....	....	....	....	....
	Fort Wayne	IHL	32	7	14	21	82	12	4	6	10	10
	Hershey	AHL	28	7	25	32	18	....	....	....	....	....
1993-94	**Philadelphia**	**NHL**	**10**	**1**	**3**	**4**	**8**	....	....	....	....	....
a	Hershey	AHL	69	8	53	61	100	9	1	4	5	8
	NHL Totals		**18**	**2**	**5**	**7**	**10**	....	....	....	....	....

a AHL Second All-Star Team (1994)

Traded to **Philadelphia** by **Detroit** for future considerations, February 2, 1993.

WILKIE, DAVID — MTL.

Defense. Shoots right. 6'3", 215 lbs. Born, Ellensburgh, WA, May 30, 1974.
(Montreal's 1st choice, 20th overall, in 1992 Entry Draft).

			Regular Season					Playoffs				
Season	Club	Lea	GP	G	A	TP	PIM	GP	G	A	TP	PIM
1990-91	Seattle	WHL	25	1	1	2	22	....	....	....	....	....
1991-92	Kamloops	WHL	71	12	28	40	153	16	6	5	11	19
1992-93	Kamloops	WHL	53	11	26	37	109	6	4	2	6	2
1993-94	Kamloops	WHL	27	11	18	29	18	....	....	....	....	....
	Regina	WHL	29	27	21	48	16	4	1	4	5	4

WILKINSON, NEIL — WPG.

Defense. Shoots right. 6'3", 190 lbs. Born, Selkirk, Man., August 15, 1967.
(Minnesota's 2nd choice, 30th overall, in 1986 Entry Draft).

			Regular Season					Playoffs				
Season	Club	Lea	GP	G	A	TP	PIM	GP	G	A	TP	PIM
1986-87	Michigan State	CCHA	19	3	4	7	18	....	....	....	....	....
1987-88	Medicine Hat	WHL	55	11	21	32	157	5	1	0	1	2
1988-89	Kalamazoo	IHL	39	5	15	20	96	....	....	....	....	....
1989-90	**Minnesota**	**NHL**	**36**	**0**	**5**	**5**	**100**	**7**	**0**	**2**	**2**	**11**
	Kalamazoo	IHL	20	6	7	13	62	....	....	....	....	....
1990-91	**Minnesota**	**NHL**	**50**	**2**	**9**	**11**	**117**	**22**	**3**	**3**	**6**	**12**
	Kalamazoo	IHL	10	0	3	3	38	....	....	....	....	....
1991-92	**San Jose**	**NHL**	**60**	**4**	**15**	**19**	**107**	....	....	....	....	....
1992-93	**San Jose**	**NHL**	**59**	**1**	**7**	**8**	**96**	....	....	....	....	....
1993-94	**Chicago**	**NHL**	**72**	**3**	**9**	**12**	**116**	**4**	**0**	**0**	**0**	**0**
	NHL Totals		**277**	**10**	**45**	**55**	**536**	**33**	**3**	**5**	**8**	**23**

Claimed by **San Jose** from **Minnesota** in Dispersal Draft, May 30, 1991. Traded to **Chicago** by **San Jose** as future considerations to complete June 18, 1993 trade for Jimmy Waite, July 9, 1993. Traded to **Winnipeg** by **Chicago** for Chicago's third round choice (previously acquired by Winnipeg) in 1995 Entry Draft, June 3, 1994.

WILLETT, PAUL

Center. Shoots right. 5'9", 180 lbs. Born, New Richmond, Que., May 10, 1969.

			Regular Season					Playoffs				
Season	Club	Lea	GP	G	A	TP	PIM	GP	G	A	TP	PIM
1988-89	Longueuil	QMJHL	60	45	67	112	89	....	....	....	....	....
1989-90	Longueuil	QMJHL	68	57	75	132	68	7	7	3	10	12
1990-91	Roanoke	ECHL	29	21	29	50	26	....	....	....	....	....
1991-92	New Haven	AHL	69	29	51	80	68	5	3	1	4	2
1992-93	Fort Wayne	IHL	74	33	52	85	109	10	*7	6	13	22
1993-94	Cornwall	AHL	56	24	34	58	60	13	2	10	12	0

Signed as a free agent by **Quebec**, July 23, 1993.

WILLIAMS, DARRYL — L.A.

Left wing. Shoots left. 5'11", 185 lbs. Born, Mt. Pearl, Nfld., February 9, 1968.

			Regular Season					Playoffs				
Season	Club	Lea	GP	G	A	TP	PIM	GP	G	A	TP	PIM
1986-87	Belleville	OHL	58	9	10	19	108	....	....	....	....	....
1987-88	Belleville	OHL	63	29	39	68	169	....	....	....	....	....
1988-89	Belleville	AHL	46	24	21	45	137	....	....	....	....	....
	New Haven	AHL	15	5	5	10	24	....	....	....	....	....
1989-90	New Haven	AHL	51	9	13	22	124	....	....	....	....	....
1990-91	New Haven	AHL	57	14	11	25	278	....	....	....	....	....
	Phoenix	IHL	12	1	2	3	53	7	1	0	1	12
1991-92	Phoenix	IHL	48	8	19	27	219	....	....	....	....	....
	New Haven	AHL	13	0	2	2	69	....	....	....	....	....
1992-93	**Los Angeles**	**NHL**	**2**	**0**	**0**	**0**	**10**	....	....	....	....	....
	Phoenix	IHL	61	18	7	25	314	....	....	....	....	....
1993-94	Phoenix	IHL	52	11	18	29	237	....	....	....	....	....
	NHL Totals		**2**	**0**	**0**	**0**	**10**	....	....	....	....	....

Signed as a free agent by **Los Angeles**, May 19, 1989.

WILLIAMS, DAVID — ANA.

Defense. Shoots right. 6'2", 195 lbs. Born, Plainfield, NJ, August 25, 1967.
(New Jersey's 12th choice, 234th overall, in 1985 Entry Draft).

			Regular Season					Playoffs				
Season	Club	Lea	GP	G	A	TP	PIM	GP	G	A	TP	PIM
1986-87	Dartmouth	ECAC	23	2	19	21	20	....	....	....	....	....
1987-88	Dartmouth	ECAC	25	8	14	22	30	....	....	....	....	....
1988-89ab	Dartmouth	ECAC	25	4	11	15	28	....	....	....	....	....
1989-90	Dartmouth	ECAC	26	3	12	15	32	....	....	....	....	....
1990-91	Muskegon	IHL	14	1	2	3	4	....	....	....	....	....
	Knoxville	ECHL	38	12	15	27	40	3	0	0	0	4
1991-92	**San Jose**	**NHL**	**56**	**3**	**25**	**28**	**40**	....	....	....	....	....
	Kansas City	IHL	18	2	3	5	22	....	....	....	....	....
1992-93	**San Jose**	**NHL**	**40**	**1**	**11**	**12**	**49**	....	....	....	....	....
	Kansas City	IHL	31	1	11	12	28	....	....	....	....	....
1993-94	**Anaheim**	**NHL**	**56**	**5**	**15**	**20**	**42**	....	....	....	....	....
	San Diego	IHL	16	1	6	7	17	....	....	....	....	....
	NHL Totals		**152**	**9**	**51**	**60**	**131**	....	....	....	....	....

a ECAC First All-Star Team (1989)
b NCAA East Second All-American Team (1989)

Signed as a free agent by **San Jose**, August 9, 1991. Claimed by **Anaheim** from **San Jose** in Expansion Draft, June 24, 1993.

WILLIS, RICK — NYR

Left wing. Shoots left. 6', 190 lbs. Born, Lynn, MA, January 12, 1972.
(NY Rangers' 5th choice, 76th overall, in 1990 Entry Draft).

			Regular Season					Playoffs				
Season	Club	Lea	GP	G	A	TP	PIM	GP	G	A	TP	PIM
1991-92	U. of Michigan	CCHA	32	1	4	5	42	....	....	....	....	....
1992-93	U. of Michigan	CCHA	39	3	8	11	67	....	....	....	....	....
1993-94	U. of Michigan	CCHA	40	8	5	13	83	....	....	....	....	....

WILLNER, BRADLEY — N.J.

Defense. Shoots right. 6'3", 191 lbs. Born, Edina, MN, January 6, 1973.
(New Jersey's 4th choice, 77th overall, in 1991 Entry Draft).

			Regular Season					Playoffs				
Season	Club	Lea	GP	G	A	TP	PIM	GP	G	A	TP	PIM
1991-92	Lake Superior	CCHA	16	0	0	0	10	....	....	....	....	....
1992-93	Lake Superior	CCHA	37	2	4	6	28	....	....	....	....	....
1993-94	Lake Superior	CCHA	45	2	13	15	42	....	....	....	....	....

WILSON, LANDON — QUE.

Right wing. Shoots right. 6'2", 202 lbs. Born, St. Louis, MO, March 13, 1975.
(Toronto's 2nd choice, 19th overall, in 1993 Entry Draft).

			Regular Season					Playoffs				
Season	Club	Lea	GP	G	A	TP	PIM	GP	G	A	TP	PIM
1992-93	Dubuque	USHL	43	29	36	65	284	....	....	....	....	....
1993-94	North Dakota	WCHA	35	18	15	33	*147	....	....	....	....	....

Traded to **Quebec** by **Toronto** with Wendel Clark, Sylvain Lefebvre and Toronto's first round choice (Jeffrey Kealty) in 1994 Entry Draft for Mats Sundin, Garth Butcher, Todd Warriner and Philadelphia's first round choice (previously acquired by Quebec — later traded to Washington — Washington selected Nolan Baumgartner) in 1994 Entry Draft, June 28, 1994.

WILSON, MIKE — VAN.

Defense. Shoots left. 6'4", 195 lbs. Born, Brampton, Ont., February 26, 1975.
(Vancouver's 1st choice, 20th overall, in 1993 Entry Draft).

			Regular Season					Playoffs				
Season	Club	Lea	GP	G	A	TP	PIM	GP	G	A	TP	PIM
1992-93	Sudbury	OHL	53	6	7	13	58	14	1	1	2	2
1993-94	Sudbury	OHL	60	4	22	26	62	9	1	3	4	8

WILSON, RON

Center. Shoots left. 5'9", 180 lbs. Born, Toronto, Ont., May 13, 1956.
(Montreal's 15th choice, 133rd overall, in 1976 Amateur Draft).

			Regular Season					Playoffs				
Season	Club	Lea	GP	G	A	TP	PIM	GP	G	A	TP	PIM
1974-75	Toronto	OMJHL	16	6	12	18	6	23	9	17	26	6
1975-76	St. Catharines	OHA	64	37	62	99	44	4	1	6	7	7
1976-77	Nova Scotia	AHL	67	15	21	36	18	6	0	0	0	0
1977-78	Nova Scotia	AHL	59	15	25	40	17	11	4	4	8	9
1978-79	Nova Scotia	AHL	77	33	42	75	91	10	5	6	11	14
1979-80	**Winnipeg**	**NHL**	**79**	**21**	**36**	**57**	**28**	....	....	....	....	....
1980-81	**Winnipeg**	**NHL**	**77**	**18**	**33**	**51**	**55**	....	....	....	....	....
1981-82	**Winnipeg**	**NHL**	**39**	**3**	**13**	**16**	**49**	....	....	....	....	....
	Tulsa	CHL	41	20	38	58	22	3	1	0	1	2
1982-83	**Winnipeg**	**NHL**	**12**	**6**	**3**	**9**	**4**	**3**	**2**	**2**	**4**	**2**
	Sherbrooke	AHL	65	30	55	85	71	....	....	....	....	....
1983-84	**Winnipeg**	**NHL**	**51**	**3**	**12**	**15**	**12**	....	....	....	....	....
	Sherbrooke	AHL	22	10	30	40	16	....	....	....	....	....
1984-85	**Winnipeg**	**NHL**	**75**	**10**	**9**	**19**	**31**	**8**	**4**	**2**	**6**	**2**
1985-86	**Winnipeg**	**NHL**	**54**	**6**	**7**	**13**	**16**	**1**	**0**	**0**	**0**	**0**
	Sherbrooke	AHL	10	9	8	17	9	....	....	....	....	....
1986-87	**Winnipeg**	**NHL**	**80**	**3**	**13**	**16**	**13**	**10**	**1**	**2**	**3**	**0**
1987-88	**Winnipeg**	**NHL**	**69**	**5**	**8**	**13**	**28**	**1**	**0**	**0**	**0**	**2**
1988-89a	Moncton	AHL	80	31	61	92	110	8	1	4	5	20
1989-90	Moncton	AHL	47	16	37	53	39	....	....	....	....	....
	St. Louis	**NHL**	**33**	**3**	**17**	**20**	**23**	**12**	**3**	**5**	**8**	**18**
1990-91	**St. Louis**	**NHL**	**73**	**10**	**27**	**37**	**54**	**7**	**0**	**0**	**0**	**28**
1991-92	**St. Louis**	**NHL**	**64**	**12**	**17**	**29**	**46**	**6**	**0**	**1**	**1**	**0**
1992-93	**St. Louis**	**NHL**	**78**	**7**	**11**	**19**	**44**	**11**	**0**	**0**	**0**	**12**
1993-94	**Montreal**	**NHL**	**48**	**2**	**10**	**12**	**12**	**4**	**0**	**0**	**0**	**0**
	NHL Totals		**832**	**109**	**216**	**326**	**415**	**63**	**10**	**12**	**22**	**64**

a AHL Second All-Star Team (1989)

Sold to **Winnipeg** by **Montreal**, October 4, 1979. Traded to **St. Louis** by **Winnipeg** for Doug Evans, January 22, 1990. Signed as a free agent by **Montreal**, August 20, 1993.

WILSON, ROSS

Right wing. Shoots right. 6'3", 197 lbs. Born, The Pas, Man., June 26, 1969.
(Los Angeles' 3rd choice, 43rd overall, in 1987 Entry Draft).

			Regular Season					Playoffs				
Season	Club	Lea	GP	G	A	TP	PIM	GP	G	A	TP	PIM
1986-87	Peterborough	OHL	66	28	11	39	91	12	3	5	8	16
1987-88	Peterborough	OHL	66	29	30	59	114	12	2	9	11	15
1988-89	Peterborough	OHL	64	48	41	89	90	15	10	13	23	23
1989-90	New Haven	AHL	61	19	14	33	39	....	....	....	....	....
1990-91	New Haven	AHL	68	29	17	46	28	....	....	....	....	....
1991-92	Phoenix	IHL	28	9	9	18	81	....	....	....	....	....
	Kalamazoo	IHL	31	18	6	24	38	11	9	1	10	6
1992-93	Kalamazoo	IHL	58	15	14	29	49	....	....	....	....	....
1993-94	Moncton	AHL	75	29	38	67	49	21	10	9	19	18

WINDSOR, NICHOLAS — QUE.

Defense. Shoots left. 6'1", 165 lbs. Born, Granby, Que., January 19, 1976.
(Quebec's 8th choice, 139th overall, in 1994 Entry Draft).

			Regular Season					Playoffs				
Season	Club	Lea	GP	G	A	TP	PIM	GP	G	A	TP	PIM
1992-93	Magog	Midget	36	12	28	40	....	....	....	....	....	....
1993-94	Cornwall	Jr. A	43	13	39	52	121	....	....	....	....	....

WINNES, CHRIS — PHI.

Right wing. Shoots right. 6', 201 lbs. Born, Ridgefield, CT, February 12, 1968.
(Boston's 9th choice, 161st overall, in 1987 Entry Draft).

			Regular Season					Playoffs				
Season	Club	Lea	GP	G	A	TP	PIM	GP	G	A	TP	PIM
1987-88	N. Hampshire	H.E.	30	17	19	36	28	....	....	....	....	....
1988-89	N. Hampshire	H.E.	30	11	20	31	22	....	....	....	....	....
1989-90	N. Hampshire	H.E.	24	10	13	23	12	....	....	....	....	....
1990-91	N. Hampshire	H.E.	33	15	16	31	24	....	....	....	....	....
	Maine	AHL	7	3	1	4	0	1	0	2	2	0
	Boston	**NHL**	....	....	....	....	....	**1**	**0**	**0**	**0**	**0**
1991-92	**Boston**	**NHL**	**24**	**1**	**3**	**4**	**6**	....	....	....	....	....
	Maine	AHL	45	12	35	47	30	....	....	....	....	....
1992-93	**Boston**	**NHL**	**5**	**0**	**1**	**1**	**0**	....	....	....	....	....
	Providence	AHL	64	23	36	59	34	4	0	2	2	5
1993-94	**Philadelphia**	**NHL**	**4**	**0**	**2**	**2**	**0**	....	....	....	....	....
	Hershey	AHL	70	29	21	50	20	7	1	3	4	0
	NHL Totals		**33**	**1**	**6**	**7**	**6**	**1**	**0**	**0**	**0**	**0**

Signed as a free agent by **Philadelphia**, August 4, 1993.

WISEMAN, BRIAN — NYR

Center. Shoots left. 5'6", 175 lbs. Born, Chatham, Ont., July 13, 1971.
(NY Rangers' 12th choice, 257th overall, in 1991 Entry Draft).

			Regular Season					Playoffs				
Season	Club	Lea	GP	G	A	TP	PIM	GP	G	A	TP	PIM
1990-91	U. of Michigan	CCHA	47	25	33	58	58	....	....	....	....	....
1991-92	U. of Michigan	CCHA	44	27	44	71	38	....	....	....	....	....
1992-93	U. of Michigan	CCHA	35	13	37	50	40	....	....	....	....	....
1993-94ab	U. of Michigan	CCHA	40	19	50	69	44	....	....	....	....	....

a CCHA First All-Star Team (1994)
b NCAA West First All-American Team (1994)

WITT, BRENDAN — WSH.

Defense. Shoots left. 6'1", 205 lbs. Born, Humbolt, Sask., February 20, 1975.
(Washington's 1st choice, 11th overall, in 1993 Entry Draft).

			Regular Season					Playoffs				
Season	Club	Lea	GP	G	A	TP	PIM	GP	G	A	TP	PIM
1991-92	Seattle	WHL	67	3	9	12	212	15	1	1	2	84
1992-93a	Seattle	WHL	70	2	26	28	239	5	1	2	3	30
1993-94ab	Seattle	WHL	56	8	31	39	235	9	3	8	11	23

a WHL West First All-Star Team (1993, 1994)
b Canadian Major Junior First All-Star Team (1994)

WOLANIN, CRAIG (wuh-LAN-ihn) QUE.

Defense. Shoots left. 6'3", 205 lbs. Born, Grosse Pointe, MI, July 27, 1967.
(New Jersey's 1st choice, 3rd overall, in 1985 Entry Draft).

			Regular Season					Playoffs				
Season	**Club**	**Lea**	**GP**	**G**	**A**	**TP**	**PIM**	**GP**	**G**	**A**	**TP**	**PIM**
1984-85	Kitchener	OHL	60	5	16	21	95	4	1	1	2	2
1985-86	**New Jersey**	**NHL**	**44**	**2**	**16**	**18**	**74**	....	....	....	....	....
1986-87	**New Jersey**	**NHL**	**68**	**4**	**6**	**10**	**109**	....	....	....	....	....
1987-88	**New Jersey**	**NHL**	**78**	**6**	**25**	**31**	**170**	**18**	**2**	**5**	**7**	**51**
1988-89	**New Jersey**	**NHL**	**56**	**3**	**8**	**11**	**69**	....	....	....	....	....
1989-90	**New Jersey**	**NHL**	**37**	**1**	**7**	**8**	**47**	....	....	....	....	....
	Utica	AHL	6	2	4	6	2	....	....	....	....	....
	Quebec	**NHL**	**13**	**0**	**3**	**3**	**10**	....	....	....	....	....
1990-91	**Quebec**	**NHL**	**80**	**5**	**13**	**18**	**89**	....	....	....	....	....
1991-92	**Quebec**	**NHL**	**69**	**2**	**11**	**13**	**80**	....	....	....	....	....
1992-93	**Quebec**	**NHL**	**24**	**1**	**4**	**5**	**49**	**4**	**0**	**0**	**0**	**4**
1993-94	**Quebec**	**NHL**	**63**	**6**	**10**	**16**	**80**	....	....	....	....	....
	NHL Totals		**532**	**30**	**103**	**133**	**777**	**22**	**2**	**5**	**7**	**55**

Traded to **Quebec** by **New Jersey** with future considerations (Randy Velischek, August 13, 1990) for Peter Stastny, March 6, 1990.

WOOD, DODY S.J.

Center. Shoots left. 5'11", 181 lbs. Born, Chetwynd, B.C., March 10, 1972.
(San Jose's 4th choice, 45th overall, in 1991 Entry Draft).

			Regular Season					Playoffs				
Season	**Club**	**Lea**	**GP**	**G**	**A**	**TP**	**PIM**	**GP**	**G**	**A**	**TP**	**PIM**
1989-90	Ft. St. John	Tier II	44	51	73	124	270	....	....	....	....	....
	Seattle	WHL	....	....	....	....	....	5	0	0	0	2
1990-91	Seattle	WHL	69	28	37	65	272	6	0	1	1	2
1991-92	Seattle	WHL	37	13	19	32	232	....	....	....	....	....
	Swift Current	WHL	3	0	2	2	14	7	2	1	3	37
1992-93	**San Jose**	**NHL**	**13**	**1**	**1**	**2**	**71**	....	....	....	....	....
	Kansas City	IHL	36	3	2	5	216	6	0	1	1	15
1993-94	Kansas City	IHL	48	5	15	20	320	....	....	....	....	....
	NHL Totals		**13**	**1**	**1**	**2**	**71**	....	....	....	....	....

WOOD, RANDY BUF.

Left wing/Center. Shoots left. 6', 195 lbs. Born, Princeton, NJ, October 12, 1963.

			Regular Season					Playoffs				
Season	**Club**	**Lea**	**GP**	**G**	**A**	**TP**	**PIM**	**GP**	**G**	**A**	**TP**	**PIM**
1982-83	Yale	ECAC	26	5	14	19	10	....	....	....	....	....
1983-84	Yale	ECAC	18	7	7	14	10	....	....	....	....	....
1984-85a	Yale	ECAC	32	25	28	53	23	....	....	....	....	....
1985-86bc	Yale	ECAC	31	25	30	55	26	....	....	....	....	....
1986-87	**NY Islanders**	**NHL**	**6**	**1**	**0**	**1**	**4**	**13**	**1**	**3**	**4**	**14**
	Springfield	AHL	75	23	24	47	57	....	....	....	....	....
1987-88	**NY Islanders**	**NHL**	**75**	**22**	**16**	**38**	**80**	**5**	**1**	**0**	**1**	**6**
	Springfield	AHL	1	0	1	1	0	....	....	....	....	....
1988-89	**NY Islanders**	**NHL**	**77**	**15**	**13**	**28**	**44**	....	....	....	....	....
	Springfield	AHL	1	1	1	2	0	....	....	....	....	....
1989-90	**NY Islanders**	**NHL**	**74**	**24**	**24**	**48**	**39**	**5**	**1**	**1**	**2**	**4**
1990-91	**NY Islanders**	**NHL**	**76**	**24**	**18**	**42**	**45**	....	....	....	....	....
1991-92	**NY Islanders**	**NHL**	**8**	**2**	**2**	**4**	**21**	....	....	....	....	....
	Buffalo	**NHL**	**70**	**20**	**16**	**36**	**65**	**7**	**2**	**1**	**3**	**6**
1992-93	**Buffalo**	**NHL**	**82**	**18**	**25**	**43**	**77**	**8**	**1**	**4**	**5**	**4**
1993-94	**Buffalo**	**NHL**	**84**	**22**	**16**	**38**	**71**	**6**	**0**	**0**	**0**	**0**
	NHL Totals		**552**	**148**	**130**	**278**	**446**	**44**	**6**	**9**	**15**	**34**

a ECAC Second All-Star Team (1985)
b ECAC First All-Star Team (1986)
c NCAA East Second All-Star Team (1986)

Signed as a free agent by **NY Islanders**, September 17, 1986. Traded to **Buffalo** by **NY Islanders** with Pat Lafontaine, Randy Hillier and NY Islanders' fourth round choice (Dean Melanson) in 1992 Entry Draft for Pierre Turgeon, Uwe Krupp, Benoit Hogue and Dave McLlwain, October 25, 1991.

WOODCROFT, CRAIG

Left wing. Shoots left. 6'1", 185 lbs. Born, Toronto, Ont., December 3, 1969.
(Chicago's 6th choice, 134th overall, in 1988 Entry Draft).

			Regular Season					Playoffs				
Season	**Club**	**Lea**	**GP**	**G**	**A**	**TP**	**PIM**	**GP**	**G**	**A**	**TP**	**PIM**
1987-88	Colgate	ECAC	29	7	10	17	28	....	....	....	....	....
1988-89	Colgate	ECAC	29	20	29	49	62	....	....	....	....	....
	Cdn. National	....	2	0	0	0	4	....	....	....	....	....
1989-90	Colgate	ECAC	37	20	26	46	108	....	....	....	....	....
1990-91	Colgate	ECAC	32	26	30	56	52	....	....	....	....	....
1991-92	Indianapolis	IHL	75	21	17	38	67	....	....	....	....	....
1992-93	Cdn. National	....	11	2	4	6	6	....	....	....	....	....
	Indianapolis	IHL	65	12	19	31	80	....	....	....	....	....
1993-94	Cdn. National	....	48	10	7	17	30	....	....	....	....	....
	PEI	AHL	33	5	9	14	41	....	....	....	....	....

WOODS, MARTIN WPG.

Defense. Shoots right. 5'10", 205 lbs. Born, Hull, Que., May 14, 1975.
(Winnipeg's 8th choice, 171st overall, in 1993 Entry Draft).

			Regular Season					Playoffs				
Season	**Club**	**Lea**	**GP**	**G**	**A**	**TP**	**PIM**	**GP**	**G**	**A**	**TP**	**PIM**
1991-92	Victoriaville	QMJHL	60	3	12	15	193	....	....	....	....	....
1992-93	Victoriaville	QMJHL	65	13	27	40	433	4	2	1	3	41
1993-94	Victoriaville	QMJHL	18	2	7	9	41	....	....	....	....	....
	Granby	QMJHL	58	8	20	28	222	3	1	2	3	17

WOODWARD, ROB VAN.

Left wing. Shoots left. 6'4", 225 lbs. Born, Evanston, IL, January 15, 1971.
(Vancouver's 2nd choice, 29th overall, in 1989 Entry Draft).

			Regular Season					Playoffs				
Season	**Club**	**Lea**	**GP**	**G**	**A**	**TP**	**PIM**	**GP**	**G**	**A**	**TP**	**PIM**
1989-90	Michigan State	CCHA	37	17	9	26	8	....	....	....	....	....
1990-91	Michigan State	CCHA	32	5	13	18	16	....	....	....	....	....
1991-92	Michigan State	CCHA	40	14	15	29	60	....	....	....	....	....
1992-93	Michigan State	CCHA	36	12	9	21	90	....	....	....	....	....
1993-94	Hamilton	AHL	60	11	14	25	45	2	0	0	0	0

WOOLLEY, JASON WSH.

Defense. Shoots left. 6', 186 lbs. Born, Toronto, Ont., July 27, 1969.
(Washington's 4th choice, 61st overall, in 1989 Entry Draft).

			Regular Season					Playoffs				
Season	**Club**	**Lea**	**GP**	**G**	**A**	**TP**	**PIM**	**GP**	**G**	**A**	**TP**	**PIM**
1988-89	Michigan State	CCHA	47	12	25	37	26	....	....	....	....	....
1989-90	Michigan State	CCHA	45	10	38	48	26	....	....	....	....	....
1990-91ab	Michigan State	CCHA	40	15	44	59	24	....	....	....	....	....
1991-92	Cdn. National	....	60	14	30	44	36	....	....	....	....	....
	Cdn. Olympic	....	8	0	5	5	4	....	....	....	....	....
	Washington	**NHL**	**1**	**0**	**0**	**0**	**0**	....	....	....	....	....
	Baltimore	AHL	15	1	10	11	6	....	....	....	....	....
1992-93	**Washington**	**NHL**	**26**	**0**	**2**	**2**	**10**	....	....	....	....	....
	Baltimore	AHL	29	14	27	41	22	1	0	2	2	0
1993-94	**Washington**	**NHL**	**10**	**1**	**2**	**3**	**4**	**4**	**1**	**0**	**1**	**4**
	Portland	AHL	41	12	29	41	14	9	2	2	4	4
	NHL Totals		**37**	**1**	**4**	**5**	**14**	**4**	**1**	**0**	**1**	**4**

a CCHA First All-Star Team (1991)
b NCAA West First All-American Team (1991)

WORTMAN, KEVIN

Defense. Shoots right. 6', 200 lbs. Born, Sagus, MA, February 22, 1969.
(Calgary's 9th choice, 168th overall, in 1989 Entry Draft).

			Regular Season					Playoffs				
Season	**Club**	**Lea**	**GP**	**G**	**A**	**TP**	**PIM**	**GP**	**G**	**A**	**TP**	**PIM**
1990-91	American Int'l	NCAA	28	21	25	46	6	....	....	....	....	....
1991-92	Salt Lake	IHL	82	12	34	46	34	5	1	0	1	0
1992-93a	Salt Lake	IHL	82	13	50	63	24	....	....	....	....	....
1993-94	**Calgary**	**NHL**	**5**	**0**	**0**	**0**	**2**	....	....	....	....	....
	Saint John	AHL	72	17	32	49	32	7	1	5	6	16
	NHL Totals		**5**	**0**	**0**	**0**	**2**	....	....	....	....	....

a IHL Second All-Star Team (1993)

WOTTON, MARK VAN.

Defense. Shoots left. 5'11", 187 lbs. Born, Foxwarren, Man., November 16, 1973.
(Vancouver's 11th choice, 237th overall, in 1992 Entry Draft).

			Regular Season					Playoffs				
Season	**Club**	**Lea**	**GP**	**G**	**A**	**TP**	**PIM**	**GP**	**G**	**A**	**TP**	**PIM**
1990-91	Saskatoon	WHL	45	4	11	15	37	....	....	....	....	....
1991-92	Saskatoon	WHL	64	11	25	36	92	....	....	....	....	....
1992-93	Saskatoon	WHL	71	15	51	66	90	9	6	5	11	18
1993-94a	Saskatoon	WHL	65	12	34	46	108	16	3	12	15	32

a WHL East Second All-Star Team (1994)

WREN, BOB L.A.

Left wing. Shoots left. 5'10", 175 lbs. Born, Preston, Ont., September 16, 1974.
(Los Angeles' 3rd choice, 94th overall, in 1993 Entry Draft).

			Regular Season					Playoffs				
Season	**Club**	**Lea**	**GP**	**G**	**A**	**TP**	**PIM**	**GP**	**G**	**A**	**TP**	**PIM**
1991-92	Detroit	OHL	62	13	36	49	58	7	3	4	7	19
1992-93a	Detroit	OHL	63	57	88	145	91	15	4	11	15	20
1993-94a	Detroit	OHL	57	45	64	109	81	17	12	18	30	20

a OHL Second All-Star Team (1993, 1994)

WRIGHT, DARREN BOS.

Defense. Shoots left. 6'1", 182 lbs. Born, Duncan, B.C., May 22, 1976.
(Boston's 4th choice, 125th overall, in 1994 Entry Draft).

			Regular Season					Playoffs				
Season	**Club**	**Lea**	**GP**	**G**	**A**	**TP**	**PIM**	**GP**	**G**	**A**	**TP**	**PIM**
1991-92	Prince Albert	WHL	2	0	0	0	2	....	....	....	....	....
1992-93	Prince Albert	WHL	53	0	4	4	131	....	....	....	....	....
1993-94	Prince Albert	WHL	56	0	5	5	151	....	....	....	....	....

WRIGHT, JAMIE DAL.

Left wing. Shoots left. 5'11", 172 lbs. Born, Kitchener, Ont., May 13, 1976.
(Dallas' 3rd choice, 98th overall, in 1994 Entry Draft).

			Regular Season					Playoffs				
Season	**Club**	**Lea**	**GP**	**G**	**A**	**TP**	**PIM**	**GP**	**G**	**A**	**TP**	**PIM**
1993-94	Guelph	OHL	65	17	15	32	34	8	2	1	3	10

WRIGHT, TYLER EDM.

Center. Shoots right. 5'11", 175 lbs. Born, Canora, Sask., April 6, 1973.
(Edmonton's 1st choice, 12th overall, in 1991 Entry Draft).

			Regular Season					Playoffs				
Season	**Club**	**Lea**	**GP**	**G**	**A**	**TP**	**PIM**	**GP**	**G**	**A**	**TP**	**PIM**
1989-90	Swift Current	WHL	67	14	18	32	139	4	0	0	0	12
1990-91	Swift Current	WHL	66	41	51	92	157	3	0	0	0	6
1991-92	Swift Current	WHL	63	36	46	82	295	8	2	5	7	16
1992-93	**Edmonton**	**NHL**	**7**	**1**	**1**	**2**	**19**	....	....	....	....	....
	Swift Current	WHL	37	24	41	65	76	17	9	17	26	*49
1993-94	**Edmonton**	**NHL**	**5**	**0**	**0**	**0**	**4**	....	....	....	....	....
	Cape Breton	AHL	65	14	27	41	160	5	2	0	2	11
	NHL Totals		**12**	**1**	**1**	**2**	**23**	....	....	....	....	....

YACHMENEV, VITALI (yach-meh-NEHV)

Right wing. Shoots left. 5'9", 180 lbs. Born, Chelyabinsk, USSR, January 8, 1975.
(Los Angeles' 3rd choice, 59th overall, in 1994 Entry Draft).

			Regular Season					Playoffs				
Season	**Club**	**Lea**	**GP**	**G**	**A**	**TP**	**PIM**	**GP**	**G**	**A**	**TP**	**PIM**
1992-93	Chelyabinsk	CIS 2	51	23	20	43	12	....	....	....	....	....
1993-94a	North Bay	OHL	66	*61	52	113	18	18	13	19	32	12

a Canadian Major Junior Rookie of the Year (1994)

YAKE, TERRY (YAYK) ANA.

Right wing. Shoots right. 5'11", 190 lbs. Born, New Westminster, B.C., October 22, 1968.
(Hartford's 3rd choice, 81st overall, in 1987 Entry Draft).

			Regular Season					Playoffs				
Season	Club	Lea	GP	G	A	TP	PIM	GP	G	A	TP	PIM
1984-85	Brandon	WHL	11	1	1	2	0	....	....	....	....	....
1985-86	Brandon	WHL	72	26	26	52	49	....	....	....	....	....
1986-87	Brandon	WHL	71	44	58	102	64	....	....	....	....	....
1987-88	Brandon	WHL	72	55	85	140	59	3	4	2	6	7
1988-89	**Hartford**	**NHL**	**2**	**0**	**0**	**0**	**0**	....	....	....	....	....
	Binghamton	AHL	75	39	56	95	57	....	....	....	....	....
1989-90	**Hartford**	**NHL**	**2**	**0**	**1**	**1**	**0**	....	....	....	....	....
	Binghamton	AHL	77	13	42	55	37	....	....	....	....	....
1990-91	**Hartford**	**NHL**	**19**	**1**	**4**	**5**	**10**	**6**	**1**	**1**	**2**	**16**
	Springfield	AHL	60	35	42	77	56	15	9	9	18	10
1991-92	**Hartford**	**NHL**	**15**	**1**	**1**	**2**	**4**	....	....	....	....	....
	Springfield	AHL	53	21	34	55	63	8	3	4	7	2
1992-93	**Hartford**	**NHL**	**66**	**22**	**31**	**53**	**46**	....	....	....	....	....
	Springfield	AHL	16	8	14	22	27	....	....	....	....	....
1993-94	**Anaheim**	**NHL**	**82**	**21**	**31**	**52**	**44**	....	....	....	....	....
	NHL Totals		**186**	**45**	**68**	**113**	**104**	**6**	**1**	**1**	**2**	**16**

Claimed by **Anaheim** from **Hartford** in Expansion Draft, June 24, 1993.

YAKOVENKO, VLADISLAV N.J.

Left wing. Shoots right. 5'11", 176 lbs. Born, Lipetsk, USSR, February 15, 1974.
(New Jersey's 12th choice, 258th overall, in 1992 Entry Draft).

			Regular Season					Playoffs				
Season	Club	Lea	GP	G	A	TP	PIM	GP	G	A	TP	PIM
1991-92	Argus	CIS 3	16	4	0	4	18	....	....	....	....	....
1992-93	Spartak	CIS	21	1	2	3	4	2	0	0	0	2
1993-94	CSKA	CIS	30	2	0	2	12	....	....	....	....	....
	Russian Pen's	IHL	6	0	6	6	10	....	....	....	....	....

YAKUBOV, RAVIL (yah-KOO-bohv, rah-VEEL) CGY.

Center. Shoots left. 6'1", 190 lbs. Born, Moscow, USSR, July 26, 1970.
(Calgary's 6th choice, 126th overall, in 1992 Entry Draft).

			Regular Season					Playoffs				
Season	Club	Lea	GP	G	A	TP	PIM	GP	G	A	TP	PIM
1990-91	Moscow D'amo	USSR	31	4	4	8	6	....	....	....	....	....
1991-92	Moscow D'amo	CIS	39	14	1	15	29	....	....	....	....	....
1992-93	Moscow D'amo	CIS	40	7	13	20	26	10	1	2	3	6
1993-94	Moscow D'amo	CIS	44	12	12	24	30	10	3	1	4	4

YASHIN, ALEXEI (YAH-shin) OTT.

Center. Shoots right. 6'3", 215 lbs. Born, Sverdlovsk, USSR, November 5, 1973.
(Ottawa's 1st choice, 2nd overall, in 1992 Entry Draft).

			Regular Season					Playoffs				
Season	Club	Lea	GP	G	A	TP	PIM	GP	G	A	TP	PIM
1990-91	Sverdlovsk	USSR	26	2	1	3	10	....	....	....	....	....
1991-92	Moscow D'amo	CIS	35	7	5	12	19	....	....	....	....	....
1992-93	Moscow D'amo	CIS	27	10	12	22	18	10	7	3	10	18
1993-94	**Ottawa**	**NHL**	**83**	**30**	**49**	**79**	**22**	....	....	....	....	....
	NHL Totals		**83**	**30**	**49**	**79**	**22**	....	....	....	....	....

Played in NHL All-Star Game (1994)

YAWNEY, TRENT CGY.

Defense. Shoots left. 6'3", 195 lbs. Born, Hudson Bay, Sask., September 29, 1965.
(Chicago's 2nd choice, 45th overall, in 1984 Entry Draft).

			Regular Season					Playoffs				
Season	Club	Lea	GP	G	A	TP	PIM	GP	G	A	TP	PIM
1982-83	Saskatoon	WHL	59	6	31	37	44	6	0	2	2	0
1983-84	Saskatoon	WHL	73	13	46	59	81	....	....	....	....	....
1984-85	Saskatoon	WHL	72	16	51	67	158	3	1	6	7	7
1985-86	Cdn. National	....	73	6	15	21	60	....	....	....	....	....
1986-87	Cdn. National	....	51	4	15	19	37	....	....	....	....	....
1987-88	Cdn. National	....	60	4	12	16	81	....	....	....	....	....
	Cdn. Olympic	....	8	1	1	2	6	....	....	....	....	....
	Chicago	**NHL**	**15**	**2**	**8**	**10**	**15**	**5**	**0**	**4**	**4**	**8**
1988-89	**Chicago**	**NHL**	**69**	**5**	**19**	**24**	**116**	**15**	**3**	**6**	**9**	**20**
1989-90	**Chicago**	**NHL**	**70**	**5**	**15**	**20**	**82**	**20**	**3**	**5**	**8**	**27**
1990-91	**Chicago**	**NHL**	**61**	**3**	**13**	**16**	**77**	**1**	**0**	**0**	**0**	**0**
1991-92	**Calgary**	**NHL**	**47**	**4**	**9**	**13**	**45**	....	....	....	....	....
	Indianapolis	IHL	9	2	3	5	12	....	....	....	....	....
1992-93	**Calgary**	**NHL**	**63**	**1**	**16**	**17**	**67**	**6**	**3**	**2**	**5**	**6**
1993-94	**Calgary**	**NHL**	**58**	**6**	**15**	**21**	**60**	**7**	**0**	**0**	**0**	**16**
	NHL Totals		**383**	**26**	**95**	**121**	**462**	**54**	**9**	**17**	**26**	**77**

Traded to **Calgary** by **Chicago** for Stephane Matteau, December 16, 1991.

YEGOROV, ALEXEI (yeh-GOH-rohv) S.J.

Center. Shoots left. 5'11", 185 lbs. Born, St. Petersburg, USSR, May 21, 1975.
(San Jose's 3rd choice, 66th overall, in 1994 Entry Draft).

			Regular Season					Playoffs				
Season	Club	Lea	GP	G	A	TP	PIM	GP	G	A	TP	PIM
1992-93	SKA St. Peterburg	CIS	17	1	2	3	10	6	3	1	4	6
1993-94	SKA St. Peterburg	CIS	23	5	3	8	18	6	0	0	0	4

YELLE, STEPHANE (YEHL-ee) QUE.

Center. Shoots left. 6'1", 162 lbs. Born, Ottawa, Ont., May 9, 1974.
(New Jersey's 8th choice, 186th overall, in 1992 Entry Draft).

			Regular Season					Playoffs				
Season	Club	Lea	GP	G	A	TP	PIM	GP	G	A	TP	PIM
1991-92	Oshawa	OHL	55	12	14	26	20	7	2	0	2	1
1992-93	Oshawa	OHL	66	24	50	74	20	10	2	4	6	4
1993-94	Oshawa	OHL	66	35	69	104	22	5	1	7	8	2

Traded to **Quebec** by **New Jersey** with New Jersey's eleventh round choice (Steven Low) in 1994 Entry Draft for Quebec's eleventh round choice (Mike Hansen) in 1994 Entry Draft, June 1, 1994.

YERESKO, YURI (yeh-REHS-koh) DET.

Defense. Shoots left. 5'11", 178 lbs. Born, Moscow, USSR, August 30, 1975.
(Detroit's 8th choice, 178th overall, in 1993 Entry Draft).

			Regular Season					Playoffs				
Season	Club	Lea	GP	G	A	TP	PIM	GP	G	A	TP	PIM
1992-93	CSKA	CIS	35	0	0	0	8	....	....	....	....	....
1993-94	CSKA	CIS	45	0	0	0	16	3	0	1	1	0

YLONEN, JUHA (YOO-lih-nehn, YOO-hah) WPG.

Center. Shoots left. 6', 180 lbs. Born, Helsinki, Finland, February 13, 1972.
(Winnipeg's 5th choice, 91st overall, in 1991 Entry Draft).

			Regular Season					Playoffs				
Season	Club	Lea	GP	G	A	TP	PIM	GP	G	A	TP	PIM
1990-91	Espoo	Fin. 2	40	12	21	33	4	....	....	....	....	....
1991-92	HPK	Fin.	43	7	11	18	8	....	....	....	....	....
1992-93	HPK	Fin.	48	8	18	26	22	12	3	5	8	2
1993-94	Jokerit	Fin.	37	5	11	16	2	12	1	3	4	8

YORK, JASON DET.

Defense. Shoots right. 6'1", 192 lbs. Born, Ottawa, Ont., May 20, 1970.
(Detroit's 6th choice, 129th overall, in 1990 Entry Draft).

			Regular Season					Playoffs				
Season	Club	Lea	GP	G	A	TP	PIM	GP	G	A	TP	PIM
1989-90	Windsor	OHL	39	9	30	39	38	....	....	....	....	....
	Kitchener	OHL	25	11	25	36	17	17	3	19	22	10
1990-91	Windsor	OHL	66	13	80	93	40	11	3	10	13	12
1991-92	Adirondack	AHL	49	4	20	24	32	5	0	1	1	0
1992-93	**Detroit**	**NHL**	**2**	**0**	**0**	**0**	**0**	....	....	....	....	....
	Adirondack	AHL	77	15	40	55	86	11	0	3	3	18
1993-94	**Detroit**	**NHL**	**7**	**1**	**2**	**3**	**2**	....	....	....	....	....
a	Adirondack	AHL	74	10	56	66	98	12	3	11	14	22
	NHL Totals		**9**	**1**	**2**	**3**	**2**	....	....	....	....	....

a AHL First All-Star Team (1994)

YOUNG, JASON BUF.

Left wing. Shoots left. 5'10", 197 lbs. Born, Sudbury, Ont., December 16, 1972.
(Buffalo's 3rd choice, 57th overall, in 1991 Entry Draft).

			Regular Season					Playoffs				
Season	Club	Lea	GP	G	A	TP	PIM	GP	G	A	TP	PIM
1989-90	Sudbury	OHL	62	26	47	73	64	7	3	2	5	8
1990-91	Sudbury	OHL	37	21	38	59	22	5	0	4	4	10
1991-92	Sudbury	OHL	55	26	56	82	49	11	3	2	5	14
1992-93	Rochester	AHL	59	20	20	40	60	14	3	4	7	31
1993-94	Rochester	AHL	68	17	26	43	84	4	2	2	4	8

YOUNG, SCOTT QUE.

Right wing. Shoots right. 6', 190 lbs. Born, Clinton, MA, October 1, 1967.
(Hartford's 1st choice, 11th overall, in 1986 Entry Draft).

			Regular Season					Playoffs				
Season	Club	Lea	GP	G	A	TP	PIM	GP	G	A	TP	PIM
1985-86	Boston U.	H.E.	38	16	13	29	31	....	....	....	....	....
1986-87	Boston U.	H.E.	33	15	21	36	24	....	....	....	....	....
1987-88	U.S. National	....	56	11	47	58	31	....	....	....	....	....
	U.S. Olympic	....	6	2	6	8	4	....	....	....	....	....
	Hartford	**NHL**	**7**	**0**	**0**	**0**	**2**	**4**	**1**	**0**	**1**	**0**
1988-89	**Hartford**	**NHL**	**76**	**19**	**40**	**59**	**27**	**4**	**2**	**0**	**2**	**4**
1989-90	**Hartford**	**NHL**	**80**	**24**	**40**	**64**	**47**	**7**	**2**	**0**	**2**	**2**
1990-91	**Hartford**	**NHL**	**34**	**6**	**9**	**15**	**8**	....	....	....	....	....
	Pittsburgh	**NHL**	**43**	**11**	**16**	**27**	**33**	**17**	**1**	**6**	**7**	**2**
1991-92	Bolzano	Italy	18	22	17	39	6	5	4	3	7	7
	U.S. National	....	10	2	4	6	21	....	....	....	....	....
	U.S. Olympic	....	8	2	1	3	2	....	....	....	....	....
1992-93	**Quebec**	**NHL**	**82**	**30**	**30**	**60**	**20**	**6**	**4**	**1**	**5**	**0**
1993-94	**Quebec**	**NHL**	**76**	**26**	**25**	**51**	**14**	....	....	....	....	....
	NHL Totals		**398**	**116**	**160**	**276**	**151**	**38**	**10**	**7**	**17**	**8**

Traded to **Pittsburgh** by **Hartford** for Rob Brown, December 21, 1990. Traded to **Quebec** by **Pittsburgh** for Bryan Fogarty, March 10, 1992.

YSEBAERT, PAUL (IGHS-bahrt) CHI.

Center. Shoots left. 6'1", 190 lbs. Born, Sarnia, Ont., May 15, 1966.
(New Jersey's 4th choice, 74th overall, in 1984 Entry Draft).

			Regular Season					Playoffs				
Season	Club	Lea	GP	G	A	TP	PIM	GP	G	A	TP	PIM
1984-85	Bowling Green	CCHA	42	23	32	55	54	....	....	....	....	....
1985-86a	Bowling Green	CCHA	42	23	45	68	50	....	....	....	....	....
1986-87a	Bowling Green	CCHA	45	27	58	85	44	....	....	....	....	....
	Cdn. National	....	5	1	0	1	4	....	....	....	....	....
1987-88	Utica	AHL	78	30	49	79	60	....	....	....	....	....
1988-89	**New Jersey**	**NHL**	**5**	**0**	**4**	**4**	**0**	....	....	....	....	....
	Utica	AHL	56	36	44	80	22	5	0	1	1	4
1989-90	**New Jersey**	**NHL**	**5**	**1**	**2**	**3**	**0**	....	....	....	....	....
bcd	Utica	AHL	74	53	52	*105	61	5	2	4	6	0
1990-91	**New Jersey**	**NHL**	**11**	**4**	**3**	**7**	**6**	....	....	....	....	....
	Detroit	**NHL**	**51**	**15**	**18**	**33**	**16**	**2**	**0**	**2**	**2**	**0**
1991-92e	**Detroit**	**NHL**	**79**	**35**	**40**	**75**	**55**	**10**	**1**	**0**	**1**	**10**
1992-93	**Detroit**	**NHL**	**80**	**34**	**28**	**62**	**42**	**7**	**3**	**1**	**4**	**2**
1993-94	**Winnipeg**	**NHL**	**60**	**9**	**18**	**27**	**18**	....	....	....	....	....
	Chicago	**NHL**	**11**	**5**	**3**	**8**	**8**	**6**	**0**	**0**	**0**	**8**
	NHL Totals		**302**	**103**	**116**	**219**	**145**	**25**	**4**	**3**	**7**	**20**

a CCHA Second All-Star Team (1986, 1987)
b AHL First All-Star Team (1990)
c Won John B. Sollenberger Trophy (Top Scorer - AHL) (1990)
d Won Les Cunningham Plaque (MVP - AHL) (1990)
e Won Alka-Seltzer Plus Award (1992)

Traded to **Detroit** by **New Jersey** for Lee Norwood and Detroit's fourth round choice (Scott McCabe) in 1992 Entry Draft, November 27, 1990. Traded to **Winnipeg** by **Detroit** with future considerations (Alan Kerr, June 18, 1993) for Aaron Ward and Toronto's fourth round choice (previously acquired by Winnipeg — later traded to Detroit — Detroit selected John Jakopin) in 1993 Entry Draft, June 11, 1993. Traded to **Chicago** by **Winnipeg** for Chicago's third round choice in 1995 Entry Draft, March 21, 1994.

YULE, STEVE HFD.

Defense. Shoots right. 6', 210 lbs. Born, Gleichen, Alta., May 27, 1972.
(Hartford's 8th choice, 163rd overall, in 1991 Entry Draft).

			Regular Season					Playoffs				
Season	Club	Lea	GP	G	A	TP	PIM	GP	G	A	TP	PIM
1990-91	Kamloops	WHL	66	7	16	23	141	6	0	1	1	8
1991-92	Kamloops	WHL	61	7	10	17	257	17	2	1	3	37
1992-93	Springfield	AHL	38	0	4	4	52	....	....	....	....	....
1993-94	Springfield	AHL	61	4	13	17	133	5	0	4	4	8

YUSHKEVICH, DIMITRI (yoosh-KAY-vihch) PHI.

Defense. Shoots right. 5'11", 208 lbs. Born, Yaroslavl, USSR, November 19, 1971.
(Philadelphia's 6th choice, 122nd overall, in 1991 Entry Draft).

			Regular Season					Playoffs				
Season	Club	Lea	GP	G	A	TP	PIM	GP	G	A	TP	PIM
1988-89	Torpedo Yaro.	USSR	23	2	1	3	8	....	....	....	....	....
1989-90	Torpedo Yaro.	USSR	41	2	3	5	39	....	....	....	....	....
1990-91	Torpedo Yaro.	USSR	41	10	4	14	22	....	....	....	....	....
1991-92	Moscow D'amo	CIS	35	5	7	12	14	....	....	....	....	....
1992-93	**Philadelphia**	**NHL**	**82**	**5**	**27**	**32**	**71**	....	....	....	....	....
1993-94	**Philadelphia**	**NHL**	**75**	**5**	**25**	**30**	**86**	....	....	....	....	....
	NHL Totals		**157**	**10**	**52**	**62**	**157**	....	....	....	....	....

YZERMAN, STEVE (IGH-zuhr-muhn) DET.

Center. Shoots right. 5'11", 185 lbs. Born, Cranbrook, B.C., May 9, 1965.
(Detroit's 1st choice, 4th overall, in 1983 Entry Draft).

			Regular Season					Playoffs				
Season	Club	Lea	GP	G	A	TP	PIM	GP	G	A	TP	PIM
1981-82	Peterborough	OHL	58	21	43	64	65	6	0	1	1	16
1982-83	Peterborough	OHL	56	42	49	91	33	4	1	4	5	0
1983-84a	**Detroit**	**NHL**	**80**	**39**	**48**	**87**	**33**	**4**	**3**	**3**	**6**	**0**
1984-85	**Detroit**	**NHL**	**80**	**30**	**59**	**89**	**58**	**3**	**2**	**1**	**3**	**2**
1985-86	**Detroit**	**NHL**	**51**	**14**	**28**	**42**	**16**	....	....	....	....	....
1986-87	**Detroit**	**NHL**	**80**	**31**	**59**	**90**	**43**	**16**	**5**	**13**	**18**	**8**
1987-88	**Detroit**	**NHL**	**64**	**50**	**52**	**102**	**44**	**3**	**1**	**3**	**4**	**6**
1988-89b	**Detroit**	**NHL**	**80**	**65**	**90**	**155**	**61**	**6**	**5**	**5**	**10**	**2**
1989-90	**Detroit**	**NHL**	**79**	**62**	**65**	**127**	**79**	....	....	....	....	....
1990-91	**Detroit**	**NHL**	**80**	**51**	**57**	**108**	**34**	**7**	**3**	**3**	**6**	**4**
1991-92	**Detroit**	**NHL**	**79**	**45**	**58**	**103**	**64**	**11**	**3**	**5**	**8**	**12**
1992-93	**Detroit**	**NHL**	**84**	**58**	**79**	**137**	**44**	**7**	**4**	**3**	**7**	**4**
1993-94	**Detroit**	**NHL**	**58**	**24**	**58**	**82**	**36**	**3**	**1**	**3**	**4**	**0**
	NHL Totals		**815**	**469**	**653**	**1122**	**512**	**60**	**27**	**39**	**66**	**38**

a NHL All-Rookie Team (1984)
b Won Lester B. Pearson Award (1989)
Played in NHL All-Star Game (1984, 1988-93)

ZALAPSKI, ZARLEY CGY.

Defense. Shoots left. 6'1", 211 lbs. Born, Edmonton, Alta., April 22, 1968.
(Pittsburgh's 1st choice, 4th overall, in 1986 Entry Draft).

			Regular Season					Playoffs				
Season	Club	Lea	GP	G	A	TP	PIM	GP	G	A	TP	PIM
1985-86	Cdn. National	....	59	22	37	59	56	....	....	....	....	....
1986-87	Cdn. National	....	74	11	29	40	28	....	....	....	....	....
1987-88	Cdn. National	....	47	3	13	16	32	....	....	....	....	....
	Cdn. Olympic	....	8	1	3	4	2	....	....	....	....	....
	Pittsburgh	**NHL**	**15**	**3**	**8**	**11**	**7**	....	....	....	....	....
1988-89a	**Pittsburgh**	**NHL**	**58**	**12**	**33**	**45**	**57**	**11**	**1**	**8**	**9**	**13**
1989-90	**Pittsburgh**	**NHL**	**51**	**6**	**25**	**31**	**37**	....	....	....	....	....
1990-91	**Pittsburgh**	**NHL**	**66**	**12**	**36**	**48**	**59**	....	....	....	....	....
	Hartford	**NHL**	**11**	**3**	**3**	**6**	**6**	**6**	**1**	**3**	**4**	**8**
1991-92	**Hartford**	**NHL**	**79**	**20**	**37**	**57**	**120**	**7**	**2**	**3**	**5**	**6**
1992-93	**Hartford**	**NHL**	**83**	**14**	**51**	**65**	**94**	....	....	....	....	....
1993-94	**Hartford**	**NHL**	**56**	**7**	**30**	**37**	**56**	....	....	....	....	....
	Calgary	**NHL**	**13**	**3**	**7**	**10**	**18**	**7**	**0**	**3**	**3**	**2**
	NHL Totals		**432**	**80**	**230**	**310**	**454**	**31**	**4**	**17**	**21**	**29**

a NHL All-Rookie Team (1989)
Played in NHL All-Star Game (1993)
Traded to **Hartford** by **Pittsburgh** with John Cullen and Jeff Parker for Ron Francis, Grant Jennings and Ulf Samuelsson, March 4, 1991. Traded to **Calgary** by **Hartford** with James Patrick and Michael Nylander for Gary Suter, Paul Ranheim and Ted Drury, March 10, 1994.

ZAMUNER, ROB (ZAM-nuhr) T.B.

Center. Shoots left. 6'2", 202 lbs. Born, Oakville, Ont., September 17, 1969.
(NY Rangers' 3rd choice, 45th overall, in 1989 Entry Draft).

			Regular Season					Playoffs				
Season	Club	Lea	GP	G	A	TP	PIM	GP	G	A	TP	PIM
1986-87	Guelph	OHL	62	6	15	21	8	....	....	....	....	....
1987-88	Guelph	OHL	58	20	41	61	18	....	....	....	....	....
1988-89	Guelph	OHL	66	46	65	111	38	7	5	5	10	9
1989-90	Flint	IHL	77	44	35	79	32	4	1	0	1	6
1990-91	Binghamton	AHL	80	25	58	83	50	9	7	6	13	35
1991-92	**NY Rangers**	**NHL**	**9**	**1**	**2**	**3**	**2**	....	....	....	....	....
	Binghamton	AHL	61	19	53	72	42	11	8	9	17	8
1992-93	**Tampa Bay**	**NHL**	**84**	**15**	**28**	**43**	**74**	....	....	....	....	....
1993-94	**Tampa Bay**	**NHL**	**59**	**6**	**6**	**12**	**42**	....	....	....	....	....
	NHL Totals		**152**	**22**	**36**	**58**	**118**	....	....	....	....	....

Signed as a free agent by **Tampa Bay**, July 13, 1992.

ZAVARUKHIN, NIKOLAI (zah-vah-RUH-khihn) N.J.

Center. Shoots left. 5'9", 167 lbs. Born, Ufa, USSR, March 18, 1975.
(New Jersey's 7th choice, 169th overall, in 1993 Entry Draft).

			Regular Season					Playoffs				
Season	Club	Lea	GP	G	A	TP	PIM	GP	G	A	TP	PIM
1991-92	Ufa Salavat	CIS Jr.	40	25	15	40	30	....	....	....	....	....
1992-93	Ufa Salavat	CIS	37	2	4	6	18	2	0	0	0	2
1993-94	Ufa Salavat	CIS	45	8	8	16	20	5	0	1	1	0

ZAVISHA, BRAD (zuh-VIH-shuh) EDM.

Left wing. Shoots left. 6'2", 205 lbs. Born, Hines Creek, Alta., January 4, 1972.
(Quebec's 3rd choice, 43rd overall, in 1990 Entry Draft).

			Regular Season					Playoffs				
Season	Club	Lea	GP	G	A	TP	PIM	GP	G	A	TP	PIM
1988-89	Seattle	WHL	52	8	13	21	43	....	....	....	....	....
1989-90	Seattle	WHL	69	22	38	60	124	13	1	6	7	16
1990-91	Seattle	WHL	24	15	12	27	40	....	....	....	....	....
	Portland	WHL	48	25	22	47	41	....	....	....	....	....
1991-92a	Portland	WHL	11	7	4	11	18	....	....	....	....	....
	Lethbridge	WHL	59	44	40	84	160	5	3	1	4	18
1992-93			DID NOT PLAY – INJURED									
1993-94	**Edmonton**	**NHL**	**2**	**0**	**0**	**0**	**0**	....	....	....	....	....
	Cape Breton	AHL	58	19	15	34	114	2	0	0	0	2
	NHL Totals		**2**	**0**	**0**	**0**	**0**	....	....	....	....	....

a WHL East First All-Star Team (1992)
Traded to **Edmonton** by **Quebec** with Ron Tugnutt for Martin Rucinsky, March 10, 1992.

ZELEPUKIN, VALERI (zeh-leh-POO-kin) N.J.

Left wing. Shoots left. 5'11", 190 lbs. Born, Voskresensk, USSR, September 17, 1968.
(New Jersey's 13th choice, 221st overall, in 1990 Entry Draft).

			Regular Season					Playoffs				
Season	Club	Lea	GP	G	A	TP	PIM	GP	G	A	TP	PIM
1984-85	Khimik	USSR	5	0	0	0	2	....	....	....	....	....
1985-86	Khimik	USSR	33	2	2	4	10	....	....	....	....	....
1986-87	Khimik	USSR	19	1	0	1	4	....	....	....	....	....
1987-88	SKA MVO	USSR 2	18	18	6	24	....	....	....	....	....	....
	CSKA	USSR	19	3	1	4	8	....	....	....	....	....
1988-89	CSKA	USSR	17	2	3	5	2	....	....	....	....	....
1989-90	Khimik	USSR	46	17	14	31	26	....	....	....	....	....
1990-91	Khimik	USSR	34	11	6	17	38	....	....	....	....	....
1991-92	**New Jersey**	**NHL**	**44**	**13**	**18**	**31**	**28**	**4**	**1**	**1**	**2**	**2**
	Utica	AHL	22	20	9	29	8	....	....	....	....	....
1992-93	**New Jersey**	**NHL**	**78**	**23**	**41**	**64**	**70**	**5**	**0**	**2**	**2**	**0**
1993-94	**New Jersey**	**NHL**	**82**	**26**	**31**	**57**	**70**	**20**	**5**	**2**	**7**	**14**
	NHL Totals		**204**	**62**	**90**	**152**	**168**	**29**	**6**	**5**	**11**	**16**

ZEMLAK, RICHARD

Right wing. Shoots right. 6'2", 190 lbs. Born, Wynard, Sask., March 3, 1963.
(St. Louis' 9th choice, 209th overall, in 1981 Entry Draft).

			Regular Season					Playoffs				
Season	Club	Lea	GP	G	A	TP	PIM	GP	G	A	TP	PIM
1980-81	Spokane	WHL	72	19	19	38	132	4	1	1	2	6
1981-82	Spokane	WHL	26	9	20	29	113	....	....	....	....	....
	Winnipeg	WHL	2	1	2	3	0	....	....	....	....	....
	Medicine Hat	WHL	41	11	20	31	70	....	....	....	....	....
	Salt Lake	CHL	6	0	0	0	2	1	0	0	0	0
1982-83	Medicine Hat	WHL	51	20	17	37	119	....	....	....	....	....
	Nanaimo	WHL	18	2	8	10	50	....	....	....	....	....
1983-84	Montana	CHL	14	2	2	4	17	....	....	....	....	....
	Toledo	IHL	45	8	19	27	101	....	....	....	....	....
1984-85	Muskegon	IHL	64	19	18	37	223	17	5	4	9	68
	Fredericton	AHL	16	3	4	7	59	....	....	....	....	....
1985-86	Fredericton	AHL	58	6	5	11	305	3	0	0	0	49
	Muskegon	IHL	3	1	2	3	36	....	....	....	....	....
1986-87	**Quebec**	**NHL**	**20**	**0**	**2**	**2**	**47**	....	....	....	....	....
	Fredericton	AHL	29	9	6	15	201	....	....	....	....	....
1987-88	**Minnesota**	**NHL**	**54**	**1**	**4**	**5**	**307**	....	....	....	....	....
1988-89	**Minnesota**	**NHL**	**3**	**0**	**0**	**0**	**13**	....	....	....	....	....
	Kalamazoo	IHL	2	1	3	4	22	....	....	....	....	....
	Pittsburgh	**NHL**	**31**	**0**	**0**	**0**	**135**	**1**	**0**	**0**	**0**	**10**
	Muskegon	IHL	18	5	4	9	55	8	1	1	2	35
1989-90	**Pittsburgh**	**NHL**	**19**	**1**	**5**	**6**	**43**	....	....	....	....	....
	Muskegon	IHL	61	17	39	56	263	14	3	4	7	105
1990-91	Salt Lake	IHL	59	14	20	34	194	3	0	1	1	14
1991-92	**Calgary**	**NHL**	**5**	**0**	**1**	**1**	**42**	....	....	....	....	....
	Salt Lake	IHL	60	5	14	19	204	3	0	0	0	0
1992-93	Milwaukee	IHL	62	3	9	12	301	2	1	1	2	6
1993-94	Milwaukee	IHL	61	3	8	11	243	2	0	0	0	16
	NHL Totals		**132**	**2**	**12**	**14**	**587**	**1**	**0**	**0**	**0**	**10**

Rights sold to **Quebec** by **St. Louis** with rights to Dan Wood and Roger Hagglund, June 22, 1984. Claimed by **Minnesota** in NHL Waiver Draft, October 5, 1987. Traded to **Pittsburgh** by **Minnesota** for the rights to Rob Gaudreau, November 1, 1988. Signed as a free agent by **Calgary**, November 8, 1990.

ZENT, JASON NYI

Left wing. Shoots left. 5'11", 180 lbs. Born, Buffalo, NY, April 15, 1971.
(NY Islanders' 3rd choice, 44th overall, in 1989 Entry Draft).

			Regular Season					Playoffs				
Season	Club	Lea	GP	G	A	TP	PIM	GP	G	A	TP	PIM
1990-91	U. Wisconsin	WCHA	39	19	18	37	51	....	....	....	....	....
1991-92a	U. Wisconsin	WCHA	39	22	17	39	128	....	....	....	....	....
1992-93	U. Wisconsin	WCHA	40	26	12	38	92	....	....	....	....	....
1993-94	U. Wisconsin	WCHA	42	20	21	41	120	....	....	....	....	....

a NCAA All-Tournament Team (1992)

ZETTLER, ROB PHI.

Defense. Shoots left. 6'3", 195 lbs. Born, Sept Iles, Que., March 8, 1968.
(Minnesota's 5th choice, 55th overall, in 1986 Entry Draft).

			Regular Season					Playoffs				
Season	Club	Lea	GP	G	A	TP	PIM	GP	G	A	TP	PIM
1985-86	S.S. Marie	OHL	57	5	23	28	92	....	....	....	....	....
1986-87	S.S. Marie	OHL	64	13	22	35	89	4	0	0	0	0
1987-88	Kalamazoo	IHL	2	0	1	1	0	7	0	2	2	2
	S.S. Marie	OHL	64	7	41	48	77	6	2	2	4	9
1988-89	**Minnesota**	**NHL**	**2**	**0**	**0**	**0**	**0**	....	....	....	....	....
	Kalamazoo	IHL	80	5	21	26	79	6	0	1	1	26
1989-90	**Minnesota**	**NHL**	**31**	**0**	**8**	**8**	**45**	....	....	....	....	....
	Kalamazoo	IHL	41	6	10	16	64	7	0	0	0	6
1990-91	**Minnesota**	**NHL**	**47**	**1**	**4**	**5**	**119**	....	....	....	....	....
	Kalamazoo	IHL	1	0	0	0	2	....	....	....	....	....
1991-92	**San Jose**	**NHL**	**74**	**1**	**8**	**9**	**99**	....	....	....	....	....
1992-93	**San Jose**	**NHL**	**80**	**0**	**7**	**7**	**150**	....	....	....	....	....
1993-94	**San Jose**	**NHL**	**42**	**0**	**3**	**3**	**65**	....	....	....	....	....
	Philadelphia	**NHL**	**33**	**0**	**4**	**4**	**69**	....	....	....	....	....
	NHL Totals		**309**	**2**	**34**	**36**	**547**	....	....	....	....	....

Claimed by **San Jose** from **Minnesota** in Dispersal Draft, May 30, 1991. Traded to **Philadelphia** by **San Jose** for Viacheslav Butsayev, February 1, 1994.

ZEZEL, PETER (ZEH-zehl) DAL.

Center. Shoots left. 5'11", 200 lbs. Born, Toronto, Ont., April 22, 1965.
(Philadelphia's 1st choice, 41st overall, in 1983 Entry Draft).

			Regular Season					Playoffs				
Season	Club	Lea	GP	G	A	TP	PIM	GP	G	A	TP	PIM
1982-83	Toronto	OHL	66	35	39	74	28	4	2	4	6	0
1983-84	Toronto	OHL	68	47	86	133	31	9	7	5	12	4
1984-85	**Philadelphia**	**NHL**	**65**	**15**	**46**	**61**	**26**	**19**	**1**	**8**	**9**	**28**
1985-86	**Philadelphia**	**NHL**	**79**	**17**	**37**	**54**	**76**	**5**	**3**	**1**	**4**	**4**
1986-87	**Philadelphia**	**NHL**	**71**	**33**	**39**	**72**	**71**	**25**	**3**	**10**	**13**	**10**
1987-88	**Philadelphia**	**NHL**	**69**	**22**	**35**	**57**	**42**	**7**	**3**	**2**	**5**	**7**
1988-89	**Philadelphia**	**NHL**	**26**	**4**	**13**	**17**	**15**	....	....	....	....	....
	St. Louis	**NHL**	**52**	**17**	**36**	**53**	**27**	**10**	**6**	**6**	**12**	**4**
1989-90	**St. Louis**	**NHL**	**73**	**25**	**47**	**72**	**30**	**12**	**1**	**7**	**8**	**4**
1990-91	**Washington**	**NHL**	**20**	**7**	**5**	**12**	**10**	....	....	....	....	....
	Toronto	**NHL**	**32**	**14**	**14**	**28**	**4**	....	....	....	....	....
1991-92	**Toronto**	**NHL**	**64**	**16**	**33**	**49**	**26**	....	....	....	....	....
1992-93	**Toronto**	**NHL**	**70**	**12**	**23**	**35**	**24**	**20**	**2**	**1**	**3**	**6**
1993-94	**Toronto**	**NHL**	**41**	**8**	**8**	**16**	**19**	**18**	**2**	**4**	**6**	**8**
	NHL Totals		**662**	**190**	**336**	**526**	**370**	**116**	**21**	**39**	**60**	**71**

Traded to **St. Louis** by **Philadelphia** for Mike Bullard, November 29, 1988. Traded to **Washington** by **St. Louis** with Mike Lalor for Geoff Courtnall, July 13, 1990. Traded to **Toronto** by **Washington** with Bob Rouse for Al Iafrate, January 16, 1991. Acquired by **Dallas** from **Toronto** with Grant Marshall as compensation for Toronto's signing of free agent Mike Craig, August 10, 1994.

ZHAMNOV, ALEXEI (ZHAHM-nahf) WPG.

Center. Shoots left. 6'1", 195 lbs. Born, Moscow, USSR, October 1, 1970.
(Winnipeg's 5th choice, 77th overall, in 1990 Entry Draft).

			Regular Season					Playoffs				
Season	Club	Lea	GP	G	A	TP	PIM	GP	G	A	TP	PIM
1988-89	Moscow D'amo	USSR	4	0	0	0	0	....	....	....	....	....
1989-90	Moscow D'amo	USSR	43	11	6	17	21	....	....	....	....	....
1990-91	Moscow D'amo	USSR	46	16	12	28	24	....	....	....	....	....
1991-92	Moscow D'amo	CIS	39	15	21	36	28	....	....	....	....	....
1992-93	**Winnipeg**	**NHL**	**68**	**25**	**47**	**72**	**58**	**6**	**0**	**2**	**2**	**2**
1993-94	**Winnipeg**	**NHL**	**61**	**26**	**45**	**71**	**62**	....	....	....	....	....
	NHL Totals		**129**	**51**	**92**	**143**	**120**	**6**	**0**	**2**	**2**	**2**

ZHITNIK, ALEXEI (ZHIHT-nihk) L.A.

Defense. Shoots left. 5'11", 190 lbs. Born, Kiev, USSR, October 10, 1972.
(Los Angeles' 3rd choice, 81st overall, in 1991 Entry Draft).

			Regular Season					Playoffs				
Season	Club	Lea	GP	G	A	TP	PIM	GP	G	A	TP	PIM
1989-90	Sokol Kiev	USSR	31	3	4	7	16	....	....	....	....	....
1990-91	Sokol Kiev	USSR	46	1	4	5	46	....	....	....	....	....
1991-92	CSKA	CIS	44	2	7	9	52	....	....	....	....	....
1992-93	**Los Angeles**	**NHL**	**78**	**12**	**36**	**48**	**80**	**24**	**3**	**9**	**12**	**26**
1993-94	**Los Angeles**	**NHL**	**81**	**12**	**40**	**52**	**101**	....	....	....	....	....
	NHL Totals		**159**	**24**	**76**	**100**	**181**	**24**	**3**	**9**	**12**	**26**

ZHOLTOK, SERGEI (ZHOL-tok) BOS.

Center. Shoots right. 6', 190 lbs. Born, Riga, Latvia, December 2, 1972.
(Boston's 2nd choice, 55th overall, in 1992 Entry Draft).

			Regular Season					Playoffs				
Season	Club	Lea	GP	G	A	TP	PIM	GP	G	A	TP	PIM
1990-91	Dynamo Riga	USSR	39	4	0	4	16	....	....	....	....	....
1991-92	Riga	CIS	27	6	3	9	6	....	....	....	....	....
1992-93	**Boston**	**NHL**	**1**	**0**	**1**	**1**	**0**	....	....	....	....	....
	Providence	AHL	64	31	35	66	57	6	3	5	8	4
1993-94	**Boston**	**NHL**	**24**	**2**	**1**	**3**	**2**	....	....	....	....	....
	Providence	AHL	54	29	33	62	16	....	....	....	....	....
	NHL Totals		**25**	**2**	**2**	**4**	**2**	....	....	....	....	....

ZHURIK, ALEXANDER (ZHUH-rihk) EDM.

Defense. Shoots left. 6'3", 195 lbs. Born, Minsk, USSR, May 29, 1975.
(Edmonton's 7th choice, 163rd overall, in 1993 Entry Draft).

			Regular Season					Playoffs				
Season	Club	Lea	GP	G	A	TP	PIM	GP	G	A	TP	PIM
1992-93	Dynamo Minsk	CIS Jr.	UNAVAILABLE									
1993-94	Kingston	OHL	59	7	23	30	92	6	0	0	0	4

ZMOLEK, DOUG (zuh-MOH-lehk) DAL.

Defense. Shoots left. 6'2", 225 lbs. Born, Rochester, MN, November 3, 1970.
(Minnesota's 1st choice, 7th overall, in 1989 Entry Draft).

			Regular Season					Playoffs				
Season	Club	Lea	GP	G	A	TP	PIM	GP	G	A	TP	PIM
1989-90	U. Minnesota	WCHA	40	1	10	11	52	....	....	....	....	....
1990-91	U. Minnesota	WCHA	34	11	6	17	38	....	....	....	....	....
1991-92ab	U. Minnesota	WCHA	41	6	20	26	84	....	....	....	....	....
1992-93	**San Jose**	**NHL**	**84**	**5**	**10**	**15**	**229**	....	....	....	....	....
1993-94	**San Jose**	**NHL**	**68**	**0**	**4**	**4**	**122**	....	....	....	....	....
	Dallas	**NHL**	**7**	**1**	**0**	**1**	**11**	**7**	**0**	**1**	**1**	**4**
	NHL Totals		**159**	**6**	**14**	**20**	**362**	**7**	**0**	**1**	**1**	**4**

a WCHA Second All-Star Team (1992)
b NCAA West Second All-American Team (1992)

Claimed by **San Jose** from **Minnesota** in Dispersal Draft, May 30, 1991. Traded to **Dallas** by **San Jose** with Mike Lalor for Ulf Dahlen and a future draft choice, March 19, 1994.

ZOLOTOV, ROMAN (ZOH-loh-tov) PHI.

Defense. Shoots left. 6'1", 191 lbs. Born, Moscow, USSR, February 13, 1974.
(Philadelphia's 5th choice, 127th overall, in 1992 Entry Draft).

			Regular Season					Playoffs				
Season	Club	Lea	GP	G	A	TP	PIM	GP	G	A	TP	PIM
1991-92	Moscow D'amo	CIS	1	0	0	0	0	....	....	....	....	....
1992-93	Moscow D'amo	CIS Jr.	UNAVAILABLE									
1993-94	Moscow D'amo	CIS	33	0	2	2	20	5	0	1	1	6

ZOLOTOV, SERGEI (ZOH-loh-tov) CGY.

Left wing. Shoots right. 5'10", 180 lbs. Born, Kazan, USSR, January 27, 1971.
(Calgary's 11th choice, 219th overall, in 1991 Entry Draft).

			Regular Season					Playoffs				
Season	Club	Lea	GP	G	A	TP	PIM	GP	G	A	TP	PIM
1988-89	Soviet Wings	USSR	34	5	1	6	4	....	....	....	....	....
1989-90	Soviet Wings	USSR	48	12	2	14	14	....	....	....	....	....
1990-91	Soviet Wings	USSR	42	9	6	15	12	....	....	....	....	....
1991-92	Soviet Wings	CIS	39	12	5	17	4	....	....	....	....	....
1992-93	Soviet Wings	CIS	42	15	6	21	14	7	3	3	6	0
1993-94	Soviet Wings	CIS	44	16	17	33	31	3	1	0	1	0

ZOMBO, RICK

Defense. Shoots right. 6'1", 195 lbs. Born, Des Plaines, IL, May 8, 1963.
(Detroit's 6th choice, 149th overall, in 1981 Entry Draft).

			Regular Season					Playoffs				
Season	Club	Lea	GP	G	A	TP	PIM	GP	G	A	TP	PIM
1981-82	North Dakota	WCHA	45	1	15	16	31	....	....	....	....	....
1982-83	North Dakota	WCHA	35	5	11	16	41	....	....	....	....	....
1983-84	North Dakota	WCHA	34	7	24	31	40	....	....	....	....	....
1984-85	**Detroit**	**NHL**	**1**	**0**	**0**	**0**	**0**	....	....	....	....	....
	Adirondack	AHL	56	3	32	35	70	....	....	....	....	....
1985-86	**Detroit**	**NHL**	**14**	**0**	**1**	**1**	**16**	....	....	....	....	....
	Adirondack	AHL	69	7	34	41	94	17	0	4	4	40
1986-87	**Detroit**	**NHL**	**44**	**1**	**4**	**5**	**59**	**7**	**0**	**1**	**1**	**9**
	Adirondack	AHL	25	0	6	6	22	....	....	....	....	....
1987-88	**Detroit**	**NHL**	**62**	**3**	**14**	**17**	**96**	**16**	**0**	**6**	**6**	**55**
1988-89	**Detroit**	**NHL**	**75**	**1**	**20**	**21**	**106**	**6**	**0**	**1**	**1**	**16**
1989-90	**Detroit**	**NHL**	**77**	**5**	**20**	**25**	**95**	....	....	....	....	....
1990-91	**Detroit**	**NHL**	**77**	**4**	**19**	**23**	**55**	**7**	**1**	**0**	**1**	**10**
1991-92	**Detroit**	**NHL**	**3**	**0**	**0**	**0**	**15**	....	....	....	....	....
	St. Louis	**NHL**	**64**	**3**	**15**	**18**	**46**	**6**	**0**	**2**	**2**	**12**
1992-93	**St. Louis**	**NHL**	**71**	**0**	**15**	**15**	**78**	**11**	**0**	**1**	**1**	**12**
1993-94	**St. Louis**	**NHL**	**74**	**2**	**8**	**10**	**85**	**4**	**0**	**0**	**0**	**11**
	NHL Totals		**562**	**19**	**116**	**135**	**651**	**57**	**1**	**11**	**12**	**125**

Traded to **St. Louis** by **Detroit** for Vincent Riendeau, October 18, 1991.

ZUBOV, SERGEI (ZOO-bahf) NYR

Defense. Shoots right. 6'1", 195 lbs. Born, Moscow, USSR, July 22, 1970.
(NY Rangers' 6th choice, 85th overall, in 1990 Entry Draft).

			Regular Season					Playoffs				
Season	Club	Lea	GP	G	A	TP	PIM	GP	G	A	TP	PIM
1988-89	CSKA	USSR	29	1	4	5	10	....	....	....	....	....
1989-90	CSKA	USSR	48	6	2	8	16	....	....	....	....	....
1990-91	CSKA	USSR	41	6	5	11	12	....	....	....	....	....
1991-92	CSKA	CIS	44	4	7	11	8	....	....	....	....	....
1992-93	CSKA	CIS	1	0	1	1	0	....	....	....	....	....
	NY Rangers	**NHL**	**49**	**8**	**23**	**31**	**4**	....	....	....	....	....
	Binghamton	AHL	30	7	29	36	14	11	5	5	10	2
1993-94	**NY Rangers**	**NHL**	**78**	**12**	**77**	**89**	**39**	**22**	**5**	**14**	**19**	**0**
	Binghamton	AHL	2	1	2	3	0	....	....	....	....	....
	NHL Totals		**127**	**20**	**100**	**120**	**43**	**22**	**5**	**14**	**19**	**0**

ZWAKMAN, GREG HFD.

Defense. Shoots left. 6'2", 182 lbs. Born, Edina, MN, September 23, 1973.
(Hartford's 9th choice, 201st overall, in 1992 Entry Draft).

			Regular Season					Playoffs				
Season	Club	Lea	GP	G	A	TP	PIM	GP	G	A	TP	PIM
1992-93	U. Minnesota	WCHA	36	0	1	1	30	....	....	....	....	....
1993-94	U. Minnesota	WCHA	42	2	6	8	36	....	....	....	....	....

Retired Players and Goaltenders Research Project

Throughout the Retired Players and Retired Goaltenders sections of this book, you will notice many players with a bullet (•) by their names. These players, according to our records, are deceased. The editors recognize that our information on the death dates of NHLers is incomplete. If you have documented information on the passing of any player not marked with a bullet (•) in this edition, we would like to hear from you. Please send this information to:

Retired Player Research Project
c/o NHL Publishing
194 Dovercourt Road
Toronto, Ontario
M6J 3C8 Canada
Fax: 416/531-3939

Many thanks to the following contributors in 1993-94:

Corey Bryant, Norman Butt, Paul R. Carroll, Jr., Raymond DeVillers, Kate Dwyer, Christopher Ellis, Alan Mann, Fred Meheden, Paul Patton, Gary J. Pearce, Robert Stanton, Reginald Varin, Stale Volleng, Jason B. Young.

Retired NHL Player Index

Abbreviations: Teams/Cities: — **Ana.** – Anaheim; **Atl.** – Atlanta; **Bos.** – Boston, **Bro.** – Brooklyn; **Buf.** – Buffalo; **Cal.** – California; **Cgy.** – Calgary; **Cle.** – Cleveland; **Col.** – Colorado; **Dal.** – Dallas; **Det.** – Detroit; **Edm.** – Edmonton; **Fla.** – Florida; **Ham.** – Hamilton; **Hfd.** – Hartford; **K.C.** – Kansas City; **L.A.** – Los Angeles; **Min.** — Minnesota; **Mtl.** – Montreal; **Mtl. M.** – Montreal Maroons; **Mtl. W.** – Montreal Wanderers; **N.J.** – New Jersey; **NYA** – NY Americans; **NYI** – New York Islanders; **NYR** – New York Rangers; **Oak.** – Oakland; **Ott.** – Ottawa; **Phi.** – Philadelphia; **Pit.** – Pittsburgh; **Que.** – Quebec; **St. L.** – St. Louis; **S.J.** – San Jose; **T.B.** – Tampa Bay; **Tor.** – Toronto; **Van.** – Vancouver; **Wpg.** – Winnipeg; **Wsh.** – Washington.

Total seasons are rounded off to the nearest full season. **A** – assists; **G** – goals; **GP** – games played; **PIM** – penalties in minutes; **TP** – total points.
• – deceased. Assists not recorded during 1917-18 season.

			Regular Schedule					Playoffs					NHL	First	Last
Name	NHL Teams	NHL Seasons	GP	G	A	TP	PIM	GP	G	A	TP	PIM	Cup Wins	NHL Season	NHL Season
A															
Abbott, Reg	Mtl.	1	3	0	0	0	0	....	....	....	....	....		1952-53	1952-53
• Abel, Clarence	NYR, Chi.	8	333	18	18	36	359	38	1	1	2	58	2	1926-27	1933-34
Abel, Gerry	Det.	1	1	0	0	0	0	....	....	....	....	....		1966-67	1966-67
Abel, Sid	Det., Chi.	14	613	189	283	472	376	96	28	30	58	77	3	1938-39	1953-54
Abgrall, Dennis	L.A.	1	13	0	2	2	4	....	....	....	....	....		1975-76	1975-76
Abrahamsson, Thommy	Hfd.	1	32	6	11	17	16	....	....	....	....	....		1980-81	1980-81
Achtymichuk, Gene	Mtl., Det.	4	32	3	5	8	2	....	....	....	....	....		1951-52	1958-59
Acomb, Doug	Tor.	1	2	0	1	1	0	....	....	....	....	....		1969-70	1969-70
Adam, Douglas	NYR	1	4	0	1	1	0	....	....	....	....	....		1949-50	1949-50
Adam, Russ	Tor.	1	8	1	2	3	11	....	....	....	....	....		1982-83	1982-83
Adams, Greg C.	Phi., Hfd., Wsh., Edm., Van., Que., Det.	10	545	84	143	227	1173	43	2	11	13	153		1980-81	1989-90
Adams, Jack	Mtl.	1	42	6	12	18	11	3	0	0	0	0		1940-41	1940-41
• Adams, Jack J.	Tor., Ott.	7	173	82	29	111	307	10	3	0	3	12	2	1917-18	1926-27
• Adams, Stewart	Chi., Tor.	4	106	9	26	35	60	11	3	3	6	14		1929-30	1932-33
Adduono, Rick	Bos., Atl.	2	4	0	0	0	2	....	....	....	....	....		1975-76	1979-80
Affleck, Bruce	St.L., Van., NYI	7	280	14	66	80	86	8	0	0	0	0		1974-75	1983-84
Ahern, Fred	Cal., Cle., Col.	4	146	31	30	61	130	2	0	1	1	2		1974-75	1977-78
Ahlin,	Chi.	1	1	0	0	0	0	....	....	....	....	....		1937-38	1937-38
Ahrens, Chris	Min.	6	52	0	3	3	14	1	0	0	0	0		1973-74	1977-78
Ailsby, Lloyd	NYR	1	3	0	0	0	2	....	....	....	....	....		1951-52	1951-52
Aitken, Brad	Pit., Edm.	2	14	1	3	4	25	....	....	....	....	....		1987-88	1990-91
Albright, Clint	NYR	1	59	14	5	19	19	....	....	....	....	....		1948-49	1948-49
Aldcorn, Gary	Tor., Det., Bos.	5	226	41	56	97	78	6	1	2	3	4		1956-57	1960-61
Alexander, Claire	Tor., Van.	4	155	18	47	65	36	16	2	4	6	4		1974-75	1977-78
• Alexandre, Art	Mtl.	2	11	0	2	2	8	4	0	0	0	0		1931-32	1932-33
Allen, George	NYR, Chi., Mtl.	8	339	82	115	197	179	41	9	10	19	32		1938-39	1946-47
Allen, Jeff	Cle.	1	4	0	0	0	2	....	....	....	....	....		1977-78	1977-78
Allen, Keith	Det.	2	28	0	4	4	8	5	0	0	0	0	1	1953-54	1954-55
Allen, Viv	NYA	1	6	0	1	1	0	....	....	....	....	....		1940-41	1940-41
Alley, Steve	Hfd.	2	15	3	3	6	11	3	0	1	1	0		1979-80	1980-81
Allison, Dave	Mtl.	1	3	0	0	0	12	....	....	....	....	....		1983-84	1983-84
Allison, Mike	NYR, Tor., L.A.	10	499	102	166	268	630	82	9	17	26	135		1980-81	1989-90
Allison, Ray	Hfd., Phi.	7	238	64	93	157	223	12	2	3	5	20		1979-80	1986-87
Allum, Bill	NYR	1	1	0	1	1	0	....	....	....	....	....		1940-41	1940-41
• Amadio, Dave	Det., L.A.	3	125	5	11	16	163	16	1	2	3	18		1957-58	1968-69
Amodeo, Mike	Wpg.	1	19	0	0	0	2	....	....	....	....	....		1979-80	1979-80
Anderson, Bill	Bos.	1	....	....	....	....	....	1	0	0	0	0		1942-43	1942-43
Anderson, Dale	Det.	1	13	0	0	0	6	2	0	0	0	0		1956-57	1956-57
Anderson, Doug	Mtl.	1	....	....	....	....	....	2	0	0	0	0	1	1952-53	1952-53
Anderson, Earl	Det., Bos.	3	109	19	19	38	22	5	0	1	1	0		1974-75	1976-77
Anderson, Jim	L.A.	1	7	1	2	3	2	....	....	....	....	....		1967-68	1967-68
Anderson, Murray	Wsh.	1	40	0	1	1	68	....	....	....	....	....		1974-75	1974-75
Anderson, Perry	St. L., N.J., S.J.	10	400	50	59	109	1051	36	2	1	3	161		1981-82	1991-92
Anderson, Ron C.	Det., L.A., St.L., Buf.	5	251	28	30	58	146	5	0	0	0	4		1967-68	1971-72
Anderson, Ron H.	Wsh.	1	28	9	7	16	8	....	....	....	....	....		1974-75	1974-75
Anderson, Russ	Pit., Hfd., L.A.	10	519	22	99	121	1086	10	0	3	3	28		1976-77	1984-85
• Anderson, Tom	Det., NYA, Bro.	8	319	62	127	189	190	16	2	7	9	62		1934-35	1941-42
Andersson, Kent-Erik	Min., NYR	7	456	72	103	175	78	50	4	11	15	4		1977-78	1983-84
Andersson, Peter	Wsh., Que.	3	172	10	41	51	80	7	0	2	2	2		1983-84	1985-86
Andrascik, Steve	NYR	1	....	....	....	....	....	1	0	0	0	0		1971-72	1971-72
Andrea, Paul	NYR, Pit., Cal., Buf.	4	150	31	49	80	12	....	....	....	....	....		1965-66	1970-71
Andrews, Lloyd	Tor.	4	53	8	5	13	10	7	2	0	2	5		1921-22	1924-25
Andruff, Ron	Mtl., Col.,	5	153	19	36	55	54	2	0	0	0	0		1974-75	1978-79
Angotti, Lou	NYR, Chi., Phi., Pit., St.L.	10	653	103	186	289	228	65	8	8	16	17		1964-65	1973-74
Anholt, Darrel	Chi.	1	1	0	0	0	0	....	....	....	....	....		1983-84	1983-84
Anslow, Bert	NYR	1	2	0	0	0	0	....	....	....	....	....		1947-48	1947-48
Antonovich, Mike	Min., Hfd., N.J.	5	87	10	15	25	37	....	....	....	....	....		1975-76	1983-84
Apps, Syl (Jr.)	NYR, Pit., L.A.	10	727	183	423	606	311	23	5	5	10	23		1970-71	1979-80
Apps, Syl (Sr.)	Tor.	10	423	201	231	432	56	69	25	28	53	16	3	1936-37	1947-48
Arbour, Al	Det., Chi., Tor., St.L.	14	626	12	58	70	617	86	1	8	9	92	3	1953-54	1970-71
• Arbour, Amos	Mtl., Ham., Tor.	6	109	51	13	64	66	....	....	....	....	....		1918-19	1923-24
Arbour, Jack	Det., Tor.	2	47	5	1	6	56	....	....	....	....	....		1926-27	1928-29
Arbour, John	Bos., Pit., Van., St.L.	5	106	1	9	10	149	5	0	0	0	0		1965-66	1971-72
Arbour, Ty	Pit., Chi.	5	207	28	28	56	112	11	2	0	2	6		1926-27	1930-31
Archambault, Michel	Chi.	1	3	0	0	0	0	....	....	....	....	....		1976-77	1976-77
Archibald, Jim	Min.	3	16	1	2	3	45	....	....	....	....	....		1984-85	1986-87
Areshenkoff, Ronald	Edm.	1	4	0	0	0	0	....	....	....	....	....		1979-80	1979-80
• Armstrong, Bob	Bos.	12	542	13	86	99	671	42	1	7	8	28		1950-51	1961-62
Armstrong, George	Tor.	21	1187	296	417	713	721	110	26	34	60	88	4	1949-50	1970-71
Armstrong, Murray	Tor., NYA, Bro., Det.	8	270	67	121	188	62	30	4	6	10	2		1937-38	1945-46
• Armstrong, Red	Tor.	1	7	1	1	2	2	....	....	....	....	....		1962-63	1962-63
Armstrong, Tim	Tor.	1	11	1	0	1	6	....	....	....	....	....		1988-89	1988-89
Arnason, Chuck	Mtl., Atl., Pit., K.C., Col., Cle., Min., Wsh.	8	401	109	90	199	122	9	2	4	6	4		1971-72	1978-79
Arthur, Fred	Hfd., Phi.	3	80	1	8	9	49	4	0	0	0	2		1980-81	1982-83
Arundel, John	Tor.	1	3	0	0	0	0	....	....	....	....	....		1949-50	1949-50
• Ashbee, Barry	Bos., Phi.	5	284	15	70	85	291	17	0	4	4	22	1	1965-66	1973-74
• Ashby, Don	Tor., Col., Edm.	6	188	40	56	96	40	12	1	0	1	4		1975-76	1980-81
Ashworth, Frank	Chi.	1	18	5	4	9	2	....	....	....	....	....		1946-47	1946-47
Asmundson, Oscar	NYR, Det., St.L., NYA, Mtl.	5	112	11	23	34	30	9	0	2	2	4	1	1932-33	1937-38
Atanas, Walt	NYR	1	49	13	8	21	40	....	....	....	....	....		1944-45	1944-45
Atcheynum, Blair	Ott.	1	4	0	1	1	0	....	....	....	....	....		1992-93	1992-93
Atkinson, Steve	Bos., Buf., Wsh.	6	302	60	51	111	104	1	0	0	0	0		1968-69	1974-75
Attwell, Bob	Col.	2	22	1	5	6	0	....	....	....	....	....		1979-80	1980-81
Attwell, Ron	St.L., NYR	1	21	1	7	8	8	....	....	....	....	....		1967-68	1967-68
Aubin, Norm	Tor.	2	69	18	13	31	30	1	0	0	0	0		1981-82	1982-83
Aubry, Pierre	Que., Det.	5	202	24	26	50	133	20	1	1	2	32		1980-81	1984-85
Aubuchon, Ossie	Bos., NYR	2	50	19	12	31	4	6	1	0	1	0		1942-43	1943-44
Auge, Les	Col.	1	6	0	3	3	4	....	....	....	....	....		1980-81	1980-81
• Aurie, Larry	Det.	12	489	147	129	276	279	24	6	9	15	10	2	1927-28	1938-39
Awrey, Don	Bos., St.L., Mtl., Pit., NYR, Col.	16	979	31	158	189	1065	71	0	18	18	150	2	1963-64	1978-79
Ayres, Vern	NYA, Mtl.M., St.L., NYR	6	211	6	14	20	350	....	....	....	....	....		1930-31	1935-36
B															
Babando, Pete	Bos., Det., Chi., NYR	6	351	86	73	159	194	17	3	3	6	6	1	1947-48	1952-53
Babcock, Bobby	Wsh.	2	2	0	0	0	2	....	....	....	....	....		1990-91	1992-93
Babe, Warren	Min.	3	21	2	5	7	23	2	0	0	0	0		1987-88	1990-91
Babin, Mitch	St.L.	1	8	0	0	0	0	....	....	....	....	....		1975-76	1975-76
Baby, John	Cle., Min.	2	26	2	8	10	26	....	....	....	....	....		1977-78	1978-79

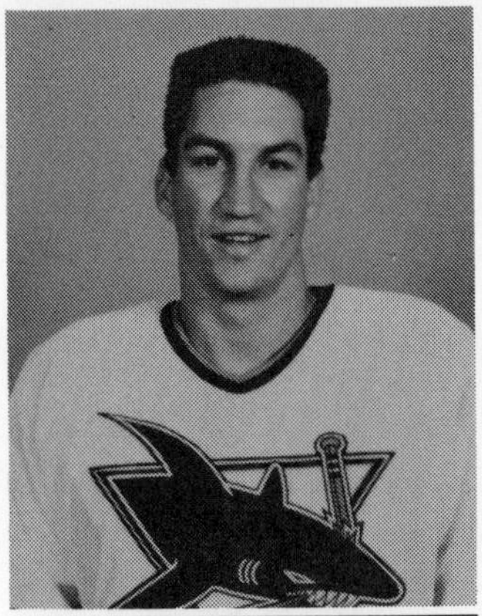
Perry Anderson

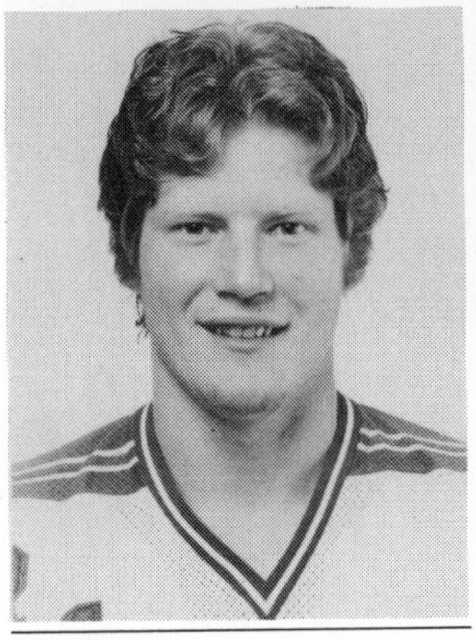
Mike Allison

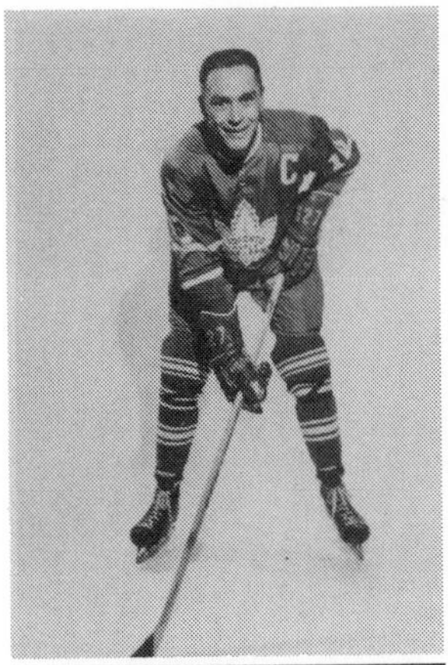
George Armstrong

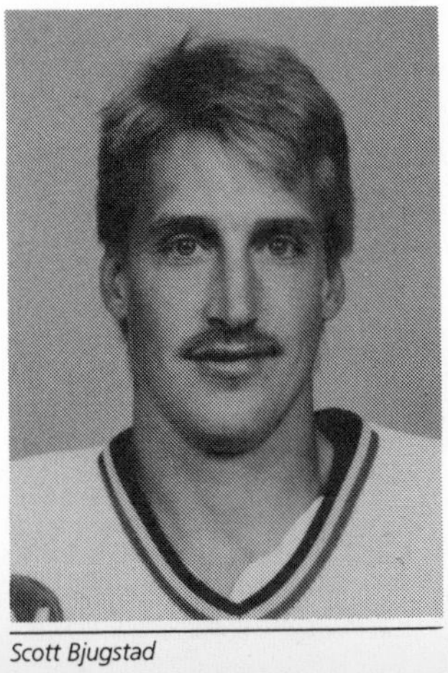
Scott Bjugstad

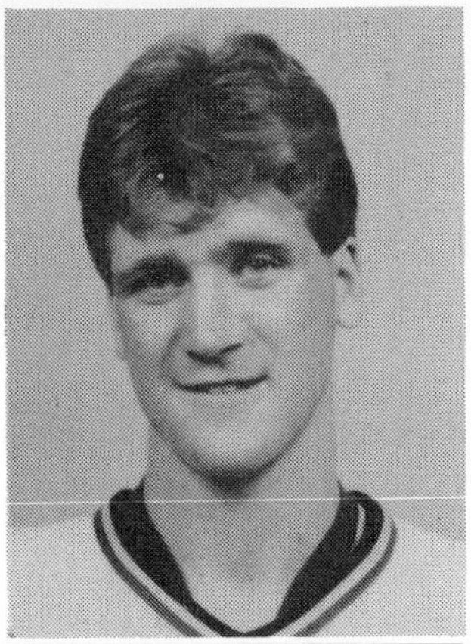

Warren Babe

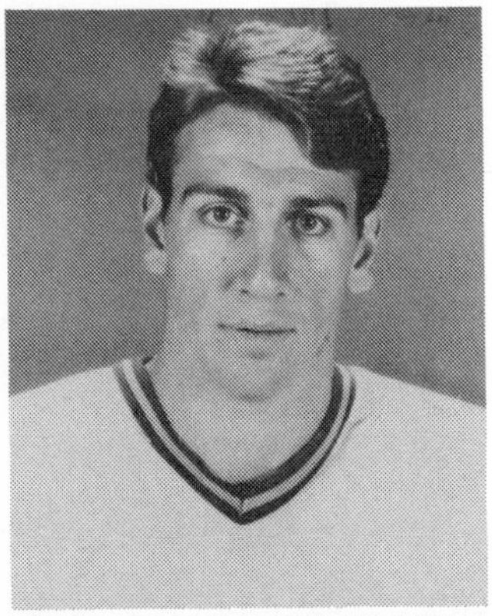

Charlie Bourgeois

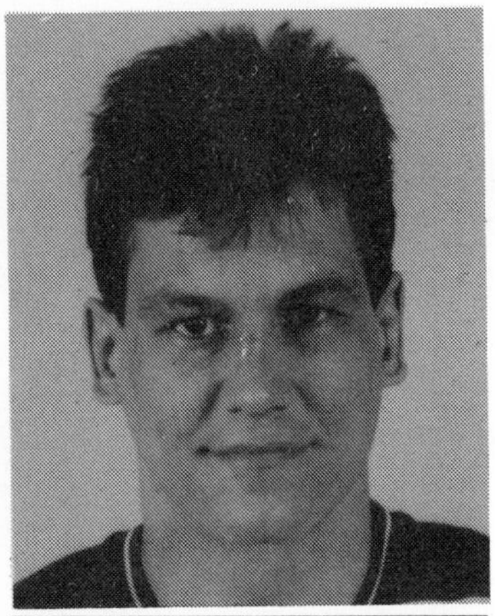

Paul Baxter

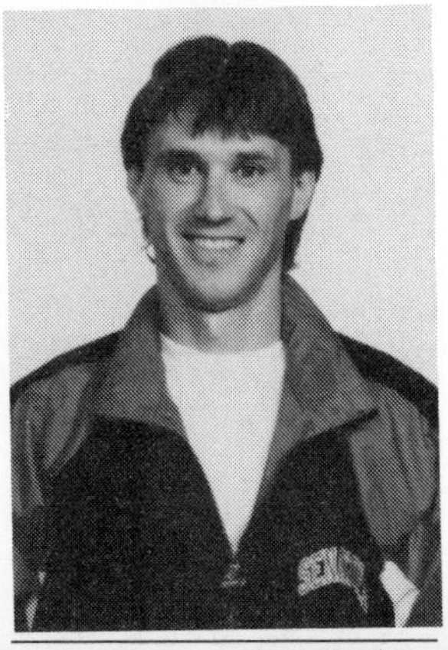

Laurie Boschman

			Regular Schedule					Playoffs							
Name	NHL Teams	NHL Seasons	GP	G	A	TP	PIM	GP	G	A	TP	PIM	NHL Cup Wins	First NHL Season	Last NHL Season
Babych, Wayne	St.L., Pit., Que., Hfd.	9	519	192	246	438	498	41	7	9	16	25		1978-79	1986-87
Backman, Mike	NYR	3	18	1	6	7	18	10	2	2	4	2		1981-82	1983-84
Backor, Peter	Tor.	1	36	4	5	9	6	....	....	....	....	....	1	1944-45	1944-45
Backstrom, Ralph	Mtl., L.A., Chi.	17	1032	278	361	639	386	116	27	32	59	68	6	1956-57	1972-73
Bailey, Ace (G.)	Bos., Det., St.L., Wsh.	10	568	107	171	278	633	15	2	4	6	28	1	1968-69	1977-78
• Bailey, Ace (I.)	Tor.	8	313	111	82	193	472	21	3	4	7	12	1	1926-27	1933-34
Bailey, Bob	Tor., Det., Chi.	4	150	15	21	36	207	15	0	4	4	22		1953-54	1957-58
Bailey, Reid	Phi., Tor., Hfd.	4	40	1	3	4	105	16	0	2	2	25		1980-81	1983-84
Baillargeon, Joel	Wpg., Que.	3	20	0	2	2	31	....	....	....	....	....		1986-87	1988-89
Baird, Ken	Cal.	1	10	0	2	2	15	....	....	....	....	....		1971-72	1971-72
Baker, Bill	Mtl., Col., St.L., NYR	3	143	7	25	32	175	6	0	0	0	0		1980-81	1982-83
Bakovic, Peter	Van.	1	10	2	0	2	48	....	....	....	....	....		1987-88	1987-88
Balderis, Helmut	Min.	1	26	3	6	9	2	....	....	....	....	....		1989-90	1989-90
Baldwin, Doug	Tor., Det., Chi.	3	24	0	1	1	8	....	....	....	....	....		1945-46	1947-48
Balfour, Earl	Tor., Chi.,	7	288	30	22	52	78	26	0	3	3	4	1	1951-52	1960-61
• Balfour, Murray	Mtl., Chi., Bos.	8	306	67	90	157	393	40	9	10	19	45	1	1956-57	1964-65
Ball, Terry	Phi., Buf.	4	74	7	19	26	26	....	....	....	....	....		1967-68	1971-72
Balon, Dave	NYR, Mtl., Min., Van.	14	776	192	222	414	607	78	14	21	35	109	2	1959-60	1972-73
Baltimore, Byron	Edm.	1	2	0	0	0	4	....	....	....	....	....		1979-80	1979-80
Baluik, Stanley	Bos.	1	7	0	0	0	2	....	....	....	....	....		1959-60	1959-60
Bandura, Jeff	NYR	1	2	0	1	1	0	....	....	....	....	....		1980-81	1980-81
Barahona, Ralph	Bos.	2	6	2	2	4	0	....	....	....	....	....		1990-91	1991-92
Barbe, Andy	Tor.	1	1	0	0	0	2	....	....	....	....	....		1950-51	1950-51
Barber, Bill	Phi.	12	903	420	463	883	623	129	53	55	108	109	2	1972-73	1984-85
Barber, Don	Min., Wpg., Que., S.J.	4	115	25	32	57	64	11	4	4	8	10		1988-89	1991-92
• Barilko, Bill	Tor.	5	252	26	36	62	456	47	5	7	12	104	4	1946-47	1950-51
Barkley, Doug	Chi., Det.	6	253	24	80	104	382	30	0	9	9	63		1957-58	1965-66
Barlow, Bob	Min.	2	77	16	17	33	10	6	2	2	4	6		1969-70	1970-71
Barnes, Blair	L.A.	1	1	0	0	0	0	....	....	....	....	....		1982-83	1982-83
Barnes, Norm	Phi., Hfd.	4	156	6	38	44	178	12	0	0	0	8		1976-77	1981-82
Baron, Normand	Mtl., St.L.	2	27	2	0	2	51	3	0	0	0	22		1983-84	1985-86
Barrett, Fred	Min., L.A.	13	745	25	123	148	671	44	0	2	2	60		1970-71	1983-84
Barrett, John	Det., Wsh., Min.	8	488	20	77	97	604	16	2	2	4	50		1980-81	1987-88
Barrie, Doug	Pit., Buf., L.A.	3	158	10	42	52	268	....	....	....	....	....		1968-69	1971-72
Barry, Ed	Bos.	1	19	1	3	4	2	....	....	....	....	....		1946-47	1946-47
• Barry, Marty	NYA, Bos., Det., Mtl.	12	509	195	192	387	231	43	15	18	33	34	2	1927-28	1939-40
Barry, Ray	Bos.	1	18	1	2	3	6	....	....	....	....	....		1951-52	1951-52
Bartel, Robin	Cgy., Van.	2	41	0	1	1	14	6	0	0	0	16		1985-86	1986-87
Bartlett, Jim	Mtl., NYR, Bos.	5	191	34	23	57	273	2	0	0	0	0		1954-55	1960-61
• Barton, Cliff	Pit., Phi., NYR	3	85	10	9	19	22	....	....	....	....	....		1929-30	1939-40
Bathe, Frank	Det., Phi.,	9	224	3	28	31	542	27	1	3	4	42		1974-75	1983-84
Bathgate, Andy	NYR, Tor., Det., Pit.	17	1069	349	624	973	624	54	21	14	35	76	1	1952-53	1970-71
Bathgate, Frank	NYR	1	2	0	0	0	2	....	....	....	....	....		1952-53	1952-53
• Bauer, Bobby	Bos.	10	327	123	137	260	36	48	11	8	19	6	2	1935-36	1951-52
Baumgartner, Mike	K.C.	1	17	0	0	0	0	....	....	....	....	....		1974-75	1974-75
Baun, Bob	Tor., Oak., Det.	17	964	37	187	224	1493	96	3	12	15	171	4	1956-57	1972-73
Baxter, Paul	Que., Pit., Cgy.	8	472	48	121	169	1564	40	0	5	5	162		1979-80	1986-87
Beadle, Sandy	Wpg.	1	6	1	0	1	2	....	....	....	....	....		1980-81	1980-81
Beaton, Frank	NYR	2	25	1	1	2	43	....	....	....	....	....		1978-79	1979-80
Beattie, Red	Bos., Det., NYA	9	335	62	85	147	137	22	4	2	6	6		1930-31	1938-39
Beaudin, Norm	St.L., Min.	2	25	1	2	3	4	....	....	....	....	....		1967-68	1970-71
Beaudoin, Serge	Atl.	1	3	0	0	0	0	....	....	....	....	....		1979-80	1979-80
Beaudoin, Yves	Wsh.	3	11	0	0	0	5	....	....	....	....	....		1985-86	1987-88
Beck, Barry	Col., NYR, L.A.	10	615	104	251	355	1016	51	10	23	33	77		1977-78	1989-90
Beckett, Bob	Bos.	4	68	7	6	13	18	....	....	....	....	....		1956-57	1963-64
Bedard, James	Chi.	2	22	1	1	2	8	....	....	....	....	....		1949-50	1950-51
Bednarski, John	NYR, Edm.	4	100	2	18	20	114	1	0	0	0	0		1974-75	1979-80
Beers, Eddy	Cgy., St.L.	5	250	94	116	210	256	41	7	10	17	47		1981-82	1985-86
Behling, Dick	Det.	2	5	1	0	1	2	....	....	....	....	....		1940-41	1942-43
Beisler, Frank	NYA	2	2	0	0	0	0	....	....	....	....	....		1936-37	1939-40
Belanger, Alain	Tor.	1	9	0	1	1	6	....	....	....	....	....		1977-78	1977-78
Belanger, Roger	Pit.	1	44	3	5	8	32	....	....	....	....	....		1984-85	1984-85
Belisle, Danny	NYR	1	4	2	0	2	0	....	....	....	....	....		1960-61	1960-61
Beliveau, Jean	Mtl.	20	1125	507	712	1219	1029	162	79	97	176	211	10	1950-51	1970-71
• Bell, Billy	Mtl.W, Mtl., Ott.	6	61	3	1	4	4	9	0	0	0	0	1	1917-18	1923-24
Bell, Bruce	Que., St. L., NYR, Edm.	5	209	12	64	76	113	34	3	5	8	41		1984-85	1989-90
Bell, Harry	NYR	1	1	0	1	1	0	....	....	....	....	....		1946-47	1946-47
Bell, Joe	NYR	2	62	8	9	17	18	....	....	....	....	....		1942-43	1946-47
Belland, Neil	Van., Pit.	6	109	13	32	45	54	21	2	9	11	23		1981-82	1986-87
• Bellefeuille, Pete	Tor., Det.	4	92	26	4	30	58	....	....	....	....	....		1925-26	1929-30
• Bellemer, Andy	Mtl.M.	1	15	0	0	0	0	....	....	....	....	....		1932-33	1932-33
Bend, Lin	NYR	1	8	3	1	4	2	....	....	....	....	....		1942-43	1942-43
Bennett, Bill	Bos., Hfd.	2	31	4	7	11	65	....	....	....	....	....		1978-79	1979-80
Bennett, Curt	St.L., NYR, Atl.	10	580	152	182	334	347	21	1	1	2	57		1970-71	1979-80
Bennett, Frank	Det.	1	7	0	1	1	2	....	....	....	....	....		1943-44	1943-44
Bennett, Harvey	Pit., Wsh., Phi., Min., St.L.	5	268	44	46	90	347	4	0	0	0	2		1974-75	1978-79
• Bennett, Max	Mtl.	1	1	0	0	0	0	....	....	....	....	....		1935-36	1935-36
Benning, Jim	Tor., Van.	9	605	52	191	243	461	7	1	1	2	2		1981-82	1989-90
Benoit, Joe	Mtl.	5	185	75	69	144	94	11	6	3	9	11	1	1940-41	1946-47
Benson, Bill	NYA, Bro.	2	67	11	25	36	35	....	....	....	....	....		1940-41	1941-42
Benson, Bobby	Bos.	1	8	0	1	1	4	....	....	....	....	....		1924-25	1924-25
• Bentley, Doug	Chi., NYR	13	566	219	324	543	217	23	9	8	17	8		1939-40	1953-54
• Bentley, Max	Chi., Tor., NYR	12	646	245	299	544	179	52	18	27	45	14	3	1940-41	1953-54
Bentley, Reggie	Chi.	1	11	1	2	3	2	....	....	....	....	....		1942-43	1942-43
Beraldo, Paul	Bos.	2	10	0	0	0	4	....	....	....	....	....		1987-88	1988-89
Berenson, Red	Mtl., NYR, St.L., Det.	17	987	261	397	658	305	85	23	14	37	49	2	1961-62	1977-78
Berezan, Perry	Cgy., Min., S.J.	9	378	61	75	136	279	31	4	7	11	34		1984-85	1992-93
Bergdinon, Fred	Bos.	1	2	0	0	0	0	....	....	....	....	....		1925-26	1925-26
Bergen, Todd	Phi.	1	14	11	5	16	4	17	4	9	13	8		1984-85	1984-85
Berger, Mike	Min.	2	30	3	1	4	67	....	....	....	....	....		1987-88	1988-89
Bergeron, Michel	Det., NYI, Wsh.	5	229	80	58	138	165	....	....	....	....	....		1974-75	1978-79
Bergeron, Yves	Pit.	2	3	0	0	0	0	....	....	....	....	....		1974-75	1976-77
Bergloff, Bob	Min.	1	2	0	0	0	5	....	....	....	....	....		1982-83	1982-83
Berglund, Bo	Que., Min., Phi.	3	130	28	39	67	40	9	2	0	2	6		1983-84	1985-86
Bergman, Gary	Det., Min., K.C.	12	838	68	299	367	1249	21	0	5	5	20		1964-65	1975-76
Bergman, Thommie	Det.	6	246	21	44	65	243	7	0	2	2	2		1972-73	1979-80
Bergqvist, Jonas	Cgy.	1	22	2	5	7	10	....	....	....	....	....		1989-90	1989-90
• Berlinquette, Louis	Mtl., Mtl.M., Pit.	8	193	44	29	73	111	16	1	1	2	0		1917-18	1925-26
Bernier, Serge	Phi., L.A., Que.	7	302	78	119	197	234	5	1	1	2	0		1968-69	1980-81
Berry, Bob	Mtl., L.A.	8	541	159	191	350	344	26	2	6	8	6		1968-69	1976-77
Berry, Doug	Col.	2	121	10	33	43	25	....	....	....	....	....		1979-80	1980-81
Berry, Fred	Det.	1	3	0	0	0	0	....	....	....	....	....		1976-77	1976-77
Berry, Ken	Edm., Van.	4	55	8	10	18	30	....	....	....	....	....		1981-82	1988-89
Besler, Phil	Bos., Chi., Det.	2	30	1	4	5	18	....	....	....	....	....		1935-36	1938-39
Bessone, Pete	Det.	1	6	0	1	1	6	....	....	....	....	....		1937-38	1937-38
Bethel, John	Wpg.	1	17	0	2	2	4	....	....	....	....	....		1979-80	1979-80
Bettio, Sam	Bos.	1	44	9	12	21	32	....	....	....	....	....		1949-50	1949-50
Beverley, Nick	Bos., Pit., NYR, Min., L.A., Col.	11	502	18	94	112	156	7	0	1	1	0		1966-67	1979-80
Bialowas, Dwight	Atl., Min.	4	164	11	46	57	46	....	....	....	....	....		1973-74	1976-77
Bianchin, Wayne	Pit., Edm.	7	276	68	41	109	137	3	0	1	1	6		1973-74	1979-80
Bidner, Todd	Wsh.	1	12	2	1	3	7	....	....	....	....	....		1981-82	1981-82
Biggs, Don	Min.	1	1	0	0	0	0	....	....	....	....	....		1984-85	1984-85
Bignell, Larry	Pit.	2	20	0	3	3	2	3	0	0	0	2		1973-74	1974-75
Bilodeau, Gilles	Que.	1	9	0	1	1	25	....	....	....	....	....		1979-80	1979-80
Bionda, Jack	Tor., Bos.	4	93	3	9	12	113	11	0	1	1	14		1955-56	1958-59
Bissett, Tom	Det.	1	5	0	0	0	0	....	....	....	....	....		1990-91	1990-91
Bjugstad, Scott	Min., Pit., L.A.	9	317	76	68	144	144	9	0	1	1	2		1983-84	1991-92
Black, Stephen	Det., Chi.	2	113	11	20	31	77	13	0	0	0	13	1	1949-50	1950-51
Blackburn, Bob	NYR., Pit.	3	135	8	12	20	105	6	0	0	0	4		1968-69	1970-71
Blackburn, Don	Bos., Phi., NYR, NYI, Min.	6	185	23	44	67	87	12	3	0	3	10		1962-63	1972-73
Blade, Hank	Chi.	2	24	2	3	5	2	....	....	....	....	....		1946-47	1947-48
Bladon, Tom	Phi., Pit., Edm., Wpg., Det.	9	610	73	197	270	392	86	8	29	37	70	2	1972-73	1980-81
Blaine, Gary	Mtl.	1	1	0	0	0	0	....	....	....	....	....		1954-55	1954-55
• Blair, Andy	Tor., Chi.	9	402	74	86	160	323	38	6	6	12	32	1	1928-29	1936-37

Name	NHL Teams	NHL Seasons	Regular Schedule GP	G	A	TP	PIM	Playoffs GP	G	A	TP	PIM	NHL Cup Wins	First NHL Season	Last NHL Season
Blair, Chuck	Tor.	2	3	0	0	0	0	....	....	....	....	....		1948-49	1950-51
Blair, George	Tor.	1	2	0	0	0	0	....	....	....	....	....		1950-51	1950-51
Blaisdell, Mike	Det., NYR, Pit., Tor.	9	343	70	84	154	166	....	....	....	....	....		1980-81	1988-89
Blake, Mickey	St.L., Bos., Tor.	2	16	1	1	2	4	....	....	....	....	....		1934-35	1935-36
Blake, Toe	Mtl.M., Mtl.	15	578	235	292	527	272	57	25	37	62	23	3	1932-33	1947-48
Blight, Rick	Van., L.A.	7	326	96	125	221	170	5	0	5	5	2		1975-76	1982-83
Blinco, Russ	Mtl.M, Chi.	6	268	59	66	125	24	19	3	3	6	4	1	1933-34	1938-39
Block, Ken	Van.	1	1	0	0	0	0	....	....	....	....	....		1970-71	1970-71
Blomqvist, Timo	Wsh., N.J.	5	243	4	53	57	293	13	0	0	0	24		1981-82	1986-87
Bloom, Mike	Wsh., Det.	3	201	30	47	77	215	....	....	....	....	....		1974-75	1976-77
Blum, John	Edm., Bos., Wsh., Det.	8	250	7	34	41	610	20	0	2	2	27		1982-83	1989-90
Bodak, Bob	Cgy., Hfd.	2	4	0	0	0	29	....	....	....	....	....		1987-88	1989-90
Boddy, Gregg	Van.	5	273	23	44	67	263	3	0	0	0	0		1971-72	1975-76
Bodnar, Gus	Tor., Chi., Bos.	12	667	142	254	396	207	32	4	3	7	10	2	1943-44	1954-55
Boehm, Ron	Oak.	1	16	2	1	3	10	....	....	....	....	....		1967-68	1967-68
Boesch, Garth	Tor.	4	197	9	28	37	205	34	2	5	7	18	3	1946-47	1949-50
Boh, Rick	Min.	1	8	2	1	3	4	....	....	....	....	....		1987-88	1987-88
Boileau, Marc	Det.	1	54	5	6	11	8	....	....	....	....	....		1961-62	1961-62
Boileau, Rene	NYA	1	7	0	0	0	0	....	....	....	....	....		1925-26	1925-26
Boimistruck, Fred	Tor.	2	83	4	14	18	45	....	....	....	....	....		1981-82	1982-83
Boisvert, Serge	Tor., Mtl.	5	46	5	7	12	8	23	3	7	10	4	1	1982-83	1987-88
Boivin, Leo	Tor., Bos., Det., Pit., Min.	19	1150	72	250	322	1192	54	3	10	13	59		1951-52	1969-70
Boland, Mike A.	Phi.	1	2	0	0	0	0	....	....	....	....	....		1974-75	1974-75
Boland, Mike J.	K.C., Buf.	2	23	1	2	3	29	3	1	0	1	2		1974-75	1978-79
Boldirev, Ivan	Bos., Cal., Chi., Atl., Van., Det.	15	1052	361	505	866	507	48	13	20	33	14		1970-71	1984-85
Bolduc, Danny	Det., Cgy.	3	102	22	19	41	33	1	0	0	0	0		1978-79	1983-84
Bolduc, Michel	Que.	2	10	0	0	0	6	....	....	....	....	....		1981-82	1982-83
Boll, Buzz	Tor., NYA, Bro., Bos.	11	436	133	130	263	148	29	7	3	10	13		1933-34	1943-44
Bolonchuk, Larry	Van., Wsh.	4	74	3	9	12	97	....	....	....	....	....		1972-73	1977-78
Bolton, Hughie	Tor.	8	235	10	51	61	221	17	0	5	5	14		1949-50	1956-57
Bonar, Dan	L.A.	3	170	25	39	64	208	14	3	4	7	22		1980-81	1982-83
Bonin, Marcel	Det., Bos., Mtl.	9	454	97	175	272	336	50	11	14	25	51	4	1952-53	1961-62
Boo, Jim	Min.	1	6	0	0	0	22	....	....	....	....	....		1977-78	1977-78
Boone, Buddy	Bos.	2	34	5	3	8	28	22	2	1	3	25		1956-57	1957-58
Boothman, George	Tor.	2	58	17	19	36	18	5	2	1	3	2		1942-43	1943-44
Bordeleau, Chris	Mtl., St.L., Chi.,	4	205	38	65	103	82	19	4	7	11	17	1	1968-69	1971-72
Bordeleau, J.P.	Chi.	10	519	97	126	223	143	48	3	6	9	12		1969-70	1979-80
Bordeleau, Paulin	Van.	3	183	33	56	89	47	5	2	1	3	0		1973-74	1975-76
Borotsik, Jack	St.L.	1	1	0	0	0	0	....	....	....	....	....		1974-75	1974-75
Boschman, Laurie	Tor., Edm., Wpg., N.J., Ott.	14	1009	229	348	577	2265	57	8	13	21	140		1979-80	1992-93
Bossy, Mike	NYI	10	752	573	553	1126	210	129	85	75	160	38	4	1977-78	1986-87
Bostrom, Helge	Chi.	4	96	3	3	6	58	13	0	0	0	16		1929-30	1932-33
Botell, Mark	Phi.	1	32	4	10	14	31	....	....	....	....	....		1981-82	1981-82
Bothwell, Tim	NYR, St.L., Hfd.	11	502	28	93	121	382	49	0	3	3	56		1978-79	1988-89
Botting, Cam	Atl.	1	2	0	1	1	0	....	....	....	....	....		1975-76	1975-76
Boucha, Henry	Det., Min., K.C., Col.	6	247	53	49	102	157	....	....	....	....	....		1971-72	1976-77
Bouchard, Dick	NYR	1	1	0	0	0	0	....	....	....	....	....		1954-55	1954-55
Bouchard, Edmond	Mtl., Ham., NYA, Pit.	8	223	19	20	39	105	....	....	....	....	....		1921-22	1928-29
Bouchard, Emile (Butch)	Mtl.	15	784	49	144	193	863	113	11	21	32	121	4	1941-42	1955-56
Bouchard, Pierre	Mtl., Wsh.	12	595	24	82	106	433	76	3	10	13	56	5	1970-71	1981-82
• Boucher, Billy	Mtl., Bos., NYA	7	213	93	35	128	391	21	9	3	12	35	1	1921-22	1927-28
• Boucher, Frank	Ott., NYR	14	557	161	262	423	119	56	16	18	34	12	2	1921-22	1943-44
• Boucher, George	Ott., Mtl.M, Chi.	15	457	122	62	184	712	44	11	4	15	84	4	1917-18	1931-32
• Boucher, Robert	Mtl.	1	12	0	0	0	0	....	....	....	....	....	1	1923-24	1923-24
Boudreau, Bruce	Tor., Chi.	8	141	28	42	70	46	9	2	0	2	0		1976-77	1985-86
Boudrias, Andre	Mtl., Min., Chi., St.L., Van.	12	662	151	340	491	218	34	6	10	16	12		1963-64	1975-76
Boughner, Barry	Oak., Cal.	2	20	0	0	0	11	....	....	....	....	....		1969-70	1970-71
Bourbonnais, Dan	Hfd.	2	59	3	25	28	11	....	....	....	....	....		1981-82	1983-84
Bourbonnais, Rick	St.L.	3	71	9	15	24	29	4	0	1	1	0		1975-76	1977-78
Bourcier, Conrad	Mtl.	1	6	0	0	0	0	....	....	....	....	....		1935-36	1935-36
Bourcier, Jean	Mtl.	1	9	0	1	1	0	....	....	....	....	....		1935-36	1935-36
• Bourgeault, Leo	Tor. NYR, Ott., Mtl.	8	307	24	20	44	269	24	1	1	2	18	1	1926-27	1934-35
Bourgeois, Charlie	Cgy., St.L., Hfd.	7	290	16	54	70	788	40	2	3	5	194		1981-82	1987-88
Bourne, Bob	NYI, L.A.	14	964	258	324	582	605	139	40	56	96	108	4	1974-75	1987-88
Boutette, Pat	Tor., Hfd., Pit.	10	756	171	282	453	1354	46	10	14	24	109		1975-76	1984-85
Boutilier, Paul	NYI, Bos., Min., NYR, Wpg.	8	288	27	83	110	358	41	1	9	10	45		1981-82	1988-89
Bowcher, Clarence	NYA	2	47	2	2	4	110	....	....	....	....	....		1926-27	1927-28
Bowman, Kirk	Chi.	3	88	11	17	28	19	7	1	0	1	0		1976-77	1978-79
• Bowman, Ralph	Ott., St.L., Det.	7	274	8	17	25	260	22	2	2	4	6	2	1933-34	1939-40
Bownass, Jack	Mtl., NYR	4	80	3	8	11	58	....	....	....	....	....		1957-58	1961-62
Bowness, Rick	Atl., Det., St. L, Wpg.	7	173	18	37	55	191	5	0	0	0	2		1975-76	1981-82
• Boyd, Bill	NYR, NYA	4	138	15	7	22	72	9	0	0	0	2	1	1926-27	1929-30
Boyd, Irwin	Bos., Det.	4	97	18	19	37	51	15	0	1	1	4		1931-32	1943-44
Boyd, Randy	Pit., Chi., NYI, Van.	8	257	20	67	87	328	13	0	2	2	26		1981-82	1988-89
Boyer, Wally	Tor., Chi., Oak. Pit.	7	365	54	105	159	163	15	1	3	4	0		1965-66	1971-72
Boyko, Darren	Wpg.	1	1	0	0	0	0	....	....	....	....	....		1988-89	1988-89
Bozek, Steve	L.A., Cgy., St. L., Van., S.J.	11	641	164	167	331	309	58	12	11	23	69		1981-82	1991-92
• Brackenborough, John	Bos.	1	7	0	0	0	0	....	....	....	....	....		1925-26	1925-26
Brackenbury, Curt	Que., Edm., St.L.	4	141	9	17	26	226	2	0	0	0	0		1979-80	1982-83
Bradley, Barton	Bos.	1	1	0	0	0	0	....	....	....	....	....		1949-50	1949-50
Bradley, Lyle	Cal. Cle.	2	6	1	0	1	2	....	....	....	....	....		1973-74	1976-77
Bragnalo, Rick	Wsh.	4	145	15	35	50	46	....	....	....	....	....		1975-76	1978-79
Brannigan, Andy	NYA, Bro.	2	26	1	2	3	31	....	....	....	....	....		1940-41	1941-42
Brasar, Per-Olov	Min., Van.	5	348	64	142	206	33	13	1	2	3	0		1977-78	1981-82
Brayshaw, Russ	Chi.	1	43	5	9	14	24	....	....	....	....	....		1944-45	1944-45
Breault, Francois	L.A.	3	27	2	4	6	42	....	....	....	....	....		1990-91	1992-93
Breitenbach, Ken	Buf.	3	68	1	13	14	49	8	0	1	1	4		1975-76	1978-79
Brennan, Dan	L.A.	2	8	0	1	1	9	....	....	....	....	....		1983-84	1985-86
Brennan, Doug	NYR	3	123	9	7	16	152	16	1	0	1	21	1	1931-32	1933-34
Brennan, Tom	Bos.	2	22	2	2	4	2	....	....	....	....	....		1943-44	1944-45
Brenneman, John	Chi., NYR, Tor., Det., Oak.	5	152	21	19	40	46	....	....	....	....	....		1964-65	1968-69
Bretto, Joe	Chi.	1	3	0	0	0	4	....	....	....	....	....		1944-45	1944-45
Brewer, Carl	Tor., Det., St.L.	12	604	25	198	223	1037	72	3	17	20	146	3	1957-58	1979-80
Briden, Archie	Det., Pit.	2	72	9	5	14	56	....	....	....	....	....		1926-27	1929-30
Bridgman, Mel	Phi., Cgy., N.J., Det., Van.	14	977	252	449	701	1625	125	28	39	67	298		1975-76	1988-89
• Briere, Michel	Pit.	1	76	12	32	44	20	10	5	3	8	17		1969-70	1969-70
Brindley, Doug	Tor.	1	3	0	0	0	0	....	....	....	....	....		1970-71	1970-71
Brink, Milt	Chi.	1	5	0	0	0	0	....	....	....	....	....		1936-37	1936-37
Brisson, Gerry	Mtl.	1	4	0	2	2	4	....	....	....	....	....		1962-63	1962-63
Britz, Greg	Tor., Hfd.	3	8	0	0	0	4	....	....	....	....	....		1983-84	1986-87
• Broadbent, Harry	Ott. Mt.M, NYA	11	302	122	45	167	553	41	13	1	14	69	4	1918-19	1928-29
Brochu, Stephane	NYR	1	1	0	0	0	0	....	....	....	....	....		1988-89	1988-89
Broden, Connie	Mtl.	3	6	2	1	3	2	7	0	1	1	0	2	1955-56	1957-58
Brooke, Bob	NYR, Min., N.J.	7	447	69	97	166	520	34	9	9	18	59		1983-84	1989-90
Brooks, Gord	St.L., Wsh.	3	70	7	18	25	37	....	....	....	....	....		1971-72	1974-75
• Brophy, Bernie	Mtl.M, Det.	3	62	4	4	8	25	2	0	0	0	2	1	1925-26	1929-30
Brossart, Willie	Phi., Tor., Wsh.	6	129	1	14	15	88	1	0	0	0	0		1970-71	1975-76
Broten, Aaron	Col., N.J., Min., Que., Tor., Wpg.	12	748	186	329	515	441	34	7	18	25	40		1980-81	1991-92
• Brown, Adam	Det. Chi. Bos.	10	391	104	113	217	358	26	2	14	6	14	1	1941-42	1951-52
Brown, Arnie	Tor. NYR, Det., NYI, Atl.	12	681	44	141	185	738	22	0	6	6	23		1961-62	1973-74
Brown, Cam	Van.	1	1	0	0	0	7	....	....	....	....	....		1990-91	1990-91
Brown, Connie	Det.	5	91	15	24	39	12	14	2	3	5	0		1938-39	1942-43
Brown, Fred	Mtl.M	1	19	1	0	1	0	9	0	0	0	0		1927-28	1927-28
Brown, George	Mtl.	3	79	6	22	28	34	7	0	0	0	2		1936-37	1938-39
Brown, Gerry	Det.	2	23	4	5	9	2	12	2	1	3	4		1941-42	1945-46
Brown, Harold	NYR	1	13	2	1	3	2	....	....	....	....	....		1945-46	1945-46
Brown, Jim	L.A.	1	3	0	1	1	5	....	....	....	....	....		1982-83	1982-83
Brown, Larry	NYR, Det., Phi., L.A.	9	455	7	53	60	180	35	0	4	4	10		1969-70	1977-78
Brown, Stan	NYR, Det.	2	48	8	2	10	18	2	0	0	0	0		1926-27	1927-28
Brown, Wayne	Bos.	1	....	....	....	....	....	4	0	0	0	2		1953-54	1953-54
• Browne, Cecil	Chi.	1	13	2	0	2	4	....	....	....	....	....		1927-28	1927-28
Brownschidle, Jack	St.L., Hfd.	9	494	39	162	201	151	26	0	5	5	18		1977-78	1985-86
Brownschidle, Jeff	Hfd.	2	7	0	1	1	2	....	....	....	....	....		1981-82	1982-83
Brubaker, Jeff	Hfd., Mtl., Cgy., Tor., Edm., NYR, Det.	8	178	16	9	25	512	2	0	0	0	27		1979-80	1988-89

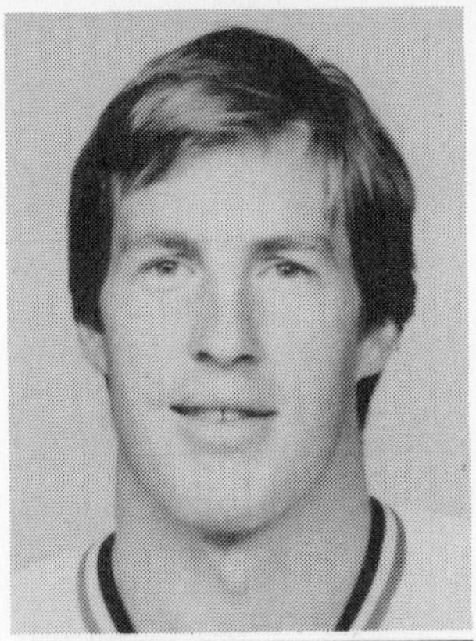

Bob Brooke

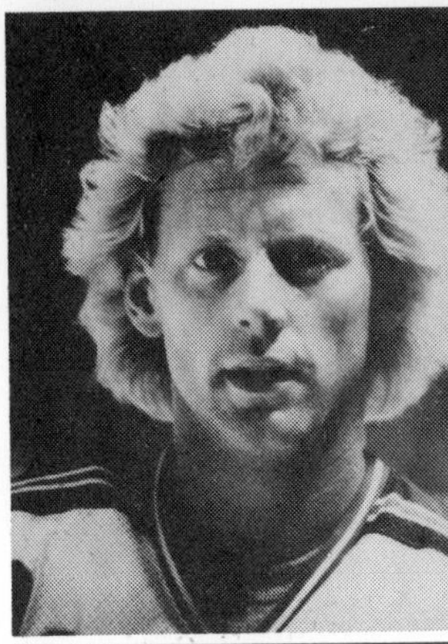

Bill Baker

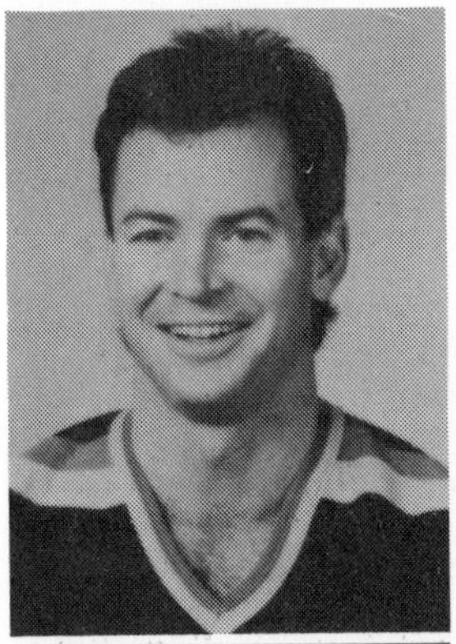

Ken Berry

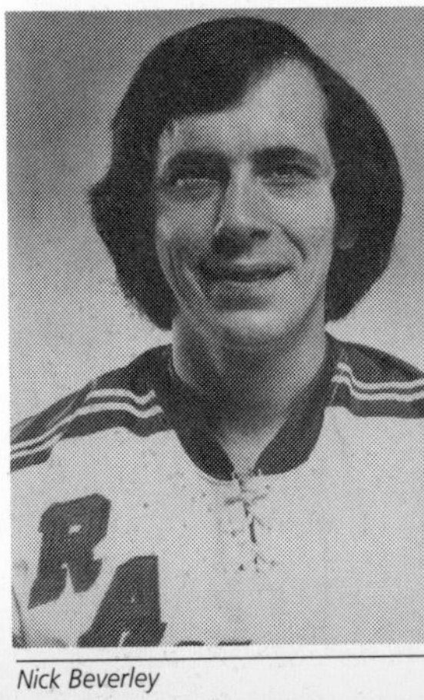

Nick Beverley

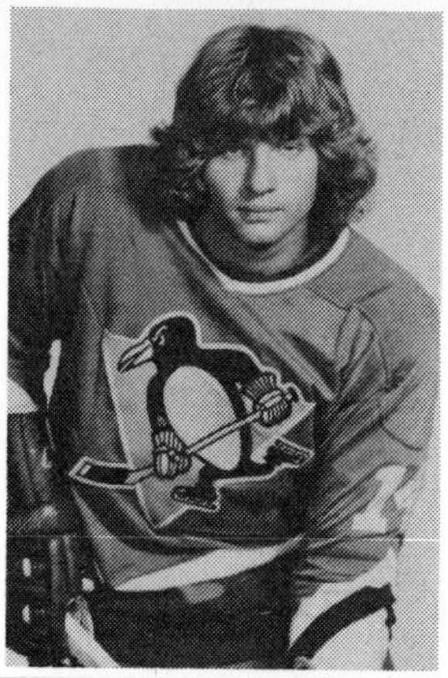

Wayne Bianchin

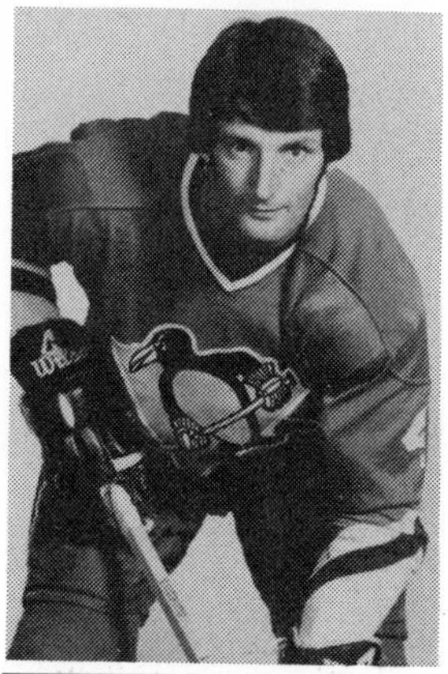

Dave Burrows

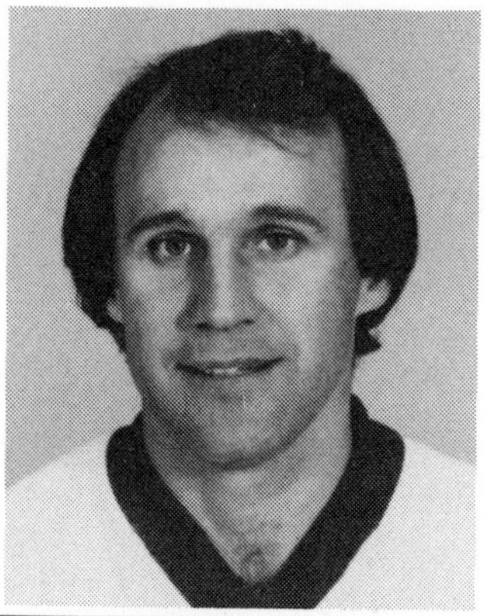

Colin Campbell

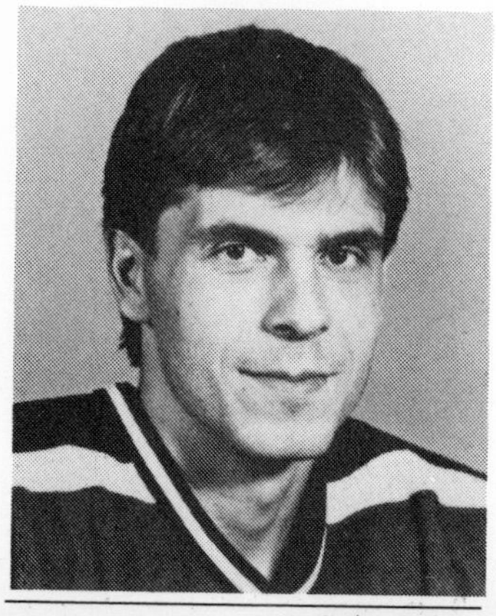

Anders Carlsson

Name	NHL Teams	NHL Seasons	Regular Schedule GP	G	A	TP	PIM	Playoffs GP	G	A	TP	PIM	NHL Cup Wins	First NHL Season	Last NHL Season
Bruce, Gordie	Bos.	3	28	4	9	13	13	7	2	3	5	4		1940-41	1945-46
Bruce, Morley	Ott.	4	72	8	1	9	27	12	0	0	0	3	2	1917-18	1921-22
Brumwell, Murray	Min., N.J.,	7	128	12	31	43	70	2	0	0	0	2		1980-81	1987-88
Bruneteau, Eddie	Det.	7	180	40	42	82	35	26	7	6	13	0		1940-41	1948-49
• Bruneteau, Mud	Det.	11	411	139	138	277	80	77	23	14	37	22	3	1935-36	1945-46
• Brydge, Bill	Tor., Det., NYA	9	368	26	52	78	506	2	0	0	0	4		1926-27	1935-36
Brydges, Paul	Buf.	1	15	2	2	4	6	....	....	....	....	....		1986-87	1986-87
• Brydson, Glenn	Mtl.M, St.L., NYR, Chi.	8	299	56	79	135	203	11	0	0	0	8		1930-31	1937-38
Brydson, Gord	Tor.	1	8	2	0	2	8	....	....	....	....	....		1929-30	1929-30
Bubla, Jiri	Van.	5	256	17	101	118	202	6	0	0	0	7		1981-82	1985-86
Buchanan, Al	Tor.	2	4	0	1	1	2	....	....	....	....	....		1948-49	1949-50
Buchanan, Bucky	NYR	1	2	0	0	0	0	....	....	....	....	....		1948-49	1948-49
Buchanan, Mike	Chi.	1	1	0	0	0	0	....	....	....	....	....		1951-52	1951-52
Buchanan, Ron	Bos., St.L.	2	5	0	0	0	0	....	....	....	....	....		1966-67	1969-70
Bucyk, John	Det., Bos.,	23	1540	556	813	1369	497	124	41	62	103	42	2	1955-56	1977-78
Bucyk, Randy	Mtl., Cgy.	2	19	4	2	6	8	2	0	0	0	0		1985-86	1987-88
Buhr, Doug	K.C.	1	6	0	2	2	4	....	....	....	....	....		1974-75	1974-75
Bukovich, Tony	Det.	2	44	7	3	10	6	6	0	1	1	0		1943-44	1944-45
• Buller, Hy	Det., NYR	5	188	22	58	80	215	....	....	....	....	....		1943-44	1953-54
Bulley, Ted	Chi., Wsh., Pit.	8	414	101	113	214	704	29	5	5	10	24		1976-77	1983-84
• Burch, Billy	Ham., NYA, Bos., Chi.	11	390	137	53	190	251	2	0	0	0	0		1922-23	1932-33
Burchell, Fred	Mtl.	2	4	0	0	0	2	....	....	....	....	....		1950-51	1953-54
Burdon, Glen	K.C.	1	11	0	2	2	0	....	....	....	....	....		1974-75	1974-75
Burega, Bill	Tor.	1	4	0	1	1	4	....	....	....	....	....		1955-56	1955-56
Burke, Eddie	Bos., NYA	4	106	29	20	49	55	....	....	....	....	....		1931-32	1934-35
• Burke, Marty	Mtl., Pit., Ott., Chi.	11	494	19	47	66	560	31	2	4	6	44	2	1927-28	1937-38
Burmeister, Roy	NYA	3	67	4	3	7	2	....	....	....	....	....		1929-30	1931-32
Burnett, Kelly	NYR	1	3	1	0	1	0	....	....	....	....	....		1952-53	1952-53
Burns, Bobby	Chi.	3	20	1	0	1	8	....	....	....	....	....		1927-28	1929-30
Burns, Charlie	Det., Bos., Oak., Pit., Min.	11	749	106	198	304	252	31	5	4	9	4		1958-59	1972-73
Burns, Gary	NYR	2	11	2	2	4	18	5	0	0	0	6		1980-81	1981-82
Burns, Norm	NYR	1	11	0	4	4	2	....	....	....	....	....		1941-42	1941-42
Burns, Robin	Pit., K.C.	5	190	31	38	69	139	....	....	....	....	....		1970-71	1975-76
Burrows, Dave	Pit., Tor.	10	724	29	135	164	377	29	1	5	6	25		1971-72	1980-81
Burry, Bert	Ott.	1	4	0	0	0	0	....	....	....	....	....		1932-33	1932-33
Burton, Cummy	Det.	3	43	0	2	2	21	3	0	0	0	0		1955-56	1958-59
Burton, Nelson	Wsh.	2	8	1	0	1	21	....	....	....	....	....		1977-78	1978-79
• Bush, Eddie	Det.	2	27	4	6	10	50	12	1	6	7	23		1938-39	1941-42
Busniuk, Mike	Phi.	2	143	3	23	26	297	25	2	5	7	34		1979-80	1980-81
Busniuk, Ron	Buf.	2	6	0	3	3	4	....	....	....	....	....		1972-73	1973-74
• Buswell, Walt	Det., Mtl.	8	368	10	40	50	164	24	2	1	3	10		1932-33	1939-40
Butler, Dick	Chi.	1	7	2	0	2	0	....	....	....	....	....		1947-48	1947-48
Butler, Jerry	NYR, St.L., Tor., Van., Wpg.	11	641	99	120	219	515	48	3	3	6	79		1972-73	1982-83
Butters, Bill	Min.	2	72	1	4	5	77	....	....	....	....	....		1977-78	1978-79
Buttrey, Gord	Chi.	1	10	0	0	0	0	10	0	0	0	0		1943-44	1943-44
Buynak, Gordon	St. L	1	4	0	0	0	2	....	....	....	....	....		1974-75	1974-75
Byce, John	Bos.	3	21	2	3	5	6	8	2	0	2	2		1989-90	1991-92
Byers, Gord	Bos.	1	1	0	1	1	0	....	....	....	....	....		1949-50	1949-50
Byers, Jerry	Min., Atl, NYR	4	43	3	4	7	10	....	....	....	....	....		1972-73	1977-78
Byers, Mike	Tor., Phi., Buf., L.A.	4	166	42	34	76	39	4	0	1	1	0		1967-68	1971-72
Byram, Shawn	NYI, Chi.	2	5	0	0	0	14	....	....	....	....	....		1990-91	1991-92

C

Name	NHL Teams	NHL Seasons	Regular Schedule GP	G	A	TP	PIM	Playoffs GP	G	A	TP	PIM	NHL Cup Wins	First NHL Season	Last NHL Season
Caffery, Jack	Tor., Bos.	3	57	3	2	5	22	10	1	0	1	4		1954-55	1957-58
Caffery, Terry	Chi., Min.	2	14	0	0	0	0	1	0	0	0	0		1969-70	1970-71
• Cahan, Larry	Tor., NYR, Oak., L.A.	13	665	38	92	130	700	29	1	1	2	38		1954-55	1970-71
Cahill, Chuck	Bos.	2	32	0	1	1	4	....	....	....	....	....		1925-26	1926-27
• Cain, Herb	Mtl.M, Mtl., Bos.	13	571	206	194	400	178	64	16	13	29	13	2	1933-34	1945-46
• Cain, Jim	Mtl.M, Tor.	2	61	4	0	4	35	....	....	....	....	....	1	1924-25	1925-26
Cairns, Don	K.C., Col.	2	9	0	1	1	2	....	....	....	....	....		1975-76	1976-77
Calder, Eric	Wsh.	2	2	0	0	0	0	....	....	....	....	....		1981-82	1982-83
Calladine, Norm	Bos.	3	63	19	29	48	8	....	....	....	....	....		1942-43	1944-45
Callander, Drew	Phi., Van.	4	39	6	2	8	7	....	....	....	....	....		1976-77	1979-80
Callighen, Brett	Edm.	3	160	56	89	145	132	14	4	6	10	8		1979-80	1981-82
Callighen, Patsy	NYR	1	36	0	0	0	32	9	0	0	0	0	1	1927-28	1927-28
Camazzola, James	Chi.	2	3	0	0	0	0	....	....	....	....	....		1983-84	1986-87
Camazzola, Tony	Wsh.	1	3	0	0	0	4	....	....	....	....	....		1981-82	1981-82
Cameron, Al	Det., Wpg.	6	282	11	44	55	356	7	0	1	1	2		1975-76	1980-81
Cameron, Billy	Mtl., NYA	2	39	0	0	0	2	6	0	0	0	0	1	1923-24	1925-26
Cameron, Craig	Det., St.L., Min., NYI	9	552	87	65	152	202	27	3	1	4	17		1966-67	1975-76
Cameron, Dave	Col., N.J.	3	168	25	28	53	238	....	....	....	....	....		1981-82	1983-84
• Cameron, Harry	Tor., Ott., Mtl.	6	127	90	27	117	120	20	7	3	10	29	3	1917-18	1922-23
Cameron, Scotty	NYR	1	35	8	11	19	0	....	....	....	....	....		1942-43	1942-43
Campbell, Bryan	L.A., Chi.	5	260	35	71	106	74	22	3	4	7	2		1967-68	1971-72
Campbell, Colin	Pit., Col., Edm., Van., Det.	11	636	25	103	128	1292	45	4	10	14	181		1974-75	1984-85
• Campbell, Dave	Mtl.	1	3	0	0	0	0	....	....	....	....	....		1920-21	1920-21
Campbell, Don	Chi.	1	17	1	3	4	8	....	....	....	....	....		1943-44	1943-44
Campbell, Scott	Wpg., St.L.	3	80	4	21	25	243	....	....	....	....	....		1979-80	1981-82
Campbell, Spiff	Ott., NYA	3	77	5	1	6	12	2	0	0	0	0		1923-24	1925-26
Campbell, Wade	Wpg., Bos.	6	213	9	27	36	305	10	0	0	0	20		1982-83	1987-88
Campeau, Tod	Mtl.	3	42	5	9	14	16	1	0	0	0	0		1943-44	1948-49
Campedelli, Dom	Mtl.	1	2	0	0	0	0	....	....	....	....	....		1985-86	1985-86
Capuano, Jack	Tor., Van., Bos.	3	6	0	0	0	0	....	....	....	....	....		1989-90	1991-92
Carbol, Leo	Chi.	1	6	0	1	1	4	....	....	....	....	....		1942-43	1942-43
Cardin, Claude	St.L.	1	1	0	0	0	0	....	....	....	....	....		1967-68	1967-68
Cardwell, Steve	Pit.	3	53	9	11	20	35	4	0	0	0	2		1970-71	1972-73
• Carey, George	Que, Ham., Tor.	5	72	22	8	30	14	....	....	....	....	....		1919-20	1923-24
Carleton, Wayne	Tor., Bos., Cal.	7	278	55	73	128	172	18	2	4	6	14	1	1965-66	1971-72
Carlin, Brian	L.A.	1	5	1	0	1	0	....	....	....	....	....		1971-72	1971-72
Carlson, Jack	Min., St.L.	6	236	30	15	45	417	25	1	2	3	72		1978-79	1986-87
Carlson, Kent	Mtl., St.L., Wsh.	5	113	7	11	18	148	8	0	0	0	13		1983-84	1988-89
Carlson, Steve	L.A.	1	52	9	12	21	23	4	1	1	2	7		1979-80	1979-80
Carlsson, Anders	N.J.	3	104	7	26	33	34	3	1	0	1	2		1986-87	1988-89
Carlyle, Randy	Tor., Pit., Wpg.	17	1055	148	499	647	1400	69	9	24	33	120		1976-77	1992-93
• Caron, Alain	Oak., Mtl.	2	60	9	13	22	18	....	....	....	....	....		1967-68	1968-69
• Carpenter, Eddie	Que, Ham.	2	44	10	4	14	23	....	....	....	....	....		1919-20	1920-21
Carr,	Que.	1	1	0	0	0	0	....	....	....	....	....		1919-20	1919-20
Carr, Al	Tor.	1	5	0	1	1	4	....	....	....	....	....		1943-44	1943-44
Carr, Gene	St.L., NYR, L.A., Pit., Atl.	8	465	79	136	215	365	35	5	8	13	66		1971-72	1978-79
Carr, Lorne	NYR, NYA, Tor.	13	580	204	222	426	132	53	10	9	19	13	1	1933-34	1945-46
Carriere, Larry	Buf. Atl, Van., L.A., Tor.	7	366	16	74	90	463	27	0	3	3	42		1972-73	1979-80
• Carrigan, Gene	NYR, StL, Det.	3	37	2	1	3	13	4	0	0	0	0		1930-31	1934-35
Carroll, Billy	NYI, Edm., Det.	7	322	30	54	84	113	71	6	12	18	18	4	1980-81	1986-87
Carroll, George	Mtl.M, Bos.	1	15	0	0	0	9	....	....	....	....	....		1924-25	1924-25
Carroll, Greg	Wsh., Det., Hfd.	2	131	20	34	54	44	....	....	....	....	....		1978-79	1979-80
Carruthers, Dwight	Det. Phi.	2	2	0	0	0	0	....	....	....	....	....		1965-66	1967-68
Carse, Bill	NYR, Chi.	4	124	28	43	71	38	16	3	2	5	0		1938-39	1941-42
Carse, Bob	Chi., Mtl.	5	167	32	55	87	52	10	0	2	2	2		1939-40	1947-48
• Carson, Bill	Tor., Bos.	4	159	54	24	78	156	11	3	0	3	14	1	1926-27	1929-30
• Carson, Frank	Mtl.M., NYA, Det.	7	248	42	48	90	166	22	0	2	2	9	1	1925-26	1933-34
• Carson, Gerry	Mtl., NYR, Mtl.M.	6	261	12	11	23	205	22	0	0	0	12	1	1928-29	1936-37
Carson, Lindsay	Phi., Hfd.	7	373	66	80	146	524	49	4	10	14	56		1981-82	1987-88
Carter, Billy	Mtl., Bos.	3	16	0	0	0	6	....	....	....	....	....		1957-58	1961-62
Carter, Ron	Edm.	1	2	0	0	0	0	....	....	....	....	....		1979-80	1979-80
• Carveth, Joe	Det., Bos., Mtl.	11	504	150	189	339	81	69	21	16	37	28	2	1940-41	1950-51
Cashman, Wayne	Bos.	17	1027	277	516	793	1041	145	31	57	88	250	2	1964-65	1982-83
Cassidy, Bruce	Chi.	6	36	4	13	17	10	1	0	0	0	0		1983-84	1989-90
Cassidy, Tom	Pit.	1	26	3	4	7	15	....	....	....	....	....		1977-78	1977-78
Cassolato, Tony	Wsh.	3	23	1	6	7	4	....	....	....	....	....		1979-80	1981-82
Ceresino, Ray	Tor.	1	12	1	1	2	2	....	....	....	....	....		1948-49	1948-49
Cernik, Frantisek	Det.	1	49	5	4	9	13	....	....	....	....	....		1984-85	1984-85
Chad, John	Chi.	3	80	15	22	37	29	10	0	1	1	2		1939-40	1945-46

Name	NHL Teams	NHL Seasons	Regular Schedule GP	G	A	TP	PIM	Playoffs GP	G	A	TP	PIM	NHL Cup Wins	First NHL Season	Last NHL Season
Chalmers, Bill	NYR	1	1	0	0	0	0	....	....	....	....	....		1953-54	1953-54
Chalupa, Milan	Det.	1	14	0	5	5	6	....	....	....	....	....		1984-85	1984-85
• Chamberlain, Murph	Tor., Mtl., Bro., Bos.	12	510	100	175	275	769	66	14	17	31	96	2	1937-38	1948-49
Champagne, Andre	Tor.	1	2	0	0	0	0	....	....	....	....	....		1962-63	1962-63
Chapdelaine, Rene	L.A.	3	32	0	2	2	32	....	....	....	....	....		1990-91	1992-93
• Chapman, Art	Bos., NYA	10	438	62	176	238	140	25	1	5	6	9		1930-31	1939-40
Chapman, Blair	Pit., St.L.	7	402	106	125	231	158	25	4	6	10	15		1976-77	1982-83
Charbonneau, Stephane	Que.	1	2	0	0	0	0	....	....	....	....	....		1991-92	1991-92
Charlebois, Bob	Min.	1	7	1	0	1	0	....	....	....	....	....		1967-68	1967-68
Charlesworth, Todd	Pit., NYR	6	93	3	9	12	47	....	....	....	....	....		1983-84	1989-90
Charron, Guy	Mtl., Det., K.C., Wsh.	12	734	221	309	530	146	....	....	....	....	....		1969-70	1980-81
Chartier, Dave	Wpg.	1	1	0	0	0	0	....	....	....	....	....		1980-81	1980-81
Chartraw, Rick	Mtl., L.A., NYR, Edm.	10	420	28	64	92	399	75	7	9	16	80	4	1974-75	1983-84
Check, Lude	Det., Chi.	2	27	6	2	8	4	....	....	....	....	....		1943-44	1944-45
Chernoff, Mike	Min.	1	1	0	0	0	0	....	....	....	....	....		1968-69	1968-69
Cherry, Dick	Bos., Phi.	3	145	12	10	22	45	4	1	0	1	4		1956-57	1969-70
Cherry, Don	Bos.	1	....	....	....	....	....	1	0	0	0	0		1954-55	1954-55
• Chevrefils, Real	Bos., Det.	8	387	104	97	201	185	30	5	4	9	20		1951-52	1958-59
Chicoine, Dan	Cle. Min.	3	31	1	2	3	12	1	0	0	0	0		1977-78	1979-80
Chinnick, Rick	Min.	2	4	0	2	2	0	....	....	....	....	....		1973-74	1974-75
Chipperfield, Ron	Edm., Que.,	2	83	22	24	46	34	....	....	....	....	....		1979-80	1980-81
Chisholm, Art	Bos.	1	3	0	0	0	0	....	....	....	....	....		1960-61	1960-61
Chisholm, Colin	Min.	1	1	0	0	0	0	....	....	....	....	....		1986-87	1986-87
• Chisholm, Les	Tor.	2	54	10	8	18	19	3	1	0	1	0		1939-40	1940-41
Chorney, Marc	Pit. L.A.	4	210	8	27	35	209	7	0	1	1	2		1980-81	1983-84
Chouinard, Gene	Ott.	1	8	0	0	0	0	....	....	....	....	....		1927-28	1927-28
Chouinard, Guy	Atl, Cgy., St.L.	10	578	205	370	575	120	46	9	28	37	12		1974-75	1983-84
Christie, Mike	Cal., Cle., Col., Van.	7	412	15	101	116	550	2	0	0	0	0		1974-75	1980-81
Christoff, Steve	Min. Cgy., L.A.	5	248	77	64	141	108	35	16	12	28	25		1979-80	1983-84
Chrystal, Bob	NYR	2	132	11	14	25	112	....	....	....	....	....		1953-54	1954-55
Church, Jack	Tor., Bro., Bos.	6	145	5	22	27	164	25	1	1	2	18		1938-39	1945-46
• Ciesla, Hank	Chi., NYR	4	269	26	51	77	87	6	0	2	2	0		1955-56	1958-59
Clackson, Kim	Pit., Que.	2	106	0	8	8	370	8	0	0	0	70		1979-80	1980-81
• Clancy, Francis (King)	Ott., Tor.	16	592	137	143	280	904	61	9	8	17	92	3	1921-22	1936-37
Clancy, Terry	Oak., Tor.	4	93	6	6	12	39	....	....	....	....	....		1967-68	1972-73
• Clapper, Dit	Bos.	20	833	228	246	474	462	86	13	17	30	50	3	1927-28	1946-47
Clark, Andy	Bos.	1	5	0	0	0	0	....	....	....	....	....		1927-28	1927-28
Clark, Dan	NYR	1	4	0	1	1	6	....	....	....	....	....		1978-79	1978-79
Clark, Dean	Edm.	1	1	0	0	0	0	....	....	....	....	....		1983-84	1983-84
Clark, Gordie	Bos.	2	8	0	1	1	0	1	0	0	0	0		1974-75	1975-76
Clarke, Bobby	Phi.	15	1144	358	852	1210	1453	136	42	77	119	152	2	1969-70	1983-84
• Cleghorn, Odie	Mtl., Pit.	10	180	95	29	124	147	23	9	2	11	2	1	1918-19	1927-28
• Cleghorn, Sprague	Ott. Tor. Mtl., Bos.	10	256	84	39	123	489	37	7	8	15	48	3	1918-19	1927-28
Clement, Bill	Phi., Wsh., Atl., Cgy.	11	719	148	208	356	383	50	5	3	8	26	2	1971-72	1981-82
Cline, Bruce	NYR	1	30	2	3	5	10	....	....	....	....	....		1956-57	1956-57
Clippingdale, Steve	L.A., Wsh.	2	19	1	2	3	9	1	0	0	0	0		1976-77	1979-80
Cloutier, Real	Que. Buf.	6	317	146	198	344	119	25	7	5	12	20		1979-80	1984-85
Cloutier, Rejean	Det.	2	5	0	2	2	2	....	....	....	....	....		1979-80	1981-82
Cloutier, Roland	Det., Que.	3	34	8	9	17	2	....	....	....	....	....		1977-78	1979-80
Clune, Wally	Mtl.	1	5	0	0	0	6	....	....	....	....	....		1955-56	1955-56
Coalter, Gary	Cal., K.C.	2	34	2	4	6	2	....	....	....	....	....		1973-74	1974-75
Coates, Steve	Det.	1	5	1	0	1	24	....	....	....	....	....		1976-77	1976-77
Cochrane, Glen	Phi., Van., Chi., Edm.	10	411	17	72	89	1556	18	1	1	2	31		1978-79	1988-89
Coflin, Hughie	Chi.	1	31	0	3	3	33	....	....	....	....	....		1950-51	1950-51
Colley, Tom	Min.	1	1	0	0	0	2	....	....	....	....	....		1974-75	1974-75
Collings, Norm	Mtl.	1	1	0	1	1	0	....	....	....	....	....		1934-35	1934-35
Collins, Bill	Min., Mtl., Det., St. L, NYR, Phi., Wsh.	11	768	157	154	311	415	18	3	5	8	12		1967-68	1977-78
Collins, Gary	Tor.	1	....	....	....	....	....	2	0	0	0	0		1958-59	1958-59
Collyard, Bob	St.L.	1	10	1	3	4	4	....	....	....	....	....		1973-74	1973-74
• Colman, Michael	S.J.	1	15	0	1	1	32	....	....	....	....	....		1991-92	1991-92
Colville, Mac	NYR	9	353	71	104	175	130	40	9	10	19	14	1	1935-36	1946-47
• Colville, Neil	NYR	12	464	99	166	265	213	46	7	19	26	33	1	1935-36	1948-49
Colwill, Les	NYR	1	69	7	6	13	16	....	....	....	....	....		1958-59	1958-59
Comeau, Rey	Mtl., Atl, Col.	9	564	98	141	239	175	9	2	1	3	8		1971-72	1979-80
Conacher, Brian	Tor., Det.	5	154	28	28	56	84	12	3	2	5	21	1	1961-62	1971-72
• Conacher, Charlie	Tor., Det., NYA	12	460	225	173	398	523	49	17	18	35	53	1	1929-30	1940-41
Conacher, Jim	Det., Chi., NYR	8	328	85	117	202	91	19	5	2	7	4		1945-46	1952-53
• Conacher, Lionel	Pit., NYA, Mtl.M., Chi.	12	500	80	105	185	882	35	2	2	4	34	2	1925-26	1936-37
Conacher, Pete	Chi., NYR, Tor.	6	229	47	39	86	57	7	0	0	0	0		1951-52	1957-58
• Conacher, Roy	Bos., Det., Chi.	11	490	226	200	426	90	42	15	15	30	14	2	1938-39	1951-52
Conn, Hugh	NYA	2	96	9	28	37	22	....	....	....	....	....		1933-34	1934-35
Connelly, Wayne	Mtl., Bos., Min., Det., St. L, Van.	10	543	133	174	307	156	24	11	7	18	4		1960-61	1971-72
Connolly, Bert	NYR, Chi.	3	87	13	15	28	37	14	1	0	1	0	1	1934-35	1937-38
Connor, Cam	Mtl., Edm., NYR	5	89	9	22	31	256	20	5	0	5	6	1	1978-79	1982-83
• Connor, Harry	Bos., NYA, Ott.	4	134	16	5	21	139	10	0	0	0	2		1927-28	1930-31
• Connors, Bobby	NYA, Det.	3	78	17	10	27	110	2	0	0	0	10		1926-27	1929-30
Contini, Joe	Col., Min.	3	68	17	21	38	34	2	0	0	0	0		1977-78	1980-81
• Convey, Eddie	NYR	3	36	1	1	2	33	....	....	....	....	....		1930-31	1932-33
• Cook, Bill	NYR	11	452	229	138	367	386	46	13	12	25	66	2	1926-27	1936-37
• Cook, Bob	Van., Det., NYI, Min.	4	72	13	9	22	22	....	....	....	....	....		1970-71	1974-75
Cook, Bud	Bos., Ott., St.L.	3	51	5	4	9	22	....	....	....	....	....		1931-32	1934-35
• Cook, Bun	NYR, Bos.	11	473	158	144	302	449	46	15	3	18	57	2	1926-27	1936-37
Cook, Lloyd	Bos.	1	4	1	0	1	0	....	....	....	....	....		1924-25	1924-25
• Cook, Tom	Chi., Mtl.M.	8	311	77	98	175	184	24	2	4	6	17	1	1929-30	1937-38
• Cooper, Carson	Bos., Mtl., Det.	8	278	110	57	167	111	4	0	0	0	2		1924-25	1931-32
Cooper, Ed	Col.	2	49	8	7	15	46	....	....	....	....	....		1980-81	1981-82
Cooper, Hal	NYR	1	8	0	0	0	2	....	....	....	....	....		1944-45	1944-45
• Cooper, Joe	NYR, Chi.	11	420	30	66	96	442	32	3	5	8	6		1935-36	1946-47
Copp, Bob	Tor.	2	40	3	9	12	26	....	....	....	....	....		1942-43	1950-51
• Corbeau, Bert	Mtl., Ham., Tor.,	10	257	64	31	95	501	14	2	0	2	10		1917-18	1926-27
Corbett, Michael	L.A.	1	....	....	....	....	....	2	0	1	1	2		1967-68	1967-68
Corcoran, Norm	Bos., Det., Chi.	4	29	1	3	4	21	4	0	0	0	6		1949-50	1955-56
Cormier, Roger	Mtl.	1	1	0	0	0	0	....	....	....	....	....		1925-26	1925-26
Corrigan, Charlie	Tor., NYA	2	19	2	2	4	2	....	....	....	....	....		1937-38	1940-41
Corrigan, Mike	L.A., Van., Pit.	10	594	152	195	347	698	17	2	3	5	20		1967-68	1977-78
Corriveau, Andre	Mtl.	1	3	0	1	1	0	....	....	....	....	....		1953-54	1953-54
Cory, Ross	Wpg.	2	51	2	10	12	41	....	....	....	....	....		1979-80	1980-81
Cossete, Jacques	Pit.	3	64	8	6	14	29	3	0	1	1	4		1975-76	1978-79
Costello, Les	Tor.	3	15	2	3	5	11	6	2	2	4	2	1	1947-48	1949-50
Costello, Murray	Chi., Bos., Det.	4	162	13	19	32	54	5	0	0	0	2		1953-54	1956-57
Costello, Rich	Tor.	2	12	2	2	4	2	....	....	....	....	....		1983-84	1985-86
Cotch, Charlie	Ham.	1	11	1	0	1	0	....	....	....	....	....		1924-25	1924-25
Cote, Alain	Que.	10	696	103	190	293	383	67	9	15	24	44		1979-80	1988-89
Cote, Ray	Edm.	3	15	0	0	0	4	14	3	2	5	0		1982-83	1984-85
• Cotton, Baldy	Pit., Tor., NYA	12	500	101	103	204	419	43	4	9	13	46	1	1925-26	1936-37
• Coughlin, Jack	Tor., Que, Mtl., Ham.	3	19	2	0	2	0	....	....	....	....	....	1	1917-18	1920-21
Coulis, Tim	Wsh., Min.	4	47	4	5	9	138	3	1	0	1	2		1979-80	1985-86
Coulson, D'arcy	Phi.	1	28	0	0	0	103	....	....	....	....	....		1930-31	1930-31
Coulter, Art	Chi., NYR	11	465	30	82	112	543	49	4	5	9	61	2	1931-32	1941-42
Coulter, Neal	NYI	3	26	5	5	10	11	1	0	0	0	0		1985-86	1987-88
Coulter, Tommy	Chi.	1	2	0	0	0	0	....	....	....	....	....		1933-34	1933-34
Cournoyer, Yvan	Mtl.	16	968	428	435	863	255	147	64	63	127	47	10	1963-64	1978-79
Courteau, Yves	Cgy., Hfd.	3	22	2	5	7	4	1	0	0	0	0		1984-85	1986-87
• Coutu, Billy	Mtl., Ham., Bos.	10	239	33	18	51	350	32	2	0	2	42	1	1917-18	1926-27
• Couture, Gerry	Det., Mtl., Chi.,	10	385	86	70	156	89	45	9	7	16	4	1	1944-45	1953-54
• Couture, Rosie	Chi., Mtl.	8	304	48	56	104	184	23	1	5	6	15		1928-29	1935-36
Cowan, Tommy	Phi.	1	1	0	0	0	0	....	....	....	....	....		1930-31	1930-31
Cowick, Bruce	Phi., Wsh., St.L.	3	70	5	6	11	43	8	0	0	0	9	1	1973-74	1975-76
• Cowley, Bill	St.L., Bos.	13	549	195	353	548	143	64	12	34	46	22	2	1934-35	1946-47
• Cox, Danny	Tor., Ott., Det., NYR, St.L.	9	329	47	49	96	110	10	0	1	1	6		1926-27	1934-35
Coxe, Craig	Van., Cgy., St. L., S.J.	8	235	14	31	45	713	5	1	0	1	18		1984-85	1991-92
Crashley, Bart	Det., K.C., L.A.	6	140	7	36	43	50	....	....	....	....	....		1965-66	1975-76
Crawford, Bob	St.L., Hfd., NYR, Wsh.	7	246	71	71	142	72	11	0	1	1	8		1979-80	1986-87

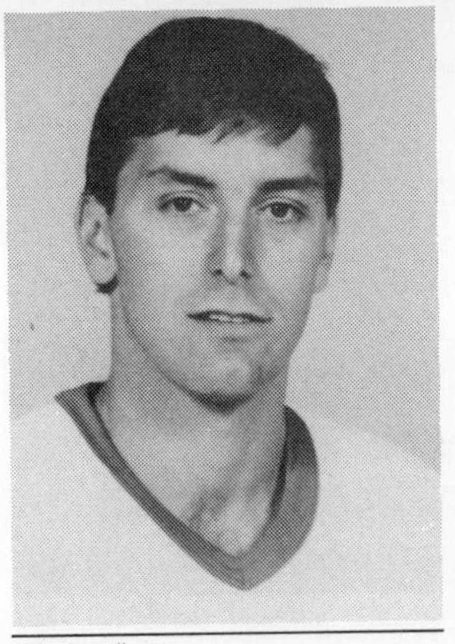

Billy Carroll

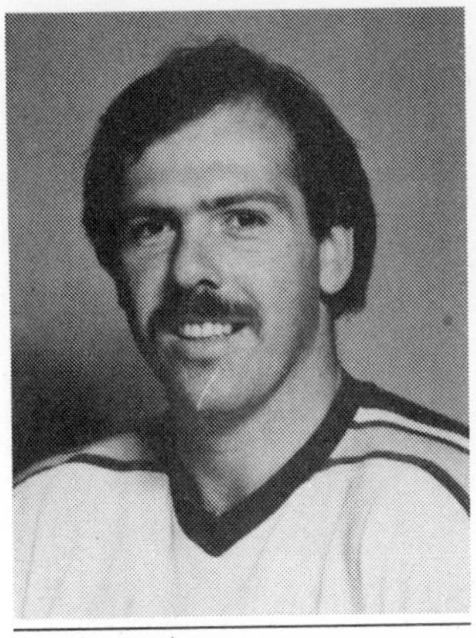

Guy Chouinard

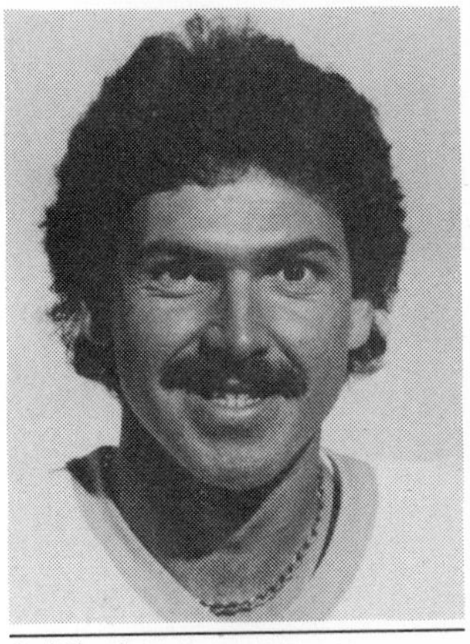

Real Cloutier

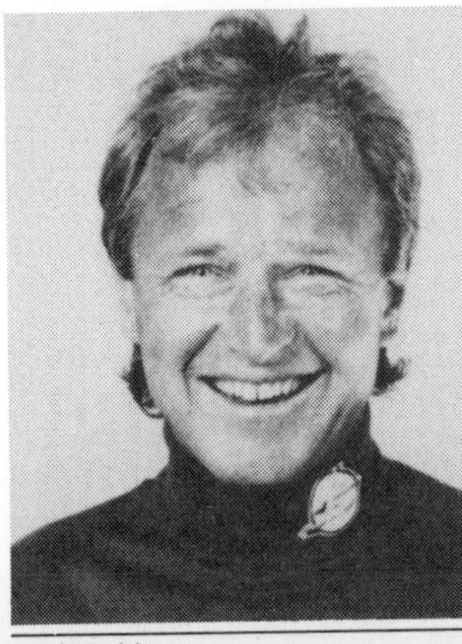

Randy Carlyle

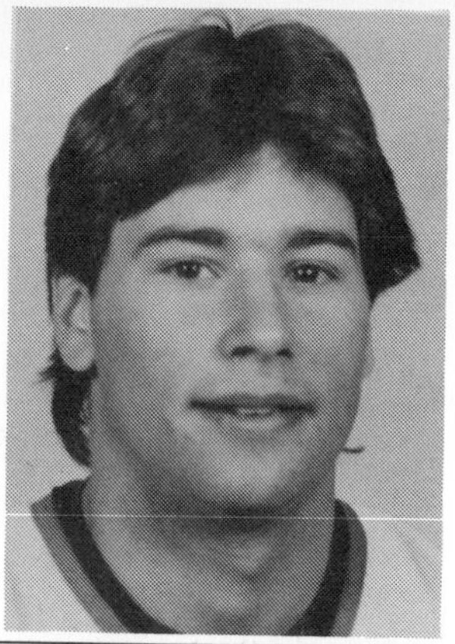
Bruce Cassidy

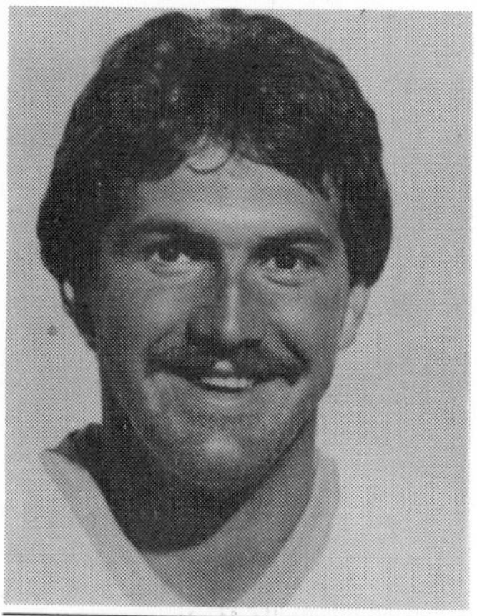
Richard David

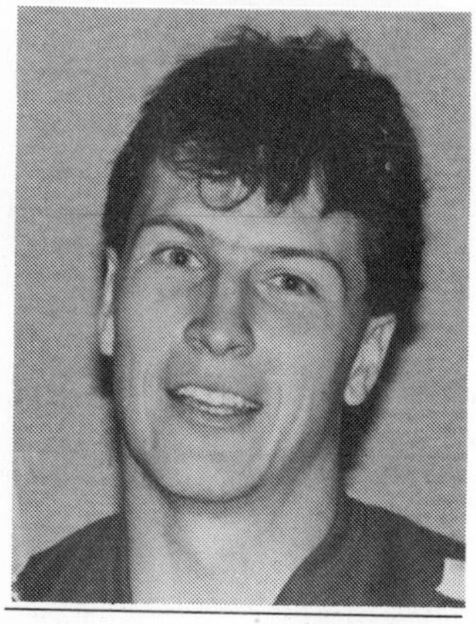
Jerome Dupont

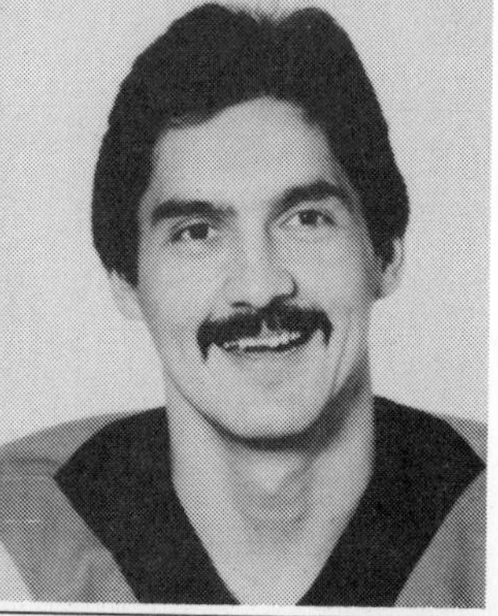
Ron Delorme

Name	NHL Teams	NHL Seasons	Regular Schedule GP	G	A	TP	PIM	Playoffs GP	G	A	TP	PIM	NHL Cup Wins	First NHL Season	Last NHL Season
Crawford, Bobby	Col., Det.	2	16	1	3	4	6	....	....	....	....	....		1980-81	1982-83
• Crawford, John	Bos.	13	547	38	140	178	202	66	4	13	17	36	2	1937-38	1949-50
Crawford, Lou	Bos.	2	26	2	1	3	29	....	....	....	....	....		1989-90	1991-92
Crawford, Marc	Van.	6	176	19	31	50	229	20	1	2	3	44		1981-82	1986-87
• Crawford, Rusty	Ott., Tor.,	2	38	10	3	13	51	2	2	1	3	0	1	1917-18	1918-19
Creighton, Dave	Bos., Chi., Tor., NYR	12	615	140	174	314	223	51	11	13	24	20		1948-49	1959-60
Creighton, Jimmy	Det.,	1	11	1	0	1	2	....	....	....	....	....		1930-31	1930-31
Cressman, Dave	Min.	2	85	6	8	14	37	....	....	....	....	....		1974-75	1975-76
Cressman, Glen	Mtl.	1	4	0	0	0	2	....	....	....	....	....		1956-57	1956-57
Crisofoli, Ed	Mtl.	1	9	0	1	1	4	....	....	....	....	....		1989-90	1989-90
Crisp, Terry	Bos., St.L., Phi., NYI	11	536	67	134	201	135	110	15	28	43	40	2	1965-66	1976-77
Croghen, Maurice	Mtl.M.	1	16	0	0	0	4	....	....	....	....	....		1937-38	1937-38
Crombeen, Mike	Cle., St.L., Hfd.	8	475	55	68	123	218	27	6	2	8	32		1977-78	1984-85
Crossett, Stan	Phi.,	1	21	0	0	0	10	....	....	....	....	....		1930-31	1930-31
Croteau, Gary	L.A., Det., Cal., K.C., Col.	12	684	144	175	319	143	11	3	2	5	8		1968-69	1979-80
Crowder, Bruce	Bos., Pit.	4	243	47	51	98	156	31	8	4	12	41		1981-82	1984-85
Crowder, Keith	Bos., L.A.	10	662	223	271	494	1346	85	14	22	36	218		1980-81	1989-90
Crowder, Troy	N.J., Det.	4	76	6	3	9	240	4	0	0	0	22		1987-88	1991-92
Crozier, Joe	Tor.,	1	5	0	3	3	2	....	....	....	....	....		1959-60	1959-60
Crutchfield, Nels	Mtl.	1	41	5	5	10	20	2	0	1	1	22		1934-35	1934-35
Culhane, Jim	Hfd.	1	6	0	1	1	4	....	....	....	....	....		1989-90	1989-90
Cullen, Barry	Tor., Det.	5	219	32	52	84	111	6	0	0	0	2		1955-56	1959-60
Cullen, Brian	Tor., NYR	7	326	56	100	156	92	19	3	0	3	2		1954-55	1960-61
Cullen, Ray	NYR, Det., Min., Van.	6	313	92	123	215	120	20	3	10	13	2		1965-66	1970-71
Cummins, Barry	Cal.	1	36	1	2	3	39	....	....	....	....	....		1973-74	1973-74
Cunningham, Bob	NYR	2	4	0	1	1	0	....	....	....	....	....		1960-61	1961-62
Cunningham, Jim	Phi.	1	1	0	0	0	4	....	....	....	....	....		1977-78	1977-78
Cunningham, Les	NYA, Chi.	2	60	7	19	26	21	1	0	0	0	2		1936-37	1939-40
Cupolo, Bill	Bos.	1	47	11	13	24	10	7	1	2	3	0		1944-45	1944-45
Currie, Glen	Wsh., L.A.	8	326	39	79	118	100	12	1	3	4	4		1979-80	1987-88
Currie, Hugh	Mtl.	1	1	0	0	0	0	....	....	....	....	....		1950-51	1950-51
Currie, Tony	St.L., Hfd., Van.	8	290	92	119	211	73	16	4	12	16	14		1977-78	1984-85
Curry, Floyd	Mtl.	11	601	105	99	204	147	91	23	17	40	38	4	1947-48	1957-58
Curtale, Tony	Cgy.	1	2	0	0	0	0	....	....	....	....	....		1980-81	1980-81
Curtis, Paul	Mtl., L.A., St.L.	4	185	3	34	37	151	5	0	0	0	2		1969-70	1972-73
Cushenan, Ian	Chi., Mtl., NYR, Det.	5	129	3	11	14	134	....	....	....	....	....		1956-57	1963-64
Cusson, Jean	Oak.	1	2	0	0	0	0	....	....	....	....	....		1967-68	1967-68
Cyr, Denis	Cgy., Chi., St.L.	6	193	41	43	84	36	4	0	0	0	0		1980-81	1985-86
Cyr, Paul	Buf., NYR, Hfd.	9	470	101	140	241	623	24	4	6	10	31		1982-83	1991-92

D

Name	NHL Teams	NHL Seasons	Regular Schedule GP	G	A	TP	PIM	Playoffs GP	G	A	TP	PIM	NHL Cup Wins	First NHL Season	Last NHL Season
Dahlin, Kjell	Mtl.	3	166	57	59	116	10	35	6	11	17	6	1	1985-86	1987-88
Dahlstrom, Cully	Chi.	8	342	88	118	206	52	29	6	8	14	4	1	1937-38	1944-45
Daigle, Alain	Chi.	6	389	56	50	106	122	17	0	1	1	0		1974-75	1979-80
Dailey, Bob	Van., Phi.	9	561	94	231	325	814	63	12	34	46	106		1973-74	1981-82
Daley, Frank	Det.	1	5	0	0	0	0	2	0	0	0	0		1928-29	1928-29
Daley, Pat	Wpg.	2	12	1	0	1	13	....	....	....	....	....		1979-80	1980-81
Dallman, Marty	Tor.	2	6	0	1	1	0	....	....	....	....	....		1987-88	1988-89
Dallman, Rod	NYI, Phi.	4	6	1	0	1	26	1	0	1	1	0		1987-88	1991-92
Dame, Bunny	Mtl.	1	34	2	5	7	4	....	....	....	....	....		1941-42	1941-42
Damore, Hank	NYR	1	4	1	0	1	2	....	....	....	....	....		1943-44	1943-44
Daoust, Dan	Mtl., Tor.	8	522	87	167	254	544	32	7	5	12	83		1982-83	1989-90
Dark, Michael	St.L.	2	43	5	6	11	14	....	....	....	....	....		1986-87	1987-88
Darragh, Harry	Pit., Phi., Bos., Tor.	8	308	68	49	117	50	16	1	3	4	4	1	1925-26	1932-33
• Darragh, Jack	Ott.	6	120	68	21	89	84	21	14	2	16	7	3	1917-18	1923-24
David, Richard	Que.	3	31	4	4	8	10	1	0	0	0	0		1979-80	1982-83
Davidson, Bob	Tor.,	12	491	94	160	254	398	82	5	17	22	79	2	1934-35	1945-46
Davidson, Gord	NYR	2	51	3	6	9	8	....	....	....	....	....		1942-43	1943-44
• Davie, Bob	Bos.	3	41	0	1	1	25	....	....	....	....	....		1933-34	1935-36
Davies, Ken	NYR	1	....	....	....	....	....	1	0	0	0	0		1947-48	1947-48
Davis, Bob	Det.	1	3	0	0	0	0	....	....	....	....	....		1932-33	1932-33
Davis, Kim	Pit., Tor.	4	36	5	7	12	12	4	0	0	0	0		1977-78	1980-81
Davis, Lorne	Mtl., Chi., Det., Bos.	6	95	8	12	20	20	18	3	1	4	10	1	1951-52	1959-60
Davis, Mal	Det., Buf.	5	100	31	22	53	34	7	1	0	1	0		1980-81	1985-86
Davison, Murray	Bos.	1	1	0	0	0	0	....	....	....	....	....		1965-66	1965-66
Dawes, Robert	Tor., Mtl.	4	32	2	7	4	6	10	0	0	0	2	1	1946-47	1950-51
• Day, Hap	Tor., NYA	14	581	86	116	202	601	53	4	7	11	56	1	1924-25	1937-38
Dea, Billy	Chi., NYR, Det., Pit.	8	397	67	54	121	44	11	2	0	2	6		1953-54	1970-71
Deacon, Don	Det.	3	30	6	4	10	6	2	2	1	3	0		1936-37	1939-40
Deadmarsh, Butch	Buf., ATL, K.C.	5	137	12	5	17	155	4	0	0	0	17		1970-71	1974-75
Dean, Barry	Col., Phi.	3	165	25	56	81	146	....	....	....	....	....		1976-77	1978-79
Debenedet, Nelson	Det., Pit.	2	46	10	4	14	13	....	....	....	....	....		1973-74	1974-75
DeBlois, Lucien	NYR, Col., Wpg., Mtl., Que., Tor.	15	993	249	276	525	814	52	7	6	13	38		1977-78	1991-92
Debol, David	Hfd.	2	92	26	26	52	4	3	0	0	0	0		1979-80	1980-81
Defazio, Dean	Pit.	1	22	0	2	2	28	....	....	....	....	....		1983-84	1983-84
DeGray, Dale	Cgy., Tor. L.A., Buf.	5	153	18	47	65	195	13	1	3	4	28		1985-86	1989-90
Delmonte, Armand	Bos.	1	1	0	0	0	0	....	....	....	....	....		1945-46	1945-46
Delorme, Gilbert	Mtl., St. L., Que., Det., Pit.	9	541	31	92	123	520	56	1	9	10	56		1981-82	1989-90
Delorme, Ron	Col., Van.	9	524	83	83	166	667	25	1	2	3	59		1976-77	1984-85
Delory, Valentine	NYR	1	1	0	0	0	0	....	....	....	....	....		1948-49	1948-49
Delparte, Guy	Col.	1	48	1	8	9	18	....	....	....	....	....		1976-77	1976-77
Delvecchio, Alex	Det.	24	1549	456	825	1281	383	121	35	69	104	29	3	1950-51	1973-74
• DeMarco, Ab	Chi., Tor., Bos., NYR	7	209	72	93	165	53	11	3	0	3	2		1938-39	1946-47
DeMarco, Albert	NYR, St.L., Pit., Van., L.A., Bos.	9	344	44	80	124	75	25	1	2	3	17		1969-70	1978-79
DeMeres, Tony	Mtl., NYR	6	83	20	22	42	23	3	0	0	0	0		1937-38	1943-44
Denis, Johnny	NYR	2	10	0	2	2	2	....	....	....	....	....		1946-47	1949-50
Denis, Lulu	Mtl.	2	3	0	1	1	0	....	....	....	....	....		1949-50	1950-51
• Denneny, Corbett	Tor., Ham., Chi.	9	175	99	29	128	130	15	7	4	11	6	2	1917-18	1927-28
• Denneny, Cy	Ott., Bos.	12	326	246	69	315	176	37	18	3	21	31	5	1917-18	1928-29
Dennis, Norm	St.L.	4	12	3	0	3	11	5	0	0	0	2		1968-69	1971-72
Denoird, Gerry	Tor.	1	15	0	0	0	0	....	....	....	....	....		1922-23	1922-23
Derlago, Bill	Van., Bos., Wpg., Que., Tor.	9	555	189	227	416	247	13	5	0	5	8		1978-79	1986-87
• Desaulniers, Gerard	Mtl.	3	8	0	2	2	4	....	....	....	....	....		1950-51	1953-54
Desilets, Joffre	Mtl., Chi.	5	192	37	45	82	57	7	1	0	1	7		1935-36	1939-40
Desjardins, Martin	Mtl.	1	8	0	2	2	2	....	....	....	....	....		1989-90	1989-90
Desjardins, Vic	Chi., NYR	2	87	6	15	21	27	16	0	0	0	0		1930-31	1931-32
Deslauriers, Jacques	Mtl.	1	2	0	0	0	0	....	....	....	....	....		1955-56	1955-56
Devine, Kevin	NYI	1	2	0	1	1	8	....	....	....	....	....		1982-83	1982-83
Dewar, Tom	NYR	1	9	0	2	2	4	....	....	....	....	....		1943-44	1943-44
Dewsbury, Al	Det., Chi.	9	347	30	78	108	365	14	1	5	6	60	1	1946-47	1955-56
Deziel, Michel	Buf.	1	....	....	....	....	....	1	0	0	0	0		1974-75	1974-75
Dheere, Marcel	Mtl.	1	11	1	2	3	2	5	0	0	0	6		1942-43	1942-43
Diachuk, Edward	Det.	1	12	0	0	0	19	....	....	....	....	....		1960-61	1960-61
Dick, Harry	Chi.	1	12	0	1	1	12	....	....	....	....	....		1946-47	1946-47
Dickens, Ernie	Tor., Chi.	6	278	12	44	56	48	13	0	0	0	4	1	1941-42	1950-51
Dickenson, Herb	NYR	2	48	18	17	35	10	....	....	....	....	....		1951-52	1952-53
Dietrich, Don	Chi., N.J.	2	28	0	7	7	10	....	....	....	....	....		1983-84	1985-86
• Dill, Bob	NYR	2	76	15	15	30	135	....	....	....	....	....		1943-44	1944-45
Dillabough, Bob	Det., Bos., Pit., Oak.	7	283	32	54	86	76	17	3	0	3	0		1961-62	1969-70
• Dillon, Cecil	NYR, Det.	10	453	167	131	298	105	43	14	9	23	14	1	1930-31	1939-40
Dillon, Gary	Col.	1	13	1	1	2	29	....	....	....	....	....		1980-81	1980-81
Dillon, Wayne	NYR, Wpg.	4	229	43	66	109	60	3	0	1	1	0		1975-76	1979-80
Dineen, Bill	Det., Chi.	5	323	51	44	95	122	37	1	1	2	18	2	1953-54	1957-58
Dineen, Gary	Min.	1	4	0	1	1	0	....	....	....	....	....		1968-69	1968-69
Dineen, Peter	L.A., Det.	2	13	0	2	2	13	....	....	....	....	....		1986-87	1989-90
Dinsmore, Chuck	Mtl.M	4	100	6	2	8	44	12	1	0	1	6	1	1924-25	1929-30
Dionne, Marcel	Det., L.A., NYR	18	1348	731	1040	1771	600	49	21	24	45	17		1971-72	1988-89
Djoos, Per	Det., NYR	3	82	2	31	33	58	....	....	....	....	....		1990-91	1992-93
Doak, Gary	Det., Bos., Van., NYR	16	789	23	107	130	908	78	2	4	6	121	1	1965-66	1980-81
Dobson, Jim	Min., Col.	3	11	0	0	0	6	....	....	....	....	....		1979-80	1981-82
• Doherty, Fred	Mtl.	1	3	0	0	0	0	....	....	....	....	....		1918-19	1918-19
Donaldson, Gary	Chi.	1	1	0	0	0	0	....	....	....	....	....	2	1973-74	1973-74
Donnelly, Babe	Mtl.M.	1	34	0	1	1	14	2	0	0	0	0		1926-27	1926-27

Name	NHL Teams	NHL Seasons	Regular Schedule					Playoffs					NHL Cup Wins	First NHL Season	Last NHL Season
			GP	G	A	TP	PIM	GP	G	A	TP	PIM			
Donnelly, Dave	Bos., Chi., Edm.	5	137	15	24	39	150	5	0	0	0	0		1983-84	1987-88
Doran, Red (I.)	Det.	1	24	3	2	5	10	....	....	....	....	....		1946-47	1946-47
• Doran, Red (J.)	NYA., Det., Mtl.	5	98	5	10	15	110	3	0	0	0	0		1933-34	1939-40
• Doraty, Ken	Chi., Tor., Det.	5	103	15	26	41	24	15	7	2	9	2		1926-27	1937-38
Dore, Andre	NYR, St.L., Que.	7	257	14	81	95	261	23	1	2	3	32		1978-79	1984-85
Dore, Daniel	Que.	2	17	2	3	5	59	....	....	....	....	....		1989-90	1990-91
Dorey, Jim	Tor., NYR	4	232	25	74	99	553	11	0	2	2	40		1968-69	1971-72
Dorion, Dan	N.J.	2	4	1	1	2	2	....	....	....	....	....		1985-86	1987-88
Dornhoefer, Gary	Bos., Phi.	14	787	214	328	542	1291	80	17	19	36	203	2	1963-64	1977-78
Dorohoy, Eddie	Mtl.	1	16	0	0	0	6	....	....	....	....	....		1948-49	1948-49
Douglas, Jordy	Hfd., Min., Wpg.	6	268	76	62	138	160	6	0	0	0	4		1979-80	1984-85
Douglas, Kent	Tor., Oak., Det.	7	428	33	115	148	631	19	1	3	4	33	1	1962-63	1968-69
Douglas, Les	Det.	4	52	6	12	18	8	10	3	2	5	0	1	1940-41	1946-47
Downie, Dave	Tor.	1	11	0	1	1	2	....	....	....	....	....		1932-33	1932-33
• Draper, Bruce	Tor.	1	1	0	0	0	0	....	....	....	....	....		1962-63	1962-63
• Drillon, Gordie	Tor., Mtl.	7	311	155	139	294	56	50	26	15	41	10	1	1936-37	1942-43
Driscoll, Pete	Edm.	2	60	3	8	11	97	3	0	0	0	0		1979-80	1980-81
Drolet, Rene	Phi., Det.	2	2	0	0	0	0	....	....	....	....	....		1971-72	1974-75
Drouillard, Clarence	Det.	1	10	0	1	1	0	....	....	....	....	....		1937-38	1937-38
Drouin, Jude	Mtl., Min., NYI, Wpg.	12	666	151	305	456	346	72	27	41	68	33		1968-69	1980-81
• Drouin, Polly	Mtl.	6	173	23	50	73	80	5	0	1	1	5		1935-36	1940-41
Drummond, John	NYR	1	2	0	0	0	0	....	....	....	....	....		1944-45	1944-45
Drury, Herb	Pit., Phi.	6	213	24	13	37	203	4	1	1	2	0		1925-26	1930-31
Dube, Gilles	Mtl., Det.	2	12	1	2	3	2	2	0	0	0	0	1	1949-50	1953-54
Dube, Norm	K.C.	2	57	8	10	18	54	....	....	....	....	....		1974-75	1975-76
Dudley, Rick	Buf., Wpg.	6	309	75	99	174	292	25	7	2	9	69		1972-73	1980-81
Duff, Dick	Tor., NYR, Mtl., L.A., Buf.	18	1030	283	289	572	743	114	30	49	79	78	6	1954-55	1971-72
Dufour, Luc	Bos., Que., St.L.	3	167	23	21	44	199	18	1	0	1	32		1982-83	1984-85
Dufour, Marc	NYR, L.A.	3	14	1	0	1	2	....	....	....	....	....		1963-64	1968-69
Duggan, Jack	Ott.	1	27	0	0	0	0	2	0	0	0	0		1925-26	1925-26
Duggan, Ken	Min.	1	1	0	0	0	0	....	....	....	....	....		1987-88	1987-88
Duguay, Ron	NYR, Det., Pit., L.A.	12	864	274	346	620	582	89	31	22	53	118		1977-78	1988-89
• Duguid, Lorne	Mtl.M, Det., Bos.	6	135	9	15	24	57	2	0	0	0	4		1931-32	1936-37
Dumart, Woody	Bos.	16	771	211	218	429	99	82	12	15	27	23	2	1935-36	1953-54
Dunbar, Dale	Van., Bos.	2	2	0	0	0	2	....	....	....	....	....		1985-86	1988-89
• Duncan, Art	Det., Tor.	5	156	18	16	34	225	5	0	0	0	4		1926-27	1930-31
Duncan, Iain	Wpg.	4	127	34	55	89	149	11	0	3	3	6		1986-87	1990-91
Dundas, Rocky	Tor.	1	5	0	0	0	14	....	....	....	....	....		1989-90	1989-90
Dunlap, Frank	Tor.	1	15	0	1	1	2	....	....	....	....	....		1943-44	1943-44
Dunlop, Blake	Min., Phi., St.L., Det.	11	550	130	274	404	172	40	4	10	14	18		1973-74	1983-84
Dunn, Dave	Van., Tor.	3	184	14	41	55	313	10	1	1	2	41		1973-74	1975-76
Dunn, Richie	Buf., Cgy., Hfd.	12	483	36	140	176	314	36	3	15	18	24		1977-78	1988-89
Dupere, Denis	Tor., Wsh., St.L., K.C., Col.	8	421	80	99	179	66	16	1	0	1	0		1970-71	1977-78
Dupont, Andre	NYR, St.L., Phi., Que.	13	810	59	185	244	1986	140	14	18	32	352	2	1970-71	1982-83
Dupont, Jerome	Chi., Tor.	6	214	7	29	36	468	20	0	2	2	56		1981-82	1986-87
Dupont, Norm	Mtl., Wpg., Hfd.	5	256	55	85	140	52	13	4	2	6	0		1979-80	1983-84
Durbano, Steve	St.L., Pit., K.C., Col.	6	220	13	60	73	1127	5	0	2	2	8		1972-73	1978-79
Duris, Vitezslav	Tor.	2	89	3	20	23	62	3	0	1	1	2		1980-81	1982-83
Dussault, Norm	Mtl.	4	206	31	62	93	47	7	3	1	4	0		1947-48	1950-51
Dutkowski, Duke	Chi., NYA, NYR	5	200	16	30	46	172	6	0	0	0	6		1926-27	1933-34
• Dutton, Red	Mtl.M, NYA	10	449	29	67	96	871	18	1	0	1	33		1926-27	1935-36
Dvorak, Miroslav	Phi.	3	193	11	74	85	51	18	0	2	2	6		1982-83	1984-85
Dwyer, Mike	Col., Cgy.	4	31	2	6	8	25	1	1	0	1	0		1978-79	1981-82
Dyck, Henry	NYR	1	1	0	0	0	0	....	....	....	....	....		1943-44	1943-44
• Dye, Babe	Tor., Ham., Chi., NYA	11	269	202	41	243	205	15	11	2	13	11	1	1919-20	1930-31
Dykstra, Steven	Buf., Edm., Pit., Hfd.	5	217	8	32	40	545	1	0	0	0	2		1985-86	1989-90
Dyte, John	Chi.	1	27	1	0	1	31	....	....	....	....	....		1943-44	1943-44

E

Name	NHL Teams	NHL Seasons	GP	G	A	TP	PIM	GP	G	A	TP	PIM	NHL Cup Wins	First NHL Season	Last NHL Season
Eakin, Bruce	Cgy., Det.	4	13	2	2	4	4	....	....	....	....	....		1981-82	1985-86
Eatough, Jeff	Buf.	1	1	0	0	0	0	....	....	....	....	....		1981-82	1981-82
Eaves, Mike	Min., Cgy.	8	324	83	143	226	80	43	7	10	17	14		1978-79	1985-86
Eaves, Murray	Wpg., Det.	8	57	4	13	17	9	4	0	1	1	2		1980-81	1989-90
Ecclestone, Tim	St.L., Det., Tor., Atl.	11	692	126	233	359	346	48	6	11	17	76		1967-68	1977-78
Edberg, Rolf	Wsh.	3	184	45	58	103	24	....	....	....	....	....		1978-79	1980-81
• Eddolls, Frank	Mtl., NYR	8	317	23	43	66	114	31	0	2	2	10	1	1944-45	1951-52
Edestrand, Darryl	St.L., Phi., Pit., Bos., L.A.	10	455	34	90	124	404	42	3	9	12	57		1967-68	1978-79
Edmundson, Garry	Mtl., Tor.	3	43	4	6	10	49	11	0	1	1	8		1951-52	1960-61
Edur, Tom	Col., Pit	2	158	17	70	87	67	....	....	....	....	....		1976-77	1977-78
Egan, Pat	Bro., Det., Bos., NYR	11	554	77	153	230	776	44	9	4	13	44		1939-40	1950-51
Egers, Jack	NYR, St.L., Wsh.	7	284	64	69	133	154	32	5	6	11	32		1969-70	1975-76
Ehman, Gerry	Bos., Det., Tor., Oak, Cal.	9	429	96	118	214	100	41	10	10	20	12	1	1957-58	1970-71
Eldebrink, Anders	Van., Que.	2	55	3	11	14	29	14	0	0	0	0		1981-82	1982-83
Elik, Boris	Det.	1	3	0	0	0	0	....	....	....	....	....		1962-63	1962-63
Elliot, Fred	Ott.	1	43	2	0	2	6	....	....	....	....	....		1928-29	1928-29
Ellis, Ron	Tor.	16	1034	332	308	640	207	70	18	8	26	20	1	1963-64	1980-81
Eloranta, Kari	Cgy., St.L.	5	267	13	103	116	155	26	1	7	8	19		1981-82	1986-87
Emberg, Eddie	Mtl.	1	....	....	....	....	....	2	1	0	1	0		1944-45	1944-45
• Emms, Hap	Mtl.M, NYA, Det., Bos.	10	320	36	53	89	311	14	0	0	0	12		1926-27	1937-38
Engblom, Brian	Mtl., Wsh., L.A., Buf., Cgy.	11	659	29	177	206	599	48	3	9	12	43	3	1976-77	1986-87
Engele, Jerry	Min.	3	100	2	13	15	162	2	0	1	1	0		1975-76	1977-78
English, John	L.A.	1	3	1	3	4	4	1	0	0	0	0		1987-88	1987-88
Ennis, Jim	Edm.	1	5	1	0	1	10	....	....	....	....	....		1987-88	1987-88
Erickson, Aut	Bos., Chi., Oak., Tor.	7	227	7	84	31	182	7	0	0	0	2	1	1959-60	1969-70
Erickson, Grant	Bos., Min.	2	6	1	0	1	4	....	....	....	....	....		1968-69	1969-70
Eriksson, Peter	Edm.	1	20	3	3	6	24	....	....	....	....	....		1989-90	1989-90
Eriksson, Rolie	Min., Van.	3	193	48	95	143	26	2	1	0	1	0		1976-77	1978-79
Eriksson, Thomas	Phi.	5	208	22	76	98	107	19	0	3	3	6		1980-81	1985-86
Erixon, Jan	NYR	10	556	57	159	216	167	58	7	7	14	16		1983-84	1992-93
Esposito, Phil	Chi., Bos., NYR	18	1282	717	873	1590	910	130	61	76	137	137	2	1963-64	1980-81
Evans, Chris	Tor., Buf., St.L., Det., K.C.	5	241	19	42	61	143	12	1	1	2	8		1969-70	1974-75
Evans, Daryl	L.A., Wsh., Tor.	6	113	22	30	52	25	11	5	8	13	12		1981-82	1986-87
Evans, Jack	NYR, Chi.	14	752	19	80	99	989	56	2	2	4	97	1	1948-49	1962-63
Evans, John	Phi.	3	103	14	25	39	34	1	0	0	0	0		1978-79	1982-83
Evans, Paul	Tor.	2	11	1	1	2	21	2	0	0	0	0		1976-77	1977-78
Evans, Shawn	St. L., NYI	2	9	1	0	1	2	....	....	....	....	....		1985-86	1989-90
Evans, Stewart	Det., Mtl.M., Mtl.	8	367	28	49	77	425	26	0	0	0	20	1	1930-31	1938-39
Ezinicki, Bill	Tor., Bos., NYR	9	368	79	105	184	713	40	5	8	13	87	3	1944-45	1954-55

F

Name	NHL Teams	NHL Seasons	GP	G	A	TP	PIM	GP	G	A	TP	PIM	NHL Cup Wins	First NHL Season	Last NHL Season
Fahey, Trevor	NYR	1	1	0	0	0	0	....	....	....	....	....		1964-65	1964-65
Fairbairn, Bill	NYR, Min. St.L.	11	658	162	261	423	173	54	13	22	35	42		1968-69	1978-79
Falkenberg, Bob	Det.	5	54	1	5	6	26	....	....	....	....	....		1966-67	1971-72
Farrant, Walt	Chi.	1	1	0	0	0	0	....	....	....	....	....		1943-44	1943-44
Farrish, Dave	NYR, Que, Tor.	7	430	17	110	127	440	14	0	2	2	24		1976-77	1983-84
Fashoway, Gordie	Chi.	1	13	3	2	5	14	....	....	....	....	....		1950-51	1950-51
Faubert, Mario	Pit.	7	231	21	90	111	292	10	2	2	4	6		1974-75	1981-82
Faulkner, Alex	Tor., Det.	3	101	15	17	32	15	12	5	0	5	2		1961-62	1963-64
Fauss, Ted	Tor.	2	28	0	2	2	15	....	....	....	....	....		1986-87	1987-88
Feamster, Dave	Chi.	4	169	13	24	37	155	33	3	5	8	61		1981-82	1984-85
Featherstone, Tony	Oak., Cal., Min.	3	130	17	21	38	65	2	0	0	0	0		1969-70	1973-74
Federko, Bernie	St.L., Det.	14	1000	369	761	1130	487	91	35	66	101	83		1976-77	1989-90
Felix, Chris	Wsh.	4	35	1	12	13	10	2	0	1	1	0		1987-88	1990-91
Feltrin, Tony	Pit., NYR	4	48	3	3	6	65	....	....	....	....	....		1980-81	1985-86
Fenton, Paul	Hfd., NYR, L.A., Wpg., Tor., Cgy., S.J.	8	411	100	83	183	198	17	4	1	5	27		1984-85	1991-92
Fenyves, David	Buf., Phi.	9	206	3	32	35	119	11	0	0	0	9		1982-83	1990-91
Fergus, Tom	Bos., Tor., Van.	12	726	235	346	581	499	65	21	17	38	48		1981-82	1992-93
Ferguson,	Chi.	1	1	0	0	0	0	....	....	....	....	....		1939-40	1939-40
Ferguson, George	Tor., Pit, Min	12	797	160	238	398	431	86	14	23	37	44		1972-73	1983-84
Ferguson, John	Mtl.	8	500	145	158	303	1214	85	20	18	38	260	5	1963-64	1970-71
Ferguson, Lorne	Bos., Det., Chi.	8	422	82	80	162	193	31	6	3	9	24		1949-50	1958-59

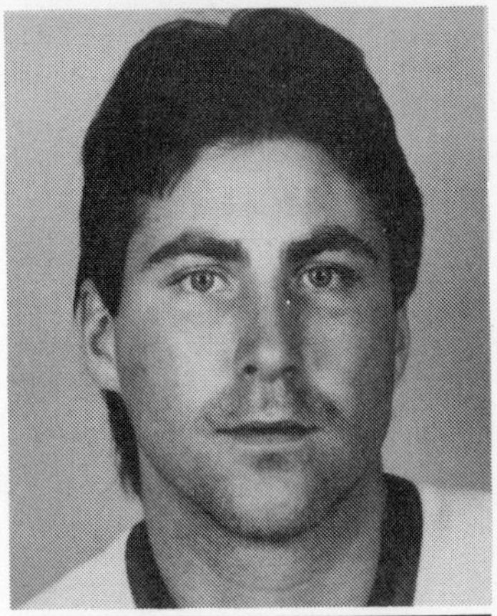

Dave Donnelly

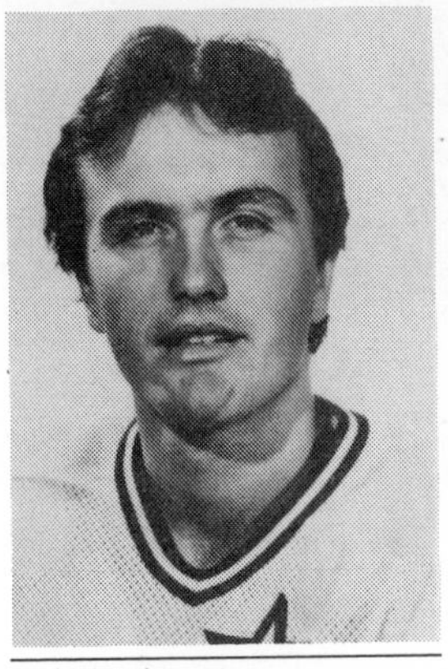

Jordy Douglas

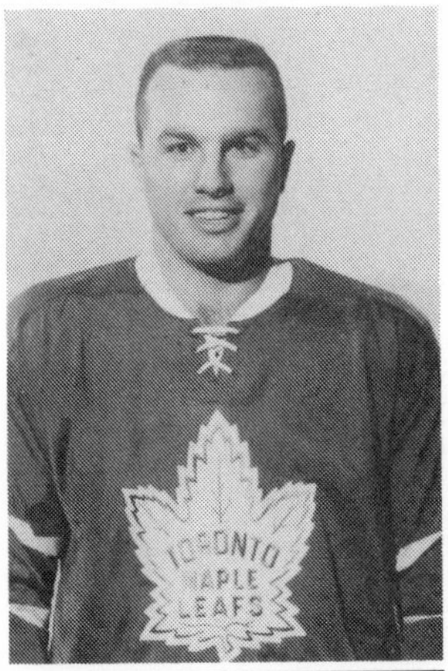

Ron Ellis

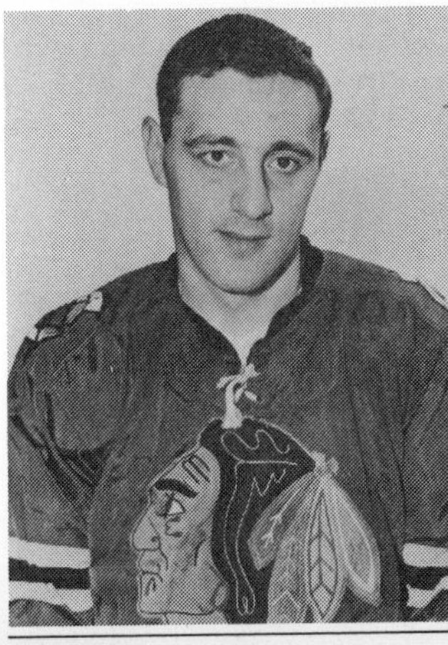

Phil Esposito

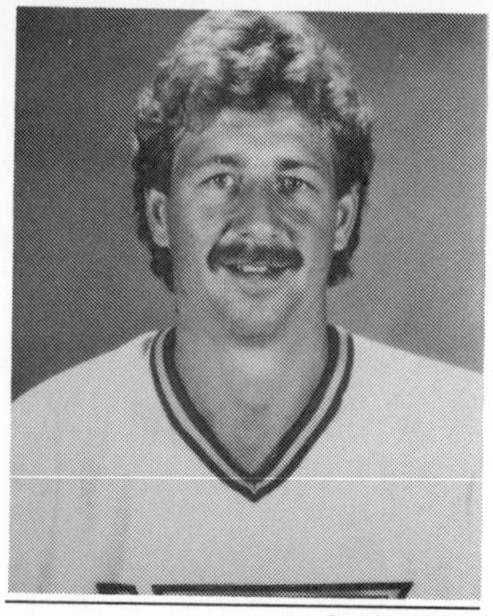

Bernie Federko

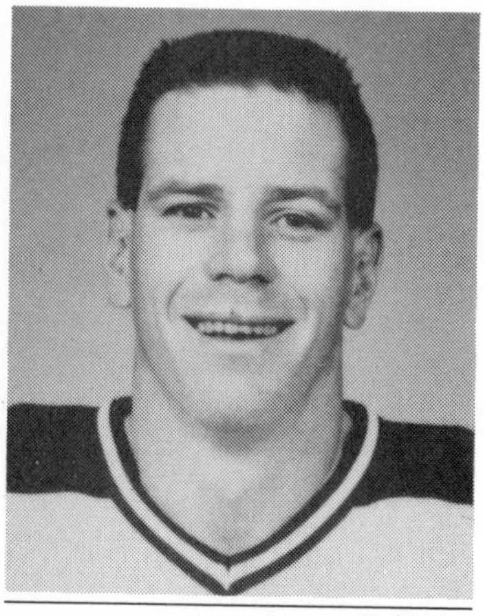

Paul Fenton

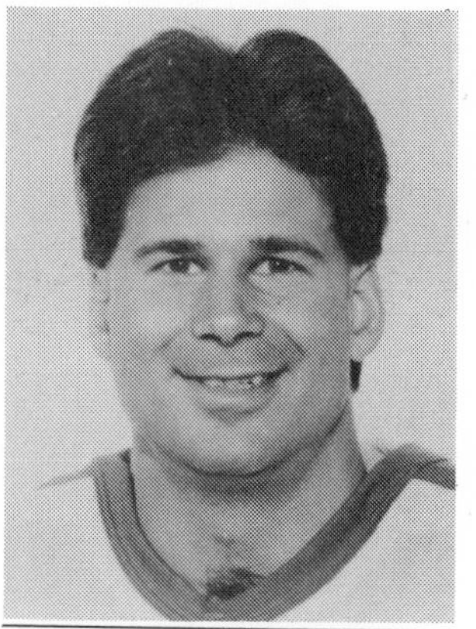

Jim Fox

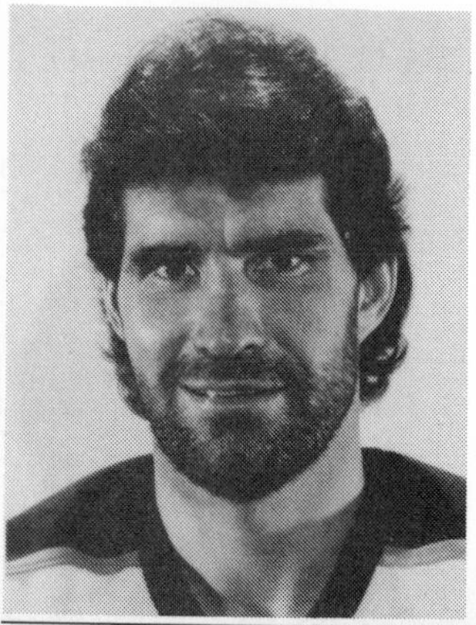

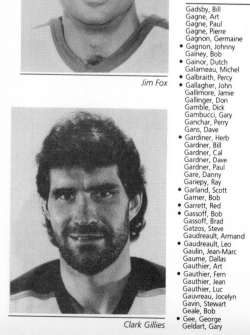

Clark Gillies

Name	NHL Teams	NHL Seasons	Regular Schedule					Playoffs					NHL Cup Wins	First NHL Season	Last NHL Season
			GP	G	A	TP	PIM	GP	G	A	TP	PIM			
Ferguson, Norm	Oak., Cal.	4	279	73	66	139	72	10	1	4	5	7		1968-69	1971-72
Fidler, Mike	Cle., Min, Hfd., Chi.	7	271	84	97	181	124	....	....	....	....	....		1976-77	1982-83
Field, Wilf	Bro., Mtl., Chi.	6	218	17	25	42	151	3	0	0	0	0		1936-37	1944-45
Fielder, Guyle	Det., Chi., Bos.	4	9	0	0	0	2	6	0	0	0	2		1950-51	1957-58
Fillion, Bob	Mtl.	7	327	42	61	103	84	33	7	4	11	10	2	1943-44	1949-50
Fillion, Marcel	Bos.	1	1	0	0	0	0	....	....	....	....	....		1944-45	1944-45
• Filmore, Tommy	Det., NYA, Bos.	4	116	15	12	27	33	....	....	....	....	....		1930-31	1933-34
Finkbeiner, Lloyd	NYA	1	1	0	0	0	0	....	....	....	....	....		1940-41	1940-41
Finney, Sid	Chi.	3	59	10	7	17	4	7	0	0	0	2		1951-52	1953-54
Finnigan, Ed	Bos.	1	3	0	0	0	0	....	....	....	....	....		1935-36	1935-36
• Finnigan, Frank	Ott., Tor., St.L.	14	555	115	88	203	405	39	6	9	15	22	2	1923-24	1936-37
Fischer, Ron	Buf.	2	18	0	7	7	6	....	....	....	....	....		1981-82	1982-83
Fisher, Alvin	Tor.	1	9	1	0	1	4	....	....	....	....	....		1924-25	1924-25
Fisher, Dunc	NYR, Bos., Det.	7	275	45	70	115	104	21	4	4	8	14		1947-48	1958-59
Fisher, Joe	Det.	4	66	8	12	20	13	15	2	1	3	6	1	1939-40	1942-43
Fitchner, Bob	Que	2	78	12	20	32	59	3	0	0	0	10		1979-80	1980-81
Fitzpatrick, Ross	Phi.	4	20	5	2	7	0	....	....	....	....	....		1982-83	1985-86
Fitzpatrick, Sandy	NYR, Min.	2	22	3	6	9	8	12	0	0	0	0		1964-65	1967-68
Flaman, Fern	Bos., Tor.	17	910	34	174	208	1370	63	4	8	12	93	1	1944-45	1960-61
Fleming, Reggie	Mtl., Chi., Bos., NYR, Phi., Buf.	12	749	108	132	240	1468	50	3	6	9	106	1	1959-60	1970-71
Flesch,	Ham.	1	1	0	0	0	0	....	....	....	....	....		1920-21	1920-21
Flesch, John	Min, Pit, Col.	4	124	18	23	41	117	....	....	....	....	....		1974-75	1979-80
Fletcher, Steven	Mtl., Wpg.	2	3	0	0	0	5	1	0	0	0	5		1987-88	1988-89
Flett, Bill	L.A., Phi., Tor., Atl, Edm.	11	689	202	215	417	501	52	7	16	23	42	1	1967-68	1979-80
Flichel, Todd	Wpg.	4	6	0	1	1	4	....	....	....	....	....		1987-88	1989-90
Flockhart, Rob	Van., Min	5	55	2	5	7	14	1	1	0	1	2		1976-77	1980-81
Flockhart, Ron	Phi., Pit., Mtl., St.L., Bos.	9	453	145	183	328	208	29	11	18	29	16		1980-81	1988-89
Floyd, Larry	N.J.	2	12	2	3	5	9	....	....	....	....	....		1982-83	1983-84
Fogolin, Lee	Buf., Edm.	13	924	44	195	239	1318	108	5	19	24	173	2	1974-75	1986-87
Fogolin, Lidio (Lee)	Det., Chi.	9	427	10	48	58	575	28	0	2	2	30	1	1947-48	1955-56
Folco, Peter	Van.	1	2	0	0	0	0	....	....	....	....	....		1973-74	1973-74
Foley, Gerry	Tor., NYR, L.A.	4	142	9	14	23	99	9	0	1	1	2		1954-55	1968-69
Foley, Rick	Chi., Phi., Det.	3	67	11	26	37	180	4	0	1	1	4		1970-71	1973-74
Folk, Bill	Det.	2	12	0	0	0	4	....	....	....	....	....		1951-52	1952-53
Fontaine, Len	Det.	2	46	8	11	19	10	....	....	....	....	....		1972-73	1973-74
Fontas, Jon	Min.	2	2	0	0	0	0	....	....	....	....	....		1979-80	1980-81
Fonteyne, Val	Det., NYR, Pit.	13	820	75	154	229	26	59	3	10	13	8		1959-60	1971-72
Fontinato, Louie	NYR, Mtl.	9	535	26	78	104	1247	21	0	2	2	42		1954-55	1962-63
Forbes, Dave	Bos., Wsh.	6	363	64	64	128	341	45	1	4	5	13		1973-74	1978-79
Forbes, Mike	Bos., Edm.	3	50	1	11	12	41	....	....	....	....	....		1977-78	1981-82
Forey, Connie	St.L.	1	4	0	0	0	2	....	....	....	....	....		1973-74	1973-74
Forsey, Jack	Tor.	1	19	7	9	16	10	3	0	1	1	0		1942-43	1942-43
Forslund, Gus	Ott.	1	48	4	9	13	2	....	....	....	....	....		1932-33	1932-33
Forslund, Tomas	Cgy.	2	44	5	11	16	12	....	....	....	....	....		1991-92	1992-93
Forsyth, Alex	Wsh.	1	1	0	0	0	0	....	....	....	....	....		1976-77	1976-77
Fortier, Charles	Mtl.	1	1	0	0	0	0	....	....	....	....	....	1	1923-24	1923-24
Fortier, Dave	Tor., NYI, Van.	4	205	8	21	29	335	20	0	2	2	33		1972-73	1976-77
Fortin, Ray	St.L.	3	92	2	6	8	33	6	0	0	0	8		1967-68	1969-70
Foster, Dwight	Bos., Col., N.J., Det.	10	541	111	163	274	420	35	5	12	17	4		1977-78	1986-87
Foster, Harry	NYR, Bos., Det.	4	83	3	2	5	32	....	....	....	....	....		1929-31	1934-35
Foster, Herb	NYR	2	5	1	0	1	5	....	....	....	....	....		1940-41	1947-48
Fotiu, Nick	NYR, Hfd., Cgy., Phi., Edm.	13	646	60	77	137	1362	38	0	4	4	67		1976-77	1988-89
• Fowler, Jimmy	Tor.	3	135	18	29	47	39	18	0	3	3	2		1936-37	1938-39
Fowler, Tom	Chi.	1	24	0	1	1	18	....	....	....	....	....		1946-47	1946-47
Fox, Greg	Atl, Chi., Pit.	8	494	14	92	106	637	44	1	9	10	67		1977-78	1984-85
Fox, Jim	L.A.	10	578	186	293	479	143	22	4	8	12	0		1980-81	1989-90
• Foyston, Frank	Det.	2	64	17	7	24	32	....	....	....	....	....		1926-27	1927-28
Frampton, Bob	Mtl.	1	2	0	0	0	0	3	0	0	0	0		1949-50	1949-50
Franceschetti, Lou	Wsh., Tor., Buf.	10	459	59	81	140	747	44	3	2	5	111		1981-82	1991-92
Francis, Bobby	Det.	1	14	2	0	2	0	....	....	....	....	....		1982-83	1982-83
Fraser, Archie	NYR	1	3	0	1	1	0	....	....	....	....	....		1943-44	1943-44
Fraser, Curt	Van., Chi., Min.	12	704	193	240	433	1306	65	15	18	33	198		1978-79	1989-90
Fraser, Gord	Chi., Det., Mtl., Pit., Phi.	5	144	24	12	36	224	2	1	0	1	6		1926-27	1930-31
Fraser, Harry	Chi.	1	21	5	4	9	0	....	....	....	....	....		1944-45	1944-45
Fraser, Jack	Ham.	1	1	0	0	0	0	....	....	....	....	....		1923-24	1923-24
Frawley, Dan	Chi., Pit.	6	273	37	40	77	674	1	0	0	0	0		1983-84	1988-89
• Frederickson, Frank	Det., Bos., Pit.	5	165	39	34	73	207	10	2	5	7	26	1	1926-27	1930-31
Frew, Irv	Mtl.M, St.L., Mtl.	3	95	2	5	7	146	4	0	0	0	6		1933-34	1935-36
Friday, Tim	Det.	1	23	0	3	3	6	....	....	....	....	....		1985-86	1985-86
Fridgen, Dan	Hfd.	2	13	2	3	5	2	....	....	....	....	....		1981-82	1982-83
Friest, Ron	Min.	3	64	7	7	14	191	6	1	0	1	7		1980-81	1982-83
Frig, Len	Chi., Cal., Cle., St.L.	7	311	13	51	64	479	14	2	1	3	0		1972-73	1979-80
Frost, Harry	Bos.	1	3	0	0	0	0	1	0	0	0	0		1938-39	1938-39
Frycer, Miroslav	Que., Tor., Det., Edm.	8	415	147	183	330	486	17	3	8	11	16		1981-82	1988-89
Fryday, Bob	Mtl.	2	5	1	0	1	0	....	....	....	....	....		1949-50	1951-52
Ftorek, Robbie	Det., Que, NYR	8	334	77	150	227	262	19	9	6	15	28		1972-73	1984-85
Fullan, Lawrence	Wsh.	1	4	1	0	1	0	....	....	....	....	....		1974-75	1974-75
Fusco, Mark	Hfd.	2	80	3	12	15	42	....	....	....	....	....		1983-84	1984-85

G

Name	NHL Teams	NHL Seasons	GP	G	A	TP	PIM	GP	G	A	TP	PIM	NHL Cup Wins	First NHL Season	Last NHL Season
Gadsby, Bill	Chi., NYR, Det.	20	1248	130	437	567	1539	67	4	23	27	92		1946-47	1965-66
Gagne, Art	Mtl., Bos., Ott., Det.	6	228	67	33	100	257	11	2	1	3	20		1926-27	1931-32
Gagne, Paul	Col., N.J., Tor., NYI	8	390	110	101	211	127	....	....	....	....	....		1980-81	1989-90
Gagne, Pierre	Bos.	1	2	0	0	0	0	....	....	....	....	....		1959-60	1959-60
Gagnon, Germaine	Mtl., NYI, Chi., K.C.	5	259	40	101	141	72	19	2	3	5	2		1971-72	1975-76
• Gagnon, Johnny	Mtl., Bos., NYA	10	454	120	141	261	295	32	12	12	24	37	1	1930-31	1939-40
Gainey, Bob	Mtl.	16	1160	239	262	501	585	182	25	48	73	151	5	1973-74	1988-89
• Gainor, Dutch	Bos., NYR, Ott., Mtl.M	7	243	51	56	107	129	25	2	1	3	14	2	1927-28	1934-35
Galarneau, Michel	Hfd.	3	78	7	10	17	34	....	....	....	....	....		1980-81	1982-83
• Galbraith, Percy	Bos., Ott.	8	347	29	31	60	223	31	4	7	11	24		1926-27	1933-34
• Gallagher, John	Mtl.M, Det., NYA	7	204	14	19	33	153	22	2	3	5	27	1	1930-31	1938-39
Gallimore, Jamie	Min.	1	2	0	0	0	0	....	....	....	....	....		1977-78	1977-78
Gallinger, Don	Bos.	5	222	65	88	153	89	23	5	5	10	19		1942-43	1947-48
Gamble, Dick	Mtl., Chi., Tor.	8	195	41	41	82	66	14	1	2	3	4	2	1950-51	1966-67
Gambucci, Gary	Min.	2	51	2	7	9	9	....	....	....	....	....		1971-72	1973-74
Ganchar, Perry	St. L., Mtl., Pit.	4	42	3	7	10	36	7	3	1	4	0		1983-84	1988-89
Gans, Dave	L.A.	2	6	0	0	0	2	....	....	....	....	....		1982-83	1985-86
• Gardiner, Herb	Mtl., Chi.	3	101	10	9	19	52	7	0	1	1	14		1926-27	1928-29
Gardner, Bill	Chi., Hfd.	9	380	73	115	188	68	45	3	8	11	17		1980-81	1988-89
Gardner, Cal	NYR, Tor., Chi., Bos.	12	696	154	238	392	517	61	7	10	17	20	2	1945-46	1956-57
Gardner, Dave	Mtl., St.L., Cal., Cle., Phi.	7	350	75	115	190	41	....	....	....	....	....		1972-73	1979-80
Gardner, Paul	Col., Tor., Pit., Wsh., Buf.	7	447	201	201	402	207	16	2	6	8	14		1976-77	1985-86
Gare, Danny	Buf., Det., Edm.	13	827	354	331	685	1285	64	25	21	46	195		1974-75	1986-87
Gariepy, Ray	Bos., Tor.	2	36	1	6	7	43	....	....	....	....	....		1953-54	1955-56
• Garland, Scott	Tor., L.A.	3	91	13	24	37	115	7	1	2	3	35		1975-76	1978-79
Garner, Bob	Pit.	1	1	0	0	0	0	....	....	....	....	....		1982-83	1982-83
• Garrett, Red	NYR	1	23	1	1	2	18	....	....	....	....	....		1942-43	1942-43
• Gassoff, Bob	St.L.	4	245	11	47	58	866	9	0	1	1	16		1973-74	1976-77
Gassoff, Brad	Van.	4	122	19	17	36	163	3	0	0	0	0		1975-76	1978-79
Gatzos, Steve	Pit.	4	89	15	20	35	83	1	0	0	0	0		1981-82	1984-85
Gaudreault, Armand	Bos.	1	44	15	9	24	27	7	0	2	2	8		1944-45	1944-45
• Gaudreault, Leo	Mtl.	3	67	8	4	12	30	....	....	....	....	....		1927-28	1932-33
Gaulin, Jean-Marc	Que.	4	26	4	3	7	8	1	0	0	0	0		1982-83	1985-86
Gaume, Dallas	Hfd.	1	4	1	1	2	0	....	....	....	....	....		1988-89	1988-89
Gauthier, Art	Mtl.	1	13	0	0	0	0	1	0	0	0	0		1926-27	1926-27
• Gauthier, Fern	NYR, Mtl., Det.	6	229	46	50	96	35	22	5	1	6	7		1943-44	1948-49
Gauthier, Jean	Mtl., Phi., Bos.	10	166	6	29	35	150	14	1	3	4	22	1	1960-61	1969-70
Gauthier, Luc	Mtl.	1	3	0	0	0	2	....	....	....	....	....		1990-91	1990-91
Gauvreau, Jocelyn	Mtl.	1	2	0	0	0	0	....	....	....	....	....		1983-84	1983-84
Gavin, Stewart	Tor., Hfd., Min.	13	768	130	155	285	584	66	14	20	34	75		1980-81	1992-93
Geale, Bob	Pit.	1	1	0	0	0	2	....	....	....	....	....		1984-85	1984-85
• Gee, George	Chi., Det.	9	551	135	183	318	345	41	6	13	19	32	1	1945-46	1953-54
Geldart, Gary	Min.	1	4	0	0	0	5	....	....	....	....	....		1970-71	1970-71

Name	NHL Teams	NHL Seasons	Regular Schedule GP	G	A	TP	PIM	Playoffs GP	G	A	TP	PIM	NHL Cup Wins	First NHL Season	Last NHL Season
Gendron, Jean-Guy	NYR, Mtl., Bos., Phi.	14	863	182	201	383	701	42	7	4	11	47		1955-56	1971-72
Geoffrion, Bernie	Mtl., NYR	16	883	393	429	822	689	132	58	60	118	88	6	1950-51	1967-68
Geoffrion, Danny	Mtl., Wpg.	3	111	20	32	52	99	2	0	0	0	7		1979-80	1981-82
• Geran, Gerry	Mtl.W., Bos.	2	37	5	1	6	6	....	....	....	....	....		1917-18	1925-26
• Gerard, Eddie	Ott.	6	128	50	30	80	94	26	7	3	10	51	4	1917-18	1922-23
Germain, Eric	L.A.	1	4	0	1	1	13	1	0	0	0	4		1987-88	1987-88
Getliffe, Ray	Bos., Mtl.	10	393	136	137	273	260	45	9	10	19	30	2	1935-36	1944-45
Giallonardo, Mario	Col.	2	23	0	3	3	6	....	....	....	....	....		1979-80	1980-81
Gibbs, Barry	Bos., Min., Atl., St.L., L.A.	13	797	58	224	282	945	36	4	2	6	67		1967-68	1979-80
Gibson, Don	Van.	1	14	0	3	3	20	....	....	....	....	....		1990-91	1990-91
Gibson, Doug	Bos., Wsh.	3	63	9	19	28	0	1	0	0	0	0		1973-74	1977-78
Gibson, John	L.A., Tor., Wpg.	3	48	0	2	2	120	....	....	....	....	....		1980-81	1983-84
Giesebrecht, Gus	Det.	4	135	27	51	78	13	17	2	3	5	0		1938-39	1941-42
Giffin, Lee	Pit.	2	27	1	3	4	9	....	....	....	....	....		1986-87	1987-88
Gilbert, Ed	K.C., Pit.	3	166	21	31	52	22	....	....	....	....	....		1974-75	1976-77
Gilbert, Jean	Bos.	2	9	0	0	0	4	....	....	....	....	....		1962-63	1964-65
Gilbert, Rod	NYR	18	1065	406	615	1021	508	79	34	33	67	43		1960-61	1977-78
Gilbertson, Stan	Cal., St.L., Wsh., Pit.	6	428	85	89	174	148	3	1	1	2	2		1971-72	1976-77
Giles, Curt	Min., NYR, St.L.	14	895	43	199	242	733	103	6	16	22	118		1979-80	1992-93
Gillen, Don	Phi., Hfd.	2	35	2	4	6	22	....	....	....	....	....		1979-80	1981-82
Gillie, Ferrand	Det.	1	1	0	0	0	0	....	....	....	....	....		1928-29	1928-29
Gillies, Clark	NYI, Buf.	14	958	319	378	697	1023	164	47	47	94	287	4	1974-75	1987-88
Gillis, Jere	Que., Buf., Phi., Van., NYR	9	386	78	95	173	230	19	4	7	11	9		1977-78	1986-87
Gillis, Mike	Col., Bos.	6	246	33	43	76	186	27	2	5	7	10		1978-79	1983-84
Gillis, Paul	Que., Chi., Hfd.	11	624	88	154	242	1498	42	3	14	17	156		1982-83	1992-93
Gingras, Gaston	Mtl., Tor., St.L.	10	476	61	174	235	161	52	6	18	24	20	1	1979-80	1988-89
Girard, Bob	Cal., Cle., Wsh.	5	305	45	69	114	140	....	....	....	....	....		1975-76	1979-80
Girard, Kenny	Tor.	3	7	0	1	1	2	....	....	....	....	....		1956-57	1959-60
Giroux, Art	Mtl., Bos., Det.	3	54	6	4	10	14	2	0	0	0	0		1932-33	1935-36
Giroux, Larry	St.L., K.C., Det., Hfd.	7	274	15	74	89	333	5	0	0	0	4		1973-74	1979-80
Giroux, Pierre	L.A.	1	6	1	0	1	17	....	....	....	....	....		1982-83	1982-83
Gladney, Bob	L.A., Pit.	2	14	1	5	6	4	....	....	....	....	....		1982-83	1983-84
Gladu, Jean	Bos.	1	40	6	14	20	2	7	2	2	4	0		1944-45	1944-45
Glennie, Brian	Tor., L.A.	10	572	14	100	114	621	32	0	1	1	66		1969-70	1978-79
Glennon, Matt	Bos.	1	3	0	0	0	2	....	....	....	....	....		1991-92	1991-92
Gloeckner, Lorry	Det.	1	13	0	2	2	6	....	....	....	....	....		1978-79	1978-79
Gloor, Dan	Van.	1	2	0	0	0	0	....	....	....	....	....		1973-74	1973-74
Glover, Fred	Det., Chi.	4	92	13	11	24	62	3	0	0	0	0		1948-49	1952-53
Glover, Howie	Chi., Det., NYR, Mtl.	5	144	29	17	46	101	11	1	2	3	2		1958-59	1968-69
Godden, Ernie	Tor.	1	5	1	1	2	6	....	....	....	....	....		1981-82	1981-82
Godfrey, Warren	Bos., Det.	16	786	32	125	157	752	52	1	4	5	42		1952-53	1967-68
Godin, Eddy	Wsh.	2	27	3	6	9	12	....	....	....	....	....		1977-78	1978-79
Godin, Sammy	Ott., Mtl.	3	83	4	3	7	36	....	....	....	....	....		1927-28	1933-34
Goegan, Peter	Det., NYR, Min.	11	383	19	67	86	365	33	1	3	4	61		1957-58	1967-68
Goertz, Dave	Pit.	1	2	0	0	0	2	....	....	....	....	....		1987-88	1987-88
• Goldham, Bob	Tor., Chi., Det.	12	650	28	143	171	400	66	3	14	17	53	4	1941-42	1955-56
Goldsworthy, Bill	Bos., Min., NYR	14	771	283	258	541	793	40	18	19	37	30		1964-65	1977-78
• Goldsworthy, Leroy	NYR, Det., Chi., Mtl., Bos., NYA	9	337	66	57	123	79	22	1	0	1	4	1	1929-30	1938-39
Goldup, Glenn	Mtl., L.A.	9	291	52	67	119	303	16	4	3	7	22		1973-74	1981-82
Goldup, Hank	Tor., NYR	6	181	63	80	143	97	26	5	1	6	6	1	1939-40	1945-46
Gooden, Bill	NYR	2	53	9	11	20	15	....	....	....	....	....		1942-43	1943-44
Goodenough, Larry	Phi., Van.	6	242	22	77	99	179	22	3	15	18	10	1	1974-75	1979-80
• Goodfellow, Ebbie	Det.	14	554	134	190	324	511	45	8	8	16	65	3	1929-30	1942-43
Gordon, Fred	Det., Bos.	2	77	8	7	15	68	1	0	0	0	0		1926-27	1927-28
Gordon, Jackie	NYR	3	36	3	10	13	0	9	1	1	2	7		1948-49	1950-51
Gorence, Tom	Phi., Edm.	6	303	58	53	111	89	37	9	6	15	47		1978-79	1983-84
Goring, Butch	L.A., NYI, Bos.	16	1107	375	513	888	102	134	38	50	88	32	4	1969-70	1984-85
Gorman, Dave	Atl.	1	3	0	0	0	0	....	....	....	....	....		1979-80	1979-80
• Gorman, Ed	Ott., Tor.	4	111	14	5	19	108	8	0	0	0	2	1	1924-25	1927-28
Gosselin, Benoit	NYR	1	7	0	0	0	33	....	....	....	....	....		1977-78	1977-78
Gosselin, Guy	Wpg.	1	5	0	0	0	6	....	....	....	....	....		1987-88	1987-88
Gotaas, Steve	Pit., Min.	3	49	6	9	15	53	3	0	1	1	5		1987-88	1990-91
• Gottselig, Johnny	Chi.	16	589	176	195	371	203	43	13	13	26	20	2	1928-29	1944-45
Gould, Bobby	Atl., Cgy., Wsh., Bos.	11	697	145	159	304	572	78	15	13	28	58		1979-80	1989-90
Gould, John	Buf., Van., Atl.	9	504	131	138	269	113	14	3	2	5	4		1971-72	1979-80
Gould, Larry	Van.	1	2	0	0	0	0	....	....	....	....	....		1973-74	1973-74
Goupille, Red	Mtl.	8	222	12	28	40	256	8	2	0	2	6		1935-36	1942-43
Goyer, Gerry	Chi.	1	40	1	2	3	4	3	0	0	0	2		1967-68	1967-68
Goyette, Phil	Mtl., NYR, St.L., Buf.	16	941	207	467	674	131	94	17	29	46	26	4	1956-57	1971-72
Graboski, Tony	Mtl.	3	66	6	10	16	18	2	0	0	0	0		1940-41	1942-43
• Gracie, Bob	Tor., Bos., NYA, Mtl.M., Mtl., Chi.	9	378	82	109	191	204	33	4	7	11	4	2	1930-31	1938-39
Gradin, Thomas	Van., Bos.	9	677	209	384	593	298	42	17	25	42	20		1978-79	1986-87
• Graham, Leth	Ott., Ham.	6	26	3	0	3	0	1	0	0	0	0	1	1920-21	1925-26
Graham, Pat	Pit., Tor.	3	103	11	17	28	136	4	0	0	0	2		1981-82	1983-84
Graham, Rod	Bos.	1	14	2	1	3	7	....	....	....	....	....		1974-75	1974-75
Graham, Ted	Chi., Mtl.M., Det., St.L., Bos., NYA	9	343	14	25	39	300	23	3	1	4	34		1927-28	1936-37
Grant, Danny	Mtl., Min., Det., L.A.	13	736	263	273	536	239	43	10	14	24	19	1	1965-66	1978-79
Gratton, Dan	L.A.	1	7	1	0	1	5	....	....	....	....	....		1987-88	1987-88
Gratton, Norm	NYR, Atl., Buf., Min.	5	201	39	44	83	64	6	0	1	1	2		1971-72	1975-76
Gravelle, Leo	Mtl., Det.	5	223	44	34	78	42	17	4	1	5	2		1946-47	1950-51
Graves, Hilliard	Cal., Atl., Van., Wpg.	9	556	118	163	281	209	2	0	0	0	0		1970-71	1979-80
Graves, Steve	Edm.	3	35	5	4	9	10	....	....	....	....	....		1983-84	1987-88
• Gray, Alex	NYR, Tor.	2	50	7	0	7	30	13	1	0	1	0	1	1927-28	1928-29
Gray, Terry	Bos., Mtl., L.A., St.L.	6	147	26	28	54	64	35	5	5	10	22		1961-62	1970-71
Green, Red	Ham., NYA, Bos., Det.	6	195	59	13	72	261	....	....	....	....	....	1	1923-24	1928-29
Green, Rick	Wsh., Mtl., Det., NYI	15	845	43	220	263	588	100	3	16	19	73	1	1976-77	1991-92
Green, Ted	Bos.	11	620	48	206	254	1029	31	4	8	12	54	1	1960-61	1971-72
• Green, Wilf	Ham., NYA	4	103	33	8	41	151	....	....	....	....	....		1923-24	1926-27
Gregg, Randy	Edm., Van.	10	474	41	152	193	333	137	13	38	51	127	5	1981-82	1991-92
Greig, Bruce	Cal.	2	9	0	1	1	46	....	....	....	....	....		1973-74	1974-75
Grenier, Lucien	Mtl., L.A.	4	151	14	14	28	18	2	0	0	0	0	1	1968-69	1971-72
Grenier, Richard	NYI	1	10	1	1	2	2	....	....	....	....	....		1972-73	1972-73
Greschner, Ron	NYR	16	982	179	431	610	1226	84	17	32	49	106		1974-75	1989-90
Grigor, George	Chi.	1	2	1	0	1	0	1	0	0	0	0		1943-44	1943-44
Grisdale, John	Tor., Van.	6	250	4	39	43	346	10	0	1	1	15		1972-73	1978-79
Gronsdahl, Lloyd	Bos.	1	10	1	2	3	0	....	....	....	....	....		1941-42	1941-42
Gronstrand, Jari	Min., NYR, Que., NYI	5	185	8	26	34	135	3	0	0	0	4		1986-87	1990-91
Gross, Llyod	Tor., NYA, Bos., Det.	3	62	11	5	16	20	1	0	0	0	0		1926-27	1934-35
• Grosso, Don	Det., Chi., Bos.	9	334	87	117	204	90	50	14	12	26	46	1	1938-39	1946-47
Grosvenar, Len	Ott., NYA, Mtl.	6	147	9	11	20	78	4	0	0	0	2		1927-28	1932-33
Groulx, Wayne	Que.	1	1	0	0	0	0	....	....	....	....	....		1984-85	1984-85
Gruen, Danny	Det., Col.	3	49	9	13	22	19	....	....	....	....	....		1972-73	1976-77
Gryp, Bob	Bos., Wsh.	3	74	11	13	24	33	....	....	....	....	....		1973-74	1975-76
Guay, Francois	Buf.	1	117	11	23	34	92	9	0	1	1	12		1989-90	1989-90
Guay, Paul	Phi., L.A., Bos., NYI	7	117	11	23	34	92	9	0	1	1	12		1983-84	1990-91
Guerard, Stephane	Que.	2	34	0	0	0	40	....	....	....	....	....		1987-88	1989-90
Guevremont, Jocelyn	Van., Buf., NYR	9	571	84	223	307	319	40	4	17	21	18		1971-72	1979-80
Guidolin, Aldo	NYR	4	182	9	15	24	117	....	....	....	....	....		1952-53	1955-56
Guidolin, Bep	Bos., Det., Chi.	9	519	107	171	278	606	24	5	7	12	35		1942-43	1951-52
Guindon, Bobby	Wpg.	1	6	0	1	1	0	....	....	....	....	....		1979-80	1979-80
Gustafsson, Bengt	Wsh.	9	629	196	359	555	196	32	9	19	28	16		1979-80	1988-89
Gustavsson, Peter	Col.	1	2	0	0	0	0	....	....	....	....	....		1981-82	1981-82

H

Name	NHL Teams	NHL Seasons	Regular Schedule GP	G	A	TP	PIM	Playoffs GP	G	A	TP	PIM	NHL Cup Wins	First NHL Season	Last NHL Season
Haanpaa, Ari	NYI	3	60	6	11	17	37	6	0	0	0	10		1985-86	1987-88
Habscheid, Marc	Edm., Min., Det., Cgy.	11	345	72	91	163	171	12	1	3	4	13		1981-82	1991-92
Hachborn, Len	Phi., L.A.	3	102	20	39	59	29	7	0	3	3	7		1983-84	1985-86
Haddon, Lloyd	Det.	1	8	0	0	0	2	1	0	0	0	0		1959-60	1959-60
Hadfield, Vic	NYR, Pit.	16	1002	323	389	712	1154	73	27	21	48	117		1961-62	1976-77
Haggarty, Jim	Mtl.	1	5	1	1	2	0	3	2	1	3	0		1941-42	1941-42
• Hagglund, Roger	Que.	1	3	0	0	0	0	....	....	....	....	....		1984-85	1984-85
Hagman, Matti	Bos., Edm.	4	237	56	89	145	36	20	5	2	7	6		1976-77	1981-82
Haidy, Gord	Det.	1	....	....	....	....	....	1	0	0	0	0	1	1949-50	1949-50

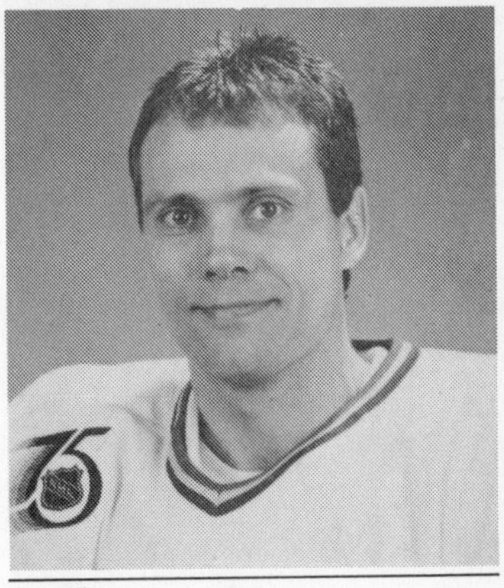
Curt Giles

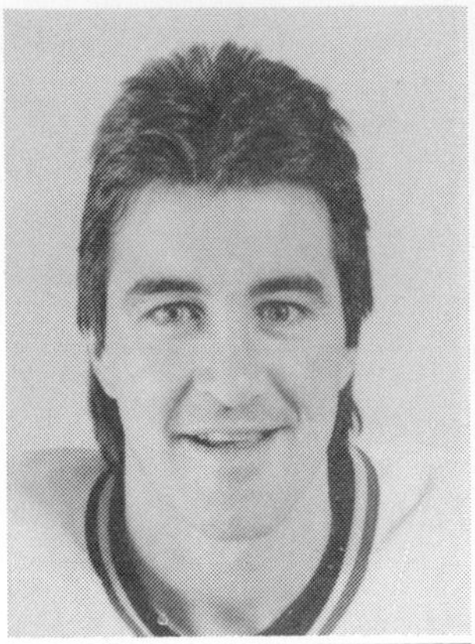
Stu Gavin

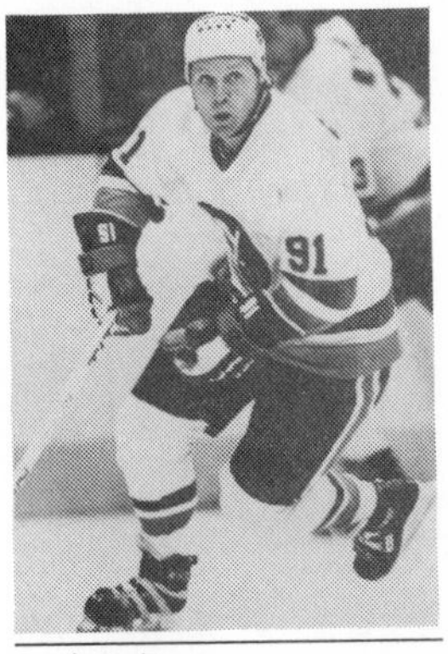
Butch Goring

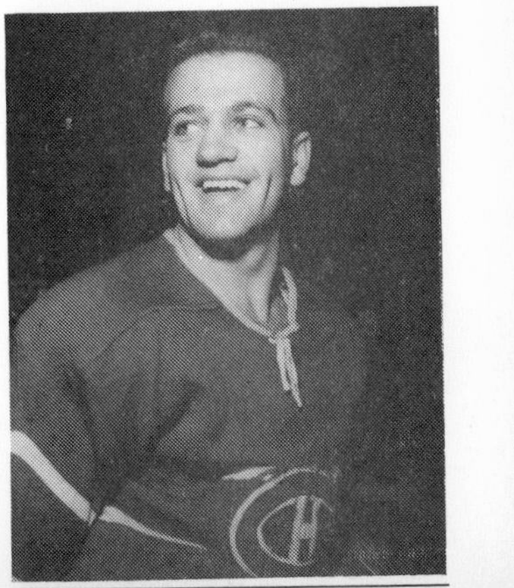
Bernie Geoffrion

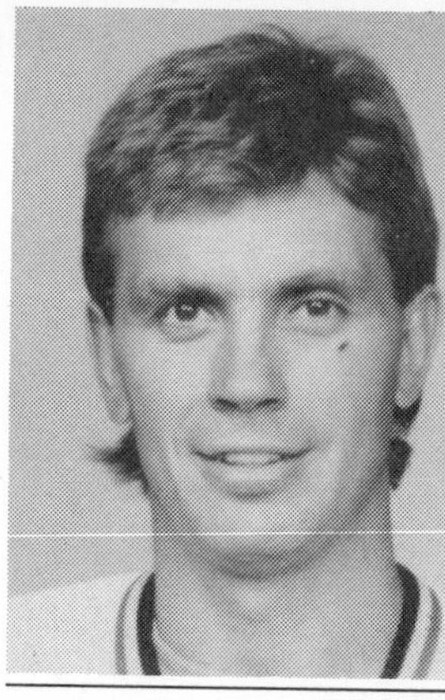

Craig Hartsburg

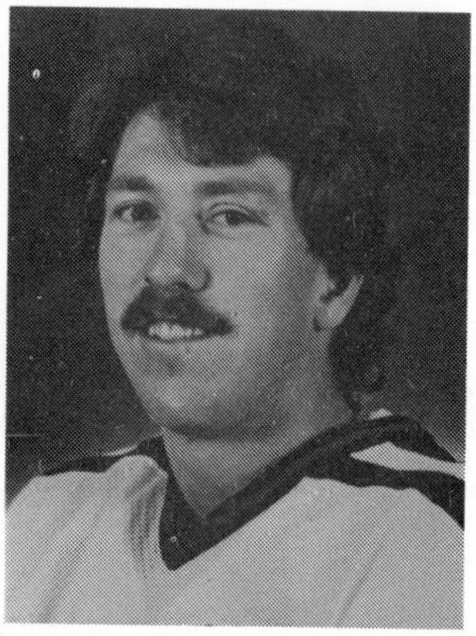

Bob Hoffmeyer

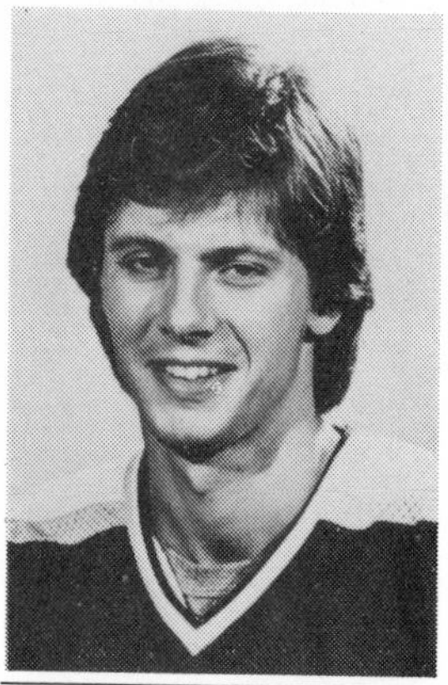

Anders Hakansson

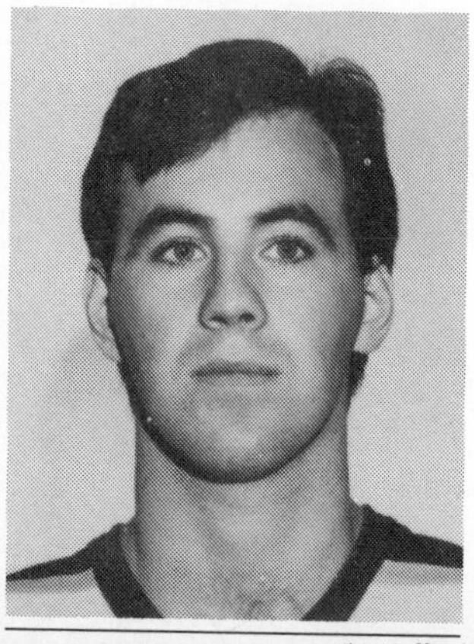

Jim Hofford

Name	NHL Teams	NHL Seasons	Regular Schedule GP	G	A	TP	PIM	Playoffs GP	G	A	TP	PIM	NHL Cup Wins	First NHL Season	Last NHL Season
Hajdu, Richard	Buf.	2	5	0	0	0	4	....	....	....	....	....		1985-86	1986-87
Hajt, Bill	Buf.	14	854	42	202	244	43	80	2	16	18	70		1973-74	1986-87
Hakansson, Anders	Min., Pit., L.A.	5	330	52	46	98	141	6	0	0	0	2		1981-82	1985-86
• Halderson, Slim	Det., Tor.	1	44	3	2	5	65	....	....	....	....	....	1	1926-27	1926-27
Hale, Larry	Phi.	4	196	5	37	42	90	8	0	0	0	12		1968-69	1971-72
Haley, Len	Det.	2	30	2	2	4	14	6	1	3	4	6		1959-60	1960-61
Hall, Bob	NYA	1	8	0	0	0	0	....	....	....	....	....		1925-26	1925-26
Hall, Del	Cal.	3	9	2	0	2	2	....	....	....	....	....		1971-72	1973-74
• Hall, Joe	Mtl.	2	37	15	1	16	85	12	0	2	2	0		1917-18	1918-19
Hall, Murray	Chi., Det., Min., Van.	9	164	35	48	83	46	6	0	0	0	0		1961-62	1971-72
Hall, Taylor	Van., Bos.	5	41	7	9	16	29	....	....	....	....	....		1983-84	1987-88
Hall, Wayne	NYR	1	4	0	0	0	0	....	....	....	....	....		1960-61	1960-61
Halliday, Milt	Ott.	3	67	1	0	1	6	6	0	0	0	0	1	1926-27	1928-29
Hallin, Mats	NYI, Min.	5	152	17	14	31	193	15	1	0	1	13	1	1982-83	1986-87
Halward, Doug	Bos., L.A., Van., Det., Edm.	14	653	69	224	293	774	47	7	10	17	113		1975-76	1988-89
Hamel, Gilles	Buf., Wpg., L.A.	9	519	127	147	274	276	27	4	5	9	10		1980-81	1988-89
Hamel, Herb	Tor.	1	2	0	0	0	14	....	....	....	....	....		1930-31	1930-31
Hamel, Jean	St.L., Det., Que., Mtl.	12	699	26	95	121	766	33	0	2	2	44		1972-73	1983-84
• Hamill, Red	Bos., Chi.	12	418	128	94	222	160	13	1	2	3	12	2	1937-38	1950-51
Hamilton, Al	NYR, Buf., Edm.	7	257	10	78	88	258	7	0	0	0	2		1965-66	1979-80
Hamilton, Chuck	Mtl., St.L.	2	4	0	2	2	2	....	....	....	....	....		1961-62	1972-73
Hamilton, Jack	Tor.	3	138	31	48	79	76	11	2	1	3	0		1942-43	1945-46
Hamilton, Jim	Pit.	8	95	14	18	32	28	6	3	0	3	0		1977-78	1984-85
• Hamilton, Reg	Tor., Chi.	12	387	21	87	108	412	64	6	6	12	54	2	1935-36	1946-47
Hammarstrom, Inge	Tor., St.L.	6	427	116	123	239	86	13	2	3	5	4		1973-74	1978-79
Hampson, Gord	Cgy.	1	4	0	0	0	5	....	....	....	....	....		1982-83	1982-83
Hampson, Ted	Tor., NYR, Det., Oak., Cal., Min.	12	676	108	245	353	94	35	7	10	17	2		1959-60	1971-72
Hampton, Rick	Cal., Cle., L.A.	6	337	59	113	172	147	2	0	0	0	0		1974-75	1979-80
Hamway, Mark	NYI	3	53	5	13	18	9	1	0	0	0	0		1984-85	1986-87
Handy, Ron	NYI, St.L.	2	14	0	3	3	0	....	....	....	....	....		1984-85	1987-88
Hangsleben, Al	Hfd., Wsh., L.A.	3	185	21	48	69	396	....	....	....	....	....		1979-80	1981-82
Hanna, John	NYR, Mtl., Phi.	5	198	6	26	32	206	....	....	....	....	....		1958-59	1967-68
• Hannigan, Gord	Tor.	4	161	29	31	60	117	9	2	0	2	8		1952-53	1955-56
Hannigan, Pat	Tor., NYR, Phi.	5	182	30	39	69	116	11	1	2	3	11		1959-60	1968-69
Hannigan, Ray	Tor.	1	3	0	0	0	2	....	....	....	....	....		1948-49	1948-49
Hansen, Ritchie	NYI, St.L.	4	20	2	8	10	6	....	....	....	....	....		1976-77	1981-82
Hanson, Dave	Det., Min.	2	33	1	1	2	65	....	....	....	....	....		1978-79	1979-80
Hanson, Emil	Det.	1	7	0	0	0	6	....	....	....	....	....		1932-33	1932-33
Hanson, Keith	Cgy.	1	25	0	2	2	77	....	....	....	....	....		1983-84	1983-84
Hanson, Ossie	Chi.	1	7	0	0	0	0	....	....	....	....	....		1937-38	1937-38
Harbaruk, Nick	Pit., St.L.	5	364	45	75	120	273	14	3	1	4	20		1969-70	1973-74
Harding, Jeff	Phi.	2	15	0	0	0	47	....	....	....	....	....		1988-89	1989-90
Hardy, Joe	Oak., Cal.	2	63	9	14	23	51	4	0	0	0	0		1969-70	1970-71
Hargreaves, Jim	Van.	2	66	1	7	8	105	....	....	....	....	....		1970-71	1972-73
Harlow, Scott	St.L.	1	1	0	1	1	0	....	....	....	....	....		1987-88	1987-88
Harmon, Glen	Mtl.	9	452	50	96	146	334	53	5	10	15	37	2	1942-43	1950-51
Harms, John	Chi.	2	44	5	5	10	21	3	3	0	3	2		1943-44	1944-45
Harnott, Happy	Bos.	1	6	0	0	0	6	....	....	....	....	....		1933-34	1933-34
Harper, Terry	Mtl., L.A., Det., St.L., Col.	19	1066	35	221	256	1362	112	4	13	17	140	5	1962-63	1980-81
Harrer, Tim	Cgy.	1	3	0	0	0	2	....	....	....	....	....		1982-83	1982-83
• Harrington, Hago	Bos., Mtl.	3	72	9	3	12	15	4	1	0	1	2		1925-26	1932-33
Harris, Billy	Tor., Det., Oak., Cal., Pit.	12	769	126	219	345	205	62	8	10	18	30	3	1955-56	1968-69
Harris, Billy	NYI, L.A., Tor.	12	897	231	327	558	394	71	19	19	38	48		1972-73	1983-84
Harris, Duke	Min., Tor.	1	26	1	4	5	4	....	....	....	....	....		1967-68	1967-68
Harris, Hugh	Buf.	1	60	12	26	38	17	3	0	0	0	0		1972-73	1972-73
Harris, Ron	Det., Oak., Atl., NYR	12	476	20	91	111	484	28	4	3	7	33		1962-63	1975-76
Harris, Smokey	Bos.	2	40	5	5	10	28	2	0	0	0	0		1924-25	1930-31
Harris, Ted	Mtl., Min., Det., St.L., Phi.	12	788	30	168	198	1000	100	1	22	23	230	5	1963-64	1974-75
Harrison, Ed	Bos., NYR	4	194	27	24	51	53	9	1	0	1	2		1947-48	1950-51
Harrison, Jim	Bos., Tor., Chi., Edm.	8	324	67	86	153	435	13	1	1	2	43		1968-69	1979-80
Hart, Gerry	Det., NYI, Que., St.L.	15	730	29	150	179	1240	78	3	12	15	175		1968-69	1982-83
• Hart, Gizzy	Det., Mtl.	3	100	6	8	14	12	8	0	1	1	0	1	1926-27	1932-33
Hartsburg, Craig	Min.	10	570	98	315	413	818	61	15	27	42	70		1979-80	1988-89
• Harvey, Doug	Mtl., NYR, Det., St.L.	20	1113	88	452	540	1216	137	8	64	72	152	6	1947-48	1968-69
Harvey, Fred	Min., Atl., K.C., Det.	7	407	90	118	208	131	14	0	2	2	8		1970-71	1976-77
Harvey, Hugh	K.C.	2	18	1	1	2	4	....	....	....	....	....		1974-75	1975-76
Hassard, Bob	Tor., Chi.	5	126	9	28	37	22	....	....	....	....	....		1949-50	1954-55
Hatoum, Ed	Det., Van.	3	47	3	6	9	25	....	....	....	....	....		1968-69	1970-71
Haworth, Alan	Buf., Wsh., Que.	8	524	189	211	400	425	42	12	16	28	28		1980-81	1987-88
Haworth, Gord	NYR	1	2	0	1	1	0	....	....	....	....	....		1952-53	1952-53
Hawryliw, Neil	NYI	1	1	0	0	0	0	....	....	....	....	....		1981-82	1981-82
Hay, Billy	Chi.	8	506	113	273	386	244	67	15	21	36	62		1959-60	1966-67
• Hay, George	Chi., Det.	7	242	74	60	134	84	8	2	3	5	14		1926-27	1933-34
Hay, Jim	Det.	3	75	1	5	6	22	9	1	0	1	2	1	1952-53	1954-55
Hayek, Peter	Min.	1	1	0	0	0	0	....	....	....	....	....		1981-82	1981-82
Hayes, Chris	Bos.	1	....	....	....	....	....	1	0	0	0	0	1	1971-72	1971-72
Haynes, Paul	Mtl.M., Bos., Mtl.	11	390	61	134	195	164	25	2	8	10	13		1930-31	1940-41
Hayward, Rick	L.A.	1	4	0	0	0	5	....	....	....	....	....		1990-91	1990-91
Hazlett, Steve	Van.	1	1	0	0	0	0	....	....	....	....	....		1979-80	1979-80
Head, Galen	Det.	1	1	0	0	0	0	....	....	....	....	....		1967-68	1967-68
Headley, Fern	Bos., Mtl.	1	27	1	1	2	6	5	0	0	0	0		1924-25	1924-25
Healey, Dick	Det.	1	1	0	0	0	2	....	....	....	....	....		1960-61	1960-61
Heaslip, Mark	NYR, L.A.	3	117	10	19	29	110	5	0	0	0	2		1976-77	1978-79
Heath, Randy	NYR	2	13	2	4	6	15	....	....	....	....	....		1984-85	1985-86
Hebenton, Andy	NYR, Bos.	9	630	189	202	391	83	22	6	5	11	8		1955-56	1963-64
Hedberg, Anders	NYR	7	465	172	225	397	144	58	22	24	46	31		1978-79	1984-85
• Heffernan, Frank	Tor.	1	17	0	0	0	4	....	....	....	....	....		1919-20	1919-20
Heffernan, Gerry	Mtl.	3	83	33	35	68	27	11	3	3	6	8	1	1941-42	1943-44
Heidt, Mike	L.A.	1	6	0	1	1	7	....	....	....	....	....		1983-84	1983-84
Heindl, Bill	Min., NYR	3	18	2	1	3	0	....	....	....	....	....		1970-71	1972-73
Heinrich, Lionel	Bos.	1	35	1	1	2	33	....	....	....	....	....		1955-56	1955-56
Heiskala, Earl	Phi.	3	127	13	11	24	294	....	....	....	....	....		1968-69	1970-71
Helander, Peter	L.A.	1	7	0	1	1	0	....	....	....	....	....		1982-83	1982-83
• Heller, Ott	NYR	15	647	55	176	231	465	61	6	8	14	61	2	1931-32	1945-46
Helman, Harry	Ott.	3	42	1	0	1	7	5	0	0	0	0	1	1922-23	1924-25
Helminen, Raimo	NYR, Min., NYI	3	117	13	46	59	16	2	0	0	0	0		1985-86	1988-89
Hemmerling, Tony	NYA	2	24	3	3	6	4	....	....	....	....	....		1935-36	1936-37
Henderson, Archie	Wsh., Min., Hfd.	3	23	3	1	4	92	....	....	....	....	....		1980-81	1982-83
Henderson, Murray	Bos.	8	405	24	62	86	305	41	2	3	5	23		1944-45	1951-52
Henderson, Paul	Det., Tor., Atl.	13	707	236	241	477	304	56	11	14	25	28		1962-63	1979-80
Hendrickson, John	Det.	3	5	0	0	0	4	....	....	....	....	....		1957-58	1961-62
Henning, Lorne	NYI	9	544	73	111	184	102	81	7	7	14	8	2	1972-73	1980-81
Henry, Camille	NYR, Chi., St.L.	14	727	279	249	528	88	47	6	12	18	7		1953-54	1969-70
Henry, Dale	NYI	6	132	13	26	39	263	....	....	....	....	....		1984-85	1989-90
Hepple, Alan	N.J.	3	3	0	0	0	7	....	....	....	....	....		1983-84	1985-86
• Herberts, Jimmy	Bos., Tor., Det.	6	206	83	29	112	250	9	3	0	3	35		1924-25	1929-30
Herchenratter, Art	Det.	1	10	1	2	3	2	....	....	....	....	....		1940-41	1940-41
Hergerts, Fred	NYA	2	19	2	4	6	2	....	....	....	....	....		1934-35	1935-36
Hergesheimer, Philip	Chi., Bos.	4	125	21	41	62	19	7	0	0	0	2		1939-40	1942-43
Hergesheimer, Wally	NYR, Chi.	7	351	114	85	199	106	5	1	0	1	0		1951-52	1958-59
Heron, Red	Tor., Bro., Mtl.	4	106	21	19	40	38	16	2	2	4	55		1938-39	1941-42
Hervey, Matt	Wpg., Bos., T.B.	3	35	0	5	5	97	5	0	0	0	6		1988-89	1992-93
Hess, Bob	St.L., Buf., Hfd.	8	329	27	95	122	178	4	1	1	2	2		1974-75	1983-84
Heximer, Orville	NYR, Bos., NYA	3	85	13	7	20	28	5	0	0	0	2		1929-30	1934-35
Hextall, Bryan Jr.	NYR, Pit., Atl., Det., Min.	8	549	99	161	260	738	18	0	4	4	59		1962-63	1975-76
• Hextall, Bryan Sr.	NYR	11	447	187	175	362	227	37	8	9	17	19	1	1936-37	1947-48
Hextall, Dennis	NYR, L.A., Cal., Min., Det., Wsh.	13	681	153	350	503	1398	22	3	3	6	45		1968-69	1979-80
Heyliger, Vic	Chi.	2	34	2	3	5	2	....	....	....	....	....		1937-38	1943-44
Hicke, Bill	Mtl., NYR, Oak.	14	729	168	234	402	395	42	3	10	13	41	2	1958-59	1971-72
Hicke, Ernie	Cal., Atl., NYI, Min., L.A.	8	520	132	140	272	407	2	1	0	1	0		1970-71	1977-78
Hickey, Greg	NYR	1	1	0	0	0	0	....	....	....	....	....		1977-78	1977-78
Hickey, Pat	NYR, Col., Tor., Que., St.L.	10	646	192	212	404	351	55	5	11	16	37		1975-76	1984-85
Hicks, Doug	Min., Chi., Edm., Wsh.	9	561	37	131	168	442	....	....	....	....	....		1974-75	1982-83
Hicks, Glenn	Det.	2	108	6	12	18	127	....	....	....	....	....		1979-80	1980-81

			Regular Schedule					Playoffs					NHL	First	Last
Name	NHL Teams	NHL Seasons	GP	G	A	TP	PIM	GP	G	A	TP	PIM	Cup Wins	NHL Season	NHL Season
• Hicks, Hal	Mtl.M., Det.	3	110	7	2	9	72	....	....	....	....	....		1928-29	1930-31
Hicks, Wayne	Chi., Bos., Mtl., Phi., Pit.	5	115	13	23	36	22	2	0	1	1	2	1	1959-60	1967-68
Hidi, Andre	Wsh.	2	7	2	1	3	9	2	0	0	0	0		1983-84	1984-85
Hiemer, Uli	N.J.	3	143	19	54	73	176	....	....	....	....	....		1984-85	1986-87
Higgins, Paul	Tor.	2	25	0	0	0	152	1	0	0	0	0		1981-82	1982-83
Higgins, Tim	Chi., N.J., Det.	11	706	154	198	352	719	65	5	8	13	77		1978-79	1988-89
Hildebrand, Ike	NYR, Chi.	2	41	7	11	18	16	....	....	....	....	....		1953-54	1954-55
Hill, Al	Phi.	8	221	40	55	95	227	51	8	11	19	43		1976-77	1987-88
Hill, Brian	Hfd.	1	19	1	1	2	4	....	....	....	....	....		1979-80	1979-80
Hill, Mel	Bos., Bro., Tor.	9	323	89	109	198	138	43	12	7	19	18	3	1937-38	1945-46
Hiller, Dutch	NYR, Det., Bos., Mtl.	9	385	91	113	204	163	48	9	8	17	21	2	1937-38	1945-46
Hillier, Randy	Bos., Pit., NYI, Buf.	11	543	16	110	126	906	28	0	2	2	93	1	1981-82	1991-92
Hillman, Floyd	Bos.	1	6	0	0	0	10	....	....	....	....	....		1956-57	1956-57
Hillman, Larry	Det., Bos., Tor., Min., Mtl., Phi., L.A., Buf.	19	790	36	196	232	579	74	2	9	11	30	4	1954-55	1972-73
• Hillman, Wayne	Chi., NYR, Min., Phi.	13	691	18	86	104	534	28	0	3	3	19	1	1960-61	1972-73
Hilworth, John	Det.	3	57	1	1	2	89	....	....	....	....	....		1977-78	1979-80
Himes, Normie	NYA	9	402	106	113	219	127	2	0	0	0	0		1926-27	1934-35
Hindmarch, Dave	Cgy.	4	99	21	17	38	25	10	0	0	0	6		1980-81	1983-84
Hinse, Andre	Tor.	1	4	0	0	0	0	....	....	....	....	....		1967-68	1967-68
Hinton, Dan	Chi.	1	14	0	0	0	16	....	....	....	....	....		1976-77	1976-77
Hirsch, Tom	Min.	3	31	1	7	8	30	12	0	0	0	6		1983-84	1987-88
Hirschfeld, Bert	Mtl.	2	33	1	4	5	2	5	1	0	1	0		1949-50	1950-51
Hislop, Jamie	Que., Cgy.	5	345	75	103	178	86	28	3	2	5	11		1979-80	1983-84
• Hitchman, Lionel	Ott., Bos.	12	413	28	33	61	523	40	4	1	5	77	2	1922-23	1933-34
Hlinka, Ivan	Van.	2	137	42	81	123	28	16	3	10	13	8		1981-82	1982-83
Hodge, Ken	Chi., Bos., NYR	13	881	328	472	800	779	97	34	47	81	120	2	1965-66	1977-78
Hodgson, Dan	Tor., Van.	4	114	29	45	74	64	....	....	....	....	....		1985-86	1988-89
Hodgson, Rick	Hfd.	1	6	0	0	0	6	1	0	0	0	0		1979-80	1979-80
Hodgson, Ted	Bos.	1	4	0	0	0	0	....	....	....	....	....		1966-67	1966-67
Hoekstra, Cecil	Mtl.	1	4	0	0	0	0	....	....	....	....	....		1959-60	1959-60
Hoekstra, Ed	Phi.	1	70	15	21	36	6	7	0	1	1	0		1967-68	1967-68
Hoene, Phil	L.A.	3	37	2	4	6	22	....	....	....	....	....		1972-73	1974-75
Hoffinger, Vic	Chi.	2	28	0	1	1	30	....	....	....	....	....		1927-28	1928-29
Hoffman, Mike	Hfd.	3	9	1	3	4	2	....	....	....	....	....		1982-83	1985-86
Hoffmeyer, Bob	Chi., Phi., N.J.	6	198	14	52	66	325	3	0	1	1	25		1977-78	1984-85
Hofford, Jim	Buf., L.A.	3	18	0	0	0	47	....	....	....	....	....		1985-86	1988-89
Hogaboam, Bill	Atl., Det., Min.	8	332	80	109	189	100	2	0	0	0	0		1972-73	1979-80
Hoganson, Dale	L.A., Mtl., Que.	7	343	13	77	90	186	11	0	3	3	12		1969-70	1981-82
Holbrook, Terry	Min.	2	43	3	6	9	4	6	0	0	0	0		1972-73	1973-74
Holland, Jerry	NYR	2	37	8	4	12	6	....	....	....	....	....		1974-75	1975-76
Hollett, Frank	Tor., Ott., Bos., Det.	13	565	132	181	313	358	79	8	26	34	38	2	1933-34	1945-46
• Hollingworth, Gord	Chi., Det.	4	163	4	14	18	201	3	0	0	0	2		1954-55	1957-58
Holloway, Bruce	Van.	1	2	0	0	0	0	....	....	....	....	....		1984-85	1984-85
• Holmes, Bill	Mtl., NYA.	2	51	6	4	10	35	....	....	....	....	....		1925-26	1929-30
Holmes, Chuck	Det.	2	23	1	3	4	10	....	....	....	....	....		1958-59	1961-62
Holmes, Lou	Chi.	2	59	1	4	5	6	2	0	0	0	2		1931-32	1932-33
Holmes, Warren	L.A.	3	45	8	18	26	7	....	....	....	....	....		1981-82	1983-84
Holmgren, Paul	Phi., Min.	10	527	144	179	323	1684	82	19	32	51	195		1975-76	1984-85
• Holota, John	Det.	2	15	2	0	2	0	....	....	....	....	....		1942-43	1945-46
Holst, Greg	NYR	3	11	0	0	0	0	....	....	....	....	....		1975-76	1977-78
Holt, Gary	Cal., Clev., St.L.	5	101	13	11	24	183	....	....	....	....	....		1973-74	1977-78
Holt, Randy	Chi., Clev., Van., L.A., Cgy., Wsh., Phi.	10	395	4	37	41	1438	21	2	3	5	83		1974-75	1983-84
• Holway, Albert	Tor., Mtl.M., Pit.	5	117	7	2	9	48	8	0	0	0	2	1	1923-24	1928-29
Homenuke, Ron	Van.	1	1	0	0	0	0	....	....	....	....	....		1972-73	1972-73
Hopkins, Dean	L.A., Edm., Que.	6	223	23	51	74	306	18	1	5	6	29		1979-80	1988-89
Hopkins, Larry	Tor., Wpg.	4	60	13	16	29	26	6	0	0	0	2		1977-78	1982-83
Horava, Miloslav	NYR	3	80	5	17	22	38	2	0	1	1	0		1988-89	1990-91
Horbul, Doug	K.C.	1	4	1	0	1	2	....	....	....	....	....		1974-75	1974-75
Hordy, Mike	NYI	2	11	0	0	0	7	....	....	....	....	....		1978-79	1979-80
Horeck, Pete	Chi., Det., Bos.	8	426	106	118	224	340	34	6	8	14	43		1944-45	1951-52
• Horne, George	Mtl.M, Tor.	3	54	9	3	12	34	4	0	0	0	4	1	1925-26	1928-29
Horner, Red	Tor.	12	490	42	110	152	1264	71	7	10	17	166	1	1928-29	1939-40
Hornung, Larry	St.L.	2	48	2	9	11	10	11	0	2	2	2		1970-71	1971-72
• Horton, Tim	Tor., NYR, Buf., Pit.	24	1446	115	403	518	1611	126	11	39	50	183	4	1949-50	1973-74
Horvath, Bronco	NYR, Mtl., Bos., Chi., Tor., Min.	9	434	141	185	326	319	36	12	9	21	18		1955-56	1967-68
Hospodar, Ed	NYR, Hfd., Phi., Min., Buf.	9	450	17	51	68	1314	44	4	1	5	206		1979-80	1987-88
Hostak, Martin	Phi.	2	55	3	11	14	24	....	....	....	....	....		1990-91	1991-92
Hotham, Greg	Tor., Pit.	6	230	15	74	89	139	5	0	3	3	6		1979-80	1984-85
Houck, Paul	Min.	3	16	1	2	3	2	....	....	....	....	....		1985-86	1987-88
Houde, Claude	K.C.	2	59	3	6	9	40	....	....	....	....	....		1974-75	1975-76
Houle, Rejean	Mtl.	11	635	161	247	408	395	90	14	34	48	66	5	1969-70	1982-83
Houston, Ken	Atl., Cgy., Wsh., L.A.	9	570	161	167	328	624	35	10	9	19	66		1975-76	1983-84
Howard, Frank	Tor.	1	2	0	0	0	0	....	....	....	....	....		1936-37	1936-37
Howatt, Garry	NYI, Hfd., N.J.	12	720	112	156	268	1836	87	12	14	26	289	2	1972-73	1983-84
Howe, Gordie	Det., Hfd.	26	1767	801	1049	1850	1685	157	68	92	160	220	4	1946-47	1979-80
Howe, Marty	Hfd., Bos.	6	197	2	29	31	99	15	1	2	3	9		1979-80	1984-85
• Howe, Syd	Ott., Phi., Tor., St.L., Det.	17	691	237	291	528	212	70	17	27	44	10	3	1929-30	1945-46
Howe, Vic	NYR	3	33	3	4	7	10	....	....	....	....	....		1950-51	1954-55
Howell, Harry	NYR, Oak., L.A.	21	1411	94	324	418	1298	38	3	3	6	32		1952-53	1972-73
Howell, Ron	NYR	2	4	0	0	0	4	....	....	....	....	....		1954-55	1955-56
Howse, Don	L.A.	1	33	2	5	7	6	2	0	0	0	0		1979-80	1979-80
Howson, Scott	NYI	2	18	5	3	8	4	....	....	....	....	....		1984-85	1985-86
Hoyda, Dave	Phi., Wpg.	4	132	6	17	23	299	12	0	0	0	17		1977-78	1980-81
Hrdina, Jiri	Cgy., Pit.	5	250	45	85	130	92	46	2	5	7	24	3	1987-88	1991-92
Hrechkosy, Dave	Cal., St.L.	4	140	42	24	66	41	3	1	0	1	2		1973-74	1976-77
Hrycuik, Jim	Wsh.	1	.21	5	5	10	12	....	....	....	....	....		1974-75	1974-75
Hrymnak, Steve	Chi., Det.	2	18	2	1	3	4	2	0	0	0	0		1951-52	1952-53
Hrynewich, Tim	Pit.	2	55	6	8	14	82	....	....	....	....	....		1982-83	1983-84
Huard, Rolly	Tor.	1	1	1	0	1	0	....	....	....	....	....		1930-31	1930-31
Huber, Willie	Det., NYR, Van., Phi.	10	655	104	217	321	950	33	5	5	10	35		1978-79	1987-88
Hubick, Greg	Tor., Van.	2	77	6	9	15	10	....	....	....	....	....		1975-76	1979-80
Huck, Fran	Mtl., St.L.	3	94	24	30	54	38	11	3	4	7	2		1969-70	1972-73
Hucul, Fred	Chi., St.L.	5	164	11	30	41	113	6	1	0	1	10		1950-51	1967-68
Hudson, Dave	NYI, K.C., Col.	6	409	59	124	183	89	2	1	1	2	0		1972-73	1977-78
Hudson, Lex	Pit.	1	2	0	0	0	0	2	0	0	0	0		1978-79	1978-79
Hudson, Ron	Det.	2	34	5	2	7	2	....	....	....	....	....		1937-38	1939-40
Huggins, Al	Mtl.M	1	20	1	1	2	2	....	....	....	....	....		1930-31	1930-31
Hughes, Al	NYA	2	60	6	8	14	22	....	....	....	....	....		1930-31	1931-32
Hughes, Brent	L.A., Phi., St.L., Det., K.C.	8	435	15	117	132	440	22	1	3	4	53		1967-68	1974-75
Hughes, Frank	Cal.	1	5	0	0	0	0	....	....	....	....	....		1971-72	1971-72
Hughes, Howie	L.A.	3	168	25	32	57	30	14	2	0	2	2		1967-68	1969-70
Hughes, Jack	Col.	2	46	2	5	7	104	....	....	....	....	....		1980-81	1981-82
Hughes, John	Van., Edm., NYR	3	70	2	14	16	211	7	0	1	1	16		1979-80	1980-81
Hughes, Pat	Mtl., Pit., Edm., Buf., St.L., Hfd.	10	573	130	128	258	646	71	8	25	33	77	3	1977-78	1986-87
Hughes, Rusty	Det.	1	40	0	1	1	48	....	....	....	....	....		1929-30	1929-30
Hull, Bobby	Chi., Wpg., Hfd.	16	1063	610	560	1170	640	119	62	67	129	102	1	1957-58	1979-80
Hull, Dennis	Chi., Det.	14	959	303	351	654	261	104	33	34	67	30		1964-65	1977-78
• Hunt, Fred	NYA, NYR	2	59	15	14	29	6	....	....	....	....	....		1940-41	1944-45
Hunter, Dave	Edm., Pit., Wpg.	10	746	133	190	323	918	105	16	24	40	211	3	1979-80	1988-89
Hunter, Mark	Mtl., St.L., Cgy., Hfd., Wsh.	12	628	213	171	384	1426	79	18	20	38	230	1	1981-82	1992-93
Huras, Larry	NYR	1	1	0	0	0	0	....	....	....	....	....		1976-77	1976-77
Hurlburt, Bob	Van.	1	1	0	0	0	2	....	....	....	....	....		1974-75	1974-75
Hurley, Paul	Bos.	1	1	0	1	1	0	....	....	....	....	....		1968-69	1968-69
Hurst, Ron	Tor.	2	64	9	7	16	7	3	0	2	2	4		1955-56	1956-57
Huston, Ron	Cal.	2	79	15	31	46	8	....	....	....	....	....		1973-74	1974-75
Hutchinson, Ronald	NYR	1	9	0	0	0	0	....	....	....	....	....		1960-61	1960-61
Hutchison, Dave	L.A., Tor., Chi., N.J.	10	584	19	97	116	1550	48	2	12	14	149		1974-75	1983-84
• Hutton, William	Bos., Ott., Phi.	2	64	3	2	5	8	2	0	0	0	0		1929-30	1930-31
• Hyland, Harry	Mtl.W, Ott.	1	16	14	0	14	0	....	....	....	....	....		1917-18	1917-18
Hynes, Dave	Bos.	2	22	4	0	4	2	....	....	....	....	....		1973-74	1974-75

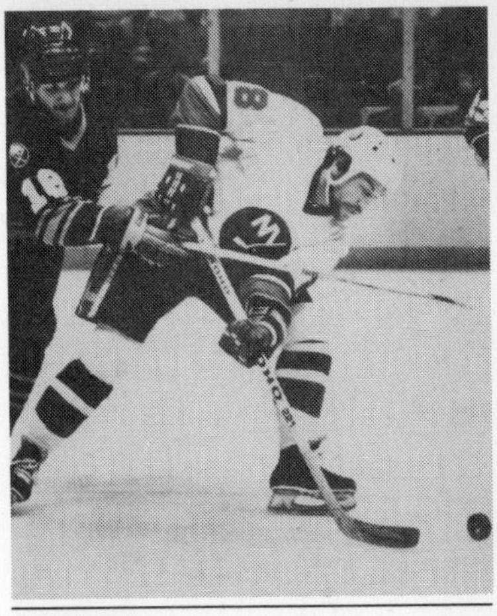
Garry Howatt

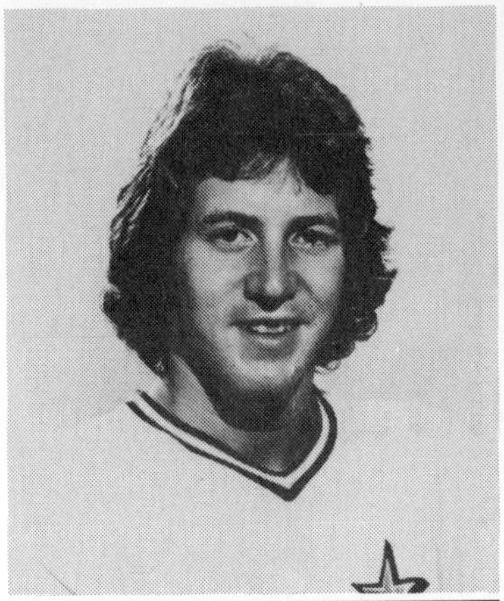
Doug Hicks

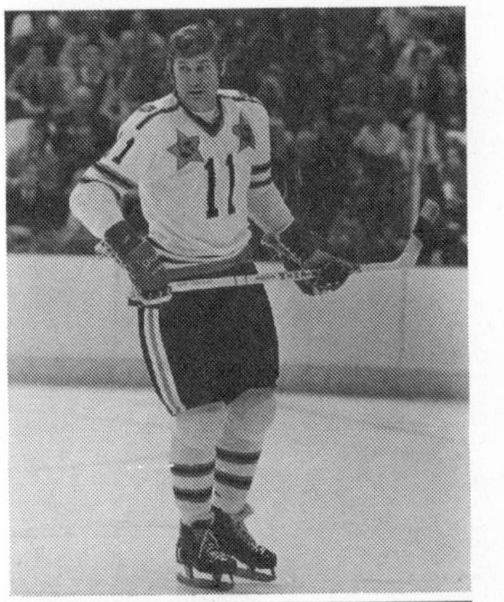
Vic Hadfield

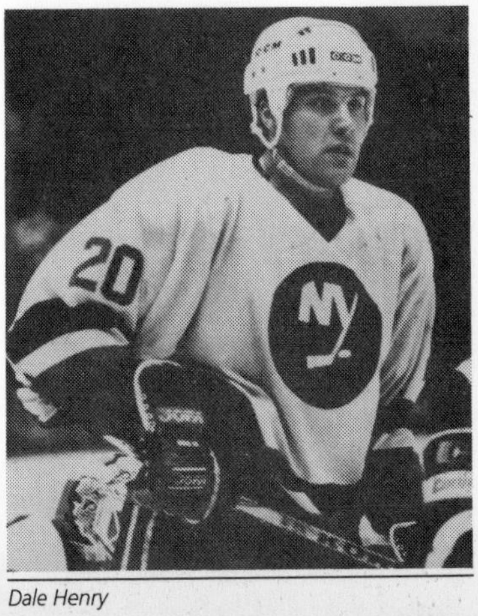
Dale Henry

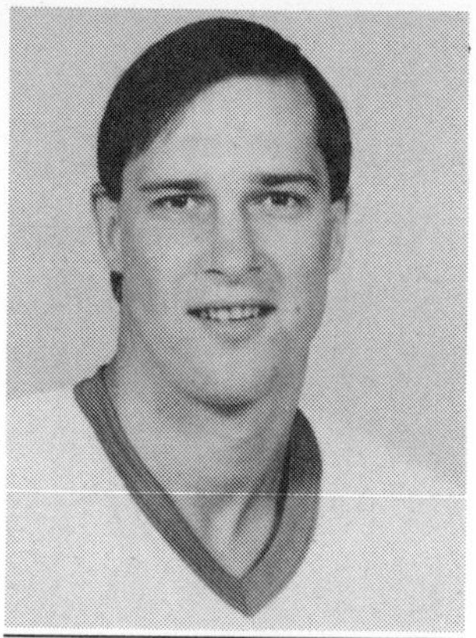

Tim Higgins

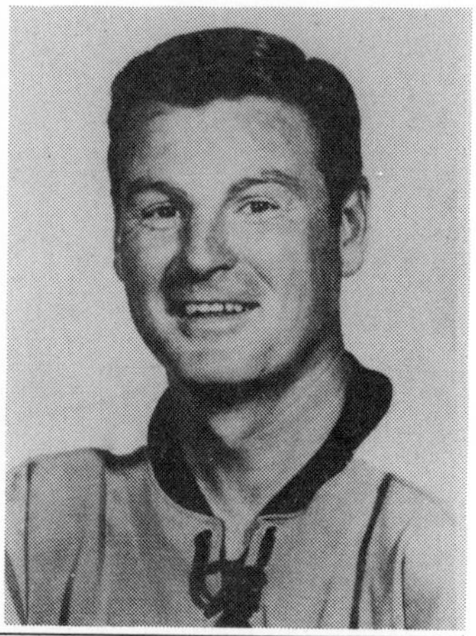

Earl Ingarfield

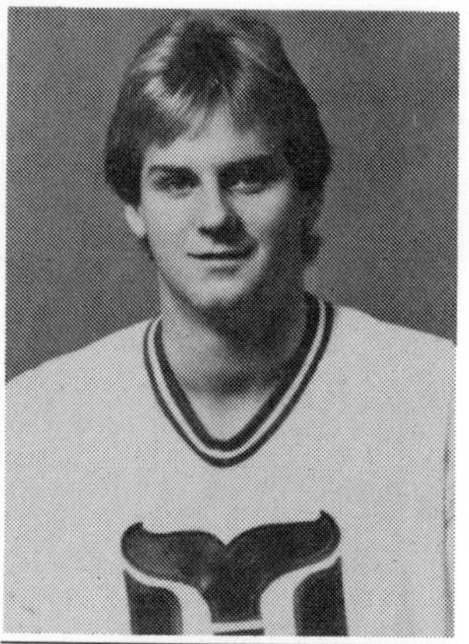

Dave Jensen

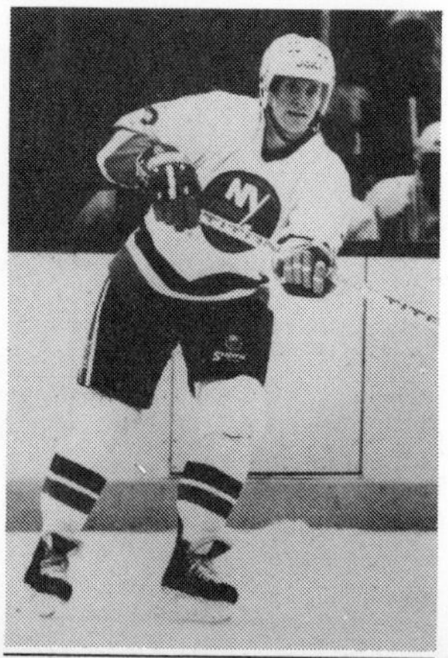

Tomas Jonsson

Name	NHL Teams	NHL Seasons	Regular Schedule					Playoffs					NHL Cup Wins	First NHL Season	Last NHL Season
			GP	G	A	TP	PIM	GP	G	A	TP	PIM			
I															
Ihnacak, Miroslav	Tor., Det.	3	56	8	9	17	39	1	0	0	0	0		1985-86	1988-89
Ihnacak, Peter	Tor.	8	417	102	165	267	175	28	4	10	14	25		1982-83	1989-90
Imlach, Brent	Tor.	2	3	0	0	0	2	....	....	....	....	....		1965-66	1966-67
Ingarfield, Earl	NYR, Pit., Oak., Cal.	13	746	179	226	405	239	21	9	8	17	10		1958-59	1970-71
Ingarfield, Earl Jr.	Atl., Cgy., Det.	2	39	4	4	8	22	2	0	1	1	0		1979-80	1980-81
Inglis, Bill	L.A., Buf.	3	36	1	3	4	4	11	1	2	3	4		1967-68	1970-71
• Ingoldsby, Johnny	Tor.	2	29	5	1	6	15	....	....	....	....	....		1942-43	1943-44
Ingram, Frank	Bos., Chi.	4	102	24	16	40	69	11	0	1	1	2		1924-25	1931-32
Ingram, Ron	Chi., Det., NYR	4	114	5	15	20	81	2	0	0	0	0		1956-57	1964-65
• Irvin, Dick	Chi.	3	94	29	23	52	76	2	2	0	2	4		1926-27	1928-29
Irvine, Ted	Bos., L.A., NYR, St.L.	11	724	154	177	331	657	83	16	24	40	115		1963-64	1976-77
Irwin, Ivan	Mtl., NYR	5	155	2	27	29	214	5	0	0	0	8		1952-53	1957-58
Isaksson, Ulf	L.A.	1	50	7	15	22	10	....	....	....	....	....		1982-83	1982-83
Issel, Kim	Edm.	1	4	0	0	0	0	....	....	....	....	....		1988-89	1988-89
J															
• Jackson, Art	Bos., Tor.	11	466	123	178	301	144	51	8	12	20	27	2	1934-35	1944-45
Jackson, Don	Min., Edm., NYR	10	311	16	52	68	640	53	4	5	9	147	2	1977-78	1986-87
Jackson, Hal	Chi., Det.	8	222	17	34	51	208	31	1	2	3	33	2	1936-37	1946-47
• Jackson, Harvey	Tor., Bos., NYA	15	636	241	234	475	437	71	18	12	30	53	1	1929-30	1943-44
Jackson, Jeff	Tor., NYR, Que., Chi.	8	263	38	48	86	313	6	1	1	2	16		1984-85	1991-92
Jackson, Jim	Cgy., Buf.	4	112	17	30	47	20	14	3	2	5	6		1982-83	1987-88
Jackson, John	Chi.	1	48	2	5	7	38	....	....	....	....	....		1946-47	1946-47
Jackson, Lloyd	NYA	1	14	1	1	2	0	....	....	....	....	....		1936-37	1936-37
Jackson, Stan	Tor., Bos., Ott.	5	84	9	4	13	74	....	....	....	....	....	1	1921-22	1926-27
Jackson, Walt	NYA	3	82	16	11	27	18	....	....	....	....	....		1932-33	1934-35
• Jacobs, Paul	Tor.	1	1	0	0	0	0	....	....	....	....	....		1918-19	1918-19
Jacobs, Tim	Cal.	1	46	0	10	10	35	....	....	....	....	....		1975-76	1975-76
Jalo, Risto	Edm.	1	3	0	3	3	0	....	....	....	....	....		1985-86	1985-86
Jalonen, Kari	Cgy., Edm.	2	37	9	6	15	4	5	1	0	1	0		1982-83	1983-84
James, Gerry	Tor.	5	149	14	26	40	257	15	1	0	1	8		1954-55	1959-60
James, Val	Buf., Tor.	2	11	0	0	0	30	....	....	....	....	....		1981-82	1986-87
Jamieson, Jim	NYR	1	1	0	1	1	0	....	....	....	....	....		1943-44	1943-44
Jankowski, Lou	Det., Chi.	4	127	19	18	37	15	1	0	0	0	0		1950-51	1954-55
Jarrett, Doug	Chi., NYR	13	775	38	182	220	631	99	7	16	23	82		1964-65	1976-77
Jarrett, Gary	Tor., Det., Oak., Cal.	7	341	72	92	164	131	11	3	1	4	9		1960-61	1971-72
Jarry, Pierre	NYR, Tor., Det., Min.	7	344	88	117	205	142	5	0	1	1	0		1971-72	1977-78
Jarvenpaa, Hannu	Wpg.	3	114	11	26	37	83	....	....	....	....	....		1986-87	1988-89
Jarvi, Iiro	Que.	2	116	18	43	61	58	....	....	....	....	....		1988-89	1989-90
Jarvis, Doug	Mtl., Wsh., Hfd.	13	964	139	264	403	263	105	14	27	41	42	4	1975-76	1987-88
Jarvis, Jim	Pit., Phi., Tor.	3	108	17	15	32	62	....	....	....	....	....		1929-30	1936-37
Jarvis, Wes	Wsh., Min., L.A., Tor.	8	237	31	55	86	98	2	0	0	0	2		1979-80	1987-88
Javanainen, Arto	Pit.	1	14	4	1	5	2	....	....	....	....	....		1984-85	1984-85
Jeffrey, Larry	Det., Tor., NYR	8	368	39	62	101	293	38	4	10	14	42	1	1961-62	1968-69
Jelinek, Tomas	Ott.	1	49	7	6	13	52	....	....	....	....	....		1992-93	1992-93
Jenkins, Dean	L.A.	1	5	0	0	0	2	....	....	....	....	....		1983-84	1983-84
Jenkins, Roger	Tor., Chi., Mtl., Bos., Mtl.M., NYA	8	328	15	39	54	279	25	1	7	8	12	2	1930-31	1938-39
Jennings, Bill	Det., Bos.	5	108	32	33	65	45	20	4	4	8	6		1940-41	1944-45
Jensen, David A.	Hfd., Wsh.	4	69	9	13	22	22	11	0	0	0	2		1983-84	1987-88
Jensen, David H.	Min.	3	18	0	2	2	11	....	....	....	....	....		1983-84	1985-86
Jensen, Steve	Min., L.A.	7	438	113	107	220	318	12	0	3	3	9		1975-76	1981-82
• Jeremiah, Ed	NYA, Bos.	1	15	0	1	1	0	....	....	....	....	....		1931-32	1931-32
Jerrard, Paul	Min.	1	5	0	0	0	4	....	....	....	....	....		1988-89	1988-89
Jerwa, Frank	Bos.	1	28	4	5	9	12	....	....	....	....	....		1931-32	1931-32
Jerwa, Joe	NYR, Bos., St.L., NYA	9	293	36	69	105	338	17	2	3	5	20		1930-31	1938-39
Jirik, Jaroslav	St.L.	1	3	0	0	0	0	....	....	....	....	....		1969-70	1969-70
Joanette, Rosario	Mtl.	1	2	0	1	1	4	....	....	....	....	....		1944-45	1944-45
Jodzio, Rick	Col., Clev.	1	70	2	8	10	71	....	....	....	....	....		1977-78	1977-78
Johannesen, Glenn	NYI	1	2	0	0	0	0	....	....	....	....	....		1985-86	1985-86
Johannson, John	N.J.	1	5	0	0	0	0	....	....	....	....	....		1983-84	1983-84
Johansen, Trevor	Tor., Col., L.A.	5	286	11	46	57	282	13	0	3	3	21		1977-78	1981-82
Johansson, Bjorn	Clev.	2	15	1	1	2	10	....	....	....	....	....		1976-77	1977-78
Johns, Don	NYR, Mtl., Min.	6	153	2	21	23	76	....	....	....	....	....		1960-61	1967-68
Johnson, Al	Mtl., Det.	4	105	21	28	49	30	11	2	2	4	6		1956-57	1962-63
Johnson, Brian	Det.	1	3	0	0	0	5	....	....	....	....	....		1983-84	1983-84
• Johnson, Danny	Tor., Van., Det.	3	121	18	19	37	24	....	....	....	....	....		1969-70	1971-72
Johnson, Earl	Det.	1	1	0	0	0	0	....	....	....	....	....		1953-54	1953-54
• Johnson, Ivan	NYR, NYA	12	435	38	48	86	808	60	5	2	7	161	2	1926-27	1937-38
Johnson, Jim	NYR, Phi., L.A.	8	302	75	111	186	73	7	0	2	2	2		1964-65	1971-72
Johnson, Mark	Pit., Min., Hfd., St.L., N.J.	11	669	203	305	508	260	37	16	12	28	10		1979-80	1989-90
Johnson, Norm	Bos., Chi.	3	61	5	20	25	41	14	4	0	4	6		1957-58	1959-60
Johnson, Terry	Que., St.L., Cgy., Tor.	9	285	3	24	27	580	38	0	4	4	118		1979-80	1987-88
Johnson, Tom	Mtl., Bos.	17	978	51	213	264	960	111	8	15	23	109	6	1947-48	1964-65
Johnson, Virgil	Chi.	3	75	2	9	11	27	19	0	3	3	4	1	1937-38	1944-45
Johnson, William	Tor.	1	1	0	0	0	0	....	....	....	....	....		1949-50	1949-50
Johnston, Bernie	Hfd.	2	57	12	24	36	44	3	0	1	1	0		1979-80	1980-81
Johnston, George	Chi.	4	58	20	12	32	2	....	....	....	....	....		1941-42	1946-47
Johnston, Greg	Bos., Tor.	9	187	26	30	56	124	22	2	1	3	12		1983-84	1991-92
Johnston, Jay	Wsh.	2	8	0	0	0	13	....	....	....	....	....		1980-81	1981-82
Johnston, Joey	Min., Cal., Chi.	6	332	85	106	191	320	....	....	....	....	....		1968-69	1975-76
Johnston, Larry	L.A., Det., K.C., Col.	7	320	9	64	73	580	....	....	....	....	....		1967-68	1976-77
Johnston, Marshall	Min., Cal.	7	251	14	52	66	58	6	0	0	0	2		1967-68	1973-74
Johnston, Randy	NYI	1	4	0	0	0	4	....	....	....	....	....		1979-80	1979-80
Johnstone, Eddie	NYR, Det.	10	426	122	136	258	375	55	13	10	23	83		1975-76	1986-87
Johnstone, Ross	Tor.	2	42	5	4	9	14	3	0	0	0	0	1	1943-44	1944-45
• Joliat, Aurel	Mtl.	16	654	270	190	460	757	54	14	19	33	89	3	1922-23	1937-38
Joliat, Bobby	Mtl.	1	1	0	0	0	0	....	....	....	....	....		1924-25	1924-25
Joly, Greg	Wsh., Det.	9	365	21	76	97	250	5	0	0	0	8		1974-75	1982-83
Joly, Yvan	Mtl.	3	2	0	0	0	0	10	0	0	0	0		1979-80	1982-83
Jonathon, Stan	Bos., Pit.	8	411	91	110	201	751	63	8	4	12	137		1975-76	1982-83
Jones, Bob	NYR	1	2	0	0	0	0	....	....	....	....	....		1968-69	1968-69
Jones, Brad	Wpg., L.A., Phi.	6	148	25	31	56	122	9	1	1	2	2		1986-87	1991-92
Jones, Buck	Det., Tor.	4	50	2	2	4	36	12	0	1	1	18		1938-39	1942-43
Jones, Jim	Cal.	1	2	0	0	0	0	....	....	....	....	....		1971-72	1971-72
Jones, Jimmy	Tor.	3	148	13	18	31	68	19	1	5	6	11		1977-78	1979-80
Jones, Ron	Bos., Pit., Wsh.	5	54	1	4	5	31	....	....	....	....	....		1971-72	1975-76
Jonsson, Tomas	NYI, Edm.	8	552	85	259	344	482	80	11	26	37	97	2	1981-82	1988-89
Joseph, Anthony	Wpg.	1	2	1	0	1	0	....	....	....	....	....		1988-89	1988-89
Joyal, Eddie	Det., Tor., L.A., Phi.	9	466	128	134	262	103	50	11	8	19	18		1962-63	1971-72
Juckes, Bing	NYR	2	16	2	1	3	6	....	....	....	....	....		1947-48	1949-50
Julien, Claude	Que.	2	14	0	1	1	25	....	....	....	....	....		1984-85	1985-86
Jutila, Timo	Buf.	1	10	1	5	6	13	....	....	....	....	....		1984-85	1984-85
Juzda, Bill	NYR, Tor.	9	393	14	54	68	398	42	0	3	3	46	2	1940-41	1951-52
K															
Kabel, Bob	NYR	2	48	5	13	18	34	....	....	....	....	....		1959-60	1960-61
Kachowski, Mark	Pit.	3	64	6	5	11	209	....	....	....	....	....		1987-88	1989-90
Kachur, Ed	Chi.	2	96	10	14	24	35	....	....	....	....	....		1956-57	1957-58
Kaese, Trent	Buf.	1	1	0	0	0	0	....	....	....	....	....		1988-89	1988-89
Kaiser, Vern	Mtl.	1	50	7	5	12	33	2	0	0	0	0		1950-51	1950-51
Kalbfleish, Walter	Ott., St.L., NYA, Bos.	4	36	0	4	4	32	5	0	0	0	2		1933-34	1936-37
• Kaleta, Alex	Chi., NYR	7	387	92	121	213	190	17	1	6	7	2		1941-42	1950-51
Kallur, Anders	NYI	6	383	101	110	211	149	78	12	23	35	32	4	1979-80	1984-85
• Kaminsky, Max	Ott., St.L., Bos., Mtl.M.	4	130	22	34	56	38	4	0	0	0	0		1933-34	1936-37
• Kampman, Bingo	Tor.	5	189	14	30	44	287	47	1	4	5	38	1	1937-38	1941-42
Kane, Frank	Det.	1	2	0	0	0	0	....	....	....	....	....		1943-44	1943-44
Kannegiesser, Gord	St.L.	2	23	0	1	1	15	....	....	....	....	....		1967-68	1971-72
Kannegiesser, Sheldon	Pit., NYR, L.A., Van.	8	366	14	67	81	292	18	0	2	2	10		1970-71	1977-78

Name	NHL Teams	NHL Seasons	Regular Schedule GP	G	A	TP	PIM	Playoffs GP	G	A	TP	PIM	NHL Cup Wins	First NHL Season	Last NHL Season
Karjalainen, Kyosti	L.A.	1	28	1	8	9	12	3	0	1	1	2		1991-92	1991-92
Karlander, Al	Det.	4	212	36	56	92	70	4	0	1	1	0		1969-70	1972-73
Kasper, Steve	Bos., L.A., Phi., T.B.	13	821	177	291	468	554	94	20	28	48	82		1980-81	1992-93
Kastelic, Ed	Wsh., Hfd.	7	220	11	10	21	719	8	1	0	1	32		1985-86	1991-92
Kaszycki, Mike	NYI, Wsh., Tor.	5	226	42	80	122	108	19	2	6	8	10		1977-78	1982-83
Kea, Ed	Atl., St.L.	10	583	30	145	175	508	32	2	4	6	39		1973-74	1982-83
Kearns, Dennis	Van.	10	677	31	290	321	386	11	1	2	3	8		1971-72	1980-81
• Keating, Jack	NYA	2	35	5	5	10	17	....	....	....	....	....		1931-32	1932-33
Keating, John	Det.	2	11	2	1	3	4	....	....	....	....	....		1938-39	1939-40
Keating, Mike	NYR	1	1	0	0	0	0	....	....	....	....	....		1977-78	1977-78
• Keats, Duke	Det., Chi.	3	80	3	19	49	113	....	....	....	....	....		1926-27	1928-29
• Keeling, Butch	Tor., NYR	12	528	157	63	220	331	47	11	11	22	32	1	1926-27	1937-38
Keenan, Larry	Tor., St.L., Buf., Phi.	6	233	38	64	102	28	46	15	16	31	12		1961-62	1971-72
Kehoe, Rick	Tor., Pit.	14	906	371	396	767	120	39	4	17	21	4		1971-72	1984-85
Keller, Ralph	NYR	1	3	1	0	1	6	....	....	....	....	....		1962-63	1962-63
Kellgren, Christer	Col.	1	5	0	0	0	0	....	....	....	....	....		1981-82	1981-82
Kelly, Bob	St.L., Pit., Chi.	6	425	87	109	196	687	23	6	3	9	40		1973-74	1978-79
Kelly, Bob	Phi., Wsh.	12	837	154	208	362	1454	101	9	14	23	172	2	1970-71	1981-82
Kelly, Dave	Det.	1	16	2	0	2	4	....	....	....	....	....		1976-77	1976-77
Kelly, John Paul	L.A.	7	400	54	70	124	366	18	1	1	2	41		1979-80	1985-86
Kelly, Pete	St.L., Det., NYA, Bro.	7	180	21	38	59	68	19	3	1	4	8	2	1934-35	1941-42
Kelly, Red	Det., Tor.	20	1316	281	542	823	327	164	33	59	92	51	8	1947-48	1966-67
• Kelly, Reg	Tor., Chi., Bro.	8	289	74	53	127	105	39	7	6	13	10		1934-35	1941-42
Kemp, Kevin	Hfd.	1	3	0	0	0	4	....	....	....	....	....		1980-81	1980-81
Kemp, Stan	Tor.	1	1	0	0	0	2	....	....	....	....	....		1948-49	1948-49
Kendall, William	Chi., Tor.	5	132	16	10	26	28	5	0	0	0	0	1	1933-34	1937-38
Kennedy, Forbes	Chi., Det., Bos., Phi., Tor.	11	603	70	108	178	988	12	2	4	6	64		1956-57	1968-69
Kennedy, Ted	Tor.	14	696	231	329	560	432	78	29	31	60	32	5	1942-43	1956-57
• Kenny, Eddie	NYR, Chi.	2	11	0	0	0	18	....	....	....	....	....		1930-31	1934-35
Keon, Dave	Tor., Hfd.	18	1296	396	590	986	117	92	32	36	68	6	4	1960-61	1981-82
Kerr, Alan	NYI, Det., Wpg.	9	391	72	94	166	826	38	5	4	9	70		1984-85	1992-93
Kerr, Reg	Cle., Chi., Edm.	6	263	66	94	160	169	7	1	0	1	7		1977-78	1983-84
Kerr, Tim	Phi., NYR, Hfd.	13	655	370	304	674	596	81	40	31	71	58		1980-81	1992-93
Kessell, Rick	Pit., Cal.	5	135	4	24	28	6	....	....	....	....	....		1969-70	1973-74
Ketola, Veli-Pekka	Col.	1	44	9	5	14	4	....	....	....	....	....		1981-82	1981-82
Ketter, Kerry	Atl.	1	41	0	2	2	58	....	....	....	....	....		1972-73	1972-73
Kharin, Sergei	Wpg.	1	7	2	3	5	2	....	....	....	....	....		1990-91	1990-91
Kidd, Ian	Van.	2	20	4	7	11	25	....	....	....	....	....		1987-88	1988-89
Kiessling, Udo	Min.	1	1	0	0	0	2	....	....	....	....	....		1981-82	1981-82
Kilrea, Brian	Det., L.A.	2	26	3	5	8	12	....	....	....	....	....		1957-58	1967-68
• Kilrea, Hec	Ott., Det., Tor.	15	633	167	129	296	438	48	8	7	15	18	3	1925-26	1939-40
Kilrea, Ken	Det.	5	88	16	23	39	8	10	2	2	4	4		1938-39	1943-44
Kilrea, Wally	Ott., Phi., NYA, Mtl.M., Det.	9	315	35	58	93	87	25	2	4	6	6		1929-30	1937-38
Kindrachuk, Orest	Phi., Pit., Wsh.	10	508	118	261	379	648	76	20	20	40	53	2	1972-73	1981-82
King, Frank	Mtl.	1	10	1	0	1	2	....	....	....	....	....		1950-51	1950-51
King, Wayne	Cal.	3	73	5	18	23	34	....	....	....	....	....		1973-74	1975-76
Kinsella, Brian	Wsh.	2	10	0	1	1	0	....	....	....	....	....		1975-76	1976-77
Kinsella, Ray	Ott.	1	14	0	0	0	0	....	....	....	....	....		1930-31	1930-31
Kirk, Bobby	NYR	1	39	4	8	12	14	....	....	....	....	....		1937-38	1937-38
Kirkpatrick, Bob	NYR	1	49	12	12	24	6	....	....	....	....	....		1942-43	1942-43
Kirton, Mark	Tor., Det., Van.	6	266	57	56	113	121	4	1	2	3	7		1979-80	1984-85
Kitchen, Bill	Mtl., Tor.	4	41	1	4	5	40	3	0	1	1	0		1981-82	1984-85
• Kitchen, Hobie	Mtl.M., Det.	2	47	5	4	9	58	....	....	....	....	....		1925-26	1926-27
Kitchen, Mike	Col., N.J.	8	474	12	62	74	370	2	0	0	0	2		1976-77	1983-84
Kjellberg, Patrik	Mtl.	1	7	0	0	0	2	....	....	....	....	....		1992-93	1992-93
Klassen, Ralph	Cal., Clev., Col., St.L.	9	497	52	93	145	120	26	4	2	6	12		1975-76	1983-84
Klein, Jim	Bos., NYA	8	169	30	24	54	68	5	0	0	0	2	1	1928-29	1937-38
Kleinendorst, Scot	NYR, Hfd., Wsh.	8	281	12	46	58	452	26	2	7	9	40		1982-83	1989-90
Klingbeil, Ike	Chi.	1	5	1	2	3	2	....	....	....	....	....		1936-37	1936-37
Klukay, Joe	Tor., Bos.	11	566	109	127	236	189	71	13	10	23	23	4	1942-43	1955-56
Kluzak, Gord	Bos.	7	299	25	98	123	543	46	6	13	19	129		1982-83	1990-91
Knibbs, Bill	Bos.	1	53	7	10	17	4	....	....	....	....	....		1964-65	1964-65
• Knott, Nick	Bro.	1	14	3	1	4	9	....	....	....	....	....		1941-42	1941-42
Knox, Paul	Tor.	1	1	0	0	0	0	....	....	....	....	....		1954-55	1954-55
Komadoski, Neil	L.A., St.L.	8	502	16	76	92	632	23	0	2	2	47		1972-73	1979-80
Konik, George	Pit.	1	52	7	8	15	26	....	....	....	....	....		1967-68	1967-68
Kopak, Russ	Bos.	1	24	7	9	16	0	....	....	....	....	....		1943-44	1943-44
Korab, Jerry	Chi., Van., Buf., L.A.	15	975	114	341	455	1629	93	8	18	26	201		1970-71	1984-85
• Kordic, John	Mtl., Tor., Wsh., Que.	7	244	17	18	35	997	41	4	3	7	131	1	1985-86	1991-92
Korn, Jim	Det., Tor., Buf., N.J., Cgy.	10	597	66	122	188	1801	16	1	2	3	109		1979-80	1989-90
Korney, Mike	Det., NYR	4	77	9	10	19	59	....	....	....	....	....		1973-74	1978-79
Koroll, Cliff	Chi.	11	814	208	254	462	376	85	19	29	48	67		1969-70	1979-80
Kortko, Roger	NYI	2	79	7	17	24	28	10	0	3	3	17		1984-85	1985-86
Kostynski, Doug	Bos.	2	15	3	1	4	4	....	....	....	....	....		1983-84	1984-85
Kotanen, Dick	Det., NYR	2	2	0	1	1	0	....	....	....	....	....		1948-49	1950-51
Kotsopoulos, Chris	NYR, Hfd.,Tor., Det.	10	479	44	109	153	827	31	1	3	4	91		1980-81	1989-90
Kowal, Joe	Buf.	2	22	0	5	5	13	2	0	0	0	0		1976-77	1977-78
Kozak, Don	L.A., Van.	7	437	96	86	182	480	29	7	2	9	69		1972-73	1978-79
Kozak, Les	Tor.	1	12	1	0	1	2	....	....	....	....	....		1961-62	1961-62
Kraftcheck, Stephen	Bos., NYR, Tor.	4	157	11	18	29	83	6	0	0	0	7		1950-51	1958-59
Krake, Skip	Bos., L.A., Buf.	7	249	23	40	63	182	10	1	0	1	17		1963-64	1970-71
Krentz, Dale	Det.	3	30	5	3	8	9	2	0	0	0	0		1986-87	1988-89
Krol, Joe	NYR, Bro.	3	26	10	4	14	8	....	....	....	....	....		1936-37	1941-42
Kromm, Rich	Cgy., NYI	9	372	70	103	173	138	36	2	6	8	22		1983-84	1992-93
Krook, Kevin	Col.	1	3	0	0	0	2	....	....	....	....	....		1978-79	1978-79
Krulicki, Jim	NYR, Det.	1	41	0	3	3	6	....	....	....	....	....		1970-71	1970-71
Krutov, Vladimir	Van.	1	61	11	23	34	20	....	....	....	....	....		1989-90	1989-90
Kryskow, Dave	Chi., Wsh., Det., Atl.	4	231	33	56	89	174	12	2	0	2	4		1972-73	1975-76
Kryznowski, Edward	Bos., Chi.	5	237	15	22	37	65	18	0	1	1	4		1948-49	1952-53
Kuhn, Gord	NYA	1	12	1	1	2	4	....	....	....	....	....		1932-33	1932-33
Kukulowicz, Adolph	NYR	2	4	1	0	1	0	....	....	....	....	....		1952-53	1953-54
Kulak, Stu	Van., Edm., NYR, Que., Wpg.	4	90	8	4	12	130	3	0	0	0	2		1982-83	1988-89
Kullman, Arnie	Bos.	2	13	0	1	1	11	....	....	....	....	....		1947-48	1949-50
Kullman, Eddie	NYR	6	343	56	70	126	298	6	1	0	1	2		1947-48	1953-54
Kumpel, Mark	Que., Det., Wpg.	6	288	38	46	84	113	39	6	4	10	14		1984-85	1990-91
Kuntz, Alan	NYR	2	45	10	12	22	12	6	1	0	1	2		1941-42	1945-46
Kuntz, Murray	St.L.	1	7	1	2	3	0	....	....	....	....	....		1974-75	1974-75
Kurtenbach, Orland	NYR, Bos., Tor., Van.	13	639	119	213	332	628	19	2	4	6	70		1960-61	1973-74
Kuryluk, Mervin	Chi.	1	....	....	....	....	....	2	0	0	0	0		1961-62	1961-62
Kuzyk, Ken	Clev.	2	41	5	9	14	8	....	....	....	....	....		1976-77	1977-78
Kwong, Larry	NYR	1	1	0	0	0	0	....	....	....	....	....		1947-48	1947-48
• Kyle, Bill	NYR	2	3	0	3	3	0	....	....	....	....	....		1949-50	1950-51
Kyle, Gus	NYR, Bos.	3	203	6	20	26	362	14	1	2	3	34		1949-50	1951-52
Kyllonen, Marku	Wpg.	1	9	0	2	2	2	....	....	....	....	....		1988-89	1988-89

L

Name	NHL Teams	NHL Seasons	Regular Schedule GP	G	A	TP	PIM	Playoffs GP	G	A	TP	PIM	NHL Cup Wins	First NHL Season	Last NHL Season
Labadie, Mike	NYR	1	3	0	0	0	0	....	....	....	....	....		1952-53	1952-53
Labatte, Neil	St.L.	2	26	0	2	2	19	....	....	....	....	....		1978-79	1981-82
L'Abbe, Moe	Chi.	1	5	0	1	1	0	....	....	....	....	....		1972-73	1972-73
Labine, Leo	Bos., Det.	11	643	128	193	321	730	60	11	12	23	82		1951-52	1961-62
Labossierre, Gord	NYR, L.A., Min.	6	215	44	62	106	75	10	2	3	5	28		1963-64	1971-72
Labovitch, Max	NYR	1	5	0	0	0	4	....	....	....	....	....		1943-44	1943-44
Labraaten, Dan	Det., Cgy.	4	268	71	73	144	47	5	1	0	1	4		1978-79	1981-82
Labre, Yvon	Pit., Wsh.	9	371	14	87	101	788	....	....	....	....	....		1970-71	1980-81
Labrie, Guy	Bos., NYR	2	42	4	9	13	16	....	....	....	....	....		1943-44	1944-45
Lach, Elmer	Mtl.	14	664	215	408	623	478	76	19	45	64	36	3	1940-41	1953-54
Lachance, Earl	Mtl.	1	1	0	0	0	0	....	....	....	....	....		1926-27	1926-27
Lachance, Michel	Col.	1	21	0	4	4	22	....	....	....	....	....		1978-79	1978-79
Lacombe, Francois	Oak., Buf., Que.	4	78	2	17	19	54	3	1	0	1	0		1968-69	1979-80
Lacombe, Normand	Buf., Edm., Phi	7	319	53	62	115	196	26	5	1	6	49	1	1984-85	1990-91
Lacroix, Andre	Phi., Chi., Hfd.	6	325	79	119	198	44	16	2	5	7	0		1967-68	1979-80
Lacroix, Pierre	Que., Hfd.	4	274	24	108	132	197	8	0	2	2	10		1979-80	1982-83
Lafleur, Guy	Mtl., NYR, Que.	17	1126	560	793	1353	399	128	58	76	134	67	5	1971-72	1990-91

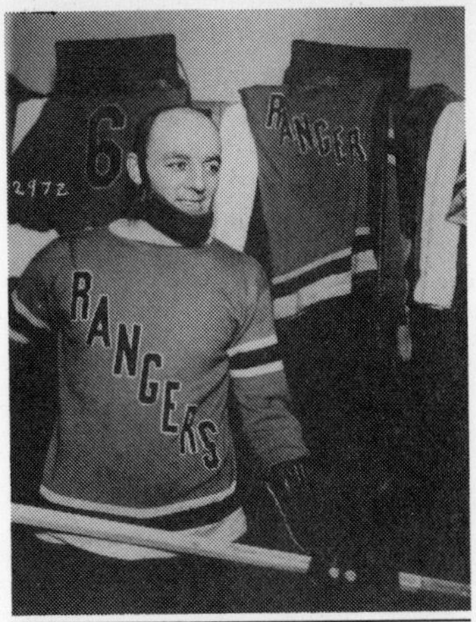

Ivan "Ching" Johnson

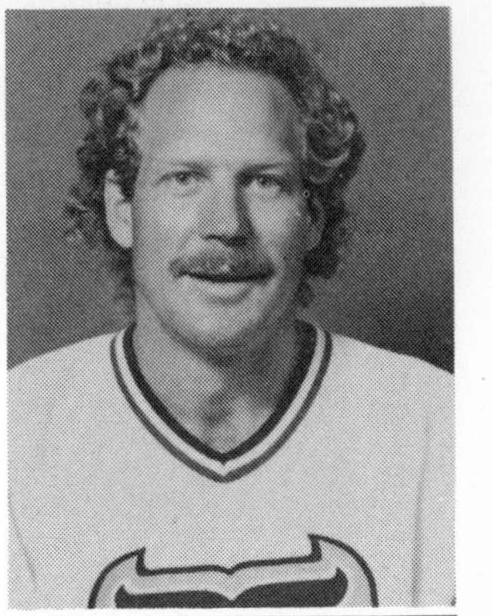
Tim Kerr

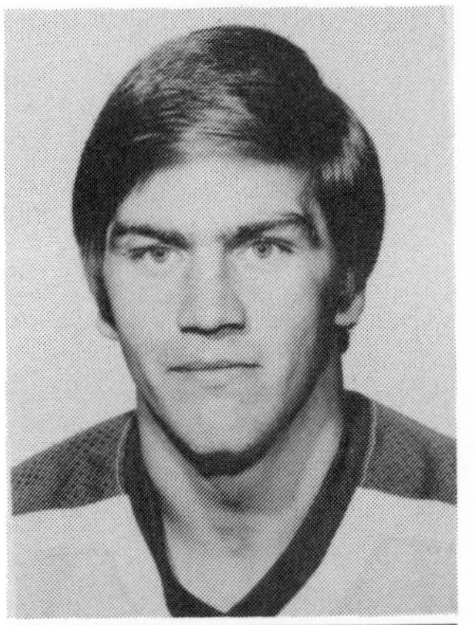
John Paul Kelly

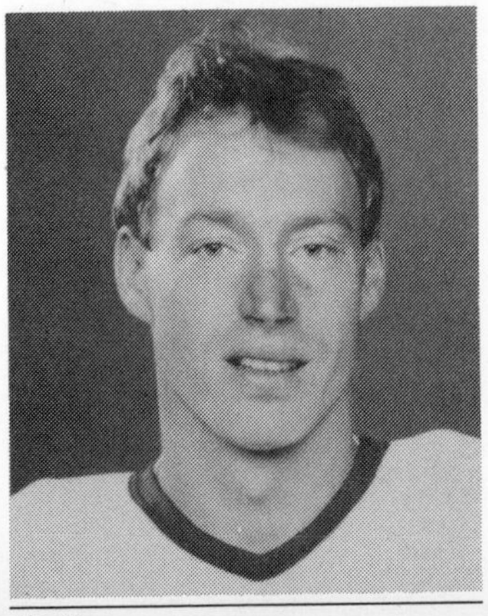
Alan Kerr

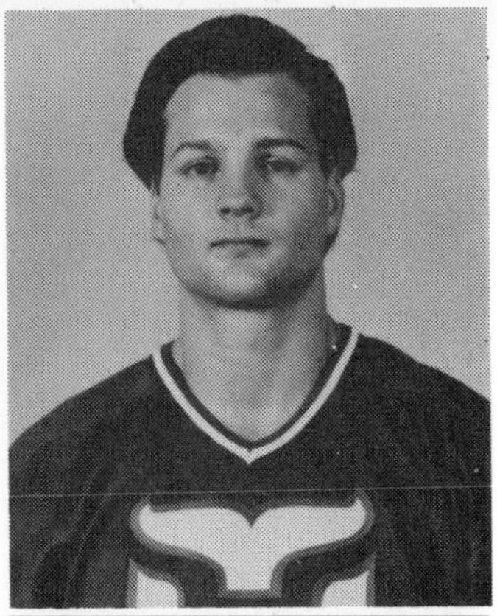

Ed Kastelic

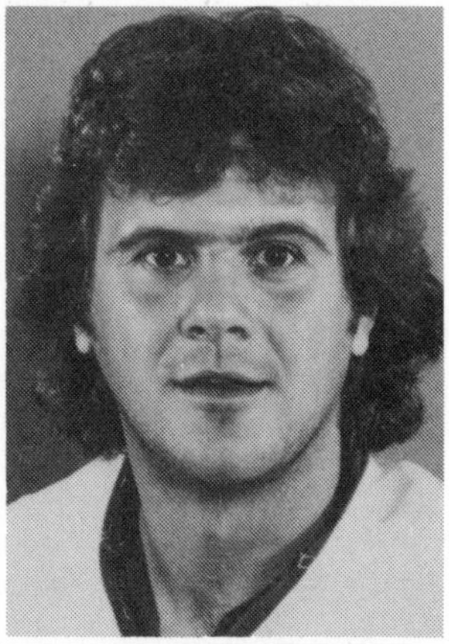

Tom Lysiak

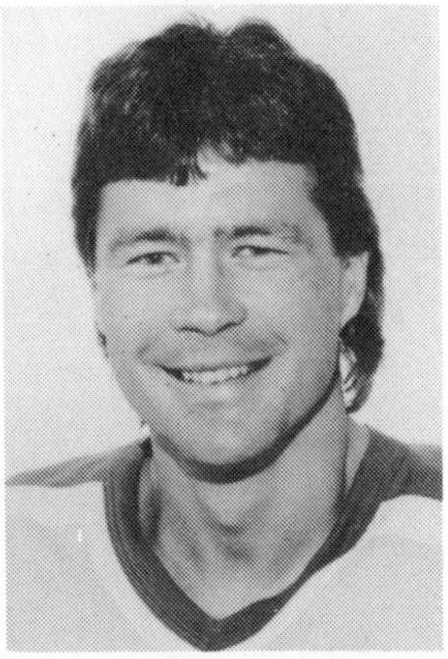

Morris Lukowich

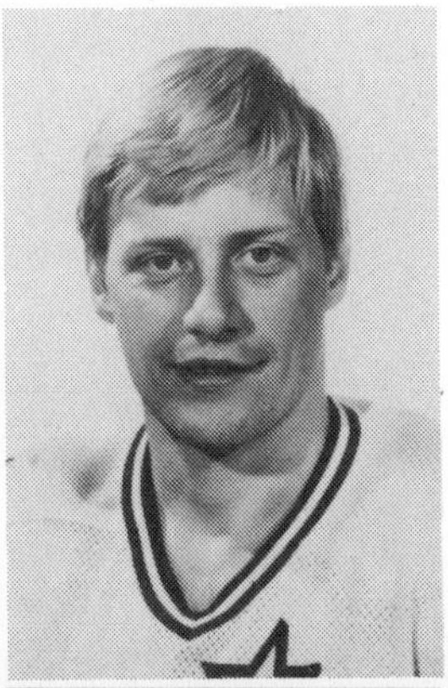

Craig Levie

			Regular Schedule					Playoffs					NHL	First	Last
Name	NHL Teams	NHL Seasons	GP	G	A	TP	PIM	GP	G	A	TP	PIM	Cup Wins	NHL Season	NHL Season
Lafleur, Rene	Mtl.	1	1	0	0	0	0	....	....	....	....	....		1924-25	1924-25
Laforce, Ernie	Mtl.	1	1	0	0	0	0	....	....	....	....	....		1942-43	1942-43
LaForest, Bob	L.A.	1	5	1	0	1	2	....	....	....	....	....		1983-84	1983-84
Laforge, Claude	Mtl., Det., Phi.	8	192	24	33	57	82	5	1	2	3	15		1957-58	1968-69
Laframboise, Pete	Cal., Wsh., Pit.	4	227	33	55	88	70	9	1	0	1	0		1971-72	1974-75
Lafrance, Adie	Mtl.	1	3	0	0	0	2	2	0	0	0	0		1933-34	1933-34
Lafrance, Leo	Mtl., Chi.	2	33	2	0	2	6	....	....	....	....	....		1926-27	1927-28
Lafreniere, Roger	Det., St.L.	2	13	0	0	0	4	....	....	....	....	....		1962-63	1972-73
Lagace, Jean-Guy	Pit., Buf., K.C.	6	187	9	39	48	251	....	....	....	....	....		1968-69	1975-76
Laidlaw, Tom	NYR, L.A.	10	705	25	139	164	717	69	4	17	21	78		1980-81	1989-90
Laird, Robbie	Min.	1	1	0	0	0	0	....	....	....	....	....		1979-80	1979-80
Lajeunesse, Serge	Det., Phi.	5	103	1	4	5	103	7	1	2	3	4		1970-71	1974-75
Lalande, Hec	Chi., Det.	4	151	21	39	60	120	....	....	....	....	....		1953-54	1957-58
Lalonde, Bobby	Van., Atl., Bos., Cgy.	11	641	124	210	334	298	16	4	2	6	6		1971-72	1981-82
• Lalonde, Edouard	Mtl., NYA	6	99	124	27	151	122	12	22	1	23	0	1	1917-18	1926-27
Lalonde, Ron	Pit., Wsh.	7	397	45	78	123	106	....	....	....	....	....		1972-73	1978-79
Lamb, Joe	Mtl.M., Ott., NYA, Bos., Mtl., St.L., Det.	11	444	108	101	209	601	18	1	1	2	51		1927-28	1937-38
Lambert, Lane	Det., NYR, Que.	6	283	58	66	124	521	17	2	4	6	40		1983-84	1988-89
Lambert, Yvon	Mtl., Buf.	10	683	206	273	479	340	90	27	22	49	67	4	1972-73	1981-82
Lamby, Dick	St.L.	3	22	0	5	5	22	....	....	....	....	....		1978-79	1980-81
• Lamirande, Jean-Paul	NYR, Mtl.	4	49	5	5	10	26	8	0	0	0	4		1946-47	1954-55
• Lamoureux, Leo	Mtl.	6	235	19	79	98	175	28	1	6	7	16	2	1941-42	1946-47
Lamoureux, Mitch	Pit., Phi.	3	73	11	9	20	59	....	....	....	....	....		1983-84	1987-88
Lampman, Mike	St.L., Van., Wsh.	4	96	17	20	37	34	....	....	....	....	....		1972-73	1976-77
Lancien, Jack	NYR	4	63	1	5	6	35	6	0	1	1	2		1946-47	1950-51
Landon, Larry	Mtl., Tor.	2	9	0	0	0	2	....	....	....	....	....		1983-84	1984-85
Lane, Gord	Wsh., NYI	10	539	19	94	113	1228	75	3	14	17	214	4	1975-76	1984-85
• Lane, Myles	NYR, Bos.	3	60	4	1	5	41	10	0	0	0	0	1	1928-29	1933-34
Langdon, Steve	Bos.	3	7	0	1	1	2	4	0	0	0	2		1974-75	1977-78
Langelle, Pete	Tor.	4	137	22	51	73	11	41	5	9	14	4	1	1938-39	1941-42
Langevin, Chris	Buf.	2	22	3	1	4	22	....	....	....	....	....		1983-84	1985-86
Langevin, Dave	NYI, Min., L.A.	8	513	12	107	119	530	87	2	15	17	106	4	1979-80	1986-87
Langlais, Alain	Min.	2	25	4	4	8	10	....	....	....	....	....		1973-74	1974-75
Langlois, Al	Mtl., NYR, Det., Bos.	9	448	21	91	112	488	53	1	5	6	60	3	1957-58	1965-66
Langlois, Charlie	Ham., NYA., Pit., Mtl.	4	151	22	3	25	201	2	0	0	0	0		1924-25	1927-28
Langway, Rod	Mtl., Wsh.	15	994	51	278	329	849	104	5	22	27	97	1	1978-79	1992-93
Lanthier, Jean-Marc	Van.	4	105	16	16	32	29	....	....	....	....	....		1983-84	1987-88
Lanyon, Ted	Pit.	1	5	0	0	0	4	....	....	....	....	....		1967-68	1967-68
Lanz, Rick	Van., Tor., Chi.	10	569	65	221	286	448	28	3	8	11	35		1980-81	1991-92
Laperriere, Jacques	Mtl.	12	691	40	242	282	674	88	9	22	31	101	6	1962-63	1973-74
Lapointe, Guy	Mtl., St.L., Bos.	16	884	171	451	622	893	123	26	44	70	138	6	1968-69	1983-84
Lapointe, Rick	Det., Phi., St.L., Que., L.A.	11	664	44	176	220	831	46	2	7	9	64		1975-76	1985-86
Lappin, Peter	Min., S.J.	2	7	0	0	0	2	....	....	....	....	....		1989-90	1991-92
Laprade, Edgar	NYR	10	501	108	172	280	42	18	4	9	13	4		1945-46	1954-55
LaPrairie, Ben	Chi.	1	7	0	0	0	0	....	....	....	....	....		1936-37	1936-37
Lariviere, Garry	Que., Edm.	4	219	6	57	63	167	14	0	5	5	8		1979-80	1982-83
Larmer, Jeff	Col., N.J., Chi.	5	158	37	51	88	57	5	1	0	1	2		1981-82	1985-86
• Larochelle, Wildor	Mtl., Chi.	12	474	92	74	166	211	34	6	4	10	24	2	1925-26	1936-37
Larocque, Denis	L.A.	1	8	0	1	1	18	....	....	....	....	....		1987-88	1987-88
Larose, Charles	Bos.	1	6	0	0	0	0	....	....	....	....	....		1925-26	1925-26
Larose, Claude	NYR	2	25	4	7	11	2	2	0	0	0	0		1979-80	1981-82
Larose, Claude	Mtl., Min., St.L.	16	943	226	257	483	887	97	14	18	32	143	5	1962-63	1977-78
Larouche, Pierre	Pit., Mtl., Hfd., NYR	14	812	395	427	822	237	64	20	34	54	16	1	1974-75	1987-88
Larson, Norman	NYA., Bro., NYR	3	89	25	18	43	12	....	....	....	....	....		1940-41	1946-47
Larson, Reed	Det., Bos., Edm., NYI, Min., Buf.	14	904	222	463	685	1391	32	4	7	11	63		1976-77	1989-90
Larter, Tyler	Wsh.	1	1	0	0	0	0	....	....	....	....	....		1989-90	1989-90
Latal, Jiri	Phi.	2	92	12	36	48	24	....	....	....	....	....		1989-90	1990-91
Latos, James	NYR	1	1	0	0	0	0	....	....	....	....	....		1988-89	1988-89
Latreille, Phil	NYR	1	4	0	0	0	2	....	....	....	....	....		1960-61	1960-61
Latta, David	Que.	4	36	4	8	12	4	....	....	....	....	....		1985-86	1990-91
Lauder, Marty	Bos.	1	3	0	0	0	2	....	....	....	....	....		1927-28	1927-28
Lauen, Mike	Wpg.	1	3	0	1	1	0	....	....	....	....	....		1983-84	1983-84
Laughlin, Craig	Mtl., Wsh., L.A., Tor.	8	549	136	205	341	364	33	6	6	12	20		1981-82	1988-89
Laughton, Mike	Oak., Cal.	4	189	39	48	87	101	11	2	4	6	0		1967-68	1970-71
Laurence, Red	Atl., St.L.	2	79	15	22	37	14	....	....	....	....	....		1978-79	1979-80
LaVallee, Kevin	Cgy., L.A., St.L., Pit.	7	366	110	125	235	85	32	5	8	13	24		1980-81	1986-87
Lavarre, Mark	Chi.	3	78	9	16	25	58	1	0	0	0	2		1985-86	1987-88
Lavender, Brian	St.L., NYI, Det., Cal.	4	184	16	26	42	174	3	0	0	0	2		1971-72	1974-75
• Laviolette, Jack	Mtl.	1	18	2	0	2	0	2	0	0	0	0		1917-18	1917-18
Lawless, Paul	Hfd., Phi., Van., Tor.	7	239	49	77	126	54	3	0	2	2	2		1982-83	1989-90
Lawson, Danny	Det., Min., Buf.	5	219	28	29	57	61	16	0	1	1	2		1967-68	1971-72
Lawton, Brian	Min., NYR, Hfd., Que., Bos., S.J.	9	483	112	154	266	401	11	1	1	2	12		1983-84	1992-93
Laxdal, Derek	Tor., NYI	6	67	12	7	19	90	1	0	2	2	2		1984-85	1990-91
Laycoe, Hal	NYR, Mtl., Bos.	11	531	25	77	102	292	40	2	5	7	39		1945-46	1955-56
Leach, Larry	Bos.	3	126	13	29	42	91	7	1	1	2	8		1958-59	1961-62
Leach, Reggie	Bos., Cal., Phi., Det.	13	934	381	285	666	387	94	47	22	69	22	1	1970-71	1982-83
Leavins, Jim	Det., NYR	2	41	2	12	14	30	....	....	....	....	....		1985-86	1986-87
LeBlanc, Fern	Det.	3	34	5	6	11	0	....	....	....	....	....		1976-77	1978-79
LeBlanc, J.P.	Chi., Det.	5	153	14	30	44	87	2	0	0	0	0		1968-69	1978-79
LeBrun, Al	NYR	2	6	0	2	2	4	....	....	....	....	....		1960-61	1965-66
Lecaine, Bill	Pit.	1	4	0	0	0	0	....	....	....	....	....		1968-69	1968-69
Leclair, Jackie	Mtl.,	3	160	20	40	60	56	20	6	0	7	6	1	1954-55	1956-57
Leclerc, Rene	Det.	2	87	10	11	21	105	....	....	....	....	....		1968-69	1970-71
Lecuyer, Doug	Chi., Wpg., Pit.	4	126	11	31	42	178	7	4	0	4	15		1978-79	1982-83
Ledingham, Walt	Chi., NYI	3	15	0	2	2	4	....	....	....	....	....		1972-73	1976-77
• LeDuc, Albert	Mtl., Ott., NYR	10	383	57	35	92	614	31	5	6	11	32	2	1925-26	1934-35
LeDuc, Rich	Bos., Que.	4	130	28	38	66	55	5	0	0	0	9		1972-73	1980-81
• Lee, Bobby	Mtl.	1	1	0	0	0	0	....	....	....	....	....		1942-43	1942-43
Lee, Edward	Que.	1	2	0	0	0	5	....	....	....	....	....		1984-85	1984-85
Lee, Peter	Pit.	6	431	114	131	245	257	19	0	8	8	4		1977-78	1982-83
Lefley, Bryan	N.Y.I., K.C., Col.	5	228	7	29	36	101	2	0	0	0	0		1972-73	1977-78
Lefley, Chuck	Mtl., St.L.	9	407	128	164	292	137	29	5	8	13	10		1970-71	1980-81
• Leger, Roger	NYR, Mtl.	5	187	18	53	71	71	20	0	7	7	14		1943-44	1949-50
Legge, Barry	Que., Wpg.	3	107	1	11	12	144	....	....	....	....	....		1979-80	1981-82
Legge, Randy	NYR	1	12	0	2	2	2	....	....	....	....	....		1972-73	1972-73
Lehmann, Tommy	Bos., Edm.	3	36	5	5	10	16	....	....	....	....	....		1987-88	1989-90
Lehto, Petteri	Pit.	1	6	0	0	0	4	....	....	....	....	....		1984-85	1984-85
Lehtonen, Antero	Wsh.	1	65	9	12	21	14	....	....	....	....	....		1979-80	1979-80
Lehvonen, Henri	K.C.	1	4	0	0	0	0	....	....	....	....	....		1974-75	1974-75
Leier, Edward	Chi.	2	16	2	1	3	2	....	....	....	....	....		1949-50	1950-51
Leinonen, Mikko	NYR, Wsh.	4	162	31	78	109	71	20	2	11	13	28		1981-82	1984-85
Leiter, Bobby	Bos., Pit., Atl.	10	447	98	126	224	144	8	3	0	3	2		1962-63	1975-76
Leiter, Ken	NYI, Min.	5	143	14	36	50	62	15	0	6	6	8		1984-85	1989-90
Lemaire, Jacques	Mtl.	12	853	366	469	835	217	145	61	78	139	63	8	1967-68	1978-79
Lemay, Moe	Van., Edm., Bos., Wpg.	8	317	72	94	166	442	28	6	3	9	55	1	1981-82	1988-89
Lemelin, Roger	K.C., Col.	4	36	1	2	3	27	....	....	....	....	....		1974-75	1977-78
Lemieux, Alain	St.L., Que., Pit.	6	119	28	44	72	38	19	4	6	10	0		1981-82	1986-87
Lemieux, Bob	Oak.	1	19	0	1	1	12	....	....	....	....	....		1967-68	1967-68
Lemieux, Jacques	L.A.	2	19	0	4	4	8	1	0	0	0	0		1967-68	1969-70
Lemieux, Jean	L.A., Atl., Wsh.	6	204	23	63	86	39	3	1	1	2	0		1969-70	1977-78
• Lemieux, Real	Det., L.A., NYR, Buf.	7	381	40	75	115	184	18	2	4	6	10		1966-67	1973-74
Lemieux, Richard	Van., K.C., Atl.	5	274	39	82	121	132	2	0	0	0	0		1971-72	1975-76
Lenardon, Tim	N.J., Van.	2	15	2	1	3	4	....	....	....	....	....		1986-87	1989-90
• Lepine, Hec	Mtl.	1	33	5	2	7	2	....	....	....	....	....		1925-26	1925-26
• Lepine, Pit	Mtl.	13	526	143	98	241	392	41	7	5	12	26	2	1925-26	1937-38
Leroux, Gaston	Mtl.	1	2	0	0	0	0	....	....	....	....	....		1935-36	1935-36
Lesieur, Art	Mtl., Chi.	4	100	4	2	6	50	14	0	0	0	4	1	1928-29	1935-36
Lesuk, Bill	Bos., Phi., L.A., Wsh., Wpg.	8	388	44	63	107	368	9	1	0	1	12	1	1968-69	1979-80
Leswick, Jack	Chi.	1	47	1	7	8	16	....	....	....	....	....	1	1933-34	1933-34
Leswick, Peter	NYA, Bos.	2	3	1	0	1	0	....	....	....	....	....		1936-37	1944-45
Leswick, Tony	NYR, Det., Chi.	12	740	165	159	324	900	59	13	10	23	91	3	1945-46	1957-58
Levandoski, Joseph	NYR	1	8	1	1	2	0	....	....	....	....	....		1946-47	1946-47
Leveille, Norm	Bos.	2	75	17	25	42	49	....	....	....	....	....		1981-82	1982-83
Lever, Don	Van., Atl., Cgy., Col., N.J., Buf.	15	1020	313	367	680	593	30	7	10	17	26		1972-73	1986-87

			Regular Schedule					Playoffs					NHL	First	Last
		NHL											Cup	NHL	NHL
Name	NHL Teams	Seasons	GP	G	A	TP	PIM	GP	G	A	TP	PIM	Wins	Season	Season
Levie, Craig	Wpg., Min., Van., St.L.	6	183	22	53	75	177	16	2	3	5	32		1981-82	1986-87
• Levinsky, Alex	Tor., Chi., NYR	9	367	19	49	68	307	34	2	1	3	2	2	1930-31	1938-39
Levo, Tapio	Col., N.J.,	2	107	16	53	69	36	....	....	....	....	....		1981-82	1982-83
Lewicki, Danny	Tor., NYR, Chi.	9	461	105	135	240	177	28	0	4	4	8	1	1950-51	1958-59
Lewis, Bob	NYR	1	8	0	0	0	0	....	....	....	....	....		1975-76	1975-76
Lewis, Dave	NYI, L.A., N.J., Det.	15	1008	36	187	223	953	91	1	20	21	143		1973-74	1987-88
Lewis, Douglas	Mtl.	1	3	0	0	0	0	....	....	....	....	....		1946-47	1946-47
• Lewis, Herbie	Det.	11	483	148	161	309	248	38	13	10	23	6	2	1928-29	1938-39
Ley, Rick	Tor., Hfd.	6	310	12	72	84	528	14	0	2	2	20		1968-69	1980-81
Liba, Igor	NYR, L.A.	1	37	7	18	25	36	2	0	0	0	2		1988-89	1988-89
Libett, Nick	Det., K.C., Pit.	14	982	237	268	505	472	16	6	2	8	2		1967-68	1980-81
Licari, Anthony	Det.	1	9	0	1	1	0	....	....	....	....	....		1946-47	1946-47
Liddington, Bob	Tor.	1	11	0	1	1	2	....	....	....	....	....		1970-71	1970-71
Lindgren, Lars	Van., Min.	6	394	25	113	138	325	40	5	6	11	20		1978-79	1983-84
Lindholm, Mikael	L.A.	1	18	2	2	4	2	....	....	....	....	....		1989-90	1989-90
Lindsay, Ted	Det., Chi.	17	1068	379	472	851	1808	133	47	49	96	194	4	1944-45	1964-65
Lindstrom, Willy	Wpg., Edm., Pit.	8	582	161	162	323	200	57	14	18	32	24	2	1979-80	1986-87
Linseman, Ken	Phi., Edm., Bos., Tor.	14	860	256	551	807	1727	113	43	77	120	325	1	1978-79	1991-92
Liscombe, Carl	Det.	9	383	137	140	277	117	59	22	19	41	20	1	1937-38	1945-46
Litzenberger, Ed	Mtl., Chi., Det., Tor.	12	618	178	238	416	283	40	5	13	18	34	4	1952-53	1963-64
• Locas, Jacques	Mtl.	2	59	7	8	15	66	....	....	....	....	....		1947-48	1948-49
Lochead, Bill	NYR, Det., Col.	6	330	69	62	131	180	7	3	0	3	6		1974-75	1979-80
Locking, Norm	Chi.	2	48	2	6	8	26	1	0	0	0	0		1934-35	1935-36
Lofthouse, Mark	Wsh., Det.	6	181	42	38	80	73	....	....	....	....	....		1977-78	1982-83
Logan, Dave	Chi., Van.	6	218	5	29	34	470	12	0	0	0	10		1975-76	1980-81
Logan, Robert	Buf., L.A.	3	42	10	5	15	0	....	....	....	....	....		1986-87	1988-89
Long, Barry	L.A., Det., Wpg.	5	280	11	68	79	250	5	0	1	1	18		1972-73	1981-82
Long, Stanley	Mtl.	1	....	....	....	....	....	3	0	0	0	0		1951-52	1951-52
Lonsberry, Ross	Phi., Pit., Bos., L.A.	15	968	256	310	566	806	100	21	25	46	87	2	1966-67	1980-81
Loob, Hakan	Cgy.	6	450	193	236	429	189	73	26	28	54	16	1	1983-84	1988-89
Loob, Peter	Que.	1	8	1	2	3	0	....	....	....	....	....		1984-85	1984-85
Lorentz, Jim	NYR, Buf., Bos., St.L.	10	659	161	238	399	208	54	12	10	22	30	1	1968-69	1977-78
Lorimer, Bob	NYI, Col., N.J.	10	529	22	90	112	431	49	3	10	13	83	2	1976-77	1985-86
Lorrain, Rod	Mtl.	6	179	28	39	67	30	11	0	3	3	0		1935-36	1941-42
Loughlin, Clem	Det., Chi.	3	101	8	6	14	77	....	....	....	....	....		1926-27	1928-29
Loughlin, Wilf	Tor.	1	14	0	0	0	2	....	....	....	....	....		1923-24	1923-24
Lovsin, Ken	Wsh.	1	1	0	0	0	0	....	....	....	....	....		1990-91	1990-91
Lowdermilk, Dwayne	Wsh.	1	2	0	1	1	2	....	....	....	....	....		1980-81	1980-81
Lowe, Darren	Pit.	1	8	1	2	3	0	....	....	....	....	....		1983-84	1983-84
Lowe, Norm	NYR	2	4	1	1	2	0	....	....	....	....	....		1948-49	1949-50
• Lowe, Ross	Bos., Mtl.	3	77	6	8	14	82	2	0	0	0	0		1949-50	1951-52
• Lowery, Fred	Mtl.M., Pit.	2	54	1	0	1	10	2	0	0	0	6	1	1924-25	1925-26
• Lowrey, Eddie	Ott., Ham.	3	24	2	0	2	3	....	....	....	....	....		1917-18	1920-21
• Lowrey, Gerry	Chi., Ott., Tor., Phi., Pit.	6	209	48	48	96	168	2	1	0	1	2		1927-28	1932-33
Lucas, Danny	Phi.	1	6	1	0	1	0	....	....	....	....	....		1978-79	1978-79
Lucas, Dave	Det.	1	1	0	0	0	0	....	....	....	....	....		1962-63	1962-63
Luce, Don	NYR, Det., Buf., L.A., Tor.	13	894	225	329	554	364	71	17	22	39	52		1969-70	1981-82
Ludvig, Jan	N.J., Buf.	7	314	54	87	141	418	....	....	....	....	....		1982-83	1988-89
Ludzik, Steve	Chi., Buf.	9	424	46	93	139	333	44	4	8	12	70		1981-82	1989-90
Lukowich, Bernie	Pit., St.L.	2	79	13	15	28	34	2	0	0	0	0		1973-74	1974-75
Lukowich, Morris	Wpg., Bos., L.A.	8	582	199	219	418	584	11	0	2	2	24		1979-80	1986-87
Luksa, Charlie	Hfd.	1	8	0	1	1	4	....	....	....	....	....		1979-80	1979-80
Lumley, Dave	Mtl., Edm., Hfd.	9	437	98	160	258	680	61	6	8	14	131	2	1978-79	1986-87
Lund, Pentti	NYR, Bos.	7	259	44	55	99	40	18	7	5	12	0		1946-47	1952-53
Lundberg, Brian	Pit.	1	1	0	0	0	2	....	....	....	....	....		1982-83	1982-83
Lunde, Len	Min., Van., Det., Chi.	8	321	39	83	122	75	20	3	2	5	2		1958-59	1970-71
Lundholm, Bengt	Wpg.	5	275	48	95	143	72	14	3	4	7	14		1981-82	1985-86
Lundrigan, Joe	Tor., Wsh.	2	52	2	8	10	22	....	....	....	....	....		1972-73	1974-75
Lundstrom, Tord	Det.	1	11	1	1	2	0	....	....	....	....	....		1973-74	1973-74
Lundy, Pat	Det. Chi.	5	150	37	32	69	31	9	1	1	2	2		1945-46	1950-51
Lupien, Gilles	Mtl., Pit., Hfd.	5	226	5	25	30	416	25	0	0	0	21	2	1977-78	1981-82
Lupul, Gary	Van.	7	293	70	75	145	243	25	4	7	11	11		1979-80	1985-86
Lyle, George	Det., Hfd.	4	99	24	38	62	51	....	....	....	....	....		1979-80	1982-83
Lynch, Jack	Pit., Det., Wsh.	7	382	24	106	130	336	....	....	....	....	....		1972-73	1978-79
Lynn, Vic	Det., Mtl., Tor., Bos., Chi.	10	326	49	76	125	274	47	7	10	17	46	3	1943-44	1953-54
Lyon, Steve	Pit.	1	3	0	0	0	2	....	....	....	....	....		1976-77	1976-77
Lyons, Ron	Bos., Phi.	1	36	2	4	6	29	5	0	0	0	0		1930-31	1930-31
Lysiak, Tom	Atl., Chi.	13	919	292	551	843	567	78	25	38	63	49		1973-74	1985-86
M															
MacAdam, Al	Phi., Cal., Cle., Min., Van.	12	864	240	351	591	509	64	20	24	44	21	1	1973-74	1984-85
MacDonald, Blair	Edm., Van.	4	219	91	100	191	65	11	0	6	6	2		1979-80	1982-83
MacDonald, Brett	Van.	1	1	0	0	0	0	....	....	....	....	....		1987-88	1987-88
• MacDonald, Kilby	NYR	4	151	36	34	70	47	15	1	2	3	4	1	1939-40	1944-45
MacDonald, Lowell	Det., L.A., Pit.	13	506	180	210	390	92	30	11	11	22	12		1961-62	1977-78
MacDonald, Parker	Tor., NYR, Det., Bos., Min.	14	676	144	179	323	253	75	14	14	28	20		1952-53	1968-69
MacDougall, Kim	Min.	1	1	0	0	0	0	....	....	....	....	....		1974-75	1974-75
MacEachern, Shane	St.L.	1	1	0	0	0	0	....	....	....	....	....		1987-88	1987-88
Macey, Hubert	NYR, Mtl.	3	30	6	9	15	0	8	0	0	0	0		1941-42	1946-47
MacGregor, Bruce	Det., NYR	14	893	213	257	470	217	107	19	28	47	44		1960-61	1973-74
MacGregor, Randy	Hfd.	1	2	1	1	2	2	....	....	....	....	....		1981-82	1981-82
MacGuigan, Garth	NYI	1	2	0	0	0	0	....	....	....	....	....		1979-80	1979-80
MacIntosh, Ian	NYR	1	4	0	0	0	4	....	....	....	....	....		1952-53	1952-53
MacIver, Don	Wpg.	1	6	0	0	0	2	....	....	....	....	....		1979-80	1979-80
MacKasey, Blair	Tor.	1	1	0	0	0	2	....	....	....	....	....		1976-77	1976-77
MacKay, Calum	Det., Mtl.	8	237	50	55	105	214	38	5	13	18	20	1	1946-47	1954-55
Mackay, Dave	Chi.	1	29	3	0	3	26	5	0	1	1	2		1940-41	1940-41
• MacKay, Mickey	Chi., Pit., Bos.	4	151	44	19	63	79	11	0	0	0	6	1	1926-27	1929-30
MacKay, Murdo	Mtl.	3	19	0	3	3	0	15	1	2	3	0		1945-46	1947-48
Mackell, Fleming	Tor., Bos.	13	665	149	220	369	562	80	22	41	63	75	2	1947-48	1959-60
MacKenzie, Barry	Min.	1	6	0	1	1	6	....	....	....	....	....		1968-69	1968-69
• MacKenzie, Bill	Chi., Mtl.M., Mtl., NYR	7	266	15	14	29	133	19	1	1	2	11	1	1932-33	1939-40
MacKey, Reggie	NYR	1	34	0	0	0	16	1	0	0	0	0		1926-27	1926-27
Mackie, Howie	Det.	2	20	1	0	1	4	8	0	0	0	0	1	1936-37	1937-38
MacKinnon, Paul	Wsh.	5	147	5	23	28	91	....	....	....	....	....		1979-80	1983-84
MacLean, Paul	St.L., Wpg., Det.	11	719	324	349	673	968	53	21	14	35	104		1980-81	1990-91
MacLeish, Rick	Phi., Hfd., Pit., Det.	14	846	349	410	759	434	114	54	53	107	38	2	1970-71	1983-84
MacLellan, Brian	L.A., NYR, Min., Cgy., Det.	10	606	172	241	413	551	47	5	9	14	42		1982-83	1991-92
MacMillan, Billy	Tor., Atl., NYI	7	446	74	77	151	184	53	6	6	12	40		1970-71	1976-77
MacMillan, Bob	NYR, St.L., Atl., Cgy., Col., N.J., Chi.	11	753	228	349	577	260	31	8	11	19	16		1974-75	1984-85
MacMillan, John	Tor., Det.	5	104	5	10	15	32	12	0	1	1	2	2	1960-61	1964-65
MacNeil, Al	Tor., Mtl., Chi., NYR, Pit.	11	524	17	75	92	617	37	0	4	4	67		1955-56	1967-68
MacNeil, Bernie	St.L.	1	4	0	0	0	0	....	....	....	....	....		1973-74	1973-74
• MacPherson, Bud	Mtl.	7	259	5	33	38	233	29	0	3	3	21	1	1948-49	1956-57
MacSweyn, Ralph	Phi.	5	47	0	5	5	10	8	0	0	0	6		1967-68	1971-72
Madigan, Connie	St.L.	1	20	0	3	3	25	5	0	0	0	4		1972-73	1972-73
Magee, Dean	Min.	1	7	0	0	0	4	....	....	....	....	....		1977-78	1977-78
Maggs, Daryl	Chi., Cal., Tor.	3	135	14	19	33	54	4	0	0	0	0		1971-72	1979-80
Magnan, Marc	Tor.	1	4	0	1	1	5	....	....	....	....	....		1982-83	1982-83
Magnuson, Keith	Chi.	11	589	14	125	139	1442	68	3	9	12	164		1969-70	1979-80
Maguire, Kevin	Tor., Buf., Phi.	6	260	29	30	59	782	11	0	0	0	86		1986-87	1991-92
Mahaffy, John	Mtl., NYR	3	37	11	25	36	4	1	0	1	1	0		1942-43	1944-45
Mahovlich, Frank	Tor., Det., Mtl.	18	1181	533	570	1103	1056	137	51	67	118	163	6	1956-57	1973-74
Mahovlich, Pete	Det., Mtl., Pit.	16	884	288	485	773	916	88	30	42	72	134	4	1965-66	1980-81
Mailhot, Jacques	Que.	1	5	0	0	0	33	....	....	....	....	....		1988-89	1988-89
Mailley, Frank	Mtl.	1	1	0	0	0	0	....	....	....	....	....		1942-43	1942-43
Mair, Jim	Phi., NYI, Van.	5	76	4	15	19	49	3	1	2	3	4		1970-71	1974-75
• Majeau, Fern	Mtl.	2	56	22	24	46	43	1	0	0	0	0	1	1943-44	1944-45
Major, Bruce	Que.	1	4	0	0	0	0	....	....	....	....	....		1990-91	1990-91
Maki, Chico	Chi.	15	841	143	292	435	345	113	17	36	53	43	1	1960-61	1975-76
• Maki, Wayne	Chi., St.L., Van.	6	246	57	79	136	184	2	1	0	1	2		1967-68	1972-73
Makkonen, Karl	Edm.	1	9	2	2	4	0	....	....	....	....	....		1979-80	1979-80
Malinowski, Merlin	Col., N.J., Hfd.	5	282	54	111	165	121	....	....	....	....	....		1978-79	1982-83

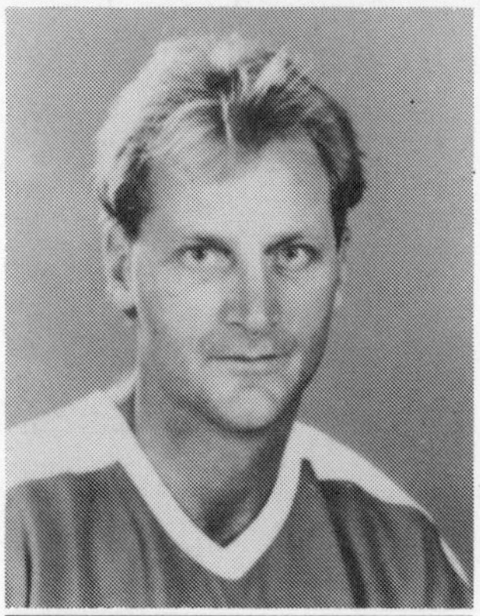
Rod Langway

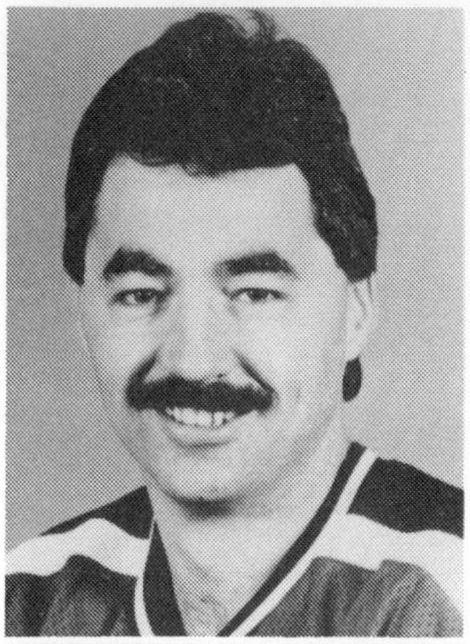
Bob Lorimer

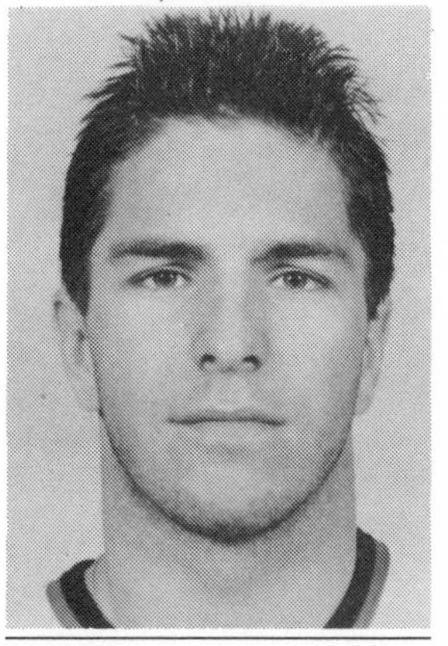
Mark Lavarre

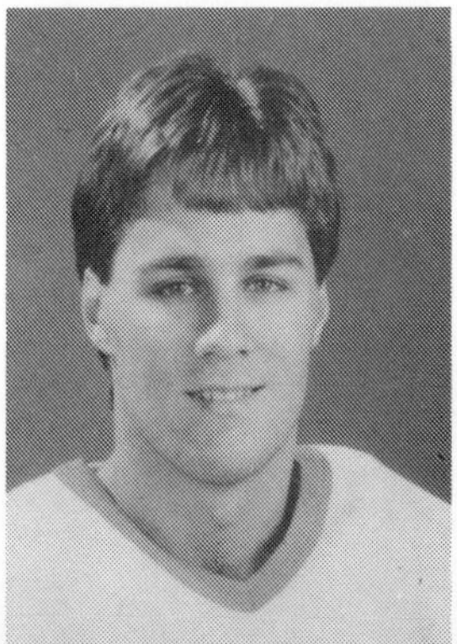
David Latta

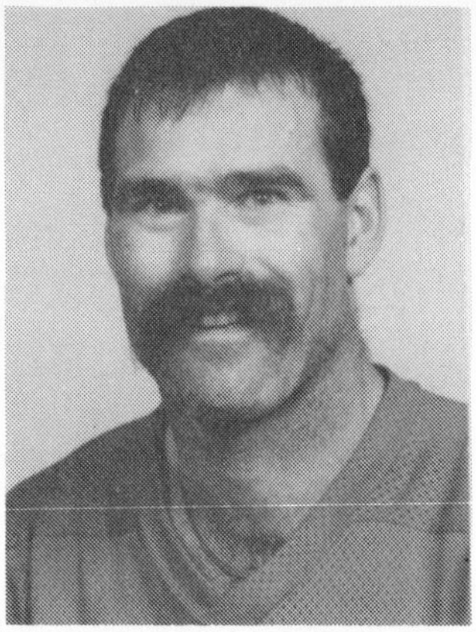
Paul MacLean

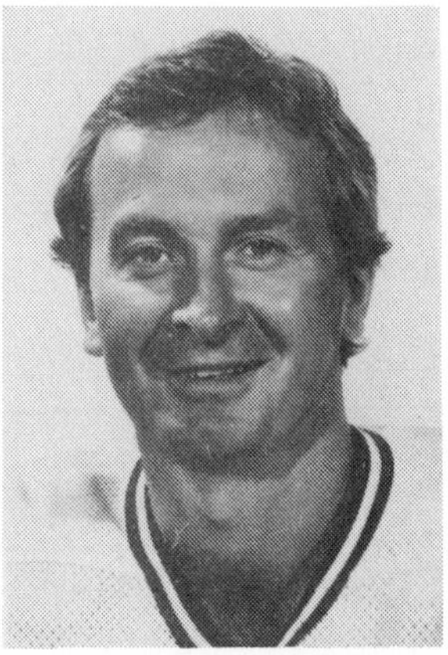
Walt McKechnie

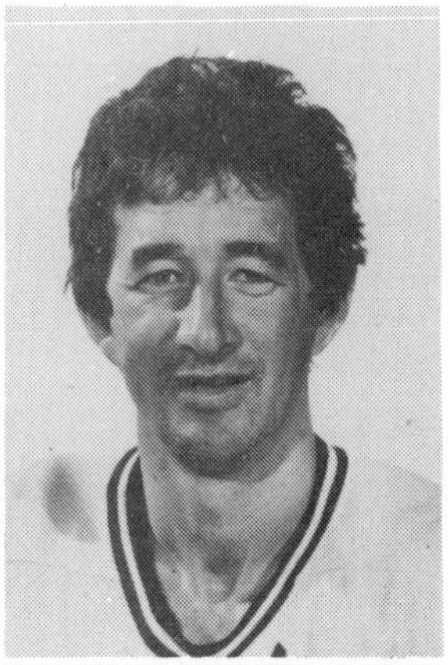
Al MacAdam

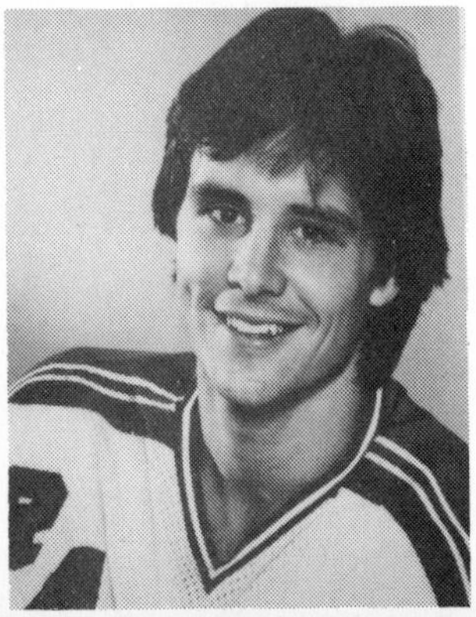
Rob McClanahan

			Regular Schedule					Playoffs					NHL	First	Last
		NHL											Cup	NHL	NHL
Name	NHL Teams	Seasons	GP	G	A	TP	PIM	GP	G	A	TP	PIM	Wins	Season	Season
Malone, Cliff	Mtl.	1	3	0	0	0	0	....	....	....	....	....		1951-52	1951-52
Malone, Greg	Pit., Hfd., Que.	11	704	191	310	501	661	20	3	5	8	32		1976-77	1986-87
• Malone, Joe	Mtl., Que., Ham.	7	125	146	21	167	23	9	5	0	5	0	1	1917-18	1923-24
Maloney, Dan	Chi., L.A., Det., Tor.	11	737	192	259	451	1489	40	4	7	11	35		1970-71	1981-82
Maloney, Dave	NYR, Buf.	11	657	71	246	317	1154	49	7	17	24	91		1974-75	1984-85
Maloney, Don	NYR, Hfd., NYI	13	765	214	350	564	815	94	22	35	57	101		1978-79	1990-91
Maloney, Phil	Bos., Tor., Chi.	5	158	28	43	71	16	6	0	0	0	0		1949-50	1959-60
Maluta, Ray	Bos.	2	25	2	3	5	6	2	0	0	0	0		1975-76	1976-77
Manastersky, Tom	Mtl.	1	6	0	0	0	11	....	....	....	....	....		1950-51	1950-51
Mancuso, Gus	Mtl., NYR	4	42	7	9	16	17	....	....	....	....	....		1937-38	1942-43
Mandich, Dan	Min.	4	111	5	11	16	303	7	0	0	0	2		1982-83	1985-86
Manery, Kris	Van., Wpg., Clev., Min.	4	250	63	64	127	91	....	....	....	....	....		1977-78	1980-81
Manery, Randy	L.A., Det., Atl.	10	582	50	206	256	415	13	0	2	2	12		1970-71	1979-80
Mann, Jack	NYR	2	9	3	4	7	0	....	....	....	....	....		1943-44	1944-45
Mann, Jimmy	Wpg., Que., Pit.	8	293	10	20	30	895	22	0	0	0	89		1979-80	1987-88
Mann, Ken	Det.	1	1	0	0	0	0	....	....	....	....	....		1975-76	1975-76
Mann, Norm	Tor.	2	31	0	3	3	4	1	0	0	0	0		1938-39	1940-41
Manners, Rennison	Pit., Phi.	2	37	3	2	5	14	....	....	....	....	....		1929-30	1930-31
Manno, Bob	Van., Tor., Det.	8	371	41	131	172	274	17	2	4	6	12		1976-77	1984-85
Manson, Ray	Bos., NYR	2	2	0	1	1	0	....	....	....	....	....		1947-48	1948-49
• Mantha, Georges	Mtl.	13	498	89	102	181	148	36	6	2	8	16	2	1928-29	1940-41
Mantha, Moe	Wpg., Pit., Edm., Min., Phi.	12	656	81	289	370	501	17	5	10	15	18		1980-81	1991-92
• Mantha, Sylvio	Mtl., Bos.	14	543	63	72	135	667	46	5	4	9	66	3	1923-24	1936-37
Maracle, Buddy	NYR	1	11	1	3	4	4	4	0	0	0	0		1930-31	1930-31
Marcetta, Milan	Tor., Min.	3	54	7	15	22	10	17	7	7	14	4	1	1966-67	1968-69
March, Mush	Chi.	17	758	153	230	383	540	48	12	15	27	41	2	1928-29	1944-45
Marchinko, Brian	Tor., NYI	4	47	2	6	8	0	....	....	....	....	....		1970-71	1973-74
Marcinyshyn, David	N.J., Que., NYR	3	16	0	1	1	49	....	....	....	....	....		1990-91	1992-93
Marcon, Lou	Det.	3	70	0	4	4	42	....	....	....	....	....		1958-59	1962-63
Marcotte, Don	Bos.	15	868	230	255	485	317	132	34	27	61	81	2	1965-66	1981-82
Marini, Hector	NYI, N.J.	5	154	27	46	73	246	10	3	6	9	14	2	1978-79	1983-84
Mario, Frank	Bos.	2	53	9	19	28	24	....	....	....	....	....		1941-42	1944-45
• Mariucci, John	Chi.	5	223	11	34	45	308	8	0	3	3	26		1940-41	1947-48
Markell, John	Wpg., St. L., Min.	4	55	11	10	21	36	....	....	....	....	....		1979-80	1984-85
Marker, Gus	Det., Mtl.M., Tor., Bro.	10	336	64	69	133	133	45	6	8	14	36	1	1932-33	1941-42
Markham, Ray	NYR	1	14	1	1	2	21	7	1	0	1	24		1979-80	1979-80
Markle, Jack	Tor.	1	8	0	1	1	0	....	....	....	....	....		1935-36	1935-36
• Marks, Jack	Mtl.W, Tor., Que.	2	7	0	0	0	4	....	....	....	....	....	1	1917-18	1919-20
Marks, John	Chi.	10	657	112	163	275	330	57	5	9	14	60		1972-73	1981-82
Markwart, Nevin	Bos., Cgy.	8	309	41	68	109	794	19	1	0	1	33		1983-84	1991-92
Marois, Mario	NYR, Van., Que., Wpg., St.L.	15	955	76	357	433	1746	100	4	34	38	182		1977-78	1991-92
Marotte, Gilles	Bos., Chi., L.A., NYR, St.L.	12	808	56	265	321	872	29	3	3	6	26		1965-66	1976-77
Marquess, Mark	Bos.	1	27	5	4	9	27	4	0	0	0	0		1946-47	1946-47
Marsh, Brad	Atl., Cgy., Phi., Tor., Det., Ott.	15	1086	23	175	198	1241	97	6	18	24	124		1978-79	1992-93
Marsh, Gary	Det., Tor.	2	7	1	3	4	4	....	....	....	....	....		1967-68	1968-69
Marsh, Peter	Wpg., Chi.	5	278	48	71	119	224	26	1	5	6	33		1979-80	1983-84
Marshall, Bert	Det., Oak., Cal., NYR, NYI	14	868	17	181	198	926	72	4	22	26	99		1965-66	1978-79
Marshall, Don	Mtl., NYR, Buf., Tor.	19	1176	265	324	589	127	94	8	15	23	14	5	1951-52	1971-72
Marshall, Paul	Pit., Tor., Hfd.	4	95	15	18	33	17	1	0	0	0	0		1979-80	1982-83
Marshall, Willie	Tor.	4	33	1	15	16	2	....	....	....	....	....		1952-53	1958-59
Marson, Mike	Wsh., L.A.	6	196	24	24	48	233	....	....	....	....	....		1974-75	1979-80
Martin, Clare	Bos., Det., Chi., NYR	6	237	12	28	40	78	22	0	2	2	6	1	1941-42	1951-52
Martin, Frank	Bos., Chi.	6	282	11	46	57	122	10	0	1	1	2		1952-53	1957-58
Martin, Grant	Van., Wsh.	4	44	0	4	4	55	1	1	0	1	2		1983-84	1986-87
Martin, Jack	Tor.	1	1	0	0	0	0	....	....	....	....	....		1960-61	1960-61
Martin, Pit	Det., Bos., Chi., Van.	17	1101	324	485	809	609	100	27	31	58	56		1961-62	1978-79
Martin, Rick	Buf., L.A.	11	685	384	317	701	477	63	24	29	53	74		1971-72	1981-82
Martin, Ron	NYA	2	94	13	16	29	36	....	....	....	....	....		1932-33	1933-34
Martin, Terry	Buf., Que., Tor., Edm., Min.	10	479	104	101	205	202	21	4	2	6	26		1975-76	1984-85
Martin, Tom	Wpg., Hfd., Min.	6	92	12	11	23	249	4	0	0	0	6		1984-85	1989-90
Martin, Tom	Tor.	1	3	1	0	1	0	....	....	....	....	....		1967-68	1967-68
Martineau, Don	Atl., Min., Det.	4	90	6	10	16	63	....	....	....	....	....		1973-74	1976-77
Martinson, Steven	Det., Mtl., Min.	4	49	2	1	3	244	1	0	0	0	10		1987-88	1991-92
Maruk, Dennis	Cal., Clev., Min., Wsh.	14	888	356	522	878	761	34	14	22	36	26		1975-76	1988-89
Masnick, Paul	Mtl., Chi., Tor.	6	232	18	41	59	139	33	4	5	9	27	1	1950-51	1957-58
Mason, Charley	NYR, NYA, Det., Chi.	4	95	7	18	25	44	4	0	1	1	0		1934-35	1938-39
Massecar, George	NYA	3	100	12	11	23	46	....	....	....	....	....		1929-30	1931-32
Masters, Jamie	St.L.	3	33	1	13	14	2	2	0	0	0	0		1975-76	1978-79
• Masterton, Bill	Min.	1	38	4	8	12	4	....	....	....	....	....		1967-68	1967-68
Mathers, Frank	Tor.	3	23	1	3	4	4	....	....	....	....	....		1948-49	1951-52
Mathiasen, Dwight	Pit.	3	33	1	7	8	18	....	....	....	....	....		1985-86	1987-88
• Matte, Joe	Tor., Ham., Bos., Mtl.	4	64	18	14	32	43	....	....	....	....	....		1919-20	1925-26
Matte, Joe	Chi.	1	12	0	1	1	0	....	....	....	....	....		1942-43	1942-43
Matte, Roland	Det.	1	12	0	1	1	0	....	....	....	....	....		1929-30	1929-30
Mattiussi, Dick	Pit., Oak., Cal.	4	200	8	31	39	124	8	0	1	1	6		1967-68	1970-71
Matz, Johnny	Mtl.	1	30	3	2	5	0	5	0	0	0	2		1924-25	1924-25
Maxner, Wayne	Bos.	2	62	8	9	17	48	....	....	....	....	....		1964-65	1965-66
Maxwell, Brad	Min., Que., Tor., Van., NYR	10	612	98	270	368	1292	79	12	49	61	178		1977-78	1986-87
Maxwell, Bryan	Min., St.L., Wpg., Pit.	8	331	18	77	95	745	15	1	1	2	86		1977-78	1984-85
Maxwell, Kevin	Min., Col., N.J.	3	66	6	15	21	61	16	3	4	7	24		1980-81	1983-84
Maxwell, Wally	Tor.	1	2	0	0	0	0	....	....	....	....	....		1952-53	1952-53
Mayer, Jim	NYR	1	4	0	0	0	0	....	....	....	....	....		1979-80	1979-80
Mayer, Pat	Pit.	1	1	0	0	0	4	....	....	....	....	....		1987-88	1987-88
Mayer, Shep	Tor.	1	12	1	2	3	4	....	....	....	....	....		1942-43	1942-43
Mazur, Eddie	Mtl., Chi.	6	107	8	20	28	120	25	4	5	9	22	1	1950-51	1956-57
McAdam, Gary	Buf., Pit., Det., Cal., Wsh., N.J., Tor.	11	534	96	132	228	243	30	6	5	11	16		1975-76	1985-86
McAdam, Sam	NYR	1	5	0	0	0	0	....	....	....	....	....		1930-31	1930-31
McAndrew, Hazen	Bro.	1	7	0	1	1	6	....	....	....	....	....		1941-42	1941-42
McAneeley, Ted	Cal.	3	158	8	35	43	141	....	....	....	....	....		1972-73	1974-75
McAtee, Jud	Det.	3	46	15	13	28	6	14	2	1	3	0		1942-43	1944-45
McAtee, Norm	Bos.	1	13	0	1	1	0	....	....	....	....	....		1946-47	1946-47
McAvoy, George	Mtl.	1	....	....	....	....	....	4	0	0	0	0		1954-55	1954-55
McBride, Cliff	Mtl.M., Tor.	2	2	0	0	0	0	....	....	....	....	....		1928-29	1929-30
McBurney, Jim	Chi.	1	1	0	1	1	0	....	....	....	....	....		1952-53	1952-53
McCabe, Stan	Det., Mtl.M.	4	78	9	4	13	49	....	....	....	....	....		1929-30	1933-34
• McCaffrey, Bert	Tor., Pit., Mtl.	7	260	42	30	72	202	8	2	1	3	12		1924-25	1930-31
McCahill, John	Col.	1	1	0	0	0	0	....	....	....	....	....		1977-78	1977-78
McCaig, Douglas	Det., Chi.	7	263	8	21	29	255	17	0	1	1	8		1941-42	1950-51
• McCallum, Dunc	NYR, Pit.	5	187	14	35	49	230	10	1	2	3	12		1965-66	1970-71
McCalmon, Eddie	Chi., Phi.	2	39	5	0	5	14	....	....	....	....	....		1927-28	1930-31
McCann, Rick	Det.	6	43	1	4	5	6	....	....	....	....	....		1967-68	1974-75
McCarthy, Dan	NYR	1	5	4	0	4	4	....	....	....	....	....		1980-81	1980-81
McCarthy, Kevin	Phi., Van., Pit.	10	537	67	191	258	527	21	2	3	5	20		1977-78	1986-87
• McCarthy, Tom	Que., Ham.	2	34	19	3	22	10	....	....	....	....	....		1919-20	1920-21
McCarthy, Tom	Det., Bos.	4	60	8	9	17	8	....	....	....	....	....		1956-57	1960-61
McCarthy, Tom	Min., Bos.	9	460	178	221	399	330	68	12	26	38	67		1979-80	1987-88
McCartney, Walt	Mtl.	1	2	0	0	0	0	....	....	....	....	....		1932-33	1932-33
McCaskill, Ted	Min.	1	4	0	2	2	0	....	....	....	....	....		1967-68	1967-68
McClanahan, Rob	Buf., Hfd., NYR	5	224	38	63	101	126	34	4	12	16	31		1979-80	1983-84
McCord, Bob	Bos., Det., Min., St.L.	7	316	58	68	126	262	14	2	5	7	10		1963-64	1972-73
McCord, Dennis	Van.	1	3	0	0	0	0	....	....	....	....	....		1973-74	1973-74
McCormack, John	Tor., Mtl., Chi.	8	311	25	49	74	35	22	1	1	2	0	1	1947-48	1954-55
McCourt, Dale	Det., Buf., Tor.	7	532	194	284	478	124	21	9	7	16	6		1977-78	1983-84
McCreary, Bill	Tor.	1	12	1	0	1	4	....	....	....	....	....		1980-81	1980-81
McCreary, Bill E.	NYR, Det., Mtl., St.L.	10	309	53	62	115	108	48	6	16	22	14		1953-54	1970-71
McCreary, Keith	Mtl., Pit., Atl.	10	532	131	112	243	294	16	0	4	4	6		1961-62	1974-75
• McCreedy, Johnny	Tor.	2	64	17	12	29	25	21	4	3	7	16	2	1941-42	1944-45
McCrimmon, Jim	St.L.	1	2	0	0	0	0	....	....	....	....	....		1974-75	1974-75
McCulley, Bob	Mtl.	1	1	0	0	0	0	....	....	....	....	....		1934-35	1934-35
McCurry, Duke	Pit.	4	148	21	11	32	119	4	0	2	2	4		1925-26	1928-29
McCutcheon, Brian	Det.	3	37	3	1	4	7	....	....	....	....	....		1974-75	1976-77
McCutheon, Darwin	Tor.	1	1	0	0	0	0	....	....	....	....	....		1981-82	1981-82
McDill, Jeff	Chi.	1	1	0	0	0	0	....	....	....	....	....		1976-77	1976-77
McDonagh, Bill	NYR	1	4	0	0	0	2	....	....	....	....	....		1949-50	1949-50
McDonald, Ab	Mtl., Chi., Bos., Det., Pit., St.L.	15	762	182	248	430	200	84	21	29	50	42	4	1957-58	1971-72

			Regular Schedule					Playoffs					NHL	First	Last
Name	NHL Teams	NHL Seasons	GP	G	A	TP	PIM	GP	G	A	TP	PIM	Cup Wins	NHL Season	NHL Season
McDonald, Brian	Chi., Buf.	2	12	0	0	0	29	8	0	0	0	2		1967-68	1970-71
• McDonald, Bucko	Det., Tor., NYR	11	448	35	88	123	206	63	6	1	7	24	3	1934-35	1944-45
McDonald, Butch	Det., Chi.	2	66	8	20	28	2	5	0	2	2	10		1939-40	1944-45
McDonald, Gerry	Hfd.	1	3	0	0	0	0	....	....	....	....	....		1981-82	1981-82
• McDonald, Jack	Mtl.W, Mtl., Que., Tor.	5	73	27	11	38	13	12	2	0	2	0		1917-18	1921-22
McDonald, John	NYR	1	43	10	9	19	6	....	....	....	....	....		1943-44	1943-44
McDonald, Lanny	Tor., Col., Cgy.	16	1111	500	506	1006	899	117	44	40	84	120	1	1973-74	1988-89
McDonald, Robert	NYR	1	1	0	0	0	0	....	....	....	....	....		1943-44	1943-44
McDonald, Terry	K.C.	1	8	0	1	1	6	....	....	....	....	....		1975-76	1975-76
McDonnell, Joe	Van., Pit.	3	50	2	10	12	34	....	....	....	....	....		1981-82	1985-86
• McDonnell, Moylan	Ham.	1	20	1	1	2	0	....	....	....	....	....		1920-21	1920-21
McDonough, Al	L.A., Pit., Atl., Det.	5	237	73	88	161	73	8	0	1	1	2		1970-71	1977-78
McDougal, Mike	NYR, Hfd.	4	61	8	10	18	43	....	....	....	....	....		1978-79	1982-83
McElmury, Jim	Min.; K.C., Col.	5	180	14	47	61	49	....	....	....	....	....		1972-73	1977-78
McEwen, Mike	NYR, Col., NYI, L.A., Wsh., Det., Hfd.	12	716	108	296	404	460	78	12	36	48	48	3	1976-77	1987-88
McFadden, Jim	Det., Chi.	7	412	100	126	226	89	49	10	9	19	30	1	1947-48	1953-54
McFadyen, Don	Chi.	4	179	12	33	45	77	12	2	2	4	5	1	1932-33	1935-36
McFall, Dan	Wpg.	2	9	0	1	1	0	....	....	....	....	....		1984-85	1985-86
McFarland, George	Chi.	1	2	0	0	0	0	....	....	....	....	....		1926-27	1926-27
McGeough, Jim	Wsh., Pit.	4	57	7	10	17	32	....	....	....	....	....		1981-82	1986-87
McGibbon, John	Mtl.	1	1	0	0	0	2	....	....	....	....	....		1942-43	1942-43
McGill, Jack	Mtl.	3	134	27	10	37	71	3	2	0	2	0		1934-35	1936-37
McGill, Jack G.	Bos.	4	97	23	36	59	42	27	7	4	11	17		1941-42	1946-47
McGregor, Sandy	NYR	1	2	0	0	0	2	....	....	....	....	....		1963-64	1963-64
McGuire, Mickey	Pit.	2	36	3	0	3	6	....	....	....	....	....		1926-27	1927-28
McIlhargey, Jack	Phi., Van., Hfd.	8	393	11	36	47	1102	27	0	3	3	68		1974-75	1981-82
McInenly, Bert	Det., NYA, Ott., Bos.	6	166	19	15	34	144	4	0	0	0	2		1930-31	1935-36
McIntosh, Bruce	Min.	1	2	0	0	0	0	....	....	....	....	....		1972-73	1972-73
McIntosh, Paul	Buf.	2	48	0	0	2	66	2	0	0	0	7		1974-75	1975-76
McIntyre, Jack	Bos., Chi., Det.	11	499	109	102	211	173	29	7	6	13	4		1949-50	1959-60
McIntyre, Larry	Tor.	2	41	0	3	3	26	....	....	....	....	....		1969-70	1972-73
McKay, Doug	Det.	1	....	....	....	....	....	1	0	0	0	0	1	1949-50	1949-50
McKay, Ray	Chi., Buf., Cal.	6	140	2	16	18	102	....	....	....	....	....		1968-69	1973-74
McKechnie, Walt	Min., Cal., Bos., Det., Wsh., Clev., Tor., Col.	16	955	214	392	606	469	15	7	5	12	9		1967-68	1982-83
McKegney, Ian	Chi.	1	3	0	0	0	2	....	....	....	....	....		1976-77	1976-77
McKegney, Tony	Buf., Que., Min., NYR, St. L., Det., Chi.	13	912	320	319	639	517	79	24	23	47	56		1978-79	1990-91
• McKell, Jack	Ott.	2	42	4	1	5	42	9	0	0	0	0	1	1919-20	1920-21
McKendry, Alex	NYI, Cgy.	4	46	3	6	9	21	6	2	2	4	0	1	1977-78	1980-81
McKenna, Sean	Buf., L.A., Tor.	9	414	82	80	162	181	15	1	2	3	2		1981-82	1989-90
McKenney, Don	Bos., NYR, Tor., Det., St.L.	13	798	237	345	582	211	58	18	29	47	10	1	1954-55	1967-68
McKenny, Jim	Tor., Min.	14	604	82	247	329	294	37	7	9	16	10		1965-66	1978-79
McKenzie, Brian	Pit.	1	6	1	1	2	4	....	....	....	....	....		1971-72	1971-72
McKenzie, John	Chi., Det., NYR, Bos.	12	691	206	268	474	917	69	15	32	47	133	2	1958-59	1971-72
McKinnon, Alex	Ham., NYA, Chi.	5	194	19	10	29	235	....	....	....	....	....		1924-25	1928-29
McKinnon, Bob	Chi.	1	2	0	0	0	0	....	....	....	....	....		1928-29	1928-29
• McKinnon, John	Mtl., Pit., Phi.	6	218	28	11	39	224	2	0	0	0	4		1925-26	1930-31
McLean, Don	Wsh.	1	9	0	0	0	6	....	....	....	....	....		1975-76	1975-76
• McLean, Fred	Que., Ham.	2	9	0	0	0	2	....	....	....	....	....		1919-20	1920-21
McLean, Jack	Tor.	3	67	14	24	38	76	13	2	2	4	8	1	1942-43	1944-45
• McLellan, John	Tor.	1	2	0	0	0	0	....	....	....	....	....		1951-52	1951-52
McLellan, Scott	Bos.	1	2	0	0	0	0	....	....	....	....	....		1982-83	1982-83
McLellan, Todd	NYI	1	5	1	1	2	0	....	....	....	....	....		1987-88	1987-88
McLenahan, Roly	Det.	1	9	2	1	3	10	2	0	0	0	0		1945-46	1945-46
McLeod, Al	Det.	1	26	2	2	4	24	....	....	....	....	....		1973-74	1973-74
McLeod, Jackie	NYR	5	106	14	23	37	12	7	0	0	0	0		1949-50	1954-55
McMahon, Mike	NYR, Min., Chi., Det., Pit., Buf.	8	224	15	68	83	171	14	3	7	10	4		1963-64	1971-72
• McMahon, Mike C.	Mtl., Bos.	3	57	7	18	25	102	13	1	2	3	30	1	1942-43	1945-46
McManama, Bob	Pit.	3	99	11	25	36	28	8	0	1	1	6		1973-74	1975-76
McManus, Sammy	Mtl.M., Bos.	2	26	0	1	1	8	1	0	0	0	0	1	1934-35	1936-37
McMurchy, Tom	Chi., Edm.	4	55	8	4	12	65	....	....	....	....	....		1983-84	1987-88
McNab, Max	Det.	4	128	16	19	35	24	25	1	0	1	4	1	1947-48	1950-51
McNab, Peter	Buf., Bos., Van., N.J.	14	954	363	450	813	179	107	40	42	82	20		1973-74	1986-87
McNabney, Sid	Mtl.	1	....	....	....	....	....	5	0	1	1	2		1950-51	1950-51
• McNamara, Howard	Mtl.	1	11	1	0	1	2	....	....	....	....	....		1919-20	1919-20
• McNaughton, George	Que.B.	1	1	0	0	0	0	....	....	....	....	....		1919-20	1919-20
McNeill, Billy	Det.	6	257	21	46	67	142	4	1	1	2	4		1956-57	1963-64
McNeill, Stu	Det.	3	10	1	1	2	2	....	....	....	....	....		1957-58	1959-60
McPhee, George	NYR, N.J.	7	115	24	25	49	257	29	5	3	8	69		1982-83	1988-89
McRae, Chris	Tor., Det.	3	21	1	0	1	122	....	....	....	....	....		1987-88	1989-90
McReavy, Pat	Bos., Det.	4	55	5	10	15	4	20	3	3	6	9	1	1938-39	1941-42
McSheffrey, Bryan	Van., Buf.	3	90	13	7	20	44	....	....	....	....	....		1972-73	1974-75
McTaggart, Jim	Wsh.	2	71	3	10	13	205	....	....	....	....	....		1980-81	1981-82
McTavish, Gordon	St.L., Wpg.	2	11	1	3	4	2	....	....	....	....	....		1978-79	1979-80
• McVeigh, Charley	Chi., NYA	9	397	84	88	172	138	4	0	0	0	2		1926-27	1934-35
McVicar, Jack	Mtl.M.	2	88	2	4	6	63	2	0	0	0	2		1930-31	1931-32
Meagher, Rick	Mtl., Hfd., N.J., St.L.	12	691	144	165	309	383	62	8	7	15	41		1979-80	1990-91
Meehan, Gerry	Tor., Phi., Buf., Van., Atl., Wsh.	10	670	180	243	423	111	10	0	1	1	0		1968-69	1978-79
Meeke, Brent	Cal., Clev.	5	75	9	22	31	8	....	....	....	....	....		1972-73	1976-77
Meeker, Howie	Tor.	8	346	83	102	185	329	42	6	9	15	50	4	1946-47	1953-54
Meeker, Mike	Pit.	1	4	0	0	0	5	....	....	....	....	....		1978-79	1978-79
• Meeking, Harry	Tor., Det., Bos.	3	63	18	3	21	42	14	4	2	6	0	1	1917-18	1926-27
Meger, Paul	Mtl.	6	212	39	52	91	112	35	3	8	11	16	1	1949-50	1954-55
Meighan, Ron	Min., Pit.	2	48	3	7	10	18	....	....	....	....	....		1981-82	1982-83
Meissner, Barrie	Min.	2	6	0	1	1	4	....	....	....	....	....		1967-68	1968-69
Meissner, Dick	Bos., NYR	5	171	11	15	26	37	....	....	....	....	....		1959-60	1964-65
Melametsa, Anssi	Wpg.	1	27	0	3	3	2	....	....	....	....	....		1985-86	1985-86
Melin, Roger	Min.	2	3	0	0	0	0	....	....	....	....	....		1980-81	1981-82
Mellor, Tom	Det.	2	26	2	4	6	25	....	....	....	....	....		1973-74	1974-75
Melnyk, Gerry	Det., Chi., St.L.	6	269	39	77	116	34	53	6	6	12	6		1955-56	1967-68
Melnyk, Larry	Bos., Edm., NYR, Van.	10	432	11	63	74	686	66	2	9	11	127	1	1980-81	1989-90
Melrose, Barry	Wpg., Tor., Det.	6	300	10	23	33	728	7	0	2	2	38		1979-80	1985-86
Menard, Hillary	Chi.	1	1	0	0	0	0	....	....	....	....	....		1953-54	1953-54
Menard, Howie	Det., L.A., Chi., Oak.	4	151	23	42	65	87	19	3	7	10	36		1963-64	1969-70
Mercredi, Vic	Atl.	1	2	0	0	0	0	....	....	....	....	....		1974-75	1974-75
Meredith, Greg	Cgy.	2	38	6	4	10	8	5	3	1	4	4		1980-81	1982-83
Merkosky, Glenn	Hfd., N.J., Det.	5	66	5	12	17	22	....	....	....	....	....		1981-82	1989-90
Meronek, Bill	Mtl.	2	19	5	8	13	0	1	0	0	0	0		1939-40	1942-43
Merrick, Wayne	St.L., Cal., Clev., NYI	12	774	191	265	456	303	102	19	30	49	30	4	1972-73	1983-84
• Merrill, Horace	Ott.	2	11	0	0	0	0	....	....	....	....	....	1	1917-18	1919-20
Messier, Mitch	Min.	4	20	0	2	2	11	....	....	....	....	....		1987-88	1990-91
Messier, Paul	Col.	1	9	0	0	0	4	....	....	....	....	....		1978-79	1978-79
Metcalfe, Scott	Edm., Buf.	3	19	1	2	3	18	....	....	....	....	....		1987-88	1989-90
Metz, Don	Tor.	8	172	20	35	55	42	47	7	8	15	10	5	1939-40	1948-49
• Metz, Nick	Tor.	12	518	131	119	250	149	76	19	20	39	31	4	1934-35	1947-48
Michaluk, Art	Chi.	1	5	0	0	0	0	....	....	....	....	....		1947-48	1947-48
Michaluk, John	Chi.	1	1	0	0	0	0	....	....	....	....	....		1950-51	1950-51
Micheletii, Pat	Min.	1	12	2	0	2	8	....	....	....	....	....		1987-88	1987-88
Micheletti, Joe	St.L., Col.	3	158	11	60	71	114	11	1	11	12	10		1979-80	1981-82
• Mickey, Larry	Chi., NYR., Tor., Mtl., L.A., Phi., Buf.	11	292	39	53	92	160	9	1	0	1	10		1964-65	1974-75
Mickoski, Nick	NYR, Chi., Det., Bos.	13	703	158	184	342	319	18	1	6	7	6		1947-48	1959-60
Middleton, Rick	NYR, Bos.	14	1005	448	540	988	157	114	45	55	100	19		1974-75	1987-88
Migay, Rudy	Tor.	10	418	59	92	151	293	15	1	0	1	20		1949-50	1959-60
Mikita, Stan	Chi.	22	1394	541	926	1467	1270	155	59	91	150	169	1	1958-59	1979-80
Mikkelson, Bill	L.A., N.Y.I., Wsh.	4	147	4	18	22	105	....	....	....	....	....		1971-72	1976-77
Mikol, Jim	Tor., NYR	2	34	1	4	5	8	....	....	....	....	....		1962-63	1964-65
Milbury, Mike	Bos.	12	754	49	189	238	1552	86	4	24	28	219		1975-76	1986-87
• Milks, Hib	Pit., Phi., NYR, Ott.	8	314	87	41	128	179	10	0	0	0	2		1925-26	1932-33
Millar, Hugh	Det.	1	4	0	0	0	0	1	0	0	0	0		1946-47	1946-47
Millar, Mike	Hfd., Wsh., Bos., Tor.	5	78	18	18	36	12	....	....	....	....	....		1986-87	1990-91
Miller, Bill	Mtl.M., Mtl.	3	95	7	3	10	16	12	0	0	0	0	1	1934-35	1936-37
Miller, Bob	Bos., Col., L.A.	6	404	75	119	194	220	36	4	7	11	27		1977-78	1984-85
• Miller, Earl	Chi., Tor.	5	116	19	14	33	124	10	1	0	1	6	1	1927-28	1931-32
Miller, Jack	Chi.	2	17	0	0	0	4	....	....	....	....	....		1949-50	1950-51

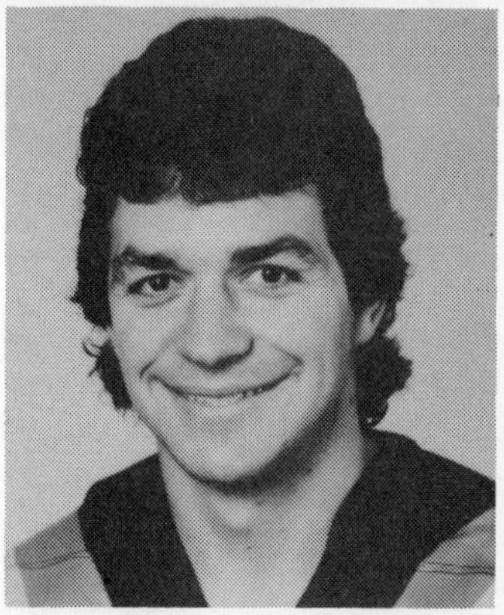
Kevin McCarthy

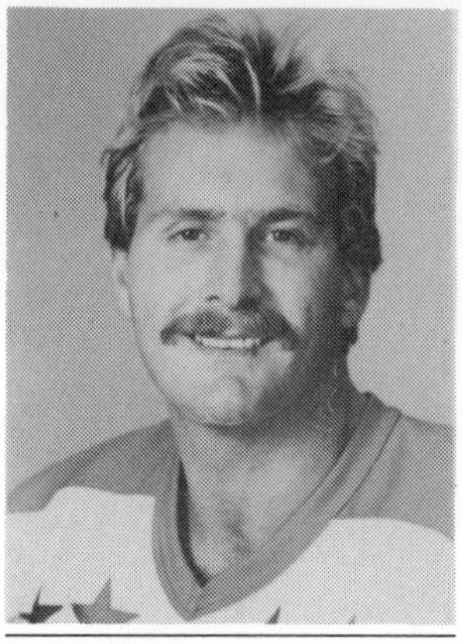
Paul MacKinnon

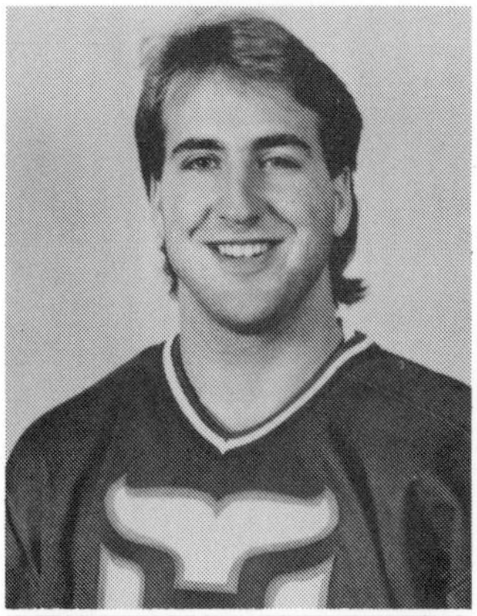
Tom Martin

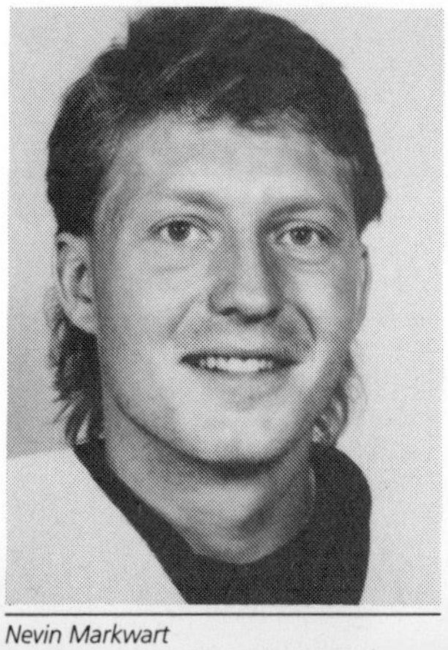
Nevin Markwart

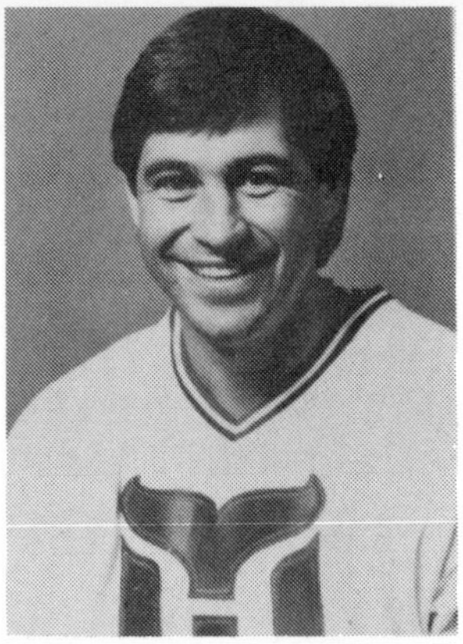

Greg Malone

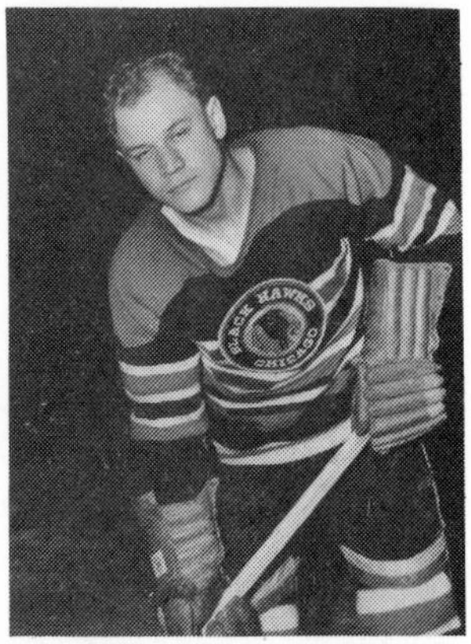

Bill Mosienko

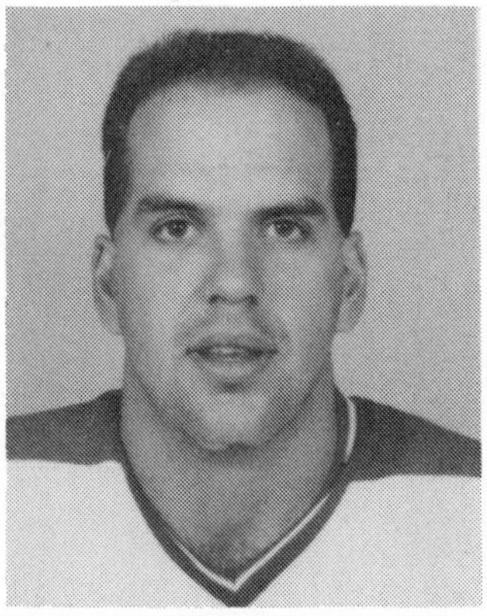

Ric Nattress

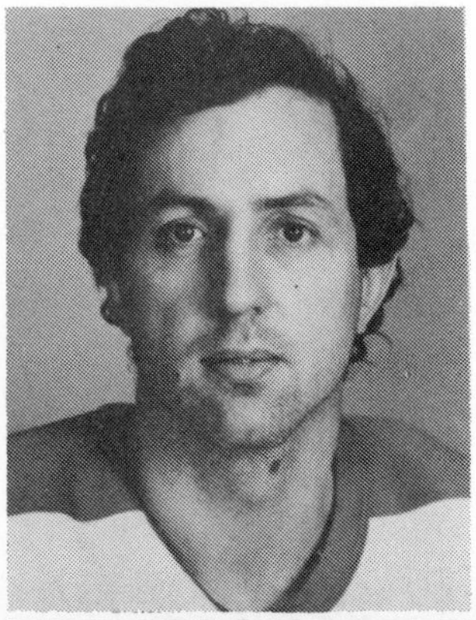

Milan Novy

Name	NHL Teams	NHL Seasons	Regular Schedule GP	G	A	TP	PIM	Playoffs GP	G	A	TP	PIM	NHL Cup Wins	First NHL Season	Last NHL Season
Miller, Jay	Bos., L.A.	7	446	40	44	84	1723	48	2	3	5	243		1985-86	1991-92
Miller, Paul	Col.	1	3	0	3	3	0	....	....	....	....	....		1981-82	1981-82
Miller, Perry	Det.	4	217	10	51	61	387	....	....	....	....	....		1977-78	1980-81
Miller, Tom	Det., NYI	4	118	16	25	41	34	....	....	....	....	....		1970-71	1974-75
Miller, Warren	NYR, Hfd.	4	262	40	50	90	137	6	1	0	1	0		1979-80	1982-83
Miner, John	Edm.	1	14	2	3	5	16	....	....	....	....	....		1987-88	1987-88
Minor, Gerry	Van.	5	140	11	21	32	173	12	1	3	4	25		1979-80	1983-84
Miszuk, John	Det., Chi., Phi., Min.	6	237	7	39	46	232	19	0	3	3	19		1963-64	1969-70
Mitchell, Bill	Det.	1	1	0	0	0	0	....	....	....	....	....		1963-64	1963-64
Mitchell, Herb	Bos.	2	53	6	0	6	38	....	....	....	....	....		1924-25	1925-26
Mitchell, Red	Chi.	3	83	4	5	9	67	....	....	....	....	....		1941-42	1944-45
Moe, Billy	NYR	5	261	11	42	53	163	1	0	0	0	0		1944-45	1948-49
Moffat, Lyle	Tor., Wpg.	3	97	12	16	28	51	....	....	....	....	....		1972-73	1979-80
Moffat, Ron	Det.	3	36	1	1	2	8	7	0	0	0	0		1932-33	1934-35
Moher, Mike	N.J.	1	9	0	1	1	28	....	....	....	....	....		1982-83	1982-83
Mohns, Doug	Bos., Chi., Min., Atl., Wsh.	22	1390	248	462	710	1250	94	14	36	50	122		1953-54	1974-75
Mohns, Lloyd	NYR	1	1	0	0	0	0	....	....	....	....	....		1943-44	1943-44
Mokosak, Carl	Cgy., L.A., Phi., Pit., Bos.	6	83	11	15	26	170	1	0	0	0	0		1981-82	1988-89
Mokosak, John	Det.	2	41	0	2	2	96	....	....	....	....	....		1988-89	1989-90
Molin, Lars	Van.	3	172	33	65	98	37	19	2	9	11	7		1981-82	1983-84
Moller, Mike	Buf., Edm.	7	134	15	28	43	41	3	0	1	1	0		1980-81	1986-87
Molloy, Mitch	Buf.	1	2	0	0	0	10	....	....	....	....	....		1989-90	1989-90
Molyneaux, Larry	NYR	2	45	0	1	1	20	3	0	0	0	8		1937-38	1938-39
Monahan, Garry	Mtl., Det., L.A., Tor., Van.	12	748	116	169	285	484	22	3	1	4	13		1967-68	1978-79
Monahan, Hartland	Cal., NYR, Wsh., Pit., L.A., St.L.	7	334	61	80	141	163	6	0	0	0	4		1973-74	1980-81
• Mondou, Armand	Mtl.	12	385	47	71	118	99	35	3	5	8	12	2	1928-29	1939-40
Mondou, Pierre	Mtl.	9	548	194	262	456	179	69	17	28	45	26	3	1976-77	1984-85
Mongrain, Bob	Buf., L.A.	6	83	13	14	27	14	11	1	2	3	2		1979-80	1985-86
Monteith, Hank	Det.	3	77	5	12	17	6	4	0	0	0	0		1968-69	1970-71
Moore, Dickie	Mtl., Tor., St.L.	14	719	261	347	608	652	135	46	64	110	122	6	1951-52	1967-68
Moran, Amby	Mtl., Chi.	2	35	1	1	2	24	....	....	....	....	....		1926-27	1927-28
• Morenz, Howie	Mtl., Chi., NYR	14	550	270	197	467	563	47	21	11	32	68	3	1923-24	1936-37
Moretto, Angelo	Clev.	1	5	1	2	3	2	....	....	....	....	....		1976-77	1976-77
Morin, Pete	Mtl.	1	31	10	12	22	7	1	0	0	0	0		1941-42	1941-42
Morris, Bernie	Bos.	1	6	2	0	2	0	....	....	....	....	....		1924-25	1924-25
Morris, Elwyn	Tor., NYR	4	135	13	29	42	58	18	4	2	6	16	1	1943-44	1948-49
Morrison, Dave	L.A., Van.	4	39	3	3	6	4	....	....	....	....	....		1980-81	1984-85
Morrison, Don	Det., Chi.	3	112	18	28	46	12	3	0	1	1	0		1947-48	1950-51
Morrison, Doug	Bos.	4	23	7	3	10	15	....	....	....	....	....		1979-80	1984-85
Morrison, Gary	Phi.	3	43	1	15	16	70	5	0	1	1	2		1979-80	1981-82
Morrison, George	St.L.	2	115	17	21	38	13	3	0	0	0	0		1970-71	1971-72
Morrison, Jim	Bos., Tor., Det., NYR, Pit.	12	704	40	160	200	542	36	0	12	12	38		1951-52	1970-71
Morrison, John	NYA	1	18	0	0	0	0	....	....	....	....	....		1925-26	1925-26
Morrison, Kevin	Col.	1	41	4	11	15	23	....	....	....	....	....		1979-80	1979-80
Morrison, Lew	Phi., Atl., Wsh., Pit.	9	564	39	52	91	107	17	0	0	0	2		1969-70	1977-78
Morrison, Mark	NYR	2	10	1	1	2	0	....	....	....	....	....		1981-82	1983-84
Morrison, Roderick	Det.	1	34	8	7	15	4	3	0	0	0	0		1947-48	1947-48
Morrow, Ken	NYI	10	550	17	88	105	309	127	11	22	33	97	4	1979-80	1988-89
Morton, Dean	Det.	1	1	1	0	1	2	....	....	....	....	....		1989-90	1989-90
Mortson, Gus	Tor., Chi., Det.	13	797	46	152	198	1380	54	5	8	13	68	4	1946-47	1958-59
Mosdell, Kenny	Bro., Mtl., Chi.	16	693	141	168	309	475	79	16	13	29	48	4	1941-42	1958-59
• Mosienko, Bill	Chi.	14	711	258	282	540	117	22	10	4	14	15		1941-42	1954-55
Mott, Morris	Cal.	3	199	18	32	50	49	....	....	....	....	....		1972-73	1974-75
Motter, Alex	Bos., Det.	8	267	39	64	103	135	40	3	9	12	41	1	1934-35	1942-43
Moxey, Jim	Cal., Clev., L.A.	3	127	22	27	49	59	....	....	....	....	....		1974-75	1976-77
Mulhern, Richard	Atl., L.A., Tor., Wpg.	6	303	27	93	120	217	7	0	3	3	5		1975-76	1980-81
Muloin, Wayne	Det., Oak., Cal., Min.	3	147	3	21	24	93	11	0	0	0	2		1963-64	1970-71
Mulvenna, Glenn	Pit., Phi.	2	2	0	0	0	4	....	....	....	....	....		1991-92	1992-93
Mulvey, Grant	Chi., N.J.	10	586	149	135	284	816	42	10	5	15	70		1974-75	1983-84
Mulvey, Paul	Wsh., Pit., L.A.	4	225	30	51	81	613	....	....	....	....	....		1978-79	1981-82
• Mummery, Harry	Tor., Que., Mtl., Ham.	6	106	33	13	46	161	7	1	4	5	0		1917-18	1922-23
• Munro, Dunc	Mtl.	8	239	28	18	46	170	25	3	2	5	24	1	1924-25	1931-32
Munro, Gerry	Mtl., Tor.	2	33	1	0	1	22	....	....	....	....	....		1924-25	1925-26
Murdoch, Bob J.	Mtl., L.A., Atl., Cgy.	12	757	60	218	278	764	69	4	18	22	92	2	1970-71	1981-82
Murdoch, Bob L.	Cal., Clev., St.L.	4	260	72	85	157	127	....	....	....	....	....		1975-76	1978-79
Murdoch, Don	NYR, Edm., Det.	5	320	121	117	238	155	24	10	8	18	16		1976-77	1981-82
Murdoch, Murray	NYR	11	507	84	108	192	197	55	9	12	21	28		1926-27	1936-37
Murphy, Brian	Det.	1	1	0	0	0	0	....	....	....	....	....		1974-75	1974-75
Murphy, Mike	St.L. NYR, L.A.	12	831	238	318	556	514	66	13	23	36	54		1971-72	1982-83
Murphy, Ron	NYR, Chi., Det., Bos.	18	889	205	274	479	460	53	7	8	15	26	1	1952-53	1969-70
Murray, Allan	NYA	7	277	5	9	14	163	14	0	0	0	8		1933-34	1939-40
Murray, Bob F.	Chi.	15	1008	132	382	514	873	112	19	37	56	0		1975-76	1989-90
Murray, Bob J.	Atl., Van.	4	194	6	16	22	98	9	1	1	2	15		1973-74	1976-77
Murray, Jim	L.A.	1	30	0	2	2	14	....	....	....	....	....		1967-68	1967-68
Murray, Ken	Tor., N.Y.I., Det., K.C.	5	106	1	10	11	135	....	....	....	....	....		1969-70	1975-76
Murray, Leo	Mtl.	1	6	0	0	0	2	....	....	....	....	....		1932-33	1932-33
Murray, Mike	Phi.	1	1	0	0	0	0	....	....	....	....	....		1987-88	1987-88
Murray, Pat	Phi.	2	25	3	1	4	15	....	....	....	....	....		1990-91	1991-92
Murray, Randy	Tor.	1	3	0	0	0	2	....	....	....	....	....		1969-70	1969-70
Murray, Terry	Cal., Phi., Det., Wsh.	8	302	4	76	80	199	18	2	2	4	10		1972-73	1981-82
Myers, Hap	Buf.	1	13	0	0	0	6	....	....	....	....	....		1970-71	1970-71
Myles, Vic	NYR	1	45	6	9	15	57	....	....	....	....	....		1942-43	1942-43

N

Name	NHL Teams	NHL Seasons	Regular Schedule GP	G	A	TP	PIM	Playoffs GP	G	A	TP	PIM	NHL Cup Wins	First NHL Season	Last NHL Season
Nachbaur, Don	Hfd., Edm., Phi.	8	223	23	46	69	465	11	1	1	2	24		1980-81	1989-90
Nahrgang, Jim	Det.	3	57	5	12	17	34	....	....	....	....	....		1974-75	1976-77
Nanne, Lou	Min.	11	635	68	157	225	356	32	4	10	14	9		1967-68	1977-78
Nantais, Richard	Min.	3	63	5	4	9	79	....	....	....	....	....		1974-75	1976-77
Napier, Mark	Mtl., Min., Edm., Buf.	11	767	235	306	541	157	82	18	24	42	11	1	1978-79	1988-89
Naslund, Mats	Mtl.	8	617	243	369	612	107	97	34	57	91	33	1	1982-83	1989-90
Nattrass, Ralph	Chi.	4	223	18	38	56	308	....	....	....	....	....		1946-47	1949-50
Nattress, Ric	Mtl., St.L., Cgy., Tor., Phi.	11	536	29	135	164	377	67	5	10	15	60	1	1982-83	1992-93
Natyshak, Mike	Que.	1	4	0	0	0	0	....	....	....	....	....		1987-88	1987-88
Nechaev, Victor	L.A.	1	3	1	0	1	0	....	....	....	....	....		1982-83	1982-83
Nedomansky, Vaclav	Det., NYR, St.L.	6	421	122	156	278	88	7	3	5	8	0		1977-78	1982-83
Neely, Bob	Tor., Col.	5	283	39	59	98	266	26	5	7	12	15		1973-74	1977-78
Neilson, Jim	NYR, Cal., Clev.	16	1023	69	299	368	904	65	1	17	18	61		1962-63	1977-78
Nelson, Gordie	Tor.	1	3	0	0	0	11	....	....	....	....	....		1969-70	1969-70
Nemeth, Steve	NYR	1	12	2	0	2	2	....	....	....	....	....		1987-88	1987-88
Nesterenko, Eric	Tor., Chi.	21	1219	250	324	574	1273	124	13	24	37	127	1	1951-52	1971-72
Nethery, Lance	NYR, Edm.	2	41	11	14	25	14	14	5	3	8	9		1980-81	1981-82
Neufeld, Ray	Hfd., Win., Bos.	11	595	157	200	357	816	28	8	6	14	55		1979-80	1989-90
• Neville, Mike	Tor., NYA	4	62	6	3	9	14	2	0	0	0	0	1	1917-18	1930-31
Nevin, Bob	Tor., NYR, Min., L.A.	18	1128	307	419	726	211	84	16	18	34	24	2	1957-58	1975-76
Newberry, John	Mtl., Hfd.	4	22	0	4	4	6	2	0	0	0	0		1982-83	1985-86
Newell, Rick	Det.	2	7	0	0	0	0	....	....	....	....	....		1972-73	1973-74
Newman, Dan	NYR, Mtl., Edm.	4	126	17	24	41	63	3	0	0	0	4		1976-77	1979-80
Newman, John	Det.	1	8	1	1	2	0	....	....	....	....	....		1930-31	1930-31
Nicholson, Al	Bos.	2	19	0	1	1	4	....	....	....	....	....		1955-56	1956-57
Nicholson, Edward	Det.	1	1	0	0	0	0	....	....	....	....	....		1947-48	1947-48
Nicholson, Graeme	Bos., Col., NYR	3	52	2	7	9	60	....	....	....	....	....		1978-79	1982-83
Nicholson, John	Chi.	1	2	1	0	1	0	....	....	....	....	....		1937-38	1937-38
Nicholson, Neil	Oak., N.Y.I.	4	39	3	1	4	23	2	0	0	0	0		1969-70	1977-78
Nicholson, Paul	Wsh.	3	62	4	8	12	18	....	....	....	....	....		1974-75	1976-77
Niekamp, Jim	Det.	2	29	0	2	2	27	....	....	....	....	....		1970-71	1971-72
Nienhui, Kraig	Bos.	3	87	20	16	36	39	2	0	0	0	14		1985-86	1987-88
• Nighbor, Frank	Ott., Tor.	13	348	136	60	196	241	36	11	9	20	27	4	1917-18	1929-30
Nigro, Frank	Tor.	2	68	8	18	26	39	3	0	0	0	2		1982-83	1983-84
Nilan, Chris	Mtl., NYR, Bos.	13	688	110	115	225	3043	111	8	9	17	541	1	1979-80	1991-92
Nill, Jim	St.L., Van., Bos., Wpg., Det.	9	524	58	87	145	854	59	10	5	15	203		1981-82	1989-90
Nilsson, Kent	Atl., Cgy., Min., Edm.	8	547	263	422	685	116	59	11	41	52	14	1	1979-80	1986-87
Nilsson, Ulf	NYR	4	170	57	112	169	85	25	8	14	22	27		1978-79	1982-83
Nistico, Lou	Col.	1	3	0	0	0	0	....	....	....	....	....		1977-78	1977-78

			Regular Schedule					Playoffs							
Name	NHL Teams	NHL Seasons	GP	G	A	TP	PIM	GP	G	A	TP	PIM	NHL Cup Wins	First NHL Season	Last NHL Season
• Noble, Reg	Tor., Mtl.M., Det.	16	526	167	79	246	807	32	4	5	9	39	3	1917-18	1932-33
Noel, Claude	Wsh.	1	7	0	0	0	0	....	....	....	....	....		1979-80	1979-80
Nolan, Pat	Tor.	1	2	0	0	0	0	....	....	....	....	....	1	1921-22	1921-22
Nolan, Ted	Det., Pit.	3	78	6	16	22	105	....	....	....	....	....		1981-82	1985-86
Nolet, Simon	Phi., K.C., Pit., Col.	10	562	150	182	332	187	34	6	3	9	8	1	1967-68	1976-77
Nordmark, Robert	St. L., Van.	4	236	13	70	83	254	7	3	2	5	8		1987-88	1990-91
Noris, Joe	Pit., St.L., Buf.	3	55	2	5	7	22	....	....	....	....	....		1971-72	1973-74
Norrish, Rod	Min.	2	21	3	3	6	2	....	....	....	....	....		1973-74	1974-75
• Northcott, Baldy	Mtl.M., Chi.	11	446	133	112	245	273	31	8	5	13	14	1	1928-29	1938-39
Norwich, Craig	Wpg., St.L., Col.	2	104	17	58	75	60	....	....	....	....	....		1979-80	1980-81
Novy, Milan	Wsh.	1	73	18	30	48	16	2	0	0	0	0		1982-83	1982-83
Nowak, Hank	Pit., Det., Bos.	4	180	26	29	55	161	3	1	0	1	8		1973-74	1976-77
Nykoluk, Mike	Tor.	1	32	3	1	4	20	....	....	....	....	....		1956-57	1956-57
Nylund, Gary	Tor., Chi., NYI	11	608	32	139	171	1235	24	0	6	6	63		1982-83	1992-93
Nyrop, Bill	Mtl., Min.	4	207	12	51	63	101	35	1	7	8	22	3	1975-76	1981-82
Nystrom, Bob	NYI	14	900	235	278	513	1248	157	39	44	83	236	4	1972-73	1985-86

O

Name	NHL Teams	NHL Seasons	GP	G	A	TP	PIM	GP	G	A	TP	PIM	NHL Cup Wins	First NHL Season	Last NHL Season
• Oatman, Russell	Det., Mtl.M., NYR	3	124	20	9	29	100	17	1	0	1	18		1926-27	1928-29
O'Brien, Dennis	Min., Col., Clev., Bos.	10	592	31	91	122	1017	34	1	2	3	101		1970-71	1979-80
O'Brien, Obie	Bos.	1	2	0	0	0	0	....	....	....	....	....		1955-56	1955-56
O'Callahan, Jack	Chi., N.J.	7	389	27	104	131	541	32	4	11	15	41		1982-83	1988-89
O'Connell, Mike	Chi., Bos., Det.	13	860	105	334	439	605	82	8	24	32	64		1977-78	1989-90
• O'Connor, Buddy	Mtl., NYR	10	509	140	257	397	34	53	15	21	36	6	2	1941-42	1950-51
Oddleifson, Chris	Bos., Van.	9	524	95	191	286	464	14	1	6	7	8		1972-73	1980-81
Odelin, Selmar	Edm.	3	18	0	2	2	35	....	....	....	....	....		1985-86	1988-89
O'Donnell, Fred	Bos.	2	115	15	11	26	98	5	0	1	1	5		1972-73	1973-74
O'Donoghue, Don	Oak., Cal.	3	125	18	17	35	35	3	0	0	0	0		1969-70	1971-72
Odrowski, Gerry	Det., Oak., St.L.	6	299	12	19	31	111	30	0	1	1	16		1960-61	1971-72
O'Dwyer, Bill	L.A., Bos.	5	120	9	13	22	113	10	0	0	0	2		1983-84	1989-90
O'Flaherty, Gerry	Tor., Van., Atl.	8	438	99	95	194	168	7	2	2	4	6		1971-72	1978-79
O'Flaherty, John	NYA, Bro.	2	21	5	1	6	0	....	....	....	....	....		1940-41	1941-42
Ogilvie, Brian	Chi., St.L.	6	90	15	21	36	29	....	....	....	....	....		1972-73	1978-79
O'Grady, George	Mtl.M.	1	4	0	0	0	0	....	....	....	....	....		1917-18	1917-18
Ogrodnick, John	Det., Que., NYR	14	928	402	425	827	260	41	18	8	26	6		1979-80	1992-93
Ojanen, Janne	N.J.	4	98	21	23	44	28	3	0	2	2	0		1988-89	1992-93
Okerlund, Todd	NYI	1	4	0	0	0	2	....	....	....	....	....		1987-88	1987-88
• Oliver, Harry	Bos., NYA	11	473	127	85	212	147	35	10	6	16	22	1	1926-27	1936-37
Oliver, Murray	Det., Bos., Tor., Min.	17	1127	274	454	728	319	35	9	16	25	10		1957-58	1974-75
Olmstead, Bert	Chi., Mtl., Tor.	14	848	181	421	602	884	115	16	42	58	1	5	1948-49	1961-62
Olson, Dennis	Det.	1	4	0	0	0	0	....	....	....	....	....		1957-58	1957-58
O'Neil, Paul	Van., Bos.	2	6	0	0	0	0	....	....	....	....	....		1973-74	1975-76
O'Neill, Jim	Bos., Mtl.	6	165	6	30	36	109	11	1	1	2	13		1933-34	1941-42
• O'Neill, Tom	Tor.	2	66	10	12	22	53	4	0	0	0	6	1	1943-44	1944-45
Orban, Bill	Chi., Min.	3	114	8	15	23	673	3	0	0	0	0		1967-68	1969-70
O'Ree, Willie	Bos.	2	45	4	10	14	26	....	....	....	....	....		1957-58	1960-61
O'Regan, Tom	Pit.	3	60	5	12	17	10	....	....	....	....	....		1983-84	1985-86
O'Reilly, Terry	Bos.	14	891	204	402	606	2095	108	25	42	67	335		1971-72	1984-85
Orlando, Gaetano	Buf.	3	98	18	26	44	51	5	0	4	4	14		1984-85	1986-87
Orlando, Jimmy	Det.	6	200	7	24	31	375	36	0	9	9	105	1	1936-37	1942-43
Orleski, Dave	Mtl.	2	2	0	0	0	0	....	....	....	....	....		1980-81	1981-82
Orr, Bobby	Bos., Chi.	12	657	270	645	915	953	74	26	66	92	107	2	1966-67	1978-79
Osborne, Keith	St.L., T.B.	2	16	1	3	4	16	....	....	....	....	....		1989-90	1992-93
Osburn, Randy	Tor., Phi.	2	27	0	2	2	0	....	....	....	....	....		1972-73	1974-75
O'Shea, Danny	Min., Chi., St.L.	5	369	64	115	179	265	39	3	7	10	62		1968-69	1972-73
O'Shea, Kevin	Buf., St.L.	3	134	13	18	31	85	12	2	1	3	10		1970-71	1972-73
Ouelette, Eddie	Chi.	1	43	3	2	5	11	1	0	0	0	0		1935-36	1935-36
Ouelette, Gerry	Bos.	1	34	5	4	9	0	....	....	....	....	....		1960-1	1960-61
Owchar, Dennis	Pit., Col.	6	288	30	85	115	200	10	1	1	2	8		1974-75	1979-80
• Owen, George	Bos.	5	192	44	33	77	151	21	2	5	7	25	1	1928-29	1932-33

P

Name	NHL Teams	NHL Seasons	GP	G	A	TP	PIM	GP	G	A	TP	PIM	NHL Cup Wins	First NHL Season	Last NHL Season
Pachal, Clayton	Bos., Col.	3	35	2	3	5	95	....	....	....	....	....		1976-77	1978-79
Paddock, John	Wsh., Phi., Que.	5	87	8	14	22	86	5	2	0	2	0		1975-76	1982-83
Paiement, Rosaire	Phi., Van.	5	190	48	52	100	343	3	3	0	3	0		1967-68	1971-72
Paiement, Wilf	K.C. Col., Tor., Que., NYR, Buf., Pit.	14	946	356	458	814	1757	69	18	17	35	185		1974-75	1987-88
Palangio, Peter	Mtl., Det., Chi.	5	71	13	10	23	28	7	0	0	0	0	1	1926-27	1937-38
Palazzari, Aldo	Bos., NYR	1	35	8	3	11	4	....	....	....	....	....		1943-44	1943-44
Palazzari, Doug	St.L.	4	108	18	20	38	23	2	0	0	0	0		1974-75	1978-79
Palmer, Brad	Min., Bos.	3	168	32	38	70	58	29	9	5	14	16		1980-81	1982-83
Palmer, Rob H.	Chi.	3	16	0	3	3	2	....	....	....	....	....		1973-74	1975-76
Palmer, Rob R.	L.A., N.J.	6	320	9	101	110	115	8	1	2	3	6		1977-78	1983-84
• Panagabko, Ed	Bos.	2	29	0	3	3	38	....	....	....	....	....		1955-56	1956-57
Papike, Joe	Chi.	3	21	3	3	6	4	5	0	2	2	0		1940-41	1944-45
Pappin, Jim	Tor., Chi., Cal., Clev.	14	767	278	295	573	667	92	33	34	67	101	2	1963-64	1976-77
Paradise, Bob	Min., Atl., Pit., Wsh.	8	368	8	54	62	393	12	0	1	1	19		1971-72	1978-79
Pargeter, George	Mtl.	1	4	0	0	0	0	....	....	....	....	....		1946-47	1946-47
Parise, J.P.	Bos., Tor., Min., NYI, Clev.	14	890	238	356	594	706	86	27	31	58	87		1965-66	1978-79
Parizeau, Michel	St.L., Phi.	1	58	3	14	17	18	....	....	....	....	....		1971-72	1971-72
Park, Brad	NYR, Bos., Det.	17	1113	213	683	896	1429	161	35	90	125	217		1968-69	1984-85
Parker, Jeff	Buf., Hfd.	5	141	16	19	35	163	5	0	0	0	26		1986-87	1990-91
Parkes, Ernie	Mtl.M.	1	17	0	0	0	2	....	....	....	....	....		1924-25	1924-25
Parsons, George	Tor.	3	64	12	13	25	17	7	3	2	5	11		1936-37	1938-39
Pasek, Dusan	Min.	1	48	4	10	14	30	2	1	0	1	0		1988-89	1988-89
Pasin, Dave	Bos., L.A.	2	76	18	19	37	50	3	0	1	1	0		1985-86	1988-89
Paterson, Joe	Det., Phi., L.A., NYR	9	291	19	37	56	829	22	3	4	7	77		1980-81	1988-89
Paterson, Mark	Hfd.	4	29	3	3	6	33	....	....	....	....	....		1982-83	1985-86
Paterson, Rick	Chi.	9	430	50	43	93	136	61	7	10	17	51		1978-79	1986-87
Patey, Doug	Wsh.	3	45	4	2	6	8	....	....	....	....	....		1976-77	1978-79
Patey, Larry	Cal., St.L., NYR	12	717	153	163	316	631	40	8	10	18	57		1973-74	1984-85
Patrick, Craig	Cal., St.L., K.C., Min. Wsh.	8	401	72	91	163	61	2	0	1	1	0		1971-72	1978-79
Patrick, Glenn	St.L., Cal., Clev.	3	38	2	3	5	72	....	....	....	....	....		1973-74	1976-77
• Patrick, Lester	NYR	1	1	0	0	0	2	....	....	....	....	....		1926-27	1926-27
• Patrick, Lynn	NYR	10	455	145	190	335	240	44	10	6	16	22	1	1934-35	1945-46
Patrick, Muzz	NYR	5	166	5	26	31	133	25	4	0	4	34	1	1937-38	1945-46
Patrick, Steve	Buf., NYR, Que.	6	250	40	68	108	242	12	0	1	1	12		1980-81	1985-86
Patterson, Colin	Cgy., Buf.	10	504	96	109	205	239	85	12	17	29	57	1	1983-84	1992-93
Patterson, Dennis	K.C., Phi.	3	138	6	22	28	67	....	....	....	....	....		1974-75	1979-80
• Patterson, George	Bos., Det., St.L., Tor., Mtl., NYA	9	289	51	27	78	218	3	0	0	0	2		1926-27	1934-35
• Paul, Butch	Det.	1	3	0	0	0	0	....	....	....	....	....		1964-65	1964-65
• Paulhus, Rollie	Mtl.	1	33	0	0	0	0	....	....	....	....	....		1925-26	1925-26
Pavelich, Mark	NYR, Min., S.J.	7	355	137	192	329	340	23	7	17	24	14		1981-82	1991-92
Pavelich, Marty	Det.	10	634	93	159	252	454	91	13	15	28	74	4	1947-48	1956-57
Pavese, Jim	St.L., NYR, Det., Hfd.	8	328	13	44	57	689	34	0	6	6	81		1981-82	1988-89
• Payer, Evariste	Mtl.	1	1	0	0	0	0	....	....	....	....	....		1917-18	1917-18
Payne, Steve	Min.	10	613	228	238	466	435	71	35	35	70	60		1978-79	1987-88
Pearson, Mel	NYR, Pit.	5	38	2	6	8	25	....	....	....	....	....		1949-50	1967-68
Pederson, Barry	Bos., Van., Pit., Hfd.	12	701	238	416	654	472	34	22	30	52	25		1980-81	1991-92
Peer, Bert	Det.	1	1	0	0	0	0	....	....	....	....	....		1939-40	1939-40
Peirson, Johnny	Bos.	11	545	153	173	326	315	49	9	17	26	26		1946-47	1957-58
Pelensky, Perry	Chi.	1	4	0	0	0	5	....	....	....	....	....		1983-84	1983-84
Pelletier, Roger	Phi.	1	1	0	0	0	0	....	....	....	....	....		1967-68	1967-68
Peloffy, Andre	Wsh.	1	9	0	0	0	2	....	....	....	....	....		1974-75	1974-75
Pelyk, Mike	Tor.	9	441	26	88	114	566	40	0	3	3	41		1967-68	1977-78
Pennington, Cliff	Mtl., Bos.	3	101	17	42	59	6	....	....	....	....	....		1960-61	1962-63
Peplinski, Jim	Cgy.	10	705	161	262	423	1456	99	15	31	46	382	1	1980-81	1989-90
Perlini, Fred	Tor.	2	8	2	3	5	0	....	....	....	....	....		1981-82	1983-84
Perreault, Fern	NYR	2	3	0	0	0	0	....	....	....	....	....		1947-48	1949-50
Perreault, Gilbert	Buf.	17	1191	512	814	1326	500	90	33	70	103	44		1970-71	1986-87
Perry, Brian	Oak., Buf.	3	96	16	29	45	24	8	1	1	2	4		1968-69	1970-71
Persson, Stefan	NYI	9	622	52	317	369	574	102	7	50	57	69	4	1977-78	1985-86

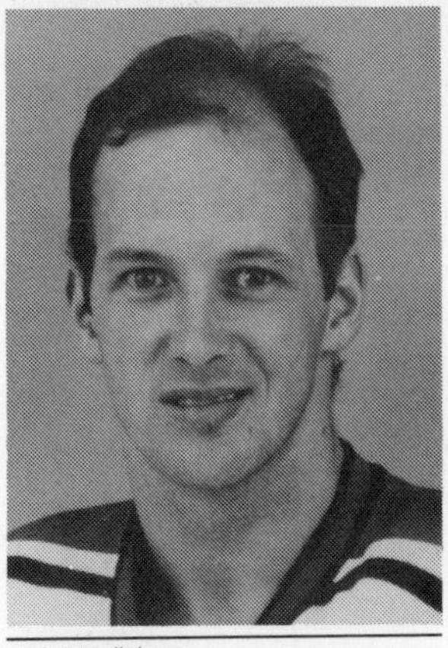
Jack O'Callahan

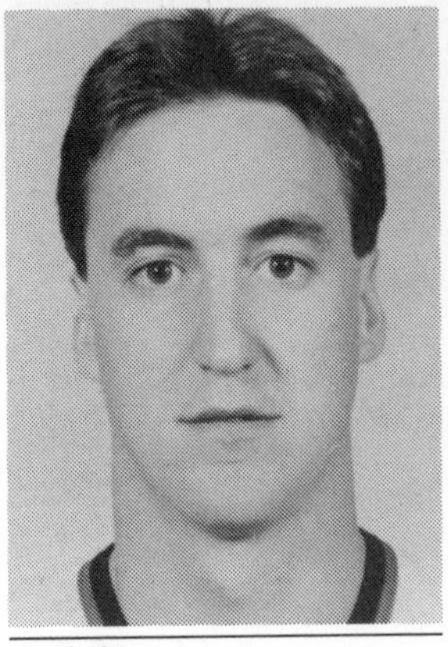
Jim Playfair

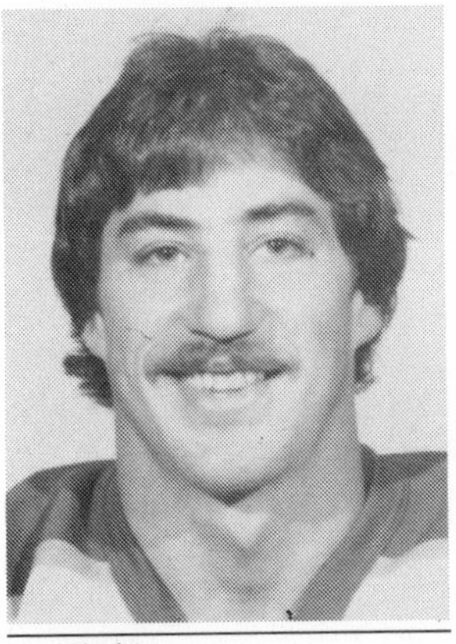
Larry Playfair

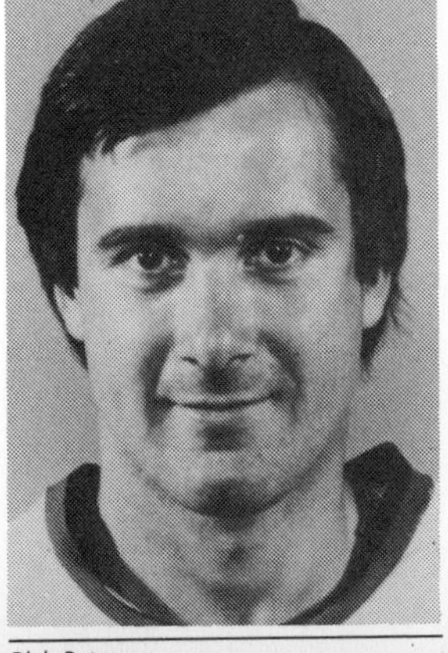
Rick Paterson

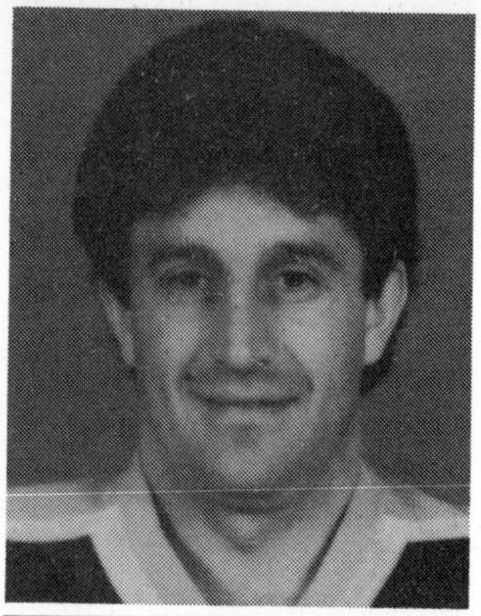

Jaroslav Pouzar

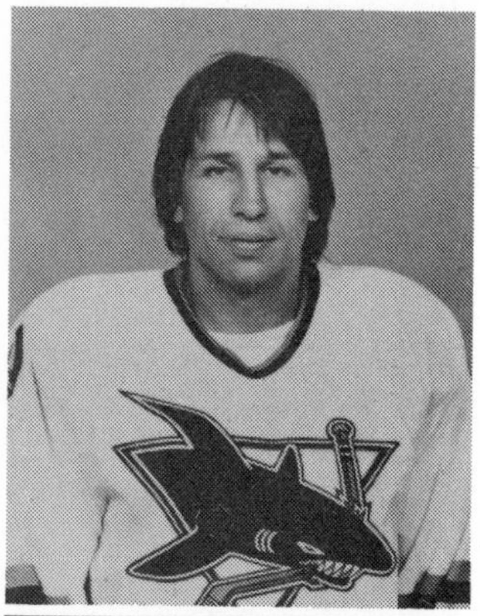

Mark Pavelich

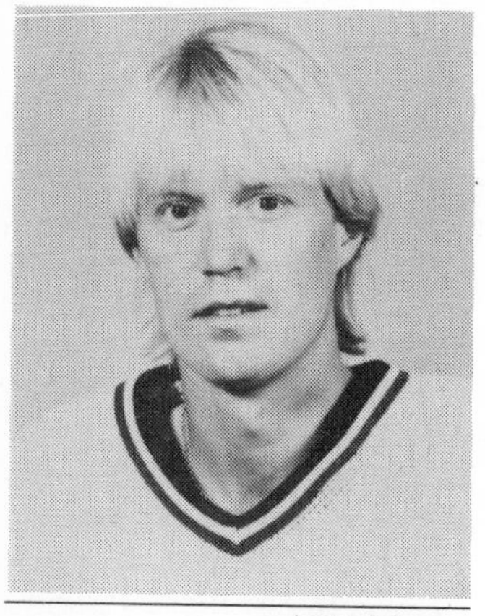

Jorgen Pettersson

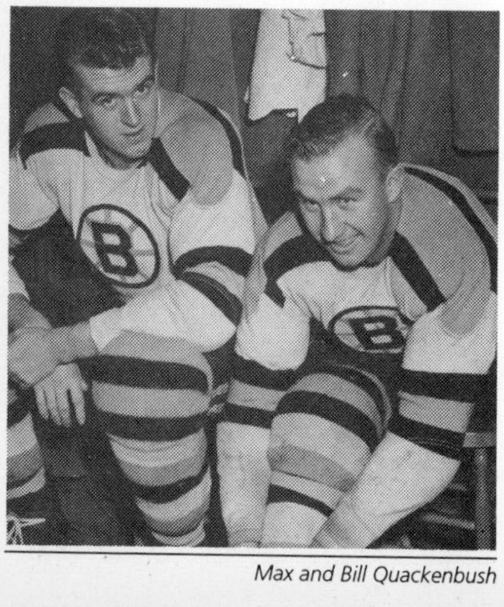

Max and Bill Quackenbush

			Regular Schedule					Playoffs							
Name	NHL Teams	NHL Seasons	GP	G	A	TP	PIM	GP	G	A	TP	PIM	NHL Cup Wins	First NHL Season	Last NHL Season
Pesut, George	Cal.	2	92	3	22	25	130	....	....	....	....	....		1974-75	1975-76
Peters, Frank	NYR	1	43	0	0	0	59	4	0	0	0	2		1930-31	1930-31
Peters, Garry	Mtl., NYR, Phi., Bos.	8	331	34	34	68	261	9	2	2	4	31	1	1964-65	1971-72
Peters, Jim	Det., Chi., Mtl., Bos.	9	574	125	150	275	186	60	5	9	14	22	3	1945-46	1953-54
Peters, Jimy	Det., L.A.	9	309	37	36	73	48	11	0	2	2	2		1964-65	1974-75
Peters, Steve	Col.	1	2	0	1	1	0	....	....	....	....	....		1979-80	1979-80
Peterson, Brent	Det., Buf., Van., Hfd.	10	620	72	141	213	484	31	4	4	8	65		1979-80	1988-89
Pettersson, Jorgen	St.L., Hfd., Wsh.	6	435	174	192	366	117	44	15	12	27	4		1980-81	1985-86
• Pettinger, Eric	Ott., Bos., Tor.	3	97	7	12	19	83	4	1	0	1	8		1928-29	1930-31
Pettinger, Gord	Det., NYR, Bos.	8	292	42	74	116	77	49	4	5	9	11	4	1932-33	1939-40
Phair, Lyle	L.A.	3	48	6	7	13	12	1	0	0	0	0		1985-86	1987-88
Phillipoff, Harold	Atl., Chi.,	3	141	26	57	83	267	6	0	2	2	9		1977-78	1979-80
Phillips, Bat	Mtl.M.	1	27	1	1	2	6	4	0	0	0	2		1929-30	1929-30
• Phillips, Bill	Mtl.M., NYA.	8	302	52	31	83	232	28	6	2	8	19	1	1925-26	1932-33
Phillips, Charlie	Mtl.	1	17	0	0	0	6	....	....	....	....	....		1942-43	1942-43
Picard, Noel	Atl., Mtl., St.L.	7	335	12	63	75	616	50	2	11	13	167	1	1964-65	1972-73
Picard, Robert	Wsh. Tor., Mtl., Wpg., Que., Det.	13	899	104	319	423	1025	36	5	15	20	39		1977-78	1989-90
Picard, Roger	St.L.	1	15	2	2	4	21	....	....	....	....	....		1967-68	1967-68
Pichette, Dave	Que., St.L., N.J., NYR	7	322	41	140	181	348	28	3	7	10	54		1980-81	1987-88
Picketts, Hal	NYA.	1	48	3	1	4	32	....	....	....	....	....		1933-34	1933-34
Pidhirny, Harry	Bos.	1	2	0	0	0	0	....	....	....	....	....		1957-58	1957-58
Pierce, Randy	Col., N.J., Hfd.	8	277	62	76	138	223	2	0	0	0	0		1977-78	1984-85
Pike, Alf	NYR	6	234	42	77	119	145	21	4	2	6	12	1	1939-40	1946-47
Pilote, Pierre	Chi., Tor.	14	890	80	418	498	1251	86	8	53	61	102	1	1955-56	1968-69
Pinder, Gerry	Chi., Cal.	3	223	55	69	124	135	17	0	4	4	6		1969-70	1971-72
Pirus, Alex	Min., Det.	4	159	30	28	58	94	2	0	1	1	2		1976-77	1979-80
• Pitre, Didier	Mtl.	6	127	64	17	81	50	14	2	2	4	0		1917-18	1922-23
• Plager, Barclay	St.L.	10	614	44	187	231	1115	68	3	20	23	182		1967-68	1976-77
Plager, Bob	NYR, St.L.	14	644	20	126	146	802	74	2	17	19	195		1964-65	1977-78
Plager, William	Min., St.L., Atl.	9	263	4	34	38	292	31	0	2	2	26		1967-68	1975-76
Plamondon, Gerry	Mtl.	5	74	7	13	20	10	11	5	2	7	2	1	1945-46	1950-51
Plante, Cam	Tor.	1	2	0	0	0	0	....	....	....	....	....		1984-85	1984-85
Plante, Pierre	NYR, Que., Phi., St.L., Chi.	9	599	125	172	297	599	33	2	6	8	51		1971-72	1979-80
Plantery, Mark	Wpg.	1	25	1	5	6	14	....	....	....	....	....		1980-81	1980-81
Plaxton, Hugh	Mtl.M.	1	15	1	2	3	4	....	....	....	....	....		1932-33	1932-33
Playfair, Jim	Edm., Chi.	3	21	2	4	6	51	....	....	....	....	....		1983-84	1988-89
Playfair, Larry	Buf., L.A.	12	688	26	94	120	1812	43	0	6	6	111		1978-79	1989-90
Pleau, Larry	Mtl.	3	94	9	15	24	27	4	0	0	0	0		1969-70	1971-72
Plett, Willi	Atl., Cgy., Min., Bos.	13	834	222	215	437	2572	83	24	22	46	466		1975-76	1987-88
Plumb, Rob	Det.	1	7	2	1	3	0	....	....	....	....	....		1977-78	1977-78
Plumb, Ron	Hfd.	1	26	3	4	7	14	....	....	....	....	....		1979-80	1979-80
Pocza, Harvie	Wsh.	2	3	0	0	0	0	....	....	....	....	....		1979-80	1981-82
Poddubny, Walt	Edm., Tor., NYR, Que., N.J.	11	468	184	238	422	454	19	7	2	9	12		1981-82	1991-92
Podloski, Ray	Bos.	1	8	0	1	1	22	....	....	....	....	....		1988-89	1988-89
Podolsky, Nels	Det.	1	1	0	0	0	0	7	0	0	0	4		1948-49	1948-49
Poeta, Anthony	Chi.	1	1	0	0	0	0	....	....	....	....	....		1951-52	1951-52
Poile, Bud	NYR, Bos., Det., Tor., Chi.,	7	311	107	122	229	91	23	4	4	8	8	1	1942-43	1949-50
Poile, Don	Det.	2	66	7	9	16	12	4	0	0	0	0		1954-55	1957-58
Poirer, Gordie	Mtl.	1	10	0	1	1	0	....	....	....	....	....		1939-40	1939-40
Polanic, Tom	Min.	2	19	0	2	2	53	5	1	1	2	4		1969-70	1970-71
Polich, John	NYR	2	3	0	1	1	0	....	....	....	....	....		1939-40	1940-41
Polich, Mike	Mtl., Min.	5	226	24	29	53	7	23	2	1	3	2	1	1976-77	1980-81
Polis, Greg	Pit., St.L., NYR, Wsh.	10	615	174	169	343	391	7	0	2	2	6		1970-71	1979-80
Poliziani, Daniel	Bos.	1	1	0	0	0	0	3	0	0	0	0		1958-59	1958-59
Polonich, Dennis	Det.	8	390	59	82	141	1242	7	1	0	1	19		1974-75	1982-83
Pooley, Paul	Wpg.	2	15	0	3	3	0	....	....	....	....	....		1984-85	1985-86
Popein, Larry	NYR, Oak.	8	449	80	141	221	162	16	1	4	5	6		1954-55	1967-68
Popiel, Paul	Bos., L.A., Det., Van., Edm.	7	224	13	41	54	210	4	1	0	1	4		1965-66	1979-80
Portland, Jack	Chi., Mtl., Bos.	10	381	15	56	71	323	33	1	3	4	25	1	1933-34	1942-43
Porvari, Jukka	Col., N.J.	2	39	3	9	12	4	....	....	....	....	....		1981-82	1982-83
Posa, Victor	Chi.	1	2	0	0	0	2	....	....	....	....	....		1985-86	1985-86
Posavad, Mike	St.L.	2	8	0	0	0	0	....	....	....	....	....		1985-86	1986-87
Potvin, Denis	NYI	15	1060	310	742	1052	1356	185	56	108	164	253	4	1973-74	1987-88
Potvin, Jean	L.A., Min., Phi., NYI, Cle.	11	613	63	224	287	478	39	2	9	11	17	1	1970-71	1980-81
Poudrier, Daniel	Que.	1	25	1	5	6	10	....	....	....	....	....		1985-86	1987-88
Poulin, Dan	Min.	1	3	1	1	2	2	....	....	....	....	....		1981-82	1981-82
Pouzar, Jaroslav	Edm.	4	186	34	48	82	135	29	6	4	10	16	3	1982-83	1986-87
Powell, Ray	Chi.	1	31	7	15	22	2	....	....	....	....	....		1950-51	1950-51
Powis, Geoff	Chi.	1	2	0	0	0	0	....	....	....	....	....		1967-68	1967-68
Powis, Lynn	Chi., K.C.	2	130	19	33	52	25	1	0	0	0	0		1973-74	1974-75
Prajsler, Petr	L.A., Bos.	4	46	3	10	13	51	4	0	0	0	0		1987-88	1991-92
• Pratt, Babe	Bos., NYR, Tor.	12	517	83	209	292	473	63	12	17	29	90	2	1935-36	1946-47
Pratt, Jack	Bos.	2	37	2	0	2	42	4	0	0	0	0		1930-31	1931-32
Pratt, Kelly	Pit.	1	22	0	6	6	15	....	....	....	....	....		1974-75	1974-75
Pratt, Tracy	Van., Col., Buf., Pit. Tor., Oak.	10	580	17	97	114	1026	25	0	1	1	62		1967-68	1976-77
Prentice, Dean	Pit., Min., Det., NYR, Bos.	22	1378	391	469	860	484	54	13	17	30	38		1952-53	1973-74
Prentice, Eric	Tor.	1	5	0	0	0	4	....	....	....	....	....		1943-44	1943-44
Preston, Rich	Chi., N.J.	8	580	127	164	291	348	47	4	18	22	56		1979-80	1986-87
Preston, Yves	Phi.	2	28	7	3	10	4	....	....	....	....	....		1978-79	1980-81
Priakin, Sergei	Cgy.	3	46	3	8	11	2	1	0	0	0	0		1988-89	1990-91
• Price, Bob	Ott.	1	1	0	0	0	0	....	....	....	....	....		1919-20	1919-20
Price, Jack	Chi.	3	57	4	6	10	24	4	0	0	0	0		1951-52	1953-54
Price, Noel	Pit., L.A., Det., Tor., NYR, Mtl., Atl.	14	499	14	114	128	333	12	0	1	1	8	1	1957-58	1975-76
Price, Pat	NYI, Edm., Pit., Que., NYR, Min.	13	726	43	218	261	1456	74	2	10	12	195		1975-76	1987-88
Price, Tom	Cal., Clev., Pit.	5	29	0	2	2	12	....	....	....	....	....		1974-75	1978-79
• Primeau, Joe	Tor.	9	310	66	177	243	105	38	5	18	23	12	1	1927-28	1935-36
Primeau, Kevin	Van.	1	2	0	0	0	4	....	....	....	....	....		1980-81	1980-81
Pringle, Ellie	NYA	1	6	0	0	0	0	....	....	....	....	....		1930-31	1930-31
• Prodgers, Goldie	Tor., Ham.	6	110	63	22	85	33	....	....	....	....	....		1919-20	1924-25
Pronovost, Andre	Mtl., Bos., Det., Min.	10	556	94	104	198	408	70	11	11	22	58	4	1956-57	1967-68
Pronovost, Jean	Wsh., Pit., Atl.	14	998	391	383	774	413	35	11	9	20	14		1968-69	1981-82
Pronovost, Marcel	Det., Tor.	21	1206	88	257	345	851	134	8	23	31	104	5	1950-51	1969-70
• Provost, Claude	Mtl.	15	1005	254	335	589	469	126	25	38	63	86	9	1955-56	1969-70
Pryor, Chris	Min., NYI	6	82	1	4	5	122	....	....	....	....	....		1984-85	1989-90
Prystai, Metro	Chi., Det.	11	674	151	179	330	231	43	12	14	26	8	2	1947-48	1957-58
• Pudas, Al	Tor.	1	3	0	0	0	0	....	....	....	....	....		1926-27	1926-27
Pulford, Bob	Tor., L.A.	16	1079	281	362	643	792	89	25	26	51	126	4	1956-57	1971-72
Pulkkinen, Dave	NYI	1	2	0	0	0	0	....	....	....	....	....		1972-73	1972-73
Purpur, Cliff	Det., Chi., St.L.	5	144	26	34	60	46	16	1	2	3	4		1934-35	1944-45
Purves, John	Wsh.	1	7	1	0	1	0	....	....	....	....	....		1990-91	1990-91
• Pusie, Jean	Mtl., NYR, Bos.	5	61	1	4	5	28	7	0	0	0	0	1	1930-31	1935-36
Pyatt, Nelson	Det., Wsh., Col.	7	296	71	63	134	69	....	....	....	....	....		1973-74	1979-80
Q															
Quackenbush, Bill	Det., Bos.	14	774	62	222	284	95	80	2	19	21	8		1942-43	1955-56
Quackenbush, Max	Bos., Chi.,	2	61	4	7	11	30	6	0	0	0	4		1950-51	1951-52
Quenneville, Joel	Tor., Col., N.J., Hfd., Wsh.	13	803	54	136	190	705	32	0	8	8	22		1978-79	1990-91
Quenneville, Leo	NYR	1	25	0	3	3	10	3	0	0	0	0		1929-30	1929-30
• Quilty, John	Mtl., Bos.	4	125	36	34	70	81	13	3	5	8	9		1940-41	1947-48
Quinn, Pat	Tor., Van., Atl.	9	606	18	113	131	950	11	0	1	1	21		1968-69	1976-77
R															
Radley, Yip	NYA, Mtl.M.	2	18	0	1	1	13	....	....	....	....	....		1930-31	1936-37
Raglan, Clare	Det., Chi.	3	100	4	9	13	52	3	0	0	0	0		1950-51	1952-53
Raleigh, Don	NYR	10	535	101	219	320	96	18	6	5	11	6		1943-44	1955-56
• Ramsay, Beattie	Tor.,	1	43	0	2	2	10	....	....	....	....	....		1927-28	1927-28
Ramsay, Craig	Buf.	14	1070	252	420	672	201	89	17	31	48	27		1971-72	1984-85
Ramsay, Wayne	Buf.	1	2	0	0	0	0	....	....	....	....	....		1977-78	1977-78
Ramsey, Les	Chi.	1	11	2	2	4	2	....	....	....	....	....		1944-45	1944-45
• Randall, Ken	Tor., Ham., NYA	10	217	67	28	95	360	13	3	1	4	19	2	1917-18	1926-27
Ranieri, George	Bos.	1	2	0	0	0	0	....	....	....	....	....		1956-57	1956-57

Name	NHL Teams	NHL Seasons	Regular Schedule					Playoffs					NHL Cup Wins	First NHL Season	Last NHL Season
			GP	G	A	TP	PIM	GP	G	A	TP	PIM			
Ratelle, Jean	NYR, Bos.	21	1281	491	776	1267	276	123	32	66	98	24		1960-61	1980-81
Rathwell, John	Bos.	1	1	0	0	0	0	....	....	....	....	....		1974-75	1974-75
Rausse, Errol	Wsh.	3	31	7	3	10	0	....	....	....	....	....		1979-80	1981-82
Rautakallio, Pekka	Atl., Cgy.	3	235	33	121	154	122	23	2	5	7	8		1979-80	1981-82
Ravlich, Matt	Bos., Chi., Det., L.A.	9	410	12	78	90	364	24	1	5	6	16		1962-63	1972-73
Raymond, Armand	Mtl.	2	22	0	2	2	10	....	....	....	....	....		1937-38	1939-40
Raymond, Paul	Mtl.	4	76	2	3	5	6	5	0	0	0	2		1932-33	1937-38
Read, Mel	NYR	1	1	0	0	0	0	....	....	....	....	....		1946-47	1946-47
Reardon, Ken	Mtl.	7	341	26	96	122	604	31	2	5	7	62	1	1940-41	1949-50
Reardon, Terry	Bos., Mtl.	7	193	47	53	100	73	30	8	10	18	12	1	1938-39	1946-47
Reaume, Marc	Tor., Det., Mtl., Van.	9	344	8	43	51	273	21	0	2	2	8		1954-55	1970-71
Reay, Billy	Det., Mtl.	10	479	105	162	267	202	63	13	16	29	43	2	1943-44	1952-53
Redahl, Gord	Bos.	1	18	0	1	1	2	....	....	....	....	....		1958-59	1958-59
Redding, George	Bos.	2	35	3	2	5	10	....	....	....	....	....		1924-25	1925-26
Redmond, Craig	L.A., Edm.	5	191	16	68	84	134	3	1	0	1	2		1984-85	1988-89
Redmond, Dick	Min., Cal., Chi., St.L., Atl., Bos.	13	771	133	312	445	504	66	9	22	31	27		1969-70	1981-82
Redmond, Mickey	Mtl., Det.	9	538	233	195	428	219	16	2	3	5	2	2	1967-68	1975-76
Reeds, Mark	St.L., Hfd.	8	365	45	114	159	135	53	8	9	17	23		1981-82	1988-89
Regan, Bill	NYR, NYA	3	67	3	2	5	67	8	0	0	0	2		1929-30	1932-33
Regan, Larry	Bos., Tor.,	5	280	41	95	136	71	42	7	14	21	18		1956-57	1960-61
Regier, Darcy	Clev., NYI	3	26	0	2	2	35	....	....	....	....	....		1977-78	1983-84
Reibel, Earl	Det., Chi., Bos.	6	409	84	161	245	75	39	6	14	20	4	2	1953-54	1958-59
Reid, Dave	Tor.	3	7	0	0	0	0	....	....	....	....	....		1952-53	1955-56
Reid, Gerry	Det.	1	....	....	....	....	....	2	0	0	0	2		1948-49	1948-49
Reid, Gordie	NYA	1	1	0	0	0	2	....	....	....	....	....		1936-37	1936-37
Reid, Reg	Tor.	2	40	2	0	2	4	2	0	0	0	0		1924-25	1925-26
Reid, Tom	Chi., Min.	11	701	17	113	130	654	42	1	13	14	49		1967-68	1977-78
Reierson, Dave	Cgy.	1	2	0	0	0	2	....	....	....	....	....		1988-89	1988-89
Reigle, Ed	Bos.	1	17	0	2	2	25	....	....	....	....	....		1950-51	1950-51
Reinhart, Paul	Atl., Cgy., Van.	11	648	133	426	559	277	83	23	54	77	42		1979-80	1989-90
Reinikka, Ollie	NYR	1	16	0	0	0	0	....	....	....	....	....		1926-27	1926-27
Reise, Leo Jr.	Chi., Det., NYR	9	494	28	81	109	399	52	8	5	13	68	2	1945-46	1953-54
• Reise, Leo Sr.	Ham., NYA, NYR	8	199	36	29	65	177	6	0	0	0	16		1920-21	1929-30
Renaud, Mark	Hfd., Buf.	5	152	6	50	56	86	....	....	....	....	....		1979-80	1983-84
Reynolds, Bobby	Tor.	1	7	1	1	2	0	....	....	....	....	....		1989-90	1989-90
Ribble, Pat	Atl., Chi., Tor., Wsh., Cgy.	8	349	19	60	79	365	8	0	1	1	12		1975-76	1982-83
Richard, Henri	Mtl.	20	1256	358	688	1046	928	180	49	80	129	181	11	1955-56	1974-75
Richard, Jacques	Alt., Buf., Que.	10	556	160	187	347	307	35	5	5	10	34		1972-73	1982-83
Richard, Jean-Marc	Que.	2	5	2	1	3	2	....	....	....	....	....		1987-88	1989-90
Richard, Maurice	Mtl.	18	978	544	421	965	1285	133	82	44	126	188	8	1942-43	1959-60
Richard, Mike	Wsh.	2	7	0	2	2	0	....	....	....	....	....		1987-88	1989-90
Richardson, Dave	NYR, Chi., Det.	4	45	3	2	5	27	....	....	....	....	....		1963-64	1967-68
Richardson, Glen	Van.	1	24	3	6	9	19	....	....	....	....	....		1975-76	1975-76
Richardson, Ken	St.L.	3	49	8	13	21	16	....	....	....	....	....		1974-75	1978-79
Richer, Bob	Buf.	1	3	0	0	0	0	....	....	....	....	....		1972-73	1972-73
Richmond, Steve	NYR, Det., N.J., L.A.	5	159	4	23	27	514	4	0	0	0	12		1983-84	1988-89
Richter, Dave	Min., Phi., Van., St.L.	9	365	9	40	49	1030	22	1	0	1	80		1981-82	1989-90
Riley, Bill	Wsh., Wpg.	5	139	31	30	61	320	....	....	....	....	....		1974-75	1979-80
Riley, Jack	Det., Mtl., Bos.,	4	104	10	22	32	8	4	0	3	3	0		1932-33	1935-36
Riley, Jim	Det.	1	17	0	2	2	14	....	....	....	....	....		1926-27	1926-27
Riopellie, Howard	Mtl.	3	169	27	16	43	73	8	1	1	2	2		1947-48	1949-50
Rioux, Gerry	Wpg.	1	8	0	0	0	6	....	....	....	....	....		1979-80	1979-80
Rioux, Pierre	Cgy.	1	14	1	2	3	4	....	....	....	....	....		1982-83	1982-83
Ripley, Vic	Chi., Bos., NYR, St.L.	7	278	51	49	100	173	20	4	1	5	10		1928-29	1934-35
Risebrough, Doug	Mtl., Cgy.	14	740	185	286	471	1542	124	21	37	58	238	4	1974-75	1986-87
Rissling, Gary	Wsh., Pit.	7	221	23	30	53	1008	5	0	1	1	4		1978-79	1984-85
Ritchie, Bob	Phi., Det.	2	29	8	4	12	10	....	....	....	....	....		1976-77	1977-78
• Ritchie, Dave	Mtl.W, Ott., Tor., Que., Mtl.	6	54	15	3	18	27	1	0	0	0	0		1917-18	1925-26
Ritson, Alex	NYR	1	1	0	0	0	0	....	....	....	....	....		1944-45	1944-45
Rittinger, Alan	Bos.	1	19	3	7	10	0	....	....	....	....	....		1943-44	1943-44
Rivard, Bob	Pit.	1	27	5	12	17	4	....	....	....	....	....		1967-68	1967-68
• Rivers, Gus	Mtl.	3	88	4	5	9	12	16	2	0	2	2	2	1929-30	1931-32
Rivers, Wayne	Det., Bos., St.L., NYR	7	108	15	30	45	94	....	....	....	....	....		1961-62	1968-69
Rizzuto, Garth	Van.	1	37	3	4	7	16	....	....	....	....	....		1970-71	1970-71
• Roach, Mickey	Tor., Ham., NYA	8	209	75	27	102	41	....	....	....	....	....		1919-20	1926-27
Roberge, Serge	Que.	1	9	0	0	0	24	....	....	....	....	....		1990-91	1990-91
Robert, Claude	Mtl.	1	23	1	0	1	9	....	....	....	....	....		1950-51	1950-51
Robert, Rene	Tor., Pit., Buf., Col.	12	744	284	418	702	597	50	22	19	41	73		1970-71	1981-82
• Robert, Sammy	Ott.	1	1	0	0	0	0	....	....	....	....	....		1917-18	1917-18
Roberto, Phil	Mtl., St.L., Det., K.C., Col., Clev.	8	385	75	106	181	464	31	9	8	17	69	1	1969-70	1976-77
Roberts, Doug	Det., Dak., Cal., Bos.	10	419	43	104	147	342	16	2	3	5	46		1965-66	1974-75
Roberts, Jim	Mtl., St.L.	15	1006	126	194	320	621	153	20	16	36	160	5	1963-64	1977-78
Roberts, Jimmy	Min.	3	106	17	23	40	33	2	0	0	0	0		1976-77	1978-79
Robertson, Fred	Tor., Det.,	2	34	1	0	1	35	7	0	0	0	0	1	1931-32	1933-34
Robertson, Geordie	Buf.	1	5	1	2	3	7	....	....	....	....	....		1982-83	1982-83
Robertson, George	Mtl.	2	31	2	5	7	6	....	....	....	....	....		1947-48	1948-49
Robertson, Torrie	Wsh., Hfd., Det.	10	442	49	99	148	1751	22	2	1	3	90		1980-81	1989-90
Robidoux, Florent	Chi.	3	52	7	4	11	75	....	....	....	....	....		1980-81	1983-84
Robinson, Doug	Chi., NYR, L.A.	7	239	44	67	111	34	11	4	3	7	0		1963-64	1970-71
Robinson, Earl	Mtl.M., Chi., Mtl.	11	418	83	98	181	123	25	5	4	9	0	1	1928-29	1939-40
Robinson, Larry	Mtl., L.A.	20	1384	208	750	958	793	227	28	116	144	211	6	1972-73	1991-92
Robinson, Moe	Mtl	1	1	0	0	0	0	....	....	....	....	....		1979-80	1979-80
Robinson, Scott	Min.	1	1	0	0	0	2	....	....	....	....	....		1989-90	1989-90
Robitaille, Mike	NYR, Det., Buf., Van.	8	382	23	105	128	280	13	0	1	1	4		1969-70	1976-77
• Roche, Earl	Mtl.M., Bos., Ott., St.L., Det.	4	146	25	27	52	48	2	0	0	0	0		1930-31	1934-35
Roche, Ernest	Mtl.	1	4	0	0	0	2	....	....	....	....	....		1950-51	1950-51
Roche, Michel	Mtl.M., Ott., St.L., Mtl., Det.	4	112	20	18	38	44	....	....	....	....	....		1930-31	1934-35
Rochefort, Dave	Det	1	1	0	0	0	0	....	....	....	....	....		1966-67	1966-67
Rochefort, Leon	NYR, Mtl., Phi., L.A., Det., Atl., Van.	15	617	121	147	268	93	39	4	4	8	16	2	1960-61	1975-76
Rockburn, Harvey	Det., Ott.	3	94	4	2	6	254	....	....	....	....	....		1929-30	1932-33
• Rodden, Eddie	Chi., Tor., Bos., NYR	4	98	6	14	20	152	2	0	1	1	0	1	1926-27	1930-31
Rogers, Alfred	Min.	2	14	2	4	6	0	....	....	....	....	....		1973-74	1974-75
Rogers, Mike	Hfd., NYR, Edm.	7	484	202	317	519	184	17	1	13	14	6		1979-80	1985-86
Rohlicek, Jeff	Van.	2	9	0	0	0	8	....	....	....	....	....		1987-88	1988-89
Rolfe, Dale	Bos., L.A., Det., NYR	9	509	25	125	150	556	71	5	24	29	89		1959-60	1974-75
Romanchych, Larry	Chi., Atl	6	298	68	97	165	102	7	2	2	4	4		1970-71	1976-77
Rombough, Doug	Buf., NYI, Min.	4	150	24	27	51	80	....	....	....	....	....		1972-73	1975-76
• Romnes, Doc	Chi., Tor., NYA	10	359	68	136	204	42	43	7	18	25	4	2	1930-31	1939-40
• Ronan, Skene	Ott.	1	11	0	0	0	0	....	....	....	....	....		1918-19	1918-19
Ronson, Len	NYR, Oak.	2	18	2	1	3	10	....	....	....	....	....		1960-61	1968-69
Ronty, Paul	Bos., NYR, Mtl.	8	488	101	211	312	103	21	1	7	8	6		1947-48	1954-55
Rooney, Steve	Mtl., Wpg., N.J.	5	154	15	13	28	496	25	3	2	5	86	1	1984-85	1988-89
Root, Bill	Mtl., Tor., St.L., Phi.	6	247	11	23	34	180	22	1	2	3	25		1982-83	1987-88
• Ross, Art	Mtl.W	1	3	1	0	1	0	....	....	....	....	....		1917-18	1917-18
Ross, Jim	NYR	2	62	2	11	13	29	....	....	....	....	....		1951-52	1952-53
Rossignol, Roland	Det., Mtl.	3	14	3	5	8	6	1	0	0	0	2		1943-44	1945-46
Rota, Darcy	Chi., Atl., Van.	11	794	256	239	495	973	60	14	7	21	147		1973-74	1983-84
Rota, Randy	Mtl., L.A., K.C., Col.	5	212	38	39	77	60	5	0	1	1	0		1972-73	1976-77
• Rothschild, Sam	Mtl.M., NYA	4	99	8	6	14	24	10	0	0	0	0	1	1924-25	1927-28
• Roulston, Rolly	Det.	3	24	0	6	6	10	....	....	....	....	....	1	1935-36	1937-38
Roulston, Tom	Edm., Pit.	6	195	47	49	96	74	21	2	2	4	2		1980-81	1985-86
Roupe, Magnus	Phi.	2	40	3	5	8	42	....	....	....	....	....		1987-88	1988-89
Rousseau, Bobby	Mtl., Min., NYR	15	942	245	458	703	359	128	27	57	84	69	4	1960-61	1974-75
Rousseau, Guy	Mtl.	2	4	0	1	1	0	....	....	....	....	....		1954-55	1956-57
Rousseau, Roland	Mtl.	1	2	0	0	0	0	....	....	....	....	....		1952-53	1952-53
Routhier, Jean-Marc	Que.	1	8	0	0	0	9	....	....	....	....	....		1989-90	1989-90
Rowe, Bobby	Bos.	1	4	1	0	1	0	....	....	....	....	....		1924-25	1924-25
Rowe, Mike	Pit.	3	11	0	0	0	11	....	....	....	....	....		1984-85	1986-87
Rowe, Ron	NYR	1	5	1	0	1	0	....	....	....	....	....		1947-48	1947-48
Rowe, Tom	Wsh., Hfd., Det.	7	357	85	100	185	615	3	2	0	2	0		1976-77	1982-83
Roy, Stephane	Min.	1	12	1	0	1	0	....	....	....	....	....		1987-88	1987-88
Rozzini, Gino	Bos.	1	31	5	10	15	20	6	1	2	3	6		1944-45	1944-45
Rucinski, Mike	Chi.	2	1	0	0	0	0	2	0	0	0	0		1987-88	1988-89
Ruelle, Bernard	Det.	1	2	1	0	1	0	....	....	....	....	....		1943-44	1943-44

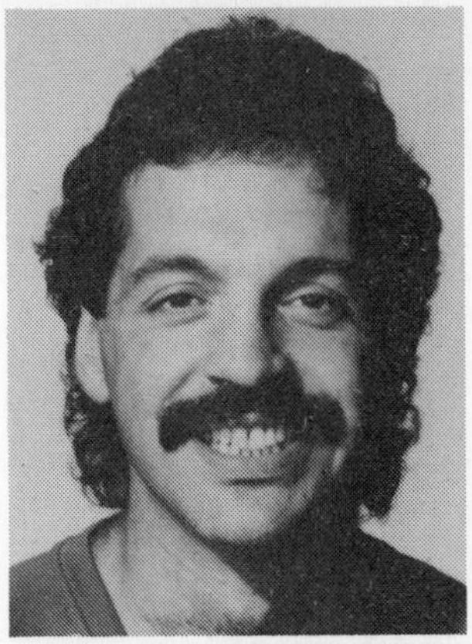
Terry Ruskowski

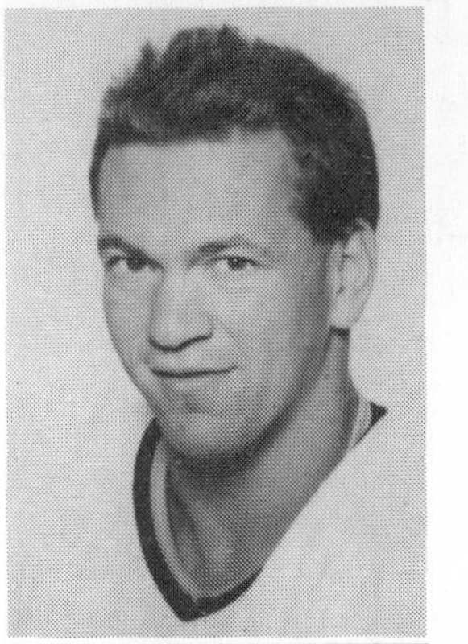
Steve Richmond

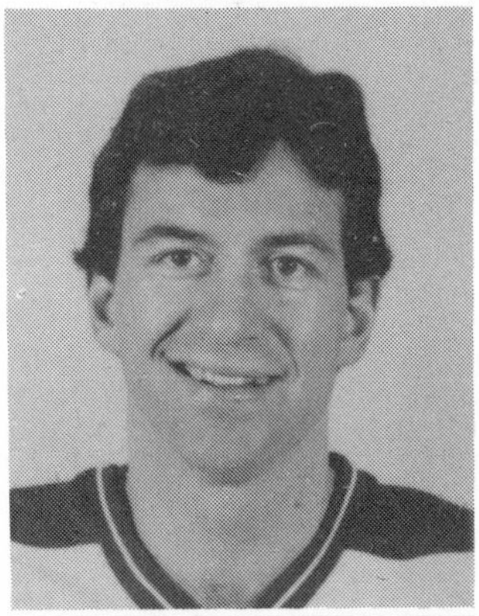
Doug Risebrough

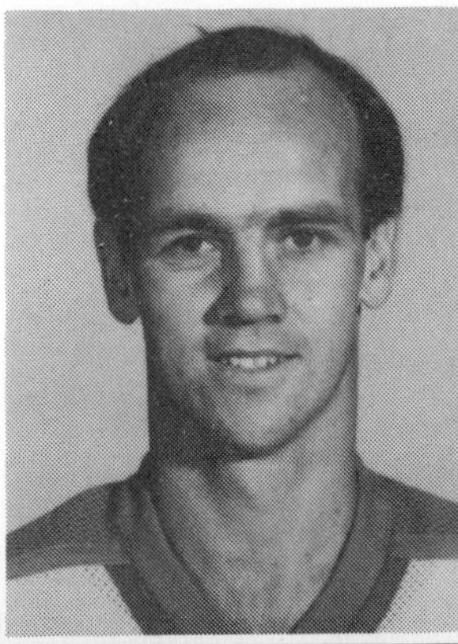
Tom Rowe

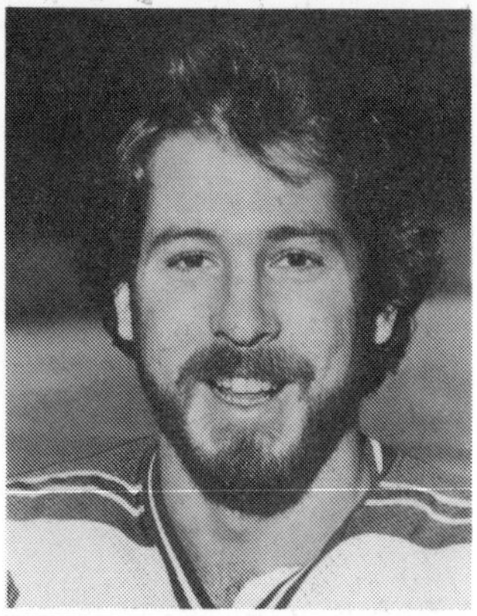

Mike Rogers

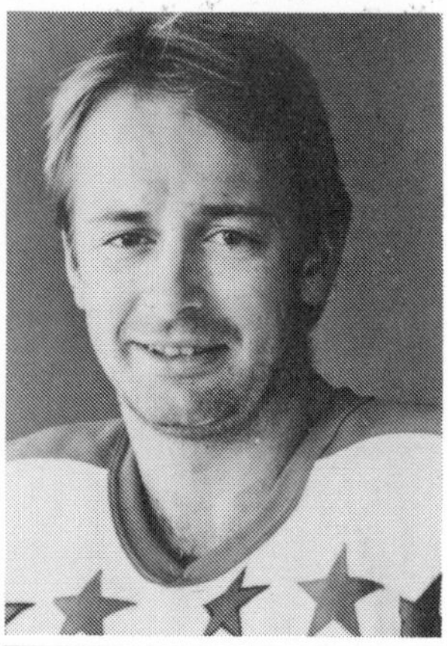

Gary Sampson

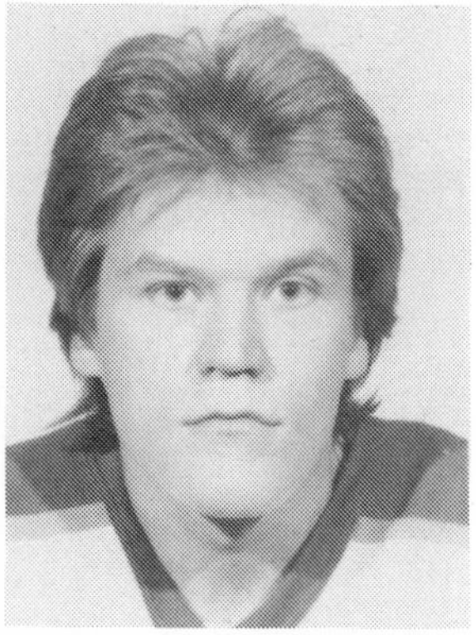

Kai Suikkawen

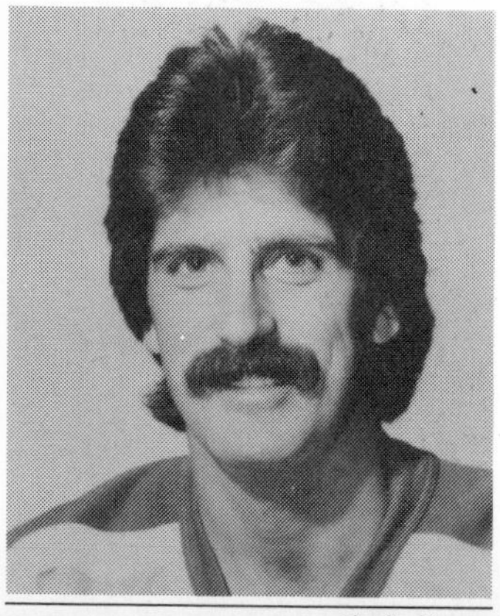

Charlie Simmer

Name	NHL Teams	NHL Seasons	Regular Schedule GP	G	A	TP	PIM	Playoffs GP	G	A	TP	PIM	NHL Cup Wins	First NHL Season	Last NHL Season
Ruff, Lindy	Buf., NYR	12	691	105	195	300	1264	52	11	13	24	193		1979-80	1990-91
Ruhnke, Kent	Bos.	1	2	0	1	1	0	....	....	....	....	....		1975-76	1975-76
Rundqvist, Thomas	Mtl.	1	2	0	1	1	0	....	....	....	....	....		1984-85	1984-85
• Runge, Paul	Bos., Mtl.M., Mtl.	7	143	18	22	40	57	7	0	0	0	6		1930-31	1937-38
Ruotsalainen, Reijo	NYR, Edm., N.J.	7	446	107	237	344	180	86	15	32	47	44	2	1981-82	1989-90
Rupp, Duane	NYR, Tor., Min., Pit.	10	374	24	93	117	220	10	2	2	4	8		1962-63	1972-73
Ruskowski, Terry	Chi., L.A., Pit., Min.	10	630	113	313	426	1354	21	1	6	7	86		1979-80	1988-89
Russell, Churchill	NYR	3	90	20	16	36	12	....	....	....	....	....		1945-46	1947-48
Russell, Phil	Chi., Atl., Cgy., N.J., Buf.	15	1016	99	325	424	2038	73	4	22	26	202		1972-73	1986-87
Rymsha, Andy	Que.	1	6	0	0	0	23	....	....	....	....	....		1991-92	1991-92

S

Name	NHL Teams	NHL Seasons	Regular Schedule GP	G	A	TP	PIM	Playoffs GP	G	A	TP	PIM	NHL Cup Wins	First NHL Season	Last NHL Season
Saarinen, Simo	NYR	1	8	0	0	0	0	....	....	....	....	....		1984-85	1984-85
Sabol, Shaun	Phi.	1	2	0	0	0	0	....	....	....	....	....		1989-90	1989-90
Sabourin, Bob	Tor.	1	1	0	0	0	2	....	....	....	....	....		1951-52	1951-52
Sabourin, Gary	St.L., Tor., Cal., Clev.	10	627	169	188	357	397	62	19	11	30	58		1967-68	1976-77
Sacharuk, Larry	NYR, St.L.	5	151	29	33	62	42	2	1	1	2	2		1972-73	1976-77
Saganiuk, Rocky	Tor., Pit.	6	259	57	65	122	201	6	1	0	1	15		1978-79	1983-84
St. Laurent, Andre	NYI, Det., L.A., Pit.	11	644	129	187	316	749	59	8	12	20	48		1973-74	1983-84
St. Laurent, Dollard	Mtl., Chi.	12	652	29	133	162	496	92	2	22	24	87	5	1950-51	1961-62
St. Marseille, Frank	St.L., L.A.	10	707	140	285	425	242	88	20	25	45	18		1967-68	1976-77
St. Sauveur, Claude	Atl.	1	79	24	24	48	23	2	0	0	0	0		1975-76	1975-76
Saleski, Don	Phi., Col.	9	543	128	125	253	629	82	13	17	30	131	2	1971-72	1979-80
Salming, Borje	Tor., Det.	17	1148	150	637	787	1344	81	12	37	49	91		1973-74	1989-90
Salovaara, John	Det.	2	90	2	13	15	70	....	....	....	....	....		1974-75	1975-76
Salvian, Dave	NYI	1	....	....	....	....	....	1	0	1	1	2		1976-77	1976-77
Samis, Phil	Tor.	2	2	0	0	0	0	5	0	1	1	2	1	1947-48	1949-50
Sampson, Gary	Wsh.	4	105	13	22	35	25	12	1	0	1	0		1983-84	1986-87
Sandelin, Scott	Mtl., Phi., Min.	4	25	0	4	4	2	....	....	....	....	....		1986-87	1991-92
Sanderson, Derek	Bos., NYR, St.L., Van., Pit.	13	598	202	250	452	911	56	18	12	30	187	2	1965-66	1977-78
Sandford, Ed	Bos., Det., Chi.	9	502	106	145	251	355	42	12	11	24	27		1947-48	1955-56
• Sands, Charlie	Tor., Bos., Mtl., NYR	12	432	99	109	208	58	44	6	6	12	4	1	1932-33	1943-44
Sanipass, Everett	Chi., Que.	5	164	25	34	59	358	5	2	0	2	4		1986-87	1990-91
Sargent, Gary	L.A., Min.	8	402	61	161	222	273	20	5	7	12	8		1975-76	1982-83
Sarner, Craig	Bos.	1	7	0	0	0	0	....	....	....	....	....		1974-75	1974-75
Sarrazin, Dick	Phi.	3	100	20	35	55	22	4	0	0	0	0		1968-69	1971-72
Saskamoose, Fred	Chi.	1	11	0	0	0	6	....	....	....	....	....		1953-54	1953-54
Sasser, Grant	Pit.	1	3	0	0	0	0	....	....	....	....	....		1983-84	1983-84
Sather, Glen	Bos., Pit., NYR, St.L., Mtl., Min.	10	658	80	113	193	724	72	1	5	6	86		1966-67	1975-76
Saunders, Bernie	Que.	2	10	0	1	1	8	....	....	....	....	....		1979-80	1980-81
Saunders, Bud	Ott.	1	19	1	3	4	4	....	....	....	....	....		1933-34	1933-34
Saunders, David	Van.	1	56	7	13	20	10	....	....	....	....	....		1987-88	1987-88
Sauve, Jenn F.	Buf., Que.	7	290	65	138	203	117	36	9	12	21	10		1980-81	1986-87
Savage, Joel	Buf.	1	3	0	1	1	0	....	....	....	....	....		1990-91	1990-91
• Savage, Tony	Bos., Mtl.	1	49	1	5	6	6	2	0	0	0	0		1934-35	1934-35
Savard, Andre	Bos., Buf., Que.	12	790	211	271	482	411	85	13	18	31	77		1973-74	1984-85
Savard, Jean	Chi, Hfd.	3	43	7	12	19	29	....	....	....	....	....		1977-78	1979-80
Savard, Serge	Mtl., Wpg.	17	1040	106	333	439	592	130	19	49	68	88	7	1966-67	1982-83
Scamurra, Peter	Wsh.	4	132	8	25	33	59	....	....	....	....	....		1975-76	1979-80
Sceviour, Darin	Chi.	1	1	0	0	0	0	....	....	....	....	....		1986-87	1986-87
Schaeffer, Butch	Chi.,	1	5	0	0	0	6	....	....	....	....	....		1936-37	1936-37
Schamehorn, Kevin	Det., L.A.	3	10	0	0	0	17	....	....	....	....	....		1976-77	1980-81
Schella, John	Van.	2	115	2	18	20	224	....	....	....	....	....		1970-71	1971-72
Scherza, Chuck	Bos., NYR	2	56	6	6	12	35	....	....	....	....	....		1943-44	1944-45
Schinkel, Ken	NYR, Pit.	12	636	127	198	325	163	19	7	2	9	4		1959-60	1972-73
Schliebener, Andy	Van.	3	84	2	11	13	74	6	0	0	0	0		1981-82	1984-85
Schmautz, Bobby	Chi., Bos., Edm., Col., Van.	13	764	271	286	557	988	73	28	33	61	92		1967-68	1980-81
Schmautz, Cliff	Buf., Phi.	1	56	13	19	32	33	....	....	....	....	....		1970-71	1970-71
Schmidt, Clarence	Bos.,	1	7	1	0	1	2	....	....	....	....	....		1943-44	1943-44
Schmidt, Jackie	Bos.	1	45	6	7	13	6	5	0	0	0	0		1942-43	1942-43
Schmidt, Joseph	Bos.	1	2	0	0	0	0	....	....	....	....	....		1943-44	1943-44
Schmidt, Milt	Bos.	16	778	229	346	575	466	86	24	25	49	60	2	1936-37	1954-55
Schmidt, Norm	Pit.	4	125	23	33	56	73	....	....	....	....	....		1983-84	1987-88
Schnarr, Werner	Bos.	2	25	0	0	0	0	....	....	....	....	....		1924-25	1925-26
Schock, Danny	Bos., Phi.	2	20	1	2	3	0	1	0	0	0	0	1	1969-70	1970-71
Schock, Ron	Bos., St.L., Pit., Buf.	15	909	166	351	517	260	55	4	16	20	29		1963-64	1977-78
Schoenfeld, Jim	Buf., Det., Bos.	13	719	51	204	255	1132	75	3	13	16	151		1972-73	1984-85
Schofield, Dwight	Det., Mtl., St.L., Wsh., Pit., Wpg.	7	211	8	22	30	631	9	0	0	0	55		1976-77	1987-88
Schreiber, Wally	Min.	2	41	8	10	18	12	....	....	....	....	....		1987-88	1988-89
• Schriner, Sweeney	NYA, Tor.	11	484	201	204	405	148	60	18	11	29	54	2	1934-35	1945-46
Schultz, Dave	Phi., L.A., Pit., Buf.	9	535	79	121	200	2294	73	8	12	20	412	2	1971-72	1979-80
Schurman, Maynard	Hfd.	1	7	0	0	0	0	....	....	....	....	....		1979-80	1979-80
Schutt, Rod	Mtl., Pit., Tor.	8	286	77	92	169	177	22	8	6	14	26		1977-78	1985-86
Sclisizzi, Enio	Det., Chi.	6	81	12	11	23	26	13	0	0	0	6		1946-47	1952-53
Scott, Ganton	Tor., Ham., Mtl.M.	3	53	1	1	2	0	....	....	....	....	....		1922-23	1924-25
• Scott, Laurie	NYA, NYR	2	62	6	3	9	28	....	....	....	....	....	1	1926-27	1927-28
Scruton, Howard	L.A.	1	4	0	4	4	9	....	....	....	....	....		1982-83	1982-83
Seabrooke, Glen	Phi.	3	19	1	6	7	4	....	....	....	....	....		1986-87	1988-89
Secord, Al	Bos., Chi., Tor, Phi.	12	766	273	222	495	2093	102	21	34	55	382		1978-79	1989-90
Sedlbauer, Ron	Van., Chi., Tor.	7	430	143	86	229	210	19	1	3	4	27		1974-75	1980-81
Seftel, Steve	Wsh.	1	4	0	0	0	2	....	....	....	....	....		1990-91	1990-91
Seguin, Dan	Min., Van.	2	37	2	6	8	50	....	....	....	....	....		1970-71	1973-74
Seguin, Steve	L.A.	1	5	0	0	0	9	....	....	....	....	....		1984-85	1984-85
• Seibert, Earl	NYR, Chi., Det.	15	652	89	187	276	768	66	8	9	19	66	2	1931-32	1945-46
Seiling, Ric	Buf., Det.	10	738	179	208	387	573	62	14	14	28	36		1977-78	1986-87
Seiling, Rod	Tor., NYR, Wsh., St.L., Atl.	17	979	62	269	331	603	77	4	8	12	55		1962-63	1978-79
Sejba, Jiri	Buf.	1	11	0	2	2	8	....	....	....	....	....		1990-91	1990-91
Selby, Brit	Tor., Phi., St.L.	8	350	55	62	117	163	16	1	1	2	8		1964-65	1971-72
Self, Steve	Wsh.	1	3	0	0	0	0	....	....	....	....	....		1976-77	1976-77
Selwood, Brad	Tor., L.A.	3	163	7	40	47	153	6	0	0	0	4		1970-71	1979-80
Semenko, Dave	Edm., Hfd., Tor.	9	575	65	88	153	1175	73	6	6	12	208	2	1979-80	1987-88
Senick, George	NYR	1	13	2	3	5	8	....	....	....	....	....		1952-53	1952-53
Seppa, Jyrki	Wpg.	1	13	0	2	2	6	....	....	....	....	....		1983-84	1983-84
Serafini, Ron	Cal.	1	2	0	0	0	2	....	....	....	....	....		1973-74	1973-74
Servinis, George	Min.	1	5	0	0	0	0	....	....	....	....	....		1987-88	1987-88
Sevcik, Jaroslav	Que.	1	13	0	2	2	2	....	....	....	....	....		1989-90	1989-90
Shack, Eddie	NYR, Tor., Bos., L.A., Buf., Pit.	17	1047	239	226	465	1437	74	6	7	13	151	4	1958-59	1974-75
• Shack, Joe	NYR	2	70	23	13	36	20	....	....	....	....	....		1942-43	1944-45
Shakes, Paul	Cal.	1	21	0	4	4	12	....	....	....	....	....		1973-74	1973-74
Shanahan, Sean	Mtl., Col., Bos.	3	40	1	3	4	47	....	....	....	....	....		1975-76	1977-78
Shand, Dave	Atl., Tor., Wsh.	8	421	19	84	103	544	26	1	2	3	83		1976-77	1984-85
Shannon, Charles	NYA	1	4	0	0	0	2	....	....	....	....	....		1939-40	1939-40
Shannon, Gerry	Ott., St.L., Bos., Mtl.M.	5	183	23	29	52	121	9	0	1	1	2		1933-34	1937-38
Sharpley, Glen	Min., Chi.	6	389	117	161	278	199	27	7	11	18	24		1976-77	1981-82
Shaunessy, Scott	Que.	2	7	0	0	0	23	....	....	....	....	....		1986-87	1988-89
Shay, Norman	Bos., Tor.	2	53	5	2	7	34	....	....	....	....	....		1924-25	1925-26
Shea, Pat	Chi.	1	14	0	1	1	0	....	....	....	....	....		1931-32	1931-32
Shedden, Doug	Pit., Det., Que., Tor.	8	416	139	186	325	176	....	....	....	....	....		1981-82	1990-91
Sheehan, Bobby	Mtl., Cal., Chi., Det., NYR, Col., L.A.	9	310	48	63	111	50	25	4	3	7	8	1	1969-70	1981-82
Sheehy, Neil	Cgy., Hfd., Wsh.	9	379	18	47	65	1311	54	0	3	3	241		1983-84	1991-92
Sheehy, Tim	Det., Hfd.	2	27	2	1	3	0	....	....	....	....	....		1977-78	1979-80
Shelton, Doug	Chi.	1	5	0	1	1	0	....	....	....	....	....		1967-68	1967-68
Sheppard, Frank	Det.	1	8	1	1	2	0	....	....	....	....	....		1927-28	1927-28
Sheppard, Gregg	Bos., Pit.	10	657	205	293	498	243	92	32	40	72	31		1972-73	1981-82
Sheppard, Johnny	Det., NYA, Bos., Chi.	8	311	68	58	126	224	10	0	0	0	0	1	1926-27	1933-34
Sherf, John	Det.	5	19	0	0	0	8	8	0	1	1	2	1	1935-36	1943-44
• Shero, Fred	NYR	3	145	6	14	20	137	13	0	2	2	8		1947-48	1949-50
Sherritt, Gordon	Det.	1	8	0	0	0	12	....	....	....	....	....		1943-44	1943-44
Sherven, Gord	Edm., Min., Hfd.	5	97	13	22	35	33	3	0	0	0	0		1983-84	1987-88
• Shewchuck, Jack	Bos.	6	187	9	19	28	160	20	0	1	1	19	1	1938-39	1944-45
Shibicky, Alex	NYR	8	317	110	91	201	159	40	12	12	24	12	1	1935-36	1945-46
Shields, Al	Ott., Phi., NYA, Mtl.M., Bos.	11	460	42	46	88	637	17	0	1	1	14	1	1927-28	1937-38
Shill, Bill	Bos.	3	79	21	13	34	18	7	1	2	3	2		1942-43	1946-47

Name	NHL Teams	NHL Seasons	Regular Schedule					Playoffs					NHL Cup Wins	First NHL Season	Last NHL Season
			GP	G	A	TP	PIM	GP	G	A	TP	PIM			
• Shill, Jack	Tor., Bos., NYA, Chi.	6	163	15	20	35	70	27	1	6	7	13	1	1933-34	1938-39
Shinske, Rick	Clev., St.L.	3	63	5	16	21	10	....	....	....	....	....		1976-77	1978-79
Shires, Jim	Det., St.L., Pit.	3	56	3	6	9	32	....	....	....	....	....		1970-71	1972-73
Shmyr, Paul	Chi., Cal., Min., Hfd.	7	343	13	72	85	528	34	3	3	6	44		1968-69	1981-82
Shoebottom, Bruce	Bos.	4	35	1	4	5	53	14	1	2	3	77		1987-88	1990-91
• Shore, Eddie	Bos., NYA	14	553	105	179	284	1047	55	6	13	19	187	2	1926-27	1939-40
• Shore, Hamby	Ott.	1	18	3	0	3	0	....	....	....	....	....		1917-18	1917-18
Shores, Aubry	Phi.	1	1	0	0	0	0	....	....	....	....	....		1930-31	1930-31
Short, Steve	L.A., Det.	2	6	0	0	0	2	....	....	....	....	....		1977-78	1978-79
Shudra, Ron	Edm.	1	10	0	5	5	6	....	....	....	....	....		1987-88	1987-88
Shutt, Steve	Mtl., L.A.	13	930	424	393	817	410	99	50	48	98	65	5	1972-73	1984-85
• Siebert, Babe	Mtl.M., NYR, Bos., Mtl.	14	592	140	156	296	982	53	8	7	15	62	2	1925-26	1938-39
Silk, Dave	NYR, Bos., Wpg., Det.	7	249	54	59	113	271	13	2	4	6	13		1979-80	1985-86
Siltala, Mike	Wsh., NYR	3	7	1	0	1	2	....	....	....	....	....		1981-82	1987-88
Siltanen, Risto	Edm., Hfd., Que.	8	562	90	265	355	266	32	6	12	18	30		1979-80	1986-87
Sim, Trevor	Edm.	1	3	0	1	1	2	....	....	....	....	....		1989-90	1989-90
Simmer, Charlie	Cal., Cle., L.A., Bos., Pit.	14	712	342	369	711	544	24	9	9	18	32		1974-75	1987-88
Simmons, Al	Cal., Bos.	3	11	0	1	1	21	1	0	0	0	0		1971-72	1975-76
Simon, Cully	Det., Chi.	3	130	4	11	15	121	14	0	1	1	6	1	1942-43	1944-45
Simon, Thain	Det.	1	3	0	0	0	0	....	....	....	....	....		1946-47	1946-47
Simonetti, Frank	Bos.	4	115	5	8	13	76	12	0	1	1	8		1984-85	1987-88
Simpson, Bobby	Atl., St.L., Pit.	5	175	35	29	64	98	6	0	1	1	2		1976-77	1982-83
• Simpson, Cliff	Det.	2	6	0	1	1	0	2	0	0	0	0		1946-47	1947-48
• Simpson, Joe	NYA	6	228	21	19	40	156	2	0	0	0	0		1925-26	1930-31
Sims, Al	Bos., Hfd., L.A.	10	475	49	116	165	286	41	0	2	2	14		1973-74	1982-83
Sinclair, Reg	NYR, Det.	3	208	49	43	92	139	3	1	0	1	0		1950-51	1952-53
Singbush, Alex	Mtl.	1	32	0	5	5	15	3	0	0	0	4		1940-41	1940-41
Sinisalo, Ilkka	Phi., Min., L.A.	11	582	204	222	426	208	68	21	11	32	6		1981-82	1991-92
Siren, Ville	Pit., Min.	5	290	14	68	82	276	7	0	0	0	6		1985-86	1989-90
Sirois, Bob	Phi., Wsh.	6	286	92	120	212	42	....	....	....	....	....		1974-75	1979-80
Sittler, Darryl	Tor., Phi., Det.	15	1096	484	637	1121	948	76	29	45	74	137		1970-71	1984-85
• Sjoberg, Lars-Erik	Wpg.	1	79	7	27	34	48	....	....	....	....	....		1979-80	1979-80
• Skaare, Bjorne	Det.	1	1	0	0	0	0	....	....	....	....	....		1978-79	1978-79
Skarda, Randy	St. L.	2	26	0	5	5	11	....	....	....	....	....		1989-90	1991-92
• Skilton, Raymie	Mtl.W	1	1	1	0	1	0	....	....	....	....	....		1917-18	1917-18
• Skinner, Alf	Tor., Bos., Mtl.M., Pit.	4	70	26	4	30	56	7	8	1	9	0	1	1917-18	1925-26
Skinner, Larry	Col.	4	47	10	12	22	8	2	0	0	0	0		1976-77	1979-80
Skov, Glen	Det., Chi., Mtl.	12	650	106	136	242	413	53	7	7	14	48	3	1949-50	1960-61
Skriko, Petri	Van., Bos., Wpg., S.J.	9	541	183	222	405	246	28	5	9	14	4		1984-85	1992-93
Sleaver, John	Chi.	2	24	2	0	2	6	....	....	....	....	....		1953-54	1956-57
Sleigher, Louis	Que., Bos.	6	194	46	53	99	146	17	1	1	2	64		1979-80	1985-86
Sloan, Tod	Tor., Chi.	13	745	220	262	482	781	47	9	12	21	47	2	1947-48	1960-61
• Slobodzian, Peter	NYA	1	41	3	2	5	54	....	....	....	....	....		1940-41	1940-41
Slowinski, Eddie	NYR	6	291	58	74	132	63	16	2	6	8	6		1947-48	1952-53
Sly, Darryl	Tor., Min., Van.	4	79	1	2	3	20	....	....	....	....	....		1965-66	1970-71
Smail, Doug	Wpg., Min., Que., Ott.	13	845	210	249	459	602	42	9	2	11	49		1980-81	1992-93
Smart, Alex	Mtl.	1	8	5	2	7	0	....	....	....	....	....		1942-43	1942-43
Smedsmo, Dale	Tor.	1	4	0	0	0	0	....	....	....	....	....		1972-73	1972-73
Smillie, Don	Bos.	1	12	2	2	4	4	....	....	....	....	....		1933-34	1933-34
• Smith, Alex	Ott., Det., Bos., NYA	11	443	41	50	91	643	19	0	2	2	40	1	1924-25	1934-35
• Smith, Arthur	Tor., Ott.	4	137	15	10	25	249	4	1	1	2	8		1927-28	1930-31
Smith, Barry	Bos., Col.	3	114	7	7	14	10	....	....	....	....	....		1975-76	1980-81
Smith, Bobby	Min., Mtl.	15	1077	357	679	1036	917	184	64	96	160	245	1	1978-79	1992-93
Smith, Brad	Van., Atl., Cgy., Det., Tor.	9	222	28	34	62	591	20	3	3	6	49		1978-79	1986-87
Smith, Brian D.	L.A., Min.	2	67	10	10	20	33	7	0	0	0	0		1967-68	1968-69
Smith, Brian S.	Det.	3	61	2	8	10	12	5	0	0	0	0		1957-58	1960-61
Smith, Carl	Det.	1	7	1	1	2	2	....	....	....	....	....		1943-44	1943-44
Smith, Clint	NYR, Chi.	11	483	161	236	397	24	44	10	14	24	2	1	1936-37	1946-47
Smith, Dallas	Bos., NYR	16	890	55	252	307	959	86	3	29	32	128	2	1959-60	1977-78
Smith, Dalton	NYA, Det.	2	11	1	2	3	0	....	....	....	....	....		1936-37	1943-44
Smith, Dennis	Wsh., L.A.	2	8	0	0	0	4	....	....	....	....	....		1989-90	1990-91
Smith, Derek	Buf., Det.	8	335	78	116	194	60	30	9	14	23	13		1975-76	1982-83
Smith, Des	Mtl.M., Mtl., Chi., Bos.	5	195	22	25	47	236	25	1	4	5	18	1	1937-38	1941-42
• Smith, Don	Mtl.	1	10	1	0	1	4	....	....	....	....	....		1919-20	1919-20
Smith, Don A.	NYR	1	11	1	1	2	0	1	0	0	0	0		1949-50	1949-50
Smith, Doug	L.A., Buf., Edm., Van., Pit.	9	535	115	138	253	624	....	....	....	....	....		1981-82	1989-90
Smith, Floyd	Bos., NYR, Det., Tor., Buf.	13	616	129	178	307	207	48	12	11	23	16		1954-55	1971-72
Smith, George	Tor.	1	9	0	0	0	0	....	....	....	....	....		1921-22	1921-22
Smith, Glen	Chi.	1	2	0	0	0	0	....	....	....	....	....		1950-51	1950-51
Smith, Glenn	Tor.	1	9	0	0	0	0	....	....	....	....	....		1922-23	1922-23
Smith, Gord	Wsh., Wpg.	6	299	9	30	39	284	....	....	....	....	....		1974-75	1979-80
Smith, Greg	Cal., Clev., Min., Det., Wsh.	13	829	56	232	288	1110	63	4	7	11	106		1975-76	1987-88
• Smith, Hooley	Ott., Mtl.M., Bos., NYA	17	715	200	215	415	1013	54	11	8	19	109	2	1924-25	1940-41
Smith, Kenny	Bos.	7	331	78	93	171	49	30	8	13	21	6		1944-45	1950-51
Smith, Randy	Min.	2	3	0	0	0	0	....	....	....	....	....		1985-86	1986-87
Smith, Rick	Bos., Cal., St.L., Det., Wsh.	11	687	52	167	219	560	78	3	23	26	73	1	1968-69	1980-81
• Smith, Roger	Pit., Phi.	6	210	20	4	24	172	4	3	0	3	0		1925-26	1930-31
Smith, Ron	NYI	1	11	1	1	2	14	....	....	....	....	....		1972-73	1972-73
Smith, Sid	Tor.	12	601	186	183	369	94	44	17	10	27	2	3	1946-47	1957-58
Smith, Stan	NYR	2	9	2	1	3	0	....	....	....	....	....	1	1939-40	1940-41
Smith, Steve	Phi., Buf.	6	78	10	47	57	214	4	0	0	0	10		1981-82	1988-89
Smith, Stu E.	Mtl.	2	4	2	2	4	2	1	0	0	0	0		1940-41	1941-42
Smith, Stu G.	Hfd.	4	77	2	10	12	95	....	....	....	....	....		1979-80	1982-83
• Smith, Tommy	Que.B.	1	10	0	0	0	9	....	....	....	....	....		1919-20	1919-20
Smith, Vern	NYI	1	1	0	0	0	0	....	....	....	....	....		1984-85	1984-85
Smith, Wayne	Chi.	1	2	1	1	2	2	1	0	0	0	0		1966-67	1966-67
Smrke, John	St.L., Que.	3	103	11	17	28	33	....	....	....	....	....		1977-78	1979-80
• Smrke, Stan	Mtl.	2	9	0	3	3	0	....	....	....	....	....		1956-57	1957-58
Smyl, Stan	Van.	13	896	262	411	673	1556	41	16	17	33	64		1978-79	1990-91
• Smylie, Rod	Tor., Ott.	6	76	4	1	5	10	9	1	2	3	2	1	1920-21	1925-26
Snell, Ron	Pit.	2	7	3	2	5	6	....	....	....	....	....		1968-69	1969-70
Snell, Ted	Pit., K.C., Det.	2	104	7	18	25	22	....	....	....	....	....		1973-74	1974-75
Snepsts, Harold	Van., Min., Det., St.L.	17	1033	38	195	223	2009	93	1	14	15	231		1974-75	1990-91
Snow, Sandy	Det.	1	3	0	0	0	2	....	....	....	....	....		1968-69	1968-69
Snuggerud, Dave	Buf., S.J., Phi.	4	265	30	54	84	127	12	1	3	4	6		1989-90	1992-93
Sobchuk, Denis	Det., Que.	2	35	5	6	11	2	....	....	....	....	....		1979-80	1982-83
Sobchuk, Gene	Van.	1	1	0	0	0	0	....	....	....	....	....		1973-74	1973-74
Solheim, Ken	Chi., Min., Det., Edm.	5	135	19	20	39	34	3	1	1	2	2		1980-81	1985-86
Solinger, Bob	Tor., Det.	5	99	10	11	21	19	....	....	....	....	....		1951-52	1959-60
• Somers, Art	Chi., NYR	6	222	33	56	89	189	30	1	5	6	20	1	1929-30	1934-35
Sommer, Roy	Edm.	1	3	1	0	1	7	....	....	....	....	....		1980-81	1980-81
Songin, Tom	Bos.	3	43	5	5	10	22	....	....	....	....	....		1978-79	1980-81
Sonmor, Glen	NYR	2	28	2	0	2	21	....	....	....	....	....		1953-54	1954-55
• Sorrell, John	Det., NYA	11	490	127	119	246	100	42	12	15	27	10	2	1930-31	1940-41
Sparrow, Emory	Bos.	1	6	0	0	0	4	....	....	....	....	....		1924-25	1924-25
Speck, Fred	Det., Van.	3	28	1	2	3	2	....	....	....	....	....		1968-69	1971-72
• Speer, Bill	Pit., Bos.	4	130	5	20	25	79	8	1	0	1	4	1	1967-68	1970-71
Speers, Ted	Det.	1	4	1	1	2	0	....	....	....	....	....		1985-86	1985-86
• Spencer, Brian	Tor., NYI, Buf., Pit.	10	553	80	143	223	634	37	1	5	6	29		1969-70	1978-79
Spencer, Irv	NYR, Bos., Det.	8	230	12	38	50	127	16	0	0	0	8		1959-60	1967-68
Speyer, Chris	Tor., NYA	3	14	0	0	0	0	....	....	....	....	....		1923-24	1933-34
Spring, Don	Wpg.	4	259	1	52	55	80	6	0	0	0	10		1980-81	1983-84
Spring, Frank	Bos., St.L., Cal., Clev.	5	61	14	20	34	12	....	....	....	....	....		1969-70	1976-77
• Spring, Jesse	Ham., Pit., Tor., NYA	6	137	11	2	13	62	2	0	2	2	2		1923-24	1929-30
Spruce, Andy	Van., Col.	3	172	31	42	73	111	2	0	2	2	2		1976-77	1978-79
Srsen, Tomas	Edm.	1	2	0	0	0	0	....	....	....	....	....		1990-91	1990-91
Stackhouse, Ron	Cal., Det., Pit.	12	889	87	372	459	824	32	5	8	13	38		1970-71	1981-82
Stackhouse, Ted	Tor.	1	12	0	0	0	2	5	0	0	0	0	1	1921-22	1921-22
Stahan, Butch	Mtl.	1	....	....	....	....	....	3	0	1	1	2		1944-45	1944-45
Staley, Al	NYR	1	1	0	1	1	0	....	....	....	....	....		1948-49	1948-49
Stamler, Lorne	L.A., Tor., Wpg.	4	116	14	11	25	16	....	....	....	....	....		1976-77	1979-80
Standing, George	Min.	1	2	0	0	0	0	....	....	....	....	....		1967-68	1967-68
Stanfield, Fred	Chi., Bos., Min., Buf.	14	914	211	405	616	134	106	21	35	56	10	2	1964-65	1977-78

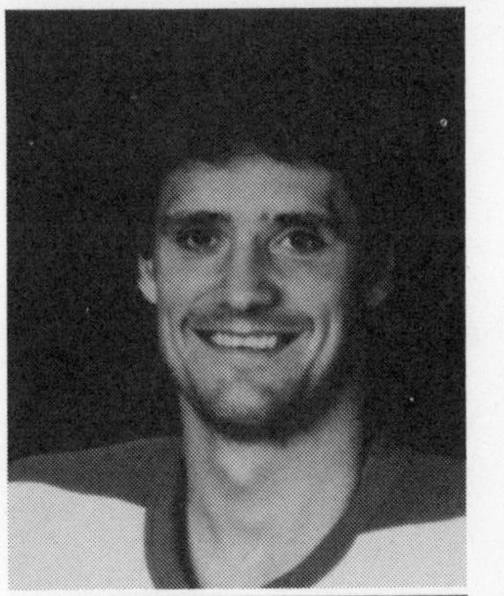

Peter Sundstrom

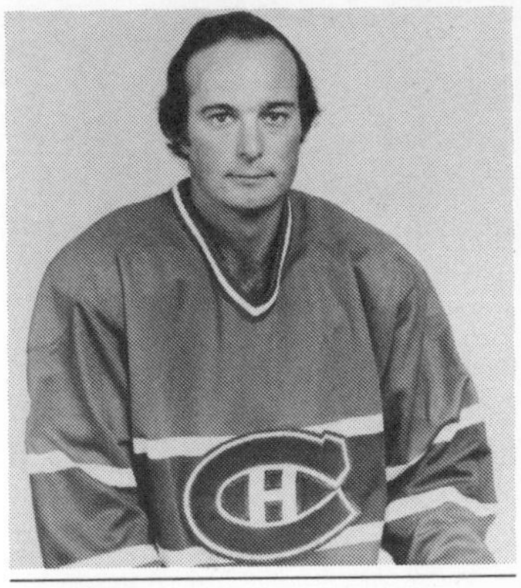

Steve Shutt

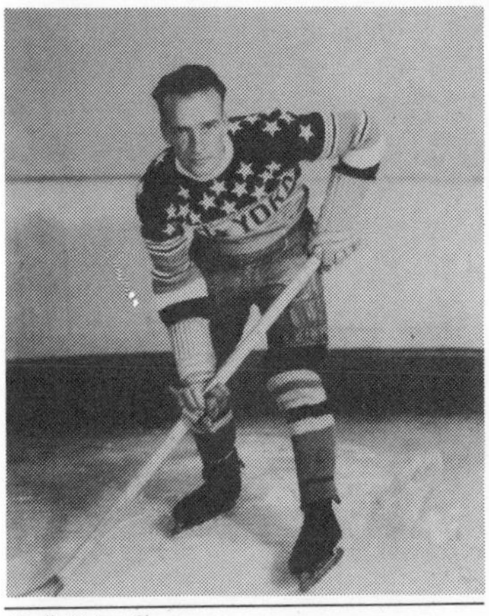

"Bullet" Joe Simpson

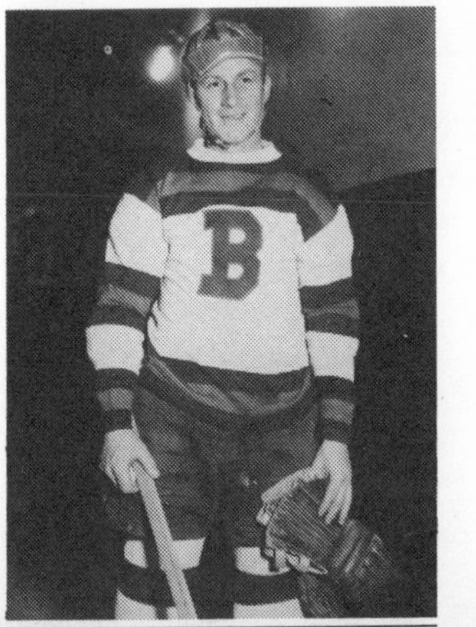

Eddie Shore

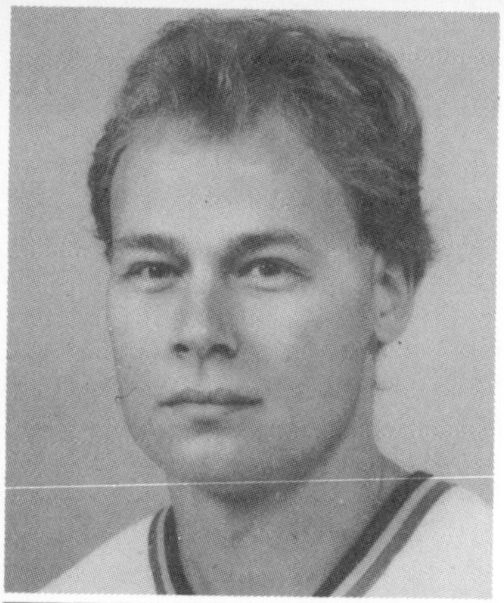

Petri Skriko

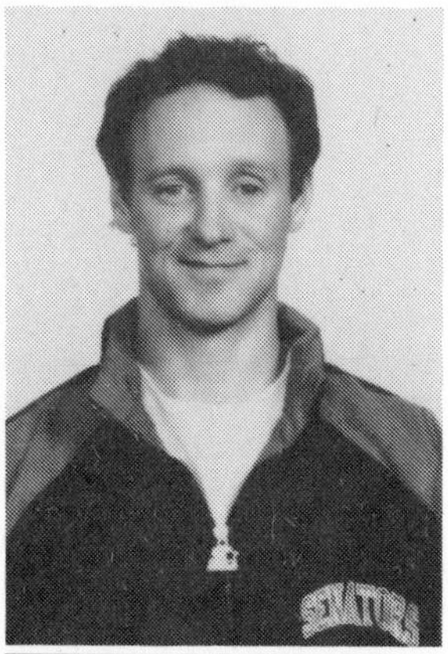

Doug Smail

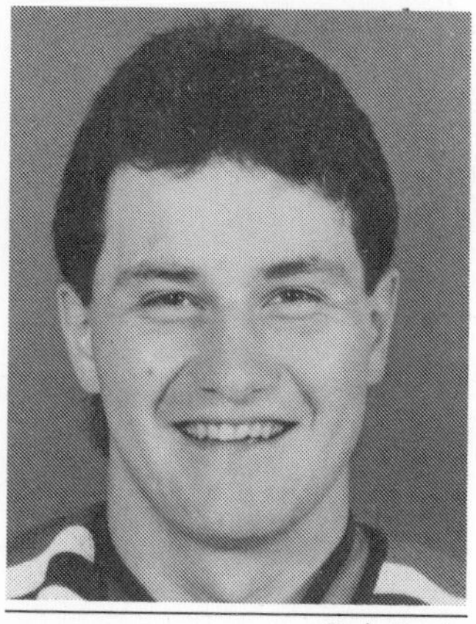

Rocky Trottier

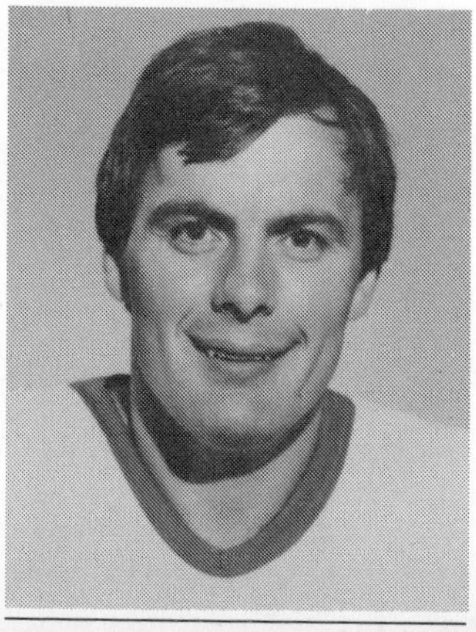

Marc Tardif

Name	NHL Teams	NHL Seasons	Regular Schedule GP	G	A	TP	PIM	Playoffs GP	G	A	TP	PIM	NHL Cup Wins	First NHL Season	Last NHL Season
Stanfield, Jack	Chi.	1	....	....	....	....	....	1	0	0	0	0		1965-66	1965-66
Stanfield, Jim	L.A.	3	7	0	1	1	0	....	....	....	....	....		1969-70	1971-72
Stankiewicz, Edward	Det.	2	6	0	0	0	2	....	....	....	....	....		1953-54	1955-56
Stankiewicz, Myron	St.L., Phi.	1	35	0	7	7	36	1	0	0	0	0		1968-69	1968-69
Stanley, Allan	NYR, Chi., Bos., Tor., Phi.	21	1244	100	333	433	792	109	7	36	43	80	4	1948-49	1968-69
• Stanley, Barney	Chi.	1	1	0	0	0	0	....	....	....	....	....		1927-28	1927-28
Stanley, Daryl	Phi., Van.	6	189	8	17	25	408	17	0	0	0	30		1983-84	1989-90
Stanowski, Wally	Tor., NYR	10	428	23	88	111	160	60	3	14	17	13	4	1939-40	1950-51
Stapleton, Brian	Wsh.	1	1	0	0	0	0	....	....	....	....	....		1975-76	1975-76
Stapleton, Pat	Bos., Chi.	10	635	43	294	337	353	65	10	39	49	38		1961-62	1972-73
Starikov, Sergei	N.J.	1	16	0	1	1	8	....	....	....	....	....		1989-90	1989-90
Starr, Harold	Ott., Mtl.M., Mtl., NYR	7	203	6	5	11	186	17	1	0	1	2		1929-30	1935-36
Starr, Wilf	NYA, Det.	4	89	8	6	14	25	7	0	2	2	2	1	1932-33	1935-36
Stasiuk, Vic	Chi., Det., Bos.	14	745	183	254	437	669	69	16	18	34	40	2	1949-50	1962-63
Stastny, Anton	Que.	9	650	252	384	636	150	66	20	32	52	31		1980-81	1988-89
Stastny, Marian	Que., Tor.	5	322	121	173	294	110	32	5	17	22	7		1981-82	1985-86
Staszak, Ray	Det.	1	4	0	1	1	7	....	....	....	....	....		1985-86	1985-86
Steele, Frank	Det.	1	1	0	0	0	0	....	....	....	....	....		1930-31	1930-31
Steen, Anders	Wpg.	1	42	5	11	16	22	....	....	....	....	....		1980-81	1980-81
Stefaniw, Morris	Atl.	1	13	1	1	2	2	....	....	....	....	....		1972-73	1972-73
Stefanski, Bud	NYR	1	1	0	0	0	0	....	....	....	....	....		1977-78	1977-78
Stemkowski, Pete	Tor., Det., NYR, L.A.	15	967	206	349	555	866	83	25	29	54	136	1	1963-64	1977-78
Stenlund, Vern	Clev.	1	4	0	0	0	0	....	....	....	....	....		1976-77	1976-77
• Stephens, Phil	Mtl.W, Mtl.	2	8	1	0	1	0	....	....	....	....	....		1917-18	1921-22
Stephenson, Bob	Hfd., Tor.	1	18	2	3	5	4	....	....	....	....	....		1979-80	1979-80
Sterner, Ulf	NYR	1	4	0	0	0	0	....	....	....	....	....		1964-65	1964-65
Stevens, Paul	Bos.	1	17	0	0	0	0	....	....	....	....	....		1925-26	1925-26
Stevenson, Shayne	Bos., T.B.	3	27	0	2	2	35	....	....	....	....	....		1990-91	1992-93
Stewart, Allan	N.J., Bos.	6	64	6	4	10	243	....	....	....	....	....		1985-86	1991-92
Stewart, Bill	Buf., St.L., Tor., Min.	8	261	7	64	71	424	13	1	3	4	11		1977-78	1985-86
Stewart, Blair	Det., Wsh., Que.	7	229	34	44	78	326	....	....	....	....	....		1973-74	1979-80
Stewart, Gaye	Tor., Chi., Det., NYR, Mtl.	11	502	185	159	344	274	25	2	9	11	16	2	1941-42	1953-54
• Stewart, Jack	Det., Chi.	12	565	31	84	115	765	80	5	14	19	143	2	1938-39	1951-52
Stewart, John	Pit., Atl., Cal., Que.	6	260	58	60	118	158	4	0	0	0	10		1970-71	1979-80
Stewart, Ken	Chi.	1	6	1	1	2	2	....	....	....	....	....		1941-42	1941-42
• Stewart, Nels	Mtl.M., Bos., NYA	15	650	324	191	515	953	54	15	11	26	61	1	1925-26	1939-40
Stewart, Paul	Que.	1	21	2	0	2	74	....	....	....	....	....		1979-80	1979-80
Stewart, Ralph	Van., NYI	7	252	57	73	130	28	19	4	4	8	2		1970-71	1977-78
Stewart, Robert	Bos., Cal., Clev., St.L., Pit.	9	510	27	101	128	809	5	1	1	2	2		1971-72	1979-80
Stewart, Ron	Tor., Bos., St.L., NYR, Van., NYI	21	1353	276	253	529	560	119	14	21	35	60	3	1952-53	1972-73
Stewart, Ryan	Wpg.	1	3	1	0	1	0	....	....	....	....	....		1985-86	1985-86
Stiles, Tony	Cgy.	1	30	2	7	9	20	....	....	....	....	....		1983-84	1983-84
Stoddard, Jack	NYR	2	80	16	15	31	31	....	....	....	....	....		1951-52	1952-53
Stoltz, Roland	Wsh.	1	14	2	2	4	14	....	....	....	....	....		1981-82	1981-82
Stone, Steve	Van.	1	2	0	0	0	0	....	....	....	....	....		1973-74	1973-74
Stothers, Mike	Phi., Tor.	4	30	0	2	2	65	5	0	0	0	11		1984-85	1987-88
Stoughton, Blaine	Pit., Tor., Hfd., NYR	8	526	258	191	449	204	8	4	2	6	2		1973-74	1983-84
Stoyanovich, Steve	Hfd.	1	23	3	5	8	11	....	....	....	....	....		1983-84	1983-84
• Strain, Neil	NYR	1	52	11	13	24	12	....	....	....	....	....		1952-53	1952-53
Strate, Gord	Det.	3	61	0	0	0	34	....	....	....	....	....		1956-57	1958-59
Stratton, Art	NYR, Det., Chi., Pit., Phi.	4	95	18	33	51	24	5	0	0	0	0		1959-60	1967-68
Strobel, Art	NYR	1	7	0	0	0	0	....	....	....	....	....		1943-44	1943-44
Strong, Ken	Tor.	3	15	2	2	4	6	....	....	....	....	....		1982-83	1984-85
Strueby, Todd	Edm.	3	5	0	1	1	2	....	....	....	....	....		1981-82	1983-84
• Stuart, Billy	Tor., Bos.	7	193	30	17	47	145	17	1	0	1	12	1	1920-21	1926-27
Stumpf, Robert	St.L., Pit.	1	10	1	1	2	20	....	....	....	....	....		1974-75	1974-75
Sturgeon, Peter	Col.	2	6	0	1	1	2	....	....	....	....	....		1979-80	1980-81
Suikkanen, Kai	Buf.	2	2	0	0	0	0	....	....	....	....	....		1981-82	1982-83
Sulliman, Doug	NYR, Hfd., N.J., Phi.	11	631	160	168	328	175	16	1	3	4	2		1979-80	1989-90
Sullivan, Barry	Det.	1	1	0	0	0	0	....	....	....	....	....		1947-48	1947-48
Sullivan, Bob	Hfd.	1	62	18	19	37	18	....	....	....	....	....		1982-83	1982-83
Sullivan, Frank	Tor., Chi.	4	8	0	0	0	2	....	....	....	....	....		1949-50	1955-56
Sullivan, Peter	Wpg.	2	126	28	54	82	40	....	....	....	....	....		1979-80	1980-81
Sullivan, Red	Bos., Chi., NYR	11	557	107	239	346	441	18	1	2	3	7		1949-50	1960-61
Summanen, Raimo	Edm., Van.	5	151	36	40	76	35	10	2	5	7	0		1983-84	1987-88
• Summerhill, Bill	Mtl., Bro.	3	72	14	17	31	70	3	0	0	0	2		1938-39	1941-42
Sundstrom, Patrik	Van., N.J.	10	679	219	369	588	349	37	9	17	26	25		1982-83	1991-92
Sundstrom, Peter	NYR, Wsh., N.J.	6	338	61	83	144	120	23	3	3	6	8		1983-84	1989-90
Suomi, Al	Chi.	1	5	0	0	0	0	....	....	....	....	....		1936-37	1936-37
Sutherland, Bill	Mtl., Phi., Tor., St.L., Det.	6	250	70	58	128	99	14	2	4	6	0		1962-63	1971-72
Sutherland, Ron	Bos.	1	2	0	0	0	0	....	....	....	....	....		1931-32	1931-32
Sutter, Brian	St.L.	12	779	303	333	636	1786	65	21	21	42	249		1976-77	1987-88
Sutter, Darryl	Chi.	8	406	161	118	279	288	51	24	19	43	26		1979-80	1986-87
Sutter, Duane	NYI, Chi.	11	731	139	203	342	1333	161	26	32	58	405	4	1979-80	1989-90
Suzor, Mark	Phi., Col.	2	64	4	16	20	60	....	....	....	....	....		1976-77	1977-78
Svensson, Leif	Wsh.	2	121	6	40	46	49	....	....	....	....	....		1978-79	1979-80
Swain, Garry	Pit.	1	9	1	1	2	0	....	....	....	....	....		1968-69	1968-69
Swarbrick, George	Oak., Pit., Phi.	4	132	17	25	42	173	....	....	....	....	....		1967-68	1970-71
• Sweeney, Bill	NYR	1	4	1	0	1	0	....	....	....	....	....		1959-60	1959-60
Sykes, Bob	Tor.	1	2	0	0	0	0	....	....	....	....	....		1974-75	1974-75
Sykes, Phil	L.A., Wpg.	10	456	79	85	164	519	26	0	3	3	29		1982-83	1991-92
Szura, Joe	Oak.	2	90	10	15	25	30	7	2	3	5	2		1967-68	1968-69

T

Name	NHL Teams	NHL Seasons	Regular Schedule GP	G	A	TP	PIM	Playoffs GP	G	A	TP	PIM	NHL Cup Wins	First NHL Season	Last NHL Season
Taft, John	Det.	1	15	0	2	2	4	....	....	....	....	....		1978-79	1978-79
Talafous, Dean	Atl., Min., NYR	8	497	104	154	258	163	21	4	7	11	11		1974-75	1981-82
Talakoski, Ron	NYR	2	9	0	1	1	33	....	....	....	....	....		1986-87	1987-88
Talbot, Jean-Guy	Mtl., Min., Det., St.L., Buf.	17	1056	43	242	285	1006	150	4	26	30	142	7	1954-55	1970-71
Tallon, Dale	Van., Chi., Pit.	10	642	98	238	336	568	33	2	10	12	45		1970-71	1979-80
Tambellini, Steve	NYI, Col., N.J., Cgy., Van.	10	553	160	150	310	105	2	0	1	1	0	1	1978-79	1987-88
Tanguay, Chris	Que.	1	2	0	0	0	0	....	....	....	....	....		1981-82	1981-82
Tannahill, Don	Van.	2	111	30	33	63	25	....	....	....	....	....		1972-73	1973-74
Tardif, Marc	Mtl., Que.	8	517	194	207	401	443	62	13	15	28	75	2	1969-70	1982-83
• Taylor, Billy	Tor., Det., Bos., NYR	7	323	87	180	267	120	33	6	18	24	13	1	1939-40	1947-48
• Taylor, Billy	NYR	1	2	0	0	0	0	....	....	....	....	....		1964-65	1964-65
• Taylor, Bob	Bos.	1	8	0	0	0	6	....	....	....	....	....		1929-30	1929-30
Taylor, Harry	Tor., Chi.	3	66	5	10	15	30	1	0	0	0	0	1	1946-47	1951-52
Taylor, Mark	Phi., Pit., Wsh.	5	209	42	68	110	73	6	0	0	0	0		1981-82	1985-86
• Taylor, Ralph	Chi., NYR	3	99	4	1	5	169	4	0	0	0	10		1927-28	1929-30
Taylor, Ted	NYR, Det., Min., Van.	6	166	23	35	58	181	....	....	....	....	....		1964-65	1971-72
Teal, Jeff	Mtl.	1	6	0	1	1	0	....	....	....	....	....		1984-85	1984-85
Teal, Skip	Bos.	1	1	0	0	0	0	....	....	....	....	....		1954-55	1954-55
Teal, Victor	NYI	1	1	0	0	0	0	....	....	....	....	....		1973-74	1973-74
Tebbutt, Greg	Que., Pit.	2	26	0	3	3	35	....	....	....	....	....		1979-80	1983-84
Terbenche, Paul	Chi., Buf.	5	189	5	26	31	28	12	0	0	0	0		1967-68	1973-74
Terrion, Greg	L.A., Tor.	8	561	93	150	243	339	35	2	9	11	41		1980-81	1987-88
Terry, Bill	Min.	1	5	0	0	0	0	....	....	....	....	....		1987-88	1987-88
Tessier, Orval	Mtl., Bos.	3	59	5	7	12	6	....	....	....	....	....		1954-55	1960-61
Thatchell, Spence	NYR	1	1	0	0	0	0	....	....	....	....	....		1942-43	1942-43
Theberge, Greg	Wsh.	5	153	15	63	78	73	4	0	1	1	0		1979-80	1983-84
Thelin, Mats	Bos.	3	163	8	19	27	107	5	0	0	0	6		1984-85	1986-87
Thelven, Michael	Bos.	5	207	20	80	100	217	34	4	10	14	34		1985-86	1989-90
Therrien, Gaston	Que.	3	22	0	8	8	12	9	0	1	1	4		1980-81	1982-83
Thibaudeau, Gilles	Mtl., NYI, Tor.	5	119	25	37	62	40	8	3	3	6	2		1986-87	1990-91
Thibeault, Laurence	Det., Mtl.	2	5	0	2	2	0	....	....	....	....	....		1944-45	1945-46
Thiffault, Leo	Min.	1	....	....	....	....	....	5	0	0	0	0		1967-68	1967-68
Thomas, Cy	Chi., Tor.	1	14	2	2	4	12	....	....	....	....	....		1947-48	1947-48
Thomas, Reg	Que.	1	39	9	7	16	6	....	....	....	....	....		1979-80	1979-80
Thompson, Cliff	Bos.	2	13	0	1	1	2	....	....	....	....	....		1941-42	1948-49
Thompson, Errol	Tor., Det., Pit.	10	599	208	185	393	184	34	7	5	12	11		1970-71	1980-81
• Thompson, Kenneth	Mtl.W	1	1	0	0	0	0	....	....	....	....	....		1917-18	1917-18
Thompson, Paul	NYR, Chi.	13	586	153	179	332	336	48	11	11	22	54	3	1926-27	1938-39
• Thoms, Bill	Tor., Chi., Bos.	13	549	135	206	341	172	44	6	10	16	6		1932-33	1944-45

Name	NHL Teams	NHL Seasons	Regular Schedule GP	G	A	TP	PIM	Playoffs GP	G	A	TP	PIM	NHL Cup Wins	First NHL Season	Last NHL Season
Thomson, Bill	Det., Chi.	2	10	2	2	4	0	2	0	0	0	0		1938-39	1943-44
Thomson, Floyd	St.L.	8	411	56	97	153	341	10	0	2	2	6		1971-72	1979-80
Thomson, Jack	NYA	3	15	1	1	2	0	2	0	0	0	0		1938-39	1940-41
• Thomson, Jimmy	Tor., Chi.	13	787	19	215	234	920	63	2	13	15	135	4	1945-46	1957-58
• Thomson, Rhys	Mtl., Tor.	2	25	0	2	2	38	....	....	....	....	....		1939-40	1942-43
Thornbury, Tom	Pit.	1	14	1	8	9	16	....	....	....	....	....		1983-84	1983-84
Thorsteinson, Joe	NYA	1	4	0	0	0	0	....	....	....	....	....		1932-33	1932-33
Thurier, Fred	NYA, Bro., NYR	3	80	25	27	52	18	....	....	....	....	....		1940-41	1944-45
Thurlby, Tom	Oak.	1	20	1	2	3	4	....	....	....	....	....		1967-68	1967-68
Thyer, Mario	Min.	1	5	0	0	0	0	1	0	0	0	2		1989-90	1989-90
Tidey, Alex	Buf., Edm.	3	9	0	0	0	8	2	0	0	0	0		1976-77	1979-80
Timgren, Ray	Tor., Chi.	6	251	14	44	58	70	30	3	9	12	6	2	1948-49	1954-55
Titanic, Morris	Buf.	2	19	0	0	0	0	....	....	....	....	....		1974-75	1975-76
Tkaczuk, Walt	NYR	14	945	227	451	678	556	93	19	32	51	119		1967-68	1980-81
Toal, Mike	Edm.	1	3	0	0	0	0	....	....	....	....	....		1979-80	1979-80
Tomalty, Glenn	Wpg.	1	1	0	0	0	0	....	....	....	....	....		1979-80	1979-80
Tomlinson, Kirk	Min.	1	1	0	0	0	0	....	....	....	....	....		1987-88	1987-88
Tonelli, John	NYI, Cgy., L.A., Chi., Que.	14	1028	325	511	836	911	172	40	75	115	200	4	1978-79	1991-92
Toomey, Sean	Min.	1	1	0	0	0	0	....	....	....	....	....		1986-87	1986-87
Toppazzini, Jerry	Bos., Chi., Det.	12	783	163	244	407	436	40	13	9	22	13		1952-53	1963-64
Toppazzini, Zellio	Bos., NYR, Chi.	5	123	21	22	43	49	2	0	0	0	0		1948-49	1956-57
Torkki, Jari	Chi.	1	4	1	0	1	0	....	....	....	....	....		1988-89	1988-89
Touhey, Bill	Mtl.M., Ott., Bos.	7	280	65	40	105	107	2	1	0	1	0		1927-28	1933-34
Toupin, Jacques	Chi.	1	8	1	2	3	0	4	0	0	0	0		1943-44	1943-44
Townsend, Art	Chi.	1	5	0	0	0	0	....	....	....	....	....		1926-27	1926-27
Trader, Larry	Det., St.L., Mtl.	4	91	5	13	18	74	3	0	0	0	0		1982-83	1987-88
Trainor, Wes	NYR	1	17	1	2	3	6	....	....	....	....	....		1948-49	1948-49
• Trapp, Bobby	Chi.	2	82	4	4	8	129	2	0	0	0	4		1926-27	1927-28
Trapp, Doug	Buf.	1	2	0	0	0	0	....	....	....	....	....		1986-87	1986-87
Traub, Percy	Chi., Det.	3	130	3	3	6	214	4	0	0	0	6		1926-27	1928-29
Tredway, Brock	L.A.	1	....	....	....	....	....	1	0	0	0	0		1981-82	1981-82
Tremblay, Brent	Wsh.	2	10	1	0	1	6	....	....	....	....	....		1978-79	1979-80
Tremblay, Gilles	Mtl.	9	509	168	162	330	161	48	9	14	23	4	2	1960-61	1968-69
Tremblay, J.C.	Mtl.	13	794	57	306	363	204	108	14	51	65	58	5	1959-60	1971-72
Tremblay, Marcel	Mtl.	1	10	0	2	2	0	....	....	....	....	....		1938-39	1938-39
Tremblay, Mario	Mtl.	12	852	258	326	584	1043	100	20	29	49	187	5	1974-75	1985-86
• Tremblay, Nels	Mtl.	2	3	0	1	1	0	2	0	0	0	0		1944-45	1945-46
Trimper, Tim	Chi., Wpg., Min.	6	190	30	36	66	153	2	0	0	0	2		1979-80	1984-85
• Trottier, Dave	Mtl.M., Det.	11	446	121	113	234	517	31	4	3	7	41	1	1928-29	1938-39
Trottier, Guy	NYR, Tor.	3	115	28	17	45	37	9	1	0	1	16		1968-69	1971-72
Trottier, Rocky	N.J.	2	38	6	4	10	2	....	....	....	....	....		1983-84	1984-85
• Trudel, Louis	Chi., Mtl.	8	306	49	69	118	122	24	1	3	4	6	2	1933-34	1940-41
Trudell, Rene	NYR	3	129	24	28	52	72	5	0	0	0	2		1945-46	1947-48
Tudin, Connie	Mtl.	1	4	0	1	1	4	....	....	....	....	....		1941-42	1941-42
Tudor, Rob	Van., St.L.	3	28	4	4	8	19	3	0	0	0	0		1978-79	1982-83
Tuer, Allan	L.A., Min., Hfd.	4	57	1	1	2	208	....	....	....	....	....		1985-86	1989-90
Turcotte, Alfie	Mtl., Wpg., Wsh.	7	112	17	29	46	49	5	0	0	0	0		1983-84	1990-91
Turlick, Gord	Bos.	1	2	0	0	0	2	....	....	....	....	....		1959-60	1959-60
Turnbull, Ian	Tor., L.A., Pit.	10	628	123	317	440	736	55	13	32	45	94		1973-74	1982-83
Turnbull, Perry	St.L., Mtl., Wpg.	9	608	188	163	351	1245	34	6	7	13	86		1979-80	1987-88
Turnbull, Randy	Cgy.	1	1	0	0	0	2	....	....	....	....	....		1981-82	1981-82
Turner, Bob	Mtl., Chi.	8	478	19	51	70	307	68	1	4	5	44	5	1955-56	1962-63
Turner, Dean	NYR, Col., L.A.	4	35	1	0	1	59	....	....	....	....	....		1978-79	1982-83
Tustin, Norman	NYR	1	18	2	4	6	0	....	....	....	....	....		1941-42	1941-42
Tuten, Audley	Chi.	2	39	4	8	12	48	....	....	....	....	....		1941-42	1942-43
Tutt, Brian	Wsh.	1	7	1	0	1	2	....	....	....	....	....		1989-90	1989-90

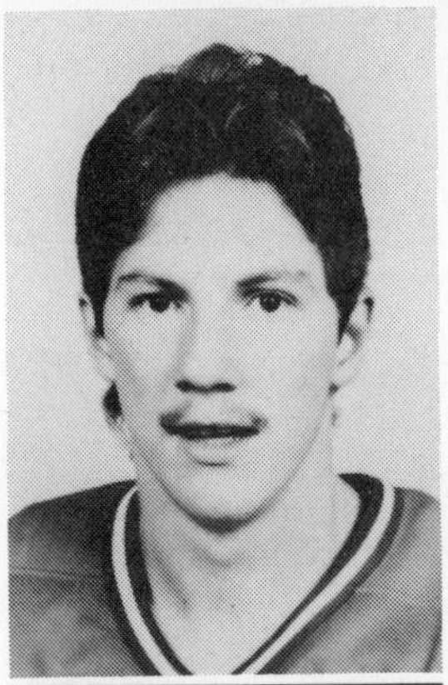

Gilles Thibaudeau

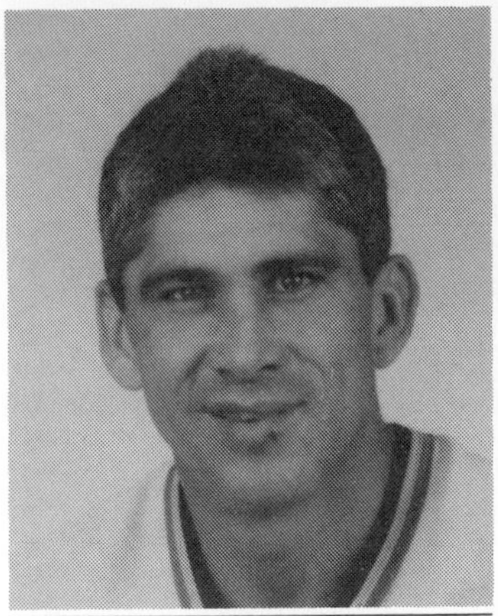

Rick Vaive

U V

Name	NHL Teams	NHL Seasons	Regular Schedule GP	G	A	TP	PIM	Playoffs GP	G	A	TP	PIM	NHL Cup Wins	First NHL Season	Last NHL Season
Ubriaco, Gene	Pit., Oak., Chi.	3	177	39	35	74	50	11	2	0	2	4		1967-68	1969-70
Ullman, Norm	Det., Tor.	20	1410	490	739	1229	712	106	30	53	83	67		1955-56	1974-75
Unger, Garry	Tor., Det., St.L., Atl., L.A., Edm.	16	1105	413	391	804	1075	52	12	18	30	105		1967-68	1982-83
Vadnais, Carol	Mtl., Oak., Cal., Bos., NYR, N.J.	17	1087	169	418	587	1813	106	10	40	50	185	2	1966-67	1982-83
Vail, Eric	Atl, Cgy., Det.	9	591	216	260	476	281	20	5	6	11	6		1973-74	1981-82
Vail, Melville	NYR	2	50	4	1	5	18	10	0	0	0	2		1928-29	1929-30
Vaive, Rick	Van., Tor., Chi., Buf.	13	876	441	347	788	1445	54	27	16	43	111		1979-80	1991-92
Valentine, Chris	Wsh.	3	105	43	52	95	127	2	0	0	0	4		1981-82	1983-84
Valiquette, Jack	Tor., Col.	7	350	84	134	218	79	23	3	6	9	4		1974-75	1980-81
Van Boxmeer, John	Mtl., Col., Buf., Que.	11	588	84	274	358	465	38	5	15	20	37		1973-74	1983-84
Van Dorp, Wayne	Edm., Pit., Chi., Que.	6	125	12	12	24	565	27	0	1	1	42		1986-87	1991-92
Van Impe, Ed	Chi., Phi., Pit.	11	700	27	126	153	1025	66	1	12	13	131	2	1966-67	1976-77
Vasko, Elmer	Chi., Min.	13	786	34	166	200	719	78	2	7	9	73	1	1956-57	1969-70
Vasko, Rick	Det.	3	31	3	7	10	29	....	....	....	....	....		1977-78	1980-81
Vautour, Yvon	NYI, Col., N.J., Que.	6	204	26	33	59	401	....	....	....	....	....		1979-80	1984-85
Vaydik, Greg	Chi.	1	5	0	0	0	0	....	....	....	....	....		1976-77	1976-77
Veitch, Darren	Wsh., Det., Tor.	10	511	48	209	257	296	33	4	11	15	33		1980-81	1990-91
Venasky, Vic	L.A.	7	430	61	101	162	66	21	1	5	6	12		1972-73	1978-79
Veneruzzo, Gary	St.L.	2	7	1	1	2	0	9	0	2	2	2		1967-68	1971-72
Verret, Claude	Buf.	2	14	2	5	7	2	....	....	....	....	....		1983-84	1984-85
Verstraete, Leigh	Tor.	3	8	0	1	1	14	....	....	....	....	....		1982-83	1987-88
Ververgaert, Dennis	Van., Phi., Wsh.	8	583	176	216	392	247	8	1	2	3	6		1973-74	1980-81
Veysey, Sid	Van.	1	1	0	0	0	0	....	....	....	....	....		1977-78	1977-78
Vickers, Steve	NYR	10	698	246	340	586	330	68	24	25	49	58		1972-73	1981-82
Vigneault, Alain	St.L.	2	42	2	5	7	82	4	0	1	1	26		1981-82	1982-83
Vincelette, Daniel	Chi., Que.	6	193	20	22	42	351	12	0	0	0	4		1986-87	1991-92
Vipond, Pete	Cal.	1	3	0	0	0	0	....	....	....	....	....		1972-73	1972-73
Virta, Hannu	Buf.	5	245	25	101	126	66	17	1	3	4	6		1981-82	1985-86
Viveiros, Emanuel	Min.	3	29	1	11	12	6	....	....	....	....	....		1985-86	1987-88
Vokes, Ed	Chi.	1	5	0	0	0	0	....	....	....	....	....		1930-31	1930-31
Volcan, Mickey	Hfd., Cgy.	4	162	8	33	41	146	....	....	....	....	....		1980-81	1983-84
Volmar, Doug	Det., L.A.	4	62	13	8	21	26	2	1	0	1	0		1969-70	1972-73
• Voss, Carl	Tor., NYR, Det., Ott., St.L., Mtl.M., NYA, Chi.	8	261	34	70	104	50	24	5	3	8	0		1926-27	1937-38
Vyazmikin, Igor	Edm.	1	4	1	0	1	0	....	....	....	....	....		1990-91	1990-91

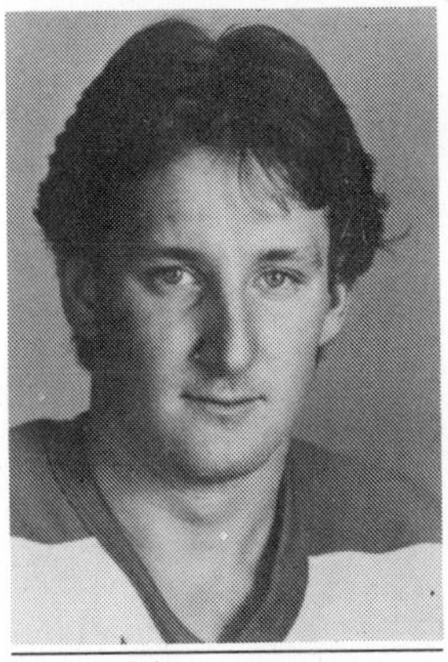

Darren Veitch

W

Name	NHL Teams	NHL Seasons	Regular Schedule GP	G	A	TP	PIM	Playoffs GP	G	A	TP	PIM	NHL Cup Wins	First NHL Season	Last NHL Season
Waddell, Don	L.A.	1	1	0	0	0	0	....	....	....	....	....		1980-81	1980-81
Waite, Frank	NYR	1	17	1	3	4	4	....	....	....	....	....		1930-31	1930-31
Walker, Gord	NYR, L.A.	4	31	3	4	7	23	....	....	....	....	....		1986-87	1989-90
Walker, Howard	Wsh., Cal.	3	83	2	13	15	133	....	....	....	....	....		1980-81	1982-83
• Walker, Jack	Det.	2	80	5	8	13	18	....	....	....	....	....		1926-27	1927-28
Walker, Kurt	Tor.	3	71	4	5	9	152	16	0	0	0	34		1975-76	1977-78
Walker, Russ	L.A.	2	17	1	0	1	41	....	....	....	....	....		1976-77	1977-78
Wall, Bob	Det., L.A., St.L.	8	322	30	55	85	155	22	0	3	3	2		1964-65	1971-72
Wallin, Peter	NYR	2	52	3	14	17	14	14	2	6	8	6		1980-81	1981-82
Walsh, Jim	Buf.	1	4	0	1	1	4	....	....	....	....	....		1981-82	1981-82
Walsh, Mike	NYI	2	14	2	0	2	4	....	....	....	....	....		1987-88	1988-89
Walter, Ryan	Wsh., Mtl., Van.	15	1003	264	382	646	946	113	16	35	51	62	1	1978-79	1992-93
Walton, Bobby	Mtl.	1	4	0	0	0	0	....	....	....	....	....		1943-44	1943-44
Walton, Mike	Tor., Bos., Van., Chi., St.L.	12	588	201	247	448	357	47	14	10	24	45	2	1965-66	1978-79
Wappel, Gord	Atl., Cgy.	3	20	1	1	2	10	2	0	0	0	4		1979-80	1981-82
Ward, Don	Chi., Bos.	2	34	0	1	1	16	....	....	....	....	....		1957-58	1959-60
• Ward, Jimmy	Mtl.M., Mtl.	12	532	147	127	274	465	31	4	4	8	18	1	1927-28	1938-39
Ward, Joe	Col.	1	4	0	0	0	2	....	....	....	....	....		1980-81	1980-81
Ward, Ron	Tor., Van.,	2	89	2	5	7	6	....	....	....	....	....		1969-70	1971-72
Ware, Michael	Edm.	2	5	0	1	1	15	....	....	....	....	....		1988-89	1989-90
Wares, Eddie	NYR, Det., Chi.	9	291	60	102	162	161	45	5	7	12	34	1	1936-37	1946-47
Warner, Bob	Tor.	2	10	1	1	2	4	4	0	0	0	0		1975-76	1976-77
Warner, Jim	Hfd.	1	32	0	3	3	10	....	....	....	....	....		1979-80	1979-80
Warwick, Bill	NYR	2	14	3	3	6	16	....	....	....	....	....		1942-43	1943-44
Warwick, Grant	NYR, Bos., Mtl.	9	395	147	142	289	220	16	2	4	6	6		1941-42	1949-50
• Wasnie, Nick	Chi., Mtl., NYA, Ott., St.L.	7	248	57	34	91	176	14	6	3	9	20	2	1927-28	1934-35

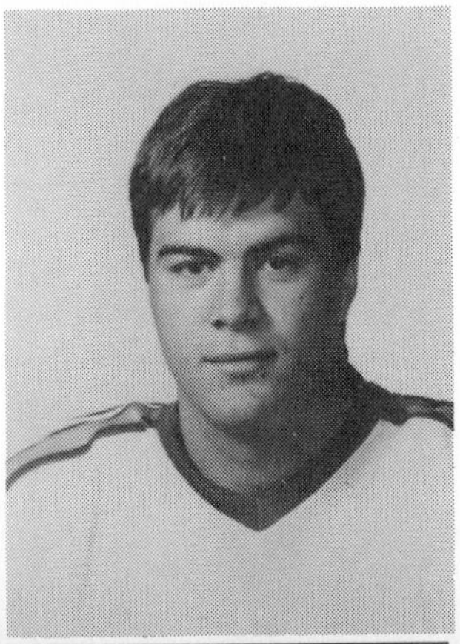

Alain Vignealt

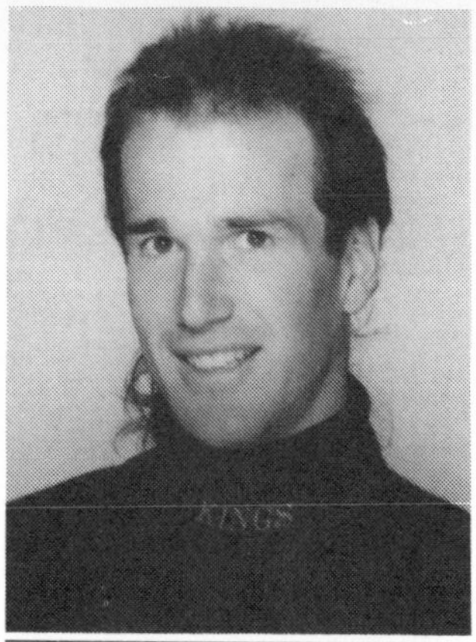

Gord Walker

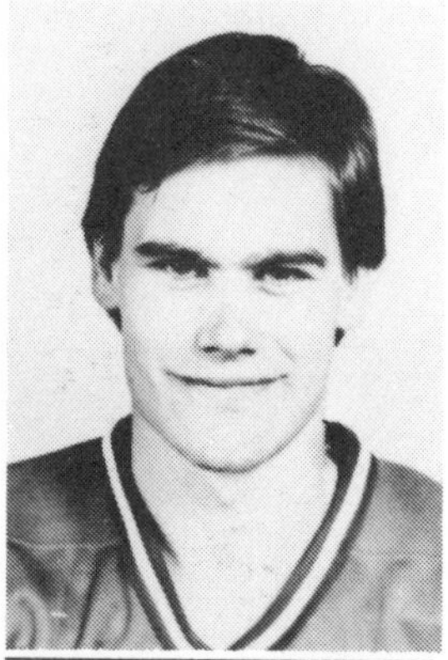

Ryan Walter

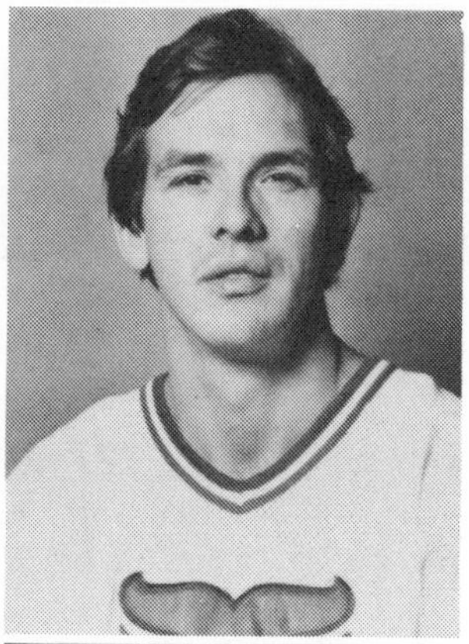

Wally Weir

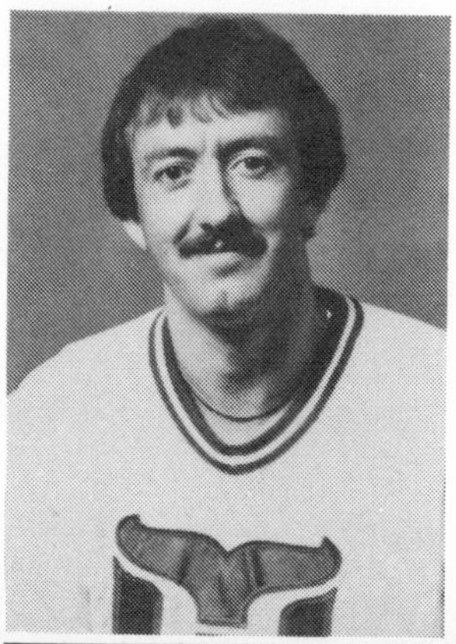

Mike Zuke

Name	NHL Teams	NHL Seasons	Regular Schedule					Playoffs					NHL Cup Wins	First NHL Season	Last NHL Season
			GP	G	A	TP	PIM	GP	G	A	TP	PIM			
Watson, Bill	Chi.	4	115	23	36	59	12	6	0	2	2	0		1985-86	1988-89
Watson, Bryan	Mtl., Oak., Pit., Det., St.L., Wsh.	16	878	17	135	152	2212	32	2	0	2	70		1963-64	1978-79
Watson, Dave	Col.	2	18	0	1	1	10	....	....	....	....	....		1979-80	1980-81
Watson, Harry	Bro., Det., Tor., Chi.	14	805	236	207	443	150	62	16	9	25	27	5	1941-42	1956-57
Watson, Jim	Det., Buf.	7	221	4	19	23	345	....	....	....	....	....		1963-64	1971-72
Watson, Jimmy	Phi.	10	613	38	148	186	492	101	5	34	39	89	2	1972-73	1981-82
Watson, Joe	Bos., Phi., Col.	14	835	38	178	216	447	84	3	12	15	82	2	1964-65	1978-79
• Watson, Phil	NYR, Mtl.	13	590	144	265	409	542	45	10	25	35	67	2	1935-36	1947-48
Watts, Brian	Det.	1	4	0	0	0	0	....	....	....	....	....		1975-76	1975-76
Webster, Aubrey	Phi., Mtl.M.	2	5	0	0	0	0	....	....	....	....	....		1930-31	1934-35
• Webster, Don	Tor.	1	27	7	6	13	28	5	0	0	0	12		1943-44	1943-44
Webster, John	NYR	1	14	0	0	0	4	....	....	....	....	....		1949-50	1949-50
Webster, Tom	Bos., Det., Cal.	5	102	33	42	75	61	1	0	0	0	0		1968-69	1979-80
• Weiland, Cooney	Bos., Ott., Det.	11	508	173	160	333	147	45	12	10	22	12		1928-29	1938-39
Weir, Stan	Cal., Tor., Edm., Col., Det.	10	642	139	207	346	183	37	6	5	11	4		1972-73	1982-83
Weir, Wally	Que., Hfd., Pit.	6	320	21	45	66	625	23	0	1	1	96		1979-80	1984-85
• Wellington, Duke	Que.	1	1	0	0	0	0	....	....	....	....	....		1919-20	1919-20
Wensink, John	Bos., Que., Col., N.J., St.L.	8	403	70	68	138	840	43	2	6	8	86		1973-74	1982-83
• Wentworth, Cy	Chi., Mtl.M., Mtl.	13	578	39	68	107	355	35	5	6	11	22	1	1927-28	1939-40
Wesley, Blake	Phi., Hfd., Que., Tor.	7	298	18	46	64	486	19	2	2	4	30		1979-80	1985-86
Westfall, Ed	Bos., NYI	18	1227	231	394	625	544	95	22	37	59	41	2	1961-62	1978-79
Wharram, Kenny	Chi.	14	766	252	281	533	222	80	16	27	43	38	1	1951-52	1968-69
Wharton, Len	NYR	1	1	0	0	0	0	....	....	....	....	....		1944-45	1944-45
Wheeldon, Simon	NYR, Wpg.	3	15	0	2	2	10	....	....	....	....	....		1987-88	1990-91
• Wheldon, Donald	St.L.	1	2	0	0	0	0	....	....	....	....	....		1974-75	1974-75
Whelton, Bill	Wpg.	1	2	0	0	0	0	....	....	....	....	....		1980-81	1980-81
Whistle, Rob	NYR, St.L.	2	51	7	5	12	16	4	0	0	0	2		1985-86	1987-88
White, Bill	L.A., Chi.	9	604	50	215	265	495	91	7	32	39	76		1967-68	1975-76
White, Moe	Mtl.	1	4	0	1	1	2	....	....	....	....	....		1945-46	1945-46
White, Sherman	NYR	2	4	0	2	2	0	....	....	....	....	....		1946-47	1949-50
• White, Tex	Pit., NYA, Phi.	6	203	33	12	45	141	4	0	0	0	2		1925-26	1930-31
White, Tony	Wsh., Min.	5	164	37	28	65	104	....	....	....	....	....		1974-75	1979-80
Whitelaw, Bob	Det.	2	32	0	2	2	2	8	0	0	0	0		1940-41	1941-42
Whitlock, Bob	Min.	1	1	0	0	0	0	....	....	....	....	....		1969-70	1969-70
Wickenheiser, Doug	Mtl., St.L., Van., NYR, Wsh.	10	556	111	165	276	286	....	....	....	....	....		1980-81	1989-90
• Widing, Juha	NYR, L.A., Clev.	8	575	144	226	370	208	8	1	2	3	2		1969-70	1976-77
• Wiebe, Art	Chi.	11	411	14	27	41	209	31	1	3	4	8	1	1932-33	1943-44
• Wilcox, Archie	Mtl.M., Bos., St.L.	6	212	8	14	22	158	12	1	0	1	10		1929-30	1934-35
Wilcox, Barry	Van.	2	33	3	2	5	15	....	....	....	....	....		1972-73	1974-75
Wilder, Arch	Det.	1	18	0	2	2	2	....	....	....	....	....		1940-41	1940-41
Wiley, Jim	Pit., Van.	5	63	4	10	14	8	....	....	....	....	....		1972-73	1976-77
Wilkins, Barry	Bos., Van., Pit.	9	418	27	125	152	663	6	0	1	1	4		1966-67	1975-76
Wilkinson, John	Bos.	1	9	0	0	0	3	....	....	....	....	....		1943-44	1943-44
Wilks, Brian	L.A.	4	48	4	8	12	27	....	....	....	....	....		1984-85	1988-89
Willard, Rod	Tor.	1	1	0	0	0	0	....	....	....	....	....		1982-83	1982-83
Williams, Burr	Det., St.L., Bos.	3	19	0	1	1	28	2	0	0	0	8		1933-34	1936-37
Williams, Dave	Tor., Van., Det., L.A., Hfd.	14	962	241	272	513	3966	83	12	23	35	455		1974-75	1987-88
Williams, Fred	Det.	1	44	2	5	7	10	....	....	....	....	....		1976-77	1976-77
Williams, Gord	Phi.	2	2	0	0	0	2	....	....	....	....	....		1981-82	1982-83
Williams, Sean	Chi.	1	2	0	0	0	4	....	....	....	....	....		1991-92	1991-92
• Williams, Tom	Bos., Min., Cal., Wsh.	13	663	161	269	430	177	10	2	5	7	2		1961-62	1975-76
Williams, Tommy	NYR, L.A.	8	397	115	138	253	73	29	8	7	15	4		1971-72	1978-79
Williams, Warren	St.L., Cal.	3	108	14	35	49	131	....	....	....	....	....		1973-74	1975-76
Willson, Don	Mtl.	2	22	2	7	9	0	3	0	0	0	0		1937-38	1938-39
Wilson, Behn	Phi., Chi.	9	601	98	260	358	1480	67	12	29	41	190		1978-79	1987-88
• Wilson, Bert	NYR, L.A., St.L., Cgy.	8	478	37	44	81	646	21	0	2	2	42		1973-74	1980-81
Wilson, Bob	Chi.	1	1	0	0	0	0	....	....	....	....	....		1953-54	1953-54
Wilson, Carey	Cgy., Hfd., NYR	10	552	169	258	427	314	52	11	13	24	14		1983-84	1992-93
Wilson, Cully	Tor., Mtl., Ham., Chi.	5	125	60	23	83	232	2	1	0	1	6		1919-20	1926-27
Wilson, Doug	Chi., S.J.	16	1024	237	590	827	830	95	19	61	80	88		1977-78	1992-93
Wilson, Gord	Bos.	1	....	....	....	....	....	2	0	0	0	0		1954-55	1954-55
Wilson, Hub	NYA	1	2	0	0	0	0	....	....	....	....	....		1931-32	1931-32
Wilson, Jerry	Mtl.	1	3	0	0	0	2	....	....	....	....	....		1956-57	1956-57
Wilson, Johnny	Det., Chi., Tor., NYR	13	688	161	171	332	190	66	14	13	27	11	4	1949-50	1961-62
• Wilson, Larry	Det., Chi.	6	152	21	48	69	75	4	0	0	0	0	1	1949-50	1955-56
Wilson, Mitch	N.J., Pit.	2	26	2	3	5	104	....	....	....	....	....		1984-85	1986-87
Wilson, Murray	Mtl., L.A.	7	386	94	95	189	162	53	5	14	19	32	4	1972-73	1978-79
Wilson, Rick	Mtl., St.L., Det.	4	239	6	26	32	165	3	0	0	0	0		1973-74	1976-77
Wilson, Rik	St.L., Cgy., Chi.	6	251	25	65	90	220	22	0	4	4	23		1981-82	1987-88
Wilson, Roger	Chi.	1	7	0	2	2	6	....	....	....	....	....		1974-75	1974-75
Wilson, Ron	Tor., Min.	7	177	26	67	93	68	20	4	13	17	8		1977-78	1987-88
Wilson, Wally	Bos.	1	53	11	8	19	18	1	0	0	0	0		1947-48	1947-48
Wing, Murray	Det.	1	1	0	1	1	0	....	....	....	....	....		1973-74	1973-74
• Wiseman, Eddie	Det., NYA, Bos.	10	454	115	164	279	137	45	10	10	20	16	1	1932-33	1941-42
Wiste, Jim	Chi., Van.	3	52	1	10	11	8	....	....	....	....	....		1968-69	1970-71
Witherspoon, Jim	L.A.	1	2	0	0	0	0	....	....	....	....	....		1975-76	1975-76
Witiuk, Steve	Chi.	1	33	3	8	11	14	....	....	....	....	....		1951-52	1951-52
Woit, Benny	Det., Chi.	7	334	7	26	33	170	41	2	6	8	18	3	1950-51	1956-57
Wojciechowski, Steven	Det.	2	54	19	20	39	17	6	0	1	1	0		1944-45	1946-47
Wolf, Bennett	Pit.	3	30	0	1	1	133	....	....	....	....	....		1980-81	1982-83
Wong, Mike	Det.	1	22	1	1	2	12	....	....	....	....	....		1975-76	1975-76
Wood, Robert	NYR	1	1	0	0	0	0	....	....	....	....	....		1950-51	1950-51
Woodley, Dan	Van.	1	5	2	0	2	17	....	....	....	....	....		1987-88	1987-88
Woods, Paul	Det.	7	501	72	124	196	276	7	0	5	5	4		1977-78	1983-84
• Woytowich, Bob	Bos., Min., Pit., L.A.	8	503	32	126	158	352	24	1	3	4	20		1964-65	1971-72
Wright, John	Van., St.L., K.C.	3	127	16	36	52	67	....	....	....	....	....		1972-73	1974-75
Wright, Keith	Phi.	1	1	0	0	0	0	....	....	....	....	....		1967-68	1967-68
Wright, Larry	Phi., Cal., Det.	5	106	4	8	12	19	....	....	....	....	....		1971-72	1977-78
Wycherley, Ralph	NYA, Bro.	2	28	4	7	11	6	....	....	....	....	....		1940-41	1941-42
Wylie, Duane	Chi.	2	14	3	3	6	2	....	....	....	....	....		1974-75	1976-77
• Wylie, William	NYR	1	1	0	0	0	0	....	....	....	....	....		1950-51	1950-51
Wyrozub, Randy	Buf.	4	100	8	10	18	10	....	....	....	....	....		1970-71	1973-74

Y Z

Yackel, Ken	Bos.	1	6	0	0	0	2	2	0	0	0	0		1958-59	1958-59
Yaremchuk, Gary	Tor.	4	34	1	4	5	28	....	....	....	....	....		1981-82	1984-85
Yaremchuk, Ken	Chi., Tor.	6	235	36	56	92	106	31	6	8	14	49		1983-84	1988-89
Yates, Ross	Hfd.	1	7	1	1	2	4	....	....	....	....	....		1983-84	1983-84
Young, Brian	Chi.	1	8	0	2	2	6	....	....	....	....	....		1980-81	1980-81
Young, C.J.	Cgy., Bos.	1	43	7	7	14	32	....	....	....	....	....		1992-93	1992-93
• Young, Doug	Mtl., Det.	10	391	35	45	80	303	28	1	5	6	16	2	1931-32	1940-41
Young, Howie	Det., Chi., Van.	8	336	12	62	74	851	19	2	4	6	46		1960-61	1970-71
Young, Tim	Min., Wpg., Phi.	10	628	195	341	536	438	36	7	24	31	27		1975-76	1984-85
Young, Warren	Min., Pit., Det.	7	236	72	77	149	472	....	....	....	....	....		1981-82	1987-88
Younghans, Tom	Min., NYR	6	429	44	41	85	373	24	2	1	3	21		1976-77	1981-82
Zabroski, Marty	Chi.	1	1	0	0	0	0	....	....	....	....	....		1944-45	1944-45
Zaharko, Miles	Atl., Chi.	4	129	5	32	37	84	3	0	0	0	0		1977-78	1981-82
Zaine, Rod	Pit., Buf.	2	61	10	6	16	25	....	....	....	....	....		1970-71	1971-72
Zanussi, Joe	NYR, Bos., St.L.	3	87	1	13	14	46	4	0	1	1	2		1974-75	1976-77
Zanussi, Ron	Min., Tor.	5	299	52	83	135	373	17	0	4	4	17		1977-78	1981-82
Zeidel, Larry	Det., Chi., Phi.	5	158	3	16	19	198	12	0	1	1	12	1	1951-52	1968-69
Zeniuk, Ed	Det.	1	2	0	0	0	0	....	....	....	....	....		1954-55	1954-55
Zetterstrom, Lars	Van.	1	14	0	1	1	2	....	....	....	....	....		1978-79	1978-79
Zuke, Mike	St.L., Hfd.	8	455	86	196	282	220	26	6	6	12	12		1978-79	1985-86
Zunich, Ruby	Det.	1	2	0	0	0	2	....	....	....	....	....		1943-44	1943-44

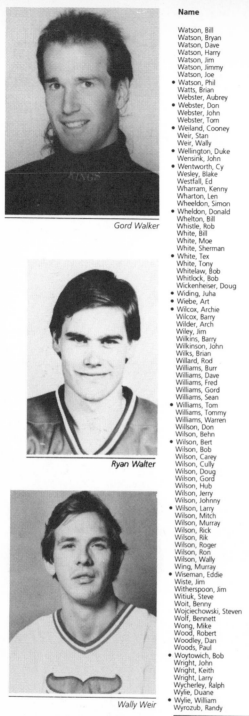

1994-95 Goaltender Register

Note: The 1994-95 Goaltender Register lists every goaltender who appeared in an NHL game in the 1993-94 season, every goaltender drafted in the first six rounds of the 1993 and 1994 Entry Drafts, goaltenders on NHL Reserve Lists and other goaltenders.

Trades and roster changes are current as of August 19, 1994

To calculate a goaltender's goals-against-per-game average **(AVG)**, divide goals against **(GA)** by minutes played **(Mins)** and multiply this result by **60**.

Abbreviations: A list of league names can be found at the beginning of the Player Register. **Avg.** – goals against per game average; **GA** – goals against; **GP** – games played; **L** – losses; **Lea** – league; **SO** – shutouts; **T** – ties; **W** – wins.

Player Register begins on page 247.

ABEL, BRETT — EDM.

Goaltender. Catches left. 6'2", 185 lbs. Born, Lynnfield, MA, June 10, 1970.
(Edmonton's 1st choice, 7th overall, in 1993 Supplemental Draft).

			Regular Season								Playoffs						
Season	Club	Lea	GP	W	L	T	Mins	GA	SO	Avg	GP	W	L	Mins	GA	SO	Avg
1989-90	N. Hampshire	H.E.	2	1	0	0	100	9	0	5.40	....	....	....	....	....	....	....
1990-91	N. Hampshire	H.E.	2	2	0	0	120	6	0	3.00	....	....	....	....	....	....	....
1991-92	N. Hampshire	H.E.	*35	20	13	2	*2030	111	0	3.28	....	....	....	....	....	....	....
1992-93	N. Hampshire	H.E.	32	15	15	2	1903	109	0	3.44	....	....	....	....	....	....	....
1993-94	Wheeling	ECHL	43	22	14	1	2358	177	1	4.50	1	0	0	20	2	0	6.00

ALLAN, SANDY

Goaltender. Catches left. 6', 175 lbs. Born, Nassau, Bahamas, January 22, 1974.
(Los Angeles' 2nd choice, 63rd overall, in 1992 Entry Draft).

			Regular Season								Playoffs						
Season	Club	Lea	GP	W	L	T	Mins	GA	SO	Avg	GP	W	L	Mins	GA	SO	Avg
1991-92	North Bay	OHL	34	18	5	4	1747	112	0	3.85	3	0	0	18	2	0	6.67
1992-93	North Bay	OHL	39	8	19	4	1845	134	0	4.36	4	0	3	180	10	0	3.33
1993-94	North Bay	OHL	45	*31	10	1	2404	131	1	*3.27	*17	*10	5	*912	58	*1	3.82

ASKEY, TOM — ANA.

Goaltender. Catches left. 6'2", 185 lbs. Born, Kenmore, NY, October 4, 1974.
(Anaheim's 8th choice, 186th overall, in 1993 Entry Draft).

			Regular Season								Playoffs						
Season	Club	Lea	GP	W	L	T	Mins	GA	SO	Avg	GP	W	L	Mins	GA	SO	Avg
1992-93	Ohio State	NCAA	25	2	19	0	1235	125	....	6.07	....	....	....	....	....	....	....
1993-94	Ohio State	NCAA	27	3	19	4	1488	103	....	4.15	....	....	....	....	....	....	....

BACH, RYAN — DET.

Goaltender. Catches left. 6'1", 180 lbs. Born, Sherwood Park, Alta., October 21, 1973.
(Detroit's 11th choice, 262nd overall, in 1992 Entry Draft).

			Regular Season								Playoffs						
Season	Club	Lea	GP	W	L	T	Mins	GA	SO	Avg	GP	W	L	Mins	GA	SO	Avg
1992-93	Colorado	WCHA	4	1	3	0	239	11	0	2.76	....	....	....	....	....	....	....
1993-94	Colorado	WCHA	30	17	7	5	1733	105	0	3.64	....	....	....	....	....	....	....

BAILEY, SCOTT — BOS.

Goaltender. Catches left. 6', 195 lbs. Born, Calgary, Alta., May 2, 1972.
(Boston's 3rd choice, 112th overall, in 1992 Entry Draft).

			Regular Season								Playoffs						
Season	Club	Lea	GP	W	L	T	Mins	GA	SO	Avg	GP	W	L	Mins	GA	SO	Avg
1990-91a	Spokane	WHL	46	33	11	0	2537	157	*4	3.71	....	....	....	....	....	....	....
1991-92a	Spokane	WHL	65	34	23	5	3798	206	1	3.30	10	5	5	605	43	0	4.26
1992-93	Johnstown	ECHL	36	13	15	3	1750	112	1	3.84	....	....	....	....	....	....	....
1993-94	Providence	AHL	7	2	2	2	377	24	0	3.82	....	....	....	....	....	....	....
	Charlotte	ECHL	36	22	11	3	2180	130	1	3.58	3	1	2	187	12	0	3.83

a WHL West Second All-Star Team (1991, 1992)

BALES, MICHAEL — OTT.

Goaltender. Catches left. 6'1", 180 lbs. Born, Prince Albert, Sask., August 6, 1971.
(Boston's 4th choice, 105th overall, in 1990 Entry Draft).

			Regular Season								Playoffs						
Season	Club	Lea	GP	W	L	T	Mins	GA	SO	Avg	GP	W	L	Mins	GA	SO	Avg
1989-90	Ohio State	CCHA	21	6	13	2	1117	95	0	5.11	....	....	....	....	....	....	....
1990-91	Ohio State	CCHA	*39	11	24	3	*2180	184	0	5.06	....	....	....	....	....	....	....
1991-92	Ohio State	CCHA	36	11	20	5	2060	180	0	5.24	....	....	....	....	....	....	....
1992-93	**Boston**	**NHL**	**1**	**0**	**0**	**0**	**25**	**1**	**0**	**2.40**	....	....	....	....	....	....	....
	Providence	AHL	44	22	17	0	2363	166	1	4.21	2	0	2	118	8	0	4.07
1993-94	Providence	AHL	33	9	15	4	1757	130	0	4.44	....	....	....	....	....	....	....
	NHL Totals		**1**	**0**	**0**	**0**	**25**	**1**	**0**	**2.40**	....	....	....	....	....	....	....

Signed as a free agent by **Ottawa**, July 4, 1994.

BARRASSO, TOM (buh-RAH-soh) — PIT.

Goaltender. Catches right. 6'3", 211 lbs. Born, Boston, MA, March 31, 1965.
(Buffalo's 1st choice, 5th overall, in 1983 Entry Draft).

			Regular Season								Playoffs						
Season	Club	Lea	GP	W	L	T	Mins	GA	SO	Avg	GP	W	L	Mins	GA	SO	Avg
1982-83	Acton-Boxboro	HS	23	....	....	....	1035	17	10	0.73	....	....	....	....	....	....	....
1983-84 abcd	**Buffalo**	**NHL**	**42**	**26**	**12**	**3**	**2475**	**117**	**2**	**2.84**	**3**	**0**	**2**	**139**	**8**	**0**	**3.45**
1984-85ef	**Buffalo**	**NHL**	**54**	**25**	**18**	**10**	**3248**	**144**	***5**	***2.66**	**5**	**2**	**3**	**300**	**22**	**0**	**4.40**
	Rochester	AHL	5	3	1	1	267	6	1	1.35	....	....	....	....	....	....	....
1985-86	**Buffalo**	**NHL**	**60**	**29**	**24**	**5**	**3561**	**214**	**2**	**3.61**	....	....	....	....	....	....	....
1986-87	**Buffalo**	**NHL**	**46**	**17**	**23**	**2**	**2501**	**152**	**2**	**3.65**	....	....	....	....	....	....	....
1987-88	**Buffalo**	**NHL**	**54**	**25**	**18**	**8**	**3133**	**173**	**2**	**3.31**	**4**	**1**	**3**	**224**	**16**	**0**	**4.29**
1988-89	**Buffalo**	**NHL**	**10**	**2**	**7**	**0**	**545**	**45**	**0**	**4.95**	....	....	....	....	....	....	....
	Pittsburgh	**NHL**	**44**	**18**	**15**	**7**	**2406**	**162**	**0**	**4.04**	**11**	**7**	**4**	**631**	**40**	**0**	**3.80**
1989-90	**Pittsburgh**	**NHL**	**24**	**7**	**12**	**3**	**1294**	**101**	**0**	**4.68**	....	....	....	....	....	....	....
1990-91	**Pittsburgh**	**NHL**	**48**	**27**	**16**	**3**	**2754**	**165**	**1**	**3.59**	**20**	**12**	**7**	**1175**	**51**	***1**	***2.60**
1991-92	**Pittsburgh**	**NHL**	**57**	**25**	**22**	**9**	**3329**	**196**	**1**	**3.53**	***21**	***16**	**5**	***1233**	**58**	**1**	**2.82**
1992-93e	**Pittsburgh**	**NHL**	**63**	***43**	**14**	**5**	**3702**	**186**	**4**	**3.01**	**12**	**7**	**5**	**722**	**35**	***2**	**2.91**
1993-94	**Pittsburgh**	**NHL**	**44**	**22**	**15**	**5**	**2482**	**139**	**2**	**3.36**	**6**	**2**	**4**	**356**	**17**	**0**	**2.87**
	NHL Totals		**546**	**266**	**196**	**60**	**31430**	**1794**	**21**	**3.42**	**82**	**47**	**33**	**4780**	**247**	**4**	**3.10**

a NHL First All-Star Team (1984)
b Won Vezina Trophy (1984)
c Won Calder Memorial Trophy (1984)
d NHL All-Rookie Team (1984)
e NHL Second All-Star Team (1985, 1993)
f Shared William Jennings Trophy with Bob Sauve (1985)

Played in NHL All-Star Game (1985)

Traded to **Pittsburgh** by **Buffalo** with Buffalo's third round choice (Joe Dziedzic) in 1990 Entry Draft for Doug Bodger and Darrin Shannon, November 12, 1988.

BEAUBIEN, FREDERICK (boh-BEE-yehn) — L.A.

Goaltender. Catches left. 6'1", 204 lbs. Born, Lauzon, Que., April 1, 1975.
(Los Angeles' 4th choice, 105th overall, in 1993 Entry Draft).

			Regular Season								Playoffs						
Season	Club	Lea	GP	W	L	T	Mins	GA	SO	Avg	GP	W	L	Mins	GA	SO	Avg
1992-93	St-Hyacinthe	QMJHL	33	8	16	3	1702	133	0	4.69	....	....	....	....	....	....	....
1993-94	St-Hyacinthe	QMJHL	47	0	0	0	2663	168	1	3.79	7	3	4	411	33	0	4.82

BEAUPRE, DON (boh-PRAY) — WSH.

Goaltender. Catches left. 5'10", 172 lbs. Born, Waterloo, Ont., September 19, 1961.
(Minnesota's 2nd choice, 32nd overall, in 1980 Entry Draft).

			Regular Season								Playoffs						
Season	Club	Lea	GP	W	L	T	Mins	GA	SO	Avg	GP	W	L	Mins	GA	SO	Avg
1978-79	Sudbury	OHA	54	....	....	....	3248	260	2	4.78	10	....	....	600	44	0	4.20
1979-80a	Sudbury	OHA	59	28	29	2	3447	248	0	4.32	9	5	4	552	38	0	4.13
1980-81	**Minnesota**	**NHL**	**44**	**18**	**14**	**11**	**2585**	**138**	**0**	**3.20**	**6**	**4**	**2**	**360**	**26**	**0**	**4.33**
1981-82	**Minnesota**	**NHL**	**29**	**11**	**8**	**9**	**1634**	**101**	**0**	**3.71**	**2**	**0**	**1**	**60**	**4**	**0**	**4.00**
	Nashville	CHL	5	2	3	0	299	25	0	5.02	....	....	....	....	....	....	....
1982-83	**Minnesota**	**NHL**	**36**	**19**	**10**	**5**	**2011**	**120**	**0**	**3.58**	**4**	**2**	**2**	**245**	**20**	**0**	**4.90**
	Birmingham	CHL	10	8	2	0	599	31	0	3.11	....	....	....	....	....	....	....
1983-84	**Minnesota**	**NHL**	**33**	**16**	**13**	**2**	**1791**	**123**	**0**	**4.12**	**13**	**6**	**7**	**782**	**40**	**1**	**3.07**
	Salt Lake	CHL	7	2	5	0	419	30	0	4.30	....	....	....	....	....	....	....
1984-85	**Minnesota**	**NHL**	**31**	**10**	**17**	**3**	**1770**	**109**	**1**	**3.69**	**4**	**1**	**1**	**184**	**12**	**0**	**3.91**
1985-86	**Minnesota**	**NHL**	**52**	**25**	**20**	**6**	**3073**	**182**	**1**	**3.55**	**5**	**2**	**3**	**300**	**17**	**0**	**3.40**
1986-87	**Minnesota**	**NHL**	**47**	**17**	**20**	**6**	**2622**	**174**	**1**	**3.98**	....	....	....	....	....	....	....
1987-88	**Minnesota**	**NHL**	**43**	**10**	**22**	**3**	**2288**	**161**	**0**	**4.22**	....	....	....	....	....	....	....
1988-89	**Minnesota**	**NHL**	**1**	**0**	**1**	**0**	**59**	**3**	**0**	**3.05**	....	....	....	....	....	....	....
	Kalamazoo	IHL	3	1	2	0	179	9	1	3.02	....	....	....	....	....	....	....
	Washington	**NHL**	**11**	**5**	**4**	**0**	**578**	**28**	**1**	**2.91**	....	....	....	....	....	....	....
	Baltimore	AHL	30	14	12	2	1715	102	0	3.57	....	....	....	....	....	....	....
1989-90	**Washington**	**NHL**	**48**	**23**	**18**	**5**	**2793**	**150**	**2**	**3.22**	**8**	**4**	**3**	**401**	**18**	**0**	**2.69**
1990-91	**Washington**	**NHL**	**45**	**20**	**18**	**3**	**2572**	**113**	***5**	**2.64**	**11**	**5**	**5**	**624**	**29**	***1**	**2.79**
	Baltimore	AHL	2	2	0	0	120	3	0	1.50	....	....	....	....	....	....	....
1991-92	**Washington**	**NHL**	**54**	**29**	**17**	**6**	**3108**	**166**	**1**	**3.20**	**7**	**3**	**4**	**419**	**22**	**0**	**3.15**
	Baltimore	AHL	3	1	1	1	184	10	0	3.26	....	....	....	....	....	....	....
1992-93	**Washington**	**NHL**	**58**	**27**	**23**	**5**	**3282**	**181**	**1**	**3.31**	**2**	**1**	**1**	**119**	**9**	**0**	**4.54**
1993-94	**Washington**	**NHL**	**53**	**24**	**16**	**8**	**2853**	**135**	**2**	**2.84**	**8**	**5**	**2**	**429**	**21**	**1**	**2.94**
	NHL Totals		**585**	**254**	**221**	**72**	**33019**	**1884**	**15**	**3.42**	**70**	**33**	**31**	**3923**	**218**	**3**	**3.33**

a OHA First All-Star Team (1980)

Played in NHL All-Star Game (1981, 1992)

Traded to **Washington** by **Minnesota** for rights to Claudio Scremin, November 1, 1988.

BEAUREGARD, STEPHANE — WPG.

Goaltender. Catches right. 5'11", 190 lbs. Born, Cowansville, Que., January 10, 1968.
(Winnipeg's 3rd choice, 52nd overall, in 1988 Entry Draft).

			Regular Season								Playoffs						
Season	Club	Lea	GP	W	L	T	Mins	GA	SO	Avg	GP	W	L	Mins	GA	SO	Avg
1986-87	St-Jean	QMJHL	13	6	7	0	785	58	0	4.43	5	1	3	260	26	0	6.00
1987-88ab	St-Jean	QMJHL	66	38	20	3	3766	229	2	3.65	7	3	4	423	34	0	4.82
1988-89	Moncton	AHL	15	4	8	2	824	62	0	4.51	....	....	....	....	....	....	....
	Fort Wayne	IHL	16	9	5	0	830	43	0	3.10	9	4	4	484	21	*1	*2.60
1989-90	**Winnipeg**	**NHL**	**19**	**7**	**8**	**3**	**1079**	**59**	**0**	**3.28**	**4**	**1**	**3**	**238**	**12**	**0**	**3.03**
	Fort Wayne	IHL	33	20	8	3	1949	115	0	3.54	....	....	....	....	....	....	....
1990-91	**Winnipeg**	**NHL**	**16**	**3**	**10**	**1**	**836**	**55**	**0**	**3.95**	....	....	....	....	....	....	....
	Moncton	AHL	9	3	4	1	504	20	1	2.38	1	1	0	60	1	0	1.00
	Fort Wayne	IHL	32	14	13	2	1761	109	0	3.71	*19	*10	9	*1158	57	0	2.95
1991-92	**Winnipeg**	**NHL**	**26**	**6**	**8**	**6**	**1267**	**61**	**2**	**2.89**	....	....	....	....	....	....	....
1992-93	**Philadelphia**	**NHL**	**16**	**3**	**9**	**0**	**802**	**59**	**0**	**4.41**	....	....	....	....	....	....	....
	Hershey	AHL	13	5	5	3	794	48	0	3.63	....	....	....	....	....	....	....
1993-94	**Winnipeg**	**NHL**	**13**	**0**	**4**	**1**	**418**	**34**	**0**	**4.88**	....	....	....	....	....	....	....
	Moncton	AHL	37	18	11	6	2082	121	1	3.49	*21	*12	9	*1305	57	*2	2.62
	NHL Totals		**90**	**19**	**39**	**11**	**4402**	**268**	**2**	**3.65**	**4**	**1**	**3**	**238**	**12**	**0**	**3.03**

a QMJHL First All-Star Team (1988)
b Canadian Major Junior Goaltender of the year (1988)

Traded to **Buffalo** by **Winnipeg** for Christian Ruuttu and future considerations, June 15, 1992. Traded to **Chicago** by **Buffalo** with Buffalo's fourth round choice (Eric Dazel) in 1993 Entry Draft for Dominik Hasek, August 7, 1992. Traded to **Winnipeg** by **Chicago** for Christian Ruuttu, August 10, 1992. Traded to **Philadelphia** by **Winnipeg** for future considerations, October 1, 1992. Traded to **Winnipeg** by **Philadelphia** for future considerations, June 11, 1993.

BELFOUR, ED — CHI.

Goaltender. Catches left. 5'11", 182 lbs. Born, Carman, Man., April 21, 1965.

			Regular Season								Playoffs						
Season	**Club**	**Lea**	**GP**	**W**	**L**	**T**	**Mins**	**GA**	**SO**	**Avg**	**GP**	**W**	**L**	**Mins**	**GA**	**SO**	**Avg**
1986-87a	North Dakota	WCHA	34	29	4	0	2049	81	3	2.43	....	....	....	....	....	....	....
1987-88bc	Saginaw	IHL	61	32	25	0	*3446	183	3	3.19	9	4	5	561	33	0	3.53
1988-89	**Chicago**	**NHL**	**23**	**4**	**12**	**3**	**1148**	**74**	**0**	**3.87**	....	....	....	....	....	....	....
	Saginaw	IHL	29	12	10	0	1760	92	0	3.10	5	2	3	298	14	0	2.82
1989-90	Cdn. National	....	33	13	12	6	1808	93	0	3.08	....	....	....	....	....	....	....
	Chicago	**NHL**	....	....	....	....	....	....	....	....	**9**	**4**	**2**	**409**	**17**	**0**	**2.49**
1990-91 defghi	**Chicago**	**NHL**	***74**	***43**	**19**	**7**	***4127**	**170**	**4**	***2.47**	**6**	**2**	**4**	**295**	**20**	**0**	**4.07**
1991-92	**Chicago**	**NHL**	**52**	**21**	**18**	**10**	**2928**	**132**	***5**	**2.70**	**18**	**12**	**4**	**949**	**39**	**1**	***2.47**
1992-93deg	**Chicago**	**NHL**	***71**	**41**	**18**	**11**	***4106**	**177**	***7**	**2.59**	**4**	**0**	**4**	**249**	**13**	**0**	**3.13**
1993-94	**Chicago**	**NHL**	**70**	**37**	**24**	**6**	**3998**	**178**	***7**	**2.67**	**6**	**2**	**4**	**360**	**15**	**0**	**2.50**
	NHL Totals		**290**	**146**	**91**	**37**	**16307**	**731**	**23**	**2.69**	**43**	**20**	**18**	**2262**	**104**	**1**	**2.76**

a WCHA First All-Star Team (1987)
b IHL First All-Star Team (1988)
c Shared Garry F. Longman Memorial Trophy with John Cullen (Top Rookie - AHL) (1988)
d NHL First All-Star Team (1991, 1993)
e Won Vezina Trophy (1991, 1993)
f Won Calder Memorial Trophy (1991)
g Won William M. Jennings Trophy (1991, 1993)
h Won Trico Goaltender Award (1991)
i NHL/Upper Deck All-Rookie Team (1991)

Played in NHL All-Star Game (1992, 1993)

Signed as a free agent by **Chicago**, September 25, 1987.

BELLEY, ROCH

Goaltender. Catches left. 5'10", 170 lbs. Born, Hull, Que., August 12, 1971.
(Chicago's 8th choice, 176th overall, in 1991 Entry Draft).

			Regular Season								Playoffs						
Season	**Club**	**Lea**	**GP**	**W**	**L**	**T**	**Mins**	**GA**	**SO**	**Avg**	**GP**	**W**	**L**	**Mins**	**GA**	**SO**	**Avg**
1990-91	Niagara Falls	OHL	45	26	8	7	2499	151	1	3.68	14	7	5	743	49	....	3.96
1991-92	Indianapolis	IHL	25	4	12	3	1270	88	0	4.16	....	....	....	....	....	....	....
1992-93	Fort Worth	CHL	33	14	13	2	1782	141	0	4.75	....	....	....	....	....	....	....
	Indianapolis	IHL	7	1	2	1	289	25	0	5.19	2	0	0	33	2	0	3.64
1993-94	Muskegon	ColHL	48	24	17	5	2703	185	1	4.11	3	0	3	176	13	0	4.42
	Indianapolis	IHL	1	0	0	0	2	1	0	29.50	....	....	....	....	....	....	....

BERGERON, JEAN-CLAUDE — T.B.

Goaltender. Catches left. 6'2", 192 lbs. Born, Hauterive, Que., October 14, 1968.
(Montreal's 5th choice, 104th overall, in 1988 Entry Draft).

			Regular Season								Playoffs						
Season	**Club**	**Lea**	**GP**	**W**	**L**	**T**	**Mins**	**GA**	**SO**	**Avg**	**GP**	**W**	**L**	**Mins**	**GA**	**SO**	**Avg**
1987-88	Verdun	QMJHL	49	13	31	3	2715	265	0	5.86	....	....	....	....	....	....	....
1988-89	Verdun	QMJHL	44	8	34	1	2417	199	0	4.94	....	....	....	....	....	....	....
	Sherbrooke	AHL	5	4	1	0	302	18	0	3.58	....	....	....	....	....	....	....
1989-90abc	Sherbrooke	AHL	40	21	8	7	2254	103	2	*2.74	9	6	2	497	28	0	3.38
1990-91	**Montreal**	**NHL**	**18**	**7**	**6**	**2**	**941**	**59**	**0**	**3.76**	....	....	....	....	....	....	....
	Fredericton	AHL	18	12	6	0	1083	59	1	3.27	10	5	5	546	32	0	3.52
1991-92	Fredericton	AHL	13	5	7	1	791	57	0	4.32	....	....	....	....	....	....	....
	Peoria	IHL	27	14	9	3	1632	96	1	3.53	6	3	3	352	24	0	4.09
1992-93	**Tampa Bay**	**NHL**	**21**	**8**	**10**	**1**	**1163**	**71**	**0**	**3.66**	....	....	....	....	....	....	....
	Atlanta	IHL	31	21	7	1	1722	92	1	3.21	6	3	3	368	19	0	3.10
1993-94	**Tampa Bay**	**NHL**	**3**	**1**	**1**	**1**	**134**	**7**	**0**	**3.13**	....	....	....	....	....	....	....
d	Atlanta	IHL	48	27	11	7	2755	141	0	3.07	2	1	1	153	6	0	2.34
	NHL Totals		**42**	**16**	**17**	**4**	**2238**	**137**	**0**	**3.67**	....	....	....	....	....	....	....

a AHL First All-Star Team (1990)
b Shared Harry "Hap" Holmes Trophy (fewest goals-against - AHL) with Andre Racicot (1990)
c Won Baz Bastien Award (Top Goaltender - AHL) (1990)
d Shared James Norris Memorial Trophy (fewest goals-against - IHL) with Mike Greenlay (1994)

Traded to **Tampa Bay** by **Montreal** for Frederic Chabot, June 19, 1992.

BERTHIAUME, DANIEL (bairt-YOHM)

Goaltender. Catches left. 5'9", 155 lbs. Born, Longueuil, Que., January 26, 1966.
(Winnipeg's 3rd choice, 60th overall, in 1985 Entry Draft).

			Regular Season								Playoffs						
Season	**Club**	**Lea**	**GP**	**W**	**L**	**T**	**Mins**	**GA**	**SO**	**Avg**	**GP**	**W**	**L**	**Mins**	**GA**	**SO**	**Avg**
1984-85	Chicoutimi	QMJHL	59	40	11	2	2177	149	0	4.11	14	8	6	770	51	0	3.97
1985-86	Chicoutimi	QMJHL	66	34	29	3	3718	286	1	4.62	9	4	5	580	36	0	3.72
	Winnipeg	**NHL**	....	....	....	....	....	....	....	....	**1**	**0**	**1**	**68**	**4**	**0**	**3.53**
1986-87	**Winnipeg**	**NHL**	**31**	**18**	**7**	**3**	**1758**	**93**	**1**	**3.17**	**8**	**4**	**4**	**439**	**21**	**0**	**2.87**
	Sherbrooke	AHL	7	4	3	0	420	23	0	3.29	....	....	....	....	....	....	....
1987-88	**Winnipeg**	**NHL**	**56**	**22**	**19**	**7**	**3010**	**176**	**2**	**3.51**	**5**	**1**	**4**	**300**	**25**	**0**	**5.00**
1988-89	**Winnipeg**	**NHL**	**9**	**0**	**8**	**0**	**443**	**44**	**0**	**5.96**	....	....	....	....	....	....	....
	Moncton	AHL	21	6	9	2	1083	76	0	4.21	3	1	2	180	11	0	3.67
1989-90	**Winnipeg**	**NHL**	**24**	**10**	**11**	**3**	**1387**	**86**	**1**	**3.72**	....	....	....	....	....	....	....
	Minnesota	**NHL**	**5**	**1**	**3**	**0**	**240**	**14**	**0**	**3.50**	....	....	....	....	....	....	....
1990-91	**Los Angeles**	**NHL**	**37**	**20**	**11**	**4**	**2119**	**117**	**1**	**3.31**	....	....	....	....	....	....	....
1991-92	**Los Angeles**	**NHL**	**19**	**7**	**10**	**1**	**979**	**66**	**0**	**4.04**	....	....	....	....	....	....	....
	Boston	**NHL**	**8**	**1**	**4**	**2**	**399**	**21**	**0**	**3.16**	....	....	....	....	....	....	....
1992-93	Graz	Alp.	28	....	....	....	....	110	0	4.07	....	....	....	....	....	....	....
	Ottawa	**NHL**	**25**	**2**	**17**	**1**	**1326**	**95**	**0**	**4.30**	....	....	....	....	....	....	....
1993-94	**Ottawa**	**NHL**	**1**	**0**	**0**	**0**	**1**	**2**	**0**	**120.00**	....	....	....	....	....	....	....
	PEI	AHL	30	8	16	3	1640	130	0	4.76	....	....	....	....	....	....	....
	Adirondack	AHL	11	7	2	0	552	35	0	3.80	11	6	4	632	30	0	2.85
	NHL Totals		**215**	**81**	**90**	**21**	**11662**	**714**	**5**	**3.67**	**14**	**5**	**9**	**807**	**50**	**0**	**3.72**

Traded to **Minnesota** by **Winnipeg** for future considerations, January 22, 1990. Traded to **Los Angeles** by **Minnesota** for Craig Duncanson, September 6, 1990. Traded to **Boston** by **Los Angeles** for future considerations, January 18, 1992. Traded to **Winnipeg** by **Boston** for Doug Evans, June 10, 1992. Signed as a free agent by **Ottawa**, December 15, 1992. Traded to **Detroit** by **Ottawa** for Steve Konroyd, March 21, 1994.

BESTER, ALLAN — ANA.

Goaltender. Catches left. 5'7", 155 lbs. Born, Hamilton, Ont., March 26, 1964.
(Toronto's 3rd choice, 48th overall, in 1983 Entry Draft).

			Regular Season								Playoffs						
Season	**Club**	**Lea**	**GP**	**W**	**L**	**T**	**Mins**	**GA**	**SO**	**Avg**	**GP**	**W**	**L**	**Mins**	**GA**	**SO**	**Avg**
1981-82	Brantford	OHL	19	4	11	0	970	68	0	4.21	....	....	....	....	....	....	....
1982-83a	Brantford	OHL	56	29	21	3	3210	188	0	3.51	8	3	3	480	20	*1	*2.50
1983-84	**Toronto**	**NHL**	**32**	**11**	**16**	**4**	**1848**	**134**	**0**	**4.35**	....	....	....	....	....	....	....
	Brantford	OHL	23	12	9	1	1271	71	1	3.35	1	0	1	60	5	0	5.00
1984-85	**Toronto**	**NHL**	**15**	**3**	**9**	**1**	**767**	**54**	**1**	**4.22**	....	....	....	....	....	....	....
	St. Catharines	AHL	30	9	18	1	1669	133	0	4.78	....	....	....	....	....	....	....
1985-86	**Toronto**	**NHL**	**1**	**0**	**0**	**0**	**20**	**2**	**0**	**6.00**	....	....	....	....	....	....	....
	St. Catharines	AHL	50	23	23	3	2855	173	1	3.64	11	7	3	637	27	0	2.54
1986-87	**Toronto**	**NHL**	**36**	**10**	**14**	**3**	**1808**	**110**	**2**	**3.65**	**1**	**0**	**0**	**39**	**1**	**0**	**1.54**
	Newmarket	AHL	3	1	0	0	190	6	0	1.89	....	....	....	....	....	....	....
1987-88	**Toronto**	**NHL**	**30**	**8**	**12**	**5**	**1607**	**102**	**2**	**3.81**	**5**	**2**	**3**	**253**	**21**	**0**	**4.98**
1988-89	**Toronto**	**NHL**	**43**	**17**	**20**	**3**	**2460**	**156**	**2**	**3.80**	....	....	....	....	....	....	....
1989-90	**Toronto**	**NHL**	**42**	**20**	**16**	**0**	**2206**	**165**	**0**	**4.49**	**4**	**0**	**3**	**196**	**14**	**0**	**4.29**
	Newmarket	AHL	5	2	1	1	264	18	0	4.09	....	....	....	....	....	....	....
1990-91	**Toronto**	**NHL**	**6**	**0**	**4**	**0**	**247**	**18**	**0**	**4.37**	....	....	....	....	....	....	....
	Newmarket	AHL	19	7	8	4	1157	58	1	3.01	....	....	....	....	....	....	....
	Detroit	**NHL**	**3**	**0**	**3**	**0**	**178**	**13**	**0**	**4.38**	**1**	**0**	**0**	**20**	**1**	**0**	**3.00**
1991-92	**Detroit**	**NHL**	**1**	**0**	**0**	**0**	**31**	**2**	**0**	**3.87**	....	....	....	....	....	....	....
b	Adirondack	AHL	22	13	8	0	1268	78	0	3.69	*19	*14	5	1174	50	*1	*2.56
1992-93	Adirondack	AHL	41	16	15	5	2268	133	1	3.52	10	7	3	633	26	*1	2.46
1993-94	San Diego	IHL	46	22	14	6	2543	150	1	3.54	8	4	4	419	28	0	4.00
	NHL Totals		**209**	**69**	**94**	**16**	**11172**	**756**	**7**	**4.06**	**11**	**2**	**6**	**508**	**37**	**0**	**4.37**

a OHL First All-Star Team (1983)
b Won Jack Butterfield Trophy (Playoff MVP - AHL) (1992)

Traded to **Detroit** by **Toronto** for Detroit's sixth round choice (Alexander Kuzminsky) in 1991 Entry Draft, March 5, 1991. Signed as a free agent by **Anaheim**, September 9, 1993.

BILLINGTON, CRAIG — OTT.

Goaltender. Catches left. 5'10", 170 lbs. Born, London, Ont., September 11, 1966.
(New Jersey's 2nd choice, 23rd overall, in 1984 Entry Draft).

			Regular Season								Playoffs						
Season	**Club**	**Lea**	**GP**	**W**	**L**	**T**	**Mins**	**GA**	**SO**	**Avg**	**GP**	**W**	**L**	**Mins**	**GA**	**SO**	**Avg**
1983-84	Belleville	OHL	44	20	19	0	2335	162	1	4.16	1	0	0	30	3	0	6.00
1984-85a	Belleville	OHL	47	26	19	0	2544	180	1	4.25	14	7	5	761	47	1	3.71
1985-86	**New Jersey**	**NHL**	**18**	**4**	**9**	**1**	**901**	**77**	**0**	**5.13**	....	....	....	....	....	....	....
	Belleville	OHL	3	2	1	0	180	11	0	3.67	20	9	6	1133	68	0	3.60
1986-87	**New Jersey**	**NHL**	**22**	**4**	**13**	**2**	**1114**	**89**	**0**	**4.79**	....	....	....	....	....	....	....
	Maine	AHL	20	9	8	2	1151	70	0	3.65	....	....	....	....	....	....	....
1987-88	Utica	AHL	*59	22	27	8	*3404	208	1	3.67	....	....	....	....	....	....	....
1988-89	**New Jersey**	**NHL**	**3**	**1**	**1**	**0**	**140**	**11**	**0**	**4.71**	....	....	....	....	....	....	....
	Utica	AHL	41	17	18	6	2432	150	2	3.70	4	1	3	220	18	0	4.91
1989-90	Utica	AHL	38	20	13	1	2087	138	0	3.97	....	....	....	....	....	....	....
1990-91	Cdn. National	....	34	17	14	2	1879	110	2	3.51	....	....	....	....	....	....	....
1991-92	**New Jersey**	**NHL**	**26**	**13**	**7**	**1**	**1363**	**69**	**2**	**3.04**	....	....	....	....	....	....	....
1992-93	**New Jersey**	**NHL**	**42**	**21**	**16**	**4**	**2389**	**146**	**2**	**3.67**	**2**	**0**	**1**	**78**	**5**	**0**	**3.85**
1993-94	**Ottawa**	**NHL**	**63**	**11**	**41**	**4**	**3319**	**254**	**0**	**4.59**	....	....	....	....	....	....	....
	NHL Totals		**174**	**54**	**87**	**12**	**9226**	**646**	**4**	**4.20**	**2**	**0**	**1**	**78**	**5**	**0**	**3.85**

a OHL First All-Star Team (1985)

Played in NHL All-Star Game (1993)

Traded to **Ottawa** by **New Jersey** with Troy Mallette and New Jersey's fourth round choice (Cosmo Dupaul) in 1993 Entry Draft for Peter Sidorkiewicz and future considerations (Mike Peluso, June 26, 1993), June 20, 1993.

BLUE, JOHN — BOS.

Goaltender. Catches left. 5'10", 185 lbs. Born, Huntington Beach, CA, February 19, 1966.
(Winnipeg's 9th choice, 197th overall, in 1986 Entry Draft).

			Regular Season								Playoffs						
Season	**Club**	**Lea**	**GP**	**W**	**L**	**T**	**Mins**	**GA**	**SO**	**Avg**	**GP**	**W**	**L**	**Mins**	**GA**	**SO**	**Avg**
1984-85	U. Minnesota	WCHA	34	23	10	0	1964	111	2	3.39	....	....	....	....	....	....	....
1985-86a	U. Minnesota	WCHA	29	20	6	0	1588	80	2	3.02	....	....	....	....	....	....	....
1986-87	U. Minnesota	WCHA	33	21	9	1	1889	99	3	3.14	....	....	....	....	....	....	....
1987-88	Kalamazoo	IHL	15	3	8	4	847	65	0	4.60	1	0	1	40	6	0	9.00
	U.S. National	....	13	3	4	1	588	33	0	3.37	....	....	....	....	....	....	....
1988-89	Kalamazoo	IHL	17	8	6	0	970	69	0	4.27	....	....	....	....	....	....	....
	Virginia	ECHL	10	....	....	....	570	38	0	4.00	....	....	....	....	....	....	....
1989-90	Phoenix	IHL	19	5	10	3	986	92	0	5.65	....	....	....	....	....	....	....
	Knoxville	ECHL	19	6	10	1	1000	85	0	5.15	....	....	....	....	....	....	....
	Kalamazoo	IHL	4	2	1	1	232	18	0	4.65	....	....	....	....	....	....	....
1990-91	Maine	AHL	10	3	4	2	545	22	0	2.42	1	0	1	40	7	0	10.50
	Albany	IHL	19	11	6	0	1077	71	0	3.96	....	....	....	....	....	....	....
	Kalamazoo	IHL	1	1	0	0	64	2	0	1.88	....	....	....	....	....	....	....
	Peoria	IHL	4	4	0	0	240	12	0	3.00	....	....	....	....	....	....	....
	Knoxville	ECHL	3	1	1	0	149	13	0	5.23	....	....	....	....	....	....	....
1991-92	Maine	AHL	43	11	23	6	2168	165	1	4.57	....	....	....	....	....	....	....
1992-93	**Boston**	**NHL**	**23**	**9**	**8**	**4**	**1322**	**64**	**1**	**2.90**	**2**	**0**	**1**	**96**	**5**	**0**	**3.13**
	Providence	AHL	19	14	4	1	1159	67	0	3.47	....	....	....	....	....	....	....
1993-94	**Boston**	**NHL**	**18**	**5**	**8**	**3**	**944**	**47**	**0**	**2.99**	....	....	....	....	....	....	....
	Providence	AHL	24	7	11	4	1298	76	1	3.51	....	....	....	....	....	....	....
	NHL Totals		**41**	**14**	**16**	**7**	**2266**	**111**	**1**	**2.94**	**2**	**0**	**1**	**96**	**5**	**0**	**3.13**

a WCHA First All-Star Team (1986)

Traded to **Minnesota** by **Winnipeg** for Winnipeg's seventh round choice (Markus Akerblom) in 1988 Entry Draft, March 7, 1988. Signed as a free agent by **Boston**, August 1, 1991.

BRATHWAITE, FRED — EDM.

Goaltender. Catches left. 5'7", 170 lbs. Born, Ottawa, Ont., November 24, 1972.

			Regular Season								Playoffs						
Season	**Club**	**Lea**	**GP**	**W**	**L**	**T**	**Mins**	**GA**	**SO**	**Avg**	**GP**	**W**	**L**	**Mins**	**GA**	**SO**	**Avg**
1989-90	Oshawa	OHL	20	11	2	1	886	43	1	2.91	10	4	2	451	22	0	*2.93
1990-91	Oshawa	OHL	39	25	6	3	1986	112	1	3.38	13	*9	2	677	43	0	3.81
1991-92	Oshawa	OHL	24	12	7	2	1248	81	0	3.89	....	....	....	....	....	....	....
	London	OHL	23	15	6	2	1325	61	*4	2.76	10	5	5	615	36	0	3.51
1992-93	Detroit	OHL	37	23	10	4	2192	134	0	3.67	15	9	6	858	48	1	3.36
1993-94	**Edmonton**	**NHL**	**19**	**3**	**10**	**3**	**982**	**58**	**0**	**3.54**	....	....	....	....	....	....	....
	Cape Breton	AHL	2	1	1	0	119	6	0	3.04	....	....	....	....	....	....	....
	NHL Totals		**19**	**3**	**10**	**3**	**982**	**58**	**0**	**3.54**	....	....	....	....	....	....	....

Signed as a free agent by **Edmonton**, October 6, 1993.

BROCHU, MARTIN — MTL.

Goaltender. Catches left. 5'11", 195 lbs. Born, Anjou, Que., March 10, 1973.

			Regular Season								Playoffs						
Season	**Club**	**Lea**	**GP**	**W**	**L**	**T**	**Mins**	**GA**	**SO**	**Avg**	**GP**	**W**	**L**	**Mins**	**GA**	**SO**	**Avg**
1991-92	Granby	QMJHL	52	15	29	2	2772	278	0	4.72	....	....	....	....	....	....	....
1992-93	Hull	QMJHL	29	9	15	1	1453	137	0	5.66	2	0	1	69	7	0	6.07
1993-94	Fredericton	AHL	32	10	11	3	1505	76	2	3.03	....	....	....	....	....	....	....

Signed as a free agent by **Montreal**, September 22, 1992.

BRODEUR, MARTIN (broh-DOOR, MAHR-tihn) N.J.

Goaltender. Catches left. 6'1", 205 lbs. Born, Montreal, Que., May 6, 1972.
(New Jersey's 1st choice, 20th overall, in 1990 Entry Draft).

			Regular Season								Playoffs						
Season	Club	Lea	GP	W	L	T	Mins	GA	SO	Avg	GP	W	L	Mins	GA	SO	Avg
1989-90	St-Hyacinthe	QMJHL	42	23	13	2	2333	156	0	4.01	12	5	7	678	46	0	4.07
1990-91	St-Hyacinthe	QMJHL	52	22	24	4	2946	162	2	3.30	4	0	4	232	16	0	4.14
1991-92	**New Jersey**	**NHL**	**4**	**2**	**1**	**0**	**179**	**10**	**0**	**3.35**	**1**	**0**	**1**	**32**	**3**	**0**	**5.63**
a	St-Hyacinthe	QMJHL	48	27	16	4	2846	161	2	3.39	5	2	3	317	14	0	2.65
1992-93	Utica	AHL	32	14	13	5	1952	131	0	4.03	4	1	3	258	18	0	4.19
1993-94bc	**New Jersey**	**NHL**	**47**	**27**	**11**	**8**	**2625**	**105**	**3**	**2.40**	**17**	**8**	**9**	**1171**	**38**	**1**	**1.95**
	NHL Totals		**51**	**29**	**12**	**8**	**2804**	**115**	**3**	**2.46**	**18**	**8**	**10**	**1203**	**41**	**1**	**2.04**

a QMJHL Second All-Star Team (1992)
b NHL/Upper Deck All-Rookie Team (1994)
c Won Calder Memorial Trophy (1994)

BROWN, CRAIG

Goaltender. Catches left. 5'11", 170 lbs. Born, Scarborough, Ont., February 29, 1972.
(Los Angeles' 9th choice, 196th overall, in 1991 Entry Draft).

			Regular Season								Playoffs						
Season	Club	Lea	GP	W	L	T	Mins	GA	SO	Avg	GP	W	L	Mins	GA	SO	Avg
1990-91	W. Michigan	CCHA	33	17	13	2	1898	111	0	3.51	....	....	....	....	....	....	....
1991-92	W. Michigan	CCHA	28	13	10	5	1668	89	0	3.20	....	....	....	....	....	....	....
1992-93	W. Michigan	CCHA	20	9	8	1	1125	72	....	3.84	....	....	....	....	....	....	....
1993-94	W. Michigan	CCHA	24	14	5	2	1324	63	0	2.85	....	....	....	....	....	....	....

BRUMBY, DAVID TOR.

Goaltender. Catches left. 6'1", 172 lbs. Born, Victoria, B.C., June 23, 1975.
(Toronto's 6th choice, 201st overall, in 1993 Entry Draft).

			Regular Season								Playoffs						
Season	Club	Lea	GP	W	L	T	Mins	GA	SO	Avg	GP	W	L	Mins	GA	SO	Avg
1992-93	Tri-City	WHL	30	13	12	0	1529	123	0	4.83	4	0	4	240	20	0	5.00
1993-94	Tri-City	WHL	28	7	16	2	1518	132	0	5.22	2	1	1	120	9	0	4.50

BURKE, SEAN HFD.

Goaltender. Catches left. 6'4", 210 lbs. Born, Windsor, Ont., January 29, 1967.
(New Jersey's 2nd choice, 24th overall, in 1985 Entry Draft).

			Regular Season								Playoffs						
Season	Club	Lea	GP	W	L	T	Mins	GA	SO	Avg	GP	W	L	Mins	GA	SO	Avg
1984-85	Toronto	OHL	49	25	21	3	2987	211	0	4.24	5	1	3	266	25	0	5.64
1985-86	Toronto	OHL	47	16	27	3	2840	233	0	4.92	4	0	4	238	24	0	6.05
1986-87	Cdn. National	....	42	27	13	2	2550	130	0	3.05	....	....	....	....	....	....	....
1987-88	Cdn. National	....	37	19	9	2	1962	92	1	2.81	....	....	....	....	....	....	....
	Cdn. Olympic	....	4	1	2	1	238	12	0	3.02	....	....	....	....	....	....	....
	New Jersey	**NHL**	**13**	**10**	**1**	**0**	**689**	**35**	**1**	**3.05**	**17**	**9**	**8**	**1001**	**57**	***1**	**3.42**
1988-89	**New Jersey**	**NHL**	**62**	**22**	**31**	**9**	**3590**	**230**	**3**	**3.84**	....	....	....	....	....	....	....
1989-90	**New Jersey**	**NHL**	**52**	**22**	**22**	**6**	**2914**	**175**	**0**	**3.60**	**2**	**0**	**2**	**125**	**8**	**0**	**3.84**
1990-91	**New Jersey**	**NHL**	**35**	**8**	**12**	**8**	**1870**	**112**	**0**	**3.59**	....	....	....	....	....	....	....
1991-92	Cdn. National	....	31	18	6	4	1721	75	1	2.61	....	....	....	....	....	....	....
	Cdn. Olympic	....	7	....	....	....	429	17	0	2.37	....	....	....	....	....	....	....
	San Diego	IHL	7	4	2	1	424	17	0	2.41	3	0	3	160	13	0	4.88
1992-93	**Hartford**	**NHL**	**50**	**16**	**27**	**3**	**2656**	**184**	**0**	**4.16**	....	....	....	....	....	....	....
1993-94	**Hartford**	**NHL**	**47**	**17**	**24**	**5**	**2750**	**137**	**2**	**2.99**	....	....	....	....	....	....	....
	NHL Totals		**259**	**95**	**117**	**31**	**14469**	**873**	**6**	**3.62**	**19**	**9**	**10**	**1126**	**65**	**1**	**3.46**

Played in NHL All-Star Game (1989)

Traded to **Hartford** by **New Jersey** with Eric Weinrich for Bobby Holik, Hartford's second round choice (Jay Pandolfo) in 1993 Entry Draft and future considerations, August 28, 1992.

BURNS, CHRIS

Goaltender. Catches left. 6'1", 185 lbs. Born, Sudbury, Ont., May 19, 1973.
(San Jose's 9th choice, 195th overall, in 1992 Entry Draft).

			Regular Season								Playoffs						
Season	Club	Lea	GP	W	L	T	Mins	GA	SO	Avg	GP	W	L	Mins	GA	SO	Avg
1992-93	U. of Denver	WCHA	12	1	2	0	433	35	0	4.85	....	....	....	....	....	....	....
1993-94	U. of Denver	WCHA	3	1	2	0	178	13	0	4.38	....	....	....	....	....	....	....

BUTLER, JEROME

Goaltender. Catches left. 5'11", 175 lbs. Born, Roseau, MN, December 14, 1972.
(Calgary's 6th choice, 107th overall, in 1991 Entry Draft).

			Regular Season								Playoffs						
Season	Club	Lea	GP	W	L	T	Mins	GA	SO	Avg	GP	W	L	Mins	GA	SO	Avg
1991-92	Minn.-Duluth	WCHA	22	9	11	2	1325	91	0	4.12	....	....	....	....	....	....	....
1992-93	Minn.-Duluth	WCHA	21	12	6	2	1183	74	0	3.75	....	....	....	....	....	....	....
1993-94	Minn. Duluth	WCHA	7	1	4	1	328	27	0	4.94	....	....	....	....	....	....	....

BUZAK, MIKE ST.L.

Goaltender. Catches left. 6'3", 183 lbs. Born, Edson, Alta., February 10, 1973.
(St. Louis' 5th choice, 167th overall, in 1993 Entry Draft).

			Regular Season								Playoffs						
Season	Club	Lea	GP	W	L	T	Mins	GA	SO	Avg	GP	W	L	Mins	GA	SO	Avg
1991-92	Michigan State	CCHA	7	4	0	0	311	22	0	4.25	....	....	....	....	....	....	....
1992-93	Michigan State	CCHA	38	22	10	2	*2090	102	0	2.93	....	....	....	....	....	....	....
1993-94a	Michigan State	CCHA	*39	21	12	5	*2297	104	....	2.72	....	....	....	....	....	....	....

a CCHA Second All-Star Team (1994)

CALLINAN, JEFF ST.L.

Goaltender. Catches left. 5'10", 169 lbs. Born, Minneapolis, MN, January 6, 1973.
(St. Louis' 5th choice, 109th overall, in 1991 Entry Draft).

			Regular Season								Playoffs						
Season	Club	Lea	GP	W	L	T	Mins	GA	SO	Avg	GP	W	L	Mins	GA	SO	Avg
1991-92	U. Minnesota	WCHA	6	2	1	0	209	15	0	4.32	....	....	....	....	....	....	....
1992-93	U. Minnesota	WCHA	21	8	5	5	1113	72	0	3.88	....	....	....	....	....	....	....
1993-94	U. Minnesota	WCHA	26	14	5	3	1491	80	0	3.22	....	....	....	....	....	....	....

CARAVAGGIO, LUCIANO N.J.

Goaltender. Catches left. 5'11", 175 lbs. Born, Etobicoke, Ont., October 3, 1975.
(New Jersey's 7th choice, 155th overall, in 1994 Entry Draft).

			Regular Season								Playoffs						
Season	Club	Lea	GP	W	L	T	Mins	GA	SO	Avg	GP	W	L	Mins	GA	SO	Avg
1993-94	Michigan Tech	WCHA	13	1	7	0	538	37	*1	4.13	....	....	....	....	....	....	....

CAREY, JIM WSH.

Goaltender. Catches left. 6'2", 190 lbs. Born, Dorchester, MA, May 31, 1974.
(Washington's 2nd choice, 32nd overall, in 1992 Entry Draft).

			Regular Season								Playoffs						
Season	Club	Lea	GP	W	L	T	Mins	GA	SO	Avg	GP	W	L	Mins	GA	SO	Avg
1992-93a	U. Wisconsin	WCHA	26	15	8	1	1525	78	1	3.07	....	....	....	....	....	....	....
1993-94	U. Wisconsin	WCHA	*40	*24	13	1	*2247	114	*1	*3.04	....	....	....	....	....	....	....

a WCHA Second All-Star Team (1993)

CASEY, JON ST.L.

Goaltender. Catches left. 5'10", 155 lbs. Born, Grand Rapids, MN, March 29, 1962.

			Regular Season								Playoffs						
Season	Club	Lea	GP	W	L	T	Mins	GA	SO	Avg	GP	W	L	Mins	GA	SO	Avg
1980-81	North Dakota	WCHA	5	3	1	0	300	19	0	3.80	....	....	....	....	....	....	....
1981-82	North Dakota	WCHA	18	15	3	0	1038	48	1	2.77	....	....	....	....	....	....	....
1982-83	North Dakota	WCHA	17	9	6	2	1020	42	0	2.51	....	....	....	....	....	....	....
1983-84	North Dakota	WCHA	37	25	10	2	2180	115	2	3.13	....	....	....	....	....	.	....
	Minnesota	**NHL**	**2**	**1**	**0**	**0**	**84**	**6**	**0**	**4.29**	....	....	....	....	....	....	....
1984-85ab	Baltimore	AHL	46	30	11	4	2646	116	*4	*2.63	*13	8	3	689	38	0	3.31
1985-86	**Minnesota**	**NHL**	**26**	**11**	**11**	**1**	**1402**	**91**	**0**	**3.89**	....	....	....	....	....	....	....
	Springfield	AHL	9	4	3	1	464	30	0	3.88	....	....	....	....	....	....	....
1986-87	Springfield	AHL	13	1	8	0	770	56	0	4.36	....	....	....	....	....	....	....
	Indianapolis	IHL	31	14	15	0	1794	133	0	4.45	....	....	....	....	....	....	....
1987-88	**Minnesota**	**NHL**	**14**	**1**	**7**	**4**	**663**	**41**	**0**	**3.71**	....	....	....	....	....	....	....
	Kalamazoo	IHL	42	24	13	5	2541	154	2	3.64	7	3	3	382	26	0	4.08
1988-89	**Minnesota**	**NHL**	**55**	**18**	**17**	**12**	**2961**	**151**	**1**	**3.06**	**4**	**1**	**3**	**211**	**16**	**0**	**4.55**
1989-90	**Minnesota**	**NHL**	**61**	***31**	**22**	**4**	**3407**	**183**	**3**	**3.22**	**7**	**3**	**4**	**415**	**21**	**1**	**3.04**
1990-91	**Minnesota**	**NHL**	**55**	**21**	**20**	**11**	**3185**	**158**	**3**	**2.98**	***23**	***14**	**7**	***1205**	**61**	***1**	**3.04**
1991-92	**Minnesota**	**NHL**	**52**	**19**	**23**	**5**	**2911**	**165**	**2**	**3.40**	**7**	**3**	**4**	**437**	**22**	**0**	**3.02**
	Kalamazoo	IHL	4	2	1	1	250	11	0	2.64	....	....	....	....	....	....	....
1992-93	**Minnesota**	**NHL**	**60**	**26**	**26**	**5**	**3476**	**193**	**3**	**3.33**	....	....	....	....	....	....	....
1993-94	**Boston**	**NHL**	**57**	**30**	**15**	**9**	**3192**	**153**	**4**	**2.88**	**11**	**5**	**6**	**698**	**34**	**0**	**2.92**
	NHL Totals		**382**	**158**	**141**	**51**	**21281**	**1141**	**16**	**3.22**	**52**	**26**	**24**	**2966**	**154**	**2**	**3.12**

a Won Baz Bastien Trophy (Top Goaltender - AHL) (1985)
b AHL First All-Star Team (1985)

Played in NHL All-Star Game (1993)

Signed as a free agent by **Minnesota**, April 1, 1984. Traded to **Boston** by **Dallas** for Andy Moog to complete June 20, 1993 trade which sent Gord Murphy to Dallas for future considerations, June 25, 1993. Signed as a free agent by **St. Louis**, June 29, 1994.

CAVICCHI, TRENT MTL.

Goaltender. Catches left. 6'3", 190 lbs. Born, Halifax, N.S., August 11, 1974.
(Montreal's 12th choice, 236th overall, in 1992 Entry Draft).

			Regular Season								Playoffs						
Season	Club	Lea	GP	W	L	T	Mins	GA	SO	Avg	GP	W	L	Mins	GA	SO	Avg
1992-93	N. Hampshire	H.E.	9	3	2	1	391	32	0	4.91	....	....	....	....	....	....	....
1993-94	N. Hampshire	H.E.	25	14	7	1	1324	65	1	2.95	....	....	....	....	....	....	....

CHABOT, FREDERIC (shah-BOH)

Goaltender. Catches right. 5'11", 177 lbs. Born, Hebertville-Station, Que., February 12, 1968.
(New Jersey's 10th choice, 192nd overall, in 1986 Entry Draft).

			Regular Season								Playoffs						
Season	Club	Lea	GP	W	L	T	Mins	GA	SO	Avg	GP	W	L	Mins	GA	SO	Avg
1986-87	Drummondville	QMJHL	62	31	29	0	3508	293	1	5.01	8	2	6	481	40	0	4.99
1987-88	Drummondville	QMJHL	58	27	24	4	3276	237	1	4.34	16	10	6	1019	56	*1	*3.30
1988-89a	Prince Albert	WHL	54	21	29	0	2957	202	2	4.10	4	1	1	199	16	0	4.82
1989-90	Sherbrooke	AHL	2	1	1	0	119	8	0	4.03	....	....	....	....	....	....	....
	Fort Wayne	IHL	23	6	13	3	1208	87	1	4.32	....	....	....	....	....	....	....
1990-91	**Montreal**	**NHL**	**3**	**0**	**0**	**1**	**108**	**6**	**0**	**3.33**	....	....	....	....	....	....	....
	Fredericton	AHL	35	9	15	5	1800	122	0	4.07	....	....	....	....	....	....	....
1991-92	Fredericton	AHL	30	17	9	4	1761	79	2	*2.69	7	3	4	457	20	0	2.63
	Winston-Salem	ECHL	24	15	7	2	1449	71	0	*2.94	....	....	....	....	....	....	....
1992-93	**Montreal**	**NHL**	**1**	**0**	**0**	**0**	**40**	**1**	**0**	**1.50**	....	....	....	....	....	....	....
	Fredericton	AHL	45	22	17	4	2544	141	0	3.33	4	1	3	261	16	0	3.68
1993-94	**Montreal**	**NHL**	**1**	**0**	**1**	**0**	**60**	**5**	**0**	**5.00**	....	....	....	....	....	....	....
	Fredericton	AHL	3	0	1	1	143	12	0	5.03	....	....	....	....	....	....	....
	Las Vegas	IHL	2	1	1	0	110	5	0	2.72	....	....	....	....	....	....	....
	Philadelphia	**NHL**	**4**	**0**	**1**	**1**	**70**	**5**	**0**	**4.29**	....	....	....	....	....	....	....
b	Hershey	AHL	28	13	5	6	1464	63	2	*2.58	11	7	4	665	32	0	2.89
	NHL Totals		**9**	**0**	**2**	**2**	**278**	**17**	**0**	**3.67**	....	....	....	....	....	....	....

a WHL First All-Star Team (1989)
b Won Baz Bastien Trophy (Top Goaltender - AHL) (1994)

Signed as a free agent by **Montreal**, January 16, 1990. Claimed by **Tampa Bay** from **Montreal** in Expansion Draft, June 18, 1992. Traded to **Montreal** by **Tampa Bay** for J.C. Bergeron, June 19, 1992. Traded to **Philadelphia** by **Montreal** for cash, February 21, 1994.

CHARBONNEAU, PATRICK OTT.

Goaltender. Catches left. 5'11", 205 lbs. Born, St-Jean sur Richelieu, Que., July 22, 1975.
(Ottawa's 3rd choice, 53rd overall, in 1993 Entry Draft).

			Regular Season								Playoffs						
Season	Club	Lea	GP	W	L	T	Mins	GA	SO	Avg	GP	W	L	Mins	GA	SO	Avg
1991-92	Victoriaville	QMJHL	37	9	23	2	1943	163	0	5.03	....	....	....	....	....	....	....
1992-93	Victoriaville	QMJHL	59	*35	22	0	3121	216	0	4.15	2	1	0	92	4	0	2.61
1993-94	Victoriaville	QMJHL	56	....	....	....	2948	261	0	5.31	5	1	4	212	24	0	6.79
	PEI	AHL	3	2	1	0	180	11	0	3.67	....	....	....	....	....	....	....

CHEVELDAE, TIM (SHEH-vehl-day) WPG.

Goaltender. Catches left. 5'10", 195 lbs. Born, Melville, Sask., February 15, 1968.
(Detroit's 4th choice, 64th overall, in 1986 Entry Draft).

			Regular Season								Playoffs						
Season	Club	Lea	GP	W	L	T	Mins	GA	SO	Avg	GP	W	L	Mins	GA	SO	Avg
1985-86	Saskatoon	WHL	36	21	10	3	2030	165	0	4.88	8	6	2	480	29	0	3.63
1986-87	Saskatoon	WHL	33	20	11	0	1909	133	2	4.18	5	4	1	308	20	0	3.90
1987-88a	Saskatoon	WHL	66	44	19	3	3798	235	1	3.71	6	4	2	364	27	0	4.45
1988-89	**Detroit**	**NHL**	**2**	**0**	**2**	**0**	**122**	**9**	**0**	**4.43**	....	....	....	....	....	....	....
	Adirondack	AHL	30	20	8	0	1694	98	1	3.47	2	1	0	99	9	0	5.45
1989-90	**Detroit**	**NHL**	**28**	**10**	**9**	**8**	**1600**	**101**	**0**	**3.79**	....	....	....	....	....	....	....
	Adirondack	AHL	31	17	8	6	1848	116	0	3.77	....	....	....	....	....	....	....
1990-91	**Detroit**	**NHL**	**65**	**30**	**26**	**5**	**3615**	**214**	**2**	**3.55**	**7**	**3**	**4**	**398**	**22**	**0**	**3.32**
1991-92	**Detroit**	**NHL**	***72**	***38**	**23**	**9**	***4236**	**226**	**2**	**3.20**	**11**	**3**	**7**	**597**	**25**	***2**	**2.51**
1992-93	**Detroit**	**NHL**	**67**	**34**	**24**	**7**	**3880**	**210**	**4**	**3.25**	**7**	**3**	**4**	**423**	**24**	**0**	**3.40**
1993-94	**Detroit**	**NHL**	**30**	**16**	**9**	**1**	**1572**	**91**	**1**	**3.47**	....	....	....	....	....	....	....
	Adirondack	AHL	2	1	0	1	125	7	0	3.36	....	....	....	....	....	....	....
	Winnipeg	**NHL**	**14**	**5**	**8**	**1**	**788**	**52**	**1**	**3.96**	....	....	....	....	....	....	....
	NHL Totals		**278**	**133**	**101**	**31**	**15813**	**903**	**10**	**3.43**	**25**	**9**	**15**	**1418**	**71**	**2**	**3.00**

a WHL East All-Star Team (1988)

Played in NHL All-Star Game (1992)

Traded to **Winnipeg** by **Detroit** with Dallas Drake for Bob Essensa and Sergei Bautin, March 8, 1994.

CLOUTIER, DAN NYR

Goaltender. Catches left. 6'1", 182 lbs. Born, Mont-Laurier, Que., April 22, 1976.
(NY Rangers' 1st choice, 26th overall, in 1994 Entry Draft).

			Regular Season								Playoffs						
Season	Club	Lea	GP	W	L	T	Mins	GA	SO	Avg	GP	W	L	Mins	GA	SO	Avg
1992-93	S.S. Marie	OHL	12	4	6	0	572	44	0	4.62	4	1	2	231	12	0	3.12
1993-94	S.S. Marie	OHL	55	28	14	6	2934	174	*2	3.56	14	*10	4	833	52	0	3.75

CLOUTIER, JACQUES (clootz-YAY)

Goaltender. Catches left. 5'7", 168 lbs. Born, Noranda, Que., January 3, 1960.
(Buffalo's 4th choice, 55th overall, in 1979 Entry Draft).

			Regular Season								Playoffs						
Season	Club	Lea	GP	W	L	T	Mins	GA	SO	Avg	GP	W	L	Mins	GA	SO	Avg
1977-78	Trois-Rivières	QJHL	71	....	....	....	4134	240	*4	3.48	13	....	....	779	40	1	3.08
1978-79a	Trois-Rivières	QJHL	72	....	....	....	4168	218	*3	*3.14	13	....	....	780	36	0	*2.77
1979-80	Trois-Rivières	QJHL	55	27	20	7	3222	231	2	4.30	7	3	4	420	33	0	4.71
1980-81	Rochester	AHL	*61	27	27	6	*3478	209	1	3.61	....	....	....	....	....	....	....
1981-82	Buffalo	NHL	7	5	1	0	311	13	0	2.51	....	....	....	....	....	....	....
	Rochester	AHL	23	14	7	2	1366	64	0	2.81	....	....	....	....	....	....	....
1982-83	Buffalo	NHL	25	10	7	6	1390	81	0	3.50	....	....	....	....	....	....	....
	Rochester	AHL	13	7	3	1	634	42	0	3.97	16	12	4	992	47	0	2.84
1983-84	Rochester	AHL	*51	26	22	1	*2841	172	1	3.63	*18	9	9	*1145	68	0	3.56
1984-85	Buffalo	NHL	1	0	0	1	65	4	0	3.69	....	....	....	....	....	....	....
	Rochester	AHL	14	10	2	1	803	36	0	2.69	....	....	....	....	....	....	....
1985-86	Buffalo	NHL	15	5	9	1	872	49	1	3.37	....	....	....	....	....	....	....
	Rochester	AHL	14	10	2	2	835	38	1	2.73	....	....	....	....	....	....	....
1986-87	Buffalo	NHL	40	11	19	5	2167	137	0	3.79	....	....	....	....	....	....	....
1987-88	Buffalo	NHL	20	4	8	2	851	67	0	4.72	....	....	....	....	....	....	....
1988-89	Buffalo	NHL	36	15	14	0	1786	108	0	3.63	4	1	3	238	10	1	2.52
	Rochester	AHL	11	2	7	0	527	41	0	4.67	....	....	....	....	....	....	....
1989-90	Chicago	NHL	43	18	15	2	2178	112	2	3.09	4	0	2	175	8	0	2.74
1990-91	Chicago	NHL	10	2	3	0	403	24	0	3.57	....	....	....	....	....	....	....
	Quebec	NHL	15	3	8	2	829	61	0	4.41	....	....	....	....	....	....	....
1991-92	Quebec	NHL	26	6	14	3	1345	88	0	3.93	....	....	....	....	....	....	....
1992-93	Quebec	NHL	3	0	2	1	154	10	0	3.90	....	....	....	....	....	....	....
1993-94	Quebec	NHL	14	3	2	1	475	24	0	3.03	....	....	....	....	....	....	....
	NHL Totals		255	82	102	24	12826	778	3	3.64	8	1	5	413	18	1	2.62

a QMJHL First All-Star Team (1979)

Traded to **Chicago** by **Buffalo** for future considerations, September 28, 1989. Traded to **Quebec** by **Chicago** for Tony McKegney, January 29, 1991.

COUSINEAU, MARCEL — TOR.

Goaltender. Catches left. 5'9", 180 lbs. Born, Delson, Que., April 30, 1973.
(Boston's 3rd choice, 62nd overall, in 1991 Entry Draft).

			Regular Season								Playoffs						
Season	Club	Lea	GP	W	L	T	Mins	GA	SO	Avg	GP	W	L	Mins	GA	SO	Avg
1990-91	Beauport	QMJHL	49	13	29	3	2739	196	1	4.29	....	....	....	....	....	....	....
1991-92	Beauport	QMJHL	*67	26	32	5	*3673	241	0	3.94	....	....	....	....	....	....	....
1992-93	Drummondville	QMJHL	60	20	32	2	3298	225	0	4.09	9	3	6	498	37	*1	4.45
1993-94	St. John's	AHL	37	13	11	9	2015	118	0	3.51	....	....	....	....	....	....	....

Signed as a free agent by **Toronto**, November 13, 1993.

COWLEY, WAYNE — EDM.

Goaltender. Catches left. 6', 185 lbs. Born, Scarborough, Ont., December 4, 1964.

			Regular Season								Playoffs						
Season	Club	Lea	GP	W	L	T	Mins	GA	SO	Avg	GP	W	L	Mins	GA	SO	Avg
1985-86	Colgate	ECAC	7	2	2	0	313	23	1	4.42	....	....	....	....	....	....	....
1986-87	Colgate	ECAC	31	21	8	1	1805	106	0	3.52	....	....	....	....	....	....	....
1987-88	Colgate	ECAC	20	11	7	1	1162	58	1	2.99	....	....	....	....	....	....	....
1988-89	Salt Lake	IHL	29	17	7	1	1423	94	0	3.96	2	1	0	69	6	0	5.22
1989-90	Salt Lake	IHL	36	15	12	5	2009	124	1	3.70	3	0	0	118	6	0	3.05
1990-91	Salt Lake	IHL	7	3	4	0	377	23	1	3.66	....	....	....	....	....	....	....
a	Cincinnati	ECHL	30	19	9	2	1680	108	1	3.85	4	1	3	249	13	*1	3.13
1991-92	Cape Breton	AHL	11	6	5	0	644	45	0	3.53	1	0	1	61	3	0	2.95
	Raleigh	ECHL	38	16	18	2	2213	137	0	3.71	....	....	....	....	....	....	....
1992-93	Cape Breton	AHL	42	14	17	6	2334	152	1	3.91	16	*14	2	1014	47	*1	2.78
	Wheeling	ECHL	1	1	0	0	60	3	0	3.00	....	....	....	....	....	....	....
1993-94	Edmonton	NHL	1	0	1	0	57	3	0	3.16	....	....	....	....	....	....	....
	Cape Breton	AHL	44	20	17	5	2486	150	0	3.62	5	1	4	0	20	0	4.66
	NHL Totals		1	0	1	0	57	3	0	3.16	....	....	....	....	....	....	....

a ECHL Second All-Star Team (1991)

Signed as a free agent by **Calgary**, May 1, 1988. Signed as a free agent by **Edmonton**, September 13, 1993.

CURRIE, JASON — HFD.

Goaltender. Catches right. 5'10", 170 lbs. Born, Brampton, Ont., April 26, 1972.
(Hartford's 10th choice, 207th overall, in 1991 Entry Draft).

			Regular Season								Playoffs						
Season	Club	Lea	GP	W	L	T	Mins	GA	SO	Avg	GP	W	L	Mins	GA	SO	Avg
1990-91	Clarkson	ECAC	21	11	3	2	968	58	0	3.59	....	....	....	....	....	....	....
1991-92	Clarkson	ECAC	18	11	6	1	965	42	2	2.61	....	....	....	....	....	....	....
1992-93	Clarkson	ECAC	12	4	6	1	642	34	1	3.18	....	....	....	....	....	....	....
1993-94a	Clarkson	ECAC	*33	*18	9	5	*1877	95	*4	3.04	....	....	....	....	....	....	....

a ECAC Second All-Star Team (1994)

DAFOE, BYRON — WSH.

Goaltender. Catches left. 5'11", 175 lbs. Born, Sussex, England, February 25, 1971.
(Washington's 2nd choice, 35th overall, in 1989 Entry Draft).

			Regular Season								Playoffs						
Season	Club	Lea	GP	W	L	T	Mins	GA	SO	Avg	GP	W	L	Mins	GA	SO	Avg
1988-89	Portland	WHL	59	29	24	3	3279	291	1	5.32	*18	10	8	*1091	81	*1	4.45
1989-90	Portland	WHL	40	14	21	3	2265	193	0	5.11	....	....	....	....	....	....	....
1990-91	Portland	WHL	8	1	5	1	414	41	0	5.94	....	....	....	....	....	....	....
	Prince Albert	WHL	32	13	12	4	1839	124	0	4.05	....	....	....	....	....	....	....
1991-92	New Haven	AHL	7	3	2	1	364	22	0	3.63	....	....	....	....	....	....	....
	Baltimore	AHL	33	12	16	4	1847	119	0	3.87	....	....	....	....	....	....	....
	Hampton Rds.	ECHL	10	6	4	0	562	26	0	2.78	....	....	....	....	....	....	....
1992-93	Washington	NHL	1	0	0	0	1	0	0	0.00	....	....	....	....	....	....	....
	Baltimore	AHL	48	16	20	7	2617	191	1	4.38	5	2	3	241	22	0	5.48
1993-94	Washington	NHL	5	2	2	0	230	13	0	3.39	2	0	2	118	5	0	2.54
ab	Portland	AHL	47	24	16	4	2661	148	1	3.34	1	0	0	9	1	0	6.79
	NHL Totals		6	2	2	0	231	13	0	3.38	2	0	2	118	5	0	2.54

a AHL First All-Star Team (1994)
b Share Harry "Hap" Holmes Trophy (fewest goals-against - AHL) with Olaf Kolzig (1994)

DAUBENSPECK, KIRK — OTT.

Goaltender. Catches left. 6'1", 170 lbs. Born, Madison, WI, July 16, 1974.
(Philadelphia's 7th choice, 151st overall, in 1992 Entry Draft).

			Regular Season								Playoffs						
Season	Club	Lea	GP	W	L	T	Mins	GA	SO	Avg	GP	W	L	Mins	GA	SO	Avg
1992-93	Sioux City	USHL	9	0	7	1	470	49	0	6.26	....	....	....	....	....	....	....
	Wisconsin	USHL	28	5	20	1	1542	123	....	4.79	....	....	....	....	....	....	....
1993-94	U. Wisconsin	WCHA	7	2	2	0	280	19	0	4.07	....	....	....	....	....	....	....

Traded to **Ottawa** by **Philadelphia** with Claude Boivin for Mark Lamb, March 5, 1994.

DAVIS, CHRIS — BUF.

Goaltender. Catches left. 6'3", 177 lbs. Born, Calgary, Alta., December 1, 1974.
(Buffalo's 8th choice, 246th overall, in 1993 Entry Draft).

			Regular Season								Playoffs						
Season	Club	Lea	GP	W	L	T	Mins	GA	SO	Avg	GP	W	L	Mins	GA	SO	Avg
1992-93	Calgary Royals	Jr. A	42	....	....	....	2374	134	3	3.39	....	....	....	....	....	....	....
1993-94	Alaska-Anch.	WCHA	9	2	4	0	390	27	0	4.15	....	....	....	....	....	....	....

DEGRACE, YANICK

Goaltender. Catches left. 5'11", 175 lbs. Born, Lameque, N.B., April 16, 1971.
(Philadelphia's 5th choice, 94th overall, in 1991 Entry Draft).

			Regular Season								Playoffs						
Season	Club	Lea	GP	W	L	T	Mins	GA	SO	Avg	GP	W	L	Mins	GA	SO	Avg
1990-91	Trois-Rivières	QMJHL	33	13	11	2	1726	97	1	3.37	4	1	0	129	11	0	5.12
1991-92	Hull	QMJHL	35	18	9	3	1970	112	0	3.41	2	0	2	31	4	0	7.64
	Hershey	AHL	2	0	1	1	125	6	0	2.88	....	....	....	....	....	....	....
1992-93	Hershey	AHL	30	10	15	2	1442	103	1	4.29	....	....	....	....	....	....	....
1993-94	Hershey	AHL	3	1	0	0	97	11	0	6.74	....	....	....	....	....	....	....

DENOMME, C. J.

Goaltender. Catches left. 5'11", 180 lbs. Born, London, Ont., April 8, 1974.
(Detroit's 9th choice, 189th overall, in 1992 Entry Draft).

			Regular Season								Playoffs						
Season	Club	Lea	GP	W	L	T	Mins	GA	SO	Avg	GP	W	L	Mins	GA	SO	Avg
1991-92	Kitchener	OHL	21	4	5	4	881	63	0	4.29	1	0	0	20	2	0	6.00
1992-93	Kitchener	OHL	45	17	20	5	2497	189	0	4.54	2	0	2	65	7	0	6.46
1993-94	Kitchener	OHL	3	1	2	0	144	9	0	3.75	....	....	....	....	....	....	....
	Ottawa	OHL	35	20	8	5	1973	108	1	3.28	13	6	7	780	48	0	3.69

DERKSEN, DUANE — WSH.

Goaltender. Catches left. 6'1", 180 lbs. Born, St. Boniface, Man., July 7, 1968.
(Washington's 4th choice, 57th overall, in 1988 Entry Draft).

			Regular Season								Playoffs						
Season	Club	Lea	GP	W	L	T	Mins	GA	SO	Avg	GP	W	L	Mins	GA	SO	Avg
1988-89	U. Wisconsin	WCHA	11	4	5	0	561	37	1	3.96	....	....	....	....	....	....	....
1989-90ab	U. Wisconsin	WCHA	*41	*31	8	1	*2345	133	*2	*3.40	....	....	....	....	....	....	....
1990-91a	U. Wisconsin	WCHA	*42	24	15	3	*2474	133	3	3.23	....	....	....	....	....	....	....
1991-92cd	U. Wisconsin	WCHA	31	18	11	2	1825	100	0	3.29	....	....	....	....	....	....	....
1992-93	Baltimore	AHL	26	6	13	3	1247	86	0	4.14	4	1	1	188	7	0	2.23
	Hampton Rds.	ECHL	13	7	5	0	747	48	0	3.86	....	....	....	....	....	....	....
1993-94	Rochester	AHL	6	2	1	1	235	14	0	3.57	....	....	....	....	....	....	....
	Adirondack	AHL	11	4	6	0	599	37	0	3.70	....	....	....	....	....	....	....
	Milwaukee	IHL	9	4	2	2	490	28	0	3.42	....	....	....	....	....	....	....

a WCHA Second All-Star Team (1990, 1991)
b NCAA Final Four All-Tournament Team, Tournament Top Goaltender (1990)
c NCAA West Second All-American Team (1992)
d WCHA First All-Star Team (1992)

DEROUVILLE, PHILIPPE — PIT.

Goaltender. Catches left. 6'1", 183 lbs. Born, Victoriaville, Que., August 7, 1974.
(Pittsburgh's 5th choice, 115th overall, in 1992 Entry Draft).

			Regular Season								Playoffs						
Season	Club	Lea	GP	W	L	T	Mins	GA	SO	Avg	GP	W	L	Mins	GA	SO	Avg
1990-91	Longueuil	QMJHL	20	13	6	0	1030	50	0	2.91	....	....	....	....	....	....	....
1991-92	Verdun	QMJHL	34	20	6	3	1854	99	2	3.20	11	7	3	593	28	1	2.83
1992-93a	Verdun	QMJHL	61	30	27	2	3491	210	1	3.61	4	....	4	256	18	....	3.61
1993-94a	Verdun	QMJHL	51	0	0	0	2845	145	1	*3.06	4	0	4	210	14	0	4.00

a QMJHL Second All-Star Team (1993, 1994)

DESCHENES, FREDERIC — DET.

Goaltender. Catches left. 5'9", 164 lbs. Born, Quebec, Que., January 12, 1976.
(Detroit's 4th choice, 114th overall, in 1994 Entry Draft).

			Regular Season								Playoffs						
Season	Club	Lea	GP	W	L	T	Mins	GA	SO	Avg	GP	W	L	Mins	GA	SO	Avg
1992-93	Ste. Foy	Midget	....	....	....	....	....	....	....	....	....	....	....	....	....	....	....
1993-94	Granby	QMJHL	35	14	15	1	1861	132	0	4.26	7	3	4	372	27	0	4.35

DOPSON, ROBERT — PIT.

Goaltender. Catches left. 6', 200 lbs. Born, Smiths Falls, Ont., August 21, 1967.

			Regular Season								Playoffs						
Season	Club	Lea	GP	W	L	T	Mins	GA	SO	Avg	GP	W	L	Mins	GA	SO	Avg
1989-90	Wilfred Laurier	OUAA	22	....	....	....	1319	57	0	2.59	....	....	....	....	....	....	....
1990-91	Muskegon	IHL	24	10	10	0	1243	90	0	4.34	....	....	....	....	....	....	....
	Louisville	ECHL	3	3	0	0	180	12	0	4.00	5	3	1	270	16	0	3.55
1991-92	Muskegon	IHL	28	13	12	2	1655	90	4	3.26	12	8	4	697	40	0	3.44
1992-93	Cleveland	IHL	50	26	15	3	2825	167	1	3.55	4	0	4	203	20	0	5.91
1993-94	Pittsburgh	NHL	2	0	0	0	45	3	0	4.00	....	....	....	....	....	....	....
	Cleveland	IHL	32	9	10	8	1681	109	0	3.89	....	....	....	....	....	....	....
	NHL Totals		2	0	0	0	45	3	0	4.00	....	....	....	....	....	....	....

Signed as a free agent by **Pittsburgh**, July 6, 1991.

DRAPER, TOM — NYI

Goaltender. Catches left. 5'11", 185 lbs. Born, Outremont, Que., November 20, 1966.
(Winnipeg's 8th choice, 165th overall, in 1985 Entry Draft).

			Regular Season								Playoffs						
Season	Club	Lea	GP	W	L	T	Mins	GA	SO	Avg	GP	W	L	Mins	GA	SO	Avg
1983-84	U. of Vermont	ECAC	20	8	12	0	1205	82	0	4.08	....	....	....	....	....	....	....
1984-85	U. of Vermont	ECAC	24	5	17	0	1316	90	0	4.11	....	....	....	....	....	....	....
1985-86	U. of Vermont	ECAC	29	15	12	1	1697	87	1	3.08	....	....	....	....	....	....	....
1986-87a	U. of Vermont	ECAC	29	16	13	0	1662	96	2	3.47	....	....	....	....	....	....	....
1987-88	Tappara	Fin.	28	16	3	9	1619	87	0	3.22	....	....	....	....	....	....	....
1988-89	**Winnipeg**	**NHL**	**2**	**1**	**1**	**0**	**120**	**12**	**0**	**6.00**	....	....	....	....	....	....	....
b	Moncton	AHL	*54	27	17	5	*2962	171	2	3.46	7	5	2	419	24	0	3.44
1989-90	**Winnipeg**	**NHL**	**6**	**2**	**4**	**0**	**359**	**26**	**0**	**4.35**	....	....	....	....	....	....	....
	Moncton	AHL	51	20	24	3	2844	167	1	3.52	....	....	....	....	....	....	....
1990-91	Moncton	AHL	30	15	13	2	1779	95	1	3.20	....	....	....	....	....	....	....
	Fort Wayne	IHL	10	5	3	1	564	32	0	3.40	....	....	....	....	....	....	....
	Peoria	IHL	10	6	3	1	584	36	0	3.70	4	2	1	214	10	0	2.80
1991-92	**Buffalo**	**NHL**	**26**	**10**	**9**	**5**	**1403**	**75**	**1**	**3.21**	**7**	**3**	**4**	**433**	**19**	**1**	**2.63**
	Rochester	AHL	9	4	3	2	531	28	0	3.16	....	....	....	....	....	....	....
1992-93	**Buffalo**	**NHL**	**11**	**5**	**6**	**0**	**664**	**41**	**0**	**3.70**	....	....	....	....	....	....	....
	Rochester	AHL	5	3	2	0	303	22	0	4.36	....	....	....	....	....	....	....
1993-94	**NY Islanders**	**NHL**	**7**	**1**	**3**	**0**	**227**	**16**	**0**	**4.23**	....	....	....	....	....	....	....
	Salt Lake	IHL	35	7	23	3	1933	140	0	4.34	....	....	....	....	....	....	....
	NHL Totals		**52**	**19**	**23**	**5**	**2773**	**170**	**1**	**3.68**	**7**	**3**	**4**	**433**	**19**	**1**	**2.63**

a ECAC First All-Star Team (1987)
b AHL Second All-Star Team (1989)

Traded to **St. Louis** by **Winnipeg** for future considerations (Jim Vesey, May 24, 1991), February 28, 1991. Traded to **Winnipeg** by **St. Louis** for future considerations, May 24, 1991. Traded to **Buffalo** by **Winnipeg** for Buffalo's seventh round choice (Artur Oktyabrev) in 1992 Entry Draft, June 22, 1991. Traded to **NY Islanders** by **Buffalo** for NY Islanders' seventh round choice (Stev Plouffe) in 1994 Entry Draft, September 30, 1993.

DUFFUS, PARRIS — (DOO-fihz, PAIR-ihz) ST.L.

Goaltender. Catches left. 6'2", 192 lbs. Born, Denver, CO, January 27, 1970.
(St. Louis' 6th choice, 180th overall, in 1990 Entry Draft).

			Regular Season								Playoffs						
Season	Club	Lea	GP	W	L	T	Mins	GA	SO	Avg	GP	W	L	Mins	GA	SO	Avg
1990-91	Cornell	ECAC	4	0	0	0	37	3	0	4.86	....	....	....	....	....	....	....
1991-92ab	Cornell	ECAC	28	14	11	3	1677	74	1	2.65	....	....	....	....	....	....	....
1992-93	Hampton Rds.	ECHL	4	3	1	0	245	13	0	3.18	....	....	....	....	....	....	....
	Peoria	IHL	37	16	15	4	2149	142	0	3.96	1	0	1	59	5	0	5.08
1993-94	Peoria	IHL	36	19	10	3	1845	141	0	4.58	2	0	1	92	6	0	3.88

a NCAA East First All-American Team (1992)
b ECAC Second All-Star Team (1992)

DUNHAM, MICHAEL — (DUHN-uhm) N.J.

Goaltender. Catches left. 6'3", 185 lbs. Born, Johnson City, NY, June 1, 1972.
(New Jersey's 4th choice, 53rd overall, in 1990 Entry Draft).

			Regular Season								Playoffs						
Season	Club	Lea	GP	W	L	T	Mins	GA	SO	Avg	GP	W	L	Mins	GA	SO	Avg
1990-91	U. of Maine	H.E.	23	14	5	2	1275	63	0	*2.96	....	....	....	....	....	....	....
1991-92	U. of Maine	H.E.	7	6	0	0	382	14	1	2.20	....	....	....	....	....	....	....
	U.S. National	....	3	0	1	1	157	10	0	3.82	....	....	....	....	....	....	....
1992-93ab	U. of Maine	H.E.	25	*21	1	1	1429	63	0	2.65	....	....	....	....	....	....	....
1993-94	U.S. National	....	33	....	....	....	1983	125	2	3.78	....	....	....	....	....	....	....
	U.S. Olympic	....	3	....	....	....	180	15	0	5.02	....	....	....	....	....	....	....
	Albany	AHL	5	2	2	1	304	26	0	5.12	....	....	....	....	....	....	....

a Hockey East First All-Star Team (1993)
b NCAA East First All-American Team (1993)

DYCK, LARRY

Goaltender. Catches left. 5'11", 180 lbs. Born, Winkler, Man., December 15, 1965.

			Regular Season								Playoffs						
Season	Club	Lea	GP	W	L	T	Mins	GA	SO	Avg	GP	W	L	Mins	GA	SO	Avg
1986-87	U. Manitoba	CWUAA	18	....	....	....	1019	61	*3	3.59	....	....	....	....	....	....	....
1987-88	U. Manitoba	CWUAA	*19	....	....	....	1118	87	0	4.78	....	....	....	....	....	....	....
1988-89	Kalamazoo	IHL	42	17	20	2	2308	168	0	4.37	....	....	....	....	....	....	....
1989-90	Kalamazoo	IHL	36	20	12	0	1959	116	0	3.55	7	2	3	353	22	0	3.74
	Knoxville	ECHL	3	1	1	1	184	12	0	3.91	....	....	....	....	....	....	....
1990-91	Kalamazoo	IHL	38	21	15	0	2182	133	1	3.66	1	0	1	60	6	0	6.00
1991-92	Kalamazoo	IHL	*56	25	23	6	*3305	195	0	3.54	12	5	7	690	43	0	3.74
1992-93	Milwaukee	IHL	40	23	9	5	2329	131	0	3.37	3	1	2	180	10	0	3.33
1993-94	Milwaukee	IHL	41	15	13	7	2145	121	0	3.38	3	0	3	120	11	0	5.47

Signed as a free agent by **Minnesota**, November 10, 1988.

ELLIS, AARON — QUE.

Goaltender. Catches left. 6'1", 170 lbs. Born, Indianapolis, IN, May 13, 1974.
(Quebec's 11th choice, 244th overall, in 1992 Entry Draft).

			Regular Season								Playoffs						
Season	Club	Lea	GP	W	L	T	Mins	GA	SO	Avg	GP	W	L	Mins	GA	SO	Avg
1992-93	Bowling Green	CCHA	25	14	10	1	1479	94	0	3.81	....	....	....	....	....	....	....
1993-94	Detroit	OHL	27	14	9	1	1425	88	0	3.71	12	6	6	694	46	0	3.98

ERICKSON, CHAD — N.J.

Goaltender. Catches right. 5'10", 175 lbs. Born, Minneapolis, MN, August 21, 1970.
(New Jersey's 8th choice, 138th overall, in 1988 Entry Draft).

			Regular Season								Playoffs						
Season	Club	Lea	GP	W	L	T	Mins	GA	SO	Avg	GP	W	L	Mins	GA	SO	Avg
1988-89	Minn.-Duluth	WCHA	15	5	7	1	821	49	0	3.58	....	....	....	....	....	....	....
1989-90ab	Minn.-Duluth	WCHA	39	19	19	1	2301	141	0	3.68	....	....	....	....	....	....	....
1990-91	Minn.-Duluth	WCHA	40	14	19	7	2393	159	0	3.99	....	....	....	....	....	....	....
1991-92	**New Jersey**	**NHL**	**2**	**1**	**1**	**0**	**120**	**9**	**0**	**4.50**	....	....	....	....	....	....	....
	Utica	AHL	43	18	19	3	2341	147	2	3.77	2	0	2	127	11	0	5.20
1992-93	Utica	AHL	9	1	7	1	505	47	0	5.58	....	....	....	....	....	....	....
	Cincinnati	IHL	10	2	6	1	516	42	0	4.88	....	....	....	....	....	....	....
	Birmingham	ECHL	14	6	6	2	856	54	0	3.79	....	....	....	....	....	....	....
1993-94	Albany	AHL	4	2	1	0	183	13	0	4.25	....	....	....	....	....	....	....
	Raleigh	ECHL	32	19	9	3	1883	101	0	3.22	6	3	1	286	21	0	4.40
	NHL Totals		**2**	**1**	**1**	**0**	**120**	**9**	**0**	**4.50**	....	....	....	....	....	....	....

a WCHA Second All-Star Team (1990)
b NCAA West First All-American Team (1990)

ESSENSA, BOB — (EH-sehn-suh) DET.

Goaltender. Catches left. 6', 185 lbs. Born, Toronto, Ont., January 14, 1965.
(Winnipeg's 5th choice, 69th overall, in 1983 Entry Draft).

			Regular Season								Playoffs						
Season	Club	Lea	GP	W	L	T	Mins	GA	SO	Avg	GP	W	L	Mins	GA	SO	Avg
1983-84	Michigan State	CCHA	17	11	4	0	946	44	2	2.79	....	....	....	....	....	....	....
1984-85	Michigan State	CCHA	18	15	2	0	1059	29	2	1.64	....	....	....	....	....	....	....
1985-86a	Michigan State	CCHA	23	17	4	1	1333	74	1	3.33	....	....	....	....	....	....	....
1986-87	Michigan State	CCHA	25	19	3	1	1383	64	2	2.78	....	....	....	....	....	....	....
1987-88	Moncton	AHL	27	7	11	1	1287	100	1	4.66	....	....	....	....	....	....	....
1988-89	**Winnipeg**	**NHL**	**20**	**6**	**8**	**3**	**1102**	**68**	**1**	**3.70**	....	....	....	....	....	....	....
	Fort Wayne	IHL	22	14	7	0	1287	70	0	3.26	....	....	....	....	....	....	....
1989-90b	**Winnipeg**	**NHL**	**36**	**18**	**9**	**5**	**2035**	**107**	**1**	**3.15**	**4**	**2**	**1**	**206**	**12**	**0**	**3.50**
	Moncton	AHL	6	3	3	0	358	15	0	2.51	....	....	....	....	....	....	....
1990-91	**Winnipeg**	**NHL**	**55**	**19**	**24**	**6**	**2916**	**153**	**4**	**3.15**	....	....	....	....	....	....	....
	Moncton	AHL	2	1	0	1	125	6	0	2.88	....	....	....	....	....	....	....
1991-92	**Winnipeg**	**NHL**	**47**	**21**	**17**	**6**	**2627**	**126**	***5**	**2.88**	**1**	**0**	**0**	**33**	**3**	**0**	**5.45**
1992-93	**Winnipeg**	**NHL**	**67**	**33**	**26**	**6**	**3855**	**227**	**2**	**3.53**	**6**	**2**	**4**	**367**	**20**	**0**	**3.27**
1993-94	**Winnipeg**	**NHL**	**56**	**19**	**30**	**6**	**3136**	**201**	**1**	**3.85**	....	....	....	....	....	....	....
	Detroit	**NHL**	**13**	**4**	**7**	**2**	**778**	**34**	**1**	**2.62**	**2**	**0**	**2**	**109**	**9**	**0**	**4.95**
	NHL Totals		**294**	**120**	**121**	**34**	**16449**	**916**	**15**	**3.34**	**13**	**4**	**7**	**715**	**44**	**0**	**3.69**

a CCHA Second All-Star Team (1986)
b NHL All-Rookie Team (1990)

Traded to **Detroit** by **Winnipeg** with Sergei Bautin for Tim Cheveldae and Dallas Drake, March 8, 1994.

FERNANDEZ, EMMANUEL — DAL.

Goaltender. Catches left. 6', 173 lbs. Born, Etobicoke, Ont., August 27, 1974.
(Quebec's 4th choice, 52nd overall, in 1992 Entry Draft).

			Regular Season								Playoffs						
Season	Club	Lea	GP	W	L	T	Mins	GA	SO	Avg	GP	W	L	Mins	GA	SO	Avg
1991-92	Laval	QMJHL	31	14	13	2	1593	99	1	3.73	9	3	5	468	39	0	5.00
1992-93	Laval	QMJHL	43	26	14	2	2347	141	1	3.60	13	*12	1	818	42	0	3.08
1993-94a	Laval	QMJHL	51	....	....	....	2776	143	*5	3.09	19	14	5	1116	49	*1	*2.63

a QMJHL First All-Star Team (1994)

Rights traded to **Dallas** by **Quebec** for Tommy Sjodin and Dallas' third round draft choice (Chris Drury) in 1994 Entry Draft, February 13, 1994.

FICHAUD, ERIC — TOR.

Goaltender. Catches left. 5'11", 165 lbs. Born, Montreal, Que., November 4, 1975.
(Toronto's 1st choice, 16th overall, in 1994 Entry Draft).

			Regular Season								Playoffs						
Season	Club	Lea	GP	W	L	T	Mins	GA	SO	Avg	GP	W	L	Mins	GA	SO	Avg
1992-93	Chicoutimi	QMJHL	43	18	13	1	2039	149	0	4.38	....	....	....	....	....	....	....
1993-94abc	Chicoutimi	QMJHL	*63	37	21	3	*3493	192	4	3.30	*26	*16	10	*1560	86	*1	3.31

a Canadian Major Junior Second All-Star Team (1994)
b Memorial Cup All-Star Team (1994)
c Won Hap Emms Memorial Trophy (Memorial Cup Tournament Top Goaltender) (1994)

FINCH, GEOFF

Goaltender. Catches left. 6', 180 lbs. Born, Oshawa, Ont., April 8, 1972.
(Minnesota's 7th choice, 137th overall, in 1991 Entry Draft).

			Regular Season								Playoffs						
Season	Club	Lea	GP	W	L	T	Mins	GA	SO	Avg	GP	W	L	Mins	GA	SO	Avg
1990-91	Brown	ECAC	22	9	9	1	1203	78	1	3.89	....	....	....	....	....	....	....
1991-92	Brown	ECAC	15	4	7	2	815	65	0	4.79	....	....	....	....	....	....	....
1992-93	Brown	ECAC	18	11	5	1	1020	56	0	3.29	....	....	....	....	....	....	....
1993-94a	Brown	ECAC	25	13	9	3	1448	78	0	3.23	....	....	....	....	....	....	....

a ECAC First All-Star Team (1994)

FISET, STEPHANE — (fih-SEHT) QUE.

Goaltender. Catches left. 6'1", 195 lbs. Born, Montreal, Que., June 17, 1970.
(Quebec's 3rd choice, 24th overall, in 1988 Entry Draft).

			Regular Season								Playoffs						
Season	Club	Lea	GP	W	L	T	Mins	GA	SO	Avg	GP	W	L	Mins	GA	SO	Avg
1987-88	Victoriaville	QMJHL	40	15	17	4	2221	146	1	3.94	2	0	2	163	10	0	3.68
1988-89ab	Victoriaville	QMJHL	43	25	14	0	2401	138	1	*3.45	12	*9	2	711	33	0	*2.78
1989-90	**Quebec**	**NHL**	**6**	**0**	**5**	**1**	**342**	**34**	**0**	**5.96**	....	....	....	....	....	....	....
	Victoriaville	QMJHL	24	14	6	3	1383	63	1	*2.73	*14	7	6	*790	49	0	3.72
1990-91	**Quebec**	**NHL**	**3**	**0**	**2**	**1**	**186**	**12**	**0**	**3.87**	....	....	....	....	....	....	....
	Halifax	AHL	36	10	15	8	1902	131	0	4.13	....	....	....	....	....	....	....
1991-92	**Quebec**	**NHL**	**23**	**7**	**10**	**2**	**1133**	**71**	**1**	**3.76**	....	....	....	....	....	....	....
	Halifax	AHL	29	8	14	6	1675	110	*3	3.94	....	....	....	....	....	....	....
1992-93	**Quebec**	**NHL**	**37**	**18**	**9**	**4**	**1939**	**110**	**0**	**3.40**	**1**	**0**	**0**	**21**	**1**	**0**	**2.86**
	Halifax	AHL	3	2	1	0	180	11	0	3.67	....	....	....	....	....	....	....
1993-94	**Quebec**	**NHL**	**50**	**20**	**25**	**4**	**2798**	**158**	**2**	**3.39**	....	....	....	....	....	....	....
	Cornwall	AHL	1	0	1	0	60	4	0	4.00	....	....	....	....	....	....	....
	NHL Totals		**119**	**45**	**51**	**12**	**6398**	**385**	**3**	**3.61**	**1**	**0**	**0**	**21**	**1**	**0**	**2.86**

a QMJHL First All-Star Team (1989)
b Canadian Major Junior Goaltender of the Year (1989)

FITZPATRICK, MARK — FLA.

Goaltender. Catches left. 6'2", 190 lbs. Born, Toronto, Ont., November 13, 1968.
(Los Angeles' 2nd choice, 27th overall, in 1987 Entry Draft).

			Regular Season								Playoffs						
Season	Club	Lea	GP	W	L	T	Mins	GA	SO	Avg	GP	W	L	Mins	GA	SO	Avg
1985-86	Medicine Hat	WHL	41	26	6	1	2074	99	1	2.86	19	12	5	986	58	0	3.53
1986-87a	Medicine Hat	WHL	50	31	11	4	2844	159	4	3.35	20	12	8	1224	71	1	3.48
1987-88a	Medicine Hat	WHL	63	36	15	6	3600	194	2	3.23	16	12	4	959	52	*1	*3.25
1988-89	**Los Angeles**	**NHL**	**17**	**6**	**7**	**3**	**957**	**64**	**0**	**4.01**	....	....	....	....	....	....	....
	New Haven	AHL	18	10	5	1	980	54	1	3.31	....	....	....	....	....	....	....
	NY Islanders	**NHL**	**11**	**3**	**5**	**2**	**627**	**41**	**0**	**3.92**	....	....	....	....	....	....	....
1989-90	**NY Islanders**	**NHL**	**47**	**19**	**19**	**5**	**2653**	**150**	**3**	**3.39**	**4**	**0**	**2**	**152**	**13**	**0**	**5.13**
1990-91	**NY Islanders**	**NHL**	**2**	**1**	**1**	**0**	**120**	**6**	**0**	**3.00**	....	....	....	....	....	....	....
	Capital Dist.	AHL	12	3	7	2	734	47	0	3.84	....	....	....	....	....	....	....
1991-92b	**NY Islanders**	**NHL**	**30**	**11**	**13**	**5**	**1743**	**93**	**0**	**3.20**	....	....	....	....	....	....	....
	Capital Dist.	AHL	14	6	5	1	782	39	0	2.99	....	....	....	....	....	....	....
1992-93	**NY Islanders**	**NHL**	**39**	**17**	**15**	**5**	**2253**	**130**	**0**	**3.46**	**3**	**0**	**1**	**77**	**4**	**0**	**3.12**
	Capital Dist.	AHL	5	1	3	1	284	18	0	3.80	....	....	....	....	....	....	....
1993-94	**Florida**	**NHL**	**28**	**12**	**8**	**6**	**1603**	**73**	**1**	**2.73**	....	....	....	....	....	....	....
	NHL Totals		**174**	**69**	**68**	**26**	**9956**	**557**	**4**	**3.36**	**7**	**0**	**3**	**229**	**17**	**0**	**4.45**

a Won Hap Emms Memorial Trophy (Memorial Cup Tournament Top Goaltender) (1987, 1988)
b Won Bill Masterton Memorial Trophy (1992)

Traded to **NY Islanders** by **Los Angeles** with Wayne McBean and future considerations (Doug Crossman, May 23, 1989) for Kelly Hrudey, February 22, 1989. Traded to **Quebec** by **NY Islanders** with NY Islanders' first round choice (Adam Deadmarsh) in 1993 Entry Draft for Ron Hextall and Quebec's first round choice (Todd Bertuzzi) in 1993 Entry Draft, June 20, 1993. Claimed by **Florida** from **Quebec** in Expansion Draft, June 24, 1993.

FITZSIMMONS, JASON — VAN.

Goaltender. Catches left. 5'11", 175 lbs. Born, Regina, Sask., June 3, 1971.
(Vancouver's 11th choice, 227th overall, in 1991 Entry Draft).

			Regular Season								Playoffs						
Season	Club	Lea	GP	W	L	T	Mins	GA	SO	Avg	GP	W	L	Mins	GA	SO	Avg
1990-91	Moose Jaw	WHL	44	15	23	2	2170	179	0	4.95	8	4	4	481	27	....	3.37
1991-92	Moose Jaw	WHL	60	29	28	1	3286	222	0	4.05	4	0	4	186	27	0	8.71
1992-93	Hamilton	AHL	14	5	8	1	788	53	0	4.04	....	....	....	....	....	....	....
	Columbus	ECHL	23	10	9	3	1340	91	0	4.07	....	....	....	....	....	....	....
1993-94	Hamilton	AHL	17	2	8	0	708	49	0	4.15	2	0	2	98	6	0	3.67

FLAHERTY, WADE — S.J.

Goaltender. Catches right. 6', 170 lbs. Born, Terrace, B.C., January 11, 1968.
(Buffalo's 10th choice, 181st overall, in 1988 Entry Draft).

			Regular Season								Playoffs						
Season	Club	Lea	GP	W	L	T	Mins	GA	SO	Avg	GP	W	L	Mins	GA	SO	Avg
1988-89	Victoria	WHL	42	21	19	0	2408	180	4	4.49	....	....	....	....	....	....	....
1989-90	Greensboro	ECHL	27	12	10	0	1308	96	0	4.40	....	....	....	....	....	....	....
1990-91	Kansas City	IHL	*56	16	31	4	2990	224	0	4.49	....	....	....	....	....	....	....
1991-92	**San Jose**	**NHL**	**3**	**0**	**3**	**0**	**178**	**13**	**0**	**4.38**	....	....	....	....	....	....	....
	Kansas City	IHL	43	26	14	3	2603	140	1	3.23	1	0	0	1	0	0	0.00
1992-93	**San Jose**	**NHL**	**1**	**0**	**1**	**0**	**60**	**5**	**0**	**5.00**	....	....	....	....	....	....	....
	Kansas City	IHL	*61	*34	19	7	*3642	195	2	3.21	*12	6	6	733	34	*1	2.78
1993-94a	Kansas City	IHL	*60	32	19	9	*3564	202	0	3.40	....	....	....	....	....	....	....
	NHL Totals		**4**	**0**	**4**	**0**	**238**	**18**	**0**	**4.54**	....	....	....	....	....	....	....

a IHL Second All-Star Team (1993, 1994)

Signed as a free agent by **San Jose**, September 3, 1991.

FORSBERG, JONAS — (FOHRS-behrg) S.J.

Goaltender. Catches left. 5'10", 150 lbs. Born, Stockholm, Sweden, June 15, 1975.
(San Jose's 11th choice, 210th overall, in 1993 Entry Draft).

			Regular Season								Playoffs						
Season	Club	Lea	GP	W	L	T	Mins	GA	SO	Avg	GP	W	L	Mins	GA	SO	Avg
1992-93	Djurgarden	Swe. Jr.	....	....	....	....	....	....	....	....	....	....	....	....	....	....	....
1993-94	Djurgarden	Swe.	1	....	....	....	60	4	....	4.00	....	....	....	....	....	....	....

FOSTER, NORM

Goaltender. Catches left. 5'9", 175 lbs. Born, Vancouver, B.C., February 10, 1965.
(Boston's 11th choice, 222nd overall, in 1983 Entry Draft).

			Regular Season								Playoffs						
Season	Club	Lea	GP	W	L	T	Mins	GA	SO	Avg	GP	W	L	Mins	GA	SO	Avg
1984-85	Michigan State	CCHA	26	22	4	0	1531	67	0	2.63	....	....	....	....	....	....	....
1985-86	Michigan State	CCHA	24	17	5	1	1414	87	0	3.69	....	....	....	....	....	....	....
1986-87	Michigan State	CCHA	24	14	7	1	1383	90	1	3.90	....	....	....	....	....	....	....
1987-88	Milwaukee	IHL	38	10	22	1	2001	170	0	5.10	....	....	....	....	....	....	....
1988-89	Maine	AHL	47	16	17	6	2411	156	1	3.88	....	....	....	....	....	....	....
1989-90	Maine	AHL	*64	23	28	10	*3664	217	3	3.55	....	....	....	....	....	....	....
1990-91	**Boston**	**NHL**	**3**	**2**	**1**	**0**	**184**	**14**	**0**	**4.57**	....	....	....	....	....	....	....
	Maine	AHL	2	1	1	0	122	7	0	3.44	....	....	....	....	....	....	....
	Cape Breton	AHL	40	15	14	7	2207	135	1	3.67	2	0	2	128	8	0	3.75
1991-92	**Edmonton**	**NHL**	**10**	**5**	**3**	**0**	**439**	**20**	**0**	**2.73**	....	....	....	....	....	....	....
	Cape Breton	AHL	29	15	13	1	1699	119	0	4.20	3	1	2	193	14	0	4.35
1992-93	Cape Breton	AHL	10	5	5	0	560	53	0	5.68	....	....	....	....	....	....	....
	Kansas City	IHL	8	6	1	1	489	28	0	3.44	1	0	0	16	0	0	0.00
1993-94	Hershey	AHL	17	5	9	1	775	58	0	4.49	....	....	....	....	....	....	....
	NHL Totals		**13**	**7**	**4**	**0**	**623**	**34**	**0**	**3.27**	....	....	....	....	....	....	....

Traded to **Edmonton** by **Boston** for Edmonton's sixth round choice (Jiri Dopita) in 1992 Entry Draft, September 11, 1991. Signed as a free agent by **Philadelphia**, August 4, 1993.

FOUNTAIN, MIKE — VAN.

Goaltender. Catches left. 6'1", 176 lbs. Born, North York, Ont., January 26, 1972.
(Vancouver's 4th choice, 69th overall, in 1992 Entry Draft).

			Regular Season								Playoffs						
Season	Club	Lea	GP	W	L	T	Mins	GA	SO	Avg	GP	W	L	Mins	GA	SO	Avg
1990-91	S.S. Marie	OHL	7	5	2	0	380	19	....	3.00	....	....	....	....	....	....	....
	Oshawa	OHL	30	17	5	1	1483	84	....	3.40	8	1	4	292	26	0	5.34
1991-92a	Oshawa	OHL	40	18	13	6	2260	149	1	3.96	7	3	4	429	26	0	3.64
1992-93	Cdn. National	....	13	7	5	1	45	37	1	2.98	....	....	....	....	....	....	....
	Hamilton	AHL	12	2	8	0	618	46	0	4.47	....	....	....	....	....	....	....
1993-94b	Hamilton	AHL	*70	*34	28	6	*4005	241	*4	3.61	3	0	2	146	12	0	4.92

a OHL First All-Star Team (1992)
b AHL Second All-Star Team (1994)

FRANEK, PETR — (FRAH-nehk) QUE.

Goaltender. Catches left. 5'11", 187 lbs. Born, Most, Czech., April 6, 1975.
(Quebec's 10th choice, 205th overall, in 1993 Entry Draft).

			Regular Season								Playoffs						
Season	Club	Lea	GP	W	L	T	Mins	GA	SO	Avg	GP	W	L	Mins	GA	SO	Avg
1992-93	Litvinov	Czech.	5	....	....	....	273	15	....	3.29	....	....	....	....	....	....	....
1993-94	Litvinov	Czech.	11	....	....	....	535	34	....	3.81	2	....	....	61	10	....	9.83

FUHR, GRANT — (FYOOR) BUF.

Goaltender. Catches right. 5'9", 190 lbs. Born, Spruce Grove, Alta., September 28, 1962.
(Edmonton's 1st choice, 8th overall, in 1981 Entry Draft).

			Regular Season								Playoffs						
Season	Club	Lea	GP	W	L	T	Mins	GA	SO	Avg	GP	W	L	Mins	GA	SO	Avg
1979-80a	Victoria	WHL	43	30	12	0	2488	130	2	3.14	8	5	3	465	22	0	2.84
1980-81a	Victoria	WHL	59	48	9	1	3448	160	*4	*2.78	15	12	3	899	45	*1	*3.00
1981-82b	**Edmonton**	**NHL**	**48**	**28**	**5**	**14**	**2847**	**157**	**0**	**3.31**	**5**	**2**	**3**	**309**	**26**	**0**	**5.05**
1982-83	**Edmonton**	**NHL**	**32**	**13**	**12**	**5**	**1803**	**129**	**0**	**4.29**	**1**	**0**	**0**	**11**	**0**	**0**	**0.00**
	Moncton	AHL	10	4	5	1	604	40	0	3.98	....	....	....	....	....	....	....
1983-84	**Edmonton**	**NHL**	**45**	**30**	**10**	**4**	**2625**	**171**	**1**	**3.91**	**16**	**11**	**4**	**883**	**44**	**1**	**2.99**
1984-85	**Edmonton**	**NHL**	**46**	**26**	**8**	**7**	**2559**	**165**	**1**	**3.87**	***18**	***15**	**3**	**1064**	**55**	**0**	**3.10**
1985-86	**Edmonton**	**NHL**	**40**	**29**	**8**	**0**	**2184**	**143**	**0**	**3.93**	**9**	**5**	**4**	**541**	**28**	**0**	**3.11**
1986-87	**Edmonton**	**NHL**	**44**	**22**	**13**	**3**	**2388**	**137**	**0**	**3.44**	**19**	**14**	**5**	**1148**	**47**	**0**	**2.46**
1987-88cd	**Edmonton**	**NHL**	***75**	***40**	**24**	**9**	***4304**	**246**	***4**	**3.43**	***19**	***16**	**2**	***1136**	**55**	**0**	**2.90**
1988-89	**Edmonton**	**NHL**	**59**	**23**	**26**	**6**	**3341**	**213**	**1**	**3.83**	**7**	**3**	**4**	**417**	**24**	**1**	**3.45**
1989-90	**Edmonton**	**NHL**	**21**	**9**	**7**	**3**	**1081**	**70**	**1**	**3.89**	....	....	....	....	....	....	....
	Cape Breton	AHL	2	2	0	0	120	6	0	3.01	....	....	....	....	....	....	....
1990-91	**Edmonton**	**NHL**	**13**	**6**	**4**	**3**	**778**	**39**	**1**	**3.01**	**17**	**8**	**7**	**1019**	**51**	**0**	**3.00**
	Cape Breton	AHL	4	2	2	0	240	17	0	4.25	....	....	....	....	....	....	....
1991-92	**Toronto**	**NHL**	**66**	**25**	**33**	**5**	**3774**	**230**	**2**	**3.66**	....	....	....	....	....	....	....
1992-93	**Toronto**	**NHL**	**29**	**13**	**9**	**4**	**1665**	**87**	**1**	**3.14**	....	....	....	....	....	....	....
	Buffalo	**NHL**	**29**	**11**	**15**	**2**	**1694**	**98**	**0**	**3.47**	**8**	**3**	**4**	**474**	**27**	**1**	**3.42**
1993-94e	**Buffalo**	**NHL**	**32**	**13**	**12**	**3**	**1726**	**106**	**2**	**3.68**	....	....	....	....	....	....	....
	Rochester	AHL	5	3	0	2	310	10	0	1.94	....	....	....	....	....	....	....
	NHL Totals		**579**	**288**	**186**	**68**	**32769**	**1991**	**14**	**3.65**	**119**	**77**	**36**	**7002**	**357**	**3**	**3.06**

a WHL First All-Star Team (1980, 1981)
b NHL Second All-Star Team (1982)
c NHL First All-Star Team (1988)
d Won Vezina Trophy (1988)
e Shared William M. Jennings Trophy with Dominik Hasek (1994)

Played in NHL All-Star Game (1982, 1984-86, 1988-89)

Traded to **Toronto** by **Edmonton** with Glenn Anderson and Craig Berube for Vincent Damphousse, Peter Ing, Scott Thornton, Luke Richardson, future considerations and cash, September 19, 1991. Traded to **Buffalo** by **Toronto** with future considerations for Dave Andreychuk, Daren Puppa and Buffalo's first round choice (Kenny Jonsson) in 1993 Entry Draft, February 2, 1993.

GAGE, JOAQUIN — EDM.

Goaltender. Catches left. 6', 200 lbs. Born, Vancouver, B.C., October 19, 1973.
(Edmonton's 6th choice, 109th overall, in 1992 Entry Draft).

			Regular Season								Playoffs						
Season	Club	Lea	GP	W	L	T	Mins	GA	SO	Avg	GP	W	L	Mins	GA	SO	Avg
1990-91	Portland	WHL	3	0	3	0	180	17	0	5.70	....	....	....	....	....	....	....
1991-92	Portland	WHL	63	27	30	4	3635	269	2	4.44	6	2	4	366	28	0	4.59
1992-93	Portland	WHL	38	21	16	1	2302	153	2	3.99	8	5	2	427	30	0	4.22
1993-94	Prince Albert	WHL	53	24	25	3	3041	212	1	4.18	....	....	....	....	....	....	....

GAGNON, DAVID

Goaltender. Catches left. 6', 185 lbs. Born, Windsor, Ont., October 31, 1967.

			Regular Season								Playoffs						
Season	Club	Lea	GP	W	L	T	Mins	GA	SO	Avg	GP	W	L	Mins	GA	SO	Avg
1987-88	Colgate	ECAC	13	6	4	2	743	43	1	3.47	....	....	....	....	....	....	....
1988-89	Colgate	ECAC	28	17	9	2	1622	102	0	3.77	....	....	....	....	....	....	....
1989-90a	Colgate	ECAC	33	28	3	1	1986	93	0	2.88	....	....	....	....	....	....	....
1990-91	**Detroit**	**NHL**	**2**	**0**	**1**	**0**	**35**	**6**	**0**	**10.29**	....	....	....	....	....	....	....
	Adirondack	AHL	24	8	8	5	1356	94	0	4.16	....	....	....	....	....	....	....
b	Hampton Rds.	ECHL	10	7	1	2	606	26	2	2.57	11	*10	1	696	27	0	*2.32
1991-92	Fort Wayne	IHL	2	2	0	0	125	7	0	3.36	....	....	....	....	....	....	....
	Toledo	ECHL	7	4	2	0	354	18	0	3.05	....	....	....	....	....	....	....
1992-93	Adirondack	AHL	1	0	1	0	60	5	0	5.00	....	....	....	....	....	....	....
	Fort Wayne	IHL	31	15	11	2	1771	116	0	3.93	1	0	0	6	0	0	0.00
1993-94	Fort Wayne	IHL	19	7	6	3	1026	58	0	3.39	....	....	....	....	....	....	....
c	Toledo	ECHL	20	13	5	0	1122	65	1	3.48	*14	*12	2	*909	41	0	*2.70
	NHL Totals		**2**	**0**	**1**	**0**	**35**	**6**	**0**	**10.29**	....	....	....	....	....	....	....

a ECAC First All-Star Team (1990)
b Playoff MVP - ECHL (Shared with Dave Flanagan) (1991)
c Playoff MVP - ECHL (1994)

Signed as a free agent by **Detroit**, June 11, 1990.

GAGNON, JOEL — (GAN-yahn) ANA.

Goaltender. Catches left. 6', 194 lbs. Born, Hearst, Ont., March 14, 1975.
(Anaheim's 4th choice, 82nd overall, in 1993 Entry Draft).

			Regular Season								Playoffs						
Season	Club	Lea	GP	W	L	T	Mins	GA	SO	Avg	GP	W	L	Mins	GA	SO	Avg
1992-93	Oshawa	OHL	48	19	19	1	2248	159	0	4.24	7	3	0	285	21	0	4.42
1993-94	Oshawa	OHL	23	4	11	3	1089	100	0	5.51	....	....	....	....	....	....	....

GALUPPO, SANDY

Goaltender. Catches . 5'10", 170 lbs. Born, Farmingdale, NY, October 4, 1969.
(Edmonton's 1st choice, 22nd overall, in 1990 Supplemental Draft).

			Regular Season								Playoffs						
Season	Club	Lea	GP	W	L	T	Mins	GA	SO	Avg	GP	W	L	Mins	GA	SO	Avg
1987-88	Boston College	H.E.	8	2	2	1	341	30	0	5.28	....	....	....	....	....	....	....
1988-89	Boston College	H.E.	12	6	3	0	525	28	0	3.20	....	....	....	....	....	....	....
1989-90	Boston College	H.E.	22	11	9	1	1235	73	0	3.55	....	....	....	....	....	....	....
1990-91	Boston College	H.E.	12	7	2	0	557	39	0	4.20	....	....	....	....	....	....	....
1991-92									UNAVAILABLE								
1992-93	Cincinnati	IHL	28	6	11	3	1356	93	0	4.12	....	....	....	....	....	....	....
	Dayton	ECHL	17	12	1	1	869	46	2	3.18	....	....	....	....	....	....	....
1993-94	Cincinnati	IHL	4	1	2	0	170	16	0	5.62	....	....	....	....	....	....	....
	Birmingham	ECHL	30	22	4	1	1700	111	1	3.92	8	5	3	477	25	0	3.14

Signed as a free agent by **Florida**, October 22, 1993.

GAMBLE, TROY

Goaltender. Catches left. 5'11", 195 lbs. Born, New Glasgow, N.S., April 7, 1967.
(Vancouver's 2nd choice, 25th overall, in 1985 Entry Draft).

			Regular Season								Playoffs						
Season	Club	Lea	GP	W	L	T	Mins	GA	SO	Avg	GP	W	L	Mins	GA	SO	Avg
1984-85a	Medicine Hat	WHL	37	27	6	2	2095	100	3	2.86	2	1	1	120	9	0	4.50
1985-86	Medicine Hat	WHL	45	28	11	0	2264	142	0	3.76	11	5	4	530	31	0	3.51
1986-87	**Vancouver**	**NHL**	**1**	**0**	**1**	**0**	**60**	**4**	**0**	**4.00**	....	....	....	....	....	....	....
	Medicine Hat	WHL	11	7	3	0	646	46	0	4.27	....	....	....	....	....	....	....
	Spokane	WHL	38	17	17	1	2155	163	0	4.54	5	0	5	298	35	0	7.05
1987-88b	Spokane	WHL	67	36	26	1	3824	235	0	3.69	15	7	8	875	56	1	3.84
1988-89	**Vancouver**	**NHL**	**5**	**2**	**3**	**0**	**302**	**12**	**0**	**2.38**	....	....	....	....	....	....	....
	Milwaukee	IHL	42	23	9	0	2198	138	0	3.77	11	5	5	640	35	0	3.28
1989-90	Milwaukee	IHL	*56	22	21	4	2779	160	2	4.21	5	2	2	216	19	0	5.28
1990-91	**Vancouver**	**NHL**	**47**	**16**	**16**	**6**	**2433**	**140**	**1**	**3.45**	**4**	**1**	**3**	**249**	**16**	**0**	**3.86**
1991-92	**Vancouver**	**NHL**	**19**	**4**	**9**	**3**	**1009**	**73**	**0**	**4.34**	....	....	....	....	....	....	....
	Milwaukee	IHL	9	2	4	2	521	31	0	3.57	....	....	....	....	....	....	....
1992-93	Hamilton	AHL	14	1	10	2	769	62	0	4.84	....	....	....	....	....	....	....
	Cincinnati	IHL	33	11	18	2	1762	134	0	4.56	....	....	....	....	....	....	....
1993-94	Kalamazoo	IHL	48	25	13	5	2607	146	*2	3.36	2	0	1	80	7	0	5.25
	NHL Totals		**72**	**22**	**29**	**9**	**3804**	**229**	**1**	**3.61**	**4**	**1**	**3**	**249**	**16**	**0**	**3.86**

a WHL East First All-Star Team (1985)
b WHL West First All-Star Team (1988)

Signed as a free agent by **Dallas**, August 28, 1993.

GAUTHIER, SEAN — WPG.

Goaltender. Catches left. 5'11", 202 lbs. Born, Sudbury, Ont., March 28, 1971.
(Winnipeg's 7th choice, 181st overall, in 1991 Entry Draft).

			Regular Season								Playoffs						
Season	Club	Lea	GP	W	L	T	Mins	GA	SO	Avg	GP	W	L	Mins	GA	SO	Avg
1990-91	Kingston	OHL	*59	16	36	3	3200	282	0	5.29	....	....	....	....	....	....	....
1991-92	Moncton	AHL	25	8	10	5	1415	88	1	3.73	2	0	0	26	2	0	4.62
	Fort Wayne	IHL	18	10	4	2	978	59	1	3.62	2	0	0	48	7	0	8.75
1992-93	Moncton	AHL	38	10	16	9	2196	145	0	3.96	2	0	1	75	6	0	4.80
1993-94	Moncton	AHL	13	3	5	1	616	41	0	3.99	....	....	....	....	....	....	....
	Fort Wayne	IHL	22	9	9	3	1139	66	0	3.48	....	....	....	....	....	....	....

GILMORE, MIKE

Goaltender. Catches left. 5'10", 173 lbs. Born, Detroit, MI, March 11, 1968.
(NY Rangers' 1st choice, 18th overall, in 1990 Supplemental Draft).

			Regular Season								Playoffs						
Season	Club	Lea	GP	W	L	T	Mins	GA	SO	Avg	GP	W	L	Mins	GA	SO	Avg
1988-89	Michigan State	CCHA	3	1	0	0	74	5	0	4.04	....	....	....	....	....	....	....
1989-90	Michigan State	CCHA	12	9	1	0	638	29	0	2.73	....	....	....	....	....	....	....
1990-91a	Michigan State	CCHA	22	9	8	3	1218	54	*2	2.66	....	....	....	....	....	....	....
1991-92	Michigan State	CCHA	33	14	9	7	1831	95	0	3.11	....	....	....	....	....	....	....
1992-93	Erie	ECHL	31	19	8	1	1762	134	0	4.56	5	2	3	300	24	0	4.80
1993-94	Binghamton	AHL	7	1	5	0	338	25	0	4.43	....	....	....	....	....	....	....
	Erie	ECHL	1	1	0	0	33	0	0	0.00	....	....	....	....	....	....	....

a CCHA Second All-Star Team (1991)

GOSSELIN, MARIO — HFD.

Goaltender. Catches left. 5'8", 160 lbs. Born, Thetford Mines, Que., June 15, 1963.
(Quebec's 3rd choice, 55th overall, in 1982 Entry Draft).

			Regular Season								Playoffs						
Season	Club	Lea	GP	W	L	T	Mins	GA	SO	Avg	GP	W	L	Mins	GA	SO	Avg
1980-81	Shawinigan	QMJHL	21	4	9	0	907	75	0	4.96	1	0	0	20	2	0	6.00
1981-82a	Shawinigan	QMJHL	60	....	....	....	3404	230	0	4.05	14	....	....	788	58	0	4.42
1982-83	Shawinigan	QMJHL	46	32	9	1	2496	133	3	3.12	8	5	3	457	29	0	3.81
1983-84	Cdn. Olympic	....	36	....	....	....	2007	126	0	3.77	....	....	....	....	....	....	....
	Quebec	**NHL**	**3**	**2**	**0**	**0**	**148**	**3**	**1**	**1.21**	....	....	....	....	....	....	....
1984-85	**Quebec**	**NHL**	**35**	**19**	**10**	**3**	**1960**	**109**	**1**	**3.34**	**17**	**9**	**8**	**1059**	**54**	**0**	**3.06**
1985-86	**Quebec**	**NHL**	**31**	**14**	**14**	**1**	**1726**	**111**	**2**	**3.86**	**1**	**0**	**1**	**40**	**5**	**0**	**7.50**
	Fredericton	AHL	5	2	2	1	304	15	0	2.96	....	....	....	....	....	....	....
1986-87	**Quebec**	**NHL**	**30**	**13**	**11**	**1**	**1625**	**86**	**0**	**3.18**	**11**	**7**	**4**	**654**	**37**	**0**	**3.39**
1987-88	**Quebec**	**NHL**	**54**	**20**	**28**	**4**	**3002**	**189**	**2**	**3.78**	....	....	....	....	....	....	....
1988-89	**Quebec**	**NHL**	**39**	**11**	**19**	**3**	**2064**	**146**	**0**	**4.24**	....	....	....	....	....	....	....
	Halifax	AHL	3	3	0	0	183	9	0	2.95	....	....	....	....	....	....	....
1989-90	**Los Angeles**	**NHL**	**26**	**7**	**11**	**1**	**1226**	**79**	**0**	**3.87**	**3**	**0**	**2**	**63**	**3**	**0**	**2.90**
1990-91	Phoenix	IHL	46	24	15	4	2673	172	1	3.86	11	7	4	670	43	0	3.83
1991-92	Springfield	AHL	47	28	11	5	2606	142	0	3.27	6	1	4	319	18	0	3.39
1992-93	**Hartford**	**NHL**	**16**	**5**	**9**	**1**	**867**	**57**	**0**	**3.94**	....	....	....	....	....	....	....
	Springfield	AHL	23	8	7	7	1345	75	0	3.35	....	....	....	....	....	....	....
1993-94	**Hartford**	**NHL**	**7**	**0**	**4**	**0**	**239**	**21**	**0**	**5.27**	....	....	....	....	....	....	....
	Springfield	AHL	2	2	0	0	120	5	0	2.50	....	....	....	....	....	....	....
	NHL Totals		**241**	**91**	**106**	**14**	**12857**	**801**	**6**	**3.74**	**32**	**16**	**15**	**1816**	**99**	**0**	**3.27**

a QMJHL Second All-Star Team (1982)

Played in NHL All-Star Game (1986)

Signed as a free agent by **Los Angeles**, June 14, 1989. Signed as a free agent by **Hartford**, September 4, 1991.

GOVERDE, DAVID

Goaltender. Catches right. 6', 210 lbs. Born, Toronto, Ont., April 9, 1970.
(Los Angeles' 4th choice, 91st overall, in 1990 Entry Draft).

			Regular Season								Playoffs						
Season	Club	Lea	GP	W	L	T	Mins	GA	SO	Avg	GP	W	L	Mins	GA	SO	Avg
1989-90	Sudbury	OHL	52	28	12	7	2941	182	0	3.71	7	3	3	394	25	0	3.81
1990-91	Phoenix	IHL	40	11	19	5	2007	137	0	4.10	....	....	....	....	....	....	....
1991-92	**Los Angeles**	**NHL**	**2**	**1**	**1**	**0**	**120**	**9**	**0**	**4.50**	....	....	....	....	....	....	....
	Phoenix	IHL	35	11	19	3	1951	129	1	3.97	....	....	....	....	....	....	....
	New Haven	AHL	5	1	3	0	248	17	0	4.11	....	....	....	....	....	....	....
1992-93	**Los Angeles**	**NHL**	**2**	**0**	**2**	**0**	**98**	**13**	**0**	**7.96**	....	....	....	....	....	....	....
	Phoenix	IHL	45	18	21	3	2569	173	1	4.04	....	....	....	....	....	....	....
1993-94	**Los Angeles**	**NHL**	**1**	**0**	**1**	**0**	**60**	**7**	**0**	**7.00**	....	....	....	....	....	....	....
	Portland	AHL	1	0	0	0	59	4	0	4.01	....	....	....	....	....	....	....
	Peoria	IHL	5	4	1	0	299	13	0	2.61	1	0	1	59	7	0	7.05
	NHL Totals		**5**	**1**	**4**	**0**	**278**	**29**	**0**	**6.26**	....	....	....	....	....	....	....

GREENLAY, MIKE — T.B.

Goaltender. Catches left. 6'3", 200 lbs. Born, Vitoria, Brazil, September 15, 1968.
(Edmonton's 9th choice, 189th overall, in 1986 Entry Draft).

			Regular Season								Playoffs						
Season	Club	Lea	GP	W	L	T	Mins	GA	SO	Avg	GP	W	L	Mins	GA	SO	Avg
1986-87	Lake Superior	CCHA	17	7	5	0	744	44	0	3.54	....	....	....	....	....	....	....
1987-88	Lake Superior	CCHA	19	10	3	3	1023	57	0	3.34	....	....	....	....	....	....	....
1988-89a	Saskatoon	WHL	20	10	8	1	1128	86	0	4.57	6	2	0	174	16	0	5.52
	Lake Superior	CCHA	2	1	1	0	85	6	0	4.23	....	....	....	....	....	....	....
1989-90	**Edmonton**	**NHL**	**2**	**0**	**0**	**0**	**20**	**4**	**0**	**12.00**	....	....	....	....	....	....	....
	Cape Breton	AHL	46	19	18	5	2595	146	2	3.38	5	1	3	306	26	0	5.09
1990-91	Cape Breton	AHL	11	5	2	0	493	33	0	4.02	....	....	....	....	....	....	....
	Knoxville	ECHL	29	17	9	2	1725	108	2	3.75	....	....	....	....	....	....	....
1991-92	Cape Breton	AHL	3	1	1	1	144	12	0	5.00	....	....	....	....	....	....	....
	Knoxville	ECHL	27	8	12	2	1415	113	0	4.79	....	....	....	....	....	....	....
1992-93	Louisville	ECHL	27	12	11	2	1437	96	1	4.01	....	....	....	....	....	....	....
	Atlanta	IHL	12	5	3	2	637	40	0	3.77	....	....	....	....	....	....	....
1993-94b	Atlanta	IHL	34	16	10	4	1741	104	0	3.58	13	*11	1	749	29	*1	*2.32
	NHL Totals		**2**	**0**	**0**	**0**	**20**	**4**	**0**	**12.00**	....	....	....	....	....	....	....

a Won Hap Emms Memorial Trophy (Memorial Cup Tournament Top Goaltender)
b Shared James Norris Memorial Trophy (fewest goals-against - IHL) with J.C. Bergeron (1994)

Signed as a free agent by **Tampa Bay**, July 29, 1992.

HACKETT, JEFF — CHI.

Goaltender. Catches left. 6'1", 180 lbs. Born, London, Ont., June 1, 1968.
(NY Islanders' 2nd choice, 34th overall, in 1987 Entry Draft).

			Regular Season								Playoffs						
Season	Club	Lea	GP	W	L	T	Mins	GA	SO	Avg	GP	W	L	Mins	GA	SO	Avg
1986-87	Oshawa	OHL	31	18	9	2	1672	85	2	3.05	15	8	7	895	40	0	2.68
1987-88	Oshawa	OHL	53	30	21	2	3165	205	0	3.89	7	3	4	438	31	0	4.25
1988-89	**NY Islanders**	**NHL**	**13**	**4**	**7**	**0**	**662**	**39**	**0**	**3.53**	....	....	....	....	....	....	....
	Springfield	AHL	29	12	14	2	1677	116	0	4.15	....	....	....	....	....	....	....
1989-90a	Springfield	AHL	54	24	25	3	3045	187	1	3.68	*17	*10	5	934	60	0	3.85
1990-91	**NY Islanders**	**NHL**	**30**	**5**	**18**	**1**	**1508**	**91**	**0**	**3.62**	....	....	....	....	....	....	....
1991-92	**San Jose**	**NHL**	**42**	**11**	**27**	**1**	**2314**	**148**	**0**	**3.84**	....	....	....	....	....	....	....
1992-93	**San Jose**	**NHL**	**36**	**2**	**30**	**1**	**2000**	**176**	**0**	**5.28**	....	....	....	....	....	....	....
1993-94	**Chicago**	**NHL**	**22**	**2**	**12**	**3**	**1084**	**62**	**0**	**3.43**	....	....	....	....	....	....	....
	NHL Totals		**143**	**24**	**94**	**6**	**7568**	**516**	**0**	**4.09**	....	....	....	....	....	....	....

a Won Jack Butterfield Trophy (Playoff MVP - AHL) (1990)

Claimed by **San Jose** from **NY Islanders** in Expansion Draft, May 30, 1991. Traded to **Chicago** by **San Jose** for Chicago's third round choice (Alexei Yegorov) in 1994 Entry Draft, July 13, 1993.

HALTIA, PATRIK — (HAHL-tih-ah) CGY.

Goaltender. Catches left. 6'1", 176 lbs. Born, Karlstad, Sweden, March 29, 1973.
(Calgary's 8th choice, 149th overall, in 1994 Entry Draft).

			Regular Season								Playoffs						
Season	Club	Lea	GP	W	L	T	Mins	GA	SO	Avg	GP	W	L	Mins	GA	SO	Avg
1993-94	Grums	Swe. 2								UNAVAILABLE							

HASEK, DOMINIK — (HAH-shihk) BUF.

Goaltender. Catches left. 5'11", 165 lbs. Born, Pardubice, Czech., January 29, 1965.
(Chicago's 11th choice, 199th overall, in 1983 Entry Draft).

			Regular Season								Playoffs						
Season	Club	Lea	GP	W	L	T	Mins	GA	SO	Avg	GP	W	L	Mins	GA	SO	Avg
1981-82	Pardubice	Czech.	12	....	....	....	661	34	....	3.09	....	....	....	....	....	....	....
1982-83	Pardubice	Czech.	42	....	....	....	2358	105	....	2.67	....	....	....	....	....	....	....
1983-84	Pardubice	Czech.	40	....	....	....	2304	108	....	2.81	....	....	....	....	....	....	....
1984-85	Pardubice	Czech.	42	....	....	....	2419	131	....	3.25	....	....	....	....	....	....	....
1985-86a	Pardubice	Czech.	45	....	....	....	2689	138	....	3.08	....	....	....	....	....	....	....
1986-87ab	Pardubice	Czech.	43	....	....	....	2515	103	....	2.46	....	....	....	....	....	....	....
1987-88ac	Pardubice	Czech.	31	....	....	....	1862	93	....	3.00	....	....	....	....	....	....	....
1988-89abc	Pardubice	Czech.	42	....	....	....	2507	114	....	2.73	....	....	....	....	....	....	....
1989-90abc	Dukla Jihlava	Czech.	40	....	....	....	2251	80	....	2.13	....	....	....	....	....	....	....
1990-91	**Chicago**	**NHL**	**5**	**3**	**0**	**1**	**195**	**8**	**0**	**2.46**	**3**	**0**	**0**	**69**	**3**	**0**	**2.61**
d	Indianapolis	IHL	33	20	11	1	1903	80	*5	*2.52	1	1	0	60	3	0	3.00
1991-92e	**Chicago**	**NHL**	**20**	**10**	**4**	**1**	**1014**	**44**	**1**	**2.60**	**3**	**0**	**2**	**158**	**8**	**0**	**3.04**
	Indianapolis	IHL	20	7	10	3	1162	69	1	3.56	....	....	....	....	....	....	....
1992-93	**Buffalo**	**NHL**	**28**	**11**	**10**	**4**	**1429**	**75**	**0**	**3.15**	**1**	**1**	**0**	**45**	**1**	**0**	**1.33**
1993-94fgh	**Buffalo**	**NHL**	**58**	**30**	**20**	**6**	**3358**	**109**	***7**	***1.95**	**7**	**3**	**4**	**484**	**13**	**2**	***1.61**
	NHL Totals		**111**	**54**	**34**	**12**	**5996**	**236**	**8**	**2.36**	**14**	**4**	**6**	**756**	**25**	**2**	**1.98**

a Czechoslovakian Goaltender-of-the-Year (1986, 1987, 1988, 1989, 1990)
b Czechoslovakian Player-of-the-Year (1987, 1989, 1990)
c Czechoslovakian First-Team All-Star (1988, 1989, 1990)
d IHL First All-Star Team (1991)
e NHL/Upper Deck All-Rookie Team (1992)
f NHL First All-Star Team (1994)
g Won Vezina Trophy (1994)
h Shared William M. Jennings Trophy with Grant Fuhr (1994)

Traded to **Buffalo** by **Chicago** for Stephane Beauregard and Buffalo's fourth round choice (Eric Daze) in 1993 Entry Draft, August 7, 1992.

HEALY, GLENN — NYR

Goaltender. Catches left. 5'10", 183 lbs. Born, Pickering, Ont., August 23, 1962.

			Regular Season								Playoffs						
Season	Club	Lea	GP	W	L	T	Mins	GA	SO	Avg	GP	W	L	Mins	GA	SO	Avg
1981-82	W. Michigan	CCHA	27	7	19	1	1569	116	0	4.44	....	....	....	....	....	....	....
1982-83	W. Michigan	CCHA	30	8	19	2	1732	116	0	4.01	....	....	....	....	....	....	....
1983-84	W. Michigan	CCHA	38	19	16	3	2241	146	0	3.90	....	....	....	....	....	....	....
1984-85	W. Michigan	CCHA	37	21	14	2	2171	118	0	3.26	....	....	....	....	....	....	....
1985-86	**Los Angeles**	**NHL**	**1**	**0**	**0**	**0**	**51**	**6**	**0**	**7.06**	....	....	....	....	....	....	....
	New Haven	AHL	43	21	15	4	2410	160	0	3.98	2	0	2	49	11	0	5.55
1986-87	New Haven	AHL	47	21	15	0	2828	173	1	3.67	7	3	4	427	19	0	2.67
1987-88	**Los Angeles**	**NHL**	**34**	**12**	**18**	**1**	**1869**	**135**	**1**	**4.33**	**4**	**1**	**3**	**240**	**20**	**0**	**5.00**
1988-89	**Los Angeles**	**NHL**	**48**	**25**	**19**	**2**	**2699**	**192**	**0**	**4.27**	**3**	**0**	**1**	**97**	**6**	**0**	**3.71**
1989-90	**NY Islanders**	**NHL**	**39**	**12**	**19**	**6**	**2197**	**128**	**2**	**3.50**	**4**	**1**	**2**	**166**	**9**	**0**	**3.25**
1990-91	**NY Islanders**	**NHL**	**53**	**18**	**24**	**9**	**2999**	**166**	**0**	**3.32**	....	....	....	....	....	....	....
1991-92	**NY Islanders**	**NHL**	**37**	**14**	**16**	**4**	**1960**	**124**	**1**	**3.80**	....	....	....	....	....	....	....
1992-93	**NY Islanders**	**NHL**	**47**	**22**	**20**	**2**	**2655**	**146**	**1**	**3.30**	**18**	**9**	**8**	**1109**	**59**	**0**	**3.19**
1993-94	**NY Rangers**	**NHL**	**29**	**10**	**12**	**2**	**1368**	**69**	**2**	**3.03**	**2**	**0**	**0**	**68**	**1**	**0**	**0.88**
	NHL Totals		**288**	**113**	**128**	**26**	**15798**	**966**	**7**	**3.67**	**31**	**11**	**14**	**1680**	**95**	**0**	**3.39**

Signed as a free agent by **Los Angeles**, June 13, 1985. Signed as a free agent by **NY Islanders**, August 16, 1989. Claimed by **Anaheim** from **NY Islanders** in Expansion Draft, June 24, 1993. Claimed by **Tampa Bay** from **Anaheim** in Phase II of Expansion Draft, June 25, 1993. Traded to **NY Rangers** by **Tampa Bay** for Tampa Bay's third round choice (previously acquired by NY Rangers — Tampa Bay selected Allan Egeland) in 1993 Entry Draft, June 25, 1993.

HEBERT, GUY — (ay-BAIR, GEE) — ANA.

Goaltender. Catches left. 5'11", 185 lbs. Born, Troy, NY, January 7, 1967.
(St. Louis' 8th choice, 159th overall, in 1987 Entry Draft).

			Regular Season								Playoffs						
Season	**Club**	**Lea**	**GP**	**W**	**L**	**T**	**Mins**	**GA**	**SO**	**Avg**	**GP**	**W**	**L**	**Mins**	**GA**	**SO**	**Avg**
1985-86	Hamilton Coll.	NCAA	18	4	12	2	1011	69	2	4.09	....	....	....	....	....	....	....
1986-87	Hamilton Coll.	NCAA	18	12	5	0	1070	40	3	2.19	2	1	1	134	6	0	2.69
1987-88	Hamilton Coll.	NCAA	9	5	3	0	510	22	1	2.58	1	0	1	60	3	0	3.00
1988-89	Hamilton Coll.	NCAA	25	18	7	0	1454	62	2	2.56	2	1	1	126	4	0	1.90
1989-90	Peoria	IHL	30	7	13	7	1706	124	1	4.36	2	0	1	76	5	0	3.95
1990-91a	Peoria	IHL	36	24	10	1	2093	100	2	2.87	8	3	4	458	32	0	4.19
1991-92	**St. Louis**	**NHL**	**13**	**5**	**5**	**1**	**738**	**36**	**0**	**2.93**	....	....	....	....	....	....	....
	Peoria	IHL	29	20	9	0	1731	98	0	3.40	4	3	1	239	9	0	2.26
1992-93	**St. Louis**	**NHL**	**24**	**8**	**8**	**2**	**1210**	**74**	**1**	**3.67**	**1**	**0**	**0**	**2**	**0**	**0**	**0.00**
1993-94	**Anaheim**	**NHL**	**52**	**20**	**27**	**3**	**2991**	**141**	**2**	**2.83**	....	....	....	....	....	....	....
	NHL Totals		**89**	**33**	**40**	**6**	**4939**	**251**	**3**	**3.05**	**1**	**0**	**0**	**2**	**0**	**0**	**0.00**

a IHL Second All-Star Team (1991)

Claimed by **Anaheim** from **St. Louis** in Expansion Draft, June 24, 1993.

HEINKE, MICHAEL — N.J.

Goaltender. Catches left. 5'11", 165 lbs. Born, Denville, NY, January 11, 1971.
(New Jersey's 5th choice, 89th overall, in 1989 Entry Draft).

			Regular Season								Playoffs						
Season	**Club**	**Lea**	**GP**	**W**	**L**	**T**	**Mins**	**GA**	**SO**	**Avg**	**GP**	**W**	**L**	**Mins**	**GA**	**SO**	**Avg**
1990-91	Providence	H.E.	14	8	7	1	923	74	0	4.81	....	....	....	....	....	....	....
1991-92	Providence	H.E.	16	10	4	0	816	48	*2	3.53	....	....	....	....	....	....	....
1992-93	N. Hampshire	H.E.	DID NOT PLAY														
1993-94	N. Hampshire	H.E.	22	11	5	2	1116	67	1	3.60	....	....	....	....	....	....	....

HERLOFSKY, DEREK — DAL.

Goaltender. Catches left. 6', 160 lbs. Born, Minneapolis, MN, October 1, 1971.
(Minnesota's 9th choice, 184th overall, in 1991 Entry Draft).

			Regular Season								Playoffs						
Season	**Club**	**Lea**	**GP**	**W**	**L**	**T**	**Mins**	**GA**	**SO**	**Avg**	**GP**	**W**	**L**	**Mins**	**GA**	**SO**	**Avg**
1991-92	Boston U.	H.E.	9	7	1	1	537	22	0	2.46	....	....	....	....	....	....	....
1992-93	Boston U.	H.E.	19	12	5	1	1060	50	*3	2.83	....	....	....	....	....	....	....
1993-94a	Boston U.	H.E.	20	15	3	0	1056	44	*4	*2.50	....	....	....	....	....	....	....

a Hockey East Second All-Star Team (1994)

HEXTALL, RON — NYI

Goaltender. Catches left. 6'3", 192 lbs. Born, Brandon, Man., May 3, 1964.
(Philadelphia's 6th choice, 119th overall, in 1982 Entry Draft).

			Regular Season								Playoffs						
Season	**Club**	**Lea**	**GP**	**W**	**L**	**T**	**Mins**	**GA**	**SO**	**Avg**	**GP**	**W**	**L**	**Mins**	**GA**	**SO**	**Avg**
1981-82	Brandon	WHL	30	12	11	0	1398	133	0	5.71	3	0	2	103	16	0	9.32
1982-83	Brandon	WHL	44	13	30	0	2589	249	0	5.77	....	....	....	....	....	....	....
1983-84	Brandon	WHL	46	29	13	2	2670	190	0	4.27	10	5	5	592	37	0	3.75
1984-85	Hershey	AHL	11	4	6	0	555	34	0	3.68	....	....	....	....	....	....	....
	Kalamazoo	IHL	19	6	11	1	1103	80	0	4.35	....	....	....	....	....	....	....
1985-86ab	Hershey	AHL	*53	30	19	2	*3061	174	*5	3.41	13	5	7	780	42	*1	3.23
1986-87 cdef	**Philadelphia**	**NHL**	***66**	**37**	**21**	**6**	***3799**	**190**	**1**	**3.00**	***26**	**15**	**11**	***1540**	**71**	***2**	**2.77**
1987-88g	**Philadelphia**	**NHL**	**62**	**30**	**22**	**7**	**3561**	**208**	**0**	**3.51**	**7**	**2**	**4**	**379**	**30**	**0**	**4.75**
1988-89h	**Philadelphia**	**NHL**	***64**	**30**	**28**	**6**	***3756**	**202**	**0**	**3.23**	**15**	**8**	**7**	**886**	**49**	**0**	**3.32**
1989-90	**Philadelphia**	**NHL**	**8**	**4**	**2**	**1**	**419**	**29**	**0**	**4.15**	....	....	....	....	....	....	....
	Hershey	AHL	1	1	0	0	49	3	0	3.67	....	....	....	....	....	....	....
1990-91	**Philadelphia**	**NHL**	**36**	**13**	**16**	**5**	**2035**	**106**	**0**	**3.13**	....	....	....	....	....	....	....
1991-92	**Philadelphia**	**NHL**	**45**	**16**	**21**	**6**	**2668**	**151**	**3**	**3.40**	....	....	....	....	....	....	....
1992-93	**Quebec**	**NHL**	**54**	**29**	**16**	**5**	**2988**	**172**	**0**	**3.45**	**6**	**2**	**4**	**372**	**18**	**0**	**2.90**
1993-94	**NY Islanders**	**NHL**	**65**	**27**	**26**	**6**	**3581**	**184**	**5**	**3.08**	**3**	**0**	**3**	**158**	**16**	**0**	**6.08**
	NHL Totals		**400**	**186**	**152**	**42**	**22807**	**1242**	**9**	**3.27**	**57**	**27**	**29**	**3335**	**184**	**2**	**3.31**

a AHL First All-Star Team (1986)
b AHL Rookie of the Year (1986)
c NHL First All-Star Team (1987)
d Won Vezina Trophy (1987)
e Won Conn Smythe Trophy (1987)
f NHL All-Rookie Team (1987)
g Scored a goal vs. Boston, December 8, 1987
h Scored a goal in playoffs vs. Washington, April 11, 1989

Played in NHL All-Star Game (1988)

Traded to **Quebec** by **Philadelphia** with Peter Forsberg, Steve Duchesne, Kerry Huffman, Mike Ricci, Chris Simon, Philadelphia's first choice in the 1993 (Jocelyn Thibault) and 1994 (later traded to Toronto — later traded to Washington — Washington selected Nolan Baumgartner) Entry Drafts and cash for Eric Lindros, June 30, 1992. Traded to **NY Islanders** by **Quebec** with Quebec's first round choice (Todd Bertuzzi) in 1993 Entry Draft for Mark Fitzpatrick and NY Islanders' first round choice (Adam Deadmarsh) in 1993 Entry Draft, June 20, 1993.

HILLEBRANDT, JON — NYR

Goaltender. Catches left. 5'10", 160 lbs. Born, Cottage Grove, WI, December 18, 1971.
(NY Rangers' 12th choice, 202nd overall, in 1990 Entry Draft).

			Regular Season								Playoffs						
Season	**Club**	**Lea**	**GP**	**W**	**L**	**T**	**Mins**	**GA**	**SO**	**Avg**	**GP**	**W**	**L**	**Mins**	**GA**	**SO**	**Avg**
1991-92a	Ill.-Chicago	CCHA	31	7	19	....	1754	121	0	4.14	....	....	....	....	....	....	....
1992-93	Ill.-Chicago	CCHA	33	8	22	2	1783	134	0	4.51	....	....	....	....	....	....	....
1993-94	U.S. National	....	2	....	....	....	120	10	0	5.00	....	....	....	....	....	....	....
	Binghamton	AHL	7	1	3	0	294	18	0	3.67	....	....	....	....	....	....	....
	Erie	ECHL	3	2	0	1	189	8	1	2.53	....	....	....	....	....	....	....

a CCHA Second All-Star Team (1992)

HIRSCH, COREY — (HUHRSH) — NYR

Goaltender. Catches left. 5'10", 160 lbs. Born, Medicine Hat, Alta., July 1, 1972.
(NY Rangers' 8th choice, 169th overall, in 1991 Entry Draft).

			Regular Season								Playoffs						
Season	**Club**	**Lea**	**GP**	**W**	**L**	**T**	**Mins**	**GA**	**SO**	**Avg**	**GP**	**W**	**L**	**Mins**	**GA**	**SO**	**Avg**
1988-89	Kamloops	WHL	32	11	12	2	1516	106	....	4.20	5	3	2	....	....	....	4.65
1989-90	Kamloops	WHL	*63	*48	13	0	3608	230	*3	3.82	*17	*14	3	*1043	60	0	*3.45
1990-91a	Kamloops	WHL	38	26	7	1	1970	100	3	*3.05	11	5	6	623	42	....	4.04
1991-92 abcd	Kamloops	WHL	48	35	10	2	2732	124	*5	*2.72	*16	*11	5	954	35	*2	*2.20
1992-93	**NY Rangers**	**NHL**	**4**	**1**	**2**	**1**	**224**	**14**	**0**	**3.75**	....	....	....	....	....	....	....
efg	Binghamton	AHL	46	*35	4	5	2692	125	1	*2.79	14	7	7	831	46	0	3.32
1993-94	Cdn. National	....	45	24	17	3	2653	124	0	2.80	....	....	....	....	....	....	....
	Cdn. Olympic	....	8	5	2	1	495	17	0	2.06	....	....	....	....	....	....	....
	Binghamton	AHL	10	5	4	1	610	38	0	3.73	....	....	....	....	....	....	....
	NHL Totals		**4**	**1**	**2**	**1**	**224**	**14**	**0**	**3.75**	....	....	....	....	....	....	....

a WHL West First All-Star Team (1991, 1992)
b Canadian Major Junior Goaltender of the Year (1992)
c Memorial Cup All-Star Team (1992)
d Won Hap Emms Memorial Trophy (Memorial Cup Tournament Top Goaltender) (1992)
e Won Dudley "Red" Garrett Memorial Trophy (Top Rookie - AHL) (1993)
f Shared Harry "Hap" Holmes Memorial Trophy (fewest goals-against - AHL) with Boris Rousson (1993)
g AHL First All-Star Team (1993)

HNILICKA, MILAN — (hih-LEECH-kah, MEE-lahn) — NYI

Goaltender. Catches left. 6', 180 lbs. Born, Litomerice, Czech., June 25, 1973.
(NY Islanders' 4th choice, 70th overall, in 1991 Entry Draft).

			Regular Season								Playoffs						
Season	**Club**	**Lea**	**GP**	**W**	**L**	**T**	**Mins**	**GA**	**SO**	**Avg**	**GP**	**W**	**L**	**Mins**	**GA**	**SO**	**Avg**
1989-90	Kladno	Czech.	24	....	....	....	1113	70	....	3.77	....	....	....	....	....	....	....
1990-91	Kladno	Czech.	40	....	....	....	2122	98	0	2.80	....	....	....	....	....	....	....
1991-92	Kladno	Czech.	38	....	....	....	2066	128	0	3.73	....	....	....	....	....	....	....
1992-93	Swift Current	WHL	*65	*46	12	2	3679	206	2	3.36	*17	*12	5	*1017	54	*2	3.19
1993-94	Richmond	ECHL	43	18	16	5	2299	155	4	4.05	....	....	....	....	....	....	....
	Salt Lake	IHL	8	5	1	0	378	25	0	3.97	....	....	....	....	....	....	....

HODSON, KEVIN — DET.

Goaltender. Catches left. 6', 178 lbs. Born, Winnipeg, Man., March 27, 1972.

			Regular Season								Playoffs						
Season	**Club**	**Lea**	**GP**	**W**	**L**	**T**	**Mins**	**GA**	**SO**	**Avg**	**GP**	**W**	**L**	**Mins**	**GA**	**SO**	**Avg**
1990-91	S.S. Marie	OHL	30	18	11	0	1638	88	0	*3.22	10	*9	1	581	28	0	*2.89
1991-92	S.S. Marie	OHL	50	28	12	4	2722	151	0	3.33	18	12	6	1116	54	1	2.90
1992-93ab	S.S. Marie	OHL	26	18	5	2	1470	76	1	*3.10	14	11	2	755	34	0	2.70
	Indianapolis	IHL	14	5	9	0	777	53	0	4.09	....	....	....	....	....	....	....
1993-94	Adirondack	AHL	37	20	10	5	2082	102	2	2.94	3	0	2	89	10	0	6.77

a Memorial Cup All-Star Team (1993)
b Won Hap Emms Memorial Trophy (Memorial Cup Tournament Top Goaltender) (1993)

Signed as a free agent by **Chicago**, August 17, 1992. Signed as a free agent by **Detroit**, June 16, 1993.

HRIVNAK, JIM — (RIV-NAK) — ST.L.

Goaltender. Catches left. 6'2", 195 lbs. Born, Montreal, Que., May 28, 1968.
(Washington's 4th choice, 61st overall, in 1986 Entry Draft).

			Regular Season								Playoffs						
Season	**Club**	**Lea**	**GP**	**W**	**L**	**T**	**Mins**	**GA**	**SO**	**Avg**	**GP**	**W**	**L**	**Mins**	**GA**	**SO**	**Avg**
1985-86	Merrimack	NCAA	21	12	8	0	1230	75	0	3.66	....	....	....	....	....	....	....
1986-87	Merrimack	NCAA	34	27	7	0	1618	58	3	2.14	....	....	....	....	....	....	....
1987-88	Merrimack	NCAA	37	31	6	0	2119	84	4	2.38	....	....	....	....	....	....	....
1988-89	Merrimack	NCAA	22	....	....	....	1295	52	4	2.41	....	....	....	....	....	....	....
	Baltimore	AHL	10	1	8	0	502	55	0	6.57	....	....	....	....	....	....	....
1989-90	**Washington**	**NHL**	**11**	**5**	**5**	**0**	**609**	**36**	**0**	**3.55**	....	....	....	....	....	....	....
a	Baltimore	AHL	47	24	19	2	2722	139	*4	3.06	6	4	2	360	19	0	3.17
1990-91	**Washington**	**NHL**	**9**	**4**	**2**	**1**	**432**	**26**	**0**	**3.61**	....	....	....	....	....	....	....
	Baltimore	AHL	42	20	16	6	2481	134	1	3.24	6	2	3	324	21	0	3.89
1991-92	**Washington**	**NHL**	**12**	**6**	**3**	**0**	**605**	**35**	**0**	**3.47**	....	....	....	....	....	....	....
	Baltimore	AHL	22	10	8	3	1303	73	0	3.36	....	....	....	....	....	....	....
1992-93	**Washington**	**NHL**	**27**	**13**	**9**	**2**	**1421**	**83**	**0**	**3.50**	....	....	....	....	....	....	....
	Winnipeg	**NHL**	**3**	**2**	**1**	**0**	**180**	**13**	**0**	**4.33**	....	....	....	....	....	....	....
1993-94	**St. Louis**	**NHL**	**23**	**4**	**10**	**0**	**970**	**69**	**0**	**4.27**	....	....	....	....	....	....	....
	NHL Totals		**85**	**34**	**30**	**3**	**4217**	**262**	**0**	**3.73**	....	....	....	....	....	....	....

a AHL Second All-Star Team (1990)

Traded to **Winnipeg** by **Washington** with Washington's second round choice (Alexei Budayev) in 1993 Entry Draft for Rick Tabaracci, March 22, 1993. Traded to **St. Louis** by **Winnipeg** for St. Louis' seventh round choice (later traded to Florida — later traded to Edmonton — later traded to Winnipeg — Winnipeg selected Chris Kibermanis) in 1994 Entry Draft and future considerations, July 29, 1993.

HRUDEY, KELLY — (ROO-dee) — L.A.

Goaltender. Catches left. 5'10", 189 lbs. Born, Edmonton, Alta., January 13, 1961.
(NY Islanders' 2nd choice, 38th overall, in 1980 Entry Draft).

			Regular Season								Playoffs						
Season	**Club**	**Lea**	**GP**	**W**	**L**	**T**	**Mins**	**GA**	**SO**	**Avg**	**GP**	**W**	**L**	**Mins**	**GA**	**SO**	**Avg**
1978-79	Medicine Hat	WHL	57	12	34	7	3093	318	0	6.17	....	....	....	....	....	....	....
1979-80	Medicine Hat	WHL	57	25	23	4	3049	212	1	4.17	13	6	6	638	48	0	4.51
1980-81a	Medicine Hat	WHL	55	32	19	1	3023	200	4	3.97	4	....	....	244	17	0	4.18
	Indianapolis	CHL	....	....	....	....	....	....	....	....	2	....	....	135	8	0	3.56
1981-82bc	Indianapolis	CHL	51	27	19	4	3033	149	1	*2.95	13	11	2	842	34	*1	*2.42
1982-83bcd	Indianapolis	CHL	47	*26	17	1	2744	139	2	3.04	10	*7	3	*637	28	0	*2.64
1983-84	**NY Islanders**	**NHL**	**12**	**7**	**2**	**0**	**535**	**28**	**0**	**3.14**	....	....	....	....	....	....	....
	Indianapolis	CHL	6	3	2	1	370	21	0	3.40	....	....	....	....	....	....	....
1984-85	**NY Islanders**	**NHL**	**41**	**19**	**17**	**3**	**2335**	**141**	**2**	**3.62**	**5**	**1**	**3**	**281**	**8**	**0**	**1.71**
1985-86	**NY Islanders**	**NHL**	**45**	**19**	**15**	**8**	**2563**	**137**	**1**	**3.21**	**2**	**0**	**2**	**120**	**6**	**0**	**3.00**
1986-87	**NY Islanders**	**NHL**	**46**	**21**	**15**	**7**	**2634**	**145**	**0**	**3.30**	**14**	**7**	**7**	**842**	**38**	**0**	**2.71**
1987-88	**NY Islanders**	**NHL**	**47**	**22**	**17**	**5**	**2751**	**153**	**3**	**3.34**	**6**	**2**	**4**	**381**	**23**	**0**	**3.62**
1988-89	**NY Islanders**	**NHL**	**50**	**18**	**24**	**3**	**2800**	**183**	**0**	**3.92**	....	....	....	....	....	....	....
	Los Angeles	**NHL**	**16**	**10**	**4**	**2**	**974**	**47**	**1**	**2.90**	**10**	**4**	**6**	**566**	**35**	**0**	**3.71**
1989-90	**Los Angeles**	**NHL**	**52**	**22**	**21**	**6**	**2860**	**194**	**2**	**4.07**	**9**	**4**	**4**	**539**	**39**	**0**	**4.34**
1990-91	**Los Angeles**	**NHL**	**47**	**26**	**13**	**6**	**2730**	**132**	**3**	**2.90**	**12**	**6**	**6**	**798**	**37**	**0**	**2.78**
1991-92	**Los Angeles**	**NHL**	**60**	**26**	**17**	**13**	**3509**	**197**	**1**	**3.37**	**6**	**2**	**4**	**355**	**22**	**0**	**3.72**
1992-93	**Los Angeles**	**NHL**	**50**	**18**	**21**	**6**	**2718**	**175**	**2**	**3.86**	**20**	**10**	**10**	**1261**	**74**	**0**	**3.52**
1993-94	**Los Angeles**	**NHL**	**64**	**22**	**31**	**7**	**3713**	**228**	**1**	**3.68**	....	....	....	....	....	....	....
	NHL Totals		**530**	**230**	**197**	**66**	**30122**	**1760**	**16**	**3.51**	**84**	**36**	**46**	**5143**	**282**	**0**	**3.29**

a WHL Second All-Star Team (1981)
b CHL First All-Star Team (1982, 1983)
c Shared Terry Sawchuk Trophy (Leading Goaltender - CHL) with Rob Holland (1982, 1983)
d Won Tommy Ivan Trophy (Most Valuable Player - CHL) (1983)

Traded to **Los Angeles** by **NY Islanders** for Mark Fitzpatrick, Wayne McBean and future considerations (Doug Crossman, May 23, 1989) February 22, 1989.

ING, PETER — DET.

Goaltender. Catches left. 6'2", 170 lbs. Born, Toronto, Ont., April 28, 1969.
(Toronto's 3rd choice, 48th overall, in 1988 Entry Draft).

			Regular Season								Playoffs						
Season	Club	Lea	GP	W	L	T	Mins	GA	SO	Avg	GP	W	L	Mins	GA	SO	Avg
1986-87	Windsor	OHL	28	13	11	3	1615	105	0	3.90	5	4	0	161	9	0	3.35
1987-88	Windsor	OHL	43	30	7	1	2422	125	2	3.10	3	2	0	225	7	0	1.87
1988-89	Windsor	OHL	19	7	7	3	1043	76	*1	4.37							
	London	OHL	32	18	11	2	1848	104	*2	3.38	21	11	9	1093	82	0	4.50
1989-90	**Toronto**	**NHL**	**3**	**0**	**2**	**1**	**182**	**18**	**0**	**5.93**							
	Newmarket	AHL	48	16	19	12	2829	184	0	3.90							
	London	OHL	8	6	2	0	480	27	0	3.38							
1990-91	**Toronto**	**NHL**	**56**	**16**	**29**	**8**	**3126**	**200**	**1**	**3.84**							
1991-92	**Edmonton**	**NHL**	**12**	**3**	**4**	**0**	**463**	**33**	**0**	**4.28**							
	Cape Breton	AHL	24	9	10	4	1411	92	0	3.91	1	0	1	60	9	0	9.00
1992-93	Detroit	ColHL	3	2	1	0	136	6	0	2.65							
	San Diego	IHL	17	11	4	1	882	53	0	3.61	4	2	2	183	13	0	4.26
1993-94	**Detroit**	**NHL**	**3**	**1**	**2**	**0**	**170**	**15**	**0**	**5.29**							
	Adirondack	AHL	7	3	3	1	425	26	1	3.67							
	Las Vegas	IHL	30	16	7	4	1627	91	0	3.36	2	0	1	40	4	0	5.87
	NHL Totals		**74**	**20**	**37**	**9**	**3941**	**266**	**1**	**4.05**							

Traded to **Edmonton** by **Toronto** with Vincent Damphousse, Scott Thornton, Luke Richardson, future considerations and cash for Grant Fuhr, Glenn Anderson and Craig Berube, September 19, 1991. Traded to **Detroit** by **Edmonton** for Detroit's seventh round choice (Chris Wickenheiser) in 1994 Entry Draft and future considerations, August 30, 1993.

IRBE, ARTURS — (UHR-bay, AHR-tuhrs) — S.J.

Goaltender. Catches left. 5'7", 180 lbs. Born, Riga, Latvia, February 2, 1967.
(Minnesota's 11th choice, 196th overall, in 1989 Entry Draft).

			Regular Season								Playoffs						
Season	Club	Lea	GP	W	L	T	Mins	GA	SO	Avg	GP	W	L	Mins	GA	SO	Avg
1986-87	Dynamo Riga	USSR	2				27	1	0	2.22							
1987-88a	Dynamo Riga	USSR	34				1870	86	4	2.69							
1988-89	Dynamo Riga	USSR	40				2460	116	4	2.85							
1989-90	Dynamo Riga	USSR	48				2880	115	2	2.42							
1990-91	Dynamo Riga	USSR	46				2713	133	5	2.94							
1991-92	**San Jose**	**NHL**	**13**	**2**	**6**	**3**	**645**	**48**	**0**	**4.47**							
bc	Kansas City	IHL	32	24	7	1	1955	80	0	*2.46	*15	*12	3	914	44	0	*2.89
1992-93	**San Jose**	**NHL**	**36**	**7**	**26**	**0**	**2074**	**142**	**1**	**4.11**							
	Kansas City	IHL	6	3	3	0	364	20	0	3.30							
1993-94	**San Jose**	**NHL**	***74**	**30**	**28**	**16**	***4412**	**209**	**3**	**2.84**	**14**	**7**	**7**	**806**	**50**	**0**	**3.72**
	NHL Totals		**123**	**39**	**60**	**19**	**7131**	**399**	**4**	**3.36**	**14**	**7**	**7**	**806**	**50**	**0**	**3.72**

a Soviet National League Rookie-of-the-Year (1988)
b IHL First All-Star Team (1992)
c Won James Norris Memorial Trophy (Top Goaltender - IHL) (1992)

Played in NHL All-Star Game (1994)

Claimed by **San Jose** from **Minnesota** in Dispersal Draft, May 30, 1991.

ISRAEL, AARON — PHI.

Goaltender. Catches left. 6'2", 176 lbs. Born, Boston, MA, June 4, 1973.
(Philadelphia's 6th choice, 166th overall, in 1993 Entry Draft).

			Regular Season								Playoffs						
Season	Club	Lea	GP	W	L	T	Mins	GA	SO	Avg	GP	W	L	Mins	GA	SO	Avg
1992-93	Harvard	ECAC	14	9	4	1	843	43	0	3.06							
1993-94a	Harvard	ECAC	18	12	2	2	1045	40	0	*2.30							

a NCAA Final Four All-Tournament Team (1994)

JABLONSKI, PAT — TOR.

Goaltender. Catches right. 6', 178 lbs. Born, Toledo, OH, June 20, 1967.
(St. Louis' 6th choice, 138th overall, in 1985 Entry Draft).

			Regular Season								Playoffs						
Season	Club	Lea	GP	W	L	T	Mins	GA	SO	Avg	GP	W	L	Mins	GA	SO	Avg
1985-86	Windsor	OHL	29	6	16	4	1600	119	1	4.46	6	0	3	263	20	0	4.56
1986-87	Windsor	OHL	41	22	14	2	2328	128	*3	3.30	12	8	4	710	38	0	3.21
1987-88	Peoria	IHL	5	2	2	1	285	17	0	3.58							
	Windsor	OHL	18	14	3	0	994	48	2	*2.90	9	*8	0	537	28	0	3.13
1988-89	Peoria	IHL	35	11	20	0	2051	163	1	4.77	3	0	2	130	13	0	6.00
1989-90	**St. Louis**	**NHL**	**4**	**0**	**3**	**0**	**208**	**17**	**0**	**4.90**							
	Peoria	IHL	36	14	17	4	2023	165	0	4.89	4	1	3	223	19	0	5.11
1990-91	**St. Louis**	**NHL**	**8**	**2**	**3**	**3**	**492**	**25**	**0**	**3.05**	**3**	**0**	**0**	**90**	**5**	**0**	**3.33**
	Peoria	IHL	29	23	3	2	1738	87	0	3.00	10	7	2	532	23	0	2.59
1991-92	**St. Louis**	**NHL**	**10**	**3**	**6**	**0**	**468**	**38**	**0**	**4.87**							
	Peoria	IHL	8	6	1	1	493	29	1	3.53							
1992-93	**Tampa Bay**	**NHL**	**43**	**8**	**24**	**4**	**2268**	**150**	**1**	**3.97**							
1993-94	**Tampa Bay**	**NHL**	**15**	**5**	**6**	**3**	**834**	**54**	**0**	**3.88**							
	St. John's	AHL	16	12	3	1	962	49	1	3.05	11	6	5	676	36	0	3.19
	NHL Totals		**80**	**18**	**42**	**10**	**4270**	**284**	**1**	**3.99**	**3**	**0**	**0**	**90**	**5**	**0**	**3.33**

Traded to **Tampa Bay** by **St. Louis** with Steve Tuttle and Darin Kimble for future considerations, June 19, 1992. Traded to **Toronto** by **Tampa Bay** for cash, February 21, 1994.

JAKS, PAULI — (YAHKS, POW-lee) — L.A.

Goaltender. Catches left. 6', 194 lbs. Born, Schaffhausen, Switz., January 25, 1972.
(Los Angeles' 5th choice, 108th overall, in 1991 Entry Draft).

			Regular Season								Playoffs						
Season	Club	Lea	GP	W	L	T	Mins	GA	SO	Avg	GP	W	L	Mins	GA	SO	Avg
1990-91	Ambri-Piotta	Switz.	22				1247	100	0	4.81							
1991-92	Ambri-Piotta	Switz.	33	25	7	1	1890	97	2	2.93							
1992-93	Ambri-Piotta	Switz.	29					92		3.17							
1993-94	Phoenix	IHL	33	16	13	1	1712	101	0	3.54							

JOSEPH, CURTIS — ST.L.

Goaltender. Catches left. 5'10", 182 lbs. Born, Keswick, Ont., April 29, 1967.

			Regular Season								Playoffs						
Season	Club	Lea	GP	W	L	T	Mins	GA	SO	Avg	GP	W	L	Mins	GA	SO	Avg
1988-89a	U. Wisconsin	WCHA	38	21	11	5	2267	94	1	2.49							
1989-90	**St. Louis**	**NHL**	**15**	**9**	**5**	**1**	**852**	**48**	**0**	**3.38**	**6**	**4**	**1**	**327**	**18**	**0**	**3.30**
	Peoria	IHL	23	10	8	2	1241	80	0	3.87							
1990-91	**St. Louis**	**NHL**	**30**	**16**	**10**	**2**	**1710**	**89**	**0**	**3.12**							
1991-92	**St. Louis**	**NHL**	**60**	**27**	**20**	**10**	**3494**	**175**	**2**	**3.01**	**6**	**2**	**4**	**379**	**23**	**0**	**3.64**
1992-93	**St. Louis**	**NHL**	**68**	**29**	**28**	**9**	**3890**	**196**	**1**	**3.02**	**11**	**7**	**4**	**715**	**27**	***2**	**2.27**
1993-94	**St. Louis**	**NHL**	**71**	**36**	**23**	**11**	**4127**	**213**	**1**	**3.10**	**4**	**0**	**4**	**246**	**15**	**0**	**3.66**
	NHL Totals		**244**	**117**	**86**	**33**	**14073**	**721**	**4**	**3.07**	**27**	**13**	**13**	**1667**	**83**	**2**	**2.99**

a WCHA First All-Star Team (1989)

Played in NHL All-Star Game (1994)

Signed as a free agent by **St. Louis**, June 16, 1989.

KETTERER, MARKUS — BUF.

Goaltender. Catches left. 5'11", 167 lbs. Born, Helsinki, Finland, August 23, 1967.
(Buffalo's 6th choice, 107th overall, in 1992 Entry Draft).

			Regular Season								Playoffs						
Season	Club	Lea	GP	W	L	T	Mins	GA	SO	Avg	GP	W	L	Mins	GA	SO	Avg
1987-88	Jokerit	Fin.	21					61	0								
1988-89	TPS	Fin.	34				2021	95	2	2.82	3			139	6	0	2.59
1989-90	TPS	Fin.	29				1709	68	1	2.38	7			422	15	1	2.13
1990-91	TPS	Fin.	36				2022	85	2	2.52	8			440	13	2	1.77
1991-92	Jokerit	Fin.	37				2128	97	1	2.73	10	7	3	634	20	3	1.89
1992-93	Jokerit	Fin.	37				2064	96	3	2.79	2	0	0	130	11	0	5.07
1993-94	Rochester	AHL	32	9	15	5	1774	110	1	3.72	4	0	3	199	13	0	3.92

KHABIBULIN, NIKOLAI — (khah-bee-BOO-lihn) — WPG.

Goaltender. Catches left. 6'1", 176 lbs. Born, Sverdlovsk, USSR, January 13, 1973.
(Winnipeg's 8th choice, 204th overall, in 1992 Entry Draft).

			Regular Season								Playoffs						
Season	Club	Lea	GP	W	L	T	Mins	GA	SO	Avg	GP	W	L	Mins	GA	SO	Avg
1988-89	Sverdlovsk	USSR	1				3	0	0	0.00							
1989-90	Sverdlovsk Jrs.	USSR	UNAVAILABLE														
1990-91	Sputnik	USSR 3	UNAVAILABLE														
1991-92	CSKA	CIS	2				34	2		3.52							
1992-93	CSKA	CIS	13				491	27		3.29							
1993-94	CSKA	CIS	46				2625	116		2.65	3			193	11		3.42
	Russian Pen's	IHL	12	2	7	2	639	47	0	4.41							

KIDD, TREVOR — CGY.

Goaltender. Catches left. 6'2", 190 lbs. Born, Dugald, Man., March 29, 1972.
(Calgary's 1st choice, 11th overall, in 1990 Entry Draft).

			Regular Season								Playoffs						
Season	Club	Lea	GP	W	L	T	Mins	GA	SO	Avg	GP	W	L	Mins	GA	SO	Avg
1988-89	Brandon	WHL	32				1509	102	0	4.06							
1989-90a	Brandon	WHL	*63	24	32	2	*3676	254	2	4.15							
1990-91	Brandon	WHL	30	10	19	1	1730	117	0	4.06							
	Spokane	WHL	14	8	3	0	749	44	0	3.52	15	*14	1	926	32	2	*2.07
1991-92	Cdn. National	....	28	18	4	4	1349	79	2	3.51							
	Cdn. Olympic	....	1	1	0	0	60	0	1	0.00							
	Calgary	**NHL**	**2**	**1**	**1**	**0**	**120**	**8**	**0**	**4.00**							
1992-93	Salt Lake	IHL	29	10	16	1	1696	111	1	3.93							
1993-94	**Calgary**	**NHL**	**31**	**13**	**7**	**6**	**1614**	**85**	**0**	**3.16**							
	NHL Totals		**33**	**14**	**8**	**6**	**1734**	**93**	**0**	**3.22**							

a WHL East First All-Star Team (1990)

KNICKLE, RICK — (kuh-NIHK-uhl)

Goaltender. Catches left. 5'10", 175 lbs. Born, Chatham, N.B., February 26, 1960.
(Buffalo's 7th choice, 116th overall, in 1979 Entry Draft).

			Regular Season								Playoffs						
Season	Club	Lea	GP	W	L	T	Mins	GA	SO	Avg	GP	W	L	Mins	GA	SO	Avg
1977-78	Brandon	WHL	49	34	5	7	2806	182	0	3.89	8			450	36	0	4.82
1978-79a	Brandon	WHL	38	26	3	8	2240	118	1	*3.16	16	12	3	886	41	*1	*2.78
1979-80	Brandon	WHL	33	11	14	1	1604	125	0	4.68							
	Muskegon	IHL	16				829	52	0	3.76	3			156	17	0	6.54
1980-81b	Erie	EHL	43				2347	125	1	*3.20	8			446	14	0	*1.88
1981-82	Rochester	AHL	31	10	12	5	1753	108	1	3.70	3	0	2	125	7	0	3.37
1982-83	Flint	IHL	27				1638	92	2	3.37	3			193	10	0	3.11
	Rochester	AHL	4				143	11	0	4.64							
1983-84c	Flint	IHL	60	32	21	5	3518	203	3	3.46	8	8	0	480	24	0	3.00
1984-85	Sherbrooke	AHL	14	7	6	0	780	53	0	4.08							
	Flint	IHL	36	18	11	3	2018	115	2	3.42	7	3	4	401	27	0	4.04
1985-86	Saginaw	IHL	39	16	15	0	2235	135	2	3.62	3	2	1	193	12	0	3.73
1986-87	Saginaw	IHL	26	9	13	0	1413	113	0	4.80	5	1	4	329	21	0	3.83
1987-88	Flint	IHL	1	0	1	0	60	4	0	4.00							
	Peoria	IHL	13	2	8	1	705	58	0	4.94	6	3	3	294	20	....	4.08
1988-89de	Fort Wayne	IHL	47	22	16	0	2716	141	1	*3.11	4	1	2	173	15	0	5.20
1989-90	Flint	IHL	55	25	24	1	2998	210	1	4.20	2	0	2	101	13	0	7.72
1990-91	Albany	IHL	14	4	6	2	679	52	0	4.59							
	Springfield	AHL	9	6	0	2	509	28	0	3.30							
1991-92c	San Diego	IHL	46	*28	13	4	2686	155	0	3.46	2	0	1	78	3	0	2.31
1992-93df	San Diego	IHL	41	33	4	4	2437	88	*4	*2.17							
	Los Angeles	**NHL**	**10**	**6**	**4**	**0**	**532**	**35**	**0**	**3.95**							
1993-94	**Los Angeles**	**NHL**	**4**	**1**	**2**	**0**	**174**	**9**	**0**	**3.10**							
	Phoenix	IHL	25	8	9	3	1292	89	1	4.13							
	NHL Totals		**14**	**7**	**6**	**0**	**706**	**44**	**0**	**3.74**							

a WHL First All-Star Team (1979)
b EHL First All-Star Team (1981)
c IHL Second All-Star Team (1984, 1992)
d IHL First All-Star Team (1989, 1993)
e Won James Norris Memorial Trophy (Top Goaltender - IHL) (1989)
f Shared James Norris Memorial Trophy (Top Goaltender - IHL) with Clint Malarchuk (1993)

Signed as a free agent by **Montreal**, February 8, 1985. Signed as a free agent by **Los Angeles**, February 16, 1993.

KOCHAN, DIETER — VAN.

Goaltender. Catches left. 6'1", 170 lbs. Born, Saskatoon, Sask., November 5, 1974.
(Vancouver's 3rd choice, 98th overall, in 1993 Entry Draft).

			Regular Season								Playoffs						
Season	Club	Lea	GP	W	L	T	Mins	GA	SO	Avg	GP	W	L	Mins	GA	SO	Avg
1992-93	Kelowna	BCJHL	44				2582	137	0	3.18							
1993-94	N. Michigan	WCHA	20	9	7	0	686	44	0	3.85							

KOLZIG, OLAF — (KOHLT-zihg, OH-lahf) — WSH.

Goaltender. Catches left. 6'3", 205 lbs. Born, Johannesburg, South Africa, April 9, 1970.
(Washington's 1st choice, 19th overall, in 1989 Entry Draft).

			Regular Season								Playoffs						
Season	Club	Lea	GP	W	L	T	Mins	GA	SO	Avg	GP	W	L	Mins	GA	SO	Avg
1987-88	N. Westminster	WHL	15	6	5	0	650	48	1	4.43	3			149	11	0	4.43
1988-89	Tri-Cities	WHL	30	16	10	2	1671	97	1	*3.48							
1989-90	**Washington**	**NHL**	**2**	**0**	**2**	**0**	**120**	**12**	**0**	**6.00**							
	Tri-Cities	WHL	48	27	27	3	2504	250	1	4.38	6	4	0	318	27	0	5.09
1990-91	Baltimore	AHL	26	10	12	1	1367	72	0	3.16							
	Hampton Rds.	ECHL	21	11	9	1	1248	71	2	3.41	3	1	2	180	14	0	4.66
1991-92	Baltimore	AHL	28	5	17	2	1503	105	1	4.19							
	Hampton Rds.	ECHL	14	11	3	0	847	41	0	2.90							
1992-93	**Washington**	**NHL**	**1**	**0**	**0**	**0**	**20**	**2**	**0**	**6.00**							
	Rochester	AHL	49	25	16	4	2737	168	0	3.68	*17	9	8	*1040	61	0	3.52
1993-94	**Washington**	**NHL**	**7**	**0**	**3**	**0**	**224**	**20**	**0**	**5.36**							
ab	Portland	AHL	29	16	8	5	1725	88	3	3.06	17	*12	5	1035	44	0	*2.55
	NHL Totals		**10**	**0**	**5**	**0**	**364**	**34**	**0**	**5.60**							

a Shared Harry "Hap" Holmes Trophy (fewest goals-against - AHL) with Byron Dafoe (1994)
b Won Jack Butterfield Trophy (Playoff MVP - IHL) (1994)

KOSECKI, JAMES — DET.

Goaltender. Catches . 6'1", 170 lbs. Born, Syracuse, NY, March 11, 1975.
(Detroit's 11th choice, 256th overall, in 1993 Entry Draft).

			Regular Season								Playoffs						
Season	Club	Lea	GP	W	L	T	Mins	GA	SO	Avg	GP	W	L	Mins	GA	SO	Avg
1992-93	Bershire	HS	16	....	....	....	....	44	....	3.00	....	....	....	....	....	....	....
1993-94										UNAVAILABLE							

KRAKE, PAUL — QUE.

Goaltender. Catches left. 6', 183 lbs. Born, Lloydminster, Sask., March 25, 1969.
(Quebec's 10th choice, 148th overall, in 1989 Entry Draft).

			Regular Season								Playoffs						
Season	Club	Lea	GP	W	L	T	Mins	GA	SO	Avg	GP	W	L	Mins	GA	SO	Avg
1988-89	Alaska-Anch.	G.N.	19	....	....	....	1111	75	0	4.05	....	....	....	....	....	....	....
1989-90	Alaska-Anch.	G.N.	18	8	6	2	937	58	0	3.87	....	....	....	....	....	....	....
1990-91	Alaska-Anch.	G.N.	37	18	15	3	2183	123	4	3.38	....	....	....	....	....	....	....
1991-92	Alaska-Anch.	G.N.	27	19	7	0	1587	87	0	3.29	....	....	....	....	....	....	....
1992-93	Oklahoma City	CHL	17	13	3	1	1029	60	0	*3.50	....	....	....	....	....	....	....
	Halifax	AHL	17	8	6	1	916	57	1	3.73	....	....	....	....	....	....	....
1993-94	Cornwall	AHL	28	8	13	4	1382	96	0	4.17	....	....	....	....	....	....	....

KUNTAR, LES — MTL.

Goaltender. Catches left. 6'2", 195 lbs. Born, Elma, NY, July 28, 1969.
(Montreal's 8th choice, 122nd overall, in 1987 Entry Draft).

			Regular Season								Playoffs						
Season	Club	Lea	GP	W	L	T	Mins	GA	SO	Avg	GP	W	L	Mins	GA	SO	Avg
1987-88	St. Lawrence	ECAC	10	6	1	0	488	27	0	3.31	....	....	....	....	....	....	....
1988-89	St. Lawrence	ECAC	14	11	2	0	786	31	0	2.37	....	....	....	....	....	....	....
1989-90	St. Lawrence	ECAC	20	7	11	1	1136	80	0	4.23	....	....	....	....	....	....	....
1990-91ab	St. Lawrence	ECAC	*33	*19	11	1	*1797	97	*1	*3.24	....	....	....	....	....	....	....
1991-92	Fredericton	AHL	11	7	3	0	638	26	0	2.45	....	....	....	....	....	....	....
	U.S. National	....	2	0	1	0	100	4	0	2.40	....	....	....	....	....	....	....
1992-93	Fredericton	AHL	42	16	14	7	2315	130	0	3.37	1	0	1	64	6	0	5.63
1993-94	**Montreal**	**NHL**	**6**	**2**	**2**	**0**	**302**	**16**	**0**	**3.18**	....	....	....	....	....	....	....
	Fredericton	AHL	34	10	17	3	1804	109	1	3.62	....	....	....	....	....	....	....
	NHL Totals		**6**	**2**	**2**	**0**	**302**	**16**	**0**	**3.18**	....	....	....	....	....	....	....

a ECAC First All-Star Team (1991)
b NCAA East First All-American Team (1991)

KVALEVOG, TOBY — OTT.

Goaltender. Catches left. 5'11", 170 lbs. Born, Fargo, ND, December 22, 1974.
(Ottawa's 8th choice, 209th overall, in 1993 Entry Draft).

			Regular Season								Playoffs						
Season	Club	Lea	GP	W	L	T	Mins	GA	SO	Avg	GP	W	L	Mins	GA	SO	Avg
1992-93	Bemidgi	HS	21	....	....	....	945	60	0	4.29	....	....	....	....	....	....	....
1993-94	North Dakota	WCHA	32	11	17	3	1813	120	0	3.97	....	....	....	....	....	....	....

LABBE, JEAN-FRANCOIS — OTT.

Goaltender. Catches left. 5'9", 170 lbs. Born, Sherbrooke, Que., June 15, 1972.

			Regular Season								Playoffs						
Season	Club	Lea	GP	W	L	T	Mins	GA	SO	Avg	GP	W	L	Mins	GA	SO	Avg
1989-90	Trois-Rivieres	QMJHL	28	....	....	....	1499	106	0	3.64	3	1	1	132	8	....	3.64
1990-91	Trois-Rivieres	QMJHL	54	*35	14	0	2870	158	....	3.30	5	1	4	230	19	....	4.96
1991-92a	Trois-Rivieres	QMJHL	48	*31	13	3	2749	142	1	3.10	*15	*10	3	791	33	*1	*2.50
1992-93	Hull	QMJHL	46	26	18	2	2701	156	2	3.46	10	6	3	518	24	*1	*2.78
1993-94bcd	Thunder Bay	ColHL	52	*35	11	4	*2900	150	*2	*3.10	8	7	1	493	18	*2	*2.19
	P.E.I.	AHL	7	4	3	0	389	22	0	3.39	....	....	....	....	....	....	....

a QMJHL First All-Star Team (1992)
b ColHL First All-Star Team (1994)
c ColHL Rookie of the Year (1994)
d ColHL Outstanding Goaltender (1994)

Signed as a free agent by **Ottawa**, May 12, 1994.

LABRECQUE, PATRICK — MTL.

Goaltender. Catches left. 6', 190 lbs. Born, Laval, Que., March 6, 1971.
(Quebec's 5th choice, 90th overall, in 1991 Entry Draft).

			Regular Season								Playoffs						
Season	Club	Lea	GP	W	L	T	Mins	GA	SO	Avg	GP	W	L	Mins	GA	SO	Avg
1990-91	St-Jean	QMJHL	59	17	34	6	3375	216	1	3.84	....	....	....	....	....	....	....
1991-92	Halifax	AHL	29	5	12	8	1570	114	0	4.36	....	....	....	....	....	....	....
1992-93	Greensboro	ECHL	11	6	3	2	650	31	0	2.86	1	0	1	59	5	0	5.08
	Halifax	AHL	20	3	12	2	914	76	0	4.99	....	....	....	....	....	....	....
1993-94	Cornwall	AHL	4	1	2	0	198	8	1	2.42	....	....	....	....	....	....	....
	Greensboro	ECHL	29	17	8	2	1609	89	0	3.32	1	0	0	22	4	0	10.80

Signed as a free agent by **Montreal**, June 21, 1994.

LACHER, BLAINE — BOS.

Goaltender. Catches left. 6'1", 205 lbs. Born, Medicine Hat, Alta., September 5, 1970.

			Regular Season								Playoffs						
Season	Club	Lea	GP	W	L	T	Mins	GA	SO	Avg	GP	W	L	Mins	GA	SO	Avg
1991-92	Lake Superior	CCHA	9	5	3	0	410	22	0	3.22	....	....	....	....	....	....	....
1992-93	Lake Superior	CCHA	34	24	5	3	1915	86	....	2.70	....	....	....	....	....	....	....
1993-94	Lake Superior	CCHA	30	20	5	4	1785	59	....	*1.98	....	....	....	....	....	....	....

Signed as a free agent by **Boston**, June 2, 1994.

LaFOREST, MARK

Goaltender. Catches left. 5'11", 190 lbs. Born, Welland, Ont., July 10, 1962.

			Regular Season								Playoffs						
Season	Club	Lea	GP	W	L	T	Mins	GA	SO	Avg	GP	W	L	Mins	GA	SO	Avg
1981-82	Niagara Falls	OHL	24	10	13	1	1365	105	1	4.62	5	1	2	300	19	0	3.80
1982-83	North Bay	OHL	54	34	17	1	3140	195	0	3.73	8	4	4	474	31	0	3.92
1983-84	Adirondack	AHL	7	3	3	1	351	29	0	4.96	....	....	....	....	....	....	....
	Kalamazoo	IHL	13	4	5	2	718	48	1	4.01	....	....	....	....	....	....	....
1984-85	Adirondack	AHL	11	2	3	1	430	35	0	4.88	....	....	....	....	....	....	....
1985-86	**Detroit**	**NHL**	**28**	**4**	**21**	**0**	**1383**	**114**	**1**	**4.95**	....	....	....	....	....	....	....
	Adirondack	AHL	19	13	5	1	1142	57	0	2.99	*17	*12	5	*1075	58	0	3.24
1986-87	**Detroit**	**NHL**	**5**	**2**	**1**	**0**	**219**	**12**	**0**	**3.29**	....	....	....	....	....	....	....
a	Adirondack	AHL	37	23	8	0	2229	105	*3	2.83	....	....	....	....	....	....	....
1987-88	**Philadelphia**	**NHL**	**21**	**5**	**9**	**2**	**972**	**60**	**1**	**3.70**	**2**	**1**	**0**	**48**	**1**	**0**	**1.25**
	Hershey	AHL	5	2	1	2	309	13	0	2.52	....	....	....	....	....	....	....
1988-89	**Philadelphia**	**NHL**	**17**	**5**	**7**	**2**	**933**	**64**	**0**	**4.12**	....	....	....	....	....	....	....
	Hershey	AHL	3	2	0	0	185	9	0	2.92	12	7	5	744	27	1	2.18
1989-90	**Toronto**	**NHL**	**27**	**9**	**14**	**0**	**1343**	**87**	**0**	**3.89**	....	....	....	....	....	....	....
	Newmarket	AHL	10	6	4	0	604	33	1	3.28	....	....	....	....	....	....	....
1990-91ab	Binghamton	AHL	45	25	14	2	2452	129	0	3.16	9	3	4	442	28	1	3.80
1991-92	Binghamton	AHL	43	25	15	3	2559	146	1	3.42	11	7	4	662	34	0	3.08
1992-93	New Haven	AHL	30	10	18	1	1688	121	1	4.30	....	....	....	....	....	....	....
	Brantford	ColHL	10	5	3	1	565	35	1	3.72	....	....	....	....	....	....	....
1993-94	**Ottawa**	**NHL**	**5**	**0**	**2**	**0**	**182**	**17**	**0**	**5.60**	....	....	....	....	....	....	....
	PEI	AHL	43	9	25	5	2359	161	0	4.09	....	....	....	....	....	....	....
	NHL Totals		**103**	**25**	**54**	**4**	**5032**	**354**	**2**	**4.22**	**2**	**1**	**0**	**48**	**1**	**0**	**1.25**

a Won Baz Bastien Trophy (Top Goaltender - AHL) (1987, 1991)
b AHL Second All-Star Team (1991)

Signed as a free agent by **Detroit**, April 29, 1983. Traded to **Philadelphia** by **Detroit** for Philadelphia's second round choice (Bob Wilkie) in 1987 Entry Draft, June 13, 1987. Traded to **Toronto** by **Philadelphia** for Toronto's sixth round choice in 1991 Entry Draft and its seventh round choice in 1991 Entry Draft, September 8, 1989. Traded to **NY Rangers** by **Toronto** with Tie Domi for Greg Johnston, June 28, 1990. Claimed by **Ottawa** from **NY Rangers** in Expansion Draft, June 18, 1992.

LAGRAND, SCOTT — PHI.

Goaltender. Catches left. 6', 165 lbs. Born, Potsdam, NY, February 11, 1970.
(Philadelphia's 5th choice, 77th overall, in 1988 Entry Draft).

			Regular Season								Playoffs						
Season	Club	Lea	GP	W	L	T	Mins	GA	SO	Avg	GP	W	L	Mins	GA	SO	Avg
1989-90	Boston College	H.E.	24	17	4	0	1268	57	0	2.70	....	....	....	....	....	....	....
1990-91a	Boston College	H.E.	23	12	8	0	1153	63	2	3.28	....	....	....	....	....	....	....
1991-92b	Boston College	H.E.	30	11	16	2	1750	108	1	3.70	....	....	....	....	....	....	....
1992-93	Hershey	AHL	32	8	17	4	1854	145	0	4.69	....	....	....	....	....	....	....
1993-94	Hershey	AHL	40	16	13	3	2032	117	2	3.45	....	....	....	....	....	....	....

a Hockey East First All-Star Team (1991)
b NCAA East Second All-American Team (1992)

LALIME, PATRICK — PIT.

Goaltender. Catches left. 6'2", 170 lbs. Born, St. Bonaventure, Que., July 7, 1974.
(Pittsburgh's 6th choice, 156th overall, in 1993 Entry Draft).

			Regular Season								Playoffs						
Season	Club	Lea	GP	W	L	T	Mins	GA	SO	Avg	GP	W	L	Mins	GA	SO	Avg
1992-93	Shawinigan	QMJHL	44	10	24	4	2467	192	0	4.67	....	....	....	....	....	....	....
1993-94	Shawinigan	QMJHL	48	....	....	....	2733	192	1	4.22	5	1	3	223	25	0	6.73

LAMBERT, JUDD — N.J.

Goaltender. Catches left. 6', 165 lbs. Born, Richmond, B.C., June 3, 1974.
(New Jersey's 9th choice, 221st overall, in 1993 Entry Draft).

			Regular Season								Playoffs						
Season	Club	Lea	GP	W	L	T	Mins	GA	SO	Avg	GP	W	L	Mins	GA	SO	Avg
1992-93	Chilliwack	Jr. A	50	....	....	....	2488	234	0	5.64	....	....	....	....	....	....	....
1993-94	Colorado	WCHA	11	6	4	0	620	33	0	3.19	....	....	....	....	....	....	....

LAMOTHE, MARC — MTL.

Goaltender. Catches left. 6'2", 187 lbs. Born, New Liskeard, Ont., February 27, 1974.
(Montreal's 6th choice, 92nd overall, in 1992 Entry Draft).

			Regular Season								Playoffs						
Season	Club	Lea	GP	W	L	T	Mins	GA	SO	Avg	GP	W	L	Mins	GA	SO	Avg
1991-92	Kingston	OHL	42	10	25	2	2378	189	1	4.77	....	....	....	....	....	....	....
1992-93	Kingston	OHL	45	23	12	6	2489	162	1	3.91	15	8	5	753	48	1	3.82
1993-94	Kingston	OHL	48	23	20	5	2828	177	*2	3.76	6	2	2	224	12	0	3.21

LANG, CHAD — DAL.

Goaltender. Catches left. 5'10", 188 lbs. Born, Newmarket, Ont., February 11, 1975.
(Dallas' 3rd choice, 87th overall, in 1993 Entry Draft).

			Regular Season								Playoffs						
Season	Club	Lea	GP	W	L	T	Mins	GA	SO	Avg	GP	W	L	Mins	GA	SO	Avg
1991-92	Peterborough	OHL	16	7	5	1	886	63	0	4.27	2	0	0	65	9	0	8.31
1992-93a	Peterborough	OHL	43	*32	6	4	2554	140	1	3.29	*21	*12	8	*1224	74	*1	3.63
1993-94	Peterborough	OHL	48	11	27	7	2732	225	0	4.94	7	3	4	391	24	0	3.68

a OHL Second All-Star Team (1993)

LANGKOW, SCOTT — WPG.

Goaltender. Catches left. 5'11", 190 lbs. Born, Sherwood Park, Alta., April 21, 1975.
(Winnipeg's 2nd choice, 31st overall, in 1993 Entry Draft).

			Regular Season								Playoffs						
Season	Club	Lea	GP	W	L	T	Mins	GA	SO	Avg	GP	W	L	Mins	GA	SO	Avg
1991-92	Portland	WHL	1	....	....	....	33	2	0	3.46	....	....	....	....	....	....	....
1992-93	Portland	WHL	34	24	8	2	2064	119	2	3.46	9	....	....	535	31	0	3.48
1993-94a	Portland	WHL	39	27	9	1	2302	121	2	3.15	10	6	4	600	34	0	3.40

a WHL West Second All-Star Team (1994)

LAROCHELLE, BRIAN — MTL.

Goaltender. Catches right. 6'1", 185 lbs. Born, Manchester, NH, August 8, 1974.
(Montreal's 12th choice, 255th overall, in 1993 Entry Draft).

			Regular Season								Playoffs						
Season	Club	Lea	GP	W	L	T	Mins	GA	SO	Avg	GP	W	L	Mins	GA	SO	Avg
1992-93	Phillips Exeter	HS	22	10	11	1	1020	76	3	4.47	....	....	....	....	....	....	....
1993-94	N. Hampshire	H.E.								DID NOT PLAY							

LEBLANC, RAYMOND

Goaltender. Catches right. 5'10", 170 lbs. Born, Fitchburg, MA, October 24, 1964.

Season	Club	Lea	Regular Season								Playoffs						
			GP	W	L	T	Mins	GA	SO	Avg	GP	W	L	Mins	GA	SO	Avg
1983-84	Kitchener	OHL	54	....	....	....	2965	185	1	3.74	....	....	....	....	....	....	....
1984-85	Pinebridge	ACHL	40	....	....	....	2178	150	0	4.13	....	....	....	....	....	....	....
1985-86	Carolina	ACHL	42	....	....	....	2505	133	3	3.19	....	....	....	....	....	....	....
1986-87	Flint	IHL	64	....	....	....	3417	222	0	3.90	....	....	....	....	....	....	....
1987-88	Flint	IHL	62	27	19	8	3269	239	1	4.39	16	10	6	925	55	1	3.57
1988-89	Flint	IHL	15	5	9	0	852	67	0	4.72	....	....	....	....	....	....	....
	New Haven	AHL	1	0	0	0	20	3	0	9.00	....	....	....	....	....	....	....
	Saginaw	IHL	29	19	7	2	1655	99	0	3.59	1	0	1	5	9	0	3.05
1989-90	Indianapolis	IHL	23	15	6	2	1334	71	2	3.19	....	....	....	....	....	....	....
	Fort Wayne	IHL	15	3	3	3	680	44	0	3.88	3	0	2	139	11	0	4.75
1990-91	Fort Wayne	IHL	21	10	8	0	1072	69	0	3.86	....	....	....	....	....	....	....
	Indianapolis	IHL	3	2	0	0	145	7	0	2.90	1	0	0	19	1	0	3.20
1991-92	U.S. National	....	17	5	10	1	891	54	0	3.63	....	....	....	....	....	....	....
	U.S. Olympic	....	8	....	....	....	463	17	2	2.20	....	....	....	....	....	....	....
	Chicago	**NHL**	**1**	**1**	**0**	**0**	**60**	**1**	**0**	**1.00**	....	....	....	....	....	....	....
	Indianapolis	IHL	25	14	9	2	1468	84	2	3.43	....	....	....	....	....	....	....
1992-93	Indianapolis	IHL	56	23	22	7	3201	206	0	3.86	5	1	4	276	23	0	5.00
1993-94	Indianapolis	IHL	2	0	1	0	112	8	0	4.25	....	....	....	....	....	....	....
	Cincinnati	IHL	34	17	9	3	1779	104	1	3.51	5	0	3	159	9	0	3.39
	NHL Totals		**1**	**1**	**0**	**0**	**60**	**1**	**0**	**1.00**	....	....	....	....	....	....	....

Signed as a free agent by **Chicago**, July 5, 1989.

LEGACE, EMMANUEL (MANNY) (leh-GAH-see) HFD.

Goaltender. Catches left. 5'9", 162 lbs. Born, Toronto, Ont., February 4, 1973.
(Hartford's 5th choice, 188th overall, in 1993 Entry Draft).

Season	Club	Lea	Regular Season								Playoffs						
			GP	W	L	T	Mins	GA	SO	Avg	GP	W	L	Mins	GA	SO	Avg
1990-91	Niagara Falls	OHL	30	13	11	2	1515	107	0	4.24	4	1	1	119	10	0	5.04
1991-92	Niagara Falls	OHL	43	21	16	3	2384	143	0	3.60	14	8	5	791	56	0	4.25
1992-93a	Niagara Falls	OHL	48	22	19	3	2630	171	0	3.90	4	0	4	240	18	0	4.50
1993-94	Cdn. National	....	16	8	6	0	859	36	2	2.51	....	....	....	....	....	....	....

a OHL First All-Star Team (1993)

LEMBKE, JEFF PIT.

Goaltender. Catches left. 5'11", 175 lbs. Born, Pembina, ND, November 29, 1972.
(Pittsburgh's 9th choice, 192nd overall, in 1991 Entry Draft).

Season	Club	Lea	Regular Season								Playoffs						
			GP	W	L	T	Mins	GA	SO	Avg	GP	W	L	Mins	GA	SO	Avg
1991-92	North Dakota	WCHA	10	3	3	0	412	41	0	5.97	....	....	....	....	....	....	....
1992-93	North Dakota	WCHA	4	0	2	0	160	16	0	5.99	....	....	....	....	....	....	....
1993-94	North Dakota	WCHA	3	0	2	0	140	10	0	4.29	....	....	....	....	....	....	....

LENARDUZZI, MIKE

Goaltender. Catches left. 6'1", 165 lbs. Born, London, Ont., September 14, 1972.
(Hartford's 3rd choice, 57th overall, in 1990 Entry Draft).

Season	Club	Lea	Regular Season								Playoffs						
			GP	W	L	T	Mins	GA	SO	Avg	GP	W	L	Mins	GA	SO	Avg
1989-90	Oshawa	OHL	12	6	3	1	444	32	0	4.32	....	....	....	....	....	....	....
	S.S. Marie	OHL	20	....	....	....	1117	66	0	3.55	....	....	....	....	....	....	....
1990-91	S.S. Marie	OHL	35	19	8	3	1966	107	0	3.27	5	3	1	268	13	*1	2.91
1991-92	S.S. Marie	OHL	9	5	3	0	486	33	0	4.07	....	....	....	....	....	....	....
	Ottawa	OHL	18	5	12	1	986	60	1	3.65	....	....	....	....	....	....	....
	Sudbury	OHL	22	11	5	4	1201	84	2	4.20	11	4	7	651	38	0	3.50
	Springfield	AHL	....	....	....	....	....	....	....	....	1	0	0	39	2	0	3.08
1992-93	**Hartford**	**NHL**	**3**	**1**	**1**	**1**	**168**	**9**	**0**	**3.21**	....	....	....	....	....	....	....
	Springfield	AHL	36	10	17	5	1945	142	0	4.38	2	1	0	100	5	0	3.00
1993-94	**Hartford**	**NHL**	**1**	**0**	**0**	**0**	**21**	**1**	**0**	**2.86**	....	....	....	....	....	....	....
	Springfield	AHL	22	5	7	2	984	73	0	4.45	....	....	....	....	....	....	....
	Salt Lake	IHL	4	0	4	0	211	22	0	6.25	....	....	....	....	....	....	....
	NHL Totals		**4**	**1**	**1**	**1**	**189**	**10**	**0**	**3.17**	....	....	....	....	....	....	....

LESLIE, LANCE OTT.

Goaltender. Catches left. 5'10", 160 lbs. Born, Dawson Creek, B.C., June 21, 1974.

Season	Club	Lea	Regular Season								Playoffs						
			GP	W	L	T	Mins	GA	SO	Avg	GP	W	L	Mins	GA	SO	Avg
1992-93	Tri-City	WHL	49	15	25	3	2620	163	3	3.73	....	....	....	....	....	....	....
1993-94	Tri-City	WHL	41	10	26	2	2273	189	2	4.99	2	0	2	120	9	0	4.50

Signed as a free agent by **Ottawa**, October 4, 1993.

LEVY, JEFF DAL.

Goaltender. Catches left. 5'11", 160 lbs. Born, Salt Lake City, UT, December 9, 1970.
(Minnesota's 7th choice, 134th overall, in 1990 Entry Draft).

Season	Club	Lea	Regular Season								Playoffs						
			GP	W	L	T	Mins	GA	SO	Avg	GP	W	L	Mins	GA	SO	Avg
1990-91ab	N. Hampshire	H.E.	24	15	7	2	1490	80	0	3.22	....	....	....	....	....	....	....
1991-92	N. Hampshire	H.E.	6	2	2	0	191	14	0	4.40	....	....	....	....	....	....	....
1992-93	Dayton	ECHL	1	0	0	1	65	3	0	2.77	2	0	2	139	9	0	3.88
	Kalamazoo	IHL	28	8	14	1	1512	115	0	4.56	....	....	....	....	....	....	....
1993-94	U.S. National	....	5	....	....	....	240	18	0	4.50	....	....	....	....	....	....	....
	Dayton	ECHL	31	10	13	3	1672	125	0	4.48	....	....	....	....	....	....	....
	Kalamazoo	IHL	2	0	1	0	59	4	0	4.06	....	....	....	....	....	....	....

a Hockey East Second All-Star Team (1991)
b NCAA East Second All-American Team (1991)

LINDFORS, SAKARI (LIHND-fohrs) QUE.

Goaltender. Catches left. 5'7", 150 lbs. Born, Helsinki, Finland, April 27, 1966.
(Quebec's 9th choice, 150th overall, in 1988 Entry Draft).

Season	Club	Lea	Regular Season								Playoffs						
			GP	W	L	T	Mins	GA	SO	Avg	GP	W	L	Mins	GA	SO	Avg
1986-87	HIFK	Fin.	20	....	....	....	1009	65	0	3.86	....	....	....	....	....	....	....
1987-88	HIFK	Fin.	39	....	....	....	2346	....	....	....	6	....	....	340	....	....	....
1988-89	HIFK	Fin.	24	11	11	2	1433	89	1	3.75	2	....	....	118	7	....	3.53
1989-90	HIFK	Fin.	42	23	15	4	2518	146	2	3.48	....	....	....	....	....	....	....
1990-91	HIFK	Fin.	41	....	....	....	2445	142	2	3.48	3	....	....	180	14	0	4.67
1991-92	HIFK	Fin.	38	....	....	....	2222	127	4	3.43	9	....	....	538	28	0	3.12
1992-93	HIFK	Fin.	39	....	....	....	2293	123	0	3.22	4	....	....	236	12	0	3.04
1993-94	HIFK	Fin.	43	0	0	0	2465	128	3	3.11	3	....	....	175	11	....	3.76

LITTLE, NEIL PHI.

Goaltender. Catches left. 6'1", 175 lbs. Born, Medicine Hat, Alta., December 18, 1971.
(Philadelphia's 11th choice, 226th overall, in 1991 Entry Draft).

Season	Club	Lea	Regular Season								Playoffs						
			GP	W	L	T	Mins	GA	SO	Avg	GP	W	L	Mins	GA	SO	Avg
1990-91	RPI	ECAC	18	9	8	0	1032	71	0	4.13	....	....	....	....	....	....	....
1991-92	RPI	ECAC	28	11	11	3	1532	96	0	3.76	....	....	....	....	....	....	....
1992-93ab	RPI	ECAC	*31	*19	9	3	*1801	88	0	2.93	....	....	....	....	....	....	....
1993-94	RPI	ECAC	27	16	7	4	1570	88	0	3.36	....	....	....	....	....	....	....
	Hershey	AHL	1	0	0	0	18	1	0	3.23	....	....	....	....	....	....	....

a ECAC First All-Star Team (1993)
b NCAA East Second All-American Team (1993)

LITTMAN, DAVID

Goaltender. Catches left. 6', 183 lbs. Born, Cranston, RI, June 13, 1967.
(Buffalo's 12th choice, 211th overall, in 1987 Entry Draft).

Season	Club	Lea	Regular Season								Playoffs						
			GP	W	L	T	Mins	GA	SO	Avg	GP	W	L	Mins	GA	SO	Avg
1985-86	Boston College	H.E.	7	4	0	1	312	18	0	3.46	....	....	....	....	....	....	....
1986-87	Boston College	H.E.	21	15	5	0	1182	68	0	3.45	....	....	....	....	....	....	....
1987-88a	Boston College	H.E.	30	11	16	2	1726	116	0	4.03	....	....	....	....	....	....	....
1988-89bc	Boston College	H.E.	*32	19	9	4	*1945	107	0	3.30	....	....	....	....	....	....	....
1989-90	Rochester	AHL	14	5	6	1	681	37	0	3.26	....	....	....	....	....	....	....
	Phoenix	IHL	18	8	7	2	1047	64	0	3.67	....	....	....	....	....	....	....
1990-91	**Buffalo**	**NHL**	**1**	**0**	**0**	**0**	**36**	**3**	**0**	**5.00**	....	....	....	....	....	....	....
d	Rochester	AHL	*56	*33	13	5	*3155	160	3	3.04	8	4	2	378	16	0	2.54
1991-92	**Buffalo**	**NHL**	**1**	**0**	**1**	**0**	**60**	**4**	**0**	**4.00**	....	....	....	....	....	....	....
ef	Rochester	AHL	*61	*29	20	9	*3558	174	*3	2.93	15	8	7	879	43	*1	2.94
1992-93	**Tampa Bay**	**NHL**	**1**	**0**	**1**	**0**	**45**	**7**	**0**	**9.33**	....	....	....	....	....	....	....
	Atlanta	IHL	44	23	12	4	2390	134	0	3.36	3	1	2	178	8	0	2.70
1993-94	Fredericton	AHL	16	8	7	0	872	63	0	4.33	....	....	....	....	....	....	....
	Providence	AHL	25	10	11	3	1385	83	0	3.60	....	....	....	....	....	....	....
	NHL Totals		**3**	**0**	**2**	**0**	**141**	**14**	**0**	**5.96**	....	....	....	....	....	....	....

a Hockey East Second All-Star Team (1988)
b Hockey East First All-Star Team (1989)
c NCAA East Second All-American Team (1989)
d AHL First All-Star Team (1991)
e Won Harry "Hap" Holmes Memorial Trophy (fewest goals against - AHL) (1992)
f AHL Second All-Star Team (1992)

Signed as a free agent by **Tampa Bay**, August 27, 1992. Signed as a free agent by **Boston**, August 6, 1993.

LORENZ, DANNY FLA.

Goaltender. Catches left. 5'10", 183 lbs. Born, Murrayville, B.C., December 12, 1969.
(NY Islanders' 4th choice, 58th overall, in 1988 Entry Draft).

Season	Club	Lea	Regular Season								Playoffs						
			GP	W	L	T	Mins	GA	SO	Avg	GP	W	L	Mins	GA	SO	Avg
1986-87	Seattle	WHL	38	12	21	2	2103	199	0	5.68	....	....	....	....	....	....	....
1987-88	Seattle	WHL	62	20	37	2	3302	314	0	5.71	....	....	....	....	....	....	....
1988-89	Springfield	AHL	4	2	1	0	210	12	0	3.43	....	....	....	....	....	....	....
a	Seattle	WHL	*68	31	33	4	*4003	240	*3	3.60	....	....	....	....	....	....	....
1989-90a	Seattle	WHL	56	37	15	2	3226	221	0	4.11	13	6	7	751	40	0	3.21
1990-91	**NY Islanders**	**NHL**	**2**	**0**	**1**	**0**	**80**	**5**	**0**	**3.75**	....	....	....	....	....	....	....
	Capital Dist.	AHL	17	5	9	2	940	70	0	4.47	....	....	....	....	....	....	....
	Richmond	ECHL	20	6	9	2	1020	75	0	4.41	....	....	....	....	....	....	....
1991-92	**NY Islanders**	**NHL**	**2**	**0**	**2**	**0**	**120**	**10**	**0**	**5.00**	....	....	....	....	....	....	....
	Capital Dist.	AHL	53	22	22	7	3050	181	2	3.56	7	3	4	442	25	0	3.39
1992-93	**NY Islanders**	**NHL**	**4**	**1**	**2**	**0**	**157**	**10**	**0**	**3.82**	....	....	....	....	....	....	....
	Capital Dist.	AHL	44	16	17	5	2412	146	1	3.63	4	0	3	219	12	0	3.29
1993-94	Salt Lake	IHL	20	4	12	0	982	91	0	5.56	....	....	....	....	....	....	....
	Springfield	AHL	14	5	7	1	801	59	0	4.42	2	0	0	35	0	0	0.00
	NHL Totals		**8**	**1**	**5**	**0**	**357**	**25**	**0**	**4.20**	....	....	....	....	....	....	....

a WHL West First All-Star Team (1989, 1990)

Signed as a free agent by **Florida**, June 14, 1994.

LOUDER, GREG EDM.

Goaltender. Catches left. 6'1", 185 lbs. Born, Concord, MA, November 16, 1971.
(Edmonton's 5th choice, 101st overall, in 1990 Entry Draft).

Season	Club	Lea	Regular Season								Playoffs						
			GP	W	L	T	Mins	GA	SO	Avg	GP	W	L	Mins	GA	SO	Avg
1990-91	Notre Dame	NCAA	33	16	5	2	1958	134	1	4.11	....	....	....	....	....	....	....
1991-92	Notre Dame	NCAA	18	5	13	0	1055	88	0	5.00	....	....	....	....	....	....	....
1992-93	Notre Dame	CCHA	24	4	16	1	1177	95	....	4.84	....	....	....	....	....	....	....
1993-94	Notre Dame	CCHA	28	7	13	4	1333	93	0	4.19	....	....	....	....	....	....	....

LUKOWSKI, BRIAN ST.L.

Goaltender. Catches left. 5'9", 180 lbs. Born, Buffalo, NY, January 8, 1971.
(St. Louis' 11th choice, 219th overall, in 1989 Entry Draft).

Season	Club	Lea	Regular Season								Playoffs						
			GP	W	L	T	Mins	GA	SO	Avg	GP	W	L	Mins	GA	SO	Avg
1989-90	Lake Superior	CCHA	4	1	0	0	114	8	0	4.20	....	....	....	....	....	....	....
1990-91	Lake Superior	CCHA	4	3	0	0	200	8	0	2.40	....	....	....	....	....	....	....
1991-92	Lake Superior	CCHA	1	0	0	0	30	2	0	4.00	....	....	....	....	....	....	....
	Geneseo State	NCAA	15	9	6	....	....	....	0	4.09	....	....	....	....	....	....	....
1992-93	Geneseo State	NCAA	15	5	8	0	745	60	0	4.83	....	....	....	....	....	....	....
1993-94										UNAVAILABLE							

MacDONALD, TODD FLA.

Goaltender. Catches left. 6', 155 lbs. Born, Charlottetown, P.E.I., July 5, 1975.
(Florida's 7th choice, 109th overall, in 1993 Entry Draft).

Season	Club	Lea	Regular Season								Playoffs						
			GP	W	L	T	Mins	GA	SO	Avg	GP	W	L	Mins	GA	SO	Avg
1992-93	Tacoma	WHL	19	6	6	0	823	59	0	4.30	....	....	....	....	....	....	....
1993-94	Tacoma	WHL	29	13	10	2	1606	109	1	4.07	....	....	....	....	....	....	....

MADELEY, DARRIN
(MAY-duh-lee) **OTT.**

Goaltender. Catches left. 5'11", 170 lbs. Born, Holland Landing, Ont., February 25, 1968.

			Regular Season								Playoffs						
Season	Club	Lea	GP	W	L	T	Mins	GA	SO	Avg	GP	W	L	Mins	GA	SO	Avg
1989-90	Lake Superior	CCHA	30	21	7	1	....	68	....	2.42	....	....	....	....	....	....	....
1990-91a	Lake Superior	CCHA	36	*29	3	3	....	93	....	*2.61	....	....	....	....	....	....	....
1991-92abc	Lake Superior	CCHA	36	23	6	4	....	69	....	*2.05	....	....	....	....	....	....	....
1992-93	**Ottawa**	**NHL**	**2**	**0**	**2**	**0**	**90**	**10**	**0**	**6.67**	....	....	....	....	....	....	....
	New Haven	AHL	41	10	16	9	2295	127	0	3.32	....	....	....	....	....	....	....
1993-94	**Ottawa**	**NHL**	**32**	**3**	**18**	**5**	**1583**	**115**	**0**	**4.36**	....	....	....	....	....	....	....
	PEI	AHL	6	0	4	0	270	26	0	5.77	....	....	....	....	....	....	....
	NHL Totals		**34**	**3**	**20**	**5**	**1673**	**125**	**0**	**4.48**	....	....	....	....	....	....	....

a NCAA West First All-American Team (1991, 1992)
b NCAA Final Four All-Tournament Team (1992)
c CCHA First All-Star Team (1992)
d AHL Second All-Star Team (1993)

Signed as a free agent by **Ottawa**, June 20, 1992.

MALARCHUK, CLINT

Goaltender. Catches left. 6', 185 lbs. Born, Grande Prairie, Alta., May 1, 1961.
(Quebec's 3rd choice, 74th overall, in 1981 Entry Draft).

			Regular Season								Playoffs						
Season	Club	Lea	GP	W	L	T	Mins	GA	SO	Avg	GP	W	L	Mins	GA	SO	Avg
1979-80	Portland	WHL	37	21	10	0	1948	147	0	4.53	1	0	0	40	3	0	4.50
1980-81	Portland	WHL	38	28	8	0	2235	142	3	3.81	4	....	....	307	21	0	4.10
1981-82	**Quebec**	**NHL**	**2**	**0**	**1**	**1**	**120**	**14**	**0**	**7.00**	....	....	....	....	....	....	....
	Fredericton	AHL	51	15	34	2	2906	247	0	5.10	....	....	....	....	....	....	....
1982-83	**Quebec**	**NHL**	**15**	**8**	**5**	**2**	**900**	**71**	**0**	**4.73**	....	....	....	....	....	....	....
	Fredericton	AHL	25	....	....	....	1506	78	0	3.11	....	....	....	....	....	....	....
1983-84	**Quebec**	**NHL**	**23**	**10**	**9**	**2**	**1215**	**80**	**0**	**3.95**	....	....	....	....	....	....	....
	Fredericton	AHL	11	5	5	1	663	40	0	3.62	....	....	....	....	....	....	....
1984-85	Fredericton	AHL	*56	26	25	4	*3347	198	2	3.55	6	2	4	379	20	0	3.17
1985-86	**Quebec**	**NHL**	**46**	**26**	**12**	**4**	**2657**	**142**	**4**	**3.21**	**3**	**0**	**2**	**143**	**11**	**0**	**4.62**
1986-87	**Quebec**	**NHL**	**54**	**18**	**26**	**9**	**3092**	**175**	**1**	**3.40**	**3**	**0**	**2**	**140**	**8**	**0**	**3.43**
1987-88	**Washington**	**NHL**	**54**	**24**	**20**	**4**	**2926**	**154**	***4**	**3.16**	**4**	**0**	**2**	**193**	**15**	**0**	**4.66**
1988-89	**Washington**	**NHL**	**42**	**16**	**18**	**7**	**2428**	**141**	**1**	**3.48**	**1**	**0**	**1**	**59**	**5**	**0**	**5.08**
	Buffalo	**NHL**	**7**	**3**	**1**	**1**	**326**	**13**	**1**	**2.39**	....	....	....	....	....	....	....
1989-90	**Buffalo**	**NHL**	**29**	**14**	**11**	**2**	**1596**	**89**	**0**	**3.35**	....	....	....	....	....	....	....
1990-91	**Buffalo**	**NHL**	**37**	**12**	**14**	**10**	**2131**	**119**	**1**	**3.35**	**4**	**2**	**2**	**246**	**17**	**0**	**4.15**
1991-92	**Buffalo**	**NHL**	**29**	**10**	**13**	**3**	**1639**	**102**	**0**	**3.73**	....	....	....	....	....	....	....
	Rochester	AHL	2	2	0	0	120	3	1	1.50	....	....	....	....	....	....	....
1992-93a	San Diego	IHL	27	17	3	3	1516	72	3	2.85	*12	6	4	668	34	0	3.05
1993-94	Las Vegas	IHL	55	*34	10	7	3076	172	1	3.35	5	1	3	257	16	0	3.74
	NHL Totals		**338**	**141**	**130**	**45**	**19030**	**1100**	**12**	**3.47**	**15**	**2**	**9**	**781**	**56**	**0**	**4.30**

a Shared James Norris Memorial Trophy (Top Goaltender - IHL) with Rick Knickle (1993)

Traded to **Washington** by **Quebec** with Dale Hunter for Gaetan Duchesne, Alan Haworth and Washington's first round choice (Joe Sakic) in 1987 Entry Draft, June 13, 1987. Traded to **Buffalo** by **Washington** with Grant Ledyard and Washington's sixth round choice (Brian Holzinger) in 1991 Entry Draft for Calle Johansson and Buffalo's second round choice (Byron Dafoe) in 1989 Entry Draft, March 7, 1989.

MARACLE, NORM
DET.

Goaltender. Catches left. 5'9", 175 lbs. Born, Belleville, Ont., October 2, 1974.
(Detroit's 6th choice, 126th overall, in 1993 Entry Draft).

			Regular Season								Playoffs						
Season	Club	Lea	GP	W	L	T	Mins	GA	SO	Avg	GP	W	L	Mins	GA	SO	Avg
1991-92	Saskatoon	WHL	29	13	6	3	1529	87	1	3.41	15	9	5	860	37	0	3.38
1992-93a	Saskatoon	WHL	53	27	18	3	1939	160	1	3.27	9	4	5	569	33	0	3.48
1993-94bcd	Saskatoon	WHL	56	*41	13	1	3219	148	2	2.76	16	*11	5	940	48	*1	3.06

a WHL East Second All-Star Team (1993)
b WHL East First All-Star Team (1994)
c Canadian Major Junior First All-Star Team (1994)
d Canadian Major Junior Goaltender of the Year (1994)

MASON, BOB

Goaltender. Catches right. 6'1", 180 lbs. Born, International Falls, MN, April 22, 1961.

			Regular Season								Playoffs						
Season	Club	Lea	GP	W	L	T	Mins	GA	SO	Avg	GP	W	L	Mins	GA	SO	Avg
1981-82	Minn.-Duluth	WCHA	26	....	....	....	1401	115	0	4.45	....	....	....	....	....	....	....
1982-83	Minn.-Duluth	WCHA	43	....	....	....	2593	151	1	3.49	....	....	....	....	....	....	....
1983-84	U.S. National	....	33	....	....	....	1895	89	0	2.82	....	....	....	....	....	....	....
	U.S. Olympic	....	3	....	....	....	160	10	0	3.75	....	....	....	....	....	....	....
	Washington	**NHL**	**2**	**2**	**0**	**0**	**120**	**3**	**0**	**1.50**	....	....	....	....	....	....	....
	Hershey	AHL	5	1	4	0	282	26	0	5.53	....	....	....	....	....	....	....
1984-85	**Washington**	**NHL**	**12**	**8**	**2**	**1**	**661**	**31**	**1**	**2.81**	....	....	....	....	....	....	....
	Binghamton	AHL	20	10	6	1	1052	58	1	3.31	....	....	....	....	....	....	....
1985-86	**Washington**	**NHL**	**1**	**1**	**0**	**0**	**16**	**0**	**0**	**0.00**	....	....	....	....	....	....	....
	Binghamton	AHL	34	20	11	2	1940	126	0	3.90	3	1	1	124	9	0	4.35
1986-87	**Washington**	**NHL**	**45**	**20**	**18**	**5**	**2536**	**137**	**0**	**3.24**	**4**	**2**	**2**	**309**	**9**	**1**	**1.75**
	Binghamton	AHL	2	1	1	0	119	4	0	2.02	....	....	....	....	....	....	....
1987-88	**Chicago**	**NHL**	**41**	**13**	**18**	**8**	**2312**	**160**	**0**	**4.15**	**1**	**0**	**1**	**60**	**3**	**0**	**3.00**
1988-89	**Quebec**	**NHL**	**22**	**5**	**14**	**1**	**1168**	**92**	**0**	**4.73**	....	....	....	....	....	....	....
	Halifax	AHL	23	11	7	1	1278	73	1	3.43	2	0	2	97	9	0	5.57
1989-90	**Washington**	**NHL**	**16**	**4**	**9**	**1**	**822**	**48**	**0**	**3.50**	....	....	....	....	....	....	....
	Baltimore	AHL	13	9	2	2	770	44	0	3.43	6	2	4	373	20	0	3.22
1990-91	**Vancouver**	**NHL**	**6**	**2**	**4**	**0**	**353**	**29**	**0**	**4.93**	....	....	....	....	....	....	....
	Milwaukee	IHL	22	8	12	1	1199	82	0	4.10	....	....	....	....	....	....	....
1991-92	Milwaukee	IHL	51	27	18	4	3024	171	1	3.39	3	1	2	179	15	0	5.03
1992-93	Hamilton	AHL	44	20	19	3	2601	159	0	3.67	....	....	....	....	....	....	....
1993-94	Milwaukee	IHL	40	21	9	8	2206	132	0	3.59	3	0	1	141	9	0	3.83
	NHL Totals		**145**	**55**	**65**	**16**	**7988**	**500**	**1**	**3.76**	**5**	**2**	**3**	**369**	**12**	**1**	**1.95**

Signed as a free agent by **Washington**, February 21, 1984. Signed as a free agent by **Chicago**, June 12, 1987. Traded to **Quebec** by **Chicago** for Mike Eagles, July 5, 1988. Traded to **Washington** by **Quebec** for future considerations, June 17, 1989. Signed as a free agent by **Vancouver**, December 1, 1990.

MASOTTA, BRYAN
OTT.

Goaltender. Catches left. 6'2", 195 lbs. Born, New Haven, CT, May 30, 1975.
(Ottawa's 3rd choice, 81st overall, in 1994 Entry Draft).

			Regular Season								Playoffs						
Season	Club	Lea	GP	W	L	T	Mins	GA	SO	Avg	GP	W	L	Mins	GA	SO	Avg
1992-93	Hotchkiss	HS	29	....	....	....	....	....	8	2.00	....	....	....	....	....	....	....
1993-94	Hotchkiss	HS	18	....	....	....	856	....	8	2.01	....	....	....	....	....	....	....

McARTHUR, MARK
NYI

Goaltender. Catches left. 5'11", 189 lbs. Born, Peterborough, Ont., November 16, 1975.
(NY Islanders' 5th choice, 112th overall, in 1994 Entry Draft).

			Regular Season								Playoffs						
Season	Club	Lea	GP	W	L	T	Mins	GA	SO	Avg	GP	W	L	Mins	GA	SO	Avg
1992-93	Guelph	OHL	35	14	14	3	1853	180	0	5.83	....	....	....	....	....	....	....
1993-94	Guelph	OHL	51	25	18	5	2936	201	0	4.11	9	4	5	561	38	0	4.06

McKERSIE, JOHN
DAL.

Goaltender. Catches left. 6', 210 lbs. Born, Madison, WI, January 23, 1972.
(Minnesota's 12th choice, 239th overall, in 1990 Entry Draft).

			Regular Season								Playoffs						
Season	Club	Lea	GP	W	L	T	Mins	GA	SO	Avg	GP	W	L	Mins	GA	SO	Avg
1991-92	Boston U.	H.E.	8	3	2	1	396	23	1	3.48	....	....	....	....	....	....	....
1992-93	Boston U.	H.E.	9	6	0	1	466	31	1	3.99	....	....	....	....	....	....	....
1993-94a	Boston U.	H.E.	24	19	4	0	1325	64	0	2.90	....	....	....	....	....	....	....

a NCAA East Second All-American Team (1994)

McLEAN, KIRK
VAN.

Goaltender. Catches left. 6', 195 lbs. Born, Willowdale, Ont., June 26, 1966.
(New Jersey's 6th choice, 107th overall, in 1984 Entry Draft).

			Regular Season								Playoffs						
Season	Club	Lea	GP	W	L	T	Mins	GA	SO	Avg	GP	W	L	Mins	GA	SO	Avg
1983-84	Oshawa	OHL	17	5	9	0	940	67	0	4.28	....	....	....	....	....	....	....
1984-85	Oshawa	OHL	47	23	17	2	2581	143	1	*3.32	5	1	3	271	21	0	4.65
1985-86	**New Jersey**	**NHL**	**2**	**1**	**1**	**0**	**111**	**11**	**0**	**5.95**	....	....	....	....	....	....	....
	Oshawa	OHL	51	24	21	2	2830	169	1	3.58	4	1	2	201	18	0	5.37
1986-87	**New Jersey**	**NHL**	**4**	**1**	**1**	**0**	**160**	**10**	**0**	**3.75**	....	....	....	....	....	....	....
	Maine	AHL	45	15	23	4	2606	140	1	3.22	....	....	....	....	....	....	....
1987-88	**Vancouver**	**NHL**	**41**	**11**	**27**	**3**	**2380**	**147**	**1**	**3.71**	....	....	....	....	....	....	....
1988-89	**Vancouver**	**NHL**	**42**	**20**	**17**	**3**	**2477**	**127**	**4**	**3.08**	**5**	**2**	**3**	**302**	**18**	**0**	**3.58**
1989-90	**Vancouver**	**NHL**	***63**	**21**	**30**	**10**	***3739**	**216**	**0**	**3.47**	....	....	....	....	....	....	....
1990-91	**Vancouver**	**NHL**	**41**	**10**	**22**	**3**	**1969**	**131**	**0**	**3.99**	**2**	**1**	**1**	**123**	**7**	**0**	**3.41**
1991-92a	**Vancouver**	**NHL**	**65**	***38**	**17**	**9**	**3852**	**176**	***5**	**2.74**	**13**	**6**	**7**	**785**	**33**	***2**	**2.52**
1992-93	**Vancouver**	**NHL**	**54**	**28**	**21**	**5**	**3261**	**184**	**3**	**3.39**	**12**	**6**	**6**	**754**	**42**	**0**	**3.34**
1993-94	**Vancouver**	**NHL**	**52**	**23**	**26**	**3**	**3128**	**156**	**3**	**2.99**	***24**	**15**	**9**	***1544**	**59**	***4**	**2.29**
	NHL Totals		**364**	**153**	**162**	**36**	**21077**	**1158**	**16**	**3.30**	**56**	**30**	**26**	**3508**	**159**	**6**	**2.72**

a NHL Second All-Star Team (1992)

Played in NHL All-Star Game (1990, 1992)

Traded to **Vancouver** by **New Jersey** with Greg Adams for Patrik Sundstrom and Vancouver's fourth round choice (Matt Ruchty) in 1988 Entry Draft, September 15, 1987.

McLENNAN, JAMIE
NYI

Goaltender. Catches left. 6', 190 lbs. Born, Edmonton, Alta., June 30, 1971.
(NY Islanders' 3rd choice, 48th overall, in 1991 Entry Draft).

			Regular Season								Playoffs						
Season	Club	Lea	GP	W	L	T	Mins	GA	SO	Avg	GP	W	L	Mins	GA	SO	Avg
1989-90	Lethbridge	WHL	34	20	4	2	1690	110	1	3.91	13	6	5	677	44	0	3.90
1990-91a	Lethbridge	WHL	56	32	18	4	3230	205	0	3.81	*16	8	8	*970	56	0	3.46
1991-92	Capital Dist.	AHL	18	4	10	2	952	60	1	3.78	....	....	....	....	....	....	....
	Richmond	ECHL	32	16	12	2	1837	114	0	3.72	....	....	....	....	....	....	....
1992-93	Capital Dist.	AHL	38	17	14	6	2171	117	1	3.23	1	0	1	20	5	0	15.00
1993-94	**NY Islanders**	**NHL**	**22**	**8**	**7**	**6**	**1287**	**61**	**0**	**2.84**	**2**	**0**	**1**	**82**	**6**	**0**	**4.39**
	Salt Lake	IHL	24	8	12	2	1320	80	0	3.64	....	....	....	....	....	....	....
	NHL Totals		**22**	**8**	**7**	**6**	**1287**	**61**	**0**	**2.84**	**2**	**0**	**1**	**82**	**6**	**0**	**4.39**

a WHL East First All-Star Team (1991)

MICHAUD, MARK

Goaltender. Catches left. 5'10", 175 lbs. Born, Quebec, Que., August 15, 1967.

			Regular Season								Playoffs						
Season	Club	Lea	GP	W	L	T	Mins	GA	SO	Avg	GP	W	L	Mins	GA	SO	Avg
1988-89	Miami-Ohio	CCHA	24	7	12	0	1241	105	0	5.08	....	....	....	....	....	....	....
1989-90	Miami-Ohio	CCHA	33	11	18	3	1753	149	0	5.10	....	....	....	....	....	....	....
1990-91	Miami-Ohio	CCHA	19	2	13	1	929	91	0	5.87	....	....	....	....	....	....	....
1991-92	Miami-Ohio	CCHA	31	14	12	4	1577	112	0	4.26	....	....	....	....	....	....	....
1992-93	New Haven	AHL	12	2	7	1	550	51	0	5.56	....	....	....	....	....	....	....
	Thunder Bay	ColHL	22	12	7	2	1280	82	1	3.84	....	....	....	....	....	....	....
1993-94a	Hampton Rds.	ECHL	*65	*38	17	8	*3723	214	1	3.45	7	3	4	420	25	*1	3.57

a ECHL Second All-Star Team (1994)

Signed as a free agent by **Ottawa**, October 8, 1992.

MIGNACCA, SONNY
VAN.

Goaltender. Catches left. 5'8", 178 lbs. Born, Winnipeg, Man., January 4, 1974.
(Vancouver's 10th choice, 213th overall, in 1992 Entry Draft).

			Regular Season								Playoffs						
Season	Club	Lea	GP	W	L	T	Mins	GA	SO	Avg	GP	W	L	Mins	GA	SO	Avg
1990-91	Medicine Hat	WHL	33	17	9	2	1743	121	0	4.17	1	0	0	13	2	0	9.23
1991-92a	Medicine Hat	WHL	56	35	19	0	3207	189	2	3.54	4	0	4	240	17	0	4.25
1992-93	Medicine Hat	WHL	50	18	25	2	2724	210	1	4.63	10	5	5	605	36	0	3.57
1993-94a	Medicine Hat	WHL	60	26	23	5	3361	183	2	3.27	3	0	3	180	17	0	5.67

a WHL East Second All-Star Team (1992, 1994)

MIKLENDA, JAROSLAV

Goaltender. Catches left. 6'1", 176 lbs. Born, Uherske Hradiste, Czech., March 7, 1974.
(Ottawa's 7th choice, 146th overall, in 1992 Entry Draft).

			Regular Season								Playoffs						
Season	Club	Lea	GP	W	L	T	Mins	GA	SO	Avg	GP	W	L	Mins	GA	SO	Avg
1991-92	Olomouc	Czech.	1	....	....	....	36	6	0	9.99	....	....	....	....	....	....	....
1992-93	Olomouc	Czech.	5	....	....	....	285	22	....	4.63	....	....	....	....	....	....	....
1993-94	TJ Vitkovice	Czech.	10	....	....	....	555	25	0	2.71	....	....	....	....	....	....	....

MOEN, JEFFREY
DAL.

Goaltender. Catches left. 6'1", 170 lbs. Born, Roseville, MN, February 9, 1974.
(Minnesota's 11th choice, 250th overall, in 1992 Entry Draft).

			Regular Season								Playoffs						
Season	Club	Lea	GP	W	L	T	Mins	GA	SO	Avg	GP	W	L	Mins	GA	SO	Avg
1992-93	U. Minnesota	WCHA	6	0	3	1	303	20	0	3.96	....	....	....	....	....	....	....
1993-94	U. Minnesota	WCHA	20	11	8	1	1083	60	0	3.32	....	....	....	....	....	....	....

MOOG, ANDY (MOHG) DAL.

Goaltender. Catches left. 5'8", 170 lbs. Born, Penticton, B.C., February 18, 1960.
(Edmonton's 6th choice, 132nd overall, in 1980 Entry Draft).

			Regular Season								Playoffs						
Season	Club	Lea	GP	W	L	T	Mins	GA	SO	Avg	GP	W	L	Mins	GA	SO	Avg
1978-79	Billings	WHL	26	13	5	4	1306	90	4	4.13	5	1	3	229	21	0	5.50
1979-80a	Billings	WHL	46	23	14	1	2435	149	1	3.67	3	2	1	190	10	0	3.16
1980-81	**Edmonton**	**NHL**	**7**	**3**	**3**	**0**	**313**	**20**	**0**	**3.83**	**9**	**5**	**4**	**526**	**32**	**0**	**3.65**
	Wichita	CHL	29	14	13	1	1602	89	0	3.33	5	3	2	300	16	0	3.20
1981-82	**Edmonton**	**NHL**	**8**	**3**	**5**	**0**	**399**	**32**	**0**	**4.81**	....	....	....	....	....	....	....
b	Wichita	CHL	40	23	13	3	2391	119	1	2.99	7	3	4	434	23	0	3.18
1982-83	**Edmonton**	**NHL**	**50**	**33**	**8**	**7**	**2833**	**167**	**1**	**3.54**	**16**	**11**	**5**	**949**	**48**	**0**	**3.03**
1983-84	**Edmonton**	**NHL**	**38**	**27**	**8**	**1**	**2212**	**139**	**1**	**3.77**	**7**	**4**	**0**	**263**	**12**	**0**	**2.74**
1984-85	**Edmonton**	**NHL**	**39**	**22**	**9**	**3**	**2019**	**111**	**1**	**3.30**	**2**	**0**	**0**	**20**	**0**	**0**	**0.00**
1985-86	**Edmonton**	**NHL**	**47**	**27**	**9**	**7**	**2664**	**164**	**1**	**3.69**	**1**	**1**	**0**	**60**	**1**	**0**	**1.00**
1986-87	**Edmonton**	**NHL**	**46**	**28**	**11**	**3**	**2461**	**144**	**0**	**3.51**	**2**	**2**	**0**	**120**	**8**	**0**	**4.00**
1987-88	Cdn. National	....	27	10	7	5	1438	86	0	3.58	....	....	....	....	....	....	....
	Cdn. Olympic	....	4	4	0	0	240	9	1	2.25	....	....	....	....	....	....	....
	Boston	**NHL**	**6**	**4**	**2**	**0**	**360**	**17**	**1**	**2.83**	**7**	**1**	**4**	**354**	**25**	**0**	**4.24**
1988-89	**Boston**	**NHL**	**41**	**18**	**14**	**8**	**2482**	**133**	**1**	**3.22**	**6**	**4**	**2**	**359**	**14**	**0**	**2.34**
1989-90c	**Boston**	**NHL**	**46**	**24**	**10**	**7**	**2536**	**122**	**3**	**2.89**	**20**	**13**	**7**	**1195**	**44**	***2**	***2.21**
1990-91	**Boston**	**NHL**	**51**	**25**	**13**	**9**	**2844**	**136**	**4**	**2.87**	**19**	**10**	**9**	**1133**	**60**	**0**	**3.18**
1991-92	**Boston**	**NHL**	**62**	**28**	**22**	**9**	**3640**	**196**	**1**	**3.23**	**15**	**8**	**7**	**866**	**46**	**1**	**3.19**
1992-93	**Boston**	**NHL**	**55**	**37**	**14**	**3**	**3194**	**168**	**3**	**3.16**	**3**	**0**	**3**	**161**	**14**	**0**	**5.22**
1993-94	**Dallas**	**NHL**	**55**	**24**	**20**	**7**	**3121**	**170**	**2**	**3.27**	**4**	**1**	**3**	**246**	**12**	**0**	**2.93**
	NHL Totals		**551**	**303**	**148**	**64**	**31078**	**1719**	**19**	**3.32**	**111**	**60**	**44**	**6252**	**316**	**3**	**3.03**

a WHL Second All-Star Team (1980)
b CHL Second All-Star Team (1982)
c Shared William Jennings Trophy with Rejean Lemelin (1990)

Played in NHL All-Star Game (1985, 1986, 1991)

Traded to **Boston** by **Edmonton** for Geoff Courtnall, Bill Ranford and Boston's second choice (Petro Koivunen) in 1988 Entry Draft, March 8, 1988. Traded to **Dallas** by **Boston** for Jon Casey to complete June 20, 1993 trade which sent Gord Murphy to Dallas for future considerations, June 25, 1993.

MOSS, TYLER T.B.

Goaltender. Catches right. 6', 168 lbs. Born, Ottawa, Ont., June 29, 1975.
(Tampa Bay's 2nd choice, 29th overall, in 1993 Entry Draft).

			Regular Season								Playoffs						
Season	Club	Lea	GP	W	L	T	Mins	GA	SO	Avg	GP	W	L	Mins	GA	SO	Avg
1992-93	Kingston	OHL	31	13	7	5	1537	97	0	3.79	6	1	2	228	19	0	5.00
1993-94	Kingston	OHL	13	6	4	3	795	42	1	3.17	3	0	2	136	8	0	3.53

MULLAHY, BRAD

Goaltender. Catches left. 5'10", 185 lbs. Born, North Easton, MA, February 12, 1970.
(Winnipeg's 1st choice, 5th overall, in 1991 Supplemental Draft).

			Regular Season								Playoffs						
Season	Club	Lea	GP	W	L	T	Mins	GA	SO	Avg	GP	W	L	Mins	GA	SO	Avg
1989-90	Providence	H.E.	5	2	1	0	207	13	0	3.77	....	....	....	....	....	....	....
1990-91	Providence	H.E.	22	14	5	1	1257	65	0	3.10	....	....	....	....	....	....	....
1991-92	Providence	H.E.	22	11	9	2	1291	80	2	3.72	....	....	....	....	....	....	....
1992-93	Providence	H.E.	25	8	8	1	1169	82	1	4.16	....	....	....	....	....	....	....
1993-94	Birmingham	ECHL	41	20	16	1	2298	150	1	3.92	2	1	1	120	9	0	4.50

MULLIN, MATT HFD.

Goaltender. Catches left. 5'3", 150 lbs. Born, Guelph, Ont., November 9, 1974.

			Regular Season								Playoffs						
Season	Club	Lea	GP	W	L	T	Mins	GA	SO	Avg	GP	W	L	Mins	GA	SO	Avg
1991-92	Windsor	OHL	45	12	16	7	2263	172	0	4.56	6	2	3	326	17	1	3.13
1992-93	Windsor	OHL	55	15	32	4	3070	249	0	4.87	....	....	....	....	....	....	....
1993-94	Windsor	OHL	21	3	9	2	910	60	1	3.96	....	....	....	....	....	....	....
	Sudbury	OHL	35	23	9	3	2113	110	1	3.12	10	5	5	646	38	0	3.53

MURRAY, SHAWN CGY.

Goaltender. Catches left. 5'9", 170 lbs. Born, St. Paul, MN, September 3, 1971.
(Calgary's 9th choice, 167th overall, in 1990 Entry Draft).

			Regular Season								Playoffs						
Season	Club	Lea	GP	W	L	T	Mins	GA	SO	Avg	GP	W	L	Mins	GA	SO	Avg
1990-91	Colgate	ECAC	6	2	2	0	311	21	0	4.06	....	....	....	....	....	....	....
1991-92	Colgate	ECAC	15	7	7	0	904	71	0	4.71	....	....	....	....	....	....	....
1992-93	Colgate	ECAC	15	5	7	1	723	50	0	4.15	....	....	....	....	....	....	....
1993-94	Colgate	ECAC	3	1	2	0	125	9	0	4.32	....	....	....	....	....	....	....

MUZZATTI, JASON (moo-ZAH-tee) CGY.

Goaltender. Catches left. 6'1", 190 lbs. Born, Toronto, Ont., February 3, 1970.
(Calgary's 1st choice, 21st overall, in 1988 Entry Draft).

			Regular Season								Playoffs						
Season	Club	Lea	GP	W	L	T	Mins	GA	SO	Avg	GP	W	L	Mins	GA	SO	Avg
1987-88a	Michigan State	CCHA	33	19	9	3	1915	109	0	3.41	....	....	....	....	....	....	....
1988-89	Michigan State	CCHA	42	32	9	1	2515	127	3	*3.03	....	....	....	....	....	....	....
1989-90bc	Michigan State	CCHA	33	*24	6	0	1976	99	0	3.01	....	....	....	....	....	....	....
1990-91	Michigan State	CCHA	22	8	10	2	1204	75	1	3.74	....	....	....	....	....	....	....
1991-92	Salt Lake	IHL	52	24	22	5	3033	167	2	3.30	4	1	3	247	18	0	4.37
1992-93	Cdn. National		16	6	9	0	880	53	0	3.84	....	....	....	....	....	....	....
	Indianapolis	IHL	12	5	6	1	707	48	0	4.07	....	....	....	....	....	....	....
	Salt Lake	IHL	13	5	6	1	747	52	0	4.18	....	....	....	....	....	....	....
1993-94	**Calgary**	**NHL**	**1**	**0**	**1**	**0**	**60**	**8**	**0**	**8.00**	....	....	....	....	....	....	....
	Saint John	AHL	51	26	21	3	2939	183	2	3.74	7	3	4	415	19	0	2.75
	NHL Totals		**1**	**0**	**1**	**0**	**60**	**8**	**0**	**8.00**	....	....	....	....	....	....	....

a CCHA Second All-Star Team (1988)
b CCHA First All-Star Team (1990)
c NCAA West Second All-American Team (1990)

NEWMAN, THOMAS

Goaltender. Catches left. 6'1", 185 lbs. Born, Golden Valley, MN, February 23, 1971.
(Los Angeles' 4th choice, 103rd overall, in 1989 Entry Draft).

			Regular Season								Playoffs						
Season	Club	Lea	GP	W	L	T	Mins	GA	SO	Avg	GP	W	L	Mins	GA	SO	Avg
1989-90	U. Minnesota	WCHA	35	19	13	2	1982	127	0	3.84	....	....	....	....	....	....	....
1990-91	U. Minnesota	WCHA	22	12	2	2	942	54	2	3.44	....	....	....	....	....	....	....
1991-92	U. Minnesota	WCHA	11	5	1	0	399	15	0	2.26	....	....	....	....	....	....	....
1992-93	Minnesota	WCHA	22	14	4	2	1172	61	3	3.12	....	....	....	....	....	....	....
1993-94	Greensboro	ECHL	39	21	12	3	2151	142	0	3.96	8	4	4	463	21	0	2.72

NOBLE, TOM CHI.

Goaltender. Catches left. 5'10", 165 lbs. Born, Quincy, MA, March 21, 1975.
(Chicago's 12th choice, 284th overall, in 1993 Entry Draft).

			Regular Season								Playoffs						
Season	Club	Lea	GP	W	L	T	Mins	GA	SO	Avg	GP	W	L	Mins	GA	SO	Avg
1992-93	Catholic Mem.	HS	21	....	....	....	1475	31	4	1.25	....	....	....	....	....	....	....
1993-94	Catholic Mem.	HS	24	....	....	....	1080	22	....	0.93	....	....	....	....	....	....	....

O'NEILL, MIKE WPG.

Goaltender. Catches left. 5'7", 160 lbs. Born, LaSalle, Que., November 3, 1967.
(Winnipeg's 1st choice, 15th overall, in 1988 Supplemental Draft).

			Regular Season								Playoffs						
Season	Club	Lea	GP	W	L	T	Mins	GA	SO	Avg	GP	W	L	Mins	GA	SO	Avg
1985-86	Yale	ECAC	6	3	1	0	389	17	0	3.53	....	....	....	....	....	....	....
1986-87a	Yale	ECAC	16	9	6	1	964	55	2	3.42	....	....	....	....	....	....	....
1987-88	Yale	ECAC	24	6	17	0	1385	101	0	4.37	....	....	....	....	....	....	....
1988-89ab	Yale	ECAC	25	10	14	1	1490	93	0	3.74	....	....	....	....	....	....	....
1989-90	Tappara	Fin.	41	23	13	5	2369	127	2	3.22	....	....	....	....	....	....	....
1990-91	Fort Wayne	IHL	8	5	2	1	490	31	0	3.80	....	....	....	....	....	....	....
	Moncton	AHL	30	13	7	6	1613	84	0	3.12	8	3	4	435	29	0	4.00
1991-92	**Winnipeg**	**NHL**	**1**	**0**	**0**	**0**	**13**	**1**	**0**	**4.62**	....	....	....	....	....	....	....
	Moncton	AHL	32	14	16	2	1902	108	1	3.41	11	4	7	670	43	*1	3.85
	Fort Wayne	IHL	33	22	6	3	1858	97	*4	3.13	....	....	....	....	....	....	....
1992-93	**Winnipeg**	**NHL**	**2**	**0**	**0**	**1**	**73**	**6**	**0**	**4.93**	....	....	....	....	....	....	....
	Moncton	AHL	30	13	10	4	1649	88	1	3.20	....	....	....	....	....	....	....
1993-94	**Winnipeg**	**NHL**	**17**	**0**	**9**	**1**	**738**	**51**	**0**	**4.15**	....	....	....	....	....	....	....
	Moncton	AHL	12	8	4	0	716	33	1	2.76	....	....	....	....	....	....	....
	Fort Wayne	IHL	11	4	4	3	642	38	0	3.55	....	....	....	....	....	....	....
	NHL Totals		**20**	**0**	**9**	**2**	**824**	**58**	**0**	**4.22**	....	....	....	....	....	....	....

a ECAC First All-Star Team (1987, 1989)
b NCAA East First All-American Team (1989)

OSGOOD, CHRIS DET.

Goaltender. Catches left. 5'10", 175 lbs. Born, Peace River, Alta., November 26, 1972.
(Detroit's 3rd choice, 54th overall, in 1991 Entry Draft).

			Regular Season								Playoffs						
Season	Club	Lea	GP	W	L	T	Mins	GA	SO	Avg	GP	W	L	Mins	GA	SO	Avg
1989-90	Medicine Hat	WHL	57	24	28	2	3094	228	0	4.42	3	0	3	173	17	0	5.91
1990-91a	Medicine Hat	WHL	46	23	18	3	2630	173	2	3.95	12	7	5	712	42	0	3.54
1991-92	Medicine Hat	WHL	15	10	3	0	819	44	0	3.22	....	....	....	....	....	....	....
	Brandon	WHL	16	3	10	1	890	60	1	4.04	....	....	....	....	....	....	....
	Seattle	WHL	21	12	7	1	1217	65	1	3.20	15	9	6	904	51	0	3.38
1992-93	Adirondack	AHL	45	19	19	4	2438	159	0	3.91	1	0	1	59	2	0	2.03
1993-94	**Detroit**	**NHL**	**41**	**23**	**8**	**5**	**2206**	**105**	**2**	**2.86**	**6**	**3**	**2**	**307**	**12**	**1**	**2.35**
	Adirondack	AHL	4	3	1	0	239	13	0	3.26	....	....	....	....	....	....	....
	NHL Totals		**41**	**23**	**8**	**5**	**2206**	**105**	**2**	**2.86**	**6**	**3**	**2**	**307**	**12**	**1**	**2.35**

a WHL East Second All-Star Team (1991)

PASSMORE, STEVE EDM.

Goaltender. Catches left. 5'9", 165 lbs. Born, Thunder Bay, Ont., January 29, 1973.
(Quebec's 9th choice, 196th overall, in 1992 Entry Draft).

			Regular Season								Playoffs						
Season	Club	Lea	GP	W	L	T	Mins	GA	SO	Avg	GP	W	L	Mins	GA	SO	Avg
1990-91	Victoria	WHL	35	3	25	1	1838	190	0	6.20	....	....	....	....	....	....	....
1991-92	Victoria	WHL	*71	15	50	5	*4228	347	0	4.92	....	....	....	....	....	....	....
1992-93a	Victoria	WHL	43	14	24	2	2402	150	1	3.75	....	....	....	....	....	....	....
	Kamloops	WHL	25	19	6	0	1479	69	1	2.80	7	4	2	401	22	1	3.29
1993-94a	Kamloops	WHL	36	22	9	2	1927	88	1	*2.74	*17	*11	6	*1051	55	0	3.14

a WHL West First All-Star Team (1993, 1994)

Traded to **Edmonton** by **Quebec** for Brad Werenka, March 21, 1994.

PERSSON, JOAKIM (PEHR-suhn) BOS.

Goaltender. Catches left. 5'11", 176 lbs. Born, Ostervala, Sweden, May 4, 1970.
(Boston's 10th choice, 259th overall, in 1993 Entry Draft).

			Regular Season								Playoffs						
Season	Club	Lea	GP	W	L	T	Mins	GA	SO	Avg	GP	W	L	Mins	GA	SO	Avg
1992-93	Hammarby	Swe. 2	40	....	....	....	....	....	....	2.71	....	....	....	....	....	....	....
1993-94	Hammarby	Swe. 2	2	....	....	....	....	59	....	2.57	....	....	....	....	....	....	....
	Providence	AHL	1	0	0	0	24	0	0	0.00	....	....	....	....	....	....	....

PIETRANGELO, FRANK (PEE-tuhr-AN-jehl-oh) NYI

Goaltender. Catches left. 5'10", 185 lbs. Born, Niagara Falls, Ont., December 17, 1964.
(Pittsburgh's 4th choice, 63rd overall, in 1983 Entry Draft).

			Regular Season								Playoffs						
Season	Club	Lea	GP	W	L	T	Mins	GA	SO	Avg	GP	W	L	Mins	GA	SO	Avg
1982-83	U. Minnesota	WCHA	25	15	6	1	1348	80	1	3.55	....	....	....	....	....	....	....
1983-84	U. Minnesota	WCHA	20	13	7	0	1141	66	0	3.47	....	....	....	....	....	....	....
1984-85	U. Minnesota	WCHA	17	8	3	3	912	52	0	3.42	....	....	....	....	....	....	....
1985-86	U. Minnesota	WCHA	23	15	7	0	1284	76	0	3.55	....	....	....	....	....	....	....
1986-87	Muskegon	IHL	35	23	11	0	2090	119	2	3.42	15	10	4	923	46	0	2.99
1987-88	**Pittsburgh**	**NHL**	**21**	**9**	**11**	**0**	**1207**	**80**	**1**	**3.98**	....	....	....	....	....	....	....
	Muskegon	IHL	15	11	3	1	868	43	2	2.97	....	....	....	....	....	....	....
1988-89	**Pittsburgh**	**NHL**	**15**	**5**	**3**	**0**	**669**	**45**	**0**	**4.04**	....	....	....	....	....	....	....
	Muskegon	IHL	13	10	1	0	760	38	1	3.00	9	*8	1	566	29	0	3.07
1989-90	**Pittsburgh**	**NHL**	**21**	**8**	**6**	**2**	**1066**	**77**	**0**	**4.33**	....	....	....	....	....	....	....
	Muskegon	IHL	12	9	2	1	691	38	0	3.30	....	....	....	....	....	....	....
1990-91	**Pittsburgh**	**NHL**	**25**	**10**	**11**	**1**	**1311**	**86**	**0**	**3.94**	**5**	**4**	**1**	**288**	**15**	***1**	**3.13**
1991-92	**Pittsburgh**	**NHL**	**5**	**2**	**1**	**0**	**225**	**20**	**0**	**5.33**	....	....	....	....	....	....	....
	Hartford	**NHL**	**5**	**3**	**1**	**1**	**306**	**12**	**0**	**2.35**	**7**	**3**	**4**	**425**	**19**	**0**	**2.68**
1992-93	**Hartford**	**NHL**	**30**	**4**	**15**	**1**	**1373**	**111**	**0**	**4.85**	....	....	....	....	....	....	....
1993-94	**Hartford**	**NHL**	**19**	**5**	**11**	**1**	**984**	**59**	**0**	**3.60**	....	....	....	....	....	....	....
	Springfield	AHL	23	9	10	2	1314	73	0	3.33	6	2	4	324	23	0	4.26
	NHL Totals		**141**	**46**	**59**	**6**	**7141**	**490**	**1**	**4.12**	**12**	**7**	**5**	**713**	**34**	**1**	**2.86**

Traded to **Hartford** by **Pittsburgh** for Hartford's third round choice (Sven Butenschon) and seventh round choice (Serge Aubin) in 1994 Entry Draft, March 10, 1992. Signed as a free agent by **NY Islanders**, July 28, 1994.

POTVIN, FELIX (PAHT-vihn) TOR.

Goaltender. Catches left. 6'1", 183 lbs. Born, Anjou, Que., June 23, 1971.
(Toronto's 2nd choice, 31st overall, in 1990 Entry Draft).

			Regular Season								Playoffs						
Season	Club	Lea	GP	W	L	T	Mins	GA	SO	Avg	GP	W	L	Mins	GA	SO	Avg
1988-89	Chicoutimi	QMJHL	*65	25	31	1	*3489	271	*2	4.66	....	....	....	....	....	....	....
1989-90a	Chicoutimi	QMJHL	*62	*31	26	2	*3478	231	*2	3.99	....	....	....	....	....	....	....
1990-91																	
bcde	Chicoutimi	QMJHL	54	33	15	4	3216	145	*6	*2.70	*16	*11	5	*992	46	0	*2.78
1991-92	Toronto	NHL	4	0	2	1	210	8	0	2.29	....	....	....	....	....	....	....
fgh	St. John's	AHL	35	18	10	6	2070	101	2	2.93	11	7	4	642	41	0	3.83
1992-93i	Toronto	NHL	48	25	15	7	2781	116	2	*2.50	*21	11	10	*1308	62	1	2.84
	St. John's	AHL	5	3	0	2	309	18	0	3.50	....	....	....	....	....	....	....
1993-94	Toronto	NHL	66	34	22	9	3883	187	3	2.89	18	9	9	1124	46	3	2.46
	NHL Totals		118	59	39	17	6874	311	5	2.71	39	20	19	2432	108	4	2.66

a QMJHL Second All-Star Team (1990)
b QMJHL First All-Star Team (1991)
c Canadian Major Junior Goaltender of the Year (1991)
d Memorial Cup All-Star Team (1991)
e Won Hap Emms Memorial Trophy (Memorial Cup Top Goaltender) (1991)
f Won Baz Bastien Trophy (Top Goaltender - AHL) (1992)
g Won Dudley "Red" Garrett Memorial Trophy (Top Rookie - AHL) (1992)
h AHL First All-Star Team (1992)
i NHL/Upper Deck All-Rookie Team (1993)

Played in NHL All-Star Game (1994)

PUPPA, DAREN (POO-puh) T.B.

Goaltender. Catches right. 6'3", 205 lbs. Born, Kirkland Lake, Ont., March 23, 1965.
(Buffalo's 6th choice, 74th overall, in 1983 Entry Draft).

			Regular Season								Playoffs						
Season	Club	Lea	GP	W	L	T	Mins	GA	SO	Avg	GP	W	L	Mins	GA	SO	Avg
1983-84	RPI	ECAC	32	24	6	0	....	....	....	2.94	....	....	....	....	....	....	....
1984-85	RPI	ECAC	32	31	1	0	1830	78	0	2.56	....	....	....	....	....	....	....
1985-86	Buffalo	NHL	7	3	4	0	401	21	1	3.14	....	....	....	....	....	....	....
	Rochester	AHL	20	8	11	0	1092	79	0	4.34	....	....	....	....	....	....	....
1986-87	Buffalo	NHL	3	0	2	1	185	13	0	4.22	....	....	....	....	....	....	....
a	Rochester	AHL	57	*33	14	0	3129	146	1	2.80	*16	*10	6	*944	48	*1	3.05
1987-88	Buffalo	NHL	17	8	6	1	874	61	0	4.19	3	1	1	142	11	0	4.65
	Rochester	AHL	26	14	8	2	1415	65	2	2.76	2	0	1	108	5	0	2.78
1988-89	Buffalo	NHL	37	17	10	6	1908	107	1	3.36	....	....	....	....	....	....	....
1989-90b	Buffalo	NHL	56	*31	16	6	3241	156	1	2.89	6	2	4	370	15	0	2.43
1990-91	Buffalo	NHL	38	15	11	6	2092	118	2	3.38	2	0	1	81	10	0	7.41
1991-92	Buffalo	NHL	33	11	14	4	1757	114	0	3.89	....	....	....	....	....	....	....
	Rochester	AHL	2	0	2	0	119	9	0	4.54	....	....	....	....	....	....	....
1992-93	Buffalo	NHL	24	11	5	4	1306	78	0	3.58	....	....	....	....	....	....	....
	Toronto	NHL	8	6	2	0	479	18	2	2.25	1	0	0	20	1	0	3.00
1993-94	Tampa Bay	NHL	63	22	33	6	3653	165	4	2.71	....	....	....	....	....	....	....
	NHL Totals		286	124	103	34	15896	851	11	3.21	12	3	6	613	37	0	3.62

a AHL First All-Star Team (1987)
b NHL Second All-Star Team (1990)

Played in NHL All-Star Game (1990)

Traded to **Toronto** by **Buffalo** with Dave Andreychuk and Buffalo's first round choice (Kenny Jonsson) in 1993 Entry Draft for Grant Fuhr and future considerations, February 2, 1993. Claimed by **Florida** from **Toronto** in Expansion Draft, June 24, 1993. Claimed by **Tampa Bay** from **Florida** in Phase II of Expansion Draft, June 25, 1993.

PYE, BILL

Goaltender. Catches left. 5'9", 180 lbs. Born, Canton, MI, April 9, 1969.
(Buffalo's 5th choice, 107th overall, in 1989 Entry Draft).

			Regular Season								Playoffs						
Season	Club	Lea	GP	W	L	T	Mins	GA	SO	Avg	GP	W	L	Mins	GA	SO	Avg
1987-88	N. Michigan	WCHA	13	....	....	....	654	49	0	4.49	....	....	....	....	....	....	....
1988-89	N. Michigan	WCHA	43	26	15	2	2533	133	1	3.15	....	....	....	....	....	....	....
1989-90	N. Michigan	WCHA	36	20	14	1	2035	149	1	4.39	....	....	....	....	....	....	....
1990-91abc	N. Michigan	WCHA	39	*32	3	4	2300	109	*4	2.84	....	....	....	....	....	....	....
1991-92	Rochester	AHL	7	0	4	0	272	13	0	2.87	1	1	0	60	2	0	2.00
	New Haven	AHL	4	0	3	1	200	19	0	5.70	....	....	....	....	....	....	....
	Fort Wayne	IHL	8	5	2	1	451	29	0	3.86	....	....	....	....	....	....	....
	Erie	ECHL	5	5	0	0	310	22	0	4.26	4	1	3	220	15	0	4.09
1992-93	Rochester	AHL	26	9	14	2	1427	107	0	4.50	....	....	....	....	....	....	....
1993-94	Rochester	AHL	19	7	7	2	980	70	0	4.29	....	....	....	....	....	....	....
	S. Carolina	ECHL	28	15	10	2	1578	95	1	3.61	3	1	2	178	12	0	4.03

a WCHA First All-Star Team (1991)
b NCAA West Second All-American Team (1991)
c NCAA Final Four All-Tournament Team (1991)

RACICOT, ANDRE (RAH-sih-KOH)

Goaltender. Catches left. 5'11", 165 lbs. Born, Rouyn-Noranda, Que., June 9, 1969.
(Montreal's 5th choice, 83rd overall, in 1989 Entry Draft).

			Regular Season								Playoffs						
Season	Club	Lea	GP	W	L	T	Mins	GA	SO	Avg	GP	W	L	Mins	GA	SO	Avg
1986-87	Longueuil	QMJHL	3	1	2	0	180	19	0	6.33	....	....	....	....	....	....	....
1987-88	Granby	QMJHL	30	15	11	1	1547	105	1	4.07	5	1	4	298	23	0	4.63
1988-89a	Granby	QMJHL	54	22	24	3	2944	198	0	4.04	4	0	4	218	18	0	4.95
1989-90	Montreal	NHL	1	0	0	0	13	3	0	13.85	....	....	....	....	....	....	....
b	Sherbrooke	AHL	33	19	11	2	1948	97	1	2.99	5	0	4	227	18	0	4.76
1990-91	Montreal	NHL	21	7	9	2	975	52	1	3.20	2	0	1	12	2	0	10.00
	Fredericton	AHL	22	13	8	1	1252	60	1	2.88	....	....	....	....	....	....	....
1991-92	Montreal	NHL	9	0	3	3	436	23	0	3.17	1	0	0	1	0	0	0.00
	Fredericton	AHL	28	14	8	5	1666	86	0	3.10	....	....	....	....	....	....	....
1992-93	Montreal	NHL	26	17	5	1	1433	81	1	3.39	1	0	0	18	2	0	6.67
1993-94	Montreal	NHL	11	2	6	2	500	37	0	4.44	....	....	....	....	....	....	....
	Fredericton	AHL	6	1	4	0	292	16	0	3.28	....	....	....	....	....	....	....
	NHL Totals		68	26	23	8	3357	196	2	3.50	4	0	1	31	4	0	7.74

a QMJHL Second All-Star Team (1989)
b Shared Harry "Hap" Holmes Trophy (fewest goals-against - AHL) with J.C. Bergeron (1990)

RACINE, BRUCE TOR.

Goaltender. Catches left. 6', 178 lbs. Born, Cornwall, Ont., August 9, 1966.
(Pittsburgh's 3rd choice, 58th overall, in 1985 Entry Draft).

			Regular Season								Playoffs						
Season	Club	Lea	GP	W	L	T	Mins	GA	SO	Avg	GP	W	L	Mins	GA	SO	Avg
1984-85	Northeastern	H.E.	26	11	14	1	1615	103	1	3.83	....	....	....	....	....	....	....
1985-86	Northeastern	H.E.	32	17	14	1	1920	147	0	4.56	....	....	....	....	....	....	....
1986-87ab	Northeastern	H.E.	33	12	18	3	1966	133	0	4.06	....	....	....	....	....	....	....
1987-88b	Northeastern	H.E.	30	15	11	4	1808	108	1	3.58	....	....	....	....	....	....	....
1988-89	Muskegon	IHL	51	*37	11	0	*3039	184	*3	3.63	5	4	1	300	15	0	3.00
1989-90	Muskegon	IHL	49	29	15	4	2911	182	1	3.75	9	5	4	566	32	1	3.34
1990-91	Albany	IHL	29	7	18	1	1567	104	0	3.98	....	....	....	....	....	....	....
	Muskegon	IHL	9	4	4	1	516	40	0	4.65	....	....	....	....	....	....	....
1991-92	Muskegon	IHL	27	13	10	3	1559	91	1	3.50	1	0	1	60	6	0	6.00
1992-93	Cleveland	IHL	35	13	16	6	1949	140	1	4.31	2	0	0	37	2	0	3.24
1993-94	St. John's	AHL	37	20	9	2	1875	116	0	3.71	1	0	0	20	1	0	0.00

a Hockey East First All-Star Team (1987)
b NCAA East First All-American Team (1987, 1988)

Signed as a free agent by **Toronto**, August 11, 1993.

RAM, JAMIE NYR

Goaltender. Catches left. 5'11", 164 lbs. Born, Scarborough, Ont., January 18, 1971.
(NY Rangers' 10th choice, 213th overall, in 1991 Entry Draft).

			Regular Season								Playoffs						
Season	Club	Lea	GP	W	L	T	Mins	GA	SO	Avg	GP	W	L	Mins	GA	SO	Avg
1990-91	Michigan Tech	WCHA	14	5	9	0	826	57	0	4.14	....	....	....	....	....	....	....
1991-92	Michigan Tech	WCHA	23	9	9	1	1144	83	0	4.35	....	....	....	....	....	....	....
1992-93ab	Michigan Tech	WCHA	*36	16	14	5	*2078	115	0	3.32	....	....	....	....	....	....	....
1993-94ab	Michigan Tech	WCHA	39	12	20	5	2192	117	*1	3.20	....	....	....	....	....	....	....

a WCHA First All-Star Team (1993, 1994)
b NCAA West First All-American Team (1993, 1994)

RANFORD, BILL EDM.

Goaltender. Catches left. 5'10", 170 lbs. Born, Brandon, Man., December 14, 1966.
(Boston's 2nd choice, 52nd overall, in 1985 Entry Draft).

			Regular Season								Playoffs						
Season	Club	Lea	GP	W	L	T	Mins	GA	SO	Avg	GP	W	L	Mins	GA	SO	Avg
1983-84	N. Westminster	WHL	27	10	14	0	1450	130	0	5.38	1	0	0	27	2	0	4.44
1984-85	N. Westminster	WHL	38	19	17	0	2034	142	0	4.19	7	2	3	309	26	0	5.05
1985-86	Boston	NHL	4	3	1	0	240	10	0	2.50	2	0	2	120	7	0	3.50
	N. Westminster	WHL	53	17	29	1	2791	225	0	4.84	....	....	....	....	....	....	....
1986-87	Boston	NHL	41	16	20	2	2234	124	3	3.33	2	0	2	123	8	0	3.90
	Moncton	AHL	3	3	0	0	180	6	0	2.00	....	....	....	....	....	....	....
1987-88	Maine	AHL	51	27	16	6	2856	165	1	3.47	....	....	....	....	....	....	....
	Edmonton	NHL	6	3	0	2	325	16	0	2.95	....	....	....	....	....	....	....
1988-89	Edmonton	NHL	29	15	8	2	1509	88	1	3.50	....	....	....	....	....	....	....
1989-90a	Edmonton	NHL	56	24	16	9	3107	165	1	3.19	*22	*16	6	*1401	59	1	2.53
1990-91	Edmonton	NHL	60	27	27	3	3415	182	0	3.20	3	1	2	135	8	0	3.56
1991-92	Edmonton	NHL	67	27	26	10	3822	228	1	3.58	16	8	8	909	51	*2	3.37
1992-93	Edmonton	NHL	67	17	38	6	3753	240	1	3.84	....	....	....	....	....	....	....
1993-94	Edmonton	NHL	71	22	34	11	4070	236	1	3.48	....	....	....	....	....	....	....
	NHL Totals		401	154	170	45	22475	1289	8	3.44	45	25	20	2688	133	3	2.97

a Won Conn Smythe Trophy (1990)

Played in NHL All-Star Game (1991)

Traded to **Edmonton** by **Boston** with Geoff Courtnall and future considerations for Andy Moog, March 8, 1988.

REDDICK, ELDON (POKEY) FLA.

Goaltender. Catches left. 5'8", 170 lbs. Born, Halifax, N.S., October 6, 1964.

			Regular Season								Playoffs						
Season	Club	Lea	GP	W	L	T	Mins	GA	SO	Avg	GP	W	L	Mins	GA	SO	Avg
1982-83	Nanaimo	WHL	66	19	38	1	3549	383	0	6.46	....	....	....	....	....	....	....
1983-84	N. Westminster	WHL	50	24	22	2	2930	215	0	4.40	9	4	5	542	53	0	5.87
1984-85	Brandon	WHL	47	14	30	1	2585	243	0	5.64	....	....	....	....	....	....	....
1985-86	Ft. Wayne	IHL	29	15	11	0	1674	86	*3	3.00	....	....	....	....	....	....	....
1986-87	Winnipeg	NHL	48	21	21	4	2762	149	0	3.24	3	0	2	166	10	0	3.61
1987-88	Winnipeg	NHL	28	9	13	3	1487	102	0	4.12	....	....	....	....	....	....	....
	Moncton	AHL	9	2	6	1	545	26	0	2.86	....	....	....	....	....	....	....
1988-89	Winnipeg	NHL	41	11	17	7	2109	144	0	4.10	....	....	....	....	....	....	....
1989-90	Edmonton	NHL	11	5	4	2	604	31	0	3.08	1	0	0	2	0	0	0.00
	Cape Breton	AHL	15	9	4	1	821	54	0	3.95	....	....	....	....	....	....	....
	Phoenix	IHL	3	2	1	0	185	7	0	2.27	....	....	....	....	....	....	....
1990-91	Edmonton	NHL	2	0	2	0	120	9	0	4.50	....	....	....	....	....	....	....
	Cape Breton	AHL	31	19	10	0	1673	97	2	3.48	2	0	2	124	10	0	4.84
1991-92	Cape Breton	AHL	16	5	3	3	765	45	0	3.53	....	....	....	....	....	....	....
	Ft. Wayne	IHL	14	6	5	2	787	40	1	3.05	7	3	4	369	18	0	2.93
1992-93a	Ft. Wayne	IHL	54	33	16	4	3043	156	3	3.08	*12	*12	0	723	18	0	*1.49
1993-94	Florida	NHL	2	0	1	0	80	8	0	6.00	....	....	....	....	....	....	....
	Cincinnati	IHL	54	31	12	6	2894	147	*2	3.05	10	6	2	498	21	*1	2.53
	NHL Totals		132	46	58	16	7162	443	0	3.71	4	0	2	168	10	0	3.57

a Won "Bud" Poile Trophy (Playoff MVP - IHL) (1993)

Signed as a free agent by **Winnipeg**, September 27, 1985. Traded to **Edmonton** by **Winnipeg** for future considerations, September 28, 1989. Signed as a free agent by **Florida**, July 12, 1993.

REESE, JEFF HFD.

Goaltender. Catches left. 5'9", 170 lbs. Born, Brantford, Ont., March 24, 1966.
(Toronto's 3rd choice, 67th overall, in 1984 Entry Draft).

			Regular Season								Playoffs						
Season	Club	Lea	GP	W	L	T	Mins	GA	SO	Avg	GP	W	L	Mins	GA	SO	Avg
1983-84	London	OHL	43	18	19	0	2308	173	0	4.50	6	3	3	327	27	0	4.95
1984-85	London	OHL	50	31	15	1	2878	186	1	3.88	8	5	2	440	20	1	2.73
1985-86	London	OHL	57	25	26	3	3281	215	0	3.93	5	0	4	299	25	0	5.02
1986-87	Newmarket	AHL	50	11	29	0	2822	193	1	4.10	....	....	....	....	....	....	....
1987-88	Toronto	NHL	5	1	2	1	249	17	0	4.10	....	....	....	....	....	....	....
	Newmarket	AHL	28	10	14	3	1587	103	0	3.89	....	....	....	....	....	....	....
1988-89	Toronto	NHL	10	2	6	1	486	40	0	4.94	....	....	....	....	....	....	....
	Newmarket	AHL	37	17	14	3	2072	132	0	3.82	....	....	....	....	....	....	....
1989-90	Toronto	NHL	21	9	6	3	1101	81	0	4.41	2	1	1	108	6	0	3.33
	Newmarket	AHL	7	3	2	2	431	29	0	4.04	....	....	....	....	....	....	....
1990-91	Toronto	NHL	30	6	13	3	1430	92	1	3.86	....	....	....	....	....	....	....
	Newmarket	AHL	3	2	1	0	180	7	0	2.33	....	....	....	....	....	....	....
1991-92	Toronto	NHL	8	1	5	1	413	20	1	2.91	....	....	....	....	....	....	....
	Calgary	NHL	12	3	2	2	587	37	0	3.78	....	....	....	....	....	....	....
1992-93	Calgary	NHL	26	14	4	1	1311	70	1	3.20	4	1	3	209	17	0	4.88
1993-94	Calgary	NHL	1	0	0	0	13	1	0	4.62	....	....	....	....	....	....	....
	Hartford	NHL	19	5	9	3	1086	56	1	3.09	....	....	....	....	....	....	....
	NHL Totals		132	41	47	15	6676	414	4	3.72	6	2	4	317	23	0	4.35

Traded to **Calgary** with Craig Berube, Alexander Godynyuk, Gary Leeman and Michel Petit for Doug Gilmour, Jamie Macoun, Ric Nattress, Rick Wamsley and Kent Manderville, January 2, 1992. Traded to **Hartford** by **Calgary** for Dan Keczmer, November 19, 1993.

RHODES, DAMIAN — TOR.

Goaltender. Catches left. 6', 175 lbs. Born, St. Paul, MN, May 28, 1969.
(Toronto's 6th choice, 112th overall, in 1987 Entry Draft).

			Regular Season								Playoffs						
Season	Club	Lea	GP	W	L	T	Mins	GA	SO	Avg	GP	W	L	Mins	GA	SO	Avg
1987-88	Michigan Tech	WCHA	29	16	10	1	1625	114	0	4.20	....	....	....	....	....	....	....
1988-89	Michigan Tech	WCHA	37	15	22	0	2216	163	0	4.41	....	....	....	....	....	....	....
1989-90	Michigan Tech	WCHA	25	6	17	0	1358	119	0	6.26	....	....	....	....	....	....	....
1990-91	**Toronto**	**NHL**	**1**	**1**	**0**	**0**	**60**	**1**	**0**	**1.00**	....	....	....	....	....	....	....
	Newmarket	AHL	38	8	24	3	2154	144	1	4.01	....	....	....	....	....	....	....
1991-92	St. John's	AHL	43	20	16	5	2454	148	0	3.62	6	4	1	331	16	0	2.90
1992-93	St. John's	AHL	*52	27	16	8	*3074	184	1	3.59	9	4	5	538	37	0	4.13
1993-94	**Toronto**	**NHL**	**22**	**9**	**7**	**3**	**1213**	**53**	**0**	**2.62**	**1**	**0**	**0**	**1**	**0**	**0**	**0.00**
	NHL Totals		**23**	**10**	**7**	**3**	**1273**	**54**	**0**	**2.55**	**1**	**0**	**0**	**1**	**0**	**0**	**0.00**

Note: Played 10 seconds in playoff game vs. San Jose, May 6, 1994.

RICHTER, MIKE — (RIHK-tuhr) NYR

Goaltender. Catches left. 5'11", 182 lbs. Born, Abington, PA, September 22, 1966.
(NY Rangers' 2nd choice, 28th overall, in 1985 Entry Draft).

			Regular Season								Playoffs						
Season	Club	Lea	GP	W	L	T	Mins	GA	SO	Avg	GP	W	L	Mins	GA	SO	Avg
1985-86	U. Wisconsin	WCHA	24	14	9	0	1394	92	1	3.96	....	....	....	....	....	....	....
1986-87a	U. Wisconsin	WCHA	36	19	16	1	2136	126	0	3.54	....	....	....	....	....	....	....
1987-88	Colorado	IHL	22	16	5	0	1298	68	1	3.14	10	5	3	536	35	0	3.92
	U.S. National	....	29	17	7	2	1559	86	0	3.31	....	....	....	....	....	....	....
	U.S. Olympic	....	4	2	2	0	230	15	0	3.91	....	....	....	....	....	....	....
1988-89	Denver	IHL	*57	23	26	0	3031	217	1	4.30	4	0	4	210	21	0	6.00
	NY Rangers	**NHL**	....	....	....	....	....	....	....	....	**1**	**0**	**1**	**58**	**4**	**0**	**4.14**
1989-90	**NY Rangers**	**NHL**	**23**	**12**	**5**	**5**	**1320**	**66**	**0**	**3.00**	**6**	**3**	**2**	**330**	**19**	**0**	**3.45**
	Flint	IHL	13	7	4	2	782	49	0	3.76	....	....	....	....	....	....	....
1990-91	**NY Rangers**	**NHL**	**45**	**21**	**13**	**7**	**2596**	**135**	**0**	**3.12**	**6**	**2**	**4**	**313**	**14**	***1**	**2.68**
1991-92	**NY Rangers**	**NHL**	**41**	**23**	**12**	**2**	**2298**	**119**	**3**	**3.11**	**7**	**4**	**2**	**412**	**24**	**1**	**3.50**
1992-93	**NY Rangers**	**NHL**	**38**	**13**	**19**	**3**	**2105**	**134**	**1**	**3.82**	....	....	....	....	....	....	....
	Binghamton	AHL	5	4	0	1	305	6	0	1.18	....	....	....	....	....	....	....
1993-94	**NY Rangers**	**NHL**	**68**	***42**	**12**	**6**	**3710**	**159**	**5**	**2.57**	**23**	***16**	**7**	**1417**	**49**	***4**	**2.07**
	NHL Totals		**215**	**111**	**61**	**23**	**12029**	**613**	**9**	**3.06**	**43**	**25**	**16**	**2530**	**110**	**6**	**2.61**

a WCHA Second All-Star Team (1987)

Played in NHL All-Star Game (1992, 1994)

RIENDEAU, VINCENT — (ree-EHN-doh) BOS.

Goaltender. Catches left. 5'10", 185 lbs. Born, St. Hyacinthe, Que., April 20, 1966.

			Regular Season								Playoffs						
Season	Club	Lea	GP	W	L	T	Mins	GA	SO	Avg	GP	W	L	Mins	GA	SO	Avg
1985-86a	Drummondville	QMJHL	57	33	20	3	3336	215	2	3.87	23	10	13	1271	106	1	5.00
1986-87b	Sherbrooke	AHL	41	25	14	0	2363	114	2	2.89	13	8	5	742	47	0	3.80
1987-88	**Montreal**	**NHL**	**1**	**0**	**0**	**0**	**36**	**5**	**0**	**8.33**	....	....	....	....	....	....	....
cd	Sherbrooke	AHL	44	27	13	3	2521	112	*4	*2.67	2	0	2	127	7	0	3.31
1988-89	**St. Louis**	**NHL**	**32**	**11**	**15**	**5**	**1842**	**108**	**0**	**3.52**	....	....	....	....	....	....	....
1989-90	**St. Louis**	**NHL**	**43**	**17**	**19**	**5**	**2551**	**149**	**1**	**3.50**	**8**	**3**	**4**	**397**	**24**	**0**	**3.63**
1990-91	**St. Louis**	**NHL**	**44**	**29**	**9**	**6**	**2671**	**134**	**3**	**3.01**	**13**	**6**	**7**	**687**	**35**	***1**	**3.06**
1991-92	**St. Louis**	**NHL**	**3**	**1**	**2**	**0**	**157**	**11**	**0**	**4.20**	....	....	....	....	....	....	....
	Detroit	**NHL**	**2**	**2**	**0**	**0**	**87**	**2**	**0**	**1.38**	**2**	**1**	**0**	**73**	**4**	**0**	**3.29**
	Adirondack	AHL	3	2	1	0	179	8	0	2.68	....	....	....	....	....	....	....
1992-93	**Detroit**	**NHL**	**22**	**13**	**4**	**2**	**1193**	**64**	**0**	**3.22**	....	....	....	....	....	....	....
1993-94	**Detroit**	**NHL**	**8**	**2**	**4**	**0**	**345**	**23**	**0**	**4.00**	....	....	....	....	....	....	....
	Adirondack	AHL	10	6	3	0	582	30	0	3.09	....	....	....	....	....	....	....
	Boston	**NHL**	**18**	**7**	**6**	**1**	**976**	**50**	**1**	**3.07**	**2**	**1**	**1**	**120**	**8**	**0**	**4.00**
	NHL Totals		**173**	**82**	**59**	**19**	**9858**	**546**	**5**	**3.32**	**25**	**11**	**12**	**1277**	**71**	**1**	**3.34**

a QMJHL Second All-Star Team (1986)
b Won Harry "Hap" Holmes Memorial Trophy (fewest goals-against - AHL) (1987)
c Shared Harry "Hap" Holmes Memorial Trophy (fewest goals-against - AHL) with Jocelyn Perreault (1988)
d AHL Second All-Star Team (1988)

Signed as a free agent by **Montreal**, October 9, 1985. Traded to **St. Louis** by **Montreal** with Sergio Momesso for Jocelyn Lemieux, Darrell May and St. Louis' second round choice (Patrice Brisebois) in 1989 Entry Draft, August 9, 1988. Traded to **Detroit** by **St. Louis** for Rick Zombo, October 18, 1991. Traded to **Boston** by **Detroit** for a conditional draft choice in 1995 Entry Draft, January 17, 1994.

ROBINS, TREVOR — S.J.

Goaltender. Catches left. 5'11", 190 lbs. Born, Brandon, Man., May 31, 1972.

			Regular Season								Playoffs						
Season	Club	Lea	GP	W	L	T	Mins	GA	SO	Avg	GP	W	L	Mins	GA	SO	Avg
1989-90	Saskatoon	WHL	51	21	21	1	2616	203	1	4.66	10	5	4	587	53	0	5.42
1990-91	Saskatoon	WHL	49	16	24	2	2560	200	2	4.69	....	....	....	....	....	....	....
1991-92a	Saskatoon	WHL	50	24	23	2	2794	163	0	3.50	9	5	3	473	32	0	4.06
1992-93a	Brandon	WHL	59	36	17	4	3470	183	2	3.16	4	1	3	258	11	0	2.56
1993-94	Kansas City	IHL	4	1	2	0	199	21	0	6.32	....	....	....	....	....	....	....
	Fort Worth	CHL	9	2	6	0	452	42	0	5.58	....	....	....	....	....	....	....

a WHL East First All-Star Team (1992, 1993)

Signed as a free agent by **San Jose**, December 5, 1992.

ROGLES, CHRIS — CHI.

Goaltender. Catches left. 5'11", 175 lbs. Born, St. Louis, MO, January 22, 1969.

			Regular Season								Playoffs						
Season	Club	Lea	GP	W	L	T	Mins	GA	SO	Avg	GP	W	L	Mins	GA	SO	Avg
1989-90	Clarkson	ECAC	7	1	0	0	142	7	0	2.97	....	....	....	....	....	....	....
1990-91a	Clarkson	ECAC	28	17	6	0	1359	76	....	3.35	....	....	....	....	....	....	....
1991-92	Clarkson	ECAC	18	11	3	0	974	49	0	3.02	....	....	....	....	....	....	....
1992-93	Clarkson	ECAC	27	16	4	4	1486	60	*3	2.42	....	....	....	....	....	....	....
1993-94	Indianapolis	IHL	44	14	20	6	2422	147	*2	3.64	....	....	....	....	....	....	....

a ECAC Second All-Star Team (1991)

Signed as a free agent by **Chicago**, June 21, 1993.

ROLOSON, DWAYNE — CGY.

Goaltenter. Catches left. 6'1", 180 lbs. Born, Simcoe, Ont., October 12, 1969.

			Regular Season								Playoffs						
Season	Club	Lea	GP	W	L	T	Mins	GA	SO	Avg	GP	W	L	Mins	GA	SO	Avg
1990-91	Lowell	H.E.	15	5	9	0	823	63	0	4.59	....	....	....	....	....	....	....
1991-92	Lowell	H.E.	12	3	8	0	660	52	0	4.73	....	....	....	....	....	....	....
1992-93	Lowell	H.E.	39	20	17	2	2342	150	0	3.84	....	....	....	....	....	....	....
1993-94	Lowell	H.E.	40	23	10	7	2305	106	0	2.76	....	....	....	....	....	....	....

Signed as a free agent by **Calgary**, August, 1994.

ROMANO, ROBERTO

Goaltender. Catches left. 5'6", 170 lbs. Born, Montreal, Que., October 10, 1962.

			Regular Season								Playoffs						
Season	Club	Lea	GP	W	L	T	Mins	GA	SO	Avg	GP	W	L	Mins	GA	SO	Avg
1979-80	Quebec	QMJHL	52	21	17	3	2411	183	0	4.55	3	1	1	150	12	0	4.80
1980-81	Quebec	QMJHL	59	24	26	2	3174	233	0	4.40	4	1	2	164	18	0	6.59
1981-82a	Hull	QMJHL	56	....	....	....	3090	194	1	3.77	13	....	....	760	50	0	3.95
1982-83	Baltimore	AHL	38	....	....	....	2163	146	0	4.05	....	....	....	....	....	....	....
	Pittsburgh	**NHL**	**3**	**0**	**3**	**0**	**155**	**18**	**0**	**6.98**	....	....	....	....	....	....	....
1983-84	**Pittsburgh**	**NHL**	**18**	**6**	**11**	**0**	**1020**	**78**	**1**	**4.59**	....	....	....	....	....	....	....
	Baltimore	AHL	31	23	6	1	1759	106	0	3.62	9	5	3	544	36	0	3.97
1984-85	**Pittsburgh**	**NHL**	**31**	**9**	**17**	**2**	**1629**	**120**	**1**	**4.42**	....	....	....	....	....	....	....
	Baltimore	AHL	12	2	8	2	719	44	0	3.67	....	....	....	....	....	....	....
1985-86	**Pittsburgh**	**NHL**	**46**	**21**	**20**	**3**	**2684**	**159**	**2**	**3.55**	....	....	....	....	....	....	....
1986-87	**Pittsburgh**	**NHL**	**25**	**9**	**11**	**2**	**1438**	**87**	**0**	**3.63**	....	....	....	....	....	....	....
	Baltimore	AHL	5	0	3	0	274	18	0	3.94	....	....	....	....	....	....	....
	Boston	**NHL**	**1**	**0**	**1**	**0**	**60**	**6**	**0**	**6.00**	....	....	....	....	....	....	....
	Moncton	AHL	1	0	0	0	65	3	0	2.77	....	....	....	....	....	....	....
1987-88	Maine	AHL	16	5	8	1	875	52	0	3.57	....	....	....	....	....	....	....
1988-89	Merano	Italy	....	....	....	....	....	....	....	....	....	....	....	....	....	....	....
1989-90	Bolzano	Italy	32	....	....	....	1778	105	0	3.54	....	....	....	....	....	....	....
1990-91	Milano Devils	Italy	10	....	....	....	538	31	0	3.45	....	....	....	....	....	....	....
1991-92	Milano Devils	Italy	29	....	....	....	1704	78	2	2.74	....	....	....	....	....	....	....
	Milano Devils	Alpen.	17	....	....	....	973	42	1	2.58	2	....	....	120	2	1	1.00
1992-93	Milano Lions	Italy	....	....	....	....	....	....	....	....	....	....	....	....	....	....	....
	Milano Devils	Alpen.	28	....	....	....	1549	73	0	2.82	....	....	....	....	....	....	....
1993-94	**Pittsburgh**	**NHL**	**2**	**1**	**0**	**1**	**125**	**3**	**0**	**1.44**	....	....	....	....	....	....	....
	Cleveland	AHL	11	2	7	2	642	45	1	4.20	....	....	....	....	....	....	....
	NHL Totals		**126**	**46**	**63**	**8**	**7111**	**471**	**4**	**3.97**	....	....	....	....	....	....	....

a QMJHL First All-Star Team (1982).

Signed as a free agent by **Pittsburgh**, December 6, 1982. Traded to **Boston** by **Pittsburgh** for Pat Riggin, February 6, 1987. Signed as a free agent by **Pittsburgh**, October 7, 1993.

RONNQVIST, PETTER

Goaltender. Catches left. 5'10", 154 lbs. Born, Stockholm, Sweden, February 7, 1973.
(Ottawa's 12th choice, 264th overall, in 1992 Entry Draft).

			Regular Season								Playoffs						
Season	Club	Lea	GP	W	L	T	Mins	GA	SO	Avg	GP	W	L	Mins	GA	SO	Avg
1992-93	Djurgarden	Swe.	7	....	....	....	380	20	0	3.15	1	....	....	60	5	0	5.00
1993-94	Djurgarden	Swe.	12	....	....	....	680	39	0	3.21	....	....	....	....	....	....	....

ROUSSEL, DOMINIC — (roo-SEHL) PHI.

Goaltender. Catches left. 6'1", 191 lbs. Born, Hull, Que., February 22, 1970.
(Philadelphia's 4th choice, 63rd overall, in 1988 Entry Draft).

			Regular Season								Playoffs						
Season	Club	Lea	GP	W	L	T	Mins	GA	SO	Avg	GP	W	L	Mins	GA	SO	Avg
1987-88	Trois-Rivières	QMJHL	51	18	25	4	2905	251	0	5.18	....	....	....	....	....	....	....
1988-89	Shawinigan	QMJHL	46	24	15	2	2555	171	0	4.02	10	6	4	638	36	0	3.39
1989-90	Shawinigan	QMJHL	37	20	14	1	1985	133	0	4.02	2	1	1	120	12	0	6.00
1990-91	Hershey	AHL	45	20	14	7	2507	151	1	3.61	7	3	4	366	21	0	3.44
1991-92	**Philadelphia**	**NHL**	**17**	**7**	**8**	**2**	**922**	**40**	**1**	**2.60**	....	....	....	....	....	....	....
	Hershey	AHL	35	15	11	6	2040	121	1	3.56	....	....	....	....	....	....	....
1992-93	**Philadelphia**	**NHL**	**34**	**13**	**11**	**5**	**1769**	**111**	**1**	**3.76**	....	....	....	....	....	....	....
	Hershey	AHL	6	0	3	3	372	23	0	3.71	....	....	....	....	....	....	....
1993-94	**Philadelphia**	**NHL**	**60**	**29**	**20**	**5**	**3285**	**183**	**1**	**3.34**	....	....	....	....	....	....	....
	NHL Totals		**111**	**49**	**39**	**12**	**5976**	**334**	**3**	**3.35**	....	....	....	....	....	....	....

ROUSSON, BORIS

Goaltender. Catches left. 6'2", 195 lbs. Born, Val D'or, Que., June 14, 1970.

			Regular Season								Playoffs						
Season	Club	Lea	GP	W	L	T	Mins	GA	SO	Avg	GP	W	L	Mins	GA	SO	Avg
1988-89	Laval	QMJHL	22	12	7	0	....	....	....	4.44	....	....	....	....	....	....	....
1989-90	Granby	QMJHL	39	10	26	0	....	....	....	4.56	....	....	....	....	....	....	....
1990-91a	Granby	QMJHL	*63	28	25	6	*3693	190	0	3.09	....	....	....	....	....	....	....
1991-92	Binghamton	AHL	38	16	15	6	2261	123	1	3.26	....	....	....	....	....	....	....
1992-93b	Binghamton	AHL	31	18	9	4	1847	115	0	3.74	1	0	0	20	2	0	6.00
1993-94	Binghamton	AHL	62	26	26	8	3598	232	0	3.87	....	....	....	....	....	....	....

a QMJHL Second All-Star Team (1991)
b Shared Harry "Hap" Holmes Memorial Trophy (fewest goals-against - AHL) with Corey Hirsch (1993)

Signed as a free agent by **NY Rangers**, March 31, 1991.

ROY, PATRICK — (WAH) MTL.

Goaltender. Catches left. 6', 192 lbs. Born, Quebec City, Que., October 5, 1965.
(Montreal's 4th choice, 51st overall, in 1984 Entry Draft).

			Regular Season								Playoffs						
Season	Club	Lea	GP	W	L	T	Mins	GA	SO	Avg	GP	W	L	Mins	GA	SO	Avg
1982-83	Granby	QMJHL	54	....	....	....	2808	293	0	6.26	....	....	....	....	....	....	....
1983-84	Granby	QMJHL	61	29	29	1	3585	265	0	4.44	4	0	4	244	22	0	5.41
1984-85	**Montreal**	**NHL**	**1**	**1**	**0**	**0**	**20**	**0**	**0**	**0.00**	....	....	....	....	....	....	....
	Granby	QMJHL	44	16	25	1	2463	228	0	5.55	....	....	....	....	....	....	....
	Sherbrooke	AHL	1	1	0	0	60	4	0	4.00	13	10	3	*769	37	0	*2.89
1985-86ab	**Montreal**	**NHL**	**47**	**23**	**18**	**3**	**2651**	**148**	**1**	**3.35**	**20**	***15**	**5**	**1218**	**39**	***1**	**1.92**
1986-87c	**Montreal**	**NHL**	**46**	**22**	**16**	**6**	**2686**	**131**	**1**	**2.93**	**6**	**4**	**2**	**330**	**22**	**0**	**4.00**
1987-88cd	**Montreal**	**NHL**	**45**	**23**	**12**	**9**	**2586**	**125**	**3**	**2.90**	**8**	**3**	**4**	**430**	**24**	**0**	**3.35**
1988-89 cefg	**Montreal**	**NHL**	**48**	**33**	**5**	**6**	**2744**	**113**	**4**	***2.47**	**19**	**13**	**6**	**1206**	**42**	**2**	***2.09**
1989-90efg	**Montreal**	**NHL**	**54**	***31**	**16**	**5**	**3173**	**134**	**3**	**2.53**	**11**	**5**	**6**	**641**	**26**	**1**	**2.43**
1990-91d	**Montreal**	**NHL**	**48**	**25**	**15**	**6**	**2835**	**128**	**1**	**2.71**	**13**	**7**	**5**	**785**	**40**	**0**	**3.06**
1991-92efh	**Montreal**	**NHL**	**67**	**36**	**22**	**8**	**3935**	**155**	***5**	***2.36**	**11**	**4**	**7**	**686**	**30**	**1**	**2.62**
1992-93a	**Montreal**	**NHL**	**62**	**31**	**25**	**5**	**3595**	**192**	**2**	**3.20**	**20**	***16**	**4**	**1293**	**46**	**0**	***2.13**
1993-94	**Montreal**	**NHL**	**68**	**35**	**17**	**11**	**3867**	**161**	***7**	**2.50**	**6**	**3**	**3**	**375**	**16**	**0**	**2.56**
	NHL Totals		**486**	**260**	**146**	**59**	**28092**	**1287**	**27**	**2.75**	**114**	**70**	**42**	**6964**	**285**	**5**	**2.46**

a Won Conn Smythe Trophy (1986, 1993)
b NHL All-Rookie Team (1986)
c Shared William Jennings Trophy with Brian Hayward (1987, 1988, 1989)
d NHL Second All-Star Team (1988, 1991)
e Won Vezina Trophy (1989, 1990, 1992)
f NHL First All-Star Team (1989, 1990, 1992)
g Won Trico Goaltending Award (1989, 1990)
h Won William M. Jennings Award (1992)

Played in NHL All-Star Game (1988, 1990-94)

RYABCHIKOV, EVGENY — (RYAB-chih-kohv) BOS.

Goaltender. Catches left. 5'11", 167 lbs. Born, Yaroslavl, Soviet Union, January 16, 1974.
(Boston's 1st choice, 21st overall, in 1994 Entry Draft).

			Regular Season								Playoffs						
Season	Club	Lea	GP	W	L	T	Mins	GA	SO	Avg	GP	W	L	Mins	GA	SO	Avg
1993-94	Molot Perm	CIS	28	....	....	....	1572	96	....	3.66	....	....	....	....	....	....	....

RYDER, DAN — S.J.

Goaltender. Catches left. 6'1", 200 lbs. Born, Kitchener, Ont., October 24, 1972.
(San Jose's 5th choice, 89th overall, in 1991 Entry Draft).

			Regular Season								Playoffs						
Season	Club	Lea	GP	W	L	T	Mins	GA	SO	Avg	GP	W	L	Mins	GA	SO	Avg
1990-91	Hamilton	OHL	1	0	0	0	40	1	0	1.50	....	....	....	....	....	....	....
	Sudbury	OHL	37	18	9	4	2089	126	....	3.62	2	0	0	26	1	0	2.31
1991-92	Sudbury	OHL	23	9	11	1	1157	91	0	4.72	....	....	....	....	....	....	....
	Ottawa	OHL	24	16	6	0	1380	55	3	*2.39	11	5	6	625	38	0	3.64
1992-93	Johnstown	ECHL	4	1	1	1	214	15	0	4.21	....	....	....	....	....	....	....
	Columbus	ECHL	1	0	1	0	60	6	0	6.00	....	....	....	....	....	....	....
	Kansas City	IHL	10	3	3	2	514	35	0	4.09	....	....	....	....	....	....	....
1993-94	Kansas City	IHL	3	1	1	0	139	11	0	4.73	....	....	....	....	....	....	....
	Roanoke	ECHL	42	22	13	0	1946	129	0	3.98	....	....	....	....	....	....	....

SAAL, JASON — L.A.

Goaltender. Catches left. 5'9", 165 lbs. Born, Detroit, MI, February 1, 1975.
(Los Angeles' 5th choice, 117th overall, in 1993 Entry Draft).

			Regular Season								Playoffs						
Season	Club	Lea	GP	W	L	T	Mins	GA	SO	Avg	GP	W	L	Mins	GA	SO	Avg
1992-93	Detroit	OHL	23	11	8	1	1289	85	0	3.96	3	0	0	42	2	0	2.86
1993-94	Detroit	OHL	45	28	11	3	2551	143	0	3.36	7	5	0	346	23	0	3.99

SALAJKO, JEFF — S.J.

Goaltender. Catches left. 6', 175 lbs. Born, Kitchener, Ont., April 18, 1975.
(San Jose's 12th choice, 236th overall, in 1993 Entry Draft).

			Regular Season								Playoffs						
Season	Club	Lea	GP	W	L	T	Mins	GA	SO	Avg	GP	W	L	Mins	GA	SO	Avg
1992-93	Ottawa	OHL	29	5	16	3	1436	109	0	4.55	....	....	....	....	....	....	....
1993-94	Ottawa	OHL	37	13	13	6	2022	114	2	3.38	9	3	1	312	17	0	3.27

SALO, TOMMY — NYI

Goaltender. Catches left. 5'11", 161 lbs. Born, Surahammar, Sweden, February 1, 1971.
(NY Islanders' 5th choice, 118th overall, in 1993 Entry Draft).

			Regular Season								Playoffs						
Season	Club	Lea	GP	W	L	T	Mins	GA	SO	Avg	GP	W	L	Mins	GA	SO	Avg
1990-91	Vasteras	Swe.	2	....	....	....	100	11	0	6.60	....	....	....	....	....	....	....
1991-92	Vasteras	Swe.					UNAVAILABLE										
1992-93	Vasteras	Swe.	24	....	....	....	1431	59	2	2.47	2	....	....	120	6	0	3.00
1993-94	Vasteras	Swe.	32	....	....	....	1896	106	0	3.31	....	....	....	....	....	....	....

SALZMAN, WADE — ST.L.

Goaltender. Catches right. 6'3", 195 lbs. Born, Duluth, MN, May 30, 1974.
(St. Louis' 12th choice, 259th overall, in 1992 Entry Draft).

			Regular Season								Playoffs						
Season	Club	Lea	GP	W	L	T	Mins	GA	SO	Avg	GP	W	L	Mins	GA	SO	Avg
1992-93	Notre Dame	CCHA						DID NOT PLAY									
1993-94	Notre Dame	CCHA	10	2	3	1	452	30	0	3.98	....	....	....	....	....	....	....

SARJEANT, GEOFF — ST.L.

Goaltender. Catches left. 5'9", 180 lbs. Born, Newmarket, Ont., November 30, 1969.
(St. Louis' 1st choice, 17th overall, in 1990 Supplemental Draft).

			Regular Season								Playoffs						
Season	Club	Lea	GP	W	L	T	Mins	GA	SO	Avg	GP	W	L	Mins	GA	SO	Avg
1988-89	Michigan Tech	WCHA	6	0	3	2	329	22	0	4.01	....	....	....	....	....	....	....
1989-90	Michigan Tech	WCHA	19	4	13	0	1043	94	0	5.41	....	....	....	....	....	....	....
1990-91	Michigan Tech	WCHA	23	5	15	3	1540	97	0	3.78	....	....	....	....	....	....	....
1991-92	Michigan Tech	WCHA	23	7	13	0	1201	90	1	4.50	....	....	....	....	....	....	....
1992-93	Peoria	IHL	41	22	14	3	2356	130	0	3.31	3	0	3	179	13	0	4.36
1993-94a	Peoria	IHL	41	25	9	2	2275	93	*2	*2.45	4	2	2	211	13	0	3.69

a IHL First All-Star Team (1994)

SAURDIFF, CORWIN — S.J.

Goaltender. Catches left. 5'11", 168 lbs. Born, Warroad, MN, October 17, 1972.
(San Jose's 9th choice, 177th overall, in 1991 Entry Draft).

			Regular Season								Playoffs						
Season	Club	Lea	GP	W	L	T	Mins	GA	SO	Avg	GP	W	L	Mins	GA	SO	Avg
1991-92	N. Michigan	WCHA	34	22	9	1	1926	110	0	3.43	....	....	....	....	....	....	....
1992-93	N. Michigan	WCHA	29	13	12	3	1629	101	1	3.72	....	....	....	....	....	....	....
1993-94	Kansas City	IHL	17	6	9	1	946	74	0	4.69	....	....	....	....	....	....	....
	Fort Worth	CHL	5	1	4	0	292	22	0	4.51	....	....	....	....	....	....	....

SCHOEN, BRYAN — (SHOH-ihn) S.J.

Goaltender. Catches left. 6'2", 180 lbs. Born, St. Paul, MN, September 9, 1970.
(Minnesota's 6th choice, 91st overall, in 1989 Entry Draft).

			Regular Season								Playoffs						
Season	Club	Lea	GP	W	L	T	Mins	GA	SO	Avg	GP	W	L	Mins	GA	SO	Avg
1989-90	U. of Denver	WCHA	18	8	9	0	1040	81	0	4.67	....	....	....	....	....	....	....
1990-91	U. of Denver	WCHA	19	4	13	2	1103	94	0	5.11	....	....	....	....	....	....	....
1991-92	U. of Denver	WCHA	36	9	25	2	2039	167	0	4.91	....	....	....	....	....	....	....
1992-93	U. of Denver	WCHA	35	*18	15	2	1860	121	0	3.90	....	....	....	....	....	....	....
1993-94	Fort Worth	CHL	4	2	1	0	211	14	0	3.98	....	....	....	....	....	....	....
	Roanoke	ECHL	6	1	4	0	279	23	0	4.94	....	....	....	....	....	....	....
	Louisville	ECHL	11	3	7	0	575	43	0	4.48	6	2	4	350	27	*1	4.62

Claimed by **San Jose** from **Minnesota** in Dispersal Draft, May 30, 1991.

SCHULMISTRA, RICHARD — QUE.

Goaltender. Catches right. 6'2", 186 lbs. Born, Sudbury, Ont., April 1, 1971.
(Quebec's 1st choice, 4th overall, in 1992 Supplemental Draft).

			Regular Season								Playoffs						
Season	Club	Lea	GP	W	L	T	Mins	GA	SO	Avg	GP	W	L	Mins	GA	SO	Avg
1990-91	Miami-Ohio	CCHA	20	2	12	2	920	80	0	5.21	....	....	....	....	....	....	....
1991-92	Miami-Ohio	CCHA	19	3	5	2	850	67	0	4.72	....	....	....	....	....	....	....
1992-93a	Miami-Ohio	CCHA	33	22	6	4	1949	88	....	2.71	....	....	....	....	....	....	....
1993-94	Miami-Ohio	CCHA	27	13	12	1	1521	74	0	2.92	....	....	....	....	....	....	....

a CCHA Second All-Star Team (1993)

SCHWAB, COREY — (SHWAHB) N.J.

Goaltender. Catches left. 6', 180 lbs. Born, North Battleford, Sask., November 4, 1970.
(New Jersey's 12th choice, 200th overall, in 1990 Entry Draft).

			Regular Season								Playoffs						
Season	Club	Lea	GP	W	L	T	Mins	GA	SO	Avg	GP	W	L	Mins	GA	SO	Avg
1988-89	Seattle	WHL	10	2	2	0	386	31	0	4.82	....	....	....	....	....	....	....
1989-90	Seattle	WHL	27	15	2	1	1150	69	1	3.60	3	0	0	49	2	0	2.45
1990-91	Seattle	WHL	*58	32	18	3	*3289	224	0	4.09	6	1	5	382	25	0	3.93
1991-92	Utica	AHL	24	9	12	1	1322	95	0	4.31	....	....	....	....	....	....	....
	Cincinnati	ECHL	8	6	0	1	450	31	0	4.13	9	6	3	540	29	0	3.22
1992-93	Utica	AHL	40	18	16	5	2387	169	*2	4.25	1	0	1	59	6	0	6.10
	Cincinnati	IHL	3	1	2	0	185	17	0	5.51	....	....	....	....	....	....	....
1993-94	Albany	AHL	51	27	21	3	3058	184	0	3.61	5	1	4	298	20	0	4.02

SELIGER, MARK — (ZEH-lih-gehr) WSH.

Goaltender. Catches left. 5'11", 165 lbs. Born, Rosenheim, Germany, May 1, 1974.
(Washington's 9th choice, 251st overall, in 1993 Entry Draft).

			Regular Season								Playoffs						
Season	Club	Lea	GP	W	L	T	Mins	GA	SO	Avg	GP	W	L	Mins	GA	SO	Avg
1992-93	Rosenheim	Ger.	42	....	....	....	1264	75	1	3.56	....	....	....	....	....	....	....
1993-94	Rosenheim	Ger.	27	....	....	....	....	....	....	....	....	....	....	....	....	....	....

SHEPARD, KEN — NYR

Goaltender. Catches left. 5'10", 192 lbs. Born, Toronto, Ont., January 20, 1974.
(NY Rangers' 10th choice, 216th overall, in 1993 Entry Draft).

			Regular Season								Playoffs						
Season	Club	Lea	GP	W	L	T	Mins	GA	SO	Avg	GP	W	L	Mins	GA	SO	Avg
1991-92	Oshawa	OHL	7	1	2	0	265	16	1	3.62	1	0	0	2	0	0	0.00
1992-93	Oshawa	OHL	31	12	7	4	1483	86	0	3.48	11	3	7	512	34	0	3.98
1993-94	Oshawa	OHL	45	20	15	5	2383	157	0	3.95	5	1	4	309	18	0	3.50

SHIELDS, STEVE — BUF.

Goaltender. Catches left. 6'3", 210 lbs. Born, Toronto, Ont., July 19, 1972.
(Buffalo's 5th choice, 101st overall, in 1991 Entry Draft).

			Regular Season								Playoffs						
Season	Club	Lea	GP	W	L	T	Mins	GA	SO	Avg	GP	W	L	Mins	GA	SO	Avg
1990-91	U. of Michigan	CCHA	37	26	6	3	1963	106	0	3.24	....	....	....	....	....	....	....
1991-92	U. of Michigan	CCHA	*37	*27	7	2	*2090	99	1	2.84	....	....	....	....	....	....	....
1992-93ab	U. of Michigan	CCHA	*39	*30	6	2	2027	75	....	*2.22	....	....	....	....	....	....	....
1993-94ab	U. of Michigan	CCHA	36	*28	6	1	1961	87	0	2.66	....	....	....	....	....	....	....

a CCHA First All-Star Team (1993, 1994)
b NCAA West Second All-American Team (1993, 1994)

SHTALENKOV, MIKHAIL — (shtuh-LEHN-kahf, mihk-HIGHL) ANA.

Goaltender. Catches left. 6'2", 180 lbs. Born, Moscow, USSR, October 20, 1965.
(Anaheim's 5th choice, 108th overall, in 1993 Entry Draft).

			Regular Season								Playoffs						
Season	Club	Lea	GP	W	L	T	Mins	GA	SO	Avg	GP	W	L	Mins	GA	SO	Avg
1986-87a	Moscow D'amo	USSR	17	....	....	....	893	36	1	2.41	....	....	....	....	....	....	....
1987-88	Moscow D'amo	USSR	25	....	....	....	1302	72	1	3.31	....	....	....	....	....	....	....
1988-89	Moscow D'amo	USSR	4	....	....	....	80	3	0	2.25	....	....	....	....	....	....	....
1989-90	Moscow D'amo	USSR	6	....	....	....	20	1	0	3.00	....	....	....	....	....	....	....
1990-91	Moscow D'amo	USSR	31	....	....	....	1568	56	2	2.14	....	....	....	....	....	....	....
1991-92	Moscow D'amo	CIS	27	....	....	....	1268	45	1	2.12	....	....	....	....	....	....	....
1992-93b	Milwaukee	IHL	47	26	14	5	2669	135	2	3.03	3	1	2	209	11	0	3.16
1993-94	Anaheim	NHL	10	3	4	1	543	24	0	2.65	....	....	....	....	....	....	....
	San Diego	IHL	28	15	11	2	1616	93	0	3.45	....	....	....	....	....	....	....
	NHL Totals		10	3	4	1	543	24	0	2.65	....	....	....	....	....	....	....

a Soviet Rookie of the Year (1987)
b Won Garry F. Longman Memorial Trophy (Rookie of the Year - IHL) (1993)

SIDORKIEWICZ, PETER — (sih-DOHR-kuh-vihch) N.J.

Goaltender. Catches left. 5'9", 180 lbs. Born, Dabrowa Bialostocka, Pol., June 29, 1963.
(Washington's 5th choice, 91st overall, in 1981 Entry Draft).

			Regular Season								Playoffs						
Season	Club	Lea	GP	W	L	T	Mins	GA	SO	Avg	GP	W	L	Mins	GA	SO	Avg
1980-81	Oshawa	OHA	7	3	3	0	308	24	0	4.68	5	2	2	266	20	0	4.52
1981-82	Oshawa	OHL	29	14	11	1	1553	123	*2	4.75	1	0	0	13	1	0	4.62
1982-83	Oshawa	OHL	60	36	20	3	3536	213	0	3.61	17	15	1	1020	60	0	3.53
1983-84	Oshawa	OHL	52	28	21	1	2966	250	1	4.15	7	3	4	420	27	*1	3.86
1984-85	Binghamton	AHL	45	31	9	5	2691	137	3	3.05	8	4	4	481	31	0	3.87
	Fort Wayne	IHL	10	4	4	2	590	43	0	4.37	....	....	....	....	....	....	....
1985-86	Binghamton	AHL	49	21	22	3	2819	150	2	*3.19	4	1	3	235	12	0	3.06
1986-87a	Binghamton	AHL	57	23	16	0	3304	161	4	2.92	13	6	7	794	36	0	*2.72
1987-88	Hartford	NHL	1	0	1	0	60	6	0	6.00	....	....	....	....	....	....	....
	Binghamton	AHL	42	19	17	3	2345	144	0	3.68	3	0	2	147	8	0	3.27
1988-89b	Hartford	NHL	44	22	18	4	2635	133	4	3.03	2	0	2	124	8	0	3.87
1989-90	Hartford	NHL	46	19	19	7	2703	161	1	3.57	7	3	4	429	23	0	3.22
1990-91	Hartford	NHL	52	21	22	7	2953	164	1	3.33	6	2	4	359	24	0	4.01
1991-92	Hartford	NHL	35	9	19	6	1995	111	2	3.34	....	....	....	....	....	....	....
1992-93	Ottawa	NHL	64	8	46	3	3388	250	0	4.43	....	....	....	....	....	....	....
1993-94	New Jersey	NHL	3	0	3	0	130	6	0	2.77	....	....	....	....	....	....	....
	Albany	AHL	15	6	7	2	907	60	0	3.97	....	....	....	....	....	....	....
	Fort Wayne	IHL	11	6	3	0	591	27	*2	2.74	*18	10	8	*1054	59	*1	3.36
	NHL Totals		245	79	128	27	13864	831	8	3.60	15	5	10	912	55	0	3.62

a AHL Second All-Star Team (1987)
b NHL All-Rookie Team (1989)

Played in NHL All-Star Game (1993)

Traded to **Hartford** by **Washington** with Dean Evason for David Jensen, March 12, 1985. Claimed by **Ottawa** from **Hartford** in Expansion Draft, June 18, 1992. Traded to **New Jersey** by **Ottawa** with future considerations (Mike Peluso, June 26, 1993) for Craig Billington, Troy Mallette and New Jersey's fourth round choice (Cosmo Dupaul) in 1993 Entry Draft, June 20, 1993.

SNOW, GARTH — QUE.

Goaltender. Catches left. 6'3", 200 lbs. Born, Wrentham, MA, July 28, 1969.
(Quebec's 6th choice, 114th overall, in 1987 Entry Draft).

			Regular Season								Playoffs						
Season	Club	Lea	GP	W	L	T	Mins	GA	SO	Avg	GP	W	L	Mins	GA	SO	Avg
1988-89	U. of Maine	H.E.	5	2	2	0	241	14	1	3.49	....	....	....	....	....	....	....
1989-90								DID NOT PLAY									
1990-91	U. of Maine	H.E.	25	*18	4	0	1290	64	2	2.98	....	....	....	....	....	....	....
1991-92a	U. of Maine	H.E.	31	*25	4	2	1792	73	*2	*2.44	....	....	....	....	....	....	....
1992-93b	U. of Maine	H.E.	23	*21	0	1	1210	42	1	*2.08	....	....	....	....	....	....	....
1993-94	U.S. National	....	23	....	....	....	1324	71	1	3.22	....	....	....	....	....	....	....
	U.S. Olympic	....	5	....	....	....	299	17	0	3.41	....	....	....	....	....	....	....
	Quebec	NHL	5	3	2	0	279	16	0	3.44	....	....	....	....	....	....	....
	Cornwall	AHL	16	6	5	3	927	51	0	3.30	13	8	5	790	42	0	3.19
	NHL Totals		5	3	2	0	279	16	0	3.44	....	....	....	....	....	....	....

a Hockey East Second All-Star Team (1992)
b NCAA Final Four All-Tournament Team (1993)

SODERSTROM, TOMMY — (SAH-duhr-struhm) PHI.

Goaltender. Catches left. 5'9", 165 lbs. Born, Stockholm, Sweden, July 17, 1969.
(Philadelphia's 14th choice, 214th overall, in 1990 Entry Draft).

			Regular Season								Playoffs						
Season	Club	Lea	GP	W	L	T	Mins	GA	SO	Avg	GP	W	L	Mins	GA	SO	Avg
1989-90	Djurgarden	Swe.	4	....	....	....	240	14	0	3.50	....	....	....	....	....	....	....
1990-91	Djurgarden	Swe.	39	....	....	....	2340	104	3	2.67	7	....	....	423	10	2	1.42
1991-92	Djurgarden	Swe.	39	....	....	....	2340	109	4	2.79	10	....	....	635	28	0	2.65
1992-93	Philadelphia	NHL	44	20	17	6	2512	143	5	3.42	....	....	....	....	....	....	....
	Hershey	AHL	7	4	1	0	373	15	0	2.41	....	....	....	....	....	....	....
1993-94	Philadelphia	NHL	34	6	18	4	1736	116	2	4.01	....	....	....	....	....	....	....
	Hershey	AHL	9	3	4	1	461	37	0	4.81	....	....	....	....	....	....	....
	NHL Totals		78	26	35	10	4248	259	7	3.66	....	....	....	....	....	....	....

SOUCY, CHRISTIAN — CHI.

Goaltender. Catches left. 5'11", 160 lbs. Born, Gatineau, Que., September 14, 1970.

			Regular Season								Playoffs						
Season	Club	Lea	GP	W	L	T	Mins	GA	SO	Avg	GP	W	L	Mins	GA	SO	Avg
1991-92	Vermont	ECAC	*30	15	11	3	*1783	81	0	2.83							
1992-93a	Vermont	ECAC	29	11	15	3	1708	90	1	3.16							
1993-94	**Chicago**	**NHL**	**1**	**0**	**0**	**0**	**3**	**0**	**0**	**0.00**							
	Indianapolis	IHL	46	14	25	1	2302	159	1	4.14							
	NHL Totals		**1**	**0**	**0**	**0**	**3**	**0**	**0**	**0.00**							

a ECAC Second All-Star Team (1993)

Signed as a free agent by **Chicago**, June 21, 1993.

STAUBER, ROBB (STAW-buhr) — L.A.

Goaltender. Catches left. 5'11", 180 lbs. Born, Duluth, MN, November 25, 1967.
(Los Angeles' 5th choice, 107th overall, in 1986 Entry Draft).

			Regular Season								Playoffs						
Season	Club	Lea	GP	W	L	T	Mins	GA	SO	Avg	GP	W	L	Mins	GA	SO	Avg
1986-87	U. Minnesota	WCHA	20	13	5	0	1072	63	0	3.53							
1987-88abc	U. Minnesota	WCHA	44	34	10	0	2621	119	5	2.72							
1988-89d	U. Minnesota	WCHA	34	26	8	0	2024	82	0	2.43							
1989-90	**Los Angeles**	**NHL**	**2**	**0**	**1**	**0**	**83**	**11**	**0**	**7.95**							
	New Haven	AHL	14	6	6	2	851	43	0	3.03	5	2	3	302	24	0	4.77
1990-91	New Haven	AHL	33	13	16	4	1882	115	1	3.67							
	Phoenix	IHL	4	1	2	0	160	11	0	4.13							
1991-92	Phoenix	IHL	22	8	12	1	1242	80	0	3.86							
1992-93	**Los Angeles**	**NHL**	**31**	**15**	**8**	**4**	**1735**	**111**	**0**	**3.84**	**4**	**3**	**1**	**240**	**16**	**0**	**4.00**
1993-94	**Los Angeles**	**NHL**	**22**	**4**	**11**	**5**	**1144**	**65**	**1**	**3.41**							
	Phoenix	IHL	3	1	1	0	121	13	0	6.42							
	NHL Totals		**55**	**19**	**20**	**9**	**2962**	**187**	**1**	**3.79**	**4**	**3**	**1**	**240**	**16**	**0**	**4.00**

a Won Hobey Baker Memorial Award (Top U.S. Collegiate Player) (1988)
b NCAA West First All-American Team (1988)
c WCHA First All-Star Team (1988)
d WCHA Second All-Star Team (1989)

STOLP, JEFFREY

Goaltender. Catches left. 6', 180 lbs. Born, Nashwauk, MN, June 20, 1970.
(Minnesota's 4th choice, 64th overall, in 1988 Entry Draft).

			Regular Season								Playoffs						
Season	Club	Lea	GP	W	L	T	Mins	GA	SO	Avg	GP	W	L	Mins	GA	SO	Avg
1988-89	U. Minnesota	WCHA	16	7	2	3	742	45	0	3.64							
1989-90	U. Minnesota	WCHA	10	5	1	0	417	33	1	4.75							
1990-91	U. Minnesota	WCHA	32	18	8	3	1766	82	2	2.79							
1991-92a	U. Minnesota	WCHA	33	25	7	0	1858	88	0	2.84							
1992-93	Dayton	ECHL	27	12	13	2	1550	99	0	3.83							
	Kalamazoo	IHL	14	2	11	1	733	62	0	5.08							
1993-94	Kalamazoo	IHL	1	0	0	0	8	0	0	0.00							
	Birmingham	ECHL	2	2	0	0	120	4	0	2.00							
	Dayton	ECHL	35	15	13	5	2017	132	0	3.93	3	1	1	207	11	0	3.18

a WCHA Second All-Star Team (1992)

STORR, JAMIE — L.A.

Goaltender. Catches left. 6'1", 192 lbs. Born, Brampton, Ont., December 28, 1975.
(Los Angeles' 1st choice, 7th overall, in 1994 Entry Draft).

			Regular Season								Playoffs						
Season	Club	Lea	GP	W	L	T	Mins	GA	SO	Avg	GP	W	L	Mins	GA	SO	Avg
1991-92	Owen Sound	OHL	34	11	16	1	1732	128	0	4.43	5	1	4	299	28	0	5.62
1992-93	Owen Sound	OHL	41	20	17	3	2362	180	0	4.57	8	4	4	454	35	0	4.63
1993-94a	Owen Sound	OHL	35	21	11	1	2004	120	1	3.59	9	4	5	547	44	0	4.83

a OHL First All-Star Team (1994)

TABARACCI, RICK (tab-uh-RA-chee) — WSH.

Goaltender. Catches left. 5'11", 179 lbs. Born, Toronto, Ont., January 2, 1969.
(Pittsburgh's 2nd choice, 26th overall, in 1987 Entry Draft).

			Regular Season								Playoffs						
Season	Club	Lea	GP	W	L	T	Mins	GA	SO	Avg	GP	W	L	Mins	GA	SO	Avg
1986-87	Cornwall	OHL	59	23	32	3	3347	290	1	5.20	5	1	4	303	26	0	3.17
1987-88a	Cornwall	OHL	58	*33	18	6	3448	200	*3	3.48	11	5	6	642	37	0	3.46
	Muskegon	IHL									1	0	0	13	1	0	4.62
1988-89	**Pittsburgh**	**NHL**	**1**	**0**	**0**	**0**	**33**	**4**	**0**	**7.27**							
b	Cornwall	OHL	50	24	20	5	2974	210	1	4.24	18	10	8	1080	65	*1	3.61
1989-90	Moncton	AHL	27	10	15	2	1580	107	2	4.06							
	Fort Wayne	IHL	22	8	9	1	1064	73	0	4.12	3	1	2	159	19	0	7.17
1990-91	**Winnipeg**	**NHL**	**24**	**4**	**9**	**4**	**1093**	**71**	**1**	**3.90**							
	Moncton	AHL	11	4	5	2	645	41	0	3.81							
1991-92	**Winnipeg**	**NHL**	**18**	**6**	**7**	**3**	**966**	**52**	**0**	**3.23**	**7**	**3**	**4**	**387**	**26**	**0**	**4.03**
	Moncton	AHL	23	10	11	1	1313	80	0	3.66							
1992-93	**Winnipeg**	**NHL**	**19**	**5**	**10**	**0**	**959**	**70**	**0**	**4.38**							
	Moncton	AHL	5	2	1	2	290	18	0	3.72							
	Washington	**NHL**	**6**	**3**	**2**	**0**	**343**	**10**	**2**	**1.75**	**4**	**1**	**3**	**304**	**14**	**0**	**2.76**
1993-94	**Washington**	**NHL**	**32**	**13**	**14**	**2**	**1770**	**91**	**2**	**3.08**	**2**	**0**	**2**	**111**	**6**	**0**	**3.24**
	Portland	AHL	3	3	0	0	176	8	0	2.72							
	NHL Totals		**100**	**31**	**42**	**9**	**5164**	**298**	**5**	**3.46**	**13**	**4**	**9**	**802**	**46**	**0**	**3.44**

a OHL First All-Star Team (1988)
b OHL Second All-Star Team (1989)

Traded to **Winnipeg** by **Pittsburgh** with Randy Cunneyworth and Dave McLlwain for Jim Kyte, Andrew McBain and Randy Gilhen, June 17, 1989. Traded to **Washington** by **Winnipeg** for Jim Hrivnak and Washington's second round choice (Alexei Budayev) in 1993 Entry Draft, March 22, 1993.

TANNER, JOHN — ANA.

Goaltender. Catches left. 6'3", 182 lbs. Born, Cambridge, Ont., March 17, 1971.
(Quebec's 4th choice, 54th overall, in 1989 Entry Draft).

			Regular Season								Playoffs						
Season	Club	Lea	GP	W	L	T	Mins	GA	SO	Avg	GP	W	L	Mins	GA	SO	Avg
1987-88a	Peterborough	OHL	26	18	4	3	1532	88	0	3.45	2	1	0	98	3	0	1.84
1988-89a	Peterborough	OHL	34	22	10	0	1923	107	2	*3.34	8	4	3	369	23	0	3.74
1989-90	**Quebec**	**NHL**	**1**	**0**	**1**	**0**	**60**	**3**	**0**	**3.00**							
	Peterborough	OHL	18	6	8	2	1037	70	0	4.05							
	London	OHL	19	12	5	1	1097	53	1	2.90	6	2	4	341	24	0	4.22
1990-91	**Quebec**	**NHL**	**6**	**1**	**3**	**1**	**228**	**16**	**0**	**4.21**							
	London	OHL	7	3	3	1	427	29	0	4.07							
	Sudbury	OHL	19	10	8	0	1043	60	0	3.45	5	1	4	274	21	0	4.60
1991-92	**Quebec**	**NHL**	**14**	**1**	**7**	**4**	**796**	**46**	**1**	**3.47**							
	Halifax	AHL	12	6	5	1	672	29	2	2.59							
	New Haven	AHL	16	7	6	2	908	57	0	3.77							
1992-93	Halifax	AHL	51	20	18	7	2852	199	0	4.19							
1993-94	Cornwall	AHL	38	14	15	4	2035	123	1	3.63							
	San Diego	IHL	13	5	3	2	629	37	0	3.53	3	0	1	118	5	0	2.53
	NHL Totals		**21**	**2**	**11**	**5**	**1084**	**65**	**1**	**3.60**							

a Won Dave Pinkney Trophy (Top Team Goaltending, OHL) shared with Todd Bojcun (1988, 1989)

Traded to **Anaheim** by **Quebec** for Anaheim's fourth round choice in 1995 Entry Draft, February 20, 1994.

TERRERI, CHRIS — N.J.

Goaltender. Catches left. 5'8", 160 lbs. Born, Providence, RI, November 15, 1964.
(New Jersey's 3rd choice, 87th overall, in 1983 Entry Draft).

			Regular Season								Playoffs						
Season	Club	Lea	GP	W	L	T	Mins	GA	SO	Avg	GP	W	L	Mins	GA	SO	Avg
1982-83	Providence	ECAC	11	7	1	0	528	17	2	1.93							
1983-84	Providence	ECAC	10	4	2	0	391	20	0	3.07							
1984-85ab	Providence	H.E.	33	15	13	5	1956	116	1	3.35							
1985-86	Providence	H.E.	22	6	16	0	1320	84	0	3.74							
1986-87	**New Jersey**	**NHL**	**7**	**0**	**3**	**1**	**286**	**21**	**0**	**4.41**							
	Maine	AHL	14	4	9	1	765	57	0	4.47							
1987-88	Utica	AHL	7	5	1	0	399	18	0	2.71							
	U.S. National	....	26	17	7	2	1430	81	0	3.40							
	U.S. Olympic	....	3	1	1	0	128	14	0	6.56							
1988-89	**New Jersey**	**NHL**	**8**	**0**	**4**	**2**	**402**	**18**	**0**	**2.69**							
	Utica	AHL	39	20	15	3	2314	132	0	3.42	2	0	1	80	6	0	4.50
1989-90	**New Jersey**	**NHL**	**35**	**15**	**12**	**3**	**1931**	**110**	**0**	**3.42**	**4**	**2**	**2**	**238**	**13**	**0**	**3.28**
1990-91	**New Jersey**	**NHL**	**53**	**24**	**21**	**7**	**2970**	**144**	**1**	**2.91**	**7**	**3**	**4**	**428**	**21**	**0**	**2.94**
1991-92	**New Jersey**	**NHL**	**54**	**22**	**22**	**10**	**3186**	**169**	**1**	**3.18**	**7**	**3**	**3**	**386**	**23**	**0**	**3.58**
1992-93	**New Jersey**	**NHL**	**48**	**19**	**21**	**3**	**2672**	**151**	**2**	**3.39**	**4**	**1**	**3**	**219**	**17**	**0**	**4.66**
1993-94	**New Jersey**	**NHL**	**44**	**20**	**11**	**4**	**2340**	**106**	**2**	**2.72**	**4**	**3**	**0**	**200**	**9**	**0**	**2.70**
	NHL Totals		**249**	**100**	**94**	**30**	**13787**	**719**	**6**	**3.13**	**26**	**12**	**12**	**1471**	**83**	**0**	**3.39**

a Hockey East All-Star Team (1985)
b NCAA All-American Team (1985)

THEODORE, JOSE — MTL.

Goaltender. Catches right. 5'10", 176 lbs. Born, Laval, Que., September 13, 1976.
(Montreal's 2nd choice, 44th overall, in 1994 Entry Draft).

			Regular Season								Playoffs						
Season	Club	Lea	GP	W	L	T	Mins	GA	SO	Avg	GP	W	L	Mins	GA	SO	Avg
1992-93	St-Jean	QMJHL	34	12	16	2	1776	112	0	3.78	3	0	2	175	11	0	3.77
1993-94	St-Jean	QMJHL	57	20	29	6	3225	194	0	3.61	5	1	4	296	18	0	3.65

THIBAULT, JOCELYN (tee-BOW) — QUE.

Goaltender. Catches left. 5'11", 170 lbs. Born, Montreal, Que., January 12, 1975.
(Quebec's 1st choice, 10th overall, in 1993 Entry Draft).

			Regular Season								Playoffs						
Season	Club	Lea	GP	W	L	T	Mins	GA	SO	Avg	GP	W	L	Mins	GA	SO	Avg
1991-92	Trois Rivieres	QMJHL	30	14	7	1	1496	77	0	3.09	3	....	....	110	4	0	2.19
1992-93abc	Sherbrooke	QMJHL	56	34	14	5	3190	159	3	2.99	15	9	6	882	57	0	3.87
1993-94	**Quebec**	**NHL**	**29**	**8**	**13**	**3**	**1504**	**83**	**0**	**3.31**							
	Cornwall	AHL	4	4	0	0	240	9	1	2.25							
	NHL Totals		**29**	**8**	**13**	**3**	**1504**	**83**	**0**	**3.31**							

a QMJHL First All-Star Team (1993)
b Canadian Major Junior First All-Star Team (1993)
c Canadian Major Junior Goaltender of the Year (1993)

TKACHENKO, SERGEI (kuh-CHEHN-koh, SAIR-gay) — VAN.

Goaltender. Catches left. 6'2", 198 lbs. Born, Kiev, USSR, June 6, 1971.
(Vancouver's 9th choice, 280th overall, in 1993 Entry Draft).

			Regular Season								Playoffs						
Season	Club	Lea	GP	W	L	T	Mins	GA	SO	Avg	GP	W	L	Mins	GA	SO	Avg
1989-90	Sokol Kiev	USSR	1	....	....	....	10	0	0	0.00							
1990-91	Sokol Kiev	USSR	14	....	....	....	220	14	0	3.37							
1991-92	Sokol Kiev	CIS	24	....	....	....	1305	91	0	4.18							
1992-93	Brantford	ColHL	4	0	1	0	96	11	0	6.88							
	Hamilton	AHL	1	1	0	0	60	3	0	3.00							
1993-94	Hamilton	AHL	2	0	1	1	125	9	0	4.32							
	Columbus	ECHL	34	18	7	4	1884	129	0	4.11	4	1	2	182	16	0	5.27

TORCHIA, MIKE (TOR-chee-ah) — DAL.

Goaltender. Catches left. 5'11", 215 lbs. Born, Toronto, Ont., February 23, 1972.
(Minnesota's 2nd choice, 74th overall, in 1991 Entry Draft).

			Regular Season								Playoffs						
Season	Club	Lea	GP	W	L	T	Mins	GA	SO	Avg	GP	W	L	Mins	GA	SO	Avg
1988-89	Kitchener	OHL	30	14	9	4	1472	102	0	4.02	2	0	2	126	8	0	3.81
1989-90ab	Kitchener	OHL	40	25	11	2	2280	136	1	3.58	*17	*11	6	*1023	60	0	3.52
1990-91	Kitchener	OHL	57	25	24	7	*3317	219	0	3.95	6	2	4	382	30	0	4.71
1991-92	Kitchener	OHL	*55	25	24	3	*3042	203	1	4.00	14	7	7	900	47	0	3.13
1992-93	Cdn. National	....	5	5	0	0	300	11	1	2.20							
	Kalamazoo	IHL	48	19	17	9	2729	173	0	3.80							
1993-94	Kalamazoo	IHL	43	23	12	2	2168	133	0	3.68	4	1	3	221	14	*1	3.80

a Memorial Cup All-Star Team (1990)
b Won Hap Emms Memorial Trophy (Memorial Cup Tournament Top Goaltender) (1990)

TRACY, TRIPP — PHI.

Goaltender. Catches right. 5'10", 170 lbs. Born, Detroit, MI, December 20, 1973.
(Philadelphia's 8th choice, 218th overall, in 1993 Entry Draft).

			Regular Season								Playoffs						
Season	Club	Lea	GP	W	L	T	Mins	GA	SO	Avg	GP	W	L	Mins	GA	SO	Avg
1992-93	Harvard	ECAC	17	13	2	2	1055	40	*3	*2.27							
1993-94	Harvard	ECAC	17	12	3	2	978	49	0	3.01							

TREFILOV, ANDREI (TREH-fee-lahf) CGY.

Goaltender. Catches left. 6', 180 lbs. Born, Kirovo-Chepetsk, USSR, August 31, 1969.
(Calgary's 14th choice, 261st overall, in 1991 Entry Draft).

			Regular Season								Playoffs						
Season	Club	Lea	GP	W	L	T	Mins	GA	SO	Avg	GP	W	L	Mins	GA	SO	Avg
1990-91	Moscow D'amo	USSR	20	....	....	....	1070	36	0	2.01	....	....	....	....	....	....	....
1991-92	Moscow D'amo	CIS	28	....	....	....	1326	35	0	1.58	....	....	....	....	....	....	....
1992-93	**Calgary**	**NHL**	**1**	**0**	**0**	**1**	**65**	**5**	**0**	**4.62**	....	....	....	....	....	....	....
	Salt Lake	IHL	44	23	17	3	2536	135	0	3.19	....	....	....	....	....	....	....
1993-94	**Calgary**	**NHL**	**11**	**3**	**4**	**2**	**623**	**26**	**2**	**2.50**	....	....	....	....	....	....	....
	Saint John	AHL	28	10	10	7	1629	93	0	3.42	....	....	....	....	....	....	....
	NHL Totals		**12**	**3**	**4**	**3**	**688**	**31**	**2**	**2.70**	....	....	....	....	....	....	....

TROFIMENKOFF, DAVE NYR

Goaltender. Catches right. 6', 177 lbs. Born, Calgary, Alta., January 20, 1975.
(NY Rangers' 6th choice, 138th overall, in 1993 Entry Draft).

			Regular Season								Playoffs						
Season	Club	Lea	GP	W	L	T	Mins	GA	SO	Avg	GP	W	L	Mins	GA	SO	Avg
1991-92	Lethbridge	WHL	21	10	8	1	1080	67	0	3.72	....	....	....	....	....	....	....
1992-93	Lethbridge	WHL	27	14	9	0	1419	103	0	4.36	....	....	....	....	....	....	....
1993-94	Lethbridge	WHL	42	18	18	1	2176	169	1	4.66	1	0	0	20	0	0	0.00

TUGNUTT, RON MTL.

Goaltender. Catches left. 5'11", 155 lbs. Born, Scarborough, Ont., October 22, 1967.
(Quebec's 4th choice, 81st overall, in 1986 Entry Draft).

			Regular Season								Playoffs						
Season	Club	Lea	GP	W	L	T	Mins	GA	SO	Avg	GP	W	L	Mins	GA	SO	Avg
1984-85	Peterborough	OHL	18	7	4	2	938	59	0	3.77	....	....	....	....	....	....	....
1985-86	Peterborough	OHL	26	18	7	0	1543	74	1	2.88	3	2	0	133	6	0	2.71
1986-87a	Peterborough	OHL	31	21	7	2	1891	88	2	*2.79	6	3	3	374	21	1	3.37
1987-88	**Quebec**	**NHL**	**6**	**2**	**3**	**0**	**284**	**16**	**0**	**3.38**	....	....	....	....	....	....	....
	Fredericton	AHL	34	20	9	4	1964	118	1	3.60	4	1	2	204	11	0	3.24
1988-89	**Quebec**	**NHL**	**26**	**10**	**10**	**3**	**1367**	**82**	**0**	**3.60**	....	....	....	....	....	....	....
	Halifax	AHL	24	14	7	2	1368	79	1	3.46	....	....	....	....	....	....	....
1989-90	**Quebec**	**NHL**	**35**	**5**	**24**	**3**	**1978**	**152**	**0**	**4.61**	....	....	....	....	....	....	....
	Halifax	AHL	6	1	5	0	366	23	0	3.77	....	....	....	....	....	....	....
1990-91	**Quebec**	**NHL**	**56**	**12**	**29**	**10**	**3144**	**212**	**0**	**4.05**	....	....	....	....	....	....	....
	Halifax	AHL	2	0	1	0	100	8	0	4.80	....	....	....	....	....	....	....
1991-92	**Quebec**	**NHL**	**30**	**6**	**17**	**3**	**1583**	**106**	**1**	**4.02**	....	....	....	....	....	....	....
	Halifax	AHL	8	3	3	1	447	30	0	4.03	....	....	....	....	....	....	....
	Edmonton	**NHL**	**3**	**1**	**1**	**0**	**124**	**10**	**0**	**4.84**	**2**	**0**	**0**	**60**	**3**	**0**	**3.00**
1992-93	**Edmonton**	**NHL**	**26**	**9**	**12**	**2**	**1338**	**93**	**0**	**4.17**	....	....	....	....	....	....	....
1993-94	**Anaheim**	**NHL**	**28**	**10**	**15**	**1**	**1520**	**76**	**1**	**3.00**	....	....	....	....	....	....	....
	Montreal	**NHL**	**8**	**2**	**3**	**1**	**378**	**24**	**0**	**3.81**	**1**	**0**	**1**	**59**	**5**	**0**	**5.08**
	NHL Totals		**218**	**57**	**114**	**23**	**11716**	**771**	**2**	**3.95**	**3**	**0**	**1**	**119**	**8**	**0**	**4.03**

a OHL First All-Star Team (1987)

Traded to **Edmonton** by **Quebec** with Brad Zavisha for Martin Rucinsky, March 10, 1992. Claimed by **Anaheim** from **Edmonton** in Expansion Draft, June 24, 1993. Traded to **Montreal** by **Anaheim** for Stephan Lebeau, February 20, 1994.

TURCO, MARTY DAL.

Goaltender. Catches left. 5'11", 175 lbs. Born, Sault Ste. Marie, Ont., August 13, 1975.
(Dallas' 4th choice, 124th overall, in 1994 Entry Draft).

			Regular Season								Playoffs						
Season	Club	Lea	GP	W	L	T	Mins	GA	SO	Avg	GP	W	L	Mins	GA	SO	Avg
1993-94	Cambridge	Jr. B	34	....	....	....	1973	114	0	3.47	....	....	....	....	....	....	....

TUREK, ROMAN (TOOR-ehk) DAL.

Goaltender. Catches right. 6'3", 190 lbs. Born, Strakonice, Czech., May 21, 1970.
(Minnesota's 6th choice, 113th overall, in 1990 Entry Draft).

			Regular Season								Playoffs						
Season	Club	Lea	GP	W	L	T	Mins	GA	SO	Avg	GP	W	L	Mins	GA	SO	Avg
1990-91	Budejovice	Czech.	26	....	....	....	1244	98	0	4.70	....	....	....	....	....	....	....
1991-92	Budejovice	Czech.2	....	....	....	....	....	....	....	....	....	....	....	....	....	....	....
1992-93	Budejovice	Czech.	43	....	....	....	2555	121	....	2.84	....	....	....	....	....	....	....
1993-94	Budejovice	Czech.	44	0	0	0	2584	111	0	2.51	3	....	....	180	12	0	4.00

VANBIESBROUCK, JOHN (van-BEES-bruhk) FLA.

Goaltender. Catches left. 5'8", 172 lbs. Born, Detroit, MI, September 4, 1963.
(NY Rangers' 5th choice, 72nd overall, in 1981 Entry Draft).

			Regular Season								Playoffs						
Season	Club	Lea	GP	W	L	T	Mins	GA	SO	Avg	GP	W	L	Mins	GA	SO	Avg
1980-81	S.S. Marie	OHA	56	31	16	1	2941	203	0	4.14	11	3	3	457	24	1	3.15
1981-82	**NY Rangers**	**NHL**	**1**	**1**	**0**	**0**	**60**	**1**	**0**	**1.00**	....	....	....	....	....	....	....
	S.S. Marie	OHL	31	12	12	2	1686	102	0	3.62	7	1	4	276	20	0	4.35
1982-83a	S.S. Marie	OHL	62	39	21	1	3471	209	0	3.61	16	7	6	944	56	*1	3.56
1983-84	**NY Rangers**	**NHL**	**3**	**2**	**1**	**0**	**180**	**10**	**0**	**3.33**	**1**	**0**	**0**	**1**	**0**	**0**	**0.00**
bcd	Tulsa	CHL	37	20	13	2	2153	124	*3	3.46	4	4	0	240	10	0	*2.50
1984-85	**NY Rangers**	**NHL**	**42**	**12**	**24**	**3**	**2358**	**166**	**1**	**4.22**	**1**	**0**	**0**	**20**	**0**	**0**	**0.00**
1985-86ef	**NY Rangers**	**NHL**	**61**	***31**	**21**	**5**	**3326**	**184**	**3**	**3.32**	**16**	**8**	**8**	**899**	**49**	***1**	**3.27**
1986-87	**NY Rangers**	**NHL**	**50**	**18**	**20**	**5**	**2656**	**161**	**0**	**3.64**	**4**	**1**	**3**	**195**	**11**	**1**	**3.38**
1987-88	**NY Rangers**	**NHL**	**56**	**27**	**22**	**7**	**3319**	**187**	**2**	**3.38**	....	....	....	....	....	....	....
1988-89	**NY Rangers**	**NHL**	**56**	**28**	**21**	**4**	**3207**	**197**	**0**	**3.69**	**2**	**0**	**1**	**107**	**6**	**0**	**3.36**
1989-90	**NY Rangers**	**NHL**	**47**	**19**	**19**	**7**	**2734**	**154**	**1**	**3.38**	**6**	**2**	**3**	**298**	**15**	**0**	**3.02**
1990-91	**NY Rangers**	**NHL**	**40**	**15**	**18**	**6**	**2257**	**126**	**3**	**3.35**	**1**	**0**	**0**	**52**	**1**	**0**	**1.15**
1991-92	**NY Rangers**	**NHL**	**45**	**27**	**13**	**3**	**2526**	**120**	**2**	**2.85**	**7**	**2**	**5**	**368**	**23**	**0**	**3.75**
1992-93	**NY Rangers**	**NHL**	**48**	**20**	**18**	**7**	**2757**	**152**	**4**	**3.31**	....	....	....	....	....	....	....
1993-94g	**Florida**	**NHL**	**57**	**21**	**25**	**11**	**3440**	**145**	**1**	**2.53**	....	....	....	....	....	....	....
	NHL Totals		**506**	**221**	**202**	**58**	**28820**	**1603**	**17**	**3.34**	**38**	**13**	**20**	**1940**	**105**	**2**	**3.25**

a OHL Second All-Star Team (1983)
b CHL First All-Star Team (1984)
c Shared Terry Sawchuk Trophy (Leading Goaltender - CHL) with Ron Scott (1984)
d Shared Tommy Ivan Trophy (Most Valuable Player - CHL) with Bruce Affleck of Indianapolis (1984)
e Won Vezina Trophy (1986)
f NHL First All-Star Team (1986)
g NHL Second All-Star Team (1994)

Played in NHL All-Star Game (1994)

Traded to **Vancouver** by **NY Rangers** for future considerations (Doug Lidster, June 25, 1993), June 20, 1993. Claimed by **Florida** from **Vancouver** in Expansion Draft, June 24, 1993.

VEISOR, MIKE (VIGH-awr) ST.L.

Goaltender. Catches right. 6'2", 195 lbs. Born, Dallas, TX, December 7, 1972.
(St. Louis' 12th choice, 263rd overall, in 1991 Entry Draft).

			Regular Season								Playoffs						
Season	Club	Lea	GP	W	L	T	Mins	GA	SO	Avg	GP	W	L	Mins	GA	SO	Avg
1992-93	Northeastern	H.E.	30	8	19	1	1699	151	0	5.33	....	....	....	....	....	....	....
1993-94	Northeastern	H.E.	15	7	3	2	775	55	0	4.26	....	....	....	....	....	....	....

VERNER, ANDREW EDM.

Goaltender. Catches left. 6', 194 lbs. Born, Weston, Ont., November 20, 1972.
(Edmonton's 3rd choice, 34th overall, in 1991 Entry Draft).

			Regular Season								Playoffs						
Season	Club	Lea	GP	W	L	T	Mins	GA	SO	Avg	GP	W	L	Mins	GA	SO	Avg
1989-90	Peterborough	OHL	13	7	3	0	624	38	1	3.65	2	....	....	121	6	0	2.98
1990-91a	Peterborough	OHL	46	22	14	7	2523	148	0	3.52	3	0	3	185	15	0	4.86
1991-92a	Peterborough	OHL	53	*34	13	6	3123	190	1	3.65	10	5	5	539	30	0	3.34
1992-93	Cape Breton	AHL	36	17	10	6	1974	126	1	3.83	....	....	....	....	....	....	....
1993-94	Cape Breton	AHL	38	11	17	8	2261	175	0	4.64	1	0	0	40	4	0	6.00

a OHL Second All-Star Team (1991, 1992)

VERNON, MIKE DET.

Goaltender. Catches left. 5'9", 165 lbs. Born, Calgary, Alta., February 24, 1963.
(Calgary's 2nd choice, 56th overall, in 1981 Entry Draft).

			Regular Season								Playoffs						
Season	Club	Lea	GP	W	L	T	Mins	GA	SO	Avg	GP	W	L	Mins	GA	SO	Avg
1980-81	Calgary	WHL	59	33	17	1	3154	198	1	3.77	22	....	....	1271	82	1	3.87
1981-82a	Calgary	WHL	42	22	14	2	2329	143	3	3.68	9	....	....	527	30	0	3.42
	Oklahoma City	CHL	....	....	....	....	....	....	....	....	1	0	1	70	4	0	3.43
1982-83	**Calgary**	**NHL**	**2**	**0**	**2**	**0**	**100**	**11**	**0**	**6.59**	....	....	....	....	....	....	....
a	Calgary	WHL	50	19	18	2	2856	155	3	3.26	16	9	7	925	60	0	3.89
1983-84	**Calgary**	**NHL**	**1**	**0**	**1**	**0**	**11**	**4**	**0**	**22.22**	....	....	....	....	....	....	....
b	Colorado	CHL	46	30	13	2	2648	148	1	*3.35	6	2	4	347	21	0	3.63
1984-85	Moncton	AHL	41	10	20	4	2050	134	0	3.92	....	....	....	....	....	....	....
1985-86	**Calgary**	**NHL**	**18**	**9**	**3**	**3**	**921**	**52**	**1**	**3.39**	***21**	**12**	***9**	**1229**	**60**	**0**	**2.93**
	Moncton	AHL	6	3	1	2	374	21	0	3.37	....	....	....	....	....	....	....
	Salt Lake	IHL	10	....	....	....	600	34	1	3.40	....	....	....	....	....	....	....
1986-87	**Calgary**	**NHL**	**54**	**30**	**21**	**1**	**2957**	**178**	**1**	**3.61**	**5**	**2**	**3**	**263**	**16**	**0**	**3.65**
1987-88	**Calgary**	**NHL**	**64**	**39**	**16**	**7**	**3565**	**210**	**1**	**3.53**	**9**	**4**	**4**	**515**	**34**	**0**	**3.96**
1988-89c	**Calgary**	**NHL**	**52**	***37**	**6**	**5**	**2938**	**130**	**0**	**2.65**	***22**	***16**	**5**	***1381**	**52**	***3**	**2.26**
1989-90	**Calgary**	**NHL**	**47**	**23**	**14**	**9**	**2795**	**146**	**0**	**3.13**	**6**	**2**	**3**	**342**	**19**	**0**	**3.33**
1990-91	**Calgary**	**NHL**	**54**	**31**	**19**	**3**	**3121**	**172**	**1**	**3.31**	**7**	**3**	**4**	**427**	**21**	**0**	**2.95**
1991-92	**Calgary**	**NHL**	**63**	**24**	**30**	**9**	**3640**	**217**	**0**	**3.58**	....	....	....	....	....	....	....
1992-93	**Calgary**	**NHL**	**64**	**29**	**26**	**9**	**3732**	**203**	**2**	**3.26**	**4**	**1**	**1**	**150**	**15**	**0**	**6.00**
1993-94	**Calgary**	**NHL**	**48**	**26**	**17**	**5**	**2798**	**131**	**3**	**2.81**	**7**	**3**	**4**	**466**	**23**	**0**	**2.96**
	NHL Totals		**467**	**248**	**155**	**51**	**26578**	**1454**	**9**	**3.28**	**81**	**43**	**33**	**4773**	**240**	**3**	**3.02**

a WHL First All-Star Team (1982, 1983)
b CHL Second All-Star Team (1984)
c NHL Second All-Star Team (1989)

Played in NHL All-Star Game (1988-91, 1993)

Traded to **Detroit** by **Calgary** for Steve Chiasson, June 29, 1994.

VEZINA, STEVE WPG.

Goaltender. Catches left. 5'10", 172 lbs. Born, St-Jean, Que., October 25, 1975.
(Winnipeg's 6th choice, 143rd overall, in 1994 Entry Draft).

			Regular Season								Playoffs						
Season	Club	Lea	GP	W	L	T	Mins	GA	SO	Avg	GP	W	L	Mins	GA	SO	Avg
1992-93	Beauport	QMJHL	19	1	13	0	770	67	0	5.22	....	....	....	....	....	....	....
1993-94	Beauport	QMJHL	46	19	15	4	2380	156	0	3.93	10	5	4	430	22	0	3.07

WAITE, JIMMY (WAYT) S.J.

Goaltender. Catches left. 6'1", 180 lbs. Born, Sherbrooke, Que., April 15, 1969.
(Chicago's 1st choice, 8th overall, in 1987 Entry Draft).

			Regular Season								Playoffs						
Season	Club	Lea	GP	W	L	T	Mins	GA	SO	Avg	GP	W	L	Mins	GA	SO	Avg
1986-87a	Chicoutimi	QMJHL	50	23	17	3	2569	209	2	4.48	11	4	6	576	54	1	5.63
1987-88	Chicoutimi	QMJHL	36	17	16	1	2000	150	0	4.50	4	1	2	222	17	0	4.59
1988-89	**Chicago**	**NHL**	**11**	**0**	**7**	**1**	**494**	**43**	**0**	**5.22**	....	....	....	....	....	....	....
	Saginaw	IHL	5	3	1	0	304	10	0	1.97	....	....	....	....	....	....	....
1989-90	**Chicago**	**NHL**	**4**	**2**	**0**	**0**	**183**	**14**	**0**	**4.59**	....	....	....	....	....	....	....
bc	Indianapolis	IHL	54	*34	14	5	*3207	135	*5	*2.53	*10	*9	1	*602	19	*1	*1.89
1990-91	**Chicago**	**NHL**	**1**	**1**	**0**	**0**	**60**	**2**	**0**	**2.00**	....	....	....	....	....	....	....
	Indianapolis	IHL	49	*26	18	4	2888	167	3	3.47	6	2	4	369	20	0	3.25
1991-92	**Chicago**	**NHL**	**17**	**4**	**7**	**4**	**877**	**54**	**0**	**3.69**	....	....	....	....	....	....	....
	Indianapolis	IHL	13	4	7	1	702	53	0	4.53	....	....	....	....	....	....	....
	Hershey	AHL	11	6	4	1	631	44	0	4.18	6	2	4	360	19	0	3.17
1992-93	**Chicago**	**NHL**	**20**	**6**	**7**	**1**	**996**	**49**	**2**	**2.95**	....	....	....	....	....	....	....
1993-94	**San Jose**	**NHL**	**15**	**3**	**7**	**0**	**697**	**50**	**0**	**4.30**	**2**	**0**	**0**	**40**	**3**	**0**	**4.50**
	NHL Totals		**68**	**16**	**28**	**6**	**3307**	**212**	**2**	**3.85**	**2**	**0**	**0**	**40**	**3**	**0**	**4.50**

a QMJHL Second All-Star Team (1987)
b IHL First All-Star Team (1990)
c Won James Norris Memorial Trophy (Top Goaltender - IHL) (1990)

Traded to **San Jose** by **Chicago** for future considerations (Neil Wilkinson, July 9, 1993), June 19, 1993.

WAKALUK, DARCY (WAHK-uh-luhk) DAL.

Goaltender. Catches left. 5'11", 180 lbs. Born, Pincher Creek, Alta., March 14, 1966.
(Buffalo's 7th choice, 144th overall, in 1984 Entry Draft).

			Regular Season								Playoffs						
Season	Club	Lea	GP	W	L	T	Mins	GA	SO	Avg	GP	W	L	Mins	GA	SO	Avg
1983-84	Kelowna	WHL	31	....	....	....	1555	163	0	6.29	....	....	....	....	....	....	....
1984-85	Kelowna	WHL	54	19	30	4	3094	244	0	4.73	5	1	4	282	22	0	4.68
1985-86	Spokane	WHL	47	21	22	1	2562	224	1	5.25	7	3	4	419	37	0	5.30
1986-87	Rochester	AHL	11	2	2	0	545	26	0	2.86	5	2	0	141	11	0	4.68
1987-88	Rochester	AHL	55	27	16	3	2763	159	0	3.45	6	3	3	328	22	0	4.02
1988-89	**Buffalo**	**NHL**	**6**	**1**	**3**	**0**	**214**	**15**	**0**	**4.21**	....	....	....	....	....	....	....
	Rochester	AHL	33	11	14	0	1566	97	1	3.72	....	....	....	....	....	....	....
1989-90	Rochester	AHL	56	31	16	4	3095	173	2	3.35	*17	*10	6	*1001	50	0	*3.01
1990-91	**Buffalo**	**NHL**	**16**	**4**	**5**	**3**	**630**	**35**	**0**	**3.33**	**2**	**0**	**1**	**37**	**2**	**0**	**3.24**
	Rochester	AHL	26	10	10	3	1363	68	4	*2.99	9	6	3	544	30	0	3.31
1991-92	**Minnesota**	**NHL**	**36**	**13**	**19**	**1**	**1905**	**104**	**1**	**3.28**	....	....	....	....	....	....	....
	Kalamazoo	IHL	1	1	0	0	60	7	0	7.00	....	....	....	....	....	....	....
1992-93	**Minnesota**	**NHL**	**29**	**10**	**12**	**5**	**1596**	**97**	**1**	**3.65**	....	....	....	....	....	....	....
1993-94	**Dallas**	**NHL**	**36**	**18**	**9**	**6**	**2000**	**88**	**3**	**2.64**	**5**	**4**	**1**	**307**	**15**	**0**	**2.93**
	NHL Totals		**123**	**46**	**48**	**15**	**6345**	**339**	**5**	**3.21**	**7**	**4**	**2**	**344**	**17**	**0**	**2.97**

Traded to **Minnesota** by **Buffalo** for Minnesota's eighth round choice (Jiri Kuntos) in 1991 Entry Draft and Minnesota's fifth round choice (later traded to Toronto — Toronto selected Chris Deruiter) in 1992 Entry Draft, May 26, 1991.

WEEKES, KEVIN FLA.

Goaltender. Catches left. 6', 158 lbs. Born, Toronto, Ont., April 4, 1975.
(Florida's 2nd choice, 41st overall, in 1993 Entry Draft).

			Regular Season								Playoffs						
Season	Club	Lea	GP	W	L	T	Mins	GA	SO	Avg	GP	W	L	Mins	GA	SO	Avg
1992-93	Owen Sound	OHL	29	9	12	5	1645	143	0	5.22	1	0	0	26	5	0	11.50
1993-94	Owen Sound	OHL	34	13	19	1	1974	158	0	4.80	....	....	....	....	....	....	....

WEIBEL, LARS   CHI.

Goaltender. Catches left. 6', 178 lbs.   Born, Rapperswil, Switz., May 20, 1974.
(Chicago's 10th choice, 248th overall, in 1994 Entry Draft).

						Regular Season								Playoffs			
Season	Club	Lea	GP	W	L	T	Mins	GA	SO	Avg	GP	W	L	Mins	GASO		Avg
1992-93	Biel-Bienne	Switz.	14	....	....	....	674	54	....	4.80	....	....	....	....	....		....
1993-94	Lugano	Switz.	25	....	....	....	....	....	....	....	9	....	....	560	23	....	2.46

WHITMORE, KAY   VAN.

Goaltender. Catches left. 5'11", 175 lbs.   Born, Sudbury, Ont., April 10, 1967.
(Hartford's 2nd choice, 26th overall, in 1985 Entry Draft).

						Regular Season								Playoffs			
Season	Club	Lea	GP	W	L	T	Mins	GA	SO	Avg	GP	W	L	Mins	GASO		Avg
1983-84	Peterborough	OHL	29	17	8	0	1471	110	0	4.49	....	....	....	....	....		....
1984-85	Peterborough	OHL	53	*35	16	2	3077	172	*2	3.35	17	10	4	1020	58	0	3.41
1985-86a	Peterborough	OHL	41	27	12	2	2467	114	*3	2.77	14	8	5	837	40	0	2.87
1986-87	Peterborough	OHL	36	14	17	5	2159	118	1	3.28	7	3	3	366	17	1	2.79
1987-88	Binghamton	AHL	38	17	15	4	2137	121	*3	3.40	2	0	2	118	10	0	5.08
1988-89	**Hartford**	**NHL**	3	2	1	0	180	10	0	3.33	2	0	2	135	10	0	4.44
	Binghamton	AHL	*56	21	29	4	*3200	241	1	4.52	....	....	....	....	....		....
1989-90	**Hartford**	**NHL**	9	4	2	1	442	26	0	3.53	....	....	....	....	....		....
	Binghamton	AHL	24	3	19	2	1386	109	0	4.72	....	....	....	....	....		....
1990-91	**Hartford**	**NHL**	18	3	9	1	850	52	0	3.67	....	....	....	....	....		....
b	Springfield	AHL	33	22	9	1	1916	98	1	3.07	*15	*11	4	*926	37	0	*2.40
1991-92	**Hartford**	**NHL**	45	14	21	6	2567	155	3	3.62	1	0	0	19	1	0	3.16
1992-93	**Vancouver**	**NHL**	31	18	8	4	1817	94	1	3.10	....	....	....	....	....		....
1993-94	**Vancouver**	**NHL**	32	18	14	0	1921	113	0	3.53	....	....	....	....	....		....
	NHL Totals		**138**	**59**	**55**	**14**	**7777**	**450**	**4**	**3.47**	**3**	**0**	**2**	**154**	**11**	**0**	**4.29**

a   OHL First All-Star Team (1986)
b   Won Jack A. Butterfield Trophy (Playoff MVP - AHL) (1991)

Traded to **Vancouver** by **Hartford** for Corrie D'Alessio and future considerations, October 1, 1992.

WILKINSON, DEREK   T.B.

Goaltender. Catches left. 6', 160 lbs.   Born, Lasalle, Que., July 29, 1974.
(Tampa Bay's 7th choice, 145th overall, in 1992 Entry Draft).

						Regular Season								Playoffs			
Season	Club	Lea	GP	W	L	T	Mins	GA	SO	Avg	GP	W	L	Mins	GASO		Avg
1991-92	Detroit	OHL	38	16	17	1	1943	138	1	4.26	7	3	2	313	28	0	5.37
1992-93	Belleville	OHL	*59	21	24	11	*3370	237	0	4.22	7	3	4	434	29	0	4.01
1993-94	Belleville	OHL	56	24	16	4	2860	179	*2	3.76	12	6	6	700	39	*1	3.34

WILLIS, JORDAN   DAL.

Goaltender. Catches left. 5'9", 155 lbs.   Born, Kincardine, Ont., February 28, 1975.
(Dallas' 8th choice, 243rd overall, in 1993 Entry Draft).

						Regular Season								Playoffs			
Season	Club	Lea	GP	W	L	T	Mins	GA	SO	Avg	GP	W	L	Mins	GASO		Avg
1992-93	London	OHL	26	13	6	3	1428	101	1	4.24	....	....	....	....	....		....
1993-94	London	OHL	44	20	19	2	2428	158	1	3.90	1	0	0	8	1	0	7.50

WREGGET, KEN   (REHG-eht)   PIT.

Goaltender. Catches left. 6'1", 195 lbs.   Born, Brandon, Man., March 25, 1964.
(Toronto's 4th choice, 45th overall, in 1982 Entry Draft).

						Regular Season								Playoffs			
Season	Club	Lea	GP	W	L	T	Mins	GA	SO	Avg	GP	W	L	Mins	GASO		Avg
1981-82	Lethbridge	WHL	36	19	12	0	1713	118	0	4.13	3	....	....	84	3	0	2.14
1982-83	Lethbridge	WHL	48	26	17	1	2696	157	0	3.49	20	14	5	1154	58	1	3.02
1983-84	**Toronto**	**NHL**	3	1	1	1	165	14	0	5.09	....	....	....	....	....		....
a	Lethbridge	WHL	53	32	20	0	3053	161	0	*3.16	4	1	3	210	18	0	5.14
1984-85	**Toronto**	**NHL**	23	2	15	3	1278	103	0	4.84	....	....	....	....	....		....
	St. Catharines	AHL	12	2	8	1	688	48	0	4.19	....	....	....	....	....		....
1985-86	**Toronto**	**NHL**	30	9	13	4	1566	113	0	4.33	10	6	4	607	32	*1	3.16
	St. Catharines	AHL	18	8	9	0	1058	78	1	4.42	....	....	....	....	....		....
1986-87	**Toronto**	**NHL**	56	22	28	3	3026	200	0	3.97	13	7	6	761	29	1	2.29
1987-88	**Toronto**	**NHL**	56	12	35	4	3000	222	2	4.44	2	0	1	108	11	0	6.11
1988-89	**Toronto**	**NHL**	32	9	20	2	1888	139	0	4.42	....	....	....	....	....		....
	Philadelphia	**NHL**	3	1	1	0	130	13	0	6.00	5	2	2	268	10	1	2.24
1989-90	**Philadelphia**	**NHL**	51	22	24	3	2961	169	0	3.42	....	....	....	....	....		....
1990-91	**Philadelphia**	**NHL**	30	10	14	3	1484	88	0	3.56	....	....	....	....	....		....
1991-92	**Philadelphia**	**NHL**	23	9	8	3	1259	75	0	3.57	....	....	....	....	....		....
	Pittsburgh	**NHL**	9	5	4	0	448	31	0	4.15	1	0	0	40	4	0	6.00
1992-93	**Pittsburgh**	**NHL**	25	13	7	2	1368	78	0	3.42	....	....	....	....	....		....
1993-94	**Pittsburgh**	**NHL**	42	21	12	7	2456	138	1	3.37	....	....	....	....	....		....
	NHL Totals		**383**	**136**	**181**	**35**	**21029**	**1383**	**3**	**3.95**	**31**	**15**	**13**	**1784**	**86**	**3**	**2.89**

a   WHL East First All-Star Team (1984)

Traded to **Philadelphia** by **Toronto** for Philadelphia's first round choice (Rob Pearson) and Calgary's first round choice (previously acquired by Philadelphia — Toronto selected Steve Bancroft in 1989 Entry Draft, March 6, 1989. Traded to **Pittsburgh** by **Philadelphia** with Rick Tocchet, Kjell Samuelsson and Philadelphia's third round choice (Dave Roche) in 1993 Entry Draft for Mark Recchi, Brian Benning and Los Angeles' first round choice (previously acquired by Pittsburgh — Philadelphia selected Jason Bowen) in 1992 Entry Draft, February 19, 1992.

YOUNG, WENDELL   T.B.

Goaltender. Catches left. 5'9", 181 lbs.   Born, Halifax, N.S., August 1, 1963.
(Vancouver's 3rd choice, 73rd overall, in 1981 Entry Draft).

						Regular Season								Playoffs			
Season	Club	Lea	GP	W	L	T	Mins	GA	SO	Avg	GP	W	L	Mins	GASO		Avg
1980-81	Kitchener	OHA	42	19	15	0	2215	164	1	4.44	14	9	1	800	42	*1	3.15
1981-82	Kitchener	OHL	60	38	17	0	3470	195	1	3.37	15	12	1	900	35	*1	*2.33
1982-83	Kitchener	OHL	61	41	19	0	3611	231	1	3.84	12	6	5	720	43	0	3.58
1983-84	Fredericton	AHL	11	7	3	0	569	39	1	4.11	....	....	....	....	....		....
	Milwaukee	IHL	6	....	....	....	339	17	0	3.01	....	....	....	....	....		....
	Salt Lake	CHL	20	11	6	0	1094	80	0	4.39	4	0	2	122	11	0	5.42
1984-85	Fredericton	AHL	22	7	11	3	1242	83	0	4.01	....	....	....	....	....		....
1985-86	**Vancouver**	**NHL**	22	4	9	3	1023	61	0	3.58	1	0	1	60	5	0	5.00
	Fredericton	AHL	24	12	8	4	1457	78	0	3.21	....	....	....	....	....		....
1986-87	**Vancouver**	**NHL**	8	1	6	1	420	35	0	5.00	....	....	....	....	....		....
	Fredericton	AHL	30	11	16	0	1676	118	0	4.22	....	....	....	....	....		....
1987-88	**Philadelphia**	**NHL**	6	3	2	0	320	20	0	3.75	....	....	....	....	....		....
abc	Hershey	AHL	51	*33	15	1	2922	135	1	2.77	12	*12	0	*767	28	*1	2.19
1988-89	**Pittsburgh**	**NHL**	22	12	9	0	1150	92	0	4.80	1	0	1	39	1	0	1.54
	Muskegon	IHL	2	....	....	....	125	7	0	3.36	....	....	....	....	....		....
1989-90	**Pittsburgh**	**NHL**	43	16	20	3	2318	161	1	4.17	....	....	....	....	....		....
1990-91	**Pittsburgh**	**NHL**	18	4	6	2	773	52	0	4.04	....	....	....	....	....		....
1991-92	**Pittsburgh**	**NHL**	18	7	6	0	838	53	0	3.79	....	....	....	....	....		....
1992-93	**Tampa Bay**	**NHL**	31	7	19	2	1591	97	0	3.66	....	....	....	....	....		....
	Atlanta	IHL	3	3	0	0	183	8	0	2.62	....	....	....	....	....		....
1993-94	**Tampa Bay**	**NHL**	9	2	3	1	480	20	1	2.50	....	....	....	....	....		....
	Atlanta	IHL	2	2	0	0	120	6	0	3.00	....	....	....	....	....		....
	NHL Totals		**177**	**56**	**80**	**12**	**8913**	**591**	**2**	**3.98**	**2**	**0**	**1**	**99**	**6**	**0**	**3.64**

a   AHL First All-Star Team (1988)
b   Won Baz Bastien Award (Most Valuable Goaltender - AHL) (1988)
c   Won Jack Butterfield Trophy (Playoff MVP - AHL) (1988)

Traded to **Philadelphia** by **Vancouver** with Vancouver's third round choice (Kimbi Daniels) in 1990 Entry Draft for Darren Jensen and Daryl Stanley, August 28, 1987. Traded to **Pittsburgh** by **Philadelphia** with Philadelphia's seventh round choice (Mika Valila) in 1990 Entry Draft for Pittsburgh's third round choice (Chris Therien) in 1990 Entry Draft, September 1, 1988. Claimed by **Tampa Bay** from **Pittsburgh** in Expansion Draft, June 18, 1992.

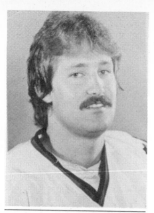

Murray Bannerman

Denis DeJordy

Markus Mattson

Johnny Bower

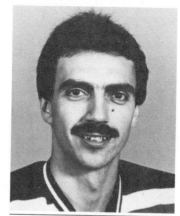

Karl Friesen

Marcel Paille

Jim Craig

Denis Herron

Pete Peeters

Roger Crozier

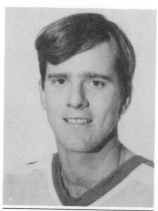

Bob Janecyk

Bill Smith

Retired NHL Goaltender Index

Abbreviations: Teams/Cities: — **Ana.** – Anaheim; **Atl.** – Atlanta; **Bos.** – Boston, **Bro.** – Brooklyn; **Buf.** – Buffalo; **Cal.** – California; **Cgy.** – Calgary; **Cle.** – Cleveland; **Col.** – Colorado; **Dal.** – Dallas; **Det.** – Detroit; **Edm.** – Edmonton; **Fla.** – Florida; **Ham.** – Hamilton; **Hfd.** – Hartford; **K.C.** – Kansas City; **L.A.** – Los Angeles; **Min.** — Minnesota; **Mtl.** – Montreal; **Mtl. M.** – Montreal Maroons; **Mtl. W.** – Montreal Wanderers; **N.J.** – New Jersey; **NYA** – NY Americans; **NYI** – New York Islanders; **NYR** – New York Rangers; **Oak.** – Oakland; **Ott.** – Ottawa; **Phi.** – Philadelphia; **Pit.** – Pittsburgh; **Que.** – Quebec; **St. L.** – St. Louis; **S.J.** – San Jose; **T.B.** – Tampa Bay; **Tor.** – Toronto; **Van.** – Vancouver; **Wpg.** – Winnipeg; **Wsh.** – Washington.

Avg. – goals against per 60 minutes played; **GA** – goals against; **GP** – games played; **Mins** – minutes played; **SO** – shutouts.
• – deceased. Assists not recorded during 1917-18 season.

			Regular Schedule								Playoffs										
Name	NHL Teams	NHL Seasons	GP	W	L	T	Mins	GA	SO	Avg	GP	W	L	T	Mins	GA	SO	Avg	NHL Cup Wins	First NHL Season	Last NHL Season
Abbott, George	Bos.	1	1	0	1	0	60	7	0	7.00	....	....	....	....	....	....	....	....		1943-44	1943-44
Adams, John	Bos., Wsh.	2	22	9	10	1	1180	85	1	4.32	....	....	....	....	....	....	....	....		1972-73	1974-75
Aiken, Don	Mtl.	1	1	0	1	0	34	6	0	10.59	....	....	....	....	....	....	....	....		1957-58	1957-58
Aitkenhead, Andy	NYR	3	106	47	43	16	6570	257	11	2.35	10	6	3	1	608	15	3	1.48	1	1932-33	1934-35
Almas, Red	Det., Chi.	3	3	0	2	1	180	13	0	4.33	5	1	3	0	263	13	0	2.97		1946-47	1952-53
• Anderson, Lorne	NYR	1	3	1	2	0	180	18	0	6.00	....	....	....	....	....	....	....	....		1951-52	1951-52
Astrom, Hardy	NYR, Col.	3	83	17	44	12	4456	278	0	3.74	....	....	....	....	....	....	....	....		1977-78	1980-81
Baker, Steve	NYR	4	57	20	20	11	3081	190	3	3.70	14	7	7	0	826	55	0	4.00		1979-80	1982-83
Bannerman, Murray	Van., Chi.	8	289	116	125	33	16470	1051	8	3.83	40	20	18	0	2322	165	0	4.26		1977-78	1986-87
Baron, Marco	Bos., L.A., Edm.	6	86	34	39	9	4822	292	1	3.63	1	0	1	0	20	3	0	9.00		1979-80	1984-85
Bassen, Hank	Chi., Det., Pit.	9	157	47	66	31	8829	441	5	3.00	5	1	4	0	274	11	0	2.41		1954-55	1967-68
• Bastien, Baz	Tor.	1	5	0	4	1	300	20	0	4.00	....	....	....	....	....	....	....	....		1945-46	1945-46
Bauman, Gary	Mtl., Min.	3	35	6	18	6	1718	102	0	3.56	....	....	....	....	....	....	....	....		1966-67	1968-69
Bedard, Jim	Wsh.	2	73	17	40	13	4232	278	1	3.94	....	....	....	....	....	....	....	....		1977-78	1978-79
Behrend, Marc	Wpg.	3	38	12	19	3	1991	164	1	4.94	7	1	3	0	312	19	0	3.65		1983-84	1985-86
Belanger, Yves	St.L., Atl., Bos.	6	78	27	36	6	4134	259	2	3.76	....	....	....	....	....	....	....	....		1974-75	1979-80
Belhumeur, Michel	Phi., Wsh.	3	65	9	36	7	3306	254	0	4.61	1	0	0	0	10	1	0	6.00		1972-73	1975-76
• Bell, Gordie	Tor., NYR	2	8	3	5	0	480	31	0	3.88	2	1	1	0	120	9	0	4.50		1945-46	1955-56
• Benedict, Clint	Ott., Mtl.M.	13	362	190	43	28	22321	863	57	2.32	48	25	18	4	2907	87	15	1.80	4	1917-18	1929-30
Bennett, Harvey	Bos.	1	24	10	12	2	1470	103	0	4.20	....	....	....	....	....	....	....	....		1944-45	1944-45
Bernhardt, Tim	Cgy., Tor.	4	67	17	36	2	3748	267	0	4.27	....	....	....	....	....	....	....	....		1982-83	1986-87
Beveridge, Bill	Det., Ott., St.L., Mtl.M., NYR	9	297	87	166	42	18375	879	18	2.87	5	2	3	0	300	11	0	2.20		1929-30	1942-43
• Bibeault, Paul	Mtl., Tor., Bos., Chi.	7	214	68	82	21	12890	785	10	3.65	20	6	14	0	1237	71	2	3.44		1940-41	1946-47
Binette, Andre	Mtl.	1	1	1	0	0	60	4	0	4.00	....	....	....	....	....	....	....	....		1954-55	1954-55
Binkley, Les	Pit.	5	196	58	94	34	11046	575	11	3.12	7	5	2	0	428	15	0	2.10		1967-68	1971-72
Bittner, Richard	Bos.	1	1	0	0	1	60	3	0	3.00	....	....	....	....	....	....	....	....		1949-50	1949-50
Blake, Mike	L.A.	3	40	13	5	15	2117	150	0	4.25	....	....	....	....	....	....	....	....		1981-82	1983-84
Boisvert, Gilles	Det.	1	3	0	3	0	180	9	0	3.00	....	....	....	....	....	....	....	....		1959-60	1959-60
Bouchard, Dan	Atl., Cgy., Que., Wpg.	14	655	286	232	113	37919	2061	27	3.26	43	13	30	0	2549	147	1	3.46		1972-73	1985-86
• Bourque, Claude	Mtl., Det.	2	62	16	38	8	3830	192	5	3.01	3	1	2	0	188	8	1	2.55		1938-39	1939-40
Boutin, Rollie	Wsh.	3	22	7	10	1	1137	75	0	3.96	....	....	....	....	....	....	....	....		1978-79	1980-81
Bouvrette, Lionel	NYR	1	1	0	1	0	60	6	0	6.00	....	....	....	....	....	....	....	....		1942-43	1942-43
Bower, Johnny	NYR, Tor.	15	552	251	196	90	32077	1347	37	2.52	74	34	35	0	4350	184	5	2.54	4	1953-54	1969-70
Brannigan, Andy	NYA	1	1	0	0	0	7	0	0	0.00	....	....	....	....	....	....	....	....		1940-41	1940-41
Brimsek, Frank	Bos., Chi.	10	514	252	182	80	31210	1404	40	2.70	68	32	36	0	4365	186	2	2.56	2	1938-39	1949-50
• Broda, Turk	Tor.	14	629	302	224	101	38173	1609	62	2.53	101	58	42	1	6389	211	13	1.98	5	1936-37	1951-52
Broderick, Ken	Min., Bos.	3	27	11	12	1	1464	74	2	3.03	....	....	....	....	....	....	....	....		1969-70	1974-75
Broderick, Len	Mtl.	1	1	1	0	0	60	2	0	2.00	....	....	....	....	....	....	....	....		1957-58	1957-58
Brodeur, Richard	NYI, Van., Hfd.	9	385	131	176	62	21968	1410	6	3.85	33	13	20	0	2009	111	1	3.32		1979-80	1987-88
Bromley, Gary	Buf., Van.	6	136	54	44	28	7427	425	7	3.43	7	2	5	0	360	25	0	4.17		1973-74	1980-81
• Brooks, Arthur	Tor.	1	4	2	1	0	220	23	0	6.27	....	....	....	....	....	....	....	....		1917-18	1917-18
Brooks, Ross	Bos.	3	54	37	7	6	3047	134	4	2.64	1	0	0	0	20	3	0	9.00		1972-73	1974-75
• Brophy, Frank	Que.	1	21	3	18	0	1247	148	0	7.12	....	....	....	....	....	....	....	....		1919-20	1919-20
Brown, Andy	Det., Pit.	3	62	22	26	9	3373	213	1	3.79	....	....	....	....	....	....	....	....		1971-72	1973-74
Brown, Ken	Chi.	1	1	0	0	0	18	1	0	3.33	....	....	....	....	....	....	....	....		1970-71	1970-71
Brunetta, Mario	Que.	3	40	12	17	1	1967	128	0	3.90	....	....	....	....	....	....	....	....		1987-88	1989-90
Bullock, Bruce	Van.	3	16	3	9	3	927	74	0	4.79	....	....	....	....	....	....	....	....		1972-73	1976-77
Buzinski, Steve	NYR	1	9	2	6	1	560	55	0	5.89	....	....	....	....	....	....	....	....		1942-43	1942-43
Caley, Don	St.L.	1	1	0	0	0	30	3	0	6.00	....	....	....	....	....	....	....	....		1967-68	1967-68
Caprice, Frank	Van.	6	102	31	40	11	5589	391	1	4.20	....	....	....	....	....	....	....	....		1982-83	1987-88
Caron, Jacques	L.A., St.L., Van.	5	72	24	29	11	3846	211	2	3.29	12	4	7	0	639	34	0	3.19		1967-68	1973-74
Carter, Lyle	Cal.	1	15	4	7	0	721	50	0	4.16	....	....	....	....	....	....	....	....		1971-72	1971-72
• Chabot, Lorne	NYR, Tor., Mtl., Chi., Mtl.M., NYA	11	411	206	140	65	25309	861	73	2.04	37	13	17	6	2558	64	5	1.50	2	1926-27	1936-37
Chadwick, Ed	Tor., Bos.	6	184	57	92	35	10980	551	14	3.01	....	....	....	....	....	....	....	....		1955-56	1961-62
Champoux, Bob	Det., Cal.	2	17	2	11	3	923	80	0	5.20	1	0	0	0	55	4	0	4.36		1963-64	1973-74
Cheevers, Gerry	Tor., Bos.	13	418	230	94	74	24394	1175	26	2.89	88	47	35	0	5396	242	8	2.69	2	1961-62	1979-80
Chevrier, Alain	N.J., Wpg., Chi., Pit., Det.	6	234	91	100	14	12202	845	2	4.16	16	9	7	0	1013	44	0	2.61		1985-86	1990-91
Clancy, Frank	Tor.	1	1	0	0	0	1	0	0	0.00	....	....	....	....	....	....	....	....		1931-32	1931-32
Cleghorn, Odie	Pit.	1	1	1	0	0	60	2	0	2.00	....	....	....	....	....	....	....	....		1925-26	1925-26
Clifford, Chris	Chi.	2	2	0	0	0	24	0	0	0.00	....	....	....	....	....	....	....	....		1984-85	1988-89
Colvin, Les	Bos.	1	1	0	1	0	60	4	0	4.00	....	....	....	....	....	....	....	....		1948-49	1948-49
Conacher, Charlie	Tor., Det.	13	3	0	0	0	9	0	0	0.00	....	....	....	....	....	....	....	....		1929-30	1940-41
• Connell, Alex	Ott., Det., NYA, Mtl.M.	12	417	199	155	59	26030	830	81	1.91	21	9	5	7	1309	26	4	1.19	2	1924-25	1936-37
Corsi, Jim	Edm.	1	26	8	14	3	1366	83	0	3.65	....	....	....	....	....	....	....	....		1979-80	1979-80
Courteau, Maurice	Bos.	1	6	2	4	0	360	33	0	5.50	....	....	....	....	....	....	....	....		1943-44	1943-44
Cox, Abbie	Mtl.M., Det., NYA, Mtl.	3	5	1	1	2	263	11	0	2.51	....	....	....	....	....	....	....	....		1929-30	1935-36
Craig, Jim	Atl., Bos., Min.	3	30	11	10	7	1588	100	0	3.78	....	....	....	....	....	....	....	....		1979-80	1983-84
Crha, Jiri	Tor.	2	69	28	27	11	3942	261	0	3.97	5	0	4	0	186	21	0	6.77		1979-80	1980-81
Crozier, Roger	Det., Buf., Wsh.	14	518	206	197	74	28567	1446	30	3.04	31	14	15	0	1769	82	1	2.78		1963-64	1976-77
• Cude, Wilf	Phi., Bos., Chi., Det., Mtl.	10	282	100	129	49	17486	796	24	2.73	19	7	11	1	1317	51	1	2.32		1930-31	1940-41
Cutts, Don	Edm.	1	6	1	2	1	269	16	0	3.57	....	....	....	....	....	....	....	....		1979-80	1979-80
• Cyr, Claude	Mtl.	1	1	0	0	0	20	1	0	3.00	....	....	....	....	....	....	....	....		1958-59	1958-59
Dadswell, Doug	Cgy.	2	27	8	8	3	1346	99	0	4.41	....	....	....	....	....	....	....	....		1986-87	1987-88
D'Alessio, Corrie	Hfd.	1	1	0	0	0	11	0	0	0.00	....	....	....	....	....	....	....	....		1992-93	1992-93
Daley, Joe	Pit., Buf., Det.	4	105	34	44	19	5836	326	3	3.35	....	....	....	....	....	....	....	....		1968-69	1971-72
Damore, Nick	Bos.	1	1	0	1	0	60	3	0	3.00	....	....	....	....	....	....	....	....		1941-42	1941-42
D'Amour, Marc	Cgy., Phi.	2	16	2	4	2	579	32	0	3.32	....	....	....	....	....	....	....	....		1985-86	1988-89
Daskalakis, Cleon	Bos.	3	12	3	4	1	506	41	0	4.86	....	....	....	....	....	....	....	....		1984-85	1986-87
Davidson, John	St.L., NYR	10	301	123	124	39	17109	1004	7	3.52	31	16	14	0	1862	77	1	2.48		1973-74	1982-83
Decourcy, Robert	NYR	1	1	0	1	0	29	6	0	12.41	....	....	....	....	....	....	....	....		1947-48	1947-48
Defelice, Norman	Bos.	1	10	3	5	2	600	30	0	3.00	....	....	....	....	....	....	....	....		1956-57	1956-57
DeJordy, Denis	Chi., L.A., Mtl., Det.	11	316	124	127	51	17798	929	15	3.13	18	6	9	0	946	55	0	3.49		1962-63	1973-74
DelGuidice, Matt	Bos.	2	11	2	5	1	434	28	0	3.87	....	....	....	....	....	....	....	....		1990-91	1991-92
Desjardins, Gerry	L.A., Chi., NYI, Buf.	10	331	122	153	44	19014	1042	12	3.29	35	15	15	0	1874	108	0	3.46		1968-69	1977-78
Dickie, Bill	Chi.	1	1	1	0	0	60	3	0	3.00	....	....	....	....	....	....	....	....		1941-42	1941-42
Dion, Connie	Det.	2	38	23	11	4	2280	119	0	3.13	5	1	4	0	300	17	0	3.40		1943-44	1944-45
Dion, Michel	Que., Wpg., Pit.	6	227	60	118	32	12695	898	2	4.24	5	2	3	0	304	22	0	4.34		1979-80	1984-85
Dolson, Clarence	Det.	3	93	35	44	13	5820	192	16	1.98	2	0	2	0	120	7	0	3.50		1928-29	1930-31
Dowie, Bruce	Tor.	1	2	0	1	0	72	4	0	3.33	....	....	....	....	....	....	....	....		1983-84	1983-84
Dryden, Dave	NYR, Chi., Buf., Edm.	9	203	48	57	24	10424	555	9	3.19	3	0	2	0	133	9	0	4.06		1961-62	1979-80
Dryden, Ken	Mtl.	8	397	258	57	74	23352	870	46	2.24	112	80	32	0	6846	274	10	2.40	6	1970-71	1978-79
Dumas, Michel	Chi.	2	8	2	1	2	362	24	0	3.98	1	0	0	0	19	1	0	3.16		1974-75	1976-77
Dupuis, Bob	Edm.	1	1	0	1	0	60	4	0	4.00	....	....	....	....	....	....	....	....		1979-80	1979-80
• Durnan, Bill	Mtl.	7	383	208	112	62	22945	901	34	2.36	45	27	18	0	2851	99	2	2.08	2	1943-44	1949-50
Dyck, Ed	Van.	3	49	8	28	5	2453	178	1	4.35	....	....	....	....	....	....	....	....		1971-72	1973-74
Edwards, Don	Buf., Cgy., Tor.	10	459	208	155	77	26181	1449	16	3.32	42	16	21	0	2302	132	1	3.44		1976-77	1985-86
Edwards, Gary	St.L., L.A., Clev., Min., Edm., Pit.	13	286	88	125	43	16002	973	10	3.65	11	5	4	0	537	34	0	3.80		1968-69	1981-82
Edwards, Marv	Pit., Tor., Cal.	4	61	15	34	7	3467	218	2	3.77	....	....	....	....	....	....	....	....		1968-69	1973-74
Edwards, Roy	Det., Pit.	7	236	92	88	38	13109	637	12	2.92	4	0	3	0	206	11	0	3.20		1967-68	1973-74
Eliot, Darren	L.A., Det., Buf.	5	89	25	41	12	4931	377	1	4.59	1	0	0	0	40	7	0	10.50		1984-85	1988-89
Ellacott, Ken	Van.	1	12	2	3	4	555	41	0	4.43	....	....	....	....	....	....	....	....		1982-83	1982-83

Name	NHL Teams	NHL Seasons	Regular Schedule								Playoffs								NHL Cup Wins	First NHL Season	Last NHL Season
			GP	W	L	T	Mins	GA	SO	Avg	GP	W	L	T	Mins	GA	SO	Avg			
Esposito, Tony	Mtl., Chi.	16	886	423	307	151	52585	2563	76	2.92	99	45	53	0	6017	308	6	3.07	1	1968-69	1983-84
• Evans, Claude	Mtl., Bos.	2	5	2	2	1	280	16	0	3.43	....	....	....	....	....	....	....	....		1954-55	1957-58
Exelby, Randy	Mtl., Edm.	2	2	0	1	0	63	5	0	4.76	....	....	....	....	....	....	....	....		1988-89	1989-90
Farr, Rocky	Buf.	3	19	2	6	3	722	42	0	3.49	....	....	....	....	....	....	....	....		1972-73	1974-75
Favell, Doug	Phi., Tor., Col.	12	373	123	153	69	20771	1096	18	3.17	21	5	16	0	1270	66	1	3.12		1967-68	1978-79
• Forbes, Jake	Tor., Ham., NYA, Phi.	13	210	84	114	11	12922	594	19	2.76	2	0	2	0	120	7	0	3.50		1919-20	1932-33
Ford, Brian	Que., Pit.	2	11	3	7	0	580	61	0	6.31	....	....	....	....	....	....	....	....		1983-84	1984-85
Fowler, Hec	Bos.	1	7	1	6	0	420	43	0	6.14	....	....	....	....	....	....	....	....		1924-25	1924-25
Francis, Emile	Chi., NYR	6	95	31	52	11	5660	355	1	3.76	....	....	....	....	....	....	....	....		1946-47	1951-52
Franks, Jim	Det., NYR, Bos.	4	43	12	23	7	2580	185	1	4.30	1	0	1	0	30	2	0	4.00	1	1936-37	1943-44
Frederick, Ray	Chi.	1	5	0	4	1	300	22	0	4.40	....	....	....	....	....	....	....	....		1954-55	1954-55
Friesen, Karl	N.J.	1	4	0	2	1	130	16	0	7.38	....	....	....	....	....	....	....	....		1986-87	1986-87
Froese, Bob	Phi., NYR	9	242	128	72	20	13451	694	13	3.10	18	3	9	0	830	55	0	3.98		1982-83	1990-91
• Gamble, Bruce	NYR, Bos., Tor., Phi.	10	327	109	139	47	18442	992	22	3.23	5	0	4	0	206	25	0	7.28		1958-59	1971-72
Gardiner, Bert	NYR, Mtl., Chi., Bos.	6	144	49	68	27	8760	554	3	3.79	9	4	5	0	647	20	0	1.85		1935-36	1943-44
• Gardiner, Chuck	Chi.	7	316	112	152	52	19687	664	42	2.02	21	12	6	3	1532	35	5	1.37	1	1927-28	1933-34
Gardner, George	Det., Van.	5	66	16	30	6	3313	207	0	3.75	....	....	....	....	....	....	....	....		1965-66	1971-72
Garrett, John	Hfd., Que., Van.	6	207	68	91	37	11763	837	1	4.27	9	4	3	0	461	33	0	4.30		1979-80	1984-85
Gatherum, Dave	Det.	1	3	2	0	1	180	3	1	1.00	....	....	....	....	....	....	....	....		1953-54	1953-54
Gauthier, Paul	Mtl.	1	1	0	0	1	70	2	0	1.71	....	....	....	....	....	....	....	....		1937-38	1937-38
Gelineau, Jack	Bos., Chi.	4	143	46	64	33	8580	447	7	3.13	4	2	2	0	260	7	1	1.62		1948-49	1953-54
Giacomin, Ed	NYR, Det.	13	610	289	206	97	35693	1675	54	2.82	65	29	35	0	3834	180	1	2.82		1965-66	1977-78
Gilbert, Gilles	Min., Bos., Det.	14	416	182	148	60	23677	1290	18	3.27	32	17	15	0	1919	97	3	3.03		1969-70	1982-83
Gill, Andre	Bos.	1	5	3	2	0	270	13	1	2.89	....	....	....	....	....	....	....	....		1967-68	1967-68
• Goodman, Paul	Chi.	3	52	23	20	9	3240	117	6	2.17	3	0	3	0	187	10	0	3.21	1	1937-38	1940-41
Gordon, Scott	Que.	2	23	2	16	0	1082	101	0	5.60	....	....	....	....	....	....	....	....		1989-90	1990-91
Grahame, Ron	Bos., L.A., Que.	4	114	50	43	15	6472	409	5	3.79	4	2	1	0	202	7	0	2.08		1977-78	1980-81
Grant, Ben	Tor., NYA., Bos.	6	50	17	26	4	2990	188	4	3.77	....	....	....	....	....	....	....	....		1928-29	1943-44
Grant, Doug	Det., St.L.	7	77	27	34	8	4199	280	2	4.00	....	....	....	....	....	....	....	....		1973-74	1979-80
Gratton, Gilles	St.L., NYR	2	47	13	18	9	2299	154	0	4.02	....	....	....	....	....	....	....	....		1975-76	1976-77
Gray, Gerry	Det., NYI	2	8	1	5	1	440	35	0	4.77	....	....	....	....	....	....	....	....		1970-71	1972-73
Gray, Harrison	Det.	1	1	0	0	0	40	5	0	7.50	....	....	....	....	....	....	....	....		1963-64	1963-64
Guenette, Steve	Pit., Cgy.	5	35	19	16	0	1958	122	1	3.74	....	....	....	....	....	....	....	....		1986-87	1990-91
• Hainsworth, George	Mtl., Tor.	11	465	246	145	74	29415	937	94	1.91	52	21	26	5	3486	112	8	1.93	2	1926-27	1936-37
Hall, Glenn	Det., Chi., St.L.	18	906	407	327	165	53484	2239	84	2.51	115	49	65	0	6899	321	6	2.79	1	1952-53	1970-71
Hamel, Pierre	Tor., Wpg.	4	69	13	41	7	3766	276	0	4.40	....	....	....	....	....	....	....	....		1974-75	1980-81
Hanlon, Glen	Van., St.L., NYR, Det.	14	477	167	202	61	26037	1561	13	3.60	35	11	15	0	1756	92	4	3.14		1977-78	1990-91
Harrison, Paul	Min., Tor., Pit., Buf.	7	109	28	53	8	5806	408	2	4.22	4	0	1	0	157	9	0	3.44		1975-76	1981-82
Hayward, Brian	Wpg., Mtl., Min., S.J.	11	357	143	156	37	20025	1242	8	3.72	37	11	18	0	1803	104	0	3.46		1982-83	1992-93
Head, Don	Bos.	1	38	9	26	3	2280	161	2	4.24	....	....	....	....	....	....	....	....		1961-62	1961-62
• Hebert, Sammy	Tor., Ott.	2	4	1	3	0	200	19	0	5.70	....	....	....	....	....	....	....	....	1	1917-18	1923-24
Heinz, Rick	St.L., Van.	5	49	14	19	5	2356	159	2	4.05	1	0	0	0	8	1	0	7.50		1980-81	1984-85
Henderson, John	Bos.	2	46	15	15	15	2700	113	5	2.51	2	0	2	0	120	8	0	4.00		1954-55	1955-56
• Henry, Gord	Bos.	4	3	1	2	0	180	5	1	1.67	5	0	4	0	283	21	0	4.45		1948-49	1952-53
Henry, Jim	NYR, Chi., Bos.	9	404	159	178	67	24240	1166	28	2.89	29	11	18	0	1741	81	2	2.79		1941-42	1954-55
Herron, Denis	Pit., K.C., Mtl.	14	462	146	203	76	25608	1579	10	3.70	15	5	10	0	901	50	0	3.33		1972-73	1985-86
Highton, Hec	Chi.	1	24	10	14	0	1440	108	0	4.50	....	....	....	....	....	....	....	....		1943-44	1943-44
Himes, Normie	NYA	2	2	0	0	1	79	3	0	2.28	....	....	....	....	....	....	....	....		1927-28	1928-29
Hodge, Charlie	Mtl., Oak., Van.	13	358	152	124	60	20593	927	24	2.70	16	6	8	0	803	32	2	2.39	4	1954-55	1970-71
Hoffort, Bruce	Phi.	2	9	4	0	3	368	22	0	3.59	....	....	....	....	....	....	....	....		1989-90	1990-91
Hoganson, Paul	Pit.	1	2	0	1	0	57	7	0	7.37	....	....	....	....	....	....	....	....		1970-71	1970-71
Hogosta, Goran	NYI, Que.	2	22	5	12	3	1208	83	1	4.12	....	....	....	....	....	....	....	....		1977-78	1979-80
Holden, Mark	Mtl., Wpg.	4	8	2	2	1	372	25	0	4.03	....	....	....	....	....	....	....	....		1981-82	1984-85
Holland, Ken	Hfd.	1	1	0	1	0	60	7	0	7.00	....	....	....	....	....	....	....	....		1980-81	1980-81
Holland, Robbie	Pit.	2	44	11	22	9	2513	171	1	4.08	....	....	....	....	....	....	....	....		1979-80	1980-81
• Holmes, Harry	Tor., Det.	4	105	41	54	10	6510	264	17	2.43	7	4	3	0	420	26	0	3.71		1917-18	1927-28
Horner, Red	Tor.	1	1	0	0	0	1	1	0	60.00	....	....	....	....	....	....	....	....		1932-33	1932-33
Inness, Gary	Pit., Phi., Wsh.	7	162	58	61	27	8710	494	2	3.40	9	5	4	0	540	24	0	2.67		1973-74	1980-81
Ireland, Randy	Buf.	1	2	0	0	0	30	3	0	6.00	....	....	....	....	....	....	....	....		1978-79	1978-79
Irons, Robbie	St.L.	1	1	0	0	0	3	0	0	0.00	....	....	....	....	....	....	....	....		1968-69	1968-69
• Ironstone, Joe	NYA, Tor.	2	2	1	1	0	110	3	0	1.64	....	....	....	....	....	....	....	....		1925-26	1927-28
Jackson, Doug	Chi.	1	6	2	3	1	360	42	0	7.00	....	....	....	....	....	....	....	....		1947-48	1947-48
Jackson, Percy	Bos., NYA, NYR	4	7	1	3	1	392	26	0	3.98	....	....	....	....	....	....	....	....		1931-32	1935-36
Janaszak, Steve	Min., Col.	2	3	0	1	1	160	15	0	5.62	....	....	....	....	....	....	....	....		1979-80	1981-82
Janecyk, Bob	Chi., L.A.	6	110	43	47	13	6250	432	2	4.15	3	0	3	0	184	10	0	3.26		1983-84	1988-89
Jenkins, Roger	NYA	1	1	0	1	0	30	7	0	14.00	....	....	....	....	....	....	....	....		1938-39	1938-39
Jensen, Al	Det., Wsh., L.A.	7	179	95	53	18	9974	557	8	3.35	12	5	5	0	598	32	0	3.21		1980-81	1986-87
Jensen, Darren	Phi.	2	30	15	10	1	1496	95	2	3.81	....	....	....	....	....	....	....	....		1984-85	1985-86
Johnson, Bob	St.L., Pit.	2	24	9	9	1	1059	66	0	3.74	....	....	....	....	....	....	....	....		1972-73	1974-75
Johnston, Eddie	Bos., Tor., St.L., Chi.	16	592	236	256	87	34209	1855	32	3.25	18	7	10	0	1023	57	1	3.34	2	1962-63	1977-78
Junkin, Joe	Bos.	1	1	0	0	0	8	0	0	0.00	....	....	....	....	....	....	....	....		1968-69	1968-69
Kaarela, Jari	Col.	1	5	2	2	0	220	22	0	6.00	....	....	....	....	....	....	....	....		1980-81	1980-81
Kampurri, Hannu	N.J.	1	13	1	10	1	645	54	0	5.02	....	....	....	....	....	....	....	....		1984-85	1984-85
• Karakas, Mike	Chi., Mtl.	8	336	114	169	53	20616	1002	28	2.92	23	11	12	0	1434	72	3	3.01	1	1935-36	1945-46
Keans, Doug	L.A., Bos.	9	210	96	64	26	11388	666	4	3.51	9	2	6	0	432	34	0	4.72		1979-80	1987-88
Keenan, Don	Bos.	1	1	0	1	0	60	4	0	4.00	....	....	....	....	....	....	....	....		1958-59	1958-59
• Kerr, Dave	Mtl.M., NYA, NYR	11	426	203	148	75	26519	960	51	2.17	40	18	19	3	2616	76	8	1.74	1	1930-31	1940-41
King, Scott	Det.	2	2	0	0	0	61	3	0	2.95	....	....	....	....	....	....	....	....		1990-91	1991-92
Kleisinger, Terry	NYR	1	4	0	2	0	191	14	0	4.40	....	....	....	....	....	....	....	....		1985-86	1985-86
Klymkiw, Julian	NYR	1	1	0	0	0	19	2	0	6.32	....	....	....	....	....	....	....	....		1958-59	1958-59
Kurt, Gary	Cal.	1	16	1	7	5	838	60	0	4.30	....	....	....	....	....	....	....	....		1971-72	1971-72
Lacroix, Al	Mtl.	1	5	1	4	0	280	16	0	3.43	....	....	....	....	....	....	....	....		1925-26	1925-26
LaFerriere, Rick	Col.	1	1	0	0	0	20	1	0	3.00	....	....	....	....	....	....	....	....		1981-82	1981-82
• Larocque, Michel	Mtl., Tor., Phi., St.L.	11	312	160	89	45	17615	978	17	3.33	14	6	6	0	759	37	1	2.92	4	1973-74	1983-84
Laskowski, Gary	L.A.	2	59	19	27	5	2942	228	0	4.65	....	....	....	....	....	....	....	....		1982-83	1983-84
Laxton, Gord	Pit.	4	17	4	9	0	800	74	0	5.55	....	....	....	....	....	....	....	....		1975-76	1978-79
LeDuc, Albert	Mtl.	1	1	0	0	0	2	1	0	30.00	....	....	....	....	....	....	....	....		1931-32	1931-32
Legris, Claude	Det.	2	4	0	1	1	91	4	0	2.64	....	....	....	....	....	....	....	....		1980-81	1981-82
• Lehman, Hugh	Chi.	2	48	20	24	4	3047	136	6	2.68	2	0	1	1	120	10	0	5.00		1926-27	1927-28
Lemelin, Reggie	Atl., Cgy., Bos.	15	507	236	162	63	28006	1613	12	3.46	59	23	25	0	3119	186	2	3.58		1978-79	1992-93
Lessard, Mario	L.A.	6	240	92	97	39	13529	843	9	3.74	20	6	12	0	1136	83	0	4.38		1978-79	1983-84
Levasseur, Louis	Min.	1	1	0	1	0	60	7	0	7.00	....	....	....	....	....	....	....	....		1979-80	1979-80
Levinsky, Alex	Tor.	1	1	0	0	0	1	1	0	60.00	....	....	....	....	....	....	....	....		1932-33	1932-33
• Lindbergh, Pelle	Phi.	5	157	87	49	15	9151	503	7	3.30	23	12	10	0	1214	63	3	3.11		1981-82	1985-86
• Lindsay, Bert	Mtl.W., Tor.	2	20	6	14	0	2219	118	0	3.19	....	....	....	....	....	....	....	....		1917-18	1918-19
Liut, Mike	St. L., Hfd., Wsh.	13	663	293	271	74	38155	2219	25	3.49	67	29	32	0	3814	215	2	3.38		1979-80	1991-92
Lockett, Ken	Van.	2	55	13	15	8	2348	131	2	3.35	1	0	1	0	60	6	0	6.00		1974-75	1975-76
• Lockhart, Howie	Tor., Que., Ham., Bos.	5	57	17	39	0	3371	282	1	5.02	....	....	....	....	....	....	....	....		1919-20	1924-25
LoPresti, Pete	Min., Edm.	6	175	43	102	20	9858	668	5	4.07	2	0	2	0	77	6	0	4.68		1974-75	1980-81
• LoPresti, Sam	Chi.	2	74	30	38	6	4530	236	4	3.13	8	3	5	0	530	17	1	1.92		1940-41	1941-42
Loustel, Ron	Wpg.	1	1	0	1	0	60	10	0	10.00	....	....	....	....	....	....	....	....		1980-81	1980-81
Low, Ron	Tor., Wsh., Det., Que., Edm., NJ	11	382	102	203	37	20502	1463	4	4.28	7	1	6	0	452	29	0	3.85		1972-73	1984-85
Lozinski, Larry	Det.	1	30	6	11	7	1459	105	0	4.32	....	....	....	....	....	....	....	....		1980-81	1980-81
Lumley, Harry	Det., NYR, Chi., Tor., Bos.	16	804	332	324	143	48107	2210	71	2.76	76	29	47	0	4759	199	7	2.51	1	1943-44	1959-60
MacKenzie, Shawn	N.J.	1	4	0	1	0	130	15	0	6.92	....	....	....	....	....	....	....	....		1982-83	1982-83
Maneluk, George	NYI	1	4	1	1	0	140	15	0	6.43	....	....	....	....	....	....	....	....		1990-91	1990-91
Maniago, Cesare	Tor., Mtl., NYR, Min., Van.	15	568	189	261	96	32570	1774	30	3.27	36	15	21	0	2245	100	3	2.67		1960-61	1977-78
Marios, Jean	Tor., Chi.	2	3	1	2	0	180	15	0	5.00	....	....	....	....	....	....	....	....		1943-44	1953-54
Martin, Seth	St.L.	1	30	8	10	7	1552	67	1	2.59	2	0	0	0	73	5	0	4.11		1967-68	1967-68
Mattson, Markus	Wpg., Min., L.A.	4	92	21	46	14	5007	343	6	4.11	....	....	....	....	....	....	....	....		1979-80	1983-84
May, Darrell	St. L.	2	6	1	5	0	364	31	0	5.11	....	....	....	....	....	....	....	....		1985-86	1987-88
Mayer, Gilles	Tor.	4	9	1	7	1	540	25	0	2.78	....	....	....	....	....	....	....	....		1949-50	1955-56
McAuley, Ken	NYR	2	96	17	64	15	5740	537	1	5.61	....	....	....	....	....	....	....	....		1943-44	1944-45
McCartan, Jack	NYR	2	12	3	7	2	680	43	1	3.79	....	....	....	....	....	....	....	....		1959-60	1960-61

Name	NHL Teams	NHL Seasons	GP	W	L	T	Mins	GA	SO	Avg	GP	W	L	T	Mins	GA	SO	Avg	NHL Cup Wins	First NHL Season	Last NHL Season
			Regular Schedule								Playoffs										
• McCool, Frank	Tor.	2	72	34	31	7	4320	242	4	3.36	13	8	5	0	807	30	4	2.23	1	1944-45	1945-46
McDuffe, Pete	St.L., NYR, K.C., Det.	5	57	11	36	6	3207	218	0	4.08	1	0	1	0	60	7	0	7.00		1971-72	1975-76
McGrattan, Tom	Det.	1	1	0	0	0	8	0	0	0.00	....	....	....	....	....	....	....	....		1947-48	1947-48
McKay, Ross	Hfd.	1	1	0	0	0	35	3	0	5.14	....	....	....	....	....	....	....	....		1990-91	1990-91
McKenzie, Bill	Det., K.C., Col.	6	91	18	49	13	4776	326	2	4.10	....	....	....	....	....	....	....	....		1973-74	1979-80
McKichan, Steve	Van.	1	1	0	0	0	20	2	0	6.00	....	....	....	....	....	....	....	....		1990-91	1990-91
McLachlan, Murray	Tor.	1	2	0	1	0	25	4	0	9.60	....	....	....	....	....	....	....	....		1970-71	1970-71
McLelland, Dave	Van.	1	2	1	1	0	120	10	0	5.00	....	....	....	....	....	....	....	....		1972-73	1972-73
McLeod, Don	Det., Phi.	2	18	3	10	1	879	74	0	5.05	....	....	....	....	....	....	....	....		1970-71	1971-72
McLeod, Jim	St.L.	1	16	6	6	4	880	44	0	3.00	....	....	....	....	....	....	....	....		1971-72	1971-72
McNamara, Gerry	Tor.	2	7	2	2	1	323	15	0	2.79	....	....	....	....	....	....	....	....		1960-61	1969-70
McNeil, Gerry	Mtl.	7	276	119	105	52	16535	650	28	2.36	35	17	18	0	2284	72	5	1.89	3	1947-48	1956-57
McRae, Gord	Tor.	5	71	21	32	10	3799	221	1	3.49	8	2	5	0	454	22	0	2.91		1972-73	1977-78
Melanson, Rollie	NYI, Min., L.A., N.J., Mtl.	11	291	129	106	33	16452	995	6	3.63	23	4	9	0	801	59	0	4.42	3	1980-81	1991-92
Meloche, Gilles	Chi., Cal., Cle., Min., Pit.	18	788	270	351	131	45401	2756	20	3.64	45	21	19	0	2464	143	2	3.48		1970-71	1987-88
Micalef, Corrado	Det.	5	113	26	59	15	5794	409	2	4.24	3	0	0	0	49	8	0	9.80		1981-82	1985-86
Middlebrook, Lindsay	Wpg., Min., N.J., Edm.	4	37	3	23	6	1845	152	0	4.94	....	....	....	....	....	....	....	....		1979-80	1982-83
• Millar, Al	Bos.	1	6	1	3	2	360	25	0	4.17	....	....	....	....	....	....	....	....		1957-58	1957-58
Millen, Greg H.	Pit., Hfd., St. L., Que., Chi., Det.	14	604	215	284	89	35377	2281	17	3.87	59	27	29	0	3383	193	0	3.42		1978-79	1991-92
• Miller, Joe	NYA, NYR, Pit., Phi.	4	130	24	90	16	7981	386	16	2.90	3	2	1	0	180	3	1	1.00		1927-28	1930-31
Mio, Eddie	Edm., NYR, Det.	7	192	83	85	31	12299	822	6	4.01	17	9	7	0	986	63	0	3.83		1979-80	1985-86
• Mitchell, Ivan	Tor.	3	21	11	9	0	1232	93	0	4.53	....	....	....	....	....	....	....	....	1	1919-20	1921-22
Moffatt, Mike	Bos.	3	19	7	7	2	979	70	0	4.29	11	6	5	0	663	38	0	3.44		1981-82	1983-84
Moore, Alfie	NYA, Det., Chi.,	4	21	7	14	0	1290	81	1	3.77	3	1	2	0	180	7	0	2.33	1	1936-37	1939-40
Moore, Robbie	Phi., Wsh.	2	6	3	1	1	257	8	2	1.87	5	3	2	0	268	18	0	4.03		1978-79	1982-83
Morisette, Jean	Mtl.	1	1	0	1	0	36	4	0	6.67	....	....	....	....	....	....	....	....		1963-64	1963-64
Mowers, Johnny	Det.	4	152	65	55	25	9350	399	15	2.56	32	19	13	0	2000	85	2	2.55	1	1940-41	1946-47
Mrazek, Jerry	Phi.	1	1	0	0	0	6	1	0	10.00	....	....	....	....	....	....	....	....		1975-76	1975-76
• Mummery, Harry	Que., Ham.	2	4	2	1	0	191	20	0	6.28	....	....	....	....	....	....	....	....		1919-20	1921-22
• Murphy, Hal	Mtl.	1	1	1	0	0	60	4	0	4.00	....	....	....	....	....	....	....	....		1952-53	1952-53
Murray, Tom	Mtl.	1	1	0	1	0	60	4	0	4.00	....	....	....	....	....	....	....	....		1929-30	1929-30
Myllys, Jarmo	Min., S.J.	4	39	4	27	1	1846	161	0	5.23	....	....	....	....	....	....	....	....		1988-89	1991-92
Mylnikov, Sergei	Que.	1	10	1	7	2	568	47	0	4.96	....	....	....	....	....	....	....	....		1989-90	1989-90
Myre, Phil	Mtl., Atl., St.L., Phi., Col., Buf.	14	439	149	198	76	25220	1482	14	3.53	12	6	5	0	747	41	1	3.29		1969-70	1982-83
Newton, Cam	Pit.	2	16	4	7	1	814	51	0	3.76	....	....	....	....	....	....	....	....		1970-71	1972-73
Norris, Jack	Bos., Chi., L.A.	4	58	19	26	4	3119	202	2	3.89	....	....	....	....	....	....	....	....		1964-65	1970-71
Oleschuk, Bill	K.C., Col.	4	55	7	28	10	2835	188	1	3.98	....	....	....	....	....	....	....	....		1975-76	1979-80
• Olesevich, Dan	NYR	1	1	0	0	1	40	2	0	3.00	....	....	....	....	....	....	....	....		1961-62	1961-62
Ouimet, Ted	St.L.	1	1	0	1	0	60	2	0	2.00	....	....	....	....	....	....	....	....		1968-69	1968-69
Pageau, Paul	L.A.	1	1	0	1	0	60	8	0	8.00	....	....	....	....	....	....	....	....		1980-81	1980-81
Paille, Marcel	NYR	7	107	33	52	21	6342	362	2	3.42	....	....	....	....	....	....	....	....		1957-58	1964-65
Palmateer, Mike	Tor., Wsh.	8	356	149	138	52	20131	1183	17	3.53	29	12	17	0	1765	89	2	3.03		1976-77	1983-84
Pang, Darren	Chi.	3	81	27	35	7	4252	287	0	4.05	6	1	3	0	250	18	0	4.32		1984-85	1988-89
Parent, Bernie	Bos., Tor., Phi.	13	608	270	197	121	35136	1493	55	2.55	71	38	33	0	4302	174	6	2.43	2	1965-66	1978-79
Parent, Bob	Tor.	2	3	0	2	0	160	15	0	5.62	....	....	....	....	....	....	....	....		1981-82	1982-83
Parro, Dave	Wsh.	4	77	21	36	10	4015	274	2	4.09	....	....	....	....	....	....	....	....		1980-81	1983-84
• Patrick, Lester	NYR	1	....	....	....	....	....	....	....	....	1	1	0	0	46	1	0	1.30		1927-28	1927-28
Peeters, Pete	Phi., Bos., Wsh.	13	489	246	155	51	27699	1424	21	3.08	71	35	35	0	4200	232	2	3.31		1978-79	1990-91
Pelletier, Marcel	Chi., NYR	2	8	1	6	1	395	33	0	5.01	....	....	....	....	....	....	....	....		1950-51	1962-63
Penney, Steve	Mtl., Wpg.	5	91	35	38	12	5194	313	1	3.62	27	15	12	0	1604	72	4	2.69		1983-84	1987-88
• Perreault, Robert	Mtl., Det., Bos.	3	31	8	16	6	1833	106	2	3.47	....	....	....	....	....	....	....	....		1955-56	1962-63
Pettie, Jim	Bos.	3	21	9	7	2	1157	71	1	3.68	....	....	....	....	....	....	....	....		1976-77	1978-79
• Plante, Jacques	Mtl., NYR, St.L., Tor., Bos.	18	837	434	246	137	49553	1965	82	2.38	112	71	37	0	6651	241	14	2.17	6	1952-53	1972-73
Plasse, Michel	St.L., Mtl., K.C., Pit., Col., Que.	11	299	92	136	54	16760	1058	2	3.79	4	1	2	0	195	9	1	2.77	1	1970-71	1981-82
Plaxton, Hugh	Mtl.M.	1	1	0	1	0	59	5	0	5.08	....	....	....	....	....	....	....	....		1932-33	1932-33
Pronovost, Claude	Bos., Mtl.	2	3	1	1	0	120	7	1	3.50	....	....	....	....	....	....	....	....		1955-56	1958-59
Pusey, Chris	Det.	1	1	0	0	0	40	3	0	4.50	....	....	....	....	....	....	....	....		1985-86	1985-86
Raymond, Alain	Wsh.	1	1	0	1	0	40	2	0	3.00	....	....	....	....	....	....	....	....		1987-88	1987-88
Rayner, Chuck	NYA, Bro., NYR	10	424	138	209	77	25491	1294	25	3.05	18	9	9	0	1134	46	1	2.43		1940-41	1952-53
Reaugh, Daryl	Edm., Hfd.	3	27	8	9	1	1246	72	1	3.47	....	....	....	....	....	....	....	....		1984-85	1990-91
Redquest, Greg	Pit.	1	1	0	0	0	13	3	0	13.85	....	....	....	....	....	....	....	....		1977-78	1977-78
Reece, Dave	Bos.	1	14	7	5	2	777	43	2	3.32	....	....	....	....	....	....	....	....		1975-76	1975-76
Resch, Glenn	NYI, Col., N.J., Phi.	14	571	231	224	82	32279	1761	26	3.27	41	17	17	0	2044	85	2	2.50	1	1973-74	1986-87
Rheaume, Herb	Mtl.	1	31	10	19	1	1889	92	0	2.92	....	....	....	....	....	....	....	....		1925-26	1925-26
Ricci, Nick	Pit.	4	19	7	12	0	1087	79	0	4.36	....	....	....	....	....	....	....	....		1979-80	1982-83
Richardson, Terry	Det., St.L.	5	20	3	11	0	906	85	0	5.63	....	....	....	....	....	....	....	....		1973-74	1978-79
Ridley, Curt	NYR, Van., Tor.	6	104	27	47	16	5498	355	1	3.87	2	0	2	0	120	8	0	4.00		1974-75	1980-81
Riggin, Dennis	Det.	2	18	5	10	2	985	54	1	3.29	....	....	....	....	....	....	....	....		1959-60	1962-63
Riggin, Pat	Atl., Cgy., Wsh., Bos., Pit.	9	350	153	120	52	19872	1135	11	3.43	25	8	13	0	1336	72	0	3.23		1979-80	1987-88
Ring, Bob	Bos.	1	1	0	0	0	34	4	0	7.06	....	....	....	....	....	....	....	....		1965-66	1965-66
Rivard, Fern	Min.	4	55	9	20	7	2865	190	2	3.98	....	....	....	....	....	....	....	....		1968-69	1974-75
• Roach, John	Tor., NYR, Det.	14	491	218	204	69	30423	1246	58	2.46	34	15	16	3	2206	69	8	1.88	1	1921-22	1934-35
• Roberts, Moe	Bos., NYA, Chi.	4	10	2	5	0	506	31	0	3.68	....	....	....	....	....	....	....	....		1925-26	1951-52
• Robertson, Earl	NYA, Bro., Det.	6	190	60	95	34	11820	575	16	2.92	15	6	7	0	995	29	2	1.75	1	1936-37	1941-42
Rollins, Al	Tor., Chi., NYR	9	430	138	205	84	25717	1196	28	2.79	13	6	7	0	755	30	0	2.38	1	1949-50	1959-60
Rupp, Pat	Det.	1	1	0	1	0	60	4	0	4.00	....	....	....	....	....	....	....	....		1963-64	1963-64
Rutherford, Jim	Det., Pit., Tor., L.A.	13	457	150	227	59	25895	1576	14	3.65	8	2	5	0	440	28	0	3.82		1970-71	1982-83
Rutledge, Wayne	L.A.	3	82	22	30	5	4325	241	2	3.34	8	2	2	0	378	20	0	3.17		1967-68	1969-70
St. Laurent, Sam	N.J., Det.	5	34	7	12	4	1572	92	1	3.51	1	0	0	0	10	1	0	6.00		1985-86	1989-90
Sands, Charlie	Mtl.	1	1	0	0	0	25	5	0	12.00	....	....	....	....	....	....	....	....		1939-40	1939-40
Sands, Mike	Min.	2	6	0	5	0	302	26	0	5.17	....	....	....	....	....	....	....	....		1984-85	1986-87
Sauve, Bob	Buf., Det., Chi., N.J.	12	405	178	149	53	22991	1321	8	3.45	34	15	16	0	1850	95	4	3.08		1976-77	1987-88
• Sawchuk, Terry	Det., Bos., Tor., L.A., NYR	21	971	435	337	188	57205	2401	103	2.52	106	54	48	0	6291	267	12	2.55	4	1949-50	1969-70
Schaefer, Joe	NYR	2	2	0	1	0	86	8	0	5.58	....	....	....	....	....	....	....	....		1959-60	1960-61
Scott, Ron	NYR, L.A.	5	28	8	13	4	1450	91	0	3.77	1	0	0	0	32	4	0	7.50		1983-84	1989-90
Sevigny, Richard	Mtl., Que.	8	176	90	44	20	9485	507	5	3.21	6	0	3	0	208	13	0	3.75	1	1979-80	1986-87
Sharples, Scott	Cgy.	1	1	0	0	1	65	4	0	3.69	....	....	....	....	....	....	....	....		1991-92	1991-92
Shields, Al	NYA	1	2	0	0	0	41	9	0	13.17	....	....	....	....	....	....	....	....		1931-32	1931-32
Simmons, Don	Bos., Tor., NYR	11	247	100	104	39	14436	705	20	2.93	24	13	11	0	1436	64	3	2.67	2	1956-57	1968-69
Simmons, Gary	Cal., Clev., L.A.	4	107	30	57	15	6162	366	5	3.56	1	0	0	0	20	1	0	3.00		1974-75	1977-78
Skidmore, Paul	St.L.	1	2	1	1	0	120	6	0	3.00	....	....	....	....	....	....	....	....		1981-82	1981-82
Skorodenski, Warren	Chi., Edm.	5	35	12	11	4	1732	100	2	3.46	2	0	0	0	33	6	0	10.91		1981-82	1987-88
Smith, Al	Tor., Pit., Det., Buf., Hfd., Col.	10	233	68	99	36	12752	735	10	3.46	6	1	4	0	317	21	0	3.97		1965-66	1980-81
Smith, Billy	L.A., NYI	18	680	305	233	105	38431	2031	22	3.17	132	88	36	0	7645	348	5	2.73	4	1971-72	1988-89
Smith, Gary	Tor., Oak., Cal., Chi., Van., Min., Wsh., Wpg.	14	532	152	237	67	29619	1675	26	3.39	20	5	13	0	1153	62	1	3.23		1965-66	1979-80
• Smith, Norman	Mtl.M., Det.	8	199	81	83	35	12297	475	17	2.32	12	9	2	0	880	18	3	1.23	2	1931-32	1944-45
Sneddon, Bob	Cal.	1	5	0	2	0	225	21	0	5.60	....	....	....	....	....	....	....	....		1970-71	1970-71
Soetaert, Doug	NYR, Wpg., Mtl.	12	284	110	103	44	15583	1030	6	3.97	5	1	2	0	180	14	0	4.67	1	1975-76	1986-87
• Spooner, Red	Pit.	1	1	0	1	0	60	6	0	6.00	....	....	....	....	....	....	....	....		1929-30	1929-30
St.Croix, Rick	Phi., Tor.	8	129	49	54	18	7275	450	2	3.71	11	4	6	0	562	29	1	3.10		1977-78	1984-85
Staniowski, Ed	St.L., Wpg., Hfd.	10	219	67	104	21	12075	818	2	4.06	8	1	6	0	428	28	0	3.93		1975-76	1984-85
Starr, Harold	Mtl.M.	1	1	0	0	0	3	0	0	0.00	....	....	....	....	....	....	....	....		1931-32	1931-32
Stefan, Greg	Det.	9	299	115	127	30	16333	1068	5	3.92	30	12	17	0	1681	99	1	3.53		1981-82	1989-90
Stein, Phil	Tor.	1	1	0	0	1	70	2	0	1.71	....	....	....	....	....	....	....	....		1939-40	1939-40
Stephenson, Wayne	St.L., Phi., Wsh.	10	328	146	93	46	18343	937	14	3.06	26	11	12	0	1522	79	2	3.11	1	1971-72	1980-81
Stevenson, Doug	NYR, Chi.	2	8	2	6	0	480	39	0	4.88	....	....	....	....	....	....	....	....		1944-45	1945-46
Stewart, Charles	Bos.	3	77	31	41	5	4737	194	10	2.46	....	....	....	....	....	....	....	....		1924-25	1926-27
Stewart, Jim	Bos.	1	1	0	1	0	20	5	0	15.00	....	....	....	....	....	....	....	....		1979-80	1979-80
Stuart, Herb	Det.	1	3	0	1	0	180	5	0	1.67	....	....	....	....	....	....	....	....		1926-27	1926-27
Sylvestri, Don	Bos.	1	3	0	0	2	102	6	0	3.53	....	....	....	....	....	....	....	....		1984-85	1984-85
Takko, Kari	Min., Edm.	6	142	37	71	14	7317	475	1	3.90	4	0	1	0	109	7	0	3.85		1985-86	1990-91
Tataryn, Dave	NYR	1	2	1	1	0	80	10	0	7.50	....	....	....	....	....	....	....	....		1976-77	1976-77
Taylor, Bobby	Phi., Pit.	5	46	15	17	6	2268	155	0	4.10	....	....	....	....	....	....	....	....	1	1971-72	1975-76

Name	NHL Teams	NHL Seasons	GP	W	L	T	Mins	GA	SO	Avg	GP	W	L	T	Mins	GA	SO	Avg	NHL Cup Wins	First NHL Season	Last NHL Season
							Regular Schedule								**Playoffs**						
Teno, Harvey	Det.	1	5	2	3	0	300	15	0	3.00										1938-39	1938-39
Thomas, Wayne	Mtl., Tor., NYR	8	243	103	93	34	13768	766	10	3.34	15	6	8	0	849	50	1	3.53		1972-73	1980-81
• Thompson, Tiny	Bos., Det.	12	553	284	194	75	34174	1183	81	2.08	44	20	22	0	2970	93	7	1.88	1	1928-29	1939-40
Tremblay, Vince	Tor., Pit.	5	58	12	26	8	2785	223	1	4.80										1979-80	1983-84
Tucker, Ted	Cal.	1	5	1	1	1	177	10	0	3.39										1973-74	1973-74
Turner, Joe	Det.	1	1	0	0	1	60	3	0	3.00										1941-42	1941-42
Vachon, Rogatien	Mtl., L.A., Det., Bos.	16	795	355	291	115	46298	2310	51	2.99	48	23	23	0	2876	133	2	2.77	3	1966-67	1981-82
Veisor, Mike	Chi., Hfd., Wpg.	10	139	41	62	26	7806	532	5	4.09	4	0	2	0	180	15	0	5.00		1973-74	1983-84
• Vezina, Georges	Mtl.	9	191	105	80	5	11564	633	13	3.28	26	19	6	0	1596	74	4	2.78	2	1917-18	1925-26
Villemure, Gilles	NYR, Chi.	10	205	98	65	27	11581	542	13	2.81	14	5	5	0	656	32	0	2.93		1963-64	1976-77
Wakely, Ernie	Mtl., St.L.	5	113	41	42	17	6344	290	8	2.74	10	2	6	0	509	37	1	4.36		1962-63	1971-72
• Walsh, James	Mtl.M., NYA	7	108	48	43	16	6461	250	12	2.32	8	2	4	2	570	16	2	1.68		1926-27	1932-33
Wamsley, Rick	Mtl., St.L., Cgy., Tor.	13	407	204	131	46	23123	1287	12	3.34	27	7	18	0	1397	81	0	3.48	1	1980-81	1992-93
Watt, Jim	St.L.	1	1	0	0	0	20	2	0	6.00										1973-74	1973-74
Weeks, Steve	NYR, Hfd., Van., NYI, L.A., Ott.	13	290	111	119	33	15879	989	5	3.74	12	3	5	0	486	27	0	3.33		1973-74	1973-74
Wetzel, Carl	Det., Min.	2	7	1	3	1	302	22	0	4.37										1964-65	1967-68
Wilson, Dunc	Phi., Van., Tor., NYR, Pit.	10	287	80	150	33	15851	988	8	3.74										1969-70	1978-79
Wilson, Lefty	Det., Tor., Bos.	3	3	0	0	1	85	1	0	0.71										1953-54	1957-58
• Winkler, Hal	NYR, Bos.	2	75	35	26	14	4739	126	21	1.60	10	2	3	5	640	18	2	1.69		1926-27	1927-28
Wolfe, Bernie	Wsh.	4	120	20	61	21	6104	424	1	4.17										1975-76	1978-79
Woods, Alec	NYA	1	1	0	1	0	70	3	0	2.57										1936-37	1936-37
Worsley, Gump	NYR, Mtl., Min.	21	862	335	353	150	50232	2432	43	2.90	70	41	25	0	4081	192	5	2.82	4	1952-53	1973-74
• Worters, Roy	Pit., NYA, Mtl.	12	484	171	233	68	30175	1143	66	2.27	11	3	6	2	690	24	3	2.09		1925-26	1936-37
Worthy, Chris	Oak., Cal.	3	26	5	10	4	1326	98	0	4.43										1968-69	1970-71
Young, Doug	Det.	1	1	0	0	0	21	1	0	2.86										1933-34	1933-34
Zanier, Mike	Edm.	1	3	1	1	1	185	12	0	3.89										1984-85	1984-85

1993-94 Transactions

August, 1993

3 – **Dave Tomlinson** traded from Florida to Winnipeg for **Jason Cirone**.

5 – **Shawn Cronin** traded from Philadelphia to San Jose for cash.

5 – **Sergei Makarov** traded from Hartford to San Jose to complete trade of June 26, 1993.

10 – **Patrik Carnback** and **Todd Ewen** traded from Montreal to Anaheim for Anaheim's 3rd round choice in 1994 Entry Draft (**Chris Murray**).

12 – **Kevin McClelland** traded from Toronto to Winnipeg for cash.

20 – **Daniel Jardemyr** traded from Winnipeg to Toronto for future considerations.

27 – **Marty McSorley** traded from Los Angeles to Pittsburgh for **Shawn McEachern**.

30 – **Peter Ing** traded from Edmonton to Detroit for Detroit's 7th round choice in 1994 Entry Draft (**Chris Wickenheiser**) and future considerations.

September

1 – **Craig Simpson** traded from Edmonton to Buffalo for **Jozef Cierny** and future considerations.

2 – **Brad Miller** and **Jeff Perry** traded from Toronto to Calgary for **Paul Holden** and **Todd Gillingham**.

7 – **Mike Hurlbut** traded from NY Rangers to Quebec for **Alexander Karpovtsev**.

9 – **Stewart Malgunas** traded from Detroit to Philadelphia for future considerations.

10 – **Link Gaetz** traded from San Jose to Edmonton for future considerations.

14 – **Brian Glynn** traded from Edmonton to Ottawa for future considerations.

24 – **Phil Housley** traded from Winnipeg to St. Louis for **Nelson Emerson** and **Stephane Quintal**.

30 – **Evgeny Davydov** and a future draft pick traded from Winnipeg to Florida for a future draft pick.

30 – **Darin Kimble** traded from Florida to Chicago for **Keith Brown**.

30 – **Tom Draper** traded from Buffalo to NY Islanders for a future draft pick.

30 – **Brent Severyn** traded from New Jersey to Winnipeg for future draft picks.

October

3 – **Brent Severyn** traded from Winnipeg to Florida for **Milan Tichy**.

5 – **Peter Ahola** traded from Tampa Bay to Calgary for cash.

5 – **Terry Carkner** traded from Philadelphia to Detroit for **Yves Racine** and Detroit's 4th round choice in 1994 Entry Draft (**Sebastien Vallee**).

6 – **Francois Leroux** claimed on waivers from Edmonton by Ottawa.

7 – **Adam Bennett** traded from Chicago to Edmonton for **Kevin Todd**.

8 – **Paul Stanton** traded from Pittsburgh to Boston for Boston's 3rd round choice in 1994 Entry Draft (**Greg Crozier**).

12 – **Jim Hiller** claimed on waivers by NY Rangers from Detroit.

22 – **Keith Acton** claimed on waivers by NY Islanders from Washington.

22 – **Pat Elynuik** traded from Washington to Tampa Bay for future draft picks.

26 – **Todd Elik** claimed on waivers by San Jose from Edmonton.

27 – **Keith Carney** and contingent draft choices traded from Buffalo to Chicago for **Craig Muni** and contingent draft choices.

28 – **Jon Morris** traded from San Jose to Boston for cash.

November

2 – **Steve Larmer** and **Bryan Marchment** traded from Chicago to Hartford for **Eric Weinrich** and **Patrick Poulin**.

2 – **Steve Larmer**, **Nick Kypreos**, **Barry Richter** and Hartford's 6th round pick in 1994 Entry Draft (**Yuri Litvinov**) traded from Hartford to NY Rangers for **Darren Turcotte** and **James Patrick**.

2 – **Jeff Chychrun** traded from Los Angeles to Edmonton for a conditional pick in the 1995 Entry Draft.

3 – **Doug Houda** traded from Hartford to Los Angeles for **Marc Potvin**.

3 – **Bob McGill** claimed on waivers by Hartford from NY Islanders.

5 – **Mike Foligno** traded from Toronto to Florida for cash.

5 – **Dave Capuano** traded from San Jose to Boston for cash.

11 – **Bob Beers** traded from Tampa Bay to Edmonton for **Chris Joseph**.

12 – **Martin Hamrlik** traded from Hartford to St. Louis for cash.

19 – **Jeff Reese** traded from Calgary to Hartford for **Dan Keczmer** and a conditional pick in the 1994 Entry Draft.

25 – **Randy Gilhen** and conditional draft picks traded from Florida to Winnipeg for **Stu Barnes** and conditional draft picks.

28 – **Rob Ramage** traded from Montreal to Philadelphia for cash.

30 – **Greg Hawgood** traded from Philadelphia to Florida for cash.

December

2 – **Mark Krys** traded from Boston to Buffalo for cash.

6 – **Fredrik Olausson** and Winnipeg's 7th round pick in 1994 Entry Draft (**Curtis Sheptak**) traded from Winnipeg to Edmonton for Edmonton's 3rd round pick in 1994 Entry Draft (**Tavis Hansen**).

6 – **Geoff Smith** traded from Edmonton to Florida for future draft picks.

7 – **Greg Smyth** traded from Florida to Toronto for cash.

9 – **Craig Fisher** traded from Edmonton to Winnipeg for cash.

15 – **Mark Laforge** traded from Edmonton to NY Islanders for **Brent Grieve**.

15 – **Gord Donnelly** traded from Buffalo to Dallas for **James Black** and a future draft choice.

16 – **Alexander Godynyuk** traded from Florida to Hartford for **Jim McKenzie**.

16 – **Jim McKenzie** traded from Florida to Dallas for Dallas's 4th round pick in 1994 or 1995 Entry Draft (Dallas's option).

January, 1994

1 – **Guy Larose** claimed on waivers by Calgary from Toronto.

6 – **Mike Sullivan** claimed on waivers by Calgary from San Jose.

6 – **Bob Kudelski** traded from Ottawa to Florida for **Evgeny Davydov**, **Scott Levins** and future draft picks.

8 – **Jimmy Carson** traded from Los Angeles to Vancouver for **Dixon Ward** and a conditional pick in the 1995 Entry Draft.

8 – **Greg Smyth** claimed on waivers by Chicago from Toronto.

15 – **Kerry Huffman** claimed on waivers by Ottawa from Quebec.

15 – **Martin Gelinas** claimed on waivers by Vancouver from Quebec.

17 – **Vincent Riendeau** traded from Detroit to Boston for a future draft pick in the 1995 Entry Draft.

23 – **Steve Duchesne** and **Denis Chasse** traded from Quebec to St. Louis for **Garth Butcher**, **Ron Sutter** and **Bob Bassen**.

23 – **David Maley** traded from San Jose to NY Islanders for cash.

24 – **Scott Morrow** traded from Hartford to Calgary for **Todd Harkins**.

25 – **Ted Crowley** traded from Toronto to Hartford for **Mark Greig** and Hartford's 6th round pick in 1995 Entry Draft.

28 – **Brad Tiley** traded from NY Rangers to Los Angeles for a future draft pick in 1994 Entry Draft.

February

1 – **Viacheslav Butsayev** traded from Philadelphia to San Jose for **Rob Zettler**.

1 – **Yan Kaminsky** traded from Winnipeg to NY Islanders for **Wayne McBean**.

5 – **Brian Glynn** claimed on waivers by Vancouver from Ottawa.

13 – **Tommy Sjodin** and a future draft pick in 1994 or 1995 Entry Draft traded from Dallas to Quebec for the rights to **Emmanuel Fernandez**.

16 – **Marty McSorley** and **Jim Paek** traded from Pittsburgh to Los Angeles for **Tomas Sandstrom** and **Shawn McEachern**.

19 – **Mike Stapleton** claimed on waivers by Edmonton from Pittsburgh.

20 – **Ron Tugnutt** traded from Anaheim to Montreal for **Stephan Lebeau**.

20 – **John Tanner** traded from Quebec to Anaheim for Anaheim's 4th round pick in 1995 Entry Draft.

21 – **Frederic Chabot** traded from Montreal to Philadelphia for cash.

21 – **Pat Jablonski** traded from Tampa Bay to Toronto for cash.

March

5 – **Mark Lamb** traded from Ottawa to Philadelphia for **Claude Boivin** and **Kirk Daubenspeck**.

8 – **Bob Essensa** and **Sergei Bautin** traded from Winnipeg to Detroit for **Tim Cheveldae** and **Dallas Drake**.

9 – **Larry DePalma** claimed on waivers by Pittsburgh from NY Islanders.

10 – **Gary Suter, Paul Ranheim** and **Ted Drury** traded from Calgary to Hartford for **James Patrick, Zarley Zalapski** and **Michael Nylander**.

11 – **Frantisek Kucera** and **Jocelyn Lemieux** traded from Chicago to Hartford for **Gary Suter, Randy Cunneyworth** and a future draft pick.

11 – **Troy Murray** traded from Chicago to Winnipeg for future considerations.

15 – **Dave Manson** and St. Louis' 6th round pick in 1994 Entry Draft (acquired previously, Winnipeg selected **Chris Kibermanis**) traded from Edmonton to Winnipeg for Boris Mironov, Mats Lindgren, Winnipeg's 1st round pick in 1994 Entry Draft and Florida's 4th round pick in 1994 Entry Draft (acquired previously, Edmonton selected **Adam Copeland**).

18 – **Jim Cummins** and Philadelphia's 4th round pick in 1995 Entry Draft traded from Philadelphia to Tampa Bay for **Rob DiMaio**.

18 – **Ken Belanger** traded from Hartford to Toronto for Toronto's 9th round pick in 1994 Entry Draft (**Matt Ball**).

19 – **Donald Dufresne** traded from Tampa Bay to Los Angeles for Los Angeles' 6th round pick in 1994 Entry Draft (**Daniel Juden**).

19 – **Jeff Daniels** traded from Pittsburgh to Florida for **Greg Hawgood**.

19 – **Doug Zmolek** and **Mike Lalor** traded from San Jose to Dallas for **Ulf Dahlen** and a future draft pick.

21 – **Joe Juneau** traded from Boston to Washington for **Al Iafrate**.

21 – **Craig Janney** traded from Vancouver to St. Louis for **Jeff Brown, Bret Hedican** and **Nathan Lafayette**.

21 – **Jim Johnson** traded from Dallas to Washington for **Alan May** and Washington's 7th round pick in 1995 Entry Draft.

21 – **Joe Reekie** traded from Tampa Bay to Washington for **Enrico Ciccone** and Washington's 3rd round pick in 1994 Entry Draft (later traded to Anaheim) and a conditional draft pick.

21 – **Steve Konroyd** traded from Detroit to Ottawa for **Daniel Berthiaume**.

21 – **Phil Bourque** traded from NY Rangers to Ottawa for future considerations.

21 – **Tony Amonte** and the rights to **Matt Oates** traded from NY Rangers to Chicago for **Stephane Matteau** and **Brian Noonan**.

21 – **Peter Andersson** traded from NY Rangers to Florida for future considerations.

21 – **Robert Dirk** traded from Vancouver to Chicago for Chicago's 4th round pick in 1994 Entry Draft (**Mike Dubinsky**).

21 – **Mike Gartner** traded from NY Rangers to Toronto for **Glenn Anderson** the rights to **Scott Malone** and Toronto's 4th round pick in 1994 Entry Draft (**Alexander Korobolin**).

21 – **Craig MacTavish** traded from Edmonton to NY Rangers for **Todd Marchant**.

21 – **Paul Ysebaert** traded from Winnipeg to Chicago for Chicago's 3rd round pick in 1995 Entry Draft.

21 – **Alexei Kasatonov** traded from Anaheim to St. Louis for **Maxim Bets** and St. Louis's 6th round pick in 1995 Entry Draft.

21 – **Mike Needham** traded from Pittsburgh to Dallas for **Jim McKenzie**.

21 – **Kevin Todd** traded from Chicago to Los Angeles for Los Angeles's 4th round pick in 1994 Entry Draft (**Steve McLaren**).

21 – **Pelle Eklund** traded from Philadelphia to Dallas for future considerations.

21 – **Roy Mitchell** and **Reid Simpson** traded from Dallas to New Jersey for future considerations.

21 – **Steve Passmore** traded from Quebec to Edmonton for **Brad Werenka**.

May

25 – **Sheldon Kennedy** traded from Detroit to Winnipeg for Winnipeg's 3rd round pick in 1995 Entry Draft.

June

1 – **Stephane Yelle** and New Jersey's 11th round choice in 1994 Entry Draft (**Steven Low**) traded from New Jersey to Quebec for Quebec's 11th round pick in 1994 Entry Draft (**Mike Hanson**).

1 – **Jeff Toms** traded from New Jersey to Tampa Bay for Vancouver's 4th round pick (previously acquired and later traded to Calgary) in 1994 Entry Draft.

3 – **Neil Wilkinson** traded from Chicago to Winnipeg for Chicago's 3rd round pick in 1995 Entry Draft (previously acquired).

25 – **Jim Paek** traded from Los Angeles to Ottawa for a conditional pick in the 1995 Entry Draft.

28 – **Garth Butcher, Mats Sundin, Todd Warriner** and the 10th overall pick in the 1994 Entry Draft (previously acquired from Philadelphia and later traded to Washington) traded from Quebec to Toronto for **Wendel Clark, Sylvain Lefebvre, Landon Wilson** and the 22nd overall pick in the 1994 Entry Draft (**Jeff Kealty**).

28 – **Ron Sutter** and the 9th overall pick in the 1994 Entry Draft (**Brett Lindros**) traded from Quebec to NY Islanders for **Uwe Krupp** and the 12th pick in the 1994 Entry Draft (**Wade Belak**).

28 – **NHL Supplemental Draft**

Sean McCann	Florida (Harvard)
Steve Rucchin	Anaheim (Western Ontario)
Stephen Guolla	Ottawa (Michigan State)
Randy Stevens	Winnipeg (Michigan Tech)
Steve Martins	Hartford (Harvard)
Chad Dameworth	Edmonton (N. Michigan)
Quinn Fair	Los Angeles (Kent State)
Francois Bouchard	Tampa Bay (Northeastern)
Reid Simonton	Quebec (Union)
Kirk Nielsen	Philadelphia (Harvard)

29 – **Sean Hill** and Anaheim's 9th round pick in the 1994 Entry Draft (**Frederic Cassivi**) traded from Anaheim to Ottawa for Ottawa's 3rd round pick in the 1994 Entry Draft (later traded to Tampa Bay).

29 – Anaheim traded the 55th overall pick in the 1994 Entry Draft (previously acquired from Ottawa) to Tampa Bay for the 67th overall pick in the 1994 Entry Draft (previously acquired from Washington) and Tampa Bay's 4th round pick in the 1995 Entry Draft. Tampa Bay selected **Vadim Epanchintsev**. Anaheim selected **Craig Reichert**.

29 – Calgary traded its 3rd round pick in the 1994 Entry Draft to New Jersey for the 77th, 91st (previously acquired from Tampa Bay) and 107th (previously acquired from Ottawa) overall picks in the 1994 Entry Draft. New Jersey selected **Sheldon Souray**. Calgary selected **Chris Clark, Ryan Duthie** and **Nils Ekman**.

29 – NY Islanders traded the 64th overall pick in the 1994 Entry Draft to Toronto for Toronto's 2nd round pick in the 1995 Entry Draft. Toronto selected **Fredrik Modin**.

29 – **Artur Oktyabrev** traded from Winnipeg to Vancouver for Vancouver's 6th round pick in the 1994 Entry Draft (**Steve Vezina**).

July

3 – **Al MacInnis** and Calgary's 4th round pick in the 1997 Entry Draft traded from Calgary to St. Louis for **Phil Housley** and St. Louis's 2nd round pick in the 1996 and 1997 Entry Draft.

11 – **Yanic Perreault** traded from Toronto to Los Angeles for a conditional pick in the 1996 Entry Draft.

12 – **Robert Dirk** traded from Chicago to Anaheim for Tampa Bay's 4th round pick in the 1995 Entry Draft (previously acquired).

24 – **Petr Nedved** traded to NY Rangers from St. Louis for **Esa Tikkanen** and **Doug Lidster**.

26 – **Doug Houda** traded from Los Angeles to Buffalo for **Sean O'Donnell**.

29 – **Rick Tocchet** and Pittsburgh's 2nd round choice in 1995 Entry Draft traded from Pittsburgh to Los Angeles for **Luc Robitaille**.

August

8 – **Ruslan Batyrshin** and Winnipeg's 2nd round choice in 1996 Entry Draft traded from Winnipeg to Los Angeles for **Brent Thompson** and future considerations.

19 – **Guy Carbonneau** traded from Montreal to St. Louis for **Jim Montgomery**.

19 – **Glen Featherstone** traded from Boston to NY Rangers for **Daniel Lacroix**.

THREE STAR SELECTION...

NHL PUBLICATIONS
ORDER FORM

Please send

☐ copies of next year's
NHL Guide & Record Book/95-96 (available Sept. 95)

☐ copies of this year's
NHL Guide & Record Book/94-95 (available now)

☐ copies of next year's
NHL Yearbook 1996 magazine (available Sept. 95)

☐ copies of this year's
NHL Yearbook 1995 magazine (available Sept. 94)

☐ copies of the
NHL Rule Book and Schedule/94-95 (available Sept. 94)

PRICES:	CANADA	U.S.A.	OVERSEAS
Guide & Record Book	$19.95	$16.95	$19.95 CDN
Postage (per copy)	$ 3.88	$ 8.00	$ 9.00 CDN
7% GST	$ 1.67	—	—
Total (per copy)	**$25.50**	**$24.95**	**$28.95** CDN
Add Extra for airmail	$ 8.00	$ 9.00	$18.00 CDN
Yearbook	$ 7.95	$ 6.95	$ 7.95 CDN
Handling (per copy)	$ 2.94	$ 3.50	$ 5.00 CDN
7% GST	$ .76	—	—
Total (per copy)	**$11.65**	**$10.45**	**$12.95** CDN
Rule Book	$ 9.95	$ 7.95	$ 9.95 CDN
Handling (per copy)	$ 1.73	$ 3.00	$ 3.50 CDN
7% GST	$ .82	—	—
Total (per copy)	**$12.50**	**$10.95**	**$13.45** CDN

☐ Enclosed is my cheque or money order.
Note to overseas customers:
Cheque must be drawn on a U.S. or a Canadian bank.

Charge my   ☐ Visa   ☐ MasterCard   ☐ Am Ex

Credit Card Account Number _____   Expiry Date (important) _____

Signature _____

Name _____

Address _____

Province/State/Country _____   Postal/Zip Code _____

IN CANADA	IN U.S.A.	OVERSEAS
Mail completed form to:	Mail completed form to:	Mail completed form to:
NHL Publishing	NHL Publishing	NHL Publishing
194 Dovercourt Rd.	194 Dovercourt Rd.	194 Dovercourt Rd.
Toronto, Ontario	Toronto, Ontario	Toronto, Ontario
M6J 3C8	M6J 3C8	CANADA M6J 3C8
	Remit in U.S. funds	**Money order or credit card only.**

Please allow up to five weeks for delivery.

NHL PUBLISHING
IS PLEASED TO OFFER THREE OF THE GAME'S LEADING ANNUAL PUBLICATIONS

1. **THE NHL OFFICIAL GUIDE & RECORD BOOK**

The NHL's authoritative information source.
63rd year in print.
448 pages.
The "Bible of Hockey".
Read worldwide.

2. **THE NHL YEARBOOK**

200-page, full-color magazine with features on each club.
Award winners, All-Stars and special statistics.

3. **THE NHL RULE BOOK**

Complete playing rules, including all changes for 1994-95.

Free Book List and NHL Schedule included with each order

CREDIT CARD HOLDERS CAN ORDER BY FAX:
416/531-3939, 24 HOURS
(PLEASE INCLUDE YOUR CARD'S EXPIRY DATE)